Interlinear Greek-English NEW TESTAMENT

Interlinear Greek-English New Testament

Third Edition

With Strong's Concordance Numbers above Each Word

Jay P. Green, Sr.
General Editor and Translator

BakerBooks
A Division of Baker Book House Co.
Grand Rapids, Michigan 49516

Published by Baker Books
a division of Baker Book House Company
P.O. Box 6287, Grand Rapids, MI 49516-6287

ISBN 0-8010-2138-3

The *Interlinear Greek-English New Testament* is volume 4 of *The Interlinear Hebrew-Greek-English Bible* and is copyright 1980, 1981, 1983, 1984 (2d ed.), and 1996 (3d ed.). *The Interlinear Hebrew-Greek-English Bible* has four volumes and is copyright 1976, 1977, 1978, 1979, 1980, 1981, 1984, and 1985 (2d ed.).

Printed in the United States of America

THE BOOKS OF

The New Testament

PREFACE TO THE FIRST EDITION

"Every Scripture (is) God-breathed, and (is) profitable for teaching, for reproof, for correction, for instruction in righteousness, so that the man of God may be fitted out, having been fully furnished for every good work" - 2 Timothy 3:16.

You now have in your hand the fourth and final volume of *The Interlinear Hebrew-Greek-English Bible*, which is presented to you and to all the Christian community with much exultation, tempered by fear and trembling and awe toward our almighty God and Savior, Jesus Christ.

It is hoped that you will discern that we have fully believed all the words of this Holy Book, handling it with reverence, knowing that *"Men shall not live by bread alone, but by every word that proceeds out of the mouth of God"* - Matthew 4:4. For we recognize that these words did not come *"by the will of man, but men spoke from God, being borne along by (the) Holy Spirit"* - 2 Peter 1:21. It also has been written that each of the sons of men shall be judged by the words of this Book: *"And if anyone hears My words, and does not believe, I do not judge him, . . . the word which I spoke is that which will judge him in the last day"* - John 12:47,48. Considering that the words of this Book are the ones that will judge every person who has lived in all the ages, then how important it must be that the very words of God, and no other, shall be contained in a portable book, to be distributed far and wide, in a form and in a commonly understood language which can be easily and immediately taken into the heart and into the consciousness of all who have the privilege to read them. With these considerations in mind, and in holy fear inculcated by our God, we have sought to provide within *The Interlinear Hebrew-Greek-English Bible* all the original God-breathed Hebrew, Aramaic and Greek words. And after much prayer and laborious study, it was concluded that this could best be done by providing you with the two attested texts that alone have been uniquely preserved whole, and accepted in all generations, in all lands, by the vast majority of God's people as their 'received texts.' Other texts have been put forth from time to time, but none have been found true and powerful enough to displace these two texts: The Masoretic Text of the Old Testament, and the Received Text of the New Testament.

WHY ANOTHER INTERLINEAR NEW TESTAMENT NOW?

The marketplace is being glutted with new books which are being represented as *versions* of the Bible. Each one claims to be the very word of God, yet there are literally thousands of differences between them - and such differences as to cause one to discern that there is much disagreement as to which Greek words are to be translated, or paraphrased. In one way the new *versions* agree: they all leave out dozens of references to the deity of Jesus Christ, and they add words which tend to question His virgin birth, His substitutionary, fully satisfying atonement. This is due to their decision to depend on an Alexandrian text-base, instead of that body of God's words which has been universally received and believed in for nineteen centuries, known to us as the Received Text. These new versions are not only marked by additions, but also by subtractions, since some four whole pages of words, phrases, sentences, and verses have been omitted by these new *versions.* And these are words attested to as God's words by overwhelming evidence contained in all the Greek manuscripts, in the ancient versions, in the writings of the early fathers - and these from every inhabited land on the earth where Christianity has been.

It is for these reasons that we conclude that another interlinear New Testament is needed, so that those who love *every* word of God, and who live by every word of God, may be able to compare *any* version to the original Greek, and to thereby know if any of the words of God are being withheld from their hearts. They will know that it is important to their spiritual life to be reading the right version, one that is true in its translation of the original language, complete with *all* the words of God.

Again, then, let this question be posed: Has Satan, like a slight-of-hand shell-game artist, finally brought God's children to the point where they are searching desperately for the true Word of God? Are we to believe that it cannot now be intact, having been run through the shredder of unholy hands and heads? Let it not be said! Let your answer be a resounding, crashing NO!

For remember that it has been written: *"For I say to you, Until the heavens and the earth pass away, in no way shall pass away one iota or one point from the Law, until all things come to pass"* - Matthew 5:18. Who, then, will you believe? If our almighty, omniscient God assures us that not even an iota, or a point, of His word shall pass away, then an original word, or phrase, or sentence, or verse surely cannot be lost! But still we see version after version pouring from the presses without hundreds and hundreds of authentic, well-attested words which have always been properly held to be the very words of God.

Then should you not ask, Who are these men who tell us these are not God's words? And what evidence do they present to you to persuade you to give up these historically accepted, venerable words that have stood the test of time - and this despite the onslaughts of emperors, heathen hordes, philosophers, popes, and all fleshly inducements men and devils could conceive? And what is the nature of the words they are so determined to steal from your Bible? How did these words come to be questioned in the first place? What is behind these omissions?

A cardinal rule for the Bible reader should be: *"Let God be true, and every man a liar"* - Romans 3:4. The Lord Jesus did not trust Himself to men, and not one of us should do so. Instead, let the Bible reader put his faith in God, for it is only by faith that the word of God can be apprehended. Being thus armed with faith toward God, depending on Him to verify the words which are truly His words, and at the same time being armed with a healthy suspicion of men, one can ask, Who are these men who are assuring us that this or that word, or phrase, or verse does not belong in our Bible? If they are learned scholars, should we not allow their scholarly minds to guide us as to what words to believe? No! For it is written: *"And we have not received the spirit of the world, but the Spirit from God, that we may know the things freely given to us by God; which things we also speak, not in words taught of human wisdom, but in (words) taught of (the) Holy Spirit"* - 1 Corinthians 2:12,13. And, again, *"But the Paraclete, the Holy Spirit which the Father will send in My name, that One will teach you all things and remind you (of) all things which I have said to you"* - John 16:13. Through faith, we believe. And through faith it is that we are equipped to judge which words to believe - faith in God, not faith in men.

What then is the evidence these Bible-alterers offer to persuade you to give up the precious words they have removed from their versions? Mainly they cite two manuscripts, admittedly old, from the fourth century AD., but also admittedly carelessly executed. One, the Sinaiticus, was so poorly executed that ten different hands of 'textual critics' can be discerned as they tried to impose their views on this already corrupted manuscript. They twisted it like a nose of wax to meet their purposes at the time. It is no wonder that it was discarded, finally found in a wastebasket fourteen centuries after it was executed. The other, the Vaticanus, manuscript lay on a shelf in the Vatican library at Rome until 1431, and was considered so corrupt that no one would use it. Erasmus, the noted Roman Catholic scholar, refused to consider it as a source when he formed the Received Text. This Vaticanus manuscript has errors so absurd that the books purporting to teach 'textual science' carefully avoid mentioning these gross errors in their favorite manuscript. They take these two corrupt, carelessly executed manuscripts, and add a handful of later manuscripts from the Alexandrian text-base - all of them loose and disrespectful in their handling of the Scriptures, and from these they give you their never-ending theories, hypotheses, glosses, and doubts. Yea, year after year there is a new crop, and the new ones explode the old theories of the past year.

But let them be known by their fruits. What are these words which they have so freely removed from their *versions* of the Scriptures? (a) They have made Joseph to be the begetter of Jesus, rather than following the Scriptures which say that God the Spirit begot the human body of the Lord Jesus (check Luke 2:33); (b) they have made Jesus to be a begotten creature, rather than the third person of the eternal Godhead (see John 1:18, where some of these proposed versions refer to an "only-begotten God" - an impossibility, since God cannot be begotten - God is an eternal Being, having always existed, and Jesus is God; *(c)* they have deleted *"Son of God"* from Mark 1:1; (d) and they have removed from their so-called versions Christ, or Jesus, or Christ Jesus, or Christ as God, twenty-five or more times; (e) and in 1 Cor. 5:7, they have Christ suffering, but not for us; (f) in 1 Peter 4:1, they have Christ sacrificed, but not *"for us"*; (g) in Luke 24:3, 6, 12, 37, 40, 51, and 52, they have systematically removed Luke's witness to the ascension of Christ - and of course they have done away entirely with Mark's witness to the ascension, simply by removing the last twelve verses of Mark (this they do, they claim, because the two oldest manuscripts do not have those verses - but note this: the Vaticanus manuscript has left an empty space at the end of Mark exactly large enough to contain those twelve verses; how did the copyist know how much space to leave if he was not looking at a still older manuscript with the last 12 verses of Mark in it? As for the Sinaiticus manuscript, it is written in the same-size letters throughout until you come to the place where the last twelve verses of Mark belong, then the letters become large and spread out, taking up enough extra space to allow the last twelve verses of Mark to appear in the smaller letters that had been used up until this time. So much for the so-called evidence from the two 'oldest' manuscripts; if anything they testify to the authenticity of the last twelve verses of Mark.) Shall we allow the words of God to be stolen from us before our very eyes by such specious reasoning?

You can see that the words they are taking away from us are very important words. Then why should we give them up without overwhelming evidence, and the inward assurance of God the Holy Spirit that they are spurious? The fact is, history is repeating itself again In the beginning, it was the old Serpent, Satan, who was the first textual critic, as well as the first murderer, when he succeeded in insinuating into the itching ear of Eve, *"You shall not surely die . . . , you shall be as God"* - Genesis 3:1-5. From that point on, men became unbelieving sinners *("only evil continually"* - Genesis 6:5). As sinners without saving grace men are disposed to believe the lie, especially if the lie suits their fancy better than what God has written for us. Like Origen, an early textual critic, too many men believe what Origen said, "that the Scriptures are of little use to those who understand them as they are written" (quoted by McClintock and Strong Cyclopedia's article on Origen). And given the opportunity, many men will do as Origen did, actually altering the manuscripts to make them say what they understand them to mean, or what they want them to mean. Such things were done as soon as the Word of God was complete. In fact the apostles, Paul, Peter and John all warned that corrupters of the word of God were already plying their trade within the first century churches. For example, God warned His children through Paul: *"I am amazed that you are quickly being transported away from Him who has called you by (the) grace of Christ, to a different gospel, which is not another, except there are some troubling you and desire to pervert the gospel of Christ"* - Galatians 1:6, 7. And borne along by God the Spirit, the apostle John wrote: *"For many false prophets have gone out into the world"* - 1 John 4:1. And through the apostle Peter we learn that perverters of Scripture were already rampant among those calling themselves Christians: *"even as our beloved brother Paul wrote to you, according to the wisdom given to him . . . among which things are some things hard to understand, which the ignorant and unsettled ones pervert, as also the other Scriptures, to their own destruction"* - 2 Peter 3:15, 16.

By these and other Scriptures we see that the apostles were not yet in the bosom of Abraham before the Bible-tinkerers began to distort and to adulterate the word of God. By the time the apostle John died, gnosticism had gotten a toehold in many Christian churches. And quickly thereafter the gnostics expanded their poisonous influence at a rapid pace. Justin Martyr, Valentinus, Clement of Alexandria, Marcion, Tatian, and a horde of others practiced their 'textual science' by operating on manuscripts, or by writing their own *versions.* To this we have many testimonies, such as this one:

"The worst corruptions to which the New Testament has ever been subjected originated within a hundred years after it was composed; that Ireneus (AD. 150), and the African fathers, and the whole Western, . . . used far inferior manuscripts to those employed by Stunica, or Erasmus, or Stephens thirteen centuries later, when molding the Textus Receptus" - *Scrivener, Introduction to the New Testament,* third edition, p. 511. And Eusebius quotes a second century father, writing shortly after the death of the apostle John: "Wherefore, they have no fear to lay hands on the divine Scriptures under pretense of correcting them . . . As for their denying their guilt, the thing is impossible, since the copies were written in their own hand; and they did not receive the Scriptures in this condition from their teachers, nor can they show the originals from which they made their copies" - Eusebius, *Ecclesiastical History,* LCS, Vol. 1, pp. 522-524. Even Origen condemned Marcion and Lucian for altering the Scriptures, though he himself can be shown to have quoted the same verse of Scripture in two contradictory words in many places. Like many 'textual critics' of our day, Origen molded the Scriptures according to his philosophy, or his fancy based on the allegory of the day, having no twinge of conscience for doing so. And it is this Origen, considered by his pupils Jerome and Eusebius, to be the master textual critic, that has left us much of the legacy of the invidious deletions from our modern versions. Do we see the Godhood of Jesus being surreptitiously removed from these modern versions? Origen believed Jesus Christ to be a created being. And by his reputation, and his influence on his pupils, the Latin Vulgate, the ornate manuscripts made for the libraries and the rulers of his day, he influenced many, such as those in the Alexandrian school. This in turn has caused many of the latter-day attackers of the Majority Text to attempt to keep out many references in the Scriptures which plainly reveal Jesus Christ to be God the Son, our original Creator *("because in Him were created all things, the things in the heavens, and the things in the earth, the visible and the invisible, whether thrones, or lordships, or rulers, or authorities, all things through Him and for Him have been created . . . "* - Colossians 1:16). We who love every word that has proceeded from the mouth of God are asked by nearly all of the modern *versions* to do without a host of testimonies to the Godhead of our Lord and Savior, Jesus Christ. For example, in John 3:13, *"who is in Heaven"* is omitted from modern *versions* because it makes the Son to be in Heaven at the same time that He is on earth. In other words, these words make Jesus Christ as God the Son to be omnipresent; that is, He was in the body on earth, yet in spirit He was also still reigning in Heaven. To this day, all the later *versions* continue to deny this attribute of omnipresence to Jesus Christ, which attribute is absolutely essential to Godhood. By omitting from the Scriptures these words, "who is in Heaven," or by putting down "whose home is in Heaven," these men throw doubt on the Scriptures which make Jesus Christ to be equal in the Godhead. The fact is, those words, "whose home is in Heaven," are a gloss, a reading that cannot be shown to appear in a single one of the 5,000 or more Greek manuscripts - it is a fraud to cover up the theft of those important four words which testify that our God, Jesus Christ, was omnipresent even while He was on earth in the body. Of the twenty best-selling New Testaments of this century, only the KJV, KJVII, New KJB, NKJV, *Modern King James Version of the Holy Bible* and Green's *Literal Translation of the Bible* retain this testimony to the coequal Godhood of Jesus Christ.

THE PROVIDENTIAL PRESERVATION OF THE SCRIPTURES

We believe wholeheartedly that God has preserved His word, that He guided His true followers to carefully copy, and to use the whole Bible, as it is represented in the vast majority of the extant manuscripts. We believe that this was done in the same way God guarded the Canon of the New Testament, using the Greek Orthodox Church and the Greek manuscripts used by the churches in all the habitable world to safeguard the deposit which He had given to us. It took the churches two centuries to finally form and to defend the Canon, the sixty-six books of the Bible as we now have them. And it took them another century and a half to finally discard those manuscripts with spurious words added, or with serious omissions of the true words of God. All modern-day critics will admit that the text as essentially displayed in the vast majority of the extant manuscripts has been virtually identical in copy after copy from the period from the fourth century until the invention of the printing press. In fact the Received Text was so widely and so completely accepted in all countries, and in all denominations except the Roman Catholic, that Westcott and Hort felt compelled to invent a mythical council of church fathers, who supposedly met and fixed the text as we now know it. Such a council is unknown to history, and being totally undemonstrable by evidence, it must be considered a myth proposed in order to deceive.

Truly God in His mercy did not leave His people to grope after the true New Testament text. Through the leading of God the Spirit He guided them to preserve it during the manuscript period. God brought this to pass through the working of His preserving and governing providence. First, many trustworthy copies were produced by faithful scribes. Secondly, these were read, used, and recopied by true believers when those original copies were worn out. Thirdly, untrustworthy copies (such as the Vaticanus and the Sinaiticus) were laid aside, not copied, but consigned to oblivion. Today there are more than 5,000 manuscripts and lectionaries in Greek as witnesses to the New Testament text. And 90% or more of these witness to the Received Text readings.

Partly due to the fact those ancient manuscripts containing the Received Text were worn out by use, while the Alexandrian text-base manuscripts were preserved by the dry conditions in Egypt, some have sought to discredit the Received Text, saying that it is not ancient. But now the manuscript portions from the second century are being unearthed, and lo and behold, many of the readings of the Received Text which had been tagged scornfully as 'late readings' by nearly unanimous consent of the 'textual scientists' are now showing up in these earliest manuscripts. Readings which were before being called *late* and *spurious* have been found in these early date manuscripts. For example, the Chester Beatty Papyri contained sixty-five readings which had before been ejected from the Bible by the critics. And Papyrus Bodmer II, of the second century, actually was found to contain thirteen percent of all the so called late readings of the critic-despised Majority Text. Yet strangely, in textual criticism classes, such discoveries are swept under the rug, not being reported to the students. And so it goes. Day by day we see the conjectures of these reputed experts being swept away, along with their hypotheses. Next, we trust, will be the discrediting of their *versions.*

In the light of these facts, should we then allow these 'scientists' (falsely so-called - "O Timothy, guard the deposit, having turned away from the profane, empty babblings and opposing theories of the falsely-named knowledge, which some having asserted have missed the mark concerning the faith"- 1 Timothy 6:20, 21). A man of faith is not spiritually blind. A true believer should not be found following these men without serious investigation of their claims that they are able to tell us which are and which are not the words of God. All who do follow the current crop of 'textual scientists' are apt to wind up in the spiritual ditch with them, being chastised by God for not putting trust in God the Spirit to preserve the words He caused the prophets and apostles to write as the Scriptures. Keep in mind that which is written: *"You shall not add to the word which I (am) commanding you, and not take away from it"* - Deuteronomy 4:2. Also, *"Do not add to His words, lest He reprove you, and you be found a liar"* - Proverbs 30:6. Also, *"If anyone take away from the words of (the) Book of this Prophecy, God will take away his part from the Book of Life"* - Revelation 22:19. Do not be misled by an appeal to your reason. Try the spirits, whether they are of God.

THE GREEK TEXT IN THIS VOLUME

The Greek text herein is purportedly that which underlies the *King James Version,* as reconstructed by F. H. A. Scrivener in 1894. It thus differs to a degree from all previously printed editions of the Received Text (there are more than 250 differences, most of them quite minor, between this text and the Stephens 1550 'standard' *Textus Receptus).* The present text was typeset in England for the Trinitarian Bible Society, and corresponds to *The New Testament in the Original Greek according to the Text Followed in the Authorized Version,* edited by F. H. A. Scrivener, and originally published by Cambridge University Press in 1894 and 1902. The present Trinitarian Bible Society edition of the Greek New Testament was published in 1976.

Careful study, however, will show that this present text does not agree 100% with the text used by the KJV translators, though virtually always it does so. In places it has a different reading than that found in the KJV *(e.g.* Matthew 12:24, 27, Gk. *"Beelzeboul";* KJV has *"Beelzebub"* - John 8:21, Gk. *"sin";* KJV, *"sins"* - John 10:16, Gk. *"one flock";* KJV, *"one fold"* - 1 Corinthians 14:10, KJV has *"of these,"* but it is omitted in the Greek - 1 Corinthians 16:1, the KJV has *"churches,"* without any MSS support at all; the Greek has *"church."* In other places the present text gives Greek words where the KJV translators indicated by italics that they had none (the following KJV italicized words are actually given in the Greek of this TBS edition: Mark 8:14, *the disciples;* Mark 9:42, *these;* John 8:6, *as though he heard them not;* Acts 1:4, *them;* 1 John 3:16; *of God.* Some of these readings do have minority MSS support.- It seems clear that these readings were not in the text chosen by the KJV translators. Nevertheless, to all intents and purposes, the TBS edition faithfully reproduces the KJV Greek text, as nearly as could be done at this date.

Although it is admitted that Erasmus has added to his Received Text two or three readings from the Latin Vulgate, without Greek manuscript authority *(e.g.,* Acts 9:5, 6); and, also one from the Complutension Bible has virtually no Greek manuscript authority (1 John 5:7). We have not deleted these from the Greek text as supplied by the Trinitarian Bible Society, though we do not accept them as part of the true deposit of the Holy Scriptures.

THE ENGLISH TRANSLATIONS

There are two translations in this volume, one appearing as the literal translation of the Greek words, with English equivalents placed directly under each of the Greek words, and the other, A *Literal Translation of the Holy Bible* on the side of the page, serving to provide a straightforward translation for the purpose of making it easy for the reader to see the proper word order in English, and thus to easily assimilate the message given in God's word on that page. Both translations are accomplished in a word-for-word translation. The 'conceptual idea' form of 'translating' the word of God has been rejected, studiously avoided because no person has the right, nor the inspiration, to rewrite God's word to conform it to his or her own concepts. Those passing off their conceptual ideas are, in our opinion, despising the words originally given, and carefully preserved, by God the Spirit through the prophets and apostles. It is only a dodge to give the paraphraser an opportunity to *"be as God,"* as Satan promised in his lie to Eve.

It is hoped that these literal word-for-word translations will demonstrate that a true, literal word-for-word translation also can be a readable and easily understood representation of the Holy Scriptures

INTERPRETATIONS

In the matter of interpretation, or as some would call it, bias, there is no hesitation on our part to admit to the fact that there are many interpretive decisions that must be made in any translation of the Bible. It has been our determination to let the text say what it says. And so no particular set of beliefs has been inserted into the text by these translations. Nevertheless, by the very fact that a true translation must take into consideration the entire context of a word, or phrase, or sentence, or verse, interpretation must be present in making that translation. This is especially so in those places where a Greek word, apart from the context, may be correctly translated by several different English words. For instance, it does make a difference whether a person is "saved," or "cured." And conceivably there could be differences of opinion in the choice of an English word to express a Greek word in such cases.

If a list of interpretive renditions were to be compiled, these at least should be noted as present in this volume: (a) Punctuation has been added, and the original manuscripts have none; (b) capitals and small letters have been added, and the original manuscripts had only capital letters. Especially we have attempted to aid the reader by capitalizing pronouns connected to a Person of the Godhead. Without a doubt, there is room for differences of opinion here. In those places quoted from the Old Testament, the New Testament writers nearly always have fixed the deity of the Persons quoted, so these are not so interpretative. But in another class of places, where we have endeavored to capitalize, or not to capitalize pronouns according to whether the persons addressing Jesus acknowledged Him as God - there is room for much difference of opinion. (c) Words have sometimes been added to aid the English reader to follow the sense, in which case, an attempt has been made to indicate those supplied words in parentheses under the Greek, or in italics in the marginal English translation.

PRESUPPOSITIONS

Being a willing slave of our God and Savior, Jesus Christ, and joyfully submitting to His higher thoughts, we gladly admit to a number of presuppositions: (a) We have acted on the premise that *"the Scriptures cannot be broken" (John 10:35),* meaning that not an iota or a point of them has been lost; and having the firm conviction that each word was God-breathed (2 Timothy 3:16 - Greek), and that having had such an origin God Himself has taken it upon Himself to also carefully preserve His words for us even to this day, we have not dared to change a word, or to supply a word without designating it as uninspired by parentheses or by italics. If God has appeared at places to use an ambiguous word, we have tried to leave it that way, etc. (b) We have presupposed that Jesus Christ is not only our personal Savior and Lord, but that the Scriptures clearly reveal Him as equal with God the Father and with God the Holy Spirit, that He is in fact one of the three Persons in the Godhead; that He came to earth to give Himself as a fully paid ransom for many; that He both lived and died as a substitute for the sins of all those who shall come to a saving knowledge and belief in Him; that He has risen to sit at the right of God the Father, ruling the world from there, interceding for and providentially guiding His own, until that day when He will destroy the earth by fire, and shall then come to receive all of them to a place at His right hand; and finally that He will sit as supreme Judge of all men of all ages, and that He will use the words of the Bible to judge the deeds of each and every person who will have inhabited the earth, casting all unbelievers into everlasting fiery punishment, and sitting all true believers at His feet to learn from Him *"the depths of the riches and of (the) wisdom and knowledge of God"* throughout all eternity.

DISTINCTIVE TRANSLATIONS

For easy apprehension, and continuity with the Old Testament, we have translated the Greek representing the names of the Old Testament characters and places by the same English names that were used there.

Due to the principle of translating each Greek word literally, a number of translations have emerged that are quite different from other versions:

The Greek word designating the mother of Jesus has always been translated "Mary," but most often the Greek word is actually MariaAM, properly meaning Mariam, or Miriam, rather than Mary. So we have given it. It is not that we think we can at this late date change her name in the mind of others from Mary to Mariam, but that we simply translated its literal meaning. It does answer to the question that some have raised, as to why there would be two Marys in one family.

In translating the Greek words for *"I am"* in certain places we have capitalized these words: *viz. I AM* (see John 8:59 and other places). It is our firm conviction that in those cases Jesus is identifying Himself as Jehovah *(Jehovah* properly translated meaning *I AM THAT I AM). Jesus* is of course the English name assigned to a word that means Jehovah is salvation.

Under the Greek we have translated literally, *"to the ages,"* though we surely believe that the words are a clear idiomatic expression for *"forever."* In the translation in the margin we have reversed this. Likewise we have translated under the Greek *"clean"* heart, but firmly believe that *"pure"* could be idiomatically used.

We have tried to translate various places in a way that would not be misleading as to sex. Many times other translators have put *"any man"* where *"anyone"* was literally correct. Male pronouns and male references abound in the Scriptures. There is no good reason for supplying additional male references.

This is now the only interlinear New Testament in current, proper English. All others continue to use Elizabethan-age English. The Bible was written in simple, common Hebrew and Greek words, with no special language used when addressing God. Why now encase the Bible in a stilted language of another age, whether it be Latin or Elizabethan English. As Tyndale wrote that every plowboy should be able to understand the Scriptures in his own language. Otherwise, why not leave it in the original languages?

Our constant aim in translation has been to represent the meaning of the Greek words in English as precisely and accurately as the English language will allow. This has included an attempt to display the meaning of compound Greek words so that the parts of them are expressed in the translation. For example, in John 8:7, Jesus did not merely rise, or stand up - He had bent down, and now he was bending back up - by which words we can visualize exactly what He was doing. This principle may have been imperfectly applied, but in succeeding editions an attempt will be made to achieve more of this type of accuracy. There has been a conscious recognition of the value of consistency in translation. And although we believe we have achieved more consistency than in other versions, there is recognition on our part that there is yet more to be done in this area.

TRANSLATION PROBLEMS AND CHALLENGES

Just as there are difficult places to understand, so there are difficult places to translate. And sometimes the difficulty is not so much in assigning meanings to the Greek words as it is in punctuating them so as to catch the apostle's meaning. One example of this is 1 Corinthians 12:2.

Among the many decisions made, some may want to challenge the choice of a translation at some place or other. For instance, in many places a Greek word has been left untranslated, usually a particle or an article, where it would be redundant or otherwise unsuitable to English transmission.

Where the Greek order or word is difficult to English readers, superior numbers have not been used, because it is believed that the reader may more easily see the English order by referring to the translation in the margin. In most cases the literal translation of each word is given, rather than an idiomatic phrase, where it was considered more explanatory of the meaning than the idiom would supply. In some places where the present tense in Greek takes an English past for proper English, the past tense has been used in translation. But in a great many cases this has not been done, depending on the reader to realize the differences in the two languages. This is also true of the aorist. In fact it is doubted that the New Testament writers themselves used the aorist in the strict (or, restricted) way that Greek grammarians interpret it today.

Due to space problems, a true translation of the participle has not always been given under the Greek. For example, where the English words "having been" would be proper, "being" has often been given. In other places where the Greek word is short, but the English equivalent is long, a substitution may have been given *(e.g.,* "by" instead of "through"). In the case of the double negative construction in the Greek, it is often left as literally translated, rather than to change one negative to a positive in order to make good English out of it. In some cases the added strength of the double-negative, as intended in the Greek, has been transmitted by the use of punctuation.

Many other problems are encountered in rendering Greek into English. The reader is referred to other introductions to the Greek New Testament, especially to those in other interlinear New Testaments.

THE MAJORITY TEXT NOTES *

A healthy debate is beginning to rage between adherents of the Alexandrian text-base (which was developed by a school of critics in Alexandria, Egypt in the early centuries, and which underlies most of the modern *versions)* and those who believe that the Byzantine/Majority text-base, as represented in nearly all cases in the Received Text, is the only true text of the New Testament. William G. Pierpont of Wichita, Kansas has prepared *The Majority Text Notes* that appear in the appendix. By the use of these notes, one can make a direct comparison between the Received Text in this volume, and the manuscript evidence. These notes represent years of research, and it is a privilege to share them with the reader here.

Not included in the 1996 edition.

JAY P. GREEN, SR.
General Editor

PREFACE TO THE SECOND EDITION

This much-improved Second Edition *of The Interlinear Greek-English New Testament* has been made more useful in many ways:

First, much credit must go to the host of serious students of the Bible who have purchased the tens of thousands of copies of the First Edition. Many of these have sent in suggestions for improvement, and most of those suggestions have been incorporated into this Second Edition.

Secondly, being convinced that they would save much more time and energy to those studying the New Testament, we have added to this volume the numbers assigned to each Greek word by James Strong in his *Strong's Exhaustive Concordance.* This has added one hundred pages to the volume, but it should prove to be well worth the extra cost.

Thirdly, the First Edition of A *Literal Translation of the Holy Bible* has been printed in the margin. This also has benefited from a host of suggestions by others who are vitally interested in achieving the most accurate Bible translation possible in the English language. Proofreading by Philip Rosenbaum, and others, has been invaluable in eliminating errors and in improving the English translation in a goodly number of places.

Fourthly, the introduction of *A Literal Translation of the Holy Bible* in the margins, and the re-typesetting of thousands of the lines of the interlinear portion of this volume, has now given it a far better appearance, and a much more readable character.

As General Editor and Translator, my heartfelt thanks must be expressed to all of you who have followed the leading of God the Spirit to participate in this effort to aid the readers and users of this volume.

SOME NOTES ON THE NUMBERING SYSTEM

In order to save both time and energy, and also to enhance general knowledge of the meaning of the individual Greek words, James Strong devised a number system for the Greek words of the New Testament, and he incorporated those numbers into his Greek Lexicon, which appeared in his *Exhaustive Concordance* in the last century. In recent years these numbers have been added to many of the Hebrew and Greek study volumes, such as *The Englishman's Greek Concordance, Thayer's Greek-English Lexicon, Englishman's Hebrew Concordance, Gesenius Hebrew-Chaldee Lexicon.* Also, the new *Concise Lexicon to the Biblical Languages* has the Strong's numbers in both the Hebrew and Greek sections. To complete the perfect circle of usefulness for serious Bible students, it was important that the Bible itself be numbered with these numbers. This has now been done in this volume, and in the other three volumes of *The Interlinear Hebrew-Greek-English Bible.*

Please note the following suggestions for the numbering system:

1. Because some Greek words are shorter than the numbers, where they appear close together, they are sometimes separated by a /. Also, in cases where many of these shorter words follow one another, there is not enough room to allow for all the numbers to be placed above the Greek words. In such a case the use of an asterisk above one or more of the words will indicate to the reader that the number for that word or words will appear in the verse margin to the left of the line.

2. In order to avoid confusion and congestion which would be caused by the numbering of the many very common, short Greek words, these numbers have not been given above the words. The reader should not have any difficulty in finding the numbers of these words, which are usually articles and/or conjunctions, nearly always the following:

NOTE: Frequent words not numbered; and, but, (1161, 2532); the (3588) **.

3. Since some combinations of Greek words, usually two or three words following one another, have a combined meaning, or an idiomatic meaning, Strong assigned different numbers to the combination. In such cases you will find equal signs preceding and following the number, so that it will be seen that the one number covers all the words between the equal signs.

Your assistance will be appreciated in the reporting of any error found in this volume.

***** All words are numbered in the 1996 edition)***

JAY P. GREEN, SR.

General Editor

RESPONSIBILITY FOR THE TRANSLATIONS

The English translations in this volume, both the literal translation under the Greek words, and the translation named A Literal Translation of the Holy Bible, are the work of Jay P. Green, Sr., improved and corrected by the suggestions of others who have reviewed these pages (both in the original manuscript, and in the many printings of this volume since). The responsibility for the assignment of English equivalents belongs to Jay P. Green, Sr., since he was the sole judge of what would, or would not, be allowed in either of the English translations.

In each printed volume an invitation will be given to all lovers of God's word to submit suggestions for improvement of these translations. May God be pleased to use us collectively to achieve the most accurate translation possible in the English language!

PREFACE TO THIS THIRD EDITION (1996)

In the sixteen years since the appearance of the first edition, the editor has been more thoroughly instructed by his Guide, God the Holy Spirit, both by a constant reading and rereading of the Scriptures, and by reference to a multitude of volumes produced by others, especially by those before the current rash of authors who persist in a cultic-like adherence to the theory that altering what God actually wrote is not a mortal sin. The editor holds the contrary belief, that any adding to, or subtracting from, the God-breathed of the Scriptures is the defining sin of our present age. The warnings contained in the preface to the first edition were not strong enough. Where in the mid-century, hundreds of words were deleted or added, beginning in the 1960's wholesale changes were introduced in modern pseudo-translations, so that actually tens of thousands of deletions, and more than 100,000 thousand man-breathed words have been added, none of which can be said to be God-breathed. This misrepresentation of what God actually wrote has fostered a scandalous confusion, and predictably, a disrespect regarding the Holy Scriptures. Surely Satan could not be more pleased in any result from his insinuations since Adam and Eve fell prey to his innocent-appearing questioning of what God actually said.

This edition has been thoroughly revised and improved by the editor, often inserting the many suggestions supplied by the thousands and thousands of readers of the first two editions. We trust that these voluntary contributions may be recorded in Heaven, as well as in this new edition. Readers will note much correspondence between the literal translations and those contained in the notes of the Geneva Bible and the Authorised, KJV Version.

This edition includes a second marginal column with the AV/KJV text on the right-hand side (1769 Cambridge edition English). This is in response to an often expressed desire of the readers of earlier editions of this work. [Because of space problems, the One Volume Edition of the INTERLINEAR HEBREW-GREEK-ENGLISH BIBLE will not contain the AV/KJV. in the right-hand margin.]

This edition has been newly typeset throughout, including the Greek, the English underneath the Greek, the English in the side columns, and the Strong's numbers. Because of the complexity and extent of this completely new typesetting, the potentiality of error in the typesetting process was multiplied. To offset this a very thorough proofreading has been applied. Volunteer proofreaders, as well as staff members, have spent thousands of hours in an attempt to make certain that no errors would remain. However, both typesetting and proofreading is done by human beings, and thus imperfection will creep in. This is particularly true in the case of the accents and breathings in the Greek typesetting (which was done by the editor, then was much improved in the proofreading by others). As in previous editions, we appeal to the readers to advise the editor of any imperfection noted. Send notes on a separate page, in care of the publisher. All this edition is stored on computer, which will permit quick and certain changes an be made, and thus to insure that future printings will not include such imperfections.

NOTES TO AID THE READER IN THE USE OF THIS EDITION

On the whole, the punctuation in the Greek text has been followed in the English wording under the Greek. Since no punctuation was present in the original manuscripts, any punctuation is editorial. The present editor has varied from the punctuation in the Greek in a few cases. An example is the emphasis added by an exclamation mark, especially after the words Behold(!), and woe (!). By these words God the Holy Spirit, the ultimate Author of the Scriptures, intends to alert the reader that a very important statement is to be made directly after these words. Another variation appears when direct speech follows the Greek word ὅτι when it precedes direct speech, no translation of this Greek word is given in such cases; instead the first word of the direct speech is capitalized, as in English compositions. Quotation marks are not used for direct speech, but the reader can discern that it is direct speech from the format.

An effort is made to retain the tenses, the figures of speech, and other distinctives of the koine Greek, at times the editor has added such English helper words as "do," to assist the reader's understanding.. The use of participles and the frequent of the aorist in Greek, which impedes the rhythm and flow of the English, yet in most cases we have retained the Greek usage. Since most readers will not be familiar with Greek grammar, it might be mentioned that there are idiomatic combinations in Greek usage. In some cases we have chosen to literally translate the words, while in most cases we have given the idiomatic. An example is in Titus 1:5, where κατα πολιν is translated "every city," or in other cases where κατα precedes a word it could have been given as "(city by) city;" "(day by) day;" "(house to) house," etc.

The double negative is common in Greek, which intends to add strong emphasis to what is being said. ου μη (not, not) is commonly translated as "not at all," "by no means," "in no way," etc. where in English one would say "never ever."

Interrogative questions in Greek are often preceded by "Not," in which case the other half of the negative is omitted.

As mentioned in the preface to the first edition (which each new reader should carefully use as an introduction to this work), capitalization is strictly interpretative in this work. The guidelines we have established include the capitalization of Deity, including pronouns, wherever it is clear that members of the Trinity, or personifications of them, plainly indicate that Deity is in mind. However, where a speaker is clearly an unbeliever (such as when a Pharisee addressed Jesus), we do not capitalize the pronouns, etc. in their statements since they plainly do not believe that Jesus is God). Other capitalizations include persons and their offices (such as Savior, Intercessor, Mediator for offices of Jesus); names (such as, the Bush, the ever-burning bush that attracted Moses), well-known Biblical events (such, as the Deluge or Flood); places (such as the Valley of Giants where David did many of his heroic deeds; Gethsemane; Mount of Olives, etc.), this in addition to the capitalization of the beginning of sentences, the first word of direct speech, etc.

And important one is the capitalization of "Heaven," the abode of God. In the Greek this word is not capitalized..There are numerous places where the Greek says, "the heaven," or even "the heavens" indicating the sky, or that part of the universe which is above the earth. However, in many of the places where these words appear in Greek the meaning is clearly "Heaven," such as may be seen in the scenes in the book of Revelation, and in a host of other places.

In the Greek the word for miracles is "signs," so we translate literally. However, the saints of God need not allow anyone to use this fact to deny the multitude of miracles which were performed by God, the prophets, and the apostles. Ultimately, of course, the laws of nature can only be suspended by God Himself, so any miracle by others (including those by

Satan, such as calling down fire), required that God give this miraculous act His personal power.

DIFFERENCES BETWEEN THE LITERAL TRANSLATION (LITV) AND INTERLINEAR

In this third edition of the LITV an effort is made to more closely relate it to the meanings under the Greek in the interlinear column. Where formerly we may have translated with a different word, yet one having an equally correct meaning, we intended to expand the understanding of the reader. Or in some cases, an alternative translation appeared. This caused some confusion. Therefore, in this edition we have endeavored to have the LITV column match closely with the interlinear section. However, sentence structure, punctuation, and other differences which do not reflect any different meaning still may be seen in the LITV side column. By far the most important aim of this work is for the reader to comprehend what God has said to him or her, and so to assimilate this knowledge into the personal life and practice of each individual reader.

As in all editions we make mention of the privilege God has granted us to feed His lambs by way of a literal English rendition of the God-breathed words in the original language, we have ever been burdened with the awesome responsibility attached to such a task. He has been most gracious to us in the past when hundreds of thousands of His saints have read and profited by previous editions of this work, yet we found that with closer examination the translation could be improved by getting even closer to the literal translation of His Word. Until we sit at the feet of Jesus in eternity, we may not know all that there is to know about what God meant in each word of the Scriptures. In the light of this obvious fact, no claim to infallibility is made by the editor-translator.

INVITATION TO THE READER TO PARTICIPATE IN FUTURE EDITIONS

Repeating our invitation in the first edition, "an invitation is given to all lovers of God's Word to submit suggestions for improvement of these translations". Although correspondence is prohibited by the volume of such suggestions, be assured that each suggestion will be carefully considered, independent study will be made, and in many cases will appear in the next edition. Put all suggestions on a separate page from any correspondence. Include your name and address for our files.

ACKNOWLEDGEMENTS

First, I want to thank my wife, Mary Virginia Green, whose patience and support have allowed me the long hours necessary to translate, edit and typeset the Interlinear Bibles.

Much recognition and praise is due to many persons who have contributed to this revised and improved edition. Among these are our staff members:

Jay P. Green, Jr., our information systems administrator, designer, typographer and stylist, without whom this volume could not have been produced on computer.

Tina Green and Tracy Funkhouser who rendered invaluable help in the nuts and bolts phases of the work, including computer keyboarding, typesetting the Strong's numbers, and proofing, etc.

Our many keen proofreaders, some of whom spent a multitude of voluntary hours to ensure the veracity of the work. These include the following, alphabetically rather than the amount of work contributed: No academic degrees are indicated lest some consider them as indication of their greater importance to the work.

Jeffery Boer

Gary Gurbikian

Robert Hamilton

Mark Langley

Dale Maddox

Phil Rosenbaum

Thomas Seaman

Paul Siechert

Stewart Traill

Paul Watkins

Cheryl Zatko

Gary Zeola

For a listing of those who gave material assistance in making the Hebrew translations, see Volume I of the INTERLINEAR HEBREW-GREEK-ENGLISH BIBLE

Literal Translation

THE GOSPEL ACCORDING TO MATTHEW

Matthew 1

1. The Book of the genealogy of Jesus Christ, (the) son of David, (the) son of Abraham:

2 Abraham fathered Isaac; and Isaac fathered Jacob; and Jacob fathered Judah and his brothers.

3 And Judah fathered Pharez and Zarah out of Tamar; and Pharez fathered Hezron, and Hezron fathered Aram;

4 and Aram fathered Amminadab; and Amminadab fathered Nahshon; and Nahshon fathered Salmon;

5 and Salmon fathered Boaz out of Rahab; and Boaz fathered Obed out of Ruth; and Obed fathered Jesse;

6 and Jesse fathered David the king. And David the king fathered Solomon out of (her who had been) the (wife) of Uriah;

7 and Solomon fathered Rehoboam; and Rehoboam fathered Abijah; and Abijah fathered Asa;

8 and Asa fathered Jehoshaphat; and Jehoshaphat fathered Jehoram; and Jehoram fathered Uzziah;

9 and Uzziah fathered Jotham; and Jotham fathered Ahaz; and Ahaz fathered Hezekiah;

10 and Hezekiah fathered Manasseh;

ΕΥΑΓΓΕΛΙΟΝ
GOSPEL

ΤΟ ΚΑΤΑ ΜΑΘΘΑΙΟΝ
THE ACCORDING TO MATTHEW

976 1078 2424 5547 5207 1138 5207
1. Βίβλος γενέσεως Ἰησοῦ Χριστοῦ, υἱοῦ Δαβίδ, υἱοῦ
(The) Book of genealogy of Jesus Christ, son of David, son
11
Ἀβραάμ.
of Abraham.

11 1080 3588 2464 2464 1161 1080 3588
2. Ἀβραὰμ ἐγέννησε τὸν Ἰσαάκ· Ἰσαὰκ δὲ ἐγέννησε τὸν
Abraham fathered Isaac, Isaac and fathered
2384 2384 1161 1080 3588 2455 2532 3588 80
Ἰακώβ· Ἰακὼβ δὲ ἐγέννησε τὸν Ἰούδαν καὶ τοὺς ἀδελφοὺς
Jacob. Jacob and fathered Judah (Judas) and the brothers
846 2455 1161 1080 3588 5329 2532 3588 2196 1537 3588
αὐτοῦ· 3 Ἰούδας δὲ ἐγέννησε τὸν Φαρὲς καὶ τὸν Ζαρὰ ἐκ τῆς
of him. Judah (Judas) and fathered Pharez (Phares) and Zarah (Zara) of
2283 5329 1161 1080 3588 2074 2074 1161 1080
Θάμαρ· Φαρὲς δὲ ἐγέννησε τὸν Ἐσρώμ· Ἐσρὼμ δὲ ἐγέννησε
Tamar. (Thamar) Pharez (Phares) and fathered Hezron; (Esrom) Hezron (Esrom) and fathered
3588 689 689 1161 1080 3588 284 284
τὸν Ἀράμ· 4 Ἀρὰμ δὲ ἐγέννησε τὸν Ἀμιναδάβ· Ἀμιναδὰβ
Aram. Aram and fathered Amminadab (Aminadab); Amminadab (Aminadab)
1161 1080 3588 3476 3476 1161 1080 3588
δὲ ἐγέννησε τὸν Ναασσών· Ναασσὼν δὲ ἐγέννησε τὸν
and fathered Nahshon, (Naasson) Nahshon (Naasson) and fathered
4533 4533 1161 1080 3588 1003 1537 3588 4477
Σαλμών· 5 Σαλμὼν δὲ ἐγέννησε τὸν Βοὸζ ἐκ τῆς Ῥαχάβ·
Salmon; Salmon and fathered Boaz (Booz) of Rahab; (Rachab)
1003 1161 1080 3588 5601 1537 3588 4503 5601 1161
Βοὸζ δὲ ἐγέννησε τὸν Ὠβὴδ ἐκ τῆς Ῥούθ· Ὠβὴδ δὲ
Boaz (Booz) and fathered Obed of Ruth; Obed and
1080 3588 2421 2421 1161 1080 3588 1138 3588
ἐγέννησε τὸν Ἰεσσαί· 6 Ἰεσσαὶ δὲ ἐγέννησε τὸν Δαβὶδ τὸν
fathered Jesse; Jesse and fathered David the
935
βασιλέα.
king.

1138 1161 3588 935 1080 3588 4672 1537 3588
Δαβὶδ δὲ ὁ βασιλεὺς ἐγέννησε τὸν Σολομῶντα ἐκ τῆς
David and the king fathered Solomon out of the
3588 3774 4672 1161 1080 3588 4497 4497
τοῦ Οὐρίου· 7 Σολομὼν δὲ ἐγέννησε τὸν Ῥοβοάμ· Ῥοβοὰμ
(wife) of Uriah; (Urias) Solomon and fathered Rehoboam; (Roboam) Rehoboam (Roboam)
1161 1080 3588 7 7 1161 1080 3588 760 760
δὲ ἐγέννησε τὸν Ἀβιά· Ἀβιὰ δὲ ἐγέννησε τὸν Ἀσά· 8 Ἀσὰ
and fathered Abijah; (Abia) Abijah (Abia) and fathered Asa; Asa
1161 1080 3588 2498 2498 1161 1080 3588
δὲ ἐγέννησε τὸν Ἰωσαφάτ· Ἰωσαφὰτ δὲ ἐγέννησε τὸν
and fathered Jehoshaphat; (Josaphat) Jehoshaphat (Josaphat) and fathered
2496 2496 1161 1080 3588 3604 3604 1161 1080
Ἰωράμ· Ἰωρὰμ δὲ ἐγέννησε τὸν Ὀζίαν· 9 Ὀζίας δὲ ἐγέννησε
Jehoram; (Joram) Jehoram (Joram) and fathered Uzziah; (Ozias) Uzziah (Ozias) and fathered
3588 2488 2488 1161 1080 3588 881 881 1161
τὸν Ἰωάθαμ· Ἰωάθαμ δὲ ἐγέννησε τὸν Ἄχάζ· Ἄχὰζ δὲ
Jotham, (Joatham) Jotham (Joatham) and fathered Ahaz, (Achaz) Ahaz (Achaz) and
1080 3588 1478 1478 1161 1080 3588 3128
ἐγέννησε τὸν Ἐζεκίαν· 10 Ἐζεκίας δὲ ἐγέννησε τὸν Μανασσῆ·
fathered Hezekiah; (Ezekias) Hezekiah (Ezekias) and fathered Manasseh; (Manasses)

King James Version

THE GOSPEL ACCORDING TO MATTHEW

Matthew 1

1. The book of the generation of Jesus Christ, the son of David, the son of Abraham.

2 Abraham begat Isaac; and Isaac begat Jacob; and Jacob begat Judas and his brethren;

3 And Judas begat Phares and Zara of Thamar; and Phares begat Esrom; and Esrom begat Aram;

4 And Aram begat Aminadab; and Aminadab begat Naasson; and Naasson begat Salmon;

5 And Salmon begat Booz of Rachab; and Booz begat Obed of Ruth; and Obed begat Jesse;

6 And Jesse begat David the king; and David the king begat Solomon of her (that had been the wife) of Urias;

7 And Solomon begat Roboam; and Roboam begat Abia; and Abia begat Asa;

8 And Asa begat Josaphat; and Josaphat begat Joram; and Joram begat Ozias;

9 And Ozias begat Joatham; and Joatham begat Achaz; and Achaz begat Ezekias;

10 And Ezekias begat Manasses;

Literal Translation | **Matthew 1:11** | ***King James Version***

and Manasseh fathered Amon; and Amon fathered Josiah;

3128 1161 1080 3588 300 300 1161 1080 3588
Μανασσῆς δὲ ἐγέννησε τὸν Ἀμών· Ἀμὼν δὲ ἐγέννησε τὸν
Manasseh (Manasses) and fathered Amon; Amon and fathered
2502 2502 1161 1080 3588 2423 2532 3588
Ἰωσίαν· 11 Ἰωσίας δὲ ἐγέννησε τὸν Ἰεχονίαν καὶ τοὺς
Josiah; (Josias) Josiah (Josias) and fathered Jehoiachin (Jechonias) and the
80 846 1909 3588 3350 897
ἀδελφοὺς αὐτοῦ, ἐπὶ τῆς μετοικεσίας Βαβυλῶνος.
brothers of him, at the deportation of Babylon.

and Manasses begat Amon; and Amon begat Josias;

11 and Josiah fathered Jehoiachin and his brothers, at the deportation of Babylon.

11 And Josias begat Jechonias and his brethren, about the time they were carried away to Babylon:

12 And after the deportation of Babylon, Jehoiachin fathered Shealtiel; and Shealtiel fathered Zerubbabel;

3326 1161 3588 3350 897 2423 1080
12.Μετὰ δὲ τὴν μετοικεσίαν Βαβυλῶνος, Ἰεχονίας ἐγέννησε
after And the deportation of Babylon, Jehoiachin fathered
3588 4528 4528 1161 1080 3588 2216
τὸν Σαλαθιήλ; Σαλαθιὴλ δὲ ἐγέννησε τὸν Ζοροβάβελ;
Shealtiel (Salathiel) Shealtiel (Salathiel) and fathered Zerubbabel (Zorobabel)

12 And after they were brought to Babylon, Jechonias begat Salathiel; and Salathiel begat Zorobabel;

13 and Zerubbabel fathered Abiud; and Abiud fathered Eliakim; and Eliakim fathered Azor;
14 and Azor fathered Sadoc; and Sadoc fathered Achim, and Achim fathered Eliud;

2216 1161 1080 3588 10 10 1161 1080
13 Ζοροβάβελ δὲ ἐγέννησε τὸν Ἀβιούδ· Ἀβιοὺδ δὲ ἐγέννησε
Zerubbabel (Zorobabel) and fathered Abiud; Abiud and fathered
3588 1662 1662 1161 1080 3588 107 107 1161
τὸν Ἐλιακείμ· Ἐλιακεὶμ δὲ ἐγέννησε τὸν Ἀζώρ· 14 Ἀζὼρ δὲ
Eliakim, Eliakim and fathered Azor; Azor and
1080 3588 4524 4524 1161 1080 3588 885 885
ἐγέννησε τὸν Σαδώκ· Σαδὼκ δὲ ἐγέννησε τὸν Ἀχείμ· Ἀχεὶμ
fathered Sadoc,; Sadoc and fathered Achim; Achim
1161 1080 3588 1664 1664 1161 1080 3588 1648
δὲ ἐγέννησε τὸν Ἐλιούδ· 15 Ἐλιοὺδ δὲ ἐγέννησε τὸν Ἐλεάζαρ·
and fathered Eliud,; Eliud and fathered Eleazar;

13 And Zorobabel begat Abiud; and Abiud begat Eliakim; and Eliakim begat Azor;
14 And Azor begat Sadoc; and Sadoc begat Achim; and Achim begat Eliud;

15 and Eliud fathered Eleazar; and Eleazar fathered Matthan; and, Matthan fathered Jacob;

1648 1161 1080 3588 3157 3157 1161 1080 3588
Ἐλεάζαρ δὲ ἐγέννησε τὸν Ματθάν· Ματθὰν δὲ ἐγέννησε τὸν
Eleazar and fathered Matthan,; Matthan and fathered

15 And Eliud begat Eleazar; and Eleazar begat Matthan; and Matthan begat Jacob.

16 and Jacob fathered Joseph; the husband (to be) of Mariam (Mary), out of whom Jesus was generated (the One) called Christ.

2384 2384 1161 1080 3588 2501 3588 435 3137
Ἰακώβ· 16 Ἰακὼβ δὲ ἐγέννησε τὸν Ἰωσὴφ τὸν ἄνδρα Μαρίας,
Jacob,; Jacob and fathered Joseph the husband of Mariam, (Mary)
1537 3739 1080 2424 3588 3004 5547
ἐξ ἧς ἐγεννήθη Ἰησοῦς ὁ λεγόμενος Χριστός.
out of whom was generated Jesus the (One) called Christ.

16 And Jacob begat Joseph the husband of Mary, of whom was born Jesus, who is called Christ.

17 So all the generations from Abraham to David (were) four-teen generations, and from David to the deportation to Babylon, fourteen generations, and from the deportation to Babylon until the Christ, fourteen generations.

3956 3767 3588 1074 575 11 2193 1138 1074
17. Πᾶσαι οὖν αἱ γενεαὶ ἀπὸ Ἀβραὰμ ἕως Δαβὶδ γενεαὶ
all Then the generations from Abraham until David, generations
1180 2532 575 1138 2193 3588 3350 897
δεκατέσσαρες· καὶ ἀπὸ Δαβὶδ ἕως τῆς μετοικεσίας Βαβυλῶνος
fourteen, and from David until the deportation of Babylon,
1074 1180 2532 575 3588 3350 897
γενεαὶ δεκατέσσαρες· καὶ ἀπὸ τῆς μετοικεσίας Βαβυλῶνος
generations fourteen, and until the deportation of Babylon
2193 3588 5547 1074 1180
ἕως τοῦ Χριστοῦ γενεαὶ δεκατέσσαρες.
until the Christ, generations fourteen.

17 So all the generations from Abraham to David (are) fourteen generations; and from David until the carrying away into Babylon (are) fourteen generations; and from the carrying away into Babylon unto Christ (are) fourteen generations

18. And the birth of Jesus Christ was this way (for His mother Mary had been betrothed to Joseph) before the joining of them, she was discovered having (become pregnant) in womb by (the) Holy Spirit.
19 But her husband (to be) Joseph being just, and not willing to expose her publicly, he purposed to put her away secretly.

3588 1161 2424 5547 3588 1083 3779 2258 3423
18.Τοῦ δὲ Ἰησοῦ Χριστοῦ ἡ γέννησις οὕτως ἦν. μνηστευθεί-
Now of Jesus Christ the birth this way was: being betrothed
1063 3588 3384 846 3137 3588 2501 4250 2228
σης γὰρ τῆς μητρὸς αὐτοῦ Μαρίας τῷ Ἰωσήφ, πρὶν ἢ
for the mother of Him, Mariam, (Mary) to Joseph, before
4905 846 2147 1722 1064 2192 1537 4151
συνελθεῖν αὐτούς, εὑρέθη ἐν γαστρὶ ἔχουσα ἐκ Πνεύματος
joining of them, she was found in womb, having by Spirit
40 2501 1161 3588 435 846 1342 5607 2532 3361 2309
Ἁγίου. 19 Ἰωσὴφ δὲ ὁ ἀνὴρ αὐτῆς, δίκαιος ὢν, καὶ μὴ θέλων
Holy. Joseph and the husband of her, just being, and not willing
846 3856 1014 2977 630 846
αὐτὴν παραδειγματίσαι, ἐβουλήθη λάθρα ἀπολῦσαι αὐτήν.
her to expose publicly, purposed secretly to put away her.

18. Now the birth of Jesus Christ was on this wise: When as his mother Mary was espoused to Joseph, before they came together, she was found with child of the Holy Ghost.
19 Then Joseph her husband, being a just (man), and not willing to make her a publick example, was minded to put her away privily.

Literal Translation

Matthew 1:20

King James Version

20 And (as) he (was) thinking about these things, behold, an angel of (the) Lord was seen by him in a dream, saying, Joseph, son of David, do not fear to take Mary (as) your wife. For that in her is generated by (the) Holy Spirit.
21 And she will bear a son, and you shall call His name Jesus, for He shall save His people from their sins.

22 And all this happened that might be fulfilled that spoken by the Lord through the prophet, saying,

23 "Behold! The virgin will conceive in (her) womb and will bear a son, and they will call His name Emmanuel" (which translated is, God with us). (Isa. 7:14)
24 And Joseph being aroused from sleep, he did as the angel of (the) Lord commanded him, and took (her as)his wife,
25 and did not know her until she bore her son, the First-born. And he called His name JESUS.

5023 1161 846 1760 2400 32 2962 2596
20 ταῦτα δὲ αὐτοῦ ἐνθυμηθέντος, ἰδού, ἄγγελος Κυρίου κατ'
these things And he meditating on, behold! An angel of (the) Lord by

3677 5316 846 3004 2501 5207 1138 3361 5399
ὄναρ ἐφάνη αὐτῷ, λέγων, Ἰωσήφ, υἱὸς Δαβίδ, μὴ φοβηθῇς
a dream was seen by him, saying, Joseph, son of David, not do fear

3880 3137 3588 1135 4675 3588 1063 1722 846
παραλαβεῖν Μαριὰμ τὴν γυναῖκά σου· τὸ γὰρ ἐν αὐτῇ
to take Mariam (Mary) (as) the wife of you; that for in her

1080 1537 4151 2076 40 5088 1161 5207 2532
γεννηθὲν ἐκ Πνεύματός ἐστιν Ἁγίου. 21τέξεται δὲ υἱόν, καὶ
begotten by (the) Spirit is Holy. she will bear And a son, and

2564 3588 3686 846 2424 846 1063 4982 3588 2992
καλέσεις τὸ ὄνομα αὐτοῦ Ἰησοῦν· αὐτὸς γὰρ σώσει τὸν λαὸν
you shall call the name of Him Jesus. He For will save the people

846 575 3588 266 846 5124 1161 3650 1096
αὐτοῦ ἀπὸ τῶν ἁμαρτιῶν αὐτῶν. 22 τοῦτο δὲ ὅλον γέγονεν,
of Him from the sins of them. this And all happened

2443 4137 3588 4483 5259 3588 2962 1223 3588 4396
ἵνα πληρωθῇ τὸ ῥηθὲν ὑπὸ τοῦ Κυρίου διὰ τοῦ προφήτου,
that be fulfilled that spoken by the Lord through the prophet

3004 2400 3588 3933 1722 1064 2192 2532 5088
λέγοντος, 23 Ἰδού, ἡ παρθένος ἐν γαστρὶ ἕξει καὶ τέξεται
saying, Behold, the virgin in womb will conceive and will bear

5207 2532 2564 3588 3686 846 1694 3739 2076
υἱόν, καὶ καλέσουσι τὸ ὄνομα αὐτοῦ Ἐμμανουήλ, ὅ ἐστι
a son, and they will call the name of Him Emmanuel, which is

3177 3326 2257 3588 2316 1326 1161 3588
μεθερμηνευόμενον, Μεθ' ἡμῶν ὁ θεός. 24 διεγερθεὶς δὲ ὁ
translated with us God. being aroused And

2501 575 3588 5258 4160 5613 4367 846 3588 32
Ἰωσὴφ ἀπὸ τοῦ ὕπνου ἐποίησεν ὡς προσέταξεν αὐτῷ ὁ ἄγγελος
Joseph from the sleep he did as commanded him the angel

2962 2532 3880 3588 1135 846 2532 3756
Κυρίου· καὶ παρέλαβε τὴν γυναῖκα αὐτοῦ, 25 καὶ οὐκ
of (the) Lord. and took (as) the wife of him, and not

1097 846 2193 3757 5088 3588 5207 846 3588
ἐγίνωσκεν αὐτὴν ἕως οὗ ἔτεκε τὸν υἱὸν αὐτῆς τὸν
did know her until she bore the son of her, the

4416 2532 2564 3588 3686 846 2424
πρωτότοκον· καὶ ἐκάλεσε τὸ ὄνομα αὐτοῦ ἸΗΣΟΨΝ.
First-born. And he called the name of Him, JESUS.

20 But while he thought on these things, behold, the angel of the Lord appeared unto him in a dream, saying, Joseph, thou son of David, fear not to take unto thee Mary thy wife: for that which is conceived in her is of the Holy Ghost.

21 And she shall bring forth a son, and thou shalt call his name JESUS: for he shall save his people from their sins.

22 Now all this was done, that it might be fulfilled which was spoken of the Lord by the prophet, saying,

23 Behold, a virgin shall be with child, and shall bring forth a son, and they shall call his name Emmanuel, which being interpreted is, God with us. {they...: or, his name shall be called}
24 Then Joseph being raised from sleep did as the angel of the Lord had bidden him, and took unto him his wife:

25 And knew her not till she had brought forth her firstborn son: and he called his name JESUS.

Matthew 2

Matthew 2

Matthew 2

1. And when Jesus had been born in Bethlehem of Judea in (the) days of Herod the king, behold, wise men arrived from (the) east to Jerusalem,

2 saying, Where is He born King of the Jews? For we saw His star in the east and have come to worship Him.

3 But Herod the king hearing (this, he) was troubled and all Jerusalem with

3588 1161 2424 1080 1722 965 3588 2449 1722
1. Τοῦ δὲ Ἰησοῦ γεννηθέντος ἐν Βηθλεὲμ τῆς Ἰουδαίας, ἐν
And Jesus having been born in Bethlehem of Judea , in

2250 2264 3588 935 2400 3097 575 395
ἡμέραις Ἡρώδου τοῦ βασιλέως, ἰδού, μάγοι ἀπὸ ἀνατολῶν
(the) days of Herod the king, behold, Magi from (the) east

3854 1519 2414 3004 4226 2076 3588 5088
παρεγένοντο εἰς Ἱεροσόλυμα, 2 λέγοντες, Ποῦ ἐστὶν ὁ τεχθεὶς
arrived into Jerusalem saying, Where is he born

935 3588 2453 1492 1063 846 3588 792 1722
βασιλεὺς τῶν Ἰουδαίων; εἴδομεν γὰρ αὐτοῦ τὸν ἀστέρα ἐν
king of the Jews? we saw For of him the star in

3588 395 2532 2064 4352 846 191 1161
τῇ ἀνατολῇ, καὶ ἤλθομεν προσκυνῆσαι αὐτῷ. 3 ἀκούσας δὲ
the east, and came to worship him. hearing And

2264 3588 935 5015 2532 956 2414 3326
Ἡρώδης ὁ βασιλεὺς ἐταράχθη, καὶ πᾶσα Ἱεροσόλυμα μετ'
Herod the king was troubled, and all Jerusalem with

1. Now when Jesus was born in Bethlehem of Judaea in the days of Herod the king, behold, there came wise men from the east to Jerusalem,

2 Saying, Where is he that is born King of the Jews? for we have seen his star in the east, and are come to worship him.
3 When Herod the king had heard (these things), he was troubled, and all Jerusalem with

Literal Translation

him.
4. And having gathered all the chief priests and scribes of the people, he inquired from them where the Christ was to be born.

5 And they said to him, In Bethlehem of Judea, for so it has been written through the prophet,
6 "And you, Bethlehem, land of Judah, in no way are you least among the governors of Judah, for out of you shall come a Governor who shall shepherd My people Israel." (Micah 5:2)
7 Then secretly calling the wise men, Herod asked of them exactly the time of the star appearing.

8 And sending them to Bethlehem, he said, Having gone, exactly inquire about the child. And when you find (him), report to me so that coming I may also worship him.

9. And having heard the king, they departed. And, behold! The star which they saw in the east went before them until it had come and stood over where the child was.
10 And seeing the star, they rejoiced exceedingly (with) a great joy.
11. And having come into the house, they saw the child with His mother Mary. And falling down, they worshiped Him. And opening their treasures, they presented gifts to Him: gold and frankincense and myrrh.

12 And having been warned by a dream not to return to Herod, they went back into their own country by another way.

Matthew 2:4

846 2532 4863 3956 3588 749 2532 1122
αὐτοῦ, 4 καὶ συναγαγὼν πάντας τοὺς ἀρχιερεῖς καὶ γραμ-
him. And having gathered all the chief priests and scribes

3588 2992 4441 3844 846 4226 3588 5547
ματεῖς τοῦ λαοῦ ἐπυνθάνετο παρ αὐτῶν ποῦ ὁ Χριστὸς
of the people, he inquired from them where the Christ

1080 3588 1161 2036 846 1722 965 3588 2449
γεννᾶται. 5 οἱ δὲ εἶπον αὐτῷ, Ἐν Βηθλεὲμ τῆς Ἰουδαίας·
was to be born. they And said to him, In Bethlehem of Judea;

3779 1063 1125 1223 3588 4396 2532 4771 965
οὕτω γὰρ γέγραπται διὰ τοῦ προφήτου· 6 Καὶ σὺ Βηθλεέμ,
thus for it has been written through the prophet, And you Bethlehem,

1093 2448 3760 1646 1488 1722 3588 2232 2448 1537
γῆ Ἰούδα, οὐδαμῶς ἐλαχίστη εἶ ἐν τοῖς ἡγεμόσιν Ἰούδα· ἐκ
land of Judah, in no way least are among the governors of Judah out of

4675 1063 1831 2233 3748 4165 3588 2992
σοῦ γὰρ ἐξελεύσεται ἡγούμενος, ὅστις ποιμανεῖ τὸν λαόν
you For will come out a Governor who will shepherd the people

3450 3588 2474 5119 2264 2977 2564 3588
μου τὸν Ἰσραήλ. 7 τότε Ἡρώδης, λάθρα καλέσας τοὺς
of Me, (even) Israel. Then Herod, secretly calling the

3097 198 3844 846 3588 5550 3588 5316
μάγους, ἠκρίβωσε παρ᾽ αὐτῶν τὸν χρόνον τοῦ φαινο-
Magi, asked exactly from them the time of the appearing

792 2532 3992 846 1519 965 2036 4198
μένου ἀστέρος, 8 καὶ πέμψας αὐτοὺς εἰς Βηθλεὲμ εἶπε, Πορευ-
star. And sending them to Bethlehem He said, Having

199 1833 4012 3588 3813 1875 1161 2147
θέντες ἀκριβῶς ἐξετάσατε περὶ τοῦ παιδίου· ἐπὰν δὲ εὕρητε,
gone exactly inquire about the child. when And you find

518 3427 3704 2504 2064 4352 846
ἀπαγγείλατέ μοι, ὅπως κἀγὼ ἐλθὼν προσκυνήσω αὐτῷ.
report to me, so that I also coming may worship him.

3588 1161 191 3588 935 4198 2532 2400 3588
9οἱ δὲ ἀκούσαντες τοῦ βασιλέως ἐπορεύθησαν· καὶ ἰδού, ὁ
they And having heard the king, departed. And behold, the

792 3739 1492 1722 3588 395 4254 846 2193
ἀστήρ, ὃν εἶδον ἐν τῇ ἀνατολῇ, προῆγεν αὐτούς, ἕως
star which they saw in the east went before them until

2064 2476 1883 3757 2258 3588 3813 1492 1161 3588 792
ἐλθὼν ἔστη ἐπάνω οὗ ἦν τὸ παιδίον. 10 ἰδόντες δὲ τὸν ἀστέρα,
coming it stood over where was the child. seeing And the star

5463 5479 3173 4970 2532 2064 1519 3588
ἐχάρησαν χαρὰν μεγάλην σφόδρα. 11 καὶ ἐλθόντες εἰς τὴν
they rejoiced a joy great exceedingly. And having come into the

3614 2147 3588 3813 3326 3137 3588 3384 846
οἰκίαν εἶδον τὸ παιδίον μετὰ Μαρίας τῆς μητρὸς αὐτοῦ,
house, they saw the child with Mary the mother of Him.

2532 4098 4352 846 2532 455 3588
καὶ πεσόντες προσεκύνησαν αὐτῷ, καὶ ἀνοίξαντες τοὺς
And falling down, they worshiped Him. And opening the

2344 846 4374 846 1435 5557 2532
θησαυροὺς αὐτῶν προσήνεγκαν αὐτῷ δῶρα, χρυσὸν καὶ
treasures of them they offered to Him gifts, gold and

3030 2532 4666 2532 5537 2596 3677 3361
λίβανον καὶ σμύρναν. 12 καὶ χρηματισθέντες κατ᾽ ὄναρ μὴ
frankincense and myrrh. And having been warned by a dream not

344 4314 2264 1223 243 3598 402 1519
ἀνακάμψαι πρὸς Ἡρώδην, δι᾽ ἄλλης ὁδοῦ ἀνεχώρησαν εἰς
to return to Herod, by another way they went back into

3588 5561 846
τὴν χώραν αὐτῶν.
the country of them.

King James Version

him.
4. And when he had gathered all the chief priests and scribes of the people together, he demanded of them where Christ should be born.

5 And they said unto him, In Bethlehem of Judaea: for thus it is written by the prophet,
6 And thou Bethlehem, (in) the land of Juda, art not the least among the princes of Juda: for out of thee shall come a Governor, that shall rule my people Israel. {rule: or, feed}

7. Then Herod, when he had privily called the wise men, enquired of them diligently what time the star appeared.

8 And he sent them to Bethlehem, and said, Go and search diligently for the young child; and when ye have found (him), bring me word again, that I may come and worship him also.

9 . When they had heard the king, they departed; and, lo, the star, which they saw in the east, went before them, till it came and stood over where the young child was.
10 When they saw the star, they rejoiced with exceeding great joy.
11. And when they were come into the house, they saw the young child with Mary his mother, and fell down, and worshipped him: and when they had opened their treasures, they presented unto him gifts; gold, and frankincense, and myrrh. {presented: or, offered}

12 And being warned of God in a dream that they should not return to Herod, they departed into their own country another way.

Literal Translation

13. And they having departed, an angel of (the) Lord appeared to Joseph by a dream, saying, Rise up! Take the child and His mother with you, and flee into Egypt. And be there until I shall tell you. For Herod is about to seek the child in order to destroy Him.

14 And rising up, he took along the child and His mother by night and withdrew into Egypt.

15 And he was there until the end of Herod, that might be fulfilled that spoken by the Lord through the prophet, saying, "Out of Egypt I have called My Son." (Hosea 11:1)

16 Then seeing that he was mocked by the wise men, Herod was greatly enraged, and having sent, he killed all the boys in Bethlehem and in all its districts, from two years old and under, according to the time which he exactly asked from the wise men.

17 Then was fulfilled that spoken by Jeremiah the prophet, saying:

18 "A voice was heard in Ramah, lamenting and wailing and great mourning, Rachel weeping (for) her children and was not willing to be comforted, because they were not." (Jer. 31:15)

19. But Herod having expired, behold, an angel of (the) Lord appears (to) Joseph by a dream in Egypt,

20 saying, Rising up, take along the child and His mother and pass over into (the) land of Israel; for those seeking the life of the child have expired.

21 And rising up, he

Matthew 2:13

402 1161 846 2400 32 2962
13 Ἀναχωρησάντων δὲ αὐτῶν, ἰδού, ἄγγελος Κυρίου
having departed And they, behold, an angel of (the) Lord

5316 2596 3677 3588 2501 3004 1453 3880
φαίνεται κατ' ὄναρ τῷ Ἰωσήφ, λέγων, Ἐγερθεὶς παράλαβε
appears by a dream to Joseph, saying, Rise up; take with (you)

3588 3813 2532 3588 3384 846 2532 5343 1519 125
τὸ παιδίον καὶ τὴν μητέρα αὐτοῦ, καὶ φεῦγε εἰς Αἴγυπτον,
the child and the mother of Him, and flee into Egypt

2532 2468 1563 2193 302 2036 4671 3195 1063 2264 2212 3588
καὶ ἴσθι ἐκεῖ ἕως ἂν εἴπω σοι· μέλλει γὰρ Ἡρώδης ζητεῖν τὸ
and be there until I shall say to you. is about For Herod to seek the

3813 3588 622 846 3588 1161 1453 3880 3588
παιδίον, τοῦ ἀπολέσαι αὐτό. 14 ὁ δὲ ἐγερθεὶς παρέλαβε τὸ
child, to destroy Him. he And rising up took along the

3813 2532 3588 3384 846 3571 2532 402 1519
παιδίον καὶ τὴν μητέρα αὐτοῦ νυκτὸς, καὶ ἀνεχώρησεν εἰς
child and the mother of Him by night, and withdrew into

125 2532 2258 1563 2193 3588 5054 2264 2443
Αἴγυπτον, 15 καὶ ἦν ἐκεῖ ἕως τῆς τελευτῆς Ἡρώδου· ἵνα
Egypt. And he was there until the death of Herod, that

4137 3588 4483 5259 3588 2962 1223 3588 4396
πληρωθῇ τὸ ῥηθὲν ὑπὸ τοῦ Κυρίου διὰ τοῦ προφήτου,
be fulfilled that spoken by the Lord through the prophet,

3004 1537 125 2564 3588 5207 3450 5119
λέγοντος, Ἐξ Αἰγύπτου ἐκάλεσα τὸν υἱόν μου. 16 τότε
saying, Out of Egypt I have called the Son of Me. Then

2264 1492 3754 1702 5259 3588 3097 2373
Ἡρώδης, ἰδὼν ὅτι ἐνεπαίχθη ὑπὸ τῶν μάγων, ἐθυμώθη
Herod, seeing that he was mocked by the Magi, was enraged

3029 2532 649 337 3956 3588 3816 3588 1722
λίαν, καὶ ἀποστείλας ἀνεῖλε πάντας τοὺς παῖδας τοὺς ἐν
greatly, and having sent, he killed all the boy-children in

965 2532 1722 3956 3588 3725 846 575 1332 2532
Βηθλεὲμ καὶ ἐν πᾶσι τοῖς ὁρίοις αὐτῆς ἀπὸ διετοῦς καὶ
Bethlehem and in all the districts of it, from two years and

2736 2596 3588 5550 3739 198 3844 3588 3097
κατωτέρω, κατὰ τὸν χρόνον ὃν ἠκρίβωσε παρὰ τῶν μάγων.
under, according to the time which he exactly asked from the Magi.

5119 4137 3588 4483 5259 2408 3588 4396
17 τότε ἐπληρώθη τὸ ῥηθὲν ὑπὸ Ἱερεμίου τοῦ προφήτου,
Then was fulfilled that spoken by Jeremiah the prophet,

3004 5456 1722 4471 191 2355 2532 2805
λέγοντος, 18 Φωνὴ ἐν Ῥαμᾶ ἠκούσθη, θρῆνος καὶ κλαυθμὸς
saying, A voice in Rama was heard, lamenting and wailing

2532 3602 4183 4478 2799 3588 5043 846 2532
καὶ ὀδυρμὸς πολύς, Ῥαχὴλ κλαίουσα τὰ τέκνα αὐτῆς, καὶ
and mourning much; Rachel weeping for the children of her, and

3756 2309 3870 3754 3756 1526 5053 1161
οὐκ ἤθελε παρακληθῆναι, ὅτι οὐκ εἰσί. 19 τελευτήσαντος δὲ
not willing to be comforted, because not they were. having expired But

3588 2264 2400 32 2962 2596 3677 5316 3588
τοῦ Ἡρώδου, ἰδού, ἄγγελος Κυρίου κατ' ὄναρ φαίνεται τῷ
Herod, behold, an angel of (the) Lord by a dream appears (to)

2501 1722 125 3004 1453 3880 3588 3813
Ἰωσὴφ ἐν Αἰγύπτῳ 20 λέγων, Ἐγερθεὶς παράλαβε τὸ παιδίον
Joseph in Egypt, saying, Rising up take along the child

2532 3588 3384 846 2532 4198 1519 1093 2474 2348
καὶ τὴν μητέρα αὐτοῦ, καὶ πορεύου εἰς γῆν Ἰσραήλ, τεθνή-
and the mother of Him, and pass over into (the) land of Israel; have

1063 3588 2212 3588 5590 3588 3813 3588 1161 1453
κασι γὰρ οἱ ζητοῦντες τὴν ψυχὴν τοῦ παιδίου. 21 ὁ δὲ ἐγερθεὶς
expired for those seeking the life of the child. he And rising up

King James Version

13. And when they were departed, behold, the angel of the Lord appeareth to Joseph in a dream, saying, Arise, and take the young child and his mother, and flee into Egypt, and be thou there until I bring thee word: for Herod will seek the young child to destroy him.

14 When he arose, he took the young child and his mother by night, and departed into Egypt:

15 And was there until the death of Herod: that it might be fulfilled which was spoken of the Lord by the prophet, saying, Out of Egypt have I called my son.

16 Then Herod, when he saw that he was mocked of the wise men, was exceeding wroth, and sent forth, and slew all the children that were in Bethlehem, and in all the coasts thereof, from two years old and under, according to the time which he had diligently enquired of the wise men.

17 Then was fulfilled that which was spoken by Jeremy the prophet, saying,

18 In Rama was there a voice heard, lamentation, and weeping, and great mourning, Rachel weeping (for) her children, and would not be comforted, because they are not.

19. But when Herod was dead, behold, an angel of the Lord appeareth in a dream to Joseph in Egypt,

20 Saying, Arise, and take the young child and his mother, and go into the land of Israel: for they are dead which sought the young child's life.

21 And he arose,

Literal Translation

Matthew 2:22

took along the child and His mother and came into (the) land of Israel.

22 But hearing that Archelaus reigns over Judea in place of his father Herod, he feared to go there. And being warned by a dream, he withdrew into the parts of Galilee.

23 And coming, he lived in a city called Nazareth, so as to fulfill that spoken by the prophets, ""He shall be called a Nazarene."

3880 3588 3813 2532 3588 3384 846 2532 2064 1519
παρέλαβε τὸ παιδίον καὶ τὴν μητέρα αὐτοῦ, καὶ ἦλθεν εἰς
took along the child and the mother of Him, and came into

1093 2474 191 1161 3754 745 936 1909 3588
γῆν Ἰσραήλ. 22 ἀκούσας δὲ ὅτι Ἀρχέλαος βασιλεύει ἐπὶ τῆς
(the) land of Israel. hearing But that Archelaus reigns over

2449 473 2264 3588 3962 846 5399 1563
Ἰουδαίας ἀντὶ Ἡρώδου τοῦ πατρὸς αὐτοῦ, ἐφοβήθη ἐκεῖ
Judea in place of Herod the father of him, he feared there

565 5537 1161 2596 3677 402 1519 3588 3313
ἀπελθεῖν· χρηματισθεὶς δὲ κατ᾽ ὄναρ, ἀνεχώρησεν εἰς τὰ μέρη
to go. being warned And by a dream, he withdrew into the parts

3588 1056 2532 2064 2730 1519 4172 3004
τῆς Γαλιλαίας, 23 καὶ ἐλθὼν κατῴκησεν εἰς πόλιν λεγομένην
of Galilee. And having come he dwelt in a city being called

3478 3704 4137 3588 4483 1223 3588 4396 3754
Ναζαρέθ· ὅπως πληρωθῇ τὸ ῥηθὲν διὰ τῶν προφητῶν ὅτι
Nazareth; thus to fulfill that spoken through the prophet:

3480 2564
Ναζωραῖος κληθήσεται.
A Nazarene He shall be called.

King James Version

took the young child and his mother, and came into the land of Israel.

22 But when he heard that Archelaus did reign in Judaea in the room of his father Herod, he was afraid to go thither: notwithstanding, being warned of God in a dream, he turned aside into the parts of Galilee:

23 And he came and dwelt in a city called Nazareth: that it might be fulfilled which was spoken by the prophets, He shall be called a Nazarene.

Matthew 3

1. Now in those days John the Baptist came proclaiming in the deserted (place) of Judea, **2** and saying, Repent! For the kingdom of Heaven has drawn near.

3 For this is he spoken of by Isaiah the prophet, saying: "A voice crying in the deserted (place): Prepare the way of (the) Lord! Make His paths straight!" (Isa. 40:3)

4 And John himself had his clothing from hairs of a camel, and a belt of leather about his loin. And his food was locusts and wild honey.

5. Then Jerusalem and all Judea went out to him, and all the neighborhood of the Jordan,

6 and were baptized by him in the Jordan, confessing their sins.

7 But seeing many of the Pharisees and Sadducees coming to his baptism,

Matthew 3

1722 1161 3588 2250 1565 3854 2491 3588
1 Ἐν δὲ ταῖς ἡμέραις ἐκείναις παραγίνεται Ἰωάννης ὁ
in And days those comes John the

910 2784 1722 3588 2048 3588 2449 2532 3004
βαπτιστὴς κηρύσσων ἐν τῇ ἐρήμῳ τῆς Ἰουδαίας 2 καὶ λέγων,
Baptist proclaiming in the deserted (place) of Judea, and saying,

3340 1488 1063 3588 932 3588 3772 3778
Μετανοεῖτε· ἤγγικε γὰρ ἡ βασιλεία τῶν οὐρανῶν. 3 ουτος
Repent! has come near For the kingdom of Heaven. this

1063 2076 3588 4483 5259 2268 3588 4396 3004
γάρ ἐστιν ὁ ῥηθεὶς ὑπὸ Ἡσαΐου τοῦ προφήτου, λέγοντος,
For is the (one) spoken of by Isaiah the prophet, saying,

5456 994 1722 3588 2048 2090 3588 3598 2962
Φωνὴ βοῶντος ἐν τῇ ἐρήμῳ, Ἑτοιμάσατε τὴν ὁδὸν Κυρίου·
A voice crying in the deserted (place),Prepare the way of (the) Lord;

2117 4160 3588 5147 846 846 1161 3588 2491 2192
εὐθείας ποιεῖτε τὰς τρίβους αὐτοῦ. 4 Αὐτὸς δὲ ὁ Ἰωάννης εἶχε
straight make the paths of Him. he And, John, had

3588 1742 846 575 2359 2574 2532 2223 1193
τὸ ἔνδυμα αὐτοῦ ἀπὸ τριχῶν καμήλου, καὶ ζώνην δερ-
the clothing of him from hairs of a camel, and a belt of

4012 3588 3751 846 3588 1161 5160 846 2258
ματίνην περὶ τὴν ὀσφὺν αὐτοῦ· ἡ δὲ τροφὴ αὐτοῦ ἦν
leather around the loin of him; the and food of him was

200 2532 3192 66 5119 1607 4314 846
ἀκρίδες καὶ μέλι ἄγριον. 5 τότε ἐξεπορεύετο πρὸς αὐτὸν
locusts and wild honey. Then went out to him

2414 2532 3956 3588 2449 2532 3956 3588 4066 3588
Ἱεροσόλυμα καὶ πᾶσα ἡ Ἰουδαία καὶ πᾶσα ἡ περίχωρος τοῦ
Jerusalem and all Judea and all the neighborhood of the

2446 2532 907 1722 3588 2446 5259 846
Ἰορδάνου· 6 καὶ ἐβαπτίζοντο ἐν τῷ Ἰορδάνῃ ὑπ᾽ αὐτοῦ,
Jordan, and were baptized in the Jordan by him

1843 3588 266 846 1492 1161 4183 3588
ἐξομολογούμενοι τὰς ἁμαρτίας αὐτῶν. 7 Ἰδὼν δὲ πολλοὺς τῶν
having confessed the sins of them. seeing And many of the

5330 2532 4523 2064 1909 3588 908
Φαρισαίων καὶ Σαδδουκαίων ἐρχομένους ἐπὶ τὸ βάπτισμα
Pharisees and Sadducees coming on the baptism

Matthew 3

1. In those days came John the Baptist, preaching in the wilderness of Judaea,
2 And saying, Repent ye: for the kingdom of heaven is at hand.

3 For this is he that was spoken of by the prophet Esaias, saying, The voice of one crying in the wilderness, Prepare ye the way of the Lord, make his paths straight.

4 And the same John had his raiment of camel's hair, and a leathern girdle about his loins; and his meat was locusts and wild honey.

5. Then went out to him Jerusalem, and all Judaea, and all the region round about Jordan,

6 And were baptized of him in Jordan, confessing their sins.

7 But when he saw many of the Pharisees and Sadducees come to his baptism,

Literal Translation | **Matthew 3:8** | **King James Version**

Literal Translation

he said to them, Offspring of vipers! Who warned you to flee from the wrath to come?

8 Then produce fruits worthy of repentance.

9 And do not think to say within yourselves, We have a father, Abraham. For I say to you that God is able to raise up children to Abraham from these stones.
10 But already the axe is even laid at the root of the trees; therefore, any tree not producing good fruit is cut off and is thrown into fire.

11 I indeed baptize you in water to repentance; but He (who is) coming after me is stronger than me,of whom I am not worthy to lift the sandals. He will baptize you in (the) Holy Spirit and fire,

12 whose fan (is) in His hand, and He will cleanse His floor and will gather His wheat into the barn. But He will burn up the chaff with fire that cannot be put out.

13. Then Jesus arrives from Galilee to the Jordan, to John, to be baptized by him.

14 But John restrained Him, saying, I have need to be baptized by You, and do You come to me?
15 But answering, Jesus said to him, Allow (it) now, for it is becoming to us this way to fulfill all righteousness. Then he allows Him.

16 And having been baptized, Jesus went up immediately from the water. And, behold! The heavens were opened to Him, and He saw

846 2036 846 1081 2191 5101 5263 5213
αὐτοῦ, εἶπεν αὐτοῖς, Γεννήματα ἐχιδνῶν, τίς ὑπέδειξεν ὑμῖν
of him, he said to them, Offspring of vipers! Who warned you

5343 575 3588 3195 3709 4160 3767 2590
φυγεῖν ἀπὸ τῆς μελλούσης ὀργῆς; 8 ποιήσατε οὖν καρποὺς
to flee from the coming wrath? Produce then fruits

514 3588 3341 2532 3361 1380 3004 1722 1438
ἀξίους τῆς μετανοίας· 9 καὶ μὴ δόξητε λέγειν ἐν ἑαυτοῖς,
worthy of repentance; and not do think to say in yourself

3962 2192 3588 11 3004 1063 5213 3754 1410 3588
Πατέρα ἔχομεν τὸν Ἀβραάμ· λέγω γὰρ ὑμῖν ὅτι δύναται ὁ
A father we have Abraham. I say For to you that is able

2316 1537 3588 3037 5130 1453 5043 3588 11 2235
θεὸς ἐκ τῶν λίθων τούτων ἐγεῖραι τέκνα τῷ Ἀβραάμ. 10 ἤδη
God out of stones these to raise up children to Abraham. already

1161/2532/3588 513 4314 3588 4491 3588 1186 2749 3956 3767
δὲ καὶ ἡ ἀξίνη πρὸς τὴν ῥίζαν τῶν δένδρων κεῖται· πᾶν οὖν
And even the axe at the root of the trees is laid. any Then

1186 3361 4160 2590 2570 1581 2532 1519 4442
δένδρον μὴ ποιοῦν καρπὸν καλὸν ἐκκόπτεται καὶ εἰς πῦρ
tree not producing fruit good is cut off and into fire

906 1473 3303 907 5209 1722 5204 1519 3341 3588
βάλλεται. 11 ἐγὼ μὲν βαπτίζω ὑμᾶς ἐν ὕδατι εἰς μετάνοιαν· ὁ
is thrown. I indeed baptize you in water to repentance. He

1161 3694 3450 2064 2478 3450 2076 3739 3756 1510
δὲ ὀπίσω μου ἐρχόμενος ἰσχυρότερός μου ἐστίν, οὗ οὐκ εἰμὶ
But after me coming stronger (than) me is, of whom not I am

2425 3588 5266 941 846 5209 907 1722
ἱκανὸς τὰ ὑποδήματα βαστάσαι· αὐτὸς ὑμᾶς βαπτίσει ἐν
worthy the sandals to bear; He you will baptize in

4151 40 2532 4442 3739 3588 4425 1722 3588 5495 846
Πνεύματι Ἁγίῳ καὶ πυρί· 12 οὗ τὸ πτύον ἐν τῇ χειρὶ αὐτοῦ,
(the) Spirit Holy and fire; of whom the fan (is) in the hand of Him,

2532 1245 3588 257 846 2532 4863 3588 4621
καὶ διακαθαριεῖ τὴν ἅλωνα αὐτοῦ, καὶ συνάξει τὸν σῖτον
And He will cleanse the floor of Him, and will gather the wheat

846 1519 3588 596 3588 1161 892 2618 4442
αὐτοῦ εἰς τὴν ἀποθήκην, τὸ δὲ ἄχυρον κατακαύσει πυρὶ
of Him into the barn, the but chaff He will burn with fire

762 5119 3854 3588 2424 575 3588 1056 1909
ἀσβέστῳ. 13. Τότε παραγίνεται ὁ Ἰησοῦς ἀπὸ τῆς Γαλιλαίας ἐπὶ
unquenchable. Then arrives Jesus from Galilee at

3588 2446 4314 3588 2491 3588 907 5259
τὸν Ἰορδάνην πρὸς τὸν Ἰωάννην, τοῦ βαπτισθῆναι ὑπ'
the Jordan to John, to be baptized by

846 3588 1161 2491 1254 846 3004 1473 5532
αὐτοῦ. 14 ὁ δὲ Ἰωάννης διεκώλυεν αὐτόν, λέγων, Ἐγὼ χρε-
him. But John restrained Him, saying I need

2192 5259 4675 907 2532 4771 2064 4314 3165 611
ίαν ἔχω ὑπὸ σοῦ βαπτισθῆναι, καὶ σὺ ἔρχῃ πρός με; 15 ἀποκ-
have by You to be baptized, and You come to me? answering

1161 3588 2424 2036 4314 846 863 737 3779
ριθεὶς δὲ ὁ Ἰησοῦς εἶπε πρὸς αὐτόν, Ἄφες ἄρτι· οὕτω
But Jesus said to him, Allow (it) now; thus

1063 4241 2076 2254 4137 3956 1343 5119
γὰρ πρέπον ἐστὶν ἡμῖν πληρῶσαι πᾶσαν δικαιοσύνην. τότε
for becoming it is to us to fulfill all righteousness. Then

863 846 2532 907 3588 2424 305 2117 575
ἀφίησιν αὐτόν. 16 καὶ βαπτισθεὶς ὁ Ἰησοῦς ἀνέβη εὐθὺς ἀπὸ
he allows Him. And being baptized, Jesus went up at once from

3588 5204 2532 2400 455 846 3588 3772 2532 1492
τοῦ ὕδατος· καὶ ἰδού, ἀνεῴχθησαν αὐτῷ οἱ οὐρανοί, καὶ εἶδε
the water. And, behold, were opened to Him the heavens, and He saw

King James Version

he said unto them, O generation of vipers, who hath warned you to flee from the wrath to come?
8 Bring forth therefore fruits meet for repentance:
9 And think not to say within yourselves, We have Abraham to (our) father: for I say unto you, that God is able of these stones to raise up children unto Abraham.
10 And now also the axe is laid unto the root of the trees: therefore every tree which bringeth not forth good fruit is hewn down, and cast into the fire.

11 I indeed baptize you with water unto repentance: but he that cometh after me is mightier than I, whose shoes I am not worthy to bear: he shall baptize you with the Holy Ghost, and (with) fire:

12 Whose fan (is) in his hand, and he will throughly purge his floor, and gather his wheat into the garner; but he will burn up the chaff with unquenchable fire.

13. Then cometh Jesus from Galilee to Jordan unto John, to be baptized of him.

14 But John forbad him, saying, I have need to be baptized of thee, and comest thou to me?
15 And Jesus answering said unto him, Suffer (it to be so) now: for thus it becometh us to fulfil all righteousness. Then he suffered him.

16 And Jesus, when he was baptized, went up straightway out of the water: and, lo, the heavens were opened unto him, and he saw

Matthew 3:17

Literal Translation

the Spirit of God coming down as a dove, and coming upon Him.

17 And behold! A voice out of the heavens saying, This is My Son, the Beloved, in whom I have found delight. (Ps. 2:7; Isa. 42:1)

3588 4151 3588 2316 2597 5616 4058 2532
τὸ Πνεῦμα τοῦ θεοῦ καταβαῖνον ὡσεὶ περιστερὰν καὶ
the Spirit of God descending as a dove, and

2064 1909 846 2532 2400 5456 1537 3588 3772
ἐρχόμενον ἐπ' αὐτόν. 17 καὶ ἰδού, φωνὴ ἐκ τῶν οὐρανῶν,
coming upon Him. And behold! A voice out of the heavens,

3004 3778 2076 3588 5207 3450 3588 27 1722 3739 2106
λέγουσα, Οὗτός ἐστιν ὁ υἱός μου ὁ ἀγαπητός, ἐν ᾧ εὐδόκησα.
saying, This is the Son of Me, the Beloved, in whom I was delighted.

King James Version

the Spirit of God descending like a dove, and lighting upon him:

17 And lo a voice from heaven, saying, This is my beloved Son, in whom I am well pleased.

Matthew 4

1. Then Jesus was led up into the wilderness by the Spirit, to be tempted by the devil.
2 And having fasted forty days and forty nights, afterwards He hungered.

3 And coming near to Him, the Tempter said, If You are (the) Son of God, speak that these stones may become loaves.
4 But answering, He said, It has been written: "Man shall not live on bread alone, but by every word going out of (the) mouth of God." (Deut. 8:3)

5 Then the devil takes Him to the holy city, and (he) set Him on the wing of the temple.

6 And (he) said to Him, If You are (the) Son of God, throw Yourself down; for it has been written: "He shall give His angels charge concerning You, and they shall bear You on (their) hands, lest You strike Your foot against a stone." (Ps. 91:11, 12)
7 Jesus said to him, Again it has been written: "You shall not tempt (the) Lord your God." (Deut. 6:16)
8 Again the devil takes Him to a very high mountain, and (he) showed to Him all the kingdoms of the world and their glory.
9 And (he) said to Him. I will give all these things to You if falling down, You

Matthew 4

5119 3588 2424 321 1519 3588 2048 5259 3588 4151
1. Τότε ὁ Ἰησοῦς ἀνήχθη εἰς τὴν ἔρημον ὑπὸ τοῦ Πνεύ-
Then Jesus was led into the deserted (place) by the Spirit,

3985 5259 3588 1228 2532 3522
ματος, πειρασθῆναι ὑπὸ τοῦ διαβόλου. 2 καὶ νηστεύσας
to be tested by the devil. and Having fasted

2250 5062 2532 3571 5062 5305
ἡμέρας τεσσαράκοντα καὶ νύκτας τεσσαράκοντα, ὕστερον
days forty and nights forty, afterward

3983 2532 4334 846 3588 3985 2036 1487 5207
ἐπείνασε. 3 Καὶ προσελθὼν αὐτῷ ὁ πειράζων εἶπεν, Εἰ υἱὸς
He hungered. And coming near to Him the tempter said, If Son

1488 3588 2316 2036 2443 3588 3037 3778 740 1096 3588 1161
εἶ τοῦ θεοῦ, εἰπὲ ἵνα οἱ λίθοι οὗτοι ἄρτοι γένωνται. 4 ὁ δὲ
You are of God, say that stones these loaves may become. He But

611 2036 1125 3756 1909 740 3441 2198
ἀποκριθεὶς εἶπε, Γέγραπται, Οὐκ ἐπ' ἄρτῳ μόνῳ ζήσεται
answering said, It has been written, Not on bread alone shall live

444 235 1909 3956 4487 1607 1223 4750
ἄνθρωπος, ἀλλ' ἐπὶ παντὶ ῥήματι ἐκπορευομένῳ διὰ στό-
man, but on every word proceeding through (the)

2316 5119 3880 846 3588 1228 1519 3588
ματος θεοῦ. 5 Τότε παραλαμβάνει αὐτὸν ὁ διάβολος εἰς τὴν
mouth of God. Then takes Him the devil into the

40 4172 2532 476 846 1909 3588 4419 3588 2411
ἁγίαν πόλιν, καὶ ἵστησιν αὐτὸν ἐπὶ τὸ πτερύγιον τοῦ ἱεροῦ,
holy city, and sets Him on the wing of the temple.

2532 3004 846 1487 5207 1488 3588 2316 906 4572 2736
6 καὶ λέγει αὐτῷ, Εἰ υἱὸς εἶ τοῦ θεοῦ, βάλε σεαυτὸν κάτω·
and says to Him, If Son you are of God, throw Yourself down;

1125 1063 3754 3588 32 846 1781 4012
γέγραπται γὰρ ὅτι Τοῖς ἀγγέλοις αὐτοῦ ἐντελεῖται περὶ
it has been written for, that the angels of Him He will give charge about

4675 2532 1909 5495 142 4571 3379 4350 4314
σοῦ, καὶ ἐπὶ χειρῶν ἀροῦσί σε, μήποτε προσκόψῃς πρὸς
You, and on hands they will bear You, that not you strike against

3037 3588 4228 4675 5346 846 3588 2424 3825 1125
λίθον τὸν πόδα σοῦ. 7 ἔφη αὐτῷ ὁ Ἰησοῦς, Πάλιν γέγραπται,
a stone the foot of You. said to him Jesus, Again it has been written,

3756 1598 2962 3588 2316 4675 3825 3880
Οὐκ ἐκπειράσεις Κύριον τὸν θεόν σου. 8 πάλιν παραλαμβάνει
Not you shall tempt (the) Lord God of you. Again takes

846 3588 1228 1519 3735 5308 3029 2532 1166 846
αὐτὸν ὁ διάβολος εἰς ὄρος ὑψηλὸν λίαν, καὶ δείκνυσιν αὐτῷ
Him the devil into a mount high exceeding, and shows Him

3956 3588 932 3588 2889 2532 3588 1391 846 2532
πάσας τὰς βασιλείας τοῦ κόσμου καὶ τὴν δόξαν αὐτῶν, 9 καὶ
all the kingdoms of the world, and the glory of them, and

3004 846 5023 3956 4671 1325 1437 4698 4352
λέγει αὐτῷ, Ταῦτα πάντα σοι δώσω, ἐὰν πεσὼν προσ-
says to Him, These things all to You I will give, if falling down you

Matthew 4

1. Then was Jesus led up of the Spirit into the wilderness to be tempted of the devil.
2 And when he had fasted forty days and forty nights, he was afterward an hungred.

3 And when the tempter came to him, he said, If thou be the Son of God, command that these stones be made bread.
4 But he answered and said, It is written, Man shall not live by bread alone, but by every word that proceedeth out of the mouth of God.

5 Then the devil taketh him up into the holy city, and setteth him on a pinnacle of the temple,

6 And saith unto him, If thou be the Son of God, cast thyself down: for it is written, He shall give his angels charge concerning thee: and in (their) hands they shall bear thee up, lest at any time thou dash thy foot against a stone.

7 Jesus said unto him, It is written again, Thou shalt not tempt the Lord thy God.
8 Again, the devil taketh him up into an exceeding high mountain, and sheweth him all the kingdoms of the world, and the glory of them;
9 And saith unto him, All these things will I give thee, if thou wilt fall down

Literal Translation

Matthew 4:10

King James Version

will worship me.
10 Then Jesus said to him, Go, Satan! For it has been written: "You shall worship (the) Lord your God, and you shall serve Him only." (Deut. 6:13)
11 Then the devil leaves Him. And behold! Angels came near and ministered to Him.
12. But Jesus having heard that John was delivered up, He withdrew into Galilee.

3427 5119 3004 846 3588 2424 5217 4567
κυνήσῃς μοι. 10 τότε λέγει αὐτῷ ὁ Ἰησοῦς, Ὕπαγε, Σατανᾶ·
will worship me. Then says to him Jesus, Go, Satan;
1125 1063 2962 3588 2316 4675 4352 2532
γέγραπται γάρ, Κύριον τὸν θεόν σου προσκυνήσεις, καὶ
it has been written For, (the) Lord God of you you shall worship, and
846 3441 3000 5119 863 846 3588 1228 2532
αὐτῷ μόνῳ λατρεύσεις. 11 τότε ἀφίησιν αὐτὸν ὁ διάβολος· καὶ
Him only you shall serve. Then leaves Him the devil. And
2400 32 4334 2532 1247 846 191 1161
ἰδού, ἄγγελοι προσῆλθον καὶ διηκόνουν αὐτῷ. 12. Ἀκούσας δὲ
behold! Angels came near and ministered to Him. having heard But
3588 2424 3754 2491 3860 402 1519 3588
ὁ Ἰησοῦς ὅτι Ἰωάννης παρεδόθη, ἀνεχώρησεν εἰς τὴν
Jesus that John was delivered up, He withdrew into

worship me.
10 Then saith Jesus unto him, Get thee hence, Satan: for it is written, Thou shalt worship the Lord thy God, and him only shalt thou serve.
11 Then the devil leaveth him, and, behold, angels came and ministered unto him.
12. Now when Jesus had heard that John was cast into prison, he departed into Galilee;

13 And leaving Nazareth, coming He lived at Capernaum, beside the sea in (the) districts of Zebulun and Naphtali,

1056 2532 2641 3588 3478 2064 2730
Γαλιλαίαν. 13 καὶ καταλιπὼν τὴν Ναζαρέθ, ἐλθὼν κατῴκησεν
Galilee. And having left Nazareth, having come, He lived
1519 2584 3588 3864 1722 3725 2194
εἰς Καπερναοὺμ τὴν παραθαλασσίαν, ἐν ὁρίοις Ζαβουλὼν
in Capernaum beside the sea, in districts of Zebulun

13 And leaving Nazareth, he came and dwelt in Capernaum, which is upon the sea coast, in the borders of Zabulon and Nephthalim:

14 that might be fulfilled that spoken through Isaiah the prophet, saying:
15 "Land of Zebulun and land of Naphtali, way of (the) sea, beyond the Jordan, Galilee of the nations:
16 the people sitting in the darkness saw a great Light; and to those sitting in (the) region and shadow of death, Light sprang up to them." (Isa. 9:1, 2)

2532 3508 2443 4137 3588 4483 1223 2268 3588 4396
καὶ Νεφθαλείμ· 14 ἵνα πληρωθῇ τὸ ῥηθὲν διὰ Ἡσαΐου τοῦ προ-
and Napthali; that may be fulfilled that spoken through Isaiah the
3004 1093 2194 2532 1093 3508 3598
φήτου, λέγοντος, 15 Γῆ Ζαβουλὼν καὶ γῆ Νεφθαλείμ, ὁδὸν
prophet, saying, Land of Zebulun and land of Napthali, way
2281 4008 3588 2446 1056 3588 1484 3588 2992
θαλάσσης, πέραν τοῦ Ἰορδάνου, Γαλιλαία τῶν ἐθνῶν, 16 ὁ λαὸς
of the sea, beyond the Jordan, Galilee of the nations, the people
3588 2521 1722 4655 1492 5457 3173 2532 3588 2521 1722
ὁ καθήμενος ἐν σκότει εἶδε φῶς μέγα, καὶ τοῖς καθημένοις ἐν
sitting in darkness saw a light great, and to those sitting in
5561 2532 4639 2288 5457 393 846
χώρᾳ καὶ σκιᾷ θανάτου, φῶς ἀνέτειλεν αὐτοῖς.
a region and shadow of death, light has sprung up to them.

14 That it might be fulfilled which was spoken by Esaias the prophet, saying,
15 The land of Zabulon, and the land of Nephthalim, (by) the way of the sea, beyond Jordan, Galilee of the Gentiles;
16 The people which sat in darkness saw great light; and to them which sat in the region and shadow of death light is sprung up.

17 From then Jesus began to proclaim and to say, Repent! For the kingdom of Heaven has drawn near.

575 5119 756 3588 2424 2784 2532 3004
17. Ἀπὸ τότε ἤρξατο ὁ Ἰησοῦς κηρύσσειν καὶ λέγειν,
From then began Jesus to proclaim and to say,
3340 1448 1063 3588 932 3588 3772
Μετανοεῖτε· ἤγγικε γὰρ ἡ βασιλεία τῶν οὐρανῶν.
Repent! has drawn near For the kingdom of Heaven.

17 From that time Jesus began to preach, and to say, Repent: for the kingdom of heaven is at hand.

18. And walking beside the sea of Galilee, Jesus saw two brothers, Simon called Peter and his brother Andrew casting a net into the sea; for they were fishers.
19 And He says to them, Come after Me, and I will make you fishers of men.
20 And leaving the nets, they immediately followed Him.
21 And going on from there, He saw two other brothers, James the (son) of Zebedee

4043 1161 3588 2424 3844 3588 2281 3588
18. Περιπατῶν δὲ ὁ Ἰησοῦς παρὰ τὴν θάλασσαν τῆς
walking about And Jesus beside the sea
1056 1492 1417 80 4613 3588 3004 4074
Γαλιλαίας εἶδε δύο ἀδελφούς, Σίμωνα τὸν λεγόμενον Πέτρον,
of Galilee, saw two brothers, Simon being called Peter,
2532 406 3588 80 846 906 293
καὶ Ἀνδρέαν τὸν ἀδελφὸν αὐτοῦ, βάλλοντας ἀμφίβληστρον
and Andrew the brother of him, casting a net
1519 3588 2281 2258 1063 231 2532 3004 846 1205
εἰς τὴν θάλασσαν· ἦσαν γὰρ ἁλιεῖς. 19 καὶ λέγει αὐτοῖς, Δεῦτε
into the sea. they were For fishers. And He says to them, Come
3694 3450 2532 4160 5209 231 444 3588 1161 2112
ὀπίσω μου, καὶ ποιήσω ὑμᾶς ἁλιεῖς ἀνθρώπων. 20. οἱ δὲ εὐθέως
after Me, and I will make you fishers of men. they And at once
863 3588 1350 190 846 2532 4260 1564
ἀφέντες τὰ δίκτυα ἠκολούθησαν αὐτῷ. 21 Καὶ προβὰς ἐκεῖθεν,
forsaking the nets followed Him. And going on from there
1492 243 1417 80 2385 3588 3588 2199 2532
εἶδεν ἄλλους δύο ἀδελφούς, Ἰάκωβον τὸν τοῦ Ζεβεδαίου καὶ
He saw other two brothers, James the (son) of Zebedee, and

18. And Jesus, walking by the sea of Galilee, saw two brethren, Simon called Peter, and Andrew his brother, casting a net into the sea: for they were fishers.
19 And he saith unto them, Follow me, and I will make you fishers of men.
20 And they straightway left (their) nets, and followed him.
21 And going on from thence, he saw other two brethren, James (the son) of Zebedee,

Literal Translation | **Matthew 4:22** | ***King James Version***

and his brother John in the boat with their father Zebedee, mending their nets. And He called them.

2491 3588 80 846 1722 3588 4143 3326 2199
Ἰωάννην τὸν ἀδελφὸν αὐτοῦ, ἐν τῷ πλοίῳ μετὰ Ζεβεδαίου
John the brother of him, in the boat with Zebedee

3588 3962 846 2675 3588 1350 846
τοῦ πατρὸς αὐτῶν, καταρτίζοντας τὰ δίκτυα αὐτῶν·
the father of them, mending the nets of them;

2532 2564 846
καὶ ἐκάλεσεν αὐτούς.
and He called them.

and John his brother, in a ship with Zebedee their father, mending their nets; and he called them.

22 And at once leaving the boat and their father, they followed Him.

3588 1161 2112 863 3588 4143 2532
22 οἱ δὲ εὐθέως ἀφέντες τὸ πλοῖον καὶ
they And at once forsaking the boat and

3588 3962 846 190 846
τὸν πατέρα αὐτῶν ἠκολούθησαν αὐτῷ.
the father of them followed Him.

22 And they immediately left the ship and their father, and followed him.

23. And Jesus went around all Galilee teaching in their synagogues and proclaiming the gospel of the kingdom, and healing every disease and every (one of the) illnesses among the people.

2532 4013 3650 3588 1056 3588 2424 1321
23. Καὶ περιῆγεν ὅλην τὴν Γαλιλαίαν ὁ Ἰησοῦς, διδάσκων
And went about all Galilee Jesus, teaching

1722 3588 4864 846 2532 2784 3588 2098
ἐν ταῖς συναγωγαῖς αὐτῶν, καὶ κηρύσσων τὸ εὐαγγέλιον
in the synagogues of them, and proclaiming the gospel

3588 932 2532 2323 3956 3554 2532 3956
τῆς βασιλείας, καὶ θεραπεύων πᾶσαν νόσον καὶ πᾶσαν
of the kingdom, and healing every disease and every

3119 1722 3588 2992
μαλακίαν ἐν τῷ λαῷ.
sickness among the people.

23. And Jesus went about all Galilee, teaching in their synagogues, and preaching the gospel of the kingdom, and healing all manner of sickness and all manner of disease among the people.

24 And the report of Him went out into all Syria. And they brought to Him all the ones having illness, suffering various diseases and torments, also (those) having been demon-possessed, and (those) having been moonstruck, and paralytics; and He healed them.

2532 565 3588 189 846 1519 3650
24 καὶ ἀπῆλθεν ἡ ἀκοὴ αὐτοῦ εἰς ὅλην
And went the report of Him into all

3588 4947 2532 4374 846 3956 3588 2560
τὴν Συρίαν· καὶ προσήνεγκαν αὐτῷ πάντας τοὺς κακῶς
Syria. And they brought to Him all those illness

2192 4164 3554 2532 931 4912 2532
ἔχοντας, ποικίλαις νόσοις καὶ βασάνοις συνεχομένους, καὶ
having, various diseases and torments suffering, and

1139 2532 4583 2532 3885
δαιμονιζομένους, καὶ σεληνιαζομένους, καὶ παραλυτικούς·
having been demon-possessed, and having been moonstruck, and paralytics.

2532 2323 846
καὶ ἐθεράπευσεν αὐτούς.
And He healed them.

24 And his fame went throughout all Syria: and they brought unto him all sick people that were taken with divers diseases and torments, and those which were possessed with devils, and those which were lunatick, and those that had the palsy; and he healed them.

25 And great crowds followed Him from Galilee and Decapolis, and Jerusalem, and Judea, and beyond the Jordan.

2532 190 846 3793
25 καὶ ἠκολούθησαν αὐτῷ ὄχλοι
And followed Him crowds

4183 575 3588 1056 2532 1179 2532 2414
πολλοὶ ἀπὸ τῆς Γαλιλαίας καὶ Δεκαπόλεως καὶ Ἱεροσολύμων
great from Galilee and Decapolis and Jerusalem

2532 2449 2532 4008 3588 2446
καὶ Ἰουδαίας καὶ πέραν τοῦ Ἰορδάνου.
and Judea, and beyond the Jordan.

25 And there followed him great multitudes of people from Galilee, and (from) Decapolis, and (from) Jerusalem, and (from) Judaea, and (from) beyond Jordan.

Matthew 5 | Matthew 5 | Matthew 5

1. But seeing the crowds, He went up into the mountain, and seating Himself, His disciples came near to Him. 2 And opening His mouth, He began to teach them, saying:

1492 1161 3588 3793 305 1519 3588 3735 2532 2523
1. Ἰδὼν δὲ τοὺς ὄχλους ἀνέβη εἰς τὸ ὄρος καὶ καθίσαντος
seeing And the crowds, He went into the mount, and sitting down

846 4334 846 3588 3101 846
αὐτοῦ, προσῆλθον αὐτῷ οἱ μαθηταὶ αὐτοῦ·
Himself, came near to Him the disciples of Him.

2532 455 3588 4750 846 1321 846 3004
2 καὶ ἀνοίξας τὸ στομα αὐτοῦ, ἐδίδασκεν αὐτούς, λέγων,
And opening the mouth of Him, He began to teach them, saying,

1. And seeing the multitudes, he went up into a mountain: and when he was set, his disciples came unto him:
2 And he opened his mouth, and taught them, saying,

3 Blessed (are) the poor in spirit! For theirs is the kingdom of Heaven.

3107 3588 4434 3588 4151 3754 846 2076 3588
3. Μακάριοι οἱ πτωχοὶ τῷ πνεύματι· ὅτι αὐτῶν ἐστιν ἡ
Blessed (are) the poor in spirit; because of them is the

932 3588 3772
βασιλέια των οὐρανῶν
kingdom of Heaven.

3 Blessed (are) the poor in spirit: for theirs is the kingdom of heaven.

4 Blessed (are) the (ones) mourning! For they shall be comforted.

3107 3588 3996 3754 846 3870
4. Μακάριοι οἱ πενθοῦντες· ὅτι αὐτοὶ παρακληθήσονται.
Blessed (are) the (ones) mourning; because they shall be comforted.

4 Blessed (are) they that mourn: for they shall be comforted.

Literal Translation | **Matthew 5:5** | **King James Version**

5 Blessed (are) the meek! For they shall inherit the earth. (Ps. 37:11)

6 Blessed (are) the (ones) hungering and thirsting after righteousness! For they shall be filled.

7 Blessed (are) the merciful! For they shall obtain mercy.

8 Blessed (are) the pure in heart! For they shall see God.

9 Blessed (are) the peacemakers! For they shall be called sons of God.

10 Blessed (are) the (ones) being persecuted for righteousness' sake! For theirs is the kingdom of Heaven.

11 Blessed are you when they shall reproach you, and persecute (you), and shall say every evil word against you, lying, on account of Me.

12 Rejoice and leap for joy, for your reward (is) great in Heaven; for in this way they persecuted the prophets who were before you.

13. You are the salt of the earth, but if the salt becomes tasteless, with what shall it be salted? For it has strength for nothing any more except to be thrown out and to be trampled under by men.

14 You are the light of the world. A city situated on a mountain cannot be hidden.

15 Nor do they light a lamp and put it under the grain measure, but on the lampstand; and it shines for all those in the house.

16 So let your light shine before men, so that they may see your good works, and may glorify

3107 3588 4239 3754 846 2816 3588 1093
5. Μακάριοι οἱ πρᾳεῖς· ὅτι αὐτοὶ κληρονομήσουσι τὴν γῆν.
Blessed (are) the meek; because they shall inherit the earth.

3107 3588 3983 2532 1372 3588 1343
6. Μακάριοι οἱ πεινῶντες καὶ διψῶντες τὴν δικαιοσύνην·
Blessed (are) the(ones) hungering and thirsting (after) righteousness;
3754 846 5526
ὅτι αὐτοὶ χορτασθήσονται.
because they shall be filled.

3107 3588 1655 3754 846 1653
7. Μακάριοι οἱ ἐλεήμονες· ὅτι αὐτοὶ ἐλεηθήσονται.
Blessed (are) the merciful; because they shall receive mercy.

3107 3588 2513 3588 2588 3754 846 3588 2316
8. Μακάριοι οἱ καθαροὶ τῇ καρδίᾳ· ὅτι αὐτοὶ τὸν Θεὸν
Blessed (are) the pure in heart; because they God
3700
ὄψονται.
shall see.

3107 3588 1518 3754 846 5207 2316 2564
9. Μακάριοι οἱ εἰρηνοποιοί· ὅτι αὐτοὶ υἱοὶ Θεοῦ κληθήσονται.
Blessed (are) the peacemakers; because they sons of God shall be called.

3107 3588 1377 1752 1343 3754 846
10. Μακάριοι οἱ δεδιωγμένοι ἕνεκεν δικαιοσύνης· ὅτι αὐτῶν
Blessed (are) those being persecuted because of righteousness; for of them
2076 3588 932 3588 3772 3107 2075 3752
ἐστιν ἡ βασιλεία τῶν οὐρανῶν. 11. Μακάριοί ἐστε, ὅταν
is the kingdom of Heaven. Blessed are you when
3679 5209 2532 1377 2532 2036 3956 4190 4487
ονειδίσωσιν υμᾶς καὶ διώξωσι, καὶ εἴπωσι πᾶν πονηρὸν ρῆμα
they will reproach you, and persecute, and shall say every evil word
2596 5216 5574 1752 1700 5463 2532 21
καθ' υμῶν ψευδομενοι, ενεκεν εμου· 12 χαιρετε καὶ ἀγαλλιᾶσθε,
against you lying, because of Me. Rejoice and be very glad,
3754 3588 3408 5216 4183 1722 3588 3772 3779 1063 1377
ὅτι ὁ μισθὸς ὑμῶν πολὺς ἐν τοῖς οὐρανοῖς· οὕτω γὰρ ἐδίω-
for the reward of you (is) great in Heaven; thus for they perse-
3588 4396 3588 4253 5216
ξαν τοὺς προφήτας τοὺς πρὸ ὑμῶν.
cuted the prophets before you.

5210 2075 3588 217 3588 1093 1437 1161 3588 217 3471 1722
13. Ὑμεῖς ἐστε τὸ ἅλας τῆς γῆς· ἐὰν δὲ τὸ ἅλας μωρανθῇ, ἐν
You are the salt of the earth; if but the salt be tasteless, by
5101 233 1519 3762 2480 2089 1487 3361 906 1854
τίνι ἁλισθήσεται; εἰς οὐδὲν ἰσχύει ἔτι, εἰ μὴ βληθῆναι ἔξω
what shall it be salted? For nothing it is strong still, except to be thrown out,
2532 2662 5259 3588 444 5210 2075 3588 5457
καὶ καταπατεῖσθαι ὑπὸ τῶν ἀνθρώπων. 14 ὑμεῖς ἐστε τὸ φῶς
and to be trampled under by men. You are the light
3588 2889 3756 1410 4172 2928 1883 3735
τοῦ κόσμου. οὐ δύναται πόλις κρυβῆναι ἐπάνω ὄρους
of the world. not is able A city to be hidden on a mount
2749 3761 2545 3088 2532 5087 846 5259 3588
κειμένη· 15 οὐδὲ καίουσι λύχνον καὶ τιθέασιν αὐτὸν ὑπὸ τὸν
situated; Nor do they light a lamp and place it under the
3426 235 1909 3588 3087 2532 2989 3956 3588 1722 3588
μόδιον, ἀλλ' ἐπὶ τὴν λυχνίαν, καὶ λάμπει πᾶσι τοῖς ἐν τῇ
grain measure, but on the lampstand, and it lightens all those in the
3614 3779 2989 3588 5457 5216 1715 3588 444
οἰκίᾳ. 16 οὕτω λαμψάτω τὸ φῶς ὑμῶν ἔμπροσθεν τῶν ἀνθρώ-
house. So let shine the light of you before men,
3704 1492 5216 3588 2570 2041 2532 1392 3588
πων, ὅπως ἴδωσιν ὑμῶν τὰ καλὰ ἔργα, καὶ δοξάσωσι τὸν
so that they may see of you the good works, and may glorify the

5 Blessed (are) the meek: for they shall inherit the earth.

6 Blessed (are) they which do hunger and thirst after righteousness: for they shall be filled.

7 Blessed (are) the merciful: for they shall obtain mercy.

8 Blessed (are) the pure in heart: for they shall see God.

9 Blessed (are) the peacemakers: for they shall be called the children of God.

10 Blessed (are) they which are persecuted for righteousness' sake: for theirs is the kingdom of heaven.

11 Blessed are ye, when (men) shall revile you, and persecute (you), and shall say all manner of evil against you falsely, for my sake.

12 Rejoice, and be exceeding glad: for great (is) your reward in heaven: for so persecuted they the prophets which were before you.

13. Ye are the salt of the earth: but if the salt have lost his savour, wherewith shall it be salted? it is thenceforth good for nothing, but to be cast out, and to be trodden under foot of men.

14 Ye are the light of the world. A city that is set on an hill cannot be hid.

15 Neither do men light a candle, and put it under a bushel, but on a candlestick; and it giveth light unto all that are in the house.

16 Let your light so shine before men, that they may see your good works, and glorify

Literal Translation | **Matthew 5:17** | ***King James Version***

your Father in heaven.

17. Think not that I come to destroy the Law, or the Prophets: I did not come to destroy, but to fulfil.
18 For truly I say to you, Till heaven and earth should pass away, one jot or one tittle shall in no way pass away from the Law, till all be fulfilled.

19 Therefore whoever relaxes one of these commandments, the least, and shall teach men so, he shall be called least in the kingdom of Heaven. But whoever does and teaches (them), this one shall be called great in the kingdom of Heaven.

20 For I say to you, If your righteousness shall not exceed (the righteousness) of the scribes and Pharisees, ye shall in no case enter into the kingdom of heaven.

21. Ye have heard that it was said by them of old time, Thou shalt not kill; and whosoever shall kill shall be in danger of the judgment:
22 But I say to you that each who is angry with his brother without a cause shall be liable to the Judgment: and whoever says to his brother, Raca, shall be liable to the Sanhedrin; and whoever says, Fool, shall be liable to the hell of fire.
23 If then you off your gift before the altar, and there remember that your brother has a thing against you,

24 leave there your gift before the altar, and go, first be reconciled to your brother,

3962 5216 3588 1722 3588 3772
πατέρα ὑμῶν τὸν ἐν τοῖς οὐρανοῖς.
Father of you in Heaven.

3361 3543 3754 2064 2647 3588 3551 2228 3588
17. Μὴ νομίσητε ὅτι ἦλθον καταλῦσαι τὸν νόμον ἢ τοὺς
Not do think that I came to disintegrate the Law or the

4396 3756 2064 2647 235 4137 281
προφήτας· οὐκ ἦλθον καταλῦσαι ἀλλὰ πληρῶσαι. 18 ἀμὴν
Prophets; not I came to disintegrate, but to fulfill. truly

1063 3004 5213 2193 302 3928 3588 3772 2532 3588 1093 2503
γὰρ λέγω ὑμῖν, ἕως ἂν παρέλθῃ ὁ οὐρανὸς καὶ η γῆ, ἰῶτα
For I say to you, Until should pass away the heaven and the earth, iota

1520 2228 3391 2762 3756 3361 3928 575 3588 3551 2193 302
ἓν ἢ μία κεραία οὐ μὴ παρέλθῃ ἀπὸ τοῦ νόμου, ἕως ἂν
one or one point in no way shall pass away from the Law, until should

3956 1096 3739 1437 3767 3089 3391 3588 1785 5130
πάντα γένηται. 19 ὃς ἐὰν οὖν λύσῃ μίαν τῶν ἐντολῶν τούτων
all things occur. Whoever, then, releases one commandments of these

3588 1646 2532 1321 3779 3588 444 1646
τῶν ἐλαχίστων, καὶ διδάξῃ οὕτω τοὺς ἀνθρώπους, ἐλά-
the least, and teaches so men,

2564 1722 3588 932 3588 3772 3739 1161 302
χιστος κληθήσεται ἐν τῇ βασιλείᾳ τῶν οὐρανῶν· ὃς δ' ἂν
least he shall be called in the kingdom of Heaven; who but ever

4160 2532 1321 3778 3173 2564 1722 3588 932
ποιήσῃ καὶ διδάξῃ, οὗτος μέγας κληθήσεται ἐν τῇ βασιλείᾳ
does (them) and teaches, this one great shall be called in the kingdom

3588 3772 3004 1063 5213 3754 1437 3361 4052 3588
τῶν οὐρανῶν. 20 λέγω γὰρ ὑμῖν ὅτι ἐὰν μὴ περισσεύσῃ ἡ
of Heaven. I say For to you that if not shall exceed the

1343 5216 4119 3588 1122 2532 5330
δικαιοσύνη ὑμῶν πλεῖον τῶν γραμματέων καὶ Φαρισαίων,
righteousness of you more (than) the scribes and Pharisees,

3756 3361 1525 1519 3588 932 3588 3772
οὐ μὴ εἰσέλθητε εἰς τὴν βασιλείαν τῶν οὐρανῶν.
in no way shall you go into the kingdom of Heaven.

191 3754 4483 3588 744 3756 5407 3739 1161
21. Ἠκούσατε ὅτι ἐρρέθη τοῖς ἀρχαίοις, Οὐ φονεύσεις· ὃς δ'
You have heard that it was said of the ancients, Not do murder; who but

302 5407 1777 2071 3588 2920 1473 1161 3004 5213
ἂν φονεύσῃ, ἔνοχος ἔσται τῇ κρίσει. 22 ἐγὼ δὲ λέγω ὑμῖν
ever has murdered, liable shall be to the Judgment. I But say to you

3754 3956 3588 3710 3588 80 846 1500 1777 2071
ὅτι πᾶς ὁ ὀργιζόμενος τῷ ἀδελφῷ αὐτοῦ εἰκῇ ἔνοχος ἔσται
that each who is angry with the brother of him without cause liable shall be

3588 2920 3739 1161 302 2036 3588 80 846 4469 1777
τῇ κρίσει· ὃς δ' ἂν εἴπῃ τῷ ἀδελφῷ αὐτοῦ, Ῥακά, ἔνοχος
to the Judgment; who and ever says to the brother of him, Raca, liable

2071 3588 4892 3739 1161 302 2036 3474 1777 2071 1519
ἔσται τῷ συνεδρίῳ· ὃς δ' ἂν εἴπῃ, Μωρέ, ἔνοχος ἔσται εἰς
shall be to the Sanhedrin; who and ever says, Fool, liable shall be into

3588 1067 3588 4442 1437 3767 4374 3588 1435 4675
τὴν γέενναν τοῦ πυρός. 23 ἐὰν οὖν προσφέρῃς τὸ δῶρόν σου
the Gehenna of fire. If then you offer the gift of you

1909 3588 2379 2546 3415 3754 3588 80 4675 2192
ἐπὶ τὸ θυσιαστήριον, κἀκεῖ μνησθῇς ὅτι ὁ ἀδελφός σου ἔχει
on the altar, and there remember that the brother of you has

5100 2596 4675 863 1563 3588 1435 4675 1715 3588 2379
τι κατὰ σοῦ, 24 ἄφες ἐκεῖ τὸ δῶρόν σου ἔμπροσθεν τοῦ θυσια-
a thing against you, leave there the gift of you before the altar,

2532 5217 4412 1259 3588 80 4675
στηρίου, καὶ ὕπαγε, πρῶτον διαλλάγηθι τῷ ἀδελφῷ σου,
and go, first be reconciled to the brother of you,

your Father which is in heaven.

17. Think not that I am come to destroy the law, or the prophets: I am not come to destroy, but to fulfil.
18 For verily I say unto you, Till heaven and earth pass, one jot or one tittle shall in no wise pass from the law, till all be fulfilled.

19 Whosoever therefore shall break one of these least commandments, and shall teach men so, he shall be called the least in the kingdom of heaven: but whosoever shall do and teach (them), the same shall be called great in the kingdom of heaven.

20 For I say unto you, That except your righteousness shall exceed (the righteousness) of the scribes and Pharisees, ye shall in no case enter into the kingdom of heaven.

21. Ye have heard that it was said by them of old time, Thou shalt not kill; and whosoever shall kill shall be in danger of the judgment:
22 But I say unto you, That whosoever is angry with his brother without a cause shall be in danger of the judgment: and whosoever shall say to his brother, Raca, shall be in danger of the council: but whosoever shall say, Thou fool, shall be in danger of hell fire.
23 Therefore if thou bring thy gift to the altar, and there rememberest that thy brother hath ought against thee;

24 Leave there thy gift before the altar, and go thy way; first be reconciled to thy brother,

Literal Translation | **Matthew 5:25** | *King James Version*

and then coming, offer your gift.
25 Be well-minded toward your opponent quickly, while you are in the way with him, that the adversary not deliver you to the judge, and the judge deliver you to the officer, and you be thrown into prison.
26 Truly, I say to you, In no way shall you come out from there until you pay the last kodrantes.

27. You have heard that it was said to the ancients: "Do not commit adultery." (Ex. 20:14; Deut. 5:18)
28 But I say to you, Everyone looking at a woman to lust after her has already committed adultery with her in his heart.
29 But if your right eye offends you, take it out and throw (it) from you, for (it is) profitable to you that one of your members should perish and all your body not be thrown into Hell.
30 And if your right hand causes you to offend, cut it off and throw (it) from you, for (it is) profitable to you that one of your members should perish and all your body not be thrown into Hell.
31. It was also said, Whoever puts away his wife, let him give her a bill of divorce. (Deut. 24:1)

32 But I say to you, Whoever puts away his wife, apart from a matter of fornication, causes her to commit adultery. And who ever shall marry the one put away commits adultery.
33. Again, you have heard that it was said to the ancients: "You shall not swear falsely, but shall give your oaths to the Lord." (Lev. 19:12; Num. 30:2)
34 But I say to you, Do not swear at all, neither by Heaven, because it is God's throne;

2532 5119 2064 4374 3588 1435 4675 2468 2132 3588
καὶ τότε ἐλθὼν πρόσφερε τὸ δῶρόν σου. 25 Ἴσθι εὐνοῶν τῷ
And then coming offer the gift of you. Be well-minded to the

476 4675 5035 2193 3755 1488 1722 3588 3598 3326 846
ἀντιδίκῳ σου ταχύ, ἕως ὅτου εἶ ἐν τῇ ὁδῷ μετ' αὐτοῦ,
opponent of you quickly, until that you are in the way with him,

3379 4571 3860 3588 476 3588 2923 2532 3588 2923 4571
μήποτέ σε παραδῷ ὁ ἀντίδικος τῷ κριτῇ, καὶ ὁ κριτής σε
that not you deliver the adversary to the judge, and the judge you

3860 3588 5257 2532 1519 5438 906 281 3004
παραδῷ τῷ ὑπηρέτῃ, καὶ εἰς φυλακὴν βληθήσῃ. 26 ἀμὴν λέγω
deliver to the officer, and into prison you be thrown. Truly I say

4671 3756 3361 1831 1564 2193 302 591 3588 2078
σοι, οὐ μὴ ἐξέλθῃς ἐκεῖθεν, ἕως ἂν ἀποδῷς τὸν ἔσχατον
to you, not ever will you come out from there, until you should pay the last

2835 191 3754 4483 3588 744 3756 3431
κοδράντην. 27. Ἠκούσατε ὅτι ἐρρέθη τοῖς ἀρχαίοις, Οὐ μοιχεύ
kodrantes. You have heard that it was said to the ancients, Not commit

1473 1161 3004 5213 3754 3956 3588 991 1135 4314 3588
σεις· 28 ἐγὼ δὲ λέγω ὑμῖν, ὅτι πᾶς ὁ βλέπων γυναικα πρὸς τὸ
adultery. I But I say to you, that everyone looking at a woman in order to

1937 846 2235 3431 846 1722 3588 2588 846
ἐπιθυμῆσαι αὐτῆς ἤδη ἐμοίχευσεν αὐτὴν ἐν τῇ καρδίᾳ αὐτοῦ.
lust after her already has commited adultery with her in the heart of him.

1487/1161/3588 3788 4675 3588 1188 4624 4571 1807 846
29 εἰ δὲ ὁ ὀφθαλμός σου ὁ δεξιὸς σκανδαλίζει σε, ἔξελε αὐτὸν
if But the eye of you right offends you, take out it

2532 906 575 4675 4851 1063 4671 2443 622 1520 3588
καὶ βάλε ἀπὸ σοῦ· συμφέρει γάρ σοι ἵνα ἀπόληται ἓν τῶν
and throw (it) from you; profitable for to you that should perish one of the

3196 4675 2532 3361 3650 3588 4983 4675 906 1519 1067 2532
μελῶν σου, καὶ μὴ ὅλον τὸ σῶμά σου βληθῇ εἰς γέενναν. 30 καὶ
parts of you, and not all the body of you be cast into Gehenna. And

1487/3588/1188/4675 5495 4624 4571 1581 846 2532 906
εἰ ἡ δεξιά σου χεὶρ σκανδαλίζει σε, ἔκκοψον αὐτὴν καὶ βάλε
if the right of you hand cause to offend you, cut off it and throw

575 4675 4851 1063 4671 2443 622 1520 3588 3196 4675
ἀπὸ σοῦ· συμφέρει γάρ σοι ἵνα ἀπόληται ἓν τῶν μελῶν σου,
from you; profitable for for you that should perish one of the parts of you,

2532 3361 3650 3588 4983 4675 906 1519 1067 4483 1161 3754
καὶ μὴ ὅλον τὸ σῶμά σου βληθῇ εἰς γέενναν. 31. ἐρρέθη δέ ὅτι
and not all the body of you be cast into Gehenna. it was said And,

3739 302 630 3588 1135 846 1325 846 647
Ὃς ἂν ἀπολύσῃ τὴν γυναῖκα αὐτοῦ, δότω αὐτῇ ἀπος-
Whoever puts away the wife of him, let him give her a bill of

1473 1161 3004 5213 3754 3739 302 630 3588 1135
τάσιον. 32 ἐγω δὲ λέγω ὑμῖν, ὅτι ὃς ἂν ἀπολύσῃ τὴν γυναῖκα
divorce. I But say to you that whoever puts away the wife

846 3924 3056 4202 4160 846 3429
αὐτοῦ, παρεκτὸς λόγου πορνείας, ποιεῖ αὐτὴν μοιχᾶσθαι·
of him apart from a matter of fornication causes her to commit adultery,

2532 3739 1437 630 1060 3429
καὶ ὃς ἐὰν ἀπολελυμένην γαμήσῃ μοιχᾶται.
and whoever the put away one shall marry commits adultery.

3825 191 3754 4483 3588 744 3756 1964
33. Πάλιν ηκούσατε ὅτι ἐρρέθη τοῖς ἀρχαίοις, Οὐκ ἐπιορκή-
Again, you have heard that it was said to the ancients, Not you shall per-,

591 1161 3588 2962 3588 3727 4675 1473 1161 3004
σεις, ἀποδώσεις δὲ τῷ Κυρίῳ τοὺς ὅρκους σου· 34 ἐγὼ δὲ λέγω
jure, shall deliver but to the Lord the oaths of you. I But say

5213 3361 3660 3654 3383 1722 3588 3772 3754 2362 2076
ὑμῖν μὴ ὀμόσαι ὅλως· μήτε ἐν τῷ οὐρανῷ, ὅτι θρόνος ἐστὶ
to you not do swear (at) all; neither by Heaven, because throne it is

and then come and offer thy gift.
25 Agree with thine adversary quickly, whiles thou art in the way with him; lest at any time the adversary deliver thee to the judge, and the judge deliver thee to the officer, and thou be cast into prison.
26 Verily I say unto thee, Thou shalt by no means come out thence, till thou hast paid the uttermost farthing.

27. Ye have heard that it was said by them of old time, Thou shalt not commit adultery:
28 But I say unto you, That whosoever looketh on a woman to lust after her hath committed adultery with her already in his heart.

29 And if thy right eye offend thee, pluck it out, and cast (it) from thee: for it is profitable for thee that one of thy members should perish, and not (that) thy whole body should be cast into hell.
30 And if thy right hand offend thee, cut it off, and cast (it) from thee: for it is profitable for thee that one of thy members should perish, and not (that) thy whole body should be cast into hell.
31. It hath been said, Whosoever shall put away his wife, let him give her a writing of divorcement:
32 But I say unto you, That whosoever shall put away his wife, saving for the cause of fornication, causeth her to commit adultery: and whosoever shall marry her that is divorced committeth adultery.
33. Again, ye have heard that it hath been said by them of old time, Thou shalt not forswear thyself, but shalt perform unto the Lord thine oaths:
34 But I say unto you, Swear not at all; neither by heaven; for it is God's throne:

Matthew 5:35

Literal Translation

35 nor by the earth, because it is the footstool of His feet; nor by Jerusalem, because it is (the) city of the great King. (Isa. 66:1; Ps. 48:2)

36 Nor shall you swear by your head, because you are not able to make one hair white or black.
37 But let your word be Yes, yes; No, no; but the excess of these is from evil.

38. You have heard that it was said: "An eye for an eye, and a tooth for a tooth;" (Ex. 21:24; Lev. 24:20; Deut. 19:21)
39 but I say to you, Do not resist the malicious (one); but whoever strikes you on your right cheek, turn the other to him also.
40 And to him desiring to sue you, and to take your tunic, allow him also (to have) the coat.
41 And whoever shall compel you to go one mile, go two with him.
42 The (one) asking you to give, and the (one) wishing to borrow from you, do not turn away.

43. You have heard that it was said, "You shall love your neighbor and hate your enemy;" (Lev. 19:18)
44 but I say to you, Love your enemies; bless those cursing you, do well to those hating you; and pray for those abusing and persecuting you,

45 so that you may be sons of your Father in Heaven. Because He causes the sun to rise on (the) evil and (the) good, and sends rain on the just and unjust.

46 For if you love those loving you,

3588 2316 3383 1722 3588 1093 3754 5286 2076 3588 4228
τοῦ Θεοῦ· 35 μήτε ἐν τῇ γῇ, ὅτι ὑποπόδιόν ἐστι τῶν ποδῶν
of God; neither by the earth, because footstool it is of the feet

846 3383 1519 2414 3754 4172 2076 3588 3173
αὐτοῦ· μήτε εἰς Ἱεροσόλυμα, ὅτι πόλις ἐστὶ τοῦ μεγάλου
of Him; neither by Jerusalem, because city it is of the great

935 3383 1722 3588 2776 4675 3660 3754/3756 1410
βασιλέως· 36 μήτε ἐν τῇ κεφαλῇ σου ὀμόσῃς, ὅτι οὐ δύνασαι
King; neither by the head of you swear, because not you can

3391 2359 3022 2228 3189 4160 2077 1161 3588 3056
μίαν τρίχα λευκὴν ἢ μέλαιναν ποιῆσαι. 37 ἔστω δὲ ὁ λόγος
one hair white or black make. let be But the word

5216 3483/3483/3756/3756/3588/1161 4053 5130 1537 3588 4190
ὑμῶν, ναὶ ναί, οὒ οὔ· τὸ δὲ περισσὸν τούτων ἐκ τοῦ πονηροῦ
of you, Yes, yes, No, no; the but excess of these from the evil

2076 191 3754 4483 3788 473 3788 2532
ἐστιν. 38. Ἠκούσατε ὅτι ἐρρέθη, Ὀφθαλμὸν ἀντὶ ὀφθαλμοῦ, καὶ
is. You have heard that it was said, An eye for an eye and

3599 473 3599 1473 1161 3004 5213 3361 436 3588
ὀδόντα ἀντὶ ὀδόντος· 39 ἐγὼ δὲ λέγω ὑμῖν μὴ ἀντιστῆναι τῷ
a tooth for a tooth; I but say to you, Not do resist the

4190 235 3748 4571 4474 1909 3588 1188 4675 4600
πονηρῷ· ἀλλ' ὅστις σε ῥαπίσει ἐπὶ τὴν δεξιὰν σου σιαγόνα,
malicious; but whoever you strikes on the right of you cheek,

4762 846 2532 3588 243 2532 3588 2309 4671 2919
στρέψον αὐτῷ καὶ τὴν ἄλλην· 40 καὶ τῷ θέλοντί σοι κριθῆναι
turn to him also the other. And the (one) wishing you to sue

2532 3588 5509 4675 2983 863 846 2532 3588 2440 2532
καὶ τὸν χιτῶνά σου λαβεῖν, ἄφες αὐτῷ καὶ τὸ ἱμάτιον· 41 καὶ
and the tunic of you take, allow him also the coat. And

3748 4571 29 3400 1520 5217 3326 846 1417 3588
ὅστις σε ἀγγαρεύσει μίλιον ἕν, ὕπαγε μετ' αὐτοῦ δύο. 42 τῷ
whoever you shall force to go mile one, go with him two. The (one)

154 4571 1325 2532 3588 2309 575 4675 1155 3361
αἰτοῦντί σε δίδου· καὶ τὸν θέλοντα ἀπὸ σοῦ δανείσασθαι μὴ
asking you to give; and the (one) wishing from you to borrow not

654
ἀποστραφῇς.
do turn away.

191 3754 4483 25 3588 4139 4675 2532
43. Ἠκούσατε ὅτι ἐρρέθη, Ἀγαπήσεις τὸν πλησίον σου, καὶ
You have heard that it was said, You shall love the neighbor of you, and

3404 3588 2190 4675 1473 1161 3004 5213 25 3588
μισήσεις τὸν ἐχθρόν σου· 44 ἐγὼ δὲ λέγω ὑμῖν, ἀγαπᾶτε τοὺς
you shall hate the enemy of you; I but say to you, Love the

2190 5216 2127 3588 2672 5209 2573
ἐχθροὺς ὑμῶν, εὐλογεῖτε τοὺς καταρωμένους ὑμᾶς, καλῶς
enemies of you, bless the ones cursing you, well

4160 3588 3404 5209 2532 4336 5228 3588
ποιεῖτε τοὺς μισοῦντας ὑμᾶς, καὶ προσεύχεσθε ὑπὲρ τῶν
do to the ones hating you, and pray on behalf of those

1908 5209 2532 1377 5209 3704 1096
ἐπηπεαζόντων ὑμᾶς, καὶ διωκόντων ὑμᾶς· 45 ὅπως γένησθε
abusing you, and persecuting you; so that you may be

5207 3588 3962 5216 3588 1722 3772 3754 3588 2246 846
υἱοὶ τοῦ πατρὸς ὑμῶν τοῦ ἐν οὐρανοῖς, ὅτι τὸν ἥλιον αὐτοῦ
sons of the Father of you in Heaven, Because the sun of Him

393 1909 4190 2532 18 2532 1026 1909
ἀνατέλλει ἐπὶ πονηροὺς καὶ ἀγαθούς, καὶ βρέχει ἐπὶ
He makes rise on (the) evil and (the) good, and sends rain on

1342 2532 94 1437 1063 25 3588 25
δικαίους καὶ ἀδίκους. 46 ἐὰν γὰρ ἀγαπήσητε τοὺς ἀγαπῶντας
(the) just and (the) unjust. if For you love the (ones) loving

King James Version

35 Nor by the earth; for it is his footstool: neither by Jerusalem; for it is the city of the great King.

36 Neither shalt thou swear by thy head, because thou canst not make one hair white or black.
37 But let your communication be, Yea, yea; Nay, nay: for whatsoever is more than these cometh of evil.
38. Ye have heard that it hath been said, An eye for an eye, and a tooth for a tooth:
39 But I say unto you, That ye resist not evil: but whosoever shall smite thee on thy right cheek, turn to him the other also.

40 And if any man will sue thee at the law, and take away thy coat, let him have (thy) cloke also.
41 And whosoever shall compel thee to go a mile, go with him twain.
42 Give to him that asketh thee, and from him that would borrow of thee turn not thou away.

43. Ye have heard that it hath been said, Thou shalt love thy neighbour, and hate thine enemy.
44 But I say unto you, Love your enemies, bless them that curse you, do good to them that hate you, and pray for them which despitefully use you, and persecute you;

45 That ye may be the children of your Father which is in heaven: for he maketh his sun to rise on the evil and on the good, and sendeth rain on the just and on the unjust.

46 For if ye love them which love you,

Literal Translation

Matthew 5:47

King James Version

what reward do you have? Do not even the tax-collectors do the same?
47 And if you only greet your brothers, what exceptional (thing) do you do? Do not the tax-collectors do so?

48 Therefore, you be perfect even as your Father in Heaven is perfect.

5209 5101 3408 2192 3780 2532 3588 5057 3588 846
ὑμᾶς, τίνα μισθὸν ἔχετε; οὐχὶ καὶ οἱ τελῶναι τὸ αὐτὸ
you, what reward have you? Not even the tax-collectors the same
4160 2532 1437 782 3588 80 5216 3440
ποιοῦσι; 47 καὶ ἐὰν ἀσπάσησθε τοὺς ἀδελφοὺς ὑμῶν μόνον,
do? And if you greet the brothers of you only,
5101 4053 4160 3780 2532 3588 5057 3779 4160
τί περισσὸν ποιεῖτε; οὐχὶ καὶ οἱ τελῶναι οὕτω ποιοῦσιν;
what exceptional do you? Not even the tax-collectors so do?
2071 3767 5210 5046 5618 3588/3962 5216/3588/1722/3588
48 ἔσεσθε οὖν ὑμεῖς τέλειοι, ὥσπερ ὁ πατὴρ ὑμῶν ὁ ἐν τοῖς
be then You perfect, even as the Father of you in
3772 5046 2076
οὐρανοῖς τέλειός ἐστι.
Heaven perfect is.

what reward have ye? do not even the publicans the same?

47 And if ye salute your brethren only, what do ye more (than others)? do not even the publicans so?

48 Be ye therefore perfect, even as your Father which is in heaven is perfect.

Matthew 6

1. Take care not to do your merciful deeds before men in order to be seen of them. Otherwise, you have no reward from your Father in Heaven.

4337 3588 1654 5216 3361 4160 1715
1. Προσέχετε τὴν ἐλεημοσύνην ὑμῶν μὴ ποιεῖν ἔμπροσθεν
Take care the merciful deeds of you not to do before
3588 444 4314 3588 2300 846 1487 1161 3361
τῶν ἀνθρώπων, πρὸς τὸ θεαθῆναι αὐτοῖς· εἰ δὲ μήγε,
men, in order to be seen of them; if but not,
3408 3756 2192 3844 3588 3962 5216 3588 1722 3588 3772
μισθὸν οὐκ ἔχετε παρὰ τῷ πατρὶ ὑμῶν τῷ ἐν τοῖς οὐρανοῖς.
reward not you have from the Father of you in Heaven.

1. Take heed that ye do not your alms before men, to be seen of them: otherwise ye have no reward of your Father which is in heaven.

2 Therefore, when you do merciful deeds, do not trumpet before you as the hypocrites do in the synagogues and in the streets, so that they may be glorified by men. Truly I say to you, they have their reward.

3 But you doing merciful deeds, do not let your left know what your right hand does,

3752 3767 4160 1654 3361 4537 1715
2. Ὅταν οὖν ποιῇς ἐλεημοσύνην, μὴ σαλπίσῃς ἔμπροσθέν
when Then you do merciful deeds, not do trumpet before
4675 5618 3588 5273 4160 1722 3588 4864 2532
σου, ὥσπερ οἱ ὑποκριταὶ ποιοῦσιν ἐν ταῖς συναγωγαῖς καὶ
you, as the hypocrites do in the synagogues and
1722 3588 4505 3704 1392 5259 3588 444
ἐν ταῖς ῥύμαις, ὅπως δοξασθῶσιν ὑπὸ τῶν ἀνθρώπων·
in the streets, so that they may be glorified by men.
281 3004 5213 568 3588 3408 846 4675 1161 4160
ἀμὴν λέγω ὑμῖν, ἀπέχουσι τὸν μισθὸν αὐτῶν. 3 σοῦ δὲ ποιοῦν-
Truly I say to you, they have the reward of them. you But doing
1654 3361 1097 3588 710 4675 5101 4160 3588
τος ἐλεημοσύνην, μὴ γνώτω ἡ ἀριστερά σου τί ποιεῖ ἡ
merciful deeds, not do let know the left of you what does the
1188 4675 3704 5600 4675 3588 1654 1722 3588 2927 2532 3588
δεξιά σου, 4 ὅπως ᾖ σου ἡ ἐλεημοσύνη ἐν τῷ κρυπτῷ· καὶ ὁ
right of you, so that may be of you the merciful deeds in secret, andthe
3962 4675 3588 991 1722 3588 2927 846 591 4671 1722
πατήρ σου ὁ βλέπων ἐν τῷ κρυπτῷ αὐτὸς ἀποδώσει σοι ἐν
Father of you seeing in secret Him(self) will repay you in
3588 5318
τῷ φανερῷ.
the open.

2 Therefore when thou doest (thine) alms, do not sound a trumpet before thee, as the hypocrites do in the synagogues and in the streets, that they may have glory of men. Verily I say unto you, They have their reward.

3 But when thou doest alms, let not thy left hand know what thy right hand doeth:

4 so that your merciful deeds may be in secret. And your Father seeing in secret Himself will repay you in the open.

4 That thine alms may be in secret: and thy Father which seeth in secret himself shall reward thee openly.

5. And when you pray, you shall not be as the hypocrites, for they love to pray standing in the synagogues and in the corners of the open streets so that they may shine to men. Truly I say to you, they have their reward.

2532 3752 4336 3756 2071 5618 3588 5273 3754
5. Καὶ ὅταν προσεύχῃ, οὐκ ἔσῃ ὥσπερ οἱ ὑποκριταί, ὅτι
And when you pray, not you shall be as the hypocrites; because
5368 1722 3588 4864 2532 1722 3588 1137 3588
φιλοῦσιν ἐν ταῖς συναγωγαῖς καὶ ἐν ταῖς γωνίαις τῶν
they love in the synagogues and in the corners of the
4113 2476 4336 3704 302 5316 3588
πλατειῶν ἑστῶτες προσεύχεσθαι, ὅπως ἂν φανῶσι τοῖς
open streets standing to pray, so that they may shine
444 281 3004 5213 3754 568 3588 3408
ἀνθρώποις· ἀμὴν λέγω ὑμῖν ὅτι ἀπέχουσι τὸν μισθὸν
to men. Truly, I say to you that they have the reward

5. And when thou prayest, thou shalt not be as the hypocrites (are): for they love to pray standing in the synagogues and in the corners of the streets, that they may be seen of men. Verily I say unto you, They have their reward.

Matthew 6:6

Literal Translation

6 But you, when you pray, enter into your room and shutting your door, pray to your Father in secret. And your Father seeing in secret will repay you in the open.

7 But when you pray, do not babble vain words, as the nations; for they think that they shall be heard in their much speaking.

8 Then do not be like them, for your Father knows what (things) you have need of before you ask Him.

9 Then you (should) pray this way: Our Father who is in Heaven, let be sanctified Your name.
10 Let Your kingdom come; let Your will be done, as (it is) in Heaven, also on the earth.

11 Give us today our daily bread,

12 and forgive us our debts as we also forgive our debtors.

13 And do not lead us into temptation, but deliver us from the evil, for Yours is the kingdom and the power and the glory to the ages. Amen.

14 For if you forgive men their offenses, your heavenly Father will also forgive you.
15 But if you do not forgive men their offenses, neither will your Father forgive your offenses.

16. And when you fast, do not be as the hypocrites, (with) sullen face, for they disfigure their faces so that

846 4771 1161 3752 4336 1525 1519 3588 5009 4675
αὐτῶν. 6 σὺ δὲ, ὅταν προσεύχῃ, εἴσελθε εἰς τὸ ταμιεῖόν σου,
of them. you But, when you pray, enter into the room of you

2532 2808 3588 2374 4675 4336 3588 3962 4675 3588
καὶ κλείσας τὴν θύραν σου, πρόσευξαι τῷ πατρί σου τῷ
and shutting the door of you, pray to the Father of you

1722 3588 2927 2532 3588 3962 4675 3588 991 1722 3588 2927
ἐν τῷ κρυπτῷ· καὶ ὁ πατήρ σου ὁ βλέπων ἐν τῷ κρυπτῷ
in secret; and the Father of you seeing in secret

591 4671 1722 3588 5318 4336 1161 3361 945
ἀποδώσει σοι ἐν τῷ φανερῷ. 7 προσευχόμενοι δὲ μὴ βαττο-
will repay you in the open. when praying But, not do use

5618 3588 1482 1380 1063 3754 1722 3588 4180
λογήσητε, ὥσπερ οἱ ἐθνικοί. δοκοῦσι γὰρ ὅτι ἐν τῇ πολυ-
vain repetition, as the nations, they think for that in the much

846 1522 3361 3767 3666 846
λογίᾳ αὐτῶν εἰσακουσθήσονται. 8 μὴ οὖν ὁμοιωθῆτε αὐτοῖς·
speaking of them they will be heard. not Then do be like them;

1492 1063 3588 3962 5216 3739 5532 2192 4253 3588 5209
οἶδε γὰρ ὁ πατὴρ ὑμῶν ὧν χρείαν ἔχετε, πρὸ τοῦ ὑμᾶς
knows for the Father of you what need you have before you

154 846 3779 3767 4336 5210 3962 2257
αἰτῆσαι αὐτόν. 9 οὕτως οὖν προσεύχεσθε ὑμεῖς· Πάτερ ἡμῶν ὁ
ask Him. So then pray you, Father of us

1722 3588 3772 37 3588 3686 4675 2064 3588
ἐν τοῖς οὐρανοῖς, ἁγιασθήτω τὸ ὄνομά σου· 10 ἐλθέτω ἡ
in Heaven, let be sanctified the name of You; let comethe

932 4675 1096 3588 2307 4675 5613 1722 3772 2532
βασιλεία σου· γενηθήτω τὸ θέλημά σου, ὡς ἐν οὐρανῷ, καὶ
kingdom of You; let be done the will of You, as in Heaven, also

1909 3588 1093 3588 740 2257 3588 1967 1325 2254
ἐπὶ τῆς γῆς· 11 τὸν ἄρτον ἡμῶν τὸν ἐπιούσιον δὸς ἡμῖν
on the earth. The bread of us daily give to us

4594 2532 863 2254 3588 3783 2257 5613 2532 2249
σήμερον· 12 καὶ ἄφες ἡμῖν τὰ ὀφειλήματα ἡμῶν, ὡς καὶ ἡμεῖς
today; and forgive us the debts of us, as also we

863 3588 3781 2257 2532 3361 1533 2248 1519
ἀφίεμεν τοῖς ὀφειλέταις ἡμῶν· 13. καὶ μὴ εἰσενέγκῃς ἡμᾶς εἰς
forgive the debtors of us; and not lead us into

3986 235 4506 2248 575 3588 4190 3754 4675
πειρασμόν, ἀλλὰ ῥῦσαι ἡμᾶς ἀπὸ τοῦ πονηροῦ. ὅτι σοῦ
temptation, but deliver us from evil; because of You

2076 3588 932 2532 3588 1411 2532 3588 1391 1519 3588 165
ἐστιν ἡ βασιλεία καὶ ἡ δύναμις καὶ ἡ δόξα εἰς τοὺς αἰῶνας.
is the kingdom, and the power, and the glory to the ages.

281 1437 1063 863 3588 444 3588 3900
ἀμήν. 14 Ἐὰν γὰρ ἀφῆτε τοῖς ἀνθρώποις τὰ παραπτώματα
Amen. if For you forgive men the trespasses

846 863 2532 5213 3588 3962 5216 3588 3770 1437 1161
αὐτῶν, ἀφήσει καὶ ὑμῖν ὁ πατὴρ ὑμῶν ὁ οὐράνιος· 15 ἐὰν δὲ
of them, will forgive also you the Father of you heavenly. if But

3361 863 3588 444 3588 3900 846 3761 3588
μὴ ἀφῆτε τοῖς ἀνθρώποις τὰ παραπτώματα αὐτῶν, οὐδὲ ὁ
not you forgive men the trespasses of them, neither the

3962 5216 863 3588 3900 5216
πατὴρ ὑμῶν ἀφήσει τὰ παραπτώματα ὑμῶν.
Father of you will forgive the trespasses of you.

3752 1161 3522 3361 1096 5618 3588 5273
16. Ὅταν δὲ νηστεύητε, μὴ γίνεσθε ὥσπερ οἱ ὑποκριταὶ
when And you fast, not do become as the hypocrites

4659 853 1063 3588 4383 846 3704
σκυθρωποί· ἀφανίζουσι γὰρ τὰ πρόσωπα αὐτῶν, ὅπως
(with) sullen face; they disfigure for the faces of them, so as

King James Version

6 But thou, when thou prayest, enter into thy closet, and when thou hast shut thy door, pray to thy Father which is in secret; and thy Father which seeth in secret shall reward thee openly.

7 But when ye pray, use not vain repetitions, as the heathen (do): for they think that they shall be heard for their much speaking.

8 Be not ye therefore like unto them: for your Father knoweth what things ye have need of, before ye ask him.

9 After this manner therefore pray ye: Our Father which art in heaven, Hallowed be thy name.
10 Thy kingdom come. Thy will be done in earth, as (it is) in heaven.

11 Give us this day our daily bread.

12 And forgive us our debts, as we forgive our debtors.

13 And lead us not into temptation, but deliver us from evil: For thine is the kingdom, and the power, and the glory, for ever. Amen.

14 For if ye forgive men their trespasses, your heavenly Father will also forgive you:
15 But if ye forgive not men their trespasses, neither will your Father forgive your trespasses.

16. Moreover when ye fast, be not, as the hypocrites, of a sad countenance: for they disfigure their faces, that

Literal Translation **Matthew 6:17** ***King James Version***

they may appear to men (to be) fasting. Truly I say to you that they have their reward.
17. But you (in) fasting, anoint your head and wash your face,
18 so as not to appear to men to be fasting, but to your Father in secret. And your Father seeing in secret will repay you in the open.

5316 3588 444 3522 281 3004 5213 3754
φανῶσι τοῖς ἀνθρώποις νηστεύοντες· ἀμὴν λέγω ὑμῖν ὅτι
they appear to men fasting; truly, I say to you that

568 3588 3408 846 4771 1161 3522 218 4675
ἀπέχουσι τὸν μισθὸν αὐτῶν. 17 σὺ δὲ νηστεύων ἄλειψαί σου
they have the reward of them. you But (in) fasting anoint of you

3588 2776 2532 3588 4383 4675 3538 3704 3361 5316
τὴν κεφαλήν, καὶ τὸ πρόσωπόν σου νίψαι, 18 ὅπως μὴ φανῇς
the head, and the face of you wash, so as not to appear

3588 444 3522 235 3588 3962 4675 3588 1722 3588
τοῖς ἀνθρώποις νηστεύων, ἀλλὰ τῷ πατρί σου τῷ ἐν τῷ
to men fasting, but to the Father of you in

2927 2532 3588 3962 4675 3588 991 1722 3588 2927 591
κρυπτῷ· καὶ ὁ πατήρ σου ὁ βλέπων ἐν τῷ κρυπτῷ ἀποδώ-
secret; and the Father of you seeing in secret will repay

4671 1722 3588 5318
σει σοι ἐν τῷ φανερῷ.
you in the open.

they may appear unto men to fast. Verily I say unto you, They have their reward.
17. But thou, when thou fastest, anoint thine head, and wash thy face;
18 That thou appear not unto men to fast, but unto thy Father which is in secret: and thy Father, which seeth in secret, shall reward thee openly.

19 Do not treasure up for you treasures on the earth, where moth and rust cause to perish, and where thieves dig through and steal.

20 But treasure up for you treasures in Heaven, where neither moth nor rust cause to perish, and where thieves do not dig through and steal.
21 For where your treasure is, there your heart will be also.

3361 2343 5213 2344 1909 3588 1093 3699 4597
19. Μὴ θησαυρίζετε ὑμῖν θησαυροὺς ἐπὶ τῆς γῆς, ὅπου σὴς
Not do treasure up for you treasures on the earth, where moth

2532 1035 853 2532 3699 2812 1358 2532
καὶ βρῶσις ἀφανίζει, καὶ ὅπου κλέπται διορύσσουσι καὶ
and rust cause to perish, and where thieves dig through and

2813 2343 1161 5213 2344 1722 3772
κλέπτουσι· 20 θησαυρίζετε δὲ ὑμῖν θησαυροὺς ἐν οὐρανῷ,
steal; treasure up But for you treasures in Heaven,

3699 3777 4597 3777 1035 853 2532 3699 2812 3756
ὅπου οὔτε σὴς οὔτε βρῶσις ἀφανίζει, καὶ ὅπου κλέπται οὐ
where neither moth nor rust cause to perish, and where thieves not

1358 3761 2813 3699 1063 2076 3588 2344
διορύσσουσιν οὐδὲ κλέπτουσιν· 21 ὅπου γάρ ἐστιν ὁ θησαυρός
dig through nor steal. where For is the treasure

5216 1563 2071 2532 3588 2588 5216 3588 3088 3588 4983
ὑμῶν, ἐκεῖ ἔσται καὶ ἡ καρδία ὑμῶν. 22 ὁ λύχνος τοῦ σώματός
of you, there will be also the heart of you. The lamp of the body

2076 3588 3788 1437 3767 3588 3788 4675 573 5600 3650
ἐστιν ὁ ὀφθαλμός· ἐὰν οὖν ὁ ὀφθαλμός σου ἁπλοῦς ᾖ, ὅλον
is the eye; if then the eye of you sound be, all

3588 4983 4675 5460 2071 1437 1161 3588 3788 4675 4190
τὸ σῶμά σου φωτεινὸν ἔσται· 23 ἐὰν δὲ ὁ ὀφθαλμός σου πονη-
the body of you full of light is. if But the eye of you evil

5600 3650 3588 4983 4675 4652 2071/1487/3767/3588/5457/3588
ρὸς ᾖ, ὅλον τὸ σῶμά σου σκοτεινὸν ἔσται. εἰ οὖν τὸ φῶς τὸ
be, all the body of you dark is. If, then the light

1722 4671 4655 2076 3588 4655 4214 3762 1410 1417
ἐν σοὶ σκότος ἐστί, τὸ σκότος πόσον; 24 οὐδεὶς δύναται δυσὶ
in you darkness is, the darkness how great! No one is able two

2962 1398 2228 1063 3588 1520 3404 2532 3588 2087
κυρίοις δουλεύειν· ἢ γὰρ τὸν ἕνα μισήσει, καὶ τὸν ἕτερον
lords to serve; either for the one he will hate, and the other

25 2228 1520 472 2532 3588 2087 2706
ἀγαπήσει· ἢ ἑνὸς ἀνθέξεται, καὶ τοῦ ἑτέρου καταφρονήσει.
he will love; or one he will cleave to, and the other he will despise.

3756 1410 2316 1398 2532 3126 1223 5124 3004
οὐ δύνασθε θεῷ δουλεύειν καὶ μαμμωνᾷ. 25 διὰ τοῦτο λέγω
not You are able God to serve and wealth. Because of this, I say

5213 3361 3309 3588 5590 5216 5101 5315 2532 5101 4095
ὑμῖν, μὴ μεριμνᾶτε τῇ ψυχῇ ὑμῶν, τί φάγητε καὶ τί πίητε·
to you, not do be anxious for the life of you, what you eat, and what drink;

3366 3588 4983 5216 5101 1746 3780 3588 5590 4119;
μηδὲ τῷ σώματι ὑμῶν, τί ἐνδύσησθε. οὐχὶ ἡ ψυχὴ πλεῖόν
nor for the body of you, what you put on. not the soul more

19 Lay not up for yourselves treasures upon earth, where moth and rust doth corrupt, and where thieves break through and steal:

20 But lay up for yourselves treasures in heaven, where neither moth nor rust doth corrupt, and where thieves do not break through nor steal:
21 For where your treasure is, there will your heart be also.

22 The lamp of the body is the eye. Then if your eye is sound, all your body is full of light.

23 But if your eye is evil, all your body is dark. If, then, the light in you is darkness, how great is the darkness!

24 No one is able to serve two lords; for either he will hate the one, and he will love the other; or he will cleave to the one, and he will despise the other. You are not able to serve God and wealth.

25 Because of this, I say to you, Do not be anxious for your life, what you eat and what you drink, nor for your body, what you put on. Is not the soul

22 The light of the body is the eye: if therefore thine eye be single, thy whole body shall be full of light.

23 But if thine eye be evil, thy whole body shall be full of darkness. If therefore the light that is in thee be darkness, how great (is) that darkness!
24 No man can serve two masters: for either he will hate the one, and love the other; or else he will hold to the one, and despise the other. Ye cannot serve God and mammon.

25 Therefore I say unto you, Take no thought for your life, what ye shall eat, or what ye shall drink; nor yet for your body, what ye shall put on. Is not the life

Matthew 6:26

Literal Translation

more than the food and the body than the clothing?
26 Look at the birds of the heaven, that they do not sow, nor do they reap, nor do (they) gather into barns, yet your heavenly Father feeds them. Do you not rather surpass them?
27 But who of you (by) being anxious is able to add one cubit onto his stature?
28 And why are you anxious about clothing? Consider the lilies of the field, how they grow. They do not labor nor do they spin,
29 but I say to you that not even Solomon in all his glory was clothed like one of these.
30 If God so enrobes the grass of the field, which is today, and is thrown into a furnace tomorrow, (will He) not much rather you, little-faiths?
31 Then do not be anxious, saying, What may we eat? Or, what may we drink? Or, what may clothe us?
32 For all these things the nations seek. For your heavenly Father knows that you have need of all these things.
33 But seek first the kingdom of God and His righteousness, and all these things will be added to you.
34 Then do not be anxious for tomorrow. For the morrow will be anxious of itself. Sufficient to (each) day is its (own) badness.

2076 3588 5160 2532 3588 4983 3588 1742 1689
ἐστι τῆς τροφῆς, καὶ τὸ σῶμα τοῦ ἐνδύματος; 26 ἐμβλέψατε
Is (than) the food, and the body (than) the clothing? Look

1519 3588 4071 3588 3772 3754 3756 4687 3761 2325
εἰς τὰ πετεινὰ τοῦ οὐρανοῦ ὅτι οὐ σπείρουσιν, οὐδὲ θερί-
at the birds of the heaven that not they sow, nor do they

3761 4863 1519 596 2532 3588 3962 5216 3588
ζουσιν, οὐδὲ συνάγουσιν εἰς ἀποθήκας, καὶ ὁ πατὴρ ὑμῶν ὁ
reap, nor gather into barns, yet the Father of you

3770 5142 846 3756 5210 3123 1308 846
οὐράνιος τρέφει αὐτά· οὐχ ὑμεῖς μᾶλλον διαφέρετε αὐτῶν;
heavenly feeds them; not do you rather surpass them?

5101 1161 1537 5216 3309 1410 4369 1909 3588
27 τίς δὲ ἐξ ὑμῶν μεριμνῶν δύναται προσθεῖναι ἐπὶ τὴν
who But of you being anxious is able to add onto the

2244 846 4083 1520 2532 4012 1742 5101 3309
ἡλικίαν αὐτοῦ πῆχυν ἕνα; 28 καὶ περὶ ἐνδύματος τί μεριμνᾶτε;
stature of him cubit one? And concerning clothing, why anxious are you?

2648 3588 2918 3588 68 4459 837 3756 2872
καταμάθετε τὰ κρίνα τοῦ ἀγροῦ, πῶς αὐξάνει· οὐ κοπιᾷ,
Consider the lilies of the field, how they grow; not they labor,

3761 3514 3004 1161 5213 3754 3761 4672 1722 3956 3588
οὐδὲ νήθει· 29 λέγω δὲ ὑμῖν ὅτι οὐδὲ Σολομὼν ἐν πάσῃ τῇ
nor spin; I say but to you that not even Solomon in all the

1391 846 4016 5613 1520 5130 1487 1161 3588 5528 3588
δόξῃ αὐτοῦ περιεβάλετο ὡς ἓν τούτων. 30 εἰ δὲ τὸν χόρτον τοῦ
glory of him was clothed as one of these. if But the grass of the

68 4594 5607 2532 839 1519 2823 906
ἀγροῦ, σήμερον ὄντα, καὶ αὔριον εἰς κλίβανον βαλλόμενον,
field today being, and tomorrow into a furnace being thrown,

3588 2316 3779 294 3756 4183 3123 5209 3640
ὁ θεὸς οὕτως ἀμφιέννυσιν, οὐ πολλῷ μᾶλλον ὑμᾶς, ὀλιγό-
God thus enrobes; not much more (Are) you, little-

3361 3767 3309 3004 5101 5315 2228 5101
πιστοι; 31 μὴ οὖν μεριμνήσητε, λέγοντες, Τί φάγωμεν, ἢ τί
faiths? not Then be anxious, saying, What may we eat, or what

4095 2228 5101 4016 3956 1063 5023 3588 1484
πίωμεν, ἢ τί περιβαλώμεθα; 32 πάντα γὰρ ταῦτα τὰ ἔθνη
may we drink, or what may clothe us? all For these things the nations

1934 1492 1063 3588 3962 5216 3588 3770 3754 5535
ἐπιζητεῖ· οἶδε γὰρ ὁ πατὴρ ὑμῶν ὁ οὐράνιος ὅτι χρῄζετε
seek; knows for the Father of you heavenly that you need

5130 537 2212 1161 4412 3588 932 3588
τούτων ἁπάντων. 33 ζητεῖτε δὲ πρῶτον τὴν βασιλείαν τοῦ
these all. seek But first the kingdom

2316 2532 3588 1343 846 2532 5023 3956 4369
θεοῦ καὶ τὴν δικαιοσύνην αὐτοῦ, καὶ ταῦτα πάντα προσ-
of God and the righteousness of Him, and these things all will be

5213 3361 3767 3309 1519 3588 839 3588 1063
τεθήσεται ὑμῖν. 34 μὴ οὖν μεριμνήσητε εἰς τὴν αὔριον· ἡ γὰρ
added to you. not Then do be anxious for the morrow; the for

839 3309 3588 1438 713 3588 2250 3588 2549
αὔριον μεριμνήσει τὰ ἑαυτῆς· ἀρκετὸν τῇ ἡμέρᾳ ἡ κακία
morrow will be anxious of itself. Sufficient to the day (is) the badness

846
αὐτῆς.
of it.

King James Version

more than meat, and the body than raiment?
26 Behold the fowls of the air: for they sow not, neither do they reap, nor gather into barns; yet your heavenly Father feedeth them. Are ye not much better than they?
27 Which of you by taking thought can add one cubit unto his stature?
28 And why take ye thought for raiment? Consider the lilies of the field, how they grow; they toil not, neither do they spin:
29 And yet I say unto you, That even Solomon in all his glory was not arrayed like one of these.
30 Wherefore, if God so clothe the grass of the field, which to day is, and to morrow is cast into the oven, (shall he) not much more (clothe) you, O ye of little faith?
31 Therefore take no thought, saying, What shall we eat? or, What shall we drink? or, Wherewithal shall we be clothed?
32 (For after all these things do the Gentiles seek:) for your heavenly Father knoweth that ye have need of all these things.
33 But seek ye first the kingdom of God, and his righteousness; and all these things shall be added unto you.
34 Take therefore no thought for the morrow: for the morrow shall take thought for the things of itself. Sufficient unto the day (is) the evil thereof.

Matthew 7

1. Do not judge, that you not be judged;
2 for with what judgment you judge,

Matthew 7

3361 2919 2443 3361 2919 1722 3739 1063 2917 2919
1. Μὴ κρίνετε, ἵνα μὴ κριθῆτε· 2 ἐν ᾧ γὰρ κρίματι κρίνετε,
Not do judge, that not you be judged; in what for judgment you judge

Matthew 7

1. Judge not, that ye be not judged.
2 For with what judgment ye judge,

Literal Translation **Matthew 7:3** ***King James Version***

and with what measure you measure, it will be measured to you.
3 But why do you look on the chip that (is) in the eye of your brother, but do not see the beam in your eye?
4 Or how will you say to your brother, Allow me to cast out the chip from your eye; and behold, the beam (is) in your eye!

2919 2532 1722 3739 3358 3354 488
κριθήσεσθε· καὶ ἐν ᾧ μέτρῳ μετρεῖτε, ἀντιμετρηθήσεται
you will be judged and in what measure you measure, it will be measured
5213 5101 1161 991 3588 2595 3588 1722 3588 3788 3588 80
ὑμῖν. 3 τί δὲ βλέπεις τὸ κάρφος τὸ ἐν τῷ ὀφθαλμῷ τοῦ ἀδελφοῦ
to you. why But do you see the chip in the eye of the brother
4675 3588 1161 1722 3588 4674 3788 1385 3756 2657 2228 4459
σου, τὴν δὲ ἐν τῷ σῷ ὀφθαλμῷ δοκὸν οὐ κατανοεῖς; 4 ἢ πῶς
of you,the but in of your eye beam not you perceive? Or how
2046 3588 80 4675 863 1544 3588 2595 575 3588
ἐρεῖς τῷ ἀδελφῷ σου, Ἄφες ἐκβάλω τὸ κάρφος ἀπὸ τοῦ
will you say to the brother of you,Permit (me) to take the chip from the,
3788 4675 2532 2400 3588 1385 1722 3588 3788 4675
ὀφθαλμοῦ σου· καὶ ἰδού, ἡ δοκὸς ἐν τῷ ὀφθαλμῷ σου;
the eye of you, and behold, the beam (is) in the eye of you?

and with what measure ye mete, it shall be measured to you again.
3 And why beholdest thou the mote that is in thy brother's eye, but considerest not the beam that is in thine own eye?
4 Or how wilt thou say to thy brother, Let me pull out the mote out of thine eye; and, behold, a beam (is) in thine own eye?

5 Hypocrite, first cast the beam out of your eye, and then you will see clearly to cast the chip out of the eye of your brother.

5273 1544 4412 3588 1385 1537 3588 3788 4675
5 ὑποκριτά, ἔκβαλε πρῶτον τὴν δοκὸν ἐκ τοῦ ὀφθαλμοῦ σου,
Hypocrite! take out First the beam out of the eye of you,
2532 5119 1227 1544 3588 2595 1537 3588 3788
καὶ τότε διαβλέψεις ἐκβαλεῖν τὸ κάρφος ἐκ τοῦ ὀφθαλμοῦ
and then you will see clearly to take out the chip out of the eye
3588 80 4675
τοῦ ἀδελφοῦ σου.
of the brother of you.

5 Thou hypocrite, first cast out the beam out of thine own eye; and then shalt thou see clearly to cast out the mote out of thy brother's eye.

6. Do not give (that which is) holy to the dogs, nor throw your pearls before the pigs, that they not trample them with their feet, and turning they charge you.

3361 1325 3588 40 3588 2965 3366 906 3588 3135
6. Μὴ δῶτε τὸ ἅγιον τοῖς κυσί· μηδὲ βάλητε τοὺς μαργαρί-
Not do give the holy to the dogs, nor throw the pearls
5216 1715 3588 5519 3379 2662
τας ὑμῶν ἔμπροσθεν τῶν χοίρων, μήποτε καταπατήσωσιν
of you before the pigs, lest they trample
846 1722 3588 4228 846 2532 4762 4486 5209
αὐτοὺς ἐν τοῖς ποσὶν αὐτῶν, καὶ στραφέντες ῥήξωσιν ὑμᾶς.
them in the feet of them, and turning they charge you.

6. Give not that which is holy unto the dogs, neither cast ye your pearls before swine, lest they trample them under their feet, and turn again and rend you.

7. Ask, and it will be given to you; seek, and you will find; knock, and it will be opened to you.
8 For each one that asks receives, and the (one) that seeks finds; and to the (one) knocking, it will be opened.
9 Or who is a man from you, who, if his son should ask a loaf of him, will he give him a stone?
10 And if he should ask a fish, will he give him a snake?
11 Therefore, if you, being evil. know to give good gifts to your children, how much more will your Father in Heaven give good things to those that ask Him?

154 2532 1325 5213 2212 2532 2147
7. Αἰτεῖτε, καὶ δοθήσεται ὑμῖν· ζητεῖτε, καὶ εὑρήσετε·
Ask and it will be given to you; seek and you will find.
2925 2532 455 5213 3956 1063 3588 154 2983
κρούετε, καὶ ἀνοιγήσεται ὑμῖν. 8 πᾶς γὰρ ὁ αἰτῶν λαμβάνει,
Knock and it will be opened to you. each For asking receives,
2532 3588 2212 2147 2532 3588 2925 455 2228 5101
καὶ ὁ ζητῶν εὑρίσκει, καὶ τῷ κρούοντι ἀνοιγήσεται. 9 ἢ τίς
and he seeking finds. And to the (one) knocking,it will be opened. Or who
2076 1537 5216 444 3739 1437 154 3588 5207 846 740
ἐστιν ἐξ ὑμῶν ἄνθρωπος, ὃν ἐὰν αἰτήσῃ ὁ υἱὸς αὐτοῦ ἄρτον,
is from you a man who if should ask the son of him a loaf,
3361 3037 1929 846 2532 1437 2486 154 3361 3789
μὴ λίθον ἐπιδώσει αὐτῷ; 10 καὶ ἐὰν ἰχθὺν αἰτήσῃ, μὴ ὄφιν
not a stone he will give him? And if a fish he should ask, not a snake
1929 846 1487 3767 5210 4190 5607 1492 1390
ἐπιδώσει αὐτῷ; 11 εἰ οὖν ὑμεῖς, πονηροὶ ὄντες, οἴδατε δόματα
he will give him? If, then , you evil being, know gifts
18 1325 3588 5043 5216 4214 3123 3588 3962
ἀγαθὰ διδόναι τοῖς τέκνοις ὑμῶν, πόσῳ μᾶλλον ὁ πατὴρ
good to give to the children of you, how much more the Father
5216 3588 1722 3588 3772 1325 18 3588 154 846
ὑμῶν ὁ ἐν τοῖς οὐρανοῖς δώσει ἀγαθὰ τοῖς αἰτοῦσιν αὐτόν;
of you in Heaven will give good things to those asking Him.

7. Ask, and it shall be given you; seek, and ye shall find; knock, and it shall be opened unto you:
8 For every one that asketh receiveth; and he that seeketh findeth; and to him that knocketh it shall be opened.
9 Or what man is there of you, whom if his son ask bread, will he give him a stone?
10 Or if he ask a fish, will he give him a serpent?
11 If ye then, being evil, know how to give good gifts unto your children, how much more shall your Father which is in heaven give good things to them that ask him?

12 Therefore, all things, whatever you desire that men should do to you, so also you should do to them; for this is the Law and

3956 3767 3745 302 2309 2443 4160 5213 3588 444
12 πάντα οὖν ὅσα ἂν θέλητε ἵνα ποιῶσιν ὑμῖν οἱ ἄνθρωποι,
all things Then,what ever you desire that may do to you, men
3779 2532 5210 4160 846 3778 1063 2076 3588 3551 2532
οὕτω καὶ ὑμεῖς ποιεῖτε αὐτοῖς· οὗτος γάρ ἐστιν ὁ νόμος καὶ
so also you do to them. this For is the Law and

12 Therefore all things whatsoever ye would that men should do to you, do ye even so to them: for this is the law

Literal Translation | **Matthew 7:13** | ***King James Version***

the Prophets.

3588 4396
οἱ προφῆται.
the Prophets.

and the prophets.

13. Go in through the narrow gate; for wide (is) the gate and broad (is) the way that leads to destruction, and many are the ones entering in through it.
14 For narrow (is) the gate, and constricted (is) the way leading away into life, and few are those finding it.

1525 1223 3588 4728 4439 3754 4116 3588 4439 2532
13. Εἰσέλθετε διὰ τῆς στενῆς πύλης· ὅτι πλατεῖα ἡ πύλη, καὶ
Enter in through the narrow gate, because wide (is) the gate, and
2149 3588 3598 3588 520 1519 3588 684 2532 4183
εὐρύχωρος ἡ ὁδὸς ἡ ἀπάγουσα εἰς τὴν ἀπώλειαν, καὶ πολλοί
broad (is) the way leading away into destruction; and many
1526 3588 1525 1223 846 3754 4728 3588 4439 2532
εἰσιν οἱ εἰσερχόμενοι δι᾽ αὐτῆς·14 ὅτι στενὴ ἡ πύλη, καὶ
are those entering in through it. Because narrow (is) the gate, and
2346 3588 3598 3588 520 1519 3588 2222 2532 3641
τεθλιμμένη ἡ ὁδὸς ἡ ἀπάγουσα εἰς τὴν ζωήν, καὶ ὀλίγοι
constricted (is) the way leading away into life; and few
1526 3588 2147 846
εἰσὶν οἱ εὑρίσκοντες αὐτήν.
are those finding it.

13. Enter ye in at the strait gate: for wide (is) the gate, and broad (is) the way, that leadeth to destruction, and many there be which go in thereat:
14 Because strait (is) the gate, and narrow (is) the way, which leadeth unto life, and few there be that find it.

15. But beware of the false prophets who come to you in sheep's clothing, but inwardly they are plundering wolves.
16 From their fruits you shall know them. Neither do they gather grapes from thorn bushes, or figs from thistles?
17 So every good tree produces good fruits, but the corrupt tree produces evil fruits.
18 A good tree cannot produce evil fruits, nor a corrupt tree produce good fruits.
19 Every tree not producing good fruit is cut down and is thrown into fire.
20 Then surely from their fruits you shall know them.

4337 1161 575 3588 5578 3748 2064
15. Προσέχετε δὲ ἀπὸ τῶν ψευδοπροφητῶν, οἵτινες ἔρχονται
beware But from the false prophets, who come
4314 5209 1722 1742 4263 2081 1161 1526 3074
πρὸς ὑμᾶς ἐν ἐνδύμασι προβάτων, ἔσωθεν δέ εἰσι λύκοι
to you in clothing of sheep; inwardly But they are wolves
727 575 3588 2590 846 1921 846
ἅρπαγες. 16 ἀπὸ τῶν καρπῶν αὐτῶν ἐπιγνώσεσθε αὐτούς·
plundering. From the fruits of them, you shall know them.
3385 4816 575 173 4718 2228 575 5146
μήτι συλλέγουσιν ἀπὸ ἀκανθῶν σταφυλήν, ἢ ἀπὸ τριβόλων
Neither do they gather from thornbushes grapes, or from thistles
4810 3779 3956 1186 18 2590 2570 4160
σῦκα; 17 οὕτω πᾶν δένδρον ἀγαθὸν καρποὺς καλοὺς ποιεῖ·
figs? So every tree good fruits good produces
3588 1161 4550 1186 2590 4190 4160 3756 1410
τὸ δὲ σαπρὸν δένδρον καρποὺς πονηροὺς ποιεῖ. 18 οὐ δύναται
the But corrupt tree fruits evil produces.. Not is able
1186 18 2590 4190 4160 3761 1186
δένδρον ἀγαθὸν καρποὺς πονηροὺς ποιεῖν, οὐδέ δένδρον
a tree good fruits evil to produce; nor a tree
4550 2590 2570 4160 3956 1186 3361 4160
σαπρὸν καρποὺς καλοὺς ποιεῖν. 19 πᾶν δένδρον μὴ ποιοῦν
corrupt fruits good to produce. Every tree not producing
2590 2570 1581 2532 1519 4442 906 686 575
καρπὸν καλὸν ἐκκόπτεται καὶ εἰς πῦρ βάλλεται. 20 ἄραγε ἀπὸ
fruits good is cut out, and into fire is thrown. Surely, from
3588 2590 846 1921 846 3756 3956 3588 3004 3427
τῶν καρπῶν αὐτῶν ἐπιγνώσεσθε αὐτούς. 21 Οὐ πᾶς ὁ λέγων μοι,
the fruits of them you will know them. Not everyone saying to Me,

15. Beware of false prophets, which come to you in sheep's clothing, but inwardly they are ravening wolves.
16 Ye shall know them by their fruits. Do men gather grapes of thorns, or figs of thistles?
17 Even so every good tree bringeth forth good fruit; but a corrupt tree bringeth forth evil fruit.
18 A good tree cannot bring forth evil fruit, neither (can) a corrupt tree bring forth good fruit.
19 Every tree that bringeth not forth good fruit is hewn down, and cast into the fire.
20 Wherefore by their fruits ye shall know them.

21. Not everyone saying to Me, Lord, Lord, will enter into the kingdom of Heaven, but the (ones) doing the will of My Father in Heaven.

2962 2962 1525 1519 3588 932 3588
Κύριε, Κύριε, εἰσελεύσεται εἰς τὴν βασιλείαν τῶν
Lord, Lord, will enter into the kingdom of
3772 235 3588 4160 3588 2307 3588 3962 3450 3588 1722
οὐρανῶν· ἀλλ᾽ ὁ ποιῶν τὸ θέλημα τοῦ πατρός μου τοῦ ἐν
Heaven, but those doing the will of the Father of Me in

21. Not every one that saith unto me, Lord, Lord, shall enter into the kingdom of heaven; but he that doeth the will of my Father which is in heaven.

22 Many will say to Me in that day, Lord, Lord, did we not prophesy in Your name, and in Your name cast out demons, and in Your name many

3772 4183 2046 3427 1722 1565 3588 2250 2962
οὐρανοῖς.22 πολλοὶ ἐροῦσί μοι ἐν ἐκείνῃ τῇ ἡμέρᾳ, Κύριε,
Heaven. Many will say to Me in that day, Lord,
2962 3756 3588 4674 3686 4395 2532 3588 4674 3686
Κύριε, οὐ τῷ σῷ ὀνόματι προεφητεύσαμεν, καὶ τῷ σῷ ὀνό-
Lord, Not in your name did we prophesy, and in your name
1140 1544 2532 3588 4674 3686 1411 4183
ματι δαιμόνια ἐξεβάλομεν, καὶ τῷ σῷ ὀνόματι δυνάμεις πολλας
demons cast out; and in your name works of power many

22 Many will say to me in that day, Lord, Lord, have we not prophesied in thy name? and in thy name have cast out devils? and in thy name done many

Literal Translation | **Matthew 7:23** | *King James Version*

works of power we performed?
23 And then I will declare to them, I never knew you; depart from Me, those working lawlessness! (Ps. 6:8)
24. Then everyone who hears these words from Me, and does them, I will compare him to a prudent man who built his house on the rock;
25 and the rain came down, and the floods came up, and the winds blew, and fell against that house; but it did not fall, for it had been founded on the rock.

4160 2532 5119 3670 846 3754 3763
ἐποιήσαμεν; 23 καὶ τότε ὁμολογήσω αὐτοῖς, ὅτι οὐδέποτε
we performed? And then I will declare to them, Never

1097 5209 672 575 1700 3588 2038 3588
ἔγνων ὑμᾶς· ἀποχωρεῖτε ἀπ' ἐμοῦ οἱ ἐργαζόμενοι τὴν
I knew you depart from Me those working

458 3956 3767 3748 191 3450 3588 3056 5128 2532
ἀνομίαν.24 Πᾶς οὖν ὅστις ἀκούει μου τοὺς λόγους τούτους καὶ
lawlessness. Everyone then who hears of Me words these, and

4160 846 3666 846 435 5429 3748 3618
ποιεῖ αὐτούς, ὁμοιώσω αὐτὸν ἀνδρὶ φρονίμῳ, ὅστις ᾠκοδό-
does them, I will compare him to a man prudent who built

3588 3614 846 1909 3588 4073 2532 2597 3588 1028
μησε τὴν οἰκίαν αὐτοῦ ἐπί τὴν πέτραν· 25 καὶ κατέβη ἡ βροχὴ
the house of him on the rock. And came down the rain,

2532 2064 3588 4215 2532 4154 3588 417 2532 4363
καὶ ἦλθον οἱ ποταμοὶ καὶ ἔπνευσαν οἱ ἄνεμοι, καὶ προσ-
and came up the floods, and blew the winds, and fell

3588 3614 1565 2532 3756 4098 2311 1063 1909
έπεσον τῇ οἰκίᾳ ἐκείνῃ, καὶ οὐκ ἔπεσε· τεθεμελίωτο γὰρ ἐπὶ
against house that; and not it fell; it had been founded for on

3588 4073 2532 3956 3588 191 3450 3588 3056 5128
τὴν πέτραν. 26 καὶ πᾶς ὁ ἀκούων μου τοὺς λόγους τούτους
the rock. And everyone hearing of Me words these

wonderful works?
23 And then will I profess unto them, I never knew you: depart from me, ye that work iniquity.
24. Therefore whosoever heareth these sayings of mine, and doeth them, I will liken him unto a wise man, which built his house upon a rock:
25 And the rain descended, and the floods came, and the winds blew, and beat upon that house; and it fell not: for it was founded upon a rock.

26 And everyone hearing these words of Me, and not doing them, (he) shall be compared to a foolish man who built his house on the sand;
27 and the rain came down, and the floods came up, and the winds blew and beat against that house; and it fell, and great was the collapse of it.

2532 3361 4160 846 3666 435 3474 3748
καὶ μὴ ποιῶν αὐτούς, ὁμοιωθήσεται ἀνδρὶ μωρῷ, ὅστις
and not doing them, will be compared to a man foolish, who

3618 3588 3614 846 1909 3588 285 2532 2597 3588
ᾠκοδόμησε τὴν οἰκίαν αὐτοῦ ἐπὶ τὴν ἄμμον·27καὶ κατέβη ἡ
built the house of him on the sand; and came down the

1028 2532 2064 3588 4215 2532 4154 3588 417 2532
βροχὴ καὶ ἦλθον οἱ ποταμοὶ καὶ ἔπνευσαν οἱ ἄνεμοι, καὶ
rain, and came up the floods, and blew the winds, and

4350 3588 3614 1565 2532 4098 2532 2258 3588 4431
προσέκοψαν τῇ οἰκίᾳ ἐκείνῃ, καὶ ἔπεσε· καὶ ἦν ἡ πτῶσις
beat against house that, and it fell, and was the collapse

846 3173
αὐτῆς μεγάλη.
of it great.

26 And every one that heareth these sayings of mine, and doeth them not, shall be likened unto a foolish man, which built his house upon the sand:
27 And the rain descended, and the floods came, and the winds blew, and beat upon that house; and it fell: and great was the fall of it.

28. And it happened, when Jesus had finished these sayings, the crowds were astonished at His doctrine.
29 For He was teaching them as having authority, and not as the scribes.

2532 1096 3753 4931 3588 2424 3588 3056 5128
28. Καὶ ἐγένετο ὅτε συνετέλεσεν ὁ Ἰησοῦς τοὺς λόγους τού-
And it happened when had finished Jesus words these

1605 3588 3793 1909 3588 1322 846 2258 1063
τους ἐξεπλήσσοντο οἱ ὄχλοι ἐπὶ τῇ διδαχῇ αὐτοῦ· 29 ἦν γὰρ
were astonished the crowds at the doctrine of Him. He was For

1321 846 5613 1849 2192 2532 3756 5613 3588 1122
διδάσκων αὐτοὺς ὡς ἐξουσίαν ἔχων, καὶ οὐχ ὡς οἱ γραμ-
teaching them as authority having, and not as the

ματεῖς.
scribes.

28. And it came to pass, when Jesus had ended these sayings, the people were astonished at his doctrine:
29 For he taught them as (one) having authority, and not as the scribes.

Matthew 8

1.. And He having come down from the mount, great crowds followed Him.
2 And behold, coming up, a leper worshiped Him, saying, Lord, If You will, You are able to cleanse me.
3 And stretching

2597 1161 846 575 3588 3735 190 846
1. Καταβάντι δὲ αὐτῷ ἀπὸ τοῦ ὄρους, ἠκολούθησαν αὐτῷ
having come down And He from the mount followed Him

3793 4183 2532 2400 3015 2064 4352 846
ὄχλοι πολλοί. 2 καὶ ἰδού, λεπρὸς ἐλθὼν προσεκύνει αὐτῷ,
crowds great. And, behold, a leper coming worshiped Him,

3004 2962 1437 2309 1410 3165 2511 2532 1614
λέγων, Κύριε, ἐὰν θέλῃς, δύνασαί με καθαρίσαι.3καὶ ἐκτείνας
saying, Lord, if You will, You are able me to cleanse. And stretching

1. When he was come down from the mountain, great multitudes followed him.
2 And, behold, there came a leper and worshipped him, saying, Lord, if thou wilt, thou canst make me clean.
3 And Jesus put forth

Literal Translation

Matthew 8:4

King James Version

and stretching out His hand, Jesus touched him, saying, I will! Be cleansed! And instantly his leprosy was cleansed.
4 And Jesus says to him, See that you tell no one, but go, show yourself to the priest and offer the gift which Moses commanded, for a testimony to them.

3588 5495 680 846 3588 2424 3004 2309 2511
τὴν χεῖρα, ἥψατο αὐτοῦ ὁ Ἰησοῦς, λέγων, Θέλω, καθαρί-
the hand, touched him Jesus, saying, I will, be

2532 2112 2511 846 3588 3014 2532 3004
σθητι. καὶ εὐθέως ἐκαθαρίσθη αὐτοῦ ἡ λέπρα. 4 καὶ λέγει
cleansed! And instantly was cleansed of Him the leprosy. And says

846 3588 2424 3708 3367 2036 235 5217 4572
αὐτῷ ὁ Ἰησοῦς, Ὅρα μηδενὶ εἴπῃς· ἀλλ' ὕπαγε, σεαυτὸν
to him Jesus, See (that) no one you tell, but go, yourself

1166 3588 2409 2532 4374 3588 1435 3739 4367
δεῖξον τῷ ἱερεῖ, καὶ προσένεγκε τὸ δῶρον ὃ προσέταξε
show to the priest and offer the gift which commanded

3475 1519 3142 846
Μωσῆς, εἰς μαρτύριον αὐτοῖς.
Moses, for a testimony to them.

(his) hand, and touched him, saying, I will; be thou clean. And immediately his leprosy was cleansed.
4 And Jesus saith unto him, See thou tell no man; but go thy way, shew thyself to the priest, and offer the gift that Moses commanded, for a testimony unto them.

5. And Jesus, entering into Capernaum, a centurion came near to Him, begging Him,
6 and saying, Lord, my child has been laid in the house, a paralytic, being terribly tormented.

7 And Jesus says to him, I will come and heal him.

8 And answering, the centurion said, Lord, I am not worthy that You should enter under my roof, but only speak a word and my child will be healed.
9 For I am also a man under authority, having soldiers under myself. And I say to this (one), Go; and he goes; and to another, Come; and he comes; and to my slave, Do this; and he does (it).

1525 1161 3588 2424 1519 2584 4334
5.Εἰσελθόντι δὲ τῷ Ἰησοῦ εἰς Καπερναούμ, προσῆλθεν
having entered And Jesus into Capernaum, came near

846 1543 3870 846 2532 3004 2962
αὐτῷ ἑκατόνταρχος παρακαλῶν αὐτόν, 6 καὶ λέγων, Κύριε,
to Him a centurion beseeching Him, and saying, Lord,

3588 3816 3450 906 1722/3588/3614 3885 1171 928
ὁ παῖς μου βέβληται ἐν τῇ οἰκίᾳ παραλυτικός, δεινῶς βασανι-
the child of me has been laid in the house a paralytic terribly

2532 3004 846 3588 2424 1473 2064 2323
ζόμενος. 7 καὶ λέγει αὐτῷ ὁ Ἰησοῦς, Ἐγὼ ἐλθὼν θεραπεύσω
tormented And says to him Jesus, I coming will heal

846 2532 611 3588 1543 5346 2962 3756 1510
αὐτόν. 8 καὶ ἀποκριθεὶς ὁ ἑκατόνταρχος ἔφη, Κύριε, οὐκ εἰμὶ
him. And answering the centurion said, Lord, not I am

2425 2443 3450 5259 3588 4721 1525 235 3440 2036
ἱκανὸς ἵνα μου ὑπὸ τὴν στέγην εἰσέλθῃς· ἀλλὰ μόνον εἰπὲ
worthy that of me under the roof You may enter, but only say

3056 2532 2390 3588 3816 3450 2532 1063 1473 444
λόγον, καὶ ἰαθήσεται ὁ παῖς μου. 9 καὶ γὰρ ἐγὼ ἄνθρωπός
a word, and will be healed the child of me also For I a man

1510 5259 1849 2192 5259 1683 4757 2532 3004
εἰμι ὑπὸ ἐξουσίαν, ἔχων ὑπ' ἐμαυτὸν στρατιώτας· καὶ λέγω
am under authority, having under myself soldiers; and I say

5129 4198 2532 4198 2532 243 2064 2532
τούτῳ, Πορεύθητι, καὶ πορεύεται· καὶ ἄλλῳ, Ἔρχου, καὶ
to this (one), Go! And he goes. And to another, Come! And

2064 2532 3588 1401 3450 4160 5124 2532 4160
ἔρχεται· καὶ τῷ δούλῳ μου, Ποίησον τοῦτο, καὶ ποιεῖ.
he comes. And to the slave of me, Do this! And he does

5. And when Jesus was entered into Capernaum, there came unto him a centurion, beseeching him,
6 And saying, Lord, my servant lieth at home sick of the palsy, grievously tormented.
7 And Jesus saith unto him, I will come and heal him.
8 The centurion answered and said, Lord, I am not worthy that thou shouldest come under my roof: but speak the word only, and my servant shall be healed.
9 For I am a man under authority, having soldiers under me: and I say to this (man), Go, and he goeth; and to another, Come, and he cometh; and to my servant, Do this, and he doeth (it).

10 And hearing, Jesus marveled, and said to those following, Truly I say to you, Not even in Israel did I find such faith.

11 But I say to you that many will come from east and west, and will recline with Abraham and Isaac and Jacob in the kingdom of Heaven,
12 but the sons of the kingdom shall be cast out into the outer darkness.

191 1161 3588 2424 2296 2532 2036 3588 190
10ἀκούσας δὲ ὁ Ἰησοῦς ἐθαύμασε, καὶ εἶπε τοῖς ἀκολουθοῦσιν,
hearing And Jesus marveled, and said to those following,

281 3004 5213 3761 1722 3588 2474 5118 4102
Ἀμὴν λέγω ὑμῖν, οὐδὲ ἐν τῷ Ἰσραὴλ τοσαύτην πίστιν
Truly, I say to you, Not even in Israel such faith

2147 3004 1161 5213 3754 4183 575 395 2532 1424
εὗρον. 11 λέγω δὲ ὑμῖν, ὅτι πολλοὶ ἀπὸ ἀνατολῶν καὶ δυσμῶν
I found. I say And to you, that many from the east and west

2240 2532 347 3326 11 2532 2464 2532
ἥξουσι, καὶ ἀνακλιθήσονται μετὰ Ἀβραὰμ καὶ Ἰσαὰκ καὶ
will come, and will recline with Abraham and Isaac and

2384 1722 3588 932 3588 3772 3588 1161 5207 3588 932
Ἰακὼβ ἐν τῇ βασιλείᾳ τῶν οὐρανῶν· 12 οἱ δὲ υἱοὶ τῆς βασιλείας
Jacob in the kingdom of the heavens. the But sons of the kingdom

1544 1519 3588 4655 3588 1857 1563 2071 3588
ἐκβληθήσονται εἰς τὸ σκότος τὸ ἐξώτερον· ἐκεῖ ἔσται ὁ
shall be cast out into the darkness outer; there shall be

10 When Jesus heard (it), he marvelled, and said to them that followed, Verily I say unto you, I have not found so great faith, no, not in Israel.
11 And I say unto you, That many shall come from the east and west, and shall sit down with Abraham, and Isaac, and Jacob, in the kingdom of heaven.
12 But the children of the kingdom shall be cast out into outer darkness:

Literal Translation | **Matthew 8:13** | *King James Version*

There shall be weeping and gnashing of the teeth.
13 And Jesus said to the centurion, Go, and as you have believed, (so) let it be to you. And his child was healed in that hour.

2805 2532 3588 1030 3588 3599 2532 2036 3588 2424
κλαυθμὸς καὶ ὁ βρυγμὸς τῶν ὀδόντων. 13 καὶ εἶπεν ὁ Ἰησοῦς
weeping and gnashing of the teeth. And said Jesus
3588 1543 5217 2532/5613 4100 1096 4671
τῷ ἑκατοντάρχῳ, Ὕπαγε, καὶ ὡς ἐπίστευσας γενηθήτω σοι.
to the centurion, Go! And as you believed, let it be to you.
2532 2390 3588 3816 846 1722 3588 5610 1565
καὶ ἰάθη ὁ παῖς αὐτοῦ ἐν τῇ ὥρᾳ ἐκείνῃ.
And was healed the child of him in hour that.

there shall be weeping and gnashing of teeth.
13 And Jesus said unto the centurion, Go thy way; and as thou hast believed, (so) be it done unto thee. And his servant was healed in the selfsame hour.

14. And coming to the house of Peter, Jesus saw his mother-in-law laid (out) and burning with fever.
15 And He touched her hand, and the fever left her. And she rose up and served them.

2532 2064 3588 2424 1519 3588 3614 4074 1492 3588
14. Καὶ ἐλθὼν ὁ Ἰησοῦς εἰς τὴν οἰκίαν Πέτρου, εἶδε τὴν
And coming Jesus into the house of Peter, He saw the
3994 846 906 2532 4445 2532 680
πενθερὰν αὐτοῦ βεβλημένην καὶ πυρέσσουσαν, 15 καὶ ἥψατο
mother-in-law of him having been laid and burning with fever. And He touched
3588 5495 846 2532 863 846 3588 4446 2532 1453
τῆς χειρὸς αὐτῆς, καὶ ἀφῆκεν αὐτὴν ὁ πυρετός· καὶ ἠγέρθη,
the hand of her, and left her the fever. And she arose
2532 1247 846
καὶ διηκόνει αὐτοῖς.
and served them.

14. And when Jesus was come into Peter's house, he saw his wife's mother laid, and sick of a fever.
15 And he touched her hand, and the fever left her: and she arose, and ministered unto them.

16. And evening having come on, they brought to Him many having been possessed by demons. And He cast out the spirits by a word, and He healed all those having illness,
17 so that it might be fulfilled that spoken by Isaiah the prophet, saying, "He took (upon Himself) our weaknesses, and He bore (our) sicknesses." (Isa. 53:4)

3798 1161 1096 4374 846
16 ὀψίας δὲ γενομένης προσήνεγκαν αὐτῷ
evening And having come, they brought to Him
1139 4183 2532 1544 3588 4151 3056
δαιμονιζομένους πολλούς· καὶ ἐξέβαλε τὰ πνεύματα λόγῳ,
having been demon-possed many. And He cast out the spirits by a word.
2532 3956 3588 2560 2192 2323 3704 4137
καὶ πάντας τοὺς κακῶς ἔχοντας ἐθεράπευσεν· 17 ὅπως πληρωθῇ
and all those illness having, He healed, so as may be fulfilled
3588 4483 1223 2268 3588 4396 3004 846 3588
τὸ ῥηθὲν διὰ Ἡσαΐου τοῦ προφήτου, λέγοντος, Αὐτὸς τὰς
that spoken through Isaiah the prophet, saying, He the
769 2257 2983 2532 3588 3554 941
ἀσθενείας ἡμῶν ἔλαβε, καὶ τὰς νόσους ἐβάστασεν.
weaknesses of us took, and the sicknesses He bore.

16. When the even was come, they brought unto him many that were possessed with devils: and he cast out the spirits with (his) word, and healed all that were sick:
17 That it might be fulfilled which was spoken by Esaias the prophet, saying, Himself took our infirmities, and bare (our) sicknesses.

18. And seeing great crowds around Him, Jesus ordered to go away to the other side.
19 And one scribe, coming near, said to Him, Teacher, I will follow You wherever you may go.
20 And Jesus says to him, The foxes have holes, and the birds of the heaven (have) roosts, but the Son of man has nowhere He may lay (His) head.

1492 1161 3588 2424 4183 3793 4012 846 2753
18. Ἰδὼν δὲ ὁ Ἰησοῦς πολλοὺς ὄχλους περὶ αὐτόν, ἐκέλευσεν
seeing And Jesus great crowds around Him, He ordered
565 1519 3588 4008 2532 4334 1520 1122 2036
ἀπελθεῖν εἰς τὸ πέραν. 19 καὶ προσελθὼν εἷς γραμματεὺς εἶπεν
to go away to the other side. And coming near one scribe said
846 1320 190 4671 3699 1437 565 2532
αὐτῷ, Διδάσκαλε, ἀκολουθήσω σοι ὅπου ἐὰν ἀπέρχῃ. 20 καὶ
to Him, Teacher, I will follow You wherever You go. And
3004 846 3588 2424 3588 258 5454 2192 2532 3588
λέγει αὐτῷ ὁ Ἰησοῦς, Αἱ ἀλώπεκες φωλεοὺς ἔχουσι, καὶ τὰ
says to him Jesus, The foxes holes have and the
4071 3588 3772 2682 3588 1161 5207 3588 444
πετεινὰ τοῦ οὐρανοῦ κατασκηνώσεις· ὁ δὲ υἱὸς τοῦ ἀνθρώ-
birds of the heavens roosts; the but Son of man
3756 2192 4226/3588 2776 2827
που οὐκ ἔχει ποῦ τὴν κεφαλὴν κλίνῃ.
not has where the head He may lay.

18. Now when Jesus saw great multitudes about him, he gave commandment to depart unto the other side.
19 And a certain scribe came, and said unto him, Master, I will follow thee whithersoever thou goest.
20 And Jesus saith unto him, The foxes have holes, and the birds of the air (have) nests; but the Son of man hath not where to lay (his) head.

21 And another of His disciples said to Him, Lord, allow me first to go away and bury my father.

2087 1161 3588 3101
21 ἕτερος δὲ τῶν μαθητῶν
another And of the disciples
846 2036 846 2962 2010 3427 4412 565
αὐτοῦ εἶπεν αὐτῷ, Κύριε, ἐπίτρεψόν μοι πρῶτον ἀπελθεῖν
of Him said to Him, Lord, allow me first to go away
2532 2290 3588 3962 3450
καὶ θάψαι τὸν πατέρα μου.
and to bury the father of me.

21 And another of his disciples said unto him, Lord, suffer me first to go and bury my father.

22 But Jesus said to him, Follow Me, and allow the dead to bury their own dead.

3588 1161 2424 2036 846 190
22 ὁ δὲ Ἰησοῦς εἶπεν αὐτῷ, Ἀκολού-
But Jesus said to him, Follow
3427 2532 863 3588 3498 2290 3588 1438 3498
θει μοι, καὶ ἄφες τοὺς νεκροὺς θάψαι τοὺς ἑαυτῶν νεκρούς.
Me, and allow the dead to bury the of themselves dead.

22 But Jesus said unto him, Follow me; and let the dead bury their dead.

23. And He entering into the boat,

2532 1684 846 1519 3588 4143 190 846 3588
23. Καὶ ἐμβάντι αὐτῷ εἰς τὸ πλοῖον, ἠκολούθησαν αὐτῷ οἱ
And entering He into the boat, followed Him the

23. And when he was entered into a ship,

Literal Translation — **Matthew 8:24** — **King James Version**

His disciples followed Him.

24 And, behold, a great shaking occurred in the sea, so that the boat was covered by the waves; but He was sleeping.

25 And coming near, His disciples aroused Him, saying, Lord, save us! We are perishing.

26 And He said to them, Why are you afraid, little-faiths? Then rising up, He rebuked the winds and the sea. And a great calm occurred.

27 And the men marveled, saying, What kind (of man) is this, that even the winds and the sea obey Him?

28. And He coming to the other side, into the country of the Gergesenes, two who had been demon-possessed met Him, coming out of the tombs, very violent, so that not any was able to pass through that way.

29 And, behold! They cried out, saying, What (is) to us and to You, Jesus, Son of God? Have You come here beforetime to torment us?

30 And at a distance from them there was a herd of many pigs feeding.

31 And the demons begged Him, saying, If You expel us, allow us to go away into the herd of pigs.

32 And He said to them, Go! And coming out, (they) went away into the herd of pigs. And, behold, all the herd of pigs rushed down the cliff into the sea, and died in the waters.

33 But those feeding (them) fled,

3101 846 2532 2400 4578 3173 1096 1722 3588
μαθηταὶ αὐτοῦ. 24 καὶ ἰδού, σεισμὸς μέγας ἐγένετο ἐν τῇ θα-
disciples of Him. And, behold, a shaking great occurred in the
2281 5620 3588 4143 2572 5259 3588 2949
λάσσῃ, ὥστε τὸ πλοῖον καλύπτεσθαι ὑπὸ τῶν κυμάτων·
sea, so that the boat was covered by the waves
846 1161 2518 2532 4334 3588 3101 846.
αὐτὸς δὲ ἐκάθευδε. 25 καὶ προσελθόντες οἱ μαθηταὶ αὐτοῦ
He But was sleeping. And having come near the disciples of Him
1453 846 3004 2962 4982 2248 622
ἤγειραν αὐτόν, λέγοντες, Κύριε, σῶσον ἡμᾶς, ἀπολλύμεθα.
aroused Him, saying, Lord, save us; we are perishing.
2532 3004 846 5101 1169 2075 3640 5119 1453
26καὶ`λέγει αὐτοῖς Τί δειλοι ἐστε, ὀλιγόπιστοι; τότε ἐγερθεὶς
And He says to them, Why afraid are you, little-faiths? Then rising up
2008 3588 417 2532 3588 2281 2532 1096 1055
ἐπετίμησε τοῖς ἀνέμοις καὶ τῇ θαλάσσῃ, καὶ ἐγένετο γαλήνη
He rebuked the winds and the sea, and occurred a calm
3173 3588 1161 444 2296 3004 4217
μεγάλη. 27 οἱ δὲ ἄνθρωποι ἐθαύμασαν, λέγοντες, Ποταπός
great. the And men marveled, saying, Of what kind
2076 3778 3754 2532 3588 417 2532 3588 2281 5219
ἐστιν οὗτος, ὅτι καὶ οἱ ἄνεμοι καὶ ἡ θάλασσα ὑπακούουσιν
is this, that even the winds and the sea obey
846
αὐτῷ;
Him?

2532 2064 846 1519 3588 4008 1519 3588 5561 3588
28. Καὶ ἐλθόντι αὐτῷ εἰς τὸ πέραν εἰς τὴν χώραν τῶν
And comi ng He to the other side into the country of the
1086 5221 846 1417 1139 1537 3588
Γεργεσηνῶν, ὑπήντησαν αὐτῷ δύο δαιμονιζόμενοι ἐκ τῶν
Gergesenes, met Him two being demon-possessed out ofthe
3419 1831 5467 3029 5620 3361 2480 5100
μνημείων ἐξερχόμενοι, χαλεποὶ λίαν, ὥστε μὴ ἰσχύειν τινὰ
tombs coming out, violent very, so as not was able any
3928 1223 3588 3598 1565 2532 2400 2896 3004
παρελθεῖν διὰ τῆς ὁδοῦ ἐκείνης. 29καὶ ἰδού, ἔκραξαν λέγοντες,
to pass through way that. And, behold, they cried out, saying
5101 2254 2532 4671 2424 5207 3588 2316 2064 5602 4253 2540
Τί ἡμῖν καὶ σοί, Ἰησοῦ, υἱὲ τοῦ θεοῦ; ἦλθες ὧδε πρὸ καιροῦ
What to us and to You, Jesus, Son of God? Come You here before time
928 2248 2258 1161 3112 575 846 34 5519
βασανίσαι ἡμᾶς; 30 ἦν δε` μακρὰν ἀπ' αὐτῶν ἀγέλη χοίρων
to torment us? was And at a distance from them a herd of pigs
4183 1006 3588 1161 1142 3870 846
πολλῶν βοσκομένη. 31 οἱ δὲ δαίμονες παρεκάλουν αὐτόν,
many feeding. the And demons begged Him,
3004 1487 1544 2248 2010 2254 565 1519 3588
λέγοντες, Εἰ ἐκβάλλεις ἡμᾶς, ἐπίτρεψον ἡμῖν ἀπελθεῖν εἰς τὴν
saying, If You expel us, allow us to go away into the
34 3588 5519 2532 2036 846 5217 3588 1161
ἀγέλην τῶν χοίρων. 32 καὶ εἶπεν αὐτοῖς, Ὑπάγετε. οἱ δὲ
herd of the pigs. And He said to them, Go! those And
1831 565 1519 3588 34 3588 5519 2532 2400
ἐξελθόντες ἀπῆλθον εἰς τὴν ἀγέλην τῶν χοίρων· καὶ ἰδού,
coming out went away into the herd of the pigs. And, behold
3729 3956 3588 34 3588 5519 2596 3588 2911 1519
ὥρμησε πᾶσα ἡ ἀγέλη τῶν χοίρων κατὰ τοῦ κρημνοῦ εἰς
rushed all the herd of the pigs down the precipice into
3588 2281 2532 599 1722 3588 5204 3588/1161 1006
τὴν θάλασσαν, καὶ ἀπέθανον ἐν τοῖς ὕδασιν. 33 οἱ δε βόσκοντες
the sea, and died in the waters. those And feeding

his disciples followed him.

24 And, behold, there arose a great tempest in the sea, insomuch that the ship was covered with the waves: but he was asleep.

25 And his disciples came to (him), and awoke him, saying, Lord, save us: we perish.

26 And he saith unto them, Why are ye fearful, O ye of little faith? Then he arose, and rebuked the winds and the sea; and there was a great calm.

27 But the men marvelled, saying, What manner of man is this, that even the winds and the sea obey him!

28. And when he was come to the other side into the country of the Gergesenes, there met him two possessed with devils, coming out of the tombs, exceeding fierce, so that no man might pass by that way.

29 And, behold, they cried out, saying, What have we to do with thee, Jesus, thou Son of God? art thou come hither to torment us before the time?

30 And there was a good way off from them an herd of many swine feeding.

31 So the devils besought him, saying, If thou cast us out, suffer us to go away into the herd of swine.

32 And he said unto them, Go. And when they were come out, they went into the herd of swine: and, behold, the whole herd of swine ran violently down a steep place into the sea, and perished in the waters.

33 And they that kept them fled,

Literal Translation | **Matthew 8:34** | *King James Version*

and going into the city (they) told all things, and of the (ones) having been demon-posessed.
34 And, behold, all the city went out to meet with Jesus. And seeing Him, they begged that He move away from their borders.

5343 2532 565 1519 3588 4172 518 3956
ἔφυγον, καὶ ἀπελθόντες εἰς τὴν πόλιν ἀπήγγειλαν πάντα,
fled, and going away into the city told all things,
2532 3588 3588 1139 2532 2400 3956 3588 4172 1831
καὶ τὰ τῶν δαιμονιζομένων. 34 καὶ ἰδού, πᾶσα ἡ πόλις ἐξῆλ-
and of the (ones) having been demon-possessed And behold, all the city went
1519 4877 3588 2424 2532 1492 846 3870
θεν εἰς συνάντησιν τῷ Ἰησοῦ· καὶ ἰδόντες αὐτόν, παρεκα-
out to meet with Jesus; and seeing Him, they
3704 3327 575 3588 3725 846
λεσαν ὅπως μεταβῇ ἀπὸ τῶν ὁρίων αὐτῶν.
begged that He move from the borders of them.

and went their ways into the city, and told every thing, and what was befallen to the possessed of the devils.
34 And, behold, the whole city came out to meet Jesus: and when they saw him, they besought (him) that he would depart out of their coasts.

Matthew 9

1 And entering into the boat, He passed over and came to (His) own city.
2 And, behold! They were bringing to Him a paralytic laid out on a cot. And seeing their faith, Jesus said to the paralytic, Be comforted, child. Your sins have been remitted to you.
3 And, behold, some of the scribes said within themselves, This one blasphemes.
4 And seeing their thoughts, Jesus said, Why do you think evil in your hearts?
5 For what is easier, to say, (Your) sins have been remitted to you; or to say, Rise up and walk?
6 But that you may know that the Son of man has authority on earth to remit sins, then He said to the paralytic, Rising up, lift up your cot and go to your house.
7 And rising up, he went away to his house.
8 And seeing, the crowds marveled, and (they) glorified God, the (One) giving such authority to men.

2532 1684 1519 3588 4143 1276 2532 2064 1519 3588 2398
1.Καὶ ἐμβὰς εἰς τὸ πλοῖον διεπέρασε καὶ ἦλθεν εἰς τὴν ἰδίαν
And entering into the boat, He passed over and came into the own
4172 2532 2400 4374 846 3885 1909 2825
πόλιν. 2 καὶ ἰδού, προσέφερον αὐτῷ παραλυτικὸν ἐπὶ κλίνης
city. And behold, they were bringing to Him a paralytic on a cot
906 2532 1492 3588 2424 3588 4102 846 2036 3588
βεβλημένον· καὶ ἰδὼν ὁ Ἰησοῦς τὴν πίστιν αὐτῶν εἶπε τῷ
laid out. And seeing Jesus the faith of them, He said to
3885 2293 5043 863 4671 3588 266
παραλυτικῷ, Θάρσει, τέκνον· ἀφέωνταί σοι αἱ ἁμαρτίαι
paralyzed (one), Be comforted, child; have been remitted to you the sins
4675 2532 2400 5100 3588 1122 2036 1722 1438
σου. 3 καὶ ἰδού, τινὲς τῶν γραμματέων εἶπον ἐν ἑαυτοῖς,
of you. And, behold! Some of the scribes said within themselves,
3778 987 2532 1492 3588 2424 3588 1761 846
Οὗτος βλασφημεῖ. 4 καὶ ἰδὼν ὁ Ἰησοῦς τὰς ἐνθυμήσεις αὐτῶν
This (one) blasphemes. And seeing Jesus the thoughts of them,
2036 2444 5210 1760 4190 1722 3588 2588 5216
εἶπεν,Ἱνατί ὑμεῖς ἐνθυμεῖσθε πονηρὰ ἐν ταῖς καρδίαις ὑμῶν;
He said, Why do you think evil in the hearts of you?
5101 1063 2076 2123 2036 863 4671 3588
5 τί γάρ ἐστιν εὐκοπώτερον, εἰπεῖν, Ἀφέωνταί σοι αἱ
what For is easier, to say, Are remitted of you the
266 2228 2036 1453 2532 4043 2443 1161 1492
ἁμαρτίαι· ἢ εἰπεῖν,Ἔγειραι και περιπάτει; 6 ἵνα δὲ εἰδῆτε,
sins, or to say, Rise up and walk around? that But you may know
3754 1849 2192 3588 5207 3588 444 1909 3588 1093 863
ὅτι ἐξουσίαν ἔχει ὁ υἱὸς τοῦ ἀνθρώπου ἐπὶ τῆς γῆς ἀφιέναι
that authority has the Son of man on the earth to remit
266 5119 3004 3588 3885 1453 142 4675
ἁμαρτίας [τότε λέγει τῷ παραλυτικῷ,] Ἐγερθεὶς ἆρόν σου
sins, then He says to the paralytic, Rising up lift your
3588 2825 2532 5217 1519 3588 3624 4675 2532 1453 565
τὴν κλίνην, καὶ ὕπαγε εἰς τὸν οἶκόν σου. 7 καὶ ἐγερθεὶς ἀπῆλ-
cot and go to the house of you. And rising up he went
1519 3588 3624 846 1492 1161 3588 3793 2296 2532
θεν εἰς τὸν οἶκον αὐτοῦ. 8 ἰδόντες δὲ οἱ ὄχλοι ἐθαύμασαν, καὶ
away to the house of him. having seen And, the crowds marveled, and
1392 3588 2316 3588 1325 1849 5108 3588
ἐδόξασαν τὸν Θεόν, τὸν δόντα ἐξουσίαν τοιαύτην τοῖς
glorified God, the (One) giving authority such
444
ἀνθρώποις.
to men.

1 And he entered into a ship, and passed over, and came into his own city.
2 And, behold, they brought to him a man sick of the palsy, lying on a bed: and Jesus seeing their faith said unto the sick of the palsy; Son, be of good cheer; thy sins be forgiven thee.
3 And, behold, certain of the scribes said within themselves, This (man) blasphemeth.
4 And Jesus knowing their thoughts said, Wherefore think ye evil in your hearts?
5 For whether is easier, to say, (Thy) sins be forgiven thee; or to say, Arise, and walk?
6 But that ye may know that the Son of man hath power on earth to forgive sins, (then saith he to the sick of the palsy,) Arise, take up thy bed, and go unto thine house.
7 And he arose, and departed to his house.
8 But when the multitudes saw (it), they marvelled, and glorified God, which had given such power unto men.

9. And passing from there, Jesus saw a man named Matthew sitting

2532 3855 3588 2424 1564 1492 444 2521
9.Καὶ παράγων ὁ Ἰησοῦς ἐκεῖθεν εἶδεν ἄνθρωπον καθήμενον
And passing by Jesus from there saw a man sitting

9. And as Jesus passed forth from thence, he saw a man, named Matthew, sitting

Literal Translation | **Matthew 9:10** | **King James Version**

at the tax office. And (He) said to him, Follow Me. And rising up, he followed Him.

1909 3588 5058 3156 3004 2532 3004 846 190
ἐπὶ τὸ τελώνιον, Ματθαῖον λεγόμενον, καὶ λέγει αὐτῷ,'Ακο-
at the tax-office, Matthew called, and says to him,

3427 2532 450 190 846
λούθει μοι. καὶ ἀναστὰς ἠκολούθησεν αὐτῷ.
Follow Me. And rising up he followed Him.

at the receipt of custom: and he saith unto him, Follow me. And he arose, and followed him.

10. And it happened as He reclined in the house, and behold, many tax collectors and sinners having come, (these) were reclining with Jesus and His disciples.
11 And seeing, the Pharisees said to His disciples, Why does your teacher eat with tax collectors and sinners?

12 But Jesus hearing, He said to them, The (ones) being strong have no need of a healer, but the (ones) having illness..

13 But going, learn what (this) is, "I desire mercy and not sacrifice." "For I did not come to call righteous (ones), but sinners to repentance." (Hosea 6:6)

2532 1096 846 345 1722 3588 3614 2532 2400
10.Καὶ ἐγένετο αὐτοῦ ἀνακειμένου ἐν τῇ οἰκίᾳ, καὶ ἰδού,
And it happened, He having reclined in the house; and behold,

4183 5057 2532 268 2064 4873 3588
πολλοὶ τελῶναι καὶ ἁμαρτωλοὶ, ἐλθόντες συνανέκειντο τῷ
many tax-collectors and sinners having come were reclining

2424 2532 3588 3101 846 2532 1492 3588 5330
'Ιησοῦ καὶ τοῖς μαθηταῖς αὐτοῦ. 11 καὶ ἰδόντες οἱ Φαρισαῖοι
with Jesus and the disciples of Him. And seeing the Pharisees

2036 3588 3101 846 1302 3326 3588 5057 2532
εἶπον τοῖς μαθηταῖς αὐτοῦ, Διατί μετὰ τῶν τελωνῶν καὶ
said to the disciples of Him, Why with the tax-collectors and

268 2068 3588 1320 5216 3588 1161 2424 191
ἁμαρτωλῶν ἐσθίει ὁ διδάσκαλος ὑμῶν; 12 ὁ δὲ'Ιησοῦς ἀκούσας
sinners eats the teacher of you? And Jesus hearing

2036 846 3756 5532 2192 3588 2480 2395 235
εἶπεν αὐτοις, Οὐ χρείαν ἔχουσιν οἱ ἰσχύοντες ἰατροῦ, ἀλλ'
He said to them, Not need have the (ones) being strong of a healer, but

3588 2560 2192 4198 1161 3129 5101 2076 1656
οἱ κακῶς ἔχοντες. 13 πορευθέντες δὲ μάθετε τί ἐστιν,"Ελεον
those illness having. having gone But learn what this is: mercy

2309 2532 3756 2378 3756 1063 2064 2564 1342 235
θέλω, καὶ οὐ θυσίαν· οὐ γὰρ ἦλθον καλέσαι δικαίους, ἀλλ'
I desire, and not sacrifice. not For I came to call righteous (ones), but

268 1519 3341
ʽμαρτωλοὺς εἰς υετάνοιαν.
sinners to repentance.

10. And it came to pass, as Jesus sat at meat in the house, behold, many publicans and sinners came and sat down with him and his disciples.

11 And when the Pharisees saw (it), they said unto his disciples, Why eateth your Master with publicans and sinners?

12 But when Jesus heard (that), he said unto them, They that be whole need not a physician, but they that are sick.

13 But go ye and learn what (that) meaneth, I will have mercy, and not sacrifice: for I am not come to call the righteous, but sinners to repentance.

14. Then the disciples of John came to Him, saying, Why do we and the Pharisees fast much, and Your disciples do not fast?

15 And Jesus said to them, Can the sons of the bridechamber mourn as long as the bridegroom is with them? But the days will come when the bridegroom will have been taken from them, and then they will fast.
16 But no one puts a patch of new cloth on an old garment. For its fullness takes away from the garment, and a worse tear occurs.

5119 4334 846 3588 3101 2491 3004
14. Τότε προσέρχονται αὐτῷ οἱ μαθηταὶ'Ιωάννου, λέγοντες,
Then came near to Him the disciples of John, saying,

1302 2249 2532 3588 5330 3522 4183 3588 1161
Διατί ἡμεῖς καὶ οἱ Φαρισαῖοι νηστεύομεν πολλά, οἱ δὲ
Why we and the Pharisees fast much, the but

3101 4675 3756 3522 2532 2036 846 3588 2424 3361
μαθηταί σου οὐ νηστεύουσι; 15 καὶ εἶπεν αὐτοῖς ὁ 'Ιησοῦς, Μὴ
disciples of You not do fast? And said to them Jesus, Not

1410 3588 5207 3588 3567 3996 1909 3745 3326 846
δύνανται οι υἱοὶ τοῦ νυμφῶνος πενθεῖν ἐφ' ὅσον μετ' αὐτῶν
are able the sons of the bridechamber to mourn as long as with them

2076 3588 3566 2064 1161 2250 3752 522 575
ἐστιν ὁ νυμφίος; ἐλεύσονται δὲ ἡμέραι ὅταν ἀπαρθῇ ἀπ'
is the bridegroom? will come But days when will have been taken from

846 3588 3566 2532 5119 3522 3762 1161 1911
αὐτῶν ὁ νυμφίος, καὶ τότε νηστεύσουσιν.16 οὐδεὶς δὲ ἐπιβάλ-
them the bridegroom,and then they will fast. no one But puts

1915 4470 46 1909 2440 3820 142
λει ἐπίβλημα ῥάκους ἀγνάφου ἐπι ἱματίῳ παλαιῷ· αἴρει
a patch of cloth unfulled on a garment old, takes away

1063 3588 4138 846 575 3588 2440 2532 5501
γὰρ τὸ πλήρωμα αὐτοῦ ἀπὸ τοῦ ἱματίου, καὶ χεῖρον
for the fullness of it from the garment, and a worse

14. Then came to him the disciples of John, saying, Why do we and the Pharisees fast oft, but thy disciples fast not?

15 And Jesus said unto them, Can the children of the bridechamber mourn, as long as the bridegroom is with them? but the days will come, when the bridegroom shall be taken from them, and then shall they fast.
16 No man putteth a piece of new cloth unto an old garment, for that which is put in to fill it up taketh from the garment, and the rent is made worse.

17 Nor do they put new wine into old wineskins; otherwise, the wineskins are burst, and the wine

4978 1096 3761 906 3631 3501 1519 779
σχίσμα γίνεται.17οὐδὲ βάλλουσιν οἶνον νέον εἰς ἀσκοὺς
tear occurs. Neither do they put wine new into wineskins

3820 1487 1161 3361 4486 3588 779 2532 3588 3631
παλαιούς· εἰ δὲ μήγε, ῥήγνυνται οἱ ἀσκοί, καὶ ὁ οἶνος
old; otherwise are burst the wineskins and the wine

17 Neither do men put new wine into old bottles: else the bottles break, and the wine

Literal Translation

pours out, and the wine-
skins will be ruined. But
they put new wine into
fresh wineskins, and
both are preserved to-
gether.

18. (As He was) speak-
ing these things to them,
behold, coming one
ruler worshiped Him,
saying, My daughter
has just now died; but
coming lay Your hand
on her, and she will live.

19 And rising up, Jesus
and His disciples fol-
lowed him.
20. And behold, a
woman who had a flow
of blood for twelve
years came near behind
(Him, and) touched the
fringe of His robe.

21 For she said within
herself, If only I shall
touch His robe, I will be
cured.
22 But turning and see-
ing her, Jesus said, Be
comforted, daughter;
your faith has healed
you. And the woman
was healed from that
hour.
23 And Jesus coming
into the house of the
ruler, and seeing the
flute-players and the
crowd causing a tumult,

24 (He) says to them,
Go back, for the little
girl has not died, but she
sleeps. And they de-
rided Him.
25 But when the crowd
had been put out, enter-
ing He took hold of her
hand, and the little girl
rose up.
26 And this report went
out into all that land.

27. And Jesus passing
on from there, two blind
ones followed Him,
crying and saying, Pity
us, Son of David.
28 And coming into the
house, the blind ones
came

Matthew 9:18

1632 2532 3588 779 622 235 906 3631
ἐκχεῖται, καὶ οἱ ἀσκοὶ ἀπολοῦνται· ἀλλὰ βάλλουσιν οἶνον
pours out, and the wineskins will be ruined. But they put wine
3501 1519 779 2537 2532 297 4933
νέον εἰς ἀσκοὺς καινούς, καὶ ἀμφότερα συντηροῦνται.
new into wineskins fresh, and both are preserved together.

5023 846 2980 846 2400 758 1520 2064
18. Ταῦτα αὐτοῦ λαλοῦντος αὐτοῖς, ἰδού, ἄρχων εἷς ἐλθὼν
These things (He) speaking to them, behold! ruler one coming
4352 846 3004 3754 3588 2364 3450 737 5053
προσεκύνει αὐτῷ, λέγων ὅτι Ἡ θυγάτηρ μου ἄρτι ἐτελεύ-
worshiped Him, saying, The daughter of me just now has
235 2064 2007 3588 5495 4675 1909 846 2532
τησεν· ἀλλὰ ἐλθὼν ἐπίθες τὴν χεῖρά σου ἐπ' αὐτήν, καὶ
died, but coming lay the hand of You on her, and
2198 2532 1453 3588 2424 190 846 2532 3588
ζήσεται. 19 καὶ ἐγερθεὶς ὁ Ἰησοῦς ἠκολούθησεν αὐτῷ καὶ οἱ
she will live. And rising up Jesus followed him, and the
3101 846 2532 2400 1135 131 1427 2094
μαθηταὶ αὐτοῦ. 20 καὶ ἰδού, γυνὴ αἱμορροοῦσα δώδεκα ἔτη,
disciples of Him. And behold! a woman having a flow of blood twelve years,
4334 3693 680 3588 2899 3588 2440
προσελθοῦσα ὄπισθεν, ἥψατο τοῦ κρασπέδου τοῦ ἱματίου
coming near behind, (she) touched the fringe of the garment
846 3004 1063 1722 1438 1437 3440 680 3588 2440
αὐτοῦ· 21 ἔλεγε γὰρ ἐν ἑαυτῇ, Ἐὰν μόνον ἅψωμαι τοῦ ἱματίου
of Him. she said For within herself, If only I shall touch the garment
846 4982 3588 1161 2424 1994 2532 1492 846
αὐτοῦ, σωθήσομαι. 22 ὁ δὲ Ἰησοῦς ἐπιστραφεὶς καὶ ἰδὼν αὐτὴν
of Him, I will be cured. But Jesus having turned and seeing her,
2036 2293 2364 3588 4102 4675 4982 , 4571 2532 4982
εἶπε, Θάρσει, θύγατερ· ἡ πίστις σου σέσωκέ σε. καὶ ἐσώθη
said, Be comforted, daughter. The faith of you has cured you. And was cured
3588 1135 575 3588 5610 1565 2532 2064 3588 2424 1519 3588
ἡ γυνὴ ἀπὸ τῆς ὥρας ἐκείνης. 23 Καὶ ἐλθὼν ὁ Ἰησοῦς εἰς τὴν
the woman from hour that. And coming Jesus into the
3614 3588 758 2532 1492 3588 834 2532 3588 3793
οἰκίαν τοῦ ἄρχοντος, καὶ ἰδὼν τοὺς αὐλητὰς καὶ τὸν ὄχλον
house of the ruler, and seeing the flute-players and the crowd
2350 3004 846 402 3756 1063 599
θορυβούμενον, 24 λέγει αὐτοῖς, Ἀναχωρεῖτε· οὐ γὰρ ἀπέθανε
causing a tumult, (He) says to them, Go back, not for has died
3588 2877 235 2518 2532 2606 846 3753 1161
τὸ κοράσιον, ἀλλὰ καθεύδει. καὶ κατεγέλων αὐτοῦ. 25 ὅτε δὲ
the girl, but she sleeps. And they derided Him. when But
1544 3588 3793 1525 2902 3588 5495 846 2532
ἐξεβλήθη ὁ ὄχλος, εἰσελθὼν ἐκράτησε τῆς χειρὸς αὐτῆς, καὶ
had been put out the crowd entering He took the hand of her, and
1453 3588 2877 2532 1831 3588 5345 3778 1519 3650 3588
ἠγέρθη τὸ κοράσιον. 26 καὶ ἐξῆλθεν ἡ φήμη αὕτη εἰς ὅλην τὴν
arose the girl. And went out report this into all
1093 1565
γῆν ἐκείνην.
land that

2532 3855 1564 3588 2424 190 846 1417
27. Καὶ παράγοντι ἐκεῖθεν τῷ Ἰησοῦ, ἠκολούθησαν αὐτῷ δύο
And passing on from there Jesus, followed Him two
5185 2896 2532 3004 1653 2248 5207 1138
τυφλοί, κράζοντες καὶ λέγοντες, Ἐλέησον ἡμᾶς, υἱὲ Δαβίδ.
blind ones, crying and saying, Pity us, son of David.
2064 1161 1519 3588 3614 4334 846 3588 5185 2532
28 ἐλθόντι δὲ εἰς τὴν οἰκίαν, προσῆλθον αὐτῷ οἱ τυφλοί, καὶ
coming And into the house, came near to Him the blind ones, and

King James Version

runneth out, and the
bottles perish: but they
put new wine into new
bottles, and both are
preserved.

18. While he spake
these things unto them,
behold, there came a
certain ruler, and wor-
shipped him, saying,
My daughter is even
now dead: but come and
lay thy hand upon her,
and she shall live.

19 And Jesus arose, and
followed him, and (so
did) his disciples.
20. And, behold, a
woman, which was dis-
eased with an issue of
blood twelve years,
came behind (him), and
touched the hem of his
garment:
21 For she said within
herself, If I may but
touch his garment, I
shall be whole.
22 But Jesus turned him
about, and when he saw
her, he said, Daughter,
be of good comfort; thy
faith hath made thee
whole. And the woman
was made whole from
that hour.
23 And when Jesus
came into the ruler's
house, and saw the min-
strels and the people
making a noise,

24 He said unto them,
Give place: for the maid
is not dead, but sleepeth.
And they laughed him
to scorn.
25 But when the people
were put forth, he went
in, and took her by the
hand, and the maid
arose.
26 And the fame hereof
went abroad into all that
land.

27. And when Jesus
departed thence, two
blind men followed
him, crying, and saying,
(Thou) Son of David,
have mercy on us.
28 And when he was
come into the house, the
blind men

Literal Translation **Matthew 9:29** *King James Version*

near to Him. And Jesus said to them, Do you believe that I am able to do this? And they say to Him, Yes, Lord.
29 Then He touched their eyes, saying, According to your faith let it be to you.
30 And their eyes were opened. And Jesus strictly ordered them, saying, See, let no one know.
31 But going out, they reported Him in all that land.

3004 846 3588 2424 4100 3754 1410 5124 4160
λέγει αὐτοῖς ὁ Ἰησοῦς, Πιστεύετε ὅτι δύναμαι τοῦτο ποιῆ-
said to them Jesus, Do you believe that I am able this to do?

3004 846 3483 2962 5119 680 3588 3788
σαι; λέγουσιν αὐτῷ, Ναί, Κύριε. 29 τότε ἥψατο τῶν ὀφθαλμῶν
They say to Him, Yes, Lord. Then He touched the eyes

846 3004 2596 3588 4102 5216 1096 5213 2532
αὐτῶν, λέγων, Κατὰ τὴν πίστιν ὑμῶν γενηθήτω ὑμῖν. 30 καὶ
of them, saying According to the faith of you let it be to you. And

455 846 3588 3788 2532 1690 846 3588
ἀνεῴχθησαν αὐτῶν οἱ ὀφθαλμοί· καὶ ἐνεβριμήσατο αὐτοῖς ὁ
were opened of them the eyes. And strictly commanded them

2424 3004 3708 3367 1097 3588 1161 1831
Ἰησοῦς, λέγων, Ὁρᾶτε μηδεὶς γινωσκέτω.31οἱ δὲ ἐξελθόντες
Jesus, saying, See, no one let know. they But going out

1310 846 1722 3650 3588 1093 1565
διεφήμισαν αὐτὸν ἐν ὅλῃ τῇ γῇ ἐκείνῃ.
reported Him in all land that.

came to him: and Jesus saith unto them, Believe ye that I am able to do this? They said unto him, Yea, Lord.
29 Then touched he their eyes, saying, According to your faith be it unto you.
30 And their eyes were opened; and Jesus straitly charged them, saying, See (that) no man know (it).
31 But they, when they were departed, spread abroad his fame in all that country.

32. And as they were going out, behold, they brought to Him a dumb man having been possessed by a demon.
33 And the demon being cast out, the dumb one spoke. And the crowds marveled, saying, Never was it seen this way in Israel.
34 But the Pharisees were saying, He casts out the demons by the ruler of the demons.

846 1161 1831 2400 4374 846 444
32. Αὐτῶν δὲ ἐξερχομένων, ἰδού, προσήνεγκαν αὐτῷ ἄνθρω-
(as) they And were going out, behold! They brought to Him a man

2974 1139 2532 1544 3588 1140
πον κωφὸν δαιμονιζόμενον. 33 καὶ ἐκβληθέντος τοῦ δαιμονίου,
dumb, having been demon-possessed. And being cast out, the demon

2980 3588 2974 2532 2296 3588 3793 3004
ἐλάλησεν ὁ κωφός· καὶ ἐθαύμασαν οἱ ὄχλοι, λέγοντες,
spoke the dumb. And marveled the crowds, saying,

3763 5316 3779 1722 3588 2474 3588 1161 5330
Οὐδέποτε ἐφάνη οὕτως ἐν τῷ Ἰσραήλ . 34 οἱ δὲ Φαρισαῖοι
Never was it seen thus in Israel. the But Pharisees

3004 1722 3588 758 3588 1140 1544 3588
ἔλεγον, Ἐν τῷ ἄρχοντι τῶν δαιμονίων ἐκβάλλει τὰ
were saying , By the ruler of the demons He casts out the

1140
δαιμόνια.
demons.

32. As they went out, behold, they brought to him a dumb man possessed with a devil.
33 And when the devil was cast out, the dumb spake: and the multitudes marvelled, saying, It was never so seen in Israel.
34 But the Pharisees said, He casteth out devils through the prince of the devils.

35. And Jesus went about all the cities and the villages teaching in their synagogues, and proclaiming the gospel of the kingdom, and healing every sickness and every weakness (of body) among the people.
36 And seeing the crowds, He was moved with pity concerning them, because they were wearyand scattered like sheep having no shepherd.
37 Then He said to His disciples, The harvest truly (is) great, but the workers few.
38 Pray then that the Lord of the harvest may send out workers into His harvest.

2532 4013 3588 2424 3588 4172 3956 2532 3588 2968
35. Καὶ περιῆγεν ὁ Ἰησοῦς τὰς πόλεις πάσας καὶ τὰς κώμας,
And went about Jesus the cities all and the villages,

1321 1722 3588 4864 846 2532 2784 3588
διδάσκων ἐν ταῖς συναγωγαῖς αὐτῶν καὶ κηρύσσων τὸ
teaching in the synagogues of them, and proclaiming the

2098 3588 932 2532 2323 3956 3554 2532
εὐαγγέλιον τῆς βασιλείας, καὶ θεραπεύων πᾶσαν νόσον καὶ
gospel of the kingdom, and healing every sickness and

3956 3119 1722 3588 2992 1492 1161 3588 3793 4697
πᾶσαν μαλακίαν ἐν τῷ λαῷ. 36 ἰδὼν δὲ τοὺς ὄχλους, ἐσπλαγ-
every weakness in the people seeing And the crowds. He was moved

4012 846 3754 2258 1590 2532 4496
χνίσθη περὶ αὐτῶν, ὅτι ἦσαν ἐκλελυμένοι καὶ ἐρριμμένοι
with pity concerning them, because they were weary and scattered

5616 4263 3361 2192 4166 5119 3004 3588 3101
ὡσεὶ πρόβατα μὴ ἔχοντα ποιμένα. 37 τότε λέγει τοῖς μαθηταῖς
as sheep not having a shepherd. Then He says to the disciples

846 3588 3303 2326 4183 3588 1161 2040 3641
αὐτοῦ, Ὁ μὲν θερισμὸς πολύς, οἱ δὲ ἐργάται ὀλίγοι·
of Him, the Truly harvest (is) great, the but workmen few;

1189 3767 3588 2962 3588 2326 3704 1544
38 δεήθητε οὖν τοῦ Κυρίου τοῦ θερισμοῦ, ὅπως ἐκβάλῃ
pray then the Lord of the harvest, that He may send

2040 1519 3588 2326 846
ἐργάτας εἰς τὸν θερισμὸν αὐτοῦ.
workmen into the harvest of Him.

35. And Jesus went about all the cities and villages, teaching in their synagogues, and preaching the gospel of the kingdom, and healing every sickness and every disease among the people.
36 But when he saw the multitudes, he was moved with compassion on them, because they fainted, and were scattered abroad, as sheep having no shepherd.
37 Then saith he unto his disciples, The harvest truly (is) plenteous, but the labourers (are) few;
38 Pray ye therefore the Lord of the harvest, that he will send forth labourers into his harvest.

Literal Translation

Matthew 10

1. And having called His twelve disciples, He gave them authority over unclean spirits, so as to throw them out, and to heal every disease and every weakness of body.

2 And the names of the twelve apostles are these: First, Simon who is called Peter and his brother Andrew, James the (son) of Zebedee and his brother John,

3 Philip, and Bartholomew, Thomas, and Matthew the tax-collector, James the (son) of Alpheus, and Lebbaeus, who was surnamed Thaddaeus,
4 Simon the Canaanite, and Judas Iscariot, who also betrayed Him.
5 Jesus sent these twelve out, charging them, saying: Do not go into the way of the nations, and do not go into a Samaritan city.

6 But rather go to the lost sheep of (the) house of Israel.
7 And going on, proclaim, saying, The kingdom of Heaven has drawn near.
8 Heal sick ones, cleanse lepers, raise dead ones, cast out demons. You freely received, freely give.

9 Do not provide gold, nor silver, nor copper in your belts,

10 nor provision bag for (the) way, nor two tunics, nor sandals, nor staves. For the worker is worthy of his food.
11 And into whatever city or village you enter, search out who in it

Matthew 10:1

2532 4341 3588 1427 3101 846 1325
1. Καὶ προσκαλεσάμενος τοὺς δώδεκα μαθητὰς αὐτοῦ, ἔδωκεν
And having called near the twelve disciples of Him, He gave

846 1849 4151 169 5620 1544
αὐτοῖς ἐξουσίαν πνευμάτων ἀκαθάρτων, ὥστε ἐκβάλλειν
to them authority (over) spirits unclean so as to cast out

846 2532 2323 3956 3554 2532 3956 3119
αὐτὰ, καὶ θεραπεύειν πᾶσαν νόσον καὶ πᾶσαν μαλακίαν.
them, and to heal every disease and every weakness.

3588 1161 1427 652 3588 3686 2076 5023
2 Τῶν δὲ δώδεκα ἀποστόλων τὰ ὀνόματά ἐστι ταῦτα·
the And twelve apostles the names are these:

4413 4613 3588 3004 4074 2532 406 3588 80
πρῶτος Σίμων ὁ λεγόμενος Πέτρος, καὶ Ἀνδρέας ὁ ἀδελφὸς
first Simon who is called Peter, and Andrew the brother

846 2385 3588 3588 2199 2532 2491 3588 80
αὐτοῦ Ἰάκωβος ὁ τοῦ Ζεβεδαίου, καὶ Ἰωάννης ὁ αδελφὸς
of him; James the (son) of Zebedee, and John the brother

846 5376 2532 918 2381 2532 3156
αὐτοῦ· 3 Φίλιππος, καὶ Βαρθολομαῖος· Θωμᾶς, καὶ Ματθαῖος
of him; Phillip, and Bartholomew, Thomas and Matthew

3588 5057 2385 3588 3588 256 2532 3002 3588
ὁ τελώνης· Ἰάκωβος ὁ τοῦ Ἀλφαίου, καὶ Λεββαῖος ὁ
the tax-collector; James the (son) of Alphaeus, and Lebbaeus who

1941 2280 4613 3588 2581 2532 2455
ἐπικληθεὶς Θαδδαῖος· 4 Σίμων ὁ Κανανίτης, καὶ Ἰούδας
was surnamed Thaddaeus; Simon the Canaanite; and Judas

2469 3588 2532 3860 846 5128 3588 1427
Ἰσκαριώτης ὁ καὶ παραδοὺς αὐτόν. 5 Τούτους τοὺς δώδεκα
Iscariot the (one) also betraying Him. These twelve

649 3588 2424 3853 846 3004
ἀπέστειλεν ὁ Ἰησοῦς παραγγείλας αὐτοῖς, λέγων,
sent out Jesus, having charged them, saying,

1519 3598 1484 3361 565 2532 1519 4172 4541
Εἰς ὁδὸν ἐθνῶν μὴ ἀπέλθητε, καὶ εἰς πόλιν Σαμαρειτῶν
Into the way of nations not do go, and into a city of the Samaritans

3361 1525 4198 1161 3123 4314 3588 4263 3588
μὴ εἰσέλθητε· 6 πορεύεσθε δὲ μᾶλλον πρὸς τὰ πρόβατα τὰ
not do enter. go But rather to the sheep the

622 3624 2474 4198 1161 2784 3004
ἀπολωλότα οἴκου Ἰσραήλ. 7 πορευόμενοι δὲ κηρύσσετε, λέγον-
lost of (the) house of Israel. going on And, proclaim, saying,

3754 1448 3588 932 3588 3772 770
τες ὅτι Ἤγγικεν ἡ βασιλεία τῶν οὐρανῶν. 8 ἀσθενοῦντας
Has drawn near the kingdom of Heaven. Sick ones

2323 3015 2511 3498 1453 1140
θεραπεύετε, λεπροὺς καθαρίζετε, νεκροὺς ἐγείρετε, δαιμόνια
heal, lepers cleanse, dead ones raise, demons

1544 1432 2983 1432 1325 3361 2932
ἐκβάλλετε δωρεὰν ἐλάβετε, δωρεὰν δότε. 9 μὴ κτήσησθε
cast out. Freely you received, freely give. Not provide

5557 3366 696 3366 5475 1519 3588 2223 5216
χρυσὸν, μηδὲ ἄργυρον, μηδὲ χαλκὸν εἰς τὰς ζώνας ὑμῶν,
gold, nor silver, nor copper for the belts of you,

3361 4082 1519 3598 3366 1417 5509 3366 5266
10 μὴ πήραν εἰς ὁδὸν, μηδὲ δύο χιτῶνας, μηδὲ ὑποδήματα,
nor a bag for (the) way, nor two tunics, nor sandals,

3366 4464 514 1063 3588 2040 3588 5160 846 2076
μηδὲ ῥάβδους· ἄξιος γὰρ ὁ ἐργάτης τῆς τροφῆς αὐτου ἐστιν.
nor staves, worthy for the worker of the food of him is

1519 3739 302 4172 3588 2968 1525 1833 5101 1722 846
11 εἰς ἣν δ ἂν πόλιν ἢ κώμην εἰσέλθητε, εξετάσατε τίς ἐν αὐτῇ
into what ever And city or village you enter, search out who in it

King James Version

Matthew 10

1. And when he had called unto (him) his twelve disciples, he gave them power (against) unclean spirits, to cast them out, and to heal all manner of sickness and all manner of disease.

2 Now the names of the twelve apostles are these; The first, Simon, who is called Peter, and Andrew his brother; James (the son) of Zebedee, and John his brother;

3 Philip, and Bartholomew; Thomas, and Matthew the publican; James (the son) of Alphaeus, and Lebbaeus, whose surname was Thaddaeus;
4 Simon the Canaanite, and Judas Iscariot, who also betrayed him.
5 These twelve Jesus sent forth, and commanded them, saying, Go not into the way of the Gentiles, and into (any) city of the Samaritans enter ye not:

6 But go rather to the lost sheep of the house of Israel.
7 And as ye go, preach, saying, The kingdom of heaven is at hand.

8 Heal the sick, cleanse the lepers, raise the dead, cast out devils: freely ye have received, freely give.

9 Provide neither gold, nor silver, nor brass in your purses,

10 Nor scrip for (your) journey, neither two coats, neither shoes, nor yet staves: for the workman is worthy of his meat.
11 And into whatsoever city or town ye shall enter,

Matthew 10:12

Literal Translation

is worthy; and remain
there until you go out.
12 But entering into the
house, greet it;
13 and if the house truly
is worthy, let your peace
come upon it. But if it is
not worthy, let your
peace return to you.

14 And whoever will
not receive you, nor will
hear your words, hav-
ing gone out of that
house or city, shake off
the dust of your feet.

15 Truly I say to you, It
will be more bearable to
the land of Sodom and
Gomorrah in Judgment
Day than for that city.

16 Behold, I send you
out as sheep in (the)
midst of wolves. There-
fore, be wise as serpents
and guileless as doves.

17 But beware from
men. For they will be-
tray you to sanhedrins,
and they will flog you in
their synagogues.

18 And also you will be
brought before gover-
nors and kings for My
sake, for a testimony to
them and to the nations.
19 But when they de-
liver you up, do not be
anxious how or what
you should say, for it is
given to you in that hour
what you should say.
20 For you are not the
ones speaking, but the
Spirit of your Father
the (One) speaking in
you.

21 But brother will be-
tray brother to death,
and (the) father (his)
child. And children will
rise up against parents
and will put them to
death.
22 And you will be
hated by all on account
of My name, but the
(one) enduring to (the)
end

514 2076 2546 3306 2193 302 1831 1525 1161
ἄξιός ἐστι·κἀκεῖ μείνατε, ἕως ἂν ἐξέλθητε.12 εἰσερχόμενοι δὲ
worthy is, and there remain, until you go out. entering But

1519 3588 3614 782 846 2532/1437/3303/5600/3588/3614
εἰς τὴν οἰκίαν, ἀσπάσασθε αὐτήν· 13 καὶ ἐὰν μὲν ᾖ ἡ οἰκία
into the house, greet it.; and if truly be the house

514 2064 3588 1515 5216 1909 846 1437 1161 3361 5600 514 3588
ἀξία, ἐλθέτω ἡ εἰρήνη ὑμῶν ἐπ' αὐτήν· ἐὰν δὲ μὴ ᾖ ἀξία, ἡ
worthy, let come the peace of you on it. if But not it is worthy, the

1515 5216 4314 5209 1994 2532 3739 1437 3361 1209
εἰρήνη ὑμῶν πρὸς ὑμᾶς ἐπιστραφήτω.14 καὶ ὃς ἐὰν μὴ δέξηται
peace of you to you let return. And whoever not will receive

5209 3366 191 3588 3056 5216 1831 3588 3614 2228
ὑμᾶς μηδὲ ἀκούσῃ τοὺς λόγους ὑμῶν, ἐξερχόμενοι τῆς οἰκίας ἢ
you, nor will hear the words of you, going out (of) the house or

3588 4172 1565 1621 3588 2868 3588 4228
τῆς πόλεως ἐκείνης ἐκτινάξατε τὸν κονιορτὸν τῶν ποδῶν
city that shake off the dust of the feet

5216 281 3004 5213 414 2071 1093 4670 2532
ὑμῶν. 15 ἀμὴν λέγω ὑμῖν, ἀνεκτότερον ἔσται γῇ Σοδόμων καὶ
of you. Truly I say to you, More bearable it will be to the land of Sodom and

1116 1722 2250 2920 2228 3588 4172 1565
Γομόρρων ἐν ἡμέρᾳ κρίσεως, ἢ τῇ πόλει ἐκείνῃ.
Gommorah in (the) day of judgment than city that.

2400 1473 649 5209 5613 4263 1722 3319 3074
16. Ἰδού, ἐγὼ ἀποστέλλω ὑμᾶς ὡς πρόβατα ἐν μέσῳ λύκων·
Behold, I send out you as sheep in (the) midst of wolves;

1096 3767 5429 5613 3588 3789 2532 185 5613 3588 4058
γίνεσθε οὖν φρόνιμοι ὡς οἱ ὄφεις, καὶ ἀκέραιοι ὡς αἱ περιστε-
you be then wise as serpents, and guileless as doves.

4337 1161 575 3588 444 3860 1063
ραι. 17 προσέχετε δὲ ἀπὸ τῶν ἀνθρώπων· παραδώσουσι γὰρ
beware And from men. they will betray For

5209 1519 4892 2532 1722 3588 4864 846 3146
ὑμᾶς εἰς συνέδρια, καὶ ἐν ταῖς συναγωγαῖς αὐτῶν μαστιγώ-
you to sanhedrins, and in the synagogues of them they will

5209 2532 1909 2232 11612532 935 71
σουσιν ὑμᾶς· 18 καὶ ἐπὶ ἡγεμόνας δὲ καὶ βασιλεῖς ἀχθήσεσθε
scourge you. And before governors and also kings you will be brought

1752 1700 1519 3142 846 2532 3588 1484 3752 1161
ἕνεκεν ἐμοῦ,εἰς μαρτύριον αὐτοῖς καὶ τοῖς ἔθνεσιν. 19 ὅταν δὲ
for the sake of Me, for a testimony to them and to the nations. when But

3860 5209 3361 3309 4459 2228 5101 2980
παραδιδῶσιν ὑμᾶς, μὴ μεριμνήσητε πῶς ἢ τί λαλήσητε·
they deliver up you, not do be anxious how or what you may say;

1325 1063 5213 1722 1565 3588 5610 5101 2980 3756 1063
δοθήσεται γὰρ ὑμῖν ἐν ἐκείνῃ τῇ ὥρᾳ τί λαλήσετε· 20 οὐ γὰρ
it is given for to you in that hour what you may say. not For

5210 2075 3588 2980 235 3588 4151 3588 3962 5216
ὑμεῖς ἐστὲ οἱ λαλοῦντες, ἀλλὰ τὸ Πνεῦμα τοῦ πατρὸς ὑμῶν
you are the (ones) speaking, but the Spirit of the Father of you

3588 2980 1722 5213 3860 1161 80 80 1519
τὸ λαλοῦν ἐν ὑμῖν. 21 παραδώσει δὲ ἀδελφὸς ἀδελφὸν εἰς
the (One) speaking in you. will deliver up But brother brother to

2288 2532 3962 5043 2532 1881 5043 1909
θάνατον, καὶ πατὴρ τέκνον· καὶ ἐπαναστήσονται τέκνα ἐπὶ
death, and father (the) child; and will rise up children against

1118 2532 2289 846 2532 2071 3404 5259
γονεῖς καὶ θανατώσουσιν αὐτούς. 22 καὶ ἔσεσθε μισούμενοι ὑπὸ
parents and put to death them. And you will be hated by

3956 1223 3588 3686 3450 3588 1161 5278 1519 5056 3778
πάντων διὰ τὸ ὄνομά μου· ὁ δὲ ὑπομείνας εἰς τέλος, οὗτος
all because of the name of Me. the (one) But enduring to (the) end this (one)

King James Version

enquire who in it is wor-
thy; and there abide till
ye go thence.
12 And when ye come
into an house, salute it.
13 And if the house be
worthy, let your peace
come upon it: but if it be
not worthy, let your
peace return to you.

14 And whosoever
shall not receive you,
nor hear your words,
when ye depart out of
that house or city, shake
off the dust of your feet.

15 Verily I say unto you,
It shall be more toler-
able for the land of
Sodom and Gomorrha
in the day of judgment,
than for that city.

16 Behold, I send you
forth as sheep in the
midst of wolves: be ye
therefore wise as ser-
pents, and harmless as
doves.

17 But beware of men:
for they will deliver you
up to the councils, and
they will scourge you in
their synagogues;

18 And ye shall be
brought before gover-
nors and kings for my
sake, for a testimony
against them and the
Gentiles.
19 But when they de-
liver you up, take no
thought how or what ye
shall speak: for it shall
be given you in that
same hour what ye shall
speak.
20 For it is not ye that
speak, but the Spirit of
your Father which
speaketh in you.
21 And the brother shall
deliver up the brother to
death, and the father the
child: and the children
shall rise up against
(their) parents, and
cause them to be put to
death.
22 And ye shall be hated
of all (men) for my
name's sake: but he that
endureth to the end

Literal Translation

shall be kept safe.
23 But when they persecute you in this city, flee to another. For truly I say to you, In no way will you have finished the cities of Israel until the Son of man comes.

24 A disciple is not above the teacher, nor a slave above his lord.

25 (It is) enough for the disciple (to) become as his teacher, and the slave as his lord. If they called the master of the house Beelzebub, how much more those of his household?

26 Therefore, you should not fear them, for nothing is covered which will not be uncovered; and hidden, which will not be made known.
27 What I say to you in the darkness, you say in the light. And what you hear in the ear, proclaim on the housetops.
28 And do not fear the (ones) killing the body, but not being able to kill the soul. But rather fear Him being able to destroy both soul and body in Hell.

29 Are not two sparrows sold for an assarion? Yet not one of them shall fall to the ground without your Father.

30 But even the hairs of your head are all numbered.
31 Then do not fear; you are better than many sparrows.

32 Then everyone who shall confess Me before men, I will also confess him before My Father in Heaven.

33 But whoever denies Me before men, I also will deny him

Matthew 10:23

4982 3752 1161 1377 5209 1722 3588 4172 3778
σωθήσεται. 23 ὅταν δὲ διώκωσιν ὑμᾶς ἐν τῇ πόλει ταύτῃ,
will be kept safe. when But they persecute you in the city this

5343 1519 3588 243 281 1063 3004 5213 3756 3361 5055
φεύγετε εἰς τὴν ἄλλην· ἀμὴν γὰρ λέγω ὑμῖν, οὐ μὴ τελέσητε
flee into another. truly For I say to you, not at all will have finished

3588 4172 3588 2474 2193 302 2064 3588 5207 3588 444
τὰς πόλεις τοῦ Ἰσραὴλ, ἕως ἂν ἔλθῃ ὁ υἱὸς τοῦ ἀνθρώπου.
the cities of Israel until may come the Son of man.

3756 2076 3101 5228 3588 1320 3761 1401
24. Οὐκ ἔστιν μαθητὴς ὑπὲρ τὸν διδάσκαλον, οὐδὲ δοῦλος
Not is a disciple above the teacher, nor a slave

5228 3588 2962 846 713 3588 3101 2443 1096 5613
ὑπὲρ τὸν κύριον αὐτοῦ. 25 ἀρκετὸν τῷ μαθητῇ ἵνα γένηται ὡς
above the Lord of him. (It is) enough for the disciple that (he) become as

3588 1320 846 2532 3588 1401 5613 3588 2962 846 1487 3588
ὁ διδάσκαλος αὐτοῦ, καὶ ὁ δοῦλος ὡς ὁ κύριος αὐτοῦ. εἰ τὸν
the teacher of him, and the slave as the Lord of him. If the

3617 954 2564 4214 3123 3588
οἰκοδεσπότην Βεελζεβοὺβ ἐκάλεσαν, πόσῳ μᾶλλον τοὺς
master of the house Beelzebub they called, how much more those

3615 846 3361 3767 5399 846 3762 1063 2076
οἰκιακοὺς αὐτοῦ; 26 μὴ οὖν φοβηθῆτε αὐτούς· οὐδὲν γάρ ἐστι
of the household of him? not Then you should fear them, nothing for is

2572 3739 3756 601 2532 2927 3739 3756
κεκαλυμμένον ὃ οὐκ ἀποκαλυφθήσεται· καὶ κρυπτὸν ὃ οὐ
covered which not will be uncovered, and hidden which not

3739 3004 5213 1722 3588 4653 2036 1722 3588 5457
γνωσθήσεται. 27 ὃ λέγω ὑμῖν ἐν τῇ σκοτίᾳ, εἴπατε ἐν τῷ φωτί·
will be made known. What I say to you in the darkness, you say in the light.

2532 3739 1519 3588 3775 191 2784 1909 3588 1430 2532 3361
καὶ ὃ εἰς τὸ οὖς ἀκούετε, κηρύξατε ἐπὶ τῶν δωμάτων. 28 καὶ μὴ
And what into the ear you hear, proclaim on the housetops. And not

5399 575 3588 615 3588 4983 3588 1161 5590
φοβηθῆτε ἀπὸ τῶν ἀποκτεινόντων τὸ σῶμα, τὴν δὲ ψυχὴν
you should fear the (ones) killing the body, the but soul

3361 1410 615 5399 1161 3123 3588 1410
μὴ δυναμένων ἀποκτεῖναι· φοβήθητε δὲ μᾶλλον τὸν δυνά-
not being able to kill. fear But rather the (one)

2532 5590 2532 4983 622 1722 1067 3780 1417
μενον καὶ ψυχὴν καὶ σῶμα ἀπολέσαι ἐν γεέννῃ. 29 οὐχὶ δύο
being able both the soul and the body to destroy in Gehenna Not (are) two

4765 787 4453 2532 1520 1537 846 3756 4098
στρουθία ἀσσαρίου πωλεῖται; καὶ ἓν ἐξ αὐτῶν οὐ πεσεῖται
sparrows (for) an assarion sold? And one out of them not shall fall

1909 3588 1093 427 3588 3962 5216 5216 1161 2532 3588 2359 3588
ἐπὶ τὴν γῆν ἄνευ τοῦ πατρὸς ὑμῶν·30ὑμῶν δὲ καὶ αἱ τρίχες τῆς
on the earth without the Father of you. of you But even the hairs of the

2776 3956 705 1526 3361 3767 5399 4183
κεφαλῆς πᾶσαι ἠριθμημέναι εἰσι. 31μὴ οὖν φοβηθῆτε· πολλῶν
head all numbered. are. not Then do fear; many

4765 1308 5210 3956 3767 3748 3670 1722
στρουθίων διαφέρετε ὑμεῖς. 32 πᾶς οὖν ὅστις ὁμολογήσει ἐν
sparrows excel you. Everyone then who shall confess in

1698 1715 3588 444 3670 2504 1722 846
ἐμοὶ ἔμπροσθεν τῶν ἀνθρώπων, ὁμολογησω κἀγὼ ἐν αὐτῷ
Me before men, will confess I also in him

1715 3588 3962 3450 3588 1722 3772 3748 1161 302
ἔμπροσθεν τοῦ πατρός μου τοῦ ἐν οὐρανοῖς. 33 ὅστις δ' ἂν
before the Father of Me in Heaven. whoever And shall

720 3165 1715 3588 444 720 846
ἀρνήσηταί με ἔμπροσθεν τῶν ἀνθρώπων, ἀρνήσομαι αὐτὸν
deny Me before men, will deny him

King James Version

shall be saved.
23 But when they persecute you in this city, flee ye into another: for verily I say unto you, Ye shall not have gone over the cities of Israel, till the Son of man be come.

24 The disciple is not above (his) master, nor the servant above his lord.
25 It is enough for the disciple that he be as his master, and the servant as his lord. If they have called the master of the house Beelzebub, how much more (shall they call) them of his household?

26 Fear them not therefore: for there is nothing covered, that shall not be revealed; and hid, that shall not be known.

27 What I tell you in darkness, (that) speak ye in light: and what ye hear in the ear, (that) preach ye upon the housetops.
28 And fear not them which kill the body, but are not able to kill the soul: but rather fear him which is able to destroy both soul and body in hell.

29 Are not two sparrows sold for a farthing? and one of them shall not fall on the ground without your Father.

30 But the very hairs of your head are all numbered.
31 Fear ye not therefore, ye are of more value than many sparrows.

32 Whosoever therefore shall confess me before men, him will I confess also before my Father which is in heaven.

33 But whosoever shall deny me before men, him

Literal Translation

before My Father in Heaven.

34 Do not think that I came to bring peace on earth. I did not come to bring peace, but a sword.
35 I came to divide a man against his father, and a daughter against her mother, and a bride against her mother-in-law.
36 And a man's enemies (shall be) those of his (own) house. (Micah 7:6)
37 The (one) loving father or mother above Me is not worthy of Me. And the (one) loving son or daughter above Me is not worthy of Me.
38 And who does not take up his cross and follow after Me is not worthy of Me.

39 The (one) finding his life shall lose it. And the (one) losing his life on account of Me shall find it.

40 The (one) receiving you receives Me, and the (one) receiving Me receives Him who sent Me.
41 The (one) receiving a prophet in the name of a prophet will receive a prophet's reward, and the (one) receiving a just (one) in the name of a just one will receive a just (one's) reward.
42 And whoever gives only a cup of cold (water to) drink to one of these little ones only in the name of a disciple, truly I say to you, In no way will he lose his reward.

Matthew 10:34

2504 1715 3588 3962 3450 3588 1722 3772
κἀγὼ ἔμπροσθεν τοῦ πατρός μου τοῦ ἐν οὐρανοῖς.
I also before the Father of Me in Heaven.

3361 3543 3754 2064 906 1515 1909 3588 1063 3756
34. Μὴ νομίσητε ὅτι ἦλθον βαλεῖν εἰρήνην ἐπὶ τὴν γῆν· οὐκ
Not think that I came to cast peace on the earth; not

2064 906 1515 235 3162 2064 1093 1369
ἦλθον βαλεῖν εἰρήνην ἀλλὰ μάχαιραν. 35 ἦλθον γὰρ διχάσαι
I came to cast peace but a sword. I came For to divide

444 2596 3588 3962 846 2532 2364 2596 3588
ἄνθρωπον κατὰ τοῦ πατρὸς αὐτοῦ, καὶ θυγατέρα κατὰ τῆς
a man against the father of him, and a daughter against the

3384 846 2532 3565 2596 3588 3994 846 2532
μητρὸς αὐτῆς, καὶ νύμφην κατὰ τῆς πενθερᾶς αὐτῆς· 36 καὶ
mother of her, and a bride against the mother-in-law of her and

2190 3588 444 3588 3615 846 3588 5368 3962 2228
ἐχθροὶ τοῦ ἀνθρώπου οἱ οἰκιακοὶ αὐτοῦ. 37 ὁ φιλῶν πατέρα ἢ
hostile (ones) of the man those of the house him The (one) loving father or

3384 5228 1691 3756 2076 3450 514 2532 3588 5368 5207 2228
μητέρα ὑπὲρ ἐμὲ, οὐκ ἔστι μου ἄξιος· καὶ ὁ φιλῶν υἱὸν ἢ
mother above Me, not is of Me worthy; and the (one) loving son or

2364 5228 1691 3756 2076 3450 514 2532 3739 3756 2983
θυγατέρα ὑπὲρ ἐμὲ, οὐκ ἔστι μου ἄξιος· 38 καὶ ὃς οὐ λαμβάνει
daughter above Me, not is of Me worthy. And who not takes up

3588 4716 846 2532 190 3694 3450 3756 2076 3450
τὸν σταυρὸν αὐτοῦ καὶ ἀκολουθεῖ ὀπίσω μου, οὐκ ἔστι μου
the cross of him and follow after me, not is of Me

. 514 3588 2147 3588 5590 846 622 846 2532 3588
ἄξιος. 39 ὁ εὑρὼν τὴν ψυχὴν αὐτοῦ ἀπολέσει αὐτήν· καὶ ὁ
worthy. The (one) finding the life of him will lose it; and he

622 3588 5590 846 1752 1700 2147 846
ἀπολέσας τὴν ψυχὴν αὐτοῦ ἕνεκεν ἐμοῦ εὑρήσει αὐτήν.
losing the life of him for sake of Me will find it.

3588 1209 5209 1691 1209 2532 3588 1691 1209
40. Ὁ δεχόμενος ὑμᾶς ἐμὲ δέχεται· καὶ ὁ ἐμὲ δεχόμενος
The (one) receiving you Me receives, and he Me receiving

1209 3588 649 3165 3588 1209 4396 1519
δέχεται τὸν ἀποστείλαντά με. 41 ὁ δεχόμενος προφήτην εἰς
receives the (one) sending Me. The (one) receiving a prophet in (the)

3686 4396 3408 4396 2983 2532 3588 1209
ὄνομα προφήτου μισθὸν προφήτου λήψεται· καὶ ὁ δεχόμενος
name of a prophet (the) reward of a prophet receives. And the (one) receiving

1342 1519 3686 1342 3408 1342 2983 2532 3739
δίκαιον εἰς ὄνομα δικαίου μισθὸν δικαίου λήψεται.42και ὃς
a just (one) in the name of a just (one), reward a just will receive. And who-

1437 4222 1520 3588 3398 5130 4221 5593 3440
ἐὰν ποτίσῃ ἕνα τῶν μικρῶν τούτων ποτήριον ψυχροῦ μόνον
ever gives drink to one little ones of these a cup of cold (water) only

1519 3686 3101 281 3004 5213 3756 3361 622 3588
εἰς ὄνομα μαθητοῦ, ἀμὴν λέγω ὑμῖν, οὐ μὴ ἀπολέσῃ τὸν
in the name of a disciple, truly I say to you, not ever will he lose the

3408 846
μισθὸν αὐτοῦ.
reward of him.

King James Version

will I also deny before my Father which is in heaven.

34 Think not that I am come to send peace on earth: I came not to send peace, but a sword.
35 For I am come to set a man at variance against his father, and the daughter against her mother, and the daughter in law against her mother in law.
36 And a man's foes (shall be) they of his own household.
37 He that loveth father or mother more than me is not worthy of me: and he that loveth son or daughter more than me is not worthy of me.

38 And he that taketh not his cross, and followeth after me, is not worthy of me.

39 He that findeth his life shall lose it: and he that loseth his life for my sake shall find it.

40 He that receiveth you receiveth me, and he that receiveth me receiveth him that sent me.
41 He that receiveth a prophet in the name of a prophet shall receive a prophet's reward; and he that receiveth a righteous man in the name of a righteous man shall receive a righteous man's reward.
42 And whosoever shall give to drink unto one of these little ones a cup of cold (water) only in the name of a disciple, verily I say unto you, he shall in no wise lose his reward.

Matthew 11

1. And it happened when Jesus finished commanding His twelve disciples, He moved from there to teach and

Matthew 11

2532 1096 3753 5055 3588 2424 1299 3588
1. Καὶ ἐγένετο ὅτε ἐτέλεσεν ὁ Ἰησοῦς διατάσσων τοῖς
And it happened when finished Jesus giving command to the

1427 3101 846 3327 1564 3588 1321 2532
δώδεκα μαθηταῖς αὐτοῦ, μετέβη ἐκεῖθεν τοῦ διδάσκειν καὶ
twelve disciples of Him, He moved from there to teach and

Matthew 11

1. And it came to pass, when Jesus had made an end of commanding his twelve disciples, he departed thence to teach and

Literal Translation

to proclaim in their cities.

2. But hearing in the prison of the works of Christ, sending two of his disciples,
3 John said to Him, Are You the (One) coming, or should we look for another?
4 And answering, Jesus said to them, Going, relate to John what you hear and see:

5 The blind receive sight, and the lame walk; lepers are cleansed, and the deaf hear; the dead are raised, and the poor are given the gospel.
6 And blessed is the (one), whoever shall not be offended in Me.
7 . But as these were going, Jesus began to say to the crowds about John, What did you go out into the wilderness to see? A reed being shaken with the wind?

8 But what did you go out to behold? A man clothed in soft things being clothed? Behold, those wearing soft things are in the houses of kings.
9 But what did you go out to see? A prophet? Yes, I say to you, and (one) more excellent than a prophet.
10 For this is (the one) about whom it has been written: "Behold, I sent out My messenger before Your face, who shall prepare Your way before You." (Mal. 3:1)

11 Truly I say to you, Not has arisen among (those) born of a woman (any) greater than John the Baptist. But the lesser in the kingdom of Heaven is greater than he is.

12 But from the days of John the Baptist until now, the

Matthew 11:2

2784 1722 3588 4172 846
κηρύσσειν ἐν ταῖς πόλεσιν αὐτῶν.
to proclaim in the cities of them.

3588 1161 2491 191 1722 3588 1201 3588 2041 3588
2. Ὁ δὲ Ἰωάννης ἀκούσας ἐν τῷ δεσμωτηρίῳ τὰ ἔργα τοῦ
But John hearing in the prison the works

5547 3992 1417 3588 3101 846 2036 846 4771
Χριστοῦ, πέμψας δύο τῶν μαθητῶν αὐτοῦ, 3 εἶπεν αὐτῷ, Σὺ
of Christ, sending two of the disciples of him, said to Him, You

1488 3588 2064 2228 2087 4328 2532 611 3588
εἶ ὁ ἐρχόμενος, ἢ ἕτερον προσδοκῶμεν; 4 καὶ ἀποκριθεὶς ὁ
are the coming (One), or another should we look for? And answering

2424 2036 846 4198 518 2491 3739
Ἰησοῦς εἶπεν αὐτοῖς, Πορευθέντες ἀπαγγείλατε Ἰωάννῃ ἃ
Jesus said to them, Going relate to John what

191 2532 991 5185 308 2532 5560 4043
ἀκούετε καὶ βλέπετε· 5 τυφλοὶ ἀναβλέπουσι, καὶ χωλοὶ περι-
you hear and see: blind ones receive sight, and lame ones walk

3015 2511 2532 2974 191 3498
πατοῦσι, λεπροὶ καθαρίζονται καὶ κωφοὶ ἀκούουσι, νεκροὶ
about; lepers are cleansed, and deaf ones hear; dead ones

1453 2532 4434 2097 2532 3107 2076
ἐγείρονται, καὶ πτωχοὶ εὐαγγελίζονται· 6 καὶ μακάριός ἐστιν,
are raised, and poor ones are given the gospel; and blessed is (he),

3739 1437 3361 4624 1722 1691 5130 1161 4198
ὃς ἐὰν μὴ σκανδαλισθῇ ἐν ἐμοί. 7 τούτων δὲ πορευομένων,
whoever not is stumbled in Me. (as) these But were going

756 3588 2424 3004 3588 3793 4012 2491 5101
ἤρξατο ὁ Ἰησοῦς λέγειν τοῖς ὄχλοις περὶ Ἰωάννου, Τί
began Jesus to say to the crowds concerning John, What

1831 1519 3588 2048 2300 2563 5259 417
ἐξήλθετε εἰς τὴν ἔρημον θεάσασθαι; κάλαμον ὑπὸ ἀνέμου
did you go out to the deserted (place) to behold? A reed by wind

4531 235 5101 1831 1492 444 1722 3120
σαλευόμενον; 8 ἀλλὰ τί ἐξήλθατε ἰδεῖν; ἄνθρωπον ἐν μαλακοῖς
being shaken? But what went you out to see? A man in soft

2440 294 2400 3588 3588 3120 5409 1722 3588
ἱματίοις ἠμφιεσμένον; ἰδού, οἱ τὰ μαλακὰ φοροῦντες ἐν τοῖς
garments having been clothed? Behold, those the soft wearing in the

3624 3588 935 1526 235 5101 1831 1492 4396
οἴκοις τῶν βασιλέων εἰσίν. 9 ἀλλὰ τί ἐξήλθετε ἰδεῖν; προφήτην;
houses of kings are, But what did you go out to see, a prophet?

3483 3004 5213 2532 4055 4396 3778 1063
ναί, λέγω ὑμῖν, καὶ περισσότερον προφήτου· 10 οὗτός γάρ
Yea, I say to you, even (one) more excellent than a prophet. this For

2076 4012 3739 1125 2400 1473 649 3588
ἐστι περὶ οὗ γέγραπται, Ἰδού, ἐγὼ ἀποστέλλω τὸν
is (he) about whom it has been written: Behold! I sent forth the

32 3450 4253 4383 4675 3739 2680 3588
ἄγγελόν μου πρὸ προσώπου σου, ὃς κατασκευάσει τὴν
messenger of Me before the face of You, who shall prepare the

3598 4675 1715 4675 281 3004 5213 3756 1453 1722
ὁδόν σου ἔμπροσθέν σου. 11 ἀμὴν λέγω ὑμῖν, οὐκ ἐγήγερται ἐν
way of You before You. Truly, I say to you, not has arisen in

1084 1135 3187 2491 3588 910 3588 1161
γεννητοῖς γυναικῶν μείζων Ἰωάννου τοῦ βαπτιστοῦ· ὁ δὲ
(those) born of a woman a greater (than) John the Baptist; the But

3398 1722 3588 932 3588 3772 3187 846 2076
μικρότερος ἐν τῇ βασιλείᾳ τῶν οὐρανῶν μείζων αὐτοῦ ἐστιν.
lesser in the kingdom of Heaven greater (than) he is.

575 1161 3588 2250 2491 3588 910 2193 737 3588
12 ἀπὸ δὲ τῶν ἡμερῶν Ἰωάννου τοῦ βαπτιστοῦ ἕως ἄρτι ἡ
from And the days of John the Baptist until now the

King James Version

to preach in their cities.

2. Now when John had heard in the prison the works of Christ, he sent two of his disciples,
3 And said unto him, Art thou he that should come, or do we look for another?
4 Jesus answered and said unto them, Go and shew John again those things which ye do hear and see:
5 The blind receive their sight, and the lame walk, the lepers are cleansed, and the deaf hear, the dead are raised up, and the poor have the gospel preached to them.
6 And blessed is (he), whosoever shall not be offended in me.
7 . And as they departed, Jesus began to say unto the multitudes concerning John, What went ye out into the wilderness to see? A reed shaken with the wind?

8 But what went ye out for to see? A man clothed in soft raiment? behold, they that wear soft (clothing) are in kings' houses.

9 But what went ye out for to see? A prophet? yea, I say unto you, and more than a prophet.
10 For this is (he), of whom it is written, Behold, I send my messenger before thy face, which shall prepare thy way before thee.

11 Verily I say unto you, Among them that are born of women there hath not risen a greater than John the Baptist: notwithstanding he that is least in the kingdom of heaven is greater than he.
12 And from the days of John the Baptist until now the

Matthew 11:13

Literal Translation

kingdom of Heaven is taken by force, and (the) violent seize it.

13 For all the Prophets and the Law prophesied until John.
14 And if you are willing to receive, he is Elijah, the (one) about to come.
15 The (one) having ears to hear, let him hear.
16 But to what shall I compare this generation? It is like little children sitting in (the) markets, and calling to their mates,

17 and saying, We piped to you, and you did not dance; we mourned to you, and you did not wail.
18 For John came neither eating nor drinking, and they say, He has a demon.
19 The Son of man came eating and drinking, and they say, Behold, a gluttonous man and a wine drinker, and a friend of tax collectors, and of sinners. And wisdom was justified by her children.

20. Then He began to reproach the cities in which most of His powerful acts had occurred, for they did not repent.
21 Woe to you, Chorazin! Woe to you, Bethsaida! For if the powerful acts which occurred in you had happened in Tyre and Sidon, they would have repented long ago in sackcloth and ashes.
22 But I say to you, It shall be more bearable for Tyre and Sidon in Judgment Day than for you.
23 And you, Capernaum, who have been exalted to the heaven, (you) will be thrown down to Hades. For if the powerful acts happening in you had taken place in Sodom, it would remain until today. (Isa. 14:13,15)
24 But I say to you,

---

932 3588 3772 971 2532 973 726
βασιλεία τῶν οὐρανῶν βιαζεταὶ, καὶ βιασταὶ ἁρπάζουσιν
kingdom of Heaven (is) taken by force, and (the) violent seize

846 3956 1063 3588 4396 2532 3588 3551 2193 2491
αὐτήν. 13 πάντες γὰρ οἱ προφῆται καὶ ὁ νόμος ἕως Ἰωάννου
it. all For the Prophets and the Law until John

4395 2532 1487 2309 1209 846 2076 2243 3588
προεφήτευσαν·14 καὶ εἰ θέλετε δέξασθαι, αὐτός ἐστιν Ἠλίας ὁ
prophesied; and if you are willing to receive, he is Elijah he

3195 2064 3588 2192 3775 191 191 5101 1161
μέλλων ἔρχεσθαι.15 ὁ ἔχων ὦτα ἀκούειν ἀκουέτω.16 τίνι δὲ
about to come. He having ears to hear, let him hear. to what But

3666 3588 1074 3778 3664 2076 3808 1722
ὁμοιώσω τὴν γενεὰν ταύτην; ὁμοία ἐστὶ παιδαρίοις ἐν
shall I compare generation this? like it is little children in

58 2521 2532 4377 3588 2083 846
ἀγοραῖς καθημένοις, καὶ προσφωνοῦσι τοῖς ἑταίροις αὐτῶν,
(the) markets sitting and calling to the mates of them,

2532 3004 832 5213 2532 3756 3738 2354
17 καὶ λέγουσιν, Ηὐλήσαμεν ὑμῖν, καὶ οὐκ ὠρχήσασθε· ἐθρηνή-
and saying, We piped to you, and not you did dance; we

5213 2532 3756 2875 2064 1063 2491 3383 2068
σαμεν ὑμῖν, καὶ οὐκ ἐκόψασθε.18ἦλθε γὰρ Ἰωάννης μήτε ἐσθίων
mourned to you, and not you did wail. came For John neither eating

3383 4095 2532 3004 1140 2192 2064 3588 5207 3588
μήτε πίνων, καὶ λέγουσι, Δαιμόνιον ἔχει. 19 ἦλθεν ὁ υἱὸς τοῦ
nor drinking, and they say, A demon he has. Came the Son

444 2068 2532 4095 2532 3004 2400 444
ἀνθρώπου ἐσθίων καὶ πίνων, καὶ λέγουσιν, Ἰδού, ἄνθρωπος
of man eating and drinking, and they say Behold a man

5314 2532 3630 5057 5384 2532 268 2532
φάγος καὶ οἰνοπότης, τελωνῶν φίλος καὶ ἁμαρτωλῶν. καὶ
gluttonous and a wine-drinker, of tax-collectors a friend and of sinners And

1344 3588 4678 575 3588 5043 846
ἐδικαιώθη ἡ σοφία ἀπὸ τῶν τεκνων αὐτῆς.
was justified wisdom by the children of her.

5119 756 3679 3588 4172 1722 3739 1096 3588
20. Τότε ἤρξατο ὀνειδίζειν τὰς πόλεις ἐν αἷς ἐγένοντο αἱ
Then He began to reproach the cities in which had occurred the

4118 1411 846 3754 3756 3340 3759 4671
πλεῖσται δυνάμεις αὐτοῦ, ὅτι οὐ μετενόησαν. 21 Οὐαί σοι,
most acts of power of His, because not they had repented. Woe to you

5523 3759 4671 966 3754 1487 1722 5184 2532 4605
Χοραζίν, οὐαί σοι, Βηθσαϊδά, ὅτι εἰ ἐν Τύρῳ καὶ Σιδῶνι
Chorazin; woe to you, Bethsaida! Because if in Tyre and Sidon

1096 3588 1411 3588 1096 1722 5213 3819 302 1722 4526
ἐγένοντο αἱ δυνάμεις αἱ γενόμεναι ἐν ὑμῖν, πάλαι ἂν ἐν σάκκῳ
occurred the acts of power happening in you, long ago in sackcloth

2532 4700 3340 4133 3004 5213 5184 2532 4605
καὶ σποδῷ μετενόησαν. 22 πλὴν λέγω ὑμῖν, Τύρῳ καὶ Σιδῶνι
and ashes they had repented. However I say to you, For Tyre and for Sidon

414 2071 1722 2250 2920 2228 5213 2532 4771 2584
ἀνεκτότερον ἔσται ἐν ἡμέρᾳ κρίσεως, ἢ ὑμῖν. 23καὶ σύ, Καπερ-
more bearable it will be in (the) day of judgment, than for you. And you Caper-

3588 2193 3588 3772 5312 2193 86 2601
ναούμ, ἡ ἕως τοῦ οὐρανοῦ ὑψωθεῖσα, ἕως ᾅδου καταβιβα-
naum, who to the heaven have been exalted, to Hades you will be cast

3754 1487 1722 4670 1096 3588 1411 3588 1096 1722
σθήσῃ·ὅτι εἰ ἐν Σοδόμοις ἐγένοντο αι δυνάμεις αἱ γενόμεναι ἐν
down, because if in Sodom had occurred the acts of power happening in

4671 3306 302 3360 3588 4594 4133 3004 5213 3754 1093
σοί, ἔμειναν ἂν μέχρι τῆς σήμερον. 24 πλὴν λέγω ὑμῖν, ὅτι γῇ
you, it would remain until today. However I say to you that (for) land

---

King James Version

kingdom of heaven suffereth violence, and the violent take it by force.

13 For all the prophets and the law prophesied until John.
14 And if ye will receive (it), this is Elias, which was for to come.
15 He that hath ears to hear, let him hear.
16 But whereunto shall I liken this generation? It is like unto children sitting in the markets, and calling unto their fellows,

17 And saying, We have piped unto you, and ye have not danced; we have mourned unto you, and ye have not lamented.
18 For John came neither eating nor drinking, and they say, He hath a devil.
19 The Son of man came eating and drinking, and they say, Behold a man gluttonous, and a winebibber, a friend of publicans and sinners. But wisdom is justified of her children.
20. Then began he to upbraid the cities wherein most of his mighty works were done, because they repented not:
21 Woe unto thee, Chorazin! woe unto thee, Bethsaida! for if the mighty works, which were done in you, had been done in Tyre and Sidon, they would have repented long ago in sackcloth and ashes.
22 But I say unto you, It shall be more tolerable for Tyre and Sidon at the day of judgment, than for you.
23 And thou, Capernaum, which art exalted unto heaven, shalt be brought down to hell: for if the mighty works, which have been done in thee, had been done in Sodom, it would have remained until this day.
24 But I say unto you, That it

Literal Translation

It will be more bearable for the land of Sodom in Judgment day than for you.

25. Answering at that time, Jesus said, I praise You, Father, Lord of Heaven and the earth, because You hid these things from (the) sophisticated and cunning and revealed them to babes.

26 Yes, Father, for so it was pleasing before You.
27 All things were yielded up to Me by My Father; and no one knows the Son except the Father; nor does anyone know the Father, except the Son, and whomever the Son purposes to reveal (Him).

28. Come to Me, all those laboring and being burdened, and I will give you rest.
29 Take My yoke upon you and learn from Me, because I am meek and lowly in heart, and you will find rest to your souls. (Jer. 6:16)

30 For My yoke (is) easy, and My burden is light.

Matthew 11:25

4670 414 2071 1722 2250 2920 2228 4671
Σοδόμων ἀνεκτότερον ἔσται ἐν ἡμέρᾳ κρίσεως, ἢ σοί.
of Sodom more bearable it will be in (the) day of judgment, than for you.

1722 1565 3588 2540 611 3588 2424 2036 1843
25 Ἐν ἐκείνῳ τῷ καιρῷ ἀποκριθεὶς ὁ Ἰησοῦς εἶπεν, Ἐξομολο-
At that time answering Jesus said, I give praise

4671 3962 2962 3588 3772 2532 3588 1093 3754
γοῦμαί σοι, πάτερ, Κύριε τοῦ οὐρανοῦ καὶ τῆς γῆς, ὅτι
to You, Father, Lord of the heaven and the earth, for

613 5023 575 4680 2532 4908 2532 601
ἀπέκρυψας ταῦτα ἀπὸ σοφῶν καὶ συνετῶν, καὶ ἀπεκάλυψας
You hid these things from sophisticated and cunning, and revealed

846 3516 3483 3588 3962 3754 3779 1096 2107
αὐτὰ νηπίοις. 26 ναί ὁ πατήρ, ὅτι οὕτως ἐγένετο εὐδοκία
them to babes; yea, Father, because thus it was well-pleasing

1715 4675 3956 3427 3860 5259 3588 3962 3450
ἔμπροσθέν σου. 27 πάντα μοι παρεδόθη ὑπὸ τοῦ πατρός μου·
before You. All things to Me were yielded by the Father of Me,

2532 3762 1921 3588 5207 1487 3361 3588 3962 3761 3588
καὶ οὐδεὶς ἐπιγινώσκει τὸν υἱόν, εἰ μὴ ὁ πατήρ· οὐδὲ τὸν
and no one knows the Son except the Father, nor the

3962 5100 1921 1487 3361 3588 5207 2532 3739 1437 1014 3588
πατέρα τις ἐπιγινώσκει, εἰ μὴ ὁ υἱός, καὶ ᾧ ἐὰν βούληται ὁ
Father anyone knows except the Son, and to whomever purposes the

5207 601 1205 4314 3165 3956 3588 2872 2532
υἱὸς ἀποκαλύψαι. 28 δεῦτε πρός με πάντες οἱ κοπιῶντες καὶ
Son to reveal. Come to Me all the (ones) laboring and

5412 2504 373 5209 142 3588 2218
πεφορτισμένοι, κἀγὼ ἀναπαύσω ὑμᾶς. 29 ἄρατε τὸν ζυγόν
being burdened, and I give rest to you. Take the yoke

3450 1909 5209 2532 3129 575 1700 3754 4235 1510 2532 5011
μου ἐφ᾽ ὑμᾶς καὶ μάθετε ἀπ᾽ ἐμοῦ, ὅτι πρᾷός εἰμι καὶ ταπεινὸς
of Me on you and learn from Me, because meek I am and lowly

3588 2588 2532 2147 372 3588 5590 5216 3588
τῇ καρδίᾳ· καὶ εὑρήσετε ἀνάπαυσιν ταῖς ψυχαῖς ὑμῶν· 30 ὁ
in heart and you will find rest to the souls of you; the

1063 2218 3450 5543 2532 3588 5413 3450 1645 2076
γὰρ ζυγός μου χρηστὸς καὶ τὸ φορτίον μου ἐλαφρόν ἐστιν.
for yoke of Me (is) easy and the burden of Me light is

King James Version

shall be more tolerable for the land of Sodom in the day of judgment, than for thee.

25. At that time Jesus answered and said, I thank thee, O Father, Lord of heaven and earth, because thou hast hid these things from the wise and prudent, and hast revealed them unto babes.

26 Even so, Father: for so it seemed good in thy sight.
27 All things are delivered unto me of my Father: and no man knoweth the Son, but the Father; neither knoweth any man the Father, save the Son, and (he) to whomsoever the Son will reveal (him).

28. Come unto me, all (ye) that labour and are heavy laden, and I will give you rest.
29 Take my yoke upon you, and learn of me; for I am meek and lowly in heart: and ye shall find rest unto your souls.

30 For my yoke (is) easy, and my burden is light.

Matthew 12

1. At that season on the sabbath, Jesus went through the grain fields. And His disciples were hungry, and began to pluck heads (of grain) and to eat.
2 But seeing, the Pharisees said to Him, Behold, your disciples are doing what it is not lawful to do on the sabbath.
3 But He said to them, Have you not read what David did, when he and those with him hungered?
4 How he entered into the house of God, and he ate the Loaves of Presentation

Matthew 12

1722 1565 3588 2540 4198 3588 2424 3588 4521
1. Ἐν ἐκείνῳ τῷ καιρῷ ἐπορεύθη ὁ Ἰησοῦς τοῖς σάββασι
At that season went Jesus on the sabbath

1223 3588 4702 3588 1161 3101 846 3983 2532 756
διὰ τῶν σπορίμων· οἱ δὲ μαθηταὶ αὐτοῦ ἐπείνασαν, καὶ ἤρξαντο
through the grainfields. the And disciples of Him hungered, and began

5089 4719 2532 2068 3588 1161 5330 1492 2036
τίλλειν στάχυας καὶ ἐσθίειν. 2 οἱ δὲ Φαρισαῖοι ἰδόντες εἶπον
to pluck heads and to eat. the But Pharisees seeing said

846 2400 3588 3101 4675 4160 3739 3756 1832 4160
αὐτῷ, Ἰδού, οἱ μαθηταί σου ποιοῦσιν ὃ οὐκ ἔξεστι ποιεῖν
to Him, Behold, the disciples of You are doing what not it is lawful to do

1722 4521 3588 1161 2036 846 3756 314 5101 4160
ἐν σαββάτῳ. 3 ὁ δὲ εἶπεν αὐτοῖς, Οὐκ ἀνέγνωτε τί ἐποίησε
in a sabbath. He But said to them, Not did you read what did

1138 3753 3983 846 2532 3588 3326 846 4459 1525
Δαβὶδ, ὅτε ἐπείνασεν αὐτὸς καὶ οἱ μετ᾽ αὐτοῦ· 4 πῶς εἰσῆλθεν
David, when he hungered himself and those with him? How he went in

1519 3588 3624 3588 2316 2532 3588 740 3588 4286
εἰς τὸν οἶκον τοῦ θεοῦ, καὶ τοὺς ἄρτους τῆς προθέσεως
into the house of God, and the loaves of the presentation

Matthew 12

1. At that time Jesus went on the sabbath day through the corn; and his disciples were an hungred, and began to pluck the ears of corn, and to eat.
2 But when the Pharisees saw (it), they said unto him, Behold, thy disciples do that which is not lawful to do upon the sabbath day.

3 But he said unto them, Have ye not read what David did, when he was an hungred, and they that were with him;
4 How he entered into the house of God, and did eat the shewbread,

Literal Translation **Matthew 12:5** *King James Version*

Literal Translation

which it was not lawful for him to eat, nor for those with him, except for the priests only?

5 Or have you not read in the Law that on the sabbaths the priests in the temple profane the sabbath and are guiltless?

6 But I say to you, (One) greater than the temple is here.

7 But if you had known what (this) is, "I desire mercy and not sacrifice," you would not have condemned the guiltless. (Hosea 6:6)

8 For the Son of man is also Lord of the sabbath.

9. And moving from there, He came into their synagogue.

10 And, behold, a man having (a) withered hand was there. And they asked Him, saying, Is it lawful to heal on the sabbaths? That they might accuse Him.

11 But He said to them, What man of you will be who will have one sheep, and if this one fall into a pit on the sabbaths, will he not lay hold of it and raise (it) up?

12 How much more, then, does a man excel a sheep! So that it is lawful to do well on the sabbaths.

13 Then He said to the man, Stretch out your hand! And he stretched out. And it was restored sound as the other.

14. But as they were leaving, the Pharisees took up a council against Him, how they might destroy Him.

15 But knowing, Jesus withdrew from there. And great crowds followed Him, and He healed them all

16 and warned them that they should not make Him manifest.

17 So that might be fulfilled

5315 3739 3756 1832 2258 846 5315 3761 3588 3326 846
ἔφαγεν, οὓς οὐκ ἐξὸν ἦν αὐτῷ φαγεῖν, οὐδὲ τοῖς μετ᾽ αὐτοῦ,
he ate, which not lawful it was for him to eat, nor for those with him,

1487 3361 3588 2409 3441 2228 3756 314 1722 3588 3551 3754
εἰ μὴ τοῖς ἱερεῦσι μόνοις; 5 ἢ οὐκ ἀνέγνωτε ἐν τῷ νόμῳ, ὅτι
except for the priest only? Or not did you read in the Law that

3588 4521 3588 2409 1722 3588 2411 3588 4521 953
τοῖς σάββασιν οἱ ἱερεῖς ἐν τῷ ἱερῷ τὸ σάββατον βεβηλοῦσι,
on the sabbaths the priests in the temple the sabbath profane,

2532 338 1526 3004 1161 5213 3754 3588 2411 3187 2076
καὶ ἀναίτιοί εἰσι; 6 λέγω δὲ ὑμῖν ὅτι τοῦ ἱεροῦ μεῖζόν ἐστιν
and guiltless are? I say But to you that the temple a greater than is

5602 1487 1161 1097 5101 2076 1656 2309 2532 3756 2378
ὧδε. 7 εἰ δὲ ἐγνώκειτε τί ἐστιν, Ἔλεον θέλω καὶ οὐ θυσίαν,
here. if But you had known what it is, Mercy I desire and not sacrifice

3756 302 2613 3588 338 2962 1063 2076/2532/3588
οὐκ ἂν κατεδικάσατε τοὺς ἀναιτίους. 8 κύριος γάρ ἐστι καὶ τοῦ
not would you have judged the guiltless. Lord For is also of the

4521 3588 5207 3588 444
σαββάτου ὁ υἱὸς τοῦ ἀνθρώπου.
sabbath the Son of man

2532 3327 1564 2064 1519 3588 4864 846 2532
9. Καὶ μεταβὰς ἐκεῖθεν ἦλθεν εἰς τὴν συναγωγὴν αὐτῶν. 10 καὶ
And moving from there He came into the synagogue of them. And

2400 444 2258 3588 5495 2192 3584 2532 1905
ἰδού, ἄνθρωπος ἦν τὴν χεῖρα ἔχων ξηράν. καὶ ἐπηρώτησαν
behold, a man was, the hand having withered, And they questioned

846 3004 1487 1832 3588 4521 2323 2443
αὐτὸν, λέγοντες, Εἰ ἔξεστι τοῖς σάββασι θεραπεύειν; ἵνα
Him, saying. If it is lawful on the Sabbaths to heal? That

2723 846 3588 1161 2036 846 5101 2071 1537
κατηγορήσωσιν αὐτοῦ. 11 ὁ δὲ εἶπεν αὐτοῖς, Τίς ἔσται ἐξ
they might accuse Him. He But said to them, What will be of

5216 444 3739 2192 4263 1520 2532 1437 1706 5124
ὑμῶν ἄνθρωπος, ὃς ἕξει πρόβατον ἕν, καὶ ἐὰν ἐμπέσῃ τοῦτο
you a man who will have sheep one, and if fall (in) this

3588 4521 1519 999 3780 2902 846 2532 1453
τοῖς σάββασιν εἰς βόθυνον, οὐχὶ κρατήσει αὐτὸ καὶ ἐγερεῖ;
on the sabbaths into a pit, not will he lay hold of it and raise (it)?

4214 3767 1308 444 4263 5620 1832 3588
12 πόσῳ οὖν διαφέρει ἄνθρωπος προβάτου. ὥστε ἔξεστι τοῖς
How much then surpasses a man a sheep! So that it is lawful on the

4521 2573 4160 5119 3004 3588 444 1614
σάββασι καλῶς ποιεῖν. 13 τότε λέγει τῷ ἀνθρώπῳ, Ἔκτεινόν
sabbaths well to do. Then He says to the man, Stretch out

3588 5495 4675 2532 1614 2532 600 5199 5613 3588
τὴν χεῖρά σου. καὶ ἐξέτεινε, καὶ ἀποκατεστάθη ὑγιὴς ὡς ἡ
the hand of you, and he stretched out and it was restored sound as the

243 3588 1161 5330 4824 2983 2596 846
ἄλλη. 14 οἱ δὲ Φαρισαῖοι συμβούλιον ἔλαβον κατ᾽ αὐτοῦ
other. the But Pharisees a council took against Him

1831 3704 846 622 3588 1161 2424 1097
ἐξελθόντες, ὅπως αὐτὸν ἀπολέσωσιν. 15 Ὁ δὲ Ἰησοῦς γνοὺς
they having left, how Him they might destroy. But Jesus knowing

402 1564 2532 190 846 3793 4183
ἀνεχώρησεν ἐκεῖθεν· καὶ ἠκολούθησαν αὐτῷ ὄχλοι πολλοί,
withdrew from there. And followed Him crowds many

2532 2323 846 3956 2532 2008 846
καὶ ἐθεράπευσεν αὐτοὺς πάντας, 16 καὶ ἐπετίμησεν αὐτοῖς,
and He healed them all, and warned them

2443 3361 5318 846 4160 3704 4137 3588
ἵνα μὴ φανερὸν αὐτὸν ποιήσωσιν· 17 ὅπως πληρωθῇ τὸ
that not manifest Him they should make; so that may be fulfilled that

King James Version

which was not lawful for him to eat, neither for them which were with him, but only for the priests?

5 Or have ye not read in the law, how that on the sabbath days the priests in the temple profane the sabbath, and are blameless?

6 But I say unto you, That in this place is (one) greater than the temple.

7 But if ye had known what (this) meaneth, I will have mercy, and not sacrifice, ye would not have condemned the guiltless.

8 For the Son of man is Lord even of the sabbath day.

9. And when he was departed thence, he went into their synagogue:

10 And, behold, there was a man which had (his) hand withered. And they asked him, saying, Is it lawful to heal on the sabbath days? that they might accuse him.

11 And he said unto them, What man shall there be among you, that shall have one sheep, and if it fall into a pit on the sabbath day, will he not lay hold on it, and lift (it) out?

12 How much then is a man better than a sheep? Wherefore it is lawful to do well on the sabbath days.

13 Then saith he to the man, Stretch forth thine hand. And he stretched (it) forth; and it was restored whole, like as the other.

14. Then the Pharisees went out, and held a council against him, how they might destroy him.

15 But when Jesus knew (it), he withdrew himself from thence: and great multitudes followed him, and he healed them all;

16 And charged them that they should not make him known:

17 That it might be fulfilled

Literal Translation

that spoken through Isaiah the prophet, saying,
18 "Behold My Servant whom I chose, My Beloved, in whom My soul has delighted! I will put My Spirit on Him, and He will declare judgment to the nations.
19 He will not strive nor cry out, nor will anyone hear His voice in the streets.
20 A bruised reed He will not break, and smoking flax He will not quench, until He bring forth the judgment to victory.

21 And (the) nations will hope in His name." (Isa. 42:1-4)
22. Then one having been demon-possessed was brought to Him, blind and dumb. And He healed him, so that the blind and dumb one both to speak and to see.
23 And all the crowds were amazed, and said, Is this not the son of David?
24 But hearing, the Pharisees said, This (one) does not cast out demons except by Beelzebul, ruler of the demons.

25 But Jesus, knowing their thoughts, He said to them, Every kingdom divided against itself is brought to ruin. And every city or house divided against itself will not stand.

26 And if Satan casts out Satan, he was divided against himself. How then will his kingdom stand?

27 And if I cast out the demons by Beelzebul, by whom do your sons throw (them) out? Because of this, they shall be your judges.
28 But if I cast out the demons by (the) Spirit of God, then the kingdom of God has come on you.
29 Or

Matthew 12:18

4483 1223 2268 3588 4396 3004 2400 3588 3816
ῥηθὲν διὰ Ἠσαΐου τοῦ προφήτου, λέγοντος, 18 Ἰδού, ὁ παῖς
spoken through Isaiah the prophet, saying, Behold, the Servant

3450 3739 140 3588 27 3450 1519 3739 2106 3588 5590
μου ὃν ᾑρέτισα· ὁ ἀγαπητός μου εἰς ὃν εὐδόκησεν ἡ ψυχή
of Me whom I chose, the Beloved of Me, in whom has delighted the soul

3450 5087 3588 4151 3450 1909 846 2532 2920 3588 1484
μου· θήσω τὸ πνεῦμά μου ἐπ' αὐτόν, καὶ κρίσιν τοῖς ἔθνεσιν
of Me I will put the Spirit of Me on Him, and judgment to the nations

518 3756 2051 3761 2905 3761 191 5100 1722
ἀπαγγελεῖ. 19 οὐκ ἐρίσει οὐδὲ κραυγάσει· οὐδὲ ἀκούσει τις ἐν
He will declare. Not He will strive, nor cry out nor will hear any in

3588 4113 3588 5456 846 2563 4937
ταῖς πλατείαις τὴν φωνὴν αὐτοῦ. 20 κάλαμον συντετριμμένον
the streets the voice of Him. A reed having been bruised

3756 2608 2532 3043 5188 3756 4570 2193 302 1544 1519
οὐ κατεάξει, καὶ λῖνον τυφόμενον οὐ σβέσει, ἕως ἂν ἐκβάλῃ εἰς
not He will break, and flax smoking not he will quench until He might expel to

3534 3588 2920 2532 1722 3588 3686 846 1484 1679
νῖκος τὴν κρίσιν. 21 καὶ ἐν τῷ ὀνόματι αὐτοῦ ἔθνη ἐλπιοῦσι.
victory the judgment. And in the name of Him nations will hope.

5119 4374 846 1139 5185 2532
22. Τότε προσηνέχθη αὐτῷ δαιμονιζόμενος, τυφλὸς καὶ
Then was brought to Him one having been demon-possessed, blind and

2974 2532 2323 846 5620 3588 5185 2532 2974
κωφός· καὶ ἐθεράπευσεν αὐτόν, ὥστε τὸν τυφλὸν καὶ κωφὸν
dumb; and He healed him, so as the blind and dumb

2532 2980 2532 991 2532 1839 3956 3588 3793 2532
καὶ λαλεῖν καὶ βλέπειν. 23 καὶ ἐξίσταντο πάντες οἱ ὄχλοι καὶ
both to speak and to see. And were amazed all the crowds, and

3004 3385 3778 2076 3588 5207 1138 3588 1161 5330
ἔλεγον, Μήτι οὗτός ἐστιν ὁ υἱὸς Δαβίδ; 24 οἱ δὲ Φαρισαῖοι
said, not this Is the Son of David? the But Pharisees

191 2036 3778 3756 1544 3588 1140 1487 3361
ἀκούσαντες εἶπον, Οὗτος οὐκ ἐκβάλλει τὰ δαιμόνια εἰ μὴ
having heard said, This one not casts out the demons. except

1722 3588 954 758 3588 1140 1492 1161 3588
ἐν τῷ Βεελζεβοὺλ ἄρχοντι τῶν δαιμονίων. 25 εἰδὼς δὲ ὁ
by Beelzebul ruler of the demons. knowing But

2424 3588 1761 846 2036 846 3956 932
Ἰησοῦς τὰς ἐνθυμήσεις αὐτῶν εἶπεν αὐτοῖς, Πᾶσα βασιλεία
Jesus the thoughts of them He said to them, Every kingdom

3307 2596 1438 2049 2532 3956 4172 2288 3614
μερισθεῖσα καθ' ἑαυτῆς ἐρημοῦται, καὶ πᾶσα πόλις ἢ οἰκία
divided against itself (is) brought to ruin, and every city or house

3307 2596 1438 3756 2476 2532/1487/3588 4567 3588
μερισθεῖσα καθ' ἑαυτῆς οὐ σταθήσεται. 26 καὶ εἰ ὁ Σατανᾶς τὸν
divided against itself not will stand. And if Satan

4567 1544 1909 1438 3307 4459 3767 2476
Σατανᾶν ἐκβάλλει, ἐφ' ἑαυτὸν ἐμερίσθη· πῶς οὖν σταθήσεται
Satan casts out, against himself he was divided; how then will stand

3588 932 846 2532 1487 1473 1722 954 1544 3588
ἡ βασιλεία αὐτοῦ; 27 καὶ εἰ ἐγὼ ἐν Βεελζεβοὺλ ἐκβάλλω τὰ
the kingdom of him? And if I by Beelzebul cast out the

1140 3588 5207 5216 1722 5101 1544 1223 5124 846
δαιμόνια, οἱ υἱοὶ ὑμῶν ἐν τίνι ἐκβάλλουσι; διὰ τοῦτο αὐτοὶ
demons, the sons of you by whom do they cast out? Because of this they

5216 2071 2923 1487/1161/1473/1722 4151 2316 1544
ὑμῶν ἔσονται κριταί. 28 εἰ δὲ ἐγὼ ἐν Πνεύματι Θεοῦ ἐκβάλλω
of you shall be judges. if But I in (the) Spirit of God cast out

3588 1140 686 5348 1909 5209 3588 932 3588 2316 2228
τὰ δαιμόνια, ἄρα ἔφθασεν ἐφ' ὑμᾶς ἡ βασιλεία τοῦ θεοῦ. 29 ἢ
the demons, then has come upon you the kingdom of God. Or

Literal Translation

which was spoken by Esaias the prophet, saying,
18 Behold my servant, whom I have chosen; my beloved, in whom my soul is well pleased: I will put my spirit upon him, and he shall shew judgment to the Gentiles.
19 He shall not strive, nor cry; neither shall any man hear his voice in the streets.
20 A bruised reed shall he not break, and smoking flax shall he not quench, till he send forth judgment unto victory.

21 And in his name shall the Gentiles trust.

22. Then was brought unto him one possessed with a devil, blind, and dumb: and he healed him, insomuch that the blind and dumb both spake and saw.
23 And all the people were amazed, and said, Is not this the son of David?
24 But when the Pharisees heard (it), they said, This (fellow) doth not cast out devils, but by Beelzebub the prince of the devils.

25 And Jesus knew their thoughts, and said unto them, Every kingdom divided against itself is brought to desolation; and every city or house divided against itself shall not stand:

26 And if Satan cast out Satan, he is divided against himself; how shall then his kingdom stand?

27 And if I by Beelzebub cast out devils, by whom do your children cast (them) out? therefore they shall be your judges.

28 But if I cast out devils by the Spirit of God, then the kingdom of God is come unto you.
29 Or

Matthew 12:30

Literal Translation

how is anyone able to enter the house of the strong one and plunder his vessels, if he does not first tie up the strong one; and then he will plunder his house?

30 The (one) not being with Me is against Me, and the (one) not gathering with Me scatters.
31 Because of this, I say to you, Every sin and blasphemy shall be forgiven to men, but blasphemy of the Spirit shall not be forgiven to men.

32 And whoever speaks a word against the Son of man, it will be forgiven him. But whoever speaks against the Holy Spirit, it will not be forgiven him, not in this age nor in the coming (one).

33 Either make the tree good and its fruit good, or make the tree corrupt and its fruit corrupt; for the tree is known by the fruit.

34 Offspring of vipers! How can you, being evil, speak good things? For out of the abundance of the heart the mouth speaks.

35 The good man out of the good treasure of the heart puts forth good things. And the evil man out of the evil treasure puts forth evil things.

36 But I say to you, that every idle word, whatever men may speak, they shall give an account of it in Judgment Day.

37 For by your words you will be justified, and by your words you will be condemned.

4459 1410 5100 1525 1519 3588 3614 3588 2478 2532 3588
πῶς δύναταί τις εἰσελθεῖν εἰς τὴν οἰκίαν τοῦ ἰσχυροῦ καὶ τὰ
how is able anyone to enter into the house of the strong one and the

4632 846 1283 1437 3361 4412 1210 3588 2478
σκεύη αὐτοῦ διαρπάσαι, ἐὰν μὴ πρῶτον δήσῃ τὸν ἰσχυρόν;
vessels of him to plunder, if not first he binds the strong one?

2532 5119 3588 3614 846 1283 3588 3361 5607 3326 1700
και τότε τὴν οἰκίαν αὐτοῦ διαρπάσει. 30 ὁ μὴ ὢν μετ' ἐμοῦ,
And then the house of him he will plunder. The (one) not being with Me,

2596 1700 2076 2532 3588 3361 4863 3326 1700 4650 1223
κατ' ἐμοῦ ἐστι, καὶ ὁ μὴ συνάγων μετ' ἐμοῦ, σκορπίζει. 31 διὰ
against Me is, and he not gathering with Me scatters. Because

5124 3004 5213 3956 266 2532 988 863
τοῦτο λέγω ὑμῖν, Πᾶσα ἁμαρτία καὶ βλασφημία ἀφεθήσεται
of this I say to you, Every sin and blasphemy shall be forgiven

3588 444 3588 1161 3588 4151 988 3756 863
τοῖς ἀνθρώποις· ἡ δὲ τοῦ Πνεύματος βλασφημία οὐκ ἀφεθή-
to men; the but of the Spirit blasphemy not will be

3588 444 2532 3739 302 2036 3056 2596 3588 5207
σεται τοῖς ἀνθρώποις· 32 καὶ ὃς ἂν εἴπῃ λόγον κατὰ τοῦ υἱοῦ
forgiven to men.; and whoever speaks a word against the Son

3588 444 863 846 3739 1161 302 2036 2596 3588
τοῦ ἀνθρώπου, ἀφεθήσεται αὐτῷ· ὃς δ' ἂν εἴπῃ κατὰ τοῦ
of man, it will be forgiven him; who but ever speaks against the

4151 3588 40 3756 863 846 3777 1722 5129
Πνεύματος τοῦ Ἁγίου, οὐκ ἀφεθήσεται αὐτῷ, οὔτε ἐν τούτῳ
Spirit the Holy, not it will be forgiven him, neither in this

3588 165 3777 1722 3588 3195 2228 4160 3588 1186
τῷ αἰῶνι οὔτε ἐν τῷ μέλλοντι. 33 ἢ ποιήσατε τὸ δένδρον
age nor in the coming (one). Either make the tree

2570 2532 3588 2590 846 2570 2228 4160 3588 1186
καλὸν, καὶ τὸν καρπὸν αὐτοῦ καλόν, ἢ ποιήσατε τὸ δένδρον
good and the fruit of it good, or make the tree

4550 2532 3588 2590 846 4550 1537 1063 3588 2590
σαπρὸν καὶ τὸν καρπὸν αὐτοῦ σαπρόν, ἐκ γὰρ τοῦ καρποῦ
corrupt and the fruit of it corrupt; from for the fruit

3588 1186 1097 1081 2191 4459 1410
το δένδρον γινώσκεται. 34 γεννήματα ἐχιδνῶν, πῶς δύνασθε
the tree is known. Offspring of vipers! How can you

18 2980 4190 5607 1537 1063 3588 4051
ἀγαθὰ λαλεῖν, πονηροὶ ὄντες; ἐκ γὰρ τοῦ περισσεύματος
good things speak, evil being? out of For the abundance

3588 2588 3588 4750 2980 3588 18 444 1537 3588
τῆς καρδίας τὸ στόμα λαλεῖ. 35 ὁ ἀγαθὸς ἄνθρωπος ἐκ τοῦ
of the heart the mouth speaks. The good man out of the

18 2344 3588 2588 1544 3588 18 2532 3588
ἀγαθοῦ θησαυρου τῆς καρδίας ἐκβάλλει τὰ ἀγαθά· καὶ ὁ
good treasure of the heart puts forth the good things; and the

4190 444 1537 3588 4190 2344 1544
πονηρὸς ἄνθρωπος ἐκ τοῦ πονηροῦ θησαυροῦ ἐκβάλλει
evil man out of the evil treasure puts forth

4190 3005 1161 5213 3754 3956 4487 692 3739 1437 2980
πονηρά. 36 λέγω δὲ ὑμῖν, ὅτι πᾶν ῥῆμα ἀργὸν, ὃ ἐὰν λαλή-
evil things. I say But to you, that every word idle, whatever may speak

3588 444 591 4012 846 3056 1722
σωσιν οἱ ἄνθρωποι, ἀποδώσουσι περὶ αὐτοῦ λόγον ἐν
men, they will give concerning it account in

2250 2920 1537 1063 3588 3056 4675 1344 2532 1537
ἡμέρᾳ κρίσεως· 37 ἐκ γὰρ τῶν λόγων σου δικαιωθήσῃ, καὶ ἐκ
(the) day of judgment; from for the words of you you will be justified, and from

3588 3056 4675 2613
τῶν λόγων σου καταδικασθήσῃ.
the words of you you will be condemned.

Literal Translation

else how can one enter into a strong man's house, and spoil his goods, except he first bind the strong man? and then he will spoil his house.

30 He that is not with me is against me; and he that gathereth not with me scattereth abroad.
31 Wherefore I say unto you, All manner of sin and blasphemy shall be forgiven unto men: but the blasphemy (against) the (Holy) Ghost shall not be forgiven unto men.

32 And whosoever speaketh a word against the Son of man, it shall be forgiven him: but whosoever speaketh against the Holy Ghost, it shall not be forgiven him, neither in this world, neither in the (world) to come.
33 Either make the tree good, and his fruit good; or else make the tree corrupt, and his fruit corrupt: for the tree is known by (his) fruit.

34 O generation of vipers, how can ye, being evil, speak good things? for out of the abundance of the heart the mouth speaketh.

35 A good man out of the good treasure of the heart bringeth forth good things: and an evil man out of the evil treasure bringeth forth evil things.

36 But I say unto you, That every idle word that men shall speak, they shall give account thereof in the day of judgment.

37 For by thy words thou shalt be justified, and by thy words thou shalt be condemned.

Literal Translation

38. Then some of the scribes and Pharisees answered, saying, Teacher, we desire to see a sign from you.
39 But answering, He said to them, An evil and adulterous generation seeks a sign, and a sign shall not be given to it, except the sign of Jonah the prophet.

40 And even as Jonah was in the belly of the huge fish three days and three nights, so shall the Son of man be in the heart of the earth three days and three nights. (Jonah 1:17)

41 Men, Ninevites, will stand up in the Judgment with this generation and will condemn it. For they repented at the preaching of Jonah, and, behold, a Greater-than-Jonah (is) here.
42 (The) queen of (the) south will be raised in the Judgment with this generation and will condemn it. For she came from the ends of the earth to hear the wisdom of Solomon, and, behold, a Greater-than-Solomon (is) here.

43 But when the unclean spirit goes from a man, he goes through dry places seeking rest and does not find (it).

44 Then he says, I will return to my house from which I came out. And coming, he finds (it) vacant, having been swept and having been decorated.
45 Then he goes and takes with him seven other spirits more evil than him(self), and entering dwells there. And the last things of that man become worse than the first. So it will be also to this evil generation.

Matthew 12:38

5119 611 5100 3588 1122 2532 5330
38. Τότε ἀπεκρίθησάν τινες τῶν γραμματέων καὶ Φαρισαίων,
Then answered some of the scribes and Pharisees,

3004 1320 2309 575 4675 4592 1492 3588 1161
λέγοντες, Διδάσκαλε, θέλομεν ἀπὸ σοῦ σημεῖον ἰδεῖν. 39 ὁ δὲ
saying, Teacher, we desire from you a sign to see. He But

611 2036 846 1074 4190 2532 3428 4592
ἀποκριθεὶς εἶπεν αὐτοῖς, Γενεὰ πονηρὰ καὶ μοιχαλὶς σημεῖον
answering said to them, generation an evil and adulterous a sign

1934 2532 4592 3756 1325 846 1487 3361 3588 4592
ἐπιζητεῖ· καὶ σημεῖον οὐ δοθήσεται αὐτῇ, εἰ μὴ τὸ σημεῖον
seeks, and a sign not will be given to it, except the sign

2495 3588 4396 5618 1063 2258 2495 1722 3588 2836
Ἰωνᾶ τοῦ προφήτου. 40 ὥσπερ γὰρ ἦν Ἰωνᾶς ἐν τῇ κοιλίᾳ
of Jonah the prophet. even as For was Jonah in the belly

3588 2785 5140 2250 2532 5140 3571 3779 2071 3588 5207
τοῦ κήτους τρεῖς ἡμέρας καὶ τρεῖς νύκτας, οὕτως ἔσται ὁ υἱὸς
of the great fish three days and three nights, so will be the Son

3588 444 1722 3588 2588 3588 1093 5140 2250 2532 5140
τοῦ ἀνθρώπου ἐν τῇ καρδίᾳ τῆς γῆς τρεῖς ἡμέρας καὶ τρεῖς
of man in the heart of the earth three days and three

3571 435 3536 450 1722 3588 2920 3326
νύκτας. 41 ἄνδρες Νινευῖται ἀναστήσονται ἐν τῇ κρίσει μετὰ
nights Men Ninevites will stand up in the judgment with

3588 1074 3778 2532 2632 846 3754 3340
τῆς γενεᾶς ταύτης καὶ κατακρινοῦσιν αὐτήν· ὅτι μετενόησαν
generation this and will condemn it; because they repented

1519 3588 2782 2495 2532 2400 4119 2495 5602 938
εἰς τὸ κήρυγμα Ἰωνᾶ· καὶ ἰδού, πλεῖον Ἰωνᾶ ὧδε. 42 βασίλισσα
at the preaching of Jonah; and behold! A Greater-than-Jonah (is) here. Queen

3558 1453 1722 3588 2920 3326 3588 1074 3778 2532
νότου ἐγερθήσεται ἐν τῇ κρίσει μετὰ τῆς γενεᾶς ταύτης καὶ
of (the) south will be raised in the judgment with generation this and

2632 846 3754 2064 1537 3588 4009 3588 1093
κατακρινεῖ αὐτήν· ὅτι ἦλθεν ἐκ τῶν περάτων τῆς γῆς
will condemn it; because she came from the ends of the earth

191 3588 4678 4672 2532 2400 4119 4672
ἀκοῦσαι τὴν σοφίαν Σολομῶνος· καὶ ἰδού, πλεῖον Σολο-
to hear the wisdom of Solomon, and, behold! A Greater-than-Solomon

5602 3752 1161 3588 169 4151 1831 575 3588
μῶνος ὧδε. 43 ὅταν δὲ τὸ ἀκάθαρτον πνεῦμα ἐξέλθῃ ἀπὸ τοῦ
(is) here when And the unclean spirit goes out from

444 1330 1223 504 5117 2212 372
ἀνθρώπου, διέρχεται δι' ἀνύδρων τόπων, ζητοῦν ἀνάπαυσιν,
a man, he goes through dry places seeking rest,

2532 3756 2147 5119 3004 1994 1519 3588 3624 3450
καὶ οὐχ εὑρίσκει. 44 τότε λέγει, Ἐπιστρέψω εἰς τὸν οἶκόν μου
and not does find. Then he says, I will return to the house of me

3606 1831 2532 2064 2147 4980 4563
ὅθεν ἐξῆλθον· καὶ ἐλθὸν εὑρίσκει σχολάζοντα, σεσαρωμένον,
from where I came out; and coming he finds (it) vacant, having been swept,

2532 2885 5119 4198 2532 3880 3326
καὶ κεκοσμημένον. 45 τότε πορεύεται καὶ παραλαμβάνει μεθ'
and having been decorated. Then he goes and takes along with

1438 2033 2087 4151 4191 1438 2532
ἑαυτοῦ ἑπτὰ ἕτερα πνεύματα πονηρότερα ἑαυτοῦ, καὶ
him seven other spirits more evil (than) himself, and

1525 2730 1563 2532 1096 3588 2078 3588 444
εἰσελθόντα κατοικεῖ ἐκεῖ· καὶ γίνεται τὰ ἔσχατα τοῦ ἀνθρώ-
entering dwells there. And becomes the last things of man

1565 5501 3588 4413 3779 2071 2532 3588 1074
που ἐκείνου χείρονα τῶν πρώτων. οὕτως ἔσται καὶ τῇ γενεᾷ
that worse (than) the first. So it will be also generation

Literal Translation

38. Then certain of the scribes and of the Pharisees answered, saying, Master, we would see a sign from thee.
39 But he answered and said unto them, An evil and adulterous generation seeketh after a sign; and there shall no sign be given to it, but the sign of the prophet Jonas:

40 For as Jonas was three days and three nights in the whale's belly; so shall the Son of man be three days and three nights in the heart of the earth.

41 The men of Nineveh shall rise in judgment with this generation, and shall condemn it: because they repented at the preaching of Jonas; and, behold, a greater than Jonas (is) here.
42 The queen of the south shall rise up in the judgment with this generation, and shall condemn it: for she came from the uttermost parts of the earth to hear the wisdom of Solomon; and, behold, a greater than Solomon (is) here.

43 When the unclean spirit is gone out of a man, he walketh through dry places, seeking rest, and findeth none.

44 Then he saith, I will return into my house from whence I came out; and when he is come, he findeth (it) empty, swept, and garnished.
45 Then goeth he, and taketh with himself seven other spirits more wicked than himself, and they enter in and dwell there: and the last (state) of that man is worse than the first. Even so shall it be also unto this wicked generation.

Literal Translation

46. But while He was yet speaking to the crowds, behold, (His) mother and brothers were standing outside, seeking to speak to Him.

47 Then one said to Him, Behold, Your mother and Your brothers are standing outside, seeking to speak to You.
48 But answering, He said to the (one) speaking to Him, Who is My mother? And who are My brothers?
49 And stretching out His hand to His disciples, He said, Behold, My mother and My brothers.

50 For whoever does the will of My Father in Heaven, that one is My brother and sister and mother.

Matthew 12:46

3778 3588 4190
ταύτῃ τῇ πονηρᾷ.
this evil.

2089 1161 846 2980 3588 3793 2400 3588 3384 2532
46. Ἔτι δὲ αὐτοῦ λαλοῦντος τοῖς ὄχλοις, ἰδού, ἡ μήτηρ καὶ
while But He is speaking to the crowds, behold, the mother and
3588 80 846 2476 1854 2212 846 2980
οἱ ἀδελφοὶ αὐτοῦ εἱστήκεισαν ἔξω, ζητοῦντες αὐτῷ λαλῆσαι.
the brothers of Him stood outside, seeking to Him to speak.

2036 1161 5100 846 2400 3588 3384 4675 2532 3588 80 4675 1854
47 εἶπε δέ τις αὐτῷ,'Ἰδού, ἡ μήτηρ σου καὶ οἱ ἀδελφοί σου ἔξω
said And one to Him, behold, the mother of You and the brothers of You out
2476 2212 4671 2980 3588 1161 611 2036 3588
ἑστήκασι, ζητοῦντές σοι λαλῆσαι. 48 ὁ δὲ ἀποκριθεὶς εἶπε τῷ
are standing, seeking to You to speak. He And answering said to him
2036 846 5101 2076 3588 3384 3450 2532 5101 1526 3588
εἰπόντι αὐτῷ, Τίς ἐστιν ἡ μήτηρ μου; καὶ τίνες εἰσὶν οἱ
speaking to Him, Who is the mother of Me? And who are the
80 3450 2532 1614 3588 5495 846 1909 3588
ἀδελφοί μου; 49 καὶ ἐκτείνας τὴν χεῖρα αὐτοῦ ἐπὶ τοὺς
brothers of Me? And stretching out the hand of Him on the
3101 846 2036 2400 3588 3384 3450 2532 3588 80 3450
μαθητὰς αὐτοῦ εἶπεν, 'Ἰδού, ἡ μήτηρ μου καὶ οἱ ἀδελφοί μου·
disciples of Him, He said, Behold, the mother of Me and the brothers of Me;

3748 1063 302 4160 3588 2307 3588 3962 3450 3588 1722
50 ὅστις γὰρ ἂν ποιήσῃ τὸ θέλημα τοῦ πατρός μου τοῦ ἐν
who for ever does the will of the Father of Me the (One) in
3772 846 3450 80 2532 79 2532 3384 2076
οὐρανοῖς αὐτός μου ἀδελφὸς καὶ ἀδελφὴ καὶ μήτηρ ἐστίν.
Heaven, he of Me brother and sister and mother is.

Literal Translation

46. While he yet talked to the people, behold, (his) mother and his brethren stood without, desiring to speak with him.

47 Then one said unto him, Behold, thy mother and thy brethren stand without, desiring to speak with thee.
48 But he answered and said unto him that told him, Who is my mother? and who are my brethren?
49 And he stretched forth his hand toward his disciples, and said, Behold my mother and my brethren!

50 For whosoever shall do the will of my Father which is in heaven, the same is my brother, and sister, and mother.

Matthew 13

1. And going out from the house in that day, Jesus sat down by the sea.

2 And great crowds were gathered to Him, so that boarding the boat, He sat down. And all the crowd stood on the shore.

3 And He spoke to them many things in parables, saying: Behold, the (one) sowing went out to sow.

4 And in his sowing, some fell by the roadside, and the birds came and ate them.

5 (And) other fell on the stony places where they did not have much earth, and it immediately sprang up because (it) had no deepness of earth.
6 And (the) sun rising, it was scorched, even because of having no root,

Matthew 13

1722 1161 3588 2250 1565 1831 3588 2424 575 3588 3614
1. Ἐν δὲ τῇ ἡμέρᾳ ἐκείνῃ ἐξελθὼν ὁ Ἰησοῦς ἀπὸ τῆς οἰκίας
in And day that going forth Jesus from the house
2521 3844 3588 2281 2532 4863 4314 846
ἐκάθητο παρὰ τὴν θάλασσαν. 2 καὶ συνήχθησαν πρὸς αὐτὸν
He sat down beside the sea. And were assembled to Him
3793 4183 5620 846 1519 3588 4143 1684 2521
ὄχλοι πολλοί, ὥστε αὐτὸν εἰς τὸ πλοῖον ἐμβάντα καθῆσθαι·
crowds great, so that He into the boat having entered sat down.
2532 3956 3588 3793 1909 3588 123 2476 2532 2980
καὶ πᾶς ὁ ὄχλος ἐπὶ τὸν αἰγιαλὸν εἱστήκει. 3 καὶ ἐλάλησεν
And all the crowd on the shore stood. And He spoke
846 4183 1722 3850 3004 2400 1831 3588
αὐτοῖς πολλὰ ἐν παραβολαῖς, λέγων, 'Ἰδού, ἐξῆλθεν ὁ
to them many things in parables, saying, Behold! went out he
4687 3588 4687 2532 1722 3588 4687 846 3739 3303 4098
σπείρων τοῦ σπείρειν. 4 καὶ ἐν τῷ σπείρειν αὐτόν, ἃ μὲν ἔπεσε
sowing to sow. And in the sowing of him, some truly fell
3844 3588 3598 2532 2064 3588 4071 2532 2719 846
παρὰ τὴν ὁδόν· καὶ ἦλθε τὰ πετεινὰ καὶ κατέφαγεν αὐτά.
beside the roadway, and came the birds and ate them.
243 1161 4098 1909 3588 4075 3699 3756 2192 1093 4183
5 ἄλλα δὲ ἔπεσεν ἐπι τὰ πετρώδη, ὅπου οὐκ εἶχε γῆν πολλήν·
other And fell on the rocky places, where not they had earth much;
2532 2112 1816 1223 3588 3361 2192 899 1093 2246 1161
καὶ εὐθέως ἐξανέτειλε, διὰ τὸ μὴ ἔχειν βάθος γῆς.6 ἡλίου δὲ
and at once it sprang up, because not having depth of earth. sun And
393 2739 2532 1233 3588 3361,2192 4491
ἀνατείλαντος ἐκαυματίσθη, καὶ διὰ τὸ μὴ ἔχειν ῥίζαν,
rising it was scorched, even because of not having root,

Matthew 13

1. The same day went Jesus out of the house, and sat by the sea side.

2 And great multitudes were gathered together unto him, so that he went into a ship, and sat; and the whole multitude stood on the shore.

3 And he spake many things unto them in parables, saying, Behold, a sower went forth to sow;

4 And when he sowed, some (seeds) fell by the way side, and the fowls came and devoured them up:
5 Some fell upon stony places, where they had not much earth: and forthwith they sprung up, because they had no deepness of earth:
6 And when the sun was up, they were scorched; and because they had no root,

Literal Translation

it was dried up.
7 And other fell on the thornbushes, and the thornbushes grew up and choked them.
8 And other fell on the good ground and yielded fruit; indeed, one a hundred(fold), and one sixty, and one thirty.
9 The (one) having ears to hear, let him hear.

10. And coming near, the disciples said to Him, Why do You speak to them in parables?
11 And answering, He said to them, Because it has been given to you to know the mysteries of the kingdom of Heaven, but it has not been given to those.
12 For whoever has, to him will be given, and he will have overabundance. But whoever does not have, even what he has will be taken from him.
13 Because of this, I speak to them in parables, because seeing they do not see, and hearing they do not hear, nor do they understand.
14 And the prophecy of Isaiah is being fulfilled on them, which says, "In hearing you will hear, yet in no way understand, and seeing you will see, yet in no way perceive.
15 For the heart of this people has grown fat, and they heard sluggishly with the ears, and they have closed their eyes, that they not see with the eyes, or hear with the ears, and understand with the heart, and be converted, and I heal them." (Isa. 6:9, 10)
16 But your eyes (are) blessed because they see; and your ears because they hear.
17 For truly I tell you that many prophets and righteous ones desired to see what you see and did not see, and to hear what you hear and

Matthew 13:7

3583 243 1161 4098 1909 3588 173 2532 305 3588
ἐξηράνθη. 7 ἄλλα δὲ ἔπεσεν ἐπὶ τὰς ἀκάνθας, καὶ ἀνέβησαν αἱ
it was dried up. other And fell on the thornbushes, and grew up the

173 2532 638 846 243 1161 4098 1909 3588 1093
ἄκανθαι καὶ ἀπέπνιξαν αὐτά. 8 ἄλλα δὲ ἔπεσεν ἐπὶ τὴν γῆν
thornbushes and choked them. other And fell on the earth

3588 2570 2532 1325 2590 3588 3303 1540 3739 1161 1835
τὴν καλὴν, καὶ ἐδίδου καρπόν, ὃ μὲν ἑκατόν, ὃ δὲ ἑξήκοντα,
good, and yielded fruit, one a hundred, one and sixty,

3739 1161 5144 3588 2192 3775 191 191
ὃ δὲ τριάκοντα. 9 ὁ ἔχων ὦτα ἀκούειν ἀκουέτω.
one and thirty. The (one) having ears to hear, let him hear.

2532 4334 3588 3101 2036 846 1302 1722
10. Καὶ προσελθόντες οἱ μαθηταὶ εἶπαν αὐτῷ, Διατί ἐν
And having come near the disciples said to Him, Why in

3850 2980 846 3588 1161 611 2036 846 3754
παραβολαῖς λαλεῖς αὐτοῖς; 11ὁ δὲ ἀποκριθεὶς εἶπεν αὐτοῖς ὅτι
parables do You speak to them? He And answering said to them,

5213 1325 1097 3588 3466 3588 932 3588 3772
Ὑμῖν δέδοται γνῶναι τὰ μυστήρια τῆς βασιλείας τῶν οὐρ-
To you it has been given to know the mysteries of the kingdom of

1565 1161 3756 1325 3748 1063 2192 1325 846
ανῶν, ἐκείνοις δὲ οὐ δέδοται.12 ὅστις γὰρ ἔχει, δοθήσεται αὐτῷ
Heaven, to those but not it has been given. whoever For has, will be given to him,

2532 4052 3748 1161 3756 2192 2532 3739 2192
καὶ περισσευθήσεται· ὅστις δὲ οὐκ ἔχει, καὶ ὃ ἔχει,
and he will have abundance; whoever but not has, even what he has,

142 575 846 1223 5124 1722 3850 846 2980
ἀρθήσεται ἀπ᾽ αὐτοῦ.13 διὰ τοῦτο ἐν παραβολαῖς αὐτοῖς λαλῶ,
will be taken from him. Because of this in parables to them I speak,

3754 991 3756 991 2532 191 3756 191
ὅτι βλέποντες οὐ βλέπουσι, καὶ ἀκούοντες οὐκ ἀκούουσιν,
because seeing not they see, and hearing not they hear,

3761 4920 2532 378 1909 846 3588 4394
οὐδὲ συνιοῦσι. 14 καὶ ἀναπληροῦται ἐπ᾽ αὐτοῖς ἡ προφητεία
neither understand. And is being fulfilled on them the prophecy

2268 3588 3004 189 191 2532 3764 3361 4920 2532
Ἠσαΐου, ἡ λέγουσα, Ἀκοῇ ἀκούσετε καὶ οὐ μὴ συνῆτε· καὶ
of Isaiah, which says, In hearing you will hear, yet in no way understand; and

991 991 2532 3756 3361 1492 3975 1063 3588 2588
βλέποντες βλέψετε, καὶ οὐ μὴ ἴδητε. 15 ἐπαχύνθη γὰρ ἡ καρδία
seeing you will see, and in no way perceive. has grown fat For the heart

3588 2992 5127 2532 3588 3775 917 191 2532 3588
τοῦ λαοῦ τούτου, καὶ τοῖς ὠσὶ βαρέως ἤκουσαν, καὶ τοὺς
of people this, and with the ears heavily they heard, and the

3788 846 2576 3379 1492 3588 3788
ὀφθαλμοὺς αὐτῶν ἐκάμμυσαν· μήποτε ἴδωσι τοῖς ὀφθαλμοῖς,
eyes of them they closed; that not they see with the eyes

2532 3588 3775 191 2532 3588 2588 4920 2532 1994
καὶ τοῖς ὠσὶν ἀκούσωσι, καὶ τῇ καρδίᾳ συνῶσι, καὶ ἐπι-
and with the ears they hear and with the heart understand, and be

2532 2390 846 5216 1161 3107 3588 3788
στρέψωσι, καὶ ἰάσομαι αὐτούς.16 ὑμῶν δὲ μακάριοι οἱ ὀφθαλ-
converted, and I heal them. of you But blessed (are) the eyes

3754 991 2532 3588 3775 5216 3754 191 281 1063
μοί, ὅτι βλέπουσι· καὶ τὰ ὦτα ὑμῶν, ὅτι ἀκούει. 17 ἀμὴν γὰρ
because they see, and the ears of you, because they hear. truly For

3004 5213 3754 4183 4396 2532 1342 1937
λέγω ὑμῖν ὅτι πολλοὶ προφῆται καὶ δίκαιοι ἐπεθύμησαν
I say to you that many prophets and righteous (ones) desired

1492 3739 991 2532 3756 1492 2532 191 3739 191 2532
ἰδεῖν ἃ βλέπετε, καὶ οὐκ εἶδον· καὶ ἀκοῦσαι ἃ ἀκούετε, καὶ
to see what you see, and not did see; and to hear what you hear, and

Literal Translation

they withered away.
7 And some fell among thorns; and the thorns sprung up, and choked them:
8 But other fell into good ground, and brought forth fruit, some an hundredfold, some sixtyfold, some thirtyfold.
9 Who hath ears to hear, let him hear.

10. And the disciples came, and said unto him, Why speakest thou unto them in parables?
11 He answered and said unto them, Because it is given unto you to know the mysteries of the kingdom of heaven, but to them it is not given.
12 For whosoever hath, to him shall be given, and he shall have more abundance: but whosoever hath not, from him shall be taken away even that he hath.
13 Therefore speak I to them in parables: because they seeing see not; and hearing they hear not, neither do they understand.
14 And in them is fulfilled the prophecy of Esaias, which saith, By hearing ye shall hear, and shall not understand; and seeing ye shall see, and shall not perceive:
15 For this people's heart is waxed gross, and (their) ears are dull of hearing, and their eyes they have closed; lest at any time they should see with (their) eyes, and hear with (their) ears, and should understand with (their) heart, and should be converted, and I should heal them.
16 But blessed (are) your eyes, for they see: and your ears, for they hear.
17 For verily I say unto you, That many prophets and righteous (men) have desired to see (those things) which ye see, and have not seen (them); and to hear (those things) which ye hear, and

Literal Translation

did not hear.
18. Then hear the parable of the sower:

19 Everyone hearing the Word of the kingdom, and not understanding, (then) the evil one comes and catches away that which was sown in his heart. This is that sown by the roadside.

20 And the (Word) sown on the stony places is this: the (one) hearing the Word, and immediately receiving it with joy,
21 but has no root in himself, but is temporary, and tribulation, or persecution occurring because of the Word, he is at once offended.
22 And that sown into the thornbushes is this: the (one) hearing the Word, and the anxiety of this age, and the deceit of riches, choke the Word, and it becomes unfruitful.

23 But that sown on the good ground is this: the (one) hearing the Word, and understanding it, who indeed bears fruit and yields one truly a hundred(fold), and one sixty, and one thirty.

24. He put before them another parable, saying: The kingdom of Heaven is compared to a man sowing good seed in his fields.
25 But while the men were sleeping, his enemy came and sowed darnel in the midst of the wheat, and went away.

26 And when the blade sprouted and produced fruit, then the darnel also appeared.
27 And coming near, the slaves of the housemaster said to him, Sir, did you not

Matthew 13:18

3756 191 5210 3767 191 3588 3850 3588
οὐκ ἤκουσαν. 18. ὑμεῖς οὖν ἀκούσατε τὴν παραβολὴν τοῦ
not did hear. You therefore hear the parable of the

4687 3956 191 3588 3056 3588 932 2532
σπείραντος. 19 παντὸς ἀκούοντος τὸν λόγον τῆς βασιλείας καὶ
sower: Anyone hearing the Word of the kingdom and

3361 4920 2064 3588 4190 2532 726 3588 4687
μὴ συνιέντος, ἔρχεται ὁ πονηρὸς, καὶ ἁρπάζει τὸ ἐσπαρ-
not understanding, comes the evil one and catches away that being

1722 3588 2588 846 3778 2076 3588 3844 3588 3598
μένον ἐν τῇ καρδίᾳ αὐτοῦ· οὗτός ἐστιν ὁ παρὰ τὴν ὁδὸν
sown in the heart of him. This is the (Word) by the way

4687 3588 1161 1909 3588 4075 4687 3778 2076 3588 3588
σπαρείς. 20 ὁ δὲ ἐπὶ τὰ πετρώδη σπαρείς, οὗτός ἐστιν ὁ τὸν
sown. the And (word) on the rocky places sown, this is the (one) the

3056 191 2532 2117 3326 5479 2983 846 3756
λόγον ἀκούων, καὶ εὐθὺς μετὰ χαρᾶς λαμβάνων αὐτόν· 21 οὐκ
Word hearing, and at once with joy receiving it; not

2192 1161 4491 1722 1438 235 4340 2076 1096 1161
ἔχει δὲ ῥίζαν ἐν ἑαυτῷ, ἀλλὰ πρόσκαιρός ἐστι· γενομένης δὲ
has but root in himself, but temporary is; occurring but

2347 2228 1375 1223 3588 3056 2117 4624 3588
θλίψεως ἢ διωγμοῦ διὰ τὸν λόγον, εὐθὺς σκανδαλίζεται. 22 ὁ
tribulation or persecution through the Word at once he is offended. the (one)

1161 1519 3588 173 4687 3778 2076 3588 3588 3056 191
δὲ εἰς τὰς ἀκάνθας σπαρείς, οὗτός ἐστιν ὁ τὸν λόγον ἀκούων,
But into the thornbushes sown, this is the(one) the Word hearing,

2532 3588 3308 3588 165 5127 2532 3588 539 3588 4149
καὶ ἡ μέριμνα τοῦ αἰῶνος τούτου καὶ ἡ ἀπάτη τοῦ πλούτου
and the anxiety age of this and the deceit of riches

4846 3588 3056 2532 175 1096 3588 1161 1909 3588 1093
συμπνίγει τὸν λόγον, καὶ ἄκαρπος γίνεται. 23 ὁ δὲ ἐπὶ τὴν γῆν
choke the Word, and unfruitful it becomes. that But on the earth

3588 2570 4687 3778 2076 3588 3588 3056 191 2532
τὴν καλὴν σπαρείς, οὗτός ἐστιν ὁ τὸν λόγον ἀκούων καὶ
good was sown, this is the (one) the Word hearing and

4920 3739 1211 2592 2532 4160 3739 3303 1540 3739 1161
συνιών· ὃς δὴ καρποφορεῖ καὶ ποιεῖ ὃ μὲν ἑκατόν, ὃ δὲ
understanding; who indeed bears fruit and yields one truly a hundred, one and

1835 3739 1161 5144
ἑξήκοντα, ὃ δὲ τριάκοντα.
sixty, one and thirty.

243 3850 3908 846 3004
24. Ἄλλην παραβολὴν παρέθηκεν αὐτοῖς, λέγων,
Another parable He put forth to them, saying

3666 3588 932 3588 3772 444 4687
Ὡμοιώθη ἡ βασιλεία τῶν οὐρανῶν ἀνθρώπῳ σπείραντι
Is compared to the kingdom of Heaven to a man sowing

2570 4690 1722 3588 68 846 1722 1161 3588 2518 3588
καλὸν σπέρμα ἐν τῷ ἀγρῷ αὐτοῦ. 25 ἐν δὲ τῷ καθεύδειν τοὺς
good seed in the fields of him; in but the sleeping of the

444 2064 846 3588 2190 2532 4687 2215 303
ἀνθρώπους, ἦλθεν αὐτοῦ ὁ ἐχθρὸς καὶ ἔσπειρε ζιζάνια ἀνὰ
men came his hostile (one) and sowed darnel in

3319 3588 4621 2532 565 3753 1161 985 3588 5528
μέσον τοῦ σίτου, καὶ ἀπῆλθεν. 26 ὅτε δὲ ἐβλάστησεν ὁ χόρτος
amidst the wheat, and went away. when And sprouted the blade

2532 2590 4160 5119 5316 2532 3588 2215 4334
καὶ καρπὸν ἐποίησε, τότε ἐφάνη καὶ τὰ ζιζάνια. 27 προσελθόντες
and fruit produced, then appeared also the darnel. coming near

1161 3588 1401 3588 3617 2036 846 2962 3780
δὲ οἱ δοῦλοι τοῦ οἰκοδεσπότου εἶπον αὐτῷ, Κύριε, οὐχὶ
And the slaves of the master of the house said to him, Lord, not

Literal Translation

have not heard (them).
18. Hear ye therefore the parable of the sower.

19 When any one heareth the word of the kingdom, and understandeth (it) not, then cometh the wicked (one), and catcheth away that which was sown in his heart. This is he which received seed by the way side.

20 But he that received the seed into stony places, the same is he that heareth the word, and anon with joy receiveth it;
21 Yet hath he not root in himself, but dureth for a while: for when tribulation or persecution ariseth because of the word, by and by he is offended.
22 He also that received seed among the thorns is he that heareth the word; and the care of this world, and the deceitfulness of riches, choke the word, and he becometh unfruitful.
23 But he that received seed into the good ground is he that heareth the word, and understandeth (it); which also beareth fruit, and bringeth forth, some an hundredfold, some sixty, some thirty.

24. Another parable put he forth unto them, saying, The kingdom of heaven is likened unto a man which sowed good seed in his field:
25 But while men slept, his enemy came and sowed tares among the wheat, and went his way.

26 But when the blade was sprung up, and brought forth fruit, then appeared the tares also.
27 So the servants of the householder came and said unto him, Sir, didst not

Literal Translation

sow good seed in your field? Then from where does it have the darnel?

28 And he said to them, A hostile man did this. And the slaves said to him, Do you desire, then, that going out we should gather them?

29 But he said, No, lest gathering the darnel you should uproot the wheat with them.
30 Allow both to grow together until the harvest. And in the time of the harvest I will say to the reapers, First gather the darnel, and bind them into bundles to burn them, but gather the wheat into my granary.

31. He set before them another parable, saying: The kingdom of Heaven is like a grain of mustard, which taking, a man sowed in his field;
32 which indeed is lesser than all the seeds, but when it is grown it is greater than the plants, and becomes a tree, so that the birds of the heaven come and roost in its branches.

33. He spoke another parable to them: The kingdom of Heaven is like leaven, which taking a woman hid in three measures of meal until the whole was leavened.

34 Jesus spoke all these things in parables to the crowds, and He did not speak to them without a parable,
35 so that was fulfilled that spoken through the prophet, saying: "I will open

Matthew 13:28

2570 4690 4687 1722 3588 4674 68 4159 3767 2192 3588
καλὸν σπέρμα ἔσπειρας ἐν τῷ σῷ ἀγρῷ; πόθεν οὖν ἔχει τὰ
good seed did you sow in the of you field? From where then has it the

2215 3588 1161 5346 846 2190 444 5124 4160
ζιζάνια; 28 ὁ δὲ ἔφη αὐτοῖς,'Εχθρὸς ἄνθρωπος τοῦτο ἐποίησεν.
darnel? he And said to them, hostile A man, this did.

3588 1161 1401 2036 846 2309 3767 565 4816
οἱ δὲ δοῦλοι εἶπον αὐτῷ, Θέλεις οὖν ἀπελθόντες συλλέξωμεν
the And slaves said to him, Will you then going out we may gather

846 3588 1161 5346 3756 3379 4816 3588 2215
αὐτά; 29 ὁ δέ ἔφη, Οὔ· μήποτε, συλλέγοντες τὰ ζιζάνια,
them? he But said, No, that not gathering the darnel,

1610 260 846 3588 4621 863 4885
ἐκριζώσητε ἅμα αὐτοῖς τὸν σῖτον. 30 ἄφετε συναυξάνεσθαι
you may uproot with them the wheat. Allow to grow together

297 3360 3588 2326 2532 1722 3588 2540 3588 2326
ἀμφότερα μέχρι τοῦ θερισμοῦ· καὶ ἐν τῷ καιρῷ τοῦ θερισμοῦ
both until the harvest; and in the time of the harvest

2046 3588 2327 4816 4412 3588 2215 2532
ἐρῶ τοῖς θερισταῖς, Συλλέξατε πρῶτον τὰ ζιζάνια, καὶ
I will say to the reapers, Gather first the darnel, and

1210 846 1519 1197 4314 3588 2618 846 3588 1161
δήσατε αὐτὰ εἰς δέσμας πρὸς τὸ κατακαῦσαι αὐτά· τὸν δὲ
bind them into bundles in order to burn them; the but

4621 4863 1519 3588 596 3450
σῖτον συναγάγετε εἰς τὴν ἀποθήκην μου.
wheat bring together into the granary of me.

243 3850 3908 846 3004 3664
31. Ἄλλην παραβολὴν παρέθηκεν αὐτοῖς, λέγων, Ὁμοία
Another parable He set before them, saying, Like

2076 3588 932 3588 3772 2848 4615 3739 2983
ἐστὶν ἡ βασιλεία τῶν οὐρανῶν κόκκῳ σινάπεως, ὃν λαβὼν
is the kingdom of Heaven to a grain of mustard, which taking

444 4687 1722 3588 68 846 3739 3398 3303
ἄνθρωπος ἔσπειρεν ἐν τῷ ἀγρῷ αὐτοῦ· 32 ὃ μικρότερον μέν
a man sowed in the field of him; which lesser truly

2076 3956 3588 4690 3752 1161 837 3173 3588
ἐστι πάντων τῶν σπερμάτων· ὅταν δὲ αὐξηθῇ, μεῖζον τῶν
is (than) all of the seeds.; when but it is grown, greater (than) the

3001 2076 2532 1096 1186 5620 2064 3588 4071
λαχάνων ἐστὶ, καὶ γίνεται δένδρον, ὥστε ἐλθεῖν τὰ πετεινὰ
plants is, and becomes a tree, so that come the birds

3588 3772 2532 2681 1722 3588 2798 846
τοῦ οὐρανοῦ καὶ κατασκηνοῦν ἐν τοῖς κλάδοις αὐτοῦ.
of the heaven and roost in the branches of it.

243 3850 2980 846 3664 2076 3588
33. Ἄλλην παραβολὴν ἐλάλησεν αὐτοῖς, Ὁμοία ἐστὶν ἡ
Another parable He spoke to them, Like is the

932 3588 3772 2219 3739 2983 1135 1470
βασιλεία τῶν οὐρανῶν ζύμῃ, ἣν λαβοῦσα γυνὴ ἐνέκρυψεν
kingdom of Heaven to leaven, which taking a woman hid

1519 224 4568 5140 2193 3757 2220 3650
εἰς ἀλεύρου σάτα τρία, ἕως οὗ ἐζυμώθη ὅλον.
in of meal measures three, until was leavened the whole.

5023 3956 2980 3588 2424 1722 3850 3588
34. Ταῦτα πάντα ἐλάλησεν ὁ Ἰησοῦς ἐν παραβολαῖς τοῖς
These things all spoke Jesus in parables to the

3793 2532 5565 3850 3756 2980 846 3704
ὄχλοις, καὶ χωρὶς παραβολῆς οὐκ ἐλάλει αὐτοῖς· 35 ὅπως
crowds, and without a parable not He spoke to them; so that

4137 3588 4483 1223 3588 4396 3004 455
πληρωθῇ τὸ ῥηθὲν διὰ τοῦ προφήτου, λέγοντος, Ανοίξω
was fulfilled that spoken through the prophet, saying, I will open

Literal Translation

thou sow good seed in thy field? from whence then hath it tares?

28 He said unto them, An enemy hath done this. The servants said unto him, Wilt thou then that we go and gather them up?

29 But he said, Nay; lest while ye gather up the tares, ye root up also the wheat with them.
30 Let both grow together until the harvest: and in the time of harvest I will say to the reapers, Gather ye together first the tares, and bind them in bundles to burn them: but gather the wheat into my barn.

31. Another parable put he forth unto them, saying, The kingdom of heaven is like to a grain of mustard seed, which a man took, and sowed in his field:
32 Which indeed is the least of all seeds: but when it is grown, it is the greatest among herbs, and becometh a tree, so that the birds of the air come and lodge in the branches thereof.

33. Another parable spake he unto them; The kingdom of heaven is like unto leaven, which a woman took, and hid in three measures of meal, till the whole was leavened.

34 All these things spake Jesus unto the multitude in parables; and without a parable spake he not unto them:
35 That it might be fulfilled which was spoken by the prophet, saying, I will open

Literal Translation | **Matthew 13:36** | ***Literal Translation***

My mouth in parables; I will speak out things hidden from (the) foundation of (the) world." (Ps. 78:2)

36. Then sending away the crowds, Jesus came into the house. And His disciples came to Him, saying, Explain to us the parable of the darnel of the field.
37 And answering, He said to them, The (one) sowing the good seed is the Son of man.

38 And the field is the world; and the good seed, these are the sons of the kingdom; but the darnel are the sons of the evil (one).

39 And the enemy who sowed them is the Devil, and the harvest is the completion of the age, and the angels are the reapers.

40 Then as the darnel is gathered and is consumed in the fire, so it will be in the completion of this age.

41 The Son of man will send forth His angels, and they will gather out of His kingdom all the offenses, and those doing lawlessness.
42 And they will throw them into the furnace of fire; there will be weeping and gnashing of the teeth.

43 Then the righteous will shine out like the sun in the kingdom of their Father. The (one) having ears to hear, let him hear.

44. Again, the kingdom of Heaven is like treasure being hidden in the field, which finding, a man hid;

1722 3850 3588 4750 3450 2044 2928 575
ἐν παραβολαῖς τὸ στόμα μου, ἐρεύξομαι κεκρυμμένα ἀπὸ
in parables the mouth of Me; I will speak out things hidden from

2602 2889
καταβολῆς κόσμου.
(the) foundation of (the) world.

5119 863 3588 3793 2064 1519 3588 3614 3588 2424
36 Τότε ἀφεὶς τοὺς ὄχλους ἦλθεν εἰς τὴν οἰκίαν ὁ Ἰησοῦς·
Then sending away the crowds came into the house Jesus;

2532 4334 846 3588 3101 846 3004 5419
καὶ προσῆλθον αὐτῷ οἱ μαθηταὶ αὐτοῦ, λέγοντες, Φράσον
and came near to Him the disciples of Him, saying, Explain

2254 3588 3850 3588 2215 3588 68 3588 1161
ἡμῖν τὴν παραβολὴν τῶν ζιζανίων τοῦ ἀγροῦ. 37 ὁ δὲ
to us the parable of the darnel of the field. He And

611 2036 846 3588 4687 3588 2570 4690 2076 3588
ἀποκριθεὶς εἶπεν αὐτοῖς, Ὁ σπείρων τὸ καλὸν σπέρμα ἐστὶν ὁ
answering said to them, The (one) sowing the good seed is the

5207 3588 444 3588 1161 68 2076 3588 2889 3588 1161 2570
υἱὸς τοῦ ἀνθρώπου· 38 ὁ δὲ ἀγρός ἐστιν ὁ κόσμος· τὸ δὲ καλὸν
Son of man the And field is the world; the and good

4690 3778 1526 3588 5207 3588 932 3588 1161 2215 1526
σπέρμα, οὗτοί εἰσιν οἱ υἱοὶ τῆς βασιλείας· τὰ δὲ ζιζάνιά εἰσιν
seed, these are the sons of the kingdom. the But darnel are

3588 5207 3588 4190 3588 1161 2190 3588 4687 846 2076 3588
οἱ υἱοὶ τοῦ πονηροῦ· 39 ὁ δὲ ἐχθρὸς ὁ σπείρας αὐτά ἐστιν ὁ
the sons of the evil (one); the And hostile (one) who sowed them is the

1228 3588 1161 2326 4930 3588 165 2076 3588 1161
διάβολος· ὁ δὲ θερισμὸς συντέλεια τοῦ αἰῶνός ἐστιν· οἱ δὲ
devil; the and harvest (the) completion of the age is; the and

2327 32 1526 5618 3767 4816 3588 2215
θερισταὶ ἄγγελοί εἰσιν. 40 ὥσπερ οὖν συλλέγεται τὰ ζιζάνια
reapers angels are. As therefore is gathered the darnel,

2532 4442 2618 3779 2071 1722 3588 4930 3588
καὶ πυρὶ κατακαίεται, οὕτως ἔσται ἐν τῇ συντελείᾳ τοῦ
and with fire is consumed So it will be in the completion

165 5127 649 3588 5207 3588 444 3588
αἰῶνος τούτου. 41 ἀποστελεῖ ὁ υἱὸς τοῦ ἀνθρώπου τοὺς
age of this. Shall send out the Son of man the

32 846 2532 4816 1537 3588 932 846 3956
ἀγγέλους αὐτοῦ, καὶ συλλέξουσιν ἐκ τῆς βασιλείας αὐτοῦ πάντα
angels of Him, and they will gather out of the kingdom of Him all

3588 4625 2532 3588 4160 3588 458 2532 906
τὰ σκάνδαλα καὶ τοὺς ποιοῦντας τὴν ἀνομίαν, 42 καὶ βαλοῦσιν
the offenses and the (ones) doing lawlessness, and they will cast

846 1519 3588 2575 3588 4442 1563 2071 3588 2805 2532
αὐτοὺς εἰς τὴν κάμινον τοῦ πυρός· ἐκεῖ ἔσται ὁ κλαυθμὸς καὶ
them into the furnace of fire; there shall be the weeping and

3588 1030 3588 3599 5119 3588 1342 1584 5613 3588
ὁ βρυγμὸς τῶν ὀδόντων. 43 Τότε οἱ δίκαιοι ἐκλάμψουσιν ὡς ὁ
the gnashing of the teeth. Then the righteous will shine forth as the

2246 1722 3588 932 3588 3962 846 3588 2192 3775 191
ἥλιος ἐν τῇ βασιλείᾳ τοῦ πατρὸς αὐτῶν. ὁ ἔχων ὦτα ἀκούειν
sun in the kingdom of the Father of them. The (one) having ears to hear

191
ἀκουέτω.
let him hear.

3825 3664 2076 3588 932 3588 3772 2344
44. Πάλιν ὁμοία ἐστὶν ἡ βασιλεία τῶν οὐρανῶν θησαυρῷ
Again like is the kingdom of Heaven to treasure

2928 1722 3588 68 3739 2147 444 2928 2532 575
κεκρυμμένῳ ἐν τῷ ἀγρῷ, ὃν εὑρὼν ἄνθρωπος ἔκρυψε· καὶ ἀπὸ
having been hidden in the field, which having found a man hid, and from

---

my mouth in parables; I will utter things which have been kept secret from the foundation of the world.

36. Then Jesus sent the multitude away, and went into the house: and his disciples came unto him, saying, Declare unto us the parable of the tares of the field.
37 He answered and said unto them, He that soweth the good seed is the Son of man;

38 The field is the world; the good seed are the children of the kingdom; but the tares are the children of the wicked (one);

39 The enemy that sowed them is the devil; the harvest is the end of the world; and the reapers are the angels.

40 As therefore the tares are gathered and burned in the fire; so shall it be in the end of this world.

41 The Son of man shall send forth his angels, and they shall gather out of his kingdom all things that offend, and them which do iniquity;
42 And shall cast them into a furnace of fire: there shall be wailing and gnashing of teeth.

43 Then shall the righteous shine forth as the sun in the kingdom of their Father. Who hath ears to hear, let him hear.

44. Again, the kingdom of heaven is like unto treasure hid in a field; the which when a man hath found, he hideth,

Literal Translation | **Matthew 13:45** | *Literal Translation*

and for the joy of it, he goes and sells all things, as many as he has, and buys that field.

45 Again, the kingdom of Heaven is like a man, a merchant seeking excellent pearls;
46 who finding one very precious pearl, going away has sold all things, as many as he had, and bought it.

47. Again, the kingdom of Heaven is like a drag net thrown into the sea, and gathering together of every kind;

48 which, when it was filled, drawing it up on the shore, and sitting down, (they) gathered the good into containers, and they threw out the rotten.
49 So it will be in the completion of the age: the angels will go out and will separate the wicked from the midst of the righteous,

50 and will throw them into the furnace of fire; there will be weeping and gnashing of the teeth.

51 Jesus says to them, Have you understood all these things? They said to Him, Yes, Lord.
52 And He said to them, Because of this, every scribe discipled to the kingdom of Heaven is like a man, a master of a house, who puts forth out of his treasure new and old.

53. And it happened, when Jesus had finished these parables, He moved from there.
54 And coming into His fatherland, He taught

3588 5479 846 5217 2532 3956 3745 2192 4453 2532
τῆς χαρᾶς αὐτοῦ ὑπάγει, καὶ πάντα ὅσα ἔχει πωλεῖ, καὶ
the joy of it he goes, and all things which he has he sells, and

59 3588 68 1565
ἀγοράζει τὸν ἀγρὸν ἐκεῖνον.
buys field that.

3825 3664 2076 3588 932 3588 3772 444
45. Πάλιν ὁμοία ἐστὶν ἡ βασιλεία τῶν οὐρανῶν ἀνθρώπῳ
Again like is the kingdom of Heaven to a man

1713 2212 2570 3135 3739 2147 1520 4186
ἐμπόρῳ ζητοῦντι καλοὺς μαργαρίτας· 46 ὃς εὑρὼν ἕνα πολύ-
a merchant, seeking excellent pearls; who finding one very

3135 565 4097 3956 3745 2192 2532
τιμον μαργαρίτην, ἀπελθὼν πέπρακε πάντα ὅσα εἶχε, καὶ
precious pearl, going away he has sold all things that he had, and

59 846
ἠγόρασεν αὐτόν.
bought it.

3825 3664 2076 3588 932 3588 3772 4522
47. Πάλιν ὁμοία ἐστὶν ἡ βασιλεία τῶν οὐρανῶν σαγήνῃ
Again like is the kingdom of Heaven to a net

906 1519 3588 2281 2532 1537 3956 1085 4863
βληθείσῃ εἰς τὴν θάλασσαν, καὶ ἐκ παντὸς γένους συναγα-
thrown into the sea, and of every kind gathering

3739 3753 4137 307 1909 3588 123
γούσῃ· 48 ἣν ὅτε ἐπληρώθη, ἀναβιβάσαντες ἐπὶ τὸν αἰγιαλὸν,
together; which when it was filled, drawing up onto the shore

2532 2523 4816 3588 2570 1519 30 3588 1161 4450
καὶ καθίσαντες, συνέλεξαν τὰ καλὰ εἰς ἀγγεῖα, τὰ δὲ σαπρὰ
and sitting down, (they) gathered the good into vessels, the and corrupt

1854 906 3779 2071 1722 3588 4930 3588 165
ἔξω ἔβαλον. 49 οὕτως ἔσται ἐν τῇ συντελείᾳ τοῦ αἰῶνος·
out they threw. So it will be in the completion of the age;

1831 3588 32 2532 873 3588 4190 1537
ἐξελεύσονται οἱ ἄγγελοι, καὶ ἀφοριοῦσι τοὺς πονηροὺς ἐκ
will go out the angels and will separate the evil from

3319 3588 1342 2532 906 846 1519 3588 2575 3588
μέσου τῶν δικαίων, 50 καὶ βαλοῦσιν αὐτοὺς εἰς τὴν κάμινον τοῦ
(the) midst of the righteous, and will throw them into the furnace of the

4442 1563 2071 3588 2805 2532 3588 1030 3588 3599
πυρός· ἐκεῖ ἔσται ὁ κλαυθμὸς καὶ ὁ βρυγμὸς τῶν ὀδόντων.
fire; there shall be the weeping and the gnashing of the teeth.

3004 846 3588 2424 4920 5023 3956 3004
51. Λέγει αὐτοῖς ὁ Ἰησοῦς, Συνήκατε ταῦτα πάντα; λέγουσιν
says to them Jesus, Did you discern these things all? They say

846 3483 2962 3588 1161 2036 846 1223 5124 3956 1122
αὐτῷ, Ναί, Κύριε. 52 ὁ δὲ εἶπεν αὐτοῖς, Διὰ τοῦτο πᾶς γραμ-
to Him, Yes, Lord. He And said to them, Because of this every scribe

3100 1519 3588 932 3588 3772 3664
ματεὺς μαθητευθεὶς εἰς τὴν βασιλείαν τῶν οὐρανῶν ὅμοιός
discipled into the kingdom of Heaven like

2076 444 3617 3748 1544 1537 3588
ἐστιν ἀνθρώπῳ οἰκοδεσπότῃ ὅστις ἐκβάλλει ἐκ τοῦ
is to a man, a master of a house, who puts forth out of the

2344 846 2537 2532 3820
θησαυροῦ αὐτοῦ καινὰ καὶ παλαιά.
treasure of him new and old.

2532 1096 3753 5055 3588 2424 3588 3850 3778
53. Καὶ ἐγένετο ὅτε ἐτέλεσεν ὁ Ἰησοῦς τὰς παραβολὰς ταύτας,
And it happened when had ended Jesus parables these,

3332 1564 2532 2064 1519 3588 3968 846 1321
μετῆρεν ἐκεῖθεν· 54καὶ ἐλθὼν εἰς τὴν πατρίδα αὐτοῦ ἐδίδασκεν
He moved from there. And coming into the fatherland of Him He taught

and for joy thereof goeth and selleth all that he hath, and buyeth that field.

45 Again, the kingdom of heaven is like unto a merchant man, seeking goodly pearls:
46 Who, when he had found one pearl of great price, went and sold all that he had, and bought it.

47. Again, the kingdom of heaven is like unto a net, that was cast into the sea, and gathered of every kind:

48 Which, when it was full, they drew to shore, and sat down, and gathered the good into vessels, but cast the bad away.

49 So shall it be at the end of the world: the angels shall come forth, and sever the wicked from among the just,

50 And shall cast them into the furnace of fire: there shall be wailing and gnashing of teeth.

51 Jesus saith unto them, Have ye understood all these things? They say unto him, Yea, Lord.
52 Then said he unto them, Therefore every scribe (which is) instructed unto the kingdom of heaven is like unto a man (that is) an householder, which bringeth forth out of his treasure (things) new and old.
53. And it came to pass, (that) when Jesus had finished these parables, he departed thence.
54 And when he was come into his own country, he taught

Literal Translation

them in their synagogue, so that they were astonished, and said, From where did this one (get) this wisdom, and the powerful works?
55 Is this not the carpenter's son? (Is) not his mother called Mary, and his brothers, James, and Joses, and Simon, and Judas?

56 And are not his sisters all with us? From where then did this one (get) all these things?
57 And they were offended in Him. But Jesus said to them, A prophet is not without honor, except in his own homeland, and in his (own) house.

58 And He did not do many works of power there because of their unbelief.

Matthew 13:55

846 1722 3588 4864 846 5620 1605 846
αὐτοὺς ἐν τῇ συναγωγῇ αὐτῶν, ὥστε ἐκπλήττεσθαι αὐτοὺς
them in the synagogue of them, so that were astounded they

2532 3004 4159 5129 3588 4678 3778 2532 3588 1411 3756
καὶ λέγειν, Πόθεν τούτῳ ἡ σοφία αὕτη καὶ αἱ δυνάμεις; 55 οὐχ
even to say, From where this one wisdom this and the works of power? Not

3778 2076 3588 3588 5045 5207 3780 3588 3384 846
οὗτός ἐστιν ὁ τοῦ τέκτονος υἱός; οὐχὶ ἡ μήτηρ αὐτοῦ
this is the of the carpenter son? (Is) not the mother of him

3004 3137 2532 3588 80 846 2385 2532 2500
λέγεται Μαριὰμ, καὶ οἱ ἀδελφοὶ αὐτοῦ Ἰάκωβος καὶ Ἰωσῆς
called Mariam, and the brothers of him James and Joseph

2532 4613 2532 2455 2532 3588 79 846 3780 3956
καὶ Σίμων καὶ Ἰούδας; 56 καὶ αἱ ἀδελφαὶ αὐτοῦ οὐχὶ πᾶσαι
and Simon and Judas? And the sisters of him not all

4314 2248 1526 4159 3767 5129 5023 3956 2532
πρὸς ἡμᾶς εἰσι; πόθεν οὖν τούτῳ ταῦτα πάντα; 57 καὶ
with us are? From where then this (one) these things all? And

4624 1722 846 3588 1161 2424 2036 846 3756
ἐσκανδαλίζοντο ἐν αὐτῷ. ὁ δὲ Ἰησοῦς εἶπεν αὐτοῖς, Οὐκ
they were offended in Him. But Jesus said to them, Not

2036 4396 820 1487 3361 1722 3588 3968 846 2532 1722 3588
ἔστι προφήτης ἄτιμος, εἰ μὴ ἐν τῇ πατρίδι αὐτοῦ καὶ ἐν τῇ
is a prophet honorless, except in the fatherland of him, and in the

3614 846 2532 3756 4160 1563 1411 4183 1223
οἰκίᾳ αὐτοῦ. 58 καὶ οὐκ ἐποίησεν ἐκεῖ δυνάμεις πολλὰς, διὰ
house of him. And not He did there works of power many, because

3588 570 846
τὴν ἀπιστίαν αὐτῶν.
of the unbelief of them.

Literal Translation

them in their synagogue, insomuch that they were astonished, and said, Whence hath this (man) this wisdom, and (these) mighty works?
55 Is not this the carpenter's son? is not his mother called Mary? and his brethren, James, and Joses, and Simon, and Judas?

56 And his sisters, are they not all with us? Whence then hath this (man) all these things?
57 And they were offended in him. But Jesus said unto them, A prophet is not without honour, save in his own country, and in his own house.

58 And he did not many mighty works there because of their unbelief.

Matthew 14

1 At that time Herod the tetrarch heard the fame of Jesus.
2 And he said to his servants, This is John the Baptist. He is risen from the dead, and because of this, powerful works (are) working in him.

3. For seizing John, Herod bound him and put (him) into prison, because of Herodias, the wife of his brother Philip.

4 For John said to him, It is not lawful for you to have her.
5 And desiring to kill him, he feared the crowd, because they held him as a prophet.
6 But a birthday (feast for) Herod being held, the daughter of Herodias danced in the midst

Matthew 14

1722 1565 3588 2540 191 2264 3588 5076 3588
1. Ἐν ἐκείνῳ τῷ καιρῷ ἤκουσεν Ἡρώδης ὁ τετραάρχης τὴν
At that time heard Herod the tetrarch the

189 2424 2532 2036 3588 3816 846 3778 2076
ἀκοὴν Ἰησοῦ, 2 καὶ εἶπε τοῖς παισὶν αὐτοῦ, Οὗτός ἐστιν
fame of Jesus, and said to the servants of him, This is

2491 3588 910 846 1453 575 3588 3498 2532
Ἰωάννης ὁ βαπτιστής· αὐτὸς ἠγέρθη ἀπὸ τῶν νεκρῶν, καὶ
John the Baptist; he is risen from the dead, and

1223 5124 3588 1411 1754 1722 846 3588 1063 2264
διὰ τοῦτο αἱ δυνάμεις ἐνεργοῦσιν ἐν αὐτῷ. 3 ὁ γὰρ Ἡρῴδης
because of this the works of power operate in him. For Herod

2902 3588 291 1210 846 2532 5087 1722 5438
κρατήσας τὸν Ἰωάννην ἔδησεν αὐτὸν καὶ ἔθετο ἐν φυλακῇ,
having seized John bound him and put in prison,

1223 2266 3588 1135 5376 3588 80 846
διὰ Ἡρῳδιάδα τὴν γυναῖκα Φιλίππου τοῦ ἀδελφοῦ αὐτοῦ.
because of Herodias the wife of Philip the brother of him.

3004 1063 846 3588 2491 3756 1832 4671 2192 846
4 ἔλεγε γὰρ αὐτῷ ὁ Ἰωάννης, Οὐκ ἔξεστί σοι ἔχειν αὐτήν.
said For to him John, Not it is lawful for you to have her.

2532 2309 846 615 5399 3588 3793 3754 5613
5 καὶ θέλων αὐτὸν ἀποκτεῖναι, ἐφοβήθη τὸν ὄχλον, ὅτι ὡς
And wishing him to kill, he feared the crowd, because as

4396 846 2192 1077 1161 71 3588 2264
προφήτην αὐτὸν εἶχον. 6 γενεσίων δὲ αγομένων τοῦ Ἡρῴδου,
a prophet him they held. a birth-feast But being held of Herod,

3738 3588 2364 3588 2266 1722 3588 3319 2532
ὠρχήσατο ἡ θυγάτηρ τῆς Ἡρῳδιάδος ἐν τῷ μέσῳ, καὶ
danced the daughter of Herodias in the midst, and

Matthew 14

1 At that time Herod the tetrarch heard of the fame of Jesus,
2 And said unto his servants, This is John the Baptist; he is risen from the dead; and therefore mighty works do shew forth themselves in him.

3. For Herod had laid hold on John, and bound him, and put (him) in prison for Herodias' sake, his brother Philip's wife.

4 For John said unto him, It is not lawful for thee to have her.
5 And when he would have put him to death, he feared the multitude, because they counted him as a prophet.
6 But when Herod's birthday was kept, the daughter of Herodias danced before them,

Literal Translation

and pleased Herod.
7 From which (act) he assented with an oath to give her whatever she should ask.
8 But she being urged on by her mother, she says, Give me here on a platter the head of John the Baptist.
9 And the king was grieved, but because of the oaths, and those who reclined with (him), he ordered (it) to be given.
10 And sending, he beheaded John in the prison.
11 And his head was brought on a platter and was given to the girl, and she brought (it) to her mother.
12 And having come, his disciples took the body and buried it; and coming, (they) reported to Jesus.

Matthew 14:7

700 3588 2264 3526 3326 3727 3670 846 1325
ἤρεσε τῷ Ἡρῴδῃ. 7 ὅθεν μεθ' ὅρκου ὡμολόγησεν αὐτῇ δοῦναι
pleased Herod. From which with an oath he assented to her to give

3588 1437 154 3588 1161 4264 5259 3588 3384
ὃ ἐὰν αἰτήσηται. 8 ἡ δὲ, προβιβασθεῖσα ὑπὸ τῆς μητρὸς
whatever she might ask. she But, being urged on by the mother

846 1325 3427 5346 5602 1909 4094 3588 2776 2491
αὐτῆς, Δός μοι, φησίν, ὧδε ἐπὶ πίνακι τὴν κεφαλὴν Ἰωάννου
of her, Give me, she says, here on a platter the head of John

3588 910 2532 3076 3588 935 1223 1161 3588 3727
τοῦ βαπτιστοῦ. 9 καὶ ἐλυπήθη ὁ βασιλεύς, διὰ δὲ τοὺς ὅρκους
the Baptist. And was grieved the king, because but of the oaths

2532 3588 4873 2753 1325 2532 3992
καὶ τοὺς συνανακειμένους ἐκέλευσε δοθῆναι· 10 καὶ πέμψας
and those who reclined with (him) he ordered (it) to be given. And sending

607 3588 2491 1722 3588 5438 2532 5342 3588
ἀπεκεφάλισε τὸν Ἰωάννην ἐν τῇ φυλακῇ· 11 καὶ ἠνέχθη ἡ
He beheaded John in the prison. And was brought the

2776 846 1909 4094 2532 1325 3588 2877 2532 5342
κεφαλὴ αὐτοῦ ἐπὶ πίνακι, καὶ ἐδόθη τῷ κορασίῳ· καὶ ἤνεγκε
head of him on a platter, and was given to the girl, and she brought

3588 3384 846 2532 4334 3588 3101 846 142
τῇ μητρὶ αὐτῆς. 12 καὶ προσελθόντες οἱ μαθηταὶ αὐτοῦ ἦραν
to the mother of her. And having come near the disciples of him took

3588 4983 2532 2290 846 2532 2064 518 3588
τὸ σῶμα, καὶ ἔθαψαν αὐτό· καὶ ἐλθόντες ἀπήγγειλαν τῷ
the body, and buried it; and coming told

2424
Ἰησοῦ.
Jesus.

Literal Translation

and pleased Herod.
7 Whereupon he promised with an oath to give her whatsoever she would ask.
8 And she, being before instructed of her mother, said, Give me here John Baptist's head in a charger.
9 And the king was sorry: nevertheless for the oath's sake, and them which sat with him at meat, he commanded (it) to be given (her).
10 And he sent, and beheaded John in the prison.
11 And his head was brought in a charger, and given to the damsel: and she brought (it) to her mother.
12 And his disciples came, and took up the body, and buried it, and went and told Jesus.

13. And having heard, Jesus withdrew privately from there in a boat, into a deserted place. And hearing, the crowds followed Him on foot out of the cities.
14 And going out, Jesus saw a great crowd and was filled with pity on them. And He healed their infirm ones.

15. And evening coming, His disciples came near to Him saying, The place is deserted, and the hour is already gone by. Dismiss the crowds, that going away into the villages they may buy provisions for themselves.

16 But Jesus said to them, They have no need to go away. You give them (food) to eat.
17 But they said to Him, We have nothing here except five loaves and two fish.
18 And He said,

2532 191 3588 2424 402 1564 1722 4143 1519
13. Καί ακούσας ὁ Ἰησοῦς ἀνεχώρησεν ἐκεῖθεν ἐν πλοίῳ εἰς
And hearing Jesus withdrew from there in a boat into

2048 5117 2596 2398 2532 191 3588 3793 190
ἔρημον τόπον κατ' ἰδίαν· καὶ ἀκούσαντες οἱ ὄχλοι ἠκολού-
a deserted place privately. And having heard the crowds followed

846 3979 575 3588 4172 2532 1831 3588 2424
θησαν αὐτῷ πεζῇ ἀπὸ τῶν πόλεων. 14 καὶ ἐξελθὼν ὁ Ἰησοῦς
Him on foot from the cities. And going out Jesus

1492 4183 3793 2532 4697 1909 846 2532
εἶδε πολὺν ὄχλον, καὶ ἐσπλαγχνίσθη ἐπ' αὐτούς, καὶ ἐθερά-
saw a great, crowd, and was filled with pity on them, and He

2323 3588 732 846 3798 1161 1096
πευσε τοὺς ἀρρώστους αὐτῶν. 15 ὀψίας δὲ γενομένης,
healed the infirm of them. evening And having come,

4334 846 3588 3101 846 3004 2048
προσῆλθον αὐτῷ οἱ μαθηταὶ αὐτοῦ, λέγοντες, Ἔρημός
came near to Him the disciples of Him, saying, Deserted

2076 3588 5117 2532 3588 5610 2235 3928 630 3588
ἐστιν ὁ τόπος, καὶ ἡ ὥρα ἤδη παρῆλθεν· ἀπόλυσον τοὺς
is the place, and the hour already is gone by. Dismiss the

3793 2443 565 1519 3588 2968 59 1438
ὄχλους, ἵνα ἀπελθόντες εἰς τὰς κώμας ἀγοράσωσιν ἑαυτοῖς
crowds, that going away into the villages they may buy for themselves

1033 3588 1161 2424 2036 846 3756 5532 2192
βρώματα. 16 ὁ δὲ Ἰησοῦς εἶπεν αὐτοῖς, Οὐ χρείαν ἔχουσιν
foods. But Jesus said to them, Not need they have

565 1325 846 5210 5315 3588 1161 3004 846
ἀπελθεῖν· δότε αὐτοῖς ὑμεῖς φαγεῖν. 17 οἱ δὲ λέγουσιν αὐτῷ,
to go away; give to them you to eat. they But say to Him,

3756 2192 5602 1487 3361 4002 740 2532 1417 2486 3588 1161 2036
Οὐκ ἔχομεν ὧδε εἰ μὴ πέντε ἄρτους καὶ δύο ἰχθύας. 18 ὁ δὲ εἶπε,
Not we have here except five loaves and two fish. He And said,

13. When Jesus heard (of it), he departed thence by ship into a desert place apart: and when the people had heard (thereof), they followed him on foot out of the cities.
14 And Jesus went forth, and saw a great multitude, and was moved with compassion toward them, and he healed their sick.
15. And when it was evening, his disciples came to him, saying, This is a desert place, and the time is now past; send the multitude away, that they may go into the villages, and buy themselves victuals.

16 But Jesus said unto them, They need not depart; give ye them to eat.
17 And they say unto him, We have here but five loaves, and two fishes.
18 He said,

Literal Translation

Bring them here to Me.
19 And commanding the crowds to recline on the grass, and taking the five loaves and two fish, looking up to Heaven, He blessed. And breaking, He gave the loaves to the disciples, and the disciples (gave) to the crowds.
20 And all ate and were satisfied. And they took up the left over pieces, twelve hand baskets full.
21 And the ones eating were about five thousand men, besides women and children.
22. And immediately Jesus made His disciples get into a boat and to go before Him to the other side until He should dismiss the crowds.
23 And having dismissed the crowds, He went up into the mountain alone to pray. And evening coming on, He was there alone.
24 But the boat was now in (the) middle of the sea, tossed by the waves, for the wind was contrary.
25 But in the fourth watch of the night, Jesus went out to them, walking on the sea.
26 And seeing Him walking on the sea, the disciples were troubled, saying, It is a phantom! And they cried out from the fear.
27 But immediately Jesus spoke to them, saying, Be comforted! I AM! Do not fear.
28 And answering, Him, Peter said, Lord, if You are (He), command me to come to You on the waters.
29 And He said,

Matthew 14:19

5342 3427 846 5602 2532 2753 3588 3793 347
Φέρετέ μοι αὐτούς ὧδε. 19 καὶ κελεύσας τοὺς ὄχλους ἀνακλι-
Bring to Me them here. And commanding the crowds to recline

1909 3588 5528 2532 2983 3588 4002 740 2532 3588
θῆναι ἐπὶ τοὺς χόρτους, καὶ λαβὼν τοὺς πέντε ἄρτους καὶ τοὺς
on the grass, and taking the five loaves and the

1417 2486 308 1519 3588 3772 2127 2532
δύο ἰχθύας, ἀναβλέψας εἰς τὸν οὐρανὸν, εὐλόγησε, καὶ
two fish, looking up into Heaven, He blessed, and

2806 1325 3588 3101 3588 740 3588 1161 3101 3588
κλάσας ἔδωκε τοῖς μαθηταῖς τοὺς ἄρτους, οἱ δὲ μαθηταὶ τοῖς
breaking He gave to the disciples the loaves, the and disciples to the

3793 2532 5315 3956 2532 5526 2532 142 3588
ὄχλοις. 20 καὶ ἔφαγον πάντες, καὶ ἐχορτάσθησαν· καὶ ἦραν τὸ
crowds. And ate all, and were satisfied; and they took the

4052 3588 2801 1427 2894 4134 3588
περισσεῦον τῶν κλασμάτων, δώδεκα κοφίνους πλήρεις. 21 οἱ
left over of the pieces, twelve handbaskets full. those

1161 2068 2258 435 5616 4000 5565 1135
δὲ ἐσθίοντες ἦσαν ἄνδρες ὡσεὶ πεντακισχίλιοι, χωρὶς γυναι-
And eating were men about five thousand, apart from women

2532 3813
κῶν καὶ παιδίων.
and children.

2532 2112 315 3588 2424 3588 3101 846
22. Καὶ εὐθέως ἠνάγκασεν ὁ Ἰησοῦς τοὺς μαθητὰς αὐτοῦ
And instantly constrained Jesus the disciples of Him

1684 1519 3588 4143 2532 4254 846 1519 3588 4008
ἐμβῆναι εἰς τὸ πλοῖον, καὶ προάγειν αὐτὸν εἰς τὸ πέραν,
to enter into the boat, and to go before Him to the other side,

2193 3759 630 3588 3793 2532 630 3588 3793
ἕως οὗ ἀπολύσῃ τοὺς ὄχλους. 23 καὶ ἀπολύσας τοὺς ὄχλους,
until He dismissed the crowds. And having dismissed the crowds

305 1519 3588 3735 2596 2398 4336 3798 1161 1096
ἀνέβη εἰς τὸ ὄρος κατ' ἰδίαν προσεύξασθαι. ὀψίας δὲ γενο-
He went into the mountain apart in order to pray. evening And

3441 2258 1563 3588 1161 4143 2235 3319 3588 2281
μένης, μόνος ἦν ἐκεῖ. 24 τὸ δὲ πλοῖον ἤδη μέσον τῆς θαλάσσης
coming, alone He was there. the And boat now amidst the sea

2258 928 5259 3588 2949 2258 1063 1727 3588
ἦν, βασανιζόμενον ὑπὸ τῶν κυμάτων· ἦν γὰρ ἐναντίος ὁ
was, being tossed by the waves; was for contrary the

417 5067 1161 5438 3588 3571 565 4314 846
ἄνεμος.25τετάρτῃ δὲ φυλακῇ τῆς νυκτὸς ἀπῆλθε πρὸς αὐτοὺς
wind. in (the) fourth But watch of the night went toward them

3588 2424 4043 1909 3588 2281 2532 1492 846
ὁ Ἰησοῦς, περιπατῶν ἐπὶ τῆς θαλάσσης. 26 καὶ ἰδόντες αὐτὸν
Jesus, walking on the sea. And seeing Him

3588 3101 1909 3588 2281 4043 5015
οἱ μαθηταὶ ἐπὶ τὴν θάλασσαν περιπατοῦντα ἐταράχθησαν,
the disciples on the sea walking about they were troubled,

3004 3754 5326 2076 2532 575 3588 5401 2896
λέγοντες ὅτι Φάντασμά ἐστι· καὶ ἀπὸ τοῦ φόβου ἔκραξαν.
saying, A phantom it is, and out of fear they cried out.

2112 1161 2980 846 3588 2424 3004 2293 1473
27 εὐθέως δὲ ἐλάλησεν αὐτοῖς ὁ Ἰησοῦς, λέγων, Θαρσεῖτε, ἐγώ
at once But spoke to them Jesus, saying, Be comforted, I

1510 3361 5399 611 1161 846 3588 4074 2036 2962
εἰμι·μὴ φοβεῖσθε. 28 ἀποκριθεὶς δὲ αὐτῷ ὁ Πέτρος εἶπε, Κύριε,
AM! not Do fear. answering And Him, Peter said, Lord,

1487 4771 1488 2753 3165 4314 4571 2064 1909 3588 5204 3588 1161 2036
εἰ σὺ εἶ, κέλευσόν με πρὸς σε ἐλθεῖν ἐπὶ τὰ ὕδατα· 29 ὁ δὲ εἶπεν,
If You are, command me to You to come on the waters. He And said,

Literal Translation

Bring them hither to me.
19 And he commanded the multitude to sit down on the grass, and took the five loaves, and the two fishes, and looking up to heaven, he blessed, and brake, and gave the loaves to (his) disciples, and the disciples to the multitude.
20 And they did all eat, and were filled: and they took up of the fragments that remained twelve baskets full.
21 And they that had eaten were about five thousand men, beside women and children.
22.And straightway Jesus constrained his disciples to get into a ship, and to go before him unto the other side, while he sent the multitudes away.
23 And when he had sent the multitudes away, he went up into a mountain apart to pray: and when the evening was come, he was there alone.
24 But the ship was now in the midst of the sea, tossed with waves: for the wind was contrary.
25 And in the fourth watch of the night Jesus went unto them, walking on the sea.
26 And when the disciples saw him walking on the sea, they were troubled, saying, It is a spirit; and they cried out for fear.
27 But straightway Jesus spake unto them, saying, Be of good cheer; it is I; be not afraid.
28 And Peter answered him and said, Lord, if it be thou, bid me come unto thee on the water.
29 And he said,

Literal Translation

Come! And going down from the boat, Peter walked on the waters to come to Jesus.
30 But seeing the strong wind, he was afraid, and beginning to sink, he cried out, saying, Lord, save me!

31 And immediately stretching out the hand, Jesus took hold of him, and says to him, Little-faith, why did you doubt?

32 And they going up into the boat, the wind ceased.

33 And those in the boat came and worshiped Him, saying, Truly, You are the Son of God.

34. And having passed over, they came to the land of Gennesaret.
35 And recognizing Him, the men of that place sent to all that neighborhood, and brought to Him all those who had illness.
36 And (they) begged Him that they might only touch the fringe of His garment. And as many as touched were made perfectly well.

Matthew 14:30

2064 2532 2597 575 3588 4143 3588 4074 4043
Ἐλθέ. καὶ καταβὰς ἀπὸ τοῦ πλοίου ὁ Πέτρος περιεπάτησεν
Come! And descending from the boat Peter walked

1909 3588 5204 2064 4314 3588 2424 991 1161 3588
ἐπὶ τὰ ὕδατα, ἐλθεῖν πρὸς τὸν Ἰησοῦν. 30 βλέπων δὲ τὸν
on the waters, to come to Jesus. seeing But the

417 2478 5399 2532 756 2670
ἄνεμον ἰσχυρὸν ἐφοβήθη· καὶ ἀρξάμενος καταποντίζεσθαι
wind strong, he was afraid; and beginning to sink

2896 3004 2962 4982 3165 2112 1161 3588 2424 1614
ἔκραξε, λέγων, Κύριε, σῶσόν με. 31 εὐθέως δὲ ὁ Ἰησοῦς ἐκτείνας
he cried out, saying, Lord, save me. instantly And Jesus stretching out

3588 5495 1949 846 2532 3004 846 3640
τὴν χεῖρα ἐπελάβετο αὐτοῦ καὶ λέγει αὐτῷ, Ὀλιγόπιστε,
the hand took hold of him, and says to him, Little-faith,

1519 5101 1365 2532 1684 846 1519 3588 4143
εἰς τί ἐδίστασας; 32 καὶ ἐμβάντων αὐτῶν εἰς τὸ πλοῖον,
why did you doubt? And going up they into the boat,

2869 3588 417 3588 1161 1722 3588 4143 2064
ἐκόπασεν ὁ ἄνεμος. 33 οἱ δὲ ἐν τῷ πλοίῳ ἐλθόντες
ceased the wind. the (ones) And in the boat coming

4352 846 3004 230 2316 5207 1488
προσεκύνησαν αὐτῷ, λέγοντες, Ἀληθῶς Θεοῦ υἱὸς εἶ.
worshiped Him, saying, Truly of God Son You are.

2532 1276 2064 1519 3588 1093 1082 2532
34.Καὶ διαπεράσαντες ἦλθον εἰς τὴν γῆν Γεννησαρέτ. 35 καὶ
And passing over they came into the land of Gennesaret. And

1921 846 3588 435 3588 5117 1565 649
ἐπιγνόντες αὐτὸν οἱ ἄνδρες τοῦ τόπου ἐκείνου ἀπέστειλαν
recognizing Him the men of place that sent

1519 3650 3588 4066 1565 2532 4374 846
εἰς ὅλην τὴν περίχωρον ἐκείνην, καὶ προσήνεγκαν αὐτῷ
into all neighborhood that, and brought to Him

3956 3588 2560 2192 2532 3870 846 2443
πάντας τοὺς κακῶς ἔχοντας, 36 καὶ παρεκάλουν αὐτὸν, ἵνα
all those illness having, and begged Him that

3440 680 3588 2899 3588 2440 846 2532
μόνον ἅψωνται τοῦ κρασπέδου τοῦ ἱματίου αὐτοῦ· καὶ
only they might touch the fringe of the garment of Him; and

3745 680 1295
ὅσοι ἥψαντο διεσώθησαν.
as many as touched were cured.

Literal Translation

Come. And when Peter was come down out of the ship, he walked on the water, to go to Jesus.
30 But when he saw the wind boisterous, he was afraid; and beginning to sink, he cried, saying, Lord, save me.

31 And immediately Jesus stretched forth (his) hand, and caught him, and said unto him, O thou of little faith, wherefore didst thou doubt?
32 And when they were come into the ship, the wind ceased.

33 Then they that were in the ship came and worshipped him, saying, Of a truth thou art the Son of God.

34. And when they were gone over, they came into the land of Gennesaret.
35 And when the men of that place had knowledge of him, they sent out into all that country round about, and brought unto him all that were diseased;
36 And besought him that they might only touch the hem of his garment: and as many as touched were made perfectly whole.

Matthew 15

1. Then the scribes and Pharisees came to Jesus from Jerusalem, saying,

2 Why do your disciples transgress the tradition of the elders? For they do not wash their hands whenever they eat bread.

3 But answering He said to them, Why do you also transgress the command of God on account of your tradition?
4 For God

Matthew 15

5119 4334 3588 2424 3588 575 2414
1. Τότε προσέρχονται τῷ Ἰησοῦ οἱ ἀπὸ Ἱεροσολύμων
Then came near to Jesus those from Jerusalem,

1122 2532 5330 3004 1302 3588 3101 4675
γραμματεῖς καὶ Φαρισαῖοι, λέγοντες, 2 Διατί οἱ μαθηταί σου
scribes and Pharisees, saying, Why the disciples of you

3845 3588 3862 3588 4245 3756 1063
παραβαίνουσι τὴν παράδοσιν τῶν πρεσβυτέρων; οὐ γὰρ
transgress the tradition of the elders? not For

3538 3588 5495 846 3752 740 2068 3588 1161
νίπτονται τὰς χεῖρας αὐτῶν, ὅταν ἄρτον ἐσθίωσιν. 3 ὁ δὲ
they wash the hands of them, when bread they eat. He But

611 2036 846 1302 2532 5210 3845 3588
ἀποκριθεὶς εἶπεν αὐτοῖς, Διατί καὶ ὑμεῖς παραβαίνετε τὴν
answering said to them, Why also you do transgress the

1785 3588 2316 1223 3588 3862 5216 3588 1063 2316
ἐντολὴν τοῦ Θεοῦ διὰ τὴν παράδοσιν ὑμῶν; 4 ὁ γὰρ Θεὸς
command of God because of the tradition of you? For God

Matthew 15

1. Then came to Jesus scribes and Pharisees, which were of Jerusalem, saying,
2 Why do thy disciples transgress the tradition of the elders? for they wash not their hands when they eat bread.

3 But he answered and said unto them, Why do ye also transgress the commandment of God by your tradition?

4 For God

Literal Translation

commanded, saying, "Honor your father and mother," and, "The (one) speaking evil of father or mother, by death let him die." (Ex. 20:12; 21:17)

5 But you say, Whoever says to the father or the mother, A gift, whatever you would gain from me;
6 and in no way he honors his father or his mother. And you annulled the command of God on account of your tradition.
7 Hypocrites! Well did Isaiah prophesy concerning you, saying:
8 "This people draws near to Me with their mouth, and with (their) lips honor Me; but their heart holds far off from Me.

9 But in vain they worship Me, teaching (as) doctrines (the) ordinances of men." (Isa. 29:13)
10. And calling near the crowd, He said to them, Hear and understand:
11 (It is) not that which has entered into the mouth that defiles the man, but that which has come out of the mouth, this defiles the man.

12 Then coming, the disciples said to Him, You know that hearing the saying, the Pharisees were offended?

13 But answering, He said, Every plant which My heavenly Father has not planted shall be rooted up.
14 Leave them (alone). They are blind leaders of the blind; and if the blind lead the blind, both will fall into a pit.
15 And answering, Peter said to Him, Explain this parable to us.

16 But Jesus said, Are you also still without understanding?
17 Do you not yet perceive

Matthew 15:5

1781 3004 5091 3588 3962 4675 2532 3588 3384
ἐνετείλατο, λέγων, Τίμα τὸν πατέρα σοῦ, καὶ τὴν μητέρα·
commanded, saying, Honor the father of you, and the mother;

2532 3588 2551 3962 2228 3384 2288 5053
καί, Ὁ κακολογῶν πατέρα ἢ μητέρα θανάτῳ τελευτάτω·
also, the (one) speaking evil of father or mother by death let him end.

5210 1161 3004 3739 302 2036 3588 3962 2228 3588 3384 1435
5 ὑμεῖς δὲ λέγετε, Ὃς ἂν εἴπῃ τῷ πατρὶ ἢ τῇ μητρί, Δῶρον,
you But say, Whoever says to the father or the mother, A gift,

3739 1437 1537/1700 5623 2532 3756 3361 5091 3588 3962
ὃ ἐὰν ἐξ ἐμοῦ ὠφεληθῇς, 6 καὶ οὐ μὴ τιμήσει τὸν πατέρα
whatever by me you would gain, and in no way he honors the father

846 2228 3588 3384 846 2532 208 3588 1785 846
αὐτοῦ ἢ τὴν μητέρα αὐτοῦ· καὶ ἠκυρώσατε τὴν ἐντολὴν τοῦ
of him or the mother of him; and you annulled the command

2316 1223 3588 3862 5216 5273 2573 4395
Θεοῦ διὰ τὴν παράδοσιν ὑμῶν. 7 ὑποκριταί, καλῶς προεφή-
of God because of traditiion your. Hypocrites! Well proph-

4012 5216 2268 3004 1448 3427 3588 2992 3778
τευσε περὶ ὑμῶν Ἠσαΐας, λέγων, 8 Ἐγγίζει μοι ὁ λαὸς οὗτος
esied concerning you Isaiah, saying, Draws near to Me people this

3588 4750 846 2532 3588 5491 3165 5091 2228 1161 2588
τῷ στόματι αὐτῶν, καὶ τοῖς χείλεσί με τιμᾷ· ἡ δὲ καρδία
with the mouth of them, and with the lips Me it honors; the but heart

846 4206 568 575 1700 3155 1161 4576 3165
αὐτῶν πόρρω ἀπέχει ἀπ' ἐμοῦ. 9 μάτην δὲ σέβονταί με, διδά-
of them far holds off from Me. in vain But they worship Me,

1321 1319 1778 444 2532 4341
σκοντες διδασκαλίας ἐντάλματα ἀνθρώπων. 10 καὶ προσκα-
teaching (as) doctrines ordinances of men. And calling

3588 3793 2036 846 191 2532 4920 3756
λεσάμενος τὸν ὄχλον, εἶπεν αὐτοῖς, Ἀκούετε καὶ συνίετε. 11 οὐ
near the crowd, He said to them, Hear and understand, not

3588 1525 1519 3588 4750 2840 3588 444 235 3588
τὸ εἰσερχόμενον εἰς τὸ στόμα κοινοῖ τὸν ἄνθρωπον· ἀλλὰ τὸ
the (thing) entering into the mouth defiles the man; but that

1607 1537 3588 4750 5124 2840 3588 444
ἐκπορευόμενον ἐκ τοῦ στόματος, τοῦτο κοινοῖ τὸν ἄνθρωπον.
coming forth from the mouth, this defiles the man.

5119 4334 3588 3101 846 2036 846 1492
12 τότε προσελθόντες οἱ μαθηταὶ αὐτοῦ εἶπον αὐτῷ, Οἶδας
Then coming the disciples of Him, they said to Him, Know (You)

3754 3588 5330 191 3588 3056 4624
ὅτι οἱ Φαρισαῖοι ἀκούσαντες τὸν λόγον ἐσκανδαλίσθησαν;
that the Pharisees hearing the saying were offended?

3588 1161 611 2036 3956 5451 3739 3756 5452 3588
13 ὁ δὲ ἀποκριθεὶς εἶπε, Πᾶσα φυτεία, ἣν οὐκ ἐφύτευσεν ὁ
He But answering said, Every plant which not has planted the

3962 3450 3588 3770 1610 863 846
πατήρ μου ὁ οὐράνιος, ἐκριζωθήσεται. 14 ἄφετε αὐτούς·
Father of Me the heavenly, shall be rooted up. Leave them;

3595 1526 5185 5185 5185 1161 5185 1437 3594
ὁδηγοί εἰσι τυφλοὶ τυφλῶν· τυφλὸς δὲ τυφλὸν ἐὰν ὁδηγῇ,
leaders they are blind of blind; blind and blind if lead,

297 1519 999 4098 611 1161 3588 4074
ἀμφότεροι εἰς βόθυνον πεσοῦνται. 15 ἀποκριθεὶς δὲ ὁ Πέτρος
both into a pit will fall. answering And Peter

2036 846 5419 2254 3588 3850 3778 3588 1161
εἶπεν αὐτῷ, Φράσον ἡμῖν τὴν παραβολὴν ταύτην. 16 ὁ δὲ
said to Him, Explain to us parable this. But

2424 2036 188 2532 5210 801 2075 3768 3539
Ἰησοῦς εἶπεν, Ἀκμὴν καὶ ὑμεῖς ἀσύνετοί ἐστε; 17 οὔπω νοεῖτε,
Jesus said,. Yet also you unintelligent are? Not yet you perceive

Literal Translation

commanded, saying, Honour thy father and mother: and, He that curseth father or mother, let him die the death.

5 But ye say, Whosoever shall say to (his) father or (his) mother, (It is) a gift, by whatsoever thou mightest be profited by me;
6 And honour not his father or his mother, (he shall be free). Thus have ye made the commandment of God of none effect by your tradition.
7 (Ye) hypocrites, well did Esaias prophesy of you, saying,
8 This people draweth nigh unto me with their mouth, and honoureth me with (their) lips; but their heart is far from me.
9 But in vain they do worship me, teaching (for) doctrines the commandments of men.
10. And he called the multitude, and said unto them, Hear, and understand:
11 Not that which goeth into the mouth defileth a man; but that which cometh out of the mouth, this defileth a man.

12 Then came his disciples, and said unto him, Knowest thou that the Pharisees were offended, after they heard this saying?
13 But he answered and said, Every plant, which my heavenly Father hath not planted, shall be rooted up.
14 Let them alone: they be blind leaders of the blind. And if the blind lead the blind, both shall fall into the ditch.
15 Then answered Peter and said unto him, Declare unto us this parable.
16 And Jesus said, Are ye also yet without understanding?
17 Do not ye yet understand,

Literal Translation

that everything entering into the mouth goes into the belly, and is expelled into (the) waste bowl?

18 But the things which come out of the mouth come forth from the heart, and these defile the man.

19 For out of the heart come forth evil reasonings, murders, adulteries, fornications, thefts, false witnessings, blasphemies.

20 These things are the (things) defiling the man. But to eat with unwashed hands does not defile the man.

21. And going out from there, Jesus withdrew to the parts of Tyre and Sidon.
22 And, behold, a woman of Canaan coming forth from those borders cried out to Him, saying, Have pity on me, Lord, Son of David! My daughter is badly demon-possessed.
23 But He did not answer her a word. And coming near, His disciples asked Him, saying, Send her away, because she cries out after us.

24 But answering, He said, I was not sent except to the lost sheep of (the) house of Israel.
25 But coming, she worshiped Him, saying, Lord, help me!
26 But answering, He said, It is not good to take the bread of the children to throw (it) to the little dogs.

27 But she said, Yes, Lord; for even the little dogs eat of the crumbs falling from the table of their lords.

28 Then answering, Jesus said to her, O woman, your faith (is) great;

Matthew 15:18

3754 3956 3588 1531 1519 3588 4750 1519 3588 2836
ὅτι πᾶν τὸ εἰσπορευόμενον εἰς τὸ στόμα εἰς τὴν κοιλίαν
that everything having entered into the mouth into the stomach

5562 2532 1519 856 1544 3588 1161 1607 1537
χωρεῖ, καὶ εἰς ἀφεδρῶνα ἐκβάλλεται; 18 τὰ δὲ ἐκπορευόμενα ἐκ
goes, and into (the) wastebowl is expelled? the things But coming out of

3588 4750 1537 3588 2588 1831 2548 2840 3588
τοῦ στόματος ἐκ τῆς καρδίας ἐξέρχεται, κἀκεῖνα κοινοῖ τὸν
the mouth from the heart come forth, and those defile the

444 1537 1063 3588 2588 1831 1261
ἄνθρωπον. 19 ἐκ γὰρ τῆς καρδίας ἐξέρχονται διαλογισμοὶ
man. out of For the heart come forth reasonings,

4190 5408 3430 4202 2829 5577
πονηροί, φόνοι, μοιχεῖαι, πορνεῖαι, κλοπαί, ψευδομαρτυρίαι,
evils, murders, adulteries, fornications, thefts, false witnessings,

988 5023 2076 3588 2840 3588 444 3588
βλασφημίαι· 20 ταῦτά ἐστι τὰ κοινοῦντα τὸν ἄνθρωπον· τὸ
blasphemies; these things are the things defiling the man;

1161 449 5495 5315 3756 2840 3588 444
δὲ ἀνίπτοις χερσί φαγεῖν οὐ κοινοῖ τὸν ἄνθρωπον.
but with unwashed hands to eat not defiles the man.

2532 1831 1564 3588 2424 402 1519 3588 3313
21. Καὶ ἐξελθὼν ἐκεῖθεν ὁ Ἰησοῦς ἀνεχώρησεν εἰς τὰ μέρη
And going out from there, Jesus withdrew into the parts

5184 2532 4605 2532 2400 1135 5478 575 3588 3725
Τύρου καὶ Σιδῶνος. 22 καὶ ἰδού, γυνὴ Χαναναία ἀπὸ τῶν ὁρίων
of Tyre and Sidon. And, behold, a woman Canaanite from borders

1565 1831 2905 846 3004 1653
ἐκείνων ἐξελθοῦσα ἐκραύγασεν αὐτῷ, λέγουσα, Ἐλέησόν
those coming forth cried out to Him, saying, Have pity on

3165 2962 5207 1138 3588 2364 3450 2560 1139 3588
με, Κύριε, υἱὲ Δαβίδ· ἡ θυγάτηρ μου κακῶς δαιμονίζεται. 23 ὁ
me, Lord, Son of David; the daughter of me badly is demon-possessed. He

1161 3756 611 846 3056 2532 4334 3588 3101
δὲ οὐκ ἀπεκρίθη αὐτῇ λόγον. καὶ προσελθόντες οἱ μαθηταὶ
But not answered her a word. And having come near the disciples

846 2065 846 3004 630 846 3754
αὐτοῦ ἠρώτων αὐτόν, λέγοντες, Ἀπόλυσον αὐτήν, ὅτι
of Him asked Him, saying, Send away her, because

2896 3693 2257 3588 1161 611 2036 3756 649
κράζει ὄπισθεν ἡμῶν. 24 ὁ δὲ ἀποκριθεὶς εἶπεν, Οὐκ ἀπεστάλην
she cries after us. He But answering said, Not I was sent

1487 3361 1519 3588 4263 3588 622 3624 2474 3588 1161
εἰ μὴ εἰς τὰ πρόβατα τὰ ἀπολωλότα οἴκου Ἰσραήλ. 25 ἡ δὲ
except to the sheep lost of (the) house of Israel. she But

2064 4352 846 3004 2962 997 3427 3588 1161
ἐλθοῦσα προσεκύνει αὐτῷ λέγουσα, Κύριε, βοήθει μοι. 26 ὁ δὲ
coming worshiped Him, saying, Lord, help me! He But

611 2036 3756 2076 2570 2983 3588 740 3588
ἀποκριθεὶς εἶπεν, Οὐκ ἔστι καλὸν λαβεῖν τὸν ἄρτον τῶν
answering said, Not it is good to take the bread of the

5043 2532 906 3588 2952 3588 1161 2036 3483 2962 2532
τέκνων, καὶ βαλεῖν τοῖς κυναρίοις. 27 ἡ δὲ εἶπε, Ναί, Κύριε· καὶ
children, and to throw to the dogs. she And said, Yes, Lord; even

1063 3588 2952 2068 575 3588 5589 3588 4098
γὰρ τὰ κυνάρια ἐσθίει ἀπο τῶν ψιχίων τῶν πιπτόντων
for the dogs eat from the crumbs falling

575 3588 5132 3588 2962 846 5119 611 3588
ἀπὸ τῆς τραπέζης τῶν κυρίων αὐτῶν. 28 τότε ἀποκριθεὶς ὁ
from the table of the lords of them. Then answering

2424 2036 846 5599 1135 3173 4675 3588 4102
Ἰησοῦς εἶπεν αὐτῇ, Ὦ γύναι, μεγάλη σου ἡ πίστις·
Jesus said to her, O woman, great (is) of you the faith;

Literal Translation

that whatsoever entereth in at the mouth goeth into the belly, and is cast out into the draught?
18 But those things which proceed out of the mouth come forth from the heart; and they defile the man.

19 For out of the heart proceed evil thoughts, murders, adulteries, fornications, thefts, false witness, blasphemies:

20 These are (the things) which defile a man: but to eat with unwashen hands defileth not a man.

21. Then Jesus went thence, and departed into the coasts of Tyre and Sidon.
22 And, behold, a woman of Canaan came out of the same coasts, and cried unto him, saying, Have mercy on me, O Lord, (thou) Son of David; my daughter is grievously vexed with a devil.
23 But he answered her not a word. And his disciples came and besought him, saying, Send her away; for she crieth after us.

24 But he answered and said, I am not sent but unto the lost sheep of the house of Israel.
25 Then came she and worshipped him, saying, Lord, help me.
26 But he answered and said, It is not meet to take the children's bread, and to cast (it) to dogs.

27 And she said, Truth, Lord: yet the dogs eat of the crumbs which fall from their masters' table.

28 Then Jesus answered and said unto her, O woman, great (is) thy faith:

Literal Translation

let it be to you as you desire. And her daughter was healed from that hour.

29. And moving from there, Jesus came beside the Sea of Galilee. And going up into the mountain, He sat there.
30 And great crowds came to Him, having with them lame ones, blind, dumb, maimed, and many others. And they flung them down at the feet of Jesus. And He healed them;

31 so that the crowds marveled, seeing the dumb speaking, the maimed whole, the lame walking, and the blind seeing. And they glorified the God of Israel.

32. But having called near His disciples, Jesus said, I am filled with pity on the crowd, because they already have remained with Me three days and have not anything they may eat. And I do not desire to send them away fasting, that they may not be weary in the way.
33 And His disciples said to Him, From where in a deserted (place will come) to us so many loaves as to satisfy so great a crowd?
34 And Jesus said to them, How many loaves do you have? And they said, Seven, and a few small fish.
35 And He ordered the crowds to recline on the ground.

36 And taking the seven loaves and the fish, giving thanks, He broke and gave to His disciples, and the disciples to the crowd.
37 And all ate and were

Matthew 15:29

1096 4671 5613 2309 2532 2390 3588 2364 846 575 3588
γενηθήτω σοι ὡς θέλεις. καὶ ἰάθη ἡ θυγάτηρ αὐτῆς ἀπὸ τῆς
let it be to you as you desire. And was healed the daughter of her from

5610 1565
ὥρας ἐκείνης.
hour that.

2532 3327 1564 3588 2424 2064 3844 3588 2281
29. Καὶ μεταβὰς ἐκεῖθεν ὁ Ἰησοῦς ἦλθε παρὰ τὴν θάλασσαν
And moving from there Jesus came beside the Sea

3588 1056 2532 305 1519 3588 3735 2521 1563 2532
τῆς Γαλιλαίας· καὶ ἀναβὰς εἰς τὸ ὄρος ἐκάθητο ἐκεῖ.30 καὶ
of Galilee; and going up into the mount He sat there. And

4334 846 3793 4183 2192 3326 1438 5560
προσῆλθον αὐτῷ ὄχλοι πολλοὶ, ἔχοντες μεθ' ἑαυτῶν χωλούς,
came to Him crowds great, having with themselves (the) lame,

5185 2974 2948 2532 2087 4183 2532 4496
τυφλούς, κωφούς, κυλλούς, καὶ ἑτέρους πολλούς, καὶ ἔρριψαν
blind, dumb, maimed, and others many. And they flung

846 3844 3588 4228 3588 2424 2532 2323 846
αὐτοὺς παρὰ τοὺς πόδας τοῦ Ἰησοῦ καὶ ἐθεράπευσεν αὐτούς·
them beside the feet of Jesus; and He healed them;

5620 3588 3793 2296 991 2974 2980
31 ὥστε τοὺς ὄχλους θαυμάσαι, βλέποντας κωφοὺς λαλοῦντας,
so that the crowds (had) to marvel, seeing dumb ones speaking,

2948 5199 5560 4043 2532 5185
κυλλοὺς ὑγιεῖς, χωλοὺς περιπατοῦντας, καὶ τυφλοὺς
maimed ones whole, lame ones walking about and blind ones

991 2532 1392 3588 2316 2474
βλέποντας· καὶ ἐδόξασαν τὸν Θεὸν Ἰσραήλ.
seeing. And they glorified the God of Israel.

3588 1161 2424 4341 3588 3101 846 2036
32. Ὁ δὲ Ἰησοῦς προσκαλεσάμενος τοὺς μαθητὰς αὐτοῦ εἶπε,
And Jesus having called near the disciples of Him said,

4697 1909 3588 3793 3754 2235 2250 5140 4357
Σπλαγχνίζομαι ἐπὶ τὸν ὄχλον, ὅτι ἤδη ἡμέρας τρεῖς προσ-
I am filled with pity on the crowd because now days three they

3427 2532 3756 2192 5101 5315 2532 630
μένουσί μοι, καὶ οὐκ ἔχουσι τί φάγωσι· καὶ ἀπολῦσαι
remain with Me, and not have anything they may eat; and to send away

846 3523 3756 2309 3379 1590 1722 3588 3598 2532
αὐτοὺς νήστεις οὐ θέλω, μήποτε ἐκλυθῶσιν ἐν τῇ ὁδῷ. 33 καὶ
them fasting not I desire, that not they be weary in the way. And

3004 846 3588 3101 846 4159 2254 1722 2047
λέγουσιν αὐτῷ οἱ μαθηταί αὐτοῦ, Πόθεν ἡμῖν ἐν ἐρημίᾳ
say to Him the disciples of Him, From where to us in a desert

740 5118 5620 5526 3793 5118 2532
ἄρτοι τοσοῦτοι, ὥστε χορτάσαι ὄχλον τοσοῦτον; 34 καὶ
loaves so many as to satisfy a crowd so great? And

3004 846 3588 2424 4214 740 2192 3588 1161 2036
λέγει αὐτοῖς ὁ Ἰησοῦς, Πόσους ἄρτους ἔχετε; οἱ δὲ εἶπον,
said to them Jesus, How many loaves have you? they And said,

2033 2532 3641 2485 2532 2753 3588 3793 377
Ἑπτά, καὶ ὀλίγα ἰχθύδια. 35 καὶ ἐκέλευσε τοῖς ὄχλοις ἀναπε-
Seven, and a few small fish. And He ordered the crowd to recline

1909 3588 1093 2532 2983 3588 2033 740 2532 3588
σεῖν ἐπὶ τὴν γῆν. 36 καὶ λαβὼν τοὺς ἑπτὰ ἄρτους καὶ τοὺς
on the ground. And taking the seven loaves and the

2486 2168 2806 2532 1325 3588 3101 846
ἰχθύας, εὐχαριστήσας ἔκλασε, καὶ ἔδωκε τοῖς μαθηταῖς αὐτοῦ,
fish, giving thanks He broke and gave to the disciples of Him,

3588 1161 3101 3588 3793 2532 5315 3956 2532 5526
οἱ δὲ μαθηταὶ τῷ ὄχλῳ. 37 καὶ ἔφαγον πάντες καὶ ἐχορτά-
the and disciples to the crowd. And ate all and were

Literal Translation

be it unto thee even as thou wilt. And her daughter was made whole from that very hour.

29. And Jesus departed from thence, and came nigh unto the sea of Galilee; and went up into a mountain, and sat down there.
30 And great multitudes came unto him, having with them (those that were) lame, blind, dumb, maimed, and many others, and cast them down at Jesus' feet; and he healed them:

31 Insomuch that the multitude wondered, when they saw the dumb to speak, the maimed to be whole, the lame to walk, and the blind to see: and they glorified the God of Israel.

32 .Then Jesus called his disciples (unto him), and said, I have compassion on the multitude, because they continue with me now three days, and have nothing to eat: and I will not send them away fasting, lest they faint in the way.
33 And his disciples say unto him, Whence should we have so much bread in the wilderness, as to fill so great a multitude?

34 And Jesus saith unto them, How many loaves have ye? And they said, Seven, and a few little fishes.

35 And he commanded the multitude to sit down on the ground.
36 And he took the seven loaves and the fishes, and gave thanks, and brake (them), and gave to his disciples, and the disciples to the multitude.
37 And they did all eat, and were

Literal Translation

filled. And they took up the left over pieces, seven lunch baskets full.
38 And the ones eating were four thousand men, besides women and children.
39 And sending away the crowds He went into the boat and came to the borders of Magdala.

Matthew 15:38

2532 142 3588 4052 3588 2801 2033
σθησαν· καὶ ἦραν τὸ περισσεῦον τῶν κλασμάτων, ἑπτὰ
filled. And they took up the excess of the pieces, seven

4711 4134 3588 1161 2068 2258 5070
σπυρίδας πλήρεις. 38 οἱ δὲ ἐσθίοντες ἦσαν τετρακισχίλιοι
lunch-baskets full. the (ones) And eating were four thousand

435 5565 1135 2532 3813 2532 630 3588
ἄνδρες, χωρὶς γυναικῶν καὶ παιδίων. 39 Καὶ ἀπολύσας τοὺς
men, apart from women and children. And sending away the

3793 1684 1519 3588 4143 2532 2064 1519 3588 3725 3093
ὄχλους ἐνέβη εἰς τὸ πλοῖον, καὶ ἦλθεν εἰς τὰ ὅρια Μαγδαλά.
crowds, He went into the boat, and came into the borders of Magdala.

Literal Translation

filled: and they took up of the broken (meat) that was left seven baskets full.
38 And they that did eat were four thousand men, beside women and children.
39 And he sent away the multitude, and took ship, and came into the coasts of Magdala.

Matthew 16

1. And coming, the Pharisees and Sadducees asked Him to show them a sign out of the heaven, tempting (Him).

2 But answering, He said to them, Evening coming on, you say, Clear sky, for the heaven is red.
3 And at morning, Today a storm, for the heaven is red, being overcast. Hypocrites! You indeed know how to discern the face of the heaven, but you cannot the signs of the times.

4 An evil and adulterous generation seeks a sign, and a sign will not be given to it, except the sign of Jonah the prophet. And leaving them, He went away.

5. And His disciples coming to the other side, they forgot to take loaves.
6 And Jesus said to them, Watch, and take heed from the leaven of the Pharisees and Sadducees.
7 And they reasoned among themselves, saying, Because we did not take loaves.
8 And knowing, Jesus said to them, Why do you reason among yourselves because you took no loaves, little-faiths?
9 Do you not

Matthew 16

2532 4334 3588 5330 2532 4523 3985
1. Καὶ προσελθόντες οἱ Φαρισαῖοι καὶ Σαδδουκαῖοι πειρά-
And having come the Pharisees and Sadducees tempting

1905 846 4592 1537 3588 3772 1925
ζοντες ἐπηρώτησαν αὐτὸν σημεῖον ἐκ τοῦ οὐρανοῦ ἐπιδεῖξαι
asked Him a sign out of the heaven to show

846 3588 1161 611 2036 846 3798 1096
αὐτοῖς. 2 ὁ δὲ ἀποκριθεὶς εἶπεν αὐτοῖς, Ὀψίας γενομένης
them. He But answering said to them, Evening coming on

3004 2105 4449 1063 3588 3772 2532 4404 4594
λέγετε, Εὐδία· πυρράζει γὰρ ὁ οὐρανός. 3 καὶ πρωΐ, Σήμερον
you say, Clear sky; is red for the heaven. And at morning, Today

5494 4449 1063 4768 3588 3772 5273
χειμών· πυρράζει γὰρ στυγνάζων ὁ οὐρανός. ὑποκριταί,
a storm; is red for being overcast the heaven Hypocrites!

3588 3303 4383 3588 3772 1097 1252 3588
τὸ μὲν πρόσωπον τοῦ οὐρανοῦ γινώσκετε διακρίνειν, τὰ
the Indeed face of the heaven you know to discern, the

1161 4592 3588 2540 3756 1410 1074 4190 2532
δὲ σημεῖα τῶν καιρῶν οὐ δύνασθε; 4 γενεὰ πονηρὰ καὶ
but signs of the times not you are able? A generation evil and

3428 4592 1934 2532 4592 3756 1325 846
μοιχαλὶς σημεῖον ἐπιζητεῖ· καὶ σημεῖον οὐ δοθήσεται αὐτῇ,
adulterous a sign seeks; and a sign not will be given to it,

1487 3361 3588 4592 2495 3588 4396 2532 2641
εἰ μὴ τὸ σημεῖον Ἰωνᾶ τοῦ προφήτου. καὶ καταλιπὼν
except the sign of Jonah the prophet. And leaving

846 565
αὐτοὺς, ἀπῆλθε.
them, He went away.

2532 2064 3588 3101 846 1519 3588 4008 1950
5. Καὶ ἐλθόντες οἱ μαθηταὶ αὐτοῦ εἰς τὸ πέραν ἐπελάθοντο
And coming the disciples of Him to the other side they forgot

740 2983 3588 1161 2424 2036 846 3708 2532 4337
ἄρτους λαβεῖν. 6 ὁ δὲ Ἰησοῦς εἶπεν αὐτοῖς, Ὁρᾶτε καὶ προσ-
loaves to take. And Jesus said to them, Beware and take

575 3588 2219 3588 5330 2532 4523 3588
έχετε ἀπὸ τῆς ζύμης τῶν Φαρισαίων καὶ Σαδδουκαίων. 7 οἱ
heed from the leaven of the Pharisees and Sadducees. they

1161 1260 1722 1438 3004 3754 740 3756
δὲ διελογίζοντο ἐν ἑαυτοῖς, λέγοντες ὅτι Ἄρτους οὐκ
But reasoned among themselves, saying, Loaves not

2983 1097 1161 3588 2424 2036 846 5101 1260
ἐλάβομεν. 8 γνοὺς δὲ ὁ Ἰησοῦς εἶπεν αὐτοῖς, Τί διαλογίζεσθε
we took. knowing And Jesus said to them, Why do you reason

1722 1438 3640 3754 740 3756 2983 3768
ἐν ἑαυτοῖς, ὀλιγόπιστοι, ὅτι ἄρτους οὐκ ἐλάβετε; 9 οὔπω
among yourselves, little-faiths, because loaves not you took? Not

Matthew 16

1. The Pharisees also with the Sadducees came, and tempting desired him that he would shew them a sign from heaven.

2 He answered and said unto them, When it is evening, ye say, (It will be) fair weather: for the sky is red.
3 And in the morning, (It will be) foul weather to day: for the sky is red and lowring. O (ye) hypocrites, ye can discern the face of the sky; but can ye not (discern) the signs of the times?

4 A wicked and adulterous generation seeketh after a sign; and there shall no sign be given unto it, but the sign of the prophet Jonas. And he left them, and departed.

5. And when his disciples were come to the other side, they had forgotten to take bread.
6 Then Jesus said unto them, Take heed and beware of the leaven of the Pharisees and of the Sadducees.
7 And they reasoned among themselves, saying, (It is) because we have taken no bread.
8 (Which) when Jesus perceived, he said unto them, O ye of little faith, why reason ye among yourselves, because ye have brought no bread?
9 Do ye not

Literal Translation

perceive nor recall the five loaves of the five thousand, and how many handbaskets you took up?
10 Nor the seven loaves of the four thousand, and how many lunch baskets you took up?

11 How do you not perceive that (it was) not about loaves that I said to you to take heed from the leaven of the Pharisees and Sadducees?
12 Then they knew that He did not say to beware of the leaven of bread, but from the teaching of the Pharisees and Sadducees.

13. And coming into the parts of Caesarea of Philip, Jesus questioned His disciples, saying, Whom do men say Me the Son of Man to be?

14 And they said, Some (say) John the Baptist, and others Elijah, and others Jeremiah, or one of the prophets.

15 He says to them, But you, who do you say Me to be?
16 And answering, Simon Peter said, You are the Christ, the Son of the living God.
17 And answering, Jesus said to him, Blessed are you, Simon, son of Jonah, for flesh and blood did not reveal (it) to you, but My Father in Heaven.

18 And I also say to you that you are Peter, and on this rock I will build My church, and (the) gates of Hades will not prevail against her.

19 And I will give to you the keys of the kingdom of Heaven. And whatever you bind on earth shall occur, having been bound in Heaven. And whatever you may loose on the earth

Matthew 16:10

3539 3761 3421 3588 4002 740 3588 4000
νοεῖτε, οὐδὲ μνημονεύετε τοὺς πέντε ἄρτους τῶν πεντακι-
you perceive nor remember the five loaves of the five

2532 4214 2894 2983 3761 3588 2033
σχιλίων, καὶ πόσους κοφίνους ἐλάβετε; 10 οὐδὲ τοὺς ἑπτὰ
thousand, and how many handbaskets you took? Neither the seven

740 3588 5070 2532 4214 4711 2983
ἄρτους τῶν τετρακισχιλίων, καὶ πόσας σπυρίδας ἐλάβετε;
loaves of the four thousand, and how many lunch-baskets you took up?

4459 3756 3539 3754 3756 4012 740 2036 5213 4337 575
11 πῶς οὐ νοεῖτε, ὅτι οὐ περὶ ἄρτου εἶπον ὑμῖν προσέχειν ἀπὸ
How not perceive that not about loaves I said to you to take heed from

3588 2219 3588 5330 2532 4523 5119 4920
τῆς ζύμης τῶν Φαρισαίων καὶ Σαδδουκαίων; 12 τότε συνῆκαν
the leaven of the Pharisees and Sadducees? Then they knew

3754 3756 2036 4337 575 3588 2219 3588 740 235 575
ὅτι οὐκ εἶπε προσέχειν ἀπὸ τῆς ζύμης τοῦ ἄρτου, ἀλλ' ἀπο
that not He said to take heed from the leaven of bread, but from

3588 1322 3588 5330 2532 4523
τῆς διδαχῆς τῶν Φαρισαίων καὶ Σαδδουκαίων.
the teaching of the Pharisees and Sadducees.

2064 1161 3588 2424 1519 3588 3313 2542 3588 376
13 Ἐλθὼν δὲ ὁ Ἰησοῦς εἰς τὰ μέρη Καισαρείας τῆς Φιλίππου
coming And Jesus into the parts of Caesarea of Philip

2065 3588 3101 846 3004 5101 3165 3004 3588
ἠρώτα τοὺς μαθητὰς αὐτοῦ, λέγων, Τίνα με λέγουσιν οἱ
He queried the disciples of Him, saying, Whom Me do say

444 1511 3588 5207 3588 444 3588 1161 2036 3588 3303
ἄνθρωποι εἶναι, τὸν υἱὸν τοῦ ἀνθρώπου; 14 οἱ δὲ εἶπον, Οἱ μὲν
men to be, the Son of man? they And said, Some truly

2491 3588 910 243 1161 2243 2087 1161
Ἰωάννην τὸν Βαπτιστήν· ἄλλοι δὲ Ἠλίαν· ἕτεροι δὲ
(say) John the Baptist; others and Elijah; others and

2408 2228 1520 3588 4396 3004 846 5210 1161 5101
Ἱερεμίαν, ἢ ἕνα τῶν προφητῶν. 15 λέγει αὐτοῖς, Ὑμεῖς δὲ τίνα
Jeremiah, or one of the prophets. He says to them, you But whom

3165 3004 1511 611 1161 4613 4074 2036 4771 1488
με λέγετε εἶναι; 16 ἀποκριθεὶς δὲ Σίμων Πέτρος εἶπε, Σὺ εἶ
Me do you say to be? answering And Simon Peter said, You are

3588 5547 3588 5207 3588 2316 3588 2198 2532 611 3588
ὁ Χριστὸς ὁ υἱὸς τοῦ Θεοῦ τοῦ ζῶντος. 17 καὶ ἀποκριθεὶς ὁ
the Christ, the Son of God the living. And answering

2424 2036 846 3107 1488 4613 920 920 3754 4561
Ἰησοῦς εἶπεν αὐτῷ, Μακάριος εἶ, Σίμων Βὰρ Ἰωνᾶ, ὅτι σὰρξ
Jesus said to him, Blessed are you, Simon Bar-jonah because flesh

2532 129 3756 601 4671 235 3588 3962 3450 3588 1722 3588
καὶ αἷμα οὐκ ἀπεκάλυψέ σοι, ἀλλ' ὁ πατήρ μου ὁ ἐν τοῖς
and blood not did reveal to you, but the Father of Me in

3772 2504 1161 4671 3004 3754 4771 1488 4074 2532 1909 3778
οὐρανοῖς. 18 κἀγὼ δέ σοι λέγω, ὅτι σὺ εἶ Πέτρος, καὶ ἐπὶ ταύτῃ
Heaven. I also And to you say, You are Peter, and on this

3588 4073 3618 3450 3588 1577 2532 4439 86
τῇ πέτρᾳ οἰκοδομήσω μου τὴν ἐκκλησίαν, καὶ πύλαι ᾅδου
rock I will build of Me the church, and (the) gates of Hades

3756 2729 846 2532 1325 4671 3588 2807 3588
οὐ κατισχύσουσιν αὐτῆς. 19 καὶ δώσω σοι τὰς κλεῖς τῆς
not will prevail against her. And I will give to you the keys of the

932 3588 3772 2532 3588 1437 1210 1909 3588 1093 2071
βασιλείας τῶν οὐρανῶν· καὶ ὃ ἐὰν δήσῃς ἐπὶ τῆς γῆς, ἔσται
kingdom of Heaven; and whatever you bind on the earth, shall be,

1210 1722 3588 3772 2532 3739 1437 3089 1909 3588 1093
δεδεμένον ἐν τοῖς οὐρανοῖς· καὶ ὃ ἐὰν λύσῃς ἐπὶ τῆς γῆς,
having been bound in Heaven; and whatever you loose on the earth,

Literal Translation

yet understand, neither remember the five loaves of the five thousand, and how many baskets ye took up?
10 Neither the seven loaves of the four thousand, and how many baskets ye took up?

11 How is it that ye do not understand that I spake (it) not to you concerning bread, that ye should beware of the leaven of the Pharisees and of the Sadducees?
12 Then understood they how that he bade (them) not beware of the leaven of bread, but of the doctrine of the Pharisees and of the Sadducees.
13. When Jesus came into the coasts of Caesarea Philippi, he asked his disciples, saying, Whom do men say that I the Son of man am?

14 And they said, Some (say that thou art) John the Baptist: some, Elias; and others, Jeremias, or one of the prophets.

15 He saith unto them, But whom say ye that I am?
16 And Simon Peter answered and said, Thou art the Christ, the Son of the living God.
17 And Jesus answered and said unto him, Blessed art thou, Simon Barjona: for flesh and blood hath not revealed (it) unto thee, but my Father which is in heaven.

18 And I say also unto thee, That thou art Peter, and upon this rock I will build my church; and the gates of hell shall not prevail against it.

19 And I will give unto thee the keys of the kingdom of heaven: and whatsoever thou shalt bind on earth shall be bound in heaven: and whatsoever thou shalt loose on earth

Literal Translation

Matthew 16:20

King James Version

shall be, having been loosed in Heaven.
20 Then He warned His disciples that they should tell no one that He is Jesus the Christ.

2071 3089 1722 3588 3772 5119 1291
ἔσται λελυμένον ἐν τοῖς οὐρανοῖς. 20 τότε διεστείλατο
shall be, having been loosed in Heaven. Then He warned

3588 3101 846 2443 3367 2036 3754 846 2076
τοῖς μαθηταῖς αὐτοῦ ἵνα μηδενὶ εἴπωσιν ὅτι αὐτός ἐστιν
the disciples of Him that to no one they may tell that He is

2424 3588 5547
Ἰησοῦς ὁ Χριστός.
Jesus the Christ..

loosed in heaven.
20 Then charged he his disciples that they should tell no man that he was Jesus the Christ.

21. From that time, Jesus began to show to His disciples that it behoves Him to go away to Jerusalem, and to suffer many things from the elders and chief priests and scribes, and to be killed, and to be raised on the third day.

575 5119 756 3588 2424 1166 3588 3101
21. Ἀπὸ τότε ἤρξατο ὁ Ἰησοῦς δεικνύειν τοῖς μαθηταῖς
From then began Jesus to show to the disciples

846 3754 1163 846 565 1519 2414 2532 4183
αὐτοῦ ὅτι δεῖ αὐτὸν ἀπελθεῖν εἰς Ἱεροσόλυμα, καὶ πολλὰ
of Him that it behoves Him to go away to Jerusalem, and many things

3958 575 3588 4245 2532 749 2532 1122
παθεῖν ἀπὸ τῶν πρεσβυτέρων καὶ ἀρχιερέων καὶ γραμ-
to suffer from the elders and chief priests and scribes,

2532 615 2532 3588 5154 2250 1453
ματέων, καὶ ἀποκτανθῆναι, καὶ τῇ τρίτῃ ἡμέρᾳ ἐγερθῆναι.
and to be killed, and on the third day to be raised

21. From that time forth began Jesus to shew unto his disciples, how that he must go unto Jerusalem, and suffer many things of the elders and chief priests and scribes, and be killed, and be raised again the third day.

22 And having taken Him near, Peter began to rebuke Him, saying, (God be) merciful to You, Lord; this shall never be to You.
23 But turning He said to Peter, Go behind Me, Satan! You are an offense to Me, for you do not think the things of God, but the things of men.

24. Then Jesus said to His disciples, If anyone desires to come after Me, let him deny himself, and let him bear his cross, and let him follow Me.
25 For whoever may desire to save his life will lose it. But whoever may lose his life for My sake will find it.

26 For what will a man be benefited if he should gain the whole world, but forfeits his soul? Or what will a man give (as) an exchange (for) his soul?

27 For the Son of man is about to come with His angels in the glory of His Father. And then He will give reward to each according to his practice. (Ps. 62:12)
28 Truly I say

2532 4355 846 3588 4074 756 2008 846.
22 καὶ προσλαβόμενος αὐτὸν ὁ Πέτρος ἤρξατο ἐπιτιμᾶν αὐτῷ
And taking near Him Peter began to rebuke Him

3004 2436 4671 2962 3756 3361 2071 4671 5124 3588 1161
λέγων, Ἵλεώς σοι, Κύριε· οὐ μὴ ἔσται σοι τοῦτο. 23 ὁ δὲ
saying, Merciful to You, Lord, not at all shall be to You this. He But

4762 2036 3588 4074 5217 3694 3450 4567
στραφεὶς εἶπε τῷ Πέτρῳ, Ὕπαγε ὀπίσω μου, Σατανᾶ,
turning said to Peter, Go behind Me, Satan.

4625 3450 1488 3754 3756 5426 3588 3588 2316 235
σκάνδαλον μου εἶ· ὅτι οὐ φρονεῖς τὰ τοῦ Θεοῦ, ἀλλὰ
an offense to Me You are, because not you think the things of God, but

3588 3588 444 5119 3588 2424 2036 3588 3101 846
τὰ τῶν ἀνθρώπων. 24 τότε ὁ Ἰησοῦς εἶπε τοῖς μαθηταῖς αὐτοῦ,
the things of men. Then Jesus said to the disciples of Him,

1487 5100 2309 3694 3450 2064 533 1438 2532 142
Εἴ τις θέλει ὀπίσω μου ἐλθεῖν, ἀπαρνησάσθω ἑαυτὸν, καὶ ἀράτω
If anyone desires after Me to come, let him deny himself, and let him bear

3588 4716 846 2532 190 3427 3739 1063 302 2309
τὸν σταυρὸν αὐτοῦ, καὶ ἀκολουθείτω μοι. 25 ὃς γὰρ ἂν θέλῃ
the cross of him, and let him follow Me. whoever For should desire

3588 5590 846 4982 622 846 3739 1161 302 622 3588
τὴν ψυχὴν αὐτοῦ σῶσαι ἀπολέσει αὐτήν· ὃς δ' ἂν ἀπολέσῃ τὴν
the life of him to save, he will lose it; Whoever And should lose the

5590 846 1752 1700 2147 846 5101 1063 5623
ψυχὴν αὐτοῦ ἕνεκεν ἐμοῦ εὑρήσει αὐτήν. 26 τί γὰρ ὠφελεῖται
life of him for the sake of Me, he will find it. what For will be benefited

444 1437 3588 2889 3650 2770 3588 1161 5590 846
ἄνθρωπος ἐὰν τὸν κόσμον ὅλον κερδήσῃ, τὴν δὲ ψυχὴν αὐτοῦ
a man if the world whole he should gain, the but soul of him

2210 3588 5102 1325 444 465 3588 5590
ζημιωθῇ; ἢ τί δώσει ἄνθρωπος ἀντάλλαγμα τῆς ψυχῆς
forfeits? Or what will give a man (as) an exchange (for) the soul

846 3195 1063 3588 5207 3588 444 2064 1722 3588
αὐτοῦ; 27 μέλλει γὰρ ὁ υἱὸς τοῦ ἀνθρώπου ἔρχεσθαι ἐν τῇ
of him? is about For the Son of man to come in the

1391 3588 3962 846 3326 3588 32 846 2532
δόξῃ τοῦ πατρὸς αὐτοῦ μετὰ τῶν ἀγγέλων αὐτοῦ, καὶ
glory of the Father of Him with the angels of Him, and

5119 591 1538 2596 3588 4234 846 281 3004
τότε ἀποδώσει ἑκάστῳ κατὰ τὴν πρᾶξιν αὐτοῦ. 28 ἀμὴν λέγω
then He will reward to each according to the practice of him. Truly I say

22 Then Peter took him, and began to rebuke him, saying, Be it far from thee, Lord: this shall not be unto thee.
23 But he turned, and said unto Peter, Get thee behind me, Satan: thou art an offence unto me: for thou savourest not the things that be of God, but those that be of men.

24. Then said Jesus unto his disciples, If any (man) will come after me, let him deny himself, and take up his cross, and follow me.
25 For whosoever will save his life shall lose it: and whosoever will lose his life for my sake shall find it.

26 For what is a man profited, if he shall gain the whole world, and lose his own soul? or what shall a man give in exchange for his soul?

27 For the Son of man shall come in the glory of his Father with his angels; and then he shall reward every man according to his works.
28 Verily I say

Literal Translation

to you, There are some standing here who in no way will taste of death until they see the Son of man coming in His kingdom.

Matthew 17:1

5213 1526 5100 3588 5602 2476 3748 3756 3361 1089
ὑμῖν, εἰσί τινες τῶν ὧδε ἑστηκότων, οἵτινες οὐ μὴ γεύ-
to you, there are some here standing, who not at all will

2288 2193 302 1492 3588 5207 3588 444
σωνται θανάτου, ἕως ἂν ἴδωσι τὸν υἱὸν τοῦ ἀνθρώπου
taste of death, until they should see the Son of man

2064 1722 3588 932 846
ἐρχόμενον ἐν τῇ βασιλείᾳ αὐτοῦ.
coming in the kingdom of Him.

King James Version

unto you, There be some standing here, which shall not taste of death, till they see the Son of man coming in his kingdom.

Matthew 17

1. And after six days, Jesus took Peter and James, and his brother John, and brought them up into a high mountain privately.

2 And He was transfigured before them, and His face shone like the sun, and His clothing became white as the light.

3 And, behold! Moses and Elijah appeared to them, talking together with Him.

4 And answering, Peter said to Jesus, Lord, it is good for us to be here. If You desire, let us make three tents here, one for You, one for Moses, and one for Elijah.
5 While he was speaking, behold, a radiant cloud overshadowed them. And, behold, a voice out of the cloud saying, This is My Son, the Beloved, in whom I have delighted; hear Him. (Ps. 2:7)

6 And hearing, the disciples fell on their face and were greatly terrified.

7 And coming near, Jesus touched them and said, Rise up, and do not be terrified.
8 And lifting up their eyes, they did not see anyone except Jesus alone.

9. And they coming down from the mountain,

Matthew 17

2532 3326 2250 1803 3880 3588 2424 3588 4074
1. Καὶ μεθ' ἡμέρας ἓξ παραλαμβάνει ὁ Ἰησοῦς τὸν Πέτρον
And after days six takes alongside(Him) Jesus Peter

2532 2385 2532 2491 3588 80 846 2532 399
καὶ Ἰάκωβον καὶ Ἰωάννην τὸν ἀδελφὸν αὐτοῦ, καὶ ἀναφέρει
and James and John the brother of him, and (He) leads

846 1519 3735 5308 2596 2398 2532 3339
αὐτοὺς εἰς ὄρος ὑψηλὸν κατ' ἰδίαν. 2 καὶ μετεμορφώθη
them into mountain a high privately. And He was transfigured

1715 846 2532 2989 3588 4383 846 5613 3588
ἔμπροσθεν αὐτῶν, καὶ ἔλαμψε τὸ πρόσωπον αὐτοῦ ὡς ὁ
before them, and shone the face of Him as the

2246 3588 1161 2440 846 1096 3022 5613 3588 5457 2532 2400
ἥλιος, τὰ δὲ ἱμάτια αὐτοῦ ἐγένετο λευκὰ ὡς τὸ φῶς. 3 καὶ ἰδού,
sun, the and garments of Him became white as the light. And behold!

3700 846 3475 2532 2243 3326 846 4814
ὤφθησαν αὐτοῖς Μωσῆς καὶ Ἠλίας, μετ' αὐτοῦ συλλαλοῦν-
Appeared to them Moses and Elijah, with Him talking to-

611 1161 3588 4074 2036 3588 2424 2962 2570
τες. 4 ἀποκριθεὶς δὲ ὁ Πέτρος εἶπε τῷ Ἰησοῦ, Κύριε, καλόν
gether. answering And Peter said to Jesus, Lord, good

2076 2248 5602 1511 1487 2309 4160 5602 5140 4633
ἐστιν ἡμᾶς ὧδε εἶναι· εἰ θέλεις, ποιήσωμεν ὧδε τρεῖς σκηνάς,
it is us here to be. If You desire, let us make here three tents,

4671 3391 2532 3475 3391 2532 3391 2243 2089 846 2980
σοὶ μίαν, καὶ Μωσῇ μίαν, καὶ μίαν Ἠλίᾳ. 5 ἔτι αὐτοῦ λαλοῦν-
for you one, and for Moses one, and one for Elijah. While he (was) speaking,

2400 3507 5460 1982 846 2532 2400
τος, ἰδού, νεφέλη φωτεινὴ ἐπεσκίασεν αὐτούς· καὶ ἰδού,
Behold! A cloud radiant overshadowed them And, behold!

5456 1537 3588 3507 3004 3778 2076 3588 5207 3450
φωνὴ ἐκ τῆς νεφέλης, λέγουσα, Οὗτός ἐστιν ὁ υἱός μου
A voice out of the cloud, saying, This is the Son of Me

3588 27 1722 3739 2106 846 191 2532 191
ὁ ἀγαπητός, ἐν ᾧ εὐδόκησα· αὐτοῦ ἀκούετε. 6 καὶ ἀκούσαντες
the Beloved, in whom I have delighted; Him hear. And hearing

3588 3101 4098 1909 4383 846 2532 5399
οἱ μαθηταὶ ἔπεσαν ἐπὶ πρόσωπον αὐτῶν, καὶ ἐφοβήθησαν
the disciples fell on the face of them, and were terrified

4970 2532 4334 3588 2424 680 846 2532 2036
σφόδρα. 7 καὶ προσελθὼν ὁ Ἰησοῦς ἥψατο αὐτῶν καὶ εἶπεν,
greatly. And having come near Jesus touched them and said,

1453 2532 3361 5399 1869 1161 3588 3788
Ἐγέρθητε καὶ μὴ φοβεῖσθε. 8 ἐπάραντες δὲ τοὺς ὀφθαλμοὺς
Rise up and not do be terrified. lifting up And the eyes

846 3762 1492 1487 3361 3588 2424 3441
αὐτῶν, οὐδένα εἶδον, εἰ μὴ τὸν Ἰησοῦν μόνον.
of them, no one they saw, except Jesus alone.

2532 2597 846 575 3588 3735 1781
9. Καὶ καταβαινόντων αὐτῶν ἀπὸ τοῦ ὄρους, ἐνετείλατο
And coming down they from the mountain, enjoined

Matthew 17

1. And after six days Jesus taketh Peter, James, and John his brother, and bringeth them up into an high mountain apart,

2 And was transfigured before them: and his face did shine as the sun, and his raiment was white as the light.

3 And, behold, there appeared unto them Moses and Elias talking with him.

4 Then answered Peter, and said unto Jesus, Lord, it is good for us to be here: if thou wilt, let us make here three tabernacles; one for thee, and one for Moses, and one for Elias.
5 While he yet spake, behold, a bright cloud overshadowed them: and behold a voice out of the cloud, which said, This is my beloved Son, in whom I am well pleased; hear ye him.

6 And when the disciples heard (it), they fell on their face, and were sore afraid.

7 And Jesus came and touched them, and said, Arise, and be not afraid.

8 And when they had lifted up their eyes, they saw no man, save Jesus only.

9. And as they came down from the mountain,

Literal Translation

Matthew 17:10

King James Version

Jesus charged them, saying, Tell the vision to no one until the Son of man is raised from the dead.
10 And His disciples questioned Him, saying, Why then do the scribes say that Elijah must come first?

11 And answering, Jesus said to them, Elijah indeed comes first and shall restore all things.

12 But I say to you, Elijah has already come, and they did not recognize him, but did by him whatever they desired. So also the Son of man is about to suffer by them.

13 Then the disciples understood that He spoke to them about John the Baptist.

14. And they having come to the crowd, a man came near to Him, kneeling down to Him, and saying,
15 Lord, pity my son. For he is moonstruck and suffers miserably. For he often falls into the fire, and often into the water.
16 And I brought him to Your disciples, and they were not able to heal him.

17 And answering, Jesus said, O faithless and perverted generation! How long will I be with you? How long shall I bear with you? Bring him here to Me.
18 And Jesus rebuked him, and the demon came out from him; and the boy was healed from that hour.

19 Then having come up to Jesus privately, the disciples said, Why were we not

846 3588 2424 3004 3367 2036 3588 3705 2193/3739/3588
αὐτοῖς ὁ Ἰησοῦς, λέγων, Μηδενὶ εἴπητε τὸ ὅραμα, ἕως οὗ ὁ
them Jesus, saying, To no one tell the vision until the

5207 3588 444 1537 3498 450 2532 1905
υἱὸς τοῦ ἀνθρώπου ἐκ νεκρῶν ἀνασθῇ. 10 καὶ ἐπηρώτησαν
Son of man from the dead is raised. And questioned

846 3588 3101 846 3004 5101 3767 3588 1122
αὐτὸν οἱ μαθηται αὐτοῦ λέγοντες, Τί οὖν οἱ γραμματεῖς
Him the disciples of Him saying, Why then the scribes

3004 3754 2243 1163 2064 4412 3588 1161 2424 611
λέγουσιν ὅτι Ἠλίαν δεῖ ἐλθεῖν πρῶτον; 11 ὁ δὲ Ἰησοῦς ἀποκρι
say that Elijah must come first? And Jesus answering

2036 846 2243 3303 2064 4412 2532 600
θεὶς εἶπεν αὐτοῖς, Ἠλίας μὲν ἔρχεται πρῶτον, καὶ ἀποκατα
said to them, Elijah indeed comes first, and shall restore

3956 3004 1161 5213 3754 2243 2235 2064 2532 3756
στήσει πάντα· 12 λέγω δὲ ὑμῖν ὅτι Ἠλίας ἤδη ἦλθε, καὶ οὐκ
all things; I say but to you that Elijah already came, and not

1921 846 235 4160 1722 846 3745 2309
ἐπέγνωσαν αὐτόν, ἀλλ᾽ ἐποίησαν ἐν αὐτῷ ὅσα ἠθέλησαν·
they recognized him, but did by him whatever they desired;

3779 2532 3588 5207 3588 444 3195 3958 5259 846
οὕτω καὶ ὁ υἱὸς τοῦ ἀνθρώπου μέλλει πάσχειν ὑπ᾽ αὐτῶν.
so also the Son of man is about to suffer by them.

5119 4920 3588 3101 3754 4012 2491 3588 910
13 τότε συνῆκαν οἱ μαθηταὶ ὅτι περὶ Ἰωάννου τοῦ βαπτιστοῦ
Then understood the disciples that about John the Baptist

2036 846
εἶπεν αὐτοῖς.
He spoke to them.

2532 2064 846 4314 3588 3793 4334 846
14. Καὶ ἐλθόντων αὐτῶν πρὸς τὸν ὄχλον, προσῆλθεν αὐτῷ
And having come they toward the crowd, came near to Him

444 1120 846 2532 3004 2962 1653 3450
ἄνθρωπος γονυπετῶν αὐτῷ 15 καὶ λέγων, Κύριε, ἐλέησόν μου
a man kneeling down to Him and saying, Lord, pity of me

3588 5207 3754 4583 2532 2560 3958 4178 1063
τὸν υἱόν, ὅτι σεληνιάζεται καὶ κακῶς πάσχει· πολλάκις γὰρ
the son, because he is moonstruck and miserably suffers. often for

4098 1519 3588 4442 2532 4178 1519 3588 5204 2532 4374
πίπτει εἰς τὸ πῦρ, καὶ πολλάκις εἰς τὸ ὕδωρ. 16 καὶ προσήνεγκα
he falls into the fire, and often into the water. And I brought

846 3588 3101 4675 2532 3756 1410 846
αὐτὸν τοῖς μαθηταῖς σου, καὶ οὐκ ἠδυνήθησαν αὐτὸν
him to the disciples of You, and not they were able him

2323 611 1161 3588 2424 2036 5599 1074 571
θεραπεῦσαι. 17 ἀποκριθεὶς δὲ ὁ Ἰησοῦς εἶπεν, Ὦ γενεὰ ἄπιστος
to heal. answering And Jesus said, O generation faithless

2532 1294 2193 4219 2071 3326 5216 2193 4219
καὶ διεστραμμένη, ἕως πότε ἔσομαι μεθ᾽ ὑμῶν; ἕως πότε
and perverted, until when shall I be with you? Until when

430 5216 5342 3427 846 5602 2532 2008 846
ἀνέξομαι ὑμῶν; φέρετέ μοι αὐτὸν ὧδε. 18 καὶ ἐπετίμησεν αὐτῷ
shall I endure you? Bring to Me him here. And rebuked it

3588 2424 2532 1831 575 846 3588 1140 2532 2323
ὁ Ἰησοῦς, καὶ ἐξῆλθεν ἀπ᾽ αὐτοῦ τὸ δαιμόνιον, καὶ ἐθεραπεύ-
Jesus, and came out from him the demon, and was healed

3588 3816 575 3588 5610 1565 5119 4334 3588
θη ὁ παῖς ἀπὸ τῆς ὥρας ἐκείνης. 19 τότε προσελθόντες οἱ
the boy from hour that. Then having come up the

3101 3588 2424 2596 2398 2036 1302 2249 3756 1410
μαθηταὶ τῷ Ἰησοῦ κατ᾽ ἰδίαν εἶπον, Διατί ἡμεῖς οὐκ ἠδυνή-
disciples to Jesus privately said, Why us not were

Jesus charged them, saying, Tell the vision to no man, until the Son of man be risen again from the dead.
10 And his disciples asked him, saying, Why then say the scribes that Elias must first come?

11 And Jesus answered and said unto them, Elias truly shall first come, and restore all things.

12 But I say unto you, That Elias is come already, and they knew him not, but have done unto him whatsoever they listed. Likewise shall also the Son of man suffer of them.

13 Then the disciples understood that he spake unto them of John the Baptist.

14. And when they were come to the multitude, there came to him a (certain) man, kneeling down to him, and saying,
15 Lord, have mercy on my son: for he is lunatick, and sore vexed: for ofttimes he falleth into the fire, and oft into the water.
16 And I brought him to thy disciples, and they could not cure him.

17 Then Jesus answered and said, O faithless and perverse generation, how long shall I be with you? how long shall I suffer you? bring him hither to me.
18 And Jesus rebuked the devil; and he departed out of him: and the child was cured from that very hour.

19 Then came the disciples to Jesus apart, and said, Why could not we

Matthew 17:20

Literal Translation

able to cast him out?
20 And Jesus said to them, Because of your unbelief. For truly I say to you, If you have faith as a grain of mustard, you will say to this mountain, Move from here to there! And it will move. And nothing shall be impossible to you.
21 But this kind does not go out except by prayer and fasting.

22. And (while) they were living in Galilee, Jesus said to them, The Son of man is about to be delivered into (the) hands of men.

23 And they will kill Him, and on the third day He will be raised. And they grieved exceedingly.

24. And they having come into Capernaum, those receiving the didrachmas came to Peter and said, Does your teacher not pay the didrachmas?
25 He said, Yes. And when he entered into the house, Jesus anticipated him, saying, What do you think, Simon? From whom do the kings of the earth receive custom or head-tax? From their sons or from strangers?

26 Peter said to Him, From strangers. Jesus said to him, Then truly the sons are free.
27 But that we may not offend them, going to the sea, throw in a hook and take the first fish coming up. And having opened its mouth, you will find a stater; having taken that, give to them for you and Me.

1544 846 3588 1161 2424 2036 846 1223 3588
θημεν ἐκβαλεῖν αὐτό; 20 ὁ δὲ Ἰησοῦς εἶπεν αὐτοῖς, Διὰ τὴν
able to cast out him? And Jesus said to them, Because of the

570 5216 281 1063 3004 5213 1437 2192 4102 5613
ἀπιστίαν ὑμῶν. ἀμὴν γὰρ λέγω ὑμῖν, ἐὰν ἔχητε πίστιν ὡς
unbelief of you. truly For I say to you, If you have faith as

2848 4615 2046 3588 3735 5129 3327 1782
κόκκον σινάπεως, ἐρεῖτε τῷ ὄρει τούτῳ, Μετάβηθι ἐντεῦθεν
a grain of mustard, you will say to mountain this, Move from here

1563 2532 3327 2532 3762 101 5213 5124 1161
ἐκεῖ, καὶ μεταβήσεται· καὶ οὐδὲν ἀδυνατήσει ὑμῖν. 21 τοῦτο δὲ
to there, and it will move, and nothing shall be impossible to you. this But

3588 1085 3756 1607 1487 3361 1722 4335 2532 3521
τὸ γένος οὐκ ἐκπορεύεται εἰ μὴ ἐν προσευχῇ καὶ νηστείᾳ.
kind not does go out except in prayer and fasting.

390 1161 846 1722 3588 1056 2036 846
22. Ἀναστρεφομένων δὲ αὐτῶν ἐν τῇ Γαλιλαίᾳ, εἶπεν αὐτοῖς
(while) were living And they in Galilee, said to them

3588 2424 3195 3588 5207 3588 444 3860 1519
ὁ Ἰησοῦς, Μέλλει ὁ υἱὸς τοῦ ἀνθρώπου παραδίδοσθαι εἰς
Jesus, is about the Son of man to be delivered up into

5495 444 2532 615 846 2532 3588 5154
χεῖρας ἀνθρώπων, 23 καὶ ἀποκτενοῦσιν αὐτόν, καὶ τῇ τρίτῃ
(the) hands of men, and they will kill Him, and on the third

2250 1453 2532 3076 4970
ἡμέρᾳ ἐγερθήσεται. καὶ ἐλυπήθησαν σφόδρα.
day He will be raised. And they grieved exceedingly.

2064 1161 846 1519 2584 4334 3588 3588
24. Ἐλθόντων δὲ αὐτῶν εἰς Καπερναοὺμ, προσῆλθον οἱ τὰ
having come And they into Capernaum, came up those the

1323 2983 3588 4074 2532 2036 3588 1320
δίδραχμα λαμβάνοντες τῷ Πέτρῳ καὶ εἶπον, Ὁ διδάσκαλος
didrachmas receiving to Peter and said, The teacher

5216 3756 5055 3588 1323 3004 3483 2532 3753 1525 1519
ὑμῶν οὐ τελεῖ τὰ δίδραχμα; 25 λέγει, Ναί. και ὅτε εἰσῆλθεν εἰς
of you not pays the didrachma? He says, Yes. And when he entered into

3588 3614 4399 846 3588 2424 3004 5101 4671
τὴν οἰκίαν, προέφθασεν αὐτὸν ὁ Ἰησοῦς, λέγων, Τί σοι
the house, anticipated him Jesus, saying, What do you

1380 4613 3588 935 3588 1093 575 5101 2983
δοκεῖ, Σίμων; οἱ βασιλεῖς τῆς γῆς ἀπὸ τίνων λαμβάνουσι
think, Simon? The kings of the earth from whom do they receive

5056 2228 2778 575 3588 5207 846 2228 575 3588
τέλη ἢ κῆνσον; ἀπὸ τῶν υἱῶν αὐτῶν, ἢ ἀπὸ τῶν
custom or head-tax? From the sons of them, or from the

245 3004 846 3588 4074 575 3588 245
ἀλλοτρίων; 26 λέγει αὐτῷ ὁ Πέτρος, Ἀπὸ τῶν ἀλλοτρίων.
strangers? says to him Peter, From the strangers.

5346 846 3588 2424 686 1658 1526 3588 5207 2443 1161
ἔφη αὐτῷ ὁ Ἰησοῦς, Ἄραγε ἐλεύθεροί εἰσιν οἱ υἱοί. 27 ἵνα δὲ
said to him Jesus, Then indeed free are the sons. that But

3361 4624 846 4198 1519 3588 2281 906
μὴ σκανδαλίσωμεν αὐτούς, πορευθεὶς εἰς τὴν θάλασσαν βάλε
not we may offend them, having gone to the sea throw

44 2532 3588 305 4412 2486 142 2532
ἄγκιστρον, καὶ τὸν ἀναβάντα πρῶτον ἰχθὺν ἆρον· καὶ
a hook, and the coming up first fish take; and

455 3588 4750 846 2147 4715 1565 2983
ἀνοίξας τὸ στόμα αὐτοῦ, εὑρήσεις στατῆρα· ἐκεῖνον λαβὼν
having opened the mouth of it, you will find a stater; that having taken

1325 846 473 1700 2532 4675
δὸς αὐτοῖς ἀντὶ ἐμοῦ καὶ σοῦ.
give to them for Me and for you.

King James Version

cast him out?
20 And Jesus said unto them, Because of your unbelief: for verily I say unto you, If ye have faith as a grain of mustard seed, ye shall say unto this mountain, Remove hence to yonder place; and it shall remove; and nothing shall be impossible unto you.
21 Howbeit this kind goeth not out but by prayer and fasting.

22. And while they abode in Galilee, Jesus said unto them, The Son of man shall be betrayed into the hands of men:

23 And they shall kill him, and the third day he shall be raised again. And they were exceeding sorry.

24. And when they were come to Capernaum, they that received tribute (money) came to Peter, and said, Doth not your master pay tribute?
25 He saith, Yes. And when he was come into the house, Jesus prevented him, saying, What thinkest thou, Simon? of whom do the kings of the earth take custom or tribute? of their own children, or of strangers?

26 Peter saith unto him, Of strangers. Jesus saith unto him, Then are the children free.
27 Notwithstanding, lest we should offend them, go thou to the sea, and cast an hook, and take up the fish that first cometh up; and when thou hast opened his mouth, thou shalt find a piece of money: that take, and give unto them for me and thee.

Literal Translation

Matthew 18

1. In that hour the disciples came to Jesus, saying, Who then is greater in the kingdom of Heaven?

2 And having called forward a little child, Jesus set him in their midst.
3 And (He) said, Truly I say to you, If not you convert and become as the little children, not at all can you enter into the kingdom of Heaven.
4 Then whoever will humble himself as this little child, this one is the greater in the kingdom of Heaven.

5 And whoever will receive one such little child in My name receives Me.
6 But whoever causes one of these little (ones) believing in Me to offend, it is gain for him that a millstone (turned by) an ass be hung on his neck, and he be sunk in the depth of the sea.

7. Woe to the world from (its) offenses! It is (a) necessity for the offenses to come, yet woe to that man through whom the offense comes!

8 And if your hand or your foot offends you, cut it off and throw (it) from you; it is good for you to enter into life lame or maimed, than having two hands or two feet to be thrown into the everlasting fire.

9 And if your eye offends you, pluck it out and throw (it) from you; for it is good for you to enter into life one eyed, than having two eyes to be thrown into the hell of fire.

10. See (that)

Matthew 18:1

1722 1565 3588 5610 4334 3588 3101 3588 2424
1. Ἐν ἐκείνῃ τῇ ὥρᾳ προσῆλθον οἱ μαθηταὶ τῷ Ἰησοῦ,
In that hour came up the disciples to Jesus,

3004 5101 687 3187 2076 1722 3588 932 3588 3772
λέγοντες, Τίς ἄρα μείζων ἐστὶν ἐν τῇ βασιλείᾳ τῶν οὐρα-
saying, Who then greater is in the kingdom of the heavens?

2532 4341 3588 2424 3813 2476
νῶν 2 καὶ προσκαλεσάμενος ὁ Ἰησοῦς παιδίον ἔστησεν
And having called forward Jesus a child He set

846 1722 3319 846 2532 2036 281 3004 5213 1437 3361
αὐτὸ ἐν μέσῳ αὐτῶν, 3 καὶ εἶπεν, Ἀμὴν λέγω ὑμῖν, ἐὰν μὴ
him in the midst of them. And (He) said, Truly, I say to you, if not

4762 2532 1096 5613 3588 3813 3756 3361 1525 1519 3588
στραφῆτε καὶ γένησθε ὡς τὰ παιδία, οὐ μὴ εἰσέλθητε εἰς τὴν
you convert and become as the children, in no way you may enter into the

932 3588 3772 3748 3767 5013 1438 5613 3588
βασιλείαν τῶν οὐρανῶν. 4 ὅστις οὖν ταπεινώσῃ ἑαυτὸν ὡς τὸ
kingdom of the heavens. Whoever then will humble himself as

3813 5124 3778 2076 3588 3187 1722 3588 932 3588
παιδίον τοῦτο, οὗτός ἐστιν ὁ μείζων ἐν τῇ βασιλείᾳ τῶν
child this, this (one) is the greater in the kingdom

3772 2532 3739 1437 1209 3813 5108 1520 1909 3588
οὐρανῶν. 5 καὶ ὃς ἐὰν δέξηται παιδίον τοιοῦτον ἓν ἐπὶ τῷ
Heaven. And whoever may receive child such one on the

3686 3450 1691 1209 3739 1161 302 4624 1520 3588
ὀνόματί μου, ἐμὲ δέχεται. 6 ὃς δ' ἂν σκανδαλίσῃ ἕνα τῶν
name of Me, Me receives. who But ever offends one

3398 5130 3588 4100 1519 1691 4851 846 2443
μικρῶν τούτων τῶν πιστευόντων εἰς ἐμέ, συμφέρει αὐτῷ ἵνα
little (ones) of these believing into Me, it is gain for him that

2910 3458 3684 1909 3588 5137 846 2532 2670
κρεμασθῇ μύλος ὀνικὸς ἐπὶ τὸν τράχηλον αὐτοῦ, καὶ κατα-
be hung a millstone of an ass on the neck of him, and he be

1722 3588 3989 3588 2281 3759 3588 2889
ποντισθῇ ἐν τῷ πελάγει τῆς θαλάσσης. 7 οὐαὶ τῷ κόσμῳ
sunk in the depth of the sea. Woe to the world

575 3588 4625 318 1063 2076 2064 3588 4625
ἀπὸ τῶν σκανδάλων· ἀνάγκη γάρ ἐστιν ἐλθεῖν τὰ σκάνδαλα·
from offenses; (a) necessity for it is to come the offenses;

4133 3759 3588 444 1565 1223 3739 3588 4625
πλὴν οὐαὶ τῷ ἀνθρώπῳ ἐκείνῳ, δι' οὗ τὸ σκάνδαλον
yet woe man (to) that through whom the offense

2064 1487 1161 3588 5495 4675 2228 3588 4228 4675 4624 4571
ἔρχεται. 8 εἰ δὲ ἡ χείρ σου ἢ ὁ πούς σου σκανδαλίζει σε,
comes! if And the hand of you or the foot of you offends you,

1581 846 2532 906 575 4675 2570 4671 2076 1525
ἔκκοψον αὐτὰ καὶ βάλε ἀπὸ σοῦ· καλόν σοι ἐστιν εἰσελθεῖν
cut off it and throw from you; good for you it is to enter

1519 3588 2222 5560 2228 2948 2228 1417 5495 2228 1417 4228
εἰς τὴν ζωὴν χωλὸν ἢ κυλλὸν, ἢ δύο χεῖρας ἢ δύο πόδας
into life lame or maimed than two hands or two feet

2192 906 1519 3588 4442 3588 166 2532 1487 3588 3788
ἔχοντα βληθῆναι εἰς τὸ πῦρ τὸ αἰώνιον. 9 καὶ εἰ ὁ ὀφθαλμός
having to be thrown into the fire everlasting. And if the eye

4675 4624 4571 1807 846 2532 906 575 4675 2570
σου σκανδαλίζει σε, ἔξελε αὐτὸν και βάλε ἀπὸ σοῦ· καλόν
of you offends you, pluck out it and throw from you; good

4671 2076 3442 1519 3588 2222 1525 2228 1417 3788
σοι ἐστι μονόφθαλμον εἰς τὴν ζωὴν εἰσελθεῖν, ἢ δύο ὀφθαλ-
for you it is one-eyed into life to enter, than two eyes

2192 906 1519 3588 1067 3588 4442 3708 3361
μοὺς ἔχοντα βληθῆναι εἰς τὴν γέενναν τοῦ πυρός. 10 ὁρᾶτε μὴ
having to be thrown into the Gehenna of fire. See (that) not

King James Version

Matthew 18

1. At the same time came the disciples unto Jesus, saying, Who is the greatest in the kingdom of heaven?

2 And Jesus called a little child unto him, and set him in the midst of them,
3 And said, Verily I say unto you, Except ye be converted, and become as little children, ye shall not enter into the kingdom of heaven.
4 Whosoever therefore shall humble himself as this little child, the same is greatest in the kingdom of heaven.

5 And whoso shall receive one such little child in my name receiveth me.
6 But whoso shall offend one of these little ones which believe in me, it were better for him that a millstone were hanged about his neck, and (that) he were drowned in the depth of the sea.

7. Woe unto the world because of offences! for it must needs be that offences come; but woe to that man by whom the offence cometh!

8 Wherefore if thy hand or thy foot offend thee, cut them off, and cast (them) from thee: it is better for thee to enter into life halt or maimed, rather than having two hands or two feet to be cast into everlasting fire.

9 And if thine eye offend thee, pluck it out, and cast (it) from thee: it is better for thee to enter into life with one eye, rather than having two eyes to be cast into hell fire.

10 .Take heed that

Literal Translation — **Matthew 18:11** — *King James Version*

you do not despise one of these little (ones), for I tell you that their angels in Heaven continually look on the face of My Father in Heaven.

11 For the Son of man has come to save the thing which has been lost.

12 What do you think? If there be to any man a hundred sheep, and one of them strays away, will he not leave the ninety nine on the mountains, (and) having gone he seeks the (one) having strayed?

13 And if he happens to find it, truly I say to you that he rejoices over it more than over the ninety nine not going astray.

14 So it is not (the) will before your Father in Heaven that one of these little (ones) should perish.

15. But if your brother may sin against you, go and reprove him between you and him alone. If he shall hear you, you have gained your brother.

16 But if he shall not hear, take one or two more with you, so that on (the) mouth of two or three witnesses every word may stand. (Deut. 19:15)

17 But if he fails to hear them, tell (it) to the church. And if he also fails to hear the church, let him be to you as the pagan and the tax collector.

18 Truly I say to you, Whatever you may bind on the earth shall occur, having been bound in Heaven. And whatever you may loose on the earth shall be, having been loosed in Heaven.

19 Again I say to you, If two of you agree

2706 1520 3588 3398 5130 3004 1063 5213
καταφρονήσητε ἑνὸς τῶν μικρῶν τούτων, λέγω γὰρ ὑμῖν
you despise one little (ones) of these, I say for to you

3754 3588 32 846 1722 3772 1223 3956 991 3588
ὅτι οἱ ἄγγελοι αὐτῶν ἐν οὐρανοῖς διὰ παντὸς βλέπουσι τὸ
that the angels of them in Heaven through all behold the

4383 3588 3962 3450 3588 1722 3772 2064 1063 3588
πρόσωπον τοῦ πατρός μου τοῦ ἐν οὐρανοῖς. 11 ἦλθε γὰρ ὁ
face of the Father of Me in Heaven. is come For the

5207 3588 444 4982 3588 622 5101 5213 1380 1437
υἱὸς τοῦ ἀνθρώπου σῶσαι τὸ ἀπολωλός. 12 τί ὑμῖν δοκεῖ; ἐὰν
Son of man to save the thing having been lost. What to you seems? If

1096 5100 444 1540 4263 2532 4105 1520 1537
γένηταί τινι ἀνθρώπῳ ἑκατὸν πρόβατα, καὶ πλανηθῇ ἓν ἐξ
there be to any man a hundred sheep, and strays one from

846 3780 863 3588 1768 1909 3588 3735 4198
αὐτῶν· οὐχὶ ἀφεὶς τὰ ἐνενήκονταἐννέα, ἐπὶ τὰ ὄρη πορευθεὶς
them; not will he leave the ninty-nine, on the mounts having gone

2212 3588 4105 2532 1437 1096 2147 846 281
ζητεῖ τὸ πλανώμενον; 13 καὶ ἐὰν γένηται εὑρεῖν αὐτό, ἀμὴν
he seeks the (one) having strayed? And if he happens to find it, truly

3004 5213 3754 5463 1909 846 3123 2228 1909 3588 1768
λέγω ὑμῖν ὅτι χαίρει ἐπ' αὐτῷ μᾶλλον, ἢ ἐπὶ τοῖς ἐννενη-
I say to you that he rejoices over it more, than over the ninety-

3588 3361 4105 3779 3756 2076 2307
κονταἐννέα τοῖς μὴ πεπλανημένοις. 14 οὕτως οὐκ ἔστι θέλημα
nine not having gone astray. So not is the will

1715 3588 3962 5216 3588 1722 3772 2443 622
ἔμπροσθεν τοῦ πατρὸς ὑμῶν τοῦ ἐν οὐρανοῖς, ἵνα ἀπόληται
before the Father of you in Heaven, that should perish

1520 3588 3398 5130
εἷς τῶν μικρῶν τούτων.
one little (ones) (of) these.

1437 1161 264 1519 4571 3588 80 4675 5217 2532
15. Ἐὰν δὲ ἁμαρτήσῃ εἰς σὲ ὁ ἀδελφός σου, ὕπαγε καὶ
if But might sin against you the brother of you, go and

1651 846 3342 4675 2532 846 3441 1437 4675
ἔλεγξον αὐτὸν μεταξὺ σοῦ καὶ αὐτοῦ μόνου. ἐάν σου
reprove him between you and him alone. If you

191 2770 3588 80 4675 1437 1161 3361 191
ἀκούσῃ, ἐκέρδησας τὸν ἀδελφόν σου· 16 ἐὰν δὲ μὴ ἀκούσῃ,
he shall hear, you have gained the brother of you; if but not he shall hear,

3880 3326 4675 2089 1520 2228 1417 2443 1909 4750 1417
παράλαβε μετὰ σοῦ ἔτι ἕνα ἢ δύο, ἵνα ἐπὶ στόματος δύο
take along with you besides one or two that upon (the) mouth of two

3144 2228 5140 2476 3956 4487 1437 1161 3878
μαρτύρων ἢ τριῶν σταθῇ πᾶν ῥῆμα. 17 ἐὰν δὲ παρακούσῃ
witnesses or three may stand every word. If But he fails to hear

846 2036 3588 1577 1437 1161 2532 3588 1577
αὐτῶν, εἰπὲ τῇ ἐκκλησίᾳ· ἐὰν δὲ καὶ τῆς ἐκκλησίας παρα-
them, tell (it to) the church; if and even the church he fails

3878 2077 4671 5618 3588 1482 2532 3588 5057 281 3004
κούσῃ, ἔστω σοι ὥσπερ ὁ ἐθνικὸς καὶ ὁ τελώνης. 18 ἀμὴν λέγω
to hear, let him be to you as the pagan and the tax-collector. Truly I say

5213 3745 1437 1210 1909 3588 1093 2071 1210 1722
ὑμῖν, ὅσα ἐὰν δήσητε ἐπὶ τῆς γῆς, ἔσται δεδεμένα ἐν
to you, whatever you may bind on the earth, will occur having been bound in

3588 3772 2532 3745 1437 3089 1909 3588 1093 2071 3089
τῷ οὐρανῷ καὶ ὅσα ἐὰν λύσητε ἐπὶ τῆς γῆς, ἔστα λελυμένα
Heaven; and whatever you may loose on the earth, will occur having been loosed

1722/3588 3722 2825 3004 5213 3754 1437 1417 5216 4856
ἐν τῷ οὐρανῷ. 19 πάλιν λέγω ὑμῖν, ὅτι ἐὰν δύο ὑμῶν συμφωνή-
in Heaven. Again I say to you, that if two of you may agree

ye despise not one of these little ones; for I say unto you, That in heaven their angels do always behold the face of my Father which is in heaven.

11 For the Son of man is come to save that which was lost.

12 How think ye? if a man have an hundred sheep, and one of them be gone astray, doth he not leave the ninety and nine, and goeth into the mountains, and seeketh that which is gone astray?

13 And if so be that he find it, verily I say unto you, he rejoiceth more of that (sheep), than of the ninety and nine which went not astray.

14 Even so it is not the will of your Father which is in heaven, that one of these little ones should perish.

15. Moreover if thy brother shall trespass against thee, go and tell him his fault between thee and him alone: if he shall hear thee, thou hast gained thy brother.

16 But if he will not hear (thee, then) take with thee one or two more, that in the mouth of two or three witnesses every word may be established.

17 And if he shall neglect to hear them, tell (it) unto the church: but if he neglect to hear the church, let him be unto thee as an heathen man and a publican.

18 Verily I say unto you, Whatsoever ye shall bind on earth shall be bound in heaven: and whatsoever ye shall loose on earth shall be loosed in heaven.

19 Again I say unto you, That if two of you shall agree

Literal Translation

on earth concerning every matter whatever they shall ask, it will occur to them from My Father in Heaven.

20 For where two or three are gathered together in My name, there I am in their midst.

21. Then having come up to Him, Peter said, Lord, how often shall my brother sin against me, and I forgive him? Until seven times?

22 Jesus says to him, I do not say to you, Until seven times, but, Until seventy times seven.

23. Because of this the kingdom of Heaven has been compared to a man, a king, who decided to take account with his slaves.

24 And having begun to reckon, one debtor of ten thousand talents was brought near to him.

25 But he not having (any) to pay, the lord commanded him to be sold, also his wife and children, and all things, as much as he had, even to pay back.

26 Then having fallen down, the slave bowed the knee to him, saying, Lord, have patience with me, and I will pay all to you.

27 And having pitied, the lord of that slave released him and forgave him the loan.

28 But having gone out, that slave found one of his fellow slaves who owed him a hundred denarii. And having seized him, he choked (him), saying, Pay me whatever you owe.

29 Then having fallen down at his feet, his fellow-slave begged him,

Matthew 18:20

1909 3588 1093 4012 3956 4229 3739 1437 154
σωσιν ἐπὶ τῆς γῆς περὶ παντὸς πράγματος οὗ ἐὰν αἰτή-
on the earth concerning every matter whatever they

1096 846 3844 3588 3962 3450 3588 1722
σωνται, γενήσεται αὐτοῖς παρὰ τοῦ πατρός μου τοῦ ἐν
may ask, it will occur to them from the Father of Me in

3772 3757 1063 1526 1417 2228 5140 4863 1519 3588 1699
οὐρανοῖς. 20 οὗ γάρ εἰσι δύο ἢ τρεῖς συνηγμένοι εἰς τὸ ἐμὸν
Heaven. where For are two or three gathered together in My

3686 1563 1510 1722 3319 846
ὄνομα, ἐκεῖ εἰμι ἐν μέσῳ αὐτῶν.
name, there I am in (the) midst of them.

5119 4334 846 3588 4074 2036 2962 4212
21. Τότε προσελθὼν αὐτῷ ὁ Πέτρος εἶπε, Κύριε, ποσάκις
Then having come up to Him Peter said, Lord, how often

264 1519 1691 3588 80 3450 2532 863 846 2193
ἁμαρτήσει εἰς ἐμὲ ὁ ἀδελφός μου, καὶ ἀφήσω αὐτῷ; ἕως
shall sin against me the brother of me, and I forgive him? Until

2034 3004 846 3588 2424 3956 3004 4671 2193 2034
ἑπτάκις; 22 λέγει αὐτῷ ὁ Ἰησοῦς, Οὐ λέγω σοι ἕως ἑπτάκις,
seven times? Says to him Jesus, Not I say to you until seven times,

235 2193 1441 2033 1223 5124 3666 3588
ἀλλ᾽ ἕως ἑβδομηκοντάκις ἑπτά. 23 διὰ τοῦτο ὡμοιώθη ἡ
but until seventy times seven. Because of this was likened the

932 3588 3772 444 935 3739 2309
βασιλεία τῶν οὐρανῶν ἀνθρώπῳ βασιλεῖ, ὃς ἠθέλησε
kingdom of the heavens to a man a king, who desired

4868 3056 3326 3588 1401 846 756 1161
συνᾶραι λόγον μετὰ τῶν δούλων αὐτοῦ. 24 ἀρξαμένου δὲ
to take account with the slaves of him. having begun And

846 4868 4374 846 1520 3781 3463
αὐτοῦ συναίρειν, προσηνέχθη αὐτῷ εἷς ὀφειλέτης μυρίων
him to reckon, was brought near to him one debtor of ten thousand

5007 3361 2192 1161 846 591 2753 846
ταλάντων. 25 μὴ ἔχοντος δὲ αὐτοῦ ἀποδοῦναι ἐκέλευσεν αὐτὸν
talents. not having And he to repay commanded him

3588 2962 846 4097 2532 3588 1135 846 2532 3588
ὁ κύριος αὐτοῦ πραθῆναι, καὶ τὴν γυναῖκα αὐτοῦ καὶ τὰ
the lord of him to be sold, also the wife of him and the

5043 2532 3956 3745 2192 2532 591 4098 3767
τέκνα, καὶ πάντα ὅσα εἶχε, καὶ ἀποδοθῆναι. 26 πεσὼν οὖν
children, and all as much as he had, and to pay back. having fallen Then

3588 1401 4352 846 3004 2962 3114 1909
ὁ δοῦλος προσεκύνει αὐτῷ, λέγων, Κύριε, μακροθύμησον ἐπ᾽
the slave bowed the knee to him, saying, Lord, have patience over

1698 2532 3956 4671 591 4697 1161 3588 2962
ἐμοί, καὶ πάντα σοι ἀποδώσω. 27 σπλαγχνισθεὶς δὲ ὁ κύριος
me, and all to you I will repay. having pitied And the lord

3588 1401 1565 630 846 2532 3588 1156 863
τοῦ δούλου ἐκείνου ἀπέλυσεν αὐτόν, καὶ τὸ δάνειον ἀφῆκεν
slave (of) that released him, and the loan forgave

846 1831 1161 3588 1401 1565 2147 1520 3588 4889
αὐτῷ. 28 ἐξελθὼν δὲ ὁ δοῦλος ἐκεῖνος εὗρεν ἕνα τῶν συνδούλων
him. having gone But slave that found one of the fellow-slaves

846 3739 3784 846 1540 1220 2532 2902
αὐτοῦ, ὃς ὤφειλεν αὐτῷ ἑκατὸν δηνάρια, καὶ κρατήσας
of him, who owed him a hundred denarii, and having seized

846 4155 3004 591 3427 3739 5100 3784 4098 3767
αὐτὸν ἔπνιγε, λέγων, Ἀπόδος μοι ὅ τι ὀφείλεις. 29 πεσὼν οὖν
him he choked, saying, Pay back to me whatever you owe. falling Then

3588 4889 846 1519 3588 4228 846 3870 846
ὁ σύνδουλος αὐτοῦ εἰς τοὺς πόδας αὐτοῦ παρεκάλει αὐτὸν,
the fellow-slave of him to the feet of him begged him,

King James Version

on earth as touching any thing that they shall ask, it shall be done for them of my Father which is in heaven.

20 For where two or three are gathered together in my name, there am I in the midst of them.

21. Then came Peter to him, and said, Lord, how oft shall my brother sin against me, and I forgive him? till seven times?

22 Jesus saith unto him, I say not unto thee, Until seven times: but, Until seventy times seven.

23. Therefore is the kingdom of heaven likened unto a certain king, which would take account of his servants.

24 And when he had begun to reckon, one was brought unto him, which owed him ten thousand talents.

25 But forasmuch as he had not to pay, his lord commanded him to be sold, and his wife, and children, and all that he had, and payment to be made.

26 The servant therefore fell down, and worshipped him, saying, Lord, have patience with me, and I will pay thee all.

27 Then the lord of that servant was moved with compassion, and loosed him, and forgave him the debt.

28 But the same servant went out, and found one of his fellowservants, which owed him an hundred pence: and he laid hands on him, and took (him) by the throat, saying, Pay me that thou owest.

29 And his fellowservant fell down at his feet, and besought him,

Literal Translation | **Matthew 18:30** | *King James Version*

saying, Have patience with me, and I will pay all to you.
30 But he would not, but having gone away he threw him into prison until he pay back the (amount) owing.
31 But his fellow slaves, having seen the things occurring, they were greatly grieved. And having come they reported to their lord all the things having occurred.
32 Then having called him near, his lord said to him, Evil slave! I forgave you all that debt, since you begged me.

3004 3114 1909 1698 2532 3956 591 4671
λέγων, Μακροθύμησον ἐπ' ἐμοί, καὶ πάντα ἀποδώσω σοι.
saying, Have patience over me, and all I will repay to you.

3588 1161 3756 2309 235 565 906 846 1519 5438
30 ὁ δὲ οὐκ ἤθελεν, ἀλλ' ἀπελθὼν ἔβαλεν αὐτὸν εἰς φυλακὴν,
he But not willed (it), but having gone away threw him into prison

2193 3757 591 3588 3784 1492 1161 3588 4889 846
ἕως οὗ ἀποδῷ τὸ ὀφειλόμενον. 31 ἰδόντες δὲ οἱ σύνδουλοι αὐτοῦ
until he pay back that owing. having seen And the fellow-slaves of him

3588 1096 3076 4970 2532 2064 1285
τὰ γενόμενα ἐλυπήθησαν σφόδρα· καὶ ἐλθόντες διεσάφησαν
the things occurring, they were grieved greatly; and having come reported

3588 2962 846 3956 3588 1096 5119 4341
τῷ κυρίῳ αυτῶν πάντα τὰ γενόμενα. 32 τότε προσκαλεσά-
to the lord of them all the things having occurred. Then having called near

846 3588 2962 846 3004 846 1401 4190
μενος αὐτὸν ὁ κύριος αὐτοῦ λέγει αὐτῷ, Δοῦλε πονηρέ,
him, the lord of him says to him, slave Evil,

3956 3588 3782 1565 863 4671 1893 3870 3165
πᾶσαν τὴν ὀφειλὴν ἐκείνην ἀφῆκά σοι, ἐπεὶ παρεκάλεσάς με·
all debt that I forgave you, since you begged me;

saying, Have patience with me, and I will pay thee all.
30 And he would not: but went and cast him into prison, till he should pay the debt.
31 So when his fellowservants saw what was done, they were very sorry, and came and told unto their lord all that was done.
32 Then his lord, after that he had called him, said unto him, O thou wicked servant, I forgave thee all that debt, because thou desiredst me:

33 Ought you not also to had mercy on your fellow slave, as I also had mercy on you?
34 And being angry, his lord delivered him up to the tormentors until he pay back all that had been owing to him.

3767 1163 2532 4571 1653 3588 4889 4675 5613 2532 1473 4571
33 οὐκ ἔδει καὶ σὲ ἐλεῆσαι τὸν σύνδουλόν σου, ὡς καὶ εγώ σε
not Ought even you to have mercy on the fellow-slave of you, as also I you

1653 2532 3710 3588 2962 846 3860 846
ἠλέησα; 34 καὶ ὀργισθεὶς ὁ κύριος αὐτοῦ παρέδωκεν αὐτὸν
had mercy? And being angry the lord of him delivered him

3588 930 2193 3757 591 3956 3588 3784 846
τοῖς βασανισταῖς ἕως οὗ ἀποδῷ πᾶν τὸ ὀφειλόμενον αὐτῷ.
to the tormentors until he should repay all that owing to him.

33 Shouldest not thou also have had compassion on thy fellowservant, even as I had pity on thee?
34 And his lord was wroth, and delivered him to the tormentors, till he should pay all that was due unto him.

35 So also My heavenly Father will do to you if not each of you from your hearts forgive his brother their trespasses.

3779 2532 3588 3962 3450 3588 2032 4160 5213 1437 3361
35 οὕτω καὶ ὁ πατήρ μου ὁ ἐπουράνιος ποιήσει ὑμῖν, ἐὰν μὴ
So also the Father of Me heavenly will do to you, if not

863 1538 3588 80 846 575 3588 2588 5216 3588
ἀφῆτε ἕκαστος τῷ ἀδελφῷ αὐτοῦ ἀπὸ τῶν καρδιῶν υμῶν τὰ
you forgive each one the brother of him from the hearts of you the

3900 846
παραπτώματα αὐτῶν.
trespasses of them.

35 So likewise shall my heavenly Father do also unto you, if ye from your hearts forgive not every one his brother their trespasses.

Matthew 19

1. And it happened when Jesus had finished these words, He moved from Galilee and came into the borders of Judea beyond the Jordan.
2 And great crowds followed Him, and He healed them there.

2532 1096 3753 5055 3588 2424 3588 3056 5128
1. Καὶ ἐγένετο ὅτε ἐτέλεσεν ὁ Ἰησοῦς τοὺς λόγους τούτους,
And it happened when ended Jesus words these,

3332 575 3588 1056 2532 2064 1519 3588 3725 3588
μετῆρεν ἀπὸ τῆς Γαλιλαίας, καὶ ἦλθεν εἰς τὰ ὅρια τῆς
He moved from Galilee, and came into the borders

2449 4008 3588 2446 2532 190 846
Ἰουδαίας πέραν τοῦ Ἰορδάνου. 2 καὶ ἠκολούθησαν αὐτῷ
of Judea across the Jordan. And followed Him

3793 4183 2532 2323 846 1563
ὄχλοι πολλοί, καὶ ἐθεράπευσεν αὐτοὺς ἐκεῖ.
crowds great, and He healed them there

1. And it came to pass, (that) when Jesus had finished these sayings, he departed from Galilee, and came into the coasts of Judaea beyond Jordan;
2 And great multitudes followed him; and he healed them there.

3. And the Pharisees came near to Him, tempting Him, and saying to Him, Is it lawful for a man to put away his wife for every reason?
4 But having answered He said

2532 4334 846 3588 5330 3985 846
3. Καὶ προσῆλθον αὐτῷ οἱ Φαρισαῖοι πειράζοντες αὐτὸν,
And came near him the Pharisees tempting Him,

2532 3004 846 1487 1832 444 630 3588
καὶ λέγοντες αὐτῷ, Εἰ ἔξεστιν ἀνθρώπῳ ἀπολῦσαι τὴν
and saying to Him, Whether it is lawful for a man to put away the

1135 846 2596 3956 156 3588 1161 611 2036
γυναῖκα αὐτοῦ κατὰ πᾶσαν αἰτίαν; 4 ὁ δὲ ἀποκριθεὶς εἶπεν
wife of him for every reason? He And having answered said

3. The Pharisees also came unto him, tempting him, and saying unto him, Is it lawful for a man to put away his wife for every cause?
4 And he answered and said

Literal Translation

to them, Did you not read that He having made (them) from the beginning created them male and female?
5 And He said, "On account of this a man shall leave father and mother, and shall be joined to his wife, and the two shall become one flesh." (Gen. 1:27; 2:24)

6 So that they are no longer two, but one flesh. Therefore, what God has yoked together, let not man separate.
7 They said to Him, Why then did Moses command to give a bill of divorce, and to put her away? (Deut. 24:1)
8 He says to them, In view of your hardheartedness, Moses allowed you to put away your wives. But from the beginning it was not so.

9 And I say to you, Whoever shall put away his wife, if not for fornication, and shall marry another, (that one) commits adultery. And the one who marries her (who was) put away commits adultery.
10. His disciples said to Him, If the case of the man be so with (his) wife, it is not gain to marry.
11 But He said to them, Not all make room for this word, but (those) to whom it is given.

12 For there are eunuchs who were generated thus from (the) womb of (their) mother, and there are eunuchs who were made eunuchs by men, and there are eunuchs who made eunuchs (of) themselves for the sake of the kingdom of Heaven. He who is able to receive, let him receive it.

13. Then little children were brought to Him, that He might lay

Matthew 19:5

846 3756 314 3754 3588 4160 575 746 730 2532
αὐτοῖς, Οὐκ ἀνέγνωτε ὅτι ὁ ποιήσας ἀπ' ἀρχῆς ἄρσεν καὶ
to them, not Did you read that He having made from beginning male and

2338 4160 846 2532 2036 1752 5127 2641
θῆλυ ἐποίησεν αὐτούς; 5 καὶ εἶπεν, Ἕνεκεν τούτου καταλείψει
female made them? And He said, For the sake of this shall leave

444 3588 3962 2532 3588 3384 2532 4347
ἄνθρωπος τὸν πατέρα καὶ τὴν μητέρα, καὶ προσκολληθή-
a man father and mother, and shall be joined to

3588 1135 846 2532 2071 3588 1417 1519 4561 3391
σεται τῇ γυναικὶ αὐτοῦ, καὶ ἔσονται οἱ δύο εἰς σάρκα μίαν.
the wife of him, and shall be the two into flesh one.

5620 3765 1526 1417 235 4561 3391 3739 3767 3588 2316
6 ὥστε οὐκέτι εἰσὶ δύο, ἀλλὰ σὰρξ μία· ὃ οὖν ὁ Θεὸς
so that no longer are they two, but flesh one; what then God

4801 444 3361 5563 3004 846 5101 3767
συνέζευξεν, ἄνθρωπος μὴ χωριζέτω. 7 λέγουσιν αὐτῷ, Τί οὖν
has yoked together man not do let separate. They say to Him, Why then

3475 1781 1325 975 647 2532
Μωσῆς ἐνετείλατο δοῦναι βιβλίον ἀποστασίου, καὶ
Moses did command to give a bill of divorce, and

630 846 3004 846 3754 3475 4314 3588
ἀπολῦσαι αὐτήν; 8 λέγει αὐτοῖς ὅτι Μωσῆς πρὸς τὴν
to put away her? He says to them that Moses in view of the

4641 5216 2010 5213 630 3588 1135
σκληροκαρδίαν ὑμῶν ἐπέτρεψεν ὑμῖν ἀπολῦσαι τὰς γυναῖκας
hardheartedness of you allowed you to put away the wives

5216 575 746 1161 3756 1096 3779 30041161 5213 3754 3739 302
ὑμῶν· ἀπ' ἀρχῆς δὲ οὐ γέγονεν οὕτω. 9 λέγω δὲ ὑμῖν ὅτι ὃς ἂν
of you; from beginning but not it was so. I sayAnd to you that whoever

630 3588 1135 846 1487 3361 1909 4202 2532 1060
ἀπολύσῃ τὴν γυναῖκα αὐτοῦ, εἰ μὴ ἐπὶ πορνείᾳ, καὶ γαμήσῃ
puts away the wife of him, if not over fornication, and shall marry

243 3429 2532 3588 630 1060 3429
ἄλλην, μοιχᾶται· 10 καὶ ὁ ἀπολελυμένην γαμήσας μοιχᾶται.
another commits adultery and he her having put away marrying commits adultery.

3004 846 3588 3101 846 1487 3779 2076 3588 156
λέγουσιν αὐτῷ οἱ μαθηταὶ αὐτοῦ, Εἰ οὕτως ἐστὶν ἡ αἰτία
Say to Him the disciples of Him, If thus is the cause

3588 444 3326 3588 1135 3756 4851 1060 35881161
τοῦ ἀνθρώπου μετὰ τῆς γυναικός, οὐ συμφέρει γαμῆσαι. 11 ὁ δὲ
of the man with the wife, not it is gain to marry. He But

2036 846 3756 3956 5562 3588 3056 5126 235
εἶπεν αὐτοῖς, Οὐ πάντες χωροῦσι τὸν λόγον τοῦτον, ἀλλ'
said to them, Not all make room for word this, only

3739 1325 1526 1063 2135 3748 1537 2836 3384
οἷς δέδοται. 12 εἰσὶ γὰρ εὐνοῦχοι οἵτινες ἐκ κοιλίας μητρὸς
to whom it is given. there are For eunuchs who from (the) womb of a mother

1080 3779 2532 1526 2135 3748 2134
ἐγεννήθησαν οὕτω· καὶ εἰσὶν εὐνοῦχοι, οἵτινες εὐνουχίσθησαν
were generated so; and there are eunuchs who were made eunuchs

5259 3588 444 2532 1526 2135 3748 2134
ὑπὸ τῶν ἀνθρώπων· καὶ εἰσὶν εὐνοῦχοι, οἵτινες εὐνούχισαν
by men; and there are eunuchs who made eunuchs

1438 1223 3588 932 3588 3772 3588 1410
ἑαυτοὺς διὰ τὴν βασιλείαν τῶν οὐρανῶν. ὁ δυνά-
(of) themselves because of the kingdom of the heavens. The (one) having

5562 5562
μενος χωρεῖν χωρείτω.
been enabled to receive, let him receive (it).

5119 4374 846 3813 2443 3588 5495 2007
13. Τότε προσηνέχθη αὐτῷ παιδία, ἵνα τὰς χεῖρας ἐπιθῇ
Then was brought to Him children, that the hands He may lay

King James Version

unto them, Have ye not read, that he which made (them) at the beginning made them male and female,
5 And said, For this cause shall a man leave father and mother, and shall cleave to his wife: and they twain shall be one flesh?

6 Wherefore they are no more twain, but one flesh. What therefore God hath joined together, let not man put asunder.
7 They say unto him, Why did Moses then command to give a writing of divorcement, and to put her away?
8 He saith unto them, Moses because of the hardness of your hearts suffered you to put away your wives: but from the beginning it was not so.
9 And I say unto you, Whosoever shall put away his wife, except (it be) for fornication, and shall marry another, committeth adultery: and whoso marrieth her which is put away doth commit adultery.
10. His disciples say unto him, If the case of the man be so with (his) wife, it is not good to marry.
11 But he said unto them, All (men) cannot receive this saying, save (they) to whom it is given.

12 For there are some eunuchs, which were so born from (their) mother's womb: and there are some eunuchs, which were made eunuchs of men: and there be eunuchs, which have made themselves eunuchs for the kingdom of heaven's sake. He that is able to receive (it), let him receive (it).

13. Then were there brought unto him little children, that he should put

Matthew 19:14

Literal Translation

hands on them and to pray. But the disciples rebuked them.

14 But Jesus said, Allow the little children and do not prevent them to come to Me, for of such is the kingdom of Heaven.

15 And having laid hands on them, He went away from there.

16. And, behold, one coming near said to Him, Good Teacher, what good thing shall I do that I may have eternal life?

17 And He said to him, Why do you call Me good? No one (is) good except One, God! But if you desire to enter into life, keep the commandments.

18 He said to Him, Which? And Jesus said, "You shall not commit murder, nor commit adultery, nor steal, nor bear false witness,

19 honor your father and your mother," and, "You shall love your neighbor as yourself." (Ex. 20:12-16; Deut. 5:16-20)

20 The young man said to Him, All these things I have kept from my youth. What do I still lack?

21 Jesus said to him, If you desire to be perfect, go sell your property and give to (the) poor, and you will have treasure in Heaven; and come, follow Me.

22 But having heard the word, being grieved, the young man went away, for he had many possessions.

23. And Jesus said to His disciples, Truly I say to you that a rich man will with difficulty enter into the kingdom of Heaven.

24 And again I say to you, It is easier for a camel to pass through a needle's eye, than for a rich man to enter the kingdom

846 2532 4336 3588 1161 3101 2008 846
αὐτοῖς, καὶ προσεύξηται· οἱ δὲ μαθηταὶ ἐπετίμησαν αὐτοῖς.
on them, and to pray; the But disciples rebuked them.

3588 1161 2424 2036 863 3588 3813 2532 3361 2967 846
14 ὁ δὲ Ἰησοῦς εἶπεν, Ἄφετε τὰ παιδία, καὶ μὴ κωλύετε αὐτὰ
But Jesus said, Permit the children, and not do prevent them

2064 4314 3165 3588 1063 5108 2076 3588 932 3588
ἐλθεῖν πρός με· τῶν γὰρ τοιούτων ἐστὶν ἡ βασιλεία τῶν
to come to Me; for of such is the kingdom

3772 2532 2007 846 3588 5495 4198 1564
οὐρανῶν. 15 καὶ ἐπιθεὶς αὐτοῖς τὰς χεῖρας, ἐπορεύθη ἐκεῖθεν.
of Heaven. And having laid on them the hands, He went away from there.

2532 2400 1520 4334 2036 846 1320 18
16. Καὶ ἰδού, εἷς προσελθὼν εἶπεν αὐτῷ, Διδάσκαλε ἀγαθέ,
And behold! One coming near said to Him, teacher Good,

5101 18 4160 2443 2192 2222 166 3588 1161 2036 846
τί ἀγαθὸν ποιήσω, ἵνα ἔχω ζωὴν αἰώνιον; 17 ὁ δὲ εἶπεν αὐτῷ,
what good shall I do, that I may have life everlasting? He And said to him,

5101 3165 3004 18 3762 18 1487/3361/1520/3588/2316 1487/1161
Τί με λέγεις ἀγαθόν; οὐδεὶς ἀγαθός, εἰ μὴ εἷς, ὁ Θεός, εἰ δὲ
Why Me you call good? No one (is) good, except One, God, if but

2309 1525 1519 3588 2222 5083 3588 1785 3004
θέλεις εἰσελθεῖν εἰς τὴν ζωήν, τήρησον τὰς ἐντολάς. 18 λέγει
you desire to enter into life, keep the commandments. He says

846 4169 3588 1161 2424 2036 3588 3756 5407 3756 3431
αὐτῷ, Ποίας; ὁ δὲ Ἰησοῦς εἶπε, Τὸ οὐ φονεύσεις· οὐ μοιχεύ-
to Him, Which? And Jesus said, not You shall murder; not commit

3756 2813 3756 5576 5091 3588 3962
σεις· οὐ κλέψεις· οὐ ψευδομαρτυρήσεις, 19 Τίμα τὸν πατέρα
adultery; not steal; not bear false witness, honor the father

4675 2532 3588 3384 2532 25 3588 4139 4675 5613
σου καὶ τὴν μητέρα· καί, ἀγαπήσεις τὸν πλησίον σου ὡς
of you and the mother; and you shall love the neighbor of you as

4572 3004 846 3588 3495 3956 5023 5442
σεαυτόν. 20 λέγει αὐτῷ ὁ νεανίσκος, Πάντα ταῦτα ἐφυλαξάμην
yourself. Says to him the young man, All these things I have kept

1537 3503 3450 5101 2089 5302 5346 846 3588 2424 1487 2309
ἐκ νεότητός μου· τί ἔτι ὑστερῶ; 21 ἔφη αὐτῷ ὁ Ἰησοῦς, Εἰ θέλεις
from youth. of me; What yet do I lack? said to him Jesus, If you desire

5046 1511 5217 4453 4675 3588 5224 2532 1325
τέλειος εἶναι, ὕπαγε, πώλησόν σου τὰ ὑπάρχοντα καὶ δὸς
perfect to be, go, sell of you the property and give

4434 2532 2192 2344 1722 3772 2532 1204 190
πτωχοῖς, καὶ ἕξεις θησαυρὸν ἐν οὐρανῷ· καὶ δεῦρο, ἀκολούθει
to (the) poor, and you will have treasure in Heaven; and come, follow

3427 191 1161 3588 3495 3588 3056 565 3076
μοι. 22 ἀκούσας δὲ ὁ νεανίσκος τὸν λόγον ἀπῆλθε λυπούμενος·
Me. having heard But the young man the word went away being grieved;

2258 1063 2192 2933 4183
ἦν γὰρ ἔχων κτήματα πολλά.
he was For having possessions many.

3588 1161 2424 2036 3588 3101 846 281 3004 5213
23. Ὁ δὲ Ἰησοῦς εἶπε τοῖς μαθηταῖς αὐτοῦ, Ἀμὴν λέγω ὑμῖν
And Jesus said to the disciples of Him, Truly I say to you

3754 1423 4145 1525 1519 3588 932 3588
ὅτι δυσκόλως πλούσιος εἰσελεύσεται εἰς τὴν βασιλείαν τῶν
that with difficulty a rich man will enter into the kingdom

3772 3825 1161 3004 5213 2123 2076 2574
οὐρανῶν. 24 πάλιν δὲ λέγω ὑμῖν, εὐκοπώτερόν ἐστιν κάμηλον
of Heaven. again And I say to you, easier it is a camel

1223 5169 4476 1330 2228 4145 1519 3588 932
διὰ τρυπήματος ῥαφίδος διελθεῖν, ἢ πλούσιον εἰς τὴν βασι-
through (the) eye of a needle to pass than a rich man into the king-

King James Version

(his) hands on them, and pray: and the disciples rebuked them.

14 But Jesus said, Suffer little children, and forbid them not, to come unto me: for of such is the kingdom of heaven.

15 And he laid (his) hands on them, and departed thence.

16. And, behold, one came and said unto him, Good Master, what good thing shall I do, that I may have eternal life?

17 And he said unto him, Why callest thou me good? (there is) none good but one, (that is), God: but if thou wilt enter into life, keep the commandments.

18 He saith unto him, Which? Jesus said, Thou shalt do no murder, Thou shalt not commit adultery, Thou shalt not steal, Thou shalt not bear false witness,

19 Honour thy father and (thy) mother: and, Thou shalt love thy neighbour as thyself.

20 The young man saith unto him, All these things have I kept from my youth up: what lack I yet?

21 Jesus said unto him, If thou wilt be perfect, go (and) sell that thou hast, and give to the poor, and thou shalt have treasure in heaven: and come (and) follow me.

22 But when the young man heard that saying, he went away sorrowful: for he had great possessions.

23. Then said Jesus unto his disciples, Verily I say unto you, That a rich man shall hardly enter into the kingdom of heaven.

24 And again I say unto you, It is easier for a camel to go through the eye of a needle, than for a rich man to enter into the kingdom

Literal Translation

Matthew 19:25

King James Version

of God.
25 And His disciples were exceedingly astonished when they heard this, saying, Who then can be saved?
26 But having looked on (them), Jesus said to them, With men this is impossible, but with God all things are possible.
27. Then answering, Peter said to Him, Behold, we left all things and followed You. What then shall be to us?
28 And Jesus said to them, Truly I say to you, You who have followed Me, in the regeneration when the Son of man sits on the throne of His glory, you also will sit on twelve thrones, judging the twelve tribes of Israel.
29 And everyone who left houses, or brothers, or sisters, or father, or mother, or wife, or children, or lands, for My name's sake, shall receive a hundredfold, and shall inherit everlasting life.
30 But many first (ones) shall be last, and last (ones) first.

3588 2316 1525 191 1161 3588 3101 846
λείαν τοῦ Θεοῦ εἰσελθεῖν. 25 ἀκούσαντες δὲ οἱ μαθηταὶ αὐτοῦ
dom of God to enter. having heard And the disciples of Him
1605 4970 3004 5101 687 1410 4982
ἐξεπλήσσοντο σφόδρα λέγοντες, Τίς ἄρα δύναται σωθῆναι;
were astonished exceedingly saying, Who then is able to be saved?
1689 1161/3588/2424 2036 846 3844 444 5124
26 ἐμβλέψας δὲ ὁ Ἰησοῦς εἶπεν αὐτοῖς, Παρὰ ἀνθρώποις τοῦτο
having looked But Jesus said to them, With men this
102 2076 3844 1161 2316 3956 1415 2076 5119
ἀδύνατόν ἐστι, παρὰ δὲ Θεῷ πάντα δυνατα ἐστί. 27 Τότε
impossible is, with but God all things possible are. Then
611 3588 4074 2036 846 2400 2249 863
ἀποκριθεὶς ὁ Πέτρος εἶπεν αὐτῷ, Ἰδού, ἡμεῖς ἀφήκαμεν
answering Peter said to Him, Behold we left
3956 2532 190 4671 5101 687 2071 2254 3588 1161
πάντα καὶ ἠκολουθήσαμέν σοι· τί ἄρα ἔσται ἡμῖν; 28 ὁ δε
all things and followed You; what then shall be to us? And
2424 2036 846 281 3004 5213 3754 5210 3588 190
Ἰησοῦς εἶπεν αὐτοῖς, Ἀμὴν λέγω ὑμῖν ὅτι ὑμεῖς οἱ ἀκολουθή-
Jesus said to them, Truly I say to you that you, those having
3427 1722 3588 3824 3752 2523 3588 5207 3588
σαντές μοι, ἐν τῇ παλιγγενεσίᾳ, ὅταν καθίσῃ ὁ υἱὸς τοῦ
followed Me, in the regeneration, when sits the Son
444 1909 2362 1391 846 2523 2532 5210 1909
ἀνθρώπου ἐπὶ θρόνου δόξης αὐτοῦ, καθήσεσθε καὶ ὑμεῖς ἐπὶ
of man on (the) throne of glory of Him, you will sit even you on
1427 2362 2919 3588 1427 5443 3588 2474
δώδεκα θρόνους, κρίνοντες τὰς δώδεκα φυλὰς τοῦ Ἰσραήλ.
twelve thrones, judging the twelve tribes of Israel.
2532 3956 3739 863 3614 2228 80 2228 79 2228
29 καὶ πᾶς ὃς ἀφῆκεν οἰκίας, ἢ ἀδελφούς, ἢ ἀδελφάς, ἢ
And everyone who left houses, or brothers, or sisters, or
3962 2228 3384 2228 1135 2228 5043 2228 68 1752 3588
πατέρα, ἢ μητέρα, ἢ γυναῖκα, ἢ τέκνα, ἢ ἀγρούς, ἕνεκεν τοῦ
father, or mother, or wife, or children, or lands, for the sake of the
3686 3450 1542 2983 2532 2222 166
ὀνόματός μου ἑκατονταπλασίονα λήψεται, καὶ ζωὴν αἰώνιον
name of Me a hundredfold shall receive, and life everlasting
2816 4183 1161 2071 4413 2078 2532
κληρονομήσει. 30 Πολλοὶ δὲ ἔσονται πρῶτοι ἔσχατοι, καὶ
shall inherit. many But shall be first last, and
2078 4413
ἔσχατοι πρῶτοι.
last first.

of God.
25 When his disciples heard (it), they were exceedingly amazed, saying, Who then can be saved?
26 But Jesus beheld (them), and said unto them, With men this is impossible; but with God all things are possible.
27. Then answered Peter and said unto him, Behold, we have forsaken all, and followed thee; what shall we have therefore?
28 And Jesus said unto them, Verily I say unto you, That ye which have followed me, in the regeneration when the Son of man shall sit in the throne of his glory, ye also shall sit upon twelve thrones, judging the twelve tribes of Israel.
29 And every one that hath forsaken houses, or brethren, or sisters, or father, or mother, or wife, or children, or lands, for my name's sake, shall receive an hundredfold, and shall inherit everlasting life.
30 But many (that are) first shall be last; and the last (shall be) first.

Matthew 20

1. For the kingdom of Heaven is like a man, a housemaster, who went out when (it was) early to hire workers into his vineyard.
2 And agreeing with the workers for a denarius (for) the day, he sent them into his vineyard.
3 And having gone out about the third hour, he saw others

Matthew 20

3664 1063 2076 3588 932 3588 3772 444
1. Ὁμοία γάρ ἐστιν ἡ βασιλεία τῶν οὐρανῶν ἀνθρώπῳ
like For is the kingdom of Heaven to a man
3617 3748 1831 260 4404 3409 2040
οἰκοδεσπότῃ, ὅστις ἐξῆλθεν ἅμα πρωι μισθώσασθαι ἐργάτας
a housemaster, who went out when early to hire workmen
1519 3588 290 846 4856 1161 3326 3588 2040 1537
εἰς τὸν ἀμπελῶνα αὐτοῦ. 2 συμφωνήσας δὲ μετὰ τῶν ἐργατῶν ἐκ
into the vineyard of him. having agreed And with the workmen (for)
1220 3588 2250 649 846 1519 3588 290
δηναρίου τὴν ἡμέραν, ἀπέστειλεν αὐτοὺς εἰς τὸν ἀμπελῶνα
a denarius the day, he sent them into the vineyard
846 2532 1831 4012 3588 5154 5610 1492 243
αὐτοῦ. 3 καὶ ἐξελθὼν περὶ τὴν τρίτην ὥραν, εἶδεν ἄλλους
of him. And having gone out about the third hour, he saw others

Matthew 20

1. For the kingdom of heaven is like unto a man (that is) an householder, which went out early in the morning to hire labourers into his vineyard.
2 And when he had agreed with the labourers for a penny a day, he sent them into his vineyard.
3 And he went out about the third hour, and saw others

Matthew 20:4

Literal Translation

standing idle in the market.
4 And he said to them, You also go into the vineyard, and I will give you whatever is just. And they went.
5 Again, having gone out about (the) sixth and ninth hour, he did the same.
6 And having gone out about the eleventh hour, he found others standing idle, and said to them, Why do you stand here idle all day?
7 They said to him, Because no one hired us. He said to them, You also go into the vineyard, and you will receive whatever is just.
8 But evening having come, the Lord of the vineyard said to his manager, Call the workers and pay them the wage, having begun from the last to the first.
9 And having come those about the eleventh hour each received a denarius.
10 And having come, the first supposed that they would receive more. And they also each received a denarius.
11 And having received (it), they grumbled against the housemaster,
12 saying, These last have performed one hour, and you have made them equal to us who have borne the burden and the heat of the day.
13 But answering, he said to one of them, Friend, I do not wrong you. Did you not agree to a denarius with me?
14 Take yours and go. But I desire to give to this last as also to you.
15 Or is it not lawful for me to do what I desire with my things? Is your eye evil because

Greek Interlinear

2476 1722 3588 58 692 2548 2036 5217 2532
ἑστῶτας ἐν τῇ ἀγορᾷ ἀργούς· 4 κἀκείνοις εἶπεν, Ὑπάγετε καὶ
standing in the market idle; and to them said, Go also

5210 1519 3588 290 2532/3588/1437/5600 1342 1325 5213 3588
ὑμεῖς εἰς τὸν ἀμπελῶνα, καὶ ὃ ἐὰν ᾖ δίκαιον δώσω ὑμῖν. 5 οἱ
you into the vineyard, and whatever may be just I will give you. they

1161 565 3825 1831 4012 1623 2532 1766 5610
δὲ ἀπῆλθον. πάλιν ἐξελθὼν περὶ ἕκτην καὶ ἐνάτην ὥραν,
And went. Again going out about the sixth and ninth hour,

4160 5615 4012 1161 3588 1734 5610 1831
ἐποίησεν ὡσαύτως. 6 περὶ δὲ τὴν ἑνδεκάτην ὥραν ἐξελθὼν,
he did the same. about And the eleventh hour going out,

2147 243 2476 692 2532 3004 846 5101 5602
εὗρεν ἄλλους ἑστῶτας ἀργούς, καὶ λέγει αὐτοῖς, Τί ὧδε
he found others standing idle, and says to them, Why here

2476 3650 3588 2250 692 3004 846 3754
ἑστήκατε ὅλην τὴν ἡμέραν ἀργοί; 7 λέγουσιν αὐτῷ, Ὅτι
do you stand all the day idle? They say to him, Because

3762 2248 3409 3004 846 5217 2532 5210
οὐδεὶς ἡμᾶς ἐμισθώσατο. λέγει αὐτοῖς, Ὑπάγετε καὶ ὑμεῖς
no one us hired. He says to them, Go also you

1519 3588 290 2532/3588/1437/5600 1342 2983 3798 1161
εἰς τὸν ἀμπελῶνα, καὶ ὃ ἐὰν ᾖ δίκαιον λήψεσθε. 8 ὀψίας δὲ
into the vineyard, and whatever may be just you will receive. evening But

1096 3004 3588 2962 3588 290 3588 2012 846
γενομένης λέγει ὁ κύριος τοῦ ἀμπελῶνος τῷ ἐπιτρόπῳ αὐτοῦ,
having come says the lord of the vineyard to the manager of him,

2564 3588 2040 2532 591 846 3588 3408
Κάλεσον τοὺς ἐργάτας, καὶ ἀπόδος αὐτοῖς τὸν μισθόν,
Call the workmen, and pay them the wage,

756 575 3588 2078 2193 3588 4413 2532 2064
ἀρξάμενος ἀπὸ τῶν ἐσχάτων ἕως τῶν πρώτων. 9 καὶ ἐλθόντες
having begun from the last ones until the first. And having come

3588 4012 3588 1734 5610 2983 303 1220 2064
οἱ περὶ τὴν ἑνδεκάτην ὥραν ἔλαβον ἀνὰ δηνάριον. 10 ἐλθόντες
those about the eleventh hour received each a denarius. having come

1161 3588 4413 3543 3754 4119 2983 2532 2983 2532
δὲ οἱ πρῶτοι ἐνόμισαν ὅτι πλείονα λήμψονται· καὶ ἔλαβον καὶ
And the first supposed that more they will receive; and they got also

846 303 1220 2983 1161 1111 2596 3588
αὐτοὶ ἀνὰ δηνάριον. 11 λαβόντες δὲ ἐγόγγυζον κατὰ τοῦ
themselves each a denarius. having received And they grumbled against the

3617 3004 3754 3778 3588 2078 3391 5610
οἰκοδεσπότου, 12 λέγοντες ὅτι Οὗτοι οἱ ἔσχατοι μίαν ὥραν
housemaster, saying, These last one hour

4160 2532 2470 2254 846 4160 3588 941
ἐποίησαν, καὶ ἴσους ἡμῖν αὐτοὺς ἐποίησας, τοῖς βαστάσασι
performed, and equal to us them you have made, those having borne

3588 922 3588 2250 2532 3588 2742 3588 1161 611
τὸ βάρος τῆς ἡμέρας καὶ τὸν καύσωνα. 13 ὁ δὲ ἀποκριθεὶς
the burden of the day and the heat. he But answering

2036 1520 846 2083 3756 91 4571 3780 1220
εἶπεν ἑνὶ αὐτῶν, Ἑταῖρε, οὐκ ἀδικῶ σε· οὐχὶ δηναρίου
said to one of them, Friend, not I wrong you; Not of a denarius

4856 3427 142 3588 4674 2532 5217 2309 1161 5129
συνεφώνησάς μοι; 14 ἆρον τὸ σὸν καὶ ὕπαγε· θέλω δὲ τούτῳ
you agreed with me? Take yours and go; I desire But to this

3588 2078 1325 5613 2532 4671 2228 3756 1832 3427 4160 3739
τῷ ἐσχάτῳ δοῦναι ὡς καὶ σοί. 15 ἢ οὐκ ἔξεστί μοι ποιῆσαι ὃ
last to give as also to you Or not is it lawful for me to do what

2309 1722 3588 1699 1487 3588 3788 4675 4190 2076 3754
θέλω ἐν τοῖς ἐμοῖς; εἰ ὁ ὀφθαλμός σου πονηρός ἐστιν, ὅτι
I desire in things my? the eye of you evil Is, because

King James Version

standing idle in the marketplace,
4 And said unto them; Go ye also into the vineyard, and whatsoever is right I will give you. And they went their way.
5 Again he went out about the sixth and ninth hour, and did likewise.
6 And about the eleventh hour he went out, and found others standing idle, and saith unto them, Why stand ye here all the day idle?
7 They say unto him, Because no man hath hired us. He saith unto them, Go ye also into the vineyard; and whatsoever is right, (that) shall ye receive.
8 So when even was come, the lord of the vineyard saith unto his steward, Call the labourers, and give them (their) hire, beginning from the last unto the first.
9 And when they came that (were hired) about the eleventh hour, they received every man a penny.
10 But when the first came, they supposed that they should have received more; and they likewise received every man a penny.
11 And when they had received (it), they murmured against the goodman of the house,
12 Saying, These last have wrought (but) one hour, and thou hast made them equal unto us, which have borne the burden and heat of the day.
13 But he answered one of them, and said, Friend, I do thee no wrong: didst not thou agree with me for a penny?
14 Take (that) thine (is), and go thy way: I will give unto this last, even as unto thee.
15 Is it not lawful for me to do what I will with mine own? Is thine eye evil, because

Literal Translation

I am good?
16 So the last shall be first, and the first last; for many are called, but few chosen.

17. And going up to Jerusalem, Jesus took along the twelve disciples privately, in the way, and said to them,

18 Behold! We are going up to Jerusalem, and the Son of man will be delivered up to the chief priests and scribes. And they will condemn Him to death.
19 And they will deliver Him up to the nations to mock, and to scourge, and to crucify. And the third day He will rise again.

20. Then the mother of the sons of Zebedee came near to Him, along with her sons worshiping, and asking something from Him.

21 And He said to her, What do you desire? She said to Him, Say that these two sons of mine may sit one off Your right, and one off (Your) left in Your Kingdom.
22 And answering, Jesus said, You do not know what you ask. Are you able to drink the cup which I am about to drink, and to be baptized with the baptism with which I am to be baptized? They said to Him, We are able.
23 And He said to them, Indeed you shall drink My cup, and you shall be baptized with the baptism with which I am baptized; but to sit off My right and off My left (hand) is not Mine to give, but (to those) for whom it was prepared by My Father.

24 And hearing, the ten were indignant about the

Matthew 20:16

1473 18 1510 3779 2071 3588 2078 4413 2532 3588
ἐγὼ ἀγαθός εἰμι; 16 οὕτως ἔσονται οἱ ἔσχατοι πρῶτοι, καὶ οἱ
I good am? So shall be the last first, and the

4413 2078 4183 1063 1526 2822 3641 1161 1588
πρῶτοι ἔσχατοι. πολλοὶ γάρ εἰσι κλητοί ὀλίγοι δὲ ἐκλεκτοί.
first last; many for are called few but elect.

2532 305 3588 2424 1519 2414 3880 3588
17. Καὶ ἀναβαίνων ὁ Ἰησοῦς εἰς Ἱεροσόλυμα παρέλαβε τοὺς
And going up Jesus into Jerusalem He took along the

1427 3101 2596 2398 1722 3588 3598 2532 2036 846
δώδεκα μαθητὰς κατ' ἰδίαν, ἐν τῇ ὁδῷ, καὶ εἶπεν αὐτοῖς,
twelve disciples privately, in the way, and (He) said to them,

2400 305 1519 2414 2532 3588 5207 3588 444
18 Ἰδού, ἀναβαίνομεν εἰς Ἱεροσόλυμα, καὶ ὁ υἱὸς τοῦ ἀνθρώπου
Behold! We are going up to Jerusalem, and the Son of man

3860 3588 749 2532 1122 2532 2632
παραδοθήσεται τοῖς ἀρχιερεῦσι καὶ γραμματεῦσι· καὶ κατα-
will be delivered up to the chief priests and scribes; and they

846 2288 2532 3860 846 3588
κρινοῦσιν αὐτὸν θανάτῳ, 19 καὶ παραδώσουσιν αὐτὸν τοῖς
will condemn Him to death, and they will deliver up Him to the

1484 1519 3588 1702 2532 3146 2532 4717
ἔθνεσιν εἰς τὸ ἐμπαῖξαι καὶ μαστιγῶσαι καὶ σταυρῶσαι·
nations in order to mock and to scourge and to crucify.

2532 3588 5154 2250 450
καὶ τῇ τρίτῃ ἡμέρᾳ ἀναστήσεται.
And the third day He will rise again.

5119 4334 846 3588 3384 3588 5207 2199 3326
20. Τότε προσῆλθεν αὐτῷ ἡ μήτηρ τῶν υἱῶν Ζεβεδαίου μετὰ
Then came near to Him the mother of the sons of Zebedee with

3588 5207 846 4352 2532 154 5100 3844 846
τῶν υἱῶν αὐτῆς προσκυνοῦσα καὶ αἰτοῦσά τι παρ' αὐτοῦ.
the sons of her worshiping and asking something from Him.

3588 1161 2036 846 5101 2309 3004 846 2036 2443 2523
21 ὁ δὲ εἶπεν αὐτῇ, Τί θέλεις; λέγει αὐτῷ, Εἰπὲ ἵνα καθίσωσιν
He And said to her, What desire you? She says to Him, Say that may sit

3778 3588 1417 5207 3450 1520 1537 1188 4675 2532 1520 1537 2176
οὗτοι οἱ δύο υἱοί μου, εἷς ἐκ δεξιῶν σου, καὶ εἷς ἐξ εὐωνύμων,
these the two sons of me, one off the right of You, and one off the left,

1722 3588 932 4675 611 1161 3588 2424 2036 3765
ἐν τῇ βασιλείᾳ σου. 22 ἀποκριθεὶς δὲ ὁ Ἰησοῦς εἶπεν, Οὐκ
in the kingdom of You. answering And Jesus said, Not

1492 5101 154 1410 4095 3588 4221 3739 1473 3195
οἴδατε τί αἰτεῖσθε, δύνασθε πιεῖν τὸ ποτήριον ὃ ἐγὼ μέλλω
you know what you ask. Are you able to drink the cup which I am about

4095 2532 3588 908 3739 1473 907 907
πίνειν, καὶ τὸ βάπτισμα ὃ ἐγὼ βαπτίζομαι βαπτισθῆναι;
to drink, and the baptism (with) which I am baptized to be baptized?

3004 846 1410 2532 3004 846 3588 3303
λέγουσιν αὐτῷ, Δυνάμεθα. 23 καὶ λέγει αὐτοῖς, Τὸ μὲν
They say to Him, We are able. And He says to them, the indeed

4221 3450 4095 2532 3588 908 3739 1473 907
ποτήριόν μου πίεσθε, καὶ τὸ βάπτισμα ὃ ἐγὼ βαπτίζομαι
cup of Me you will drink, and the baptism (with) which I am baptized

907 3588 1161 2523 1537 1188 3450 2532 1537 2176
βαπτισθήσεσθε· τὸ δὲ καθίσαι ἐκ δεξιῶν μου καὶ ἐξ εὐωνύμων
you will be baptized; but to sit off (the) right of Me and off (the) left

3450 3756 2076 1699 1325 235 3739 2090 5259 3588 3962
μου, οὐκ ἔστιν ἐμὸν δοῦναι, ἀλλ οἷς ἡτοίμασται ὑπὸ τοῦ πατρός
of Me, not is Mine to give, but for whom it was prepared by the Father

3450 2532 191 3588 1176 23 4012 3588
μου. 24 καὶ ἀκούσαντες οἱ δέκα ἠγανάκτησαν περὶ τῶν
of Me And having heard the ten were indignant about the

King James Version

I am good?
16 So the last shall be first, and the first last: for many be called, but few chosen.

17. And Jesus going up to Jerusalem took the twelve disciples apart in the way, and said unto them,

18 Behold, we go up to Jerusalem; and the Son of man shall be betrayed unto the chief priests and unto the scribes, and they shall condemn him to death,
19 And shall deliver him to the Gentiles to mock, and to scourge, and to crucify (him): and the third day he shall rise again.

20. Then came to him the mother of Zebedee's children with her sons, worshipping (him), and desiring a certain thing of him.

21 And he said unto her, What wilt thou? She saith unto him, Grant that these my two sons may sit, the one on thy right hand, and the other on the left, in thy kingdom.
22 But Jesus answered and said, Ye know not what ye ask. Are ye able to drink of the cup that I shall drink of, and to be baptized with the baptism that I am baptized with? They say unto him, We are able.

23 And he saith unto them, Ye shall drink indeed of my cup, and be baptized with the baptism that I am baptized with: but to sit on my right hand, and on my left, is not mine to give, but (it shall be given to them) for whom it is prepared of my Father.
24 And when the ten heard (it), they were moved with indignation against the

Literal Translation

Matthew 20:25

King James Version

two brothers.
25 But having called them, Jesus said, You know that the rulers of the nations exercise lordship over them, and the great ones exercise authority over them.
26 But it will not be so among you. But whoever desires to become great among you, let him be your servant.
27 And whoever desires to be first among you, he will be your servant;
28 Even as the Son of man did not come to be served, but to serve, and to give His life a ransom for many.

1417 80 3588 1161 2424 4341 846 2036
δύο ἀδελφῶν. 25 ὁ δὲ Ἰησοῦς προσκαλεσάμενος αὐτοὺς εἶπεν,
two brothers. But Jesus having called near them said,

1492 3754 3588 758 3588 1484 2634 846
Οἴδατε ὅτι οἱ ἄρχοντες τῶν ἐθνῶν κατακυριεύουσιν αὐτῶν,
You know that the rulers of the nations exercise lordship over them,

2532 3588 3173 2715 846 3756 3779 1161 2071
καὶ οἱ μεγάλοι κατεξουσιάζουσιν αὐτῶν. 26 οὐχ οὕτως δὲ ἔσται
and the great ones exercise authority over them. not so But it will be

1722 5213 235 3739 1437 2309 1722 5213 3173 1096 2077 5216
ἐν ὑμῖν· ἀλλ' ὃς ἐὰν θέλῃ ἐν ὑμῖν μέγας γενέσθαι ἔστω ὑμῶν
among you, but whoever desires among you great to become will be of you

1249 2532 3739 1437 2309 1722 5213 1511 4413 2077 5216
διάκονος· 27 καὶ ὃς ἐὰν θέλῃ ἐν ὑμῖν εἶναι πρῶτος ἔστω ὑμῶν
a servant. And whoever desires among you to be first he will be of you

1401 561 3588 5207 3588 444 3756 2064 1247
δοῦλος· 28 ὥσπερ ὁ υἱὸς τοῦ ἀνθρώπου οὐκ ἦλθε διακονηθῆναι,
a slave; even as the Son of man not did come to be served,

235 1247 2532 1325 3588 5590 846 3083 473
ἀλλὰ διακονῆσαι, καὶ δοῦναι τὴν ψυχὴν αὐτοῦ λύτρον ἀντὶ
but to serve, and to give the life of Him a ransom instead of

4183
πολλῶν.
many.

two brethren.
25 But Jesus called them (unto him), and said, Ye know that the princes of the Gentiles exercise dominion over them, and they that are great exercise authority upon them.
26 But it shall not be so among you: but whosoever will be great among you, let him be your minister;
27 And whosoever will be chief among you, let him be your servant:
28 Even as the Son of man came not to be ministered unto, but to minister, and to give his life a ransom for many.

29. And (as) they (were) going out from Jericho, a great crowd followed Him.
30 And, behold! Two blind ones sitting beside the way, hearing that Jesus is passing by, (they) cried out, saying, Have pity on us, Lord, Son of David!
31 But the crowd rebuked them that they be silent. But they cried out the more, saying, Have pity on us, Lord, Son of David!
32 And stopping, Jesus called them, and said, What do you desire that I may do to you?
33 They said to Him, Lord, that our eyes may be opened.
34 And being moved with pity, Jesus touched their eyes. And instantly their eyes saw again, and they followed Him.

2532 1607 846 575 2410 190
29. Καὶ ἐκπορευομένων αὐτῶν ἀπὸ Ἰεριχώ, ἠκολούθησεν
And (as were) going out they from Jericho, followed

846 3793 4183 2532 2400 1417 5185 2521 3844
αὐτῷ ὄχλος πολύς. 30 καὶ ἰδού, δύο τυφλοὶ καθήμενοι παρὰ
Him a crowd great. And behold! Two blind (ones) sitting beside

3588 3598 191 3754 2424 3855 2896
τὴν ὁδόν, ἀκούσαντες ὅτι Ἰησοῦς παράγει, ἔκραξαν,
the roadway, hearing that Jesus is passing by, cried out,

3004 1653 2248 2962 5207 1138 3588 1161 3793
λέγοντες, Ἐλέησον ἡμᾶς, Κύριε, υἱὸς Δαβίδ. 31 ὁ δὲ ὄχλος
saying, Have pity on us, Lord, son of David. the But crowd

2008 846 2443 4623 3588 1161 3185 2896
ἐπετίμησεν αὐτοῖς ἵνα σιωπήσωσιν, οἱ δὲ μεῖζον ἔκραξον,
rebuked them that they be silent. they But the more cried out,

3004 1653 2248 2962 5207 1138 2532 2476 3588
λέγοντες, Ἐλέησον ἡμᾶς, Κύριε, υἱὸς Δαβίδ. 32 καὶ στὰς ὁ
saying, Have pity on us, Lord, son of David. And stopping

2424 5455 846 2532 2036 5101 2309 4160 5213
Ἰησοῦς ἐφώνησεν αὐτούς, καὶ εἶπε, Τί θέλετε ποιήσω ὑμῖν;
Jesus called them, and said, What you desire I may do to you?

3004 846 2962 2443 455 2257 3588 3788
33 λέγουσιν αὐτῷ, Κύριε, ἵνα ἀνοιχθῶσιν ἡμῶν οἱ ὀφθαλμοί.
They say to Him, Lord, that may be opened of us the eyes.

4697 1161 3588 2424 680 3588 3788 846
34 σπλαγχνισθεὶς δὲ ὁ Ἰησοῦς ἥψατο τῶν ὀφθαλμῶν αὐτῶν·
being moved with pity And Jesus touched the eyes of them;

2532 2112 308 846 3588 3788 2532 190
καὶ εὐθέως ἀνέβλεψαν αὐτῶν οἱ ὀφθαλμοί, καὶ ἠκολούθησαν
and instantly saw again of them the eyes, and they followed

846
αὐτῷ.
Him.

29. And as they departed from Jericho, a great multitude followed him.
30 And, behold, two blind men sitting by the way side, when they heard that Jesus passed by, cried out, saying, Have mercy on us, O Lord, (thou) Son of David.
31 And the multitude rebuked them, because they should hold their peace: but they cried the more, saying, Have mercy on us, O Lord, (thou) Son of David.
32 And Jesus stood still, and called them, and said, What will ye that I shall do unto you?
33 They say unto him, Lord, that our eyes may be opened.
34 So Jesus had compassion (on them), and touched their eyes: and immediately their eyes received sight, and they followed him.

Matthew 21

1. And when they drew near to Jerusalem and came into Bethphage

Matthew 21

2532 3753 1448 1519 2414 2532 2064 1519 967
1. Καὶ ὅτε ἤγγισαν εἰς Ἱεροσόλυμα, καὶ ἦλθον εἰς Βηθφαγῆ
And when they drew near to Jerusalem, and came into Bethphage

Matthew 21

1. And when they drew nigh unto Jerusalem, and were come to Bethphage,

Literal Translation | **Matthew 21:2** | **King James Version**

toward the Mount of Olives, then Jesus sent two disciples,

2 saying to them, Go into the village opposite you, and immediately you will find an ass tied, and a colt with her; Loosening lead (them) to Me.
3 And if anyone says anything to you, you shall say, The Lord has need of them. And he will send them at once.

4 But all this happened that might be fulfilled that spoken through the prophet, saying:
5 "Tell the daughter of Zion, Behold! Your King comes to you, meek and mounted on an ass, even a colt, (the) son of an ass." (Isa. 62:11; Zech. 9:9)
6 And the disciples, going and doing as Jesus ordered them,
7 they led the ass and the colt. And (they) put on them their garments, and He sat on them.

8 And the very great crowd strewed their garments on the road. And others were cutting branches from the trees and were spreading (them) in the way.

9 And the crowd, the ones going before and the ones following, were crying out, saying, Hosanna to the Son of David! Blessed (is) He coming in (the) name of (the) Lord! Hosanna in the highest! (Ps. 118:25, 26)

10. And having entered into Jerusalem, all the city was shaken, saying, Who is this?
11 And the crowds said, This is Jesus, the Prophet, the (one) from Nazareth of Galilee.

4314 3588 3735 3588 1636 5119 3588 2424 649 1417
πρὸς τὸ ὄρος τῶν ἐλαιῶν, τότε ὁ Ἰησοῦς ἀπέστειλε δύο
toward the Mount of the Olives, then Jesus sent two

3101 3004 846 4198 1519 3588 2968 3588 561
μαθητὰς, 2 λέγων αὐτοῖς, Πορεύθητε εἰς τὴν κώμην τὴν ἀπέ-
disciples, saying to them, You go into the village the (one)

5216 2532 2112 2147 3688 1210 2532 4454
ναντι ὑμῶν, καὶ εὐθέως εὑρήσετε ὄνον δεδεμένην, καὶ πῶλον
opposite you, and at once you will find an ass tied, and a colt

3326 846 3089 71 3427 2532 1437 5100 5213 2036 5100
μετ᾽αὐτῆς·λύσαντες ἀγάγετέ μοι. 3 καὶ ἐάν τις ὑμῖν εἴπῃ τι,
with her; loosening lead to Me. And if anyone to you says a thing,

2046 3754 3588 2962 846 5532 2192 2112 1161 649
ἐρεῖτε ὅτι Ὁ Κύριος αὐτῶν χρείαν ἔχει· εὐθέως δὲ ἀποστελεῖ
you will say, The Lord of them need has; at once and he will send

846 5124 1161 3650 1096 2443 4137 3588 4483 1223
αὐτούς. 4 τοῦτο δὲ ὅλον γέγονεν, ἵνα πληρωθῇ τὸ ῥηθὲν διὰ
them. this But all occurred that may be fulfilled that spoken through

3588 4396 3004 2036 3588 2364 4622 2400
τοῦ προφήτου, λέγοντος, 5 Εἴπατε τῇ θυγατρὶ Σιών, Ἰδού,
the prophet, saying, Tell the daughter of Zion, behold!

3588 935 4675 2064 4671 4239 2532 1910 1909 3688
ὁ βασιλεύς σου ἔρχεταί σοι, πραυς καὶ ἐπιβεβηκὼς ἐπὶ ὄνον
The king of you comes to you, meek and mounted on an ass

2532 4454 5207 5268 4198 1161 3588 3101 2532
καὶ πῶλον υἱὸν ὑποζυγίου. 6 πορευθέντες δὲ οἱ μαθηταὶ, καὶ
even a colt (the) son of an ass. having gone And the disciples, and

4160 2531 4367 846 3588 2424 71
ποιήσαντες καθὼς προσέταξεν αὐτοῖς ὁ Ἰησοῦς, 7 ἤγαγον
having done as ordered them Jesus, they led

3588 3688 2532 3588 4454 2532 2007 1883 846 3588
τὴν ὄνον καὶ τὸν πῶλον, καὶ ἐπέθηκαν ἐπάνω αὐτῶν τὰ
the ass and the colt, and put upon them the

2440 846 2532 1940 1883 846 3588 1161 4118
ἱμάτια αὐτῶν, καὶ ἐπεκάθισεν ἐπάνω αὐτῶν. 8 ὁ δὲ πλεῖστος
garments of them, and He sat on them. the And very great

3793 4766 1438 3588 2440 1722 3588 3598 243 1161
ὄχλος ἔστρωσαν ἑαυτῶν τὰ ἱμάτια ἐν τῇ ὁδῷ· ἄλλοι δὲ
crowd strewed of themselves the garments in the way. others And

2875 2798 575 3588 1186 2532 4766 1722 3588
ἔκοπτον κλάδους ἀπὸ τῶν δένδρων, καὶ ἐστρώννυον ἐν τῇ
were cutting branches from the trees, and were spreading in the

3598 3588 1161 3793 3588 4254 2532 3588 190
ὁδῷ. 9 οἱ δὲ ὄχλοι οἱ προάγοντες καὶ οἱ ἀκολουθοῦντες
way. the And crowds those going before and those following,

2896 3004 5614 3588 5207 1138 2127 3588
ἔκραζον, λέγοντες, Ὡσαννὰ τῷ υἱῷ Δαβίδ· Εὐλογημένος ὁ
were crying out, saying, Hosanna to the Son of David! Blessed (is) He

2064 1722 3686 2962 5614 1722 3588 5310
ἐρχόμενος ἐν ὀνόματι Κυρίου· Ὡσαννὰ ἐν τοῖς ὑψίστοις.
coming in (the) name of the Lord! Hosanna in the highest!

2532 1525 846 1519 2424 4579 3956 3588
10 καὶ εἰσελθόντος αὐτοῦ εἰς Ἱεροσόλυμα, ἐσείσθη πᾶσα ἡ
And having entered of Him into Jerusalem, was shaken all the

4172 3004 5101 2076 3778 3588 1161 3793 3004
πόλις λέγουσα, Τίς ἐστιν οὗτος; 11 οἱ δὲ ὄχλοι ἔλεγον,
city saying, Who is this? the And crowds were saying,

3778 2076 2424 3588 4396 3588 575 3478 3588
Οὗτός ἐστιν Ἰησοῦς ὁ προφήτης, ὁ ἀπὸ Ναζαρὲθ τῆς
This is Jesus the prophet, the (one) from Nazareth

1056
Γαλιλαίας.
of Galilee.

---

unto the mount of Olives, then sent Jesus two disciples,

2 Saying unto them, Go into the village over against you, and straightway ye shall find an ass tied, and a colt with her: loose (them), and bring (them) unto me.
3 And if any (man) say ought unto you, ye shall say, The Lord hath need of them; and straightway he will send them.

4 All this was done, that it might be fulfilled which was spoken by the prophet, saying,
5 Tell ye the daughter of Sion, Behold, thy King cometh unto thee, meek, and sitting upon an ass, and a colt the foal of an ass.

6 And the disciples went, and did as Jesus commanded them,
7 And brought the ass, and the colt, and put on them their clothes, and they set (him) thereon.

8 And a very great multitude spread their garments in the way; others cut down branches from the trees, and strawed (them) in the way.

9 And the multitudes that went before, and that followed, cried, saying, Hosanna to the Son of David: Blessed (is) he that cometh in the name of the Lord; Hosanna in the highest.

10. And when he was come into Jerusalem, all the city was moved, saying, Who is this?
11 And the multitude said, This is Jesus the prophet of Nazareth of Galilee.

Literal Translation

12. And Jesus entered into the temple of God and threw out all those selling and buying in the temple. And He overthrew the tables of the money changers and the seats of those selling the doves.

13 And He said to them, It has been written, "My house shall be called a house of prayer," but you have made it a den of plunderers. (Isa. 56:7; Jer. 7:11)
14 And blind and lame ones came to Him in the temple, and He healed them.

15 But the chief priests and the scribes, having seen the wonders which He did, and the children crying out in the temple, and saying, Hosanna to the Son of David, they were incensed.
16 And (they) said to Him, Do you hear what these say? And Jesus said to them, Yes. Did you never read, "Out of (the) mouth of babes and sucklings You have perfected praise"? (Ps. 8:2)

17 And leaving them, He went out of the city to Bethany, and spent the night there.

18. And returning early to the city, He hungered.
19 And seeing one fig tree by the way, He went up (to) it, and found nothing on it except leaves only. And He said to it, Let there be no more fruit from you forever. And the fig tree immediately dried up.

20 And having seen, the disciples marveled, saying, How quickly the fig tree is dried up!
21 And answering, Jesus said to them, Truly I say to you, If you have faith and do not

Matthew 21:12

2532 1525 3588 2424 1519 3588 2411 3588 2316 2532
12. Καὶ εἰσῆλθεν ὁ Ἰησοῦς εἰς τὸ ἱερόν τοῦ Θεοῦ, καὶ
And went in Jesus into the temple of God, and

1544 3956 3588 4453 2532 59 1722 3588 2411
ἐξέβαλε πάντας τοὺς πωλοῦντας καὶ ἀγοράζοντας ἐν τῷ ἱερῷ,
threw out all those selling and buying in the temple.

2532 3588 5132 3588 2855 2690 2532 3588
καὶ τὰς τραπέζας τῶν κολλυβιστῶν κατέστρεψε, καὶ τὰς
And the tables of the moneychangers He overthrew, and the

2515 3588 4453 3588 4058 2532 3004 846
καθέδρας τῶν πωλούντων τὰς περιστεράς, 13 καὶ λέγει αὐτοῖς,
seats of those selling the doves. And He says to them,

1125 3588 3624 3450 3624 4335 2564
Γέγραπται, Ὁ οἶκός μου οἶκος προσευχῆς κληθήσεται·
it has been written, The house of Me a house of prayer shall be called;

5210 1161 846 4160 4693 3027 2532 4334
ὑμεῖς δὲ αὐτὸν ἐποιήσατε σπήλαιον λῃστῶν. 14 καὶ προσῆλθον
you but it have made a den of plunderers. And came near

846 5185 2532 5560 1722 3588 2411 2532 2323 846
αὐτῷ τυφλοὶ καὶ χωλοὶ ἐν τῷ ἱερῷ· καὶ ἐθεράπευσεν αὐτούς.
to Him blind and lame in the temple; and He healed them.

1492 1161 3588 749 2532 3588 1122 3588 2297 3739
15 ἰδόντες δὲ οἱ ἀρχιερεῖς καὶ οἱ γραμματεῖς τὰ θαυμάσια ἃ
having seen But the chief priests and the scribes the wonders which

4160 2532 3588 3816 2896 1722 3588 2411 2532 3004
ἐποίησε, καὶ τοὺς παῖδας κράζοντας ἐν τῷ ἱερῷ, καὶ λέγον-
He did, and the children crying out in the temple, and saying,

5614 3588 5207 1138 23 2532 2036 846
τας, Ὡσαννὰ τῷ υἱῷ Δαβίδ, ἠγανάκτησαν, 16 καὶ εἶπον αὐτῷ,
Hosanna to the Son of David, they were incensed, and said to Him,

191 5101 3778 3004 3588 1161 2424 3004 846 3483
Ἀκούεις τί οὗτοι λέγουσιν; ὁ δὲ Ἰησοῦς λέγει αὐτοῖς, Ναί·
Do you hear what these say? And Jesus says to them, Yes;

3763 314 3754 1537 4750 3516 2532 2337
οὐδέποτε ἀνέγνωτε ὅτι Ἐκ στόματος νηπίων καὶ θηλα-
never Did you read, Out of the mouth of babes and sucking

2675 136 2532 2641 846 1831
ζόντων κατηρτίσω αἶνον; 17 καὶ καταλιπὼν αὐτοὺς ἐξῆλθεν
(ones) You have perfected praise? And leaving them He went

1854 3588 4172 1519 963 2532 835 1563
ἔξω τῆς πόλεως εἰς Βηθανίαν, καὶ ηὐλίσθη ἐκεῖ.
out of the city to Bethany, and lodged there.

4405 1161 1877 1519 3588 4172 3983 2532 1492
18. Πρωιας δὲ ἐπανάγων εἰς τὴν πόλιν, ἐπείνασε. 19 καὶ ἰδὼν
early And returning into the city, He hungered. And seeing

4808 3391 1909 3588 3598 2064 1909 846 2532 3762 2147
συκῆν μίαν ἐπὶ τῆς ὁδοῦ, ἦλθεν ἐπ' αὐτήν, καὶ οὐδὲν εὗρεν
fig-tree one on the way, He went up (to) it, and nothing found

1722 846 1487 3361 5444 3440 2532 3004 846 3371 1537 4675
ἐν αὐτῇ εἰ μὴ φύλλα μόνον· καὶ λέγει αὐτῇ, Μηκέτι ἐκ σοῦ
in it except leaves only. And He says to it, No longer from you

2590 1096 1519 3588 165 2532 3583 3916 3588
καρπὸς γένηται εἰς τὸν αἰῶνα. καὶ ἐξηράνθη παραχρῆμα ἡ
fruit may be to the age. And was dried up instantly the

4808 2532 1492 3588 3101 2296 3004 4459
συκῆ. 20 καὶ ἰδόντες οἱ μαθηταὶ ἐθαύμασαν, λέγοντες, Πῶς
fig-tree. And having seen the disciples marveled, saying, How

3916 3583 3588 4808 611 1161 3588 2424
παραχρῆμα ἐξηράνθη ἡ συκῆ; 21 ἀποκριθεὶς δὲ ὁ Ἰησοῦς
instantly was dried up the fig-tree? answering And Jesus

2036 846 281 3004 5213 1437 2192 4102 2532 3361
εἶπεν αὐτοῖς, Ἀμὴν λέγω ὑμῖν, ἐὰν ἔχητε πίστιν, καὶ μὴ
said to them, Truly I say to you, If you have faith, and not

King James Version

12. And Jesus went into the temple of God, and cast out all them that sold and bought in the temple, and overthrew the tables of the money-changers, and the seats of them that sold doves,

13 And said unto them, It is written, My house shall be called the house of prayer; but ye have made it a den of thieves.

14 And the blind and the lame came to him in the temple; and he healed them.

15 And when the chief priests and scribes saw the wonderful things that he did, and the children crying in the temple, and saying, Hosanna to the Son of David; they were sore displeased,
16 And said unto him, Hearest thou what these say? And Jesus saith unto them, Yea; have ye never read, Out of the mouth of babes and sucklings thou hast perfected praise?

17 And he left them, and went out of the city into Bethany; and he lodged there.

18. Now in the morning as he returned into the city, he hungered.
19 And when he saw a fig tree in the way, he came to it, and found nothing thereon, but leaves only, and said unto it, Let no fruit grow on thee henceforward for ever. And presently the fig tree withered away.
20 And when the disciples saw (it), they marvelled, saying, How soon is the fig tree withered away!
21 Jesus answered and said unto them, Verily I say unto you, If ye have faith, and doubt not,

Literal Translation | **Matthew 21:22** | **King James Version**

Literal Translation

doubt, not only will you do (the miracle) of the fig tree, but even if you should say to this mountain, Be taken up and thrown into the sea, it will be so.
22 And all things, whatever you may ask in prayer, believing, you shall receive.

23. And He, having come into the temple, the chief priests and elders of the people came near to Him (as He was) teaching, saying, By what authority do you do these things? And who gave this authority to you?

24 And answering, Jesus said to them, I also will ask you one thing, which if you tell Me, I also will tell you by what authority I do these things.
25 The baptism of John, from where was it? From Heaven, or from men? And they reasoned among themselves, saying, If we shall say, From Heaven, He will say to us, Why then did you not believe him?
26 But if we should say, From men, we fear the crowd. For all hold John to be a prophet.

27 And answering Jesus, they said, We do not know. And He said to them, Neither do I tell you by what authority I do these things.

28. But what does it seem to you? A man had two children, and coming to the first he said, Child, go today; work in my vineyard.

29 And answering, he said, I will not. But afterward, having regretted, he went.
30 And having come to the second, he said the same. And answering, he said, I (go),

1252 3756 3440 3588 3588 4808 4160 235 2579 3588
διακριθῆτε, οὐ μόνον τὸ τῆς συκῆς ποιήσετε, ἀλλὰ κἂν τῷ
do doubt, not only that of the fig-tree you will do, but also if

3735 5129 2036 142 2532 906 1519 3588 2281
ὄρει τούτῳ εἴπητε, Ἄρθητι καὶ βλήθητι εἰς τὴν θάλασσαν,
mountain to this you say, Be taken and thrown into the sea,

1096 2532 3956 3745 302 154 1722 3588 4335
γενήσεται· 22 καὶ πάντα ὅσα ἂν αἰτήσητε ἐν τῇ προσευχῇ
it will happen; and all things whatever you ask in prayer

4100 2983
πιστεύοντες λήμψεσθε.
believing, you will receive.

2532 2064 846 1519 3588 2411 4334 846 1321
23. Καὶ ἐλθόντι αὐτῷ εἰς τὸ ἱερὸν προσῆλθον αὐτῷ διδά-
And having come Him into the temple, came near to Him teach-

3588 749 2532 3588 4245 3588 2992 3004
σκοντι οἱ ἀρχιερεῖς καὶ οἱ πρεσβύτεροι τοῦ λαοῦ, λέγοντες,
ing the chief priests and the elders of the people, saying,

1722 4169 1849 5023 4160 2532 5101 4671 1325 3588
Ἐν ποίᾳ ἐξουσίᾳ ταῦτα ποιεῖς; καὶ τίς σοι ἔδωκε τὴν
By what authority these things do you? And who to you gave

1849 3778 611 1161 3588 2424 2036 846
ἐξουσίαν ταύτην; 24 ἀποκριθεὶς δὲ ὁ Ἰησοῦς εἶπεν αὐτοῖς,
authority this? answering And Jesus said to them,

2065 5209 2504 3056 1520 3739 1437 2036 3427 2504
Ἐρωτήσω ὑμᾶς κἀγὼ λόγον ἕνα, ὃν ἐὰν εἴπητέ μοι, κἀγὼ
will question you I also word one, which if you tell me, I also

5213 2046 1722 4169 1849 5023 4160 3588 908 2491
ὑμῖν ἐρῶ ἐν ποίᾳ ἐξουσίᾳ ταῦτα ποιῶ. 25 τὸ βάπτισμα Ἰωάννου
you will tell by what authority these things I do The baptism of John,

4159 2258 1537 3772 2228 1537 444 3588 1161 1260
πόθεν ἦν; ἐξ οὐρανοῦ ἢ ἐξ ἀνθρώπων; οἱ δὲ διελογίζοντο
from where was it? From Heaven or from men? they And reasoned

3844 1438 3004 1437 2036 1537 3772 2046 2254
παρ' ἑαυτοῖς, λέγοντες, Ἐὰν εἴπωμεν, ἐξ οὐρανοῦ, ἐρεῖ ἡμῖν,
by themselves, saying, If we say from Heaven, He will say to us,

1302 3767 3756 4100 846 1437 1161 2036 1537 444
Διατί οὖν οὐκ ἐπιστεύσατε αὐτῷ; 26 ἐὰν δὲ εἴπωμεν, ἐξ ἀνθρώ-
Why then not you believed him? if But we say, From men,

5399 3588 3793 3956 1063 2192 3588 2491
πων, φοβούμεθα τὸν ὄχλον· πάντες γὰρ ἔχουσι τὸν Ἰωάννην
we fear the crowd; all for they hold John

5613 4396 2532 611 3588 2424 2036 3756
ὡς προφήτην. 27 καὶ ἀποκριθέντες τῷ Ἰησοῦ εἶπον, Οὐκ
as a prophet. And answering Jesus they said, Not

1492 5346 846 2532 846 3761 1473 3004 5213 1722 4169
οἴδαμεν. ἔφη αὐτοῖς καὶ αὐτός, Οὐδὲ ἐγὼ λέγω ὑμῖν ἐν ποίᾳ
we know. said to them And He, Neither I do tell you by what

1849 5023 4160 5101 1161 5213 1380 444 2192
ἐξουσίᾳ ταῦτα ποιῶ. 28 τί δὲ ὑμῖν δοκεῖ; ἄνθρωπος εἶχε
authority these things I do. what But to you (it) seems? A man had

5043 1417 2532 4334 3588 4413 2036 5043 5217
τέκνα δύο, καὶ προσελθὼν τῷ πρώτῳ εἶπε, Τέκνον, ὕπαγε,
children two, and having come to the first he said, Child, go,

4594 2038 1722 3588 290 3450 3588 1161 611 2036
σήμερον ἐργάζου ἐν τῷ ἀμπελῶνι μου. 29 ὁ δὲ ἀποκριθεὶς εἶπεν,
today work in the vineyard of me. he And answering said

3756 2309 5305 1161 3338 565 2532 4334
Οὐ θέλω· ὕστερον δὲ μεταμεληθεὶς ἀπῆλθε. 30 καὶ προσελθὼν
Not I will; afterwards but having regretted he went. And having come

3588 1208 2036 5615 3588 1161 611 2036 1473
τῷ δευτέρῳ εἶπεν ὡσαύτως. ὁ δὲ ἀποκριθεὶς εἶπεν, Ἐγώ,
to the second he said likewise. he And answering said I (go),

King James Version

ye shall not only do this (which is done) to the fig tree, but also if ye shall say unto this mountain, Be thou removed, and be thou cast into the sea; it shall be done.
22 And all things, whatsoever ye shall ask in prayer, believing, ye shall receive.

23. And when he was come into the temple, the chief priests and the elders of the people came unto him as he was teaching, and said, By what authority doest thou these things? and who gave thee this authority?

24 And Jesus answered and said unto them, I also will ask you one thing, which if ye tell me, I in like wise will tell you by what authority I do these things.
25 The baptism of John, whence was it? from heaven, or of men? And they reasoned with themselves, saying, If we shall say, From heaven; he will say unto us, Why did ye not then believe him?

26 But if we shall say, Of men; we fear the people; for all hold John as a prophet.

27 And they answered Jesus, and said, We cannot tell. And he said unto them, Neither tell I you by what authority I do these things.

28. But what think ye? A (certain) man had two sons; and he came to the first, and said, Son, go work to day in my vineyard.

29 He answered and said, I will not: but afterward he repented, and went.
30 And he came to the second, and said likewise. And he answered and said, I (go),

Literal Translation | **Matthew 21:31** | ***King James Version***

sir; but (he) did not leave.
31 Who out of the two did the will of the father? They said to Him, The first. Jesus said to them, Truly I say to you, the tax collectors and the harlots go before you into the kingdom of God.

32 For John came to you in (the) way of righteousness, and you did not believe him. But the tax-collectors and the harlots believed him. And having seen you did not regret afterwards to believe him.

2962 2532 3756 565 5101 1537 3588 1417 4160 3588 2307
κύριε· καὶ οὐκ ἀπῆλθε. 31 τίς ἐκ τῶν δύο ἐποίησε τὸ θέλημα
lord; and not he did leave. Who out of the two did the will

3588 3962 3004 846 3588 4413 3004 846 3588
τοῦ πατρός; λέγουσιν αὐτῷ, Ὁ πρῶτος. λέγει αὐτοῖς ὁ
of the father? They say to Him, The first. says to them

2424 281 3004 5213 3754 3588 5057 2532 3588 4204
Ἰησοῦς, Ἀμὴν λέγω ὑμῖν, ὅτι οἱ τελῶναι καὶ αἱ πόρναι
Jesus, Truly I say to you, that the tax-collectors and the harlots

4254 5209 1519 3588 932 3588 2316 2064 1063
προάγουσιν ὑμᾶς εἰς τὴν βασιλείαν τοῦ Θεοῦ. 32 ἦλθε γὰρ
go before you into the kingdom of God. came For

4314 5209 2491 1722 3598 1343 2532 3756 4100
πρὸς ὑμᾶς Ἰωάννης ἐν ὁδῷ δικαιοσύνης, καὶ οὐκ ἐπιστεύ-
to you John in (the) way of righteousness, and not did you

846 3588 1161 5057 2532 3588 4204 4100 846
σατε αὐτῷ· οἱ δὲ τελῶναι καὶ αἱ πόρναι ἐπίστευσαν αὐτῷ·
believe him; the But tax-collecters and the harlots believed him.

5210 1161 1492 3756 3338 5305 3588 4100
ὑμεῖς δὲ ἰδόντες οὐ μετεμελήθητε ὕστερον τοῦ πιστεῦσαι
you And having seen not regretted afterwards to believe

846
αὐτῷ.
him.

sir: and went not.
31 Whether of them twain did the will of (his) father? They say unto him, The first. Jesus saith unto them, Verily I say unto you, That the publicans and the harlots go into the kingdom of God before you.
32 For John came unto you in the way of righteousness, and ye believed him not: but the publicans and the harlots believed him: and ye, when ye had seen (it), repented not afterward, that ye might believe him.

33. Hear another parable: There was a certain man, a housemaster, who planted a vineyard and placed a hedge around it; and (he) dug a winepress in it, and built a tower. And (he) rented it to vinedressers and left the country.
34 And when the season of the fruits drew near, he sent his slaves to the vinedressers to receive its fruits.

243 3850 191 444 5100 2258 3617
33. Ἄλλην παραβολὴν ἀκούσατε. Ἄνθρωπος τις ἦν οἰκοδε-
Another parable hear: A man certain was a house-

3748 5452 290 2532 5418 846
σπότης, ὅστις ἐφύτευσεν ἀμπελῶνα, καὶ φραγμὸν αὐτῷ
master, who planted a vineyard, and a hedge it

4060 2532 3736 1722 846 3025 2532 3618 4444
περιέθηκε, καὶ ὤρυξεν ἐν αὐτῷ ληνόν, καὶ ᾠκοδόμησε πύργον,
put around, and dug in it a winepress, and built a tower,

2532 1554 846 1092 2532 589 3753 1161
καὶ ἐξέδετο αὐτὸν γεωργοῖς, καὶ ἀπεδήμησεν. 34 ὅτε δὲ
and rented out it to vinedressers, and departed. when And

1448 3588 2540 3588 2590 649 3588 1401
ἤγγισεν ὁ καιρὸς τῶν καρπῶν, ἀπέστειλε τοὺς δούλους
drew near the season of the fruits, he sent the slaves

846 4314 3588 1092 2983 3588 2590 846
αὐτοῦ πρὸς τοὺς γεωργούς, λαβεῖν τοὺς καρποὺς αὐτοῦ·
of him to the vinedressers to receive the fruits of it.

33. Hear another parable: There was a certain householder, which planted a vineyard, and hedged it round about, and digged a winepress in it, and built a tower, and let it out to husbandmen, and went into a far country:
34 And when the time of the fruit drew near, he sent his servants to the husbandmen, that they might receive the fruits of it.

35 And the vinedressers, having taken his slaves, they beat this one, and they killed one, and they stoned one.
36 Again he sent other slaves, more (than) the first. And they did the same to them.

37 And later he sent his son to them, saying, They will respect my son.
38 But having seen the son, the vinedressers said among themselves, This is the heir. Come, let us kill him and possess his inheritance.

2532 2983 3588 1092 3588 1401 846 3739 3303 1194
35καὶ λαβόντες οἱ γεωργοὶ τοὺς δούλους αὐτοῦ, ὃν μὲν ἔδειραν,
And having taken the vinedressers the slaves of him, this one they beat,

3739 1161 1615 3739 1161 3036 3825 649
ὃν δὲ ἀπέκτειναν, ὃν δὲ ἐλιθοβόλησαν. 36 πάλιν ἀπέστειλεν
one and they killed, one and they stoned. Again he sent

243 1401 4119 3588 4413 2532 4160 846
ἄλλους δούλους πλείονας τῶν πρώτων, καὶ ἐποίησαν αὐτοῖς
other slaves more (than) the last, and they did to them

5615 5305 1161 649 4314 846 3588 5207
ὡσαύτως. 37 ὕστερον δὲ ἀπέστειλε πρὸς αὐτοὺς τὸν υἱὸν
likewise. later But he sent to them the son

846 3004 1788 3588 5207 3450 3588 1161 1092
αὐτοῦ, λέγων, Ἐντραπήσονται τὸν υἱόν μου. 38 οἱ δὲ γεωργοὶ
of him, saying, They will respect the son of me. the But vinedressers

1492 3588 5207 2036 1722 1438 3778 2076 3588 2818
ἰδόντες τὸν υἱὸν εἶπον ἐν ἑαυτοῖς, Οὗτός ἐστιν ὁ κληρονόμος·
having seeen the son said among themselves, This is the heir;

1205 615 846 2532 2722 3588 2817
δεῦτε, ἀποκτείνωμεν αὐτόν, καὶ κατάσχωμεν τὴν κληρονο-
come, let us kill him, and let us possess the inheritance

35 And the husbandmen took his servants, and beat one, and killed another, and stoned another.
36 Again, he sent other servants more than the first: and they did unto them likewise.

37 But last of all he sent unto them his son, saying, They will reverence my son.
38 But when the husbandmen saw the son, they said among themselves, This is the heir; come, let us kill him, and let us seize on his inheritance.

Literal Translation

39 And taking him, they threw (him) out of the vineyard and killed (him).
40 Therefore, when the lord of the vineyard comes, what will he do to these vinedressers?
41 They said to Him, Bad men! He will miserably destroy them, and he will give out the vineyard to other vinedressers who will give to him the fruits in their seasons.

42 Jesus said to them, Did you never read in the Scriptures, "A Stone which the builders rejected, this One became the head of (the) corner. This was from the Lord, and it is a wonder in our eyes"? (Ps. 118:22, 23)

43 Because of this I say to you, The kingdom of God will be taken from you, and it will be given to a nation producing the fruits of it.
44 And he who falls on this Stone will be broken; but on whomever it falls, it will pulverize him.
45 And hearing His parables, the chief priests and the Pharisees knew that He was speaking about them.

46 And seeking to lay hold of Him, they feared the crowds, because they held Him as a prophet.

Matthew 21:39

846 2532 2983 846 1544 1854 3588 290
μίαν αὐτοῦ. 39 καὶ λαβόντες αὐτὸν ἐξέβαλον ἔξω τοῦ ἀμπε-
of him. And taking him they threw out from the vine-

2532 615 3752 3767 2064 3588 2962 3588
λῶνος καὶ ἀπέκτειναν. 40 ὅταν οὖν ἔλθῃ ὁ κύριος τοῦ
yard and killed (him). When therefore comes the lord of the

290 5101 4160 3588 1092 1565 3004
ἀμπελῶνος, τί ποιήσει τοῖς γεωργοῖς ἐκείνοις; 41 λέγουσιν
vineyard, what will he do vinedressers to those? They say

846 2556 2560 622 846 2532 3588 290
αὐτῷ, Κακοὺς κακῶς ἀπολέσει αὐτούς, καὶ τὸν ἀμπελῶνα
to Him, Bad men, badly he will destroy them, and the vineyard

1554 243 1092 3748 591 846
ἐκδώσεται ἄλλοις γεωργοῖς, οἵτινες ἀποδώσουσιν αὐτῷ
he will give out to other vinedressers, who will give over to him

3588 2590 1722 3588 2540 846 3004 846 3588 2424
τοὺς καρποὺς ἐν τοῖς καιροῖς αὐτῶν. 42 λέγει αὐτοῖς ὁ Ἰησοῦς,
the fruits in the seasons of them. says to them Jesus,

3763 314 1722 3588 1124 3037 3739 593
Οὐδέποτε ἀνέγνωτε ἐν ταῖς γραφαῖς, Λίθον ὃν ἀπεδοκί-
Never did you read in the Scriptures, A stone which rejected

3588 3618 3778 1096 1519 2776
μασαν οἱ οἰκοδομοῦντες, οὗτος ἐγενήθη εἰς κεφαλὴν
the builders, this (One) became head

1137 3844 2962 1096 3778 2532 2076 2298 1722
γωνίας· παρὰ Κυρίου ἐγένετο αὕτη, καὶ ἔστι θαυμαστὴ ἐν
of corner; from (the) Lord happened this, and it is a wonder in

3788 2257 1223 5124 3004 5213 3754 142 575
ὀφθαλμοῖς ἡμῶν; 43 διὰ τοῦτο λέγω ὑμῖν ὅτι ἀρθήσεται ἀφ'
(the) eyes of us? Because of this I say to you that will be taken from

5216 3588 932 3588 2316 2532 1325 1484 4160
ὑμῶν ἡ βασιλεία τοῦ Θεοῦ, καὶ δοθήσεται ἔθνει ποιοῦντι
you the kingdom of God, and will be given to a nation producing

3588 2590 846 2532 3588 4098 1909 3588 3037 5126
τοὺς καρποὺς αὐτῆς. 44 καὶ ὁ πεσὼν ἐπὶ τὸν λίθον τοῦτον
the fruits of it. And the (one) falling on Stone this

4917 1909 3739 1161 302 4098 3039 846 2532
συνθλασθήσεται· ἐφ' ὃν δ' ἂν πέσῃ, λικμήσει αὐτόν. 45 καὶ
will be broken up; upon whom but ever it fall, it will pulverize him. And

191 3588 749 2532 3588 5330 3588 3850
ἀκούσαντες οἱ ἀρχιερεῖς καὶ οἱ Φαρισαῖοι τὰς παραβολὰς
hearing the chief priests and the Pharisees the parables

846 1097 3754 4012 846 3004 2532 2212 846
αὐτοῦ ἔγνωσαν ὅτι περὶ αὐτῶν λέγει· 46 καὶ ζητοῦντες αὐτὸν
of Him, they knew that about them He speaks. And seeking Him

2902 5399 3588 3793 1894 5613 4396
κρατῆσαι, ἐφοβήθησαν τοὺς ὄχλους, ἐπειδὴ ὡς προφήτην
to seize, they feared the crowds, because as a prophet

846 2192
αὐτὸν εἶχον.
Him they held.

King James Version

39 And they caught him, and cast (him) out of the vineyard, and slew (him).
40 When the lord therefore of the vineyard cometh, what will he do unto those husbandmen?
41 They say unto him, He will miserably destroy those wicked men, and will let out (his) vineyard unto other husbandmen, which shall render him the fruits in their seasons.
42 Jesus saith unto them, Did ye never read in the scriptures, The stone which the builders rejected, the same is become the head of the corner: this is the Lord's doing, and it is marvellous in our eyes?

43 Therefore say I unto you, The kingdom of God shall be taken from you, and given to a nation bringing forth the fruits thereof.
44 And whosoever shall fall on this stone shall be broken: but on whomsoever it shall fall, it will grind him to powder.
45 And when the chief priests and Pharisees had heard his parables, they perceived that he spake of them.
46 But when they sought to lay hands on him, they feared the multitude, because they took him for a prophet.

Matthew 22

1. And answering, Jesus again spoke to them in parables, saying:
2 The kingdom of Heaven is compared to a man, a king, who made a wedding feast for his son.
3 And he sent

Matthew 22

2532 611 3588 2424 3825 2036 846 1722 3850
1. Καὶ ἀποκριθεὶς ὁ Ἰησοῦς πάλιν εἶπεν αὐτοῖς ἐν παρα-
And answering Jesus again spoke to them in parables

3004 3666 3588 932 3588 3772 444
βολαῖς, λέγων, 2 Ὡμοιώθη ἡ βασιλεία τῶν οὐρανῶν ἀνθρώπῳ
saying, is compared to the kingdom of Heaven to a man

935 3748 4160 1062 3588 5207 846 2532 649
βασιλεῖ, ὅστις ἐποίησε γάμους τῷ υἱῷ αὐτοῦ· 3 καὶ ἀπέστειλε
a king, who made a wedding-feast to the son of him. And he sent

Matthew 22

1. And Jesus answered and spake unto them again by parables, and said,
2 The kingdom of heaven is like unto a certain king, which made a marriage for his son,
3 And sent

Literal Translation

his slaves to call those who had been invited to the wedding feast, but they did not desire to come.
4 Again, he sent other slaves, saying, Tell the ones invited, Behold, I have prepared my supper; my oxen, and the fatlings (are) killed, and all things ready; come to the wedding feast.

5 But not caring they went away, one to (his) own field, and one to his trading.

6 And the rest, seizing his slaves, insulted and killed (them).

7 And hearing, the king became angry. And sending his troops, (he) destroyed those murderers and burned their city.

8 Then he said to his slaves, Indeed, the wedding feast is ready, but those invited were not worthy.

9 Then go onto the exits of the highways and call to the wedding feast as many as you may find.
10 And going out into the highways, those slaves gathered all, as many as they found, both evil and good. And the wedding feast was filled with (those) reclining.

11 And the king coming in to look over (those) reclining, he saw a man there not having been dressed (in) a wedding garment.
12 And he said to him, Friend, how did you come in here, not having a wedding garment? But he was silenced.
13 Then the king said to the servants, Binding his feet and hands, take him away and throw (him) out into the outer darkness. There shall be weeping

Matthew 22:4

3588 1401 846 2564 3588 2564 1519 3588
τοὺς δούλους αὐτοῦ καλέσαι τοὺς κεκλημένους εἰς τοὺς
the slaves of him to call the (ones) being called to the

1062 2532 3756 2309 2064 3825 649 243
γάμους, καὶ οὐκ ἤθελον ἐλθεῖν. 4 πάλιν ἀπέστειλεν ἄλλους
wedding feast. And not they desired to come. Again he sent other

1401 3004 2036 3588 2564 2400 3588 712
δούλους, λέγων, Εἴπατε τοῖς κεκλημένοις, Ἰδού, τὸ ἄριστόν
slaves, saying, Tell the (ones) called, Behold, the supper

3450 2090 3588 5022 3450 2532 3588 4619 2380 2532
μου ἡτοίμασα, οἱ ταῦροί μου καὶ τὰ σιτιστὰ τεθυμένα, καὶ
of me I have readied, the oxen of me and the fatted beasts are killed, and

3956 2092 1205 1519 3588 1062 3588 1161 272
πάντα ἕτοιμα· δεῦτε εἰς τοὺς γάμους. 5 οἱ δὲ ἀμελήσαντες
all things ready. Come to the wedding-feast. they But not caring

565 3588 3303 1519 3588 2398 68 3588 1161 1519 3588 1711
ἀπῆλθον, ὁ μὲν εἰς τὸν ἴδιον ἀγρόν, ὁ δὲ εἰς τὴν ἐμπορίαν
went off, one to the own field, one and to the trading

846 3588 1161 3062 2902 3588 1401 846
αὐτοῦ· 6 οἱ δὲ λοιποὶ κρατήσαντες τοὺς δούλους αὐτοῦ
of him; the and rest seizing the slaves of him

5195 2532 615 191 1161 3588 935 3710
ὕβρισαν καὶ ἀπέκτειναν. 7 ἀκούσας δὲ ὁ βασιλεὺς ὠργίσθη,
insulted and killed. hearing And the king became angry,

2532 3992 3588 4753 846 622 3588 5406
καὶ πέμψας τὰ στρατεύματα αὐτοῦ ἀπώλεσε τοὺς φονεῖς
and sending the troops of him destroyed murderers

1565 2532 3588 4172 846 1714 5119 3004 3588
ἐκείνους καὶ τὴν πόλιν αὐτῶν ἐνέπρησε. 8 τότε λέγει τοῖς
those, and the city of them burned. Then he says to the

1401 846 3588 3303 1062 2092 2076 3588 1161 2564
δούλοις αὐτοῦ, Ὁ μὲν γάμος ἕτοιμός ἐστιν, οἱ δὲ κεκλημένοι
slaves of him, the Indeed wedding ready is, those but called

3756 2258 514 4198 3767 1909 3588 1327 3588 3598
οὐκ ἦσαν ἄξιοι. 9 πορεύεσθε οὖν ἐπὶ τὰς διεξόδους των ὁδῶν,
not were worthy. You go therefore onto the exits of the ways,

2532 3745 302 2147 2564 1519 3588 1062 2532 1831
καὶ ὅσους ἂν εὕρητε, καλέσατε εἰς τοὺς γάμους. 10 καὶ ἐξελ-
and as many as you find, call to the wedding-feast. And having

3588 1401 1565 1519 3588 3598 4863 3956
θόντες οἱ δοῦλοι ἐκεῖνοι εἰς τὰς ὁδοὺς συνήγαγον πάντας
gone out slaves those into the ways gathered all

3745 2147 4190 5037 2532 18 2532 4130 3588
ὅσους εὗρον, πονηρούς τε καὶ ἀγαθούς· καὶ ἐπλήσθη ὁ
as many as they found, evil both and good; and was filled the

1062 345 1525 1161 3588 935 2300 3588
γάμος ἀνακειμένων. 11 εἰσελθὼν δὲ ὁ βασιλεὺς θεάσασθαι τοὺς
wedding feast with (those) reclining. coming in And the king to look over those

345 1492 1563 444 3756 1746 1742
ἀνακειμένους εἶδεν ἐκεῖ ἄνθρωπον οὐκ ἐνδεδυμένον ἔνουμα
reclining he saw there a man not being dressed (in) a dress

1062 2532 3004 846 2083 4459 1525 5602 3361 2192
γάμου· 12 καὶ λέγει αὐτῷ, Ἑταῖρε, πῶς εἰσῆλθες ὧδε μὴ ἔχων
of wedding. And he said to him, Friend, how did you enter here not having

1742 1062 3588 1161 5392 5119 2036 3588 932 3588
ἔνδυμα γάμου; ὁ δὲ ἐφιμώθη. 13 τότε εἶπεν ὁ βασιλεὺς τοῖς
a dress of wedding? he But was silenced. Then said the king to the

1249 1210 846 4228 2532 5495 142 846
διακόνοις, Δήσαντες αὐτοῦ πόδας καὶ χεῖρας, ἄρατε αὐτὸν
servants, Binding of him (the) feet and hands, take away him

2532 1544 1519 3588 4655 3588 1857 1563 2071 3588 2805
καὶ ἐκβάλετε εἰς τὸ σκότος τὸ ἐξώτερον· ἐκεῖ ἔσται ὁ κλαυθμὸς
and throw out into the darkness outer, There shall be the weeping

King James Version

forth his servants to call them that were bidden to the wedding: and they would not come.
4 Again, he sent forth other servants, saying, Tell them which are bidden, Behold, I have prepared my dinner: my oxen and (my) fatlings (are) killed, and all things (are) ready: come unto the marriage.

5 But they made light of (it), and went their ways, one to his farm, another to his merchandise:

6 And the remnant took his servants, and entreated (them) spitefully, and slew (them).
7 But when the king heard (thereof), he was wroth: and he sent forth his armies, and destroyed those murderers, and burned up their city.
8 Then saith he to his servants, The wedding is ready, but they which were bidden were not worthy.

9 Go ye therefore into the highways, and as many as ye shall find, bid to the marriage.
10 So those servants went out into the highways, and gathered together all as many as they found, both bad and good: and the wedding was furnished with guests.

11 And when the king came in to see the guests, he saw there a man which had not on a wedding garment:
12 And he saith unto him, Friend, how camest thou in hither not having a wedding garment? And he was speechless.
13 Then said the king to the servants, Bind him hand and foot, and take him away, and cast (him) into outer darkness; there shall be weeping

Literal Translation | **Matthew 22:14** | **King James Version**

and gnashing of the teeth.
14 For many are called, but few chosen.

15. Then going, the Pharisees took counsel so as they might trap Him in speech.
16 And they sent to Him their disciples with the Herodians, saying, Teacher, we know that you are true, and teach the way of God in truth, and it does not concern you about anyone, for you do not look to (the) face of men.

17 Then tell us, what do you think? Is it allowed to give tribute to Caesar, or not?
18 But knowing their wickedness, Jesus said, Why do you test Me, hypocrites?

19 Show Me the tribute coin. And they brought a denarius to Him.

20 And He said to them, Whose image and inscription is this?

21 They said to Him, Caesar's. Then He said to them, Then give to Caesar the things of Caesar, and to God the things of God.

22 And hearing, they marveled. And leaving Him, they went away.

23. On that day, Sadducees, who say there is no resurrection, came to Him. And they questioned Him,

24 saying, Teacher, Moses said, If any should die not having children, his brother shall take his wife, and shall raise up seed to his brother. (Deut. 25:5)
25 And

2532 3588 1030 3588 3599 4183 1063 1526 2822 3641
καὶ ὁ βρυγμὸς τῶν ὀδόντων. 14 πολλοὶ γάρ εἰσι κλητοί, ὀλίγοι
and the gnashing of the teeth. many For are called, few
1161 1588
δὲ ἐκλεκτοί.
but chosen.

5119 4198 3588 5330 4824 2983 3704
15. Τότε πορευθέντες οἱ Φαρισαῖοι συμβούλιον ἔλαβον ὅπως
Then going the Pharisees counsel took so as
846 3802 1722 3056 2532 649 846
αὐτὸν παγιδεύσωσιν ἐν λόγῳ. 16 καὶ ἀποστέλλουσιν αὐτῷ
Him they might ensnare in discourse. And they send forth to Him
3588 3101 846 3326 3588 2265 3004
τοὺς μαθητὰς αὐτῶν μετὰ τῶν Ἡρῳδιανῶν, λέγοντες,
the disciples of them with the Herodians, saying,
1320 1492 3754 227 1488 2532 3588 3598 3588 2316
Διδάσκαλε, οἴδαμεν ὅτι ἀληθὴς εἶ, καὶ τὴν ὁδὸν τοῦ Θεοῦ
Teacher, we know that truthful you are, and the way of God
1722 225 1321 2532 3756 3199 4671 4012 3762 3756 1063
ἐν ἀληθείᾳ διδάσκεις, καὶ οὐ μέλει σοι περὶ οὐδενός, οὐ γὰρ
in truth you teach, and not it concerns you about no one; not for

991 1519 4383 444 2036 3767 2254 5101 4671
βλέπεις εἰς πρόσωπον ἀνθρώπων. 17 εἰπὲ οὖν ἡμῖν, τί σοι
you look to (the) face of men. tell Then us, what you
1380 1832 1325 2778 2541 2228 3756 1097/1161/3588
δοκεῖ; ἔξεστι δοῦναι κῆνσον Καίσαρι, ἢ οὔ; 18 γνοὺς δὲ ὁ
think: Is it allowed to give tribute to Caesar, or not? knowing But
2424 3588 4189 846 2036 5101 3165 3985 5273
Ἰησοῦς τὴν πονηρίαν αὐτῶν εἶπε, Τί με πειράζετε, ὑπο-
Jesus the wickedness of them said, Why Me you tempt, Hypo-
1925 3427 3588 3546 3588 2778 3588 1161 4374
κριταί; 19 ἐπιδείξατέ μοι τὸ νόμισμα τοῦ κήνσου. οἱ δὲ προσ-
crites? Show Me the coin of the tribute. they And brought
846 1220 2532 3004 846 5101 3588 1504
ήνεγκαν αὐτῷ δηνάριον. 20 καὶ λέγει αὐτοῖς, Τίνος ἡ εἰκὼν
to Him a denarius. And He says to them, Of whom image
3778 2532 3588 1923 3004 846 2541 5519 3004
αὕτη καὶ ἡ ἐπιγραφή; 21 λέγουσιν αὐτῷ, Καίσαρος. τότε λέγει
this and inscription? They say to Him, Of Caesar. Then He says
846 591 3767 3588 2541 2541 2532 3588 3588
αὐτοῖς, Ἀπόδοτε οὖν τὰ Καίσαρος Καίσαρι· καὶ τὰ τοῦ
to them, Give over then the things of Caesar to Caesar, and the things
2316 3588 2316 2532 191 2296 2532 863 846
Θεοῦ τῷ Θεῷ. 22 καὶ ἀκούσαντες ἐθαύμασαν· καὶ ἀφέντες αὐτὸν
of God to God. And hearing they marveled and leaving Him
565
ἀπῆλθαν.
they went away.

1722 1565 3588 2250 4334 846 4523 3588
23. Ἐν ἐκείνῃ τῇ ἡμέρᾳ προσῆλθον αὐτῷ Σαδδουκαῖοι, οἱ
In that day coming near to Him Sadducees, who
3004 3361 1511 386 2532 1905 846
λέγοντες μὴ εἶναι ἀνάστασιν, καὶ ἐπηρώτησαν αὐτὸν,
are saying not to be a resurrection. And they questioned Him,
3004 1320 3475 2036 1437 5100 599 3361
24 λέγοντες, Διδάσκαλε, Μωσῆς εἶπεν, Ἐάν τις ἀποθάνῃ μὴ
saying, Teacher, Moses said, If any (man) die not
2192 5043 1918 3588 80 846 3588 1135
ἔχων τέκνα, ἐπιγαμβρεύσει ὁ ἀδελφὸς αὐτοῦ τὴν γυναῖκα
having children, shall take to wife the brother of him the wife
846 2532 450 4690 3588 80 846 2258 1161
αὐτοῦ, καὶ ἀναστήσει σπέρμα τῷ ἀδελφῷ αὐτοῦ. 25 ἦσαν δὲ
of him, and shall raise up seed to the brother of him. were And

and gnashing of teeth.
14 For many are called, but few (are) chosen.

15. Then went the Pharisees, and took counsel how they might entangle him in (his) talk.
16 And they sent out unto him their disciples with the Herodians, saying, Master, we know that thou art true, and teachest the way of God in truth, neither carest thou for any (man): for thou regardest not the person of men.

17 Tell us therefore, What thinkest thou? Is it lawful to give tribute unto Caesar, or not?
18 But Jesus perceived their wickedness, and said, Why tempt ye me, (ye) hypocrites?

19 Shew me the tribute money. And they brought unto him a penny.
20 And he saith unto them, Whose (is) this image and superscription?
21 They say unto him, Caesar's. Then saith he unto them, Render therefore unto Caesar the things which are Caesar's; and unto God the things that are God's.
22 When they had heard (these words), they marvelled, and left him, and went their way.
23. The same day came to him the Sadducees, which say that there is no resurrection, and asked him,

24 Saying, Master, Moses said, If a man die, having no children, his brother shall marry his wife, and raise up seed unto his brother.

25 Now there were

Matthew 22:26

Literal Translation

seven brothers were with us. And having married, the first expired, and not having seed left his wife to his brother.

26 In the same way also the second, and the third, until the seven.
27 And last of all, the woman also died.
28 Then in the resurrection, of which of the seven will she be wife? For all had her.

29 And answering, Jesus said to them, You err, not knowing the Scriptures nor the power of God.
30 For in the resurrection they neither marry nor are given in marriage, but they are as the angels of God in Heaven.
31 But concerning the resurrection of the dead, have you not read that spoken to you by God, saying:
32 "I am the God of Abraham, and the God of Isaac, and the God of Jacob"? God is not God of the dead, but of the living. (Ex. 3:6)
33 And hearing, the crowds were amazed at His doctrine.

34. But hearing that He had silenced the Sadducees, the Pharisees were gathered together.
35 And one of them, a lawyer, questioned (Him), testing Him, and saying,
36 Teacher, which (is the) great commandment in the Law?
37 And Jesus said to him, "You shall love the Lord your God in all, your heart, and in all your soul, and in all your mind." (Deut. 6:5)

38 This is the first and great commandment.
39 And the second (is) like it: "You shall love your neighbor as yourself." (Lev. 19:18)
40 On these

3844 2254 2033 80 2532 3588 4413 1060 5053
παρ' ἡμῖν ἑπτὰ ἀδελφοί· καὶ ὁ πρῶτος γαμήσας ἐτελεύτησε,
with us seven brothers. And the first having married expired,

2532 3361 2192 4690 863 3588 1135 846 3588 80
καὶ μὴ ἔχων σπέρμα, ἀφῆκεν τὴν γυναῖκα αὐτοῦ τῷ ἀδελφῷ
and not having seed, left the wife of him to the brother

846 3668 2532 3588 1208 2532 3588 5154 2193 3588 2033
αὐτοῦ. 26 ὁμοίως καὶ ὁ δεύτερος, καὶ ὁ τρίτος, ἕως τῶν ἑπτά.
of him; likewise also the second, and the third, until the seven.

5305 1161 3956 599 2532/3588/1135 1722/3588/3767 386
27 ὕστερον δὲ πάντων ἀπέθανε καὶ ἡ γυνή. 28ἐν τῇ οὖν ἀναστάσει,
last And of all died also the woman. in the Then resurrection,

5101 3588 2033 2071 1135 3956 1063 2192 846
τίνος τῶν ἑπτὰ ἔσται γυνή; πάντες γὰρ ἔσχον αὐτήν.
of which of the seven will be wife? all For had her.

611 1161 3588 2424 2036 846 4105 3361 1492
29 ἀποκριθεὶς δὲ ὁ'Ιησοῦς εἶπεν αὐτοῖς, Πλανᾶσθε, μὴ εἰδότες
answering And Jesus said to them, You err, not knowing

3588 1124 3366 3588 1411 3588 2316 1722 1063 3588 386
τὰς γραφὰς, μηδὲ τὴν δύναμιν τοῦ Θεοῦ. 30 ἐν γὰρ τῇ ἀναστά-
the Scriptures, nor the power of God. in For the resurrection

3777 1060 3777 1547 235 5613 32 3588
σει οὔτε γαμοῦσιν, οὔτε ἐκγαμίζονται, ἀλλ' ὡς ἄγγελοι τοῦ
neither marry, nor are given in marriage; but as angels

2316 1722 3772 1526 4012 1161 3588 386 3588 3498
Θεοῦ ἐν οὐρανῷ εἰσι. 31 περὶ δὲ τῆς ἀναστάσεως τῶν νεκρῶν,
of God in Heaven they are. concerning But the resurrection of the dead,

3756 314 3588 4483 5213 5259 3588 2316 3004 1473
οὐκ ἀνέγνωτε τὸ ῥηθὲν ὑμῖν ὑπὸ τοῦ Θεοῦ, λέγοντος, 32 'Εγώ
not have you read that spoken to you by God, saying, I

1510 3588 2316 11 2532 3588 2316 2464 2532 3588 2316 2384
εἰμι ὁ Θεὸς 'Αβραὰμ, καὶ ὁ Θεὸς 'Ισαὰκ, καὶ ο Θεὸς 'Ιακώβ;
am the God of Abraham, and the God of Isaac, and the God of Jacob?

3756 2076 3588 2316 2316 3498 235 2198 2532 191
οὐκ ἔστιν ὁ Θεὸς Θεὸς νεκρῶν, ἀλλὰ ζώντων. 33 καὶ ἀκού
not is God God of the dead, but of (the) living. And having

3588 3793 1605 1909 3588 1322 846
σαντες οἱ ὄχλοι ἐξεπλήσσοντο ἐπὶ τῇ διδαχῇ αὐτοῦ.
heard, the crowds were amazed at the doctrine of Him.

3588 1161 5330 191 3754 5392 3588 4523
34. Οἱ δὲ Φαρισαῖοι ἀκούσαντες ὅτι ἐφίμωσε τοὺς Σαδδου-
the But Pharisees hearing that He silenced the Sadducees

4863 1909 3588 846 2532 1905 1520 1537
καίους, συνήχθησαν ἐπὶ τὸ αὐτό. 35 καὶ ἐπηρώτησεν εἷς ἐξ
were assembled together. And questioned one of

846 3544 3985 846 2532 3004 1320
αὐτῶν νομικὸς, πειράζων αὐτόν, καὶ λέγων, 36 Διδάσκαλε,
them, a lawyer, tempting Him, and saying, Teacher

4169 1785 3173 1722 3588 3551 3588 1161 2424 2036 846
ποία ἐντολὴ μεγάλη ἐν τῷ νόμῳ; 37 ὁ δὲ'Ιησοῦς εἶπεν αὐτῷ,
which command (is) great in the Law? And Jesus said to him,

25 2962 3588 2316 4675 1722 3650 3588 2588 4675
Αγαπήσεις Κύριον τὸν Θεόν σου, ἐν ὅλῃ τῇ καρδίᾳ σου,
You shall love the Lord the God of you with all the heart of you,

2532 1722 3650 3588 5590 4675 2532 1722 3650 3588 1271 4675 3778
καὶ ἐν ὅλῃ τῇ ψυχῇ σου καὶ ἐν ὅλῃ τῇ διανοίᾳ σου. 38 αὕτη
and with all the soul of you and with all the mind of you This

2076 4413 2532 3173 1785 1208 1161 3664 846
ἐστὶ πρώτη καὶ μεγάλη ἐντολή. 39 δευτέρα δὲ ὁμοία αὐτῇ,
is the first and great commandment. the second And (is) like to it,

25 3588 4139 4675 5613 4572 1722 3778 3588
'Αγαπήσεις τὸν πλησίον σου ὡς σεαυτόν. 40 ἐν ταύταις ταῖς
You shall love the neighbor of you as yourself. In these

King James Version

with us seven brethren: and the first, when he had married a wife, deceased, and, having no issue, left his wife unto his brother:

26 Likewise the second also, and the third, unto the seventh.
27 And last of all the woman died also.
28 Therefore in the resurrection whose wife shall she be of the seven? for they all had her.

29 Jesus answered and said unto them, Ye do err, not knowing the scriptures, nor the power of God.
30 For in the resurrection they neither marry, nor are given in marriage, but are as the angels of God in heaven.
31 But as touching the resurrection of the dead, have ye not read that which was spoken unto you by God, saying,
32 I am the God of Abraham, and the God of Isaac, and the God of Jacob? God is not the God of the dead, but of the living.
33 And when the multitude heard (this), they were astonished at his doctrine.

34. But when the Pharisees had heard that he had put the Sadducees to silence, they were gathered together.
35 Then one of them, (which was) a lawyer, asked (him a question), tempting him, and saying,
36 Master, which (is) the great commandment in the law?
37 Jesus said unto him, Thou shalt love the Lord thy God with all thy heart, and with all thy soul, and with all thy mind.
38 This is the first and great commandment.
39 And the second (is) like unto it, Thou shalt love thy neighbour as thyself.
40 On these

Literal Translation

two commandments all the Law and the Prophets hang.

41. But the Pharisees having been gathered, Jesus questioned them,
42 saying, What do you think about the Christ? Whose son is He? They say to Him, David's.
43 He said to them, Then how does David in Spirit call Him Lord, saying,
44 "The Lord said to my Lord, Sit on My right until I place Your enemies as a footstool for Your feet"? (Ps. 110:1)

45 Then if David calls Him Lord, how is He his son?
46 And no one was able to answer Him a word, nor did anyone dare from that day to question Him any more.

Matthew 22:41

1417 1785 3650 3588 3551 2532 3588 4396 2910
δυσὶν ἐντολαῖς ὅλος ὁ νόμος καὶ οἱ προφῆται κρέμαται.
two commandments all the Law and the Prophets hang.

4863 1161 3588 5330 1905 846 3588
41. Συνηγμένων δὲ τῶν Φαρισαίων, ἐπηρώτησεν αὐτοὺς ὁ
having been assembled But the Pharisees questioned them

2424 3004 5101 5213 1380 4012 3588 5547 5101 5207
Ἰησοῦς, 42 λέγων, Τί ὑμῖν δοκεῖ περὶ τοῦ Χριστοῦ; τίνος υἱός
Jesus, saying, What to you seems about the Christ? Of whom son

2076 3004 846 3588 1138 3004 846 4459 3767
ἐστι; λέγουσιν αὐτῷ, Τοῦ Δαβίδ. 43 λέγει αὐτοῖς, Πῶς οὖν
is He? They say to Him, Of David. He says to them, How then

1138 1722 4151 2962 846 2564 3004 2036 3588
Δαβὶδ ἐν πνεύματι Κύριον αὐτὸν καλεῖ, λέγων, 44 Εἶπεν ὁ
David in (the) Spirit Lord Him calls, saying, Said the

2962 3588 2962 3450 2521 1537 1188 3450 2193 302 5087 3588
Κύριος τῷ κυρίῳ μου, Κάθου ἐκ δεξιῶν μου, ἕως ἂν θῶ τοὺς
Lord to the Lord of me, Sit off the right of Me until I should put the

2190 4675 5286 3588 4228 4675 1487 3767 1138
ἐχθρούς σου ὑποπόδιον τῶν ποδῶν σου; 45 εἰ οὖν Δαβὶδ
hostile (ones) of You (as) a footstool of the feet of You? If, then, David

2564 846 2962 4459 5207 846 2076 2532 3762 1410
καλεῖ αὐτὸν Κύριον, πῶς υἱὸς αὐτοῦ ἐστι; 46 καὶ οὐδεὶς ἐδύνατο
calls Him Lord, how a son of him is He? And no one was able

846 611 3056 3761 5111 5100 575 1565 3588
αὐτῷ ἀποκριθῆναι λόγον· οὐδὲ ἐτόλμησέ τις ἀπ' ἐκείνης τῆς
Him to answer a word, nor dared anyone from that

2250 1905 846 3765
ἡμέρας ἐπερωτῆσαι αὐτὸν οὐκέτι.
day to question Him no more.

King James Version

two commandments hang all the law and the prophets.

41. While the Pharisees were gathered together, Jesus asked them,
42 Saying, What think ye of Christ? whose son is he? They say unto him, (The Son) of David.
43 He saith unto them, How then doth David in spirit call him Lord, saying,
44 The LORD said unto my Lord, Sit thou on my right hand, till I make thine enemies thy footstool?
45 If David then call him Lord, how is he his son?
46 And no man was able to answer him a word, neither durst any (man) from that day forth ask him any more (questions).

Matthew 23

1. Then Jesus spoke to the crowd and to His disciples,

2 saying, The scribes and the Pharisees sat down on Moses' seat.
3 Then all things, whatever they tell you to keep, keep and do. But do not do according to their works, for they say, and do not do.

4 For they bind heavy and hard to bear burdens, and lay (them) on the shoulders of men, but they do not desire to move them with their finger.

5 And they do all their works to be seen by men; even they broaden their phylacteries and enlarge the fringes of their robes.

6 And they love

Matthew 23

5119 3588 2424 2980 3588 3793 2532 3588 3101
1. Τότε ὁ Ἰησοῦς ἐλάλησε τοῖς ὄχλοις καὶ τοῖς μαθηταῖς
Then Jesus spoke to the crowd and to the disciples

846 3004 1909 3588 3475 2515 2523 3588
αὐτοῦ, 2 λέγων, Ἐπὶ τῆς Μωσέως καθέδρας ἐκάθισαν οἱ
of Him, saying, On the of Moses seat sat the

1122 2532 3588 5330 3956 3967 3745 302 2036
γραμματεῖς καὶ οἱ Φαρισαῖοι. 3 πάντα οὖν ὅσα ἂν εἴπωσιν
scribes and the Pharisees. All things then whatever they tell

5213 5083 5083 2532 4160 2596 1161 3588 2041 846 3361
ὑμῖν τηρεῖν, τηρεῖτε καὶ ποιεῖτε· κατὰ δὲ τὰ ἔργα αὐτῶν μὴ
you to keep, keep and do; according to but the works of them not

4160 3004 1063 2532 3756 4160 1195 1063 5413
ποιεῖτε, λέγουσι γὰρ καὶ οὐ ποιοῦσι. 4 δεσμεύουσι γὰρ φορτία
do. they say For and not do. they bind For burdens

926 2532 1419 2532 2007 1909 3588 5606
βαρέα καὶ δυσβάστακτα, καὶ ἐπιτιθέασιν ἐπὶ τοὺς ὤμους
heavy, and hard to bear, and lay (them) on the shoulders

3588 444 3588 1161 1147 846 3756 2309 2795
τῶν ἀνθρώπων, τῷ δὲ δακτύλῳ αὐτῶν οὐ θέλουσι κινῆσαι
of men, with the But finger of them not they desire to move

846 3956 1161 3588 2041 846 4160 4314 3588 2300
αὐτά. 5 πάντα δὲ τὰ ἔργα αὐτῶν ποιοῦσι πρὸς τὸ θεαθῆναι
them. all But the works of them they do in order to be seen

3588 444 4115 1161 3588 5440 846 2532
τοῖς ἀνθρώποις· πλατύνουσι δὲ τὰ φυλακτήρια αὐτῶν, καὶ
by men. they broaden And the phylacteries of them, and

3170 3588 2899 3588 2440 846 5368 5037
μεγαλύνουσι τὰ κράσπεδα τῶν ἱματίων αὐτῶν· 6 φιλοῦσί τε
enlarge the fringes of the garments of them. they love And

Matthew 23

1. Then spake Jesus to the multitude, and to his disciples,

2 Saying, The scribes and the Pharisees sit in Moses' seat:
3 All therefore whatsoever they bid you observe, (that) observe and do; but do not ye after their works: for they say, and do not.

4 For they bind heavy burdens and grievous to be borne, and lay (them) on men's shoulders; but they (themselves) will not move them with one of their fingers.

5 But all their works they do for to be seen of men: they make broad their phylacteries, and enlarge the borders of their garments,

6 And love

Literal Translation **Matthew 23:7** ***King James Version***

the first couch in the
suppers, and the first
seats in the synagogues,
7 and the greetings in
the markets, and to be
called by men, Rabbi,
Rabbi.
8 But do not you be
called Rabbi, for One is
your Leader, the Christ,
and you are all brothers.

3588 4411 1722 3588 1173 2532 3588 4410
τὴν πρωτοκλισίαν ἐν τοῖς δείπνοις, καὶ τὰς πρωτοκαθεδρίας
the first couch in the suppers, and the first seats
1722 3588 4864 2532 3588 783 1722 3588 58
ἐν ταῖς συναγωγαῖς, 7 καὶ τοὺς ἀσπασμοὺς ἐν ταῖς ἀγοραῖς,
in the synagogues, and the greetings in the markets,
2532 2564 5259 3588 444 4461 4461 5210 1161 3361
καὶ καλεῖσθαι ὑπὸ τῶν ἀνθρώπων, Ῥαββι, Ραββι. 8 ὑμεῖς δὲ μὴ
and to be called by men, Rabbi, Rabbi! you But not
2564 4461 1520 1063 2076 5216 3588 2519 3588 5547
κληθῆτε ῥαββί· εἷς γάρ ἐστιν ὑμῶν ὁ καθηγητής, ὁ Χριστός·
be called Rabbi; one For is of you the leader, the Christ,

the uppermost rooms at
feasts, and the chief
seats in the synagogues,
7 And greetings in the
markets, and to be
called of men, Rabbi,
Rabbi.
8 But be not ye called
Rabbi: for one is your
Master, (even) Christ;
and all ye are brethren.

9 And call no one your
father on earth, for One
is your Father, the (One)
in Heaven.

3956 1161 5210 80 2075 2532 3962 3361 2564 5216
πάντες δὲ ὑμεῖς ἀδελφοί ἐστε. 9 καὶ πατέρα μὴ καλέσητε ὑμῶν
all and of you brothers are. And Father not call of you
1909 3588 1093 1520 1063 2076 3588 3962 5216 3588 1722 3588 3772
ἐπὶ τῆς γης· εἷς γάρ ἐστιν ὁ πατὴρ ὑμῶν, ὁ ἐν τοῖς οὐρανοῖς.
on the earth, One for is the Father of you, the (One) in Heaven.

9 And call no (man)
your father upon the
earth: for one is your Fa-
ther, which is in heaven.

10 Nor be called lead-
ers, for One is your
Leader, the Christ.
11 But the greater of you
shall be your servant.
12 And whoever will
exalt himself shall be
humbled, and whoever
will humble himself
shall be exalted.

3366 2564 2519 1520 1063 5216 2076 3588 2519
10 μηδὲ κληθῆτε καθηγηταί· εἷς γὰρ ὑμῶν ἐστιν ὁ καθηγητής,
Neither be called leaders, One for of you is the Leader,
3588 5547 3588 1161 3187 5216 2071 5216 1249 3748 1161
ὁ Χριστός. 11 ὁ δὲ μείζων ὑμῶν ἔσται ὑμῶν διάκονος. 12 ὅστις δὲ
the Christ. the And greater of you shall be of you a servant. whoever But
5312 1438 5013 2532 3748 5013
ὑψώσει ἑαυτὸν, ταπεινωθήσεται· καὶ ὅστις ταπεινώσει
will exalt himself shall be humbled; and whoever will humble
1438 5312
ἑαυτὸν, ὑψωθήσεται.
himself shall be exalted.

10 Neither be ye called
masters: for one is your
Master, (even) Christ.
11 But he that is greatest
among you shall be
your servant.
12 And whosoever
shall exalt himself shall
be abased; and he that
shall humble himself
shall be exalted.

13. But woe to you,
scribes and Pharisees,
hypocrites! Because
you shut up the king-
dom of Heaven before
men; for you do not en-
ter, nor do you allow
those entering to go in.

3759 1161 5213 1122 2532 5330 5273 3754
13. Οὐαὶ δὲ ὑμῖν, γραμματεῖς καὶ Φαρισαῖοι, ὑποκριταί, ὅτι
woe But to you, scribes and Pharisees, hypocrites! Because
2808 3588 932 3588 3772 1715 3588 444
κλείετε τὴν βασιλείαν τῶν οὐρανῶν ἔμπροσθεν τῶν ἀνθρώ-
you shut the kingdom of the heavens before men
5210 1063 3756 1525 3761 3588 1525
πων· ὑμεῖς γὰρ οὐκ εἰσέρχεσθε, οὐδὲ τοὺς εἰσερχομένους
you for not do enter, nor the (ones) entering
863 1525
ἀφίετε εἰσελθεῖν.
do you allow to enter.

13. But woe unto you,
scribes and Pharisees,
hypocrites! for ye shut
up the kingdom of
heaven against men: for
ye neither go in (your-
selves), neither suffer ye
them that are entering to
go in.

14 Woe to you, scribes
and Pharisees, hypo-
crites! Because you de-
vour the houses of wid-
ows, and pray at length
as a pretext. Because of
this you will receive
more abundant judg-
ment.

3759 5213 1122 2532 5330 5273 3754
14 Οὐαὶ ὑμῖν, γραμματεῖς, καὶ Φαρισαῖοι, ὑποκριταί, ὅτι
Woe to you, scribes and Pharisees, hypocrites! Because
2719 3588 3614 3588 5503 2532 4392 3117
κατεσίετε τὰς οἰκίας τῶν χηρῶν, καὶ προφάσει μακρὰ
you devour the houses of the widows, and as a pretext (are) long
4336 1223 5124 2983 4055 2917
προσευχόμενοι· διὰ τοῦτο λήψεσθε περισσότερον κρίμα.
praying. Because of this you will receive more abundant judgment.

14 Woe unto you,
scribes and Pharisees,
hypocrites! for ye de-
vour widows' houses,
and for a pretence make
long prayer: therefore
ye shall receive the
greater damnation.

15 Woe to you, scribes
and Pharisees, hypo-
crites! Because you go
about the sea and the dry
(land) to make one
proselyte; and when he
has become so, you
make him twofold
more a son of Hell than
yourselves.

3759 5213 1122 2532 5330 5273 3754
15. Οὐαὶ ὑμῖν, γραμματεῖς καὶ Φαρισαῖοι, ὑποκριταί, ὅτι
Woe to you, scribes and Pharisees, hypocrites! Because
4013 3588 2281 2532 3588 3584 4160 1520 4339
περιάγετε τὴν θάλασσαν καὶ τὴν ξηρὰν ποιῆσαι ἕνα προσή-
you go about the sea and the dry (land) to make one prose-
2532 3752 1096 4160 846 5207 1067
λυτον, καὶ ὅταν γένηται ποιεῖτε αὐτὸν υἱὸν γεέννης
lyte, and when he becomes you make him a son of Gehenna
1362 5216
διπλότερον ὑμῶν.
two fold more (than) you.

15 Woe unto you,
scribes and Pharisees,
hypocrites! for ye com-
pass sea and land to
make one proselyte,
and when he is made, ye
make him twofold
more the child of hell
than yourselves.

Literal Translation **Matthew 23:16** *King James Version*

16 Woe to you, blind guides, who say, Whoever swears by the temple, it is nothing; but whoever swears by the gold of the temple is a debtor.
17 Fools and blind! For what is greater, the gold, or the temple that sanctifies the gold?
18 And (you say), Whoever swears by the altar, it is nothing; but whoever swears by the gift on it, (he is) a debtor.
19 Fools and blind! For which (is) greater, the gift, or the altar that sanctifies the gift?
20 Then the (one) swearing by the altar swears by it, and by all things on it.

3759 5213 3595 5185 3588 3004 3739 302 3660 1722
16. Οὐαὶ ὑμῖν, ὁδηγοὶ τυφλοὶ, οἱ λέγοντες, "Ὃς ἂν ὀμόσῃ ἐν
Woe to you, leaders blind, the (ones) saying, Whoever swears by
3588 3485 3762 2076 3739 1161 302 3660 1722 3588 5557 3588 3485
τῷ ναῷ, οὐδέν ἐστιν· ὃς δ' ἂν ὀμόσῃ ἐν τῷ χρυσῷ τοῦ ναοῦ
the temple, nothing it is, who but ever swears by the gold of the temple
3784 3474 2532 5185 5101 1063 3187 2076 3588 5557 2228
ὀφείλει. 17 μωροὶ καὶ τυφλοί· τίς γὰρ μείζων ἐστίν, ὁ χρυσὸς, ἢ
is a debtor. Fools and blind! what For greater is, the gold or
3588 3485 3588 37 3588 5557 2532 3739 1437 3660 1722 3588
ὁ ναὸς ὁ ἁγιάζων τὸν χρυσόν; 18 καί, "Ὃς ἐὰν ὀμόσῃ ἐν τῷ
the temple sanctifying the gold? And, Whoever swears by the
2379 3762 2076 3739 3588 302 3660 1722 3588 1435 3588
θυσιαστηρίῳ, οὐδέν ἐστιν· ὃς δ' ἂν ὀμόσῃ ἐν τῷ δώρῳ τῷ
altar, nothing it is, who but ever swears by the gift
1883 846 3784 3474 2532 5185 5101 1063 3173
ἐπάνω αὐτοῦ ὀφείλει. 19 μωροὶ καὶ τυφλοί· τί γὰρ μεῖζον,
on it is a debtor. Fools and blind! what For is greater,
3588 1435 2228 3588 2379 3588 37 3588 1435 3588 3767
τὸ δῶρον, ἢ τὸ θυσιαστήριον τὸ ἁγιάζον τὸ δῶρον; 20 ὁ οὖν
the gift, or the altar sanctifying the gift? he Then
3660 1722 3588 2379 3660 1722 846 2532 1722 3956 3588
ὀμόσας ἐν τῷ θυσιαστηρίῳ ὀμνύει ἐν αὐτῷ καὶ ἐν πᾶσι τοῖς
swearing by the altar swears by it and by all the things

16 Woe unto you, (ye) blind guides, which say, Whosoever shall swear by the temple, it is nothing; but whosoever shall swear by the gold of the temple, he is a debtor!
17 (Ye) fools and blind: for whether is greater, the gold, or the temple that sanctifieth the gold?
18 And, Whosoever shall swear by the altar, it is nothing; but whosoever sweareth by the gift that is upon it, he is guilty.
19 (Ye) fools and blind: for whether (is) greater, the gift, or the altar that sanctifieth the gift?
20 Whoso therefore shall swear by the altar, sweareth by it, and by all things thereon.

21 And the (one) swearing by the temple swears by it, and by the One dwelling in it.
22 And the (one) swearing by Heaven swears by the throne of God, and by the (One) sitting on it.

1883 846 2532 3588 3660 1722 3588 3485 3660 1722 846 2532 1722
ἐπάνω αὐτοῦ· 21 καὶ ὁ ὀμόσας ἐν τῷ ναῷ ὀμνύει ἐν αὐτῷ καὶ ἐν
on it; and he swearing by the temple swears by it and by
3588 2730 846 2532 3588 3660 1722 3588 3772 3660
τῷ κατοικοῦντι αὐτόν· 22 καὶ ὁ ὀμόσας ἐν τῷ οὐρανῷ ὀμνύει
the (One) inhabiting it. And he swearing by Heaven swears
1722 3588 2362 3588 2316 2532 1722 3588 2521 1883 846
ἐν τῷ θρόνῳ τοῦ Θεοῦ καὶ ἐν τῷ καθημένῳ ἐπάνω αὐτοῦ.
by the throne of God and by the (One) sitting on it.

21 And whoso shall swear by the temple, sweareth by it, and by him that dwelleth therein.
22 And he that shall swear by heaven, sweareth by the throne of God, and by him that sitteth thereon.

23 Woe to you, scribes and Pharisees, hypocrites! For you pay tithes of mint and dill and cummin, and you have left aside the weightier things of the Law: judgment, and mercy, and faith. It was right to do these, and not to have left those aside.

3759 5213 1122 2532 5330 5273 3754
23. Οὐαὶ ὑμῖν, γραμματεῖς καὶ Φαρισαῖοι, ὑποκριταί, ὅτι
Woe to you, scribes and Pharisees, hypocrites! Because
586 3588 2238 2532 3588 432 2532 3588 2951
ἀποδεκατοῦτε τὸ ἡδύοσμον καὶ τὸ ἄνηθον καὶ τὸ κύμινον,
you tithe the mint and the dill and the cummim,
2532 863 3588 926 3588 3551 3588 2920 2532 3588
καὶ ἀφήκατε τὰ βαρύτερα τοῦ νόμου, τὴν κρίσιν καὶ τὸν
and you have left the weightier things of the Law, judgment and
1656 2532 3588 4102 5023 1163 4160 2548 3361
ἔλεον καὶ τὴν πίστιν· ταῦτα ἔδει ποιῆσαι, κἀκεῖνα μὴ
mercy and faith. These things it is right to do, and those not

23 Woe unto you, scribes and Pharisees, hypocrites! for ye pay tithe of mint and anise and cummin, and have omitted the weightier (matters) of the law, judgment, mercy, and faith: these ought ye to have done, and not to leave the other undone.

24 Blind guides, straining out the gnat, but swallowing the camel!

863 3595 5185 3588 1368 3588 2971 3588 1161
ἀφιέναι. 24 ὁδηγοὶ τυφλοί, οἱ διυλίζοντες τὸν κώνωπα, τὴν δὲ
to leave. leaders Blind, the (ones) straining out the gnat, the but
2574 2666
κάμηλον καταπίνοντες.
camel swallowing.

24 (Ye) blind guides, which strain at a gnat, and swallow a camel.

25 Woe to you, scribes and Pharisees, hypocrites! Because you cleanse the outside of the cup and of the dish, but within they are full of robbery and self-indulgence.
26 Blind Pharisee! First cleanse the inside of the cup and the dish,

3759 5213 1122 2532 5330 5273 3754
25. Οὐαὶ ὑμῖν, γραμματεῖς καὶ Φαρισαῖοι, ὑποκριταί, ὅτι
Woe to you, scribes and Pharisees, hypocrites! Because
2511 3588 1855 3588 4221 2532 3588 3953
καθαρίζετε τὸ ἔξωθεν τοῦ ποτηρίου καὶ τῆς παροψίδος,
you cleanse the outside of the cup and the dish,
2081 1161 1073 1537 724 2532 192 5330 5185
ἔσωθεν δὲ γέμουσιν ἐξ ἁρπαγῆς καὶ ἀκρασίας. 26 Φαρισαῖε τυφλέ,
within but they are full of robbery and self-indulgence. Pharisees Blind,
2511 4412 3588 1787 3588 4221 2532 3588 3953
καθάρισον πρῶτον τὸ ἐντὸς τοῦ ποτηρίου, καὶ τῆς παροψί-
cleanse first the inside of the cup and the dish,

25 Woe unto you, scribes and Pharisees, hypocrites! for ye make clean the outside of the cup and of the platter, but within they are full of extortion and excess.
26 (Thou) blind Pharisee, cleanse first that (which is) within the cup and platter,

Literal Translation **Matthew 23:27** *King James Version*

that the outside of them may become clean also.

27 Woe to you, scribes and Pharisees, hypocrites! Because you are like graves being whitewashed, which outwardly indeed appear beautiful, but within are full of bones of (the) dead, and of all uncleanness.

28 So you also indeed outwardly appear righteous to men, but within are full of hypocrisy and lawlessness.

29 Woe to you, scribes and Pharisees, hypocrites! Because you build the graves of the prophets, and adorn the monuments of the righteous.
30 And you say, If we had been in the days of our fathers, we would not have been sharers with them in the blood of the prophets.

31 So you witness to yourselves that you are the sons of those who murdered the prophets.
32 And you fill up the measure of your fathers.
33 Serpents! Offspring of vipers! How shall you escape from the judgment of Hell?
34 Because of this, behold, I send to you prophets and wise ones and scribes. And (some) of them you will kill and crucify, and (some) of them you will flog in your synagogues and persecute from city to city;

35 so that should come on you all (the) righteous blood poured out on the earth, from the blood of righteous Abel to the blood of Zechariah the son of Berechiah whom

2443 1096 2532 3588 1623 846 2813
δος, ἵνα γένηται καὶ τὸ ἐκτὸς αὐτῶν καθαρόν.
that may become also the outside of them clean.

3759 5213 1122 2532 5330 5273 3754
27. Οὐαὶ ὑμῖν, γραμματεῖς καὶ Φαρισαῖοι, ὑποκριταί, ὅτι
Woe to you, scribes and Pharisees, hypocrites! Because

3945 5028 2867 3748 1855 3303
παρομοιάζετε τάφοις κεκονιαμένοις, οἵτινες ἔξωθεν μὲν
you are like graves being whitewashed, who outwardly indeed

5316 5611 2081 1161 1073 3747 3498 2532
φαίνονται ὡραῖοι, ἔσωθεν δὲ γέμουσιν ὀστέων νεκρῶν καὶ
appear beautiful, within but are full of bones of the dead and

3956 167 3779 2532 5210 1855 3303 5316 3588
πάσης ἀκαθαρσίας. 28 οὕτω καὶ ὑμεῖς ἔξωθεν μὲν φαίνεσθε τοῖς
all uncleanness. So also you outwardly indeed appear

444 1342 2081 1161 3324 2075 5212 2532
ἀνθρώποις δίκαιοι, ἔσωθεν δέ μεστοὶ ἐστε ὑποκρίσεως καὶ
to men righteous, within but full are of hypocrisy and

458
ἀνομίας.
lawlessness.

3759 5213 1122 2532 5330 5273 3754
29. Οὐαὶ ὑμῖν, γραμματεῖς καὶ Φαρισαῖοι, ὑποκριταί, ὅτι
Woe to you, scribes and Pharisees, hypocrites! Because

3618 3588 5028 3588 4396 2532 2885 3588
οἰκοδομεῖτε τοὺς τάφους τῶν προφητῶν, καὶ κοσμεῖτε τὰ
you build the graves of the prophets, and adorn the

3419 3588 1342 2532 3004 1487 2258 1722 3588 2250
μνημεῖα τῶν δικαίων, 30 καὶ λέγετε, Εἰ ἤμεθα ἐν ταῖς ἡμέραις
monuments of the righteous, and say, If we had been in the days

3588 3962 2257 3756 302 2258 2844 846 1722 3588
τῶν πατέρων ἡμῶν, οὐκ ἂν ἤμεν κοινωνοὶ αὐτῶν ἐν τῷ
of the fathers of us, not would we have been sharers of them in the

129 3588 4396 5620 3140 1438 3754 5207
αἵματι τῶν προφητῶν. 31 ὥστε μαρτυρεῖτε ἑαυτοῖς ὅτι υἱοί
blood of the prophets. So you witness to yourselves that sons

2075 3588 5407 3588 4396 2532 5210 4137
ἐστε τῶν φονευσάντων τοὺς προφήτας· 32 καὶ ὑμεῖς πληρώσατε
you are of the ones murdering the prophets, and you fill up

3588 3358 3588 3962 5216 3789 1081 2191
τὸ μέτρον τῶν πατέρων ὑμῶν. 33 ὄφεις, γεννήματα ἐχιδνῶν,
the measure of the fathers of you. Serpents! Offspring of vipers!

4459 5343 575 3588 2920 3588 1067 1223 5124 2400
πῶς φύγητε ἀπὸ τῆς κρίσεως τῆς γεέννης; 34 διὰ τοῦτο, ἰδού,
How escape you from the judgment of Gehenna? Through this, behold,

1473 649 4314 5209 4396 2532 4680 2532 1122
ἐγὼ ἀποστέλλω πρὸς ὑμᾶς προφήτας καὶ σοφοὺς καὶ γραμ-
I send to you prophets and sophisticated and scribes

2532 1537 846 615 2532 4717 2532 1537
ματεῖς· καὶ ἐξ αὐτῶν ἀποκτενεῖτε καὶ σταυρώσετε, καὶ ἐξ
and of them you will kill and crucify, and of

846 3146 1722 3588 4864 5216 2532 1377
αὐτῶν μαστιγώσετε ἐν ταῖς συναγωγαῖς ὑμῶν καὶ διώξετε
them you will scourge in the synagogues of you, and persecute

575 4172 1519 4172 3704 2064 1909 5209 3956 129 1342
ἀπὸ πόλεως εἰς πόλιν· 35 ὅπως ἔλθῃ ἐφ' ὑμᾶς πᾶν αἷμα δίκαιον
from city to city; so that comes on you all blood righteous

1632 1909 3588 1093 575 3588 129 6 3588
ἐκχυνόμενον ἐπὶ τῆς γῆς, ἀπὸ τοῦ αἵματος Ἄβελ τοῦ
being poured out on the earth from the blood of Abel the

1342 2193 3588 129 2197 5207 914 3739
δικαίου, ἕως τοῦ αἵματος Ζαχαρίου υἱοῦ Βαραχίου, ὃν
righteous until the blood of Zechariah (the) son of Barachiah, whom

that the outside of them may be clean also.

27 Woe unto you, scribes and Pharisees, hypocrites! for ye are like unto whited sepulchres, which indeed appear beautiful outward, but are within full of dead (men's) bones, and of all uncleanness.

28 Even so ye also outwardly appear righteous unto men, but within ye are full of hypocrisy and iniquity.

29 Woe unto you, scribes and Pharisees, hypocrites! because ye build the tombs of the prophets, and garnish the sepulchres of the righteous,
30 And say, If we had been in the days of our fathers, we would not have been partakers with them in the blood of the prophets.

31 Wherefore ye be witnesses unto yourselves, that ye are the children of them which killed the prophets.
32 Fill ye up then the measure of your fathers.
33 (Ye) serpents, (ye) generation of vipers, how can ye escape the damnation of hell?
34 Wherefore, behold, I send unto you prophets, and wise men, and scribes: and (some) of them ye shall kill and crucify; and (some) of them shall ye scourge in your synagogues, and persecute (them) from city to city:

35 That upon you may come all the righteous blood shed upon the earth, from the blood of righteous Abel unto the blood of Zacharias son of Barachias, whom

Literal Translation

you murdered between the temple and the altar.
36 Truly I say to you, All these things will come on this generation.

37 Jerusalem, Jerusalem, the (one) killing the prophets and stoning those sent to her. How often I desired to gather your children in the way a bird gathers her young under (her) wings! And you did not desire (it).

38 Behold, your house is being left to you desolate. (Jer. 22:5)
39 For I say to you, In no way shall you see Me from now on, until you say, "Blessed (is) He who comes in (the) name of (the) Lord." (Ps. 118:26)

Matthew 23:36

5407 3342 3588 3485 2532 3588 2379 281
ἐφονεύσατε μεταξὺ τοῦ ναοῦ καὶ τοῦ θυσιαστηρίου. 36 ἀμὴν
you murdered between the temple and the altar. Truly

3004 5213 2240 5023 3956 1909 3588 1074 3778
λέγω ὑμῖν, ἥξει ταῦτα πάντα ἐπὶ τὴν γενεὰν ταύτην.
I say to you, will come these things all on generation this.

2419 2419 3588 615 3588 4396
37. Ἰερουσαλὴμ, Ἰερουσαλήμ, ἡ ἀποκτείνουσα τοὺς προφή-
Jerusalem, Jerusalem, the (one) killing the prophets

2532 3036 3588 649 4314 846
τας καὶ λιθοβολοῦσα τοὺς ἀπεσταλμένους πρὸς αὐτήν,
and stoning the (ones) sent to her,

4212 2309 1996 3588 5043 4675 3739 5158
ποσάκις ἠθέλησα ἐπισυναγαγεῖν τὰ τέκνα σου, ὃν τρόπον
how often I desired to gather together the children of you in the way

1996 3733 3588 3556 1438 5259 3588 4420 2532
ἐπισυνάγει ὄρνις τὰ νοσσία ἑαυτῆς ὑπὸ τὰς πτέρυγας, καὶ
gathers together a bird the young of her under the wings, and

3756 2309 2400 863 5213 3588 3624 5216 2048
οὐκ ἠθελήσατε. 38 ἰδοὺ, ἀφίεται ὑμῖν ὁ οἶκος ὑμῶν ἔρημος.
not you desired. Behold, is being left to you the house of you desolate;

3004 1063 5213 3756 3361 3165 1492 575 737 2193 302
39 λέγω γὰρ ὑμῖν, οὐ μή με ἴδητε ἀπ' ἄρτι, ἕως ἂν
I say For to you, not at all Me you will see from now until you

2036 2127 3588 2064 1722 3686 2962
εἴπητε, Εὐλογημένος ὁ ἐρχόμενος ἐν ὀνόματι Κυρίου.
may say, Blessed (is) the (One) coming in (the) name of the Lord.

King James Version

ye slew between the temple and the altar.
36 Verily I say unto you, All these things shall come upon this generation.

37 O Jerusalem, Jerusalem, (thou) that killest the prophets, and stonest them which are sent unto thee, how often would I have gathered thy children together, even as a hen gathereth her chickens under (her) wings, and ye would not!

38 Behold, your house is left unto you desolate.

39 For I say unto you, Ye shall not see me henceforth, till ye shall say, Blessed (is) he that cometh in the name of the Lord.

Matthew 24

Literal Translation

1. And going out, Jesus went away from the temple. And His disciples came to show Him the buildings of the temple.

2 But Jesus said to them, Do you not see all these things? Truly I say to you, There will not at all be left one stone on a stone which in no way will not be thrown down.

3. And He was sitting on the Mount of Olives, the disciples came to Him privately, saying, Tell us, when will these things be? And, What (is) the sign of Your coming and of the end of the age?

4 And answering, Jesus said to them, See (that) not any misleads you.

5 For many will come in My name, saying, I am the Christ, and

Matthew 24

2532 1831 3588 2424 4198 575 3588 2411 2532
1. Καὶ ἐξελθὼν ὁ Ἰησους ἐπορεύετο ἀπὸ τοῦ ἱεροῦ· καὶ
And going forth Jesus went away from the temple and

4334 3588 3101 846 1925 846 3588 3619
προσῆλθον οἱ μαθηταὶ αὐτοῦ ἐπιδεῖξαι αὐτῷ τὰς οἰκοδομὰς
came up the disciples of Him to show Him the buildings

3588 2411 3588 1161 2424 2036 846 3756 991 3956
τοῦ ἱεροῦ. 2 ὁ δὲ Ἰησοῦς εἶπεν αὐτοῖς, Οὐ βλέπετε πάντα
of the Temple. And Jesus said to them, Not you see all

5023 281 3004 5213 3756 3361 863 5602 3037 1909 3037 3739
ταῦτα; ἀμὴν λέγω ὑμῖν, οὐ μὴ ἀφεθῇ ὧδε λίθος ἐπὶ λίθον, ὃς
these? Truly I say to you, Not at all will be left here stone on stone which

3756 3361 2647
οὐ μὴ καταλυθήσεται.
not at all shall be thrown down.

2521 1161 846 1909 3588 3735 3588 1636 4334
3. Καθημένου δὲ αὐτοῦ ἐπὶ τοῦ ὄρους τῶν ἐλαιῶν, προσῆλ-
sitting And He on the Mount of the Olives, came

846 3588 3101 2596 2398 3004 2036 2254 4129
θον αὐτῷ οἱ μαθηταὶ κατ' ἰδίαν, λέγοντες, Εἰπὲ ἡμῖν, πότε
up to Him the disciples privately, saying, Tell us, when

5023 2071 2532 5101 3588 4592 3588 4674 3952 2532 3588
ταῦτα ἔσται, καὶ τί τὸ σημεῖον τῆς σῆς παρουσίας, καὶ τῆς
these things will be, and what (is) the sign of your coming, and of the

4930 3588 165 2532 611 3588 2424 2036 846
συντελείας τοῦ αἰῶνος. 4 καὶ ἀποκριθεὶς ὁ Ἰησοῦς εἶπεν αὐτοῖς,
termination of the age? And answering Jesus said to them

911 3361 5100 5209 4105 4183 1063 2064 1909
Βλέπετε, μή τις ὑμᾶς πλανήσῃ. 5 πολλοὶ γὰρ ἐλεύσονται ἐπὶ
See (that) not any of you misleads. many For will come on

3588 3686 3450 3004 1473 1510 3588 5547 2532 4183
τῷ ὀνόματί μου, λέγοντες, Ἐγώ εἰμι ὁ Χριστός· καὶ πολλοὺς
the name of Me, saying, I am the Christ, and many

King James Version

Matthew 24

1. And Jesus went out, and departed from the temple: and his disciples came to (him) for to shew him the buildings of the temple.

2 And Jesus said unto them, See ye not all these things? Verily I say unto you, There shall not be left here one stone upon another, that shall not be thrown down.

3. And as he sat upon the mount of Olives, the disciples came unto him privately, saying, Tell us, when shall these things be? and what (shall be) the sign of thy coming, and of the end of the world?

4 And Jesus answered and said unto them, Take heed that no man deceive you.
5 For many shall come in my name, saying, I am Christ; and

Literal Translation — **Matthew 24:6** — *King James Version*

(they) will cause many to err.
6 But you are going to hear of wars and rumors of wars. See, do not be terrified. For all things must happen, but the end is not yet.
7 For nation will be raised against nation, and kingdom against kingdom; and there will be famines and plagues and earthquakes against (many) places.
8 But all these (are) a beginning of throes.
9 Then they will deliver you up to affliction, and will kill you, and you will be hated by all nations for My name's sake.

10 And then many will be ensnared, and they will deliver up one another and will hate one another.
11 And many false prophets will be raised and will cause many to err.
12 And because lawlessness shall have been multiplied, the love of the many will grow cold.
13 But the (one) who endures to (the) end, that one will be kept safe.
14 And this gospel of the Kingdom shall be preached in all the earth for a testimony to all the nations, and then will come the end.

15 Then when you see the abomination of desolation, which was spoken of by Daniel the prophet, standing in (the) holy place (the (one) reading, let him understand),
16 then let those in Judea flee on the mountains;
17 the (one) on the housetop, let him not come down to take anything out of his house;
18 and the (one) in the field, let him not turn back to take his garment.
19 But woe to the (woman) having (a child) in womb, and

4105 3195 1161 191 4171 2532 189
πλανήσουσι. 6 μελλήσετε δὲ ἀκούειν πολέμους καὶ ἀκοὰς
will cause to err. you are going But to hear of wars and rumors

4171 3708 3361 2360 1163 1063 3956 1096 235
πολέμων· ὁρᾶτε, μὴ θροεῖσθε· δεῖ γὰρ πάντα γενέσθαι· ἀλλ᾽
of wars. See, not do be not terrified; must for all these things happen. But

3768 2076 3588 5056 1453 1063 1484 1909 1484 2532
οὔπω ἐστὶ τὸ τέλος. 7 ἐγερθήσεται γὰρ ἔθνος ἐπὶ ἔθνος, καὶ
not yet is the end. will be raised For nation against nation, and

932 1909 932 2532 2071 3042 2532 3061 2532
βασιλεία ἐπὶ βασιλείαν· καὶ ἔσονται λιμοὶ καὶ λοιμοὶ καὶ
kingdom against kingdom, and there will be famines and plagues and

4578 2596 5117 3956 1161 5023 746 5604 5119
σεισμοὶ κατὰ τόπους. 8 πάντα δὲ ταῦτα ἀρχὴ ὠδίνων. 9 τότε
earthquakes against places. all But these (are) beginning of throes. Then

3860 5209 1519 2347 2532 615 5209 2532
παραδώσουσιν ὑμᾶς εἰς θλίψιν, καὶ ἀποκτενοῦσιν ὑμᾶς· καὶ
they will deliver up you to affliction, and will kill you and

2071 3404 5259 3956 3588 1484 1223 3588 3686 3450
ἔσεσθε μισούμενοι ὑπὸ πάντων τῶν ἐθνῶν διὰ τὸ ὄνομά μου.
you will be hated by all the nations because of name My.

2532 5119 4624 4183 2532 240 3860
10 καὶ τότε σκανδαλισθήσονται πολλοί, καὶ ἀλλήλους παραδώ-
And then will be ensnared many, and one another will deliver

2532 3404 240 2532 4183 5578
σουσι, καὶ μισήσουσιν ἀλλήλους· 11 καὶ πολλοὶ ψευδοπρο-
up, and they will hate one another. And many false

1453 2532 4105 4183 2532 1223 3588
φῆται ἐγερθήσονται, καὶ πλανήσουσι πολλούς. 12 καὶ διὰ τὸ
prophets will be raised up, and will cause to err many. And because

4129 3588 458 5594 3588 26 3588
πληθυνθῆναι τὴν ἀνομίαν, ψυγήσεται ἡ ἀγάπη τῶν
will have been multiplied the lawlessness, will grow cold the love of the

4183 3588 1161 5278 1519 5056 3778 4982 2532
πολλῶν· 13 ὁ δὲ ὑπομείνας εἰς τέλος, οὗτος σωθήσεται. 14 καὶ
many. the (one) But enduring to (the) end, this one will be kept safe. And

2784 5124 3588 2098 3588 932 1722 3650
κηρυχθήσεται τοῦτο τὸ εὐαγγέλιον τῆς βασιλείας ἐν ὅλῃ
will be proclaimed this gospel of the kingdom in all

3588 3625 1519 3142 3956 3588 1484 2532 5119 2240
τῇ οἰκουμένῃ εἰς μαρτύριον πᾶσι τοῖς ἔθνεσι· καὶ τότε ἥξει
the inhabited earth for a testimony to all the nations, and then will come

3588 5056
τὸ τέλος.
the end.

3752 3767 1492 3588 946 3588 2050 3588 4483 1223
15 Ὅταν οὖν ἴδητε τὸ βδέλυγμα τῆς ἐρημώσεως τὸ ῥηθὲν διὰ
When, therefore you see the abomination of desolation spoken through

1158 3588 4396 2476 1722 5117 40 3588 314
Δανιὴλ τοῦ προφήτου, ἑστὼς ἐν τόπῳ ἁγίῳ [ὁ ἀναγινώ-
Daniel the prophet, standing in place (the) holy the (one) reading

3539 5119 3588 1722 3588 2449 5343 1909
σκων νοείτω], 16 τότε οἱ ἐν τῇ Ἰουδαίᾳ φευγέτωσαν εἰς
let him understand; then the (ones) in Judea, let them flee on

3588 3735 3588/1909/3588 1430 3361 2597 142 5100 1537
τὰ ὄρη· 17 ὁ ἐπὶ τοῦ δώματος μὴ καταβαινέτω ἆραι τι ἐκ
mountains; he on the housetops not let him go down to take anything from

3588 3614 846 2532/3588/1722/3588/68 3361 1994 2594
τῆς οἰκίας αὐτοῦ, 18 καὶ ὁ ἐν τῷ ἀγρῷ μὴ ἐπιστρεψάτω ὀπίσω
the house of him. And he in the field not let him turn behind

142 3588 2440 846 3759 1161 3588 1722 1064 2192 2532
ἆραι τὰ ἱμάτια αὐτοῦ. 19 οὐαὶ δὲ ταῖς ἐν γαστρὶ ἐχούσαις καὶ
to take the garment of him. woe And to the (ones) in womb having, and

shall deceive many.
6 And ye shall hear of wars and rumours of wars: see that ye be not troubled: for all (these things) must come to pass, but the end is not yet.
7 For nation shall rise against nation, and kingdom against kingdom: and there shall be famines, and pestilences, and earthquakes, in divers places.
8 All these (are) the beginning of sorrows.
9 Then shall they deliver you up to be afflicted, and shall kill you: and ye shall be hated of all nations for my name's sake.

10 And then shall many be offended, and shall betray one another, and shall hate one another.
11 And many false prophets shall rise, and shall deceive many.

12 And because iniquity shall abound, the love of many shall wax cold.
13 But he that shall endure unto the end, the same shall be saved.
14 And this gospel of the kingdom shall be preached in all the world for a witness unto all nations; and then shall the end come.

15 When ye therefore shall see the abomination of desolation, spoken of by Daniel the prophet, stand in the holy place, (whoso readeth, let him understand:)
16 Then let them which be in Judaea flee into the mountains:
17 Let him which is on the housetop not come down to take any thing out of his house:
18 Neither let him which is in the field return back to take his clothes.
19 And woe unto them that are with child, and

Literal Translation

to those suckling in those days!
20 And pray that your flight will not be in winter nor on a sabbath.

21 For there will be great affliction, such as has not happened from (the) beginning of (the) world until now, no, nor ever will be.
22 And except those days were shortened, not any flesh would be saved. But on account of the elect, those days will be shortened.
23 Then if anyone says to you, Behold, here (is) the Christ! Or, Here! Do not believe.

24 For false christs and false prophets will rise up. And (they) will give great signs and wonders, so as to cause to err. if possible, even the elect.
25 Behold, I tell you beforehand.
26 Then if they say to you, Behold, (He is) in the wilderness; do not go out. Behold, (He is) in the inner rooms; do not believe.
27 For as the lightning comes forth from (the) east and shines as far as (the) west, so also will be the coming of the Son of man.
28 For wherever the dead body may be, there the vultures will be gathered.

29. And immediately after the affliction of those days the sun will be darkened and the moon will not give her light, and the stars will fall from the heaven, and the powers of the heavens will be shaken.

30 And then the sign of the Son of man will appear in the heavens. And then all the tribes of the land will wail. And they will see the Son

Matthew 24:20

3588 2337 1722 1565 3588 2250 4336 1161
ταῖς θηλαζούσαις ἐν ἐκείναις ταῖς ἡμέραις. 20προσεύχεσθε δὲ
to the (ones) suckling in those days. pray And

2443 3361 1096 3588 5437 5216 5494 3366 1722 4521
ἵνα μὴ γένηται ἡ φυγὴ ὑμῶν χειμῶνος, μηδὲ ἐν σαββάτῳ.
that not will occur the flight of you of winter, nor in a sabbath.

2071 1063 5119 2347 3173 3634 3756 1096 575 746
21 ἔσται γὰρ τότε θλίψις μεγάλη, οἵα οὐ γέγονεν ἀπ ἀρχῆς
will be For then affliction great, such as not has occurred from (the) beginning

2889 2193 3588 3568 3761 3756 3361 1096 2532 1487 3361 2856
κόσμου ἕως τοῦ νῦν, οὐδ' οὐ μὴ γένηται. 22 καὶ εἰ μὴ ἐκολοβώ-
of world until now, neither never occur. And except were cut

3588 2250 1565 3756 302 4982 3956 4561 1223 1161
θησαν αἱ ἡμέραι ἐκεῖναι, οὐκ ἂν ἐσώθη πᾶσα σάρξ· διὰ δὲ
short days those not would be saved any flesh; because of but

3588 1588 2856 3588 2250 1565 5119 1437
τοὺς ἐκλεκτοὺς κολοβωθήσονται αἱ ἡμέραι ἐκεῖναι. 23τότε ἐάν
the elect will be cut short days those. Then if

5100 5213 2036 2400 5602 3588 5547 2228 5602 3361 4100
τις ὑμῖν εἴπῃ, Ἰδοὺ, ὧδε ὁ Χριστός, ἤ ὧδε, μὴ πιστεύσητε.
anyone of you says, Behold, here the Christ; or, Here; not do believe.

1453 1063 5580 2532 5578 2532
24 ἐγερθήσονται γὰρ ψευδόχριστοι καὶ ψευδοπροφῆται, καὶ
will rise up For false christs and false prophets, and

1325 4592 3173 2532 5059 5620 4105 1487
δώσουσι σημεῖα μεγάλα καὶ τέρατα, ὥστε πλανῆσαι, εἰ
they will give signs great and wonders, so as to cause to err, if

1415 2532 3588 1588 2400 4280 5213 1437 3767
δυνατόν, καὶ τοὺς ἐκλεκτούς. 25 ἰδού, προείρηκα ὑμῖν. 26 ἐὰν οὖν
possible, even the elect. Behold, I have before told you. If, then,

2036 5213 2400 1722 3588 2048 2076 3361 1831 2400
εἴπωσιν ὑμῖν, Ἰδοὺ, ἐν τῇ ἐρήμῳ ἐστί, μὴ ἐξέλθητε· Ἰδοὺ,
they say to you, Behold, in the desert He is! Not do go forth; behold,

1722 3588 5009 3361 4100 5618 1063 3588 796
ἐν τοῖς ταμείοις, μὴ πιστεύσητε. 27 ὥσπερ γὰρ ἡ ἀστραπὴ
in the private rooms! Not do believe. as For the lightning

1831 575 395 2532 5316 2193 1424 3779
ἐξέρχεται ἀπὸ ἀνατολῶν καὶ φαίνεται ἕως δυσμῶν, οὕτως
comes forth from (the) east and shines as far as (the) west, so

2071 2532 3588 3952 3588 5207 3588 444 3699 1063
ἔσται καὶ ἡ παρουσία τοῦ υἱοῦ τοῦ ἀνθρώπου. 28 ὅπου γὰρ
will be also the coming of the Son of man. wherever For

14375600/3588/4430 1563 4863 3588 105
ἐὰν ᾖ τὸ πτῶμα, ἐκεῖ συναχθήσονται οἱ ἀετοί.
if may be the carcase, there will be gathered the vultures.

2112 1161 3326 3588 2347 3588 2250 1565 3588 2246
29. Εὐθέως δὲ μετὰ τὴν θλίψιν τῶν ἡμερῶν ἐκείνων, ὁ ἥλιος
Immediately And after the affliction of days those, the sun

4654 2532 3588 4582 3756 1325 3588 5338 846
σκοτισθήσεται, καὶ ἡ σελήνη οὐ δώσει τὸ φέγγος αὐτῆς,
will be darkened, and the moon not will give the light of her,

2532 3588 792 4098 575 3588 3772 2532 3588 1411
καὶ οἱ ἀστέρες πεσοῦνται ἀπὸ τοῦ οὐρανοῦ, καὶ αἱ δυνάμεις
and the stars will fall from the heaven, and the powers

3588 3772 4531 2532 5119 5316 3588
τῶν οὐρανῶν σαλευθήσονται. 30 καὶ τότε φανήσεται τὸ
of the heavens will be shaken. And then will appear the

4592 3588 5207 3588 444 1722 3588 3772 2532 5119
σημεῖον τοῦ υἱοῦ τοῦ ἀνθρώπου ἐν τῷ οὐρανῷ· καὶ τότε
sign of the Son of man in the heavens, and then

2875 3956 3588 5443 3588 1093 2532 3700 3588 5207 3588
κόψονται πᾶσαι αἱ φυλαὶ τῆς γῆς, καὶ ὄψονται τὸν υἱὸν τοῦ
will wail all the tribes of the land, and they will see the Son

King James Version

to them that give suck in those days!
20 But pray ye that your flight be not in the winter, neither on the sabbath day:

21 For then shall be great tribulation, such as was not since the beginning of the world to this time, no, nor ever shall be.
22 And except those days should be shortened, there should no flesh be saved: but for the elect's sake those days shall be shortened.
23 Then if any man shall say unto you, Lo, here (is) Christ, or there; believe (it) not.

24 For there shall arise false Christs, and false prophets, and shall shew great signs and wonders; insomuch that, if (it were) possible, they shall deceive the very elect.
25 Behold, I have told you before.
26 Wherefore if they shall say unto you, Behold, he is in the desert; go not forth: behold, (he is) in the secret chambers; believe (it) not.
27 For as the lightning cometh out of the east, and shineth even unto the west; so shall also the coming of the Son of man be.
28 For wheresoever the carcase is, there will the eagles be gathered together.

29. Immediately after the tribulation of those days shall the sun be darkened, and the moon shall not give her light, and the stars shall fall from heaven, and the powers of the heavens shall be shaken:

30 And then shall appear the sign of the Son of man in heaven: and then shall all the tribes of the earth mourn, and they shall see the Son

Literal Translation

of man coming on the clouds of heaven with power and much glory. (Dan. 7:13)
31 And He will send His angels with a great sound of a trumpet, and they will gather His elect from the four winds, from the ends of (the) heavens to their ends.

32. But learn the parable from the fig-tree: When its tender shoot becomes tender and it puts out leaves, you know that the summer (is) near;
33 so also you, when you see all these things, know that it is near at (the) doors.
34 Truly I say to you, In no way will this generation pass away until all these things shall occur.
35 The heaven and the earth will pass away, but not at all My words will pass away.
36. But as to that day and that hour, no one knows, neither the angels of Heaven, except My Father only.
37 But as the days of Noah, so also will be the coming of the Son of man.
38 For as they were in the days before the flood: eating, and drinking, marrying, and giving in marriage, until (the) day (when) Noah went into the ark.
39 And they did not know until the flood came and took all away. So also will be the coming of the Son of man.
40 Then two will be out in the field; the one is taken away, and the one is left;
41 two grinding in

Matthew 24:31

444 2064 1909 3588 3507 3588 3772 3326
ἀνθρώπου ἐρχόμενον ἐπὶ τῶν νεφελῶν τοῦ οὐρανοῦ μετὰ
of man coming on the clouds of heaven with

1411 2532 1391 4183 2532 649 3588 32
δυνάμεως καὶ δόξης πολλῆς. 31 καὶ ἀποστελεῖ τοὺς ἀγγέλους
power and glory much. And He will send the angels

846 3326 4536 5456 3173 2532 1996
αὐτοῦ μετὰ σάλπιγγος φωνῆς μεγάλης, καὶ ἐπισυνάξουσι
of Him with of a trumpet sound a great, and they will gather

3588 1588 846 1537 3588 5064 417 575 206
τοὺς ἐκλεκτοὺς αὐτοῦ ἐκ τῶν τεσσάρων, ἀνέμων, ἀπ᾿ ἄκρων
the elect of Him out of the four winds from (the) ends

3772 2193 206 846
οὐρανῶν ἕως ἄκρων αὐτῶν.
of (the) heavens to (the) ends of them.

575 1161 3588 4808 3129 3588 3850 3752 2235 3588
32. Ἀπὸ δὲ τῆς συκῆς μάθετε τὴν παραβολήν· ὅταν ἤδη ὁ
from And the fig-tree learn the parable: When now the

2798 846 1096 527 2532 3588 5444 1631 1097
κλάδος αὐτῆς γένηται ἁπαλὸς καὶ τὰ φύλλα ἐκφύῃ, γινώ-
tender shoot of it becomes tender, and the leaves it puts out, you

3754 1451 3588 2330 3779 2532 5210 3752 1492 3956
σκετε ὅτι ἐγγὺς τὸ θέρος· 33 οὕτω καὶ ὑμεῖς, ὅταν ἴδητε πάντα
know that near (is) the summer; so also you when you see all

5023 1097 3754 1451 2076 1909 2374 281 3004
ταῦτα, γινώσκετε ὅτι ἐγγύς ἐστιν ἐπὶ θύραις. 34 ἀμὴν λέγω
these things know that near it is on (the) doors. Truly I say

5213 3756 3361 3928 3588 1074 3778 2193 302 3956 5023
ὑμῖν, οὐ μὴ παρέλθῃ ἡ γενεὰ αὕτη, ἕως ἂν πάντα ταῦτα
to you, not at all passes away generation this until should all these things

1096 3588 3772 2532 3588 1093 3928 3588 1161 3056
γένηται. 35 ὁ οὐρανὸς καὶ ἡ γῆ παρελεύσεται, οἱ δὲ λόγοι
occur. The heavens and the earth will pass away, the but words

3450 3756 3361 3928 4012 1161 3588 2250 1565 2532 3588
μου οὐ μὴ παρέλθωσι. 36 περὶ δὲ τῆς ἡμέρας ἐκείνης καὶ τῆς
of Me not at all may pass away. about But day that and the

5610 3762 1492 3761 3588 32 3588 3772 1487 3361 3588
ὥρας οὐδεὶς οἶδεν, οὐδὲ οἱ ἄγγελοι τῶν οὐρανῶν, εἰ μὴ ὁ
hour no one knows, neither the angels of the heavens, except the

3962 3450 3441 5618 1161 3588 2250 3588 3575 3779
πατήρ μου μόνος. 37 ὥσπερ δὲ αἱ ἡμέραι τοῦ Νῶε, οὕτως
Father of Me only. as But the days of Noah, so

2071 2532 3588 3952 3588 5207 3588 444 5618 1063
ἔσται καὶ ἡ παρουσία τοῦ υἱοῦ τοῦ ἀνθρώπου. 38 ὥσπερ γὰρ
will be also the coming of the Son of man. as For

2258 1722 3588 2250 3588 4253 3588 2627 5176
ἦσαν ἐν ταῖς ἡμέραις ταῖς πρὸ τοῦ κατακλυσμοῦ τρώγοντες
they were in the days before the flood, eating,

2532 4095 1060 2532 1547 891 3739 2250
καὶ πίνοντες, γαμοῦντες καὶ ἐκγαμίζοντες, ἄχρι ἧς ἡμέρας
and drinking, marrying and giving in marriage, until which day

1525 3575 1519 3588 2787 2532 3756 1097 2193 2064
εἰσῆλθε Νῶε εἰς τὴν κιβωτόν, 39 καὶ οὐκ ἔγνωσαν, ἕως ἦλθεν
entered Noah into the ark, and not (they)knew until came

3588 2627 2532 142 537 3779 2071 2532 3588 3952
ὁ κατακλυσμὸς καὶ ἦρεν ἅπαντας, οὕτως ἔσται καὶ ἡ παρου-
the flood and took all, so will be the coming

3588 5207 3588 444 5119 1417 2071 1722 3588 68
σία τοῦ υἱοῦ τοῦ ἀνθρώπου. 40 τότε δύο ἔσονται ἐν τῷ ἀγρῷ·
of the Son of man. Then two will be in the field,

3588 1520 3880 2532/3588/1520 863 1417 229 1722
ὁ εἷς παραλαμβάνεται, και ὁ εἷς ἀφίεται. 41 δύο ἀλήθουσαι ἐν
the one is taken away, and the one is left; two grinding in

King James Version

of man coming in the clouds of heaven with power and great glory.
31 And he shall send his angels with a great sound of a trumpet, and they shall gather together his elect from the four winds, from one end of heaven to the other.

32. Now learn a parable of the fig tree; When his branch is yet tender, and putteth forth leaves, ye know that summer (is) nigh:
33 So likewise ye, when ye shall see all these things, know that it is near, (even) at the doors.
34 Verily I say unto you, This generation shall not pass, till all these things be fulfilled.
35 Heaven and earth shall pass away, but my words shall not pass away.
36. But of that day and hour knoweth no (man), no, not the angels of heaven, but my Father only.
37 But as the days of Noe (were), so shall also the coming of the Son of man be.
38 For as in the days that were before the flood they were eating and drinking, marrying and giving in marriage, until the day that Noe entered into the ark,
39 And knew not until the flood came, and took them all away; so shall also the coming of the Son of man be.
40 Then shall two be in the field; the one shall be taken, and the other left.
41 Two (women shall be) grinding at

Literal Translation

the mill; one is taken away, and one is left.
42. Watch, then, because you do not know in what hour your Lord comes.

43 But know this, that if the housemaster had known in what watch the thief is coming, he would have watched and not have allowed his house to be dug through.
44 Because of this, you also be ready, for in that hour you think not, the Son of man comes.

45 Who then is the faithful and prudent servant whom his lord has set over his care, to give to them the food in season?

46 Blessed (is) that servant whom his lord shall find so doing when he comes.
47 Truly I say to you, He will set him over all his substance.

48 But if that bad servant says in his heart, My lord delays to come,
49 and begins to beat (his) fellow servants, and to eat and to drink with the (ones) drinking,

50 the lord of that slave will come in a day in which he does not expect and in an hour which he does not know,
51 and will cut him in two, and will appoint his portion with the hypocrites. There will be weeping and gnashing of the teeth.

Matthew 24:42

3588 3459 3391 3880 2532 3391 863 1127
τῷ μύλωνι· μία παραλαμβάνεται καὶ μία ἀφίεται. 42 γρηγο-
the mill, one is taken away, and one is left. Watch

3767 3754 3756 1492 4169 5610 3588 2962 5216 2064
ρεῖτε οὖν, ὅτι οὐκ οἴδατε ποίᾳ ὥρᾳ ὁ Κύριος ὑμῶν ἔρχεται.
then because not you know on what hour the Lord of you is coming.

1565 1161 1097 3754 1487 1492 3588 3617 4169
43 ἐκεῖνο δὲ γινώσκετε, ὅτι εἰ ᾔδει ὁ οἰκοδεσπότης ποίᾳ
this And know, that if knew the housemaster in what

5438 3588 2812 2064 1127 302 2532 3756 302 1439
φυλακῇ ὁ κλέπτης ἔρχεται, ἐγρηγόρησεν ἄν, καὶ οὐκ ἂν εἴασε
watch the thief is coming, he would have watched and not might allow

1358 3588 3614 846 1223 5124 2532 5210 1096
διορυγῆναι τὴν οἰκίαν αὐτοῦ. 44 διὰ τοῦτο καὶ ὑμεῖς γίνεσθε
to be dug through the house of him. Because of this also you become

2092 3754 3739 5610 3756 1380 3588 5207 3588 444 2064
ἕτοιμοι· ὅτι ᾗ ὥρᾳ οὐ δοκεῖτε, ὁ υἱὸς τοῦ ἀνθρώπου ἔρχεται.
ready; because that hour not you think, the Son of man comes.

5101 687 2076 3588 4103 1401 2532 5429 3739 2525
45 τίς ἄρα ἐστὶν ὁ πιστὸς δοῦλος καὶ φρόνιμος, ὃν κατέστησεν
Who then is the faithful slave and prudent, whom appointed

3588 2962 846 1909 3588 2322 846 3588 1325
ὁ κύριος αὐτοῦ ἐπὶ τῆ θεραπείας αὐτοῦ, τοῦ διδόναι
the lord of him over the care of him, to give

846 3588 5160 1722 2540 3107 3588 1401 1565 3739
αὐτοῖς τὴν τροφὴν ἐν καιρῷ; 46 μακάριος ὁ δοῦλος ἐκεῖνος, ὃν
to them the food in season? Blessed (is) slave that whom

2064 3588 2962 846 2147 4160 3779 281 3004
ἐλθὼν ὁ κύριος αὐτοῦ εὑρήσει ποιοῦντα οὕτως. 47 ἀμὴν λέγω
coming the lord of him will find doing so. Truly I say

5213 3754 1909 3956 3588 5224 846 2525
ὑμῖν, ὅτι ἐπὶ πᾶσι τοῖς ὑπάρχουσιν αὐτοῦ καταστήσει
to you that over all the substance of him he will appoint

846 1437 1161 2036 3588 2556 1401 1565 1722 3588 2588
αὐτόν. 48 ἐὰν δὲ εἴπῃ ὁ κακὸς δοῦλος ἐκεῖνος ἐν τῇ καρδίᾳ
him. if But says bad slave that in the heart

846 5549 3588 2962 3450 2064 2532 756 5180
αὐτοῦ, Χρονίζει ὁ κύριός μου ἐλθεῖν, 49 καὶ ἄρξηται τύπτειν
of him delays the lord of me to come, and should begin to beat

3588 4889 2068 1161 2532 4095 3326 3588 3184
τοὺς συνδούλους, ἐσθίειν δὲ καὶ πίνειν μετὰ τῶν μεθυόντων,
the fellow-slaves, to eat and also to drink with the (ones) drinking,

2040 3588 2962 3588 1401 1565 1161 2250 3739 3756
50 ἥξει ὁ κύριος τοῦ δούλου ἐκείνου ἐν ἡμέρᾳ ᾗ οὐ
comes the lord slave of that in a day which not

4328 2532 1722 5610 3739 3756 1097 2532 1371
προσδοκᾷ, καὶ ἐν ὥρᾳ ᾗ οὐ γινώσκει, 51 καὶ διχοτομήσει
he expects and in an hour which not he knows, and will cut in two

846 2532 3588 3313 846 3326 3588 5273 5087 1563
αὐτὸν, καὶ τὸ μέρος αὐτοῦ μετὰ τῶν ὑποκριτῶν θήσει· ἐκεῖ
him, and the portion of him with the hypocrites will put. There

2071 3588 2805 2532 3588 1030 3588 3599
ἔσται ὁ κλαυθμὸς καὶ ὁ βρυγμὸς τῶν ὀδόντων.
will be the weeping and the gnashing of the teeth.

King James Version

the mill; the one shall be taken, and the other left.
42. Watch therefore: for ye know not what hour your Lord doth come.

43 But know this, that if the goodman of the house had known in what watch the thief would come, he would have watched, and would not have suffered his house to be broken up.
44 Therefore be ye also ready: for in such an hour as ye think not the Son of man cometh.

45 Who then is a faithful and wise servant, whom his lord hath made ruler over his household, to give them meat in due season?

46 Blessed (is) that servant, whom his lord when he cometh shall find so doing.
47 Verily I say unto you, That he shall make him ruler over all his goods.

48 But and if that evil servant shall say in his heart, My lord delayeth his coming;
49 And shall begin to smite (his) fellowservants, and to eat and drink with the drunken;

50 The lord of that servant shall come in a day when he looketh not for (him), and in an hour that he is not aware of,
51 And shall cut him asunder, and appoint (him) his portion with the hypocrites: there shall be weeping and gnashing of teeth.

Matthew 25

1. Then the kingdom of Heaven shall be compared to ten virgins who taking their torches, went out to

5119 3666 3588 932 3588 3772 1176 3933
1. Τότε ὁμοιωθήσεται ἡ βασιλεία τῶν οὐρανῶν δέκα παρθέ-
Then shall be compared the kingdom of the heavens to ten virgins.

3748 2983 3588 2985 846 1831 1519
νοις, αἵτινες λαβοῦσαι τὰς λαμπάδας αὐτῶν ἐξῆλθον εἰς
who taking the torches of them went out to

1. Then shall the kingdom of heaven be likened unto ten virgins, which took their lamps, and went forth to

Literal Translation

a meeting of the bridegroom.
2 And five of them were prudent, and five foolish,
3 who being foolish, having taken their torches, did not take oil with them.
4 But the prudent took oil in their vessels with their torches.
5 But the bridegroom delaying, all nodded and slept.
6 And at midnight, a cry occurred, (saying), Behold, the bridegroom comes! Go out to a meeting with him.
7 Then all those virgins arose and prepared their torches.
8 And the foolish said to the wise, Give us from your oil, for our torches are being snuffed out.
9 But the wise answered, saying, (No), lest there not be enough for us and you. But rather, go to those who sell and buy for yourselves.
10 But they going away to buy, the bridegroom came. And those ready went in with him to the wedding feast, and the door was shut.
11 And later, the rest of the virgins also came, saying, Lord, Lord, open to us.
12 But answering, he said, Truly I say to you, I do not know you.
13 Therefore, watch, for you do not know the day nor the hour in which the Son of man comes.
14. For (it is) as if a man going abroad called (his) own slaves and delivered his goods to them.
15 And

Matthew 25:2

529 3588 3566 4002 1161 2258 1537 846 5429
ἀπάντησιν τοῦ νυμφίου. 2 πέντε δὲ ἦσαν ἐξ αὐτῶν φρόνιμοι,
a meeting of the bridegroom. five And were to them prudent

2532 3588 4002 3474 3748 3474 2983 3588 2985
καὶ αἱ πέντε μωραὶ. 3 αἵτινεσ μωραί, λαβοῦσαι τὰς λαμπάδας
and the five foolish (ones), who (being) foolish having taken the torches

1438 3756 2983 3326 1438 1637 3588 1161 5429
ἑαυτῶν, οὐκ ἔλαβον μεθ᾽ ἑαυτῶν, ἔλαιον· 4 αἱ δὲ φρόνιμοι
of them not did take with themselves oil. the But prudent

2983 1637 1722 3588 30 846 3326 3588 2985
ἔλαβον ἔλαιον ἐν τοῖς ἀγγείοις αὐτῶν μετὰ τῶν λαμπάδων
took oil in the vessels of them with the torches.

846 5549 1161 3588 3566 3573 3956 2532
αυτῶν. 5 χρονίζοντος δὲ τοῦ νυμφίου, ἐνύσταξαν πᾶσαι καὶ
of them. delaying But the bridegroom, nodded all and

2518 3319 1161 3571 2906 1096 2400 3588
ἐκάθευδον. 6 μέσης δὲ νυκτὸς κραυγὴ γέγονεν, Ἰδού, ὁ
slept. (at) mid- And night a cry occurred, Behold! The

3566 2064 1831 1519 529 846 5119
νυμφίος ἔρχεται, ἐξέρχεσθε εἰς ἀπάντησιν αὐτοῦ. 7 τότε
bridegroom comes. Go out to a meeting of him. Then

1453 3956 3588 3933 1565 2532 2885 3588
ἠγέρθησαν πᾶσαι αἱ παρθένοι ἐκεῖναι, καὶ ἐκόσμησαν τὰς
rose up all virgins those and prepared the

2985 846 3588 1161 3474 3588 5429 2036 1325
λαμπάδας αυτῶν. 8 αἱ δὲ μωραὶ ταῖς φρονίμοις εἶπον, Δότε
torches of them. the And foolish to the prudent said, Give

2254 1537 3588 1637 5216 3754 3588 2985 2257 4570
ἡμῖν ἐκ τοῦ ἐλαίου ὑμῶν, ὅτι αἱ λαμπάδες ἡμῶν σβέννυνται.
us from the oil of you, because the torches of us are being snuffed.

611 1161 3588 5429 3004 3379 3756
9 ἀπεκρίθησαν δὲ αἱ φρόνιμοι, λέγουσαι, Μήποτε οὐκ
answered But the prudent saying, (No,) lest not

714 2254 2532 5213 4198 1161 3123 4314 3588
ἀρκέσῃ ἡμῖν καὶ ὑμῖν· πορεύεσθε δὲ μᾶλλον πρὸς τοὺς
it suffices to us and to you. go But rather to the (ones)

4453 2532 59 1438 565 1161 846
πωλοῦντας καὶ ἀγοράσατε ἑαυταῖς. 10 ἀπερχομένων δὲ αὐτῶν
selling and buy for yourselves. going away And they

59 2064 3588 3566 2532 3588 2092 1525 3326
ἀγοράσαι, ἦλθεν ὁ νυμφίος· καὶ αἱ ἕτοιμοι εἰσῆλθον μετ᾽
to buy, came the bridegroom and the ready (ones) went in with

846 1519 3588 1062 2532 2808 3588 2374 5305 1161
αὐτοῦ εἰς τοὺς γάμους, καὶ ἐκλείσθη ἡ θύρα. 11 ὕστερον δὲ
him to the wedding-feast, and was shut the door. later And

2064 2532 3588 3062 3933 3004 2962 2962
ἔρχονται καὶ αἱ λοιπαὶ παρθένοι, λέγουσαι, Κύριε, κύριε,
come also the remaining virgins, saying, Lord, Lord,

455 2254 3588 1161 611 2036 281 3004 5213 3750
ἄνοιξον ἡμῖν. 12 ὁ δὲ ἀποκριθεὶς εἶπεν, Ἀμὴν λέγω ὑμῖν, οὐκ
open to us. he But answering said, Truly I say to you, not

1492 5209 1127 3767 3754 3756 1492 3588 2250 3761
οἶδα ὑμᾶς. 13 γρηγορεῖτε οὖν, ὅτι οὐκ οἴδατε τὴν ἡμέραν οὐδὲ
I know you. Watch, therefore, for not you know the day nor

3588 5610 1722 3739 3588 5207 3588 444 2064
τὴν ὥραν. ἐν ᾗ ὁ υἱὸς τοῦ ἀνθρώπου ἔρχεται.
the hour in which the Son of man comes.

5618 1063 444 589 2564 3588 2398
14. Ὥσπερ γὰρ ἄνθρωπος ἀποδημῶν ἐκάλεσε τοὺς ἰδίους
(it is) as if For a man going abroad called the own

1401 2532 3860 846 3588 5224 846 2532
δούλους, καὶ παρέδωκεν αὐτοῖς τὰ ὑπάρχοντα αὐτοῦ· 15 καὶ
slaves, and delivered to them the goods of him. And

King James Version

meet the bridegroom.
2 And five of them were wise, and five (were) foolish.
3 They that (were) foolish took their lamps, and took no oil with them:
4 But the wise took oil in their vessels with their lamps.
5 While the bridegroom tarried, they all slumbered and slept.
6 And at midnight there was a cry made, Behold, the bridegroom cometh; go ye out to meet him.
7 Then all those virgins arose, and trimmed their lamps.
8 And the foolish said unto the wise, Give us of your oil; for our lamps are gone out.
9 But the wise answered, saying, (Not so); lest there be not enough for us and you: but go ye rather to them that sell, and buy for yourselves.
10 And while they went to buy, the bridegroom came; and they that were ready went in with him to the marriage: and the door was shut.
11 Afterward came also the other virgins, saying, Lord, Lord, open to us.
12 But he answered and said, Verily I say unto you, I know you not.
13 Watch therefore, for ye know neither the day nor the hour wherein the Son of man cometh.
14. For (the kingdom of heaven is) as a man travelling into a far country, (who) called his own servants, and delivered unto them his goods.
15 And

Literal Translation

to one he gave five talents, and to one, two, and to one, one, to each according to his ability. And (he) went abroad at once.
16 And going, the (one) who received the five talents worked with them and made another five talents.
17 In the same way, the (one with) the two also (did); he also gained another two.
18 But going away, the (one) who received the one dug in the earth and hid his lord's silver.
19 And after much time, the lord of those slaves came and took account with them.
20 And coming up, the (one) who received five talents brought another five talents near, saying, Lord, you delivered five talents to me. Behold, I gained another five talents above them.
21 And his lord said to him, Well (done), good and faithful slave. You were faithful over a few things; I will set you over many. Enter into the joy of your lord.
22 And the (one) who received two talents also coming up, (he) said, Lord, you delivered two talents to me. Behold, I have gained two other talents above them.
23 His lord said to him, Well (done), good and faithful slave. You were faithful over a few things, I will set you over many. Enter into the joy of your lord.
24 And the (one) who received the one talent also coming up, (he) said, Lord, I knew you, that you are a hard man, reaping where you did not sow, and gathering where you did not scatter;
25 and being afraid, going away,

Matthew 25:16

3739/3303 1325 4002 5007 3739/1161/1417/3739/1161/1520 1538 2596
ᾧ μὲν ἔδωκε πέντε τάλαντα, ᾧ δὲ δύο, ᾧ δὲ ἕν, ἑκάστῳ κατὰ
to one he gave five talents; to one and two; to one and one, to each to

3588 2398 1411 2532 589 2112 4198 1161 3588
τὴν ἰδίαν δύναμιν· καὶ ἀπεδήμησεν εὐθέως. 16 πορευθεὶς δὲ ὁ
the own ability, and went abroad at once. going And he

3588 4002 5007 2983 2038 1722 846 2532 4160
τὰ πέντε τάλαντα λαβὼν εἰργάσατο ἐν αὐτοῖς, καὶ ἐποίησεν
the five talents receiving worked in them, and made

243 4002 5007 5615 2532 3588 3588 1417 2770 2532
ἄλλα πέντε τάλαντα. 17 ὡσαύτως καὶ ὁ τὰ δύο ἐκέρδησε καὶ
other five talents. Likewise, also the (one) the two gained also

846 243 1417 3588 1161 3588 1520 2983 565 3736 1722 3588
αὐτος ἄλλα δύο. 18 ὁ δὲ τὸ ἓν λαβὼν ἀπελθὼν ὤρυξεν ἐν τῇ
he other two. he But the one receiving, going away, dug in the

1093 2532 613 3588 694 3588 2962 846 3326 1161
γῇ, καὶ ἀπέκρυψε τὸ ἀργύριον τοῦ κυρίου αὐτοῦ. 19 μετὰ δὲ
earth and hid the silver of the lord of him. after And

5550 4183 2064 3588 2962 3588 1401 1565 2532
χρόνον πολὺν ἔρχεται ὁ κύριος τῶν δούλων ἐκείνων, καὶ
time much comes the lord slaves of those, and

4868 3326 846 3056 2532 4334 3588 3588 4002
συναίρει μετ᾽ αὐτῶν λόγον. 20 καὶ προσελθὼν ὁ τὰ πέντε
takes with them account. And coming up he the (one) five

5007 2983 4374 243 4002 5007 3004
τάλαντα λαβὼν προσήνεγκεν ἄλλα πέντε τάλαντα, λέγων,
talent receiving brought near other five talents, saying,

2962 4002 5007 3427 3860 2396 243 4002
Κύριε, πέντε τάλαντά μοι παρέδωκας· ἴδε, ἄλλα πέντε
Lord, five talents to me you delivered. Behold, other five

5007 2770 1909 846 5346 1161 846 3588 2962 846
τάλαντα ἐκέρδησα ἐπ᾽ αὐτοῖς. 21 ἔφη δὲ αὐτῷ ὁ κύριος αὐτοῦ,
talents I gained over them. said And to him the lord to him,

2095 1401 18 2532 4103 1909 3641 2258 4103 1909 4183
Εὖ, δοῦλε ἀγαθὲ καὶ πιστέ, ἐπὶ ὀλίγα ἦς πιστός, ἐπὶ πολλῶν
Well, slave good and faithful, over a few you were faithful, over many

4571 2525 1525 1519 3588 5479 3588 2962 4675
σε καταστήσω· εἴσελθε εἰς τὴν χαρὰν τοῦ κυρίου σου.
you I will set. Enter into the joy of the lord of you.

4334 1161 2532 3588 3588 1417 5007 2983 2036 2962
22 προσελθὼν δὲ καὶ ὁ τὰ δύο τάλαντα λαβὼν εἶπε, Κύριε,
coming up And also he the two talents receiving said, Lord

1417 5007 3427 3860 2396 243 1417 5007
δύο τάλαντά μοι παρέδωκας· ἴδε, ἄλλα δύο τάλαντα
two talents to me you delivered. Behold, other two talents

2770 1909 846 5346 846 3588 2962 846 2095 1401
ἐκέρδησα ἐπ᾽ αὐτοῖς. 23 ἔφη αὐτῷ ὁ κύριος αὐτοῦ, Εὖ, δοῦλε
I gained over them. said to him The lord of him, Well, slave

18 2532 4103 1909 3641 2258 4103 1909 4183 4571
ἀγαθὲ καὶ πιστέ, ἐπὶ ὀλίγα ἦς πιστός, ἐπὶ πολλῶν σε
good and faithful, over a few you were faithful, over many you

2525 1525 1519 3588 5479 3588 2962 4675 4334
καταστήσω· εἴσελθε εἰς τὴν χαρὰν τοῦ κυρίου σου. 24 προσ-
I will set. Enter into the joy of the lord of you. coming

1161 2532 3588 3588 1520 5007 2983 2036 2962 1097
ελθὼν δὲ καὶ ὁ τὸ ἓν τάλαντον εἰληφὼς εἶπε, Κύριε, ἔγνων
up And also he the one talent receiving, said, Lord, I knew

4571 3754 4642 1488 444 2325 3699 3756 4687 2532
σε ὅτι σκληρὸς εἶ ἄνθρωπος ,θερίζων ὅπου οὐκ ἔσπειρας, καὶ
you, that hard you are a man, reaping where not you sowed, and

4863 3606 3756 1287 2532 5399 565
συνάγων ὅθεν οὐ διεσκόρπισας· 25 καὶ φοβηθεὶς, ἀπελθὼν
gathering from where not you scattered; and fearing, going away,

King James Version

unto one he gave five talents, to another two, and to another one; to every man according to his several ability; and straightway took his journey.
16 Then he that had received the five talents went and traded with the same, and made (them) other five talents.
17 And likewise he that (had received) two, he also gained other two.
18 But he that had received one went and digged in the earth, and hid his lord's money.
19 After a long time the lord of those servants cometh, and reckoneth with them.
20 And so he that had received five talents came and brought other five talents, saying, Lord, thou deliveredst unto me five talents: behold, I have gained beside them five talents more.
21 His lord said unto him, Well done, (thou) good and faithful servant: thou hast been faithful over a few things, I will make thee ruler over many things: enter thou into the joy of thy lord.
22 He also that had received two talents came and said, Lord, thou deliveredst unto me two talents: behold, I have gained two other talents beside them.
23 His lord said unto him, Well done, good and faithful servant; thou hast been faithful over a few things, I will make thee ruler over many things: enter thou into the joy of thy lord.
24 Then he which had received the one talent came and said, Lord, I knew thee that thou art an hard man, reaping where thou hast not sown, and gathering where thou hast not strawed:
25 And I was afraid, and went and

Literal Translation — **Matthew 25:26** — ***King James Version***

I hid your talent in the earth. Behold, you have yours.

26 And answering, his lord said to him, Evil and slothful slave! You knew that I reap where I did not sow, and gather where I did not I scatter.
27 Then you ought to have put my silver to the bankers, and coming I would have received my own with interest.

28 Therefore, take the talent from him and give (it) to him who has the ten talents.
29 For to each who has, (more) will be given, and he will abound. But from him who does not have, even that which he has will be taken from him.
30 And throw the worthless slave out into the outer darkness. There will be weeping and gnashing of the teeth.

31. But when the Son of man comes in His glory, and all the holy angels with Him, then He will sit on the throne of His glory.

32 And before Him shall be gathered all the nations; and He will separate them from one another, as the shepherd separates the sheep from the goats.
33 And indeed (He) will set the sheep off His right, but the goats off (the) left (hand).

34 Then the King will say to those off His right, Come, the (ones) having been blessed of My Father. Inherit the kingdom prepared for you from (the) foundation of (the) world.
35 For I hungered, and you gave Me to eat; I thirsted, and you gave Me drink; I was an alien,

---

2928 3588 5007 4675 1722 3588 1093 2396 2192 3588 4674
ἔκρυψα τὸ τάλαντόν σου ἐν τῇ γῇ· ἴδε, ἔχεις τὸ σόν.
I hid the talent of you in the earth. Behold, you have yours.

611 1161 3588 2962 846 2036 846 4190 1401 2532
26 ἀποκριθεὶς δὲ ὁ κύριος αὐτοῦ εἶπεν αὐτῷ, Πονηρὲ δοῦλε καὶ
answering And the lord of him said to him, Evil slave and

3636 1492 3754 2325 3699 3756 4687 2532 4863 3606
ὀκνηρέ, ᾔδεις ὅτι θερίζω ὅπου οὐκ ἔσπειρα, καὶ συνάγω ὅθεν
slothful, you knew that I reap where not I sowed, and I gather where

3756 1287 1163 3767 4571 906 3588 694 3450 3588
οὐ διεσκόρπισα; 27 ἔδει οὖν σε βαλεῖν τὸ ἀργύριόν μου τοῖς
not I scattered. It behoved then you to put the silver of me to the

5133 2532 2064 1473 2865 302 3588 1699 4862
τραπεζίταις, καὶ ἐλθὼν ἐγὼ ἐκομισάμην ἂν τὸ ἐμὸν σὺν
bankers, and coming I would have received again mine with

5110 142 3767 675 846 3588 5007 2532 1325 3588
τόκῳ. 28 ἄρατε οὖν ἀπ' αὐτοῦ τὸ τάλαντον, καὶ δότε τῷ
interest. Take, therefore, from him the talent, and give to him

2192 3588 1176 5007 3588 1063 2192 3956 1325
ἔχοντι τὰ δέκα τάλαντα· 29 τῷ γὰρ ἔχοντι παντὶ δοθήσεται,
having the ten talents. the (one) For having to everyone will be given,

2532 4052 575 1161 3588 3361 2192 2532 3739 2192
καὶ περισσευθήσεται· ἀπὸ δὲ τοῦ μὴ ἔχοντος, καὶ ὃ ἔχει,
and he will abound. from But the (one) not having, even what he has

142 575 846 2532 3588 888 1401 1544
ἀρθήσεται ἀπ' αὐτοῦ. 30 καὶ τὸν ἀχρεῖον δοῦλον ἐκβάλλετε
will be taken from him. And the worthless slave throw out

1519 3588 4655 3588 1857 1563 2071 3588 2805 2532 3588
εἰς τὸ σκότος τὸ ἐξώτερον. ἐκεῖ ἔσται ὁ κλαυθμὸς καὶ ὁ
into the darkness outer. There will be the weeping and the

1030 3588 3599
βρυγμὸς τῶν ὀδόντων.
gnashing of the teeth.

3752 1161 2064 3588 5207 3588 444 1722 3588 1391 846
31. Ὅταν δὲ ἔλθῃ ὁ υἱὸς τοῦ ἀνθρώπου ἐν τῇ δόξῃ αὐτοῦ,
when And comes the Son · of man in the glory of Him,

2532 3956 3588 40 32 3326 846 5119 2523 1909
καὶ πάντες οι ἅγιοί ἄγγελοι μετ' αὐτοῦ, τότε καθίσει ἐπὶ
and all the holy angels with Him, then He will sit on

2362 1391 846 2532 4863 1715 846
θρόνου δόξης αὐτοῦ, 32 καὶ συναχθήσεται ἔμπροσθεν αὐτοῦ
a throne of glory of Him, and will be assembled before Him

3956 3588 1484 2532 873 846 575 240 5618 3588
πάντα τὰ ἔθνη, καὶ ἀφοριεῖ αὐτοὺς ἀπ' ἀλλήλων, ὥσπερ ὁ
all the nations, and He will part them from one another, as the

4166 873 3588 4263 575 3588 2056 2532 2476
ποιμὴν ἀφορίζει τὰ πρόβατα ἀπὸ τῶν ἐρίφων· 33 καὶ στήσει
shepherd parts the sheep from the goats, and will set

3588 3303 4263 1537 1188 846 3588 1161 2055 1537 2176
τὰ μὲν πρόβατα ἐκ δεξιῶν αὐτοῦ, τὰ δὲ ἐρίφια ἐξ εὐωνύμων.
the indeed sheep off the right of Him, the and goats off the left.

5119 2046 3588 935 3588 1537 1188 846 1205 3588 2127
34 τότε ἐρεῖ ὁ βασιλεὺς τοῖς ἐκ δεξιῶν αὐτοῦ, Δεῦτε, οἱ εὐλογη-
Then will say the King to those off the right of Him, Come, those having

3588 3962 3450 2816 3588 2090
μένοι τοῦ πατρός μου, κληρονομήσατε τὴν ἡτοιμασμένην
been blessed the Father of Me; inherit the having been prepared

5213 932 575 2602 2889 3983 1063 2532
ὑμῖν βασιλείαν ἀπὸ καταβολῆς κόσμου. 35 ἐπείνασα γάρ, καὶ
for you kingdom from foundation of (the) world. I hungered For, and

1325 3427 5315 1372 2532 4222 3165 3581 2252
ἐδώκατέ μοι φαγεῖν· ἐδίψησα, καὶ ἐποτίσατέ με· ξένος ἤμην,
you gave Me to eat; I thirsted, and you gave drink Me; an alien I was

---

hid thy talent in the earth: lo, (there) thou hast (that is) thine.

26 His lord answered and said unto him, (Thou) wicked and slothful servant, thou knewest that I reap where I sowed not, and gather where I have not strawed:
27 Thou oughtest therefore to have put my money to the exchangers, and (then) at my coming I should have received mine own with usury.
28 Take therefore the talent from him, and give (it) unto him which hath ten talents.
29 For unto every one that hath shall be given, and he shall have abundance: but from him that hath not shall be taken away even that which he hath.
30 And cast ye the unprofitable servant into outer darkness: there shall be weeping and gnashing of teeth.

31. When the Son of man shall come in his glory, and all the holy angels with him, then shall he sit upon the throne of his glory:

32 And before him shall be gathered all nations: and he shall separate them one from another, as a shepherd divideth (his) sheep from the goats:
33 And he shall set the sheep on his right hand, but the goats on the left.

34 Then shall the King say unto them on his right hand, Come, ye blessed of my Father, inherit the kingdom prepared for you from the foundation of the world:
35 For I was an hungred, and ye gave me meat: I was thirsty, and ye gave me drink: I was a stranger,

Literal Translation

and you took Me in;
36 naked, and you clothed Me; I was sick, and you visited Me; I was in prison, and you came to Me.

37 Then the righteous will answer, saying, Lord, when did we see You hungering, and fed (You); or thirsting, and gave (You) drink?
38 And when did we see You an alien, and took (You) in; or naked, and clothed (You)?
39 And when did we see You sick, or in prison, and came to You?
40 And answering, the King will say to them, Truly I say to you, Inasmuch as you did (it) to one of these, the least of My brothers, you did (it) to Me.
41 Then He will also say to those on (His) left, Go away from Me, cursed ones, into the everlasting fire having been prepared for the Devil and his angels.

42 For I hungered, and you gave Me nothing to eat; I thirsted, and you gave me nothing to drink;
43 I was an alien, and you did not gather Me in; naked, and you did not clothe Me; sick, and in prison, and you did not visit Me.
44 Then they also will answer Him, saying, Lord, when did we see You hungering, or thirsting, or an alien, or naked, or sick, or in prison, and did not minister to You?

45 Then He will answer them, saying, Truly I say to you, Inasmuch as you did not do (it) to one of these, the least, neither did you do (it) to Me.
46 And these shall go away into everlasting punishment, but the righteous into everlasting life.

Matthew 25:36

2532 4863 3165 1131 2532 4016 3165 770
καὶ συνηγάγετέ με· 36 γυμνὸς, καὶ περιεβάλετέ με· ἠσθένησα,
and you took in Me; naked, and you clothed Me; I was sick,
2532 1980 3165 1722 5438 2252 2532 2064 4314 3165
καὶ ἐπεσκέψασθέ με· ἐν φυλακῇ ἤμην, καὶ ἤλθετε πρός με.
and you visited Me; in prison I was, and you came to Me.
5119 611 846 3588 1342 3004 2962
37 τότε ἀποκριθήσονται αὐτῷ οἱ δίκαιοι, λέγοντες, Κύριε,
Then will answer Him the righteous, saying, Lord,
4219 4571 1492 3983 2532 5142 2228 1372 2532
πότε σε εἴδομεν πεινῶντα, καὶ ἐθρέψαμεν; ἢ διψῶντα, καὶ
when You did we see hungering and (we) fed; or thirsting, and
4222 4219 1161 4571 1492 581 2532 4863
ἐποτίσαμεν; 38 πότε δέ σε εἴδομεν ξένον, καὶ συνηγάγομ εν;
gave drink? when And You did we see an alien, and gathered (You) in,
2228 1131 2532 4016 4219 1161 4571 1492 722 2228 1722
ἢ γυμνὸν, καὶ περιεβάλομεν; 39 πότε δέ σε εἴδομεν ἀσθενῆ, ἢ ἐν
or naked, and clothed (You)? when And You did we see sick, or in
5438 2532 2064 4314 4571 2532 611 3588 935 2046
φυλακῇ, καὶ ἤλθομεν πρός σε; 40 καὶ ἀποκριθεὶς ὁ βασιλεὺς ἐρεῖ
prison, and came to You? And answering the King will say
846 281 3004 5213 1909 3745 4160 1520 5130 3588
αὐτοῖς, Ἀμὴν λέγω ὑμῖν, ἐφ᾽ ὅσον ἐποιήσατε ἑνὶ τούτων τῶν
to them, Truly, I say to you, in so far as you did to one of these the
80 3450 3588 1646 1698 4160 5119 2046 2532
ἀδελφῶν μου τῶν ἐλαχίστων, ἐμοὶ ἐποιήσατε. 41 τότε ἐρεῖ καὶ
brothers of Me the least, to Me you did. Then He says also
3588 1537 2176 4198 575 1700 3588 2672 1519
τοῖς ἐξ εὐωνύμων, Πορεύεσθε ἀπ᾽ ἐμοῦ, οἱ κατηραμένοι εἰς
to those off the left, Go from Me, the (ones) cursed into
3588 4442 3588 166 3588 2090 3588 1228 2532 3588
τὸ πῦρ τὸ αἰώνιον, τὸ ἡτοιμασμένον τῷ διαβόλῳ καὶ τοῖς
the fire everlasting, having been prepared for the devil and the
32 846 3983 1063 2532 3756 1325 3427 5315
ἀγγέλοις αὐτοῦ. 42 ἐπείνασα γὰρ, καὶ οὐκ ἐδώκατέ μοι φαγεῖν·
angels of him. I hungered For, and not you gave Me to eat;
1372 2532 3756 4222 3165 3581 2252 2532 3756 4863
ἐδίψησα, καὶ οὐκ ἐποτίσατέ με· 43 ξένος ἤμην, καὶ οὐ συνηγά-
I thirsted, and not you gave drink to Me; an alien I was, and not you gathered
3165 1131 2532 3756 4016 3165 772 2532 1722
γετέ με· γυμνὸς, καὶ οὐ περιεβάλετέ με· ἀσθενὴς, καὶ ἐν
in Me; naked, and not you clothed Me; sick, and in
5438 2532 3756 1980 3165 5119 611
φυλακῇ, καὶ οὐκ ἐπεσκέψασθέ με. 44 τότε ἀποκριθήσονται
prison, and not you visited Me. Then will answer
846 2532 846 3004 2962 4219 4571 1492 3983
αὐτῷ καὶ αὐτοὶ, λέγοντες, Κύριε, πότε σε εἴδομεν πεινῶντα,
Him also them, saying, Lord, when You did we see hungering,
2228 1372 2228 3581 2228 1131 2228 772 2228 1722 5438 2532
ἢ διψῶντα, ἢ ξένον, ἢ γυμνὸν, ἢ ἀσθενῆ, ἢ ἐν φυλακῇ, καὶ
or thirsting, or an alien, or naked, or sick, or in prison, and
3756 1247 4671 5119 611 846 3004
οὐ διηκονήσαμέν σοι; 45 τότε ἀποκριθήσεται αὐτοῖς, λέγων,
not we did minister to You? Then He will answer them, saying,
281 3004 5213 1909 3785 3756 4160 1520 5130 3588
Ἀμὴν λέγω ὑμῖν, ἐφ ὅσον οὐκ ἐποιήσατε ἑνὶ τούτων τῶν
Truly I say to you, in as much as not you did to one of these the
1646 3761 1698 4160 2532 565 3778
ἐλαχίστων, οὐδὲ ἐμοὶ ἐποιήσατε. 46 καὶ ἀπελεύσονται οὗτοι
least (ones), neither to Me you did. And will go away these
1519 2851 166 3588 1161 1342 1519 2222 166
εἰς κόλασιν αἰώνιον· οἱ δὲ δίκαιοι εἰς ζωὴν αἰώνιον.
into punishment everlasting, the but righteous into life everlasting.

King James Version

and ye took me in:
36 Naked, and ye clothed me: I was sick, and ye visited me: I was in prison, and ye came unto me.

37 Then shall the righteous answer him, saying, Lord, when saw we thee an hungred, and fed (thee)? or thirsty, and gave (thee) drink?
38 When saw we thee a stranger, and took (thee) in? or naked, and clothed (thee)?
39 Or when saw we thee sick, or in prison, and came unto thee?
40 And the King shall answer and say unto them, Verily I say unto you, Inasmuch as ye have done (it) unto one of the least of these my brethren, ye have done (it) unto me.
41 Then shall he say also unto them on the left hand, Depart from me, ye cursed, into everlasting fire, prepared for the devil and his angels:

42 For I was an hungred, and ye gave me no meat: I was thirsty, and ye gave me no drink:
43 I was a stranger, and ye took me not in: naked, and ye clothed me not: sick, and in prison, and ye visited me not.

44 Then shall they also answer him, saying, Lord, when saw we thee an hungred, or athirst, or a stranger, or naked, or sick, or in prison, and did not minister unto thee?

45 Then shall he answer them, saying, Verily I say unto you, Inasmuch as ye did (it) not to one of the least of these, ye did (it) not to me.

46 And these shall go away into everlasting punishment: but the righteous into life eternal.

Literal Translation

Matthew 26

1. And it happened, when Jesus finished all these sayings, He said to His disciples,
2 You know that the Passover comes after two days, and the Son of man is delivered up to be crucified.

3. Then the chief priests and the scribes and the elders of the people were assembled to the court of the high priest, the (one) named Caiaphas.
4 And (they) plotted together in order that they might seize Jesus by guile and kill (Him).

5 But they said, Not during the feast, that there be no uproar among the people.

6. And Jesus being in Bethany, in Simon the leper's house,
7 a woman came to Him having an alabaster vial of ointment, very precious. And (she) poured (it) on His head as He reclined.
8 But seeing, His disciples were indignant, saying, For what (is) this waste?
9 For this ointment could have been sold for much and be given to (the) poor.
10 But knowing, Jesus said to them, Why do you cause trouble to the woman? For she worked a good work toward Me.
11 For you always have the poor with you, but you do not always have Me.
12 For pouring this ointment on My body, she did (it) in order to bury Me.

13 Truly I say to you, Wherever this gospel is proclaimed in all the world, what she did

Matthew 26:1

2532 1096 3753 5055 3588 2424 3956 3588 3956
1. Καὶ ἐγένετο ὅτε ἐτέλεσεν ὁ Ἰησοῦς πάντας τοὺς λόγους
And it was, when ended Jesus all sayings

5128 2036 3588 3101 846 1492 3754 3326 1417
τούτους, εἶπε τοῖς μαθηταῖς αὐτοῦ, 2 Οἴδατε ὅτι μετὰ δύο
these, He said to the disciples of Him, You know that after two

2250 3588 3857 1096 2532 3588 5207 3588 444 3860
ἡμέρας τὸ πάσχα γίνεται, καὶ ὁ υἱὸς τοῦ ἀνθρώπου παραδί-
days the Passover comes, and the Son of man delivered

1519 3588 4717 5119 4863 3588 749
δοται εἰς τὸ σταυρωθῆναι. 3 τότε συνήχθησαν οἱ ἀρχιερεῖς
up to be crucified. Then were assembled the chief priests

2532 3588 1122 2532 3588 4245 3588 2992 1519 3588
καὶ οἱ γραμματεῖς καὶ οἱ πρεσβύτεροι τοῦ λαοῦ εἰς τὴν
and the scribes and the elders of the people to the

833 3588 749 3588 3004 2533 2532 4823
αὐλὴν τοῦ ἀρχιερέως τοῦ λεγομένου Καιάφα, 4 καὶ συνεβου-
court of the high priest being named Caiaphas, and consulted

2443 3588 2424 2902 1388 2532 615
λεύσαντο ἵνα τὸν Ἰησοῦν κρατήσωσι δόλῳ καὶ ἀπο-
together that Jesus they might seize by guile and

3004 1161 3361 1722 3588 1859 2443 3361 2351
κτείνωσιν. 5 ἔλεγον δέ, Μὴ ἐν τῇ ἑορτῇ, ἵνα μὴ θόρυβος
kill (Him). they said And, Not at the feast, that not a turmoil

1096 1722 3588 2992
γένηται ἐν τῷ λαῷ.
occur among the people.

3588 1161 2424 1096 1722 963 1722 3614 4613 3588
6. Τοῦ δὲ Ἰησοῦ γενομένου ἐν Βηθανίᾳ ἐν οἰκίᾳ Σίμωνος τοῦ
And Jesus being in Bethany in house of Simon the

3015 4334 846 1135 211 3414 2192
λεπροῦ, 7 προσῆλθεν αὐτῷ γυνὴ ἀλάβαστρον μύρου ἔχουσα
leper, came up to Him a woman an alabaster vial of ointment having

927 2532 2708 1909 3588 2776 846 345
βαρυτίμου, καὶ κατέχεεν ἐπὶ τὴν κεφαλὴν αὐτοῦ ἀνακει-
very precious, and poured (it) over the head of Him (He) having

1492 1161 3588 3101 846 23 3004
μένου. 8 ἰδόντες δὲ οἱ μαθηταὶ αὐτοῦ ἠγανάκτησαν, λέγοντες,
reclined. seeing And the disciples of Him were indignant, saying,

1519 5101 3588 684 3778 1410 1063 5124 3588 3464
Εἰς τί ἡ ἀπώλεια αὕτη; 9 ἠδύνατο γὰρ τοῦτο τὸ μύρον
To what waste this? was able For this ointment

4097 4183 2532 1325 4434 1097 1161 3588 2424
πραθῆναι πολλοῦ, καὶ δοθῆναι πτωχοῖς. 10 γνοὺς δὲ ὁ Ἰησοῦς
have been sold of much, and to be given to (the) poor. knowing But Jesus

2036 846 5101 2873 3930 3588 1135 2041 1063
εἶπεν αὐτοῖς, Τί κόπους παρέχετε τῇ γυναικί; ἔργον γὰρ
said to them, Why trouble do you cause to the woman? work For

2570 2038 1519 1691 3842 1063 3588 4434 2192
καλὸν εἰργάσατο εἰς ἐμέ· 11 πάντοτε γὰρ τοὺς πτωχοὺς ἔχετε
a good she worked toward Me. always For the poor you have

3326 1438 1691 1161 3756 3842 2192 906 1063 846
μεθ' ἑαυτῶν, ἐμὲ δὲ οὐ πάντοτε ἔχετε. 12 βαλοῦσα γὰρ αὕτη
with yourselves. Me But not always you have. pouring For she

3588 3464 5124 1909 3588 4983 3450 4314 3588 1779
τὸ μύρον τοῦτο ἐπὶ τοῦ σώματός μου, πρὸς τὸ ἐνταφιάσαι
ointment this over the body of Me in order to bury

3165 4160 281 3004 5213 3699 1437 2784 3588 2098
με ἐποίησεν. 13 ἀμὴν λέγω ὑμῖν, ὅπου ἐὰν κηρυχθῇ τὸ εὐαγ-
Me she did (it). Truly I say to you, wherever is proclaimed gospel

5124 1722 3650 3588 2889 2980 2532 3739 4160
γέλιον τοῦτο ἐν ὅλῳ τῷ κόσμῳ, λαληθήσεται καὶ ὃ ἐποίησεν
this in all the world, will be spoken also what did

King James Version

Matthew 26

1. And it came to pass, when Jesus had finished all these sayings, he said unto his disciples,
2 Ye know that after two days is (the feast of) the passover, and the Son of man is betrayed to be crucified.

3. Then assembled together the chief priests, and the scribes, and the elders of the people, unto the palace of the high priest, who was called Caiaphas,
4 And consulted that they might take Jesus by subtilty, and kill (him).

5 But they said, Not on the feast (day), lest there be an uproar among the people.

6. Now when Jesus was in Bethany, in the house of Simon the leper,
7 There came unto him a woman having an alabaster box of very precious ointment, and poured it on his head, as he sat (at meat).
8 But when his disciples saw (it), they had indignation, saying, To what purpose (is) this waste?
9 For this ointment might have been sold for much, and given to the poor.
10 When Jesus understood (it), he said unto them, Why trouble ye the woman? for she hath wrought a good work upon me.
11 For ye have the poor always with you; but me ye have not always.

12 For in that she hath poured this ointment on my body, she did (it) for my burial.

13 Verily I say unto you, Wheresoever this gospel shall be preached in the whole world, (there) shall also this, that

Literal Translation | **Matthew 26:14** | **King James Version**

of as a memorial of her.

846 1519 3422 846
αὐτη, εἰς μνημόσυνον αὐτῆς.
she for a memorial of her.

for a memorial of her.

14. Then one of the twelve going to the chief priests, the (one) being named Judas Iscariot,
15 said, What will you give to me, and I will deliver Him up to you? And they weighed to him thirty silver pieces. (Zech. 11:12)

16 And from then he sought opportunity that he might deliver up Him.

5119 4198 1520 3588 1427 3588 3004 2455
14. Τότε πορευθεὶς εἷς τῶν δώδεκα, ὁ λεγόμενος Ἰούδας
Then going one of the Twelve, he being named Judas
2469 4314 3588 749 2036 5101 2309 3427 1325
Ἰσκαριώτης, πρὸς τοὺς ἀρχιερεῖς, 15 εἶπε, Τί θέλετέ μοι δοῦναι,
Iscariot, to the chief priests, said, What will you me give
2504 5213 3860 846 3588 1161 2476 846 5144
κἀγὼ ὑμῖν παραδώσω αὐτόν; οἱ δὲ ἔστησαν αὐτῷ τριά-
and I to you will deliver up Him? they And weighed him thirty
694 2532 575 5119 2212 2120 2443 846
κοντα ἀργύρια. 16 καὶ ἀπὸ τότε ἐζήτει εὐκαιρίαν ἵνα αὐτὸν
silver pieces. And from then he sought opportunity that Him
3860
παραδῷ.
he might deliver up.

14. Then one of the twelve, called Judas Iscariot, went unto the chief priests,
15 And said (unto them), What will ye give me, and I will deliver him unto you? And they covenanted with him for thirty pieces of silver.
16 And from that time he sought opportunity to betray him.

17. And on the first (day of) the (Feast of) Unleavened (Bread), the disciples came to Jesus, saying to Him, Where do you desire we should prepare for You to eat the Passover?
18 And He said, Go into the city to a certain one and say to him, The Teacher says, My time is near; with you I will prepare the Passover with My disciples.

3588 1161 4413 3588 106 4334 3588 3101 3588
17. Τῇ δὲ πρώτῃ τῶν ἀζύμων προσῆλθον οἱ μαθηταὶ τῷ
on the And first (day) of the unleavened (bread) came the disciples
2424 3004 846 4226 2309 2090 4671 5315
Ἰησοῦ, λέγοντες αὐτῷ, Ποῦ θέλεις ἑτοιμάσωμέν σοι φαγεῖν
to Jesus, saying to Him, Where desire You we may prepare for You to eat
3588 3957 3588 1161 2036 5217 1519 3588 4172 4314 3588
τὸ πάσχα; 18 ὁ δὲ εἶπεν, Ὑπάγετε εἰς τὴν πόλιν πρὸς τὸν
the Passover? He And said, Go into the city to
1170 2532 2036 846 3588 1320 3004 3588 2540 3450
δεῖνα, καὶ εἴπατε αὐτῷ, Ὁ διδάσκαλος λέγει, Ὁ καιρός μου
a certain one, and say to him, The Teacher says, The time of Me
1451 2076 4314 4571 4160 3588 3957 3326 3588 3101 3450
ἐγγύς ἐστι· πρὸς σὲ ποιῶ τὸ πάσχα μετὰ τῶν μαθητῶν μου.
near is; with you I make the Passover with the disciples of Me.

17. Now the first (day) of the (feast of) unleavened bread the disciples came to Jesus, saying unto him, Where wilt thou that we prepare for thee to eat the passover?
18 And he said, Go into the city to such a man, and say unto him, The Master saith, My time is at hand; I will keep the passover at thy house with my disciples.

19 And the disciples did as Jesus ordered them, and prepared the Passover.
20. And evening coming, He reclined with the Twelve.
21 And (as) they were eating, He said, Truly I say to you that one of you will betray Me.
22 And grieving exceedingly, they began to say to Him, each of them, Lord, not I am (the one)?
23 But answering, He said, The (one) dipping the hand with Me in the dish, this one will betray Me.
24 Indeed, the Son of man goes, as it has been written about Him. But woe to that man by whom the Son of man is betrayed. It were good for him if that man was never born.

25 And answering, the (one)

2532 4160 3588 3101 5613 4929 846 3588 2424 2532
19 καὶ ἐποίησαν οἱ μαθηταὶ ὡς συνέταξεν αὐτοῖς ὁ Ἰησοῦς, καὶ
And did the disciples as ordered them Jesus, and
2090 3588 3957 3798 1161 1096 345 3326 3588
ἡτοίμασαν τὸ πάσχα. 20 ὀψίας δὲ γενομένης ἀνέκειτο μετὰ τῶν
prepared the Passover. evening And having come He reclined with the
1427 2532 2068 846 2036 281 3004 5213 3754
δώδεκα. 21 καὶ ἐσθιόντων αὐτῶν εἶπεν, Ἀμὴν λέγω ὑμῖν ὅτι
Twelve. And eating they He said, Truly I say to you that
1520 1537 5216 3860 3165 2532 3076 4970 756
εἷς ἐξ ὑμῶν παραδώσει με. 22 καὶ λυπούμενοι σφόδρα ἤρξαντο
one out of you will betray Me. And grieving exceedingly they began
3004 846 1538 846 3385 1473 1510 2962 3588 1161
λέγειν αὐτῷ ἕκαστος αὐτῶν, Μήτι ἐγώ εἰμι, Κύριε; 23 ὁ δὲ
to say to Him each of them, Not I am (he), Lord? He But
611 2036 3588 1686 3326 1700 1722 3588 5165 3588
ἀποκριθεὶς εἶπεν, Ὁ ἐμβάψας μετ᾽ ἐμοῦ ἐν τῷ τρυβλίῳ τὴν
answering said, The (one) dipping with Me in the dish the
5495 3778 3165 3860 3588/3303/5207 3588 444 5217
χεῖρα, οὗτός με παραδώσει. 24 ὁ μὲν υἱὸς του ἀνθρώπου ὑπάγει,
hand, this one Me will betray. the Truly Son of man goes,
2531 1125 4012 846 3759 1161 3588 444 1565
καθὼς γέγραπται περὶ αὐτοῦ· οὐαὶ δὲ τῷ ἀνθρώπῳ ἐκείνῳ,
even as it has been written about Him; woe But man to that,
1223 3739 3588 5207 3588 444 3860 2570 2258 846 1487
δι᾽ οὗ ὁ υἱὸς τοῦ ἀνθρώπου παραδίδοται· καλὸν ἦν αὐτῷ εἰ
by whom the Son of man is betrayed; good were it if
3756 1080 3588 444 1565 611 1161 2455 3588
οὐκ ἐγεννήθη ὁ ἄνθρωπος ἐκεῖνος. 25 ἀποκριθεὶς δὲ Ἰούδας ὁ
not was born man that. answering And Judas who

19 And the disciples did as Jesus had appointed them; and they made ready the passover.
20. Now when the even was come, he sat down with the twelve.
21 And as they did eat, he said, Verily I say unto you, that one of you shall betray me.
22 And they were exceeding sorrowful, and began every one of them to say unto him, Lord, is it I?
23 And he answered and said, He that dippeth (his) hand with me in the dish, the same shall betray me.
24 The Son of man goeth as it is written of him: but woe unto that man by whom the Son of man is betrayed! it had been good for that man if he had not been born.

25 Then Judas, which

Matthew 26:26

Literal Translation

betraying Him, Judas,
said, Not I am (the one),
Rabbi? He said to him,
You said (it).
26. And as they ate,
taking the bread and
blessing (it), Jesus
broke and gave to the
disciples, and said,
Take, eat; this is My
body.
27 And taking the cup,
and giving thanks, He
gave to them, saying,
Drink all of it.

28 For this is My blood
of the New Covenant
which concerning
many is being poured
out for remission of
sins.

29 But I say to you, I will
not at all drink of this
fruit of the vine after this
until that day when I
drink it new with you in
the kingdom of My Father.

30. And having sung a
hymn, they went to the
Mount of Olives.

31 Then Jesus said to
them, You all will be offended
in Me during
this night. For it has
been written, "I will
smite the Shepherd, and
the sheep of the flock
will be scattered."
(Zech. 13:7)

32 But after My being
raised I will go before
you into Galilee.

33 And answering, Peter
said to Him, Even if
all will be offended in
You, I will never be offended.

34 Jesus said to him,
Truly I say to you, During
this night, before a
cock crows, you will
deny Me three times.
35 Peter said to Him,
Even if it were necessary
for me to die with
You, I will in no way
deny You. And all the
disciples said the same.

3860 846 2036 3385 1473 1510 4461 3004 846
παραδιδοὺς αὐτὸν εἶπε, Μήτι ἐγώ εἰμι, ῥαββί; λέγει αὐτῷ,
was betraying Him said, Not I am (he), Rabbi? He says to him,

4771 2036 2068 1161 846 2983 3588 2424 3588 740
Σὺ εἶπας. 26 ἐσθιόντων δὲ αὐτῶν, λαβὼν ὁ Ἰησοῦς τὸν ἄρτον,
You have said. eating And they, taking Jesus the bread

2532 2127 2806 2532 1325 3588 3101 2532 2036
καὶ εὐλογήσας, ἔκλασε καὶ ἐδίδου τοῖς μαθηταῖς, καὶ εἶπε,
and blessing, He broke and gave to the disciples, and said,

2983 5315 5124 2076 3588 4983 3450 2532 2983 3588
Λάβετε, φάγετε· τοῦτό ἐστι τὸ σῶμά μου. 27 καὶ λαβὼν τὸ
Take, eat, this is the body of Me. And taking the

4221 2532 2168 1325 846 3004 4095
ποτήριον καὶ εὐχαριστήσας, ἔδωκεν αὐτοῖς, λέγων, Πίετε
cup and giving thanks, He gave to them, saying, Drink

1537 846 3956 5124 1063 2076 3588 129 3450 3588 3588 2537
ἐξ αὐτοῦ πάντες· 28 τοῦτο γάρ ἐστι τὸ αἷμά μου, τὸ τῆς καινῆς
of it all; this for is the blood of Me of the New

1242 3588 4012 4183 1632 1519 859 266
διαθήκης τὸ περὶ πολλῶν ἐκχυνόμενον εἰς ἄφεσιν ἁμαρτιῶν.
Covenant, that concerning many is being poured out for remission of sins.

3004 1161 5213 3754 3756 3361 4095 575 737 1537 5127 3588 1081
29 λέγω δὲ ὑμῖν ὅτι οὐ μὴ πίω ἀπ' ἄρτι ἐκ τούτου τοῦ γεννή-
I say And to you that not at all will I drink from now of this fruit

3588 288 2193 3588 2250 1565 3752 846 4095
ματος τῆς ἀμπέλου, ἕως τῆς ἡμέρας ἐκείνης ὅταν αὐτὸ πίνω
of the vine until day that when it I drink

3326 5216 2537 1722 3588 932 3588 3962 3450
μεθ' ὑμῶν καινὸν ἐν τῇ βασιλείᾳ τοῦ πατρός μου.
with you new in the kingdom of the Father of Me.

2532 5214 1831 1519 3588 3735 3588 1636
30 Καὶ ὑμνήσαντες ἐξῆλθον εἰς τὸ ὄρος τῶν ἐλαιῶν.
And having hymned they went to the Mount of the Olives.

5119 3004 846 3588 2424 3956 5210 4624
31. Τότε λέγει αὐτοῖς ὁ Ἰησοῦς, Πάντες ὑμεῖς σκανδαλισθή-
Then says to them Jesus, All you will be offended

1722 1698 1722 3588 3571 3778 1125 1063 3960
σεσθε ἐν ἐμοὶ ἐν τῇ νυκτὶ ταύτῃ· γέγραπται γάρ, Πατάξω
in Me in night this; it has been written for, I will strike

3588 4166 2532 1287 3588 4263 3588
τὸν ποιμένα, καὶ διασκορπισθήσεται τὰ πρόβατα τῆς
the Shepherd, and will be scattered the sheep of the

4167 3326 1161 3588 1453 3165 4254 5209 1519 3588
ποίμνης. 32 μετὰ δὲ τὸ ἐγερθῆναί με, προάξω ὑμᾶς εἰς τὴν
flock; after But being raised Me, I will go before you into

1056 611 1161/3588 4074 2036 846 1487/2532
Γαλιλαίαν. 33 ἀποκριθεὶς δὲ ὁ Πέτρος εἶπεν αὐτῷ, Εἰ καὶ
Galilee. answering And Peter said to Him, If even

3956 4624 1722 4671 1473 3763 4624
πάντες σκανδαλισθήσονται ἐν σοί, ἐγὼ οὐδέποτε σκανδαλισ-
all be offended in You, i never will be offended.

5346 846 3588 2424 281 3004 4671 3754 1722 1778
θήσομαι. 34 ἔφη αὐτῷ ὁ Ἰησοῦς, Ἀμὴν λέγω σοι ὅτι ἐν ταύτῃ
said to him Jesus, Truly I say to you that in this

3588 3571 4250 220 5455 5151 533 3165 3004
τῇ νυκτί, πρὶν ἀλέκτορα φωνῆσαι τρὶς ἀπαρνήσῃ με. 35 λέγει
night, before (the) cock crows, thrice you will deny Me. says

846 3588 4074 2579 1163 3165 4862 4671 599 3756/3361/4571
αὐτῷ ὁ Πέτρος, Κἂν δέῃ με σὺν σοὶ ἀποθανεῖν, οὐ μή σε
to him Peter, Even if must me with You to die, in no way You

533 3668 2532 3956 3588 3101 2036
ἀπαρνήσομαι. ὁμοίως καὶ πάντες οἱ μαθηταὶ εἶπον.
I will deny. Likewise also all the disciples said.

King James Version

betrayed him, answered
and said, Master,
is it I? He said unto
him, Thou hast said.
26. And as they were
eating, Jesus took bread,
and blessed (it), and
brake (it), and gave (it)
to the disciples, and said,
Take, eat; this is my
body.
27 And he took the cup,
and gave thanks, and
gave (it) to them, saying,
Drink ye all of it;

28 For this is my blood
of the new testament,
which is shed for many
for the remission of
sins.

29 But I say unto you, I
will not drink henceforth
of this fruit of the
vine, until that day
when I drink it new with
you in my Father's
kingdom.

30. And when they had
sung an hymn, they
went out into the mount
of Olives.
31 Then saith Jesus
unto them, All ye shall
be offended because of
me this night: for it is
written, I will smite the
shepherd, and the sheep
of the flock shall be
scattered abroad.

32 But after I am risen
again, I will go before
you into Galilee.

33 Peter answered and
said unto him, Though
all (men) shall be offended
because of thee,
(yet) will I never be offended.

34 Jesus said unto him,
Verily I say unto thee,
That this night, before
the cock crow, thou
shalt deny me thrice.
35 Peter said unto him,
Though I should die
with thee, yet will I not
deny thee. Likewise
also said all the disciples.

Literal Translation

36. Then Jesus came with them to a place called Gethsemane. And He said to the disciples, Sit here, until going away, I shall pray there.
37 And taking along Peter and the two sons of Zebedee, He began to grieve and to be deeply troubled.

38 Then He said to them, My soul is deeply grieved unto death. Stay here and watch with Me.
39 And going forward a little, He fell on His face, praying, and saying, My Father, if it is possible, let this cup pass from Me; yet not as I will, but as You (will).

40 And He came to the disciples and found them sleeping. And (He) said to Peter, So! Were you not able to watch one hour with Me?

41 Watch and pray, that you do not enter into temptation. The spirit indeed (is) ready, but the flesh (is) weak.

42 Again, going away a second time, He prayed, saying, My Father, if this cup cannot pass away from Me without My drinking it, let Your will be done.

43 And coming, He again found them sleeping, for their eyes were weighed down.
44 And leaving them, going away again, He prayed a third time, saying the same word.

45 Then He came to His disciples and said to them, Sleep on, and rest. Behold,

Matthew 26:36

5119 2064 3326 846 3588 2424 1519 5564 3004
36. Τότε ἔρχεται μετ' αὐτῶν ὁ Ἰησοῦς εἰς χωρίον λεγόμενον
Then comes with them Jesus to a place being called

1068 2532 3004 3588 3101 2523 846 2193 3757
Γεθσημανῆ, καὶ λέγει τοῖς μαθηταῖς, Καθίσατε αὐτοῦ, ἕως οὗ
Gethsemane, and says to the disciples, You sit here until

565 4336 1563 2532 3880 3588 4074 2532
ἀπελθὼν προσεύξωμαι ἐκεῖ. 37 καὶ παραλαβὼν τὸν Πέτρον καὶ
going away I shall pray there. And taking along Peter and

3588 1417 5207 2199 756 3076 2532 85
τοὺς δύο υἱοὺς Ζεβεδαίου, ἤρξατο λυπεῖσθαι καὶ ἀδημονεῖν.
the two sons of Zebedee, He began to grieve and to be distressed.

5119 3004 846 4036 2076 3588 5590 3450 2193 2288
38 τότε λέγει αὐτοῖς, Περίλυπός ἐστιν ἡ ψυχή μου ἕως θανάτου·
Then He says to them, Deeply grieved is the soul of Me unto death;

3306 5602 2532 1127 3326 1700 2532 4281 3397
μείνατε ὧδε καὶ γρηγορεῖτε μετ' ἐμοῦ. 39 καὶ προελθὼν μικρὸν,
remain here and watch with Me. And going forward a little,

4098 1909 4383 846 4336 2532 3004
ἔπεσεν ἐπὶ πρόσωπον αὐτοῦ προσευχόμενος καὶ λέγων,
He fell on (the) face of Him, praying and saying,

3962 3450 1487 1415 2076 3928 575 1700 3588 4221
Πάτερ μου, εἰ δυνατόν ἐστι, παρελθάτω ἀπ' ἐμοῦ τὸ ποτή-
Father of Me, If possible it is, let pass from Me cup

5124 4133 3756 5613 1473 2309 235 5613 4771 2532 2064
ριον τοῦτο· πλὴν οὐχ ὡς ἐγὼ θέλω, ἀλλ' ὡς σύ. 40 καὶ ἔρχεται
this; yet not as I will, but as You And He comes

4314 3588 3101 2532 2147 846 2518 2532
πρὸς τοὺς μαθητάς, καὶ εὑρίσκει αὐτοὺς. καθεύδοντας, καὶ
to the disciples and finds them sleeping, and

3004 3588 4074 3779 3756 2480 3391 5610 1127
λέγει τῷ Πέτρῳ, Οὕτως οὐκ ἰσχύσατε μίαν ὥραν γρηγορῆ-
says to Peter, So not had you strength one hour to watch

3326 1700 1127 2532 4336 2443 3361
σαι μετ' ἐμοῦ; 41 γρηγορεῖτε καὶ προσεύχεσθε, ἵνα μὴ
with Me? Watch and pray, that not

1525 1519 3986 3588 3303 4151 4289 3588 1161
εἰσέλθητε εἰς πειρασμόν· τὸ μὲν πνεῦμα πρόθυμον, ἡ δὲ
you enter into temptation; the indeed spirit (is) eager, the but

4561 772 3825 1537 1208 565 4336
σὰρξ ἀσθενής. 42 πάλιν ἐκ δευτέρου ἀπελθὼν προσηύξατο,
flesh (is) weak. Again a second (time) going away He prayed,

3004 3962 3450 1487 3756 1410 5124 3588 4221
λέγων, Πάτερ μου, εἰ οὐ δύναται τοῦτο τὸ ποτήριον
saying, Father of Me, if not (it is) possible this cup

3928 575 1700 1437 3361 846 4095 1096 3588 2307
παρελθεῖν ἀπ' ἐμοῦ, ἐὰν μὴ αὐτὸ πίω, γενηθήτω τὸ θέλημά
to pass away from Me, if not it I drink, let be done the will

4675 2532 2064 2147 846 3825 2518 2258
σου. 43 καὶ ἐλθὼν εὑρίσκει αὐτοὺς πάλιν καθεύδοντας, ἦσαν
of You. And coming He finds them again sleeping, were

1063 846 3588 3788 916 2532 863 846
γὰρ αὐτῶν οἱ ὀφθαλμοὶ βεβαρημένοι. 44 καὶ ἀφεὶς αὐτοὺς
for of them the eyes weighed down. And leaving them

565 3825 4336 1537 5154 3588 846 3056
ἀπελθὼν πάλιν προσηύξατο ἐκ τρίτου, τὸν αὐτὸν λόγον
going away again, He prayed a third (time), the same word

2036 5119 2064 4314 3588 3101 846 2532 3004
εἰπών. 45 τότε ἔρχεται πρὸς τοὺς μαθητὰς αὐτοῦ, καὶ λέγει
saying. Then He comes to the disciples of Him, and says

846 2518 3588 3063 2532 373 2400 1448
αὐτοῖς, Καθεύδετε τὸ λοιπὸν καὶ ἀναπαύεσθε; ἰδού, ἤγγικεν
to them, Sleep on now and rest. Behold! draws near

King James Version

36. Then cometh Jesus with them unto a place called Gethsemane, and saith unto the disciples, Sit ye here, while I go and pray yonder.

37 And he took with him Peter and the two sons of Zebedee, and began to be sorrowful and very heavy.

38 Then saith he unto them, My soul is exceeding sorrowful, even unto death: tarry ye here, and watch with me.
39 And he went a little further, and fell on his face, and prayed, saying, O my Father, if it be possible, let this cup pass from me: nevertheless not as I will, but as thou (wilt).
40 And he cometh unto the disciples, and findeth them asleep, and saith unto Peter, What, could ye not watch with me one hour?

41 Watch and pray, that ye enter not into temptation: the spirit indeed (is) willing, but the flesh (is) weak.

42 He went away again the second time, and prayed, saying, O my Father, if this cup may not pass away from me, except I drink it, thy will be done.

43 And he came and found them asleep again: for their eyes were heavy.
44 And he left them, and went away again, and prayed the third time, saying the same words.

45 Then cometh he to his disciples, and saith unto them, Sleep on now, and take (your) rest: behold,

Literal Translation — **Matthew 26:46** — *King James Version*

the hour draws near, and the Son of man is betrayed into (the) hands of sinners.
46 Rise up, let us go. Behold, the (one) betraying Me draws near.

47. And as He was yet speaking, behold, Judas came, one of the Twelve. And with him was a numerous crowd with swords and clubs, from the chief priests and elders of the people.
48 And the (one) betraying Him gave them a sign, saying, Whomever I may kiss, it is He; seize Him.

49 And coming up at once to Jesus, he said, Hail, Rabbi. And (he) ardently kissed Him.

50 But Jesus said to him, Friend, why are you here? Then coming up, they laid hands on Jesus and seized Him.

51 And, behold, one of those with Jesus, stretching out the hand, drew his sword and striking the slave of the high priest took off his ear.
52 Then Jesus said to him, Put your sword back into its place. For all who take (the) sword shall perish by a sword.

53 Or do you think that I am not able now to call on My Father, and He will place beside Me more than twelve legions of angels?
54 How then should the Scriptures be fulfilled, that it must happen this way?
55 In that hour, Jesus said to the crowds, Did you come out together to take Me with swords and clubs, as against a plunderer?

3588 5610 2532 3588 5207 3588 444 3860 1519 5495
ἡ ὥρα, καὶ ὁ υἱὸς τοῦ ἀνθρώπου παραδίδοται εἰς χεῖρας
the hour, and the Son of man is delivered up into hands

268 1453 71 2400 1448 3588 3860
ἁμαρτωλῶν. 46 ἐγείρεσθε, ἄγωμεν. ἰδού, ἤγγικεν ὁ παραδι-
of sinners. Rise, let us go. Behold! draws near The (one)

3165
δούς με.
betraying Me.

2532 2089 846 2980 2400 2455 1520 3588 1427
47. Καὶ ἔτι αὐτοῦ λαλοῦντος, ἰδού, Ἰούδας εἷς τῶν δώδεκα
And while He was speaking, behold, Judas, one to the twelve

2064 2532 3326 846 3793 4183 3326 3162 2532
ἦλθε, καὶ μετ᾽ αὐτοῦ ὄχλος πολὺς μετὰ μαχαιρῶν καὶ
came, and with him a crowd numerous with swords and

3586 575 3588 749 2532 4245 3588 2992 3588
ξύλων, ἀπὸ τῶν ἀρχιερέων καὶ πρεσβυτέρων τοῦ λαοῦ. 48 ὁ
clubs, from the chief priests and elders of the people. he

1161 3860 846 1325 846 4592 3004 3739
δὲ παραδιδοὺς αὐτὸν ἔδωκεν αὐτοῖς σημεῖον, λέγων, Ὃν
And delivering up Him gave to them a sign, saying, Whom-

302 5368 846 2076 2902 846 2532 2112
ἂν φιλήσω, αὐτός ἐστι· κρατήσατε αὐτόν. 49 καὶ εὐθέως
ever I may kiss, He it is; seize Him. And at once

4334 3588 2424 2036 5463 4461 2532 2705
προσελθὼν τῷ Ἰησοῦ εἶπε, Χαῖρε, ῥαββί· καὶ κατεφίλησεν
coming up to Jesus, he said, Hail, Rabbi, and ardently kissed

846 3588 1161 2424 2036 846 2083 1909 3739 3918 5119
αὐτόν. 50 ὁ δὲ Ἰησοῦς εἶπεν αὐτῷ, Ἑταῖρε, ἐφ᾽ ᾧ πάρει; τότε
Him. But Jesus said to him, Friend, why are you here? Then

4334 1911 3588 5495 1909 3588 2424 2532
προσελθόντες ἐπέβαλον τὰς χεῖρας ἐπὶ τὸν Ἰησοῦν, καὶ
coming up, they laid the hands on Jesus, and

2902 846 2532 2400 1520 3588 3326 2424 1614
ἐκράτησαν αὐτόν. 51 καὶ ἰδού, εἷς τῶν μετὰ Ἰησοῦ, ἐκτείνας
seized Him. And, behold, one of those with Jesus, stretching

3588 5495 645 3588 3162 846 2532 3960 3588
τὴν χεῖρα, ἀπέσπασε τὴν μάχαιραν αὐτοῦ, καὶ πατάξας τὸν
the hand, drew the sword of him, and striking the

1401 3588 749 851 846 3588 5621 5119 3004
δοῦλον τοῦ ἀρχιερέως ἀφεῖλεν αὐτοῦ τὸ ὠτίον. 52 τότε λέγει
slave of the high priest took off to him the ear. Then says

846 3588 2424 654 4675 3588 3162 1519 3588
αὐτῷ ὁ Ἰησοῦς, Ἀπόστρεψόν σου τὴν μάχαιράν εἰς τὸν
to him Jesus, Put back of you the sword to the

5117 846 3956 1063 3588 2983 3162 1722 3162
τόπον αὐτῆς· πάντες γὰρ οἱ λαβόντες μάχαιραν ἐν μαχαίρᾳ
place of it; all for those taking (the) sword by a sword

622 2228 1380 3754 3756 1410 737 3870 3588
ἀπολοῦνται. 53 ἢ δοκεῖς ὅτι οὐ δύναμαι ἄρτι παρακαλέσαι τὸν
shall perish. Or think you that not I am able now to call upon the

3962 3450 2532 3936 3427 4119 2228 1427 3003
πατέρα μου, καὶ παραστήσει μοι πλείους ἢ δώδεκα λεγεῶνας
Father of Me, and He will place near Me more than twelve legions

32 4459 3767 4137 3588 1124 3754 3779 1163
ἀγγέλων; 54 πῶς οὖν πληρωθῶσιν αἱ γραφαί, ὅτι οὕτω δεῖ
of angels? How, then, should be fulfilled the Scriptures, that so it must

1096 1722 1565 3588 5610 2036 3588 2424 3588 3793 5613
γενέσθαι; 55 ἐν ἐκείνῃ τῇ ὥρᾳ εἶπεν ὁ Ἰησοῦς τοῖς ὄχλοις, Ὡς
happen? In that hour said Jesus to the crowds, As

1909 3027 1831 3326 3162 2532 3586 4815
ἐπὶ λῃστὴν ἐξήλθετε μετὰ μαχαιρῶν καὶ ξύλων συλλαβεῖν
on a plunderer came you with swords and clubs together to take

---

the hour is at hand, and the Son of man is betrayed into the hands of sinners.
46 Rise, let us be going: behold, he is at hand that doth betray me.

47. And while he yet spake, lo, Judas, one of the twelve, came, and with him a great multitude with swords and staves, from the chief priests and elders of the people.
48 Now he that betrayed him gave them a sign, saying, Whomsoever I shall kiss, that same is he: hold him fast.
49 And forthwith he came to Jesus, and said, Hail, master; and kissed him.

50 And Jesus said unto him, Friend, wherefore art thou come? Then came they, and laid hands on Jesus, and took him.

51 And, behold, one of them which were with Jesus stretched out (his) hand, and drew his sword, and struck a servant of the high priest's, and smote off his ear.
52 Then said Jesus unto him, Put up again thy sword into his place: for all they that take the sword shall perish with the sword.

53 Thinkest thou that I cannot now pray to my Father, and he shall presently give me more than twelve legions of angels?
54 But how then shall the scriptures be fulfilled, that thus it must be?
55 In that same hour said Jesus to the multitudes, Are ye come out as against a thief with swords and staves for to take

Literal Translation **Matthew 26:56** ***King James Version***

I sat with you daily
teaching in the temple,
and you did not lay hold
of Me.
56 But all this has oc-
curred that the Scrip-
tures of the prophets
may be fulfilled. Then
all the disciples ran
away, forsaking Him.

57. And those seizing
Jesus led (Him) away to
Caiaphas the high
priest, where the scribes
and the elders were as-
sembled.
58 And Peter followed
Him from a distance,
even to the court of the
high priest. And going
inside, (he) sat with the
under-officers to see the
end.
59 And the chief priests
and the elders and the
whole sanhedrin sought
false testimony against
Jesus, so that they might
put Him to death,
60 but did not find
(any), even though
(there were) many false
witnesses coming for-
ward, they did not find
any. But at last, coming
up two false witnesses
61 said, This one said, I
am able to destroy the
temple of God, and
through three days to
build it.
62 And standing up, the
high priest said to Him,
Do you answer noth-
ing? What do these wit-
ness against you?
63 But Jesus kept silent.
And answering, the
high priest said to Him,
I put you on oath by the
living God that you tell
us if you are the Christ,
the Son of God.
64 Jesus says to him,
You said (it). I tell you
more. From this time
you shall see the Son of
man sitting off (the)
right (hand) of power,
and

3165 2596 2250 4314 5209 2516 1321 1722 3588 2411
με; καθ' ἡμέραν πρὸς ὑμᾶς ἐκαθεζόμην διδάσκων ἐν τῷ ἱερῷ,
Me? Daily with you I sat teaching in the Temple,

2532 3756 2902 3165 5124 1161 3650 1096 2443 4137
καὶ οὐκ ἐκρατήσατέ με. 56 τοῦτο δὲ ὅλον γέγονεν, ἵνα πληρωθῶ-
and not you seized Me. this But all has occurred that may be ful-

3588 1124 3588 4396 5119 3588 3101 3956
σιν αἱ γραφαὶ τῶν προφητῶν. τότε οἱ μαθηταὶ πάντες
filled the Scriptures of the prophets. Then the disciples all

863 846 5343
ἀφέντες αὐτὸν ἔφυγον.
forsaking Him fled.

3588 1161 2902 3588 2424 520 4314 2533
57. Οἱ δὲ κρατήσαντες τὸν Ἰησοῦν ἀπήγαγον πρὸς Καϊάφαν
The (ones) But seizing Jesus led away to Caiaphas

3588 749 3699 3588 1122 2532 3588 4245
τὸν ἀρχιερέα, ὅπου οἱ γραμματεῖς καὶ οἱ πρεσβύτεροι
the high priest, where the scribes and the elders

4863 3588 1161 4074 190 846 575 3113
συνήχθησαν. 58 ὁ δὲ Πέτρος ἠκολούθει αὐτῷ ἀπὸ μακρόθεν,
were assembled. And Peter followed Him from a distance

2193 3588 833 3588 749 2532 1525 2080 2521
ἕως τῆς αὐλῆς τοῦ ἀρχιερέως, καὶ εἰσελθὼν ἔσω ἐκάθητο
up to the court of the high priest; and going inside (he) sat

3326 3588 5257 1492 3588 5056 3588 1161 749 2532 3588
μετὰ τῶν ὑπηρετῶν, ἰδεῖν τὸ τέλος. 59 οἱ δὲ ἀρχιερεῖς καὶ οἱ
with the under-officers to see the end. the And chief priests and the

4245 2532 3588 4892 3650 2212 5577
πρεσβύτεροι καὶ τὸ συνέδριον ὅλον ἐζήτουν ψευδομαρτυ-
elders and the Sanhedrin whole sought false testimony

2596 3588 2424 3704 846 2289 2532 3756
ρίαν κατὰ τοῦ Ἰησοῦ ὅπως αὐτὸν θανατώσωσι, 60 καὶ οὐχ
against Jesus so as Him they might put to death. And not

2147 2532 4183 5575 4334 3756
εὗρον· καὶ πολλῶν ψευδομαρτύρων προσελθόντων, οὐχ
they found , even (though) many false witnesses (were) coming forward, not

2147 5305 1161 4334 1417 5575 2036
εὗρον. ὕστερον δὲ προσελθόντες δύο ψευδομάρτυρες 61 εἶπον,
did find. at last But coming up two false witnesses said,

3778 5346 1410 2647 3588 3485 3588 2316 2532 1223
Οὗτος ἔφη, Δύναμαι καταλῦσαι τὸν ναὸν τοῦ Θεοῦ, καὶ διὰ
This one said, I am able to destroy the temple of God, and through

5140 2250 3618 846 2532 450 3588 749
τριῶν ἡμερῶν οἰκοδομῆσαι αὐτόν. 62 καὶ ἀναστὰς ὁ ἀρχιερεὺς
three days to build it. And standing up the high priest

2036 846 3762 611 5101 3778 4675 2649
εἶπεν αὐτῷ, Οὐδὲν ἀποκρίνῃ; τι΄ οὗτοί σου καταμαρτυροῦ-
said to Him, Nothing do you reply of what these you do witness

3588 1161 2424 4623 2532 611 3588 749 2036
σιν; 63 ὁ δὲ Ἰησοῦς ἐσιώπα. καὶ ἀποκριθεὶς ὁ ἀρχιερεὺς εἶπεν
against? But Jesus kept silent. And answering the high priest said

846 1844 4571 2596 3588 2316 3588 2198 2443 2254
αὐτῷ, Ἐξορκίζω σε κατὰ τοῦ Θεοῦ τοῦ ζῶντος, ἵνα ἡμῖν
to Him, I on oath put you by God the living, that us

2036 1487 4771 1488 3588 5547 3588 5207 3588 2316 3004 846/3588
εἴπῃς εἰ σὺ εἶ ὁ Χριστός, ὁ υἱός, τοῦ Θεοῦ. 64 λέγει αὐτῷ ὁ
You tell if You are the Christ, the Son of God. Says to him

2424 4771 2036 4133 3004 5213 575 737 3700 3588
Ἰησοῦς, Σὺ εἶπας. πλὴν λέγω ὑμῖν, ἀπ' ἄρτι ὄψεσθε τὸν
Jesus, You said (it). More I tell you from now you will see the

5207 3588 444 2521 1537 1188 3588 1411 2532
υἱὸν τοῦ ἀνθρώπου καθήμενον ἐκ δεξιῶν τῆς δυνάμεως καὶ
Son of man sitting off the right (hand) of power and

me? I sat daily with you
teaching in the temple,
and ye laid no hold on
me.
56 But all this was done,
that the scriptures of the
prophets might be ful-
filled. Then all the disci-
ples forsook him, and
fled.

57. And they that had
laid hold on Jesus led
(him) away to Caiaphas
the high priest, where
the scribes and the eld-
ers were assembled.
58 But Peter followed
him afar off unto the
high priest's palace, and
went in, and sat with the
servants, to see the end.
59 Now the chief
priests, and elders, and
all the council, sought
false witness against Je-
sus, to put him to death;
60 But found none: yea,
though many false wit-
nesses came, (yet)
found they none. At the
last came two false wit-
nesses,
61 And said, This (fel-
low) said, I am able to
destroy the temple of
God, and to build it in
three days.
62 And the high priest
arose, and said unto
him, Answerest thou
nothing? what (is it
which) these witness
against thee?
63 But Jesus held his
peace. And the high
priest answered and
said unto him, I adjure
thee by the living God,
that thou tell us whether
thou be the Christ, the
Son of God.
64 Jesus saith unto him,
Thou hast said: never-
theless I say unto you,
Hereafter shall ye see
the Son of man sitting
on the right hand of
power, and

Literal Translation

coming on the clouds of the heavens. (Ps. 110:1; Dan. 7:13)
65 Then the high priest tore his garments, saying, He blasphemed! Why do we have any more need of witnesses? Behold, now you have heard his blasphemy.
66 What does it seem to you? And answering, they said, He is liable to death.
67 Then they spat in His face, and beat Him with the fist, and they slapped (Him),
68 saying, Prophesy to us, Christ. Who is the (one) that struck you?

69. And Peter sat outside in the court. And one slave-girl came near to him, saying, And you were with Jesus the Galilean.

70 But he denied before all, saying, I do not know what you say.

71 And he, going out into the porch, another saw him and said to those there, And this one was with Jesus the Nazarene.

72 And again he denied with an oath, I do not know the man.
73 And after a little, coming near, those standing by said to Peter, Truly you also are of them, for even your speech makes you known.
74 Then he began to curse and to swear, I do not know the man. And immediately a cock crowed.

75 And Peter recalled the word of Jesus, saying to him, Before a cock crows, you will deny Me three times. And going out, he wept bitterly.

Matthew 26:65

2064 1909 3588 3507 3588 3772 5119 3588 749
ἐρχόμενον ἐπὶ τῶν νεφελῶν τοῦ οὐρανοῦ. 65 τότε ὁ ἀρχιερεὺς
coming on the clouds of the heaven. Then the high priest

1284 3588 2440 846 3004 3754 987 5101 2089
διέρρηξε τὰ ἱμάτια αὐτοῦ, λέγων ὅτι Ἐβλασφήμησε· τί ἔτι
tore the garments of him, saying, He blasphemed! Why yet

5532 2192 3144 2396 3568 191 3588 988
χρείαν ἔχομεν μαρτύρων; ἴδε, νῦν ἠκούσατε τὴν βλασφημίαν
need have we of witnesses? Behold, now, you heard the blasphemy

846 5101 5213 1380 3588 1161 611 2036 1777
αὐτοῦ· 66 τί ὑμῖν δοκεῖ; οἱ δὲ ἀποκριθέντες εἶπον, Ἔνοχος
of Him. What to you seems it? they And answering said, Liable

2288 2076 5119 1716 1519 3588 4383 846 2532
θανάτου ἐστί. 67 τότε ἐνέπτυσαν εἰς τὸ πρόσωπον αὐτοῦ καὶ
to death He is. Then they spat into the face of Him, and

2852 846 3588 1161 4474 3004 4395
ἐκολάφισαν αὐτόν· οἱ δὲ ἐρράπισαν, 68 λέγοντες, Προφή-
beat with the fist Him. they And slapped (Him), saying, Prophesy

2254 5547 5101 2076 3588 3817 4571
τευσον ἡμῖν, Χριστέ, τίς ἐστιν ὁ παίσας σε;
to us, Christ; who is it, the (one) striking you?

3588 1161 4074 1854 2521 1722 3588 833 2532 4334
69. Ὁ δὲ Πέτρος ἔξω ἐκάθητο ἐν τῇ αὐλῇ· καὶ προσῆλθεν
And Peter outside sat in the courtyard. And came near

846 3391 3814 3004 2532 4771 2588 3326 2424 3588
αὐτῷ μία παιδίσκη λέγουσα, Καὶ σὺ ἦσθα μετὰ Ἰησοῦ τοῦ
to him one slave-girl saying, And you were with Jesus the

1057 3588 1161 720 1715 3956 3004 3756
Γαλιλαίου. 70 ὁ δὲ ἠρνήσατο ἔμπροσθεν πάντων, λέγων, Οὐκ
Galilean. he But denied before all, saying, not

1492 5101 3004 1831 1161 846 1519 3588 4440 1492
οἶδα τί λέγεις. 71 ἐξελθόντα δὲ αὐτὸν εἰς τὸν πυλῶνα, εἶδεν
I know what you say. going out And he into the portal, saw

846 243 2532 3004 3588 1563 2532 3778 2258 3326 2424
αὐτὸν ἄλλη, καὶ λέγει τοῖς ἐκεῖ, Καὶ οὗτος ἦν μετὰ Ἰησοῦ
him another, and says to those there, And this one was with Jesus

3588 3480 2532 3825 720 3326 3727 3754 3756
τοῦ Ναζωραίου. 72 καὶ πάλιν ἠρνήσατο μεθ' ὅρκου ὅτι Οὐκ
the Nazaraean. And again he denied, with an oath, Not

1492 3588 444 3326 3397 1161 4334 3588 2476
οἶδα τὸν ἄνθρωπον. 73 μετὰ μικρὸν δὲ προσελθόντες οἱ ἑστῶτες
I know the man. after a little And coming near those standing

2036 3588 4074 230 2532 4771 1537 846 1488 2532 1063 3588
εἶπον τῷ Πέτρῳ, Ἀληθῶς καὶ σὺ ἐξ αὐτῶν εἶ· καὶ γὰρ ἡ
said to Peter, Truly, also you of them are, even for the

2981 4675 1212 4571 4160 5119 756 2653 2532
λαλιά σου δῆλόν σε ποιεῖ. 74 τότε ἤρξατο καταναθεματίζειν καὶ
speech of you manifest you makes. Then he began to curse and

3660 3754 3756 1492 3588 444 2532 2112 220
ὀμνύειν ὅτι Οὐκ οἶδα τὸν ἄνθρωπον. καὶ εὐθέως ἀλέκτωρ
to swear, Not I know the man. And at once a cock

5455 2532 3415 3588 4074 3588 4487 3588 2424
ἐφώνησε. 75 καὶ ἐμνήσθη ὁ Πέτρος τοῦ ῥήματος τοῦ Ἰησοῦ
crowed. And remembered Peter the word of Jesus

2046 846 3754 4250 220 5455 5151 533
εἰρηκότος αὐτῷ ὅτι Πρὶν ἀλέκτορα φωνῆσαι, τρὶς ἀπαρνήσῃ
saying to him Before a cock crows thrce you will deny

3165 2532 1831 1854 2799 4090
με· καὶ ἐξελθὼν ἔξω ἔκλαυσε πικρῶς.
Me. And going forth outside he wept bitterly.

King James Version

coming in the clouds of heaven.
65 Then the high priest rent his clothes, saying, He hath spoken blasphemy; what further need have we of witnesses? behold, now ye have heard his blasphemy.
66 What think ye? They answered and said, He is guilty of death.

67 Then did they spit in his face, and buffeted him; and others smote (him) with the palms of their hands,
68 Saying, Prophesy unto us, thou Christ, Who is he that smote thee?

69. Now Peter sat without in the palace: and a damsel came unto him, saying, Thou also wast with Jesus of Galilee.

70 But he denied before (them) all, saying, I know not what thou sayest.
71 And when he was gone out into the porch, another (maid) saw him, and said unto them that were there, This (fellow) was also with Jesus of Nazareth.
72 And again he denied with an oath, I do not know the man.
73 And after a while came unto (him) they that stood by, and said to Peter, Surely thou also art (one) of them; for thy speech bewrayeth thee.

74 Then began he to curse and to swear, (saying), I know not the man. And immediately the cock crew.

75 And Peter remembered the word of Jesus, which said unto him, Before the cock crow, thou shalt deny me thrice. And he went out, and wept bitterly.

Literal Translation

Matthew 27

1. And early morning occurring, all the chief priests and the elders of the people took counsel together against Jesus, so as to put Him to death.

2 And binding Him, they led (Him) away and delivered Him to Pontius Pilate the governor.

3 . Then Judas, the (one) betraying Him, seeing that He was condemned, sorrowing, returned the thirty pieces of silver to the chief priests and the elders,
4 saying, I sinned, betraying innocent blood. But they said, What (is it) to us? You see (to it).
5 And tossing the silver pieces in the temple, he left. And going away (he) hanged himself.

6 And taking the pieces of silver, the chief priests said, It is not lawful to put them into the treasury, since it is (the) price of blood.
7 And taking counsel, they bought of them the potter's field, for burial of the aliens.
8 So that field was called Field of Blood until today.
9 Then was fulfilled that spoken through Jeremiah the prophet, saying, "And I took the thirty pieces of silver, the price of Him who had been priced, on whom they of the sons of Israel set a price,

10 and gave them for the potter's field, as the Lord directed me." (Zech. 11:12, 13)

11. And Jesus stood before the governor. And the governor questioned Him, saying, Are you the king of the Jews? And Jesus said to him, You say (it).

12 And when

Matthew 27:1

4405 1161 1096 4824 2983 3956 3588
1. Πρωΐας δὲ γενομένης, συμβούλιον ἔλαβον πάντες οἱ
early morning And occurring, counsel together took all the
749 2532 3588 4245 3588 2992 2596 3588 2424
ἀρχιερεῖς καὶ οἱ πρεσβύτεροι τοῦ λαοῦ κατὰ τοῦ Ἰησοῦ,
chief priests and the others of the people against Jesus
5620 2289 846 2532 1210 846 520 2532
ὥστε θανατῶσαι αὐτόν· 2 καὶ δήσαντες αὐτὸν ἀπήγαγον καὶ
so as to put to death Him. And having bound Him, they led away and
3860 846 4194 4091 3588 2232
παρέδωκαν αὐτον Ποντίῳ Πιλάτῳ τῷ ἡγεμόνι.
delivered Him to Pontius Pilate the governor.

5119 1492 2455 3588 3860 846 3754 2632
3. Τότε ἰδὼν Ἰούδας ὁ παραδιδοὺς αὐτὸν ὅτι κατεκρίθη,
Then seeing Judas the (one) betraying Him, that He was condemned,
3338 654 3588 5144 694 3588 749
μεταμεληθεὶς ἀπέστρεψε τὰ τριάκοντα ἀργύρια τοῖς ἀρχιε-
sorrowing returned the thirty pieces of silver to the chief
2532 3588 4245 3004 264 3860
ρεῦσι καὶ τοῖς πρεσβυτέροις, 4 λέγων, Ἥμαρτον παραδοὺς
priests and the elders, saying, I sinned, betraying
129 121 3588 1161 2036 5101 4314 2248 4771 3700 2532 4496
αἷμα ἀθῶον. οἱ δὲ εἶπον, Τί πρὸς ἡμᾶς; σὺ ὄψει. 5 καὶ ῥίψας
blood innocent. they But said, What to us? You see (to it). And tossing
3588 694 1722 3588 3485 402 2532 565 519
τὰ ἀργύρια ἐν τῷ ναῷ, ἀνεχώρησε· καὶ ἀπελθὼν ἀπήγξατο.
the silver pieces in the temple, he left; and going away hanged himself.

3588 1161 749 2963 3588 694 2036 3756 1832
6 οἱ δὲ ἀρχιερεῖς λαβόντες τὰ ἀργύρια εἶπον, Οὐκ ἔξεστι
the But chief priests taking the silver pieces said, Not it is lawful
846 1519 3588 2878 1893 5092 129 2076 4824
βαλεῖν αὐτὰ εἰς τὸν κορβανᾶν, ἐπεὶ τιμὴ αἵματός ἐστι. 7 συμ-
to put them into the treasury, since price of blood it is.
1161 2983 59 1537 846 3588 68 3588
βούλιον δὲ λαβόντες ἠγόρασαν ἐξ αὐτῶν τὸν ἀγρὸν τοῦ
counsel And taking they bought of them the field of the
2763 1519 5027 3588 3581 1352 2564 3588 68 1565
κεραμέως, εἰς ταφὴν τοῖς ξένοις. 8 διὸ ἐκλήθη ὁ ἀγρὸς ἐκεῖνος
potter for burial of the aliens. So was called field that
68 129 2193 3588 4594 5119 4137 3588 4483
ἀγρὸς αἵματος, ἕως τῆς σήμερον. 9 τότε ἐπληρώθη τὸ ῥηθὲν
Field of Blood, until today Then was fulfilled that spoken
1223 2408 3588 4396 3004 2532 2983 3588
διὰ Ἱερεμίου τοῦ προφήτου, λέγοντος, Καὶ ἔλαβον τὰ
through Jeremiah the prophet, saying, And I took the
5144 694 3588 5092 3588 5091 3739 5091
τριάκοντα ἀργύρια, τὴν τιμὴν τοῦ τετιμημένου, ὃν ἐτιμή-
thirty pieces of silver, the price of the (One) having been priced, whom they
575 5207 2474 2532 1325 846 1519 3588 68
σαντο ἀπὸ υἱῶν Ἰσραήλ· 10 καὶ ἔδωκαν αὐτὰ εἰς τὸν ἀγρὸν
priced from sons of Israel, and gave them for the field
3588 2763 2505 4929 3427 2962
τοῦ κεραμέως, καθὰ συνέταξέ μοι Κύριος.
of the potter, as directed me (the) Lord.

3588 1161 2424 2476 1715 3588 2232 2532 1905
11. Ὁ δὲ Ἰησοῦς ἔστη ἔμπροσθεν τοῦ ἡγεμόνος· καὶ ἐπηρώ-
And Jesus stood before the governor, and questioned
846 3588 2232 3004 4771 1488 3588 935 3588
τησεν αὐτὸν ὁ ἡγεμὼν, λέγων, Σὺ εἶ ὁ βασιλεὺς τῶν
Him the governor, saying, You are the king of the
2453 3588 1161 2424 5346 846 4771 3004 2532 1722 3588
Ἰουδαίων; ὁ δὲ Ἰησοῦς ἔφη αὐτῷ, Σὺ λέγεις. 12 καὶ ἐν τῷ
Jews? And Jesus said to him, You say (it). And during the

King James Version

Matthew 27

1. When the morning was come, all the chief priests and elders of the people took counsel against Jesus to put him to death:

2 And when they had bound him, they led (him) away, and delivered him to Pontius Pilate the governor.

3. Then Judas, which had betrayed him, when he saw that he was condemned, repented himself, and brought again the thirty pieces of silver to the chief priests and elders,
4 Saying, I have sinned in that I have betrayed the innocent blood. And they said, What (is that) to us? see thou (to that).
5 And he cast down the pieces of silver in the temple, and departed, and went and hanged himself.
6 And the chief priests took the silver pieces, and said, It is not lawful for to put them into the treasury, because it is the price of blood.
7 And they took counsel, and bought with them the potter's field, to bury strangers in.
8 Wherefore that field was called, The field of blood, unto this day.
9 Then was fulfilled that which was spoken by Jeremy the prophet, saying, And they took the thirty pieces of silver, the price of him that was valued, whom they of the children of Israel did value;

10 And gave them for the potter's field, as the Lord appointed me.

11. And Jesus stood before the governor: and the governor asked him, saying, Art thou the King of the Jews? And Jesus said unto him, Thou sayest.

12 And when

Literal Translation — **Matthew 27:13** — ***King James Version***

accusing (of) Him by the chief priests and the elders, He answered nothing.
13 Then Pilate said to Him, Do you not hear how many things they testify against you?
14 And He did not answer him, not even to one word, so that the governor greatly marveled.

15. And at a feast, the governor customarily released one prisoner to the crowd, whom they wished.
16 And they had then a notorious prisoner named Barabbas.
17 Then they, having been assembled, Pilate said to them, Whom do you wish I may release to you, Barabbas, or Jesus being called Christ?
18 For he knew they delivered Him up through envy.

19. But as he was sitting on the judgment seat, his wife sent to him, saying, Let nothing (be) to you and that just one. For I have suffered many things today by a dream because of him.

20 But the chief priests and the elders had persuaded the crowds, that they should ask (for) Barabbas, and to destroy Jesus.

21 And answering, the governor said to them, From the two, which do you wish that I release (to) you? And they said, Barabbas.

22 Pilate said to them, What then should I do to Jesus being called Christ? They all said to him, Let him be crucified.
23 But the governor said, For what wrong did he do? But they the more cried out, saying, Let him be crucified.
24 And seeing that nothing is gained, but rather an uproar occurs, taking water,

---

2723 846 5259 3588 749 2532 3588 4245
κατηγορεῖσθαι αὐτὸν ὑπὸ τῶν ἀρχιερέων καὶ τῶν πρε-
accusing (of) Him by the chief priests and the

3762 611 5119 3004 846 3588 4091
σβυτέρων οὐδὲν ἀπεκρίνατο. 13 τότε λέγει αὐτῷ ὁ Πιλᾶτος,
elders nothing He answered. Then says to Him Pilate,

3756 191 4214 5675 2649 2532 3756 611
Οὐκ ἀκούεις πόσα σοῦ καταμαρτυροῦσι; 14 καὶ οὐκ ἀπεκρίθη
Not do you hear what you they witness against? And not He answered

846 4314 3761 1520 4487 5620 2296 3588 2232 3029
αὐτῷ πρὸς οὐδὲ ἓν ῥῆμα, ὥστε θαυμάζειν τὸν ἡγεμόνα λίαν.
him, to not even one word, so as to marvel the governor much.

2596 1161 1859 1486 3588 2232 630 1520 3588 3793
15 κατὰ δὲ ἑορτὴν εἰώθει ὁ ἡγεμὼν ἀπολύειν ἕνα τῷ ὄχλῳ
at And a feast used the governor to release one to the crowd

1198 3739 2309 2192 1161 5119 1198 1978 3004
δέσμιον, ὃν ἤθελον. 16 εἶχον δὲ τότε δέσμιον ἐπίσημον, λεγό-
prisoner, whom they wished. they had And then a prisoner notorious, having

912 4863 3767 846 2036 846 3588
μενον Βαραββᾶν. 17 συνηγμένων οὖν αὐτῶν, εἶπεν αὐτοῖς ὁ
been called Barabbas. having assembled Then they, said to them

4091 5101 2309 630 5213 912 2228 2424
Πιλάτος, Τίνα θέλετε ἀπολύσω ὑμῖν; βαραββᾶν, ἤ Ἰησοῦν
Pilate, Whom wish you I may release to you, Barabbas, or Jesus

3588 3004 5547 1492 1063 3754 1223 5355 3860
τὸν λεγόμενον Χριστόν; 18 ᾔδει γὰρ ὅτι διὰ φθόνον παρέδωκαν
having been called Christ? he knew For that through envy they delivered

846 2521 1161 846 1909 3588 968 649
αὐτόν. 19 καθημένου δὲ αὐτοῦ ἐπὶ τοῦ βήματος, ἀπέστειλε
Him. having sat And he on the tribunal, sent

4314 846 3588 1135 846 3004 3367 4671 2532 3588
πρὸς αὐτὸν ἡ γυνὴ αὐτοῦ, λέγουσα, Μηδέν σοι καὶ τῷ
to him the wife of him, saying, Nothing to you and

1342 1565 4183 1063 3958 4594 2596 3577 1223
δικαίῳ ἐκείνῳ· πολλὰ γὰρ ἔπαθον σήμερον κατ᾽ ὄναρ δι᾽
just one to that. many things For I suffered today by a dream because

846 3588 1161 1749 2532 3588 4245 3982 3588
αὐτόν. 20 οἱ δὲ ἀρχιερεῖς καὶ οἱ πρεσβύτεροι ἔπεισαν τοὺς
of Him. the But chief priests and the elders having persuaded the

3793 2443 154 3588 912 3588 1161 2424
ὄχλους ἵνα αἰτήσωνται τὸν Βαραββᾶν, τὸν δὲ Ἰησοῦν
crowds that they should ask Barabbas, and Jesus

622 611 1161 3588 2232 2036 846 5101
ἀπολέσωσιν. 21 ἀποκριθεὶς δὲ ὁ ἡγεμὼν εἶπεν αὐτοῖς, Τίνα
destroy. answering And the governor said to them, Which

2309 575 3588 1417 630 5213 3588 1161 2036 912
θέλετε ἀπὸ τῶν δύο ἀπολύσω ὑμῖν; οἱ δὲ εἶπον, Βαραββᾶν.
do you wish from the two I may release to you? they And said, Barabbas.

3004 846 3588 4091 5101 3767 4160 2424 3588 3004
22 λέγει αὐτοῖς ὁ Πιλᾶτος, Τί οὖν ποιήσω Ἰησοῦν τὸν λεγό-
Says to them Pilate, What then should I do to Jesus having

5547 3004 846 3956 4717 3588
μενον Χριστόν; λέγουσιν αὐτῷ πάντες, Σταυρωθήτω. 23 ὁ
been called Christ? They say to him all, Let him be crucified. the

1161 2232 5346 5101 1063 2556 4160 3588 1161 4057
δὲ ἡγεμὼν ἔφη, Τί γὰρ κακὸν ἐποίησεν; οἱ δὲ περισσῶς
But governor said, what For badness did he do? they But more

2896 3004 4717 1492 1161 3588 4091 3754
ἔκραζον, λέγοντες, Σταυρωθήτω. 24 ἰδὼν δὲ ὁ Πιλάτος ὅτι
cried out, saying, Let him be crucified! seeing And Pilate that

3762 5623 235 3123 2351 1096 2983 5204
οὐδὲν ὠφελεῖ, ἀλλὰ μᾶλλον θόρυβος γίνεται, λαβὼν ὕδωρ,
nothing is gained, but rather an uproar occurs, taking water

---

he was accused of the chief priests and elders, he answered nothing.
13 Then said Pilate unto him, Hearest thou not how many things they witness against thee?
14 And he answered him to never a word; insomuch that the governor marvelled greatly.

15. Now at (that) feast the governor was wont to release unto the people a prisoner, whom they would.
16 And they had then a notable prisoner, called Barabbas.
17 Therefore when they were gathered together, Pilate said unto them, Whom will ye that I release unto you? Barabbas, or Jesus which is called Christ?
18 For he knew that for envy they had delivered him.
19. When he was set down on the judgment seat, his wife sent unto him, saying, Have thou nothing to do with that just man: for I have suffered many things this day in a dream because of him.

20 But the chief priests and elders persuaded the multitude that they should ask Barabbas, and destroy Jesus.

21 The governor answered and said unto them, Whether of the twain will ye that I release unto you? They said, Barabbas.
22 Pilate saith unto them, What shall I do then with Jesus which is called Christ? (They) all say unto him, Let him be crucified.
23 And the governor said, Why, what evil hath he done? But they cried out the more, saying, Let him be crucified.
24 When Pilate saw that he could prevail nothing, but (that) rather a tumult was made, he took water,

Literal Translation | **Matthew 27:25** | **King James Version**

Pilate washed (his) hands before the crowd, saying, I am innocent of the blood of this just one; you will see.
25 And answering, all the people said, His blood (be) on us and on our children.

26 Then he released Barabbas to them. But having flogged Jesus, he delivered (Him) up that He might be crucified.

27. Then taking Jesus into the praetorium, the soldiers of the governor gathered all the cohort' against Him.

28 And stripping Him, they put a scarlet cloak around Him.

29.And plaiting a crown of thorns, they placed (it) on His head, and a reed in His right (hand). And bowing the knee before Him, they mocked at Him, saying, Hail, King of the Jews.

30 And spitting at Him, (they) took the reed and struck at His head.

31. And when they mocked Him, they stripped off His cloak, and they put His garments on Him and led Him away to crucify (Him).

32 And going out, they found a man, a Cyrenean, named Simon. They forced this one to bear His cross.
33 And coming to a place called Golgotha, which is called, Place of a Skull,
34 they gave Him vinegar mingled with gall to drink. And having tasted, He would not drink.
35. And having crucified

633 3588 5495 561 3588 3793 3004 121
ἀπενίψατο τὰς χεῖρας ἀπέναντι τοῦ ὄχλου, λέγων, Ἀθῷός
he washed the hands before the crowd, saying, innocent

1510 575 3588 129 3588 1342 5127 5210 3700 2532
εἰμι ἀπὸ τοῦ αἵματος τοῦ δικαίου τούτου· ὑμεῖς ὄψεσθε. 25 καὶ
I am from the blood righteous one of this; you will see. And

611 3956 3588 2992 2036 3588 129 846 1909 2248 2532 1909
ἀποκριθεὶς πᾶς ὁ λαὸς εἶπε, Τὸ αἷμα αὐτοῦ ἐφ' ἡμᾶς καὶ ἐπὶ
answering all the people said, The blood of him on us and on

3588 5043 2257 5119 630 846 3588 912 3588
τὰ τέκνα ἡμῶν. 26 τότε ἀπέλυσεν αὐτοῖς τὸν Βαραββᾶν, τὸν
the children of us. Then he released to them Barabbas.

1161 2424 5417 3860 2443 4717
δὲ Ἰησοῦν φραγελλώσας παρέδωκεν ἵνα σταυρωθῇ.
But Jesus having flogged he delivered that He might be crucified.

5119 3588 4757 3588 2232 3880 3588
27. Τότε οἱ στρατιῶται τοῦ ἡγεμόνος, παραλαβόντες τὸν
Then the soldieers of the governor, having taken

2424 1519 3588 4232 4863 1909 846 3650 3588
Ἰησοῦν εἰς τὸ πραιτώριον, συνήγαγον ἐπ' αὐτὸν ὅλην τὴν
Jesus into the praetorium, gathered against Him all the

4686 2532 1562 846 4060 846 5511
σπεῖραν. 28 καὶ ἐκδύσαντες αὐτὸν, περιέθηκαν αὐτῷ χλαμύδα
cohort. And stripping Him, they put around Him a cloak

2847 2532 4120 4735 1537 173 2007
κοκκίνην. 29 καὶ πλέξαντες στέφανον ἐξ ἀκανθῶν, ἐπέθηκαν
scarlet, and having plaited a crown of thorns, they placed

1909 3588 2776 846 2532 2563 1909 3588 1188 846
ἐπὶ τὴν κεφαλὴν αὐτοῦ, καὶ κάλαμον ἐπὶ τὴν δεξιὰν αὐτοῦ·
on the head of Him, and a reed on the right of Him.

2532 1120 1715 846 1702 846
καὶ γονυπετήσαντες ἔμπροσθεν αὐτοῦ ἐνέπαιζον αὐτῷ,
And bowing the knee in front of Him, they mocked at Him,

3004 5463 3588 935 3588 2453 2532 1715
λέγοντες, Χαῖρε, ὁ βασιλεὺς τῶν Ἰουδαίων· 30 καὶ ἐμπτύσαντες
saying, Hail, king of the Jews. And spitting

1519 846 2983 3588 2563 2532 5180 1519 3588 2776
εἰς αὐτὸν, ἔλαβον τὸν κάλαμον, καὶ ἔτυπτον εἰς τὴν κεφαλὴν
at Him, (they) took the reed and struck at the head

846 2532 3753 1702 846 1562 846 3588
αὐτοῦ. 31 καὶ ὅτε ἐνέπαιξαν αὐτῷ, ἐξέδυσαν αὐτὸν τὴν
of Him. And when they mocked at Him, they stripped off Him the

5511 2532 1746 846 3588 2440 846 2532 520
χλαμύδα, καὶ ἐνέδυσαν αὐτὸν τὰ ἱμάτια αὐτοῦ, καὶ ἀπή-
cloak and put on Him the garments of Him, and led

846 1519 3588 4717
γαγον αὐτὸν εἰς τὸ σταυρῶσαι.
away Him in order to crucify (Him).

1831 1161 2147 444 2956 3686
32. Ἐξερχόμενοι δὲ εὗρον ἄνθρωπον Κυρηναῖον, ὀνόματι
going forth And they found a man, a Cyrenian, by name

4613 5126 29 2443 142 3588 4716 846 2532
Σίμωνα· τοῦτον ἠγγάρευσαν ἵνα ἄρῃ τὸν σταυρὸν αὐτοῦ. 33καὶ
Simon. This one they compelled, that he bear the cross of Him. And

2064 1519 5117 3004 1115 3739 2076 3004
ἐλθόντες εἰς τόπον λεγόμενον Γολγοθᾶ, ὅς ἐστι λεγόμενος
coming to a place called Golgotha, which is saying

2898 5117 1325 846 4095 3690 3326 5521
κρανίου τόπος, 34ἔδωκαν αὐτῷ πιεῖν ὄξος μετὰ χολῆς
Of a skull place, they gave Him to drink vinegar with gall

3396 2532 1089 3756 2309 4095 4717
μεμιγμένον· καὶ γευσάμενος οὐκ ἤθελε πιεῖν. 35 σταυρώσαντες
being mixed. And having tasted, not He would drink. having crucified

and washed (his) hands before the multitude, saying, I am innocent of the blood of this just person: see ye (to it).
25 Then answered all the people, and said, His blood (be) on us, and on our children.

26 Then released he Barabbas unto them: and when he had scourged Jesus, he delivered (him) to be crucified.

27. Then the soldiers of the governor took Jesus into the common hall, and gathered unto him the whole band (of soldiers).

28 And they stripped him, and put on him a scarlet robe.

29. And when they had platted a crown of thorns, they put (it) upon his head, and a reed in his right hand: and they bowed the knee before him, and mocked him, saying, Hail, King of the Jews!

30 And they spit upon him, and took the reed, and smote him on the head.

31. And after that they had mocked him, they took the robe off from him, and put his own raiment on him, and led him away to crucify (him).

32 And as they came out, they found a man of Cyrene, Simon by name: him they compelled to bear his cross.
33 And when they were come unto a place called Golgotha, that is to say, a place of a skull,
34 They gave him vinegar to drink mingled with gall: and when he had tasted (thereof), he would not drink.
35. And they crucified him,

Literal Translation **Matthew 27:36** ***King James Version***

Him, they divided His garments, casting a lot, that might be fulfilled that spoken by the prophet, "They divided My garments (to) themselves, and they cast a lot over My clothing." (Ps. 22:18)

36 And sitting down, they guarded Him there.
37 And they put up over His head His charge, (it) having been written: THIS IS JESUS, THE KING OF THE JEWS.
38 Then two robbers were crucified with Him, one off (the) right, and one off (the) left (of Him).
39. But those passing by, blasphemed Him, shaking their heads,

40 and saying, The (one) razing the temple and building (it) in three days, if you are the Son of God, come down from the cross.

41 And in the same way, the chief priests with the scribes and elders, mocking, spoke,

42 He saved others; he is not able to save himself. If he is the king of Israel, let him come down now from the cross, and we will believe him.
43 He trusted on God. Let Him rescue him now, if He desires him. For he said, I am Son of God.
44 And also the robbers crucified with Him reviled Him, (saying) the same.

1161 846 1266 3588 2440 846 906 2819
δε αὐτόν, διεμερίσαντο τὰ ἱμάτια αὐτοῦ, βάλλοντες κλῆρον·
and Him, they divided the garments of Him, casting a lot,

2443 4137 3588 4483 5259 3588 4396 1266 3588
ἵνα πληρωθῇ τὸ ῥηθὲν ὑπὸ τοῦ προφήτου, Διεμερίσαντο τὰ
that may be fulfilled that spoken by the prophet, They divided the

2440 3450 1438 2532 1909 3588 2441 3450 906 2819
ἱμάτιά μου ἑαυτοῖς, καὶ ἐπὶ τὸν ἱματισμόν μου ἔβαλον κλῆρον.
garments of Me themselves, and over the clothing of Me they cast a lot.

2532 2521 5083 846 1563 2532 2007 1883
36 καὶ καθήμενοι ἐτήρουν αὐτὸν ἐκεῖ. 37 καὶ ἐπέθηκαν ἐπάνω
And having sat down, they guarded Him there. And they placed above

3588 2776 846 3588 156 846 1125 3778 2076
τῆς κεφαλῆς αὐτοῦ τὴν αἰτίαν αὐτοῦ γεγραμμένην, Οὗτός ἐστιν
the head of Him the charge of Him, (it) having been written, This is

2424 3588 935 3588 2453 5119 4717 4862
Ἰησοῦς ὁ βασιλεὺς τῶν Ἰουδαίων. 38 τότε σταυροῦνται σὺν
JESUS THE KING OF THE JEWS. Then are crucified with

846 1417 3027 1520 1537 1188 2532 1520 1537 2176 3588 1161
αὐτῷ δύο λησταί, εἷς ἐκ δεξιῶν καὶ εἷς ἐξ εὐωνύμων. 39 οἱ δὲ
Him two robbers, one off the right, and one off the left. those And

3899 987 846 2795 3588 2776
παραπορευόμενοι ἐβλασφήμουν αὐτὸν κινοῦντες τὰς κεφα-
passing by blasphemed Him, shaking the heads

846 2532 3004 3588 2647 3588 3485 2532 1722
λὰς αὐτῶν, 40 καὶ λέγοντες, Ὁ καταλύων τὸν ναὸν καὶ ἐν
of them, and saying, The (one) razing the temple and in

5140 2250 3618 4982 4572 1487 5207 1488 3588
τρισὶν ἡμέραις οἰκοδομῶν, σῶσον σεαυτόν· εἰ υἱὸς εἶ τοῦ
three days building (it), save yourself. If Son You are

2316 2597 575 3588 4716 3668 1161 2532 3588
Θεοῦ, κατάβηθι ἀπὸ τοῦ σταυροῦ. 41 ὁμοίως δὲ καὶ οἱ
of God, come down from the cross. likewise And also the

749 1702 3326 3588 1122 2532 4245
ἀρχιερεῖς ἐμπαίζοντες μετὰ τῶν γραμματέων καὶ πρεσ-
chief priests mocking with the scribes and elders

3004 243 4982 1438 3756 1410 4982
βυτέρων ἔλεγον, 42 Ἄλλους ἔσωσεν, ἑαυτὸν οὐ δύναται σῶσαι·
spoke, Others he saved, himself not he is able to save.

1487 935 2474 2076 2597 3568 575 3588 4617
εἰ βασιλεὺς Ἰσραήλ ἐστι, καταβάτω νῦν ἀπὸ τοῦ σταυροῦ
If king of Israel he is, let him come down now from the cross,

2532 4100 846 3983 1909 3588 2316 4506
καὶ πιστεύσομεν αὐτῷ. 43 πέποιθεν ἐπὶ τὸν Θεόν· ῥυσάσθω
and we will believe Him. He trusted on God; let Him rescue

3568 846 1487 2309 846 2036 1063 3754 2316 1510 5207 3588
νῦν αὐτον, εἰ θέλει αὐτόν. εἶπε γὰρ ὅτι Θεοῦ εἰμι υἱός. 44 τὸ
now Him, if He desires him. He said For of God I am Son. the

1161 846 2532 3588 3027 3588 4957 846 3679
δ' αὐτὸ καὶ οἱ λησταὶ οἱ συσταυρωθέντες αὐτῷ ὠνείδιζον
And same also the robbers crucified together with Him reproached

846
αὐτῷ.
Him.

and parted his garments, casting lots: that it might be fulfilled which was spoken by the prophet, They parted my garments among them, and upon my vesture did they cast lots.

36 And sitting down they watched him there;
37 And set up over his head his accusation written, THIS IS JESUS THE KING OF THE JEWS.
38 Then were there two thieves crucified with him, one on the right hand, and another on the left.
39. And they that passed by reviled him, wagging their heads,

40 And saying, Thou that destroyest the temple, and buildest (it) in three days, save thyself. If thou be the Son of God, come down from the cross.
41 Likewise also the chief priests mocking (him), with the scribes and elders, said,

42 He saved others; himself he cannot save. If he be the King of Israel, let him now come down from the cross, and we will believe him.
43 He trusted in God; let him deliver him now, if he will have him: for he said, I am the Son of God.
44 The thieves also, which were crucified with him, cast the same in his teeth.

45. And from (the) sixth hour darkness occurred over all the land until (the) ninth hour.
46 And about the ninth hour, Jesus cried out with a loud voice, saying, Eli, Eli, lama sabachthani;

575 1161 1623 5610 4655 1096 1909 3956 3588 1093
45. Ἀπὸ δὲ ἕκτης ὥρας σκότος ἐγένετο ἐπὶ πᾶσαν τὴν γῆν
from And sixth hour darkness occurred over all the land

2193 5610 1766 4012 1161 3588 1766 5610 310 3588
ἕως ὥρας ἐννάτης· 46 περὶ δὲ τὴν ἐνάτην ὥραν ἀνεβόησεν ὁ
until hour (the) ninth. about And the ninth hour cried out

2424 5456 3173 3004 2241 2241 2982 4518
Ἰησοῦς φωνῇ μεγάλῃ, λέγων, Ηλι, Ηλι, λεμα σαβαχθανι;
Jesus voice a great, saying, Eli, Eli, lama sabachthani?

45. Now from the sixth hour there was darkness over all the land unto the ninth hour.
46 And about the ninth hour Jesus cried with a loud voice, saying, Eli, Eli, lama sabachthani?

Literal Translation

that is, My God, My God, why did You forsake Me? (Ps. 22:1)
47 And hearing, some of those standing there said, This One calls Elijah.

48 And at once, one of them running and taking a sponge, and filling (it) with vinegar, put (it) on a reed and gave drink to Him. (Ps. 69:21)
49 But the rest said, Let be; let us see if Elijah is coming to save him.

50. And crying again with a loud voice, Jesus released (His) spirit.

51 And, behold! The veil of the temple was torn into two from top to bottom. And the earth was shaken, and the rocks were sheared!

52 And the tombs were opened, and many bodies of the saints who had fallen asleep were raised.
53 And coming forth out of the tombs after His resurrection, (they) entered into the holy city and appeared to many.
54 But the centurion and those with him guarding Jesus, seeing the earthquake and the things happening, (they) feared exceedingly, saying, Truly this One was Son of God.

55 And many women were there, beholding from afar away, (those) who followed Jesus from Galilee, ministering to Him;

56 among whom was Mary Magdalene, and Mary the mother of James and Joses, and the mother of the sons of Zebedee.

57. And evening having come, a rich man named Joseph, from Arimathea who also himself was discipled

Matthew 27:47

5124 2076 2316 3450 2316 3450 2444 3165 1459 5100
τοῦτ' ἔστι, Θεέ μου, Θεέ μου, ἱνατί με ἐγκατέλιπες; 47 τινὲς
this is, God of Me, God of Me, why Me did You forsake? some

1161 3588 1563 2476 191 3004 3754 2243 5455
δὲ τῶν ἐκεῖ ἑστώτων ἀκούσαντες ἔλεγον ὅτι Ἠλίαν φωνεῖ
And of those there standing hearing said, Elijah calls

3778 2532 2112 5143 1520 1537 846 2532 2983 4699
οὗτος. 48 καὶ εὐθέως δραμὼν εἷς ἐξ αὐτῶν, καὶ λαβὼν σπόγγον,
This One. And at once running one of them and taking a sponge,

4130 5037 3690 2532 4060 2563 4222 846 3588 1161
πλήσας τε ὄξους, καὶ περιθεὶς καλάμῳ, ἐπότιζεν αὐτόν. 49 οἱ δὲ
filling (it) and with vinegar, and put on a reed, gave drink to Him. the But

3062 3004 863 1492 1487 2064 2243 4982 846
λοιποὶ ἔλεγον, Ἄφες, ἴδωμεν εἰ ἔρχεται Ἠλίας σώσων αὐτόν.
rest said, Leave! Let us see if is coming Elijah to save Him.

3588 1161 2424 3825 2896 5456 3173 863 3588 4151
50 ὁ δὲ Ἰησοῦς πάλιν κράξας φωνῇ μεγάλῃ ἀφῆκε τὸ πνεῦμα.
And Jesus again crying voice with a great released the spirit

2532 2400 3588 2665 3588 3485 4977 1519 1417 575
51 καὶ ἰδού, τὸ καταπέτασμα τοῦ ναοῦ ἐσχίσθη εἰς δύο ἀπὸ
And behold! The veil of the temple was torn into two, from

509 2193 2736 2532 3588 1093 4579 2532 3588 4073 4977
ἄνωθεν ἕως κάτω· καὶ ἡ γῆ ἐσείσθη· καὶ αἱ πέτραι ἐσχίσθη-
above until below, and the earth was shaken, and the rocks were torn,

2532 3588 3419 455 2532 4183 4983 3588
σαν, 52 καὶ τὰ μνημεῖα ἀνεῴχθησαν καὶ πολλὰ σώματα τῶν
and the tombs were opened, and many bodies of the

2837 40 1453 2532 1831 1537 3588
κεκοιμημένων ἁγίων ἠγέρθη· 53 καὶ ἐξελθόντες ἐκ τῶν
having fallen asleep saints were raised; and coming forth out of the

3419 3326 3588 1454 846 1525 1519 3588 40
μνημείων μετὰ τὴν ἔγερσιν αὐτοῦ εἰσῆλθον εἰς τὴν ἁγίαν
tombs after the resurrection of Him entered into the holy

4172 2532 1718 4183 3588/1161 1543 2532/3588
πόλιν, καὶ ἐνεφανίσθησαν πολλοῖς. 54 ὁ δὲ ἑκατόνταρχος καὶ οἱ
city and appeared to many. the And centurion and those

3326 846 5083 3588 2424 1492 3588 4578 2532/3588
μετ' αὐτοῦ τηροῦντες τὸν Ἰησοῦν, ἰδόντες τὸν σεισμὸν καὶ τὰ
with him guarding Jesus, seeing the earthquake and the

1096 5399 4970 3004 230 2316 5207
γενόμενα, ἐφοβήθησαν σφόδρα, λέγοντες, Ἀληθῶς Θεοῦ υἱὸς
happenings, feared exceedingly, saying, Truly of God Son

2258 3778 2258 1161 1563 1135 4183 575 3113
ἦν οὗτος. 55 ἦσαν δὲ ἐκεῖ γυναῖκες πολλαὶ ἀπὸ μακρόθεν
was This One. were And there women many from far away

2334 3748 190 3588 2424 575 3588
θεωροῦσαι, αἵτινες ἠκολούθησαν τῷ Ἰησοῦ ἀπὸ τῆς
beholding who followed Jesus from

1056 1247 846 1722 3739 2258 3137 3588
Γαλιλαίας, διακονοῦσαι αὐτῷ· 56 ἐν αἷς ἦν Μαρία ἡ
Galilee, ministering to Him; among whom was Mary the

3094 2532 3137 3588 3588 2385 2532 2500 3384
Μαγδαληνη, και Μαρία ἡ τοῦ Ἰακώβου καὶ Ἰωσῆ μήτηρ,
Magdalene, and Mary the of James and of Joseph mother,

2532/3588/3384 3588 5207 2199
καὶ ἡ μήτηρ τῶν υἱῶν Ζεβεδαίου.
and the mother of the lifesons of Zebedee.

3798 1161 1096 2064 444 4145 575
57. Ὀψίας δὲ γενομένης, ἦλθεν ἄνθρωπος πλούσιος ἀπὸ
evening And having come, came a man rich from

707 5122 2501 3739 2532 846 3100 3588
Ἀριμαθαίας, τοὔνομα Ἰωσήφ, ὃς καὶ αὐτὸς ἐμαθήτευσε τῷ
Arimathea, by name Joseph, who also himself was discipled

King James Version

that is to say, My God, my God, why hast thou forsaken me?
47 Some of them that stood there, when they heard (that), said, This (man) calleth for Elias.

48 And straightway one of them ran, and took a spunge, and filled (it) with vinegar, and put (it) on a reed, and gave him to drink.
49 The rest said, Let be, let us see whether Elias will come to save him.

50. Jesus, when he had cried again with a loud voice, yielded up the ghost.
51 And, behold, the veil of the temple was rent in twain from the top to the bottom; and the earth did quake, and the rocks rent;

52 And the graves were opened; and many bodies of the saints which slept arose,
53 And came out of the graves after his resurrection, and went into the holy city, and appeared unto many.

54 Now when the centurion, and they that were with him, watching Jesus, saw the earthquake, and those things that were done, they feared greatly, saying, Truly this was the Son of God.

55 And many women were there beholding afar off, which followed Jesus from Galilee, ministering unto him:

56 Among which was Mary Magdalene, and Mary the mother of James and Joses, and the mother of Zebedee's children.

57. When the even was come, there came a rich man of Arimathaea, named Joseph, who also himself was

Literal Translation | **Matthew 27:58** | *King James Version*

to Jesus,
58 coming up (to) Pilate, this one asked (for) the body of Jesus. Then Pilate commanded the body to be given.

59 And taking the body, Joseph wrapped it in clean linen,

60 and laid it in his new tomb, which he had cut out in the rock. And rolling a great stone to the door of the tomb, he went away.

61 And there was Mary Magdalene and the other Mary, sitting across from the grave.

2424 3778 4334 3588 4091 154 3588 4983
Ἰησοῦ· 58 οὗτος προσελθὼν τῷ Πιλάτῳ ᾐτήσατο τὸ σῶμα
to Jesus; this one coming up (to) Pilate asked the body

3588 2424 5119 3588 4091 2753 591 3588 4983
τοῦ Ἰησοῦ. τότε ὁ Πιλάτος ἐκέλευσεν ἀποδοθῆναι τὸ σῶμα.
of Jesus. Then Pilate commanded to be given the body.

2532 2983 3588 4983 3588 2501 1794 846 4616
59 καὶ λαβὼν τὸ σῶμα ὁ Ἰωσὴφ ἐνετύλιξεν αὐτὸ σινδόνι
and taking the body Joseph wrapped it in linen

2513 2532 5087 846 1722 3588 2537 846 3419 3739
καθαρᾷ, 60 καὶ ἔθηκεν αὐτὸ ἐν τῷ καινῷ αὐτοῦ μνημείῳ, ὃ
clean, and placed it in the new of him tomb, which

2998 1722 3588 4073 2532 4351 3037 3173 3588
ἐλατόμησεν ἐν τῇ πέτρᾳ· καὶ προσκυλίσας λίθον μέγαν τῇ
he had hewed in the rock, and having rolled a stone large to the

2374 3588 3419 565 2258 1161 1563 3137 3588 3094
θύρᾳ τοῦ μνημείου ἀπῆλθεν. 61 ἦν δὲ ἐκεῖ Μαριὰ ἡ Μαγδαληνή,
door of the tomb, (he) went away. was And there Mary the Magdalene,

2532 3588 243 3137 2521 561 3588 5028
καὶ ἡ ἄλλη Μαρία, καθήμεναι ἀπέναντι τοῦ τάφου.
and the other Mary, sitting opposite the grave.

Jesus' disciple:
58 He went to Pilate, and begged the body of Jesus. Then Pilate commanded the body to be delivered.

59 And when Joseph had taken the body, he wrapped it in a clean linen cloth,
60 And laid it in his own new tomb, which he had hewn out in the rock: and he rolled a great stone to the door of the sepulchre, and departed.
61 And there was Mary Magdalene, and the other Mary, sitting over against the sepulchre.

62. And on the morrow, which is after the Preparation, were assembled the chief priests and the Pharisees to Pilate,
63 saying, Sir, we have recalled that that deceiver while living said, After three days I will rise.
64 Therefore, command that the grave be secured until the third day, that his disciples may not come by night and steal him away, and may say to the people, He is raised from the dead. And the last deception will be worse than the first.

3588 1161 1887 3748 2076 3326 3588 3904 4863
62. Τῇ δὲ ἐπαύριον, ἥτις ἐστὶ μετὰ τὴν παρασκευήν, συνή-
on the And morrow which is after the Preparation were

3588 749 2532 3588 5330 4314 4091 3004
χθησαν οἱ ἀρχιερεῖς καὶ οἱ Φαρισαῖοι πρὸς Πιλάτον, 63 λέγ-
assembled the chief priests and the Pharisees to Pilate,

2962 3415 3754 1565 3588 4108 2036 2089 2198
οντες, Κύριε, ἐμνήσθημεν ὅτι ἐκεῖνος ὁ πλάνος εἶπεν ἔτι ζῶν,
saying, Sir, we have recalled that that deceiver said yet living,

3326 5140 2250 1453 2753 3767 805
Μετὰ τρεῖς ἡμέρας ἐγείρομαι. 64 κέλευσον οὖν ἀσφαλισθῆναι
After three days I arise. Command, then, to be made secure

3588 5028 2193 3588 5154 2250 3379 2064 3588 3101
τὸν τάφον ἕως τῆς τρίτης ἡμέρας· μήποτε ἐλθόντες οἱ μαθηταὶ
the grave until the third day, lest coming the disciples

848 3571 2813 846 2532 2036 3588 2092 1453
αὐτοῦ νυκτὸς κλέψωσιν αὐτόν, καὶ εἴπωσι τῷ λαῷ, Ἠγέρ-
of him by night may steal him, and may say to the people, He is

575 3588 3498 2532 2071 3588 2078 4106 5501 3588
θη ἀπὸ τῶν νεκρῶν· καὶ ἔσται ἡ ἐσχάτη πλάνη χείρων τῆς
raised from the dead, and will be the last deceit worse than the

62. Now the next day, that followed the day of the preparation, the chief priests and Pharisees came together unto Pilate,
63 Saying, Sir, we remember that that deceiver said, while he was yet alive, After three days I will rise again.
64 Command therefore that the sepulchre be made sure until the third day, lest his disciples come by night, and steal him away, and say unto the people, He is risen from the dead: so the last error shall be worse than the first.

65 And Pilate said to them, You have a guard, go away, make (it as) secure as you know (how).
66 And going along with the guard, they made the grave secure, sealing the stone.

4413 5346 1161 846 3588 4091 2192 2892
πρώτης. 65 ἔφη δὲ αὐτοῖς ὁ Πιλάτος, Ἔχετε κουστωδίαν·
first. said And to them Pilate, You have a guard;

5217 805 5613 1492 3588 1161 4198 805
ὑπάγετε, ἀσφαλίσασθε ὡς οἴδατε. 66 οἱ δὲ πορευθέντες ἠσφαλί-
go, make secure as you know. they And going made

3588 5028 4972 3588 3037 3326 3588
σαντο τὸν τάφον, σφραγίσαντες τὸν λίθον, μετὰ τῆς
secure the grave, sealing the stone, with the

2892
κουστωδίας.
guard.

65 Pilate said unto them, Ye have a watch: go your way, make (it) as sure as ye can.
66 So they went, and made the sepulchre sure, sealing the stone, and setting a watch.

Matthew 28

1. And at evening (of the) sabbath, at the dawning into the first of (the) week, Mary Magdalene and the other Mary came to see

3796 1161 4521 3588 2020 1519 3391 4521
1. Ὀψὲ δὲ σαββάτων, τῇ ἐπιφωσκούσῃ εἰς μίαν σαββάτων,
late in But the week, at the dawning into the first of (the) week,

2064 3137 3588 3094 2532 3588 243 3137 2334
ἦλθεν Μαριὰ ἡ Μαγδαληνή, καὶ ἡ ἄλλη Μαρία, θεωρῆσαι
came Mary the Magdalene and the other Mary to view

1. In the end of the sabbath, as it began to dawn toward the first (day) of the week, came Mary Magdalene and the other Mary to see

Literal Translation

the grave.
2 And, behold! A great earthquake had occurred! For descending from Heaven and coming near, an angel of (the) Lord rolled away the stone from the door and (was) sitting on it.
3 And his appearance was as lightning and his clothing white as snow.

4 And those keeping guard were shaken from the fear of him, and they became as dead.
5 But answering, the angel said to the women, You (must) not fear, for I know that you seek Jesus who has been crucified.
6 He is not here, for He was raised, as He said. Come, see the place where the Lord lay.
7 And going quickly say to His disciples that He was raised from the dead. And behold! He goes before you into Galilee. You will see Him there. Behold! I told you.

8 And going away from the tomb quickly, with fear and great joy, they ran to report to His disciples.

9. But as they were going to report to His disciples, behold, Jesus also met them, saying, Hail! And coming near, they seized His feet and worshiped Him.

10 Then Jesus said to them, Do not fear. Go tell your brothers that they may go into Galilee, and there they will see Me.

11. And they, having gone, behold, some of the guard

Matthew 28:2

3588 5028 2532 2400 4578 1096 3173 32 1063
τὸν τάφον. 2 καὶ ἰδού, σεισμὸς ἐγένετο μέγας· ἄγγελος γὰρ
the grave. And, behold! An earthquake had occurred great; an angel for

2962 2597 1537 3772 4334 617 3588
Κυρίου καταβὰς ἐξ οὐρανοῦ, προσελθὼν ἀπεκύλισε τὸν
of (the) Lord descending from Heaven, and coming up, rolled away the

3037 575 3588 2374 2532 2521 1883 846 2258 1161 3588
λίθον ἀπὸ τῆς θύρας, καὶ ἐκάθητο ἐπάνω αὐτοῦ. 3 ἦν δὲ ἡ
stone from the door, and sitting on it. was And the

2397 846 5613 796 2532 3588 1742 846 3022 5616
ἰδέα αὐτοῦ ὡς ἀστραπή, καὶ τὸ ἔνδυμα αὐτοῦ λευκὸν ὡσεὶ
look of him as lightning, and the dress of him white as

5510 575 1161 3588 5401 846 4579 3588 5083
χιών. 4 ἀπὸ δὲ τοῦ φόβου αὐτοῦ ἐσείσθησαν οἱ τηροῦντες
snow. from And the fear of him were shaken those guarding,

2532 1096 5616 3498 611 1161 3588 32 2036 3588
καὶ ἐγένοντο ὡσεὶ νεκροί. 5 ἀποκριθεὶς δὲ ὁ ἄγγελος εἶπε ταῖς
and they became as dead. answering And the angel said to the

1135 3361 5399 5210 1492 1063 3754 2424 3588
γυναιξί, Μὴ φοβεῖσθε ὑμεῖς· οἶδα γὰρ ὅτι Ἰησοῦν τὸν
women, Not do fear you; I know for that Jesus the (One)

4717 2212 3756 2076 5602 1453 1063 2531
ἐσταυρωμένον ζητεῖτε· 6 οὐκ ἔστιν ὧδε· ἠγέρθη γάρ, καθὼς
having been crucified you seek. not He is here; He was raised for, even as

2036 1205 1492 3588 5117 3699 2749 3588 2962 2532 5053
εἶπε. δεῦτε, ἴδετε τὸν τόπον ὅπου ἔκειτο ὁ Κύριος. 7 καὶ ταχὺ
He said. Come, see the place where lay the Lord. And quickly

4198 2036 3588 3101 846 3754 1453 575
πορευθεῖσαι εἴπατε τοῖς μαθηταῖς αὐτοῦ ὅτι Ἠγέρθη ἀπὸ
going to tell the disciples of Him that He was raised from

3588 3498 2532 2400 4254 5209 1519 3588 1056 1563
τῶν νεκρῶν, καὶ ἰδού, προάγει ὑμᾶς εἰς τὴν Γαλιλαίαν· ἐκεῖ
the dead. And behold! He goes before you into Galilee. There

846 3700 2400 2036 5213 2532 1831 5035 575
αὐτὸν ὄψεσθε· ἰδού, εἶπον ὑμῖν. 8 καὶ ἐξελθοῦσαι ταχὺ ἀπὸ
Him you will see. Behold, I told you. And going away quickly from

3588 3419 3326 5401 2532 5479 3173 5143
τοῦ μνημείου μετὰ φόβου καὶ χαρᾶς μεγάλης, ἔδραμον
the tomb, with fear and joy great, they ran

518 3588 3101 846 5613 1161 4198 518
ἀπαγγεῖλαι τοῖς μαθηταῖς αὐτοῦ. 9 ὡς δὲ ἐπορεύοντο ἀπαγ-
to report to the disciples of Him. as But they were going to

3588 3101 846 2532 2400 3588 2424 528
γεῖλαι τοῖς μαθηταῖς αὐτοῦ, καὶ ἰδού, ὁ Ἰησοῦς ἀπήντησεν
report to the disciples of Him, even behold, Jesus met

846 3004 5463 3588 1161 4334 2902
αὐταῖς, λέγων, Χαίρετε. αἱ δὲ προσελθοῦσαι ἐκράτησαν
them, saying, Hail! they And coming near seized

846 3588 4228 2532 4352 846 5119 3004
αὐτοῦ τοὺς πόδας, καὶ προσεκύνησαν αὐτῷ. 10 τότε λέγει
of Him the feet and worshiped Him. Then says

846 3588 2424 3361 5399 5217 518 3588
αὐταῖς ὁ Ἰησοῦς· Μὴ φοβεῖσθε· ὑπάγετε ἀπαγγείλατε τοῖς
to them Jesus, Not do fear. Go, announce to the

80 3450 2443 565 1519 3588 1056 2546 3165
ἀδελφοῖς μου ἵνα ἀπέλθωσιν εἰς τὴν Γαλιλαίαν, κἀκεῖ με
brothers of Me that they may go into Galilee, and there Me

3700
ὄψονται.
they will see.

4198 1161 846 2400 5100 3588 2892
11 Πορευομένων δὲ αὐτῶν, ἰδού, τινες τῆς κουστωδίας
going And they, behold, some of the guard

King James Version

the sepulchre.
2 And, behold, there was a great earthquake: for the angel of the Lord descended from heaven, and came and rolled back the stone from the door, and sat upon it.
3 His countenance was like lightning, and his raiment white as snow:

4 And for fear of him the keepers did shake, and became as dead (men).

5 And the angel answered and said unto the women, Fear not ye: for I know that ye seek Jesus, which was crucified.
6 He is not here: for he is risen, as he said. Come, see the place where the Lord lay.
7 And go quickly, and tell his disciples that he is risen from the dead; and, behold, he goeth before you into Galilee; there shall ye see him: lo, I have told you.

8 And they departed quickly from the sepulchre with fear and great joy; and did run to bring his disciples word.

9. And as they went to tell his disciples, behold, Jesus met them, saying, All hail. And they came and held him by the feet, and worshipped him.

10 Then said Jesus unto them, Be not afraid: go tell my brethren that they go into Galilee, and there shall they see me.

11. Now when they were going, behold, some of the watch

Literal Translation

coming into the city reported to the chief priests all things that occurred.

12 And being assembled with the elders, and taking counsel, (they) gave enough silver to the soldiers,

13 saying, Say that his disciples came (and) stole him by night, we being asleep.

14 And if this is heard by the governor, we will persuade him and will make you free from anxiety.

15 And taking the silver, they did as they were taught. And this report was spread by the Jews until today.

16. But the eleven disciples went into Galilee, to the mount where Jesus appointed them.

17 And seeing Him, they worshiped Him. But they doubted.

18 And coming up Jesus talked with them, saying, All authority in Heaven and on earth was given to Me.

19 Going, then, disciple all nations, baptizing them into the name of the Father and of the Son and of the Holy Spirit,

20 teaching them to observe all things, whatever I commanded you. And, behold, I am with you all the days until the completion of the age. Amen.

Matthew 28:12

2064 1519 3588 4172 518 3588 749 537
ἐλθόντες εἰς τὴν πόλιν ἀπήγγειλαν τοῖς ἀρχιερεῦσιν ἅπαντα
coming into the city reported to the chief priests all things

3588 1096 2532 4863 3326 3588 4245 4824
τὰ γενόμενα. 12 καὶ συναχθέντες μετὰ τῶν πρεσβυτέρων, συμ-
that occurred. And being assembled with the elders,

5037 2983 694 2425 1325 3588 4757
βούλιόν τε λαβόντες, ἀργύρια ἱκανὰ ἔδωκαν τοῖς στρατιώ-
counsel and taking, silver enough gave to the soldiers,

3004 2036 3754 3588 3101 846 3571
ταις, 13 λέγοντες, Εἴπατε ὅτι Οἱ μαθηταὶ αὐτοῦ νυκτὸς
saying, Say that the disciples of him by night

2064 2813 846 2257 2837 2532 1437 191
ἐλθόντες ἔκλεψαν αὐτὸν ἡμῶν κοιμωμένων. 14 καὶ ἐὰν ἀκουσθῇ
coming stole him, we being asleep. And if is heard

5124 1909 3588 2232 2249 3982 846 2532 5209
τοῦτο ἐπὶ τοῦ ἡγεμόνος, ἡμεῖς πείσομεν αὐτὸν, καὶ ὑμᾶς
this before the governor, we will persuade him, and you

275 4160 3588 1161 2983 3588 694 4160
ἀμερίμνους ποιήσομεν. 15 οἱ δὲ λαβόντες τὰ ἀργύρια ἐποίη-
free from anxiety we will make. they And taking the silver did

5613 1321 2532 1310 3588 3056 3778 3844
σαν ὡς ἐδιδάχθησαν. καὶ διεφημίσθη ὁ λόγος οὗτος παρὰ
as they were taught. And was spread saying this by

2453 3360 3588 4594
Ἰουδαίοις μέχρι τῆς σήμερον.
Jews until today.

3588 1161 1733 3101 4198 1519 3588 1056
16. Οἱ δὲ ἕνδεκα μαθηταὶ ἐπορεύθησαν εἰς τὴν Γαλιλαίαν,
the And eleven disciples went into Galilee,

1519/3588/3735/3757 5021 846 3588 2424 2532 1492 846
εἰς τὸ ὄρος οὗ ἐτάξατο αὐτοῖς ὁ Ἰησοῦς. 17 καὶ ἰδόντες αὐτὸν
to the mount where appointed them Jesus. And seeing Him,

4352 846 3588 1161 1365 2532 4334 3588
προσεκύνησαν αὐτῷ, οἱ δὲ ἐδίστασαν. 18 καὶ προσελθὼν ὁ
they worshiped Him, they but doubted. And coming up

2424 2980 846 3004 1325 3427 3956 1849
Ἰησοῦς ἐλάλησεν αὐτοῖς, λέγων, Ἐδόθη μοι πᾶσα ἐξουσία
Jesus talked with them, saying, has been given to Me All authority

1722 3772 2532/1909/1093 4198 3767 3100 3956
ἐν οὐρανῷ καὶ ἐπὶ γῆς. 19 πορευθέντες οὖν μαθητεύσατε πάντα
in Heaven and on earth. Having gone, then, disciple all

3588 1484 907 846 1519 3588 3686 3588 3962 2532
τὰ ἔθνη, βαπτίζοντες αὐτοὺς εἰς τὸ ὄνομα τοῦ Πατρὸς καὶ
the nations, baptizing them into the name of the Father and

3588 5207 2532 3588 40 4151 1321 846
τοῦ Υἱοῦ καὶ τοῦ Ἁγίου Πνεύματος, 20 διδάσκοντες αὐτοὺς
of the Son and of the Holy Spirit, teaching them

5083 3956 3745 1781 5213 2532 2400 1473 3326
τηρεῖν πάντα ὅσα ἐνετειλάμην ὑμῖν· καὶ ἰδού, ἐγὼ μεθ'
to observe all things whatever I commanded you; and, behold, I with

5216 1510 3956 3588 2250 2193 3588 4930 3588 165
ὑμῶν εἰμι πάσας τὰς ἡμέρας ἕως τῆς συντελείας τοῦ αἰῶνος.
you am all the days until the completion of the age.

281
Ἀμήν.
Amen.

King James Version

came into the city, and shewed unto the chief priests all the things that were done.

12 And when they were assembled with the elders, and had taken counsel, they gave large money unto the soldiers,

13 Saying, Say ye, His disciples came by night, and stole him (away) while we slept.

14 And if this come to the governor's ears, we will persuade him, and secure you.

15 So they took the money, and did as they were taught: and this saying is commonly reported among the Jews until this day.

16. Then the eleven disciples went away into Galilee, into a mountain where Jesus had appointed them.

17 And when they saw him, they worshipped him: but some doubted.

18 And Jesus came and spake unto them, saying, All power is given unto me in heaven and in earth.

19 Go ye therefore, and teach all nations, baptizing them in the name of the Father, and of the Son, and of the Holy Ghost:

20 Teaching them to observe all things whatsoever I have commanded you: and, lo, I am with you alway, (even) unto the end of the world. Amen.

Literal Translation
THE GOSPEL ACCORDING TO MARK

Mark 1

1. The beginning of the
gospel of Jesus Christ,
(the) Son of God,

2 as it has been written
in the Prophets, "Be-
hold, I send My mes-
senger before Your
face, who will prepare
Your way before You;
3 (the) voice of one cry-
ing in the wilderness.
Prepare the way of (the)
Lord, make His paths
straight." (Mal. 3:1; Isa.
40:3)

4. John came baptizing
in the wilderness and
proclaiming a baptism
of repentance to remis-
sion of sins.
5 And all the Judean
country and (those of)
Jerusalem went out to
him, and were all bap-
tized by him in the Jor-
dan River, having con-
fessed their sins.

6 And John was being
clothed in camel's hairs,
and a leather girdle
about his loin, and eat-
ing locusts and wild
honey.

7 And he proclaimed,
saying, He who comes
after me is stronger than
I, of whom I am not fit
stooping to loosen the
thong of His sandals.
8 I indeed baptized you
in water, but He will
baptize you in (the)
Holy Spirit.

9. And it happened in
those days, Jesus came
from Nazareth of Gali-
lee, and was baptized by
John in the Jordan.
10 And going up from
the water, immediately
He saw

ΕΥΑΓΓΕΛΙΟΝ
GOSPEL
ΤΟ ΚΑΤΑ ΜΑΡΚΟΝ
THE ACCORDING TO MARK

Mark 1

746 3588 2098 2424 5547 5207 3588 2316
1. Ἀρχὴ τοῦ εὐαγγελίου Ἰησοῦ Χριστοῦ, υἱοῦ τοῦ Θεοῦ.
(The) beginning of the gospel of Jesus Christ, Son of God.
5613 1125 1722 3588 4396 2400 1473 649
2. Ὡς γέγραπται ἐν τοῖς προφήταις, Ἰδού, ἐγὼ ἀποστέλλω
As it has been written in the prophets, Behold! I send
3588 32 3450 4253 4383 4675 3739 2680 3588
τὸν ἄγγελόν μου πρὸ προσώπου σου, ὃς κατασκευάσει τὴν
the messenger of Me before (the) face of You, who will prepare the
3598 4675 1715 4675 5456 994 1722 3588 2048
ὁδόν σου ἔμπροσθέν σου. 3 φωνὴ βοῶντος ἐν τῇ ἐρήμῳ,
way of You before You. (The) voice of one crying in the wilderness,
2090 3588 3598 2912 2117 4160 3588 5147
Ἑτοιμάσατε τὴν ὁδὸν Κυρίου· εὐθείας ποιεῖτε τὰς τρίβους
Prepare the way of (the) Lord; straight make the paths
846 1096 2491 907 1722 3588 2048 2532 2784
αὐτοῦ. 4 ἐγένετο Ἰωάννης βαπτίζων ἐν τῇ ἐρήμῳ, καὶ κηρύσ-
of Him. came John baptizing in the wilderness, and proclaim-
908 3341 1519 859 266 2532 1607
σων βάπτισμα μετανοίας εἰς ἄφεσιν ἁμαρτιῶν. 5 καὶ ἐξεπορεύ-
ing a baptism of repentance to remission of sins. And went out
4314 846 3956 3588 2449 5561 2532 3588 2415
ετο πρὸς αὐτὸν πᾶσα ἡ Ἰουδαία χώρα, καὶ οἱ Ἱεροσολυμῖται,
to him all the Judean country, and the Jerusalemites,
2532 907 3956 1722 3588 2446 4215 5259 846
καὶ ἐβαπτίζοντο πάντες ἐν τῷ Ἰορδάνῃ ποταμῷ ὑπ' αὐτοῦ,
and were baptized all in the Jordan River by him,
1843 3588 266 848 2258 1161 2491
ἐξομολογούμενοι τὰς ἁμαρτίας αὐτῶν. 6 ἦν δὲ Ἰωάννης
having confessed the sins of them. was And John
1746 2359 2574 2532 2223 1193 4012
ἐνδεδυμένος τρίχας καμήλου, καὶ ζώνην δερματίνην περὶ
being clothed in hairs of a camel, and a girdle leather around
3588 3751 846 2532 2068 200 2532 3192 66
τὴν ὀσφὺν αὐτοῦ, καὶ ἐσθίων ἀκρίδας καὶ μέλι ἄγριον.
the loin of him, and eating locusts and honey wild.
2532 2784 3004 2064 3588 2478 3450 3694
7 καὶ ἐκήρυσσε, λέγων, Ἔρχεται ὁ ἰσχυρότερός μου ὀπίσω
And he proclaimed, saying, Comes He stronger than me after
3450 3739 3756 1510 2425 2955 3089 3588 2438 3588
μου, οὗ οὐκ εἰμὶ ἱκανὸς κύψας λῦσαι τὸν ἱμάντα τῶν
me, of whom not I am worthy stooping to loosen the thong of the
5266 846 1473 3303 907 5209 1722 5204 846
ὑποδημάτων αὐτοῦ. 8 ἐγὼ μὲν ἐβάπτισα ὑμᾶς ἐν ὕδατι· αὐτὸς
sandals of Him. I indeed baptized you in water; He
1161 907 5209 1722 4151 40
δὲ βαπτίσει ὑμᾶς ἐν Πνεύματι Ἁγίῳ.
but will baptize you in (the) Spirit Holy.
2532 1096 1722 1565 3588 2250 2064 2424 575
9. Καὶ ἐγένετο ἐν ἐκείναις ταῖς ἡμέραις, ἦλθεν Ἰησοῦς ἀπὸ
And it happened in those days, came Jesus from
3478 3588 1056 2532 907 5259 2491 1519 3588
Ναζαρὲθ τῆς Γαλιλαίας, καὶ ἐβαπτίσθη ὑπὸ Ἰωάννου εἰς τὸν
Nazareth of Galilee, and was baptized by John in the
2446 2532 2112 305 575 3588 5204 1492
Ἰορδάνην. 10 καὶ εὐθέως ἀναβαίνων ἀπὸ τοῦ ὕδατος εἶδε
Jordan. And immediately going up from the water, he saw

King James Version
THE GOSPEL ACCORDING TO MARK

Mark 1

1. The beginning of the
gospel of Jesus Christ,
the Son of God;

2 As it is written in the
prophets, Behold, I
send my messenger be-
fore thy face, which
shall prepare thy way
before thee.
3 The voice of one cry-
ing in the wilderness,
Prepare ye the way of
the Lord, make his
paths straight.

4. John did baptize in
the wilderness, and
preach the baptism of
repentance for the re-
mission of sins.
5 And there went out
unto him all the land of
Judaea, and they of Je-
rusalem, and were all
baptized of him in the
river of Jordan, con-
fessing their sins.

6 And John was clothed
with camel's hair, and
with a girdle of a skin
about his loins; and he
did eat locusts and wild
honey;

7 And preached, say-
ing, There cometh one
mightier than I after me,
the latchet of whose
shoes I am not worthy to
stoop down and un-
loose.
8 I indeed have baptized
you with water: but he
shall baptize you with
the Holy Ghost.

9. And it came to pass
in those days, that Jesus
came from Nazareth of
Galilee, and was bap-
tized of John in Jordan.
10 And straightway
coming up out of the
water, he saw

Literal Translation | **Mark 1:11** | **King James Version**

the heavens being torn, and the Spirit coming down as a dove upon Him.
11 And a voice occurred out of Heaven, You are My Son, the Beloved, in whom I take delight. (Ps. 2:7; Isa. 42:1)

4977 3588 3772 2532 3588 4151 5616 4058
σχιζομένους τοὺς οὐρανούς, καὶ τὸ Πνεῦμα ὡσεὶ περιστερὰν
being torn the heavens, and the Spirit as a dove
2597 1909 846 2532 5456 1096 1537 3588 3772
καταβαῖνον ἐπ' αὐτόν· 11 καὶ φωνὴ ἐγένετο ἐκ τῶν οὐρανῶν,
coming down upon Him. And a voice occurred out of Heaven,
4571 1488 3588 5207 3450 3588 27 1722 3739 2106
Σὺ εἶ ὁ υἱός μου ὁ ἀγαπητός, ἐν ᾧ εὐδόκησα.
You are the Son of Me the Beloved, in whom I take delight.

the heavens opened, and the Spirit like a dove descending upon him:
11 And there came a voice from heaven, (saying), Thou art my beloved Son, in whom I am well pleased.

12. And the Spirit at once thrusts Him out into the deserted (place).
13 And He was there in the deserted (place) forty days, being tempted by Satan, and was with the wild beasts. And the angels ministered to Him.

2532 2117 3588 4151 846 1544 1519 3588 2048 2532
12. Καὶ εὐθὺς τὸ Πνεῦμα αὐτὸν ἐκβάλλει εἰς τὴν ἔρημον. 13 καὶ
And at once the Spirit Him thrusts into the deserted (place). And
2258 1563 1722 3588 2048 2250 5062 3985
ἦν ἐκεῖ ἐν τῇ ἐρήμῳ ἡμέρας τεσσαράκοντα πειραζόμενος
He was there in the deserted (place) days forty being tempted
5259 3588 4567 2532 2258 3326 3588 2342 2532 3588 32
ὑπὸ τοῦ Σατανᾶ, καὶ ἦν μετὰ τῶν θηρίων, καὶ οἱ ἄγγελοι διη-
by Satan, and was with the wild beasts, and the angels
1247 846
κόνουν αὐτῷ.
ministered to Him.

12. And immediately the Spirit driveth him into the wilderness.
13 And he was there in the wilderness forty days, tempted of Satan; and was with the wild beasts; and the angels ministered unto him.

14. And after John was delivered up, Jesus came into Galilee proclaiming the gospel of the kingdom of God,
15 and saying, The time has been fulfilled, and the kingdom of God draws near. Repent and believe in the gospel.

3326 1161 3588 3860 3588 2491 2064 3588 2424
14. Μετὰ δὲ τὸ παραδοθῆναι τὸν Ἰωάννην, ἦλθεν ὁ Ἰησοῦς
after And was delivered up John, came Jesus
1519 3588 1056 2784 3588 2098 3588 932
εἰς τὴν Γαλιλαίαν, κηρύσσων τὸ εὐαγγέλιον τῆς βασιλείας
into Galilee, proclaiming the gospel of the kingdom
3588 2316 2532 3004 3754 4137 3588 2540 2532 1448
τοῦ Θεοῦ, 15 καὶ λέγων ὅτι Πεπλήρωται ὁ καιρός, καὶ ἤγγικεν
of God, and saying, Has been fulfilled the time, and draws near
3588 932 3588 2316 3340 2532 4100 1722 3588
ἡ βασιλεία τοῦ θεοῦ· μετανοεῖτε, καὶ πιστεύετε ἐν τῷ
the kingdom of God; repent, and believe in the
2098
εὐαγγελίῳ.
gospel.

14. Now after that John was put in prison, Jesus came into Galilee, preaching the gospel of the kingdom of God,
15 And saying, The time is fulfilled, and the kingdom of God is at hand: repent ye, and believe the gospel.

16. And walking along beside the Sea of Galilee, He saw Simon and his brother Andrew casting a small net in the sea; for they were fishers.
17 And Jesus said to them, Come after Me, and I will make you to become fishers of men.
18 And leaving their nets, they at once followed Him.
19 And going forward from there a little, He saw James the (son) of Zebedee, and his brother John. And they were in the boat mending the nets.
20 And at once He called them. And leaving their father

4043 1161 3844 3588 2281 3588 1056 1492
16. Περιπατῶν δὲ παρὰ τὴν θάλασσαν τῆς Γαλιλαίας εἶδε
walking along And beside the sea of Galilee, He saw
4613 2532 406 3588 80 846 906
Σίμωνα καὶ Ἀνδρέαν τὸν ἀδελφὸν αὐτοῦ, βάλλοντας
Simon and Andrew the brother of him, casting
293 1722 3588 2281 2258 1063 231 2532 2036
ἀμφίβληστρον ἐν τῇ θαλάσσῃ· ἦσαν γὰρ ἁλιεῖς. 17 καὶ εἶπεν
a small net in the sea; they were for fishers. And said
846 3588 2424 1205 3694 3450 2532 4160 5209
αὐτοῖς ὁ Ἰησοῦς, Δεῦτε ὀπίσω μου, καὶ ποιήσω ὑμᾶς
to them Jesus, Come after Me, and I will make you
1096 231 444 2532 2112 863 3588 1350
γενέσθαι ἁλιεῖς ἀνθρώπων. 18 καὶ εὐθέως ἀφέντες τὰ δίκτυα
to become fishers of men. And at once leaving the nets
846 190 846 2532 4260 1564 3641
αὐτῶν, ἠκολούθησαν αὐτῷ. 19 Καὶ προβὰς ἐκεῖθεν ὀλίγον,
of them, they followed Him. And going forward from there a bit,
1492 2385 3588 3588 2199 2532 2491 3588
εἶδεν Ἰάκωβον τὸν τοῦ Ζεβεδαίου, καὶ Ἰωάννην τὸν
He saw James the (son) of Zebedee, and John the
80 846 2532 846 1722 3588 4143 2675 3588 1350
ἀδελφὸν αὐτοῦ, καὶ αὐτοὺς ἐν τῷ πλοίῳ καταρτίζοντας τα δικ-
brother of him, and they in the boat mending the
2532 2112 2564 846 2532 863 3588 3962
τυα, 20 καὶ εὐθέως ἐκάλεσεν αὐτούς· καὶ ἀφέντες τὸν πατέρα
nets. And at once He called them. And leaving the father

16. Now as he walked by the sea of Galilee, he saw Simon and Andrew his brother casting a net into the sea: for they were fishers.
17 And Jesus said unto them, Come ye after me, and I will make you to become fishers of men.
18 And straightway they forsook their nets, and followed him.
19 And when he had gone a little further thence, he saw James the (son) of Zebedee, and John his brother, who also were in the ship mending their nets.
20 And straightway he called them: and they left their father

Literal Translation

Zebedee in the boat with the hired servants, they went after Him.

21. And they passed along into Capernaum. And entering into the synagogue, at once He taught on the sabbaths.
22 And they were astounded at His doctrine, for He was teaching them as having authority, and not as the scribes.
23 And a man with an unclean spirit was in their synagogue. And he cried out,

24 saying, Ah! What (is) to us and to You, Jesus, Nazarene? Did You come to destroy us? I know You, who You are, the Holy (One) of God.
25 And Jesus rebuked him, saying, Be quiet, and come out of him.

26 And the unclean spirit convulsing him, and crying out with a loud voice, he came out of him.
27 And all were astonished, so as to discuss to themselves, saying, What is this? What new teaching (is) this, that He commands even the unclean spirits with authority, and they obey Him?

28 And His fame went out at once into all the neighborhood of Galilee.

29. And at once going out of the synagogue, they came into the house of Simon and Andrew, with James and John.
30 And the mother-in-law of Simon was laid out, stricken by fever. And at once they spoke to Him about her.
31 And coming near, He raised her up,

Mark 1:21

846 2199‘ 1722 3588 4143 3326 3588 3411 565
αὐτῶν Ζεβεδαῖον ἐν τῷ πλοίῳ μετὰ τῶν μισθωτῶν ἀπῆλθον
of them Zebedee, in the boat with the hired servants, they went
3694 846
ὀπίσω αὐτοῦ.
after Him.

2532 1531 1519 2584 2532 2112 3588
21. Καὶ εἰσπορεύονται εἰς Καπερναούμ· καὶ εὐθέως τοῖς
And they passed along into Capernaum; and at once on the
4521 1525 1519 3588 4864 1321 2532
σάββασιν εἰσελθὼν εἰς τὴν συναγωγήν, ἐδίδασκε. 22 καὶ
sabbaths entering into the synagogue, He taught. And
1605 1909 3588 1322 846 2258 1063 1321
ἐξεπλήσσοντο ἐπὶ τῇ διδαχῇ αὐτοῦ· ἦν γὰρ διδάσκων
they were astounded at the doctrine of Him. He was For teaching
846 5613 1849 2192 2532 3756 5613 3588 1122 2532
αὐτοὺς ὡς ἐξουσίαν ἔχων, καὶ οὐχ ὡς οἱ γραμματεῖς. 23 καὶ
them as authority having, and not as the scribes. And
2258 1722 3588 4864 846 444 1722 4151 169
ἦν ἐν τῇ συναγωγῇ αὐτῶν ἄνθρωπος ἐν πνεύματι ἀκαθάρτῳ,
was in the synagogue of them a man with a spirit unclean,
2532 349 3004 1436 5101 2254 2532 4671 2424 3479
καὶ ἀνέκραξε, 24 λέγων, Ἔα, τί ἡμῖν καὶ σοί, Ἰησοῦ Ναζαρηνέ;
and he cried out, saying, Ah! What to us and to You, Jesus, Nazarene?
2064 622 2248 1492 4571 5101 1488 3588 40 3588 2316 2532
ἦλθες ἀπολέσαι ἡμᾶς; οἶδά σε τίς εἶ, ὁ ἅγιος τοῦ Θεοῦ. 25 καὶ
Came You to destroy us? I know You, who you are, the Holy of God. And
2008 846 3588 2424 3004 5392 2532 1831
ἐπετίμησεν αὐτῷ ὁ Ἰησοῦς, λέγων, Φιμώθητι, καὶ ἔξελθε
rebuked him Jesus, saying, Be quiet, and come
1537 846 2532 4682 846 3588 4151 3588 169 2532
ἐξ αὐτοῦ. 26 καὶ σπαράξαν αὐτὸν τὸ πνεῦμα τὸ ἀκάθαρτον καὶ
out of him. And convulsing him the spirit unclean and
2896 5456 3173 183 1537 846 2532 2284
κράξαν φωνῇ μεγάλῃ, ἐξῆλθεν ἐξ αὐτοῦ. 27 καὶ ἐθαμβήθησαν
crying out with a voice great, he came out of him. And were astonished
3956 5620 4802 4314 846 3004 5101 2076
πάντες, ὥστε συζητεῖν πρὸς αὐτούς, λέγοντας, Τί ἐστι
all, so as to discuss to themselves, saying, What is
5124 5101 3588 1322 3588 2537 3778 3754 2596 1849 2532
τοῦτο; τίς ἡ διδαχὴ ἡ καινὴ αὕτη, ὅτι κατ' ἐξουσίαν καὶ
this? What teaching new (is) this, that with authority even
3588 4151 3588 169 2004 2532 5219
τοῖς πνεύμασι τοῖς ἀκαθάρτοις ἐπιτάσσει, καὶ ὑπακούουσιν
the spirits unclean he commands, and they obey
846 1831 1161 3588 189 846 2117 1519 3650 3588 4066
αὐτῷ; 28 ἐξῆλθε δὲ ἡ ἀκοὴ αὐτοῦ εὐθὺς εἰς ὅλην τὴν περίχωρον
Him? went out And the fame of Him at once into all the neighborhood
3588 1056
τῆς Γαλιλαίας.
of Galilee.

2532 2112 1537 3588 4864 1831 2064 1519 3588
29. Καὶ εὐθέως ἐκ τῆς συναγωγῆς ἐξελθόντες, ἦλθον εἰς τὴν
And at once out of the synagogue going forth, they came into the
3614 4613 2532 406 3326 2385 2532 2491
οἰκίαν Σίμωνος καὶ Ἀνδρέου, μετὰ Ἰακώβου καὶ Ἰωάννου.
house of Simon and Andrew, with James and John.
3588 1161 3994 4163 2621 4445 2532 2112
30 ἡ δὲ πενθερὰ Σίμωνος κατέκειτο πυρέσσουσα, καὶ εὐθέως
the And mother-in-law of Simon was laid fever-stricken, and at once
3004 846 4012 846 2532 4334 1453 846
λέγουσιν αὐτῷ περὶ αὐτῆς· 31 καὶ προσελθὼν ἤγειρεν αὐτήν,
they speak to Him about her.. And coming near He raised her

King James Version

Zebedee in the ship with the hired servants, and went after him.

21. And they went into Capernaum; and straightway on the sabbath day he entered into the synagogue, and taught.
22 And they were astonished at his doctrine: for he taught them as one that had authority, and not as the scribes.
23 And there was in their synagogue a man with an unclean spirit; and he cried out,

24 Saying, Let (us) alone; what have we to do with thee, thou Jesus of Nazareth? art thou come to destroy us? I know thee who thou art, the Holy One of God.
25 And Jesus rebuked him, saying, Hold thy peace, and come out of him.
26 And when the unclean spirit had torn him, and cried with a loud voice, he came out of him.
27 And they were all amazed, insomuch that they questioned among themselves, saying, What thing is this? what new doctrine (is) this? for with authority commandeth he even the unclean spirits, and they do obey him.

28 And immediately his fame spread abroad throughout all the region round about Galilee.
29. And forthwith, when they were come out of the synagogue, they entered into the house of Simon and Andrew, with James and John.
30 But Simon's wife's mother lay sick of a fever, and anon they tell him of her.
31 And he came and took her by the hand, and lifted her up;

Literal Translation

holding her hand. And the fever left her instantly, and she served them.

32. And evening coming, when the sun sank, they brought to Him all the (ones) badly having (illness) and the (ones) having been demon-possessed.
33 And having gathered the whole city was at the door.
34 And He healed many badly having (illness) of various diseases. And he cast out many demons, and (He) did not allow the demons to speak, because they knew Him.

35. And rising up quite early in (the) night, He went out and went away into a deserted place. And (He) was praying there.
36 And Simon and those with him searched for Him.
37 And finding Him, they say to Him, All are seeking You.
38 And He says to them, Let us go into the neighboring towns, that I may proclaim there also. For to this I came forth.
39 And He was proclaiming in their synagogues in all Galilee, and casting out the demons.
40. And a leper came to Him, begging Him, and falling on (his) knees to Him, and saying to Him, If You desire, You are able to make me clean.
41 And Jesus being filled with pity, reaching out the hand, He touched him, and said to him, I am willing. Be made clean!
42 And (He) having spoken to him, instantly the leprosy departed from him, and he was made clean.
43 And having strictly warned him, He at once put him out,

Mark 1:32

2902 3588 5495 846 2532 863 846 3588 4446
κρατήσας τῆς χειρός αὐτῆς· καὶ ἀφῆκεν αὐτὴν ὁ πυρετὸς
holding the hand of her, and left her the fever

2112 2532 1247 846
εὐθέως, καὶ διηκόνει αὐτοῖς.
instantly. And she served them.

3798 1161 1096 3753 1416 3588 2246 5342 4314 846
32 Ὀψίας δὲ γενομένης, ὅτε ἔδυ ὁ ἥλιος, ἔφερον πρὸς αὐτὸν
evening And having come when sank the sun, they brought to Him

3956 3588 2560 2192 2532 3588 1139 2532
πάντας τοὺς κακῶς ἔχοντας καὶ τοὺς δαιμονιζομένους· 33 καὶ
all those badly (illness) having and those having been demon-possessed; and

3588 4172 3650 1996 2258 4314 3588 2374 2532
ἡ πόλις ὅλη ἐπισυνηγμένη ἦν πρὸς τὴν θύραν. 34 καὶ
the city whole having gathered was at the door. And

2323 4183 2560 2192 4164 3554 2532
ἐθεράπευσε πολλοὺς κακῶς ἔχοντας ποικίλαις νόσοις, καὶ
He healed many badly (illness) having of various diseases, and

1140 4183 1544 2532 3756 863 2980 3588 1140 3754
δαιμόνια πολλὰ ἐξέβαλε, καὶ οὐκ ἤφιε λαλεῖν τὰ δαιμόνια, ὅτι
demons many he cast out, and not allowed to speak the demons, because

1492 846
ᾔδεισαν αὐτόν.
they knew Him.

2532 4404 1773 3029 450 1831 2532 565 1519
35. Καὶ πρωῒ ἔννυχον λίαν ἀναστὰς ἐξῆλθε, καὶ ἀπῆλθεν εἰς
And early in (the) night quite rising up He went out, and went away into

2048 5117 2546 4336 2532 2614 846 3588
ἔρημον τόπον, κἀκεῖ προσηύχετο. 36 καὶ κατεδίωξαν αὐτὸν ὁ
a deserted place, and there (He) was praying. And searched for him

4613 2532 3588 3326 846 2532 2147 846 3004 846
Σίμων καὶ οἱ μετ' αὐτοῦ· 37 καὶ εὑρόντες αὐτὸν λέγουσιν αὐτῷ
Simon and those with him; and finding Him they say to Him,

3754 3956 2122 4571 2532 3004 846 71 1519 3588
ὅτι Πάντες ζητοῦσί σε. 38 καὶ λέγει αὐτοῖς, Ἄγωμεν εἰς τὰς
All are seeking You. And He says to them, Let us go into the

2192 2969 2443 2546 2784 1519 5124 1063
ἐχομένας κωμοπόλεις, ἵνα κἀκεῖ κηρύξω· εἰς τοῦτο γὰρ
neighboring towns, that there also I may proclaim; to this for

1831 2532 2258 2784 1722 3588 4864 846 1519
ἐξελήλυθα. 39 καὶ ἦν κηρύσσων ἐν ταῖς συναγωγαῖς αὐτῶν εἰς
I came forth. And He was proclaiming in the synagogues of them in

3650 3588 1056 2532 3588 1140 1544
ὅλην τὴν Γαλιλαίαν, καὶ τὰ δαιμόνια ἐκβάλλων.
all Galilee, and the demons casting out.

2532 2064 4314 846 3015 3870 846 2532
40. Καὶ ἔρχεται πρὸς αὐτὸν λεπρός, παρακαλῶν αὐτὸν καὶ
And comes to Him a leper, begging Him and

1120 846 2532 3004 846 3754 1437 2309 1410
γονυπετῶν αὐτόν, καὶ λέγων αὐτῷ ὅτι Ἐὰν θέλῃς, δύνασαί
falling on knees to Him, and saying to Him, If You desire, You are able

3165 2511 3588 1161 2424 4697 1614 3588
με καθαρίσαι. 41 ὁ δὲ Ἰησοῦς σπλαγχνισθείς, ἐκτείνας τὴν
me to make clean. And Jesus being filled with pity, reaching out the

5495 680 846 2532 3004 846 2309 2511
χεῖρα, ἥψατο αὐτοῦ καὶ λέγει αὐτῷ. Θέλω, καθαρίσθητι.
hand, He touched him and says to him, I am willing, be made clean.

2532 2036 846 2112 565 575 846 3588 3014
42 καὶ εἰπόντος αὐτοῦ, εὐθέως ἀπῆλθεν ἀπ' αὐτοῦ ἡ λέπρα,
And having spoken to him, instantly departed from him the leprosy,

2532 2511 2532 1690 846 2112 1544
καὶ ἐκαθαρίσθη.43καὶ ἐμβριμησάμενος αὐτῷ, εὐθέως ἐξέβαλεν
and he was cleansed. And having strictly warned him, at once He put out

King James Version

and immediately the fever left her, and she ministered unto them.

32. And at even, when the sun did set, they brought unto him all that were diseased, and them that were possessed with devils.
33 And all the city was gathered together at the door.
34 And he healed many that were sick of divers diseases, and cast out many devils; and suffered not the devils to speak, because they knew him.

35. And in the morning, rising up a great while before day, he went out, and departed into a solitary place, and there prayed.
36 And Simon and they that were with him followed after him.
37 And when they had found him, they said unto him, All (men) seek for thee.
38 And he said unto them, Let us go into the next towns, that I may preach there also: for therefore came I forth.
39 And he preached in their synagogues throughout all Galilee, and cast out devils.

40. And there came a leper to him, beseeching him, and kneeling down to him, and saying unto him, If thou wilt, thou canst make me clean.
41 And Jesus, moved with compassion, put forth (his) hand, and touched him, and saith unto him, I will; be thou clean.
42 And as soon as he had spoken, immediately the leprosy departed from him, and he was cleansed.
43 And he straitly charged him, and forthwith sent

Literal Translation

44 and said to him, See, tell no one, not a thing, but go show yourself to the priest, and offer what Moses directed concerning your cleansing, for a testimony to them.

45 But going out he began to proclaim much, and to spread about the matter, so that He no longer was able to openly enter into a city. But He was outside in deserted places. And they came to Him from every quarter.

Mark 1:44

846 2532 3004 846 3708 3367 3367 2036 235
αὐτόν, 44 καὶ λέγει αὐτῷ, Ὅρα, μηδενὶ μηδὲν εἴπῃς· ἀλλ'
him, and says to him, See, no one, not a thing, tell; but

5217 4572 1166 3588 2409 2532 4374 4012 3588
ὕπαγε σεαυτὸν δεῖξον τῷ ἱερεῖ, καὶ προσένεγκε περὶ τοῦ
go yourself show to the priest and offer concerning the

2512 4675 3739 4367 3475 1519 3142 846
καθαρισμοῦ σου ἃ προσέταξε Μωσῆς, εἰς μαρτύριον αὐτοῖς.
cleansing of you what ordered Moses, for a testimony to them.

3588 1161 1831 756 2784 4183 2532 1310 3588
45 ὁ δὲ ἐξελθὼν ἤρξατο κηρύσσειν πολλὰ καὶ διαφημίζειν τὸν
he But going out began to proclaim much and to spread about the

3056 5620 3371 846 1410 5320 1519 4172
λόγον, ὥστε μηκέτι αὐτὸν δύνασθαι φανερῶς εἰς πόλιν
matter, so as no longer He to be able openly into a city

1525 235 1854 1722 2048 5117 2258 2532 2064 4314
εἰσελθεῖν, ἀλλ ἔξω ἐν ἐρήμοις τόποις ἦν· καὶ ἤρχοντο πρὸς
to enter, but outside in deserted places He was, and they came to

846 3836
αὐτὸν πάνταχόθεν.
Him from every quarter.

King James Version

him away;

44 And saith unto him, See thou say nothing to any man: but go thy way, shew thyself to the priest, and offer for thy cleansing those things which Moses commanded, for a testimony unto them.

45 But he went out, and began to publish (it) much, and to blaze abroad the matter, insomuch that Jesus could no more openly enter into the city, but was without in desert places: and they came to him from every quarter.

Mark 2

1. And again He entered into Capernaum through (some) days. And it was heard that He was in (a) house.

2 And at once many were gathered, so as none any longer had room, not even to the door. And He spoke the Word to them.

3 And they came to Him carrying a paralytic, being borne by four.

4 And not being able to draw near to Him, because of the crowd, they unroofed the roof where He was. And digging through, they lower the cot on which the paralytic was lying.

5 And seeing their faith, Jesus says to the paralytic, Child, your sins are remitted to you.

6 But some of the scribes were sitting there ,and reasoning in their hearts,

7 Why does this one speak blasphemies this way? Who is able to remit sins, except One, God?

8 And instantly knowing in His spirit

Mark 2

2532 3825 1525 1519 2584 1223 2250 2532
1. Καὶ πάλιν εἰσῆλθεν εἰς Καπερναοὺμ δι' ἡμερῶν· καὶ
And again He entered into Capernaum through days; and

191 3754 1519 3624 2076 2532 2112 4863 4183
ἠκούσθη ὅτι εἰς οἶκόν ἐστι. 2 καὶ εὐθέως συνήχθησαν πολλοί,
it was heard that into (a) house He is. And at once were assembled many,

5620 3371 5562 3366 3588 4314 3588 2374 2532 2980
ὥστε μηκέτι χωρεῖν μηδὲ τὰ πρὸς τὴν θύραν· καὶ ἐλάλει
so as no longer to have room not even to the door; and He spoke

846 3588 3056 2532 2064 4314 846 3885
αὐτοῖς τὸν λόγον. 3 καὶ ἔρχονται πρὸς αὐτόν, παραλυτικὸν
to them the Word. And they come to Him a paralytic

5342 142 5259 5064 2532 3361 1410
φέροντες, αἰρόμενον ὑπὸ τεσσάρων. 4 καὶ μὴ δυνάμενοι
carrying, being borne by four. And not being able

4331 846 1223 3588 3793 648 3588 4721
προσεγγίσαι αὐτῷ διὰ τὸν ὄχλον, ἀπεστέγασαν τὴν στέγην
to draw near to Him because of the crowd, they unroofed the roof

3699 2258 2532 1846 5465 3588 2895 1909 3759 3588
ὅπου ἦν, καὶ ἐξορύξαντες χαλῶσι τὸν κράβαττον ἐφ' ᾧ ὁ
where He was, and digging through they lower the cot on which the

3885 2621 1492 1161 3588 2424 3588 4102 846
παραλυτικὸς κατέκειτο. 5 ἰδὼν δὲ ὁ Ἰησοῦς τὴν πίστιν αὐτῶν
paralytic was lying. seeing And Jesus the faith of them

3004 3588 3885 5043 863 4671 3588 266
λέγει τῷ παραλυτικῷ, Τέκνον, ἀφέωνταί σοι αἱ ἁμαρτίαι
He says to the paralytic, Child, are remitted to you the sins

4675 2258 1161 5100 3588 1122 1563 2521 2532
σου. 6 ἦσαν δέ τινες τῶν γραμματέων ἐκεῖ καθήμενοι, καὶ
of you. were But some of the scribes there sitting, and

1260 1722 3588 2588 846 5101 3778 3779
διαλογιζόμενοι ἐν ταῖς καρδίαις αὐτῶν, 7 Τί οὗτος οὕτω
reasoning in the hearts of them. Why this one thus

2980 988 5101 1410 863 266 1487 3361 1520
λαλεῖ βλασφημίας; τίς δύναται ἀφιέναι ἁμαρτίας εἰ μὴ εἷς,
speaks blasphemies? Who is able to remit sins except One,

3588 2316 2532 2112 1921 3588 2424 3588 4151 846
ὁ Θεός; 8 καὶ εὐθέως ἐπιγνοὺς ὁ Ἰησοῦς τῷ πνεύματι αὐτοῦ
God? And instantly knowing Jesus in the spirit of Him

Mark 2

1. And again he entered into Capernaum after (some) days; and it was noised that he was in the house.

2 And straightway many were gathered together, insomuch that there was no room to receive (them), no, not so much as about the door: and he preached the word unto them.

3 And they come unto him, bringing one sick of the palsy, which was borne of four.

4 And when they could not come nigh unto him for the press, they uncovered the roof where he was: and when they had broken (it) up, they let down the bed wherein the sick of the palsy lay.

5 When Jesus saw their faith, he said unto the sick of the palsy, Son, thy sins be forgiven thee.

6 But there were certain of the scribes sitting there, and reasoning in their hearts,

7 Why doth this (man) thus speak blasphemies? who can forgive sins but God only?

8 And immediately when Jesus perceived in his spirit

Literal Translation

that they reason this way within themselves, Jesus said to them, Why do you reason these things in your hearts?
9 Which is easier? To say to the paralytic, (Your) sins are remitted to you, or to say, Rise up and take up your cot and walk?
10 But that you may know that the Son of man has authority to remit sins on the earth, He said to the paralytic,
11 I say to you, Rise up and take up your cot and go to your house.
12 And at once he rose up. And taking up his cot, he went out before all, so as to be all astonished and to glorify God, saying, Never did we see (it) this way.
13. And he went out by the sea again. And all the crowd kept coming to Him, and He kept on teaching them.
14 And passing along He saw Levi the (son) of Alphaeus sitting at the tax office. And (He) says to him, Follow Me. And rising up, he followed Him.
15. And it happened (as) He reclined in his house, even many tax collectors and sinners reclined with Jesus and His disciples, for they were many. And they followed Him.
16 And the scribes and Pharisees seeing Him eating with tax collectors and sinners, (they) said to His disciples, Why (is it) that He eats and drinks with the tax-collectors and sinners?
17 And hearing, Jesus said

Mark 2:9

3754 3779 1260 1722 1438 2036 846 5101 5023
ὅτι οὕτως διαλογίζονται ἐν ἑαυτοῖς, εἶπεν αὐτοῖς, Τί ταῦτα
that so they reason within themselves, He says to them,Why these things

1260 1722 3588 2588 5216 5101 2076 2123
διαλογίζεσθε ἐν ταῖς καρδίαις ὑμῶν; 9 τί ἐστιν εὐκοπώτερον,
do you reason in the hearts of you? What is easier,

2036 3588 3885 863 4671 3588 266 2228 2036
εἰπεῖν τῷ παραλυτικῷ, Ἀφέωνταί σου αἱ ἁμαρτίαι, ἢ εἰπεῖν,
to say to the paralytic, Are remitted to you the sins, or to say,

1453 2532 142 4675 3588 2895 2532 4043 2443
Ἔγειραι, καὶ ἆρόν σου τὸν κράβαττον, καὶ περιπάτει; 10 ἵνα
Rise up, and take up of you the cot, and walk? that

1161 1492 3754 1849 2192 3588 5207 3588 444 863
δὲ εἰδῆτε ὅτι ἐξουσίαν ἔχει ὁ υἱὸς τοῦ ἀνθρώπου ἀφιέναι
But you may know that authority has the Son of man to remit

1909 3588 1093 266 3004 3588 3885 4671 3004
ἐπὶ τῆς γῆς ἁμαρτίας [λέγει τῷ παραλυτικῷ], 11 Σοὶ λέγω,
on the earth sins, He says to the paralytic, To you I say,

1453 2532 142 3588 2895 4675 2532 5217 1519 3588
ἔγειραι, καὶ ἆρον τὸν κράβαττόν σου, καὶ ὕπαγε εἰς τὸν
Rise up and take up the cot of you, and go to the

3624 4675 2532 1453 2112 2532 142 3588 2895
οἶκόν σου. 12 καὶ ἠγέρθη εὐθέως, καὶ ἄρας τὸν κράβαττον,
house of you. And he rose up at once, and taking up the cot,

1831 1726 3956 5620 1839 3956 2532
ἐξῆλθεν ἐναντίον πάντων· ὥστε ἐξίστασθαι πάντας, καὶ
he went out before all; so as to be astonished all, and

1392 3588 2316 3004 3754 3763 3779 1492
δοξάζειν τὸν Θεόν, λέγοντας ὅτι Οὐδέποτε οὕτως εἴδομεν.
to glorify God, saying, Never this way we saw.

2532 1831 3825 3844 3588 2281 2532 3956 3588 3793
13. Καὶ ἐξῆλθε πάλιν παρὰ τὴν θάλασσαν· καὶ πᾶς ὁ ὄχλος
And He went out again beside the sea.; and all the crowd

2064 4314 846 2532 1321 846 2532 3855
ἤρχετο πρὸς αὐτόν, καὶ ἐδίδασκεν αὐτούς. 14 καὶ παράγων
kept coming to Him, and He kept on teaching them. And passing along

1492 3018 3588 3588 256 2521 1909 3588 5058 2532
εἶδε Λευΐν τὸν τοῦ Ἀλφαίου καθήμενον ἐπὶ τὸ τελώνιον, καὶ
He saw Levi the (son) of Alphaeus sitting at the tax-office, and

3004 846 190 3427 2532 450 190
λέγει αὐτῷ, Ἀκολούθει μοι. καὶ ἀναστὰς ἠκολούθησεν
says to him, Follow Me. And rising up he followed

846 2532 1096 1722 3588 2621 846 1722 3588 3614
αὐτῷ. 15 Καὶ ἐγένετο ἐν τῷ κατακεῖσθαι αὐτὸν ἐν τῇ οἰκίᾳ
Him. And it was during the reclining He in the house

846 2532 4183 5057 2532 268 4873 3588
αὐτοῦ, καὶ πολλοὶ τελῶναι καὶ ἁμαρτωλοὶ συνανέκειντο τῷ
of him, even many tax-collectors and sinners reclined with

2424 2532 3588 3101 846 2258 1063 4183 2532
Ἰησοῦ καὶ τοῖς μαθηταῖς αὐτοῦ· ἦσαν γὰρ πολλοί, καὶ
Jesus and the disciples of Him; they were for many, and

190 846 2532 3588 1122 2532 3588 5330
ἠκολούθησαν αὐτῷ. 16 καὶ οἱ γραμματεῖς καὶ οἱ Φαρισαῖοι,
they followed Him. And the scribes and the Pharisees

1492 846 2068 3326 3588 5057 2532 268
ἰδόντες αὐτὸν ἐσθίοντα μετὰ τῶν τελωνῶν καὶ ἁμαρτωλῶν,
seeing Him eating with tax-collectors and sinners,

3004 3588 3101 846 5101 3754 3326 3588 5057 2532
ἔλεγον τοῖς μαθηταῖς αὐτοῦ, Τί ὅτι μετὰ τῶν τελωνῶν καὶ
said to the disciples of Him,Why that with the tax-collectors and

268 2068 2532 4095 2532 191 3588 2424 3004
ἁμαρτωλῶν ἐσθίει καὶ πίνει; 17 καὶ ἀκούσας ὁ Ἰησοῦς λέγει
sinners does He eat and drink? And hearing Jesus says

King James Version

that they so reasoned within themselves, he said unto them, Why reason ye these things in your hearts?
9 Whether is it easier to say to the sick of the palsy, (Thy) sins be forgiven thee; or to say, Arise, and take up thy bed, and walk?
10 But that ye may know that the Son of man hath power on earth to forgive sins, (he saith to the sick of the palsy,)
11 I say unto thee, Arise, and take up thy bed, and go thy way into thine house.
12 And immediately he arose, took up the bed, and went forth before them all; insomuch that they were all amazed, and glorified God, saying, We never saw it on this fashion.
13. And he went forth again by the sea side; and all the multitude resorted unto him, and he taught them.
14 And as he passed by, he saw Levi the (son) of Alphaeus sitting at the receipt of custom, and said unto him, Follow me. And he arose and followed him.
15. And it came to pass, that, as Jesus sat at meat in his house, many publicans and sinners sat also together with Jesus and his disciples: for there were many, and they followed him.
16 And when the scribes and Pharisees saw him eat with publicans and sinners, they said unto his disciples, How is it that he eateth and drinketh with publicans and sinners?
17 When Jesus heard (it), he saith

Literal Translation | **Mark 2:18** | ***King James Version***

to them, Those who are strong have no need of a healer, but those badly having (illness). I did not come to call righteous ones to repentance, but sinners.

846 3756 5532 2192 3588 2480 2395 235 3588
αὐτοῖς, Οὐ χρείαν ἔχουσιν οἱ ἰσχύοντες ἰατροῦ, ἀλλ' οἱ
to them, Not need have those being strong of a healer, but those
2560 2192 3756 2064 2564 1342 235 268
κακῶς ἔχοντες. οὐκ ἦλθον καλέσαι δικαίους, ἀλλὰ ἁμαρ-
badly (illness) having. Not I came to call righteous ones, but sinners
1519 3341
τωλούς εἰς μετάνοιαν.
to repentance.

unto them, They that are whole have no need of the physician, but they that are sick: I came not to call the righteous, but sinners to repentance.

18. And John's disciples, and those of the Pharisees, were fasting. And they came and say to Him, Why do John's disciples and those of the Pharisees fast, but your disciples do not fast?

2532 2258 3588 3101 2491 2532 3588 3588 5330
18. Καὶ ἦσαν οἱ μαθηταὶ Ἰωάννου καὶ οἱ τῶν Φαρισαίων
And were the disciples of John, and those of the Pharisees
3522 2532 2064 2532 3004 846 1302 3588
νηστεύοντες· καὶ ἔρχονται καὶ λέγουσιν αὐτῷ, Διατί οἱ
fasting; and they come and say to Him, Why do the
3101 2491 2532 3588 3588 5330 3522 3588
μαθηταὶ Ἰωάννου καὶ οἱ τῶν Φαρισαίων νηστεύουσιν, οἱ
disciples of John and those of the Pharisees fast, the
1161 4674 3101 3756 3522 2532 2036 846 3588 2424
δὲ σοὶ μαθηταὶ οὐ νηστεύουσι; 19 καὶ εἶπεν αὐτοῖς ὁ Ἰησοῦς,
but of you disciples not do fast? And said to them Jesus,

18. And the disciples of John and of the Pharisees used to fast: and they come and say unto him, Why do the disciples of John and of the Pharisees fast, but thy disciples fast not?

19 And Jesus said to them, Not are able to make the sons of the bridechamber to fast while the bridegroom is with them? What time they have the bridegroom with them, they are not able to fast.

3361 1410 3588 5207 3588 3567 1722 3739 3588 3566 3326
Μὴ δύνανται οἱ υἱοὶ τοῦ νυμφῶνος, ἐν ᾧ ὁ νυμφίος μετ'
Not are able the sons of the bridechamber, while the bridegroom with
846 2076 3522 3745 5550 3326 1438 2192 3588
αὐτῶν ἐστι, νηστεύειν; ὅσον χρόνον μεθ' ἑαυτῶν ἔχουσι τὸν
them is to fast? What time with them they have the
3566 3756 1410 3522 2064 1161 2250 3752
νυμφίον, οὐ δύνανται νηστεύειν· 20 ἐλεύσονται δὲ ἡμέραι ὅταν
bridegroom, not they are able to fast. will come But days when

19 And Jesus said unto them, Can the children of the bridechamber fast, while the bridegroom is with them? as long as they have the bridegroom with them, they cannot fast.

20 But the days will come when the bridegroom will be taken away from them, and then they will fast in those days.

522 575 846 3588 3566 2532 5119 3522 1722
ἀπαρθῇ ἀπ' αὐτῶν ὁ νυμφίος, καὶ τότε νηστεύσουσιν ἐν
will be taken from them the bridegroom, and then they will fast in
1565 3588 2250 2532 3762 1915 4470 46
ἐκείναις ταῖς ἡμέραις. 21 καὶ οὐδεὶς ἐπίβλημα ῥάκους ἀγνάφου
those days. And no one a patch of cloth unfulled

20 But the days will come, when the bridegroom shall be taken away from them, and then shall they fast in those days.

21 And no one sews a patch of unmilled cloth on an old garment, else (it) takes away its fullness, the new (from) the old, and a worse tear occurs.

1976 1909 2440 3820 1487 1161 3361 142 3588 4138
ἐπιρράπτει ἐπὶ ἱματίῳ παλαιῷ· εἰ δὲ μή, αἴρει τὸ πλήρωμα
sews on a garment old; otherwise takes away the fullness
846 3588 2537 3588 3820 2532 5501 4978 1096
αὐτοῦ τὸ καινὸν τοῦ παλαιοῦ, καὶ χεῖρον σχίσμα γίνεται.
of it the new (from) the old, and a worse tear occurs.

21 No man also seweth a piece of new cloth on an old garment: else the new piece that filled it up taketh away from the old, and the rent is made worse.

22 And no one puts new wine into old wineskins, else the new wine will burst the wineskins, and the wine pours out, and the wineskins will be destroyed. But new wine is to be put into fresh wineskins.

2532 3762 906 3631 3501 1519 779 3820 1487 1161
22 καὶ οὐδεὶς βάλλει οἶνον νέον εἰς ἀσκοὺς παλαιούς· εἰ δὲ
And no one puts wine new into wineskins old; other-
3361 4486 3588 3631 3588 3501 3588 779 2532 3588 3631 1632 2532
μή, ῥήσσει ὁ οἶνος ὁ νέος τοὺς ἀσκούς, καὶ ὁ οἶνος ἐκχεῖται καὶ
wise, burst the wine new the wineskins, and the wine pours out and
3588 779 622 235 3631 3501 1519 779 2537
οἱ ἀσκοὶ ἀπολοῦνται· ἀλλὰ οἶνον νέον εἰς ἀσκοὺς καινοὺς
the wineskins will be destroyed; but wine new into wineskins fresh
992
βλητέον.
is to be put.

22 And no man putteth new wine into old bottles: else the new wine doth burst the bottles, and the wine is spilled, and the bottles will be marred: but new wine must be put into new bottles.

23. And it happened, He went along through the grain fields in the sabbaths. And His disciples began to make way, plucking the heads (of grain).
24 And the Pharisees said to Him,

2532 1096 3899 846 1722 3588 4521 1223
23. Καὶ ἐγένετο παραπορεύεσθαι αὐτὸν ἐν τοῖς σάββασι διὰ
And it happened (that) went along He in the sabbaths through
3588 4702 2532 756 3588 3101 846 3598 4160
τῶν σπορίμων, καὶ ἤρξαντο οἱ μαθηταὶ αὐτοῦ ὁδὸν ποιεῖν
the grainfields, and began the disciples of Him (a) way to make
5089 3588 4719 2532 3588 5330 3004 846
τίλλοντες τοὺς στάχυας. 24 καὶ οἱ Φαρισαῖοι ἔλεγον αὐτῷ,
plucking the heads (of grain). And the Pharisees said to Him,

23. And it came to pass, that he went through the corn fields on the sabbath day; and his disciples began, as they went, to pluck the ears of corn.
24 And the Pharisees said unto him,

Literal Translation

Mark 2:25

King James Version

Behold! Why do they do what is not lawful on the sabbaths?
25 And He said to them, Did you never read what David did when he had need and hungered, he and those with him?
26 How he entered the house of God in (the days of) Abiathar (who afterwards became) the high priest, and ate the Loaves of the Presentation, which it is not lawful to eat, except for the priests, and (he) even gave to those being with him?
27 And He said to them, The sabbath came into being because of man, not man because of the sabbath.
28 So then the Son of man is Lord of the sabbath also.

2396 5101 4160 1722 3588 4521 3739 3756 1832 2532 846
Ἴδε, τί ποιοῦσιν ἐν τοῖς σάββασιν ὃ οὐκ ἔξεστι; 25 καὶ αὐτὸς
Behold! Why do they in the sabbaths what not is lawful? And He

3004 846 3763 314 5101 4160 1138 3753
ἔλεγεν αὐτοῖς, Οὐδέποτε ἀνέγνωτε τί ἐποίησε Δαβίδ, ὅτε
said to them, never Did you read what did David when

5532 2192 2532 3983 846 2532 3588 3326 846 4459
χρείαν ἔσχε καὶ ἐπείνασεν αὐτὸς καὶ οἱ μετ' αὐτοῦ; 26 πῶς
need he had, and hungered he and those with him? How

1525 1519 3588 3624 3588 2316 1909 8 3588 749
εἰσῆλθεν εἰς τὸν οἶκον τοῦ Θεοῦ ἐπὶ Ἀβιάθαρ τοῦ ἀρχιερέως,
he entered the house of God on Abiathar the high priest,

2532 3588 740 3588 4286 5315 3739 3756 1832
καὶ τοὺς ἄρτους τῆς προθέσεως ἔφαγεν, οὓς οὐκ ἔξεστι
and the Loaves of the Presentation ate, which not is lawful

5315 1487 3361 3588 2409 2532 1325 2532 3588 4862 846 5607
φαγεῖν εἰ μὴ τοῖς ἱερεῦσι, καὶ ἔδωκε καὶ τοῖς σὺν αὐτῷ οὖσι;
to eat except the priests, and gave also to those with him being?

2532 3004 846 3588 4521 1223 3588 444 1096
27 καὶ ἔλεγεν αὐτοῖς, Τὸ σάββατον διὰ τὸν ἄνθρωπον ἐγένετο,
And He said to them, The sabbath because of man came into being,

3756 3588 444 1223 3588 4521 5620 2962 2076 3588 5207
οὐχ ὁ ἄνθρωπος διὰ τὸ σάββατον· 28 ὥστε Κύριός ἐστιν ὁ υἱὸς
not man because of the sabbath; so then Lord is the Son

3588 444 2532 3588 4521
τοῦ ἀνθρώπου καὶ τοῦ σαββάτου.
of man also of the sabbath.

Behold, why do they on the sabbath day that which is not lawful?
25 And he said unto them, Have ye never read what David did, when he had need, and was an hungred, he, and they that were with him?
26 How he went into the house of God in the days of Abiathar the high priest, and did eat the shewbread, which is not lawful to eat but for the priests, and gave also to them which were with him?
27 And he said unto them, The sabbath was made for man, and not man for the sabbath:
28 Therefore the Son of man is Lord also of the sabbath.

Mark 3

1. And again He entered into the synagogue. And there was a man who had a withering (of) the hand.
2 And they watched Him, whether He will heal him on the sabbaths, that they might accuse Him.
3 And He said to the man having a withering (of) the hand, Rise up into the middle.
4 And He says to them, (Is it) lawful to do good on the sabbaths, or to do evil? To save a soul, or to kill? But they were silent.
5 And having looked around on them with anger, being greatly grieved over the hardness of their heart, He said to the man, Stretch out your hand! And he stretched out, and his hand was restored sound as the other.
6 And going out, immediately the Pharisees took counsel with the Herodians

Mark 3

2532 1525 3825 1519 3588 4864 2532 2258 1563 444
1. Καὶ εἰσῆλθε πάλιν εἰς τὴν συναγωγήν, καὶ ἦν ἐκεῖ ἄνθρω-
And He entered again into the synagogue, and was there a

3583 2192 3588 5495 2532 3906 846 1487
πος ἐξηραμμένην ἔχων τὴν χεῖρα. 2 καὶ παρετήρουν αὐτὸν εἰ
man a withering having (of) the hand. And they watched Him if

3588 4521 2323 846 2443 2723 846
τοῖς σάββασι θεραπεύσει αὐτόν, ἵνα κατηγορήσωσιν αὐτοῦ.
on the sabbath He will heal him, that they might accuse Him.

2532 3004 3588 444 3588 3583 2192 3588 5495
3 καὶ λέγει τῷ ἀνθρώπῳ τῷ ἐξηραμμένην εχοντι τὴν χεῖρα,
And He says to the man a withering having of the hand,

1453 1519 3588 3319 2532 3004 846 1832 3588 4521
Ἔγειραι εἰς τὸ μέσον. 4 καὶ λέγει αὐτοῖς, Ἔξεστι τοῖς σάββασιν
Rise up into the middle. And He says to them, Lawful on the sabbaths

15 2228 2554 5590 4982 2228 615
ἀγαθοποιῆσαι, ἢ κακοποιῆσαι; ψυχὴν σῶσαι, ἢ ἀπο-
to do good, or to do evil? A soul to save, or to

3588 1161 4623 2532 4017 846 3326
κτεῖναι; οἱ δὲ ἐσιώπων. 5 καὶ περιβλεψάμενος αὐτοὺς μετ'
kill? they But were silent. And having looked around (on) them with

3709 4818 1909 3588 4457 3588 2588 846
ὀργῆς, συλλυπούμενος ἐπὶ τῇ πωρώσει τῆς καρδίας αὐτῶν,
anger, being greatly grieved over the hardness of the heart of them,

3004 3588 444 1614 3588 5495 4675 2532 1614
λέγει τῷ ἀνθρώπῳ, Ἔκτεινον τὴν χεῖρά σου. καὶ ἐξέτεινε,
He says to the man, Stretch out the hand of you. And he stretched,

2532 600 3588 5495 846 5199 5613 3588 243 2532
καὶ ἀποκατεστάθη ἡ χεὶρ αὐτοῦ ὑγιὴς ὡς ἡ ἄλλη. 6 καὶ
and was restored the hand of him sound as the other. And

1831 3588 5330 2112 3326 3588 2265
ἐξελθόντες οἱ Φαρισαῖοι εὐθέως μετὰ τῶν Ἡρωδιανῶν
having gone out the Pharisees immediately with the Herodians

Mark 3

1. And he entered again into the synagogue; and there was a man there which had a withered hand.
2 And they watched him, whether he would heal him on the sabbath day; that they might accuse him.
3 And he saith unto the man which had the withered hand, Stand forth.
4 And he saith unto them, Is it lawful to do good on the sabbath days, or to do evil? to save life, or to kill? But they held their peace.
5 And when he had looked round about on them with anger, being grieved for the hardness of their hearts, he saith unto the man, Stretch forth thine hand. And he stretched (it) out: and his hand was restored whole as the other.
6 And the Pharisees went forth, and straightway took counsel with the Herodians

Literal Translation | **Mark 3:7** | **King James Version**

Literal Translation

against Him, how they might destroy Him.

7. And Jesus withdrew to the sea with His disciples; and a great multitude from Galilee and from Judea followed Him,

8 also (some) from Jerusalem, and from Idumea, and beyond the Jordan, also those around Tyre and Sidon. A great multitude came to Him, hearing how much He was doing.

9 And He spoke to His disciples that a small boat should stay near to Him because of the crowd, that they might not press upon Him.

10 For He healed many, so that (they) fell on Him, that they might touch Him, as many as had plagues.

11 And when the unclean spirits saw Him, (they) fell before Him, and cried out, saying, You are the Son of God!

12 And he warned them very much that they should not make Him manifest.

13. And He went up into the mountain, and He called near whom He desired. And they went to Him.

14 And He made (disciples of) twelve, that they might be with Him; and that He might send them to proclaim,

15 and to have authority to heal diseases, and to cast out the demons.

16 And He put on Simon (the) name Peter.

17 And on James the (son) of Zebedee, and John the brother of James, He put on them (the) names Boanerges, which is, Sons of Thunder.

18 Also (He appointed) Andrew, and Philip, and Bartholomew,

4824 4160 2596 846 3704 846 622
συμβούλιον ἐποίουν κατ' αὐτοῦ, ὅπως αὐτὸν ἀπολέσωσι.
counsel made against Him, how that Him they might destroy.

2532 3588 2424 402 3326 3588 3101 846 4314
7. Καὶ ὁ Ἰησοῦς ἀνεχώρησε μετὰ τῶν μαθητῶν αὐτοῦ πρὸς
And Jesus withdrew with the disciples of Him to

3588 2281 2532 4183 4128 575 3588 1056 190
τὴν θάλασσαν· καὶ πολὺ πλῆθος ἀπὸ τῆς Γαλιλαίας ἠκολού-
the sea; and a great multitude from Galilee followed

846 2532 575 3588 2449 2532 575 2414
θησαν αὐτῷ καὶ ἀπὸ τῆς Ἰουδαίας, 8 καὶ ἀπὸ Ἱεροσολύμων,
Him also from Judea, also from Jerusalem,

2532 575 3588 2401 2532 4008 3588 2446 2532 3588
καὶ ἀπὸ τῆς Ἰδουμαίας, καὶ πέραν τοῦ Ἰορδάνου, καὶ οἱ
and from Idumea, and beyond the Jordan, and those

4012 5184 2532 4605 4128 4183 191 3745
περὶ Τύρον καὶ Σιδῶνα, πλῆθος πολύ, ἀκούσαντες ὅσα
around Tyre and Sidon, multitude a great, hearing how much

4160 2064 4314 846 2532 2036 3588 3101 846
ἐποίει, ἦλθον πρὸς αὐτόν. 9 καὶ εἶπε τοῖς μαθηταῖς αὐτοῦ
He was doing, came to Him. And He spoke to the disciples of Him

2443 4142 4342 846 1223 3588 3793 2443 3361
ἵνα πλοιάριον προσκαρτερῇ αὐτῷ διὰ τὸν ὄχλον, ἵνα μὴ
that a small boat should stay near Him because of the crowd, that not

2346 846 4183 1063 2323 5620 1968
θλίβωσιν αὐτόν· 10 πολλοὺς γὰρ ἐθεράπευσεν, ὥστε ἐπιπίπτειν
they press on Him. many For He healed, so that (they) fell

846 2443 846 680 3745 2192 3148 2532 3588
αὐτῷ, ἵνα αὐτοῦ ἅψωνται, ὅσοι εἶχον μάστιγας. 11 καὶ τὰ
on Him, that Him they might touch, as many as had plagues. And the

4151 3588 169 3752 846 2334 4363
πνεύματα τὰ ἀκάθαρτα, ὅταν αὐτὸν ἐθεώρει, προσέπιπτεν
spirits unclean, when Him they saw, fell before

846 2532 2896 3004 3754 4771 1488 3588 5207 3588 2316 2532
αὐτῷ καὶ ἔκραζε, λέγοντα ὅτι Σὺ εἶ ὁ υἱὸς τοῦ Θεοῦ. 12 καὶ
Him and cried out, saying, You are the Son of God! And

4183 2008 846 2443 3361 846 5318 4160
πολλὰ ἐπετίμα αὐτοῖς ἵνα μὴ αὐτὸν φανερὸν ποιήσωσι.
much He warned them that not Him manifest they should make.

2532 305 1519 3588 3735 2532 4341 3739 2309
13. Καὶ ἀναβαίνει εἰς τὸ ὄρος, καὶ προσκαλεῖται οὓς ἤθελεν
And He goes up into the mount, and called near whom desired

846 2532 565 4314 846 2532 4160 1427 2443
αὐτός· καὶ ἀπῆλθον πρὸς αὐτόν. 14 καὶ ἐποίησε δώδεκα, ἵνα
He. And they went to Him. And He made twelve, that

5600 3326 846 2532 2443 649 846 2784 2532
ὦσι μετ' αὐτοῦ καὶ ἵνα ἀποστέλλῃ αὐτοὺς κηρύσσειν 15 καὶ
they be with Him, and that He might send them to proclaim and

2192 1849 2323 3588 3554 2532 1544 3588
ἔχειν ἐξουσίαν θεραπεύειν τὰς νόσους, καὶ ἐκβάλλειν τὰ
to have authority to heal the diseases, and to cast out the

1140 2532 2007 3588 4613 3686 4074 2532 2385
δαιμόνια· 16 καὶ ἐπέθηκε τῷ Σίμωνι ὄνομα Πέτρον; 17 καὶ Ἰάκω-
demons. And He put on Simon a name, Peter. And James

3588 3588 2199 2532 2491 3588 80 3588 2385
βον τὸν τοῦ Ζεβεδαίου καὶ Ἰωάννην τὸν ἀδελφὸν τοῦ Ἰακώβου,
the (son) of Zebedee, and John the brother of James,

2532 2007 846 3686 993 3739 2076 5207
καὶ ἐπέθηκεν αὐτοῖς ὀνόματα Βοανηργές, ὅ ἐστιν, Υἱοὶ
also He put on them names, Boanerges, which is, Sons

1027 2532 406 2532 5376 2532 918
Βροντῆς· 18 καὶ Ἀνδρέαν, καὶ Φίλιππον, καὶ Βαρθολομαῖον,
of Thunder; also Andrew, and Phillip, and Bartholomew,

King James Version

against him, how they might destroy him.

7. But Jesus withdrew himself with his disciples to the sea: and a great multitude from Galilee followed him, and from Judaea,

8 And from Jerusalem, and from Idumaea, and (from) beyond Jordan; and they about Tyre and Sidon, a great multitude, when they had heard what great things he did, came unto him.

9 And he spake to his disciples, that a small ship should wait on him because of the multitude, lest they should throng him.

10 For he had healed many; insomuch that they pressed upon him for to touch him, as many as had plagues.

11 And unclean spirits, when they saw him, fell down before him, and cried, saying, Thou art the Son of God.

12 And he straitly charged them that they should not make him known.

13. And he goeth up into a mountain, and calleth (unto him) whom he would: and they came unto him.

14 And he ordained twelve, that they should be with him, and that he might send them forth to preach,

15 And to have power to heal sicknesses, and to cast out devils:

16 And Simon he surnamed Peter;

17 And James the (son) of Zebedee, and John the brother of James; and he surnamed them Boanerges, which is, The sons of thunder:

18 And Andrew, and Philip, and Bartholomew,

Mark 3:19

Literal Translation

and Matthew, and Thomas, and James the (son) of Alphaeus, and Thaddaeus, and Simon the Canaanite,
19 and Judas Iscariot, who also betrayed Him.

20. And He comes into a house; and again a crowd comes together, so as they were not able to eat, not even bread.
21 And hearing, those with Him went out to take hold (of) Him; for they said, He is out of wits.
22 And coming down from Jerusalem, the scribes said, He has Beelzebul; also that He casts out demons by the ruler of the demons.

23 And having called them near, He spoke to them in parables, (saying), How is Satan able to cast out Satan?

24 And if a kingdom is divided against itself, that kingdom cannot stand.
25 And if a house is divided against itself, that house is not able to stand.
26 And if Satan rises upon himself, and has been divided, he is not able to stand, but (he) has an end.

27 No one is able, not one, to plunder the vessels of the strong one, entering into his house, unless he first tie up the strong one; and then he will plunder his house.

28 Truly I say to you, All the sins will be remitted to the sons of men, and whatever blasphemies they have blasphemed;

29 but whoever commits blasphemy against the Holy Spirit has no remission to eternity, but is liable

Mark 3:19

2532 3156 2532 2381 2532 2385 3588 3588 256
καὶ Ματθαῖον, καὶ Θωμᾶν, καὶ Ἰάκωβον τὸν τοῦ Ἀλφαίου,
and Matthew, and Thomas, and James the (son) of Alphaeus,

2532 2280 2532 4613 3588 2581 2532 2455
καὶ Θαδδαῖον, καὶ Σίμωνα τὸν Κανανaῖον, 19 καὶ Ἰούδαν
and Thaddaeus, and Simon the Canaanite, and Judas

2469 3739 2532 3860 846
Ἰσκαριώθ, ὃς καὶ παρέδωκεν αὐτόν.
Iscariot, who also betrayed Him.

2532 2064 1519 3624 2532 4905 3825 3793 5620
20. Καὶ ἔρχονται εἰς οἶκον· καὶ συνέρχεται πάλιν ὄχλος, ὥστε
And He comes into a house, and comes together again a crowd, so as

3361 1410 846 3383 740 5315 2532 191 3588
μὴ δύνασθαι αὐτοὺς μητὲ ἄρτον φαγεῖν. 21 καὶ ἀκούσαντες οἱ
not to be able they not even bread to eat. And having heard those

3844 846 1831 2902 846 3004 1063 3754
παρ᾽ αὐτοῦ ἐξῆλθον κρατῆσαι αὐτόν, ἔλεγον γὰρ ὅτι
with Him went forth to take hold of Him; they said for,

1839 2532 3588 1122 3588 575 2414 2597
Ἐξέστη. 22 καὶ οἱ γραμματεῖς οἱ ἀπὸ Ἱεροσολύμων καταβάντες
He is out of wits. And the scribes those from Jerusalem coming down

3004 3754 954 2192 2532 3754 1722 3588 758 3588
ἔλεγον ὅτι Βεελζεβοὺλ ἔχει, καὶ ὅτι Ἐν τῷ ἄρχοντι τῶν
said, Beelzebul he has, also that by the ruler of the

1140 1544 3588 1140 2532 4341
δαιμονίων ἐκβάλλει τὰ δαιμόνια. 23 καὶ προσκαλεσάμενος
demons he casts out the demons. And having called near

846 1722 3850 3004 846 4459 1410 4567
αὐτοὺς ἐν παραβολαῖς ἔλεγεν αὐτοῖς, Πῶς δύναται Σατανᾶς
them in parables He spoke to them, How is able Satan

4567 1544 2532 1437 932 1909 1438 3307 3756
Σατανᾶν ἐκβάλλειν; 24 καὶ ἐὰν βασιλεία ἐφ᾽ ἑαυτὴν μερισθῇ, οὐ
Satan to cast out? And if a kingdom against itself is divided,

1410 2476 3588 932 1565 2532 1437 3614 1909
δύναται σταθῆναι ἡ βασιλεία ἐκείνη· 25 καὶ ἐὰν οἰκία ἐφ᾽
not is able to stand kingdom that. And if a house against

1438 3307 3756 1410 2476 3588 3614 1565 2532
ἑαυτὴν μερισθῇ, οὐ δύναται σταθῆναι ἡ οἰκία ἐκείνη. 26 καὶ
itself is divided, not is able to stand house that. And

1487 3588 4567 450 1909 1438 2532 3307 3756 1410
εἰ ὁ Σατανᾶς ἀνέστη ἐφ᾽ ἑαυτὸν καὶ μεμέρισται, οὐ δύναται
if Satan rises upon himself and has been divided, not he is able

2476 235 5056 2192 3756 1410 3762 3588 4632 3588
σταθῆναι, ἀλλὰ τέλος ἔχει. 27 οὐ δύναται οὐδεὶς τὰ σκεύη τοῦ
to stand, but an end has. Not is able, no one, the vessels of the

478 1525 1519 3588 3614 846 1283 1437 3361
ἰσχυροῦ, εἰσελθὼν εἰς τὴν οἰκίαν αὐτοῦ, διαρπάσαι, ἐὰν μὴ
strong one, having entered into the house of him, to plunder, unless

4412 3588 2478 1210 2532 5119 3588 3614 846 1283
πρῶτον τὸν ἰσχυρὸν δήσῃ, καὶ τότε τὴν οἰκίαν αὐτοῦ διαρ-
first the strong one he bind, and then the house of him he will

281 3004 5213 3754 3956 863 3588 265
πάσει. 28 ἀμὴν λέγω ὑμῖν, ὅτι πάντα ἀφεθήσεται τὰ ἁμαρτή-
plunder. Truly I say to you, that all will be remitted the sins

3588 5207 3588 444 2532 988 3745 302
ματα τοῖς υἱοῖς τῶν ἀνθρώπων, καὶ βλασφημίαι ὅσας ἂν
of the sons of men, and blasphemies whatever

987 3739 1161 302 987 1519 3588 4151 3588
βλασφημήσωσιν· 29 ὃς δ᾽ ἂν βλασφημήσῃ εἰς τὸ Πνεῦμα τὸ
they have blasphemed; who but ever blasphemes against the Spirit

40 3756 2192 859 1519 3588 165 235 1777 2076
Ἅγιον, οὐκ ἔχει ἄφεσιν εἰς τὸν αἰῶνα, ἀλλ᾽ ἔνοχός ἐστιν
Holy, not has remission to the age, but liable is

King James Version

and Matthew, and Thomas, and James the (son) of Alphaeus, and Thaddaeus, and Simon the Canaanite,
19 And Judas Iscariot, which also betrayed him: and they went into an house.

20. And the multitude cometh together again, so that they could not so much as eat bread.
21 And when his friends heard (of it), they went out to lay hold on him: for they said, He is beside himself.
22 And the scribes which came down from Jerusalem said, He hath Beelzebub, and by the prince of the devils casteth he out devils.

23 And he called them (unto him), and said unto them in parables, How can Satan cast out Satan?

24 And if a kingdom be divided against itself, that kingdom cannot stand.
25 And if a house be divided against itself, that house cannot stand.
26 And if Satan rise up against himself, and be divided, he cannot stand, but hath an end.

27 No man can enter into a strong man's house, and spoil his goods, except he will first bind the strong man; and then he will spoil his house.

28 Verily I say unto you, All sins shall be forgiven unto the sons of men, and blasphemies wherewith soever they shall blaspheme:

29 But he that shall blaspheme against the Holy Ghost hath never forgiveness, but is in danger

Literal Translation

to eternal judgment,
30 because they were saying, He has an unclean spirit.

31. Then His mother and brothers came. And standing outside, (they) sent to Him, calling Him.
32 And a crowd sat around Him. And they said to Him, Behold, Your mother and Your brothers seek You outside.
33 And He answered them, saying, Who is My mother or My brothers?
34 And having looked around on those sitting around Him in a circle, He said, Behold, My mother and My brothers!
35 For whoever does the will of God, this one is My brother, and My sister, and mother.

Mark 3:30

166 2920 3754 3004 4151 169 2192
αἰωνίου κρίσεως. 30 ὅτι ἔλεγον, Πνεῦμα ἀκάθαρτον ἔχει.
to eternal judgment. Because they were saying, A spirit unclean He has.

2064 3767 3588 80 2532 3588 3384 846 2532 1854
31. Ἔρχονται οὖν οἱ ἀδελφοὶ καὶ ἡ μήτηρ αὐτοῦ, καὶ ἔξω
come Then the brothers and the mother of Him, and outside

2476 649 4314 846 5455 846 2532
ἑστῶτες ἀπέστειλαν πρὸς αὐτὸν, φωνοῦντες αὐτόν. 32 καὶ
standing sent to Him, calling Him. And

2521 3793 4012 846 2036 1161 846 2400 3588 3384
ἐκάθητο ὄχλος περὶ αὐτὸν· εἶπον δὲ αὐτῷ, Ἰδού, ἡ μήτηρ
sat a crowd around Him. they said And to Him, Behold, the mother

4675 2532 3588 80 4675 1854 2212 4571 2532 611 846
σου καὶ οἱ ἀδελφοί σου ἔξω ζητοῦσί σε. 33 καὶ ἀπεκρίθη αὐτοῖς
of You and the brothers of You outside seek You. And He answered them,

3004 5101 2076 3588 3384 3450 2228 3588 80 3450 2532
λέγει, Τίς ἐστιν ἡ μήτηρ μου ἢ οἱ ἀδελφοί μου; 34 καὶ
saying, Who is the mother of Me and the brothers of Me? And

4017 2945 3588 4012 846 2521 3004
περιβλεψάμενος κύκλῳ τοὺς περὶ αὐτὸν καθημένους, λέγει,
having looked around in a circle (at) those about Him sitting, He says,

2396 3588 3384 3450 2532 3588 80 3450 3739 1063 302 4160 3588
Ἴδε ἡ μήτηρ μου καὶ οἱ ἀδελφοί μου. 35 ὃς γὰρ ἂν ποιήσῃ τὸ
Behold the mother of Me and the brothers of Me! who For ever does the

2307 3588 2316 3778 80 3450 2532 79 3450 2532
θέλημα τοῦ Θεοῦ, οὗτος ἀδελφός μου καὶ ἀδελφή μού καὶ
will of God, this one brother of Me and sister of Me and

3384 2076
μήτηρ ἐστί.
mother is.

King James Version

of eternal damnation:
30 Because they said, He hath an unclean spirit.

31. There came then his brethren and his mother, and, standing without, sent unto him, calling him.
32 And the multitude sat about him, and they said unto him, Behold, thy mother and thy brethren without seek for thee.
33 And he answered them, saying, Who is my mother, or my brethren?
34 And he looked round about on them which sat about him, and said, Behold my mother and my brethren!

35 For whosoever shall do the will of God, the same is my brother, and my sister, and mother.

Mark 4

1. And again He began to teach by the sea. And a large crowd was gathered to Him, so that He entered into the boat in order to sit in the sea. And all the crowd were on the land toward the sea.

2 And He taught them many things in parables, and said to them in His teaching:
3 Hear! Behold, the (one) sowing went out to sow.
4 And it happened during the sowing that one indeed fell by the wayside; and the birds of the heaven came and devoured it.
5 And another fell on the rocky (places) where it did not have much earth. And it sprang up at once, due to not having deepness of earth.
6 And (the) sun having risen,

Mark 4

2532 3825 756 1321 3844 3588 2281 2532
1. Καὶ πάλιν ἤρξατο διδάσκειν παρὰ τὴν θάλασσαν. καὶ
And again He began to teach beside the sea. And

4863 4314 846 3793 4183 5620 846 1684 1519
συνήχθη πρὸς αὐτὸν ὄχλος πολύς, ὥστε αὐτὸν ἐμβάντα εἰς
is assembled to Him a crowd large, so that he entering into

3588 4143 2521 1722 3588 2281 2532 3956 3588 3793 4314
τὸ πλοῖον καθῆσθαι ἐν τῇ θαλάσσῃ· καὶ πᾶς ὁ ὄχλος πρὸς
the boat (had) to sit in the sea, and all the crowd toward

3588 2281 1909 3588 1093 2258 2532 1321 846 1722
τὴν θάλασσαν ἐπὶ τῆς γῆς ἦν. 2 καὶ ἐδίδασκεν αὐτοὺς ἐν
the sea on the land were. And He taught them in

3850 4183 2532 3004 846 1722 3588 1322 846
παραβολαῖς πολλά, καὶ ἔλεγεν αὐτοῖς ἐν τῇ διδαχῇ αὐτοῦ,
parables many things, and said to them in the teaching of Him,

191 2400 1831 3588 4687 3588 4687 2532 1096
3 Ἀκούετε· ἰδού, ἐξῆλθεν ὁ σπείρων τοῦ σπεῖραι. 4 καὶ ἐγένετο
Hear! Behold, went out the (one) sowing to sow. And it was

1722 3588 4687 3739 3303 4098 3844 3588 3598 2532 2064 3588
ἐν τῷ σπείρειν, ὃ μὲν ἔπεσε παρὰ τὴν ὁδόν, καὶ ἦλθε τὰ
during the sowing one indeed fell beside the wayside, and came the

4071 3588 3772 2532 2719 846 243 1161 4098
πετεινὰ τοῦ οὐρανοῦ καὶ κατέφαγεν αὐτό. 5 ἄλλο δὲ ἔπεσεν
birds of the heaven and devoured it. other And fell

1909 3588 4075 3699 3756 2192 1093 4183 2532 2112
ἐπὶ τὸ πετρῶδες, ὅπου οὐκ εἶχε γῆν πολλήν· καὶ εὐθέως
on the rocky (place), where not it had earth much, and at once

1816 1223 3588 3361 2192 899 1093 2246 1161 393
ἐξανέτειλε, διὰ τὸ μὴ ἔχειν βάθος γῆς· 6 ἡλίου δὲ ἀνατείλαντος
it sprang up, through not having depth of earth; sun and having risen,

Mark 4

1. And he began again to teach by the sea side: and there was gathered unto him a great multitude, so that he entered into a ship, and sat in the sea; and the whole multitude was by the sea on the land.

2 And he taught them many things by parables, and said unto them in his doctrine,

3 Hearken; Behold, there went out a sower to sow:
4 And it came to pass, as he sowed, some fell by the way side, and the fowls of the air came and devoured it up.
5 And some fell on stony ground, where it had not much earth; and immediately it sprang up, because it had no depth of earth:
6 But when the sun was up,

Literal Translation

it was scorched; and through not having root, it dried up.
7 And another fell into the thornbushes, and the thornbushes grew up and choked it; and it did not give fruit.
8 And another fell into the good earth, and gave fruit, going up and increasing; and bore one thirty, and one sixty, and one a hundred(fold).

9 And He said to them, The (one) having ears to hear, let him hear.

10. And when He was alone, those around Him, with the Twelve, asked Him (as to) the parable.
11 And He said to them, To you has been given to know the mystery of the kingdom of God. But to these, the (ones) outside, all things come to be in parables,

12 that seeing they may see and not perceive; and hearing they may hear, and not understand, lest they should convert, and their sins be remitted. (Isa. 6:9, 10)
13 And He said to them, Do you not know this parable? And how will you know all parables?

14. The (one) sowing sows the Word.
15 And these are those by the wayside where the Word is sown. And when they hear immediately Satan comes and takes away the Word having been sown in their hearts.

16 And likewise, these are the ones being sown on the rocky (places), who, when they hear the Word, (they) at once receive it with joy,

17 yet they have no root in themselves, but are temporary. Then

Mark 4:7

2739 2532 1223 3588 3361 2192 4491 3583 2532 243
ἐκαυματίσθη, καὶ διὰ τὸ μὴ ἔχειν ῥίζαν ἐξηράνθη. 7 καὶ ἄλλο
it was scorched, and through not having root it dried up. And other

4098 1519 3588 173 2532 305 3588 173 2532 4846
ἔπεσεν εἰς τὰς ἀκάνθας, καὶ ἀνέβησαν αἱ ἄκανθαι, καὶ συνέ-
fell into the thornbushes, and grew the thornbushes and choked

846 2532 2590 3756 1325 2532 243 4098 1519 3588
πνιξαν αὐτό, καὶ καρπὸν οὐκ ἔδωκε. 8 καὶ ἄλλο ἔπεσεν εἰς τὴν
it, and fruit not it gave. And other fell into the

1093 3588 2570 2532 1325 2590 305 2532
γῆν τὴν καλήν· καὶ ἐδίδου καρπὸν ἀναβαίνοντα καὶ
earth good, and gave fruit going up and

837 2532 5342 1722 5144 2532 1722 1835 2532
αὐξάνοντα, καὶ ἔφερεν ἓν τριάκοντα, καὶ ἓν ἑξήκοντα, καὶ
increasing, and bore one thirty, and one sixty, and

1520 1540 2532 3004 846 3588 2192 3775 191 191
ἓν ἑκατόν. 9 καὶ ἔλεγεν αὐτοῖς, Ὁ ἔχων ὦτα ἀκούειν ἀκουέτω.
one a hundred. And He said to them, The (one) having ears to hear, let him hear.

3753 1161 1096 2651 2065 846 3588 4012
10. Ὅτε δὲ ἐγένετο καταμόνας, ἠρώτησαν αὐτὸν οἱ περὶ
when And He became alone, asked Him those around

846 4862 3588 1427 3588 3850 2532 3004 846
αὐτὸν σὺν τοῖς δώδεκα τὰς παραβολήν. 11 καὶ ἔλεγεν αὐτοῖς,
Him with the twelve the parable. And He said to them,

5213 1325 1097 3588 3466 3588 932 3588
Ὑμῖν δέδοται γνῶναι τὸ μυστήριον τῆς βασιλείας τοῦ
To you has been given to know the mystery of the kingdom

2316 1565 1161 3588 1854 1722 3850 3588 3956 1096
Θεοῦ· ἐκείνοις δὲ τοῖς ἔξω, ἐν παραβολαῖς τὰ πάντα γίνεται·
of God; to these but the (ones) outside in parables all things come to be,

2443 991 991 2532 3361 1492 2532 191
12 ἵνα βλέποντες βλέπωσι, καὶ μὴ ἴδωσι, καὶ ἀκούοντες
that seeing they may see, and not perceive, and hearing

191 2532 3361 4920 3379 1994 2532
ἀκούωσι, καὶ μὴ συνιῶσι· μήποτε ἐπιστρέψωσι, καὶ
they may hear, and not understand, that not they convert and

863 846 3588 265 2532 3004 846 3756 1492
ἀφεθῇ αὐτοῖς τὰ ἁμαρτήματα. 13 καὶ λέγει αὐτοῖς, Οὐκ οἴδατε
be remitted of them the sins And He says to them, Not know you

3588 3850 3778 2532 4459 3956 3588 3850
τὴν παραβολὴν ταύτην; καὶ πῶς πάσας τὰς παραβολὰς
parable this? And how all the parables

1097 3588 4687 3588 3056 4687 3778 1161 1526 3588
γνώσεσθε; 14 ὁ σπείρων τὸν λόγον σπείρει. 15 οὗτοι δέ εἰσιν οἱ
will you know? He sowing the Word sows. these And are those

3844 3588 3598 3699 4687 3588 3056 2532 3752 191
παρὰ τὴν ὁδὸν, ὅπου σπείρεται ὁ λόγος, καὶ ὅταν ἀκούσω-
beside the wayside where is sown the Word. And when they hear

2112 2064 3588 4567 2532 142 3588 3056 3588
σιν, εὐθέως ἔρχεται ὁ Σατανᾶς καὶ αἴρει τὸν λόγον τὸν
immediately comes Satan and takes the Word

4687 1722 3588 2588 846 2532 3778 1526 3668
ἐσπαρμένον ἐν ταῖς καρδίαις αὐτῶν. 16 καὶ οὗτοί εἰσιν ὁμοίως
having been sown in the hearts of them. And these are likewise

3588 1909 3588 4075 4687 3739 3752 191 3588
οἱ ἐπὶ τὰ πετρώδη σπειρόμενοι, οἳ, ὅταν ἀκούσωσι τὸν
those on the rocky (places) having been sown, who when they hear the

3056 2112 3326 5479 2983 846 2532 3756
λόγον, εὐθέως μετὰ χαρᾶς λαμβάνουσιν αὐτόν, 17 καὶ οὐκ
Word, at once with joy they receive it, yet not

2192 4491 1722 1438 235 4340 1526 1534 1096
ἔχουσι ῥίζαν ἐν ἑαυτοῖς, ἀλλὰ πρόσκαιροί εἰσιν· εἶτα γενο-
they have root in themselves, but temporary are; then having

King James Version

it was scorched; and because it had no root, it withered away.
7 And some fell among thorns, and the thorns grew up, and choked it, and it yielded no fruit.
8 And other fell on good ground, and did yield fruit that sprang up and increased; and brought forth, some thirty, and some sixty, and some an hundred.

9 And he said unto them, He that hath ears to hear, let him hear.

10. And when he was alone, they that were about him with the twelve asked of him the parable.
11 And he said unto them, Unto you it is given to know the mystery of the kingdom of God: but unto them that are without, all (these) things are done in parables:

12 That seeing they may see, and not perceive; and hearing they may hear, and not understand; lest at any time they should be converted, and (their) sins should be forgiven them.
13 And he said unto them, Know ye not this parable? and how then will ye know all parables?
14. The sower soweth the word.
15 And these are they by the way side, where the word is sown; but when they have heard, Satan cometh immediately, and taketh away the word that was sown in their hearts.

16 And these are they likewise which are sown on stony ground; who, when they have heard the word, immediately receive it with gladness;
17 And have no root in themselves, and so endure but for a time: when

Literal Translation | **Mark 4:18** | **King James Version**

trouble or persecution having occurred through the Word, immediately they are offended.

18 These are those being sown into the thornbushes, those having heard the Word,

19 and the anxieties of this age, and the deceitfulness of riches, and the lusts about other things entering in, (they) choke the Word, and it becomes unfruitful.

20 And these are those being sown on the good ground, who hear and welcome the Word and bring forth fruit, one thirty, and one sixty, and one a hundred(fold).

21. And He said to them, Does the lamp come that it may be put under the (grain) measure, or under the couch? (Is it) not that it may be put on the lampstand?

22 For not anything is hidden which may not be revealed, nor (anything) become covered but that it will come to light.

23 If anyone has ears to hear, let him hear.

24 And He said to them, Watch what you hear. In what measure you measure, it will be measured to you; and it will be added to you, the (ones) hearing.

25 For whoever may have, (more) will be given to him; and (the one) who does not have, even what he has will be taken from him.

26. And He said, So is the kingdom of God, as if a man should cast seed on the earth,

27 and should sleep, and rise night and day; and the seed should sprout and lengthen of itself, as he does not know.

28 For of itself the earth bears fruit: first greenery, then a head, then full grain in

---

2347 2228 1375 1223 3588 3056 2112 4624
μένης θλίψεως ἢ διωγμοῦ διὰ τόν λόγον, ευθεως σκανδαλι-
occurred trouble or persecution through the Word, immediately they are

2532 3778 1526 3588 1519 3588 173 4687 3588
ζονται. 18 καὶ οὗτοι εἰσὶν οἱ εἰς τὰς ἀκάνθας σπειρόμενοι, οἱ
stumbled. And these are those into the thornbushes having been sown, those

3588 3056 191 2532/3588 3308 3588 165 5127
τὸν λόγον ἀκούσαντες, 19 καὶ αἱ μέριμναι τοῦ αἰῶνος τούτου,
the Word having heard, and the anxieties age of this,

2532/3588 539 3588 4149 2532 3588 4012 3588 3062 1939
καὶ ἡ ἀπάτη τοῦ πλούτου καὶ αἱ περὶ τὰ λοιπὰ ἐπιθυμίαι
and the deceitfulness of riches, and the about the other things lusts

1531 4846 3588 3056 2532 175
εἰσπορευόμεναι συμπνίγουσι τὸν λόγον, καὶ ἄκαρπος
entering in choke the Word, and unfruitful

1096 2532 3778 1526 3588 1909 3588 1093 3588 2570 4687
γίνεται. 20καὶ οὗτοί εἰσιν οἱ ἐπὶ τὴν γῆν τὴν καλὴν σπαρέντες,
it becomes. And these are those on the earth good being sown,

3748 191 3588 3056 2532 3858 2532 2592
οἵτινες ἀκούουσι τὸν λόγον, καὶ παραδέχονται, καὶ καρ-
who hear the Word and welcome (it), and bring

1520 5144 2532 1520 1835 2532 1520 1540
ποφοροῦσιν, ἓν τριάκοντα, καὶ ἓν ἑξήκοντα, καὶ ἓν ἑκατόν.
forth fruit, one thirty, and one sixty, and one a hundred.

2532 3004 846 3385 3588 3088 2064 2443 5259 3588
21. Καὶ ἔλεγεν αὐτοῖς, Μήτι ὁ λύχνος ἔρχεται ἵνα ὑπὸ τὸν
And He said to them, Not (is) the lamp come that under the

3426 5087 2228 5259 3588 2825 3756 2443 1909 3588 3087
μόδιον τεθῇ ἢ ὑπὸ τὴν κλίνην; οὐχ ἵνα ἐπὶ τὴν λυχνίαν
measure be put, or under the couch? (Is it) not that on the lampstand

2007 3756 1063 2076 5101 2927 3739 - 3362 - 5319 3761
ἐπιτεθῇ; 22 οὐ γάρ ἐστι τι κρυπτὸν, ὃ ἐὰν μὴ φανερωθῇ· οὐδὲ
it be put? not For is a thing hidden which if not it may be revealed nor

1096 614 235 2443 1519 5318 2064 -1536- 2192
ἐγένετο ἀπόκρυφον, ἀλλ᾽ ἵνα εἰς φανερόν ἔλθῃ. 23 εἴ τις ἔχει
come to be covered, but that to light it may come. If any has

3775 191 191 2532 3004 846 991 5101 191
ὦτα ἀκούειν ἀκουέτω. 24 καὶ ἔλεγεν αὐτοῖς, Βλέπετε τί ἀκούετε.
ears to hear let him hear. And He said to them, Watch what you hear.

1722 3739 3354 3354 3354 5213 2532 4359
ἐν ᾧ μέτρῳ μετρεῖτε μετρηθήσεται ὑμῖν, καὶ προστεθήσεται
In what measure you measure, it will be measured to you, and it will be added

5213 3588 191 3739 1063 302 2192 1325 846 2532
ὑμῖν τοῖς ἀκούουσιν. 25 ὃς γὰρ ἂν ἔχῃ, δοθήσεται αὐτῷ· καὶ
to you the (ones) hearing. who For ever may have, it will be given to him, and

3739 3756 2192 2532 3739 2192 142 575 846
ὃς οὐκ ἔχει, καὶ ὃ ἔχει ἀρθήσεται ἀπ᾽ αὐτοῦ.
who not has, even what he has will be taken from him.

2532 3004 3779 2076 3588 932 3588 2316 5613 1437
26. Καὶ ἔλεγεν, Οὕτως ἐστὶν ἡ βασιλεία τοῦ Θεοῦ, ὡς ἐὰν
And He said, So is the kingdom of God, as if

444 906 3588 4703 1909 3588 1093 2532 2518
ἄνθρωπος βάλῃ τὸν σπόρον ἐπὶ τῆς γῆς, 27 καὶ καθεύδῃ
a man should cast the seed on the earth, and should sleep and

2532 1453 3571 2532 2250 2532 3588 4703 985 2532
καὶ,ἐγείρηται νύκτα καὶ ἡμέραν, καὶ ὁ σπόρος βλαστάνῃ καὶ
rise night and day, and the seed should sprout and

3373 5613 3756 1492 846 844 1063 3588 1093 2592
μηκύνηται ὡς οὐκ οἶδεν αὐτός. 28 αὐτομάτη γὰρ ἡ γῆ καρπο-
lengthen as not knows he. of itself For the earth bears

4412 5528 1534 4719 1534 4134 4621 1722
φορεῖ, πρῶτον χόρτον, εἶτα στάχυν, εἶτα πλήρη σῖτον ἐν
fruit, first greenery, then a head, then full grain in

---

affliction or persecution ariseth for the word's sake, immediately they are offended.

18 And these are they which are sown among thorns; such as hear the word,

19 And the cares of this world, and the deceitfulness of riches, and the lusts of other things entering in, choke the word, and it becometh unfruitful.

20 And these are they which are sown on good ground; such as hear the word, and receive (it), and bring forth fruit, some thirtyfold, some sixty, and some an hundred.

21. And he said unto them, Is a candle brought to be put under a bushel, or under a bed? and not to be set on a candlestick?

22 For there is nothing hid, which shall not be manifested; neither was any thing kept secret, but that it should come abroad.

23 If any man have ears to hear, let him hear.

24 And he said unto them, Take heed what ye hear: with what measure ye mete, it shall be measured to you: and unto you that hear shall more be given.

25 For he that hath, to him shall be given: and he that hath not, from him shall be taken even that which he hath.

26. And he said, So is the kingdom of God, as if a man should cast seed into the ground;

27 And should sleep, and rise night and day, and the seed should spring and grow up, he knoweth not how.

28 For the earth bringeth forth fruit of herself; first the blade, then the ear, after that the full corn in

Mark 4:29

Literal Translation

the head.
29 And when the fruit yields, immediately he sends forth the sickle, for the harvest stands ready. (Joel 3:13)

30. And He said, To what shall we compare the kingdom of God? Or in what parable shall we compare it?
31 (It is) like a grain of mustard, which, when it is sown on the earth, it is lesser than all the seeds of those on the earth.

32 And when it is sown, (it) comes up and becomes greater than all the plants, and produces great branches, so as to be able the birds of the heaven to roost under its shade.

33. And with many such parables He spoke the Word to them, even as they were able to hear.
34 But He did not speak to them without a parable, but He explained all things to His disciples privately.

35. And evening having come, He said to them on that day, Let us go through to the other side.
36 And dismissing the crowd, they took Him along in the boat as He was. And other small boats also were with Him.
37 And a great windstorm occurred, and the waves thrust into the boat so that it was filled already.

38 And He was on the stern, sleeping on the headrest. And they awaken Him, and say to Him, Teacher, does it not matter to You that we are perishing?
39 And being awakened, He rebuked the

Greek interlinear

3588 4719 3752 1161 3860 3588 2590 2112 649
τῷ στάχυι. 29 ὅταν δὲ παραδῷ ὁ καρπός, εὐθέως ἀποστέλλει
the head. when But yields the fruit, at once he sends forth

3588 1407 3754 3936 3588 2326
τὸ δρέπανον, ὅτι παρέστηκεν ὁ θερισμός.
the sickle, because stands ready the harvest.

2532 3004 5101 3666 3588 932 3588 2316
30. Καὶ ἔλεγε, Τίνι ὁμοιώσωμεν τὴν βασιλείαν τοῦ Θεοῦ;
And He said, To what may we compare the kingdom of God?

3588 1722 4169 3850 3846 846 5613 2848
ἢ ἐν ποίᾳ παραβολῇ παραβάλωμεν αὐτήν; 31 ὡς κόκκῳ
Or in what parable may we compare it? As to a grain

4615 3739 3752 4687 1909 3588 1093 3398 3956
σινάπεως, ὃς ὅταν σπαρῇ ἐπὶ τῆς γῆς, μικρότερος πάντων
of mustard, which when it is sown on the earth, lesser than all

3588 4690 2076 3588 1909 3588 1093 2532 3752 4687
τῶν σπερμάτων ἐστὶ τῶν ἐπὶ τῆς γῆς, 32 καὶ ὅταν σπαρῇ,
the seeds it is of those on the earth. And when it is sown

305 2532 1096 3956 3588 3001 3187 2532
ἀναβαίνει, καὶ γίνεται πάντων τῶν λαχάνων μείζων, καὶ
it comes up and becomes all the plants greater than, and

4160 2798 2173 5620 1410 5259 3588 4639
ποιεῖ κλάδους μεγάλους, ὥστε δύνασθαι ὑπὸ τὴν σκιὰν
makes branches great, so as to be able under the shade

846 3588 4071 3588 3772 2681
αὐτοῦ τὰ πετεινὰ τοῦ οὐρανοῦ κατασκηνοῦν.
of it the birds of the heaven to roost.

2532 5108 3850 4183 2980 846 3588
33. Καὶ τοιαύταις παραβολαῖς πολλαῖς ἐλάλει αὐτοῖς τὸν
And such parables many He spoke to them the

3056 2531 1410 191 5565 1161 3850 3756
λόγον, καθὼς ἠδύναντο ἀκούειν· 34 χωρὶς δὲ παραβολῆς· οὐκ
Word, even as they were able to hear; without and a parable not

2980 846 2596 2398 1161 3588 3101 846 1966
ἐλάλει αὐτοῖς· κατ' ἰδίαν δὲ τοῖς μαθηταῖς αὐτοῦ ἐπέλυε
He spoke to them, privately but to the disciples of Him, He explained

3956
πάντα.
all things.

2532 3004 846 1722 1565 3588 2250 3798 1096
35. Καὶ λέγει αὐτοῖς ἐν ἐκείνῃ τῇ ἡμέρᾳ, ὀψίας γενομένης,
And He says to them in that day, evening having come,

1330 1519 3588 4008 2532 863 3588 3793 3880
Διέλθωμεν εἰς τὸ πέραν. 36 καὶ ἀφέντες τὸν ὄχλον, παραλαμ-
Let us go through to the other side. And dismissing the crowd, they take

846 5613 2258 1722 3588 4143 2532 243 1161 4142
βάνουσιν αὐτὸν ὡς ἦν ἐν τῷ πλοίῳ. καὶ ἄλλα δὲ πλοιάρια
along Him as He was in the boat. And other also small boats

2258 3326 846 2532 1096 2978 417 3173 3588 1161
ἦν μετ' αὐτοῦ. 37 καὶ γίνεται λαῖλαψ ἀνέμου μεγάλη· τὰ δὲ
were with Him. And occurs a storm of wind great; , the and

2949 1911 1519 3588 4143 5620 846 2235 1072
κύματα ἐπέβαλλεν εἰς τὸ πλοῖον, ὥστε αὐτὸ ἤδη γεμίζεσθαι.
waves thrust into the boat, so as it already was filled.

2532 2258 846 1909 3588 4403 1909 3588 4344 2518
38 καὶ ἦν αὐτὸς ἐπὶ τῇ πρύμνῃ ἐπὶ τὸ προσκεφάλαιον καθεύδων·
And was He on the stern, on the headrest sleeping.

2532 1326 846 2532 3004 846 1320 3756
καὶ διεγείρουσιν αὐτὸν, καὶ λέγουσιν αὐτῷ, Διδάσκαλε, οὐ
And they awaken Him, and say to Him, Teacher, not

3199 4671 3754 622 2532 1326 2008 3588
μέλει σοι ὅτι ἀπολλύμεθα; 39 καὶ διεγερθεὶς ἐπετίμησε τῷ
it matters to you that we are perishing? And being awakened He rebuked the

King James Version

the ear.
29 But when the fruit is brought forth, immediately he putteth in the sickle, because the harvest is come.

30. And he said, Whereunto shall we liken the kingdom of God? or with what comparison shall we compare it?
31 (It is) like a grain of mustard seed, which, when it is sown in the earth, is less than all the seeds that be in the earth:
32 But when it is sown, it groweth up, and becometh greater than all herbs, and shooteth out great branches; so that the fowls of the air may lodge under the shadow of it.

33. And with many such parables spake he the word unto them, as they were able to hear (it).
34 But without a parable spake he not unto them: and when they were alone, he expounded all things to his disciples.

35. And the same day, when the even was come, he saith unto them, Let us pass over unto the other side.
36 And when they had sent away the multitude, they took him even as he was in the ship. And there were also with him other little ships.
37 And there arose a great storm of wind, and the waves beat into the ship, so that it was now full.
38 And he was in the hinder part of the ship, asleep on a pillow: and they awake him, and say unto him, Master, carest thou not that we perish?
39 And he arose, and rebuked the

Literal Translation

wind, and said to the sea, Be Silent! Be still! And the wind sank, and there was a great calm.

40 And He said to them, Why are you so fearful? How do you not have faith?

41 And they feared a great fear and said to one another, Who then is this One, that even the wind and the sea obey Him?

Mark 4:40

417 2532 2036 3588 2281 4623 5392 2532 2896
ἀνέμῳ, καὶ εἶπε τῇ θαλάσσῃ, Σιώπα, πεφίμωσο. καὶ ἐκόπα-
wind, and said to the sea, Be Silent! Be still! And sank

3588 417 2532 1096 1055 3173 2532 2036 846
σεν ὁ ἄνεμος, καὶ ἐγένετο γαλήνη μεγάλη. 40 καὶ εἶπεν αὐτοῖς,
the wind, and there was a calm great. And He said to them,

5101 1169 2075 3779 4459 3756 2192 4102 2532 5399
Τί δειλοί ἐστε οὕτω; πῶς οὐκ ἔχετε πίστιν; 41 καὶ ἐφοβήθησαν
Why fearful are you so? How not you have faith? And they feared

5401 3173 2532 3004 4314 240 5101 686 3778
φόβον μέγαν, καὶ ἔλεγον πρὸς ἀλλήλους, Τίς ἄρα οὗτός
fear a great, and said to one another, Who then this One

2078 3754 2532 3588 417 2532 3588 2281 5219 846
ἐστιν, ὅτι καὶ ὁ ἄνεμος καὶ ἡ θάλασσα ὑπακούουσιν αὐτῷ;
is, that even the wind and the sea obey Him?

King James Version

wind, and said unto the sea, Peace, be still. And the wind ceased, and there was a great calm.

40 And he said unto them, Why are ye so fearful? how is it that ye have no faith?

41 And they feared exceedingly, and said one to another, What manner of man is this, that even the wind and the sea obey him?

Mark 5

1. And they came to the other side of the sea, to the country of the Gadarenes.

2 And He coming out from the boat, at once out of the tombs a man with an unclean spirit met Him,

3 who had (his) abode among the tombs; and no one was able to bind him, not even with chains.

4 Because he had often been bound with fetters and chains, and the chains had been torn by him, and the fetters had been shattered. And no one had strength to subdue him.

5 And through all night and day in the hills, and among the tombs, he was crying and cutting himself with stones.

6 And seeing Jesus from a distance, he ran and fell down before Him.

7 And crying with a loud voice, he said, What (is) to me and to You, Jesus, Son of the Most High God? I adjure You by God, do not torment me.

8 For He said to him, Unclean spirit, come out of the man!

9 And He asked him, What (is) your name? And he answered, saying, My name (is) Legion,

Mark 5

2532 2064 1519 3588 4008 3588 2281 1519 3588 5561 3588
1. Καὶ ἦλθον εἰς τὸ πέραν τῆς θαλάσσης, εἰς τὴν χώραν τῶν
And they came to the other side of the sea, into the country of the

1046 2532 1831 846 1537 3588 4143 2112
Γαδαρηνῶν. 2 καὶ ἐξελθόντι αὐτῷ ἐκ τοῦ πλοίου, εὐθέως
Gadarenes. And coming out He from the boat, at once

528 846 1537 3588 3419 444 1722 4151
ἀπήντησεν αὐτῷ ἐκ τῶν μνημείων ἄνθρωπος ἐν πνεύματι
met Him out of the tombs a man in a spirit

169 3739 3588 2731 2192 1722 3588 3419 2532
ἀκαθάρτῳ, 3 ὃς τὴν κατοίκησιν εἶχεν ἐν τοῖς μνημείοις· καὶ
unclean, who the abode had among the tombs; even

3777 254 3762 1410 846 1210 1223 3588 846
οὔτε ἁλύσεσιν οὐδεὶς ἠδύνατο αὐτὸν δῆσαι, 4 διὰ τὸ αὐτὸν
not with chains no one was able him to bind, because that he

4178 3976 2532 254 1210 2532 1288 5259
πολλάκις πέδαις καὶ ἁλύσεσι δεδέσθαι, καὶ διεσπᾶσθαι ὑπ'
often with fetters and chains had been bound, and had been torn by

846 3588 254 2532 3588 3976 4937 2532 3762
αὐτοῦ τὰς ἁλύσεις καὶ τὰς πέδας συντετρῖφθαι· καὶ οὐδεὶς
him the chains, and the fetters had been shattered, and no one

846 2480 1150 2532 1223 3956 3571 2532 2250
αὐτὸν ἴσχυε δαμάσαι· 5 καὶ διὰ παντὸς, νυκτὸς καὶ ἡμέρας,
him had strength to subdue. And through all night and day

1722 3588 3735 2532 1722 3588 3418 2258 2896 2532 2629
ἐν τοῖς ὄρεσι καὶ ἐν τοῖς μνήμασιν ἦν κράζων καὶ κατακόπτων
among the hills and in the tombs he was crying and cutting

1438 3037 1492 1161 3588 2424 575 3113 5143
ἑαυτὸν λίθοις. 6 ἰδὼν δὲ τὸν Ἰησοῦν ἀπὸ μακρόθεν, ἔδραμε
himself with stones. seeing And Jesus from a distance, he ran

2532 4352 846 2532 2896 5456 3173 2036 5101
καὶ προσεκύνησεν αὐτῷ, 7 καὶ κράξας φωνῇ μεγάλῃ εἶπε, Τί
and fell down before Him. And crying with a voice great said, What

1698 2532 4671 2424 5207 3588 2316 3588 5310 3726 4571
ἐμοὶ καὶ σοί, Ἰησοῦ, υἱὲ τοῦ Θεοῦ τοῦ ὑψίστου; ὁρκίζω σε
to me and to you, Jesus, Son of God the Most High? I adjure You

3588 2316 3361 3165 928 3004 1063 846 1831 3588
τὸν Θεόν, μή με βασανίσῃς. 8 ἔλεγε γὰρ αὐτῷ, Ἔξελθε, τὸ
(by) God, not me you may torment. He said For to him, Come out, the

4151 3588 169 1537 3588 444 2532 1905
πνεῦμα τὸ ἀκάθαρτον, ἐκ τοῦ ἀνθρώπου. 9 καὶ ἐπηρώτα
spirit unclean, out of the man! And He asked

846 5101 4671 3686 2532 611 3004 3003 3686
αὐτόν, Τί σοι ὄνομά; καὶ ἀπεκρίθη, λέγων, Λεγιὼν ὄνομά
him, What of you the name? And he answered, saying, Legion (the) name

Mark 5

1. And they came over unto the other side of the sea, into the country of the Gadarenes.

2 And when he was come out of the ship, immediately there met him out of the tombs a man with an unclean spirit,

3 Who had (his) dwelling among the tombs; and no man could bind him, no, not with chains:

4 Because that he had been often bound with fetters and chains, and the chains had been plucked asunder by him, and the fetters broken in pieces: neither could any (man) tame him.

5 And always, night and day, he was in the mountains, and in the tombs, crying, and cutting himself with stones.

6 But when he saw Jesus afar off, he ran and worshipped him,

7 And cried with a loud voice, and said, What have I to do with thee, Jesus, (thou) Son of the most high God? I adjure thee by God, that thou torment me not.

8 For he said unto him, Come out of the man, (thou) unclean spirit.

9 And he asked him, What (is) thy name? And he answered, saying, My name (is) Legion:

Literal Translation — **Mark 5:10** — **King James Version**

because we are many.
10 And he begged Him
very much that He
would not send them
outside the country.
11 And a great herd of
pigs were feeding there
near the mountain.
12 And all the demons
begged Him, saying,
Send us into the pigs,
that we may enter into
them.

13 And immediately
Jesus allowed them.
And coming out, the,
unclean spirits entered
into the pigs. And the
herd rushed down the
precipice into the sea,
and they were about
two thousand, and
(they) were choked in
the sea.

14 And those who fed
the pigs fled, and (they)
told (it) in the city, and
in the fields. And they
came out to see what (it)
is that had happened.
15 And they came to Je-
sus, and to behold the
(one) who had been
demon-possessed, sit-
ting and being clothed,
and being in his senses,
the (one) who had the
legion. And they feared.

16 And those seeing (it)
related to them how it
happened to the (one)
who had been demon-
possessed, and about
the pigs.
17 And they began to
beg Him to depart from
their borders.
18 And He having en-
tered into the boat, the
(former) demoniac
begged Him, that he be
with Him.
19 But Jesus did not
permit him, but said to
him, Go to your house,
to your own, and report
to them what things the
Lord has done to you
and had mercy on you.
20 And he left and be-
gan to proclaim in De-
capolis what things Je-
sus did to him.

3427 3754 4183 2070 2532 3870 846 4183 2443 3361
μοι, ὅτι πολλοί ἐσμεν. 10 καὶ παρεκάλει αὐτὸν πολλὰ, ἵνα μὴ
of me, for many we are. And he begged Him much, that not

846 649 1854 3588 5561 2258 1161 1563 4314 3588 3735
αὐτοὺς ἀποστείλῃ ἔξω τῆς χώρας. 11 ἦν δὲ ἐκεῖ πρὸς τὰ ὄρη
them He would send outside the country. was And there near the mount

34 5519 3173 1006 2532 3870 846
ἀγέλη χοίρων μεγάλη βοσκομένη· 12 καὶ παρεκάλεσαν αὐτὸν
herd of pigs a great feeding. And begged Him

3956 3588 1142 3004 3992 2248 1519 3588 5519
πάντες οἱ δαίμονες, λέγοντες, Πέμψον ἡμᾶς εἰς τοὺς χοίρους,
all the demons, saying, Send us into the pigs,

2443 1519 846 1525 2532 2010 846 2112 3588
ἵνα εἰς αὐτοὺς εἰσέλθωμεν. 13 καὶ ἐπέτρεψεν αὐτοῖς εὐθέως ὁ
that into them we may enter. And allowed them immediately

2424 2532 1831 3588 4151 3588 169 1525
Ἰησοῦς. καὶ ἐξελθόντα τὰ πνεύματα τὰ ἀκάθαρτα εἰσῆλθον
Jesus. And coming out the spirits unclean entered

1519 3588 5519 2532 3729 3588 34 2592 3588 2911
εἰς τοὺς χοίρους· καὶ ὥρμησεν ἡ ἀγέλη κατὰ τοῦ κρημνοῦ
into the pigs; and rushed the herd down the precipice

1519 3588 2281 2258 1161 5613 1367 2532 4155 1722 3588
εἰς τὴν θάλασσαν· ἦσαν δὲ ὡς δισχίλιοι· καὶ ἐπνίγοντο ἐν τῇ
into the sea. they were And about two thousand, and were choked in the

2281 3588 1161 1006 3588 5519 5343 2532 312
θαλάσσῃ. 14 οι δὲ βόσκοντες τοὺς χοίρους ἔφυγον, καὶ ἀνήγ-
sea. those And feeding the pigs fled and told

1519 3588 4172 2532 1519 3588 68 2532 1831 1492
γειλαν εἰς τὴν πόλιν καὶ εἰς τοὺς ἀγρούς· καὶ ἐξῆλθον ἰδεῖν
(it) in the city and in the fields. And they came out to see

5101 2076 3588 1096 2532 2064 4314 3588 2424 2532
τί ἐστι τὸ γεγονός· 15 καὶ ἔρχονται πρὸς τὸν Ἰησοῦν, καὶ
what is that having occurred. And they come to Jesus, and

2334 3588 1139 2521 2532 2439
θεωροῦσι τὸν δαιμονιζόμενον καθήμενον καὶ ἱματισμένον
to behold the (one) having been demon-possessed sitting and having been robed

2532 4993 3588 2192 3588 3003 2532 5399
καὶ σωφρονοῦντα, τὸν ἐσχηκότα τὸν λεγεῶνα· καὶ ἐφοβήθη-
and being in his senses, the (one) having had the legion; and they feared.

2532 1334 846 3588 1492 4459 1096 3588
σαν. 16 καὶ διηγήσαντο αὐτοῖς οἱ ἰδόντες πῶς ἐγένετο τῷ
And related to them those seeing how it occurred to him

1139 2532 4012 3588 5519 2532 756 3870
δαιμονιζομένῳ καὶ περὶ τῶν χοίρων. 17 καὶ ἤρξαντο παρα-
having been demon-possessed, and about the pigs. And they began to

846 565 575 3588 3725 846 2532 1684
καλεῖν αὐτὸν ἀπελθεῖν ἀπὸ τῶν ὁρίων αὐτῶν. 18 καὶ ἐμβάντος
beg Him to depart from the borders of them. And entering

846 1519 3588 4143 3870 846 3588 1139 2443 3588
αὐτοῦ εἰς τὸ πλοῖον, παρεκάλει αὐτὸν ὁ δαιμονισθεὶς, ἵνα ᾖ
Him into the boat, begged Him the demoniac that he be

3326 846 3588 1161 2424 3756 863 846 235 3004 846
μετ᾽ αὐτοῦ. 19 ὁ δὲ Ἰησοῦς οὐκ ἀφῆκεν αὐτόν, ἀλλὰ λέγει αὐτῷ,
with Him. But Jesus not did permit him, but says to him,

5217 1519 3588 3624 4675 4314 3588 4674 2532 312
Ὕπαγε εἰς τὸν οἶκόν σου πρὸς τοὺς σούς, καὶ ἀπάγγειλον
Go into the house of you to those of you, and report

846 3745 4671/3588/2962 4160 2532 1653 1161 2532 565
αὐτοῖς ὅσα σοι ὁ Κύριός εποίησε, καὶ ἠλέησέ σε. 20 καὶ ἀπῆλθε
to them what things to you the Lord has done, and pitied you. And he left

2532 756 2784 1722 3588 1179 3745 4160 846 3588
καὶ ἤρξατο κηρύσσειν ἐν τῇ Δεκαπόλει ὅσα ἐποίησεν αὐτῷ ὁ
and began to proclaim in Decapolis what things did to him

for we are many.
10 And he besought
him much that he would
not send them away out
of the country.
11 Now there was there
nigh unto the mountains
a great herd of swine
feeding.
12 And all the devils be-
sought him, saying,
Send us into the swine,
that we may enter into
them.

13 And forthwith Jesus
gave them leave. And
the unclean spirits went
out, and entered into the
swine: and the herd ran
violently down a steep
place into the sea, (they
were about two thou-
sand;) and were choked
in the sea.

14 And they that fed the
swine fled, and told (it)
in the city, and in the
country. And they went
out to see what it was
that was done.
15 And they come to Je-
sus, and see him that
was possessed with the
devil, and had the le-
gion, sitting, and
clothed, and in his right
mind: and they were
afraid.

16 And they that saw (it)
told them how it befell
to him that was pos-
sessed with the devil,
and (also) concerning
the swine.
17 And they began to
pray him to depart out of
their coasts.
18 And when he was
come into the ship, he
that had been possessed
with the devil prayed
him that he might be
with him.
19 Howbeit Jesus suf-
fered him not, but saith
unto him, Go home to
thy friends, and tell
them how great things
the Lord hath done for
thee, and hath had com-
passion on thee.
20 And he departed,
and began to publish in
Decapolis how great
things Jesus had done
for him:

Literal Translation

And all marveled.

21. And Jesus having crossed over in the boat again to the other side, a large crowd gathered upon Him; and He was beside the sea.

22 And, behold, one of the synagogue rulers named Jairus comes. And seeing Him, (he) fell at His feet.

23 And (he) begged Him very much, saying, My little daughter has (faded) extremely. (I pray) that coming You will lay hands on her, that (she) may be cured and may live.
24 And He went with him. And a large crowd were following Him and were pressing on Him.

25. And a certain woman being with an issue of blood twelve years,
26 and suffering many things under many healers, and having spent all things with herself, and having gained nothing, but rather having come to worse,
27 hearing about Jesus, coming in the crowd behind (Him), she touched His garment.
28 For she said, If I may but touch His garments, I will be cured.
29 And instantly the fountain of her blood was dried up, and she knew in (her) body that she is healed from the plague.
30 And knowing instantly within Himself that power had gone forth out of Him, turning in the crowd, Jesus said, Who touched My garments?

31 And His disciples said to Him, You see the crowd pressing on You, and do You say, Who touched Me?
32 And He looked

Mark 5:21

2424 2532 3956 2296
Ἰησοῦς· καὶ πάντες ἐθαύμαζον.
Jesus. And all marveled.

2532 1276 3588 2424 1722 3588 4143 3825 1519 3588
21. Καὶ διαπεράσαντος τοῦ Ἰησοῦ ἐν τῷ πλοίῳ πάλιν εἰς τὸ
And crossing over Jesus in the boat again to the
4008 4863 3793 4183 1909 846 2532 2258 3844 3588
πέραν, συνήχθη ὄχλος πολὺς ἐπ' αὐτόν, καὶ ἦν παρὰ τὴν
other side, was collected a crown large upon Him, and He was by the
2281 2532 2400 2064 1520 3588 752
θάλασσαν. 22 καὶ ἰδού, ἔρχεται εἷς τῶν ἀρχισυναγώγων,
sea. And, behold! comes One of the synagogue rulers,
3686 2383 2532 1492 846 4098 4314 3588 4228
ὀνόματι Ἰάϊρος, καὶ ἰδὼν αὐτὸν, πίπτει πρὸς τοὺς πόδας
by name Jairus. And seeing Him, he falls at the feet
846 2532 3870 846 4183 3004 3754 3588 2365
αὐτοῦ, 23 καὶ παρακαλεῖ αὐτὸν πολλὰ, λέγων ὅτι Τὸ θυγάτριόν
of Him, and begs Him much, saying, The little daughter
3450 2079 2192 2443 2064 2007 846 3588 5495 3704
μου ἐσχάτως ἔχει· ἵνα ἐλθὼν ἐπιθῇς αὐτῇ τὰς χεῖρας, ὅπως
of me extremely has (faded); that coming You may lay on her the hands, that (she)
4982 2532 2198 2532 565 3326 846 2532 190
σωθῇ καὶ ζήσεται. 24 καὶ ἀπῆλθε μετ' αὐτοῦ· καὶ ἠκολούθει
be cured and may live. And He went with him; and followed
846 3793 4183 2532 4918 846
αὐτῷ ὄχλος πολύς, καὶ συνέθλιβον αὐτόν.
Him a crowd large, and were pressing on Him.

2532 1135 5100 5607 1722 4511 129 2094 1427 2532
25. Καὶ γυνὴ τις οὖσα ἐν ῥύσει αἵματος ἔτη δώδεκα, 26 καὶ
And a woman certain being in a flow of blood years twelve, and
4183 3958 5259 4183 2395 2532 1159 3588
πολλὰ παθοῦσα ὑπὸ πολλῶν ἰατρῶν, καὶ δαπανήσασα τὰ
many things suffering under many healers, and having spent the
3844 1438 3956 2532 3367 5623 235 3123
παρ' ἑαυτῆς πάντα, καὶ μηδὲν ὠφεληθεῖσα, ἀλλὰ μᾶλλον
with herself all things, and nothing having been gained, but rather
1519 3588 5501 2064 191 4012 3588 2424 2064
εἰς τὸ χεῖρον ἐλθοῦσα, 27 ἀκούσασα περὶ τοῦ Ἰησοῦ, ἐλθοῦσα
to the worse having come, hearing about Jesus, coming
1722 3588 3793 3693 680 3588 2440 846 3004 1063
ἐν τῷ ὄχλῳ ὄπισθεν, ἥψατο τοῦ ἱματίου αὐτοῦ· 28 ἔλεγε γὰρ
in the crowd behind, she touched the garment of Him; she said for
3754 2579 3588 2440 846 680 4982 2532
ὅτι Κἂν τῶν ἱματίων αὐτοῦ ἅψωμαι, σωθήσομαι. 29 καὶ
If but the garments of Him I may touch, I will be cured. And
2112 3583 3588 4077 3588 129 846 2532 1097 3588
εὐθέως ἐξηράνθη ἡ πηγὴ τοῦ αἵματος αὐτῆς, καὶ ἔγνω τῷ
instantly dried up the fountain of the blood of her, and she knew in the
4983 3754 2390 575 3588 3148 2532 2112 3588 2424
σώματι ὅτι ἴαται ἀπὸ τῆς μάστιγος. 30 καὶ εὐθέως ὁ Ἰησοῦς
body that she is healed from the plague. And instantly Jesus
1994 1722 1438 3588 1537 846 1411 1831
ἐπιγνοὺς ἐν ἑαυτῷ τὴν ἐξ αὐτοῦ δύναμιν ἐξελθοῦσαν,
knowing within Himself that out of Him power had gone forth,
1994 1722 3588 3739 3004 5101 3450 630 3588 2440
ἐπιστραφεὶς ἐν τῷ ὄχλῳ, ἔλεγε, Τίς μου ἥψατο τῶν ἱματίων;
turning in the crowd (He) said, Who of Me touched the garments?

2532 3004 846 3588 3101 846 991 3588 3793
31 καὶ ἔλεγον αὐτῷ οἱ μαθηταὶ αὐτοῦ, Βλέπεις τὸν ὄχλον
And said to Him the disciples of Him, You see the crowd
4918 4571 2532 3004 5101 3450 680 2532 4017
συνθλίβοντά σε, καὶ λέγεις, Τίς μου ἥψατο; 32 καὶ περιεβλέ-
pressing on You, and You say, Who of Me touched? And He looked

King James Version

and all (men) did marvel.

21. And when Jesus was passed over again by ship unto the other side, much people gathered unto him: and he was nigh unto the sea.

22 And, behold, there cometh one of the rulers of the synagogue, Jairus by name; and when he saw him, he fell at his feet,

23 And besought him greatly, saying, My little daughter lieth at the point of death: (I pray thee), come and lay thy hands on her, that she may be healed; and she shall live.
24 And (Jesus) went with him; and much people followed him, and thronged him.

25. And a certain woman, which had an issue of blood twelve years,
26 And had suffered many things of many physicians, and had spent all that she had, and was nothing bettered, but rather grew worse,
27 When she had heard of Jesus, came in the press behind, and touched his garment.
28 For she said, If I may touch but his clothes, I shall be whole.
29 And straightway the fountain of her blood was dried up; and she felt in (her) body that she was healed of that plague.

30 And Jesus, immediately knowing in himself that virtue had gone out of him, turned him about in the press, and said, Who touched my clothes?

31 And his disciples said unto him, Thou seest the multitude thronging thee, and sayest thou, Who touched me?
32 And he looked

Literal Translation

Mark 5:33

King James Version

around to see the (one) who had done this.
33 And the woman, fearing and trembling, knowing what had happened on her, she came and fell down before Him and told Him all the truth.
34 And He said to her, Daughter, your faith has healed you. Go in peace and be whole from your plague.

35. While He was speaking, they came from the synagogue ruler saying, Your daughter has died. Why do you still trouble the Teacher?

36 But hearing the word spoken, at once Jesus said to the synagogue ruler, Do not fear, only believe.

37 And He did not allow anyone to go with Him except Peter and James and John, the brother of James.

38 And they come into the synagogue ruler's house. And He sees a tumult, and weeping and much wailing.
39 And going in, He said to them, Why do you make a tumult and weep? The child has not died, but is sleeping.

40 And they laughed at Him. But putting all out, (He) takes along the father and the mother of the child, and those with Him, and goes into where the child was lying.

41 And taking hold of the child's hand, He said to her, Talitha koumi; which is, being translated, Little girl, I say to you, Rise up!

42 And immediately the little girl rose up and walked. For she was

1492 3588 5124 4160 3588 1161 1135 5399 2532
πετο ἰδεῖν τὴν τοῦτο ποιήσασαν. 33 ἡ δὲ γυνὴ φοβηθεῖσα καὶ
around to see the (one) this having done. the And woman fearing and

5141 1492 3588 1096 1909 846 2064 2532 4363
τρέμουσα, εἰδυῖα ὃ γέγονεν ἐπ' αὐτῇ, ἦλθε καὶ προσέπεσεν
trembling, knowing what happened on her, came and fell before

846 2532 2036 846 3956 3588 225 3588 1161 2036 846
αὐτῷ, καὶ εἶπεν αὐτῷ πᾶσαν τὴν ἀλήθειαν. 34 ὁ δὲ εἶπεν αὐτῇ,
Him, and told Him all the truth. And He said to her,

2364 3588 4102 4675 4982 4571 5217 1519 1515 2532
Θυγάτηρ, ἡ πίστις σου σέσωκέ σε· ὕπαγε εἰς εἰρήνην, καὶ
Daughter, the faith of you has healed you. Go in peace, and

2468 5199 575 3588 3148 4675
ἴσθι ὑγιὴς ἀπὸ τῆς μάστιγός σου.
be whole from the plague of you.

2089 846 2980 2064 575 3588 752
35. Ἔτι αὐτοῦ λαλοῦντος, ἔρχονται ἀπὸ τοῦ ἀρχισυναγώ-
While He was speaking, they come from the synagogue

3004 3754 2364 4675 599 5101 2089 4660
γου, λέγοντες ὅτι Ἡ θυγάτηρ σου ἀπέθανε· τί ἔτι σκύλλεις
ruler, saying, The daughter of you has died. Why still trouble

3588 1320 3588 1161 2424 2112 191 3588 3056
τὸν διδάσκαλον; 36 ὁ δὲ Ἰησοῦς εὐθέως ἀκούσας τὸν λόγον
the Teacher? But Jesus at once, hearing the word

2980 3004 3588 752 3361 5399 3440
λαλούμενον λέγει τῷ ἀρχισυναγώγῳ, Μὴ φοβοῦ, μόνον
spoken, says to the synagogue ruler, Not do fear; only

4100 2532 3756 863 3762 846 4870 1488 3361
πίστευε. 37 καὶ οὐκ ἀφῆκεν οὐδένα αὐτῷ συνακολουθῆσαι, εἰ μὴ
believe. And not He allowed no one Him to accompany, except

4074 2532 2385 2532 2491 3588 80 2385
Πέτρον καὶ Ἰάκωβον καὶ Ἰωάννην τὸν ἀδελφὸν Ἰακώβου.
Peter and James and John the brother of James.

2532 2064 1519 3588 3624 3588 752 2532 2334
38 καὶ ἔρχεται εἰς τὸν οἶκον τοῦ ἀρχισυναγώγου, καὶ θεωρεῖ
And they come into the house of the synagogue ruler, and He sees

2351 2532 2799 2532 214 4183 2532
θόρυβον, καὶ κλαίοντας καὶ ἀλαλάζοντας πολλά, 39 καὶ
a tumult, and weeping and wailing much. And

1525 3004 846 5101 2350 2532 2799 3588
εἰσελθὼν λέγει αὐτοῖς, Τί θορυβεῖσθε καὶ κλαίετε; τὸ
entering He says to them, Why do you make a tumult and weep? The

3813 3756 599 235 2518 2532 2606 846
παιδίον οὐκ ἀπέθανεν, ἀλλὰ καθεύδει. 40 καὶ κατεγέλων αὐτοῦ.
child not has died, but sleeps. And they laughed at Him.

3588 1161 1544 537 3880 3588 3962 3588
ὁ δέ, ἐκβαλὼν ἅπαντας παραλαμβάνει τὸν πατέρα τοῦ
He But having put out all (He) takes along the father of the

3813 2532 3588 3384 2532 3588 3326 846 2532 1531
παιδίου καὶ τὴν μητέρα καὶ τοὺς μετ' αὐτοῦ, καὶ εἰσπορεύε-
child and the mother, and those with Him, and goes into

3699 2258 3588 3813 345 2532 2902 3588
ται ὅπου ἦν τὸ παιδίον ἀνακείμενον. 41 καὶ κρατήσας τῆς
where was the child lying. And taking hold of the

5495 3588 3813 3004 846 5008 2891 3739 2076
χειρὸς τοῦ παιδίου, λέγει αὐτῇ, Ταλιθα κοῦμι· ὅ ἐστι
hand of the child, He says to her, Talitha koumi, which is,

3177 3588 2877 4671 3004 1453 2532
μεθερμηνευόμενον, Τὸ κοράσιον, σοὶ λέγω, ἔγειραι. 42 καὶ
being translated, Little girl, to you I say, Rise up! And

2112 450 3588 2877 2532 4043 2258 1063 2094
εὐθέως ἀνέστη τὸ κοράσιον καὶ περιεπάτει, ἦν γὰρ ἐτῶν
instantly rose up the little girl and walked about. she was For of years

round about to see her that had done this thing.
33 But the woman fearing and trembling, knowing what was done in her, came and fell down before him, and told him all the truth.
34 And he said unto her, Daughter, thy faith hath made thee whole; go in peace, and be whole of thy plague.

35. While he yet spake, there came from the ruler of the synagogue's (house certain) which said, Thy daughter is dead: why troublest thou the Master any further?
36 As soon as Jesus heard the word that was spoken, he saith unto the ruler of the synagogue, Be not afraid, only believe.
37 And he suffered no man to follow him, save Peter, and James, and John the brother of James.

38 And he cometh to the house of the ruler of the synagogue, and seeth the tumult, and them that wept and wailed greatly.
39 And when he was come in, he saith unto them, Why make ye this ado, and weep? the damsel is not dead, but sleepeth.
40 And they laughed him to scorn. But when he had put them all out, he taketh the father and the mother of the damsel, and them that were with him, and entereth in where the damsel was lying.
41 And he took the damsel by the hand, and said unto her, Talitha cumi; which is, being interpreted, Damsel, I say unto thee, arise.

42 And straightway the damsel arose, and walked; for she was (of the age)

Literal Translation

twelve years (old). And they were amazed with great ecstasy..
43 And very much He ordered them that no one should know this. And He said to give her something to eat.

Mark 5:43

1427 2532 1839 1611 3173 2532 1291
δώδεκα· καὶ ἐξέστησαν ἐκστάσει μεγάλῃ. 43 καὶ διεστείλατο
twelve. And they were amazed with ecstasy great. And He ordered
846 4183 2443 3367 1097 5124 2532 2036 1325
αὐτοῖς πολλὰ ἵνα μηδεὶς γνῷ τοῦτο· καὶ εἶπε δοθῆναι
them much that no one should know this, and said to be given
846 5315
αὐτῇ φαγεῖν.
her to eat.

King James Version

of twelve years. And they were astonished with a great astonishment.
43 And he charged them straitly that no man should know it; and commanded that something should be given her to eat.

Mark 6

1. And He went out from there and came to His native-place. And His disciples followed Him.
2 And a sabbath occurring, He began to teach in the synagogue. And hearing, many were amazed, saying, From where (has) this one these things? And what (is) the wisdom given to him, that even such works of power occur through his hands?
3 Is this one not the carpenter, the son of Mary, and brother of James and Joseph and Judas and Simon? And are not his sisters here with us? And they were offended in Him.
4 And Jesus said to them, A prophet is not without honor, except in his native-place, and among the relatives, and in his house.
5 And He could do no work of power there, except He healed a few infirm ones, laying on (His) hands.
6 And He marveled because of their unbelief.
And He went around the villages in a circuit, teaching.
7. And He calls near the Twelve and began to send them out two (by) two. And He gave them authority (over) the

Mark 6

2532 1831 1564 2532 2064 1519 3588 3968 846
1. Καὶ ἐξῆλθεν ἐκεῖθεν, καὶ ἦλθεν εἰς τὴν πατρίδα αὐτοῦ·
And He went out from there, and comes into the native-place of Him;
2532 190 846 3588 3101 846 2532 1096
καὶ ἀκολουθοῦσιν αὐτῷ οἱ μαθηταὶ αὐτοῦ. 2 καὶ γενομένου
and follow Him the disciples of Him. And having come
4521 756 1722 3588 4864 1322 2532 4183
σαββάτου, ἤρξατο ἐν τῇ συναγωγῇ διδάσκειν· καὶ πολλοὶ
a sabbath, He began in the synagogue to teach. And many
191 1605 3004 4159 5129 5023
ἀκούοντες ἐξεπλήσσοντο, λέγοντες, Πόθεν τούτῳ ταῦτα;
hearing were amazed, saying, From where this one these things?
2532 5101 3588 4678 3588 1325 846 3754 2532 1411 5108
καὶ τίς ἡ σοφία ἡ δοθεῖσα αὐτῷ, ὅτι καὶ δυνάμεις τοιαῦται
and what the wisdom given to Him, that even powerful works such
1223 3588 5495 846 1096 3756 3778 2076 3588 5045
διὰ τῶν χειρῶν αὐτοῦ γίνονεται; 3 οὐχ οὗτός ἐστιν ὁ τέκτων,
through the hands of Him occur? Not this one is the carpenter,
3588 5207 3137 80 1161 2385 2532 2500 2532 2455
ὁ υἱὸς Μαρίας, ἀδελφὸς δὲ Ἰακώβου καὶ Ἰωσῆ καὶ Ἰούδα
the son of Mary, brother and of James and Joseph and Judas
2532 4613 2532 3756 1526 3588 79 846 5612 4314 2248
καὶ Σίμωνος; καὶ οὐκ εἰσὶν αἱ ἀδελφαὶ αὐτοῦ ὧδε πρὸς ἡμᾶς;
and Simon? And not are the sisters of Him here with us?
2532 4624 1722 846 3004 1161 846 3588 2424 3754
καὶ ἐσκανδαλίζοντο ἐν αὐτῷ. 4 ἔλεγε δὲ αὐτοῖς ὁ Ἰησοῦς ὅτι
And they were offended in Him. said But to them Jesus,
3756 2076 4396 820 -1508 1722 3588 3968 846 2532
Οὐκ ἔστι προφήτης ἄτιμος, εἰ μὴ ἐν τῇ πατρίδι αὐτοῦ, καὶ
Not is a prophet unhonored, except in the native-place of him, and
1722 3588 4773 2532/1722/3588/3614 846 2532 3756 1410
ἐν τοῖς συγγενέσι καὶ ἐν τῇ οἰκίᾳ αὐτοῦ. 5 καὶ οὐκ ἠδύνατο
among the relatives and in the house of Him. And not he could
1563 3762 1411 4160 -1508 - 3641 732
ἐκεῖ οὐδεμίαν δύναμιν ποιῆσαι, εἰ μὴ ὀλίγοις ἀρρώστοις
there no work of power do, except a few infirm ones
2007 3588 5495 2323 2532 2296 1223 3588
ἐπιθεὶς τὰς χεῖρας ἐθεράπευσε. 6. καὶ ἐθαύμαζε διὰ τὴν
laying on the hands, He healed. And He marveled through the
570 846
ἀπιστίαν αὐτῶν.
unbelief of them.

2532 4013 3588 2968 2945 1321
Καὶ περιῆγε τὰς κώμας κύκλῳ διδάσκων.
And He went about the villages in circuit teaching.

2532 4341 3588 1427 2532 756 846
7. καὶ προσκαλεῖται τοὺς δώδεκα, καὶ ἤρξατο αὐτοὺς
And He calls near the twelve, and began them
649 1417 1417 2532 1325 846 1849 3588
ἀποστέλλειν δύο δύο, καὶ ἐδίδου αὐτοῖς ἐξουσίαν τῶν
to send out two (by) two, and gave to them authority (over) the

Mark 6

1. And he went out from thence, and came into his own country; and his disciples follow him.
2 And when the sabbath day was come, he began to teach in the synagogue: and many hearing (him) were astonished, saying, From whence hath this (man) these things? and what wisdom (is) this which is given unto him, that even such mighty works are wrought by his hands?
3 Is not this the carpenter, the son of Mary, the brother of James, and Joses, and of Juda, and Simon? and are not his sisters here with us? And they were offended at him.
4 But Jesus said unto them, A prophet is not without honour, but in his own country, and among his own kin, and in his own house.
5 And he could there do no mighty work, save that he laid his hands upon a few sick folk, and healed (them).
6 And he marvelled because of their unbelief. And he went round about the villages, teaching.
7. And he called (unto him) the twelve, and began to send them forth by two and two; and gave them power over

Literal Translation	**Mark 6:8**	***King James Version***

Literal Translation:
unclean spirits,
8 and charged them that they take nothing in (the) way, except only a staff; not a bag, not bread, not copper in the belt;

4151 3588 169 2532 3853 846 2443
πνευμάτων τῶν ἀκαθάρτων. 8 καὶ παρήγγειλεν αὐτοῖς ἵνα
spirits the unclean. And (He) charged them that

3367 142 1519 3598 - 1508 - 4464 3440 3361 4082 3361
μηδὲν αἴρωσιν εἰς ὁδόν, εἰ μὴ ῥάβδον μόνον· μὴ πήραν, μὴ
nothing they take in (the) way, except a staff only; not a bag, not

740 3361 1519 3588 2223 5475 235 5265
ἄρτον, μὴ εἰς τὴν ζώνην χαλκόν· 9 ἀλλ' ὑποδεδεμένους
bread, not in the belt copper; but having tied under

King James Version:
unclean spirits;
8 And commanded them that they should take nothing for (their) journey, save a staff only; no scrip, no bread, no money in (their) purse:

Literal Translation:
9 but having tied under sandals, and not to put on two tunics.
10 And He said to them, Wherever you enter into a house, remain there until you go out from there.

4547 2532 3361 1746 1417 5509 2532 3004
σανδάλια· καὶ μὴ ἐνδύσασθαι δύο χιτῶνας. 10 καὶ ἔλεγεν
sandals, and not to put on two tunics. And He said

846 3699 1437 1525 1519 3614 1563 3306 2193 302
αὐτοῖς, Ὅπου ἐὰν εἰσέλθητε εἰς οἰκίαν, ἐκεῖ μένετε ἕως ἂν
to them, Wherever you enter into a house, there remain until

King James Version:
9 But (be) shod with sandals; and not put on two coats.
10 And he said unto them, In what place soever ye enter into an house, there abide till ye depart from that place.

Literal Translation:
11 And as many as will not receive you, nor hear from you, having gone out from there, shake off the dust under your feet for a testimony to them. Truly I say to you, it will be more bearable for Sodom or Gomorrah in Judgment Day than for that city.

1831 1564 2532 3745 302 3361 1209 5209 3366
ἐξέλθητε ἐκεῖθεν. 11 καὶ ὅσοι ἂν μὴ δέξωνται ὑμᾶς, μηδὲ
you go out from there. And as many as not will receive you, nor

191 5216 1607 1564 1621 3588
ἀκούσωσιν ὑμῶν, ἐκπορευόμενοι ἐκεῖθεν, ἐκτινάξατε τὸν
hear from you, having gone out from there, shake off the

5522 3588 5270 3588 4228 5216 1519 3142 846
χοῦν τὸν ὑποκάτω τῶν ποδῶν ὑμῶν εἰς μαρτύριον αὐτοῖς.
dust under the feet of you for a testimony to them.

281 3004 5213 414 2071 4670 2228 1116 1722
ἀμὴν λέγω ὑμῖν, ἀνεκτότερον ἔσται Σοδόμοις ἢ Γομόρροις ἐν
Truly I say to you, more bearable it will be for Sodom or Gomorrah in

King James Version:
11 And whosoever shall not receive you, nor hear you, when ye depart thence, shake off the dust under your feet for a testimony against them. Verily I say unto you, It shall be more tolerable for Sodom and Gomorrha in the day of judgment, than for that city.

Literal Translation:
12 And having gone out, they proclaimed that (men) should repent.
13 And they cast out many demons, and anointed with oil and healed many sick ones.

2250 2920 2228/3588/4172 1565 2532 1831 2784
ἡμέρᾳ κρίσεως, ἢ τῇ πόλει ἐκείνῃ. 12 καὶ ἐξελθόντες ἐκήρυσ-
the Day of Judgment than for city that. And having gone out they proclaimed

2443 3340 2532 1140 4183 1544 2532
σον ἵνα μετανοήσωσι· 13 καὶ δαιμόνια πολλὰ ἐξέβαλλον, καὶ
that (men) should repent. And demons many they cast out, and

218 1637 4183 732 2532 2323
ἤλειφον ἐλαίῳ πολλοὺς ἀρρώστους καὶ ἐθεράπευον.
anointed with oil many sick ones, and healed.

King James Version:
12 And they went out, and preached that men should repent.
13 And they cast out many devils, and anointed with oil many that were sick, and healed (them).

Literal Translation:
14. And Herod the king heard, for His name became public. And he said, John the Baptizing (one) is risen from the dead, and because of this the works of power operate in him.

2532 191 3588 935 2264 5318 1063 1096
14. Καὶ ἤκουσεν ὁ βασιλεὺς Ἡρώδης, φανερὸν γὰρ ἐγένετο
And heard the king Herod, public for became

3588 3686 846 2532 3004 3754 2491 3588 907 1537 3498
τὸ ὄνομα αὐτοῦ, καὶ ἔλεγεν ὅτι Ἰωάννης ὁ βαπτίζων ἐκ νεκρῶν
the name of Him. And he said, John the Baptizing (one) from the dead

1453 2532 1223 5124 1754 3588 1411 1722 846
ἠγέρθη, καὶ διὰ τοῦτο ἐνεργοῦσιν αἱ δυνάμεις ἐν αὐτῷ.
is risen, and because of this operate the works of power in him.

King James Version:
14. And king Herod heard (of him); (for his name was spread abroad:) and he said, That John the Baptist was risen from the dead, and therefore mighty works do shew forth themselves in him.

Literal Translation:
15 Others said, He is Elijah; and others said, He is a prophet or as one of the prophets.
16 But hearing, Herod said, This one is John whom I beheaded. This one is risen from the dead.

243 3004 3754 2243 2076 243 1161 3004 3754
15 ἄλλοι ἔλεγον ὅτι Ἠλίας ἐστίν· ἄλλοι δὲ ἔλεγον ὅτι
Others said that Elijah he is; others and said that

4396 2076 2228/5613/1519/3588 4396 191 1161/3588
Προφήτης ἐστίν, ἢ ὡς εἷς τῶν προφητῶν. 16 ἀκούσας δὲ ὁ
a prophet he is, or as one of the prophets. having heard But

2264 2036 3754 3739/1473 607 2491 3778 2076
Ἡρῴδης εἶπεν ὅτι Ὃν ἐγὼ ἀπεκεφάλισα Ἰωάννην, οὗτος ἐστιν·
Herod said (he) whom I beheaded, John, this one is

846 1453 1537 3498 848 1063/3588 2264 649
αὐτὸς ἠγέρθη ἐκ νεκρῶν. 17 αὐτὸς γὰρ ὁ Ἡρώδης ἀποστείλας
he is risen from the dead. himself For Herod having sent

King James Version:
15 Others said, That it is Elias. And others said, That it is a prophet, or as one of the prophets.
16 But when Herod heard (thereof), he said, It is John, whom I beheaded: he is risen from the dead.

Literal Translation:
17 For having sent, Herod himself had seized John and bound him in the prison, because of Herodias the wife of his brother Philip,

2902 3588 2491 2532 1210 846 1722 3588 5438
ἐκράτησε τὸν Ἰωάννην, καὶ ἔδησεν αὐτὸν ἐν τῇ φυλακῇ,
had seized John, and bound him in the prison,

1223 2266 3588 1135 5376 3588 80 846
διὰ Ἡρωδιάδα τὴν γυναῖκα Φιλίππου τοῦ ἀδελφοῦ αὐτοῦ,
because of Herodias the wife of Philip, the brother of him,

King James Version:
17 For Herod himself had sent forth and laid hold upon John, and bound him in prison for Herodias' sake, his brother Philip's wife:

Literal Translation

because he had married her.
18 For John had said to Herod, It is not lawful for you to have the wife of your brother.
19 And Herodias held it against him, and desired to kill him, and was not able.
20 For Herod feared John, knowing him (to be) a holy and just man, and kept him safe. And hearing him, he did many things, and gladly heard from him.
21 And a suitable day having come, when on his birth-feast Herod made a supper for his great ones, also the chiliarchs, and the first ones of Galilee.
22 And the daughter of Herodias herself entering, and she having danced and pleased Herod and those reclining with (him), the king said to the girl, Ask me whatever you wish, and I will give it to you.
23 And he swore to her, Whatever you ask me, I will give to you, up to half of my kingdom.
24 And going out, she said to her mother, What shall I ask? And she said, The head of John the Baptist.
25 And immediately going in with haste to the king, she asked, saying, I desire that at once you give to me the head of John the Baptist on a platter.
26 And having become deeply grieved, because of the oaths and those reclining together, the king did not wish to refuse her.
27 And at once the king sending an executioner,

Mark 6:18

3754 846 1060 3004 1063 3588 2491 3588 2264
ὅτι αὐτὴν ἐγάμησεν. 18 ἔλεγε γὰρ ὁ Ἰωάννης τῷ Ἡρώδῃ
because her he had married. had said For John to Herod,

3754 3756 1832 4671 2192 3588 1135 3588 80 4675
ὅτι Οὐκ ἔξεστί σοι ἔχειν τὴν γυναῖκα τοῦ ἀδελφοῦ σου.
Not it is lawful for you to have the wife of the brother of you.

3588/1161 2266 1758 846 2532 2309 846 615
19 ἡ δὲ Ἡρῳδιὰς ἐνεῖχεν αὐτῷ, καὶ ἤθελεν αὐτὸν ἀποκτεῖναι·
And Herodias held it against him. And (she) desired him to kill,

2532 3756 1410 3588 1063 2264 5399 3588 2491
καὶ οὐκ ἠδύνατο· 20 ὁ γὰρ Ἡρώδης ἐφοβεῖτο τὸν Ἰωάννην,
and not was able. For Herod feared John,

1492 846 435 1342 2532 40 2532 4933 846
εἰδὼς αὐτὸν ἄνδρα δίκαιον καὶ ἅγιον, καὶ συνετήρει αὐτόν·
knowing him a man just and holy, and kept safe him,

2532 191 846 4183 4160 2532 2234 846 191
καὶ ἀκούσας αὐτοῦ, πολλὰ ἐποίει, καὶ ἡδέως αὐτοῦ ἤκουε.
and having heard him, many things he did, and gladly from him heard.

2532 1096 2250 2121 3753 2264 3588 1077
21 καὶ γενομένης ἡμέρας εὐκαίρου, ὅτε Ἡρώδης τοῖς γενεσίοις
And having come a day suitable, when Herod on the birth-feast

846 1173 4160 3588 3175 846 2532 3588
αὐτοῦ δεῖπνον ἐποίει τοῖς μεγιστᾶσιν αὐτοῦ καὶ τοῖς
of him a supper made for the great ones of him, and the

5506 2532 3588 4413 3588 1056 2532 1525
χιλιάρχοις καὶ τοῖς πρώτοις τῆς Γαλιλαίας, 22 καὶ εἰσελθούσης
chiliarchs, and the first ones of Galilee. And entering

3588 2364 846 2266 2532 3738 2532
τῆς θυγατρὸς αὐτοῦ Ἡρωδιάδος καὶ ὀρχησαμένης, καὶ
the daughter of her, of Herodias, and she having danced and

700 3588 2264 2532 3588 4873 2036 3588
ἀρεσάσης τῷ Ἡρώδῃ καὶ τοῖς συνανακειμένοις, εἶπεν ὁ
pleased Herod and the (ones) having reclined with him, said the

935 3588 2877 154 3165/3588/1437 2309 2532 1325
βασιλεὺς τῷ κορασίῳ, Αἴτησόν με ὃ ἐὰν θέλῃς, καὶ δώσω
king to the girl, Ask me whatever you wish, and I will give

4671 2532 3660 846 3754 3739 1437 3165 154 1325 4671
σοι· 23 καὶ ὤμοσεν αὐτῇ ὅτι Ὃ ἐάν με αἰτήσῃς, δώσω σοι,
to you. And he swore to her, Whatever me you ask, I will give to you,

2193 2255 3588 932 3450 3588 1161 1831 2036 3588
ἕως ἡμίσους τῆς βασιλείας μου. 24 ἡ δὲ ἐξελθοῦσα εἶπε τῇ
up to half of the kingdom of me. she And going out said to the

3384 846 5101 154 3588 1161 2036 3588 2776
μητρὶ αὐτῆς, Τί αἰτήσομαι; ἡ δὲ εἶπε, Τὴν κεφαλὴν
mother of her, What shall I ask? she And said, The head

2491 3588 910 2532 1525 2112 3326
Ἰωάννου τοῦ βαπτιστοῦ. 25 καὶ εἰσελθοῦσα εὐθέως μετὰ
of John the Baptist. And entering immediately with

4710 4314 3588 935 154 3004 2309 2443
σπουδῆς πρὸς τὸν βασιλέα, ᾐτήσατο, λέγουσα, Θέλω ἵνα
haste to the king, she asked, saying, I desire that

3427 1325 1824 1909 4094 3588 2776 2491 3588
μοι δῷς ἐξαυτῆς ἐπὶ πίνακι τὴν κεφαλὴν Ἰωάννου τοῦ
to me you give at once on a platter the head of John the

910 2532 4036 1096 3588 935 1223 3588
βαπτιστοῦ. 26 καὶ περίλυπος γενόμενος ὁ βασιλεὺς, διὰ τους
Baptist. And deeply grieved having become the king, because of the

3727 2532 3588 4873 3756 2309 846 114
ὅρκους καὶ τοὺς συνανακειμένους οὐκ ἠθέλησεν αὐτὴν ἀθε-
oaths and the ones having reclined with (him) not did wish her to

2532 2112 649 3588 935 4688
τῆσαι. 27 καὶ εὐθέως ἀποστείλας ὁ βασιλεὺς σπεκουλάτωρα
refuse. And at once sending the king an executioner

King James Version

for he had married her.
18 For John had said unto Herod, It is not lawful for thee to have thy brother's wife.
19 Therefore Herodias had a quarrel against him, and would have killed him; but she could not:
20 For Herod feared John, knowing that he was a just man and an holy, and observed him; and when he heard him, he did many things, and heard him gladly.
21 And when a convenient day was come, that Herod on his birthday made a supper to his lords, high captains, and chief (estates) of Galilee;
22 And when the daughter of the said Herodias came in, and danced, and pleased Herod and them that sat with him, the king said unto the damsel, Ask of me whatsoever thou wilt, and I will give (it) thee.
23 And he sware unto her, Whatsoever thou shalt ask of me, I will give (it) thee, unto the half of my kingdom.
24 And she went forth, and said unto her mother, What shall I ask? And she said, The head of John the Baptist.
25 And she came in straightway with haste unto the king, and asked, saying, I will that thou give me by and by in a charger the head of John the Baptist.
26 And the king was exceeding sorry; (yet) for his oath's sake, and for their sakes which sat with him, he would not reject her.
27 And immediately the king sent an executioner,

Literal Translation | **Mark 6:28** | **King James Version**

he ordered his head to be brought. And going, he beheaded him in the prison,
28 and brought his head on a platter and gave it to the girl. And the girl gave it to her mother.

29 And having heard his disciples went, and took his corpse and placed it in a tomb.

30. And the apostles assembled to Jesus, and reported to Him all things, even what they did and what they taught.

31 And He said to them, You yourselves come privately into a deserted place, and rest a little. For those coming and those going were many, and they did not even have opportunity to eat.

32 And they went away by the boat privately into a deserted place.

33 And the crowds saw them going, and many recognized Him. And (they) ran together on foot there from all the cities, and came before them, and came together to Him.
34 And going out, Jesus saw a huge crowd, and had pity on them, because they were as sheep not having a shepherd. And He began to teach them many things. (Num. 27:17; Eze. 34:5)
35 And (it) now becoming a late hour, drawing near to Him, the disciples said, The place is deserted, and (it is) now a late hour.

36 Send them away, that going away to the surrounding fields and villages

2004 5342 3588 2776 846 3588 1161 565
ἐπέταξεν ἐνεχθῆναι τὴν κεφαλὴν αὐτοῦ. ὁ δὲ ἀπελθὼν
ordered to be brought the head of him. he And going,

607 846 1722 3588 5438 2532 5342 3588 2776
ἀπεκεφάλισεν αὐτὸν ἐν τῇ φυλακῇ, 28 καὶ ἤνεγκε τὴν κεφαλὴν
beheaded him in the prison, and brought the head

846 1909 4094 2532 1325 846 3588 2877 2532 3588
αὐτοῦ ἐπὶ πίνακι, καὶ ἔδωκεν αὐτὴν τῷ κορασίῳ· καὶ τὸ
of him on a platter,. and gave it to the girl; and the

2877 1325 846 3588 3384 846 2532 191
κοράσιον ἔδωκεν αὐτὴν τῇ μητρὶ αὐτῆς. 29 καὶ ἀκούσαντες
girl gave it to the mother of her. And having heard

3588 3101 846 2064 2532 142 3588 4430 846 2532
οἱ μαθηταὶ αὐτοῦ ἦλθον, καὶ ἦραν τὸ πτῶμα αὐτοῦ, καὶ
the disciples of him went, and took the corpse of him, and

5087 846 1722 3419
ἔθηκαν αὐτὸ ἐν μνημείῳ.
placed it in a tomb.

2532 4863 3588 652 4314 3588 2424 2532
30. Καὶ συνάγονται οἱ ἀπόστολοι πρὸς τὸν Ἰησοῦν, καὶ
And assembled the apostles to Jesus, and

518 846 3956 2532 3745 4160 2532 3745 1321
ἀπήγγειλαν αὐτῷ πάντα, καὶ ὅσα ἐποίησαν καὶ ὅσα ἐδί-
reported to Him all things, even what they did and what they

2532 2036 846 1205 5210 846 2596 2398 1519
δαξαν. 31 καὶ εἶπεν αὐτοῖς, Δεῦτε ὑμεῖς αὐτοὶ κατ᾽ ἰδίαν εἰς
taught. And He said to them, Come you yourselves privately into

2048 5117 2532 373 3641 2258 1063 3588
ἔρημον τόπον, καὶ ἀναπαύεσθε ὀλίγον. ἦσαν γὰρ οἱ
a deserted place, and rest a little. were For those

2064 2532 3588 5217 4183 2532 3761 5315 2119
ἐρχόμενοι καὶ οἱ ὑπάγοντες πολλοί, καὶ οὐδὲ φαγεῖν ηὐκαί-
coming and those going many, and not even to eat they had

2532 565 1519 2048 5117 3588 4143 2596 2398
ρουν. 32 καὶ ἀπῆλθον εἰς ἔρημον τόπον τῷ πλοίῳ κατ᾽ ἰδίαν.
opportunity.And they went away to a deserted place by the boat privately.

2532 1492 846 5217 3588 3793 2532 1921 846
33 καὶ εἶδον αὐτοὺς ὑπάγοντας οἱ ὄχλοι, καὶ ἐπέγνωσαν αὐτὸν
And saw them going the crowds, and recognized Him

4183 2532 3979 575 3956 3588 4172 4936 1563
πολλοί, καὶ πεζῇ ἀπὸ πασῶν τῶν πόλεων συνέδραμον ἐκεῖ,
many, and on foot from all the cities ran together there,

2532 4281 846 2532 4905 4314 846 2532
καὶ προῆλθον αὐτούς, καὶ συνῆλθον πρὸς αὐτόν. 34 καὶ
and came before them, and came together to Him. And

1831 1492 3588 2424 4183 3793 2532 4697
ἐξελθὼν εἶδεν ὁ Ἰησοῦς πολὺν ὄχλον, καὶ ἐσπλαγχνίσθη
going out saw Jesus huge a crowd and had compassion

1909 846 3754 2258 5613 4263 3361 2192 4166 2532
ἐπ᾽ αὐτοῖς, ὅτι ἦσαν ὡς πρόβατα μὴ ἔχοντα ποιμένα· καὶ
on them, because they were as sheep not having a shepherd. And

756 1321 846 4183 2532 2235 5610 4183
ἤρξατο διδάσκειν αὐτοὺς πολλά. 35 καὶ ἤδη ὥρας πολλῆς
He began to teach them many things. And now an hour a much

1096 4334 846 3588 3101 846 3004
γενομένης, προσελθόντες αὐτῷ οἱ μαθηταὶ αὐτοῦ λέγουσιν
having occurred, drawing near to Him the disciples of Him said,

3754 2048 2076 3588 5119 2532 2235 5610 4183 630
ὅτι Ἔρημός ἐστιν ὁ τόπος, καὶ ἤδη ὥρα πολλή· 36 ἀπόλυσον
deserted is The place, and now an hour much. Send away

846 2443 565 1519 3588 2945 68 2532 2968
αὐτούς, ἵνα ἀπελθόντες εἰς τοὺς κύκλῳ ἀγροὺς καὶ κώμας
them, that going away to the surrounding fields and villages

and commanded his head to be brought: and he went and beheaded him in the prison,
28 And brought his head in a charger, and gave it to the damsel: and the damsel gave it to her mother.

29 And when his disciples heard (of it), they came and took up his corpse, and laid it in a tomb.

30. And the apostles gathered themselves together unto Jesus, and told him all things, both what they had done, and what they had taught.

31 And he said unto them, Come ye yourselves apart into a desert place, and rest a while: for there were many coming and going, and they had no leisure so much as to eat.

32 And they departed into a desert place by ship privately.

33 And the people saw them departing, and many knew him, and ran afoot thither out of all cities, and outwent them, and came together unto him.
34 And Jesus, when he came out, saw much people, and was moved with compassion toward them, because they were as sheep not having a shepherd: and he began to teach them many things.

35 And when the day was now far spent, his disciples came unto him, and said, This is a desert place, and now the time (is) far passed:

36 Send them away, that they may go into the country round about, and into the villages,

Literal Translation

they may buy bread for themselves. For they do not have what they may eat.
37 And answering He said to them, You give them (food) to eat. And they said to Him, Going, should we buy two hundred denarii of loaves and give them to eat?
38 And He said to them, How many loaves do you have? Go and see. And knowing, they said, Five, and two fish.
39 And He ordered them all to recline, groups (by) groups on the green grass.
40 And they reclined, rows (by) rows, by hundred and by fifty.
41 And taking the five loaves and the two fish, looking up to Heaven, He blessed, and having broken the loaves, and giving out to His disciples, that they might set before them. And He divided the two fish to all.
42 And all ate and were satisfied.
43 And they took up twelve hand-baskets full (of) fragments, also from the fish.
44 And the (ones) eating the loaves were about five thousand men.
45. And at once He constrained His disciples to enter into the boat, and to go before to the other side, to Bethsaida, until He should dismiss the crowd.
46 And taking leave (of) them, He went away to the mountain to pray.
47 And evening having come, the boat was in (the) middle of the sea, and He alone on the land.
48 And He saw them being distressed in the row(ing),

Mark 6:37

59 1438 740 5101 1063 5315 3756 2192
ἀγοράσωσιν ἑαυτοῖς ἄρτους. τί γὰρ φάγωσιν οὐκ ἔχουσιν.
they may buy for themselves bread. what For they may eat not they have.

3588/1161 611 2036 846 1325 846 5210 5315 2532
37 ὁ δὲ ἀποκριθεὶς εἶπεν αὐτοῖς, Δότε αὐτοῖς ὑμεῖς φαγεῖν. καὶ
He But answering said to them, Give them you to eat. And

3004 846 565 59 1250 1220
λέγουσιν αὐτῷ, Ἀπελθόντες ἀγοράσωμεν διακοσίων δηνα-
they say to Him, going should we buy two hundred denarii

740 2532 1325 846 5315 3588 1161 3004 846
ρίων ἄρτους, καὶ δῶμεν αὐτοῖς φαγεῖν; 38 ὁ δὲ λέγει αὐτοῖς,
of loaves and give to them to eat? He And says to them,

4214 740 2192 5217 2532 1492 2532 1097
Πόσους ἄρτους ἔχετε; ὑπάγετε καὶ ἴδετε. καὶ γνόντες
How many loaves do you have? Go and see. And knowing

3004 4002 2532 1417 2486 2532 2004 846 347
λέγουσι, Πέντε, καὶ δύο ἰχθύας. 39 καὶ ἐπέταξεν αὐτοῖς ἀνα-
they say, Five, and two fish. And He ordered them to

3956 4849 4849 1909 3588 5515 5528
κλῖναι πάντας συμπόσια συμπόσια ἐπὶ τῷ χλωρῷ χόρτῳ.
recline all groups (by) groups on the green grass.

2532 377 4237 4237 302 1540 2532 303 4004
40 καὶ ἀνέπεσον πρασιαὶ πρασιαι, ἀνὰ ἑκατὸν καὶ ἀνὰ πεντή-
And they reclined rows (by) rows, by hundred and by fifty.

2532 2983 3588 4002 740 2532 3588 1417 2486
κοντα. 41 καὶ λαβὼν τοὺς πέντε ἄρτους καὶ τοὺς δύο ἰχθύας,
And taking the five loaves and the two fish,

308 1519 3588 3772 2127 2532 2622 3588
ἀναβλέψας εἰς τὸν οὐρανόν, εὐλόγησε, καὶ κατέκλασε τοὺς
looking up into Heaven, He blessed and breaking the

740 2532 1325 3588 3101 846 2443 3908
ἄρτους, καὶ ἐδίδου τοῖς μαθηταῖς αὐτοῦ ἵνα παραθῶσιν
loaves, and giving out to the disciples of Him that they may set before

846 2532 3588 1417 2486 3307 3956 2532 5315
αὐτοῖς· καὶ τοὺς δύο ἰχθύας ἐμέρισε πᾶσι. 42 καὶ ἔφαγον
them. And the two fish He divided to all. And ate,

3956 2532 5526 2532 142 280 1427
πάντες, καὶ ἐχορτάσθησαν· 43 καὶ ἦραν κλασμάτων δώδεκα
all, and were satisfied. And they took of fragments twelve

2894 4134 2532 575 3588 2486 2532 2258 3588 5315
κοφίνους πλήρεις, καὶ ἀπὸ τῶν ἰχθύων. 44 καὶ ἦσαν οἱ φαγόντες
hand-baskets full, also from the fish. And were the (ones) eating

3588 740 5616 4000 435
τοὺς ἄρτους ὡσεὶ πεντακισχίλιοι ἄνδρες.
the loaves about five thousand men.

2532 2112 315 3588 3101 846 1684 1519 3588
45. Καὶ εὐθέως ἠνάγκασε τοὺς μαθητὰς αὐτοῦ ἐμβῆναι εἰς τὸ
And at once He constrained the disciples of Him to enter into the

4143 2532 4254 1519 3588 4008 4314 966 2193
πλοῖον, καὶ προάγειν εἰς τὸ πέραν πρὸς Βηθσαϊδά, ἕως
boat, and to go before to the other side to Bethsaida, until

846 630 3588 3793 2532 657 846
αὐτὸς ἀπολύσῃ τὸν ὄχλον. 46 καὶ ἀποταξάμενος αὐτοῖς,
He should dismiss the crowd. And having taken leave (of) them,

565 1519 3588 3735 4336 2532 3798 1096
ἀπῆλθεν εἰς τὸ ὄρος προσεύξασθαι. 47 καὶ ὀψίας γενομένης,
He went away into the mount to pray. And evening occurring,

2258 3588 4143 1722 3319 3588 2281 2532 846 3441 1909 3588
ἦν τὸ πλοῖον ἐν μέσῳ τῆς θαλάσσης, καὶ αὐτὸς μόνος ἐπὶ τῆς
was the boat in (the) midst of the sea, and He alone on the

1093 2532 1492 846 928 1722 3588 1643 2258
γῆς. 48 καὶ εἶδεν αὐτοὺς βασανιζομένους ἐν τῷ ἐλαύνειν, ἦν
land. And He saw them being distressed in the row(ing), was

King James Version

and buy themselves bread: for they have nothing to eat.
37 He answered and said unto them, Give ye them to eat. And they say unto him, Shall we go and buy two hundred pennyworth of bread, and give them to eat?
38 He saith unto them, How many loaves have ye? go and see. And when they knew, they say, Five, and two fishes.
39 And he commanded them to make all sit down by companies upon the green grass.
40 And they sat down in ranks, by hundreds, and by fifties.
41 And when he had taken the five loaves and the two fishes, he looked up to heaven, and blessed, and brake the loaves, and gave (them) to his disciples to set before them; and the two fishes divided he among them all.
42 And they did all eat, and were filled.
43 And they took up twelve baskets full of the fragments, and of the fishes.
44 And they that did eat of the loaves were about five thousand men.
45. And straightway he constrained his disciples to get into the ship, and to go to the other side before unto Bethsaida, while he sent away the people.
46 And when he had sent them away, he departed into a mountain to pray.
47 And when even was come, the ship was in the midst of the sea, and he alone on the land.
48 And he saw them toiling in rowing;

Mark 6:49

Literal Translation

for the wind was contrary to them. And about the fourth watch of the night He came toward them, walking on the sea. And (He) willed to go by them.

49 But seeing Him walking on the sea, they thought it to be a phantom, and (they) cried out.

50 For all saw Him, and were troubled. And immediately He spoke to them and said to them, Have courage. I AM! Do not fear.

51 And He went up to them into the boat, and the wind sank. And they were amazed, exceedingly beyond measure within themselves, and marveled.

52 For they did not understand (the miracle of) the loaves, for their hearts were hardened.

53 And crossing over, they came into the land of Gennesaret and anchored near.

54 And they, coming out of the boat, at once knowing Him,

55 running around all that neighborhood. they began to carry about those badly (illness) having on cots to where they heard that He is.

56 And wherever He entered into villages or cities or fields, they laid the ailing (ones) in the markets, and begged Him that even they may touch the fringe of His garment. And as many as touched Him were healed.

1063 3588 417 1727 846 2532 4012 5067 5438
γὰρ ὁ ἄνεμος ἐναντίος αὐτοῖς, καὶ περὶ τετάρτην φυλακὴν
for the wind contrary to them. And about the fourth watch

3588 3571 2064 4314 846 4043 1909 3588
τῆς νυκτὸς ἔρχεται πρὸς αὐτούς, περιπατῶν ἐπὶ τῆς
of the night He comes toward them, walking on the

2281 2532 2309 3928 846 3588 1161 1492 846
θαλάσσης· καὶ ἤθελε παρελθεῖν αὐτούς. 49 οἱ δέ, ἰδόντες αὐτὸν
sea; and (He) willed to go by them. they But, seeing Him

4043 1909 3588 2281 1380 5326 1511
περιπατοῦντα ἐπὶ τῆς θαλάσσης, ἔδοξαν φάντασμα εἶναι,
walking around on the sea, thought a phantom it to be,

2532 349 3956 1063 846 1492 2532 5015
καὶ ἀνέκραξαν· 50 πάντες γὰρ αὐτὸν εἶδον, καὶ ἐταράχθησαν.
and cried out. all For Him saw, and were troubled.

2532 2112 2980 3326 846 2532 3004 846 2293
καὶ εὐθέως ἐλάλησε μετ' αὐτῶν, καὶ λέγει αὐτοῖς, Θαρσεῖτε·
And immediately He spoke with them, and says to them, Have courage;

1473 1510 3361 5399 2532 305 4314 846 1519 3588 4143
ἐγώ εἰμι, μὴ φοβεῖσθε. 51 καὶ ἀνέβη πρὸς αὐτοὺς εἰς τὸ πλοῖον,
I AM! not Do fear. And He went up to them into the boat,

2532 2869 3588 417 2532 3029 1537 4053 1722 1438
καὶ ἐκόπασεν ὁ ἄνεμος· καὶ λίαν ἐκ περισσοῦ ἐν ἑαυτοῖς
and sank the wind. And greatly beyond measure in themselves,

1839 2532 2296 3756 1063 4920 1909 3588 740
ἐξίσταντο, καὶ ἐθαύμαζον. 52 οὐ γὰρ συνῆκαν ἐπὶ τοῖς ἄρτοις·
they were amazed, and marveled. not For they understood about the loaves,

2258 1063 3588 2588 846 4456
ἦν γὰρ ἡ καρδία αὐτῶν πεπωρωμένη.
was for the hearts of them hardened.

2532 1276 2064 1909 3588 1093 1082 2532
53. Καὶ διαπεράσαντες ἦλθον ἐπὶ τὴν γῆν Γεννησαρέτ, καὶ
And crossing over they came onto the land of Gennesaret, and

4358 2532 1831 846 1537 3588 4143
προσωρμίσθησαν. 54 καὶ ἐξελθόντων αὐτῶν ἐκ τοῦ πλοίου,
anchored near. And coming out they from the boat,

2112 1921 846 4063 3650 3588 4066
εὐθέως ἐπιγνόντες αὐτόν, 55 περιδραμόντες ὅλην τὴν περίχω-
at once knowing Him, running around all neighborhood

1565 756 1909 3588 2895 3588 2560
ρον ἐκείνην, ἤρξαντο ἐπὶ τοῖς κραββάτοις τοὺς κακῶς
that., they began on the cots those badly (illness)

2192 4064 3699 191 3754 1563 2076 2532 3699 302
ἔχοντας περιφέρειν, ὅπου ἤκουον ὅτι ἐκεῖ ἐστι. 56 καὶ ὅπου ἂν
having to carry about, where they heard that there He is. And wherever

1531 1519 2968 2228 4172 2228 68 1722 3588 58
εἰσεπορεύετο εἰς κώμας ἢ πόλεις ἢ ἀγρούς, ἐν ταῖς ἀγοραῖς
He entered into villages or cities or fields, in the markets

5087 3588 770 2532 3870 846 2443 2579
ἐτίθουν τοὺς ἀσθενοῦντας, καὶ παρεκάλουν αὐτὸν ἵνα κἂν
they laid the ailing (ones), and begged Him that even

3588 2899 3588 2440 846 680 2532 3745 302
τοῦ κρασπέδου τοῦ ἱματίου αὐτοῦ ἅψωνται· καὶ ὅσοι ἂν
the fringe of the garment of Him they may touch; and as many as

680 846 4982
ἥπτοντο αὐτοῦ ἐσῴζοντο.
touched Him were healed.

King James Version

for the wind was contrary unto them: and about the fourth watch of the night he cometh unto them, walking upon the sea, and would have passed by them.

49 But when they saw him walking upon the sea, they supposed it had been a spirit, and cried out:

50 For they all saw him, and were troubled. And immediately he talked with them, and saith unto them, Be of good cheer: it is I; be not afraid.

51 And he went up unto them into the ship; and the wind ceased: and they were sore amazed in themselves beyond measure, and wondered.

52 For they considered not (the miracle) of the loaves: for their heart was hardened.

53 And when they had passed over, they came into the land of Gennesaret, and drew to the shore.

54 And when they were come out of the ship, straightway they knew him,

55 And ran through that whole region round about, and began to carry about in beds those that were sick, where they heard he was.

56 And whithersoever he entered, into villages, or cities, or country, they laid the sick in the streets, and besought him that they might touch if it were but the border of his garment: and as many as touched him were made whole.

Mark 7

Mark 7

1. And the Pharisees were assembled to Him, and some of the

2532 4863 4314 846 3588 5330 2532 5100 3588
1. Καὶ συνάγονται πρὸς αὐτὸν οἱ Φαρισαῖοι, καί τινες τῶν
And were assembled to Him the Pharisees, and some of the

Mark 7

1. Then came together unto him the Pharisees, and certain of the

Literal Translation

scribes, coming from Jerusalem.
2 And having seen some of His disciples eating loaves with unclean, that is unwashed hands, they found fault.

3 For the Pharisees and all the Jews do not eat unless they wash the hands with (the) fist, holding the tradition of the elders.

4 And (coming) from the market, they do not eat if not they dip themselves. And there are many other things which they received to hold: immersings of cups, and of utensils, and of copper vessels, and couches.
5 Then the Pharisees and scribes questioned Him, Why do your disciples not walk according to the tradition of the elders, but eat bread with unwashed hands?

6 And answering, He said to them, Well did Isaiah prophesy concerning you, hypocrites; as it has been written: "This people honors Me with the lips, but their heart is far away from Me;

7 but in vain they worship Me, teaching (as) doctrines commandments of men." (Isa. 29:13)
8 For forsaking the commandment of God, you hold the tradition of men: immersings of utensils and cups, and many other such like things you do.
9 And He said to them, Do you do well to set aside the commandment of God, that you may keep your tradition?
10 For Moses said, "Honor your father and your mother;" and, "The (one speaking)

Mark 7:2

1122 2065 575 2414 2532 1492 5100
γραμματέων, ἐλθόντες ἀπὸ Ἱεροσολύμων· 2 καὶ ἰδόντες τινὰς
scribes, coming from Jerusalem. And having seen some

3588 3101 846 2839 5495 ---5123--- 449
τῶν μαθητῶν αὐτοῦ κοιναῖς χερσί, τοῦτ᾽ ἔστιν ἀνίπτοις,
of the disciples of Him with unclean hands, that is unwashed,

2068 740 3201 3588 1063 5330 2532 3956
ἐσθίοντας ἄρτους ἐμέμψαντο. 3 οἱ γὰρ Φαρισαῖοι καὶ πάντες
eating loaves they found fault. the For Pharisees and all

3588 2453 - 3362 - 4435 3538 3588 5495 3756
οἱ Ἰουδαῖοι, ἐὰν μὴ πυγμῇ νίψωνται τὰς χεῖρας, οὐκ
the Jews if not (with the) fist they wash the hands, not

2068 2902 3588 3862 3588 4245
ἐσθίουσι, κρατοῦντες τὴν παράδοσιν τῶν πρεσβυτέρων·
do they eat, holding the tradition of the elders;

2532 575 58 - 3362 - 907 3756 2068 2532
4 καὶ ἀπὸ ἀγορᾶς, ἐὰν μὴ βαπτίσωνται, οὐκ ἐσθίουσι· καὶ
and from market if not they may dip themselves, not they eat; and

243 4183 2076 3588 3880 2902 909
ἄλλα πολλά ἐστιν ἃ παρέλαβον κρατεῖν, βαπτισμοὺς
other many things there are which they received to hold, immersings

1905 2532 3582 2532 5473 2532 2825 1899
ποτηρίων καὶ ξεστῶν καὶ χαλκίων καὶ κλινῶν. 5 ἔπειτα
of cups and of utensils and of copper (things) and couches. Then

1905 846 3588 5330 2532 3588 1122 1302 3588
ἐπερωτῶσιν αὐτὸν οἱ Φαρισαῖοι καὶ οἱ γραμματεῖς, Διατί οἱ
question Him the Pharisees and the scribes, Why the

3101 4675 3756 4043 2596 3588 3862 3588
μαθηταί σου οὐ περιπατοῦσι κατὰ τὴν παράδοσιν τῶν
disciples of you not walk according to the tradition of the

4245 235 449 5495 2098 3588 740
πρεσβυτέρων, ἀλλὰ ἀνίπτοις χερσὶν ἐσθίουσι τὸν ἄρτον;
elders, but with unwashed hands eat the bread?

3588 1161 611 2036 846 3754 2573 4395
6 ὁ δὲ ἀποκριθεὶς εἶπεν αὐτοῖς ὅτι Καλῶς προεφήτευσεν
He And answering said to them, Well prophesied

2268 4012 5216 3588 5273 5613 1125 3778 3588
Ἠσαΐας περὶ ὑμῶν τῶν ὑποκριτῶν, ὡς γέγραπται, Οὗτος ὁ
Isaiah concerning you hypocrites, as it has been written, This

2992 3588 5491 3165 5091/3588/1161 2588 846 4206 568
λαὸς τοῖς χείλεσί με τιμᾷ, ἡ δὲ καρδία αὐτῶν πόρρω ἀπέχει
people with the lips Me honors, the but heart of them far is away

575 1700 3155 1161 4576 3165 1321 1319
ἀπ᾽ ἐμοῦ. 7 μάτην δὲ σέβονταί με, διδάσκοντες διδασκαλίας
from Me; in vain but they worship Me, teaching (as) doctrines

1778 444 863 1063 3588 1785 3588 2316
ἐντάλματα ἀνθρώπων. 8 ἀφέντες γὰρ τὴν ἐντολὴν τοῦ Θεοῦ,
commandments of men. forsaking For the commandment of God,

2902 3588 3862 3588 444 909
κρατεῖτε τὴν παράδοσιν τῶν ἀνθρώπων, βαπτισμοὺς
you hold the tradition of men, immersings

3582 2532 4221 2532 243 3946 5108 4183
ξεστῶν καὶ ποτηρίων· καὶ ἄλλα παρόμοια τοιαῦτα πολλὰ
of utensils and cups, and other like things such many

4160 2532 3004 846 2573 114 3588 1785 3588
ποιεῖτε. 9 καὶ ἔλεγεν αὐτοῖς, Καλῶς ἀθετεῖτε τὴν ἐντολὴν τοῦ
you do. And He said to them, Well do you set aside the commandment

2316 2443 3588 3862 4216 5083 3475 1063 2036
Θεου, ἵνα τὴν παράδοσιν ὑμῶν τηρήσητε. 10 Μωσῆς γὰρ εἶπε,
of God, that the tradition of you you may keep. Moses For said,

5091 3588 3962 4675 2532 3588 3384 4675 2532 3588 2551
Τίμα τὸν πατέρα σου καὶ τὴν μητέρα σου· καί, Ὁ κακο-
Honor the father of you and the mother of you; and He speak-

King James Version

scribes, which came from Jerusalem.
2 And when they saw some of his disciples eat bread with defiled, that is to say, with unwashen, hands, they found fault.
3 For the Pharisees, and all the Jews, except they wash (their) hands oft, eat not, holding the tradition of the elders.

4 And (when they come) from the market, except they wash, they eat not. And many other things there be, which they have received to hold, (as) the washing of cups, and pots, brasen vessels, and of tables.
5 Then the Pharisees and scribes asked him, Why walk not thy disciples according to the tradition of the elders, but eat bread with unwashen hands?

6 He answered and said unto them, Well hath Esaias prophesied of you hypocrites, as it is written, This people honoureth me with (their) lips, but their heart is far from me.

7 Howbeit in vain do they worship me, teaching (for) doctrines the commandments of men.
8 For laying aside the commandment of God, ye hold the tradition of men, (as) the washing of pots and cups: and many other such like things ye do.

9 And he said unto them, Full well ye reject the commandment of God, that ye may keep your own tradition.
10 For Moses said, Honour thy father and thy mother; and, Whoso

Literal Translation | **Mark 7:11** | **King James Version**

evil of father or mother, let him end by death." (Ex. 21:17; Deut. 5:16)
11 But you say, If a man, says to (his) father or mother, Corban, (which is, A gift!) whatever you may profit by me.
12 And you no longer allow him to do anything for (his) father or his mother,
13 making void the Word of God by your tradition which you delivered. And many such like things you do.

14. And having called all the crowd near, He said to them, All hear Me and understand.

15 There is nothing from outside the man, having entered into him, which is able to defile (him). But the things passing out from him, those are the things defiling the man.

16 If anyone has ears to hear, let him hear.
17 And when He went into a house from the crowd, His disciples questioned Him about the parable.
18 And He said to them, Are you also so undiscerning? Do you not perceive that everything having entered from the outside into the man is not able to defile him?
19 (This is) because it does not enter into his heart, but into the belly, and goes out into the toilet bowl, purging all the foods.

20 And He said, That passing out of the man, it is the thing that defiles the man.
21 For from within, out of the heart of men, pass out the depraved thoughts, adulteries, fornications, murders,
22 thefts, greedy desires,

3962 2228 3384 2288 5053 5210 1161 3004
λογῶν πατέρα ἢ μητέρα θανάτῳ τελευτάτω· 11 ὑμεῖς δὲ λέγετε,
ing evil of father or mother by death let him end. you But say,

1437 2036 444 3588 3962 2228 3588 3384 2878 3603 2076
Ἐὰν εἴπῃ ἄνθρωπος τῷ πατρὶ ἢ τῇ μητρί, Κορβᾶν, ὅ ἐστι,
If says a man to the father or the mother, Corban (which is,

1435 3588 1437 1537 1700 5623 2532 3765 863 846
δῶρον, ὃ ἐὰν ἐξ ἐμοῦ ὠφεληθῇς· 12 καὶ οὐκέτι ἀφίετε αὐτὸν
a gift), whatever by me you might profit; and no longer you allow him

3762 4160 3588 3962 846 2228 3588 3384 846 208
οὐδὲν ποιῆσαι τῷ πατρὶ αὐτοῦ ἢ τῇ μητρὶ αὐτοῦ, 13 ἀκυ-
nothing to do for the father of him or the mother of him, making

3588 3056 3588 2316 3588 3862 5216 3739 3860
ροῦντες τὸν λόγον τοῦ Θεοῦ τῇ παραδόσει ὑμῶν ἣ παρεδώ-
void the Word of God by the tradition of you which you

2532 3946 5108 4183 4160 2532 4341
κατε· καὶ παρόμοια τοιαῦτα πολλὰ ποιεῖτε. 14 καὶ προσκαλε-
delivered. And like things such many you do. And having called

3956 3588 3793 3004 846 191 3450
σάμενος πάντα τὸν ὄχλον, ἔλεγεν αὐτοῖς, Ἀκούετέ μου
near all the crowd, He said to them, Hear Me

3956 2532 4920 3762 2076 1855 3588 444
πάντες, καὶ συνίετε. 15 οὐδέν ἐστιν ἔξωθεν τοῦ ἀνθρώπου
all, and understand. nothing There is from outside the man

1531 1519 846 3739 1410 846 2840 235
εἰσπορευόμενον εἰς αὐτόν, ὃ δύναται αὐτὸν κοινῶσαι· ἀλλὰ
having entered into him, which is able him to defile; but

3588 1607 575 846 1565 2076 3588 2840 3588
τὰ ἐκπορευόμενα ἀπ᾽ αὐτοῦ, ἐκεῖνά ἐστι τὰ κοινοῦντα τὸν
the things going out from him, those are the things defiling the

444 -1536- 2192 3775 191 191 2532 3753
ἄνθρωπον. 16 εἴ τις ἔχει ὦτα ἀκούειν ἀκουέτω. 17 καὶ ὅτε
man. If anyone has ears to hear let him hear. And when

1525 1519 3624 575 3588 3793 1905 846 3588 3101
εἰσῆλθεν εἰς οἶκον ἀπὸ τοῦ ὄχλου, ἐπηρώτων αὐτὸν οἱ μαθηταὶ
he went into a house from the crowd, questioned Him the disciples

846 4012 3588 3850 2532 3004 846 3779 2532
αὐτοῦ περὶ τῆς παραβολῆς. 18 καὶ λέγει αὐτοῖς, Οὕτω καὶ
of Him about the parable. And He says to them. So also

5210 801 2075 3756 3539 3754/3956/3588 1855 1531
ὑμεῖς ἀσύνετοί ἐστε; οὐ νοεῖτε ὅτι πᾶν τὸ ἔξωθεν εἰσπορευό-
you undiscerning are? Not perceive you that every thing from outside having

1519 3588 444 3756 1410 846 2840 3754
μενον εἰς τὸν ἄνθρωπον οὐ δύναται αὐτὸν κοινῶσαι, 19 ὅτι
entered into the man not is able him to defile, because

3756 1531 846 1519 3588 2588 235 1519 3588
οὐκ εἰσπορεύεται αὐτοῦ εἰς τὴν καρδίαν, ἀλλ᾽ εἰς τὴν
not it does enter of him into the heart, but into the

2836 2532 1519 3588 856 1607 2511
κοιλίαν· καὶ εἰς τὸν ἀφεδρῶνα ἐκπορεύεται, καθαρίζον
belly, and into the toilet bowl goes out, purging

3956 3588 1033 3004 1161 3754 3588 1537 3588 444
πάντα τὰ βρώματα. 20 ἔλεγε δὲ ὅτι Τὸ ἐκ τοῦ ἀνθρώπου
all the foods. He said And, The thing out of the man

1607 1565 2840 3588 444 2081 1063
ἐκπορευόμενον, ἐκεῖνο κοινοῖ τὸν ἄνθρωπον· 21 ἔσωθεν γάρ,
passing out, (it is) that defiles the man. from within For,

1537 3588 2588 3588 444 3588 1261 3588 2556
ἐκ τῆς καρδίας τῶν ἀνθρώπων, οἱ διαλογισμοὶ οἱ κακοὶ
out of the heart of men, thoughts depraved

1607 3430 4202 5408 2829 4124
ἐκπορεύονται, μοιχεῖαι, πορνεῖαι, φόνοι, 22 κλοπαί, πλεονεξίαι,
pass out, adulteries, fornications, murders, thefts, greedy desires,

---

curseth father or mother, let him die the death:
11 But ye say, If a man shall say to his father or mother, (It is) Corban, that is to say, a gift, by whatsoever thou mightest be profited by me; (he shall be free).
12 And ye suffer him no more to do ought for his father or his mother;
13 Making the word of God of none effect through your tradition, which ye have delivered: and many such like things do ye.
14. And when he had called all the people (unto him), he said unto them, Hearken unto me every one (of you), and understand:
15 There is nothing from without a man, that entering into him can defile him: but the things which come out of him, those are they that defile the man.

16 If any man have ears to hear, let him hear.
17 And when he was entered into the house from the people, his disciples asked him concerning the parable.
18 And he saith unto them, Are ye so without understanding also? Do ye not perceive, that whatsoever thing from without entereth into the man, (it) cannot defile him;
19 Because it entereth not into his heart, but into the belly, and goeth out into the draught, purging all meats?

20 And he said, That which cometh out of the man, that defileth the man.
21 For from within, out of the heart of men, proceed evil thoughts, adulteries, fornications, murders,
22 Thefts, covetousness,

Literal Translation | **Mark 7:23** | **King James Version**

iniquities, deceit, lustful desires, a wicked eye, blasphemy, pride, foolishness.
23 All these evil things pass out from within and defile the man.

4189 1388 766 3788 4190 988
πονηρίαι, δόλος, ἀσέλγεια, ὀφθαλμὸς πονηρός, βλασφημία,
iniquities, deceit, lustful desires, an eye wicked, blasphemy,
5243 877 3956 5023 3588 4190 2081
ὑπερηφανία, ἀφροσύνη· 23 πάντα ταῦτα τὰ πονηρὰ ἔσωθεν
pride, foolishness; all these things evil from within
1607 2532 2840 3588 444
ἐκπορεύεται, καὶ κοινοῖ τὸν ἄνθρωπον.
pass out and defile the man.

wickedness, deceit, lasciviousness, an evil eye, blasphemy, pride, foolishness:
23 All these evil things come from within, and defile the man.

24. And rising up from there, he went away into the borders of Tyre and Sidon. And entering into the house, no one He desired to know, but He could not be hidden.
25 For having heard about Him, a woman came up, (one) whose little daughter had an unclean spirit, (and) she fell down at His feet.

26 And the woman was a Greek, a Syro-phenician by race. And she asked Him, that He would cast out the demon from her little daughter.
27 And Jesus said to her, First, allow the children to be satisfied, for it is not good to take the children's bread and to throw (it) to the dogs.

28 But she answered and said to Him, Yes, Lord; for even the little dogs under the table eat from the crumbs of the children.

2532 1564 450 565 1519 3588 3181 5184 2532
24. Καί ἐκεῖθεν ἀναστὰς ἀπῆλθεν εἰς τὰ μεθόρια Τύρου καὶ
And from there rising up He went away into the borders of Tyre and
4605 2532 1525 1519 3588 3614 3762 2309 1097
Σιδῶνος. καὶ εἰσελθὼν εἰς τὴν οἰκίαν, οὐδένα ἤθελε γνῶναι,
Sidon. And entering into the house, no one He desired to know,
2532/3756 1410 2990 191 1063 1135 4012 846 3739
καὶ οὐκ ἠδυνήθη λαθεῖν. 25 ἀκούσασα γὰρ γυνὴ περὶ αὐτοῦ, ἧς
but not He could be hidden. having heard For a woman about Him, of whom
2192 3588 2365 846 4151 169 2064
εἶχε τὸ θυγάτριον αὐτῆς πνεῦμα ἀκάθαρτον, ἐλθοῦσα
had the little daughter of her a spirit unclean, coming
4363 4314 3588 4228 846 2258/1161/3588/1135 1674
προσέπεσε πρὸς τοὺς πόδας αὐτοῦ· 26 ἦν δὲ ἡ γυνὴ Ἑλληνίς,
(she) fell down at the feet of Him. was And the woman a Greek,
4949 3588 1085 2532 2065 846 2443 3588 1140
Συροφοίνισσα τῷ γένει· καὶ ἠρώτα αὐτὸν ἵνα τὸ δαιμόνιον
a Syro-phoenician by race. And she asked Him that the demon
1544 1537 3588 2364 846 3588 1161 2424 2036 846
ἐκβάλλῃ ἐκ τῆς θυγατρὸς αὐτῆς. 27 ὁ δὲ Ἰησοῦς εἶπεν αὐτῇ,
He cast out from the little daughter of her. But Jesus said to her,
863 4412 5526 3588 5043 3756 1063 2570 2076
Ἄφες πρῶτον χορτασθῆναι τὰ τέκνα· οὐ γὰρ καλόν ἐστι
Allow first to be satisfied the children. not For good is
2983 3588 740 3588 5043 2532 906 3588 2952 3588
λαβεῖν τὸν ἄρτον τῶν τέκνων καὶ βαλεῖν τοῖς κυναρίοις.28 ἡ
to take the bread of the children and to throw (it) to the dogs. she
1161 611 2532 3004 846 3483 2962 2532 1063 3588 2952
δὲ ἀπεκρίθη καὶ λέγει αὐτῷ, Ναί, Κύριε· καὶ γὰρ τὰ κυνάρια
But answered and said to Him, Yes, Lord; even for the little dogs
5270 3588 5132 2068 575 3588 5589 3588 3813
ὑποκάτω τῆς τραπέζης ἐσθίει ἀπὸ τῶν ψιχίων τῶν παιδίων.
under the table eat from the crumbs of the children.

24. And from thence he arose, and went into the borders of Tyre and Sidon, and entered into an house, and would have no man know (it): but he could not be hid.
25 For a (certain) woman, whose young daughter had an unclean spirit, heard of him, and came and fell at his feet:

26 The woman was a Greek, a Syrophenician by nation; and she besought him that he would cast forth the devil out of her daughter.
27 But Jesus said unto her, Let the children first be filled: for it is not meet to take the children's bread, and to cast (it) unto the dogs.

28 And she answered and said unto him, Yes, Lord: yet the dogs under the table eat of the children's crumbs.

29 And He said to her, Because of this word, go. The demon has gone out from your daughter.
30 And going away to her house, she found the demon had gone out, and her little daughter was thrown upon the couch.

2532 2036 846 1223 5126 3588 3056 5217 1831 3588
29 καὶ εἶπεν αὐτῇ, Διὰ τοῦτον τὸν λόγον ὕπαγε· ἐξελήλυθε τὸ
And He said to her, Because of this word go; has gone out the
1140 1537/3588 2364 4675 2532 565 1519/3588 3624
δαιμόνιον ἐκ τῆς θυγατρός σου. 30καὶ ἀπελθοῦσα εἰς τὸν οἶκον
demon from the little daughter of you .And going away into the house
846 2147 3588 1140 1831 2532 3588 2364
αὐτῆς, εὗρε τὸ δαιμόνιον ἐξεληλυθός, καὶ τὴν θυγατέρα
of her, she found the demon had gone out, and the little daughter
906 1909 3588 2825
βεβλημένην ἐπὶ τῆς κλίνης.
was thrown upon the couch.

29 And he said unto her, For this saying go thy way; the devil is gone out of thy daughter.
30 And when she was come to her house, she found the devil gone out, and her daughter laid upon the bed.

31. And again going out from the borders of Tyre and Sidon, He came to the Sea of Galilee, in the midst of the borders of Decapolis.
32 And they bring a deaf one to Him, hardly speaking. And

2532 3825 1831 1537 3588 3725 5184 2532 4605 2064
31.Καὶ πάλιν ἐξελθὼν ἐκ τῶν ὁρίων Τύρου καὶ Σιδῶνος, ἦλθε
And again going out from the borders of Tyre and Sidon, He came
4314 3588 2281 3588 1056 303 3319 3588 3725
πρὸς τὴν θάλασσαν τῆς Γαλιλαίας, ἀνὰ μέσον τῶν ὁρίων
to the Sea of Galilee, in the midst of the borders
1179 2532 5342 846 2974 3424 2532
Δεκαπόλεως. 32 καὶ φέρουσιν αὐτῷ κωφὸν μογιλάλον, καὶ
of (the) Decapolis. And they bring to Him a deaf one, hardly speaking, and

31. And again, departing from the coasts of Tyre and Sidon, he came unto the sea of Galilee, through the midst of the coasts of Decapolis.
32 And they bring unto him one that was deaf, and had an impediment in his speech; and

Literal Translation | **Mark 7:33** | *King James Version*

they begged Him, that He put (His) hand on him.
33 And taking him away from the crowd privately, He put His fingers into his ears; and having spit, He touched his tongue;

34 and looking up into the heaven, He groaned and said to him, Ephphatha! (which is, Be opened!)
35 And instantly his ears were opened, and the bond of his tongue was loosened, and he spoke correctly.

36 And He ordered them that they should tell no one. But as much as He ordered them, much more abundantly they proclaimed.

37 And they were most exceedingly amazed, saying, He has done all things well. He makes even the deaf to hear, and the dumb to speak.

3870 846 2443 2007 846 3588 5495 2532 618
παρακαλοῦσιν αὐτὸν ἵνα ἐπιθῇ αὐτῷ τὴν χεῖρα. 33 καὶ ἀπολα-
they begged Him that He put on him the hands. And taking

846 575 3588 3793 2596 2398 906 3588 1147
βόμενος αὐτὸν ἀπὸ τοῦ ὄχλου κατ' ἰδίαν, ἔβαλε τοὺς δα-
away him from the crowd privately, He put the

846 1519 3588 3775 846 2532 4429 680 3588
κτύλους αὐτοῦ εἰς τὰ ὦτα αὐτοῦ, καὶ πτύσας ἥψατο τῆς
fingers of Him into the ears of him, and having spit He touched the

1100 846 2532 308 1519 3588 3772 4727
γλώσσης αὐτοῦ, 34 καὶ ἀναβλέψας εἰς τὸν οὐρανόν, ἐστέναξε,
tongue of him, and looking up into the heaven, He groaned,

2532 3004 846 2188 3739 2076 1272 2532 2112
καὶ λέγει αὐτῷ, Ἐφφαθά, ὅ ἐστι, Διανοίχθητι. 35 καὶ εὐθέως
and says to him, Ephphatha! which is, Be opened! And instantly

1272 846 3588 189 2532 3089 3588 1199 3588 1100
διηνοίχθησαν αὐτοῦ αἱ ἀκοαί· καὶ ἐλύθη ὁ δεσμὸς τῆς γλώσ-
were opened of him the ears; and was loosened the bond of the tongue

846 2532 2980 3723 2532 1291 846 2443
σης αὐτοῦ, καὶ ἐλάλει ὀρθῶς. 36 καὶ διεστείλατο αὐτοῖς ἵνα
of him, and he spoke correctly. And He ordered them that

3367 2036 3745 1161 846 846 1291 3123
μηδενὶ εἴπωσιν· ὅσον δὲ αὐτὸς αὐτοῖς διεστέλλετο, μᾶλλον
no one they should tell. as much as But He them ordered, much

4053 2784 2532 5249 1605
περισσότερον ἐκήρυσσον. 37 καὶ ὑπερπερισσῶς ἐξεπλήσσοντο,
more abundantly they proclaimed. And most exceedingly they were amazed,

3004 2573 3956 4160 2532 3588 2974 4160
λέγοντες, Καλῶς πάντα πεποίηκε· καὶ τοὺς κωφοὺς ποιεῖ
saying, well all things He has done; even the deaf He makes

191 2532 3588 216 2980
ἀκούειν, καὶ τοὺς ἀλάλους λαλεῖν.
to hear, and the dumb to speak.

they beseech him to put his hand upon him.
33 And he took him aside from the multitude, and put his fingers into his ears, and he spit, and touched his tongue;

34 And looking up to heaven, he sighed, and saith unto him, Ephphatha, that is, Be opened.
35 And straightway his ears were opened, and the string of his tongue was loosed, and he spake plain.

36 And he charged them that they should tell no man: but the more he charged them, so much the more a great deal they published (it);
37 And were beyond measure astonished, saying, He hath done all things well: he maketh both the deaf to hear, and the dumb to speak.

Mark 8

1. The crowd being very great in those days, and not having anything they may eat, Jesus, having called nearHis disciples, said to them,
2 I have pity on the crowd because now three days they continue with Me, and they do not have what they may eat.

3 And if I send them away fasting to their house, they will faint in the way, for some of them come from afar.
4 And His disciples answered Him, From where will anyone here be able to satisfy these (with) loaves in a deserted (place)?

5 And He asked them, How many loaves do you have? And they said, Seven.

Mark 8

1722 1565 3588 2250 3827 3793 5607 2532
1. Ἐν ἐκείναις ταῖς ἡμέραις, παμπόλλου ὄχλου ὄντος, καὶ
In those days, very great the crowd being, and

3361 2192 5101 5315 4341 3588 2424 3588
μὴ ἐχόντων τί φάγωσι, προσκαλεσάμενος ὁ Ἰησοῦς τοὺς
not having anything they may eat, having called near Jesus the

3101 846 3004 846 4697 1909 3588 3793
μαθητὰς αὐτοῦ λέγει αὐτοῖς, 2 Σπλαγχνίζομαι ἐπὶ τὸν ὄχλον·
disciples of Him He says to them, I have pity on the crowd,

3754 2235 2250 5140 4357 3427 2532 3756 2192 5101
ὅτι ἤδη ἡμέρας τρεῖς προσμένουσί μοι, καὶ οὐκ ἔχουσι τί
because now days three they continue with Me, and not have what

5315 2532 1437 630 846 3523 1519 3624 846
φάγωσι· 3 καὶ ἐὰν ἀπολύσω αὐτοὺς νήστεις εἰς οἶκον αὐτῶν,
they may eat. And if I send away them fasting to (the) house of them,

1590 1722 3588 3598 5100 1063 846 3113 2240
ἐκλυθήσονται ἐν τῇ ὁδῷ· τινὲς γὰρ αὐτῶν μακρόθεν ἥκασι.
they will faint in the way; some for of them from afar are come.

2532 611 846 3588 3101 846 4159 5128
4 καὶ ἀπεκρίθησαν αὐτῷ οἱ μαθηταὶ αὐτοῦ, Πόθεν τούτους
And answered Him the disciples of Him, From where these

1410 5100 5602 5526 740 1909 2047 2532
δυνήσεταί τις ὧδε χορτάσαι ἄρτων ἐπ' ἐρημίας; 5 καὶ
will be able anyone here to satisfy (with) loaves on a deserted (place); and

1905 846 4214 2192 740 3588/1161/2036 2033
ἐπηρώτα αὐτούς, Πόσους ἔχετε ἄρτους; οἱ δὲ εἶπον, Ἑπτά.
He asked them, How many have you loaves? they And said, Seven.

Mark 8

1. In those days the multitude being very great, and having nothing to eat, Jesus called his disciples (unto him), and saith unto them,
2 I have compassion on the multitude, because they have now been with me three days, and have nothing to eat:

3 And if I send them away fasting to their own houses, they will faint by the way: for divers of them came from far.
4 And his disciples answered him, From whence can a man satisfy these (men) with bread here in the wilderness?
5 And he asked them, How many loaves have ye? And they said, Seven.

Literal Translation **Mark 8:6** ***King James Version***

6 And He ordered the crowd to recline on the ground. And taking the seven loaves, giving thanks, He broke and gave to His disciples, that they might serve. And they served the crowd.
7 And they had a few fish. And blessing, He said for these also to be served.
8 And they ate, and were satisfied. And (they) took up over and above seven lunch baskets (of) fragments.
9 And those eating were about four thousand. And He sent them away.
10. And at once entering into the boat with His disciples, He came into the region of Dalmanutha.

2532 3853 3588 3793 377 1909 3588 1093 2532 2983
6 καὶ παρήγγειλε τῷ ὄχλῳ ἀναπεσεῖν ἐπὶ τῆς γῆς· καὶ λαβὼν
And He ordered the crowd to recline on the ground. And taking
3588 2033 740 2168 2806 2532 1325 3588
τοὺς ἑπτὰ ἄρτους, εὐχαριστήσας ἔκλασε καὶ ἐδίδου τοῖς
the seven loaves, having given thanks, He broke and gave to the
3101 846 2443 3908 2532 3908 3588 3793
μαθηταῖς αὐτοῦ, ἵνα παραθῶσι· καὶ παρέθηκαν τῷ ὄχλῳ.
disciples of Him, that they may serve. And they served the crowd.
2532 2192 2485 3641 2532 2127 2036 3908 2532
7 καὶ εἶχον ἰχθύδια ὀλίγα· καὶ εὐλογήσας εἶπε παραθεῖναι καὶ
And they had fish a few. And having blessed He said to be served also
846 5315 1161 2532 5526 2532 142 4051
αὐτά. 8 ἔφαγον δέ, καὶ ἐχορτάσθησαν· καὶ ἦραν περισσεύματα
these. they ate And, and were satisfied, and took up over and above
2801 2033 4711 2258 1161 3588 5315 5613
κλασμάτων ἑπτὰ σπυρίδας. 9 ἦσαν δὲ οἱ φαγόντες ὡς
of fragments seven lunch-baskets. were And those eating about
5070 2532 630 846 2532 2112 1684 1519
τετρακισχίλιοι· καὶ ἀπέλυσεν αὐτούς. 10 καὶ εὐθέως ἐμβὰς εἰς
four thousand; and He sent away them. And at once entering into
3588 4143 3326 3588 3101 846 2064 1519 3588 3313
τὸ πλοῖον μετὰ τῶν μαθητῶν αὐτοῦ, ἦλθεν εἰς τὰ μέρη
the boat with the disciples of Him, He came into the region
1148
Δαλμανουθά.
of Dalmanutha.

6 And he commanded the people to sit down on the ground: and he took the seven loaves, and gave thanks, and brake, and gave to his disciples to set before (them); and they did set (them) before the people.
7 And they had a few small fishes: and he blessed, and commanded to set them also before (them).
8 So they did eat, and were filled: and they took up of the broken (meat) that was left seven baskets.
9 And they that had eaten were about four thousand: and he sent them away.
10. And straightway he entered into a ship with his disciples, and came into the parts of Dalmanutha.

11 And the Pharisees went out and began to argue with Him, seeking from Him a sign from Heaven, tempting Him.
12 And groaning in His spirit, He said, Why does this generation seek a sign? Truly I say to you, (As) if this generation will be given a sign!
13 And leaving them, again entering into the boat, He went away to the other side.

2532 1831 3588 5330 2532 756 4802 846
11. Καὶ ἐξῆλθον οἱ Φαρισαῖοι, καὶ ἤρξαντο συζητεῖν αὐτῷ,
And went out the Pharisees, and began to argue with Him,
2212 3844 846 4592 575 3588 3772 3985
ζητοῦντες παρ' αὐτοῦ σημεῖον ἀπὸ τοῦ οὐρανοῦς, πειρά-
seeking from Him a sign from Heaven, tempting
846 2532 389 3588 4151 846 3004
ζοντες αὐτόν. 12 καὶ ἀναστενάξας τῷ πνεύματι αὐτοῦ λέγει,
Him. And groaning in the spirit of Him He says,
5101 3588 1074 3778 4592 1934 281 3004 5213 1487
Τί ἡ γενεὰ αὕτη σημεῖον ἐπιζητεῖ; ἀμὴν λέγω ὑμῖν, εἰ
Why generation this a sign seeks? Truly I say to you, (As) if
1325 3588 1074 3778 4592 2532 863 846 1684
δοθήσεται τῇ γενεᾷ ταύτῃ σημεῖον. 13 καὶ ἀφεὶς αὐτούς, ἐμβὰς
will be given generation to this a sign! And leaving them, entering
3825 1519 3588 4143 565 1519 3588 4008
πάλιν εἰς τὸ πλοῖον, ἀπῆλθεν εἰς τὸ πέραν.
again into the boat, He went away to the other side.

11 And the Pharisees came forth, and began to question with him, seeking of him a sign from heaven, tempting him.
12 And he sighed deeply in his spirit, and saith, Why doth this generation seek after a sign? verily I say unto you, There shall no sign be given unto this generation.
13 And he left them, and entering into the ship again departed to the other side.

14. And the disciples forgot to take loaves. And they did not have (any) with themselves in the boat, except one loaf.
15 And He charged them, saying, See! Look out from the leaven of the Pharisees, and of the leaven of Herod.
16 And they reasoned with one another, saying, Because we have no loaves.
17 And knowing, Jesus said to them, Why do you reason because you have no loaves?

2532 1950 3588 3101 2983 740 2532 1487 3361 1520
14. Καὶ ἐπελάθοντο οἱ μαθηταὶ λαβεῖν ἄρτους, καὶ εἰ μὴ ἕνα
And forgot the disciples to take loaves, and except one
740 3756 2192 3326 1438 1722 3588 4143 2532 1291
ἄρτον οὐκ εἶχον μεθ' ἑαυτῶν ἐν τῷ πλοίῳ. 15 καὶ διεστέλλετο
loaf not they had with themselves in the boat. And he charged
846 3004 3708 991 575 3588 2219 3588
αὐτοῖς, λέγων, Ὁρᾶτε, βλέπετε ἀπὸ τῆς ζύμης τῶν
them, saying, See, look out from the leaven of the
5330 2532 3588 2219 2264 2532 1260 4314
Φαρισαίων καὶ τῆς ζύμης Ἡρώδου. 16 καὶ διελογίζοντο πρὸς
Pharisees and of the leaven of Herod. And they reasoned with
240 3004 3754 740 3756 2192 2532 1097 3588
ἀλλήλους, λέγοντες ὅτι Ἄρτους οὐκ ἔχομεν. 17 καὶ γνοὺς ὁ
one another, saying, Because loaves not we have. And knowing
2424 3004 846 5101 1260 3754 740 3756 2192
Ἰησοῦς λέγει αὐτοῖς, Τί διαλογίζεσθε ὅτι ἄρτους οὐκ ἔχετε;
Jesus says to them, Why do you reason because loaves not you have?

14. Now (the disciples) had forgotten to take bread, neither had they in the ship with them more than one loaf.
15 And he charged them, saying, Take heed, beware of the leaven of the Pharisees, and (of) the leaven of Herod.
16 And they reasoned among themselves, saying, (It is) because we have no bread.
17 And when Jesus knew (it), he saith unto them, Why reason ye, because ye have no bread?

Literal Translation **Mark 8:18** *King James Version*

Do you not yet perceive nor realize? Have you still hardened your heart?
18 Having eyes, do you not see? And having ears, do you not hear? And do you not remember? (Jer. 5:21)
19 When I broke the five loaves to the five thousand, how many hand-baskets full of fragments did you take up? They said to Him, Twelve.
20 And when the seven to the four thousand, how many lunch-baskets did you take up (with the) fillings of fragments? And they said, Seven.
21 And He said to them, How do you not understand?

3768 3539 3761 4920 2089 4456 2192 3588
οὔπω νοεῖτε, οὐδὲ συνίετε; ἔπι πεπωρωμένην ἔχετε τὴν
not yet Do you perceive, nor realize? still hardened have you the

2588 5216 3788 2192 3756 991 2532 3775
καρδίαν ὑμῶν; 18 ὀφθαλμοὺς ἔχοντες οὐ βλέπετε; καὶ ὦτα
heart of you? eyes Having not do you see? And ears

2192 3756 191 2532 3756 3421 3753 3588 4002
ἔχοντες οὐκ ἀκούετε; καὶ οὐ μνημονεύετε; 19 ὅτε τοὺς πέντε
having not do you hear? And not do you remember? When the five

740 2806 1519 3588 4000 4214 2894
ἄρτους ἔκλασα εἰς τοὺς πεντακισχιλίους, πόσους κοφίνους
loaves I broke to the five thousand, how many hand-baskets

4134 2801 142 3004 846 1427 3753
πλήρεις κλασμάτων ἤρατε; λέγουσιν αὐτῷ, Δώδεκα. 20 Ὅτε
full of fragments you took up? They say to Him, Twelve. when

1161 3588 2033 1519 3588 5070 4214 4711
δὲ τοὺς ἑπτὰ εἰς τοὺς τετρακισχιλίους, πόσων σπυρίδων
And the seven to the four thousand, how many lunch-baskets

4138 2801 142 3588 1161 2036 2033 2532
πληρώματα κλασμάτων ἤρατε; οἱ δὲ εἶπον, Ἑπτά. 21 καὶ
(the) fillings of fragments you took up? they And said, Seven. And

3004 846 4459 3756 4920
ἔλεγεν αὐτοῖς, Πῶς οὐ συνίετε;
He said to them, How not do you understand?

perceive ye not yet, neither understand? have ye your heart yet hardened?
18 Having eyes, see ye not? and having ears, hear ye not? and do ye not remember?
19 When I brake the five loaves among five thousand, how many baskets full of fragments took ye up? They say unto him, Twelve.
20 And when the seven among four thousand, how many baskets full of fragments took ye up? And they said, Seven.
21 And he said unto them, How is it that ye do not understand?

22. And He came to Bethsaida. And they carried a blind one to Him, and they beg Him that He would touch him.
23 And having laid hold of the blind one's hand, He led him forth outside the village. And spitting into his eyes, having laid (His) hands on him, He asked him if he sees anything.
24 And having looked, he said, I see men as trees walking.
25 Then again He placed (His) hands on his eyes again, and made him look up. And he was restored and saw all clearly.

2532 2064 1519 966 2532 5342 846 5185
22. Καὶ ἔρχεται εἰς Βηθσαϊδά. καὶ φέρουσιν αὐτῷ τυφλόν,
And He comes into Bethsaida. And they carry to Him a blind one.

2532 3870 846 2443 846 680 2532 1949
καὶ παρακαλοῦσιν αὐτὸν ἵνα αὐτοῦ ἅψηται. 23 καὶ ἐπιλαβό-
And they beg him that He would touch. And having laid

3588 5495 3588 5185 1806 846 1854 3588
μενος τῆς χειρὸς τοῦ τυφλοῦ, ἐξήγαγεν αὐτὸν ἔξω τῆς
hold of the hand of the blind one, He led forth him outside the

2968 2532 4429 1519 3588 3659 846 2007 3588 5495
κώμης· καὶ πτύσας εἰς τὰ ὄμματα αὐτοῦ, ἐπιθεὶς τὰς χεῖρας
village. And having spit into the eyes of him, having laid the hands

846 1905 846 1487 5100 991 2532 308 3004
αὐτῷ, ἐπηρώτα αὐτὸν εἴ τι βλέπει. 24 καὶ ἀναβλέψας ἔλεγε,
on him, He asked him if anything he sees? And having looked he said,

991 3588 444 5613 1186 4043 1534
Βλέπω τοὺς ἀνθρώπους ὡς δένδρα περιπατοῦντας. 25 εἶτα
I see men as trees walking around. Then

3825 2007 3588 5495 1909 3588 3788 846 2532
πάλιν ἐπέθηκε τὰς χεῖρας ἐπὶ τοὺς ὀφθαλμοὺς αὐτοῦ, καὶ
again He placed the hands on the eyes of him, and

4160 846 308 2532 600 2532 1689
ἐποίησεν αὐτὸν ἀναβλέψαι. καὶ ἀποκατεστάθη, καὶ ἐνέβλεψε
made him look up. And he was restored, and saw

5081 537 2532 649 846 1519 3588 3624
τηλαυγῶς ἅπαντας. 26 καὶ ἀπέστειλεν αὐτὸν εἰς τὸν οἶκον
clearly all. And He sent him to the house

846 3004 3366 1519 3588 2968 1525 3366 2036
αὐτοῦ, λέγων, Μηδὲ εἰς τὴν κώμην εἰσέλθῃς, μηδὲ εἴπῃς
of him, saying, Not into the village you may go in, nor may tell

5100 1722 3588 2968
τινὶ ἐν τῇ κώμῃ.
anyone in the village.

22. And he cometh to Bethsaida; and they bring a blind man unto him, and besought him to touch him.
23 And he took the blind man by the hand, and led him out of the town; and when he had spit on his eyes, and put his hands upon him, he asked him if he saw ought.
24 And he looked up, and said, I see men as trees, walking.
25 After that he put (his) hands again upon his eyes, and made him look up: and he was restored, and saw every man clearly.

26 And He sent him to his house, saying, You may not go into the village, nor may tell anyone in the village.

26 And he sent him away to his house, saying, Neither go into the town, nor tell (it) to any in the town.

27. And Jesus and His disciples went out to the villages of Caesarea of Philip. And in the way, He questioned

2532 1831 3588 2424 2532 3588 3101 846 1519 3588
27. Καὶ ἐξῆλθεν ὁ Ἰησοῦς καὶ οἱ μαθηταὶ αὐτοῦ εἰς τὰς
And went out Jesus and the disciples of Him into the

2968 2542 3588 5376 2532/1722/3588/3598 1905
κώμας Καισαρείας τῆς Φιλίππου· καὶ ἐν τῇ ὁδῷ ἐπηρώτα
villages of Caesarea of Philip. And in the way He questioned

27. And Jesus went out, and his disciples, into the towns of Caesarea Philippi: and by the way he asked

Literal Translation

His disciples, saying to them, Whom do men say Me to be?

28 And they answered, John the Baptist, and others (say) Elijah; but others, one of the prophets.
29 And He said to them, And you, whom do you say Me to be? And answering, Peter said to Him, You are the Christ.

30 And He warned them that they may tell no one about Him.
31. And He began to teach them that it is necessary for the Son of man to suffer many things and to be rejected of the elders and chief priests and scribes, and to be killed, and after three days to rise again.

32 And He spoke the word openly. And taking Him aside, Peter began to rebuke Him.
33 But turning around and seeing His disciples, He rebuked Peter, saying, Go behind Me, Satan, because you do not mind the things of God, but the things of men.

34. And having calledl near the crowd with His disciples, He said to them, Whoever desires to come after Me, let him deny himself and take his cross, and let him follow Me.

35 For whoever desires to save his life, (he) shall lose it. But whoever shall lose his life for My sake and the gospel, that one shall save it.

36 For what shall it profit a man if he gain the whole world, yet damage his soul?
37 Or what shall a man give

Mark 8:28

3588 3101 846 3004 846 5101 3165 3004 3588
τοὺς μαθητὰς αὐτοῦ, λέγων αὐτοῖς, Τίνα με λέγουσιν οἱ
the disciples of Him, saying to them, Whom Me say

‘ 444 ‘ 1511 3588 1161 611 2491 3588 910
ἄνθρωποι εἶναι; 28 οἱ δὲ ἀπεκρίθησαν, Ἰωάννην τὸν βαπτι-
men to be? they And answered, John the Baptist;

2532 243 2243 243 1161 1520 3588 4396 2532
στήν· καὶ ἄλλοι, Ἠλίαν, ἄλλοι δὲ ἕνα τῶν προφητῶν. 29 καὶ
and others, Elijah, others but one of the prophets. And

846 3004 846 5210 1161 5101 3165 3004 1511 611
αὐτὸς λέγει αὐτοῖς, Ὑμεῖς δὲ τίνα με λέγετε εἶναι; ἀποκριθεὶς
He says to them, you And whom Me say you to be? answering

1161 3588 4074 3004 846 4771 1488 3588 5547 2532 2008
δὲ ὁ Πέτρος λέγει αὐτῷ, Σὺ εἶ ὁ Χριστός. 30 καὶ ἐπετίμησεν
And Peter says to Him, You are the Christ! And He warned

846 2443 3367 3004 4012 846 2532 756 1321
αὐτοῖς,ἵνα μηδενὶ λέγωσι περὶ αὐτοῦ. 31 καὶ ἤρξατο διδάσκειν
them, that no one they may tell about Him. And He began to teach

846 3754 1163 3588 5207 3588 444 4183 3958 2532
αὐτούς, ὅτι δεῖ τὸν υἱὸν τοῦ ἀνθρώπου πολλὰ παθεῖν, καὶ
them, that must the Son of man many things to suffer, and

593 575 3588 4245 2532 749 2532
ἀποδοκιμασθῆναι ἀπὸ τῶν πρεσβυτέρων καὶ ἀρχιερέων καὶ
to be rejected from the elders and chief priests and

1122 2532 615 2532 3326 5140 2250
γραμματέων, καὶ ἀποκτανθῆναι, καὶ μετὰ τρεῖς ἡμέρας
scribes, and to be killed, and after three days

450 2532 3954 3588 3056 2980 2532 4355
ἀναστῆναι· 32 καὶ παρρησίᾳ τὸν λόγον ἐλάλει. καὶ προσλαβό-
to rise again. And openly the word He spoke. And having taken

846 3588 4074 756 2008 846 3588 1161 1994
μενος αὐτὸν ὁ Πέτρος ἤρξατο ἐπιτιμᾷν αὐτῷ. 33 ὁ δὲ ἐπιστρα-
aside Him Peter began to rebuke Him. He But turning

2532 1492 3588 3101 846 2008 3588 4074
φεὶς, καὶ ἰδὼν τοὺς μαθητὰς αὐτοῦ, ἐπετίμησε τῷ Πέτρῳ,
around and seeing the disciples of Him rebuked Peter,

3004 5217 3694 3450 4567 3754 3756 5426 3588 3588
λέγων, Ὕπαγε ὀπίσω μου, Σατανᾶ, ὅτι οὐ φρονεῖς τὰ τοῦ
saying, Go behind Me, Satan, because not you mind the things

2316 235 3588 3588 444 2532 4341 3588
Θεοῦ, ἀλλὰ τὰ τῶν ἀνθρώπων. 34 καὶ προσκαλεσάμενος τὸν
of God, but the things of men. And having called near the

3793 4862 3588 3101 846 2036 846 3748 2309
ὄχλον σὺν τοῖς μαθηταῖς αὐτοῦ, εἶπεν αὐτοῖς, Ὅστις θέλει
crowd with the disciples of Him, He said to them, Whoever desires

3694 3450 2064 533 1438 2532 142 3588
ὀπίσω μου ἐλθεῖν, ἀπαρνησάσθω ἑαυτὸν, καὶ ἀράτω τὸν
after Me to come, let him deny himself, and take the

4716 846 2532 190 3427 3739 1063 302 2309 3588
σταυρὸν αὐτοῦ, καὶ ἀκολουθείτω μοι. 35 ὃς γὰρ ἂν θέλῃ τὴν
cross of him, and let him follow Me. who For ever desires the

5590 846 4982 622 846 3739 1161 302 622 3588
ψυχὴν αὐτοῦ σῶσαι, ἀπολέσει αὐτήν· ὃς δ' ἂν ἀπολέσῃ τὴν
life of him to save, shall lose it. who But ever may lose the

5590 846 1752 1700 2532 3588 2098 3778 4982
ψυχὴν αὐτοῦ ἕνεκεν ἐμοῦ καὶ τοῦ εὐαγγελίου, οὗτος σώσει
life of him for the sake of Me and the gospel, this one will save

846 5101 1063 5623 444 1437 2770 3588
αὐτήν. 36 τί γὰρ ὠφελήσει ἄνθρωπον, ἐὰν κερδήσῃ τὸν
it. what For shall it profit a man, if he gain the

2889 3650 2532 2210 3588 5590 846 2228 5101 4982
κόσμον ὅλον, καὶ ζημιωθῇ τὴν ψυχὴν αὐτοῦ; 37 ἢ τί δώσει
world whole, yet damage the soul of him? Or what shall give

King James Version

his disciples, saying unto them, Whom do men say that I am?

28 And they answered, John the Baptist: but some (say), Elias; and others, One of the prophets.
29 And he saith unto them, But whom say ye that I am? And Peter answereth and saith unto him, Thou art the Christ.
30 And he charged them that they should tell no man of him.
31. And he began to teach them, that the Son of man must suffer many things, and be rejected of the elders, and (of) the chief priests, and scribes, and be killed, and after three days rise again.

32 And he spake that saying openly. And Peter took him, and began to rebuke him.
33 But when he had turned about and looked on his disciples, he rebuked Peter, saying, Get thee behind me, Satan: for thou savourest not the things that be of God, but the things that be of men.

34. And when he had called the people (unto him) with his disciples also, he said unto them, Whosoever will come after me, let him deny himself, and take up his cross, and follow me.

35 For whosoever will save his life shall lose it; but whosoever shall lose his life for my sake and the gospel's, the same shall save it.

36 For what shall it profit a man, if he shall gain the whole world, and lose his own soul?
37 Or what shall a man give

Literal Translation | **Mark 8:38** | ***King James Version***

(as) an exchange (for) his soul?
38 For whoever may be ashamed of Me and My words in this adulterous and sinful generation, the Son of man will also be ashamed of him when He comes in the glory of His Father, along with the holy angels.

444 465 3588 5590 846 3739 1063 302 1870
ἄνθρωπος ἀντάλλαγμα τῆς ψυχῆς αὐτοῦ; 38 ὃς γὰρ ἂν ἐπαι-
a man (as) an exchange (for) the soul of him? who For ever may be

3165 2532 3588 1699 3056 1722 3588 1074 3778 3588
σχυνθῇ με καὶ τοὺς ἐμοὺς λόγους ἐν τῇ γενεᾷ ταύτῃ τῇ
ashamed of Me and My words in generation this

3428 2532 268 2532 3588 5207 3588 444 1870
μοιχαλίδι καὶ ἁμαρτωλῷ, καὶ ὁ υἱὸς τοῦ ἀνθρώπου ἐπαι-
adulterous and sinful, also the Son of man will

846 3752 2064 1722 3588 1391 3588 3962
σχυνθήσεται αὐτὸν, ὅταν ἔλθῃ ἐν τῇ δόξῃ τοῦ πατρὸς
be ashamed of him, when He comes in the glory of the Father

846 3326 3588 32 3588 40
αὐτοῦ μετὰ τῶν ἀγγέλων τῶν ἁγίων.
of Him with the angels holy.

in exchange for his soul?
38 Whosoever therefore shall be ashamed of me and of my words in this adulterous and sinful generation; of him also shall the Son of man be ashamed, when he cometh in the glory of his Father with the holy angels.

Mark 9

1. And He said to them, Truly I say to you, There are some of those standing here who in no way shall taste of death until (they) see the kingdom of God coming in power.

2. And after six days Jesus takes along Peter and James and John, and leads them up into a high mountain privately, alone. And He was transfigured before them.

3 And His garments became shining, very white like snow, such as a fuller on earth is not able to whiten.

4 And Elijah with Moses was seen by them, and they were speaking with Jesus.
5 And answering, Peter said to Jesus, Rabbi, it is good (for) us to be here; and, Let us make three tents, one for You, and one for Moses, and one for Elijah.
6 For he did not know what to say, for they were very fearful.
7 And a cloud was overshadowing them, and a voice came out of the cloud, saying, This is My Son, the Beloved; hear Him. (Ps. 2:7)

8 And suddenly,

Mark 9

2532 3004 846 281 3004 5213 3754 1526 5100 3588
1. Καὶ ἔλεγεν αὐτοῖς, Ἀμὴν λέγω ὑμῖν, ὅτι εἰσί τινες τῶν
And He said to them, Truly I say to you, that are some of the ones

5602 2476 3748 3756 3361 1089 2288 2193 302
ὧδε ἑστηκότων, οἵτινες οὐ μὴ γεύσωνται θανάτου, ἕως ἂν
here standing, who in no way shall taste of death, until may

1492 3588 932 3588 2316 2064 1722 1411
ἴδωσι τὴν βασιλείαν τοῦ Θεοῦ ἐληλυθυῖαν ἐν δυνάμει.
see the kingdom of God coming in power.

2532 3326 2250 1803 3880 3588 2424 3588 4074
2. Καὶ μεθ᾿ ἡμέρας ἓξ παραλαμβάνει ὁ Ἰησοῦς τὸν Πέτρον
And after days six takes along Jesus Peter

2532 3588 2385 2532 3588 2491 2532 399 846
καὶ τὸν Ἰάκωβον καὶ τὸν Ἰωάννην, καὶ ἀναφέρει αὐτοὺς
and James and John, and brings up them

1519 3735 5308 2596 2398 3441 2532 3339 1715
εἰς ὄρος ὑψηλὸν κατ᾿ ἰδίαν μόνους· καὶ μετεμορφώθη ἔμπρο-
into a mount high privately alone. And He was transfigured before

846 2532 3588 2440 846 1096 4744 3022
σθεν αὐτῶν, 3 καὶ τὰ ἱμάτια αὐτοῦ ἐγένετο στίλβοντα, λευκὰ
them. And the garments of Him became shining, white

3029 5613 5510 3634 1102 1909 3588 1093 3756 1410 3021
λίαν ὡς χιών, οἷα γναφεὺς ἐπὶ τῆς γῆς οὐ δύναται λευκᾶναι.
very as snow, such as a fuller on the earth not is able to whiten.

2532 3700 846 2243 4862 3475 2532 2258 4814
4 καὶ ὤφθη αὐτοῖς Ἠλίας σὺν Μωσεῖ, καὶ ἦσαν συλλαλοῦντε
And was seen by them Elijah with Moses, and were they speaking with

3588 2424 2532 611 3588 4074 3004 3588 2424 4461
τῷ Ἰησοῦ. 5 καὶ ἀποκριθεὶς ὁ Πέτρος λέγει τῷ Ἰησοῦ, Ῥαββί,
Jesus. And answering Peter says to Jesus, Rabbi,

2570 2076 2248 5602 1511 2532 4160 4633 5140
καλόν ἐστιν ἡμᾶς ὧδε εἶναι· καὶ ποιήσωμεν σκηνάς τρεῖς,
good it is us here to be; and, Let us make tents three,

4671 3391 2532 3475 3391 2532 2243 3391 3756 1063 1492 5101
σοὶ μίαν, καὶ Μωσεῖ μίαν, καὶ Ἠλίᾳ μίαν. 6 οὐ γὰρ ᾔδει τί
for You one, and for Moses one, and for Elijah one. not For he knew what

2980 2258 1063 1630 2532 1096 3507 1982
λαλήσῃ· ἦσαν γὰρ ἔκφοβοι. 7 καὶ ἐγένετο νεφέλη ἐπισκιάζουσα
to say; they were for very fearful. And came to be a cloud overshadowing

846 2532 2064 5456 1537 3588 3507 3004 3778 2076
αὐτοῖς· καὶ ἦλθε φωνὴ ἐκ τῆς νεφέλης, λέγουσα, Οὗτός ἐστιν
them; and came a voice out of the cloud, saying, This is

3588 5207 3450 3588 27 846 191 2532 1819
ὁ υἱός μου ὁ ἀγαπητός· αὐτοῦ ἀκούετε. 8 καὶ ἐξάπινα
the Son of Me, the Beloved. Him Hear! And suddenly

Mark 9

1. And he said unto them, Verily I say unto you, That there be some of them that stand here, which shall not taste of death, till they have seen the kingdom of God come with power.

2. And after six days Jesus taketh (with him) Peter, and James, and John, and leadeth them up into an high mountain apart by themselves: and he was transfigured before them.

3 And his raiment became shining, exceeding white as snow; so as no fuller on earth can white them.

4 And there appeared unto them Elias with Moses: and they were talking with Jesus.
5 And Peter answered and said to Jesus, Master, it is good for us to be here: and let us make three tabernacles; one for thee, and one for Moses, and one for Elias.
6 For he wist not what to say; for they were sore afraid.
7 And there was a cloud that overshadowed them: and a voice came out of the cloud, saying, This is my beloved Son: hear him.
8 And suddenly,

Literal Translation | **Mark 9:9** | *King James Version*

looking around, they saw no one any longer, but Jesus alone with themselves.

4017 3765 3762 1492 235 3588 2424
περιβλεψάμενοι, οὐκέτι οὐδένα εἶδον, ἀλλὰ τὸν Ἰησοῦν
having looked around, no longer no one they saw, but Jesus
3441 3326 1438
μόνον μεθ' ἑαυτῶν.
alone with themselves.

when they had looked round about, they saw no man any more, save Jesus only with themselves.

9 And as they were coming down from the mountain, He commanded them that they should tell no one what they saw, except when the Son of man should rise from (the) dead.
10 And they held the word to themselves, debating what (it) is to rise from (the) dead.

2597 1161 846 575 3588 3735 1291
9. καταβαινόντων δὲ αὐτῶν ἀπὸ τοῦ ὄρους, διεστείλατο
(as) were descending And they from the mountain, He commanded
846 2443 3367 1334 3739 1492 1487 3361 3752 3588 5207
αὐτοῖς ἵνα μηδενὶ διηγήσωνται ἃ εἶδον, εἰ μὴ ὅταν ὁ υἱὸς
them that to no one they should tell what they saw, except when the Son
3588 444 1537 3498 450 2532 3588 3056 2902
τοῦ ἀνθρώπου ἐκ νεκρῶν ἀναστῇ. 10 καὶ τὸν λόγον ἐκράτησαν
of man from (the) dead may rise. And the word they held
4314 1438 4802 5101 2076 3588 1537 3498 450
πρὸς ἑαυτοὺς συζητοῦντες τί ἐστι τὸ ἐκ νεκρῶν ἀναστῆναι.
to themselves debating what is (it) from (the) dead to rise.

9 And as they came down from the mountain, he charged them that they should tell no man what things they had seen, till the Son of man were risen from the dead.
10 And they kept that saying with themselves, questioning one with another what the rising from the dead should mean.

11. And they asked Him, saying, Do the scribes say that Elijah must come first?
12 And answering, He said to them, Indeed, Elijah coming first restores all things. And how it has been written on the Son of man that He may suffer many things and be despised!

13 But I say to you, Elijah also has come and they did to him whatever they desired, even as it has been written of him.

2532 1905 846 3004 3754 3004 3588 1122
11 καὶ ἐπηρώτων αὐτὸν, λέγοντες ὅτι Λέγουσιν οἱ γραμματεῖς
And they asked Him, saying, Say the scribes
3754 2243 1163 2064 4412 3588 1161 611 2036 846
ὅτι Ἠλίαν δεῖ ἐλθεῖν πρῶτον; 12 ὁ δὲ ἀποκριθείς, εἶπεν αὐτοῖς,
that Elijah must come first? He And answering, said to them,
2243 3303 2064 4412 600 3956 2532 4459
Ἠλίας μὲν ἐλθὼν πρῶτον, ἀποκαθιστᾷ πάντα· καὶ πῶς
Elijah indeed coming first, restores all things. And how
1125 1909 3588 5207 3588 444 2443 4183 3958
γέγραπται ἐπὶ τὸν υἱὸν τοῦ ἀνθρώπου, ἵνα πολλὰ πάθῃ
has it been written on the Son of man, that many things He may suffer
2532 1847 235 3004 5213 3754 2532 2243 2064
καὶ ἐξουδενηθῇ; 13 ἀλλὰ λέγω ὑμῖν ὅτι καὶ Ἠλίας ἐλήλυθε,
and be despised? But I say to you that also Elijah has come,
2532 4160 846 3745 2309 2531 1125 1909
καὶ ἐποίησαν αὐτῷ ὅσα ἠθέλησαν, καθὼς γέγραπται ἐπ'
and they did to him whatever they desired, even as it has been written on
846
αὐτόν.
him.

11. And they asked him, saying, Why say the scribes that Elias must first come?
12 And he answered and told them, Elias verily cometh first, and restoreth all things; and how it is written of the Son of man, that he must suffer many things, and be set at nought.

13 But I say unto you, That Elias is indeed come, and they have done unto him whatsoever they listed, as it is written of him.

14. And coming to the disciples, He saw a great crowd around them, and scribes arguing with them.
15 And at once all the crowd seeing Him were greatly amazed. And running up, (they) greeted Him.

16 And He questioned the scribes, What are you arguing with them?
17 And one answered out of the crowd, saying, Teacher, I brought my son to You, having a dumb spirit.

18 And wherever it seizes him, it dashes him; and he foams and gnashes his teeth. And

2532 2064 4314 3588 3101 1492 3793 4183 4012
14. Καὶ ἐλθὼν πρὸς τοὺς μαθητὰς, εἶδον ὄχλον πολὺν περὶ
And coming to the disciples, He saw a crowd great around
846 2532 1122 4802 846 2532 2112
αὐτοὺς, καὶ γραμματεῖς συζητοῦντας αὐτοῖς. 15 καὶ εὐθέως
them, and scribes arguing with them. And at once
3956 3588 3793 1492 846 1568 2532 4370
πᾶς ὁ ὄχλος ἰδὼν αὐτὸν ἐξεθαμβήθη, καὶ προστρέχοντες
all the crowd seeing Him were greatly amazed. And running up
782 846 2532 1905 3588 1122 5101
ἠσπάζοντο αὐτόν. 16 καὶ ἐπηρώτησε τοὺς γραμματεῖς, Τί
(they) greeted Him. And He questioned the scribes, What
4802 4314 846 2532 611 1520 1537 3588 3793
συζητεῖτε πρὸς αὐτούς; 17 καὶ ἀποκρίθεὶς εἷς ἐκ τοῦ ὄχλου
are you arguing with them? And answered one out of the crowd,
2036 1320 5342 3588 5207 3450 4314 4571 2192
εἶπε, Διδάσκαλε, ἤνεγκα τὸν υἱόν μου πρὸς σέ, ἔχοντα
saying, Teacher, I brought the son of me to You, having
4151 216 2532 3699 302 846 2638 4486
πνεῦμα ἄλαλον· 18 καὶ ὅπου ἂν αὐτὸν καταλάβῃ, ῥήσσει
a spirit dumb; and wherever him it seizes, it dashes
846 2532 875 2532 5149 3588 3599 846 2532
αὐτόν· καὶ ἀφρίζει, καὶ τρίζει τοὺς ὀδόντας αὐτοῦ, καὶ
him; and he foams and gnashes the teeth of him, and

14. And when he came to (his) disciples, he saw a great multitude about them, and the scribes questioning with them.
15 And straightway all the people, when they beheld him, were greatly amazed, and running to (him) saluted him.
16 And he asked the scribes, What question ye with them?
17 And one of the multitude answered and said, Master, I have brought unto thee my son, which hath a dumb spirit;

18 And wheresoever he taketh him, he teareth him: and he foameth, and gnasheth with his teeth, and

Literal Translation

he wastes away. And I told Your disciples, that they might expel it. And they were not able.

19 And answering them, He said, O unbelieving generation! Until when will I be with you? Until when shall I endure you? Bring him to Me.
20 And they brought him to Him. And seeing Him, the spirit immediately convulsed him. And falling on the ground, he wallowed, foaming.
21 And He questioned his father, How long a time is it while this has happened to him? And he said, From childhood.
22 And often it threw him both into fire and into water, that it might destroy him. But if You are able to do anything, help us, having pity on us.
23 And Jesus said to him, If you are able to believe, all things (are) possible to those believing.

24 And immediately crying out, the father of the child said with tears, Lord, I believe! Help my unbelief!

25 And seeing that a crowd is running together, Jesus rebuked the unclean spirit, saying to it, Dumb and deaf spirit, I command you, Come out from him, and you may no more go into him!

26 And crying out, and convulsing him very much, it came out. And he became as if dead, so as (for) many to say that he died.

27 But taking hold of his hand, Jesus raised him up, and he stood up.
28 And He entering into a house, His disciples questioned Him privately, (Why) were we not

Mark 9:19

3583 2532 2036 3588 3101 4675 2443 846 1544
ξηραίνεται· καὶ εἶπον τοῖς μαθηταῖς σου ἵνα αὐτὸ ἐκβάλωσι,
he wastes away. And I told the disciples of You that it they might expel,
2532 3756 2480 3588 1161 611 846 3004 5599 1074
καὶ οὐκ ἴσχυσαν. 19 ὁ δὲ ἀποκριθεὶς αὐτοῖς λέγει, Ὦ γενεὰ
and not they were able. He And answering them says, O generation
571 2193 4219 4314 5209 2071 2193 4219 430
ἄπιστος, ἕως πότε πρὸς ὑμᾶς ἔσομαι; ἕως πότε ἀνέξομαι
unbelieving, until when with you will I be? Until when shall I endure
5216 5342 846 4314 3165 2532 5342 846 4314 846
ὑμῶν; φέρετε αὐτὸν πρός με. 20 καὶ ἤνεγκαν αὐτὸν πρὸς αὐτόν.
you? Bring him to Me. And they brought him to Him.
2532 1492 846 2112 3588 4151 4682 846 2532
καὶ ἰδὼν αὐτὸν, εὐθέως τὸ πνεῦμα εσπάραξεν αὐτόν· καὶ
And seeing Him, immediately the spirit convulsed him; and
4098 1909 3588 1093 2947 875 2532 1905 3588
πεσὼν ἐπὶ τῆς γῆς, ἐκυλίετο ἀφρίζων. 21 καὶ ἐπηρώτησε τὸν
falling on the ground, he wallowed, foaming. And He questioned the
3962 846 4214 5550 2076 5613 5124 1096 846
πατέρα αὐτοῦ, Πόσος χρόνος ἐστὶν, ὡς τοῦτο γέγονεν αὐτῷ;
father of him, How long a time is it, while this has happened to him?
3588 1161 2036 3812 2532 4178 846 2532 1519 4442 906
ὁ δὲ εἶπε, Παιδιόθεν. 22 καὶ πολλάκις αὐτὸν καὶ εἰς πῦρ ἔβαλε
he And said, From childhood. And often him both into fire it threw
2532 1519 5204 2443 622 846 235 1487 5100 1410
καὶ εἰς ὕδατα, ἵνα ἀπολέσῃ αὐτόν· ἀλλ' εἴ τι δύνασαι,
and into water, that it might destroy him. But if anything You can do,
997 2254 4697 1909 2248 3588 1161 2424 2036
βοήθησον ἡμῖν σπλαγχνισθεὶς ἐφ' ἡμᾶς. 23 ὁ δὲ Ἰησοῦς εἶπεν
help us having pity on us. And Jesus said
846 3588 1487 1410 4100 3956 1415 3588
αὐτῷ τὸ, Εἰ δύνασαι πιστεῦσαι, πάντα δυνατὰ τῷ
to him, If you are able to believe, all things possible to the
4100 2532 2112 2896 3588 3962 3588 3813 3326
πιστεύοντι. 24 καὶ εὐθέως κράξας ὁ πατὴρ τοῦ παιδίου, μετὰ
believing (are). And at once crying out the father of the child, with
1144 3004 4100 2962 997 3450 3588 570
δακρύων ἔλεγε, Πιστεύω, Κύριε, βοήθει μου τῇ ἀπιστίᾳ.
tears said, I believe, Lord, help of me the unbelief!
1492 1161 3588 2424 3754 1998 3793 2008 3588
25 ἰδὼν δὲ ὁ Ἰησοῦς ὅτι ἐπισυντρέχει ὄχλος, ἐπετίμησε τῷ
seeing And Jesus that is running together a crowd, rebuked the
4151 3588 169 3004 846 3588 4151 3588 216
πνεύματι τῷ ἀκαθάρτῳ, λέγων αὐτῷ, Τὸ πνεῦμα τὸ ἄλαλον
spirit unclean, saying to it, spirit Dumb
2532 2974 1473 4671 2004 1831 1537 846 2532 3371
καὶ κωφὸν, ἐγώ σοι ἐπιτάσσω, ἔξελθε ἐξ αὐτοῦ, καὶ μηκέτι
and deaf, I you command, Come out from him, and no more
1525 1519 846 2532 2896 2532 4183 4682 846
εἰσέλθῃς εἰς αὐτόν. 26 καὶ κράξας, καὶ πολλὰ σπαράξαν αὐτόν,
may you go into him. And crying out, and much convulsing him,
1831 2532 1096 5616 3498 5620 4183 3004 3754
ἐξῆλθε· καὶ ἐγένετο ὡσεὶ νεκρός, ὥστε πολλοὺς λέγειν ὅτι
it came out. And he became as dead, so as many to say that
599 3588 1161 2424 2902 846 3588 5495 1453
ἀπέθανεν. 27 ὁ δὲ Ἰησοῦς κρατήσας αὐτόν τῆς χειρὸς, ἤγειρεν
he died. But Jesus, taking hold of him of the hand, raised up
846 2532 450 2532 1525 846 1519 3624 3588
αὐτόν· καὶ ἀνέστη. 28 καὶ εἰσελθόντα αὐτὸν εἰς οἶκον, οἱ
him; and he stood up. And entering He into a house, the
3101 846 1905 846 2596 2398/3754 2249 3756
μαθηταὶ αὐτοῦ ἐπηρώτων αὐτὸν κατ' ἰδίαν ὅτι Ἡμεῖς οὐκ
disciples of Him questioned Him privately, (Why) we not

King James Version

pineth away: and I spake to thy disciples that they should cast him out; and they could not.
19 He answereth him, and saith, O faithless generation, how long shall I be with you? how long shall I suffer you? bring him unto me.
20 And they brought him unto him: and when he saw him, straightway the spirit tare him; and he fell on the ground, and wallowed foaming.

21 And he asked his father, How long is it ago since this came unto him? And he said, Of a child.

22 And ofttimes it hath cast him into the fire, and into the waters, to destroy him: but if thou canst do any thing, have compassion on us, and help us.
23 Jesus said unto him, If thou canst believe, all things (are) possible to him that believeth.

24 And straightway the father of the child cried out, and said with tears, Lord, I believe; help thou mine unbelief.

25 When Jesus saw that the people came running together, he rebuked the foul spirit, saying unto him, (Thou) dumb and deaf spirit, I charge thee, come out of him, and enter no more into him.

26 And (the spirit) cried, and rent him sore, and came out of him: and he was as one dead; insomuch that many said, He is dead.

27 But Jesus took him by the hand, and lifted him up; and he arose.
28 And when he was come into the house, his disciples asked him privately, Why could not

Literal Translation | **Mark 9:29** | ***King James Version***

able to cast it out?
29 And He said to them, This kind can go out by nothing except by prayer and fasting.

1410 1544 846 2532 2036 846 5124 3588
ἠδυνήθημεν ἐκβαλεῖν αὐτό; 29 καὶ εἶπεν αὐτοῖς, Τοῦτο τὸ
were able to cast out it? And He said to them, This
1085 1722 3762 1410 1831 1487 3361 1722 4335 2532
γένος ἐν οὐδενὶ δύναται ἐξελθεῖν, εἰ μὴ ἐν προσευχῇ καὶ
kind by nothing can go out, except by prayer and
3521
νηστείᾳ.
fasting.

we cast him out?
29 And he said unto them, This kind can come forth by nothing, but by prayer and fasting.

30. And going forth from there, they passed by through Galilee. And He desired that no one know.
31 For He taught His disciples, and said to them, The Son of man is delivered up into (the) hands of men, and they will kill Him. And having been slain, He will rise up the third day.

32 But they did not know the word, and feared to question Him.

2532 1564 1831 3899 1223 3588 1056
30.Καὶ εκεῖθεν ἐξελθόντες παρεπορεύοντο διὰ τῆς Γαλι-
And from there going forth they passed by through Galilee.
2532 3756 2309 2443 5100 1097 1321 1063 3588
λαίας· καὶ οὐκ ἤθελεν ἵνα τις γνῷ. 31 ἐδίδασκε γὰρ τοὺς
And not He desired that anyone know. He taught For the
3101 846 2532 3004 846 3754 3588 5207 3588 444
μαθητὰς αὐτοῦ, καὶ ἔλεγεν αὐτοῖς ὅτι Ὁ υἱὸς τοῦ ἀνθρώπου
disciples of Him, and said to them, The Son of man
3860 1519 5495 444 2532 615 846
παραδίδοται εἰς χεῖρας ἀνθρώπων, καὶ ἀποκτενοῦσιν αὐτόν·
is delivered up into hands of men, and they will kill Him;
2532 615 3588 5154 2250 450 3588 1161
καὶ ἀποκτανθεὶς, τῇ τρίτῃ ἡμέρᾳ ἀναστήσεται. 32 οἱ δὲ
and having been slain, the third day He will rise up. they But
50 3588 4487 2532 5399 846 1905
ἠγνόουν τὸ ῥῆμα, καὶ ἐφοβοῦντο αὐτὸν ἐπερωτῆσαι.
knew not the word, and feared Him to question.

30. And they departed thence, and passed through Galilee; and he would not that any man should know (it).
31 For he taught his disciples, and said unto them, The Son of man is delivered into the hands of men, and they shall kill him; and after that he is killed, he shall rise the third day.

32 But they understood not that saying, and were afraid to ask him.

33. And they came to Capernaum. And having come into the house, He questioned them, What were you discussing to yourselves in the way?
34 And they were quiet, for they reasoned with one another in the way (as to) who (was) greater.
35 And sitting, He called the Twelve and said to them, If anyone desires to be first, he shall be last of all and servant of all.
36 And taking a child, He set it in their midst, and having embraced it, He said to them,

2532 2064 1519 2584 2532 1722 3588 3614 1096
33. Καὶ ἦλθεν εἰς Καπερναούμ· καὶ ἐν τῇ οἰκίᾳ γενόμενος
And they came into Capernaum. And in the house having come,
1905 846 5101 1722 3588 3598 4314 1438 1260
ἐπηρώτα αὐτούς, Τί ἐν τῇ ὁδῷ πρὸς ἑαυτοὺς διελογίζεσθε;
He questioned them, What in the way to yourselves you were discussing?
3588 1161 4623 4314 240 1063 1256 1722 3588 3598
34 οἱ δὲ ἐσιώπων· πρὸς ἀλλήλους γὰρ διελέχθησαν ἐν τῇ ὁδῷ,
they And they were quiet to one another, for they reasoned in the way
5101 3187 2532 2523 5455 3588 1427 2532 3004
τίς μείζων. 35 καὶ καθίσας ἐφώνησε τοὺς δώδεκα, καὶ λέγει
who (was) greater. And sitting He called the twelve, and says
846 1487 5100 2309 4413 1511 2071 3956 2078
αὐτοῖς, Εἴ τις θέλει πρῶτος εἶναι, ἔσται πάντων ἔσχατος,
to them, If anyone desires first to be, he shall be of all last,
2532 3956 1249 2532 2983 3813 2476 846
καὶ πάντων διάκονος. 36 καὶ λαβὼν παιδίον, ἔστησεν αὐτὸ
and of all servant. And taking a child, He set it
1722 3319 846 2532 1723 846 2036 846
ἐν μέσῳ αὐτῶν· καὶ ἐναγκαλισάμενος αὐτὸ, εἶπεν αὐτοῖς,
in(the) midst of them. And having embraced it, He said to them,

33. And he came to Capernaum: and being in the house he asked them, What was it that ye disputed among yourselves by the way?
34 But they held their peace: for by the way they had disputed among themselves, who (should be) the greatest.
35 And he sat down, and called the twelve, and saith unto them, If any man desire to be first, (the same) shall be last of all, and servant of all.
36 And he took a child, and set him in the midst of them: and when he had taken him in his arms, he said unto them,

37 Whoever receives one of such children on My name receives Me. And whoever receives Me does not receives Me, but the (One) having sent Me.

3739 1437 1520 3588 5108 3813 1209 1909 3588 3686
37 Ὃς ἂν ἓν τῶν τοιούτων παιδίων δέξηται ἐπὶ τῷ ὀνόματί
Whoever one of such children receives on the name
3450 1691 1209 2532 3739 1437 1691 1209 3756 1691 1209
μου, ἐμὲ δέχεται· καὶ ὃς ἐὰν ἐμὲ δέχηται, οὐκ ἐμὲ δέχεται
of Me, Me receives. And whoever Me receives, not Me receives
235 3588 649 3165
ἀλλὰ τὸν ἀποστείλαντά με.
but the (One) having sent Me.

37 Whosoever shall receive one of such children in my name, receiveth me: and whosoever shall receive me, receiveth not me, but him that sent me.

38. And John answered Him, saying, Teacher, we saw someone in Your name casting out demons, who

611 1161 846 3588 2491 3004 1320
38. Ἀπεκρίθη δὲ αὐτῷ ὁ Ἰωάννης, λέγων, Διδάσκαλε,
answered And Him John, saying, Teacher,
1492 5100 1722 3588 3686 4675 1544 1140 3739
εἴδομέν τινα ἐν τῷ ὀνόματί σου ἐκβάλλοντα δαιμόνια, ὃς
we saw someone in the name of You casting out demons, who

38. And John answered him, saying, Master, we saw one casting out devils

Mark 9:39

Literal Translation

in Your name, who does not follow us. And we stopped him, because he does not follow us.
39 But Jesus said, Do not stop him. For there is no one who shall do a work of power in My name, yet be able to speak evil of Me quickly.
40 For who is not against us is for us.

41 For whoever gives you a cup of water to drink in My name, because you are of Christ, truly I say to you, In no way he will lose his reward.
42 And whoever causes one of (these) little ones that believe in Me to stumble, it is good for him if rather a millstone be laid around his neck, and he be thrown into the sea.

43 And if your hand causes you to offend, cut it off. For it is profitable for you to enter into life maimed, than having two hands to go away into Hell, into the unquenchable fire,

44 where their worm does not die, and the fire is not put out.
45 And if your foot causes you to offend, cut it off, for it is profitable for you to enter into life lame, than having two feet to be thrown into Hell, into the unquenchable fire,

46 where their worm does not die, and the fire is not put out.

47 And if your eye causes you to offend, cast it out. For it is profitable for you to enter into the kingdom of God one-eyed, than having two eyes to be thrown into the Hell of fire,

3756 190 2254 2532 2967 846 3754 3756
οὐκ ἀκολουθεῖ ἡμῖν· καὶ ἐκωλύσαμεμ αὐτόν, ὅτι οὐκ
not does follow us; and we stopped him, because not

190 2254 3588 1161 2424 2036 3361 2967 846
ἀκολουθεῖ ἡμῖν. 39 ὁ δὲ Ἰησοῦς εἶπε, Μὴ κωλύετε αὐτόν·
he follows us. But Jesus said, Not do stop him;

3762 1063 2076 3739 4160 1411 1909 3588 3686 3450
οὐδεὶς γάρ ἐστιν ὃς ποιήσει δύναμιν ἐπὶ τῷ ὀνόματί μου,
no one for is who shall do a work of power on the name of Me,

2532 1410 5035 2551 3165 3739 1063 3756 2076 2596
καὶ δυνήσεται ταχὺ κακολογῆσαί με. 40 ὃς γὰρ οὐκ ἔστι καθ'
yet be able quickly to speak evil of Me. who For not is against

5216 5228 5216 2076 3739 1063 302 4222 5209 4221
ἡμῶν, ὑπὲρ ἡμῶν ἐστιν. 41 ὃς γὰρ ἂν ποτίσῃ ὑμᾶς ποτήριον
us, for us is. who For ever gives drink you a cup

5204 1722 3588 3686 3450 3754 5547 2075 281 3004
ὕδατος ἐν τῷ ὀνόματι μου, ὅτι Χριστοῦ ἐστε, ἀμὴν λέγω
of water in the name of Me, because of Christ you are, truly I say

5213 3756 3361 622 3588 3408 846 2532 3739 302 4624
ὑμῖν, οὐ μὴ ἀπολέσῃ τὸν μισθὸν αὐτοῦ. 42 καὶ ὃς ἂν σκαν-
to you, in no way he will lose the reward of him. And whoever causes

1520 3588 3398 5130 3588 4100 1519 1691
δαλίσῃ ἕνα τῶν μικρῶν τούτων τῶν πιστευόντων εἰς ἐμέ,
to stumble one little (ones) of these believing into Me,

2570 2076 846 3123 1487 4029 3037 3457 4012
καλόν ἐστιν αὐτῷ μᾶλλον εἰ περίκειται λίθος μύλικὸς περὶ
good it is for him rather if be laid about of a stone of a mill around

3588 5137 846 2532 906 1519 3588 2281 2532
τὸν τράχηλον αὐτοῦ, καὶ βέβληται εἰς τὴν θάλασσαν. 43 καὶ
the neck of him, and he be thrown into the sea. And

1437 4624 4571 3588 5495 4675 609 846 2570 4671
ἐὰν σκανδαλίζῃ σε ἡ χείρ σου, ἀπόκοψον αὐτήν· καλόν σοι
if offend you the hand of you, cut off it; good for you

2076 2948 1519 3588 2222 1525 2228 3588 1417 5495 2192
ἐστὶ κυλλὸν εἰς τὴν ζωὴν εἰσελθεῖν, ἢ τὰς δύο χεῖρας ἔχοντα
is it maimed into life to enter, than the two hands having

565 1519 3588 1067 1519 3588 4442 3588 762 3699 3588
ἀπελθεῖν εἰς τὴν γέενναν, εἰς τὸ πῦρ τὸ ἄσβεστον, 44 ὅπου ὁ
to go away into Gehenna, into the fire unquenchable, where the

4663 846 3756 5053 2532 3588 4442 3756 4570 2532
σκώληξ αὐτῶν οὐ τελευτᾷ, καὶ τὸ πῦρ οὐ σβέννυται. 45 καὶ
worm of them not has an end, and the fire not is quenched. And

1437 3588 4228 4675 4624 4571 609 846 2570 2076
ἐὰν ὁ πούς σου σκανδαλίζῃ σε, ἀπόκοψον αὐτόν· καλόν ἐστί
if the foot of you causes to offend you, cut off it; good is it

4671 1525 1519 3588 2222 5560 2228 3588 1417 4228 2192
σοι εἰσελθεῖν εἰς τὴν ζωὴν χωλὸν ἢ τοὺς δύο πόδας ἔχοντα
you to enter into life lame than the two feet having

906 1519 3588 1067 1519 3588 4442 3588 762 3699
βληθῆναι εἰς τὴν γέενναν, εἰς τὸ πῦρ τὸ ἄσβεστον, 46 ὅπου
to be thrown into Gehenna, into the fire unquenchable, where

3588 4663 846 3756 5053 2532 3588 4442 3756 4570 2532
ὁ σκώληξ αὐτῶν οὐ τελευτᾷ, καὶ τὸ πῦρ οὐ σβέννυται. 47 καὶ
the worm of them not has an end, and the fire not is quenched. And

1437/3588 3788 4675 4624 4571 1544 846 2570
ἐὰν ὁ ὀφθαλμός σου σκανδαλίζῃ σε, ἔκβαλε αὐτόν· καλόν
if the eye of you causes to offend you, cast out it; good

4671 2076 3442 1525 1519 3588 932 3588 2316
σοι ἐστι μονόφθαλμον εἰσελθεῖν εἰς τὴν βασιλείαν τοῦ Θεοῦ,
for you it is one-eyed to enter into the kingdom of God,

2228 1417 3788 2192 906 1519 3588 1067 3588
ἢ δύο ὀφθαλμοὺς ἔχοντα βληθῆναι εἰς τὴν γέενναν τοῦ
than two eyes having to be thrown into the Gehenna

King James Version

in thy name, and he followeth not us: and we forbad him, because he followeth not us.
39 But Jesus said, Forbid him not: for there is no man which shall do a miracle in my name, that can lightly speak evil of me.

40 For he that is not against us is on our part.

41 For whosoever shall give you a cup of water to drink in my name, because ye belong to Christ, verily I say unto you, he shall not lose his reward.
42 And whosoever shall offend one of (these) little ones that believe in me, it is better for him that a millstone were hanged about his neck, and he were cast into the sea.

43 And if thy hand offend thee, cut it off: it is better for thee to enter into life maimed, than having two hands to go into hell, into the fire that never shall be quenched:

44 Where their worm dieth not, and the fire is not quenched.
45 And if thy foot offend thee, cut it off: it is better for thee to enter halt into life, than having two feet to be cast into hell, into the fire that never shall be quenched:

46 Where their worm dieth not, and the fire is not quenched.

47 And if thine eye offend thee, pluck it out: it is better for thee to enter into the kingdom of God with one eye, than having two eyes to be cast into hell fire:

Literal Translation | **Mark 9:48** | ***King James Version***

48 where their worm does not die and the fire is not put out. (Isa. 66:24)
49 For everyone will be salted with fire, and every sacrifice will be salted with salt.
50 Salt (is) good, but if the salt becomes saltless, by what will you season? Have salt in yourselves and be at peace with one another.

4442 3699 3588 4663 846 3756 5053 2532 3588 4442 3756
πυρός, 48 ὅπου ὁ σκώληξ αὐτῶν οὐ τελευτᾷ, καὶ τὸ πῦρ οὐ
of fire, where the worm of them not has an end, and the fire not
4570 3956 1063 4442 233 2532 3956 2378 251
σβέννυται. 49 πᾶς γὰρ πυρὶ ἁλισθήσεται, καὶ πᾶσα θυσία ἁλὶ
is quenched. everyone For with fire will be salted, and every sacrifice with salt
233 2570 3588 217 1437 1161 3588 217 358 1096
ἁλισθήσεται. 50 καλὸν τὸ ἅλας· ἐὰν δὲ τὸ ἅλας ἄναλον γένηται,
will be salted. Good (is) salt, if but the salt saltless becomes,
1722 5101 846 741 2192 1722 1438 217 2532 1514
ἐν τίνι αὐτὸ ἀρτύσετε; ἔχετε ἐν ἑαυτοῖς ἅλας, καὶ εἰρηνεύετε
by what it will you season? Have in yourselves salt, and be at peace
1722 240
ἐν ἀλλήλοις.
among one another.

48 Where their worm dieth not, and the fire is not quenched.

49 For every one shall be salted with fire, and every sacrifice shall be salted with salt.
50 Salt (is) good: but if the salt have lost his saltness, wherewith will ye season it? Have salt in yourselves, and have peace one with another.

Mark 10

Mark 10 | **Mark 10**

1. And rising up from there, He came into the borders of Judea through the other side of the Jordan. And again crowds came together to Him, and as He usually did, He again taught them.
2. And coming near, the Pharisees asked Him, if it is lawful for a man to put away a wife, testing Him.

2547 450 2064 1519 3588 3725 3588 2449 1223
1. Κἀκεῖθεν ἀναστὰς ἔρχεται εἰς τὰ ὅρια τῆς Ἰουδαίας διὰ
And from there arising, He comes into the borders of Judea by
3588 4008 3588 2446 2532 4848 3825 3793
τοῦ πέραν τοῦ Ἰορδάνου· καὶ συμπορεύονται πάλιν ὄχλοι
the other side of the Jordan. And came together again crowds
4314 846 2532 5613 1486 3825 1321 846 2532
πρὸς αὐτόν· καὶ, ὡς εἰώθει, πάλιν ἐδίδασκεν αὐτούς. 2 καὶ
to Him. And as He did usually, again He taught them. And
4334 3588 5330 1905 846 1487 1832
προσελθόντες οἱ Φαρισαῖοι ἐπηρώτησαν αὐτόν, Εἰ ἔξεστιν
coming near the Pharisees questioned Him, if it is lawful
435 1135 630 3985 846 3588 1161 611
ἀνδρὶ γυναῖκα ἀπολῦσαι, πειράζοντες αὐτόν. 3 ὁ δὲ ἀποκρι-
for a man a wife to dismiss, testing Him. He And answer-

1. And he arose from thence, and cometh into the coasts of Judaea by the farther side of Jordan: and the people resort unto him again; and, as he was wont, he taught them again.
2. And the Pharisees came to him, and asked him, Is it lawful for a man to put away (his) wife? tempting him.

3 But answering, He said to them, What did Moses command you?
4 And they said, Moses allowed to write a bill of divorce, and to put away. (Deut. 24:1)

2036 846 5101 5213 1781 3475 3588 1161 2036
θεὶς εἶπεν αὐτοῖς, Τί ὑμῖν ἐνετείλατο Μωσῆς; 4 οἱ δὲ εἶπον,
ing said to them, What you did command Moses? they And said
3475 2010 975 647 1125 2532 630
Μωσῆς ἐπέτρεψε βιβλίον ἀποστασίου γράψαι, καὶ ἀπολῦ-
Moses allowed a roll of divorce to write, and to dismiss.

3 And he answered and said unto them, What did Moses command you?
4 And they said, Moses suffered to write a bill of divorcement, and to put (her) away.

5 And answering, Jesus said to them, With respect to your hardheartedness he wrote this command to you.

2532 611 3588 2424 2036 846 4314 3588
σαι. 5 καὶ ἀποκριθεὶς ὁ Ἰησοῦς εἶπεν αὐτοῖς, Πρὸς τὴν
And answering Jesus said to them, For the
4641 5216 1125 5213 3588 1785 3778
σκληροκαρδίαν ὑμῶν ἔγραψεν ὑμῖν τὴν ἐντολὴν ταύτην·
hardheartedness of you he wrote to you commandment this.

5 And Jesus answered and said unto them, For the hardness of your heart he wrote you this precept.

6 But from the beginning of creation God made them male and female. (Gen. 1:27)
7 Because of this, a man shall leave his father and mother and shall be joined to his wife,

575 1161 746 2937 730 2532 2338 4160 846 3588
6 ἀπὸ δὲ ἀρχῆς κτίσεως, ἄρσεν καὶ θῆλυ ἐποίησεν αὐτοὺς ὁ
from But the beginning of creation male and female made them
2316 1752 5127 2641 444 3588 3962 846
Θεός. 7 ἕνεκεν τούτου καταλείψει ἄνθρωπος τὸν πατέρα αὐτοῦ
God. Because of this shall leave a man the father of him
2532 3588 3384 2532 4347 4314 3588 1135
καὶ τὴν μητέρα· καὶ προσκολληθήσεται πρὸς τὴν γυναῖκα
and the mother and shall be joined to the wife

6 But from the beginning of the creation God made them male and female.
7 For this cause shall a man leave his father and mother, and cleave to his wife;

8 and the two shall be one flesh; so that they no longer are two, but one flesh. (Gen. 2:24)
9 Therefore, what God yoked together, let not man put apart.
10 And again, in the house His disciples asked Him about the

846 2532 2071 3588 1417 1519 4561 3391 5620 3765 1526
αὐτοῦ, 8 καὶ ἔσονται οἱ δύο εἰς σάρκα μίαν, ὥστε οὐκέτι εἰσὶ
of him, and shall become the two into flesh one, so as no longer are they
1417 235 3391 4561 3739 3767 3588 2316 4801 444 3361
δύο, ἀλλὰ μία σάρξ. 9 ὃ οὖν ὁ Θεὸς συνέζευξεν, ἄνθρωπος μὴ
two, but one flesh. What then God yoked together, man not
5563 2532 1722 3588 3614 3825 3588 3101 846 4012 3588
χωριζέτω. 10 καὶ ἐν τῇ οἰκίᾳ πάλιν οἱ μαθηταὶ αὐτοῦ περὶ τοῦ
let put apart. And in the house again the disciples of Him about the

8 And they twain shall be one flesh: so then they are no more twain, but one flesh.
9 What therefore God hath joined together, let not man put asunder.
10 And in the house his disciples asked him again of the

Mark 10:11

Literal Translation

same.
11 And He said to them, Whoever shall put away his wife and marries another commits adultery against her.

12 And if a woman puts away her husband and marries another, she commits adultery.

13. And they brought children to Him, that He might touch them. But the disciples rebuked the (ones)bringing (them).
14 But seeing, Jesus was indignant. And He said to them, Permit the children to come to Me, and do not stop them. For of such is the kingdom of God.

15 Truly I say to you, Whoever does not receive the kingdom of God as a child may in no way enter into it.

16 And having taken them in (His) arms, laying hands on them, He blessed them.

17. And He having gone out into (the) way, running up and kneeling down to Him, one questioned Him, Good Teacher, what shall I do that I may inherit everlasting life?
18 But Jesus said to him, Why do you call Me good? No one is good except One, God.

19 You know the commandments: Do not commit adultery, do not commit murder, do not steal, do not bear false witness, do not defraud, honor your father and mother. (Ex. 20:12-16)
20 And answering, he said to Him, Teacher, I observed all these from my youth.
21 And looking at him, Jesus loved him, and said to him,

---

846 1905 846 2532 3004 846 3739 1437 630
αὐτοῦ ἐπηρώτησαν αὐτόν. 11 καὶ λέγει αὐτοῖς, Ὃς ἐὰν ἀπο-
same questioned Him. And He says to them, Whoever may

3588 1135 846 2532 1060 243 3429 1909
λύσῃ τὴν γυναῖκα αὐτοῦ καὶ γαμήσῃ ἄλλην, μοιχᾶται ἐπ’
dismiss the wife of him, and marries another, commits adultery against

846 2532 1437 1135 630 3588 435 846 2532 1060
αὐτήν· 12 καὶ ἐὰν γυνὴ ἀπολύσῃ τὸν ἄνδρα αὐτῆς καὶ γαμηθῇ
her. And if a woman may dismiss the husband of her, and marries

243 3429
ἄλλῳ, μοιχᾶται.
another she commits adultery.

2532 4374 846 3813 2443 680 846 3588 1161
13. Καὶ προσέφερον αὐτῷ παιδία ἵνα ἅψηται αὐτῶν· οἱ δὲ
And they brought to Him children, that He may touch them. the But

3101 2008 3588 4374 1492 1161 3588 2424
μαθηταὶ ἐπετίμων τοῖς προσφέρουσιν. 14 ἰδὼν δὲ ὁ Ἰησοῦς
disciples rebuked those bringing (them). seeing But Jesus

23 2532 2036 846 863 3588 3813 2064
ἠγανάκτησε, καὶ εἶπεν αὐτοῖς, Ἄφετε τὰ παιδία ἔρχεσθαι
was indignant, and He said to them, Permit the children to come

4314 3165 2532 3361 2967 846 3588 1063 5108 2076 3588
πρός με, καὶ μὴ κωλύετε αὐτά· τῶν γὰρ τοιούτων ἐστὶν ἡ
to Me, and not stop them. (as) these For of such is the

932 3588 2316 281 3004 5213 3739 1437 3361 1209 3588
βασιλεία τοῦ Θεοῦ. 15 ἀμὴν λέγω ὑμῖν, ὃς ἐὰν μὴ δέξηται τὴν
kingdom of God. Truly I say to you, whoever not receives the

932 3588 2316 5613 3813 3756 3361 1525 1519 846
βασιλείαν τοῦ Θεοῦ ὡς παιδίον, οὐ μὴ εἰσέλθῃ εἰς αὐτήν.
kingdom of God as a child in no way may enter into it.

2532 1723 846 5087 3588 5495 1909 846
16 καὶ ἐναγκαλισάμενος αὐτὰ, τιθεὶς τὰς χεῖρας ἐπ’ αὐτὰ,
And having taken in arms them, laying the hands on them,

2127 846
ηὐλόγει αὐτά.
He blessed them.

2532 1607 846 1519 3598 4370 1520 2532
17. Καὶ ἐκπορευομένου αὐτοῦ εἰς ὁδόν, προσδραμὼν εἷς καὶ
And having gone forth Him into (the) way, running up one and

1120 846 1905 846 1320 18 5101
γονυπετήσας αὐτὸν ἐπηρώτα αὐτόν, Διδάσκαλε ἀγαθέ, τί
kneeling down to Him questioned Him, Teacher Good, What

4160 2443 2222 166 2816 3588 1161 2424
ποιήσω ἵνα ζωὴν αἰώνιον κληρονομήσω; 18 ὁ δὲ Ἰησοῦς
shall I do that life everlasting I may inherit? And Jesus

2036 846 5101 3165 3004 18 3762 18 1487 3361 1520 3588
εἶπεν αὐτῷ, Τί με λέγεις ἀγαθόν; οὐδεὶς ἀγαθός, εἰ μὴ εἷς, ὁ
said to him, Why Me call you good? No one (is) good, except One,

2316 3588 1785 1492 3361 3431 3361 5407 3361
Θεός. 19 τὰς ἐντολὰς οἶδας, Μὴ μοιχεύσῃς, μὴ φονεύσῃς, μὴ
God. The commandments you know: Not commit adultery, not do murder, not

2813 3361 5576 3361 650 5091 3588
κλέψῃς, μὴ ψευδομαρτυρήσῃς, μὴ ἀποστερήσῃς, τίμα τὸν
steal, not do bear false witness, not defraud, honor the

3962 4675 2532 3588 3384 3588 1161 611 2036 846
πατέρα σου καὶ τὴν μητέρα. 20 ὁ δὲ ἀποκριθεὶς εἶπεν αὐτῷ,
father of you and the mother. he And answering said to Him,

1320 5023 3956 5442 1537 3503 3450 3588 1161
Διδάσκαλε, ταῦτα πάντα ἐφυλαξάμην ἐκ νεότητός μου. 21 ὁ δὲ
Teacher, these things all I observed from youth of me. And

2424 1689 846 25 846 2532 2036 846
Ἰησοῦς ἐμβλέψας αὐτῷ ἠγάπησεν αὐτὸν, καὶ εἶπεν αὐτῷ,
Jesus looking at him loved him, and said to him,

King James Version

same (matter).
11 And he saith unto them, Whosoever shall put away his wife, and marry another, committeth adultery against her.

12 And if a woman shall put away her husband, and be married to another, she committeth adultery.

13. And they brought young children to him, that he should touch them: and (his) disciples rebuked those that brought (them).
14 But when Jesus saw (it), he was much displeased, and said unto them, Suffer the little children to come unto me, and forbid them not: for of such is the kingdom of God.
15 Verily I say unto you, Whosoever shall not receive the kingdom of God as a little child, he shall not enter therein.

16 And he took them up in his arms, put (his) hands upon them, and blessed them.

17. And when he was gone forth into the way, there came one running, and kneeled to him, and asked him, Good Master, what shall I do that I may inherit eternal life?
18 And Jesus said unto him, Why callest thou me good? (there is) none good but one, (that is), God.

19 Thou knowest the commandments, Do not commit adultery, Do not kill, Do not steal, Do not bear false witness, Defraud not, Honour thy father and mother.
20 And he answered and said unto him, Master, all these have I observed from my youth.
21 Then Jesus beholding him loved him, and said unto him,

Literal Translation

Mark 10:22

King James Version

One (thing) is lacking to you. Go, sell what things you have, and give to the poor. And you will have treasure in Heaven. And come, follow Me, taking up the cross.
22 But being sad at the word, he went away grieving; for he had many possessions.

23. And looking around, Jesus said to His disciples, How hardly those having riches will enter into the kingdom of God!

24 And the disciples were astonished at His words. And answering again, Jesus said to them, Children, how hard it is for those trusting on riches to enter into the kingdom of God!

25 It is easier (for) a camel to pass through the eye of the needle, than (for) a rich one to enter into the kingdom of God.

26 And they were exceedingly astonished, saying to themselves, And who is able to be saved?
27 But looking at them, Jesus said, From men (it is) impossible, but not from God. For all things are possible from God.
28. And Peter began to say to Him, Behold, we left all and followed You.

29 But answering, Jesus said, Truly I say to you, There is no one who forsook house, or brothers, or sisters, or father, or mother, or wife, or children, or lands, for My sake and the gospel,

30 that will not receive a hundredfold

1520 4671 5302 5217 3745 2192 4453 2532 1325 3588
Ἕν σοι ὑστερεῖ· ὕπαγε, ὅσα ἔχεις πώλησον, καὶ δὸς τοῖς
One to you is lacking; go; what things you have sell, and give to the
4434 2532 2192 2344 1722 3772 2532 1204 190
πτωχοῖς, καὶ ἕξεις θησαυρὸν ἐν οὐρανῷ· καὶ δεῦρο, ἀκολούθει
poor; and you will have treasure in Heaven; and come, follow
3427 142 3588 4716 3588 1161 4768 1909 3588 3056 565
μοι, ἄρας τὸν σταυρόν. 22 ὁ δὲ στυγνάσας ἐπὶ τῷ λόγῳ ἀπῆλθε
Me, taking up the cross. he But, being sad at the word went away
3076 2258 1063 2192 2933 4183
λυπούμενος· ἦν γὰρ ἔχων κτήματα πολλά.
grieving; he was for having possessions many.

2532 4017 3588 2424 3004 3588 3101 846
23. Καὶ περιβλεψάμενος ὁ Ἰησοῦς λέγει τοῖς μαθηταῖς αὐτοῦ,
And having looked around, Jesus says to the disciples of Him,
4459 1423 3588 3588 5536 2192 1519 3588 932 3588
Πῶς δυσκόλως οἱ τὰ χρήματα ἔχοντες εἰς τὴν βασιλείαν τοῦ
How hardly those the riches having into the kingdom
2316 1525 3588 1161 3101 2284 1909 3588
Θεοῦ εἰσελεύσονται. 24 οἱ δὲ μαθηταὶ ἐθαμβοῦντο ἐπὶ τοῖς
of God will enter! the But disciples were amazed at the
3056 846 3588 1161 2424 3825 611 3004 846
λόγοις αὐτοῦ. ὁ δὲ Ἰησοῦς πάλιν ἀποκριθεὶς λέγει αὐτοῖς,
words of Him. And Jesus again answering says to them,
5043 4459 1422 2076 3588 3982 1909 3588
Τέκνα, πῶς δύσκολόν ἐστι τοὺς πεποιθότας ἐπὶ τοῖς
Children, how hard it is for those trusting on the
5536 1519 3588 932 3588 2316 1525 2123
χρήμασιν εἰς τὴν βασιλείαν τοῦ Θεοῦ εἰσελθεῖν. 25 εὐκοπώ-
riches into the kingdom of God to enter. Easier
2076 2574 1223 3588 5168 3588 4476
τερόν ἐστι κάμηλον διὰ τῆς τρυμαλιᾶς τῆς ῥαφίδος
it is (for) a camel through the eye of the needle
1525 2228 4145 1519 3588 932 3588 2316 1525
διελθεῖν, ἢ πλούσιον εἰς τὴν βασιλείαν τοῦ Θεοῦ εἰσελθεῖν.
to pass, than (for) a rich one into the kingdom of God to enter.

3588 1161 4057 1605 3004 4314 1438 2532
26 οἱ δὲ περισσῶς ἐξεπλήσσοντο, λέγοντες πρὸς ἑαυτούς, Καὶ
they But exceedingly were astonished, saying to themselves, And
5101 1410 4982 1689 1161 846 3588 2424 3004
τίς δύναται σωθῆναι; 27 ἐμβλέψας δὲ αὐτοῖς ὁ Ἰησοῦς λέγει,
who is able to be saved? looking at them Jesus says,
3844 444 102 235 3756 3844 3588 2316 3956
Παρὰ ἀνθρώποις ἀδύνατον, ἀλλ' οὐ παρὰ τῷ Θεῷ· πάντα
From men (it is) impossible; but not from God; all things
1063 1415 2076 3844 3588 2316 2532 2756 3588 4074
γὰρ δυνατά ἐστι παρὰ τῷ Θεῷ. 28 καὶ ἤρξατο ὁ Πέτρος
for possible are from God. And began Peter
3004 846 2400 2249 863 3956 2532 190
λέγειν αὐτῷ, Ἰδού ἡμεῖς ἀφήκαμεν πάντα καὶ ἠκολουθήσαμέν
to say to Him, Behold! We forsook all things and have followed

4671 611 1161 3588 2424 2036 281 3004 5213
σοι. 29 ἀποκριθεὶς δὲ ὁ Ἰησοῦς εἶπεν, Ἀμὴν λέγω ὑμῖν,
You. answering But Jesus said, Truly I say to you,
3762 2076 3739 863 3614 2228 80 2228 79 2228
οὐδείς ἐστιν ὃς ἀφῆκεν οἰκίαν, ἢ ἀδελφούς, ἢ ἀδελφάς, ἢ
no one there is who forsook house, or brothers, or sisters, or
3962 2228 3384 2228 1135 2228 5043 2228 68 1752
πατέρα, ἢ μητέρα, ἢ γυναῖκα, ἢ τέκνα, ἢ ἀγρούς, ἕνεκεν
father, or mother, or wife, or children, or fields, for the sake
1700 2532 3588 2098 1437 3361 2983 1542
ἐμοῦ καὶ τοῦ εὐαγγελίου, 30 ἐὰν μὴ λάβῃ ἑκατονταπλασίονα
of Me and the gospel, if not he receives a hundredfold

One thing thou lackest: go thy way, sell whatsoever thou hast, and give to the poor, and thou shalt have treasure in heaven: and come, take up the cross, and follow me.
22 And he was sad at that saying, and went away grieved: for he had great possessions.

23. And Jesus looked round about, and saith unto his disciples, How hardly shall they that have riches enter into the kingdom of God!

24 And the disciples were astonished at his words. But Jesus answereth again, and saith unto them, Children, how hard is it for them that trust in riches to enter into the kingdom of God!

25 It is easier for a camel to go through the eye of a needle, than for a rich man to enter into the kingdom of God.

26 And they were astonished out of measure, saying among themselves, Who then can be saved?
27 And Jesus looking upon them saith, With men (it is) impossible, but not with God: for with God all things are possible.
28. Then Peter began to say unto him, Lo, we have left all, and have followed thee.

29 And Jesus answered and said, Verily I say unto you, There is no man that hath left house, or brethren, or sisters, or father, or mother, or wife, or children, or lands, for my sake, and the gospel's,

30 But he shall receive an hundredfold

Literal Translation | **Mark 10:31** | **King James Version**

now in this time, houses and brothers and sisters and mothers and children, and lands, amidst persecutions; and in the coming age, eternal life.

31 But many first shall be last, and the last (shall be) first.

32. And they were in the way, going up to Jerusalem. And Jesus was going before them, and following they were astonished and were afraid. And taking the Twelve again, He began to tell them the things about to happen to Him:

33 Behold, we are going up to Jerusalem. And the Son of man will be delivered up to the chief priests and to the scribes. And they will condemn Him to death and will deliver up Him to the nations.

34 And they will mock Him and will flog Him and will spit at Him, and will kill Him. And on the third day He will rise again.

35. And coming up to Him, James and John, the sons of Zebedee, said, Teacher, we desire that whatever we may ask You would do for us.

36 And He said to them, What do you desire for Me to do for you?

37 And they said to Him, Give us that we may sit one off (the) right of You and one off (the) left of You in Your glory.

38 But Jesus said to them, You do not know what you ask. Are you able to drink the cup which I drink, and to be baptized

3568 1722 3588 2540 5129 3614 2532 80 2532 80
νῦν ἐν τῷ καιρῷ τούτῳ οἰκίας καὶ ἀδελφοὺς καὶ ἀδελφὰς
now in time this, houses and brothers and sisters

2532 3384 2532 5043 2532 68 3326 1375 2532 1722 3588
καὶ μητέρας καὶ τέκνα καὶ ἀγρούς, μετὰ διωγμῶν, καὶ ἐν τῷ
and mothers and children and fields, amidst persecutions, and in the

165 3588 2064 2222 166 4183 1161 2071
αἰῶνι τῷ ἐρχομένῳ ζωὴν αἰώνιον. 31 πολλοὶ δὲ ἔσονται
age coming life everlasting. many And will be

4413 2078 2532 3588 2078 4413
πρῶτοι ἔσχατοι, καὶ οἱ ἔσχατοι πρῶτοι.
first last, and the last first.

2258 1161 1722 3588 3598 305 1519 2414
32. Ἦσαν δὲ ἐν τῇ ὁδῷ ἀναβαίνοντες εἰς Ἱεροσόλυμα·
they were And in the way, going up into Jerusalem.

2532 2258 4254 846 3588 2424 2532 2284 2532
καὶ ἦν προάγων αὐτοὺς ὁ Ἰησοῦς, καὶ ἐθαμβοῦντο, καὶ
And was going before them Jesus. And they were amazed, and

190 5399 2532 5631 3825 3588
ἀκολουθοῦντες ἐφοβοῦντο. καὶ παραλαβὼν πάλιν τοὺς
following were afraid. And taking again the

1427 756 846 3004 3588 3195 846 5721
δώδεκα, ἤρξατο αὐτοῖς λέγειν τὰ μέλλοντα αὐτῷ συμβαίνειν,
twelve, He began them to tell the things about to Him to happen,

3754 2400 305 1519 2414 2532 3588 5207 3588
33 ὅτι Ἰδού, ἀναβαίνομεν εἰς Ἱεροσόλυμα, καὶ ὁ υἱὸς τοῦ
Behold! We are going up into Jerusalem, and the Son

444 3860 3588 749 2532 3588 3146
ἀνθρώπου παραδοθήσεται τοῖς ἀρχιερεῦσι καὶ τοῖς γραμ-
of man will be delivered up to the chief priests and to the scribes,

2532 3860 846 2288 2532 3860
ματεῦσι, καὶ κατακρινοῦσιν αὐτὸν θανάτῳ, καὶ παραδώ-
and they will condemn Him to death, and will deliver

846 3588 1484 2532 1716 846 2532
σουσιν αὐτὸν τοῖς ἔθνεσι, 34 καὶ ἐμπαίξουσιν αὐτῷ, καὶ
up Him to the nations. And they will mock Him, and

3146 846 2532 1716 846 2532 615
μαστιγώσουσιν αὐτόν, καὶ ἐμπτύσουσιν αὐτῷ, καὶ ἀπο-
will scourge Him, and will spit at Him, and will

846 2532 3588 5154 2250 450
κτενοῦσιν αὐτόν· καὶ τῇ τρίτῃ ἡμέρᾳ ἀναστήσεται.
kill Him; and on the third day He will rise again.

2532 4365 846 2385 2532 2491 3588
35. Καὶ προσπορεύονται αὐτῷ Ἰάκωβος καὶ Ἰωάννης οἱ
And came up to Him James and John, the

5207 2199 3004 1320 2309 2443 3739 1437
υἱοὶ Ζεβεδαίου, λέγοντες, Διδάσκαλε, θέλομεν ἵνα ὃ ἐὰν
sons of Zebedee, saying, Teacher, we desire that whatever

154 4160 2254 3588 1161 2036 846 5101 2309
αἰτήσωμεν, ποιήσῃς ἡμῖν. 36 ὁ δὲ εἶπεν αὐτοῖς, Τί θέλετε
we may ask You would do for us. He And He said to them, What desire

4160 3165 5213 3588 1161 2036 846 1325 2254 2443 1520 1537
ποιῆσαί με ὑμῖν; 37 οἱ δὲ εἶπον αὐτῷ, Δὸς ἡμῖν, ἵνα εἷς ἐκ
to do Me for you? they And said to Him, Give us that one off

1188 4675 2532 1520 1537 2176 4675 2523 1722 3588 1391
δεξιῶν σου καὶ εἷς ἐξ εὐωνύμων σου καθίσωμεν ἐν τῇ δόξῃ
(the) right of You and one off (the) left of You we may sit in the glory

4675 3588 1161 2424 2036 846 3756 1492 5101 154
σου. 38 ὁ δὲ Ἰησοῦς εἶπεν αὐτοῖς, Οὐκ οἴδατε τί αἰτεῖσθε.
of You. And Jesus said to them, Not you know what you ask.

1410 4095 3588 4221 3739 1473 4095 2532 3588 908 3739
δύνασθε πιεῖν τὸ ποτήριον ὃ ἐγὼ πίνω, καὶ τὸ βάπτισμα ὃ
Can you drink the cup which I drink, and the baptism which

now in this time, houses, and brethren, and sisters, and mothers, and children, and lands, with persecutions; and in the world to come eternal life.

31 But many (that are) first shall be last; and the last first.

32. And they were in the way going up to Jerusalem; and Jesus went before them: and they were amazed; and as they followed, they were afraid. And he took again the twelve, and began to tell them what things should happen unto him,

33 (Saying), Behold, we go up to Jerusalem; and the Son of man shall be delivered unto the chief priests, and unto the scribes; and they shall condemn him to death, and shall deliver him to the Gentiles:

34 And they shall mock him, and shall scourge him, and shall spit upon him, and shall kill him: and the third day he shall rise again.

35. And James and John, the sons of Zebedee, come unto him, saying, Master, we would that thou shouldest do for us whatsoever we shall desire.

36 And he said unto them, What would ye that I should do for you?

37 They said unto him, Grant unto us that we may sit, one on thy right hand, and the other on thy left hand, in thy glory.

38 But Jesus said unto them, Ye know not what ye ask: can ye drink of the cup that I drink of? and be baptized

Literal Translation

(with) the baptism I am baptized (with)?
39 And they said to Him, We are able. But Jesus said to them, Indeed you will drink the cup which I drink, and you will be baptized (with) the baptism (with) which I am baptized.
40 But to sit off My right and off My left is not Mine to give, but for whom it has been prepared.
41 And hearing, the ten began to be indignant about James and John.
42 But having called them near, Jesus said to them, You know that those seeming to rule the nations lord it over them, and their great ones exercise authority over them.
43 But it shall not be so among you, but whoever desires to become great among you shall be your servant.
44 And whoever of you desires to become first, (he) shall be slave of all.
45 For even the Son of man did not come to be served, but to serve, and to give His life (as) a ransom on behalf of many.

46. And they came to Jericho. And He and His disciples and a large crowd having gone out from Jericho, a son of Timaeus, Bartimaeus the blind, sat beside the way begging.
47 And hearing that it was Jesus the Nazarene, he began to cry out and to say, Son of David, Jesus, pityme!
48 And many warned him that he be quiet. But he much more cried out, Son of David, have mercy on me!
49 And standing still, Jesus

Mark 10:39

1473 907 5683 3588 1161 2036 846 1410
ἐγὼ βαπτίζομαι βαπτισθῆναι;39 οἱ δὲ εἶπον αὐτῷ, Δυνάμεθα.
I am baptized to be baptized (with)? they And say to Him, We are able.

3588 1161 2424 2036 846 3588 3303 4221 3739 1473 4095
ὁ δὲ Ἰησοῦς εἶπεν αὐτοῖς, Τὸ μὲν ποτήριον ὃ ἐγὼ πίνω
And Jesus said to them, the indeed cup which I drink

4095 2532 3588 908 3739 1473 907 907
πίεσθε· καὶ τὸ βάπτισμα ὃ ἐγὼ βαπτίζομαι βαπτισθήσεσθε·
you will drink,and the baptism which I am baptized (with) you will be baptized;

3588 1161 2523 1537 1188 3450 2532 1537 2176 3450 3756 2076
40 τὸ δὲ καθίσαι ἐκ δεξιῶν μου καὶ ἐξ εὐωνύμων μου οὐκ ἔστιν
but to sit off (the) right of Me and off (the) left of Me not is

1699 1325 235 3739 2090 2532 191 3588 1176
ἐμὸν δοῦναι, ἀλλ᾽ οἷς ἡτοίμασται. 41 καὶ ἀκούσαντες οἱ δέκα
Mine to give, but for whom it has been prepared. And having heard the ten

756 23 4012 2385 2532 2491 3588 1161 2424
ἤρξαντο ἀγανακτεῖν περὶ Ἰακώβου καὶ Ἰωάννου. 42 ὁ δὲ Ἰησοῦς
began to be indignant about James and John. But Jesus

4341 846 3004 846 1492 3754 3588 1380
προσκαλεσάμενος αὐτοὺς λέγει αὐτοῖς, Οἴδατε ὅτι οἱ δοκοῦν-
having called near them says to them, You know that those seeming

757 3588 1484 2634 846 2532 3588 3173
τες ἄρχειν τῶν ἐθνῶν κατακυριεύουσιν αὐτῶν· καὶ οἱ μεγάλοι
to rule the nations lord it over them, and those great

846 2715 846 3756 3779 1161 2071 1722
αὐτῶν κατεξουσιάζουσιν αὐτῶν. 43 οὐχ οὕτω δὲ ἔσται ἐν
of them exercise authority over them. not so But to be among

5213 235/3739/1437 2309 1096 3173 1722 5213 2071 1249
ὑμῖν· ἀλλ᾽ ὃς ἐὰν θέλῃ γενέσθαι μέγας ἐν ὑμῖν, ἔσται διάκονος
you; but whoever desires to become great among you shall be servant

5216 2532/3739/302/ 2309 5216 1096 4413 2071 3956
ὑμῶν· 44 καὶ ὃς ἂν θέλῃ ὑμῶν γενέσθαι πρῶτος ἔσται πάντων
of you. And whoever desires of you to become first shall be of all

1401 2532 1063 3588 5207 3588 444 3756 2064
δοῦλος. 45 καὶ γὰρ ὁ υἱὸς τοῦ ἀνθρώπου οὐκ ἦλθε
slave . even For the Son of man not did come

1247 235 1247 2532 1325 3588 5590
διακονηθῆναι, ἀλλὰ διακονῆσαι, καὶ δοῦναι τὴν ψυχὴν
to be served, but to serve, and to give the life

846 3083 473 4183
αὐτοῦ λύτρον ἀντὶ πολλῶν.
of Him a ransom instead of many.

2532 2064 1519 2410 2532 1607 846 575
46. Καὶ ἔρχονται εἰς Ἰεριχώ· καὶ ἐκπορευομένου αὐτοῦ ἀπὸ
And they come into Jericho. And having gone out He from

2410 2532 3588 3101 846 2532 3793 2425 5207
Ἰεριχώ, καὶ τῶν μαθητῶν αὐτοῦ, καὶ ὄχλου ἱκανοῦ, υἱὸς
Jericho, and the disciples of Him, and a crowd considerable, son

5090 924 3588 5185 2521 3844 3588 3598
Τιμαίου Βαρτίμαιος ὁ τυφλὸς ἐκάθητο παρὰ τὴν ὁδὸν
of Timaeus Bartimaeus the blind sat by the way

4319 2532 191 3754 2424 3588 3480 2076
προσαιτῶν. 47 καὶ ἀκούσας ὅτι Ἰησοῦς ὁ Ναζωραῖός ἐστιν,
begging. And hearing that Jesus the Nazarene it is,

756 2896 2532 3004 3588 5207 1138 2424 1653
ἤρξατο κράζειν καὶ λέγειν, Ὁ υἱὸς Δαβὶδ, Ἰησοῦ, ἐλέησόν
he began to cry out and to say, Son of David, Jesus, pity

3165 2532 2008 846 4183 2443 4623 3588 1161 4319
με. 48 καὶ ἐπετίμων αὐτῷ πολλοὶ, ἵνα σιωπήσῃ· ὁ δὲ πολλῷ
me. And warned him many, that he be quiet. he But much

2896 5207 1138 1653 3165 2532 2476/3588 2424
μᾶλλον ἔκραζεν, Υἱὲ Δαβίδ, ἐλέησόν με. 49 καὶ στὰς ὁ Ἰησοῦς
more cried out, Son of David, pity me. And standing Jesus

King James Version

with the baptism that I am baptized with?
39 And they said unto him, We can. And Jesus said unto them, Ye shall indeed drink of the cup that I drink of; and with the baptism that I am baptized withal shall ye be baptized:
40 But to sit on my right hand and on my left hand is not mine to give; but (it shall be given to them) for whom it is prepared.
41 And when the ten heard (it), they began to be much displeased with James and John.
42 But Jesus called them (to him), and saith unto them, Ye know that they which are accounted to rule over the Gentiles exercise lordship over them; and their great ones exercise authority upon them.
43 But so shall it not be among you: but whosoever will be great among you, shall be your minister:
44 And whosoever of you will be the chiefest, shall be servant of all.
45 For even the Son of man came not to be ministered unto, but to minister, and to give his life a ransom for many.

46. And they came to Jericho: and as he went out of Jericho with his disciples and a great number of people, blind Bartimaeus, the son of Timaeus, sat by the highway side begging.
47 And when he heard that it was Jesus of Nazareth, he began to cry out, and say, Jesus, (thou) Son of David, have mercy on me.
48 And many charged him that he should hold his peace: but he cried the more a great deal, (Thou) Son of David, have mercy on me.
49 And Jesus stood still,

Mark 10:50

Literal Translation

said for him to be called. And they called the blind (one), saying to him, Be comforted, rise up, He calls you.
50 And throwing away his garment, rising up, he came to Jesus.
51 And answering, Jesus said to him, What do you desire I should do to you? And the blind (one) said to Him, My Lord, that I may see again.
52 And Jesus said to him, Go, your faith has healed you. And instantly he saw again, and followed Jesus in the way.

2036 846 5455 2532 5455 3588 5185 3004
εἶπεν αὐτὸν φωνηθῆναι· καὶ φωνοῦσι τὸν τυφλόν, λέγοντες
said for him to be called. And they call the blind (one), saying

846 2293 1453 5455 4571 3588 1161 577 3588 2440
αὐτῷ, Θάρσει· ἔγειραι, φωνεῖ σε. 50 ὁ δὲ ἀποβαλὼν τὸ ἱμάτιον
to him, Be comforted! Rise up, He calls you. he And casting away the garment

846 450 2064 4314 3588 2424 2532 611 3004
αὐτοῦ ἀναστὰς ἦλθε πρὸς τὸν Ἰησοῦν. 51 καὶ ἀποκριθεὶς λέγει
of him, rising up came to Jesus. And answering says

846 3588 2424 5101 2309 4160 4671 3588 1161 5185 2036
αὐτῷ ὁ Ἰησοῦς, Τί θέλεις ποιήσω σοί; ὁ δὲ τυφλὸς εἶπεν
to him Jesus, What desire you I do for you? the And blind (one) said

846 4462 2443 308 3588 1161 2424 2036 846
αὐτῷ, Ῥαββονί, ἵνα ἀναβλέψω. 52 ὁ δὲ Ἰησοῦς εἶπεν αὐτῷ,
to Him, My Lord, that I may see again. And Jesus said to him,

5217 3588 4102 4675 4982 4571 2532 2112 308 2532
Ὕπαγε· ἡ πίστις σου σέσωκέ σε. καὶ εὐθέως ἀνέβλεψε, καὶ
Go! The faith of you has healed you. And instantly he saw again, and

190 3588 2424 1722 3588 3598
ἠκολούθει τῷ Ἰησοῦ ἐν τῇ ὁδῷ.
followed Jesus in the way.

King James Version

and commanded him to be called. And they call the blind man, saying unto him, Be of good comfort, rise; he calleth thee.
50 And he, casting away his garment, rose, and came to Jesus.
51 And Jesus answered and said unto him, What wilt thou that I should do unto thee? The blind man said unto him, Lord, that I might receive my sight.
52 And Jesus said unto him, Go thy way; thy faith hath made thee whole. And immediately he received his sight, and followed Jesus in the way.

Mark 11

1. And when they drew near to Jerusalem, to Bethphage and Bethany, toward the Mount of Olives, He sent two of His disciples,
2 and said to them, Go into the village opposite you. And going into it, at once you will find a colt being tied, on which no one of men has sat. Having loosed it, bring (it).
3 And if anyone says to you, Why do you do this? say, The Lord has need of it. And he will at once send it here.
4 And they departed and found the colt being tied at the door outside, on the crossway; and they loosed it.
5 And some of those standing there said to them, What are you doing, loosening the colt?
6 And they said to them as Jesus commanded, and they let them go.
7 And they led the colt to Jesus. And they threw their garments on it,

2532 3753 1448 1519 2419 1519 967 2532
1. Καὶ ὅτε ἐγγίζουσιν εἰς Ἱερουσαλήμ, εἰς Βηθφαγὴ καὶ
And when they draw near to Jerusalem, to Bethphage and

963 4314 3588 3735 3588 1636 649 1417 3588
Βηθανίαν, πρὸς τὸ ὄρος τῶν ἐλαιῶν, ἀποστέλλει δύο τῶν
Bethany, toward the Mount of the Olives, He sends two of the

3101 846 2532 3004 846 5217 1519 3588 2968
μαθητῶν αὐτοῦ, 2 καὶ λέγει αὐτοῖς, Ὑπάγετε εἰς τὴν κώμην
disciples of Him, and says to them, Go into the village

3588 2713 5216 2532 2112 1531 1519 846
τὴν κατέναντι ὑμῶν· καὶ εὐθέως εἰσπορευόμενοι εἰς αὐτὴν
opposite you, and at once entering into it

2147 4454 1210 1909 3739 3762 444 2523
εὑρήσετε πῶλον δεδεμένον, ἐφ' ὃν οὐδεὶς ἀνθρώπων κεκάθικε·
you will find a colt being tied, on which no one of men has sat.

3089 846 71 2532 1437 5100 5213 2036 5101 4160
λύσαντες αὐτὸν ἀγάγετε. 3 καὶ ἐάν τις ὑμῖν εἴπῃ, Τί ποιεῖτε
Having loosed it lead (it) And if anyone to you says, Why do you do

5124 2036 3754 3588 2962 846 5532 2192 2532 2112
τοῦτο; εἴπατε ὅτι Ὁ κύριος αὐτοῦ χρείαν ἔχει· καὶ εὐθέως
this? Say, the Lord of it need has. And at once

846 649 5602 565 1161 2532 2147 3588 4454
αὐτὸν ἀποστελεῖ ὧδε. 4 ἀπῆλθον δὲ καὶ εὗρον τὸν πῶλον
he will send (it) here. they departed And and found the colt

1210 4314 3588 2374 1854 1909 3588 296 2532
δεδεμένον πρὸς τὴν θύραν ἔξω ἐπὶ τοῦ ἀμφόδου, καὶ
being tied to the door outside on the crossway, and

3089 846 2532 5100 3588 1563 2476 3004 846
λύουσιν αὐτόν. 5 καί τινες τῶν ἐκεῖ ἑστηκότων ἔλεγον αὐτοῖς,
they loosen it. And some of those there standing said to them,

5101 4160 3089 3588 4454 3588 1161 2036 846 2531
Τί ποιεῖτε λύοντες τὸν πῶλον; 6 οἱ δὲ εἶπον αὐτοῖς καθὼς
What do you do loosening the colt. they And said to them even as

1781 3588 2424 2532 863 846 2532 71 3588
ἐνετείλατο ὁ Ἰησοῦς· καὶ ἀφῆκαν αὐτούς. 7 καὶ ἤγαγον τὸν
commanded Jesus; and they let go them. And they led the

4454 4314 3588 2424 2532 1911 846 3588 2440
πῶλον πρὸς τὸν Ἰησοῦν, καὶ ἐπέβαλον αὐτῷ τὰ ἱμάτια
colt to Jesus, and they throw on it the garments

1 . And when they came nigh to Jerusalem, unto Bethphage and Bethany, at the mount of Olives, he sendeth forth two of his disciples,
2 And saith unto them, Go your way into the village over against you: and as soon as ye be entered into it, ye shall find a colt tied, whereon never man sat; loose him, and bring (him).
3 And if any man say unto you, Why do ye this? say ye that the Lord hath need of him; and straightway he will send him hither.
4 And they went their way, and found the colt tied by the door without in a place where two ways met; and they loose him.
5 And certain of them that stood there said unto them, What do ye, loosing the colt?
6 And they said unto them even as Jesus had commanded: and they let them go.
7 And they brought the colt to Jesus, and cast their garments on him;

Literal Translation

Mark 11:8

King James Version

and He sat on it.
8 And many spread their garments on the highway, and others were cutting branches from the trees and were spreading (them) on the highway.
9 And those going before, and those following after, cried out, saying, Hosanna! Blessed (is) the (One) having come in (the) name of (the) Lord!
10 Blessed (is) the coming kingdom of our father David in (the) name of (the) Lord! Hosanna in the highest! (Ps. 118:25, 26)

846 2532 2523 1909 846 4183 1161 3588 2440 846
αὐτῶν, καὶ ἐκάθισεν ἐπ' αὐτῷ. 8 πολλοὶ δὲ τὰ ἱμάτια αὐτῶν
of them; and He sat on it. many And the garments of them
4766 1519 3588 3598 243 1161 4746 2875 1537
ἔστρωσαν εἰς τὴν ὁδόν· ἄλλοι δὲ στοιβάδας ἔκοπτον ἐκ
scattered into the way, others and branches were cutting from
3588 1186 2532 4766 1519 3588 3598 2532 3588 4254
τῶν δένδρων, καὶ ἐστρώννυον εἰς τὴν ὁδόν. 9 καὶ οἱ προάγον-
the trees, and were scattering into the way. And those going
2532 3588 190 2896 3004 5614
τες καὶ οἱ ἀκολουθοῦντες ἔκραζον, λέγοντες, Ὡσαννά·
before and those following, cried out, saying, Hosanna!
2127 3588 2064 1722 3686 2962 2127
εὐλογημένος ὁ ἐρχόμενος ἐν ὀνόματι Κυρίου· 10 εὐλογημένη
Has been blessed the having come in the name of (the) Lord! Blessed (be)
(One)
2228 2064 932 1722 3686 2962 3588 3962 2257
ἡ ἐρχομένη βασιλεία ἐν ὀνόματι Κυρίου τοῦ πατρὸς ἡμῶν
the coming kingdom in (the) name of (the) Lord, of the father of us,
1138 5614 1722 3588 5310
Δαβίδ· Ὡσαννὰ ἐν τοῖς ὑψίστοις.
David. Hosanna in the highest!

and he sat upon him.
8 And many spread their garments in the way: and others cut down branches off the trees, and strawed (them) in the way.
9 And they that went before, and they that followed, cried, saying, Hosanna; Blessed (is) he that cometh in the name of the Lord:
10 Blessed (be) the kingdom of our father David, that cometh in the name of the Lord: Hosanna in the highest.

11 And Jesus entered into Jerusalem, and into the temple. And having looked around at all things, the hour already being late, He went out to Bethany with the Twelve.

2532 1525 1519 2414 3588 2424 2532 1519 3588 2411
11. Καὶ εἰσῆλθεν εἰς Ἱεροσόλυμα ὁ Ἰησοῦς, καὶ εἰς τὸ ἱερόν·
And entered into Jerusalem Jesus, and into the temple.
2532 4017 3956 3798 2235 5607 3588 5610
καὶ περιβλεψάμενος πάντα, ὀψίας ἤδη οὔσης τῆς ὥρας,
And having looked around at all things, late already being the hour,
1831 1519 963 3326 3588 1427
ἐξῆλθεν εἰς Βηθανίαν μετὰ τῶν δώδεκα.
He went out to Bethany with the twelve.

11 And Jesus entered into Jerusalem, and into the temple: and when he had looked round about upon all things, and now the eventide was come, he went out unto Bethany with the twelve.

12. And on the morrow, they having gone out from Bethany, He hungered.
13 And seeing afar off a fig tree having leaves, He went (toward it), if perhaps He would find anything on it. And coming on it, He found nothing except leaves, for it was not (the) season of figs.
14 And answering, Jesus said to it, Let no one eat fruit of you any more to the age. And His disciples heard.

2532 3588 1887 1831 846 575 963
12. Καὶ τῇ ἐπαύριον ἐξελθόντων αὐτῶν ἀπὸ Βηθανίας,
And on the morrow, having gone out they from Bethany,
3983 2532 1492 4808 3113 2192 5444 2064
ἐπείνασε. 13 καὶ ἰδὼν συκῆν μακρόθεν, ἔχουσαν φύλλα, ἦλθεν
He hungered. And seeing a fig-tree afar off having leaves, He came
1487 686 2147 5100 1722 846 2532 2064 1909 846 3762
εἰ ἄρα εὑρήσει τι ἐν αὐτῇ· καὶ ἐλθὼν ἐπ' αὐτήν, οὐδὲν
if perhaps He will find something in it. And coming upon it, nothing
2147 1487 3361 5444 3756 1063 2258 2540 4810 2532 611
εὗρεν εἰ μὴ φύλλα· οὐ γὰρ ἦν καιρὸς σύκων. 14 καὶ ἀποκριθεὶς
He found except leaves; not for it was season of figs And answering
3588 2424 2036 846 3371 1537 4675 1519 3588 165 3367
ὁ Ἰησοῦς εἶπεν αὐτῇ, Μηκέτι ἐκ σοῦ εἰς τὸν αἰῶνα μηδεὶς
Jesus said to it, No more from you to the age no one
2590 5315 2532 191 3588 3101 846
καρπὸν φάγοι. καὶ ἤκουον οἱ μαθηταὶ αὐτοῦ.
fruit may eat. And heard the disciples of Him.

12. And on the morrow, when they were come from Bethany, he was hungry:
13 And seeing a fig tree afar off having leaves, he came, if haply he might find any thing thereon: and when he came to it, he found nothing but leaves; for the time of figs was not (yet).
14 And Jesus answered and said unto it, No man eat fruit of thee hereafter for ever. And his disciples heard (it).

15. And they came to Jerusalem. And entering into the temple, Jesus began to throw out those selling and buying in the temple; also He overturned the tables of the moneychangers and the seats of those selling the doves.
16 And (He) did not allow any to carry a vessel through the temple.
17 And (He)

2532 2064 1519 2414 2532 1525 3588 2424 1519
15. Καὶ ἔρχονται εἰς Ἱεροσόλυμα· καὶ εἰσελθὼν ὁ Ἰησοῦς εἰς
And they come into Jerusalem. And entering Jesus into
3588 2411 756 1544 3588 4453 2532 59
τὸ ἱερὸν ἤρξατο ἐκβάλλειν τοὺς πωλοῦντας καὶ ἀγοράζοντας
the temple, He began to throw out those selling and buying
1722 3588 2411 2532 3588 5132 3588 2855 2532 3588
ἐν τῷ ἱερῷ· καὶ τὰς τραπέζας τῶν κολλυβιστῶν, καὶ τὰς
in the temple; and the tables of the moneychangers, and the
2515 3588 4453 3588 4058 2690 2532
καθέδρας τῶν πωλούντων τὰς περιστερὰς κατέστρεψε· 16 καὶ
seats of those selling the doves He overturned; and
3756 863 2443 5100 1308 4632 1223 3588 2411 2532 1321
οὐκ ἤφιεν ἵνα τις διενέγκῃ σκεῦος διὰ τοῦ ἱεροῦ. 17 καὶ εδι-
not He allowed that any may carry a vessel through the temple. And (He)

15. And they come to Jerusalem: and Jesus went into the temple, and began to cast out them that sold and bought in the temple, and overthrew the tables of the moneychangers, and the seats of them that sold doves;
16 And would not suffer that any man should carry (any) vessel through the temple.
17 And he

Literal Translation **Mark 11:18** **King James Version**

taught, saying to them, Has it not been written, "My house shall be called a house of prayer for all the nations"? But you have made it a den of plunderers. (Isa. 56:7; Jer. 7:11)
18 And the scribes and the chief priests heard. And they sought how they might destroy Him, for they feared Him, because all the crowd was astounded at His doctrine.

3004 846 3756 1125 3754 3588 3624 3450 3624
δασκε, λέγων αὐτοις, Οὐ γέγραπται ὅτι Ὁ οἶκός μου οἶκος
taught, saying to them, not Has it been written that the house of Me a house

4335 2564 3956 3588 1484 5210 1161 4160
προσευχῆς κληθήσεται πᾶσι τοῖς ἔθνεσιν; ὑμεῖς δὲ ἐποιή-
of prayer shall be called for all the nations? you But have

846 4693 3027 2532 191 3588 1122
σατε αὐτὸν σπήλαιον ληστῶν. 18 καὶ ἤκουσαν οἱ γραμματεῖς
made it a den of plunderers. And heard the scribes

2532 3588 749 2532 2212 4459 846 622
καὶ οἱ ἀρχιερεῖς, καὶ ἐζήτουν πῶς αὐτὸν ἀπολέσουσιν·
and the chief priests, and they sought how Him they might destroy.

5399 1063 846 3754 3956 3588 3793 1605 1909
ἐφοβοῦντο γὰρ αὐτόν, ὅτι πᾶς ὁ ὄχλος ἐξεπλήσσετο ἐπὶ
they feared For Him, because all the crowd was astounded at

3588 1322 846
τῇ διδαχῇ αὐτοῦ.
the doctrine of Him

taught, saying unto them, Is it not written, My house shall be called of all nations the house of prayer? but ye have made it a den of thieves.

18 And the scribes and chief priests heard (it), and sought how they might destroy him: for they feared him, because all the people was astonished at his doctrine.

19 And when (it) was evening, He went outside the city.

2532 3753 3796 1096 1607 1854 3588 4172
19. Καὶ ὅτε ὀψὲ ἐγένετο, ἐξεπορεύετο ἔξω τῆς πόλεως.
And when evening (it) was, He went forth out of the city.

19 And when even was come, he went out of the city.

20. And passing along early, they saw the fig-tree withered from (the) roots.
21 And remembering, Peter said to Him, Rabbi, behold, the fig tree which You cursed has withered.
22 And answering, Jesus said to them, Have faith of God.
23 For truly I say to you, Whoever says to this mountain, Be taken up and be thrown into the sea, and does not doubt in his heart, but believes that what he says occurs, it will be to him, whatever he says.
24 Because of this I say to you, All things, whatever you ask, having prayed, believe that you will receive, and it will be to you.
25 And when you stand having prayed, if you have anything against anyone, forgive (it), so that your Father in Heaven may also forgive your transgressions.
26 But if you do not forgive, neither will your Father in Heaven forgive your transgressions.

2532 4404 3899 1492 3588 4808 3583
20. Καὶ πρωῒ παραπορευόμενοι, εἶδον τὴν συκῆν ἐξηραμ-
And early passing along, they saw the fig-tree having been

1537 4491 2532 363 3588 4074 3004 846
μένην ἐκ ῥιζῶν. 21 καὶ ἀναμνησθεὶς ὁ Πέτρος λέγει αὐτῷ,
dried out from (the) roots. And remembering Peter says to Him,

4461 2396 3588 4808 3739 2672 3583 2532 611
Ῥαββί, ἴδε ἡ συκῆ ἣν κατηράσω ἐξήρανται. 22 καὶ ἀποκριθεὶς
Rabbi, behold the fig-tree which You cursed has withered. And answering

2424 3004 846 2192 4102 2316 281 1063 3004 5213
Ἰησοῦς λέγει αὐτοῖς, Ἔχετε πίστιν Θεοῦ. 23 ἀμὴν γὰρ λέγω ὑμῖν
Jesus says to them, Have faith of God. truly For I say to you

3754 3739 302 2036 3588 3735 5139 142 2532 906 1519 3588
ὅτι ὃς ἂν εἴπῃ τῷ ὄρει τούτῳ, Ἄρθητι, καὶ βλήθητι εἰς τὴν
that whoever says mountain to this, Be taken up, and be cast into the

2281 2532 3361 1252 1722 3588 2588 846 235 4100
θάλασσαν, καὶ μὴ διακριθῇ ἐν τῇ καρδίᾳ αὐτοῦ, ἀλλὰ πιστεύσῃ
sea, and not does doubt in the heart of him, but believes

3754 3739 3004 1096 2071 846 3739 1437 2036 1223 5124 3004
ὅτι ἃ λέγει γίνεται· ἔσται αὐτῷ ὃ ἐὰν εἴπῃ. 24 διὰ τοῦτο λέγω
that what he says occurs, it will be to him whatever he says. Because of this I say

5213 3956 3745 302 4336 154 4100 3754
ὑμῖν, Πάντα ὅσα ἂν προσευχόμενοι αἰτεῖσθε, πιστεύετε ὅτι
to you, All things whatever having prayed you ask, believe that

2983 2532 2071 5213 2532 3752 4739 4336
λαμβάνετε, καὶ ἔσται ὑμῖν. 25 καὶ ὅταν στήκητε προσευχόμενοι,
you receive, and it will be to you. And when you stand having prayed,

863 1487 5100 2192 2596 5100 2443 2532 3588 3962 5216/3588/ 1722
ἀφίετε εἴ τι ἔχετε κατά τινος· ἵνα καὶ ὁ πατὴρ ὑμῶν ὁ ἐν
forgive if anything you have against any, that also the Father of you in

3588 3772 863 5213 3588 3900 5216 1487 1161 5210
τοῖς οὐρανοῖς ἀφῇ ὑμῖν τὰ παραπτώματα ὑμῶν. 26 εἰ δὲ ὑμεῖς
Heaven may forgive you the transgressions of you. if But you

3756 863 3761 3588 3962 5216 3588 1722 3588 3772 863 3588
οὐκ ἀφίετε, οὐδὲ ὁ πατὴρ ὑμῶν ὁ ἐν τοῖς οὐρανοῖς ἀφήσει τὰ
not do forgive, neither the Father of you in Heaven will forgive the

3900 5216
παραπτώματα ὑμῶν.
transgressions of you..

20. And in the morning, as they passed by, they saw the fig tree dried up from the roots.
21 And Peter calling to remembrance saith unto him, Master, behold, the fig tree which thou cursedst is withered away.
22 And Jesus answering saith unto them, Have faith in God.
23 For verily I say unto you, That whosoever shall say unto this mountain, Be thou removed, and be thou cast into the sea; and shall not doubt in his heart, but shall believe that those things which he saith shall come to pass; he shall have whatsoever he saith.
24 Therefore I say unto you, What things soever ye desire, when ye pray, believe that ye receive (them), and ye shall have (them).
25 And when ye stand praying, forgive, if ye have ought against any: that your Father also which is in heaven may forgive you your trespasses.
26 But if ye do not forgive, neither will your Father which is in heaven forgive your trespasses.

27. And they came again to Jerusalem. And as He was walking in the temple,

2532 2064 3825 1519 2414 2532 1722 3588 2411
27. Καὶ ἔρχονται πάλιν εἰς Ἱεροσόλυμα· καὶ ἐν τῷ ἱερῷ
And they come again into Jerusalem. And in the temple

27. And they come again to Jerusalem: and as he was walking in the temple,

Literal Translation | **Mark 11:28** | **King James Version**

the chief priests and the scribes and the elders came to Him.

28 And they said to Him, By what authority do you do these things? And who gave you this authority that you do these things?

29 And answering, Jesus said to them, I will also ask you one thing, and answer Me, and I will tell you by what authority I do these things:

30 The baptism of John, was (it) from Heaven, or from men? Answer Me.

31 And they argued to themselves, saying, If we say, From Heaven, he will say, Why then did you not believe him?

32 But if we say, From men, they feared the people. For all held that John really was a prophet.

33 And answering, they said to Jesus, We do not know. And answering, Jesus said to them, Neither do I tell you by what authority I do these things.

4043 846 2064 4314 846 3588 749
περιπατοῦντος αὐτοῦ, ἔρχονται πρὸς αὐτὸν οἱ ἀρχιερεῖς
walking around Him, come to Him the chief priests

2532 3588 1122 2532 3588 4245 2532 3004 846
καὶ οἱ γραμματεῖς καὶ οἱ πρεσβύτεροι, 28 καὶ λέγουσιν αὐτῷ,
and the scribes and the elders. And they say to Him,

1722 4169 1849 5023 5160 2532 5101 4671 3588 1849
Ἐν ποίᾳ ἐξουσίᾳ ταῦτα ποιεῖς; καὶ τίς σοι τὴν ἐξουσίαν
By what authority these things you do? And who you authority

3778 1325 2443 5023 4160 3588 1161 2424 611
ταύτην ἔδωκεν ἵνα ταῦτα ποιῇς; 29 ὁ δὲ Ἰησοῦς ἀποκριθεὶς
this gave that these things you do? But Jesus answering

2036 846 1905 5209 2504 1520 3056 2532
εἶπεν αὐτοῖς, Ἐπερωτήσω ὑμᾶς κἀγὼ ἕνα λόγον, καὶ
said to them, I will ask you I also one word, and

611 3427 2532 2046 5213 1722 4169 1849 5023 4160
ἀποκρίθητέ μοι, καὶ ἐρῶ ὑμῖν ἐν ποίᾳ ἐξουσίᾳ ταῦτα ποιῶ.
answer to Me, and I will tell you by what authority these things I do.

3588 908 2491 1537 3772 2258 2228 1537 444
30 τὸ βάπτισμα Ἰωάννου ἐξ οὐρανοῦ ἦν, ἢ ἐξ ἀνθρώπων;
The baptism of John, from Heaven was (it), or from men?

611 3427 2532 3049 4314 1438 3004
ἀποκρίθητέ μοι. 31 καὶ ἐλογίζοντο πρὸς ἑαυτούς, λέγοντες,
Answer Me. And they argued with themselves, saying,

1437 2036 1537 3772 2046 1302 3767 3756 4100
Ἐὰν εἴπωμεν, Ἐξ οὐρανοῦ, ἐρεῖ, Διατί οὖν οὐκ ἐπιστεύσατε
If we say, From Heaven, He will say, Why then not you did believe

846 235 1437 2036 1537 444 5399 3588
αὐτῷ; 32 ἀλλ' ἐὰν εἴπωμεν, Ἐξ ἀνθρώπων, ἐφοβοῦντο τὸν
him? But if we say, From men, they feared the

2992 537 1063 2192 3588 2491 3754 3689 4396
λαόν· ἅπαντες γὰρ εἶχον τὸν Ἰωάννην, ὅτι ὄντως προφήτης
people, all for held John, that really a prophet

2258 2532 611 3004 3588 2424 3756 1492 2532/3588
ἦν. 33 καὶ ἀποκριθέντες λέγουσι τῷ Ἰησοῦ, Οὐκ οἴδαμεν. καὶ ὁ
he was. And answering they say to Jesus, Not we know. And

2424 611 3004 846 3761 1473 3004 5213 1722 4169
Ἰησοῦς ἀποκριθεὶς λέγει αὐτοῖς, Οὐδὲ ἐγὼ λέγω ὑμῖν ἐν ποίᾳ
Jesus answering says to them, Neither I tell you by what

1849 5023 4160
ἐξουσίᾳ ταῦτα ποιῶ.
authority these things I do.

there come to him the chief priests, and the scribes, and the elders,

28 And say unto him, By what authority doest thou these things? and who gave thee this authority to do these things?

29 And Jesus answered and said unto them, I will also ask of you one question, and answer me, and I will tell you by what authority I do these things.

30 The baptism of John, was (it) from heaven, or of men? answer me.

31 And they reasoned with themselves, saying, If we shall say, From heaven; he will say, Why then did ye not believe him?

32 But if we shall say, Of men; they feared the people: for all (men) counted John, that he was a prophet indeed.

33 And they answered and said unto Jesus, We cannot tell. And Jesus answering saith unto them, Neither do I tell you by what authority I do these things.

Mark 12

1. And He began to speak to them in parables: A man planted a vineyard, and put a fence around (it), and dug a winevat, and built a tower. And (he) gave it out to vinedressers and went away. (Isa. 5:1, 2)

2 And at the season, he sent a slave to the vinedressers, that he might receive from the vinedressers the fruit of the vineyard.

3 But taking him, they beat (him), and

2532 756 846 1722 3850 3004 290
1. Καὶ ἤρξατο αὐτοῖς ἐν παραβολαῖς λέγειν, Ἀμπελῶνα
And He began to them in parables to speak, A vineyard

5452 444 2532 4060 5418 2532 3736
ἐφύτευσεν ἄνθρωπος, καὶ περιέθηκε φραγμόν, καὶ ὤρυξεν
planted a man, and put around (it) a fence, and dug

5276 2532 3618 4444 2532 1554 846
ὑπολήνιον, καὶ ᾠκοδόμησε πύργον, καὶ ἐξέδοτο αὐτὸν
a winevat, and built a tower, and gave out it

1092 2532 589 2532 649 4314 3588 1092
γεωργοῖς, καὶ ἀπεδήμησε. 2 καὶ ἀπέστειλε πρὸς τοὺς γεωργοὺς
to vinedressers, and went away. And he sent to the vinedressers

3588 2540 1401 2443 3844 3588 1092 2983 575 3588
τῷ καιρῷ δοῦλον, ἵνα παρὰ τῶν γεωργῶν λάβῃ ἀπὸ τοῦ
(at) the season a slave, that from the vinedressers he receive from the

2590 3588 290 3588 1161 2983 846 1194 2532
καρποῦ τοῦ ἀμπελῶνος. 3 οἱ δὲ λαβόντες αὐτὸν ἔδειραν, καὶ
fruit to the vineyard. they But having taken him, beat (him) and

1. And he began to speak unto them by parables. A (certain) man planted a vineyard, and set an hedge about (it), and digged (a place for) the winefat, and built a tower, and let it out to husbandmen, and went into a far country.

2 And at the season he sent to the husbandmen a servant, that he might receive from the husbandmen of the fruit of the vineyard.

3 And they caught (him), and beat him, and

Literal Translation

Mark 12:4

sent (him) away empty.
4 And again he sent to them another slave; having stoned that one, they struck (him) in the head and sent (him) away, insulting him.

5 And again, he sent another, (and) they killed that one; also many others, indeed beating these, and killing these.

6 Yet having one son, his own beloved, then he sent him to them also, last (of all), saying, They will have respect for my son.

7 But these vinedressers said to themselves, This is the heir; come, let us kill him and the inheritance will be ours.

8 And taking (him), they killed him and threw (him) outside the vineyard.
9 What, then, will the lord of the vineyard do? He will come and will destroy the vinedressers and will give the vineyard to others.
10 Did you not even read this Scripture: "(The) Stone which the builders rejected, this one came to be Head of (the) corner;

11 this came to be from (the) Lord, and it is marvelous in our eyes"? (Ps. 118:22, 23)

12 And they sought to seize Him, yet feared the crowd. For they knew that He spoke the parable against them. And leaving Him, they went away.

13. And they sent to Him some of the Pharisees and of the Herodians, that they might catch Him in a word.
14 And coming, they said to Him, Teacher, we know that you are true,

---

649 2756 2532 3825 649 4314 846 243
ἀπέστειλαν κενόν. 4 καὶ πάλιν ἀπέστειλε πρὸς αὐτοὺς ἄλλον
sent (him) away empty. And again he sent to them another

1401 2548 3036 2775 2532 649
δοῦλον· κἀκεῖνον λιθοβολήσαντες ἐκεφαλαίωσαν, καὶ ἀπέ-
slave; that one having stoned they struck in the head, and

821 2532 3825 243 649 2548
στειλαν ἠτιμωμένον. 5 καὶ πάλιν ἄλλον ἀπέστειλε· κἀκεῖνον
sent away insulting him. And again another he sent. That one

615 2532 4183 243 3588 3303 1194 3588
ἀπέκτειναν· καὶ πολλοὺς ἄλλους, τοὺς μὲν δέροντες, τοὺς
they killed; and many others these indeed beating these

1161 615 2089 3767 1520 5207 2192 27 846
δὲ ἀποκτείνοντες. 6 ἔτι οὖν ἕνα υἱὸν ἔχων ἀγαπητὸν αὐτοῦ,
and killing. Still then one son having beloved his, own,

649 2532 846 4314 846 2078 3004 3754
ἀπέστειλε καὶ αὐτὸν πρὸς αὐτοὺς ἔσχατον, λέγων ὅτι
he sent also him to them last, saying,

1788 3588 5207 3450 1565 1161 3588 1092 2036
Ἐντραπήσονται τὸν υἱόν μου. 7 ἐκεῖνοι δὲ οἱ γεωργοὶ εἶπον
They will respect the son of me. those But vinedressers said

4314 1438 3754 3778 2076 3588 2818 1205 615
πρὸς ἑαυτοὺς ὅτι Οὗτός ἐστιν ὁ κληρονόμος· δεῦτε, ἀπο-
to themselves, This is the heir; come, let

846 2532 2257 2071 2228 2817 2532 2983
κτείνωμεν αὐτόν, καὶ ἡμῶν ἔσται ἡ κληρονομία. 8 καὶ λαβόντες
us kill him, and of us will be the inheritance. And taking

846 615 2532 1544 1854 3588 290 5101 3767
αὐτὸν ἀπέκτειναν, καὶ ἐξέβαλον ἔξω τοῦ ἀμπελῶνος. 9 τί οὖν
him they killed, and threw (him) outside the vineyard. What then

4160 3588 2962 3588 290 2064 2532 622
ποιήσει ὁ κύριος τοῦ ἀμπελῶνος; ἐλεύσεται καὶ ἀπολέσει
will do the lord of the vineyard? He will come and will destroy

3588 1092 2532 1325 3588 290 243 3761 3588
τοὺς γεωργούς, καὶ δώσει τὸν ἀμπελῶνα ἄλλοις. 10 οὐδὲ τὴν
the vinedressers, and will give the vineyard to others, not even

1124 3778 314 3037 3739 593 3588
γραφὴν ταύτην ἀνέγνωτε, Λίθον ὃν ἀπεδοκίμασαν οἱ
scripture this Did you read, (The) Stone which rejected those

3618 3778 1096 1519 2776 1137 3844
οἰκοδομοῦντες, οὗτος ἐγενήθη εἰς κεφαλὴν γωνίας· 11 παρὰ
building, this One came to be for the Head of (the) corner; from

2962 1096 846 2532 2076 2298 1722 3788
Κυρίου ἐγένετο αὕτη, καὶ ἔστι θαυμαστὴ ἐν ὀφθαλμοῖς
(the) Lord came to be this, and it is marvelous in eyes

2257 2532 2212 846 2902 2532 5399 3588
ἡμῶν; 12 καὶ ἐζήτουν αὐτὸν κρατῆσαι, καὶ ἐφοβήθησαν τὸν
of us? And they sought Him to seize, and feared the

3793 1097 1063 3754 4314 846 3588 3850
ὄχλον· ἔγνωσαν γὰρ ὅτι πρὸς αὐτοὺς τὴν παραβολὴν
crowd. they knew For that against them the parable

2036 2532 863 846 565
εἶπε· καὶ ἀφέντες αὐτὸν ἀπῆλθον.
He told. And leaving Him they went away.

2532 649 4314 846 5100 3588 5330 2532
13. Καὶ ἀποστέλλουσι πρὸς αὐτόν τινας τῶν Φαρισαίων καὶ
And they send to Him some of the Pharisees and

3588 2265 2443 846 64 3056 3588 1161
τῶν Ἡρωδιανῶν, ἵνα αὐτὸν ἀγρεύσωσι λόγῳ. 14 οἱ δὲ
the Herodians, that Him they might catch in a word. they And

2064 3004 846 1320 1492 3754 227
ἐλθόντες λέγουσιν αὐτῷ, Διδάσκαλε, οἴδαμεν ὅτι ἀληθὴς
coming say to Him, Teacher, we know that true

King James Version

sent (him) away empty.
4 And again he sent unto them another servant; and at him they cast stones, and wounded (him) in the head, and sent (him) away shamefully handled.
5 And again he sent another; and him they killed, and many others; beating some, and killing some.

6 Having yet therefore one son, his wellbeloved, he sent him also last unto them, saying, They will reverence my son.

7 But those husbandmen said among themselves, This is the heir; come, let us kill him, and the inheritance shall be ours.

8 And they took him, and killed (him), and cast (him) out of the vineyard.
9 What shall therefore the lord of the vineyard do? he will come and destroy the husbandmen, and will give the vineyard unto others.
10 And have ye not read this scripture; The stone which the builders rejected is become the head of the corner:

11 This was the Lord's doing, and it is marvelous in our eyes?

12 And they sought to lay hold on him, but feared the people: for they knew that he had spoken the parable against them: and they left him, and went their way.

13. And they send unto him certain of the Pharisees and of the Herodians, to catch him in (his) words.
14 And when they were come, they say unto him, Master, we know that thou art true,

Literal Translation

and there is not a care to you about anyone, for you do not look to (the) face of men, but on truth teach the way of God: Is it lawful to give tribute to Caesar, or not?

15 Should we give, or should we not give? But knowing their hypocrisy, He said to them, Why do you tempt Me? Bring Me a denarius that I may see.
16 And they brought (one). And He said to them, Whose image and inscription is this? And they said to Him, Caesar's.
17 And answering, Jesus said to them, Give back the things of Caesar to Caesar, and the things of God to God. And they marveled at Him.

18. And Sadducees came to Him, who say there is no resurrection. And they questioned Him, saying,

19 Teacher, Moses wrote to us that if a brother of anyone should die and leave behind a wife, and leave no children, that his brother should take his wife and raise up seed to his brother. (Deut. 25:5)

20 Then there were seven brothers. And the first took a wife, and dying, (he) left no seed.

21 And the second took her, and died, and neither did he leave seed; and the third likewise.
22 And all seven took her and left no seed. Last of all the woman also died.

23 Then in the resurrection, when they rise again, of which of them will she be the wife? For the seven had her as wife.

Mark 12:15

1488 2532 3756 3199 4671 4012 3762 3756 1063 991 1519
εἶ, καὶ οὐ μέλει σοι περὶ οὐδενός· οὐ γὰρ βλέπεις εἰς
you are, and not a care to you about no one; not for you look to

4383 444 235 1909 225 3588 3598 3588 2316
πρόσωπον ἀνθρώπων, ἀλλ' ἐπ' ἀληθείας τὴν ὁδὸν τοῦ Θεοῦ
(the) face of men, but on truth the way of God

1321 1832 2778 2541 1325 2228 3756 1325
διδάσκεις· ἔξεστι κῆνσον Καίσαρι δοῦναι ἢ οὔ; δῶμεν,
teach. Is it lawful tribute to Caesar to give, or not? Should we give

2228 3361 1325 3588 1161 1492 846 3588 5272 2036 846
ἢ μὴ δῶμεν; 15 ὁ δὲ εἰδὼς αὐτῶν τὴν ὑπόκρισιν εἶπεν αὐτοῖς,
or not give? He But knowing their hypocrisy said to them,

5101 3165 3985 5342 3427 1220 2443 1492 3588/1161
Τί με πειράζετε; φέρετέ μοι δηνάριον, ἵνα ἴδω. 16 οἱ δὲ
Why Me tempt you? Bring Me a denarius, that I may see. they And

5342 2532 3004 846 5101 2228 1504 846 2532 2228
ἤνεγκαν. καὶ λέγει αὐτοῖς, Τίνος ἡ εἰκὼν αὕτη καὶ ἡ
brought. And He says to them, Whose (is) image this and

1923 3588 1161 2036 846 2541 2532 611 3588
ἐπιγραφή; οἱ δὲ εἶπον αὐτῷ, Καίσαρος. 17 καὶ ἀποκριθεὶς ὁ
inscription? they And said to Him, Caesar's. And answering

2424 2036 846 591 3588 2541 2541 2532
Ἰησοῦς εἶπεν αὐτοῖς, Ἀπόδοτε τὰ Καίσαρος Καίσαρι, καὶ
Jesus said to them, Give back the things of Caesar to Caesar, and

3588 3588 2316 3588 2316 2532 2296 1909 846
τὰ τοῦ Θεοῦ τῷ Θεῷ. καὶ ἐθαύμασαν ἐπ' αὐτῷ.
the things of God to God And they marveled at Him.

2532 2064 4523 4314 846 3748 3004
18. Καὶ ἔρχονται Σαδδουκαῖοι πρὸς αὐτόν, οἵτινες λέγουσιν
And come Sadducees to Him, who say

386 3361 1511 2532 1905 846 1320
ἀνάστασιν μὴ εἶναι· καὶ ἐπηρώτησαν αὐτόν, λέγοντες,
a resurrection not to be, and questioned Him, saying,

1320 3475 1125 2254 3754 1437 5100 80
19 Διδάσκαλε, Μωσῆς ἔγραψεν ἡμῖν, ὅτι ἐάν τινος ἀδελφὸς
Teacher, Moses wrote to us that if anyone a brother

599 2532 2641 1135 2532 5043 3361 863 2443
ἀποθάνῃ, καὶ καταλίπῃ γυναῖκα, καὶ τέκνα μὴ ἀφῇ, ἵνα
should die and leave behind a wife, and children not leave, that

2983 3588 80 846 3588 1135 846 2532 1817
λάβῃ ὁ ἀδελφὸς αὐτοῦ τὴν γυναῖκα αὐτοῦ, καὶ ἐξαναστήσῃ
should take the brother of him the wife of him, and should raise up

4690 3588 80 846 2033 3736 80 2258 2532 3588
σπέρμα τῷ ἀδελφῷ αὐτοῦ· 20 ἑπτὰ οὖν ἀδελφοὶ ἦσαν· καὶ ὁ
seed to the brother of him. seven Then brothers were, and the

4413 2983 1135 2532 599 3756 863 4690
πρῶτος ἔλαβε γυναῖκα, καὶ ἀποθνῄσκων οὐκ ἀφῆκε σπέρμα·
first took a wife, and dying not did leave seed.

2532 3588 1208 2983 846 2532 599 2532 3761 846
21 καὶ ὁ δεύτερος ἔλαβεν αὐτήν, καὶ ἀπέθανε, καὶ οὐδὲ αὐτὸς
And the second took her, and died, and neither he

863 4690 2532 3588 5154 5615 2532 2983 846
ἀφῆκε σπέρμα· καὶ ὁ τρίτος ὡσαύτως. 22 καὶ ἔλαβον αὐτὴν
left behind seed. And the third likewise. And took her

3588 2033 2532 3756 863 4690 2078 3956 599
οἱ ἑπτὰ, καὶ οὐκ ἀφῆκαν σπέρμα. ἐσχάτη πάντων ἀπέθανε
the seven, and not did leave seed. Last of all died

2532 3588 1135 1722 3588 3767 386 3752 450 5101
καὶ ἡ γυνή. 23 ἐν τῇ οὖν ἀναστάσει, ὅταν ἀναστῶσι, τίνος
also the wife. in the Then resurrection, when they rise again, of which

846 2071 1135 3588 1063 2033 2192 846 1135
αὐτῶν ἔσται γυνή; οἱ γὰρ ἑπτὰ ἔσχον αὐτὴν γυναῖκα.
of them will she be wife? the For seven had her (as) wife.

King James Version

and carest for no man: for thou regardest not the person of men, but teachest the way of God in truth: Is it lawful to give tribute to Caesar, or not?

15 Shall we give, or shall we not give? But he, knowing their hypocrisy, said unto them, Why tempt ye me? bring me a penny, that I may see (it).
16 And they brought (it). And he saith unto them, Whose (is) this image and superscription? And they said unto him, Caesar's.
17 And Jesus answering said unto them, Render to Caesar the things that are Caesar's, and to God the things that are God's. And they marvelled at him.

18. Then come unto him the Sadducees, which say there is no resurrection; and they asked him, saying,

19 Master, Moses wrote unto us, If a man's brother die, and leave (his) wife (behind him), and leave no children, that his brother should take his wife, and raise up seed unto his brother.

20 Now there were seven brethren: and the first took a wife, and dying left no seed.

21 And the second took her, and died, neither left he any seed: and the third likewise.
22 And the seven had her, and left no seed: last of all the woman died also.

23 In the resurrection therefore, when they shall rise, whose wife shall she be of them? for the seven had her to wife.

Literal Translation

24 And answering, Jesus said to them, Do you not err because of this, not knowing the Scriptures nor the power of God?

25 For when they rise again from (the) dead, they neither marry nor are given in marriage, but are as angels in Heaven.

26 But concerning the dead, that they are raised, have you not read in the book of Moses, as God spoke to him at the Bush, saying, "I am the God of Abraham, and the God of Isaac, and the God of Jacob"? (Ex. 3:6)
27 He is not the God of (the) dead, but God of (the) living. Therefore, you greatly err.

28. And coming up, one of the scribes, hearing them debating, knowing that He answered them well, he questioned Him, What is (the) first commandment of all?
29 And Jesus answered him, The first of all the commandments (is): "Hear, Israel. (The) Lord our God is one Lord,
30 and you shall love (the) Lord your God with all your heart, and with all your soul and with all your mind, and with all your strength." This is the first commandment. (Deut. 6:4, 5)

31 And (the) second (is) like this, "You shall love your neighbor as yourself." There is not another commandment greater than these. (Lev. 19:18)
32 And the scribe said to Him, You say well, Teacher. By truth You say that God is one,, and there is no other besides Him;

33 and to love

Mark 12:24

2532 611 3588 2424 2036 846 3756 1223 5124
24 καὶ ἀποκριθεὶς ὁ Ἰησοῦς εἶπεν αὐτοῖς, Οὐ διὰ τοῦτο
And answering Jesus said to them, Not because of this

4105 3361 1492 3588 1124 3366 3588 1411 3588
πλανᾶσθε, μὴ εἰδότες τὰς γραφάς, μηδὲ τὴν δύναμιν τοῦ
do you err, not knowing the Scriptures, nor the power

2316 3752 1063 1537 3498 450 3777 1060
Θεοῦ; 25 ὅταν γὰρ ἐκ νεκρῶν ἀναστῶσιν, οὔτε γαμοῦσιν,
of God? when For from (the) dead they rise again, they neither marry

3777 1061 235 1526 5613 32 3588 1722 3588
οὔτε γαμίσκονται, ἀλλ' εἰσὶν ὡς ἄγγελοι οἱ ἐν τοῖς
nor are given in marriage, but are as angels in

3772 4012 1161 3588 3498 3754 1453 3756 314
οὐρανοῖς. 26 περὶ δὲ τῶν νεκρῶν, ὅτι ἐγείρονται, οὐκ ἀνέγνωτε
Heaven. about But the dead, that they are raised, not did you read

1722 3588 976 3475 1909 3588 942 5613 2036 846 3588 2316
ἐν τῇ βίβλῳ Μωσέως, ἐπὶ τῆς βάτου, ὡς εἶπεν αὐτῷ ὁ Θεὸς,
in the roll of Moses, at the Bush, as spoke to him God,

3004 1473 3588 2316 11 2532 3588 2316 2464 2532 3588 2316
λέγων, Ἐγὼ ὁ Θεὸς Ἀβραάμ, καὶ ὁ Θεὸς Ἰσαάκ, καὶ ὁ Θεὸς
saying, I (am) the God of Abraham, and the God of Isaac, and the God

2384 3756 2076 3588 2316 3498 235 2316 2198 5210
Ἰακώβ; 27 οὐκ ἔστιν ὁ Θεὸς νεκρῶν, ἀλλὰ Θεὸς ζώντων· ὑμεῖς
of Jacob? not He is the God of (the) dead, but God of (the) living. you

4183 3767 4105
οὖν πολὺ πλανᾶσθε.
Therefore much err.

2532 4334 1520 3588 1122 191 846
28. Καὶ προσελθὼν εἷς τῶν γραμματέων, ἀκούσας αὐτῶν
And coming up one of the scribes, hearing them

4802 1492 3754 2573 846 611 1905
συζητούντων, εἰδὼς ὅτι καλῶς αὐτοῖς ἀπεκρίθη, ἐπηρώ-
debating, knowing that well to them He answered, asked

846 4169 2076 4413 3956 1785 3588 1161
τησεν αὐτόν, Ποία ἐστὶ πρώτη πασῶν ἐντολή; 29 ὁ δὲ
Him, What is (the) first of all commandment? And

2424 611 846 3754 4413 3956 3588 1785
Ἰησοῦς ἀπεκρίθη αὐτῷ ὅτι Πρώτη πασῶν τῶν ἐντολῶν,
Jesus answered him, (The) first of all the commandments:

191 2474 2962 3588 2316 2257 2962 1520 2076 2532
Ἄκουε, Ἰσραήλ· Κύριος ὁ Θεὸς ἡμῶν, Κύριος εἷς ἐστί· 30 καὶ
Hear, Israel, Lord the God of us Lord one is; and,

25 2962 3588 2316 4675 1537 3650 3588 2588 4675
ἀγαπήσεις Κύριον τὸν Θεόν σου ἐξ ὅλης τῆς καρδίας σου,
You shall love the Lord the God of you with all the heart of you,

2532 1537 3650 3588 5590 4675 2532 1537 3650 3588 1271 4675
καὶ ἐξ ὅλης τῆς ψυχῆς σου, καὶ ἐξ ὅλης τῆς διανοίας σου,
and with all the soul of you, and with all the mind of you,

2532 1537 3650 3588 2479 4675 846 4413 1785 2532
καὶ ἐξ ὅλης τῆς ἰσχύος σου. αὕτη πρώτη ἐντολή. 31 καὶ
and with all the strength of you. This (is the) first commandment. And

1208 3664 846 25 3588 4139 4675 5613 4572
δευτέρα ὁμοία αὕτη, Ἀγαπήσεις τὸν πλησίον σου ὡς σεαυτόν.
(the) second like this, You shall love the neighbor of you as yourself.

3187 5130 243 1785 3756 2076 2532 2036 846 3588
μείζων τούτων ἄλλη ἐντολὴ οὐκ ἔστι. 32 καὶ εἶπεν αὐτῷ ὁ
Greater (than) these other command not is. And said to Him the

1122 2573 1320 1909 225 2036 3754 1520 2076
γραμματεύς, Καλῶς, διδάσκαλε, ἐπ' ἀληθείας εἶπας ὅτι εἷς ἐστι
scribe, Well, Teacher, by truth you say that one is

2316 2532 3756 2076 243 4133 846 2532 3588 25
Θεός, καὶ οὐκ ἔστιν ἄλλος πλὴν αὐτοῦ. 33 καὶ τὸ ἀγαπᾶν
God, and not there is another besides Him; and to love

King James Version

24 And Jesus answering said unto them, Do ye not therefore err, because ye know not the scriptures, neither the power of God?

25 For when they shall rise from the dead, they neither marry, nor are given in marriage; but are as the angels which are in heaven.

26 And as touching the dead, that they rise: have ye not read in the book of Moses, how in the bush God spake unto him, saying, I (am) the God of Abraham, and the God of Isaac, and the God of Jacob?

27 He is not the God of the dead, but the God of the living: ye therefore do greatly err.

28. And one of the scribes came, and having heard them reasoning together, and perceiving that he had answered them well, asked him, Which is the first commandment of all?
29 And Jesus answered him, The first of all the commandments (is), Hear, O Israel; The Lord our God is one Lord:
30 And thou shalt love the Lord thy God with all thy heart, and with all thy soul, and with all thy mind, and with all thy strength: this (is) the first commandment.

31 And the second (is) like, (namely) this, Thou shalt love thy neighbour as thyself. There is none other commandment greater than these.
32 And the scribe said unto him, Well, Master, thou hast said the truth: for there is one God; and there is none other but he:

33 And to love

Literal Translation | **Mark 12:34** | ***King James Version***

Him from all the heart, and from all the understanding, and from all the soul, and from all the strength; and to love one's neighbor as oneself is more than all the burnt offerings and the sacrifices. (Deut. 35:4, 5; Lev. 19:18)

846 1537 3650 3588 2588 2532 1537 3650 3588 4907 2532 1537
αὐτὸν ἐξ ὅλης τῆς καρδίας, καὶ ἐξ ὅλης τῆς συνέσεως, καὶ ἐξ
Him out of all the heart, and out of all the understanding, and out of
3650 3588 5590 2532 1537 3650 3588 2479 2532 3588 25 3588
ὅλης τῆς ψυχῆς, καὶ ἐξ ὅλης τῆς ἰσχύος, καὶ τὸ ἀγαπᾶν τὸν
all the soul, and out of all the strength, and to love the
4139 5613 1438 4119 2076 3956 3588 3646
πλησίον ὡς ἑαυτόν, πλεῖόν ἐστι πάντων τῶν ὁλοκαυτωμάτων
neighbor as oneself, more is than all the burnt offerings
2532 3588 2378 2532 3588 2424 1492 846 3754 3562
καὶ τῶν θυσιῶν. 34 καὶ ὁ Ἰησοῦς ἰδὼν αὐτὸν ὅτι νουνεχῶς
and the sacrifices. And Jesus seeing him that intelligently
611 2036 846 3756 3112 1488 575 3588 932 3588
ἀπεκρίθη, εἶπεν αὐτῷ, Οὐ μακρὰν εἶ ἀπὸ τῆς βασιλείας τοῦ
he answered, said to him, Not far are you from the kingdom
2316 2532 3762 3765 5111 846 1905
Θεοῦ. καὶ οὐδεὶς οὐκέτι ἐτόλμα αὐτὸν ἐπερωτῆσαι.
of God. And no one no more dared Him to question.

him with all the heart, and with all the understanding, and with all the soul, and with all the strength, and to love (his) neighbour as himself, is more than all whole burnt offerings and sacrifices.

34 And seeing that he answered intelligently, Jesus said to him, You are not far from the kingdom of God. And no one dared to question Him any more.

34 And when Jesus saw that he answered discreetly, he said unto him, Thou art not far from the kingdom of God. And no man after that durst ask him (any question).

35. And teaching in the temple, answering Jesus said, How do the scribes say that Christ is the son of David?

2532 611 3588 2424 3004 1321 1722 3588 2411
35. Καὶ ἀποκριθεὶς ὁ Ἰησοῦς ἔλεγε, διδάσκων ἐν τῷ ἱερῷ,
And answering Jesus said, teaching in the temple,
4459 3004 3588 1122 3754/3588 5547 5207 2076 1138
Πῶς λέγουσιν οἱ γραμματεῖς ὅτι ὁ Χριστὸς υἱός ἐστι Δαβίδ;
How say the scribes that the Christ son is of David?
846 1063 1138 2036 1722 3588 4151 3588 40 2036 3588
36 αὐτὸς γὰρ Δαβὶδ εἶπεν ἐν τῷ Πνεύματι τῷ Ἁγίῳ, Εἶπεν ὁ
himself For David said in the Spirit Holy, Said the
2962 3588 2962 3450 2521 1537 1188 3450 2193 302 5087 3588
Κύριος τῷ Κυρίῳ μου, Κάθου ἐκ δεξιῶν μου, ἕως ἂν θῶ τοὺς
Lord to the Lord of me, Sit off the right of Me, until I put the
2190 4675 5286 3588 4228 4675 848 3767 1138
ἐχθρούς σου ὑποπόδιον τῶν ποδῶν σου. 37 Αὐτὸς οὖν Δαβὶδ
enemies of You (as) a footstool of the feet of You. himself Then David
3004 846 2962 2532 4159 5207 846 2076 2532 3588 4183
λέγει αὐτὸν Κύριον· καὶ πόθεν υἱὸς αὐτοῦ ἐστι; καὶ ὁ πολὺς
says Him (to be) Lord; and from where son of him is He? And the large
3793 191 846 2234
ὄχλος ἤκουεν αὐτοῦ ἡδέως.
crowd heard Him gladly.

35. And Jesus answered and said, while he taught in the temple, How say the scribes that Christ is the Son of David?

36 For David himself said by the Holy Spirit "The Lord said to my Lord, Sit off My right until I place Your enemies as a footstool for Your feet." (Ps. 110:1)
37 Then David himself calls Him Lord. And from where is He his son? And the large crowd heard Him gladly.

36 For David himself said by the Holy Ghost, The LORD said to my Lord, Sit thou on my right hand, till I make thine enemies thy footstool.
37 David therefore himself calleth him Lord; and whence is he (then) his son? And the common people heard him gladly.

38. And He said to them in His teaching, Look out from the scribes, those desiring to walk about in robes, and greetings in the markets,
39 and chief seats in the synagogues, and chief couches in the dinners,

40 those devouring the houses of widows, and for a pretense praying at length. These will receive more abundant judgment.

2532 3004 846 1722 3588 1322 846 991 575 3588
38. Καὶ ἔλεγεν αὐτοῖς ἐν τῇ διδαχῇ αὐτοῦ, Βλέπετε ἀπὸ τῶν
And He said to them in the teaching of Him, Look out from the
1122 3588 2309 1722 4749 4043 2532
γραμματέων, τῶν θελόντων ἐν στολαῖς περιπατεῖν, καὶ
scribes, the (ones) desiring in robes to walk about, and
783 1722 3588 58 2532 4410 1722 3588
ἀσπασμοὺς ἐν ταῖς ἀγοραῖς, 39 καὶ πρωτοκαθεδρίας ἐν ταῖς
greetings in the markets, and chief seats in the
4864 2532 4411 1722 3588 1173 3588 2719
συναγωγαῖς, καὶ πρωτοκλισίας ἐν τοῖς δείπνοις· 40 οἱ κατε-
synagogues, and chief couches in the dinners; the (ones)
3588 3614 3588 5503 2532 4392 3117
σθίοντες τὰς οἰκίας τῶν χηρῶν, καὶ προφάσει μακρὰ
devouring the houses of the widows, and for a pretense long
4336 3778 2983 4055 2917
προσευχόμενοι· οὗτοι λήψονται περισσότερον κρίμα.
praying; these will receive more abundant judgment.

38. And he said unto them in his doctrine, Beware of the scribes, which love to go in long clothing, and (love) salutations in the marketplaces,
39 And the chief seats in the synagogues, and the uppermost rooms at feasts:
40 Which devour widows' houses, and for a pretence make long prayers: these shall receive greater damnation.

41. And sitting down opposite the treasury, Jesus watched how the crowd threw copper (coins) into the treasury.

2532 2523 3588 2424 2713 3588 1049
41. Καὶ καθίσας ὁ Ἰησοῦς κατέναντι τοῦ γαζοφυλακίου
And sitting Jesus opposite the treasury,
2334 4459 3588 3793 906 5475 1519 3588 1049
ἐθεώρει πῶς ὁ ὄχλος βάλλει χαλκὸν εἰς τὸ γαζοφυλάκιον·
He watched how the crowd cast copper (coins) into the treasury.

41. And Jesus sat over against the treasury, and beheld how the people cast money into the treasury:

Literal Translation **Mark 12:42** *King James Version*

And many rich ones threw in much.
42 And coming, one poor widow threw in two lepta (which is a quadrans).
43 And having called His disciples near, He said to them, Truly I say to you that this poor widow has thrown (in) more than all of those casting into the treasury.
44 For all threw in out of that abounding to them, but she out of her poverty threw (in) all, as much as she had, her whole livelihood.

2532 4183 4145 906 4183 2532 2064 3391
καὶ πολλοὶ πλούσιοι ἔβαλλον πολλά. 42 καὶ ἐλθοῦσα μία
And many rich ones cast in much. And coming one

5503 4434 906 3016 1417 3588 2076 2835 2532
χήρα πτωχὴ ἔβαλε λεπτὰ δύο, ὅ ἐστι κοδράντης. 43 καὶ
widow poor cast in lepta two, which is a quadrans. And

4341 3588 3101 846 3004 846 281
προσκαλεσάμενος τοὺς μαθητὰς αὐτοῦ, λέγει αὐτοῖς, Ἀμὴν
having called near the disciples of Him, He says to them, Truly

3004 5213 3754 3588 5503 846 3588 4434 4119 3956
λέγω ὑμῖν ὅτι ἡ χήρα αὕτη ἡ πτωχὴ πλεῖον πάντων
I say to you that widow this poor more than all

906 3588 906 1519 3588 1049 3956 1063
βέβληκε τῶν βαλόντων εἰς τὸ γαζοφυλάκιον· 44 πάντες γὰρ
has cast in the (ones) casting into the treasury; all for

1537 3588 4052 846 906 846 1161 1537 3588
ἐκ τοῦ περισσεύοντος αὐτοῖς ἔβαλον· αὕτη δὲ ἐκ τῆς
out of that abounding to them cast in; she but out of the

5304 846 3956 3745 2192 906 3650 3588 979
ὑστερήσεως αὐτῆς πάντα ὅσα εἶχεν ἔβαλεν, ὅλον τὸν βίον
poverty of her all as much as she had cast in, all the living

846
αὐτῆς.
of her.

and many that were rich cast in much.
42 And there came a certain poor widow, and she threw in two mites, which make a farthing.
43 And he called (unto him) his disciples, and saith unto them, Verily I say unto you, That this poor widow hath cast more in, than all they which have cast into the treasury:
44 For all (they) did cast in of their abundance; but she of her want did cast in all that she had, (even) all her living.

Mark 13 Mark 13 Mark 13

1. And He having gone out of the temple, one of His disciples said to Him, Teacher, Behold! What kind of stones and what kind of buildings!
2 And answering, Jesus said to him, Do you see these great buildings? Not at all one stone shall be left upon a stone which shall not be demolished, none.

2532 1607 846 1537 3588 2411 3004 846 1520
1. Καὶ ἐκπορευομένου αὐτοῦ ἐκ τοῦ ἱεροῦ, λέγει αὐτῷ εἷς
And having gone forth He out of the temple, says to Him one

3588 3101 846 1320 2396 4217 3037 2532
τῶν μαθητῶν αὐτοῦ, Διδάσκαλε, ἴδε, ποταποὶ λίθοι καὶ
of the disciples of Him, Teacher, behold, what kind of stones and,

4217 3619 2532 3588 2424 611 2036 846
ποταπαὶ οἰκοδομαί. 2 καὶ ὁ Ἰησοῦς ἀποκριθεὶς εἶπεν αὐτῷ,
what kind of buildings! And Jesus answering said to him,

991 3778 3588 3173 3619 3756 3361 863 3037
Βλέπεις ταύτας τὰς μεγάλας οἰκοδομάς; οὐ μὴ ἀφεθῇ λίθος
Do you see these great buildings? Not at all will be left stone

1909 3037 3739 3756 3361 2647
ἐπὶ λίθῳ ὃς οὐ μὴ καταλυθῇ.
on stone which not at all (will) be demolished.

1. And as he went out of the temple, one of his disciples saith unto him, Master, see what manner of stones and what buildings (are here)!
2 And Jesus answering said unto him, Seest thou these great buildings? there shall not be left one stone upon another, that shall not be thrown down.

3 And (as) He (was) sitting in the Mount of Olives opposite the temple, Peter and James and John and Andrew questioned Him privately:
4 Tell us when these things shall be? And what (is) the sign when all these things are about to be completed?
5 And answering, Jesus began to say to them, Look out that no one lead you astray.
6 For many will come on My name, saying, I AM! And they will lead many astray.
7 But when

2532 2521 846 1519 3588 3735 3588 1636 2713
3. Καὶ καθημένου αὐτοῦ εἰς τὸ ὄρος τῶν ἐλαιῶν κατέναντι
And sitting He in the Mount of the Olives opposite

3588 2411 1905 846 2596 2398 4074 2532 2385
τοῦ ἱεροῦ, ἐπηρώτων αὐτὸν κατ' ἰδίαν Πέτρος καὶ Ἰάκωβος
the temple, questioned Him privately Peter and James

2532 2491 2532 406 2036 2254 4219 5023 2071
καὶ Ἰωάννης καὶ Ἀνδρέας, 4 Εἰπὲ ἡμῖν, πότε ταῦτα ἔσται;
and John and Andrew, Tell us, when these things will be?

2532 51013588 4592 3752 3195 3956 5023 4931
καὶ τί τὸ σημεῖον ὅταν μέλλῃ πάντα ταῦτα συντελεῖσθαι;
And what (is) the sign when are about all these things to be completed?

3588 1161 2424 611 846 756 3004 991 3361 5100
5 ὁ δὲ Ἰησοῦς ἀποκριθεὶς αὐτοῖς ἤρξατο λέγειν, Βλέπετε μή τις
And Jesus answering to them began to say, Beware not anyone

5209 4105 4183 1063 2064 1909 3588 3686 3450
ὑμᾶς πλανήσῃ. 6 πολλοὶ γὰρ ἐλεύσονται ἐπὶ τῷ ὀνόματί μου,
you lead astray. many For will come on the name of Me,

3004 3754 1473 1510 2532 4183 4105 3752 1161
λέγοντες ὅτι Ἐγώ εἰμι· καὶ πολλοὺς πλανήσουσιν. 7 ὅταν δὲ
saying, I AM! And many they will lead astray. when But

3 And as he sat upon the mount of Olives over against the temple, Peter and James and John and Andrew asked him privately,
4 Tell us, when shall these things be? and what (shall be) the sign when all these things shall be fulfilled?
5 And Jesus answering them began to say, Take heed lest any (man) deceive you:
6 For many shall come in my name, saying, I am (Christ); and shall deceive many.
7 And when

Literal Translation | **Mark 13:8** | **King James Version**

you hear (of) wars and rumors of wars, do not be alarmed, for it must occur; but the end (is) not yet.
8 For nation will be aroused against nation, and kingdom against kingdom. And there shall be earthquakes (in) various places. And there shall be famines and agitations. These things (are) the beginnings of travails.

191 4171 2532 189 4171 3361 2360 1163
ἀκούσητε πολέμους καὶ ἀκοὰς πολέμων, μὴ θροεῖσθε· δεῖ
you hear (of) wars and rumors of wars, not be alarmed; it must
1063 1096 235 3768 3588 5056 1453 1063 1484
γὰρ γενέσθαι· ἀλλ' οὔπω τὸ τέλος. 8 ἐγερθήσεται γὰρ ἔθνος
for occur; but not yet the end. will be aroused For nation
1909 1484 2532 932 1909 932 2532 2071 4578
ἐπὶ ἔθνος, καὶ βασιλεία ἐπὶ βασιλείαν· καὶ ἔσονται σεισμοὶ
against nation. and kingdom against kingdom. And shall be earthquakes
2596 5117 2532 2071 3042 2532 5016 746 5604
κατὰ τόπους, καὶ ἔσονται λιμοὶ καὶ ταραχαί· ἀρχαὶ ὠδίνων
(in) various places, and shall be famines and agitations; beginnings of travails
5023
ταῦτα.
These things (are).

ye shall hear of wars and rumours of wars, be ye not troubled: for (such things) must needs be; but the end (shall) not (be) yet.
8 For nation shall rise against nation, and kingdom against kingdom: and there shall be earthquakes in divers places, and there shall be famines and troubles: these (are) the beginnings of sorrows.

9. But you yourselves look out, for they will deliver you up to sanhedrins and to synagogues. You will be flogged, and you will be led before rulers and kings for My sake, for a testimony to them.

10 And the gospel must first be proclaimed to all the nations.
11 But whenever they lead (you) away, delivering (you), do not be anxious beforehand, what you should say, nor meditate. But whatever may be given to you in that hour, speak that. For you are not those speaking, but the Holy Spirit.
12 And a brother will deliver up a brother to death, and a father a child. And children will rise up on parents and will put them to death.

13 And you will be hated by all on account of My name. But the (one) enduring to the end, this (one) will be kept safe.

991 1161 5210 1438 3860 1063 5209 1519
9. βλέπετε δὲ ὑμεῖς ἑαυτούς· παραδώσουσι γὰρ ὑμᾶς εἰς
look out But you yourselves; they will deliver up for you to
4892 2532 1519 4864 1194 2532 1909 2232
συνέδρια, καὶ εἰς συναγωγὰς δαρήσεσθε, καὶ ἐπὶ ἡγεμόνων
sanhedrins, and to synagogues you will be flogged, and before rulers
2532 935 2476 1752 1700 1519 3142 846
καὶ βασιλέων ἀχθήσεσθε ἕνεκεν ἐμοῦ, εἰς μαρτύριον αὐτοῖς.
and kings you will be led for the sake of Me, for a testimony to them.
2532 1519 3956 3588 1484 1163 4412 2784 3588 2098
10 καὶ εἰς πάντα τὰ ἔθνη δεῖ πρῶτον κηρυχθῆναι τὸ εὐαγγέλιον.
And to all the nations must first be proclaimed the gospel.
3752 1161 71 5209 3860 3361 4305 5101
11 ὅταν δὲ ἀγάγωσιν ὑμᾶς παραδιδόντες, μὴ προμεριμνᾶτε τί
when And they lead away you, delivering (you), not be anxious before what
2980 3366 3191 235 3739 1437 1325 5213 1722 1565 3588
λαλήσητὲ, μηδὲ μελετᾶτε· ἀλλ' ὃ ἐὰν δοθῇ ὑμῖν ἐν ἐκείνῃ τῇ
you shall say, nor meditate; but whatever is given to you in that
5610 5124 2980 3756 1063 2075 5210 3588 2980 235
ὥρᾳ, τοῦτο λαλεῖτε· οὐ γάρ ἐστε ὑμεῖς οἱ λαλοῦντες, ἀλλὰ
hour, this speak; not for are you the (one) speaking, but
3588 4151 3588 40 3860 1161 80 80 1519
τὸ Πνεῦμα τὸ Ἅγιον. 12 παραδώσει δὲ ἀδελφὸς ἀδελφὸν εἰς
the Spirit Holy. will deliver up But a brother a brother to
2288 2532 3962 5043 2532 1881 5043 1909
θάνατον, καὶ πατὴρ τέκνον· καὶ ἐπαναστήσονται τέκνα ἐπὶ
death, and a father a child; and will rise up children upon
1118 2532 2289 846 2532 2071 3404
γονεῖς, καὶ θανατώσουσιν αὐτούς· 13 καὶ ἔσεσθε μισούμενοι
parents, and put to death them. And you will be hated
5259 3956 1223 3588 3686 3450 3588 1161 5278 1519 5056
ὑπὸ πάντων διὰ τὸ ὄνομά μου· ὁ δὲ ὑπομείνας εἰς τέλος,
by all on account of the name of Me. he But enduring to the end,
3778 4982
οὗτος σωθήσεται.
this (one) will be kept safe.

9. But take heed to yourselves: for they shall deliver you up to councils; and in the synagogues ye shall be beaten: and ye shall be brought before rulers and kings for my sake, for a testimony against them.

10 And the gospel must first be published among all nations.
11 But when they shall lead (you), and deliver you up, take no thought beforehand what ye shall speak, neither do ye premeditate: but whatsoever shall be given you in that hour, that speak ye: for it is not ye that speak, but the Holy Ghost.
12 Now the brother shall betray the brother to death, and the father the son; and children shall rise up against (their) parents, and shall cause them to be put to death.
13 And ye shall be hated of all (men) for my name's sake: but he that shall endure unto the end, the same shall be saved.

14. But when you see the abomination of desolation, the (one) spoken of by Daniel the prophet, standing where it ought not (he reading, let him understand), then let those in Judea flee into the mountains. (Dan. 11:31; 12:11)
15 And he on the housetop, let him not go down into the house,

3752 1161 1492 3588 946 3588 2050 3588 4483
14. Ὅταν δὲ ἴδητε τὸ βδέλυγμα τῆς ἐρημώσεως, τὸ ῥηθὲν
when But you see the abomination of desolation, that spoken
5259 1158 3588 4396 2476 3699 3756 1163 3588 314
ὑπὸ Δανιὴλ τοῦ προφήτου, ἑστὼς ὅπου οὐ δεῖ [ὁ ἀναγινώ-
by Daniel the prophet, standing where not it ought (he reading,
3539 5119 3588 1722 3588 2449 5343 1519 3588
σκων νοείτω], τότε οἱ ἐν τῇ Ἰουδαίᾳ φευγέτωσαν εἰς τὰ
let him understand), then those in Judea let them flee into the
3735 3588 1161 1909 3588 1430 3361 2597 1519 3588 3614
ὄρη· 15 ὁ δὲ ἐπὶ τοῦ δώματος μὴ καταβάτω εἰς τὴν οἰκίαν,
mounts; he and on the housetop not let him descend into the house,

14. But when ye shall see the abomination of desolation, spoken of by Daniel the prophet, standing where it ought not, (let him that readeth understand,) then let them that be in Judaea flee to the mountains:
15 And let him that is on the housetop not go down into the house,

Literal Translation

nor go in to take anything out of his house.
16 And the one in the field, let him not return to the things behind to take his garment.

17 But woe to those holding (a babe) in womb, and to those giving suck in those days!
18 And pray that your flight may not occur in winter;
19 for there will be affliction (in) those days, such as has not been the like from (the) beginning of creation which God created until now, and not at all may be.
20 And if (the) Lord had not shortened the days, not any flesh would be saved; but because of the elect whom He elected, He shortened the days.
21 And then if anyone says to you, Behold, here (is) the Christ! Or, Behold, there! Do not believe.

22 For false christs and false prophets will be raised, and they will give signs and wonders in order to lead astray, if possible, even the elect.

23 But you be careful. Behold, I have foretold you all things.

24. But in those days, after that affliction, the sun will be darkened, and the moon will not give her light;

25 and the stars of the heaven will be falling, and the powers in the heavens will be shaken.
26 And then they will see the Son of man coming in clouds with much power and glory. (Dan. 7:13)

27 And then He will send His angels and will gather His elect from

Mark 13:16

3366 1525 142 5100 1537 3588 3614 846 2532 3588 1519 3588
μηδὲ εἰσελθέτω ἆραί τι ἐκ τῆς οἰκίας αὐτοῦ· 16 καὶ ὁ εἰς τὸν
nor let him enter to take a thing out of the house of him. And the (one) in the

68 5607 3361 1994 1519 3588 3694 142 3588 2440
ἀγρὸν ὢν μὴ ἐπιστρεψάτω εἰς τὰ ὀπίσω, ἆραι τὸ ἱμάτιον
field being, not let him go back to the things behind, to take the garment

846 3759 1161 3588 1722 1064 2192 2532 3588 2337
αὐτοῦ. 17 οὐαὶ δὲ ταῖς ἐν γαστρὶ ἐχούσαις καὶ ταῖς θηλαζού-
of him. woe But to those in womb holding, and to those giving

1722 1565 3588 2250 4336 1161 2443 3361 1096
σαις ἐν ἐκείναις ταῖς ἡμέραις. 18 προσεύχεσθε δὲ ἵνα μὴ γένηται
suck in those days. pray But that not may occur

3588 5437 5216 5494 2071 1063 3588 2250 1565 2347
ἡ φυγὴ ὑμῶν χειμῶνος. 19 ἔσονται γὰρ αἱ ἡμέραι ἐκεῖναι θλίψις,
the flight of you in winter. will be For days those affliction

3634 3756 1096 5108 575 746 2937 3739 2936 3588
οἵα οὐ γέγονε τοιαύτη ἀπ' ἀρχῆς κτίσεως ἧς ἔκτισεν ὁ
such as not has been the like from beginning of creation which created

2316 2193 3588 3568 2532 3756 3361 1096 2532 1487 3361 2962
Θεὸς ἕως τοῦ νῦν, καὶ οὐ μὴ γένηται. 20 καὶ εἰ μὴ Κύριος
God until now, and not at all may be. And except (the) Lord

2856 3588 2250 3756 302 4982 3956 4561 235 1223
ἐκολόβωσε τὰς ἡμέρας, οὐκ ἂν ἐσώθη πᾶσα σάρξ· ἀλλὰ διὰ
had shortened the days, not would be saved any flesh; but because of

3588 1588 3739 1586 2856 3588 2250 2532
τοὺς ἐκλεκτούς, οὓς ἐξελέξατο, ἐκολόβωσε τὰς ἡμέρας. 21 καὶ
the elect, whom He elected, He shortened the days. And

5119 1437 5100 5213 2036 2400 5602 3588 5547 2228 2400 1563 3361
τότε ἐάν τις ὑμῖν εἴπῃ, Ἰδού, ὧδε ὁ Χριστός, ἤ Ἰδού, ἐκεῖ, μὴ
then if anyone to you says, Behold! Here (is) the Christ, or, behold, there, not

4100 1453 1063 5580 2532 5578
πιστεύσητε. 22 ἐγερθήσονται γὰρ ψευδόχριστοι καὶ ψευδο-
do believe. will be raised For false christs and false

2532 1325 4592 2532 5059 4314 3588 635
προφῆται, καὶ δώσουσι σημεῖα καὶ τέρατα, πρὸς τὸ ἀπο-
prophets, and they will give signs and wonders in order to lead

1487 1415 2532 3588 1588 5210 1161 991
πλανᾷν, εἰ δυνατόν, καὶ τοὺς ἐκλεκτούς. 23 ὑμεῖς δὲ βλέπετε·
astray, if it could be, even the elect. you But look out.

2400 4280 5213 3956
ἰδού, προείρηκα ὑμῖν πάντα.
Behold! I have told before you all things.

235 1722 1565 3588 2250 3326 3588 2347 1565
24.'Ἀλλ' ἐν ἐκείναις ταῖς ἡμέραις, μετὰ τὴν θλίψιν ἐκείνην,
But in those days, after affliction that,

3588 2246 4654 2532 3588 4582 3756 1325 3588 5338
ὁ ἥλιος σκοτισθήσεται, καὶ ἡ σελήνη οὐ δώσει τὸ φέγγος
the sun will be darkened, and the moon not will give the light

846 2532 3588 792 3588 3772 2071 1601
αὐτῆς, 25 καὶ οἱ ἀστέρες τοῦ οὐρανοῦ ἔσονται ἐκπίπτοντες,
of her, and the stars of the heaven will be falling,

2532 3588 1411 3588 1722 3588 3772 4531 2532 5119
καὶ αἱ δυνάμεις αἱ ἐν τοῖς οὐρανοῖς σαλευθήσονται. 26 καὶ τότε
and the powers in the heavens will be shaken. And then

3700 3588 5207 3588 444 2064 1722 3507
ὄψονται τὸν υἱὸν τοῦ ἀνθρώπου ἐρχόμενον ἐν νεφέλαις
they will see the Son of man coming in clouds

3326 1411 4183 2532 1391 2532 5119 649 3588
μετὰ δυνάμεως πολλῆς καὶ δόξης. 27 καὶ τότε ἀποστελεῖ τοὺς
with power much and glory. And then He will send the

32 846 2532 1996 3588 1588 846 1537
ἀγγέλους αὐτοῦ, καὶ ἐπισυνάξει τοὺς ἐκλεκτοὺς αὐτοῦ ἐκ
angels of Him, and they will gather the elect of Him out of

King James Version

neither enter (therein), to take any thing out of his house:
16 And let him that is in the field not turn back again for to take up his garment.

17 But woe to them that are with child, and to them that give suck in those days!
18 And pray ye that your flight be not in the winter.
19 For (in) those days shall be affliction, such as was not from the beginning of the creation which God created unto this time, neither shall be.
20 And except that the Lord had shortened those days, no flesh should be saved: but for the elect's sake, whom he hath chosen, he hath shortened the days.
21 And then if any man shall say to you, Lo, here (is) Christ; or, lo, (he is) there; believe (him) not:

22 For false Christs and false prophets shall rise, and shall shew signs and wonders, to seduce, if (it were) possible, even the elect.

23 But take ye heed: behold, I have foretold you all things.

24. But in those days, after that tribulation, the sun shall be darkened, and the moon shall not give her light,

25 And the stars of heaven shall fall, and the powers that are in heaven shall be shaken.
26 And then shall they see the Son of man coming in the clouds with great power and glory.

27 And then shall he send his angels, and shall gather together his elect from

Mark 13:28

Literal Translation

the four winds, from (the) end of earth to (the) end of (the) heaven.

28 And from the fig tree learn the parable: When its branch becomes tender and puts out leaves, you know the summer is near.

29 So you also, when you see these things happening, know that it is near, at (the) doors.
30 Truly I say to you, Not at all will this generation pass away until all these things occur.

31 The heaven and the earth will pass away, but My words will not pass away, never!
32. But concerning that day and the hour, no one knows, not the angels, those in Heaven, nor the Son, except the Father.

33 Watch! Be wakeful, and pray. For you do not know when the time is.
34 As a man going away, leaving his house, and giving his slaves authority, and to each his work (and he commanded the doorkeeper, that he should watch),

35 then you watch, for you do not know when the lord of the house is coming, (at) evening, or midnight, or at cock-crowing, or at dawn;

36 so that not coming suddenly he find you sleeping.

37 And what I say to you, I say to all. Watch!

Greek Interlinear

3588 5064 417 575 206 1093 2193 206 3772
τῶν τεσσάρων ἀνέμων, ἀπ' ἄκρου γῆς ἕως ἄκρου οὐρανοῦ.
the four winds, from (the) end of earth until (the) end of (the) heaven.

575 1161 3588 4808 3129 3588 3850 3752 846
28. Ἀπὸ δὲ τῆς συκῆς μάθετε τὴν παραβολήν· ὅταν αὐτῆς
from And the fig-tree learn the parable: when of it

2235 3588 2798 527 1096 2532 1631 3588 5444 1097
ἤδη ὁ κλάδος ἁπαλὸς γένηται καὶ ἐκφύῃ τὰ φύλλα, γινώ-
now the branch tender becomes and puts out the leaves, you

3754 1451 3588 2330 2076 3779 2532 5210 3752 5023
σκετε ὅτι ἐγγὺς τὸ θέρος ἐστίν· 29 οὕτω καὶ ὑμεῖς, ὅταν ταῦτα
know that near the summer is. So also you, when these things

1492 1096 1097 3754 1451 2076 1909 2374 281
ἴδητε γινόμενα, γινώσκετε ὅτι ἐγγύς ἐστιν ἐπὶ θύραις. 30 ἀμὴν
you see happening, know that near it is, at (the) doors. Truly

3004 5213 3754 3756 3361 3928 3588 1074 846 3360 3756
λέγω ὑμῖν ὅτι οὐ μὴ παρέλθῃ ἡ γενεὰ αὕτη, μέχρις οὗ
I say to you that in no way will pass away generation this until

3956 5023 1096 3588 3772 2532 3588 1093 3928
πάντα ταῦτα γένηται. 31 ὁ οὐρανὸς καὶ ἡ γῆ παρελεύσονται·
all these things occur. The heaven and the earth will pass away;

3588 1161 3056 3450 3756 3361 3928 4012 1161 3588 2250
οἱ δὲ λόγοι μου οὐ μὴ παρέλθωσι. 32 περὶ δὲ τῆς ἡμέρας
the but words of Me in no way will pass away. concerning But day

1565 2532 3588 5610 3762 1492 3761 3588 32 3588 1722
ἐκείνης καὶ τῆς ὥρας οὐδεὶς οἶδεν, οὐδὲ οἱ ἄγγελοι οἱ ἐν
that and the hour no one knows, not the angels in

3772 3761 3588 5207 1487 3361 3588 3962 991 69
οὐρανῷ, οὐδὲ ὁ υἱός, εἰ μὴ ὁ πατήρ. 33 βλέπετε, ἀγρυπνεῖτε
Heaven, nor the Son, except the Father. Look out!, Be wakeful

2532 4336 3756 1492 1063 4219 3588 2540 2076 5613
καὶ προσεύχεσθε· οὐκ οἴδατε γὰρ πότε ὁ καιρός ἐστιν. 34 ὡς
and pray! not you know For when the time is. As

444 590 863 3588 3614 846 2532 1325 3588
ἄνθρωπος ἀπόδημος ἀφεὶς τὴν οἰκίαν αὐτοῦ, καὶ δοὺς τοῖς
a man going away leaving the house of him, and giving to the

1401 846 3588 1849 2532 1538 3588 2041 846
δούλοις αὐτοῦ τὴν ἐξουσίαν, καὶ ἑκάστῳ τὸ ἔργον αὐτοῦ,
slaves of him the authority, and to each the work of him,

2532 3588 2377 1781 2443 1127 1127 3767
καὶ τῷ θυρωρῷ ἐνετείλατο ἵνα γρηγορῇ. 35 γρηγορεῖτε οὖν·
and the doorkeeper he ordered that he should watch. You watch then;

3756 1492 1063 4219 3588 2962 3588 3614 2064 3796 2228
οὐκ οἴδατε γὰρ πότε ὁ κύριος τῆς οἰκίας ἔρχεται, ὀψέ, ἢ
not you know for when the lord of the house comes, evening or

3317 2228 219 2228 4404 3361 2064 1810
μεσονυκτίου, ἢ ἀλεκτοροφωνίας, ἢ πρωΐ· 36 μὴ ἐλθὼν ἐξαίφνης
midnight, or at cock-crowing, or at dawn; (that) not coming suddenly

2147 5209 2518 3739 1161 5213 3004 3956 3004
εὕρῃ ὑμᾶς καθεύδοντας. 37 ἃ δὲ ὑμῖν λέγω πᾶσι λέγω,
he find you sleeping. what And to you I say, to all I say:

1127
Γρηγορεῖτε.
Watch!

King James Version

the four winds, from the uttermost part of the earth to the uttermost part of heaven.

28 Now learn a parable of the fig tree; When her branch is yet tender, and putteth forth leaves, ye know that summer is near:

29 So ye in like manner, when ye shall see these things come to pass, know that it is nigh, (even) at the doors.
30 Verily I say unto you, that this generation shall not pass, till all these things be done.

31 Heaven and earth shall pass away: but my words shall not pass away.
32. But of that day and (that) hour knoweth no man, no, not the angels which are in heaven, neither the Son, but the Father.

33 Take ye heed, watch and pray: for ye know not when the time is.
34 (For the Son of man is) as a man taking a far journey, who left his house, and gave authority to his servants, and to every man his work, and commanded the porter to watch.

35 Watch ye therefore: for ye know not when the master of the house cometh, at even, or at midnight, or at the cock-crowing, or in the morning:
36 Lest coming suddenly he find you sleeping.

37 And what I say unto you I say unto all, Watch.

Mark 14

Literal Translation

1. And it was the Passover, and (the Feast) of Unleavened (Bread) after two days. And the chief priests and the scribes were seeking how they might get hold of Him by guile,

Greek Interlinear

2258 1161 3588 3957 2532 3588 106 3326 1417 2250 2532
1. Ἦν δὲ τὸ πάσχα καὶ τὰ ἄζυμα μετὰ δύο ἡμέρας· καὶ
it was And the Passover and the unleavened (bread) after two days. And

2212 3588 749 2532 3588 1122 4459 846 1722 1388
ἐζήτουν οἱ ἀρχιερεῖς καὶ οἱ γραμματεῖς πῶς αὐτὸν ἐν δόλῳ
sought the chief priests and the scribes how Him by guile

King James Version

1 After two days was (the feast of) the passover, and of unleavened bread: and the chief priests and the scribes sought how they might take him by craft,

Literal Translation | **Mark 14:2** | **King James Version**

(to) kill (Him).
2 But they said, Not during the Feast, thatt not will be a tumult of the people.

3. And He being in Bethany, in the house of Simon the leper, He having reclined, a woman came having an alabaster vial of pure, costly ointment of nard. And breaking the alabaster vial, she poured (it) down His head.
4 And some were being indignant to themselves, and saying, To what has this waste of the ointment occurred?

5 For this could be sold (for) over three hundred denarii, and to be given to the poor. And they were incensed with her.

6 But Jesus said, Let her alone. Why do you cause her troubles? She worked a good work toward Me.

7 For you have the poor with yourselves always, and when you wish, you can do well toward them, but you do not have Me always.

8 What this one held, she did. She took beforehand to anoint My body for the burial.
9 Truly I say to you, Wherever this gospel is proclaimed into all the world, what this woman did will also be spoken of for a memorial of her.

10. And Judas Iscariot, one of the Twelve, went away to the chief priests, that he might betray Him to them.
11 And hearing, they rejoiced and promised to give him silver. And he sought how he might opportunely betray Him.

2902 615 3004 1161 3361 1722 3588 1859
κρατήσαντες ἀποκτείνωσιν· 2 ἔλεγον δέ, Μὴ ἐν τῇ ἑορτῇ,
having seized they might kill. they said But, Not in the Feast,
3379 2351 2071 3588 2992
μήποτε θόρυβος ἔσται τοῦ λαοῦ.
that not a tumult will be of the people.

2532 5607 846 1722 963 1722 3588 3614 4613 3588
3. Καὶ ὄντος αὐτοῦ ἐν Βηθανίᾳ, ἐν τῇ οἰκίᾳ Σίμωνος τοῦ
And being He in Bethany, in the house of Simon the
3015 2621 846 2064 1135 2192 211
λεπροῦ, κατακειμένου αὐτοῦ ἦλθε γυνὴ ἔχουσα ἀλάβαστρον
leper, having reclined He came a woman having an alabaster vial
3464 3487 4101 4185 2532 4937 3588
μύρου νάρδου πιστικῆς πολυτελοῦς· καὶ συντρίψασα τὸ
of ointment of nard pure costly. And breaking the
211 2708 846 2596 3588 2776 2258 1161
ἀλάβαστρον, κατέχεεν αὐτοῦ κατὰ τῆς κεφαλῆς. 4 ἦσαν δέ
alabaster vial, she poured (it) of Him down the head. were And
5100 23 4314 1438 2532 3004 1519 5101 3588
τινες ἀγανακτοῦντες πρὸς ἑαυτούς, καὶ λέγοντες, Εἰς τί ἡ
some being indignant to themselves, and saying, To what
684 846 3588 3464 1096 1410 1063 5124
ἀπώλεια αὕτη τοῦ μύρου γέγονεν; 5 ἠδύνατο γὰρ τοῦτο
waste this of the ointment has occurred? could For this
4097 1883 5145 1220 2532 1325 3588
πραθῆναι ἐπάνω τριακοσίων δηναρίων, καὶ δοθῆναι τοῖς
be sold (for) over three hundred denarii, and to be given to the
4434 2532 1690 846 3588 1161 2424 2036 863
πτωχοῖς. καὶ ἐνεβριμῶντο αὐτῇ. 6 ὁ δὲ Ἰησοῦς εἶπεν, Ἄφετε
poor. And they were incensed with her. But Jesus said, Let alone
846 5101 846 2873 3930 2570 2041 2038
αὐτήν· τί αὐτῇ κόπους παρέχετε; καλὸν ἔργον εἰργάσατο
her. Why to her troubles do you cause? a good work She worked
1519 1691 3842 1063 3588 4434 2192 3326 1438 2532
εἰς ἐμέ. 7 πάντοτε γὰρ τοὺς πτωχοὺς ἔχετε μεθ' ἑαυτῶν, καὶ
to Me. always For the poor you have with yourselves, and
3752 2309 1410 846 2095 4160 1691 1161 3756 3842
ὅταν θέλητε δύνασθε αὐτοὺς εὖ ποιῆσαι· ἐμὲ δὲ οὐ πάντοτε
when you desire you are able (to) them well to do; Me but not always
2192 3739 2192 846 4160 4301 3462 3450 3588
ἔχετε. 8 ὃ εἶχεν αὕτη ἐποίησε· προέλαβε μυρίσαι μου τὸ
you have. What held this one,she did; she took beforehand to anoint of Me the
4983 1519 3588 1780 281 3004 5213 3699 302
σῶμα εἰς τὸν ἐνταφιασμόν. 9 ἀμὴν λέγω ὑμῖν, ὅπου ἂν
body for the burial. Truly I say to you, wherever
2784 3588 2098 5124 1519 3650 3588 2889 2532/3739
κηρυχθῇ τὸ εὐαγγέλιον τοῦτο εἰς ὅλον τὸν κόσμον, καὶ ὃ
is proclaimed gospel this into all the world, also what
4160 846 2980 151 3422 846
ἐποίησεν αὕτη λαληθήσεται εἰς μνημόσυνον αὐτῆς.
did this woman will be spoken for a memorial of her.

2532 3588 2455 3588 2469 1520 3588 1427 565 4314
10. Καὶ ὁ Ἰούδας ὁ Ἰσκαριώτης, εἷς τῶν δώδεκα, ἀπῆλθε πρὸς
And Judas Iscariot, one of the twelve, went away
3588 749 2443 3860 846 846 3588 1161 191
τοὺς ἀρχιερεῖς, ἵνα παραδῷ αὐτὸν αὐτοῖς. 11 οἱ δὲ ἀκού-
to the chief priests, that he may betray Him to them. they And
5463 2532 1861 846 694 1325
σαντες ἐχάρησαν, καὶ ἐπηγγείλαντο αὐτῷ ἀργύριον δοῦναι·
hearing rejoiced and promised him silver to give.
2532 2212 4459 2122 846 3860
καὶ ἐζήτει πῶς εὐκαίρως αὐτὸν παραδῷ.
And he sought how opportunely Him he might betray.

---

and put (him) to death.
2 But they said, Not on the feast (day), lest there be an uproar of the people.

3. And being in Bethany in the house of Simon the leper, as he sat at meat, there came a woman having an alabaster box of ointment of spikenard very precious; and she brake the box, and poured (it) on his head.
4 And there were some that had indignation within themselves, and said, Why was this waste of the ointment made?

5 For it might have been sold for more than three hundred pence, and have been given to the poor. And they murmured against her.

6 And Jesus said, Let her alone; why trouble ye her? she hath wrought a good work on me.

7 For ye have the poor with you always, and whensoever ye will ye may do them good: but me ye have not always.

8 She hath done what she could: she is come aforehand to anoint my body to the burying.
9 Verily I say unto you, Wheresoever this gospel shall be preached throughout the whole world, (this) also that she hath done shall be spoken of for a memorial of her.

10. And Judas Iscariot, one of the twelve, went unto the chief priests, to betray him unto them.
11 And when they heard (it), they were glad, and promised to give him money. And he sought how he might conveniently betray him.

Literal Translation | **Mark 14:12** | **King James Version**

12. And on the first day of the Unleavened (Bread), when they killed the passover, His disciples said to Him, Where do You desire (that) going we may prepare that You eat the passover?
13 And He sent two of His disciples, and said to them, Go into the city, and you will meet a man carrying a pitcher of water. Follow him.
14 And wherever he enters, tell the housemaster, The Teacher says, Where is the guestroom where I may eat the passover with My disciples?
15 And he will show you a large upper room, having been spread (and) made ready. Prepare for us there.
16 And His disciples went out and came into the city and found (it) as He told them. And they prepared the Passover.

2532 3588 4413 2250 3588 106 3753 3588 3957 2380
12. Καὶ τῇ πρώτῃ ἡμέρᾳ τῶν ἀζύμων, ὅτε τὸ πάσχα ἔθυον,
And on the first day of the unleavened, when the passover they killed,
3004 846 3588 3101 846 4226 2309 565
λέγουσιν αὐτῷ οἱ μαθηταὶ αὐτοῦ, Ποῦ θέλεις ἀπελθόντες
say to Him the disciples of Him, Where do you wish going
2090 2443 5315 3588 3957 2532 649 1417 3588
ἑτοιμάσωμεν ἵνα φάγῃς τὸ πάσχα; 13 καὶ ἀποστέλλει δύο τῶν
we may prepare that You eat the Passover? And He sends two of the
3101 846 2532 3004 846 5217 1519 3588 4172
μαθητῶν αὐτοῦ, καὶ λέγει αὐτοῖς, Ὑπάγετε εἰς τὴν πόλιν,
disciples of Him, and says to them, Go into the city,
2532 528 5213 444 2765 5204 941
καὶ ἀπαντήσει ὑμῖν ἄνθρωπος κεράμιον ὕδατος βαστάζων·
and will meet you a man a pitcher of water carrying;
190 846 2532 3699 1437 1525 2036 3588
ἀκολουθήσατε αὐτῷ, 14 καὶ ὅπου ἐὰν εἰσέλθῃ, εἴπατε τῷ
follow him. And where ever he enters, tell the
3617 3754 3588 1320 3004 4226 2076 3588 2646
οἰκοδεσπότῃ ὅτι Ὁ διδάσκαλος λέγει, Ποῦ ἐστι τὸ κατά-
housemaster, The Teacher says, Where is the guest-
3699 3588 3957 3326 3588 3101 3450 5315 2532
λυμά, ὅπου τὸ πάσχα μετὰ τῶν μαθητῶν μου φάγω; 15 καὶ
room where the passover with the disciples of Me I may eat? And
846 5213 1166 508 3173 4766 2092 1563
αὐτὸς ὑμῖν δείξει ἀνώγεον μέγα ἐστρωμένον ἕτοιμον· ἐκεῖ
he you will show an upper room large being spread ready. There
2090 2254 2532 1831 3588 3101 846 2532 2064
ἑτοιμάσατε ἡμῖν. 16 καὶ ἐξῆλθον οἱ μαθηταὶ αὐτοῦ, καὶ ἦλθον
you prepare for us. And went out the disciples of Him, and came
1519 3588 4172 2532 2147 2531 2036 846 2532 2090
εἰς τὴν πόλιν, καὶ εὗρον καθὼς εἶπεν αὐτοῖς, καὶ ἡτοίμασαν
into the city, and found even as He said to them. And they prepared
3588 3957
τὸ πάσχα.
the passover.

12. And the first day of unleavened bread, when they killed the passover, his disciples said unto him, Where wilt thou that we go and prepare that thou mayest eat the passover?
13 And he sendeth forth two of his disciples, and saith unto them, Go ye into the city, and there shall meet you a man bearing a pitcher of water: follow him.
14 And wheresoever he shall go in, say ye to the goodman of the house, The Master saith, Where is the guestchamber, where I shall eat the passover with my disciples?
15 And he will shew you a large upper room furnished (and) prepared: there make ready for us.
16 And his disciples went forth, and came into the city, and found as he had said unto them: and they made ready the passover.

17 And evening having come, He came with the Twelve.
18 And they having reclined and having eaten, Jesus said, Truly I say to you, One of you will betray Me, the (one) eating with Me.
19 And they began to be grieved, and to say to Him one by one, Not at all I, (is it)? And another, Not at all I, (is it)?
20 But answering, He said to them, (It is) one from the Twelve, the (one) dipping in the dish with Me.

2532 3798 1096 2064 3326 3588 1427 2532
17. Καὶ ὀψίας γενομένης ἔρχεται μετὰ τῶν δώδεκα. 18 καὶ
And evening occurring, He comes with the twelve. And
345 846 2532 2068 2036 3588 2424 281 3004
ἀνακειμένων αὐτῶν καὶ ἐσθιόντων, εἶπεν ὁ Ἰησοῦς, Ἀμὴν λέγω
having reclined they and having eaten, said Jesus, Truly I say
5213 3754 1520 1537 5216 3860 3165 3588 2068 3326 1700 3588
ὑμῖν, ὅτι εἷς ἐξ ὑμῶν παραδώσει με, ὁ ἐσθίων μετ' ἐμοῦ. 19 οἱ
to you that one from you will betray Me, he eating with Me. they
1161 756 3076 2532 3004 846 1520 2596 1520 =3385=
δὲ ἤρξαντο λυπεῖσθαι, καὶ λέγειν αὐτῷ εἷς καθ' εἷς, Μή, τι
And began to be grieved, and to say to Him one by one, Not at all
1473 2532 243 - - =3385=-1473 3588 1161 611 2036 846
ἐγώ; καὶ ἄλλος Μή τι ἐγώ; 20 ὁ δὲ ἀποκριθεὶς εἶπεν αὐτοῖς,
I? And another, Not at all I? He And answering said to them,
1520 1537 3588 1427 3588 1686 3326 1700 1519 3588 5165
Εἷς ἐκ τῶν δώδεκα, ὁ ἐμβαπτόμενος μετ' ἐμοῦ εἰς τὸ τρύβλιον.
One out of the twelve, the (one) dipping with Me in the dish.

17 And in the evening he cometh with the twelve.
18 And as they sat and did eat, Jesus said, Verily I say unto you, One of you which eateth with me shall betray me.
19 And they began to be sorrowful, and to say unto him one by one, (Is) it I? and another (said, Is) it I?
20 And he answered and said unto them, (It is) one of the twelve, that dippeth with me in the dish.

21 Truly the Son of man goes as it has been written concerning Him, but woe to that man by whom the Son of man is betrayed! It were good for him if that man had never been born.

3588 3303 5207 3588 444 5217 2531 1125 4012
21 ὁ μὲν υἱὸς τοῦ ἀνθρώπου ὑπάγει, καθὼς γέγραπται περὶ
the Truly Son of man goes, even as it has been written about
846 3759 1161 3588 444 1565 1223 3739 3588 5207 3588
αὐτοῦ· οὐαὶ δὲ τῷ ἀνθρώπῳ ἐκείνῳ δι' οὗ ὁ υἱὸς τοῦ
Him, woe but man (to) that through whom the Son
444 3860 2570 2258 846 1487 3756 1080 3588
ἀνθρώπου παραδίδοται· καλὸν ἦν αὐτῷ εἰ οὐκ ἐγεννήθη ὁ
of man is betrayed; good were it if not was born

21 The Son of man indeed goeth, as it is written of him: but woe to that man by whom the Son of man is betrayed! good were it for that man if he had never been born.

Literal Translation | **Mark 14:22** | **King James Version**

444 1565
ἄνθρωπος ἐκεῖνος.
man that!

22. And (as) they (were) eating, Jesus taking a loaf, blessing, He broke and gave to them. And He said, Take, eat, this is My body.

2532 2068 846 2983 3588 2424 740 2127
22. Καὶ ἐσθιόντων αὐτῶν, λαβὼν ὁ Ἰησοῦς ἄρτον εὐλογήσας
And eating they, taking Jesus a loaf blessing,
2806 2532 1325 846 2532 2036 2983 5315 5124
ἔκλασε, καὶ ἔδωκεν αὐτοῖς, καὶ εἶπε, Λάβετε, φάγετε· τοῦτό
He broke and gave to them, and said, Take, eat, this
2076 3588 4983 3450 2532 2983 3588 4221 2168
ἐστι τὸ σῶμά μου. 23 καὶ λαβὼν τὸ ποτήριον εὐχαριστήσας
is the body of Me. And taking the cup, giving thanks,
1325 846 2532 4095 1537 846 3956 2532 2036 846
ἔδωκεν αὐτοῖς· καὶ ἔπιον ἐξ αὐτοῦ πάντες. 24 καὶ εἶπεν αὐτοῖς,
He gave to them; and drank from it all. And He said to them,
5124 2076 3588 129 3450 3588 3588 2537 1242 3588 4012
Τοῦτό ἐστι τὸ αἷμά μου, τὸ τῆς καινῆς διαθήκης τὸ περὶ
This is the blood of Me, that of the New Covenant concerning
4183 1632 281 3004 5213 3754 3765 3756 3361
πολλῶν ἐκχυνόμενον. 25 ἀμὴν λέγω ὑμῖν ὅτι οὐκέτι οὐ μὴ
many being poured out. Truly I say to you that no more, not at all
4095 1537 3588 1081 3588 288 2193 3588 2250 1565
πίω ἐκ τοῦ γεννήματος τῆς ἀμπέλου, ἕως τῆς ἡμέρας ἐκείνης
I may drink from the offspring of the vine, until day that
3752 846 4095 2537 1722 3588 932 3588 2316
ὅταν αὐτὸ πίνω καινὸν ἐν τῇ βασιλείᾳ τοῦ Θεοῦ.
when it I drink new in the kingdom of God.

22. And as they did eat, Jesus took bread, and blessed, and brake (it), and gave to them, and said, Take, eat: this is my body.

23 And taking the cup, giving thanks, He gave to them; and all drank from it.

23 And he took the cup, and when he had given thanks, he gave (it) to them: and they all drank of it.

24 And He said to them, This is My blood, that of the New Covenant, (which is) being poured out concerning many.

24 And he said unto them, This is my blood of the new testament, which is shed for many.

25 Truly I say to you that no more, not at all I may not drink of the offspring of the vine any more until that day when I drink it new in the kingdom of God.

25 Verily I say unto you, I will drink no more of the fruit of the vine, until that day that I drink it new in the kingdom of God.

26. And havings sung a hymn, they went into the Mount of Olives.

2532 5214 1831 1519 3588 3735 3588 1636
26. Καὶ ὑμνήσαντες ἐξῆλθον εἰς τὸ ὄρος τῶν Ἐλαιῶν.
And having sung a hymn they went into the Mount of the Olives.

26. And when they had sung an hymn, they went out into the mount of Olives.

27 And Jesus said to them, All of you will be offended in Me in this night, because it has been written: "I will strike the Shepherd, and the sheep will be scattered." (Zech. 13:7)

28 But after the rising of Me, I will go before you into Galilee.

29 But Peter said to Him, Even if all shall be offended, yet not I.

2532 3004 846 3588 2424 3754 3956 4624
27. Καὶ λέγει αὐτοῖς ὁ Ἰησοῦς ὅτι Πάντες σκανδαλισθήσεσθε
And says to them Jesus, All you will be offended
1722 1698 1722 3588 3571 5026 3754 1125 3960 3588
ἐν ἐμοὶ ἐν τῇ νυκτὶ ταύτῃ· ὅτι γέγραπται, Πατάξω τὸν
in Me in night this, because it has been written, I will strike the
4166 2532 1287 3588 4263 , 235 3326
ποιμένα, καὶ διασκορπισθήσεται τὰ πρόβατα. 28 ἀλλὰ μετὰ
Shepherd, and will be scattered the sheep. But after
3588 1453 3165 4254 5209 1519 3588 1056 3588 1161
τὸ ἐγερθῆναί με, προάξω ὑμᾶς εἰς τὴν Γαλιλαίαν. 29 ὁ δὲ
the rising up of Me, I will go before you into Galilee. And
4074 5346 846 2532 1487 3956 4624 235
Πέτρος ἔφη αὐτῷ, Καὶ εἰ πάντες σκανδαλισθήσονται, ἀλλ᾽
Peter said to Him, Even if all shall be offended, yet
3756 1473 2532 3004 846 3588 2424 281 3004 4671 3754
οὐκ ἐγώ. 30 καὶ λέγει αὐτῷ ὁ Ἰησοῦς, Ἀμὴν λέγω σοι, ὅτι
not I. And says to him Jesus, Truly I say to you,
4594 1722 3588 3571 3778 4250 2228 1364 220 5455
σήμερον ἐν τῇ νυκτι ταύτῃ, πρὶν ἢ δὶς ἀλέκτορα φωνῆσαι,
Today, in night this, before twice (the) cock sounds,
5151 533 3165 3588/1161/1537 4053 3004 3123 1437 3165
τρίς ἀπαρνήσῃ με. 31 ὁ δὲ ἐκ περισσοῦ ἔλεγε μᾶλλον, Ἐάν με
trice you will deny Me. he And more exceedingly said much, If me
1163 4880 4671 3756 3361 4571 533 5615
δέῃ συναποθανεῖν σοι, οὐ μή σε ἀπαρνήσομαι. ὡσαύτως
must die with You, in no way You I will deny. likewise
1161 2532 3956 3004
δὲ καὶ πάντες ἔλεγον.
And also all said.

27 And Jesus saith unto them, All ye shall be offended because of me this night: for it is written, I will smite the shepherd, and the sheep shall be scattered.

28 But after that I am risen, I will go before you into Galilee.

29 But Peter said unto him, Although all shall be offended, yet (will) not I.

30 And Jesus said to him, Truly I say to you, Today, in this night, before a cock crows twice, you will deny Me three times.

30 And Jesus saith unto him, Verily I say unto thee, That this day, (even) in this night, before the cock crow twice, thou shalt deny me thrice.

31 But he said much more fervently, If it were needful for me to die with You, in no way will I deny You. And also all said the same.

31 But he spake the more vehemently, If I should die with thee, I will not deny thee in any wise. Likewise also said they all.

32. And they came to a place which (was) named Gethsemane. And

2532 2064 1519 5564 3739 3588 3686 1068 2532
32. Καὶ ἔρχονται εἰς χωρίον οὗ τὸ ὄνομα Γεθσημανῆ· καὶ
And they come into a place of which the name (was) Gethsemane. And

32. And they came to a place which was named Gethsemane: and

Literal Translation | **Mark 14:33** | *King James Version*

He said to His disciples, Sit here while I pray.

33 And He took along Peter and James and John with Him. And He began to be much amazed and to be distressed.

34 And (He) said to them, My soul is deeply grieved, unto death. Remain here and watch.
35 And going forward a little, He fell on the earth and prayed that if it were possible, the hour might pass from Him.

36 And He said, Abba, Father, all things (are) possible to You; take this cup from Me. Yet not what I desire, but what You (desire).

37 And He came and found them sleeping. And (He) said to Peter, Simon, do you sleep? Were you not strong (enough) to watch one hour?
38 Watch and pray, that you may not enter into temptation. Truly the spirit (is) ready, but the flesh (is) weak.

39 And going away again, He prayed, saying the same word.
40 And returning, He found them sleeping again, for their eyes were weighing heavily. And they did not know what to answer Him.

41 And He came a third time, and said to them, Sleep now, and rest. It is enough. The hour has come. Behold! The Son of man is delivered up into the hands of sinners.

42 Rise up, let us go. Behold, the (one) delivering up Me has drawn near.

43. And at once, as He was yet speaking, Judas came up,

3004 3588 3101 846 2523 5602 2193 4336
λέγει τοῖς μαθηταῖς αὐτοῦ, Καθίσατε ὧδε ἕως προσεύξω-
He says to the disciples of Him, Sit here while I pray.

2532 3880 3588 4074 2532 3588 2385 2532
μαι. 33 καὶ παραλαμβάνει τὸν Πέτρον καὶ τὸν Ἰάκωβον καὶ
And He takes along Peter and James and

2491 3326 1438 2532 756 1568 2532 85
Ἰωάννην μεθ᾽ ἑαυτοῦ, καὶ ἤρξατο ἐκθαμβεῖσθαι καὶ ἀδη-
John with Him. And He began to be much amazed and to be

2532 3004 846 4036 2076 3588 5590 3450 2193
μονεῖν, 34 καὶ λέγει αὐτοῖς, Περίλυπός ἐστιν ἡ ψυχή μου ἕως
distressed. And He says to them, Deeply grieved is the soul of Me unto

2288 3306 5602 2532 1127 2532 4281 3397
θανάτου· μείνατε ὧδε καὶ γρηγορεῖτε. 35 καὶ προελθὼν μικρὸν,
death. Remain here and watch. And going forward a little,

4098 1909 3588 1093 2532 4336 2443 1487 1415 2076
ἔπεσεν ἐπὶ τῆς γῆς, καὶ προσηύχετο ἵνα, εἰ δυνατόν ἐστι,
He fell on the earth and prayed that, if possible it is,

3928 575 846 3588 5610 2532 3004 5 3588 3962
παρέλθῃ ἀπ᾽ αὐτοῦ ἡ ὥρα. 36 καὶ ἔλεγεν, Αββα, ὁ πατήρ,
might pass from Him the hour. And He said, Abba, Father,

3956 1415 4671 3911 3588 4221 575 1700 5124
πάντα δυνατά σοι· παρένεγκε τὸ ποτήριον ἀπ᾽ ἐμοῦ τοῦτο·
all things (are) possible to You; remove cup from Me this;

235 3756 5101 1473 2309 235 5101 4771 2532 2064 2532 2147
ἀλλ᾽ οὐ τί ἐγὼ θέλω, ἀλλὰ τί σύ. 37 καὶ ἔρχεται καὶ εὑρίσκει
but not what I desire, but what You. And He comes and finds

846 2518 2532 3004 3588 4074 4613 2518
αὐτοὺς καθεύδοντας, καὶ λέγει τῷ Πέτρῳ, Σίμων, καθεύδεις;
them sleeping, and says to Peter, Simon, do you sleep?

3756 2480 3391 5610 1127 1127 2532
οὐκ ἴσχυσας μίαν ὥραν γρηγορῆσαι; 38 γρηγορεῖτε καὶ
Not were you strong one hour to watch? Watch and

4336 2443 3361 1525 1519 3986 3588 3303 4151
προσεύχεσθε, ἵνα μὴ εἰσέλθητε εἰς πειρασμόν. τὸ μὲν πνεῦμα
pray, that not you enter into temptation. the Indeed spirit

4289 3588 1161 4561 772 2532 3825 565 4336
πρόθυμον, ἡ δὲ σὰρξ ἀσθενής. 39 καὶ πάλιν ἀπελθὼν προσηύ-
(is) ready, the but flesh is weak. And again going away He prayed,

3588 846 3056 2036 2532 5290 2147 846
ξατο, τὸν αὐτὸν λόγον εἰπών. 40 καὶ ὑποστρέψας εὗρεν αὐτοὺς
the same word saying. And returnimg He found them

3825 2518 2258 1063 3588 3788 846 916
πάλιν καθεύδοντας· ἦσαν γὰρ οἱ ὀφθαλμοὶ αὐτῶν βεβαρη-
again sleeping; were for the eyes of them weighing

2532 3756 1492 5101 846 611 2532 2064 3588
μένοι, καὶ οὐκ ᾔδεισαν τί αὐτῷ ἀποκριθῶσι. 41 καὶ ἔρχεται τὸ
heavily. And not they knew what Him to answer. And He comes the

5154 2532 3004 846 2518 3588 3063 2532 373
τρίτον, καὶ λέγει αὐτοῖς, Καθεύδετε τὸ λοιπὸν καὶ ἀναπαύε-
third (time) and says to them, Sleep now and rest.

566 2064 3588 5610 2400 3860 3588 5207 3588
σθε. ἀπέχει· ἦλθεν ἡ ὥρα· ἰδού, παραδίδοται ὁ υἱὸς τοῦ
It is enough; has come the hour. Behold! is delivered up The Son

444 1519 3588 5495 3588 268 1453 71
ἀνθρώπου εἰς τὰς χεῖρας τῶν ἁμαρτωλῶν. 42 ἐγείρεσθε ἄγωμεν·
of man into the hands of the sinners. Rise up; let us go.

2400 3588 3860 3165 1448
ἰδού, ὁ παραδιδούς με ἤγγικε.
Behold! He delivering up Me has drawn near.

2532 2112 2089 846 2980 3854 2455
43. Καὶ εὐθέως, ἔτι αὐτοῦ λαλοῦντος, παραγίνεται Ἰούδας
And at once, yet He speaking, comes up Judas

---

he saith to his disciples, Sit ye here, while I shall pray.

33 And he taketh with him Peter and James and John, and began to be sore amazed, and to be very heavy;

34 And saith unto them, My soul is exceeding sorrowful unto death: tarry ye here, and watch.
35 And he went forward a little, and fell on the ground, and prayed that, if it were possible, the hour might pass from him.
36 And he said, Abba, Father, all things (are) possible unto thee; take away this cup from me: nevertheless not what I will, but what thou wilt.
37 And he cometh, and findeth them sleeping, and saith unto Peter, Simon, sleepest thou? couldest not thou watch one hour?

38 Watch ye and pray, lest ye enter into temptation. The spirit truly (is) ready, but the flesh (is) weak.

39 And again he went away, and prayed, and spake the same words.
40 And when he returned, he found them asleep again, (for their eyes were heavy,) neither wist they what to answer him.

41 And he cometh the third time, and saith unto them, Sleep on now, and take (your) rest: it is enough, the hour is come; behold, the Son of man is betrayed into the hands of sinners.

42 Rise up, let us go; lo, he that betrayeth me is at hand.

43. And immediately, while he yet spake, cometh Judas,

Mark 14:44

Literal Translation

being one of the Twelve. And with him (was) a large crowd with swords and clubs, from the chief priests and the scribes and the elders.

44 And the (one) betraying Him had given them a signal, saying, Whomever I kiss, (it) is He; seize Him and lead (Him) away securely.

45 And coming, at once drawing near to Him, he said, Rabbi, Rabbi! And (he) ardently kissed Him.

46 And they laid their hands on Him and seized Him.

47 But a certain one of those standing by, drawing the sword, struck the slave of the high priest and took off his ear.
48 And answering Jesus said to them, Have you come out with swords and clubs to take Me, as against a plunderer?

49 I was with you day after day teaching in the temple, and you did not seize Me. But (it is) that the Scriptures may be fulfilled.

50 And abandoning Him, all fled.

51 And one, a certain young man, was following Him, having thrown a linen cloth about (his) naked (body). And the young men seized him.
52 But leaving the linen cloth, he fled from them naked.
53. And they led away Jesus to the high priest. And all the chief priests and the elders and the scribes came together to him.

54 And Peter followed Him from a distance, until (he was) inside the court of the high priest. And he was sitting with

1520 5607 3588 1427 2532 3326 846 3793 4183 3326 3162
εἷς ὢν τῶν δώδεκα, καὶ μετ᾽ αὐτοῦ ὄχλος πολὺς μετὰ μαχαι-
one being of the twelve, and with him a crowd large with swords

2532 3586 3844 3588 749 2532 3588 1122
ρῶν καὶ ξύλων, παρὰ τῶν ἀρχιερέων καὶ τῶν γραμματέων
and clubs, from the chief priests and the scribes

2532 3588 4245 1325 1161 3588 3860 846
καὶ τῶν πρεσβυτέρων. 44 δεδώκει δὲ ὁ παραδιδοὺς αὐτὸν
and the elders. had given And the (one) betraying Him

4953 846 3004 3739 302 5368 846 2076 2902
σύσσημον αὐτοῖς, λέγων, Ὃν ἂν φιλήσω, αὐτός ἐστι· κρατή-
a signal them, saying, Whomever I kiss, He it is; seize

846 2532 520 806 2532 2064 2112
σατε αὐτὸν, καὶ ἀπαγάγετε ἀσφαλῶς. 45 καὶ ἐλθών, εὐθέως
Him and lead away securely. And coming, at once

4334 846 3004 4461 4461 2532 2705
προσελθὼν αὐτῷ λέγει, Ῥαββί, ῥαββί· καὶ κατεφίλησεν
coming near to Him, he says, Rabbi, Rabbi; and ardently kissed

846 3588 1161 1911 1909 846 3588 5495 846 2532
αὐτόν. 46 οἱ δὲ ἐπέβαλον ἐπ᾽ αὐτὸν τὰς χεῖρας αὐτῶν, καὶ
Him. they And laid on Him the hands of them, and

2902 846 1520 1161 5100 3588 3936 4685
ἐκράτησαν αὐτόν. 47 εἷς δέ τις τῶν παρεστηκότων σπασά-
seized Him. one But a certain of those standing by drawing

3588 3162 3817 3588 1401 3588 749 2532
μενος τὴν μάχαιραν ἔπαισε τὸν δοῦλον τοῦ ἀρχιερέως, καὶ
the sword struck the slave of the high priest, and

851 846 3588 5621 2532 611 3588 2424 2036
ἀφεῖλεν αὐτοῦ τὸ ὠτίον. 48 καὶ ἀποκριθεὶς ὁ Ἰησοῦς εἶπεν
took off of him the ear. And answering Jesus said

846 5613 1909 3027 1831 3326 3162 2532 3586
αὐτοῖς, Ὡς ἐπὶ λῃστὴν ἐξήλθετε μετὰ μαχαιρῶν καὶ ξύλων
to them, As against a plunderer come you out with swords and clubs

4815 3165 2596 2250 2252 4314 5209 1722 3588 2411
συλλαβεῖν με; 49 καθ ἡμέραν ἤμην πρὸς ὑμᾶς ἐν τῷ ἱερῷ
to take Me? Day after day I was with you in the temple

1321 2532 3756 2902 3165 235 2443 4137 3588
διδάσκων, καὶ οὐκ ἐκρατήσατέ με· ἀλλ᾽ ἵνα πληρωθῶσιν αἱ
teaching, and not you did seize Me; but that may be fulfilled the

1124 2532 863 846 3956 5343
γραφαί. 50 καὶ ἀφέντες αὐτὸν πάντες ἔφυγον.
Scriptures. And abandoning Him all fled.

2532 1520 5100 3495 190 846 4016
51. Καὶ εἷς τις νεανίσκος ἠκολούθει αὐτῷ περιβεβλημένος
And one a certain young man was following Him having thrown about

4616 1909 1131 2532 2902 846 3588 3495 3588
σινδόνα ἐπὶ γυμνοῦ, καὶ κρατοῦσιν αὐτόν οἱ νεανίσκοι· 52 ὁ
a linen cloth upon (his) naked (body). And seized him the young men. he

1161 2641 3588 4905 1131 5343 575 846
δὲ καταλιπὼν τὴν σινδόνα γυμνὸς ἔφυγεν ἀπ᾽ αὐτῶν.
But leaving the linen cloth naked fled from them.

2532 520 3588 2424 4314 3588 749 2532 4905
53. Καὶ ἀπήγαγον τὸν Ἰησοῦν πρὸς τὸν ἀρχιερέα· καὶ συνέρ-
And they led away Jesus to the high priest. And come

846 3956 3588 749 2532 3588 4245 2532 3588
χονται αὐτῷ πάντες οἱ ἀρχιερεῖς καὶ οἱ πρεσβύτεροι καὶ οἱ
together to him all the chief priests and the elders and the

1122 2532 3588 4074 575 3113 190 846
γραμματεῖς. 54 καὶ ὁ Πέτρος ἀπὸ μακρόθεν ἠκολούθησεν αὐτῷ
scribes. And Peter from afar followed Him

2193 2080 1519 3588 833 3588 749 2532 2258 4775
ἕως ἔσω εἰς τὴν αὐλὴν τοῦ ἀρχιερέως· καὶ ἦν συγκαθήμενος
until inside in the court of the high priest; and (he) was sitting together

King James Version

one of the twelve, and with him a great multitude with swords and staves, from the chief priests and the scribes and the elders.

44 And he that betrayed him had given them a token, saying, Whomsoever I shall kiss, that same is he; take him, and lead (him) away safely.
45 And as soon as he was come, he goeth straightway to him, and saith, Master, master; and kissed him.

46 And they laid their hands on him, and took him.

47 And one of them that stood by drew a sword, and smote a servant of the high priest, and cut off his ear.

48 And Jesus answered and said unto them, Are ye come out, as against a thief, with swords and (with) staves to take me?

49 I was daily with you in the temple teaching, and ye took me not: but the scriptures must be fulfilled.

50 And they all forsook him, and fled.

51 And there followed him a certain young man, having a linen cloth cast about (his) naked (body); and the young men laid hold on him:
52 And he left the linen cloth, and fled from them naked.
53. And they led Jesus away to the high priest: and with him were assembled all the chief priests and the elders and the scribes.

54 And Peter followed him afar off, even into the palace of the high priest: and he sat with

Literal Translation

the under-officers, also warming himself near the light.
55 And the chief priests and the whole sanhedrin sought testimony against Jesus, to put Him to death. And not did find any.

56 For many falsely testified against Him, but the testimonies were not identical.
57 And standing up, some falsely testified against Him, saying,
58 We heard Him saying, I will throw down this temple made with hands, and through three days I will build another not made with hands.
59 And neither in this was their testimony identical.
60 And standing up in the middle, the high priest questioned Jesus, saying, Do you not answer? Nothing? What (do) these testify against you?

61 But He was silent and answered nothing. Again the high priest questioned Him, and said to Him, Are you the Christ, the Son of the Blessed?
62 And Jesus said, I AM! And you will see the Son of man sitting, off (the) right (hand) of power, and coming with the clouds of the heaven. (Ps. 110:1; Dan. 7:13)

63 And tearing his garments, the high priest said, Why do we still have need of witnesses?

64 You heard the blasphemy. What does it seem to you? And they all condemned Him to be liable, (even) of death.
65 And some began to spit at Him, and to cover His face, and to beat Him with a fist, and to say to Him, Prophesy! And

Mark 14:55

3326 3588 5257 2532 2328 4314 3588 5457 3588 1161
μετὰ τῶν ὑπηρετῶν, καὶ θερμαινόμενος πρὸς τὸ φῶς. 55 οἱ δὲ
with the under-officers, and warming himself toward the light. the And

749 2532 3650 3588 4892 2212 2596 3588 2424
ἀρχιερεῖς καὶ ὅλον τὸ συνέδριον ἐζήτουν κατὰ τοῦ Ἰησοῦ
chief priests and all the Sanhedrin sought against Jesus

3141 1519 3588 2289 846 2532 3756 2147
μαρτυρίαν, εἰς τὸ θανατῶσαι αὐτόν· καὶ οὐχ εὕρισκον.
testimony for the putting to death Him, and not did find.

4183 1063 5576 2596 846 2532 2470 3588
56 πολλοὶ γὰρ ἐψευδομαρτύρουν κατ' αὐτοῦ, καὶ ἴσαι αἱ
many For falsely testified against Him, but identical the

3141 3756 2258 2532 5100 450 5576
μαρτυρίαι οὐκ ἦσαν. 57 καί τινες ἀναστάντες ἐψευδομαρτύρουν
testimonies not were. And some standing up falsely testified

2596 846 3004 3754 2249 191 846 3004
κατ' αὐτοῦ, λέγοντες 58 ὅτι Ἡμεῖς ἠκούσαμεν αὐτοῦ λέγοντος
against Him, saying, We heard Him saying

3754 1473 2647 3588 348 5126 3588 5499 2532
ὅτι Ἐγὼ καταλύσω τὸν ναὸν τοῦτον τὸν χειροποίητον, καὶ
I will throw down temple this made with hands, and

1223 5140 2250 243 886 3618 2532
διὰ τριῶν ἡμερῶν ἄλλον ἀχειροποίητον οἰκοδομήσω. 59 καὶ
through three days another not made with hands I will build. And

3761 3779 2470 2258 3588 3141 846 2532 450 3588 749
οὐδὲ οὕτως ἴση ἦν ἡ μαρτυρία αὐτῶν. 60 καὶ ἀναστὰς ὁ ἀρχιε-
neither thus identical was the witness of them. And standing up the high

1519 3588 3319 1905 3588 2424 3004 3756 611
ρεὺς εἰς τὸ μέσον ἐπηρώτησε τὸν Ἰησοῦν, λέγων, Οὐκ ἀπο-
priest into the midst, he questioned Jesus, saying, Do not you

3762 5101 3778 4675 2649 3588 1161 4623
κρίνῃ οὐδέν; τί οὗτοί σου καταμαρτυροῦσιν; 61 ὁ δὲ ἐσιώπα,
answer? Nothing? What these you testify against? He But was silent,

2532 3762 611 3825 3588 749 1905 846 2532
καὶ οὐδὲν ἀπεκρίνατο. πάλιν ὁ ἀρχιερεὺς ἐπηρώτα αὐτόν, καὶ
and nothing answered. Again the high priest questioned Him and

3004 846 4771 1488 3588 5547 3588 5207 3588 2128 3588 1161
λέγει αὐτῷ, Σὺ εἶ ὁ Χριστὸς, ὁ υἱὸς τοῦ εὐλογητοῦ; 62 ὁ δὲ
says to Him, You are the Christ, the Son of the Blessed (One)? And

2424 2036 1473 1510 2532 3700 3588 5207 3588 444
Ἰησοῦς εἶπεν, Ἐγώ εἰμι. καὶ ὄψεσθε τὸν υἱὸν τοῦ ἀνθρώπου
Jesus said, I AM! And you will see the Son of man

2521 1537 1188 3588 1411 2532 2064 3326 3588
καθήμενον ἐκ δεξιῶν τῆς δυνάμεως, καὶ ἐρχόμενον μετὰ τῶν
having sat off (the) right of the Power, and coming with the

3507 3588 3772 3588 1161 749 1284 3588
νεφελῶν τοῦ οὐρανοῦ. 63 ὁ δὲ ἀρχιερεὺς διαρρήξας τοὺς
clouds of the heaven. the And high priest, tearing the

5509 846 3004 5101 2089 5532 2192 3144
χιτῶνας αὐτοῦ λέγει, Τί ἔτι χρείαν ἔχομεν μαρτύρων;
garments of him says, Why still need do we have of witnesses?

191 3588 988 5101 5213 5316 3588 1161 3956
64 ἠκούσατε τῆς βλασφημίας· τί ὑμῖν φαίνεται; οἱ δὲ πάντες
You heard the blasphemy. What to you appears it? they And all

846 1511 1777 2288 2532 756 5100
κατέκριναν αὐτὸν εἶναι ἔνοχον θανάτου. 65 καὶ ἤρξαντό τινες
condemned Him to be liable of death. And began some

1716 846 2532 4028 3588 4383 846
ἐμπτύειν αὐτῷ, καὶ περικαλύπτειν τὸ πρόσωπον αὐτοῦ,
to spit at Him, and to cover the face of Him,

2532 2852 846 2532 3004 846 4395 2532
καὶ κολαφίζειν αὐτὸν, καὶ λέγειν αὐτῷ, Προφήτευσον· καὶ
and to beat with a fist Him, and to say to Him, Prophesy! And

King James Version

the servants, and warmed himself at the fire.
55 And the chief priests and all the council sought for witness against Jesus to put him to death; and found none.

56 For many bare false witness against him, but their witness agreed not together.
57 And there arose certain, and bare false witness against him, saying,
58 We heard him say, I will destroy this temple that is made with hands, and within three days I will build another made without hands.
59 But neither so did their witness agree together.
60 And the high priest stood up in the midst, and asked Jesus, saying, Answerest thou nothing? what (is it which) these witness against thee?

61 But he held his peace, and answered nothing. Again the high priest asked him, and said unto him, Art thou the Christ, the Son of the Blessed?
62 And Jesus said, I am: and ye shall see the Son of man sitting on the right hand of power, and coming in the clouds of heaven.

63 Then the high priest rent his clothes, and saith, What need we any further witnesses?

64 Ye have heard the blasphemy: what think ye? And they all condemned him to be guilty of death.
65 And some began to spit on him, and to cover his face, and to buffet him, and to say unto him, Prophesy: and

Literal Translation | **Mark 14:66** | **King James Version**

the under-officers struck Him with slaps.

66. And Peter being in the court below, one of the high priest's female slaves came.
67 And seeing Peter warming himself, looking at him, she said, And you were with Jesus the Nazarene.

68 But he denied, saying, I do not know nor understand what you say. And he went out into the forecourt. And a cock crowed.

69 And seeing him again, the female slave began to say to those standing by, This one is of them.

70 And again he denied. And after a little, those standing by again said to Peter, Truly you are from them, for you are even a Galilean and your speech agrees.
71 But he began to curse and to swear, I do not know this man (of) whom you speak.

72 And a second time a cock crowed. And Peter remembered the word Jesus said to him, Before a cock crows twice, you will deny Me three times. And putting (his mind) on (it), he was weeping.

3588 5257 4475 846 906
οἱ ὑπηρέται ῥαπίσμασιν αὐτὸν ἔβαλλον.
the under-officers with slaps Him struck.

2532 5607 3588 4074 1722 3588 833 2736 2064 3391 3588
66. Καὶ ὄντος τοῦ Πέτρου ἐν τῇ αὐλῇ κάτω, ἔρχεται μία τῶν
And being Peter in the court below, comes one of the

3814 3588 749 2532 1492 3588 4074 2328
παιδισκῶν τοῦ ἀρχιερέως, 67 καὶ ἰδοῦσα τὸν Πέτρον θερμαινό-
female slaves of the high priest; and seeing Peter warming

1689 846 3004 2532 4771 3326 3588 3479
μενον, ἐμβλέψασα αὐτῷ λέγει, Καὶ σὺ μετὰ τοῦ Ναζαρηνοῦ
himself, looking at him, says, And you with the Nazarene

2424 2258 3588 1161 720 3004 3756 1492 3761
Ἰησοῦ ἦσθα. 68 ὁ δὲ ἠρνήσατο, λέγων, Οὐκ οἶδα, οὐδὲ
Jesus were. he And denied, saying, Not I know, nor

1987 5101 4771 3004 2532 1831 1854 1519 3588 4259
ἐπίσταμαι τί σὺ λέγεις. καὶ ἐξῆλθεν ἔξω εἰς τὸ προαύλιον·
understand what you say. And he went out into the forecourt.

2532 220 5455 2532 3588 3814 1492 846 3825
καὶ ἀλέκτωρ ἐφώνησε. 69 καὶ ἡ παιδίσκη ἰδοῦσα αὐτὸν πάλιν
And a cock sounded. And the female slave seeing him again

756 3004 3588 3936 3754 3778 1537 846 2076
ἤρξατο λέγειν τοῖς παρεστηκόσιν ὅτι Οὗτος ἐξ αὐτῶν ἐστιν.
began to say to those standing by, This one from them is.

3588 1161 3825 720 2532 3326 3397 3825 3588 3936
70 ὁ δὲ πάλιν ἠρνεῖτο. καὶ μετὰ μικρὸν πάλιν οἱ παρεστῶτες
he But again denied. And after a little again those standing by

3004 3588 4074 230 1537 846 1488 2532 1063 1057
ἔλεγον τῷ Πέτρῳ, Ἀληθῶς ἐξ αὐτῶν εἶ· καὶ γὰρ Γαλιλαῖος
said to Peter, Truly from them you are, even for a Galilean

1488 2532 3588 2981 4675 3662 3588 1161 756 332
εἶ, καὶ ἡ λαλιά σου ὁμοιάζει. 71 ὁ δὲ ἤρξατο ἀναθεματίζειν
you are and the speech of you agrees. he And began to curse

2532 3660 3754 3756 1492 3588 444 5126 3739 3004
καὶ ὀμνύναι ὅτι Οὐκ οἶδα τὸν ἄνθρωπον τοῦτον ὃν λέγετε.
and to swear, Not I know man this whom you say.

2532 1537 1208 220 5455 2532 363 3588 4074
72 καὶ ἐκ δευτέρου ἀλέκτωρ ἐφώνησε. καὶ ἀνεμνήσθη ὁ Πέτρος
And a second time a cock sounded. And remembered Peter

3588 4487 3739 2036 846 3588 2424 3754 4250 220
τοῦ ῥήματος οὗ εἶπεν αὐτῷ ὁ Ἰησοῦς ὅτι Πρὶν ἀλέκτορα
the word that said to him Jesus Before a cock

5455 1364 533 3165 5151 2532 1911 2799
φωνῆσαι δὶς, ἀπαρνήσῃ με τρίς. καὶ ἐπιβαλὼν ἔκλαιε.
sounds twice, you will deny Me thrice. And putting (his mind) on (it) he wept.

the servants did strike him with the palms of their hands.

66. And as Peter was beneath in the palace, there cometh one of the maids of the high priest:
67 And when she saw Peter warming himself, she looked upon him, and said, And thou also wast with Jesus of Nazareth.

68 But he denied, saying, I know not, neither understand I what thou sayest. And he went out into the porch; and the cock crew.

69 And a maid saw him again, and began to say to them that stood by, This is (one) of them.

70 And he denied it again. And a little after, they that stood by said again to Peter, Surely thou art (one) of them: for thou art a Galilaean, and thy speech agreeth (thereto).
71 But he began to curse and to swear, (saying), I know not this man of whom ye speak.

72 And the second time the cock crew. And Peter called to mind the word that Jesus said unto him, Before the cock crow twice, thou shalt deny me thrice. And when he thought thereon, he wept.

Mark 15

1. And immediately in the morning, the chief priests with the elders and scribes and all the sanhedrin forming a council, having bound Jesus, (they) led (Him) away and delivered (Him) to Pilate.

2 And Pilate questioned Him, Are you the king of the Jews? And answering, He said to him, You

2532 2112 1909 3588 4404 4824 4160 3588
1. Καὶ εὐθέως ἐπὶ τὸ πρωῒ συμβούλιον ποιήσαντες οἱ
And immediately on the early (morn) a council having made the

749 3326 3588 4245 2532 1122 2532 3650
ἀρχιερεῖς μετὰ τῶν πρεσβυτέρων καὶ γραμματέων, καὶ ὅλον
chief priests with the elders and scribes, and all

3588 4892 1210 3588 2424 667 2532 3860
τὸ συνέδριον, δήσαντες τὸν Ἰησοῦν ἀπήνεγκαν καὶ παρέδω-
the Sanhedrin, having bound Jesus, led (Him) away and delivered

3588 4091 2532 1905 846 3588 4091 4771/1488/3588
καν τῷ Πιλάτῳ. 2 καὶ ἐπηρώτησεν αὐτὸν ὁ Πιλάτος, Σὺ εἶ ὁ
up (Him) to Pilate. And questioned Him Pilate, You are the

935 3588 2453 3588 1161 611 2036 846 4771
βασιλεὺς τῶν Ἰουδαίων; ὁ δὲ ἀποκριθεὶς εἶπεν αὐτῷ, Σὺ
king of the Jews? He And answering said to him, You

1. And straightway in the morning the chief priests held a consultation with the elders and scribes and the whole council, and bound Jesus, and carried (him) away, and delivered (him) to Pilate.

2 And Pilate asked him, Art thou the King of the Jews? And he answering said unto him, Thou

Literal Translation — **Mark 15:3** — *King James Version*

say (it).
3 And the chief priests urgently accused Him (of) many things. But He answered nothing.
4 But Pilate again questioned Him, saying, Do you answer nothing? Behold, how many things they testify against you.
5 But Jesus answered nothing any more, so as (for) Pilate to marvel.

3004 2532 2723 846 3588 749 4183 846 1161
λέγεις. 3 καὶ κατηγόρουν αὐτοῦ οἱ ἀρχιερεῖς πολλά· αὐτὸς δὲ
say (it). And accused Him the chief priests many things. He But
3762 611 3588 1161 4091 3825 1905 846
οὐδὲν ἀπεκρίνατο. 4 ὁ δὲ Πιλάτος πάλιν ἐπηρώτησεν αὐτὸν,
nothing answered. But Pilate again questioned Him,
3004 3756 611 3762 2396 4214 4675 2649
λέγων, Οὐκ ἀποκρίνῃ οὐδέν; ἴδε, πόσα σου καταυατυ-
saying, not Do you answer, nothing? Behold, how many things you they testify
3588 1161 2424 3765 3762 611 5620 2296
ροῦσιν. 5 ὁ δὲ Ἰησοῦς οὐκέτι οὐδὲν ἀπεκρίθη, ὥστε θαυμάζειν
against. But Jesus no more nothing answered, so as to marvel
3588 4091
τὸν Πιλάτον.
Pilate.

sayest (it).
3 And the chief priests accused him of many things: but he answered nothing.
4 And Pilate asked him again, saying, Answerest thou nothing? behold how many things they witness against thee.
5 But Jesus yet answered nothing; so that Pilate marvelled.

6. And at a feast, he released to them one prisoner, whomever they asked.
7 And there was the (one) called Barabbas, having been bound with the insurgents, who in the insurrection had committed murder.
8 And crying aloud, the crowd began to beg (him to do) as he always did to them.
9 But Pilate answered them, saying, Do you desire I should release to you the king of the Jews?
10 For he knew that the chief priests had delivered Him up through envy.
11 But the chief priests stirred up the crowd, that rather he should release Barabbas to them.
12 But answering again, Pilate said to them, What then do you desire I do (with him) whom you call king of the Jews?
13 And again they cried out, Crucify him!
14 But Pilate said to them, For what bad (thing) did he do? But they much more cried out, Crucify him!
15 And deciding to do the easiest (to) the crowd, Pilate released Barabbas to them. And having flogged (Him), he delivered up Jesus, that He might be crucified.

2596 1161 1859 630 846 1520 1198 3746
6. Κατὰ δὲ ἑορτὴν ἀπέλυεν αὐτοῖς ἕνα δέσμιον, ὅνπερ
at And a feast he released to them one prisoner, whomever
154 2258 1161 3588 3004 912 3326 3588 4955
ᾐτοῦντο. 7 ἦν δὲ ὁ λεγόμενος Βαραββᾶς μετὰ τῶν συστασια-
they asked. was And the (one) called Barabbas with the insurgents
1210 3748 1722 3588 4714 5408 4160
στῶν δεδεμένος, οἵτινες ἐν τῇ στάσει φόνον πεποιήκεισαν.
having been bound, who in the insurrection murder had committed.
2532 310 3588 3793 756 154 2531 104 4160
8 καὶ ἀναβοήσας ὁ ὄχλος ἤρξατο αἰτεῖσθαι καθὼς ἀεὶ ἐποίει
And crying aloud the crowd began to beg even as always he did
846 3588 1161 4091 611 846 3004 2309
αὐτοῖς. 9 ὁ δὲ Πιλάτος ἀπεκρίθη αὐτοῖς, λέγων, Θέλετε
for them. And Pilate answered them, saying, Desire you
630 5213 3588 935 3588 2453 1097 1063/3754
ἀπολύσω ὑμῖν τὸν βασιλέα τῶν Ἰουδαίων; 10 ἐγίνωσκε γὰρ ὅτι
I release to you the king of the Jews? he knew For that
1223 5355 3860 846 3588 749 3588 1161
διὰ φθόνον παραδεδώκεισαν αὐτὸν οἱ ἀρχιερεῖς. 11 οἱ δὲ
through envy had delivered over Him the chief priests. the But
749 383 3588 3793 2443 3123 3588 912
ἀρχιερεῖς ἀνέσεισαν τὸν ὄχλον, ἵνα μᾶλλον τὸν Βαραββᾶν
chief priests stirred up the crowd, that rather Barabbas
630 846 3588 1161 4091 611 3825 2036
ἀπολύσῃ αὐτοῖς. 12 ὁ δὲ Πιλάτος ἀποκριθεὶς πάλιν εἶπεν
he may release to them. And Pilate answering again said
846 5101 3767 2309 4160 3739 3004 935 3588 2453
αὐτοῖς, Τί οὖν θέλετε ποιήσω ὃν λέγετε βασιλέα τῶν Ἰουδαίων;
to them, What then wish you I do (with) whom you call king of the Jews?
3588 1161 3825 2896 4717 846 3588 1161 4091
13 οἱ δὲ πάλιν ἔκραξαν, Σταύρωσον αὐτόν. 14 ὁ δὲ Πιλάτος
they And again cried out, Crucify Him! But Pilate
3004 846 5101 1063 2556 4160 3588 1161 4056
ἔλεγεν αὐτοῖς, Τί γὰρ κακὸν ἐποίησεν; οἱ δὲ περισσοτέρως
said to them, what For bad (thing) did He do? they But much more
2896 4717 846 3588 1161 4091 1014 3588
ἔκραξαν, Σταύρωσον αὐτόν. 15 ὁ δὲ Πιλάτος βουλόμενος τῷ
cried out, Crucify Him! And Pilate, having decided the
3793 3588 2425 4160 630 846 3588 912 2532
ὄχλῳ τὸ ἱκανὸν ποιῆσαι, ἀπέλυσεν αὐτοῖς τὸν Βαραββᾶν· καὶ
crowd the easiest to do, released to them Barabbas, and
3860 3588 2424 5417 2443 4717
παρέδωκε τὸν Ἰησοῦν, φραγελλώσας ἵνα σταυρωθῇ.
delivered up Jesus, having flogged (Him) that He might be crucified.

6. Now at (that) feast he released unto them one prisoner, whomsoever they desired.
7 And there was (one) named Barabbas, (which lay) bound with them that had made insurrection with him, who had committed murder in the insurrection.
8 And the multitude crying aloud began to desire (him to do) as he had ever done unto them.
9 But Pilate answered them, saying, Will ye that I release unto you the King of the Jews?
10 For he knew that the chief priests had delivered him for envy.
11 But the chief priests moved the people, that he should rather release Barabbas unto them.
12 And Pilate answered and said again unto them, What will ye then that I shall do (unto him) whom ye call the King of the Jews?
13 And they cried out again, Crucify him.
14 Then Pilate said unto them, Why, what evil hath he done? And they cried out the more exceedingly, Crucify him.
15 And (so) Pilate, willing to content the people, released Barabbas unto them, and delivered Jesus, when he had scourged (him), to be crucified.

16. And the soldiers led Him away inside the court, which is

3588 1161 4757 520 846 2080 3588 833 3739 2076
16. Οἱ δὲ στρατιῶται ἀπήγαγον αὐτὸν ἔσω τῆς αὐλῆς, ὅ ἐστι
the And soldiers led away Him inside the court, which is

16. And the soldiers led him away into the hall, called

Literal Translation **Mark 15:17** *King James Version*

(the) praetorium. And they called together all the cohort.
17 And they put a purple (robe) on Him, and they plaited and placed a crown of thorns on Him.
18 And they began to salute Him, Hail, king of the Jews!
19 And they struck His head with a reed, and spat at Him. And placing the knees, (they) did homage to Him.
20 And when they had mocked Him, they took the purple off Him, and put His own garments on Him. And they bring Him out, that they might crucify Him.
21 And they forced one passing by, Simon, a Cyrenian, coming from a field, the father of Alexander and Rufus, that he bear His cross.
22 And they brought Him onto Golgotha Place, which translated is Place of a Skull.
23 And they gave him wine spiced with myrrh to drink. But He did not take (it).
24 And crucifying Him, they divided His garments, casting a lot on them, who and what (each) should take. (Ps. 22:18)
25 And it was (the) third hour, and they crucified Him.
26 And the inscription of His charge was written over (Him), THE KING OF THE JEWS.
27 And they crucified two plunderers with Him, one off (the) right, and one off (the) left of Him.
28 And the Scripture was fulfilled which says, "And He was counted with (the) lawless." (Isa. 53:12)
29. And those passing by blasphemed Him, shaking their heads, and saying, Aha! (You) razing the temple, and in three

4232 2532 4779 3650 3588 4686 2532
πραιτώριον, καὶ συγκαλοῦσιν ὅλην τὴν σπεῖραν. 17 καὶ
(the) praetorium. And they call together all the cohort. And

1746 846 4209 2532 4060 846 4120
ἐνδυούσιν αὐτὸν πορφύραν, καὶ περιτιθέασιν αὐτῷ πλέξαντες
they put on Him a purple (robe),and place around Him having plaited,

174 4735 2532 756 782 846 5463
ἀκάνθινον στέφανον, 18 καὶ ἤρξαντο ἀσπάζεσθαι αὐτόν, Χαῖρε,
a thorny crown. And they began to salute Him, Hail,

935 3588 2453 2532 5180 846 3588 2776
βασιλεῦ τῶν Ἰουδαίων· 19 καὶ ἔτυπτον αὐτοῦ τὴν κεφαλὴν
King of the Jews! And they struck of Him the head

2563 2532 1716 846 2532 5087 3588 1119
καλάμῳ, καὶ ἐνέπτυον αὐτῷ, καὶ τιθέντες τὰ γόνατα
with a reed, and spit at Him, and placing the knees,

4352 846 2532 3753 1702 846 1562
προσεκύνουν αὐτῷ. 20 καὶ ὅτε ἐνέπαιξαν αὐτῷ, ἐξέδυσαν
did homage to Him. And when they had mocked Him, they took off

846 3588 4209 2532 1746 846 3588 2440 3588 2398
αὐτὸν τὴν πορφύραν, καὶ ἐνέδυσαν αὐτὸν τὰ ἱμάτια τὰ ἴδια.
Him the purple (robe), and put on Him garments the own.

2532 1806 846 2443 4717 846 2532
Καὶ ἐξάγουσιν αὐτὸν ἵνα σταυρώσωσιν αὐτόν. 21 καὶ
And they bring out Him that they might crucify Him. And

29 3855 5100 4613 2956 2064
ἀγγαρεύουσι παράγοντά τινα Σίμωνα Κυρηναῖον, ἐρχόμενον
they compel passing by a certain Simon a Cyrenian coming

575 68 3588 3962 223 2532 4504 2443 142
ἀπ᾽ ἀγροῦ, τὸν πατέρα Ἀλεξάνδρου καὶ Ῥούφου, ἵνα ἄρῃ
from a field, the father of Alexander and of Rufus, that he bear

3588 4716 846 2532 5342 846 1909 1115 5117
τὸν σταυρὸν αὐτοῦ. 22 καὶ φέρουσιν αὐτὸν ἐπὶ Γολγοθᾶ τόπον,
the cross of Him. And they bring Him onto Golgotha place,

3739 2076 3177 2898 5117 2532 1325 846
ὅ ἐστι μεθερμηνευόμενον, κρανίου τόπος. 23 καὶ ἐδίδουν αὐτῷ
which is, being translated, Of a Skull Place. And they gave Him

4095 4669 3631 3588 1161 3756 2983 2532 4717
πιεῖν ἐσμυρνισμένον οἶνον· ὁ δὲ οὐκ ἔλαβε. 24 καὶ σταυρώσαντες
to drink spiced with myrrh wine. He But not did take. And having crucified

846 1266 3588 2440 846 906 2819 1909 846
αὐτὸν, διεμερίζον τὰ ἱμάτια αὐτοῦ, βάλλοντες κλῆρον ἐπ᾽ αὐτὰ,
Him, they divided the garments of Him, casting a lot on them,

5101 5101 142 2258 1161 5610 5154 2532 4717 846
τίς τί ἄρῃ. 25 ἦν δὲ ὥρα τρίτη, καὶ ἐσταύρωσαν αὐτόν.
who what may take. was And hour third, and they crucified Him.

2532 2258 3588 1923 3588 156 846 1924 3588
26 καὶ ἦν ἡ ἐπιγραφὴ τῆς αἰτίας αὐτοῦ ἐπιγεγραμμένη, Ὁ
And was the inscription of the accusation of Him written over (Him): THE

935 3588 2453 2532 4862 846 4717 1417 3027
βασιλεὺς τῶν Ἰουδαίων. 27 καὶ σὺν αὐτῷ σταυροῦσι δύο λῃστάς,
KING OF THE JEWS. And with Him they crucify two plunderers,

1520 1537 1188 2532 1520 1537 2176 846 2532 4137 3588
ἕνα ἐκ δεξιῶν καὶ ἕνα ἐξ εὐωνύμων αὐτοῦ. 28 καὶ ἐπληρώθη ἡ
one off (the) right and one off (the) left of Him. And was fulfilled the

1124 3588 3004 2532 3326 459 3049 2532 3588
γραφὴ ἡ λέγουσα, Καὶ μετὰ ἀνόμων ἐλογίσθη. 29 καὶ οἱ
Scripture which says, And with(the) lawless He was counted. And those

3899 987 846 2975 3588 2776
παραπορευόμενοι ἐβλασφήμουν αὐτὸν, κινοῦντες τὰς κεφαλὰς
passing by blasphemed Him, shaking the head

846 2532 3004 3758 3588 2647 3588 3485 2532 1722 5140
αὐτῶν, καὶ λέγοντες, Οὐὰ, ὁ καταλύων τὸν ναόν, καὶ ἐν τρισὶν
of them, and saying, Aha, the (one) razing the temple, and in three

Praetorium; and they call together the whole band.
17 And they clothed him with purple, and platted a crown of thorns, and put it about his (head),
18 And began to salute him, Hail, King of the Jews!
19 And they smote him on the head with a reed, and did spit upon him, and bowing (their) knees worshipped him.
20 And when they had mocked him, they took off the purple from him, and put his own clothes on him, and led him out to crucify him.
21 And they compel one Simon a Cyrenian, who passed by, coming out of the country, the father of Alexander and Rufus, to bear his cross.
22 And they bring him unto the place Golgotha, which is, being interpreted, The place of a skull.
23 And they gave him to drink wine mingled with myrrh: but he received (it) not.
24 And when they had crucified him, they parted his garments, casting lots upon them, what every man should take.
25 And it was the third hour, and they crucified him.
26 And the superscription of his accusation was written over, THE KING OF THE JEWS.
27 And with him they crucify two thieves; the one on his right hand, and the other on his left.
28 And the scripture was fulfilled, which saith, And he was numbered with the transgressors.
29. And they that passed by railed on him, wagging their heads, and saying, Ah, thou that destroyest the temple, and buildest (it) in three

Literal Translation **Mark 15:30** *King James Version*

days building (it),
30 save yourself and
come down from the
cross.
31 And the chief priests
and the scribes mock-
ing to one another said
the same, He saved oth-
ers; he is not able to save
himself.

32 The Christ, the King
of Israel, let him now
come down from the
cross, that we may see
and believe. And the
ones crucified with
Him insulted Him.

2250 3618 4982 4572 2532 2597 575 3588
ἡμέραις οἰκοδομῶν, 30 σῶσον σεαυτόν, καὶ κατάβα ἀπὸ τοῦ
days building, save yourself, and come down from the

4716 3668 2532 3588 749 1702 4314
σταυροῦ. 31 ὁμοίως καὶ οἱ ἀρχιερεῖς ἐμπαίζοντες πρὸς
cross. likewise And the chief priests mocking to

240 3326 3588 1122 3004 243 4982
ἀλλήλους μετὰ τῶν γραμματέων ἔλεγον, Ἄλλους ἔσωσεν,
one another with the scribes, said, Others he saved,

1438 3756 1410 4982 3588 5547 3588 935 3588 2474
ἑαυτὸν οὐ δύναται σῶσαι. 32 ὁ Χριστὸς ὁ βασιλεὺς τοῦ Ἰσραὴλ
himself not he is able to save. The Christ the king of Israel

2597 3568 575 3588 4716 2443 1492 2532 4100
καταβάτω νῦν ἀπὸ τοῦ σταυροῦ, ἵνα ἴδωμεν καὶ πιστεύσωμεν.
let him come down now from the cross, that we may see and believe.

2532 3588 4957 846 3679 846
καὶ οἱ συνεσταυρωμένοι αὐτῷ ὠνείδιζον αὐτόν.
And the (ones) being crucified with Him insulted Him.

days,
30 Save thyself, and
come down from the
cross.
31 Likewise also the
chief priests mocking
said among themselves
with the scribes, He
saved others; himself he
cannot save.

32 Let Christ the King
of Israel descend now
from the cross, that we
may see and believe.
And they that were cru-
cified with him reviled
him.

33. And the sixth hour
occurring, darkness
came over all the land
until (the) ninth hour.
34 And at the ninth hour
Jesus cried with a loud
voice, saying, Eloi,
Eloi, lama sabachthani?
(Which being trans-
lated is, My God, My
God, why did You for-
sake Me?) (Ps. 22:1;
69:21)

35 And hearing, some
of those standing by
said, Behold! He calls
Elijah.
36 And one running up,
and filling a sponge
with vinegar, and put-
ting (it) on a reed, gave
Him to drink. (But they)
said, Leave alone, let us
see if Elijah comes to
take Him down.
37 And letting out a
great cry, Jesus expired.
38 And the veil of the
Holy Place was torn
into two, from top to
bottom.
39. And standing off
across from Him, see-
ing that (He) had cried
out so, (and) He expired,
the centurion said,
Truly, this Man was Son
of God.

40 And also women
were watching from far
away, among whom
also was Mary Mag-
dalene; also Mary the
mother of James the
less, and of Joses, and
Salome,
41 who also

1096 1161 5610 1623 4655 1096 1909 3650 3588
33. Γενομένης δὲ ὥρας ἕκτης, σκότος ἐγένετο ἐφ' ὅλην τὴν
occurring And hour sixth, darkness came to be over all the

1093 2193 5610 1766 2532 3588 5610 3588 1766 994 3588
γῆν ἕως ὥρας ἐννάτης. 34 καὶ τῇ ὥρᾳ τῇ ἐννάτῃ ἐβόησεν ὁ
land until hour (the) ninth. And at the hour ninth cried

2424 5456 3173 3004 1682 1682 2982 4518
Ἰησοῦς φωνῇ μεγάλῃ, λέγων, Ἐλωι, Ἐλωι, λαμμᾶ σαβαχθανι;
Jesus with a voice great, saying, Eloi, Eloi, Lama sabachthani?

3739 2076 3177 3588 2316 3450 3588 2316 3450 1519 5101 3165
ὅ ἐστι μεθερμηνευόμενον, Ὁ Θεός μου, ὁ Θεός μου, εἰς τί με
which is, being translated, The God of Me, the God of Me, why Me

1459 2532 5100 3588 3936 191
ἐγκατέλιπές; 35 καί τινες τῶν παρεστηκότων ἀκούσαντες
did You forsake? And some of the (ones) standing by hearing

3004 2400 2243 5455 5143 1161 1520 2532 1072
ἔλεγον, Ἰδού, Ἠλίαν φωνεῖ. 36 δραμὼν δέ εἷς καὶ γεμίσας
said, Behold! Elijah He calls. running And one and filling

4699 3690 4060 5037 2563 4222 846 3004
σπόγγον ὄξους, περιθείς τε καλάμῳ, ἐπότιζεν αὐτόν, λέγων,
a sponge of vinegar, putting it and on a reed, gave to drink Him, saying,

863 1492 1487 2064 2243 2507 846 3588 1161
Ἄφετε, ἴδωμεν εἰ ἔρχεται Ἠλίας καθελεῖν αὐτόν. 37 ὁ δὲ
Leave, let us see if comes Elijah to take down Him. But

2400 863 5456 3173 1606 2532 3588 2665
Ἰησοῦς ἀφεὶς φωνὴν μεγάλην ἐξέπνευσε. 38 καὶ τὸ καταπέτασμα
Jesus letting out a voice great expired. And the veil

3588 3485 4977 1519 1417 575 509 2193 2736 1492 1161
τοῦ ναοῦ ἐσχίσθη εἰς δύο ἀπὸ ἄνωθεν ἕως κάτω. 39 Ἰδὼν δὲ
of the temple was torn into two from top to bottom. seeing And

3588 2760 3588 3936 1537 1727 846 3754 3779
ὁ κεντυρίων ὁ παρεστηκὼς ἐξ ἐναντίας αὐτοῦ ὅτι οὕτω
the centurion standing near from across Him, that thus

2896 1606 2036 230 3588 444 3778 5207
κράξας ἐξέπνευσεν, εἶπεν, Ἀληθῶς ὁ ἄνθρωπος οὗτος υἱὸς
crying out He expired, said, Truly Man this Son

2258 2316 2258 1161 2532 1135 575 3113 2334
ἦν Θεοῦ. 40 ἦσαν δὲ καὶ γυναῖκες ἀπὸ μακρόθεν θεωροῦσαι,
was of God. were And also women from afar watching,

1722 3739 2258 2532 3137 3588 3094 2532 3137 3588 3588
ἐν αἷς ἦν καὶ Μαρία ἡ Μαγδαληνὴ, καὶ Μαρία ἡ τοῦ
among whom was also Mary the Magdalene, and Mary the

2385 3588 3398 2532 2499 3384 2532 4539 3739 2532
Ἰακώβου τοῦ μικροῦ καὶ Ἰωσῆ μήτηρ, καὶ Σαλώμη, 41 αἳ καὶ,
of James the less and of Joses mother, and Salome, who also

33. And when the sixth
hour was come, there
was darkness over the
whole land until the
ninth hour.
34 And at the ninth hour
Jesus cried with a loud
voice, saying, Eloi,
Eloi, lama sabachthani?
which is, being inter-
preted, My God, my
God, why hast thou for-
saken me?

35 And some of them
that stood by, when they
heard (it), said, Behold,
he calleth Elias.
36 And one ran and
filled a spunge full of
vinegar, and put (it) on a
reed, and gave him to
drink, saying, Let alone;
let us see whether Elias
will come to take him
down.
37 And Jesus cried with
a loud voice, and gave
up the ghost.
38 And the veil of the
temple was rent in twain
from the top to the bot-
tom.
39. And when the cen-
turion, which stood over
against him, saw that he
so cried out, and gave up
the ghost, he said, Truly
this man was the Son of
God.

40 There were also
women looking on afar
off: among whom was
Mary Magdalene, and
Mary the mother of
James the less and of
Joses, and Salome;
41 (Who also,

Literal Translation | **Mark 15:42** | **King James Version**

had followed Him and ministered to Him when He was in Galilee; and many (other) women who came up to Jerusalem with Him.

3753 2258 1722 3588 1056 190 846 2532 1247
ὅτε ἦν ἐν τῇ Γαλιλαίᾳ, ἠκολούθουν αὐτῷ, καὶ διηκόνουν
when He was in Galilee had followed Him and ministered

846 2532 243 4183 3588 4872 846 1519
αὐτῷ, καὶ ἄλλαι πολλαὶ αἱ συναναβᾶσαι αὐτῷ εἰς
to Him, and other (women) many who came up with Him into

2414
Ἱεροσόλυμα.
Jerusalem.,

when he was in Galilee, followed him, and ministered unto him;) and many other women which came up with him unto Jerusalem.

42. And it becoming evening already, since it was (the) preparation, that is, (the) day before sabbath,
43 Joseph of Arimathea came, an honorable councillor, who himself was also waiting for the kingdom of God. (And) taking courage, (he) went in to Pilate and asked the body of Jesus.
44 And Pilate marveled if He had already died. And having called near the centurion, he questioned him if He died already.

45 And knowing from the centurion, he granted the body to Joseph.
46 And having bought a linen cloth, and having taken Him down, he wrapped (Him) in the linen, and laid Him in a tomb which was cut out of rock. And (he) rolled a stone against the door of the tomb.

47 And Mary Magdalene, and Mary of Joses, saw where He was laid.

2532 2235 3798 1096 1893 2258 3904 3739 2076
42. Καὶ ἤδη ὀψίας γενομένης, ἐπεὶ ἦν Παρασκευή, ὅ ἐστι
And now evening occurring, since it was (the) preparation which is

4315 2064 2501 3588 575 707 2158
προσάββατον, 43 ἦλθεν Ἰωσὴφ ὁ ἀπὸ Ἀριμαθαίας, εὐσχήμων
day before sabbath, coming Joseph from Arimathea, an honorable

1010 3739 2532 846 2258 4327 3588 932
βουλευτής, ὃς καὶ αὐτὸς ἦν προσδεχόμενος τὴν βασιλείαν
councillor, who also (him)self was expecting the kingdom

3588 2316 5111 1525 4314 4091 2532 154
τοῦ Θεοῦ· τολμήσας εἰσῆλθε πρὸς Πιλάτον, καὶ ᾐτήσατο
of God, taking courage went in to Pilate, and asked

3588 4983 3588 2424 3588 1161 4091 2296 1487 2235
τὸ σῶμα τοῦ Ἰησοῦ. 44 ὁ δὲ Πιλάτος ἐθαύμασεν εἰ ἤδη
the body of Jesus. And Pilate marveled if already

2348 2532 4341 3588 2760 1905
τέθνηκε· καὶ προσκαλεσάμενος τὸν κεντυρίωνα, ἐπηρώτησεν
He had died. And having called near the centurion, he questioned

846 1487 3819 599 2532 1097 575 3588 2760
αὐτὸν εἰ πάλαι ἀπέθανε. 45 καὶ γνοὺς ἀπὸ τοῦ κεντυρίωνος
him if long ago He died. And knowing from the centurion

1433 3588 4983 3588 2501 2532 59 4616
ἐδωρήσατο τὸ σῶμα τῷ Ἰωσήφ. 46 καὶ ἀγοράσας σινδόνα,
he granted the body to Joseph. And having bought a linen cloth,

2532 2507 846 1750 3588 4616 2532 2698 846
καὶ καθελὼν αὐτὸν, ἐνείλησε τῇ σινδόνι, καὶ κατέθηκεν αὐτὸν
and taking down Him, he wrapped in linen, and laid Him

1722 3419 3739 2258 2998 1537 4073 2532 4351
ἐν μνημείῳ, ὃ ἦν λελατομημένον ἐκ πέτρας· καὶ προσεκύλισε
in a tomb, which was (one) being hewn out of rock; and rolled

3037 1909 3588 2374 3588 3419 3588 1161 3137 3588 3094
λίθον ἐπὶ τὴν θύραν τοῦ μνημείου. 47 ἡ δὲ Μαρία ἡ Μαγδαληνὴ
a stone against the door of the tomb And Mary the Magdalene

2532 3137 3588 2499 2334 4225 5087
καὶ Μαρία ἡ Ἰωσῆ ἐθεώρουν ποῦ τέθεται.
and Mary of Joses beheld where He had been laid.

42. And now when the even was come, because it was the preparation, that is, the day before the sabbath,
43 Joseph of Arimathaea, an honourable counsellor, which also waited for the kingdom of God, came, and went in boldly unto Pilate, and craved the body of Jesus.

44 And Pilate marvelled if he were already dead: and calling (unto him) the centurion, he asked him whether he had been any while dead.
45 And when he knew (it) of the centurion, he gave the body to Joseph.
46 And he bought fine linen, and took him down, and wrapped him in the linen, and laid him in a sepulchre which was hewn out of a rock, and rolled a stone unto the door of the sepulchre.

47 And Mary Magdalene and Mary (the mother) of Joses beheld where he was laid.

Mark 16

1. And the sabbath having passed, Mary Magdalene and Mary the (mother) of James and Salome, bought spices, so that coming they might anoint Him.
2 And very early on the first of the sabbaths, the sun having risen, they came upon the tomb.

3 And they said to themselves, Who will roll away the

2532 1230 3588 4521 3137 3588 3094
1. Καὶ διαγενομένου τοῦ σαββάτου, Μαρία ἡ Μαγδαληνὴ
And having passed the sabbath Mary the Magdalene

2532 3137 3588 3588 2385 2532 4539 59 759
καὶ Μαρία ἡ τοῦ Ἰακώβου καὶ Σαλώμη ἠγόρασαν ἀρώματα,
and Mary the (mother) of James and Salome bought spices,

2443 2064 218 846 2532 3029 4404 3588 3391
ἵνα ἐλθοῦσαι ἀλείψωσιν αὐτόν. 2 καὶ λίαν πρωι τῆς μιᾶς
that coming they might anoint Him. And very early on the first

4521 2064 1909 3588 3419 393 3588
σαββάτων ἔρχονται ἐπὶ τὸ μνημεῖον, ἀνατείλαντος τοῦ
of the sabbaths they come upon the tomb, having risen the

2246 2532 3004 4314 1438 5101 617 2254 3588
ἡλίου. 3 καὶ ἔλεγον πρὸς ἑαυτάς, Τίς ἀποκυλίσει ἡμῖν τὸν
sun. And they said to themselves, Who will roll away for us the

1. And when the sabbath was past, Mary Magdalene, and Mary the (mother) of James, and Salome, had bought sweet spices, that they might come and anoint him.
2 And very early in the morning the first (day) of the week, they came unto the sepulchre at the rising of the sun.
3 And they said among themselves, Who shall roll us away the

Literal Translation

stone from the door of the tomb for us?
4 And looking up, they saw that the stone had been rolled back; for it was very large.

5 And havng entered into the tomb, they saw a young man sitting on the right, having been clothed (in) a white robe. And they were much amazed.
6 But He said to them, Do not be much amazed. You seek Jesus, the Nazarene who has been crucified. He was raised. He is not here. Behold! The place where they put Him.
7 But go, tell the disciples and to Peter, He goes before you into Galilee. You will see Him there, even as He said to you.

8 And going out quickly, they fled from the tomb. And trembling and ecstasy took hold of them. And they told no one, not a thing, for they were afraid.

9. And having risen early on the first of the week, He first appeared to Mary Magdalene, from whom He had cast out seven demons.
10 That (one who) had gone (and) reported to those who had been with Him, (who were) mourning and weeping.
11 And those hearing that He lives, and was seen by her, they did not believe.

12. And after these things, He was revealed in a different form to two of them walking, having gone into the country.
13 And going, those reported to the rest. Neither did they believe those.
14. Later, as they reclined, He was revealed to the Eleven.

Mark 16:4

3037 1537 3588 2374 3588 3419 2532 308
λίθον ἐκ τῆς θύρας τοῦ μνημείου; 4 καὶ ἀναβλέψασαι
stone from the door of the tomb? And looking up

2334 3754 617 3588 3037 2258 1063 3173
θεωροῦσιν ὅτι ἀποκεκύλισται ὁ λίθος, ἦν γὰρ μέγας
they see that has been rolled back the stone; it was for great

4970 2532 1525 1519 3588 3419 1492 3495
σφόδρα. 5 καὶ εἰσελθοῦσαι εἰς τὸ μνημεῖον, εἶδον νεανίσκον
exceedingly. And having entered into the tomb, they saw a young man

2521 1722 3588 1188 4016 4749 3022
καθήμενον ἐν τοῖς δεξιοῖς, περιβεβλημένον στολὴν λευκήν·
sitting on the right, having been clothed (in) a robe white;

2532 1568 3588 1161 3004 846 3361 1568
καὶ ἐξεθαμβήθησαν. 6 ὁ δὲ λέγει αὐταῖς, Μὴ ἐκθαμβεῖσθε·
and they were much amazed But he says to them, not Be much amazed;

2424 2212 3588 3479 3588 4717 1453
Ἰησοῦν ζητεῖτε τὸν Ναζαρηνὸν τὸν ἐσταυρωμένον· ἠγέρθη,
Jesus you seek the Nazarene; having been crucified He was raised,

3756 2076 5602 2396 3588 5117 3699 5087 846 235
οὐκ ἔστιν ὧδε· ἴδε, ὁ τόπος ὅπου ἔθηκαν αὐτόν. 7 ἀλλ'
not He is here. Behold, the place where they put Him. But

5217 2036 3588 3101 846 2532 3588 4074 3754
ὑπάγετε, εἴπατε τοῖς μαθηταῖς αὐτοῦ καὶ τῷ Πέτρῳ ὅτι
go, tell the disciples of Him and Peter,

4254 5209 1519 3588 1056 1563 846 3700 2531
Προάγει ὑμᾶς εἰς τὴν Γαλιλαίαν· ἐκεῖ αὐτὸν ὄψεσθε, καθὼς
He goes before you into Galilee; there Him you will see, even as

2036 5213 2532 1831 5035 5343 575 3588 3419
εἶπεν ὑμῖν. 8 καὶ ἐξελθοῦσαι ταχὺ ἔφυγον ἀπὸ τοῦ μνημείου·
He said to you. And going out quickly, they fled from the tomb.

2192 1161 846 5156 2532 1161 2532 3762 3762 2036
εἶχε δὲ αὐτὰς τρόμος καὶ ἔκστασις· καὶ οὐδενὶ οὐδὲν εἶπον,
held And them trembling and ecstasy; and no one nothing they told,

5399 1063
ἐφοβοῦντο γάρ.
they were afraid for.

450 1161 4404 4413 4521 5316 4412
9. Ἀναστὰς δὲ πρωῒ πρώτῃ σαββάτου ἐφάνη πρῶτον
having risen And early on the first of the week, He appeared first

3137 3588 3094 575 3739 1544 2033 1140
Μαρίᾳ τῇ Μαγδαληνῇ, ἀφ' ἧς ἐκβεβλήκει ἑπτὰ δαιμόνια.
to Mary the Magdalene, from whom He had cast out seven demons.

1565 4198 518 3588 3326 846 1096
10 ἐκείνη πορευθεῖσα ἀπήγγειλε τοῖς μετ' αὐτοῦ γενομένοις,
That (one) having gone reported to those with Him having been,

3996 2532 2799 2548 191 3754 2198 2532
πενθοῦσι καὶ κλαίουσι. 11 κἀκεῖνοι ἀκούσαντες ὅτι ζῇ καὶ
mourning and weeping. And those hearing that He lives and

2300 5259 846 569
ἐθεάθη ὑπ' αὐτῆς ἠπίστησαν.
was seen by her, they disbelieved.

3326 1161 5023 5319 1537 846 4043 5319
12. Μετὰ δὲ ταῦτα δυσὶν ἐξ αὐτῶν περιπατοῦσιν ἐφανερώθη
after And these things to two of them walking He was revealed

1722 2087 3444 4198 1519 68 2548 565
ἐν ἑτέρᾳ μορφῇ, πορευομένοις εἰς ἀγρόν. 13 κἀκεῖνοι ἀπελθόντες
in a different form, having gone into the country. And those going

518 3588 3062 3761 1565 4100
ἀπήγγειλαν τοῖς λοιποῖς· οὐδὲ ἐκείνοις ἐπίστευσαν.
reported to the rest; neither those they believed

5305 345 846 3588 1733 5319
14. Ὕστερον ἀνακειμένοις αὐτοῖς τοῖς ἕνδεκα ἐφανερώθη,
Later as reclined they, to the eleven He was revealed

King James Version

stone from the door of the sepulchre?
4 And when they looked, they saw that the stone was rolled away: for it was very great.
5 And entering into the sepulchre, they saw a young man sitting on the right side, clothed in a long white garment; and they were affrighted.
6 And he saith unto them, Be not affrighted: Ye seek Jesus of Nazareth, which was crucified: he is risen; he is not here: behold the place where they laid him.

7 But go your way, tell his disciples and Peter that he goeth before you into Galilee: there shall ye see him, as he said unto you.

8 And they went out quickly, and fled from the sepulchre; for they trembled and were amazed: neither said they any thing to any (man); for they were afraid.

9. Now when (Jesus) was risen early the first (day) of the week, he appeared first to Mary Magdalene, out of whom he had cast seven devils.
10 (And) she went and told them that had been with him, as they mourned and wept.
11 And they, when they had heard that he was alive, and had been seen of her, believed not.

12. After that he appeared in another form unto two of them, as they walked, and went into the country.
13 And they went and told (it) unto the residue: neither believed they them.

14. Afterward he appeared unto the eleven

Literal Translation

And (He) reproached
their unbelief and hard-
ness of heart, because
they did not believe
those who had seen
Him, having been
raised.
15 And He said to them,
Going into all the world,
preach the gospel to all
the creation.

16 The (one) believing
and being baptized will
be saved. And the (one)
not believing will be
condemned.
17 And to those believ-
ing these signs will fol-
low: they will cast out
demons in My name;
they will speak new lan-
guages;
18 they will take up
snakes; and if they drink
anything deadly, not at
all it will hurt them; they
will lay hands on infirm
ones, and they will be
well.

19. Then indeed, after
speaking to them, the
Lord was taken up into
Heaven, and sat off
(the) right of God. (Ps.
110:1)
20 And having gone
out, they preached eve-
rywhere, the Lord
working with (them)
and confirming the
Word through the signs
following. Amen.

Mark 16:15

2532 3679 3588 518 846 2532 4641 3754 3588
καὶ ὠνείδισε τὴν ἀπιστίαν αὐτῶν καὶ σκληροκαρδίαν ὅτι τοῖς
and reproached the unbelief of them and hardness of heart, because those

2300 846 1453 3756 4100 2532 2036
θεασαμένοις αὐτὸν ἐγηγερμένον οὐκ ἐπίστευσαν. 15 καὶ εἶπεν
having seen Him having been raised not they believed. And He said

846 4198 1519 3588 2889 537 2784 3588
αὐτοῖς, Πορευθέντες εἰς τὸν κόσμον ἅπαντα, κηρύξατε τὸ
to them, Going into the world all, proclaim the

2098 3956 3588 2937 3588 4100 2532 907
εὐαγγέλιον πάσῃ τῇ κτίσει. 16 ὁ πιστεύσας καὶ βαπτισθεὶς
gospel to all the creation. The (one) believing and being baptized

4982 3588 1161 569 2632 4592 1161
σωθήσεται· ὁ δὲ ἀπιστήσας κατακριθήσεται. 17 σημεῖα δὲ
will be saved. he But not believing will be condemned. signs And

3588 4100 5023 3877 1722 3588 3686 3450
τοῖς πιστεύσασι ταῦτα παρακολουθήσει· ἐν τῷ ὀνόματί μου
to those believing these will follow; in the name of Me

1140 1544 1100 2980 2537 3789
δαιμόνια ἐκβαλοῦσι· γλώσσαις λαλήσουσι καιναῖς, 18 ὄφεις
demons they will cast out; languages they will speak new; snakes

142 2579 2286 5100 4095 3756 3361 846 984 1909
ἀροῦσι· κἂν θανάσιμόν τι πίωσιν, οὐ μὴ αὐτοὺς βλάψει· ἐπὶ
they will take; and if deadly anything they drink, not at all them it will hurt; on

732 5495 2007 2532 2573 2192
ἀρρώστους χεῖρας ἐπιθήσουσι, καὶ καλῶς ἕξουσιν.
infirm ones hands they will place, and wellness they will have.

3588 3303 3767 2962 3326 3588 2980 846 353 1519
19. Ὁ μὲν οὖν Κύριος, μετὰ τὸ λαλῆσαι αὐτοῖς, ἀνελήφθη εἰς
the indeed Then Lord, after the speaking to them, was taken up into

3588 3772 2532 2523 1537 1188 3588 2316 1565 1161
τὸν οὐρανὸν, καὶ ἐκάθισεν ἐκ δεξιῶν τοῦ Θεοῦ. 20 ἐκεῖνοι δὲ
Heaven, and sat off (the) right of God. they But

1831 2784 3837 3588 2962 4903
ἐξελθόντες ἐκήρυξαν πανταχοῦ, τοῦ Κυρίου συνεργοῦντος,
having gone out preached everywhere, the Lord working with (them),

2532 3588 3056 950 1223 3588 1872
καὶ τὸν λόγον βεβαιοῦντος διὰ τῶν ἐπακολουθούντων
and the Word confirming through the accompanying

4592 281
σημείων. Ἀμήν.
signs. Amen.

King James Version

as they sat at meat, and
upbraided them with
their unbelief and hard-
ness of heart, because
they believed not them
which had seen him af-
ter he was risen.
15 And he said unto
them, Go ye into all the
world, and preach the
gospel to every crea-
ture.
16 He that believeth and
is baptized shall be
saved; but he that be-
lieveth not shall be
damned.
17 And these signs shall
follow them that be-
lieve; In my name shall
they cast out devils;
they shall speak with
new tongues;
18 They shall take up
serpents; and if they
drink any deadly thing,
it shall not hurt them;
they shall lay hands on
the sick, and they shall
recover.

19. So then after the
Lord had spoken unto
them, he was received
up into heaven, and sat
on the right hand of
God.
20 And they went forth,
and preached every
where, the Lord work-
ing with (them), and
confirming the word
with signs following.
Amen.

Literal Translation

THE GOSPEL ACCORDING TO LUKE

Luke 1

1. Since many took in hand to draw up an account concerning the matters having been fully borne out among us,
2 as those from (the) beginning delivered to us, having become eyewitnesses and ministers of the Word,
3 it seemed good also to me, having traced out all things accurately from the first, to write in order to you, most excellent Theophilus,
4 that you may fully know the certainty of (the) words about which you were taught.
5. In the days of Herod the king of Judea, there was a certain priest named Zacharias, of (the) daily course of Abijah; and his wife (was) of the daughters of Aaron, and her name (was) Elizabeth.

6 And they were both righteous before God, walking blameless in all the commandments and ordinances of the Lord.

7 And no child was (born) to them, because Elizabeth was barren. And both were advanced in their days.

8 And it happened in his serving as priest in the order of his course before God,
9 according to the custom of the priests, entering into the temple of the Lord, (it was his) lot to burn incense.
10 And all the multitude of the people was praying outside at the hour of incense.
11 And an angel (of the) Lord appeared to him, standing on

ΕΥΑΓΓΕΛΙΟΝ ΤΟ ΚΑΤΑ
THE GOSPEL ACCORDING TO

ΛΟΥΚΑΝ
LUKE

Luke 1

1895 4183 2021 392 1335
1. Ἐπειδήπερ πολλοὶ ἐπεχείρησαν ἀνατάξασθαι διήγησιν
Since many took in hand to draw up an account

4012 3588 4135 1722 2254 4229 2531
περὶ τῶν πεπληροφορημένων ἐν ἡμῖν πραγμάτων, 2 καθὼς
concerning the having been borne out among us matters, even as

3860 2254 3588 575 746 845 2532 5257 1096
παρέδοσαν ἡμῖν οἱ ἀπ' ἀρχῆς αὐτόπται καὶ ὑπηρέται γενόμενοι
delivered to us the from beginning eyewitnesses and ministers having become

3588 3056 1380 2504 3877 509 3956
τοῦ λόγου, 3 ἔδοξε κἀμοί, παρηκολουθηκότι ἄνωθεν πᾶσιν
of the Word, it seemed good also to me, having traced out from the first all things

199 2517 4671 1125 2903 2321 2443 1921
ἀκριβῶς, καθεξῆς σοι γράψαι, κράτιστε Θεόφιλε, 4 ἵνα ἐπι-
accurately, in order to you write, most excellent Theophilus, that you may

4012 3739 2729 3056 3588 803
γνῷς περὶ ὧν κατηχήθης λόγων τὴν ἀσφάλειαν.
know about which you were taught of (the) words the certainty.

1096 1722 3588 2250 2264 3588 935 3588
5. Ἐγένετο ἐν ταῖς ἡμέραις Ἡρῴδου τοῦ βασιλέως τῆς
There was in the days of Herod the king

2449 2409 5100 3686 2197 1537 2183 7
Ἰουδαίας ἱερεύς τις ὀνόματι Ζαχαρίας, ἐξ ἐφημερίας Ἀβιά·
of Judea, a priest certain by name Zacharias, of (the) daily course of Abia;

2532 3588 1135 846 15373588 2364 2 2532 3588 3686
καὶ ἡ γυνὴ αὐτοῦ ἐκ τῶν θυγατέρων Ἀαρών, καὶ τὸ ὄνομα
and the wife of him from the daughters of Aaron; and the name

846 1665 2258 1161 1342 297 1799 3588
αὐτῆς Ἐλισάβετ. 6 ἦσαν δὲ δίκαιοι ἀμφότεροι ἐνώπιον τοῦ
of her (was) Elizabeth. they were And righteous both before

2316 4198 1722 3956 3588 1785 2532 1345
Θεοῦ, πορευόμενοι ἐν πάσαις ταῖς ἐντολαῖς καὶ δικαιώμασι
God, walking in all the commandments and ordinances

3588 2962 273 2532 3756 2258 846 5043 2530
τοῦ Κυρίου ἄμεμπτοι. 7 καὶ οὐκ ἦν αὐτοῖς τέκνον, καθότι
the Lord blameless. And not was to them a child, because

3588 1665 2258 4723 2532 297 4260 1722 3588
ἡ Ἐλισάβετ ἦν στεῖρα, καὶ ἀμφότεροι προβεβηκότες ἐν ταῖς
Elizabeth was barren, and both advanced in age in the

2250 846 2258
ἡμέραις αὐτῶν ἦσαν.
days of them were.

1096 1161 1722 3588 2407 846 1722 3588 5010 3588
8 Ἐγένετο δὲ ἐν τῷ ἱερατεύειν αὐτὸν ἐν τῇ τάξει τῆς ἐφη-
it was And in the serving as priest of him in the order of the

2183 846 1725 3588 2316 2596 3588 1485 3588 2405
μερίας αὐτοῦ ἔναντι τοῦ Θεοῦ, 9 κατὰ τὸ ἔθος τῆς ἱερατείας,
course of him before God, according to the custom of the priests,

2975 3588 2370 1525 1519 3588 3485 3588 2962 2532
ἔλαχε τοῦ θυμιάσαι εἰσελθὼν εἰς τὸν ναὸν τοῦ Κυρίου· 10 καὶ
(his) lot to burn incense entering into the temple of the Lord. And

3956 3588 4128 3588 2992 2258 4336 1854 3588 5610
πᾶν τὸ πλῆθος τοῦ λαοῦ ἦν προσευχόμενον ἔξω τῇ ὥρᾳ
all the multitude of the people was praying outside at the hour

3588 2368 3700 1161 846 32 2962 2476 1537
τοῦ θυμιάματος. 11 ὤφθη δὲ αὐτῷ ἄγγελος Κυρίου, ἑστὼς ἐκ
of incense. appeared And to him an angel of (the) Lord standing on

King James Version

THE GOSPEL ACCORDING TO LUKE

Luke 1

1. Forasmuch as many have taken in hand to set forth in order a declaration of those things which are most surely believed among us,
2 Even as they delivered them unto us, which from the beginning were eyewitnesses, and ministers of the word;
3 It seemed good to me also, having had perfect understanding of all things from the very first, to write unto thee in order, most excellent Theophilus,
4 That thou mightest know the certainty of those things, wherein thou hast been instructed.
5. There was in the days of Herod, the king of Judaea, a certain priest named Zacharias, of the course of Abia: and his wife (was) of the daughters of Aaron, and her name (was) Elisabeth.
6 And they were both righteous before God, walking in all the commandments and ordinances of the Lord blameless.

7 And they had no child, because that Elisabeth was barren, and they both were (now) well stricken in years.

8 And it came to pass, that while he executed the priest's office before God in the order of his course,
9 According to the custom of the priest's office, his lot was to burn incense when he went into the temple of the Lord.
10 And the whole multitude of the people were praying without at the time of incense.
11 And there appeared unto him an angel of the Lord standing on

Luke 1:12

Literal Translation

(the) right of the altar of incense.

12 And seeing (this), Zacharias was troubled, and fear fell on him.

13 But the angel said to him, Do not fear, Zacharias, because your petition was heard, and your wife Elizabeth will bear a son to you, and you shall call his name John.

14 And he will be joy and exultation to you, and many will rejoice over his birth.

15 For he will be great in the eyes of the Lord, and he shall not at all drink wine or strong drink. And he will be filled of (the) Holy Spirit, even from his mother's womb.

16 And he will turn many of the sons of Israel to (the) Lord their God.

17 And he will go out before Him in (the) spirit and power of Elijah to turn (the) hearts of fathers to (their) children, and disobedient (ones) in (the) wisdom of (the) just, to make ready a people having been prepared for (the) Lord. (Mal. 4:5, 6)

18 And Zacharias said to the angel, By what shall I know this? For I am old and my wife is advanced in her days.

19 And answering, the angel said to him, I am Gabriel the (one) standing by before God, and I was sent to speak to you and to proclaim to you (the) good news (of) these things.

20 And behold! You shall be silent and not able to speak until the day these things occur, because you did not believe my words which shall be fulfilled in their time.

1188 3588 2379 3588 2368 2532 5015
δεξιῶν τοῦ θυσιαστηρίου τοῦ θυμιάματος. 12 καὶ ἐταράχθη
(the) right of the altar of incense. And was troubled

2197 1492 2532 5401 1968 1909 846 2036 1161 4314
Ζαχαρίας ἰδών, καὶ φόβος ἐπέπεσεν ἐπ' αὐτόν. 13 εἶπε δὲ πρὸς
Zacharias seeing, and fear fell upon him. said But to

846 3588 32 3361 5399 2197 1360 1522 3588
αὐτὸν ὁ ἄγγελος, Μὴ φοβοῦ, Ζαχαρία· διότι εἰσηκούσθη ἡ
him the angel, Do not fear, Zacharias; because was heard the

1162 4675 2532 3588 1135 4675 1665 1080 5207 4671 2532
δέησίς σου, καὶ ἡ γυνή σου Ἐλισάβετ γεννήσει υἱόν σοι, καὶ
petition of you, and the wife of you. Elizabeth will bear a son to you, and

2564 3588 3686 846 2491 2532 2071 5479 4671 2532
καλέσεις τὸ ὄνομα αὐτοῦ Ἰωάννην. 14 καὶ ἔσται χαρά σοι καὶ
you shall call the name of him John. And he shall be joy to you and

20 2532 4183 1909 3588 1083 846 5463
ἀγαλλίασις, καὶ πολλοὶ ἐπὶ τῇ γεννήσει αὐτοῦ χαρήσονται.
exultation, and many over the birth of him will rejoice.

2071 1063 3173 1799 3588 2962 2532 3651 2532 4608
15 ἔσται γὰρ μέγας ἐνώπιον τοῦ Κυρίου, καὶ οἶνον καὶ σίκερα
he will be For great in the eyes of the Lord, and wine and strong drink

3756 3361 4095 2532 4151 40 4130 2089 1537 2836
οὐ μὴ πίῃ, καὶ Πνεύματος Ἁγίου πλησθήσεται ἔτι ἐκ κοιλίας
never may he drink, and of Spirit (the) Holy he will be filled even from womb

3384 846 2532 4183 3588 5207 2474 1994
μητρὸς αὐτοῦ. 16 καὶ πολλοὺς τῶν υἱῶν Ἰσραὴλ ἐπιστρέψει
of mother of him. And many of the sons of Israel he will turn

1909 2962 3588 2316 846 2532 846 4281
ἐπὶ Κύριον τὸν Θεὸν αὐτῶν· 17 καὶ αὐτὸς προελεύσεται
onto (the) Lord, the God of them; and he will go ahead

1799 846 1722 4151 2532 1411 2243 1994
ἐνώπιον αὐτοῦ ἐν πνεύματι καὶ δυνάμει Ἠλίου, ἐπιστρέψαι
before Him in (the) spirit and power of Elijah, to turn

2588 3962 1909 5043 2532 545 1722 5428
καρδίας πατέρων ἐπὶ τέκνα, καὶ ἀπειθεῖς ἐν φρονήσει
(the) hearts of fathers onto chilldren, and disobedient in (the) wisdom

1342 2090 2962 2992 2680 2532 2036
δικαίων, ἑτοιμάσαι Κυρίῳ λαὸν κατεσκευασμένον. 18 καὶ εἶπε
of (the) just, to make ready for (the) Lord a people having been prepared. And said

2197 4314 3588 32 2596 5101 1097 5124
Ζαχαρίας πρὸς τὸν ἄγγελον, Κατὰ τί γνώσομαι τοῦτο;
Zacharias to the angel, By what shall I know this?

1473 1063 1510 4246 2532 3588 1135 3450 4260 1722
ἐγὼ γάρ εἰμι πρεσβύτης καὶ ἡ γυνή μου προβεβηκυῖα ἐν
I For am old, and the wife of me is advanced in

3588 2250 846 2532 611 3588 32 2036 846
ταῖς ἡμέραις αὐτῆς. 19 καὶ ἀποκριθεὶς ὁ ἄγγελος εἶπεν αὐτῷ,
the days of her. And answering the angel said to him,

1473 1510 1043 3588 3936 1799 3588 2316 2532
Ἐγώ εἰμι Γαβριὴλ ὁ παρεστηκὼς ἐνώπιον τοῦ Θεοῦ· καὶ
I am Gabriel the (one) standing by before God; and

649 2980 4314 4571 2532 2097 4671
ἀπεστάλην λαλῆσαι πρός σε, καὶ εὐαγγελίσασθαί σοι
I was sent to speak to you, and to proclaim good news to you

5023 2532 2400 2071 4623 2532 3361 1410 2980
ταῦτα. 20 καὶ ἰδού, ἔσῃ σιωπῶν καὶ μὴ δυνάμενος λαλῆσαι
these things. And behold! you will be silent and not being able to speak

891 3739 2250 1096 5023 473 3739 3756 4100
ἄχρι ἧς ἡμέρας γένηται ταῦτα, ἀνθ' ὧν οὐκ ἐπίστευσας
until which day occur these things, because not you believed

3588 3056 3450 3748 4137 1519 3588 2540
τοῖς λόγοις μου, οἵτινες πληρωθήσονται εἰς τὸν καιρὸν
the words of me, which will be fulfilled in the time

King James Version

the right side of the altar of incense.

12 And when Zacharias saw (him), he was troubled, and fear fell upon him.

13 But the angel said unto him, Fear not, Zacharias: for thy prayer is heard; and thy wife Elisabeth shall bear thee a son, and thou shalt call his name John.

14 And thou shalt have joy and gladness; and many shall rejoice at his birth.

15 For he shall be great in the sight of the Lord, and shall drink neither wine nor strong drink; and he shall be filled with the Holy Ghost, even from his mother's womb.

16 And many of the children of Israel shall he turn to the Lord their God.

17 And he shall go before him in the spirit and power of Elias, to turn the hearts of the fathers to the children, and the disobedient to the wisdom of the just; to make ready a people prepared for the Lord.

18 And Zacharias said unto the angel, Whereby shall I know this? for I am an old man, and my wife well stricken in years.

19 And the angel answering said unto him, I am Gabriel, that stand in the presence of God; and am sent to speak unto thee, and to shew thee these glad tidings.

20 And, behold, thou shalt be dumb, and not able to speak, until the day that these things shall be performed, because thou believest not my words, which shall be fulfilled in their season.

Literal Translation

Luke 1:21

King James Version

21 And the people were expecting Zach-arias, and they wondered at his delay in the temple.
22 But coming out, he was not able to speak to them, and they recog-nized that he had seen a vision in the Holy Place. And he was signaling to them and remained dumb.

23 And it occurred as the days of his service were fulfilled, he went away to his house.

24 And after these days his wife Elizabeth con-ceived. And (she) hid herself five months, saying,
25 So has the Lord done to me in (the) days in which He looked on (me) to take away my reproach among men.

26. And in the sixth month, the angel Gabriel was sent by God to a city of Galilee named Nazareth,

27 to a virgin who had been betrothed to a man whose name was Joseph, of (the) house of David; and the vir-gin's name (was) Mariam.
28 And entering, the an-gel said to her, Hail, (one) having received grace! The Lord (is) with you. Blessed (are) you among women!
29 And seeing (this), she was disturbed at his word, and considered what kind of greeting this may be.
30 And the angel said to her, Do not fear, Mariam, for you found favor from God.
31 And behold! You will conceive in (your) womb and bear a Son, and you will call His name Jesus.
32 This One will be great and will be called Son of (the) Most High.

846 2532 2258 3588 2992 4328 3588 2197 2532
αὐτῶν. 21 καὶ ἦν ὁ λαὸς προσδοκῶν τὸν Ζαχαρίαν· καὶ
of them. And were the people expecting Zacharias, and

2296 1722 3588 5549 3588 1722 3588 3485 1831 1161 3756
ἐθαύμαζον ἐν τῷ χρονίζειν αὐτὸν ἐν τῷ ναῷ. 22 ἐξελθὼν δὲ οὐκ
they wondered at the delay of him in the temple. coming out And not

1410 2980 846 2532 1921 3754 3701
ἠδύνατο λαλῆσαι αὐτοῖς· καὶ ἐπέγνωσαν ὅτι ὀπτασίαν
he was able to speak to them, and they recognized that a vision

3708 1722 3588 3485 2532 846 2258 1269 846 2532
ἑώρακεν ἐν τῷ ναῷ· καὶ αὐτὸς ἦν διανεύων αὐτοῖς, καὶ
he had seen in the temple. And he was signaling to them, and

1265 2974 2532 1096 5613 4130 3588 2250 3588
διέμενε κωφός. 23 καὶ ἐγένετο, ὡς ἐπλήσθησαν αἱ ἡμέραι τῆς
remained dumb. And it occurred as were fulfilled the days of the

3009 846 565 1519 3588 3624 846
λειτουργίας αὐτοῦ, ἀπῆλθεν εἰς τὸν οἶκον αὐτοῦ.
service of him, he went away to the house of him.

3326 1161 3778 3588 2250 4815 1665 3588 1135
24. Μετὰ δὲ ταύτας τὰς ἡμέρας συνέλαβεν Ἐλισάβετ ἡ γυνὴ
after And these days conceived Elizabeth the wife

846 2532 4032 1438 3376 4002 3004 3754
αὐτοῦ, καὶ περιέκρυβεν ἑαυτὴν μῆνας πέντε, λέγουσα 25 ὅτι
of him, and hid herself months five, saying,

3779 3427 4160 3588 2962 1722 2250 3739 1896 851
Οὕτω μοι πεποίηκεν ὁ Κύριος ἐν ἡμέραις αἷς ἐπεῖδεν ἀφελεῖν
So to me has done the Lord in days in which He looked to remove

3588 3681 3450 1722 444
τὸ ὄνειδός μου ἐν ἀνθρώποις.
the reproach of me among men.

1722 1161 3588 3376 3588 1623 649 3588 32 1043
26. Ἐν δὲ τῷ μηνὶ τῷ ἕκτῳ ἀπεστάλη ὁ ἄγγελος Γαβριὴλ
in And the month sixth was sent the angel Gabriel

5259 3588 2316 1519 4172 3588 1056 3739 3686 3478
ὑπὸ τοῦ Θεοῦ εἰς πόλιν τῆς Γαλιλαίας, ᾗ ὄνομα Ναζαρὲθ,
by God to a city of Galilee to which the name, Nazareth,

4314 3933 3423 435 3739 3686 2501
27 πρὸς παρθένον μεμνηστευμένην ἀνδρὶ, ᾧ ὄνομα Ἰωσὴφ,
to a virgin having been betrothed to a man whose name, Joseph

1537 3624 1138 2532 3588 3686 3588 3933 3137 2532
ἐξ οἴκου Δαβίδ· καὶ τὸ ὄνομα τῆς παρθένου Μαριάμ. 28 καὶ
of (the) house of David; and the name of the virgin (was) Mariam. (Mary) And

1525 3588 32 4314 846 2036 5463 5487
εἰσελθὼν ὁ ἄγγελος πρὸς αὐτὴν εἶπε, Χαῖρε, κεχαριτωμένη·
entering the angel to her said, Hail, (one) receiving grace,

3588 2962 3326 4675 2127 4771 1722 1135 3588 1161 1492
ὁ Κύριος μετά σοῦ, εὐλογημένη σὺ ἐν γυναιξίν. 29 ἡ δὲ ἰδοῦσα
the Lord (is) with you. Blessed (are) you among women. she And seeing

1298 1909 3588 3056 846 2532 1260 4217
διεταράχθη ἐπὶ τῷ λόγῳ αὐτοῦ, καὶ διελογίζετο ποταπὸς
was disturbed at the word of him, and considered of what kind

1498 3588 783 3778 2532 2036 3588 32 846 3361 5399
εἴη ὁ ἀσπασμὸς οὗτος. 30 καὶ εἶπεν ὁ ἄγγελος αὐτῇ, Μὴ φοβοῦ,
may be greeting this. And said the angel to her, Do not fear,

3137 2147 1063 5485 3844 3588 2316 2532 2400 4815
Μαριάμ· εὗρες γὰρ χάριν παρὰ τῷ Θεῷ. 31 καὶ ἰδοὺ, συλ-
Mariam, (Mary) you found for favor with God. And behold! You will con-

4815 1722 1064 2532 5088 5207 2532 2564 3588 3686 846
λήψῃ ἐν γαστρὶ, καὶ τέξῃ υἱόν, καὶ καλέσεις τὸ ὄνομα αὐτοῦ
ceive in womb, and bear a son, and you will call the name of Him

2424 3778 2071 3173 2532 5207 5310 2564
Ἰησοῦν. 32 οὗτος ἔσται μέγας, καὶ υἱὸς ὑψίστου κληθήσεται·
Jesus. This One will be great, and Son of Most High will be called;

21 And the people waited for Zacharias, and marvelled that he tarried so long in the temple.
22 And when he came out, he could not speak unto them: and they perceived that he had seen a vision in the tem-ple: for he beckoned unto them, and re-mained speechless.

23 And it came to pass, that, as soon as the days of his ministration were accomplished, he de-parted to his own house.

24 And after those days his wife Elisabeth con-ceived, and hid herself five months, saying,
25 Thus hath the Lord dealt with me in the days wherein he looked on (me), to take away my reproach among men.

26. And in the sixth month the angel Gabriel was sent from God unto a city of Galilee, named Nazareth,
27 To a virgin espoused to a man whose name was Joseph, of the house of David; and the virgin's name (was) Mary.
28 And the angel came in unto her, and said, Hail, (thou that art) highly favoured, the Lord (is) with thee: blessed (art) thou among women.
29 And when she saw (him), she was troubled at his saying, and cast in her mind what manner of salutation this should be.
30 And the angel said unto her, Fear not, Mary: for thou hast found favour with God.
31 And, behold, thou shalt conceive in thy womb, and bring forth a son, and shalt call his name JESUS.
32 He shall be great, and shall be called the Son of the Highest:

Literal Translation

And (the) Lord God will give to Him the throne of His father David.

33 And He will reign over the house of Jacob to the ages; and of His kingdom there will be no end.
34 But Mariam said to the angel, How will this be since I do not know a man?

35 And answering, the angel said to her, The Holy Spirit will come upon you, and (the) power of (the) Most High will overshadow you, and for this reason that Holy (One) being born of you will be called Son of God.
36 And behold! Your kinswoman Elizabeth. She also conceived a son in her old age, and this is (the) sixth month with her, she being called barren;
37 for not will be impossible with God every word..
38 And Mariam said, Behold, the slave of (the) Lord! May it be to me according to your word. And the angel departed from her.

39. And rising up in these days, Mariam went into the hill country with haste to a city of Judah.
40 And (she) entered into the house of Zacharias and greeted Elizabeth.
41 And it happened, as Elizabeth heard the greeting of Mariam, the babe in her womb leaped, and Elizabeth was filled of the Holy Spirit.
42 And (she) cried out with a loud voice and said, Having been blessed you (are) among women, also being blessed (is) the fruit of your womb!
43 And from where (is) this to me that the mother of my Lord comes to me?
44 For behold, as the sound

Luke 1:33

2532 1325 846 2962 3588 2316 3588 2362 1138 3588 3962
καὶ δώσει αὐτῷ Κύριος ὁ Θεὸς τὸν θρόνον Δαβὶδ τοῦ πατρὸς
and will give to Him (the) Lord God the throne of David the Father

846 2532 936 1909 3588 3624 2384 1519 3588 165
αὐτοῦ, 33 καὶ βασιλεύσει ἐπὶ τὸν οἶκον Ἰακὼβ εἰς τοὺς αἰῶνας,
of Him. And He will reign over the house of Jacob to the ages,

2532 3588 932 846 3756 2071 5056 2036 1161 3137
καὶ τῆς βασιλείας αὐτοῦ οὐκ ἔσται τέλος. 34 εἶπε δὲ Μαριὰμ
and of the kingdom of Him not will be an end. said And Mariam (Mary)

4314 3588 32 4459 2071 5124 1893 435 3756 1097
πρὸς τὸν ἄγγελον, Πῶς ἔσται τοῦτο, ἐπεὶ ἄνδρα οὐ γινώσκω;
to the angel, How will be this, since a man not I know?

2532 611 3588 32 2036 846 4151 40
35 καὶ ἀποκριθεὶς ὁ ἄγγελος εἶπεν αὐτῇ, Πνεῦμα Ἅγιον
And answering the angel said to her, (The) Spirit Holy

1904 1909 4571 2532 1411 5310 1982 4671 1352
ἐπελεύσεται ἐπὶ σέ, καὶ δύναμις ὑψίστου ἐπισκιάσει σοι· διὸ
will come up upon you, and power of (the) Most High will overshadow you; so

2532 3588 1080 1537 4675 40 2564 5207 2316 2532
καὶ τὸ γεννώμενον ἐκ σοῦ ἅγιον κληθήσεται υἱὸς Θεοῦ. 36 καὶ
also that having been born of you Holy (One) will be called Son of God. And

2400 1665 3588 4773 4675 2532 846 4815 5207 1722
ἰδού, Ἐλισάβετ ἡ συγγενής σου, καὶ αὐτὴ συνειληφυῖα υἱὸν ἐν
behold! Elizabeth the kinswoman of you, also she conceived a son in

1094 846 2532 3778 3376 1623 2076 846 3588 2564
γήρᾳ αὐτῆς· καὶ οὗτος μὴν ἕκτος ἐστὶν αὐτῇ τῇ καλουμένῃ
old age of her, and this month sixth is with her, she being called

4723 3754 3756 101 3844 3588 2316 3956 4487 2036
στείρᾳ. 37 ὅτι οὐκ ἀδυνατήσει παρὰ τῷ Θεῷ πᾶν ῥῆμα. 38 εἶπε
barren; because not is impossible with God every word. said

1161 3137 2400 3588 1399 2962 1096 3427 2596 3588 4487
δὲ Μαριάμ, Ἰδού, ἡ δούλη Κυρίου· γένοιτό μοι κατὰ τὸ ῥῆμά
And Mariam (Mary), behold, the slave of (the) Lord! May it be to me according the word

4675 2532 565 575 846 3588 32
σου. καὶ ἀπῆλθεν ἀπ' αὐτῆς ὁ ἄγγελος.
of you. And went away from her the angel.

450 1161 3137 1722 3588 2250 3778 4198
39. Ἀναστᾶσα δὲ Μαριὰμ ἐν ταῖς ἡμέραις ταύταις ἐπορεύθη
rising up And Mariam (Mary) in days these, she went

1519 3588 3714 3326 4710 1519 4172 2448 2532 1525
εἰς τὴν ὀρεινὴν μετὰ σπουδῆς εἰς πόλιν Ἰούδα, 40 καὶ εἰσῆλθεν
to the hill-country with haste, to a city of Judah, and entered

1519 3588 3624 2197 2532 782 3588 1665 2532
εἰς τὸν οἶκον Ζαχαρίου, καὶ ἠσπάσατο τὴν Ἐλισάβετ. 41 καὶ
into the house of Zacharias, and greeted Elizabeth. And

1096 5613 191 3588 1665 3588 783 3588 3137
ἐγένετο ὡς ἤκουσεν ἡ Ἐλισάβετ τὸν ἀσπασμὸν τῆς Μαρίας,
it was as heard Elizabeth the greeting of Mariam

4640 3588 1025 1722 3588 2836 846 2532 4130 4151
ἐσκίρτησε τὸ βρέφος ἐν τῇ κοιλίᾳ αὐτῆς· καὶ ἐπλήσθη Πνεύ-
leaped the babe in the womb of her, and was filled of (the)

40 3588 1665 2532 400 3456 3173
ματος Ἁγίου ἡ Ἐλισάβετ, 42 καὶ ἀνεφώνησε φωνῇ μεγάλῃ,
Spirit Holy Elizabeth. And she cried out with a voice great,

2532 2036 2137 4771 1722 1135 2532 2127 3588
καὶ εἶπεν, Εὐλογημένη σὺ ἐν γυναιξί, καὶ εὐλογημένος ὁ
and said, Having been blessed you (are) among women, and being blessed the

2590 3588 2836 4675 2532 4159 3427 5124 2443 2064 3588
καρπὸς τῆς κοιλίας σου. 43 καὶ πόθεν μοι τοῦτο, ἵνα ἔλθῃ ἡ
fruit of the womb of you. And from where to me this, that comes the

3384 3588 2962 3450 4314 3165 2400 1063 5613 1096 3588 5456
μήτηρ τοῦ Κυρίου μου πρός με; 44 ἰδοὺ γάρ, ὡς ἐγένετο ἡ φωνὴ
mother of the Lord of me to me? behold For, as came to be the sound

King James Version

and the Lord God shall give unto him the throne of his father David:

33 And he shall reign over the house of Jacob for ever; and of his kingdom there shall be no end.
34 Then said Mary unto the angel, How shall this be, seeing I know not a man?

35 And the angel answered and said unto her, The Holy Ghost shall come upon thee, and the power of the Highest shall overshadow thee: therefore also that holy thing which shall be born of thee shall be called the Son of God.
36 And, behold, thy cousin Elisabeth, she hath also conceived a son in her old age: and this is the sixth month with her, who was called barren.
37 For with God nothing shall be impossible.
38 And Mary said, Behold the handmaid of the Lord; be it unto me according to thy word. And the angel departed from her.

39. And Mary arose in those days, and went into the hill country with haste, into a city of Juda;
40 And entered into the house of Zacharias, and saluted Elisabeth.
41 And it came to pass, that, when Elisabeth heard the salutation of Mary, the babe leaped in her womb; and Elisabeth was filled with the Holy Ghost:

42 And she spake out with a loud voice, and said, Blessed (art) thou among women, and blessed (is) the fruit of thy womb.
43 And whence (is) this to me, that the mother of my Lord should come to me?
44 For, lo, as soon as the voice

Literal Translation

of your greeting came into my ears, the babe in my womb leaped in exultation.
45 And blessed (is) the (one) believing, because there will be a completion to the things spoken to her from (the) Lord.
46. And Mariam said, My soul magnifies the Lord,
47 and my spirit exulted on God My Savior.
48 For He looked upon the humiliation of His slave woman. For, behold, from now on all generations will count me blessed. (1 Sam. 1:11)
49 For the Mighty One did great things to me, and holy (is) His name.
50 And His mercy (is) to generations of generations to those having feared Him. (Ps. 103:17)
51 He has done might(ily) with His arm; He scattered proud ones in (the) thought of their heart.
52 He pulled down powerful ones from thrones, and exalted lowly ones.
53 He filled (the) hungering ones (with) good things, and He sent (the) rich ones away empty.
54 He helped His servant Israel in order to remember mercy,
55 even as He spoke to our fathers, to Abraham, and to his seed to the age.
56 And Mariam remained with her about three months, and returned to her house.
57. And the time was fulfilled to Elizabeth (for) her to bear, and she bore a son.
58 And the neighbors and her relatives heard that (the) Lord magnified His mercy with

Luke 1:45

3588 783 4675 1519 3588 3775 3450 4640 1722 20
τοῦ ἀσπασμοῦ σου εἰς τὰ ὦτά μου, ἐσκίρτησεν ἐν ἀγαλλιάσει
of the greeting of you into the ears of me, leaped in exultation
3588 1025 1722 3588 2836 3450 2532 3107 3588 4100 3754
τὸ βρέφος ἐν τῇ κοιλίᾳ μου. 45 καὶ μακαρία ἡ πιστεύσασα, ὅτι
the babe in the womb of me. And blessed (is) the (one) believing, for
2071 5050 3588 2980 846 3844 2962 2532
ἔσται τελείωσις τοῖς λελαλημένοις αὐτῇ παρὰ Κυρίου. 46 καὶ
will be a completion to the things being spoken to her from (the) Lord. And
2036 3137 3170 3588 5590 3450 3588 2962 2532
εἶπε Μαριάμ, 47 Μεγαλύνει ἡ ψυχή μου τὸν Κύριον, καὶ
said Mariam,, (Mary) magnifies The soul of me the Lord, and
21 3588 4151 3450 1909 3588 2316 3588 4990 3450 3754
ἠγαλλίασε τὸ πνεῦμά μου ἐπὶ τῷ Θεῷ τῷ σωτῆρί μου. 48 ὅτι
exulted the spirit of me on God the Savior of me; because
1914 1909 3588 5014 3588 1399 846 2400 1063
ἐπέβλεψεν ἐπὶ τὴν ταπείνωσιν τῆς δούλης αὐτοῦ. ἰδοὺ γάρ,
He looked upon the humiliaton of the slave woman of Him. behold, For,
575 3588 3568 3106 3165 3956 3588 1074 3754 4160 3427
ἀπὸ τοῦ νῦν μακαριοῦσί με πᾶσαι αἱ γενεαί. 49 ὅτι ἐποίησέ μοι
from now will count blessed me all the generations; because did to me
3167 3588 1415 2532 40 3588 3686 846 2532 3588
μεγαλεῖα ὁ δυνατός, καὶ ἅγιον τὸ ὄνομα αὐτοῦ. 50 καὶ τὸ
great things the Mighty One, and holy the name of Him, and the
1656 846 1519 1074 1074 3588 5399 846
ἔλεος αὐτοῦ εἰς γενεὰς γενεῶν τοῖς φοβουμένοις αὐτόν.
mercy of Him to generations of generations to those having feared Him.

4160 2904 1722 1023 846 1287 5244
51 ἐποίησε κράτος ἐν βραχίονι αὐτοῦ· διεσκόρπισεν ὑπερη-
He has done might(ily) with (the) arm of Him. He has scattered proud
1271 2588 846 2507 1413 575
φάνους διανοίᾳ καρδίας αὐτῶν. 52 καθεῖλε δυνάστας ἀπὸ
ones in (the) thought of the heart of them; He pulled down potentates from
2362 2532 5312 5011 3983 1705
θρόνων, καὶ ὕψωσε ταπεινούς. 53 πεινῶντας ἐνέπλησεν
thrones, and exalted lowly ones. hungering ones He filled
18 2532 4147 1821 2756 482
ἀγαθῶν, καὶ πλουτοῦντας ἐξαπέστειλε κενούς. 54 ἀντελάβετο
of good things and rich ones He sent away empty. He helped
2474 3816 846 3415 1656 2531 2980
Ἰσραὴλ παιδὸς αὐτοῦ, μνησθῆναι ἐλέους, 55 [καθὼς ἐλάλησε
Israel, (the) servant of Him to remember mercy, even as He spoke
4314 3588 3962 2257 3588 11 2532 3588 4690
πρὸς τοὺς πατέρας ἡμῶν] τῷ Ἀβραὰμ καὶ τῷ σπέρματι
to the fathers of us, to Abraham and to the seed
846 1519 3588 165
αὐτοῦ εἰς τὸν αἰῶνα.
of him to the age.

3306 1161 3137 4862 846 5616 3376 5140 2532
56. Ἔμεινε δὲ Μαριὰμ σὺν αὐτῇ ὡσεὶ μῆνας τρεῖς, καὶ ὑπέ-
remained And Mariam (Mary) with her about months three, and
5290 1519 3588 3624 846
στρεψεν εἰς τὸν οἶκον αὐτῆς.
returned to the house of her.

3588 1161 1665 4130 3588 5550 3588 5088 846
57. Τῇ δὲ Ἐλισάβετ ἐπλήσθη ὁ χρόνος τοῦ τεκεῖν αὐτήν,
And to Elizaabeth was fulfilled the time to bear (for) her,
2532 1080 5207 2532 191 3588 4040 2532 3588
καὶ ἐγέννησεν υἱόν. 58 καὶ ἤκουσαν οἱ περίοικοι καὶ οἱ συγ-
and she bore a son. And heard the neighbors and the
4773 846 3754 3170 2962 3588 1656 846 3326
γενεῖς αὐτῆς ὅτι ἐμεγάλυνε Κύριος τὸ ἔλεος αὐτοῦ μετ'
relatives of her that magnified (the) Lord the mercy of Him with

King James Version

of thy salutation sounded in mine ears, the babe leaped in my womb for joy.
45 And blessed (is) she that believed: for there shall be a performance of those things which were told her from the Lord.
46. And Mary said, My soul doth magnify the Lord,
47 And my spirit hath rejoiced in God my Saviour.
48 For he hath regarded the low estate of his handmaiden: for, behold, from henceforth all generations shall call me blessed.
49 For he that is mighty hath done to me great things; and holy (is) his name.
50 And his mercy (is) on them that fear him from generation to generation.
51 He hath shewed strength with his arm; he hath scattered the proud in the imagination of their hearts.
52 He hath put down the mighty from (their) seats, and exalted them of low degree.
53 He hath filled the hungry with good things; and the rich he hath sent empty away.
54 He hath holpen his servant Israel, in remembrance of (his) mercy;
55 As he spake to our fathers, to Abraham, and to his seed for ever.
56 And Mary abode with her about three months, and returned to her own house.
57. Now Elisabeth's full time came that she should be delivered; and she brought forth a son.
58 And her neighbours and her cousins heard how the Lord had shewed great mercy upon

Literal Translation

her, and they rejoiced
with her.
59 And it happened on
the eighth day, they
came to circumcise the
child, and were calling
it by his father's name,
Zacharias.
60 And answering his
mother said, Not so, but
he shall be called John.

61 And they said to her,
No one is among your
kindred who is called by
this name.

62 And they signaled to
his father, what he
might desire him to be
called.
63 And asking for a tab-
let, he wrote, saying,
John is his name. And
all wondered.

64 And instantly his
mouth was opened and
his tongue (loosed), and
he spoke, blessing God.
65 And fear came on all
those living around
them. And in all the hill
country of Judea all
these things were talked
over.

66 And all the (ones)
hearing laid (them) up
in their hearts, saying,
What then will this child
be? And the hand of
(the) Lord was with
him.

67. And his father
Zacharias was filled of
(the) Holy Spirit and
prophesied, saying,
68 Blessed (be the)
Lord, the God of Israel,
because He visited and
worked redemption for
His people.

69 And (He) raised up a
Horn of salvation for us
in the house of His ser-
vant David;
70 even as He spoke
through the mouth of
His holy prophets from
the age (before):
71 Salvation from

Luke 1:59

846 2532 4796 846 2532 1096 1722 3588 3590 2250
αὐτῆς, καὶ συνέχαιρον αὐτῇ. 59καὶ ἐγένετο ἐν τῇ ὀγδόῃ ἡμέρᾳ,
her, and they rejoiced with her. And it was in the eighth day,

2064 4059 3588 3813 2532 2564 846 1909 3588
ἦλθον περιτεμεῖν τὸ παιδίον· καὶ ἐκάλουν αὐτὸ ἐπὶ τῷ
they came to circumcise the child, and were calling it on the

3686 3588 3962 846 2197 2532 611 3588
ὀνόματι τοῦ πατρὸς αὐτοῦ Ζαχαρίαν. 60 καὶ ἀποκριθεῖσα ἡ
name of the father of him, Zacharias. And answering the

3384 846 2036 3780 235 2564 2491 2532
μήτηρ αὐτοῦ εἶπεν, Οὐχί, ἀλλὰ κληθήσεται Ἰωάννης. 61 καὶ
mother of him said, Not so, but he shall be called John. And

2036 4314 846 3754 3762 2076 1722 3588 4772 4675
εἶπον πρὸς αὐτὴν ὅτι Οὐδείς ἐστιν ἐν τῇ συγγενείᾳ σου
they said to her, No one there is in the kindred of you

3739 2564 3588 3686 5129 1770 1161 3588 3962 846
ὃς καλεῖται τῷ ὀνόματι τούτῳ. 62 ἐνένευον δὲ τῷ πατρὶ αὐτοῦ,
who is called by name this. they signaled And to the father of him

3588 5101 302 2309 2564 846 2532 154 4093
τὸ τί ἂν θέλοι καλεῖσθαι αὐτόν. 63 καὶ αἰτήσας πινακίδιον
what may he desire to be called him. And asking for a tablet,

1125 3004 2491 2076 3588 3686 846 2532
ἔγραψε, λέγων, Ἰωάννης ἐστὶ τὸ ὄνομα αὐτοῦ· καὶ ἐθαύ-
he wrote, saying, John is the name of him. And

2296 3956 455 1161 3588 4750 846 3916
μασαν πάντες. 64 ἀνεῴχθη δὲ τὸ στόμα αὐτοῦ παραχρῆμα
wondered all. was opened And the mouth of him instantly,

2532 3588 1100 846 2532 2980 2127 3588 2316 2532
καὶ ἡ γλῶσσα αὐτοῦ, καὶ ἐλάλει εὐλογῶν τὸν Θεόν. 65 καὶ
and the tongue of him, and he spoke blessing God. And

1096 1909 3956 5401 3588 4039 846 2532
ἐγένετο ἐπὶ πάντας φόβος τοὺς περιοικοῦντας αὐτούς· καὶ
was upon all fear, those living around them, and

1722 3650 3588 3714 3588 2449 1255 3956 3588 4487
ἐν ὅλῃ τῇ ὀρεινῇ τῆς Ἰουδαίας διελαλεῖτο πάντα τὰ ῥήματα
in all the hill-country of Judea were talked over all things

5023 2532 5087 3956 3588 191 1722 3588 5023 846
ταῦτα. 66 καὶ ἔθεντο πάντες οἱ ἀκούσαντες ἐν τῇ καρδίᾳ αὐτῶν,
these. And laid up all the (ones) hearing in the heart of them,

3004 5101 687 3588 3813 2124 2071 2532 5495 2962
λέγοντες, Τί ἄρα τὸ παιδίον τοῦτο ἔσται; καὶ χεὶρ Κυρίου
saying, What then child this will be? And (the) hand of (the) Lord

2258 3326 846
ἦν μετ' αὐτοῦ.
was with him.

2532 2197 3588 3962 846 4130 4151
67. Καὶ Ζαχαρίας ὁ πατὴρ αὐτοῦ ἐπλήσθη Πνεύματος
And Zacharias the father of him was filled of (the) Spirit

40 2532 4395 3004 2128 2962 3588
Ἁγίου, καὶ προεφήτευσε, λέγων, 68 Εὐλογητὸς Κύριος ὁ
Holy, and prophesied, saying, Blessed (be the) Lord the

2316 3588 2474 3754 1980 2532 4160 3085 3588
Θεὸς τοῦ Ἰσραήλ, ὅτι ἐπεσκέψατο καὶ ἐποίησε λύτρωσιν τῷ
God of Israel, because He visited and worked redemption for the

2992 846 2532 1453 2768 4991 2254 1722 3588 3624
λαῷ αὐτοῦ, 69 καὶ ἤγειρε κέρας σωτηρίας ἡμῖν ἐν τῷ οἴκῳ
people of Him, and raised a Horn of Salvation for us in the house

1138 3588 3816 846 2531 2980 1223 4750
Δαβὶδ τοῦ παιδὸς αὐτοῦ, 70 [καθὼς ἐλάλησε διὰ στόματος
of David the servant of Him; even as He spoke through (the) mouth

3588 40 3588 575 165 4396 846 4991 1537
τῶν ἁγίων τῶν ἀπ' αἰῶνος προφητῶν αὐτοῦ], 71 σωτηρίαν ἐξ
the holy from (the) age prophets of Him, Salvation from

King James Version

her; and they rejoiced
with her.
59 And it came to pass,
that on the eighth day
they came to circum-
cise the child; and they
called him Zacharias,
after the name of his fa-
ther.
60 And his mother an-
swered and said, Not
(so); but he shall be
called John.
61 And they said unto
her, There is none of thy
kindred that is called by
this name.

62 And they made signs
to his father, how he
would have him called.

63 And he asked for a
writing table, and
wrote, saying, His
name is John. And they
marvelled all.

64 And his mouth was
opened immediately,
and his tongue (loosed),
and he spake, and
praised God.
65 And fear came on all
that dwelt round about
them: and all these say-
ings were noised
abroad throughout all
the hill country of
Judaea.

66 And all they that
heard (them) laid
(them) up in their
hearts, saying, What
manner of child shall
this be! And the hand of
the Lord was with him.

67. And his father
Zacharias was filled
with the Holy Ghost,
and prophesied, saying,
68 Blessed (be) the
Lord God of Israel; for
he hath visited and re-
deemed his people,
69 And hath raised up
an horn of salvation for
us in the house of his
servant David;
70 As he spake by the
mouth of his holy
prophets, which have
been since the world be-
gan:
71 That we should be
saved from

Literal Translation

our enemies, and from (the) hand of all the (ones) hating us,

72 to execute mercy with our fathers, and to remember His holy covenant,
73 (the) oath which He swore to our father Abraham,
74 to give to us, being delivered out of our enemies' hand, in order to serve Him without fear,
75 in consecration and righteousness before Him all the days of our life.

76 And you, child, will be called a prophet of (the) Most High, for you will go before (the) face of (the) Lord to prepare His ways, (Mal. 3:1)
77 to give a knowledge of salvation to His people by remission of their sins,
78 through (the) tender bowels of mercy of our God, in which (the) Dayspring from on high has looked upon us,
79 to appear to those sitting in darkness and in a shadow of death, to direct our feet into (the) way of peace. (Isa. 9:2)

80 And the child grew, and became strong in spirit. And he was in deserted (places) until (the) day of his showing to Israel.

Luke 1:72

2190 2257 2532 1537 5495 3956 3588 3404 2248
ἐχθρῶν ἡμῶν, καὶ ἐκ χειρὸς πάντων τῶν μισούντων ἡμᾶς·
(the) enemies of us, and out of the hand of all the (ones) hating us,

4160 1656 3326 3588 3962 2257 2532 3415
72 ποιῆσαι ἔλεος μετὰ τῶν πατέρων ἡμῶν, καὶ μνησθῆναι
to execute mercy with the fathers of us, and to remember

1242 40 846 3727 3739 3660 4314 11 3588
διαθήκης ἁγίας αὐτοῦ, 73 ὅρκον ὃν ὤμοσε πρὸς Ἀβραὰμ τὸν
(the) covenant holy of Him, (the) oath which He swore to Abraham the

3962 2257 3588 1325 2254 870 1537 5495 3588
πατέρα ἡμῶν, τοῦ δοῦναι ἡμῖν, 74 ἀφόβως, ἐκ χειρὸς τῶν
father of us, to give to us, without fear from (the) hand of the

2190 2257 4506 3000 846 1722 3742 2532
ἐχθρῶν ἡμῶν ῥυσθέντας, λατρεύειν αὐτῷ 75 ἐν ὁσιότητι καὶ
enemies of us being delivered, to serve Him in consecration and

1343 1799 846 3956 3588 2250 3588 2222
δικαιοσύνῃ ἐνώπιον αὐτοῦ πάσας τὰς ἡμέρας τῆς ζωῆς
righteousness before Him all the days of the life

2257 2532 4771 3813 4396 5310 2564
ἡμῶν. 76 καὶ σύ, παιδίον, προφήτης ὑψίστου κληθήσῃ·
of us. And you, child, a prophet of (the) Most High will be called,

4313 1063 4253 4383 2962 2090 3598
προπορεύσῃ γὰρ πρὸ προσώπου Κυρίου ἑτοιμάσαι ὁδοὺς
you will go for before (the) face of (the) Lord to prepare (the) ways

846 3588 1325 1108 4991 3588 2992 846 1722
αὐτοῦ· 77 τοῦ δοῦναι γνῶσιν σωτηρίας τῷ λαῷ αὐτοῦ ἐν
of Him, to give a knowledge of salvation to the people of Him by

859 266 846 1223 4698 1656 2316 2257
ἀφέσει ἁμαρτιῶν αὐτῶν, 78 διὰ σπλάγχνα ἐλέους Θεοῦ ἡμῶν,
remission of sins of them, through (the) bowels of mercy of God to us,

1722 3739 1980 2248 395 1537 5311 2014 3588 1722
ἐν οἷς ἐπεσκέψατο ἡμᾶς ἀνατολὴ ἐξ ὕψους, 79 ἐπιφᾶναι τοῖς ἐν
in which has looked on us (the) Dayspring from on high, to appear to those in

4655 2532 4639 2288 2521 3588 2720 3588
σκότει καὶ σκιᾷ θανάτου καθημένοις, τοῦ κατευθῦναι τοὺς
darkness and in a shadow of death sitting, to direct the

4228 2257 1519 3598 1515
πόδας ἡμῶν εἰς ὁδὸν εἰρήνης.
feet of us into a way of peace.

3588 1161 3813 837 2532 2901 4151 2532 2258
80. Τὸ δὲ παιδίον ηὔξανε καὶ ἐκραταιοῦτο πνεύματι, καὶ ἦν
the And child grew and became strong in spirit, and was

1722 3588 2048 2193 2250 323 846 4314 3588
ἐν ταῖς ἐρήμοις ἕως ἡμέρας ἀναδείξεως αὐτοῦ πρὸς τὸν
in deserted (places) until days of showing of him to

2474
Ἰσραήλ.
Israel.

King James Version

our enemies, and from the hand of all that hate us;

72 To perform the mercy (promised) to our fathers, and to remember his holy covenant;
73 The oath which he sware to our father Abraham,
74 That he would grant unto us, that we being delivered out of the hand of our enemies might serve him without fear,
75 In holiness and righteousness before him, all the days of our life.

76 And thou, child, shalt be called the prophet of the Highest: for thou shalt go before the face of the Lord to prepare his ways;

77 To give knowledge of salvation unto his people by the remission of their sins,
78 Through the tender mercy of our God; whereby the dayspring from on high hath visited us,
79 To give light to them that sit in darkness and (in) the shadow of death, to guide our feet into the way of peace.

80 And the child grew, and waxed strong in spirit, and was in the deserts till the day of his shewing unto Israel.

Luke 2

1. And it happened in those days, a decree went out from Caesar Augustus (for) all the habitable world to be registered.
2 This registration first occurred (during) the governing of Syria (by) Cyrenius.
3 And all went to be registered,

1096 1161 1722 3588 2250 1565 1831 1378 3844
1. Ἐγένετο δὲ ἐν ταῖς ἡμέραις ἐκείναις, ἐξῆλθε δόγμα παρὰ
it happened And in days those, went out a decree from

2541 828 583 3956 3588 3625
Καίσαρος Αὐγούστου, ἀπογράφεσθαι πᾶσαν τὴν οἰκου-
Caesar Augustus to be registered all the habitable

3778 582 4413 1096 2230 3588
μένην. 2 αὕτη ἡ ἀπογραφὴ πρώτη ἐγένετο ἡγεμονεύοντος τῆς
earth. This registration first occurred (during the) governing

4947 2958 2532 4198 3956 583
Συρίας Κυρηνίου. 3 καὶ ἐπορεύοντο πάντες ἀπογράφεσθαι,
(of) Syria (by) Cyrenius. And went all to be registered,

1. And it came to pass in those days, that there went out a decree from Caesar Augustus, that all the world should be taxed.
2 ((And) this taxing was first made when Cyrenius was governor of Syria.)
3 And all went to be taxed,

Literal Translation

each to (his) own city.
4 And Joseph also went up from Galilee, out of (the) city of Nazareth to Judea, to (the) city of David which is called Bethlehem, because of his being of (the) house and family of David,

5 to be registered with Mariam, (she) having been betrothed to him as wife, (she) being pregnant.
6 And it happened as they were there, the days were fulfilled (for) her to bear.
7 And she bore her son, the First-born. And she wrapped Him in a navel band and laid Him in the manger, because there was no place for them in the inn.

8. And shepherds were in the same country living in the fields and keeping guard over their flock (by) night.

9 And, behold! An angel of (the) Lord came on them. And (the) glory of (the) Lord shone around them. And they feared with a great fear.
10 And the angel said to them, Do not fear. For, behold, I proclaim good news to you, a great joy, which will be to all people,
11 because today a Savior, who is Christ (the) Lord, was born to you in (the) city of David.
12 And this (is) a sign to you: You will find a babe having been wrapped in a navel band, lying in a manger.
13 And suddenly there was with the angel a multitude of (the) heavenly host, praising God and saying,

14 Glory to God in the highest, and peace on earth, good will among men.

Luke 2:4

1538 1519 3588 2398 4172 305 1161 2532 2501 575 3588
ἕκαστος εἰς τὴν ἰδίαν πόλιν. 4 ἀνέβη δὲ καὶ Ἰωσὴφ ἀπὸ τῆς
each one into the own city. went up And also Joseph from

1056 1537 4172 3478 1519 3588 2449 1519 4172
Γαλιλαίας, ἐκ πόλεως Ναζαρὲθ, εἰς τὴν Ἰουδαίαν, εἰς πόλιν
Galilee, out of (the) city of Nazareth into Judea, into (the) city

1138 3748 2564 965 1223 3588 1511 846 1537 3624 2532
Δαβὶδ, ἥτις καλεῖται Βηθλεέμ, διὰ τὸ εἶναι αὐτὸν ἐξ οἴκου καὶ
of David, which is called Bethlehem, because of being him out of house and

3965 1138 583 4862 3137 3588 3423
πατριᾶς Δαβίδ, 5 ἀπογράψασθαι σὺν Μαριὰμ τῇ μεμνηστευ-
family of David, to be registered with Mariam (Mary) (the) one having been

846 1135 5607 1471 1096 1161 1722 3588 1511
μένῃ αὐτῷ γυναικί, οὔσῃ ἐγκύῳ. 6 ἐγένετο δὲ ἐν τῷ εἶναι
betrothed to him (as) wife, being pregnant. it happened And in being

846 1563 4130 3588 2250 3588 5088 846 2532
αὐτοὺς ἐκεῖ, ἐπλήσθησαν αἱ ἡμέραι τοῦ τεκεῖν αὐτήν. 7 καὶ
they there, were fulfilled the days (for) the bearing (of) her. And

5088 3588 5207 846 3588 4416 2532 4683
ἔτεκε τὸν υἱὸν αὐτῆς τὸν πρωτότοκον, καὶ ἐσπαργάνωσεν
she bore the son of her, the First-born, and she wrapped in a navel band

846 2532 347 846 1722 3588 5336 1360 3756 2258 846
αὐτὸν, καὶ ἀνέκλινεν αὐτὸν ἐν τῇ φάτνῃ, διότι οὐκ ἦν αὐτοῖς
Him and laid Him in the manger, because not was for them

5117 1722 3588 2646
τόπος ἐν τῷ καταλύματι.
a place in the inn.

2532 4166 2258 1722 3588 5561 3588 846 63 2532
8. Καὶ ποιμένες ἦσαν ἐν τῇ χώρᾳ τῇ αὐτῇ ἀγραυλοῦντες καὶ
And shepherds were in the country same living in the fields and

5442 5441 3588 3571 1909 3588 4167 846
φυλάσσοντες φυλακὰς τῆς νυκτὸς ἐπὶ τὴν ποίμνην αὐτῶν.
keeping guard of the night over the flock of them.

2532 2400 32 2962 2186 846 2532 1391 2962
9 καὶ ἰδού, ἄγγελος Κυρίου ἐπέστη αὐτοῖς, καὶ δόξα Κυρίου
And behold! An angel of (the) Lord came on them, and glory of (the) Lord

4034 846 2532 5399 5401 3173 2532
περιέλαμψεν αὐτούς· καὶ ἐφοβήθησαν φόβον μέγαν. 10 καὶ
shone around them; and they feared (with) a fear great. And

2036 846 3588 32 3361 5399 2400 1063 2097
εἶπεν αὐτοῖς ὁ ἄγγελος, Μὴ φοβεῖσθε· ἰδοὺ γὰρ, εὐαγγελ-
said to them the angel, Do not fear, behold for, I proclaim

5213 5479 3173 3748 2071 3956 3588 2992 3754
ίζομαι ὑμῖν χαρὰν μεγάλην, ἥτις ἔσται παντὶ τῷ λαῷ· 11 ὅτι
good news to you, a joy great, which will be to all the people, because

5088 5213 5494 4990 3739 2076 5547 2962 1722 4172
ἐτέχθη ὑμῖν σήμερον Σωτὴρ, ὅς ἐστι Χριστὸς Κύριος, ἐν πόλει
was born to you today a Savior, who is Christ (the) Lord, in the city

1138 2532 5124 5213 3588 4592 2147 1025 4683
Δαβίδ. 12 καὶ τοῦτο ὑμῖν τὸ σημεῖον· εὑρήσετε βρέφος ἐσπαρ-
of David. And this to you a sign: you will find a babe having

2749 1722 3588 5336 2532 1810 1096 4862
γανωμένον, κείμενον ἐν τῇ φάτνῃ. 13 καὶ ἐξαίφνης ἐγένετο σὺν
been wrapped, lying in a manger. And suddenly there was with

3588 32 4128 4756 3770 134 3588
τῷ ἀγγέλῳ πλῆθος στρατιᾶς οὐρανίου, αἰνούντων τὸν
the angel a multitude of (the) host heavenly. praising

2316 2532 3004 1391 1722 5310 2316 2532 1909 1093
Θεὸν, καὶ λεγόντων, 14 Δόξα ἐν ὑψίστοις Θεῷ, καὶ ἐπὶ γῆς
God, and saying, Glory in the highest to God, and on earth

1515 1722 444 2107
εἰρήνη· ἐν ἀνθρώποις εὐδοκία.
peace, among men good will.

King James Version

every one into his own city.
4 And Joseph also went up from Galilee, out of the city of Nazareth, into Judaea, unto the city of David, which is called Bethlehem; (because he was of the house and lineage of David:)

5 To be taxed with Mary his espoused wife, being great with child.
6 And so it was, that, while they were there, the days were accomplished that she should be delivered.
7 And she brought forth her firstborn son, and wrapped him in swaddling clothes, and laid him in a manger; because there was no room for them in the inn.

8. And there were in the same country shepherds abiding in the field, keeping watch over their flock by night.

9 And, lo, the angel of the Lord came upon them, and the glory of the Lord shone round about them: and they were sore afraid.
10 And the angel said unto them, Fear not: for, behold, I bring you good tidings of great joy, which shall be to all people.
11 For unto you is born this day in the city of David a Saviour, which is Christ the Lord.

12 And this (shall be) a sign unto you; Ye shall find the babe wrapped in swaddling clothes, lying in a manger.
13 And suddenly there was with the angel a multitude of the heavenly host praising God, and saying,
14 Glory to God in the highest, and on earth peace, good will toward men.

Literal Translation | **Luke 2:15** | **King James Version**

15 And it happened as the angels departed from them into the heaven, even the men, the shepherds, said to one another, Indeed, let us go as far as Bethlehem, and see this thing which has occurred, which the Lord made known to us.
16 And hurrying, they came and sought out both Mariam and Joseph, and the babe lying in the manger.

2532 1096 5613 565 575 846 1519 3588 3772 3588
15. Καὶ ἐγένετο, ὡς ἀπῆλθον ἀπ' αὐτῶν εἰς τὸν οὐρανὸν οἱ
And it happened, as departed from them into the heaven the
32 2532 3588 444 3588 4166 2036 4314 240
ἄγγελοι, καὶ οἱ ἄνθρωποι οἱ ποιμένες εἶπον πρὸς ἀλλήλους,
angels, even the men, the shepherds, said to one another,
1330 1211 2193 965 2532 1492 3588 4487 5124 3588
Διέλθωμεν δὴ ἕως Βηθλεέμ, καὶ ἴδωμεν τὸ ῥῆμα τοῦτο τὸ
Let us go indeed as far as Bethlehem and see thing this
1096 3739 3588 2962 1107 2254 2532 2064 4692
γεγονός, ὃ ὁ Κύριος ἐγνώρισεν ἡμῖν. 16 καὶ ἦλθον σπεύσαντες,
occurring which the Lord made known to us. And they came hurrying,
2532 429 3588 5037 3137 2532 3588 2501 2532 3588 1025
καὶ ἀνεῦρον τήν τε Μαριὰμ καὶ τὸν Ἰωσήφ, καὶ τὸ βρέφος
and sought out both Mariam (Mary) and Joseph, and the babe
2749 1722 3588 5336 1492 1161 1232 4012 3588
κείμενον ἐν τῇ φάτνῃ. 17 ἰδόντες δὲ διεγνώρισαν περὶ τοῦ
lying in the manger. seeing And they publicly told about the

15 And it came to pass, as the angels were gone away from them into heaven, the shepherds said one to another, Let us now go even unto Bethlehem, and see this thing which is come to pass, which the Lord hath made known unto us.
16 And they came with haste, and found Mary, and Joseph, and the babe lying in a manger.

17 And seeing, they publicly told about the word spoken to them about this Child.

4487 3588 2980 846 4012 3588 3813 5127
ῥήματος τοῦ λαληθέντος αὐτοῖς περὶ τοῦ παιδίου τούτου.
word spoken to them about Child this.

17 And when they had seen (it), they made known abroad the saying which was told them concerning this child.

18 And all those hearing wondered about the things spoken to them by the shepherds.
19 And Mariam kept all these words, meditating in her heart.

2532 3956 3588 191 2296 4012 3588 2980
18 καὶ πάντες οἱ ἀκούσαντες ἐθαύμασαν περὶ τῶν λαληθέντων
And all those hearing wondered concerning the things spoken
5259 3588 4166 4314 846 3588 1161 3137 3956
ὑπὸ τῶν ποιμένων πρὸς αὐτούς. 19 ἡ δὲ Μαριὰμ πάντα
by the shepherds to them. And Mariam (Mary) all
4933 3588 4487 5023 4820 1722 3588 2588
συνετήρει τὰ ῥήματα ταῦτα, συμβάλλουσα ἐν τῇ καρδίᾳ
kept words these, meditating in the heart
846 2532 1994 3588 4166 1392 2532
αὐτῆς. 20 καὶ ἐπέστρεψαν οἱ ποιμένες, δοξάζοντες καὶ
of her. And returned the shepherds, glorifying and

18 And all they that heard (it) wondered at those things which were told them by the shepherds.
19 But Mary kept all these things, and pondered (them) in her heart.

20 And the shepherds returned, glorifying and praising God (for) all things which they heard and saw, even as was spoken to them.

134 3588 2316 1909 3956 3739 191 2532 1492 2531
αἰνοῦντες τὸν Θεὸν ἐπὶ πᾶσιν οἷς ἤκουσαν καὶ εἶδον, καθὼς
praising God at all things which they heard and saw, even as
2980 4314 846
ἐλαλήθη πρὸς αὐτούς.
was spoken to them.

20 And the shepherds returned, glorifying and praising God for all the things that they had heard and seen, as it was told unto them.

21. And when eight days were fulfilled to circumcise the child, His name was called Jesus, (the name) that was called by the angel before He was conceived in the womb.

2532 3753 4130 2250 3638 3588 4059 3588
21. Καὶ ὅτε ἐπλήσθησαν ἡμέραι ὀκτὼ τοῦ περιτεμεῖν τὸ
And when were fulfilled days eight to circumcise the
3813 2532 2564 3588 3686 846 2424 3588 2564 5259
παιδίον, καὶ ἐκλήθη τὸ ὄνομα αὐτοῦ Ἰησοῦς, τὸ κληθὲν ὑπὸ
Child, and was called the name of Him Jesus, that called by
3588 32 4253 3588 4815 846 1722 3588 2836
τοῦ ἀγγέλου πρὸ τοῦ συλληφθῆναι αὐτὸν ἐν τῇ κοιλίᾳ.
the angel before was conceived Him in the womb.

21. And when eight days were accomplished for the circumcising of the child, his name was called JESUS, which was so named of the angel before he was conceived in the womb.

22 And were fulfilled when the days of her cleansing according to the Law of Moses, they took Him up to Jerusalem to present (Him) to the Lord,
23 as it has been written in (the) Law of the Lord: "Every male opening a womb shall be called holy to the Lord;" (Ex. 13:2)
24 and to give a sacrifice according to that said in the Law

2532 3753 4130 3588 2250 3588 2512 846
22. Καὶ ὅτε ἐπλήσθησαν αἱ ἡμέραι τοῦ καθαρισμοῦ αὐτῆς
And when were fulfilled the days of the cleansing of her
2596 3588 3551 3475 321 846 1519 2414
κατὰ τὸν νόμον Μωσέως, ἀνήγαγον αὐτὸν εἰς Ἱεροσόλυμα,
according to the Law of Moses, they took up Him to Jerusalem,
3936 3588 2962 2531 1125 1722 3551 2962
παραστῆσαι τῷ Κυρίῳ 23 [καθὼς γέγραπται ἐν νόμῳ Κυρίου
to present to the Lord, even as it has been written in (the) Law of the Lord:
3754 3956 730 1272 3388 40 3588 2962 2564
ὅτι Πᾶν ἄρσεν διανοῖγον μήτραν ἅγιον τῷ Κυρίῳ κληθήσε-
Every male opening a womb holy to the Lord shall be
2532 3588 1325 2378 2596 3588 2046 1722 3551
ται], 24 καὶ τοῦ δοῦναι θυσίαν κατὰ τὸ εἰρημένον ἐν νόμῳ
called; and to give a sacrifice according to that said in the Law

22 And when the days of her purification according to the law of Moses were accomplished, they brought him to Jerusalem, to present (him) to the Lord;
23 (As it is written in the law of the Lord, Every male that openeth the womb shall be called holy to the Lord;)
24 And to offer a sacrifice according to that which is said in the law

Literal Translation **Luke 2:25** ***King James Version***

of (the) Lord, a pair of turtledoves, or two nestlings of doves. (Lev. 12:8)
25 And behold! There was a man in Jerusalem whose name (was) Simeon. And this man (was) righteous and devout, eagerly expecting (the) Consolation of Israel. And (the) Holy Spirit was upon him.

26 And (it) was to him, having been alerted by the Holy Spirit, (he was), not to see death before he sees the Christ of (the) Lord.

27 And by the Spirit he came into the temple. And (as) the parents (were) bringing in the child Jesus (for) them to do according to the custom of the Law concerning Him,
28 even (Simeon) received Him into his arms. And (he) blessed God and said,

29 Now, Master, You will let Your slave go in peace according to Your word;
30 because my eyes saw Your Salvation,
31 which You prepared before (the) face of all the peoples;
32 a Light for revelation (to the) nations, and a glory of Your people Israel.
33 And Joseph was wondering, also His mother, at the things being spoken concerning Him.
34 And Simeon blessed them and said to His mother Mariam, Behold! This (One) is set for (the) fall and rising of many in Israel, and for a sign spoken against;

35 a sword also will pierce your own soul, so that (the) thoughts of many hearts may be revealed.
36. And there was Anna, a prophetess, a daughter of Phanuel,

2962 2201 5167 2228 1417 3502 4058 2532
Κυρίου, Ζεῦγος τρυγόνων ἢ δύο νεοσσοὺς περιστερῶν. 25 καὶ
of (the) Lord, a pair of turtledoves, or two nestlings of doves. And

2400 2258 444 1722 2419 3739 3686 4826 2532 3588
ἰδοὺ, ἦν ἄνθρωπος ἐν Ἱερουσαλὴμ, ᾧ ὄνομα Σιμεών, καὶ ὁ
behold! was a man in Jerusalem, to whom name (was) Simeon, and

444 3778 1342 2532 2126 4327
ἄνθρωπος οὗτος δίκαιος καὶ εὐλαβής, προσδεχόμενος
man this (was) righteous and devout, eagerly expecting

3874 3588 2474 2532 4151 40 2258 1909 846
παράκλησιν τοῦ Ἰσραήλ, καὶ Πνεῦμα Ἅγιον ἦν ἐπ' αὐτόν.
(the) Consolation of Israel, and (the) Spirit Holy was upon him.

2532 2258 846 5537 5259 3588 4151 3588
26 καὶ ἦν αὐτῷ κεχρηματισμένον ὑπὸ τοῦ Πνεύματος τοῦ
And was to him, having been alerted by the Spirit

40 3361 1492 2288 4250 2228 1492 3588 5547 2962
Ἁγίου, μὴ ἰδεῖν θάνατον πρὶν ἢ ἴδη τὸν Χριστὸν Κυρίου.
Holy, not to see death before he sees the Christ of (the) Lord.

2532 2064 1722 3588 4151 1519 3588 2411 2532 1722 3588 1521
27 καὶ ἦλθεν ἐν τῷ Πνεύματι εἰς τὸ ἱερόν· καὶ ἐν τῷ εἰσαγαγεῖν
And he came in the Spirit into the temple; and in the bringing in

3588 1118 3588 3813 2424 3588 4160 846 2596
τοὺς γονεῖς τὸ παιδίον Ἰησοῦν, τοῦ ποιῆσαι αὐτοὺς κατὰ
the parents the child Jesus, to do them according to

3588 1480 3588 3551 4012 846 2532 846 1209 846
τὸ εἰθισμένον τοῦ νόμου περὶ αὐτοῦ, 28 καὶ αὐτὸς ἐδέξατο αὐτὸ
the custom of the Law concerning Him, even he received Him

1519 3588 43 846 2532 2127 3588 2316 2532 2036
εἰς τὰς ἀγκάλας αὐτοῦ, καὶ εὐλόγησε τὸν Θεὸν, καὶ εἶπε,
into the arms of him, and blessed God, and said,

3568 630 3588 1401 4675 1203 2596 3588 4487 4675
29. Νῦν ἀπολύεις τὸν δοῦλόν σου, δέσποτα, κατὰ τὸ ῥῆμά σου,
Now let go the slave of You, Master, according to the word of You

1722 1515 3754 1492 3588 3788 3450 3588 4992 4675 3739
ἐν εἰρήνη· 30 ὅτι εἶδον οἱ ὀφθαλμοί μου τὸ σωτήριόν σου, 31 ὃ
in peace; because saw the eyes of me the Salvation of You which

2090 2596 4383 3956 3588 2992 5457 1519
ἡτοίμασας κατὰ πρόσωπον πάντων τῶν λαῶν· 32 φῶς εἰς
You prepared before (the) face of all the peoples, a Light for

602 1484 2532 1391 2992 4675 2474 2532 2258
ἀποκάλυψιν ἐθνῶν, καὶ δόξαν λαοῦ σου Ἰσραήλ. 33 καὶ ἦν
revelation (to the) nations, and a glory of people of You, Israel. And was

2501 2532 3588 3384 846 2296 1909 3588 2980
Ἰωσὴφ καὶ ἡ μήτηρ αὐτοῦ θαυμάζοντες ἐπὶ τοῖς λαλου-
Joseph and the mother of Him wondering at the things being

4012 846 2532 2127 846 4826 2532 2036
μένοις περὶ αὐτοῦ. 34 καὶ εὐλόγησεν αὐτοὺς Σιμεὼν, καὶ εἶπε
spoken about Him. And blessed them Simeon, and said

4314 3137 3588 3384 846 2400 778 2749 1519
πρὸς Μαριὰμ τὴν μητέρα αὐτοῦ, Ἰδοὺ, οὗτος κεῖται εἰς
to Mariam (Mary) the mother of Him, Behold! This (One) is set for

4431 2532 386 4183 1722 3588 2474 2532 1519 4592
πτῶσιν καὶ ἀνάστασιν πολλῶν ἐν τῷ Ἰσραὴλ, καὶ εἰς σημεῖον
the fall and rising of many in Israel, and for a sign

483 2532 6751161 846 3588 5590 1330
ἀντιλεγόμενον· 35 καὶ σοῦ δὲ αὐτῆς τὴν ψυχὴν διελεύσεται
spoken against; also of you And of her the soul will pierce

4501 3704 302 601 1537 4183 2588
ῥομφαία· ὅπως ἂν ἀποκαλυφθῶσιν ἐκ πολλῶν καρδιῶν
a sword so as may be revealed out of many hearts

1261 2532 2258 451 4398 2364 5323
διαλογισμοί. 36 καὶ ἦν Ἄννα προφῆτις, θυγάτηρ Φανουήλ,
(the) thoughts. And was Anna a prophetess, a daughter of Phanuel,

of the Lord, A pair of turtledoves, or two young pigeons.
25 And, behold, there was a man in Jerusalem, whose name (was) Simeon; and the same man (was) just and devout, waiting for the consolation of Israel: and the Holy Ghost was upon him.

26 And it was revealed unto him by the Holy Ghost, that he should not see death, before he had seen the Lord's Christ.

27 And he came by the Spirit into the temple: and when the parents brought in the child Jesus, to do for him after the custom of the law,

28 Then took he him up in his arms, and blessed God, and said,

29 Lord, now lettest thou thy servant depart in peace, according to thy word:
30 For mine eyes have seen thy salvation,
31 Which thou hast prepared before the face of all people;
32 A light to lighten the Gentiles, and the glory of thy people Israel.
33 And Joseph and his mother marvelled at those things which were spoken of him.

34 And Simeon blessed them, and said unto Mary his mother, Behold, this (child) is set for the fall and rising again of many in Israel; and for a sign which shall be spoken against;

35 (Yea, a sword shall pierce through thy own soul also,) that the thoughts of many hearts may be revealed.
36. And there was one Anna, a prophetess, the daughter of Phanuel,

Literal Translation

of (the) tribe of Asher. She was advanced in many days, having lived seven years with a husband from her virginity;

37 and she (was) a widow (of) eighty-four years, who did not depart from the temple, serving night and day with fastings and petitions.

38 And coming on at the same hour, she gave thanks to the Lord, and spoke concerning Him to all those in Jerusalem eagerly expecting redemption.

39 And as they finished all things according to (the) Law of (the) Lord, they returned to Galilee, to Nazareth their city.

40 And the Child grew, and became strong in spirit, being filled with wisdom. And the grace of God was on Him.

41. And His parents went into Jerusalem year by year at the Feast of the Passover.

42 And when He was twelve years (old), they, going up to Jerusalem according to the custom of the Feast,

43 and fulfilling the days, in their returning, the boy Jesus remained in Jerusalem. And Joseph and His mother did not know.

44 But supposing Him to be in the company, they went a day on the way. And (they) looked for Him among the relatives and among the friends

45 And not finding Him, they returned to Jerusalem looking for Him.

46 And it happened after three days they found Him in the temple having sat in the midst

Luke 2:37

1537 5443 768 846 4260 1722 2250 4183
ἐκ φυλῆς ᾿Ασήρ· [αὕτη προβεβηκυῖα ἐν ἡμέραις πολλαῖς,
out of (the) tribe of Asher; she (was) advanced in days many,

2198 2094 3326 435 2033 575 3588 3932 846
ζήσασα ἔτη μετὰ ἀνδρὸς ἑπτὰ ἀπὸ τῆς παρθενίας αὐτῆς,
having lived years with a husband seven from the virginity of her,

2532 846 5503 5613 2094 3589 3739 3756
37 καὶ αὕτὴ χήρα ὡς ἐτῶν ὀγδοήκοντατεσσάρων], ἣ οὐκ ἀφί-
and she a widow about years eighty-four, who not

868 575 3588 2411 3521 2532 1162 3000
στατο ἀπὸ τοῦ ἱεροῦ, νηστείαις καὶ δεήσεσι λατρεύουσα
departed from the temple, with fastings and petitions serving

3571 2532 2250 2532 846 846 3588 5610 2186 437
νύκτα καὶ ἡμέραν. 38 καὶ αὕτη αὐτῇ τῇ ὥρᾳ ἐπιστᾶσα ἀνθω-
night and day. And she at the same hour coming on, gave

3588 2962 2532 2980 4012 846 3956 3588
μολογεῖτο τῷ Κυρίῳ, καὶ ἐλάλει περὶ αὐτοῦ πᾶσι τοῖς
thanks to the Lord, and spoke concerning Him to all those

4327 3085 1722 2419 2532 5613 5055
προσδεχομένοις λύτρωσιν ἐν Ἱερουσαλήμ. 39 καὶ ὡς ἐτέλεσαν
expecting redemption in Jerusalem. And as they finished

537 3588 2596 3588 3551 2962 5290 1519 3588
ἅπαντα τὰ κατὰ τὸν νόμον Κυρίου, ὑπέστρεψαν εἰς τὴν
all things according to the Law of (the) Lord, they returned into

1056 1519 3588 4172 846 3478
Γαλιλαίαν, εἰς τὴν πόλιν αὐτῶν Ναζαρέθ.
Galilee, into the city of them Nazareth.

3588 1161 3813 837 2532 2901 4151 4137
40 Τὸ δὲ παιδίον ηὔξανε, καὶ ἐκραταιοῦτο πνεύματι, πληρού-
the And Child grew and became strong in spirit, having been

4678 2532 5485 2316 2258 1909 846
μενον σοφίας· καὶ χάρις Θεοῦ ἦν ἐπ᾽ αὐτό.
filled with wisdom; and the grace of God was on Him.

2532 4198 3588 1118 846 2596 2094 1519 2419
41. Καὶ ἐπορεύοντο οἱ γονεῖς αὐτοῦ κατ᾽ ἔτος εἰς Ἱερουσαλὴμ
And went the parents of Him year by year into Jerusalem

3588 1859 3588 3957 2532 3753 1096 2094 1427 305
τῇ ἑορτῇ τοῦ πάσχα. 42 καὶ ὅτε ἐγένετο ἐτῶν δώδεκα, ἀναβάν-
at the Feast of the Passover. And when He was years twelve, going up

846 1519 2414 2596 3588 1485 3588 1859 2532
των αὐτῶν εἰς Ἱεροσόλυμα κατὰ τὸ ἔθος τῆς ἑορτῆς, 43 καὶ
them into Jerusalem according to the custom of the Feast, and

5048 3588 2250 1722 3588 5290 846
τελειωσάντων τὰς ἡμέρας, ἐν τῷ ὑποστρέφειν αὐτούς, ὑπέ-
fulfilling the days, in the returning of them,

5278 2424 3588 3816 1722 2419 2532 3756 1097 2501
μεινεν Ἰησοῦς ὁ παῖς ἐν Ἱερουσαλήμ· καὶ οὐκ ἔγνω Ἰωσὴφ
remained Jesus the boy in Jerusalem. And not did know Joseph

2532 3588 3384 846 3543 1161 846 1722 3588 4923
καὶ ἡ μήτηρ αὐτοῦ· 44 νομίσαντες δὲ αὐτὸν ἐν τῇ συνοδίᾳ
and the mother of Him; supposing but Him in the company

1511 2064 2250 3598 2532 327 846 1722 3588
εἶναι, ἦλθον ἡμέρας ὁδόν, καὶ ἀνεζήτουν αὐτὸν ἐν τοῖς
to be, they went a day on the way, and looked for Him among the

4773 2532 1722 3588 1110 2532 3361 2147 846
συγγενέσι καὶ ἐν τοῖς γνωστοῖς· 45 καὶ μὴ εὑρόντες αὐτόν,
relatives and among the friends, and not finding Him,

5290 1519 2419 2212 846 2532 1096
ὑπέστρεψαν εἰς Ἱερουσαλὴμ, ζητοῦντες αὐτόν. 46 καὶ ἐγένετο,
they returned to Jerusalem looking for Him. And it was

3326 2250 5140 2147 846 1722 3588 2411 2516 1722 3319
μεθ᾽ ἡμέρας τρεῖς εὗρον αὐτὸν ἐν τῷ ἱερῷ, καθεζόμενον ἐν μέσῳ
after days three they found Him in the temple, having sat amidst

King James Version

of the tribe of Aser: she was of a great age, and had lived with an husband seven years from her virginity;

37 And she (was) a widow of about fourscore and four years, which departed not from the temple, but served (God) with fastings and prayers night and day.

38 And she coming in that instant gave thanks likewise unto the Lord, and spake of him to all them that looked for redemption in Jerusalem.

39 And when they had performed all things according to the law of the Lord, they returned into Galilee, to their own city Nazareth.

40 And the child grew, and waxed strong in spirit, filled with wisdom: and the grace of God was upon him.

41. Now his parents went to Jerusalem every year at the feast of the passover.

42 And when he was twelve years old, they went up to Jerusalem after the custom of the feast.

43 And when they had fulfilled the days, as they returned, the child Jesus tarried behind in Jerusalem; and Joseph and his mother knew not (of it).

44 But they, supposing him to have been in the company, went a day's journey; and they sought him among (their) kinsfolk and acquaintance.

45 And when they found him not, they turned back again to Jerusalem, seeking him.

46 And it came to pass, that after three days they found him in the temple, sitting in the midst

Literal Translation

Luke 2:47

King James Version

of the teachers, even hearing them and questioning them.

47 And all those hearing Him were amazed at His intelligence and answers.
48 And seeing Him, they were astonished. And His mother said to Him, Child, why did You do so to us? Behold, Your father and I were looking for You, greatly distressed.

49 And He said to them, Why did you look for me? Did you not know that I must be (busy) in the (affairs) of My Father?
50 And they did not understand the word which He spoke to them.
51 And He went with them and came to Nazareth and was being subject to them. And His mother carefully kept all these words in her heart.

3588 1320 2532 191 846 2532 1905
τῶν διδασκάλων, καὶ ἀκούοντα αὐτῶν, καὶ ἐπερωτῶντα
the teachers, even hearing them, and questioning

846 1839 1161 3956 3588 191 846 1909 3588
αὐτούς. 47 ἐξίσταντο δὲ πάντες οἱ ἀκούοντες αὐτοῦ ἐπὶ τῇ
them. were amazed And all those hearing Him at the

4907 2532 3588 612 846 2532 1492 846
συνέσει καὶ ταῖς ἀποκρίσεσιν αὐτοῦ. 48 καὶ ἰδόντες αὐτὸν
intelligence and the answers of Him. And seeing Him,

1605 2532 4314 846 3588 3384 846 2036 5043 5101
ἐξεπλάγησαν· καὶ πρὸς αὐτὸν ἡ μήτηρ αὐτοῦ εἶπε, Τέκνον, τί
they were astonished, and to Him the mother of Him said, Child, why

4160 2254 3779 2400 3588 3962 4675 2504 3600
ἐποίησας ἡμῖν οὕτως; ἰδού, ὁ πατήρ σου κἀγὼ ὀδυνώμενοι
did You do to us so? Behold, the father of you and I very distressed

2212 4571 2532 2036 4314 846 5101 3754 2212 3165 3756
ἐζητοῦμέν σε. 49 καὶ εἶπε πρὸς αὐτούς, Τί ὅτι ἐζητεῖτέ με; οὐκ
are looking for You. And He said to them, Why that you looked for Me? Not

1492 3754 1722 3588 3588 3962 3450 1163 1511 3165 2532 846 3756
ᾔδειτε ὅτι ἐν τοῖς τοῦ πατρός μου δεῖ εἶναί με; 50 καὶ αὐτοὶ οὐ
knew you that in the (affairs) of the Father of Me must be Me? And they not

4920 3588 4487 3739 2980 846 2532 2597 3326 846
συνῆκαν τὸ ῥῆμα ὃ ἐλάλησεν αὐτοῖς. 51 καὶ κατέβη μετ᾽ αὐτῶν,
understood the word which He spoke to them. And He went with them

2532 2064 1519 3478 2532 2258 5293 846 2532 3588
καὶ ἦλθεν εἰς Ναζαρέθ· καὶ ἦν ὑποτασσόμενος αὐτοῖς· καὶ ἡ
and came into Nazareth, and was being subject to them. And the

3384 846 1301 3956 3588 4487 5023 1722 3588
μήτηρ αὐτοῦ διετήρει πάντα τὰ ῥήματα ταῦτα ἐν τῇ
mother of Him carefully kept all sayings these in the

2588 846
καρδίᾳ αὐτῆς.
heart of her.

of the doctors, both hearing them, and asking them questions.
47 And all that heard him were astonished at his understanding and answers.
48 And when they saw him, they were amazed: and his mother said unto him, Son, why hast thou thus dealt with us? behold, thy father and I have sought thee sorrowing.

49 And he said unto them, How is it that ye sought me? wist ye not that I must be about my Father's business?
50 And they understood not the saying which he spake unto them.
51 And he went down with them, and came to Nazareth, and was subject unto them: but his mother kept all these sayings in her heart.

52 And Jesus progressed (in) wisdom and stature and favor before God and men. (see 1 Sam. 2:26)

2532 2424 4298 4678 2532 2244 2532 5485 3844
52. Καὶ Ἰησοῦς προέκοπτε σοφίᾳ καὶ ἡλικίᾳ, καὶ χάριτι παρὰ
And Jesus progressed (in) wisdom and stature and favor before

2316 2532 444
Θεῷ καὶ ἀνθρώποις.
God and men.

52 And Jesus increased in wisdom and stature, and in favour with God and man.

Luke 3

1. And in (the) fifteenth year of the government of Tiberius Caesar, Pontius Pilate governing Judea, and Herod ruling as tetrarch of Galilee, and his brother Philip ruling as tetrarch of Iturea and (the) Trachonitis country, and Lysanias ruling as tetrarch of Abilene,

2 upon (the) high priesthood of Anna(s) and Caiaphas, the word of God came on John the son of Zacharias in the desert.
3 And

1722 2094 1161 4003 3588 2231 5086
1. Ἐν ἔτει δὲ πεντεκαιδεκάτῳ τῆς ἡγεμονίας Τιβερίου
in (the) year And fifteenth of the government of Tiberius

2541 2230 4194 4091 3588 2449
Καίσαρος, ἡγεμονεύοντος Ποντίου Πιλάτου τῆς Ἰουδαίας,
Caesar, (during the) governing of Pontius Pilate of Judea,

2532 5075 3588 1056 2264 5376 1161
καὶ τετραρχοῦντος τῆς Γαλιλαίας Ἡρῴδου, Φιλίππου δὲ
and ruling as tetrarch of Galilee Herod, Phillip And

3588 80 846 5075 3588 2484 2532
τοῦ ἀδελφοῦ αὐτοῦ τετραρχοῦντος τῆς Ἰτουραίας καὶ
the brother of him ruling as tetrarch of Iturea and

5139 5561 2532 3078 3588 9 5075
Τραχωνίτιδος χώρας, καὶ Λυσανίου τῆς Ἀβιληνῆς τετραρ-
of Trachonitis country, And Lysanias of Abilene ruling as

1909 749 452 2532 2533 1096 4487
χοῦντος, 2 ἐπ᾽ ἀρχιερέων Ἄννα καὶ Καιάφα, ἐγένετο ῥῆμα
tetrarch, at high priesthood of Anna and Caiaphas, came to be a word

2316 1909 2491 3588 3588 2197 5207 1722 3588 2048 2532
Θεοῦ ἐπὶ Ἰωάννην τὸν τοῦ Ζαχαρίου υἱὸν ἐν τῇ ἐρήμῳ. 3 καὶ
of God upon John the of Zacharias son in the desert. And

1. Now in the fifteenth year of the reign of Tiberius Caesar, Pontius Pilate being governor of Judaea, and Herod being tetrarch of Galilee, and his brother Philip tetrarch of Ituraea and of the region of Trachonitis, and Lysanias the tetrarch of Abilene,

2 Annas and Caiaphas being the high priests, the word of God came unto John the son of Zacharias in the wilderness.
3 And

Literal Translation **Luke 3:4** ***King James Version***

he came into the neighborhood of the Jordan, proclaiming a baptism of repentance for remission of sins,
4 as it has been written in (the) roll of (the) words of Isaiah the prophet, saying: "(the) voice of (one) crying in the wilderness, Prepare the way of (the) Lord, make His paths straight;

5 every valley shall be filled up, and every mountain and hill shall be laid low; and the crooked (places) shall be made into straight, and the rough into smooth ways;
6 and all flesh shall see the salvation of God." (Isa. 40:35)

7 Then he said to the crowds having gone out to be baptized by him, Offspring of vipers! Who warned you to flee from the coming wrath?
8 Then produce fruits worthy of repentance, and do not begin to say within yourselves, We have Abraham (as) father. For I say to you that God is able to raise up children (to) Abraham out of these stones.
9 And also the axe is already laid to the root of the trees; therefore, every tree not producing good fruit is being cut down and being thrown into (the) fire.
10 And the crowd asked him, saying, What then shall we do?
11 And answering, he said to them, The (one) having two tunics, let him give to the (one) not having. And the (one) having foods, let him do the same.
12 And tax collectors also came to be baptized. And they said to him, Teacher, what shall we do?
13 And he said to them, Continue to do no

2064 1519 3956 3588 4066 3588 2446 2784
ἦλθεν εἰς πᾶσαν τὴν περίχωρον τοῦ Ἰορδάνου, κηρύσσων
he came into all the neighborhood the Jordan, proclaiming

908 3341 1519 859 266 5613 1125 1722
βάπτισμα μετανοίας εἰς ἄφεσιν ἁμαρτιῶν· 4 ὡς γέγραπται ἐν
a baptism of repentance for remission of sins, as it has been written in

976 3056 2268 3588 4396 3004 5456
βίβλῳ λόγων Ἡσαΐου τοῦ προφήτου, λέγοντος, Φωνὴ
(the) roll of (the) words of Isaiah the prophet, saying, (The) voice

994 1722 3588 2048 2090 3588 3598 2962 2117
βοῶντος ἐν τῇ ἐρήμῳ, Ἑτοιμάσατε τὴν ὁδὸν Κυρίου· εὐθείας
of crying in the wilderness, prepare the way of (the) Lord, straight

4160 3588 5147 846 3956 5327 4137
ποιεῖτε τὰς τρίβους αὐτοῦ. 5 πᾶσα φάραγξ πληρωθήσεται,
make the paths of Him; every valley shall be filled up

2532 3956 3735 2532 1015 5013 2532 2071 3588
καὶ πᾶν ὄρος καὶ βουνὸς ταπεινωθήσεται· καὶ ἔσται τὰ
and every mountain and hill shall be laid low; and shall be the

4646 1519 2117 2532 3588 5138 1519 3598 3006 2532
σκολιὰ εἰς εὐθείαν, καὶ αἱ τραχεῖαι εἰς ὁδοὺς λείας· 6 καὶ
crooked into straight, and the rough (places) into ways smooth; and

3700 3956 4561 3588 4992 3588 2316
ὄψεται πᾶσα σὰρξ τὸ σωτήριον τοῦ Θεοῦ.
shall see all flesh the salvation of God.

3004 3767 3588 1607 3793 907 5259
7. Ἔλεγεν οὖν τοῖς ἐκπορευομένοις ὄχλοις βαπτισθῆναι ὑπ'
he said Then to the having gone out crowds to be baptized by

846 1081 2191 5101 5263 5213 5343 575
αὐτοῦ, Γεννήματα ἐχιδνῶν, τίς ὑπέδειξεν ὑμῖν φυγεῖν ἀπὸ
him, Offspring of vipers! Who warned you to flee from

3588 3195 3709 4160 3767 2590 514 3588
τῆς μελλούσης ὀργῆς; 8 ποιήσατε οὖν καρποὺς ἀξίους τῆς
the coming wrath? produce Then fruits worthy

3341 2532 3361 756 3004 1722 1438 3962 2192
μετανοίας· καὶ μὴ ἄρξησθε λέγειν ἐν ἑαυτοῖς, Πατέρα ἔχομεν
of repentance; and not do begin to say within yourselves,(As) father we have

3588 11 3004 1063 5213 3754 1410 3588 2316 1537 3588
τὸν Ἀβραάμ· λέγω γὰρ ὑμῖν ὅτι δύναται ὁ Θεὸς ἐκ τῶν
Abraham. I say For to you that is able God out of

3037 5130 1453 5043 3588 11 2235 1161 2532 3588 513
λίθων τούτων ἐγεῖραι τέκνα τῷ Ἀβραάμ. 9 ἤδη δὲ καὶ ἡ ἀξίνη
stones these to raise up children (to) Abraham. already And also the axe

4314 3588 4491 3588 1186 2749 3956 3767 1186 3361
πρὸς τὴν ῥίζαν τῶν δένδρων κεῖται· πᾶν οὖν δένδρον μὴ
to the root of the trees is laid; every therefore tree not

4160 2590 2570 1581 2532 1519 4442 906 2532
ποιοῦν καρπὸν καλὸν ἐκκόπτεται καὶ εἰς πῦρ βάλλεται. 10 καὶ
producing fruit good is being cut down and into fire being cast. And

1905 846 3588 3793 3004 5101 3767 4160
ἐπηρώτων αὐτὸν οἱ ὄχλοι λέγοντες, Τί οὖν ποιήσωμεν;
asked him the crowd, saying, What, then, shall we do?

611 1161 3004 846 3588 2192 1417 5509 3330
11 ἀποκριθεὶς δὲ λέγει αὐτοῖς, Ὁ ἔχων δύο χιτῶνας μεταδότω
answering And he said to them, He having two tunics, let him give

3588 3361 2192 2532 3588 2192 1033 3668 4160 2064
τῷ μὴ ἔχοντι· καὶ ὁ ἔχων βρώματα ὁμοίως ποιείτω. 12 ἦλθον
to the (one) not having; and he having foods the same let him do. came

1161 2532 5057 907 2532 2036 4314 846
δὲ καὶ τελῶναι βαπτισθῆναι, καὶ εἶπον πρὸς αὐτόν,
And also tax-collectors to be baptized, and said to him,

1320 5101 4160 3588 1161 2036 4314 846 3367
Διδάσκαλε, τί ποιήσομεν; 13 ὁ δὲ εἶπε πρὸς αὐτούς, Μηδὲν
Teacher, what shall we do? And he said to them, Nothing

he came into all the country about Jordan, preaching the baptism of repentance for the remission of sins;
4 As it is written in the book of the words of Esaias the prophet, saying, The voice of one crying in the wilderness, Prepare ye the way of the Lord, make his paths straight.

5 Every valley shall be filled, and every mountain and hill shall be brought low; and the crooked shall be made straight, and the rough ways (shall be) made smooth;
6 And all flesh shall see the salvation of God.

7 Then said he to the multitude that came forth to be baptized of him, O generation of vipers, who hath warned you to flee from the wrath to come?
8 Bring forth therefore fruits worthy of repentance, and begin not to say within yourselves, We have Abraham to (our) father: for I say unto you, That God is able of these stones to raise up children unto Abraham.
9 And now also the axe is laid unto the root of the trees: every tree therefore which bringeth not forth good fruit is hewn down, and cast into the fire.
10 And the people asked him, saying, What shall we do then?
11 He answereth and saith unto them, He that hath two coats, let him impart to him that hath none; and he that hath meat, let him do likewise.
12 Then came also publicans to be baptized, and said unto him, Master, what shall we do?
13 And he said unto them, Exact no

Literal Translation **Luke 3:14** ***King James Version***

more besides that commanded to you.
14 And also ones serving as soldiers asked him, saying, And we, what shall we do? And he said to them, Do not forcibly extort anyone nor accuse falsely, and be satisfied with your pay.

15. But the people expecting, and all reasoning in their hearts about John, lest perhaps he is the Christ,

16 John answered to all, saying, I indeed baptize you in water; but He stronger than I comes, of whom I am not worthy to loosen the thong of His sandals. He will baptize you in (the) Holy Spirit and fire,

17 whose sifting fan (is) in His hand; and He will fully purge His threshing-floor, and will gather the wheat into His barn; but the chaff He will burn up with unquenchable fire.

18 And then indeed exhorting many different things, he proclaimed the gospel to the people.
19. But Herod the tetrarch, having been reproved by him concerning the wife of his brother, Herodias, and concerning all (the) evil things Herod did,
20 he also added this above all, he even shut up John in the prison.

21. And it happened, in the baptizing (of) all the people, Jesus also being baptized, and praying,

4119 3844 3588 1299 5213 4238 1905
πλέον παρὰ τὸ διατεταγμένον ὑμῖν πράσσετε. 14 ἐπηρώ-
more besides that commanded to you keep doing. asked

1161 846 2532 4754 3004 2532 2249 5101
των δὲ αὐτὸν καὶ στρατευόμενοι, λέγοντες, Καὶ ἡμεις τί
And him also ones serving as soldiers, saying, And we, what

4160 2532 2036 4314 846 3367 1286
ποιήσομεν; καὶ εἶπε πρὸς αὐτοῖς, Μηδένα διασείσητε,
shall we do? And he said to them, No one forcibly extort,

3366 4811 2532 714 3588 3800 5216
μηδὲ συκοφαντήσητε· καὶ ἀρκεῖσθε τοῖς ὀψωνίοις ὑμῶν.
nor accuse falsely; and be satisfied with the pay of you.

4328 1161 3588 2992 2532 1260 3956
15. Προσδοκῶντος δὲ τοῦ λαοῦ, καὶ διαλογιζομένων πάντων
expecting But the people, and reasoning all

1722 3588 2588 846 4012 3588 2491 3379 846
ἐν ταῖς καρδίαις αὐτῶν περὶ τοῦ Ἰωάννου, μήποτε αὐτὸς
in the hearts of them concerning John,, lest perhaps he

1498 3588 5547 611 3588 2491 537 3004 1473
εἴη ὁ Χριστός, 16 ἀπεκρίνατο ὁ Ἰωάννης, ἅπασι λέγων, Ἐγὼ
is the Christ, answered John to all, saying, I

3303 5204 907 5209 2064 1161 3588 2478 3450 3739
μὲν ὕδατι βαπτίζω ὑμᾶς· ἔρχεται δὲ ὁ ἰσχυρότερός μου, οὗ
indeed in water baptize you; comes But He stronger than me, of whom

3756 1510 2425 3089 3588 2438 3588 5266 846
οὐκ εἰμὶ ἱκανὸς λῦσαι τὸν ἱμάντα τῶν ὑποδημάτων αὐτοῦ·
not I am worthy to loose the thong of the sandals of Him;

846 5209 907 1722 4151 40 2532 4442 3739 3588
αὐτὸς ὑμᾶς βαπτίσει ἐν Πνεύματι Ἁγίῳ καὶ πυρί· 17 οὗ τὸ
He you will baptize in (the) Spirit Holy and fire; of whom the

4425 1722 3588 5495 846 2532 1245 3588 257 846
πτύον ἐν τῇ χειρὶ αὐτοῦ, καὶ διακαθαριεῖ τὴν ἅλωνα αὐτοῦ,
fan (is) in the hand of Him, and He will fully purge the threshing floor of Him,

2532 4863 3588 4621 1519 3588 596 846 3588 1161 892
καὶ συνάξει τὸν σῖτον εἰς τὴν ἀποθήκην αὐτοῦ, τὸ δὲ ἄχυρον
and will gather the wheat into the barn of Him; the but chaff

2618 4442 762
κατακαύσει πυρὶ ἀσβέστῳ.
He will burn up with fire unquenchable.

4183 3303 3767 2532 2087 3870 2097
18 Πολλὰ μὲν οὖν καὶ ἕτερα παρακαλῶν εὐηγγελίζετο
Many things indeed then and different exhorting, he proclaimed the gospel

3588 2992 3588 1161 2264 3588 5076 1651 5259 846
τὸν λαόν· 19 ὁ δὲ Ἡρώδης ὁ τετράρχης, ἐλεγχόμενος ὑπ' αὐτοῦ
to the people. But Herod the tetrarch, having been reproved by him

4012 2266 3588 1135 5376 3588 80 846
περὶ Ἡρωδιάδος τῆς γυναικὸς Φιλίππου τοῦ ἀδελφοῦ αὐτοῦ,
concerning Herodias the wife of Phillip the brother of him,

2532 4012 3956 3739 4160 4190 3588 2264 4369
καὶ περὶ πάντων ὧν ἐποίησε πονηρῶν ὁ Ἡρώδης, 20 προσέ-
and concerning all things which did evil Herod, he

2532 4124 1909 3956 2532 2623 3588 2491 1722 3588
θηκε καὶ τοῦτο ἐπὶ πᾶσι, καὶ κατέκλεισε τὸν Ἰωάννην ἐν τῇ
added also this above all, even he shut up John in the

5438
φυλακῇ.
prison.

1096 1161 1722 3588 907 537 3588 2992 2532
21. Ἐγένετο δὲ ἐν τῷ βαπτισθῆναι ἅπαντα τὸν λαόν, καὶ
it was And in the baptizing (of) all the people, also

2424 907 2532 4336 455 3588
Ἰησοῦ βαπτισθέντος καὶ προσευχομένου, ἀνεῳχθῆναι τὸν
Jesus being baptized and praying, was opened the

more than that which is appointed you.
14 And the soldiers likewise demanded of him, saying, And what shall we do? And he said unto them, Do violence to no man, neither accuse (any) falsely; and be content with your wages.

15. And as the people were in expectation, and all men mused in their hearts of John, whether he were the Christ, or not;

16 John answered, saying unto (them) all, I indeed baptize you with water; but one mightier than I cometh, the latchet of whose shoes I am not worthy to unloose: he shall baptize you with the Holy Ghost and with fire:

17 Whose fan (is) in his hand, and he will throughly purge his floor, and will gather the wheat into his garner; but the chaff he will burn with fire unquenchable.

18 And many other things in his exhortation preached he unto the people.
19. But Herod the tetrarch, being reproved by him for Herodias his brother Philip's wife, and for all the evils which Herod had done,
20 Added yet this above all, that he shut up John in prison.

21. Now when all the people were baptized, it came to pass, that Jesus also being baptized, and praying, the heaven was opened,
22 And the Holy Ghost descended in a bodily

Literal Translation

the heaven was opened;
22 and the Holy Spirit came down in a bodily form as a dove upon Him. And a voice out of Heaven occurred, saying, You are My Son, the Beloved; I am delighted in You. (Ps. 2:7; Isa. 42:1)

23. And Jesus Himself was beginning to be about thirty years (old), being, as was supposed, the son of Joseph, (the son) of Heli,
24 (the son) of Matthat, (the son) of Levi, (the son) of Melchi, (the son) of Janna, (the son) of Joseph,
25 (the son) of Mattathias, (the son) of Amos, (the son) of Nahum, (the son) of Esli, (the son) of Naggai,
26 (the son) of Maath, (the son) of Mattathias, (the son) of Semei, (the son) of Joseph, (the son) of Judah,
27 (the son) of Joannas, (the son) of Rhesa, (the son) of Zerubbabel, (the son) of Shealtiel, (the son) of Neri,

28 (the son) of Melchi, (the son) of Addi, (the son) of Cosam, (the son) of Elmodam, (the son) of Er,
29 (the son) of Joses, (the son) of Eliezer, (the son) of Jorim, (the son) of Matthat, (the son) of Levi,
30 (the son) of Simeon, (the son) of Judah, (the son) of Joseph, (the son) of Jonan, (the son) of Eliakim,
31 (the son) of Melea, (the son) of Menan, (the son) of Mattatha, (the son) of Nathan, (the son) of David,
32 (the son) of Jesse, (the son) of Obed, (the son) of Boaz, (the son) of Salmon, (the son) of Nahshon,
33 (the son) of Amminadab, (the son) of Aram, (the son) of Hezron, (the son) of Pharez, (the son) of Judah,
34 (the son) of Jacob, (the son) of Isaac, (the son) of Abraham, (the son) of Terah, (the son) of Nahor,
35 (the son) of Serug, (the son) of Reu, (the son) of Peleg, (the son) of Eber, (the son) of Salah,
36 (the son) of Cainan, (the son) of Arphaxad, (the son) of Shem, (the son) of Noah, (the son) of Lamech,
37 (the son) of Methuselah, (the son) of Enoch, (the son) of Jared, (the son) of Mahalaleel, (the son) of Cainan;
38 (the son)

Luke 3:22

3772 2532 2597 3588 4151 3588 40 4984
οὐρανόν, 22 καὶ καταβῆναι τὸ Πνεῦμα τὸ Ἅγιον σωματικῷ
heaven, and came down the Spirit Holy in a bodily

1491 5616 4058 1909 846 2532 5456 1537 3772
εἴδει ὡσεὶ περιστερὰν ἐπ' αὐτόν, καὶ φωνὴν ἐξ οὐρανοῦ
form as a dove upon Him, and a voice out of Heaven

1096 3004 4771 1488 3588 5207 3450 3588 27 1722 4671
γενέσθαι, λέγουσαν, Σὺ εἶ ὁ υἱός μου ὁ ἀγαπητός, ἐν σοὶ
occurred, saying, You are the Son of Me, the Beloved; in You

2106
ηὐδόκησα.
I am delighted.

2532 846 2258 3588 2424 5616 2094 5144 756
23. Καὶ αὐτὸς ἦν ὁ Ἰησοῦς ὡσεὶ ἐτῶν τριάκοντα ἀρχόμενος,
And Himself was Jesus about years (old) thirty beginning

5607 5613 3543 5207 2501 3588 2242 3588 3158 3588
ὢν [ὡς ἐνομίζετο] υἱὸς Ἰωσήφ, τοῦ Ἡλί, 24 τοῦ Ματθάτ, τοῦ
being, as was supposed son of Joseph, of Heli, of Mattatha,

3017 3588 3197 3588 2388 3588 2501 3588 3161
Λευΐ, τοῦ Μελχί, τοῦ Ἰαννά, τοῦ Ἰωσήφ, 25 τοῦ Ματταθίου,
of Levi, of Melchi, of Janna, of Joseph, of Mattathias,

,3588 301 3588 3486 3588 2069 3588 3477 3588 3092
τοῦ Ἀμώς, τοῦ Ναούμ, τοῦ Ἑσλί, τοῦ Ναγγαί 26 τοῦ Μαάθ,
of Amos, of Nahum, of Esli, of Naggai, of Maath

3588 3161 3588 4584 3588 2501 3588 2455 3588
τοῦ Ματταθίου, τοῦ Σεμεΐ, τοῦ Ἰωσήφ, τοῦ Ἰούδα, 27 τοῦ
of Mattathias, of Semei, of Joseph, of Judah,

2490 3588 4488 3588 2216 3588 4528 3588
Ἰωαννᾶ, τοῦ Ῥησά, τοῦ Ζοροβάβελ, τοῦ Σαλαθιήλ, τοῦ
of Joannes, of Rhesa, of Zerubbabel, of Salathiel,

3518 3588 3197 3588 78 3588 2973 3588 1678
Νηρί, 28 τοῦ Μελχί, τοῦ Ἀδδί, τοῦ Κωσάμ, τοῦ Ἐλμωδάμ,
of Neri, of Melchi, of Addi, of Cosam, of Elmodam,

3588 2262 3588 2499 3588 1663 3588 2497 3588 3158
τοῦ Ἤρ, 29 τοῦ Ἰωσή, τοῦ Ἐλιέζερ, τοῦ Ἰωρείμ, τοῦ Ματθάτ,
of Er, of Joses, of Eliezer, of Jorim, of Matthai,

3588 3017 3588 4826 3588 2455 3588 2501 3588 2494
τοῦ Λευΐ, 30 τοῦ Σιμεών, τοῦ Ἰούδα, τοῦ Ἰωσήφ, τοῦ Ἰωνάν,
of Levi. of Simeon, of Judah, of Joseph, of Jonan,

3588 1662 3588 3190 3588 3104 3588 3160 3588
τοῦ Ἐλιακείμ, 31 τοῦ Μελεᾶ, τοῦ Μενάμ, τοῦ Ματταθά, τοῦ
of Eliakim, of Melea, of Menam, of Mattatha,

3481 3588 1138 3588 2421 3588 5601 3588 1003 3588
Ναθάν, τοῦ Δαβίδ, 32 τοῦ Ἰεσσαί, τοῦ Ὠβήδ, τοῦ Βοόζ, τοῦ
of Nathan, of David, of Jesse, of Obed, of Boaz,

4533 3588 3476 3588 284 3588 689 3588
Σαλμών, τοῦ Ναασσών, 33 τοῦ Ἀμιναδάβ, τοῦ Ἀράμ, τοῦ
of Salmon, of Nahshon, of Amminadab, of Ram,

2074 3588 5329 3588 2455 3588 2384 3588 2464
Ἑσρώμ, τοῦ Φαρές, τοῦ Ἰούδα, 34 τοῦ Ἰακώβ, τοῦ Ἰσαάκ,
of Hezron, of Pharez, of Judah, of Jacob, of Isaac,

3588 11 3588 2291 3588 3493 3588 4562 3588
τοῦ Ἀβραάμ, τοῦ Θάρα, τοῦ Ναχώρ, 35 τοῦ Σαρούχ, τοῦ
of Abraham, of Terah, of Nahor, of Serug,

4466 3588 5317 3588 1443 3588 4527 3588 2536 3588
Ῥαγαῦ, τοῦ Φαλέκ, τοῦ Ἑβέρ, τοῦ Σαλά, 36 τοῦ Καϊνάν, τοῦ
of Reu, of Peleg, of Eber, of Salah, of Cainan,

742 3588 4590 3588 5575 3588 2984 3588 3103
Ἀρφαξάδ, τοῦ Σήμ, τοῦ Νῶε, τοῦ Λάμεχ, 37 τοῦ Μαθουσάλα,
or Arphaxad, of Shem, of Noah, of Lamech, of Mathuselah,

3588 1802 3588 2391 3588 3121 3588 2536 3588
τοῦ Ἑνώχ, τοῦ Ἰαρέδ, τοῦ Μαλελεήλ, τοῦ Καϊνάν, 38 τοῦ
of Enoch, of Jared, of Mahalaleel, of Cainan,

King James Version

shape like a dove upon him, and a voice came from heaven, which said, Thou art my beloved Son; in thee I am well pleased.
23. And Jesus himself began to be about thirty years of age, being (as was supposed) the son of Joseph, which was (the son) of Heli, **24** Which was (the son) of Matthat, which was (the son) of Levi, which was (the son) of Melchi, which was (the son) of Janna, which was (the son) of Joseph, **25** Which was (the son) of Mattathias, which was (the son) of Amos, which was (the son) of Naum, which was (the son) of Esli, which was (the son) of Nagge, **26** Which was (the son) of Maath, which was (the son) of Mattathias, which was (the son) of Semei, which was (the son) of Joseph, which was (the son) of Juda, **27** Which was (the son) of Joanna, which was (the son) of Rhesa, which was (the son) of Zorobabel, which was (the son) of Salathiel, which was (the son) of Neri,
28 Which was (the son) of Melchi, which was (the son) of Addi, which was (the son) of Cosam, which was (the son) of Elmodam, which was (the son) of Er, **29** Which was (the son) of Jose, which was (the son) of Eliezer, which was (the son) of Jorim, which was (the son) of Matthat, which was (the son) of Levi,
30 Which was (the son) of Simeon, which was (the son) of Juda, which was (the son) of Joseph, which was (the son) of Jonan, which was (the son) of Eliakim, **31** Which was (the son) of Melea, which was (the son) of Menan, which was (the son) of Mattatha, which was (the son) of Nathan, which was (the son) of David, **32** Which was (the son) of Jesse, which was (the son) of Obed, which was (the son) of Booz, which was (the son) of Salmon, which was (the son) of Naasson,
33 Which was (the son) of Aminadab, which was (the son) of Aram, which was (the son) of Esrom, which was (the son) of Phares, which was (the son) of Juda,
34 Which was (the son) of Jacob, which was (the son) of Isaac, which was (the son) of Abraham, which was (the son) of Thara, which was (the son) of Nachor, **35** Which was (the son) of Saruch, which was (the son) of Ragau, which was (the son) of Phalec, which was (the son) of Heber, which was (the son) of Sala, **36** Which was (the son) of Cainan, which was (the son) of Arphaxad, which was (the son) of Sem, which was (the son) of Noe, which was (the son) of Lamech,
37 Which was (the son) of Mathusala, which was (the son) of Enoch, which was (the son) of Jared, which was (the son) of Maleleel, which was (the son) of Cainan,

Literal Translation

of Enos, (the son) of Seth, (the son) of Adam, (the son) of God.

Luke 4

1. And full of (the) Holy Spirit, Jesus returned from the Jordan, and was led by the Spirit into the wilderness,
2 forty days being tried by the devil. And He ate nothing in those days, and they being ended, afterwards He hungered.

3 And the devil said to Him, If You are Son of God, speak to this stone that it become a loaf.

4 And Jesus answered to him, saying, It has been written: "Man shall not live on bread alone, but on every word of God." (Deut. 8:3)
5 And the devil bringing Him up into a high mountain, he showed Him all the kingdoms of the inhabited earth in a moment of time.
6 And the devil said to Him, I will give all this authority and their glory to You, because it has been delivered to me, and I give it to whomever I desire.

7 Then if You worship before me, all will be Yours.
8 And answering, to him, Jesus said, Go behind Me, Satan! For it has been written: "You shall worship (the) Lord your God, and Him only you shall serve." (Deut. 6:13)

9 And he brought Him to Jerusalem, and stood Him on the wing of the temple, and said to Him, If You are the Son of God, throw Yourself down from here;

Luke 4:1

1800 3588 4589 3588 76 3588 2316
Ἐνώς, τοῦ Σήθ, τοῦ Ἀδάμ, τοῦ Θεοῦ.
of Enos, of Seth, of Adam, of God.

Luke 4

2424 1161 4151 40 4134 5290 575 3588
1. Ἰησοῦς δὲ Πνεύματος Ἁγίου πλήρης ὑπέστρεψεν ἀπὸ τοῦ
Jesus And of (the) Spirit Holy full returned from the
2446 2532 71 1722 3588 4151 1519 3588 2048 2250
Ἰορδάνου, καὶ ἤγετο ἐν τῷ Πνεύματι εἰς τὴν ἔρημον, 2 ἡμέρας
Jordan, and was led by the Spirit into the wilderness; days
5062 3985 5259 3588 1228 2532 3756
τεσσαράκοντα πειραζόμενος ὑπὸ τοῦ διαβόλου. καὶ οὐκ
forty being tried by the devil. And not
5315 3762 1722 3588 2250 1565 2532 4931
ἔφαγεν οὐδὲν ἐν ταῖς ἡμέραις ἐκείναις· καὶ συντελεσθεισῶν
He ate nothing, in days those; and being ended
846 5305 3983 2532 2036 846 3588 1228 1487
αὐτῶν, ὕστερον ἐπείνασε. 3 καὶ εἶπεν αὐτῷ ὁ διάβολος, Εἰ
them, afterwards He hungered. And said to Him the devil, If
5207 1488 3588 2316 2036 3588 3037 5129 2443 1096 740
υἱὸς εἶ τοῦ Θεοῦ, εἰπὲ τῷ λίθῳ τούτῳ ἵνα γένηται ἄρτος.
Son You are of God, speak to stone this that it become a loaf.
2532 611 2424 4314 846 3004 1125 3754
4 καὶ ἀπεκρίθη Ἰησοῦς πρὸς αὐτόν, λέγων, Γέγραπται ὅτι
And answered Jesus to him, saying, It has been written,
3756 1909 740 3441 2198 3588 444 235 1909 3956
Οὐκ ἐπ' ἄρτῳ μόνῳ ζήσεται ὁ ἄνθρωπος, ἀλλ' ἐπὶ παντὶ
Not on bread alone shall live man, but on every
4487 2316 2532 321 846 3588 1228 1519 3735
ῥήματι Θεοῦ. 5 καὶ ἀναγαγὼν αὐτὸν ὁ διάβολος εἰς ὄρος
word of God. And bringing up Him the devil into a mount
5308 1166 846 3956 3588 932 3588 3625
ὑψηλὸν ἔδειξεν αὐτῷ πάσας τὰς βασιλείας τῆς οἰκουμένης
high, he showed him all the kingdoms of the inhabited earth
1722 4743 5550 2532 2036 846 3588 1228 4671 1325 3588
ἐν στιγμῇ χρόνου. 6 καὶ εἶπεν αὐτῷ ὁ διάβολος, Σοὶ δώσω τὴν
in a moment of time. And said to Him the devil, To You I will give
1849 3778 537 2532 3588 1391 846 3754 1698
ἐξουσίαν ταύτην ἅπασαν καὶ τὴν δόξαν αὐτῶν· ὅτι ἐμοὶ
authority this all, and the glory of them, because to me
3860 2532 3739 1437 2309 1325 846 4771 3767 1437
παραδέδοται, καὶ ᾧ ἐὰν θέλω δίδωμι αὐτήν. 7 σὺ οὖν ἐὰν
it has been delivered, and to whomever I desire I give it. You then if
4352 1799 3450 2071 4675 3956 2532 611
προσκυνήσῃς ἐνώπιόν μου, ἔσται σου πάντα. 8 καὶ ἀποκριθεὶς
You worship before me, will be of You all. And answering
846 2036 3588 2424 5217 3694 3450 4567
αὐτῷ εἶπεν ὁ Ἰησοῦς, Ὕπαγε ὀπίσω μου, Σατανᾶ·
to him said Jesus, Go behind Me, Satan!
1125 1063 4352 2962 3588 2316 4675 2532
γέγραπται γάρ, Προσκυνήσεις Κύριον τὸν Θεόν σου, καὶ
it has been written For, You shall worship (the) Lord the God of you, and
846 3441 3000 2532 71 846 519 2419
αὐτῷ μόνῳ λατρεύσεις. 9 καὶ ἤγαγεν αὐτὸν εἰς Ἱερουσαλήμ,
Him only your shall serve. And he brought Him to Jerusalem
2532 2476 846 1909 3588 4419 3588 2411 2532 2036
καὶ ἔστησεν αὐτὸν ἐπὶ τὸ πτερύγιον τοῦ ἱεροῦ, καὶ εἶπεν
and stood Him on the wing of the temple, and said
846 1487 3588 5207 1488 3588 2316 906 4572 1782 2736
αὐτῷ, Εἰ ὁ υἱὸς εἶ τοῦ Θεοῦ, βάλε σεαυτὸν ἐντεῦθεν κάτω·
to Him, If the Son You are of God, throw Yourself from here down

King James Version

38 Which was (the son) of Enos, which was (the son) of Seth, which was (the son) of Adam, which was (the son) of God.

Luke 4

1. And Jesus being full of the Holy Ghost returned from Jordan, and was led by the Spirit into the wilderness,
2 Being forty days tempted of the devil. And in those days he did eat nothing: and when they were ended, he afterward hungered.

3 And the devil said unto him, If thou be the Son of God, command this stone that it be made bread.

4 And Jesus answered him, saying, It is written, That man shall not live by bread alone, but by every word of God.

5 And the devil, taking him up into an high mountain, shewed unto him all the kingdoms of the world in a moment of time.
6 And the devil said unto him, All this power will I give thee, and the glory of them: for that is delivered unto me; and to whomsoever I will I give it.

7 If thou therefore wilt worship me, all shall be thine.
8 And Jesus answered and said unto him, Get thee behind me, Satan: for it is written, Thou shalt worship the Lord thy God, and him only shalt thou serve.

9 And he brought him to Jerusalem, and set him on a pinnacle of the temple, and said unto him, If thou be the Son of God, cast thyself down from hence:

Literal Translation | **Luke 4:10** | **King James Version**

10 for it has been written: "He will command His angels about You, even to protect You,
11 that on (their) hands they shall bear You, lest you strike Your foot against a stone." (Ps. 91:11, 12)
12 And answering, Jesus said to him, It has been said: "You shall not tempt (the) Lord your God." (Deut. 6:16)
13 And having finished every trial, the devil departed from Him until a season.

1125 1063 3754 3588 32 846 1781 4012
10 γέγραπται γὰρ ὅτι Τοῖς ἀγγέλοις αὐτοῦ ἐντελεῖται περὶ
it has been written for, To the angels of Him He will command about
4675 3588 1314 4571 2532 3754 1909 5495 142 4571
σοῦ τοῦ διαφυλάξαι σε· 11 καὶ ὅτι Ἐπὶ χειρῶν ἀροῦσί σε,
You to protect You, even that on (their) hands they will bear You
3379 4350 4314 3037 3588 4228 4675 2532 611
μήποτε προσκόψῃς πρὸς λίθον τὸν πόδα σου. 12 καὶ ἀπο-
that not You strike against a stone the foot of You. And
2036 846 3588 2424 3754 2046 3756 1598
κριθεὶς εἶπεν αὐτῷ ὁ Ἰησοῦς ὅτι Εἴρηται, Οὐκ ἐκπειράσεις
answering said to him Jesus, it has been said, Not you shall tempt
2962 3588 2316 4675 2532 4931 3956 3986 3588
Κύριον τὸν Θεόν σου. 13 καὶ συντελέσας πάντα πειρασμὸν ὁ
(the) Lord the God of you. And having finished every trial , the
1228 868 · 575 846 891 2540
διάβολος ἀπέστη ἀπ' αὐτοῦ ἄχρι καιροῦ.
devil departed from Him until a season.

10 For it is written, He shall give his angels charge over thee, to keep thee:
11 And in (their) hands they shall bear thee up, lest at any time thou dash thy foot against a stone.
12 And Jesus answering said unto him, It is said, Thou shalt not tempt the Lord thy God.
13 And when the devil had ended all the temptation, he departed from him for a season.

14. And Jesus returned in the power of the Spirit into Galilee. And a report went out through all the neighborhood about Him.
15 And He taught in their synagogues, being glorified by all.

2532 5290 3588 2424 1722 3588 1411 3588 4151
14. Καὶ ὑπέστρεψεν ὁ Ἰησοῦς ἐν τῇ δυνάμει τοῦ Πνεύματος
And returned Jesus in the power of the Spirit
1519 3588 1056 2532 5345 1831 2596 3650 3588 4066
εἰς τὴν Γαλιλαίαν· καὶ φήμη ἐξῆλθε καθ' ὅλης τῆς περιχώρου
into Galilee. And a report went out through all the neighborhood
4012 846 2532 846 1321 1722 3588 4864
περὶ αὐτοῦ. 15 καὶ αὐτὸς ἐδίδασκεν ἐν ταῖς συναγωγαῖς
about Him. And He taught in the synagogues
846 1392 5259 3956
αὐτῶν, δοξαζόμενος ὑπὸ πάντων.
of them, being glorifed by all.

14. And Jesus returned in the power of the Spirit into Galilee: and there went out a fame of him through all the region round about.
15 And he taught in their synagogues, being glorified of all.

16. And He came into Nazareth where He was brought up. And according to His custom, He went in on the day of the sabbaths, into the synagogue, and (He) stood up to read.
17 And a scroll of Isaiah the prophet was handed to Him. And unrolling the scroll, He found the place where (it) was written:
18 "(The) Spirit of (the) Lord (is) upon Me. Because of this He anointed Me to proclaim the gospel to (the) poor; He has sent Me to heal the (ones) broken (in) heart, to preach deliverance, to captives and to (the) blind to see again, to send away (the ones) having been crushed in deliverance,
19 to proclaim an acceptable year of (the) Lord." (Isa. 61:1, 2)
20 And rolling up the scroll, returning (it) to the attendant, He sat down. And the eyes of all in the synagogue were

2532 2064 1519 3478 3757 2258 5142 2532
16. Καὶ ἦλθεν εἰς τὴν Ναζαρέθ, οὗ ἦν τεθραμμένος· καὶ
And He came into Nazareth, where He was brought up. And
1525 2596 3588 1486 846 1722 3588 2250 3588 4521
εἰσῆλθε κατὰ τὸ εἰωθὸς αὐτῷ, ἐν τῇ ἡμέρᾳ τῶν σαββάτων
He went in according to the custom to Him in the day of the sabbaths,
1519 3588 4864 2532 450 314 2532 1922
εἰς τὴν συναγωγήν, καὶ ἀνέστη ἀναγνῶναι. 17 καὶ ἐπεδόθη
into the synagogue and stood up to read. And was handed
846 975 2268 3588 4396 2532 380 3588
αὐτῷ βιβλίον Ἠσαΐου τοῦ προφήτου. καὶ ἀναπτύξας τὸ
to Him a roll of Isaiah the prophet And unrolling the
975 2147 3588 5117 3757 2258 1125 4151 2962
βιβλίον, εὗρε τὸν τόπον οὗ ἦν γεγραμμένον, 18 Πνεῦμα Κυρίου
roll He found the place where was being written,(The) Spirit of (the) Lord
1909 1691 3739 1752 5548 3165 2097 4434 649
ἐπ' ἐμέ, οὗ ἕνεκεν ἔχρισέ με εὐαγγελίζεσθαι πτωχοῖς· ἀπέ-
(is) on Me, because of this He anointed Me to proclaim the gospel to (the) poor;
3165 2390 3588 4937 3588 2588
σταλκέ με ἰάσασθαι τοὺς συντετριμμένους τὴν καρδίαν·
He has sent Me to heal the (ones) having been broken (in) heart;
2784 164 859 2532 5185 309
κηρύξαι αἰχμαλώτοις ἄφεσιν, καὶ τυφλοῖς ἀνάβλεψιν,
to preach to captives deliverance, and to (the) blind to see again.
649 2352 1722 859 2784 1763
ἀποστεῖλαι τεθραυσμένους ἐν ἀφέσει, 19 κηρύξαι ἐνιαυτὸν
to send away having been crushed (ones) in deliverance, to proclaim a year
2962 1184 2532 4428 3588 975 591 3588 5257
Κυρίου δεκτόν. 20 καὶ πτύξας τὸ βιβλίον, ἀποδοὺς τῷ ὑπηρέτῃ,
(the) Lord acceptable to. And rolling up the roll, returning (it) to the attendant,
2523 2532 3956 1722 3588 4864 3588 3788 2258
ἐκάθισε· καὶ πάντων ἐν τῇ συναγωγῇ οἱ ὀφθαλμοὶ ἦσαν
He sat. And of all in the synagogue the eyes were

16. And he came to Nazareth, where he had been brought up: and, as his custom was, he went into the synagogue on the sabbath day, and stood up for to read.
17 And there was delivered unto him the book of the prophet Esaias. And when he had opened the book, he found the place where it was written,
18 The Spirit of the Lord (is) upon me, because he hath anointed me to preach the gospel to the poor; he hath sent me to heal the brokenhearted, to preach deliverance to the captives, and recovering of sight to the blind, to set at liberty them that are bruised,
19 To preach the acceptable year of the Lord.
20 And he closed the book, and he gave (it) again to the minister, and sat down. And the eyes of all them that were in the synagogue were

Luke 4:21

Literal Translation

fixed on Him.
21 And He began to say to them, Today this Scripture has been fulfilled in your ears.

22 And all bore witness to Him, and wondered at the words of grace coming out of His mouth. And they said, Is this not the son of Joseph?
23 And He said to them, undoubtedly you will speak this parable to Me, Healer heal yourself. What things (we) heard (were) happening in Capernaum, do also here in your native place.

24 But He said, Truly I say to you that no prophet is acceptable in his native-place.

25 But on a truth I say to you, There were many widows in Israel in the days of Elijah when the heaven was shut up over three years and six months, when a great famine came to be on all the land;

26 and yet Elijah was sent to not one of them except to Zarephath of Sidon, to a widow woman.
27 And many lepers were in Israel during the (time of) Elisha the prophet, and not one of them was made clean, except Naaman the Syrian.

28 And all were filled (with) anger, hearing these things in the synagogue.
29 And rising up, they threw Him outside the city, and brought Him up to the brow of the hill on which their city was built, in order to throw Him down.
30 But He went away, passing through their midst.

816 846 756 1161 3004 4314 846 3754
ἀτενίζοντες αὐτῷ. 21 ἤρξατο δὲ λέγειν πρὸς αὐτοὺς ὅτι
fixed on Him. He began And to say to them,

4594 4137 3588 1124 3778 1722 3588 3775 5216
Σήμερον πεπλήρωται ἡ γραφὴ αὕτη ἐν τοῖς ὠσὶν ὑμῶν.
Today has been fulfilled Scripture this in the ears of you.

2532 3956 3140 846 2532 2296 1909 3588 3056
22 καὶ πάντες ἐμαρτύρουν αὐτῷ, καὶ ἐθαύμαζον ἐπὶ τοῖς λόγοις
And all bore witness to Him and wondered at the words

3588 5485 3588 1607 1537 3588 4750 846 2532
τῆς χάριτος τοῖς ἐκπορευομένοις ἐκ τοῦ στόματος αὐτοῦ, καὶ
of grace coming from the mouth of Him.And

3004 3756 3778 2076 3588 5207 2501 2532 2036 4314
ἔλεγον, Οὐχ οὗτός ἐστιν ὁ υἱός Ἰωσήφ; 23 καὶ εἶπε πρὸς
they said, Not this is the son of Joseph? And He said to

846 3843 2046 3427 3588 3850 3778 2395
αὐτούς, Πάντως ἐρεῖτέ μοι τὴν παραβολὴν ταύτην, Ἰατρέ,
them, No doubt you will say to Me parable this, Healer,

2323 4572 3745 191 1096 1722 3588
θεράπευσον σεαυτόν· ὅσα ἠκούσαμεν γενόμενα ἐν τῇ
heal yourself! What things we heard happening in

2584 4160 2532 5602 1722 3588 3968 467 2036 1161
Καπερναούμ, ποίησον καὶ ὧδε ἐν τῇ πατρίδι σου. 24 εἶπε δέ,
Capernaum, do also here in the native-place of you. He said And

281 3004 5213 3754 3762 4396 1184 2076 1722 3588
Ἀμὴν λέγω ὑμῖν ὅτι οὐδεὶς προφήτης δεκτός ἐστιν ἐν τῇ
Truly, I say to you that no prophet acceptable is in the

3968 846 1909 225 1161 3004 5213 4183 5503 2258
πατρίδι αὐτοῦ. 25 ἐπ' ἀληθείας δὲ λέγω ὑμῖν, πολλαὶ χῆραι ἦσαν
native-place of him. on a truth But I say to you, Many widows were

1722 3588 2250 2243 1722 3588 2474 3753 2808 3588
ἐν ταῖς ἡμέραις Ἠλίου ἐν τῷ Ἰσραήλ, ὅτε ἐκλείσθη ὁ
in the days of Elijah in Israel when was shut up the

3772 1909 2094 5140 2532 3376 1803 5613 1096 3042 3173 1909
οὐρανὸς ἐπὶ ἔτη τρία καὶ μῆνας ἕξ, ὡς ἐγένετο λιμὸς μέγας ἐπὶ
heaven over years three and months six, when occurred a famine great on

3956 3588 1093 2532 4314 3762 846 3992 2243
πᾶσαν τὴν γῆν· 26 καὶ πρὸς οὐδεμίαν αὐτῶν ἐπέμφθη Ἠλίας,
all the land. And to not one of them was sent Elijah

1487 3361 1519 4558 3588 4605 4314 1135 5503 2532
εἰ μὴ εἰς Σάρεπτα τῆς Σιδῶνος πρὸς γυναῖκα χήραν. 27 καὶ
except to Zarephath of Sidon, to a woman a widow. And

4183 3015 2258 1909 1666 3588 4396 1722 3588
πολλοὶ λεπροὶ ἦσαν ἐπὶ Ἐλισσαίου τοῦ προφήτου ἐν τῷ
many lepers were during Elisha the prophet in

2474 2532 3762 846 2511 1487 3361 3497 3588 4948
Ἰσραήλ· καὶ οὐδεὶς αὐτῶν ἐκαθαρίσθη εἰ μὴ Νεεμὰν ὁ Σύρος.
Israel, yet not one of them was cleansed except Naaman the Syrian.

2532 4130 3956 2372 1722 3588 4864 191
28 καὶ ἐπλήσθησαν πάντες θυμοῦ ἐν τῇ συναγωγῇ ἀκούοντες
And were filled all (with) anger in the synagogue hearing

5023 2532 450 1544 846 1854 3588 4172 2532
ταῦτα, 29 καὶ ἀναστάντες ἐξέβαλον αὐτὸν ἔξω τῆς πόλεως, καὶ
these things. And rising up they threw Him outside the city, and

71 846 2193 3588 3790 3588 3735 1909 3739 3588 4172
ἤγαγον αὐτὸν ἕως τῆς ὀφρύος τοῦ ὄρους ἐφ' οὗ ἡ πόλις
brought Him up to the brow of the hill on which the city

846 3618 1519 3588 2630 846 846 1161
αὐτῶν ᾠκοδόμητο, εἰς τὸ κατακρημνίσαι αὐτόν. 30 αὐτὸς δὲ
of them was built in order to throw down Him. He But

1330 1223 3319 846 4198
διελθὼν διὰ μέσου αὐτῶν ἐπορεύετο.
passing through (the) midst of them went away.

King James Version

fastened on him.
21 And he began to say unto them, This day is this scripture fulfilled in your ears.

22 And all bare him witness, and wondered at the gracious words which proceeded out of his mouth. And they said, Is not this Joseph's son?
23 And he said unto them, Ye will surely say unto me this proverb, Physician, heal thyself: whatsoever we have heard done in Capernaum, do also here in thy country.

24 And he said, Verily I say unto you, No prophet is accepted in his own country.

25 But I tell you of a truth, many widows were in Israel in the days of Elias, when the heaven was shut up three years and six months, when great famine was throughout all the land;

26 But unto none of them was Elias sent, save unto Sarepta, (a city) of Sidon, unto a woman (that was) a widow.
27 And many lepers were in Israel in the time of Eliseus the prophet; and none of them was cleansed, saving Naaman the Syrian.

28 And all they in the synagogue, when they heard these things, were filled with wrath,
29 And rose up, and thrust him out of the city, and led him unto the brow of the hill whereon their city was built, that they might cast him down headlong.
30 But he passing through the midst of them went his way,

Literal Translation **Luke 4:31** ***King James Version***

31 And He went down to Capernaum, a city of Galilee. And He was teaching them (on) the sabbaths.
32 And they were astonished at His doctrine, because His word was with authority.
33. And in the synagogue was a man having a spirit of an unclean demon. And he cried out with a loud voice,
34 saying, Aha! What is to us and to You, Jesus, Nazarene? Did You come to destroy us? I know You, who You are, the Holy One of God.
35 And Jesus rebuked him, saying, Be silent, and come out from him!, And throwing him into the midst, the demon came out from him, not harming him.

2532 2718 1519 2584 4172 3588 105 2532
31. Καὶ κατῆλθεν εἰς Καφαρναοὺμ πόλιν τῆς Γαλιλαίας· καὶ
And He went down into Capernaum, a city of Galilee. And
2258 1321 846 1722 3588 4521 2532 1605
ἦν διδάσκων αὐτοὺς ἐν τοῖς σάββασι. 32 καὶ ἐξεπλήσσοντο
He was teaching them in the sabbaths. And they were amazed
1909 3588 1322 846 3754 1722 1849 2258 3588 3056 846 2532
ἐπὶ τῇ διδαχῇ αὐτοῦ, ὅτι ἐν ἐξουσίᾳ ἦν ὁ λόγος αὐτοῦ. 33 καὶ
at the doctrine of Him, because with authority was the word of Him. And
1722 3588 4864 2258 444 2192 4151 1140
ἐν τῇ συναγωγῇ ἦν ἄνθρωπος ἔχων πνεῦμα δαιμονίου
in the synagogue was a man having a spirit of a demon
169 2532 349 5456 3173 3004 1436 5101 2254
ἀκαθάρτου, καὶ ἀνέκραξεν φωνῇ μεγάλῃ, λέγων, 34 Ἔα, τί ἡμῖν
unclean, and (he) cried out with a voice loud, saying, Aha! What to us
2532 4671 2424 3479 2064 622 2248 1492
καὶ σοί, Ἰησοῦ Ναζαρηνέ; ἦλθες ἀπολέσαι ἡμᾶς; οἶδά
and to You, Jesus, Nazarene? Did You come to destroy us? I know
4571 5101 1488 3588 40 3588 2316 2532 2008 846 3588
σε τίς εἶ, ὁ ἅγιος τοῦ Θεοῦ. 35 καὶ ἐπετίμησεν αὐτῷ ὁ
You, who You are, the Holy One of God. And rebuked him
2424 3004 5392 2532 1831 1537 846 2532 4496 846
Ἰησοῦς λέγων, Φιμώθητι, καὶ ἔξελθε ἐξ αὐτοῦ. καὶ ῥίψαν αὐτὸν
Jesus, saying, Be silent, and come out from him. And throwing him
3588 1140 1519 3588 3319 1831 575 846 3367 984
τὸ δαιμόνιον εἰς τὸ μέσον ἐξῆλθεν ἀπ' αὐτοῦ, μηδὲν βλάψαν
the demon into the midst came out from him, nothing harming

31 And came down to Capernaum, a city of Galilee, and taught them on the sabbath days.
32 And they were astonished at his doctrine: for his word was with power.
33. And in the synagogue there was a man, which had a spirit of an unclean devil, and cried out with a loud voice,
34 Saying, Let (us) alone; what have we to do with thee, (thou) Jesus of Nazareth? art thou come to destroy us? I know thee who thou art; the Holy One of God.
35 And Jesus rebuked him, saying, Hold thy peace, and come out of him. And when the devil had thrown him in the midst, he came out of him, and hurt him not.

36 And astonishment came on all. And they spoke with one another, saying, What word (is) this, that He commands the unclean spirits with authority and power, and they come out?

846 2532 1096 2285 1909 3956 2532 4814 4314
αὐτόν. 36 καὶ ἐγένετο θάμβος ἐπὶ πάντας, καὶ συνελάλουν πρὸς
him. And came to be astonishment on all and they spoke with
240 3004 5101 3588 3056 3778 3754 1722 1849 2532
ἀλλήλους, λέγοντες, Τίς ὁ λόγος οὗτος, ὅτι ἐν ἐξουσίᾳ καὶ
one another, saying, What (is) word this, that with authority and
1411 2004 3588 169 4151 2532 1831
δυνάμει ἐπιτάσσει τοῖς ἀκαθάρτοις πνεύμασι, καὶ ἐξέρχον-
power He commands the unclean spirits, and they come

36 And they were all amazed, and spake among themselves, saying, What a word (is) this! for with authority and power he commandeth the unclean spirits, and they come out.

37 And a report about Him went out into every place of the neighborhood.

2532 1607 2279 4012 846 1519 3956 5117 3588
ται; 37 καὶ ἐξεπορεύετο ἦχος περὶ αὐτοῦ εἰς πάντα τόπον τῆς
out? And went out a report about Him into every place of the
4066
περιχώρου.
neighborhood.

37 And the fame of him went out into every place of the country round about.

38. And rising up from the synagogue, He went into the house of Simon. And the mother-in-law of Simon was being seized with a great fever. And they asked Him concerning her.
39 And standing over her, He rebuked the fever; and it left her. And instantly rising up, she served them.

450 1161 1537 3588 4864 1525 1519 3588 3614
38. Ἀναστὰς δὲ ἐκ τῆς συναγωγῆς, εἰσῆλθεν εἰς τὴν οἰκίαν
rising up And from the synagogue, He went into the house
4613 3588 3994 1161 3588 4613 2258 4912 4446
Σίμωνος· ἡ πενθερὰ δὲ τοῦ Σίμωνος ἦν συνεχομένη πυρετῷ
of Simon. the mother-in-law And of Simon was being seized with a fever
3173 2532 2065 846 4012 846 2532 2186
μεγάλῳ· καὶ ἠρώτησαν αὐτὸν περὶ αὐτῆς. 39 καὶ ἐπιστὰς
great, and they ask Him concerning her. And standing.
1883 846 2008 3588 4446 2532 863 846
ἐπάνω αὐτῆς, ἐπετίμησε τῷ πυρετῷ, καὶ ἀφῆκεν αὐτήν·
over her, He rebuked the fever, and it left her;
3916 1161 450 1247 846
παραχρῆμα δὲ ἀναστᾶσα διηκόνει αὐτοῖς.
instantly And rising up she served them.

38. And he arose out of the synagogue, and entered into Simon's house. And Simon's wife's mother was taken with a great fever; and they besought him for her.
39 And he stood over her, and rebuked the fever; and it left her: and immediately she arose and ministered unto them.

40. And the sun sinking, all, as many as had sick ones with various diseases, brought them to Him. And

1416 1161 3588 2246 3956 3745 2192 770
40 Δύνοντος δὲ τοῦ ἡλίου, πάντες ὅσοι εἶχον ἀσθενοῦντας
sinking And the sun, all, as many as had sick ones
3554 4164 5627 846 4314 846 3588 1161 1520
νόσοις ποικίλαις ἤγαγον αὐτοὺς πρὸς αὐτόν· ὁ δὲ ἑνὶ
with various diseases brought them to Him. He And one

40. Now when the sun was setting, all they that had any sick with divers diseases brought them unto him; and he

Literal Translation | **Luke 4:41** | ***King James Version***

laying hands on each one of them, He healed them.

41 And also demons came out from many, crying out and saying, You are the Christ, the Son of God! And rebuking (them), He did not allow them to say that they knew Him to be the Christ.

42 And day coming, going out, He went into a deserted place. And the crowds looked for Him, and came up to Him, and held Him fast, not to pass on from them.
43 But He said to them, It is right for Me to proclaim the gospel, the kingdom of God, to the other cities, because to this I was sent.

44 And He was proclaiming in the synagogues of Galilee.

1538 846 3588 5495 2007 2323 846
ἑκάστῳ αὐτῶ τὰς χεῖρας ἐπιθεὶς ἐθεράπευσεν αὐτούς.
each of them the hands laying on healed them.

1831 1161 2532 1140 575 4183 2896 2532 3004
41 ἐξήρχετο δὲ καὶ δαιμόνια ἀπὸ πολλῶν, κράζοντα καὶ λέγοντα
came out And also demons from many, crying out and saying

3754 4771 1488/3588 5547 3588 5207 3588 2316 2532 2008 3759
ὅτι Σὺ εἶ ὁ Χριστὸς ὁ υἱὸς τοῦ Θεοῦ. καὶ ἐπιτιμῶν οὐκ
You are the Christ, the Son of God, And rebuking not

1439 846 2980 3754 1492 3588 5547 846 1511
εἴα αὐτὰ λαλεῖν, ὅτι ᾔδεισαν τὸν Χριοτὸν αὐτὸν εἶναι.
He allowed them to speak, for they knew the Christ Him to be.

1096 1161 2250 1831 4198 1519 2048
42. Γενομένης δὲ ἡμέρας ἐξελθὼν ἐπορεύθη εἰς ἔρημον
having come And day, going out He went into a deserted

5117 2532/3588 3793 2212 846 2532 2064 2193 846
τόπον, καὶ οἱ ὄχλοι ἐπεζήτουν αὐτόν, καὶ ἦλθον ἕως αὐτοῦ,
place. And the crowds looked for Him, and came up to Him,

2532 2722 846 3588/3361 4198 575 846 3588/1161 2036
καὶ κατεῖχον αὐτὸν τοῦ μὴ πορεύεσθαι ἀπ' αὐτῶν. 43 ὁ δὲ εἶπε
and held fast Him, not to pass on from them. He And said

4314 846 3754 2532 3588 2087 4172 2097
πρὸς αὐτοὺς ὅτι Καὶ ταῖς ἑτέραις πόλεσιν εὐαγγελίσασθαί
to them, Also to the other cities to proclaim the gospel

3165 1163 3588 932 3588 2316 3754 1519 5124 649
με δεῖ τὴν βασιλείαν τοῦ Θεοῦ, ὅτι εἰς τοῦτο ἀπέσταλμαι.
Me it behooves the kingdom of God, because to this I was sent.

2532 2258 2784 1722 3588 4864 3588 1056
44 Καὶ ἦν κηρύσσων ἐν ταῖς συναγωγαῖς τῆς Γαλιλαίας.
And He was proclaiming in the synagogues of Galilee.

laid his hands on every one of them, and healed them.

41 And devils also came out of many, crying out, and saying, Thou art Christ the Son of God. And he rebuking (them) suffered them not to speak: for they knew that he was Christ.

42 And when it was day, he departed and went into a desert place: and the people sought him, and came unto him, and stayed him, that he should not depart from them.
43 And he said unto them, I must preach the kingdom of God to other cities also: for therefore am I sent.

44 And he preached in the synagogues of Galilee.

Luke 5

1. And it happened in the crowd pressing on Him to hear the Word of God, even He was standing beside Lake Gennesaret.

2 And He saw two boats standing by the lake, but the fishermen having gone from them had been washing the nets.

3 And entering into one of the boats, which was Simon's, He asked him to put out a little from the land. And sitting down, He taught the crowd from the boat.
4 And as He quit speaking, He said to Simon, Put out into the deep and let down your nets for a haul.

5 And answering Simon said to Him, Master, laboring all through the night

Luke 5

1096 1161 1722 3588 3588 3793 1945 846 3588 191
1. Ἐγένετο δὲ ἐν τῷ τὸν ὄχλον ἐπικεῖσθαι αὐτῷ τοῦ ἀκούειν
it was And in the crowd pressing on Him to hear

3588 3056 3588 2316 2532 846 2258 2476 3844 3588 3041
τὸν λόγον τοῦ Θεοῦ, καὶ αὐτὸς ἦν ἑστὼς παρὰ τὴν λίμνην
the Word of God, even He was standing beside the lake,

1082 2532 1492 1417 4143 2476 3844 3588 3041
Γεννησαρέτ, 2 καὶ εἶδε δύο πλοῖα ἑστῶτα παρὰ τὴν λίμνην·
Gennesaret. And He saw two boats standing beside the lake,

3588 1161 231 576 575 846 637 3588 1350
οἱ δὲ ἁλιεῖς ἀποβάντες ἀπ' αὐτῶν ἀπέπλυναν τὰ δίκτυα.
the but fishermen having gone from them, had been washing the nets.

1684 1161 1519 1520 3588 4143 3739 2258 3588 4613 2065
3 ἐμβὰς δὲ εἰς ἓν τῶν πλοίων, ὃ ἦν τοῦ Σίμωνος. ἠρώτησεν
entering And into one of the boats, which was Simon's, He asked

846 575 3588 1093 1877 3641 2532 2523
αὐτὸν ἀπὸ τῆς γῆς ἐπαναγαγεῖν ὀλίγον. καὶ καθίσας
him from the land to put out a little. And sitting

1321 1537 3588 4143 3588 3793 5613 1161 3973
ἐδίδασκεν ἐκ τοῦ πλοίου τοὺς ὄχλους. 4 ὡς δὲ ἐπαύσατο
He taught from the boat the crowd. as And He quit

2980 2036 4314 3588 4613 1877 1519 3588 899
λαλῶν, εἶπε πρὸς τὸν Σίμωνα, Ἐπανάγαγε εἰς το βάθος
speaking, He said to Simon, Put out into the deep

2532 5465 3588 1350 5216 1519 61 2532 611 3588
καὶ χαλάσατε τὰ δίκτυα ὑμῶν εἰς ἄγραν. 5 καὶ ἀποκριθεὶς ὁ
and let down the nets of you for a haul. And answering

4613 2036 846 1988 1223 3650 3588 3571 2872
Σίμων εἶπεν αὐτῷ, Ἐπιστάτα, δι' ὅλης τῆς νυκτὸς κοπιά-
Simon said to him, Master, through all the night laboring

Luke 5

1. And it came to pass, that, as the people pressed upon him to hear the word of God, he stood by the lake of Gennesaret,

2 And saw two ships standing by the lake: but the fishermen were gone out of them, and were washing (their) nets.

3 And he entered into one of the ships, which was Simon's, and prayed him that he would thrust out a little from the land. And he sat down, and taught the people out of the ship.
4 Now when he had left speaking, he said unto Simon, Launch out into the deep, and let down your nets for a draught.

5 And Simon answering said unto him, Master, we have toiled all the night,

Luke 5:6

Literal Translation

we took nothing. But at Your word I will let down the net.

6 And doing this, they enclosed a great multitude of fish; and their net was being torn.
7 And they signaled the partners, those in the other boat, to come (and) help them. And they came and filled both the boats, so that they were sinking.

8 And seeing Simon Peter fell at the knees of Jesus, saying, Depart from me, for I am a sinful man, Lord.

9 For astonishment took hold of him, and all those with him, at the haul of fish which they took;

10 and likewise James and John, (the) sons of Zebedee, who were sharers with Simon. And Jesus said to Simon, Do not fear. From now on you will be taking men alive.

11 And bringing the boats down onto the land, forsaking all things, they followed Him.

12. And it happened, in His being in one of the cities, even behold, a man full of leprosy! And seeing Jesus, falling on (his) face, he begged Him, saying, Lord, if You choose, You are able to cleanse me.

13 And stretching out the hand He touched him, saying, I will! Be cleansed! And instantly the leprosy departed from him.

14 And He charged him to tell no one. But going away, show yourself to the priest and offer concerning

3762 2983 1909 1161 3588 4487 4675 5465 3588
σαντες οὐδὲν ἐλάβομεν· ἐπὶ δὲ τῷ ῥήματί σου χαλάσω τὸ
nothing we took, on but the word of you I will let down the

1350 2532 5124 4160 4788 2486 4128
δίκτυον. 6 καὶ τοῦτο ποιήσαντες συνέκλεισαν ἰχθύων πλῆθος
net. And this doing, they enclosed of fish a multitude

4183 1284 1161 3588 1350 846 2532 2656
πολύ· διερρήγνυτο δὲ τὸ δίκτυον αὐτῶν. 7 καὶ κατένευσαν
much, was being torn and the net of them. And they signaled

3588 3353 3588 1722 3588 2087 4143 3588 2064 4815
τοῖς μετόχοις τοις ἐν τῷ ἑτέρῳ πλοίῳ, τοῦ ἐλθόντας συλ-
the partners, those in the other boat coming to

846 2532 2064 2532 4130 297 3588
λαβέσθαι αὐτοῖς· καὶ ἦλθον, καὶ ἔπλησαν ἀμφότερα τὰ
help them. And they came and filled both the

4143 5620 1036 846 1492 1161 4613 4074
πλοῖα, ὥστε βυθίζεσθαι αὐτά. 8 ἰδὼν δὲ Σίμων Πέτρος
boats, so as were sinking they. seeing And Simon Peter

4363 3588 1119 3588 2424 3004 1831 575 1700
προσέπεσε τοῖς γόνασι τοῦ Ἰησοῦ λέγων, Ἔξελθε ἀπ' ἐμοῦ,
fell at the knees of Jesus, saying, Depart from me,

3754 435 268 1510 2962 2285 1063 4023
ὅτι ἀνὴρ ἁμαρτωλός εἰμι, Κύριε. 9 θάμβος γὰρ περιέσχεν
because a man sinful I am, Lord. astonishment For seized

846 2532 3956 3588 4862 846 1909 3588 61 3588 2486 3739
αὐτὸν καὶ πάντας τοὺς σὺν αὐτῷ, ἐπὶ τῇ ἄγρᾳ τῶν ἰχθύων ᾗ
him and all the (ones) with him at the haul of the fish which

4815 3668 1161 2532 2385 2532 2491 5207
συνέλαβον· 10 ὁμοίως δὲ καὶ Ἰάκωβον καὶ Ἰωάννην, υἱοὺς
they took. likewise And also James and John, sons

2199 3739 2258 2844 3588 4613 2532 2036 4314 3588
Ζεβεδαίου, οἳ ἦσαν κοινωνοὶ τῷ Σίμωνι. καὶ εἶπε πρὸς τὸν
of Zebedee, who were sharers with Simon. And said to

4613 3588 2424 3361 5399 575 3588 3568 444 2071
Σίμωνα ὁ Ἰησοῦς, Μὴ φοβοῦ· ἀπὸ τοῦ νῦν ἀνθρώπους ἔσῃ
Simon Jesus, Not do fear, from now men you will be

2221 2532 2609 3588 4143 1909 3588 1093 863
ζωγρῶν. 11 καὶ καταγαγόντες τὰ πλοῖα ἐπὶ τὴν γῆν, ἀφέντες
taking alive. And bringing down the boats onto the land, forsaking

537 190 846
ἅπαντα, ἠκολούθησαν αὐτῷ.
all things, they followed Him.

2532 1096 1722 3588 1511 846 1722 3391 3588 4172 2532
12. Καὶ ἐγένετο ἐν τῷ εἶναι αὐτὸν ἐν μιᾷ τῶν πόλεων, καὶ
And it happened in the being of Him in one of the cities, and

2400 435 4134 3014 2532 1492 3588 2424 4098
ἰδοὺ, ἀνὴρ πλήρης λέπρας· καὶ ἰδὼν τὸν Ἰησοῦν, πεσὼν
behold, a man full of leprosy. And seeing Jesus, falling

1909 4383 1189 846 3004 2962 1437 2309
ἐπὶ πρόσωπον, ἐδεήθη αὐτοῦ, λέγων, Κύριε, ἐὰν θέλῃς,
on (his) face, the begged Him, saying, Lord, if You choose

1410 3165 2511 2532 1614 3588 5495 680 846
δύνασαί με καθαρίσαι. 13 καὶ ἐκτείνας τὴν χεῖρα ἥψατο αὐτοῦ,
You are able me to cleanse. And stretching out the hand He touched him,

2036 2309 2511 2532 2112 3588 3014 565 575
εἰπών, Θέλω, καθαρίσθητι. καὶ εὐθέως ἡ λέπρα ἀπῆλθεν ἀπ'
saying, I choose, Be cleansed! And instantly the leprosy departed from

846 2532 846 3853 846 3367 2036 235
αὐτοῦ. 14 καὶ αὐτὸς παρήγγειλεν αὐτῷ μηδενὶ εἰπεῖν· ἀλλὰ
him. And He charged him no one to tell, but

565 1166 4572 3588 2409 2532 4374 4012 3588
ἀπελθὼν δεῖξον σεαυτὸν τῷ ἱερεῖ, καὶ προσένεγκε περὶ τοῦ
going away show yourself to the priest, and offer concerning the

King James Version

and have taken nothing: nevertheless at thy word I will let down the net.
6 And when they had this done, they inclosed a great multitude of fishes: and their net brake.
7 And they beckoned unto (their) partners, which were in the other ship, that they should come and help them. And they came, and filled both the ships, so that they began to sink.
8 When Simon Peter saw (it), he fell down at Jesus' knees, saying, Depart from me; for I am a sinful man, O Lord.

9 For he was astonished, and all that were with him, at the draught of the fishes which they had taken:

10 And so (was) also James, and John, the sons of Zebedee, which were partners with Simon. And Jesus said unto Simon, Fear not; from henceforth thou shalt catch men.

11 And when they had brought their ships to land, they forsook all, and followed him.

12. And it came to pass, when he was in a certain city, behold a man full of leprosy: who seeing Jesus fell on (his) face, and besought him, saying, Lord, if thou wilt, thou canst make me clean.

13 And he put forth (his) hand, and touched him, saying, I will: be thou clean. And immediately the leprosy departed from him.

14 And he charged him to tell no man: but go, and shew thyself to the priest, and offer for thy

Literal Translation | **Luke 5:15** | **King James Version**

your cleansing, as Moses commanded for a testimony to them.

2512 4675 2531 4367 3475 1519 3142
καθαρισμοῦ σου, καθὼς προσέταξε Μωσῆς, εἰς μαρτύριον
cleansing of you, even as commanded Moses for a testimony

846 1330 1161 3123 3588 3056 4012 846 2532 4905
αὐτοῖς. 15 διήρχετο δὲ μᾶλλον ὁ λόγος περὶ αὐτοῦ· καὶ συν-
to them. spread But even more the word concerning Him. And were

cleansing, according as Moses commanded, for a testimony unto them.

15. But the word about Him spread even more. And large crowds were coming to hear and to be healed from their infirmities by Him.
16 But He was drawing back in the deserted (places), and praying.

3793 4183 191 2532 2323 5259 846
ήρχοντο ὄχλοι πολλοὶ ἀκούειν, καὶ θεραπεύεσθαι ὑπ' αὐτοῦ
coming crowds large to hear, and to be healed by Him

575 3588 769 846 846 1161 2258 5298 1722 3588
ἀπὸ τῶν ἀσθενειῶν αὐτῶν· 16 αὐτὸς δὲ ἦν ὑποχωρῶν ἐν ταῖς
from the infirmities of them. He But was withdrawing in the

2048 2532 4336
ἐρήμοις καὶ προσευχόμενος.
deserted (places) and praying.

15. But so much the more went there a fame abroad of him: and great multitudes came together to hear, and to be healed by him of their infirmities.
16 And he withdrew himself into the wilderness, and prayed.

17. And it happened on one of the days, and He was teaching. And Pharisees and teachers of (the) Law were sitting by, who were coming out of every village of Galilee and Judea, and Jerusalem. And (the) power of (the) Lord was there, for the curing (of) them.

2532 1096 1722 3391 3588 2250 2532 846 2258 1321
17. Καὶ ἐγένετο ἐν μιᾷ τῶν ἡμερῶν, καὶ αὐτὸς ἦν διδάσκων·
And it was in one of the days, and He was teaching.

2532 2258 2521 5330 2532 3547 3739 2258
καὶ ἦσαν καθήμενοι Φαρισαῖοι καὶ νομοδιδάσκαλοι, οἳ ἦσαν
And were sitting Pharisees and teachers of the Law, who were

2064 1537 3956 2968 3588 1056 2532 2449 2532
ἐληλυθότες ἐκ πάσης κώμης τῆς Γαλιλαίας καὶ Ἰουδαίας καὶ
coming out of every village of Galilee and Judea and

2419 2532 1411 2962 2258 1519 3588 2390 846
Ἱερουσαλήμ· καὶ δύναμις Κυρίου ἦν εἰς τὸ ἰᾶσθαι αὐτούς.
Jerusalem. And power of (the) Lord was, to the curing (of) them.

17. And it came to pass on a certain day, as he was teaching, that there were Pharisees and doctors of the law sitting by, which were come out of every town of Galilee, and Judaea, and Jerusalem: and the power of the Lord was (present) to heal them.

18. And, behold, men carrying on a cot a man who was (one) having been paralyzed. And they sought to bring him in and to lay (him) before Him.
19 And not finding what way they might bring him in through the crowd, going up on the housetop, they let him down with the cot through the tiles into the midst, in front of Jesus.
20 And seeing their faith, He said to him, Man, your sins have been remitted to you.
21 And the scribes and Pharisees began to reason, saying, Who is this who speaks blasphemies? Who is able to remit sins except God alone?

2532 2400 435 5342 1909 2825 444 3449 2253 886
18 καὶ ἰδού, ἄνδρες φέροντες ἐπὶ κλίνης ἄνθρωπον ὃς ἦν παρα-
And, behold, men carrying on a cot a man who was (one)

2532 2212 846 1533 2532 5087 1799
λελυμένος, καὶ ἐζήτουν αὐτὸν εἰσενεγκεῖν καὶ θεῖναι ἐνώπιον
having been paralyzed, and they sought Him to bring in and to lay before

846 2532 3361 2147 1223 4169 1533 846 1223
αὐτοῦ· 19 καὶ μὴ εὑρόντες διὰ ποίας εἰσενέγκωσιν αὐτὸν διὰ
Him. And not finding by what way they may bring in him through

3588 3793 305 1909 3588 1430 1223 3588 2766
τὸν ὄχλον ἀναβάντες ἐπὶ τὸ δῶμα, διὰ τῶν κεράμων
the crowd, going up on the housetop through the tiles

2524 846 4862 3588 2826 1519 3588 3319 1715 3588
καθῆκαν αὐτὸν σὺν τῷ κλινιδίῳ εἰς τὸ μέσον ἔμπροσθεν τοῦ
they let down him with the cot into the midst in front of

2424 2532 1492 3588 4102 846 2036 846 444
Ἰησοῦ. 20 καὶ ἰδὼν τὴν πίστιν αὐτῶν, εἶπεν αὐτῷ, Ἄνθρωπε,
Jesus. And seeing the faith of them, He said to him, Man,

863 4671 3588 266 4675 2532 756 1260
ἀφέωνταί σοι αἱ ἁμαρτίαι σου. 21 καὶ ἤρξαντο διαλογίζεσθαι
have been remitted to you the sins of you. And began to reason

3588 1122 2532 3588 5330 3004 5101 2076 3778
οἱ γραμματεῖς καὶ οἱ Φαρισαῖοι, λέγοντες, Τίς ἐστιν οὗτος
the scribes and the Pharisees, saying, Who is this one

3739 2980 988 5101 1410 863 266 1487 3361
ὃς λαλεῖ βλασφημίας; τίς δύναται ἀφιέναι ἁμαρτίας, εἰ μὴ
who speaks blasphemies? Who is able to remit sins, except

18. And, behold, men brought in a bed a man which was taken with a palsy: and they sought (means) to bring him in, and to lay (him) before him.
19 And when they could not find by what (way) they might bring him in because of the multitude, they went upon the housetop, and let him down through the tiling with (his) couch into the midst before Jesus.
20 And when he saw their faith, he said unto him, Man, thy sins are forgiven thee.
21 And the scribes and the Pharisees began to reason, saying, Who is this which speaketh blasphemies? Who can forgive sins, but God alone?

22 But knowing their reasonings, answering Jesus said to them, Why do you reason in your hearts?
23 What is easier, to say, Your sins have been remitted

3441 3588 2316 1921 1161 3588 2424 3588 1261
μόνος ὁ Θεός; 22 ἐπιγνοὺς δὲ ὁ Ἰησοῦς τοὺς διαλογισμοὺς
only God? knowing But Jesus the reasonings

846 611 2036 4314 846 5101 1260 1722 3588
αὐτῶν ἀποκριθεὶς εἶπε πρὸς αὐτούς, Τί διαλογίζεσθε ἐν ταῖς
of them, answering said to them, Why do you reason in the

2588 5216 5101 2076 2123 2036 863
καρδίαις ὑμῶν; 23 τί ἐστιν εὐκοπώτερον, εἰπεῖν, Ἀφέωνταί
hearts of you? What is easier, to say, Have been remitted

22 But when Jesus perceived their thoughts, he answering said unto them, What reason ye in your hearts?
23 Whether is easier, to say, Thy sins be forgiven thee;

Literal Translation

to you, or to say, Rise up and walk?
24 But that you may know that the Son of man has authority on the earth to remit sins, He said to the one who had been paralyzed, I say to you, Rise up, and taking your cot go to your house.

25 And at once rising up before them, taking (that) on which he was lying, he went to his house glorifying God.

26 And amazement seized all, and they glorified God, and were filled (with) fear, saying, We saw wonderful things today.

27. And after these things, He went out and saw a tax collector named Levi, sitting at the tax office. And (He) said to him, Follow Me!

28 And leaving all things, rising up he followed Him.

29 And Levi made a great feast for Him in his house. And there was a crowd of many tax collectors reclining, and of others who were with them.
30 And their scribes and the Pharisees murmured at His disciples, saying, Why do you eat and drink with tax collectors and sinners?

31 And answering, Jesus said to them, Those being sound have no need of a healer, but the (ones) having illness.

32 I have not come to call righteous ones, but sinners to repentance.
33. But they said to Him, Why do John's disciples fast often,

Luke 5:24

4671 3588 266 4675 2228 2036 1453 2532 4043 2443
σοι αἱ ἁμαρτίαι σου, ἢ εἰπεῖν, Ἔγειραι καὶ περιπάτει; 24 ἵνα
to you the sins of you, or to say, Rise up and walk? that

1161 1492 3754 1849 2192 3588 5207 3588 444 1909 3588 1093
δὲ εἰδῆτε ὅτι ἐξουσίαν ἔχει ὁ υἱὸς τοῦ ἀνθρώπου ἐπὶ τῆς γῆς
But you know that authority has the Son of man on the earth

863 266 2036 3588 3886 4671 3004
ἀφιέναι ἁμαρτίας [εἶπε τῷ παραλελυμένῳ,] Σοὶ λέγω,
to remit sins, He said to the (one) having been paralyzed, To you I say,

1453 2532 142 3588 2826 4675 4198 1519 3588 3624
ἔγειραι, καὶ ἄρας τὸ κλινίδιόν σου, πορεύου εἰς τὸν οἶκόν
Rise up, and taking the cot of you; go to the house

4675 2532 3916 450 1799 846 142 1909 3739
σου. 25 καὶ παραχρῆμα ἀναστὰς ἐνώπιον αὐτῶν, ἄρας ἐφ᾽ ᾧ
of you. And at once rising up before them, taking on which

2621 565 1519 3588 3624 846 1392 3588 2316
κατέκειτο, ἀπῆλθεν εἰς τὸν οἶκον αὐτοῦ, δοξάζων τὸν θεόν.
he was lying, he went to the house of him, glorifying God.

2532 1611 2983 537 2532 1392 3588 2316 2532
26 καὶ ἔκστασις ἔλαβεν ἅπαντας, καὶ ἐδόξαζον τὸν Θεόν, καὶ
And amazement seized all, and they glorified God, and

4130 5401 3004 3754 1492 3861
ἐπλήσθησαν φόβου, λέγοντες ὅτι Εἴδομεν παράδοξα
were filled (with) fear, saying, We saw wonderful things

4594
σήμερον.
today.

2532 3326 5023 1831 2532 2300 5057 3686
27. Καὶ μετὰ ταῦτα ἐξῆλθε, καὶ ἐθεάσατο τελώνην, ὀνόματι
And after these things He went out and saw a tax-collector, by name

3018 2521 1909 3588 5058 2532 2036 846 190
Λευΐν, καθήμενον ἐπὶ τὸ τελώνιον, καὶ εἶπεν αὐτῷ, Ἀκολού-
Levi, sitting at the tax office, and said to him, Follow

3427 2532 2641 537 450 190
θει μοι. 28 καὶ καταλιπὼν ἅπαντα, ἀναστὰς ἠκολούθησεν
Me! And leaving all things rising up he followed

846 2532 4160 1403 3173 3018 846 1722 3588 3614
αὐτῷ. 29 καὶ ἐποίησε δοχὴν μεγάλην Λευὶς αὐτῷ ἐν τῇ οἰκίᾳ
Him. And made a feast great Levi for Him in the house

846 2532 2258 3793 5057 4183 2532 243 3739 2258
αὐτοῦ· καὶ ἦν ὄχλος τελωνῶν πολύς, καὶ ἄλλων οἳ ἦσαν
of him; and was a crowd of tax-collectors large, and of others who were

3326 846 2621 2532 1111 3588 1122
μετ᾽ αὐτῶν κατακείμενοι. 30 καὶ ἐγόγγυζον οἱ γραμματεῖς
with them reclining And murmured the scribes

846 2532 3588 5330 4314 3588 3101 846 3004
αὐτῶν καὶ οἱ Φαρισαῖοι πρὸς τοὺς μαθητὰς αὐτοῦ, λέγοντες,
of them and the Pharisees to the disciples of Him, saying,

1302 3326 5057 2532 268 2068 2532 4095 2532
Διατί μετὰ τελωνῶν καὶ ἁμαρτωλῶν ἐσθίετε καὶ πίνετε; 31 καὶ
Why with tax-collectors and sinners do you eat and drink? And

611 3588 2424 2036 4314 846 3756 5532 2192
ἀποκριθεὶς ὁ Ἰησοῦς εἶπε πρὸς αὐτούς, Οὐ χρείαν ἔχουσιν
answering Jesus said to them, Not need have

3588 5198 2395 235 3588 2560 2192 3756 2064
οἱ ὑγιαίνοντες ἰατροῦ ἀλλ᾽ οἱ κακῶς ἔχοντες· 32 οὐκ ἐλήλυθα
those being sound of a healer, but those badly (illness) having. Not I have come

2564 1342 235 268 1519 3341 3588 1161
καλέσαι δικαίους, ἀλλὰ ἁμαρτωλοὺς εἰς μετάνοιαν. 33 οἱ δὲ
to call righteous ones, but sinners to repentance. they But

2036 4314 846 1302 3588 3101 2491 3522
εἶπον πρὸς αὐτόν, Διατί οἱ μαθηταὶ Ἰωάννου νηστεύουσι
said to Him, Why the disciples of John fast

King James Version

or to say, Rise up and walk?
24 But that ye may know that the Son of man hath power upon earth to forgive sins, (he said unto the sick of the palsy,) I say unto thee, Arise, and take up thy couch, and go into thine house.

25 And immediately he rose up before them, and took up that whereon he lay, and departed to his own house, glorifying God.

26 And they were all amazed, and they glorified God, and were filled with fear, saying, We have seen strange things to day.

27. And after these things he went forth, and saw a publican, named Levi, sitting at the receipt of custom: and he said unto him, Follow me.

28 And he left all, rose up, and followed him.

29 And Levi made him a great feast in his own house: and there was a great company of publicans and of others that sat down with them.

30 But their scribes and Pharisees murmured against his disciples, saying, Why do ye eat and drink with publicans and sinners?

31 And Jesus answering said unto them, They that are whole need not a physician; but they that are sick.

32 I came not to call the righteous, but sinners to repentance.
33. And they said unto him, Why do the disciples of John fast

Luke 5:34

Literal Translation

and make prayers, and likewise those of the Pharisees, but those (close) to You eat and drink?
34 But He said to them, Not are able to make the sons of the bridechamber to fast while the bridegroom is with them, (are you)?

35 But days will come, even when the bridegroom is taken away from them, then in those days they will fast.

36. And He also told a parable to them: No one puts a piece of a new garment on an old garment; otherwise both the new will tear, and with the old will not agree (the) piece from the new.

37 And no one puts new wine into old wineskins; otherwise, the new wine will burst the wineskins, and it will be poured out, and the wineskins will perish.

38 But new wine is to be put into new wineskins, and both are preserved together.
39 and no one drinking old (wine) immediately desires new; for he says, the old is better.

4437 2532 1162 4160 3668 2532 3588 3588 5330
πυκνὰ, καὶ δεήσεις ποιοῦνται, ὁμοίως καὶ οἱ τῶν Φαρισαίων,
often, and prayers make; likewise and those of the Pharisees,

3588 1161 4674 2068 2532 4095 3588 1161 2036 4314 846 3361
οἱ δὲ σοὶ ἐσθίουσι καὶ πίνουσιν. 34 ὁ δὲ εἶπε πρὸς αὐτούς, Μὴ
those but to You eat and drink? He But said to them, Not

1410 3588 5207 3588 3567 1722 3739 3588 3566 3326 846
δύνασθε τοὺς υἱοὺς τοῦ νυμφῶνος, ἐν ᾧ ὁ νυμφίος μετ' αὐτῶν
are able the sons of the bride-chamber while the groom with them

2076 4160 3522 2064 1161 2250 2532 3752
ἐστι ποιῆσαι νηστεύειν; 35 ἐλεύσονται δὲ ἡμέραι, καὶ ὅταν
is to make to fast? will come But days and when

522 575 846 3588 3566 5119 3522 1722
ἀπαρθῇ ἀπ' αὐτῶν ὁ νυμφίος, τότε νηστεύσουσιν ἐν
is taken away from them the bridegroom, then they will fast in

1565 3588 2250 3004 1161 2532 3850 4314 846
ἐκείναις ταῖς ἡμέραις. 36 ἔλεγε δὲ καὶ παραβολὴν πρὸς αὐτοὺς
those days. He told And also a parable to them,

3754 3762 1915 2440 2537 1911 1909 2440
ὅτι Οὐδεὶς ἐπίβλημα ἱματίου καινοῦ ἐπιβάλλει ἐπὶ ἱμάτιον
No one a piece of a garment new puts on a garment

3820 1487 1161 3361 2532 3588 2537 4977 2532 3588 3820
παλαιόν· εἰ δὲ μήγε, καὶ τὸ καινὸν σχίσει, καὶ τῷ παλαιῷ
old, otherwise both the new will tear, and with the old

3756 4856 1915 3588 575 3588 2537 2532 3762 906
οὐ συμφωνεῖ ἐπίβλημα τὸ ἀπὸ τοῦ καινοῦ. 37 καὶ οὐδεὶς βάλλει
not will agree (the) piece from the new. And no one puts

3631 3501 1519 779 3820 1487 1161 3361 4486 3588 3501 3631
οἶνον νέον εἰς ἀσκοὺς παλαιούς· εἰ δὲ μήγε, ῥήξει ο νέος οἶνος
wine new into wineskins old, otherwise will burst the new wine

3588 779 2532 846 1632 2532 3588 779 622
τοὺς ἀσκούς, καὶ αὐτὸς ἐκχυθήσεται, καὶ οἱ ἀσκοὶ ἀπολοῦν-
the wineskins, and it will be poured out, and the wineskins will perish.

235 3631 3501 1519 779 2537 992 2532
ται· 38 ἀλλὰ οἶνον νέον εἰς ἀσκοὺς καινοὺς βλητέον, 39 καὶ
But wine new into wineskins new is to be put, and

297 4933 2532 3762 4095 3820 2112 2309
ἀμφότεροι συντηροῦνται. καὶ οὐδεὶς πιὼν παλαιὸν εὐθέως θέλει
both are preserved together. And no one drinking old at once desires

3501 3004 1063 3588 3820 5543 2076
νέον· λέγει γάρ, Ὁ παλαιὸς χρηστότερός ἐστιν.
new; he says for, The old better is.

King James Version

often, and make prayers, and likewise (the disciples) of the Pharisees; but thine eat and drink?
34 And he said unto them, Can ye make the children of the bridechamber fast, while the bridegroom is with them?

35 But the days will come, when the bridegroom shall be taken away from them, and then shall they fast in those days.
36. And he spake also a parable unto them; No man putteth a piece of a new garment upon an old; if otherwise, then both the new maketh a rent, and the piece that was (taken) out of the new agreeth not with the old.

37 And no man putteth new wine into old bottles; else the new wine will burst the bottles, and be spilled, and the bottles shall perish.

38 But new wine must be put into new bottles; and both are preserved.
39 No man also having drunk old (wine) straightway desireth new: for he saith, The old is better.

Luke 6

1. And it happened on the second chief sabbath, He passed along through the sown fields. And His disciples plucked the heads and were eating, rubbing with the hands.
2 But some of the Pharisees said to them, Why do you do that which is not lawful to do on the sabbaths?

3 And answering, Jesus said to them, Have you not read this, what David did when he hungered,

1096 1161 1722 4521 1207 1279
1. Ἐγένετο δὲ ἐν σαββάτῳ δευτεροπρώτῳ διαπορεύεσθαι
it happened And in a sabbath the second chief passed along

846 1223 3588 4702 2532 5089 3588 3101 846
αὐτὸν διὰ τῶν σπορίμων· καὶ ἔτιλλον οἱ μαθηταὶ αὐτοῦ
He through the sown fields. And plucked the disciples of Him

3588 4719 2532 2068 5597 3588 5495 5100 1161 3588
τοὺς στάχυας, καὶ ἤσθιον, ψώχοντες ταῖς χερσί. 2 τινὲς δὲ τῶν
the heads, and were eating, rubbing with the hands. some And of the

5330 2036 846 5101 4160 3739 3756 1832 4160 1722
Φαρισαίων εἶπον αὐτοῖς, Τί ποιεῖτε ὃ οὐκ ἔξεστι ποιεῖν ἐν
Pharisees said to them, Why do you what not is lawful to do in

3588 4521 2532 611 4314 846 2036 3588 2424
τοῖς σάββασι; 3 καὶ ἀποκριθεὶς πρὸς αὐτοὺς εἶπεν ὁ Ἰησοῦς,
the sabbaths? And answering to them said Jesus,

3761 5124 314 3739 4160 1138 3698 3983
Οὐδὲ τοῦτο ἀνέγνωτε, ὃ ἐποίησε Δαβίδ, ὁπότε ἐπείνασεν
Not this did you read, what did David when he hungered,

1. And it came to pass on the second sabbath after the first, that he went through the corn fields; and his disciples plucked the ears of corn, and did eat, rubbing (them) in (their) hands.
2 And certain of the Pharisees said unto them, Why do ye that which is not lawful to do on the sabbath days?
3 And Jesus answering them said, Have ye not read so much as this, what David did, when himself was an hungred,

Literal Translation | **Luke 6:4** | **King James Version**

and those being with him?
4 How he went into the house of God, and he took of the Loaves of Arrangement, and ate, and even gave to those with him, which it is not lawful to eat, except only the priests?
5 And He said to them, The Son of man is Lord of the sabbath also.

846 2532 3588 3326 846 5607 5613 1525 1519 3588 3624 3588
αὐτὸς καὶ οἱ μετ' αὐτοῦ ὄντες; 4 ὡς εἰσῆλθεν εἰς τὸν οἶκον τοῦ
he and those with him being? As he went into the house
2316 2532 3588 740 3588 4286 2983 5315 2532
Θεοῦ, καὶ τοὺς ἄρτους τῆς προθέσεως ἔλαβε, καὶ ἔφαγε, καὶ
of God, and the loaves of the setting forth he took and ate, and
1325 2532 3588 3326 846 3739 3756 1832 5315 1487 3361 3441
ἔδωκε καὶ τοῖς μετ' αὐτοῦ, οὓς οὐκ ἔξεστι φαγεῖν εἰ μὴ μόνους
gave even to those with him, which not is lawful to eat except only
3588 2409 2532 3004 846 3754 2962 2076 3588 5207 3588
τοὺς ἱερεῖς; 5 καὶ ἔλεγεν αὐτοῖς ὅτι Κύριός ἐστιν ὁ υἱὸς τοῦ
the priests? And He said to them, Lord is The Son
444 2532 3588 4521
ἀνθρώπου καὶ τοῦ σαββάτου.
of man also of the sabbath.

and they which were with him;
4 How he went into the house of God, and did take and eat the shewbread, and gave also to them that were with him; which it is not lawful to eat but for the priests alone?
5 And he said unto them, That the Son of man is Lord also of the sabbath.

6. And it also happened on another sabbath, He going into the synagogue and teaching. And a man was there, and his right hand was withered.
7 And the scribes and the Pharisees kept close by Him, (to see) if He would heal on the sabbath, so that they might find an accusation of Him.
8 But He knew their reasonings. And (He) said to the man having the withered hand, Rise up and stand into the middle! And rising up, he stood.
9 Then Jesus said to them, I will ask you one thing, Is it lawful to do good on the sabbaths, or to do ill, to save a life, or to destroy (it)?

1096 1161 1722 2087 4521 1525 846 1519 3588
6. Ἐγένετο δὲ ἐν ἑτέρῳ σαββάτῳ εἰσελθεῖν αὐτὸν εἰς τὴν
it was And in another sabbath, entering He into the
4864 2532 1321 2532 2258 444 2532 3588 5495
συναγωγὴν καὶ διδάσκειν· καὶ ἦν ἄνθρωπος, καὶ ἡ χεὶρ
synagogue and teaching; and was there a man, and the hand
846 3588 1188 2258 3584 3906 1161 846 3588 1122
αὐτοῦ ἡ δεξιὰ ἦν ξηρά· 7 παρετήρουν δὲ αὐτὸν οἱ γραμματεῖς
of him, the right, was withered. kept close by And Him the scribes
2532 3588 5330 1487 1722 3588 4521 2323 2443 2147
καὶ οἱ Φαρισαῖοι, εἰ ἐν τῷ σαββάτῳ θεραπεύει· ἵνα εὕρωσι
and the Pharisees, if in the sabbath He will heal, that they may find
2724 846 846 1161 1492 3588 1261 846
κατηγορίαν αὐτοῦ. 8 αὐτὸς δὲ ᾔδει τοὺς διαλογισμοὺς αὐτῶν,
an accusation of Him. He But knew the reasonings of them,
2532 2036 3588 444 3588 3584 2192 3588 5495 1453
καὶ εἶπε τῷ ἀνθρώπῳ τῷ ξηρὰν ἔχοντι τὴν χεῖρα, Ἔγειραι
and said to the man withered having the hand, Rise up
2532 2476 1519 3588 3319 3588 1161 450 2476 2036 3767 3588 2424
καὶ στῆθι εἰς τὸ μέσον. ὁ καὶ ἀναστὰς ἔστη. 9 εἶπεν οὖν ὁ Ἰησοῦς
and stand into the middle! he And rising up stood. said Then Jesus
4314 846 1905 5209 5101 1832 3588 4521
πρὸς αὐτούς, Ἐπερωτήσω ὑμᾶς τί, Ἔξεστι τοῖς σάββασιν,
to them, I will ask you a thing, Is it lawful on the sabbaths
15 2228 2554 5590 4982 2228 622
ἀγαθοποιῆσαι ἢ κακοποιῆσαι, ψυχὴν σῶσαι ἢ ἀπολέσαι;
to do good, or to do ill, a life to save or to destroy?

6. And it came to pass also on another sabbath, that he entered into the synagogue and taught: and there was a man whose right hand was withered.
7 And the scribes and Pharisees watched him, whether he would heal on the sabbath day; that they might find an accusation against him.
8 But he knew their thoughts, and said to the man which had the withered hand, Rise up, and stand forth in the midst. And he arose and stood forth.
9 Then said Jesus unto them, I will ask you one thing; Is it lawful on the sabbath days to do good, or to do evil? to save life, or to destroy (it)?

10 And having looked around at them all, He said to the man, Stretch out your hand! And he did so. And his hand was restored sound as the other.
11 But they were filled (with) madness and talked to one another (as to) what they might do to Jesus.

2532 4017 3956 846 2036 3588 444
10 καὶ περιβλεψάμενος πάντας αὐτούς, εἶπε τῷ ἀνθρώπῳ,
And having looked around at all (of) them, He said to the man,
1614 3588 5495 4675 3588 1161 4160 3779 2532 600
Ἔκτεινον τὴν χεῖρά σου. ὁ δὲ ἐποίησεν οὕτω. καὶ ἀπεκατε-
Stretch out the hand of you! he And did so. And was restored
3588 5495 846 5199 5613 3588 243 846 1161 4130
στάθη ἡ χεὶρ αὐτοῦ ὑγιὴς ὡς ἡ ἄλλη. 11 αὐτοὶ δὲ ἐπλήσθησαν
the hand of him sound as the other. they But were filled (of)
454 2532 1255 4314 240 5101 302 4160 3588
ἀνοίας· καὶ διελάλουν πρὸς ἀλλήλους, τί ἂν ποιήσαιεν τῷ
madness, and talked to one another, what might they do
2424
Ἰησοῦ.
to Jesus.

10 And looking round about upon them all, he said unto the man, Stretch forth thy hand. And he did so: and his hand was restored whole as the other.
11 And they were filled with madness; and communed one with another what they might do to Jesus.

12. And it happened in these days, He went out into the mountain to pray. And He was spending the night in prayer

1096 1161 1722 3588 2250 3778 1831 1519 3588 3735
12. Ἐγένετο δὲ ἐν ταῖς ἡμέραις ταύταις ἐξῆλθεν εἰς τὸ ὄρος
it happened And in days, these He went out into the mount
4336 2532 2258 1273 1722 3588 4335 3588
προσεύξασθαι· καὶ ἦν διανυκτερεύων ἐν τῇ προσευχῇ τοῦ
to pray. And He was spending the night in prayer

12. And it came to pass in those days, that he went out into a mountain to pray, and continued all night in prayer

Luke 6:13

Literal Translation

to God.
13 And when it became day, He called to His disciples, also choosing out twelve from them, whom He also named apostles:

14 Simon, whom He also named Peter; and his brother Andrew; James and John; Philip and Bartholomew;

15 Matthew and Thomas; James the (son) of Alphaeus, and, Simon, the one being called Zealot;
16 Judas (brother) of James; and Judas Iscariot, who also became (the) betrayer.

17. And coming down with them, he stood on a level place. And a crowd of His disciples, and a great multitude of the people were there from all Judea and Jerusalem, and (from) the coast country of Tyre and Sidon, who came to hear Him, and to be healed from their diseases;
18 also those who had been tormented by unclean spirits. And (they) were healed.

19 And all the crowd sought to touch Him, because power went out from Him and healed all.

20. And lifting up His eyes to His disciples, He said: Blessed (are) the poor, for the kingdom of God is yours.

21 Blessed (are) those hungering now, for you will be filled. Blessed (are) those weeping now, for you will laugh.
22 Blessed (are) you when men hate you, and when they cut you off, and will reproach (you), and will cast out your name

2316 2532 3753 1096 2250 4377 3588 3101
Θεοῦ. 13 καὶ ὅτε ἐγένετο ἡμέρα, προσεφώνησε τοὺς μαθητὰς
of God. And when it became day, He called to the disciples

846 2532 1586 575 846 1427 3739 2532 652
αὐτοῦ· καὶ ἐκλεξάμενος ἀπ' αὐτῶν δώδεκα, οὓς καὶ ἀποστό-
of Him, and having chosen out from them twelve, whom also apostles

3687 4613 3739 2532 3687 4074 2532 406
λους ὠνόμασε, 14 Σίμωνα ὃν καὶ ὠνόμασε Πέτρον, καὶ Ἀνδρέαν
He named: Simon, whom also He named Peter; and Andrew

3588 80 846 2385 2532 2491 5376 2532
τὸν ἀδελφὸν αὐτοῦ, Ἰάκωβον καὶ Ἰωάννην, Φίλιππον καὶ
the brother of him; James and John; Philip and

918 3156 2532 2381 2385 3588 3588
Βαρθολομαῖον, 15 Ματθαῖον καὶ Θωμᾶν, Ἰάκωβον τὸν τοῦ
Bartholomew; Matthew and Thomas; James the (son)

256 2532 4613 3588 2564 2207 2455
Ἀλφαίου, καὶ Σίμωνα τὸν καλούμενον Ζηλωτήν, 16 Ἰούδαν
of Alphaeus; and Simon the (one) being called Zealot; Judas

2385 2532 2455 2469 3739 2532 1096 4273
Ἰακώβου, καὶ Ἰούδαν Ἰσκαριώτῃ, ὃς καὶ ἐγένετο προδό-
of James; and Judas Iscariot, who also came to be betrayer.

2532 2597 3326 846 2476 1909 5117 3977 2532
της, 17 καὶ καταβὰς μετ' αὐτῶν, ἔστη ἐπὶ τόπου πεδινοῦ, καὶ
And coming down with them, He stood on a place level, and

3793 3101 846 2532 4128 4183 3588 2992 575
ὄχλος μαθητῶν αὐτοῦ, καὶ πλῆθος πολὺ τοῦ λαοῦ ἀπὸ
a crowd of disciples of Him, and a multitude great of the people from

3956 3588 2449 2532 2419 2532 3588 3882
πάσης τῆς Ἰουδαίας καὶ Ἱερουσαλήμ, καὶ τῆς παραλίου
all Judea and Jerusalem, and the coast country

5184 2532 4605 3739 2064 191 846 2532 2390
Τύρου καὶ Σιδῶνος, 18 οἳ ἦλθον ἀκοῦσαι αὐτοῦ, καὶ ἰαθῆναι
of Tyre and Sidon, who came to hear Him, and to be healed

575 3588 3554 846 2532 3588 3791 5259 4151
ἀπὸ τῶν νόσων αὐτῶν· καὶ οἱ ὀχλούμενοι ἀπὸ πνευμάτων
from the diseases of them; also those having been tormented by spirits

169 2532 2323 2532 3956 3588 3793 2212
ἀκαθάρτων καὶ ἐθεραπεύοντο. 19 καὶ πᾶς ὁ ὄχλος ἐζήτει
unclean; and were healed. And all the crowd sought

680 846 3754 1411 3844 846 1831 2532 2390
ἅπτεσθαι αὐτοῦ· ὅτι δύναμις παρ' αὐτοῦ ἐξήρχετο καὶ ἰᾶτο
to touch Him, because power from Him went out and healed

3956
πάντας.
all.

2532 846 1869 3588 3788 846 1519 3588
20. Καὶ αὐτὸς ἐπάρας τοὺς ὀφθαλμοὺς αὐτοῦ εἰς τοὺς
And He lifting up the eyes of Him to the

3101 846 3004 3107 3588 4434 3754 5212 2076/3588
μαθητὰς αὐτοῦ ἔλεγε, Μακάριοι οἱ πτωχοί, ὅτι ὑμετέρα ἐστὶν ἡ
disciples of Him said, Blessed (are) the poor, because yours is the

932 3588 2316 3107 3588 3983 3568 3754 5526
βασιλεία τοῦ Θεοῦ. 21 μακάριοι οἱ πεινῶντες νῦν, ὅτι χορτασθή-
kingdom of God. Blessed (are) those hungering now, because you will

3107 3588 2799 3568 3754 1070 3107
σεσθε. μακάριοι οἱ κλαίοντες νῦν, ὅτι γελάσετε. 22 μακάριοί
be filled. Blessed (are) those weeping now, because you will laugh. Blessed

2075 3752 3404 5209 3588 444 2532 3752 873
ἐστε, ὅταν μισήσωσιν ὑμᾶς οἱ ἄνθρωποι, καὶ ὅταν ἀφο-
are you when hate you men, and when they

5209 2532 3679 2532 1544 3588 3686 5216
ρίσωσιν ὑμᾶς, καὶ ὀνειδίσωσι καὶ ἐκβάλωσι τὸ ὄνομα ὑμῶν
cut off you, and will reproach, and cast out the name of you

King James Version

to God.
13 And when it was day, he called (unto him) his disciples: and of them he chose twelve, whom also he named apostles;

14 Simon, (whom he also named Peter,) and Andrew his brother, James and John, Philip and Bartholomew,

15 Matthew and Thomas, James the (son) of Alphaeus, and Simon called Zelotes,
16 And Judas (the brother) of James, and Judas Iscariot, which also was the traitor.

17. And he came down with them, and stood in the plain, and the company of his disciples, and a great multitude of people out of all Judaea and Jerusalem, and from the sea coast of Tyre and Sidon, which came to hear him, and to be healed of their diseases;
18 And they that were vexed with unclean spirits: and they were healed.

19 And the whole multitude sought to touch him: for there went virtue out of him, and healed (them) all.

20. And he lifted up his eyes on his disciples, and said, Blessed (be ye) poor: for yours is the kingdom of God.

21 Blessed (are ye) that hunger now: for ye shall be filled. Blessed (are ye) that weep now: for ye shall laugh.
22 Blessed are ye, when men shall hate you, and when they shall separate you (from their company), and shall reproach (you), and cast out your name

Literal Translation

as evil, on account of the Son of man;
23 rejoice in that day, and leap for joy; for, behold, your reward (is) much in Heaven! For their fathers did according to these things to the prophets.

24. But woe to you, rich ones, for you have your comfort!
25 Woe to you, those having been filled, for you will hunger! Woe to you, those laughing now, for you will mourn and lament!

26 Woe to you when all men speak well (of) you, for their fathers did according to these things to the false prophets.

27. But I say to you, those hearing: Love your enemies, do good to those hating you,
28 bless those having cursed you and pray for those insulting you.

29 To those striking you on the cheek, turn the other also. And from those taking your garment, do not keep back the tunic also.

30 And to everyone asking you, give. And do not ask back from those taking your things.
31 And even as you desire that men should do to you, you also do likewise to them.
32 And if you love those loving you, what thanks is there to you? For even sinners love those loving them.

33 And if you do good to those doing good to you, what thanks is there to you? For even the sinners

Luke 6:23

5613 4190 1752 3588 5207 3588 444 5463 1722
ὡς πονηρὸν, ἕνεκα τοῦ υἱοῦ τοῦ ἀνθρώπου· 23 χαίρετε ἐν
as evil, on account of the Son of man. Rejoice in

1565 3588 2250 2532 4640 2400 1063 3588 3408 5216
ἐκείνῃ τῇ ἡμέρᾳ καὶ σκιρτήσατε· ἰδοὺ γάρ, ὁ μισθὸς ὑμῶν
that day and leap (for joy). behold For, the reward of you

4183 1722 3588 3772 2596 5024 1063 4160 3588 4396
πολὺς ἐν τῷ οὐρανῷ· κατὰ ταῦτα γὰρ ἐποίουν τοῖς προφήταις
much in Heaven; according to these things For did to the prophets

3588 3962 846 4133 3759 5213 3588 4145
οἱ πατέρες αὐτῶν. 24 πλὴν οὐαὶ ὑμῖν τοῖς πλουσίοις,
the fathers of them. But woe to you, the rich ones,

3754 568 3588 3874 5216 3759 5213 3588 1705
ὅτι ἀπέχετε τὴν παράκλησιν ὑμῶν. 25 οὐαὶ ὑμῖν, οἱ ἐμπεπλη-
because you have the comfort of you! Woe to you, those having

3754 3983 3759 5213 3588 1070 3568 3754
σμένοι, ὅτι πεινάσετε. οὐαι ὑμῖν, οἱ γελῶντες νῦν, ὅτι
been filled, because you will hunger! Woe to you, those laughing now, because

3996 2532 2799 3759 5213 3752 2573 5209 2036
πενθήσετε καὶ κλαύσετε. 26 οὐαὶ υμῖν, ὅταν καλῶς ὑμᾶς εἴπωσι
you will mourn and lament! Woe to you when well of you speak

3956 3588 444 2596 5024 1063 4160 3588 5578
πάντες οἱ ἄνθρωποι· κατὰ ταῦτα γὰρ ἐποίουν τοῖς ψευδο-
all men; according to these things for did the false

3588 3962 846
προφήταις οἱ πατέρες αὐτῶν.
prophets the fathers of them.

235 5213 3004 3588 191 25 3588 2190
27. Ἀλλ' ὑμῖν λέγω τοῖς ἀκούουσιν, Ἀγαπᾶτε τοὺς ἐχθροὺς
But to you I say, those hearing, Love the hostile (ones)

5216 2573 4160 3588 3404 5209 2127 3588
ὑμῶν, καλῶς ποιεῖτε τοῖς μισοῦσιν ὑμᾶς, 28 εὐλογεῖτε τοὺς
of you; well do to those hating you; bless those

2672 5213 2532 4336 5228 3588 1908
καταρωμένους ὑμῖν, καὶ προσεύχεσθε ὑπὲρ τῶν ἐπηρεαζόν-
having cursed you; and pray for those insulting

5209 3588 5180 4571 1909 3588 4600 3930 2532 3588
των ὑμᾶς. 29 τῷ τύπτοντί σε ἐπὶ τὴν σιαγόνα πάρεχε καὶ τὴν
you. To those striking you on the cheek, turn also the

243 2532 575 3588 142 4675 3588 2440 2532 3588
ἄλλην· καὶ ἀπὸ τοῦ αἴροντός σου τὸ ἱμάτιον, καὶ τὸν
other; and from the (one) taking of you the garment, also the

5509 3361 2967 3956 1161 3588 154 4571 1325 2532
χιτῶνα μὴ κωλύσῃς. 30 παντὶ δὲ τῷ αἰτοῦντί σε δίδου· καὶ
tunic not do keep back. to everyone And asking you, give; and

575 3588 142 3588 4674 3361 523 2532 2531 2309 2443
ἀπὸ τοῦ αἴροντος τὰ σὰ μὴ ἀπαίτει. 31 καὶ καθὼς θέλετε ἵνα
from the (ones) taking the things of you not do ask back. And even as you desire that

4160 5213 3588 444 2532 5210 4160 846 3668
ποιῶσιν ὑμῖν οἱ ἄνθρωποι, καὶ ὑμεῖς ποιεῖτε αὐτοῖς ὁμοίως.
may do to you men, also you do to them likewise.

2532 1487 25 3588 25 5209 4169 5213 5485
32 καὶ εἰ ἀγαπᾶτε τοὺς ἀγαπῶντας ὑμᾶς, ποία ὑμῖν χάρις
And if you love those loving you, what to you thanks

2076 2532 1063 3588 268 3588 25 846 25
ἐστί; καὶ γὰρ οἱ ἁμαρτωλοὶ τοὺς ἀγαπῶντας αὐτοὺς ἀγα-
is? even For the sinners those loving them love.

2532 1437 15 3588 15 5209
πῶσι. 33 καὶ ἐὰν ἀγαθοποιῆτε τοὺς ἀγαθοποιοῦντας ὑμᾶς,
And if you good do to those doing good to you,

4169 5213 5485 2076 2532 1063 3588 268 3588 846
ποία ὑμῖν χάρις ἐστί; καὶ γὰρ οἱ ἁμαρτωλοὶ τὸ αὐτὸ
what to you thanks is? even For the sinners the same

King James Version

as evil, for the Son of man's sake.
23 Rejoice ye in that day, and leap for joy: for, behold, your reward (is) great in heaven: for in the like manner did their fathers unto the prophets.

24. But woe unto you that are rich! for ye have received your consolation.
25 Woe unto you that are full! for ye shall hunger. Woe unto you that laugh now! for ye shall mourn and weep.

26 Woe unto you, when all men shall speak well of you! for so did their fathers to the false prophets.

27. But I say unto you which hear, Love your enemies, do good to them which hate you,
28 Bless them that curse you, and pray for them which despitefully use you.

29 And unto him that smiteth thee on the (one) cheek offer also the other; and him that taketh away thy cloke forbid not (to take thy) coat also.
30 Give to every man that asketh of thee; and of him that taketh away thy goods ask (them) not again.
31 And as ye would that men should do to you, do ye also to them likewise.

32 For if ye love them which love you, what thank have ye? for sinners also love those that love them.

33 And if ye do good to them which do good to you, what thank have ye? for sinners also do

Luke 6:34

Literal Translation

do the same.
34 And if you lend (to those) from whom you hope to receive, what thanks is there to you? For the sinners lend to sinners so that they may receive the same.
35 But love your enemies, and do good, and lend, causing no one to despair, and your reward will be much; and you will be sons of the Most High, for He is kind to the unthankful and evil (ones).

36 Therefore, be merciful, even as your Father also is merciful.

37 Judge not, and in no way be judged. Do not condemn, and in no way you will be condemned. Forgive, and you will be forgiven.
38 Give, and good measure will be given to you, pressed down and shaken together, and running over, they will give into your bosom. For the same measure which you measure, it will be measured back to you.

39 And He spoke a parable to them: A blind (one) is not able to guide a blind (one). Will they not both fall into a pit?
40 A disciple is not above his teacher, but everyone who has been perfected will be like his teacher.

41 But why do you see the twig in the eye of your brother, but do not consider the log in (your) own eye?

42 Or how can you say to your brother, Brother, allow me to take out the twig in your eye, not yourself seeing the log in your eye? Hypocrite!

4160 2532 1437 1155 3844 3739 1679 618
ποιοῦσι. 34 καὶ ἐὰν δανείζητε παρ᾽ ὧν ἐλπίζετε ἀπολαβεῖν,
do. And if you lend from whom you hope to receive,

4169 5213 5485 2076 2532 1063 3588 268 268
ποία ὑμῖν χάρις ἐστί; καὶ γὰρ οἱ ἁμαρτωλοὶ ἁμαρτωλοῖς
what to you thanks is? even For the sinners to sinners

1155 2443 618 3588 2470 4133 25 3588
δανίζουσιν ἵνα ἀπολάβωσι τὰ ἴσα. 35 πλὴν ἀγαπᾶτε τοὺς
lend that they may receive the things equal. But love the

2190 5216 2532 15 2532 1155 3367
ἐχθροὺς ὑμῶν καὶ ἀγαθοποιεῖτε καὶ δανίζετε, μηδὲν ἀπελ-
hostile (ones) of you, and do good and lend, none causing

560 2532 2071 3588 3408 5216 4183 2532 2071 5207 3588
πίζοντες· καὶ ἔσται ὁ μισθὸς ὑμῶν πολύς, καὶ ἔσεσθε υἱοὶ τοῦ
to despair; and will be the reward of you much, and you will be sons of the

5310 3754 846 5543 2076 1909 3588 884 2532
ὑψίστου· ὅτι αὐτὸς χρηστός ἐστιν ἐπὶ τοὺς ἀχαρίστους καὶ
Most High; because He kind is to the unthankful and

4190 1096 3767 3629 2531 2532 3588 3962
πονηρούς. 36 γίνεσθε οὖν οἰκτίρμονες, καθὼς καὶ ὁ πατὴρ
evil. be Therefore merciful even as also the Father

5216 3629 2076 3361 2919 2532 3756 3361 2919 3361 2613
ὑμῶν οἰκτίρμων ἐστί. 37 μὴ κρίνετε, καὶ οὐ μὴ κριθῆτε. μὴ κατα-
of you merciful is. not Judge, and in no way be judged. Not do

2532 3756 3361 2613 630 2532 630
δικάζετε, καὶ οὐ μὴ καταδικασθῆτε· ἀπολύετε, καὶ ἀπολυθή-
condemn, and in no way you will be condemned; forgive, and you will be

1325 2532 1325 5213 3358 2570 4085
σεσθε· 38 δίδοτε, καὶ δοθήσεται ὑμῖν· μέτρον καλὸν, πεπιε-
forgiven. Give, and will be given to you measure good, pressed

2532 4531 2532 5240 1325
σμένον καὶ σεσαλευμένον καὶ ὑπερεκχυνόμενον δώσουσιν
down and having been shaken together and running over shall they give

1519 3588 2859 5216 3588 1063 846 3358 3739 3354 488
εἰς τὸν κόλπον ὑμῶν· τῷ γὰρ αὐτῷ μέτρῳ ᾧ μετρεῖτε ἀντι-
into the bosom of you. the For same measure which you mete, it will

5213
μετρηθήσεται ὑμῖν.
be measured back to you.

2036 1161 3850 846 3385 1410 5185 5185
39. Εἶπε δὲ παραβολὴν αὐτοῖς· Μήτι δύναται τυφλὸς τυφλὸν
He spoke And a parable to them, Not is able a blind (one) a blind (one)

3594 3780 297 1519 999 4098 3756 2076
ὁδηγεῖν; οὐχὶ ἀμφότεροι εἰς βόθυνον πεσοῦνται; 40 οὐκ ἔστι
to guide. not Will they both into a pit fall ? Not is

3101 5228 3588 1320 846 2675 1161
μαθητὴς ὑπὲρ τὸν διδάσκαλον αὐτοῦ· κατηρτισμένος δὲ
a disciple above the teacher of him; having been perfected but

3956 2071 5613 3588 1320 846 5101 1161 991 3588 2595 3588
πᾶς ἔσται ὡς ὁ διδάσκαλος αὐτοῦ. 41 τί δὲ βλέπεις τὸ κάρφος τὸ
every one will be as the teacher of him. why And do you see the twig 1722

1722 3588 3788 3588 80 4675 3588 1161 1385 3588/ 1722/3588
ἐν τῷ ὀφθαλμῷ τοῦ ἀδελφοῦ σου, τὴν δὲ δοκὸν τὴν ἐν τῷ
in the eye of the brother of you, the but log in the

2398 3788 3756 2657 2228 4459 1410 3004 3588 80
ἰδίῳ ὀφθαλμῷ οὐ κατανοεῖς; 42 ἢ πῶς δύνασαι λέγειν τῷ ἀδελφῷ
own eye not do consider? Or how are you able to say to the brother

4675 80 863 1544 3588 2595 3588 1722 3588 3788 4675
σου, Ἀδελφέ, ἄφες ἐκβάλω τὸ κάρφος τὸ ἐν τῷ ὀφθαλμῷ σου,
of you, Brother, allow I may take out the twig in the eye of you,

846 3588 1722 3588 3788 4675 1385 3756 991 5273
αὐτὸς τὴν ἐν τῷ ὀφθαλμῷ σοῦ δοκὸν οὐ βλέπων; ὑποκριτά,
yourself the in the eye of you log not seeing? Hypocrite!

King James Version

even the same.
34 And if ye lend (to them) of whom ye hope to receive, what thank have ye? for sinners also lend to sinners, to receive as much again.

35 But love ye your enemies, and do good, and lend, hoping for nothing again; and your reward shall be great, and ye shall be the children of the Highest: for he is kind unto the unthankful and (to) the evil.

36 Be ye therefore merciful, as your Father also is merciful.

37 Judge not, and ye shall not be judged: condemn not, and ye shall not be condemned: forgive, and ye shall be forgiven:
38 Give, and it shall be given unto you; good measure, pressed down, and shaken together, and running over, shall men give into your bosom. For with the same measure that ye mete withal it shall be measured to you again.

39 And he spake a parable unto them, Can the blind lead the blind? shall they not both fall into the ditch?
40 The disciple is not above his master: but every one that is perfect shall be as his master.

41 And why beholdest thou the mote that is in thy brother's eye, but perceivest not the beam that is in thine own eye?

42 Either how canst thou say to thy brother, Brother, let me pull out the mote that is in thine eye, when thou thyself beholdest not the beam that is in thine own eye? Thou hypocrite,

Literal Translation | **Luke 6:43** | ***King James Version***

First take the log out of your eye, and then you will see clearly to take out the twig in your brother's eye.

1544 4412 3588 1385 1537 3588 3788 4675 2532 5119
ἔκβαλε πρῶτον τὴν δοκὸν ἐκ τοῦ ὀφθαλμοῦ σου, καὶ τότε
take out first the log from the eye of you, and then
1227 1544 3588 2595 3588 1722 3588 3788 3588
διαβλέψεις ἐκβαλεῖν τὸ κάρφος τὸ ἐν τῷ ὀφθαλμῷ τοῦ
you will see clearly to take out the twig in the eye of the
80 4675 3756 1063 2076 1186 2570 4160 2590
ἀδελφοῦ σου. 43 οὐ γάρ ἐστι δένδρον καλὸν ποιοῦν καρπὸν
brother of you. not For is a tree good producing fruit
4550 3761 1186 4550 4160 2590 2570
σαπρόν· οὐδὲ δένδρον σαπρὸν ποιοῦν καρπὸν καλόν.
a bad. nor tree a bad producing fruit good.

cast out first the beam out of thine own eye, and then shalt thou see clearly to pull out the mote that is in thy brother's eye.

43 For there is not a good tree producing bad fruit, nor a bad tree producing good fruit.

43 For a good tree bringeth not forth corrupt fruit; neither doth a corrupt tree bring forth good fruit.

44 For each tree is known from (its) own fruit. For they do not gather figs from thornbushes, nor do they gather grapes from a bramble bush.
45 The good man brings forth good out of the good treasure of his heart. And the evil man brings forth evil out of the evil treasure of his heart, for his mouth speaks out of the abundance of his heart.

1538 1063 1186 1537 3588 2398 2590 1097 3756
44 ἕκαστον γὰρ δένδρον ἐκ τοῦ ἰδίου καρποῦ γινώσκεται. οὐ
each For tree from the own fruit is known. not
1063 1537 173 4816 4810 3761 1537 942 5166
γὰρ ἐξ ἀκανθῶν συλλέγουσι σῦκα, οὐδὲ ἐκ βάτου τρυγῶσι
For from thornbushes do they gather figs, nor from a bramble gather
4718 3588 18 444 1537 3588 18 2344
σταφυλήν. 45 ὁ ἀγαθὸς ἄνθρωπος ἐκ τοῦ ἀγαθοῦ θησαυροῦ
a cluster of grapes. The good man out of the good treasure
3588 2588 846 4393 3588 18 2532 3588 4190
τῆς καρδίας αὐτοῦ προφέρει τὸ ἀγαθόν, καὶ ὁ πονηρὸς
of the heart of him brings forth the good, and the evil
444 1537 3588 4190 2344 3588 2588 846
ἄνθρωποσς ἐκ τοῦ πονηροῦ θησαυροῦ τῆς καρδίας αὐτοῦ
man out of the evil treasure of the heart of him
4393 3588 4190 1537 1063 3588 4051 3588
προφέρει τὸ πονηρόν· ἐκ γὰρ τοῦ περισσεύματος τῆς
brings forth the evil. out of For the abundance of the
2588 2980 3588 4750 846
καρδίας λαλεῖ τὸ στόμα αὐτοῦ.
heart speaks the mouth of him.

44 For every tree is known by his own fruit. For of thorns men do not gather figs, nor of a bramble bush gather they grapes.
45 A good man out of the good treasure of his heart bringeth forth that which is good; and an evil man out of the evil treasure of his heart bringeth forth that which is evil: for of the abundance of the heart his mouth speaketh.

46. And why do you call Me Lord, Lord, and do not do what I say?

47 Everyone coming to Me and hearing My words, and doing them, I will show you to whom he is like:
48 He is like a man building a house, who dug and deepened, and laid a foundation on the rock. And a flood occurring, the stream burst against that house and was not able to shake it, for it had been founded on the rock.

49 But he who heard and not (is) doing, (he) is like a man having built (his) house on the earth without a foundation, on which the stream burst, and it immediately fell; and the ruin

5101 1161 3165 2564 2962 2962 2532 3756 4160 3739 3004
46. Τί δέ με καλεῖτε, Κύριε, Κύριε, καὶ οὐ ποιεῖτε ἃ λέγω;
why And Me do you call Lord, Lord, and not do which I say?
3056 3588 2064 4313 3165 2532 191 3450 3588 3056 2532
47 πᾶς ὁ ἐρχόμενος πρός με καὶ ἀκούων μου τῶν λόγων καὶ
Everyone coming to Me and hearing of Me the words, and
4160 846 5263 5213 5101 2076 3664 3664 2076
ποιῶν αὐτούς, ὑποδείξω ὑμῖν τίνι ἐστὶν ὅμοιος· 48 ὅμοιός ἐστιν
doing them, I will show you to whom he is like; like He is
444 3618 3614 3739 4626 2532 900 2532
ἀνθρώπῳ οἰκοδομοῦντι οἰκίαν, ὃς ἔσκαψε, καὶ ἐβάθυνε, καὶ
a man building a house, who dug and deepened, and
5087 2310 1909 3588 4073 4132 1161 1096
ἔθηκε θεμέλιον ἐπὶ τὴν πέτραν· πλημμύρης δὲ γενομένης,
laid a foundation on the rock; a flood and occurring,
4366 3588 4215 3588 3614 1565 2532 3756 2480
προσέρρηξεν ὁ ποταμὸς τῇ οἰκίᾳ ἐκείνῃ, καὶ οὐκ ἴσχυσε
burst against the stream house of that, and not was able
4531 846 2311 1063 1909 3588 4073 3588 1161
σαλεῦσαι αὐτήν· τεθεμελίωτο γὰρ ἐπὶ τὴν πέτραν. 49 ὁ δὲ
to shake it, it had been founded for on the rock. he But
191 2532 3361 4160 3664 2076 444 3618
ἀκούσας καὶ μὴ ποιήσας ὅμοιός ἐστιν ἀνθρώπῳ οἰκοδομή-
(who) heard and not doing like is to a man (who) has
3614 1909 3588 1093 5565 2310 3739 4366 3588
σαντι οἰκίαν ἐπὶ τὴν γῆν χωρὶς θεμελίου· ᾗ προσέρρηξεν ὁ
built a house on the earth without a foundation, on which burst the
4215 2532 2112 4098 2532 1096 3588 4485 3588
ποταμός, καὶ εὐθέως ἔπεσε, καὶ ἐγένετο τὸ ῥῆγμα τῆς
stream, and immediately it fell, and became the ruin

46. And why call ye me, Lord, Lord, and do not the things which I say?
47 Whosoever cometh to me, and heareth my sayings, and doeth them, I will shew you to whom he is like:
48 He is like a man which built an house, and digged deep, and laid the foundation on a rock: and when the flood arose, the stream beat vehemently upon that house, and could not shake it: for it was founded upon a rock.

49 But he that heareth, and doeth not, is like a man that without a foundation built an house upon the earth; against which the stream did beat vehemently, and immediately it fell; and the ruin

Literal Translation | **Luke 7:1** | ***King James Version***

of that house was great.

3614 1565 3173
οἰκίας ἐκείνης μέγα.
house of that great.

of that house was great.

Luke 7

1. And when He completed all His words in the ears of the people, He went into Capernaum.

2 And a certain slave of a centurion, who was dear to him, badly (illness) having, was about to expire.
3 And hearing about Jesus, he sent elders of the Jews to Him, asking Him that coming He might cure his slave.
4 And having come to Jesus, they earnestly begged Him, saying, He to whom You give this is worthy.

5 For he loves our nation, and he built the synagogue for us.
6 And Jesus went with them. But He being yet not far away from the house, the centurion sent friends to Him, saying to Him, Lord, do not trouble, for I am not worthy that You enter under my roof.

7 For this reason I did not deem (it) fit myself to come to You. But say a word, and my servant will be cured.
8 For I also am a man having been set under authority, having soldiers under myself. And I say to this one, Go! And he goes. And to another, Come! And he comes. And to my slave, Do this! And he does (it).

9 And hearing these things, Jesus marveled

Luke 7

1893 1161 4137 3956 3588 4487 846 1519 3588 189
1. Ἐπει δὲ ἐπλήρωσε πάντα τὰ ῥήματα αὐτοῦ εἰς τὰς ἀκοὰς
when And He completed all the words of Him in the ears

3588 2992 1525 1519 2584
τοῦ λαοῦ, εἰσῆλθεν εἰς Καφαρναούμ.
of the people, He went into Capernaum.

1543 1161 5100 1401 2560 2192 3195
2 Ἑκατοντάρχου δέ τινος δοῦλος κακῶς ἔχων ἤμελλε
of a centurion And a certain slave badly (illness) having was about

5053 3739 2258 846 1784 191 1161 4012 3588 2424
τελευτᾶν, ὃς ἦν αὐτῷ ἔντιμος. 3 ἀκούσας δὲ περὶ τοῦ Ἰησοῦ
to expire, who was to him dear. hearing And about Jesus,

649 4314 846 4245 3588 2453
ἀπέστειλε πρὸς αὐτὸν πρεσβυτέρους τῶν Ἰουδαίων,
he sent to Him elders of the Jews,

2065 846 3704 2064 1295 3588 1401 846 3588
ἐρωτῶν αὐτὸν ὅπως ἐλθὼν διασώσῃ τὸν δοῦλον αὐτοῦ. 4 οἱ
asking Him that coming He may cure the slave of him. they

1161 3854 4314 3588 2424 3870 846
δὲ παραγενόμενοι πρὸς τὸν Ἰησοῦν, παρεκάλουν αὐτὸν
And having come to Jesus begged Him

4709 3004 3754 514 2076 3739 3930 5124
σπουδαίως, λέγοντες ὅτι ἄξιός ἐστιν ᾧ παρέξει τοῦτο,
earnestly, saying that worthy he is for whom you give this.

25 1063 3588 1484 2257 2532 3588 4864 846
5 ἀγαπᾷ γὰρ τὸ ἔθνος ἡμῶν, καὶ τὴν συναγωγὴν αὐτὸς
he loves For the nation of us, and the synagogue he

3618 2254 3588 1161 2424 4198 4862 846 2235
ᾠκοδόμησεν ἡμῖν. 6 ὁ δὲ Ἰησοῦς ἐπορεύετο σὺν αὐτοῖς. ἤδη
built for us. And Jesus went with them. yet

1161 846 3756 3112 568 575 3588 3614 3992 4314
δὲ αὐτοῦ οὐ μακρὰν ἀπέχοντος ἀπὸ τῆς οἰκίας, ἔπεμψε πρὸς
And Him not far being away from the house, sent to

846 3588 1543 5384 3004 846 2962 3361
αὐτὸν ὁ ἑκατόνταρχος φίλους, λέγων αὐτῷ, Κύριε, μὴ
Him the centurion friends, saying to Him, Lord, not

4660 3756 1063 1510 2425 2443 5259 3588 4721 3450
σκύλλου· οὐ γὰρ εἰμι ἱκανός ἵνα ὑπὸ τὴν στέγην μου
do trouble, not for I am worthy that under the roof of me

1525 1352 3761 1683 515 4314 4571 2064 235
εἰσέλθῃς· 7 διὸ οὐδὲ ἐμαυτὸν ἠξίωσα πρὸς σὲ ἐλθεῖν· ἀλλὰ
You enter. So not myself deem (it) fit to You to come, but

2036 3056 2532 2390 3588 3816 3450 2532 1063 1473 444
εἰπὲ λόγῳ, καὶ ἰαθήσεται ὁ παῖς μου. 8 καὶ γὰρ ἐγὼ ἄνθρωπός
say a word, and will be healed the servant of me. also For I a man

1510 5259 1849 5021 2192 5259 1683 4757
εἰμι ὑπὸ ἐξουσίαν τασσόμενος, ἔχων ὑπ' ἐμαυτὸν στρατιώ-
am under authority having been set, having under myself soldiers,

2532 3004 5129 4198 2532 4198 2532 243
τας, καὶ λέγω τούτῳ, Πορεύθητι, καὶ πορεύεται· καὶ ἄλλῳ,
and I say to this one, Go, and he goes, and another,

2064 2532 2064 2532 3588 1401 3450 4160 5124 2532
Ἔρχου, καὶ ἔρχεται· καὶ τῷ δούλῳ μου, Ποίησον τοῦτο, καὶ
Come, and he comes; and the slave of me, Do this, and

4160 191 1161 5023 3588 2424 2296 846 2532
ποιεῖ. 9 ἀκούσας δὲ ταῦτα ὁ Ἰησοῦς ἐθαύμασεν αὐτόν, καὶ
he does. hearing And these things Jesus marveled at him, and

Luke 7

1. Now when he had ended all his sayings in the audience of the people, he entered into Capernaum.

2 And a certain centurion's servant, who was dear unto him, was sick, and ready to die.
3 And when he heard of Jesus, he sent unto him the elders of the Jews, beseeching him that he would come and heal his servant.
4 And when they came to Jesus, they besought him instantly, saying, That he was worthy for whom he should do this:

5 For he loveth our nation, and he hath built us a synagogue.
6 Then Jesus went with them. And when he was now not far from the house, the centurion sent friends to him, saying unto him, Lord, trouble not thyself: for I am not worthy that thou shouldest enter under my roof:

7 Wherefore neither thought I myself worthy to come unto thee: but say in a word, and my servant shall be healed.
8 For I also am a man set under authority, having under me soldiers, and I say unto one, Go, and he goeth; and to another, Come, and he cometh; and to my servant, Do this, and he doeth (it).

9 When Jesus heard these things, he marvelled at him,

Literal Translation **Luke 7:10** ***King James Version***

at him. And turning to the crowd following Him, He said, I say to you, I did not find such faith in Israel.
10 And the (ones) sent, returning to the house, found the sick slave well.

4762 3588 190 846 3793 2036 3004 5213 3761
στραφεὶς τῷ ἀκολουθοῦντι αὐτῷ ὄχλῳ εἶπε, Λέγω ὑμῖν, οὐδὲ
turning to the following Him crowd said, I say to you, not
1722 3588 2474 5118 4102 2147 2532 5290 3588
ἐν τῷ Ἰσραὴλ τοσαύτην πίστιν εὗρον. 10 καὶ ὑποστρέψαντες οἱ
in Israel such faith I found. And returning the (ones)
3992 1519 3588 3624 2147 3588 770 1401
πεμφθέντες εἰς τὸν οἶκον εὗρον τὸν ἀσθενοῦντα δοῦλον
sent to the house found the sick slave
5198
ὑγιαίνοντα.
well.

and turned him about, and said unto the people that followed him, I say unto you, I have not found so great faith, no, not in Israel.
10 And they that were sent, returning to the house, found the servant whole that had been sick.

11. And it was in the next day, He went into a city being called Nain. And many of His disciples went with Him; also a large crowd.
12 And as He drew near to the gate of the city, even behold! (One) having died was being borne, an only son born to his mother; and she was a widow. And a considerable crowd of the city was with her.
13 And seeing her, the Lord felt pity on her and said to her, Stop weeping.
14 And coming up, He touched the coffin; and those carrying (it) stood still. And He said, Young man, I say to you, Rise up!
15 And the dead one sat up and began to speak. And He gave him to his mother.
16 And fear took hold of all; and they glorified God, saying, A great prophet has risen up among us; and, God has visited His people.
17 And this word about Him went out in all Judea, and in all the neighborhood.

2532 1096 1722 3588 1836 4198 1519 4172 2564
11. Καὶ ἐγένετο ἐν τῷ ἑξῆς ἐπορεύθη εἰς πόλιν καλουμένην
And it was in the next (day) He went into a city being called
3484 2532 4848 846 3588 3101 846 2425
Ναΐν· καὶ συνεπορεύοντο αὐτῷ οἱ μαθηταὶ αὐτοῦ ἱκανοί,
Nain; and went with Him the disciples of Him many,
2532 3793 4183 5613 1161 1448 3588 4439 3588 4172 2532 2400
καὶ ὄχλος πολύς. 12 ὡς δὲ ἤγγισε τῇ πύλῃ τῆς πόλεως, καὶ ἰδού,
and a crowd large. as And He drew to the gate of the city even behold!
1580 2348 5207 3439 3588 3384 846 2532
ἐξεκομίζετο τεθνηκὼς υἱὸς μονογενὴς τῇ μητρὶ αὐτοῦ, καὶ
was being borne having died son an only-born to the mother of him, and
846 2258 5503 2532 3793 3588 4172 2425 2258 4862 846
αὐτὴ ἦν χήρα· καὶ ὄχλος τῆς πόλεως ἱκανὸς ἦν σὺν αὐτῇ.
she was a widow. And a crowd of the city considerable was with her.
2532 1492 846 3588 2962 4697 1909 846 2532 2036
13 καὶ ιδὼν αὐτήν, ὁ Κύριος ἐσπλαγχνίσθη ἐπ' αὐτῇ, καὶ εἶπεν
And seeing her, the Lord felt pity on her, and said
846 3361 2799 2532 4334 680 3588 4673 3588 1161
αὐτῇ, Μὴ κλαῖε. 14 καὶ προσελθὼν ἥψατο τῆς σοροῦ, οἱ δὲ
to her, Not do weep. And coming up He touched the bier, those and
941 2476 2532 2036 3495 4671 3004
βαστάζοντες ἔστησαν, καὶ εἶπε, Νεανίσκε, σοὶ λέγω,
bearing stood still. And He said, Young man, to you I say,
1453 2532 339 3588 3498 2532 756 2980 2532
ἐγέρθητι. 15 καὶ ἀνεκάθισεν ὁ νεκρός, καὶ ἤρξατο λαλεῖν, καὶ
Rise up! And sat up the dead one and began to speak; and
1325 846 3588 3384 846 2983 1161 5401 537 2532
ἔδωκεν αὐτὸν τῇ μητρὶ αὐτοῦ. 16 ἔλαβε δὲ φόβος ἅπαντας, καὶ
He gave him to the mother of him. took And fear all, and
1392 3588 2316 3004 3754 4396 3173 1453
ἐδόξαζον τὸν Θεόν, λέγοντες ὅτι Προφήτης μέγας ἐγήγερται
they glorified God, saying, A prophet great has risen
1722 2254 2532 3754 1980 3588 2316 3588 2992 846 2532
ἐν ἡμῖν, καὶ ὅτι Ἐπεσκέψατο ὁ Θεὸς τὸν λαὸν αὐτοῦ. 17 καὶ
among us, and, has visited God the people of Him. And
1831 3588 3056 3778 1722 3650 3588 2449 4012 846 2532
ἐξῆλθεν ὁ λόγος οὗτος ἐν ὅλῃ τῇ Ἰουδαίᾳ περὶ αὐτοῦ, καὶ
went out word this in all Judea about Him, and
1722 3956 3588 4066
ἐν πάσῃ τῇ περιχώρῳ.
in all the neighborhood.

11. And it came to pass the day after, that he went into a city called Nain; and many of his disciples went with him, and much people.
12 Now when he came nigh to the gate of the city, behold, there was a dead man carried out, the only son of his mother, and she was a widow: and much people of the city was with her.
13 And when the Lord saw her, he had compassion on her, and said unto her, Weep not.
14 And he came and touched the bier: and they that bare (him) stood still. And he said, Young man, I say unto thee, Arise.
15 And he that was dead sat up, and began to speak. And he delivered him to his mother.
16 And there came a fear on all: and they glorified God, saying, That a great prophet is risen up among us; and, That God hath visited his people.
17 And this rumour of him went forth throughout all Judaea, and throughout all the region round about.

18. And His disciples reported to John about all these things.
19 And having called near a certain two of his disciples, John sent to Jesus, saying, Are You the

2532 518 2491 3588 3101 846 4012 3956
18. Καὶ ἀπήγγειλαν Ἰωάννῃ οἱ μαθηταὶ αὐτοῦ περὶ πάντων
And reported to John the disciples of him about all
5130 2532 4341 1417 5100 3588 3101 846
τούτων. 19 καὶ προσκαλεσάμενος δύο τινὰς τῶν μαθητῶν αὐτοῦ
these things. And having called near two a certain of the disciples of him,
3588 2491 3992 4314 3588 2424 3004 4771 1488 3588
ὁ Ἰωάννης ἔπεμψε πρὸς τὸν Ἰησοῦν, λέγων, Σὺ εἶ ὁ
John sent to Jesus, saying, You Are He

18. And the disciples of John shewed him of all these things.
19 And John calling (unto him) two of his disciples sent (them) to Jesus, saying, Art thou he

Literal Translation

(One) coming? Or should we expect another?
20 And having come to Him, the men said, John the Baptist sent us to You, saying, Are You the (One) coming, or should we expect another?

21 And in the same hour He healed many from diseases and plagues and evil spirits. And He freely gave to many blind ones (ability) to see.
22 And answering, Jesus said to them, Going, report to John what you saw and heard: Blind ones (are) seeing again; lame ones (are) walking about; lepers (are) being cleansed; deaf ones (are) hearing; dead ones (are) being raised; poor ones (are) given the gospel. (Isa. 35:5, 6; 61:1)

23 And blessed is (he) who is not offended in Me.

24. And John's messengers going away, He began to speak to the crowds about John: What did you go out to the wilderness to see? A reed being shaken by the wind?
25 But what did you go out to see? A man who had been dressed in soft clothing? Behold, those in splendid clothing and being in luxury are in king's palaces.

26 But what did you go out to see? A prophet? Yes, I say to you, more than a prophet.

27 This is he about whom it has been written: "Behold, I send My messenger before Your face, who will prepare Your way before You." (Mal. 3:1)
28 For I say to you,

Luke 7:20

2064 2228 243 4328 3854 1161 4314
ἐρχόμενος ἢ ἄλλον προσδοκῶμεν; 20 παραγενόμενοι δὲ πρὸς
coming or another should we expect? having come And to

846 3588 435 2036 2491 3588 910 649
αὐτὸν οἱ ἄνδρες εἶπον, Ἰωάννης ὁ βαπτιστὴς ἀπέσταλκεν
Him the men said, John the Baptist sent

2249 4314 4571 3004 4771 1488 3588 2064 2228 243 4328
ἡμᾶς πρὸς σὲ λέγων, Σὺ εἶ ὁ ἐρχόμενος, ἢ ἄλλον προσδοκῶμεν;
us to You saying, You Are the (One) coming, or another should we expect?

1722 846 1161 3588 5610 2323 4183 575 3554 2532
21 ἐν αὐτῇ δὲ τῇ ὥρᾳ ἐθεράπευσε πολλοὺς ἀπὸ νόσων καὶ
in the same And hour He healed many from diseases and

3148 2532 4151 4190 2532 5185 4183
μαστίγων καὶ πνευμάτων πονηρῶν, καὶ τυφλοῖς πολλοῖς
plagues and spirits evil, and blind ones to many

5483 3588 991 2532 611 3588 2424 2036 846
ἐχαρίσατο τὸ βλέπειν. 22 καὶ ἀποκριθεὶς ὁ Ἰησοῦς εἶπεν αὐτοῖς,
He freely gave to see. And answering Jesus said to them,

4198 518 2491 3739 1492 2532 191
Πορευθέντες ἀπαγγείλατε Ἰωάννῃ ἃ εἴδετε καὶ ἠκούσατε·
Going report to John what you saw and heard:

3754 5185 308 5560 4043 3015
ὅτι τυφλοὶ ἀναβλέπουσι, χωλοὶ περιπατοῦσι, λεπροὶ
Blind ones seeing again; lame ones walking about; lepers

2511 2974 191 3498 1453 4434
καθαρίζονται, κωφοὶ ἀκούουσι, νεκροὶ ἐγείρονται, πτωχοὶ
are being cleansed, deaf ones hearing; dead ones are raised; poor ones

2097 2532 3107 2076 3739 1437 3361 4624
εὐαγγελίζονται· 23 καὶ μακάριός ἐστιν, ὃς ἐὰν μὴ σκανδαλισθῇ
are being given the gospel; and blessed is whoever not is offended

1722 1698
ἐν ἐμοί.
in Me.

565 1161 3588 32 2491 756 3004
24 Ἀπελθόντων δὲ τῶν ἀγγέλων Ἰωάννου, ἤρξατο λέγειν
going away And the messengers of John, He began to speak

4314 3588 3793 4012 2491 5101 1831 1519 3588
πρὸς τοὺς ὄχλους περὶ Ἰωάννου, Τί ἐξεληλύθατε εἰς τὴν
to the crowds concerning John. What did you go out to the

2048 2300 2563 5259 417 4531 235
ἔρημον θεάσασθαι; κάλαμον ὑπὸ ἀνέμου σαλευόμενον; 25 ἀλλὰ
wilderness to behold? A reed by wind being shaken? But

5101 1831 1492 444 1722 3120 2440
τί ἐξεληλύθατε ἰδεῖν; ἄνθρωπον ἐν μαλακοῖς ἱματίοις
what did you go out to see? A man in soft clothing

294 2400 3588 1722 2441 1741 2532 5172
ἠμφιεσμένον; ἰδού, οἱ ἐν ἱματισμῷ ἐνδόξῳ καὶ τρυφῇ
being dressed? Behold! Those in clothing splendid and in luxury

5225 1722 3588 934 1526 235 5101 1831
ὑπάρχοντες ἐν τοῖς βασιλείοις εἰσίν. 26 ἀλλὰ τί ἐξεληλύθατε
being in king's palaces are. But what did you go out

1492 4396 3483 3004 5213 2532 4053 4396
ἰδεῖν; προφήτην; ναί, λέγω ὑμῖν, καὶ περισσότερον προ-
to see? A prophet? Yes, I say to you, and more than a

4396 3778 2076 4012 3739 1125 2400 1473 649
φήτου. 27 οὗτός ἐστι περὶ οὗ γέγραπται, Ἰδού, ἐγὼ ἀπο-
prophet! This is (he) about whom it has been written, Behold! I send

649 3588 32 3450 4253 4383 4675 3739 2680
στέλλω τὸν ἄγγελόν μου πρὸ προσώπου σου, ὃς κατα-
the messenger of Me before (the) face of you, who will

2680 3588 3598 4675 1715 4675 3004 1063 5213 3187
σκευάσει τὴν ὁδόν σου ἔμπροσθέν σου. 28 λέγω γὰρ ὑμῖν, μείζων
prepare the way of You before You. I say For to you, greater

King James Version

that should come? or look we for another?
20 When the men were come unto him, they said, John Baptist hath sent us unto thee, saying, Art thou he that should come? or look we for another?

21 And in that same hour he cured many of (their) infirmities and plagues, and of evil spirits; and unto many (that were) blind he gave sight.
22 Then Jesus answering said unto them, Go your way, and tell John what things ye have seen and heard; how that the blind see, the lame walk, the lepers are cleansed, the deaf hear, the dead are raised, to the poor the gospel is preached.

23 And blessed is (he), whosoever shall not be offended in me.

24. And when the messengers of John were departed, he began to speak unto the people concerning John, What went ye out into the wilderness for to see? A reed shaken with the wind?
25 But what went ye out for to see? A man clothed in soft raiment? Behold, they which are gorgeously apparelled, and live delicately, are in kings' courts.

26 But what went ye out for to see? A prophet? Yea, I say unto you, and much more than a prophet.

27 This is (he), of whom it is written, Behold, I send my messenger before thy face, which shall prepare thy way before thee.

28 For I say unto you,

Literal Translation

Luke 7:29

King James Version

Among (those) born of a woman, no prophet is greater than John the Baptist. But the least (one) in the kingdom of God is greater than he is.

29 And all the people and the tax collectors hearing, (they) justified God, being baptized (in) the baptism of John.

30 But the Pharisees and the lawyers set aside God's counsel as to themselves, not being baptized by him.

31. And the Lord said, Then to what shall I compare the men of this generation? And to what are they like?

32 They are like children sitting in a market and calling to one another, and saying, We piped to you, and you did not dance; we mourned to you, and you did not weep.

33 For John the Baptist has come neither eating bread nor drinking wine, and you say, He has a demon.

34 The Son of man has come eating and drinking, and you say, Behold, a man, a glutton and a drunkard, a friend of tax collectors and sinners.

35 But wisdom was justified from all her children.

36. And a certain one of the Pharisees asked Him that He eat with him. And going into the Pharisee's house, He reclined.

37 And, behold, a woman who was a sinner in the city, knowing that He had reclined in the Pharisee's house, taking an alabaster vial of ointment,

38 and standing at His feet, weeping behind (Him),

1722 1084 1135 4396 2491 3588 910
ἐν γεννητοῖς γυναικῶν προφήτης Ἰωάννου τοῦ βαπτιστοῦ
among (those) born of a woman prophet (than) John the Baptist

3762 2076 3588 1161 3398 1722 3588 932 3588 2316
οὐδείς ἐστιν· ὁ δὲ μικρότερος ἐν τῇ βασιλείᾳ τοῦ Θεοῦ
no one is. the But least (one) in the kingdom of God

3187 846 2076 2532 3956 3588 2992 191 2532 3588 5057
μείζων αὐτοῦ ἐστι. 29 καὶ πᾶς ὁ λαὸς ἀκούσας καὶ οἱ τελῶναι
greater he is. And all the people hearing, also the tax-collectors,

1344 3588 2316 907 3588 908 2491
ἐδικαίωσαν τὸν Θεόν, βαπτισθέντες τὸ βάπτισμα Ἰωάννου·
justified God, having been baptized (in) the baptism of John.

3588 1161 5330 2532 3588 3544 3588 1012 3588 2316
30 οἱ δὲ Φαρισαῖοι καὶ οἱ νομικοὶ τὴν βουλὴν τοῦ Θεοῦ
the But Pharisees and the lawyers the counsel of God

114 1519 1438 3361 907 5259 846 2036 1161
ἠθέτησαν εἰς ἑαυτούς, μὴ βαπτισθέντες ὑπ' αὐτοῦ. 31. εἶπε δὲ
set aside, for themselves, not have been baptized by him. said And

3588 2962 5101 3767 3666 3588 444 3588 1074
ὁ Κύριος, Τίνι οὖν ὁμοιώσω τοὺς ἀνθρώπους τῆς γενεᾶς
the Lord, To what then shall I liken the men generation

3778 2532 5101 1526 3664 3664 1526 3813 3588 1722
ταύτης, καὶ τίνι εἰσὶν ὅμοιοι; 32 ὅμοιοί εἰσι παιδίοις τοῖς ἐν
of this, and to what are they like? like They are (to) children in

58 2521 2532 4377 240 2532
ἀγορᾷ καθημένοις, καὶ προσφωνοῦσιν ἀλλήλοις, καὶ
a market sitting and calling to one another, and

3004 832 5213 2532 3756 3738 2354
λέγουσιν, Ηὐλήσαμεν ὑμῖν καὶ οὐκ ὠρχήσασθε· ἐθρηνή-
saying, We piped to you and not you danced; we

5213 2532 3756 2799 2064 1063 2491 3588
σαμεν ὑμῖν, καὶ οὐκ ἐκλαύσατε. 33 ἐλήλυθε γὰρ Ἰωάννης ὁ
mourned to you, and not you wept. has come For John the

910 3383 740 2068 3383 3631 4095 2532 3004
βαπτιστὴς μήτε ἄρτον ἐσθίων μήτε οἶνον πίνων, καὶ λέγετε,
Baptist neither bread eating nor wine drinking, and you say,

1140 2192 2064 3588 5207 3588 444 2068 2532
Δαιμόνιον ἔχει· 34 ἐλήλυθεν ὁ υἱὸς τοῦ ἀνθρώπου ἐσθίων καὶ
A demon he has. has come The Son of man eating and

4095 2532 3004 2400 444 5314 2532 3630
πίνων, καὶ λέγετε, Ἰδού, ἄνθρωπος φάγος καὶ οἰνοπότης,
drinking, and you say, Behold, a man, a glutton and a winebibber,

5057 5384 2532 268 2532 1344 3588 4678 575
τελωνῶν φίλος καὶ ἁμαρτωλῶν. 35 καὶ ἐδικαιώθη ἡ σοφία ἀπὸ
of tax-collectors friend and sinners. And was justified the wisdom from

3588 5043 846 3956
τῶν τέκνων αὐτῆς πάντων.
the children of her all.

2065 1161 5100 846 3588 5330 2443 5315 3326
36. Ἠρώτα δέ τις αὐτὸν τῶν Φαρισαίων ἵνα φάγῃ μετ'
asked And one Him of the Pharisees, that He eat with

846 2532 1525 1519 3588 3614 3588 5330 347
αὐτοῦ· καὶ εἰσελθὼν εἰς τὸν οἶκον τοῦ Φαρισαίου ἀνεκλίθη.
him. And going into the house of the Pharisee He reclined.

2532 2400 1135 1722 3588 4172 3748 2258 268 1921
37 καὶ ἰδού, γυνὴ ἐν τῇ πόλει, ἥτις ἦν ἁμαρτωλός, ἐπιγνοῦσα
And behold! A woman in the city, who was a sinner, knowing

3754 345 1722 3588 3614 3588 5330 2865 211
ὅτι ἀνάκειται ἐν τῇ οἰκίᾳ τοῦ Φαρισαίου, κομίσασα ἀλά-
that He had reclined in the house of the Pharisee, taking an

3464 2532 2476 3844 3588 4228 846 3694
βαστρον μύρου, 38 καὶ στᾶσα παρὰ τοὺς πόδας αὐτοῦ ὀπίσω
alabaster vial of ointment, and standing at the feet of Him behind

Among those that are born of women there is not a greater prophet than John the Baptist: but he that is least in the kingdom of God is greater than he.

29 And all the people that heard (him), and the publicans, justified God, being baptized with the baptism of John.

30 But the Pharisees and lawyers rejected the counsel of God against themselves, being not baptized of him.

31. And the Lord said, Whereunto then shall I liken the men of this generation? and to what are they like?

32 They are like unto children sitting in the marketplace, and calling one to another, and saying, We have piped unto you, and ye have not danced; we have mourned to you, and ye have not wept.

33 For John the Baptist came neither eating bread nor drinking wine; and ye say, He hath a devil.

34 The Son of man is come eating and drinking; and ye say, Behold a gluttonous man, and a winebibber, a friend of publicans and sinners!

35 But wisdom is justified of all her children.

36. And one of the Pharisees desired him that he would eat with him. And he went into the Pharisee's house, and sat down to meat.

37 And, behold, a woman in the city, which was a sinner, when she knew that (Jesus) sat at meat in the Pharisee's house, brought an alabaster box of ointment,

38 And stood at his feet behind (him)

Luke 7:39

Literal Translation

she began to wet His feet with tears. And she was wiping with the hairs of her head. And (she) ardently kissed His feet and was anointing (them) with the ointment.

39 But seeing, the Pharisee who had invited Him spoke within himself, saying, This one, if he was a prophet, would have known who and what the woman who touches him (is); for she is a sinner.

40 And answering, Jesus said to the man, Simon, I have a thing to say to you. And he said, Teacher, say (it).

41 There were two debtors to a certain creditor: the one owed five hundred denarii and (the) other fifty.
42 But they not having (a thing) to repay, he freely forgave both. Then which of them do (you) say will love him most?
43 And answering, Simon said, I suppose (the one) to whom he freely forgave the most. And He said to him, You judged rightly.

44 And turning to the woman, He said to Simon, Do you see this woman? I came into your house. You did not give water for My feet, but she washed My feet with tears and wiped off with the hairs of her head.

45 You gave Me no kiss, but she from (when) I entered did not stop fervently kissing My feet.

46 You did not anoint My head with oil, but she anointed My feet with ointment.
47 For this reason I say to you, her many sins are forgiven, for she loved much. But to whom little

2799 756 1026 3588 4228 846 3588 1144
κλαίουσα, ἤρξατο βρέχειν τοὺς πόδας αὐτοῦ τοῖς δάκρυσι,
weeping, began to wet the feet of Him with the tears,

2532 3588 2359 3588 2776 846 1591 2532 2705
καὶ ταῖς θριξὶ τῆς κεφαλῆς αὐτῆς ἐξέμασσε, καὶ κατεφίλει
and with the hairs of the head of her she was wiping, and kissing

3588 4228 846 2532 218 3588 3464 1492 1161 3588 5330
τοὺς πόδας αὐτοῦ, καὶ ἤλειφε τῷ μύρῳ. 39 ἰδὼν δὲ ὁ Φαρισαῖος
the feet of Him, and anointing with the ointment. seeing And the Pharisee

3588 2564 846 2036 1722 1438 3004 3778 148 2258
ὁ καλέσας αὐτὸν εἶπεν ἐν ἑαυτῷ λέγων, Οὗτος, εἰ ἦν
having invited Him, he spoke within himself, saying, This one, if He was

4396 1097 302 5101 2532 4217 3588 1135 3748
προφήτης, ἐγίνωσκεν ἂν τίς καὶ ποταπὴ ἡ γυνὴ ἥτις
a prophet, would have known who and what sort the woman (is) who

680 846 3754 268 2076 2532 611 3588
ἅπτεται αὐτοῦ, ὅτι ἁμαρτωλός ἐστι. 40 καὶ ἀποκριθεὶς ὁ
touches him, that a sinner she is. And answering

2424 2036 4314 846 4613 2192 4671 5100 2036 3588 1161 5346
Ἰησοῦς εἶπε πρὸς αὐτόν, Σίμων, ἔχω σοί τι εἰπεῖν. ὁ δέ φησι,
Jesus said to him, Simon, I have to you a thing to say. he And says,

1320 2036 1417 5533 2258 1157 5100/3588
Διδάσκαλε, εἰπέ. 41 Δύο χρεοφειλέται ἦσαν δανειστῇ τινι· ὁ
Teacher, speak. Two debtors were to a creditor certain. The

1520 3784 1220 4001 3588/1161 2087 4004 3361
εἷς ὤφειλε δηνάρια πεντακόσια, ὁ δὲ ἕτερος πεντήκοντα. 42 μὴ
one owed denarii five hundred, the and other fifty. not

2192 1161 846 591 297 5483 5101
ἐχόντων δὲ αὐτῶν ἀποδοῦναι, ἀμφοτέροις ἐχαρίσατο. τίς
having And them (a thing) to repay, both he freely forgave. Who

3767 846 2036 4119 846 25 611 1161/3588
οὖν αὐτῶν, εἰπέ, πλεῖον αὐτὸν ἀγαπήσει; 43 ἀποκριθεὶς δὲ ὁ
then of them say (you) more him will love. answering And

4613 2036 5274 3754 3739 3588 4119 5483 3588
Σίμων εἶπεν, Ὑπολαμβάνω ὅτι ᾧ τὸ πλεῖον ἐχαρίσατο. ὁ
Simon said, I suppose (it was) to whom the more he freely forgave. He

1161 2036 846 3723 2919 2532 4762 4314 3588
δὲ εἶπεν αὐτῷ, Ὀρθῶς ἔκρινας. 44 καὶ στραφεὶς πρὸς τὴν
And said to him, Rightly you judged. And turning to the

1135 3588 4613 5346 991 3778 3588 1135
γυναῖκα τῷ Σίμωνι ἔφη, Βλέπεις ταύτην τὴν γυναῖκα;
woman, to Simon He said, See this woman?

1525 4675 1519 3588 3614 5204 1909 3588 4228 3450 3756
εἰσῆλθόν σου εἰς τὴν οἰκίαν, ὕδωρ ἐπὶ τοὺς πόδας μου οὐκ
I went of you into the house, water on the feet of Me not

1325 846 1161 3588 1144 1026 3450 3588 4228 2532 3588
ἔδωκας· αὕτη δὲ τοῖς δάκρυσιν ἔβρεξέ μου τοὺς πόδας, καὶ ταῖς
you gave. she But with the tears wet of Me the feet, and with the

2359 3588 2776 846 1591 5370 3427 3756 1325
θριξὶ τῆς κεφαλῆς αὐτῆς ἐξέμαξε. 45 φίλημά μοι οὐκ ἔδωκας·
hairs head of her wiped off. A kiss to Me not you gave,

846 1161 575 3739 1525 3756 1257 2705 3450 3588
αὕτη δέ, ἀφ᾽ ἧς εἰσῆλθον οὐ διέλιπε καταφιλοῦσά μου τοὺς
she but from (when) I came in not did cease fervently kissing of Me the

4228 1637 3588 2776 3450 3756 218 846 1161 3464
πόδας. 46 ἐλαίῳ τὴν κεφαλήν μου οὐκ ἤλειψας· αὕτη δὲ μύρῳ
feet. With oil the head of Me not you anointed. she But with ointment

218 3450 3588 4228 3739 5484 3004 4671 863
ἤλειψε μου τοὺς πόδας. 47 οὗ χάριν, λέγω σοι, ἀφέωνται
anointed of Me the feet. Of which (for this cause) I say to you, are remitted

3588 266 846 3588 4183 3754 25 4183 3739 1161 3641
αἱ ἁμαρτίαι αὐτῆς αἱ πολλαί, ὅτι ἠγάπησε πολύ· ᾧ δὲ ὀλίγον
the sins of her many, because she loved much; to whom but little

King James Version

weeping, and began to wash his feet with tears, and did wipe (them) with the hairs of her head, and kissed his feet, and anointed (them) with the ointment.
39 Now when the Pharisee which had bidden him saw (it), he spake within himself, saying, This man, if he were a prophet, would have known who and what manner of woman (this is) that toucheth him: for she is a sinner.

40 And Jesus answering said unto him, Simon, I have somewhat to say unto thee. And he saith, Master, say on.

41 There was a certain creditor which had two debtors: the one owed five hundred pence, and the other fifty.
42 And when they had nothing to pay, he frankly forgave them both. Tell me therefore, which of them will love him most?
43 Simon answered and said, I suppose that (he), to whom he forgave most. And he said unto him, Thou hast rightly judged.

44 And he turned to the woman, and said unto Simon, Seest thou this woman? I entered into thine house, thou gavest me no water for my feet: but she hath washed my feet with tears, and wiped (them) with the hairs of her head.

45 Thou gavest me no kiss: but this woman since the time I came in hath not ceased to kiss my feet.
46 My head with oil thou didst not anoint: but this woman hath anointed my feet with ointment.
47 Wherefore I say unto thee, Her sins, which are many, are forgiven; for she loved much: but to whom little

Literal Translation

Luke 7:48

King James Version

is forgiven, he loves lit-tle.
48 And He said to her, Your sins are remitted.
49 And those reclining with (Him) began to say within themselves, Who is this who even remits sins?
50 But He said to the woman, Your faith has saved you. Go in peace.

863 3641 25 2036 1161 846 863 4675 3588
ἀφίεται, ὀλίγον ἀγαπᾷ. 48 εἶπε δὲ αὐτῇ, Ἀφέωνταί σου αἱ
is forgiven, little he loves. He said And to her, are remitted of you the
266 2532 756 3588 4873 3004 1722 1438
ἁμαρτίαι. 49 καὶ ἤρξαντο οἱ συνανακείμενοι λέγειν ἐν ἑαυτοῖς,
sins. And began those reclining with (Him) to say within themselves,
5101 3778 2076 3739 2532 266 863 2036 1161 4314 3588
Τίς οὗτός ἐστιν ὃς καὶ ἁμαρτίας ἀφίησιν; 50 εἶπε δὲ πρὸς τὴν
Who this is who even sins remits? He said But to the
1135 3588 4102 4675 4982 4571 4198 1519 1515
γυναῖκα, Ἡ πίστις σου σέσωκέ σε· πορεύου εἰς εἰρήνην.
woman, The faith of you has saved you. Go in peace.

is forgiven, (the same) loveth little.
48 And he said unto her, Thy sins are forgiven.
49 And they that sat at meat with him began to say within themselves, Who is this that forgiveth sins also?
50 And he said to the woman, Thy faith hath saved thee; go in peace.

Luke 8

Luke 8

Luke 8

1. And it happened afterwards, even He traveled in every city and village, preaching and announcing the gospel of the kingdom of God. And the Twelve (were) with Him;
2 also certain women who were healed from evil spirits and infirmities: Mary, having been called Magdalene, from whom seven demons had gone out,
3 and Joanna, wife of Chuza, Herod's steward, and Susanna, and many others, who were ministering to Him of their possessions.

2532 1096 1722 3588 2517 2532 846 1353 2596 4172
1. Καὶ ἐγένετο ἐν τῷ καθεξῆς, καὶ αὐτὸς διώδευε κατὰ πόλιν
And it was in the afterwards, and He traveled through city by city
2532 2968 2784 2532 2097 3588 932 3588
καὶ κώμην, κηρύσσων καὶ εὐαγγελιζόμενος τὴν βασιλείαν τοῦ
and village, preaching and announcing the gospel of the kingdom
2316 2532 3588 1427 4862 846 2532 1135 5100 3739 2258
Θεοῦ· καὶ οἱ δώδεκα σὺν αὐτῷ, 2 καὶ γυναῖκές τινες αἳ ἦσαν
of God, and the twelve with him, also women certain who were
2323 575 4151 4190 2532 769
τεθεραπευμέναι ἀπὸ πνευμάτων πονηρῶν καὶ ἀσθενειῶν,
healed from spirits evil and infirmities:
3137 3588 2564 3094 575 3739 1140 2033
Μαρία ἡ καλουμένη Μαγδαληνή, ἀφ' ἧς δαιμόνια ἑπτὰ
Mary having been called Magdalene, from whom demons seven
1831 2532 2489 1135 5529 2012 2264 2532
ἐξεληλύθει, 3 καὶ Ἰωάννα γυνὴ Χουζᾶ ἐπιτρόπου Ἡρώδου, καὶ
had gone out; and Joanna wife of Chuza steward of Herod; and
4677 2532 2087 4183 3748 1247 846 575 3588
Σουσάννα, καὶ ἕτεραι πολλαί, αἵτινες διηκόνουν αὐτῷ ἀπὸ τῶν
Susanna; and others many who ministered to Him from the
5224 846
ὑπαρχόντων αὐταῖς.
possessions of them.

1. And it came to pass afterward, that he went throughout every city and village, preaching and shewing the glad tidings of the kingdom of God: and the twelve (were) with him,
2 And certain women, which had been healed of evil spirits and infirmities, Mary called Magdalene, out of whom went seven devils,
3 And Joanna the wife of Chuza Herod's steward, and Susanna, and many others, which ministered unto him of their substance.

4. And a large crowd coming together, and those in each city coming to Him, He spoke through a parable:
5. The sower went out to sow his seed. And as he sowed, some fell by the roadway and was trampled; and the birds of the heaven ate it.
6 And other fell on the rock; and sprouting, it dried up because of not having moisture.
7 And other fell in (the) midst of the thorns; and springing up with the thornbushes, (they) choked it.
8 And other fell on the

4896 1161 3793 4183 2532 3588 2596 4172 1975
4. Συνιόντος δὲ ὄχλου πολλοῦ καὶ τῶν κατὰ πόλιν ἐπιπο-
coming together And crowd a large, and those in each city having
4314 846 2036 1223 3850 1831 3588
ρευομένων πρὸς αὐτὸν, εἶπε διὰ παραβολῆς, 5 Ἐξῆλθεν ὁ
come to Him, He said through a parable: Went out the
4687 3588 4687 3588 4703 846 2532 1722 3588 4687
σπείρων τοῦ σπεῖραι τὸν σπόρον αὐτοῦ. καὶ ἐν τῷ σπείρειν
(one) sowing to sow the seed of him. And in the sowing
846 3739 3303 4098 3844 3588 3598 2532 2662 2532 3588
αὐτὸν, ὃ μὲν ἔπεσε παρὰ τὴν ὁδόν, καὶ κατεπατήθη, καὶ τὰ
of him, one indeed fell beside the way, and was trampled; and the
4071 3588 3772 2719 846 2532 2087 4098 1909
πετεινὰ τοῦ οὐρανοῦ κατέφαγεν αὐτό. 6 καὶ ἕτερον ἔπεσεν ἐπὶ
birds of the heaven ate it. And other fell on
3588 4073 2532 5453 3583 1223 3588 3361 2192 2429
τὴν πέτραν, καὶ φυὲν ἐξηράνθη, διὰ τὸ μὴ ἔχειν ἰκμάδα.
the rock, and growing it dried up because of not having moisture.
2532 2087 4098 1722 3319 3588 173 2532 4855 3588
7 καὶ ἕτερον ἔπεσεν ἐν μέσῳ τῶν ἀκανθῶν, καὶ συμφυεῖσαι αἱ
And other fell in the middle of the thorns, and growing up with the
173 638 846 2532 2087 4098 1909 3588
ἄκανθαι ἀπέπνιξαν αὐτό. 8 καὶ ἕτερον ἔπεσεν ἐπὶ τὴν
thornbushes choked it. And other fell on

4. And when much people were gathered together, and were come to him out of every city, he spake by a parable:
5. A sower went out to sow his seed: and as he sowed, some fell by the way side; and it was trodden down, and the fowls of the air devoured it.
6 And some fell upon a rock; and as soon as it was sprung up, it withered away, because it lacked moisture.
7 And some fell among thorns; and the thorns sprang up with it, and choked it.
8 And other fell on

Literal Translation	Luke 8:9	*King James Version*

Literal Translation

good ground; and springing up, it produced fruit a hundredfold. Saying these things, He cried out, The one having ears to hear, let him hear.

9. And His disciples questioned Him, saying, What might this parable be?

10 And He said, To you it has been given to know the mysteries of the kingdom of God, but to the rest in parables, that seeing they might not see, and hearing, they might not understand. (Isa. 6:9)

11 And this is the parable: The seed is the Word of God.

12 And those beside the way are those hearing, then the devil comes and takes away the Word from their heart, lest believing they may be saved.

13 And those on the rock (are) those who, when they hear, receive the Word with joy; but these have no root, who believe for a time, and in time of trial draw back.

14 And those falling in the thornbushes, these are those hearing, but under anxieties and riches and pleasures of life, having moved along, they are choked, and do not bear to maturity.

15 And those in the good ground, these are the (ones) who in a right and good heart, hearing the Word, they hold (it) and bear fruit in patience.

16. But no one lighting a lamp covers it with a vessel, or puts (it) underneath a couch, but sets (it) on a lampstand, that those coming in may see the light.

17 For nothing is hidden which will not be revealed,

Luke 8:9

1093 3588 18 2532 5453 4160 2590 1542
γῆν τὴν ἀγαθήν, καὶ φυὲν ἐποίησε καρπὸν ἑκατονταπλασίονα.
earth the good, and growing it produced fruit a hundredfold.

5023 3004 5455 3588 2192 3775 191 191
ταῦτα λέγων ἐφώνει, Ὁ ἔχων ὦτα ἀκούειν ἀκουέτω.
These things saying He cried, Those having ears to hear, let him hear.

1905 1161 846 3588 3101 846 3004 5101
9. Ἐπηρώτων δὲ αὐτὸν οἱ μαθηταὶ αὐτοῦ, λέγοντες, Τίς
questioned And Him the disciples of Him, saying, What

1498 3588 3850 3778 3588 1161 2036 5213 1325 1097 3588
εἴη ἡ παραβολὴ αὕτη; 10 ὁ δὲ εἶπεν, Ὑμῖν δέδοται γνῶναι τὰ
might be parable this? He And said, To you it was given to know the

3466 3588 932 3588 2316 3588 1161 3062 1722
μυστήρια τῆς βασιλείας τοῦ Θεοῦ· τοῖς δὲ λοιποῖς ἐν
mysteries of the kingdom of God, to the but rest in

3850 2443 991 3361 991 2532 191 3361
παραβολαῖς, ἵνα βλέποντες μὴ βλέπωσι, καὶ ἀκούοντες μὴ
parables, that seeing not they may see, and hearing not

4920 2076 1161 3778 3588 3850 3588 4703 2076 3588
συνιῶσιν. 11 ἔστι δὲ αὕτη ἡ παραβολή· ὁ σπόρος ἐστὶν ὁ
they might know. is And this the parable: The seed is the

3056 3588 2316 3588 1161 3844 3588 3598 1526 3588 191
λόγος τοῦ Θεοῦ. 12 οἱ δὲ παρὰ τὴν ὁδόν εἰσιν οἱ ἀκούοντες,
Word of God. those And beside the way are those hearing,

1534 2064 3588 1228 2532 142 3588 3056 575 3588 2588
εἶτα ἔρχεται ὁ διάβολος καὶ αἴρει τὸν λόγον ἀπὸ τῆς καρδίας
then comes the devil and takes the Word from the heart

846 2443 3361 4100 4982 3588 1161 1909 3588
αὐτῶν, ἵνα μὴ πιστεύσαντες σωθῶσιν. 13 οἱ δὲ ἐπὶ τῆς
of them, lest believing they may be saved. those And on the

4073 3739 3752 191 3326 5479 1209 3588 3056
πέτρας οἳ, ὅταν ἀκούσωσι, μετὰ χαρᾶς δέχονται τὸν λόγον,
rock who, when they hear, with joy (they) receive the Word,

2532 3778 4491 3756 2192 3739 4314 2540 4100
καὶ οὗτοι ῥίζαν οὐκ ἔχουσιν, οἳ πρὸς καιρὸν πιστεύουσι,
but these root not do have, who for a time believe,

2532 1722 2540 3986 868 3588 1161/1519/3588 173
καὶ ἐν καιρῷ πειρασμοῦ ἀφίστανται. 14 τὸ δὲ εἰς τὰς ἀκάνθας
and in time of trial draw back. the (one) And into the thornbushes

4098 3778 1526 3588 191 2532 5259 3308 2532
πεσόν, οὗτοί εἰσιν οἱ ἀκούσαντες, καὶ ὑπὸ μεριμνῶν καὶ
falling, these are those hearing, and under anxieties and

4149 2532 2237 3588 979 4198 4846
πλούτου καὶ ἡδονῶν τοῦ βίου πορευόμενοι συμπνίγονται,
riches and pleasures of life moving along, they are choked,

2532 3756 5052 3588 1161 1722 3588 2570 1093 3778 1526
καὶ οὐ τελεσφοροῦσι. 15 τὸ δὲ ἐν τῇ καλῇ γῇ, οὗτοί εἰσιν
and not do bear to maturity. the (one) And in the good earth, these are

3748 1722 2588 2570 2532 18 191 3588 3056
οἵτινες ἐν καρδίᾳ καλῇ καὶ ἀγαθῇ ἀκούσαντες τὸν λόγον
(those) who in a heart right and good hearing the Word,

2722 2532 2592 1722 5281
κατέχουσι, καὶ καρποφοροῦσιν ἐν ὑπομονῇ.
they hold (it), and bear fruit in patience.

3762 1161 3088 681 2572 846 4632 2228 5270
16.Οὐδεὶς δὲ λύχνον ἅψας καλύπτει αὐτὸν σκεύει, ἢ ὑποκάτω
no one But a lamp having lit covers it with a vessel, or beneath

2825 5087 235 1909 3087 2007 2443/3588 1531
κλίνης τίθησιν, ἀλλ' ἐπὶ λυχνίας ἐπιτίθησιν, ἵνα οἱ εἰσπορ-
a couch puts (it), but on a lampstand puts (it), that those coming

991 3588/5457 3756/1063 2076 2927 3739/3756 5318
ευόμενοι βλέπωσι τὸ φῶς. 17οὐ γάρ ἐστι κρυπτὸν, ὃ οὐ φανερὸν
in may see the light. not For is hidden which not revealed

King James Version

good ground, and sprang up, and bare fruit an hundredfold. And when he had said these things, he cried, He that hath ears to hear, let him hear.

9. And his disciples asked him, saying, What might this parable be?

10 And he said, Unto you it is given to know the mysteries of the kingdom of God: but to others in parables; that seeing they might not see, and hearing they might not understand.

11 Now the parable is this: The seed is the word of God.

12 Those by the way side are they that hear; then cometh the devil, and taketh away the word out of their hearts, lest they should believe and be saved.

13 They on the rock (are they), which, when they hear, receive the word with joy; and these have no root, which for a while believe, and in time of temptation fall away.

14 And that which fell among thorns are they, which, when they have heard, go forth, and are choked with cares and riches and pleasures of (this) life, and bring no fruit to perfection.

15 But that on the good ground are they, which in an honest and good heart, having heard the word, keep (it), and bring forth fruit with patience.

16. No man, when he hath lighted a candle, covereth it with a vessel, or putteth (it) under a bed; but setteth (it) on a candlestick, that they which enter in may see the light.

17 For nothing is secret, that shall not be made manifest;

Literal Translation | **Luke 8:18** | *King James Version*

nor secret which will not be known and come to be revealed.

1096 3761 614 3739 3756 1097 2532 1519
γενήσεται· οὐδὲ ἀπόκρυφον, ὃ οὐ γνωσθήσεται καὶ εἰς
will be, nor secret which not will be known and to (be)
5318 2064 991 3767 4459 191 3739 1063 302 2192
φανερὸν ἔλθῃ. 18 βλέπετε οὖν πῶς ἀκούετε· ὃς γὰρ ἂν ἔχῃ,
revealed come. see Therefore how you hear; who for ever has,
1325 846 2532 3739 302 3361 2192 2532 3739 1380 2192 142
δοθήσεται αὐτῷ· καὶ ὃς ἂν μὴ ἔχῃ, καὶ ὃ δοκεῖ ἔχειν ἀρθή-
it will be given to him; and who ever not has, even what he seems to have will
575 846
σεται ἀπ' αὐτοῦ.
be taken from him.

neither (any thing) hid, that shall not be known and come abroad.

18 Therefore observe how you hear; for whoever may have, it will be given to him; and whoever may not have, even what he seems to have will be taken from him.

18 Take heed therefore how ye hear: for whosoever hath, to him shall be given; and whosoever hath not, from him shall be taken even that which he seemeth to have.

19. And His mother and (His) brothers came to Him, and were not able to come up with Him through the crowd.

3854 1161 4314 846 3588 3384 2532 3588 80
19. Παρεγένοντο δὲ πρὸς αὐτὸν ἡ μήτηρ καὶ οἱ ἀδελφοὶ
came And to Him the mother and the brothers
846 2532 3756 1410 4940 846 1223 3588 3739
αὐτοῦ, καὶ οὐκ ἠδύναντο συντυχεῖν αὐτῷ διὰ τὸν ὄχλον.
of Him, and not were able to come up with Him through the crowd.

19. Then came to him (his) mother and his brethren, and could not come at him for the press.

20 And it was told to Him, saying Your mother and Your brothers are standing outside wishing to see You.
21 And answering, He said to them, My mother and My brothers are these: the (ones) hearing the Word of God, and doing it.

2532 518 846 3004 3588 3384 4675 2532 3588
20 καὶ ἀπηγγέλη αὐτῷ, λεγόντων, Ἡ μήτηρ σου καὶ οἱ
And it was told Him, saying, The mother of You and the
80 4675 2476 1854 1492 4571 2309 3588 1161
ἀδελφοί σου ἑστήκασιν ἔξω, ἰδεῖν σε θέλοντές. 21 ὁ δὲ
brothers of you are standing outside, to see You desiring. He And
611 2036 4314 846 3384 3450 2532 80 3450
ἀποκριθεὶς εἶπε πρὸς αὐτούς, Μήτηρ μου καὶ ἀδελφοί μου
answering said to them, mother My and brothers My
3778 1526 3588 3588 3056 3588 2316 191 2532 4160
οὗτοί εἰσιν, οἱ τὸν λόγον τοῦ Θεοῦ ἀκούοντες καὶ ποιοῦντες
these are, the (ones) the Word of God hearing and doing
846
αὐτόν.
it.

20 And it was told him (by certain) which said, Thy mother and thy brethren stand without, desiring to see thee.
21 And he answered and said unto them, My mother and my brethren are these which hear the word of God, and do it.

22. And it happened on one of the days that He and His disciples entered into a boat. And He said to them, Let us go over to the other side of the lake. And they set sail.

2532 1096 1722 3391 3588 2250 2532 846 1684 1519
22. Καὶ ἐγένετο ἐν μιᾷ τῶν ἡμερῶν, καὶ αὐτὸς ἐνέβη εἰς
And it was in one of the days, and He entered into
4143 2532 3588 3101 846 2532 2036 4314 846
πλοῖον καὶ οἱ μαθηταὶ αὐτοῦ, καὶ εἶπε πρὸς αὐτούς,
a boat, also the disciples with Him. And He said to them,
1330 1519 3588 4008 3588 3041 2532 321
Διέλθωμεν εἰς τὸ πέραν τῆς λίμνης· καὶ ἀνήχθησαν.
Let us go over to the other side of the lake. And they set sail.

22. Now it came to pass on a certain day, that he went into a ship with his disciples: and he said unto them, Let us go over unto the other side of the lake. And they launched forth.

23 And as they sailed He fell asleep. And a storm of wind came down onto the lake, and they were being filled and were in danger.
24 And coming near they awakened Him, saying, Master! Master! We are perishing! And being aroused, He rebuked the wind and the roughness of the water; and they ceased, and there was a calm.

4126 1161 846 879 2532 2597 2978 417 1519
23 πλεόντων δὲ αὐτῶν ἀφύπνωσε· καὶ κατέβη λαῖλαψ ἀνέμου εἰς
sailing And them, He fell asleep. And came down a storm of wind onto
3588 3041 2532 4845 2532 2793 4334
τὴν λίμνην, καὶ συνεπληροῦντο καὶ ἐκινδύνευον. 24 προσελ-
the lake, and they were being filled and were in danger. coming
1161 1326 846 3004 1988 1988
θόντες δὲ διήγειραν αὐτὸν, λέγοντες, Ἐπιστάτα, ἐπιστάτα,
near And they awakened Him, saying, Master! Master!
622 3588 1161 1453 2008 3588 417 2532 3588
ἀπολλύμεθα. ὁ δὲ εγερθεὶς ἐπετίμησε τῷ ἀνέμῳ καὶ τῷ
We are perishing. He And being aroused rebuked the wind and
2830 3588 5204 2532 3973 2532 1096 1055
κλύδωνι τοῦ ὕδατος· καὶ ἐπαύσαντο, καὶ ἐγένετο γαλήνη.
the roughness of the water, and they ceased, and there was a calm.

23 But as they sailed he fell asleep: and there came down a storm of wind on the lake; and they were filled (with water), and were in jeopardy.
24 And they came to him, and awoke him, saying, Master, master, we perish. Then he arose, and rebuked the wind and the raging of the water: and they ceased, and there was a calm.

25 And He said to them, Where is your faith? And being afraid, they marveled, saying to one another, Who then is this One, that

2036 1161 846 4226 2076 3588 4102 5216 5399 1161
25 εἶπε δὲ αὐτοῖς, Ποῦ ἐστιν ἡ πίστις ὑμῶν; φοβηθέντες δὲ
He said And to them, Where is the faith of you? fearing And
2296 3004 4314 240 5101 687 3778 2076 3754
ἐθαύμασαν, λέγοντες πρὸς ἀλλήλους, Τίς ἄρα οὗτός ἐστιν, ὅτι
they marveled, saying to one another, Who then this One is, that

25 And he said unto them, Where is your faith? And they being afraid wondered, saying one to another, What manner of man is this!

Literal Translation | **Luke 8:26** | **King James Version**

He commands even the wind and the water, and they obey Him?

26. And they sailed down to the country of the Gadarenes, which is opposite Galilee.
27 And He going out onto the land, a certain man out of the city met Him, who had demons from a long time. (And he put no garment on; and he did not stay in a house, but among the tombs).

28 And seeing Jesus, and crying out, he fell down before Him, and, with a loud voice said, What to me and to You, Jesus, Son of God the Most High? I beg You, do not torment me.

29 For He charged the unclean spirit to come out of the man. For many times it had seized him, and he was bound with chains and fetters, being guarded. And tearing apart the bonds, he was driven by the demons into the deserted (places).

30 And Jesus asked him, saying, What is your name? And he said, Legion (because many demons entered into him).

31 And they begged Him that He not order them to go away into the abyss.
32 And there was a herd of many pigs feeding there in the mount. And they begged Him that He allow them to enter into those. And He allowed them.

33 And coming out from the man, the demons entered into the pigs; and the herd rushed down the

2532 3588 417 2004 2532 3588 5204 2532 5219
καὶ τοῖς ἀνέμοις ἐπιτάσσει καὶ τῷ ὕδατι, καὶ ὑπακούουσιν
even the wind He commands and the water, and they obey
846
αὐτῷ;
Him.

2532 2668 1519 3588 5561 3588 1046 3748
26. Καὶ κατέπλευσαν εἰς τὴν χώραν τῶν Γαδαρηνῶν, ἥτις
And they sailed down to the country of the Gadarenes, which
2076 495 3588 1056 1831 1161 846 1909 3588
ἐστὶν ἀντιπέραν τῆς Γαλιλαίας. 27 ἐξελθόντι δὲ αὐτῷ ἐπὶ τὴν
is opposite Galilee. going out And Him onto the
1093 5221 846 435 5100 1537 3588 4172 3739 2192 1140
γῆν ὑπήντησεν αὐτῷ ἀνήρ τις ἐκ τῆς πόλεως, ὃς εἶχε δαι-
land, met Him a man certain out of the city, who had demons
1537 5550 2425 2532 2440 3756 1737 2532
μόνια ἐκ χρόνων ἱκανῶν, καὶ ἱμάτιον οὐκ ἐνεδιδύσκετο, καὶ
from a time long, and a garment not he put on,
1722 3614 3756 3306 235 1722 3588 3418 1492 1161 3588
ἐν οἰκίᾳ οὐκ ἔμενεν, ἀλλ᾽ ἐν τοῖς μνήμασιν. 28 ἰδὼν δὲ τὸν
and in a house not he abode, but among the tombs seeing And .
2424 2532 349 4363 846 2532 5456 3173
Ἰησοῦν, καὶ ἀνακράξας, προσέπεσεν αὐτῷ, καὶ φωνῇ μεγάλῃ
Jesus, and crying out, he fell down before Him, and with a voice loud
2036 5101 1698 2532 4671 2424 5207 3588 2316 3588 5310
εἶπε, Τί ἐμοὶ καὶ σοί, Ἰησοῦ, υἱὲ τοῦ Θεοῦ τοῦ ὑψίστου;
said, What to me and to You, Jesus, Son of God the Most High?
1189 4675 3361 3165 928 3852 1063 3588 4151
δέομαί σου, μή με βασανίσῃς. 29 παρήγγειλε γὰρ τῷ πνεύματι
I beg You, not me do torment. He had charged For the spirit
3588 169 1831 575 3588 444 4183 1063
τῷ ἀκαθάρτῳ ἐξελθεῖν ἀπὸ τοῦ ἀνθρώπου· πολλοῖς γὰρ
unclean to come out from the man. many For
5550 4884 846 2532 1196 254 2532 3976
χρόνοις συνηρπάκει αὐτόν, καὶ ἐδεσμεῖτο ἁλύσεσι καὶ πέδαις
times it had seized him, and he was bound with chains and fetters,
5442 2532 1284 3588 1199 1643 5259 3588
φυλασσόμενος, καὶ διαρρήσσων τὰ δεσμὰ ἠλαύνετο ὑπὸ τοῦ
being guarded; and tearing apart the bonds, he was driven by the
1142 1519 3588 2048 1905 1161 846 3588 2424
δαίμονος εἰς τὰς ἐρήμους. 30 ἐπηρώτησε δὲ αὐτὸν ὁ Ἰησοῦς,
demons into deserted (places). questioned And him Jesus
3004 5101 4671 2076 3686 3588 1161 2036 3003 3754 1140
λέγωμ, Τί σοι ἐστιν ὄνομά; ὁ δὲ εἶπε, Λεγεών· ὅτι δαιμόνια
saying, What to you is (the) name? he And said, Legion; because demons
4183 1525 1519 846 2532 3870 846 2443 3361
πολλὰ εἰσῆλθεν εἰς αὐτόν. 31 καὶ παρεκάλουν αὐτὸν ἵνα μὴ
many entered into him. And they begged Him that not
2004 846 1519 3588 12 565 2258 1161 1563 34
ἐπιτάξῃ αὐτοῖς εἰς τὴν ἄβυσσον ἀπελθεῖν. 32 ἦν δὲ ἐκεῖ ἀγέλη
He order them into the abyss to go away. was And there a herd
5519 2425 1006 1722 3588 3735 2532 3870
χοίρων ἱκανῶν βοσκομένωη ἐν τῷ ὄρει· καὶ παρεκάλουν
pigs of many feeding in the mountain. And they begged
846 2443 2010 846 1519 1565 1525 2532 2010
αὐτὸν ἵνα ἐπιτρέψῃ αὐτοῖς εἰς ἐκείνους εἰσελθεῖν. καὶ ἐπέτρε-
Him that He allow them into those to enter. And He allowed
846 1831 1161 3588 1140 575 3588 444
ψεν αὐτοῖς. 33 ἐξελθόντα δὲ τὰ δαιμόνια ἀπὸ τοῦ ἀνθρώπου
them. coming out And the demons from the man
1525 1519 3588 5519 2532 3729 3588 34 2596 3588
εἰσῆλθεν εἰς τοὺς χοίρους· καὶ ὥρμησεν ἡ ἀγέλη κατὰ τοῦ
they entered into the pigs. And rushed the herd down the

for he commandeth even the winds and water, and they obey him.

26. And they arrived at the country of the Gadarenes, which is over against Galilee.
27 And when he went forth to land, there met him out of the city a certain man, which had devils long time, and ware no clothes, neither abode in (any) house, but in the tombs.

28 When he saw Jesus, he cried out, and fell down before him, and with a loud voice said, What have I to do with thee, Jesus, (thou) Son of God most high? I beseech thee, torment me not.

29 (For he had commanded the unclean spirit to come out of the man. For oftentimes it had caught him: and he was kept bound with chains and in fetters; and he brake the bands, and was driven of the devil into the wilderness.)

30 And Jesus asked him, saying, What is thy name? And he said, Legion: because many devils were entered into him.

31 And they besought him that he would not command them to go out into the deep.
32 And there was there an herd of many swine feeding on the mountain: and they besought him that he would suffer them to enter into them. And he suffered them.

33 Then went the devils out of the man, and entered into the swine: and the herd ran violently down a

Literal Translation

Luke 8:34

precipice into the lake and was choked.
34 And seeing the (thing that) had happened, those feeding (the pigs) fled. And leaving, (they) reported to the city and to the farms.
35 And they went out to see the (thing that) had happened, and came to Jesus. And (they) found the man from whom the demons had gone out, sitting at the feet of Jesus, clothed and of sound mind. And they were afraid.

36 And those seeing also related to them how he having been demon-possessed was healed.
37. And all the multitude of the neighborhood of the Gadarenes were seized with a great fear. And (they) asked Him to depart from them. And entering into the boat, He returned.

38 And the man from whom the demons had gone out begged Him, (desiring) to be with Him. But Jesus dismissed him, saying,

39 Return to your house and relate what things God did to you. And he went away proclaiming through all the city what things Jesus did to him.

40 And it happened (as) Jesus returned, the crowd gladly received Him, for they were all waiting for Him.
41 And, behold! A man named Jairus came, and this one was a synagogue ruler. And falling at the feet of Jesus, he begged Him to come into his house,

42 because an only-born daughter was born to him, about twelve years (old); and she was dying.

2911 1519 3588 3041 2532 638 1492 1161 3588
κρημνοῦ εἰς τὴν λίμνην, καὶ ἀπεπνίγη. 34 ἰδόντες δὲ οἱ
precipice into the lake, and was choked. seeing And those

1006 3588 1096 5343 2532 565 518
βόσκοντες τὸ γεγενημένον ἔφυγον, καὶ ἀπελθόντες ἀπήγ-
feeding the thing having happened, they fled. And leaving (they)

1519 3588 4172 2532 1519 3588 68 1831 1161 1492
γειλαν εἰς τὴν πόλιν καὶ εἰς τοὺς ἀγρούς. 35 ἐξῆλθον δὲ ἰδεῖν
reported to the city and to the farms. they went out And to see

3588 1096 2532 2064 4314 3588 2424 2532 2147 2521
τὸ γεγονός· καὶ ἦλθον πρὸς τὸν Ἰησοῦν, καὶ εὗρον καθή-
that happening, and came to Jesus, and found sitting

3588 444 575 3739 3588 1140 1831 2439
μενον τὸν ἄνθρωπον ἀφ' οὗ τὰ δαιμόνια ἐξεληλύθει, ἱματι-
the man from whom the demons had gone out, clothed

2532 4993 3844 3588 3844 3588 2424
σμένον καὶ σωφρονοῦντα, παρὰ τοὺς πόδας τοῦ Ἰησοῦ·
and of sound mind, at the feet of Jesus.

2532 5399 518 1161 846 2532 1161 1492 4459
καὶ ἐφοβήθησαν. 36 ἀπήγγειλαν δὲ αὐτοῖς καὶ οἱ ἰδόντες πῶς
And they were afraid. related And to them also those having seen how

4982 3588 1139 2532 2065 846 537 3588 4128
ἐσώθη ὁ δαιμονισθείς. 37 καὶ ἠρώτησαν αὐτὸν ἅπαν τὸ πλῆθος
was healed he having been demon-possessed. And asked Him all the multitude

3588 4066 3588 1046 565 575 846 3754 5401
τῆς περιχώρου τῶν Γαδαρηνῶν ἀπελθεῖν ἀπ' αὐτῶν, ὅτι φόβῳ
of the neighborhood of the Gadarenes to depart from them, for with a fear

3173 4912 846 1161 1684 1519 3588 4143 5290
μεγάλῳ συνείχοντο· αὐτὸς δὲ ἐμβὰς εἰς τὸ πλοιον ὑπέστρεψεν.
great they were seized; He And entering into the boat returned.

1189 1161 846 3588 435 575 3739 1831 3588 1140
38 ἐδέετο δὲ αὐτοῦ ὁ ἀνὴρ ἀφ' οὗ ἐξεληλύθει τὰ δαιμόνια
begged And Him the man, from whom had gone out the demons,

1511 4862 846 630 1161 846 3588 2424 3004
εἶναι σὺν αὐτῷ. ἀπέλυσε δὲ αὐτὸν ὁ Ἰησοῦς λέγων,
to be with Him. dismissed But him Jesus, saying,

5290 1519 3588 3624 4675 2532 1334 3745 4160 4671
39 Ὑπόστρεφε εἰς τὸν οἰκόν σου, καὶ διηγοῦ ὅσα ἐποίησε σοι
Return to the house of you and relate what things did to you

3588 2316 2532 565 2596 3650 3588 4172 2784 3745
ὁ Θεός. καὶ ἀπῆλθε, καθ' ὅλην τὴν πόλιν κηρύσσων ὅσα
God. And he went away through all the city proclaiming what things

4160 846 3588 2424
ἐποίησεν αὐτῷ ὁ Ἰησοῦς.
did to him Jesus.

1096 1161 1722 3588 5290 3588 2424 588
40. Ἐγένετο δὲ ἐν τῷ ὑποστρέψαι τὸν Ἰησοῦν, ἀπεδέξατο
it happened And in the returning of Jesus, gladly received

846 3588 3793 2258 1063 3956 4328 846 2532
αὐτὸν ὁ ὄχλος· ἦσαν γὰρ πάντες προσδοκῶντες αὐτόν. 41 καὶ
Him the crowd; they were for all watching for Him. And,

2400 2064 435 3739 3686 2383 2532 846 758 3588
ἰδού, ἦλθεν ἀνὴρ ᾧ ὄνομα Ἰάειρος, καὶ αὐτὸς ἄρχων τῆς
behold! came A man to whom name Jairus, and this one a ruler of the

4864 5225 2532 4098 3844 3588 4228 3588 2424
συναγωγῆς ὑπῆρχε, καὶ πεσὼν παρὰ τοὺς πόδας τοῦ Ἰησοῦ
synagogue was. And falling at the feet of Jesus,

3870 846 1525 1519 3588 3624 846 3754 2364
παρεκάλει αὐτὸν εἰσελθεῖν εἰς τὸν οἶκον αὐτοῦ· 42 ὅτι θυγάτηρ
he begged Him to come into the house of him, because daughter

3439 2258 846 5613 2094 1427 2532 846 599
μονογενὴς ἦν αὐτῷ ὡς ἐτῶν δώδεκα, καὶ αὐτὴ ἀπέθνησκεν.
an only-born was to him, about years twelve, and she was dying.

King James Version

steep place into the lake, and were choked.
34 When they that fed (them) saw what was done, they fled, and went and told (it) in the city and in the country.

35 Then they went out to see what was done; and came to Jesus, and found the man, out of whom the devils were departed, sitting at the feet of Jesus, clothed, and in his right mind: and they were afraid.

36 They also which saw (it) told them by what means he that was possessed of the devils was healed.
37. Then the whole multitude of the country of the Gadarenes round about besought him to depart from them; for they were taken with great fear: and he went up into the ship, and returned back again.
38 Now the man out of whom the devils were departed besought him that he might be with him: but Jesus sent him away, saying,

39 Return to thine own house, and shew how great things God hath done unto thee. And he went his way, and published throughout the whole city how great things Jesus had done unto him.

40 And it came to pass, that, when Jesus was returned, the people (gladly) received him: for they were all waiting for him.
41. And, behold, there came a man named Jairus, and he was a ruler of the synagogue: and he fell down at Jesus' feet, and besought him that he would come into his house:
42 For he had one only daughter, about twelve years of age, and she lay a dying.

Literal Translation **Luke 8:43** ***King James Version***

Literal Translation

And in His going, the crowd pressed on Him.

43. And a woman being in a flow of blood from twelve years, who had spent her whole living on healers, (and) could not be cured by anyone,
44 coming up behind she touched the border of His garment. And instantly the flow of her blood stopped.

45 And Jesus said, Who (was) touching Me? And all denying (it) Peter and those with Him said, Master, the crowds press on You and jostle. And do You say, Who (was) touching Me?

46. But Jesus said, Someone touched Me, for I knew power had gone out from Me.

47 And seeing that she was not hidden, the woman came trembling, and falling down before Him, she declared to Him before all the people for what cause she touched Him, and how she was instantly cured.

48 And He said to her, Daughter, be comforted. Your faith has healed you. Go in peace.

49. (As) He (was) yet speaking, someone came from the synagogue ruler, saying to him, Your daughter has expired. Do not trouble the Teacher.
50 But hearing, Jesus answered him, saying, Do not fear; only believe and she will be cured.

51. And coming into the house, He did not allow anyone to enter, except Peter and James and John, and the father of the girl and

1722 1161 3588 5217 846 3588 3793 4846 846
ἐν δὲ τῷ ὑπάγειν αὐτὸν οἱ ὄχλοι συνέπνιγον αὐτόν.
in And the going of Him the crowd pressed upon Him.

2532 1135 5607 1722 4511 129 575 2094 1427 3748
43. Καὶ γυνὴ οὖσα ἐν ῥύσει αἵματος ἀπὸ ἐτῶν δώδεκα, ἥτις
And a woman being in a flow of blood from years twelve, who

1519 2395 4321 3650 3588 979 3756 2480
εἰς ἰατροὺς προσαναλώσασα ὅλον τὸν βίον οὐκ ἴσχυσεν
to healers had spent whole (her) living, not was able

5259 3762 2323 4334 3693 680
ὑπ' οὐδενὸς θεραπευθῆναι, 44 προσελθοῦσα ὄπισθεν, ἥψατο
by no one be cured. Having come up behind, she touched

3588 2899 3588 2440 846 2532 3916 2476
τοῦ κρασπέδου τοῦ ἱματίου αὐτοῦ· καὶ παραχρῆμ ἔστη
the border of the garment of Him, and instantly stopped

3588 4511 3588 129 846 2532 2036 3588 2424 5101 3588
ἡ ῥύσις τοῦ αἵματος αὐτης. 45 καὶ εἶπεν ὁ Ἰησοῦς, Τίς ὁ
the flow of the blood of her. And said Jesus, Who

680 3450 720 1161 3956 2036 3588 4074 2532
ἁψάμενός μου; ἀρνουμένων δὲ πάντων, εἶπεν ὁ Πέτρος καὶ
(was) touching Me? denying And all, said Peter and

3588 3326 846 1988 3588 3793 4912 4571 2532
οἱ μετ ' αὐτοῦ, Ἐπιστάτα, οἱ ὄχλοι συνέχουσί σε καὶ
those with Him, Master, the crowds press upon You and

598 2532 3004 5101 3588 680 3450 3588 1161 2424
ἀποθλίβουσι. καὶ λέγεις, Τίς ὁ ἁψάμενός μου; 46 ὁ δὲ Ἰησοῦς
jostle; and do You say, Who (was) touching Me? But Jesus

2036 680 3450 5100 1473 1063 1097 1411 1831
εἶπεν, Ἥψατό μού τις· ἐγὼ γὰρ ἔγνων δύναμιν ἐξελθοῦσαν
said, touched Me Someone, I for knew power (was) going

575 1700 1492 1161 3588 1135 3754 3756 2990 5141 2064
ἀπ' ἐμοῦ. 47 ἰδοῦσα δὲ ἡ γυνὴ ὅτι οὐκ ἔλαθε, τρέμουσα ἦλθε,
from Me. seeing And the woman that not she was hidden, trembling came,

2532 4363 846 1223 3739 156 680 846
καὶ προσπεσοῦσα αὐτῷ, δι' ἣν αἰτίαν ἥψατο αὐτοῦ
and falling down before Him, for what cause she touched Him

518 846 1799 3956 3588 2992 2532 5613 2390
ἀπήγγειλεν αὐτῷ ἐνώπιον παντὸς τοῦ λαοῦ, καὶ ὡς ἰάθη
she declared to Him before all of the people, and how she was cured

3916 3588 1161 2036 846 2293 2364 3588 4102
παραχρῆμα. 48 ὁ δὲ εἶπεν αὐτῇ, Θάρσει, θυγάτερ, ἡ πίστις
instantly. He And said to her, Be comforted, daughter, the faith

4675 4982 4571 4198 1519 1515
σου σέσωκέ σε· πορεύου εἰς εἰρήνην.
of you has healed you; go in peace.

2089 846 2980 2064 5100 3844 3588 752
49. Ἔτι αὐτοῦ λαλοῦντος, ἔρχεταί τις παρὰ τοῦ ἀρχισυναγώ-
Yet Him speaking, comes someone from the synagogue ruler

3004 846 3754 2348 3588 2364 4675 3361 4660
γου, λέγων αὐτῷ ὅτι Τέθνηκεν ἡ θυγάτηρ σου· μὴ σκύλλε
saying to Him, has expired The daughter of you; not do trouble

3588 1320 3588 1161 2424 191 611 846
τὸν διδάσκαλον. 50 ὁ δὲ Ἰησοῦς ἀκούσας ἀπεκρίθη αὐτῷ
the Teacher. But Jesus hearing answered him,

3004 3361 5399 3440 4100 2532 4982 1525
λέγων, Μὴ φοβοῦ· μόνον πίστευε, καὶ σωθήσεται. 51 εἰσελθὼν
saying, not Do fear, only believe, and she will be cured. coming

1161 1519 3588 3614 3756 863 1525 3762 1487 3361 4074
δὲ εἰς τὴν οἰκίαν, οὐκ ἀφῆκεν εἰσελθεῖν οὐδένα, εἰ μὴ Πέτρον
And into the house, not He allowed to enter no one except Peter

2532 2385 2532 249 1 2532 3588 3962 3588 3816 2532
καὶ Ἰάκωβον καὶ Ἰωάννην, καὶ τὸν πατέρα τῆς παιδὸς καὶ
and James and John, and the father of the girl and

King James Version

But as he went the people thronged him.

43. And a woman having an issue of blood twelve years, which had spent all her living upon physicians, neither could be healed of any,

44 Came behind (him), and touched the border of his garment: and immediately her issue of blood stanched.

45 And Jesus said, Who touched me? When all denied, Peter and they that were with him said, Master, the multitude throng thee and press (thee), and sayest thou, Who touched me?

46. And Jesus said, Somebody hath touched me: for I perceive that virtue is gone out of me.

47 And when the woman saw that she was not hid, she came trembling, and falling down before him, she declared unto him before all the people for what cause she had touched him, and how she was healed immediately.
48 And he said unto her, Daughter, be of good comfort: thy faith hath made thee whole; go in peace.

49. While he yet spake, there cometh one from the ruler of the synagogue's (house), saying to him, Thy daughter is dead; trouble not the Master.
50 But when Jesus heard (it), he answered him, saying, Fear not: believe only, and she shall be made whole.
51. And when he came into the house, he suffered no man to go in, save Peter, and James, and John, and the father and

Literal Translation

the mother of the child.
52 And all were weeping and bewailing her. But He said, Do not weep. She did not die, but is sleeping.
53 And they ridiculed Him, knowing that she died.
54 But having thrust all outside, and having taken hold of her hand, He called out, saying, Child, rise up!

55 And her spirit returned, and she rose up immediately. And He ordered (something) to eat be given to her.
56 And her parents were amazed. But He charged them to tell no one of that which occurred.

Luke 8:52

3588 3384 2799 1161 3956 2532 2875 846 3588 1161
τὴν μητέρα. 52 ἔκλαιον δὲ πάντες, καὶ ἐκόπτοντο αὐτήν. ὁ δὲ
the mother. were weeping And all, and bewailing her. He But

2036 3361 2799 3756 599 235 2518 2532 2606
εἶπε, Μὴ κλαίετε· οὐκ ἀπέθανεν, ἀλλὰ καθεύδει. 53 καὶ κατε-
said, Not do weep; not she died, but (is) sleeping. And they

846 1492 3754 599 846 1161 1544 1854
γέλων αὐτοῦ, εἰδότες ὅτι ἀπέθανεν. 54 αὐτὸς δὲ ἐκβαλὼν ἔξω
ridiculed Him, knowing that she died. He But having thrust out

3956 2532 2902 3588 5495 846 5455 3004
πάντας, καὶ κρατήσας τῆς χειρὸς αὐτῆς, ἐφώνησε λέγων,
all, and having taken hold of the hand of her, He called, saying,

3588 3816 1453 2532 1994 3588 4151 846 2532 450
Ἡ παῖς ἔγειρου. 55 καὶ ἐπέστρεψε τὸ πνεῦμα αὐτῆς, καὶ ἀνέστη
Child, rise up! And returned the spirit of her, and she rose up

3853 2532 1299 846 1325 5315 2532 1839
παραχρῆμα· καὶ διέταξεν αὐτῇ δοθῆναι φαγεῖν. 56 καὶ ἐξέστη-
immediately. And He ordered her to be given to eat. And were

3588 1118 846 3588 1161 3853 846 3367 2036
σαν οἱ γονεῖς αὐτῆς· ὁ δὲ παρήγγειλεν αὐτοῖς μηδενὶ εἰπεῖν
amazed the parents of her. He But charged them to no one to tell

3588 1096
τὸ γεγονός.
that (which) had occurred.

King James Version

the mother of the maiden.
52 And all wept, and bewailed her: but he said, Weep not; she is not dead, but sleepeth.
53 And they laughed him to scorn, knowing that she was dead.
54 And he put them all out, and took her by the hand, and called, saying, Maid, arise.

55 And her spirit came again, and she arose straightway: and he commanded to give her meat.
56 And her parents were astonished: but he charged them that they should tell no man what was done.

Luke 9

1. And having called together His twelve disciples, He gave them power and authority over all the demons, and to heal diseases.

2 And (He) sent them to proclaim the kingdom of God, and to heal the ones being sick.
3 And He said to them, Take nothing for the way, neither staffs, nor money bag, nor bread, nor silver, nor each to have two tunics.

4 And into whatever house you enter, remain there, and go out from there.
5 And as many as may not receive you, going out from that city even shake off the dust from your feet, for a testimony against them.

6 And going out, they passed through the villages, preaching the gospel, and healing everywhere.

Luke 9

4779 1161 3588 1427 3101 846 1325
1. Συγκαλεσάμενος δὲ τοὺς δώδεκα μαθητὰς αὐτοῦ, ἔδωκεν
having called together And the twelve disciples of Him, He gave

846 1411 2532 1849 1909 3956 3588 1140 2532
αὐτοῖς δύναμιν καὶ ἐξουσίαν ἐπὶ πάντα τὰ δαιμόνια, καὶ
to them power and authority over all the demons, and

3554 2323 2532 649 846 2784 3588
νόσους θεραπεύειν, 2 καὶ ἀπέστειλεν αὐτοὺς κηρύσσειν τὴν
diseases to heal. And He sent them to proclaim the

932 3588 2316 2532 2390 3588 770 2532 2036
βασιλείαν τοῦ Θεοῦ, καὶ ἰᾶσθαι τοὺς ἀσθενοῦντας. 3 καὶ εἶπε
kingdom of God, and to heal those being sick. And He said

4314 846 3367 142 1519 3588 3598 3383 4464
πρὸς αὐτούς, Μηδὲν αἴρετε εἰς τὴν ὁδόν· μήτε ῥάβδους,
to them, Nothing take for the way, neither staffs,

3383 4082 3383 740 3383 694 3383 303 1417
μήτε πήραν, μήτε ἄρτον, μήτε ἀργύριον, μήτε ἀνὰ δύο
nor money bag, nor bread, nor silver, nor each two

5509 2192 2532 1519 3739 302 3614 1525 1563 3306
χιτῶνας ἔχειν. 4 καὶ εἰς ἣν ἂν οἰκίαν εἰσέλθητε, ἐκεῖ μένετε,
tunics to have. And into whatever house you enter, there remain,

2532 1564 1831 2532 3745 302 3361 1209 5209
καὶ ἐκεῖθεν ἐξέρχεσθε. 5 καὶ ὅσοι ἂν μὴ δέξωνται ὑμᾶς,
and from there go out. And as many as not may receive you,

1831 575 3588 4172 1565 2532 3588 2868 575
ἐξερχόμενοι ἀπὸ τῆς πόλεως ἐκείνης καὶ τὸν κονιορτὸν ἀπὸ
going out from city that even the dust from

3588 4228 5216 660 1519 3142 1909 846
τῶν ποδῶν ὑμῶν ἀποτινάξατε εἰς μαρτύριον ἐπ' αὐτούς.
the feet of you shake off, for a testimony against them.

1831 1161 1330 2596 3588 2968 2097
6 ἐξερχόμενοι δὲ διήρχοντο κατὰ τὰς κώμας, εὐαγγελιζόμενοι
going out And they passed through the villages preaching the gospel

2532 2323 3837
καὶ θεραπεύοντες πανταχοῦ.
and healing everywhere.

Luke 9

1. Then he called his twelve disciples together, and gave them power and authority over all devils, and to cure diseases.

2 And he sent them to preach the kingdom of God, and to heal the sick.
3 And he said unto them, Take nothing for (your) journey, neither staves, nor scrip, neither bread, neither money; neither have two coats apiece.

4 And whatsoever house ye enter into, there abide, and thence depart.
5 And whosoever will not receive you, when ye go out of that city, shake off the very dust from your feet for a testimony against them.

6 And they departed, and went through the towns, preaching the gospel, and healing every where.

Literal Translation | **Luke 9:7** | **King James Version**

7. And Herod the tetrarch heard all the things happening by Him, and was perplexed, because of the saying by some that John had been raised from (the) dead, **8** and by some that Elijah had appeared. And others that a prophet of the ancients rose again.

191 1161 2264 3588 5076 3588 1096 5259 846
7. Ἤκουσε δὲ Ἡρῴδης ὁ τετράρχης τὰ γινόμενα ὑπ᾽ αὐτοῦ
hearing And Herod the tetrarch the things happening by Him

3956 2532 1280 1223 3588 3004 5259 5100 3754
πάντα· καὶ διηπόρει διὰ τὸ λέγεσθαι ὑπό τινων ὅτι
all, and was perplexed, because of the saying by some that

2491 1453 1537 3498 5259 5100 1161 3754 2243
Ἰωάννης ἐγήγερται ἐκ νεκρῶν· 8 ὑπό τινων δὲ ὅτι Ἠλίας
John has been raised from (the) dead, by some and that Elijah

5316 243 1161 3754 4396 1520 3588 744 450
ἐφάνη· ἄλλων δὲ ὅτι Προφήτης εἷς τῶν ἀρχαίων ἀνέστη.
had appeared; others and that a prophet of the ancients rose again.

7. Now Herod the tetrarch heard of all that was done by him: and he was perplexed, because that it was said of some, that John was risen from the dead;
8 And of some, that Elias had appeared; and of others, that one of the old prophets was risen again.

9 And Herod said, I beheaded John, but who is this about whom I hear such things? And he sought to see Him.

2532 2036 3588 2264 2491 1473 607 5101 1161
9 καὶ εἶπεν ὁ Ἡρῴδης, Ἰωάννην ἐγὼ ἀπεκεφάλισα· τίς δέ
And said Herod, John I beheaded, who but

2076 3778 4012 3739 1473 191 5108 2532 2212 1492
ἐστιν οὗτος, περὶ οὗ ἐγὼ ἀκούω τοιαῦτα; καὶ ἐζήτει ἰδεῖν
is this about whom I hear such things? And he sought to see

846
αὐτόν.
Him.

9 And Herod said, John have I beheaded: but who is this, of whom I hear such things? And he desired to see him.

10. And returning, the apostles told Him what things they did. And taking them He withdrew privately to a deserted place of a city being called Bethsaida.
11 But knowing (this), the crowds followed Him. And having received them, He spoke to them about the kingdom of God. And He cured those having need of healing.

2532 5290 3588 652 1334 846 3745
10. Καὶ ὑποστρέψαντες οἱ ἀπόστολοι διηγήσαντο αὐτῷ ὅσα
And having returned the apostles told Him what things

4160 2532 3880 846 5298 2596 2398
ἐποίησαν. καὶ παραλαβὼν αὐτούς, ὑπεχώρησε κατ᾽ ἰδίαν
they did. And taking them He withdrew privately

1519 5117 2048 4172 2564 966 3588 1161 3793
εἰς τόπον ἔρημον πόλεως καλουμένης Βηθσαιδά. 11 οἱ δὲ ὄχλοι
to a place deserted of a city being called Bethsaida. the And crowds

1097 190 846 2532 1209 846 2980
γνόντες ἠκολούθησαν αὐτῷ· καὶ δεξάμενος αὐτούς, ἐλάλει
knowing followed Him. And having received them, He spoke

846 4012 3588 932 3588 2316 2532 3588 5532
αὐτοῖς περὶ τῆς βασιλείας τοῦ Θεοῦ, καὶ τοὺς χρείαν
to them about the kingdom of God, and those need

2192 2322 2390 3588 1161 2250 756 2827 4334
ἔχοντας θεραπείας ἰᾶτο. 12 ἡ δὲ ἡμέρα ἤρξατο κλίνειν· προσ-
having of healing He cured. the But day began to decline. coming

10. And the apostles, when they were returned, told him all that they had done. And he took them, and went aside privately into a desert place belonging to the city called Bethsaida.
11 And the people, when they knew (it), followed him: and he received them, and spake unto them of the kingdom of God, and healed them that had need of healing.

12. But the day began to decline. And coming up the Twelve said to Him, Let the crowd go that going to the surrounding villages and the farms they may lodge and find food supplies, because here we are in a deserted place.

1161 3588 1427 2036 846 630 3588 3793
ελθόντες δὲ οἱ δώδεκα εἶπον αὐτῷ, Ἀπόλυσον τὸν ὄχλον,
up And the twelve said to Him, Let go the crowd

2443 565 1519 3588 2945 2968 2532 3588 68 2647
ἵνα ἀπελθόντες εἰς τὰς κύκλῳ κώμας καὶ τοὺς ἀγροὺς κατα-
that going into the around villages and the farms they

2532 2147 1979 3754 5602 1722 2048 5117
λύσωσι, καὶ εὕρωσιν ἐπισιτισμόν· ὅτι ὧδε ἐν ἐρήμῳ τόπῳ
may lodge and may find food supplies, because here in deserted a place

12. And when the day began to wear away, then came the twelve, and said unto him, Send the multitude away, that they may go into the towns and country round about, and lodge, and get victuals: for we are here in a desert place.

13 But He said to them, You give them to eat. But they said, There are not to us more than five loaves and two fish, unless going we buy foods for all this people.

2070 2036 1161 4314 846 1325 846 5210 5315 3588 1161
ἐσμέν. 13 εἶπε δὲ πρὸς αὐτούς, Δότε αὐτοῖς ὑμεῖς φαγεῖν. οἱ δὲ
we are. He said And to them, Give them You to eat. they But

2036 3756 1526 2254 4119 2228 4002 740 2532 1417 2486
εἶπον, Οὐκ εἰσὶν ἡμῖν πλεῖον ἢ πέντε ἄρτοι καὶ δύο ἰχθύες,
said, Not is to us more than five loaves and two fish,

1487 3385 4198 2249 59 1519 3956 3588 2992
εἰ μήτι πορευθέντες ἡμεῖς ἀγοράσωμεν εἰς πάντα τὸν λαὸν
if not going we may buy for all people

13 But he said unto them, Give ye them to eat. And they said, We have no more but five loaves and two fishes; except we should go and buy meat for all this people.

14 For there were about five thousand men. But He said to His disciples, cause them to recline

5126 1033 2258 1063 5616 435 4000
τοῦτον βρώματα. 14 ἦσαν γὰρ ὡσεὶ ἄνδρες πεντακισχίλιοι.
this foods. there were For about men five thousand.

2036 1161 4314 3588 3101 846 2625 846
εἶπε δὲ πρὸς τοὺς μαθητὰς αὐτοῦ, Κατακλίνατε αὐτοὺς
He said And to the disciples of Him, Cause to recline them

14 For they were about five thousand men. And he said to his disciples, Make them sit down

Literal Translation | **Luke 9:15** | **King James Version**

in groups, by fifties.
15 And they did so, and made all recline.

16 And taking the five loaves and the two fish, looking up to Heaven, He blessed them, and broke, and gave to the disciples to set before the crowd.
17 And they ate and were all -filled. And twelve hand baskets of fragments of that left over to them were taken up.

18. And it happened (as) He was praying alone, the disciples were with Him. And He questioned them, saying, Whom do the crowds say Me to be?
19 And answering, they said, John the Baptist; and others Elijah; and, others that some prophet of the ancients has risen again.

20 And He said to them, But whom do you say Me to be? And answering, Peter said, The Christ of God.

21 And strictly warning them, He ordered no one to tell this,
22 saying, It behoves the Son of man to suffer many things and be rejected by the elders and chief priests and scribes, and be killed, and be raised the third day.

23. And He said to all, If anyone desires to come after Me, let him deny himself and take up his cross daily. And let him follow Me.

24 For whoever desires to save his life, he will lose it. But whoever may lose his life for My sake, this one will save it.

2828 303 4004 2532 4160 3779 2532 347
κλισίας ἀνὰ πεντήκοντα. 15 καὶ ἐποίησαν οὕτω, καὶ ἀνέκλιναν
in groups by fifties. And they did so, and made recline
537 2983 1161 3588 4002 740 2532 3588 1417 2486
ἅπαντας. 16 λαβὼν δὲ τοὺς πέντε ἄρτους καὶ τοὺς δύο ἰχθύας
all. taking And the five loaves and the two fish,
308 1519 3588 3772 2127 846 2532 2622
ἀναβλέψας εἰς τὸν οὐρανὸν, εὐλόγησεν αὐτοὺς, καὶ κατέκλασε,
looking up to Heaven, He blessed them, and broke
2532 1325 3588 3101 3908 3588 3793 2532
καὶ ἐδίδου τοῖς μαθηταῖς παρατιθέναι τῷ ὄχλῳ. 17 καὶ
and gave to the disciples to set before the crowd. And
5315 2532 5526 3956 2532 142 3588 4052
ἔφαγον καὶ ἐχορτάσθησαν πάντες· καὶ ἤρθη τὸ περισσεῦσαν
they ate and were filled all. And were taken the excess
846 2801 2894 1427
αὐτοῖς κλασμάτων, κόφινοι δώδεκα.
to them of fragments hand-baskets twelve.

2532 1096 1722 3588 1511 846 4336 2651
18. Καὶ ἐγένετο ἐν τῷ εἶναι αὐτὸν προσευχόμενον καταμόνας
And it happened (as) was Him praying alone,
4895 846 3588 3101 2532 1905 846 3004
συνῆσαν αὐτῷ οἱ μαθηταί· καὶ ἐπηρώτησεν αὐτούς, λέγων,
were with Him the disciples. And He questioned them, saying,
5101 3165 3004 3588 3793 1511 3588 1161 611 2036
Τίνα με λέγουσιν οἱ ὄχλοι εἶναι; 19 οἱ δὲ ἀποκριθέντες εἶπον,
Whom Me say the crowds to be? they And answering said,
2491 3588 910 243 1161 2243 243 1161 3754
Ἰωάννην τὸν βαπτιστήν· ἄλλοι δὲ Ἠλίαν· ἄλλοι δὲ, ὅτι
John the Baptist; others but Elijah; others and that
4396 5100 3588 744 450 2036 1161 846 5210
προφήτης τις τῶν ἀρχαίων ἀνέστη. 20 εἶπε δὲ αὐτοῖς, Ὑμεῖς
a prophet certain of the ancients rose again. He said And to them, you
1161 5101 3165 3004 1511 611 1161 3588 4074 2036 3588
δὲ τίνα με λέγετε εἶναι; ἀποκριθεὶς δὲ ὁ Πέτρος εἶπε, Τὸν
And, whom Me say to be? answering And Peter said, The
5547 3588 2316 3588 1161 2008 846 3853
Χριστὸν τοῦ Θεοῦ. 21 ὁ δὲ ἐπιτιμήσας αὐτοῖς παρήγγειλε
Christ of God. He But warning them ordered
3367 2036 5124 2036 3754 1163 3588 5207 3588 444
μηδενὶ εἰπεῖν τοῦτο, 22 εἰπὼν ὅτι Δεῖ τὸν υἱὸν τοῦ ἀνθρώπου
no one to tell this, saying, that it behoves the Son of man
4183 3958 2532 593 575 3588 4245
πολλὰ παθεῖν, καὶ ἀποδοκιμασθῆναι ἀπὸ τῶν πρεσβυτέρων
many things to suffer, and to be rejected from the elders
2532 749 2532 1122 2532 615 2532 3588
καὶ ἀρχιερέων καὶ γραμματέων, καὶ ἀποκτανθῆναι, καὶ τῇ
and chief priests and scribes, and to be killed, and the
5154 2250 1453 3004 1161 4314 3956 1487 5100
τρίτῃ ἡμέρᾳ ἐγερθῆναι. 23 Ἔλεγε δὲ πρὸς πάντας, Εἴ τις
third day to be raised. He said And to all, If anyone
2309 3694 3450 2064 533 1438 2532 142
θέλει ὀπίσω μου ἐλθεῖν, ἀπαρνησάσθω ἑαυτὸν, καὶ ἀράτω
desires after Me to come, let him deny himself, and take up
3588 4716 846 2596 2250 2532 190 3427 3739
τὸν σταυρὸν αὐτοῦ καθ' ἡμέραν, καὶ ἀκολουθείτω μοι. 24 ὃς
the cross of him day by day. And let him follow Me. whoever
1063 302 2309 3588 5590 846 4982 622 846 3739
γὰρ ἂν θέλῃ τὴν ψυχὴν αὐτοῦ σῶσαι, ἀπολέσει αὐτήν· ὃς
For may desire the life of him to save, he will lose it. whoever
1161 302 622 3588 5590 846 1752 1700 3778 4982
δ' ἂν ἀπολέσῃ τὴν ψυχὴν αὐτοῦ ἕνεκεν ἐμοῦ, οὗτος σώσει
But may lose the life of him for the sake of Me, this one will save

by fifties in a company.
15 And they did so, and made them all sit down.

16 Then he took the five loaves and the two fishes, and looking up to heaven, he blessed them, and brake, and gave to the disciples to set before the multitude.
17 And they did eat, and were all filled: and there was taken up of fragments that remained to them twelve baskets.

18. And it came to pass, as he was alone praying, his disciples were with him: and he asked them, saying, Whom say the people that I am?

19 They answering said, John the Baptist; but some (say), Elias; and others (say), that one of the old prophets is risen again.

20 He said unto them, But whom say ye that I am? Peter answering said, The Christ of God.

21 And he straitly charged them, and commanded (them) to tell no man that thing;
22 Saying, The Son of man must suffer many things, and be rejected of the elders and chief priests and scribes, and be slain, and be raised the third day.

23. And he said to (them) all, If any (man) will come after me, let him deny himself, and take up his cross daily, and follow me.

24 For whosoever will save his life shall lose it: but whosoever will lose his life for my sake, the same shall save it.

Literal Translation | **Luke 9:25** | **King James Version**

25 For what is a man profited gaining the whole world, but destroying himself or suffering loss?
26 For whoever may be ashamed of Me and My words, the Son of man will be ashamed of that one when He comes in His glory, and (that) of the Father, and of the holy angels.
27 But truly I say to you, There are some of those standing here who in no way shall taste of death until they see the kingdom of God.

28. And about eight days after these sayings, it happened: also taking Peter and John and James, He went into the mountain to pray.
29 And in His praying, the appearance of His face became different, and His clothing (was) dazzling white.
30 And, behold, two men talked with Him, who were Moses and Elijah,
31 who appearing in glory, (they) spoke of His exodus, which He was about to fulfill in Jerusalem.
32 But Peter and those with him were pressed down with sleep. But fully awakening, they saw His glory, and the two men standing with Him.
33 And it happened in their departing from Him, Peter said to Jesus, Master, it is good for (us) to be here. And, Let us make three tents, one for You, and one for Moses, and one for Elijah, not knowing what he said.
34 And he saying these things,

846 5101 1063 5623 444 2770 3588 2889
αὐτήν. 25 τί γὰρ ὠφελεῖται ἄνθρωπος, κερδήσας τὸν κόσμον
it. what For is profited a man gaining the world

3650 1438 1161 622 2228 2210 3739 1063 302
ὅλον, ἑαυτὸν δὲ ἀπολέσας ἢ ζημιωθείς; 26 ὃς γὰρ ἂν
whole, himself but destroying or suffering loss? whoever for may

1870 3165 2532 3588 1699 3056 5126 3588 5207 3588
ἐπαισχυνθῇ με καὶ τοὺς ἐμοὺς λόγους, τοῦτον ὁ υἱὸς τοῦ
be ashamed of Me and the of Me words, this one the Son

444 1870 3752 2064 1722 3588 1391 846 2532
ἀνθρώπου ἐπαισχυνθήσεται, ὅταν ἔλθῃ ἐν τῇ δόξῃ αὐτοῦ καὶ
of man will be ashamed of when He comes in the glory of Him, and

3588 3962 2532 3588 40 32 3004 1161 5213 230
τοῦ πατρὸς καὶ τῶν ἁγίων ἀγγέλων. 27 λέγω δὲ ὑμῖν ἀληθῶς,
of the Father, and of the holy angels. I say But to You truly

1526 5100 3588 5602 2476 3739 3756 3361 1089 2288
εἰσί τινες τῶν ὧδε ἑστηκότων, οἳ οὐ μὴ γεύσονται θανάτου,
are some of those here standing who in no way shall taste of death

2193 302 1492 3588 932 3588 2316
ἕως ἂν ἴδωσι τὴν βασιλείαν τοῦ Θεοῦ.
until may they see the kingdom of God.

1096 1161 3326 3588 3056 5128 5616 2250 3638
28. Ἐγένετο δὲ μετὰ τοὺς λόγους τούτους ὡσεὶ ἡμέραι ὀκτώ,
it was And after sayings these, about days eight,

2532 3880 3588 4074 2532 2491 2532 2385
καὶ παραλαβὼν τὸν Πέτρον καὶ Ἰωάννην καὶ Ἰάκωβον,
also taking Peter and John and James

305 1519 3588 3735 4336 2532 1096 1722 3588
ἀνέβη εἰς τὸ ὄρος προσεύξασθαι. 29 καὶ ἐγένετο ἐν τῷ
He went into the mountain to pray. And it came to be in the

4336 846 3588 1491 3588 4383 846 2087
προσεύχεσθαι αὐτὸν τὸ εἶδος τοῦ προσώπου αὐτοῦ ἕτερον,
prayng of Him the appearance of the face of Him different

2532 3588 2441 846 3022 1823 2532 2400
καὶ ὁ ἱματισμὸς αὐτοῦ λευκὸς ἐξαστράπτων. 30 καὶ ἰδού,
and the clothing of Him white dazzling. And behold!

435 1417 4814 846 3748 2258 3475 2532
ἄνδρες δύο συνελάλουν αὐτῷ, οἵτινες ἦσαν Μωσῆς καὶ
men Two talked with Him, who were Moses and

2243 3739 3700 1722 1391 3004 3588 1841 846 3739
Ἡλίας, 31 οἳ ὀφθέντες ἐν δόξῃ ἔλεγον τὴν ἔξοδον αὐτοῦ ἣν
Elijah, who appearing in glory spoke of the exodus of Him, which

3195 4137 1722 2419 3588 1161 4074 2532 3588 4862 846
ἔμελλε πληροῦν ἐν Ἱερουσαλήμ. 32 ὁ δὲ Πέτρος καὶ οἱ σὺν αὐτῷ
He was about to fulfill in Jerusalem. And Peter and those with Him

2258 916 5258 1235 1161 1492 3588
ἦσαν βεβαρημένοι ὕπνῳ· διαγρηγορήσαντες δὲ εἶδον τὴν
were being pressed down with sleep. awakening fully But they saw the

1391 846 2532 3588 1417 435 3588 4921 846
δόξαν αὐτοῦ, καὶ τοὺς δύο ἄνδρας τοὺς συνεστῶτας αὐτῷ.
glory of Him, and the two men standing with Him.

2532 1096 1722 3588 1316 846 575 846 2036
33 καὶ ἐγένετο, ἐν τῷ διαχωρίζεσθαι αὐτοὺς ἀπ᾽ αὐτοῦ, εἶπεν
And it happened in the departing of them from Him,, said

3588 4074 4314 3588 2424 1988 2570 2076 2248
ὁ Πέτρος πρὸς τὸν Ἰησοῦν, Ἐπιστάτα, καλόν ἐστιν ἡμᾶς
Peter to Jesus, Master, good it is us

5602 1511 2532 4160 4633 5140 3391 4671 2532
ὧδε εἶναι· καὶ ποιήσωμεν σκηνὰς τρεῖς, μίαν σοί, καὶ
here to be; and let us make tents three, one for You, and

3475 3391 2532 3391 2243 3361 1492 3739 3004 5023 1161
Μωσεῖ μίαν, καὶ μίαν Ἡλίᾳ· μὴ εἰδὼς ὃ λέγει. 34 ταῦτα δὲ
Moses one, and one for Elijah, not knowing what he says. these things And

25 For what is a man advantaged, if he gain the whole world, and lose himself, or be cast away?
26 For whosoever shall be ashamed of me and of my words, of him shall the Son of man be ashamed, when he shall come in his own glory, and (in his) Father's, and of the holy angels.
27 But I tell you of a truth, there be some standing here, which shall not taste of death, till they see the kingdom of God.

28. And it came to pass about an eight days after these sayings, he took Peter and John and James, and went up into a mountain to pray.
29 And as he prayed, the fashion of his countenance was altered, and his raiment (was) white (and) glistering.
30 And, behold, there talked with him two men, which were Moses and Elias:
31 Who appeared in glory, and spake of his decease which he should accomplish at Jerusalem.
32 But Peter and they that were with him were heavy with sleep: and when they were awake, they saw his glory, and the two men that stood with him.
33 And it came to pass, as they departed from him, Peter said unto Jesus, Master, it is good for us to be here: and let us make three tabernacles; one for thee, and one for Moses, and one for Elias: not knowing what he said.
34 While he thus spake,

Literal Translation | **Luke 9:35** | **King James Version**

a cloud came and overshadowed them. And they feared (as) those entered into the cloud.

846 3004 1096 3507 2532 1982 846
αὐτοῦ λέγοντος, ἐγένετο νεφέλη καὶ ἐπεσκίασεν αὐτούς·
him saying, came a cloud and overshadowed them,
5399 1161 1722 3588 1565 1525 1519 3588 3507
ἐφοβήθησαν δὲ ἐν τῷ ἐκείνους εἰσελθεῖν εἰς τὴν νεφέλην.
they feared and in the of those entering into the cloud.

there came a cloud, and overshadowed them: and they feared as they entered into the cloud.

35 And a voice came out of the cloud, saying, This is My Son, the Beloved; hear Him! (Ps. 2:7; Deut. 18:15)
36 And as the voice occurred, Jesus was found alone. And they were quiet. And (they) reported to no one in those days, nothing which they had seen.

2532 5456 1096 1537 3588 3507 3004 3778 2076 3588
35 καὶ φωνὴ ἐγένετο ἐκ τῆς νεφέλης λέγουσα, Οὗτός ἐστιν ὁ
And a voice came out of the cloud, saying, This is the
5207 3450 3588 27 846 191 2532 1722 3588 1096 3588
υἱός μου ὁ ἀγαπητός αὐτοῦ ἀκούετε. 36 καὶ ἐν τῷ γενέσθαι τὴν
Son of Me, the Beloved; Him hear. And in the occurring of the
5456 2147 3588 2424 3441 2532 846 4601 2532
φωνὴν, εὑρέθη ὁ Ἰησοῦς μόνος. καὶ αὐτοὶ ἐσίγησαν, καὶ
voice, was found Jesus alone. And they were quiet, and
3762 518 1722 1565 3588 2250 3762 3739
οὐδενὶ ἀπήγγειλαν ἐν ἐκείναις ταῖς ἡμέραις οὐδὲν ὧν
to no one reported in those days, nothing which
3708
ἑώρακασιν.
they had seen.

35 And there came a voice out of the cloud, saying, This is my beloved Son: hear him.
36 And when the voice was past, Jesus was found alone. And they kept (it) close, and told no man in those days any of those things which they had seen.

37. And it happened on the next day, they coming down from the mountain, a large crowd met Him.
38 And, behold! A man called aloud from the crowd, saying, Teacher, I beg You to look upon my son, because he is my only born.
39 And, behold! A spirit takes hold of him, and (he) suddenly cries out, and (it) convulses him, with foam. And (it) departs from him with difficulty, bruising him.

1096 1161 1722 3588 1836 2250 2718 846 575
37. Ἐγένετο δὲ ἐν τῇ ἑξῆς ἡμέρᾳ, κατελθόντων αὐτῶν ἀπὸ
it was And in the next day, coming down them from
3588 3735 4876 846 3793 4183 2532 2400 435
τοῦ ὄρους, συνήντησεν αὐτῷ ὄχλος πολύς. 38 καὶ ἰδού, ἀνὴρ
the mountain, met Him a crowd large. And, behold! A man
575 3588 3793 310 3004 1320 1189 4675
ἀπὸ τοῦ ὄχλου ἀνεβόησε, λέγων, Διδάσκαλε, δέομαί σου,
from the crowd cried out, saying, Teacher, I beg You
1914 1909 3588 5207 3450 3754 3439 2076 3427 2532
ἐπιβλέψον ἐπὶ τὸν υἱόν μου, ὅτι μονογενής ἐστί μοι. 39 καὶ
to look upon the son of me, because only born he is of me. And
2400 4151 2983 846 2532 1810 2896 2532
ἰδού, πνεῦμα λαμβάνει αὐτόν, καὶ ἐξαίφνης κράζει, καὶ
behold! A spirit takes hold of him, and suddenly he cries out, and
672 846 3326 876 2532 3425 672 575
σπαράσσει αὐτὸν μετὰ ἀφροῦ, καὶ μόγις ἀποχωρεῖ ἀπ'
convulses him with foam, and with difficulty departs from

37. And it came to pass, that on the next day, when they were come down from the hill, much people met him.
38 And, behold, a man of the company cried out, saying, Master, I beseech thee, look upon my son: for he is mine only child.
39 And, lo, a spirit taketh him, and he suddenly crieth out; and it teareth him that he foameth again, and bruising him hardly departeth from him.

40 And I begged Your disciples, that they cast it out. And they were not able.
41 And answering, Jesus said, O unbelieving and having been perverted generation, until when shall I be with you and endure you? Bring your son here.

846 4937 846 2532 1189 3588 3101 4675
αὐτοῦ, συντρίβον αὐτόν. 40 καὶ ἐδεήθην τῶν μαθητῶν σου
him, bruising him. And I begged the disciples of You
2443 1544 846 2532 3756 1410 611 1161
ἵνα ἐκβάλλωσιν αὐτό, καὶ οὐκ ἠδυνήθησαν. 41 ἀποκριθεὶς δὲ
that they cast out it, and not they were able. answering And
3588 2424 2036 5599 1074 571 2532 1294 2193
ὁ Ἰησοῦς εἶπεν, Ὦ γενεὰ ἄπιστος καὶ διεστραμμένη, ἕως
Jesus said, O generation unbelieving and having been perverted, until
4219 2071 4314 5209 2532 430 5216 4317
πότε ἔσομαι πρὸς ὑμᾶς, καὶ ἀνέξομαι ὑμῶν; προσάγαγε
when shall I be with you and endure you? Bring

40 And I besought thy disciples to cast him out; and they could not.
41 And Jesus answering said, O faithless and perverse generation, how long shall I be with you, and suffer you? Bring thy son hither.

42 But as (he) yet coming near, the demon tore him and violently convulsed (him). But Jesus rebuked the unclean spirit, and healed the child, and gave him back to his father.

5602 3588 5207 4675 2089 1161 4334 846 4486
ὧδε τὸν υἱόν σου. 42 ἔτι δὲ προσερχομένου αὐτοῦ, ἔρρηξεν
here the son of you. yet But coming near him, tore
846 3588 1140 2532 4952 2008 1161 3588
αὐτὸν τὸ δαιμόνιον καὶ συνεσπάραξεν· ἐπετίμησε δὲ ὁ
him the demon and violently convulsed. rebuked But
2424 3588 4151 3588 169 2532 2390 3588 3816
Ἰησοῦς τῷ πνεύματι τῷ ἀκαθάρτῳ, καὶ ἰάσατο τὸν παῖδα,
Jesus the spirit unclean, and healed the child,
2532 591 846 3588 3962 846 1605 1161
καὶ ἀπέδωκεν αὐτὸν τῷ πατρὶ αὐτοῦ. 43 ἐξεπλήσσοντο δὲ
and gave back him to the father of him. were astounded And

42 And as he was yet a coming, the devil threw him down, and tare (him). And Jesus rebuked the unclean spirit, and healed the child, and delivered him again to his father.

43. And all were astounded

43. And they were all amazed

Literal Translation **Luke 9:44** *King James Version*

at the majesty of God. And (as) all (were) marveling at all things which He did, Jesus said to His disciples,

3956 1909 3588 3168 3588 2316
πάντες ἐπὶ τῇ μεγαλειότητι τοῦ Θεοῦ.
all at the majesty of God.

3956 1161 2296 1909 3956 3739 4160 3588
Πάντων δὲ θαυμαζόντων ἐπὶ πᾶσιν οἷς ἐποίησεν ὁ
all And marveling at all things which He did,

2424 2036 4314 3588 3101 846 5087 5210 1519 3588
Ἰησους, εἶπε πρὸς τοὺς μαθητὰς αὐτοῦ, 44 Θέσθε ὑμεῖς εἰς τὰ
Jesus said to the disciples of Him, Lay you into the

at the mighty power of God. But while they wondered every one at all things which Jesus did, he said unto his disciples,

44 You lay into your ears these sayings, for the Son of man is about to be betrayed into (the) hands of men.

3775 5216 3588 3056 5128 3588 1063 5207 3588 444
ὦτα ὑμῶν τοὺς λόγους τούτους· ὁ γὰρ υἱὸς τοῦ ἀνθρώπου
ears of you sayings these. the For Son of man

3195 3860 1519 5495 444 3588 1161 50
μέλλει παραδίδοσθαι εἰς χεῖρας ἀνθρώπων. 45 οἱ δὲ ἠγνόουν
is about to be betrayed into (the) hands of men. they But knew not

44 Let these sayings sink down into your ears: for the Son of man shall be delivered into the hands of men.

45 But they did not know this word, and it was veiled from them so that they not perceive it. And they feared to ask Him about this word.

3588 4487 5124 2532 2258 3871 575 846 2443
τὸ ῥῆμα τοῦτο, καὶ ἦν παρακεκαλυμμένον ἀπ' αὐτῶν, ἵνα
word this, and it was being veiled from them, so that

3361 143 846 2532 5399 2065 846 4012
μὴ αἴσθωνται αὐτό· καὶ ἐφοβοῦντο ἐρωτῆσαι αὐτὸν περὶ
not they perceive it. And they feared to ask Him about

3588 4487 5127
τοῦ ῥήματος τούτου.
word this.

45 But they understood not this saying, and it was hid from them, that they perceived it not: and they feared to ask him of that saying.

46. But a reasoning came in among them, who might be (the) greater of them.
47 And seeing the reasoning of their heart, laying hold of a child, Jesus stood it beside Himself,

1525 1161 1261 1722 846 3588 5101 302 1498 3187
46. Εἰσῆλθε δὲ διαλογισμὸς ἐν αὐτοῖς, τὸ τίς ἂν εἴη μείζων
came in But a reasoning among them, who might be greater

846 3588 1161 2424 1492 3588 1261 3588 2588
αὐτῶν. 47 ὁ δὲ Ἰησοῦς ἰδὼν τὸν διαλογισμὸν τῆς καρδίας
of them. And Jesus having seen the reasoning of the heart

846 1949 3813 2476 846 3844 1438
αὐτῶν, ἐπιλαβόμενος παιδίον, ἔστησεν αὐτὸ παρ' ἑαυτῷ,
of them, having laid hold of a child, stood it beside Himself,

46. Then there arose a reasoning among them, which of them should be greatest.
47 And Jesus, perceiving the thought of their heart, took a child, and set him by him,

48 and said to them, Whoever receives this child on My name receives Me. And whoever receives Me receives the (One) who has sent Me. For the one being lesser among you all, this one shall be great.

2532 2036 846 3739 1437 1209 5124 3588 3813 1909 3588
48 καὶ εἶπεν αὐτοῖς, Ὃς ἐὰν δέξηται τοῦτο τὸ παιδίον ἐπὶ τῷ
and said to them, Whoever receives this child on the

3686 3450 1691 1209 2532 3739 1437 1691 1209 1209 3588
ὀνόματί μου ἐμὲ δέχεται· καὶ ὃς ἐὰν ἐμὲ δέξηται δέχεται τὸν
name of Me, Me receives. And whoever Me receives receives the (One)

649 3165 3588 1063 3398 1722 3956 5213 5225
ἀποστείλαντά με· ὁ γὰρ μικρότερος ἐν πᾶσιν ὑμῖν ὑπάρχων
having sent Me. the For lesser among all you being,

3778 2071 3173
οὗτός ἔσται μέγας.
this one will be great.

48 And said unto them, Whosoever shall receive this child in my name receiveth me: and whosoever shall receive me receiveth him that sent me: for he that is least among you all, the same shall be great.

49 And answering, John said, Master, we saw someone casting out demons on Your name, and we stopped him because he does not follow with us.
50 And Jesus said to them, Do not stop (them) for whoever is not against us is for us.

611 1161 3588 2491 2036 1988 1492 5100
49. Ἀποκριθεὶς δὲ ὁ Ἰωάννης εἶπεν, Ἐπιστάτα, εἴδομέν τινα
answering And John said, Master, we saw someone

1909 3588 3686 4675 1544 3588 1140 2532
ἐπὶ τῷ ὀνόματί σου ἐκβάλλοντα τὰ δαιμόνια· καὶ
on the Name of You casting out demons, and

2967 846 3754 3756 190 3326 2257 2532 2036
ἐκωλύσαμεν αὐτὸν, ὅτι οὐκ ἀκολουθεῖ μεθ' ἡμῶν. 50 καὶ εἶπε
stopped him, because not he follows with us. And said

4314 846 3588 2424 3361 2967 3739 1063 3756 2076 2596
πρὸς αὐτὸν ὁ Ἰησοῦς, Μὴ κωλύετε, ὃς γὰρ οὐκ ἔστι καθ'
to them Jesus, Not do stop (them), whoever for not is against

2257 5228 2257 2076
ἡμῶν ὑπὲρ ἡμῶν ἐστιν.
us for us is.

49 And John answered and said, Master, we saw one casting out devils in thy name; and we forbad him, because he followeth not with us.
50 And Jesus said unto him, Forbid (him) not: for he that is not against us is for us.

51. And it happened in the fulfilling (of) the days of His

1096 1161 1722 3588 4845 3588 2250 3588
51. Ἐγένετο δὲ ἐν τῷ συμπληροῦσθαι τὰς ἡμέρας τῆς
it happened And in the fulfilling of the days of the

51. And it came to pass, when the time was come that he

Literal Translation | **Luke 9:52** | **King James Version**

taking up, even He set His face to go to Jerusalem.

354 846 2532 846 3588 4383 846 4741
ἀναλήψεως αὐτοῦ, καὶ αὐτὸς τὸ πρόσωπον αὐτοῦ ἐστήριξε
taking up of Him, even He the face of Him set

3588 4198 1519 2419 2532 649 32
τοῦ πορεύεσθαι εἰς Ἱερουσαλήμ, 52 καὶ ἀπέστειλεν ἀγγέλους
to go to Jerusalem. And (He) sent messengers

4253 4383 846 2532 4198 1525 1519 2968
πρὸ προσώπου αὐτοῦ· καὶ πορευθέντες εἰσῆλθον εἰς κώμην
before the face of Him. And going they went into a village

4541 5620 2090 846 2532 3756 1209 846
Σαμαρειτῶν, ὥστε ἑτοιμάσαι αὐτῷ· 53 καὶ οὐκ ἐδέξαντο αὐτόν,
of Samaritans, so as to make ready for Him. And not they received Him,

3754 3588 4383 846 2258 4198 1519 2419
ὅτι τὸ πρόσωπον αὐτοῦ ἦν πορευόμενον εἰς Ἱερουσαλήμ.
because the face of Him was going to Jerusalem.

should be received up, he stedfastly set his face to go to Jerusalem,

52 And (He) sent messengers before His face. And going they went into a village of Samaritans, so as to make ready for Him.
53 And they did not receive Him, because His face was going toward Jerusalem.

52 And sent messengers before his face: and they went, and entered into a village of the Samaritans, to make ready for him.
53 And they did not receive him, because his face was as though he would go to Jerusalem.

54 And seeing, His disciples James and John said, Lord, do You desire (that) we tell fire to come down from Heaven, and to destroy them, even as Elijah did? (2 K. 1:10-12)
55 But turning He rebuked them. And He said, You do not know of what spirit you are.

1492 1161 3588 3101 846 2385 2532 2491 2036
54 ἰδόντες δὲ οἱ μαθηταὶ αὐτοῦ Ἰάκωβος καὶ Ἰωάννης εἶπον,
seeing And the disciples of Him, James and John said,

2962 2309 2036 4442 2597 575 3588 3772 2532
Κύριε, θέλεις εἴπωμεν πῦρ καταβῆναι ἀπὸ τοῦ οὐρανοῦ, καὶ
Lord, do You desire (that) we tell fire to come down from Heaven and

355 846 5613 2532 2243 4160 4762 1161
ἀναλῶσαι αὐτούς, ὡς καὶ Ἠλίας ἐποίησε; 55 στραφεὶς δὲ
to destroy them, as also Elijah did? turning But

2008 846 2532 2036 3756 1492 3634 4151
ἐπετίμησεν αὐτοῖς, καὶ εἶπεν, Οὐκ οἴδατε οἵου πνεύματός
He rebuked them, and said, Not you know of what spirit

54 And when his disciples James and John saw (this), they said, Lord, wilt thou that we command fire to come down from heaven, and consume them, even as Elias did?
55 But he turned, and rebuked them, and said, Ye know not what manner of spirit ye are of.

56 For the Son of man did not come to destroy men's souls, but to save. And they went to another village.

2075 5210 3588 1063 5207 3588 444 3756 2064 5590
ἐστε ὑμεῖς· 56 ὁ γὰρ υἱὸς τοῦ ἀνθρώπου οὐκ ἦλθε ψυχὰς
are you. the For Son of man not did come the souls

444 622 235 4982 2532 4198 1519
ἀνθρώπων ἀπολέσαι, ἀλλὰ σῶσαι. καὶ ἐπορεύθησαν εἰς
of men to destroy, but to save. And they went to

2087 2968
ἑτέραν κώμην.
another village.

56 For the Son of man is not come to destroy men's lives, but to save (them). And they went to another village.

57. And it happened (as) they (were) going in the way, one said to Him, I will follow You everywhere You may go, Lord.
58 And Jesus said to him, The foxes have holes, and the birds of the heaven nests, but the Son of man has nowhere He may lay (His) head.

1096 1161 4198 846 1722 3588 3598 2036 5100 4314
57. Ἐγένετο δὲ πορευομένων αὐτῶν ἐν τῇ ὁδῷ, εἶπέ τις πρός
it happened And, going them in the way, said one to

846 190 4671 3699 302 565 2962 2532 2036
αὐτόν, Ἀκολουθήσω σοι ὅπου ἂν ἀπέρχῃ, Κύριε. 58 καὶ εἶπεν
Him, I will follow You wherever may You go, Lord. And said

846 3588 2424 3588 258 5454 2192 2532 3588
αὐτῷ ὁ Ἰησοῦς, Αἱ ἀλώπεκες φωλεοὺς ἔχουσι, καὶ τὰ
to Him Jesus, The foxes holes have, and the

4071 3588 3772 2682 3588 1161 5207 3588 444
πετεινὰ τοῦ οὐρανοῦ κατασκηνώσεις· ὁ δὲ υἱὸς τοῦ ἀνθρώπου
birds of the heaven nests; the but Son of man

3756 2192 4226 3588 2776 2827 2036 1161 4314 2087
οὐκ ἔχει ποῦ τὴν κεφαλὴν κλίνῃ. 59 εἶπε δὲ πρὸς ἕτερον,
not has where the head He may lay. He said And to another,

190 3427 3588 1161 2036 2962 2010 3427 565
Ἀκολούθει μοι. ὁ δὲ εἶπε, Κύριε, ἐπίτρεψόν μοι ἀπελθόντι
Follow Me. he But said, Lord, allow me having gone

4412 2290 3588 3962 3450 2036 1161 846 3588 2424
πρῶτον θάψαι τὸν πατέρα μου. 60 εἶπε δὲ αὐτῷ, ὁ Ἰησοῦς
first to bury the father of me. said But to him Jesus,

863 3588 3498 2290 3588 1438 3498 4771 1161
Ἄφες τοὺς νεκροὺς θάψαι τοὺς ἑαυτῶν νεκρούς· σὺ δὲ
Leave the dead to bury the of themselves dead, you but

565 1229 3588 932 3588 2316 2036 1161 2532
ἀπελθὼν διάγγελλε τὴν βασιλείαν τοῦ Θεοῦ. 61 εἶπε δὲ καὶ
going out announce the kingdom of God. said And also

57. And it came to pass, that, as they went in the way, a certain (man) said unto him, Lord, I will follow thee whithersoever thou goest.
58 And Jesus said unto him, Foxes have holes, and birds of the air (have) nests; but the Son of man hath not where to lay (his) head.

59 And He said to another, Follow Me. But he said, Lord, allow me, to go first to bury my father.

60 But Jesus said to him, Leave the dead to bury their dead, but going out, you announce the kingdom of God.

61 And also another said,

59 And he said unto another, Follow me. But he said, Lord, suffer me first to go and bury my father.

60 Jesus said unto him, Let the dead bury their dead: but go thou and preach the kingdom of God.

61 And another also said,

Literal Translation

Luke 9:62

King James Version

I will follow You, Lord, but first allow me to take leave of those in my house.
62 But Jesus said to him, No one putting his hand on the plow, and looking at the things behind, is fit for the kingdom of God.

2087 190 4671 2962 4412 1161 2010 3427
ἕτερος, Ἀκολουθήσω σοι, Κύριε· πρῶτον δὲ ἐπίτρεψόν μοι
another, I will follow You, Lord, first but allow me

657 3588 1519 3588 3624 3450 2036 1161 4314 846 3588
ἀποτάξασθαι τοῖς εἰς τὸν οἶκόν μου. 62 εἶπε δὲ πρὸς αὐτὸν ὁ
to take leave of those in the house of me. said But to him

2424 3762 1911 3588 5495 846 1909 723
Ἰησοῦς, Οὐδεὶς, ἐπιβαλὼν τὴν χεῖρα αὐτοῦ ἐπ' ἄροτρον
Jesus, No one putting the hand of him on the plow

2532 991 1519 3588 3694 2111 2076 1519 3588 932
καὶ βλέπων εἰς τὰ ὀπίσω, εὔθετός ἐστιν εἰς τὴν βασιλείαν
and looking to the things behind fit is for the kingdom

3588 2316
τοῦ Θεοῦ.
of God.

Lord, I will follow thee; but let me first go bid them farewell, which are at home at my house.
62 And Jesus said unto him, No man, having put his hand to the plough, and looking back, is fit for the kingdom of God.

Luke 10

1. And after these things, the Lord also appointed seventy others, and sent them two by two before His face into every city and place, even (to) where He was about to come.

3326 1161 5023 332 3588 2962 2532 2087
1. Μετὰ δὲ ταῦτα ἀνέδειξεν ὁ Κύριος καὶ ἑτέρους
after And these things, appointed the Lord also others

1440 2532 649 846 303 1417 4253 4383
ἑβδομήκοντα, καὶ ἀπέστειλεν αὐτοὺς ἀνὰ δύο πρὸ προσώπου
seventy and sent them two by two before (the) face

846 1519 3956 4172 2532 5117 3739 3195 846 2064
αὐτοῦ εἰς πᾶσαν πόλιν καὶ τόπον οὗ ἔμελλεν αὐτὸς ἔρχεσθαι.
of Him into every city and place where was about He to come.

1. After these things the Lord appointed other seventy also, and sent them two and two before his face into every city and place, whither he himself would come.

2 Then He said to them, Indeed the harvest (is) much, but the workers (are) few. Then pray (to) the Lord of the harvest, that He send out workers into His harvest.
3 Go! Behold! I send you out as lambs in (the) midst of wolves.
4 Do not carry a purse, nor a money bag, nor sandals; and greet no one by the way.

3004 3767 4314 846 3588 3303 2326 4183 3588 1161 2040
2 ἔλεγεν οὖν πρὸς αὐτούς, Ὁ μὲν θερισμὸς πολύς, οἱ δὲ ἐργάται
He said Then to them, The indeed harvest (is) much, the but workers

3641 1189 3767 3588 2962 3588 2326 3704 1544
ὀλίγοι· δεήθητε οὖν τοῦ Κυρίου τοῦ θερισμοῦ, ὅπως ἐκβάλλῃ
few; pray then to the Lord of the harvest, that He send out

2040 1519 3588 2326 846 5217 2400 1473 649
ἐργάτας εἰς τὸν θερισμὸν αὐτοῦ. 3 ὑπάγετε· ἰδοὺ, ἐγὼ ἀπο-
workers into the harvest of Him. Go! Behold! I send

5209 5613 704 1722 3319 3074 3391 941 905
στέλλω ὑμᾶς ὡς ἄρνας ἐν μέσῳ λύκων. 4 μὴ βαστάζετε βαλάν-
out you as lambs in amidst wolves. Not do carry a purse,

3361 4082 3366 5266 2532 3367 2596 3588
τιον, μὴ πήραν, μηδὲ ὑποδήματα· καὶ μηδένα κατὰ τὴν
nor a money bag, nor sandals, and no one by the

2 Therefore said he unto them, The harvest truly (is) great, but the labourers (are) few: pray ye therefore the Lord of the harvest, that he would send forth labourers into his harvest.
3 Go your ways: behold, I send you forth as lambs among wolves.
4 Carry neither purse, nor scrip, nor shoes: and salute no man by the way.

5 And into whatever house you may enter, first say, Peace to this house.
6 And if a son of peace is indeed there, your peace shall rest on it; but if not so, it shall return on you.

3598 782 1519 3739 1161 302 3614 1525 4412
ὁδὸν ἀσπάσησθε. 5 εἰς ἣν δ' ἂν οἰκίαν εἰσέρχησθε, πρῶτον
way greet. Into whatever house you may enter, first

3004 1515 3588 3624 5129 2532 1437 3303 5600 1563 3588 5207
λέγετε, Εἰρήνη τῷ οἴκῳ τούτῳ. 6 καὶ ἐὰν μὲν ᾖ ἐκεῖ ὁ υἱὸς
say, Peace house to this. And if indeed is there a son

1515 1879 1909 846 3588 1515 5216 1487 1161
εἰρήνης, ἐπαναπαύσεται ἐπ' αὐτὸν ἡ εἰρήνη ὑμῶν· εἰ δὲ
of peace, shall rest upon it the peace of you. if But

3361 1909 5209 344 1722 846 1161 3588 3614 3306
μήγε, ἐφ' ὑμᾶς ἀνακάμψει. 7 ἐν αὐτῇ δὲ τῇ οἰκίᾳ μένετε,
not so, on you it shall return. in same And the house remain,

5 And into whatsoever house ye enter, first say, Peace (be) to this house.
6 And if the son of peace be there, your peace shall rest upon it: if not, it shall turn to you again.

7 And remain in the same house, eating and drinking the things (shared) with them; for the worker is worthy of his hire. Do not move from house to house.

2068 2532 4095 3588 3844 846 514 1063 3588 2040 3588
ἐσθίοντες καὶ πίνοντες τὰ παρ' αὐτῶν· ἄξιος γὰρ ὁ ἐργάτης τοῦ
eating and drinking the things with them; worthy for the worker of the

3408 846 2076 3361 3327 1537 3614 1519 3614 2532
μισθοῦ αὐτοῦ ἐστι. μὴ μεταβαίνετε ἐξ οἰκίας εἰς οἰκίαν. 8 καὶ
pay of him is. Not do move from house to house. And

7 And in the same house remain, eating and drinking such things as they give: for the labourer is worthy of his hire. Go not from house to house.

8 And into whatever city you enter, and they receive you, eat the things

1519 3739 1161 302 4172 1525 2532 1209 5209 2068 3588
εἰς ἣν δ' ἂν πόλιν εἰσέρχησθε, καὶ δέχωνται ὑμᾶς, ἐσθίετε τὰ
into whatever city you may enter, and they receive you, eat the things

8 And into whatsoever city ye enter, and they receive you, eat such things

Literal Translation

set before you.
9 And heal the sick in it, and say to them, The kingdom of God has drawn near on you.

10 But into whatever city you enter, and they do not receive you, going out into its streets, say,
11 Even the dust clinging to us out of your city, we shake off against you! Yet know this, that the kingdom of God has drawn near to you!

12 And I say to you that it shall be more bearable for Sodom in that day than for that city!
13 Woe to you, Chorazin! Woe to you, Bethsaida! For if the works of power which have been occurring in you had occurred in Tyre and Sidon, they would have repented long ago sitting in sackcloth and ashes!
14 But it will be more bearable for Tyre and Sidon in the Judgment than for you.
15 And you, Capernaum, have been exalted to the heaven. Unto Hades you will be thrust down! (Isa. 14:13, 15)
16 The one hearing you hears Me, and the one rejecting you also rejects Me, and the one rejecting Me rejects the One having sent Me.

17. And the seventy returned with joy, saying, Lord, even the demons are subject to us through Your Name.

18 And He said to them, I beheld Satan falling out of Heaven as lightning!
19 Behold! I give you the authority to tread on snakes and scorpions, and on all the power of the enemy, and nothing shall hurt you, in no way.
20 But

Luke 10:9

3908 5213 2532 2323 3588 1722 846 772
παρατιθέμενα ὑμῖν, 9 καὶ θεραπεύετε τοὺς ἐν αὐτῇ ἀσθενεῖς,
being set before you. And heal the in it sick,

2532 3004 846 1448 1909 5209 3588 932 3588 2316
καὶ λέγετε αὐτοῖς, Ἤγγικεν ἐφ' ὑμᾶς ἡ βασιλεία τοῦ Θεοῦ.
and say to them, has drawn near on you the kingdom of God.

1519 3739 1161 302 4172 1525 2532 3361 1209 5209 1831
10 εἰς ἣν δ' ἂν πόλιν εἰσέρχησθε, καὶ μὴ δέχωνται ὑμᾶς, ἐξελ-
into what And ever city you enter, and not they receive you, going

1519 3588 4113 846 2036 2532 3588 2868
θόντες εἰς τὰς πλατείας αὐτῆς εἴπατε, 11 Καὶ τὸν κονιορτὸν
into the streets of it say, Even the dust

3588 2853 2254 1537 3588 4172 5216 631 5213
τὸν κολληθέντα ἡμῖν ἐκ τῆς πόλεως ὑμῶν ἀπομασσόμεθα ὑμῖν·
clinging to us out of the city of you we shake off to you;

4133 5124 1097 3754 1448 1909 5209 3588 932 3588
πλὴν τοῦτο γινώσκετε, ὅτι ἤγγικεν ἐφ' ὑμᾶς ἡ βασιλεία τοῦ
yet this know, that has drawn near on you the kingdom

2316 3004 1161 5213 3754 4670 1722 3588 2250 1565 414
Θεοῦ. 12 λέγω δὲ ὑμῖν, ὅτι Σοδόμοις ἐν τῇ ἡμέρᾳ ἐκείνῃ ἀνε-
of God. I say And to you that for Sodom in day that more

2071 2228 3588 4172 1565 3759 4671 5523 3759
κτότερον ἔσται, ἢ τῇ πόλει ἐκείνῃ. 13 οὐαί σοι, Χωραζίν, οὐαί
bearable it will be than city for that. Woe to you, Chorazin! Woe

4671 966 3754 1487 1722 5184 2532 4605 1096 3588 1411
σοι, Βηθσαϊδά· ὅτι εἰ ἐν Τύρῳ καὶ Σιδῶνι ἐγένοντο αἱ δυνά-
to you, Bethsaida! Because if in Tyre and Sidon occurred the works

3588 1096 1722 5213 3819 3588 1722 4526 2532 4700
μεις αἱ γενόμεναι ἐν ὑμῖν, πάλαι ἂν ἐν σάκκῳ καὶ σποδῷ
of power occurring in you, long ago in sackcloth and ashes

2521 3340 4133 5184 2532 4605 414
καθήμεναι μετενόησαν. 14 πλὴν Τύρῳ καὶ Σιδῶνι ἀνεκτότερον
sitting they would have repented. But for Tyre and Sidon more bearable

2071 1722 3588 2920 2228 5213 2532 4771 2584 3588 2193 3588
ἔσται ἐν τῇ κρίσει, ἢ ὑμῖν. 15 καὶ σύ, Καπερναούμ, ἡ ἕως τοῦ
it will be in the Judgment than you. And you, Capernaum, which unto the

3772 5312 2193 86 2601 3588 191
οὐρανοῦ ὑψωθεισα; ἕως ᾅδου καταβιβασθήσῃ. 16 ὁ ἀκούων
heaven have been exalted? unto Hades you will be brought down. He hearing

5216 1700 191 2532 3588 114 5209 1691 114 3588 1161
ὑμῶν ἐμοῦ ἀκούει· καὶ ὁ ἀθετῶν ὑμᾶς ἐμὲ ἀθετεῖ· ὁ δὲ
you Me hears and he rejecting you Me rejects. he And

1691 114 114 3588 649 3165
ἐμὲ ἀθετῶν ἀθετεῖ τὸν ἀποστείλαντά με.
Me rejecting rejects the (One) having sent Me.

5290 1161 3588 1440 3326 5479 3004
17. Ὑπέστρεψαν δὲ οἱ ἑβδομήκοντα μετὰ χαρᾶς, λέγοντες,
returned And the seventy with joy, saying,

2962 2532 3588 1140 5293 2254 1722 3588 3686
Κύριε, καὶ τὰ δαιμόνια ὑποτάσσεται ἡμῖν ἐν τῷ ὀνόματί
Lord, even the demons are subject to us in the name

4675 2036 1161 846 2334 3588 4567 5613 796
σου. 18 εἶπε δὲ αὐτοῖς, Ἐθεώρουν τὸν Σατανᾶν ὡς ἀστραπὴν
of You. He said And to them, I beheld Satan as lightning

1537 3588 3772 4098 2400 1325 5213 3588 1849
ἐκ τοῦ οὐρανοῦ πεσόντα. 19 ἰδού, δίδωμι ὑμῖν τὴν ἐξουσίαν
out of Heaven fall. Behold! I give you the authority

3588 3961 1883 3789 2532 4651 2532 1909 3956 3588
τοῦ πατεῖν ἐπάνω ὄφεων καὶ σκορπίων, καὶ ἐπὶ πᾶσαν τὴν
to tread on snakes and scorpions, and on all the

1411 3588 2190 2532 3762 5209 3756 3361 91 4133
δύναμιν τοῦ ἐχθροῦ· καὶ οὐδὲν ὑμᾶς οὐ μὴ ἀδικήσει. 20 πλὴν
power of the enemy, and nothing you in no way shall hurt. But

King James Version

as are set before you:
9 And heal the sick that are therein, and say unto them, The kingdom of God is come nigh unto you.

10 But into whatsoever city ye enter, and they receive you not, go your ways out into the streets of the same, and say,
11 Even the very dust of your city, which cleaveth on us, we do wipe off against you: notwithstanding be ye sure of this, that the kingdom of God is come nigh unto you.

12 But I say unto you, that it shall be more tolerable in that day for Sodom, than for that city.
13 Woe unto thee, Chorazin! woe unto thee, Bethsaida! for if the mighty works had been done in Tyre and Sidon, which have been done in you, they had a great while ago repented, sitting in sackcloth and ashes.
14 But it shall be more tolerable for Tyre and Sidon at the judgment, than for you.
15 And thou, Capernaum, which art exalted to heaven, shalt be thrust down to hell.
16 He that heareth you heareth me; and he that despiseth you despiseth me; and he that despiseth me despiseth him that sent me.

17. And the seventy returned again with joy, saying, Lord, even the devils are subject unto us through thy name.

18 And he said unto them, I beheld Satan as lightning fall from heaven.
19 Behold, I give unto you power to tread on serpents and scorpions, and over all the power of the enemy: and nothing shall by any means hurt you.
20 Notwithstanding

Literal Translation

Luke 10:21

King James Version

not do rejoice in this, that the (evil) spirits submit to you. But rather rejoice that your names are written in Heaven.

1722 5129 3361 5463 3754 3588 4151 5213 5293
ἐν τούτῳ μὴ χαίρετε ὅτι τὰ πνεύματα ὑμῖν ὑποτάσσεται·
in this not do rejoice that the spirits to you submit,

5463 1161 3123 3754 3588 3686 5216 1125 1722 3588
χαίρετε δὲ μᾶλλον ὅτι τὰ ὀνόματα ὑμῶν ἐγράφη ἐν τοῖς
rejoice but rather that the names of you are written in

3772
οὐρανοῖς.
Heaven.

in this rejoice not, that the spirits are subject unto you; but rather rejoice, because your names are written in heaven.

21. In the same hour Jesus exulted in the Spirit, and said, I praise You, Father, Lord of the heaven and of the earth, that You hid these things from (the) sophisticated and cunning and revealed them to babes; yes, Father, because so it was pleasing before You.

1722 846 3588 5610 21 3588 4151 3588 2424
21. Ἐν αὐτῇ τῇ ὥρᾳ ἠγαλλιάσατο τῷ πνεύματι ὁ Ἰησοῦς,
In the same hour exulted in the Spirit Jesus,

2532 2036 1843 4671 3962 2962 3588 3772
καὶ εἶπεν, Ἐξομολογοῦμαί σοι, πάτερ, Κύριε τοῦ οὐρανοῦ
and said, I praise You, Father, Lord of the heaven

2532 3588 1093 3754 613 5023 575 4680 2532 4908
καὶ τῆς γῆς, ὅτι ἀπέκρυψας ταῦτα ἀπὸ σοφῶν καὶ συνετῶν,
and the earth, because You hid these things from sophisticated and cunning,

2532 601 846 3516 3483 3588 3962 3754 3779
καὶ ἀπεκάλυψας αὐτὰ νηπίοις· ναί, ὁ πατήρ, ὅτι οὕτως
and revealed them to babes; Yes, Father, because so

1096 2107 1715 4675 3956 3860 3427 5259
ἐγένετο εὐδοκία ἔμπροσθέν σου. 22 πάντα παρεδόθη μοι ὑπὸ
it was well-pleasing before You. All things were delivered to Me from

21. In that hour Jesus rejoiced in spirit, and said, I thank thee, O Father, Lord of heaven and earth, that thou hast hid these things from the wise and prudent, and hast revealed them unto babes: even so, Father; for so it seemed good in thy sight.

22 All things were delivered to Me by My Father, and no one knows who the Son is except the Father; and who is the Father, except the Son, and to whomever the Son purposes to reveal (Him).

3588 3962 3450 2532 3762 1097 5101 2076 3588 5207 1487 3361 3588
τοῦ πατρός μου· καὶ οὐδεὶς γινώσκει τίς ἐστιν ὁ υἱὸς εἰ μὴ ὁ
the Father of Me, and no one knows who is the Son except the

3962 2532 5101 2076 3588 3962 1487 3361 3588 5207 2532 3739 1437 1014
πατήρ, καὶ τίς ἐστιν ὁ πατὴρ, εἰ μὴ ὁ υἱὸς, καὶ ᾧ ἐὰν βούληται
Father, and who is the Father except the Son, and to whomever purposes

3588 5207 601 2532 4762 4314 3588 3101
ὁ υἱὸς ἀποκαλύψαι. 23 καὶ στραφεὶς πρὸς τοὺς μαθητὰς
the Son to reveal (Him). And turning to the disciples

22 All things are delivered to me of my Father: and no man knoweth who the Son is, but the Father; and who the Father is, but the Son, and (he) to whom the Son will reveal (him).

23. And having turned to the disciples privately, He said, Blessed (are) the eyes seeing what you see.

2596 2398 2036 3107 3588 3788 3588 991 3739 991
κατ᾽ ἰδίαν εἶπε, Μακάριοι οἱ ὀφθαλμοὶ οἱ βλέποντες ἃ βλέπετε.
privately, He said, Blessed the eyes seeing what you see

23. And he turned him unto (his) disciples, and said privately, Blessed (are) the eyes which see the things that ye see:

24 For I say to you that many prophets and kings desired to see what you see, and did not see, and to hear what you hear, and did not hear.

3004 1063 5213 3754 4183 4396 2532 935 2309
24 λέγω γὰρ ὑμῖν, ὅτι πολλοὶ προφῆται καὶ βασιλεῖς ἠθέλησαν
I say For to you that many prophets and kings desired

1492 3739 5210 991 2532 3756 1492 2532 191 3739 191 2532
ἰδεῖν ἃ ὑμεῖς βλέπετε, καὶ οὐκ εἶδαν· καὶ ἀκοῦσαι ἃ ἀκούετε καὶ
to see what you see, and not did see, and to hear what you hear, and

3756 191
οὐκ ἤκουσαν.
not did hear.

24 For I tell you, that many prophets and kings have desired to see those things which ye see, and have not seen (them); and to hear those things which ye hear, and have not heard (them).

25. And behold, a certain lawyer stood up, testing Him and saying, Teacher, What doing may I inherit eternal life?

2532 2400 3544 5100 450 1598 846 2532
25. Καὶ ἰδοὺ, νομικός τις ἀνέστη, ἐκπειράζων αὐτὸν, καὶ
And, behold! lawyer A certain stood up, testing Him, and

3004 1320 5101 4160 2222 166 2816
λέγων, Διδάσκαλε, τί ποιήσας ζωὴν αἰώνιον κληρονομήσω;
saying, Teacher, what having done life eternal I may inherit?

3588 1161 2036 4314 846 1722 3588 3551 5101 1125 4459
26 ὁ δὲ εἶπε πρὸς αὐτόν, Ἐν τῷ νόμῳ τί γέγραπται; πῶς
He And said to him, In the Law what has beenwritten? How

25. And, behold, a certain lawyer stood up, and tempted him, saying, Master, what shall I do to inherit eternal life?

26 And He said to him, What has been written in the Law? How do you read (it)?

27 And answering, he said, You shall love (the) Lord your God from all your heart, and from all your soul, and from all your strength, and from all

314 3588 1161 611 2036 25 2962
ἀναγινώσκεις; 27 ὁ δὲ ἀποκριθεὶς εἶπεν, Ἀγαπήσεις Κύριον
do you read? he And answering said, You shall love (the) Lord

3588 2316 4675 1537 3650 3588 2588 4675 2532 1537 3650 3588
τὸν Θεόν σου, ἐξ ὅλης τῆς καρδίας σου, καὶ ἐξ ὅλης τῆς
the God of you from all the heart of you, and from all the

5590 4675 2532 1537 3650 3588 2479 4675 2532 1537 3650 3588
ψυχῆς σου, καὶ ἐξ ὅλης τῆς ἰσχύι σου, καὶ ἐξ ὅλης τῆς
soul of you, and from all the strength of you, and from all the

26 He said unto him, What is written in the law? how readest thou?

27 And he answering said, Thou shalt love the Lord thy God with all thy heart, and with all thy soul, and with all thy strength, and with all

Literal Translation

your mind, and your neighbor as yourself. (Deut. 6:5; Lev. 19:18)
28 And He said to him, You have answered rightly; do this, and you will live.
29 But desiring to justify himself, he said to Jesus, And who is my neighbor?

30 And taking (it) up, Jesus said, A certain man was going down from Jerusalem to Jericho, and fell in with plunderers, who both stripping him and laying on blows, went away, leaving (him) being half dead.

31 And by a coincidence, a certain priest was going on that road; and seeing him, he passed on (the) opposite (side).

32 And in the same way, a Levite, also being at the place, coming and seeing (him), he passed on (the) opposite (side).
33 But a certain traveling Samaritan came upon him, and seeing him, he was filled with pity.
34 And coming near, (he) bound up his wounds, pouring on oil and wine. And putting him on (his) own animal, (he) brought him to an inn and cared for him.
35 And going out on the morrow, taking out two denarii, he gave (them) to the innkeeper, and said to him, Care for him, and whatever more you spend, in my return I will repay to you.

36 Who, then, of these three seems to you to have been a neighbor to the (one) falling among the plunderers?
37 And he said, The (one) doing the (deed of) mercy with him. Then Jesus said to him, Go, and you do likewise.

Luke 10:28

1271 4675 2532 3588 4139 4675 5613 4572 2036 1161
διανοίας σου· καὶ τὸν πλησίον σου ὡς σεαυτόν. 28 εἶπε δὲ
mind of you, and the neightbor of you as yourself. He said, And

846 3723 611 5124 4160 2532 2198 3588 1161 2309
αὐτῷ, Ὀρθῶς ἀπεκρίθης· τοῦτο ποίει, καὶ ζήσῃ. 29 ὁ δὲ θέλων
to him, Rightly you answered; this do, and you will live.he But desiring

1344 1438 2036 4314 3588 2424 2532 5101 2076 3450
δικαιοῦν ἑαυτὸν εἶπε πρὸς τὸν Ἰησοῦν, Καὶ τίς ἐστί μου
to justify himself said to Jesus, And who is of me

4139 5274 1161 3588 2424 2036 444 5100
πλησίον; 30 ὑπολαβὼν δὲ ὁ Ἰησοῦς εἶπεν, Ἄνθρωπός τις
neighbor? taking (it) up And Jesus said, man A certain

2597 575 2419 1519 2410 2532 3027 4045
κατέβαινεν ἀπὸ Ἱερουσαλὴμ εἰς Ἱεριχώ, καὶ λῃσταῖς περιέ-
was going down from Jerusalem to Jericho, and plunderers fell in

3739 2532 1562 846 2532 4127 2007
πεσεν, οἳ καὶ ἐκδύσαντες αὐτὸν καὶ πληγὰς ἐπιθέντες
with, who both stripping him and blows laying on

565 863 2253 5177 2596 4795
ἀπῆλθον ἀφέντες ἡμιθανῆ τυγχάνοντα. 31 κατὰ συγκυρίαν
went away, leaving (him) half-dead being. by a coincidence

1161 2409 5100 2597 1722 3588 3598 1565 2532 1492 846
δὲ ἱερεύς τις κατέβαινεν ἐν τῇ ὁδῷ ἐκείνῃ· καὶ ἰδὼν αὐτὸν
And priest a certain was going in way that; and seeing him

492 3668 1161 2532 3019 1096 2596 3588
ἀντιπαρῆλθεν· 32 ὁμοίως δὲ καὶ Λευΐτης γενόμενος κατὰ τὸν
(he) passed opposite. likewise And also a Levite being at the

5117 2064 2532 1492 492 4541 1161 5100
τόπον ἐλθὼν καὶ ἰδὼν ἀντιπαρῆλθε. 33 Σαμαρείτης δέ τις
place, coming and seeing, passed opposite. Samaritan But a certain

3593 2064 2596 846 2532 1492 846 4697
ὁδεύων ἦλθε κατ' αὐτὸν, καὶ ἰδὼν αὐτὸν ἐσπλαγχνίσθη,
traveling came upon him, and seeing him, (he) was filled with pity,

2532 4334 2611 3588 5134 846 2022
34 καὶ προσελθὼν κατέδησε τὰ τραύματα αὐτοῦ ἐπιχέων
and coming near bound up the wounds of him, pouring on

1637 2532 3631 1913 1161 846 1909 358 2398 2934
ἔλαιον καὶ οἶνον· ἐπιβιβάσας δὲ αὐτὸν ἐπὶ τὸ ἴδιον κτῆνος,
oil and wine. putting And him on the own animal

71 846 1519 3829 2532 1959 846 2532 1909
ἤγαγεν αὐτὸν εἰς πανδοχεῖον, καὶ ἐπεμελήθη αὐτοῦ. 35 καὶ ἐπὶ
(he) took him to an inn and cared for him. And on

3588 839 1831 1544 1417 1220 1325 3588 3830
τὴν αὔριον ἐξελθών, ἐκβαλὼν δύο δηνάρια ἔδωκε τῷ παν-
the morrow going out, taking out two denarii, he gave to the inn-

2532 2036 846 1959 846 2532 3588 5100 302
δοχεῖ καὶ εἶπεν αὐτῷ, Ἐπιμελήθητι αὐτοῦ· καὶ ὅ τι ἂν
keeper, and said to him, Care for him, and whatever

4325 1473 1722 3588 1880 3165 591 4671
προσδαπανήσῃς ἐγὼ ἐν τῷ ἐπανέρχεσθαί με ἀποδώσω σοι.
you spend more, I in the returning (of) me will repay you.

5101 3767 5130 3588 5140 1380 4671 4139 1096
36 τίς οὖν τούτων τῶν τριῶν δοκεῖ σοι πλησίον γεγονέναι
Who, then, of these three seems it to you neighbor to have been

3588 1706 1519 3588 3027 3588 1161 2036 3588 4160 3588
τοῦ ἐμπεσόντος εἰς τοὺς λῃστάς; 37 ὁ δὲ εἶπεν, Ὁ ποιήσας τὸ
the (one) falling into the plunderers? he And said, the (one) doing the

1656 3326 846 2036 3767 846 3588 2424 4198 2532
ἔλεος μετ' αὐτοῦ. εἶπεν οὖν αὐτῷ ὁ Ἰησοῦς, Πορεύου καὶ
mercy with him. said Then to him Jesus, Go, and

4771 4160 3668
σὺ ποίει ὁμοίως.
you do likewise.

King James Version

thy mind; and thy neighbour as thyself.
28 And he said unto him, Thou hast answered right: this do, and thou shalt live.
29 But he, willing to justify himself, said unto Jesus, And who is my neighbour?

30 And Jesus answering said, A certain (man) went down from Jerusalem to Jericho, and fell among thieves, which stripped him of his raiment, and wounded (him), and departed, leaving (him) half dead.

31 And by chance there came down a certain priest that way: and when he saw him, he passed by on the other side.

32 And likewise a Levite, when he was at the place, came and looked (on him), and passed by on the other side.
33 But a certain Samaritan, as he journeyed, came where he was: and when he saw him, he had compassion (on him),
34 And went to (him), and bound up his wounds, pouring in oil and wine, and set him on his own beast, and brought him to an inn, and took care of him.
35 And on the morrow when he departed, he took out two pence, and gave (them) to the host, and said unto him, Take care of him; and whatsoever thou spendest more, when I come again, I will repay thee.

36 Which now of these three, thinkest thou, was neighbour unto him that fell among the thieves?
37 And he said, He that shewed mercy on him. Then said Jesus unto him, Go, and do thou likewise.

Luke 10:38

Literal Translation

38. And as they went on, it happened, He also entered into a certain village. And a certain woman, Martha by name, received Him into her house.
39 And this one was a sister being called Mary, who also was sitting alongside, at the feet of Jesus, (and) heard His word.

40 But Martha was distracted about much serving. And coming on she said, Lord, (Is it) not a care to You that my sister left me alone to serve? Then tell her that she should help me.

41 But answering Jesus said to her, Martha, Martha, you are anxious and troubled about many things,
42 But there is need of (only) one; and Mary chose the good part, which shall not be taken from her.

1096 1161 1722 3588 4198 846 2532 846 1525
38.᾿Εγένετο δὲ ἐν τῷ πορεύεσθαι αὐτοὺς, καὶ αὐτὸς εἰσῆλθεν
it occurred And in the going (of) them, also He went

1519 2968 5100 1135 1161 5100 3686 3136 5264
εἰς κώμην τινά· γυνὴ δέ τις ὀνόματι Μάρθα ὑπεδέξατο
into village a certain. woman And a certain by name Martha received

846 1519 3588 3624 846 2532 3592 2258 79 2564
αὐτόν εἰς τὸν οικον αὐτῆς. 39 καὶ τῇδε ἦν ἀδελφὴ καλουμένη
him into the house of her. And to this was a sister being called

3137 3739 2532 3869 3844 3588 4228 3588 2424
Μαριά, ἣ καὶ παρακαθισασα παρὰ τοὺς πόδας τοῦ ᾿Ιησοῦ
Mary, who also sitting alongside at the feet of Jesus,

191 3588 3056 846 3588 1161 3136 4049 4012
ἤκουε τὸν λόγον αὐτοῦ. 40 ἡ δὲ Μάρθα περιεσπᾶτο περὶ
heard the word of Him. But Martha was distracted about

4183 1248 2186 1161 2036 2962 3756 3199 4671 3754
πολλὴν διακονίαν· ἐπιστᾶσα δὲ εἶπε, Κύριε, οὐ μέλει σοι ὅτι
much serving. coming on and she said, Lord, not a care to You that

3588 79 3450 3441 3165 2641 1247 2036 3767 846 2443
ἡ ἀδελφή μου μόνην με κατέλιπε διακονεῖν; εἰπὲ οὖν αὐτῇ ἵνα
the sister of me alone me left to serve? tell Then her

3427 4878 611 1161 2036 846 3588 2424
μοι συναντιλάβηται. 41 ἀποκριθεὶς δὲ εἶπεν αὐτῇ ὁ ᾿Ιησοῦς,
that me she should help. answering And said to her Jesus,

3136 3136 3309 2532 5182 4012 4183 1520
Μάρθα Μάρθα, μεριμνᾷς καὶ τυρβάζῃ περὶ πολλά· 42 ἑνὸς
Martha, Martha, you are anxious and troubled about many things; of one

1161 2076 5532 3137 1161 3588 18 3310 1586 3748
δέ ἐστι χρεία· Μαριὰ δὲ τὴν ἀγαθὴν μερίδα ἐξελέξατο ἥτις
but is need, Mary and the good part chose, which

3756 851 575 846
οὐκ ἀφαιρεθήσεται ἀπ᾿ αὐτῆς.
not will be taken from her.

King James Version

38. Now it came to pass, as they went, that he entered into a certain village: and a certain woman named Martha received him into her house.
39 And she had a sister called Mary, which also sat at Jesus' feet, and heard his word.

40 But Martha was cumbered about much serving, and came to him, and said, Lord, dost thou not care that my sister hath left me to serve alone? bid her therefore that she help me.

41 And Jesus answered and said unto her, Martha, Martha, thou art careful and troubled about many things:
42 But one thing is needful: and Mary hath chosen that good part, which shall not be taken away from her.

Luke 11

1. And it happened in His being in a certain place praying, when He ceased, one of His disciples said to Him, Lord teach us to pray, even as John also taught his disciples.

2 And He said to them: When you pray, say, Our Father who (is) in Heaven, hallowed be Your name, let Your kingdom come, let Your will be done on the earth as (it) also (is) in Heaven.

3 Give us our needed bread day by day;

4 and forgive us our sins, for we ourselves also forgive everyone

2532 1096 1722 3588 1511 846 1722 5117 5100 4336
1. Καὶ ἐγένετο ἐν τῷ εἶναι αὐτὸν ἐν τόπῳ τινὶ προσευχό-
And it happened in the being of Him in place a certain praying,

5613 3973 2036 5100 3588 3101 846 4314
μενον, ὡς ἐπαύσατο, εἶπέ τις τῶν μαθητῶν αὐτοῦ πρὸς
as He ceased, said a certain of the disciples of Him to

846 2962 1321 2248 4336 2531 2532
αὐτόν, Κύριε, δίδαξον ἡμᾶς προσεύχεσθαι, καθὼς καὶ
Him, Lord, teach us to pray, even as also

2491 1321 3588 3101 846 2036 1161 846
᾿Ιωάννης ἐδίδαξε τοὺς μαθητὰς αὐτοῦ. 2 εἶπε δὲ αὐτοῖς,
John taught the disciples of him. He said And to them,

3752 4336 3004 3962 2257 3588 1722 3588 3772
῞Οταν προσεύχησθε, λέγετε, Πάτερ ἡμῶν ὁ ἐν τοῖς οὐρανοῖς,
When you pray, say, Father Our who in Heaven (is),

37 3588 3686 4675 2064 3588 932 4675 1096
ἁγιασθήτω τὸ ὄνομά σου. ἐλθέτω ἡ βασιλεία σου. γενηθήτω
holy be the name of You; let come the kingdom of You; let be done

3588 2307 4675 5613 1722 3772 2532 1909 3588 1093 3588 740
τὸ θέλημά σου, ὡς ἐν οὐρανῷ, καὶ ἐπὶ τῆς γῆς, 3 τὸν ἄρτον
the will of You, as in Heaven, also on the earth; the bread

2257 3588 1967 1325 2254 3588 2596 2250 2532 863
ἡμῶν τὸν ἐπιούσιον δίδου ἡμῖν τὸ καθ᾿ ἡμέραν. 4 καὶ ἄφες
of us the needed give us day by day; and forgive

2254 3588 266 2257 2532 1063 846 863 3956
ἡμῖν τὰς ἁμαρτίας ἡμῶν, καὶ γὰρ αὐτοὶ ἀφίομεν παντὶ
us the sins of us; also for ourselves we forgive everyone

1. And it came to pass, that, as he was praying in a certain place, when he ceased, one of his disciples said unto him, Lord, teach us to pray, as John also taught his disciples.

2 And he said unto them, When ye pray, say, Our Father which art in heaven, Hallowed be thy name. Thy kingdom come. Thy will be done, as in heaven, so in earth.

3 Give us day by day our daily bread.

4 And forgive us our sins; for we also forgive every one

Literal Translation | **Luke 11:5** | **King James Version**

indebted to us. And lead
us not into temptation,
but deliver us from evil.

5. And He said to them,
Who of you shall have
a friend, and will come
to him at midnight and
say to him, Friend, lend
me three loaves.
6 (For) a friend of mine
arrived to me from a
journey, and I do not
have what I may set be-
fore him.
7 And answering from
within that one may say,
Do not cause me trou-
bles. The door has al-
ready been shut, and my
children are in bed with
me. I am not able to rise
up to give to you.
8 I say to you, even if
risng up he will not give
to him because he is a
friend, yet because of
his shameless insis-
tence, rising up he will
give him as many as he
needs.
9. And I say to you,
Ask, and it will be given
to you; seek, and you
will find; knock, and it
will be opened to you.
10 For everyone asking
receives, and the (one)
seeking finds, and to the
(one) knocking, it will
be opened.
11 And what father of
you, (if) the son asks
(for) a loaf, will he give
him a stone? And if a
fish, will he give him a
snake instead of a fish?
12 And if he should ask
an egg, will he give him
a scorpion?
13 Then if you being
evil know to give good
gifts to your children,
how much more the Fa-
ther out of Heaven will
give (the) Holy Spirit to
those asking Him.
14. And He was cast-
ing out a demon, and it
was dumb. And it hap-
pened

3784 2254 2532 3361 1533 2248 1519 3986 235
ὀφείλοντι ἡμῖν. καὶ μὴ εἰσενέγκῃς ἡμᾶς εἰς πειρασμόν, ἀλλὰ
indebted to us; and not do lead us into temptation, but
4506 2248 575 3588 4190
ῥῦσαι ἡμᾶς ἀπὸ τοῦ πονηροῦ.
deliver us from evil.

2532 2036 4314 846 5101 1537 5216 2192 5384 2532 4198
5. Καὶ εἶπε πρὸς αὐτούς, Τίς ἐξ ὑμῶν ἕξει φίλον, καὶ πορεύ-
And He said to them, Who out of you shall have a friend, and will
4314 846 3317 2532 2036 846 5384
σεται πρὸς αὐτὸν μεσονυκτίου καὶ εἴπῃ αὐτῷ, Φίλε,
come to him at midnight and say to him, Friend,
5531 3427 5140 740 1894 5384 3450 3854 1537
χρῆσόν μοι τρεῖς ἄρτους, 6 ἐπειδὴ φίλος μου παρεγένετο ἐξ
lend me three loaves, since a friend of me arrived from
3598 4314 3165 2532 3756 2192 3739 3908 846 2548
ὁδοῦ πρός με, καὶ οὐκ ἔχω ὃ παραθήσω αὐτῷ· 7 κἀκεῖνος
a journey to me, and not I have what I may set before him. that one
2081 611 2036 3361 3427 2873 3930 2235 3588
ἔσωθεν ἀποκριθεὶς εἴπῃ, Μή μοι κόπους πάρεχε· ἤδη ἡ
within answering may say, Not me troubles cause; already the
2374 2808 2532 3588 3813 3450 3326 1700 1519 3588 2845
θύρα κέκλεισται, καὶ τὰ παιδία μου μετ᾽ ἐμοῦ εἰς τὴν κοίτην
door has been shut, and the children of me with me in the bed
1526 3756 1410 450 1325 4671 3004 5213 1487 2532
εἰσίν· οὐ δύναμαι ἀναστὰς δοῦναί σοι. 8 λέγω ὑμῖν, εἰ καὶ
are; not I am able rising up to give to you. I say to you, if even
3756 1325 846 450 1223 3588 1511 846 5384 1223 1065 3588
οὐ δώσει αὐτῷ ἀναστάς, διὰ τὸ εἶναι αὐτοῦ φίλον, διά γε τὴν
not he will give him, rising up because of being of him friend, because yet of the
335 846 1453 1325 846 3745 5535 2504
ἀναίδειαν αὐτοῦ ἐγερθεὶς δώσει αὐτῷ ὅσων χρῄζει. 9 κἀγὼ
shameless insisting of him rising he will give him as many as he needs. And I
5213 3004 154 2532 1325 5213 2212 2532 2147
ὑμῖν λέγω, Αἰτεῖτε, καὶ δοθήσεται ὑμῖν· ζητεῖτε, καὶ εὑρήσετε·
to you say, Ask, and it will be given to you; seek, and you will find;
2925 2532 455 5213 3956 1063 3588 154 2983
κρούετε, καὶ ἀνοιγήσεται ὑμῖν. 10 πᾶς γὰρ ὁ αἰτῶν λαμβάνει·
knock, and it will be opened to you. everyone For asking receives,
2532 3588 2212 2147 2532 3588 2925 455 5101 1161
καὶ ὁ ζητῶν εὑρίσκει· καὶ τῷ κρούοντι ἀνοιγήσεται. 11 τίνα δὲ
and the (one) seeking finds; and to the (one) knocking, it will be opened. what And
5216 3588 3962 154 3588 5207 740 3361 3037 1929
ὑμῶν τὸν πατέρα αἰτήσει ὁ υἱὸς ἄρτον, μὴ λίθον ἐπιδώσει
of you father (of whom) asks the son a loaf, not a stone will he give
846 1487 2532 2486 3361 473 2486 3789 1929 846 2228 2532
αὐτῷ; εἰ καὶ ἰχθύν μὴ ἀντὶ ἰχθύος ὄφιν ἐπιδώσει αὐτῷ; 12 ἢ καὶ
him? if And a fish, not instead of a fish a snake will he give him? Or also
1437 154 5609 3361 1929 846 4651 1487 3767 5210
ἐὰν αἰτήσει ᾠόν, μὴ ἐπιδώσει αὐτῷ σκορπίον; 13 εἰ οὖν ὑμεῖς
if he should ask an egg, not will he give to him a scorpion? If then you
4190 5225 1492 18 1390 1325 3588
πονηροὶ ὑπάρχοντες οἴδατε ἀγαθὰ δόματα διδόναι τοῖς
evil being know good gifts to give to the
5043 5216 4214 3123 3588 3962 3588 1537 3772 1325
τέκνοις ὑμῶν, πόσῳ μᾶλλον ὁ πατὴρ ὁ ἐξ οὐρανοῦ δώσει
children of you, how much more the Father of Heaven will give
4151 40 3588 154 846
Πνεῦμα Ἅγιον τοῖς αἰτοῦσιν αὐτόν;
(the) Spirit Holy to the (ones) asking Him.

2532 2258 1544 1140 2532 846 2258 2974 1096
14. Καὶ ἦν ἐκβάλλων δαιμόνιον, καὶ αὐτὸ ἦν κωφόν. ἐγένετο
And He was casting out a demon, and it was dumb. it happened

that is indebted to us.
And lead us not into
temptation; but deliver
us from evil.

5. And he said unto
them, Which of you
shall have a friend, and
shall go unto him at mid-
night, and say unto him,
Friend, lend me three
loaves;
6 For a friend of mine in
his journey is come to
me, and I have nothing
to set before him?
7 And he from within
shall answer and say,
Trouble me not: the
door is now shut, and
my children are with me
in bed; I cannot rise and
give thee.
8 I say unto you,
Though he will not rise
and give him, because
he is his friend, yet be-
cause of his importunity
he will rise and give him
as many as he needeth.
9. And I say unto you,
Ask, and it shall be given
you; seek, and ye shall
find; knock, and it shall
be opened unto you.
10 For every one that
asketh receiveth; and he
that seeketh findeth;
and to him that knock-
eth it shall be opened.
11 If a son shall ask
bread of any of you that
is a father, will he give
him a stone? or if (he
ask) a fish, will he for a
fish give him a serpent?
12 Or if he shall ask an
egg, will he offer him a
scorpion?
13 If ye then, being evil,
know how to give good
gifts unto your children:
how much more shall
(your) heavenly Father
give the Holy Spirit to
them that ask him?

14. And he was casting
out a devil, and it was
dumb. And it came to
pass,

Literal Translation

as the demon (was) go-
ing out, the dumb one
spoke. And the crowds
marveled.
15 But some of them
said, He casts out the
demons by Beelzebul
the chief of the demons.
16 And tempting
(Him), others were
seeking a sign from
Heaven from Him.
17 But knowing their
thoughts, He said to
them, Every kingdom
divided against itself is
brought to ruin, and a
house against a house
falls.
18 And also if Satan
was divided against
himself, how shall his
kingdom stand? Be-
cause you say I cast out
the demons by Beelze-
bul.
19 And if I cast out the
demons by Beelzebul,
by whom do your sons
cast out? Because of
this they shall be your
judges.
20 But if I cast out the
demons by (the) finger
of God, then the king-
dom of God has come
upon you.
21 When the strong one,
having been armed,
guards his (dwelling),
his goods are in peace.
22 But when one
stronger than him
comes, (he) overcomes
him; he takes away his
armor on which he
trusted, and gives over
his arms.
23 The (one) not being
with Me is against Me.
And the (one) not gath-
ering with me scatters.
24 When the unclean
spirit goes out from the
man, he goes through
waterless places seek-
ing rest. And not find-
ing, he says, I will return
to my house from
where I came out.
25 And coming, he
finds (it) having been
swept and having
beendecorated.
26 Then

Luke 11:15

1161 3588 1140 1831 2980 3588 2974 2532
δὲ, τοῦ δαιμονίου ἐξελθόντος, ἐλάλησεν ὁ κωφός· καὶ
And, the demon going out, spoke the dumb one. And

2296 3588 3793 5100 1161 1537 846 2036 1722 954
ἐθαύμασαν οἱ ὄχλοι. 15 τινὲς δὲ ἐξ αὐτῶν εἶπον, Ἐν Βεελζεβοὺλ
marveled the crowds. some But of them said, By Beelzebul

758 3588 1140 1544 3588 1140 2087 1161
ἄρχοντι τῶν δαιμονίων ἐκβάλλει τὰ δαιμόνια· 16 ἕτεροι δὲ
the chief of the demons He casts out the demons. others And

3985 4592 3844 846 2212 1537 3772 846
πειράζοντες σημεῖον παρ' αὐτοῦ ἐζήτουν ἐξ οὐρανοῦ. 17 αὐτὸς
tempting, a sign from Him were seeking out of Heaven. He

1161 1492 846 3588 1270 2036 846 3956 932
δὲ εἰδὼς αὐτῶν τὰ διανοήματα εἶπεν αὐτοῖς, Πᾶσα βασιλεία
But knowing of them the thoughts said to them, Every kingdom

1909 1438 1266 2049 2532 3624 1909 3624
ἐφ' ἑαυτὴν διαμερισθεῖσα ἐρημοῦται· καὶ οἶκος ἐπὶ οἶκον,
against itself divided is brought to ruin, and a house against a house

4098 1487 1161 2532 3588 4567 1909 1438 1266 4459
πίπτει. 18 εἰ δὲ καὶ ὁ Σατανᾶς ἐφ' ἑαυτὸν διεμερίσθη, πῶς
falls. if And also Satan against himself was divided, how

2476 3588 932 846 3754 3004 1722 954
σταθήσεται ἡ βασιλεία αὐτοῦ; ὅτι λέγετε, ἐν Βεελζεβοὺλ
shall stand the kingdom of him? Because you say by Beelzebul

1544 3165 3588 1140 1487 1161 1473 1722 954 1544
ἐκβάλλειν με τὰ δαιμόνια. 19 εἰ δὲ ἐγὼ ἐν Βεελζεβοὺλ ἐκβάλλω
casting out me the demons. if But I by Beelzebul cast out

3588 1140 3588 5207 5216 1722 5101 1544 1223 5124
τὰ δαιμόνια, οἱ υἱοὶ ὑμῶν ἐν τίνι ἐκβάλλουσι; διὰ τοῦτο
the demons, the sons of you, by what do they cast out? Because of this

2923 5216 846 2071 1487 1161 1722 1147 2316 1544
κριταὶ ὑμῶν αὐτοὶ ἔσονται. 20 εἰ δὲ ἐν δακτύλῳ Θεοῦ ἐκβάλλω
judges of you they shall be. if But by (the) finger of God I cast out

3588 1140 686 5348 1909 5209 3588 932 3588 2316
τὰ δαιμόνια, ἄρα ἔφθασεν ἐφ' ὑμᾶς ἡ βασιλεία τοῦ Θεοῦ.
the demons, then has come upon you the kingdom of God.

3752 3588 2478 2528 5442 3588 1438 833
21 ὅταν ὁ ἰσχυρὸς καθωπλισμένος φυλάσσῃ τὴν ἑαυτοῦ αὐλήν,
When the strong one having been armed guards the of himself dwelling,

1722 1515 2076 3588 5224 846 1875 1161 3588 2478
ἐν εἰρήνῃ ἐστὶ τὰ ὑπάρχοντα αὐτοῦ· 22 ἐπὰν δὲ ὁ ἰσχυρότερος
in peace are the goods of him. when But he stronger than

846 1904 3528 846 3588 3833 846 142
αὐτοῦ ἐπελθὼν νικήσῃ αὐτόν, τὴν πανοπλίαν αὐτοῦ αἴρει
him coming overcomes him, the armor of him he takes.

1909 3739 3982 2532 3588 4661 846 1239 3588 3361 5607
ἐφ' ᾗ ἐπεποίθει, καὶ τὰ σκῦλα αὐτοῦ διαδίδωσιν. 23 ὁ μὴ ὢν
on which he trusted, and the arms of him gives over. He not being

3326 1700 2596 1700 2076 2532 3588 3361 4863 3326 1700 4650
μετ' ἐμοῦ κατ' ἐμοῦ ἐστι· καὶ ὁ μὴ συνάγων μετ' ἐμοῦ σκορπί-
with Me against Me is. And he not gathering with Me scatters.

3752 3588 169 4151 1831 575 3588 444
ζει. 24 Ὅταν τὸ ἀκάθαρτον πνεῦμα ἐξέλθῃ ἀπὸ τοῦ ἀνθρώπου,
When the unclean spirit goes out from the man,

1330 1223 504 5117 2212 372 2532 3361
διέρχεται δι' ἀνύδρων τόπων, ζητοῦν ἀνάπαυσιν· καὶ μὴ
he goes through waterless places seeking rest; and not

2147 3004 5290 1519 3588 3624 3450 3606 1831
εὑρίσκον, λέγει, Ὑποστρέψω εἰς τὸν οἶκόν μου ὅθεν ἐξῆλθον·
finding, he says, I will return to the house of me from where I came.

2532 2064 2147 4563 2532 2885 5119
25 καὶ ἐλθὸν εὑρίσκει σεσαρωμένον καὶ κεκοσμημένον. 26 τότε
And coming he finds (it) having been swept and having been decorated. Then

King James Version

when the devil was
gone out, the dumb
spake; and the people
wondered.
15 But some of them
said, He casteth out
devils through Beelze-
bub the chief of the
devils.
16 And others, tempt-
ing (him), sought of
him a sign from
heaven.
17 But he, knowing
their thoughts, said
unto them, Every
kingdom divided
against itself is
brought to desolation;
and a house (divided)
against a house falleth.
18 If Satan also be di-
vided against himself,
how shall his kingdom
stand? because ye say
that I cast out devils
through Beelzebub.
19 And if I by Beelze-
bub cast out devils, by
whom do your sons
cast (them) out? there-
fore shall they be your
judges.
20 But if I with the fin-
ger of God cast out
devils, no doubt the
kingdom of God is
come upon you.
21 When a strong man
armed keepeth his pal-
ace, his goods are in
peace:
22 But when a
stronger than he shall
come upon him, and
overcome him, he
taketh from him all his
armour wherein he
trusted, and divideth
his spoils.
23 He that is not with
me is against me: and
he that gathereth not
with me scattereth.
24 When the unclean
spirit is gone out of a
man, he walketh
through dry places,
seeking rest; and find-
ing none, he saith, I
will return unto my
house whence I came
out.
25 And when he
cometh, he findeth (it)
swept and garnished.
26 Then

Literal Translation **Luke 11:27** *King James Version*

he goes and takes seven other spirits more wicked than himself, and entering he dwells there. And the last things of that man become worse than the first.

4198 2532 3880 2033 2087 4151 4190
πορεύεται καὶ παραλαμβάνει ἑπτὰ ἕτερα πνεύματα πονηρό-
he goes and takes along seven other spirits more evil
1438 2532 1525 2730 1563 2532 1096 3588
τερα ἑαυτοῦ, καὶ εἰσελθόντα κατοικεῖ ἐκεῖ· καὶ γίνεται τὰ
than himself, and entering he dwells there; and becomes the
2078 3588 444 1565 5501 3588 4413
ἔσχατα τοῦ ἀνθρώπου ἐκείνου χείρονα τῶν πρώτων.
last things man of that worse (than) the first.

goeth he, and taketh (to him) seven other spirits more wicked than himself; and they enter in, and dwell there: and the last (state) of that man is worse than the first.

27. And (as) He spoke these things, it happened that a certain woman lifting up (her) voice out of the crowd said to Him, Blessed (is) the womb having borne You and (the) breasts which You sucked.
28 But He said, No rather blessed (are) the (ones) hearing the Word of God, and keeping it.

1096 1161 1722 3588 3004 846 5023 1869 5100
27. Ἐγένετο δὲ ἐν τῷ λέγειν αὐτὸν ταῦτα, ἐπάρασά τις
it happened And in the saying (of) Him these things, lifting up a certain
1135 5456 1537 3588 3793 2036 846 3107 3588 2836 3588
γυνὴ φωνὴν ἐκ τοῦ ὄχλου εἶπεν αὐτῷ, Μακαρία ἡ κοιλία ἡ
woman (her) voice out of the crowd said to Him, Blessed the womb
941 4571 2532 3149 3739 2337 846 1161 2036
βαστάσασά σε καὶ μαστοὶ οὓς ἐθήλασας. 28 αὐτὸς δὲ εἶπε,
having borne You and breasts which You sucked. He But said,
3304 3107 3588 191 3588 3056 3588 2316 2532
Μενοῦνγε μακάριοι οἱ ἀκούοντες τὸν λόγον τοῦ Θεοῦ καὶ
No, rather blessed the (ones) hearing the Word of God and
5442 846
φυλάσσοντες αὐτόν.
keeping it.

27. And it came to pass, as he spake these things, a certain woman of the company lifted up her voice, and said unto him, Blessed (is) the womb that bare thee, and the paps which thou hast sucked.
28 But he said, Yea rather, blessed (are) they that hear the word of God, and keep it.

29. But the crowds having pressed, He began to say, This is an evil generation. It seeks a sign, and a sign will not be given to it, except the sign of Jonah the prophet.
30 For even as Jonah became a sign to the Ninevites, so also the Son of man will be to this generation.
31 (The) queen of (the) south will be raised in the Judgment with the men of this generation, and will condemn them, because she came from the ends of the earth to hear the wisdom of Solomon. And, behold! A Greater-than-Solomon (is) here.

3588 1161 3793 1865 756 3004 3588 1074
29. Τῶν δὲ ὄχλων ἐπαθροιζομένων ἤρξατο λέγειν, Ἡ γενεὰ
the And crowds having pressed together He began to say, generation
3778 4190 2076 4592 1934 2532 4592 3756 1325
αὕτη πονηρά ἐστι· σημεῖον ἐπιζητεῖ, καὶ σημεῖον οὐ δοθή-
This an evil is; a sign it seeks, and a sign not will be
846 1487 3361 3588 4592 2495 3588 4396 2531
σεται αὐτῇ εἰ μὴ τὸ σημεῖον Ἰωνᾶ τοῦ προφήτου. 30 καθὼς
given to it, except the sign of Jonah the prophet. even as
1063 1096 2495 4592 3588 3536 3779 2071
γὰρ ἐγένετο Ἰωνᾶς σημεῖον τοῖς Νινευΐταις, οὕτως ἔσται
For came to be Jonah a sign to the Ninevites, so will be
2532 3588 5207 3588 444 3588 1074 3778 938 3558
καὶ ὁ υἱὸς τοῦ ἀνθρώπου τῇ γενεᾷ ταύτῃ. 31 βασίλισσα νότου
also the Son of man generation to this. (The) queen of south
1453 1722 3588 2920 3326 3588 435 3588 1074 3778
ἐγερθήσεται ἐν τῇ κρίσει μετὰ τῶν ἀνδρῶν τῆς γενεᾶς ταύτης,
will be raised in the Judgment with the men generation of this,
2532 2632 846 3754 2064 1537 3588 4009 3588 1093
καὶ κατακρινεῖ αὐτούς· ὅτι ἦλθεν ἐκ τῶν περάτων τῆς γῆς
and will condemn them; because she came from the ends of the earth
191 3588 4678 4672 2532 2400 4119 4672
ἀκοῦσαι τὴν σοφίαν Σολομῶνος, καὶ ἰδού, πλεῖον Σολομῶν-
to hear the wisdom of Solomon, and, behold! A Greater-than-Solomon

29. And when the people were gathered thick together, he began to say, This is an evil generation: they seek a sign; and there shall no sign be given it, but the sign of Jonas the prophet.
30 For as Jonas was a sign unto the Ninevites, so shall also the Son of man be to this generation.
31 The queen of the south shall rise up in the judgment with the men of this generation, and condemn them: for she came from the utmost parts of the earth to hear the wisdom of Solomon; and, behold, a greater than Solomon (is) here.

32 Men, Ninevites will rise up in the Judgment with this generation, and will condemn it, because they repented at the preaching of Jonah. And, behold, a Greater-than-Jonah (is) here.

5602 435 3535 450 1722 3588 2920 3326 3588
τος ὧδε. 32 ἄνδρες Νινευΐ ἀναστήσονται ἐν τῇ κρίσει μετὰ τῆς
(is) here. Men Ninevites will rise up in the Judgment with
107 3778 2532 2632 846 3754 3340
γενεᾶς ταύτης, καὶ κατακρινοῦσιν αὐτήν· ὅτι μετενόησαν
generation this, and will condemn it; because they repented
1519 3588 2782 2495 2532 2400 4119 2495 5602
εἰς τὸ κήρυγμα Ἰωνᾶ, καὶ ἰδού, πλεῖον Ἰωνᾶ ὧδε.
at the preaching of Jonah, and, behold! A Greater-than-Jonah (is) here.

32 The men of Nineve shall rise up in the judgment with this generation, and shall condemn it: for they repented at the preaching of Jonas; and, behold, a greater than Jonas (is) here.

33 But no one having lit a lamp places (it) in secret, nor under the grain-measure, but on the lampstand, that the ones entering

3762 1161 3088 681 1519 2927 5087 3761 5259
33. Οὐδεὶς δὲ λύχνον ἅψας εἰς κρυπτὸν τίθησιν, οὐδὲ ὑπὸ
no one But a lamp having lit in secret places it, nor under
3588 3426 235 1909 3588 3087 2443 3588 1531 3588
τὸν μόδιον, ἀλλ' ἐπὶ τὴν λυχνίαν, ἵνα οἱ εἰσπορευόμενοι τὸ
the grain-measure, but on the lampstand, that those having entered the

33 No man, when he hath lighted a candle, putteth (it) in a secret place, neither under a bushel, but on a candlestick, that they which come in

Literal Translation | **Luke 11:34** | *King James Version*

may see the light.
34 The lamp of the body is the eye. Then when your eye is sound, also all your body is full of light. But when it is evil, also your body (is) darkness.

5338 991 3588 3088 3588 4983 2076 3588 3788
φέγγος βλέπωσιν. 34ὁ λύχνος τοῦ σώματός ἐστιν ὁ ὀφθαλμός·
light may see. The lamp of the body is the eye;
3752 3767 3588 3788 4675 573 5600 2532 3650 3588 4983 4675
ὅταν οὖν ὁ ὀφθαλμός σου ἁπλοῦς ᾖ, καὶ ὅλον τὸ σῶμά σου
when then the eye of you single is, also all the body of you
5460 2076 1875 1161 4190 5600 2532 3588 4983 4675
φωτεινόν ἐστιν· ἐπὰν δὲ πονηρὸς ᾖ, καὶ τὸ σῶμά σου σκο-
full of light is; when but evil it is, also the body of you (is)

may see the light.
34 The light of the body is the eye: therefore when thine eye is single, thy whole body also is full of light; but when (thine eye) is evil, thy body also (is) full of darkness.

35 Then watch that the light in you is not darkness.
36 If, then, your whole body (is) full of light, not having any part dark, all will be full of light, as when the lamp enlightens you with (its) shining.

4652 4648 3767/3361/3588/5457/3588/1722/4671 4655 2076 1487
τεινόν. 35 σκόπει οὖν μὴ τὸ φῶς τὸ ἐν σοὶ σκότος ἐστίν. 36 εἰ
darkness. Watch, then, not the light in you darkness is. If
3767 3588 4983 4675 3650 5460 3361 2192 5100 3313 4652
οὖν τὸ σῶμά σου ὅλον φωτεινόν, μὴ ἔχον τι μέρος σκοτεινόν,
then the body of you whole (is) full of light, not having any part darkness,
2071 5460 3650 5613 3752 3588 3088 3588 796
ἔσται φωτεινὸν ὅλον, ὡς ὅταν ὁ λύχνος τῇ ἀστραπῇ
will be full of light all, as when the lamp with the shining
5461 4571
φωτίζῃ σε.
enlightens you.

35 Take heed therefore that the light which is in thee be not darkness.
36 If thy whole body therefore (be) full of light, having no part dark, the whole shall be full of light, as when the bright shining of a candle doth give thee light.

37. And (as He) was speaking, a certain Pharisee asked Him that He would dine with him. And going in, He reclined.
38 But perceiv0ing, the Pharisee marveled that He did not wash first before the dinner.

1722 1161 3588 2980 2065 846 5330 5100 3704
37. Ἐν δὲ τῷ λαλῆσαι ἠρώτα αὐτὸν Φαρισαῖος τις ὅπως
(as) And (He) was speaking, asked Him Pharisee a certain that
709 3844 846 1525 1161 377 3588 1161 5330
ἀριστήσῃ παρ᾽ αὐτῷ· εἰσελθὼν δὲ ἀνέπεσεν. 38 ὁ δὲ Φαρισαῖος
He would dine with him. going in And He reclined. the But Pharisee
1492 2296 3754 3756 4412 907 4253 3588 712
ἰδὼν ἐθαύμασεν ὅτι οὐ πρῶτον ἐβαπτίσθη πρὸ τοῦ ἀρίστου.
perceiving marveled that not first he washed before the dinner.

37. And as he spake, a certain Pharisee besought him to dine with him: and he went in, and sat down to meat.
38 And when the Pharisee saw (it), he marvelled that he had not first washed before dinner.

39 But the Lord said to him, Now you Pharisees cleanse the outside of the cup and of the dish, but your inside is full of robbery and evil.
40 Fools! Did not the (One) making the outside also make the inside?
41 But give alms (of) the things which are within, and behold, all things (are) clean to you.

2036 1161 3588 2962 4314 846 3568 5210 3588 5330 3588
39 εἶπε δὲ ὁ Κύριος πρὸς αὐτόν, Νῦν ὑμεῖς οἱ Φαρισαῖοι τὸ
said But the Lord to him, Now you Pharisees the
1855 3588 4221 2532 3588 4094 2511 3588 1161
ἔξωθεν τοῦ ποτηρίου καὶ τοῦ πίνακος καθαρίζετε, τὸ δὲ
outside of the cup and of the dish cleanse, the but
2081 5216 1073 724 2532 4189 878 3756
ἔσωθεν ὑμῶν γέμει ἁρπαγῆς καὶ πονηρίας. 40 ἄφρονες, οὐχ
inside of you is full of robbery and evil. Fools! Did not
3588 4160 3588 1855 2532 3588 2081 4160 4133
ὁ ποιήσας τὸ ἔξωθεν καὶ τὸ ἔσωθεν ἐποίησε; 41 πλὴν
the (One) making the outside also the inside make? But (of)
3588 1751 1325 1654 2532 2400 3956 2513
τὰ ἐνόντα δότε ἐλεημοσύνην· καὶ ἰδού, πάντα καθαρὰ
the things being within give alms; and behold, all things clean
5213 2076
ὑμῖν ἐστιν.
to you is.

39 And the Lord said unto him, Now do ye Pharisees make clean the outside of the cup and the platter; but your inward part is full of ravening and wickedness.
40 (Ye) fools, did not he that made that which is without make that which is within also?
41 But rather give alms of such things as ye have; and, behold, all things are clean unto you.

42 But woe to you, Pharisees! For you pay tithes of the mint, and the rue, and every plant, and pass by the judgment and the love of God. These things you m■st do, but not to leave aside those.

235 3759 5213 3588 5330 3754 586 3588
42. Ἀλλ᾽ οὐαὶ ὑμῖν τοῖς Φαρισαίοις, ὅτι ἀποδεκατοῦτε τὸ
But woe to you Pharisees! Because you tithe the
2238 2532 3588 4076 2532 3956 3001 2532 3928
ἡδύοσμον καὶ τὸ πήγανον καὶ πᾶν λάχανον, καὶ παρέρ-
mint and the rue and every plant, and pass
3588 2920 2532 3588 26 3588 2316 5023 1163
χεσθε τὴν κρίσιν καὶ τὴν ἀγάπην τοῦ Θεοῦ· ταῦτα ἔδει
by the judgment and the love of God; these things must
4160 2548 3361 863 3759 5213 3588 5330
ποιῆσαι, κἀκεῖνα μὴ ἀφιέναι. 43 οὐαὶ ὑμῖν τοῖς Φαρισαίοις,
(you) do, and those not to leave aside. Woe to you Pharisees!

42 But woe unto you, Pharisees! for ye tithe mint and rue and all manner of herbs, and pass over judgment and the love of God: these ought ye to have done, and not to leave the other undone.

43 Woe to you, Pharisees! Because you love the chief seats in the synagogues

3754 25 3588 4410 1722 3588 4864
ὅτι ἀγαπᾶτε τὴν πρωτοκαθεδρίαν ἐν ταῖς συναγωγαῖς
Because you love the chief seats in the synagogues

43 Woe unto you, Pharisees! for ye love the uppermost seats in the synagogues,

Literal Translation

Luke 11:44

King James Version

and the greetings in the marketplaces.
44 Woe to you, scribes and Pharisees, hypocrites! For you are as the unseen tombs, and the men walking about over (them) do not know.

45 And answering, one of the lawyers said to Him, Teacher, saying these things you also insult us.
46 And He said, Woe to you also, lawyers! Because you burden men (with) burdens hard to bear, and (you) yourselves will not touch the burdens with one of your fingers.

47 Woe to you! Because you build the tombs of the prophets, and your fathers killed them.

48 So then (you are) witnesses and consent to the works of your fathers; for they indeed killed them, and you build their tombs.

49 And because of this, the Wisdom of God said, I will send prophets and apostles to them, and they will kill and drive out (some) of them,
50 that the blood of all the prophets which has been shed from (the) foundation of the world may be required from this generation,

51 from the blood of Abel until the blood of Zechariah (who) perished between the altar and the House. Yea, I say to you, it will be required from this generation.

52 Woe to you, lawyers! Because you took the key of knowledge; you yourselves did not enter, and you kept out the ones entering.

2532 3588 783 1722 3588 58 3759 5213 1122
καὶ τοὺς ἀσπασμοὺς ἐν ταῖς ἀγοραῖς. 44 οὐαὶ ὑμῖν, γραμματεῖς
and the greetings in the markets. Woe to you, scribes

2532 5330 5273 3754 2075 5613 3588 3419 3588 82
καὶ Φαρισαῖοι, ὑποκριταί, ὅτι ἐστὲ ὡς τὰ μνημεῖα τὰ ἄδηλα,
and Pharisees, hypocrites! Because you are as the tombs unseen,

2532 3588 444 3588 4043 1883 3756 1492
καὶ οἱ ἄνθρωποι οἱ περιπατοῦντες ἐπάνω οὐκ οἴδασιν.
and the men walking about over (them) not do know.

611 1161 5100 3588 3544 3004 846 1320
45. Ἀποκριθεὶς δέ τις τῶν νομικῶν λέγει αὐτῷ, Διδάσκαλε,
answering And one of the lawyers says to Him, Teacher,

5023 3004 2532 2248 5195 3588 1161 2036 2532 5213 3588
ταῦτα λέγων καὶ ἡμᾶς ὑβρίζεις. 46 ὁ δὲ εἶπε, Καὶ ὑμῖν τοῖς
these things saying also us You insult. He And said, Also to you,

3544 3759 3754 5412 3588 444 5413
νομικοῖς οὐαί, ὅτι φορτίζετε τοὺς ἀνθρώπους φορτία
lawyers woe! Because you burden men (with) burdens

1419 2532 846 1520 3588 11 5216 3756
δυσβάστακτα, καὶ αὐτοὶ ἑνὶ τῶν δακτύλων ὑμῶν οὐ
difficult to bear, and yourselves with one of the fingers of you not

4379 3588 5413 3759 5213 3754 3618 3588
προσψαύετε τοῖς φορτίοις. 47 οὐαὶ ὑμῖν, ὅτι οἰκοδομεῖτε τὰ
you will touch the burdens. Woe to you! Because you build the

3419 3588 4396 3588 1161 3962 5216 615
μνημεῖα τῶν προφητῶν, οἱ δὲ πατέρες ὑμῶν ἀπέκτειναν
tombs of the prophets, the and fathers of you killed

846 686 3140 2532 4909 3588 2041 3588
αὐτούς. 48 ἄρα μαρτυρεῖτε καὶ συνευδοκεῖτε τοῖς ἔργοις τῶν
them. So then witnesses (you are) and consent to the works of the

3962 5216 3754 846 3303 615 846 5210 1161
πατέρων ὑμῶν· ὅτι αὐτοὶ μὲν ἀπέκτειναν αὐτούς, ὑμεῖς δὲ
fathers of you; because they indeed killed them, you and

3618 846 3588 3419 1223 5124 2532 3588 4678 3588
οἰκοδομεῖτε αὐτῶν τὰ μνημεῖα. 49 διὰ τοῦτο καὶ ἡ σοφία τοῦ
build of them the tombs. Because of this also the Wisdom

2316 2036 649 1519 846 4396 2532 652
Θεοῦ εἶπεν, Ἀποστελῶ εἰς αὐτοὺς προφήτας καὶ ἀποστό-
of God said, I will send to them prophets and apostles,

2532 1537 846 615 2532 1559 2443
λους, καὶ ἐξ αὐτῶν ἀποκτενοῦσι καὶ ἐκδιώξουσιν· 50 ἵνα
and out of them they will kill and drive out; that

1567 3588 129 3956 3588 4396 3588 1632
ἐκζητηθῇ τὸ αἷμα πάντων τῶν προφητῶν τὸ ἐκκεχυμένον
may be required the blood of all the prophets having been shed

575 2602 2889 575 3588 1074 3778 575 3588
ἀπὸ καταβολῆς κόσμου ἀπὸ τῆς γενεᾶς ταύτης, 51 ἀπὸ τοῦ
from (the) foundation of (the) world from generation this, from the

129 6 2193 3588 129 2197 3588 622
αἵματος Ἄβελ ἕως τοῦ αἵματος Ζαχαρίου τοῦ ἀπολομένου
blood of Abel until the blood of Zachariah, (who) perished

3342 3588 2379 2532 3588 3624 3483 3004 5213
μεταξὺ τοῦ θυσιαστηρίου καὶ τοῦ οἴκου· ναί, λέγω ὑμῖν,
between the altar and the House; yea, I say to you,

1567 575 3588 1074 3778 3759 5213 3588
ἐκζητηθήσεται ἀπὸ τῆς γενεᾶς ταύτης. 52 οὐαὶ ὑμῖν τοῖς
it will be required from generation this. Woe to you

3544 3754 142 3588 2807 3588 1108 846 3756
νομικοῖς, ὅτι ἤρατε τὴν κλεῖδα τῆς γνώσεως· αὐτοὶ οὐκ
lawyers! Because you took the key of knowledge; yourselves not

1525 2532 3588 1525 2967
εἰσήλθετε, καὶ τοὺς εἰσερχομένους ἐκωλύσατε.
you entered, and the (ones) entering you kept out.

and greetings in the markets.
44 Woe unto you, scribes and Pharisees, hypocrites! for ye are as graves which appear not, and the men that walk over (them) are not aware (of them).

45 Then answered one of the lawyers, and said unto him, Master, thus saying thou reproachest us also.
46 And he said, Woe unto you also, (ye) lawyers! for ye lade men with burdens grievous to be borne, and ye yourselves touch not the burdens with one of your fingers.

47 Woe unto you! for ye build the sepulchres of the prophets, and your fathers killed them.

48 Truly ye bear witness that ye allow the deeds of your fathers: for they indeed killed them, and ye build their sepulchres.

49 Therefore also said the wisdom of God, I will send them prophets and apostles, and (some) of them they shall slay and persecute:
50 That the blood of all the prophets, which was shed from the foundation of the world, may be required of this generation;

51 From the blood of Abel unto the blood of Zacharias, which perished between the altar and the temple: verily I say unto you, It shall be required of this generation.

52 Woe unto you, lawyers! for ye have taken away the key of knowledge: ye entered not in yourselves, and them that were entering in ye hindered.

Luke 11:53

Literal Translation

53 And as He was saying these things to them, the scribes and the Pharisees began to be terribly angry, and to draw (Him) out concerning many things,
54 lying in wait for Him, and seeking to catch something out of His mouth that they might accuse Him.

3004 1161 846 5023 4314 846 756 3588
53. Λέγοντος δὲ αὐτοῦ ταῦτα πρὸς αὐτούς, ἤρξαντο οἱ
as was saying And Him these things to them, began the

1122 2532 3588 5330 1171 1758 2532 653
γραμματεῖς καὶ οἱ Φαρισαῖοι δεινῶς ἐνέχειν, καὶ ἀποστο-
scribes and the Pharisees terribly to be angry, and to draw

846 4012 4119 1748 846 2532
ματίζειν αὐτὸν περὶ πλειόνων, 54 ἐνεδρεύοντες αὐτὸν, καὶ
out Him concerning many things, lying in wait for Him, and

2212 2340 5100 1537 3588 4750 846 2443 2723
ζητοῦντες θηρεῦσαί τι ἐκ τοῦ στόματος αὐτοῦ, ἵνα κατηγορή-
seeking to catch something out of the mouth of Him, that they might

846
σωσιν αὐτοῦ.
accuse Him.

King James Version

53 And as he said these things unto them, the scribes and the Pharisees began to urge (him) vehemently, and to provoke him to speak of many things:
54 Laying wait for him, and seeking to catch something out of his mouth, that they might accuse him.

Luke 12

1. During which (time) the myriads of the crowd being gathered together, so as to trample on one another, He began to say to His disciples first, Take heed to yourselves of the leaven of the Pharisees, which is hypocrisy.
2 But there is nothing which has been completely concealed which will not be uncovered, nor hidden which will not be known.
3 Therfore what things you said in the darkness will be heard in the light; and what you spoke in the ear in the secret rooms will be proclaimed on the housetops.
4 But I say to you, My friends, do not be afraid of the (ones) killing the body, and after these things not having anything more (they can) do.
5 But I will warn you whom you should fear; fear the (One) who after the killing have authority to cast into Hell; yes, I say to you, fear that One!
6 Are not five sparrows sold (for) two assaria? And not one of them is being forgotten before God.
7 But even the hairs of your head have all been

1722 3739 1996 3588 3461 3588 3793 5620
1. Ἐν οἷς ἐπισυναχθεισῶν τῶν μυριάδων τοῦ ὄχλου, ὥστε
During which being assembled the myriads of the crowd, so as

2662 240 756 3004 4314 3588 3101
καταπατεῖν ἀλλήλους, ἤρξατο λέγειν πρὸς τοὺς μαθητὰς
to trample on one another, He began to say to the disciples

846 4412 4337 1438 575 3588 2219 3588
αὐτοῦ πρῶτον, Προσέχετε ἑαυτοῖς ἀπὸ τῆς ζύμης τῶν
of Him first, Take heed to yourselves from the leaven of the

5330 3748 2076 5272 3762 1161 4780
Φαρισαίων ἥτις ἐστὶν ὑπόκρισις. 2 οὐδὲν δὲ συγκεκαλυμ-
Pharisees, which is hypocrisy. nothing And being completely

2076 3739 3756 601 2532 2927 3739 3756
μένον ἐστὶν, ὃ οὐκ ἀποκαλυφθήσεται, καὶ κρυπτὸν, ὃ οὐ
concealed is, which not will be uncovered, and hidden, which not

1097 473 3739 3745 1722 3588 4653 2036 1722 3588 5457
γνωσθήσεται. 3 ἀνθ᾽ ὧν ὅσα ἐν τῇ σκοτίᾳ εἴπατε, ἐν τῷ φωτὶ
will be known. Therefore what in the darkness you said, in the light

191 2532 3739 4314 3588 3775 2980 1722 3588 5009
ἀκουσθήσεται· καὶ ὃ πρὸς τὸ οὖς ἐλαλήσατε ἐν τοῖς ταμείοις,
it will be heard; and what to the ear you spoke in the secret rooms,

2784 1909 3588 1430 3004 1161 5213 3588 5384
κηρυχθήσεται ἐπὶ τῶν δωμάτων. 4 λέγω δὲ ὑμῖν τοῖς φίλοις
will be proclaimed on the housetops. I say But to you the friends

3450 3361 5399 575 3588 615 3588 4983 2532
μου, Μὴ φοβηθῆτε ἀπὸ τῶν ἀποκτεινόντων τὸ σῶμα, καὶ
of Me, Not do be afraid from the (ones) killing the body, and

3326 5023 3361 2192 4053 5100 4160 5263
μετὰ ταῦτα μὴ ἐχόντων περισσότερόν τι ποιῆσαι. 5 ὑποδείξω
after these things not having more anything to do. I will warn

1161 5213 5101 5399 5399 3588 3326 3588 615
δὲ ὑμῖν τίνα φοβηθῆτε· φοβήθητε τὸν μετὰ τὸ ἀποκτεῖναι
But you whom you should fear; fear the (One) after the killing

1849 2192 1685 1519 3588 1067 3483 3004 5213
ἐξουσίαν ἔχοντα ἐμβαλεῖν εἰς τὴν γέενναν· ναί, λέγω ὑμῖν,
authority having to cast into Hell Yes, I say to you

5126 5399 3780 4002 4765 4453 787
τοῦτον φοβήθητε. 6 οὐχὶ πέντε στρουθία πωλεῖται ἀσσαρίων
this One fear! not five sparrows Are sold (for) assaria

1417 2532 1520 1537 846 3756 2076 1950 1799 3588
δύο; καὶ ἓν ἐξ αὐτῶν οὐκ ἔστιν ἐπιλελησμένον ἐνώπιον τοῦ
two? And one of them not is being forgotten before

2316 235 2532 3588 2359 3588 2776 5216 3956
Θεοῦ. 7 ἀλλὰ καὶ αἱ τρίχες τῆς κεφαλῆς ὑμῶν πᾶσαι ἠρίθ-
God But even the hairs of the head of you all have been

1. In the mean time, when there were gathered together an innumerable multitude of people, insomuch that they trode one upon another, he began to say unto his disciples first of all, Beware ye of the leaven of the Pharisees, which is hypocrisy.
2 For there is nothing covered, that shall not be revealed; neither hid, that shall not be known.
3 Therefore whatsoever ye have spoken in darkness shall be heard in the light; and that which ye have spoken in the ear in closets shall be proclaimed upon the housetops.
4 And I say unto you my friends, Be not afraid of them that kill the body, and after that have no more that they can do.
5 But I will forewarn you whom ye shall fear: Fear him, which after he hath killed hath power to cast into hell; yea, I say unto you, Fear him.
6 Are not five sparrows sold for two farthings, and not one of them is forgotten before God?
7 But even the very hairs of your head are all

Literal Translation | **Luke 12:8** | *King James Version*

numbered. Then do not be afraid; you differ from many sparrows.
8 And I say to you, everyone who may confess Me before men, the Son of man will also confess him before the angels of God.

9 But he that denies me before man shall be denied before the angels of God.

10 And everyone who shall say a word against the Son of man, it will be forgiven Him; but the ones blaspheming against the Holy Spirit, will not be forgiven.

11 But when they bring you in before synagogues and rulers and the authorities, do not be anxious how or what you shall reply, or what you should answer;
12 for the Holy Spirit will teach you in the same hour what you ought to say.

13. And one from the crowd said to Him, Teacher, speak to my brother to divide the inheritance with me.
14 But He said to him, Man, who appointed Me a judge or a divider over you?

15 And He said to them, Beware, and keep back from covetousness; for one's life is not in the abundance of the things which are his.
16 And He spoke a parable to them, saying, A certain rich man produced well (from) the land.
17 And he reasoned within himself, saying, What may I do, for I have nowhere I may gather my fruits?

18 And he said, I will do this; I will raze my barns and I will build larger; and I will gather

705 3361 3767 5399 4183 4765 1308
μηνται. μὴ οὖν φοβεῖσθε· πολλῶν στρουθίων διαφέρετε.
numbered. not Then do be afraid; (from) many sparrows you differ.

3004 1161 5213 3956 3739 302 3670 1722 698 1715 3588
8 λέγω δὲ ὑμῖν, πᾶς ὃς ἂν ὁμολογήσῃ ἐν ἐμοὶ ἔμπροσθεν τῶν
I say And to you, Everyone who may confess Me before

444 2532 3588 5207 3588 444 3670 1722 846
ἀνθρώπων, καὶ ὁ υἱὸς τοῦ ἀνθρώπου ὁμολογήσει ἐν αὐτῷ
men, also the Son of man will confess him

1715 3588 32 3588 2316 3588 1161 720 3165
ἔμπροσθεν τῶν ἀγγέλων τοῦ Θεοῦ· 9 ὁ δὲ ἀρνησάμενός με
before the angels of God. The (one) But denying Me

1799 3588 444 533 1799 3588
ἐνώπιον τῶν ἀνθρώπων ἀπαρνηθήσεται ἐνώπιον τῶν
before men will be denied before the

32 3588 2316 2532 3956 3739 2046 3056 1519 3588 5207 3588
ἀγγέλων τοῦ Θεοῦ. 10 καὶ πᾶς ὃς ἐρεῖ λόγον εἰς τὸν υἱὸν τοῦ
angels of God. And everyone who shall say a word against the Son

444 863 846 3588 1161 1519 3588 40 4151
ἀνθρώπου, ἀφεθήσεται αὐτῷ· τῷ δὲ εἰς τὸ Ἅγιον Πνεῦμα
of man, it will be forgiven him; the (ones) but against the Holy Spirit

987 3756 863 3752 1161 4374 5209
βλασφημήσαντι οὐκ ἀφεθήσεται. 11 ὅταν δὲ προσφέρωσιν ὑμᾶς
blaspheming not will be forgiven. when And they bring in you

1909 3588 4864 2532 3588 746 2532 3588 1849 3361
ἐπὶ τὰς συναγωγὰς καὶ τὰς ἀρχὰς καὶ τὰς ἐξουσίας, μὴ
before synagogues and rulers and authorities, do not

3309 4459 2228 5101 626 2228 510 2036 3588 1063
μεριμνᾶτε πῶς ἢ τί ἀπολογήσησθε, ἢ τί εἴπητε· 12 τὸ γὰρ
be anxious how or what you may answer, or what you may say; the for

40 4151 1321 5209 1722 846 3588 5610 3739 1163 2036
Ἅγιον Πνεῦμα διδάξει ὑμᾶς ἐν αὐτῇ τῇ ὥρα, ἃ δεῖ εἰπεῖν.
Holy Spirit will teach you in same the hour what must you say.

2036 1161 5100 846 1537 3588 3793 1320 2036 3588 80
13. Εἶπε δέ τις αὐτῷ ἐκ τοῦ ὄχλου, Διδάσκαλε, εἰπὲ τῷ ἀδελφῷ
said And one to Him out of the crowd, Teacher, speak to the brother

3450 3307 3326 1700 3588 2817 3588 1161 2036 846
μου μερίσασθαι μετ' ἐμοῦ τὴν κληρονομίαν. 14 ὁ δὲ εἶπεν αὐτῷ,
of me to divide with me the inheritance. He But said to him,

444 5101 3165 2525 1348 2228 3312 1909 5209
Ἄνθρωπε, τίς με κατέστησε δικαστὴν ἢ μεριστὴν ἐφ' ὑμᾶς;
Man, who Me appointed a judge or a divider over you?

2036 1161 4314 846 3708 2532 5442 575 3588 4124
15 εἶπε δὲ πρὸς αὐτούς, Ὁρᾶτε καὶ φυλάσσεσθε ἀπὸ τῆς πλεονε-
He said And to them, Beware and keep back from covetous-

3754 3756 1722 3588 4052 5100 3588 2222 846 2076 1537
ξίας· ὅτι οὐκ ἐν τῷ περισσεύειν τινὶ ἡ ζωὴ αὐτοῦ ἐστιν ἐκ
ness; because not in the abundance to anyone the life of him is out of

3588 5224 846 2036 1161 3850 4314 846
τῶν ὑπαρχόντων αὐτοῦ. 16 εἶπε δὲ παραβολὴν πρὸς αὐτούς,
the things existing of him. He spoke And a parable to them,

3004 444 5100 4145 2164 3588 5561 2532
λέγων, Ἀνθρώπου τινὸς πλουσίου εὐφόρησεν ἡ χώρα· 17 καὶ
saying, A man certain rich produced well the land; and

1260 1722 1438 3004 5101 4160 3754 3756 2192 4226
διελογίζετο ἐν ἑαυτῷ λέγων, Τί ποιήσω, ὅτι οὐκ ἔχω ποῦ
he reasoned within himself, saying, What may I do, because not I have where

4863 3588 2890 3450 2532 2036 5124 4160 2507
συνάξω τοὺς καρπούς μου; 18 καὶ εἶπε, Τοῦτο ποιήσω· καθελῶ
I may gather the fruit of me. And he said, This I will do; I will raze

3450 3588 596 2532 3173 3618 2532 4863
μου τὰς ἀποθήκας καὶ μείζονας οἰκοδομήσω, καὶ συνάξω
of me the barns, and larger I will build, and I will gather

numbered. Fear not therefore: ye are of more value than many sparrows.
8 Also I say unto you, Whosoever shall confess me before men, him shall the Son of man also confess before the angels of God:

9 But he that denieth me before men shall be denied before the angels of God.

10 And whosoever shall speak a word against the Son of man, it shall be forgiven him: but unto him that blasphemeth against the Holy Ghost it shall not be forgiven.
11 And when they bring you unto the synagogues, and (unto) magistrates, and powers, take ye no thought how or what thing ye shall answer, or what ye shall say:
12 For the Holy Ghost shall teach you in the same hour what ye ought to say.

13. And one of the company said unto him, Master, speak to my brother, that he divide the inheritance with me.
14 And he said unto him, Man, who made me a judge or a divider over you?

15 And he said unto them, Take heed, and beware of covetousness: for a man's life consisteth not in the abundance of the things which he possesseth.
16 And he spake a parable unto them, saying, The ground of a certain rich man brought forth plentifully:
17 And he thought within himself, saying, What shall I do, because I have no room where to bestow my fruits?
18 And he said, This will I do: I will pull down my barns, and build greater; and there will I bestow

Literal Translation

Luke 12:19

King James Version

there all my produce and my goods.
19 And I will say to my soul, Soul, you have many goods laid (up) for many years; take rest, eat, drink, (and) be glad.
20 But God said to him, Foolish (one)! This night they demand your soul from you; and what things you prepared, to whom will it be?
21 So (is) the (one) treasuring up for himself, and not being rich toward God.

1563 3956 3588 1081 3450 2532 3588 18 3450 2532 2046
ἐκεῖ πάντα τὰ γενήματά μου καὶ τὰ ἀγαθά μου, 19 καὶ ἐρῶ
there all the produce of me and the goods of me, and I will say

3588 5590 3450 5590 2192 4183 18 2749 1519 2094
τῇ ψυχῇ μου, Ψυχή, ἔχεις πολλὰ ἀγαθὰ κείμενα εἰς ἔτη
to the soul of me. Soul, you have many goods laid (up) for years

4183 373 5315 4095 2165 2036 1161 846 3588
πολλά· ἀναπαύου, φάγε, πίε, εὐφραίνου. 20 εἶπε δὲ αὐτῷ ὁ
many; take rest, eat, drink, be glad. said But to him

2316 878 5026 3588 3571 3588 5590 4675 523
Θεός, Ἄφρον, ταύτῃ τῇ νυκτὶ τὴν ψυχήν σου ἀπαιτοῦσιν
God, Foolish (one)! This night the soul of you they demand

573 4675 3739 1161 2090 5101 2071 3779 3588 2343
ἀπὸ σοῦ· ἃ δὲ ἡτοίμασας, τίνι ἔσται; 21 οὕτως ὁ θησαυρίζων
from you. what And you prepared, to whom will it be? So (is) the (one) treasuring

1438 2532 3361 1519 2316 4147
ἑαυτῷ, καὶ μὴ εἰς Θεὸν πλουτῶν.
for himself, and not to God being rich.

all my fruits and my goods.
19 And I will say to my soul, Soul, thou hast much goods laid up for many years; take thine ease, eat, drink, (and) be merry.
20 But God said unto him, (Thou) fool, this night thy soul shall be required of thee: then whose shall those things be, which thou hast provided?
21 So (is) he that layeth up treasure for himself, and is not rich toward God.

22. And He said to His disciples, Because of this I say to you, do not be anxious as to your life, what you should eat; nor for the body, what you should put on.
23 The life is more than the food and the body than the clothing.
24 Consider the ravens, that they do not sow, nor do they reap; to which there is no storehouse or barn, and God feeds them. How much rather you do differ from the birds!

2036 1161 4314 3588 3101 846 1223 5124 5213 3004
22. Εἶπε δὲ πρὸς τοὺς μαθητὰς αὐτοῦ, Διὰ τοῦτο ὑμῖν λέγω,
He said And to the disciples of Him, Because of this to you I say,

3361 3309 3588 5590 5216 5101 5315 3366 3588 4983
μὴ μεριμνᾶτε τῇ ψυχῇ ὑμῶν, τί φάγητε· μηδὲ τῷ σώματι,
Not do be anxious the life of you, what you eat; nor for the body,

5101 1746 3588 5590 4119 2076 3588 5160 2532 3588 4983
τί ἐνδύσησθε. 23 ἡ ψυχὴ πλεῖόν ἐστι τῆς τροφῆς, καὶ τὸ σῶμα
what you put on. The life more is (than) the food, and the body

3588 1742 2657 3588 2876 3754 3756
τοῦ ἐνδύματος. 24 κατανοήσατε τοὺς κόρακας, ὅτι οὐ σπεί-
(than) the clothing. Consider the ravens, that not they

4687 3761 2325 3739 3756 2076 5009 3761 596
ρουσιν οὐδὲ θερίζουσιν, οἷς οὐκ ἔστι ταμεῖον οὐδὲ ἀποθήκη,
sow, nor do they reap, to which not is a storehouse nor barn,

2532 3588 2316 5142 846 4214 3123 210 1308 3588
καὶ ὁ Θεὸς τρέφει αὐτούς· πόσῳ μᾶλλον ὑμεῖς διαφέρετε τῶν
and God feeds them; how much rather you do differ from the

22. And he said unto his disciples, Therefore I say unto you, Take no thought for your life, what ye shall eat; neither for the body, what ye shall put on.
23 The life is more than meat, and the body (is more) than raiment.
24 Consider the ravens: for they neither sow nor reap; which neither have storehouse nor barn; and God feedeth them: how much more are ye better than the fowls?

25 And who of you (by) being anxious is able to add one cubit onto his stature?
26 Then if you are not able to do even (the) least, why are you anxious about the rest?
27 Consider the lilies, how they grow: they do not labor, nor spin, but I say to you, not even Solomon in all his glory was clothed as one of these.

4071 5101 1161 537 5216 3308 1410 4369 1909
πετεινῶν; 25 τίς δὲ ἐξ ὑμῶν μεριμνῶν δύναται προσθεῖναι ἐπὶ
birds? who And of you being anxious is able to add onto

3588 2244 846 4083 1520 1487 3767 3777 1646
τὴν ἡλικίαν αὐτοῦ πῆχυν ἕνα; 26 εἰ οὖν οὔτε ἐλάχιστον
the stature of him cubit one? If then not (the) least

1410 5101 4012 3588 3062 3309 2657 3588
δύνασθε, τί περὶ τῶν λοιπῶν μεριμνᾶτε; 27 κατανοήσατε τὰ
you are able, why about the rest are you anxious? Consider the

2918 4459 837 3756 2872 3761 3514 3004 1161 5213 3761
κρίνα πῶς αὐξάνει· οὐ κοπιᾷ, οὐδὲ νήθει· λέγω δὲ ὑμῖν, οὐδὲ
lilies, how they grow; not they labor, nor spin; I say but to you, Not

4672 1722 3956 3588 1391 846 4016 5613 1520 5130
Σολομὼν ἐν πάσῃ τῇ δόξῃ αὐτοῦ περιεβάλετο ὡς ἓν τούτων.
Solomon in all the glory of him was clothed as one of these.

25 And which of you with taking thought can add to his stature one cubit?
26 If ye then be not able to do that thing which is least, why take ye thought for the rest?
27 Consider the lilies how they grow: they toil not, they spin not; and yet I say unto you, that Solomon in all his glory was not arrayed like one of these.

28 But if God so clothes the grass, which today (is) in the field and tomorrow is thrown into the oven, how much rather you, little-faiths?
29 And you, do not seek what you shall eat, or what you drink, and do not be in anxiety.
30 For all the nations of the

1487 1161 3588 5528 1722 3588 68 4594 5607 2532 839 1519
28 εἰ δὲ τὸν χόρτον ἐν τῷ ἀγρῷ σήμερον ὄντα, καὶ αὔριον εἰς
if And the grass in the field today (is) which, and tomorrow into

2823 906 3588 2316 3779 294 4214 3123
κλίβανον βαλλόμενον, ὁ Θεὸς οὕτως ἀμφιέννυσι, πόσῳ μᾶλλον
an oven is thrown, God so clothes, how much rather

5209 3640 2532 5210 3361 2212 5101 5315 2228 5101
ὑμᾶς, ὀλιγόπιστοι. 29 καὶ ὑμεῖς μὴ ζητεῖτε τί φάγητε, ἢ τί
you, little-faiths. And you not do seek what you eat, or what

4095 2532 3361 3349 5023 1063 3956 3588 1484 3588
πίητε· καὶ μὴ μετεωρίζεσθε. 30 ταῦτα γὰρ πάντα τὰ ἔθνη τοῦ
you drink; and not do be in anxiety. these things For all the nations of the

28 If then God so clothe the grass, which is to day in the field, and to morrow is cast into the oven; how much more (will he clothe) you, O ye of little faith?
29 And seek not ye what ye shall eat, or what ye shall drink, neither be ye of doubtful mind.
30 For all these things do the nations of the

Literal Translation

world seek after these things, and your Father knows that you need these things.
31 But seek the kingdom of God and all these things will be added to you.
32 Do not be fear, little flock, because your Father was pleased to give you the kingdom.

33 Sell your possessions and give alms. Make for yourselves purses that do not grow old, an unfailing treasure in Heaven, where a thief cannot come near, nor moth can corrupt.

34 For where your treasure is, there your heart will be also.

35. Let your loins be having been girded, and the lamps burning,

36 and you (be) like men awaiting their ord when he returns from the feasts, so that (he) coming and knocking, they will open to him at once.
37 Blessed (are) those slaves whom the Lord will find watching when (he) comes. Truly I say to you that he will gird himself and will make them recline, and coming up (he) will serve them.

38 And if he comes in the second watch, (if) even he come in the third watch, and find (it) so, blessed are those slaves.

39 But know this, that if the housemaster had known what hour the thief is coming, he would have watched and would not have allowed his house to be dug through.
40 And you, then, be prepared; because (in) the hour you think not, the Son of man

Luke 12:31

2889 1934 5216 1161 3588 3962 1492 3754 5535 5130
κόσμου ἐπιζητεῖ· ὑμῶν δὲ ὁ πατὴρ οἶδεν ὅτι χρῄζετε τούτων.
world seek after; of you but the Father knows that you need these.

4133 2212 3588 932 3588 2316 2532 5023 3956
31 πλὴν ζητεῖτε τὴν βασιλείαν τοῦ Θεοῦ, καὶ ταῦτα πάντα
But you seek the kingdom of God, and these things all

4369 5213 3361 5399 3588 3398 4168 3754
προστεθήσεται ὑμῖν. 32 μὴ φοβοῦ, τὸ μικρὸν ποίμνιον· ὅτι
will be added to you. Not do fear, little flock; because

2106 3588 3962 5216 1325 5213 3588 932
εὐδόκησεν ὁ πατὴρ ὑμῶν δοῦναι ὑμῖν τὴν βασιλείαν.
was pleased the Father of you to give you the kingdom.

4453 3588 5224 5216 2532 1325 1654
33 πωλήσατε τὰ ὑπάρχοντα ὑμῶν καὶ δότε ἐλεημοσύνην.
Sell the possessions of you and give alms.

4160 1438 905 3361 3822 2344
ποιήσατε ἑαυτοῖς βαλάντια μὴ παλαιούμενα, θησαυρὸν
Make for yourselves purses not growing old, a treasure

413 1722 3588 3772 3699 2812 3756 1448 3761
ἀνέκλειπτον ἐν τοῖς οὐρανοῖς, ὅπου κλέπτης οὐκ ἐγγίζει, οὐδὲ
unfailing in Heaven, where a thief not can approach, nor

4597 1311 3699 1063 2076 3588 2344 5216 1563 2532
σὴς διαφθείρει· 34 ὅπου γάρ ἐστιν ὁ θησαυρὸς ὑμῶν, ἐκεῖ καὶ
moth can corrupt; where for is the treasure of you, there also

3588 2588 5216 2071
ἡ καρδία ὑμῶν ἔσται.
the heart of you will be.

2077 5216 3588 3751 4024 2532 3588 3088
35. Ἔστωσαν ὑμῶν αἱ ὀσφύες περιεζωσμέναι, καὶ οἱ λύχνοι
Let be of you the loins having been girded, and the lamps

2545 2532 5210 3664 444 4327 3588
καιόμενοι· 36 καὶ ὑμεῖς ὅμοιοι ἀνθρώποις προσδεχομένοις τὸν
burning; and you like men awaiting the

2962 1438 4219 360 1537 3588 1062 2443 2064
κύριον ἑαυτῶν, πότε ἀναλύσει ἐκ τῶν γάμων, ἵνα, ἐλθόντος
lord of themselves, when he returns from the feasts, that coming

2532 2925 2112 455 846 3107 3588 1401
καὶ κρούσαντος εὐθέως ἀνοίξωσιν αὐτῷ. 37 μακάριοι οἱ δοῦλοι
and having knocked at once they will open to him. Blessed slaves

1565 3739 2064 3588 2962 2147 1127 281
ἐκεῖνοι, οὓς ἐλθὼν ὁ κύριος εὑρήσει γρηγοροῦντας· ἀμὴν
those, whom having come the lord will find watching; truly

3004 5213 3754 4024 2532 347 846 2532
λέγω ὑμῖν ὅτι περιζώσεται καὶ ἀνακλινεῖ αὐτούς, καὶ παρ-
I say to you that he will gird himself and cause to recline them, and coming

3928 1247 846 2532 1437 2064 1722 3588 1208
ελθὼν διακονήσει αὐτοῖς. 38 καὶ ἐὰν ἔλθῃ ἐν τῇ δευτέρᾳ
up will serve them. And if he come in the second

5438 2532 1722 3588 5154 5438 2064 2532 2147 3779 3107
φυλακῇ, καὶ ἐν τῇ τρίτῃ φυλακῇ ἔλθῃ, καὶ εὕρῃ οὕτω μακάριοί
watch, (if) even in the third watch he come, and find (it) so, blessed

1526 3588 1401 1565 5124 1161 1097 3754 1487 1492
εἰσιν οἱ δοῦλοι ἐκεῖνοι. 39 τοῦτο δὲ γινώσκετε, ὅτι εἰ ᾔδει
are slaves those. this But know, that if had known

3588 3617 4169 5610 3588 2812 2064 1127 302
ὁ οἰκοδεσπότης ποίᾳ ὥρᾳ ὁ κλέπτης ἔρχεται, ἐγρηγόρησεν ἄν,
the housemaster what hour the thief is coming, he would have watched

2532 3756 302 863 1358 3588 3624 846 2532 5210 3767
καὶ οὐκ ἂν ἀφῆκε διορυγῆναι τὸν οἶκον αὐτοῦ. 40 καὶ ὑμεῖς οὖν
and not have allowed to be dug through the house of him. And you then,

1096 2092 3754 3739 5610 3756 1380 3588 5207 3588 444
γίνεσθε ἕτοιμοι· ὅτι ᾗ ὥρᾳ οὐ δοκεῖτε ὁ υἱὸς τοῦ ἀνθρώπου
be prepared; because the hour not you think the Son of man

King James Version

world seek after: and your Father knoweth that ye have need of these things.
31 But rather seek ye the kingdom of God; and all these things shall be added unto you.
32 Fear not, little flock; for it is your Father's good pleasure to give you the kingdom.

33 Sell that ye have, and give alms; provide yourselves bags which wax not old, a treasure in the heavens that faileth not, where no thief approacheth, neither moth corrupteth.

34 For where your treasure is, there will your heart be also.

35. Let your loins be girded about, and (your) lights burning;

36 And ye yourselves like unto men that wait for their lord, when he will return from the wedding; that when he cometh and knocketh, they may open unto him immediately.
37 Blessed (are) those servants, whom the lord when he cometh shall find watching: verily I say unto you, that he shall gird himself, and make them to sit down to meat, and will come forth and serve them.
38 And if he shall come in the second watch, or come in the third watch, and find (them) so, blessed are those servants.

39 And this know, that if the goodman of the house had known what hour the thief would come, he would have watched, and not have suffered his house to be broken through.
40 Be ye therefore ready also: for the Son of man

Literal Translation **Luke 12:41** *King James Version*

comes.

41. And Peter said to Him, Lord, do You speak this parable to us, or also to all?
42 And the Lord said, Who then is the faithful and prudent steward whom the lord will appoint over his houseservants, to give the portion of food in season?

43 Blessed (is) that slave whom his lord coming will find (him) so doing.
44 Truly I say to you, he will appoint him over all his possessions.
45 But if that slave says in his heart, My lord delays to come, and should begin to beat the men servants and the female servants, and to eat and to drink and become drunk,

46 the lord of that slave will come in the day in which he does not expect, and in an hour which he does not know. And he will cut him apart and will put his portion with the unbelievers.

47 But that slave having known the will of his lord, and not preparing, nor doing according to His will, will be beaten with many (stripes).

48 But he not knowing, and doing (things) worthy of stripes, will be beaten with few. And everyone to whom is given much, much will be demanded from him. And to whom much was deposited, more exceedingly they will ask (of) him.
49. I came to hurl fire into the earth, and what will I if already it was lit?
50 But I have a baptism to be immersed in, and how am I compressed until

2064
ἔρχεται.
comes.

2036 1161 846 3588 4074 2962 4314 2248 3588 3850
41. Εἶπε δὲ αὐτῷ ὁ Πέτρος, Κύριε, πρὸς ἡμᾶς τὴν παραβολὴν
said And to Him Peter, Lord, to us parable

3778 3004 2228 2532 4314 3956 2036 1161 3588 2962 5101 687
ταύτην λέγεις, ἢ καὶ πρὸς πάντας; 42εἶπε δὲ ὁ Κύριος, Τίς ἄρα
this do You say, or also to all? said And the Lord, Who then

2076 3588 103 3623 2532 5429 3739 2525 3588
ἐστὶν ὁ πιστὸς οἰκονόμος καὶ φρόνιμος, ὃν καταστήσει ὁ
is the faithful steward and prudent, whom will appoint the

2962 1909 3588 2322 846 3588 1325 1722 2540 3588
κύριος ἐπὶ τῆς θεραπείας αὐτοῦ, τοῦ διδόναι ἐν καιρῷ τὸ
lord over the houseservants of him, to give in season the

4620 3107 3588 1401 1565 3739 2064 3588 2962
σιτομέτριον; 43 μακάριος ὁ δοῦλος ἐκεῖνος, ὃν ἐλθὼν ὁ κύριος
portion of food? Blessed slave that, whom having come the lord

846 2147 4160 3779 230 3004 5213 3754 1909
αὐτοῦ εὑρήσει ποιοῦντα οὕτως. 44 ἀληθῶς λέγω ὑμῖν ὅτι ἐπὶ
of him will find doing so. truly I say to you that over

3956 3588 5224 846 2525 846 1437 1161 2036
πᾶσι τοῖς ὑπάρχουσιν αὐτοῦ καταστήσει αὐτόν. 45 ἐὰν δὲ εἴπῃ
all the possessions of him he will appoint him. if But says

3588 1401 1565 1722 3588 2588 846 5549 3588 2962 3450
ὁ δοῦλος ἐκεῖνος ἐν τῇ καρδίᾳ αὐτοῦ, Χρονίζει ὁ κύριός μου
slave of that in the heart of him, Delays the lord of me

2064 2532 756 5180 3588 3816 2532 3588 3814
ἔρχεσθαι, καὶ ἄρξηται τύπτειν τοὺς παῖδας καὶ τὰς παιδί-
to come, and begins to beat the men servants and the maid-

2068 5037 2532 4095 2532 3182 2240 3588 2962
σκας, ἐσθίειν τε καὶ πίνειν καὶ μεθύσκεσθαι· 46 ἥξει ὁ κύριος
servants, to eat both and to drink and to become drunk; will come the lord

3588 1401 1565 1722 2250 3739 3756 4328 2532/1722/5610/3588/3756
τοῦ δούλου ἐκείνου ἐν ἡμέρᾳ ᾗ οὐ προσδοκᾷ, καὶ ἐν ὥρᾳ ᾗ οὐ
slave that in a day in which not he expects, and in an hour which not

1097 2532 1371 846 2532 3588 3313 846 3326
γινώσκει· καὶ διχοτομήσει αὐτὸν, καὶ τὸ μέρος αὐτοῦ μετὰ
he knows; and will cut in two him, and the portion of him with

3588 571 5087 1565 1161 3588 1401 3588 1097 3588 2307
τῶν ἀπίστων θήσει. 47 ἐκεῖνος δὲ ὁ δοῦλος ὁ γνοὺς τὸ θέλημα
the unbelievers will put. that But slave having known the will

3588 2962 1438 2532 3361 2090 2228 4160 4314 3588
τοῦ κυρίου ἑαυτοῦ, καὶ μὴ ἑτοιμάσας ἢ ποιήσας πρὸς τὸ
of the lord of himself, and not did prepare, nor did according to the

2307 846 1194 4183 3588 1161 3361 1097 4160
θέλημα αὐτοῦ δαρήσεται πολλάς· 48 ὁ δὲ μὴ γνούς, ποιήσας
will of him will be beaten with many; he but not having known having done

1161 514 4127 1194 3641 3956 1161 3739 1325
δὲ ἄξια πληγῶν, δαρήσεται ὀλίγας· παντὶ δε` ᾧ ἐδόθη
and worthy of stripes will be beaten with few. everyone And to whom is given

4183 4183 2212 3844 846 2532 3739 3908 4183
πολύ, πολὺ ζητηθήσεται παρ᾽ αὐτοῦ· καὶ ᾧ παρέθεντο πολύ,
much, much will be demanded from him; and to whom was set much,

4053 154 846
περισσότερον αἰτήσουσιν αὐτόν.
more exceedingly they will ask him.

4442 2064 906 1519 3588 1093 2532 5101 2309 1487 2235 381
49. Πῦρ ἦλθον βαλεῖν ἐις τὴν γῆν, καὶ τί θέλω εἰ ἤδη ἀνήφθη;
Fire I came to cast into the earth, and what will I if already it was lit?

908 1161 2192 907 2532 4459 4912 2193 3757
50 βάπτισμα δὲ ἔχω βαπτισθῆναι, καὶ πῶς συνέχομαι ἕως οὗ
a baptism And I have to be immersed in,,and how I am compressed until

cometh at an hour when ye think not.

41. Then Peter said unto him, Lord, speakest thou this parable unto us, or even to all?
42 And the Lord said, Who then is that faithful and wise steward, whom (his) lord shall make ruler over his household, to give (them their) portion of meat in due season?
43 Blessed (is) that servant, whom his lord when he cometh shall find so doing.
44 Of a truth I say unto you, that he will make him ruler over all that he hath.
45 But and if that servant say in his heart, My lord delayeth his coming; and shall begin to beat the menservants and maidens, and to eat and drink, and to be drunken;

46 The lord of that servant will come in a day when he looketh not for (him), and at an hour when he is not aware, and will cut him in sunder, and will appoint him his portion with the unbelievers.

47 And that servant, which knew his lord's will, and prepared not (himself), neither did according to his will, shall be beaten with many (stripes).
48 But he that knew not, and did commit things worthy of stripes, shall be beaten with few (stripes). For unto whomsoever much is given, of him shall be much required: and to whom men have committed much, of him they will ask the more.

49. I am come to send fire on the earth; and what will I, if it be already kindled?
50 But I have a baptism to be baptized with; and how am I straitened till

Literal Translation — **Luke 12:51** — *King James Version*

it is finished!
51 Do you think that I came to give peace in the earth? No, I say to you, but rather division.
52 For from now on five in one house will have been divided, three against two, and two against three.

53 Father will be divided against son, and son against father; mother against daughter, and daughter against mother; mother-in-law against her daughter-in-law, and (the) daughter-in-law against her mother-in-law. (Mic. 7:6)
54. And He also said to the crowds, When you see the cloud rising up from (the) west, you immediately say, A rainstorm is coming; and it happens so.
55 And when a south wind (is) blowing, you say that there will be heat; and it occurs.
56 Hypocrites! You know to discern the face of the earth and of the heaven, but how (is it) you do not discern this time?
57 And why do you not judge what is right even from yourselves?

58. For as you go with your adversary to a magistrate, give pains in the way to be set free from him, that he not drag you to the judge, and the judge deliver you to the officer, and the officer throw you into prison.

59 I say to you, in no way may you leave there until you pay even the last lepton.

5055 1380 3754 515 3854 1325 1722 3588 1093
τελεσθῇ. 51 δοκεῖτε ὅτι εἰρήνην παρεγενόμην δοῦναι ἐν τῇ γῇ;
it is finished! Think that peace I came to give in the earth?

3780 3004 5213 235 2228 1267 2071 1063 575 3588 3568
οὐχί, λέγω ὑμῖν, ἀλλ' ἢ διαμερισμόν. 52 ἔσονται γὰρ ἀπὸ τοῦ νῦν
No, I say to you, but rather division. will be For from now

4002 1722 3624 1520 1266 5140 1909 1417 2532 1417 1909
πέντε ἐν οἴκῳ ἑνὶ διαμεμερισμένοι, τρεῖς ἐπὶ δυσί, καὶ δύο ἐπὶ
five in house one having been divided, three against two, and two against

5140 1266 3962 1909 5207 2532 5207 1909 3962
τρισί. 53 διαμερισθήσονται πατὴρ ἐφ' υἱῷ, καὶ υἱὸς ἐπὶ πατρί·
three. will be divided Father against son, and son against father;

3384 1909 2364 2532 2364 1909 3384 3994 1909
μήτηρ ἐπὶ θυψατρί, καὶ θυψάτηρ ἐπὶ μητρί· πενθερὰ ἐπὶ
mother against daughter, and daughter against mother; mother-in-law against

3588 565 846 2532 3565 1909 3588 3994 846
τὴν νύμφην αὐτῆς, καὶ νύμφη ἐπὶ τὴν πενθεράν αὐτῆς.
the daughter-in-law of her, and daughter-in-law against the mother-in-law of her.

3004 1161 2532 3588 3793 3752 1492 3588 3507
54. Ἔλεγε δὲ καὶ τοῖς ὄχλοις, Ὅταν ἴδητε τὴν νεφέλην
He said And also to the crowds, When you see the cloud

393 575 1424 2112 3004 3655 2064
ἀνατέλλουσαν ἀπὸ δυσμῶν, εὐθέως λέγετε Ὄμβρος ἔρχεται·
rising up from (the) west, at once you say, A rainstorm is coming;

2532 1096 3779 2532 3752 3558 4154 3004 3754
καὶ γίνεται οὕτω. 55 καὶ ὅταν νότον πνέοντα, λέγετε ὅτι
and it happens so. And when a south wind (is) blowing, you say that

2742 2071 2532 1096 5273 3588 4383 3588
Καύσων ἔσται· καὶ γίνεται. 56 ὑποκριταί, τὸ πρόσωπον τοῦ
heat will be; and it occurs. Hypocrites! The face of the

3772 2532 3588 1093 1492 1381 3588 1161 2540
οὐρανοῦ καὶ τῆς γῆς οἴδατε δοκιμάζειν· τὸν δὲ καιρὸν
heaven and the earth you know to discern; but time

5126 4459 3756 1381 5101 1161 2532 575 1438 3756 2919
τοῦτον πῶς οὐ δοκιμάζετε; 57 τί δὲ καὶ ἀφ' ἑαυτῶν οὐ κρίνετε
this how not do you discern? why And even from yourselves not do judge

3588 1342 5613 1063 5217 3326 3588 476 4675 1909
τὸ δίκαιον; 58 ὡς γὰρ ὑπάγεις μετὰ τοῦ ἀντιδίκου σου ἐπ'
the righteous? as For you go with the adversary of you to

758 1722 3588 3598 1325 2039 525 575 846
ἄρχοντα, ἐν τῇ ὁδῷ δὸς ἐργασίαν ἀπηλλάχθαι ἀπ' αὐτοῦ·
a magistrate, in the way give pains to be freed from him;

3379 2694 4571 4314 3588 2923 2532 3588 2923 4571
μήποτε κατασύρῃ σε πρὸς τὸν κριτήν, καὶ ὁ κριτής σε
that not he drag you to the judge, and the judge you

3860 3588 4233 2532 3588 4233 4571 906 1519 5438
παραδῷ τῷ πράκτορι, καὶ ὁ πράκτωρ σε βάλλῃ εἰς φυλακήν.
will deliver to the officer, and the officer you throw into prison.

3004 4671 3756 3361 1831 1564 2193 3757 2532 3588 2078
59 λέγω σοι, οὐ μὴ ἐξέλθῃς ἐκεῖθεν, ἕως οὗ καὶ τὸ ἔσχατον
I say to you, in no way may you leave there until even the last

3016 591
λεπτὸν ἀποδῷς.
lepton you pay.

it be accomplished!
51 Suppose ye that I am come to give peace on earth? I tell you, Nay; but rather division:
52 For from henceforth there shall be five in one house divided, three against two, and two against three.

53 The father shall be divided against the son, and the son against the father; the mother against the daughter, and the daughter against the mother; the mother in law against her daughter in law, and the daughter in law against her mother in law.
54. And he said also to the people, When ye see a cloud rise out of the west, straightway ye say, There cometh a shower; and so it is.
55 And when (ye see) the south wind blow, ye say, There will be heat; and it cometh to pass.
56 (Ye) hypocrites, ye can discern the face of the sky and of the earth; but how is it that ye do not discern this time?

57 Yea, and why even of yourselves judge ye not what is right?

58. When thou goest with thine adversary to the magistrate, (as thou art) in the way, give diligence that thou mayest be delivered from him; lest he hale thee to the judge, and the judge deliver thee to the officer, and the officer cast thee into prison.

59 I tell thee, thou shalt not depart thence, till thou hast paid the very last mite.

Luke 13

1. And some were present during the same time reporting to Him about the Galileans, whose blood Pilate mixed with

3918 1161 5100 1722 846 3588 2540 518
1. Παρῆσαν δέ τινες ἐν αὐτῷ τῷ καιρῷ ἀπαγγέλλοντες
were present And some during same the time reporting

846 4012 3588 1057 3739 3588 129 4091 3396 3326
αὐτῷ περὶ τῶν Γαλιλαίων, ὧν τὸ αἷμα Πιλᾶτος ἔμιξε μετὰ
to Him about the Galileans, of whom the blood Pilate mixed with

1. There were present at that season some that told him of the Galilaeans, whose blood Pilate had mingled with

Literal Translation | **Luke 13:2** | **King James Version**

their sacrifices.
2 And answering, Jesus said to them, Do you think that these Galileans were sinners beyond all the Galileans, because they suffered such things?
3 No, I say to you; but if you do not repent, you will all perish in the same way.

4 Or those eighteen on whom the tower in Siloam fell, and killed them, do you think that these were debtors beyond all men who lived in Jerusalem?

5 No, I say to you; but if you do not repent, you will all perish in the same way.
6. And He spoke this parable: A certain one had planted a fig tree in his vineyard. And he came seeking fruit on it and did not find (any).

7 And he said to the vinedresser, Behold, three years I come seeking for fruit on this fig tree, and found none. Cut it down, and why even does it waste the ground?
8 And the vinedresser said to him, Sir, leave it also this year until I shall dig around it and throw manure;

9 and (see) if it indeed makes fruit. But if not, hereafter you may cut it down.

10. And He was teaching in one of the synagogues on (one of) the sabbaths.
11 And, behold! There was a woman having a spirit of infirmity eighteen years, and was bent together and was not able to be completely erect.
12 And seeing her, Jesus called (her) near and said to her,

3588 2378 846 2532 611 3588 2424 2036 846
τῶν θυσιῶν αὐτῶν. 2 καὶ ἀποκριθεὶς ὁ Ἰησοῦς εἶπεν αὐτοῖς,
the sacrifices of them. And answering Jesus said to them,

1380 3754 3588 1057 3778 268 3844 3956
Δοκεῖτε ὅτι οἱ Γαλιλαῖοι οὗτοι ἁμαρτωλοὶ παρὰ πάντας
Do you think that Galileans these sinners above all

3588 1057 1096 3754 5108 3958 3780
τοὺς Γαλιλαίους ἐγένοντο, ὅτι τοιαῦτα πεπόνθασιν; 3 οὐχί,
the Galileans were, because these things they have suffered? No,

3004 5213 235 1437 3361 3340 3956 5615
λέγω ὑμῖν· ἀλλ᾽ ἐὰν μὴ μετανοῆτε, πάντες ὡσαύτως
I say to you; but if not you repent, all likewise

622 2228 1565 3588 1176 2532 3638 1909 3739 4098 3588
ἀπολεῖσθε. 4 ἢ ἐκεῖνοι οἱ δέκα καὶ ὀκτώ, ἐφ᾽ οὓς ἔπεσεν ὁ
will perish. Or those ten and eight, on whom fell the

4444 1722 3588 4611 2532 615 846 1380 3754
πύργος ἐν τῷ Σιλωὰμ καὶ ἀπέκτεινεν αὐτούς, δοκεῖτε ὅτι
tower in Siloam, and killed them, do you think that

3778 3781 1096 3844 3956 444 3588
οὗτοι ὀφειλέται ἐγένοντο παρὰ πάντας ἀνθρώπους τοὺς
these debtors were above all men the (ones)

2730 1722 2419 3780 3004 5213 235 1437
κατοικοῦντας ἐν Ἱερουσαλήμ; 5 οὐχί, λέγω ὑμῖν· ἀλλ᾽ ἐὰν
dwelling in Jerusalem? No, I say to you, but if

3361 3340 3956 3668 622 3004 1161 3778
μὴ μετανοῆτε, πάντες ὡμοίως ἀπολεῖσθε. 6 ελεγε δὲ ταύτην
not you repent, all likewise will perish. He told And this

3588 3850 4808 2192 5100 1722 3588 290 846
τὴν παραβολήν· Συκῆν εἶχέ τις ἐν τῷ ἀμπελῶνι αὐτοῦ
parable: a fig-tree had A certain one in the vineyard of him

5452 2532 2064 2590 2212 1722 846 2532 3756
πεφυτευμένην· καὶ ἦλθε καρπὸν ζητῶν ἐν αὐτῇ, καὶ οὐχ
planted; and (he) came fruit seeking in it, and not

2147 2036 1161 4314 3588 289 2400 5140 2094
εὗρεν. 7 εἶπε δὲ πρὸς τὸν ἀμπελουργόν, Ἰδού, τρία ἔτη
he found. he said And to the vinedresser, Behold, three years

2064 2212 590 1722 3588 4808 3778 2532 3756 2147
ἔρχομαι ζητῶν καρπὸν ἐν τῇ συκῇ ταύτῃ, καὶ οὐχ εὑρίσκω·
I come seeking fruit in fig-tree this, and not do find;

1581 846 2444 2532 3588 1093 2673 3588 1161 611
ἔκκοψον αὐτήν· ἱνατί καὶ τὴν γῆν καταργεῖ; 8 ὁ δὲ ἀποκριθεὶς
cut down it; why even the ground it wastes? he And answering

3004 846 2962 863 846 2532 5124 3588 2094 2193 3755
λέγει αὐτῷ, Κύριε, ἄφες αὐτὴν καὶ τοῦτο τὸ ἔτος, ἕως ὅτου
said to him, Sir, leave it also this year, until

4626 4012 846 2532 906 2874 2579 3303 4160
σκάψω περὶ αὐτήν, καὶ βάλω κόπριαν· 9 κἂν μὲν ποιήσῃ
I may dig around it, and throw manure; and if indeed it makes

2590 1487 1161 3361 1519 3588 3195 1581 846
καρπὸν εἰ δὲ μέγε, εἰς τὸ μέλλον ἐκκόψεις αὐτήν.
fruit if but not, hereafter you may cut down it.

2258 1161 1321 1722 3391 3588 4864 1722 3588 4521
10. Ἦν δὲ διδάσκων ἐν μιᾷ τῶν συναγωγῶν ἐν τοῖς σάββασι.
He was And teaching in one of the synagogues on the sabbaths.

2532 2400 1135 2258 4151 2192 769 2094 1176 2532
11 καὶ ἰδού, γυνὴ ἦν πνεῦμα ἔχουσα ἀσθενείας ἔτη δέκα καὶ
And, behold! A woman was a spirit having of infirmity years ten and

3638 2532 2258 4794 2532 3361 1410 352 1519
ὀκτώ, καὶ ἦν συγκύπτουσα, καὶ μὴ δυναμένη ἀνακύψαι εἰς
eight, and was bent together, and not was able to be erect com-

3588 3838 1492 1161 846 3588 2424 4377 2532
τὸ παντελές. 12 ἰδὼν δὲ αὐτὴν ὁ Ἰησοῦς προσεφώνησε, καὶ
pletely. seeing And her Jesus called near and

---

their sacrifices.
2 And Jesus answering said unto them, Suppose ye that these Galilaeans were sinners above all the Galilaeans, because they suffered such things?
3 I tell you, Nay: but, except ye repent, ye shall all likewise perish.

4 Or those eighteen, upon whom the tower in Siloam fell, and slew them, think ye that they were sinners above all men that dwelt in Jerusalem?

5 I tell you, Nay: but, except ye repent, ye shall all likewise perish.

6. He spake also this parable; A certain (man) had a fig tree planted in his vineyard; and he came and sought fruit thereon, and found none.

7 Then said he unto the dresser of his vineyard, Behold, these three years I come seeking fruit on this fig tree, and find none: cut it down; why cumbereth it the ground?
8 And he answering said unto him, Lord, let it alone this year also, till I shall dig about it, and dung (it):

9 And if it bear fruit, (well): and if not, (then) after that thou shalt cut it down.

10. And he was teaching in one of the synagogues on the sabbath.
11 And, behold, there was a woman which had a spirit of infirmity eighteen years, and was bowed together, and could in no wise lift up (herself).
12 And when Jesus saw her, he called (her to him), and said unto her,

Literal Translation — **Luke 13:13** — *King James Version*

Woman, you have been loosed from your infirmity.
13 And He laid hands on her. And instantly she was made erect and glorified God.

14 But answering, being angry that Jesus healed on the sabbath, the synagogue ruler said to the crowd, There are six days in which it is right to work. Then coming in these, be healed, and not on the sabbath day.

15 Then the Lord answered him and said, Hypocrites! Each one of you on the sabbath, does he not loose his ox or ass from the manger, and leading (it) away, give (it) drink?
16 And this one being a daughter of Abraham, whom Satan bound, lo, eighteen years, was (it) not right to loose from this bond on the sabbath day?

17 And (on) His saying these things, all having opposed Him were ashamed. And all the crowd rejoiced over all the glorious things happening by Him.

18. And He said, What is the kingdom of God like? And to what may I compare it?
19 It is like a grain of mustard which a man having taken threw into his garden. And it grew and became a great tree, and the birds of the heaven roosted in its branches.

20. And again He said, To what shall I compare the kingdom of God?
21 It is like leaven, which taking, a woman hid in three measures of meal until all was leavened.

2036 846 1135 630 3588 769 4675 2532
εἶπεν αὐτῇ, Γύναι, ἀπολέλυσαι τῆς ἀσθενείας σου, 13 καὶ
said to her, Woman, you have been loosed from the infirmity of you. And

2007 846 3588 5495 2532 3916 461
ἐπέθηκεν αὐτῇ τὰς χεῖρας· καὶ παραχρῆμα ἀνωρθώθη,
He laid on her the hands; and instantly she was made erect

2532 1392 3588 2316 611 1161 3588 752
καὶ ἐδόξαζε τὸν Θεόν. 14 ἀποκριθεὶς δὲ ὁ ἀρχισυνάγωγος,
and glorified God. answering But the synagogue ruler,

23 3754 3588 4521 2323 3588 2424 3004
ἀγανακτῶν ὅτι τῷ σαββάτῳ ἐθεράπευσεν ὁ Ἰησοῦς, ἔλεγε
being angry that on the sabbath healed Jesus, said

3588 3793 1803 2250 1526 1722 3739 1163 2038 1722 3778
τῷ ὄχλῳ, Ἓξ ἡμέραι εἰσὶν ἐν αἷς δεῖ ἐργάζεσθαι· ἐν ταύταις
to the crowd, Six days there are in which it is right to work; in these

3767 2064 2323 2532 3361 3588 2250 3588 4521
οὖν ἐρχόμενοι θεραπεύεσθε καὶ μὴ τῇ ἡμέρᾳ τοῦ σαββάτου.
then coming be healed and not on the day of the sabbath.

611 3767 846 3588 2962 2532 2036 5273 1538
15 ἀπεκρίθη οὖν αὐτῷ ὁ Κύριος, καὶ εἶπεν, Ὑποκριτά, ἕκαστος
answered Then him the Lord, and said, Hypocrites! Each one

5216 3588 4521 3756 3089 3588 1016 846 2228 3588 3688 575
ὑμῶν τῷ σαββάτῳ οὐ λύει τὸν βοῦν αὐτοῦ ἢ τὸν ὄνον ἀπὸ
of you on the sabbath, not do loose the ox of him or the ass from

3588 5336 2532 520 4222 3778 1161 2364
τῆς φάτνης, καὶ ἀπαγαγὼν ποτίζει; 16 ταύτην δὲ, θυγατέρα
the manger, and leading away give drink? this one And, a daughter

11 5607 3739 1210 3588 4567 2400 1176 2532 3638
Ἀβραὰμ οὖσαν, ἣν ἔδησεν ὁ Σατανᾶς, ἰδού, δέκα καὶ ὀκτὼ
of Abraham being, whom bound Satan, lo, ten and eight

2094 3756 1163 3089 575 3588 1199 5127 3588 2250 3588
ἔτη, οὐκ ἔδει λυθῆναι ἀπὸ τοῦ δεσμοῦ τούτου τῇ ἡμέρᾳ τοῦ
years, not was right to loose from bond this on the day of the

4521 2532 5023 3004 846 2617
σαββάτου; 17 καὶ ταῦτα λέγοντος αὐτοῦ, κατῃσχύνοντο
sabbath? And these things saying Him, were put to shame

3956 3588 480 846 2532 3956 3588 3793 5463 1909
πάντες οἱ ἀντικείμενοι αὐτῷ· καὶ πᾶς ὁ ὄχλος ἔχαιρεν ἐπὶ
all those having opposed Him. And all the crowd rejoiced over

3956 3588 1741 3588 1096 5259 846
πᾶσι τοῖς ἐνδόξοις τοῖς γινομένοις ὑπ' αὐτοῦ.
all the glorious things happening by Him.

3004 1161 5101 3664 2076 3588 932 3588 2316 2532 5101
18. Ἔλεγε δὲ, Τίνι ὁμοία ἐστὶν ἡ βασιλεία τοῦ Θεοῦ; καὶ τίνι
He said And, To what like is the kingdom of God? And to what

3666 846 3664 2076 2848 4615 3739 2983
ὁμοιώσω αὐτήν; 19 ὁμοία ἐστὶ κόκκῳ σινάπεως, ὃν λαβὼν
may I compare it? like It is a grain of mustard, which taking

444 906 1519 2779 1438 2532 837 2532 1096
ἄνθρωπος ἔβαλεν εἰς κῆπον ἑαυτοῦ· καὶ ηὔξησε, καὶ ἐγένετο
a man threw into a garden of himself; and it grew, and became

1519 1186 3173 2532 3588 4071 3588 3772 2681
εἰς δένδρον μέγα, καὶ τὰ πετεινὰ τοῦ οὐρανοῦ κατεσκήνωσεν
into a tree great, and the birds of the heaven roosted

1722 3588 2798 846 2532 3825 2036 5101 3666 3588
ἐν τοῖς κλάδοις αὐτοῦ. 20 καὶ πάλιν εἶπε, Τίνι ὁμοιώσω τὴν
in the branches of it. And again He said, To what may I liken the

932 3588 2316 3664 2076 2219 3739 2983 1135
βασιλείαν τοῦ Θεοῦ; 21 ὁμοία ἐστὶ ζύμῃ, ἣν λαβοῦσα γυνὴ
kingdom of God? like It is leaven, which taking a woman

1470 1519 224 4568 5140 2193 3757 2220 3650
ἐνέκρυψεν εἰς ἀλεύρου σάτα τρία, ἕως οὗ ἐζυμώθη ὅλον.
hid in of meal measures three, until were leavened all.

Woman, thou art loosed from thine infirmity.
13 And he laid (his) hands on her: and immediately she was made straight, and glorified God.

14 And the ruler of the synagogue answered with indignation, because that Jesus had healed on the sabbath day, and said unto the people, There are six days in which men ought to work: in them therefore come and be healed, and not on the sabbath day.

15 The Lord then answered him, and said, (Thou) hypocrite, doth not each one of you on the sabbath loose his ox or (his) ass from the stall, and lead (him) away to watering?
16 And ought not this woman, being a daughter of Abraham, whom Satan hath bound, lo, these eighteen years, be loosed from this bond on the sabbath day?

17 And when he had said these things, all his adversaries were ashamed: and all the people rejoiced for all the glorious things that were done by him.

18. Then said he, Unto what is the kingdom of God like? and whereunto shall I resemble it?
19 It is like a grain of mustard seed, which a man took, and cast into his garden; and it grew, and waxed a great tree; and the fowls of the air lodged in the branches of it.

20. And again he said, Whereunto shall I liken the kingdom of God?
21 It is like leaven, which a woman took and hid in three measures of meal, till the whole was leavened.

Literal Translation | **Luke 13:22** | **King James Version**

Literal Translation

22 And He traveled throughout cities and villages teaching, and making progress toward Jerusalem.
23. And one said to Him, Lord, (are) the ones being saved few? But He said to them,
24 Strive to enter in through the narrow gate, for I say to you that many will seek to enter in and will not have strength.
25 From (the time) when the Master of the house shall have risen up, and He shuts the door, and you begin to stand outside and to knock at the door, saying, Lord, Lord, open to us. And answering, He will say to you, I do not know you. From where you are.

26 Then you will begin to say, We ate and drank in Your presence, and You taught in our streets.
27 And He will say, I say to you I do not know you, from where you are. Stand back from Me all the workers of unrighteousness! (Ps. 6:8)
28 There will be weeping and gnashing of the teeth when you see Abraham and Isaac and Jacob and all the prophets in the kingdom of God, but you being thrust outside.

29 And they will come from east and west, and from north and south, and will recline in the kingdom of God.

30 And, behold! There are last ones who will be first, and there are first ones who will be last.

31. In the same day, certain Pharisees came near saying to Him, Go out and go on from here, because Herod desires to kill you.
32 And He said to them, Going say

2532 1279 2596 4172 2532 2968 1321 2532
22. Καὶ διεπορεύετο κατὰ πόλεις καὶ κώμας διδάσκων, καὶ
And He traveled throughout cities and villages teaching, and

4197 4160 1519 2419 2036 1161 5100 846 2962
πορείαν ποιούμενος εἰς Ἱερουσαλήμ. 23 εἶπε δέ τις αὐτῷ, Κύριε,
progress having made toward Jerusalem. said And one to Him, Lord

1487 3641 3588 4982 3588 1161 2036 4314 846 75
εἰ ὀλίγοι οἱ σῳζόμενοι; ὁ δὲ εἶπε πρὸς αὐτούς, 24 Ἀγωνίζεσθε
if few the (ones) being saved? He But said to them, Strive

1525 1223 3588 4728 4439 3754 4183 3004 5213
εἰσελθεῖν διὰ τῆς στενῆς θύρας, ὅτι πολλοί, λέγω ὑμῖν,
to enter in through the narrow gate, that many, I say to you,

2212 1525 2532 3756 2480 575 3739 302 1453
ζητήσουσιν εἰσελθεῖν, καὶ οὐκ ἰσχύσουσιν. 25 ἀφ' οὗ ἂν ἐγερθῇ
will seek to enter in, and not will have strength. From when is risen

3588 3617 2532 608 3588 2374 2532 756 1854
ὁ οἰκοδεσπότης καὶ ἀποκλείσῃ τὴν θύραν, καὶ ἄρξησθε ἔξω
the housemaster and he shuts the door, and you begin outside

2476 2532 2925 3588 2374 3004 2962 2962
ἑστάναι καὶ κρούειν τὴν θύραν, λέγοντες, Κύριε, Κύριε,
to stand and to knock at the door, saying, Lord, Lord.

455 2254 2532 611 2046 5213 3756 1492 5209 4159
ἄνοιξον ἡμῖν· καὶ ἀποκριθεὶς ἐρεῖ ὑμῖν, Οὐκ οἶδα ὑμᾶς, πόθεν
open to us; and answering He will say to you, Not I know you, from where

2075 5119 756 3004 5315 1799 4675 2532
ἐστέ· 26 τότε ἄρξεσθε λέγειν, Ἐφάγομεν ἐνώπιόν σου καὶ
you are. Then you will begin to say, We ate before You and

4095 2532 1722 3588 113 2257 1321 2532 2046
ἐπίομεν, καὶ ἐν ταῖς πλατείαις ἡμῶν ἐδίδαξας· 27 καὶ ἐρεῖ,
drank, and in the streets of us You taught. And He will say,

3004 5213 3756 1492 5209 4159 2075 868 575 1700
λέγω ὑμῖν, Οὐκ οἶδα ὑμᾶς πόθεν ἐστέ· ἀπόστητε ἀπ' ἐμοῦ
I say to you, Not I know you from where you are; stand back from Me

3956 3588 2040 93 1563 2071 3588 2805 2532 3588
πάντες οἱ ἐργάται ἀδικίας. 28 ἐκεῖ ἔσται ὁ κλαυθμὸς καὶ ὁ
all the workers of unrighteousness. There will be the weeping and the

1030 3588 3599 3752 3700 11 2532 2464
βρυγμὸς τῶν ὀδόντων, ὅταν ὄψεσθε Ἀβραὰμ καὶ Ἰσαὰκ
gnashing of the teeth, when you see Abraham and Isaac

2532 2384 2532 3956 3588 4396 1722 3588 932 3588
καὶ Ἰακὼβ καὶ πάντας τοὺς προφήτας ἐν τῇ βασιλείᾳ τοῦ
and Jacob and all the prophets in the kingdom

2316 5209 1161 1544 1854 2532 2240 575 395
Θεοῦ, ὑμᾶς δὲ ἐκβαλλομένους ἔξω. 29 καὶ ἥξουσιν ἀπὸ ἀνατο-
of God, you but being thrust outside. And they will come from east

2532 1424 2532 575 1005 2532 3558 2532 347
λῶν καὶ δυσμῶν καὶ ἀπὸ βορρᾶ καὶ νότου, καὶ ἀνακλιθή-
and west and from north and south, and will recline

1722 3588 932 3588 2316 2532 2400 1526 2078 3739
σονται ἐν τῇ βασιλείᾳ τοῦ Θεοῦ. 30 καὶ ἰδού, εἰσὶν ἔσχατοι οἳ
in the kingdom of God. And, behold! There are last ones who

2071 4413 2532 1526 4413 3739 2071 2078
ἔσονται πρῶτοι, καὶ εἰσὶ πρῶτοι οἳ ἔσονται ἔσχατοι.
will be first, and there are first ones who will be last.

1722 846 3588 2250 4334 5100 5330 3004
31. Ἐν αὐτῇ τῇ ἡμέρᾳ προσῆλθόν τινες Φαρισαῖοι, λέγοντες
In same the day came near certain Pharisees, saying

846 831 2532 4198 1782 3754 2264 2309 4571
αὐτῷ, Ἔξελθε καὶ πορεύου ἐντεῦθεν, ὅτι Ἡρῴδης θέλει σε
to Him, Go out and go on from here, because Herod desires you

615 2532 2036 846 4198 2036 3588
ἀποκτεῖναι. 32 καὶ εἶπεν αὐτοῖς, Πορευθέντες εἴπατε τῇ
to kill. And He said to them, Going say

King James Version

22 And he went through the cities and villages, teaching, and journeying toward Jerusalem.
23. Then said one unto him, Lord, are there few that be saved? And he said unto them,
24 Strive to enter in at the strait gate: for many, I say unto you, will seek to enter in, and shall not be able.

25 When once the master of the house is risen up, and hath shut to the door, and ye begin to stand without, and to knock at the door, saying, Lord, Lord, open unto us; and he shall answer and say unto you, I know you not whence ye are:

26 Then shall ye begin to say, We have eaten and drunk in thy presence, and thou hast taught in our streets.
27 But he shall say, I tell you, I know you not whence ye are; depart from me, all (ye) workers of iniquity.
28 There shall be weeping and gnashing of teeth, when ye shall see Abraham, and Isaac, and Jacob, and all the prophets, in the kingdom of God, and you (yourselves) thrust out.

29 And they shall come from the east, and (from) the west, and from the north, and (from) the south, and shall sit down in the kingdom of God.
30 And, behold, there are last which shall be first, and there are first which shall be last.

31. The same day there came certain of the Pharisees, saying unto him, Get thee out, and depart hence: for Herod will kill thee.
32 And he said unto them, Go

Literal Translation

to that fox, Behold! To-
day and tomorrow I cast
out demons and I com-
plete cures, and the third
(day) I am perfected.
33 But today and to-
morrow and on the fol-
lowing (day) I must
travel on; because it is
not accepted (for) a
prophet to be perish out-
side Jerusalem.
34 Jerusalem! Jerusa-
lem! The (one) killing
the prophets, and ston-
ing those having been
sent to her, how often I
desired to gather your
children in the way a
hen (gathers) her brood
under the wings, and
you did not desire (it).

35 Behold! Your house
is left to you desolate.
And truly I say to you,
You shall not at all see
Me until it come when
you say, Blessed (is) the
One coming in (the)
name of (the) Lord. (Jer.
22:5; Ps. 118:26)

Luke 13:33

258 3778 2400 1544 1140 2532 2392 2005
ἀλώπεκι ταύτῃ, Ἰδού, ἐκβάλλω δαιμόνια καὶ ἰάσεις ἐπιτελῶ
fox to that, Behold! I cast out demons and cures I finish

4594 2532 839 2532 3588 5154 5048 4133 1163 3165
σήμερον καὶ αὔριον, καὶ τῇ τρίτῃ τελειοῦμαι. 33 πλὴν δεῖ με
today and tomorrow, and the third (day) I am perfected. But must Me

4594 2532 839 2532 3588 2192 4198 3754 3756
σήμερον καὶ αὔριον καὶ τῇ ἐχομένῃ πορεύεσθαι· ὅτι οὐκ ἐν-
today and tomorrow and on the following travel on; because not it is

1735 4396 622 1854 2419 2419
δέχεται προφήτην ἀπολέσθαι ἔξω Ἱερουσαλήμ. 34 Ἱερουσαλήμ,
accepted a prophet to perish outside Jerusalem. Jerusalem!

2419 3588 15 3588 4396 2532 3036
Ἱερουσαλήμ, ἡ ἀποκτείνουσα τοὺς προφήτας, καὶ λιθοβολοῦσα
Jerusalem! The (one) killing the prophets, and stoning

3588 649 4314 846 4212 2309 1996
τοὺς ἀπεσταλμένους πρὸς αὐτήν, ποσάκις ἠθέλησα ἐπισυνά-
the (ones) having been sent to her, how often I desired to gather

3588 5043 4675 3739 5158 3733 3588 1438 3555 5259
ξαι τὰ τέκνα σου, ὃν τρόπον ὄρνις τὴν ἑαυτῆς νοσσιὰν ὑπὸ
the children of you, (in the) way a bird (gathers) her brood under

3588 4420 2532 3756 2309 2400 863 5213/3588/3614
τὰς πτέρυγας, καὶ οὐκ ἠθελήσατε. 35 ἰδού, ἀφίεται ὑμῖν ὁ οἶκος
the wings, and not you desired (it). Behold! Is left to you the house

5216 2048 281 1161 3004 5213 3754 3756 3361 3165 1492 2193 302
ὑμῶν ἔρημος· ἀμὴν δὲ λέγω ὑμῖν ὅτι Οὐ μή με ἴδητέ ἕως ἂν
of you desolate. truly And I say to you Never not Me you will see until may

2240 3753 2036 2127 3588 2064 1722 3686 2962
ἥξῃ, ὅτε εἴπητε, Εὐλογημένος ὁ ἐρχόμενος ἐν ὀνόματι Κυρίου.
it come when you say, Blessed the (One) coming in the name of (the) Lord.

King James Version

ye, and tell that fox, Be-
hold, I cast out devils,
and I do cures to day and
to morrow, and the third
(day) I shall be per-
fected.
33 Nevertheless I must
walk to day, and to mor-
row, and the (day) fol-
lowing: for it cannot be
that a prophet perish out
of Jerusalem.
34 O Jerusalem, Jerusa-
lem, which killest the
prophets, and stonest
them that are sent unto
thee; how often would I
have gathered thy chil-
dren together, as a hen
(doth gather) her brood
under (her) wings, and
ye would not!

35 Behold, your house
is left unto you desolate:
and verily I say unto
you, Ye shall not see
me, until (the time)
come when ye shall say,
Blessed (is) he that
cometh in the name of
the Lord.

Luke 14

1. And it occurred, at
His going into a house
of one of the Pharisee
leaders on a sabbath to
eat bread, even they
were intently watching
Him.
2 And behold! A certain
man was dropsical be-
fore Him.

3 And answering, Jesus
spoke to the lawyers
and Pharisees, saying, if
it is lawful to heal on the
sabbath?

4 And they were silent.
And having taken (the
man), He healed him
and let him go.
5 And answering to
them He said, Whose
ass or ox of yours shall
fall into a pit, and he will
not at once pull it up on
the sabbath day?
6 And theydid not have
strength to answer back
to Him to these things.

Luke 14

2532 1096 1722 3588 2064 846 1519 3624 5100 3588
1. Καὶ ἐγένετο ἐν τῷ ἐλθεῖν αὐτὸν εἰς οἶκόν τινος τῶν
And it was at the going Him into a house of one of the

758 3588 5330 4521 5315 740 2532
ἀρχόντων τῶν Φαρισαίων σαββάτῳ φαγεῖν ἄρτον, καὶ
leaders of the Pharisees on a sabbath to eat bread, and

846 2258 3906 846 2532 2400 444 5100
αὐτοὶ ἦσαν παρατηρούμενοι αὐτόν. 2 καὶ ἰδού, ἄνθρωπός τις
they were intently watching Him. And behold! man A certain

2258 5203 1715 846 2532 611 3588 2424
ἦν ὑδρωπικὸς ἔμπροσθεν αὐτοῦ. 3 καὶ ἀποκριθεὶς ὁ Ἰησοῦς
was dropsical before Him. And answering Jesus

2036 4314 3588 3544 2532 5330 3004 1487 1832
εἶπε πρὸς τοὺς νομικοὺς καὶ Φαρισαίους, λέγων, Εἰ ἔξεστι
said to the lawyers and Pharisees, saying, If it is lawful

3588 4521 2323 3588 1161 2270 2532 1949
τῷ σαββάτῳ θεραπεύειν; 4 οἱ δὲ ἡσύχασαν. καὶ ἐπιλαβόμενος
on the sabbath to heal? they And were silent. And having taken (him)

2390 846 2532 630 2532 611 4314 846
ἰάσατο αὐτὸν, καὶ ἀπέλυσε. 5 καὶ ἀποκριθεὶς πρὸς αὐτοὺς
He healed him and set him loose. And answering to them

2036 5101 5216 3681 2228 1016 1519 5421 1706 2532 3756
εἶπε, Τίνος ὑμῶν ὄνος ἢ βοῦς εἰς φρέαρ ἐμπεσεῖται, καὶ οὐκ
He said, Of whom of you an ass or ox into a pit should fall, and not

2112 385 846 1722 3588 2250 3588 4521 2532
εὐθέως ἀνασπάσει αὐτὸν ἐν τῇ ἡμέρᾳ τοῦ σαββάτου; 6 καὶ
at once he will pull up it in the day of the sabbath? And

3756 2480 470 4314 5023
οὐκ ἴσχυσαν ἀνταποκριθῆναι πρὸς ταῦτα.
not they had strength to answer back to these things.

Luke 14

1. And it came to pass,
as he went into the house
of one of the chief Phari-
sees to eat bread on the
sabbath day, that they
watched him.

2 And, behold, there
was a certain man be-
fore him which had the
dropsy.
3 And Jesus answering
spake unto the lawyers
and Pharisees, saying,
Is it lawful to heal on the
sabbath day?

4 And they held their
peace. And he took
(him), and healed him,
and let him go;
5 And answered them,
saying, Which of you
shall have an ass or an
ox fallen into a pit, and
will not straightway
pull him out on the sab-
bath day?
6 And they could not
answer him again to
these things.

Literal Translation **Luke 14:7** *King James Version*

7. And He spoke a parable to those who had been invited, noting how they were choosing out the chief seats, saying to them,
8 When you are invited by anyone to wedding feasts, do not recline at the chief seat lest (one) more honorable (than) you be invited by him,
9 and coming, he who invited you will say to you, Give this one place. And then you begin with shame to take the last place.
10 But when you are invited, going in, recline at the last place, so that when he who has invited you may come, he (may) say to you, Friend, go up higher. Then glory will be to you before those reclining with you.

11 For everyone exalting himself will be humbled, and the one humbling himself will be exalted.

12. And He also said to him who had invited Him, When you make a dinner or supper, do not call your friends, nor your brothers, nor your relatives, nor rich neighbors, lest they also should invite you in return, and it become a repayment to you.

13 But when you make a banquet, call the poor, the crippled, the lame, the blind;
14 and then you will be blessed, for they have nothing to repay you. For it will be repaid to you in the resurrection of the just.

15. And one of those reclining with (Him), hearing these things, (he) said to Him, Blessed (are) those eating bread in the kingdom of God.
16 But He

3004 1161 4314 3588 2564 3850 1907 4459
7. Ἔλεγε δὲ πρὸς τοὺς κεκλημένους παραβολήν, ἐπέχων πῶς
He told And to the (ones) having been invited a parable, noting how

3588 4411 1586 3004 4314 846 3752
τὰς πρωτοκλισίας ἐξελέγοντο, λέγων πρὸς αὐτούς, 8 Ὅταν
the chief seats they were choosing, saying to them, When

2564 5259 5100 1519 1062 3361 2625 1519 3588 4411
κληθῇς ὑπό τινος εἰς γάμους, μὴ κατακλιθῇς εἰς τὴν πρωτοκλι-
you are invited by anyone to feasts, do not recline at the chief seat,

3379 1784 4675 5600 2564 5259 846 2532
σίαν· μήποτε ἐντιμότερός σου ᾖ κεκλημένος ὑπ' αὐτοῦ, 9 καὶ
lest (a) more honorable than you be invited by him, and

2064 3588 4571 2532 846 2564 2046 4671 1325 5129 5117 2532
ἐλθὼν ὁ σὲ καὶ αὐτὸν καλέσας ἐρεῖ σοι, Δὸς τούτῳ τόπον· καὶ
coming he to you and him inviting will say to you, Give this one place. And

5119 756 3326 152 3588 2078 5117 2722 235
τότε ἄρξῃ μετ' αἰσχύνης τὸν ἔσχατον τόπον κατέχειν. 10 ἀλλ'
then you begin with shame the last place to take. But

3752 2564 4198 377 1519 3588 2078 5117
ὅταν κληθῇς πορευθεὶς ἀνάπεσον εἰς τὸν ἔσχατον τόπον·
when you are invited, going recline in the last place,

2443 3752 2064 3588 2564 4571 2036 4671 5384 4320
ἵνα, ὅταν ἔλθῃ ὁ κεκληκώς σε, εἴπῃ σοι, Φίλε, προσανάβηθι
that when comes he having invited you, he say to you, Friend, go up

511 5119 2071 4671 1391 1799 3588 4873
ἀνώτερον· τότε ἔσται σοι δόξα ἐνώπιον τῶν συνανακειμένων
higher; then will be to you glory before the (ones) reclining with

4671 3754 3956 3588 5312 1438 5013 2532 3588 5013
σοι. 11 ὅτι πᾶς ὁ ὑψῶν ἑαυτὸν ταπεινωθήσεται, καὶ ὁ ταπεινῶν
you. For everyone who exalts himself will be humbled, and the (one) humbling

1438 5312
ἑαυτὸν ὑψωθήσεται.
himself will be exalted.

3004 1161 2532 3588 2564 846 3752 4160 712 2228
12 Ἔλεγε δὲ καὶ τῷ κεκληκότι αὐτόν, Ὅταν ποιῇς ἄριστον ἢ
He spoke And also to those having invited Him, When you make a dinner or

1173 3361 5455 3588 5384 4675 3366 3588 80 4675
δεῖπνον, μὴ φώνει τοὺς φίλους σου, μηδὲ τοὺς ἀδελφούς σου,
a supper, do not call the friends of you, nor the brothers of you,

3366 3588 4773 4675 3366 1069 4145 3379
μηδὲ τοὺς συγγενεῖς σου, μηδὲ γείτονας πλουσίους· μήποτε
nor the relatives of you, nor neighbors rich; that not

2532 846 4571 479 2532 1096 4671 468
καὶ αὐτοί σε ἀντικαλέσωσί, καὶ γένηται σοι ἀνταπόδομα.
also they you invite in return, and it becomes to you a repayment.

235 3752 4160 1403 2564 4434 376 5560
13 ἀλλ' ὅταν ποιῇς δοχὴν, κάλει πτωχούς, ἀναπείρους, χωλούς,
But when you make a banquet, invite poor ones, disabled ones, lame ones,

5185 2532 3107 2071 3754 3756 2192 467
τυφλούς· 14 καὶ μακάριος ἔσῃ, ὅτι οὐκ ἔχουσιν ἀνταπο-
blind ones; and blessed you will be, because not they have (a thing) to

4671 467 1063 4671 1722 3588 386 3588
δοῦναί σοι· ἀνταποδοθήσεται γάρ σοι ἐν τῇ ἀναστάσει τῶν
repay you; it will be repaid for to you in the resurrection of the

1342
δικαίων.
just.

191 1161 5100 3588 4873 5023 2036 846
15. Ἀκούσας δέ τις τῶν συνανακειμένων ταῦτα εἶπεν αὐτῷ,
hearing And one of those reclining with (Him) these things said to Him,

3107 3739 5315 740 1722 3588 932 3588 2316 3588 1161
Μακάριος, ὅς φάγεται ἄρτον ἐν τῇ βασιλείᾳ τοῦ Θεοῦ. 16 ὁ δὲ
Blessed, (he) who eats bread in the kingdom of God. He But

7. And he put forth a parable to those which were bidden, when he marked how they chose out the chief rooms; saying unto them,
8 When thou art bidden of any (man) to a wedding, sit not down in the highest room; lest a more honourable man than thou be bidden of him;
9 And he that bade thee and him come and say to thee, Give this man place; and thou begin with shame to take the lowest room.
10 But when thou art bidden, go and sit down in the lowest room; that when he that bade thee cometh, he may say unto thee, Friend, go up higher: then shalt thou have worship in the presence of them that sit at meat with thee.

11 For whosoever exalteth himself shall be abased; and he that humbleth himself shall be exalted.

12. Then said he also to him that bade him, When thou makest a dinner or a supper, call not thy friends, nor thy brethren, neither thy kinsmen, nor (thy) rich neighbours; lest they also bid thee again, and a recompence be made thee.

13 But when thou makest a feast, call the poor, the maimed, the lame, the blind:
14 And thou shalt be blessed; for they cannot recompense thee: for thou shalt be recompensed at the resurrection of the just.

15. And when one of them that sat at meat with him heard these things, he said unto him, Blessed (is) he that shall eat bread in the kingdom of God.
16 Then

Literal Translation

Luke 14:17

King James Version

said to him, A certain man made a great supper and invited many.
17 And he sent his slave at the supper hour to say to those who had been invited, Come, for now all is ready.

18 And all with one (mind) began to beg off. The first said to him, I have bought a field, and I have need to go out and see it; I ask you, have me excused.

19 And another said, I bought five yoke of oxen and I am going to try them out; I ask you, have me excused.

20 And another said, I married a wife, and for this reason I am not able to come.

21 And having come up that slave reported these things to his lord. Then being angry, the housemaster said to his slave, Go out quickly into the streets and lanes of the city, and bring in here the poor and disabled and lame and blind ones.

22 And the slave said, Sir, (it) has been done as you ordered, and still there is room.
23 And the lord said to the slave, Go out into the highways and hedges and compel (them) to come in, so that my house may be filled.
24 For I say to you that not one of those men who had been invited shall taste of my supper.

25. And great crowds came together to Him. And turning, He said to them,
26 If anyone comes to Me and does not hate his father,

2036 846 444 5100 4160 1173 3173 2532
εἶπεν αὐτῷ, Ἄνθρωπός τις ἐποίησε δεῖπνον μέγα, καὶ
said to him, man A certain made a supper great, and
2564 4183 2532 649 3588 1401 846 3588 5610
ἐκάλεσε πολλούς· 17 καὶ ἀπέστειλε τὸν δοῦλον αὐτοῦ τῇ ὥρᾳ
(he) invited many. And (he) sent the slave of him at the hour
3588 1173 2036 3588 2564 2064 3754 2235
τοῦ δείπνου εἰπεῖν τοῖς κεκλημένοις, Ἔρχεσθε, ὅτι ἤδη
of the supper to say to those having been invited, Come, because now
2092 2076 3956 2532 756 575 1520 3868
ἕτοιμά ἐστι πάντα. 18 καὶ ἤρξαντο ἀπὸ μιᾶς παραιτεῖσθαι
ready it is all. And they began from one (mind) to beg off
3956 3588 4413 2036 846 68 59 2532 2192 318
πάντες. ὁ πρῶτος εἶπεν αὐτῷ, Ἀγρὸν ἠγόρασα, καὶ ἔχω ἀνάγκην
all. The first said to him, A field I have bought, and I have need
1831 2532 492 846 2065 4571 2192 3165 3868 2532
ἐξελθεῖν καὶ ἰδεῖν αὐτόν· ἐρωτῶ σε, ἔχε με παρῃτημένον. 19 καὶ
to go out and to see it; I ask you, have me excused. And
2087 2036 2201 1016 59 4002 2532 4198
ἕτερος εἶπε, Ζεύγη βοῶν ἠγόρασα πέντε, καὶ πορεύομαι
another said, yoke of oxen I have bought five, and I am going
1381 846 2065 4571 2192 3165 3868 2532
δοκιμάσαι αὐτά· ἐρωτῶ σε, ἔχε με παρῃτημένον. 20 καὶ
to try out them; I ask you, have me excused. And
2087 2036 1135 1060 2532 1223 5124 3756 1410 2064
ἕτερος εἶπε, Γυναῖκα ἔγημα, καὶ διὰ τοῦτο οὐ δύναμαι ἐλθεῖν.
another said, A wife I married, and because of this not I am able to come.
2532 3854 3588 1401 1565 518 3588 2962
21 καὶ παραγενόμενος ὁ δοῦλος ἐκεῖνος ἀπήγγειλε τῷ κυρίῳ
And having come near slave that reported to the lord
846 5023 5119 3710 3588 3617 2036 3588 1401
αὐτοῦ ταῦτα. τότε ὀργισθεὶς ὁ οἰκοδεσπότης εἶπε τῷ δούλῳ
of him these things. Then being angry the housemaster said to the slave
846 1831 5030 1519 3588 4113 2532 4505 3588 4172
αὐτοῦ, Ἔξελθε ταχέως εἰς τὰς πλατείας καὶ ῥύμας τῆς πόλεως,
of him, Go out quickly into the streets and lanes of the city,
2532 3588 4434 2532 376 2532 5560 2532 5185
καὶ τοὺς πτωχοὺς καὶ ἀναπήρους καὶ χωλοὺς καὶ τυφλοὺς
and the poor and disabled and lame and blind
1521 5602 2532 2036 3588 1401 2962 1096 5613
εἰσάγαγε ὧδε. 22 καὶ εἶπεν ὁ δοῦλος, Κύριε, γέγονεν ὡς
bring in here. And said the slave, Lord, has occurred as
2004 2532 2089 5117 2076 2532 2036 3588 2962 4314 3588
ἐπέταξας, καὶ ἔτι τόπος ἐστί. 23 καὶ εἶπεν ὁ κύριος πρὸς τὸν
you ordered, and still room there is. And said the lord to the
1401 1831 1519 3588 3598 2532 5418 2532 315
δοῦλον, Ἔξελθε εἰς τὰς ὁδοὺς καὶ φραγμούς, καὶ ἀνάγκασον
slave, Go out into the ways and hedges, and compel (them)
1525 2443 1072 3588 3624 3450 3004 1063 5213 3754 3762
εἰσελθεῖν, ἵνα γεμισθῇ ὁ οἶκός μου. 24 λέγω γὰρ ὑμῖν ὅτι οὐδεὶς
to come in, that may be filled the house of me. I say For to you that not one
3588 435 1565 3588 2564 1089 3450 3588
τῶν ἀνδρῶν ἐκείνων τῶν κεκλημένων γεύσεταί μου τοῦ
men of those having been invited shall taste of me the
1173
δείπνου.
supper.
4848 1161 846 3793 4183 2532 4762 2036
25. Συνεπορεύοντο δὲ αὐτῷ ὄχλοι πολλοί· καὶ στραφεὶς εἶπε
came together And to Him crowds great. And turning He said
4314 846 1487 5100 2064 4314 3165 2532 3756 3404 3588 3962
πρὸς αὐτούς, 26 Εἴ τις ἔρχεται πρός με, καὶ οὐ μισεῖ τὸν πατέρα
to them, If anyone comes to Me, and not hates the father

said he unto him, A certain man made a great supper, and bade many:
17 And sent his servant at supper time to say to them that were bidden, Come; for all things are now ready.

18 And they all with one (consent) began to make excuse. The first said unto him, I have bought a piece of ground, and I must needs go and see it: I pray thee have me excused.
19 And another said, I have bought five yoke of oxen, and I go to prove them: I pray thee have me excused.

20 And another said, I have married a wife, and therefore I cannot come.

21 So that servant came, and shewed his lord these things. Then the master of the house being angry said to his servant, Go out quickly into the streets and lanes of the city, and bring in hither the poor, and the maimed, and the halt, and the blind.

22 And the servant said, Lord, it is done as thou hast commanded, and yet there is room.
23 And the lord said unto the servant, Go out into the highways and hedges, and compel (them) to come in, that my house may be filled.

24 For I say unto you, That none of those men which were bidden shall taste of my supper.

25. And there went great multitudes with him: and he turned, and said unto them,
26 If any (man) come to me, and hate not his father,

Literal Translation | **Luke 14:27** | *King James Version*

and mother, and wife, and children, and brothers and sisters, and besides, even his (own) life, he cannot be My disciple.

27 And whoever does not bear his cross and come after Me, he cannot be My disciple.

28 For who of you desiring to build a tower does not first sit down (and) count the cost, whether he has the things to bring to completion;
29 that having laid a foundation, and not having strength to finish, all those seeing begin to mock him,

30 saying, This man began to build, and did not have strength to finish.

31 Or what king going to attack another king in war does not first sit down (and) take counsel whether he is able with ten thousand to meet those coming upon him with twenty thousands?

32 But if not, he being still far off, sending a delegation, he asks the things for peace.

33 So then every one of you who does not separate from all his possessions is not able to be My disciple.

34. The salt (is) good, but if the salt becomes tasteless, with what will it be seasoned?
35 It is not fit for soil nor for fertilizer; they throw it out. The (one) having ears to hear, let him hear.

1438 2532 3588 3384 2532 3588 1135 2532 3588 5043 2532
ἑαυτοῦ, καὶ τὴν μητέρα, καὶ τὴν γυναῖκα, καὶ τὰ τέκνα, καὶ
of himself, and the mother, and the wife, and the children, and

3588 80 2532 3588 79 2089 1161 2532 3588 1438 5590
τοὺς ἀδελφοὺς, καὶ τὰς ἀδελφάς, ἔτι δὲ καὶ τὴν ἑαυτοῦ ψυχὴν,
the brothers, and the sisters, besides and even the of himself soul,

3756 1410 3450 3101 1511 2532 3748 3756 941 3588
οὐ δύναταί μου μαθητής εἶναί. 27 καὶ ὅστις οὐ βαστάζει τὸν
not he is able of Me a disciple to be. And whoever not does bear the

4716 846 2532 2064 3694 3450 3756 1410 3450
σταυρὸν αυτοῦ καὶ ἔρχεται ὀπίσω μου, οὐ δύναταί μου
cross of him and comes after Me, not he is able of Me

1511 3101 5101 1063 1537 5216 2309 4444 3618
εἶναί μαθητής. 28 τίς γὰρ ἐξ ὑμῶν, θέλων πύργον οἰκοδομῆσαι,
to be a disciple. who For of you, desiring a tower to build,

3780 4412 2523 5585 3588 1160 1487 2192 3588 4314
οὐχὶ πρῶτον καθίσας ψηφίζει τὴν δαπάνην, εἰ ἔχει τὰ πρὸς
not first sitting count the cost, if he has the things to

535 2443 3379 5087 846 2310 2532 3361
ἀπαρτισμόν; 29 ἵνα μήποτε, θέντος αὐτοῦ θεμέλιον καὶ μὴ
bring to completion? So that not when, having laid him foundation, and not

2480 1615 3956 3588 2334 756 1702
ἰσχύοντος ἐκτελέσαι, πάντες οἱ θεωροῦντες ἄρξωνται ἐμπαί-
having strength to finish, all those seeing begin to

846 3004 3754 3778 3588 444 756 3618
ζειν αὐτῷ, 30 λέγοντες ὅτι Οὗτος ὁ ἄνθρωπος ἤρξατο οἰκοδο-
mock him, saying, This man began to build

2532 3756 5656 1615 2228 5101 935 4198
μεῖν καὶ οὐκ ἴσχυσεν ἐκτελέσαι. 31 ἢ τίς βασιλεὺς πορευόμενος
and not had strength to finish. Or what king having gone

4820 2087 935 1519 4171 3780 2523 4412
συμβαλεῖν ἑτέρῳ βασιλεῖ εἰς πόλεμον οὐχὶ καθίσας πρῶτον
to encounter another king at war not sitting first

1011 1487 1415 2076 1722 1176 5505 528
βουλεύεται εἰ δυνατός ἐστιν ἐν δέκα χιλιάσιν ἀπαντῆσαι
take counsel whether able he is with ten thousands to meet

3588 3326 501 5505 2064 1909 846 1487 1161 3361
τῷ μετὰ εἴκοσι χιλιάδων ἐρχομένῳ ἐπ' αὐτόν; 32 εἰ δὲ μήγε,
the (one) with twenty thousands coming upon him? if And not,

2089 846 4206 5607 4242 649 2065 3588
ἔτι αὐτοῦ πόρρω ὄντος, πρεσβείαν ἀποστείλας ἐρωτᾷ τὰ
yet him far off being, a delegation sending he asks the things

4314 1515 3779 3767 3956 1537 5216 3739 3756 657
πρὸς εἰρήνην. 33 οὕτως οὖν πᾶς ἐξ ὑμῶν ὃς οὐκ ἀποτάσσεται
for peace. So then everyone of you who not separates from

3956 3588 1438 5224 3756 1410 3450 1511
πᾶσι τοῖς ἑαυτοῦ ὑπάρχουσιν οὐ δύναται μου εἶναί
all the of himself possessions not is able of Me to be

3101 2570 3588 217 1437 1161 3588 217 3471 1722
μαθητής. 34 καλὸν τὸ ἅλας· ἐὰν δὲ τὸ ἅλας μωρανθῇ, ἐν
a disciple. Good (is) the salt; if but the salt becomes tasteless, with

5101 741 3777 1519 1093 3777 1519 2874 2111
τίνι ἀρτυθήσεται; 35 οὔτε εἰς γῆν οὔτε εἰς κοπρίαν εὔθετόν
what will it be seasoned? neither For soil nor for manure fit

2076 1854 906 846 3588 2192 3775 191 191
ἐστιν· ἔξω βάλλουσιν αὐτό. ὁ ἔχων ὦτα ἀκούειν ἀκουέτω.
it is; out they throw it. The (one) having ears to hear, let him hear.

and mother, and wife, and children, and brethren, and sisters, yea, and his own life also, he cannot be my disciple.

27 And whosoever doth not bear his cross, and come after me, cannot be my disciple.

28 For which of you, intending to build a tower, sitteth not down first, and counteth the cost, whether he have (sufficient) to finish (it)?

29 Lest haply, after he hath laid the foundation, and is not able to finish (it), all that behold (it) begin to mock him,

30 Saying, This man began to build, and was not able to finish.

31 Or what king, going to make war against another king, sitteth not down first, and consulteth whether he be able with ten thousand to meet him that cometh against him with twenty thousand?

32 Or else, while the other is yet a great way off, he sendeth an ambassage, and desireth conditions of peace.

33 So likewise, whosoever he be of you that forsaketh not all that he hath, he cannot be my disciple.

34. Salt (is) good: but if the salt have lost his savour, wherewith shall it be seasoned?
35 It is neither fit for the land, nor yet for the dunghill; (but) men cast it out. He that hath ears to hear, let him hear.

Luke 15 | **Luke 15** | **Luke 15**

1. And all the tax collectors and

2258 1161 1448 846 3956 3588 5057 2532 3588
1. Ἦσαν δὲ ἐγγίζοντες αὐτῷ πάντες οἱ τελῶναι καὶ οἱ
were And drawing near to Him all the tax-collectors and the

1. Then drew near unto him all the publicans

Literal Translation | **Luke 15:2** | **King James Version**

sinners were coming near to Him, to hear Him.
2 And the Pharisees and the scribes murmured, saying, This one receives sinners and eats with them.

268 191 846 2532 1234 3588 5330
ἁμαρτωλοὶ ἀκούειν αὐτοῦ. 2 καὶ διεγόγγυζον οἵ Φαρισαῖοι
sinners to hear Him. And murmured the Pharisees
2532 3588 1122 3004 3754 3778 268 4327
καὶ οἱ γραμματεῖς λέγοντες ὅτι Οὗτος ἁμαρτωλοὺς προσδέ-
and the scribes saying, This one sinners receives,
2532 4906 846
χεται, καὶ συνεσθίει αὐτοῖς.
and eats with them.

and sinners for to hear him.
2 And the Pharisees and scribes murmured, saying, This man receiveth sinners, and eateth with them.

3. And He spoke to them this parable, saying,
4 What man of you having a hundred sheep, and losing one of them, does not leave the ninety nine in the deserted (place) and go after the lost (one) until he finds it?
5 And finding (it), he puts (it) on his shoulders, rejoicing.
6 And coming to the house, he calls together the friends and neighbors, saying to them, Rejoice with me, for I have found my sheep that had been lost.

2036 1161 4314 846 3588 3850 3778 3004 5101
3. Εἶπε δὲ πρὸς αὐτοὺς τὴν παραβολὴν ταύτην, λέγων, 4 Τίς
He spoke And to them parable this, saying, What
444 1537 5216 2192 1540 4263 2532 622 1520
ἄνθρωπος ἐξ ὑμῶν ἔχων ἑκατὸν πρόβατα, καὶ ἀπολέσας ἓν
man of you having a hundred sheep, and losing one
1537 846 3756 2641 3588 1768 1722 3588 2048
ἐξ αὐτῶν, οὐ καταλείπει τὰ ἐννενηκονταεννέα ἐν τῇ ἐρήμῳ,
of them, not does leave the ninety-nine in the desert,
2532 4198 1909 3588 622 2193 2147 846 2532 2147
καὶ πορεύεται ἐπὶ τὸ ἀπολωλὸς, ἕως εὕρῃ αὐτό; 5 καὶ εὑρὼν
and go after the lost (one), until he finds it? And finding
2007 1909 3588 5606 1438 5463 2532 2064 1519 3588
ἐπιτίθησιν ἐπὶ τοὺς ὤμους ἑαυτοῦ χαίρων. 6 καὶ ἐλθὼν εἰς τὸν
puts it on the shoulders of himself rejoicing. And coming to the
3624 4779 3588 5384 2532 3588 1069 3004 846
οἶκον συγκαλεῖ τοὺς φίλους καὶ τοὺς γείτονας λέγων αὐτοῖς,
house he summons the friends and the neighbors saying to them,
4796 3427 3754 2147 3588 4263 3450 3588 622
Συγχάρητέ μοι, ὅτι εὗρον τὸ πρόβατόν μου τὸ ἀπολωλός.
Rejoice with me, because I have found the sheep of me, the (one) being lost.

3. And he spake this parable unto them, saying,
4 What man of you, having an hundred sheep, if he lose one of them, doth not leave the ninety and nine in the wilderness, and go after that which is lost, until he find it?
5 And when he hath found (it), he layeth (it) on his shoulders, rejoicing.
6 And when he cometh home, he calleth together (his) friends and neighbours, saying unto them, Rejoice with me; for I have found my sheep which was lost.

7 I say to you that so is joy in Heaven over one sinner repenting, than over ninety nine righteous ones who have no need of repentance.

3004 5213 3754 3779 5479 2071 1722 3588 3772 1909 1520 268
7 λέγω ὑμῖν ὅτι οὕτω χαρὰ ἔσται ἐν τῷ οὐρανῷ ἐπὶ ἑνὶ ἁμαρ-
I say to you that thus joy is in Heaven over one sinner
3340 2228 1909 1768 1342 3748
τωλῷ μετανοοῦντι, ἢ ἐπὶ ἐννενηκονταεννέα δικαίοις, οἵτινες
repenting, than over ninety-nine righteous ones who
3756 5532 2192 3341
οὐ χρείαν ἔχουσι μετανοίας.
no need have of repentance.

7 I say unto you, that likewise joy shall be in heaven over one sinner that repenteth, more than over ninety and nine just persons, which need no repentance.

8. Or what woman having ten drachmas, if she loses one drachma does not light a lamp and sweep the house, and look carefully until she finds it?
9 And finding (it), she calls together the friends and neighbors, saying, Rejoice with me, for I have found the drachma which I lost.
10 I say to you, so there is joy before the angels of God over one sinner repenting.

2228 5101 1135 1406 2192 1176 1437 622 1406
8. Ἢ τίς γυνὴ δραχμὰς ἔχουσα δέκα, ἐὰν ἀπολέσῃ δραχμὴν
Or what woman drachmas having ten, if she loses drachma
1520 3780 681 3088 2532 4563 3588 3614 2532 2212
μίαν, οὐχὶ ἅπτει λύχνον, καὶ σαροῖ τὴν οἰκίαν, καὶ ζητεῖ
one, not does light a lamp and sweep the house, and seek
1960 2193 3755 2147 2532 2147 4779 3588
ἐπιμελῶς ἕως ὅτου εὕρῃ; 9 καὶ εὑροῦσα συγκαλεῖται τὰς
carefully until she finds? And finding she summons the
5384 2532 3588 1069 3004 4796 3427 3754 2147
φίλας καὶ τὰς γείτονας, λέγουσα, Συγχάρητέ μοι, ὅτι εὗρον
friends and the neighbors, saying, Rejoice with me, because I found
3588 1406 3739 622 3779 3004 5213 5479 1096
τὴν δραχμὴν ἣν ἀπώλεσα. 10 οὕτω, λέγω ὑμῖν, χαρὰ γίνεται
the drachma which I lost. So, I say to you, joy there is
1799 3588 32 3588 2316 1909 1520 268
ἐνώπιον τῶν ἀγγέλων τοῦ Θεοῦ ἐπὶ ἑνὶ ἁμαρτωλῷ
before the angels of God over one sinner
3340
μετανοοῦντι.
repenting.

8. Either what woman having ten pieces of silver, if she lose one piece, doth not light a candle, and sweep the house, and seek diligently till she find (it)?
9 And when she hath found (it), she calleth (her) friends and (her) neighbours together, saying, Rejoice with me; for I have found the piece which I had lost.
10 Likewise, I say unto you, there is joy in the presence of the angels of God over one sinner that repenteth.

11. And He said, A certain man had two sons.
12 And the

2036 1161 444 5100 2192 1417 5207 2532 2036 3588
11. Εἶπε δέ, Ἄνθρωπός τις εἶχε δύο υἱούς· 12 καὶ εἶπεν ὁ
He said And, man a certain had two sons; and said the

11. And he said, A certain man had two sons:
12 And the

Luke 15:13

Literal Translation

younger of them said to the father, Father give me that part of the property falling (to me). And he divided the living to them.
13 And not many days after, gathering up all things, the younger son went away to a distant country. And there he wasted his property, living dissolutely.
14 But having spent all his things, a severe famine came throughout that country, and he began to be in need.
15 And going, he was joined to one of the citizens of that country. And he sent him into his fields to feed pigs.
16 And he longed to fill his stomach from the husks which the pigs ate, but no one gave to him.
17 But coming to himself he said, How many servants of my father have plenty of loaves, and I am perishing with famine.
18 Rising up, I will go to my father, and I will say to him, Father, I sinned against Heaven and before you,
19 and I am no longer worthy to be called your son. Make me as one of your hired servants.
20 And rising up, he came to his father. But he yet being far away, his father saw him and was moved with pity. And running, (he) fell on his neck and fervently kissed him.
21 And the son said to him, Father, I have sinned against Heaven and before you, and no longer am I worthy to be called your son.
22 But the father said to his slaves, Bring

3501 846 3588 3962 3962 1325 3427 3588 1911 3313
νεώτερος αὐτῶν τῷ πατρί, Πάτερ, δός μοι τὸ ἐπιβάλλον μέρος
younger of them to the father, Father, give to me the falling (to me) share

3588 3776 2532 1244 846 3588 979 2532 3326 3756 4183
τῆς οὐσίας. καὶ διεῖλεν αὐτοῖς τὸν βίον. 13 καὶ μετ' οὐ πολλὰς
of the property. And he divided to them the living. And after not many

2250 4863 537 3588 3501 5207 589 1519
ἡμέρας συναγαγὼν ἅπαντα ὁ νεώτερος υἱὸς ἀπεδήμησεν εἰς
days gathering together all things the younger son went away into

5561 117 2532 1563 1287 3588 3776 846 2198
χώραν μακράν, καὶ ἐκεῖ διεσκόρπισε τὴν οὐσίαν αὐτοῦ, ζῶν
a country distant, and there (he) dissipated the property of him, living

811 1159 1161 846 3956 1096 3042
ἀσώτως. 14 δαπανήσαντος δὲ αὐτοῦ πάντα, ἐγένετο λιμὸς
dissolutely. having spent But him all things, occurred famine

2478 2596 3588 5561 1565 2532 846 756 5302
ἰσχυρὸς κατὰ τὴν χώραν ἐκείνην, καὶ αὐτὸς ἤρξατο ὑστερεῖ-
a severe throughout country that, and he began to be in

2532 4198 2853 1520 3588 4177 3588 5561
σθαι. 15 καὶ πορευθεὶς ἐκολλήθη ἑνὶ τῶν πολιτῶν τῆς χώρας
need. And going he was joined to one of the citizens country

1565 2532 3992 846 1519 3588 68 846 1006
ἐκείνης· καὶ ἔπεμψεν αὐτὸν εἰς τοὺς ἀγροὺς αὐτοῦ βόσκειν
of that. And he sent him into the fields of him to feed

5519 2532 1937 1072 3588 2836 846 575 3588
χοίρους· 16 καὶ ἐπεθύμει γεμίσαι τὴν κοιλίαν αὐτοῦ ἀπὸ τῶν
pigs. And he longed to fill the belly of him from the

2769 3739 2068 3588 5519 2532 3762 1325 846 1519
κερατίων ὧν ἤσθιον οἱ χοῖροι· καὶ οὐδεὶς ἐδίδου αὐτῷ. 17 εἰς
husks which ate the pigs; and no one gave to him. to

1438 1161 2064 2036 4214 3407 3588 3962 3450
ἑαυτὸν δὲ ἐλθὼν εἶπε, Πόσοι μίσθιοι τοῦ πατρός μου περισ-
himself But coming he said, How many of the servants of the father of me

4052 740 1473 1161 3042 622 450 4198
σεύουσιν ἄρτων, ἐγὼ δὲ λιμῷ ἀπόλλυμαι· 18 ἀναστὰς πορεύ-
abound in loaves, I but with famine am perishing. Rising up I will

4314 3588 3962 3450 2532 2046 846 3962 264
σομαι πρὸς τὸν πατέρα μου, καὶ ἐρῶ αὐτῷ, Πάτερ, ἥμαρτον
go to the father of me, and I will say to him, Father, I sinned

1519 3588 3772 2532 1799 4675 2532 3765 1510 514
εἰς τὸν οὐρανὸν καὶ ἐνώπιόν σου· 19 καὶ οὐκέτι εἰμὶ ἄξιος
against Heaven and before you; and no longer am I worthy

2564 5207 4675 4160 3165 5613 1520 3588 3407 4675 2532
κληθῆναι υἱός σου· ποίησόν με ὡς ἕνα τῶν μισθίων σου. 20 καὶ
to be called son of you; make me as one of the servants of you. And

450 2064 4314 3588 3962 1438 2089 1161 846 3112
ἀναστὰς ἦλθε πρὸς τὸν πατέρα ἑαυτοῦ. ἔτι δὲ αὐτοῦ μακρὰν
rising up he came to the father of himself. yet But him afar

568 1492 846 3588 3962 846 2532 4697
ἀπέχοντος, εἶδεν αὐτὸν ὁ πατὴρ αὐτοῦ, καὶ ἐσπλαγχνίσθη,
being away, saw him the father of him, and was moved with pity,

2532 5143 1968 1909 3588 5137 846 2532
καὶ δραμὼν ἐπέπεσεν ἐπὶ τὸν τράχηλον αὐτοῦ, καὶ κατε-
and running fell on the neck of him, and fervently

2705 846 2036 1161 846 3588 5207 3962 264 1519 3588
φίλησεν αὐτόν. 21 εἶπε δε αὐτῷ ὁ υἱὸς, Πάτερ, ἥμαρτον εἰς τὸν
kissed him. said And to him the son, Father, I sinned against

3772 2532 1799 4675 2532 3765 1510 514 2564
οὐρανὸν καὶ ἐνώπιόν σου, καὶ οὐκέτι εἰμὶ ἄξιος κληθῆναι
Heaven and before you, and no longer I am worthy to be called

5207 4675 2036 1161 3588 3962 4314 3588 1401 846
υἱός σου. 22 εἶπε δὲ ὁ πατὴρ πρὸς τοὺς δούλους αὐτοῦ, Ἐξε-
son of you. said But the father to the slaves of him, Bring

King James Version

younger of them said to (his) father, Father, give me the portion of goods that falleth (to me). And he divided unto them (his) living.
13 And not many days after the younger son gathered all together, and took his journey into a far country, and there wasted his substance with riotous living.
14 And when he had spent all, there arose a mighty famine in that land; and he began to be in want.
15 And he went and joined himself to a citizen of that country; and he sent him into his fields to feed swine.
16 And he would fain have filled his belly with the husks that the swine did eat: and no man gave unto him.
17 And when he came to himself, he said, How many hired servants of my father's have bread enough and to spare, and I perish with hunger!
18 I will arise and go to my father, and will say unto him, Father, I have sinned against heaven, and before thee,
19 And am no more worthy to be called thy son: make me as one of thy hired servants.
20 And he arose, and came to his father. But when he was yet a great way off, his father saw him, and had compassion, and ran, and fell on his neck, and kissed him.
21 And the son said unto him, Father, I have sinned against heaven, and in thy sight, and am no more worthy to be called thy son.
22 But the father said to his servants, Bring

Literal Translation

out the best robe and clothe him, and give a ring for his hand and sandals for (his) feet.

23 And bring the fattened calf, slaughter and let us eat and be merry;
24 for this son of mine was dead, and lived again, and was lost, and was found. And they began to be merry.

25. But his older son was in a field. And coming, as he drew near to the house, he heard music and dances.
26 And having called to (him) one of the children, he inquired what this may be.
27 And he said to him, Your brother came, and your father killed the fattened calf, because he received him back in health.

28 But he was angry and did not desire to go in. Then coming out, his father begged him.
29 But answering, he said to the father, Behold, so many years I serve you, and never have I transgressed a command of you. And you never gave a goat (to me), so that I might be merry with my friends.
30 But when this son of yours came, the one having devoured your living with harlots, you killed the fattened calf for him.

31 But he said to him, Child, you are always with me, and all of my things are yours.

32 But to be merry and to rejoice was right, for this brother of yours was dead, and lived again; and having been lost, also (he) was found.

Luke 15:23

1627 3588 4749 3588 4413 2532 1746 846 2532
νέγκατε τὴν στολὴν τὴν πρώτην καὶ ἐνδύσατε αὐτόν, καὶ
out robe the first and clothe him, and

1325 1146 1519 3588 5495 846 2532 5266 1519 3588
δότε δακτύλιον εἰς τὴν χεῖρα αὐτοῦ, καὶ ὑποδήματα εἰς τοὺς
give a ring to the hand of him, and sandals to the

4228 2532 5342 3588 3448 3588 4618 2380 2532
πόδας· 23 καὶ ἐνέγκαντες τὸν μόσχον τὸν σιτευτόν θύσατε, καὶ
feet; and having brought the calf fattened kill (it), and

5315 2165 3754 3778 3588 5207 3450 3498 2258 2532
φαγόντες εὐφρανθῶμεν· 24 ὅτι οὗτος ὁ υἱός μου νεκρὸς ἦν, καὶ
having eaten let us be merry; because this the son of me dead was, and

326 2532 622 2258 2532 2147 2532 756
ἀνέζησε· καὶ ἀπολωλὼς ἦν, καὶ εὑρέθη. καὶ ἤρξαντο
lived again; and lost was, and was found. And they began

2165 2258 1161 3588 5207 846 3588 4245 1722 68
εὐφραίνεσθαι. 25 ἦν δὲ ὁ υἱὸς αὐτοῦ ὁ πρεσβύτερος ἐν ἀγρῷ·
to be merry. was And the son of him older in a field;

2532 5613 2064 1448 3588 3614 191 4858 2532
καὶ ὡς ἐρχόμενος ἤγγισε τῇ οἰκίᾳ, ἤκουσε συμφωνίας καὶ
and as coming he drew near to the house, he heard music and

5525 2532 4341 1520 3588 3816 4441
χορῶν, 26 καὶ προσκαλεσάμενος ἕνα τῶν παίδων, ἐπυνθάνετο
dances, and having called to (him) one of the children, he inquired

5101 1498 5023 3588 1161 2036 846 3754 3588 80 4675 2240
τί εἴη ταῦτα. 27 ὁ δὲ εἶπεν αὐτῷ ὅτι Ὁ ἀδελφός σου ἥκει·
what may be these things. he And said to him, The brother of you came.;

2532 2380 3588 3962 4675 3588 3448 3588 4618 3754
καὶ ἔθυσεν ὁ πατήρ σου τὸν μόσχον τὸν σιτευτόν, ὅτι
and killed the father of you the calf fattened, because

5198 846 618 3710 1161 2532 3756 2309
ὑγιαίνοντα αὐτὸν ἀπέλαβεν. 28 ὠργίσθη δὲ καὶ οὐκ ἤθελεν
being in health him he received back. he was angry But and not desired

1525 3588 3767 3962 846 1831 3870 846 3588 1161
εἰσελθεῖν· ὁ οὖν πατὴρ αὐτοῦ ἐξελθὼν παρεκάλει αὐτόν. 29 ὁ δὲ
to go in; the then father of him coming out begged him. he But

611 2036 3588 3962 2400 5118 2094 1398 4671
ἀποκριθεὶς εἶπε τῷ πατρὶ, Ἰδού, τοσαῦτα ἔτη δουλεύω σοι,
answering said to the father, Behold, so many years I serve you,

2532 3763 1785 4675 3928 2532 1698 3763
καὶ οὐδέποτε ἐντολήν σου παρῆλθον, καὶ ἐμοὶ οὐδέποτε
and never a command of you I transgressed, and to me never

1325 2056 2443 3326 3588 5384 3450 2165 3753 1161 3588
ἔδωκας ἔριφον, ἵνα μετὰ τῶν φίλων μου εὐφρανθῶ· 30 ὅτε δὲ ὁ
you gave a goat that with the friends of me I might be merry; when but

5207 4675 3778 3588 2719 4675 3588 979 3326 4204
υἱός σου οὗτος ὁ καταφαγών σου τὸν βίον μετὰ πορνῶν
son of you this the (one) having devoured of you the living with harlots

2064 2380 846 3588 3448 3588 4618 3588 1161 2036
ἦλθεν, ἔθυσας αὐτῷ τὸν μόσχον τὸν σιτευτὸν. 31 ὁ δὲ εἶπεν
came, you killed for him the calf fattened. he And said

846 5043 4771 3842 3326 1700 1488 2532 3956 3588 1699 4674
αὐτῷ, Τέκνον, σὺ πάντοτε μετ᾽ ἐμοῦ εἶ, καὶ πάντα τὰ ἐμὰ σά
to him, Child, you always with me are, and all the things of me yours

2076 2165 1161 2532 5463 1163 3754 3588 80 4675
ἐστιν· 32 εὐφρανθῆναι δὲ καὶ χαρῆναι ἔδει· ὅτι ὁ ἀδελφός σου
are; to be merry and also to rejoice it is right; because brother of you

3778 3498 2258 2532 326 2532 622 2258 2532 2147
οὗτος νεκρὸς ἦν, καὶ ἀνέζησε· καὶ ἀπολωλὼς ἦν, καὶ εὑρέθη.
this dead was, and lived again; also (he) being lost was, and was found.

King James Version

forth the best robe, and put (it) on him; and put a ring on his hand, and shoes on (his) feet:

23 And bring hither the fatted calf, and kill (it); and let us eat, and be merry:
24 For this my son was dead, and is alive again; he was lost, and is found. And they began to be merry.

25. Now his elder son was in the field: and as he came and drew nigh to the house, he heard musick and dancing.

26 And he called one of the servants, and asked what these things meant.
27 And he said unto him, Thy brother is come; and thy father hath killed the fatted calf, because he hath received him safe and sound.
28 And he was angry, and would not go in: therefore came his father out, and intreated him.
29 And he answering said to (his) father, Lo, these many years do I serve thee, neither transgressed I at any time thy commandment: and yet thou never gavest me a kid, that I might make merry with my friends:
30 But as soon as this thy son was come, which hath devoured thy living with harlots, thou hast killed for him the fatted calf.
31 And he said unto him, Son, thou art ever with me, and all that I have is thine.

32 It was meet that we should make merry, and be glad: for this thy brother was dead, and is alive again; and was lost, and is found.

Literal Translation

Luke 16

1. And He also said to His disciples, A certain man was rich; who had a steward, and this one was accused to him as wasting his possessions.

2 And having called him, he said to him, What (is) this I hear about you? Give the account of your stewardship, for you are not able still to be steward.
3 And the steward said within himself, What shall I do, for my Lord is taking away the stewardship from me? I am not able to dig, and I am ashamed to beg.

4 I know what I will do, that when I am removed (from) the stewardship, they will receive me into their houses.
5 And having called to him each one of the debtors of his lord, he said to the first, How much do you owe my lord?

6 And he said, A hundred baths of oil. And he said to him, Take your statement and sitting quickly write fifty.
7 Then he said to another, And you, how much do you owe? And he said, a hundred cors of wheat. And he said to him, Take your statement and write eighty.

8 And the lord praised the steward of unrighteousness because he acted prudently. For the sons of this age are more prudent than the sons of light themselves are in their generation.
9 And I say to you, Make to yourselves friends by the mammon of unrighteousness, that when you fail they may receive you into the eternal dwellings.
10 The (one) faithful in (the) least is also faithful in

Luke 16:1

3004 1161 2532 4314 3588 3101 846 444 5100 2258
1. Ἔλεγε δὲ καὶ πρὸς τοὺς μαθητάς αὐτοῦ, Ἄνθρωπός τις ἦν
He said And also to the disciples of Him, man A certain was

4145 3739 2192 3623 2532 3778 1225 846 5613
πλούσιος, ὃς εἶχεν οἰκονόμον· καὶ οὗτος διεβλήθη αὐτῷ ὡς
rich, who had a steward; and this one was accused to him as

1287 3588 5224 846 2532 5455 846
διασκορπίζων τὰ ὑπάρχοντα αὐτοῦ. 2 καὶ φωνήσας αὐτὸν
wasting the possessions of him. And having called him

2036 846 5101 5124 191 4012 4675 591 3588 3056
εἶπεν αὐτῷ, Τί τοῦτο ἀκούω περὶ σοῦ; ἀπόδος τὸν λόγον
he said to him, What (is) this I hear about you? Give the account

3588 3622 4675 3756 1063 1410 2089 3621 2036 1161
τῆς οἰκονομίας σου· οὐ γὰρ δύνήσῃ ἔτι οἰκονομεῖν. 3 εἶπε δὲ
of the stewardship of you; not for you are able still to be steward. said And

1722 1438 3588 3623 5101 4160 3754 3588 2962 3450 851
ἐν ἑαυτῷ ὁ οἰκονόμος, Τί ποιήσω, ὅτι ὁ κύριός μου ἀφαι-
within himself the steward, What may I do, because the lord of me takes

851 3588 3622 575 1700 4626 3756 2480 1871
ρεῖται τὴν οἰκονομίαν ἀπ᾽ ἐμοῦ; σκάπτειν οὐκ ἰσχύω, ἐπαι-
away the stewardship from me? to dig not I am able, to

153 1097 5101 4160 2443 3752 3179
τεῖν αἰσχύνομαι. 4 ἔγνων τί ποιήσω, ἵνα, ὅταν μετασταθῶ
beg I am ashamed. I know what I may do, that when I am removed

3588 3622 209 3165 1519 3588 3624 846 2532
τῆς οἰκονομίας, δέξωνταί με εἰς τοὺς οἴκους αὐτῶν. 5 καὶ
(from) the stewardship, they receive me into the houses of them. And

4341 1520 1538 3588 5533 3588 2962
προσκαλεσάμενος ἕνα ἕκαστον τῶν χρεωφειλετῶν τοῦ κυρίου
having called to (him) one each of the debtors of the lord

1438 3004 3588 4413 4214 3784 3588 2962 3450
ἑαυτοῦ, ἔλεγε τῷ πρώτῳ, Πόσον ὀφείλεις τῷ κυρίῳ μου;
of himself, he said to the first, How much do you owe to the lord of me?

3588 1161 2036 1540 943 1637 2532 2036 846 1209 4675
6 ὁ δὲ εἶπεν, Ἑκατὸν βάτους ἐλαίου. καὶ εἶπεν αὐτῷ, Δέξαι σου
he And said, A hundred baths of oil. And he said to him, Take of you

3588 1121 2532 2523 5030 1125 4004 1899
τὰ γράμμα, καὶ καθίσας ταχέως γράψον πεντήκοντα. 7 ἔπειτα
the statement and sitting quickly write fifty. Then

2087 2036 4771 1161 4214 3784 3588 1161 2036 1540 2884
ἑτέρῳ εἶπε, Σὺ δὲ πόσον ὀφείλεις; ὁ δὲ εἶπεν, Ἑκατὸν κόρους
to another he said, you And how much owe you? he And said, a hundred cors

4621 2532 3004 846 1209 4675 3588 1121 2532 1125
σίτου. καὶ λέγει αὐτῷ, Δέξαι σου τὸ γράμμα, καὶ γράψον
of wheat. And he said to him, take of you the statement, and write

3589 2532 1867 3588 2962 3588 3623 3588
ὀγδοήκοντα. 8 καὶ ἐπῄνεσεν ὁ κύριος τὸν οἰκονόμον τῆς
eighty. And praised the lord the steward

93 3754 5430 4160 3754 3588 5207 3588 165 5127
ἀδικίας ὅτι φρονίμως ἐποίησεν· ὅτι οἱ υἱοὶ τοῦ αἰῶνος τούτου
of unrighteousness that prudently he acted; because the sons age of this

5429 5228 3588 5207 3588 5457 1519 3588 1074
φρονιμώτεροι ὑπὲρ τοὺς υἱοὺς τοῦ φωτὸς εἰς τὴν γενεὰν
more prudent than the sons of the light in the generation

1438 1526 2504 5213 3004 4160 1438 5384 1537
ἑαυτῶν εἰσι. 9 κἀγὼ ὑμῖν λέγω, Ποιήσατε ἑαυτοῖς φίλους ἐκ
of themselves are. And I to you say, Make to yourselves friends from

3588 3126 3588 93 2443 3752 1587 1209 5209
τοῦ μαμωνᾶ τῆς ἀδικίας, ἵνα, ὅταν ἐκλίπητε. δέξωνται ὑμᾶς
the mammon of unrighteousness, that, when you fail, they may receive you

1519 3588 166 4633 3588 4103 1722 1646 2532 1722
εἰς τὰς αἰωνίους σκηνάς. 10 ὁ πιστὸς ἐν ἐλαχίστῳ καὶ ἐν
into the everlasting dwellings. The (one) faithful in least also in

King James Version

Luke 16

1. And he said also unto his disciples, There was a certain rich man, which had a steward; and the same was accused unto him that he had wasted his goods.
2 And he called him, and said unto him, How is it that I hear this of thee? give an account of thy stewardship; for thou mayest be no longer steward.
3 Then the steward said within himself, What shall I do? for my lord taketh away from me the stewardship: I cannot dig; to beg I am ashamed.

4 I am resolved what to do, that, when I am put out of the stewardship, they may receive me into their houses.
5 So he called every one of his lord's debtors (unto him), and said unto the first, How much owest thou unto my lord?

6 And he said, An hundred measures of oil. And he said unto him, Take thy bill, and sit down quickly, and write fifty.
7 Then said he to another, And how much owest thou? And he said, An hundred measures of wheat. And he said unto him, Take thy bill, and write fourscore.
8 And the lord commended the unjust steward, because he had done wisely: for the children of this world are in their generation wiser than the children of light.

9 And I say unto you, Make to yourselves friends of the mammon of unrighteousness; that, when ye fail, they may receive you into everlasting habitations.
10 He that is faithful in that which is least is faithful also in

Literal Translation

much. And he unrighteous in the least is also unrighteous in much.
11 Then if you were not faithful in the unrighteous mammon, who will entrust the true to you?
12 And if you were not faithful in that of another, who will give to you that (which is) yours?
13 No houseslave is able to serve two lords; for either he will hate the one, and he will love the other; or he will cling to one, and he will despise the other. You are unable to serve God and mammon.

14. And being lovers of money, the Pharisees also heard all these things; and they derided Him.
15 And He said to them, You are those justifying, yourselves before men, but God knows your hearts; for the thing highly prized among men is a hateful thing before God.

16 The Law and the Prophets (were) until John; from then the kingdom of God is being preached, and (to get) into it everyone is taking (it) by force..
17 But it is easier (for) the heaven and the earth to pass away than one horn-like stroke of the Law to fail.

18 Everyone putting away his wife, and marrying another, commits adultery. And everyone marrying her having been put away from a husband commits adultery.
19. And there was a certain rich man; and customarily put on a purple robe and fine linen, making merry luxuriously day by day.
20 And there was a certain poor one named Lazarus who had been laid at

Luke 16:11

4183 4103 2076 2532 3588 1722 646 94 2532 1722 4183
πολλῷ πιστός ἐστι, καὶ ὁ ἐν ἐλαχίστῳ ἄδικος καὶ ἐν πολλῷ
much faithful is, and the (one) in least unrighteous also in much

94 2076 1487 3767 1722 3588 94 3126 4103 3756
ἄδικός ἐστιν. 11 εἰ οὖν ἐν τῷ ἀδίκῳ μαμωνᾷ πιστοὶ οὐκ
unrighteous is. if Then in the unrighteous mammon faithful not

1096 3588 228 5101 5213 4100 2532/1487/1722/3588/245
ἐγένεσθε, τὸ ἀληθινὸν τίς ὑμῖν πιστεύσει; 12 καὶ εἰ ἐν τῷ ἀλλο-
you were, the true who to you will entrust? And if in that of

4103 3756 1096 3588 5212 5101 5213 1325 3762
τρίῳ πιστοὶ οὐκ ἐγένεσθε, τὸ ὑμέτερον τίς ὑμῖν δώσει; 13 οὐδεὶς
another faithful not you were, (that) being yours who to you will give? No

3610 1410 1417 2962 1398 2228 1063 3588 1520
οἰκέτης δύναται δυσὶ κυρίοις δουλεύειν· ἢ γὰρ τὸν ἕνα
houseslave is able two lords to serve; either for the one

3404 2532 3588 2087 25 2228 1520 472 2532 3588
μισήσει, καὶ τὸν ἕτερον ἀγαπήσει· ἢ ἑνὸς ἀνθέξεται, καὶ τοῦ
he will hate, and the other he will love; or one he will cling to, and the

2087 2706 3756 1410 2316 1398 2532 3126
ἑτέρου καταφρονήσει. οὐ δύνασθε Θεῷ δουλεύειν καὶ μαμωνᾷ.
other he will despise. not You are able God to serve and mammon.

191 1161 5023 3956 2532 3588 5330 5366
14. Ἤκουον δὲ ταῦτα πάντα καὶ οἱ Φαρισαῖοι φιλάργυροι
heard And these things all also the Pharisees money-lovers

5225 2532 1592 846 2532 2036 846
ὑπάρχοντες, καὶ ἐξεμυκτήριζον αὐτόν. 15 καὶ εἶπεν αὐτοῖς,
being, and they derided Him. And He said to them,

5210 2075 3588 1344 1438 1799 3588 444
Ὑμεῖς ἐστε οἱ δικαιοῦντες ἑαυτοὺς ἐνώπιον τῶν ἀνθρώπων,
You are those justifying yourselves before men,

3588 1161 2316 1097 3588 2588 5216 3754 3588 1722 444
ὁ δὲ Θεὸς γινώσκει τὰς καρδίας ὑμῶν· ὅτι τὸ ἐν ἀνθρώποις
but God knows the hearts of you; because that among men

5308 946 1799 3588 2316 2076 3588 3551 2532 3588
ὑψηλὸν βδέλυγμα ἐνώπιον τοῦ Θεοῦ ἐστιν. 16 ὁ νόμος καὶ οἱ
highly prized an abomination before God is. The Law and the

4396 2193 2491 575 5119 3588 932 3588 2316
προφῆται εως Ἰωάννου· ἀπὸ τότε ἡ βασιλεία τοῦ Θεοῦ
prophets (were) until John; from then the kingdom of God

2097 2532 3956 1519 846 971 2123 1161
εὐαγγελίζεται, καὶ πᾶς εἰς αὐτὴν βιάζεται. 17 εὐκοπώτερον δέ
is being preached, and everyone into it is taking by force. easier But

2076 3588 3772 2532 3588 1093 3928 2228 3588 3551 3391
ἐστι τὸν οὐρανὸν καὶ τὴν γῆν παρελθεῖν, ἢ τοῦ νόμου μίαν
it is the heaven and the earth to pass away,than of the Law one

2762 4098 3956 3588 630 3588 1135 846 2532
κεραίαν πεσεῖν. 18 πᾶς ὁ ἀπολύων τὴν γυναῖκα αὐτοῦ καὶ
little horn to fail. Everyone putting away the wife of him and

1060 2087 3431 2532 3956 3588 630 575
γαμῶν ἑτέραν μοιχεύει· και πᾶς ὁ ἀπολελυμένην ἀπὸ
marrying another commits adultery and everyone having put her away from

435 1060 3431
ἀνδρὸς γαμῶν μοιχεύει.
a husband marrying commits adultery.

444 1161 5100 2258 4145 2532 1737
19. Ἄνθρωπος δέ τις ἦν πλούσιος, καὶ ἐνεδιδύσκετο
man And a certain was rich, and customarily put on

4209 2532 1040 2165 2596 2250 2988
πορφύραν καὶ βύσσον, εὐφραινόμενος καθ' ἡμέραν λαμπρῶς.
a purple robe and fine linen, being merry day by day luxuriously.

4434 1161 5100 2258 3686 2976 3739 906 4314 3588
20 πτωχὸς δέ τις ἦν ὀνόματι Λάζαρος, ὃς ἐβέβλητο πρὸς τὸν
poor one And a certain was by name Lazarus, who had been laid at the

King James Version

much: and he that is unjust in the least is unjust also in much.

11 If therefore ye have not been faithful in the unrighteous mammon, who will commit to your trust the true (riches)?
12 And if ye have not been faithful in that which is another man's, who shall give you that which is your own?
13 No servant can serve two masters: for either he will hate the one, and love the other; or else he will hold to the one, and despise the other. Ye cannot serve God and mammon.

14. And the Pharisees also, who were covetous, heard all these things: and they derided him.
15 And he said unto them, Ye are they which justify yourselves before men; but God knoweth your hearts: for that which is highly esteemed among men is abomination in the sight of God.

16 The law and the prophets (were) until John: since that time the kingdom of God is preached, and every man presseth into it.
17 And it is easier for heaven and earth to pass, than one tittle of the law to fail.

18 Whosoever putteth away his wife, and marrieth another, committeth adultery: and whosoever marrieth her that is put away from (her) husband committeth adultery.

19. There was a certain rich man, which was clothed in purple and fine linen, and fared sumptuously every day:
20 And there was a certain beggar named Lazarus, which was laid at

Literal Translation | **Luke 16:21** | **King James Version**

Literal Translation

his doorway, having been ulcerated,
21 and longing to be filled from the crumbs that were falling from the table of the rich one. But coming, even the dogs licked his sores.

22 And it happened, the poor one died and was carried away by the angels into the bosom of Abraham. And the rich one also died and was buried.
23 And being in torments in Hades, lifting up his eyes, he sees Abraham afar off and Lazarus in his bosoms.

24 And having called he said, Father Abraham, pity me and send Lazarus that he may dip the tip of his finger in water and may cool my tongue, for I am anguished in this flame.

25 But Abraham said, Child, remember that you fully received your good things in your lifetime, and Lazarus likewise the bad things. But now he is comforted, but you are suffering.
26 And besides all these things, a great chasm has been fixed between us and you, so that those desiring to pass from here to you are not able, nor can those cross over from there to us.

27 And he said, Then I beg you, father, that you send him to my father's house;

28 for I have five brothers, so that he may witness to them, that they not also come to this place of torment.
29 Abraham said to him, They have Moses and the

4440 846 1669 2532 937 5526 575
πυλῶνα αὐτοῦ ἡλκωμένος 21 καὶ ἐπιθυμῶν χορτασθῆναι ἀπὸ
door of him having been ulcerated and longing to be filled from

3588 5589 3588 4098 575 3588 5132 3588 4145
τῶν ψιχίων τῶν πιπτόντων ἀπὸ τῆς τραπέζης τοῦ πλουσίου·
the crumbs that were falling from the table of the rich (one).

235 2532 3588 2965 2064 621 3588 1668 846
ἀλλὰ καὶ οἱ κύνες ἐρχόμενοι ἀπέλειχον τὰ ἕλκη αὐτοῦ.
But even the dogs coming licked the sores of him.

1096 1161 599 3588 4434 2532 667 846
22 ἐγένετο δὲ ἀποθανεῖν τὸν πτωχὸν, καὶ ἀπενεχθῆναι αὐτὸν
it came to be And to die the poor (one). and to be carried away him

5259 3588 32 1519 3588 2859 3588 11 599 1161
ὑπὸ τῶν ἀγγέλων εἰς τὸν κόλπον τοῦ Ἀβραάμ· ἀπέθανε δὲ
by the angels into the bosom of Abraham; died and

2532 3588 4145 2532 2290 2532 1722 3588 86 1869 3588
καὶ ὁ πλούσιος καὶ ἐτάφη. 23 καὶ ἐν τῷ ᾅδῃ ἐπάρας τοὺς
also the rich one, and was buried. And in Hades lifting up the

3788 846 5225 1722 931 3708 3588 11
ὀφθαλμοὺς αὐτοῦ, ὑπάρχων ἐν βασάνοις, ὁρᾷ τὸν Ἀβραὰμ
eyes of him, being in torments, he sees Abraham

575 3113 2532 2976 1722 3588 2859 846 2532 846
ἀπὸ μακρόθεν, καὶ Λάζαρον ἐν τοῖς κόλποις αὐτοῦ. 24 καὶ αὐτὸς
from afar, and Lazarus in the bosoms of him. And he

5455 2036 3962 11 1653 3165 2532 3992
φωνήσας εἶπε, Πάτερ Ἀβραάμ, ἐλέησόν με, καὶ πέμψον
having called said, Father Abraham, pity me, and send

2976 2443 911 3588 206 3588 1147 846 5204
Λάζαρον, ἵνα βάψῃ τὸ ἄκρον τοῦ δακτύλου αὐτοῦ ὕδατος
Lazarus, that he may dip the tip of the finger of him of water

2532 2711 3588 1100 3450 3754 3600 1722 3588
καὶ καταψύξῃ τὴν γλῶσσάν μου· ὅτι ὀδυνῶμαι ἐν τῇ
and may cool the tongue of me; because I am anguished in

5395 3778 2036 1161 11 5043 3415 3754 618
φλογὶ ταύτῃ. 25 εἶπε δὲ Ἀβραάμ, Τέκνον, μνήσθητι ὅτι ἀπέ-
flame this. said But Abraham, Child, remember that fully

4771 3588 18 4675 1722 3588 2222 4675 2532 2976 3668
λαβες σὺ τὰ ἀγαθά σου ἐν τῇ ζωῇ σου, καὶ Λάζαρος ὁμοίως
received you the good of you in the life of you, and Lazarus likewise

3588 2556 3568 1161 3592 3870 4771 1161 3600 2532 1909
τὰ κακά· νῦν δὲ ὅδε παρακαλεῖται, σὺ δὲ ὀδυνᾶσαι. 26 καὶ ἐπὶ
the bad. now But here he is comforted, you but are suffering. And over

3956 5125 3342 2257 2532 5216 5490 3173 4741
πᾶσι τούτοις, μεταξὺ ἡμῶν καὶ ὑμῶν χάσμα μέγα ἐστή-
all these things, between us and you a chasm great being

3704 3588 2309 1224 1782 4314 5209 3361
ρικται, ὅπως οἱ θέλοντες διαβῆναι ἐντεῦθεν πρὸς ὑμᾶς μὴ
fixed, so that the (ones) desiring to pass from here to you not

1410 3366 3588 1564 4314 2248 1276 2036 1161
δύνωνται, μηδὲ οἱ ἐκεῖθεν πρὸς ἡμᾶς διαπερῶσιν. 27 εἶπε δέ,
are able, nor those from there to us may cross over. he said And,

2065 3767 4571 3962 2443 3992 846 1519 3588 3624 3588
Ἐρωτῶ οὖν σε, πάτερ, ἵνα πέμψῃς αὐτὸν εἰς τὸν οἶκον τοῦ
I ask Then you, father, that you send him to the house of the

3962 3450 2192 1063 4002 80 3704 1263
πατρός μου, 28 ἔχω γὰρ πέντε ἀδελφούς, ὅπως διαμαρτύρηται
father of me, I have for five brothers, so that he may witness

846 2443 3361 2532 846 2064 1519 3588 5117 5126 3588
αὐτοῖς, ἵνα μὴ καὶ αὐτοὶ ἔλθωσιν εἰς τὸν τόπον τοῦτον τῆς
to them, that not also they come into place this

931 3004 846 11 2192 3475 2532 3588
βασάνου. 29 λέγει αὐτῷ Ἀβραάμ, Ἔχουσι Μωσέα καὶ τοὺς
of torment. says to him Abraham, They have Moses and the

King James Version

his gate, full of sores,
21 And desiring to be fed with the crumbs which fell from the rich man's table: moreover the dogs came and licked his sores.

22 And it came to pass, that the beggar died, and was carried by the angels into Abraham's bosom: the rich man also died, and was buried;
23 And in hell he lift up his eyes, being in torments, and seeth Abraham afar off, and Lazarus in his bosom.

24 And he cried and said, Father Abraham, have mercy on me, and send Lazarus, that he may dip the tip of his finger in water, and cool my tongue; for I am tormented in this flame.

25 But Abraham said, Son, remember that thou in thy lifetime receivedst thy good things, and likewise Lazarus evil things: but now he is comforted, and thou art tormented.
26 And beside all this, between us and you there is a great gulf fixed: so that they which would pass from hence to you cannot; neither can they pass to us, that (would come) from thence.

27 Then he said, I pray thee therefore, father, that thou wouldest send him to my father's house:

28 For I have five brethren; that he may testify unto them, lest they also come into this place of torment.
29 Abraham saith unto him, They have Moses and the

Literal Translation

Prophets, let them hear them.
30 But he said, No, father Abraham, but if, one should go from (the) dead to them, they will repent.

31 And he said to him, If they will not hear Moses and the Prophets, they will not be persuaded even if one from (the) dead should rise.

Luke 16:30

4396 191 846 3588 1161 2036 3780 3962
προφήτας· ἀκουσάτωσαν αὐτῶν. 30 ὁ δὲ εἶπεν, Οὐχί, πάτερ
Prophets; let them hear them. he But said, No, father
11 235 1437 5100 575 3498 4198 4314 846
Ἀβραάμ, ἀλλ᾽ ἐάν τις ἀπὸ νεκρῶν πορευθῇ πρὸς αὐτοὺς,
Abraham, but if anyone from (the) dead should go to them,
3340 2036 1161 846 1487 3475 2532 3588 4396
μετανοήσουσιν. 31 εἶπε δὲ αὐτῷ, Εἰ Μωσέως καὶ τῶν προφη-
they will repent. he said And to him, If Moses and the Prophets
3756 191 3761 1437 5100 1537 3498 450
τῶν οὐκ ἀκούουσιν, οὐδε, ἐάν τις ἐκ νεκρῶν ἀναστῇ
not they will hear, not even, if anyone from (the) dead should rise
3982
πεισθήσονται.
will they be persuaded.

King James Version

prophets; let them hear them.
30 And he said, Nay, father Abraham: but if one went unto them from the dead, they will repent.

31 And he said unto him, If they hear not Moses and the prophets, neither will they be persuaded, though one rose from the dead.

Luke 17

1. And He said to the disciples, It is impossible that the offenses not to come, but woe (to him) by whom they come!
2 It is profitable for him if a millstone of an ass is put around his neck, and he be thrown into the sea, than that he should offend one of these little ones.

3. Take heed to yourselves. And if your brother sins against you, rebuke him; and if he repents, forgive him.

4 And if seven times of the day he sins against you, and seven times of the day turns to you saying, I repent, you shall forgive him.

5. And the apostles said to the Lord, Give us more faith.

6 But the Lord said, If you have faith as a grain of mustard, you may say to this sycamine tree, Be rooted up and be planted in the sea! And it would obey you.
7 But who of you having a slave plowing or feeding will say at once (to him) coming out of the field, Coming up, recline?

8 But will he not say

Luke 17

2036 1161 4314 3588 3101 418 2076 3588 3361
1. Εἶπε δὲ πρὸς τοὺς μαθητὰς, Ἀνένδεκτόν ἐστι τοῦ μὴ
He said And to the disciples, impossible It is not
2064 3588 4625 3759 1161 1223 3739 2064 3081 846
ἐλθεῖν τὰ σκάνδαλα· οὐαὶ δὲ δι᾽ οὗ ἔρχεται. 2 λυσιτελεῖ αὐτῷ
to come the offenses; woe but through whom they come. It profits him
1487 3458 3684 4029 4012 3588 5137 846 2532
εἰ μύλος ὀνικὸς περίκειται περὶ τὸν τράχηλον αὐτοῦ, καὶ
if a millstone of an ass is put around the neck of him, and
4496 1519 3588 2281 2228 2443 4624 1520 3588
ἔρριπται εἰς τὴν θάλασσαν, ἢ ἵνα σκανδαλίσῃ ἕνα τῶν
had been thrown into the sea, than that he should offend one
3398 5130 4337 1438 1437 1161 264 1519 4571 3588
μικρῶν τούτων. 3 προσέχετε ἑαυτοῖς. ἐὰν δὲ ἁμάρτῃ εἰς σὲ ὁ
little ones of these. Take heed to yourselves. if And sins against you the
80 4675 2008 846 2532 1437 3340 863
ἀδελφός σου, ἐπιτίμησον αὐτῷ· καὶ ἐὰν μετανοήσῃ, ἄφες
brother of you, rebuke him; and if he repents, forgive
846 2532 1437 2034 3588 2250 264 1519 4571 2532
αὐτῷ· 4 καὶ ἐὰν ἑπτάκις τῆς ἡμέρας ἁμάρτῃ εἰς σὲ, καὶ
him. And if seven times of the day he sins against you, and
2034 3588 2250 1994 1909 4571 3004 3340
ἑπτάκις τῆς ἡμέρας ἐπιστρέψῃ ἐπί σε, λέγων, Μετανοῶ,
seven times of the day should turn to you, sayng, I repent,
863 846
ἀφήσεις αὐτῷ.
you shall forgive him.

2532 2036 3588 652 3588 2962 4369 2254 4102
5. Καὶ εἶπον οἱ ἀπόστολοι τῷ Κυρίῳ, Πρόσθες ἡμῖν πίστιν.
And said the apostles of the Lord, Increase to us faith.
2036 1161 3588 2962 1487 2192 4102 5613 2848 4615
6 εἶπε δὲ ὁ Κύριος, Εἰ εἴχετε πίστιν ὡς κόκκον σινάπεως,
said And the Lord, If you have faith as a grain of mustard,
3004 302 3588 4807 3778 1610 2532 5452
ἐλέγετε ἂν τῇ συκαμίνῳ ταύτῃ, Ἐκριζώθητι καὶ φυτεύθητι
you may say sycamine to this, Be rooted up, and be planted
1722 3588 2281 2532 5219 302 5213 5101 1161 1537 5216 1401
ἐν τῇ θαλάσσῃ· καὶ ὑπήκουσεν ἂν ὑμῖν. 7 τίς δὲ ἐξ ὑμῶν δοῦλον
in the sea; and it would obey you. who But of you a slave
2192 722 2228 4165 3739 1525 1537 3588
ἔχων ἀροτριῶντα ἢ ποιμαίνοντα, ὃς εἰσελθόντι ἐκ τοῦ
having plowing or shepherding, who (to him) having come from the
68 2046 2112 3928 377 235 3780 2046
ἀγροῦ ἐρεῖ εὐθέως, παρελθὼν ἀνάπεσαι· 8 ἀλλ᾽ οὐχὶ ἐρεῖ
field will say immediately, Coming up recline; but not will say

Luke 17

1. Then said he unto the disciples, It is impossible but that offences will come: but woe (unto him), through whom they come!
2 It were better for him that a millstone were hanged about his neck, and he cast into the sea, than that he should offend one of these little ones.

3. Take heed to yourselves: If thy brother trespass against thee, rebuke him; and if he repent, forgive him.

4 And if he trespass against thee seven times in a day, and seven times in a day turn again to thee, saying, I repent; thou shalt forgive him.

5. And the apostles said unto the Lord, Increase our faith.
6 And the Lord said, If ye had faith as a grain of mustard seed, ye might say unto this sycamine tree, Be thou plucked up by the root, and be thou planted in the sea; and it should obey you.
7 But which of you, having a servant plowing or feeding cattle, will say unto him by and by, when he is come from the field, Go and sit down to meat?
8 And will not rather say

Literal Translation | **Luke 17:9** | *King James Version*

to him, Prepare something I may eat, and having girded yourself, serve me until I eat and drink, and after these things you eat and drink?
9 (Does) he not have thanks to that slave because he did the things commanded of him? I think not.
10 So also when you have done all things commanded you, you say, We are unprofitable slaves, for we have done what we ought to do.

11. And it happened in His going into Jerusalem even He passed through (the) midst of Samaria and Galilee.
12 And He entering into a certain village, ten leprous men met Him, who stood afar off.
13 And they lifted (their) voice, saying, Jesus, Master, pity us.

14 And having seen (them), He said to them, Having gone, show yourselves to the priests. And it happened in their going they were cleansed.
15 And one of them, having seen that he was cured, returned glorifying God with a loud voice.

16 And (he) fell on (his) face at His feet, giving thanks to Him. And he was a Samaritan.

17 And answering, Jesus said, Were not the ten cleansed? But where (are) the nine?
18 Were not (any) found having returned to give glory to God except this foreign (one)?
19 And He said to him, Having risen, go! Your faith has cured you.

20. And having been questioned by the Pharisees (as to) when the

846 2090 5101 1172 2532 4024 1247
αὐτῷ, Ἑτοίμασον τί δειπνήσω, καὶ περιζωσάμενος διακόνει
to him, Prepare something I may eat, and having girded yourself serve

3427 2193 5315 2532 4095 2532 3326 5023 5315 2532 4095
μοι, ἕως φάγω καὶ πίω· καὶ μετὰ ταῦτα φάγεσαι καὶ πίεσαι
me until I eat and drink; and after these things eat and drink

4771 3361 5485 2192 3588 1401 1565 3754 4160 3588
σύ; 9 μὴ χάριν ἔχει τῷ δούλῳ ἐκείνῳ ὅτι ἐποίησε τὰ δια-
you? Not thanks has he slave to that because he did the things

1299 846 3756 1380 3779 2532 5210 3752 4160
ταχθέντα αὐτῷ; οὐ δοκῶ. 10 οὕτω καὶ ὑμεῖς, ὅταν ποιήσητε
commanded of him? not I think. So also you, when you have done

3956 3588 1299 5213 300 3754 1401 888 2070
πάντα τὰ διαταχθέντα ὑμῖν, λέγετε ὅτι Δοῦλοι ἀχρεῖοί ἐσμεν·
all the things commanded you, say, slaves Unprofitable we are;

3754 3739 3784 4160 4160
ὅτι ὃ ὠφείλομεν ποιῆσαι πεποιήκαμεν.
what we ought to do we have done.

2532 1096 1722 3588 4198 846 1519 2419
11. Καὶ ἐγένετο ἐν τῷ πορεύεσθαι αὐτὸν εἰς Ἱερουσαλὴμ,
And it happened in the (trip) to go Him into Jerusalem,

2532 846 1330 1223 3319 4540 2532 1056 2532
καὶ αὐτὸς διήρχετο διὰ μέσου Σαμαρείας καὶ Γαλιλαίας. 12 καὶ
even He passed through (the) midst of Samaria and Galilee. And

1525 846 1519 5100 2968 528 846 1176
εἰσερχομένου αὐτοῦ εἴς τινα κώμην, ἀπήντησαν αὐτῷ δέκα
having entered Him into certain a village, met Him ten

3015 435 3739 2476 4207 2532 846 142 5456
λεπροὶ ἄνδρες, οἳ ἔστησαν πόρρωθεν, 13 καὶ αὐτοὶ ἦραν φωνὴν,
leprous men, who stood afar off, and they lifted voice,

3004 2424 1988 1653 2248 2532 1492 2036
λέγοντες, Ἰησοῦ, ἐπιστάτα, ἐλέησον ἡμᾶς. 14 καὶ ἰδὼν εἶπεν
saying, Jesus, Master, pity us. And seeing He said

846 4198 1925 1438 3588 2409 2532
αὐτοῖς, Πορευθέντες ἐπιδείξατε ἑαυτοὺς τοῖς ἱερεῦσι. καὶ
to them, Having gone show yourselves to the priests. And

1096 1722 3588 5217 846 2511 1520 1161 1537
ἐγένετο ἐν τῷ ὑπάγειν αὐτοὺς, ἐκαθαρίσθησαν. 15 εἷς δὲ ἐξ
it happened in the (way) to go them, they were cleansed. one But of

846 1492 3754 2390 5290 3326 5456 3137
αὐτῶν, ἰδὼν ὅτι ἰάθη, ὑπέστρεψε μετὰ φωνῆς μεγάλης
them, having seen that he was cured, returned with a voice great

1392 3588 2316 2532 4098 1909 4383 3844 3588
δοξάζων τὸν Θεόν· 16 καὶ ἔπεσεν ἐπὶ πρόσωπον παρὰ τοὺς
glorifying God; and fell on (his) face at the

4228 846 2168 846 2532 846 2258 4541
πόδας αὐτου, εὐχαριστῶν αὐτῷ· καὶ αὐτὸς ἦν Σαμαρείτης.
feet of Him, giving thanks to Him; and he was a Samaritan.

611 1161 3588 2424 2036 3780 3588 1176 2511
17 ἀποκριθεὶς δὲ ὁ Ἰησοῦς εἶπεν, Οὐχὶ οἱ δέκα ἐκαθαρίσθησαν;
answering And Jesus said, Not the ten were cleansed?

3588 1161 1767 4226 3756 2147 5290 1325
οἱ δὲ ἐννέα ποῦ; 18 ουχ εὑρέθησαν ὑποστρέψαντες δουναι
the But nine where? Not were found having returned to give

1391 3588 2316 1487 3361 3588 241 3778 2532 2036 846
δόξαν τῷ Θεῷ, εἰ μὴ ὁ ἀλλογενὴς οὗτος, 19 καὶ εἶπεν αὐτῷ,
glory to God, except foreign (one) this. And He said to him,

450 4198 3588 4102 4675 4982 4571
Ἀναστὰς πορεύου· ἡ πίστις σου σέσωκέ σε.
Having risen go; the faith of you has cured you.

1905 1161 5259 3588 5330 4219 2064 3588
20. Ἐπερωτηθεὶς δὲ ὑπὸ τῶν Φαρισαίων, πότε ἔρχεται ἡ
having been questioned And by the Pharisees, when comes the

unto him, Make ready wherewith I may sup, and gird thyself, and serve me, till I have eaten and drunken; and afterward thou shalt eat and drink?
9 Doth he thank that servant because he did the things that were commanded him? I trow not.
10 So likewise ye, when ye shall have done all those things which are commanded you, say, We are unprofitable servants: we have done that which was our duty to do.

11. And it came to pass, as he went to Jerusalem, that he passed through the midst of Samaria and Galilee.
12 And as he entered into a certain village, there met him ten men that were lepers, which stood afar off:
13 And they lifted up (their) voices, and said, Jesus, Master, have mercy on us.
14 And when he saw (them), he said unto them, Go shew yourselves unto the priests. And it came to pass, that, as they went, they were cleansed.
15 And one of them, when he saw that he was healed, turned back, and with a loud voice glorified God,

16 And fell down on (his) face at his feet, giving him thanks: and he was a Samaritan.

17 And Jesus answering said, Were there not ten cleansed? but where (are) the nine?
18 There are not found that returned to give glory to God, save this stranger.
19 And he said unto him, Arise, go thy way: thy faith hath made thee whole.
20. And when he was demanded of the Pharisees, when the

Literal Translation **Luke 17:21** ***King James Version***

kingdom of God comes, He answered them and said, The kingdom of God does not come with observation;
21 nor will they say, Behold, here! Or, Behold, there! For behold the kingdom of God is in your midst.

932 3588 2316 611 846 2532 2036 3756 2064
βασιλεία τοῦ Θεοῦ, ἀπεκρίθη αὐτοῖς καὶ εἶπεν, Οὐκ ἔρχεται
kingdom of God, He answered them and said, Not comes
3588 932 3588 2316 3326 3907 3761 2046
ἡ βασιλεία τοῦ Θεοῦ μετὰ παρατηρήσεως, 21 οὐδὲ ἐροῦσιν,
the kingdom of God with observation, nor will they say,
2400 5602 2228 2400 1563 2400 1063 3588 932 3588 2316 1787
Ἰδοὺ ὧδε, ἤ, ἰδοὺ ἐκεῖ. ἰδοὺ γάρ, ἡ βασιλεία τοῦ Θεοῦ ἐντὸς
Behold, here! Or, Behold there! behold For, the kingdom of God within
5216 2076
ὑμῶν ἐστιν.
you is.

kingdom of God should come, he answered them and said, The kingdom of God cometh not with observation:
21 Neither shall they say, Lo here! or, lo there! for, behold, the kingdom of God is within you.

22. And He said to the disciples, Days will come when you will long to see one of the days of the Son of man, and will not see.
23 And they will say to you, Behold, here! Or, Behold, there! Do not go away, nor follow.
24 For as the lightning which lights up out of that under heaven and shines to the (other part) under heaven, so also will the Son of man be in His day.
25 But first He must suffer many things and be rejected from this generation.
26 And as it was in the days of Noah, so also it will be in the days of the Son of man.

2036 1161 4314 3588 3101 2064 2250 3753
22. Εἶπε δὲ πρὸς τοὺς μαθητάς, Ἐλεύσονται ἡμέραι ὅτε
He said And to the disciples, will come Days when
1937 3391 3588 2250 3588 5207 3588 444 1492
ἐπιθυμήσετε μίαν τῶν ἡμερῶν τοῦ υἱοῦ τοῦ ἀνθρώπου ἰδεῖν,
you will long one of the days of the Son of man to see,
2532 3756 3700 2532 2046 52 2400 5602 2228 2400 1563
καὶ οὐκ ὄψεσθε. 23 καὶ ἐροῦσιν ὑμῖν, Ἰδοὺ ὧδε, ἤ, ἰδοὺ ἐκεῖ·
and not will see. And they will say to you, Behold, here!, or, Behold, there!
3361 565 3366 1377 5618 1063 3588 796 3588 797
μὴ ἀπέλθητε, μηδὲ διώξητε. 24 ὥσπερ γὰρ ἡ ἀστραπὴ ἡ ἀστρά-
Not do go away, nor follow. as For the lightning lighting up
1537 3588 5259 3772 1519 3588 5259 3772 2989 3779
πτουσα ἐκ τῆς ὑπ' οὐρανὸν εἰς τὴν ὑπ οὐρανὸν λάμπει, οὕτως
out of (one part) under heaven to (one part) under heaven shines, so
2071 2532 3588 5207 3588 444 1722 3588 2250 846 4412
ἔσται καὶ ὁ υἱὸς τοῦ ἀνθρώπου ἐν τῇ ἡμέρᾳ αὐτοῦ. 25 πρῶτον
will be also the Son of man in the day of Him. first
1161 1163 846 4183 3958 2532 593 575 3588
δὲ δεῖ αὐτὸν πολλὰ παθεῖν καὶ ἀποδοκιμασθῆναι ἀπὸ τῆς
But must Him many things to suffer and to be rejected from
1074 3778 2532 2531 1096 1722 3588 2250 3588 3575
γενεᾶς ταύτης. 26 καὶ καθὼς ἐγένετο ἐν ταῖς ἡμέραις τοῦ Νῶε,
generation this. And even as it was in the days of Noah,
3779 2071 2532 1722 3588 2250 3588 5207 3588 444
οὕτως ἔσται καὶ ἐν ταῖς ἡμέραις τοῦ υἱοῦ τοῦ ἀνθρώπου.
so it will be also in the days of the Son of man.

22. And he said unto the disciples, The days will come, when ye shall desire to see one of the days of the Son of man, and ye shall not see (it).
23 And they shall say to you, See here; or, see there: go not after (them), nor follow (them).
24 For as the lightning, that lighteneth out of the one (part) under heaven, shineth unto the other (part) under heaven; so shall also the Son of man be in his day.
25 But first must he suffer many things, and be rejected of this generation.
26 And as it was in the days of Noe, so shall it be also in the days of the Son of man.

27 They were eating, drinking, marrying, giving in marriage, until (the) day Noah went into the ark. And the Flood came and destroyed all.
28 And likewise, as it was in the days of Lot, they were eating, drinking, buying, selling, planting, building;
29 but on (the) day Lot went out from Sodom, it rained fire and brimstone from the heaven and destroyed all.
30 Even so it will be in the day the Son of man is revealed.

2068 4095 1060 1547 891 3739 2250
27 ἤσθιον, ἔπινον, ἐγάμουν, ἐξεγαμίζοντο, ἄχρι ἧς ἡμέρας
they were eating, drinking, marrying, giving in marriage, until which day
1525 3575 1519 3588 2787 2532 2064 3588 2627 2532
εἰσῆλθε Νῶε εἰς τὴν κιβωτόν, καὶ ἦλθεν ὁ κατακλυσμὸς, καὶ
went in Noah into the ark, and came the Flood, and
622 537 3668 2532 5613 1096 1722 3588 2250
ἀπώλεσεν ἅπαντας. 28 ὁμοίως καὶ ὡς ἐγένετο ἐν ταῖς ἡμέραις
destroyed all. Likewise also as it was in the day
3091 2068 4095 59 4453 5452
Λώτ· ἤσθιον, ἔπινον, ἠγόραζον, ἐπώλουν, ἐφύτευον,
of Lot; they were eating, drinking, buying, selling, planting,
3618 3739 1161 2250 1831 3091 575 4670 1026
ᾠκοδόμουν· 29 ᾗ δὲ ἡμέρᾳ ἐξῆλθε Λὼτ ἀπὸ Σοδόμων, ἔβρεξε
building; on which but day went out Lot from Sodom, it rained
4442 2532 2303 575 3772 2532 622 537 2596
πῦρ καὶ θεῖον ἀπ' οὐρανοῦ, καὶ ἀπώλεσεν ἅπάντας. 30 κατὰ
fire and brimstone from heaven, and destroyed all. According to
5024 2071 3739 2250 3588 5207 3588 444 601
ταὐτὰ ἔσται ᾗ ἡμέρᾳ ὁ υἱὸς τοῦ ἀνθρώπου ἀποκαλύπτεται.
the same will be in the day the Son of man is revealed.

27 They did eat, they drank, they married wives, they were given in marriage, until the day that Noe entered into the ark, and the flood came, and destroyed them all.
28 Likewise also as it was in the days of Lot; they did eat, they drank, they bought, they sold, they planted, they builded;
29 But the same day that Lot went out of Sodom it rained fire and brimstone from heaven, and destroyed (them) all.
30 Even thus shall it be in the day when the Son of man is revealed.

31 In that day, (he) who will be on the housetop,

1722 1565 3588 2250 3739 2071 1909 3588 1430 2532 3588
31 ἐν ἐκείνῃ τῇ ἡμέρᾳ, ὃς ἔσται ἐπὶ τοῦ δώματος, καὶ τὰ
In that day, who(ever) will be on the housetop, and the

31 In that day, he which shall be upon the housetop, and

Literal Translation

Luke 17:32

King James Version

let him not come down to take his goods (from) the house. And likewise, he in the field, let him not turn back to the things behind.
32 Remember Lot's wife.
33 Whoever seeks to save his life, (he) will lose it. And whoever will lose it, he will preserve it.

34 I say to you, In that night two will be on one bed; the one will be taken and the other will be left.

35 Two will be grinding together; the one will be taken and the other will be left.
36 Two will be in the field; the one will be taken and the other will be left.

37 And answering, they said to Him, Where, Lord? And He said to them, Where the body (is), there the eagles will be gathered together.

4632 846 1722 3588 3614 3361 2597 142 846 2532 3588
σκεύη αὐτοῦ ἐν τῇ οἰκίᾳ, μὴ καταβάτω ἆραι αὐτά· καὶ ὁ
goods of him in the house, not let him go down to take them; and he

1722 3588 68 3668 3361 1994 1519 3588 3694 3421
ἐν τῷ ἀγρῷ ὁμοίως μὴ ἐπιστρεψάτω εἰς τὰ ὀπίσω. 32 μνη-
in the field likewise not let him turn back into the things behind. Re-

3588 1135 3091 3739 1437 2212 3588 5590
μονεύετε τῆς γυναικὸς Λώτ. 33 ὃς ἐὰν ζητήσῃ τὴν ψυχὴν
member the wife of Lot. Whoever seeks the life

846 4982 622 846 2532 3739 1437 622 846
αὐτοῦ σῶσαι ἀπλέσει αὐτήν· καὶ ὃς ἐὰν ἀπολέσῃ αὐτὴν
of him to save he will lose it; and whoever will lose it

2225 3004 5213 3778 3588 3571 2071 1417
ζωογονήσει. 34 λέγω ὑμῖν, ταύτῃ τῇ νυκτὶ ἔσονται δύο
will preserve it. I say to you in that night will be two

1909 2825 3391 3588 1520 3880 2532 3588 2087 863
ἐπὶ κλίνης μιᾶς· ὁ εἷς παραληφθήσεται καὶ ὁ ἕτερος ἀφεθή-
on bed one; the one will be taken, and the other will be

1417 2071 229 1909 3588 846 3588 3391 3880
σεται. 35 δύο ἔσονται ἀλήθουσαι ἐπὶ τὸ αὐτό· ἡ μία παρα-
left. Two will be grinding together; the one will be

2532 3588 2087 863 1417 2071 1722 3588
ληφθήσεται, καὶ ἡ ἑτέρα ἀφεθήσεται. 36 δύο ἔσονται ἐν τῷ
taken, and the other will be left. Two will be in the

68 3588 1520 3880 2532 3588 2086 863 2532
ἀγρῷ· ὁ εις παραληφθήσεται, καὶ ὁ ἕτερος ἀφεθήσεται. 37 καὶ
field; the one will be taken, and the other will be left. And

611 3004 846 4226 2962 3588 1161 2036 846
ἀποκριθέντες λέγουσιν αὐτῷ, Ποῦ, Κύριε; ὁ δὲ εἶπεν αὐτοῖς,
answering they say to Him, Where, Lord? He And said to them,

3699 3588 4983 1563 4863 3588 105
Ὅπου τὸ σῶμα, ἐκεῖ συναχθήσονται οἱ ἀετοί.
Where the body (is), there will be gathered the eagles.

his stuff in the house, let him not come down to take it away: and he that is in the field, let him likewise not return back.
32 Remember Lot's wife.
33 Whosoever shall seek to save his life shall lose it; and whosoever shall lose his life shall preserve it.

34 I tell you, in that night there shall be two (men) in one bed; the one shall be taken, and the other shall be left.

35 Two (women) shall be grinding together; the one shall be taken, and the other left.
36 Two (men) shall be in the field; the one shall be taken, and the other left.
37 And they answered and said unto him, Where, Lord? And he said unto them, Wheresoever the body (is), thither will the eagles be gathered together.

Luke 18

Luke 18

1. And He also spoke a parable to them to (teach) it is always right to pray, and not to faint,
2 saying, A certain judge was in a certain city, not fearing God and not respecting man.

3 And a widow was in that city, and she came to him, saying, Avenge me from my adversary.
4 And for a time he would not. But after these things he said within himself, Even if I do not fear God, and do not respect man,

5 yet because this widow causes me trouble, I will avenge her, that not coming to (the) end, she subdue me.
6 And the Lord said,

3004 1161 2532 3850 846 4314 3588 1163 3842
1. Ἔλεγε δὲ καὶ παραβολὴν αὐτοῖς πρὸς τὸ δεῖν πάντοτε
He told And also a parable to them to (teach) to behoove always

4336 2532 3361 1573 3004 2923 5100/2258/1722/5100
προσεύχεσθαι, καὶ μὴ ἐκκακεῖν, 2 λέγων, Κριτής τις ἦν ἔν τινι
to pray, and not to faint, saying, A judge certain was in a

4172 3588 2316 3361 5399 2532 444 3361 1788
πόλει, τὸν Θεὸν μὴ φοβούμενος, καὶ ἄνθρωπον μὴ ἐντρεπό-
city, God not fearing, and man not respecting;

5503 1161 2258 1722 3588 4172 1565 2532 2064 4314 846
μενος· 3 χήρα δὲ ἦν ἐν τῇ πόλει ἐκείνῃ, καὶ ἤρχετο πρὸς αὐτὸν
a widow and was in city that, and she came to him,

3004 1556 3165 575 3588 476 3450 2532 3756
λέγουσα, Ἐκδίκησόν με ἀπὸ τοῦ ἀντιδίκου μου. 4 καὶ οὐκ
saying, Avenge me from the adversary of me. And not

2309 1909 5550 3326 1161 5023 2036 1722 1438 1487
ἠθέλησεν ἐπὶ χρόνον· μετὰ δὲ ταῦτα εἶπεν ἐν ἑαυτῷ, Εἰ
he would (for) a time; after but these things he said within himself, If

2532 3588 2316 3756 5399 2532 444 3756 1788
καὶ τὸν θεὸν οὐ φοβοῦμαι, καὶ ἄνθρωπον οὐκ ἐντρέπομαι·
even God not I fear, and man not respect;

1223 1065 3588 3930 3427 2873 3588 5503 3778 1556
5 διά γε τὸ παρέχειν μοι κόπον τὴν χήραν ταύτην, ἐκδικήσω
because yet causes me trouble widow this, I will avenge

846 2443 3361 1519 5056 2064 5299 3165 2036 1161 3588
αὐτήν, ἵνα μὴ εἰς τέλος ἐρχομένη ὑπωπιάζῃ με. 6 εἶπε δὲ ὁ
her, that not to (the) end coming she subdue me. said And the

Luke 18

1. And he spake a parable unto them (to this end), that men ought always to pray, and not to faint;
2 Saying, There was in a city a judge, which feared not God, neither regarded man:

3 And there was a widow in that city; and she came unto him, saying, Avenge me of mine adversary.
4 And he would not for a while: but afterward he said within himself, Though I fear not God, nor regard man;

5 Yet because this widow troubleth me, I will avenge her, lest by her continual coming she weary me.
6 And the Lord said,

Literal Translation | **Luke 18:7** | *King James Version*

Hear what the unrighteous judge says.
7 But will God not at all execute the avenging of His elect, those crying to Him day and night, also being patient over them?

2962 191 5101 3588 2923 3588 93 3004 3588 1161 2316
Κύριος, Ἀκούσατε τί ὁ κριτὴς τῆς ἀδικίας λέγει. 7 ὁ δὲ Θεὸς
Lord, Hear what the judge of unrighteousness says. But God

3756 3361 4160 3588 1557 3588 1588 846 3588
οὐ μὴ ποιήσει τὴν ἐκδίκησιν τῶν ἐκλεκτῶν αὐτοῦ τῶν
not at all will execute the avenging of the elect of Him those

994 4314 846 2250 2532 3571 2532 3114
βοώντων πρὸς αὐτὸν ἡμέρας καὶ νυκτός, καὶ μακροθυμῶν
crying to Him day and night, also being patient

Hear what the unjust judge saith.
7 And shall not God avenge his own elect, which cry day and night unto him, though he bear long with them?

8 I say to you that He will execute the avenging of them speedily. But the Son of man coming then, will He find faith on the earth?

1909 846 3004 5213 3754 4160 3588 1557 846 1722
ἐπ' αὐτοῖς; 8 λέγω ὑμῖν ὅτι ποιήσει τὴν ἐκδίκησιν αὐτῶν ἐν
over them? I say to you that He will execute the avenging of them

5034 4133 3588 5207 3588 444 2064 687 2147 3588
τάχει. πλὴν ὁ υἱὸς τοῦ ἀνθρώπου ἐλθὼν ἆρα εὑρήσει τὴν
speedily. But the Son of man having come then, will He find

4102 1909 3588 1093
πίστιν ἐπὶ τῆς γῆς;
faith on the earth?

8 I tell you that he will avenge them speedily. Nevertheless when the Son of man cometh, shall he find faith on the earth?

9. And He also spoke this parable to some of those having relied on themselves, that they are righteous, and despising the rest:
10 Two men went up into the temple to pray, the one a Pharisee, and the other a tax collector.
11 The Pharisee (was) standing, praying these things to himself: God, I thank You that I am not as the rest of men, rapacious, unrighteous, adulterers, or even as this tax collector.

2036 1161 2532 4314 5100 3588 3982 1909 1438 3754
9. Εἶπε δὲ καὶ πρός τινας τοὺς πεποιθότας ἐφ' ἑαυτοῖς ὅτι
He said And also to some (of) those having relied on themselves that

1526 1342 2532 1848 3588 3062 3588 3850
εἰσὶ δίκαιοι, καὶ ἐξουθενοῦντας τοὺς λοιπούς, τὴν παρα-
they are righteous, and despising the rest, parable

3778 444 1417 305 1519 3588 2411
βολὴν ταύτην· 10 Ἄνθρωποι δύο ἀνέβησαν εἰς τὸ ἱερὸν
this: men Two went up into the temple

4336 3588 1520 5330 2532 3588 2087 5057 3588
προσεύξασθαι· ὁ εἷς Φαρισαῖος, καὶ ὁ ἕτερος τελώνης. 11 ὁ
to pray; the one a Pharisee, and the other a tax-collector. The

5330 2476 4314 1438 5023 4336 3588
Φαρισαῖος σταθεὶς πρὸς ἑαυτὸν ταῦτα προσηύχετο, Ὁ
Pharisee standing, to himself these things praying,

2316 2168 4671 3754 3756 1510 5618 3588 3062 3588
Θεός, εὐχαριστῶ σοι ὅτι οὐκ εἰμὶ ὥσπερ οἱ λοιποὶ τῶν
God, I thank you that not I am as the rest

444 727 94 3432 2228 2532 5613 3778 3588
ἀνθρώπων, ἅρπαγες, ἄδικοι, μοιχοί, ἢ καὶ ὡς οὗτος ὁ
of men, rapacious, unrighteous, adulterers, or even as this

9. And he spake this parable unto certain which trusted in themselves that they were righteous, and despised others:
10 Two men went up into the temple to pray; the one a Pharisee, and the other a publican.
11 The Pharisee stood and prayed thus with himself, God, I thank thee, that I am not as other men (are), extortioners, unjust, adulterers, or even as this publican.

12 I fast twice (in) the week; I tithe all things, as many as I get.
13 And standing at a distance, the tax collector would not even lift up (his) eyes to Heaven, but smote on his breast, saying, God, be merciful to me, the sinner!

5057 3522 1364 3588 4521 586 3956
τελώνης. 12 νηστεύω δὶς τοῦ σαββάτου, ἀποδεκατῶ πάντα
tax-collector. I fast twice (in) the week, I tithe all things

3745 2932 2532 3588 5057 3113 2476 3756 2309 3761
ὅσα κτῶμαι. 13 καὶ ὁ τελώνης μακρόθεν ἑστὼς οὐκ ἤθελεν οὐδὲ
as many as I get. And the tax-collector afar off standing, not would even

3588 3788 1519 3588 3772 1869 235 5180 1519/3588
τοὺς ὀφθαλμοὺς εἰς τὸν οὐρανὸν ἐπᾶραι, ἀλλ' ἔτυπτεν εἰς τὸ
the eyes to Heaven lift up, but smote on the

4738 846 3004 3588 2316 2433 3427 3588 268
στῆθος αὐτοῦ, λέγων, Ὁ Θεός, ἱλάσθητί μοι τῷ ἁμαρτωλῷ.
breast of him, saying, God, be merciful to me, the sinner.

12 I fast twice in the week, I give tithes of all that I possess.
13 And the publican, standing afar off, would not lift up so much as (his) eyes unto heaven, but smote upon his breast, saying, God be merciful to me a sinner.

14 I say to you, this one went down to his house having been justified, (rather) than that one. For everyone exalting himself will be humbled. And the (one) humbling himself will be exalted.
15. And they brought infants to Him also, that He might touch them.

3004 5213 2597 3778 1344 1519 3588 3624
14 λέγω ὑμῖν, κατέβη οὗτος δεδικαιωμένος εἰς τὸν οἶκον
I say to you, went down this one having been justified into the house

846 2228 1565 3754 3956 3588 5312 1438 5013 3588 1161
αὐτοῦ ἢ ἐκεῖνος· ὅτι πᾶς ὁ ὑψῶν ἑαυτὸν ταπεινωθήσεται, ὁ δὲ
of him, than that one, for everyone exalting himself will be humbled. he And

5013 1438 5312
ταπεινῶν ἑαυτὸν ὑψωθήσεται.
humbling himself will be exalted.

4374 1161 846 2532 3588 1025 2443 846 680
15. Προσέφερον δὲ αὐτῷ καὶ τὰ βρέφη, ἵνα αὐτῶν ἅπτηται·
they brought And to Him also the babes, that them He may touch;

14 I tell you, this man went down to his house justified (rather) than the other: for every one that exalteth himself shall be abased; and he that humbleth himself shall be exalted.
15. And they brought unto him also infants, that he would touch them:

Literal Translation

But seeing, the disciples rebuked them.
16 But Jesus called them near, saying, Allow the children to come to Me, and do not prevent them. For of such is the kingdom of God.

17 Truly I say to you, whoever does not receive the kingdom of God like a child, not at all will enter into it.

18. And a certain ruler questioned Him saying, Good Teacher, what having done may I inherit everlasting life?
19 But Jesus said to him, Why do you say Me (to be) good? No one (is) good, except One: God.

20 You know the commandments: Do not commit adultery, do not murder, do not steal, do not bear false witness, honor your father and your mother. (Ex. 20:12-16)
21 And he said, I have kept all these from my youth.
22 But having heard these things Jesus said to him, Yet one thing is lacking to you: sell all, as much as you have, and distribute to (the) poor; and you will have treasure in Heaven. And come, follow Me.
23 But having heard these things, he became very grieved, for he was exceedingly rich.
24 And having seen him having become very grieved, Jesus said, How hardly those having riches shall enter into the kingdom of God!
25 For it is easier (for) a camel to go in through a needle's eye than for a rich one to enter into the kingdom of God.

26 And having heard those said, And who is able to be saved?
27 But He said, The things impossible with men are possible

Luke 18:16

1492 1161 3588 3101 2008 846 3588 1161 2424
ἰδόντες δὲ οἱ μαθηταὶ ἐπετίμησαν αὐτοῖς. 16 ὁ δὲ Ἰησοῦς
seeing but the disciples rebuked them. But Jesus

4341 846 2036 863 3588 3813 2064
προσκαλεσάμενος αὐτὰ εἶπεν, Ἄφετε τὰ παιδία ἔρχεσθαι
having called near them said, Allow the children to come

4314 3165 2532 3361 2967 846 3588 1063 5108 2076 3588
πρός με, καὶ μὴ κωλύετε αὐτά· τῶν γὰρ τοιούτων ἐστὶν ἡ
to Me, and not do prevent them; for of such is the

932 3588 2316 281 3004 5213 3739 1437 3361 1209 3588
βασιλεία τοῦ θεοῦ. 17 ἀμὴν λέγω ὑμῖν, ὃς ἐὰν μὴ δέξηται τὴν
kingdom of God. Truly I say to you, whoever not receives the

932 3588 2316 5613 3813 3756 3361 1525 1519 846
βασιλείαν τοῦ Θεοῦ ὡς παιδίον, οὐ μὴ εἰσέλθῃ εἰς αὐτήν.
kingdom of God as a child, not at all enters into it.

2532 1905 5100 846 758 3004 1320
18. Καὶ ἐπηρώτησέ τις αὐτὸν ἄρχων, λέγων, Διδάσκαλε
And questioned a certain Him ruler, saying, Teacher

18 5101 4160 2222 166 816 2036 1161
ἀγαθέ, τί ποιήσας ζωὴν αἰώνιον κληρονομήσω; 19 εἶπε δὲ
good what having done life everlasting I may inherit? said And

846 3588 2424 5101 3165 3004 18 3762 18 1487 3361
αὐτῷ ὁ Ἰησοῦς, Τί με λέγεις ἀγαθόν; οὐδεὶς ἀγαθὸς εἰ μὴ
to him Jesus, Why Me you say (is) good? No one (is) good except

1520 3588 2316 3588 1785 1492 3361 3431 3361 5407
εἷς, ὁ Θεός. 20 τὰς ἐντολὰς οἶδας, Μὴ μοιχεύσῃς, μὴ φονεύσῃς,
One, God. The commands you know, Not do adultery, not do murder,

3361 2813 3361 5576 5091 3588 3962 4675 2532
μὴ κλέψῃς, μὴ ψευδομαρτυρήσῃς, τίμα τὸν πατέρα σου καὶ
not do steal, not do bear false witness, honor the father of you and

3588 3384 4675 3588 1161 2036 5023 3956 5442 1537
τὴν μητέρα σου. 21 ὁ δὲ εἶπε, Ταῦτα πάντα ἐφυλαξάμην ἐκ
the mother of you. he And said, These things all I have kept from

3503 3450 191 1161 5023 3588 2424 2036 846 2089
νεότητος μου. 22 ἀκούσας δὲ ταῦτα ὁ Ἰησοῦς εἶπεν αὐτῷ, Ἔτι
youth my. having heard But these things Jesus said to him, Yet

1520 4671 3007 3956 3745 2192 4453 2532 1239 4434
ἕν σοι λείπει· πάντα ὅσα ἔχεις πώλησον, καὶ διάδος πτωχοῖς,
one to you is lacking; all as much as you have sell, and distribute to the poor,

2532 2192 2344 1722 3772 2532 1204 190 3427 3588
καὶ ἕξεις θησαυρὸν ἐν οὐρανῷ· καὶ δεῦρο, ἀκολούθει μοι. 23 ὁ
and you will have treasure in Heaven; and come, follow Me. he

1161 191 5023 4036 1096 2258 1063 4145 4970
δὲ ἀκούσας ταῦτα περίλυπος ἐγένετο· ἦν γὰρ πλούσιος σφόδρα.
But hearing these things very grieved became, he was for rich exceedingly.

1492 1161 846 3588 2424 4036 1096 2036 4459
24 ἰδὼν δὲ αὐτὸν ὁ Ἰησοῦς περίλυπον γενόμενον εἶπε, Πῶς
having seen And him, Jesus very grieved having become said, How

1423 3588 3588 5536 2192 1525 1519 3588
δυσκόλως οἱ τὰ χρήματα ἔχοντες εἰσελεύσονται εἰς τὴν
hardly those riches having shall enter into the

932 3588 2316 2123 1063 2076 2574 1223
βασιλείαν τοῦ Θεοῦ. 25 εὐκοπώτερον γάρ ἐστι κάμηλον διὰ
kingdom of God. easier For it is (for) a camel through

5168 4476 1525 2228 4145 1519 3588 932
τρυμαλιᾶς ῥαφίδος εἰσελθεῖν, ἢ πλούσιον εἰς τὴν βασιλείαν
(the) eye of a needle to go in, than a rich one into the kingdom

3588 2316 1525 2036 1161 3588 191 2532 5101 1410
τοῦ Θεοῦ εἰσελθεῖν. 26 εἶπον δὲ οἱ ἀκούσαντες, Καὶ τίς δύναται
of God to enter. said And those having heard, And who is able

4982 3588 1161 2036 3588 102 3844 444 1415
σωθῆναι; 27 ὁ δὲ εἶπε, Τὰ ἀδύνατα παρὰ ἀνθρώποις δυνατὰ
to be saved? He And said, The things impossible with men possible

King James Version

but when (his) disciples saw (it), they rebuked them.
16 But Jesus called them (unto him), and said, Suffer little children to come unto me, and forbid them not: for of such is the kingdom of God.

17 Verily I say unto you, Whosoever shall not receive the kingdom of God as a little child shall in no wise enter therein.

18. And a certain ruler asked him, saying, Good Master, what shall I do to inherit eternal life?
19 And Jesus said unto him, Why callest thou me good? none (is) good, save one, (that is), God.

20 Thou knowest the commandments, Do not commit adultery, Do not kill, Do not steal, Do not bear false witness, Honour thy father and thy mother.
21 And he said, All these have I kept from my youth up.
22 Now when Jesus heard these things, he said unto him, Yet lackest thou one thing: sell all that thou hast, and distribute unto the poor, and thou shalt have treasure in heaven: and come, follow me.
23 And when he heard this, he was very sorrowful: for he was very rich.

24 And when Jesus saw that he was very sorrowful, he said, How hardly shall they that have riches enter into the kingdom of God!

25 For it is easier for a camel to go through a needle's eye, than for a rich man to enter into the kingdom of God.
26 And they that heard (it) said, Who then can be saved?
27 And he said, The things which are impossible with men are possible

Literal Translation — **Luke 18:28** — **King James Version**

with God.
28. And Peter said, Behold! We left all and followed You.

29 And He said to them, Truly I say to you, There is no one who has left house, or parents, or brothers, or wife, or children, for the sake of the kingdom of God,

30 who shall not at all receive many times more in this time, and in the age coming everlasting life.

31. And having taken aside the Twelve, He said to them, Behold! We are going up to Jerusalem, and all things will be fulfilled which have been written through the prophets to the Son of man.

32 For He will be delivered up to the nations, and will be mocked, and will be insulted, and will be spat upon.
33 And having flogged (Him), they will kill Him. And on the third day He will rise again.

34 And they understood none of these things. And this saying had been hidden from them, and they did not know the things being said.

35. And it happened (as) He drew near to Jericho, a certain blind one was sitting by the highway, begging.
36 And a crowd passing through, he asked what this might be.
37 And they reported to him that Jesus the Nazarene is passing by.
38 And he cried out, saying, Jesus, son of David, pity me!
39 And those going before rebuked him, that he be quiet. But he much more cried out, Son of David, pity me!

40 And standing, Jesus commanded him

2076 3844 3588 2316 2036 1161 3588 4074 2400 2249 863
ἐστι παρὰ τῷ Θεῷ. 28 εἶπε δὲ ὁ Πέτρος, Ἰδού, ἡμεῖς ἀφή-
is with God. said And Peter, Behold! We left

3956 2532 190 4671 3588 1161 2036 846
καμεν πάντα, καὶ ἠκολουθήσαμέν σοι. 29 ὁ δὲ εἶπεν αὐτοῖς,
all, and followed You. He And said to them,

281 3004 5213 3754 3762 2076 3739 863 3614 2228
Ἀμὴν λέγω ὑμῖν ὅτι οὐδείς ἐστιν ὃς ἀφῆκεν οἰκίαν, ἢ
Truly I say to you that no one there is who has left house, or

1118 2228 80 2228 1135 2228 5043 1752 3588 932
γονεῖς, ἢ ἀδελφούς, ἢ γυναῖκα, ἢ τέκνα, ἕνεκεν τῆς βασιλείας
parents, or brothers, or wife, or children, for the sake ot the kingdom

3588 2316 3739 3756 3361 618 4179 1722 3588 2540
τοῦ Θεοῦ, 30 ὃς οὐ μὴ ἀπολάβῃ πολλαπλασίονα ἐν τῷ καιρῷ
of God, who not at all receive many times more in time

5129 2532 1722 3588 165 3588 2064 2222 166
τούτῳ, καὶ ἐν τῷ αἰῶνι τῷ ἐρχομένῳ ζωὴν αἰώνιον.
this, and in the age coming life everlasting.

3880 1161 3588 1427 2036 4314 846 2400
31. Παραλαβὼν δὲ τοὺς δώδεκα, εἶπε πρὸς αὐτούς, Ἰδού,
having taken aside And the Twelve, He said to them, Behold!

305 1519 2414 2532 5055 3956 3588
ἀναβαίνομεν εἰς Ἱεροσόλυμα, καὶ τελεσθήσεται πάντα τὰ
We are going up to Jerusalem, and will be fulfilled all things

1125 1223 3588 4396 3588 5207 3588 444
γεγραμμένα διὰ τῶν προφητῶν τῷ υἱῷ τοῦ ἀνθρώπου.
having been written through the prophets to the Son of man.

3860 1063 3588 1484 2532 1702 2532
32 παραδοθήσεται γὰρ τοῖς ἔθνεσι, καὶ ἐμπαιχθήσεται, καὶ
He will be delivered up For to the nations, and will be mocked, and

5195 2532 1716 2532 3146
ὑβρισθήσεται καὶ ἐμπτυσθήσεται, 33 καὶ μαστιγώσαντες
will be insulted and will be spat upon, and having flogged

615 846 2532 3588 2250 3588 5154 450
ἀποκτενοῦσιν αὐτόν· καὶ τῇ ἡμέρᾳ τῇ τρίτῃ ἀναστήσεται.
they will kill Him; and on the day third He will rise again.

2532 846 3762 5130 4920 2532 2258 3588 4487 5124
34 καὶ αὐτοὶ οὐδὲν τούτων συνῆκαν, καὶ ἦν τὸ ῥῆμα τοῦτο
And they none of these things understood, and was saying this

2928 575 846 2532 3756 1097 3588 3004
κεκρυμμένον ἀπ' αὐτῶν, καὶ οὐκ ἐγίνωσκον τὰ λεγόμενα.
having been hidden from them, and not they knew the things being said.

1096 161 1722 3588 1448 846 1519 2410 5185 5100
35. Ἐγένετο δὲ ἐν τῷ ἐγγίζειν αὐτὸν εἰς Ἱεριχώ, τυφλός τις
it happened And in the to draw near Him to Jericho, blind (one) a certain

2521 3844 3588 3598 4319 191 1161 3793
ἐκάθητο παρὰ τὴν ὁδὸν προσαιτῶν. 36 ἀκούσας δὲ ὄχλου
was sitting by the way begging. hearing And a crowd

1279 4441 5101 1498 5124 518 1161
διαπορευομένου, ἐπυνθάνετο τί εἴη τοῦτο. 37 ἀπήγγειλαν δὲ
passing through, he asked what might be this. they reported And

846 3754 2424 3588 3480 3928 2532 994
αὐτῷ ὅτι Ἰησοῦς ὁ Ναζωραῖος παρέρχεται. 38 καὶ ἐβόησε
to him that Jesus the Nazarene is passing by. And he cried

3004 2424 5207 138 1653 3165 2532 3588 4254
λέγων, Ἰησοῦ, υἱὲ Δαβίδ, ἐλέησόν με. 39 καὶ οἱ προάγοντες
saying, Jesus, son of David, pity me. And those going before

2008 846 2443 4623 846 1161 4183 3123 2896
ἐπετίμων αὐτῷ ἵνα σιωπήσῃ· αὐτὸς δὲ πολλῷ μᾶλλον ἔκραζεν,
rebuked him, that he be quiet. he But much more cried out,

5207 1138 1653 3165 2476 1161 3588 2424 2753 846
Υἱὲ Δαβίδ, ἐλέησόν με. 40 σταθεὶς δὲ ὁ Ἰησοῦς ἐκέλευσεν αὐτὸν
Son of David, pity me. Standing And Jesus commanded him

---

with God.
28. Then Peter said, Lo, we have left all, and followed thee.

29 And he said unto them, Verily I say unto you, There is no man that hath left house, or parents, or brethren, or wife, or children, for the kingdom of God's sake,

30 Who shall not receive manifold more in this present time, and in the world to come life everlasting.

31. Then he took (unto him) the twelve, and said unto them, Behold, we go up to Jerusalem, and all things that are written by the prophets concerning the Son of man shall be accomplished.

32 For he shall be delivered unto the Gentiles, and shall be mocked, and spitefully entreated, and spitted on:
33 And they shall scourge (him), and put him to death: and the third day he shall rise again.
34 And they understood none of these things: and this saying was hid from them, neither knew they the things which were spoken.
35. And it came to pass, that as he was come nigh unto Jericho, a certain blind man sat by the way side begging:
36 And hearing the multitude pass by, he asked what it meant.
37 And they told him, that Jesus of Nazareth passeth by.
38 And he cried, saying, Jesus, (thou) Son of David, have mercy on me.
39 And they which went before rebuked him, that he should hold his peace: but he cried so much the more, (Thou) Son of David, have mercy on me.
40 And Jesus stood, and commanded him

Literal Translation

to be brought to Him. And he drawing near, He asked him,

41 saying, What do you desire I do to you? And he said, Lord, that I may see again.
42 And Jesus said to him, See again! Your faith has healed you.
43 And instantly he saw again. And (he) followed Him, glorifying God. And having seen, all the people gave praise to God.

Luke 19

1. And having gone in, He passed through Jericho.
2 And, behold! A man being called by name Zaccheus; and he was a chief tax collector, and he was rich.
3 And he sought to see Jesus, who He is. And he was not able from the crowd, because he was little in stature.

4 And having run ahead before (Him), he went up onto a sycamore-tree, so that he might see Him; for He was going to pass through that (way).
5 And as He came to the place, having looked up, Jesus saw him, and said to him, Zaccheus, having hastened, come down, for today I must stay in your house.
6 And hastening, he came down and welcomed Him, rejoicing.
7 And seeing, all murmured, saying, He has gone in to lodge with a sinful man.
8 But standing, Zaccheus said to the Lord, Behold, Lord! Half of my possessions I give to the poor. And if (in) anything I accused anyone falsely, I restore (it) fourfold.

9 And Jesus said to him, Today salvation has come to this house,

Luke 18:41

71 4314 846 1448 1161 846 1905 846
ἀχθῆναι πρὸς αὐτόν· ἐγγίσαντος δὲ αὐτοῦ ἐπηρώτησεν αὐτόν,
to be brought to Him. drawing near And him He asked him,

3004 5101 4671 2309 4160 3588 1161 2036 2962 2443 308
λέγων, 41 Τί σοι θέλεις ποιήσω; ὁ δὲ εἶπε, Κύριε, ἵνα ἀναβλέψω.
saying, What to you wish (that) I do? he And said, Lord, that I may see again.

2532 3588 2424 2036 846 308 3588 4102 4675 4982
42 καὶ ὁ Ἰησοῦς εἶπεν αὐτῷ, Ἀνάβλεψον· ἡ πίστις σου σέσωκέ
And Jesus said to him, See again! The faith of you has cured

4571 2532 3916 308 2532 190 846 1392
σε. 43 καὶ παραχρῆμα ἀνέβλεψε, καὶ ἠκολούθει αὐτῷ, δοξάζων
you. And at once he saw again, and followed Him, glorifying

3588 2316 2532 3956 3588 2992 1492 1325 136 3588 2316
τὸν Θεόν· καὶ πᾶς ὁ λαὸς ἰδὼν ἔδωκεν αἶνον τῷ Θεῷ.
God; and all the people having seen gave praise to God.

Luke 19

2532 1525 1330 3588 2410 2532 2400 435
1. Καὶ εἰσελθὼν διήρχετο τὴν Ἰεριχώ. 2 καὶ ἰδού, ἀνὴρ
And having entered He passed through Jericho. And, behold! A man

3686 2564 2195 2532 846 2258 754
ὀνόματι καλούμενος Ζακχαῖος, καὶ αὐτὸς ἦν ἀρχιτελώνης,
by name having been called Zaccheus; and he was a chief tax-collector.

2532 3778 2258 4145 2532 2212 1492 3588 2424 5101 2076
καὶ αὐτὸς ἦν πλούσιος. 3 καὶ ἐζήτει ἰδεῖν τὸν Ἰησοῦν τίς ἐστι,
and he was rich. And he sought to see Jesus who He is.

2532 3756 1410 575 3588 3793 3754 3588 2244 3398 2258
καὶ οὐκ ἠδύνατο ἀπὸ τοῦ ὄχλου, ὅτι τῇ ἡλικίᾳ μικρὸς ἦν.
And not he was able from the crowd, because in stature little he was.

2532 4390 1715 305 1909 4809 2443 1492
4 καὶ προδραμὼν ἔμπροσθεν ἀνέβη ἐπὶ συκομωραίαν ἵνα ἴδῃ
And having run ahead before he went up onto a sycamore-tree, that he see

846 3754 1223 1565 3195 1330 2532 5613 2064 1909
αὐτόν· ὅτι δι' ἐκείνης ἤμελλε διέρχεσθαι. 5 καὶ ὡς ἦλθεν ἐπὶ
Him; because through that (way) He was going to pass. And as He came on

3588 5117 308 3588 2424 1492 846 2532 2036 4314
τὸν τόπον, ἀναβλέψας ὁ Ἰησοῦς εἶδεν αὐτόν, καὶ εἶπε πρὸς
the place, having looked up Jesus saw him, and He said to

846 2195 4692 2597 4594 1063 1722 3588
αὐτόν, Ζακχαῖε, σπεύσας κατάβηθι, σήμερον γὰρ ἐν τῷ
him, Zaccheus, having hastened come down; today for in the

3624 4675 1163 3165 3306 2532 4692 2597 2532 5264
οἴκῳ σου δεῖ με μεῖναι. 6 καὶ σπεύσας κατέβη, καὶ ὑπεδέξατο
house of you must Me to stay. And hastening he came down, and welcomed

846 5463 2532 1492 537 1234 3004
αὐτὸν χαίρων. 7 καὶ ἰδόντες απαντες διεγόγγυζον, λέγοντες
Him rejoicing. And having seen all murmured, saying,

3754 3844 268 435 1525 2647 2476 1161
ὅτι Παρὰ ἁμαρτωλῷ ἀνδρὶ εἰσῆλθε καταλῦσαι. 8 σταθεὶς δὲ
With a sinful man He went in to lodge. standing And

2195 2036 4314 3588 2962 2400 3588 2255 3588
Ζακχαῖος εἶπε πρὸς τὸν Κύριον, Ἰδού, τὰ ἡμίση τῶν
Zaccheus said to the Lord, Behold! The half of the

5224 3450 2962 325 3588 4434 2532 1487 5100
ὑπαρχόντων μου, Κύριε, δίδωμι τοῖς πτωχοῖς· καὶ εἴ τινός
possessions of me, Lord, I give to the poor; And if anyone

5100 4811 591 5073 2036 1161 4314
τι ἐσυκοφάντησα, ἀποδίδωμι τετραπλοῦν. 9 εἶπε δὲ πρὸς
anything I accused falsely, I give back fourfold. said And to

846 3588 2424 3754 4594 4991 3588 3624 5129 1096
αὐτὸν ὁ Ἰησοῦς ὅτι Σήμερον σωτηρία τῷ οἴκῳ τούτῳ ἐγέ-
him Jesus, Today salvation house to this has

King James Version

to be brought unto him: and when he was come near, he asked him,
41 Saying, What wilt thou that I shall do unto thee? And he said, Lord, that I may receive my sight.
42 And Jesus said unto him, Receive thy sight: thy faith hath saved thee.
43 And immediately he received his sight, and followed him, glorifying God: and all the people, when they saw (it), gave praise unto God.

Luke 19

1. And (Jesus) entered and passed through Jericho.
2 And, behold, (there was) a man named Zacchaeus, which was the chief among the publicans, and he was rich.
3 And he sought to see Jesus who he was; and could not for the press, because he was little of stature.

4 And he ran before, and climbed up into a sycomore tree to see him: for he was to pass that (way).
5 And when Jesus came to the place, he looked up, and saw him, and said unto him, Zacchaeus, make haste, and come down; for to day I must abide at thy house.

6 And he made haste, and came down, and received him joyfully.
7 And when they saw (it), they all murmured, saying, That he was gone to be guest with a man that is a sinner.
8 And Zacchaeus stood, and said unto the Lord; Behold, Lord, the half of my goods I give to the poor; and if I have taken any thing from any man by false accusation, I restore (him) fourfold.

9 And Jesus said unto him, This day is salvation come to this house,

Literal Translation

because he also is a son of Abraham.
10 For the Son of man came to seek and to save the (one) being lost.

11. But (as they were) hearing these things, He spoke, adding a parable, because He was near to Jerusalem, and they thought that the kingdom of God was about to immediately be revealed.

12 Then He said: A certain wellborn man went to a distant country to receive a kingdom for himself, and to return.
13 And calling ten of his slaves, He gave to them ten minas and said to them, Trade until I come.

14 But his citizens hated him and sent a delegation after him, saying, We do not desire this one to reign over us.

15 And it happened at his returning, having received the kingdom, he even said (for) those slaves to be called to him, those to whom he gave the silver, that he might know what each had gained by trading.
16 And the first came, saying, Lord, your mina has gained ten minas.

17 And he said to him, Well (done), good slave! Because you were faithful in a least thing, (you will) be having authority over ten cities.
18 And the second came, saying, Lord, your mina has made five minas.
19 And he said to this one also, And you be over five cities.
20 And another came, saying, Lord, behold your mina which I had stored up in a cloth.
21 For I feared you,

Luke 19:10

2530 2532 846 5207 11 2076 2064 1063 3588 5207
νετο, καθότι καὶ αὐτὸς υἱὸς Ἀβραάμ ἐστιν· 10 ἦλθε γὰρ ὁ υἱὸς
come to be, because also he a son of Abraham is; came for the Son
3588 444 2212 2532 4982 3588 622
τοῦ ἀνθρώπου ζητῆσαι καὶ σῶσαι τὸ ἀπολωλός.
of man to seek and to save the (one) being lost.

191 1161 846 5023 4369 2036 3850
11. Ἀκουόντων δὲ αὐτῶν ταῦτα, προσθεὶς εἶπε παραβολήν,
hearing And them these things, adding He spoke a parable,
1223 3588 1451 846 1511 2419 2532 1380 846 3754
διὰ τὸ ἐγγὺς αὐτὸν εἶναι Ἱερουσαλήμ, καὶ δοκεῖν αὐτοὺς ὅτι
because near Him to be to Jerusalem, and to think they that
3916 3195 3588 932 3588 2316 398
παραχρῆμα μέλλει ἡ βασιλεία τοῦ Θεοῦ ἀναφαίνεσθαι.
immediately was about the kingdom of God to be revealed.

2036 3767 444 5100 2104 4198 1519 5561
12 εἶπεν οὖν, Ἄνθρωπός τις εὐγενὴς ἐπορεύθη εἰς χώραν
He said Then, man a certain well-born went into a country
3117 2983 1438 932 2532 5290 2564
μακράν, λαβεῖν ἑαυτῷ βασιλείαν, καὶ ὑποστρέψαι. 13 καλέσας
distant, to receive to himself a kingdom, and to return. having called
1161 1176 1401 1438 1325 846 1176 3414 2532 2036
δὲ δέκα δούλους ἑαυτοῦ, ἔδωκεν αὐτοῖς δέκα μνᾶς, καὶ εἶπε
And ten slaves of himself, He gave to them ten minas, and said
4314 846 4231 2193 2064 3588 1161 4177
πρὸς αὐτούς, Πραγματεύσασθε ἕως ἔρχομαι. 14 οἱ δὲ πολῖται
to them, Trade until I come. the But citizens
846 3404 846 2532 649 4242 3694
αὐτοῦ ἐμίσουν αὐτόν, καὶ ἀπέστειλαν πρεσβείαν ὀπίσω
of him hated him, and (they) sent a delegation after
846 3004 3756 2309 5126 936 1909 2248
αὐτοῦ, λέγοντες, Οὐ θέλομεν τοῦτον βασιλεῦσαι ἐφ' ἡμᾶς.
him, saying, Not we desire this one to reign over us.

2532 1096 1722 3588 1880 846 2983 3588 932
15 καὶ ἐγένετο ἐν τῷ ἐπανελθεῖν αὐτὸν λαβόντα τὴν βασιλείαν,
And it happened at the (time) to return Him having received the kingdom,
2532 2036 5455 846 3588 1401 5128 3739 1325
καὶ εἶπε φωνηθῆναι αὐτῷ τοὺς δούλους τούτους, οἷς ἔδωκε
even he said to be called to him slaves those, to whom he gave
3588 694 2443 1097 5101 5101 1281 3854
τὸ ἀργύριον, ἵνα γνῷ τίς τί διεπραγματεύσατο. 16 παρε-
the silver, that he know any what had gained by trading. came
1161 3588 4413 3004 2962 3588 3414 4675 4333
γένετο δὲ ὁ πρῶτος λέγων, Κύριε, ἡ μνᾶ σου προσειργάσατο
And the first, saying, Lord, the mina of you has gained
1176 3414 2532 2036 846 2095 18 1401 3754 1722 1646
δέκα μνᾶς. 17 καὶ εἶπεν αὐτῷ, Εὖ, ἀγαθὲ δοῦλε· ὅτι ἐν ἐλαχίστῳ
ten minas. And he said to him, Well, good slave; because in a least (thing)
4103 1096 2468 1849 2192 883 1176 4172 2532
πιστὸς ἐγένου, ἴσθι ἐξουσίαν ἔχων ἐπάνω δέκα πόλεων. 18 καὶ
faithful you were, be authority having over ten cities. And
2064 3588 1208 3004 2962 3588 3414 4675 4160 4002
ἦλθεν ὁ δεύτερος, λέγων, Κύριε, ἡ μνᾶ σου ἐποίησε πέντε
came the second, saying, Lord, the mina of you has made five
3414 2036 1161 2532 5129 2532 4771 1096 1883 4002 4172
μνᾶς. 19 εἶπε δὲ καὶ τούτῳ, Καὶ σὺ γίνου ἐπάνω πέντε πόλεων.
minas. he said And also to this, And you be over five cities.
2532 2087 2064 3004 2962 2400 3588 3414 4675 3739 2192
20 καὶ ἕτερος ἦλθε, λέγων, Κύριε, ἰδού, ἡ μνᾶ σου, ἣν εἶχον
And another came, saying, Lord, Behold! The mina of you which I have
606 1722 4676 5399 1063 4571 3754 444
ἀποκειμένην ἐν σουδαρίῳ· 21 ἐφοβούμην γάρ σε, ὅτι ἄνθρωπος
stored up in a cloth; I feared for you because a man

King James Version

forsomuch as he also is a son of Abraham.
10 For the Son of man is come to seek and to save that which was lost.

11. And as they heard these things, he added and spake a parable, because he was nigh to Jerusalem, and because they thought that the kingdom of God should immediately appear.

12 He said therefore, A certain nobleman went into a far country to receive for himself a kingdom, and to return.
13 And he called his ten servants, and delivered them ten pounds, and said unto them, Occupy till I come.

14 But his citizens hated him, and sent a message after him, saying, We will not have this (man) to reign over us.

15 And it came to pass, that when he was returned, having received the kingdom, then he commanded these servants to be called unto him, to whom he had given the money, that he might know how much every man had gained by trading.
16 Then came the first, saying, Lord, thy pound hath gained ten pounds.
17 And he said unto him, Well, thou good servant: because thou hast been faithful in a very little, have thou authority over ten cities.
18 And the second came, saying, Lord, thy pound hath gained five pounds.
19 And he said likewise to him, Be thou also over five cities.
20 And another came, saying, Lord, behold, (here is) thy pound, which I have kept laid up in a napkin:
21 For I feared thee, because thou art an austere man:

Literal Translation **Luke 19:22** ***King James Version***

because you are an exacting man, taking what you did not lay down, and reaping what you did not sow.

22 But he said to him, I will judge you out of your mouth, wicked slave. You knew that I am an exacting man, taking what I did not lay down, and reaping what I did not sow.
23 And why did you not give my silver on the (bank) table? And having come, I might have exacted it with interest.
24 And to those standing by, he said, Take the mina from him, and give to the (one) having ten minas.
25 And they said to him, Lord, he has ten minas.
26 For I say to you, To everyone who has, it will be given. And from the (one) who does not have, even what he has will be taken from him.
27 But these enemies of mine, the (ones) not desiring me to reign over them, bring them here and execute (them) before me.

840 1488 142 3739 3756 5087 2532 2325 3739 3756
αὐστηρὸς εἶ· αἴρεις ὃ οὐκ ἔθηκας, καὶ θερίζεις ὃ οὐκ
exacting you are; taking what not you lay, and reaping what not

4687 3004 1161 846 1537 3588 4750 4675 2919 4571
ἔσπειρας. 22λέγει δὲ αὐτῷ, Ἐκ τοῦ στόματός σου κρίνῶ σε,
you sowed. he says And to him, From the mouth of you I will judge you,

4190 1401 1492 3754 1473 444 840 1510 142 3739
πονηρὲ δοῦλε. ᾔδεις ὅτι ἐγὼ ἄνθρωπος αὐστηρός εἰμι, αἴρων ὃ
wicked slave. You knew that I a man exacting am, taking what

3756 5087 2532 2325 3739 3756 4687 2532 1302 3756 1325
οὐκ ἔθηκα, καὶ θερίζων ὃ οὐκ ἔσπειρα· 23 καὶ διατί οὐκ ἔδωκάς
not I laid, and reaping what not I sowed; and why not did you give

3588 694 3450 1909 3588 5132 2532 1473 2064 4862 5110 302
τὸ ἀργύριόν μου ἐπὶ τὴν τράπεζαν, καὶ ἐγὼ ἐλθὼν σὺν τόκῳ ἂν
the silver of me on the (bank) table, and I having come with interest may

4238 846 2532 3588 3936 2036 142 575 846
ἔπραξα αὐτό. 24 καὶ τοῖς παρεστῶσιν εἶπεν, Ἄρατε ἀπ' αὐτοῦ
have exacted it. And to those standing by he said, Take from him

3588 3414 2532 1325 3588 3588 1176 3414 2192 2532 2036 846
τὴν μνᾶν, καὶ δότε τῷ τὰς δέκα μνᾶς ἔχοντι. 25 καὶ εἶπον αὐτῷ,
the mina, and give to the (one) ten minas having. And they said to him,

2962 2192 1176 3414 3004 1063 5213 3754 3956 3588 2192
Κύριε, ἔχει δέκα μνᾶς. 26 λέγω γάρ ὑμῖν, ὅτι παντὶ τῷ ἔχοντι
Lord, he has ten minas. I say For to you, that to every one having

1325 575 1161 3588 3361 2192 2532 3739 2192 142
δοθήσεται· ἀπὸ δὲ τοῦ μὴ ἔχοντος, καὶ ὃ ἔχει ἀρθήσεται
it will be given; from and the (one) not having, even what he has will be taken

575 846 4133 3588 2190 3450 1565 3588 3361 2309
ἀπ' αὐτοῦ. 27 πλὴν τοὺς ἐχθρούς μου ἐκείνους, τοὺς μὴ θελή-
from him. But enemies of me these, the (ones) not

3165 936 1909 846 71 5602 2532 2695
σαντάς με βασιλεῦσαι ἐπ' αὐτοὺς, ἀγάγετε ὧδε, καὶ κατα-
desiring me to reign over them, bring here and exe-

1715 3450
σφάξατε ἔμπροσθέν μου.
cute before me.

thou takest up that thou layedst not down, and reapest that thou didst not sow.
22 And he saith unto him, Out of thine own mouth will I judge thee, (thou) wicked servant. Thou knewest that I was an austere man, taking up that I laid not down, and reaping that I did not sow:
23 Wherefore then gavest not thou my money into the bank, that at my coming I might have required mine own with usury?
24 And he said unto them that stood by, Take from him the pound, and give (it) to him that hath ten pounds.
25 (And they said unto him, Lord, he hath ten pounds.)
26 For I say unto you, That unto every one which hath shall be given; and from him that hath not, even that he hath shall be taken away from him.
27 But those mine enemies, which would not that I should reign over them, bring hither, and slay (them) before me.

28 And having said these things, He went in before (them), going up to Jerusalem.

2532 2036 5023 4198 1715 305 1519
28. Καὶ εἰπὼν ταῦτα, ἐπορεύετο ἔμπροσθεν, ἀναβαίνων εἰς
And having said these things, He went before (them), going up into

2414
Ἱεροσόλυμα.
Jerusalem.

28 And when he had thus spoken, he went before, ascending up to Jerusalem.

29. And it happened as He drew near to Bethphage and Bethany toward the Mount being called Of Olives, He sent two of His disciples,
30 saying, Go into the village opposite (you), in which having entered you will find a colt having been tied up, on which no one of men ever yet sat. Having loosed it, bring (it).
31 And if anyone asks, Why do you loose (it)? You shall say to them, The Lord has need of it.
32 And having gone, those having been sent

2532 1096 5613 1448 1519 967 2532 963 4314
29. Καὶ ἐγένετο ὡς ἤγγισεν εἰς Βηθφαγὴ καὶ Βηθανίαν πρὸς
And it happened as He drew near to Bethphage and Bethany toward

3588 3735 3588 2564 1636 649 1417 3588 3101
τὸ ὄρος τὸ καλούμενον Ἐλαιῶν, ἀπέστειλε δύο τῶν μαθητῶν
the mount being called, Of Olives, He sent two of the disciples

846 2036 5217 1519 3588 2713 2968 1722 3739
αὐτοῦ, 30 εἰπών, Ὑπάγετε εἰς τὴν κατέναντι κώμην· ἐν ᾗ
of Him, saying, Go into the opposite village, in which

1531 2147 4454 1210 1909 3739 3762
εἰσπορευόμενοι εὑρήσετε πῶλον δεδεμένον, ἐφ' ὃν οὐδεὶς
having entered you will find a colt having been tied, on which no one

4455 444 2523 3089 846 71 2532 1437
πώποτε ἀνθρώπων ἐκάθισε· λύσαντες αὐτὸν ἀγάγετε. 31 καὶ ἐάν
ever yet of men sat; having loosed it, bring (it). And if

5100 5209 2065 1302 3089 3779 2046 846 3754 3588
τις ὑμᾶς ἐρωτᾷ, Διατί λύετε; οὕτως ἐρεῖτε αὐτῷ ὅτι Ὁ
anyone you asks, Why do you loose? Thus you shall say to them, The

2962 846 5532 2192 565 1161 3588 649
Κύριος αὐτοῦ χρείαν ἔχει. 32 ἀπελθόντες δὲ οἱ ἀπεσταλμένοι
Lord of it need has. having gone And, those being sent

29. And it came to pass, when he was come nigh to Bethphage and Bethany, at the mount called (the mount) of Olives, he sent two of his disciples,
30 Saying, Go ye into the village over against (you); in the which at your entering ye shall find a colt tied, whereon yet never man sat: loose him, and bring (him hither).
31 And if any man ask you, Why do ye loose (him)? thus shall ye say unto him, Because the Lord hath need of him.
32 And they that were sent went their way,

Literal Translation — **Luke 19:33** — **King James Version**

found as He told them.
33 And (as they were) loosing the colt, its owners said to them, Why do you loose the colt?
34 And they said, The Lord has need of it.
35 And they led it to Jesus. And having thrown on their garments on the colt, they put Jesus on (it).

36 And (as He was) going they were spreading their garments in the roadway.

37 And as He was already drawing near to the descent of the Mount of Olives, all the multitude of the disciples began rejoicing, to praise God with a loud voice concerning all (the) works of power which they saw,

38 saying, Blessed (is) the One coming in the name of (the) Lord, the King. Peace in Heaven, and glory in (the) highest places! (Ps. 118:26)

39 And some of the Pharisees from the crowd said to Him, Teacher, rebuke your disciples.
40 And answering, He said to them, I say to you, If these should be silent, the stones will cry out.

41. And as He drew near, seeing the city, He wept over it,
42 saying, If you knew, also you, even at least in this day of yours, the things for your peace! But now they were hidden from your eyes.
43 For the days will come on you, and your enemies will raise up a rampart to you and will encircle you and will keep you in on every

2147 2531 2036 846 3089 1161 846 3588 4454
εὗρον καθὼς εἶπεν αὐτοῖς. 33 λυόντων δὲ αὐτῶν τὸν πῶλον,
found even as He told them. loosing And them the colt,

2036 3588 2962 846 4314 846 5101 3089 3588 4454 3588
εἶπον οἱ κύριοι αὐτοῦ πρὸς αὐτούς, Τί λύετε τὸν πῶλον; 34 οἱ
said the owners of it to them, Why do you loose the colt? they

1161 2036 3754 3588 2962 846 5532 2192 2532 71 846
δὲ εἶπον, ὅτι Ὁ Κύριος αὐτοῦ χρείαν ἔχει. 35 καὶ ἤγαγον αὐτὸν
And they said, The Lord of it need. has And they led it

4314 3588 2424 2532 1977 1438 3588 2440 1909
πρὸς τὸν Ἰησοῦν· καὶ ἐπιρρίψαντες ἑαυτῶν τὰ ἱμάτια ἐπὶ
to Jesus; and having thrown on of themselves the garments on

3588 4454 1913 3588 2424 4198 1161 846
τὸν πῶλον, ἐπεβίβασαν τὸν Ἰησοῦν. 36 πορευομένου δὲ αὐτοῦ,
the colt, they put on (it) Jesus. going And Him,

5291 3588 2440 846 1722 3588 3598
ὑπεστρώννυον τὰ ἱμάτια αὐτῶν ἐν τῇ ὁδῷ.
they spread out the garments of them in the way.

1448 1161 846 2235 4314 3588 2600 3588 3735
37 ἐγγίζοντος δὲ αὐτοῦ ἤδη πρὸς τῇ καταβάσει τοῦ ὄρους
drawing near And Him already to the descent of the Mount

3588 1636 756 537 3588 4128 3588 3101 5463
τῶν ἐλαιῶν, ἤρξαντο ἅπαν τὸ πλῆθος τῶν μαθητῶν χαίροντες
of the Olives, began all the multitude of the disciples rejoicing

134 3588 2316 5456 3173 4012 3956 3739 1492 1411
αἰνεῖν τὸν Θεὸν φωνῇ μεγάλῃ περὶ πασῶν ὧν εἶδον δυνά-
to praise God with a voice loud concerning all which they saw works

3004
μεων, 38 λέγοντες,
of power, saying,

2127 3588 2064 935 1722 3686 2962
Εὐλογημένος ὁ ἐρχομένος βασιλεὺς ἐν ὀνόματι Κυρίου·
Blessed the coming (One) the King in the name of (the) Lord;

1515 1722 3772 2532 1391 1722 5310
εἰρήνη ἐν οὐρανῷ, καὶ δόξα ἐν ὑψίστοις.
peace in Heaven, and glory in the highest places.

2532 5100 3588 5330 575 3588 3793 2036 4314
39. καί τινες τῶν Φαρισαίων ἀπὸ τοῦ ὄχλου εἶπον πρὸς
And some of the Pharisees from the crowd said to

846 1320 2008 3588 3101 4675 2532
αὐτόν, Διδάσκαλε, ἐπιτίμησον τοῖς μαθηταῖς σου. 40 καὶ
Him, Teacher, rebuke the disciples of you. And

611 2036 846 3004 5213 3754 1437 3778
ἀποκριθεὶς εἶπεν αὐτοῖς, Λέγω ὑμῖν ὅτι, ἐὰν οὗτοι
answering He said to them, I say to you, If these

4623 3588 3037 2896
σιωπήσωυσιν, οἱ λίθοι κεκράξονται.
should be silent, the stones will cry out.

2532 5613 1448 1492 3588 4172 2799 1909 846
41. Καὶ ὡς ἤγγισεν, ἰδὼν τὴν πόλιν, ἔκλαυσεν ἐπ' αὐτῇ,
And as they drew near, having seen the city, He wept over it,

3004 3754 1487 1097 2532 4771 2532 1065 1722 2250 4675 3778
42 λέγων ὅτι Εἰ ἔγνως καὶ σύ, καί γε ἐν τῇ ἡμέρᾳ σου ταύτῃ,
saying, If you knew also you, even at least in day of you this,

3588 4314 1515 4675 3568 1161 2928 575 3788 4675 3754
τὰ πρὸς εἰρήνην σου· νῦν δὲ ἐκρύβη ἀπὸ ὀφθαλμῶν σου. 43 ὅτι
the things for peace of you, now but were hid from the eyes of you. Because

2240 2250 1909 4571 2532 4016 3588 2190 4675 5482
ἥξουσιν ἡμέραι ἐπὶ σὲ, καὶ περιβαλοῦσιν οἱ ἐχθροί σου χάρακά
will come days on you, and will raise up the enemies of you a rampart

4671 2532 4033 4571 2532 4912 4571 3840
σοι, καὶ περικυκλώσουσί σε, καὶ συνέξουσί σε πάντοθεν,
to you, and will encircle you, and will keep in you on all sides,

and found even as he had said unto them.
33 And as they were loosing the colt, the owners thereof said unto them, Why loose ye the colt?
34 And they said, The Lord hath need of him.
35 And they brought him to Jesus: and they cast their garments upon the colt, and they set Jesus thereon.

36 And as he went, they spread their clothes in the way.

37 And when he was come nigh, even now at the descent of the mount of Olives, the whole multitude of the disciples began to rejoice and praise God with a loud voice for all the mighty works that they had seen;

38 Saying, Blessed (be) the King that cometh in the name of the Lord: peace in heaven, and glory in the highest.

39 And some of the Pharisees from among the multitude said unto him, Master, rebuke thy disciples.
40 And he answered and said unto them, I tell you that, if these should hold their peace, the stones would immediately cry out.

41. And when he was come near, he beheld the city, and wept over it,
42 Saying, If thou hadst known, even thou, at least in this thy day, the things (which belong) unto thy peace! but now they are hid from thine eyes.
43 For the days shall come upon thee, that thine enemies shall cast a trench about thee, and compass thee round, and keep thee in on every

Literal Translation

Luke 19:44

sides,
44 and will tear you down, and your children in you, and will not leave a stone on a stone, because you did not know the time of your visitation.

2532 1474 4571 2532 3588 5043 4675 1722 4671 2532 3756
44 καὶ ἐδαφιοῦσίν σε καὶ τὰ τέκνα σου ἐν σοί, καὶ οὐκ
and will tear down you and the children of you in you, and not
863 1722 4671 3037 1909 3037 473 3739 3756 1097 3588
ἀφήσουσιν ἐν σοὶ λίθον ἐπὶ λίθῳ· ἀνθ᾽ ὧν οὐκ ἔγνως τὸν
will leave in you stone upon stone because not you knew the
2540 3588 1984 4675
καιρὸν τῆς ἐπισκοπῆς σου.
time of the visitation of you.

King James Version

side,
44 And shall lay thee even with the ground, and thy children within thee; and they shall not leave in thee one stone upon another; because thou knewest not the time of thy visitation.

45 And having entered into the temple, He began to throw out those selling and buying in it,
46 saying to them, It has been written, "My house is a house of prayer," but you made it a den of plunderers. (Isa. 56:7; Jer. 7:11)

2532 1525 1519 3588 2411 756 1544 3588
45.Καὶ εἰσελθὼν εἰς τὸ ἱερὸν, ἤρξατο ἐκβάλλειν τοὺς
And having entered into the temple, He began to throw out those
4453 1722 846 2532 59 3004 846
πωλοῦντας ἐν αὐτῷ καὶ ἀγοράζοντας, 46 λέγων αὐτοῖς,
selling in it and buying, saying to them,
1125 3588 3624 3450 3624 4335 2076 5210 1161 846
Γέγραπται,῾Ο οἶκός μου οἶκος προσευχῆς ἐστίν· ὑμεῖς δὲ αὐτὸν
it has been written, The house of me a house of prayer is; you but it
4160 4693 3027 2532 2258 1321 3588 2596
ἐποιήσατε σπήλαιον λῃστῶν. 47 καὶ ἦν διδάσκων τὸ καθ᾽
made a den of plunderers. And He was teaching (day by)

45 And he went into the temple, and began to cast out them that sold therein, and them that bought;
46 Saying unto them, It is written, My house is the house of prayer: but ye have made it a den of thieves.

47 And He was teaching day by day in the temple. But the chief priests and the scribes and the chief men of the people sought to kill Him.
48 And (they) did not find what they might do; for all the people hung on Him, listening.

2250 1722 3588 2411 3588 1161 749 2532 3588 1122 2212
ἡμέραν ἐν τῷ ἱερῷ· οἱ δὲ ἀρχιερεῖς καὶ οἱ γραμματεῖς ἐζήτουν
day in the temple; the but chief priests and the scribes sought
846 622 2532 3588 4413 3588 2992 2532 3756 2147 3588
αὐτὸν ἀπολέσαι, καὶ οἱ πρῶτοι τοῦ λαοῦ· 48 καὶ οὐχ εὕρισκον τὸ
Him to kill, also the chief men of the people; and not (they) found
5101 4160 3588 2992 1063 537 1582 846 191
τί ποιήσωσιν, ὁ λαὸς γὰρ ἅπας ἐξεκρέματο αὐτοῦ ἀκούων.
what they might do, the people for all hung upon Him hearing.

47 And he taught daily in the temple. But the chief priests and the scribes and the chief of the people sought to destroy him,
48 And could not find what they might do: for all the people were very attentive to hear him.

Luke 20

1. And it happened on one of those days, as He was teaching the people and proclaiming the gospel in the temple, the chief priests and the scribes came up, along with the elders,
2 and spoke to Him, saying, Tell us by what authority you do these things, or who is it who gave to you this authority?
3 And answering, He said to them, I will also ask you one word, and you tell me:

2532 1096 1722 3391 3588 2250 1565 1321
1. Καὶ ἐγένετο ἐν μιᾷ τῶν ἡμερῶν ἐκείνων, διδάσκοντος
And it happened on one days of those, teaching
846 3588 2992 1722 3588 2411 2532 2097 2186 3588
αὐτοῦ τὸν λαὸν ἐν τῷ ἱερῷ καὶ εὐαγγελιζομένου, ἐπέστησαν οἱ
Him the people in the temple and proclaiming the gospel, came upon the
749 2532 3588 1122 4862 3588 4245 2532 2036
ἀρχιερεῖς καὶ οἱ γραμματεῖς σὺν τοῖς πρεσβυτέροις, 2 καὶ εἶπον
chief priests and the scribes with the elders, and spoke
4314 846 3004 2036 2254 1722 4169 1849 5023
πρὸς αὐτόν, λέγοντες, Εἰπὲ ἡμῖν, ἐν ποίᾳ ἐξουσίᾳ ταῦτα
to Him, saying, Tell us, by what authority these things
4160 2228 5101 2076 3588 325 4671 3588 1849 3778
ποιεῖς, ἢ τίς ἐστιν ὁ δούς σοι τὴν ἐξουσίαν ταύτην. 3 ἀπο-
you do, or who is the (one) giving you authority this.
611 1161 2036 4314 846 2065 5209 2504 1520
κριθεὶς δὲ εἶπε πρὸς αὐτούς, ᾽Ερωτήσω ὑμᾶς κἀγὼ ἕνα
answering And He said to them, will ask you I also one
3056 2532 2036 3427 3588 908 2491 1537 3772
λόγον, καὶ εἴπατέ μοι· 4 Τὸ βάπτισμα ᾽Ιωάννου ἐξ οὐρανοῦ
word, and you tell Me: The baptism of John, from Heaven

1. And it came to pass, (that) on one of those days, as he taught the people in the temple, and preached the gospel, the chief priests and the scribes came upon (him) with the elders,
2 And spake unto him, saying, Tell us, by what authority doest thou these things? or who is he that gave thee this authority?
3 And he answered and said unto them, I will also ask you one thing; and answer me:

4 The baptism of John, was it from Heaven, or from men?
5 And they debated to themselves, saying, If we say, From Heaven, he will say, Then why did you not believe him?
6 But if we say, From men, all the

2258 2228 1537 444 3588 1161 4817 4314 1438
ἦν, ἢ ἐξ ἀνθρώπων; 5 οἱ δὲ συνελογίσαντο πρὸς ἑαυτοὺς,
was, or from men? they And debated to themselves,
3004 3754 1437 2036 1537 3772 2046 1302 3767 3756
λέγοντες ὅτι ᾽Εὰν εἴπωμεν, ᾽Εξ οὐρανοῦ, ἐρεῖ, Διατί οὖν οὐκ
saying, If we say, Out of Heaven, he will say, Why then not
4100 846 1437 1161 2036 1537 444 3956 3588
ἐπιστεύσατε αὐτῷ; 6 ἐὰν δὲ εἴπωμεν, ᾽Εξ ἀνθρώπων, πᾶς ὁ
you believed him? if And we say, From men, all the

4 The baptism of John, was it from heaven, or of men?
5 And they reasoned with themselves, saying, If we shall say, From heaven; he will say, Why then believed ye him not?
6 But and if we say, Of men; all the

Literal Translation

people will stone us, for it is (that they) have been convinced (that) John was a prophet.
7 And they answered, they did not know from where.
8 And Jesus said to them, Neither do I tell you by what authority I do these things.

9 And He began to speak this parable to the people: A certain man planted a vineyard and let it out to vinedressers. and went away for long periods (of time).

10 And in season, he sent a slave to the vinedressers, that they would give him the fruit from the vineyard. But the vinedressers having beaten him sent (him) away empty.

11 And he again sent another slave. But they also sent that one away empty, having beaten and having insulted (him).
12 And he again sent a third. But they also threw this one out, having wounded (him).
13 And the lord of the vineyard said, What shall I do? I will send my beloved son. Perhaps having seen this one, they will respect (him).
14 And having seen him, the vinedressers reasoned to themselves, saying, This is the heir. Come let us kill him so that the inheritance may become ours.

15 And having thrown him out of the vineyard, they killed (him). Therefore, what will the Lord of the vineyard do to them?
16 He will come and will destroy these vinedressers and will give the vineyard to others. And hearing this, they said, Let it not be!
17 And

Luke 20:7

2992 2642 2248 3982 1063 2076 2491
λαὸς καταλιθάσει ἡμᾶς· πεπεισμένος γάρ ἐστιν Ἰωάννην
people will stone us; having been convinced for it is John

4396 1511 2532 611 3361 1492 4159 2532 3588
προφήτην εἶναι. 7 καὶ ἀπεκρίθησαν μὴ εἰδέναι πόθεν. 8 καὶ ὁ
a prophet to be. And they answered (claiming) not to know from where. And

2424 2036 846 3761 1473 3004 5213 1722 4169 1849
Ἰησοῦς εἶπεν αὐτοῖς, Οὐδὲ ἐγὼ λέγω ὑμῖν ἐν ποίᾳ ἐξουσίᾳ
Jesus said to them, Neither do I tell you by what authority

5023 4160
ταῦτα ποιῶ.
these things I do.

756 1161 4314 3588 2992 3004 3588 3850 3778
9. Ἤρξατο δὲ πρὸς τὸν λαὸν λέγειν τὴν παραβολὴν ταύτην·
He began And to the people to speak parable this:

444 5100 5452 290 2532 1554 846
Ἄνθρωπός τις ἐφύτευσεν ἀμπελῶνα, καὶ ἐξέδοτο αὐτὸν
man A certain planted a vineyard, and let out it

1092 2532 589 5550 2425 2532 1722 2540
γεωργοῖς, καὶ ἀπεδήμησε χρόνους ἱκανούς· 10 καὶ ἐν καιρῷ
to vinedressers, and went away periods for considerable. And in time

649 4314 3588 1092 1401 2443 575 3588 2590
ἀπέστειλε πρὸς τοὺς γεωργοὺς δοῦλον, ἵνα ἀπὸ τοῦ καρποῦ
he sent to the vinedressers a slave, that from the fruit

3588 290 1325 846 3588 1161 1092 1194 846
τοῦ ἀμπελῶνος δῶσιν αὐτῷ· οἱ δὲ γεωργοὶ δείραντες αὐτὸν
of the vineyard they will give him; the but vinedressers having beaten him

1821 2756 2532 4369 3992 2087 1401
ἐξαπέστειλαν κενόν. 11 καὶ προσέθετο πέμψαι ἕτερον δοῦλον·
sent (him) away empty. And he added to send another slave,

3588 1161 2548 1194 2532 818 1821 2756
οἱ δὲ κἀκεῖνον δείραντες καὶ ἀτιμάσαντες ἐξαπέστειλαν κενόν.
they but that one also having beaten and having insulted sent away empty.

2532 4369 3992 5154 3588 1161 2532 5126 5135
12 καὶ προσέθετο πέμψαι τρίτον· οἱ δὲ καὶ τοῦτον τραυματί-
And he added to send a third; they but also this one wounding

1544 2036 1161 3588 2962 3588 290 5101
σαντες ἐξέβαλον. 13 εἶπε δὲ ὁ κύριος τοῦ ἀμπελῶνος, Τί
(him) threw out. said And the lord of the vineyard, What

4160 3992 3588 5207 3450 3588 27 2481 5126
ποιήσω; πέμψω τὸν υἱόν μου τὸν ἀγαπητόν· ἴσως τοῦτον
may I do? I will send the son of me, the beloved; perhaps this one

1492 1788 1492 1161 846 3588 1092
ἰδόντες ἐντραπήσονται. 14 ἰδόντες δὲ αὐτὸν οἱ γεωργοὶ
having seen they will respect. having seen And him the vinedressers

1260 4314 1438 3004 3778 2076 3588
διελογίζοντο πρὸς ἑαυτούς, λέγοντες, Οὗτός ἐστιν ὁ
reasoned to themselves, saying, This is the

2818 1205 615 846 2443 2257 1096 3588
κληρονόμος· δεῦτε, ἀποκτείνωμεν αὐτόν, ἵνα ἡμῶν γένηται ἡ
heir; come, let us kill him, that of us may be the

2817 2532 1544 846 1854 3588 290
κληρονομία. 15 καὶ ἐκβαλόντες αὐτὸν ἔξω τοῦ ἀμπελῶνος,
inheritance. And having thrown out him out of the vineyard,

615 5101 3767 4160 846 3588 2962 3588 290
ἀπέκτειναν. τί οὖν ποιήσει αὐτοῖς ὁ κύριος τοῦ ἀμπελῶνος;
they killed (him). What then will do to them the lord of the vineyard?

2064 2532 622 3588 1092 5128 2532 1325
16 ἐλεύσεται καὶ ἀπολέσει τοὺς γεωργοὺς τούτους, καὶ δώσει
He will come and will destroy vinedressers these, and will give

3588 290 243 191 1161 2036 3361 1096 3588 1161
τὸν ἀμπελῶνα ἄλλοις. ἀκούσαντες δὲ εἶπον, Μὴ γένοιτο. 17 ὁ δὲ
the vineyard to others. having heard And they said, Not let it be! He And

King James Version

people will stone us: for they be persuaded that John was a prophet.
7 And they answered, that they could not tell whence (it was).
8 And Jesus said unto them, Neither tell I you by what authority I do these things.

9 Then began he to speak to the people this parable; A certain man planted a vineyard, and let it forth to husbandmen, and went into a far country for a long time.
10 And at the season he sent a servant to the husbandmen, that they should give him of the fruit of the vineyard: but the husbandmen beat him, and sent (him) away empty.

11 And again he sent another servant: and they beat him also, and entreated (him) shamefully, and sent (him) away empty.
12 And again he sent a third: and they wounded him also, and cast (him) out.
13 Then said the lord of the vineyard, What shall I do? I will send my beloved son: it may be they will reverence (him) when they see him.
14 But when the husbandmen saw him, they reasoned among themselves, saying, This is the heir: come, let us kill him, that the inheritance may be ours.

15 So they cast him out of the vineyard, and killed (him). What therefore shall the lord of the vineyard do unto them?
16 He shall come and destroy these husbandmen, and shall give the vineyard to others. And when they heard (it), they said, God forbid.
17 And he

Literal Translation

looking at them He said, What then is this which has been written, "(The) Stone that the (ones) building rejected, this One came to be for (the) Head of (the) corner"? (Ps. 118:22)
18 Everyone having fallen on that Stone will be broken in pieces, but on whomever it falls, it will crush him.
19 And the chief priests and the scribes sought to lay hands on Him in the same hour. And (they) feared the people, for they knew that He told this parable against them.

20. And having watched carefully, they sent spies, pretending themselves to be righteous, that they might seize upon a word of His, so as to deliver up Him to the power and to the authority of the governor.

21 And they questioned Him, saying, Teacher, we know that you speak and teach rightly, and do not receive a face, but you teach the way of God on truth.

22 Is it lawful for us to give tribute to Caesar, or not?
23 But having perceived their slyness, He said to them, Why do you tempt Me?
24 Show Me a denarius. Whose image and inscription does it have? And answering, they said, Caesar's.
25 And He said to them, Then give back the things of Caesar to Caesar, and the things of God to God.
26 And they were not able to lay hold of His speech before the people. And having marveled at His answer, they were silent.
27. And some of the Sadducees coming up, those speaking against

Luke 20:18

1689 846 2036 5101 3767 2076 3588 1125 5124
ἐμβλέψας αὐτοῖς εἶπε, Τί οὖν ἐστι τὸ γεγραμμένον τοῦτο,
having looked at them said, What then is having been written this,
3037 3739 593 3588 3618 3778 1096 1519
Λίθον ὃν ἀπεδοκίμασαν οἱ οἰκοδομοῦντες, οὗτος ἐγενήθη εἰς
(The) Stone which rejected those building, this One came to be for
2776 1137 3956 3588 4098 1909 1565 3588 3037
κεφαλὴν γωνίας; 18 πᾶς ὁ πεσὼν ἐπ' ἐκεῖνον τὸν λίθον
Head of (the) corner? Everyone having fallen on that Stone
4917 1909 3739 1161 302 4098 3039 846
συνθλασθήσεται· ἐφ' ὃν δ' ἂν πέσῃ, λικμήσει αὐτόν.
will be broken in pieces, but on whomever it falls, (it) will crush him.
2532 2212 3588 749 2532 3588 1122 1911
19 Καὶ ἐζήτησαν οἱ ἀρχιερεῖς καὶ οἱ γραμματεῖς ἐπιβαλεῖν
And sought the chief priests and the scribes to lay
1909 846 3588 5495 1722 846 3588 5610 2532 5399 3588
ἐπ' αὐτὸν τὰς χεῖρας ἐν αὐτῇ τῇ ὥρᾳ, καὶ ἐφοβήθησαν τὸν
on Him the hands in same the hour, and feared the
2992 1097 1063 3754 4314 846 3588 3850 3778
λαόν· ἔγνωσαν γὰρ ὅτι πρὸς αὐτοὺς τὴν παραβολὴν ταύτην
people; they knew for that against them parable this
2036 2532 3906 649 1455 5271
εἶπε. 20 καὶ παρατηρήσαντες ἀπέστειλαν ἐγκαθέτους ὑπο-
He told. And having watched carefully they sent spies pre-
1438 1342 1511 2443 1949 846
κρινομένους ἑαυτοὺς δικαίους εἶναι, ἵνα ἐπιλάβωνται αὐτοῦ
tending themselves righteous to be, that they might seize of Him
3056 1519 3588 3860 846 3588 746 2532 3588 1849
λόγου, εἰς τὸ παραδοῦναι αὐτὸν τῇ ἀρχῇ καὶ τῇ ἐξουσίᾳ
a word, to deliver up Him to the power and to the authority
3588 2232 2532 1905 846 3004 1320
τοῦ ἡγεμόνος. 21 καὶ ἐπηρώτησαν αὐτὸν, λέγοντες, Διδάσκαλε,
of the governor. And they questioned Him, saying, Teacher,
1492 3754 3723 3004 2532 1321 2532 3756 2983
οἴδαμεν ὅτι ὀρθῶς λέγεις καὶ διδάσκεις, καὶ οὐ λαμβάνεις
we know that rightly you speak and teach, and not do receive
4383 235 1909 225 3588 3598 3588 2316 1321
πρόσωπον, ἀλλ' ἐπ' ἀληθείας τὴν ὁδὸν τοῦ Θεοῦ διδάσκεις.
a face, but upon truth the way of God you teach.
1832 2254 2541 5411 1325 2228 3756 2657 1161
22 ἔξεστιν ἡμῖν Καίσαρι φόρον δοῦναι, ἢ οὔ; 23 κατανοήσας δὲ
Is it lawful for us to Caesar tribute to give, or not? perceiving And
846 3588 3834 2036 4314 846 5101 3165 3985
αὐτῶν τὴν πανουργίαν, εἶπε πρὸς αὐτούς, Τί με πειράζετε;
of them the slyness, He said to them, Why Me do you tempt?
1925 3427 1220 5101 2192 1504 2532 1923
24 ἐπιδείξατέ μοι δηνάριον· τίνος ἔχει εἰκόνα καὶ ἐπιγραφήν;
Show Me a denarius; of whom has it an image and inscription?
611 1161 2036 2541 3588 1161 2036 846
ἀπρκριθέντες δὲ εἶπον, Καίσαρος. 25 ὁ δὲ εἶπεν αὐτοῖς,
answering And they said, Of Caesar. He And said to them,
59 5106 3588 2541 2541 2532 3588 3588 2316 3588
Ἀπόδοτε τοίνυν τὰ Καίσαρος Καίσαρι, καὶ τὰ τοῦ Θεοῦ τῷ
Give back then the things of Caesar to Caesar, and the things of God
2316 2532 3756 2480 1949 846 4487 1726
Θεῷ. 26 καὶ οὐκ ἴσχυσαν ἐπιλαβέσθαι αὐτοῦ ῥήματος ἐναντίον
to God. And not they were able to lay hold of Him (the) speech before
3588 2992 2532 2296 1909 3588 612 846 4601
τοῦ λαοῦ· καὶ θαυμάσαντες ἐπὶ τῇ ἀποκρίσει αὐτοῦ, ἐσίγησαν.
the people; and having marveled at the answer of Him, they were silent.
4334 1161 5100 3588 4523 3588 483
27.Προσελθόντες δέ τινες τῶν Σαδδουκαίων, οἱ ἀντιλέγοντες
having come up And some of the Sadducees, those speaking against

King James Version

beheld them, and said, What is this then that is written, The stone which the builders rejected, the same is become the head of the corner?
18 Whosoever shall fall upon that stone shall be broken; but on whomsoever it shall fall, it will grind him to powder.

19 And the chief priests and the scribes the same hour sought to lay hands on him; and they feared the people: for they perceived that he had spoken this parable against them.

20. And they watched (him), and sent forth spies, which should feign themselves just men, that they might take hold of his words, that so they might deliver him unto the power and authority of the governor.

21 And they asked him, saying, Master, we know that thou sayest and teachest rightly, neither acceptest thou the person (of any), but teachest the way of God truly:
22 Is it lawful for us to give tribute unto Caesar, or no?
23 But he perceived their craftiness, and said unto them, Why tempt ye me?
24 Shew me a penny. Whose image and superscription hath it? They answered and said, Caesar's.
25 And he said unto them, Render therefore unto Caesar the things which be Caesar's, and unto God the things which be God's.
26 And they could not take hold of his words before the people: and they marvelled at his answer, and held their peace.
27. Then came to (him) certain of the Sadducees, which deny that there is

Literal Translation

a resurrection, (that it was) not to be, they questioned Him,
28 saying, Teacher, Moses wrote to us, If anyone's brother dies having a wife, and this one should die childless, that his brother should take the wife and raise up seed to his brother. (Deut. 25:5)
29 Then there were seven brothers. And having taken a wife, the first died childless.
30 And the second took the wife, and this one died childless.
31 And the third took her, and likewise also the seven did not leave children, and died.
32 And last of all the woman died.
33 Then in the resurrection, of which of them does she become wife? For the seven had her (as) wife.
34 And answering, Jesus said to them, The sons of this age marry, and are given in marriage.
35 But the (ones) counted worthy to attain that age, and the resurrection from (the) dead, neither marry nor are given in marriage.
36 For they are not able to die (any) more; they are angel-like, and are sons of God, being sons of the resurrection.
37 But that the dead are raised, even Moses pointed out at the Bush, when he calls (the) Lord the God of Abraham, and the God of Isaac, and the God of Jacob. (Ex. 3:6)
38 But He is not God of dead ones, but of living ones, for all live to Him.
39 And answering, some of the scribes said, Teacher, you speak well.
40 And they did not dare

Luke 20:28

386 3361 1511 1905 846 3004 1320
ἀνάστασιν μὴ εἶναι, ἐπηρώτησαν αὐτὸν, 28 λέγοντες, Διδά-
a resurrection (it) not to be, they questioned Him, saying, Teacher,

3475 1125 2254 1437 5100 80 815 599
σκαλε, Μωσῆς ἔγραψεν ἡμῖν, ἐάν τινος ἀδελφὸς ἀποθάνῃ
Moses wrote to us, if of anyone a brother dies

2192 1135 2532 3778 815 599 2443 2983 3588
ἔχων γυναῖκα, καὶ οὗτος ἄτεκνος ἀποθάνῃ, ἵνα λάβῃ ὁ
having a wife, and this one childless should die, that should take the

80 846 3588 1135 2532 1817 4690 3588
ἀδελφὸς αὐτοῦ τὴν γυναῖκα, καὶ ἐξαναστήσῃ σπέρμα τῷ
brother of him the wife, and raise up seed to the

80 846 2033 3767 80 2258 2532 3588 4413
ἀδελφῷ αὐτοῦ. 29 ἑπτὰ οὖν ἀδελφοὶ ἦσαν· καὶ ὁ πρῶτος
brother of him. seven Then brothers there were; and the first

2983 1135 599 815 2532 2983 3588 1208
λαβὼν γυναῖκα ἀπέθανεν ἄτεκνος· 30 και ἔλαβεν ὁ δεύτερος
having taken a wife died childless; and took the second

3588 1135 2532 3778 599 815 2532 3588 5154
τὴν γυναῖκα, καὶ οὗτος ἀπέθανεν ἄτεκνος. 31 καὶ ὁ τρίτος
the wife, and this one died childless. And the third

2983 846 5615 1161 2532 3588 2033 2532 3756 2641
ἔλαβεν αὐτήν. ὡσαύτως δὲ καὶ οἱ ἑπτὰ· καὶ οὐ κατέλιπον
took her. likewise And also the seven; even not did leave

5043 2532 599 5305 3956 599 2532 3588 1135
τέκνα, καὶ ἀπέθανον. 32 ὕστερον πάντων ἀπέθανε καὶ ἡ γυνὴ.
children, and died. Last of all died also the woman.

1722 3588 3767 386 5101 846 1096 1135 3588 1063
33 ἐν τῇ οὖν ἀναστάσει, τίνος αὐτῶν γίνεται γυνή; οἱ γὰρ
in the Then resurrection, of which of them she becomes wife? the For

2033 2192 846 1135 2532 611 2036 846 3588
ἑπτὰ ἔσχον αὐτὴν γυναῖκα. 34 και ἀποκριθεὶς εἶπεν αὐτοῖς ὁ
seven had her (for) wife. And answering said to them

2424 3588 5207 3588 165 5127 1060 2532 1548
Ἰησοῦς, Οἱ υἱοὶ τοῦ αἰῶνος τούτου γαμοῦσι καὶ ἐκγαμί-
Jesus, The sons age of this marry and are given

3588 1161 2261 3588 165 1565 5177 2532
σκονται· 35 οἱ δὲ καταξιωθέντες τοῦ αἰῶνος ἐκείνου τυχεῖν καὶ
in marriage; the (ones) but counted worthy age (of) that to attain and

3588 386 3588 1537 3498 3777 1060 3777 1548
τῆς ἀναστάσεως τῆς ἐκ νεκρῶν οὔτε γαμοῦσιν οὔτε ἐκγαμί-
(of) the resurrection out of (the) dead neither marry nor are given

3777 1063 599 2089 1410 2465 1063
σκονται· 36 οὐδὲ γὰρ ἀποθανεῖν ἔτι δύνανται· ἰσάγγελοι γάρ
in marriage; not even for to die (any) more are they able; angel-like for

1526 2532 5207 1526 3588 2316 3588 386 5207 5607 3754
εἰσι, καὶ υἱοί εἰσι τοῦ Θεοῦ, τῆς ἀναστάσεως υἱοὶ ὄντες. 37 ὅτι
they are, and sons are of God, ot the resurrection sons being. that

1161 1453 3588 3498 2532 3475 3377 1909 3588 942
δὲ ἐγείρονται οἱ νεκροὶ, καὶ Μωσῆς ἐμήνυσεν ἐπὶ τῆς βάτου,
But are raised the dead, even Moses pointed out at the Bush,

5613 3004 2962 3588 2316 11 2532 3588 2316 2464 2532
ὡς λέγει Κύριον τὸν Θεὸν Ἀβραὰμ και τὸν Θεὸν Ἰσαὰκ και
as he calls (the) Lord the God of Abraham and the God of Isaac and

3588 2316 2384 2316 1161 3756 2076 3498 235 2198
τὸν Θεὸν Ἰακώβ. 38 Θεὸς δὲ οὐκ ἔστι νεκρῶν, ἀλλὰ ζώντων·
the God of Jacob. God But not He is of dead ones, but of living ones;

3956 1063 846 2198 611 1161 5100 3588 1122
πάντες γὰρ αὐτῷ ζῶσιν. 39 ἀποκριθέντες δέ τινες τῶν γραμ-
all for to Him live. answering And some of the scribes

2036 1320 2573 2036 3765 1161 5111
ματέων εἶπον, Διδάσκαλε, καλῶς εἶπας· 40 Οὐκέτι δὲ ἐτόλμων
said, Teacher, Well you speak. no more And they dared

King James Version

any resurrection; and they asked him,
28 Saying, Master, Moses wrote unto us, If any man's brother die, having a wife, and he die without children, that his brother should take his wife, and raise up seed unto his brother.
29 There were therefore seven brethren: and the first took a wife, and died without children.
30 And the second took her to wife, and he died childless.
31 And the third took her; and in like manner the seven also: and they left no children, and died.
32 Last of all the woman died also.
33 Therefore in the resurrection whose wife of them is she? for seven had her to wife.
34 And Jesus answering said unto them, The children of this world marry, and are given in marriage:
35 But they which shall be accounted worthy to obtain that world, and the resurrection from the dead, neither marry, nor are given in marriage:
36 Neither can they die any more: for they are equal unto the angels; and are the children of God, being the children of the resurrection.
37 Now that the dead are raised, even Moses shewed at the bush, when he calleth the Lord the God of Abraham, and the God of Isaac, and the God of Jacob.
38 For he is not a God of the dead, but of the living: for all live unto him.
39 Then certain of the scribes answering said, Master, thou hast well said.
40 And after that they durst not

Literal Translation

to question Him any more, not a thing.

41. And He said to them, How do they say the Christ is David's son?
42 Even David himself said in (the) scroll of Psalms, "The Lord said to my Lord, Sit at My right (hand)
43 until I place Your enemies (as) a footstool of Your feet." (Ps. 110:1)
44 Then David calls Him Lord. And how is He his son?

45. And (as) all the people (were) hearing, He said to His disciples,
46 Be on guard from the scribes, those desiring to walk about in long robes, and liking greetings in the markets, and chief seats in the synagogues, and chief couches in the suppers,

47 the (ones) devouring the houses of the widows, and under pretense pray long. These will receive a more severe judgment.

Luke 20:41

1905 846 3762
ἐπερωτᾷν αὐτὸν οὐδέν.
to question Him, nothing!

2036 1161 4314 846 4459 3004 3588 5547 5207
41. Εἶπε δὲ πρὸς αὐτούς, Πῶς λέγουσι τὸν Χριστὸν υἱὸν
He said And to them, How do they say the Christ son

1138 1511 2532 846 1138 3004 1722 976 5568
Δαβὶδ εἶναι; 42 καὶ αὐτὸς Δαβὶδ λέγει ἐν βίβλῳ ψαλμῶν,
of David to be? Even himself David says in (the) scroll of Psalms,

2036 3588 2962 3588 2962 3450 2521 1537 1188 3450 2193 302
Εἶπεν ὁ Κύριος τῷ Κυρίῳ μου, Κάθου ἐκ δεξιῶν μου, 43 ἕως ἂν
Said the Lord to the Lord of Me, Sit at (the) right of Me, until may

5087 3588 2190 4675 5286 3588 4228 4675 1138
θῶ τοὺς ἐχθρούς σου ὑποπόδιον τῶν ποδῶν σου. 44 Δαβὶδ
I put the enemies of You a footstool of the foot of You. David

3767 846 2962 2564 2532 4459 5207 846 2076
οὖν αὐτὸν Κύριον καλεῖ, καὶ πῶς υἱὸς αὐτοῦ ἐστιν;
Then Him Lord calls, and how son of him is He?

191 1161 3956 3588 2992 2036 3588 3101
45. Ἀκούοντος δὲ παντὸς τοῦ λαοῦ, εἶπε τοῖς μαθηταῖς
hearing And all the people, He said to the disciples

846 4337 575 3588 1122 3588 2309
αὐτοῦ, 46 Προσέχετε ἀπὸ τῶν γραμματέων τῶν θελόντων
of Him, Be on guard from the scribes those desiring

4043 1722 4749 2532 5368 783 1722 3588
περιπατεῖν ἐν στολαῖς, καὶ φιλούντων ἀσπασμοὺς ἐν ταῖς
to walk about in robes, and loving greetings in the

58 2532 4410 1722 3588 4864 2532
ἀγοραῖς, καὶ πρωτοκαθεδρίας ἐν ταῖς συναγωγαῖς, καὶ
markets, and chief seats in the synagogues, and

4411 1722 3588 1173 3739 2719 3588 3614
πρωτοκλισίας ἐν τοῖς δείπνοις· 47 οἳ κατεσθίουσι τὰς οἰκίας
chief couches in the suppers; who devour the houses

3588 5503 2532 4392 3117 4336 3778 2983
τῶν χηρῶν, καὶ προφάσει μακρὰ προσεύχονται· οὗτοι λήψονται
of the widows, and under pretense long pray. These will receive

4053 2917
περισσότερον κρίμα.
a more severe judgment.

King James Version

ask him any (question at all).

41. And he said unto them, How say they that Christ is David's son?

42 And David himself saith in the book of Psalms, The LORD said unto my Lord, Sit thou on my right hand,
43 Till I make thine enemies thy footstool.
44 David therefore calleth him Lord, how is he then his son?

45. Then in the audience of all the people he said unto his disciples,
46 Beware of the scribes, which desire to walk in long robes, and love greetings in the markets, and the highest seats in the synagogues, and the chief rooms at feasts;

47 Which devour widows' houses, and for a shew make long prayers: the same shall receive greater damnation.

Luke 21

1. And having looked up, He saw the rich (ones) putting their gifts into the treasury.
2 And He also saw a certain poor widow putting two lepta there.
3 And He said, Truly I say to you this poor widow put (in) more than all.

4 For all these out of their abundance put into the gifts to God, but she out of her poverty put (in) all the living which she had.

Luke 21

308 1161 1492 3588 906 3588 1435 846 1519
1. Ἀναβλέψας δὲ εἶδε τοὺς βάλλοντας τὰ δῶρα αὐτῶν εἰς
having looked up And He saw those putting the gifts of them into

3588 1049 4145 1492 1161 2532 5100 5503
τὸ γαζοφυλάκιον πλουσίους· 2 εἶδε δέ καὶ τινα χήραν
the treasury rich (ones); He saw and also a certain widow

3998 906 1563 1417 3016 2532 2036 230
πενιχρὰν βάλλουσαν ἐκεῖ δύο λεπτὰ, 3 καὶ εἶπεν, Ἀληθῶς
poor putting there two lepta, And He said, Truly

3004 5213 3754 3588 5503 3588 4434 3778 4119 3956 906
λέγω ὑμῖν, ὅτι ἡ χήρα ἡ πτωχὴ αὕτη πλεῖον πάντων ἔβαλεν·
I say to you, widow poor This more (than) all put in;

537 1063 3778 1537 3588 4052 846 906 1519
4 ἅπαντες γὰρ οὗτοι ἐκ τοῦ περισσεύοντος αὐτοῖς ἔβαλον εἰς
all for these out of the abundance to them cast into

3588 1435 3588 2316 846 1161 1537 3588 5303 846
τὰ δῶρα τοῦ Θεοῦ, αὕτη δὲ ἐκ τοῦ ὑστερήματος αὐτῆς
the gifts to God, she but out of the poverty of her

537 3588 979 3739 2192 906
ἅπαντα τὸν βίον ὃν εἶχεν ἔβαλε.
all the living which she had put in.

Luke 21

1. And he looked up, and saw the rich men casting their gifts into the treasury.
2 And he saw also a certain poor widow casting in thither two mites.
3 And he said, Of a truth I say unto you, that this poor widow hath cast in more than they all:

4 For all these have of their abundance cast in unto the offerings of God: but she of her penury hath cast in all the living that she had.

Literal Translation

5. And as some were speaking about the temple, that it had been adorned with beautiful stones and gifts, He said,
6 (As to) these things that you see, days will come in which a stone will not be left on a stone, which will not be thrown down.
7 And they questioned Him, saying, Teacher, then when will these things be? And what (will be) the sign when these things (are) about to occur?
8 And He said, Watch that you not be led astray. For many will come on My name, saying, I AM! Also, The time has come! Do not go after them.
9 And when you hear of wars and disturbances, do not be afraid. For these things must first occur, but the end (is) not at once.

10 Then He said to them, Nation will be lifted up against nation, and kingdom against kingdom.
11 Also there will be great earthquakes from place to place, and famines, and plagues. And also there will be terrors and great signs from Heaven.
12 But before all these things, they will lay their hands on you, and will persecute (you), delivering (you) into synagogues and prisons, being led away before kings and governors on account of My name.
13 But it will return to you for a testimony.
14 Then put in your hearts not to premeditate to make a defense.
15 For I will give you a mouth and wisdom which all those opposing you will not be able to withstand nor contradict.
16 But you will be delivered up also by parents,

Luke 21:5

2532 5100 3004 4012 3588 2411 3754 3037 2570
5. Καί τινων λεγόντων περὶ τοῦ ἱεροῦ, ὅτι λίθοις καλοῖς
And some speaking about the temple, that with stones beautiful

2532 334 2885 2036 5023 3739 2334 2064
καὶ ἀναθήμασι κεκόσμηται, εἶπε, 6 ταῦτα ἃ θεωρεῖτε, ἐλεύ-
and gifts it had been adorned, He said, These things that you see, will

2250 1722 3739 3756 863 3037 1909 3037 3739 3756
σονται ἡμέραι ἐν αἷς οὐκ ἀφεθήσεται λίθος ἐπὶ λίθῳ, ὃς οὐ
come days in which not will be left stone on stone which not

2647 1905 1161 846 3004 1320
καταλυθήσεται. 7 ἐπηρώτησαν δὲ αὐτὸν, λέγοντες, Διδά-
will be thrown down. questioned And they, saying, Teacher,

4219 3767 5023 2071 2532 5101 3588 4592 3752 3195
σκαλε, πότε οὖν ταῦτα ἔσται; καὶ τί τὸ σημεῖον, ὅταν μέλλῃ
when then these things will be? And what the sign, when about

5023 1096 3588 1161 2036 991 3361 4105 4183
ταῦτα γίνεσθαι; 8 ὁ δὲ εἶπε, Βλέπετε μὴ πλανηθῆτε· πολλοὶ
these things to occur? He And said, Watch lest you be led astray; many

1063 2064 1909 3588 3686 3450 3004 3754 1473 1510
γὰρ ἐλεύσονται ἐπὶ τῷ ὀνόματί μου, λέγοντες ὅτι Ἐγώ εἰμι·
for will come on the name of Me, saying, I AM,

2532 3588 2540 1448 3361 3767 4198 3694 846 3752
καί, Ὁ καιρὸς ἤγγικε· μὴ οὖν πορευθῆτε ὀπίσω αὐτῶν. 9 ὅταν
also, The time has come near; not then go after them. when

1161 191 4171 2532 181 3361 4422
δὲ ἀκούσητε πολέμους καὶ ἀκαταστασίας, μὴ πτοηθῆτε·
And you hear of wars and disturbances, not do be afraid;

1163 1063 5023 1096 4412 235 3756 2112 3588 5056
δεῖ γὰρ ταῦτα γενέσθαι πρῶτον, ἀλλ' οὐκ εὐθέως τὸ τέλος.
must for these things to occur first, but not at once the end.

5119 3004 846 1453 1484 1909 1484 2532
10. Τότε ἔλεγεν αὐτοῖς, Ἐγερθήσεται ἔθνος ἐπὶ ἔθνος, καὶ
Then He said to them, will be raised Nation against nation, and

932 1909 932 4578 5037 3173 2596 5117
βασιλεία ἐπὶ βασιλείαν· 11 σεισμοί τε μεγάλοι κατὰ τόπους
kingdom against kingdom; earthquakes and great from place to place

2532 3042 2532 3061 2071 5400 5037 2532 4592 575
καὶ λιμοὶ καὶ λοιμοὶ ἔσονται, φόβητρά τε καὶ σημεῖα ἀπ'
and famines and plagues there will be; terrors and also signs from

3772 3173 2071 4253 1161 5130 537 1911
οὐρανοῦ μεγάλα ἔσται. 12 πρὸ δὲ τούτων πάντων ἐπι-
Heaven great will be. before But these things all they

1909 5209 3588 5495 846 2532 1377 3860
βαλοῦσιν ἐφ' ὑμᾶς τὰς χεῖρας αὐτῶν, καὶ διώξουσι, παραδι-
will lay on you the hands of them, and will persecute, delivering

1519 4864 2532 5438 71 1909 935
δόντες εἰς συναγωγὰς καὶ φυλακάς, ἀγομένους ἐπὶ βασιλεῖς
into synagogues and prisons, being led away before kings

2532 2232 1752 3588 3686 3450 576 1161
καὶ ἡγεμόνας, ἕνεκεν τοῦ ὀνόματός μου. 13 ἀποβήσεται δὲ
and governors, on account of the name of Me. it will return But

5213 1519 3142 5087 3767 1519 3588 2588 5216 3361
ὑμῖν εἰς μαρτύριον. 14 θέσθε οὖν ἐν τὰς καρδίαις ὑμῶν μὴ
to you for a testimony. put Then in the hearts of you not

4304 626 1473 1063 1325 5213 4750 2532
προμελετᾶν ἀπολογηθῆναι, 15 ἐγὼ γὰρ δώσω ὑμῖν στόμα καὶ
to premeditate to make a defense; I for will give you a mouth and

4678 3739 3756 1410 471 3761 436 3956
σοφίαν, ᾗ οὐ δυνήσονται ἀντειπεῖν οὐδὲ ἀντιστῆναι παντες
wisdom, which not (they) will be able to withstand nor contradict all

3588 480 5213 3860 1161 2532 5259 1118
οἱ ἀντικείμενοι ὑμῖν. 16 παραδοθήσεσθε δὲ καὶ ὑπὸ γονέων
those opposing you. you will be delivered up But also by parents

King James Version

5. And as some spake of the temple, how it was adorned with goodly stones and gifts, he said,
6 (As for) these things which ye behold, the days will come, in the which there shall not be left one stone upon another, that shall not be thrown down.
7 And they asked him, saying, Master, but when shall these things be? and what sign (will there be) when these things shall come to pass?
8 And he said, Take heed that ye be not deceived: for many shall come in my name, saying, I am (Christ); and the time draweth near: go ye not therefore after them.
9 But when ye shall hear of wars and commotions, be not terrified: for these things must first come to pass; but the end (is) not by and by.

10 Then said he unto them, Nation shall rise against nation, and kingdom against kingdom:
11 And great earthquakes shall be in divers places, and famines, and pestilences; and fearful sights and great signs shall there be from heaven.
12 But before all these, they shall lay their hands on you, and persecute (you), delivering (you) up to the synagogues, and into prisons, being brought before kings and rulers for my name's sake.
13 And it shall turn to you for a testimony.

14 Settle (it) therefore in your hearts, not to meditate before what ye shall answer:
15 For I will give you a mouth and wisdom, which all your adversaries shall not be able to gainsay nor resist.
16 And ye shall be betrayed both by parents,

Literal Translation — **Luke 21:17** — **King James Version**

Literal Translation

and brothers, and relatives, and friends. And they will put (some) of you to death.
17 And you will be (as ones) being hated by all because of My name.
18 But a hair of your head in no way shall perish.
19 In your patience you will gain your souls.

20 And when you see Jerusalem being encircled by armies, then know that its destruction has drawn near.

21 Then those in Judea, let them flee into the mountains; and those in its midst, let them go out. And those in the open spaces, let them not go into it,
22 because these are days of vengeance (so as) to be fulfilled all the things having been written.
23 But woe to the (ones) having (a child) in womb, and the (ones) giving suck in those days! For great distress will be on the earth and wrath on this people.

24 And they will fall by (the) mouth of (the) sword and will be led captive into all the nations. And Jerusalem will be trodden down by nations, until (the) times of (the) nations are fulfilled.
25. And there will be signs in sun and moon and stars. And on the earth (will be) anxiety of nations in perplexity of (the) sound of sea and of surf,

26 men fainting from fear, and expectation of the things coming on the inhabited earth. For the powers of the heavens will be shaken.
27 And then they will see the Son of man coming in a cloud with power and much glory. (Dan. 7:13)
28 And beginning

2532 80 2532 4773 2532 5384 2532 2289
καὶ ἀδελφῶν καὶ συγγενῶν καὶ φίλων, καὶ θανατώσουσιν
and brothers and relatives and friends, and they will put to death

1537 5216 2532 2071 3404 5259 3956 1223 3588 3686
ἐξ ὑμῶν, 17 καὶ ἔσεσθε μισούμενοι ὑπὸ πάντων διὰ τὸ ὄνομά
(some) of you. And you will be being hated by all because of the name

3450 2532 2359 1537 3588 2776 5216 3756 3361 622 1722 3588
μου. 18 καὶ θρὶξ ἐκ τῆς κεφαλῆς ὑμῶν οὐ μὴ ἀπόληται. 19 ἐν τῇ
of Me. But a hair from the head of you in no way shall perish. In the

5281 5216 2932 3588 5590 5216
ὑπομονῇ ὑμῶν κτήσασθε τὰς ψυχὰς ὑμῶν.
patience of you you will gain the souls of you.

3752 1161 1492 2944 5259 4760 3588
20. Ὅταν δὲ ἴδητε κυκλουμένην ὑπὸ στρατοπέδων τὴν
when And you see being encircled by armies

2419 5119 1097 3754 1448 3588 2050 846
Ἱερουσαλήμ, τότε γνῶτε ὅτι ἤγγικεν ἡ ἐρήμωσις αὐτῆς.
Jerusalem, then know that has drawn near the destruction of it.

5119 3588 1722 3588 2449 5343 1519/3588/3735/2532/3588/1722
21 τότε οἱ ἐν τῇ Ἰουδαίᾳ φευγέτωσαν εἰς τὰ ὄρη· καὶ οἱ ἐν
Then those in Judea, let them flee into the mounts; and those in

3319 846 1633 2532 3588 1722 3588 5561 3361 1525
μέσῳ αὐτῆς ἐκχωρείτωσαν· καὶ οἱ ἐν ταῖς χώραις μὴ εἰσερχέ-
midst of it let them go out; and those in the open spaces not let them

1519 846 3754 2250 1557 3778 1526 3588
σθωσαν εἰς αὐτήν, 22 ὅτι ἡμέραι ἐκδικήσεως αὗταί εἰσι, τοῦ
enter into it, because days of vengeance these are, (so as)

4137 3956 3588 1125 3759 1161 3588 1722 1064
πλησθῆναι πάντα τὰ γεγραμμένα. 23 οὐαὶ δὲ ταῖς ἐν γαστρὶ
to be fulfilled all the things having been written. woe But to (ones) in womb

2192 2532 3588 2337 1722 1565 3588 2250
ἐχούσαις καὶ ταῖς θηλαζούσαις ἐν ἐκείναις ταῖς ἡμέραις·
having and the(ones) giving suck in those days;

2071 1063 318 3173 1909 3588 1093 2532 3709 1722 3588 2992
ἔσται γὰρ ἀνάγκη μεγάλη ἐπὶ τῆς γῆς, καὶ ὀργὴ ἐν τῷ λαῷ
will be for distress great on the earth, and wrath on people

5129 2532 4098 4750 3162 2532 163
τούτῳ, 24 καὶ πεσοῦνται στόματι μαχαίρας, καὶ αἰχμαλω-
this. And they will fall by (the) mouth of (the) sword, and will be led

1519 3956 3588 1484 2532 2419 2071
τισθήσονται εἰς πάντα τὰ ἔθνη· καὶ Ἱερουσαλὴμ ἔσται
captive into all the nations; and Jerusalem will be

3961 5259 1484 891 4137 2540 1484 2532
πατουμένη ὑπὸ ἐθνῶν, ἄχρι πληρωθῶσι καιροὶ ἐθνῶν. 25 καὶ
trodden down by nations, until are fulfilled (the) times of nations. And

2071 4592 1722 2246 2532 4582 2532 798 2532 1909 3588
ἔσται σημεῖα ἐν ἡλίῳ καὶ σελήνῃ καὶ ἄστροις, καὶ ἐπὶ τῆς
will be signs in sun and moon and stars. And on the

1093 4928 1484 1722 640 2278 2281 2532 4535
γῆς συνοχὴ ἐθνῶν ἐν ἀπορίᾳ, ἠχούσης θαλάσσης καὶ σάλου,
earth anxiety of nations in perplexity of sound of sea and of surf,

674 444 575 5401 2532 4329 3588
26 ἀποψυχόντων ἀνθρώπων ἀπὸ φόβου καὶ προσδοκίας τῶν
fainting men from fear and expectation of the

1904 3588 3625 3588 1063 1411 3588 3772
ἐπερχομένων τῇ οἰκουμένῃ· αἱ γὰρ δυνάμεις τῶν οὐρανῶν
things coming on the inhabited earth; the for powers of the heavens

4531 2532 5119 3700 3588 5207 3588 444
σαλευθήσονται. 27 καὶ τότε ὄψονται τὸν υἱὸν τοῦ ἀνθρώπου
will be shaken. And then they will see the Son of man

2064 1722 3507 3326 1411 2532 1391 4183 756
ἐρχόμενον ἐν νεφέλῃ μετὰ δυνάμεως καὶ δόξης πολλῆς. 28 ἀρχο-
coming in a cloud with power and glory much. begin-

King James Version

and brethren, and kinsfolks, and friends; and (some) of you shall they cause to be put to death.
17 And ye shall be hated of all (men) for my name's sake.
18 But there shall not an hair of your head perish.
19 In your patience possess ye your souls.

20 And when ye shall see Jerusalem compassed with armies, then know that the desolation thereof is nigh.

21 Then let them which are in Judaea flee to the mountains; and let them which are in the midst of it depart out; and let not them that are in the countries enter thereinto.
22 For these be the days of vengeance, that all things which are written may be fulfilled.
23 But woe unto them that are with child, and to them that give suck, in those days! for there shall be great distress in the land, and wrath upon this people.

24 And they shall fall by the edge of the sword, and shall be led away captive into all nations: and Jerusalem shall be trodden down of the Gentiles, until the times of the Gentiles be fulfilled.
25. And there shall be signs in the sun, and in the moon, and in the stars; and upon the earth distress of nations, with perplexity; the sea and the waves roaring;
26 Men's hearts failing them for fear, and for looking after those things which are coming on the earth: for the powers of heaven shall be shaken.
27 And then shall they see the Son of man coming in a cloud with power and great glory.
28 And when these things begin

Literal Translation

these things to happen, stand erect and lift up your heads, because your redemption draws near.

29 And He spoke a parable to them: You see the fig-tree and all the trees;
30 When they sprout leaves now, seeing (it), you will know from yourselves that now the summer is near.
31 So also when you see these things occurring, know that the kingdom of God is near.

32 Truly I say to you, In no way will this generation pass away until all (these) things shall occur.
33 The heaven and the earth will pass away, but My words in no way will pass away.

34. But take heed to yourselves that your hearts not be loaded down in headaches, and intoxication, and anxieties of life, and that day come suddenly upon you
35 as a snare, for it will come in on all those sitting on (the) face of all the earth. (Isa. 24:17)

36 Then be watchful at every time, begging that you be counted worthy to escape all these things the things being about to occur, and to stand before the Son of man.

37 And (in) the days, He was teaching in the temple. And going out (in) the nights, He lodged in the Mount having been called Of Olives.
38 And all the people rose early to Him in the temple, to hear Him.

Luke 22

1. And the Feast of Unleavened (Bread), being called Passover, drew near.

Luke 21:29

1161 5130 1096 352 2532 1869 3588
μένων δὲ τούτων γίνεσθαι, ἀνακύψατε καὶ ἐπάρατε τὰς
ning And these things to happen, stand erect and lift up the
2776 5216 1360 1448 3588 629 5216
κεφαλὰς ὑμῶν· διότι ἐγγίζει ἡ ἀπολύτρωσις ὑμῶν.
heads of you; because draws near the redemption of you.

2532 2036 3850 846 1492 3588 4808 2532 3956
29. Καὶ εἶπε παραβολὴν αὐτοῖς, Ἴδετε τὴν συκῆν καὶ πάντα
And He told a parable to them: You see the fig-tree and all
3588 1186 3752 4261 2235 991 575 1438
τὰ δένδρα· 30 ὅταν προβάλωσιν ἤδη, βλέποντες ἀφ' ἑαυτῶν
the trees; when they sprout leaves now, seeing from yourselves
1097 3754 2235 1451 3588 2330 2076 3779 2532 5210
γινώσκετε ὅτι ἤδη ἐγγὺς τὸ θέρος ἐστίν· 31 οὕτω καὶ ὑμεῖς,
you know that now near the summer is; so also you
3752 1492 5023 1096 1097 3754 1451 2076 3588
ὅταν ἴδητε ταῦτα γινόμενα, γινώσκετε ὅτι ἐγγύς ἐστιν ἡ
when you see these things occurring, know that near is the
932 3588 2316 281 3004 5213 3754 3756 3361 3928 3588
βασιλεία τοῦ Θεοῦ. 32 ἀμὴν λέγω ὑμῖν ὅτι οὐ μὴ παρέλθῃ ἡ
kingdom of God. Truly I say to you In no way will pass away
1074 3778 2193 302 3956 1096 3588 3772 2532 3588 1093
γενεὰ αὕτη, ἕως ἂν πάντα γένηται. 33 ὁ οὐρανὸς καὶ ἡ γῆ
generation this, until all things occur. The heaven and the earth
3928 3588 1161 3056 3450 3756 3361 3928
παρελεύσονται, οἱ δὲ λόγοι μου οὐ μὴ παρέλθωσι.
shall pass away, the but words of Me in no way will pass away.

4337 1161 1438 3379 925 5216 3588
34. Προσέχετε δὲ ἑαυτοῖς, μήποτε βαρυνθῶσιν ὑμῶν αἱ
take heed But to yourselves, that not be loaded down of you the
2588 1722 2897 2532 3178 2532 3308 982 2532
καρδίαι ἐν κραιπάλῃ καὶ μέθῃ καὶ μερίμναις βιωτικαῖς, καὶ
hearts in headaches and intoxication and anxieties of life, and
160 1909 5209 2186 3588 2250 1565 5613 3803 1063
αἰφνίδιος ἐφ' ὑμᾶς ἐπιστῇ ἡ ἡμέρα ἐκείνη· 35 ὡς παγὶς γὰρ
suddenly on you come day that; as a snare for
1904 1909 3956 3588 2521 1909 4383
ἐπελεύσεται ἐπὶ πάντας τοὺς καθημένους ἐπὶ πρόσωπον
it will come in on all those sitting on (the) face
3956 3588 1093 69 3767 1722 3956 2540 1189 2443
πάσης τῆς γῆς. 36 ἀγρυπνεῖτε οὖν ἐν παντὶ καιρῷ δεόμενοι, ἵνα
of all the earth. you be watchful Then in every time, begging that
2661 1628 5023 3956 3588 3195 1096
καταξιωθῆτε ἐκφυγεῖν ταῦτα πάντα τὰ μέλλοντα γίνεσθαι,
you be counted worthy to escape these things all the things being about to occur,
2532 2476 1715 3588 5207 3588 444
καὶ σταθῆναι ἔμπροσθεν τοῦ υἱοῦ τοῦ ἀνθρώπου.
and to stand before the Son of man.

2258 1161 3588 2250 1722 3588 2411 1321 3588 1161 3571
37. Ἦν δὲ τὰς ἡμέρας ἐν τῷ ἱερῷ διδάσκων· τὰς δὲ νύκτας
He was And (in) the days in the temple teaching; (in) the and nights
1831 835 1519 3588 3735 3588 2564 1636 2532
ἐξερχόμενος ηὐλίζετο εἰς τὸ ὄρος τὸ καλούμενον ἐλαιῶν. 38 καὶ
going out He lodged in the mountain having been called Of Olives. And
3956 3588 2992 3719 4314 846 1722 3588 2411 191 846
πᾶς ὁ λαὸς ὤρθριζε πρὸς αὐτὸν ἐν τῷ ἱερῷ ἀκούειν αὐτοῦ.
all the people rose early to Him in the temple to hear Him.

Luke 22

1448 1161 3588 1859 3588 106 3588 3004 3957
1. Ἤγγιζε δὲ ἡ ἑορτὴ τῶν ἀζύμων, ἡ λεγομένη πάσχα.
drew near And the Feast of the Unleavened (Bread), being called Passover.

King James Version

to come to pass, then look up, and lift up your heads; for your redemption draweth nigh.

29 And he spake to them a parable; Behold the fig tree, and all the trees;
30 When they now shoot forth, ye see and know of your own selves that summer is now nigh at hand.
31 So likewise ye, when ye see these things come to pass, know ye that the kingdom of God is nigh at hand.
32 Verily I say unto you, This generation shall not pass away, till all be fulfilled.
33 Heaven and earth shall pass away: but my words shall not pass away.

34. And take heed to yourselves, lest at any time your hearts be overcharged with surfeiting, and drunkenness, and cares of this life, and (so) that day come upon you unawares.
35 For as a snare shall it come on all them that dwell on the face of the whole earth.

36 Watch ye therefore, and pray always, that ye may be accounted worthy to escape all these things that shall come to pass, and to stand before the Son of man.

37 And in the day time he was teaching in the temple; and at night he went out, and abode in the mount that is called (the mount) of Olives.
38 And all the people came early in the morning to him in the temple, for to hear him.

Luke 22

1. Now the feast of unleavened bread drew nigh, which is called the Passover.

Literal Translation

2 And the chief priests and the scribes sought how to destroy Him; for they feared the people.

3. And Satan entered into Judas, the (one) being called Iscariot, being of the number of the Twelve.
4 And going he talked with the chief priests and the commanders (as to) how he might deliver up Him.
5 And they exulted, and they agreed to give him silver.

6 And he fully consented and sought opportunity to deliver up Him to them, away from (the) crowd.

7. And the day of the Unleavened (Bread) came, in which the Passover must be killed.
8 And He sent Peter and John, saying, Having gone, prepare for us the Passover, that we may eat.
9 And they said to Him, Where do You desire (that) we prepare?
10 And He said to them, Behold! You going into the city, you will meet a man carrying a pitcher of water. Follow him into the house where he goes in.

11 And you will say to the housemaster of (that) house, The Teacher says to you, Where is the guest room where I may eat the Passover with My disciples?
12 And that one will show you a large upper room which he has spread. Prepare there.
13 And having gone, they found even as He had told them, and they prepared the Passover.
14 And when the hour came, He reclined, and the twelve apostles with Him.
15 And He said to them, With desire I desired

Luke 22:2

2532 2212 3588 749 2532 3588 1122 3588 4459 337
2 καὶ ἐζήτουν οἱ ἀρχιερεῖς καὶ οἱ γραμματεῖς τὸ πῶς ἀνέλωσιν
And sought the chief priests and the scribes how might kill

846 5399 1063 3588 2992
αὐτόν· ἐφοβοῦντο γὰρ τὸν λαόν.
Him; they feared for the people.

1525 1161 3588 4567 1519 2455 3588 1941
3 Εἰσῆλθε δὲ ὁ Σατανᾶς εἰς Ἰούδαν τὸν ἐπικαλούμενον
entered And Satan into Judas the (one) being called

2469 5607 1537 3588 706 3588 1427 2532 565
Ἰσκαριώτην, ὄντα ἐκ τοῦ ἀριθμοῦ τῶν δώδεκα. 4 καὶ ἀπελθὼν
Iscariot, being of the number of the Twelve. And going

4814 3588 749 2532 3588 4755 3588 4459
συνελάλησε τοῖς ἀρχιερεῦσι καὶ τοῖς στρατηγοῖς τὸ πῶς
he talked with the chief priests and the commanders (as to) how

846 3860 846 2532 5463 2532 4934 846
αὐτὸν παραδῷ αὐτοῖς. 5 καὶ ἐχάρησαν καὶ συνέθεντο αὐτῷ
he might deliver up Him. And they exulted and they agreed him

694 1325 2532 1843 2532 2212 2120 3588
ἀργύριον δοῦναι. 6 καὶ ἐξωμολόγησε, καὶ ἐζήτει εὐκαιρίαν τοῦ
silver to give. And he fully consented, and sought opportunity

3860 846 846 817 3793
παραδοῦναι αὐτὸν αὐτοῖς ἄτερ ὄχλου.
to deliver up Him to them away from (the) crowd.

2064 1161 3588 2250 3588 106 1722 3739 1163 2380 3588 3957
7. Ἦλθε δὲ ἡ ἡμέρα τῶν ἀζύμων, ἐν ᾗ ἔδει θύεσθαι τὸ πάσχα.
came And the day of the Unleavened, in which must be killed the Passover.

2532 649 4074 2532 2491 2036 4198
8 καὶ ἀπέστειλε Πέτρον καὶ Ἰωάννην, εἰπών, Πορευθέντες
And He sent Peter and John, saying, having gone,

2090 2254 3588 3957 2443 5315 3588 1161 2036 846
ἑτοιμάσατε ἡμῖν τὸ πάσχα, ἵνα φάγωμεν. 9 οἱ δὲ εἶπον αὐτῷ,
prepare for us the Passover, that we may eat. they And said to Him,

4226 2309 2090 3588 1161 2036 846 2400
Ποῦ θέλεις ἑτοιμάσωμεν; 10 ὁ δὲ εἶπεν αὐτοῖς, Ἰδοὺ εἰσ-
Where do You desire we prepare? He And said to them, Behold! Go-

1525 5216 1519 3588 4172 4876 5213 444
ελθόντων ὑμῶν εἰς τὴν πόλιν, συναντήσει ὑμῖν ἄνθρωπος
ing in You into the city, will meet you a man

3765 5204 941 190 846 1519 3588 3614
κεράμιον ὕδατος βαστάζων· ἀκολουθήσατε αὐτῷ εἰς τὴν οἰκίαν
a pitcher of water carrying; follow him into the house

3757 1531 2532 2046 3588 3617 3588 3614
οὗ εἰσπορεύεται. 11 καὶ ἐρεῖτε τῷ οἰκοδεσπότῃ τῆς οἰκίας,
where he goes in. And you will say to the housemaster of the house,

3004 4671 3588 1320 4226 2076 3588 2646 3699 3588
Λέγει σοι ὁ διδάσκαλος, Ποῦ ἐστι τὸ κατάλυμα, ὅπου τὸ
Says to you the Teacher, Where is the guest room where the

3957 3326 3588 3101 3450 5315 2548 5213 1166
πάσχα μετὰ τῶν μαθητῶν μου φάγω; 12 κἀκεῖνος ὑμῖν δείξει
Passover with the disciples of Me I may eat? And that one you will show

508 3173 4766 1563 2090 565 1161
ἀνώγεον μέγα ἐστρωμένον· ἐκεῖ ἑτοιμάσατε. 13 ἀπελθόντες δὲ
an upper room large having been spread; there prepare. having gone And

2147 2531 2046 846 2532 2090 3588 3957
εὗρον καθὼς εἰρήκεν αὐτοῖς· καὶ ἡτοίμασαν τὸ πάσχα.
they found even as He had told them; and they prepared the Passover.

2532 3753 1096 3588 5610 377 2532 3588 1427 652
14. Καὶ ὅτε ἐγένετο ἡ ὥρα, ἀνέπεσε, καὶ οἱ δώδεκα ἀπόσ-
And when came to be the hour, He reclined, and the twelve apostles

4862 846 2532 2036 4314 846 1939 1937
τολοι σὺν αὐτῷ. 15 καὶ εἶπε πρὸς αὐτούς, Ἐπιθυμίᾳ ἐπεθύμησα
with Him. And He said to them, With desire I desired

King James Version

2 And the chief priests and scribes sought how they might kill him; for they feared the people.

3. Then entered Satan into Judas surnamed Iscariot, being of the number of the twelve.
4 And he went his way, and communed with the chief priests and captains, how he might betray him unto them.
5 And they were glad, and covenanted to give him money.
6 And he promised, and sought opportunity to betray him unto them in the absence of the multitude.

7. Then came the day of unleavened bread, when the passover must be killed.
8 And he sent Peter and John, saying, Go and prepare us the passover, that we may eat.
9 And they said unto him, Where wilt thou that we prepare?
10 And he said unto them, Behold, when ye are entered into the city, there shall a man meet you, bearing a pitcher of water; follow him into the house where he entereth in.
11 And ye shall say unto the goodman of the house, The Master saith unto thee, Where is the guestchamber, where I shall eat the passover with my disciples?
12 And he shall shew you a large upper room furnished: there make ready.
13 And they went, and found as he had said unto them: and they made ready the passover.
14 And when the hour was come, he sat down, and the twelve apostles with him.
15 And he said unto them, With desire I have desired

Literal Translation | **Luke 22:16** | **King James Version**

to eat this Passover with you before the (time for) Me to suffer.
16 For I say to you that no more, no never will I eat of it until when it is fulfilled in the kingdom of God.

17 And having taken a cup, having given thanks, He said, Take this and divide (it) among yourselves.
18 For I say to you that in no way will I drink from the produce of the vine until when the kingdom of God comes.
19. And having taken a loaf, having given thanks, He broke, and gave to them, saying, This is My body being given for you. Do this for My remembrance.

20 And like manner the cup, after having supped, saying, This cup (is) the New Covenant in My blood, being poured out for you.

21. But behold the hand of the (one) betraying Me on the table with Me.
22 And, indeed, the Son of man goes according as it has been determined, but woe to that man by whom He is betrayed!

23 And they began to examine with themselves who then it may be of them, the (one) being about to do this.

24. And there came to be also a dispute among them, who of them seems to be greater.
25 And He said to them, The kings of the nations lord it over them, and the (ones) wielding authority over them are called benefactors.
26 But you (be) not so, but the greater among you, let him be as the lesser; and the one governing as the (one) serving.
27 For

5124 3588 3957 5315 3326 5216 4253 3588 3165 3958 3004
τοῦτο τὸ πάσχα φαγεῖν μεθ' ὑμῶν πρὸ τοῦ με παθεῖν· 16 λέγω
this Passover to eat with you before the Me to suffer; I say

1063 5213 3754 3765 3756 3361 5315 1537 846 2193 3755 4137 1722
γὰρ ὑμῖν ὅτι οὐκέτι οὐ μὴ φάγω ἐξ αὐτοῦ, ἕως ὅτου πληρωθῇ ἐν
for to you that no more no never will I eat of it, until when it is fulfilled in

3588 932 3588 2316 2532 1209 4221 2168
τῇ βασιλείᾳ τοῦ Θεοῦ. 17 καὶ δεξάμενος ποτήριον, εὐχαριστή-
the kingdom of God. And having taken a cup, having given thanks

2036 2983 5124 2532 1266 1438 3004 1063
σας εἶπε, Λάβετε τοῦτο, καὶ διαμερίσατε ἑαυτοῖς· 18 λέγω γὰρ
He said, Take this, and divide among yourselves; I say for

5213 3754 3756 3361 4095 575 3588 1081 3588 288 2193
ὑμῖν ὅτι οὐ μὴ πίω ἀπὸ τοῦ γεννήματος τῆς ἀμπέλου, ἕως
to you that in no way will I drink from the produce of the vine until

3755 3588 932 3588 2316 2064 2532 2983 740 2168
ὅτου η βασιλεία τοῦ Θεοῦ ἔλθῃ. 19 καὶ λαβὼν ἄρτον, εὐχαρ-
when the kingdom of God comes. And having taken a loaf, having

2806 2532 1325 846 3004 5124 2076 3588 4983
ιστήσας ἔκλασε, καὶ ἔδωκεν αὐτοῖς, λέγων, Τοῦτό ἐστι τὸ σῶμά
given thanks, He broke and gave to them, saying, This is the body

3450 3588 5228 5216 1325 5124 4160 1519 3588 1699
μου, τὸ ὑπὲρ ὑμῶν διδόμενον· τοῦτο ποιεῖτε εἰς τὴν ἐμὴν
of Me, for you being given; this do for My

364 5615 2532 3588 4221 3326 3588 1172
ἀνάμνησιν. 20 ὡσαύτως καὶ τὸ ποτήριον μετὰ τὸ δειπνῆσαι,
remembrance. In like manner And the cup after to sup,

3004 5124 3588 4221 3588 2537 1242 1722 3588 129
λέγων, Τοῦτο τὸ ποτήριον ἡ καινὴ διαθήκη ἐν τῷ αἵματί
saying, This cup (is) the New Covenant in the blood

3450 3588 5228 5216 1632 4133 2400 3588 5495 3588
μου, τὸ ὑπὲρ ὑμῶν ἐκχυνόμενον. 21 πλὴν ἰδού, ἡ χεὶρ τοῦ
of Me, for you being poured out. But behold the hand of the

3860 3165 3326 1700 1909 3588 5132 2532 3588 3303 5207
παραδιδόντος με μετ' ἐμοῦ ἐπὶ τῆς τραπέζης. 22 καὶ ὁ μὲν υἱὸς
(one) betraying Me with Me on the table. And the indeed Son

3588 444 4198 2596 3588 3724 4133 3759 3588
τοῦ ἀνθρώπου πορεύεται κατὰ τὸ ὡρισμένον· πλὴν οὐαὶ τῷ
of man goes according as it has been determined; but woe

444 1565 1223 3739 3860 2532 846 756
ἀνθρώπῳ ἐκείνῳ δι' οὗ παραδίδοται. 23 καὶ αὐτοὶ ἤρξαντο
man to that through whom He is betrayed! And they began

4802 4314 1438 3588 5101 687 1498 1537 846 3588 5124
συζητεῖν πρὸς ἑαυτοὺς τὸ τίς ἄρα εἴη ἐξ αὐτῶν ὁ τοῦτο
to examine with themselves who then it may be out of them the (one) this

3195 4238
μέλλων πράσσειν.
being about to do.

1096 1161 2532 5379 1722 846 3588 5101 846 1380
24. Ἐγένετο δὲ καὶ φιλονεικία ἐν αὐτοῖς τὸ τίς αὐτῶν δοκεῖ
came to be And also a dispute among them who of them seems

1511 3187 3588 1161 2036 846 3588 935 3588 1484
εἶναι μείζων. 25 ὁ δὲ εἶπεν αὐτοῖς, Οἱ βασιλεῖς τῶν ἐθνῶν
to be greater. He And said to them, The kings of the nations

2961 846 2532 3588 1850 846 2110
κυριεύουσιν αὐτῶν, καὶ οἱ ἐξουσιάζοντες αὐτῶν εὐεργέται
lord it over them, and the (ones) wielding authority over them benefactors

2564 5210 1161 3756 3779 235 3588 3187 1722 5213
καλοῦνται. 26 ὑμεῖς δὲ οὐχ οὕτως· ἀλλ' ὁ μείζων ἐν ὑμῖν
are called. you But not so; but the greater among you

1096 5613 3588 3501 2532 3588 2233 5613/3588 1247 5101
γινέσθω ὡς ὁ νεώτερος· καὶ ὁ ἡγούμενος ὡς ὁ διακονῶν. 27τίς
let him be as the lesser; and (the) one governing as the (one) serving. who

---

to eat this passover with you before I suffer:
16 For I say unto you, I will not any more eat thereof, until it be fulfilled in the kingdom of God.

17 And he took the cup, and gave thanks, and said, Take this, and divide (it) among yourselves:
18 For I say unto you, I will not drink of the fruit of the vine, until the kingdom of God shall come.
19. And he took bread, and gave thanks, and brake (it), and gave unto them, saying, This is my body which is given for you: this do in remembrance of me.

20 Likewise also the cup after supper, saying, This cup (is) the new testament in my blood, which is shed for you.

21. But, behold, the hand of him that betrayeth me (is) with me on the table.
22 And truly the Son of man goeth, as it was determined: but woe unto that man by whom he is betrayed!

23 And they began to enquire among themselves, which of them it was that should do this thing.

24. And there was also a strife among them, which of them should be accounted the greatest.
25 And he said unto them, The kings of the Gentiles exercise lordship over them; and they that exercise authority upon them are called benefactors.
26 But ye (shall) not (be) so: but he that is greatest among you, let him be as the younger; and he that is chief, as he that doth serve.
27 For

Literal Translation

Luke 22:28

King James Version

who (is) greater, the (one) serving, or the (one) reclining? (Is it) not the (one) reclining? But I am in your midst as (One) serving.
28 But you are the (ones) continuing with Me in My trials.

29 And I appoint a kingdom to you, as My Father appointed to Me,

30 that you may eat and drink at My table in My kingdom; and you will sit on thrones judging the twelve tribes of Israel.

31. And the Lord said, Simon, Simon, behold! Satan asked for you, to sift (you) as wheat;

32 but I entreated concerning you, that your faith might not fail. And you having once turned back, confirm your brothers.

33 And he said to Him, Lord, I am ready to go both to prison and into death with You.
34 And He said, Peter, I say to you, a cock will not crow today before you will deny knowing Me three times.

35. And He said to them, When I sent you without a purse, and a wallet, and sandals, did you lack anything? And they said, Nothing.
36 Then He said to them, But now, the (one) having a purse, let him take (it); likewise also a wallet. And the (one) not having, let him sell his garment, and let him buy a sword.
37 For I say to you that this that has been written must yet be fulfilled in Me: "And He was counted with the lawless." (Isa. 53:12) For the things concerning Me also have an end.
38 And they

1063 3187 3588 345 2228 3588 1247 3780 3588 345
γὰρ μείζων, ὁ ἀνακείμενος ἢ ὁ διακονῶν; οὐχὶ ὁ ἀνακεί-
For (is) greater, the (one) reclining or the (one) serving? (Is it) not the (one) re-

1473 1161 1510 1722 3319 5216 5613 3588 1247 5210 1161
μενος; ἐγὼ δὲ εἰμι ἐν μέσῳ ὑμῶν ὡς ὁ διακονῶν. 28 ὑμεῖς δέ
clining? I But am in (the) midst of you as (one) serving. you But

2075 3588 1265 3326 1700 1722 3588 3986 3450
ἐστε οἱ διαμεμενηκότες μετ᾽ ἐμοῦ ἐν τοῖς πειρασμοῖς μου·
are the (ones) having continued with Me in the trials of Me;

2504 1303 5213 2531 1303 3427 3588 3962 3450
29 κἀγὼ διατίθεμαι ὑμῖν, καθὼς διέθετό μοι ὁ πατήρ μου,
and I appoint to you, even as appointed to Me the Father of Me,

932 2443 2068 2532 4095 1909 3588 5132 3450
βασιλείαν, 30 ἵνα ἔσθίητε καὶ πίνητε ἐπὶ τῆς τραπέζης μου
a kingdom, that you may eat and drink at the table of Me

1722 3588 932 3450 2532 2523 1909 2362 2919
ἐν τῇ βασιλείᾳ μου, καὶ καθίσησθε ἐπὶ θρόνων, κρίνοντες
in the kingdom of Me; and you will sit on thrones judging

3588 1427 5443 3588 2474 2036 1161 3588 2962 4613
τὰς δώδεκα φυλὰς τοῦ Ἰσραήλ. 31 εἶπε δὲ ὁ Κύριος, Σίμων
the twelve tribes of Israel. said And the Lord, Simon

4613 2400 3588 4567 1809 5209 3588 4617 5613
Σίμων, ἰδού, ὁ Σατανᾶς ἐξῃτήσατο ὑμᾶς, τοῦ σινιάσαι ὡς
Simon, behold! Satan asked for you, to sift (you) as

3588 4621 1473 1161 1189 4012 4675 2443 3361 1587 3588 4102
τὸν σῖτον· 32 ἐγὼ δὲ ἐδεήθην περὶ σοῦ, ἵνα μὴ ἐκλείπῃ ἡ πίστις
the wheat; I but entreated about you, that not might fail the faith

4675 2532 4771 4218 1994 4741 3588 80 4675
σου· καὶ σύ ποτε ἐπιστρέψας στήρισον τοὺς ἀδελφούς σου.
of you. And you once have turned confirm the brothers of you.

3588 1161 2036 846 2962 3326 4675 2092 1510 2532 1519
33 ὁ δὲ εἶπεν αὐτῷ, Κύριε, μετὰ σοῦ ἕτοιμός εἰμι καὶ εἰς
he And said to Him, Lord, with You ready I am both into

5438 2532 1519 2288 4198 3588 1161 2036 3004 4671
φυλακὴν καὶ εἰς θάνατον πορεύεσθαι. 34 ὁ δὲ εἶπε, Λέγω σοι,
prison and into death to go. He But said, I say to you,

4074 3756 3361 5455 4594 220 4250 2228 5151 533
Πέτρε, οὐ μὴ φωνήσει σήμερον ἀλέκτωρ, πρὶν ἢ τρίς ἀπαρνήσῃ
Peter, not at all will sound today a cock before thrice you will deny

3361 1492 3165
μὴ εἰδέναι με.
not to know Me.

2532 2036 846 3753 649 5209 817 905
35. Καὶ εἶπεν αὐτοῖς, Ὅτε ἀπέστειλα ὑμᾶς ἄτερ βαλαντίου
And He said to them, When I sent you without a purse

2532 4082 2532 5266 3361 5100 5302 3588 1161 2036
καὶ πήρας καὶ ὑποδημάτων, μή τινος ὑστερήσατε; οἱ δὲ εἶπον,
and a wallet and sandals, not anything you lacked? they And said,

3762 2036 3767 846 235 3568 3588 2192 905
Οὐθενός. 36 εἶπεν οὖν αὐτοῖς, Ἀλλὰ νῦν ὁ ἔχων βαλάντιον
Nothing. He said Then to them, But now the (one) having a purse

142 3668 2532 4082 2532 3588 3361 2192 4453 3588
ἀράτω, ὁμοίως καὶ πήραν· καὶ ὁ μὴ ἔχων, πωλησάτω τὸ
let him take, likewise also a wallet; and (the) one not having, let him sell the

2440 846 2532 59 3162 3004 1063 5213
ἱμάτιον αὐτοῦ, καὶ ἀγορασάτω μάχαιραν. 37 λέγω γὰρ ὑμῖν
garment of him, and let him buy a sword. I say For to you

3754 2089 5124 3588 1125 1163 5055 1722 1698 3588 2532
ὅτι ἔτι τοῦτο τὸ γεγραμμένον δεῖ τελεσθῆναι ἐν ἐμοί, τὸ Καὶ
that yet this that has been written must be fulfilled in Me, and

3326 459 3049 2532 1063 3588 4012 1700 5056 2192 3588
μετὰ ἀνόμων ἐλογίσθη· καὶ γὰρ τὸ περὶ ἐμοῦ τέλος ἔχει. 38 οἱ
with (the) lawless He was counted; also for that about Me an end has. they

whether (is) greater, he that sitteth at meat, or he that serveth? (is) not he that sitteth at meat? but I am among you as he that serveth.
28 Ye are they which have continued with me in my temptations.

29 And I appoint unto you a kingdom, as my Father hath appointed unto me;
30 That ye may eat and drink at my table in my kingdom, and sit on thrones judging the twelve tribes of Israel.

31. And the Lord said, Simon, Simon, behold, Satan hath desired (to have) you, that he may sift (you) as wheat:

32 But I have prayed for thee, that thy faith fail not: and when thou art converted, strengthen thy brethren.

33 And he said unto him, Lord, I am ready to go with thee, both into prison, and to death.
34 And he said, I tell thee, Peter, the cock shall not crow this day, before that thou shalt thrice deny that thou knowest me.

35. And he said unto them, When I sent you without purse, and scrip, and shoes, lacked ye any thing? And they said, Nothing.
36 Then said he unto them, But now, he that hath a purse, let him take (it), and likewise (his) scrip: and he that hath no sword, let him sell his garment, and buy one.
37 For I say unto you, that this that is written must yet be accomplished in me, And he was reckoned among the transgressors: for the things concerning me have an end.
38 And they

Literal Translation

Luke 22:39

King James Version

said, Lord, behold, here (are) two swords. And He said to them, It is enough.

1161 2036 2962 2400 3162 5602 1417 3588 1161 2036 846
δὲ εἶπον, Κύριε, ἰδού, μάχαιραι ὧδε δύο. ὁ δὲ εἶπεν αὐτοῖς,
And said, Lord, behold, swords here (are) two. He And said to them,
2425 2076
Ἱκανόν ἐστι.
enough It is.

said, Lord, behold, here (are) two swords. And he said unto them, It is enough.

39. And going out, according to (His) custom, He went to the Mount of Olives; and His disciples also followed Him.
40 And having come on the place, He said to them, Pray you (will) not enter into temptation.
41 And He was withdrawn from them, about a stone's throw. And having placed the knees, He prayed,
42 saying, Father, if You will, take away this cup from Me; but let not My will be done, but Your (will).
43 And an angel from Heaven appeared to Him, strengthening Him.
44 And having come to be in an agony, He prayed more fervently. And His sweat became as drops of blood falling down onto the earth.
45 And having risen from the prayer, having come to His disciples, He found them sleeping from grief.
46 And (He) said to them, Why do you sleep? Rising up pray, that you do not enter into temptation.

2532 1831 4198 2596 3588 1485 1519 3588 3735 3588
39. Καὶ ἐξελθὼν ἐπορεύθη κατὰ τὸ ἔθος εἰς τὸ ὄρος τῶν
And having gone out He went according to the custom to the Mount of the
1636 190 1161 846 2532 3588 3101 846 1096
ἐλαιῶν· ἠκολούθησαν δὲ αὐτῷ καὶ οἱ μαθηταί αὐτοῦ. 40 γενό-
Olives; followed and Him also the disciples of Him. having
1161 1909 3588 5117 2036 846 4336 3361 1525
μενος δὲ ἐπὶ τοῦ τόπου, εἶπεν αὐτοῖς, Προσεύχεσθε μὴ εἰσελ-
come And on the place, He said to them, Pray you not to enter
1519 3986 2532 846 645 575 846 5616
θεῖν εἰς πειρασμόν. 41 καὶ αὐτὸς ἀπεσπάσθη ἀπ' αὐτῶν ὡσεὶ
into temptation. And He was withdrawn from them about
3037 1000 2532 5087 3588 1119 4336 3004 3962
λίθου βολήν, καὶ θεὶς τὰ γόνατα προσηύχετο, 42 λέγων, Πάτερ,
a stone's throw, and having placed the knees He prayed, saying, Father,
1487 1014 3911 3588 4221 5124 575 1700 4133 3361
εἰ βούλει, παρένεγκε τὸ ποτήριον τοῦτο ἀπ' ἐμοῦ· πλὴν μὴ
if You will, take away cup this from Me; but not
3588 2307 3450 235 3588 4674 1096 3700 1161 846 32
τὸ θέλημά μου, ἀλλὰ τὸ σὸν γινέσθω. 43 ὤφθη δὲ αὐτῷ ἄγγελος
the will of Me, but You let it be. appeared And to Him an angel
575 3772 1765 846 2532 1096 1722 74
ἀπ' οὐρανοῦ ἐνισχύων αὐτόν. 44 καὶ γενόμενος ἐν ἀγωνίᾳ
from Heaven strengthening Him. And having become in an agony
1617 4336 1096 1161 3588 2402 846 5616
ἐκτενέστερον προσηύχετο. ἐγένετο δὲ ὁ ἱδρὼς αὐτοῦ ὡσεὶ
more fervently He prayed. came to be And the sweat of Him as
2361 129 2597 1909 3588 1093 2532 450
θρόμβοι αἵματος καταβαίνοντος ἐπὶ τὴν γῆν. 45 καὶ ἀναστὰς
drops of blood falling down onto the earth. And having risen
575 3588 4335 2064 4314 3588 3101 846
ἀπὸ τῆς προσευχῆς, ἐλθὼν πρὸς τοὺς μαθητὰς αὐτοῦ,
from the prayer, having come to the disciples of Him,
2147 846 2837 575 3588 3077 2532 2036 846
εὗρεν αὐτοὺς κοιμωμένους ἀπὸ τῆς λύπης, 46 καὶ εἶπεν αὐτοῖς,
He found them being asleep from the grief, and said to them,
5101 2518 450 4336 2443 3361 1525
Τί καθεύδετε; ἀναστάντες προσεύχεσθε, ἵνα μὴ εἰσέλθητε
Why do you sleep? Rising up pray, that not you enter
1519 3986
εἰς πειρασμόν.
into temptation.

39. And he came out, and went, as he was wont, to the mount of Olives; and his disciples also followed him.
40 And when he was at the place, he said unto them, Pray that ye enter not into temptation.
41 And he was withdrawn from them about a stone's cast, and kneeled down, and prayed,
42 Saying, Father, if thou be willing, remove this cup from me: nevertheless not my will, but thine, be done.
43 And there appeared an angel unto him from heaven, strengthening him.
44 And being in an agony he prayed more earnestly: and his sweat was as it were great drops of blood falling down to the ground.
45 And when he rose up from prayer, and was come to his disciples, he found them sleeping for sorrow,
46 And said unto them, Why sleep ye? rise and pray, lest ye enter into temptation.

47. And (as) He (was) yet speaking, behold, a crowd! And the (one) called Judas, one of the Twelve, came in front of them and drew near to Jesus in order to kiss Him.
48 And Jesus said to him, Judas, do you betray the Son of man with a kiss?
49 And those around Him seeing that about to occur, (they) said to Him, Lord, shall we strike with

2089 1161 846 2980 2400 3793 2532 3588 3004
47. Ἔτι δὲ αὐτοῦ λαλοῦντος, ἰδού, ὄχλος, καὶ ὁ λεγόμενος
yet And Him speaking, Behold! A crowd! And he being called
2455 1520 3588 1427 4281 846 2532 1448 3588
Ἰούδας, εἷς τῶν δώδεκα, προήρχετο αὐτῶν, καὶ ἤγγισε τῷ
Judas, one of the Twelve, came before them, and drew near to
2424 5368 846 3588 1161 2424 2036 846 2455
Ἰησοῦ φιλῆσαι αὐτόν. 48 ὁ δὲ Ἰησοῦς εἶπεν αὐτῷ, Ἰούδα,
Jesus (in order) to kiss Him. But Jesus said to him, Judas,
5370 3588 5207 3588 444 3860 1492 1161 3588
φιλήματι τὸν υἱὸν τοῦ ἀνθρώπου παραδίδως; 49 ἰδόντες δὲ οἱ
with a kiss the Son of man do you betray? having seen and those
4012 846 3588 2071 2036 846 2962 1487 3960 1722
περὶ αὐτὸν τὸ ἐσόμενον εἶπον αὐτῷ, Κύριε, εἰ πατάξομεν ἐν
around Him, that about to occur said to Him, Lord, if we shall strike with

47. And while he yet spake, behold a multitude, and he that was called Judas, one of the twelve, went before them, and drew near unto Jesus to kiss him.
48 But Jesus said unto him, Judas, betrayest thou the Son of man with a kiss?
49 When they which were about him saw what would follow, they said unto him, Lord, shall we smite with

Literal Translation **Luke 22:50** *King James Version*

the sword?
50. And a certain one of them struck the slave of the high priest and cut off his right ear.
51 And answering, Jesus said, Allow (it) until this. And having touched his ear, He healed him.

52 And Jesus said to those having come upon Him, chief priests, and commanders of the temple, and elders, Have you come out with swords and clubs as against a plunderer?

53 I being with you day by day in the temple, you did not stretch out your hand on Me. But this is your hour and the authority of the darkness.

54. And having seized Him, they led (Him) away and led Him into the house of the high priest. And Peter followed at a distance.

55 And lighting a fire in (the) middle of the court, and they having sat together, Peter sat in their midst.
56 And a certain slave woman having seen him sitting near the light, and having stared at him, (she) said, And this one was with Him.
57 But he denied Him, saying, Woman, I do not know Him.
58 And after a while, another having seen him said, You also are of them. But Peter said, Man, I am not.

59 And about an hour having elapsed, a certain other one boldly charged, saying, Truly this one also was with Him, for he also is a Galilean.
60 And Peter said, Man, I do not know what you say. And immediately, while he yet spoke, the cock sounded.

3162 2532 3960 1520 5100 1537 846 3588 1401 3588
μαχαίρῃ; 50 καὶ ἐπάταξεν εἷς τις ἐξ αὐτῶν τὸν δοῦλον τοῦ
(the) sword? And struck one a certain of them the slave of the

749 2532 851 846 3588 3775 3588 1188 611
ἀρχιερέως, καὶ ἀφεῖλεν αὐτοῦ τὸ οὖς τὸ δεξιόν. 51 ἀποκριθεὶς
high priest, and cut off of him the ear, the right. answering

1161 3588 2424 2036 1439 2193 5127 2532 680 3588
δὲ ὁ Ἰησοῦς εἶπεν, Ἐᾶτε ἕως τούτου· καὶ ἁψάμενος τοῦ
And Jesus said, Allow (it) until this; and having touched the

5621 846 2390 846 2036 1161 2424 4314 3588
ὠτίου αὐτοῦ, ἰάσατο αὐτόν. 52 εἶπε δὲ ὁ Ἰησοῦς πρὸς τοὺς
ear of him, He healed him. said And Jesus to those

3854 1909 846 749 2532 4755 3588
παραγενομένους ἐπ' αὐτὸν ἀρχιερεῖς καὶ στρατηγοὺς τοῦ
having come upon Him chief priests and commanders of the

2411 2532 4245 5613 1909 3027 1831 3326
ἱεροῦ καὶ πρεσβυτέρους, Ὡς ἐπὶ λῃστὴν ἐξεληλύθατε μετὰ
temple and elders, As against a plunderer did you come out with

3162 2532 3586 2596 2250 5607 3450 3326 5216
μαχαιρῶν καὶ ξύλων; 53 καθ' ἡμέραν ὄντος μου μεθ' ὑμῶν
swords and clubs? Day after day being Me with you

1722 3588 2411 3756 1614 3588 5495 1909 1691 235 3778
ἐν τῷ ἱερῷ οὐκ ἐξετείνατε τὰς χεῖρας ἐπ' ἐμέ. ἀλλ' αὕτη
in the temple not you stretched out the hand on Me. But this

5216 2076 3588 5610 2532 3588 1849 3588 4655
ὑμῶν ἐστὶν ἡ ὥρα, καὶ ἡ ἐξουσία τοῦ σκότους.
of you is hour, and the authority of the darkness.

4815 1161 846 71 2532 1521 846
54. Συλλαβόντες δὲ αὐτὸν ἤγαγον, καὶ εἰσήγαγον αὐτὸν
having seized And Him, they led away, and brought Him

1519 3588 3624 3588 749 3588 1161 4074 190 3113
εἰς τὴν οἰκίαν τοῦ ἀρχιερέως. ὁ δὲ Πέτρος ἠκολούθει μακρόθεν.
into the house of the high priest. And Peter followed afar off.

681 1161 4442 1722 3319 3588 833 2532 4776
55 ἁψάντων δὲ πῦρ ἐν μέσῳ τῆς αὐλῆς, καὶ συγκαθισάντων
lighting And a fire in (the) midst of the court, and having sat together

846 2521 3588 4074 1722 3319 846 1492 1161 846
αὐτῶν, ἐκάθητο ὁ Πέτρος ἐν μέσω αὐτῶν. 56 ἰδοῦσα δὲ αὐτὸν
of them, sat Peter in (the) midst of them. having seen And him

3814 5100 2521 4314 3588 5457 2532 816 846
παιδίσκη τις καθήμενον πρὸς τὸ φῶς, καὶ ἀτενίσασα αὐτῷ
female slave a certain sitting near the light, and having stared at him

2036 2532 3778 4862 846 2258 3588 1161 720 846 3004
εἶπε, Καὶ οὗτος σὺν αὐτῷ ἦν· 57 ὁ δὲ ἠρνήσατο αὐτόν, λέγων,
said, And this one with Him was; he but denied Him, saying,

1135 3756 1492 846 2532 3326 1024 2087 1492 846
Γύναι, οὐκ οἶδα αὐτόν. 58 καὶ μετὰ βραχὺ ἕτερος ἰδὼν αὐτὸν
Woman, not I know Him. And after a while another having seen him

5346 2532 4771 1537 846 1488 3588 1161 4074 2036 444 3756
ἔφη, Καὶ σὺ ἐξ αὐτῶν εἶ. ὁ δὲ Πέτρος εἶπεν, Ἄνθρωπε, οὐκ
said, And you of them are. But Peter said, Man, not

1510 2532 1339 5616 5610 3391 243 5100 1340
εἰμί. 59 καὶ διαστάσης ὡσεὶ ὥρας μιᾶς, ἄλλος τις διϊσχυρίζετο,
I am. And having elapsed about hour one, other a certain boldly charged,

3004 1909 225 2532 3778 3326 846 2258 2532 1063
λέγων, Ἐπ' ἀληθείας καὶ οὗτος μετ' αὐτοῦ ἦν· καὶ γὰρ
saying, In truth also this one with Him was; also for

1057 2076 2036 1161 3588 4074 444 3756 1492 3739
Γαλιλαῖός ἐστιν· 60 εἶπε δὲ ὁ Πέτρος, Ἄνθρωπε, οὐκ οἶδα ὃ
a Galilean he is. said And Peter, Man, not I know what

3004 2532 3916 2089 2980 846 5455 3588
λέγεις. καὶ παραχρῆμα, ἔτι λαλοῦντος αὐτοῦ, ἐφώνησεν ὁ
you say. And immediately, yet speaking him, sounded the

the sword?
50. And one of them smote the servant of the high priest, and cut off his right ear.
51 And Jesus answered and said, Suffer ye thus far. And he touched his ear, and healed him.

52 Then Jesus said unto the chief priests, and captains of the temple, and the elders, which were come to him, Be ye come out, as against a thief, with swords and staves?

53 When I was daily with you in the temple, ye stretched forth no hands against me: but this is your hour, and the power of darkness.

54. Then took they him, and led (him), and brought him into the high priest's house. And Peter followed afar off.

55 And when they had kindled a fire in the midst of the hall, and were set down together, Peter sat down among them.
56 But a certain maid beheld him as he sat by the fire, and earnestly looked upon him, and said, This man was also with him.
57 And he denied him, saying, Woman, I know him not.
58 And after a little while another saw him, and said, Thou art also of them. And Peter said, Man, I am not.

59 And about the space of one hour after another confidently affirmed, saying, Of a truth this (fellow) also was with him: for he is a Galilaean.
60 And Peter said, Man, I know not what thou sayest. And immediately, while he yet spake, the cock crew.

Literal Translation

Luke 22:61

King James Version

61 And turning, the Lord looked at Peter. And Peter remembered the word of the Lord, as He told him, Before a cock would crow, you will deny Me three times.
62 And having gone outside, Peter wept bitterly.

220 2532 4762 3588 2962 1689 3588 4074 2532
ἀλέκτωρ. 61 καὶ στραφεὶς ὁ Κύριος ἐνέβλεψε τῷ Πέτρῳ. καὶ
cock. And turning the Lord looked at Peter. And
5279 3588 4074 3588 3056 3588 2962 5613 2036 846
ὑπεμνήσθη ὁ Πέτρος τοῦ λόγου τοῦ Κυρίου, ὡς εἶπεν αὐτῷ
remembered Peter the word of the Lord, as He told him
3754 4250 220 5455 533 3165 5151 2532 1831
ὅτι Πρὶν ἀλέκτορα φωνῆσαι, ἀπαρνήσῃ με τρίς. 62 καὶ ἐξελθὼν
that before a cock would crow, you will deny Me thrice. And having gone
1854 3588 4074 2799 4090
ἔξω ὁ Πέτρος ἔκλαυσε πικρῶς.
outside Peter wept bitterly.

61 And the Lord turned, and looked upon Peter. And Peter remembered the word of the Lord, how he had said unto him, Before the cock crow, thou shalt deny me thrice.
62 And Peter went out, and wept bitterly.

63. And the men having Jesus in charge mocked Him, beating (Him).
64 And having blindfolded Him, (they were) striking His face and questioning Him, saying, Prophesy, who is the one stinging you?
65 And blaspheming, many other things they said to Him.

2532 3588 435 3588 4912 3588 2424 1702 846
63. Καὶ οἱ ἄνδρες οἱ συνέχοντες τὸν Ἰησοῦν ἐνέπαιζον αὐτῷ,
And the men those having in charge Jesus mocked Him,
1194 2532 4028 846 5180 846 3588
δέροντες, 64 καὶ περικαλύψαντες αὐτὸν, ἔτυπτον αὐτοῦ τό
beating (Him), and having blindfolded Him, striking of Him the
4383 2532 1905 846 3004 4395 5101
πρόσωπον, καὶ ἐπηρώτων αὐτόν, λέγοντες, Προφήτευσον· τίς
face, and questioning Him, saying, Prophesy; who
2076 3588 3817 4571 2532 2087 4183 987 3004
ἐστιν ὁ παίσας σε; 65 καὶ ἕτερα πολλὰ βλασφημοῦντες ἔλεγον
is the (one) stinging you? And other things many blaspheming they
1519 846
εἰς αὐτόν.
said to Him.

63. And the men that held Jesus mocked him, and smote (him).
64 And when they had blindfolded him, they struck him on the face, and asked him, saying, Prophesy, who is it that smote thee?
65 And many other things blasphemously spake they against him.

66. And as day occurred, was assembled the body of elders of the people, both the chief priests and scribes. And they led Him away to the Sanhedrin of them, saying,
67 If you are the Christ, tell us. And He said to them, If I tell you, you will not at all believe.

2532 5613 1096 2250 4863 3588 4244 3588
66. Καὶ ὡς ἐγένετο ἡμέρα, συνήχθη τὸ πρεσβυτέριον τοῦ
And as occurred day, was assembled the body of elders of the
2992 749 5037 2532 1122 2532 321 846 1519
λαοῦ, ἀρχιερεῖς τε καὶ γραμματεῖς, καὶ ἀπήγαγον αὐτὸν εἰς
people, chief priests both and scribes, and led away Him into
3588 4892 1438 3004 1487 4771 1488 3588 5547 2036
τὸ συνέδριον ἑαυτῶν, 67 λέγοντες, Εἰ σὺ εἶ ὁ Χριστός, εἰπὲ
the Sanhedrin of themselves, saying, If you are the Christ, tell
2254 2036 1161 846 1437 5213 2036 3756 3361 4100
ἡμῖν. εἶπε δὲ αὐτοῖς, Ἐὰν ὑμῖν εἴπω, οὐ μὴ πιστεύσητε·
us. He said And to them, If you I tell, not at all will you believe;

66. And as soon as it was day, the elders of the people and the chief priests and the scribes came together, and led him into their council, saying,
67 Art thou the Christ? tell us. And he said unto them, If I tell you, ye will not believe:

68 And also if I ask, not at all will you answer Me, or let Me go.
69 From now on the Son of man will be sitting at (the) right of the power of God. (Ps. 110:1)
70 And they all said, Then are you the Son of God? And He said to them, You say (it), because I AM!
71 And they said, Why do we yet have need of witness? For we ourselves heard (it) from his mouth.

1437 1161 2532 2065 3756 3361 611 3427 2228 630
68 ἐὰν δὲ καὶ ἐρωτήσω, οὐ μὴ ἀποκριθῆτέ μοι, ἢ ἀπολύσητε.
if and also I ask, not at all will you answer Me, or let (Me) go.
575 3588 3568 2071 3588 5207 3588 444 2521 1537
69 ἀπὸ τοῦ νῦν ἔσται ὁ υἱὸς τοῦ ἀνθρώπου καθήμενος ἐκ
From now will be the Son of man sitting at
1188 3588 1411 3588 2316 2036 1161 3956 4771 3767 1488 3588
δεξιῶν τῆς δυνάμεως τοῦ Θεοῦ. 70 εἶπον δὲ πάντες, Σὺ οὖν εἶ ὁ
(the) right of the power of God. they said And all, you then Are the
5207 3588 2316 3588 1161 4314 846 5346 5210 3004 3754 1473
υἱὸς τοῦ Θεοῦ; ὁ δὲ πρὸς αὐτοὺς ἔφη, Ὑμεῖς λέγετε ὅτι ἐγώ
Son of God? He And to them said, You say (it), because I
1510 3588 1161 2036 5101 2089 5532 2192 3141 846 1063
εἰμι. 71 οἱ δὲ εἶπον, Τί ἔτι χρέαν ἔχομεν μαρτυρίας; αὐτοὶ γὰρ
AM! they And said, Why yet need have we of witness? ourselves For
191 575 3588 4750 846
ἠκούσαμεν ἀπὸ τοῦ στόματος αὐτοῦ.
we heard from the mouth of Him.

68 And if I also ask (you), ye will not answer me, nor let (me) go.
69 Hereafter shall the Son of man sit on the right hand of the power of God.
70 Then said they all, Art thou then the Son of God? And he said unto them, Ye say that I am.
71 And they said, What need we any further witness? for we ourselves have heard of his own mouth.

Luke 23

1. And having risen, all the multitude of them led Him before

2532 450 537 3588 4128 846 71 846 1909
1. Καὶ ἀναστὰν ἅπαν τὸ πλῆθος αὐτῶν, ἤγαγον αὐτὸν ἐπὶ
And having risen all the multitude of them led Him to

1. And the whole multitude of them arose, and led him unto

Literal Translation

Pilate.
2 And they began to accuse Him, saying, We found this one perverting the nation, and forbidding to give tribute to Caesar, saying himself to be a king, Christ.
3 And Pilate questioned Him, saying, Are you the king of the Jews? And answering, him, He said, You say (it).

4 And Pilate said to the chief priests and the crowds, I find nothing blameable in this man.

5 But they insisted, saying, He stirs up the people, teaching throughout all Judea, beginning from Galilee to here.

6 And hearing Galilee, Pilate asked if the man is a Galilean.

7 And having known that He is from Herod's jurisdiction, he sent Him up to Herod, he also being in Jerusalem in these days.

8. And having seen Jesus, Herod greatly rejoiced, for he was wishing to see Him (for) a long time, because (he wished) to hear many things about Him. And he hoped to see some sign happen by Him.

9 And he questioned Him in many words. But He answered him not a thing.
10 And the chief priests and the scribes stood vehemently accusing Him.
11 And having humiliated Him with his soldiery, and having mocked (Him) by putting around Him luxurious clothing, Herod sent Him back

Luke 23:2

3588 4091 756 1161 2723 846 3004 5126
τὸν Πιλάτον. 2 ἤρξαντο δὲ κατηγορεῖν αὐτοῦ, λέγοντες, Τοῦ-
Pilate. they began And to accuse Him, saying, This

2147 1294 3588 1484 2532 2967 2541
τον εὕραμεν διαστρέφοντα τὸ ἔθνος, καὶ κωλύοντα Καίσαρι
one we found perverting the nation, and forbidding Caesar

5411 1325 3004 1438 5547 937 1511 3588 1161
φόρους διδόναι, λέγοντα ἑαυτὸν Χριστὸν βασιλέα εἶναι. 3 ὁ δὲ
tribute to give, saying himself Christ a king to be. And

4091 1905 846 3004 4771 1488 3588 935 3588
Πιλάτος ἐπηρώτησεν αὐτόν, λέγων, Σὺ εἶ ὁ βασιλεὺς τῶν
Pilate questioned Him, saying, You Are the king of the

2453 3588 1161 611 846 5346 4771 3004 3588 1161 4091
Ἰουδαίων; ὁ δὲ ἀποκριθεὶς αὐτῷ ἔφη, Σὺ λέγεις. 4 ὁ δὲ Πιλάτος
Jews? He And answering him said, You say (it). And Pilate

2036 4314 3588 749 2532 3588 3793 3762
εἶπε πρὸς τοὺς ἀρχιερεῖς καὶ τοὺς ὄχλους, Οὐδὲν
said to the chief priests and the crowds, Nothing

2147 158 1722 3588 444 5129 3588 1161 2001
εὑρίσκω αἴτιον ἐν τῷ ἀνθρώπῳ τούτῳ. 5 οἱ δὲ ἐπίσχυον,
I find blameable in man this. they But insisted,

3004 3754 383 3588 2992 1321 2596 3650 3588
λέγοντες ὅτι Ἀνασείει τὸν λαόν, διδάσκων καθ᾽ ὅλης τῆς
saying, He stirs up the people, teaching throughout all

2449 756 575 3588 1056 2193 5602 4091 1161
Ἰουδαίας, ἀρξάμενος ἀπὸ τῆς Γαλιλαίας ἕως ὧδε. 6 Πιλάτος δὲ
Judea, beginning from Galilee to here. Pilate And

191 1056 1905 1487 3588 444 1057
ἀκούσας Γαλιλαίν ἐπηρώτησεν εἰ ὁ ἄνθρωπος Γαλιλαῖός
having heard Galilee, (he) asked if the man a Galilean

2076 2532 1921 3754 1537 3588 1849 2264 2076 375
ἐστι. 7 καὶ ἐπιγνοὺς ὅτι ἐκ τῆς ἐξουσίας Ἡρῴδου ἐστὶν, ἀνέ-
is. And having known that from the jurisdiction of Herod He is, he

846 4314 2264 5607 2532 846 1722 2414
πεμψεν αὐτὸν πρὸς Ἡρῴδην, ὄντα καὶ αὐτὸν ἐν Ἱεροσολύ-
sent up Him to Herod, being also him in Jerusalem

1722 3778 3588 2250
μοις ἐν ταύταις ταῖς ἡμέραις.
in these days.

3588 1161 2264 1492 3588 2424 5463 3029 2258 1063
8. ὁ δε``Ηρῴδης ἰδὼν τὸν Ἰησοῦν ἐχάρη λίαν· ἦν γὰρ
And Herod having seen Jesus rejoiced greatly, he was for

2309 1537 2425 1492 846 1223 3588 191 4183 4012
θέλων ἐξ ἱκανοῦ ἰδεῖν αὐτὸν, διὰ τὸ ἀκούειν πολλὰ περὶ
wishing of a long (time) to see Him, because to hear many things about

846 2532 1679 5100 4592 1492 5259 846 1096
αὐτοῦ· καὶ ἤλπιζέ τι σημεῖον ἰδεῖν ὑπ᾽ αὐτοῦ γινόμενον.
Him; and he hoped some sign to see by Him happen.

1905 1161 846 1722 3056 2425 846 1161 3762 611
9 ἐπηρώτα δὲ αὐτὸν ἐν λόγοις ἱκανοῖς· αὐτὸς δὲ οὐδὲν ἀπεκρί-
He questioned And Him in words many; He but nothing answered

846 2476 1161 3588 749 2532 3588 1122
νατο αὐτῷ. 10 εἱστήκεισαν δὲ οἱ ἀρχιερεῖς καὶ οἱ γραμματεῖς,
him. stood And the chief priests and the scribes,

2159 2723 846 1848 1161 846 3588
εὐτόνως κατηγοροῦντες αὐτοῦ. 11 ἐξουθενήσας δὲ αὐτὸν ὁ
vehemently accusing Him. having humiliated And Him

2264 4862 3588 4753 846 2532 1702
Ἡρῴδης σὺν τοῖς στρατεύμασιν αὐτοῦ, καὶ ἐμπαίξας,
Herod with the soldiery of him, and having mocked,

4016 846 2066 2986 375 846 3588
περιβαλὼν αὐτὸν ἐσθῆτα λαμπρὰν, ἀνέπεμψεν αὐτὸν τῷ
putting around Him clothing luxurious, sent back Him

King James Version

Pilate.
2 And they began to accuse him, saying, We found this (fellow) perverting the nation, and forbidding to give tribute to Caesar, saying that he himself is Christ a King.
3 And Pilate asked him, saying, Art thou the King of the Jews? And he answered him and said, Thou sayest (it).

4 Then said Pilate to the chief priests and (to) the people, I find no fault in this man.

5 And they were the more fierce, saying, He stirreth up the people, teaching throughout all Jewry, beginning from Galilee to this place.

6 When Pilate heard of Galilee, he asked whether the man were a Galilaean.

7 And as soon as he knew that he belonged unto Herod's jurisdiction, he sent him to Herod, who himself also was at Jerusalem at that time.

8. And when Herod saw Jesus, he was exceeding glad: for he was desirous to see him of a long (season), because he had heard many things of him; and he hoped to have seen some miracle done by him.

9 Then he questioned with him in many words; but he answered him nothing.
10 And the chief priests and scribes stood and vehemently accused him.

11 And Herod with his men of war set him at nought, and mocked (him), and arrayed him in a gorgeous robe, and sent him again

Literal Translation

Luke 23:12

King James Version

to Pilate.
12. And on that same day, both Pilate and Herod came to be friends with each other, for before they (had been) at enmity (between) themselves.

13. And having called together the chief priests and the leaders and the people,
14 Pilate said to them, You brought this man to me as perverting the people. And, behold! Having examined him before you, I found nothing blameable in this man (regarding that) which you bring charge against him.

15 But neither did Herod, for I sent you up to him; and, behold! Nothing worthy of death having been done by him.
16 Therefore having chastised him, I will release (him).

17 And he had to release to them one at the Feast.

18 And they all together shouted, saying, Take this one, and release Barabbas to us
19 (the one) who had been thrown into prison due to some revolt and murder having occurred in the city.

20 Then Pilate again called out, desiring to release Jesus.
21 But they shouted, saying, Crucify! Crucify him!

22 But a third (time) he said to them, For what evil did this one do? I found no cause of death in him. Therefore, having chastised him, I will release (him).
23 But with loud voices they pressed on (him), asking for Him to be crucified. And their voices, and (that) of the chief priests, prevailed.
24 And Pilate adjudged their request to be done.

4091 1096 1161 5384 3588 5037 4091 2532 3588 2264 1722
Πιλάτῳ. 12 ἐγένοντο δὲ φίλοι ὅ τε Πιλάτος καὶ ὁ Ἡρῴδης ἐν
to Pilate. came to be And friends both Pilate and Herod in
846 3588 2250 3326 240 4391 1063 1722 2189
αὐτῇ τῇ ἡμέρᾳ μετ' ἀλλήλων· προυπῆρχον γὰρ ἐν ἔχθρᾳ
same the day with each other; they before for at enmity
5607 4314 1438
ὄντες πρὸς ἑαυτούς.
being with themselves.

4091 1161 4779 3588 749 2532 3588
13. Πιλάτος δὲ συγκαλεσάμενος τοὺς ἀρχιερεῖς καὶ τοὺς
PIlate And having called together the chief priests and the
758 2532 3588 2992 2036 4314 846 4374 3427
ἄρχοντας καὶ τὸν λαὸν, 14 εἶπε πρὸς αὐτούς, Προσηνέγκατέ μοι
leaders and the people, said to them, You brought to me
3588 444 5126 5613 654 3588 2992 2532 2400
τὸν ἄνθρωπον τοῦτον, ὡς ἀποστρέφοντα τὸν λαόν· καὶ ἰδού,
man this, as perverting the people; and behold!
1473 1799 5216 350 3762 2147 1722 3588 444
ἐγὼ ἐνώπιον ὑμῶν ἀνακρίνας οὐθὲν εὗρον ἐν τῷ ἀνθρώπῳ
I before you having examined nothing I found in man
5129 158 3739 2723 2596 846 235 3761
τούτῳ αἴτιον ὧν κατηγορεῖτε κατ' αὐτοῦ· 15 ἀλλ' οὐδε
this blameable of which you bring charge against Him. But neither
2264 375 1063 5209 4314 846 2532 2400 3762
Ἡρῴδης· ἀνέπεμψα γὰρ ὑμᾶς πρὸς αὐτόν, καὶ ἰδού, οὐδὲν
Herod; I sent up for you to him, and, behold! Nothing
514 2288 2076 4238 846 3811 3767
ἄξιον θανάτου ἐστὶ πεπραγμένον αὐτῷ. 16 παιδεύσας οὖν
worthy of death is being done by Him. Having chastised then
846 630 318 1161 2192 630 846 2596
αὐτὸν ἀπολύσω. 17 ἀνάγκην δὲ εἶχεν ἀπολύειν αὐτοῖς κατὰ
Him I will release. need And he had to release to them at
1859 1520 349 1161 3826 3004 142 5126
ἑορτὴν ἕνα. 18 ἀνέκραξαν δὲ παμπληθεὶ, λέγοντες, Αἶρε τοῦτον,
(the) Feast one. they shouted And all together, saying, Take this one
630 1161 2254 3588 912 3748 2258 1223 4714 5100
ἀπόλυσον δὲ ἡμῖν τὸν Βαραββᾶν· 19 ὅστις ἦν διὰ στάσιν τινὰ
release and to us Barabbas; who was through revolt some
1096 1722 3588 4172 2532 5408 906 1519 5438
γενομένην ἐν τῇ πόλει καὶ φόνον βεβλημένος εἰς φυλακήν.
having occurred in the city and murder having been thrown into prison.

3825 3767 3588 4091 4377 2309 630 3588
20 πάλιν οὖν ὁ Πιλάτος προσεφώνησε, θέλων ἀπολῦσαι τὸν
again Then Pilate called (to them), desiring to release
2424 3588 1161 2019 3004 4717 4717
Ἰησουν. 21 οἱ δὲ ἐπεφώνουν, λέγοντες, Σταύρωσον σταύρωσον
Jesus. they But shouted, saying, Crucify! Crucify
846 3588 1161 5154 2036 4314 846 5101 1063 2556 4160
αὐτόν. 22 ὁ δὲ τρίτον εἶπε πρὸς αὐτούς, Τί γὰρ κακὸν ἐποίησεν
him! he but a third (time) said to them, what For evil did
3778 3762 158 2288 2147 1722 846 3811 3767
οὗτος; οὐδὲν αἴτιον θανάτου εὗρον ἐν αὐτῷ· παιδεύσας οὖν
this one? Nothing (as) cause of death I found in him; having chastised then
846 630 3588 1161 1945 5456 3173 154
αὐτὸν ἀπολύσω. 23 οἱ δὲ ἐπέκειντο φωναῖς μεγάλαις, αἰτού-
Him I will release. they But pressed on (him) voices with loud, asking
846 4717 2532 2729 3588 5456 846
μενοι αὐτὸν σταυρωθῆναι· καὶ κατίσχυον αἱ φωναὶ αὐτῶν
Him to be crucified; and prevailed the voices of them,
2532 3588 749 3588 1161 4091 1948 1096 3588
καὶ τῶν ἀρχιερέων. 24 ὁ δὲ Πιλάτος ἐπέκρινε γενέσθαι τὸ
and of the chief priests. And Pilate adjudged to be done the

to Pilate.
12. And the same day Pilate and Herod were made friends together: for before they were at enmity between themselves.

13. And Pilate, when he had called together the chief priests and the rulers and the people,
14 Said unto them, Ye have brought this man unto me, as one that perverteth the people: and, behold, I, having examined (him) before you, have found no fault in this man touching those things whereof ye accuse him:

15 No, nor yet Herod: for I sent you to him; and, lo, nothing worthy of death is done unto him.

16 I will therefore chastise him, and release (him).

17 (For of necessity he must release one unto them at the feast.)
18 And they cried out all at once, saying, Away with this (man), and release unto us Barabbas:
19 (Who for a certain sedition made in the city, and for murder, was cast into prison.)

20 Pilate therefore, willing to release Jesus, spake again to them.
21 But they cried, saying, Crucify (him), crucify him.
22 And he said unto them the third time, Why, what evil hath he done? I have found no cause of death in him: I will therefore chastise him, and let (him) go.
23 And they were instant with loud voices, requiring that he might be crucified. And the voices of them and of the chief priests prevailed.
24 And Pilate gave sentence that it should be

Luke 23:25

Literal Translation

25 And he released to them the (one) through revolt and murder to have been cast into prison, whom they asked. But he delivered Jesus to their will.

26. And as they led Him away, having laid hold on a certain Simon, a Cyrenian, coming from a field, they put the cross on him, to bear (it) behind Jesus.

27 And a great multitude of people were following Him, and of women who also were bewailing and lamenting Him.
28 And having turned to them, Jesus said, Daughters of Jerusalem, do not weep over Me, but weep over yourselves and over your children.
29 For behold! Days will come in which they will say, Blessed (are) the barren, and the wombs that did not bear, and breasts that did not suckle.

30 Then they will begin to say to the mountains, Fall on us! And to the hills, Cover us! (Hosea 10:8)
31 For if they do these things in the sappy tree, what may happen in the dry?

32. And also two others, two criminals, were led with Him to be executed.

33 And when they came on the place being called Skull, there they crucified Him and the criminals, one off (the) right, and one off (the) left.
34 And Jesus said, Father, forgive them, for they do not know what they are doing. And dividing His

Greek Interlinear

155 846 630 1161 846 3588 1223 4714 2532 5408
αἴτημα αὐτῶν· 25 ἀπέλυσε δὲ αὐτοῖς τὸν διὰ στάσιν καὶ φόνον
request of them.; he released and to them the (one) through revolt and murder

906 1519 5438 3739 154 3588 1161 2424
βεβλημένον εἰς φυλακήν, ὃν ᾐτοῦντο· τὸν δὲ Ἰησοῦν
having been cast into prison, (him) whom they asked; but Jesus

3860 3588 2307 846
παρέδωκε τῷ θελήματι αὐτῶν.
he delivered to the will of them.

2532 5613 520 846 1949 4613 5100
26. Καὶ ὡς ἀπήγαγον αὐτόν, ἐπιλαβόμενοι Σίμωνός τινος
And as they led Him, having laid hold on Simon a certain

2956 2064 575 68 2007 846 3588
Κυρηναίου ἐρχόμενον ἀπ' ἀγροῦ, ἐπέθηκαν αὐτῷ τὸν
Cyrenian coming from a field, they put on him the

4716 5342 3693 3588 2424
σταυρὸν φέρειν ὄπισθεν τοῦ Ἰησοῦ.
cross to bear (it) behind Jesus.

190 1161 846 4183 4128 3588 2992 2532 1135
27 Ἠκολούθει δὲ αὐτῷ πολὺ πλῆθος τοῦ λαοῦ, καὶ γυναικῶν
were following And Him a great multitude of the people, and of women,

3739 2532 2875 2532 2354 846 4762 1161 4314
αἳ καὶ ἐκόπτοντο καὶ ἐθρήνουν αὐτόν. 28 στραφεὶς δὲ πρὸς
who also were bewailing and lamenting Him. having turned and to

846 3588 2424 2036 2364 2419 3361 2799
αὐτὰς ὁ Ἰησοῦς εἶπε, Θυγατέρες Ἱερουσαλήμ, μὴ κλαίετε
them Jesus said, Daughters of Jerusalem, not do weep

1909 1691 4133 1909 1438 2799 2532 1909 3588 5043 5216 3754
ἐπ' ἐμέ, πλὴν ἐφ' ἑαυτὰς κλαίετε καὶ ἐπὶ τὰ τέκνα ὑμῶν, 29 ὅτι
over Me, but over yourselves weep and over the children of you, because

2400 2064 2250 1722 3739 2046 3107 3588 4723
ἰδού, ἔρχονται ἡμέραι ἐν αἷς ἐροῦσι, Μακάριαι αἱ στεῖραι,
behold! will come Days in which they will say, Blessed the barren,

2532 2836 3739 3756 1080 2532 3149 3739 3756 2337
καὶ κοιλίαι αἳ οὐκ ἐγέννησαν, καὶ μαστοὶ οἳ οὐκ ἐθήλασαν.
and the wombs which not did bear, and breasts that not did give suck.

5119 756 3004 3588 3735 4098 1909 2248 2532 3588
30 τότε ἄρξονται λέγειν τοῖς ὄρεσι, Πέσετε ἐφ' ἡμᾶς· καὶ τοῖς
Then they will begin to say to the mountains, Fall on us! And to the

1015 2572 2248 3754 1487 1722 3588 5200 3586 5023
βουνοῖς, Καλύψατε ἡμᾶς. 31 ὅτι εἰ ἐν τῷ ὑγρῷ ξύλῳ ταῦτα
hills, Cover us. Because if in the sappy tree these things

4160 1722 3588 3584 5101 1096
ποιοῦσιν, ἐν τῷ ξηρῷ τί γένηται;
they do, in the dry what may happen?

71 1161 2532 2087 1417 2557 4862 846
32. Ἤγοντο δὲ καὶ ἕτεροι δύο κακοῦργοι σὺν αὐτῷ ἀναι-
were led And also others two criminals with Him to be

337
ρεθῆναι.
executed.

2532 3753 565 1909 3588 5117 3588 2564 2898
33. καὶ ὅτε ἀπῆλθον ἐπὶ τὸν τόπον τὸν καλούμενον Κρανίον,
And when they came on the place being called Skull,

1563 4717 846 2532 3588 2557 3739 3303 1537
ἐκεῖ ἐσταύρωσαν αὐτὸν, καὶ τοὺς κακούργους, ὃν μὲν ἐκ
there they crucified Him, and the criminals, one off

1188 3739 1161 1537 710 3588 1161 2424 3004 3962 863
δεξιῶν, ὃν δὲ ἐξ ἀριστερῶν. 34 ὁ δὲ Ἰησοῦς ἔλεγε, Πάτερ, ἄφες
(the) right, one and off (the) left. And Jesus said, Father, forgive

846 3756 1063 1492 5101 4160 1266 1161 3588
αὐτοῖς· οὐ γὰρ οἴδασι τί ποιοῦσι. διαμεριζόμενοι δὲ τὰ
them; not for they know what they are doing. having divided And the

King James Version

as they required.
25 And he released unto them him that for sedition and murder was cast into prison, whom they had desired; but he delivered Jesus to their will.

26. And as they led him away, they laid hold upon one Simon, a Cyrenian, coming out of the country, and on him they laid the cross, that he might bear (it) after Jesus.

27 And there followed him a great company of people, and of women, which also bewailed and lamented him.
28 But Jesus turning unto them said, Daughters of Jerusalem, weep not for me, but weep for yourselves, and for your children.
29 For, behold, the days are coming, in the which they shall say, Blessed (are) the barren, and the wombs that never bare, and the paps which never gave suck.

30 Then shall they begin to say to the mountains, Fall on us; and to the hills, Cover us.
31 For if they do these things in a green tree, what shall be done in the dry?

32. And there were also two other, malefactors, led with him to be put to death.

33 And when they were come to the place, which is called Calvary, there they crucified him, and the malefactors, one on the right hand, and the other on the left.
34 Then said Jesus, Father, forgive them; for they know not what they do. And they parted his

Literal Translation | **Luke 23:35** | **King James Version**

garments, they cast a lot. (Ps. 22:18)
35 And the people stood watching. And the rulers with them also scoffed, saying, He saved others; let him save himself, if this one is the Christ, the elect of God.

36 And coming near, the soldiers also mocked Him and (were) offering vinegar to Him,
37 and saying, If you are the king of the Jews, save yourself.
38 And also an inscription was written over Him, in Greek and Latin and Hebrew letters: THIS IS THE KING OF THE JEWS.

2440 846 906 2819 2532 2476 3588 2992 2334
ἱμάτια αὐτοῦ, ἔβαλον κλῆρον. 35 καὶ εἱστήκει ὁ λαὸς θεωρῶν.
garments of Him, they cast a lot. And stood the people watching.

1592 1161 2532 3588 758 4862 846 3004
ἐξεμυκτήριζον δὲ καὶ οἱ ἄρχοντες σὺν αὐτοῖς, λέγοντες,
scoffed And also the rulers with them, saying,

243 4982 4982 1438 1487 3778 2076 3588 5547 3588
Ἄλλους ἔσωσε, σωσάτω ἑαυτόν, εἰ οὗτός ἐστιν ὁ Χριστὸς, ὁ
Others he saved, let him save himself, if this one is the Christ, the

3588 2316 1588 1702 1161 846 2532 3588 4757
τοῦ Θεοῦ ἐκλεκτός. 36 ἐνέπαιξον δὲ αὐτῷ καὶ οἱ στρατιῶται,
of God Elect. mocked And Him also the soldiers,

4334 2532 3690 4374 846 2532 3004
προσερχόμενοι καὶ ὄξος προσφέροντες αὐτῷ, 37 καὶ λέγοντες,
coming near and vinegar offering to Him, and saying,

1487 4771 1488 3588 935 3588 2453 4982 4572 2258 1161 2532
Εἰ σὺ εἶ ὁ βασιλεὺς τῶν Ἰουδαίων, σῶσον σεαυτόν. 38 ἦν δὲ καὶ
If you are the king of the Jews, save yourself. was And also

1923 1125 1909 846 1121 1673 2532
ἐπιγραφὴ γεγραμμένη ἐπ' αὐτῷ γράμμασιν Ἑλληνικοῖς καὶ
an inscription written over Him in letters Greek and

4513 2532 1444 3778 2076 3588 935 3588
Ῥωμαικοῖς καὶ Ἑβραικοῖς, Οὗτός ἐστιν ὁ βασιλεὺς τῶν
Latin and Hebrew, THIS IS THE KING OF THE

2453
Ἰουδαίων.
JEWS.

raiment, and cast lots.
35 And the people stood beholding. And the rulers also with them derided (him), saying, He saved others; let him save himself, if he be Christ, the chosen of God.

36 And the soldiers also mocked him, coming to him, and offering him vinegar,
37 And saying, If thou be the king of the Jews, save thyself.
38 And a superscription also was written over him in letters of Greek, and Latin, and Hebrew, THIS IS THE KING OF THE JEWS.

39. And one of the hanged criminals blasphemed Him, saying, If you are the Christ, save yourself and us.
40 But answering the other rebuked him, saying, Do you not fear God, because you are in the same judgment?

41 And we indeed justly, for we receive things worthy of what we did. But this One did nothing wrong.

42 And he said to Jesus, Lord, remember me when You come in Your kingdom.
43 And Jesus said to him, Truly I say to you, Today you will be with Me in Paradise.

1520 1161 3588 2910 2557 987 846
39. Εἷς δὲ τῶν κρεμασθέντων κακούργων ἐβλασφήμει αὐτὸν,
one And of the hanged criminals blasphemed Him,

3004 1487 4771 1488 3588 5547 4982 4572 2532 2248 611
λέγων, Εἰ σὺ εἶ ὁ Χριστός; σῶσον σεαυτὸν καὶ ἡμᾶς. 40 ἀπο-
saying, If you are the Christ,? Save yourself and us.

1161 3588 2087 2008 846 3004 3761 5399 4771 3588
κριθεὶς δὲ ὁ ἕτερος ἐπιτίμα αὐτῷ, λέγων, Οὐδὲ φοβῇ σὺ τὸν
answering And the other rebuked him, saying, Do not fear you

2316 3754 1722 3588 846 2917 1488 2532 2249 3303 1346 514
Θεόν, ὅτι ἐν τῷ αὐτῷ κρίματι εἶ; 41 καὶ ἡμεῖς μὲν δικαίως, ἄξια
God, because in the same judgment you are? And we indeed justly, things worthy

1063 3739 4238 618 3778 1161 3762 824
γὰρ ὧν ἐπράξαμεν ἀπολαμβάνομεν· οὗτος δὲ οὐδὲν ἄτοπον
for of what we did we receive; this One but nothing amiss

4238 2532 3004 2424 3415 3450 2962 3752
ἔπραξε. 42 καὶ ἔλεγε, Ἰησοῦ, μνήσθητί μου, Κύριε, ὅταν
did. And he said to Jesus, Remember me, Lord, when

2064 1722 3588 932 4675 2532 2036 846 3588 2424 281
ἔλθῃς ἐν τῇ βασιλείᾳ σου. 43 καὶ εἶπεν αὐτῷ ὁ Ἰησοῦς, Ἀμὴν
You come in the kingdom of You. And said to him Jesus, Truly

3004 4671 4594 3326 1700 2071 1722 3588 3857
λέγω σοι, σήμερον μετ' ἐμοῦ ἔσῃ ἐν τῷ παραδείσῳ.
I say to you, Today with Me you will be in Paradise.

39. And one of the malefactors which were hanged railed on him, saying, If thou be Christ, save thyself and us.
40 But the other answering rebuked him, saying, Dost not thou fear God, seeing thou art in the same condemnation?
41 And we indeed justly; for we receive the due reward of our deeds: but this man hath done nothing amiss.

42 And he said unto Jesus, Lord, remember me when thou comest into thy kingdom.
43 And Jesus said unto him, Verily I say unto thee, To day shalt thou be with me in paradise.

44. And it was about (the) sixth hour, and darkness came to be over all the land until (the) ninth hour.
45 And the sun was darkened, and the veil of the Holy Place was torn in the middle.
46 And crying with a great voice, Jesus said, Father, into Your hands I commit My spirit.

2258 1161 5616 5610 1623 2532 4655 1096 1909 3650 3588
44. Ἦν δὲ ὡσεὶ ὥρα ἕκτη, καὶ σκότος ἐγένετο ἐφ' ὅλην τὴν
it was And about hour sixth, and darkness came to be over all the

1093 2193 5610 1766 2532 4654 3588 2246 2532 4977
γῆν ἕως ὥρας ἐννάτης. 45 καὶ εσκοτίσθη ὁ ἥλιος, καὶ ἐσχίσθη
land until hour (the) ninth. And was darkened the sun, and was torn

3588 2665 3588 3485 3319 2532 5455 5456 3173
τὸ καταπέτασμα τοῦ ναοῦ μέσον. 46 καὶ φωνήσας φωνῇ μεγάλῃ
the veil of the temple in the middle. And crying with a voice great

3588 2424 2036 3962 1519 5495 4675 3908 3588 4151
ὁ Ἰησοῦς εἶπε, Πάτερ, εἰς χεῖράς σου παραθήσομαι τὸ πνεῦμά
Jesus said, Father, into the hands of You I commit the spirit

44. And it was about the sixth hour, and there was a darkness over all the earth until the ninth hour.
45 And the sun was darkened, and the veil of the temple was rent in the midst.
And when Jesus had cried with a loud voice, he said, Father, into thy hands I commend my spirit:

Literal Translation

And saying this, He breathed out the spirit. (Ps. 31:5)
47. And having seen the thing having happened, the centurion glorified God, saying, Truly, this Man was righteous.

48 And all the crowd having arrived together at this sight, watching the things having happened, beating their breasts, (they) returned.

49 And all those known to Him stood at a distance, and (the) women, those having accompanied Him from Galilee, (were) seeing these things.

Luke 23:47

3450 2532 5023 2036 1606 1492 1161 3588 1543
μου· καὶ ταῦτα εἰπὼν ἐξέπνευσεν, 47 Ἰδὼν δὲ ὁ ἑκατόνταρχος
of Me. And this saying He breathed out the spirit. having seen And the centurion

3588 1096 1392 3588 2316 3004 3689 3588 444
τὸ γενόμενον ἐδόξασε τὸν Θεὸν, λέγων, Ὄντως ὁ ἄνθρωπος
the thing happening glorified God, saying, Truly man

3778 1342 2258 2532 3956 3588 4836 3793
οὗτος δίκαιος ἦν. 48 καὶ πάντες οἱ συμπαραγενόμενοι ὄχλοι
this righteous was. And all the having arrived together crowd

1909 3588 2335 3778 2334 3588 1096 5180
ἐπὶ τὴν θεωρίαν ταύτην, θεωροῦντες τὰ γενόμενα, τύπτοντες
at sight this, watching the things happening, beating

1438 3588 4738 5290 2476 1161 3956 3588
ἑαυτῶν τὰ στήθη ὑπέστρεφον. 49 εἱστήκεισαν δὲ πάντες οἱ
of themselves the breasts returned. stood But all those

1110 846 3113 2532 1135 3588 4870
γνωστοὶ αὐτοῦ μακρόθεν, καὶ γυναῖκες αἱ συνακολουθήσασαι
known of Him at a distance, and women the (ones) having accompanied

846 575 3588 1056 3708 5023
αὐτῷ ἀπὸ τῆς Γαλιλαίας, ὁρῶσαι ταῦτα.
Him from Galilee, (were) seeing these things.

King James Version

and having said thus, he gave up the ghost.
47. Now when the centurion saw what was done, he glorified God, saying, Certainly this was a righteous man.

48 And all the people that came together to that sight, beholding the things which were done, smote their breasts, and returned.

49 And all his acquaintance, and the women that followed him from Galilee, stood afar off, beholding these things.

Literal Translation

50. And, behold! A man named Joseph, being a councillor, a good and righteous man.
51 This one was not agreeing with their counsel and deed; he was from Arimathea, a city of the Jews, and who himself was eagerly expecting the kingdom of God,

52 drawing near to Pilate, this one asked (for) the body of Jesus.
53 And taking it down, he wrapped it in linen, and placed it in a quarried tomb, where no one was ever yet laid.

54 And it was Preparation Day, and a sabbath was dawning.
55. And also having followed women who had accompanied Him out of Galilee, watched the tomb, and how His body was placed.
56 And having returned, (they) prepared spices and ointment. And indeed they rested (on) the sabbath, according to the commandment.

2532 2400 435 3686 2501 1010 5225
50. Καὶ ἰδού, ἀνὴρ ὀνόματι Ἰωσὴφ, βουλευτὴς ὑπάρχων,
And, behold! A man by name Joseph, a councillor being,

435 18 2532 1342 3778 3756 2258 4784
ἀνὴρ ἀγαθὸς καὶ δίκαιος 51 [οὗτος οὐκ ἦν συγκατατεθειμένος
a man good and righteous, this one not was agreeing with

3588 1012 2532 3588 4234 846 575 707 4172
τῇ βουλῇ καὶ τῇ πράξει αὐτῶν], ἀπὸ Ἀριμαθαίας πόλεως
the counsel and the action of them, from Arimathea a city

3588 2453 3739 2532 4327 2532 846 3588 932
τῶν Ἰουδαίων, ὃς καὶ προσεδέχετο καὶ αὐτὸς τὴν βασιλείαν
of the Jews, who and was eagerly expecting also himself the kingdom

3588 2316 3778 4334 3588 4091 154 3588 4983
τοῦ Θεοῦ· 52 οὗτος προσελθὼν τῷ Πιλάτῳ ᾐτήσατο τὸ σῶμα
of God; this one having drawn near to Pilate asked the body

3588 2424 2532 2507 846 1794 846 4616 2532
τοῦ Ἰησοῦ, 53 καὶ καθελὼν αὐτὸ ἐνετύλιξεν αὐτὸ σινδόνι, καὶ
of Jesus. And taking down it he wrapped it in linen, and

5087 846 1722 3418 2991 3757 3756 2258 3764 3762
ἔθηκεν αὐτὸ ἐν μνήματι λαξευτῷ, οὗ οὐκ ἦν οὐδέπω οὐδεὶς
placed it in a tomb quarried, where not was not yet no one

2749 2532 2250 2258 3904 2532 4521 2020
κείμενος. 54 καὶ ἡμέρα ἦν παρασκευή, καὶ σάββατον ἐπέφωσκε.
laid. And day it was of preparation, and a sabbath dawning

2628 1161 2532 1135 3748 2258
55 κατακολουθήσασαι δὲ καὶ γυναῖκες, αἵτινες ἦσαν
having followed And also women who were

4905 846 1537 3588 1056 2300 3588 3419
συνεληλυθυῖαι αὐτῷ ἐκ τῆς Γαλιλαίας, ἐθεάσαντο τὸ μνημεῖον,
accompanying Him out of Galilee, watched the tomb,

2532 5613 5087 3588 4983 846 5290 1161 2090
καὶ ὡς ἐτέθη τὸ σῶμα αὐτοῦ, 56 ὑποστρέψασαι δὲ ἡτοίμασαν
and how was placed the body of Him, having returned and (they) prepared

759 2532 3464
ἀρώματα καὶ μύρα.
spices and ointment.

King James Version

50. And, behold, (there was) a man named Joseph, a counsellor; (and he was) a good man, and a just:
51 (The same had not consented to the counsel and deed of them;) (he was) of Arimathaea, a city of the Jews: who also himself waited for the kingdom of God.

52 This (man) went unto Pilate, and begged the body of Jesus.
53 And he took it down, and wrapped it in linen, and laid it in a sepulchre that was hewn in stone, wherein never man before was laid.

54 And that day was the preparation, and the sabbath drew on.
55. And the women also, which came with him from Galilee, followed after, and beheld the sepulchre, and how his body was laid.

56 And they returned, and prepared spices and ointments; and rested the sabbath day according to the commandment.

Luke 24

Literal Translation

1. (See Luke 23:56) And

2532 3588 3303 4521 2270 2596 3588 1785 3588 1161
1. Καὶ τὸ μὲν σάββατον ἡσύχασαν κατὰ τὴν ἐντολήν. τῇ δὲ
And indeed (on the) sabbath they rested according to the command. the But

King James Version

1. (See Luke 23:56) Now

Literal Translation

the first of the week, while still very early, they came on the tomb, carrying spices which they prepared; and some (were) with them.
2 But they found the stone having been rolled away from the tomb.
3 And having gone in, they did not find the body of the Lord Jesus.
4 And it happened, as they were perplexed about this, even behold! Two men in shining clothing stood by them.

5 And they having become terrified, and bending (their) faces to the ground, they said to them, Why do you seek the Living (One) with the dead?
6 He is not here, but was raised. Remember how He spoke to you, yet being in Galilee,
7 saying, The Son of man must be delivered up into (the) hands of sinful men, and to be crucified, and the third day to rise again.

8 And they remembered His words.
9 And having returned from the tomb, (they) reported all these things to the Eleven, and to all the rest.

10 And they were Mary Magdalene, and Joanna, and Mary the (mother) of James, and the rest with them, who told these things to the apostles.
11 And their words seemed like idle talk before them, and they did not believe them.

12 But having risen, Peter ran to the tomb, and bending down he sees the linen lying alone. And (he) went away wondering to himself (at what) had happened.

Luke 24:2

3391 3588 4521 3722 901 2064 1909 3588 3418
μιᾷ τῶν σαββάτων, ὄρθρου βαθέος, ἦλθον ἐπὶ τὸ μνῆμα,
one of the week, while still very early, they came on the tomb,

5342 3739 2090 759 2532 5100 4862 846 2147
φέρουσαι ἃ ἡτοίμασαν ἀρώματα, καί τινες σὺν αὐταῖς. 2 εὗρον
carrying which they prepared spices, and some with them. They found

1161 3588 3037 617 575 3588 3419 2532
δὲ τὸν λίθον ἀποκεκυλισμένον ἀπὸ τοῦ μνημείου, 3 καὶ
But the stone having been rolled away from the tomb, and

1525 3756 2147 3588 4983 3588 2962 2424 2532
εἰσελθοῦσαι οὐχ εὗρον τὸ σῶμα τοῦ Κυρίου Ἰησοῦ. 4 καὶ
having gone in not they found the body of the Lord Jesus. And

1096 1722 3588 1280 846 4012 5127 2532 2400
ἐγένετο ἐν τῷ διαπορεῖσθαι αὐτὰς περὶ τούτου, καὶ ἰδού,
it happened at the in the perplexed (of) them concerning this, and, behold!

1417 435 2186 846 1722 2067 797
δύο ἄνδρες ἐπέστησαν αὐταῖς ἐν ἐσθήσεσιν ἀστραπτούσσαις·
Two men stood by them in clothing shining;

1719 1161 1096 846 2532 2827 3588 4383
5 ἐμφόβων δὲ γενομένων αὐτῶν, καὶ κλινουσῶν τὸ πρόσωπον
terrified and having become them, and bending the faces

1519 3588 1093 2036 4314 846 5101 2212 3588 2198 3326
εἰς τὴν γῆν, εἶπον πρὸς αὐτάς, Τί ζητεῖτε τὸν ζῶντα μετὰ
to the ground, they said to them, Why do you seek the Living (One) with

3588 3498 3756 2076 5602 235 1453 3415 5613
τῶν νεκρῶν; 6 οὐκ ἔστιν ὧδε, ἀλλ᾽ ἠγέρθη· μνήσθητε ὡς
the dead? not He is here, but was raised. Remember how

2980 5213 2089 5607 1722 3588 1056 3004 3754 1163 3588 5207
ἐλάλησεν ὑμῖν, ἔτι ὢν ἐν τῇ Γαλιλαίᾳ, 7 λέγων ὅτι δεῖ τὸν υἱὸν
He spoke to you, yet being in Galilee, saying, must The Son

3588 444 3860 1519 5495 444 268
τοῦ ἀνθρώπου παραδοθῆναι εἰς χεῖρας ἀνθρώπων ἁμαρτω-
of man to be delivered up into (the) hands men of sinful

2532 4717 2532 3588 5154 2250 450
λῶν, καὶ σταυρωθῆναι, καὶ τῇ τρίτῃ ἡμέρᾳ ἀναστῆναι.
and to be crucified, and the third day to rise again.

2532 3415 3588 4487 846 2532 5290
8 καὶ ἐμνήσθησαν τῶν ῥημάτων αὐτοῦ, 9 καὶ ὑποστρέψασαι
And they remembered the words of Him, and having returned

575 3588 3419 518 5023 3956 3588 1733
ἀπὸ τοῦ μνημείου, ἀπήγγειλαν ταῦτα πάντα τοῖς ἕνδεκα
from the tomb, (they) reported these things all to the Eleven

2532 3956 3588 3062 2258 1161 3588 3094 3137 2532
καὶ πᾶσι τοῖς λοιποῖς. 10 ἦσαν δὲ ἡ Μαγδαληνὴ Μαρία καὶ
and to all the rest. they were And the Magdalene Mary, and

2489 2532 3137 3588 2385 2532 3588 3062 4862 846 3739
Ἰωάννα καὶ Μαρία ἡ Ἰακώβου, καὶ αἱ λοιπαὶ σὺν αὐταῖς, αἳ
Joanna and Mary the of James, and the rest with them, who

3004 4314 3588 652 5023 2532 5316 1799
ἔλεγον πρὸς τοὺς ἀποστόλους ταῦτα. 11 καὶ ἐφάνησαν ἐνώπιον
told to the apostles these things. And seemed before

846 5616 3026 3588 4487 846 2532 569 846
αὐτῶν ὡσεὶ λῆρος τὰ ῥήματα αὐτῶν, καὶ ἠπίστουν αὐταῖς.
them as idle talk the words of them, and they disbelieved them.

3588 1161 4074 450 5143 1909 3588 3419 2532 3879
12 Ὁ δὲ Πέτρος ἀναστὰς ἔδραμεν ἐπὶ τὸ μνημεῖον, καὶ παρα-
And Peter having risen ran to the tomb, and bending

991 3588 3608 2749 3441 2532 565 4314
κύψας βλέπει τὰ ὀθόνια κείμενα μόνα· καὶ ἀπῆλθε πρὸς
down he sees the linen lying alone, and went away to

1438 2296 3588 1096
ἑαυτὸν θαυμάζων τὸ γεγονός.
himself wondering (at what) had happened.

King James Version

upon the first (day) of the week, very early in the morning, they came unto the sepulchre, bringing the spices which they had prepared, and certain (others) with them.
2 And they found the stone rolled away from the sepulchre.
3 And they entered in, and found not the body of the Lord Jesus.
4 And it came to pass, as they were much perplexed thereabout, behold, two men stood by them in shining garments:

5 And as they were afraid, and bowed down (their) faces to the earth, they said unto them, Why seek ye the living among the dead?
6 He is not here, but is risen: remember how he spake unto you when he was yet in Galilee,
7 Saying, The Son of man must be delivered into the hands of sinful men, and be crucified, and the third day rise again.

8 And they remembered his words,
9 And returned from the sepulchre, and told all these things unto the eleven, and to all the rest.

10 It was Mary Magdalene, and Joanna, and Mary (the mother) of James, and other (women that were) with them, which told these things unto the apostles.
11 And their words seemed to them as idle tales, and they believed them not.

12 Then arose Peter, and ran unto the sepulchre; and stooping down, he beheld the linen clothes laid by themselves, and departed, wondering in himself at that which was come to pass.

Literal Translation | **Luke 24:13** | ***King James Version***

13. And, behold! Two of them were going on the same day to a village being sixty stadia distant from Jerusalem, which was named Emmaus.
14 And they talked to each other about all these things having happened.
15 And it occurred in the conversing and discussing (of) them, having drawn near even Jesus Himself accompanied them;

16 but their eyes were held so as) not to recognize Him.

17 And He said to them, What words (are) these which you exchange with each other (while) walking, and are sad of face?

18 And one answering, whose name was Cleopas, said to Him, (Are) you only a visitor in Jerusalem and do not know the things having occurred in it in these days?

19 And He said to them, What things? And they said to Him, The things concerning Jesus the Nazarean, who was a man, a prophet mighty in work and word before God and all the people;

20 how both the chief priests and our rulers delivered up Him to (the) judgment of death, and crucified (Him).

21 But we were hoping that He is the (One) going to redeem Israel. But yet with all these things, this third day comes today since these things occurred.
22 But also some of our women astounded us, having been early at the tomb,

23 and not finding His body, (they) came saying to have

2532 2400 1417 1537 846 2258 4198 1722 846 3588
13. Καὶ ἰδοὺ, δύο ἐξ αὐτῶν ἦσαν προευόμενοι ἐν αὐτῇ τῇ
And, behold! Two of them were going in same the

2250 1519 2968 568 4712 1835 575
ἡμέρᾳ εἰς κώμην ἀπέχουσαν σταδίους ἑξήκοντα ἀπὸ
day to a village being distant stadia sixty from

2419 3739 3686 1695 2532 846 3656 4314
Ἱερουσαλήμ, ᾗ ὄνομα Ἐμμαοῦς, 14 καὶ αὐτοὶ ὡμίλουν πρὸς
Jerusalem, to which name (was) Emmaus; and they conversed to

240 4012 3956 3588 4819 5130 2532
ἀλλήλους περὶ πάντων τῶν συμβεβηκότων τούτων. 15 καὶ
one another concerning all having happened these things. And

1096 1722 3588 3656 846 2532 4802 2532 846 3588
ἐγένετο ἐν τῷ ὁμιλεῖν αὐτοὺς καὶ συζητεῖν, καὶ αὐτὸς ὁ
it occurred in the to converse them and to discuss, even Himself

2424 1448 4848 846 3588 1161 3788 846
Ἰησοῦς ἐγγίσας συνεπορεύετο αὐτοῖς, 16 οἱ δὲ ὀφθαλμοὶ αὐτῶν
Jesus drawing near accompanied them, the and eyes of them

2902 3588 3361 1921 846 2036 1161 4314 846
ἐκρατοῦντο τοῦ μὴ ἐπιγνῶναι αὐτόν. 17 εἶπε δὲ πρὸς αὐτούς,
were held not to recognize Him. He said And to them,

5101 3588 3056 3778 3739 474 4314 240
Τίνες οἱ λόγοι οὗτοι οὓς ἀντιβάλλετε πρὸς ἀλλήλους
What words (are) these which you exchange with each other

4043 2532 2075 4659 611 1161 3588 1520
περιπατοῦντες, καὶ ἐστε σκυθρωποί; 18 ἀποκριθεὶς δὲ ὁ εἷς,
(while) walking, and are sad of face? answering And one,

3739 3686 2810 2036 4314 846 4771 3441 3939 1722
ᾧ ὄνομα Κλεόπας, εἶπε πρὸς αὐτόν, Σὺ μόνος παροικεῖς ἐν
whose name (was) Cleopas, said to Him, Are you only a visitor in

2419 2532 3756 1097 3588 1096 1722 846 1722 3588
Ἱερουσαλὴμ, καὶ οὐκ ἔγνως τὰ γενόμενα ἐν αὐτῇ ἐν ταῖς
Jerusalem, and not do know the things having occurred in it in

2250 3778 2532 2036 846 4169 3588 1161 2036 846
ἡμέραις ταύταις; 19 καὶ εἶπεν αὐτοῖς, Ποῖα; οἱ δὲ εἶπον αὐτῷ,
days these? And He said to them, What? they And said to Him,

3588 4012 2424 3588 3480 3739 1096 435 4396
Τὰ περὶ Ἰησοῦ τοῦ Ναζαραίου, ὃς ἐγένετο ἀνὴρ προφήτης
The things about Jesus the Nazarene, who was a man, a prophet

1415 1722 2041 2532 3056 1726 3588 2316 2532 3956
δυνατὸς ἐν ἔργῳ καὶ λόγῳ ἐναντίον τοῦ Θεοῦ καὶ παντὸς
powerful in work and word before God and all

3588 2992 3704 5037 3860 846 3588 749 2532 3588
τοῦ λαοῦ, 20 ὅπως τε παρέδωκαν αὐτὸν οἱ ἀρχιερεῖς καὶ οἱ
the people, how both delivered up Him the chief priests and the

758 2257 1519 2917 2288 2532 4717 846
ἄρχοντες ἡμῶν εἰς κρίμα θανάτου, καὶ ἐσταύρωσαν αὐτόν.
rulers of us to (the) judgment of death, and crucified Him.

2249 1161 1679 3754 846 2076 3588 3195 3084 3588
21 ἡμεῖς δὲ ἠλπίζομεν ὅτι αὐτός ἐστιν ὁ μέλλων λυτροῦσθαι τὸν
we But were hoping that He is the (One) going to redeem

2474 235 1065 4862 3956 5125 5154 3778 2250 71
Ἰσραήλ. ἀλλά γε σὺν πᾶσι τούτοις τρίτην ταύτην ἡμέραν ἄγει
Israel. But yet with all these things third this day comes

4594 575 3739 5023 1096 235 2532 1135 5100 1537
σήμερον ἀφ᾽ οὗ ταῦτα ἐγένετο. 22 ἀλλὰ και γυναῖκές τινες ἐξ
today since these things occurred. But also women some of

2257 1839 2248 1096 3721 1909 3588 3419
ἡμῶν ἐξέστησαν ἡμᾶς, γενόμεναι ὀρθριαὶ ἐπὶ τὸ μνημεῖον·
us astounded us, having been early at the tomb;

2532 3361 2147 3588 4983 846 2064 3004 2532 3701
23 καὶ μὴ εὑροῦσαι τὸ σῶμα αὐτοῦ, ἦλθον λέγουσαι καὶ ὀπτα-
and not finding the body of Him, came saying also a

13. And, behold, two of them went that same day to a village called Emmaus, which was from Jerusalem (about) threescore furlongs.

14 And they talked together of all these things which had happened.
15 And it came to pass, that, while they communed (together) and reasoned, Jesus himself drew near, and went with them.

16 But their eyes were holden that they should not know him.

17 And he said unto them, What manner of communications (are) these that ye have one to another, as ye walk, and are sad?

18 And the one of them, whose name was Cleopas, answering said unto him, Art thou only a stranger in Jerusalem, and hast not known the things which are come to pass there in these days?

19 And he said unto them, What things? And they said unto him, Concerning Jesus of Nazareth, which was a prophet mighty in deed and word before God and all the people:

20 And how the chief priests and our rulers delivered him to be condemned to death, and have crucified him.

21 But we trusted that it had been he which should have redeemed Israel: and beside all this, to day is the third day since these things were done.
22 Yea, and certain women also of our company made us astonished, which were early at the sepulchre;
23 And when they found not his body, they came, saying, that they had also

Literal Translation | **Luke 24:24** | **King James Version**

seen a vision of angels also, who say Him to be alive.
24. And some of those with us went to the tomb, and found (it so), even as the women also said; but they did not see Him.

25 And He said to them, O foolish (ones), and slow in heart to believe on all things which the prophets spoke!

26 Must not the Christ suffer these things, and to enter into His glory?

27 And having begun from Moses, and from all the Prophets, He explained to them the things about Himself in all the Scriptures.

28 And they drew near to the village where they were going, and He appeared to be going further.
29 And they constrained Him, saying, Stay with us, for it is toward evening, and the day has declined. And He went in to stay with them.
30 And it happened (as) He reclined with them, having taken the loaf, He blessed, and having broken He gave to them.
31. And their eyes were opened, and they recognized Him. And He became invisible from them.

32 And they said to one another, Was not our heart burning in us as He spoke to us in the roadway, and as He opened up to us the Scriptures?
33 And rising up in the same hour, they went back to Jerusalem, and (they) found the Eleven, and those with them, having been gathered,

34 saying, The Lord really was raised and appeared to Simon.

---

32 3708 3739 3004 846 2198 2532
σίαν ἀγγέλων ἑωρακέναι, οἳ λέγουσιν αὐτὸν ζῆν. 24 καὶ ἀπ-
vision of angels to have seen, who say Him to live. And

565 5100 3588 4862 2254 1909 3588 3419 2532 2147 3779
ῆλθόν τινες τῶν σὺν ἡμῖν ἐπὶ τὸ μνημεῖον, καὶ εὗρον οὕτω
went some of those with us to the tomb, and found so

2531 2532 3588 1135 2036 846 1161 3756 1492 2532 846
καθὼς καὶ αἱ γυναῖκες εἶπον· αὐτὸν δὲ οὐκ εἶδον. 25 καὶ αὐτὸς
even as also the women said; Him but not they saw. And He

2036 4314 846 5599 453 2532 1021 3588 2588 3588
εἶπε πρὸς αὐτούς, Ὦ ἀνόητοι καὶ βραδεῖς τῇ καρδίᾳ τοῦ
said to them, O foolish (ones) and slow in heart

4100 1909 3956 3739 2980 3588 4396 3780 5023
πιστεύειν ἐπὶ πᾶσιν οἷς ἐλάλησαν οἱ προφῆται· 26 οὐχὶ ταῦτα
to believe on all things which spoke the prophets! Not these things

1163 3958 3588 5547 2532 1525 1519 3588 1391 846
ἔδει παθεῖν τὸν Χριστὸν, καὶ εἰσελθεῖν εἰς τὴν δόξαν αὐτοῦ;
must suffer the Christ, and to enter into the glory of Him?

2532 756 575 3475 2532 575 3956 3588 4396
27 καὶ ἀρξάμενος ἀπὸ Μωσέως καὶ ἀπὸ πάντων τῶν προφητῶν,
And having begun from Moses and from all the Prophets,

1329 846 1722 3956 3588 1124 3588 4012 1438
διηρμήνευεν αὐτοῖς ἐν πάσαις ταῖς γραφαῖς τὰ περὶ ἑαυτοῦ.
He explained to them in all the Scriptures the things about Himself.

2532 1448 1519 3588 2968 3757 4198 2532 846
28. καὶ ἤγγισαν εἰς τὴν κώμην οὗ ἐπορεύοντο· καὶ αὐτὸς
And they drew near to the village where they were going; and He

4364 4208 4198 2532 3849
προσεποιεῖτο πορρωτέρω πορεύεσθαι. 29 καὶ παρεβιάσαντο
appeared further to be going. And they constrained

846 3004 3306 3326 2257 3754 4314 2073 2076
αὐτὸν, λέγοντες, Μεῖνον μεθ' ἡμῶν, ὅτι πρὸς ἑσπέραν ἐστὶ,
Him, saying, Stay with us, because toward evening it is,

2532 2827 3588 2250 2532 1525 3588 3306 4862 846 2532
καὶ κέκλικεν ἡ ἡμέρα. καὶ εἰσῆλθε τοῦ μεῖναι σὺν αὐτοῖς. 30 καὶ
and has declined the day. And He went in to stay with them. And

1096 1722 3588 2625 846 3326 846 2983 3588
ἐγένετο ἐν τῷ κατακλιθῆναι αὐτὸν μετ' αὐτῶν, λαβὼν τὸν
it happened in the reclining (of) Him with them, having taken the

740 2127 2532 2806 1929 846 846 1161
ἄρτον εὐλόγησε, καὶ κλάσας ἐπεδίδου αὐτοῖς. 31 αὐτῶν δὲ
loaf He blessed; and having broken, He gave to them. of them And

1272 3588 3788 2532 1921 846 2532
διηνοίχθησαν οἱ ὀφθαλμοὶ, καὶ ἐπέγνωσαν αὐτόν· καὶ
was opened the eyes, and they recognized Him; and

846 855 1096 575 846 2532 2036 4314 240
αὐτὸς ἄφαντος ἐγένετο ἀπ' αὐτῶν. 32 καὶ εἶπον πρὸς ἀλλή-
He invisible became from them. And they said to one

3780 3588 2588 2257 2545 2258 1722 2254 5613 2980
λους, Οὐχὶ ἡ καρδία ἡμῶν καιομένη ἦν ἐν ἡμῖν, ὡς ἐλάλει
another, Not the heart of us burning was in us as He spoke

2254 1722 3588 3598 2532 5613 1272 2254 3588 1124 2532
ἡμῖν ἐν τῇ ὁδῷ, καὶ ὡς διήνοιγεν ἡμῖν τὰς γραφάς; 33 καὶ
to us in the way, and as He opened up to us the Scriptures? And

450 846 3588 5610 5290 1519 2419 2532
ἀναστάντες αὐτῇ τῇ ὥρᾳ ὑπέστρεψαν εἰς Ἱερουσαλήμ, καὶ
having risen same in the hour, they went back to Jerusalem, and

2147 4867 3588 1733 2532 3588 4862 846
εὗρον συνηθροισμένους τοὺς ἕνδεκα καὶ τοὺς σὺν αὐτοῖς,
found having been gathered the Eleven and those with them,

3004 3754 1453 3588 2962 3689 2532 3700 4613
34 λέγοντας ὅτι Ἠγέρθη ὁ Κύριος ὄντως, καὶ ὤφθη Σίμωνι.
saying, was raised the Lord really, and appeared to Simon.

---

seen a vision of angels, which said that he was alive.
24. And certain of them which were with us went to the sepulchre, and found (it) even so as the women had said: but him they saw not.
25 Then he said unto them, O fools, and slow of heart to believe all that the prophets have spoken:

26 Ought not Christ to have suffered these things, and to enter into his glory?

27 And beginning at Moses and all the prophets, he expounded unto them in all the scriptures the things concerning himself.

28 And they drew nigh unto the village, whither they went: and he made as though he would have gone further.
29 But they constrained him, saying, Abide with us: for it is toward evening, and the day is far spent. And he went in to tarry with them.
30 And it came to pass, as he sat at meat with them, he took bread, and blessed (it), and brake, and gave to them.
31. And their eyes were opened, and they knew him; and he vanished out of their sight.

32 And they said one to another, Did not our heart burn within us, while he talked with us by the way, and while he opened to us the scriptures?
33 And they rose up the same hour, and returned to Jerusalem, and found the eleven gathered together, and them that were with them,

34 Saying, The Lord is risen indeed, and hath appeared to Simon.

Literal Translation **Luke 24:35** *King James Version*

35. And they related the things in the roadway, and how He was known to them in the breaking of the loaf.

36. And (as) they (were) saying these things, Jesus Himself stood in their midst, and said to them, Peace to you!
37 But having been terrified and having been filled with fear, they thought they beheld a spirit.
38 And He said to them, Why are you being troubled? And why do reasonings come up in your hearts.
39. See My hands and My feet, that I am He? Feel Me and see, because a spirit does not have flesh and bones, as you behold Me having.
40 And having said this, He showed them (His) hands and feet.

41 But yet they not believing from the joy, and marveling, He said to them, Have you anything edible here?

42 And they gave a broiled part (of) a fish to Him, and from a honeycomb.
43 And having taken (these) before them, He ate.

44 And He said to them, These (are) the words which I spoke to you yet being with you, that must be fulfilled all the things having been written in the Law of Moses, and the Prophets, and the Psalms, concerning Me.
45 Then He opened up their mind to understand the Scriptures,
46 and said to them, So it has been written, and so the Christ must suffer, and to rise from (the) dead the third day.
47 And repentance and remission

2532 846 1834 3588/1722/3588/3598/2532/5613/1097 846
35 καὶ αὐτοὶ ἐξηγοῦντο τὰ ἐν τῇ ὁδῷ, καὶ ὡς ἐγνώσθη αὐτοῖς
And they related the things in the way, and how He was known to them
1722 3588 2800 3588 740
ἐν τῇ κλάσει τοῦ ἄρτου.
in the breaking of the loaf

5023 1161 846 2980 846 3588 2424 2476 1722
36. Ταῦτα δὲ αὐτῶν λαλούντων, αὐτὸς ὁ Ἰησοῦς ἔστη ἐν
these things And them saying, Himself Jesus stood in
3319 846 2532 3004 846 1515 5213 4422 1161
μέσῳ αὐτῶν, καὶ λέγει αὐτοῖς, Εἰρήνη ὑμῖν. 37 πτοηθέντες δὲ
(the) midst of them, and says to them, Peace to you. having been terrified But
2532 1719 1096 1380 4151 2334 2532 2036
καὶ ἔμφοβοι γενόμενοι ἐδόκουν πνεῦμα θεωρεῖν. 38 καὶ εἶπεν
and filled with fear having been, they thought a spirit they beheld. And He said
846 5101 5015 2075 2532 1302 1261
αὐτοῖς, Τί τεταραγμένοι ἐστέ; καὶ διατί διαλογισμοὶ
to them, Why being troubled are you? And why do reasonings
305 1722 3588 2588 5216 1492 3588 5495 3450
ἀναβαίνουσιν ἐν ταῖς καρδίαις ὑμῶν; 39 ἴδετε τὰς χεῖράς μου
come up in the hearts of you? See the hands of Me
2532 3588 4228 3450 3754 846 1473 1510 5584 3165 2532
καὶ τοὺς πόδας μου, ὅτι αὐτὸς ἐγώ εἰμι· ψηλαφήσατέ με καὶ
and the feet of Me, that He I am. Feel Me and
1492 3754 4151 4561 2532 3747 3756 2192 2531 1691
ἴδετε, ὅτι πνεῦμα σάρκα καὶ ὀστέα οὐκ ἔχει, καθὼς ἐμὲ
see, because a spirit flesh and bones not has, even as Me
2334 2192 2532 5124 2036 1925 846 3588
θεωρεῖτε ἔχοντα. 40 καὶ τοῦτο εἰπὼν ἐπέδειξεν αὐτοῖς τὰς
you behold having. And this having said He showed them the
5495 2532 3588 4228 2089 1161 569 846 575 3588
χεῖρας καὶ τοὺς πόδας. 41 ἔτι δὲ ἀπιστούντων αὐτῶν ἀπὸ τῆς
hands and the feet. yet And disbelieving them from the
5479 2532 2296 2036 846 2192 5100 1034
χαρᾶς καὶ θαυμαζόντων, εἶπεν αὐτοῖς, Ἔχετέ τι βρώσιμον
joy and marveling, He said to them, Have you anything edible
1759 3588 1161 1929 846 2486 3702 3313 2532 575
ἐνθάδε; 42 οἱ δὲ ἐπέδωκαν αὐτῷ ἰχθύος ὀπτοῦ μέρος, 43 καὶ ἀπὸ
here? they And gave to Him a fish broiled part (of), and from
3193 2781 2532 2983 1799 846 5315
μελισσίου κηρίου. και λαβὼν ἐνώπιον αὐτῶν ἔφαγεν.
a honey comb. And having taken befor them, He ate.

2036 1161 846 3778 3588 3056 3739 2980 4314 5209
44. Εἶπε δὲ αὐτοῖς, Οὗτοι οἱ λόγοι, οὓς ἐλάλησα πρὸς ὑμᾶς
He said And to them, These words which I spoke to you,
2089 5607 4862 5213 3754 1163 4137 3956 3588 1125
ἔτι ὢν σὺν ὑμῖν, ὅτι δεῖ πληρωθῆναι πάντα τὰ γεγραμμένα
yet being with you, that must be fulfilled all the things having been written
1722 3588 3551 3475 2532 4396 2532 5568 4012 1700
ἐν τῷ νόμῳ Μωσέως καὶ προφήταις καὶ ψαλμοῖς περὶ ἐμοῦ.
in the Law of Moses and (the) Prophets and (the) Psalms about Me.
5119 1272 846 3588 3563 3588 4920 3588 1124
45 τότε διήνοιξεν αὐτῶν τὸν νοῦν, τοῦ συνιέναι τὰς γραφάς·
Then He opened up of them the mind to understand the Scriptures;
2532 2036 846 3754 3779 1125 2532 3779 1163 3958
46 καί εἶπεν αὐτοῖς ὅτι οὕτω γέγραπται, καί οὕτως ἔδει παθεῖν
and said to them, Thus it has been written, and thus must suffer
3588 5547 2532 450 1537 3498 3588 5154 2250 2532
τὸν Χριστὸν, καὶ ἀναστῆναι ἐκ νεκρῶν τῇ τρίτῃ ἡμέρᾳ, 47 καὶ
the Christ, and to rise up out of (the) dead the third day, and
2784 1909 3588 3686 846 3341 2532 859
κηρυχθῆναι ἐπὶ τῷ ὀνόματι αὐτοῦ μετάνοιαν καὶ ἄφεσιν
to be proclaimed on the name of Him repentance and remission

35. And they told what things (were done) in the way, and how he was known of them in breaking of bread.

36. And as they thus spake, Jesus himself stood in the midst of them, and saith unto them, Peace (be) unto you.
37 But they were terrified and affrighted, and supposed that they had seen a spirit.
38 And he said unto them, Why are ye troubled? and why do thoughts arise in your hearts?
39. Behold my hands and my feet, that it is I myself: handle me, and see; for a spirit hath not flesh and bones, as ye see me have.

40 And when he had thus spoken, he shewed them (his) hands and (his) feet.
41 And while they yet believed not for joy, and wondered, he said unto them, Have ye here any meat?
42 And they gave him a piece of a broiled fish, and of an honeycomb.
43 And he took (it), and did eat before them.
44 And he said unto them, These (are) the words which I spake unto you, while I was yet with you, that all things must be fulfilled, which were written in the law of Moses, and (in) the prophets, and (in) the psalms, concerning me.
45 Then opened he their understanding, that they might understand the scriptures,
46 And said unto them, Thus it is written, and thus it behoved Christ to suffer, and to rise from the dead the third day:
47 And that repentance and remission

Literal Translation **Luke 24:48** *King James Version*

of sins (must) be preached on His name to all the nations, having begun from Jerusalem.
48 And you are witnesses of these things.
49. And, behold! I send forth the promise of My Father on you. But you sit in the city of Jerusalem until you are clothed with power from on high.

266 1519 3956 3588 1484 756 575 2419
ἁμαρτιῶν εἰς πάντα τὰ ἔθνη, ἀρξάμενοι ἀπὸ Ἱερουσαλήμ.
of sins to all the nations, having begun from Jerusalem.

5210 1161 2075 3144 5130 2532 2400 1473 649
48 ὑμεῖς δέ ἐστε μάρτυρες τούτων. 49 καὶ ἰδοὺ, ἐγὼ ἀποστέλλω
you And are witnesses of these things. And, behold! I send forth

3588 1860 3588 3962 3450 1909 5209 5210 1161 2523
τὴν ἐπαγγελίαν τοῦ πατρός μου ἐφ' ὑμᾶς· ὑμεῖς δὲ καθίσατε
the promise of the Father of Me on you; you but sit

1722 3588 4172 2419 2193 3757 746 1411 1537
ἐν τῇ πόλει Ἱερουσαλήμ, ἕως οὗ ἐνδύσησθε δύναμιν ἐξ
in the city of Jerusalem, until you are clothed with power from

5311
ὕψους.
on high.

of sins should be preached in his name among all nations, beginning at Jerusalem.
48 And ye are witnesses of these things.
49. And, behold, I send the promise of my Father upon you: but tarry ye in the city of Jerusalem, until ye be endued with power from on high.

50. And He led them out as far as to Bethany. And having lifted up His hands, He blessed them.
51 And it happened as He blessed them, He withdrew from them and was carried into Heaven.

52 And having worshiped Him, they returned to Jerusalem with great joy,
53 and were through all in the temple, praising and blessing God. Amen.

1806 1161 846 1854 2193 1519 963 2532 1869
50. Ἐξήγαγε δὲ αὐτοὺς ἔξω ἕως εἰς Βηθανίαν· καὶ ἐπάρας
He led And them out as far as to Bethany; and lifting up

3588 5495 846 2127 846 2532 1096 1722 3588
τὰς χεῖρας αὐτοῦ εὐλόγησεν αὐτούς. 51 καὶ ἐγένετο ἐν τῷ
the hands of Him, He blessed them. And it happened, in the

2127 846 846 1339 575 846 2532 399 1519
εὐλογεῖν αὐτὸν αὐτοὺς, διέστη ἀπ' αὐτῶν, καὶ ἀνεφέρετο εἰς
blessing of Him them, He withdrew from them, and was carried into

3588 3772 2532 846 4352 846 5290
τὸν οὐρανόν. 52 καὶ αὐτοὶ προσκυνήσαντες αὐτὸν, ὑπέστρεψαν
Heaven. And they, having worshiped Him, returned

1519 2419 3326 5479 3173 2532 2258 1275 1722
εἰς Ἱερουσαλὴμ μετὰ χαρᾶς μεγάλης· 53 καὶ ἦσαν διαπαντὸς ἐν
into Jerusalem with joy great; and were through all in

3588 2411 134 2532 2127 3588 2316 281
τῷ ἱερῷ , αἰνοῦντες καὶ εὐλογοῦντες τὸν Θεόν. Ἀμὴν.
the temple, praising and blessing God. Amen.

50. And he led them out as far as to Bethany, and he lifted up his hands, and blessed them.
51 And it came to pass, while he blessed them, he was parted from them, and carried up into heaven.

52 And they worshipped him, and returned to Jerusalem with great joy:
53 And were continually in the temple, praising and blessing God. Amen.

Literal Translation

THE GOSPEL ACCORDING TO JOHN

John 1

1. In (the) beginning was the Word, and the Word was with God, and the Word was God.
2 This One was in beginning with God.
3 All things came into being through Him, and without Him not even one (thing) came into being that has come into being.
4 In Him was life, and the life was the light of men;
5 and the light shines in the darkness, and the darkness did not overtake it.
6. There was a man having been sent from God; his name (was) John.
7 This one came for a witness, that (he) might witness concerning the Light, that all might believe through Him.
8 He was not that Light, but that (he) might witness concerning the Light.
9 He was the true Light which enlightens every man coming into the world.
10 He was in the world, and the world came into being through Him, yet the world did not know Him.
11 He came to (His) own, and (His) own did not receive Him.
12 But as many as received Him, to them He gave authority to become children of God, to the ones believing into His name,
13 who were generated not of bloods, nor of (the) will of (the) flesh, nor of (the) will of man, but of God (were generated).
14 And the Word became flesh and tabernacled among us. And we beheld His glory, glory as of an only begotten from (the) Father, full of grace and of truth.
15. John witnesses concerning Him,

ΕΥΑΓΓΕΛΙΟΝ ΤΟ ΚΑΤΑ
THE GOSPEL ACCORDING TO

ΙΩΑΝΝΗΝ
JOHN

John 1

1722 746 2258 3588 3056 2532 3588 3056 2258 4314 3588 2316 2532
1.Ἐν ἀρχῇ ἦν ὁ λόγος, καὶ ὁ λόγος ἦν πρὸς τὸν θεόν, καὶ
In (the) beginning was the word, and the Word was with God, and
2316 2258 3588 3056 3778 2258 1722 746 4314 3588 2316 3956
θεὸς ἦν ὁ λόγος. 2 οὗτος ἦν ἐν ἀρχῇ πρὸς τὸν θεόν. 3 πάντα
God was the Word. This One was in beginning with God. All things
1223 846 1096 2532 5565 846 1096 3761 1520 3739 1096
δι' αὐτοῦ ἐγένετο, καὶ χωρὶς αὐτοῦ ἐγένετο οὐδὲ ἕν ὃ γέγονεν.
through Him came into being, and without Him came into being not even one (thing) that came into being
1722 846 2222 2258 2532 3588 2222 2258 3588 5457 3588 444 2532
4 ἐν αὐτῷ ζωὴ ἦν, καὶ ἡ ζωὴ ἦν τὸ φῶς τῶν ἀνθρώπων, 5 καὶ
In Him life was, and the life was the light of men, and
3588 5457 1722 3588 4653 5316 2532 3588 4653 846 3756 2638
τὸ φῶς ἐν τῇ σκοτίᾳ φαίνει, καὶ ἡ σκοτία αὐτὸ οὐ κατέλαβεν.
the light in the darkness shines, and the darkness it not did overtake
1096 444 649 3844 2316 3686 846
6 ἐγένετο ἄνθρωπος ἀπεσταλμένος παρὰ θεοῦ, ὄνομα αὐτῷ
There was a man having been sent from God, name to him,
2491 3778 2064 1519 3141 2443 3140 4012
Ἰωάννης. 7 οὗτος ἦλθεν εἰς μαρτυρίαν, ἵνα μαρτυρήσῃ περὶ
John; this one came for a witness, that (he) might witness about
3588 5457 2443 3956 4100 1223 846 3756 2258 1565
τοῦ φωτός, ἵνα πάντες πιστεύσωσι δι' αὐτοῦ. 8 οὐκ ἦν ἐκεῖνος
the Light, that all might believe through Him, not He was that
3588 5457 235 2443 3140 4012 3588 5457 2258/3588 5457 3588
τὸ φῶς, ἀλλ' ἵνα μαρτυρήσῃ περὶ τοῦ φωτός. 9 ἦν τὸ φῶς τὸ
Light, but that (he) might witness about the Light. He was the Light
228 3739 5461 3956 444 2064 1519 3588
ἀληθινόν, ὃ φωτίζει πάντα ἄνθρωπον, ἐρχόμενον εἰς τὸν
true, which enlightens every man, coming into the
2889 1722 3588 2889 2258 2532 3588 2889 1223 846 1096 2532
κόσμον. 10 ἐν τῷ κόσμῳ ἦν, καὶ ὁ κόσμος δι' αὐτοῦ ἐγένετο, καὶ
world. In the world He was, and the world through Him came into being, and
3588 2889 846 3756 1097 1519 3588 2398 2064 2532 3588 2398 846
ὁ κόσμος αὐτὸν οὐκ ἔγνω.11 εἰς τὰ ἴδια ἦλθε, καὶ οἱ ἴδιοι αὐτὸν
the world Him did not know. To (His) own He came, and (His) own Him
3756 3880 3745 1161 2983 846 1325 846 1849
οὐ παρέλαβον.12 ὅσοι δὲ ἔλαβον αὐτόν, ἔδωκεν αὐτοῖς ἐξουσίαν
not did receive. as many as But received Him, He gave to them authority
5043 2316 1096 3588 4100 1519 3588 3686 846
τέκνα θεοῦ γενέσθαι, τοῖς πιστεύουσιν εἰς τὸ ὄνομα αὐτοῦ.
children of God to become, to the (ones) believing into the name of Him,
3739 3756 1537 129 3761 1537 2307 4561 3761 1537
13 οἳ οὐκ ἐξ αἱμάτων, οὐδὲ ἐκ θελήματος σαρκός, οὐδὲ ἐκ
who not of bloods, nor of (the) will of (the) flesh, nor of
2307 435 235 1537 2316 1080 2532 3588 3056
θελήματος ἀνδρός, ἀλλ' ἐκ θεοῦ ἐγεννήθησαν. 14 καὶ ὁ λόγος
(the) will of man, but of God were generated And the Word
4561 1096 2532 4637 1722 2254 2532 2300 3588
σὰρξ ἐγένετο, καὶ ἐσκήνωσεν ἐν ἡμῖν [καὶ ἐθεασάμεθα τὴν
flesh became, and tabernacled among us, and we beheld the
1391 846 1391 5613 3439 3844 3962 4134
δόξαν αὐτοῦ, δόξαν ὡς μονογενοῦς παρὰ πατρός], πλήρης
glory of Him, glory as of an only-begotten from (the) Father,) full
5485 2532 225 2491 3140 4012 846 2532
χάριτος καὶ ἀληθείας. 15. Ἰωάννης μαρτυρεῖ περὶ αὐτοῦ, καὶ
of grace and of truth. John witnesses concerning Him, and

King James Version

THE GOSPEL ACCORDING TO JOHN

John 1

1. In the beginning was the Word, and the Word was with God, and the Word was God.
2 The same was in the beginning with God.
3 All things were made by him; and without him was not any thing made that was made.
4 In him was life; and the life was the light of men.
5 And the light shineth in darkness; and the darkness comprehended it not.
6. There was a man sent from God, whose name (was) John.
7 The same came for a witness, to bear witness of the Light, that all (men) through him might believe.
8 He was not that Light, but (was sent) to bear witness of that Light.
9 (That) was the true Light, which lighteth every man that cometh into the world.
10 He was in the world, and the world was made by him, and the world knew him not.
11 He came unto his own, and his own received him not.
12 But as many as received him, to them gave he power to become the sons of God, (even) to them that believe on his name:
13 Which were born, not of blood, nor of the will of the flesh, nor of the will of man, but of God.
14 And the Word was made flesh, and dwelt among us, (and we beheld his glory, the glory as of the only begotten of the Father,) full of grace and truth.
15. John bare witness of him,

Literal Translation | **John 1:16** | *King James Version*

and has cried out, saying, This One was (He) of whom I said, He coming after me has been before me, for He was first of me.
16 And out of His fullness we all received, and grace on top of grace.
17 For the Law was given through Moses, (but) grace and truth has come into being through Jesus Christ.
18 No one has seen God at any time; the only begotten Son, who is in the bosom of the Father, that One explains (Him).

2896 3004 3778 2258 3739 2036 3588 3964 3450 2064
κέκραγε λέγων, Οὗτος ἦν ὃν εἶπον,῾Ο ὀπίσω μου ἐρχόμενος
has cried out, saying, This One was of whom I said, He after Me coming

1715 3450 1096 3754 4413 3450 2258 2532 1537 3588
ἔμπροσθέν μου γέγονεν· ὅτι πρῶτός μου ἦν. 16 καὶ ἐκ τοῦ
before Me has been, for first of me He was. And out of the

4138 846 2249 3956 2983 2532 5485 473
πληρώματος αὐτοῦ ἡμεῖς πάντες ἐλάβομεν, καὶ χάριν ἀντὶ
fullness of Him we all received, and grace upon

5485 3754 3588 3551 1223 3475 1325 3588 5485 2532 3588
χάριτος. 17 ὅτι ὁ νόμος διὰ Μωσέως ἐδόθη, ἡ χάρις καὶ ἡ
grace, because the Law through Moses was given, grace and

225 1223 2424 5547 1096 2316 3762 3708
ἀλήθεια διὰ ᾿Ιησοῦ Χριστοῦ ἐγένετο. 18 θεὸν οὐδεὶς ἑώρακε
truth through Jesus Christ has come into being. God No one has seen

4455 3588 3439 5207 3588 5607 1519 3588 2859 3588 3962
πώποτε· ὁ μονογενὴς υἱός, ὁ ὢν εἰς τὸν κόλπον τοῦ πατρὸς,
at any time; the Only-begotten Son, who is in the bosom of the Father,

1565 1834
ἐκεῖνος ἐξηγήσατο.
that One explains (Him).

and cried, saying, This was he of whom I spake, He that cometh after me is preferred before me: for he was before me.
16 And of his fulness have all we received, and grace for grace.
17 For the law was given by Moses, (but) grace and truth came by Jesus Christ.
18 No man hath seen God at any time; the only begotten Son, which is in the bosom of the Father, he hath declared (him).

19. And this is the witness of John, when the Jews sent priests and Levites that they might ask him, Who are you?
20 And he acknowledged and did not deny; even (he) acknowledged, I am not the Christ.
21 And they asked him, What, then? Are you Elijah? And he says, I am not. Are you the Prophet? And he answered, No.
22 Then they said to him, Who are you, that we may give an answer to those having sent us? What do you say about yourself?
23 He said, "I (am) a voice crying in the wilderness: Make straight the way of the Lord," even as Isaiah the prophet said. (Isa. 40:3)
24 And those who had been sent were from the Pharisees.
25 And they asked him and said to him, Why then do you baptize, if you are not the Christ, nor Elijah, nor the Prophet?
26 John answered them, saying, I baptize in water, but (One) stands in your midst whom you do not know;
27 This One it is who has come after me,

2532 3778 2076 3588 3141 3588 2491 3753 649
19.Καὶ αὕτη ἐστὶν ἡ μαρτυρία τοῦ ᾿Ιωάννου, ὅτε ἀπέστειλαν
And this is the witness of John, when sent

3588 2453 1537 2414 2409 2532 3019 2443 2065
οἱ ᾿Ιουδαῖοι ἐξ ῾Ιεροσολύμων ἱερεῖς καὶ Λευίτας ἵνα ἐρωτή-
the Jews from Jerusalem priests and Levites, that they might

846 4771 5101 1488 2532 3670 2532 3756 720
σωσιν αὐτόν, Σὺ τίς εἶ; 20 καὶ ὡμολόγησε, καὶ οὐκ ἠρνήσατο·
ask him, you, Who are? And he acknowledged and not did deny,

2532 3670 3754 3756 1510 1473 3588 5547 2532 2065
καὶ ὡμολόγησεν ὅτι Οὐκ εἰμὶ ἐγὼ ὁ Χριστός. 21 καὶ ἠρώτησαν
even he acknowledged, Not am I the Christ. And they asked

846 5101 3767 2243 1488 4771 2532 3004 3756 1510 3588 4396
αὐτόν, Τί οὖν; ᾿Ηλίας εἶ σύ; καὶ λέγει, Οὐκ εἰμί. ῾Ο προφή-
him, What, then? Elijah, are you? And he says, Not I am. The Prophet

1488 4771 2532 611 3756 2036 3767 846 5101 1488 2443
της εἶ σύ; καὶ ἀπεκρίθη, Οὔ. 22 εἶπον οὖν αὐτῷ, Τίς εἶ; ἵνα
are you? And he answered, No. they said Then to him, Who are you? that

612 1325 3588 3992 2248 5101 3004 4012
ἀπόκρισιν δῶμεν τοῖς πέμψασιν ἡμᾶς. τί λέγεις περὶ
an answer we may give to those having sent us. What do you say about

4572 5346 1473 5456 994 1722 3588 2048 2116
σεαυτοῦ; 23 ἔφη, ᾿Εγὼ φωνὴ βοῶντος ἐν τῇ ἐρήμῳ, Εὐθύνατε
yourself? He said, I am a voice crying in the wilderness, Make straight

3588 3598 2962 2531 2036 2268 3588 4396 2532 3588
τὴν ὁδὸν Κυρίου, καθὼς εἶπεν ᾿Ησαΐας ὁ προφήτης. 24καὶ οἱ
the way of (the) Lord, even as said Isaiah the prophet. And those

649 2258 1537 3588 5330 2532 2065
ἀπεσταλμένοι ἦσαν ἐκ τῶν Φαρισαίων. 25 καὶ ἠρώτησαν
having been sent were from the Pharisees. And they asked

846 2532 2036 846 5101 3767 907 1487 4771 3756 1488 3588
αὐτὸν, καὶ εἶπον αὐτῷ, Τί οὖν βαπτίζεις, εἰ σὺ οὐκ εἶ ὁ
him, and said to him, Why then do you baptize, if you not are the

5547 3777 2243 3777 3588 4396 611 846 3588
Χριστὸς, οὔτε ᾿Ηλίας, οὔτε ὁ προφήτης; 26 ἀπεκρίθη αὐτοῖς ὁ
Christ, nor Elijah, nor the Prophet? answered them

2491 3004 1473 907 1722 5204 3319 1161 5216
᾿Ιωάννης λέγων, ᾿Εγὼ βαπτίζω ἐν ὕδατι· μέσος δὲ ὑμῶν
John saying, I baptize in water; amidst but you

2476 3739 5210 3756 1492 846 2076 3588 3694 3450
ἕστηκεν ὃν ὑμεῖς οὐκ οἴδατε. 27 αὐτός ἐστιν ὁ ὀπίσω μου
stands (one) whom you not do know. This One it is who after me

19. And this is the record of John, when the Jews sent priests and Levites from Jerusalem to ask him, Who art thou?
20 And he confessed, and denied not; but confessed, I am not the Christ.
21 And they asked him, What then? Art thou Elias? And he saith, I am not. Art thou that prophet? And he answered, No.
22 Then said they unto him, Who art thou? that we may give an answer to them that sent us. What sayest thou of thyself?
23 He said, I (am) the voice of one crying in the wilderness, Make straight the way of the Lord, as said the prophet Esaias.
24 And they which were sent were of the Pharisees.
25 And they asked him, and said unto him, Why baptizest thou then, if thou be not that Christ, nor Elias, neither that prophet?
26 John answered them, saying, I baptize with water: but there standeth one among you, whom ye know not;
27 He it is, who coming after me

Literal Translation **John 1:28** *King James Version*

who has been before me, of whom I am not worthy that I should loose the thong of His sandal.
28 These things occurred in Bethabara beyond the Jordan, where John was baptizing.

2064 3739 1715 3450 1096 3739 1473 3756 1510 514
ἐρχόμενος, ὃς ἔμπροσθέν μου γέγονεν· οὗ ἐγὼ οὐκ εἰμὶ ἄξιος
coming, who before me has been, of whom I not am worthy

2443 3089 846 3588 2438 3588 5266 5023 1722
ἵνα λύσω αὐτοῦ τὸν ἱμάντα τοῦ ὑποδήματος. 28 ταῦτα ἐν
that I may loose of Him the thong of the sandal. These things in

962 1096 4008 3588 2446 3699 2258 2491
Βηθαβαρᾶ ἐγένετο πέραν τοῦ Ἰορδάνου, ὅπου ἦν Ἰωάννης
Bethabara occurred, beyond the Jordan, where was John

907
βαπτίζων.
baptizing.

is preferred before me, whose shoe's latchet I am not worthy to unloose.
28 These things were done in Bethabara beyond Jordan, where John was baptizing.

29. On the morrow, John sees Jesus coming toward him and says, Behold! The Lamb of God, taking away the sin of the world!

30 This is He about whom I said, After me comes a Man who has been before me, for He was first of me.

31 And I did not know Him; but that He be revealed to Israel, for this reason I came baptizing in water.

32 And John witnessed, saying, I have seen the Spirit coming down as a dove out of Heaven, and He abode on Him.

33 And I did not know Him, but the (One) sending me to baptize in water, that One said to me, On whomever you see the Spirit coming down and abiding on Him, this is the (One) baptizing in the Holy Spirit.

34 And I have seen and have witnessed that this One is the Son of God.

3588 1887 991 3588 2491 3588 2424 2064
29.Τῇ ἐπαύριον βλέπει ὁ Ἰωάννης τὸν Ἰησοῦν ἐρχόμενον
On the morrow sees John Jesus coming

4314 846 2532 3004 2396 3588 286 3588 2316 3588 142 3588
πρὸς αὐτόν, καὶ λέγει, Ἴδε ὁ ἀμνὸς τοῦ θεοῦ, ὁ αἴρων τὴν
toward him, and says, Behold! the Lamb of God! He taking away the

266 3588 2889 3778 2076 4012 3739 1473 2036
ἁμαρτίαν τοῦ κόσμου. 30 οὗτός ἐστι περὶ οὗ ἐγὼ εἶπον,
sin of the world! This is He about whom I said,

3694 3450 2064 435 3739 1715 3450 1096 3754
Ὀπίσω μου ἔρχεται ἀνὴρ ὃς ἔμπροσθέν μου γέγονεν, ὅτι
After me comes a Man who before me has been, for

4413 3450 2258 2504 3756 1492 846 235 2443 5319
πρῶτός μου ἦν. 31 κἀγὼ οὐκ ᾔδειν αὐτόν· ἀλλ᾽ ἵνα φανερωθῇ
first of me He was. And I not did know Him, but that He be revealed

3588 2474 1223 5124 2064 1473 1722 3588 5204 907
τῷ Ἰσραὴλ, διὰ τοῦτο ἦλθον ἐγὼ ἐν τῷ ὕδατι βαπτίζων.
to Israel; because of this came I in the water baptizing.

2532 3140 2491 3004 3754 2300 3588 4151
32 καὶ ἐμαρτύρησεν Ἰωάννης λέγων ὅτι Τεθέαμαι τὸ Πνεῦμα
And witnessed John, saying, I have beheld the Spirit

2597 5616 4058 1537 3772 2532 3306 1909
καταβαῖνον ὡσεὶ περιστερὰν ἐξ οὐρανοῦ, καὶ ἔμεινεν ἐπ᾽
coming down as a dove out of Heaven, and He abode on

846 2504 3956 1492 846 235 3588 3992 3165 907
αὐτόν· 33 κἀγὼ οὐκ ᾔδειν αὐτόν· ἀλλ᾽ ὁ πέμψας με βαπτίζειν
Him. And I not did know Him, but the (One) sending me to baptize

1722 5204 1565 3450 2036 1909 3739 302 1492 3588 4151 2597
ἐν ὕδατι, ἐκεῖνός μοι εἶπεν, Ἐφ᾽ ὃν ἂν ἴδῃς τὸ Πνεῦμα κατα-
in water, that One to me said, On whomever you see the Spirit coming

2532 3306 1909 846 3778 2076 3588 907 1722
βαῖνον καὶ μένον ἐπ᾽ αὐτόν, οὗτός ἐστιν ὁ βαπτίζων ἐν
down and abiding on Him, this is the (One) baptizing in

4151 40 2504 3708 2532 3140 3754 3778
Πνεύματι Ἁγίῳ. 34 κἀγὼ ἑώρακα, καὶ μεμαρτύρηκα ὅτι οὗτός
(the) Spirit Holy. And I have seen, and have witnessed, that this One

2076 3588 5207 3588 2316
ἐστιν ὁ υἱὸς τοῦ θεοῦ.
is the Son of God.

29. The next day John seeth Jesus coming unto him, and saith, Behold the Lamb of God, which taketh away the sin of the world.

30 This is he of whom I said, After me cometh a man which is preferred before me: for he was before me.

31 And I knew him not: but that he should be made manifest to Israel, therefore am I come baptizing with water.

32 And John bare record, saying, I saw the Spirit descending from heaven like a dove, and it abode upon him.

33 And I knew him not: but he that sent me to baptize with water, the same said unto me, Upon whom thou shalt see the Spirit descending, and remaining on him, the same is he which baptizeth with the Holy Ghost.

34 And I saw, and bare record that this is the Son of God.

35. Again on the morrow John and two from his disciples stood.
36 And looking at Jesus walking, he says, Behold! The Lamb of God!
37 And the two disciples heard him speaking, and they followed Jesus.
38 Turning

3588 1887 3825 2476 3588 2491 2532 1537 3588
35. Τῇ ἐπαύριον πάλιν εἱστήκει ὁ Ἰωάννης, καὶ ἐκ τῶν
On the morrow again stood John, and out of the

3101 846 1417 2532 1689 3588 2424 4043
μαθητῶν αὐτοῦ δύο· 36 καὶ ἐμβλέψας τῷ Ἰησοῦ περιπατοῦντι
disciples of him two. And looking at Jesus walking about,

3004 2396 3588 286 3588 2316 2532 191 846 3588 1417
λέγει, Ἴδε ὁ ἀμνὸς τοῦ θεοῦ. 37 καὶ ἤκουσαν αὐτοῦ οἱ δύο
he says, Behold! The Lamb of God! And heard him the two

3101 2980 2532 190 3588 2424 4762
μαθηταὶ λαλοῦντος, καὶ ἠκολούθησαν τῷ Ἰησοῦ. 38 στραφεὶς
disciples speaking, and they followed Jesus. Turning

35. Again the next day after John stood, and two of his disciples;
36 And looking upon Jesus as he walked, he saith, Behold the Lamb of God!
37 And the two disciples heard him speak, and they followed Jesus.

Literal Translation | **John 1:39** | **King James Version**

and having seen them following, Jesus said to them, What do you seek? And they said to Him, Rabbi (which being translated is called Teacher), where do You stay?
39 He says to them, Come and see. They went and saw where He stayed, and (they) remained with Him that day. And (the) hour was about the tenth.
40 Andrew the brother of Simon Peter was one of the two who heard, from John and was following Him.

1161 3588 2424 2532 2300 846 190 3004
δὲ ὁ Ἰησοῦς καὶ θεασάμενος αὐτοὺς ἀκολουθοῦντας, λέγει
and Jesus and beholding them following, He says
846 5101 2212 3588 1161 2036 846 4461 3739 3004
αὐτοῖς, Τί ζητεῖτε; οἱ δὲ εἶπον αὐτῷ, Ῥαββί [ὃ λέγεται
to them, What do you seek? they And said to Him, Rabbi (which is called
2059 1320 4226 3306 3004 846 2064
ἑρμηνευόμενον, Διδάσκαλε], ποῦ μένεις; 39 λέγει αὐτοῖς, Ἔρχε-
being translated, Teacher), where do you stay? He says to them, Come
2532 1492 2064 2532 1492 4225 3306 2532 3844 846
σθε καὶ ἴδετε. ἦλθον καὶ εἶδον ποῦ μένει· καὶ παρ᾽ αὐτῷ
and see. They went and saw where He stayed, and with Him
3306 3588 2250 1565 5610 1161 2258 5613 1182 2258
ἔμειναν τὴν ἡμέραν ἐκείνην· ὥρα δὲ ἦν ὡς δεκάτη. 40 ἦν
remained day that. (the) hour And was about (the) tenth. was
406 3588 80 4613 4074 1520 1537 3588 1417 3588
Ἀνδρέας ὁ ἀδελφὸς Σίμωνος Πέτρου εἷς ἐκ τῶν δύο τῶν
Andrew the brother of Simon Peter one of the two
191 3844 2491 2532 190 846
ἀκουσάντων παρὰ Ἰωάννου καὶ ἀκολουθησάντων αὐτῷ.
hearing from John, and following Him.

38 Then Jesus turned, and saw them following, and saith unto them, What seek ye? They said unto him, Rabbi, (which is to say, being interpreted, Master,) where dwellest thou?
39 He saith unto them, Come and see. They came and saw where he dwelt, and abode with him that day: for it was about the tenth hour.
40 One of the two which heard John (speak), and followed him, was Andrew, Simon Peter's brother.

41 This one first finds (his) own brother Simon and tells him, We have found the Messiah (which being translated is, the Christ).
42 And he led him to Jesus. And looking at him, Jesus said, You are Simon the son of Jonah; you shall be called Cephas (which translated is Peter).

2147 3778 4413 3588 80 3588 2398 4613 2532
41 εὑρίσκει οὗτος πρῶτος τὸν ἀδελφὸν τὸν ἴδιον Σίμωνα, καὶ
finds This one first the brother the own, Simon, and
3004 846 2147 3588 3323 3739 2076 3177
λέγει αὐτῷ, Εὑρήκαμεν τὸν Μεσσίαν [ὅ ἐστι μεθερμηνευό-
says to him, We have found the Messiah, which is being translated,
3588 5547 2532 71 846 4314 3588 2424
μενον, ὁ Χριστός]. 42 καὶ ἤγαγεν αὐτὸν πρὸς τὸν Ἰησοῦν.
the Christ. And he led him to Jesus.
1689 1161 846 3588 2424 2036 4771 1488 4613 3588 5207 2495
ἐμβλέψας δὲ αὐτῷ ὁ Ἰησοῦς εἶπε, Σὺ εἶ Σίμων ὁ υἱὸς Ἰωνᾶ·
looking at And him, Jesus said, You are Simon the son of Jonah;
4771 2564 2786 3588 2059 4074
σὺ κληθήσῃ Κηφᾶς [ὃ ἑρμηνεύεται Πέτρος].
you shall be called Cephas, which translated (is) Peter.

41 He first findeth his own brother Simon, and saith unto him, We have found the Messias, which is, being interpreted, the Christ.
42 And he brought him to Jesus. And when Jesus beheld him, he said, Thou art Simon the son of Jona: thou shalt be called Cephas, which is by interpretation, A stone.

43. And on the morrow, Jesus desired to go out into Galilee. And He found Philip, and says to him, Follow me!
44 And Philip was from Bethsaida, of the city of Andrew and Peter.
45 Philip finds Nathanael and says to him, We have found the (One of) whom Moses wrote in the Law and the Prophets, Jesus the son of Joseph, from Nazareth.

3588 1887 2309 3588 2424 1831 1519 3588
43. Τῇ ἐπαύριον ἠθέλησεν ὁ Ἰησοῦς ἐξελθεῖν εἰς τὴν
On the morrow desired Jesus to go out into
1056 2532 2147 5376 2532 3004 846 190
Γαλιλαίαν, καὶ εὑρίσκει Φίλιππον, καὶ λέγει αὐτῷ, Ἀκολούθει
Galilee. And He finds Philip, and says to him, Follow
3427 2258 1161 3588 5376 575 966 1537 3588 4172
μοι. 44 ἦν δὲ ὁ Φίλιππος ἀπὸ Βηθσαϊδά, ἐκ τῆς πόλεως
Me. was And Philip from Bethsaida, of the city
406 2532 4074 2147 5376 3588 3482 2532
Ἀνδρέου καὶ Πέτρου. 45 εὑρίσκει Φίλιππος τὸν Ναθαναήλ, καὶ
of Andrew and Peter. finds Philip Nathanael, and
3004 846 3739 1125 3475 1722 3588 3551 2532 3588 4396
λέγει αὐτῷ, Ὃν ἔγραψε Μωσῆς ἐν τῷ νόμῳ καὶ οἱ προφῆται
says to him, The (One) wrote Moses in the Law and the Prophets,
2147 2424 3588 5207 3588 2501 3588 575 3478
εὑρήκαμεν, Ἰησοῦν τὸν υἱὸν τοῦ Ἰωσὴφ τὸν ἀπὸ Ναζαρέθ.
we have found, Jesus the son of Joseph, from Nazareth.

43. The day following Jesus would go forth into Galilee, and findeth Philip, and saith unto him, Follow me.
44 Now Philip was of Bethsaida, the city of Andrew and Peter.
45 Philip findeth Nathanael, and saith unto him, We have found him, of whom Moses in the law, and the prophets, did write, Jesus of Nazareth, the son of Joseph.

46 And Nathanael said to him, Can anything good be out of Nazareth? Philip says to him, Come and see.
47 Jesus saw Nathanael coming toward Him and says concerning him,

2532 2036 846 3482 1537 3478 1410 5101 18
46 καὶ εἶπεν αὐτῷ Ναθαναήλ, Ἐκ Ναζαρὲθ δύναταί τι ἀγαθὸν
And said to him Nathanael, Out of Nazareth can anything good
1511 3004 846 5376 2064 2532 1492 1492 3588 2424
εἶναι; λέγει αὐτῷ Φίλιππος, Ἔρχου καὶ ἴδε. 47 εἶδεν ὁ Ἰησοῦς
be? says to him Philip, Come and see. saw Jesus
3588 3482 2064 4314 846 2532 3004 4012 846 2396
τὸν Ναθαναὴλ ἐρχόμενον πρὸς αὐτὸν, καὶ λέγει περὶ αὐτοῦ, Ἴδε
Nathanael coming toward Him, and says concernig him, Behold!

46 And Nathanael said unto him, Can there any good thing come out of Nazareth? Philip saith unto him, Come and see.
47 Jesus saw Nathanael coming to him, and saith of him, Behold

Literal Translation — **John 1:48** — ***King James Version***

Behold, truly an Israelite in whom is no guile! **48** Nathanael says to Him, From where do You know me? Jesus answered and says to him, Before Philip called, you being under the fig -tree, I saw you.

49 Nathanael answered and says to Him, Rabbi, You are the Son of God; You are the King of Israel.

50 Jesus answered and said to him, Because I said to you I saw you under the fig tree, do you believe? You will see greater (things) than these.
51 And He says to him, Truly, truly, I say to you, from now on you will see Heaven opened, and the angels of God ascending and descending on the Son of man. (Gen. 28:12)

230 2475 1722 3739 1388 3756 2076 3004 846
ἀληθῶς Ἰσραηλίτης, ἐν ᾧ δόλος οὐκ ἔστι. 48 λέγει αὐτῷ
Truly an Israelite in whom guile not is. says to Him

3482 4159 3165 1097 611 3588 2424 2532
Ναθαναήλ, Πόθεν με γινώσκεις; ἀπεκρίθη ὁ Ἰησοῦς καὶ
Nathanael, From where me do You know? answered Jesus and

2036 846 4253 3588 4571 5376 5455 5607 5259 3588
εἶπεν αὐτῷ, Πρὸ τοῦ σε Φίλιππον φωνῆσαι, ὄντα ὑπὸ τὴν
said to him, Before you Philip called, being under the

4808 1492 4571 611 3482 2532 3004 846 4461
συκῆν, εἶδόν σε. 49 ἀπεκρίθη Ναθαναὴλ καὶ λέγει αὐτῷ, Ῥαββί,
fig-tree, I saw you. answered Nathanael and says to Him, Rabbi,

4771 1488 3588 5207 3588 2316 4771 1488 3588 935 3588 2474
σὺ εἶ ὁ υἱὸς τοῦ θεοῦ, σὺ εἶ ὁ βασιλεὺς τοῦ Ἰσραήλ.
You are the Son of God;You are the King of Israel.

611 2424 2532 2036 846 3754 2036 4671 1492 4571
50 ἀπεκρίθη Ἰησοῦς καὶ εἶπεν αὐτῷ, Ὅτι εἶπόν σοι, εἶδόν σε
answered Jesus and said to him, Because I told you I saw you

5270 3588 4808 4100 3187 5130 3700 2532
ὑποκάτω τῆς συκῆς, πιστεύεις; μείζω τούτων ὄψει. 51 καὶ
underneath the fig-tree, do you believe? Greater than these you will see. And

3004 846 281 281 3004 5213 575 737 3700 3588 3772
λέγει αὐτῷ, Ἀμὴν ἀμὴν λέγω ὑμῖν, ἀπ' ἄρτι ὄψεσθε τὸν οὐρανὸν
He says to him, Truly , truly, I say to you, From now you will see the heaven

455 2532 3588 32 3588 2316 305 2532
ἀνεῳγότα, καὶ τοὺς ἀγγέλους τοῦ θεοῦ ἀναβαίνοντας καὶ κατα-
opened and the angels of God ascending and

2597 1909 3588 5207 3588 444
βαίνοντας ἐπὶ τὸν υἱὸν τοῦ ἀνθρώπου.
descending on the Son of man.

an Israelite indeed, in whom is no guile!
48 Nathanael saith unto him, Whence knowest thou me? Jesus answered and said unto him, Before that Philip called thee, when thou wast under the fig tree, I saw thee.

49 Nathanael answered and saith unto him, Rabbi, thou art the Son of God; thou art the King of Israel.

50 Jesus answered and said unto him, Because I said unto thee, I saw thee under the fig tree, believest thou? thou shalt see greater things than these.
51 And he saith unto him, Verily, verily, I say unto you, Hereafter ye shall see heaven open, and the angels of God ascending and descending upon the Son of man.

John 2

1. And on the third day a wedding occurred in Cana of Galilee, and the mother of Jesus was there.
2 And Jesus and His disciples also were invited to the wedding.
3 And being short of wine, the mother of Jesus says to Him, They have no wine.

4 Jesus says to her, What (is that) to Me and to you, woman? My hour has not yet come.
5 His mother says to the servants, Whatever He says to you, do.
6 And there were six stone waterpots standing, according to the purification of the Jews, each containing two or three measures.
7 Jesus says to them, Fill the waterpots with water. And they filled them to (the) top.

8 And He says

John 2

2532 3588 2250 3588 5154 1062 1096 1722 2580 3588
1. Καὶ τῇ ἡμέρᾳ τῇ τρίτῃ γάμος ἐγένετο ἐν Κανᾷ τῆς
And on the day third a wedding occurred in Cana

1056 2532 2258 3588 3384 3588 2424 1563 2564 1161 2532 3588
Γαλιλαίας, καὶ ἦν ἡ μήτηρ τοῦ Ἰησοῦ ἐκεῖ· 2 ἐκλήθη δὲ καὶ ὁ
of Galilee, and was the mother of Jesus there. was invited And also

2424 2532 3588 3101 846 1519 3588 1062 2532 5302
Ἰησοῦς καὶ οἱ μαθηταὶ αὐτοῦ εἰς τὸν γάμον. 3 καὶ ὑστερή-
Jesus and the disciples of Him to the wedding. And being

3631 3004 3588 3384 3588 2424 4314 846 3631
σαντος οἴνου, λέγει ἡ μήτηρ τοῦ Ἰησοῦ πρὸς αὐτόν, Οἶνον
short of wine, says the mother of Jesus to Him, wine

3756 2192 3004 846 3588 2424 5101 1698 2532 4671 1135
οὐκ ἔχουσι. 4 λέγει αὐτῇ ὁ Ἰησοῦς, Τί ἐμοὶ καὶ σοί, γύναι;
not They have. says to her Jesus, What to Me and to you, woman?

3768 2240 3588 5610 3450 3004 3588 3384 846 3588 1249
οὔπω ἥκει ἡ ὥρα μου. 5 λέγει ἡ μήτηρ αὐτοῦ τοῖς διακόνοις,
Not yet is come the hour of Me. says The mother of Him to the servants,

3739 5100 302 3004 5213 4160 2258 1161 1563 5201 3035
Ὅ τι ἂν λέγῃ ὑμῖν, ποιήσατε. 6 ἦσαν δὲ ἐκεῖ ὑδρίαι λίθιναι
Whatever He says to you, do. were And there waterpots stone

1803 2749 2596 3588 2512 3588 2453 5562
ἓξ κείμεναι κατὰ τὸν καθαρισμὸν τῶν Ἰουδαίων, χωροῦσαι
six standing according to the purification of the Jews, containing

303 3355 1417 2228 5140 3004 846 3588 2424 1072
ἀνὰ μετρητὰς δύο ἢ τρεῖς. 7 λέγει αὐτοῖς ὁ Ἰησοῦς, Γεμίσατε
each measures two or three. says to them Jesus, Fill

3588 5201 5204 2532 1072 846 2193 507 2532 3004
τὰς ὑδρίας ὕδατος. καὶ ἐγέμισαν αὐτὰς ἕως ἄνω. 8 καὶ λέγει
the waterpots with water. And they filled them up to (the) top. And says

John 2

1. And the third day there was a marriage in Cana of Galilee; and the mother of Jesus was there:
2 And both Jesus was called, and his disciples, to the marriage.
3 And when they wanted wine, the mother of Jesus saith unto him, They have no wine.

4 Jesus saith unto her, Woman, what have I to do with thee? mine hour is not yet come.
5 His mother saith unto the servants, Whatsoever he saith unto you, do (it).
6 And there were set there six waterpots of stone, after the manner of the purifying of the Jews, containing two or three firkins apiece.
7 Jesus saith unto them, Fill the waterpots with water. And they filled them up to the brim.
8 And he saith

Literal Translation | **John 2:9** | **King James Version**

to them, Now draw out and carry to the master of the feast. And they carried it.
9 But when the master of the feast tasted the water having become wine, and did not know from where it was, but the servants drawing the water knew, the master of the feast called the bridegroom,

846 501 3568 2532 5342 3588 755 2532
αὐτοῖς, Ἀντλήσατε νῦν, καὶ φέρετε τῷ ἀρχιτρικλίνῳ. καὶ
to them, Draw out now, and carry to the master of the feast. And
5342 5613 1161 1089 3588 755 3588 5204 3631
ἤνεγκαν. 9 ὡς δὲ ἐγεύσατο ὁ ἀρχιτρίκλινος τὸ ὕδωρ οἶνον
they carried. as But tasted the master of the feast the water wine
1096 2532 3756 1492 4159 2076 3588 1161 1249
γεγενημένον, καὶ οὐκ ᾔδει πόθεν ἐστίν, [οἱ δὲ διάκονοι
having become, and not knew from where it is the but servants
1492 3588 501 3588 5204 5455 3588 3566 3588
ᾔδεισαν οἱ ἠντληκότες τὸ ὕδωρ], φωνεῖ τὸν νυμφίον ὁ
knew, the (ones) having drawn the water, calls the bridegroom the
755
ἀρχιτρίκλινος,
master of the feast,

unto them, Draw out now, and bear unto the governor of the feast. And they bare (it).
9 When the ruler of the feast had tasted the water that was made wine, and knew not whence it was: (but the servants which drew the water knew;) the governor of the feast called the bridegroom,

10 and (he) says to him, Every man first sets on the good wine, and when they have drunk freely, then the worse. You have kept the good wine until now.
11 This beginning of the signs Jesus did in Cana of Galilee. And (it) revealed His glory, and His disciples believed in Him.

2532 3004 846 3956 444 4412 3588
10 καὶ λέγει αὐτῷ, Πᾶς ἄνθρωπος πρῶτον τὸν
and says to him, Every man first the
2570 3631 5087 2532 3752 3184 5119 3588 1640
καλὸν οἶνον τίθησι, καὶ ὅταν μεθυσθῶσι τότε τὸν ἐλάσσω·
good wine sets on, and when they have drunk, then the worse;
4771 5083 3588 2570 3631 2193 737 5026 4160
σὺ τετήρηκας τὸν καλὸν οἶνον ἕως ἄρτι. 11 Ταύτην ἐποίησε
you have kept the good wine until now. This did
3588 746 3588 4592 3588 2424 1722 2580 3588 1056
τὴν ἀρχὴν τῶν σημείων ὁ Ἰησοῦς ἐν Κανᾷ τῆς Γαλιλαίας
the beginnng of the signs Jesus in Cana of Galilee.
2532 5319 3588 1391 846 2532 4100 1519 846 3588
καὶ ἐφανέρωσε τὴν δόξαν αὐτοῦ· καὶ ἐπίστευσαν εἰς αὐτὸν οἱ
And (it) revealed the glory of Him. And believed into Him the
3101 846
μαθηταὶ αὐτοῦ.
disciples of Him.

10 And saith unto him, Every man at the beginning doth set forth good wine; and when men have well drunk, then that which is worse: (but) thou hast kept the good wine until now.
11 This beginning of miracles did Jesus in Cana of Galilee, and manifested forth his glory; and his disciples believed on him.

12. After this He went down into Capernaum, He and His mother and His brothers and His disciples. And He remained there not many days.

3326 5124 2597 1519 2584 846 2532 3588 3384
12. Μετὰ τοῦτο κατέβη εἰς Καπερναούμ, αὐτὸς καὶ ἡ μήτηρ
After this went down into Capernaum He, and the mother
846 2532 3588 80 846 2532 3588 3101 846 2532 1563
αὐτοῦ, καὶ οἱ ἀδελφοὶ αὐτοῦ, καὶ οἱ μαθηταὶ αὐτοῦ· καὶ ἐκεῖ
of Him, and the brothers of Him, and the disciples of Him. And there
3306 3756 4183 2250
ἔμειναν οὐ πολλὰς ἡμέρας.
He abode not many days.

12. After this he went down to Capernaum, he, and his mother, and his brethren, and his disciples: and they continued there not many days.

13. And the Passover of the Jews was near. And Jesus went up to Jerusalem.
14 And He found those selling oxen and sheep and doves in the temple, and the money-merchants sitting.

2532 1451 2258 3588 3957 3588 2453 2532 305 1519
13. Καὶ ἐγγὺς ἦν τὸ πάσχα τῶν Ἰουδαίων, καὶ ἀνέβη εἰς
And near was the Passover of the Jews. And went up into
2414 3588 2424 2532 2147 1722 3588 2411 3588 4453
Ἱεροσόλυμα ὁ Ἰησοῦς. 14 καὶ εὗρεν ἐν τῷ ἱερῷ τοὺς πωλοῦντας
Jerusalem Jesus. And He found in the temple those selling
1016 2532 4263 2532 4058 2532 3588 2773
βόας καὶ πρόβατα καὶ περιστεράς, καὶ τοὺς κερματιστὰς
oxen and sheep and doves, and the money-merchants
2521
καθημένους.
sitting.

13. And the Jews' passover was at hand, and Jesus went up to Jerusalem,
14 And found in the temple those that sold oxen and sheep and doves, and the changers of money sitting:

15 And making a whip out of ropes, He threw all out of the temple, both the sheep, and the oxen, and the money-changers, pouring out the money and overturning the tables.

2532 4160 5416 1537 4979 3956
15 καὶ ποιήσας φραγέλλιον ἐκ σχοινίων πάντας
And having made a whip out of ropes, all
1544 1537 3588 2411 3588 5037 4263 2532 3588 1016 2532 3588
ἐξέβαλεν ἐκ τοῦ ἱεροῦ, τά τε πρόβατα καὶ τοὺς βόας· καὶ τῶν
He threw out of the temple, the both sheep and the oxen, and the
2855 1632 3588 2772 2532 3588 5132 390
κολλυβιστῶν ἐξέχεε τὸ κέρμα, καὶ τὰς τραπέζας ἀνέστρεψε·
money-changers, pouring out the money, and the tables overturning.

15 And when he had made a scourge of small cords, he drove them all out of the temple, and the sheep, and the oxen; and poured out the changers' money, and overthrew the tables;

16 And to the ones selling the doves, He said, Take these things from here! Do not make My Father's house a house

2532 3588 3588 4058 4453 2036 142 5023
16 καὶ τοῖς τὰς περιστερὰς πωλοῦσιν εἶπεν, Ἄρατε ταῦτα
And to those the doves selling He said, Take these things
1782 3361 4160 3588 3624 3588 3962 3450 3624
ἐντεῦθεν· μὴ ποιεῖτε τὸν οἶκον τοῦ πατρός μου οἶκον
from here! Do not make the house the Father of Me a house

16 And said unto them that sold doves, Take these things hence; make not my Father's house an house

Literal Translation | **John 2:17** | **King James Version**

of merchandise.
17 And His disciples remembered that it was written, "The zeal of Your house has consumed Me." (Ps.69:9)
18. Then the Jews answered and said to Him, What sign do you show to us, since you do these things?
19 Jesus said to them, Destroy this temple, and in three days I will raise it up.

1712 3415 1161 3588 3101 846 3754 1125
ἐμπορίου. 17 ᾿εμνήσθησαν δὲ οἱ μαθηταὶ αὐτοῦ ὅτι γεγραμ-
of merchandise. remembered And the disciples of Him that having

2076 3588 2205 3588 3624 4675 2719 3165 611
μένον ἐστίν, ῾Ο ζῆλος τοῦ οἴκου σου κατέφαγε με. 18 ἀπεκρίθη-
been written is: The zeal of the house of You has consumed Me. answered

3767 3588 2453 2532 2036 846 5101 4592 1166
σαν οὖν οἱ ᾿Ιουδαῖοι καὶ εἶπον αὐτῷ, Τί σημεῖον δεικνύεις
Then the Jews and said to Him, What sign do you show

2254 3754 5023 4160 611 3588 2424 2532 2036 846
ἡμῖν, ὅτι ταῦτα ποιεῖς; 19 ἀπεκρίθη ὁ ᾿Ιησοῦς καὶ εἶπεν αὐτοῖς,
to us, since the things You do? answered Jesus and said to them,

3089 3588 3485 5126 2532 1722 5140 2250 1453 846
Λύσατε τὸν ναὸν τοῦτον, καὶ ἐν τρισὶν ἡμέραις ἐγερῶ αὐτόν.
Destroy temple this, and in three days I will raise it.

of merchandise.
17 And his disciples remembered that it was written, The zeal of thine house hath eaten me up.
18. Then answered the Jews and said unto him, What sign shewest thou unto us, seeing that thou doest these things?
19 Jesus answered and said unto them, Destroy this temple, and in three days I will raise it up.

20 Then the Jews said, This temple was forty and six years being built, and will you raise it up in three days?

2036 3767 3588 2453 5062 2532 1803 2094 3618
20 εἶπον οὖν οἱ ᾿Ιουδαῖοι, Τεσσαράκοντα καὶ ἓξ ἔτεσιν ᾠκο-
said Then the Jews, Forty and six years was being

3588 3485 3778 2532 4771 1722 5140 2250 1453 846
δομήθη ὁ ναὸς οὗτος, καὶ σὺ ἐν τρισὶν ἡμέραις ἐγερεῖς αὐτόν;
built temple this, and you in three days will raise it?

20 Then said the Jews, Forty and six years was this temple in building, and wilt thou rear it up in three days?

21 But He spoke about the temple of His body.
22 Then when He was raised from the dead, His disciples recalled that He said this to them. And they believed the Scripture, and the word which Jesus spoke.

1565 1161 3004 4012 3588 3485 3588 4983 846 3753
21 ἐκεῖνος δὲ ἔλεγε περὶ τοῦ ναοῦ τοῦ σώματος αὐτοῦ. 22 ὅτε
that One But spoke about the temple of the body of Him. When

3767 1453 1537 3498 3415 3588 3101 846 3754
οὖν ἠγέρθη ἐκ νεκρῶν, ἐμνήσθησαν οἱ μαθηταὶ αὐτοῦ ὅτι
then, He was raised from (the) dead, recalled the disciples of Him that

5124 3004 846 2532 4100 3588 1124 2532 3588 3056
τοῦτο ἔλεγεν αὐτοῖς· καὶ ἐπίστευσαν τῇ γραφῇ, καὶ τῷ λόγῳ
this He said to them; and they believed the Scripture and the word

3739 2036 3588 2424
ᾧ εἶπεν ὁ ᾿Ιησοῦς.
which said Jesus.

21 But he spake of the temple of his body.
22 When therefore he was risen from the dead, his disciples remembered that he had said this unto them; and they believed the scripture, and the word which Jesus had said.

23. And as He was in Jerusalem, at the Passover, at the Feast, many believed into His name, beholding the signs which He did.
24 But Jesus Himself did not commit Himself to them, because He knew all,
25 and because He had no need that anyone should witness concerning man, for He knew what was in man.

5613 1161 2258 1722 2414 1722 3588 3957 1722 3588 1859
23 ῾Ως δὲ ἦν ἐν ῾Ιεροσολύμοις ἐν τῷ πάσχα, ἐν τῇ ἑορτῇ,
as And was in Jerusalem, at the Passover, at the feast,

4183 4100 1519 3588 3686 846 2334 846 3588
πολλοὶ ἐπίστευσαν εἰς τὸ ὄνομα αὐτοῦ, θεωροῦντες αὐτοῦ τὰ
many believed into the name of Him, beholding of Him the

4592 3739 4160 846 1161 3588 2424 3756 4100 1438
σημεῖα ἃ ἐποίει. 24 αὐτὸς δὲ ὁ᾿Ιησοῦς οὐκ ἐπίστευεν ἑαυτὸν
signs which He did. Himself But Jesus not did commit Himself

846 1223 3588 846 1097 3956 2532 3754 3756 5532
αὐτοῖς, διὰ τὸ αὐτὸν γινώσκειν πάντας, 25 καὶ ὅτι οὐ χρείαν
to them, because (of) Him knowing all, and because no need

2192 2443 5100 3140 4012 3588 444 846 1063
εἶχεν ἵνα τις μαρτυρήσῃ περὶ τοῦ ἀνθρώπου· αὐτὸς γὰρ
He had that any should witness concerning man, He for

1097 5101 2258 1722 3588 444
ἐγίνωσκε τί ἦν ἐν τῷ ἀνθρώπῳ.
knew what was in man.

23. Now when he was in Jerusalem at the passover, in the feast (day), many believed in his name, when they saw the miracles which he did.
24 But Jesus did not commit himself unto them, because he knew all (men),
25 And needed not that any should testify of man: for he knew what was in man.

John 3

1. But there was a man from the Pharisees, Nicodemus his name, a ruler of the Jews.
2 This one came to Jesus by night and said to Him, Rabbi, we know that You

2258 1161 444 1537 3588 5330 3530 3686
1 ῏Ην δὲ ἄνθρωπος ἐκ τῶν Φαρισαίων. Νικόδημος ὄνομα
was And a man from the Pharisees, Nicodemus (the) name

846 758 3588 2453 3778 2064 4314 3588 2424
αὐτῷ, ἄρχων τῶν᾿Ιουδαίων· 2 οὗτος ἦλθε πρὸς τὸν ᾿Ιησοῦν
to him, a ruler of the Jews. This one came to Jesus

3571 2532 2036 846 4461 1492 3754 575 2316 2064
νυκτὸς, καὶ εἶπεν αὐτῷ, ῾Ραββί, οἴδαμεν ὅτι ἀπὸ θεοῦ ἐλή-
by night, and said to Him, Rabbi, we know that from God You

1. There was a man of the Pharisees, named Nicodemus, a ruler of the Jews:
2 The same came to Jesus by night, and said unto him, Rabbi, we know that thou art

Literal Translation

have come (as) a teacher from God. For no one is able to do these signs which You do, except God be with Him.
3 Jesus answered and said to him, Truly, truly, I say to you, if one is not generated from above, he is not able to see the kingdom of God.

4 Nicodemus said to Him, How is a man able to be generated, being old? Not he is able to enter into his mother's womb a second (time) and be generated?
5 Jesus answered, Truly, truly, I say to you, if not one is generated of water and of Spirit, he is not able to enter into the kingdom of God.

6 That having been generated out of the flesh is flesh, and that having been generated out of the Spirit is spirit.
7 Do not wonder because I said to you, You must be generated from above.
8 The Spirit breathes where He desires, and you hear His voice; but you do not know from where He comes, and where He goes; so is everyone who has been generated from the Spirit.
9 Nicodemus answered and said to Him, How is able these things to occur?
10 Jesus answered and said to him, Are you the teacher of Israel, and you do not know these things?
11 Truly, truly, I say to you, That which we know, we speak; and that which we have seen, we testify. And you do not receive our testimony.
12 If I told you earthly things, and you do not believe, how will you believe if I tell you heavenly things?
13 And no one has gone

John 3:3

1320 3762 1063 5023 3588 4592 1410
λυθας διδάσκαλος· οὐδεὶς γὰρ ταῦτα τὰ σημεῖα δύναται
have come a teacher; no one for these signs is able

4160 3739 4771 4160 1437 3362 5600 3588 2316 3326 846 611 3588
ποιεῖν ἃ σὺ ποιεῖς, ἐὰν μὴ ᾖ ὁ θεὸς μετ' αὐτοῦ. 3 ἀπεκρίθη ὁ
to do which You do, if not be God with him. answered

2424 2532 2036 846 281 281 3004 4671 1437 3362 5100
Ἰησοῦς καὶ εἶπεν αὐτῷ. Ἀμὴν ἀμὴν λέγω σοι, ἐὰν μή τις
Jesus and said to him, Truly, truly, I say to you, If not one

1080 509 3756 1410 1492 3588 932 3588 2316
γεννηθῇ ἄνωθεν, οὐ δύναται ἰδεῖν τὴν βασιλείαν τοῦ θεοῦ.
be generated from above not he is able to see the kingdom of God.

3004 4314 846 3588 3530 4459 1410 444
4 λέγει πρὸς αὐτὸν ὁ Νικόδημος, Πῶς δύναται ἄνθρωπος
says to Him Nicodemus, How is able a man

1080 1088 5607 3361 1410 1519 3588 2836 3588
γεννηθῆναι γέρων ὤν; μὴ δύναται εἰς τὴν κοιλίαν τῆς
to be generated, old being? Not he is able into the womb of the

3384 846 1208 1525 2532 1080 611
μητρὸς αὐτοῦ δεύτερον εἰσελθεῖν καὶ γεννηθῆναι; 5 ἀπεκρίθη
mother of him a second (time) to enter and be generated. answered

3588 2424 281 281 3004 4671 1437 3362 5100 1080 1537
ὁ Ἰησοῦς, Ἀμὴν ἀμὴν λέγω σοι, ἐὰν μή τις γεννηθῇ ἐξ
Jesus, Truly, truly, I say to you, If not one be generated of

5204 2532 4151 3756 1410 1525 1519 3588 932
ὕδατος καὶ πνεύματος, οὐ δύναται εἰσελθεῖν εἰς τὴν βασιλείαν
water and of Spirit, not he is able to enter into the kngdom

3588 2316 3588 1080 1537 3588 4561 4561 2076 532 3588
τοῦ θεοῦ. 6 τὸ γεγεννημένον ἐκ τῆς σαρκὸς σάρξ ἐστι· καὶ τὸ
of God. That having been generated out of the flesh, flesh is. And that

1080 1537 3588 4151 4151 2076 3361 2296
γεγεννημένον ἐκ τοῦ πνεύματος πνεῦμά ἐστι. 7 μὴ θαυμάσῃς
having been generated out of the Spirit, spirit is. Not do wonder

3754 2036 4671 1163 5209 1080 509 3588 4151 3699
ὅτι εἶπόν σοι, Δεῖ ὑμᾶς γεννηθῆναι ἄνωθεν. 8 τὸ πνεῦμα ὅπου
that I said to you, must You be generated from above. The Spirit where

2309 4154 2532 3588 5456 846 191 235 3756 1492
θέλει πνεῖ, καὶ τὴν φωνὴν αὐτοῦ ἀκούεις, ἀλλ' οὐκ οἶδας
He desires breathes, and the voice of Him you hear, but not you know

4159 2064 2532 4226 5217 3779 2076 3956 3588 1080
πόθεν ἔρχεται καὶ ποῦ ὑπάγει· οὕτως ἐστὶ πᾶς ὁ γεγεννη-
from where He comes and where He goes; so is everyone having been

1537 3588 4151 611 3530 2532 2036 846
μένος ἐκ τοῦ πνεύματος. 9 ἀπεκρίθη Νικόδημος καὶ εἶπεν αὐτῷ,
generated from the Spirit. answered Nicodemus and said to Him,

4459 1410 5023 1096 611 3588 2424 2532 2036
Πῶς δύναται ταῦτα γενέσθαι; 10 ἀπεκρίθη ὁ Ἰησοῦς καὶ εἶπεν
How is able these things to occur? answered Jesus and said

846 4771 1488 3588 1320 3588 2474 2532 5023 3756
αὐτῷ, Σὺ εἶ ὁ διδάσκαλος τοῦ Ἰσραήλ, καὶ ταῦτα οὐ
to him, you Are the teacher of Israel, and these things not

1097 281 281 3004 4671 3754 3739 1492 2980 2532
γινώσκεις; 11 ἀμὴν ἀμὴν λέγω σοι ὅτι ὃ οἴδαμεν λαλοῦμεν, καὶ
you know? Truly, truly, I say to you, What we know we speak, and

3739 3708 3140 2532 3588 3141 2257 3756
ὃ ἑωράκαμεν μαρτυροῦμεν· καὶ τὴν μαρτυρίαν ἡμῶν οὐ
what we have seen we witness, and the witness of us not

2983 1487 3588 1919 2036 5213 2532 3756 4100 4459
λαμβάνετε. 12 εἰ τὰ ἐπίγεια εἶπον ὑμῖν καὶ οὐ πιστεύετε, πῶς,
you receive. If the things earthly I told you and not you believe, how

1437 2036 5213 3588 2032 4100 2532 3762 305
ἐὰν εἴπω ὑμῖν τὰ ἐπουράνια, πιστεύσετε; 13 καὶ οὐδεὶς ἀναβέ-
if I tell you the things heavenly will you believe? And no one has gone

King James Version

a teacher come from God: for no man can do these miracles that thou doest, except God be with him.
3 Jesus answered and said unto him, Verily, verily, I say unto thee, Except a man be born again, he cannot see the kingdom of God.

4 Nicodemus saith unto him, How can a man be born when he is old? can he enter the second time into his mother's womb, and be born?
5 Jesus answered, Verily, verily, I say unto thee, Except a man be born of water and (of) the Spirit, he cannot enter into the kingdom of God.

6 That which is born of the flesh is flesh; and that which is born of the Spirit is spirit.
7 Marvel not that I said unto thee, Ye must be born again.
8 The wind bloweth where it listeth, and thou hearest the sound thereof, but canst not tell whence it cometh, and whither it goeth: so is every one that is born of the Spirit.

9 Nicodemus answered and said unto him, How can these things be?
10 Jesus answered and said unto him, Art thou a master of Israel, and knowest not these things?

11 Verily, verily, I say unto thee, We speak that we do know, and testify that we have seen; and ye receive not our witness.
12 If I have told you earthly things, and ye believe not, how shall ye believe, if I tell you (of) heavenly things?
13 And no man hath ascended

Literal Translation — **John 3:14** — **King James Version**

Literal Translation

up into Heaven, except He having come down out of Heaven, the Son of Man who is in Heaven.
14 And even as Moses lifted up the serpent in the wilderness, so must the Son of man be lifted up,

15 that everyone believing into Him should not perish, but may have everlasting life.

16 For God so loved the world that He gave His only begotten Son, that everyone believing into Him should not perish, but have everlasting life.
17 For God did not send His Son into the world that He judge the world, but that the world may be saved through Him.

18 The (one) believing into Him is not condemned; but the one not believing already has been condemned, for he has not believed into the name of the only begotten Son of God.
19 But this is the judgment, that the Light has come into the world, and men having loved the darkness more than the Light, for their works were evil.

20 For everyone practicing wickedness hates the Light, and does not come to the Light, that his works may not be exposed.

21 But the (one) doing the truth comes to the Light, that his works may be revealed, that they exist, having been worked in God.

22. After these things Jesus and His disciples came into the land of Judea. And (He) continued there with them and baptized.

1519 3588 3772 1487 3361 3588 1537 3588 3772 2597 3588
βηκεν εἰς τὸν οὐρανόν, εἰ μὴ ὁ ἐκ τοῦ οὐρανοῦ καταβάς, ὁ
up into Heaven, except He out of Heaven has come down, the

5207 3588 444 3588 5607 1722 3588 3772 2532 2531 3475
υἱὸς τοῦ ἀνθρώπου ὁ ὢν ἐν τῷ οὐρανῷ. 14 καὶ καθὼς Μωσῆς
Son of man, who is in Heaven. And even as Moses

5312 3588 3789 1722 3588 2048 3779 5312 1163 3588 5207
ὕψωσε τὸν ὄφιν ἐν τῇ ἐρήμῳ, οὕτως ὑψωθῆναι δεῖ τὸν υἱὸν
lifted up the serpent in the wilderness, so be lifted up must the Son

3588 444 2443 3956 3588 4100 1519 846 3361 622
τοῦ ἀνθρώπου· 15 ἵνα πᾶς ὁ πιστεύων εἰς αὐτὸν μὴ ἀπόληται
of man, that everyone believing into Him not may perish,

235 2192 2222 166
ἀλλ' ἔχῃ ζωὴν αἰώνιον.
but may have life everlasting.

3779 1063 25 3588 2316 3588 2889 5620 3588 5207
16. Οὕτω γὰρ ἠγάπησεν ὁ Θεὸς τὸν κόσμον, ὥστε τὸν υἱὸν
so For loved God the world, so as the Son

846 3588 3439 1325 2443 3956 3588 4100 1519 846
αὐτοῦ τὸν μονογενῆ ἔδωκεν, ἵνα πᾶς ὁ πιστεύων εἰς αὐτὸν
of Him, the Only-begotten, He gave, that everyone believing into Him

3361 622 235 2192 2222 166 3756 1063 649 3588
μὴ ἀπόληται, ἀλλ' ἔχῃ ζωὴν αἰώνιον. 17 οὐ γὰρ ἀπέστειλεν ὁ
not may perish, but have life everlasting. not For sent

2316 3588 5207 846 1519 3588 2889 2443 2919 3588 2889
Θεὸς τὸν υἱὸν αὐτοῦ εἰς τὸν κόσμον ἵνα κρίνῃ τὸν κόσμον,
God the Son of Him into the world that He judge the world,

235 2443 4982 3588 2889 1223 846 3588 4100 1519 846 3756
ἀλλ' ἵνα σωθῇ ὁ κόσμος δι' αὐτοῦ. 18 ὁ πιστεύων εἰς αὐτὸν οὐ
but that may be saved the world through Him. The (one) believing into Him not

2919 3588 1161 3361 4100 2235 2919 3754 3361 4100
κρίνεται· ὁ δὲ μὴ πιστεύων ἤδη κέκριται, ὅτι μὴ πεπί-
is judged; the (one) but not believing already has been judged, because not he

1519 3588 3686 3588 3439 5207 3588 2316 3778 1161
στευκεν εἰς τὸ ὄνομα τοῦ μονογενοῦς υἱοῦ τοῦ Θεοῦ. 19 αὕτη δέ
has believed into the name of the only-begotten Son of God. this But

2076 3588 2920 3754 3588 5457 2064 1519 3588 2889 2532
ἐστιν ἡ κρίσις, ὅτι τὸ φῶς ἐλήλυθεν εἰς τὸν κόσμον, καὶ
is the judgment, that the Light has come into the world, and

25 3588 444 3123 3588 4655 2228 3588 5457 2258
ἠγάπησαν οἱ ἄνθρωποι μᾶλλον τὸ σκότος ἢ τὸ φῶς, ἦν
loved men more the darkness than the Light; were

1063 4190 846 3588 2041 3956 1063 3588 5337 4238
γὰρ πονηρὰ αὐτῶν τὰ ἔργα. 20 πᾶς γὰρ ὁ φαῦλα πράσσων
for evil of them the works. everyone For wickedness practicing

3404 3588 5457 2532 3756 2064 4314 3588 5457 2443 3361 1651
μισεῖ τὸ φῶς, καὶ οὐκ ἔρχεται πρὸς τὸ φῶς, ἵνα μὴ ἐλεγχθῇ
hates the Light, and not does come to the Light, that not be reproved

3588 2041 846 3588 1161 4160 3588 225 2064 4314 3588
τὰ ἔργα αὐτοῦ. 21 ὁ δὲ ποιῶν τὴν ἀλήθειαν ἔρχεται πρὸς τὸ
the works of him. the (one) But doing the truth comes to the

5457 2443 5319 846 3588 2041 3754 1722 2316 2076
φῶς, ἵνα φανερωθῇ αὐτοῦ τὰ ἔργα, ὅτι ἐν Θεῷ ἐστιν
Light, that may be revealed of him the works, that in God they exist,

2038
εἰργασμένα.
having been worked.

3326 5023 2064 3588 2424 2532 3588 3101 846 1519
22. Μετὰ ταῦτα ἦλθεν ὁ Ἰησοῦς καὶ οἱ μαθηταὶ αὐτοῦ εἰς
After these things came Jesus and the disciples of Him into

3588 2453 1093 2532 1563 1304 3326 846 2532 907
τὴν Ἰουδαίαν γῆν· καὶ ἐκεῖ διέτριβε μετ' αὐτῶν καὶ ἐβάπτιζεν.
the Judean land, and there continued with them and baptized.

King James Version

up to heaven, but he that came down from heaven, (even) the Son of man which is in heaven.
14 And as Moses lifted up the serpent in the wilderness, even so must the Son of man be lifted up:

15 That whosoever believeth in him should not perish, but have eternal life.

16 For God so loved the world, that he gave his only begotten Son, that whosoever believeth in him should not perish, but have everlasting life.
17 For God sent not his Son into the world to condemn the world; but that the world through him might be saved.

18 He that believeth on him is not condemned: but he that believeth not is condemned already, because he hath not believed in the name of the only begotten Son of God.
19 And this is the condemnation, that light is come into the world, and men loved darkness rather than light, because their deeds were evil.

20 For every one that doeth evil hateth the light, neither cometh to the light, lest his deeds should be reproved.

21 But he that doeth truth cometh to the light, that his deeds may be made manifest, that they are wrought in God.

22. After these things came Jesus and his disciples into the land of Judaea; and there he tarried with them, and baptized.

Literal Translation | **John 3:23** | *King James Version*

23 And John was also baptizing in Aenon, near Salim, for many waters were there. And they came and were being baptized.

24 For John had not yet been thrown into the prison.
25. Then a question from John's disciples arose with the Jews about purifying.
26 And they came to John and said to him, Master, (the one) who was with you beyond the Jordan, to whom you have witnessed, behold, this one baptizes, and all are coming to Him.

27 John answered and said, A man is able to receive nothing unless it has been given to him from Heaven.

28 You (your)selves witness to me that I said, I am not the Christ, but that having been sent, I am going before that One.

29 The (one) having the bride is (the) bridegroom. But the friend of the bridegroom, standing and hearing him, rejoices with joy because of the bridegroom's voice. Then this my joy has been fulfilled.
30 That One must increase, but me to decrease.

31 The (One) having come from above is above all. The (one) being of the earth is of the earth, and speaks of the earth. The (One) having come from Heaven is above all.
32 And what He has seen and heard, this He testifies, and no one receives His testimony.

33 The (one) receiving His testimony has sealed that God is true.
34 For the (One) whom God sent speaks the words of God,

2258 1161 2532 2491 907 1722 137 1451 3588 4530
23 ἦν δὲ καὶ Ἰωάννης βαπτίζων ἐν Αἰνὼν ἐγγὺς τοῦ Σαλείμ,
was And also John baptizing in Aenon near Salem,
3754 5204 4183 2258 1563 2532 3854 2532 907
ὅτι ὕδατα πολλὰ ἦν ἐκεῖ· καὶ παρεγίνοντο καὶ ἐβαπτίζοντο.
because waters many were there; and they came and were being baptized.
3768 1063 2258 906 1519 3588 5438 3588 2491
24 οὔπω γὰρ ἦν βεβλημένος εἰς τὴν φυλακὴν ὁ Ἰωάννης.
not yet For was having been cast into prison John.
1096 3767 2214 1537 3588 3101 2491 3326
25 ἐγένετο οὖν ζήτησις ἐκ τῶν μαθητῶν Ἰωάννου μετὰ
came to be Then a questioning from the disciples of John with
2453 4012 2512 2532 2064 4314 3588 2491
Ἰουδαίων περὶ καθαρισμοῦ. 26 καὶ ἦλθον πρὸς τὸν Ἰωάννην
Jews concerning purifying. And they came to John
2532 2036 846 4461 3739 2258 3326 4675 4008 3588 2446
καὶ εἶπον αὐτῷ, Ῥαββί, ὃς ἦν μετὰ σοῦ πέραν τοῦ Ἰορδάνου,
and said to him, Rabbi, (He) who was with you beyond the Jordan,
3739 4771 3140 2396 3778 907 2532 3956 2064
ᾧ σὺ μεμαρτύρηκας, ἴδε οὗτος βαπτίζει, καὶ πάντες ἔρχονται
to whom you witnessed, behold, this one baptizes, and all are coming
4314 846 611 2491 2532 2036 3756 1410
πρὸς αὐτόν. 27 ἀπεκρίθη Ἰωάννης καὶ εἶπεν, Οὐ δύναται
to Him. answered John and said, Not is able
444 2983 3762 1437 3361 5600 1325 846 1537 3588
ἄνθρωπος λαμβάνειν οὐδέν, ἐὰν μὴ ᾖ δεδομένον αὐτῷ ἐκ τοῦ
a man to receive nothing, if not it is, having been given to him from
3772 846 5210 3427 3140 3754 2036 3756 1510
οὐρανοῦ. 28 αὐτοὶ ὑμεῖς μοι μαρτυρεῖτε ὅτι εἶπον, Οὐκ εἰμὶ
Heaven. (your)selves You to me witness that I said, Not am
1473 3588 5547 235 3754 649 1510 1715
ἐγὼ ὁ Χριστός, ἀλλ' ὅτι ἀπεσταλμένος εἰμὶ ἔμπροσθεν
I the Christ, but that having been sent I am before
1565 3588 2192 3588 3565 3566 2076 3588 1161 5384 3588
ἐκείνου. 29 ὁ ἔχων τὴν νύμφην νυμφίος ἐστίν· ὁ δὲ φίλος τοῦ
that One. (The) one having the bride (the) bridegroom is, the but friend of the
3566 3588 2476 2532 191 846 5479 5463 1223 3588
νυμφίου, ὁ ἑστηκὼς καὶ ἀκούων αὐτοῦ, χαρᾷ χαίρει διὰ τὴν
bridegroom, standing and hearing him, with joy rejoices because of the
5456 3588 3566 3778 3767 3588 5479 3588 1699 4137
φωνὴν τοῦ νυμφίου· αὕτη οὖν ἡ χαρὰ ἡ ἐμὴ πεπλήρωται.
voice of the bridegroom. this Then the joy (he) of me has been fulfilled.
1565 1163 837 1691 1161 1642
30 ἐκεῖνον δεῖ αὐξάνειν, ἐμὲ δὲ ἐλαττοῦσθαι.
That One must increase, me but to decrease.
3588 509 2064 1883 3956 2076 3588 5607 1537 3588
31 Ὁ ἄνωθεν ἐρχόμενος ἐπάνω πάντων ἐστίν. ὁ ὢν ἐκ τῆς
The (One) from above having come above all is. The (one) being of the
1093 1537 3588 1093 2076 2532 1537 3588 1093 2980 3588 1537 3588 3772
γῆς, ἐκ τῆς γῆς ἐστι, καὶ ἐκ τῆς γῆς λαλεῖ· ὁ ἐκ τοῦ οὐρανοῦ
earth, of the earth is, and of the earth speaks. He from Heaven
2064 1883 3956 2076 2532 3739 3708 2532 191
ἐρχόμενος ἐπάνω πάντων ἐστί. 32 καὶ ὃ ἑώρακε καὶ ἤκουσε,
having come above all is. And what He has seen and heard,
5124 3140 2532 3588 3141 846 3762 2983
τοῦτο μαρτυρεῖ· καὶ τὴν μαρτυρίαν αὐτοῦ οὐδεὶς λαμβάνει.
this He witnesses, and the witness of Him no one receives.
3588 2983 846 3588 3141 4972 3754 3588 2316 227
33 ὁ λαβὼν αὐτοῦ τὴν μαρτυρίαν ἐσφράγισεν ὅτι ὁ Θεὸς ἀληθής
T he (one) receiving of Him the testimony has sealed that God true
2076 3739 1063 649 3588 2316 3588 4487 3588 2316 2980
ἐστιν. 34 ὃν γὰρ ἀπέστειλεν ὁ Θεός, τὰ ῥήματα τοῦ Θεοῦ λαλεῖ·
is the (One) For sent God, the words of God speaks.

23 And John also was baptizing in Aenon near to Salim, because there was much water there: and they came, and were baptized.
24 For John was not yet cast into prison.

25. Then there arose a question between (some) of John's disciples and the Jews about purifying.
26 And they came unto John, and said unto him, Rabbi, he that was with thee beyond Jordan, to whom thou barest witness, behold, the same baptizeth, and all (men) come to him.

27 John answered and said, A man can receive nothing, except it be given him from heaven.

28 Ye yourselves bear me witness, that I said, I am not the Christ, but that I am sent before him.

29 He that hath the bride is the bridegroom: but the friend of the bridegroom, which standeth and heareth him, rejoiceth greatly because of the bridegroom's voice: this my joy therefore is fulfilled.
30 He must increase, but I (must) decrease.

31 He that cometh from above is above all: he that is of the earth is earthly, and speaketh of the earth: he that cometh from heaven is above all.
32 And what he hath seen and heard, that he testifieth; and no man receiveth his testimony.

33 He that hath received his testimony hath set to his seal that God is true.
34 For he whom God hath sent speaketh the words of God:

John 3:35

Literal Translation

for God does not give the Spirit by measure.
35 The Father loves the Son and has given all things into His hand.
36 The (one) believing into the Son has everlasting life; but the (one) disobeying the Son will not see life, but the wrath of God remains on him.

3756 1063 1537 3358 1325 3588 2316 3588 4151 3588 3962 25
οὐ γὰρ ἐκ μέτρου δίδωσιν ὁ Θεὸς τὸ Πνεῦμα. 35 ὁ πατὴρ ἀγαπᾷ
not for by measure gives God the Spirit. The Father loves

3588 5207 2532 3956 1325 1722 3588 5495 846 3588 4100
τὸν υἱόν, καὶ πάντα δέδωκεν ἐν τῇ χειρὶ αὐτοῦ. 36 ὁ πιστεύων
the Son, and all things has given into the hand of Him. The (one) believing

1519 3588 5207 2192 2222 166 3588 1161 544 3588 5207 3756
εἰς τὸν υἱὸν ἔχει ζωὴν αἰώνιον· ὁ δὲ ἀπειθῶν τῷ υἱῷ οὐκ
into the Son has life everlasting; the (one) but disbelieving the Son not

3700 2222 235 3588 3709 3588 2316 3306 1909 846
ὄψεται ζωήν, ἀλλ' ἡ ὀργὴ τοῦ Θεοῦ μένει ἐπ' αὐτόν.
will see life, but the wrath of God remains on him.

King James Version

for God giveth not the Spirit by measure (unto him).
35 The Father loveth the Son, and hath given all things into his hand.
36 He that believeth on the Son hath everlasting life: and he that believeth not the Son shall not see life; but the wrath of God abideth on him.

John 4

1. Then when the Lord knew that the Pharisees heard that Jesus was making more disciples and baptizing (more) than John,

2 though truly Jesus Himself did not baptize, but His disciples,

3 He left Judea and went away into Galilee again.

4. And it was needful for Him to pass through Samaria.

5 And He came to a Samaritan city being called Sychar, near the piece of land Jacob had given to his son Joseph.

6 And Jacob's fountain was there. Then being wearied by the journey, Jesus was sitting thus on the fountain. (It) was about (the) sixth hour.

7 A woman came out of Samaria to draw water. Jesus said to her, Give Me (some) to drink.
8 For His disciples had gone away into the city that they might buy provisions.
9 Then the Samaritan woman said to Him, How do you, being a Jew, ask to drink from me, (I) being a Samaritan woman? For Jews do not have dealings with Samaritans.

10 Jesus answered and said to her, If you knew the gift of God, and who is the (One) saying

John 4

5613 3767 1097 3588 2962 3754 191 3588 5330 3754
1. Ὡς οὖν ἔγνω ὁ Κύριος ὅτι ἤκουσαν οἱ Φαρισαῖοι ὅτι
as Then knew the Lord that heard the Pharisees that

2424 4119 3101 4160 2532 907 2228 2491
Ἰησοῦς πλείονας μαθητὰς ποιεῖ καὶ βαπτίζει ἢ Ἰωάννης
Jesus more disciples making and baptizing than John

2544 2424 846 3756 907 235 3588 3101
2 [καίτοιγε Ἰησοῦς αὐτὸς οὐκ ἐβάπτιζεν, ἀλλ' οἱ μαθηταὶ
though Jesus Himself not baptized, but the disciples

846 863 3588 2449 2532 565 3825 1519 3588
αὐτοῦ], 3 ἀφῆκε τὴν Ἰουδαίαν, καὶ ἀπῆλθε πάλιν εἰς τὴν
of Him, He left Judea and went away again into

1056 1163 1161 846 1330 1223 3588 4540
Γαλιλαίαν. 4 ἔδει δὲ αὐτὸν διέρχεσθαι διὰ τῆς Σαμαρείας.
Galilee. it behoved And Him to pass through Samaria.

2064 3767 1519 4172 3588 4540 3004 4965
5 ἔρχεται οὖν εἰς πόλιν τῆς Σαμαρείας λεγομένην Συχάρ,
He comes Then into a city of Samaria being called Sychar

4139 3588 5564 3739 1325 2384 2501 3588 5207 846
πλησίον τοῦ χωρίου ὃ ἔδωκεν Ἰακὼβ Ἰωσὴφ τῷ υἱῷ αὐτοῦ·
near the piece of land that had given Jacob to Joseph the son of him.

2258 1161 1563 4077 3588 2384 3588 3767 2424 2872 1537 3588
6 ἦν δὲ ἐκεῖ πηγὴ τοῦ Ἰακώβ. ὁ οὖν Ἰησοῦς κεκοπιακὼς ἐκ τῆς
was And there a fountain of Jacob. Then Jesus being wearied from the

3597 2516 3779 1909 3588 4077 5610 2258 5616
ὁδοιπορίας ἐκαθέζετο οὕτως ἐπὶ τῇ πηγῇ. ὥρα ἦν ὡσεὶ
journey was, sitting thus on the well; (the) hour was about

1623 2064 1135 1537 3588 4540 501 5204 3004
ἕκτη. 7 ἔρχεται γυνὴ ἐκ τῆς Σαμαρείας ἀντλῆσαι ὕδωρ· λέγει
(the) sixth. comes A woman of Samaria to draw water. says

846 3588 2424 1325 3427 4095 3588 1063 3101 846 565
αὐτῇ ὁ Ἰησοῦς, Δός μοι πιεῖν. 8 οἱ γὰρ μαθηταὶ αὐτοῦ ἀπελη-
to her Jesus, Give Me to drink. the For disciples of Him had gone

1519 3588 4172 2443 5160 59 3004 3767
λύθεισαν εἰς τὴν πόλιν, ἵνα τροφὰς ἀγοράσωσι. 9 λέγει οὖν
away into the city, that foods they might buy. says Then

846 3588 1135 3588 4542 4459 4771 2453 5607 3844 1700
αὐτῷ ἡ γυνὴ ἡ Σαμαρεῖτις, Πῶς σὺ Ἰουδαῖος ὢν παρ' ἐμοῦ
to Him the woman of Samaria, How do you, a Jew being, from me

4095 154 5607 1135 4542 3756 1063 4798
πιεῖν αἰτεῖς, οὔσης γυναικὸς Σαμαρείτιδος; [οὐ γὰρ συγ-
to drink ask, (I) being a woman of Samaria? not For deal

2453 4541 611 2424 2532 2036
χρῶνται Ἰουδαῖοι Σαμαρείταις.] 10 ἀπεκρίθη Ἰησοῦς καὶ εἶπεν
with Jews Samaritans.) answered Jesus and said

846 1487 1492 3588 1431 3588 2316 2532 5101 2076 3588 3004
αὐτῇ, Εἰ ᾔδεις τὴν δωρεὰν τοῦ Θεοῦ, καὶ τίς ἐστιν ὁ λέγων
to her, If you knew the gift of God, and who is the (One) saying

John 4

1. When therefore the Lord knew how the Pharisees had heard that Jesus made and baptized more disciples than John,

2 (Though Jesus himself baptized not, but his disciples,)

3 He left Judaea, and departed again into Galilee.

4. And he must needs go through Samaria.

5 Then cometh he to a city of Samaria, which is called Sychar, near to the parcel of ground that Jacob gave to his son Joseph.

6 Now Jacob's well was there. Jesus therefore, being wearied with (his) journey, sat thus on the well: (and) it was about the sixth hour.

7 There cometh a woman of Samaria to draw water: Jesus saith unto her, Give me to drink.
8 (For his disciples were gone away unto the city to buy meat.)
9 Then saith the woman of Samaria unto him, How is it that thou, being a Jew, askest drink of me, which am a woman of Samaria? for the Jews have no dealings with the Samaritans.

10 Jesus answered and said unto her, If thou knewest the gift of God, and who it is that saith

Literal Translation

John 4:11

King James Version

to you, Give Me to drink, you would have asked Him, and He would give you living water.
11 The woman said to Him, Sir, you have no vessel, and the well is deep. From where then do you have living water?
12 Are you greater than our father Jacob who gave us the well, and he and his sons and his livestock drank out of it?
13 Jesus answered and said to her, Everyone drinking of this water will thirst again;
14 but whoever may drink of the water which I will give him will never ever thirst, but the water which I will give to him will become a fountain of water in him, springing up into everlasting life.
15 The woman said to Him, Sir, give me this water, that I may not thirst, nor come here to draw.
16 Jesus said to her, Go, call your husband and come here.
17 And the woman answered and said, I have no husband. Jesus said to her, Well did you say, I have no husband.
18 For you have had five husbands, and now (he) whom you have is not your husband. You have spoken this truly.
19 The woman said to Him, Sir, I perceive that you are a prophet.
20 Our fathers worshiped in this mountain, and you say that in Jerusalem is the place where it is necessary to worship.
21 Jesus said to her, Woman, believe Me that an hour is coming when you will worship the Father neither in this mountain nor in Jerusalem.

4671 1325 3427 4095 4771 302 154 846 2532 1325 302 4671
σοι, Δός μοι πιεῖν, σὺ ἂν ᾔτησας αὐτὸν, καὶ ἔδωκεν ἂν σοι
to you, Give Me to drink, you would have asked Him, and He would give you

5204 2198 3004 846 3588 1135 2962 3777 502 2192 2532
ὕδωρ ζῶν. 11 λέγει αὐτῷ ἡ γυνή, Κύριε, οὔτε ἄντλημα ἔχεις, καὶ
water living. says to Him the woman, Sir, no vessel You have, and

3588 5421 2076 901 4159 3767 2192 3588 5204 3588 2198 3361/4771
τὸ φρέαρ ἐστὶ βαθύ· πόθεν οὖν ἔχεις τὸ ὕδωρ τὸ ζῶν; 12 μὴ σὺ
the well is deep; from where then have you water living? Not you

3187 1488 3588 3962 2257 2384 3739 1325 2254 3588 5421
μείζων εἶ τοῦ πατρὸς ἡμῶν Ἰακώβ, ὃς ἔδωκεν ἡμῖν τὸ φρέαρ,
greater are (than) the father of us, Jacob, who gave us the well,

2532 846 1537 846 4095 2532 3588 5207 846 2532 3588 2353
καὶ αὐτὸς ἐξ αὐτοῦ ἔπιε, καὶ οἱ υἱοὶ αὐτοῦ, καὶ τὰ θρέμματα
and he out of it drank, and the sons of him, and the livestock

846 611 3588 2424 2532 2036 846 3956 3588 4095 1537
αὐτοῦ; 13 ἀπεκρίθη ὁ Ἰησοῦς καὶ εἶπεν αὐτῇ, Πᾶς ὁ πίνων ἐκ
of him? answered Jesus and said to her, Everyone drinking of

3588 5204 5127 1372 3825 3739 1161 302 4095 1537 3588
τοῦ ὕδατος τούτου, διψήσει πάλιν· 14 ὃς δ' ἂν πίῃ ἐκ τοῦ
water this will thirst again. who But ever drinks of the

5204 3739 1473 1325 846 3756 3361 1372 1519 3588 165
ὕδατος οὗ ἐγὼ δώσω αὐτῷ, οὐ μὴ διψήσῃ εἰς τὸν αἰῶνα·
water which I will give him, not ever will thirst unto the age,

235 3588 5204 3739 1325 846 1096 1722 846 4077
ἀλλὰ τὸ ὕδωρ ὃ δώσω αὐτῷ γενήσεται ἐν αὐτῷ πηγὴ
but the water which I will give him will come to be in him a fountain

5204 242 1519 2222 166 3004 4314 846 3588
ὕδατος ἁλλομένου εἰς ζωὴν αἰώνιον. 15 λέγει πρὸς αὐτὸν ἡ
of water springing up into life everlasting. says to Him the

1135 2962 1325 3427 5124 3588 5204 2443 3361 1372 3366
γυνή, Κύριε, δός μοι τοῦτο τὸ ὕδωρ, ἵνα μὴ διψῶ, μηδε
woman, Lord, give me this water, that not I thirst, nor

2064 1759 501 3004 846 3588 2424 5217
ἔρχωμαι ἐνθάδε ἀντλεῖν. 16 λέγει αὐτῇ ὁ Ἰησοῦς, Ὕπαγε,
come here to draw. says to her Jesus, Go,

5455 3588 435 4675 2532 2064 1759 611 3588 1135
φώνησον τὸν ἄνδρα σοῦ, καὶ ἐλθὲ ἐνθάδε. 17 ἀπεκρίθη ἡ γυνὴ
call the husband of you, and come here. answered the woman

2532 2036 3756 2192 435 3004 846 3588 2424 2573 2036
καὶ εἶπεν, Οὐκ ἔχω ἄνδρα. λέγει αὐτῇ ὁ Ἰησοῦς, Καλῶς εἶπας
and said, Not I have a husband. says to her Jesus, Well you say,

3754 435 3756 2192 4002 1063 435 2192 2532 3568 3739
ὅτι Ἄνδρα οὐκ ἔχω· 18 πέντε γὰρ ἄνδρας ἔσχες, καὶ νῦν ὃν
A husband not I have. five For husbands you had, and now whom

2192 3756 2076 4675 435 5124 227 2046 3004 846
ἔχεις οὐκ ἔστι σου ἀνήρ· τοῦτο ἀληθὲς εἴρηκας. 19 λέγει αὐτῷ
you have not is your husband; this truly you have said. says to Him

3588 1135 2962 2334 3754 4396 1488 4771 3588 3962 2257
ἡ γυνή, Κύριε, θεωρῶ ὅτι προφήτης εἶ σύ. 20 οἱ πατέρες ἡμῶν
the woman, Lord, I perceive that a prophet are You. The fathers of us

1722 5129 3588 3735 4352 2532 5210 3004 3754 1722
ἐν τούτῳ τῷ ὄρει προσεκύνησαν· καὶ ὑμεῖς λέγετε ὅτι ἐν
in this mountain worshiped, and you say that in

2414 2076 3588 5117 3699 1163 4352 3004
Ἱεροσολύμοις ἐστὶν ὁ τόπος ὅπου δεῖ προσκυνεῖν. 21 λέγει
Jerusalem is the place where it is right to worship. says

846 3588 2424 1135 4100 3427 3754 2064 5610
αὐτῇ ὁ Ἰησοῦς, Γύναι, πίστευσόν μοι, ὅτι ἔρχεται ὥρα,
to her Jesus, Woman, believe Me that comes an hour

3753 3777 1722 3588 3735 5129 3777 1722 2414 4352
ὅτε οὔτε ἐν τῷ ὄρει τούτῳ οὔτε ἐν Ἱεροσολύμοις προσκυνή-
when not in mountain this nor in Jerusalem will you worship

to thee, Give me to drink; thou wouldest have asked of him, and he would have given thee living water.
11 The woman saith unto him, Sir, thou hast nothing to draw with, and the well is deep: from whence then hast thou that living water?
12 Art thou greater than our father Jacob, which gave us the well, and drank thereof himself, and his children, and his cattle?
13 Jesus answered and said unto her, Whosoever drinketh of this water shall thirst again:
14 But whosoever drinketh of the water that I shall give him shall never thirst; but the water that I shall give him shall be in him a well of water springing up into everlasting life.
15 The woman saith unto him, Sir, give me this water, that I thirst not, neither come hither to draw.
16 Jesus saith unto her, Go, call thy husband, and come hither.
17 The woman answered and said, I have no husband. Jesus said unto her, Thou hast well said, I have no husband:
18 For thou hast had five husbands; and he whom thou now hast is not thy husband: in that saidst thou truly.
19 The woman saith unto him, Sir, I perceive that thou art a prophet.
20 Our fathers worshipped in this mountain; and ye say, that in Jerusalem is the place where men ought to worship.
21 Jesus saith unto her, Woman, believe me, the hour cometh, when ye shall neither in this mountain, nor yet at Jerusalem,

Literal Translation — **John 4:22** — ***King James Version***

22 You worship what you do not know; we worship what we know, for salvation is of the Jews.

23 But an hour is coming, and now is, when the true worshipers will worship the Father in spirit and in truth. For the Father also seeks such, (the ones) worshiping Him.

24 God (is) spirit, and the (ones) worshiping Him must worship in spirit and truth.
25 The woman said to Him, I know that Messiah is coming, the (One) called Christ. When that One comes, He will announce to us all things.
26 Jesus said to her, I AM, the (One) speaking to you.

27. And on this His disciples came and marveled that He was speaking with a woman; though no one said, What do you seek? Or, Why do You speak with her?
28 Then the woman left her waterpot and went away into the city and said to the men,

29 Come, see a Man who told me all things, whatever I did. Is this One not the Christ?
30 Therefore, they went out of the city and came to Him.
31. But in the meantime the disciples asked Him, saying, Master, eat?
32 But He said to them, I have food to eat which you do not know.
33 Then the disciples said to one another, No one brought Him (food) to eat?

34 Jesus said to them, My food is that I should do the

3588 3962 5210 4352 3739 3756 1492 2249
σετε τῷ πατρί. 22 ὑμεῖς προσκυνεῖτε ὃ οὐκ οἴδατε· ἡμεῖς
the Father. You worship what not you know; we

4352 3739 1492 3754 3588 4991 1537 3588 2453
προσκυνοῦμεν ὃ οἴδαμεν· ὅτι ἡ σωτηρία ἐκ τῶν Ἰουδαίων
worship what we know; since salvation of the Jews

2076 235 2064 5610 2532 3568 2076 3753 3588 228
ἐστίν. 23 ἀλλ᾽ ἔρχεται ὥρα καὶ νῦν ἐστιν, ὅτε οἱ ἀληθινοὶ
is. But is coming an hour, and now is, when the true

4353 4352 3588 3962 1722 4151 2532
προσκυνηταὶ προσκυνήσουσι τῷ πατρὶ ἐν πνεύματι καὶ
worshipers will worship the Father in spirit and

225 2532 1063 3588 3962 5108 2212 3588 4352
ἀληθείᾳ· καὶ γὰρ ὁ πατὴρ τοιούτους ζητεῖ τοὺς προσ-
truth; also for the Father such seeks the (ones)

846 4151 3588 2316 2532 3588 4352
κυνοῦντας αὐτόν. 24 Πνεῦμα ὁ Θεός· καὶ τοὺς προσκυνοῦντας
worshiping Him. spirit God (is); and the (ones) worshiping

846 1722 4151 2532 225 1163 4352 3004 846
αὐτόν, ἐν πνεύματι καὶ ἀληθείᾳ δεῖ προσκυνεῖν. 25 λέγει αὐτῷ
Him in spirit and truth need to worship. says to Him

3588 1135 1492 3754 3323 2064 3588 3004 5547
ἡ γυνή, Οἶδα ὅτι Μεσσίας ἔρχεται [ὁ λεγόμενος Χριστός]·
The woman, I know that Messiah is coming, the (one) being called Christ;

3752 2064 1565 312 2254 3956 3004 846 3588
ὅταν ἔλθῃ ἐκεῖνος, ἀναγγελεῖ ἡμῖν πάντα. 26 λέγει αὐτῇ ὁ
when comes that One, He will announce to us all things. says to her

2424 1473 1510 3588 2980 4671
Ἰησοῦς, Ἐγώ εἰμι, ὁ λαλῶν σοι.
Jesus, I AM!, the (One) speaking to you.

2532 1909 5129 2064 3588 3101 846 2532 2296
27. Καὶ ἐπὶ τούτῳ ἦλθον οἱ μαθηταὶ αὐτοῦ, καὶ ἐθαύμασαν
And on this came the disciples of Him, and marveled

3754 3326 1135 2980 3762 3305 2036 5101 2212
ὅτι μετὰ γυναικὸς ἐλάλει· οὐδεὶς μέντοι εἶπε, Τί ζητεῖς;
that with a woman He was speaking; no one though said, What seek you?

2228 5101 2980 3326 846 863 3767 3588 5201 846 3588
ἤ, Τί λαλεῖς μετ᾽ αὐτῆς; 28 ἀφῆκεν οὖν τὴν ὑδρίαν αὐτῆς ἡ
Or, Why speak You with her? left Then the waterpot of her the

1135 2532 565 1519 3588 4172 2532 3004 3588 444
γυνή, καὶ ἀπῆλθεν εἰς τὴν πόλιν, καὶ λέγει τοῖς ἀνθρώποις,
woman, and went away into the city, and says to the men,

1205 1492 444 3739 2036 3427 3956 3745 4160 3385
29 Δεῦτε, ἴδετε ἄνθρωπον, ὃς εἶπέ μοι πάντα ὅσα ἐποίησα· μήτι
Come! See a Man who told me all things whatever I did; not

3778 2076 3588 5547 1831 3767 1537 3588 4172 2532
οὗτός ἐστιν ὁ Χριστός; 30 ἐξῆλθον οὖν ἐκ τῆς πόλεως, καὶ
this One Is the Christ? They went out, then, from the city, and

2064 4314 846 1722 1161 3588 3342 2065 846 3588
ἤρχοντο πρὸς αὐτόν. 31 ἐν δὲ τῷ μεταξὺ ἠρώτων αὐτὸν οἱ
came to Him. in But the meantime asked Him the

3101 3004 4461 5315 3588 1161 2036 846 1473
μαθηταί, λέγοντες, Ῥαββί, φάγε. 32 ὁ δὲ εἶπεν αὐτοῖς, Ἐγὼ
disciples, saying, Rabbi, eat. He But said to them, I

1035 2192 5315 3739 5210 3756 1492 3004 3767 3588
βρῶσιν ἔχω φαγεῖν ἣν ὑμεῖς οὐκ οἴδατε. 33 ἔλεγον οὖν οἱ
food have to eat which you not do know. said Then the

3101 4314 240 3387 5342 846 5315
μαθηταὶ πρὸς ἀλλήλους, Μήτις ἤνεγκεν αὐτῷ φαγεῖν;
disciples to one another, No one brought Him to eat?

3004 846 3588 2424 1699 1033 2076 2443 4160 3588
34 λέγει αὐτοῖς ὁ Ἰησοῦς, Ἐμὸν βρῶμά ἐστιν, ἵνα ποιῶ τὸ
says to them Jesus, My food is that I do the

---

worship the Father.
22 Ye worship ye know not what: we know what we worship: for salvation is of the Jews.

23 But the hour cometh, and now is, when the true worshippers shall worship the Father in spirit and in truth: for the Father seeketh such to worship him.

24 God (is) a Spirit: and they that worship him must worship (him) in spirit and in truth.
25 The woman saith unto him, I know that Messias cometh, which is called Christ: when he is come, he will tell us all things.

26 Jesus saith unto her, I that speak unto thee am (he).

27. And upon this came his disciples, and marvelled that he talked with the woman: yet no man said, What seekest thou? or, Why talkest thou with her?
28 The woman then left her waterpot, and went her way into the city, and saith to the men,

29 Come, see a man, which told me all things that ever I did: is not this the Christ?
30 Then they went out of the city, and came unto him.
31. In the mean while his disciples prayed him, saying, Master, eat.
32 But he said unto them, I have meat to eat that ye know not of.

33 Therefore said the disciples one to another, Hath any man brought him (ought) to eat?

34 Jesus saith unto them, My meat is to do the

Literal Translation | **John 4:35** | *King James Version*

will of (Him) who sent Me, and that I may finish His work.
35 Do you not say, It is yet four months and the harvest comes? Behold! I say to you, Lift up your eyes and behold the fields, because they are already white to harvest.
36 And the one reaping receives reward, and gathers fruit to everlasting life, so that both the (one) sowing and the (one) reaping may rejoice together.
37 For in this the word is true, that another (is) the (one) sowing, and another the (one) reaping.
38 I sent you to reap what you have not labored over. Others have labored, and you have entered into their labor.

39. And many of the Samaritans out of that city believed into Him, because of the word of the woman testifying, He told me all things, whatever I did.
40 Then as the Samaritans came to Him, they asked Him to remain with them. And He remained there two days.
41 And many more believed through His Word.
42 And they said to the woman, We no longer believe because of your speaking; for we (our)selves have heard, and we know that this One is truly the Savior of the world, the Christ.

43. But after the two days, He went out from there, and went away into Galilee.
44 For Jesus (Him)self testified that a prophet has no honor in (his) own native-place.
45 Therefore, when He came

2307 3588 3992 3165 2532 5048 846 3588 2041 3756
θέλημα τοῦ πέμψαντός με, καὶ τελειώσω αὐτοῦ τὸ ἔργον. 35 οὐχ
will of the (One) having sent Me, and I may finish of Him the work. Not

5210 3004 3754 2089 5072 2076 2532 3588 2326 2064
ὑμεῖς λέγετε ὅτι Ἔτι τετράμηνόν ἐστι, καὶ ὁ θερισμὸς ἔρχεται;
do you say, Yet four months, and the harvest comes?

2400 3004 5213 1869 3588 3788 5216 2532
ἰδού, λέγω ὑμῖν, Ἐπάρατε τοὺς ὀφθαλμοὺς ὑμῶν, καὶ
Behold! I say to you, Lift up the eyes of you, and

2300 3588 5561 3754 3022 1526 4314 2326 2235
θεάσασθε τὰς χώρας, ὅτι λευκαί εἰσι πρὸς θερισμόν ἤδη.
behold the fields, because white they are to harvest already.

2532 3588 2325 3408 2983 2532 4863 2590 1519 2222
36 καὶ ὁ θερίζων μισθὸν λαμβάνει, καὶ συνάγει καρπὸν εἰς ζωὴν
And the (one) reaping reward receives, and gathers fruit to life

166 2443 2532 3588 4687 3674 5463 2532 3588 2325
αἰώνιον· ἵνα καὶ ὁ σπείρων ὁμοῦ χαίρῃ καὶ ὁ θερίζων.
everlasting, that also the (one) sowing together may rejoice and he reaping.

1722 1063 5129 3588 3056 2076 228 3754 243 2076 3588
37 ἐν γὰρ τούτῳ ὁ λόγος ἐστὶν ἀληθινός, ὅτι ἄλλος ἐστὶν ὁ
in For this the word is true, that another is the (one)

4687 2532 243 3588 2325 1473 649 5209 2325
σπείρων, καὶ ἄλλος ὁ θερίζων. 38 ἐγὼ ἀπέστειλα ὑμᾶς θερίζειν
sowing, and another the (one) reaping. I sent you to reap

3739 3756 5210 2872 243 2872 2532 5210 1519 3588
ὃ οὐχ ὑμεῖς κεκοπιάκατε· ἄλλοι κεκοπιάκασι, καὶ ὑμεῖς εἰς τὸν
what not you have labored over. Others have labored, and you into the

2873 846 1525
κόπον αὐτῶν εἰσεληλύθατε.
labor of them have entered.

1537 1161 3588 4172 1565 4183 4100 1519 846
39. Ἐκ δὲ τῆς πόλεως ἐκείνης πολλοὶ ἐπίστευσαν εἰς αὐτὸν
out of And city that many believed into Him

3588 4541 1223 3588 3056 3588 1135 3140
τῶν Σαμαρειτῶν διὰ τὸν λόγον τῆς γυναικὸς μαρτυρούσης
of the Samaritans because of the word of the woman witnessing,

3754 2036 3427 3956 3745 4160 5613 3767 2064 4314 846
ὅτι Εἶπέ μοι πάντα ὅσα ἐποίησα. 40 ὡς οὖν ἦλθον πρὸς αὐτὸν
He told me all things whatever I did. as Then came to Him

3588 4541 2065 846 3306 3844 846 2532 3306
οἱ Σαμαρεῖται, ἠρώτων αὐτὸν μεῖναι παρ' αὐτοῖς· καὶ ἔμεινεν
the Samaritans, they asked Him to stay with them. And He stayed

1563 1417 2250 2532 4183 4119 4100 1223 3588
ἐκεῖ δύο ἡμέρας. 41 καὶ πολλῷ πλείους ἐπίστευσαν διὰ τὸν
there two days. And many more believed through the

3056 846 3588 5037 1135 3004 3754 3765 1223 3588 4674
λόγον αὐτοῦ, 42 τῇ τε γυναικὶ ἔλεγον ὅτι Οὐκέτι διὰ τὴν σὴν
Word of Him. to the And woman they said, No longer because of your

.2981 4100 846 1063 191 2532 1492 3754
λαλιὰν πιστεύομεν· αὐτοὶ γὰρ ἀκηκόαμεν, καὶ οἴδαμεν ὅτι
speaking we believe; (our)selves for we have heard, and we know that

3778 2076 230 3588 4990 3588 2889 3588 5547
οὗτός ἐστιν ἀληθῶς ὁ Σωτὴρ τοῦ κόσμου, ὁ Χριστός.
this One is truly the Savior of the world, the Christ.

3326 1161 3588 1417 2250 1831 1564 2532 565
43. Μετὰ δὲ τὰς δύο ἡμέρας ἐξῆλθεν ἐκεῖθεν, καὶ ἀπῆλθεν
after And the two days, He went our from there, and went

1519 3588 1056 846 1063 3588 2424 3140 3754
εἰς τὴν Γαλιλαίαν. 44 αὐτὸς γὰρ ὁ Ἰησοῦς ἐμαρτύρησεν ὅτι
into Galilee. (Him)self For Jesus testified that

4396 1722 3588 2398 3968 5092 3756 2192 3753 3767 2064
προφήτης ἐν τῇ ἰδίᾳ πατρίδι τιμὴν οὐκ ἔχει. 45 ὅτε οὖν ἦλθεν
a prophet in the own native-place honor not has. When, then, He came

will of him that sent me, and to finish his work.
35 Say not ye, There are yet four months, and (then) cometh harvest? behold, I say unto you, Lift up your eyes, and look on the fields; for they are white already to harvest.
36 And he that reapeth receiveth wages, and gathereth fruit unto life eternal: that both he that soweth and he that reapeth may rejoice together.
37 And herein is that saying true, One soweth, and another reapeth.
38 I sent you to reap that whereon ye bestowed no labour: other men laboured, and ye are entered into their labours.

39. And many of the Samaritans of that city believed on him for the saying of the woman, which testified, He told me all that ever I did.
40 So when the Samaritans were come unto him, they besought him that he would tarry with them: and he abode there two days.
41 And many more believed because of his own word;
42 And said unto the woman, Now we believe, not because of thy saying: for we have heard (him) ourselves, and know that this is indeed the Christ, the Saviour of the world.

43. Now after two days he departed thence, and went into Galilee.
44 For Jesus himself testified, that a prophet hath no honour in his own country.
45 Then when he was come

John 4:46

Literal Translation

into Galilee, the Galileans received Him, seeing all things which He did in Jerusalem at the Feast. For they also went to the Feast.

46. Then Jesus came again to Cana of Galilee where He made the water wine. And there was a certain nobleman whose son was sick in Capernaum.
47 Hearing that Jesus (was) coming from Judea into Galilee, this one went out to Him and asked Him that He would come and heal his son, for he was about to die.

48 Then Jesus said to him, Unless you see signs and wonders, you will not at all believe.
49 The nobleman said to Him, Sir, come down before my child dies.

50 Jesus said to him, Go! Your son lives. And the man believed the word which Jesus said to him, and went away.

51 But already, as he was going down, his slaves met him and reported, saying, Your child lives.

52 He then asked from them the hour in which he had gotten better. And they said to him, Yesterday, (at the) seventh hour, the fever left him.
53 Then the father knew that (it was) at that hour in which Jesus said to him, Your son lives. And he himself, and his whole household, believed.
54 Again, this second sign Jesus did, coming from Judea

1519 3588 1056 1209 846 3588 1057 3956
εἰς τὴν Γαλιλαίαν, ἐδέξαντο αὐτὸν οἱ Γαλιλαῖοι, πάντα
into Galilee, received Him the Galileans, all things

3708 3739 4160 1722 2414 1722 3588 1859 2532 846
ἑωρακότες ἃ ἐποίησεν ἐν Ἱεροσολύμοις ἐν τῇ ἑορτῇ. καὶ αὐτοὶ
having seen which He did in Jerusalem at the feast. also they

1063 2064 1519 3588 1859
γὰρ ἦλθον εἰς τὴν ἑορτήν.
For went to the feast.

2064 3767 3588 2424 3825 1519 3588 2580 3588 1056
46. Ἦλθεν οὖν ὁ Ἰησοῦς πάλιν εἰς τὴν Κανὰ τῆς Γαλιλαίας,
came Then Jesus again into Cana of Galilee,

3699 4160 3588 5204 3631 2532 2258 5100 937 3739 3588 5207
ὅπου ἐποίησε τὸ ὕδωρ οἶνον. καὶ ἦν τις βασιλικός, οὗ ὁ υἱὸς
where He made the water wine. And was one noble of whom the son

770 1722 2584 3778 191 3754 2424 240 1537
ἠσθένει ἐν Καπερναούμ. 47 οὗτος ἀκούσας ὅτι Ἰησοῦς ἥκει ἐκ
was ill in Capernaum. This one hearing that Jesus comes from

3588 2449 1519 3588 1056 565 4314 846 2532
τῆς Ἰουδαίας εἰς τὴν Γαλιλαίαν, ἀπῆλθε πρὸς αὐτόν, καὶ
Judea into Galilee went out to Him, and

2065 846 2443 2597 2532 2390 846 3588 5207
ἠρώτα αὐτὸν ἵνα καταβῇ καὶ ἰάσηται αὐτοῦ τὸν υἱόν·
asked Him that He would come and heal of him the son;

3195 1063 599 2036 3767 3588 2424 4314 846
ἤμελλε γὰρ ἀποθνήσκειν. 48 εἶπεν οὖν ὁ Ἰησοῦς πρὸς αὐτόν,
he was for about to die. said Then Jesus to him,

1437 3361 4592 2532 5059 1492 3756 3361 4100 3004
Ἐὰν μὴ σημεῖα καὶ τέρατα ἴδητε, οὐ μὴ πιστεύσητε. 49 λέγει
If not signs and wonders you see, not at all will you believe. says

4314 846 3588 937 2962 2597 4250 599
πρὸς αὐτὸν ὁ βασιλικός, Κύριε, κατάβηθι πρὶν ἀποθανεῖν
to him The noble, Lord, come down before dies

3588 3813 3450 3004 846 3588 2424 4198 3588 5207 4675
τὸ παιδίον μου. 50 λέγει αὐτῷ ὁ Ἰησοῦς, Πορεύου· ὁ υἱός σου
the child of me. says to him Jesus, Go, the son of you

2198 2532 4100 3588 444 3588 3056 3739 2036 846
ζῇ. καὶ ἐπίστευσεν ὁ ἄνθρωπος τῷ λόγῳ ᾧ εἶπεν αὐτῷ
lives. And believed the man the word which said to him

2424 2532 4198 2235 1161 846 2597 3588
Ἰησοῦς, καὶ ἐπορεύετο. 51 ἤδη δὲ αὐτοῦ καταβαίνοντος, οἱ
Jesus, and went away. already And (as) he was going down, the

1401 846 528 846 2532 518 3004
δοῦλοι αὐτοῦ ἀπήντησαν αὐτῷ, καὶ ἀπήγγειλαν λέγοντες
slaves of him met him, and reported, saying,

3754 3588 3816 4675 2198 4441 3767 3844 846 3588 5610 1722
ὅτι Ὁ παῖς σου ζῇ. 52 ἐπύθετο οὖν παρ' αὐτῶν τὴν ὥραν ἐν
The child of you lives. he asked Then from them the hour in

3739 2866 2192 2532 2036 846 3754 5504 5610 1442
ᾗ κομψότερον ἔσχε· καὶ εἶπον αὐτῷ ὅτι Χθὲς ὥραν ἑβδόμην
which become better he had. And they said to him, Yesterday (at) hour seventh

863 846 3588 4446 1097 3767 3588 3962 3754 1722 1565 3588
ἀφῆκεν αὐτὸν ὁ πυρετός. 53 ἔγνω οὖν ὁ πατὴρ ὅτι ἐν ἐκείνῃ τῇ
left him the fever. knew Then the father that in that

5610 1722 3739 2036 846 3588 2424 3754 3588 5207 4675 2198 2532
ὥρᾳ, ἐν ᾗ εἶπεν αὐτῷ ὁ Ἰησοῦς ὅτι Ὁ υἱός σου ζῇ· καὶ
hour in which said to him Jesus, The son of you lives, and

4100 846 2532 3588 3614 846 3650 5124 3825
ἐπίστευσεν αὐτὸς καὶ ἡ οἰκία αὐτοῦ ὅλη. 54 τοῦτο πάλιν
he believed, himself and the house of him whole. This again

1208 4592 4160 3588 2424 2064 1537 3588 2449
δεύτερον σημεῖον ἐποίησεν ὁ Ἰησοῦς ἐλθὼν ἐκ τῆς Ἰουδαίας
a second sign did Jesus, coming from Judea

King James Version

into Galilee, the Galilaeans received him, having seen all the things that he did at Jerusalem at the feast: for they also went unto the feast.

46. So Jesus came again into Cana of Galilee, where he made the water wine. And there was a certain nobleman, whose son was sick at Capernaum.
47 When he heard that Jesus was come out of Judaea into Galilee, he went unto him, and besought him that he would come down, and heal his son: for he was at the point of death.

48 Then said Jesus unto him, Except ye see signs and wonders, ye will not believe.
49 The nobleman saith unto him, Sir, come down ere my child die.

50 Jesus saith unto him, Go thy way; thy son liveth. And the man believed the word that Jesus had spoken unto him, and he went his way.
51 And as he was now going down, his servants met him, and told (him), saying, Thy son liveth.

52 Then enquired he of them the hour when he began to amend. And they said unto him, Yesterday at the seventh hour the fever left him.

53 So the father knew that (it was) at the same hour, in the which Jesus said unto him, Thy son liveth: and himself believed, and his whole house.
54 This (is) again the second miracle (that) Jesus did, when he was come out of Judaea

Literal Translation

into Galilee.

John 5:1

1519 3588 1056
εἰς τὴν Γαλιλαίαν.
into Galilee.

King James Version

into Galilee.

John 5

1. After these things, there was a feast of the Jews, and Jesus went up to Jerusalem.

2 And at Jerusalem is a pool at the Sheep Gate which (is) called in Hebrew, Bethesda, having five porches.

3 In these was a great multitude of the infirm lying, blind (ones), lame (ones), withered (ones), awaiting the stirring of the water.

4 For an angel from time to time descended in the pool and agitated the water. Then the (one) first entering after the agitation of the water became well, whatever disease he was held by.

5. But a certain man was there, being in infirmity thirty-eight years.

6 Seeing him lying, and knowing that he had already (spent) much time, Jesus said to him, Do you desire to become whole?

7 The infirm one answered Him, Lord, I do not have a man, that when the water is agitated he may throw me into the pool; but while I am coming, another goes down before me.

8 Jesus said to him, Rise up, Take up your cot and walk!

9 And instantly the man became whole, and took up his cot and walked. And it was a sabbath that day.

10. Then the

John 5

3326 5023 2258 1859 3588 2453 2532 305 3588
1 Μετὰ ταῦτα ἦν ἑορτὴ τῶν Ἰουδαίων, καὶ ἀνέβη ὁ
After these things was a feast of the Jews, and went up
2424 1519 2414
Ἰησοῦς εἰς Ἱεροσόλυμα.
Jesus into Jerusalem.

2076 1161 1722 3588 2414 1909 3588 4262 2861
2 Ἔστι δὲ ἐν τοῖς Ἱεροσολύμοις ἐπὶ τῇ προβατικῇ κολυμ-
is And in Jerusalem at the Sheep Gate a pool
3588 1951 1447 964 4002 4745
βήθρα ἡ ἐπιλεγομένη Ἑβραϊστὶ Βηθεσδά, πέντε στοὰς
which is being called in Hebrew Bethesda, five porches
2192 1722 5015 2621 4128 4183 3588 770
ἔχουσα. 3 ἐν ταύταις κατέκειτο πλῆθος πολὺ τῶν ἀσθενούν-
having. In these were lying a multitude great of the infirm,
5185 5560 3584 1551 3588 3588 5204
των, τυφλῶν, χωλῶν, ξηρῶν, ἐκδεχομένων τὴν τοῦ ὕδατος
blind, lame, withered (ones), awaiting the of the water
2796 32 1063 2596 2540 2597 1722 3588
κίνησιν. 4 ἄγγελος γὰρ κατὰ καιρὸν κατέβαινεν ἐν τῇ
stirring. an angel For at a time descended in the
2861 2532 5015 3588 5204 3588 3767 4413 1684
κολυμβήθρᾳ, καὶ ἐτάρασσε τὸ ὕδωρ· ὁ οὖν πρῶτος ἐμβὰς
pool, and agitated the water. he Then first entering
3326 3588 5016 3588 5204 5199 1096 3739 1221
μετὰ τὴν ταραχὴν τοῦ ὕδατος, ὑγιὴς ἐγίνετο, ᾧ δήποτε
after the agitation of the water whole became to whatever
2722 3553 2258 1161 5100 444 1563 5144 2532
κατείχετο νοσήματι. 5 ἦν δέ τις ἄνθρωπος ἐκεῖ τριάκοντα καὶ
he was held by disease. was But a certain man there thirty and
3638 2094 2192 1722 3588 769 5126 1492 3588 2424
ὀκτὼ ἔτη ἔχων ἐν τῇ ἀσθενείᾳ. 6 τοῦτον ἰδὼν ὁ Ἰησοῦς
eight years being in infirmity. this one seeing Jesus
2621 2532 1097 3754 4183 2235 5550 2192 3004
κατακείμενον, καὶ γνοὺς ὅτι πολὺν ἤδη χρόνον ἔχει, λέγει
lying (there), and knowing that much already time he has, says
846 2309 5199 1096 611 846 3588 770
αὐτῷ, Θέλεις ὑγιὴς γενέσθαι; 7 ἀπεκρίθη αὐτῷ ὁ ἀσθενῶν,
to him, Desire you whole to become? answered him The infirm one,
2962 444 3756 2192 2443 3752 5015 3588 5204
Κύριε, ἄνθρωπον οὐκ ἔχω ἵνα ὅταν ταραχθῇ τὸ ὕδωρ
Lord, a man not I have that when is agitated the water
906 3165 1519 3588 2861 1722 3739 1161 2064 1473 243
βάλλῃ με εἰς τὴν κολυμβήθραν· ἐν ᾧ δὲ ἔρχομαι ἐγώ, ἄλλος
he throw me into the pool; while but am coming I, another
4253 1700 2597 3004 846 3588 2424 1453 142
πρὸ ἐμοῦ καταβαίνει. 8 λέγει αὐτῷ ὁ Ἰησοῦς, Ἔγειραι, ἆρον
before me goes down. says to him Jesus, Rise up! Take up
3588 2895 4675 2532 4043 2532 2112 1096 5199
τὸν κράββατόν σου, καὶ περιπάτει. 9 καὶ εὐθέως ἐγένετο ὑγιὴς
the mattress of you, and walk. And instantly became whole
3588 444 2532 142 3588 2895 846 2532 4043
ὁ ἄνθρωπος, καὶ ἦρε τὸν κράββατον αὐτοῦ καὶ περιεπάτει.
the man, and took up the mattress of him and walked.
2258 1161 4521 1722 1565 3588 2250 3004 3767 3588
10 Ἦν δὲ σάββατον ἐν ἐκείνῃ τῇ ἡμέρᾳ. ἔλεγον οὖν οἱ
it was And a sabbath on that day. said Then the

John 5

1. After this there was a feast of the Jews; and Jesus went up to Jerusalem.

2 Now there is at Jerusalem by the sheep (market) a pool, which is called in the Hebrew tongue Bethesda, having five porches.

3 In these lay a great multitude of impotent folk, of blind, halt, withered, waiting for the moving of the water.

4 For an angel went down at a certain season into the pool, and troubled the water: whosoever then first after the troubling of the water stepped in was made whole of whatsoever disease he had.

5. And a certain man was there, which had an infirmity thirty and eight years.

6 When Jesus saw him lie, and knew that he had been now a long time (in that case), he saith unto him, Wilt thou be made whole?

7 The impotent man answered him, Sir, I have no man, when the water is troubled, to put me into the pool: but while I am coming, another steppeth down before me.

8 Jesus saith unto him, Rise, take up thy bed, and walk.

9 And immediately the man was made whole, and took up his bed, and walked: and on the same day was the sabbath.

10. Therefore the Jews said unto him that was cured, It is the sabbath day:

John 5:11

Literal Translation

Jews said to the (one) having been healed, It is a sabbath; it is not lawful for you to take up the cot.
11 He answered them, The (One) making me whole, that One said to me, Take up your cot and walk.

12 Then they asked him, Who is the man who told you, Take up your cot and walk?
13 But the (one) healed did not know who it is, for a crowd being in the place, Jesus had withdrawn.

14. After these things, Jesus finds him in the temple and said to him, Behold, you have become whole, sin no more that a worse thing not happen to you.
15 The man went away and told the Jews that Jesus is the (One) making him whole.

16 And because of this, the Jews persecuted Jesus, and sought to kill Him, because He did these things on a sabbath.

17. But Jesus answered them, My Father works until now, and I work.
18 Because of this, therefore, the Jews sought the more to kill Him, for not only did He break the sabbath, but also called God (His) own Father, making Himself equal to God.

19. Then Jesus answered and said to them, Truly, truly, I say to you, the Son is not able to do (anything) from Himself, nothing; except what He may see the Father doing; for whatever that One does, these things also the Son does the same way.
20 For the Father loves the Son

2453 3588 2323 4521 2076 3756 1832
Ἰουδαῖοι τῷ τεθεραπευμένῳ, Σάββατόν ἐστιν· οὐκ ἔξεστί
Jews to the (one) having been healed, A sabbath it is; not it is lawful

4671 142 3588 2895 611 846 3588 4160 3165
σοι ἆραι τὸν κράββατον. 11 ἀπεκρίθη αὐτοῖς, Ὁ ποιήσας με
for you to take up the mattress. He answered them, The (One) making me

5199 1565 3427 2036 142 3588 2895 4675 2532
ὑγιῆ, ἐκεῖνός μοι εἶπεν, Ἆρον τὸν κράββατόν σου καὶ
whole, that One to me said, Take up the mattress of you, and

4043 2065 3767 846 5101 2076 3588 444 3588
περιπάτει. 12 ἠρώτησαν οὖν αὐτόν, Τίς ἐστιν ὁ ἄνθρωπος ὁ
walk. they asked Then him, Who is the man who

2036 4671 142 3588 2895 4675 2532 4043 3588 1161
εἰπών σοι, Ἆρον τὸν κράββατόν σου καὶ περιπάτει; 13 ὁ δὲ
told you, Take up the mattress of you and walk? the (one) But

2390 3756 1492 5101 2076 3588 1063 2424 1593 3793
ἰαθεὶς οὐκ ᾔδει τίς ἐστιν· ὁ γὰρ Ἰησοῦς ἐξένευσεν, ὄχλου
healed not did know who it is. For Jesus had withdrawn, a crowd

5607 1722 3588 5117 3326 5023 2147 846 3588 2424
ὄντος ἐν τῷ τόπῳ. 14 μετὰ ταῦτα εὑρίσκει αὐτὸν ὁ Ἰησοῦς
being in the place. After these things finds him Jesus

1722 3588 2411 2532 2036 846 2396 5199 1096 3371
ἐν τῷ ἱερῷ, καὶ εἶπεν αὐτῷ, Ἴδε ὑγιὴς γέγονας· μηκέτι
in the temple, and said to him, Behold! whole you have become; no more

264 2443 3361 5501 5100 4671 1096 565 3588 444
ἁμάρτανε, ἵνα μὴ χεῖρόν τί σοι γένηται. 15 ἀπῆλθεν ὁ ἄνθρω-
sin, that not a worse thing to you occur. went away The man

2532 312 3588 2453 3754 2424 2076 3588 4160
πος, καὶ ἀνήγγειλε τοῖς Ἰουδαίοις ὅτι Ἰησοῦς ἐστιν ὁ ποιή-
and reported to the Jews that Jesus is He making

846 5199 2532 1223 5124 1377 3588 2424 3588
σας αὐτὸν ὑγιῆ. 16 καὶ διὰ τοῦτο ἐδίωκον τὸν Ἰησοῦν οἱ
him whole. And because of this persecuted Jesus the

2453 2532 2212 846 615 3754 5023 4160
Ἰουδαῖοι, καὶ ἐζήτουν αὐτὸν ἀποκτεῖναι, ὅτι ταῦτα ἐποίει
Jews, and sought Him to kill, because these things He did

1722 4521 3588 1161 2424 611 846 3588 3962 3450
ἐν σαββάτῳ. 17 ὁ δὲ Ἰησοῦς ἀπεκρίνατο αὐτοῖς, Ὁ πατήρ μου
on a sabbath. But Jesus answered to them, The Father of Me

2193 737 2038 2504 2038 1223 5124 3767 3123
ἕως ἄρτι ἐργάζεται, κἀγὼ ἐργάζομαι. 18 διὰ τοῦτο οὖν μᾶλλον
until now works, and I work. Because of this, then, the more

2212 846 3588 2453 615 3754 3756 3440 3089 3588
ἐζήτουν αὐτὸν οἱ Ἰουδαῖοι ἀποκτεῖναι, ὅτι οὐ μόνον ἔλυε τὸ
sought Him the Jews to kill, because not only He broke the

4521 235 2532 3962 2398 3004 3588 2316 2470
σάββατον, ἀλλὰ καὶ πατέρα ἴδιον ἔλεγε τὸν Θεόν, ἴσον
sabbath, but also Father the own called God, equal

1438 4160 3588 2316
ἑαυτὸν ποιῶν τῷ Θεῷ.
Himself making to God.

611 3767 3588 2424 2532 2036 846 281 281
19. Ἀπεκρίνατο οὖν ὁ Ἰησοῦς καὶ εἶπεν αὐτοῖς, Ἀμὴν ἀμὴν
answered Then Jesus and said to them, Truly, truly,

3004 5213 3756 1410 3588 5207 4160 575 1438 3762 1437
λέγω ὑμῖν, οὐ δύναται ὁ υἱὸς ποιεῖν ἀφ' ἑαυτοῦ οὐδέν, ἐὰν
I say to you, not is able the Son to do from Himself nothing, ex-

3361 5100 991 3588 3962 4160 3739 1063 302 1565 4160
μή τι βλέπῃ τὸν πατέρα ποιοῦντα· ἃ γὰρ ἂν ἐκεῖνος ποιῇ,
cept what He may see the Father doing. what For ever that One does,

5023 2532 3588 5207 3668 4160 3588 1063 3962 5368 3588 5207
ταῦτα καὶ ὁ υἱὸς ὁμοίως ποιεῖ. 20 ὁ γὰρ πατὴρ φιλεῖ τὸν υἱόν,
these things also the Son likewise does. the For Father loves the Son,

---

King James Version

it is not lawful for thee to carry (thy) bed.
11 He answered them, He that made me whole, the same said unto me, Take up thy bed, and walk.

12 Then asked they him, What man is that which said unto thee, Take up thy bed, and walk?
13 And he that was healed wist not who it was: for Jesus had conveyed himself away, a multitude being in (that) place.
14. Afterward Jesus findeth him in the temple, and said unto him, Behold, thou art made whole: sin no more, lest a worse thing come unto thee.
15 The man departed, and told the Jews that it was Jesus, which had made him whole.

16 And therefore did the Jews persecute Jesus, and sought to slay him, because he had done these things on the sabbath day.

17. But Jesus answered them, My Father worketh hitherto, and I work.
18 Therefore the Jews sought the more to kill him, because he not only had broken the sabbath, but said also that God was his Father, making himself equal with God.

19. Then answered Jesus and said unto them, Verily, verily, I say unto you, The Son can do nothing of himself, but what he seeth the Father do: for what things soever he doeth, these also doeth the Son likewise.
20 For the Father loveth the Son,

Literal Translation

John 5:21

King James Version

and shows to Him all things which He does. And He will show Him greater works (than) these in order that you may marvel.
21 For even as the Father raises the dead, and gives life, so also the Son makes alive whomever He wills.
22 For the Father judges no one, but has given all judgment to the Son,
23 so that all may honor the Son, even as they honor the Father. The (one) not honoring the Son does not honor the Father who has sent Him.
24 Truly, truly, I say to you, the (one) who hears My word, and believing the (One) having sent Me, has everlasting life, and does not come into judgment, but has passed out of death into life.
25 Truly, truly, I say to you that an hour comes, and now is when the dead will hear the voice of the Son of God, and the (ones) hearing will live.
26 For even as the Father has life in Himself, so He gave also to the Son to have life in Himself.
27 And He also gave authority to Him to execute judgment, for He is (the) Son of man.
28 Do not marvel (at) this, for an hour comes in which all the (ones) in the tombs will hear His voice.
29 And (they) will come out, the ones having done good into a resurrection of life; and the ones having practiced evil into a resurrection of judgment.
30 Not I am able to do (anything) from Myself, nothing; even as I hear, I judge; and My judgment is just, for I do not seek

2532 3956 1166 846 3739 846 4160 2532 3187 5130
καὶ πάντα δείκνυσιν αὐτῷ ἃ αὐτὸς ποιεῖ· καὶ μείζονα τούτων
and all things shows to Him which He does; and greater (than) these

1166 846 2041 2443 5210 2296 5618 1063 3588 3962
δείξει αὐτῷ ἔργα, ἵνα ὑμεῖς θαυμάζητε. 21 ὥσπερ γὰρ ὁ πατὴρ
He will show Him works, that you may marvel. even as For the Father

1453 3588 3498 2532 2227 3779 2532 3588 5207 3739 2309
ἐγείρει τοὺς νεκροὺς καὶ ζῳοποιεῖ, οὕτω καὶ ὁ υἱὸς οὓς θέλει
raises up the dead and makes alive, so also the Son whom He wills

2227 3761 1063 3588 3962 2919 3762 235 3588 2920
ζῳοποιεῖ. 22 οὐδὲ γὰρ ὁ πατὴρ κρίνει οὐδένα, ἀλλὰ τὴν κρίσιν
He makes alive. not For the Father judges, no one. But judgment

3956 1325 3588 5207 2443 3956 5091 3588 5207 2531
πᾶσαν δέδωκε τῷ υἱῷ· 23 ἵνα πάντες τιμῶσι τὸν υἱόν καθὼς
all He has given to the Son, that all may honor the Son even as

5091 3588 3962 3588 3361 5091 3588 5207 3756 5091 3588
τιμῶσι τὸν πατέρα. ὁ μὴ τιμῶν τὸν υἱόν, οὐ τιμᾷ τὸν
they honor the Father. The (one) not honoring the Son not honors the

3962 3588 3992 846 281 281 3004 5213 3754 3588
πατέρα τὸν πέμψαντα αὐτόν. 24 ἀμὴν ἀμὴν λέγω ὑμῖν ὅτι ὁ
Father, the (One) having sent Him. Truly, truly, I say to you, the (one)

3588 3056 3450 191 2532 4100 3588 3992 3165 2192
τὸν λόγον μου ἀκούων, καὶ πιστεύων τῷ πέμψαντί με, ἔχει
the Word of me hearing, and believing the (One) having sent Me, has

2222 166 2532 1519 2920 3756 2064 235 3327
ζωὴν αἰώνιον· καὶ εἰς κρίσιν οὐκ ἔρχεται, ἀλλὰ μεταβέβηκεν
life everlasting; and into judgment not comes, but has passed

1537 3588 2288 1519 3588 2222 281 281 3004 5213 3754 2064
ἐκ τοῦ θανάτου εἰς τὴν ζωήν. 25 ἀμὴν ἀμὴν λέγω ὑμῖν ὅτι ἔρχε-
out of death into life. Truly truly I say to you, comes

5610 2532 3568 2076 3753 3588 3498 191 3588 5456
ται ὥρα καὶ νῦν ἐστιν, ὅτε οἱ νεκροὶ ἀκούσονται τῆς φωνῆς
An hour and now is, when the dead will hear the voice

3588 5207 3588 2316 2532 3588 191 2198 5618 1063 3588
τοῦ υἱοῦ τοῦ Θεοῦ, καὶ οἱ ἀκούσαντες ζησονται. 26 ὥσπερ γὰρ ὁ
of the Son of God, and the (ones) hearing will live. even as For the

3962 2192 2222 1722 1438 3779 1325 2532 3588 5207 2222
πατὴρ ἔχει ζωὴν ἐν ἑαυτῷ, οὕτως ἔδωκε καὶ τῷ υἱῷ ζωὴν
Father has life in Himself, so He gave also to the Son life

2192 1722 1438 2532 1849 1325 846 2532 2920 4160
ἔχειν ἐν ἑαυτῷ. 27 καὶ ἐξουσίαν ἔδωκεν αὐτῷ καὶ κρίσιν ποιεῖν,
to have in Himself. And authority He gave to Him also judgment to do,

3754 5207 444 2076 3361 2296 5124 3754 2064
ὅτι υἱὸς ἀνθρώπου ἐστί. 28 μὴ θαυμάζετε τοῦτο· ὅτι ἔρχεται
because Son of man He is. not Marvel (at) this; because comes

5610 1722 3739 3956 3588 1722 3588 3419 191 3588 5456
ὥρα, ἐν ᾗ πάντες οἱ ἐν τοῖς μνημείοις ἀκούσονται τῆς φωνῆς
an hour in which all the (ones) in the tombs will hear the voice

846 2532 1607 3588 3588 18 4160 1519 386
αὐτοῦ, 29 καὶ ἐκπορεύσονται, οἱ τὰ ἀγαθὰ ποιήσαντες, εἰς ἀνά-
of Him, and will come out, those the good having done, into a resur-

2222 3588 1161 3588 5337 4238 1519 386 2920
στασιν ζωῆς. οἱ δὲ τὰ φαῦλα πράξαντες, εἰς ἀνάστασιν κρίσεως.
rection of life; those And the evil having done, into a resurrection of judgment.

3756 1410 1473 4160 575 1683 3762 2531 191
30 Οὐ δύναμαι ἐγὼ ποιεῖν ἀπ' ἐμαυτοῦ οὐδέν· καθὼς ἀκούω,
Not am able I to do from Myself nothing! Even as I hear,

2919 2532 3588 2920 3588 1699 1342 2076 3754 3756 2212 3588
κρίνω· καὶ ἡ κρίσις ἡ ἐμὴ δικαία ἐστίν· ὅτι οὐ ζητῶ τὸ
I judge; and the judgment of Me just is; because not I seek the

and sheweth him all things that himself doeth: and he will shew him greater works than these, that ye may marvel.
21 For as the Father raiseth up the dead, and quickeneth (them); even so the Son quickeneth whom he will.
22 For the Father judgeth no man, but hath committed all judgment unto the Son:
23 That all (men) should honour the Son, even as they honour the Father. He that honoureth not the Son honoureth not the Father which hath sent him.
24 Verily, verily, I say unto you, He that heareth my word, and believeth on him that sent me, hath everlasting life, and shall not come into condemnation; but is passed from death unto life.
25 Verily, verily, I say unto you, The hour is coming, and now is, when the dead shall hear the voice of the Son of God: and they that hear shall live.
26 For as the Father hath life in himself; so hath he given to the Son to have life in himself;
27 And hath given him authority to execute judgment also, because he is the Son of man.
28 Marvel not at this: for the hour is coming, in the which all that are in the graves shall hear his voice,
29 And shall come forth; they that have done good, unto the resurrection of life; and they that have done evil, unto the resurrection of damnation.
30 I can of mine own self do nothing: as I hear, I judge: and my judgment is just; because I seek

Literal Translation

My will, but the will of the (One) sending Me, (the) Father.

31 If I witness concerning Myself, My witness is not true;
32 it is Another witnessing concerning Me, and I know that the witness which He witnesses concerning Me is true.
33 You have sent to John, and he has testified to the truth.

34 But I do not receive witness from man, but I say these things that you may be saved.
35 That one was the burning and shining lamp, and you were willing to exult in his light for an hour.

36 But I have the greater witness than John's, for the works which the Father has given Me, that I should finish them, the works which I do themselves witness concerning Me, that the Father has sent Me.

37 And the Father, He sending Me, has Himself witnessed concerning Me. You have neither heard His voice at any time, nor have you seen His form.
38 And you do not have His Word abiding in you, for (the One) whom that One sent, this One you do not believe.

39. You search the Scriptures, because you think in them you have everlasting life. And they are the ones witnessing concerning Me.
40 And you do not desire to come to Me that you may have life.
41 I do not receive glory from men;
42 but I have known you, that you do not have the love of God in yourselves.
43 I have come in the name of My Father, and you do not receive Me.

John 5:31

2307 3588 1699 235 3588 2307 3588 3992 3165 3962
θέλημα τὸ ἐμὸν, ἀλλὰ τὸ θέλημα τοῦ πέμψαντός με πατρός.
will of Me, but the will of the (One) sending Me, (the) Father.

1437 1473 3140 4012 1683 3588 3141 3450 3756 2076
31 ἐὰν ἐγὼ μαρτυρῶ περὶ ἐμαυτοῦ, ἡ μαρτυρία μου οὐκ ἔστιν
if I witness concerning Myself, the witness of Me not is

227 243 2076 3588 3140 4012 1700 2532 1492 3754
ἀληθής. 32 ἄλλος ἐστὶν ὁ μαρτυρῶν περὶ ἐμοῦ, καὶ οἶδα ὅτι
true. another There is witnessing concerning Me, and I know that

227 2076 3588 3141 3739 3140 4012 1700 5210
ἀληθής ἐστιν ἡ μαρτυρία ἣν μαρτυρεῖ περὶ ἐμοῦ. 33 ὑμεῖς
true is the witness which He witnesses concerning Me. You

649 4314 2491 2532 3140 3588 225
ἀπεστάλκατε πρὸς Ἰωάννην, καὶ μεμαρτύρηκε τῇ ἀληθείᾳ.
have sent to John, and he has witnessed to the truth.

1473 1161 3756 3844 444 3588 3141 2983 235
34 ἐγὼ δὲ οὐ παρὰ ἀνθρώπου τὴν μαρτυρίαν λαμβάνω, ἀλλὰ
I But not from man the witness receive, but

5023 3004 2443 5210 4982 1565 2258 3588 3088 3588 2545
ταῦτα λέγω ἵνα ὑμεῖς σωθῆτε. 35 ἐκεῖνος ἦν ὁ λύχνος ὁ καιό-
these things I say that you may be saved. That one was the lamp burning

2532 5316 5210 1161 2309 21 4314
μενος καὶ φαίνων, ὑμεῖς δὲ ἠθελήσατε ἀγαλλιασθῆναι πρὸς
and shining, you and were willing to exult for

5610 1722 3588 5457 846 1473 1161 2192 3588 3141 3187
ὥραν ἐν τῷ φωτὶ αὐτοῦ. 36 ἐγὼ δὲ ἔχω τὴν μαρτυρίαν μείζω
an hour in the light of him. I But have the witness greater

3588 2491 3588 1063 2041 3739 1325 3427 3588 3962 2443
τοῦ Ἰωάννου· τὰ γὰρ ἔργα ἃ ἔδωκέ μοι ὁ πατὴρ ἵνα
than of John; the for works which has given Me the Father, that

5048 846 846 3588 2041 3739 1473 4160 3140 4012
τελειώσω αὐτά, αὐτὰ τὰ ἔργα ἃ ἐγὼ ποιῶ, μαρτυρεῖ περὶ
I may finish them, themselves the works that I do witness concerning

1700 3754 3588 3962 3165 649 2532 3588 3992 3165 3962
ἐμοῦ ὅτι ὁ πατήρ με ἀπέσταλκε. 37 καὶ ὁ πέμψας με πατήρ,
Me, that the Father Me has sent. And He sending Me (the) Father,

846 3140 4012 1700 3777 456 846 191
αὐτὸς μεμαρτύρηκε περὶ ἐμοῦ. οὔτε φωνὴν αὐτοῦ ἀκηκόατε
He has witnessed concerning Me. Neither (the) voice of Him have you heard

4455 3777 1491 846 3708 2532 3588 3056 846
πώποτε, οὔτε εἶδος αὐτοῦ ἑωράκατε. 38 καὶ τὸν λόγον αὐτοῦ
at any time, nor form His have you seen. And the Word of Him

3756 2192 3306 1722 5213 3754 3739 649 1565 5129
οὐκ ἔχετε μένοντα ἐν ὑμῖν, ὅτι ὃν ἀπέστειλεν ἐκεῖνος, τούτῳ
not you have abiding in you, for whom sent that (One), this (One)

5210 3756 4100 2045 3588 1124 3754 5210 1380
ὑμεῖς οὐ πιστεύετε. 39 ἐρευνᾶτε τὰς γραφάς, ὅτι ὑμεῖς δοκεῖτε
you not do believe. You search the Scriptures, because you think

1722 846 2222 166 2192 2532 1565 1526 3588 3140
ἐν αὐταῖς ζωὴν αἰώνιον ἔχειν, καὶ ἐκεῖναί εἰσιν αἱ μαρτυ-
in them life everlasting you have, and those are the (ones) wit-

4012 1700 2532 3756 2309 2064 4314 3165 2443 2222
ροῦσαι περὶ ἐμοῦ· 40 καὶ οὐ θέλετε ἐλθεῖν πρός με, ἵνα ζωὴν
nessing about Me. And not you desire to come to. Me, that life

2192 1391 3844 444 3756 2983 235 1097
ἔχητε. 41 δόξαν παρὰ ἀνθρώπων οὐ λαμβάνω· 42 ἀλλ' ἔγνωκα
you may have. glory from men not I receive; but I have known

5209 3754 3588 26 3588 2316 3756 2192 1722 1438
ὑμᾶς, ὅτι τὴν ἀγάπην τοῦ Θεοῦ οὐκ ἔχετε ἐν ἑαυτοῖς.
you, that the love of God not you have in yourselves.

1473 2064 1722 3588 3686 3588 3962 3450 2532 3756
43 ἐγὼ ἐλήλυθα ἐν τῷ ὀνόματι τοῦ πατρός μου, καὶ οὐ
I have come in the name of the Father of Me, and not

King James Version

not mine own will, but the will of the Father which hath sent me.

31 If I bear witness of myself, my witness is not true.
32 There is another that beareth witness of me; and I know that the witness which he witnesseth of me is true.
33 Ye sent unto John, and he bare witness unto the truth.

34 But I receive not testimony from man: but these things I say, that ye might be saved.
35 He was a burning and a shining light: and ye were willing for a season to rejoice in his light.

36 But I have greater witness than (that) of John: for the works which the Father hath given me to finish, the same works that I do, bear witness of me, that the Father hath sent me.

37 And the Father himself, which hath sent me, hath borne witness of me. Ye have neither heard his voice at any time, nor seen his shape.

38 And ye have not his word abiding in you: for whom he hath sent, him ye believe not.

39. Search the scriptures; for in them ye think ye have eternal life: and they are they which testify of me.

40 And ye will not come to me, that ye might have life.
41 I receive not honour from men.
42 But I know you, that ye have not the love of God in you.
43 I am come in my Father's name, and ye receive me not:

Literal Translation

If another comes in (his) own name, you will receive that one.
44 How are you able to believe, (you who) receive glory from one another, and the glory which (is) from the only God you do not seek?

45 Do not think that I will accuse you to the Father; there is (one) accusing you, Moses, into whom you have hoped.

46 For if you believed Moses, you would then believe Me; for that one wrote concerning Me.
47 But if you do not believe the writings of that one, how will you believe My words?

John 5:44

2983 3165 1437 243 2064 1722 3588 3686 3588 2398 1565
λαμβάνετέ με· ἐὰν ἄλλος ἔλθῃ ἐν τῷ ὀνόματι τῷ ἰδίῳ, ἐκεῖνον
you receive Me; if another comes in name the own, that one

2983 4459 1410 5210 4100 1391 3844 240
λήψεσθε. 44 πῶς δύνασθε ὑμεῖς πιστεῦσαι, δόξαν παρὰ ἀλλή-
you will receive. How can you believe, glory from one

2983 2532 3588 1391 3588 3844 3588 3441 2316
λων λαμβάνοντες, καὶ τὴν δόξαν τὴν παρὰ τοῦ μόνου Θεοῦ
another receiving, and the glory from the only God

3756 2212 3361 1380 3754 1473 2723 5216 4314 3588
οὐ ζητεῖτε; 45 μὴ δοκεῖτε ὅτι ἐγὼ κατηγορήσω ὑμῶν πρὸς τὸν
not you seek? not Think that I will accuse you to the

3962 2076 3588 2723 5216 3475 1519 3739 5210
πατέρα· ἔστιν ὁ κατηγορῶν ὑμῶν, Μωσῆς, εἰς ὃν ὑμεῖς
Father; there is the (one) accusing you, Moses, into whom you

1679 1487 1063 4100 3475 4100 302 1698
ἠλπίκατε. 46 εἰ γὰρ ἐπιστεύετε Μωσῇ, ἐπιστεύετε ἂν ἐμοί·
have hoped. if For you believed Moses, you would have believed Me;

4012 1063 1700 1565 1125 1487 1161 3588 1565 1121
περὶ γὰρ ἐμοῦ ἐκεῖνος ἔγραψεν. 47 εἰ δὲ τοῖς ἐκείνου γράμμασιν
about For Me that one wrote. if But the of that one writings

3756 4100 4459 3588 1699 4487 4100
οὐ πιστεύετε, πῶς τοῖς ἐμοῖς ῥήμασι πιστεύσετε;
not you believe, how the My words will you believe?

King James Version

if another shall come in his own name, him ye will receive.
44 How can ye believe, which receive honour one of another, and seek not the honour that (cometh) from God only?

45 Do not think that I will accuse you to the Father: there is (one) that accuseth you, (even) Moses, in whom ye trust.
46 For had ye believed Moses, ye would have believed me: for he wrote of me.
47 But if ye believe not his writings, how shall ye believe my words?

John 6

1. After these things, Jesus went away over the Sea of Galilee, the Tiberian (Sea).
2 And a great crowd followed Him, because they saw His signs which He did on the sick ones.

3 And Jesus went up into the mountain and sat there with His disciples.
4 And the Passover was near, the feast of the Jews.
5 Then Jesus lifting up (His) eyes and seeing that a great crowd is coming to Him, He said to Philip, From where may we buy loaves that these may eat?

6 But He said this to test him, for He knew what He was going to do.
7 Philip answered Him, Loaves for two hundred denarii are not enough for them, that each of them may receive a little.

8 One of His disciples said to Him,

John 6

3326 5023 565 3588 2424 4008 3588 2281 3588
1. Μετὰ ταῦτα ἀπῆλθεν ὁ Ἰησοῦς πέραν τῆς θαλάσσης τῆς
After these things went away Jesus across the Sea

1056 3588 5085 2532 190 846 3793 4183
Γαλιλαίας, τῆς Τιβεριάδος. 2 καὶ ἠκολούθει αὐτῷ ὄχλος πολύς,
of Galilee, the (Sea) of Tiberias. And followed Him a crowd great,

3754 3708 846 3588 4592 3739 4160 1909 3588
ὅτι ἑώρων αὐτοῦ τὰ σημεῖα ἃ ἐποίει ἐπὶ τῶν
because they saw of Him the signs which He did on the (ones)

770 424 1161 1519 3588 3735 3588 2424 2532 1563
ἀσθενούντων. 3 ἀνῆλθε δὲ εἰς τὸ ὄρος ὁ Ἰησοῦς, καὶ ἐκεῖ
being sick. went up And into the mountain Jesus, and there

2521 3326 3588 3101 846 2258 1161 1451 3588 3957 3588
ἐκάθητο μετὰ τῶν μαθητῶν αὐτοῦ. 4 ἦν δὲ ἐγγὺς τὸ πάσχα, ἡ
sat with the disciples of Him. was And near the Passover, the

1859 3588 2453 1869 3767 3588 2424 3588 3788
ἑορτὴ τῶν Ἰουδαίων. 5 ἐπάρας οὖν ὁ Ἰησοῦς τοὺς ὀφθαλμούς,
feast of the Jews. lifting up Then Jesus the eyes,

2532 2300 3754 4183 3793 2064 4314 846 3004 4314
καὶ θεασάμενος ὅτι πολὺς ὄχλος ἔρχεται πρὸς αὐτόν, λέγει πρὸς
and beholding that a great crowd is coming to Him, He says to

3588 5376 4159 59 740 2443 5315
τὸν Φίλιππον, Πόθεν ἀγοράσομεν ἄρτους, ἵνα φάγωσιν
Philip, From where may we buy loaves that may eat

3778 5124 1161 3004 3985 846 846 1063 1492 5101
οὗτοι; 6 τοῦτο δὲ ἔλεγε πειράζων αὐτόν· αὐτὸς γὰρ ᾔδει τί
these? this But He said testing him; He For knew what

3195 4160 611 846 5376 1250
ἔμελλε ποιεῖν. 7 ἀπεκρίθη αὐτῷ Φίλιππος, Διακοσίων
He was going to do. answered Him Philip, Of two hundred

1220 740 3756 714 846 2443 1538 846
δηναρίων ἄρτοι οὐκ ἀρκοῦσιν αὐτοῖς, ἵνα ἕκαστος αὐτῶν
denarii loaves not are enough for them, that each of them

1024 5100 2983 3004 846 1520 1537 3588 3101 846
βραχύ τι λάβῃ. 8 λέγει αὐτῷ εἷς ἐκ τῶν μαθητῶν αὐτοῦ,
a little may receive. says to Him, one out of the disciples of Him,

John 6

1. After these things Jesus went over the sea of Galilee, which is (the sea) of Tiberias.
2 And a great multitude followed him, because they saw his miracles which he did on them that were diseased.

3 And Jesus went up into a mountain, and there he sat with his disciples.
4 And the passover, a feast of the Jews, was nigh.
5 When Jesus then lifted up (his) eyes, and saw a great company come unto him, he saith unto Philip, Whence shall we buy bread, that these may eat?

6 And this he said to prove him: for he himself knew what he would do.
7 Philip answered him, Two hundred pennyworth of bread is not sufficient for them, that every one of them may take a little.

8 One of his disciples,

Literal Translation | **John 6:9** | *King James Version*

Andrew the brother of Simon Peter,
9 A little boy is here who has five barley loaves and two fish; but what are these for so many?

10 And Jesus said, Make the men to recline. And much grass was in the place. Then the men reclined, the number (was) about five thousand.

406 3588 80 4613 4074 2076 3808 1520
Ἀνδρέας ὁ ἀδελφὸς Σίμωνος Πέτρου, 9 Ἔστι παιδάριον ἓν
Andrew, the brother of Simon Peter, There is little boy one

5602 3739 2192 4002 740 2916 2532 1417 3795 235 5023
ὧδε, ὃ ἔχει πέντε ἄρτους κριθίνους καὶ δύο ὀψάρια· ἀλλὰ ταῦτα
here who has five loaves barley and two fish; but these

5101 2076 1519 5118 2036 1161 3588 2424 4160
τί ἐστιν εἰς τοσούτους; 10 εἶπε δὲ ὁ Ἰησοῦς, Ποιήσατε
what are to so many? said But Jesus, Make

3588 444 377 2258 1161 5528 4183 1722 3588 5117
τοὺς ἀνθρώπους ἀναπεσεῖν. ἦν δὲ χόρτος πολὺς ἐν τῷ τόπῳ.
the men to recline. was And grass much in the place.

377 3767 3588 435 3588 706 5616 4000
ἀνέπεσον οὖν οἱ ἄνδρες τὸν ἀριθμὸν ὡσεὶ πεντακισχίλιοι.
reclined, therefore the men the number about five thousand.

Andrew, Simon Peter's brother, saith unto him,
9 There is a lad here, which hath five barley loaves, and two small fishes: but what are they among so many?

10 And Jesus said, Make the men sit down. Now there was much grass in the place. So the men sat down, in number about five thousand.

11 And Jesus took the loaves, and having given thanks distributed to the disciples, and the disciples to the (ones) reclining. And in the same way the fish, as much as they desired.
12 And as they were filled, He said to His disciples, Gather up the fragments left over, that not anything be lost.

13 Then they gathered and filled twelve hand baskets with fragments of the five barley loaves which had been left over to those who had eaten.

14. Then seeing what sign Jesus did, the men said, This is truly the Prophet, the (one) coming into the world.

15 Then knowing that they were about to come and seize Him, that they might make Him king, Jesus withdrew again to the mountain alone (by) Himself.

2983 1161 3588 740 3588 2424 2532 2168 1239
11 ἔλαβε δὲ τοὺς ἄρτους ὁ Ἰησοῦς, καὶ εὐχαριστήσας διέδωκε
took And the loaves Jesus, and having given thanks gave out

3588 3101 3588 1161 3101 3588 345 3668 2532 1537
τοῖς μαθηταῖς, οἱ δὲ μαθηταὶ τοῖς ἀνακειμένοις· ὁμοίως καὶ ἐκ
to the disciples, the and disciples to the (ones) reclining; likewise and of

3588 3795 3745 2309 5613 1161 1705 3004 3588
τῶν ὀψαρίων ὅσον ἤθελον. 12 ὡς δὲ ἐνεπλήσθησαν, λέγει τοῖς
the fish as much as they desired. as And they were filled, He says to the

3101 846 4863 3588 4052 2801
μαθηταῖς αὐτοῦ, Συναγάγετε τὰ περισσεύσαντα κλάσματα,
disciples of Him, Gather together the left over fragments,

2443 33615100 622 4863 3767 2532 1072 1427
ἵνα μή τι ἀπόληται. 13 συνήγαγον οὖν, καὶ ἐγέμισαν δώδεκα
that not anything be lost. they gathered Then, and filled twelve

2894 2801 1537 3588 4002 740 3588 2916 3739
κοφίνους κλασμάτων ἐκ τῶν πέντε ἄρτων τῶν κριθίνων, ἃ
handbaskets with fragments of the five loaves of the barley, which

4052 3588 977 3588 3767 444 1492 3739
ἐπερίσσευσε τοῖς βεβρωκόσιν. 14 οἱ οὖν ἄνθρωποι ἰδόντες ὃ
had been left over to the (ones) having eaten. the Then men seeing what

4160 4592 3588 2424 3004 3754 3778 2076 230 3588
ἐποίησε σημεῖον ὁ Ἰησοῦς, ἔλεγον ὅτι Οὗτός ἐστιν ἀληθῶς ὁ
did sign Jesus, said, This is truly the

4396 3588 2064 1519 3588 2889 2424 3767 1097
προφήτης ὁ ἐρχόμενος εἰς τὸν κόσμον. 15 Ἰησοῦς οὖν γνοὺς
Prophet, the (one) coming into the world. Jesus Then knowing

3754 3195 2064 2532 726 846 2443 4160
ὅτι μέλλουσιν ἔρχεσθαι καὶ ἁρπάζειν αὐτὸν, ἵνα ποιήσωσιν
that they are about to come and seize Him, that they may make

846 935 402 3825 1519 3588 3735 846 3441
αὐτὸν βασιλέα, ἀνεχώρησε πάλιν εἰς τὸ ὄρος αὐτὸς μόνος.
Him a king, withdrew again into the mountain Himself alone.

11 And Jesus took the loaves; and when he had given thanks, he distributed to the disciples, and the disciples to them that were set down; and likewise of the fishes as much as they would.
12 When they were filled, he said unto his disciples, Gather up the fragments that remain, that nothing be lost.
13 Therefore they gathered (them) together, and filled twelve baskets with the fragments of the five barley loaves, which remained over and above unto them that had eaten.
14. Then those men, when they had seen the miracle that Jesus did, said, This is of a truth that prophet that should come into the world.
15 When Jesus therefore perceived that they would come and take him by force, to make him a king, he departed again into a mountain himself alone.

16. And when it became evening, His disciples went down on the sea.
17 And entering into the boat, they were going across the sea to Capernaum. And darkness now had occurred, and Jesus had not come to them.
18 And the sea was aroused by a great wind blowing.
19 Then having rowed about

5613 1161 3798 1096 2597 3588 3101 846 1909 3588
16 Ὡς δὲ ὀψία ἐγένετο, κατέβησαν οἱ μαθηταὶ αὐτοῦ ἐπὶ τὴν
when And evening it was, went down the disciples of Him on the

2281 2532 1684 1519 3588 4143 2064 4008 3588
θάλασσαν, 17 καὶ ἐμβάντες εἰς τὸ πλοῖον, ἤρχοντο πέραν τῆς
sea, and entering into the boat, they were going across the

2281 1519 2584 2532 4653 2235 1096 2532 3756
θαλάσσης εἰς Καπερναούμ. καὶ σκοτία ἤδη ἐγεγόνει, καὶ οὐκ
sea to Capernaum. And darkness now had occurred, and not

2064 4314 846 3588 2424 3588 5037 2281 417 3173
ἐληλύθει πρὸς αὐτοὺς ὁ Ἰησοῦς. 18 ἥ τε θάλασσα ἀνέμου μεγά-
had come to them Jesus. the And sea by a wind great

4154 1326 1643 3767 5613 4712
λου πνέοντος διηγείρετο. 19 ἐληλακότες οὖν ὡς σταδίους
blowing was aroused. having rowed Then about stadia

16. And when even was (now) come, his disciples went down unto the sea,
17 And entered into a ship, and went over the sea toward Capernaum. And it was now dark, and Jesus was not come to them.
18 And the sea arose by reason of a great wind that blew.
19 So when they had rowed about

Literal Translation | **John 6:20** | **King James Version**

twenty-five or thirty stadia, they behold Jesus walking on the sea. And (He) having come near the boat, they were afraid.

1501 2228 5144 2334 3588 2424 4043
εἴκοσιπέντε ἢ τριάκοντα, θεωροῦσι τὸν Ἰησοῦν περιπατοῦντα
twenty-five or thirty, they behold Jesus walking
1909 3588 2281 2532 1451 3588 4143 1096 2532
ἐπὶ τῆς θαλάσσης, καὶ ἐγγὺς τοῦ πλοίου γινόμενον· καὶ
on the sea, and near the boat having become; and
5399 3588 1161 3004 846 1473 1510 3361 5399
ἐφοβήθησαν. 20 ὁ δὲ λέγει αὐτοῖς, Ἐγώ εἰμι· μὴ φοβεῖσθε.
they were afraid. He But says to them, I AM; not do fear.

five and twenty or thirty furlongs, they see Jesus walking on the sea, and drawing nigh unto the ship: and they were afraid.

20 But He said to them, I AM! Do not fear.

20 But he saith unto them, It is I; be not afraid.

21 Then they desired to take Him into the boat. And the boat was instantly at the land to which they were going.

2309 3767 2983 846 1519 3588 4143 2532 2112 3588
21 ἤθελον οὖν λαβεῖν αὐτὸν εἰς τὸ πλοῖον· καὶ εὐθέως τὸ
they desired Then to take Him into the boat. And instantly the
4143 1096 1909 3588 1093 1519 3739 5217
πλοῖον ἐγένετο ἐπὶ τῆς γῆς εἰς ἣν ὑπῆγον.
boat came to be at the land to which they were going.

21 Then they willingly received him into the ship: and immediately the ship was at the land whither they went.

22. On the morrow, the crowd standing on the other side of the sea had seen that no other little boat was there except one, that one into which His disciples entered, and that Jesus did not go with His disciples into the little boat, but (that) the disciples went away alone.

3588 1887 3588 3793 3588 2476 4008 3588 2281
22. Τῇ ἐπαύριον ὁ ὄχλος ὁ ἑστηκὼς πέραν τῆς θαλάσσης,
On the morrow the crowd standing across the sea
1492 3754 4142 243 3756 2258 1563 1487 3361 1520 1565 1519 3739
ἰδὼν ὅτι πλοιάριον ἄλλο οὐκ ἦν ἐκεῖ εἰ μὴ ἓν ἐκεῖνο εἰς ὃ
seeing that little boat another not was there, except one, that into which
1684 3588 3101 846 2532 3754 3756 4897 3588
ἐνέβησαν οἱ μαθηταὶ αὐτοῦ, καὶ ὅτι οὐ συνεισῆλθε τοῖς
entered the disciples of Him, and that not went with the
3101 846 3588 2424 1519 3588 4142 235 3441 3588
μαθηταῖς αὐτοῦ ὁ Ἰησοῦς εἰς τὸ πλοιάριον, ἀλλὰ μόνοι οἱ
disciples of Him Jesus into the little boat, but alone the
3101 846 565
μαθηταὶ αὐτοῦ ἀπῆλθον,
disciples of Him went away,

22. The day following, when the people which stood on the other side of the sea saw that there was none other boat there, save that one whereinto his disciples were entered, and that Jesus went not with his disciples into the boat, but (that) his disciples were gone away alone;

23 But other small boats came from Tiberias near the place where they ate the loaves, the Lord having given thanks.

243 1161 2064 4142 1537
23 [ἄλλα δὲ ἦλθε πλοιάρια ἐκ
other but came little boats from
5085 1451 3588 5117 3699 5315 3588 740
Τιβεριάδος ἐγγὺς τοῦ τόπου ὅπου ἔφαγον τὸν ἄρτον,
Tiberias near the place where they ate the bread,
2168 3588 2962
εὐχαριστήσαντος τοῦ Κυρίου]·
having given thanks the Lord;

23 (Howbeit there came other boats from Tiberias nigh unto the place where they did eat bread, after that the Lord had given thanks:)

24 Therefore, when the crowd saw that Jesus was not there nor His disciples, they themselves also entered into the boats and came to Capernaum seeking Jesus.

3753 3767 1492 3588 3793 3754
24 ὅτε οὖν εἶδεν ὁ ὄχλος ὅτι
when therefore saw the crowd that
2424 3756 2076 1563 3761 3588 3101 846 1684 2532
Ἰησοῦς οὐκ ἔστιν ἐκεῖ οὐδὲ οἱ μαθηταὶ αὐτοῦ, ἐνέβησαν καὶ
Jesus not is there, nor the disciples of Him, they entered also
846 1519 3588 4143 2532 2064 1519 2584 2212 3588
αὐτοὶ εἰς τὰ πλοῖα, καὶ ἦλθον εἰς Καπερναούμ, ζητοῦντες τὸν
themselves into the boats and came into Capernaum, seeking
2424
Ἰησοῦν.
Jesus.

24 When the people therefore saw that Jesus was not there, neither his disciples, they also took shipping, and came to Capernaum, seeking for Jesus.

25 And having found Him across the sea, they said to Him, Rabbi, when did you come here?

2532 2147 846 4008 3588 2281 2036
25 καὶ εὑρόντες αὐτὸν πέραν τῆς θαλάσσης, εἶπον
And having found Him across the sea, they said
846 4461 4219 5602 1096
αὐτῷ, Ῥαββί, πότε ὧδε γέγονας;
to Him, Rabbi, when here did you come?

25 And when they had found him on the other side of the sea, they said unto him, Rabbi, when camest thou hither?

26 Jesus answered them and said, Truly, truly, I say to you, you seek Me not because you saw signs, but because you ate of the loaves and were satisfied.

611 846 3588
26 ἀπεκρίθη αὐτοῖς ὁ
answered them
2424 2532 2036 281 281 3004 5213 2212 3165 3756 3754
Ἰησοῦς καὶ εἶπεν, Ἀμὴν ἀμὴν λέγω ὑμῖν, ζητεῖτέ με, οὐχ ὅτι
Jesus and said, Truly truly I say to you, You seek Me, not because
1492 4592 235 3754 5315 1537 3588 740 2532 5526
εἴδετε σημεῖα, ἀλλ᾽ ὅτι ἐφάγετε ἐκ τῶν ἄρτων καὶ ἐχορτά-
you saw signs, but because you ate of the loaves and were
σθητε.
satisfied.

26 Jesus answered them and said, Verily, verily, I say unto you, Ye seek me, not because ye saw the miracles, but because ye did eat of the loaves, and were filled.

27 Do not labor (for) the food (which is) perishing, but for the food enduring to everlasting life, which the Son of man will give to you; for God the Father sealed this One.

2038 3361 3588 1035 3588 622 235
27 ἐργάζεσθε μὴ τὴν βρῶσιν τὴν ἀπολλυμένην, ἀλλὰ
work Do not (for) the food (which is) perishing, but
3588 1035 3588 3306 1519 2222 166 3739 3588 5207 3588
τὴν βρῶσιν τὴν μένουσαν εἰς ζωὴν αἰώνιον, ἣν ὁ υἱὸς τοῦ
the food enduring to life everlasting, which the Son
444 5213 1325 5126 1063 3588 3962 4972
ἀνθρώπου ὑμῖν δώσει· τοῦτον γὰρ ὁ πατὴρ ἐσφράγισεν,
of man to you will give; this (one) for the Father sealed,

27 Labour not for the meat which perisheth, but for that meat which endureth unto everlasting life, which the Son of man shall give unto you: for him hath God the Father sealed.

Literal Translation **John 6:28** ***King James Version***

28 Then they said to Him, What may we do that we may work the works of God?
29 Jesus answered and said to them, This is the work of God, that you believe into (Him) whom that One sent.

30 Then they said to Him, Then what sign do you do that we may see and may believe you? What do you work?
31 Our fathers ate the manna in the wilderness, even as has been written "He gave to them bread out of the heaven to eat." (Ps. 78:24)

32 Then Jesus said to them, Truly, truly, I say to you, Moses has not given you the bread out of Heaven, but My Father gives you the true bread out of Heaven.

33 For the bread of God is the (One) coming down out of Heaven and giving life to the world.
34 Then they said to Him, Lord, always give us this bread.

35 Jesus said to them, I am the Bread of life; the (one) coming to Me will not hunger, never; and the (one) believing into Me will not ever will thirst, never!

36But I said to you that you also have seen Me and did not believe.

37 All that the Father gives to Me shall come to Me, and the (one) coming to Me I will not cast out, never.
38 For I have come down out of Heaven, not that I should do My will, but the will of the (One) who has sent Me.
39 And this is the will of the Father having sent Me, that of all which He has given Me, I shall not lose

3588 2316 2036 3767 4314 846 5101 4160 2443 2038
ὁ Θεός. 28 εἶπον οὖν πρὸς αὐτόν, Τί ποιῶμεν, ἵνα ἐργαζώμεθα
God. they said Then to Him, What may we do, that we may work

3588 2041 3588 2316 611 3588 2424 2532 2036 846
τὰ ἔργα τοῦ Θεοῦ; 29 ἀπεκρίθη ὁ Ἰησοῦς καὶ εἶπεν αὐτοῖς,
the works of God? answered Jesus and said to them,

5124 2076 3588 2041 3588 2316 2443 4100 1519 3739
Τοῦτό ἐστι τὸ ἔργον τοῦ Θεοῦ, ἵνα πιστεύσητε εἰς ὃν
This is the work of God, that you believe into whom

649 1565 2036 3767 846 5101 3767 4160 4771
ἀπέστειλεν ἐκεῖνος. 30 εἶπον οὖν αὐτῷ, Τί οὖν ποιεῖς σὺ
sent that One they said Then to Him, what Then do you

4592 2443 1492 2532 4100 4671 5101 2038 3588
σημεῖον, ἵνα ἴδωμεν καὶ πιστεύσωμέν σοι; τί ἐργάζῃ; 31 οἱ
sign, that we may see and believe You? What do you work? The

3962 2257 3588 3131 5315 1722 3588 2048 2531 2076
πατέρες ἡμῶν τὸ μάννα ἔφαγον ἐν τῇ ἐρήμῳ, καθώς ἐστι
fathers of us the manna ate in the wilderness, even as it is

1125 740 1537 3588 3772 1325 846 5315
γεγραμμένον, Ἄρτον ἐκ τοῦ οὐρανοῦ ἔδωκεν αὐτοῖς φαγεῖν.
having been written, Bread out of the heaven He gave to them to eat.

2036 3767 846 3588 2424 281 281 3004 5213 3756
32 εἶπεν οὖν αὐτοῖς ὁ Ἰησοῦς, Ἀμὴν ἀμὴν λέγω ὑμῖν, Οὐ
said Then to them Jesus, Truly, truly, I say to you, not

3475 1325 5213 3588 740 1537 3588 3772 235 3588
Μωσῆς δέδωκεν ὑμῖν τὸν ἄρτον ἐκ τοῦ οὐρανοῦ· ἀλλ' ὁ
Moses has given to you the bread out of Heaven; but the

3962 3450 1325 5213 3588 740 1537 3588 3772 3588
πατήρ μου δίδωσιν ὑμῖν τὸν ἄρτον ἐκ τοῦ οὐρανοῦ τὸν
Father of Me gives to you the bread out of Heaven

228 3588 1063 740 3588 2316 2076 3588 2597 1537 3588
ἀληθινόν. 33 ὁ γὰρ ἄρτος τοῦ Θεοῦ ἐστιν ὁ καταβαίνων ἐκ τοῦ
true. the For bread of God is the (One) coming down out of

3772 2532 2222 1325 3588 2889 2036 3767 4314 846
οὐρανοῦ καὶ ζωὴν διδοὺς τῷ κόσμῳ. 34 εἶπον οὖν πρὸς αὐτόν,
Heaven and life giving to the world. they said Then to Him,

2962 3842 1325 2254 3588 740 5126 2036 1161 846
Κύριε, πάντοτε δὸς ἡμῖν τὸν ἄρτον τοῦτον. 35 εἶπε δὲ αὐτοῖς
Lord, always give us bread this. said And to them

3588 2424 1473 1510 3588 740 3588 2222 3588 2064 4314 3165
ὁ Ἰησοῦς, Ἐγώ εἰμι ὁ ἄρτος τῆς ζωῆς· ὁ ἐρχόμενος πρός με
Jesus, I am the Bread of Life; the (one) coming to Me

3756 3361 3983 2532 3588 4100 1519 1691 3756 3361 1372
οὐ μὴ πεινάσῃ· καὶ ὁ πιστεύων εἰς ἐμὲ οὐ μὴ διψήσῃ
not everwill hunger; and the (one) believing into Me not ever will thirst,

4455 235 2036 5213 3754 2532 3708 3165 2532 3756
πώποτε. 36 ἀλλ' εἶπον ὑμῖν ὅτι καὶ ἑωράκατέ με, καὶ οὐ
never! But I said to you that both you have seen Me, and not

4100 3956 3739 1325 3427 3588 3962 4314 1691 2240 2532 3588
πιστεύετε. 37 πᾶν ὃ δίδωσί μοι ὁ πατὴρ πρὸς ἐμὲ ἥξει· καὶ τὸν
do believe. All that gives to Me the Father to Me will come; and he

2064 4314 3165 3756 3361 1544 1854 3754 2597 1537
ἐρχόμενον πρός με οὐ μὴ ἐκβάλω ἔξω 38 ὅτι καταβέβηκα ἐκ
coming to Me not ever I will cast out. Because I have descended from

3588 3772 3756 2443 4160 3588 2307 3588 1699 235 3588
τοῦ οὐρανοῦ, οὐχ ἵνα ποιῶ τὸ θέλημα τὸ ἐμόν, ἀλλὰ τὸ
Heaven, not that I should do the will of Me, but the

2307 3588 3992 3165 5124 1161 2076 3588 2307 3588
θέλημα τοῦ πέμψαντός με. 39 τοῦτο δέ ἐστι τὸ θέλημα τοῦ
will of the (One) having sent Me. this And is the will of the

3992 3165 3962 2443 3956 3739 1325 3427 3361 622
πέμψαντός με πατρός, ἵνα πᾶν ὃ δέδωκέ μοι, μὴ ἀπολέσω
having sent Me Father, that all which He has given Me, not I shall lose

28 Then said they unto him, What shall we do, that we might work the works of God?
29 Jesus answered and said unto them, This is the work of God, that ye believe on him whom he hath sent.

30 They said therefore unto him, What sign shewest thou then, that we may see, and believe thee? what dost thou work?
31 Our fathers did eat manna in the desert; as it is written, He gave them bread from heaven to eat.

32 Then Jesus said unto them, Verily, verily, I say unto you, Moses gave you not that bread from heaven; but my Father giveth you the true bread from heaven.

33 For the bread of God is he which cometh down from heaven, and giveth life unto the world.
34 Then said they unto him, Lord, evermore give us this bread.
35 And Jesus said unto them, I am the bread of life: he that cometh to me shall never hunger; and he that believeth on me shall never thirst.

36 But I said unto you, That ye also have seen me, and believe not.

37 All that the Father giveth me shall come to me; and him that cometh to me I will in no wise cast out.
38 For I came down from heaven, not to do mine own will, but the will of him that sent me.

39 And this is the Father's will which hath sent me, that of all which he hath given me I should lose

Literal Translation **John 6:40** *King James Version*

(any) of it, but shall raise it up in the last day.
40 And this is the will of the (One) who has sent Me, that everyone seeing the Son and believing into Him should have everlasting life; and I will raise him up at the last day.

41 Therefore the Jews murmured about Him, because He said, I am the Bread coming down out of Heaven.
42 And they said, Is this not Jesus the son of Joseph, of whom we know the father and the mother? How does this one say, I have come down out of Heaven?

43 Then Jesus answered and said to them, Do not murmur with one another.
44 No one is able to come to Me if not the Father who sent Me draws him, and I will raise him up in the last day.
45 It is having been written in the Prophets, "They shall all be taught of God." (Isa. 54:13) So then everyone hearing and learning from the Father comes to Me;
46 not that anyone has seen the Father, except the (One) being from God, this One has seen the Father.

47 Truly, truly, I say to you, the (one) believing into Me has everlasting life.
48 I am the Bread of life.
49 Your fathers ate the manna in the wilderness and died.

50 This is the Bread coming down out of Heaven, that anyone may eat of it and not die.
51 I am the Living Bread that came down from Heaven. If anyone eats of this Bread,

---

1537 846 235 450 846 1722 3588 2078 2250 5124
ἐξ αὐτοῦ, ἀλλὰ ἀναστήσω αὐτὸ ἐν τῇ ἐσχάτῃ ἡμέρᾳ. 40 τοῦτο
of it, but shall raise up it in the last day. this

1161 2076 3588 2307 3588 3992 3165 2443 3956 3588 2334 3588
δέ ἐστι τὸ θέλημα τοῦ πέμψαντός με, ἵνα πᾶς ὁ θεωρῶν τὸν
And is the will of the (One) having sent Me, that everyone seeing the

5207 2532 4100 1519 846 2192 2222 166 2532 450
υἱὸν καὶ πιστεύων εἰς αὐτόν ἔχῃ ζωὴν αἰώνιον, καὶ ἀναστήσω
Son and believing into Him should have life everlasting, and will raise up

846 1473 3588 2078 2250
αὐτὸν ἐγὼ τῇ ἐσχάτῃ ἡμέρᾳ.
him I at the last day.

1111 3767 3588 2453 4012 846 3754 2036 1473
41 Ἐγόγγυζον οὖν οἱ Ἰουδαῖοι περὶ αὐτοῦ, ὅτι εἶπεν, Ἐγώ
murmured Therefore the Jews concerning Him, because He said, I

1510 3588 740 3588 2597 1537 3588 3772 2532 3004 3756
εἰμι ὁ ἄρτος ὁ καταβὰς ἐκ τοῦ οὐρανοῦ. 42 καὶ ἔλεγον, Οὐχ
am the Bread coming down out of Heaven. And they said, Not

3778 2076 2424 3588 5207 2501 3739 2249 1492 3588
οὗτός ἐστιν Ἰησοῦς ὁ υἱὸς Ἰωσήφ, οὗ ἡμεῖς οἴδαμεν τὸν
this is Jesus the son of Joseph, of whom we know the

3962 2532 3588 3384 4459 3767 3004 3778 3754 1537 3588
πατέρα καὶ τὴν μητέρα; πῶς οὖν λέγει οὗτος ὅτι Ἐκ τοῦ
father and the mother? How then says this one, Out of

3772 2597 611 3767 3588 2424 2532 2036
οὐρανοῦ καταβέβηκα; 43 ἀπεκρίθη οὖν ὁ Ἰησοῦς καὶ εἶπεν
Heaven I have come down? answered Then Jesus and said

846 3361 1111 3326 240 3762 1410 2064
αὐτοῖς, Μὴ γογγύζετε μετ' ἀλλήλων. 44 οὐδεὶς δύναται ἐλθεῖν
to them, Not do murmur with one another. No one is able to come

4314 3165 1437 3361 3588 3962 3588 3992 3165 1670 846 2532 1473
πρός με, ἐὰν μὴ ὁ πατὴρ ὁ πέμψας με ἑλκύσῃ αὐτόν, καὶ ἐγὼ
to Me, if not the Father who sent Me draws him, and I

450 846 3588 2078 2250 2076 1125 1722 3588
ἀναστήσω αὐτὸν τῇ ἐσχάτῃ ἡμέρᾳ. 45 ἔστι γεγραμμένον ἐν τοῖς
will raise up him in the last day. It is having been written in the

4396 2532 2071 3956 1318 3588 2316 3956 3767 3588
προφήταις, Καὶ ἔσονται πάντες διδακτοὶ τοῦ Θεοῦ. πᾶς οὖν ὁ
Prophets, And they shall be all taught of God. everyone Then

191 3844 3588 3962 2532 3129 2064 4314 3165 3756
ἀκούσας παρὰ τοῦ πατρὸς καὶ μαθών, ἔρχεται πρός με. 46 οὐχ
hearing from the Father and learning, comes to Me. Not

3754 3588 3962 5100 3708 1487 3361 3588 5607 3844 3588 2316
ὅτι τὸν πατέρα τις ἑώρακεν, εἰ μὴ ὁ ὢν παρὰ τοῦ Θεοῦ,
that the Father anyone has seen, except He being from God,

3778 3708 3588 3962 281 281 3004 5213 3588 4100
οὗτος ἑώρακε τὸν πατέρα. 47 ἀμὴν ἀμὴν λέγω ὑμῖν, ὁ πιστεύων
this One has seen the Father. Truly truly I say to you, the (one) believing

1519 1691 2192 222 166 1473 1510 3588 740 3588 2222 3588
εἰς ἐμέ, ἔχει ζωὴν αἰώνιον. 48 ἐγώ εἰμι ὁ ἄρτος τῆς ζωῆς. 49 οἱ
into Me has life everlasting. I am the Bread of Life. The

3962 5216 5315 3588 3131 1722 3588 2048 2532 599
πατέρες ὑμῶν ἔφαγον τὸ μάννα ἐν τῇ ερημῳ, καὶ ἀπέθανον.
fathers of you ate the manna in the wilderness, and died.

3778 2076 3588 740 3588 1537 3588 3772 2597 2443 5100
50 οὗτός ἐστιν ὁ ἄρτος ὁ ἐκ τοῦ οὐρανοῦ καταβαίνων, ἵνα τις
This is the Bread out of Heaven coming down, that anyone

1537 846 5315 2532 3361 599 1473 1510 3588 740 3588 2198 3588 1537
ἐξ αὐτοῦ φάγῃ καὶ μὴ ἀποθάνῃ. 51 ἐγώ εἰμι ὁ ἄρτος ὁ ζῶν, ὁ ἐκ
of it may eat and not die. I am the Bread Living, that from

3588 3772 2597 1437 5100 5315 1537 5127 3588 740
τοῦ οὐρανοῦ καταβάς· ἐάν τις φάγῃ ἐκ τούτου τοῦ ἄρτου,
Heaven came down; if anyone eat of this Bread,

---

nothing, but should raise it up again at the last day.
40 And this is the will of him that sent me, that every one which seeth the Son, and believeth on him, may have everlasting life: and I will raise him up at the last day.

41 The Jews then murmured at him, because he said, I am the bread which came down from heaven.
42 And they said, Is not this Jesus, the son of Joseph, whose father and mother we know? how is it then that he saith, I came down from heaven?

43 Jesus therefore answered and said unto them, Murmur not among yourselves.
44 No man can come to me, except the Father which hath sent me draw him: and I will raise him up at the last day.
45 It is written in the prophets, And they shall be all taught of God. Every man therefore that hath heard, and hath learned of the Father, cometh unto me.
46 Not that any man hath seen the Father, save he which is of God, he hath seen the Father.

47 Verily, verily, I say unto you, He that believeth on me hath everlasting life.
48 I am that bread of life.
49 Your fathers did eat manna in the wilderness, and are dead.

50 This is the bread which cometh down from heaven, that a man may eat thereof, and not die.
51 I am the living bread which came down from heaven: if any man eat of this bread,

Literal Translation | **John 6:52** | **King James Version**

he will live to the age. And indeed the bread which I will give is My flesh, which I will give on behalf of the life of the world.

52 Then the Jews argued with one another, saying, How is this one able to give us (his) flesh to eat?
53 Then Jesus said to them, Truly, truly, I say to you, If not you eat the flesh of the Son of man, and drink His blood, you do not have life in yourselves.

54 The one eating of My flesh and drinking of My blood has everlasting life, and I will raise him up at the last day.

55 For My flesh is truly food, and My blood is truly drink.

56 The (one) eating of My flesh and drinking of My blood abides in Me, and I in him.

57 Even as the living Father sent Me, and I live through the Father; also the (one) eating Me, even that one will live through Me.
58 This is the Bread which came down out of Heaven, not as your fathers ate the manna, and died; the (one) eating of this Bread will live to the age.

59 He said these things teaching in a synagogue in Capernaum.

60 Therefore many of His disciples having heard, (they) said, This word is hard; who is able to hear it?

61 But Jesus knowing within Himself that His disciples were murmuring about this, He said to them, Does this offend you?

2198 1519 3588 165 2532 3588 740 1161 3739 1473 1325 3588 4561
ζήσεται εἰς τὸν αἰῶνα. καὶ ὁ ἄρτος δὲ ὃν ἐγὼ δώσω, ἡ σάρξ
he will live to the age. indeed the bread And which I give, the flesh

3450 2076 3739 1473 1325 5228 3588 3588 2889 2222
μου ἐστιν, ἣν ἐγὼ δώσω ὑπὲρ τῆς τοῦ κόσμου ζωῆς.
of Me is, which I will give on behalf of the of the world life.

3164 3767 4314 240 3588 2453 3004 4459
52. Ἐμάχοντο οὖν πρὸς ἀλλήλους οἱ Ἰουδαῖοι λέγοντες, Πῶς
argued Then with one another the Jews, saying, How

1410 3778 2254 1325 3588 4561 5315 2036 3767
δύναται οὗτος ἡμῖν δοῦναι τὴν σάρκα φαγεῖν; 53 εἶπεν οὖν
is able this one us give the flesh to eat? said Then

846 3588 2424 281 281 3004 5213 1437 3361 5315 3588
αὐτοῖς ὁ Ἰησοῦς, Ἀμὴν ἀμὴν λέγω ὑμῖν, ἐὰν μὴ φάγητε τὴν
to them Jesus, Truly, truly, I say to you, If not you eat the

4561 3588 5207 3588 444 2532 4095 846 3588 129
σάρκα τοῦ υἱοῦ τοῦ ἀνθρώπου καὶ πίητε αὐτοῦ τὸ αἷμα,
flesh of the Son of man and drink of Him the blood,

3756 2192 2222 1722 1438 3588 5176 3450 3588 4561 2532
οὐκ ἔχετε ζωὴν ἐν ἑαυτοῖς. 54 ὁ τρώγων μου τὴν σάρκα καὶ
not do you have life in yourselves. The (one) eating of Me the flesh and

4095 3450 3588 129 2192 2222 166 2532 1473 450
πίνων μου τὸ αἷμα, ἔχει ζωὴν αἰώνιον, καὶ ἐγὼ ἀναστήσω
drinking of Me the blood, has life everlasting, and I will raise up

846 3588 2078 2250 3588 1063 4561 3450 230 2076
αὐτὸν τῇ ἐσχάτῃ ἡμέρᾳ. 55 ἡ γὰρ σάρξ μου ἀληθῶς ἐστι
him at the last day. the For flesh of Me truly is

1035 2532 3588 129 3450 230 2076 4213 3588 5176 3450
βρῶσις, καὶ τὸ αἷμά μου ἀληθῶς ἐστι πόσις. 56 ὁ τρώγων μου
food, and the blood of Me truly is drink. The (one) eating of Me

3588 4561 2532 4095 3450 3588 129 1722 1698 3306 2504 1722
τὴν σάρκα καὶ πίνων μου τὸ αἷμα, ἐν ἐμοὶ μένει, κἀγὼ ἐν
the flesh and drinking of Me the blood in Me abides, and I in

846 2531 649 3165 3588 2198 3962 2504 2198 1223 3588
αὐτῷ. 57 καθὼς ἀπέστειλέ με ὁ ζῶν πατήρ, κἀγὼ ζῶ διὰ τὸν
him. Even as sent Me the living Father, and I live through the

3962 2532 3588 5176 3165 2548 2198 1223 1691 3778
πατέρα· καὶ ὁ τρώγων με, κἀκεῖνος ζήσεται δι' ἐμέ. 58 οὗτός
Father also the (one) eating of Me even that one will live through Me. This

2076 3588 740 3588 1537 3588 3772 2597 3756 2531 5315
ἐστιν ὁ ἄρτος ὁ ἐκ τοῦ οὐρανοῦ καταβάς· οὐ καθὼς ἔφαγον
is the Bread which out of Heaven came down, not as ate

3588 3962 5216 3588 3131 2532 599 3588 5176 5126
οἱ πατέρες ὑμῶν τὸ μάννα, καὶ ἀπέθανον· ὁ τρώγων τοῦτον
the fathers of you the manna, and died; the (one) eating this

3588 740 2198 1519 3588 165 5023 2036 1722 4864
τὸν ἄρτον, ζήσεται εἰς τὸν αἰῶνα. 59 Ταῦτα εἶπεν ἐν συναγωγῇ
bread will live to the age. These things He said in a synagogue

1321 1722 2584
διδάσκων ἐν Καπερναούμ.
teaching in Capernaum.

4183 3767 191 1722 3588 3101 846 2036
60. Πολλοὶ οὖν ἀκούσαντες ἐκ τῶν μαθητῶν αὐτοῦ εἶπον,
many Therefore having heard of the disciples of Him said,

4642 2076 3778 3588 3056 5101 1410 846 191
Σκληρός ἐστιν οὗτος ὁ λόγος· τίς δύναται αὐτοῦ ἀκούειν;
hard is This word; who is able it to hear?

1492 1161 3588 2424 1722 1438 3754 1111 4012 5127
61 εἰδὼς δὲ ὁ Ἰησοῦς ἐν ἑαυτῷ ὅτι γογγύζουσι περὶ τούτου
knowing But Jesus within Himself that are murmuring about this

3588 3101 846 2036 846 5124 5209 4624
οἱ μαθηταὶ αὐτοῦ, εἶπεν αὐτοῖς, Τοῦτο ὑμᾶς σκανδαλίζει;
the disciples of Him, He said to them, this you Does offend?

---

he shall live for ever: and the bread that I will give is my flesh, which I will give for the life of the world.

52 The Jews therefore strove among themselves, saying, How can this man give us (his) flesh to eat?
53 Then Jesus said unto them, Verily, verily, I say unto you, Except ye eat the flesh of the Son of man, and drink his blood, ye have no life in you.

54 Whoso eateth my flesh, and drinketh my blood, hath eternal life; and I will raise him up at the last day.

55 For my flesh is meat indeed, and my blood is drink indeed.

56 He that eateth my flesh, and drinketh my blood, dwelleth in me, and I in him.

57 As the living Father hath sent me, and I live by the Father: so he that eateth me, even he shall live by me.
58 This is that bread which came down from heaven: not as your fathers did eat manna, and are dead: he that eateth of this bread shall live for ever.

59 These things said he in the synagogue, as he taught in Capernaum.

60 Many therefore of his disciples, when they had heard (this), said, This is an hard saying; who can hear it?

61 When Jesus knew in himself that his disciples murmured at it, he said unto them, Doth this offend you?

Literal Translation **John 6:62** ***King James Version***

62 Then (what) if you behold the Son of man going up where He was at first?
63 It is the Spirit (who) gives life. The flesh does not profit, nothing! The words which I speak to you are spirit and are life.
64 But there are some of you who are not believing. For Jesus knew from (the) beginning who they are the (ones) not believing, and who is the (one) betraying Him.
65 And He said, Because of this, I have told you that no one is able to come to Me if not it is given to him from My Father.

1437 3767 2334 3588 5207 3588 444 305 3699
62 ἐὰν οὖν θεωρῆτε τὸν υἱὸν τοῦ ἀνθρώπου ἀναβαίνοντα ὅπου
if Then you behold the Son of man going up where

2258 3588 4386 3588 4151 2076 3588 2227 3588 4561 3756
ἦν τὸ πρότερον; 63 τὸ πνεῦμά ἐστι τὸ ζωοποιοῦν, ἡ σὰρξ οὐκ
He was at first? the Spirit It is (who) makes alive, the flesh not

5623 3762 3588 4487 3739 1473 2980 5213 4151 2076
ὠφελεῖ οὐδέν· τὰ ῥήματα ἃ ἐγὼ λαλῶ ὑμῖν, πνεῦμά ἐστι
profits, nothing! The words which I speak to you, spirit are

2532 2222 2076 235 1526 1537 5216 5100 3739 3756 4100
καὶ ζωή ἐστιν. 64 ἀλλ' εἰσὶν ἐξ ὑμῶν τινες οἳ οὐ πιστεύουσιν.
and life are. But are of you some who not are believing.

1492 1063 1537 746 3588 2424 5101 1526 3588 3361 4100
ᾔδει γὰρ ἐξ ἀρχῆς ὁ Ἰησοῦς, τίνες εἰσὶν οἱ μὴ πιστεύοντες,
knew For from beginning Jesus, who are the (ones) not believing,

2532 5101 2076 3588 3860 846 2532 3004 1223 5124
καὶ τίς ἐστιν ὁ παραδώσων αὐτόν. 65 καὶ ἔλεγε, Διὰ τοῦτο
and who is the (one) betraying Him. And He said, Because of this

2046 5213 3754 3762 1410 2064 4314 3165 1437 3361 5600
εἴρηκα ὑμῖν, ὅτι οὐδεὶς δύναται ἐλθεῖν πρός με, ἐὰν μὴ ᾖ
I have told you, that no one is able to come to Me, if not it be

1325 846 1537 3588 3962 3450
δεδομένον αὐτῷ ἐκ τοῦ πατρός μου.
given to him from the Father of Me.

62 (What) and if ye shall see the Son of man ascend up where he was before?
63 It is the spirit that quickeneth; the flesh profiteth nothing: the words that I speak unto you, (they) are spirit, and (they) are life.
64 But there are some of you that believe not. For Jesus knew from the beginning who they were that believed not, and who should betray him.
65 And he said, Therefore said I unto you, that no man can come unto me, except it were given unto him of my Father.

66. From this (time) many of His disciples went away into the things behind, and no longer walked with Him.
67 Therefore, Jesus said to the Twelve, Do you also wish to go?
68 Then Simon Peter answered to Him, Lord, to whom shall we go? You have (the) words of everlasting life.
69 And we have believed and have known that You are the Christ, the Son of the living God.
70 Jesus answered them, Did I not choose you, the Twelve? Yet one (of) you is a devil!
71 But He spoke (of) Judas Iscariot, (son) of Simon, for this one was about to betray Him, being one of the Twelve.

1537 5127 4183 565 3588 3101 846 1519
66. Ἐκ τούτου πολλοὶ ἀπῆλθον τῶν μαθητῶν αὐτοῦ εἰς
From this (time) many went away of the disciples of Him into

3588 3694 2532 3765 3326 846 4043 2036 3767 3588
τὰ ὀπίσω, καὶ οὐκέτι μετ' αὐτοῦ περιεπάτουν. 67 εἶπεν οὖν ὁ
the things behind, and no longer with Him walked. said Then

2424 3588 1427 3361 2532 5210 2309 5217 611
Ἰησοῦς τοῖς δώδεκα, Μὴ καὶ ὑμεῖς θέλετε ὑπάγειν; 68 ἀπεκρίθη
Jesus to the Twelve, Not also do you wish to go? answered

3767 846 4613 4074 2962 4314 5101 565
οὖν αὐτῷ Σίμων Πέτρος, Κύριε, πρὸς τίνα ἀπελευσόμεθα;
Then to Him Simon Peter, Lord, to whom shall we go?

4487 2222 166 2192 2532 2249 4100 2532
ῥήματα ζωῆς αἰωνίου ἔχεις. 69 καὶ ἡμεῖς πεπιστεύκαμεν καὶ
words of life everlasting You have. And we have believed and

1097 3754 4771 1488 3588 5547 3588 5207 3588 2316 3588 2198
ἐγνώκαμεν ὅτι σὺ εἶ ὁ Χριστὸς ὁ υἱὸς τοῦ Θεοῦ τοῦ ζῶντος.
have known that You are the Christ the Son of God the living.

611 846 3588 2424 3756 1473 5209 3588 1427
70 ἀπεκρίθη αὐτοῖς ὁ Ἰησοῦς, Οὐκ ἐγὼ ὑμᾶς τοὺς δώδεκα
answered them Jesus, Not I you the Twelve

1586 2532 1537 5216 1520 1228 2076 3004 1161 3588
ἐξελεξάμην, καὶ ἐξ ὑμῶν εἷς διάβολός ἐστιν; 71 ἔλεγε δὲ τὸν
choose out, and out of you one a devil is? He spoke But

2455 4613 2469 3778 1063 3195 846
Ἰούδαν Σίμωνος Ἰσκαριώτην· οὗτος γὰρ ἤμελλεν αὐτὸν
(of) Judas of Simon Iscariot; this one for was about Him

3860 1520 5607 1537 3588 1427
παραδιδόναι, εἷς ὢν ἐκ τῶν δώδεκα.
to betray, one being of the Twelve.

66. From that (time) many of his disciples went back, and walked no more with him.
67 Then said Jesus unto the twelve, Will ye also go away?
68 Then Simon Peter answered him, Lord, to whom shall we go? thou hast the words of eternal life.
69 And we believe and are sure that thou art that Christ, the Son of the living God.
70 Jesus answered them, Have not I chosen you twelve, and one of you is a devil?
71 He spake of Judas Iscariot (the son) of Simon: for he it was that should betray him, being one of the twelve.

John 7

1. And after these things Jesus was walking in Galilee; for He did not desire to walk in Judea, because the Jews were lusting to kill Him.

2532 4043 3588 2424 3326 5023 1722 3588 1056 3756
1. Καὶ περιεπάτει ὁ Ἰησοῦς μετὰ ταῦτα ἐν τῇ Γαλιλαίᾳ· οὐ
And was walking Jesus after these things in Galilee. not

1063 2309 1722 3588 2449 4043 3754 2212 846
γὰρ ἤθελεν ἐν τῇ Ἰουδαίᾳ περιπατεῖν, ὅτι ἐζήτουν αὐτὸν
for He desired in Judea to walk, because were seeking Him

1. After these things Jesus walked in Galilee: for he would not walk in Jewry, because the Jews sought to kill him.

Literal Translation **John 7:2** *King James Version*

2 . And the Jewish Feast of the Tabernacles was near.

3 Then His brothers said to Him, Move away from here and go to Judea, that your disciples will also behold your works which you do,

4 for no one does anything in secret and himself seeks to be in public. If you do these things, reveal yourself to the world.

5 For not even His brothers believed into Him.

6 Then Jesus said to them, My time is not yet here, but your time is always ready.

7 The world is not able to hate you; but it hates Me because I witness concerning it, that its works are evil.

8 You go up to this feast. I am not yet going up to this feast, because My time has not yet been fulfilled.

9 And having said these things to them, He remained in Galilee.

10. But when His brothers went up, then He also went up to the feast, not openly, but as in secret.

11 Then the Jews sought Him in the feast, and said, Where is that (One)?

12 And much murmuring about Him was in the crowds. Indeed some said, He is a good one; but others said, No, but he deceives the crowd.

13 However, no one publicly spoke about Him, because of the fear of the Jews.

3588 2453 615 2258 1161 1451 3588 1859 3588 2453
οἱ Ἰουδαῖοι ἀποκτεῖναι. 2 ἦν δὲ ἐγγὺς ἡ ἑορτὴ τῶν Ἰουδαίων
the Jews to kill. was And near the feast of the Jews

3588 4634 2036 3767 4314 846 3588 80 846
ἡ σκηνοπηγία. 3 εἶπον οὖν πρὸς αὐτὸν οἱ ἀδελφοὶ αὐτοῦ,
The Tabernacles. said Therefore to Him the brothers of Him,

3327 1782 2532 5217 1519 3588 2449 2443 2532 3588
Μετάβηθι ἐντεῦθεν, καὶ ὕπαγε εἰς τὴν Ἰουδαίαν, ἵνα καὶ οἱ
Depart from here, and go into Judea, that also the

3101 4675 2334 3588 2041 4675 3739 4160 3762 1063
μαθηταί σου θεωρήσωσι τὰ ἔργα σου ἃ ποιεῖς. 4 οὐδεὶς γὰρ
disciples of You will behold the works of You which You do. no one For

1722 2927 5100 4160 2532 2212 846 1722 3954 1511 1487
ἐν κρυπτῷ τι ποιεῖ, καὶ ζητεῖ αὐτὸς ἐν παρρησίᾳ εἶναι. εἰ
in secret anything does, and seeks himself in public to be. If

5023 4160 5319 4572 3588 2889 3761 1063 3588
ταῦτα ποιεῖς, φανέρωσον σεαυτὸν τῷ κόσμῳ. 5 οὐδὲ γὰρ οἱ
these things you do, reveal yourself to the world. not even For the

80 846 4100 1519 846 3004 3767 846 3588
ἀδελφοὶ αὐτοῦ ἐπίστευον εἰς αὐτόν. 6 λέγει οὖν αὐτοῖς ὁ
brothers of Him believed into Him. says Then to them

2424 3588 2540 3588 1699 3768 3918 3588 1161 2540 3588
Ἰησοῦς, Ὁ καιρὸς ὁ ἐμὸς οὔπω πάρεστιν, ὁ δὲ καιρὸς ὁ
Jesus, time My not yet is present, but time

5212 3842 2076 2092 3756 1410 3588 2889
ὑμέτερος πάντοτέ ἐστιν ἕτοιμος. 7 οὐ δύναται ὁ κόσμος
your always is ready. not is able The world

3404 5209 1691 1161 3404 3754 1473 3140 4012 846 3754
μισεῖν ὑμᾶς· ἐμὲ δὲ μισεῖ, ὅτι ἐγὼ μαρτυρῶ περὶ αὐτοῦ, ὅτι
to hate you; Me but it hates, because I witness concerning it, that

3588 2041 846 4190 2076 5210 305 1519 3588 1859
τὰ ἔργα αὐτοῦ πονηρά ἐστιν. 8 ὑμεῖς ἀνάβητε εἰς τὴν ἑορτὴν
the works of it evil are. You go up to feast

3778 1473 3768 305 1519 3588 1859 3778 3754 3588
ταύτην· ἐγὼ οὔπω ἀναβαίνω εἰς τὴν ἑορτὴν ταύτην, ὅτι ὁ
this; I not yet am going up to feast this, because the

2540 3588 1699 3768 4137 5023 1161 2036 846
καιρὸς ὁ ἐμὸς οὔπω πεπλήρωται. 9 ταῦτα δὲ εἰπὼν αὐτοῖς,
time of Me not yet has been fulfilled. these things And having said to them,

3306 1722 3588 1056
ἔμεινεν ἐν τῇ Γαλιλαίᾳ.
He remained in Galilee.

5613 1161 305 3588 80 846 5119 2532 846 305
10 Ὡς δὲ ἀνέβησαν οἱ ἀδελφοὶ αὐτοῦ, τότε καὶ αὐτὸς ἀνέβη
when But went up the brothers of Him, then also He went up

1519 3588 1859 3756 5320 235 5613 1722 2927 3588 3767
εἰς τὴν ἑορτήν, οὐ φανερῶς, ἀλλ' ὡς ἐν κρυπτῷ. 11 οἱ οὖν
to the feast, not openly, but as in secret. the Then

2453 2212 846 1722 3588 1859 2532 3004 4226 2076
Ἰουδαῖοι ἐζήτουν αὐτὸν ἐν τῇ ἑορτῇ, καὶ ἔλεγον, Ποῦ ἐστιν
Jews sought Him in the feast, and said, Where is

1565 2532 1112 4183 4012 846 2258 1722 3588 3793
ἐκεῖνος; 12 καὶ γογγυσμὸς πολὺς περὶ αὐτοῦ ἦν ἐν τοῖς ὄχλοις·
that One? And murmuring much about Him was in the crowds;

3588 3303 3004 3754 18 2076 243 1161 3004 3756 235
οἱ μὲν ἔλεγον ὅτι Ἀγαθός ἐστιν· ἄλλοι δὲ ἔλεγον, Οὔ, ἀλλὰ
Some indeed said, A good one He is; others but said, No, but

4105 3588 3793 3762 3305 3954 2980 4012 846
πλανᾷ τὸν ὄχλον. 13 οὐδεὶς μέντοι παρρησίᾳ ἐλάλει περὶ αὐτοῦ
he deceives the crowd. No one however publicly spoke about Him

1223 3588 5401 3588 2453
διὰ τὸν φόβον τῶν Ἰουδαίων.
because of the fear of the Jews.

2. Now the Jews' feast of tabernacles was at hand.

3 His brethren therefore said unto him, Depart hence, and go into Judaea, that thy disciples also may see the works that thou doest.

4 For (there is) no man (that) doeth any thing in secret, and he himself seeketh to be known openly. If thou do these things, shew thyself to the world.

5 For neither did his brethren believe in him.

6 Then Jesus said unto them, My time is not yet come: but your time is alway ready.

7 The world cannot hate you; but me it hateth, because I testify of it, that the works thereof are evil.

8 Go ye up unto this feast: I go not up yet unto this feast; for my time is not yet full come.

9 When he had said these words unto them, he abode (still) in Galilee.

10. But when his brethren were gone up, then went he also up unto the feast, not openly, but as it were in secret.

11 Then the Jews sought him at the feast, and said, Where is he?

12 And there was much murmuring among the people concerning him: for some said, He is a good man: others said, Nay; but he deceiveth the people.

13 Howbeit no man spake openly of him for fear of the Jews.

Literal Translation

14. But the feast now being in the middle, Jesus went up to the temple and taught.
15 And the Jews marveled, saying, How does this one know letters, not having learned?
16 Jesus answered, them and said, My doctrine is not Mine, but of the (One) who has sent Me.
17 If anyone desires to do His will, he will know concerning the doctrine, whether it is of God, or I speak from Myself.
18 The (one) speaking from himself seeks (his) own glory. But the (one) seeking the glory of the (One) who has sent Him, this One is true, and unrighteousness is not in Him.
19 Did not Moses give you the Law, and not one of you does the Law? Why do you seek to kill Me?
20 The crowd answered and said, You have a demon. Who lusts to kill you?
21 Jesus answered and said to them, I did one work, and you all marvel.
22 Because of this Moses has given you circumcision; not that it is of Moses, but of the fathers; and on a sabbath, you circumcise a man.
23 If a man receives circumcision on a sabbath, that the Law of Moses is not broken, are you angry with Me because I made a man entirely healthy on a sabbath?
24 Do not judge according to sight, but judge righteous judgment.
25 Then some of the Jerusalemites said, Is it not this one one they are seeking to kill?
26 And, behold, He speaks publicly, and

John 7:14

2235 1161 3588 1859 3322 305 3588 2424 1519 3588
14 Ἤδη δὲ τῆς ἑορτῆς μεσούσης, ἀνέβη ὁ Ἰησοῦς εἰς τὸ
now But the feast being in middle, went up Jesus into the
2411 2532 1321 2532 2296 3588 2453 3004
ἱερόν, καὶ ἐδίδασκε. 15 καὶ ἐθαύμαζον οἱ Ἰουδαῖοι λέγοντες,
temple and taught. And marveled the Jews saying,
4459 3778 1121 1492 3361 3129 611 846 3588
Πῶς οὗτος γράμματα οἶδε, μὴ μεμαθηκώς; 16 ἀπεκρίθη αὐτοῖς ὁ
How this one letters knows, not having learned? answered to them
2424 2532 2036 3588 1699 1322 3756 2076 1699 235 3588
Ἰησοῦς καὶ εἶπεν, Ἡ ἐμὴ διδαχὴ οὐκ ἔστιν ἐμή, ἀλλὰ τοῦ
Jesus and said, My teaching not is Mine, but of the (One)
3992 3165 1437 5100 2309 3588 2307 846 4160
πέμψαντός με. 17 ἐάν τις θέλῃ τὸ θέλημα αὐτοῦ ποιεῖν,
having sent Me. If anyone desires the will of Him to do,
1097 4012 3588 1322 4220 1537 3588 2316 2076 2228
γνώσεται περὶ τῆς διδαχῆς, πότερον ἐκ τοῦ Θεοῦ ἐστιν, ἢ
he will know about the teaching, whether of God it is, or
1473 575 1683 2980 3588 575 1683 2980 3588 1391 3588
ἐγὼ ἀπ' ἐμαυτοῦ λαλῶ. 18 ὁ ἀφ' ἑαυτοῦ λαλῶν, τὴν δόξαν τὴν
I from Myself speak. The (one) from himself speaking, the glory the
2398 2212 3588 1161 2212 3588 1391 3588 3992 846 3778
ἰδίαν ζητεῖ· ὁ δὲ ζητῶν τὴν δόξαν τοῦ πέμψαντος αὐτόν, οὗτος
own seeks. the (one) But seeking the glory of (Him) having sent Him, this One
227 2076 2532 93 1722 846 3756 2076 3756 3475
ἀληθής ἐστι, καὶ ἀδικία ἐν αὐτῷ οὐκ ἔστιν. 19 οὐ Μωσῆς
true is, and unrighteousness in Him not is. not Did Moses
1325 5213 3588 3551 2532 3762 1537 5216 4160 3588 3551 5101
δέδωκεν ὑμῖν τὸν νόμον, καὶ οὐδεὶς ἐξ ὑμῶν ποιεῖ τὸν νόμον; τί
give you the Law, and no one of you does the Law? Why
3165 2212 615 611 3588 3793 2532 2036 1140
με ζητεῖτε ἀποκτεῖναι; 20 ἀπεκρίθη ὁ ὄχλος καὶ εἶπε, Δαιμόνιον
Me seek you to kill? answered The crowd and said, a demon
2192 5101 4571 2212 615 611 3588 2424 2532 2036
ἔχεις· τίς σε ζητεῖ ἀποκτεῖναι; 21 ἀπεκρίθη ὁ Ἰησοῦς καὶ εἶπεν
You have; who you seeks to kill? answered Jesus and said,
846 1520 2041 4160 2532 3956 2296 1223 5124
αὐτοῖς, Ἓν ἔργον ἐποίησα, καὶ πάντες θαυμάζετε. 22 διὰ τοῦτο
to them, One work I did, and all you marvel. Because of this
3475 1325 5213 3588 4061 3756 3754 1537 3588 3475
Μωσῆς δέδωκεν ὑμῖν τὴν περιτομήν [οὐχ ὅτι ἐκ τοῦ Μωσέως
Moses has given you circumcision; not that of Moses
2076 235 1537 3588 3962 2532 1722 4521 4059
ἐστίν, ἀλλ' ἐκ τῶν πατέρων]· καὶ ἐν σαββάτῳ περιτέμνετε
it is, but of the fathers; and in a sabbath you circumcise
444 1487 4061 2983 444 1722 4521
ἄνθρωπον. 23 εἰ περιτομὴν λαμβάνει ἄνθρωπος ἐν σαββάτῳ,
a man. If circumcision receives a man in a sabbath,
2443 3361 3089 3588 3551 3475 1698 5520 3754 3650 444
ἵνα μὴ λυθῇ ὁ νόμος Μωσέως, ἐμοὶ χολᾶτε ὅτι ὅλον ἄνθρωπον
that not is broken the Law of Moses, with Me are you angry that whole a man
5199 4160 1722 4521 3361 2919 2596 3799 235 3588
ὑγιῆ ἐποίησα ἐν σαββάτῳ; 24 μὴ κρίνετε κατ' ὄψιν, ἀλλὰ τὴν
healthy I made in a sabbath? not Do judge by sight, but
1342 2920 2919
δικαίαν κρίσιν κρίνατε.
righteous judgment judge.

3004 3767 5100 1537 3588 2415 3756 3778
25 Ἔλεγον οὖν τινες ἐκ τῶν Ἱεροσολυμιτῶν, Οὐχ οὗτός
said Then some of the Jerusalemites, Not this one
2076 3739 12 615 2532 2396 3954 2980 2532
ἐστιν ὃν ζητοῦσιν ἀποκτεῖναι; 26 καὶ ἴδε παρρησίᾳ λαλεῖ, καὶ
is it whom they are seeking to kill? And, behold! publicly He speaks, and

King James Version

14. Now about the midst of the feast Jesus went up into the temple, and taught.
15 And the Jews marvelled, saying, How knoweth this man letters, having never learned?
16 Jesus answered them, and said, My doctrine is not mine, but his that sent me.
17 If any man will do his will, he shall know of the doctrine, whether it be of God, or (whether) I speak of myself.
18 He that speaketh of himself seeketh his own glory: but he that seeketh his glory that sent him, the same is true, and no unrighteousness is in him.
19 Did not Moses give you the law, and (yet) none of you keepeth the law? Why go ye about to kill me?
20 The people answered and said, Thou hast a devil: who goeth about to kill thee?
21 Jesus answered and said unto them, I have done one work, and ye all marvel.
22 Moses therefore gave unto you circumcision; (not because it is of Moses, but of the fathers;) and ye on the sabbath day circumcise a man.
23 If a man on the sabbath day receive circumcision, that the law of Moses should not be broken; are ye angry at me, because I have made a man every whit whole on the sabbath day?
24 Judge not according to the appearance, but judge righteous judgment.
25 Then said some of them of Jerusalem, Is not this he, whom they seek to kill?
26 But, lo, he speaketh boldly, and

John 7:27

Literal Translation

they say nothing to him. Perhaps the rulers truly knew that this is truly the Christ?
27 But we know this one, from where he is. But when the Christ comes, no one knows from where He is.

28 Then teaching, Jesus cried out in the temple, and saying, You both know Me, and you know from where I am. And I have not come from Myself, but He wo has sent Me is true, whom you do not know.

29 But I know Him, because I am from Him; and He sent Me.
30 Then they sought to seize Him; yet no one laid (a) hand on Him, because His hour had not yet come.

31. But many of the crowd believed into Him, and said, The Christ, when He comes will He do more signs than these which this One did?

32. The Pharisees heard the crowd murmuring these things concerning Him, and the Pharisees and the chief priests sent (their) under-officers, that they might seize Him.

33 Then Jesus said to them, Yet a little while I am with you, and I go to the (One) who has sent Me.
34 You will seek Me, and will not find (Me); and where I am, you are not able to come.

35 Then the Jews said to themselves, Where is this one about to go that we will not find him? Is he about to go to the Dispersion of the Greeks, and to teach the Greeks?

36 What is this word which he said, You will seek

3762 846 3004 3379 230 1097 3588 758
οὐδὲν αὐτῷ λέγουσι. μήποτε ἀληθῶς ἔγνωσαν οἱ ἄρχοντες
nothing to Him they say. Perhaps truly knew the rulers

3754 3778 2076 230 3588 5547 235 5126 1492
ὅτι οὗτός ἐστιν ἀληθῶς ὁ Χριστός; 27 ἀλλὰ τοῦτον οἴδαμεν
that this is truly the Christ? But this one we know

4159 2076 3588 1161 5547 3752 2064 3762 1097 4159
πόθεν ἐστίν· ὁ δὲ Χριστὸς ὅταν ἔρχηται, οὐδεὶς γινώσκει πόθεν
from where he is; the but Christ when comes, no one knows from where

2076 2896 3767 1722 3588 2411 1321 3588 2424 2532 3004
ἐστίν. 28 ἔκραξεν οὖν ἐν τῷ ἱερῷ διδάσκων ὁ Ἰησοῦς καὶ λέγων,
He is. cried out Then in the temple teaching Jesus and saying,

2504 5723 2532 1492 4159 1510 2532 575 1683 3756
Κἀμὲ οἴδατε, καὶ οἴδατε πόθεν εἰμί· καὶ ἀπ᾽ ἐμαυτοῦ οὐκ
Both Me you know, and you know from where I am; and from Myself not

2064 235 2076 228 3588 3992 3165 3739 5210 3756
ἐλήλυθα, ἀλλ᾽ ἔστιν ἀληθινὸς ὁ πέμψας με, ὃν ὑμεῖς οὐκ
I have come, but He is true, (He) having sent Me, whom you not

1492 1473 1161 1492 846 3754 3844 846 1510 2548 3165
οἴδατε. 29 ἐγὼ δὲ οἶδα αὐτόν, ὅτι παρ᾽ αὐτοῦ εἰμι, κἀκεῖνός με
do know. I But know Him, because from Him I am, and that (One) Me

649 2212 3767 846 4084 2532 3762 1911
ἀπέστειλεν. 30 ἐζήτουν οὖν αὐτὸν πιάσαι. καὶ οὐδεὶς ἐπέβαλεν
sent. they sought Then Him to seize,.And no one laid

1909 846 3588 5495 3754 3768 2064 3588 5610 846
ἐπ᾽ αὐτὸν τὴν χεῖρα, ὅτι οὔπω ἐληλύθει ἡ ὥρα αὐτοῦ.
on Him the hand, because not yet had come the hour of Him.

4183 1161 1537 3588 3793 4100 1519 846 2532 3004
31 πολλοὶ δὲ ἐκ τοῦ ὄχλου ἐπίστευσαν εἰς αὐτόν, καὶ ἔλεγον
many But of the crowd believed into Him, and said

3754 3588 5547 3752 2064 3385 4119 4592 5130
ὅτι Ὁ Χριστὸς ὅταν ἔλθῃ, μήτι πλείονα σημεῖα τούτων
The Christ when He comes, not greater signs than these

4160 3739 3778 4160 191 3588 5330 3588
ποιήσει ὧν οὗτος ἐποίησεν; 32 ἤκουσαν οἱ Φαρισαῖοι τοῦ
will He do which this One did? heard The Pharisees the

3793 1111 4012 846 5023 2532 649 3588
ὄχλου γογγύζοντος περὶ αὐτοῦ ταῦτα· καὶ ἀπέστειλαν οἱ
crowd murmuring concerning Him these things, and sent the

5330 2532 3588 749 5257 2443 4084 846
Φαρισαῖοι καὶ οἱ ἀρχιερεῖς ὑπηρέτας ἵνα πιάσωσιν αὐτόν.
Pharisees and the chief priests under-officers, that they might seize Him.

2036 3767 846 3588 2424 2089 3398 5550 3326 5216
33 εἶπεν οὖν αὐτοῖς ὁ Ἰησοῦς, Ἔτι μικρὸν χρόνον μεθ᾽ ὑμῶν
said Then to them Jesus, Yet a little time with you

1510 2532 5217 4314 3588 3992 3165 2212 3165 2532
εἰμι, καὶ ὑπάγω πρὸς τὸν πέμψαντά με. 34 ζητήσετέ με, καὶ
I am, and I go to the (One) having sent Me. You will seek Me, and

3756 2147 2532 3699 1510 1473 5210 3756 1410 2064
οὐχ εὑρήσετε· καὶ ὅπου εἰμὶ ἐγώ, ὑμεῖς οὐ δύνασθε ἐλθεῖν.
not will find; and where am I, you not are able to come.

2036 3767 3588 2453 4314 1438 4226 3778 3195
35 εἶπον οὖν οἱ Ἰουδαῖοι πρὸς ἑαυτούς, Ποῦ οὗτος μέλλει
said Then the Jews to themselves, Where this one is about

4198 3754 2249 3756 2147 846 3361 1519 3588
πορεύεσθαι ὅτι ἡμεῖς οὐχ εὑρήσομεν αὐτόν; μὴ εἰς τὴν
to go that we not will find Him? Not to the

1290 3588 1672 3195 4198 2532 1321
διασπορὰν τῶν Ἑλλήνων μέλλει πορεύεσθαι καὶ διδάσκειν
Dispersion of the Greeks is he about to go and to teach

3588 1672 5101 2076 3778 3588 3056 3739 2036 2212
τοὺς Ἕλληνας; 36 τίς ἐστιν οὗτος ὁ λόγος ὃν εἶπε, Ζητήσετέ
the Greeks? What is this word which He said, You will seek

King James Version

they say nothing unto him. Do the rulers know indeed that this is the very Christ?
27 Howbeit we know this man whence he is: but when Christ cometh, no man knoweth whence he is.

28 Then cried Jesus in the temple as he taught, saying, Ye both know me, and ye know whence I am: and I am not come of myself, but he that sent me is true, whom ye know not.

29 But I know him: for I am from him, and he hath sent me.
30 Then they sought to take him: but no man laid hands on him, because his hour was not yet come.

31. And many of the people believed on him, and said, When Christ cometh, will he do more miracles than these which this (man) hath done?

32. The Pharisees heard that the people murmured such things concerning him; and the Pharisees and the chief priests sent officers to take him.

33 Then said Jesus unto them, Yet a little while am I with you, and (then) I go unto him that sent me.
34 Ye shall seek me, and shall not find (me): and where I am, (thither) ye cannot come.

35 Then said the Jews among themselves, Whither will he go, that we shall not find him? will he go unto the dispersed among the Gentiles, and teach the Gentiles?

36 What (manner of) saying is this that he said, Ye shall seek me,

Literal Translation

Me and will not find (Me), and, Where I am, you are not able to come?

37. And in the last day of the great feast, Jesus stood and cried out, saying, If anyone thirsts, let him come to Me and drink.

38 The (one) believing into Me, as the Writing said, "Out of his belly will flow rivers of living water."

39 But He said this concerning the Spirit, whom the ones believing into Him were about to receive; for (the) Holy Spirit was not yet (given), because Jesus was not yet glorified.

40 Therefore hearing the word, many of the crowd said, This is truly the Prophet.

41 Others said, This is the Christ. But others said, (No!) For does the Christ come out of Galilee?

42 Has not the Scripture said that the Christ comes from the seed of David, and from Bethlehem, the village where David was?

43 Then a division occurred in the crowd because of Him.

44 And some of them desired to seize Him, but no one laid hands on Him.

45. Then came the under-officers to the chief priests and Pharisees. And they said to them, Why did you not bring him?

46 The under-officers answered, Never did a man so speak as does this man.

47 Then the Pharisees answered them, Have you not also been deceived?

48 Not any from the

John 7:37

3165 2532 3756 2147 2532 3699 1510 1473 5210 3756 1410
με, καὶ οὐχ εὑρήσετε· καὶ ὅπου εἰμὶ ἐγώ, ὑμεῖς οὐ δύνασθε
Me, and not you will find; and where am I, you not are able
2064
ἐλθεῖν;
to come?

1722 1161 3588 2078 2250 3588 3173 3588 1859 2476
37 Ἐν δὲ τῇ ἐσχάτῃ ἡμέρᾳ τῇ μεγάλῃ τῆς ἑορτῆς εἱστήκει
in And the last day the great of the feast stood
3588 2424 2532 2896 3004 1437 5100 1372 2064 4314
ὁ Ἰησοῦς καὶ ἔκραξε, λέγων, Ἐάν τις διψᾷ, ἐρχέσθω πρός
Jesus and cried out, saying, If anyone thirst, let him come to
3165 2532 4095 3588 4100 1519 1691 2531 2036 3588 1124
με καὶ πινέτω. 38 ὁ πιστεύων εἰς ἐμέ, καθὼς εἶπεν ἡ γραφή,
Me and drink. The (one) believing into Me, even as said the Writing,
4215 1537 3588 2836 846 4482 5204 2198
ποταμοὶ ἐκ τῆς κοιλίας αὐτοῦ ῥεύσουσιν ὕδατος ζῶντος.
Rivers out of the belly of him will flow water of living.
5124 1161 2036 4012 3588 4151 3739 3195 2983 3588
39 τοῦτο δὲ εἶπε περὶ τοῦ Πνεύματος οὗ ἔμελλον λαμβάνειν οἱ
this But He said about the Spirit whom were about to receive those
4100 1519 846 3768 1063 2258 4151 40 3754
πιστεύοντες εἰς αὐτόν· οὔπω γὰρ ἦν Πνεῦμα Ἅγιον, ὅτι
believing into Him; not yet for was (given the) Spirit Holy, because
3588 2424 3764 1392 4183 3767 1537 3588 3793
ὁ Ἰησοῦς οὐδέπω ἐδοξάσθη. 40 πολλοὶ οὖν ἐκ τοῦ ὄχλου
Jesus not yet was glorified. many Therefore of the crowd
191 3588 3056 3004 3778 2076 230 3588 4396
ἀκούσαντες τὸν λόγον ἔλεγον, Οὗτός ἐστιν ἀληθῶς ὁ προφή-
having heard the Word said, This is truly the Prophet.
243 3004 3778 2076 3588 5547 243 1161 3004
της. 41 ἄλλοι ἔλεγον, Οὗτός ἐστιν ὁ Χριστός. ἄλλοι δὲ ἔλεγον,
Others said, This is the Christ. others But said,
3361 1063 1537 3588 1056 3588 5547 2064 3780 3588 1124
Μὴ γὰρ ἐκ τῆς Γαλιλαίας ὁ Χριστὸς ἔρχεται; 42 οὐχὶ ἡ γραφὴ
not, For out of Galilee the Christ comes? Not (has) the Scripture
2036 3754 1537 3588 4690 1138 2532 575 965 3588
εἶπεν ὅτι ἐκ τοῦ σπέρματος Δαβίδ, καὶ ἀπὸ Βηθλεέμ, τῆς
said that out of the seed of David, and from Bethlehem, the
2968 3699 2258 1138 3588 5547 2064 4978 3767 1722
κώμης ὅπου ἦν Δαβίδ, ὁ Χριστὸς ἔρχεται; 43 σχίσμα οὖν ἐν
village where was David, the Christ comes? a division Then in
3588 3793 1096 1223 846 5100 1161 2309 1537 846
τῷ ὄχλῳ ἐγένετο δι᾽ αὐτόν. 44 τινὲς δὲ ἤθελον ἐξ αὐτῶν
the crowd occurred, because of Him. some And desired of them
4084 846 235 3762 1911 1909 846 3588 5495
πιάσαι αὐτόν, ἀλλ᾽ οὐδεὶς ἐπέβαλεν ἐπ᾽ αὐτὸν τὰς χεῖρας.
to seize Him, but no one laid on Him the hands.

2064 3767 3588 5257 4314 3588 749 2532 5330
45 Ἦλθον οὖν οἱ ὑπηρέται πρὸς τοὺς ἀρχιερεῖς καὶ Φαρι-
came Then the under-officers to the chief priests and Phari-
2532 2036 846 1565 1302 3756 71 846
σαίους· καὶ εἶπον αὐτοῖς ἐκεῖνοι, Διατί οὐκ ἠγάγετε αὐτόν;
sees; and said to them those, Why not did you bring him?
611 3588 5257 3763 3779 2980
46 ἀπεκρίθησαν οἱ ὑπηρέται, Οὐδέποτε οὕτως ἐλάλησεν
answered The under-officers, Never so spoke
444 5613 3778 3588 444 611 3767 846
ἄνθρωπος, ὡς οὗτος ὁ ἄνθρωπος. 47 ἀπεκρίθησαν οὖν αὐτοῖς
a man as this man. answered Then them
3588 5330 3361 2532 5210 4105 3361 5100 1537 3588
οἱ Φαρισαῖοι, Μὴ καὶ ὑμεῖς πεπλάνησθε; 48 μή τις ἐκ τῶν
the Pharisees, not also you Have been deceived? Not any of the

King James Version

and shall not find (me): and where I am, (thither) ye cannot come?

37. In the last day, that great (day) of the feast, Jesus stood and cried, saying, If any man thirst, let him come unto me, and drink.

38 He that believeth on me, as the scripture hath said, out of his belly shall flow rivers of living water.

39 (But this spake he of the Spirit, which they that believe on him should receive: for the Holy Ghost was not yet (given); because that Jesus was not yet glorified.)

40 Many of the people therefore, when they heard this saying, said, Of a truth this is the Prophet.

41 Others said, This is the Christ. But some said, Shall Christ come out of Galilee?

42 Hath not the scripture said, That Christ cometh of the seed of David, and out of the town of Bethlehem, where David was?

43 So there was a division among the people because of him.

44 And some of them would have taken him; but no man laid hands on him.

45 . Then came the officers to the chief priests and Pharisees; and they said unto them, Why have ye not brought him?

46 The officers answered, Never man spake like this man.

47 Then answered them the Pharisees, Are ye also deceived?

48 Have any of the

John 7:49

Literal Translation

rulers or from the Pharisees believed into him?
49 But not knowing the Law, this crowd is cursed.

50 Nicodemus said to them, the (one) having come (by) night to Him, being one of themselves,
51 Does our Law judge the Man unless it hear from him first, and know what he does?

52 They answered and said to him, Are you also from Galilee? Search and see that a prophet has not been raised out of Galilee.

53. And they each one went to his house.

758 4100 1519 846 2228 1537 3588 5330 235
ἀρχόντων ἐπίστευσεν εἰς αὐτόν, ἢ ἐκ τῶν Φαρισαίων; 49 ἀλλ'
rulers have believed into Him, or from the Pharisees? But

3588 3793 3778 3588 3361 1097 3588 3551 1944 1526
ὁ ὄχλος οὗτος ὁ μὴ γινώσκων τὸν νόμον ἐπικατάρατοί εἰσι.
crowd this not knowing the Law cursed upon are.

3004 3530 4314 846 3588 2064 3571 4314 846
50 λέγει Νικόδημος πρὸς αὐτούς [ὁ ἐλθὼν νυκτὸς πρὸς αὐτόν,
says Nicodemus to them, he having come by night to Him,

1520 5607 1537 846 3361 3588 3551 2257 2919 3588 444
εἷς ὢν ἐξ αὐτῶν], 51 Μὴ ὁ νόμος ἡμῶν κρίνει τὸν ἄνθρωπον,
one being of them, Not the Law of us judge the man,

1437 3361 191 3844 846 4386 2532 1097 5101 4160
ἐὰν μὴ ἀκούσῃ παρ' αὐτοῦ πρότερον καὶ γνῷ τί ποιεῖ;
if not it hear from him first and know what he does?

611 2532 2036 846 3361 2532 4771 1537 3588 1056 1488
52 ἀπεκρίθησαν καὶ εἶπον αὐτῷ, Μὴ καὶ σὺ ἐκ τῆς Γαλιλαίας εἶ;
They answered, and said to him, not also you of Galilee Are?

2045 2532 2396 3754 4396 1537 3588 1056 3756
ἐρεύνησον καὶ ἴδε ὅτι προφήτης ἐκ τῆς Γαλιλαίας οὐκ
Search and see that a prophet out of Galilee not

1453
ἐγήγερται. 53 *(In some texts, the first sentence of John 8:1 is John 7:53)*
has been raised.

King James Version

rulers or of the Pharisees believed on him?
49 But this people who knoweth not the law are cursed.

50 Nicodemus saith unto them, (he that came to Jesus by night, being one of them,)
51 Doth our law judge (any) man, before it hear him, and know what he doeth?

52 They answered and said unto him, Art thou also of Galilee? Search, and look: for out of Galilee ariseth no prophet.
53. And every man went unto his own house.

John 8

Literal Translation

1 But Jesus went to the Mount of Olives.

2 And at dawn He again arrived into the temple; and all the people came to Him. And sitting down, He was teaching them.

3 And the scribes and the Pharisees brought to Him a woman having been taken in adultery. And standing her in (the) middle,
4 they said to Him, Teacher, this woman has been taken in the very act, committing adultery.
5 And in the Law, Moses commanded to us that such should be stoned. You, then, what do you say?
6 But they said this, tempting Him, that they may have (reason) to accuse Him. But bending down, Jesus wrote with the finger in the earth, not appearing (to hear).
7 But as they continued questioning Him, bending back up, He said to them,

2532 4198 1538 1519 3588 3624 846 2424 1161
1. Καὶ ἐπορεύθη ἕκαστος εἰς τὸν οἶκον αὐτοῦ· Ἰησοῦς δὲ
And they went each one to the house of him; Jesus but

4198 1519 3588 3735 3588 1636 3722 1161 3825 3854
ἐπορεύθη εἰς τὸ ὄρος τῶν ἐλαιῶν. 2 ὄρθρου δὲ πάλιν παρε-
went to the Mount of the Olives. at dawn And again He

1519 3588 2411 2532 3956 3588 2992 2064 4314 846 2532
γένετο εἰς τὸ ἱερόν, καὶ πᾶς ὁ λαὸς ἤρχετο πρὸς αὐτόν· καὶ
arrived into the temple, and all the people came to Him; and

2523 1321 846 71 1161 3588 1122 2532 3588
καθίσας ἐδίδασκεν αὐτούς. 3 ἄγουσι δὲ οἱ γραμματεῖς καὶ οἱ
sitting He was teaching them. bring And the scribes and the

5330 4314 846 1135 1722 3430 2638
Φαρισαῖοι πρὸς αὐτὸν γυναῖκα ἐν μοιχείᾳ κατειλημμένην,
Pharisees to Him a woman in adultery having been taken.

2532 2476 846 1722 3319 3004 846 1320
καὶ στήσαντες αὐτὴν ἐν μέσῳ, 4 λέγουσιν αὐτῷ, Διδάσκαλε,
And standing her in (the) midst, they say to Him, Teacher,

846 3588 1135 2638 1888 3431 1722 1161 3588
αὕτη ἡ γυνὴ κατειλήφθη ἐπαυτοφώρῳ μοιχευομένη. 5 ἐν δὲ τῷ
this woman has been taken in the very act committing adultery. in And the

3551 3475 2254 1781 3588 5108 3036
νόμῳ Μωσῆς ἡμῖν ἐνετείλατο τὰς τοιαύτας λιθοβολεῖσθαι·
Law Moses to us commanded such (women) to be stoned;

4771 3767 5101 3004 5124 1161 3004 3985 846 2443
σὺ οὖν τί λέγεις; 6 τοῦτο δὲ ἔλεγον πειράζοντες αὐτόν, ἵνα
you then what say you? this But they said tempting Him, that

2192 2723 846 3588 1161 2424 2736 2955 3588
ἔχωσι κατηγορεῖν αὐτοῦ. ὁ δὲ Ἰησοῦς κάτω κύψας, τῷ
they have to accuse Him. But Jesus down bending with the

1147 1125 1519 3588 1093 3361 4364 5613 1161
δακτύλῳ ἔγραφεν εἰς τὴν γῆν, 7 μὴ προσποιούμενος. ὡς δὲ
finger wrote in the earth, not appearing (to hear). as And

1961 2065 846 352 2036 4314 846
ἐπέμενον ἐρωτῶντες αὐτόν, ἀνακύψας εἶπε πρὸς αὐτούς,
they continued questioning Him, bending back up He said to them,

King James Version

1 Jesus went unto the mount of Olives.

2 And early in the morning he came again into the temple, and all the people came unto him; and he sat down, and taught them.

3 And the scribes and Pharisees brought unto him a woman taken in adultery; and when they had set her in the midst,

4 They say unto him, Master, this woman was taken in adultery, in the very act.
5 Now Moses in the law commanded us, that such should be stoned: but what sayest thou?

6 This they said, tempting him, that they might have to accuse him. But Jesus stooped down, and with (his) finger wrote on the ground, (as though he heard them not).
7 So when they continued asking him, he lifted up himself, and said unto them,

Literal Translation | **John 8:8** | **King James Version**

The (one) of you without sin, let him cast the first stone on her.
8 And bending down again, He wrote in the earth.
9 But having heard, and being convicted by the conscience, they went out one by one, beginning from the older ones, until the last. And Jesus was left alone, and the woman standing in (the) middle.

10 And Jesus bending back up, and having seen no one but the woman, He said to her, Woman, where are those the accusers of you? Did not one give judgment against you?
11 And she said, No one, Lord. And Jesus said to her, Neither do I give judgment. Go, and sin no more.

12. Then Jesus again spoke to them, saying, I am the Light of the world. The (one) following Me will in no way walk in the darkness, but will have the light of Life.
13 Then the Pharisees said to Him, You witnessed about yourself; your witness is not true.

14 Jesus answered and said to them, Even if I witness concerning Myself, My witness is true; for I know from where I came, and where I go. But you do not know from where I came, and where I go.

15 You judge according to the flesh. I judge no one.

16 But even if I judge, My judgment is true, because I am not alone, but I and (the) Father who has sent Me.

17 And in your Law it has been written

3588 361 5216 4413 3588 3037 1909 846 906
Ὁ ἀναμάρτητος ὑμῶν, πρῶτος τὸν λίθον ἐπ' αὐτῇ βαλέτω.
The (one) sinless of you, first the stone on her cast.

2532 3825 2736 2955 1125 1519 3588 1093 3588 1161 191
8 καὶ πάλιν κάτω κύψας ἔγραφεν εἰς τὴν γῆν. 9 οἱ δέ, ἀκούσαν-
And again down bending He wrote in the earth. they But, having

2532 5259 3588 4893 1651 1831 1520 2596
τες, καὶ ὑπὸ τῆς συνειδήσεως ἐλεγχόμενοι, ἐξήρχοντο εἷς καθ'
heard, and by the conscience being convicted, went out one by

1520 756 575 3588 4245 2193 3588 2078 2532
εἷς, ἀρξάμενοι ἀπὸ τῶν πρεσβυτέρων ἕως τῶν ἐσχάτων· καὶ
one, beginning from the older ones until the last. And

2641 3441 3588 2424 2532 3588 1135 1722 3319 2476
κατελείφθη μόνος ὁ Ἰησοῦς, καὶ ἡ γυνὴ ἐν μέσῳ ἑστῶσα.
was left alone Jesus, and the woman in (the) midst standing.

352 1161 3588 2424 2532 3367 2300 4133 3588
10 ἀνακύψας δὲ ὁ Ἰησοῦς, καὶ μηδένα θεασάμενος πλὴν τῆς
bending back up And Jesus, and no one having seen but the

1135 2036 846 3588 1135 4226 1526 1565 3588 2725
γυναικός, εἶπεν αὐτῇ Ἡ γυνή ποῦ εἰσιν ἐκεῖνοι οἱ κατήγοροί
woman, He said to her, Woman where are those the accusers

4675 3762 4571 2623 3588 1161 2036 3762 2962 2036 1161
σου; οὐδείς σε κατέκρινεν; 11 ἡ δὲ εἶπεν, Οὐδείς, Κύριε. εἶπε δὲ
of you? No one you judged? she And said. No one, Lord. said And

846 3588 2424 3761 1473 4571 2632 4198 2532 3371
αὐτῇ ὁ Ἰησοῦς, Οὐδὲ ἐγώ σε κατακρίνω· πορεύου καὶ μηκέτι
to her Jesus, Neither I you judge; go, and no more

264
ἁμάρτανε.
sin.

3825 3767 3588 2424 846 2980 3004 1473 1510 3588
12. Πάλιν οὖν ὁ Ἰησοῦς αὐτοῖς ἐλάλησε λέγων, Ἐγώ εἰμι τὸ
again Then Jesus to them spoke, saying, I am the

5457 3588 2889 3588 190 1698 3756 3361 4043 1722 3588
φῶς τοῦ κόσμου· ὁ ἀκολουθῶν ἐμοὶ οὐ μὴ περιπατήσει ἐν τῇ
Light of the world; the (one) following Me in no way will walk in the

4653 235 2192 3588 5457 3588 2222 2036 3767 846 3588
σκοτίᾳ, ἀλλ' ἕξει τὸ φῶς τῆς ζωῆς. 13 εἶπον οὖν αὐτῷ οἱ
darkness, but will have the light of Life. said Then to Him the

5330 4771 4012 4572 3140 3588 3141 4675 3756
Φαρισαῖοι, Σὺ περὶ σεαυτοῦ μαρτυρεῖς· ἡ μαρτυρία σου οὐκ
Pharisees, You about yourself witnessed. The witness of you not

2076 227 611 2424 2532 2036 846 2579
ἔστιν ἀληθής. 14 ἀπεκρίθη Ἰησοῦς καὶ εἶπεν αὐτοῖς, Κἂν
is true. answered Jesus and said to them, Even if

1473 3140 4012 1683 227 2076 3588 3141 3450
ἐγὼ μαρτυρῶ περὶ ἐμαυτοῦ, ἀληθής ἐστιν ἡ μαρτυρία μου·
I witness concerning Myself, true is the witness of Me;

3754 1492 4159 2064 2532 4226 5217 5210 1161 3756 1492
ὅτι οἶδα πόθεν ἦλθον, καὶ ποῦ ὑπάγω· ὑμεῖς δὲ οὐκ οἴδατε
because I know from where I came, and where I go. you But not do know

4159 2064 2532 4226 5217 5210 2596 3588 4561
πόθεν ἔρχομαι, καὶ ποῦ ὑπάγω. 15 ὑμεῖς κατὰ τὴν σάρκα
from where I come, and where I go. You according to the flesh

2919 1473 3756 2919 3762 2532 1437 2919 1161 1473 3588
κρίνετε· ἐγὼ οὐ κρίνω οὐδένα. 16 καὶ ἐὰν κρίνω δὲ ἐγώ, ἡ
judge. I not do judge, no one. even if judge But I, the

2920 3588 1699 227 2076 3754 3441 3756 1510 235 1473 2532
κρίσις ἡ ἐμὴ ἀληθής ἐστιν· ὅτι μόνος οὐκ εἰμί, ἀλλ' ἐγὼ καὶ
judgment My true is, because alone not I am, but I and

3588 3992 3165 3962 2532 1722 3588 3551 1161 3588 5212 1125
ὁ πέμψας με πατήρ. 17 καὶ ἐν τῷ νόμῳ δὲ τῷ ὑμετέρῳ γέγρα-
He having sent Me (the) Father. also in Law And your it has been

he that is without sin among you, let him first cast a stone at her.
8 And again he stooped down, and wrote on the ground.
9 And they which heard (it), being convicted by (their own) conscience, went out one by one, beginning at the eldest, (even) unto the last: and Jesus was left alone, and the woman standing in the midst.

10 When Jesus had lifted up himself, and saw none but the woman, he said unto her, Woman, where are those thine accusers? hath no man condemned thee?
11 She said, No man, Lord. And Jesus said unto her, Neither do I condemn thee: go, and sin no more.

12. Then spake Jesus again unto them, saying, I am the light of the world: he that followeth me shall not walk in darkness, but shall have the light of life.
13 The Pharisees therefore said unto him, Thou bearest record of thyself; thy record is not true.

14 Jesus answered and said unto them, Though I bear record of myself, (yet) my record is true: for I know whence I came, and whither I go; but ye cannot tell whence I come, and whither I go.

15 Ye judge after the flesh; I judge no man.

16 And yet if I judge, my judgment is true: for I am not alone, but I and the Father that sent me.

17 It is also written in your law,

Literal Translation

that the witness of two
men is true.
18 I am the (One) wit-
nessing concerning
Myself, and He who has
sent Me, the Father, wit-
nesses concerning Me.

19 Then they said to
Him, Where is your fa-
ther? Jesus answered,
You neither know Me,
nor My Father. If you
had known Me, then
you also would have
known My Father.
20 Jesus spoke these
words in the treasury,
teaching in the temple;
and no one seized Him,
for His hour had not yet
come.

21 Then Jesus said to
them again, I go, and
you will seek Me. And
you will die in your sin.
Where I go, you are not
able to come.

22 Then the Jews said,
Will he kill himself, be-
cause he says, Where I
go, you are not able to
come?

23 And He said to them,
You are from below; I
am from above. You are
from this world; I am
not from this world.

24 Therefore, I said to
you that you will die in
your sins. For if you do
not believe that I AM,
you will die in your sins.

25 Then they said to
Him, Who are you?
And Jesus said to them,
(At) the first what I also
say to you.

26 I have many things to
say and to judge con-
cerning you; but the
(One) who has sent Me
is true, and what I heard
from Him, these things
I say to the world.
27 They did not know

John 8:18

3754 1417 444 3588 3141 227 2076 1473 1510
πται ὅτι δύο ἀνθρώπων ἡ μαρτυρία ἀληθής ἐστιν. 18 ἐγώ εἰμι
written that of two men the witness true is. I am

3588 3140 4012 1683 2532 3140 4012 1700 3588 3992
ὁ μαρτυρῶν περὶ ἐμαυτοῦ, καὶ μαρτυρεῖ περὶ ἐμοῦ ὁ πέμψας
the (One) witnessing about Myself, and witnesses about Me He having sent

3165 3962 3004 3767 846 4226 2076 3588 3962 4675
με πατήρ. 19 ἔλεγον οὖν αὐτῷ, Ποῦ ἐστιν ὁ πατήρ σου;
Me, (the) Father. they said Then to Him, Where is the father of you?

611 3588 2424 3777 1691 1492 3777 3588 3962 3450
ἀπεκρίθη ὁ Ἰησοῦς, Οὔτε ἐμὲ οἴδατε, οὔτε τὸν πατέρα μου·
answered Jesus, Neither Me you know, nor the Father of Me;

1487 1691 1492 2532 3588 3962 3450 1492 302 5023 3588
εἰ ἐμὲ ᾔδειτε, καὶ τὸν πατέρα μου ᾔδειτε ἄν. 20 ταῦτα τὰ
if Me you had known, also the Father of Me you would have known. these

4487 2980 3588 2424 1722 3588 1049 1321
ῥήματα ἐλάλησεν ὁ Ἰησοῦς ἐν τῷ γαζοφυλακίῳ, διδάσκων
words spoke Jesus in the treasury, teaching

1722 3588 2411 2532 3762 4084 846 3754 3768 2064 3588
ἐν τῷ ἱερῷ· καὶ οὐδεὶς ἐπίασεν αὐτόν, ὅτι οὔπω ἐληλύθει ἡ
in the temple; and no one seized Him, because not yet had come the

5610 846
ὥρα αὐτοῦ.
hour of Him.

2036 3767 3825 846 3588 2424 1473 5217 2532
21 Εἶπεν οὖν πάλιν αὐτοῖς ὁ Ἰησοῦς, Ἐγὼ ὑπάγω, καὶ
said Then again to them Jesus, I go, and

2212 3165 2532 1722 3588 266 5216 599 3699
ζητήσετέ με, καὶ ἐν τῇ ἁμαρτίᾳ ὑμῶν ἀποθανεῖσθε· ὅπου
you will seek Me, and in the sin of you you will die. Where

1473 5217 5210 3756 1410 2064 3004 3767 3588 2453
ἐγὼ ὑπάγω, ὑμεῖς οὐ δύνασθε ἐλθεῖν. 22 ἔλεγον οὖν οἱ Ἰουδαῖοι,
I go, you not are able to come. said Then the Jews,

3385 615 1438 3754 3004 3699 1473 5217
Μήτι ἀποκτενεῖ ἑαυτόν, ὅτι λέγει, Ὅπου ἐγὼ ὑπάγω,
Not will he kill Himself, because He says, Where I go,

5210 3756 1410 2064 2532 2036 846 5210 1537 3588
ὑμεῖς οὐ δύνασθε ἐλθεῖν; 23 καὶ εἶπεν αὐτοῖς, Ὑμεῖς ἐκ τῶν
you not are able to come? And He said to them, You from

2736 2075 1473 1537 3588 507 1510 5210 1537 3588 2889 5127
κάτω ἐστέ, ἐγὼ ἐκ τῶν ἄνω εἰμί· ὑμεῖς ἐκ τοῦ κόσμου τούτου
below are. I from above am; you from world this

2075 1473 3756 1510 1537 3588 2889 5127 2036 3767 5213 3754
ἐστέ, ἐγὼ οὐκ εἰμὶ ἐκ τοῦ κόσμου τούτου. 24 εἶπον οὖν ὑμῖν ὅτι
are; I not am from world this. I said Therefore to you that

599 1722 3588 266 5216 1437 1063 3361 4100
ἀποθανεῖσθε ἐν ταῖς ἁμαρτίαις ὑμῶν· ἐὰν γὰρ μὴ πιστεύσητε
you will die in the sins of you; if for not you believe

3754 1473 1510 599 1722 3588 266 5216 3004
ὅτι ἐγώ εἰμι, ἀποθανεῖσθε ἐν ταῖς ἁμαρτίαις ὑμῶν. 25 ἔλεγον
that I AM, you will die in the sins of you. they said

3767 846 4771 5101 1488 2532 2036 846 3588 2424 3588
οὖν αὐτῷ, Σὺ τίς εἶ; καὶ εἶπεν αὐτοῖς ὁ Ἰησοῦς, Τὴν
Then to Him, you Who are? And said to them Jesus, (At) the

746 3739 5100 2532 2980 5213 4183 2192 4012 5216 2980 2532
ἀρχὴν ὅ τι καὶ λαλῶ ὑμῖν. 26 πολλὰ ἔχω περὶ ὑμῶν λαλεῖν καὶ
first what also I say to you. Many things I have about you to say and

2919 235 3588 3992 3165 227 2076 2504 3739 191 3844
κρίνειν· ἀλλ᾽ ὁ πέμψας με ἀληθής ἐστι, κἀγὼ ἃ ἤκουσα παρ᾽
to judge, but He having sent Me true is, and I what I heard from

846 5023 3004 1519 3588 2889 3756 1097 3754 3588
αὐτοῦ, ταῦτα λέγω εἰς τὸν κόσμον. 27 οὐκ ἔγνωσαν ὅτι τὸν
Him, these things I say to the world. not They knew that (of) the

King James Version

that the testimony of
two men is true.
18 I am one that bear
witness of myself, and
the Father that sent me
beareth witness of me.

19 Then said they unto
him, Where is thy Fa-
ther? Jesus answered,
Ye neither know me,
nor my Father: if ye had
known me, ye should
have known my Father
also.
20 These words spake
Jesus in the treasury, as
he taught in the temple:
and no man laid hands
on him; for his hour was
not yet come.

21 Then said Jesus
again unto them, I go
my way, and ye shall
seek me, and shall die in
your sins: whither I go,
ye cannot come.

22 Then said the Jews,
Will he kill himself? be-
cause he saith, Whither
I go, ye cannot come.

23 And he said unto
them, Ye are from be-
neath; I am from above:
ye are of this world; I am
not of this world.

24 I said therefore unto
you, that ye shall die in
your sins: for if ye be-
lieve not that I am (he),
ye shall die in your sins.

25 Then said they unto
him, Who art thou? And
Jesus saith unto them,
Even (the same) that I
said unto you from the
beginning.

26 I have many things to
say and to judge of you:
but he that sent me is
true; and I speak to the
world those things
which I have heard of
him.
27 They understood not

Literal Translation

that He spoke to them (of) the Father.
28 Then Jesus said to them, When you lift up the Son of man, then you will know that I AM; and from Myself I do nothing; but as My Father taught Me, these things I speak.

29 And the (One) who has sent Me is with Me. The Father did not leave Me alone, for I do the things pleasing to Him always.

30 He saying these things, many believed into Him.

31. Then Jesus said to the Jews who had believed in Him, If you continue in My Word, you are truly My disciples.

32 And you will know the truth, and the truth will set you free.

33 They answered Him, We are Abraham's seed, and we have been in slavery to no one, never! How do you say, You will become free?
34 Jesus answered them, Truly, truly, I say to you, everyone practicing sin is a slave of sin.

35 But the slave does not remain in the house to the age; the son remains to the age.
36 Therefore, if the Son sets you free, really you are free.
37 I know that you are Abraham's seed, but you seek to kill Me, because My Word is given no room in you.

38 I speak what I have seen with My Father. And you therefore do what you have seen with your father.
39 They answered and said to Him, Abraham is our father. Jesus said to them,

John 8:28

3962 846 3004 2036 3767 846 3588 2424 3752
πατέρα αὐτοῖς ἔλεγεν. 28 εἶπεν οὖν αὐτοῖς ὁ Ἰησοῦς, Ὅταν
Father to them He spoke. said Then to them Jesus, When

5312 3588 5207 3588 444 5119 1097 3754 1473
ὑψώσητε τὸν υἱὸν τοῦ ἀνθρώπου, τότε γνώσεσθε ὅτι ἐγώ
you lift up the Son of man, then you will know that I

1510 2532 575 1683 4160 3762 235 2531 1321 3165 3588
εἰμι, καὶ ἀπ' ἐμαυτοῦ ποιῶ οὐδέν, ἀλλὰ καθὼς ἐδίδαξέ με ὁ
AM! And from Myself I do nothing, but even as taught Me the

3962 3450 5023 2980 2532 3588 3992 3165 3326 1700 2076
πατήρ μου, ταῦτα λαλῶ. 29 καὶ ὁ πέμψας με μετ' ἐμοῦ ἐστιν·
Father of Me, these things I speak. And He having sent Me with Me is.

3756 863 3165 3441 3588 3962 3754 1473 3588 701 846 4160
οὐκ ἀφῆκέ με μόνον ὁ πατήρ, ὅτι ἐγὼ τὰ ἀρεστὰ αὐτῷ ποιῶ
not left Me alone the Father, because I the things pleasing to Him do

3842 5023 846 2980 4183 4100 1519
πάντοτε. 30 ταῦτα αὐτοῦ λαλοῦντος πολλοὶ ἐπίστευσαν εἰς
always. These things He saying many believed into

846
αὐτόν.
Him.

3004 3767 3588 2424 4314 3588 4100 846
31 Ἔλεγεν οὖν ὁ Ἰησοῦς πρὸς τοὺς πεπιστευκότας αὐτῷ
said Then Jesus to the having believed in Him

2453 1437 5210 3306 1722 3588 3056 3588 1699 230
Ἰουδαίους, Ἐὰν ὑμεῖς μείνητε ἐν τῷ λόγῳ τῷ ἐμῷ, ἀληθῶς
Jews, If you continue in the Word My, truly

3101 3450 2075 2532 1097 3588 225 2532 3588 225
μαθηταί μου ἐστέ· 32 καὶ γνώσεσθε τὴν ἀλήθειαν, καὶ ἡ ἀλήθεια
disciples of Me you are. And you will know the truth, and the truth

1659 5209 611 846 4690 11
ἐλευθερώσει ὑμᾶς. 33 ἀπεκρίθησαν αὐτῷ, Σπέρμα Ἀβραάμ
will set free you. They answered to Him, seed of Abraham

2070 2532 3762 1398 4455 4459 4771 3004 3754
ἐσμεν, καὶ οὐδενὶ δεδουλεύκαμεν πώποτε· πῶς σὺ λέγεις ὅτι
We are, and to no one have we been enslaved; never! How do you say,

1658 1096 611 846 3588 2424 281
Ἐλεύθεροι γενήσεσθε; 34 ἀπεκρίθη αὐτοῖς ὁ Ἰησοῦς, Ἀμὴν
free You will become? answered to them Jesus, Truly,

281 3004 5213 3754 3956 3588 4160 3588 266 1401 2076
ἀμὴν λέγω ὑμῖν, ὅτι πᾶς ὁ ποιῶν τὴν ἁμαρτίαν δοῦλός ἐστι
truly I say to you, that everyone practicing sin a slave is

3588 266 3588 1161 1401 3756 3306 1722 3588 3614 1519 3588
τῆς ἁμαρτίας. 35 ὁ δὲ δοῦλος οὐ μένει ἐν τῇ οἰκίᾳ εἰς τὸν
of sin. the But slave not abides in the house to the

165 3588 5207 3306 1519 3588 165 1437 3767 3588 5207 5209
αἰῶνα· ὁ υἱὸς μένει εἰς τὸν αἰῶνα. 36 ἐὰν οὖν ὁ υἱὸς ὑμᾶς
age; the son abides to the age. if Therefore the Son you

1659 3689 1658 2071 1492 3754 4690
ἐλευθερώσῃ, ὄντως ἐλεύθεροι ἔσεσθε. 37 οἶδα ὅτι σπέρμα
sets free, really free you are. I know that the seed

11 2075 235 2212 3165 615 3754 3588 3056 3588 1699 3756
Ἀβραάμ ἐστε· ἀλλὰ ζητεῖτέ με ἀποκτεῖναι, ὅτι ὁ λόγος ὁ ἐμὸς οὐ
of Abraham you are; but you seek Me to kill, because the Word My not

5562 1722 5213 1473 3739 3708 3844 3588 3962 3450 2980 2532
χωρεῖ ἐν ὑμῖν. 38 ἐγὼ ὃ ἑώρακα παρὰ τῷ πατρί μου, λαλῶ· καὶ
is given room in you. I what I have seen with the Father of Me I speak; and

5210 3767 3708 3962 3588 3962 5216 4160 611
ὑμεῖς οὖν ὃ ἑωράκατε παρὰ τῷ πατρί ὑμῶν, ποιεῖτε. 39 ἀπεκρίθη-
you then what you have seen with the father of you, you do. They answered

2532 2532 846 3588 3962 2257 11 2076 3004 846
σαν καὶ εἶπον αὐτῷ, Ὁ πατὴρ ἡμῶν Ἀβραάμ ἐστι. λέγει αὐτοῖς
and said to Him, The father of us Abraham is. says to them

King James Version

that he spake to them of the Father.
28 Then said Jesus unto them, When ye have lifted up the Son of man, then shall ye know that I am (he), and (that) I do nothing of myself; but as my Father hath taught me, I speak these things.

29 And he that sent me is with me: the Father hath not left me alone; for I do always those things that please him.

30 As he spake these words, many believed on him.

31. Then said Jesus to those Jews which believed on him, If ye continue in my word, (then) are ye my disciples indeed;

32 And ye shall know the truth, and the truth shall make you free.

33 They answered him, We be Abraham's seed, and were never in bondage to any man: how sayest thou, Ye shall be made free?

34 Jesus answered them, Verily, verily, I say unto you, Whosoever committeth sin is the servant of sin.

35 And the servant abideth not in the house for ever: (but) the Son abideth ever.
36 If the Son therefore shall make you free, ye shall be free indeed.
37 I know that ye are Abraham's seed; but ye seek to kill me, because my word hath no place in you.

38 I speak that which I have seen with my Father: and ye do that which ye have seen with your father.
39 They answered and said unto him, Abraham is our father. Jesus saith unto them,

Literal Translation

If you were children of Abraham, you would do the works of Abraham.
40 But now you seek to kill Me, a man who has spoken the truth to you, which I heard alongside (of) God. Abraham did not do this.

41 You do the works of your father. They said to Him, We were not generated of fornication; we have one father, God.
42 Then Jesus said to them, If God were your Father, you would love Me, for I went forth and have come from God. For I have not come from Myself, but that One sent Me.

43 Why do you not know My speech? (It is) because you are not able to hear My Word.
44 You are from (your) father the devil, and the lusts of your father you desire to do. That one was a manslayer from (the) beginning, and he has not stood in the truth, because there is no truth in him. When he speaks (a) lie, he speaks from (his) own, because he is a liar, and the father of it.

45 But because I speak the truth, you do not believe Me.
46 Who of you reproves Me concerning sin? But if I speak truth, why do you not believe Me?
47 The (one) being of God hears the words of God; because of this you do not hear, because you are not of God.

48 Then the Jews answered and said to Him, Do we not say well that you are a Samaritan and have a demon?

49 Jesus answered, I do not have a demon;

John 8:40

3588 2424 1487 5043 3588 11 2258 3588 2041 3588 11
ὁ Ἰησοῦς, Εἰ τέκνα τοῦ Ἀβραὰμ ἦτε, τὰ ἔργα τοῦ Ἀβραὰμ
Jesus, If children of Abraham you were, the works of Abraham

4160 302 3568 1161 2212 3165 615 444 3739 3588
ἐποιεῖτε ἄν. 40 νῦν δὲ ζητεῖτέ με ἀποκτεῖναι, ἄνθρωπον ὃς τὴν
you would do. now But you seek Me to kill, a man who the

225 5213 2980 3739 191 3844 3588 2316 5124
ἀλήθειαν ὑμῖν λελάληκα, ἣν ἤκουσα παρὰ τοῦ Θεοῦ· τοῦτο
truth to you has spoken, which I heard alongside of God; this

11 3756 4160 5210 4160 3588 2041 3588 3962
Ἀβραὰμ οὐκ ἐποίησεν. 41 ὑμεῖς ποιεῖτε τὰ ἔργα τοῦ πατρὸς
Abraham not did. You do the works of the father

5216 2036 3767 846 2249 1537 4202 3756 1080
ὑμῶν. εἶπον οὖν αὐτῷ, Ἡμεῖς ἐκ πορνείας οὐ γεγεννήμεθα·
of you. they said Then to Him, We of fornication not were generated;

1520 3962 2192 3588 2316 2036 846 3588 2424 1487 3588
ἕνα πατέρα ἔχομεν, τὸν Θεόν. 42 εἶπεν αὐτοῖς ὁ Ἰησοῦς, Εἰ ὁ
one father we have, God. said to them Jesus, If

2316 3962 5216 2258 25 302 1691 1473 1063 1537 3588 2316
Θεὸς πατὴρ ὑμῶν ἦν, ἠγαπᾶτε ἂν ἐμέ· ἐγὼ γὰρ ἐκ τοῦ Θεοῦ
God (the) father of you were, you would love Me; I for from God

1683 2532 2240 3761 1063 575 1683 2064 235
ἐξῆλθον καὶ ἥκω· οὐδὲ γὰρ ἀπ' ἐμαυτοῦ ἐλήλυθα, ἀλλ'
went out, and have come; not for from Myself I have come, but

1565 3165 649 1302 3588 2981 3588 1699 3756 1097
ἐκεῖνός με ἀπέστειλε. 43 διατί τὴν λαλιὰν τὴν ἐμὴν οὐ γινώ-
that One me sent. Why the speech My not you

3754 3756 1410 191 3588 3056 3588 1699 5210
σκετε; ὅτι οὐ δύνασθε ἀκούειν τὸν λόγον τὸν ἐμόν. 44 ὑμεῖς
know? (It is) because not you are able to hear the Word My. You

1537 3962 3588 1228 2075 2532 3588 1939 3588 3962
ἐκ πατρὸς τοῦ διαβόλου ἐστέ, καὶ τὰς ἐπιθυμίας τοῦ πατρὸς
from (your) father the devil are, and the lusts of the father

5216 2309 4160 1565 443 2258 575 746
ὑμῶν θέλετε ποιεῖν. ἐκεῖνος ἀνθρωποκτόνος ἦν ἀπ' ἀρχῆς,
of you you desire to do. That one a manslayer was from (the) first,

2532 1722 3588 225 3756 2476 3754 3756 2076 225 1722 846
καὶ ἐν τῇ ἀληθείᾳ οὐχ ἕστηκεν, ὅτι οὐκ ἔστιν ἀλήθεια ἐν αὐτῷ.
and in the truth not has stood, because not is truth in him.

3752 2980 3588 5579 1537 3588 2398 2980 3754 5583 2076
ὅταν λαλῇ τὸ ψεῦδος, ἐκ τῶν ἰδίων λαλεῖ· ὅτι ψεύστης ἐστὶ
When he speaks the lie, out of the own he speaks; because a liar he is,

2532 3588 3962 846 1473 1161 3754 3588 225 3004 3756 4100
καὶ ὁ πατὴρ αὐτοῦ. 45 ἐγὼ δὲ ὅτι τὴν ἀλήθειαν λέγω, οὐ πι-
and the father of it. I But because the truth I say, not you

3427 5101 1537 5216 1651 3165 4012 266 1487 1161 225
στεύετέ μοι. 46 τίς ἐξ ὑμῶν ἐλέγχει με περὶ ἁμαρτίας; εἰ δὲ ἀλή-
believe Me. Who of you reproves Me concerning sin? if But

3004 1302 5210 3756 4100 3427 3588 5607 1537 3588 2316
θειαν λέγω, διατί ὑμεῖς οὐ πιστεύετέ μοι; 47 ὁ ὢν ἐκ τοῦ Θεοῦ
truth I say, why you not do believe Me? The (one) being of God

3588 4487 3588 2316 191 1223 5124 5210 3756 191
τὰ ῥήματα τοῦ Θεοῦ ἀκούει· διὰ τοῦτο ὑμεῖς οὐκ ἀκούετε,
the words of God hears; because of this you not do hear,

3754 1537 3588 2316 3756 2075 611 3767 3588 2453 2532
ὅτι ἐκ τοῦ Θεοῦ οὐκ ἐστέ. 48 ἀπεκρίθησαν οὖν οἱ Ἰουδαῖοι καὶ
since from God not you are. answered Then the Jews and

2036 846 3756 2573 3004 2249 3754 4541 1488 4771
εἶπον αὐτῷ, Οὐ καλῶς λέγομεν ἡμεῖς ὅτι Σαμαρείτης εἶ σύ,
said to Him, Not well say we that a Samaritan are you,

2532 1140 2192 611 2424 1473 1140 3756
καὶ δαιμόνιον ἔχεις; 49 ἀπεκρίθη Ἰησοῦς, Ἐγὼ δαιμόνιον οὐκ
and a demon you have? answered Jesus, I a demon not

King James Version

If ye were Abraham's children, ye would do the works of Abraham.

40 But now ye seek to kill me, a man that hath told you the truth, which I have heard of God: this did not Abraham.

41 Ye do the deeds of your father. Then said they to him, We be not born of fornication; we have one Father, (even) God.
42 Jesus said unto them, If God were your Father, ye would love me: for I proceeded forth and came from God; neither came I of myself, but he sent me.

43 Why do ye not understand my speech? (even) because ye cannot hear my word.
44 Ye are of (your) father the devil, and the lusts of your father ye will do. He was a murderer from the beginning, and abode not in the truth, because there is no truth in him. When he speaketh a lie, he speaketh of his own: for he is a liar, and the father of it.

45 And because I tell (you) the truth, ye believe me not.
46 Which of you convinceth me of sin? And if I say the truth, why do ye not believe me?
47 He that is of God heareth God's words: ye therefore hear (them) not, because ye are not of God.

48 Then answered the Jews, and said unto him, Say we not well that thou art a Samaritan, and hast a devil?

49 Jesus answered, I have not a devil;

Literal Translation

but I honor My Father, and you dishonor Me.

50 But I do not seek My glory; there is One who seeks and judges.

51 Truly, truly, I say to you, If anyone keeps My Word, he will not ever behold death to the age.

52 Then the Jews said to Him, Now we know that you have a demon. Abraham died, and the prophets, and you say, If anyone keeps My Word, he will not ever taste of death to the age.

53 Are you greater than our father Abraham who died? And the prophets died! Whom do you make yourself?

54 Jesus answered, If I glorify Myself, My glory is nothing; it is My Father glorifying Me, whom you say is your God.

55 And you have not known Him; but I know Him, And if I say that I do not know Him, I shall be like you, a liar. But I know Him, and I keep His Word.

56 Your father Abraham leaped for joy that he should see My day, and he saw, and rejoiced.

57 Then the Jews said to Him, You do not yet have fifty years, and have you seen Abraham?

58 Jesus said to them, Truly, truly, I say to you, before Abraham came into being, I AM.

59 Then they took up stones that they might throw (them) on Him. But Jesus was hidden, and went forth out of the temple, going through (the) midst of them, and so passed by.

John 8:50

2192 235 5091 3588 3962 3450 2532 5210 818 3165
ἔχω, ἀλλὰ τιμῶ τὸν πατέρα μου, καὶ ὑμεῖς ἀτιμάζετέ με.
have, but I honor the Father of Me, and you dishonor Me.

1473 1161 3756 2212 3588 1391 3450 2076 3588 2212 2532 2919
50 ἐγὼ δὲ οὐ ζητῶ τὴν δόξαν μου· ἔστιν ὁ ζητῶν καὶ κρίνων.
I But not seek the glory of Me; is One seeking and judging.

281 281 3004 5213 1437 5100 3588 3056 3588 1699 5083
51 ἀμὴν ἀμὴν λέγω ὑμῖν, ἐάν τις τὸν λόγον τὸν ἐμὸν τηρήσῃ,
Truly truly I say to you, If anyone the Word My keeps,

2288 3756 3361 2334 1519 3588 165 2036 3767 846
θάνατον οὐ μὴ θεωρήσῃ εἰς τὸν αἰῶνα. 52 εἶπον οὖν αὐτῷ
death not ever will he behold to the age. said Then to Him

3588 2453 3568 1097 3754 1140 2192 11
οἱ Ἰουδαῖοι, Νῦν ἐγνώκαμεν ὅτι δαιμόνιον ἔχεις. Ἀβραὰμ
the Jews, Now we have known that a demon you have. Abraham

599 2532 3588 4396 2532 4771 3004 1437 5100 3588 3056
ἀπέθανε καὶ οἱ προφῆται, καὶ σὺ λέγεις, Ἐάν τις τὸν λόγον
died also the prophets, and you say, If anyone the Word

3450 5083 3756 3361 1089 2288 1519 3588 165 3361 4771
μου τηρήσῃ, οὐ μὴ γεύσεται θανάτου εἰς τὸν αἰῶνα. 53 μὴ σὺ
of Me keeps, not ever will he taste of death to the age. Not you

3187 1488 3588 3962 2257 11 3748 599 2532
μείζων εἶ τοῦ πατρὸς ἡμῶν Ἀβραάμ, ὅστις ἀπέθανε; καὶ
greater are (than) the father of us Abraham, who died? Also

3588 4396 599 5101 4572 4771 4160 611
οἱ προφῆται ἀπέθανον· τίνα σεαυτὸν σὺ ποιεῖς; 54 ἀπεκρίθη
the prophets died. Whom yourself you do make? answered

2424 1437 1473 1392 1683 3588 1391 3450 3762 2076
Ἰησοῦς, Ἐὰν ἐγὼ δοξάζω ἐμαυτόν, ἡ δόξα μου οὐδέν ἐστιν·
Jesus, If I glorify Myself, the glory of Me nothing is;

2076 3588 3962 3450 3588 1392 3165 3739 5210 3004 3754 2316
ἔστιν ὁ πατήρ μου ὁ δοξάζων με, ὃν ὑμεῖς λέγετε ὅτι Θεὸς
it is the Father of Me glorifying Me, whom you say that God

5216 2076 2532 3756 1097 846 1473 1161 1492 846
ὑμῶν ἐστι, 55 καὶ οὐκ ἐγνώκατε αὐτόν· ἐγὼ δὲ οἶδα αὐτόν.
of you is, and not you have known Him; I but know Him.

2532 1437 2036 3754 3756 1492 846 2071 3664 5216
καὶ ἐὰν εἴπω ὅτι οὐκ οἶδα αὐτόν, ἔσομαι ὅμοιος ὑμῶν,
And if I say that not I know Him, I shall be like you,

5583 235 1492 846 2532 3588 3056 846 5083
ψεύστης· ἀλλ' οἶδα αὐτόν καὶ τὸν λόγον αὐτοῦ τηρῶ.
a liar; but I know Him, and the Word of Him I keep.

11 3588 3962 5216 21 2443 1492 3588 2250
56 Ἀβραὰμ ὁ πατὴρ ὑμῶν ἠγαλλιάσατο ἵνα ἴδῃ τὴν ἡμέραν
Abraham the father of you leaped for joy that he may see day

3588 1699 2532 1492 2532 5463 2036 3767 3588 2453 4314
τὴν ἐμήν, καὶ εἶδε καὶ ἐχάρη. 57 εἶπον οὖν οἱ Ἰουδαῖοι πρὸς
My, and he saw and rejoiced. said Then the Jews to

846 4004 2094 3768 2192 2532 11 3708
αὐτόν, Πεντήκοντα ἔτη οὔπω ἔχεις, καὶ Ἀβραὰμ ἑώρακας;
Him, fifty years not yet You have, and Abraham you have seen?

2036 846 3588 2424 281 281 3004 5213 4250 11
58 εἶπεν αὐτοῖς ὁ Ἰησοῦς, Ἀμὴν ἀμὴν λέγω ὑμῖν, πρὶν Ἀβραὰμ
said to them Jesus, Truly truly I say to you, Before Abraham

1096 1473 1510 142 3767 3037 2443 906 1909 846
γενέσθαι, ἐγώ εἰμι. 59 ἦραν οὖν λίθους ἵνα βάλωσιν ἐπ' αὐτόν·
came to be, I AM! they took Then stones that they might cast on Him.

2424 1161 2928 2532 1831 1537 3588 2411 1330 1223
Ἰησοῦς δὲ ἐκρύβη, καὶ ἐξῆλθεν ἐκ τοῦ ἱεροῦ, διελθὼν διὰ
Jesus But was hidden, and went forth out of the temple, going through

3319 846 2532 3855 3779
μέσου αὐτῶν· καὶ παρῆγεν οὕτως.
(the) midst of them, and passed by so.

King James Version

but I honour my Father, and ye do dishonour me.

50 And I seek not mine own glory: there is one that seeketh and judgeth.

51 Verily, verily, I say unto you, If a man keep my saying, he shall never see death.

52 Then said the Jews unto him, Now we know that thou hast a devil. Abraham is dead, and the prophets; and thou sayest, If a man keep my saying, he shall never taste of death.

53 Art thou greater than our father Abraham, which is dead? and the prophets are dead: whom makest thou thyself?

54 Jesus answered, If I honour myself, my honour is nothing: it is my Father that honoureth me; of whom ye say, that he is your God:

55 Yet ye have not known him; but I know him: and if I should say, I know him not, I shall be a liar like unto you: but I know him, and keep his saying.

56 Your father Abraham rejoiced to see my day: and he saw (it), and was glad.

57 Then said the Jews unto him, Thou art not yet fifty years old, and hast thou seen Abraham?

58 Jesus said unto them, Verily, verily, I say unto you, Before Abraham was, I am.

59 Then took they up stones to cast at him: but Jesus hid himself, and went out of the temple, going through the midst of them, and so passed by.

Literal Translation

John 9

1. And passing by, He saw a man blind from birth.
2 And His disciples asked Him, saying, Teacher, who sinned, this one, or his parents, that he was born blind?
3 Jesus answered, Neither this one nor his parents sinned, but that the works of God might be revealed in him.
4 It is necessary for Me to work the works of Him who sent Me while it is day. Night comes when no one is able to work.
5 While I am in the world, I am (the) Light of the world.
6 Saying these things, He spat on the ground and made clay out of the spittle, and anointed clay on the blind one's eyes.
7 And He said to him, Go, wash in the pool of Siloam, which translated is Sent. Then he went and washed, and came seeing.
8. Then the neighbors and those who formerly saw him that he was blind, said, Is this one not the (one) who had sat and begged?
9 Some said, It is he; and others, He is like him. That one said, I am the (one).
10 Then they said to him, How were your eyes opened?
11 He answered and said, A man called Jesus made clay and anointed my eyes, and told me, Go to the pool of Siloam and wash. And going and washing I saw again.
12 Then they said to him, Where

John 9:1

2532 3855 1492 444 5185 1537 1079 2532
1. Καὶ παράγων εἶδεν ἄνθρωπον τυφλὸν ἐκ γενετῆς. 2 καὶ
And passing by He saw a man blind from birth. And
2065 846 3588 3101 846 3004 4461 5101
ἠρώτησαν αὐτὸν οἱ μαθηταὶ αὐτοῦ λέγοντες, Ῥαββί, τίς
asked Him the disciples of Him, saying, Rabbi, who
264 3778 2228 3588 1118 846 2443 5185 1080
ἥμαρτεν, οὗτος ἢ οἱ γονεῖς αὐτοῦ, ἵνα τυφλὸς γεννηθῇ;
sinned, this one, or the parents of him, that blind he was born?
611 3588 2424 3777 3778 264 3777 3588 1118
3 ἀπεκρίθη ὁ Ἰησοῦς, Οὔτε οὗτος ἥμαρτεν οὔτε οἱ γονεῖς
answered Jesus, niether this one sinned nor the parents
846 235 2443 5319 3588 2041 3588 2316 1722 846
αὐτοῦ· ἀλλ' ἵνα φανερωθῇ τὰ ἔργα τοῦ Θεοῦ ἐν αὐτῷ.
of him; but that might be revealed the works of God in him.
1691 1163 2038 3588 2041 3588 3992 3165 2193 2250
4 ἐμὲ δεῖ ἐργάζεσθαι τὰ ἔργα τοῦ πέμψαντός με ἕως ἡμέρα
Me It behooves to work the works of the (One) sending Me while day
2076 2064 3571 3753 3762 1410 2038 3752 1722
ἐστίν· ἔρχεται νύξ, ὅτε οὐδεὶς δύναται ἐργάζεσθαι. 5 ὅταν ἐν
it is. comes Night, when no one is able to work. When in
3588 2889 5600 5457 1510 3588 2889 5023 2036 4429
τῷ κόσμῳ ὦ, φῶς εἰμι τοῦ κόσμου. 6 ταῦτα εἰπών, ἔπτυσε
the world I am, (the) light I am of the world. These things saying, He spat
5476 2532 4160 4081 1537 3588 4427 2532 2025
χαμαί, καὶ ἐποίησε πηλὸν ἐκ τοῦ πτύσματος, καὶ ἐπέχρισε
on earth and made clay out of the spittle, and anointed
3588 4081 1909 3588 3788 3588 5185 2532 2036 846
τὸν πηλὸν ἐπὶ τοὺς ὀφθαλμοὺς τοῦ τυφλοῦ, 7 καὶ εἶπεν αὐτῷ,
the clay on the eyes of the blind one, and said to him,
5217 3538 1519 3588 2861 3588 4611 3739 2059
Ὕπαγε νίψαι εἰς τὴν κολυμβήθραν τοῦ Σιλωάμ [ὃ ἑρμη-
Go, wash in the pool of Sliloam (which is
649 565 3767 2532 3538 2532 2064
νεύεται, ἀπεσταλμένος]. ἀπῆλθεν οὖν καὶ ἐνίψατο, καὶ ἦλθε
translated, having been sent). he went Then and washed and came
991 3588 3767 1069 2532 3588 2334 846 3588 4386
βλέπων. 8 οἱ οὖν γείτονες καὶ οἱ θεωροῦντες αὐτὸν τὸ πρό-
seeing. the Then neighbors and the (ones) beholding him formerly
3754 5185 2258 3004 3756 3778 2076 3588 2521
τερον ὅτι τυφλὸς ἦν, ἔλεγον, Οὐχ οὗτός ἐστιν ὁ καθή-
that blind he was, said, Not this one is the (one) sit-
2532 4319 243 3004 3754 3778 2076 243
μενος καὶ προσαιτῶν; 9 ἄλλοι ἔλεγον ὅτι Οὗτός ἐστιν· ἄλλοι
ting and begging? Others said, This is he. others
1161 3754 3664 846 2076 1565 3004 3754 1473 1510
δὲ ὅτι Ὅμοιος αὐτῷ ἐστιν. ἐκεῖνος ἔλεγεν ὅτι Ἐγώ εἰμι.
And, like him he is. That one said, I am.
3004 3767 846 4459 455 4675 3588 3788
10 ἔλεγον οὖν αὐτῷ, Πῶς ἀνεῴχθησάν σου οἱ ὀφθαλμοί;
they said Then to him, How were opened of you the eyes?
611 1565 2532 2036 444 3004 2424
11 ἀπεκρίθη ἐκεῖνος καὶ εἶπεν, Ἄνθρωπος λεγόμενος Ἰησοῦς
answered That one and said, (The) man being called Jesus
4081 4160 2532 2025 3450 3588 3788 2532 2036
πηλὸν ἐποίησε, καὶ ἐπέχρισέ μου τοὺς ὀφθαλμούς, καὶ εἶπέ
clay made, and anointed of me the eyes, and told
3427 5217 1519 3588 2861 3588 4611 2532 3538
μοι, Ὕπαγε εἰς τὴν κολυμβήθραν τοῦ Σιλωάμ, καὶ νίψαι.
me, Go to the pool of Siloam, and wash.
565 1161 2532 3538 308 2036 3767 846 4226
ἀπελθὼν δὲ καὶ νιψάμενος, ἀνέβλεψα. 12 εἶπον οὖν αὐτῷ, Ποῦ
going And, and washing, I looked up. they said Then to him, Where

King James Version

John 9

1 . And as (Jesus) passed by, he saw a man which was blind from (his) birth.
2 And his disciples asked him, saying, Master, who did sin, this man, or his parents, that he was born blind?
3 Jesus answered, Neither hath this man sinned, nor his parents: but that the works of God should be made manifest in him.
4 I must work the works of him that sent me, while it is day: the night cometh, when no man can work.
5 As long as I am in the world, I am the light of the world.
6 When he had thus spoken, he spat on the ground, and made clay of the spittle, and he anointed the eyes of the blind man with the clay,
7 And said unto him, Go, wash in the pool of Siloam, (which is by interpretation, Sent.) He went his way therefore, and washed, and came seeing.
8. The neighbours therefore, and they which before had seen him that he was blind, said, Is not this he that sat and begged?
9 Some said, This is he: others (said), He is like him: (but) he said, I am (he).
10 Therefore said they unto him, How were thine eyes opened?
11 He answered and said, A man that is called Jesus made clay, and anointed mine eyes, and said unto me, Go to the pool of Siloam, and wash: and I went and washed, and I received sight.
12 Then said they unto him, Where

Literal Translation | **John 9:13** | **King James Version**

is that one? He said, I do not know.

2076 1565 3004 3756 1492
ἐστιν ἐκεῖνος; λέγει, Οὐκ οἶδα.
is that one? He says, Not I know.

is he? He said, I know not.

13. They brought him to the Pharisees, the (one) once blind.
14 And it was a sabbath when Jesus made the clay and opened his eyes.
15 Then also the Pharisees again asked him how he received sight. And he said to them, He put clay on my eyes, and I washed, and I see.

71 846 4314 3588 5330 3588 4218 5185
13 Ἄγουσιν αὐτὸν πρὸς τοὺς Φαρισαίους, τόν ποτε τυφλόν.
They lead him to the Pharisees, the (one) once blind.

2258 1161 4521 3753 3588 4081 4160 3588 2424 2532
14 ἦν δὲ σάββατον ὅτε τὸν πηλὸν ἐποίησεν ὁ Ἰησοῦς, καὶ
it was And a sabbath when the clay made Jesus, and

455 846 3588 3788 3825 3767 2065 846
ἀνέῳξεν αὐτοῦ τοὺς ὀφθαλμούς. 15 πάλιν οὖν ἠρώτων αὐτὸν
opened of him the eyes. Again therefore, asked him

2532 3588 5330 4459 308 3588 1161 2036 846 4081
καὶ οἱ Φαρισαῖοι, πῶς ἀνέβλεψεν. ὁ δὲ εἶπεν αὐτοῖς, Πηλὸν
also the Pharisees how he saw again. he And said to them, Clay

2007 1909 3588 3788 3450 2532 3538 2532
ἐπέθηκεν ἐπὶ τοὺς ὀφθαλμούς μου, καὶ ἐνιψάμην, καὶ
he put on the eyes of me, and I washed, and

991 3004 3767 1537 3588 5330 5100 3778 3588 444
βλέπω. 16 ἔλεγον οὖν ἐκ τῶν Φαρισαίων τινές, Οὗτος ὁ ἄνθρω-
I see. said Then of the Pharisees some, This man

13. They brought to the Pharisees him that aforetime was blind.
14 And it was the sabbath day when Jesus made the clay, and opened his eyes.
15 Then again the Pharisees also asked him how he had received his sight. He said unto them, He put clay upon mine eyes, and I washed, and do see.

16 Then some of the Pharisees said, This man is not from God, because He does not keep the sabbath. Others said, How can a man, a sinner, do such miracles? And there was a division among them.

3756 2076 3844 3588 2316 3754 3588 4521 3756 5083
πος οὐκ ἔστι παρὰ τοῦ Θεοῦ, ὅτι τὸ σάββατον οὐ τηρεῖ.
not is from God, because the sabbath not he keeps

243 3004 4459 1410 444 268 5108
ἄλλοι ἔλεγον, Πῶς δύναται ἄνθρωπος ἁμαρτωλὸς τοιαῦτα
Others said, How is able a man, a sinner, such

4592 4160 2532 4978 2258 1722 846 3004 3588 5185
σημεῖα ποιεῖν; καὶ σχίσμα ἦν ἐν αὐτοῖς. 17 λέγουσι τῷ τυφλῷ
signs do? And a division was among them. They say to the blind

16 Therefore said some of the Pharisees, This man is not of God, because he keepeth not the sabbath day. Others said, How can a man that is a sinner do such miracles? And there was a division among them.

17 They said to the blind one again, What do you say about him, because he opened your eyes? And he said, He is a prophet.

3825 4771 5101 3004 4012 846 3754 455 4675 3588 3788
πάλιν, Σὺ τί λέγεις περὶ αὐτοῦ, ὅτι ἤνοιξέ σου τοὺς ὀφθαλ-
again, you What say concerning him, that he opened of you the eyes?

3588 1161 2036 3754 4396 2076 3756 4100 3767 3588
μούς; ὁ δὲ εἶπεν ὅτι Προφήτης ἐστίν. 18 οὐκ ἐπίστευσαν οὖν οἱ
he And said, a prophet He is. Not did believe then the

17 They say unto the blind man again, What sayest thou of him, that he hath opened thine eyes? He said, He is a prophet.

18 Then the Jews did not believe concerning him, that he was blind and received sight, until they called the parents of him having received sight.
19 And they asked them, saying, Is this your son, whom you say that he was born blind? Then how does he now see?

2453 4012 846 3754 5185 2258 2532 308 2193
Ἰουδαῖοι περὶ αὐτοῦ, ὅτι τυφλὸς ἦν καὶ ἀνέβλεψεν, ἕως
Jews concerning him, that blind he was and looked up, until

3755 5455 3588 1118 846 3588 308 2532
ὅτου ἐφώνησαν τοὺς γονεῖς αὐτοῦ τοῦ ἀναβλέψαντος, 19 καὶ
when they called the parents of him looking up. And

2065 846 3004 3778 2076 3588 5207 5216 3739
ἠρώτησαν αὐτοὺς λέγοντες, Οὗτός ἐστιν ὁ υἱὸς ὑμῶν, ὃν
they asked them, saying, this Is the son of you, whom

5210 3004 3754 5185 1080 4459 3767 737 991
ὑμεῖς λέγετε ὅτι τυφλὸς ἐγεννήθη; πῶς οὖν ἄρτι βλέπει;
you say that blind he was born? How, then, just now he sees?

18 But the Jews did not believe concerning him, that he had been blind, and received his sight, until they called the parents of him that had received his sight.
19 And they asked them, saying, Is this your son, who ye say was born blind? how then doth he now see?

20 His parents answered them and said, We know that this is our son, and that he was born blind.
21 But how he now sees, we do not know; or who opened his eyes, we do not know. He is of age, ask him. He will speak about himself.

611 846 3588 1118 846 2532 2036 1492 3754
20 ἀπεκρίθησαν αὐτοῖς οἱ γονεῖς αὐτοῦ καὶ εἶπον, Οἴδαμεν ὅτι
answered them The parents of him and said, We know that

3778 2076 3588 5207 2257 2532 3754 5185 1080 4459 1161
οὗτός ἐστιν ὁ υἱὸς ἡμῶν, καὶ ὅτι τυφλὸς ἐγεννήθη· 21 πῶς δὲ
this is the son of us, and that blind he was born. how But

3568 991 3756 1492 2228 5101 455 846 3588 3788
νῦν βλέπει, οὐκ οἴδαμεν· ἢ τίς ἤνοιξεν αὐτοῦ τοὺς ὀφθαλμούς,
now he sees, not we know, or who opened of him the eyes,

2249 3756 1492 846 2244 2192 846 2065
ἡμεῖς οὐκ οἴδαμεν· αὐτὸς ἡλικίαν ἔχει· αὐτὸν ἐρωτήσατε,
we not do know. He age has, him ask.

20 His parents answered them and said, We know that this is our son, and that he was born blind:
21 But by what means he now seeth, we know not; or who hath opened his eyes, we know not: he is of age; ask him: he shall speak for himself.

22 His parents said these things because

846 4012 846 2980 5023 2036 3588 1118 846 3754
αὐτὸς περὶ ἀυτοῦ λαλήσει. 22 ταῦτα εἶπον οἱ γονεῖς αὐτοῦ, ὅτι
He concerning him will speak. These things said the parents of him because

22 These (words) spake his parents, because

Literal Translation

they feared the Jews; for the Jews had already agreed that if anyone should confess Him (as) Christ, he would be expelled from the synagogue.
23 Because of this, his parents said, He is of age, ask him.

24 Then a second time they called the man who was blind, and (they) said to him, Give glory to God. We know that this man is a sinner.

25 Then he answered and said, Whether He is a sinner, I do not know. One (thing) I do know; that being blind, now I see.
26 And they said to him again, What did he do to you? How did he open your eyes?

27 He answered them, I told you already, and you did not hear. Why do you wish to hear again? Do you also desire to become disciples of Him?
28 Then they reviled him and said, You are a disciple of that one, but we are disciples of Moses.
29 We know that God has spoken by Moses, but this one, we do not know from where he is.

30 The man answered and said to them, For there is a marvel in this, that you do not know from where He is, and He opened my eyes.

31 But we know that God does not hear sinful ones, but if anyone is God fearing, and does His will, He hears that one.
32 From (the beginning of) the age it was never heard that anyone opened the eyes of one having been born blind.
33 If this One was not from God, He could not do anything.
34 They answered

John 9:23

5399 3588 2453 2235 1063 4934 3588
ἐφοβοῦντο τοὺς Ἰουδαίους· ἤδη γὰρ συνετέθειντο οἱ
they feared the Jews; already for had agreed the

2453 2443 1437 5100 846 3670 5547 656
Ἰουδαῖοι, ἵνα ἐάν τις αὐτὸν ὁμολογήσῃ Χριστόν, ἀποσυνά-
Jews, that if anyone Him should confess (as) Christ, expelled from

1096 1223 5124 3588 1118 846 2036 3754
γωγος γένηται. 23 διὰ τοῦτο οἱ γονεῖς αὐτοῦ εἶπον ὅτι
the synagogue he would be. Because of this the parents of him said,

2244 2192 846 2065 5455 3767 1537 1208
Ἡλικίαν ἔχει, αὐτὸν ἐρωτήσατε. 24 ἐφώνησαν οὖν ἐκ δευτέρου
of age He is; him ask. they called Then out a second time

3588 444 3739 2258 5185 2532 2036 846 1325 1391 3588
τὸν ἄνθρωπον ὃς ἦν τυφλός, καὶ εἶπον αὐτῷ, Δὸς δόξαν τῷ
the man who was blind, and said to him, Give glory to

2316 2249 1492 3754 3588 444 3778 268 2076
Θεῷ· ἡμεῖς οἴδαμεν ὅτι ὁ ἄνθρωπος οὗτος ἁμαρτωλός ἐστιν.
God; we know that man this a sinner is.

611 3767 1565 2532 2036 1487 268 2076 3756
25 ἀπεκρίθη οὖν ἐκεῖνος καὶ εἶπεν, Εἰ ἁμαρτωλός ἐστιν, οὐκ
answere Then that one and said, If a sinner He is, not

1492 1520 1492 3754 5185 5607 737 991 2036 1161 846
οἶδα· ἓν οἶδα, ὅτι τυφλὸς ὤν, ἄρτι βλέπω. 26 εἶπον δὲ αὐτῷ
I know; one I know, that blind being, just now I see. they said And to him

3825 5101 4160 4671 4459 455 4675 3588 3788
πάλιν, Τί ἐποίησέ σοι; πῶς ἤνοιξέ σου τοὺς ὀφθαλμούς;
again, What did He to you; how opened of you the eyes?

611 846 2036 5213 2235 2532 3756 191 5101
27 ἀπεκρίθη αὐτοῖς, Εἶπον ὑμῖν ἤδη, καὶ οὐκ ἠκούσατε· τί
He answered them, I told you already, and not you heard. Why

3825 2309 191 3361 2532 5210 2309 846 3101
πάλιν θέλετε ἀκούειν; μὴ καὶ ὑμεῖς θέλετε αὐτοῦ μαθηταὶ
again do you wish to hear? Not also you wish of Him disciples

1096 3058 3767 846 2532 2036 4771 1488 3101
γενέσθαι; 28 ἐλοιδόρησαν οὖν αὐτόν, καὶ εἶπον, Σὺ εἶ μαθητὴς
to become? they reviled Then him, and said, You are a disciple

1565 2249 1161 3588 3475 2070 3101 2249 1492
ἐκείνου· ἡμεῖς δὲ τοῦ Μωσέως ἐσμὲν μαθηταί. 29 ἡμεῖς οἴδαμεν
of that one, we but of Moses are disciples. We know

3754 3475 2980 3588 2316 5126 1161 3756 1492 4159
ὅτι Μωσῇ λελάληκεν ὁ Θεός· τοῦτον δὲ οὐκ οἴδαμεν πόθεν
that by Moses has spoken God; this one but not we know from where

2076 611 3588 444 2532 2036 846 1722 1063
ἐστίν. 30 ἀπεκρίθη ὁ ἄνθρωπος καὶ εἶπεν αὐτοῖς, Ἐν γὰρ
he is. answered The man and said to them, in For

5129 2298 2076 3754 5210 3756 1492 4159 2076 2532
τούτῳ θαυμαστόν ἐστιν, ὅτι ὑμεῖς οὐκ οἴδατε πόθεν ἐστί, καὶ
this a marvel is, that you not know from where He is, and

455 3450 3588 3788 1492 1161 3754 268 3588
ἀνέῳξέ μου τοὺς ὀφθαλμούς. 31 οἴδαμεν δὲ ὅτι ἁμαρτωλῶν ὁ
He opened of Me the eyes. we know And that sinful ones

2316 3756 191 235 1437 5100 2318 5600 2532 3588 2307
Θεὸς οὐκ ἀκούει· ἀλλ' ἐάν τις θεοσεβὴς ᾖ, καὶ τὸ θέλημα
God not hears, but if anyone God-fearing is, and the will

846 4160 5127 191 1537 3588 165 3756 191
αὐτοῦ ποιῇ, τούτου ἀκούει. 32 ἐκ τοῦ αἰῶνος οὐκ ἠκούσθη
of Him does, this one He hears. From the age not it was heard

3754 455 5100 3788 5185 1080 1487 3361 2258
ὅτι ἤνοιξέ τις ὀφθαλμοὺς τυφλοῦ γεγεννημένου· 33 εἰ μὴ ἦν
that opened anyone eyes of one blind having been born. If not was

3778 3844 2316 3756 1410 4160 3762 611
οὗτος παρὰ Θεοῦ, οὐκ ἠδύνατο ποιεῖν οὐδέν. 34 ἀπεκρίθησαν
this One from God, not He could do nothing. They answered

King James Version

they feared the Jews: for the Jews had agreed already, that if any man did confess that he was Christ, he should be put out of the synagogue.
23 Therefore said his parents, He is of age; ask him.

24 Then again called they the man that was blind, and said unto him, Give God the praise: we know that this man is a sinner.

25 He answered and said, Whether he be a sinner (or no), I know not: one thing I know, that, whereas I was blind, now I see.
26 Then said they to him again, What did he to thee? how opened he thine eyes?

27 He answered them, I have told you already, and ye did not hear: wherefore would ye hear (it) again? will ye also be his disciples?
28 Then they reviled him, and said, Thou art his disciple; but we are Moses' disciples.
29 We know that God spake unto Moses: (as for) this (fellow), we know not from whence he is.

30 The man answered and said unto them, Why herein is a marvellous thing, that ye know not from whence he is, and (yet) he hath opened mine eyes.
31 Now we know that God heareth not sinners: but if any man be a worshipper of God, and doeth his will, him he heareth.
32 Since the world began was it not heard that any man opened the eyes of one that was born blind.
33 If this man were not of God, he could do nothing.
34 They answered

Literal Translation | **John 9:35** | **King James Version**

and said to him, You were born wholly in sins, and do you teach us? And they threw him outside.

35. Jesus heard that they threw him outside, and finding him, He said to him, Do you believe into the Son of God?
36 And he answered and said, Who is He, Lord, that I may believe into Him?

37 And Jesus said to him, Even you have seen Him, and He speaking with you is that One.
38 And he said, I believe, Lord! And he worshiped Him.
39. And Jesus said, I came into this world for judgment, that the ones who do not see may see, and they who see may become blind.
40 And (those) of the Pharisees who were with Him heard these things, and said to Him, Are we also blind?

41 Jesus said to them, If you were blind, you would have no sin. But now you say, We see; therefore, your sin remains.

2532 2036 846 1722 266 4771 1080 3650 2532 4771
καὶ εἶπον αὐτῷ, Ἐν ἁμαρτίαις σὺ ἐγεννήθης ὅλος, καὶ σὺ
and said to him, in sins you were born Wholly, and you
1321 2248 2532 1544 846 1854
διδάσκεις ἡμᾶς; καὶ ἐξέβαλον αὐτὸν ἔξω.
teach us? And they threw him outside.

191 3588 2424 3754 1544 846 1854 2532 2147
35 Ἤκουσεν ὁ Ἰησοῦς ὅτι ἐξέβαλον αὐτὸν ἔξω· καὶ εὑρὼν
heard Jesus that they threw him outside; and finding
846 2036 846 4771 4100 1519 3588 5207 3588 2316 611
αὐτόν, εἶπεν αὐτῷ, Σὺ πιστεύεις εἰς τὸν υἱὸν τοῦ Θεοῦ; 36 ἀπε-
him, He said to him, You do believe into the Son of God?
1565 2532 2036 5101 2076 2962 2443 4100 1519
κρίθη ἐκεῖνος καὶ εἶπε, Τίς ἐστι, Κύριε, ἵνα πιστεύσω εἰς
answered That one and said, Who is He, Lord, that I may believe into
846 2036 1161 846 3588 2424 2532 3708 846 2532 3588
αὐτόν; 37 εἶπε δὲ αὐτῷ ὁ Ἰησοῦς, Καὶ ἑώρακας αὐτόν, καὶ ὁ
Him? said And to him Jesus, Even you have seen Him, and He
2980 3326 4675 1565 2076 3588 1161 5346 4100 2962
λαλῶν μετὰ σοῦ ἐκεῖνός ἐστιν. 38 ὁ δὲ ἔφη, Πιστεύω, Κύριε·
speaking with you that One is. he And said, I believe, Lord.
2532 4352 846 2532 2036 3588 2424 1519 2917 1473
καὶ προσεκύνησεν αὐτῷ. 39 καὶ εἶπεν ὁ Ἰησοῦς, Εἰς κρίμα ἐγὼ
And he worshiped him. And said Jesus, For judgment I
1519 3588 2889 5126 2064 2443 3588 3361 991 991
εἰς τὸν κόσμον τοῦτον ἦλθον, ἵνα οἱ μὴ βλέποντες βλέπω-
into world this I came, that the (ones) not seeing may see,
2532 3588 991 5185 1096 2532 191 1537 3588
σι καὶ οἱ βλέποντες τυφλοὶ γένωνται. 40 καὶ ἤκουσαν ἐκ τῶν
and those seeing blind may become. And heard of the
5330 5023 3588 5607 3326 846 2532 2036 846 3361
Φαρισαίων ταῦτα οἱ ὄντες μετ' αὐτοῦ, καὶ εἶπον αὐτῷ, Μὴ
Pharisees these things those being with Him, and said to Him, Not
2532 2249 5185 2070 2036 846 3588 2424 1487 5185
καὶ ἡμεῖς τυφλοί ἐσμεν; 41 εἶπεν αὐτοῖς ὁ Ἰησοῦς, Εἰ τυφλοὶ
also we blind are? said to them Jesus, If blind
2258 3756 302 2192 266 3568 1161 3004 3754 991
ἦτε, οὐκ ἂν εἴχετε ἁμαρτίαν· νῦν δὲ λέγετε ὅτι Βλέπομεν·
you were, not would you have sin; now But you say, We see;
3588 3767 266 5216 3306
ἡ οὖν ἁμαρτία ὑμῶν μένει.
the then sin of you remains.

and said unto him, Thou wast altogether born in sins, and dost thou teach us? And they cast him out.

35. Jesus heard that they had cast him out; and when he had found him, he said unto him, Dost thou believe on the Son of God?
36 He answered and said, Who is he, Lord, that I might believe on him?

37 And Jesus said unto him, Thou hast both seen him, and it is he that talketh with thee.
38 And he said, Lord, I believe. And he worshipped him.
39. And Jesus said, For judgment I am come into this world, that they which see not might see; and that they which see might be made blind.
40 And (some) of the Pharisees which were with him heard these words, and said unto him, Are we blind also?

41 Jesus said unto them, If ye were blind, ye should have no sin: but now ye say, We see; therefore your sin remaineth.

John 10

1. Truly, truly, I say to you, the (one) not entering through the door into the sheepfold, but going up by another way, that one is a thief and a robber.
2 But the (one) entering through the door is the shepherd of the sheep.

3 The doorkeeper opens to him, and the sheep hear his voice, and he calls (his) own sheep by name, and leads them out.

4 And when

281 281 3004 5213 3588 3361 1525 1223 3588 2374
1 Ἀμὴν ἀμὴν λέγω ὑμῖν, ὁ μὴ εἰσερχόμενος διὰ τῆς θύρας
Truly, truly I say to you, he not entering through the door
1519 3588 833 3588 4263 235 305 237
εἰς τὴν αὐλὴν τῶν προβάτων, ἀλλὰ ἀναβαίνων ἀλλαχόθεν,
into the fold of the sheep, but going up by another way,
1565 2812 2076 2532 3027 3588 1161 1525 1223 3588
ἐκεῖνος κλέπτης ἐστὶ καὶ λῃστής· 2 ὁ δὲ εἰσερχόμενος διὰ τῆς
that one a thief is and a robber. he But entering through the
2374 4166 2076 3588 4263 5129 3588 2377
θύρας ποιμήν ἐστι τῶν προβάτων. 3 τούτῳ ὁ θυρωρὸς
door shepherd is of the sheep. To this one the doorkeeper
455 2532 3588 4263 3588 5456 846 191 2532 3588
ἀνοίγει, καὶ τὰ πρόβατα τῆς φωνῆς αὐτοῦ ἀκούει, καὶ τὰ
opens, and the sheep the voice of him hear, and the
2398 4263 2564 2596 3686 2532 1806 846 2532 3752
ἴδια πρόβατα καλεῖ κατ' ὄνομα, καὶ ἐξάγει αὐτά. 4 καὶ ὅταν
own sheep he calls by name, and leads out them. And when

1. Verily, verily, I say unto you, He that entereth not by the door into the sheepfold, but climbeth up some other way, the same is a thief and a robber.
2 But he that entereth in by the door is the shepherd of the sheep.

3 To him the porter openeth; and the sheep hear his voice: and he calleth his own sheep by name, and leadeth them out.

4 And when

Literal Translation

he puts forth his own sheep, he goes in front of them, and the sheep follow him because they know his voice.

5 But they never follow a stranger, but will flee from him, because they do not know the voice of the strangers.
6 Jesus spoke this allegory to them, but they did not know what it was which He spoke to them.

7 Then Jesus again said to them, Truly, truly, I say to you that I am the door of the sheep.
8 All who came before Me are thieves and robbers, but the sheep did not hear them.

9 I am the door. If anyone enters through Me, he will be saved, and will go in, and will go out, and will find pasture.

10 The thief does not come except that he may steal, and kill, and destroy. I came that they may have life and may have (it) abundantly.

11 I am the Good Shepherd! The Good Shepherd lays down His life for the sheep.
12 But the hireling, not even being a shepherd, who does not own the sheep, sees the wolf coming and forsakes the sheep and flees. And the wolf seizes them, and scatters the sheep.

13 But the hireling flees because he is a hireling, and there is not a care to him concerning the sheep.
14 I am the Good Shepherd, and I know those that (are) Mine, and I am known by the (ones that are) Mine.
15 Even as the Father knows Me,

John 10:5

3588 2398 4263 1544 1715 846 4198 2532
τὰ ἴδια πρόβατα ἐκβάλῃ, ἔμπροσθεν αὐτῶν πορεύεται· καὶ
the own sheep he puts forth, in front of them he passes, and

3588 4263 846 190 3754 1492 3588 5456 846
τὰ πρόβατα αὐτῷ ἀκολουθεῖ, ὅτι οἴδασι τὴν φωνὴν αὐτοῦ·
the sheep him follow, because they know the voice of him.

245 1161 3756 3361 190 235 5343 575
5 ἀλλοτρίῳ δὲ οὐ μὴ ἀκολουθήσωσιν, ἀλλὰ φεύξονται ἀπ'
a stranger But not ever they should follow, but will flee from

846 3754 3756 1492 3588 245 3588 5456 3778
αὐτοῦ· ὅτι οὐκ οἴδασι τῶν ἀλλοτρίων τὴν φωνήν. 6 ταύτην
him, because not they know of the strangers the voice. This

3588 3942 2036 846 3588 2424 1565 1161 3756 1097
τὴν παροιμίαν εἶπεν αὐτοῖς ὁ Ἰησοῦς· ἐκεῖνοι δὲ οὐκ ἔγνωσαν
allegory said to them Jesus. those But not knew

5101 2258 3739 2980 846
τίνα ἦν ἃ ἐλάλει αὐτοις.
what it was which He spoke to them.

2036 3767 3825 846 3588 2424 281 281 3004 5213
7 Εἶπεν οὖν πάλιν αὐτοῖς ὁ Ἰησοῦς, Ἀμὴν ἀμὴν λέγω ὑμῖν
said Therefore again to them Jesus, Truly, truly, I say to you

3754 1473 1510 3588 2374 3588 4263 3956 3745 4253 1700
ὅτι ἐγώ εἰμι ἡ θύρα τῶν προβάτων. 8 πάντες ὅσοι πρὸ ἐμοῦ
that I am the door of the sheep. All who before Me

2064 2812 1526 2532 3027 235 3756 191 846 3588
ἦλθον κλέπται εἰσὶ καὶ λησταί· ἀλλ' οὐκ ἤκουσαν αὐτῶν τὰ
came thieves are and robbers; but not did hear them the

4263 1473 1510 3588 2374 1223 1700 1437 5100 1525 4982
πρόβατα. 9 ἐγώ εἰμι ἡ θύρα· δι' ἐμοῦ ἐάν τις εἰσέλθῃ, σωθησε-
sheep. I am the door; through Me if anyone enter, he will

2532 1525 2532 1831 2532 3542 2147
ται, καὶ εἰσελεύσεται καὶ ἐξελεύσεται, καὶ νομὴν εὑρήσει.
be saved, and will go in and will go out, and pasture will find.

3588 2812 3756 2064 1487 3361 2443 2813 2532 2380 2532
10 ὁ κλέπτης οὐκ ἔρχεται εἰ μὴ ἵνα κλέψῃ καὶ θύσῃ καὶ
The thief not domes except that he may steal and slay and

622 1473 2064 2443 2222 2192 2532 4053 2192
ἀπολέσῃ· ἐγὼ ἦλθον ἵνα ζωὴν ἔχωσι, καὶ περισσὸν ἔχωσιν.
destroy. I came that life they may have, and abundantly may have.

1473 1510 3588 4166 3588 2570 3588 4166 3588 2570 3588 5590
11 ἐγώ εἰμι ὁ ποιμὴν ὁ καλός· ὁ ποιμὴν ὁ καλὸς τὴν ψυχὴν
I am the Shepherd Good; the Shepherd Good the life

846 5087 5228 3588 4263 3588 3411 1161 2532 3756
αὐτοῦ τίθησιν ὑπὲρ τῶν προβάτων· 12 ὁ μισθωτὸς δέ, καὶ οὐκ
of Him lays down on behald of the sheep. the hireling And, even not

5607 4166 3739 3756 1526 3588 4263 2398 2334 3588 3074
ὢν ποιμήν, οὗ οὐκ εἰσὶ τὰ πρόβατα ἴδια, θεωρεῖ τὸν λύκον
being a shepherd, whose not are the sheep own, beholds the wolf

2064 2532 863 3588 4263 2532 5343 2532 3588 3074
ἐρχόμενον, καὶ ἀφίησι τὰ πρόβατα, καὶ φεύγει· καὶ ὁ λύκος
coming, and abandons the sheep, and flees; and the wolf

726 846 2532 4650 3588 4263 3588 1161 3411
ἁρπάζει αὐτά, καὶ σκορπίζει τὰ πρόβατα. 13 ὁ δὲ μισθωτὸς
seizes them and scatters the sheep. the And hireling

5343 3754 3411 2076 2532 3756 3199 846 4012 3588
φεύγει, ὅτι μισθωτός ἐστι, καὶ οὐ μέλει αὐτῷ περὶ τῶν
flees because a hireling he is, and not it matters to him concerning the

4263 1473 1510 3588 4166 3588 2570 2532 1097 3588 1699
προβάτων. 14 ἐγώ εἰμι ὁ ποιμὴν ὁ καλός, καὶ γινώσκω τὰ ἐμά,
sheep. I am the Shepherd Good, and I know the ones of Me,

2532 1097 5259 3588 1699 2531 1097 3165 3588 3962
καὶ γινώσκομαι ὑπὸ τῶν ἐμῶν. 15 καθὼς γινώσκει με ὁ πατήρ,
and I am know by the ones of Me. Even as knows Me the Father,

King James Version

he putteth forth his own sheep, he goeth before them, and the sheep follow him: for they know his voice.

5 And a stranger will they not follow, but will flee from him: for they know not the voice of strangers.
6 This parable spake Jesus unto them: but they understood not what things they were which he spake unto them.

7 Then said Jesus unto them again, Verily, verily, I say unto you, I am the door of the sheep.
8 All that ever came before me are thieves and robbers: but the sheep did not hear them.

9 I am the door: by me if any man enter in, he shall be saved, and shall go in and out, and find pasture.

10 The thief cometh not, but for to steal, and to kill, and to destroy: I am come that they might have life, and that they might have (it) more abundantly.
11 I am the good shepherd: the good shepherd giveth his life for the sheep.
12 But he that is an hireling, and not the shepherd, whose own the sheep are not, seeth the wolf coming, and leaveth the sheep, and fleeth: and the wolf catcheth them, and scattereth the sheep.
13 The hireling fleeth, because he is an hireling, and careth not for the sheep.

14 I am the good shepherd, and know my (sheep), and am known of mine.
15 As the Father knoweth me,

Literal Translation

I also know the Father; and I lay down My life for the sheep.

16 And I have other sheep which are not of this fold. I must also lead those, and they will hear My voice; and there will be one flock, one Shepherd.
17 For this reason My Father loves Me, because I lay down My life, that I may take it again.

18 No one takes it from Me, but I lay it down from Myself. I have authority to lay it down, and I have authority to take it again. I received this commandment from My Father.

19. Then a division occurred again among the Jews, because of these words.
20 And many of them said, He has a demon and is insane. Why do you hear him?
21 Others said, These are not words of one having been possessed by a demon. A demon is not able to open (the) eyes of blind ones.

22. And (the Feast) of Dedication took place in Jerusalem, and it was winter.
23 And Jesus was walking in the temple, in Solomon's Porch.
24 Then the Jews encircled Him, and said to Him, How long do you lift up our soul? If you are the Christ, tell us publicly.

25 Jesus answered them, I told you, and you did not believe. The works which I do in the name of My Father, these bear witness about Me.
26 But

John 10:16

2504 1097 3588 3962 2532 3588 5590 3450 5087 5228
κἀγὼ γινώσκω τὸν πατέρα· καὶ τὴν ψυχήν μου τίθημι ὑπὲρ
I also know the Father, and the life of Me I lay down for

3588 4263 2532 243 4263 2192 3739 3756 2076 1537 3588
τῶν προβάτων. 16 καὶ ἄλλα πρόβατα ἔχω, ἃ οὐκ ἔστιν ἐκ τῆς
the sheep. And other sheep I have, which not are of

833 3778 2548 3165 1163 71 2532 3588 5456 3450
αὐλῆς ταύτης· κἀκεῖνά με δεῖ ἀγαγεῖν, καὶ τῆς φωνῆς μου
fold this; those also Me it behooves to lead, and of the voice of Me

191 2532 1096 3391 4167 1520 4166 1223 5124
ἀκούσουσι· καὶ γενήσεται μία ποίμνη, εἷς ποιμήν. 17 διὰ τοῦτο
they will hear, and will become one flock, one Shepherd. Because of this

3588 3962 3165 25 3754 1473 5087 3588 5590 3450 2443
ὁ πατήρ με ἀγαπᾷ, ὅτι ἐγὼ τίθημι τὴν ψυχήν μου, ἵνα
the Father of Me loves, because I lay down the life of Me, that

3825 2983 846 3762 142 846 575 1700 235 1473
πάλιν λάβω αὐτήν. 18 οὐδεὶς αἴρει αὐτὴν ἀπ' ἐμοῦ, ἀλλ' ἐγὼ
again I may take it. No one takes it from Me, but I

5087 846 575 1683 1849 2192 5087 846 2532
τίθημι αὐτὴν ἀπ' ἐμαυτοῦ. ἐξουσίαν ἔχω θεῖναι αὐτήν, καὶ
lay down it from Myself. authority I have to lay down it, and

1849 2192 3825 2983 846 3778 3588 1785
ἐξουσίαν ἔχω πάλιν λαβεῖν αὐτήν· ταύτην τὴν ἐντολὴν
authority I have again to take it. This commandment

2983 3844 3588 3962 3450
ἔλαβον παρὰ τοῦ πατρός μου.
I received from the Father of Me.

4978 3767 3825 1096 1722 3588 2453 1223 3588
19 Σχίσμα οὖν πάλιν ἐγένετο ἐν τοῖς Ἰουδαίοις διὰ τοὺς
a division Therefore again occurred among the Jews, because of

3056 5128 3004 1161 4183 1537 846 1140 2192
λόγους τούτους. 20 ἔλεγον δὲ πολλοὶ ἐξ αὐτῶν, Δαιμόνιον ἔχει
words these. said And many of them, A demon he has

2532 3105 5101 846 191 243 3004 5023 3588
καὶ μαίνεται· τί αὐτοῦ ἀκούετε; 21 ἄλλοι ἔλεγον, Ταῦτα τὰ
and is insane. Why him do you hear? Others said, These

4487 3756 2076 1139 3361 1140 1410
ῥήματα οὐκ ἔστι δαιμονιζομένου· μὴ δαιμόνιον δύναται
words not are of one having been demon-possessed. not A demon is able

5185 3788 455
τυφλῶν ὀφθαλμοὺς ἀνοίγειν;
of blind ones eyes to open?

1096 1161 3588 1456 1722 3588 2414 2532
22 Ἐγένετο δὲ τὰ ἐγκαίνια ἐν τοῖς Ἱεροσολύμοις, καὶ
occurred And the Dedication in Jerusalem, and

5494 2258 2532 4043 3588 2424 1722 3588 2411 1722 3588 4745
χειμὼν ἦν· 23 καὶ περιεπάτει ὁ Ἰησοῦς ἐν τῷ ἱερῷ ἐν τῇ στοᾷ
winter it was. And walked Jesus in the temple in the porch

3588 4672 2944 3767 846 3588 2453 2532
τοῦ Σολομῶντος. 24 ἐκύκλωσαν οὖν αὐτὸν οἱ Ἰουδαῖοι, καὶ
of Solomon. encircled Then Him the Jews, and

3004 846 2193 4219 3588 5590 2257 142 1487 4771 1488 3588
ἔλεγον αὐτῷ, Ἕως πότε τὴν ψυχὴν ἡμῶν αἴρεις; εἰ σὺ εἶ ὁ
said to Him, Until when the soul of us you lift up? If you are the

5547 2036 2254 3954 611 846 3588 2424
Χριστός, εἰπὲ ἡμῖν παρρησίᾳ. 25 ἀπεκρίθη αὐτοῖς ὁ Ἰησοῦς,
christ, tell us publicly. answered them Jesus,

2036 5213 2532 3756 4100 3588 2041 3739 1473 4160 1722 3588
Εἶπον ὑμῖν, καὶ οὐ πιστεύετε· τὰ ἔργα ἃ ἐγὼ ποιῶ ἐν τῷ
I said to you, and not you believe; the works whcih I do in the

3686 3588 3962 3450 5023 3140 4012 1700 235
ὀνόματι τοῦ πατρός μου, ταῦτα μαρτυρεῖ περὶ ἐμοῦ· 26 ἀλλ'
name of the Father of Me, these witness concerning Me. But

King James Version

even so know I the Father: and I lay down my life for the sheep.

16 And other sheep I have, which are not of this fold: them also I must bring, and they shall hear my voice; and there shall be one fold, (and) one shepherd.
17 Therefore doth my Father love me, because I lay down my life, that I might take it again.

18 No man taketh it from me, but I lay it down of myself. I have power to lay it down, and I have power to take it again. This commandment have I received of my Father.

19. There was a division therefore again among the Jews for these sayings.
20 And many of them said, He hath a devil, and is mad; why hear ye him?
21 Others said, These are not the words of him that hath a devil. Can a devil open the eyes of the blind?

22. And it was at Jerusalem the feast of the dedication, and it was winter.
23 And Jesus walked in the temple in Solomon's porch.
24 Then came the Jews round about him, and said unto him, How long dost thou make us to doubt? If thou be the Christ, tell us plainly.

25 Jesus answered them, I told you, and ye believed not: the works that I do in my Father's name, they bear witness of me.
26 But

John 10:27

Literal Translation

you do not believe for you are not of My sheep, as I said to you.

27 My sheep hear My voice, and I know them, and they follow Me.
28 And I give eternal life to them, and they shall never perish to the age, and not anyone shall pluck them out of My hand.

29 My Father who has given (them) to Me is greater than all, and no one is able to pluck out of My Father's hand.

30 I and the Father are one!

31. Then again the Jews took up stones, that they might stone Him.
32 Jesus answered them, I showed you many good works from My Father. For which work of them do you stone Me?

33 The Jews answered Him, saying, We do not stone you concerning a good work, but concerning blasphemy; and because you, being a man, make yourself God.
34 Jesus answered them, Has it not been written in your Law, "I said, you are gods"? (Ps.82:6)

35 If He called those gods with whom the Word of God was, and the Scripture cannot be broken,
36 do you say (of Him) whom the Father sanctified and sent into the world, You blaspheme, because I said, I am Son of God?
37 If I do not do the works of My Father, do not believe Me.
38 But if I do, even if you do not believe Me, believe the works, that you may know and may believe that the Father (is) in Me, and I in Him.
39. Then again they sought

5210 3756 4100 3756 1063 2075 1537 3588 4263 3588 1699
ὑμεῖς οὐ πιστεύετε· οὐ γάρ ἐστε ἐκ τῶν προβάτων τῶν ἐμῶν,
you not do believe, not for you are of the sheep of Me,

2531 2036 5213 3588 4263 3588 1699 3588 5456 3450 191
27 καθὼς εἶπον ὑμῖν. τὰ πρόβατα τὰ ἐμὰ τῆς φωνῆς μου ἀκούει,
Even as I said to you, the sheep of Me the voice of Me hear,

2504 1097 846 2532 190 3427 2504 2222
κἀγὼ γινώσκω αὐτά, καὶ ἀκολουθοῦσί μοι· 28 κἀγὼ ζωὴν
and I know them and they follow Me. And I life

166 1325 846 2532 3756 3361 622 1519 3588 165
αἰώνιον δίδωμι αὐτοῖς· καὶ οὐ μὴ ἀπόλωνται εἰς τὸν αἰῶνα,
everlasting give to them, and not ever shall they perish to the age,

2532 3756 726 5100 846 1537 3588 5495 3450 3588 3962 3450
καὶ οὐχ ἁρπάσει τις αὐτὰ ἐκ τῆς χειρός μου. 29 ὁ πατήρ μου
and not shall pluck anyone them out of the hand of Me. The Father of Me

3739 1325 3427 3187 3956 2076 2532 3762 1410
ὃς δέδωκέ μοι, μείζων πάντων ἐστί· καὶ οὐδεὶς δύναται
who has given to Me, greater than all is, and no one is able

726 1537 3588 5495 3588 3962 3450 1473 2532 3588 3962
ἁρπάζειν ἐκ τῆς χειρὸς τοῦ πατρός μου. 30 ἐγὼ καὶ ὁ πατὴρ
to pluck out of the hand of the Father of Me. I and the Father

1520 2070 941 3767 3825 3037 3588 2453 2443
ἕν ἐσμεν. 31 ἐβάστασαν οὖν πάλιν λίθους οἱ Ἰουδαῖοι ἵνα
one are. took up Therefore again stones the Jews, that

3034 846 611 846 3588 2424 4183 2570
λιθάσωσιν αὐτόν. 32 ἀπεκρίθη αὐτοῖς ὁ Ἰησοῦς, Πολλὰ καλὰ
they might stone Him. answered them Jesus, Many good

2041 1166 5213 1537 3588 3962 3450 1223 4169 846 2041
ἔργα ἔδειξα ὑμῖν ἐκ τοῦ πατρός μου· διὰ ποῖον αὐτῶν ἔργον
works I showed you from the Father of Me, because of which of them work

3034 3165 611 846 3588 2453 3004 4012
λιθάζετέ με; 33 ἀπεκρίθησαν αὐτῷ οἱ Ἰουδαῖοι λέγοντες, Περὶ
do you stone Me? answered Him The Jews, saying, Concerning

2570 2041 3756 3034 4571 235 4012 988 2532
καλοῦ ἔργου οὐ λιθάζομέν σε, ἀλλὰ περὶ βλασφημίας, καὶ
a good work not we stone you, but concerning blasphemy, and

3754 4771 444 5607 4160 4572 2316 611 846
ὅτι σὺ ἄνθρωπος ὢν ποιεῖς σεαυτὸν Θεόν. 34 ἀπεκρίθη αὐτοῖς
that you a man being make yourself God. answered them

3588 2424 3756 2076 1125 1722 3588 3551 5216 1473
ὁ Ἰησοῦς, Οὐκ ἔστι γεγραμμένον ἐν τῷ νόμῳ ὑμῶν, Ἐγὼ
Jesus, not Is it having been written in the Law of you, I

2036 2316 2075 1487 1565 2036 2316 4314 3739 3588 3056
εἶπα, Θεοί ἐστε; 35 εἰ ἐκείνους εἶπε θεούς, πρὸς οὓς ὁ λόγος
said, gods you are? If those He said to be gods, with whom the Word

3588 2316 1096 2532 3756 1410 3089 3588 1124 3739 3588
τοῦ θεοῦ ἐγένετο [καὶ οὐ δύναται λυθῆναι ἡ γραφή], 36 ὃν ὁ
of God was (and not can be broken the Scripture), whom the

3962 37 2532 649 1519 3588 2889 5210 3004
πατὴρ ἡγίασε καὶ ἀπέστειλεν εἰς τὸν κόσμον, ὑμεῖς λέγετε
Father sanctified and sent into the world, you say,

3754 987 3754 2036 5207 3588 2316 1510 1487 3756 4160
ὅτι Βλασφημεῖς, ὅτι εἶπον, Υἱὸς τοῦ Θεοῦ εἰμι; 37 εἰ οὐ ποιῶ
You blaspheme, because I said Son of God I am? If not I do

3588 2041 3588 3962 3450 3361 4100 3427 1487 1161 4160 2579
τὰ ἔργα τοῦ πατρός μου, μὴ πιστεύετέ μοι· 38 εἰ δὲ ποιῶ, κἂν
the works of the Father of Me, not do believe Me. if But I do, even if

1698 3361 4100 3588 2041 4100 2443 1097 2532
ἐμοὶ μὴ πιστεύητε, τοῖς ἔργοις πιστεύσατε· ἵνα γνῶτε καὶ
Me not you believe, the works believe, that you may know and

4100 3754 1722 1698 3588 3962 2504 1722 846 2212
πιστεύσητε ὅτι ἐν ἐμοὶ ὁ πατήρ, κἀγὼ ἐν αὐτῷ. 39 ἐζήτουν
may believe that in Me the Father (is) and I in Him. they sought

King James Version

ye believe not, because ye are not of my sheep, as I said unto you.

27 My sheep hear my voice, and I know them, and they follow me:
28 And I give unto them eternal life; and they shall never perish, neither shall any (man) pluck them out of my hand.

29 My Father, which gave (them) me, is greater than all; and no (man) is able to pluck (them) out of my Father's hand.

30 I and (my) Father are one.

31. Then the Jews took up stones again to stone him.
32 Jesus answered them, Many good works have I shewed you from my Father; for which of those works do ye stone me?

33 The Jews answered him, saying, For a good work we stone thee not; but for blasphemy; and because that thou, being a man, makest thyself God.
34 Jesus answered them, Is it not written in your law, I said, Ye are gods?

35 If he called them gods, unto whom the word of God came, and the scripture cannot be broken;
36 Say ye of him, whom the Father hath sanctified, and sent into the world, Thou blasphemest; because I said, I am the Son of God?
37 If I do not the works of my Father, believe me not.
38 But if I do, though ye believe not me, believe the works: that ye may know, and believe, that the Father (is) in me, and I in him.
39. Therefore they sought

Literal Translation

to seize Him. And He went forth out of their hand.

40 And He went away again across the Jordan to the place where John was at first baptizing and remained there.
41 And many came to Him and said, John indeed did no miracle, but all things that John said concerning this One were true.

42 And many believed into Him there.

John 10:40

3767 3825 846 4084 2532 1831 1537 3588 5495 846
οὖν πάλιν αὐτὸν πιάσαι· καὶ ἐξῆλθεν ἐκ τῆς χειρὸς αὐτῶν.
Then again Him to seize. And He went out from the hand of them.

2532 565 3825 4008 3588 2446 1519 3588 5117
40 Καὶ ἀπῆλθε πάλιν πέραν τοῦ Ἰορδάνου εἰς τὸν τόπον
And He went away again across the Jordan to the place

3699 2258 2491 3588 4413 907 2532 3306 1563 2532
ὅπου ἦν Ἰωάννης τὸ πρῶτον βαπτίζων· καὶ ἔμεινεν ἐκεῖ. 41 καὶ
where was John at first baptizing; and remained there. And

4183 2064 4314 846 2532 3004 3745 2491 3303
πολλοὶ ἦλθον πρὸς αὐτόν, καὶ ἔλεγον ὅτι Ἰωάννης μὲν
many came to Him, and said, John in deed

4592 4160 3762 3956 1161 3745 2036 2491 4012
σημεῖον ἐποίησεν οὐδέν· πάντα δὲ ὅσα εἶπεν Ἰωάννης περὶ
sign did none, all things but whatever said John concerning

5127 227 2258 2532 4100 4183 1563 1519 846
τούτου, ἀληθῆ ἦν. 42 καὶ ἐπίστευσαν πολλοὶ ἐκεῖ εἰς αὐτόν.
this One true were. And believed many there into Him.

King James Version

again to take him: but he escaped out of their hand,

40 And went away again beyond Jordan into the place where John at first baptized; and there he abode.
41 And many resorted unto him, and said, John did no miracle: but all things that John spake of this man were true.

42 And many believed on him there.

John 11

1. And there was a certain sick one, Lazarus from Bethany, of the village of Mary and her sister Martha.
2 And it was Mary who anointed the Lord with ointment and wiped His feet with her hair, whose brother Lazarus was sick.
3 Then the sisters sent to Him, saying, Lord, behold, (the one) whom You love is sick.

4 And hearing, Jesus said, This is not sickness to death, but for the glory of God, that the Son of God be glorified by it.

5 And Jesus loved Martha and her sister and Lazarus.

6 Therefore, when He heard that he is sick, then, indeed, He remained in the place where He was two days.
7 Then after this He said to the disciples, Let us go to Judea again.
8 The disciples said to Him, Rabbi, just now the Jews were seeking to stone You, and do You go there again?
9 Jesus answered, Are there not twelve hours in the day? If anyone walks

2258 1161 5100 770 2976 575 963 1537 3588 2968
1. Ἦν δέ τις ἀσθενῶν Λάζαρος ἀπὸ Βηθανίας, ἐκ τῆς κώμης
was And a certain sick one, Lazarus from Bethany, of the village

3137 2532 3136 3588 79 846 2258 1161 3137 3588
Μαρίας καὶ Μάρθας τῆς ἀδελφῆς αὐτῆς. 2 ἦν δὲ Μαρία ἡ
of Mary and Martha the sister of her. (it) was And Mary, she

218 3588 2962 3464 2532 1591 3588 4228 846
ἀλείψασα τὸν Κύριον μύρῳ, καὶ ἐκμάξασα τοὺς πόδας αὐτοῦ
anointing the Lord with ointment, and wiping off the feet of Him

3588 2359 846 3739 3588 80 2976 770 649
ταῖς θριξὶν αὐτῆς, ἧς ὁ ἀδελφὸς Λάζαρος ἠσθένει. 3 ἀπέστειλαν
with the hairs of her, of whom the brother Lazarus was sick. sent

3767 3588 79 4314 846 3004 2962 2396 3739 5368
οὖν αἱ ἀδελφαὶ πρὸς αὐτὸν λέγουσαι, Κύριε, ἴδε ὃν φιλεῖς
Then the sisters to Him, saying, Lord, behold, whom You love

770 191 1161 3588 2424 2036 3778 3588 769 3756
ἀσθενεῖ. 4 ἀκούσας δὲ ὁ Ἰησοῦς εἶπεν, Αὕτη ἡ ἀσθένεια οὐκ
is sick. hearing And Jesus said, This sickness not

2076 4314 2288 235 5228 3588 1391 3588 2316 2443 1392
ἔστι πρὸς θάνατον, ἀλλ' ὑπὲρ τῆς δόξης τοῦ Θεοῦ, ἵνα δοξασθῇ
is to death, but for the sake of the glory of God, that be glorified

3588 5207 3588 2316 1223 846 25 1161 3588 2424 3588 3136 2532
ὁ υἱὸς τοῦ Θεοῦ δι' αὐτῆς. 5 ἠγάπα δὲ ὁ Ἰησοῦς τὴν Μάρθαν καὶ
the Son of God through it. loved And Jesus Martha and

3588 79 846 2532 3588 2976 5613 3767 191 3754
τὴν ἀδελφὴν αὐτῆς καὶ τὸν Λάζαρον. 6 ὡς οὖν ἤκουσεν ὅτι
the sister of her and Lazarus. As, then, He heard that

770 5119 3303 3306 1722 3739 2258 5117 1417 2250 1899
ἀσθενεῖ, τότε μὲν ἔμεινεν ἐν ᾧ ἦν τόπῳ δύο ἡμέρας· 7 ἔπειτα
he is sick, then, indeed, He abode in which was place two days. Then

3326 5124 3004 3588 3101 71 1519 3588 2449
μετὰ τοῦτο λέγει τοῖς μαθηταῖς, Ἄγωμεν εἰς τὴν Ἰουδαίαν
after this He says to the disciples, Let us go to Judea

3825 3004 846 3588 3101 4461 3568 2212 4571
πάλιν. 8 λέγουσιν αὐτῷ οἱ μαθηταί, Ῥαββί, νῦν ἐζήτουν σε
again. say to Him The disciples, Rabbi, now were seeking You

3034 3588 2453 2532 3825 5217 1563 611 3588
λιθάσαι οἱ Ἰουδαῖοι, καὶ πάλιν ὑπάγεις ἐκεῖ; 9 ἀπεκρίθη ὁ
to stone the Jews, and again do You go there? answered

2424 3780 1427 1526 5610 3588 2250 1437 5100 4043
Ἰησοῦς, Οὐχὶ δώδεκά εἰσιν ὧραι τῆς ἡμέρας; ἐάν τις περι-
Jesus, not twelve Are hours in the day? If anyone walks

1. Now a certain (man) was sick, (named) Lazarus, of Bethany, the town of Mary and her sister Martha.
2 (It was (that) Mary which anointed the Lord with ointment, and wiped his feet with her hair, whose brother Lazarus was sick.)
3 Therefore his sisters sent unto him, saying, Lord, behold, he whom thou lovest is sick.

4 When Jesus heard (that), he said, This sickness is not unto death, but for the glory of God, that the Son of God might be glorified thereby.
5 Now Jesus loved Martha, and her sister, and Lazarus.

6 When he had heard therefore that he was sick, he abode two days still in the same place where he was.
7 Then after that saith he to (his) disciples, Let us go into Judaea again.

8 (His) disciples say unto him, Master, the Jews of late sought to stone thee; and goest thou thither again?
9 Jesus answered, Are there not twelve hours in the day? If any man walk

John 11:10

Literal Translation

in the day, he does not stumble because he sees the light of the world.
10 But if anyone walks in the night, he stumbles because the light is not in him.
11 He said these things. And after this, He said to them, Our friend Lazarus has fallen asleep, but I am going that I may awaken him.
12 Then His disciples said, Lord, if he has fallen asleep, he will recover.
13 But Jesus had spoken about his death, but they thought that He spoke of the sleep of slumber.

14 Therefore, then Jesus said to them plainly, Lazarus has died.
15 And I rejoice because of you, in order that you may believe, that I was not there. But let us go to him.
16 Then Thomas, (he) having been called Twin, said to the fellow-disciples, Let us go, even we, that we may die with Him.

17 Then coming, Jesus found him already being held in the tomb four days.
18 And Bethany was near Jerusalem, (about) fifteen stadia off.

19 And many of the Jews had come to those around Martha and Mary, that they might console them concerning their brother.
20 Then when Martha heard that Jesus is coming, she met Him; but Mary was sitting in the house.

21 Then Martha said to Jesus, Lord, if You were here, my brother would not be dead.

22 But even now I know that whatever You may ask God,

1722 3588 2250 3756 4350 3754 3588 5457 3588 2889
πατῇ ἐν τῇ ἡμέρᾳ, οὐ προσκόπτει, ὅτι τὸ φῶς τοῦ κόσμου
in the day, not he stumbles, becaue the light world

5127 991 1437 1161 5100 4043 1722 3588 3571 4350
τούτου βλέπει. 10 ἐὰν δέ τις περιπατῇ ἐν τῇ νυκτί, προσκόπτει,
of this he sees. if But anyone walk in the night, he stumbles,

3754 3588 5457 3756 2076 1722 846 5023 2036 2532 3326 5124
ὅτι τὸ φῶς οὐκ ἔστιν ἐν αὐτῷ. 11 ταῦτα εἶπε, καὶ μετὰ τοῦτο
because the light not is in him. These things He said, and after this

3004 846 2976 3588 5384 2257 2837 235
λέγει αὐτοῖς, Λάζαρος ὁ φίλος ἡμῶν κεκοίμηται· ἀλλὰ
He says to them, Lazarus the friend of us has fallen asleep, but

4198 2443 1852 846 2036 3767 3588 3101 846
πορεύομαι ἵνα ἐξυπνίσω αὐτόν. 12 εἶπον οὖν οἱ μαθηταὶ αὐτοῦ,
I am going that I may awaken him. said Then the disciples of Him,

2962 1487 2837 4982 2046 1161 3588 2424 4012
Κύριε, εἰ κεκοίμηται, σωθήσεται. 13 εἰρήκει δὲ ὁ Ἰησοῦς περὶ
Lord, if he has fallen asleep, he will recover. had spoken But Jesus about

3588 2288 846 1565 1161 1380 3754 4012 3588 2838
τοῦ θανάτου αὐτοῦ· ἐκεῖνοι δὲ ἔδοξαν ὅτι περὶ τῆς κοιμήσεως
the death of him; those but thought that about the sleep

3588 5258 3004 5119 3767 2036 846 3588 2424 3954
τοῦ ὕπνου λέγει. 14 τότε οὖν εἶπεν αὐτοῖς ὁ Ἰησοῦς παρρησίᾳ,
of slumber He says. then Therefore said to them Jesus openly,

2976 599 2532 5463 1223 5209 2443 4100 3754
Λάζαρος ἀπέθανε. 15 καὶ χαίρω δι' ὑμᾶς, ἵνα πιστεύσητε, ὅτι
Lazarus has died. And I rejoice because of you, that you may believe, that

3756 2252 1563 235 71 4314 846 2036 3767 2381 3588
οὐκ ἤμην ἐκεῖ· ἀλλ' ἄγωμεν πρὸς αὐτόν. 16 εἶπεν οὖν Θωμᾶς, ὁ
not I was there. But let us go to him. said Then Thomas,

3004 1324 3588 4827 71 2532 2249 2443
λεγόμενος Δίδυμος, τοῖς συμμαθηταῖς, Ἄγωμεν καὶ ἡμεῖς, ἵνα
being called Twin, to the fellow-disciples, Let us go, even we, that

599 3326 846
ἀποθάνωμεν μετ' αὐτοῦ.
we may die with Him.

2064 3767 3588 2424 2147 846 5064 2250 2235
17 Ἐλθὼν οὖν ὁ Ἰησοῦς εὗρεν αὐτὸν τέσσαρας ἡμέρας ἤδη
coming Then Jesus found him four days already

2192 1722 3588 3419 2258 1161 3588 963 1451 3588 2414
ἔχοντα ἐν τῷ μνημείῳ. 18 ἦν δὲ ἡ Βηθανία ἐγγὺς τῶν Ἱεροσολύ-
being held in the tomb. was and Bethany near Jerusalem,

5613 575 4712 1178 2532 4183 1537 3588
μων, ὡς ἀπὸ σταδίων δεκαπέντε. 19 καὶ πολλοὶ ἐκ τῶν
as from stadia fifteen. And many of the

2453 2064 4314 3588 4012 3136 2532 3137
Ἰουδαίων ἐληλύθεισαν πρὸς τὰς περὶ Μάρθαν καὶ Μαρίαν,
Jews had come to those around Martha and Mary,

2443 3888 846 4012 3588 80 846 3588
ἵνα παραμυθήσωνται αὐτὰς περὶ τοῦ ἀδελφοῦ αὐτῶν. 20 ἡ
that they might console them concerning the brother of them.

3767 3136 5613 191 3754 3588 2424 2064 5221
οὖν Μάρθα, ὡς ἤκουσεν ὅτι ὁ Ἰησοῦς ἔρχεται, ὑπήντησεν
Then Martha, when she heard that Jesus is coming, met

846 3137 1161 1722 3588 3624 2516 2036 3767 3588 3136
αὐτῷ· Μαριὰ δὲ ἐν τῷ οἴκῳ ἐκαθέζετο. 21 εἶπεν οὖν ἡ Μάρθα
Him; Mary but in the house was sitting. said Then Martha

4314 3588 2424 2962 1487 2258 5602 3588 80 3450 3756 302
πρὸς τὸν Ἰησοῦν, Κύριε, εἰ ἦς ὧδε, ὁ ἀδελφός μου οὐκ ἂν
to Jesus, Lord, if You were here, the brother of me not would

2348 235 2532 3568 1492 3754 3745 302 154 3588 2316
ἐτεθνήκει. 22 ἀλλὰ καὶ νῦν οἶδα ὅτι ὅσα ἂν αἰτήσῃ τὸν Θεόν,
be dead. But also now I know that whatever You may ask God,

King James Version

in the day, he stumbleth not, because he seeth the light of this world.
10 But if a man walk in the night, he stumbleth, because there is no light in him.
11 These things said he: and after that he saith unto them, Our friend Lazarus sleepeth; but I go, that I may awake him out of sleep.
12 Then said his disciples, Lord, if he sleep, he shall do well.

13 Howbeit Jesus spake of his death: but they thought that he had spoken of taking of rest in sleep.

14 Then said Jesus unto them plainly, Lazarus is dead.
15 And I am glad for your sakes that I was not there, to the intent ye may believe; nevertheless let us go unto him.
16 Then said Thomas, which is called Didymus, unto his fellowdisciples, Let us also go, that we may die with him.

17 Then when Jesus came, he found that he had (lain) in the grave four days already.
18 Now Bethany was nigh unto Jerusalem, about fifteen furlongs off:
19 And many of the Jews came to Martha and Mary, to comfort them concerning their brother.

20 Then Martha, as soon as she heard that Jesus was coming, went and met him: but Mary sat (still) in the house.

21 Then said Martha unto Jesus, Lord, if thou hadst been here, my brother had not died.

22 But I know, that even now, whatsoever thou wilt ask of God,

Literal Translation

God will give You.
23 Jesus said to her, Your brother will rise again.
24 Martha said to Him, I know that he will rise again in the resurrection in the last day.
25 Jesus said to her, I am the Resurrection and the Life. The (one) believing into Me, though he die, he shall live.

26 And everyone living and believing into Me shall not ever die forever. Do you believe this?
27 She said to Him, Yes, Lord, I have believed that You are the Christ, the Son of God who is coming into the world.

28. And saying these things, she went away and called her sister Mary secretly, saying, The Teacher is here and calls you.

29 That one, when she heard, rose up quickly and came to Him.
30 And Jesus had not yet come into the village, but was in the place where Martha met Him.

31 Then the Jews who were with her in the house, and consoling her, seeing that Mary quickly rose up and went out, (they) followed her, saying, She is going to the tomb so that she may weep there.

32 Then Mary, when she came where Jesus was, seeing Him, she fell at His feet, saying to Him, Lord, if You were here, my brother would not have died.

33 Then when He saw her weeping, and the Jews who came down with her weeping, Jesus groaned in the spirit and troubled Himself.

John 11:23

1325 4671 3588 2316 3004 846 3588 2424 450 3588
δώσει σοι ὁ Θεός. 23 λέγει αὐτῇ ὁ Ἰησοῦς, Ἀναστήσεται ὁ
will give You God. says to her Jesus, will rise again The

80 4675 3004 846 3136 1492 3754 450 1722
ἀδελφός σου. 24 λέγει αὐτῷ Μάρθα, Οἶδα ὅτι ἀναστήσεται ἐν
brother of you. says to Him Martha, I know that he will rise again in

3588 386 1722 3588 2078 2250 2036 846 3588 2424
τῇ ἀναστάσει ἐν τῇ ἐσχάτῃ ἡμέρᾳ. 25 εἶπεν αὐτῇ ὁ Ἰησοῦς,
the resurrection in the last day. said to her Jesus,

1473 1510 3588 386 2532 3588 2222 3588 4100 1519 1691 2579
Ἐγώ εἰμι ἡ ἀνάστασις καὶ ἡ ζωή· ὁ πιστεύων εἰς ἐμέ, κἂν
I am the resurrection and the life; the (one) believing into Me, though

599 2198 2532 3956 3588 2198 2532 4100 1519 1691 3756
ἀποθάνῃ, ζήσεται· 26 καὶ πᾶς ὁ ζῶν καὶ πιστεύων εἰς ἐμὲ, οὐ
he die, he shall live. And everyone living and believing into Me, not

3361 599 1519 3588 165 4100 5124 3004 846
μὴ ἀποθάνῃ εἰς τὸν αἰῶνα. πιστεύεις τοῦτο; 27 λέγει αὐτῷ,
ever shall die to the age. Do you believe this? She says to Him,

3483 2962 1473 4100 3754 4771 1488 3588 5547 3588 5207 3588
Ναί, Κύριε· ἐγὼ πεπίστευκα, ὅτι σὺ εἶ ὁ Χριστὸς, ὁ υἱὸς τοῦ
Yes, Lord, I have believed that You are the Christ, the Son

2316 3588 1519 3588 2889 2064 2532 5023 2036
Θεοῦ, ὁ εἰς τὸν κόσμον ἐρχόμενος. 28 καὶ ταῦτα εἰποῦσα
of God, who into the (one) world coming. And these things having said,

565 2532 5455 3137 3588 79 846 2977
ἀπῆλθε, καὶ ἐφώνησε Μαριὰν τὴν ἀδελφὴν αὐτῆς λάθρᾳ,
she left, and (she) called Mary the sister of her secretly,

2036 3588 1320 3918 2532 5455 4571 1565 5613
εἰποῦσα, Ὁ διδάσκαλος πάρεστι καὶ φωνεῖ σε. 29 ἐκείνη ὡς
saying, The Teacher is here and calls you. That one as

191 1453 5035 2532 2064 4314 846 3768
ἤκουσεν, ἐγείρεται ταχὺ καὶ ἔρχεται πρὸς αὐτόν. 30 [οὔπω
she heard, rises up quickly and comes to Him. (not yet

1161 2064 3588 2424 1519 3588 2968 235 2258 1722 3588 5117
δὲ ἐληλύθει ὁ Ἰησοῦς εἰς τὴν κώμην, ἀλλ' ἦν ἐν τῷ τόπῳ
And had come Jesus into the village, but was in the place

3699 5221 846 3588 3136 3588 3767 2453 3588 5607
ὅπου ὑπήντησεν αὐτῷ ἡ Μάρθα.] 31 οἱ οὖν Ἰουδαῖοι οἱ ὄντες
where met Him Martha.) the Then Jews, those being

3326 846 1722 3588 3614 2532 3888 846 1492
μετ' αὐτῆς ἐν τῇ οἰκίᾳ καὶ παραμυθούμενοι αὐτήν, ἰδόντες
with her in the house and consoling her, seeing

3588 3137 3754 5030 450 2532 1831 190
τὴν Μαρίαν ὅτι ταχέως ἀνέστη καὶ ἐξῆλθεν, ἠκολούθησαν
Mary, that quickly she rose and went out, followed

846 3004 3754 5217 1519 3588 3419 2443 2799 1563
αὐτῇ, λέγοντες ὅτι ὑπάγει εἰς τὸ μνημεῖον, ἵνα κλαύσῃ ἐκεῖ.
her, saying, She goes to the tomb, that she may weep there.

3588 3767 3137 5613 2064 3699 2258 3588 2424 1492 846
32 ἡ οὖν Μαριὰ, ὡς ἦλθεν ὅπου ἦν ὁ Ἰησοῦς, ἰδοῦσα αὐτόν,
Then Mary, when she came where was Jesus, seeing Him,

4098 1519 3588 4228 846 3004 846 2962 1487 2258
ἔπεσεν εἰς τοὺς πόδας αὐτοῦ, λέγουσα αὐτῷ, Κύριε, εἰ ἦς
fell at the feet of Him, saying to Him, Lord, if You were

5602 3756 302 599 3450 3588 80 2424 3767 5613 1492
ὧδε, οὐκ ἂν ἀπέθανέ μου ὁ ἀδελφός. 33 Ἰησοῦς οὖν ὡς εἶδεν
here, not would have died of me the brother. Jesus Then, as He saw

846 2799 2532 3588 4905 846 2453
αὐτὴν κλαίουσαν, καὶ τοὺς συνελθόντας αὐτῇ Ἰουδαίους
her weeping, and the coming down with her Jews

2799 1690 3588 4151 2532 5015 1438
κλαίοντας, ἐνεβριμήσατο τῷ πνεύματι, καὶ ἐτάραξεν ἑαυτόν,
weeping, (He) groaned in the spirit and troubled Himself,

King James Version

God will give (it) thee.
23 Jesus saith unto her, Thy brother shall rise again.
24 Martha saith unto him, I know that he shall rise again in the resurrection at the last day.
25 Jesus said unto her, I am the resurrection, and the life: he that believeth in me, though he were dead, yet shall he live:

26 And whosoever liveth and believeth in me shall never die. Believest thou this?
27 She saith unto him, Yea, Lord: I believe that thou art the Christ, the Son of God, which should come into the world.

28. And when she had so said, she went her way, and called Mary her sister secretly, saying, The Master is come, and calleth for thee.
29 As soon as she heard (that), she arose quickly, and came unto him.
30 Now Jesus was not yet come into the town, but was in that place where Martha met him.

31 The Jews then which were with her in the house, and comforted her, when they saw Mary, that she rose up hastily and went out, followed her, saying, She goeth unto the grave to weep there.

32 Then when Mary was come where Jesus was, and saw him, she fell down at his feet, saying unto him, Lord, if thou hadst been here, my brother had not died.
33 When Jesus therefore saw her weeping, and the Jews also weeping which came with her, he groaned in the spirit, and was troubled,

Literal Translation | **John 11:34** | ***King James Version***

34 And (He) said, Where have you put him? They said to Him, Lord, come and see.
35 Jesus wept.
36 Then the Jews said, See how He loved him!
37 But some of them said, Was this One, the (one) opening the eyes of the blind, not able to have caused that this one should not die?

2532 2036 4226 5087 846 3004 846 2962
34 καὶ εἶπε, Ποῦ τεθείκατε αὐτόν; λέγουσιν αὐτῷ, Κύριε,
and said, Where have you put him? They say to Him, Lord,

2064 2532 1492 1145 3588 2424 3004 3767 3588
ἔρχου καὶ ἴδε. 35 ἐδάκρυσεν ὁ Ἰησοῦς. 36 ἔλεγον οὖν οἱ
come and see. shed tears Jesus. said Therefore the

2453 2396 4459 5368 846 5100 1161 1537 846 2036 3756
Ἰουδαῖοι, Ἴδε πῶς ἐφίλει αὐτόν. 37 τινὲς δὲ ἐξ αὐτῶν εἶπον, Οὐκ
Jews, See how He loved him. some And of them said, Not

1410 3778 3588 455 3588 3788 3588 5185 4160
ἠδύνατο οὗτος, ὁ ἀνοίξας τοὺς ὀφθαλμοὺς τοῦ τυφλοῦ, ποιῆσαι
was able this One, He opening the eyes of the blind, to have caused

2443 2532 3778 3361 599 2424 3767 3825 1690
ἵνα καὶ οὗτος μὴ ἀποθάνῃ; 38 Ἰησοῦς οὖν πάλιν ἐμβριμώμενος
that also this one not should die? Jesus Then again groaning

34 And said, Where have ye laid him? They said unto him, Lord, come and see.
35 Jesus wept.
36 Then said the Jews, Behold how he loved him!
37 And some of them said, Could not this man, which opened the eyes of the blind, have caused that even this man should not have died?

38 Then groaning again within Himself, Jesus came to the tomb. And it was a cave, and a stone was lying on it.

1722 1438 2064 1519 3588 3419 2258 1161 4693 2532 3037
ἐν ἑαυτῷ ἔρχεται εἰς τὸ μνημεῖον. ἦν δὲ σπήλαιον, καὶ λίθος
in Himself comes to the tomb,. it was And a cave, and a stone

1945 1909 846 3004 3588 2424 142 3588 3037 3004
ἐπέκειτο ἐπ' αὐτῷ. 39 λέγει ὁ Ἰησοῦς, Ἄρατε τὸν λίθον. λέγει
was lying on it. says Jesus, Lift the stone. says

38 Jesus therefore again groaning in himself cometh to the grave. It was a cave, and a stone lay upon it.

39 Jesus said, Lift the stone. Martha, the sister of the one that had died, said to Him, Lord, he already smells, for it is (the) fourth (day).

846 3588 79 3588 2348 3136 2962 2235 3605
αὐτῷ ἡ ἀδελφὴ τοῦ τεθνηκότος Μάρθα, Κύριε, ἤδη ὄζει·
to Him the sister of the (one) having died, Martha, Lord, already he smells,

5066 1063 2076 3004 846 3588 2424 3756 2036 4671
τεταρταῖος γάρ ἐστι. 40 λέγει αὐτῇ ὁ Ἰησοῦς, Οὐκ εἶπόν σοι,
(the) fourth day for it is. says to her Jesus, Did not I say to you

39 Jesus said, Take ye away the stone. Martha, the sister of him that was dead, saith unto him, Lord, by this time he stinketh: for he hath been (dead) four days.

40 Jesus said to her, Did I not say to you that if you would believe you will see the glory of God?
41 Then they lifted the stone where the dead one was laid. And Jesus lifted (His) eyes upward and said, Father, I thank You that You heard Me.

3754 1437 4100 3700 3588 1391 3588 2316 142 3767 3588
ὅτι ἐὰν πιστεύσῃς, ὄψει τὴν δόξαν τοῦ Θεοῦ; 41 ἦραν οὖν τὸν
that if you believe you will see the glory of God? they lifted Then the

3037 3757 2258 3588 2348 2749 3588 1161 2424 142 3588
λίθον, οὗ ἦν ὁ τεθνηκὼς κείμενος. ὁ δὲ Ἰησοῦς ἦρε τοὺς
stone, where was the dead one laid. And Jesus lifted the

3788 507 2532 2036 3962 2168 4671 3754 191
ὀφθαλμοὺς ἄνω, καὶ εἶπε, Πάτερ, εὐχαριστῶ σοι ὅτι ἤκουσάς
eyes upward, and said, Father, I thank You that You heard

40 Jesus saith unto her, Said I not unto thee, that, if thou wouldest believe, thou shouldest see the glory of God?
41 Then they took away the stone (from the place) where the dead was laid. And Jesus lifted up (his) eyes, and said, Father, I thank thee that thou hast heard me.

42 And I know that you always hear Me, but because of the crowd standing around, I said (it), that they might believe that You sent Me.

3450 1473 1161 1492 3754 3842 3450 191 235 1223 3588
μου. 42 ἐγὼ δὲ ᾔδειν ὅτι πάντοτέ μου ἀκούεις· ἀλλὰ διὰ τὸν
Me. I And know that always Me You hear. But because of the

3793 3588 4026 2036 2443 4100 3754 4771 3165
ὄχλον τὸν περιεστῶτα εἶπον, ἵνα πιστεύσωσιν ὅτι σύ με
crowd standing around I said, so that they might believed that You Me

649 2532 5023 2036 5456 3173 2905
ἀπέστειλας. 43 καὶ ταῦτα εἰπών, φωνῇ μεγάλῃ ἐκραύγασε,
sent. And these things saying, with a voice great, He cried out,

42 And I knew that thou hearest me always: but because of the people which stand by I said (it), that they may believe that thou hast sent me.

43 And saying these things, He cried out with a loud voice, Lazarus! Here! Outside!
44 And the (one) who had died came out, the feet and the hands having been bound with sheets, and his face being bound with a cloth. Jesus said to them, Loosen him and let (him) go.

2976 1204 1854 2532 1831 3588 2348 1210 3588
Λάζαρε, δεῦρο ἔξω. 44 καὶ ἐξῆλθεν ὁ τεθνηκώς, δεδεμένος τοὺς
Lazarus! Here! Outside! And came out he having died, being bound the

4228 2532 3588 5495 2750 2532 3588 3799 846 4676
πόδας καὶ τὰς χεῖρας κειρίαις, καὶ ἡ ὄψις αὐτοῦ σουδαρίῳ
feet and the hands with sheets, and the face of him with a cloth

4019 3004 846 3588 2424 3089 846 2532 863
περιεδέδετο. λέγει αὐτοῖς ὁ Ἰησοῦς, Λύσατε αὐτὸν, καὶ ἄφετε
being bound. says to them Jesus, Loosen him, and allow (him)

5217
ὑπάγειν.
to go.

43 And when he thus had spoken, he cried with a loud voice, Lazarus, come forth.
44 And he that was dead came forth, bound hand and foot with graveclothes: and his face was bound about with a napkin. Jesus saith unto them, Loose him, and let him go.

45 Then many of the Jews, those coming to Mary, and having seen what Jesus did, believed into Him.

4183 3767 1537 3588 2453 3588 2064 4314 3588
45. Πολλοὶ οὖν ἐκ τῶν Ἰουδαίων, οἱ ἐλθόντες πρὸς τὴν
many Therefore of the Jews, those having come to

3137 2532 2300 3739 4160 3588 2424 4100 1519
Μαρίαν καὶ θεασάμενοι ἃ ἐποίησεν ὁ Ἰησοῦς, ἐπίστευσαν εἰς
Mary, and having beheld what did Jesus, believed into

45 Then many of the Jews which came to Mary, and had seen the things which Jesus did, believed on him.

Literal Translation **John 11:46** ***King James Version***

46 But some of them went away to the Pharisees and told them what Jesus had done.

47. Then the chief priests and the Pharisees assembled a sanhedrin, and said, What are we doing, for this man does many miracles?

48 If we let him alone this way, all will believe into him, and the Romans will come and will take away from us both the place and the nation.

49 But a certain one of them, Caiaphas being high priest of that year, said to them, You know nothing,

50 nor consider that it is profitable for us that one man die for the people, and not all the nation to perish.

51 But he did not say this from himself, but being high priest that year, he prophesied that Jesus was about to die on behalf of the nation,

52 and not only on behalf of the nation, but that He also might gather into one the children of God who had been scattered.

53 Then from that day, they took counsel that they might kill Him.

54 Then Jesus no longer walked publicly among the Jews, but went away, from there into the country near (*a*) deserted (place), to a city being called Ephraim, and stayed there with His disciples.

55. And the Passover of the Jews was near. And many went up to Jerusalem out of the country before the Passover,

846 5100 1161 1537 846 565 4314 3588 5330
αὐτόν. 46 τινὲς δὲ ἐξ αὐτῶν ἀπῆλθον πρὸς τοὺς Φαρισαίους,
Him. some But of them went away to the Pharisees,
2532 2036 846 3739 4160 3588 2424
καὶ εἶπον αὐτοῖς ἃ ἐποίησεν ὁ Ἰησοῦς.
and told them what did Jesus.

4863 3767 3588 749 2532 3588 5330 4892
47 Συνήγαγον οὖν οἱ ἀρχιερεῖς καὶ οἱ Φαρισαῖοι συνέδριον,
assembled Then the chief priests and the Pharisees a sanhedrin,
2532 3004 5101 4160 3754 3778 3588 444 4183
καὶ ἔλεγον, Τί ποιοῦμεν; ὅτι οὗτος ὁ ἄνθρωπος πολλὰ
and said, What are we doing, because this man many
4592 4160 1437 863 846 3779 3956 4100
σημεῖα ποιεῖ. 48 ἐὰν ἀφῶμεν αὐτὸν οὕτω, πάντες πιστεύσουσιν
signs does? If we leave him thus, all will believe
1519 846 2532 2064 3588 4514 2532 142 2257 2532
εἰς αὐτόν, καὶ ἐλεύσονται οἱ Ῥωμαῖοι καὶ ἀροῦσιν ἡμῶν καὶ
into him, and will come the Romans and will take of us both
3588 5117 2532 3588 1484 1520 1161 5100 1537 846 2533
τὸν τόπον καὶ τὸ ἔθνος. 49 εἷς δέ τις ἐξ αὐτῶν Καϊάφας,
the place and the nation. one But a certain of them, Caiaphas,
749 5607 3588 1763 1565 2036 846 5210 3756
ἀρχιερεὺς ὢν τοῦ ἐνιαυτοῦ ἐκείνου, εἶπεν αὐτοῖς, Ὑμεῖς οὐκ
high priest being of year that, said to them, You not
1492 3762 3761 1260 3754 4851 2254 2443 1520
οἴδατε οὐδέν, 50 οὐδὲ διαλογίζεσθε ὅτι συμφέρει ἡμῖν ἵνα εἷς
do know, nothing! Nor (do you) consider that it is profitable for us that one
444 599 5228 3588 2992 2532 3361 3650 3588 1484
ἄνθρωπος ἀποθάνῃ ὑπὲρ τοῦ λαοῦ, καὶ μὴ ὅλον τὸ ἔθνος
man die on behalf of the people, and not all the nation
622 5124 1161 575 1438 3756 2036 235 749 5607
ἀπόληται. 51 τοῦτο δὲ ἀφ' ἑαυτοῦ οὐκ εἶπεν, ἀλλὰ ἀρχιερεὺς ὢν
to perish. this But of himself not he said, but high priest being
3588 1763 1565 4395 3754 3195 3588 2424
τοῦ ἐνιαυτοῦ ἐκείνου, προεφήτευσεν ὅτι ἔμελλεν ὁ Ἰησοῦς
year that, he prophesied that was about Jesus
599 5228 3588 1484 2532 3756 5228 3588 1484
ἀποθνήσκειν ὑπὲρ τοῦ ἔθνους, 52 καὶ οὐχ ὑπὲρ τοῦ ἔθνους
to die on behalf of the nation, and not on behalf of the nation
3440 235 2443 2532 3588 5043 3588 2316 3588 1287
μόνον, ἀλλ' ἵνα καὶ τὰ τέκνα τοῦ Θεοῦ τὰ διεσκορπισμένα
only, but that also the children of God having been scattered
4863 1519 1520 575 1565 3767 3588 2250 4823
συναγάγῃ εἰς ἕν. 53 ἀπ' ἐκείνης οὖν τῆς ἡμέρας συνεβου-
He might gather into one. from that Therefore day they
2443 615 846
λεύσαντο ἵνα ἀποκτείνωσιν αὐτόν.
took counsel that they might kill Him.

2424 3767 3756 3954 4043 1722 3588
54 Ἰησοῦς οὖν οὐκέτι παρρησίᾳ περιεπάτει ἐν τοῖς
Jesus Therefore no longer publicly walked among the
2453 235 565 1564 1519 3588 5561 1451 3588
Ἰουδαίοις, ἀλλὰ ἀπῆλθεν ἐκεῖθεν εἰς τὴν χώραν ἐγγὺς τῆς
Jews, but went away from there into the country near the
2048 1519 2187 3004 4172 2546 1304 3326 3588
ἐρήμου, εἰς Ἐφραὶμ λεγομένην πόλιν, κἀκεῖ διέτριβε μετὰ τῶν
deserted (place) to Ephraim being called a city, and there stayed with the
3101 846 2258 1161 1451 3588 3957 3588 2453 2532
μαθητῶν αὐτοῦ. 55 ἦν δὲ ἐγγὺς τὸ πάσχα τῶν Ἰουδαίων· καὶ
disciples of Him. was And near the Passover of the Jews, and
305 4183 1519 2414 1537 3588 5561 4253 3588 3957
ἀνέβησαν πολλοὶ εἰς Ἱεροσόλυμα ἐκ τῆς χώρας πρὸ τοῦ πάσχα,
went up many to Jerusalem out of the country before the Passover,

46 But some of them went their ways to the Pharisees, and told them what things Jesus had done.

47. Then gathered the chief priests and the Pharisees a council, and said, What do we? for this man doeth many miracles.

48 If we let him thus alone, all (men) will believe on him: and the Romans shall come and take away both our place and nation.

49 And one of them, (named) Caiaphas, being the high priest that same year, said unto them, Ye know nothing at all,

50 Nor consider that it is expedient for us, that one man should die for the people, and that the whole nation perish not.

51 And this spake he not of himself: but being high priest that year, he prophesied that Jesus should die for that nation;

52 And not for that nation only, but that also he should gather together in one the children of God that were scattered abroad.

53 Then from that day forth they took counsel together for to put him to death.

54 Jesus therefore walked no more openly among the Jews; but went thence unto a country near to the wilderness, into a city called Ephraim, and there continued with his disciples.

55. And the Jews' passover was nigh at hand: and many went out of the country up to Jerusalem before the passover,

Literal Translation

John 11:56

that they might purify themselves.
56 Then they sought Jesus, and said with one another, standing in the temple, What does it seem to you? That He does not at all come to the Feast?
57 And also the chief priests and the Pharisees had given commands that if anyone knew where He is, he should inform so that they might seize Him.

2443 48 1438 2212 3767 3588 2424 2532
ἵνα ἁγνίσωσιν ἑαυτούς. 56 ἐζήτουν οὖν τὸν Ἰησοῦν, καὶ
that they might purify themselves. they sought Then Jesus, and

3004 3326 240 1722 3588 2411 2476 5101 1380 5213 3754
ἔλεγον μετ' ἀλλήλων ἐν τῷ ἱερῷ ἑστηκότες, Τί δοκεῖ ὑμῖν; ὅτι
said with one another in the temple standing, what seems it to you? That

3756 3361 2064 1519 3588 1859 1325 1161 2532 3588 749
οὐ μὴ ἔλθη εἰς τὴν ἑορτήν; 57 δεδώκεισαν δὲ καὶ οἱ ἀρχιερεῖς
not at all He comes to the fast? had given And also the chief priests

2532 3588 5330 1785 2443 1437 5100 1097 4226 2076 3377
καὶ οἱ Φαρισαῖοι ἐντολήν, ἵνα ἐάν τις γνῷ ποῦ ἐστι, μηνύσῃ,
and thePharisees commands that if anyone knew where He is, he should inform

3704 4084 846
ὅπως πιάσωσιν αὐτόν.
so that they might seize Him.

King James Version

to purify themselves.
56 Then sought they for Jesus, and spake among themselves, as they stood in the temple, What think ye, that he will not come to the feast?
57 Now both the chief priests and the Pharisees had given a commandment, that, if any man knew where he were, he should shew (it), that they might take him.

John 12

1. Then six days before the Passover, Jesus came to Bethany, where Lazarus was, who had died, whom He raised from (the) dead.

2 Then they made Him a supper there, and Martha served. But Lazarus was one of those reclining with Him.
3 Then taking a pound of ointment of pure, costly spikenard, Mary anointed the feet of Jesus and wiped off His feet with her hairs. And the house was filled with the odor of the ointment.

4 Then Simon's (son), one of His disciples, Judas Iscariot, who was about to betray Him, said,
5 Why was this ointment not sold (for) three hundred denarii and given to (the) poor?

6 But he said this, not that he was caring for the poor, but that he was a thief and held the moneybag and carried away the things being put (in).
7 Then Jesus said, Allow her, for she has kept it for the day of My burial.
8 For you always have the poor with you, but you do not always have Me.

John 12

3588 3767 2424 4253 1803 2250 3588 3957 2064 1519
1 Ὁ οὖν Ἰησοῦς πρὸ ἓξ ἡμερῶν τοῦ πάσχα ἦλθεν εἰς
Therefore Jesus before six days the Passover came to

963 3699 2258 2976 3588 2348 3739 1453 1537
Βηθανίαν, ὅπου ἦν Λάζαρος ὁ τεθνηκώς, ὃν ἤγειρεν ἐκ
Bethany, where was Lazarus, who had died, whom He raised out of

3498 4160 3767 846 1173 1563 2532 3588 3136
νεκρῶν. 2 ἐποίησαν οὖν αὐτῷ δεῖπνον ἐκεῖ, καὶ ἡ Μάρθα
(the) dead. they made Then Him a supper there, and Martha

1247 3588 1161 2976 1520 2258 3588 4873 846 3588
διηκόνει· ὁ δὲ Λάζαρος εἷς ἦν τῶν συνανακειμένων αὐτῷ. 3 ἡ
served. But Lazarus one was of the (ones) reclining with Him.

3767 3137 2983 3046 3464 3487 4101 4186
οὖν Μαρία λαβοῦσα λίτραν μύρου νάρδου πιστικῆς πολυτίμου,
Then Mary, taking a pound of ointment of spikenard pure costly,

218 3588 4228 3588 2424 2532 1591 3588 2359 846
ἤλειψε τοὺς πόδας τοῦ Ἰησοῦ, καὶ ἐξέμαξε ταῖς θριξὶν αὐτῆς
rubbed the feet of Jesus, and wiped off with the hairs of her

3588 4228 846 3588 1161 3614 4137 1537 3588 3744 3588
τοὺς πόδας αὐτοῦ· ἡ δὲ οἰκία ἐπληρώθη ἐκ τῆς ὀσμῆς τοῦ
the feet of Him. the And house was filled of the odor of the

3464 3004 3767 1520 1537 3588 3101 846 2455 4613
μύρου. 4 λέγει οὖν εἷς ἐκ τῶν μαθητῶν αὐτοῦ, Ἰούδας Σιμωνος
ointment. says Then one of the disciples of Him, Judas of Simon

2469 3588 3195 846 3860 1302 5124 3588
Ἰσκαριώτης, ὁ μέλλων αὐτὸν παραδιδόναι, 5 Διατί τοῦτο τὸ
Iscariot, the (one) going Him to betray, Why this

3464 3756 4097 5145 1220 2532 1325 4434
μύρον οὐκ ἐπράθη τριακοσίων δηναρίων, καὶ ἐδόθη πτωχοῖς;
ointment not was sold (for) three hundred denarii, and given to (the) poor?

2036 1161 5124 3756 3754 4012 3588 4434 3199 846
6 εἶπε δὲ τοῦτο, οὐχ ὅτι περὶ τῶν πτωχῶν ἔμελεν αὐτῷ,
he said But this, not because concerning the poor was caring he,

235 3754 2812 2258 2532 3588 1101 2192 2532 3588
ἀλλὰ ὅτι κλέπτης ἦν, καὶ τὸ γλωσσόκομον εἶχε, καὶ τὰ
but that a thief he was, and the money bag held, and that

906 941 2036 3767 3588 2424 863 846
βαλλόμενα ἐβάσταζεν. 7 εἶπεν οὖν ὁ Ἰησοῦς, Ἄφες αὐτήν·
being put (in) carried away. said Therefore Jesus, Allow her;

1519 3588 2250 3588 1780 3450 5083 846 3588
εἰς τὴν ἡμέραν τοῦ ἐνταφιασμοῦ μου τετήρηκεν αὐτό· 8 τοὺς
for the day of the burial of Me she has kept it. the

4434 1063 3842 2192 3326 1438 1691 1161 3756 3842
πτωχοὺς γὰρ πάντοτε ἔχετε μεθ' ἑαυτῶν, ἐμὲ δὲ οὐ πάντοτε
poor For always you have with yourselves, Me but not always

John 12

1. Then Jesus six days before the passover came to Bethany, where Lazarus was which had been dead, whom he raised from the dead.

2 There they made him a supper; and Martha served: but Lazarus was one of them that sat at the table with him.
3 Then took Mary a pound of ointment of spikenard, very costly, and anointed the feet of Jesus, and wiped his feet with her hair: and the house was filled with the odour of the ointment.

4 Then saith one of his disciples, Judas Iscariot, Simon's (son), which should betray him,
5 Why was not this ointment sold for three hundred pence, and given to the poor?

6 This he said, not that he cared for the poor; but because he was a thief, and had the bag, and bare what was put therein.

7 Then said Jesus, Let her alone: against the day of my burying hath she kept this.
8 For the poor always ye have with you; but me ye have not always.

Literal Translation | **John 12:9** | *King James Version*

9. Then a great crowd of the Jews learned that He was there. And they did not come because of Jesus alone, but that they also might see Lazarus whom He raised from (the) dead.
10 But the chief priests took counsel that they might put Lazarus to death also,
11 because through him many of the Jews went away and believed into Jesus.

12. On the morrow, coming to the Feast, hearing that Jesus is coming to Jerusalem, a great crowd
13 took palm branches and went out to a meeting with Him, and (they) were crying out, "Hosanna! Blessed (is) He coming in (the) name of (the) Lord, the King of Israel!" (Ps. 118:25,26)
14 And finding an ass colt, Jesus sat on it, even as it had been written,

15 "Do not fear, daughter of Zion. Behold, your King comes sitting on the foal of an ass." (Isa.40:9; Zech.9:9)

16 But His disciples did not know these things at the first, but when Jesus was glorified, then they recalled that these things had been written on Him, and (that) they did these things to Him.

17 Then the crowd which was with Him when He called Lazarus out of the tomb and raised him from (the) dead, witnessed.
18 Because of this also the crowd met Him, because it heard (of) this miracle He had done.
19 Then the Pharisees said to themselves, Observe that you gain nothing. Behold, the world

2192
ἔχετε.
you have.

1097 3767 3793 4183 1537 3588 2453 3754 1563 2076
9 Ἔγνω οὖν ὄχλος πολὺς ἐκ τῶν Ἰουδαίων ὅτι ἐκεῖ ἐστι·
knew Then crowd (the) great of the Jews that there He is;

2532 2064 3756 1223 3588 2424 3440 235 2443 2532 3588
καὶ ἦλθον οὐ διὰ τὸν Ἰησοῦν μόνον, ἀλλ᾽ ἵνα καὶ τὸν
and they came not because of Jesus alone, but that also

2976 1492 3739 1453 1537 3498 1011 1161 3588
Λάζαρον ἴδωσιν, ὃν ἤγειρεν ἐκ νεκρῶν. 10 ἐβουλεύσαντο δὲ οἱ
Lazarus they might see, whom He raised out of (the) dead. took counsel But the

749 2443 2532 3588 2976 615 3754 4183 1223
ἀρχιερεῖς ἵνα καὶ τὸν Λάζαρον ἀποκτείνωσιν· 11 ὅτι πολλοὶ δι᾽
chief priests that also Lazarus they might kill, because many through

846 5217 3588 2453 2532 4100 1519 3588 2424
αὐτὸν ὑπῆγον τῶν Ἰουδαίων, καὶ ἐπίστευον εἰς τὸν Ἰησοῦν.
him went away (from) the Jews and believed into Jesus.

3588 1887 3793 4183 3588 2064 1519 3588 1859 191
12 Τῇ ἐπαύριον ὄχλος πολὺς ὁ ἐλθὼν εἰς τὴν ἑορτήν, ἀκού-
On the morrow a crowd great coming to the feast, hearing

3754 2064 3588 2424 1519 2414 2983 3588
σαντες ὅτι ἔρχεται ὁ Ἰησοῦς εἰς Ἱεροσόλυμα, 13 ἔλαβον τὰ
that is coming Jesus into Jerusalem, took the

902 3588 5404 2532 1831 1519 5222 846 2532
βαΐα τῶν φοινίκων, καὶ ἐξῆλθον εἰς ὑπάντησιν αὐτῷ, καὶ
branches of the palm-trees, and went out to a meeting with Him, and

2896 5614 2127 3588 2064 1722 3686
ἔκραζον, Ὡσαννά· εὐλογημένος ὁ ἐρχόμενος ἐν ὀνόματι
cried out, Hosanna! being blessed The (One) coming in (the) name

2962 3588 935 3588 2474 2147 1161 3588 2424
Κυρίου, ὁ βασιλεὺς τοῦ Ἰσραήλ. 14 εὑρὼν δὲ ὁ Ἰησοῦς
of (the) Lord, the King of Israel. finding And Jesus

3678 2523 1909 846 2531 2076 1125 3361
ὀνάριον, ἐκάθισεν ἐπ᾽ αὐτό, καθώς ἐστι γεγραμμένον, 15 Μὴ
an ass colt, He sat on it, even as it is having been written, Not

5399 2364 4622 2400 3588 935 4675 2064 2521
φοβοῦ, θύγατερ Σιών· ἰδού, ὁ βασιλεύς σου ἔρχεται, καθήμενος
do fear, daughter of Zion. Behold! The King of you comes, sitting

1909 4454 3688 5023 1161 3756 1097 3588 3101 846 3588
ἐπὶ πῶλον ὄνου. 16 ταῦτα δὲ οὐκ ἔγνωσαν οἱ μαθηταὶ αὐτοῦ τὸ
on the foal of an ass. these things But not knew the disciples of Him at the

4413 235 3753 1392 3588 2424 5119 3415 3754
πρῶτον· ἀλλ᾽ ὅτε ἐδοξάσθη ὁ Ἰησοῦς, τότε ἐμνήσθησαν ὅτι
first, but when was glorified Jesus, they they remembered that

5023 2258 1909 846 1125 2532 5023 4160 846
ταῦτα ἦν ἐπ᾽ αὐτῷ γεγραμμένα, καὶ ταῦτα ἐποίησαν αὐτῷ.
these things were on Him having been written, and these things they did to Him.

3140 3767 3588 3793 3588 5607 3326 846 3753 3588 2976
17 ἐμαρτύρει οὖν ὁ ὄχλος ὁ ὢν μετ᾽ αὐτοῦ ὅτε τὸν Λάζαρον
witnessed Therefore the crowd which was with Him when Lazarus

5455 1537 3588 3419 2532 1453 846 1537 3498 1223
ἐφώνησεν ἐκ τοῦ μνημείου, καὶ ἤγειρεν αὐτὸν ἐκ νεκρῶν. 18 διὰ
He called out of the tomb, and raised him out of (the) dead. Because

5124 2532 5221 846 3588 3793 3754 191 5124
τοῦτο καὶ ὑπήντησεν αὐτῷ ὁ ὄχλος, ὅτι ἤκουσε τοῦτο
of this also met with Him the crowd, because it heard this

846 4160 3588 4592 3588 3767 5330 2036 4314
αὐτὸν πεποιηκέναι τὸ σημεῖον. 19 οἱ οὖν Φαρισαῖοι εἶπον πρὸς
(that) Him to have done sign. the Then Pharisees said to

1438 2334 3754 3756 5623 3762 2396 3588 2889
ἑαυτούς, Θεωρεῖτε ὅτι οὐκ ὠφελεῖτε οὐδέν· ἴδε ὁ κόσμος
themselves, Observe that not you profit, nothing! Behold! the world

9. Much people of the Jews therefore knew that he was there: and they came not for Jesus' sake only, but that they might see Lazarus also, whom he had raised from the dead.
10 But the chief priests consulted that they might put Lazarus also to death;
11 Because that by reason of him many of the Jews went away, and believed on Jesus.

12. On the next day much people that were come to the feast, when they heard that Jesus was coming to Jerusalem,
13 Took branches of palm trees, and went forth to meet him, and cried, Hosanna: Blessed (is) the King of Israel that cometh in the name of the Lord.

14 And Jesus, when he had found a young ass, sat thereon; as it is written,
15 Fear not, daughter of Sion: behold, thy King cometh, sitting on an ass's colt.

16 These things understood not his disciples at the first: but when Jesus was glorified, then remembered they that these things were written of him, and (that) they had done these things unto him.

17 The people therefore that was with him when he called Lazarus out of his grave, and raised him from the dead, bare record.
18 For this cause the people also met him, for that they heard that he had done this miracle.
19 The Pharisees therefore said among themselves, Perceive ye how ye prevail nothing? behold, the world

John 12:20

Literal Translation

has gone after Him.

20. And there were some Greeks among those coming up, that they might worship at the Feast.
21 Then these came to Philip, the one from Bethsaida of Galilee, and asked him, saying, Sir, we desire to see Jesus.
22 Philip came and told Andrew, and again Andrew and Philip told Jesus.

23. But Jesus answered them, saying, The hour has come that the Son of man should be glorified.

24 Truly, truly, I say to you, unless the grain of wheat that falls into the earth dies, it remains alone. But if it dies, it bears much fruit.

25 The (one) who loves his life loses it, and the (one) who hates his life in this world will keep it to everlasting life.

26 If anyone serves Me, let him follow Me; and where I am, there My servant will also be. And if anyone serves Me, the Father will honor him.
27 And My soul is troubled, and what may I say? Father, save Me out of this hour? But on this account I came to this hour.

28 Father, glorify Your name. Then a voice came out of the heaven: I both glorified (it), and I will glorify (it) again.

29 Then standing and hearing, the crowd said that thunder occurred. Others said, An angel has spoken to Him.
30 Jesus answered and said, This voice has not occurred because of Me,

3694 846 565
ὀπίσω αὐτοῦ ἀπῆλθεν.
after Him have gone.

2258 1161 5100 1672 1537 3588 305 2443 4352
20 Ἦσαν δὲ τινες Ἕλληνες ἐκ τῶν ἀναβαινόντων ἵνα προσ-
were And some Greeks of those going up that they

1722 3588 1859 3778 3767 4334 5376
κυνήσωσιν ἐν τῇ ἑορτῇ· 21 οὗτοι οὖν προσῆλθον Φιλίππῳ
might worship at the feast. these Then came near to Philip

3588 575 966 3588 1056 2532 2065 846
τῷ ἀπὸ Βηθσαϊδὰ τῆς Γαλιλαίας, καὶ ἠρώτων αὐτὸν
the (one) from Bethsaida of Galilee, and asked him,

3004 2962 2309 3588 2424 1492 2064
λέγοντες, Κύριε, θέλομεν τὸν Ἰησοῦν ἰδεῖν. 22 ἔρχεται
saying Sir, We desire Jesus to see. comes

5376 2532 3004 3588 406 2532 3825 406 2532
Φίλιππος καὶ λέγει τῷ Ἀνδρέᾳ· καὶ πάλιν Ἀνδρέας καὶ
Philip and tells to Andrew, and again Andrew and

5376 3004 3588 2424 3588 1161 2424 611 846
Φίλιππος λέγουσι τῷ Ἰησοῦ. 23 ὁ δὲ Ἰησοῦς ἀπεκρίνατο αὐτοῖς
Philip tell Jesus. But Jesus answers them,

3004 2064 3588 5610 2443 1392 3588 5207 3588 444
λέγων, Ἐλήλυθεν ἡ ὥρα ἵνα δοξασθῇ ὁ υἱὸς τοῦ ἀνθρώπου.
saying, has come the hour that should be glorified the Son of man.

281 281 3004 5213 1437 3361 3588 2848 3588 4621 4098 1519
24 ἀμὴν ἀμὴν λέγω ὑμῖν, ἐὰν μὴ ὁ κόκκος τοῦ σίτου πεσὼν εἰς
Truly, truly, I say to you, If not the grain of wheat falling into

3588 1093 599 846 3441 3306 1437 1161 599 4183
τὴν γῆν ἀποθάνῃ, αὐτὸς μόνος μένει· ἐὰν δὲ ἀποθάνῃ, πολὺν
the earth dies, it alone remains; if but it die, much

2590 5342 3588 5368 3588 5590 846 622 846
καρπὸν φέρει. 25 ὁ φιλῶν τὴν ψυχὴν αὐτοῦ ἀπολέσει αὐτήν,
fruit it bears. The (one) loving the life of Him loses it;

2532 3588 3404 3588 5590 846 1722 3588 2889 5129 1519 2222
καὶ ὁ μισῶν τὴν ψυχὴν αὐτοῦ ἐν τῷ κόσμῳ τούτῳ εἰς ζωὴν
and the (one) hating the life of him in world this, to life

166 5442 846 1437 1698 1247 5100 1698 190
αἰώνιον φυλάξει αὐτήν. 26 ἐὰν ἐμοὶ διακονῇ τις, ἐμοὶ ἀκολου-
everlasting will keep it. If Me serves anyone, Me let him

2532 3699 1510 1473 1563 2532 3588 1249 3588 1699 2071
θείτω· καὶ ὅπου εἰμὶ ἐγώ, ἐκεῖ καὶ ὁ διάκονος ὁ ἐμὸς ἔσται·
follow; and where am I, there also the servant of Me will be.

2532 1437 5100 1698 1247 5091 846 3588 3962 3568 3588 5590
καὶ ἐάν τις ἐμοὶ διακονῇ, τιμήσει αὐτὸν ὁ πατήρ. 27 νῦν ἡ ψυχή
And if anyone Me serves, will honor him the Father. Now the soul

3450 5015 2532 5101 2036 3962 4982 3165 1537 3588 5610
μου τετάρακται· καὶ τί εἴπω; Πάτερ, σῶσόν με ἐκ τῆς ὥρας
of Me is agitated, and what may I say? Father, save Me out of hour

3778 235 1223 5124 2064 1519 3588 5610 3778 3962
ταύτης. ἀλλὰ διὰ τοῦτο ἦλθον εἰς τὴν ὥραν ταύτην. 28 πάτερ,
this. But because of this I came to hour this. Father,

1392 4675 3588 3686 2064 3767 5456 1537 3588 3772
δόξασόν σου τὸ ὄνομα. ἦλθεν οὖν φωνὴ ἐκ τοῦ οὐρανοῦ,
glorify of You the name. came Then a voice out of Heaven:

2532 1392 2532 3825 1392 3588 3767 3793 3588 2476 2532
Καὶ ἐδόξασα, καὶ πάλιν δοξάσω. 29 ὁ οὖν ὄχλος ὁ ἑστὼς καὶ
Both I glorified, and again I will glorify. the Then crowd standing and

191 3004 1027 1096 243 3004 32
ἀκούσας ἔλεγε βροντὴν γεγονέναι· ἄλλοι ἔλεγον, Ἄγγελος
hearing said thunder to have occurred. Others said, An angel

846 2980 611 3588 2424 2532 2036 3756 1223 1691
αὐτῷ λελάληκεν. 30 ἀπεκρίθη ὁ Ἰησοῦς καὶ εἶπεν, Οὐ δι' ἐμὲ
to Him has spoken. answered Jesus and said, Not because of Me

King James Version

is gone after him.

20. And there were certain Greeks among them that came up to worship at the feast:
21 The same came therefore to Philip, which was of Bethsaida of Galilee, and desired him, saying, Sir, we would see Jesus.
22 Philip cometh and telleth Andrew: and again Andrew and Philip tell Jesus.

23. And Jesus answered them, saying, The hour is come, that the Son of man should be glorified.

24 Verily, verily, I say unto you, Except a corn of wheat fall into the ground and die, it abideth alone: but if it die, it bringeth forth much fruit.
25 He that loveth his life shall lose it; and he that hateth his life in this world shall keep it unto life eternal.

26 If any man serve me, let him follow me; and where I am, there shall also my servant be: if any man serve me, him will (my) Father honour.
27 Now is my soul troubled; and what shall I say? Father, save me from this hour: but for this cause came I unto this hour.

28 Father, glorify thy name. Then came there a voice from heaven, (saying), I have both glorified (it), and will glorify (it) again.

29 The people therefore, that stood by, and heard (it), said that it thundered: others said, An angel spake to him.
30 Jesus answered and said, This voice came not because of me,

Literal Translation | **John 12:31** | **King James Version**

but because of you.
31 Now is (the) judgment of this world; now the ruler of this world shall be cast out.

32 And I, if I be lifted up from the earth, I will draw all to Myself.

33 But He said this, signifying by what kind (of) death He was about to die.
34 The crowd answered Him, We heard out of the Law that the Christ remains forever. And how do you say that the Son of man must be lifted up? Who is this Son of man?

35 Then Jesus said to them, Yet a little while the Light is with you. Walk while you have the Light, that darkness not overtake you. And the (one) walking in the darkness does not know where he is going.

36 While you have the Light, believe into the Light, that you may become sons of Light. Jesus spoke these things, and going away (He) was hidden from them.

37. But (though) He had done so many miracles before them, they did not believe into Him,
38 so that the word of Isaiah the prophet might be fulfilled, which he said, "Lord, who has believed our report? And the arm of the Lord, to whom was it revealed"? (Isa.53:1)
39 Because of this they could not believe, because Isaiah said again,
40 "He has blinded their eyes and has hardened their heart, that they might not see with the eyes and understand with the heart, and be converted, and I should heal them." (Isa.6:10)
41 Isaiah said these

3778 3588 5456 1096 235 1223 5209 3568 2920 2076 3588
αὕτη ἡ φωνὴ γέγονεν, ἀλλὰ δι᾽ ὑμᾶς. 31 νῦν κρίσις ἐστὶ τοῦ
this voice occurred, but because of you. Now judgment is

2889 5127 3568 3588 758 3588 2889 5127 1544
κόσμου τούτου· νῦν ὁ ἄρχων τοῦ κόσμου τούτου ἐκβληθή-
of world this; now the ruler of world this shall be

1854 2504 1437 5312 1537 3588 1093 3956 1670
σεται ἔξω· 32 κἀγὼ ἐὰν ὑψωθῶ ἐκ τῆς γῆς, πάντας ἑλκύσω
cast out. And I, if I be lifted up from the earth, all I will draw

4314 1683 5124 1161 3004 4591 4169 2288
πρὸς ἐμαυτόν. 33 τοῦτο δὲ ἔλεγε, σημαίνων ποίῳ θανάτῳ
to Myself. this And He said, signifying by what kind (of) death

3195 599 611 846 3588 3793 2249 191
ἤμελλεν ἀποθνήσκειν. 34 ἀπεκρίθη αὐτῷ ὁ ὄχλος, Ἡμεῖς ἠκού-
He was about to die. answered Him the crowd, We heard

1537 3588 3551 3754 3588 5547 3306 1519 3588 165 2532 4459
σαμεν ἐκ τοῦ νόμου ὅτι ὁ Χριστὸς μένει εἰς τὸν αἰῶνα· καὶ πῶς
out of the Law that the Christ abides to the age; and how

4771 3004 3754 1163 5312 3588 5207 3588 444 5101
σὺ λέγεις ὅτι Δεῖ ὑψωθῆναι τὸν υἱὸν τοῦ ἀνθρώπου; τίς
do you say that it behooves to be lifted up the Son of man? Who

2076 3778 3588 5207 3588 444 2036 3767 846 3588
ἐστιν οὗτος ὁ υἱὸς τοῦ ἀνθρώπου; 35 εἶπεν οὖν αὐτοῖς ὁ
is this Son of man? said Then to them

2424 2089 3398 5550 3588 5457 3326 5216 2076 4043
Ἰησοῦς, Ἔτι μικρὸν χρόνον τὸ φῶς μεθ᾽ ὑμῶν ἐστι. περιπατεῖτε
Jesus, Yet a little time the Light with you is. Walk

2193 3588 5457 2192 2443 3361 4653 5209 2638 2532 3588 4043
ἕως τὸ φῶς ἔχετε, ἵνα μὴ σκοτία ὑμᾶς καταλάβῃ· καὶ ὁ περιπα-
while the Light you have, that not darkness you overtake; and the (one) walk-

3588 1722 3588 4653 3756 1492 4226 5217 2193 3588 5457 2192
τῶν ἐν τῇ σκοτίᾳ οὐκ οἶδε ποῦ ὑπάγει. 36 ἕως τὸ φῶς ἔχετε,
ing in the darkness not knows where he is going. While the Light you have,

4100 1519 3588 5457 2443 5207 5457 1096
πιστεύετε εἰς τὸ φῶς, ἵνα υἱοὶ φωτὸς γένησθε.
believe into the Light, that sons of light you may become.

5023 2980 3588 2424 2532 565 2928 575
Ταῦτα ἐλάλησεν ὁ Ἰησοῦς, καὶ ἀπελθὼν ἐκρύβη ἀπ᾽
These things spoke Jesus, and going away was hidden from

846 5118 1161 846 4592 4160 1715
αὐτῶν. 37 τοσαῦτα δὲ αὐτοῦ σημεῖα πεποιηκότος ἔμπροσθεν
them. so many But He signs having done before

846 3756 4100 1519 846 2443 3588 3056 2268 3588
αὐτῶν, οὐκ ἐπίστευον εἰς αὐτόν· 38 ἵνα ὁ λόγος Ἠσαΐου τοῦ
them, not they believed into Him, that the word of Isaiah the

4396 4137 3739 2036 2962 5101 4100 3588 189
προφήτου πληρωθῇ, ὃν εἶπε, Κύριε, τίς ἐπίστευσε τῇ ἀκοῇ
prophet might be fulfilled, which he said: Lord, who has believed the report

2257 2532 3588 1023 2962 5101 601 1223 5124
ἡμῶν; καὶ ὁ βραχίων Κυρίου τίνι ἀπεκαλύφθη; 39 διὰ τοῦτο
of us? And the arm of (the) Lord, to whom was it revealed? Because of this

3756 1410 4100 3754 3825 2036 2268 5186
οὐκ ἠδύναντο πιστεύειν, ὅτι πάλιν εἶπεν Ἠσαΐας, 40 Τετύ-
not they were able to believe, because again said Isaiah, He has

846 3588 3788 2532 4456 846 3588
φλωκεν αὐτῶν τοὺς ὀφθαλμούς, καὶ πεπώρωκεν αὐτῶν τὴν
blinded of them the eyes, and hardened of them the

2588 2443 3361 1492 3588 3788 2532 3539 3588
καρδίαν· ἵνα μὴ ἴδωσι τοῖς ὀφθαλμοῖς, καὶ νοήσωσι τῇ
heart, that not they might see with the eyes, and understand with the

2588 2532 1994 2532 2390 846 5023 2036
καρδίᾳ, καὶ ἐπιστραφῶσι, καὶ ἰάσωμαι αὐτούς. 41 ταῦτα εἶπεν
heart, and be converted, and I should heal them. These things said

but for your sakes.
31 Now is the judgment of this world: now shall the prince of this world be cast out.

32 And I, if I be lifted up from the earth, will draw all (men) unto me.

33 This he said, signifying what death he should die.

34 The people answered him, We have heard out of the law that Christ abideth for ever: and how sayest thou, The Son of man must be lifted up? who is this Son of man?

35 Then Jesus said unto them, Yet a little while is the light with you. Walk while ye have the light, lest darkness come upon you: for he that walketh in darkness knoweth not whither he goeth.

36 While ye have light, believe in the light, that ye may be the children of light. These things spake Jesus, and departed, and did hide himself from them.

37. But though he had done so many miracles before them, yet they believed not on him:
38 That the saying of Esaias the prophet might be fulfilled, which he spake, Lord, who hath believed our report? and to whom hath the arm of the Lord been revealed?
39 Therefore they could not believe, because that Esaias said again,
40 He hath blinded their eyes, and hardened their heart; that they should not see with (their) eyes, nor understand with (their) heart, and be converted, and I should heal them.

41 These things said

Literal Translation **John 12:42** *King James Version*

things when he saw His glory, and spoke about Him.

4 2 . Still, however, even out of the rulers, many did believe into Him. But because of the Pharisees, they were not confessing, so that they not be put out of the synagogue.
43 For they loved the glory of men more than the glory of God.

44. But Jesus cried out and said, The (one) believing into Me does not believe into Me, but into the (One) sending Me.
45 And the (one) beholding Me beholds the (One) who sent Me.
46 I have come (as) a Light to the world, that everyone who believes into Me may not remain in the darkness.

47 And if anyone hears My words and does not believe, I do not judge him; for I did not come that I might judge the world, but that I might save the world.
48 The (one) who rejects Me and does not receive My words has that judging him: the Word which I spoke, that will judge him in the last Day.
49 For I did not speak from Myself, but He who sent Me, (the) Father, He has given Me command, what I should say, and what I should speak.
50 And I know that His command is everlasting life. Then what things I speak, as the Father has said to Me, so I speak.

2268 3753 1492 3588 1391 846 2532 2980 4012 846
Ἠσαΐας, ὅτε εἶδε τὴν δόξαν αὐτοῦ, καὶ ἐλάλησε περὶ αὐτοῦ.
Isaiah when he saw the glory of Him, and spoke concerning Him.

3676 3305 2532 1537 3588 758 4183 4100 1519
42 ὅμως μέντοι καὶ ἐκ τῶν ἀρχόντων πολλοὶ ἐπίστευσαν εἰς
Still, however, even of the rulers many believed into

846 235 1223 3588 5330 3756 3670 2443 3361
αὐτόν· ἀλλὰ διὰ τοὺς Φαρισαίους οὐχ ὡμολόγουν, ἵνα μὴ
Him, but because of the Pharisees not they were confessing, that not

656 1096 25 1063 3588 1391 3588
ἀποσυνάγωγοι γένωνται· 43 ἠγάπησαν γὰρ τὴν δόξαν τῶν
put out of the synagogue they be. they loved For the glory

444 3123 2260 3588 1391 3588 2316
ἀνθρώπων μᾶλλον ἤπερ τὴν δόξαν τοῦ Θεοῦ.
of man more than the glory of God.

2424 1161 2896 2532 2036 3588 4100 1519 1691 3756
44 Ἰησοῦς δὲ ἔκραξε καὶ εἶπεν, Ὁ πιστεύων εἰς ἐμέ, οὐ
Jesus But cried out and said, The (one) believing into Me not

4100 1519 1691 235 1519 3588 3992 3165 2532 3588 2334
πιστεύει εἰς ἐμέ, ἀλλ' εἰς τὸν πέμψαντά με· 45 καὶ ὁ θεωρῶν
believes into Me, but into the (One) sending Me; and the (one) beholding

1691 2334 3588 3992 3165 1473 5457 1519 3588 2889
ἐμὲ, θεωρεῖ τὸν πέμψαντά με. 46 ἐγὼ φῶς εἰς τὸν κόσμον
Me beholds the (One) sending Me. I a light into the world

2064 2443 3956 3588 4100 1519 1691 1722 3588 4653 3361 3306
ἐλήλυθα, ἵνα πᾶς ὁ πιστεύων εἰς ἐμέ, ἐν τῇ σκοτίᾳ μὴ μείνῃ.
have come, that everyone believing into Me in the darkness not may abide.

2532 1437 5100 3450 191 3588 4487 2532 3361 4100
47 καὶ ἐάν τις μου ἀκούσῃ τῶν ῥημάτων καὶ μὴ πιστεύσῃ,
And if anyone of Me hears the words, and not believes,

1473 3756 2919 846 3756 1063 2064 2443 2919 3588 2889
ἐγὼ οὐ κρίνω αὐτόν· οὐ γὰρ ἦλθον ἵνα κρίνω τὸν κόσμον,
I not do judge him; not for I came that I might judge the world,

235 2443 4982 3588 2889 3588 114 1691 2532 3361 2983
ἀλλ' ἵνα σώσω τὸν κόσμον. 48 ὁ ἀθετῶν ἐμὲ καὶ μὴ λαμβάνων
but that I might save the world. The (one) rejecting Me and not receiving

3588 4487 3450 2192 3588 2919 846 3588 3056 3739
τὰ ῥήματά μου, ἔχει τὸν κρίνοντα αὐτόν· ὁ λόγος ὃν
the words of Me, has that judging him, the Word which

2980 1565 2919 846 1722 3588 2078 2250 3754 1473
ἐλάλησα, ἐκεῖνος κρινεῖ αὐτὸν ἐν τῇ ἐσχάτῃ ἡμέρα. 49 ὅτι ἐγὼ
I spoke, that will judge him in the last Day. Because I

1537 1683 3756 2980 235 3588 3992 3165 3962 846 3427
ἐξ ἐμαυτοῦ οὐκ ἐλάλησα· ἀλλ' ὁ πέμψας με πατήρ, αὐτός μοι
from Myself not spoke, but He sending Me, (the) Father, He to Me

1785 1325 5101 2036 2532 5101 2980 2532 1492 3754 3588
ἐντολὴν ἔδωκε, τί εἴπω καὶ τί λαλήσω. 50 καὶ οἶδα ὅτι ἡ
command has given, what I may say and what I may speak. And I know that the

1785 846 2222 166 2076 3739 3767 2980 1473 2531
ἐντολὴ αὐτοῦ ζωὴ αἰώνιός ἐστιν· ἃ οὖν λαλῶ ἐγώ, καθὼς
command of Him life everlasting is. what things Then speak I, even as

2046 3427 3588 3962 3779 2980
εἴρηκέ μοι ὁ πατήρ, οὕτω λαλῶ.
has said to Me the Father, so I speak.

Esaias, when he saw his glory, and spake of him.

42. Nevertheless among the chief rulers also many believed on him; but because of the Pharisees they did not confess (him), lest they should be put out of the synagogue:
43 For they loved the praise of men more than the praise of God.

44. Jesus cried and said, He that believeth on me, believeth not on me, but on him that sent me.
45 And he that seeth me seeth him that sent me.
46 I am come a light into the world, that whosoever believeth on me should not abide in darkness.

47 And if any man hear my words, and believe not, I judge him not: for I came not to judge the world, but to save the world.
48 He that rejecteth me, and receiveth not my words, hath one that judgeth him: the word that I have spoken, the same shall judge him in the last day.
49 For I have not spoken of myself; but the Father which sent me, he gave me a commandment, what I should say, and what I should speak.
50 And I know that his commandment is life everlasting: whatsoever I speak therefore, even as the Father said unto me, so I speak.

John 13

John 13

1. And before the Feast of the Passover, Jesus knowing that His hour had come that He should move from this world

4253 1161 3588 1859 3588 3957 1492 3588 2424 3754
1 Πρὸ δὲ τῆς ἑορτῆς τοῦ πάσχα, εἰδὼς ὁ Ἰησοῦς ὅτι
before And the feast of the Passover, knowing Jesus that

2064 846 3588 5610 2443 3327 1537 3588 2889 5127
ἐλήλυθεν αὐτοῦ ἡ ὥρα ἵνα μεταβῇ ἐκ τοῦ κόσμου τούτου
had come of Him the hour that He should move from world this

John 13

1. Now before the feast of the passover, when Jesus knew that his hour was come that he should depart out of this world

Literal Translation | **John 13:2** | **King James Version**

to the Father, loving (His) own in the world, He loved them to (the) end.
2 And supper having occurred, the Devil having put already into the heart of Simon's (son) Judas Iscariot that he should betray Him,
3 Jesus knowing that the Father has given all things into (His) hands, and that He came out from God, and goes away to God,
4 He rose up from the supper and laid aside (His) garments. And taking a towel, He girded Himself.
5 Then He put water into the basin and began to wash the feet of the disciples, and to wipe off with the towel with which He was girded.
6 He then came to Simon Peter. And that one said to Him, Lord, do You wash my feet?
7 Jesus answered and said to him, What I am doing, you do not yet know. But you will know after these things.
8 Peter said to Him, You may in no way wash my feet to the age. Jesus answered him, Unless I wash you, you have no part with Me.
9 Simon Peter said to Him, Lord, not my feet only, but also the hands and the head.
10 Jesus said to him, The (one) having been bathed has no need (other) than to wash the feet, but is wholly clean. And you are clean, but not all.
11 For He knew the (one) betraying Him. For this reason He said, You are not all clean.
12 Then when He had washed their feet and had taken His garments,

4314 3588 3962 25 3588 2398 3588 1722 3588 2889
πρὸς τὸν πατέρα, ἀγαπήσας τοὺς ἰδίους τοὺς ἐν τῷ κόσμῳ,
to the Father, having loved the own in the world,

1519 5056 25 846 2532 1173 1096 3588
εἰς τέλος ἠγάπησεν αὐτούς. 2 καὶ δείπνου γενομένου, τοῦ
to the end He loved them. And supper having occurred, the

1228 2235 906 1519 3588 2588 2455 4613
διαβόλου ἤδη βεβληκότος εἰς τὴν καρδίαν Ἰούδα Σίμωνος
devil already having put into the heart of Judas of Simon

2469 2443 846 3860 1492 3588 2424 3754 3956
Ἰσκαριώτου ἵνα αὐτὸν παραδῷ, 3 εἰδὼς ὁ Ἰησοῦς ὅτι πάντα
Iscariot that Him he should betray, knowing Jesus that all things

1325 846 3588 3962 1519 3588 5495 2532 3754 575 2316
δέδωκεν αὐτῷ ὁ πατὴρ εἰς τὰς χεῖρας, καὶ ὅτι ἀπὸ Θεοῦ
has given Him the Father into the hands, and that from God

1831 2532 4314 3588 2316 5217 1453 1537 3588 1173
ἐξῆλθε καὶ πρὸς τὸν Θεὸν ὑπάγει, 4 ἐγείρεται ἐκ τοῦ δείπνου,
He came out and to God departs, He rises from the supper

2532 5087 3588 2440 2532 2983 3012 1241 1438
καὶ τίθησι τὰ ἱμάτια, καὶ λαβὼν λέντιον διέζωσεν ἑαυτόν.
and lays aside the garments, and taking a towel He girded Himself.

1534 906 5204 1519 3588 3537 2532 756 3538 3588
5 εἶτα βάλλει ὕδωρ εἰς τὸν νιπτῆρα, καὶ ἤρξατο νίπτειν τοὺς
Then He puts water into the basin, and began to wash the

4228 3588 3101 2532 1591 3588 3012 3739 2258 1241
πόδας τῶν μαθητῶν, καὶ ἐκμάσσειν τῷ λεντίῳ ᾧ ἦν διεζω-
feet of the disciples, and to wipe off with the towel with which He was gird-

2064 3767 4314 4613 4074 2532 3004 846
σμένος. 6 ἔρχεται οὖν πρὸς Σίμωνα Πέτρον· καὶ λέγει αὐτῷ
ed He comes then to Simon Peter. And said to Him

1565 2962 4771 3450 3538 3588 4228 611 2424
εκεῖνος, Κύριε, σύ μου νίπτεις τοὺς πόδας; 7 ἀπεκρίθη Ἰησοῦς
that one, Lord, Do You of me wash the feet? answered Jesus

2532 2036 846 3739 1473 4160 4771 3756 1492 737 1097
καὶ εἶπεν αὐτῷ, Ὃ ἐγὼ ποιῶ, σὺ οὐκ οἶδας ἄρτι, γνώσῃ
and said to him, What I am doing, you not know yet, you will know

1161 3326 5023 3004 846 4074 3756 3361 3538 3588 4228
δὲ μετὰ ταῦτα. 8 λέγει αὐτῷ Πέτρος, Οὐ μὴ νίψῃς τοὺς πόδας
But after these things. says to Him Peter, Not at all may you wash the feet

3450 1519 3588 165 611 846 3588 2424 1437 3361 3538
μου εἰς τὸν αἰῶνα. ἀπεκρίθη αὐτῷ ὁ Ἰησοῦς, Ἐὰν μὴ νίψω
of me to the age. answered him Jesus, If not I wash

4571 3756 2192 3313 3326 1700 3004 846 4613 4074
σε, οὐκ ἔχεις μέρος μετ' ἐμοῦ. 9 λέγει αὐτῷ Σίμων Πέτρος,
you, not you have part with Me. says to Him Simon Peter,

2962 3361 3588 4228 3450 3440 235 2532 3588 5495 2532
Κύριε, μὴ τοὺς πόδας μου μόνον, ἀλλὰ καὶ τὰς χεῖρας καὶ
Lord, not the feet of me only, but also the hands and

3588 2776 3004 846 3588 2424 3588 3068 3756 5532
τὴν κεφαλήν. 10 λέγει αυτῷ ὁ Ἰησοῦς, Ὁ λελουμένος οὐ χρείαν
the head. says to him Jesus, He having been bathed no need

2192 2228 3588 4228 3538 235 2076 2513 3650 2532
ἔχει ἢ τοὺς πόδας νίψασθαι, ἀλλ' ἔστι καθαρὸς ὅλος· καὶ
has than the feet to wash, but is clean wholly; and

5210 2513 2075 235 3780 3956 1492 1063 3588 3860
ὑμεῖς καθαροί ἐστε, ἀλλ' οὐχὶ πάντες. 11 ᾔδει γὰρ τὸν παραδι-
you clean are, but not all. He knew For the (one) betray-

846 1223 5124 2036 3780 3956 2513 2075
δόντα αὐτόν· διὰ τοῦτο εἶπεν, Οὐχὶ πάντες καθαροί ἐστε.
ing Him; because of this He said, Not all clean are.

3753 3767 3538 3588 4228 846 2532 2983 3588 2440
12 Ὅτε οὖν ἔνιψε τοὺς πόδας αὐτῶν, καὶ ἔλαβε τὰ ἱμάτια
When, then, He washed the feet of them, and took the garments

unto the Father, having loved his own which were in the world, he loved them unto the end.
2 And supper being ended, the devil having now put into the heart of Judas Iscariot, Simon's (son), to betray him;
3 Jesus knowing that the Father had given all things into his hands, and that he was come from God, and went to God;
4 He riseth from supper, and laid aside his garments; and took a towel, and girded himself.
5 After that he poureth water into a bason, and began to wash the disciples' feet, and to wipe (them) with the towel wherewith he was girded.
6 Then cometh he to Simon Peter: and Peter saith unto him, Lord, dost thou wash my feet?
7 Jesus answered and said unto him, What I do thou knowest not now; but thou shalt know hereafter.
8 Peter saith unto him, Thou shalt never wash my feet. Jesus answered him, If I wash thee not, thou hast no part with me.
9 Simon Peter saith unto him, Lord, not my feet only, but also (my) hands and (my) head.
10 Jesus saith to him, He that is washed needeth not save to wash (his) feet, but is clean every whit: and ye are clean, but not all.
11 For he knew who should betray him; therefore said he, Ye are not all clean.
12 So after he had washed their feet, and had taken his garments,

Literal Translation **John 13:13** *King James Version*

reclining again, He said to them, Do you know what I have done to you?
13 You call Me The Teacher, and, The Lord. And you say well, for I AM.
14 If then I washed your feet, the Lord and the Teacher, you also ought to wash the feet of one another.
15 For I gave you an example, that as I did to you, you also should do.
16 Truly, truly, I say to you, a slave is not greater than his lord, nor a messenger greater than the (one) sending him.
17 If you know these things, blessed are you if you do them.
18. I do not speak concerning all of you; I know whom I chose out; but that the Scripture might be fulfilled, "The (one) eating the bread with Me lifted up his heel against Me." (Ps. 41:9)
19 From this time I tell you before (it) happens, that when it happens you may believe that I AM.
20 Truly, truly, I say to you, the (one) receiving whomever I may send receives Me; and the (one) receiving Me receives the (One) sending Me.

846 377 3825 2036 846 1097 5101 4160
αὐτοῦ, ἀναπεσὼν πάλιν, εἶπεν αὐτοῖς, Γινώσκετε τί πεποίη-
of Him. Reclining again, He said to them, Do you know what I have

5213 5210 5455 3165 3588 1320 2532 3588 2962 2532
κα ὑμῖν; 13 ὑμεῖς φωνεῖτέ με, Ὁ διδάσκαλος, καὶ Ὁ κύριος· καὶ
done to you? You call Me, The Teacher, and, The Lord; and

2573 3004 1510 1063 1487 3767 1473 3538 5216 3588 4228
καλῶς λέγετε, εἰμὶ γάρ. 14 εἰ οὖν ἐγὼ ἔνιψα ὑμῶν τοὺς πόδας,
well you say; I am for. If, then, I washed of you the feet,

3588 2962 2532 3588 1320 2532 5210 3784 240
ὁ κύριος καὶ ὁ διδάσκαλος, καὶ ὑμεῖς ὀφείλετε ἀλλήλων
the Lord and the Teacher, also you ought of one another

3538 3588 4228 5262 1063 1325 5213 2443 2531
νίπτειν τοὺς πόδας. 15 ὑπόδειγμα γὰρ ἔδωκα ὑμῖν, ἵνα καθὼς
to wash the feet. an example For I gave to you, that even as

1473 4160 5213 2532 5210 4160 281 281 3004 5213
ἐγὼ ἐποίησα ὑμῖν, καὶ ὑμεῖς ποιῆτε. 16 ἀμὴν ἀμὴν λέγω ὑμῖν,
I did to you, also you should do. Truly, truly. I say to you,

3756 2076 1401 3187 3588 2962 846 3761 652
Οὐκ ἔστι δοῦλος μείζων τοῦ κυρίου αὐτοῦ, οὐδὲ ἀπόστολος
not is A slave greater than the lord of him, nor a messenger

3187 3588 3992 846 1487 5023 1492 3107
μείζων τοῦ πέμψαντος αὐτόν. 17 εἰ ταῦτα οἴδατε, μακάριοί
greater than the (one) sending him. If these things you know, blessed

2075 1437 4160 846 3756 4012 3956 5216 3004 1473
ἐστε ἐὰν ποιῆτε αὐτά. 18 οὐ περὶ πάντων ὑμῶν λέγω· ἐγὼ
are you if you do them. Not concerning all of you I speak. I

1492 3739 1586 235 2443 3588 1124 4137 3588 5176
οἶδα οὓς ἐξελεξάμην· ἀλλ' ἵνα ἡ γραφὴ πληρωθῇ, Ὁ τρώγων
know whom I chose out; but that the Scripture be fulfilled, The (one) eating

3326 1700 3588 740 1869 1909 1691 3588 4418 846 575
μετ' ἐμοῦ τὸν ἄρτον ἐπῆρεν ἐπ' ἐμὲ τὴν πτέρναν αὐτοῦ. 19 ἀπ'
with Me the loaf lifted up against Me the heel of him. From

737 3004 5213 4253 3588 1096 2443 3752 1096
ἄρτι λέγω ὑμῖν πρὸ τοῦ γενέσθαι, ἵνα, ὅταν γένηται,
now I say to you before the happening, that when it happens

4100 3754 1473 1510 281 281 3004 5213 3588 2983
πιστεύσητε ὅτι ἐγώ εἰμι. 20 ἀμὴν ἀμὴν λέγω ὑμῖν, Ὁ λαμβάνων
you may believe that I AM. Truly, truly, I say to you, he receiving

1437 5100 3992 1691 2983 3588 1161 1691 2983 2983
ἐάν τινα πέμψω, ἐμὲ λαμβάνει· ὁ δὲ ἐμὲ λαμβάνων, λαμβάνει
whomever I may send, Me receives; the (one) and Me receiving, receives

3588 3992 3165
τὸν πέμψαντά με.
the (One) sending Me.

and was set down again, he said unto them, Know ye what I have done to you?
13 Ye call me Master and Lord: and ye say well; for (so) I am.
14 If I then, (your) Lord and Master, have washed your feet; ye also ought to wash one another's feet.
15 For I have given you an example, that ye should do as I have done to you.
16 Verily, verily, I say unto you, The servant is not greater than his lord; neither he that is sent greater than he that sent him.
17 If ye know these things, happy are ye if ye do them.
18. I speak not of you all: I know whom I have chosen: but that the scripture may be fulfilled, He that eateth bread with me hath lifted up his heel against me.
19 Now I tell you before it come, that, when it is come to pass, ye may believe that I am (he).
20 Verily, verily, I say unto you, He that receiveth whomsoever I send receiveth me; and he that receiveth me receiveth him that sent me.

21 Saying these things, Jesus was troubled in spirit and testified and said, Indeed I tell you truly that one of you will betray Me.
22 Then the disciples looked upon one another, being perplexed about whom He spoke.
23 But there was one of His disciples reclining at the bosom of Jesus, whom Jesus loved.
24 Then Simon Peter nodded to him to ask whom it might be

5023 2036 3588 2424 5015 3588 4151 2532
21 Ταῦτα εἰπὼν ὁ Ἰησοῦς ἐταράχθη τῷ πνεύματι, καὶ
These things saying, Jesus was agitated in the spirit, and

3140 2532 2036 281 281 3004 5213 3754 1520 1537 5216
ἐμαρτύρησε καὶ εἶπεν, Ἀμὴν ἀμὴν λέγω ὑμῖν ὅτι εἷς ἐξ ὑμῶν
witnessed and said, Truly truly I say to you that one of you

3860 3165 991 3767 1519 240 3588 3101
παραδώσει με. 22 ἔβλεπον οὖν εἰς ἀλλήλους οἱ μαθηταί,
will betray Me. looked Then to one another the disciples,

639 4012 5101 3004 2258 1161 345 1520 3588
ἀπορούμενοι περὶ τίνος λέγει. 23 ἦν δὲ ἀνακείμενος εἷς τῶν
being perplexed about whom He speaks. was And reclining one of the

3101 846 1722 3588 2859 3588 2424 3739 25 3588
μαθητῶν αὐτοῦ ἐν τῷ κόλπῳ τοῦ Ἰησοῦ, ὃν ἠγάπα ὁ
disciples of Him in the bosom of Jesus, whom loved

2424 3506 3767 5129 4613 4074 4441 5101 302 1498
Ἰησοῦς· 24 νεύει οὖν τούτῳ Σίμων Πέτρος πυθέσθαι τίς ἂν εἴη
Jesus. nods Then to this one Simon Peter to ask who it may be

21 When Jesus had thus said, he was troubled in spirit, and testified, and said, Verily, verily, I say unto you, that one of you shall betray me.
22 Then the disciples looked one on another, doubting of whom he spake.
23 Now there was leaning on Jesus' bosom one of his disciples, whom Jesus loved.
24 Simon Peter therefore beckoned to him, that he should ask who it should be

Literal Translation

of whom He spoke.
25 And that one leaning on the breast of Jesus, he said to Him, Lord, who is it?
26 Jesus answered, It is that one to whom I, having dipped the morsel, shall give (it). And dipping the morsel, He gave (it) to Judas Iscariot, (son) of Simon.
27 And after the morsel, then Satan entered into that one. Then Jesus said to him, What you do, do quickly.

28 But no one of those reclining knew this, for what He spoke to him;

29 for some thought, since Judas held the money bag, that Jesus was saying to him, Buy what things we have need (of) for the feast; or that he give something to the poor.

30 Then, receiving the morsel, that one immediately went out. And it was night.

31. Then when he had gone out, Jesus said, Now the Son of man was glorified, and God was glorified in Him.
32 If God was glorified in Him, God also will glorify Him in Himself, and immediately will glorify Him.
33 Little children, yet a little (while) I am with you. You will seek Me; and, even as I said to the Jews, Where I go, you are not able to come; I also say to you now.
34 I give a new commandment to you, that you should love one another; according as I loved you, you should also love one another.

35 In this all shall know that you are My disciples, if you have love among one another.

John 13:25

4012 3739 3004 1968 1161 1565 1909 3588 4738 3588
περὶ οὗ λέγει. 25 ἐπιπεσὼν δὲ ἐκεῖνος ἐπὶ τὸ στῆθος τοῦ
about whom He speaks. leaning And that one on the breast

2424 3004 846 2962 5101 2076 611 3588 2424
Ἰησοῦ, λέγει αὐτῷ, Κύριε, τίς ἐστιν; 26 ἀποκρίνεται ὁ Ἰησοῦς,
of Jesus, he said to Him, Lord, who is it? answers Jesus,

1565 2076 3739 1473 911 3588 5596 1929 2532 1686
Ἐκεῖνός ἐστιν ᾧ ἐγὼ βάψας τὸ ψωμίον ἐπιδώσω. καὶ ἐμβά-
That one it is to whom I having dipped the morsel shall give it. And dipping

3588 5596 1325 2455 4613 2469 2532
ψας τὸ ψωμίον, δίδωσιν Ἰούδᾳ Σίμωνος Ἰσκαριώτῃ. 27 καὶ
the morsel, He gave (it) to Judas of Simon Iscariot. And

3326 3588 5596 5119 1525 1519 1565 3588 4567 3004
μετὰ τὸ ψωμίον, τότε εἰσῆλθεν εἰς ἐκεῖνον ὁ Σατανᾶς. λέγει
after the morsel, then entered into that one Satan. says

3767 846 3588 2424 3739 4160 4160 5032 5124 1161
οὖν αὐτῷ ὁ Ἰησοῦς, Ὃ ποιεῖς, ποίησον τάχιον. 28 τοῦτο δὲ
Then to him Jesus, What you do, do quickly. this But

3762 1097 3588 345 4314 5101 2036 846 5100 1063
οὐδεὶς ἔγνω τῶν ἀνακειμένων πρὸς τί εἶπεν αὐτῷ· 29 τινὲς γὰρ
no one knew of those reclining for what He spoke to him; some for

1380 1893 3588 1101 2192 3588 2455 3754 3004
ἐδόκουν, ἐπεὶ τὸ γλωσσόκομον εἶχεν ὁ Ἰούδας, ὅτι λέγει
thought, since the money bag held Judas, that tells

846 3588 2424 59 3739 5532 2192 1519 3588
αὐτῷ ὁ Ἰησοῦς, Ἀγόρασον ὧν χρείαν ἔχομεν εἰς τὴν
him Jesus, Buy of what things need we have for the

1859 2228 3588 4434 2443 5100 1325 2983 3767 3588 5596
ἑορτήν· ἢ τοῖς πτωχοῖς ἵνα τι δῷ. 30 λαβὼν οὖν τὸ ψωμίον
feast; or, to the poor that a thing he give. Receiving then the morsel

1565 2112 1831 2258 1161 3571
ἐκεῖνος, εὐθέως ἐξῆλθεν· ἦν δὲ νύξ.
that one, at once (he) went out. it was And night.

3753 3767 1831 3004 3588 2424 3568 1392 3588 5207 3588
31 Ὅτε οὖν ἐξῆλθε, λέγει ὁ Ἰησοῦς, Νῦν ἐδοξάσθη ὁ υἱὸς τοῦ
when Then he went, says Jesus, Now was glorified the Son

444 2532 3588 2316 1392 1722 846 1487 3588 2316 1392
ἀνθρώπου, καὶ ὁ Θεὸς ἐδοξάσθη ἐν αὐτῷ. 32 εἰ ὁ Θεὸς ἐδοξάσθη
of man, and God was glorified in Him. If God was glorified

1722 846 2532 3588 2316 1392 846 1722 1438 2532 2117
ἐν αὐτῷ, καὶ ὁ Θεὸς δοξάσει αὐτὸν ἐν ἑαυτῷ, καὶ εὐθὺς
in Him, also God will glorify Him in Himself, and at once

1392 846 5040 2089 3397 3326 5216 1510 2212
δοξάσει αὐτόν. 33 τεκνία, ἔτι μικρὸν μεθ' ὑμῶν εἰμι. ζητήσετέ
will glorify Him. Children, yet a little with you I am. You willl seek

3165 2532 2531 2036 3588 2453 3754 3699 5217 1473
με, καὶ καθὼς εἶπον τοῖς Ἰουδαίοις ὅτι Ὅπου ὑπάγω ἐγώ,
Me, and even as I said to the Jews, Where go I,

5210 3756 1410 2064 2532 5213 3004 737 1785
ὑμεῖς οὐ δύνασθε ἐλθεῖν, καὶ ὑμῖν λέγω ἄρτι. 34 ἐντολὴν
you not are able to come, also to you I say now, command

2537 1325 5213 2443 25 240 2531 25
καινὴν δίδωμι ὑμῖν, ἵνα ἀγαπᾶτε ἀλλήλους· καθὼς ἠγά-
A new I give you, that you love one another even as I

5209 2443 2532 5210 25 240 1722 5129 1097
πησα ὑμᾶς, ἵνα καὶ ὑμεῖς ἀγαπᾶτε ἀλλήλους. 35 ἐν τούτῳ γνώ-
loved you, that also you should love one another. In this will

3956 3754 1698 3101 2075 1437 26 2192 1722
σονται πάντες ὅτι ἐμοὶ μαθηταί ἐστε, ἐὰν ἀγάπην ἔχητε ἐν
know all that to Me disciples you are, if love you have among

240
ἀλλήλοις.
one another.

King James Version

of whom he spake.
25 He then lying on Jesus' breast saith unto him, Lord, who is it?
26 Jesus answered, He it is, to whom I shall give a sop, when I have dipped (it). And when he had dipped the sop, he gave (it) to Judas Iscariot, (the son) of Simon.
27 And after the sop Satan entered into him. Then said Jesus unto him, That thou doest, do quickly.

28 Now no man at the table knew for what intent he spake this unto him.
29 For some (of them) thought, because Judas had the bag, that Jesus had said unto him, Buy (those things) that we have need of against the feast; or, that he should give something to the poor.

30 He then having received the sop went immediately out: and it was night.

31. Therefore, when he was gone out, Jesus said, Now is the Son of man glorified, and God is glorified in him.
32 If God be glorified in him, God shall also glorify him in himself, and shall straightway glorify him.
33 Little children, yet a little while I am with you. Ye shall seek me: and as I said unto the Jews, Whither I go, ye cannot come; so now I say to you.
34 A new commandment I give unto you, That ye love one another; as I have loved you, that ye also love one another.

35 By this shall all (men) know that ye are my disciples, if ye have love one to another.

John 13:36

Literal Translation

36. Simon Peter said to Him, Lord, where do You go? Jesus answered him, Where I go you are not able to follow Me now, but afterwards you shall follow Me.
37 Peter said to Him, Lord, why am I not able to follow You now? I will lay down my life for You!

38 Jesus answered him, Will you lay down your life for Me? Indeed, I tell you truly, in no way shall a cock crow until you deny Me three times.

3004 846 4613 4074 2962 4226 5217 611
36 Λέγει αὐτῷ Σίμων Πέτρος, Κύριε, ποῦ ὑπάγεις; ἀπεκρίθη
says to Him Simon Peter, Lord, where do You go? answered
846 3588 2424 3699 5217 3756 1410 3427 3568 190
αὐτῷ ὁ Ἰησοῦς, Ὅπου ὑπάγω, οὐ δύνασαί μοι νῦν ἀκο-
him Jesus, Where I go, not you are able Me now to
5305 1161 190 3427 3004 846 3588
λουθῆσαι, ὕστερον δὲ ἀκολουθήσεις μοι. 37 λέγει αὐτῷ ὁ
follow, later but you will follow Me. says to Him
4074 2962 1302 3756 1410 4671 190 737
Πέτρος, Κύριε, διατί οὐ δύναμαί σοι ἀκολουθῆσαι ἄρτι;
Peter, Lord, why not I am able You to follow now?
3588 5590 3450 5228 4675 5087 611 846 3588 2424
τὴν ψυχήν μου ὑπὲρ σοῦ θήσω. 38 ἀπεκρίθη αὐτῷ ὁ Ἰησοῦς,
The life of me for You I wil l lay down. answers him Jesus,
3588 5590 4675 5228 1700 5087 281 281 3004 4671 3756
Τὴν ψυχήν σου ὑπὲρ ἐμοῦ θήσεις; ἀμὴν ἀμὴν λέγω σοι, οὐ
The life of you for Me you will lay down? Truly, truly, I say to you, not
3361 220 5455 2193 3757 533 3165 5151
μὴ ἀλέκτωρ φωνήσει ἕως οὗ ἀπαρνήσῃ με τρίς.
at all a cock will crow until you deny Me three times.

King James Version

36. Simon Peter said unto him, Lord, whither goest thou? Jesus answered him, Whither I go, thou canst not follow me now; but thou shalt follow me afterwards.
37 Peter said unto him, Lord, why cannot I follow thee now? I will lay down my life for thy sake.

38 Jesus answered him, Wilt thou lay down thy life for my sake? Verily, verily, I say unto thee, The cock shall not crow, till thou hast denied me thrice.

John 14

1. Do not let your heart be troubled; you believe in God, believe also in Me.
2 In My Father's house are many dwelling places. But if not, I would have told you. I go to prepare a place for you!

3 And if I go and prepare a place for you, I am coming again and will receive you to Myself, that where I am you may be also.
4 And where I go you know, and the way you know.
5. Thomas said to Him, Lord, we do not know where You go, and how can we know the way?
6 Jesus said to him, I am the Way, and the Truth, and the Life. No one comes to the Father except through Me.

7 If you had known Me, you would have known My Father also; and from now on you do know Him, and have seen Him.

8. And Philip said to Him, Lord, show us the Father, and it is enough for us.
9 Jesus said to him,

3361 5015 5216 3588 2588 4100 1519 3588 2316
1 Μὴ ταρασσέσθω ὑμῶν ἡ καρδία· πιστεύετε εἰς τὸν Θεόν,
Not do let be agitated of you the heart; believe into God,
2532 1519 1691 4100 1722 3588 3614 3588 3962 3450 3438
καὶ εἰς ἐμὲ πιστεύετε. 2 ἐν τῇ οἰκίᾳ τοῦ πατρός μου μοναὶ
and into Me believe. In the house of the Father of Me dwellings
4183 1526 1487 1161 3361 2036 302 5213 4198 2090
πολλαί εἰσιν· εἰ δὲ μή, εἶπον ἂν ὑμῖν· πορεύομαι ἑτοιμάσαι
many are. if And not, I would have told you. I go to prepare
5117 5213 2532 1437 4198 2532 2090 5213 5117
τόπον ὑμῖν. 3 καὶ ἐὰν πορευθῶ καὶ ἑτοιμάσω ὑμῖν τόπον,
a place for you, and if I go and prepare for you a place,
3825 2064 2532 3880 5209 4314 1683 2443
πάλιν ἔρχομαι καὶ παραλήψομαι ὑμᾶς πρὸς ἐμαυτόν· ἵνα
again I am coming and will receive you to Myself, that
3699 1510 1473 2532 5210 5600 2532 3699 1473 5217 1492
ὅπου εἰμὶ ἐγώ, καὶ ὑμεῖς ἦτε. 4 καὶ ὅπου ἐγὼ ὑπάγω οἴδατε,
where am I, also you may be. And where I go, you know,
2532 3588 3598 1492 3004 846 2381 2962 3756 1492
καὶ τὴν ὁδὸν οἴδατε. 5 λέγει αὐτῷ Θωμᾶς, Κύριε, οὐκ οἴδαμεν
and the way you know. says to Him Thomas, Lord, not we know
4226 5217 2532 4459 1410 3588 3598 1492 3004
ποῦ ὑπάγεις· καὶ πῶς δυνάμεθα τὴν ὁδὸν εἰδέναι; 6 λέγει
where you go, and how are we able the way to know? says
846 3588 2424 1473 1510 3588 3598 2532 3588 225 2532 3588 2222
αὐτῷ ὁ Ἰησοῦς, Ἐγώ εἰμι ἡ ὁδὸς καὶ ἡ ἀλήθεια καὶ ἡ ζωή·
to him Jesus, I am the Way, and the Truth, and the Life;
3762 2064 4314 3588 3962 1487 3361 1223 1700 1487 1097
οὐδεὶς ἔρχεται πρὸς τὸν πατέρα, εἰ μὴ δι᾽ ἐμοῦ. 7 εἰ ἐγνώκειτέ
no one comes to the Father except through Me. If you had known
3165 2532 3588 3962 3450 1097 302 2532 575 737 1097
με, καὶ τὸν πατέρα μου ἐγνώκειτε ἄν· καὶ ἀπ᾽ ἄρτι γινώ-
Me, also the Father of Me you would have known, and from now you
846 2532 3708 846 3004 846 5376
σκετε αὐτὸν, καὶ ἑωράκατε αὐτόν. 8 λέγει αὐτῷ Φίλιππος,
know Him, and have seen Him. says to Him Phillip,
2962 1166 2254 3588 3962 2532 714 2254 3004 846
Κύριε, δεῖξον ἡμῖν τὸν πατέρα, καὶ ἀρκεῖ ἡμῖν. 9 λέγει αὐτῷ
Lord, show us the Father, and it is enough for us. says to him

1. Let not your heart be troubled: ye believe in God, believe also in me.
2 In my Father's house are many mansions: if (it were) not (so), I would have told you. I go to prepare a place for you.

3 And if I go and prepare a place for you, I will come again, and receive you unto myself; that where I am, (there) ye may be also.

4 And whither I go ye know, and the way ye know.
5. Thomas saith unto him, Lord, we know not whither thou goest; and how can we know the way?
6 Jesus saith unto him, I am the way, the truth, and the life: no man cometh unto the Father, but by me.
7 If ye had known me, ye should have known my Father also: and from henceforth ye know him, and have seen him.

8. Philip saith unto him, Lord, shew us the Father, and it sufficeth us.
9 Jesus saith unto him,

Literal Translation

Am I so long a time with you, and you have not known Me, Philip? The (one) seeing Me has seen the Father! And how do you say, Show us the Father?
10 Do you not believe that I (am) in the Father and the Father is in Me? The words which I speak to you I do not speak from Myself, but the Father who abides in Me, He does the works.

11 Believe Me that I (am) in the Father, and the Father (is) in Me; but if not, believe Me because of the works themselves.

12 Indeed, I tell you truly, the (one) believing into Me, the works which I do, that one shall do also, and greater than these he will do, because I go to My Father.
13 And whatever you may ask in My Name, this I will do, that the Father may be glorified in the Son.

14 If you ask anything in My Name, I will do (it).
15. If you love Me, keep My commandments.
16 And I will petition the Father, and He will give you another Comforter, that He may remain with you forever,
17 the Spirit of Truth, whom the world cannot receive because it does not see Him nor know Him. But you know Him, because He abides with you and shall be within you.

18 I will not leave you orphans; I am coming to you.
19 Yet a little (while) and the world no longer beholds Me, but you behold Me. Because I live, you also shall live.
20 In that day you shall know that I (am) in My Father, and you in Me,

John 14:10

3588 2424 5118 5550 3326 5216 1510 2532 3756 1097
ὁ Ἰησοῦς, Τοσοῦτον χρόνον μεθ᾽ ὑμῶν εἰμι, καὶ οὐκ ἔγνωκάς
Jesus so long a time with you I am, and not you know
3165 5376 3588 3708 1691 3708 3588 3962 2532 4459 4771
με, Φίλιππε; ὁ ἑωρακὼς ἐμὲ, ἑώρακε τὸν πατέρα· καὶ πῶς σὺ
Me, Phillip? The (one) seeing Me has seen the Father; and how do you
3004 1166 2254 3588 3962 3756 4100 3754 1473 1722 3588
λέγεις, Δεῖξον ἡμῖν τὸν πατέρα; 10 οὐ πιστεύεις ὅτι ἐγὼ ἐν τῷ
say, Show us the Father? Not do you believe that I in the
3962 2532 3588 3962 1722 1698 2076 3588 4487 3739 1473 2980
πατρὶ, καὶ ὁ πατὴρ ἐν ἐμοί ἐστι; τὰ ῥήματα ἃ ἐγὼ λαλῶ
Father (am), and the Father in Me is? The words which I speak
5213 575 1683 3756 2980 3588 1161 3962 3588 1722 1698 3306
ὑμῖν, ἀπ᾽ ἐμαυτοῦ οὐ λαλῶ· ὁ δὲ πατὴρ ὁ ἐν ἐμοὶ μένων,
to you, from Myself not I speak the but Father who in Me abides,

846 4160 3588 2041 4100 3427 3754 1473 1722 3588 3962
αὐτὸς ποιεῖ τὰ ἔργα. 11 πιστεύετέ μοι ὅτι ἐγὼ ἐν τῷ πατρὶ,
He does the works. Believe Me that I (am) in the Father,
2532 3588 3962 1722 1698 1487 1161 3361 1223 3588 2041 846 4100
καὶ ὁ πατὴρ ἐν ἐμοί· εἰ δὲ μή, διὰ τὰ ἔργα αὐτὰ πιστεύετέ
and the Father (is) in Me. if But not, because of the works themselves believe
3427 281 281 3004 5213 3588 4100 1519 1691 3588 2041 3739 1473
μοι. 12 ἀμὴν ἀμὴν λέγω ὑμῖν, ὁ πιστεύων εἰς ἐμέ, τὰ ἔργα ἃ ἐγὼ
Me. Truly truly I say to you, the (one) believing into Me, the works that I
4160 2548 4160 2532 3173 5130 4160 3754
ποιῶ κἀκεῖνος ποιήσει, καὶ μείζονα τούτων ποιήσει· ὅτι
do also that one does, and greater (than) these he will do; because
1473 4314 3588 3962 3450 4198 2532 3739 5100 302 154
ἐγὼ πρὸς τὸν πατέρα μου πορεύομαι. 13 καὶ ὅ τι ἂν αἰτήσητε
I to the Father of Me go. And whatever you may ask
1722 3588 3686 3450 5124 4160 2443 1392 3588 3962 1722
ἐν τῷ ὀνόματί μου, τοῦτο ποιήσω, ἵνα δοξασθῇ ὁ πατὴρ ἐν
in the name of Me, this I will do, that may be glorified the Father in
3588 5207 1437 5100 154 1722 3588 3686 3450 1473 4160
τῷ υἱῷ. 14 ἐάν τι αἰτήσητε ἐν τῷ ὀνόματί μου, ἐγὼ ποιήσω.
the Son. If anything you ask in the name of Me, I will do.
1437 25 3165 3588 1785 3588 1699 5083 2532 1473
15 ἐὰν ἀγαπᾶτέ με, τὰς ἐντολὰς τὰς ἐμὰς τηρήσατε. 16 καὶ ἐγὼ
If you love Me, the commandments of Me keep. And I
2065 3588 3962 2532 243 3875 1325 5213
ἐρωτήσω τὸν πατέρα, καὶ ἄλλον παράκλητον δώσει ὑμῖν,
will petition the Father, and another Comforter He will give you,
2443 3306 3326 5216 1519 3588 165 3588 4151 3588 225 3739
ἵνα μένῃ μεθ᾽ ὑμῶν εἰς τὸν αἰῶνα, 17 τὸ πνεῦμα τῆς ἀληθείας, ὃ
that He abide with you to the age, the Spirit of Truth, whom
3588 2889 3756 1410 2983 3754 3756 2334 846 3761 1097
ὁ κόσμος οὐ δύναται λαβεῖν, ὅτι οὐ θεωρεῖ αὐτό, οὐδὲ γινώ-
the world not is able to receive, because not it sees Him, nor knows
846 5210 1161 1097 846 3754 3844 5213 3306 2532
σκει αὐτό· ὑμεῖς δὲ γινώσκετε αὐτό, ὅτι παρ᾽ ὑμῖν μένει, καὶ
Him; you but know Him, because with you He abides, and
1722 5213 2071 3756 863 5209 3737 2064 4314
ἐν ὑμῖν ἔσται. 18 οὐκ ἀφήσω ὑμᾶς ὀρφανούς· ἔρχομαι πρὸς
within you will be. Not I will leave you orphans; I am coming to
5209 2089 3397 2532 3588 2889 3165 3765 2334 5210 1161 2334
ὑμᾶς. 19 ἔτι μικρὸν καὶ ὁ κόσμος με οὐκέτι θεωρεῖ, ὑμεῖς δὲ θεω-
you. Yet a little and the world Me no longer beholds. you But
3165 3754 1473 2198 2532 5210 2198 1722 1565 3588 2250
ρεῖτέ με· ὅτι ἐγὼ ζῶ, καὶ ὑμεῖς ζήσεσθε. 20 ἐν ἐκείνῃ τῇ ἡμέρᾳ
behold Me; because I live, also you will live. In that day
1097 5210 3754 1473 1722 3588 3962 3450 2532 5210 1722 1698
γνώσεσθε ὑμεῖς ὅτι ἐγὼ ἐν τῷ πατρί μου, καὶ ὑμεῖς ἐν ἐμοὶ,
will know you that I (am) in the Father of Me, and you in Me,

King James Version

Have I been so long time with you, and yet hast thou not known me, Philip? he that hath seen me hath seen the Father; and how sayest thou (then), Shew us the Father?
10 Believest thou not that I am in the Father, and the Father in me? the words that I speak unto you I speak not of myself: but the Father that dwelleth in me, he doeth the works.

11 Believe me that I (am) in the Father, and the Father in me: or else believe me for the very works' sake.

12 Verily, verily, I say unto you, He that believeth on me, the works that I do shall he do also; and greater (works) than these shall he do; because I go unto my Father.
13 And whatsoever ye shall ask in my name, that will I do, that the Father may be glorified in the Son.

14 If ye shall ask any thing in my name, I will do (it).
15. If ye love me, keep my commandments.
16 And I will pray the Father, and he shall give you another Comforter, that he may abide with you for ever;
17 (Even) the Spirit of truth; whom the world cannot receive, because it seeth him not, neither knoweth him: but ye know him; for he dwelleth with you, and shall be in you.

18 I will not leave you comfortless: I will come to you.
19 Yet a little while, and the world seeth me no more; but ye see me: because I live, ye shall live also.
20 At that day ye shall know that I (am) in my Father, and ye in me, and I in you.

Literal Translation — **John 14:21** — **King James Version**

and I in you.
21 The (one) having My commandments and keeping them, that one is the (one) loving Me; and the (one) loving Me will be loved by My Father, and I will love him and will reveal Myself to him.

2504 1722 5213 3588 2192 3588 1785 3450 2532 5083 846
κἀγὼ ἐν ὑμῖν. 21 ὁ ἔχων τὰς ἐντολάς μου καὶ τηρῶν αὐτάς,
and I in you. The (one) having the commandments of Me and keeping them,

1565 2076 3588 25 3165 3588 1161 25 3165 25
ἐκεῖνός ἐστιν ὁ ἀγαπῶν με· ὁ δὲ ἀγαπῶν με, ἀγαπηθήσεται
that one is the (one) loving Me. he And loving Me will be loved

5259 3588 3962 3450 2532 1473 25 846 2532 1718
ὑπὸ τοῦ πατρός μου· καὶ ἐγὼ ἀγαπήσω αὐτόν, καὶ ἐμφανίσω
by the Father of Me, and I will love him, and will reveal

21 He that hath my commandments, and keepeth them, he it is that loveth me: and he that loveth me shall be loved of my Father, and I will love him, and will manifest myself to him.

22 Judas said to Him, not the Iscariot, Lord, what has happened that You are about to reveal Yourself to us and not to the world?

846 1683 3004 846 2455 3756 3588 2469
αὐτῷ ἐμαυτόν. 22 λέγει αὐτῷ Ἰούδας, οὐχ ὁ Ἰσκαριώτης,
to him Myself. says to Him Judas, not the Iscariot,

2962 5101 1096 3754 2254 3195 1718 4572 2532
Κύριε, τί γέγονεν ὅτι ἡμῖν μέλλεις ἐμφανίζειν σεαυτὸν, καὶ
Lord, what has occurred that to us You are about to reveal Yourself, and

22 Judas saith unto him, not Iscariot, Lord, how is it that thou wilt manifest thyself unto us, and not unto the world?

23 Jesus answered and said to him, If anyone loves Me, he will keep My Word, and My Father will love him. And We will come to him and will make an abode with him.

3780 3588 2889 611 3588 2424 2532 2036 846 1437
οὐχὶ τῷ κόσμῳ; 23 ἀπεκρίθη ὁ Ἰησοῦς καὶ εἶπεν αὐτῷ, Ἐάν
not to the world? answered Jesus and said to him, If

5100 25 3165 3588 3056 3450 5083 2532 3588 3962 3450
τις ἀγαπᾷ με, τὸν λόγον μου τηρήσει, καὶ ὁ πατήρ μου
anyone loves Me, the Word of Me he will keep, and the Father of Me

25 846 2532 4314 846 2064 2532 3438
ἀγαπήσει αὐτόν, καὶ πρὸς αὐτὸν ἐλευσόμεθα, καὶ μονὴν
will love him, and to him We will come, and abode

23 Jesus answered and said unto him, If a man love me, he will keep my words: and my Father will love him, and we will come unto him, and make our abode with him.

24 The (one) not loving Me does not keep My words. And the Word which you hear is not Mine but of the (One) having sent Me, (the) Father.

3844 846 4160 3588 3361 25 3165 3588 3056 3450
παρ' αὐτῷ ποιήσομεν. 24 ὁ μὴ ἀγαπῶν με, τοὺς λόγους μου
with him We will make. The(one) not loving Me, the words of Me

3756 5083 2532 3588 3056 3739 191 3756 2076 1699 235 3588
οὐ τηρεῖ· καὶ ὁ λόγος ὃν ἀκούετε οὐκ ἔστιν ἐμὸς, ἀλλὰ τοῦ
not keeps; and the Word which you hear not is Mine, but of Him

3992 3165 3962
πέμψαντός με πατρός.
having sent Me (the) Father.

24 He that loveth me not keepeth not my sayings: and the word which ye hear is not mine, but the Father's which sent me.

25 I have spoken these things to you, abiding with you;
26 but the Comforter, the Holy Spirit, whom the Father will send in My name, He shall teach you all things and shall remind you (of) all things that I said to you.

5023 2980 5213 3844 5213 3306 3588 1161 3875
25.Ταῦτα λελάληκα ὑμῖν παρ' ὑμῖν μένων· 26 ὁ δὲ παράκλη-
These things I have spoken to you, with you abiding. the But Helper,

3588 4151 3588 40 3739 3992 3588 3962 1722 3588 3686 3450
τος, τὸ Πνεῦμα τὸ Ἅγιον, ὃ πέμψει ὁ πατὴρ ἐν τῷ ὀνόματί μου,
the Spirit Holy, which will send the Father in the name of Me,

1565 5209 1321 3956 2532 5279 5209 3956 3739
ἐκεῖνος ὑμᾶς διδάξει πάντα, καὶ ὑπομνήσει ὑμᾶς πάντα ἃ
that One you will teach all things, and remind you (of) all things which

25 These things have I spoken unto you, being (yet) present with you.
26 But the Comforter, (which is) the Holy Ghost, whom the Father will send in my name, he shall teach you all things, and bring all things to your remembrance, whatsoever I have said unto you.

27 I leave peace to you; My peace I give to you. Not as the world gives I give to you. Let not your heart be agitated, nor let it be fearful.

2036 5213 1515 863 5213 1515 3588 1699 1325
εἶπον ὑμῖν. 27 εἰρήνην ἀφίημι ὑμῖν, εἰρήνην τὴν ἐμὴν δίδωμι
I told you. Peace I leave to you; peace My I give

5213 3756 2531 3588 2889 1325 1473 1325 5213 3361
ὑμῖν· οὐ καθὼς ὁ κόσμος δίδωσιν, ἐγὼ δίδωμι ὑμῖν. μὴ
you; not as the world gives, I give to you. not

5015 5216 3588 2588 3366 1168 191 3754
ταρασσέσθω ὑμῶν ἡ καρδία, μηδὲ δειλιάτω. 28 ἠκούσατε ὅτι
Let be agitated of you the heart, nor let (it) be fearful. You heard that

27 Peace I leave with you, my peace I give unto you: not as the world giveth, give I unto you. Let not your heart be troubled, neither let it be afraid.

28 You heard that I said to you, I go away, and I come (again) to you. If you loved Me, you would have rejoiced that I said, I am going to the Father; for My Father is greater than I am.

1473 2036 5213 5217 2532 2064 4314 5209 1487 25
ἐγὼ εἶπον ὑμῖν, Ὑπάγω καὶ ἔρχομαι πρὸς ὑμᾶς. εἰ ἠγαπᾶτέ
I told you, I go and come to you. If you loved

3165 5463 302 3754 2036 4198 4314 3588 3962
με, ἐχάρητε ἂν ὅτι εἶπον, Πορεύομαι πρὸς τὸν πατέρα·
Me, you would have rejoiced that I said, I am going to the Father;

28 Ye have heard how I said unto you, I go away, and come (again) unto you. If ye loved me, ye would rejoice, because I said, I go unto the Father: for my Father is greater than I.

29 And now I have told you before (it) happens, that when it happens you may believe.
30 No longer many things

3754 3588 3962 3450 3187 3450 2076 2532 3568 2046 5213 4250
ὅτι ὁ πατήρ μου μείζων μού ἐστι. 29 καὶ νῦν εἴρηκα ὑμῖν πρὶν
because the Father of Me greater than Me is. And now I have told you before

1096 2443 3752 1096 4100 3765 4183
γενέσθαι· ἵνα, ὅταν γένηται, πιστεύσητε. 30 οὐκέτι πολλὰ
(it) happens; that when it happens you may believe. No longer many things

29 And now I have told you before it come to pass, that, when it is come to pass, ye might believe.
30 Hereafter I will not talk

Literal Translation

I will speak with you, for the ruler of this world is coming, and (he) has nothing in Me.
31 But that the world may know that I love the Father, even as the Father commanded Me, so I do. Rise up, let us go from here.

John 14:31

2980 3326 5216 2064 1063 3588 3588 2889 5127
λαλήσω μεθ᾽ ὑμῶν· ἔρχεται γὰρ ὁ τοῦ κόσμου τούτου
I will speak with you; is coming for the of world this

758 2532 1722 1698 3756 2192 3762 235 2443 1097 3588 2889
ἄρχων, καὶ ἐν ἐμοὶ οὐκ ἔχει οὐδέν· 31 ἀλλ᾽ ἵνα γνῷ ὁ κόσμος
ruler, and in Me not has nothing. But that may know the world

3754 25 3588 3962 2532 2531 1781 3427 3588 3962
ὅτι ἀγαπῶ τὸν πατέρα, καὶ καθὼς ἐνετείλατο μοι ὁ πατήρ,
that I love the Father, and as commanded Me the Father,

3779 4160 1453 71 1782
οὕτω ποιῶ. ἐγείρεσθε, ἄγωμεν ἐντεῦθεν.
so I do. Rise up, let us go from here.

King James Version

much with you: for the prince of this world cometh, and hath nothing in me.
31 But that the world may know that I love the Father; and as the Father gave me commandment, even so I do. Arise, let us go hence.

John 15

1. I am the True Vine, and My Father is the Vinedresser.
2 Every branch in Me not bearing fruit, He takes it away; and each one bearing fruit, He prunes, so that it may bear more fruit.
3 You are already clean because of the Word which I have spoken to you.
4 Abide in Me, and I in you. As the branch is not able to bear fruit of itself, if not it abide in the vine, so neither (can) you if not you abide in Me.
5 I am the Vine; you (are) the branches. He that remains in Me, and I in him, this one bears much fruit. For apart from Me you are not able to do anything.
6 If not anyone abides in Me, he is cast out as the branch and is dried out; and they gather and throw (them) into a fire, and they are burned.
7 If you abide in Me, and My words abide in you, whatever you desire you will ask, and it will happen to you.
8 In this My Father is glorified of Me, that you will bear much fruit; and you will be My disciples.
9 As the Father loved Me, I also loved you; abide in My love.

John 15

1473 1510 3588 288 3588 228 2532 3588 3962 3450 3588
1 Ἐγώ εἰμι ἡ ἄμπελος ἡ ἀληθινή, καὶ ὁ πατήρ μου ὁ
I am the vine true, and the Father of Me the

1092 2076 3956 2814 1722 1698 3361 5342 2590 142
γεωργός ἐστι. 2 πᾶν κλῆμα ἐν ἐμοὶ μὴ φέρον καρπόν, αἴρει
Vinedresser is. Every branch in Me not bearing fruit, He takes

846 2532 3956 3588 2590 5342 2508 846 2443 4119
αὐτό· καὶ πᾶν τὸ καρπὸν φέρον, καθαίρει αὐτό, ἵνα πλείονα
it; and every (branch) fruit bearing, He prunes it, so that more

2590 5342 2235 5210 2513 2075 1223 3588 3056 3739
καρπὸν φέρῃ. 3 ἤδη ὑμεῖς καθαροί ἐστε διὰ τὸν λόγον ὃν
fruit it may bear. Already you clean are because of the Word which

2980 5213 3306 1722 1698 2504 1722 5213 2531 3588
λελάληκα ὑμῖν. 4 μείνατε ἐν ἐμοί, κἀγὼ ἐν ὑμῖν. καθὼς τὸ
I have spoken to you. Abide in Me, and I in you. Even as the

2814 3756 1410 2590 5342 575 1438 1437 3361 3306
κλῆμα οὐ δύναται καρπὸν φέρειν ἀφ᾽ ἑαυτοῦ, ἐὰν μὴ μείνῃ
branch not is able fruit to bear from itself, if not it abide

1722 3588 288 3779 3761 5210 1437 3361 1722 1698 3306 1473
ἐν τῇ ἀμπέλῳ, οὕτως οὐδὲ ὑμεῖς ἐὰν μὴ ἐν ἐμοὶ μείνητε. 5 ἐγώ
in the vine, so neither you if not in Me you abide. I

1510 3588 288 5210 3588 2814 3588 3306 1722 1698 2504 1722
εἰμι ἡ ἄμπελος, ὑμεῖς τὰ κλήματα. ὁ μένων ἐν ἐμοί, κἀγὼ ἐν
am the Vine, you (are) the branches. the (one) abiding in Me, and I in

846 3778 5342 2590 4183 3754 5565 1700 3756 1410
αὐτῷ οὗτος φέρει καρπὸν πολύν· ὅτι χωρὶς ἐμοῦ οὐ δύνασθε
him, this one bears fruit much; because apart from Me not you are able

4160 3762 1437 3361 5100 3306 1722 1698 906 1854 5613 3588
ποιεῖν οὐδέν. 6 ἐὰν μή τις μείνῃ ἐν ἐμοί, ἐβλήθη ἔξω ὡς τὸ
to do, nothing. If not anyone abides in Me, he is cast out as the

2814 2532 3583 2532 4863 846 2532 1519 4442
κλῆμα, καὶ ἐξηράνθη, καὶ συνάγουσιν αὐτὰ καὶ εἰς πῦρ
branch, and is dried out, and they gather them and into fire

906 2532 2545 1437 3306 1722 1698 2532 3588 4487
βάλλουσι, καὶ καίεται. 7 ἐὰν μείνητε ἐν ἐμοὶ, καὶ τὰ ῥήματά
they throw, and they are burned. If you abide in Me, and the words

3450 1722 5213 3306 3739 1437 2309 154 2532 1096
μου ἐν ὑμῖν μείνῃ, ὃ ἐὰν θέλητε αἰτήσεσθε, καὶ γενήσεται
of Me in you abide, what ever you desire you will ask, and it will happen

5213 1722 5129 1392 3588 3962 3450 2443 2590 4183
ὑμῖν. 8 ἐν τούτῳ ἐδοξάσθη ὁ πατήρ μου, ἵνα καρπὸν πολὺν
to you. In this is glorified the Father of Me, that fruit much

5342 2532 1096 1698 3101 2531 25 3165 3588
φέρητε· καὶ γενήσεσθε ἐμοὶ μαθηταί. 9 καθὼς ἠγάπησέ με ὁ
you will bear, and you will be to Me disciples. Even as loved Me the

3962 2504 25 5209 3306 1722 3588 26 3588 1699
πατήρ, κἀγὼ ἠγάπησα ὑμᾶς· μείνατε ἐν τῇ ἀγάπῃ τῇ ἐμῇ.
Father, I also loved you; abide in the love of Me.

John 15

1. I am the true vine, and my Father is the husbandman.
2 Every branch in me that beareth not fruit he taketh away: and every (branch) that beareth fruit, he purgeth it, that it may bring forth more fruit.
3 Now ye are clean through the word which I have spoken unto you.
4 Abide in me, and I in you. As the branch cannot bear fruit of itself, except it abide in the vine; no more can ye, except ye abide in me.
5 I am the vine, ye (are) the branches: He that abideth in me, and I in him, the same bringeth forth much fruit: for without me ye can do nothing.
6 If a man abide not in me, he is cast forth as a branch, and is withered; and men gather them, and cast (them) into the fire, and they are burned.
7 If ye abide in me, and my words abide in you, ye shall ask what ye will, and it shall be done unto you.
8 Herein is my Father glorified, that ye bear much fruit; so shall ye be my disciples.
9 As the Father hath loved me, so have I loved you: continue ye in my love.

Literal Translation

John 15:10

King James Version

10 If you keep My commandments, you will abide in My love, as I have kept My Father's commandments and abide in His love.

11 I have spoken these things to you that My joy may abide in you, and your joy may be filled.

12 This is My commandment, that you love one another as I loved you.

13 Greater love than this has no one, that anyone should lay down his life for his friends.

14 You are My friends if you do whatever I command you.

15 I no longer call you slaves, because the slave does not know what his lord does. But I called you friends, because all things which I heard from beside My Father I made known to you.

16 You have not chosen Me, but I chose you out and planted you, that you should go and should bear fruit, and your fruit abide, that whatever you should ask the Father in My name, He may give you.

17 These things I command you, that you love one another.

18. If the world hates you, you know that it has hated Me before (it has hated) you.

19 If you were of the world, the world would love (its) own. But because you are not of the world, but I chose you out of the world, for this reason the world hates you.

20 Remember the word which I said to you, A slave is not greater than his lord. If they persecuted Me, they also will persecute you. If they kept My Word, they also will keep yours.

1437 3588 1785 3450 5083 3306 1722 3588 26 3450
10 ἐὰν τὰς ἐντολάς μου τηρήσητε, μενεῖτε ἐν τῇ ἀγάπῃ μου·
If the commandments of Me you keep, you will abide in the love of Me,

2531 1473 3588 1785 3588 3962 3450 5083 2532 3306
καθὼς ἐγὼ τὰς ἐντολὰς τοῦ πατρός μου τετήρηκα καὶ μένω
even as I the commandments of the Father of Me have kept, and abide

846 1722 3588 26 5023 2980 5213 2443 3588 5479 3588
αὐτοῦ ἐν τῇ ἀγάπῃ. 11 Ταῦτα λελάληκα ὑμῖν, ἵνα ἡ χαρὰ ἡ
of Him in the love. These things I have spoken to you, that the joy

1699 1722 5213 3306 2532 3588 5479 5216 4137 3778 2076 3588
ἐμὴ ἐν ὑμῖν μείνῃ, καὶ ἡ χαρὰ ὑμῶν πληρωθῇ. 12 αὕτη ἐστὶν ἡ
of Me in you abide, and the joy of you may be filled. This is the

1785 3588 1699 2443 25 240 2531 25
ἐντολὴ ἡ ἐμή, ἵνα ἀγαπᾶτε ἀλλήλους, καθὼς ἠγάπησα
commandment of Me, that you love one another, even as I loved

5209 3173 3778 26 3762 2192 2443 5100 3588 5590
ὑμᾶς. 13 μείζονα ταύτης ἀγάπην οὐδεὶς ἔχει, ἵνα τις τὴν ψυχὴν
you. Greater than this love no one has, that anyone the life

846 5087 5228 3588 5384 846 5210 5384 3450 2075 1437
αὐτοῦ θῇ ὑπὲρ τῶν φίλων αὐτοῦ. 14 ὑμεῖς φίλοι μου ἐστέ, ἐὰν
of him lay down for the friends of him. You friends of Me are, if

4160 3745 1473 1781 5213 3765 5209 3004 1401
ποιῆτε ὅσα ἐγὼ ἐντέλλομαι ὑμῖν. 15 οὐκέτι ὑμᾶς λέγω δούλους,
you do whatever I command you. No longer you I call slaves,

3754 3588 1401 3756 1492 5101 4160 846 3588 2962 5209 1161 2046
ὅτι ὁ δοῦλος οὐκ οἶδε τί ποιεῖ αὐτοῦ ὁ κύριος· ὑμᾶς δὲ εἴρηκα
because the slave not knows what does of him the lord; you but I called

5384 3754 3956 3739 191 3844 3588 3962 3450 1107
φίλους, ὅτι πάντα ἃ ἤκουσα παρὰ τοῦ πατρός μου ἐγνώ-
friends because all things which I heard from beside the Father of Me I made

5213 3756 5210 3165 1586 235 1473 1586
ρισα ὑμῖν. 16 οὐχ ὑμεῖς με ἐξελέξασθε, ἀλλ' ἐγὼ ἐξελεξάμην
known to you. Not you Me have chosen, but I chose out

5209 2532 5087 5209 2443 5210 5217 2532 2590 5342 2532
ὑμᾶς, καὶ ἔθηκα ὑμᾶς, ἵνα ὑμεῖς ὑπάγητε καὶ καρπὸν φέρητε, καὶ
you, and planted you, that you should go and fruit should bear, and

3588 2590 5216 3306 2443 3739 5100 302 154 3588 3962 1722 3588
ὁ καρπὸς ὑμῶν μένῃ· ἵνα ὅ τι ἂν αἰτήσητε τὸν πατέρα ἐν τῷ
the fruit of you abide; that whatever you may ask the Father in the

3686 3450 1325 5213 5023 1781 5213 2443
ὀνόματί μου, δῷ ὑμῖν. 17 ταῦτα ἐντέλλομαι ὑμῖν, ἵνα
name of Me, He may give you. These things I command you, that

25 240 1487 3588 2889 5209 3404 1097 3754
ἀγαπᾶτε ἀλλήλους. 18 εἰ ὁ κόσμος ὑμᾶς μισεῖ, γινώσκετε ὅτι
you love one another. If the world you hates, you know that

1691 4412 5216 3404 1487 1537 3588 2889 2258 3588 2889
ἐμὲ πρῶτον ὑμῶν μεμίσηκεν. 19 εἰ ἐκ τοῦ κόσμου ἦτε, ὁ κόσμος
Me before you it has hated. If of the world you were, the world

302 3588 2398 5368 3754 1161 1537 3588 2889 3756 2075 235 1473
ἂν τὸ ἴδιον ἐφίλει· ὅτι δὲ ἐκ τοῦ κόσμου οὐκ ἐστέ, ἀλλ' ἐγὼ
would the own have loved. that But of the world not you are, but I

1586 5209 1537 3588 2889 1223 5124 3404 5209 3588
ἐξελεξάμην ὑμᾶς ἐκ τοῦ κόσμου, διὰ τοῦτο μισεῖ ὑμᾶς ὁ
chose out you out of the world, because of this hates you the

2889 3421 3588 3056 3739 1473 2036 5213 3756 2076
κόσμος. 20 μνημονεύετε τοῦ λόγου οὗ ἐγὼ εἶπον ὑμῖν, Οὐκ ἔστι
world. Remember the word which I spoke to you; Not is

1401 3187 3588 2962 846 1487 1691 1377 2532 5209
δοῦλος μείζων τοῦ κυρίου αὐτοῦ. εἰ ἐμὲ ἐδίωξαν, καὶ ὑμᾶς
a slave greater than the lord of him. If Me they persecuted, also you

1377 1487 3588 3056 3450 5083 2532 3588 5212
διώξουσιν· εἰ τὸν λόγον μου ἐτήρησαν, καὶ τὸν ὑμέτερον
they will persecute. If the Word of Me they kept, also yours

10 If ye keep my commandments, ye shall abide in my love; even as I have kept my Father's commandments, and abide in his love.

11 These things have I spoken unto you, that my joy might remain in you, and (that) your joy might be full.

12 This is my commandment, That ye love one another, as I have loved you.

13 Greater love hath no man than this, that a man lay down his life for his friends.

14 Ye are my friends, if ye do whatsoever I command you.

15 Henceforth I call you not servants; for the servant knoweth not what his lord doeth: but I have called you friends; for all things that I have heard of my Father I have made known unto you.

16 Ye have not chosen me, but I have chosen you, and ordained you, that ye should go and bring forth fruit, and (that) your fruit should remain: that whatsoever ye shall ask of the Father in my name, he may give it you.

17 These things I command you, that ye love one another.

18. If the world hate you, ye know that it hated me before (it hated) you.

19 If ye were of the world, the world would love his own: but because ye are not of the world, but I have chosen you out of the world, therefore the world hateth you.

20 Remember the word that I said unto you, The servant is not greater than his lord. If they have persecuted me, they will also persecute you; if they have kept my saying, they will keep yours also.

Literal Translation

John 15:21

King James Version

21 But all these things they will do to you because of My name, because they do not know the (One) sending Me.
22 If I had not come and spoken to them, they had no sin. But now they do not have excuse concerning their sin.
23 The (one) hating Me also hates My Father.

24 If I did not do the works among them which no other did, they had no sin. But now they both have seen and also have hated Me and My Father.

25 But that may be fulfilled the Word having been written in their Law, "They hated Me without a cause." (Ps. 69:4)

5083 235 5023 3956 4160 5213 1223 3588
τηρήσουσιν. 21 ἀλλὰ ταῦτα πάντα ποιήσουσιν ὑμῖν διὰ τὸ
they will keep. But these things all they will do to you because of

3686 3450 3754 3756 1492 3588 3992 3165 1487 3361 2064 2532
ὄνομά μου, ὅτι οὐκ οἴδασι τὸν πέμψαντά με. 22 εἰ μὴ ἦλθον καὶ
name My, because not they know the (One) sending Me. If not I came and

2980 846 266 3756 2192 3568 1161 4392 3756
ἐλάλησα αὐτοῖς, ἁμαρτίαν οὐκ εἶχον· νῦν δὲ πρόφασιν οὐκ
had spoken to them, sin not they had.; now but an excuse not

2192 4012 3588 266 846 3588 1691 3404 2532 3588
ἔχουσι περὶ τῆς ἁμαρτίας αὐτῶν. 23 ὁ ἐμὲ μισῶν, καὶ τὸν
they have concerning the sin of them. The (one) Me hating, also the

3962 3450 3404 1487 3588 2041 3361 4160 1722 846 3739 3762
πατέρα μου μισεῖ. 24 εἰ τὰ ἔργα μὴ ἐποίησα ἐν αὐτοῖς ἃ οὐδεὶς
Father of Me hates. If the works not I did among them which none

243 4160 266 3756 2192 3568 1161 2532 3708
ἄλλος πεποίηκεν, ἁμαρτίαν οὐκ εἶχον· νῦν δὲ καὶ ἑωράκασι
other did, sin not they had; now but both they have seen

2532 3404 2532 1691 2532 3588 3962 3450 235 2443 4137
καὶ μεμισήκασι καὶ ἐμὲ καὶ τὸν πατέρα μου. 25 ἀλλ' ἵνα πλη-
and have hated both Me and the Father of Me. But that may be

3588 3056 3588 1125 1722 3588 3551 846 3754 3404
ρωθῇ ὁ λόγος ὁ γεγραμμένος ἐν τῷ νόμῳ αὐτῶν ὅτι 'Εμίση-
fulfilled the Word having been written in the Law of them, They

3404 3165 1432
σάν με δωρεάν.
hated Me freely.

21 But all these things will they do unto you for my name's sake, because they know not him that sent me.
22 If I had not come and spoken unto them, they had not had sin: but now they have no cloke for their sin.

23 He that hateth me hateth my Father also.

24 If I had not done among them the works which none other man did, they had not had sin: but now have they both seen and hated both me and my Father.
25 But (this cometh to pass), that the word might be fulfilled that is written in their law, They hated me without a cause.

26 And when the Comforter comes, whom I will send to you from the Father, the Spirit of truth who proceeds from the Father, that One will witness concerning Me.
27 And you also witness, because from (the) beginning you are with Me.

3752 1161 2064 3588 3875 3739 1473 3992 5213
26 Ὅταν δὲ ἔλθῃ ὁ παράκλητος, ὃν ἐγὼ πέμψω ὑμῖν
when And comes the Comforter, whom I will send to you from

3844 3588 3962 3588 4151 3588 225 3739 3844 3588 3962
παρὰ τοῦ πατρός, τὸ πνεῦμα τῆς ἀληθείας, ὃ παρὰ τοῦ πατρὸς
the Father, the Spirit of truth, who from the Father

1607 1565 3140 4012 1700 2532 5210 1161
ἐκπορεύεται, ἐκεῖνος μαρτυρήσει περὶ ἐμοῦ· 27 καὶ ὑμεῖς δὲ
proceeds, that One will witness concerning Me; also you and

3140 3754 575 746 3326 1700 2075
μαρτυρεῖτε, ὅτι ἀπ' ἀρχῆς μετ' ἐμοῦ ἐστε.
witness, because from (the) beginning with Me you are.

26 But when the Comforter is come, whom I will send unto you from the Father, (even) the Spirit of truth, which proceedeth from the Father, he shall testify of me:
27 And ye also shall bear witness, because ye have been with me from the beginning.

John 16

1. I have spoken these things to you so that you may not be stumbled.
2 They will put you out of (the) synagogue, but an hour is coming that everyone killing you will think to bear a service before God.
3 And they will do these things to you because they did not know the Father nor Me.
4 But I have spoken these things to you so that when the hour comes you may recall them, that I told you these things; and I did not say these things to you from (the) beginning because I was with you.
5 But now I am going to

John 16

5023 2980 5213 2443 3361 4624 656
1. Ταῦτα λελάληκα ὑμῖν, ἵνα μὴ σκανδαλισθῆτε. 2 ἀπο-
These things I have spoken to you, that not you may be stumbled. Out of

4160 5209 235 2064 5610 2443 3956
συναγώγους ποιήσουσιν ὑμᾶς· ἀλλ' ἔρχεται ὥρα, ἵνα πᾶς
(the) synagogue they will make you (to be); but comes an hour that everyone

3588 615 5209 1380 2999 4374 3588 2316 2532
ὁ ἀποκτείνας ὑμᾶς δόξῃ λατρείαν προσφέρειν τῷ θεῷ. 3 καὶ
killing you will think a service to bear before God. And

5023 4160 5213 3754 3756 1097 3588 3962 3761
ταῦτα ποιήσουσιν ὑμῖν, ὅτι οὐκ ἔγνωσαν τὸν πατέρα οὐδὲ
these things they will do to you, because not they knew the Father nor

1691 235 5023 2980 5213 2443 3752 2064 3588 5610
ἐμέ. 4 ἀλλὰ ταῦτα λελάληκα ὑμῖν, ἵνα ὅταν ἔλθῃ ἡ ὥρα,
Me. But these things I have spoken to you, that when comes the hour

3421 846 3754 1473 2036 5213 5023 1161 5213 1537
μνημονεύητε αὐτῶν, ὅτι ἐγὼ εἶπον ὑμῖν. ταῦτα δὲ ὑμῖν ἐξ
you may recall them, that I told you these things and to you from

746 3756 2036 3754 3326 5216 2252 3568 1161 5217 4314
ἀρχῆς οὐκ εἶπον, ὅτι μεθ' ὑμῶν ἤμην. 5 νῦν δὲ ὑπάγω πρὸς
(the) first not I said, because with you I was. now But I am going to

John 16

1. These things have I spoken unto you, that ye should not be offended.
2 They shall put you out of the synagogues: yea, the time cometh, that whosoever killeth you will think that he doeth God service.
3 And these things will they do unto you, because they have not known the Father, nor me.
4 But these things have I told you, that when the time shall come, ye may remember that I told you of them. And these things I said not unto you at the beginning, because I was with you.
5 But now I go my way to

Literal Translation | **John 16:6** | *King James Version*

going to the (One) sending Me. And not one of you asks Me, Where are you going?
6 But because I have said these things to you, grief has filled your heart.
7 But I tell you the truth, it is advantageous for you that I should go; for if I do not go away, the Comforter will not come to you. But if I go, I will send Him to you.
8 And having come that One, He will convict the world concerning sin, and concerning righteousness, and concerning judgment.
9 Truly concerning sin, because they do not believe into Me;
10 and concerning righteousness, because I am going to My Father, and you no longer see Me;
11 and concerning judgment, because the ruler of this world has been judged.
12 I have yet many things to tell you, but you are not able to bear now.
13 But when that One comes, the Spirit of truth, He will guide you into all truth, for He will not speak from Himself, but whatever He hears, He will speak; and He will announce the coming things to you.
14 That One will glorify Me, for He will receive from Mine and will announce to you.
15 All things, as many as the Father has, are Mine. For this reason I said that He receives from Mine, and will announce to you.
16 A little (while) and you do not behold Me. And again a little (while), and you will see Me, because I go away to the Father.
17 Then His disciples said to one another, What is this which He says to us, A little (while), and you do not behold me; and again, A little and you will see Me?

3588 3992 3165 2532 3762 1537 5216 2065 3165 4226 5217
τὸν πέμψαντά με, καὶ οὐδεὶς ἐξ ὑμῶν ἐρωτᾷ με, Ποῦ ὑπάγεις;
the (One) sending Me, and not one of you asks Me, Where are you going?
235 3754 5023 2980 5213 3588 3077 4137 5216
6 ἀλλ' ὅτι ταῦτα λελάληκα ὑμῖν, ἡ λύπη πεπλήρωκεν ὑμῶν
But because these things I have said to you, grief has filled of you
3588 2588 235 1473 3588 225 3004 5213 4851
τὴν καρδίαν. 7 ἀλλ' ἐγὼ τὴν ἀλήθειαν λέγω ὑμῖν· συμφέρει
the heart. But I the truth tell you, it is profitable
5213 2443 1473 565 1437 1063 3361 565 3588 3875
ὑμῖν ἵνα ἐγὼ ἀπέλθω· ἐὰν γὰρ μὴ ἀπέλθω, ὁ παράκλητος
for you that I should go away. if For not I go away, the Comforter
3756 2064 4314 5209 1437 1161 4198 3992 846
οὐκ ἐλεύσεται πρὸς ὑμᾶς· ἐὰν δὲ πορευθῶ, πέμψω αὐτὸν
not will come to you. if But I go I will send Him
4314 5209 2532 2064 1565 1651 3588 2889 4012 266
πρὸς ὑμᾶς. 8 καὶ ἐλθὼν ἐκεῖνος ἐλέγξει τὸν κόσμον περὶ ἁμαρ-
to you. And having come that One will convict the world concerning sin
2532 4012 1343 2532 4012 2920 4012 266
τίας καὶ περὶ δικαιοσύνης καὶ περὶ κρίσεως· 9 περὶ ἁμαρτίας
and concerning righteousness and concerning judgment. Concerning sin
3303 3754 3756 4100 1519 1691 4012 1343 1161 3754
μέν, ὅτι οὐ πιστεύουσιν εἰς ἐμέ· 10 περὶ δικαιοσύνης δέ, ὅτι
truly, because not they believe into Me. concerning righteousness And, because
4314 3588 3962 3450 5217 2532 3765 2334 3165 4012
πρὸς τὸν πατέρα μου ὑπάγω, καὶ οὐκέτι θεωρεῖτέ με· 11 περὶ
to the Father of Me I am going, and no longer you see Me. concerning
1161 2920 3754 3588 758 3588 2889 5127 2919 2089
δὲ κρίσεως, ὅτι ὁ ἄρχων τοῦ κόσμου τούτου κέκριται. 12 ἔτι
And judgment, because the ruler of world this has been judged. Yet
4183 2192 3004 5213 235 3756 1410 941 737
πολλὰ ἔχω λέγειν ὑμῖν, ἀλλ' οὐ δύνασθε βαστάζειν ἄρτι.
many things I have to tell you, but not you are able to bear now.
3752 1161 2064 1565 3588 4151 3588 225 3594
13 ὅταν δὲ ἔλθῃ ἐκεῖνος, τὸ πνεῦμα τῆς ἀληθείας, ὁδηγήσει
when But comes that One, the Spirit of truth, He will guide
5209 1519 3956 3588 225 3756 1063 2980 575 1438
ὑμᾶς εἰς πᾶσαν τὴν ἀλήθειαν· οὐ γὰρ λαλήσει ἀφ' ἑαυτοῦ,
you into all the truth; not for He will speak from Himself,
235 3745 302 191 2980 2532 3588 2064 312
ἀλλ' ὅσα ἂν ἀκούσῃ λαλήσει, καὶ τὰ ἐρχόμενα ἀναγγελεῖ
but whatever He hears He will speak, and the coming things will announce
5213 1565 1691 1392 3754 1537 3588 1700 2983 2532
ὑμῖν. 14 ἐκεῖνος ἐμὲ δοξάσει, ὅτι ἐκ τοῦ ἐμοῦ λήψεται καὶ
to you. That One Me will glorify, because from Mine He will receive and
312 5213 3956 3745 2192 3588 3962 1699 2076 1223
ἀναγγελεῖ ὑμῖν. 15 πάντα ὅσα ἔχει ὁ πατὴρ ἐμά ἐστι· διὰ
will announce to you. All things, as many as has the Father Mine are; because
5124 2036 3754 1537 3588 1700 2983 2532 312 5213
τοῦτο εἶπον, ὅτι ἐκ τοῦ ἐμοῦ λήψεται, καὶ ἀναγγελεῖ ὑμῖν.
of this I said, From Mine He receives, and will announce to you.
3397 2532 3756 2334 3165 2532 3825 3397 2532 3700 3165
16 μικρὸν καὶ οὐ θεωρεῖτέ με, καὶ πάλιν μικρὸν καὶ ὄψεσθέ με,
A little and not you behold Me, and again a little and you will see Me,
3754 1473 5217 4314 3588 3962 2036 3767 1537 3588
ὅτι ἐγὼ ὑπάγω πρὸς τὸν πατέρα. 17 εἶπον οὖν ἐκ τῶν
because I go to the Father. said Therefore of the
3101 846 4314 240 5101 2076 5124 3739 3004 2254
μαθητῶν αὐτοῦ πρὸς ἀλλήλους, Τί ἐστι τοῦτο ὃ λέγει ἡμῖν,
disciples of Him to one another, What is this which He says to us;
3397 2532 3756 2334 3165 2532 3825 3397 2532 3700 3165
Μικρὸν καὶ οὐ θεωρεῖτέ με, καὶ πάλιν μικρὸν καὶ ὄψεσθέ με;
A little and not you behold Me, and again a little and you will see Me?

him that sent me; and none of you asketh me, Whither goest thou?
6 But because I have said these things unto you, sorrow hath filled your heart.
7 Nevertheless I tell you the truth; It is expedient for you that I go away: for if I go not away, the Comforter will not come unto you; but if I depart, I will send him unto you.
8 And when he is come, he will reprove the world of sin, and of righteousness, and of judgment:
9 Of sin, because they believe not on me;
10 Of righteousness, because I go to my Father, and ye see me no more;
11 Of judgment, because the prince of this world is judged.
12 I have yet many things to say unto you, but ye cannot bear them now.
13 Howbeit when he, the Spirit of truth, is come, he will guide you into all truth: for he shall not speak of himself; but whatsoever he shall hear, (that) shall he speak: and he will shew you things to come.
14 He shall glorify me: for he shall receive of mine, and shall shew (it) unto you.
15 All things that the Father hath are mine: therefore said I, that he shall take of mine, and shall shew (it) unto you.
16 A little while, and ye shall not see me: and again, a little while, and ye shall see me, because I go to the Father.
17 Then said (some) of his disciples among themselves, What is this that he saith unto us, A little while, and ye shall not see me: and again, a little while, and ye shall see me:

Literal Translation

Also, Because I go away to the Father?
18 Therefore they said, What is this that He says, The little? We do not know what He says.
19 Then Jesus knew that they desired to question Him. And (He) said to them, Do you seek answers with one another concerning this, because I said, A little (while), and you do not behold Me; and again a little and you will see Me?
20 Truly, truly, I say to you that you will weep and will lament, but the world will exult. And you will be grieved, but your grief will become into joy.
21 The woman has grief when she bears, because her hour came, but when she produces the child, she no longer remembers the distress, because of the joy that a man was generated into the world.
22 And you, then, truly have grief now; but I will see you again, and your heart will rejoice, and no one takes your joy from you.
23 And in that day you will ask Me nothing. Truly, truly, I say to you, Whatever you may ask the Father in My name, He will give to you.
24 Until now you asked nothing in My name; ask, and you will receive, so that your joy may be full.
25 I have spoken these things to you in allegories. An hour comes when I will no longer speak to you in allegories, but I will reveal the Father plainly to you.
26 In that day you will ask in My name, and I do not tell you that I will petition the Father

John 16:18

2532 3754 1473 5217 4314 3588 3962 3004 3767 5124
καί ὅτι Ἐγὼ ὑπάγω πρὸς τὸν πατέρα; 18 ἔλεγον οὖν, Τοῦτο
Also, Because I go to the Father? they said Therefore, this

5101 2076 3739 3004 3588 3397 3756 1492 5101 2980 1097 3767
τί ἐστιν ὃ λέγει, τὸ μικρόν; οὐκ οἴδαμεν τί λαλεῖ. 19 ἔγνω οὖν
What is that He says, The little? do not We know what He says. knew Then

3588 2424 3754 2309 846 2065 2532 2036 846 4012
ὁ Ἰησοῦς ὅτι ἤθελον αὐτὸν ἐρωτᾷν, καὶ εἶπεν αὐτοῖς, Περὶ
Jesus that they desired Him to question, and He said to them, About

5127 2212 3326 240 3754 2036 3397 2532 3756
τούτου ζητεῖτε μετ᾽ ἀλλήλων, ὅτι εἶπον, Μικρὸν καὶ οὐ
this do you seek with one another, because I said, A little and not

2334 3165 2532 3825 3397 2532 3700 3165 281 281
θεωρεῖτέ με, καὶ πάλιν μικρὸν καὶ ὄψεσθέ με; 20 ἀμὴν ἀμὴν
you behold Me, and again a little and you will see Me? Truly truly

3004 5213 3754 2799 2532 2354 5210 3588 1161 2889
λέγω ὑμῖν ὅτι κλαύσετε καὶ θρηνήσετε ὑμεῖς, ὁ δὲ κόσμος
I say to you that will weep and will lament you, the and world

5463 5210 1161 3076 235 3588 3077 5216 1519
χαρήσεται· ὑμεῖς δὲ λυπηθήσεσθε, ἀλλ᾽ ἡ λύπη ὑμῶν εἰς
will exult. you And will be grieved, but the grief of you into

5479 1096 3588 1135 3752 5088 3077 2192 3754 2064
χαρὰν γενήσεται. 21 ἡ γυνὴ ὅταν τίκτῃ λύπην ἔχει, ὅτι ἦλθεν
joy will become. The woman when she bears grief has, because came

3588 5610 846 3752 1161 1080 3588 3813 3765 3421
ἡ ὥρα αὐτῆς· ὅταν δὲ γεννήσῃ τὸ παιδίον, οὐκέτι μνημονεύει
the hour of her; when but she produces the child, no longer she remembers

3588 2347 1223 3588 5479 3754 1080 444 1519
τῆς θλίψεως, διὰ τὴν χαρὰν ὅτι ἐγεννήθη ἄνθρωπος εἰς
the distress, because of the joy that was generated a man into

3588 2889 2532 5210 3767 3077 3303 3568 2192 3825 1161
τὸν κόσμον. 22 καὶ ὑμεῖς οὖν λύπην μὲν νῦν ἔχετε· πάλιν δὲ
the world. And you therefore grief truly now have; again but

3700 5209 2532 5463 5216 3588 2588 2532 3588 5479
ὄψομαι ὑμᾶς, καὶ χαρήσεται ὑμῶν ἡ καρδία, καὶ τὴν χαρὰν
I will see you, and will rejoice of you the heart, and the joy

5216 3762 142 575 5216 2532 1722 1565 3588 2250 1691 3756
ὑμῶν οὐδεὶς αἴρει ἀφ᾽ ὑμῶν. 23 καὶ ἐν ἐκείνῃ τῇ ἡμέρᾳ ἐμὲ οὐκ
of you no one takes from you. And in that day Me not

2065 3762 281 281 3004 5213 3754 3745 302 154
ἐρωτήσετε οὐδέν. ἀμὴν ἀμὴν λέγω ὑμῖν ὅτι ὅσα ἄν αἰτή-
you will ask nothing. Truly, truly, I say to you that whatever you may

3588 3962 1722 3588 3686 3450 1325 5213 2193 737
σητε τὸν πατέρα ἐν τῷ ὀνόματί μου, δώσει ὑμῖν. 24 ἕως ἄρτι
ask the Father in the name of Me, He will give to you. Until now

3756 154 3762 1722 3588 3686 3450 154 2532 2983
οὐκ ἠτήσατε οὐδὲν ἐν τῷ ὀνόματί μου· αἰτεῖτε, καὶ λήψεσθε,
not you asked, nothing, in the name of Me; ask, and you will receive,

2443 3588 5479 5216 3588 4137
ἵνα ἡ χαρὰ ὑμῶν ᾖ πεπληρωμένη.
that the joy of you may be filled.

5023 1722 3942 2980 5213 2064 5610 3753
25. Ταῦτα ἐν παροιμίαις λελάληκα ὑμῖν· ἔρχεται ὥρα ὅτε
These things in allegories I have spoken to you. comes An hour when

3765 1722 3942 2980 5213 235 3954 4012 3588
οὐκέτι ἐν παροιμίαις λαλήσω ὑμῖν, ἀλλὰ παρρησίᾳ περὶ τοῦ
no longer in allegories I will speak to you, but plainly concerning the

3962 312 5213 1722 1565 3588 2250 1722 3588 3686 3450
πατρὸς ἀναγγελῶ ὑμῖν. 26 ἐν ἐκείνῃ τῇ ἡμέρᾳ ἐν τῷ ὀνόματί μου
Father I will announce to you. In that day in the name of Me

154 2532 3756 3004 5213 3754 1473 2065 3588 3962
αἰτήσεσθε· καὶ οὐ λέγω ὑμῖν ὅτι ἐγὼ ἐρωτήσω τὸν πατέρα
you will ask; and not I say to you that I will petition the Father

King James Version

and, Because I go to the Father?
18 They said therefore, What is this that he saith, A little while? we cannot tell what he saith.
19 Now Jesus knew that they were desirous to ask him, and said unto them, Do ye enquire among yourselves of that I said, A little while, and ye shall not see me: and again, a little while, and ye shall see me?
20 Verily, verily, I say unto you, That ye shall weep and lament, but the world shall rejoice: and ye shall be sorrowful, but your sorrow shall be turned into joy.
21 A woman when she is in travail hath sorrow, because her hour is come: but as soon as she is delivered of the child, she remembereth no more the anguish, for joy that a man is born into the world.
22 And ye now therefore have sorrow: but I will see you again, and your heart shall rejoice, and your joy no man taketh from you.
23 And in that day ye shall ask me nothing. Verily, verily, I say unto you, Whatsoever ye shall ask the Father in my name, he will give (it) you.
24 Hitherto have ye asked nothing in my name: ask, and ye shall receive, that your joy may be full.
25 These things have I spoken unto you in proverbs: but the time cometh, when I shall no more speak unto you in proverbs, but I shall shew you plainly of the Father.
26 At that day ye shall ask in my name: and I say not unto you, that I will pray the Father for you:

Literal Translation | **John 16:27** | *King James Version*

concerning you.
27 for the Father Himself loves you, because you have loved Me, and have believed that I came forth from God.

28 I came forth from the Father and have come into the world; I leave the world again and go to the Father.

29. His disciples say to Him, Behold, now You speak with clarity, and You say not one allegory.
30 Now we know that You know all things and have no need that anyone question You. By this we believe that You came out from God.
31 Jesus answered them, Do you believe now?
32 Behold! An hour is coming, and now has come, that you are scattered each one to (his) own things, and you will leave Me alone. Yet I am not alone, because the Father is with Me.
33 I have spoken these things to you that you may have peace in Me. You have distress in the world; but be encouraged, I have overcome the world.

4012 5216 846 1063 3588 3962 5368 5209 3754 5210 1691
περὶ ὑμῶν· 27 αὐτὸς γὰρ ὁ πατὴρ φιλεῖ ὑμᾶς, ὅτι ὑμεῖς ἐμὲ
concerning you; Himself for the Father loves you, because you Me

5368 2532 4100 3754 1473 3844 3588 2316
πεφιλήκατε, καὶ πεπιστεύκατε ὅτι ἐγὼ παρὰ τοῦ Θεοῦ
have loved, and have believed that I from God

1831 1831 3844 3588 3962 2532 2064 1519 3588
ἐξῆλθον. 28 ἐξῆλθον παρὰ τοῦ πατρός, καὶ ἐλήλυθα εἰς τὸν
came forth. I came forth from the Father, and have come into the

2889 3825 863 3588 2889 2532 4198 4314 3588
κόσμον· πάλιν ἀφίημι τὸν κόσμον, καὶ πορεύομαι πρὸς τὸν
world. Again I leave the world, and go to the

3962 3004 846 3588 3101 846 2396 3568 3954
πατέρα. 29 λέγουσιν αὐτῷ οἱ μαθηταὶ αὐτοῦ, Ἴδε, νῦν παρ-
Father. say to Him The disciples of Him, Behold! Now with

2980 2532 3942 3762 3004 3568 1492
ρησίᾳ λαλεῖς, καὶ παροιμίαν οὐδεμίαν λέγεις. 30 νῦν οἴδαμεν
clarity You speak, and allegory not one You say. Now we know

3754 1492 3956 2532 3756 5532 2192 2443 5100 4571 2065 1722
ὅτι οἶδας πάντα, καὶ οὐ χρείαν ἔχεις ἵνα τίς σε ἐρωτᾷ· ἐν
that You know all things, and no need have that anyone You question. By

5129 4100 3754 575 2316 1831 611 846 3588
τούτῳ πιστεύομεν ὅτι ἀπὸ Θεοῦ ἐξῆλθες. 31 ἀπεκρίθη αὐτοῖς ὁ
this we believe that from God You came forth. answered them

2424 737 4100 2400 2064 5610 2532 3568 2064
Ἰησοῦς, Ἄρτι πιστεύετε; 32 ἰδού, ἔρχεται ὥρα καὶ νῦν ἐλή-
Jesus, Now do you believe? Behold! is coming An hour and now has

2443 4650 1538 1519 3588 2398 2532 1691 3441
λυθεν, ἵνα σκορπισθῆτε ἕκαστος εἰς τὰ ἴδια, καὶ ἐμὲ μόνον
come, that you are scattered each one to the own things, and Me alone

863 2532 3756 1510 3441 3754 3588 3962 3326 1700 2076 5023
ἀφῆτε· καὶ οὐκ εἰμὶ μόνος, ὅτι ὁ πατὴρ μετ' ἐμοῦ ἐστι. 33 ταῦτα
you leave. Yet not I am alone, because the Father with Me is. These things

2980 5213 2443 1722 1698 1515 2192 1722 3588 2889
λελάληκα ὑμῖν. ἵνα ἐν ἐμοὶ εἰρήνην ἔχητε. ἐν τῷ κόσμῳ
I have spoken to you, that in Me peace you may have. In the world

2347 2192 235 2293 1473 3528 3588 2889
θλῖψιν ἕξετε· ἀλλὰ θαρσεῖτε, ἐγὼ νενίκηκα τὸν κόσμον.
distress you have, but be encouraged, I have overcome the world.

27 For the Father himself loveth you, because ye have loved me, and have believed that I came out from God.

28 I came forth from the Father, and am come into the world: again, I leave the world, and go to the Father.

29. His disciples said unto him, Lo, now speakest thou plainly, and speakest no proverb.
30 Now are we sure that thou knowest all things, and needest not that any man should ask thee: by this we believe that thou camest forth from God.
31 Jesus answered them, Do ye now believe?
32 Behold, the hour cometh, yea, is now come, that ye shall be scattered, every man to his own, and shall leave me alone: and yet I am not alone, because the Father is with me.
33 These things I have spoken unto you, that in me ye might have peace. In the world ye shall have tribulation: but be of good cheer; I have overcome the world.

John 17

1. Jesus spoke these things and lifted up His eyes to Heaven, and said, Father, the hour has come. Glorify Your Son, that Your Son may also glorify You,
2 Even as You gave to Him authority over all flesh, so that to all which You gave to Him, He may give to them everlasting life.
3 And this is everlasting life, that they may know You, the only true God, and Jesus Christ, whom You have sent.
4 I have glorified You on the earth,

5023 2980 3588 2424 2532 1869 3588 3788
1 Ταῦτα ἐλάλησεν ὁ Ἰησοῦς, καὶ ἐπῆρε τοὺς ὀφθαλμοὺς
These things spoke Jesus, and lifted up the eyes

846 1519 3588 3772 2532 2036 3962 2064 3588 5610
αὐτοῦ εἰς τὸν οὐρανόν, καὶ εἶπε, Πάτερ, ἐλήλυθεν ἡ ὥρα·
of Him into Heaven, and said, Father, has come the hour.

1392 4675 3588 5207 2443 2532 3588 5207 4675 1392 4571 2531
δόξασόν σου τὸν υἱόν, ἵνα καὶ ὁ υἱός σου δοξάσῃ σε· 2 καθὼς
Glorify of You the Son, that also the Son of You may glorify You. Even as

1325 846 1849 3956 4561 2443 3956 3739 1325
ἔδωκας αὐτῷ ἐξουσίαν πάσης σαρκός, ἵνα πᾶν ὃ δέδωκας
You gave Him authority of all flesh, that all which You have given

846 1325 846 2222 166 3778 1161 2076 3588 166
αὐτῷ, δώσῃ αὐτοῖς ζωὴν αἰώνιον. 3 αὕτη δέ ἐστιν ἡ αἰώνιος
Him He may give to them life everlasting. this And is everlasting

2222 2443 1097 4571 3588 3441 228 2316 2532 3739
ζωή, ἵνα γινώσκωσί σε τὸν μόνον ἀληθινὸν Θεόν, καὶ ὃν
life, that they may know You the only true God, and whom

649 2424 5547 1473 4571 1392 1909 3588 1093
ἀπέστειλας Ἰησοῦν Χριστόν. 4 ἐγώ σε ἐδόξασα ἐπὶ τῆς γῆς·
You sent Jesus Christ. I You glorified on the earth,

1. These words spake Jesus, and lifted up his eyes to heaven, and said, Father, the hour is come; glorify thy Son, that thy Son also may glorify thee:
2 As thou hast given him power over all flesh, that he should give eternal life to as many as thou hast given him.
3 And this is life eternal, that they might know thee the only true God, and Jesus Christ, whom thou hast sent.
4 I have glorified thee on the earth:

Literal Translation

perfecting the work that You gave to Me that I should do.
5 And now Father, glorify Me with Yourself, along with the glory which I had with You before the existence of the world.
6 I revealed Your name to the men whom You gave to Me out of the world. They were Yours, and You gave them to Me; and they have kept Your Word.

7 Now they have known that all things, whatever You gave to Me, are from You.
8 For the words which You gave to Me, I have given to them. And they received and truly knew that I came out from beside You, and they believed that You sent Me.
9 I petition concerning them; I do not petition concerning the world, but for those whom You gave to Me, for they are Yours.
10 And all My things are Yours, and Your things (are) Mine; and I have been glorified in them.
11 And no longer I am in the world, yet these are in the world; and I come to You. Holy Father, keep them in Your name, those whom You gave to Me, that (they) may be one as We (are).

12 While I was with them in the world, I was keeping them in Your name; I guarded those whom You gave to Me, and not one of them perished, but the son of perdition (perished), that the Scripture might be fulfilled.

13 And now I come to You, and I speak these things in the world, that they have My joy being fulfilled in them.

14 I have given them Your Word, and the world hated them because they are not of the

John 17:5

3588 2041 5048 3739 1325 3427 2443 4160 2532 3568
τὸ ἔργον ἐτελείωσα ὃ δέδωκάς μοι ἵνα ποιήσω. 5 καὶ νῦν
the work perfecting which You gave to Me that I should do. And now

1392 3165 4771 3962 3844 4572 3588 1391 3739 2192 4253
δόξασόν με σύ, πάτερ, παρὰ σεαυτῷ τῇ δόξῃ ᾗ εἶχον πρὸ
glorify Me You, Father, along with Yourself with the glory that I had before

3588 3588 2889 1511 3844 4671 5319 4675 3588 3686
τοῦ τὸν κόσμον εἶναι παρὰ σοί. 6 ἐφανέρωσά σου τὸ ὄνομα
the of the world existence along with You. I revealed of You the name

3588 444 3739 1325 3427 1537 3588 2889 4674 2258
τοῖς ἀνθρώποις οὓς δέδωκάς μοι ἐκ τοῦ κόσμου· σοὶ ἦσαν,
to the men whom You gave to Me out of the world. To You they were,

2532 1698 846 1325 2532 3588 3056 4675 5083
καὶ ἐμοὶ αὐτοὺς δέδωκας· καὶ τὸν λόγον σου τετηρήκασι.
and to Me them You gave; and the Word of You they have kept.

3568 1097 3754 3956 3745 1325 3427 3844 4675 2076
7 νῦν ἔγνωκαν ὅτι πάντα ὅσα δέδωκάς μοι, παρὰ σοῦ ἐστιν·
Now they have known that all things whatever You gave to Me, from You is;

3754 3588 4487 3739 1325 3427 1325 846 2532 846
8 ὅτι τὰ ῥήματα ἃ δέδωκάς μοι, δέδωκα αὐτοῖς· καὶ αὐτοὶ
because the words which You gave to Me, I have given to them, and they

2983 2532 1097 230 3754 3844 4675 1831 2532
ἔλαβον, καὶ ἔγνωσαν ἀληθῶς ὅτι παρὰ σοῦ ἐξῆλθον, καὶ
received, and knew truly that from beside You I came forth, and

4100 3754 4771 3165 649 1473 4012 846 2065
ἐπίστευσαν ὅτι σύ με ἀπέστειλας. 9 ἐγὼ περὶ αὐτῶν ἐρωτῶ·
they believed that You Me sent. I concerning them petition;

3756 4012 3588 2889 2065 235 4012 3739 1325 3427 3754
οὐ περὶ τοῦ κόσμου ἐρωτῶ, ἀλλὰ περὶ ὧν δέδωκάς μοι, ὅτι
not concerning the world I petition, but concerning whom You gave to Me, for

4671 1526 2532 3588 1699 3956 4674 2076 2532 3588 4674 1699 2532
σοί εἰσι· 10 καὶ τὰ ἐμὰ πάντα σά ἐστι, καὶ τὰ σὰ ἐμά· καὶ
to You they are. And things My all Yours are, and things Your Mine; and

1392 1722 846 2532 3765 1510 1722 3588 2889 2532
δεδόξασμαι ἐν αὐτοῖς. 11 καὶ οὐκέτι εἰμὶ ἐν τῷ κόσμῳ, καὶ
I have been glorified in them. And no longer I am in the world, and

3778 1722 3588 2889 1526 2532 1473 4314 4571 2064 3962
οὗτοι ἐν τῷ κόσμῳ εἰσί, καὶ ἐγὼ πρός σε ἔρχομαι. πάτερ
those in the world are, and I to You come. Father

40 5083 846 1722 3588 3686 4675 3739 1325 3427
ἅγιε, τήρησον αὐτοὺς ἐν τῷ ὀνόματί σου, οὓς δέδωκάς μοι,
Holy, keep them in the name of You, whom You gave to Me,

2443 5600 1520 2531 2249 3753 2252 3326 846 1722 3588 2889
ἵνα ὦσιν ἕν, καθὼς ἡμεῖς. 12 ὅτε ἤμην μετ' αὐτῶν ἐν τῷ κόσμῳ,
that they may be one, even as We. While I was with them in the world,

1473 5083 846 1722 3588 3686 4675 3739 1325 3427
ἐγὼ ἐτήρουν αὐτοὺς ἐν τῷ ὀνόματί σου· οὓς δέδωκάς μοι
I was keeping them in the name of You; whom You gave to Me

5442 2532 3762 1537 846 622 1487 3361 3588 5207 3588
ἐφύλαξα, καὶ οὐδεὶς ἐξ αὐτῶν ἀπώλετο, εἰ μὴ ὁ υἱὸς τῆς
I guarded, and not one of them perished, but the son

684 2443 3588 1124 4137 3568 1161 4314 4571 2064
ἀπωλείας, ἵνα ἡ γραφὴ πληρωθῇ. 13 νῦν δὲ πρὸς σε ἔρχομαι,
of perdition, that the Scripture might be fulfilled. now And to You I come,

2532 5023 2980 1722 3588 2889 2443 2192 3588 5479 3588
καὶ ταῦτα λαλῶ ἐν τῷ κόσμῳ, ἵνα ἔχωσι τὴν χαρὰν τὴν
and these things I speak in the world, that they have joy

1699 4137 1722 846 1473 1325 846 3588
ἐμὴν πεπληρωμένην ἐν αυτοῖς. 14 ἐγὼ δέδωκα αὐτοῖς τὸν
My having been fulfilled in them. I have given them the

3056 4675 2532 3588 2889 3404 846 3754 3756 1526 1537
λόγον σου, καὶ ὁ κόσμος ἐμίσησεν αὐτούς, ὅτι οὐκ εἰσὶν ἐκ
Word of You, and the world hated them, because not they are of

King James Version

I have finished the work which thou gavest me to do.
5 And now, O Father, glorify thou me with thine own self with the glory which I had with thee before the world was.
6 I have manifested thy name unto the men which thou gavest me out of the world: thine they were, and thou gavest them me; and they have kept thy word.

7 Now they have known that all things whatsoever thou hast given me are of thee.
8 For I have given unto them the words which thou gavest me; and they have received (them), and have known surely that I came out from thee, and they have believed that thou didst send me.
9 I pray for them: I pray not for the world, but for them which thou hast given me; for they are thine.
10 And all mine are thine, and thine are mine; and I am glorified in them.
11 And now I am no more in the world, but these are in the world, and I come to thee. Holy Father, keep through thine own name those whom thou hast given me, that they may be one, as we (are).
12 While I was with them in the world, I kept them in thy name: those that thou gavest me I have kept, and none of them is lost, but the son of perdition; that the scripture might be fulfilled.

13 And now come I to thee; and these things I speak in the world, that they might have my joy fulfilled in themselves.

14 I have given them thy word; and the world hath hated them, because they are not of the

Literal Translation

world, as I am not of the world.
15 I do not petition that You take them out of the world, but that You keep them from evil.

16 They are not of the world, even as I am not of the world.

17 Sanctify them in Your truth; Your Word is truth.
18 Even as You have sent Me into the world, I also have sent them into the world.
19 And I sanctify Myself for them, that they also may be sanctified in truth.

20 And I do not petition concerning these only, but also concerning those who will believe into Me through their word;
21 that all may be one, as You (are) in Me, Father, and I in You, that they also may be one in Us, that the world may believe that You sent Me.

22 And the glory which You have given Me, I have given to them, that they may be one, even as We are one:
23 I in them, and You in Me, that they may be perfected in one; and that the world may know that You sent Me and loved them, even as You loved Me.
24 Father, I desire that (those) whom You have given Me, that where I am, they may be with Me also, that they may behold My glory which You gave to Me, because You loved Me before (the) foundation of (the) world.
25 Righteous Father, indeed the world did not know You, but I knew You; and these knew that You sent Me.
26 And I made known to them Your name, and will make (it) known, that the love (with) which

John 17:15

3588 2889 2531 1473 3756 1510 1537 3588 2889 3756 2065
τοῦ κόσμου, καθὼς ἐγὼ οὐκ εἰμὶ ἐκ τοῦ κόσμου. 15 οὐκ ἐρωτῶ
the world, even as I not am of the world. Not I petition

2443 142 846 1537 3588 2889 235 2443 5083 846
ἵνα ἄρῃς αὐτοὺς ἐκ τοῦ κόσμου, ἀλλ' ἵνα τηρήσῃς αὐτοὺς
that You take them out of the world, but that You keep them

1537 3588 4190 1537 3588 2889 3756 1526 2531 1473 1537 3588
ἐκ τοῦ πονηροῦ. 16 ἐκ τοῦ κόσμου οὐκ εἰσὶ, καθὼς ἐγὼ ἐκ τοῦ
from evil. of the world Not they are, even as I of the

2889 3756 1510 37 846 1722 3588 225 4675 3588
κόσμου οὐκ εἰμί. 17 ἁγίασον αὐτοὺς ἐν τῇ ἀληθείᾳ σου· ὁ
world not am. Sanctify them in the truth of You;

3056 3588 4674 225 2076 2531 1691 649 1519 3588
λόγος ὁ σὸς ἀλήθειά ἐστι. 18 καθὼς ἐμὲ ἀπέστειλας εἰς τὸν
Word Your truth is. Even as Me You sent into the

2889 2504 649 846 1519 3588 2889 2532 5228
κόσμον, κἀγὼ ἀπέστειλα αὐτοὺς εἰς τὸν κόσμον. 19 καὶ ὑπὲρ
world, I also sent them into the world. And for

846 1473 37 1683 2443 2532 846 5600 37
αὐτῶν ἐγὼ ἁγιάζω ἐμαυτόν, ἵνα καὶ αὐτοὶ ὦσιν ἡγιασμένοι
them I sanctify Myself, that also they may be sanctified

1722 225 3756 4012 5130 1161 2065 3440 235 2532 4012
ἐν ἀληθείᾳ. 20 Οὐ περὶ τούτων δὲ ἐρωτῶ μόνον, ἀλλὰ καὶ περὶ
in truth. not concerning these And I petition only, but also concerning

3588 4100 1223 3588 3056 846 1519 1691 2443 3956
τῶν πιστευσόντων διὰ τοῦ λόγου αὐτῶν εἰς ἐμέ, 21 ἵνα πάντες
those who shall believe through the word of them into Me, that all

1520 5600 2531 4771 3962 1722 1698 2504 1722 4671 2443 2532 846
ἓν ὦσι· καθὼς σύ, πάτερ, ἐν ἐμοί, κἀγὼ ἐν σοί, ἵνα καὶ αὐτοὶ
one may be, even as You, Father, in Me, and I in You, that also they

1722 2254 1520 5600 2443 3588 2889 4100 3754 4771 3165 649
ἐν ἡμῖν ἓν ὦσιν· ἵνα ὁ κόσμος πιστεύσῃ ὅτι σύ με ἀπέστειλας.
in Us one may be; that the world may believe that You Me sent.

2532 1473 3588 1391 3739 1325 3427 1325 846 2443
22 καὶ ἐγὼ τὴν δόξαν ἣν δέδωκάς μοι, δέδωκα αὐτοῖς, ἵνα
And I the glory which You have given Me, I have given to them, that

5600 1520 2531 2249 1520 2070 1473 1722 846 2532 4771 1722 1698
ὦσιν ἕν, καθὼς ἡμεῖς ἕν ἐσμεν, 23 ἐγὼ ἐν αὐτοῖς, καὶ σὺ ἐν ἐμοί,
they may be one, even as We one are; I in them, and You in Me,

2443 5600 5048 1519 1520 2532 2443 1097 3588 2889 3754
ἵνα ὦσι τετελειωμένοι εἰς ἕν, καὶ ἵνα γινώσκῃ ὁ κόσμος ὅτι
that they may be perfected into one, and that may know the world that

4771 3165 649 2532 25 846 2531 1691 25
σύ με ἀπέστειλας, καὶ ἠγάπησας αὐτούς, καθὼς ἐμὲ ἠγάπη-
You Me sent, and loved them, even as Me You loved.

3962 3739 1325 3427 2309 2443 3699 1510 1473
σας. 24 πάτερ, οὓς δέδωκάς μοι, θέλω ἵνα ὅπου εἰμὶ ἐγώ,
Father, whom You have given Me, I desire that where am I,

2548 5600 3326 1700 2443 2334 3588 1391 3588 1699
κἀκεῖνοι ὦσι μετ' ἐμοῦ· ἵνα θεωρῶσι τὴν δόξαν τὴν ἐμὴν,
those also may be with Me, that they may behold the glory of Me,

3739 1325 3427 3754 25 3165 4253 2602 2889
ἣν ἔδωκάς μοι, ὅτι ἠγάπησάς με πρὸ καταβολῆς κόσμου.
which you gave to Me, because You loved Me before foundation of (the) world.

3962 1342 2532 3588 2889 4571 3756 1097 1473 1161 4571 1097
25 πάτερ δίκαιε, καὶ ὁ κόσμος σε οὐκ ἔγνω, ἐγὼ δέ σε ἔγνων,
Father Righteous, indeed the world You not knew, I but You knew,

2532 3778 1097 3754 4771 3165 649 2532 1107
καὶ οὗτοι ἔγνωσαν ὅτι σύ με ἀπέστειλας· 26 καὶ ἐγνώρισα
and these knew that You Me sent; and I made known

846 3588 3686 4675 2532 1107 2443 3588 26 3739
αὐτοῖς τὸ ὄνομά σου, καὶ γνωρίσω· ἵνα ἡ ἀγάπη, ἣν
to them the name of You, and will make known; that the love (with) which

King James Version

world, even as I am not of the world.
15 I pray not that thou shouldest take them out of the world, but that thou shouldest keep them from the evil.
16 They are not of the world, even as I am not of the world.

17 Sanctify them through thy truth: thy word is truth.
18 As thou hast sent me into the world, even so have I also sent them into the world.
19 And for their sakes I sanctify myself, that they also might be sanctified through the truth.

20 Neither pray I for these alone, but for them also which shall believe on me through their word;
21 That they all may be one; as thou, Father, (art) in me, and I in thee, that they also may be one in us: that the world may believe that thou hast sent me.

22 And the glory which thou gavest me I have given them; that they may be one, even as we are one:
23 I in them, and thou in me, that they may be made perfect in one; and that the world may know that thou hast sent me, and hast loved them, as thou hast loved me.
24 Father, I will that they also, whom thou hast given me, be with me where I am; that they may behold my glory, which thou hast given me: for thou lovedst me before the foundation of the world.
25 O righteous Father, the world hath not known thee: but I have known thee, and these have known that thou hast sent me.
26 And I have declared unto them thy name, and will declare (it): that the love wherewith

Literal Translation

You loved Me may be in them, and I in them.

John 18:1

25 3165 1722 846 5600 2504 1722 846
ἠγάπησάς με, ἐν αὐτοῖς ᾖ, κἀγὼ ἐν αὐτοῖς.
You love Me in them may be, and I in them.

King James Version

thou hast loved me may be in them, and I in them.

John 18

1. Having said these things, Jesus went out with His disciples across the torrent of Kidron, where there was a garden into which He and His disciples entered.
2 And Judas, the (one) betraying Him, also knew the place, because Jesus many times assembled there with His disciples.
3 Therefore receiving a cohort and under-officers from the chief priests and the Pharisees, Judas came there with torches and lamps and weapons.
4 Then knowing all the things coming upon Him, going forth Jesus said to them, Whom do you seek?
5 They answered Him, Jesus the Nazarene. Jesus said to them, I AM! And Judas, the (one) betraying Him, also stood with them.
6 Then when He said to them, I AM, they went away into the rear and fell to earth.
7 Then again He inquired, Whom do you seek? And they said, Jesus the Nazarene.
8 Jesus answered, I told you that I AM! Then if you seek Me, allow these to go,
9 that the Word might be fulfilled which He said, "(Of) those whom You gave to Me, I lost no one of them."
10 Then having a sword, Simon Peter drew it and struck the slave of the high priest and cut off his right ear. And the slave's name was

John 18

5023 2036 3588 2424 1831 4862 3588 3101 846
1 Ταῦτα εἰπὼν ὁ Ἰησοῦς ἐξῆλθε σὺν τοῖς μαθηταῖς αὐτοῦ
These things having said, Jesus went out with the disciples of Him

4008 3588 5493 3588 2748 3699 2258 2779 1519 3739
πέραν τοῦ χειμάρρου τῶν Κέδρων, ὅπου ἦν κῆπος, εἰς ὃν
across the torrent of Kidron, where was a garden, into which

1525 846 2532 3588 3101 846 1492 1161 2532 2455 3588
εἰσῆλθεν αὐτὸς καὶ οἱ μαθηταὶ αὐτοῦ. 2 ᾔδει δὲ καὶ Ἰούδας, ὁ
entered He and the disciples of Him. knew And also Judas, he

3860 846 3588 5117 3754 4178 4863 3588
παραδιδοὺς αὐτόν, τὸν τόπον· ὅτι πολλάκις συνήχθη ὁ
betraying Him, the place; because many times assembled

2424 1563 3326 3588 3101 846 3588 3767 2455 2983
Ἰησοῦς ἐκεῖ μετὰ τῶν μαθητῶν αὐτοῦ. 3 ὁ οὖν Ἰούδας, λαβὼν
Jesus there with the disciples of Him. Therefore Judas, receiving

3588 4686 2532 1537 3588 749 2532 5330 5257
τὴν σπεῖραν, καὶ ἐκ τῶν ἀρχιερέων καὶ Φαρισαίων ὑπηρέτας,
the cohort, and from the chief priests and Pharisees under-officers,

2064 1563 3326 5322 2532 2985 2532 3696 2424
ἔρχεται ἐκεῖ μετὰ φανῶν καὶ λαμπάδων καὶ ὅπλων. 4 Ἰησοῦς
comes there with torches and lamps and weapons. Jesus

3767 1492 3956 3588 2064 1909 846 1831 2036
οὖν, εἰδὼς πάντα τὰ ἐρχόμενα ἐπ' αὐτὸν, ἐξελθὼν εἶπεν
Then, knowing all the things coming on Him, going forth said

846 5101 2212 611 846 2424 3588
αὐτοῖς, Τίνα ζητεῖτε; 5 ἀπεκρίθησαν αὐτῷ, Ἰησοῦν τὸν
to them, Whom do you seek? They answered Him, Jesus the

3480 3004 846 3588 2424 1473 1510 2476 1161
Ναζωραῖον. λέγει αὐτοῖς ὁ Ἰησοῦς, Ἐγώ εἰμι. εἱστήκει δὲ
Nazarene. says to them Jesus, I AM! stood And

2532 2455 3588 3860 846 3326 846 5613 3767 2036
καὶ Ἰούδας ὁ παραδιδοὺς αὐτὸν μετ' αὐτῶν. 6 ὡς οὖν εἶπεν
also Judas the (one) betraying Him with them. as Then He said to

846 3754 1473 1510 565 1519 3588 3694 2532 4098
αὐτοῖς ὅτι Ἐγώ εἰμι, ἀπῆλθον εἰς τὰ ὀπίσω, καὶ ἔπεσον
them, I AM! they went away into the rear, and fell

5476 3825 3767 846 1905 5101 2212 3588 1161
χαμαί. 7 πάλιν οὖν αὐτοὺς ἐπηρώτησε, Τίνα ζητεῖτε; οἱ δὲ
to earth. Again, then, He inquired, Whom do you seek? they And

2036 2424 3588 3480 611 3588 2424 2036
εἶπον, Ἰησοῦν τὸν Ναζωραῖον. 8 ἀπεκρίθη ὁ Ἰησοῦς, Εἶπον
said, Jesus the Nazarene. answered Jesus, I told

5213 3754 1473 1510 1487 3767 1691 2212 863 5128 5217
ὑμῖν ὅτι ἐγώ εἰμι· εἰ οὖν ἐμὲ ζητεῖτε, ἄφετε τούτους ὑπάγειν·
you that I AM! If then Me you seek, allow these to go;

2443 4137 3588 3056 3739 2036 3754 3739 1325 3427 3756
9 ἵνα πληρωθῇ ὁ λόγος ὃν εἶπεν ὅτι Οὓς δέδωκάς μοι, οὐκ
that might be fulfilled the Word which said, Whom You gave to Me, not

622 1537 846 3762 4613 3767 4074 2192 3162
ἀπώλεσα ἐξ αὐτῶν οὐδένα. 10 Σίμων οὖν Πέτρος ἔχων μάχαιραν
I lost of them, no one. Simon Then Peter having a sword,

1670 846 2532 3817 3588 3588 749 1401 2532
εἵλκυσεν αὐτήν, καὶ ἔπαισε τὸν τοῦ ἀρχιερέως δοῦλον, καὶ
drew it, and struck the of the high priest slave, and

609 846 3588 5621 3588 1188 2258 1161 3686 3588 1401
ἀπέκοψεν αὐτοῦ τὸ ὠτίον τὸ δεξιόν. ἦν δὲ ὄνομα τῷ δούλῳ
cut off of him the ear right. was And a name to the slave,

John 18

1. When Jesus had spoken these words, he went forth with his disciples over the brook Cedron, where was a garden, into the which he entered, and his disciples.
2 And Judas also, which betrayed him, knew the place: for Jesus ofttimes resorted thither with his disciples.
3 Judas then, having received a band (of men) and officers from the chief priests and Pharisees, cometh thither with lanterns and torches and weapons.
4 Jesus therefore, knowing all things that should come upon him, went forth, and said unto them, Whom seek ye?
5 They answered him, Jesus of Nazareth. Jesus saith unto them, I am (he). And Judas also, which betrayed him, stood with them.
6 As soon then as he had said unto them, I am (he), they went backward, and fell to the ground.
7 Then asked he them again, Whom seek ye? And they said, Jesus of Nazareth.
8 Jesus answered, I have told you that I am (he): if therefore ye seek me, let these go their way:
9 That the saying might be fulfilled, which he spake, Of them which thou gavest me have I lost none.
10 Then Simon Peter having a sword drew it, and smote the high priest's servant, and cut off his right ear. The servant's name

Literal Translation **John 18:11** ***King James Version***

Malchus.
11 Then Jesus said to Peter, Put your sword into the sheath: the cup which the Father has given Me, shall I not at all drink it?

3124 2036 3767 3588 2424 3588 4074 906 3588 3162
Μάλχος. 11 εἶπεν οὖν ὁ Ἰησοῦς τῷ Πέτρῳ, Βάλε τὴν μάχαιράν
Malchus. said Then Jesus to Peter, Put the sword
4675 1519 3588 2336 3588 4221 3739 1325 3427 3588 3962 3756 3361
σου εἰς τὴν θήκην· τὸ ποτήριον ὃ δέδωκέ μοι ὁ πατήρ, οὐ μὴ
of you into the sheath; the cup which has given Me the Father, not at all
4095 846
πίω αὐτό;
shall I drink it?

was Malchus.
11 Then said Jesus unto Peter, Put up thy sword into the sheath: the cup which my Father hath given me, shall I not drink it?

12 Then the cohort and the chiliarch and the under-officers of the Jews together, seized Jesus, and bound Him.
13 And they led Him away first to Annas, for he was (the) father-in-law of Caiaphas, who was high priest of that year.
14 And Caiaphas was the (one) having counseled the Jews that it was profitable (for) one man to perish on behalf of the people.

3588 3767 4686 2532 3588 5506 2532 3588 5257 3588 2453
12 Ἡ οὖν σπεῖρα καὶ ὁ χιλίαρχος καὶ οἱ ὑπηρέται τῶν Ἰου-
the Then cohort and the chiliarch and the under-officers of the
4815 3588 2424 2532 1210 846 2532 520
δαίων συνέλαβον τὸν Ἰησοῦν, καὶ ἔδησαν αὐτόν, 13 καὶ ἀπή-
Jews together seized Jesus, and bound Him, and led
846 4314 452 4412 2258 1063 3995 3588
γαγον αὐτὸν πρὸς Ἄνναν πρῶτον· ἦν γὰρ πενθερὸς τοῦ
away Him to Annas first; he was for father-in-law
2533 3739 2258 749 3588 1763 1565 2258 1161
Καϊάφα, ὃς ἦν ἀρχιερεὺς τοῦ ἐνιαυτοῦ ἐκείνου. 14 ἦν δὲ
of Caiaphas, who was high priest of year that. was And
2533 3588 4823 3588 2453 3754 4851 1520
Καϊάφας ὁ συμβουλεύσας τοῖς Ἰουδαίοις, ὅτι συμφέρει ἕνα
Caiaphas the (one) having counseled the Jews that it is profitable for one
444 622 5228 3588 2992
ἄνθρωπον ἀπολέσθαι ὑπὲρ τοῦ λαοῦ.
man to perish on behalf of the people.

12 Then the band and the captain and officers of the Jews took Jesus, and bound him,
13 And led him away to Annas first; for he was father in law to Caiaphas, which was the high priest that same year.
14 Now Caiaphas was he, which gave counsel to the Jews, that it was expedient that one man should die for the people.

15. And Simon Peter and another disciple followed Jesus, and that disciple was known to the high priest and went in with Jesus into the courtyard of the high priest,
16 but Peter stood at the entrance outside. The other disciple who was known to the high priest went out and spoke to the portress, and brought Peter in.
17 Then the slave woman, the portress, said to Peter, Are you not also of the disciples of this man? That one said, I am not.
18 Now the slaves and the under-officers were standing and warming (themselves), having made a fire of coals, for it was cold; and Peter was with them, standing and warming (himself).

190 1161 3588 2424 4613 4074 2532 243
15. Ἠκολούθει δὲ τῷ Ἰησοῦ Σίμων Πέτρος, καὶ ἄλλος
followed And Jesus Simon Peter, and another
3101 3588 1161 3101 1565 2258 1110 3588 749 2532
μαθητής. ὁ δὲ μαθητὴς ἐκεῖνος ἦν γνωστὸς τῷ ἀρχιερεῖ, καὶ
disciple. And disciple that was known to the high priest, and
4897 3588 2424 1519 3588 833 3588 749 3588 1161
συνεισῆλθε τῷ Ἰησοῦ εἰς τὴν αὐλὴν τοῦ ἀρχιερέως· 16 ὁ δὲ
went in with Jesus into the courtyard of the high priest; but
4074 2476 4314 3588 2374 1854 1831 3767 3588 3101 3588
Πέτρος εἱστήκει πρὸς τῇ θύρᾳ ἔξω. ἐξῆλθεν οὖν ὁ μαθητὴς ὁ
Peter stood at the entrance outside. went out Then the disciple the
243 3739 2258 1110 3588 749 2532 2036 3588 2377 2532
ἄλλος ὃς ἦν γνωστὸς τῷ ἀρχιερεῖ, καὶ εἶπε τῇ θυρωρῷ, καὶ
other who was known to the high priest, and spoke to the portress, and
1521 3588 4074 3004 3767 3588 3814 3588 2377 3588
εἰσήγαγε τὸν Πέτρον. 17 λέγει οὖν ἡ παιδίσκη ἡ θυρωρός τῷ
brought in Peter. says Then the slave woman, the portress,
4070 3361 2532 4771 1537 3588 3101 1488 3588 444 5127
Πέτρῳ, Μὴ καὶ σὺ ἐκ τῶν μαθητῶν εἶ τοῦ ἀνθρώπου τούτου;
to Peter, Not also you of the disciples are of man this?
3004 1565 3756 1510 2476 1161 3588 1401 2532 3588
λέγει ἐκεῖνος, Οὐκ εἰμί. 18 εἱστήκεισαν δὲ οἱ δοῦλοι καὶ οἱ
says That one, Not I am. were standing And the slaves and the
5257 439 4160 3754 5592 2258 2532
ὑπηρέται ἀνθρακιὰν πεποιηκότες, ὅτι ψῦχος ἦν, καὶ
under-officers, a fire of coals having made, because cold it was, and
2328 2258 1161 3326 846 3588 4074 2476 2532
ἐθερμαίνοντο· ἦν δὲ μετ᾽ αὐτῶν ὁ Πέτρος ἑστὼς καὶ
were warming. was And with them Peter, standing and
2328
θερμαινόμενος.
warming (himself).

15. And Simon Peter followed Jesus, and (so did) another disciple: that disciple was known unto the high priest, and went in with Jesus into the palace of the high priest.
16 But Peter stood at the door without. Then went out that other disciple, which was known unto the high priest, and spake unto her that kept the door, and brought in Peter.
17 Then saith the damsel that kept the door unto Peter, Art not thou also (one) of this man's disciples? He saith, I am not.
18 And the servants and officers stood there, who had made a fire of coals; for it was cold: and they warmed themselves: and Peter stood with them, and warmed himself.

19. Then the high priest questioned Jesus about His disciples

3588 3767 749 2065 3588 2424 4012 3588 3101
19 Ὁ οὖν ἀρχιερεὺς ἠρώτησε τὸν Ἰησοῦν περὶ τῶν μαθητῶν
the Then high priest questioned Jesus concerning the disciples

19. The high priest then asked Jesus of his disciples,

Literal Translation

and about His doctrine.
20 Jesus answered him, I publicly spoke to the world; I always taught in the synagogue and in the temple where the Jews always come together, and I spoke nothing in secret.

21 Why do you question Me? Question those hearing what I spoke to them. Behold! These know what I said!

22 But (on) His saying these things, one of the under-officers standing by gave Jesus a slap, saying, Do you answer the high priest this way?
23 Jesus answered him, If I spoke evilly, bear witness concerning the evil; but if well, why do you beat Me?

24 Then having bound (Him), Annas sent Him to Caiaphas the high priest.

25. And Simon Peter was standing and warming (himself). Then they said to him, Are you not also of His disciples? That one denied and said, I am not.
26 One of the slaves of the high priest, being a relative (of the one) whose ear Peter cut off, said, Did I not see you in the garden with Him?

27 Then again Peter denied, and at once a cock crowed.

28. Then they led Jesus from Caiaphas into the praetorium, and it was early. And they did not enter into the praetorium that they not be defiled, but that they might eat the Passover.
29 Then Pilate coming out to them, and said, What accusation

John 18:20

846 2532 4012 3588 1322 846 611 846 3588
αὐτοῦ, καὶ περὶ τῆς διδαχῆς αὐτοῦ. 20 ἀπεκρίθη αὐτῷ ὁ
of Him, and concerning the doctrine of Him. answered him

2424 1473 3954 2980 3588 2889 1473 3842
Ἰησοῦς, Ἐγὼ παρρησίᾳ ἐλάλησα τῷ κόσμῳ· ἐγὼ πάντοτε
Jesus, I publicly spoke to the world; I always

1321 1722 3588 4864 2532 1722 3588 2411 3699 3842 3588
ἐδίδαξα ἐν τῇ συναγωγῇ καὶ ἐν τῷ ἱερῷ, ὅπου πάντοτε οἱ
taught in the synagogue and in the temple, where always the

2453 4905 2532 1722 2927 2980 3762 5101 3165
Ἰουδαῖοι συνέρχονται, καὶ ἐν κρυπτῷ ἐλάλησα οὐδέν. 21 τί με
Jews come together, and in secret I spoke nothing. Why Me

1905 1905 3588 191 5101 2980 846
ἐπερωτᾷς; ἐπερώτησον τοὺς ἀκηκοότας, τί ἐλάλησα αὐτοῖς·
do you question? Question those having heard what I spoke to them.

2396 3778 1492 3739 2036 1473 5023 1161 846 2036
ἴδε, οὗτοι οἴδασιν ἃ εἶπον ἐγώ. 22 ταῦτα δὲ αὐτοῦ εἰπόντος,
Behold! These know what said I. these things But (on His) saying,

1520 3588 5257 3936 1325 4475 3588 2424
εἷς τῶν ὑπηρετῶν παρεστηκὼς ἔδωκε ῥάπισμα τῷ Ἰησοῦ,
one of the under-officers standing by gave a slap to Jesus,

2036 3779 611 3588 749 611 846 3588
εἰπών, Οὕτως ἀποκρίνῃ τῷ ἀρχιερεῖ; 23 ἀπεκρίθη αὐτῷ ὁ
saying, this way answer you the high priest? answered to him

2424 1487 2560 2980 3140 4012 3588 2556
Ἰησοῦς, Εἰ κακῶς ἐλάλησα, μαρτύρησον περὶ τοῦ κακοῦ·
Jesus, If evilly I spoke, bear witness concerning the evil;

1487 1161 2573 5101 3165 1194 649 3767 846 3588 452
εἰ δὲ καλῶς, τί με δέρεις; 24 ἀπέστειλεν οὖν αὐτὸν ὁ Ἄννας
if but well, why Me do you beat? sent Then Him Annas

1210 4314 2533 3588 749
δεδεμένον πρὸς Καϊάφαν τὸν ἀρχιερέα.
having bound to Caiaphas the high priest.

2258 1161 4613 4074 2476 2532 2328 2036 3767
25 Ἦν δὲ Σίμων Πέτρος ἑστὼς καὶ θερμαινόμενος· εἶπον οὖν
was And Simon Peter standing and warming himself. they said Then

846 3361 2532 4771 1537 3588 3101 846 1488 720
αὐτῷ, Μὴ καὶ σὺ ἐκ τῶν μαθητῶν αὐτοῦ εἶ; ἠρνήσατο
to him, Not also You of the disciples of Him are? denied

1565 2532 2036 3756 1510 3004 1520 1537 3588 1401 3588
ἐκεῖνος, καὶ εἶπεν, Οὐκ εἰμί. 26 λέγει εἷς ἐκ τῶν δούλων τοῦ
That one, and said, not I am. says One of the slaves of the

749 4773 5607 3739 609 4074 3588 5621
ἀρχιερέως, συγγενὴς ὢν οὗ ἀπέκοψε Πέτρος τὸ ὠτίον,
high priest, a relative being of whom cut off Peter the ear,

3756 1473 4571 1492 1722 3588 2779 3326 846 3825 3767
Οὐκ ἐγώ σε εἶδον ἐν τῷ κήπῳ μετ' αὐτοῦ; 27 πάλιν οὖν
Not I you did see in the garden with him? again Then

720 3588 4074 2532 2112 220 5455
ἠρνήσατο ὁ Πέτρος, καὶ εὐθέως ἀλέκτωρ ἐφώνησεν.
denied Peter. And at once a cock sounded.

71 3767 3588 2424 575 3588 2533 1519 3588 4232
28. Ἄγουσιν οὖν τὸν Ἰησοῦν ἀπὸ τοῦ Καϊάφα εἰς τὸ πραιτώ-
they lead Then Jesus from Caiaphas into the praetorium.

2258 1161 4405 2532 846 3756 1525 1519 3588 4232
ριον· ἦν δὲ πρωΐα, καὶ αὐτοὶ οὐκ εἰσῆλθον εἰς τὸ πραιτώ-
it was And early; and they not did enter into the praetorium,

2443 3361 3392 235 2443 5315 3588 3957 1831
ριον, ἵνα μὴ μιανθῶσιν, ἀλλ' ἵνα φάγωσι τὸ πάσχα. 29 ἐξῆλθεν
that not they be defiled, but that they may eat the Passover. coming out

3767 3588 4091 4314 846 2532 2036 5101 2724
οὖν ὁ Πιλάτος πρὸς αὐτούς, καὶ εἶπε, Τίνα κατηγορίαν
Then Pilate to them, and said, What accusation

King James Version

and of his doctrine.
20 Jesus answered him, I spake openly to the world; I ever taught in the synagogue, and in the temple, whither the Jews always resort; and in secret have I said nothing.

21 Why askest thou me? ask them which heard me, what I have said unto them: behold, they know what I said.

22 And when he had thus spoken, one of the officers which stood by struck Jesus with the palm of his hand, saying, Answerest thou the high priest so?
23 Jesus answered him, If I have spoken evil, bear witness of the evil: but if well, why smitest thou me?

24 Now Annas had sent him bound unto Caiaphas the high priest.

25. And Simon Peter stood and warmed himself. They said therefore unto him, Art not thou also (one) of his disciples? He denied (it), and said, I am not.
26 One of the servants of the high priest, being (his) kinsman whose ear Peter cut off, saith, Did not I see thee in the garden with him?

27 Peter then denied again: and immediately the cock crew.

28. Then led they Jesus from Caiaphas unto the hall of judgment: and it was early; and they themselves went not into the judgment hall, lest they should be defiled; but that they might eat the passover.
29 Pilate then went out unto them, and said, What accusation

John 18:30

Literal Translation

do you bring against this man?
30 They answered and said to him, If this one were not an evildoer, then we would not have delivered him to you.
31 Then Pilate said to them, You take him and judge him according to your own Law. Then the Jews said to him, It is not lawful for us to putto death, no one;
32(that the word of Jesus which He said might be fulfilled, signifying by what kind (of) death He was about to die.

33 Then Pilate again went into the praetorium and called Jesus, and said to Him, Are you the king of the Jews?

34 Jesus answered him, Do you say this from yourself, or did others tell you about Me?
35 Pilate answered, Am I a Jew? Your nation, even the chief priests, delivered you up to me! What did you do?

36 Jesus answered, My kingdom is not of this world. If My kingdom were of this world, My servants would have fought that I might not be delivered up to the Jews. But now My kingdom is not from here.

37 Then Pilate said to Him, Really not a king, are you? Jesus answered, You say that I am a king. For this (purpose) I have been born, and for this I have come into the world, that I might witness to the Truth. Everyone being of the Truth hears My voice.

38 Pilate said to Him,

5342 2596 3588 444 5127 611 2532 2036
φέρετε κατὰ τοῦ ἀνθρώπου τούτου; 30 ἀπεκρίθησαν καὶ εἶπον
bring you against man this? They answered and said

846 1487 3361 2258 3778 2555 3756 302 4671 3860
αὐτῷ, Εἰ μὴ ἦν οὗτος κακοποιός, οὐκ ἂν σοι παρεδώκαμεν
to him, If not was this one an evildoer, not would to you we had delivered

846 2036 3767 846 3588 4091 2983 846 5210 2532
αὐτόν. 31 εἶπεν οὖν αὐτοῖς ὁ Πιλᾶτος, Λάβετε αὐτὸν ὑμεῖς, καὶ
him. said Then to them Pilate, take him You, and

2596 3588 3551 5216 2919 846 2036 3767 846 3588
κατὰ τὸν νόμον ὑμῶν κρίνατε αὐτόν. εἶπον οὖν αὐτῷ οἱ
according to the law of you judge him. said Then to him the

2453 2254 3756 1832 615 3762 2443 3588 3056
Ἰουδαῖοι, Ἡμῖν οὐκ ἔξεστιν ἀποκτεῖναι οὐδένα· 32 ἵνα ὁ λόγος
Jews, for us Not it is lawful to put to death no one that the word

3588 2424 4137 3739 2036 4591 4169 2288
τοῦ Ἰησοῦ πληρωθῇ, ὃν εἶπε, σημαίνων ποίῳ θανάτῳ
of Jesus might be fulfilled, which He said, signifying by what kind (of) death

3195 599
ἤμελλεν ἀποθνήσκειν.
He was about to die.

1525 3767 1519 3588 4232 3825 3588 4091 2532
33 Εἰσῆλθεν οὖν εἰς τὸ πραιτώριον πάλιν ὁ Πιλᾶτος, καὶ
went Then into the praetorium again Pilate, and

5455 3588 2424 2532 2036 846 4771/1488 3588 935 3588
ἐφώνησε τὸν Ἰησοῦν, καὶ εἶπεν αὐτῷ, Σὺ εἶ ὁ βασιλεὺς τῶν
called Jesus, and said to Him, you Are the king of the

2453 611 846 3588 2424 575 1438 4771 5124
Ἰουδαίων; 34 ἀπεκρίθη αὐτῷ ὁ Ἰησοῦς, Ἀφ' ἑαυτοῦ σὺ τοῦτο
Jews? answered him Jesus, From yourself you this

3004 2228 243 4671 2036 4012 1700 611 3588 4091
λέγεις ἢ ἄλλοι σοι εἶπον περὶ ἐμοῦ; 35 ἀπεκρίθη ὁ Πιλᾶτος,
say, or others you said about Me? answered Pilate,

3385 1473 2453 1510 3588 1484 3588 4674 2532 3588 749
Μήτι ἐγὼ Ἰουδαῖός εἰμι; τὸ ἔθνος τὸ σὸν καὶ οἱ ἀρχιερεῖς
Not I a Jew am? The nation of you and the chief priests

3860 4571 1698 5101 4160 611 3588 2424 3588
παρέδωκάν σε ἐμοί· τί ἐποίησας; 36 ἀπεκρίθη ὁ Ἰησοῦς, Ἡ
delivered up you to me; what did you do? answered Jesus, The

932 3588 1699 3756 2076 1537 3588 2889 5127 1487 1537 3588
βασιλεία ἡ ἐμὴ οὐκ ἔστιν ἐκ τοῦ κόσμου τούτου· εἰ ἐκ τοῦ
kingdom of Me not is of world this. If of

2889 5127 2258 3588 932 3588 1699 3588 5257 302 3588 1698
κόσμου τούτου ἦν ἡ βασιλεία ἡ ἐμή, οἱ ὑπηρέται ἂν οἱ ἐμοὶ
world this was the kingdom of Me, the servants would they of Me

75 2443 3361 3860 3588 2453 3568 1161 3588
ἠγωνίζοντο, ἵνα μὴ παραδοθῶ τοῖς Ἰουδαίοις· νῦν δὲ ἡ
have fought, that not I should be delivered to the Jews. now But the

932 3588 1699 3756 2076 1782 2036 3767 846 3588
βασιλεία ἡ ἐμὴ οὐκ ἔστιν ἐντεῦθεν. 37 εἶπεν οὖν αὐτῷ ὁ
kingdom of Me not is from here. said Then to Him

4091 3766 935 1488 4771 611 3588 2424 4771 3004
Πιλᾶτος, Οὐκοῦν βασιλεὺς εἶ σύ; ἀπεκρίθη ὁ Ἰησοῦς, Σὺ λέγεις
Pilate, Really not a king are you? answered Jesus, You say

3754 935 1510 1473 1473 1519 5124 1080 2532 1519 5124
ὅτι βασιλεύς εἰμι ἐγώ. ἐγὼ εἰς τοῦτο γεγέννημαι, καὶ εἰς τοῦτο
that a king am I. I For this have been born, and for this

2064 1519 3588 2889 2443 3140 3588 225 3956 3588
ἐλήλυθα εἰς τὸν κόσμον, ἵνα μαρτυρήσω τῇ ἀληθείᾳ. πᾶς ὁ
I have come into the world, that I might witness to the truth; everyone

5607 1537 3588 225 191 3450 3588 5456 3004 846 3588
ὢν ἐκ τῆς ἀληθείας ἀκούει μου τῆς φωνῆς. 38 λέγει αὐτῷ ὁ
being of the truth hears of Me the voice. says to Him

King James Version

bring ye against this man?
30 They answered and said unto him, If he were not a malefactor, we would not have delivered him up unto thee.
31 Then said Pilate unto them, Take ye him, and judge him according to your law. The Jews therefore said unto him, It is not lawful for us to put any man to death:
32 That the saying of Jesus might be fulfilled, which he spake, signifying what death he should die.

33 Then Pilate entered into the judgment hall again, and called Jesus, and said unto him, Art thou the King of the Jews?

34 Jesus answered him, Sayest thou this thing of thyself, or did others tell it thee of me?
35 Pilate answered, Am I a Jew? Thine own nation and the chief priests have delivered thee unto me: what hast thou done?
36 Jesus answered, My kingdom is not of this world: if my kingdom were of this world, then would my servants fight, that I should not be delivered to the Jews: but now is my kingdom not from hence.

37 Pilate therefore said unto him, Art thou a king then? Jesus answered, Thou sayest that I am a king. To this end was I born, and for this cause came I into the world, that I should bear witness unto the truth. Every one that is of the truth heareth my voice.

38 Pilate saith unto him,

Literal Translation | **John 18:39** | **King James Version**

What is truth? And having said this, he again went out to the Jews and said to them, I do not find one crime in him!

39 But there is a common custom to you that I should release one (prisoner) to you at the Passover. Then you decide: should I release the king of the Jews to you?

40 Then all cried out again, saying, Not this one, but Barabbas! But Barabbas was a plunderer.

4091 5101 2076 225
Πιλάτος, Τί ἐστιν ἀλήθεια;
Pilate, What is truth?

2532 5124 2036 3825 1831 4314 3588 2453 2532
Καὶ τοῦτο εἰπών, πάλιν ἐξῆλθε πρὸς τοὺς Ἰουδαίους, καὶ
And this having said, again he went out to the Jews, and

3004 846 1473 3762 156 2147 1722 846 2076
λέγει αὐτοῖς, Ἐγὼ οὐδεμίαν αἰτίαν εὑρίσκω ἐν αὐτῷ. 39 ἔστι
said to them, I not one crime find in him. is

1161 4914 5213 2443 1520 5213 630 1722 3588 3957
δὲ συνήθεια ὑμῖν, ἵνα ἕνα ὑμῖν ἀπολύσω ἐν τῷ πάσχα·
But a custom to you, that one to you I release at the Passover;

1014 3767 5213 630 3588 935 3588 2453
βούλεσθε οὖν ὑμῖν ἀπολύσω τὸν βασιλέα τῶν Ἰουδαίων;
you decide then to you should I release the king of the Jews?

2905 3767 3825 3956 3004 3361 5126 235
40 ἐκραύγασαν οὖν πάλιν πάντες, λέγοντες, Μὴ τοῦτον, ἀλλὰ
cried out Then again all, saying, Not this one, but

3588 912 2258 1161 3588 912 3027
τὸν Βαραββᾶν· ἦν δὲ ὁ Βαραββᾶς λῃστής.
Barabbas.; was but Barabbas a plunderer.

What is truth? And when he had said this, he went out again unto the Jews, and saith unto them, I find in him no fault (at all).

39 But ye have a custom, that I should release unto you one at the passover: will ye therefore that I release unto you the King of the Jews?

40 Then cried they all again, saying, Not this man, but Barabbas. Now Barabbas was a robber.

John 19

John 19

1. Then, therefore, Pilate took Jesus and flogged (Him).

2 And having plaited a wreath out of thorns, the soldiers put (it) on His head. And they threw a purple garment around Him,

3 and said, Hail, king of the Jews! And they gave Him slaps with the palm.
4 Then Pilate went outside again and said to them, Behold, I bring Him out to you that you may know that I do not find one crime in Him!
5 Then Jesus came outside, wearing the thorny wreath and the purple garment. And he said to them, Behold! The Man!

6 Then when the chief priests and the underofficers saw Him, they cried out, saying, Crucify! Crucify! Pilate said to them, You take him and crucify (him), for I do not find (one) crime in him!

7 Then the Jews answered him, We have a law, and

5119 3767 2983 3588 4091 3588 2424 2532 3146
1. Τότε οὖν ἔλαβεν ὁ Πιλάτος τὸν Ἰησοῦν, καὶ ἐμαστίγωσε.
Then therefore took Pilate Jesus and scourged (Him).

2532 3588 4757 4120 4735 1537 173 2007
2 καὶ οἱ στρατιῶται πλέξαντες στέφανον ἐξ ἀκανθῶν ἐπέθηκαν
And the soldiers, having plaited a wreath out of thorns, put (it) on

846 3588 2776 2532 2440 4210 4016 846
αὐτοῦ τῇ κεφαλῇ, καὶ ἱμάτιον πορφυροῦν περιέβαλον αὐτόν,
of Him the head, and a garment purple threw around Him,

2532 3004 5463 3588 935 3588 2453 2532 1325
3 καὶ ἔλεγον, Χαῖρε, ὁ βασιλεὺς τῶν Ἰουδαίων· καὶ ἐδίδουν
and said, Hail, king of the Jews! And they gave

846 4475 1831 3767 3825 1854 3588 4091 2532
αὐτῷ ῥαπίσματα. 4 ἐξῆλθεν οὖν πάλιν ἔξω ὁ Πιλάτος, καὶ
Him slaps. went out Then again outside Pilate and

3004 846 2396 71 5213 846 1854 2443 1097 3754 1722
λέγει αὐτοῖς, Ἴδε, ἄγω ὑμῖν αὐτὸν ἔξω, ἵνα γνῶτε ὅτι ἐν
said to them, Behold! I bring to you him outside, that you may know that in

846 3762 156 2147 1831 3767 3588 2424 1854
αὐτῷ οὐδεμίαν αἰτίαν εὑρίσκω. 5 ἐξῆλθεν οὖν ὁ Ἰησοῦς ἔξω,
him not one crime I find. came out Then Jesus outside,

5409 3588 174 4735 2532 3588 4210 2440
φορῶν τὸν ἀκάνθινον στέφανον καὶ τὸ πορφυροῦν ἱμάτιον.
wearing the thorny wreath and the purple garment.

2532 3004 846 2396 3588 444 3753 3767 1492 846 3588
καὶ λέγει αὐτοῖς, Ἴδε, ὁ ἄνθρωπος. 6 ὅτε οὖν εἶδον αὐτὸν οἱ
And he says to them, Behold! The Man! when Then saw Him the

749 2532 3588 5257 2905 3004 4717
ἀρχιερεῖς καὶ οἱ ὑπηρέται, ἐκραύγασαν λέγοντες, Σταύρω-
chief priests and the under-officers, they cried out, saying, Crucify!

4717 3004 846 3588 4091 2983 846
σον, σταύρωσον. λέγει αὐτοῖς ὁ Πιλᾶτος, Λάβετε αὐτὸν
Crucify! says to them Pilate, take him

5210 2532 4717 1473 1063 3756 2147 1722 846 156
ὑμεῖς καὶ σταυρώσατε· ἐγὼ γὰρ οὐχ εὑρίσκω ἐν αὐτῷ αἰτίαν.
You and crucify, I for not do find in him a crime.

611 846 3588 2453 2249 3551 2192 2532
7 ἀπεκρίθησαν αὐτῷ οἱ Ἰουδαῖοι, Ἡμεῖς νόμον ἔχομεν, καὶ
answered him The Jews, We a law have, and

John 19

1. Then Pilate therefore took Jesus, and scourged (him).

2 And the soldiers platted a crown of thorns, and put (it) on his head, and they put on him a purple robe,

3 And said, Hail, King of the Jews! and they smote him with their hands.
4 Pilate therefore went forth again, and saith unto them, Behold, I bring him forth to you, that ye may know that I find no fault in him.
5 Then came Jesus forth, wearing the crown of thorns, and the purple robe. And (Pilate) saith unto them, Behold the man!

6 When the chief priests therefore and officers saw him, they cried out, saying, Crucify (him), crucify (him). Pilate saith unto them, Take ye him, and crucify (him): for I find no fault in him.

7 The Jews answered him, We have a law, and

Literal Translation **John 19:8** *King James Version*

according to our Law he ought to die because he has made himself Son of God!
8. Then when Pilate heard this word, he was more afraid.
9 And (he) entered into the praetorium again and said to Jesus, From where are you? But Jesus did not give him an answer.

10 So Pilate said to Him, Do you not speak to me? Do you not know that I have authority to crucify you, and I have authority to release you?
11 Jesus answered, You would have no authority against Me, not any, if it was not being given to you from above. Because of this, the (one) delivering Me to you has a greater sin.
12 From this (time), Pilate sought to release Him. But the Jews cried out, saying, If you release this one, you are not a friend of Caesar. Everyone making himself a king speaks against Caesar.

13. Then hearing this word, Pilate led Jesus outside. And (he) sat down on the judgment seat, at a place being called (The) Pavement, but in Hebrew, Gabbatha.
14 And it was (the) Preparation of the Passover, and about (the) sixth hour. And he said to the Jews, Behold, your king!
15 But they cried out, Away, Away! Crucify him! Pilate said to them, Shall I crucify your king? The chief priests answered, We have no king except Caesar.

16 Therefore, then, he delivered Him up to them, that He might be crucified.

2596 3588 3551 2257 3784 599 3754 1438 5207 3588
κατὰ τὸν νόμον ἡμῶν ὀφείλει ἀποθανεῖν, ὅτι ἑαυτὸν υἱὸν τοῦ
according to the law of us he ought to die, because himself Son

2316 4160 3753 3767 191 3588 4091 5126 3588
Θεοῦ ἐποίησεν. 8 ὅτε οὖν ἤκουσεν ὁ Πιλάτος τοῦτον τὸν
of God has made. when Then heard Pilate this

3056 3123 5399 2532 1525 1519 3588 4232
λόγον, μᾶλλον ἐφοβήθη, 9 καὶ εἰσῆλθεν εἰς τὸ πραιτώριον
word, more he was afraid, and entered into the praetorium

3825 2532 3004 3588 2424 4159 1488 4771 3588 1161 2424 612
πάλιν, καὶ λέγει τῷ Ἰησοῦ, Πόθεν εἶ σύ; ὁ δὲ Ἰησοῦς ἀπό-
again and said to Jesus, From where are you? But Jesus an

3756 1325 846 3004 3767 846 3588 4091 1698
κρισιν οὐκ ἔδωκεν αὐτῷ. 10 λέγει οὖν αὐτῷ ὁ Πιλάτος, Ἐμοὶ
answer not did give him. says Then to Him Pilate, To me

3756 2980 3756 1492 3754 1849 2192 4717 4571 2532
οὐ λαλεῖς; οὐκ οἶδας ὅτι ἐξουσίαν ἔχω σταυρῶσαί σε, καὶ
not you speak? Not do you know that authority I have to crucify you, and

1849 2192 630 4571 611 3588 2424 3756 2192
ἐξουσίαν ἔχω ἀπολῦσαί σε; 11 ἀπεκρίθη ὁ Ἰησοῦς, Οὐκ εἶχες
authority I have to release you? answered Jesus, Not you had

1849 3762 2596 1700 1487 3361 2258 4671 1325 509
ἐξουσίαν οὐδεμίαν κατ᾽ ἐμοῦ, εἰ μὴ ἦν σοι δεδομένον ἄνωθεν·
authority, not any, against Me, if not it was to you being given from above;

1223 5124 3588 3860 3165 4671 3173 266 2192 1537
διὰ τοῦτο ὁ παραδιδούς μέ σοι μείζονα ἁμαρτίαν ἔχει. 12 ἐκ
because of this he delivering up Me to you a greater sin has. From

5127 2212 3588 4091 630 846 3588 1161 2453
τούτου εζήτει ὁ Πιλάτος ἀπολῦσαι αὐτόν. οἱ δὲ Ἰουδαῖοι
this sought Pilate to release Him, the but Jews

2896 3004 1437 5126 630 3756 1488 5384 3588
ἔκραζον λέγοντες, Ἐὰν τοῦτον ἀπολύσῃς, οὐκ εἶ φίλος τοῦ
cried out, saying, If this one you release, not you are friend

2541 3956 3588 935 846 4160 483 3588
Καίσαρος· πᾶς ὁ βασιλέα αὐτὸν ποιῶν, ἀντιλέγει τῷ
of Caesar. Everyone a king himself making speaks against

2541 3588 3767 4091 191 5126 3588 3056 71
Καίσαρι. 13 ὁ οὖν Πιλάτος ἀκούσας τοῦτον τὸν λόγον ἤγαγεν
Caesar. Then Pilate hearing this word led

1854 3588 2424 2532 2523 1909 3588 968 1519 5117
ἔξω τὸν Ἰησοῦν, καὶ ἐκάθισεν ἐπὶ τοῦ βήματος, εἰς τόπον
outside Jesus, and sat down on the judgment seat, at a place

3004 3038 1447 1161 1042 2258 1161
λεγόμενον Λιθόστρωτον, Ἑβραϊστὶ δὲ Γαββαθᾶ· 14 ἦν δὲ
being called (The) Pavement, in Hebrew but Gabbatha. it was And

3904 3588 3957 5610 1161 5616 1623 2532 3004 3588
Παρασκευὴ τοῦ πάσχα, ὥρα δὲ ὡσεὶ ἕκτη· καὶ λέγει τοῖς
preparation of the Passover, hour and about (the) sixth. And he says to the

2453 2396 3588 935 5216 3588 1161 2905 142
Ἰουδαίοις, Ἴδε, ὁ βασιλεὺς ὑμῶν. 15 οἱ δὲ ἐκραύγασαν, Ἆρον
Jews, Behold! The king of you!. they But cried out, Away!

142 4717 846 3004 846 3588 4091 3588
ἆρον, σταύρωσον αὐτόν. λέγει αὐτοῖς ὁ Πιλάτος, Τὸν
Away! Crucify him! says to them Pilate, The

935 5216 4717 611 3588 749 3756
βασιλέα ὑμῶν σταυρώσω; ἀπεκρίθησαν οἱ ἀρχιερεῖς, Οὐκ
king of you shall I crucify? answered The chief priests, Not

2192 935 1487 3361 2541 5119 3767 3860 846
ἔχομεν βασιλέα εἰ μὴ Καίσαρα. 16 τότε οὖν παρέδωκεν αὐτὸν
we have a king except Caesar. Then, therefore, he delivered up Him

846 2443 4717
αὐτοῖς ἵνα σταυρωθῇ.
to them, that He might be crucified.

by our law he ought to die, because he made himself the Son of God.
8. When Pilate therefore heard that saying, he was the more afraid;
9 And went again into the judgment hall, and saith unto Jesus, Whence art thou? But Jesus gave him no answer.

10 Then saith Pilate unto him, Speakest thou not unto me? knowest thou not that I have power to crucify thee, and have power to release thee?
11 Jesus answered, Thou couldest have no power (at all) against me, except it were given thee from above: therefore he that delivered me unto thee hath the greater sin.
12 And from thenceforth Pilate sought to release him: but the Jews cried out, saying, If thou let this man go, thou art not Caesar's friend: whosoever maketh himself a king speaketh against Caesar.

13. When Pilate therefore heard that saying, he brought Jesus forth, and sat down in the judgment seat in a place that is called the Pavement, but in the Hebrew, Gabbatha.
14 And it was the preparation of the passover, and about the sixth hour: and he saith unto the Jews, Behold your King!
15 But they cried out, Away with (him), away with (him), crucify him. Pilate saith unto them, Shall I crucify your King? The chief priests answered, We have no king but Caesar.

16 Then delivered he him therefore unto them to be crucified.

Literal Translation

And they took Jesus and led (Him) away.
17 And He went out bearing His cross, to the place being called Of a Skull, which is called in Hebrew, Golgotha,
18 where they crucified Him, and two others with Him, on this side and on that side, and Jesus in the middle.

19. And Pilate also wrote a title and put (it) on the cross. And having been written, it was: JESUS THE NAZARENE, THE KING OF THE JEWS.
20 Therefore, many of the Jews read this title, because the place where Jesus was crucified was near the city. And it was having been written in Hebrew, in Greek, in Latin.

21 Then the chief priests of the Jews said to Pilate, Do not write, The king of the Jews, but, That one said, I am king of the Jews.

22 Pilate answered, What I have written, I have written.

23. Then when they crucified Jesus, the soldiers took His garments and made four parts, a part to each soldier, also the tunic. And the tunic was seamless, woven from the top throughout.

24 Then they said to one another, Let us not tear it, but let us cast lots about it, whose it will be (that the Scripture might be fulfilled which said, "They divided My garments to themselves, and they threw a lot (for) My garment" (Ps.22:18).

John 19:17

3880 1161 3588 2424 2532 520 2532 941
Παρέλαβον δὲ τὸν Ἰησοῦν καὶ ἀπήγαγον· 17 καὶ βαστάζων
they took And Jesus and led away, and bearing

3588 4716 846 1831 1519 3588 3004 2898
τὸν σταυρὸν αὐτοῦ ἐξῆλθεν εἰς τὸν λεγόμενον Κρανίου
the cross of Him, He went out to the being called,Of a Skull

5117 3739 3004 1447 1115 3699 846 4717
τόπον, ὃς λέγεται Ἑβραϊστὶ Γολγοθᾶ· 18 ὅπου αὐτὸν ἐσταύ-
place, which is called in Hebrew, Golgotha, where Him they

2532 3326 846 243 1417 1782 2532 1782
ρωσαν, καὶ μετ' αὐτοῦ ἄλλους δύο, ἐντεῦθεν καὶ ἐντεῦθεν,
crucified, and with Him others two, on this side and on that side,

3319 1161 3588 2424 1125 1161 2532 5102 3588 4091
μέσον δὲ τὸν Ἰησοῦν. 19 ἔγραψε δὲ καὶ τίτλον ὁ Πιλάτος,
in middle and Jesus. wrote And also a title Pilate,

2532 5087 1909 3588 4716 2258 1161 1125 2424 3588
καὶ ἔθηκεν ἐπὶ τοῦ σταυροῦ· ἦν δὲ γεγραμμένον, Ἰησοῦς ὁ
and put (it) on the cross; it was And having been written, JESUS THE

3480 3588 935 3588 2453 5126 3767 3588
Ναζωραῖος ὁ βασιλεὺς τῶν Ἰουδαίων. 20 τοῦτον οὖν τὸν
NAZARENE, THE KING OF THE JEWS. This, therefore

5102 4183 314 3588 2453 3754 1451 2258
τίτλον πολλοὶ ἀνέγνωσαν τῶν Ἰουδαίων, ὅτι ἐγγὺς ἦν
title many read of the Jews, because near was

3588 4172 3588 5117 3699 4717 3588 2424 2532 2258
τῆς πόλεως ὁ τόπος ὅπου ἐσταυρώθη ὁ Ἰησοῦς· καὶ ἦν
the city the place where was crucified Jesus. And it was

1125 1447 1676 4515 3004
γεγραμμένον Ἑβραϊστί, Ἑλληνιστί, Ῥωμαϊστί. 21 ἔλεγον
having been written in Hebrew, in Greek, in Latin. said

3767 3588 4091 3588 749 3588 2453 3361 1125
οὖν τῷ Πιλάτῳ οἱ ἀρχιερεῖς τῶν Ἰουδαίων, Μὴ γράφε,
Then to Pilate the chief priests of the Jews, Not do write

3588 935 3588 2453 235 3754 1565 2036 935
Ὁ βασιλεὺς τῶν Ἰουδαίων· ἀλλ' ὅτι ἐκεῖνος εἶπε, Βασιλεύς
The king of the Jews, but that that one said, king

1510 3588 2453 611 3588 4091 3739 1125
εἰμι τῶν Ἰουδαίων. 22 ἀπεκρίθη ὁ Πιλάτος, Ὃ γέγραφα,
I am of the Jews. answered Pilate, What I have written

1125
γέγραφα.
I have written.

3588 3767 4757 3753 4717 3588 2424 2983
23 Οἱ οὖν στρατιῶται, ὅτε ἐσταύρωσαν τὸν Ἰησοῦν, ἔλαβον
the Then soldiers, when they crucified Jesus, took

3588 2440 846 2532 4160 5064 3313 1538
τὰ ἱμάτια αὐτοῦ, καὶ ἐποίησαν τέσσαρα μέρη, ἑκάστῳ
the garments of Him, and made four parts, to each

4757 3313 2532 3588 5509 2258 1161 3588 5509 729
στρατιώτῃ μέρος, καὶ τὸν χιτῶνα· ἦν δὲ ὁ χιτὼν ἄρραφος,
soldier a part, also the tunic. was And the tunic seamless,

1537 3588 509 5307 1223 3650 2036 3767 4314 240
ἐκ τῶν ἄνωθεν ὑφαντὸς δι' ὅλου. 24 εἶπον οὖν πρὸς ἀλλήλους,
from the top woven through all. they said Then to one another,

3361 4977 846 235 2975 4012 846 5101
Μὴ σχίσωμεν αὐτόν, ἀλλὰ λάχωμεν περὶ αὐτοῦ, τίνος
Not let us tear it, but let us cast lots about it, whose

2071 2443 3588 1124 4137 3588 3004 1266 3588
ἔσται· ἵνα ἡ γραφὴ πληρωθῇ ἡ λέγουσα, Διεμερίσαντο τὰ
it will be; that the Scripture might be fulfilled which said, They divided the

2440 3450 1438 2532 1909 3588 2441 3450 906 2819
ἱμάτιά μου ἑαυτοῖς, καὶ ἐπὶ τὸν ἱματισμόν μου ἔβαλον κλῆρον.
garments of Me to themselves, and on the garment of Me cast a lot.

King James Version

And they took Jesus, and led (him) away.
17 And he bearing his cross went forth into a place called (the place) of a skull, which is called in the Hebrew Golgotha:
18 Where they crucified him, and two other with him, on either side one, and Jesus in the midst.

19. And Pilate wrote a title, and put (it) on the cross. And the writing was, JESUS OF NAZARETH THE KING OF THE JEWS.

20 This title then read many of the Jews: for the place where Jesus was crucified was nigh to the city: and it was written in Hebrew, (and) Greek, (and) Latin.

21 Then said the chief priests of the Jews to Pilate, Write not, The King of the Jews; but that he said, I am King of the Jews.

22 Pilate answered, What I have written I have written.

23. Then the soldiers, when they had crucified Jesus, took his garments, and made four parts, to every soldier a part; and also (his) coat: now the coat was without seam, woven from the top throughout.

24 They said therefore among themselves, Let us not rend it, but cast lots for it, whose it shall be: that the scripture might be fulfilled, which saith, They parted my raiment among them, and for my vesture they did cast lots.

Literal Translation | **John 19:25** | **King James Version**

Then indeed the soldiers did these things.
25. And His mother, and His mother's sister Mary, the (wife) of Clopas, and Mary Magdalene stood by the cross of Jesus.

3588 3303 3767 4757 5023 4160 2476 1161
οἱ μὲν οὖν στρατιῶται ταῦτα ἐποίησαν. 25 εἱστήκεισαν δὲ
the indeed Then soldiers these things did. there stood But

3844 3588 4716 3588 2424 3588 3384 846 2532 3588 79
παρὰ τῷ σταυρῷ τοῦ Ἰησοῦ ἡ μήτηρ αὐτοῦ, καὶ ἡ ἀδελφὴ
by the cross of Jesus the mother of Him, and the sister

3588 3384 846 3137 3588 3588 2832 2532 3137 3588
τῆς μητρὸς αὐτοῦ, Μαρία ἡ τοῦ Κλωπᾶ, καὶ Μαρία ἡ
of the mother of Him, Mary the (wife) of Clopas, and Mary the

These things therefore the soldiers did.
25. Now there stood by the cross of Jesus his mother, and his mother's sister, Mary the (wife) of Cleophas, and Mary Magdalene.

26 Then seeing (His) mother, and the disciple whom He loved standing by, Jesus said to His mother, Woman, behold your son!

27 Then He said to the disciple, Behold, your mother! And from that hour, the disciple took her into (his) own (home).

3094 2424 3767 1492 3588 3384 2532 3588 3101
Μαγδαληνή. 26 Ἰησοῦς οὖν ἰδὼν τὴν μητέρα, καὶ τὸν μαθητὴν
Magdalene. Jesus Then seeing the mother, and the disciple

3936 3739 25 3004 3588 3384 846 1135 2400 3588
παρεστῶτα ὃν ἠγάπα, λέγει τῇ μητρὶ αὐτοῦ, Γύναι, ἰδοὺ ὁ
standing by, whom He loved, says to the mother of Him, Woman, behold the

5207 4675 1534 3004 3588 3101 2400 3588 3384 4675 2532
υἱός σου. 27 εἶτα λέγει τῷ μαθητῇ, Ἰδοὺ ἡ μήτηρ σου. καὶ
son of you. Then He says to the disciple, Behold the mother of you. And

575 1565 3588 5610 2983 846 3588 3101 1519 3588 2398
ἀπ' ἐκείνης τῆς ὥρας ἔλαβεν αὐτὴν ὁ μαθητὴς εἰς τὰ ἴδια.
from that hour took her the disciple into the own (home).

26 When Jesus therefore saw his mother, and the disciple standing by, whom he loved, he saith unto his mother, Woman, behold thy son!

27 Then saith he to the disciple, Behold thy mother! And from that hour that disciple took her unto his own (home).

28. After this, knowing that all things now have been finished that the Scripture be fulfilled, Jesus said, I thirst. (Ps.69:21)
29 Then a vessel full of vinegar was set, and having filled a sponge (with) vinegar, and putting hyssop around, (they) brought (it) to His mouth.
30 Then when Jesus took the vinegar, He said, It has been finished. And bowing (His) head, He yielded up the spirit.

3326 5124 1492 3588 2424 3754 3956 2235 5055
28 Μετὰ τοῦτο εἰδὼς ὁ Ἰησοῦς ὅτι πάντα ἤδη τετέλεσται,
After this knowing Jesus that all things now have been done

2443 5048 3588 1124 3004 1372 4632 3767 2749 3690
ἵνα τελειωθῇ ἡ γραφή, λέγει, Διψῶ. 29 σκεῦος οὖν ἔκειτο ὄξους
that be fulfilled the Scripture, says, I thirst. a vessel Then was set of vinegar

3324 3588 1161 4130 4699 3690 2532 5301
μεστόν· οἱ δὲ, πλήσαντες σπόγγον ὄξους, καὶ ὑσσώπῳ
full. they And, filling a sponge (with) vinegar, and hyssop

4060 4374 846 3588 4750 3753 3767 2983
περιθέντες, προσήνεγκαν αὐτοῦ τῷ στόματι. 30 ὅτε οὖν ἔλαβε
putting around, brought of Him to the mouth. when Then took

3588 3690 3588 2424 2036 5055 2532 2827 3588 2776
τὸ ὄξος ὁ Ἰησοῦς, εἶπε, Τετέλεσται· καὶ κλίνας τὴν κεφαλήν,
the vinegar Jesus, He said, It has been finished; and bowing the head

3860 3588 4151
παρέδωκε τὸ πνεῦμα.
He yielded up the spirit.

28. After this, Jesus knowing that all things were now accomplished, that the scripture might be fulfilled, saith, I thirst.
29 Now there was set a vessel full of vinegar: and they filled a spunge with vinegar, and put (it) upon hyssop, and put (it) to his mouth.
30 When Jesus therefore had received the vinegar, he said, It is finished: and he bowed his head, and gave up the ghost.

31. Then, since it was Preparation, that the bodies not remain on the cross on the sabbath, for great was the day of that sabbath, the Jews asked Pilate that their legs might be broken and they be taken away.

32 Then the soldiers came and broke the legs of the first, and of the other crucified with Him.

3588 3767 2453 1893 3904 2258 2443 3361 3306 1909
31. Οἱ οὖν Ἰουδαῖοι, ἐπεὶ Παρασκευὴ ἦν, ἵνα μὴ μείνῃ ἐπὶ
the Then Jews, since Preparation it was, that not remain on

3588 4716 3588 4983 1722 3588 4521 2258 1063 3173 3588
τοῦ σταυροῦ τὰ σώματα ἐν τῷ σαββάτῳ [ἦν γὰρ μεγάλη ἡ
the cross the bodies on the sabbath, was for great the

2250 1565 3588 4521 2065 3588 4091 2443
ἡμέρα ἐκείνου τοῦ σαββάτου], ἠρώτησαν τὸν Πιλάτον ἵνα
day of that sabbath, they asked Pilate that

2608 846 3588 4628 2532 142 2064 3767 3588
κατεαγῶσιν αὐτῶν τὰ σκέλη, καὶ ἀρθῶσιν. 32 ἦλθον οὖν οἱ
might be broken of them the legs, and they be taken away. came Then the

4757 2532 3588 3303 4413 2608 3588 4628 2532 3588
στρατιῶται, καὶ τοῦ μὲν πρώτου κατέαξαν τὰ σκέλη καὶ τοῦ
soldiers, and of the indeed first broke the legs, and of the

31. The Jews therefore, because it was the preparation, that the bodies should not remain upon the cross on the sabbath day, (for that sabbath day was an high day,) besought Pilate that their legs might be broken, and (that) they might be taken away.

32 Then came the soldiers, and brake the legs of the first, and of the other which was crucified with him.

33 But (on) coming to Jesus, when they saw He was dead already, they did not break His legs.
34 But one of the soldiers pierced His side (with) a lance,

243 3588 4957 846 1909 1161 3588 2424 2064
ἄλλου τοῦ συσταυρωθέντος αὐτῷ· 33 ἐπὶ δὲ τὸν Ἰησοῦν ἐλ-
other crucified with Him. on But Jesus

5613 1492 846 2235 2348 3756 2608 846
θόντες, ὡς εἶδον αὐτὸν ἤδη τεθνηκότα, οὐ κατέαξαν αὐτοῦ
coming, when they saw He already was dead, not they broke of Him

3588 4628 235 1520 3588 4757 3057 846 3588 4125
τὰ σκέλη· 34 ἀλλ' εἷς τῶν στρατιωτῶν λόγχῃ αὐτοῦ τὴν πλευ-
the legs, but one of the soldiers a lance of Him the side

33 But when they came to Jesus, and saw that he was dead already, they brake not his legs:

34 But one of the soldiers with a spear pierced his side,

Literal Translation

John 19:35

King James Version

and at once blood and water came out.
35 And the (one) seeing has borne witness and his witness is true; and that one knows that he speaks true, that you may believe.
36 For these things happened that the Scripture might be fulfilled, "Not a bone of Him shall be broken." (Ex.12:46; Ps. 34:20)

37 And again, a different Scripture says, "They shall look at (Him) whom they have pierced." (Zech. 12:10)

38. And after these things, Joseph from Arimathea, being a disciple of Jesus, but being hidden because of fear of the Jews, asked Pilate that he might take the body of Jesus. And Pilate allowed (it). Then he came and took the body of Jesus.

39 And Nicodemus also came, the (one) coming at first to Jesus by night, bearing a mixture of myrrh and aloes, about a hundred litrae. .

40 Then they took the body of Jesus and bound it in linens, with the spices, as is usual with the Jews to bury.

41 And there was a garden in the place where He was crucified, and a new tomb in the garden, in which no one yet ever had been placed.
42 There, then, because of the Preparation of the Jews, because the tomb was near, they put Jesus.

3572 2532 2117 1831 129 2532 5204 2532 3588 3708
ρὰν ἔνυξε, καὶ εὐθὺς ἐξῆλθεν αἷμα καὶ ὕδωρ. 35 καὶ ὁ ἑωρακὼς
pierced, and at once came out blood and water. And he seeing
3140 2532 228 846 2076 3588 3141 2548
μεμαρτύρηκε, καὶ ἀληθινὴ αὐτοῦ ἐστιν ἡ μαρτυρία, κἀκεῖνος
has witnessed, and true of him is the witness, and that one
1492 3754 227 3004 2443 5210 4100 1096 1063
οἶδεν ὅτι ἀληθῆ λέγει, ἵνα ὑμεῖς πιστεύσητε. 36 ἐγένετο γὰρ
knows that true he speaks, that you may believe. happened For
5023 2443 3588 1124 4137 3747 3756 4937
ταῦτα ἵνα ἡ γραφὴ πληρωθῇ, Ὀστοῦν οὐ συντριβήσεται
these things that the Scripture might be fulfilled: A bone not shall be splintered
846 2532 3825 2087 1124 3004 3700 1519 3739
αὐτοῦ. 37 καὶ πάλιν ἑτέρα γραφὴ λέγει, Ὄψονται εἰς ὃν
of Him. And again a different Scripture says, They shall look at whom
1574
ἐξεκέντησαν.
they have pierced.

3326 1161 5023 2065 3588 4091 3588 2501 3588 575
38 Μετὰ δὲ ταῦτα ἠρώτησε τὸν Πιλάτον ὁ Ἰωσὴφ ὁ ἀπὸ
after And these things asked Pilate Joseph from
707 5607 3101 3588 2424 2928 1161 1223
Ἀριμαθαίας, ὢν μαθητὴς τοῦ Ἰησοῦ, κεκρυμμένος δὲ διὰ
Arimathea, being a disciple of Jesus, having been hidden but through
3588 5401 3588 2453 2443 142 3588 4983 3588 2424 2532
τὸν φόβον τῶν Ἰουδαίων, ἵνα ἄρῃ τὸ σῶμα τοῦ Ἰησοῦ· καὶ
the fear of the Jews, that he take the body of Jesus. And
2010 3588 4091 2064 3767 2532 142 3588 4983 3588 2424
ἐπέτρεψεν ὁ Πιλάτος. ἦλθεν οὖν καὶ ἦρε τὸ σῶμα τοῦ Ἰησοῦ.
allowed (it) Pilate. he came Then and took the body of Jesus.

2064 1161 2532 3530 3588 2064 4314 3588 2424 3571 3588
39 ἦλθε δὲ καὶ Νικόδημος, ὁ ἐλθὼν πρὸς τὸν Ἰησοῦν νυκτὸς τὸ
came And also Nicodemus, he coming to Jesus (by) night
4413 5342 3395 4666 2532 250 5616 3046 1540
πρῶτον, φέρων μίγμα σμύρνης καὶ ἀλόης ὡσεὶ λίτρας ἑκατόν.
at first, bearing a mixture of myrrh and aloes, about litrae a hundred.
2983 3767 3588 4983 3588 2424 2532 1210 846 3608
40 ἔλαβον οὖν τὸ σῶμα τοῦ Ἰησοῦ, καὶ ἔδησαν αὐτὸ ὀθονίοις
they took Then the body of Jesus, and bound it in linens
3326 3588 759 2531 1485 2076 3588 2453 1779
μετὰ τῶν ἀρωμάτων, καθὼς ἔθος ἐστὶ τοῖς Ἰουδαίοις ἐντα-
with the spices, even as custom is of the Jews
2258 1161 1722 3588 5117 3699 4717 2779 2532 1722
φιάζειν. 41 ἦν δὲ ἐν τῷ τόπῳ ὅπου ἐσταυρώθη κῆπος, καὶ ἐν
bury. was And in the place where He was crucified a garden, and in
3588 2779 3419 2537 1722 3739 3764 3762 5087 1563
τῷ κήπῳ μνημεῖον καινόν, ἐν ᾧ οὐδέπω οὐδεὶς ἐτέθη. 42 ἐκεῖ
the garden a tomb new, in which never yet no one was put. There
3767 1223 3588 3904 3588 2453 3754 1451 2258 3588
οὖν διὰ τὴν παρασκευὴν τῶν Ἰουδαίων, ὅτι ἐγγὺς ἦν τὸ
then because of the Preparation of the Jews, because near was the
3419 5087 3588 2424
μνημεῖον, ἔθηκαν τὸν Ἰησοῦν.
tomb, they put Jesus.

and forthwith came there out blood and water.
35 And he that saw (it) bare record, and his record is true: and he knoweth that he saith true, that ye might believe.
36 For these things were done, that the scripture should be fulfilled, A bone of him shall not be broken.

37 And again another scripture saith, They shall look on him whom they pierced.

38. And after this Joseph of Arimathaea, being a disciple of Jesus, but secretly for fear of the Jews, besought Pilate that he might take away the body of Jesus: and Pilate gave (him) leave. He came therefore, and took the body of Jesus.

39 And there came also Nicodemus, which at the first came to Jesus by night, and brought a mixture of myrrh and aloes, about an hundred pound (weight).
40 Then took they the body of Jesus, and wound it in linen clothes with the spices, as the manner of the Jews is to bury.
41 Now in the place where he was crucified there was a garden; and in the garden a new sepulchre, wherein was never man yet laid.
42 There laid they Jesus therefore because of the Jews' preparation (day); for the sepulchre was nigh at hand.

John 20

1. But on the first of the week, Mary Magdalene came early to the tomb, darkness yet being (on it). And (she) saw the

3588 1161 3391 3588 4521 3137 3588 3094 2064
1 Τῇ δὲ μιᾷ τῶν σαββάτων Μαρία ἡ Μαγδαληνὴ ἔρχεται
on the And first of the week, Mary the Magdalene comes
4404 4653 2089 5607 1519 3588 3419 2532 991 3588
πρωΐ, σκοτίας ἔτι οὔσης, εἰς τὸ μνημεῖον, καὶ βλέπει τὸν
early, darkness yet being to the tomb, and sees the

1. The first (day) of the week cometh Mary Magdalene early, when it was yet dark, unto the sepulchre, and seeth the

Literal Translation | **John 20:2** | **King James Version**

stone had been removed from the tomb.
2 Then she ran and came to Simon Peter, and to the other disciple whom Jesus loved, and said to them, They took away the Lord out of the tomb, and we do not know where they put Him.
3 Then Peter and the other disciple went out and came to the tomb.
4 And the two ran together, and the other disciple ran in front more quickly than Peter and came first to the tomb.
5 And bending down, he saw the linens lying; however, he did not go in.
6 Then Simon Peter came following him, and went into the tomb, and he beholds the linens lying.
7 And the face cloth which was on His head (was) not lying with the linens, but apart, having been wrapped up in one place by itself.
8 Therefore, then the other disciple also went in, the (one) coming first to the tomb, even he saw and believed.
9 For they did not yet know the Scripture, that it was necessary for Him to rise from (the) dead.
10 Then the disciples went away again to themselves.
11. But Mary stood at the tomb, weeping outside. Then as she wept, she bent down into the tomb.
12 And (she) beholds two angels in white, sitting one at the head, and one at the feet, where the body of Jesus had lain.
13 And they say to her, Woman, why do you weep? She said to them, Because

3037 142 1537 3588 3419 5143 3767 2532 2064 4314
λίθον ἠρμένον ἐκ τοῦ μνημείου. 2 τρέχει οὖν καὶ ἔρχεται πρὸς
stone being removed from the tomb. she runs Then and comes to

4613 4074 2532 4314 3588 243 3101 3739 5368 3588
Σίμωνα Πέτρον καὶ πρὸς τὸν ἄλλον μαθητὴν ὃν ἐφίλει ὁ
Simon Peter and to the other disciple whom loved

2424 2532 3004 846 142 3588 2962 1537 3588 3419
Ἰησοῦς, καὶ λέγει αὐτοῖς, Ἦραν τὸν Κύριον ἐκ τοῦ μνημείου,
Jesus, and says to them, They took the Lord out of the tomb,

2532 3756 1492 4226 5087 846 1831 3767 3588 4074 2532
καὶ οὐκ οἴδαμεν ποῦ ἔθηκαν αὐτόν. 3 ἐξῆλθεν οὖν ὁ Πέτρος καὶ
and not we know where they put Him. went out Then Peter and

3588 243 3101 2532 2064 1519 3588 3419 5143 1161 3588
ὁ ἄλλος μαθητής, καὶ ἤρχοντο εἰς τὸ μνημεῖον. 4 ἔτρεχον δὲ οἱ
the other disciple, and came to the tomb. ran And the

1417 3674 2532 3588 243 3101 4390 5032 3588
δύο ὁμοῦ· καὶ ὁ ἄλλος μαθητὴς προέδραμε τάχιον τοῦ
two together. And the other disciple ran in front more quickly than

4074 2532 2064 4413 1519 3588 3419 2532 3879
Πέτρου, καὶ ἦλθε πρῶτος εἰς τὸ μνημεῖον, 5 καὶ παρακύψας
Peter, and came first to the tomb, and bending to look in

991 2749 3588 3608 3756 3305 1525 2064 3767
βλέπει κείμενα τὰ ὀθόνια, οὐ μέντοι εἰσῆλθεν. 6 ἔρχεται οὖν
sees lying the linens. Not, however, he went in. comes Then

4613 4074 190 846 2532 1525 1519 3588 3419
Σίμων Πέτρος ἀκολουθῶν αὐτῷ, καὶ εἰσῆλθεν εἰς τὸ μνημεῖον,
Simon Peter following him, and entered into the tomb.

2532 2334 3588 3608 2749 2532 3588 4676 3739 2258 1909 3588
καὶ θεωρεῖ τὰ ὀθόνια κείμενα, 7 καὶ τὸ σουδάριον ὃ ἦν ἐπὶ τῆς
And he beholds the linens lying, and the face cloth which was on the

2776 846 3756 3326 3588 3608 2749 235 5565
κεφαλῆς αὐτοῦ, οὐ μετὰ τῶν ὀθονίων κείμενον, ἀλλὰ χωρὶς
head of Him, not with the linens lying, but apart

1794 1519 1520 5117 5119 3767 1525 2532 3588 243
ἐντετυλιγμένον εἰς ἕνα τόπον. 8 τότε οὖν εἰσῆλθε καὶ ὁ ἄλλος
having been wrapped up into one place. Then, therefore, went in also the other

3101 3588 2064 4413 1519 3588 3419 2532 1492 2532
μαθητὴς ὁ ἐλθὼν πρῶτος εἰς τὸ μνημεῖον, καὶ εἶδε, καὶ
disciple, the (one) coming first to the tomb; and he saw and

4100 3764 1063 1492 3588 1124 3754 1163
ἐπίστευσεν· 9 οὐδέπω γὰρ ᾔδεισαν τὴν γραφήν, ὅτι δεῖ
believed. not yet For they knew the Scripture, that must

846 1537 3498 450 565 3767 3825 4314
αὐτὸν ἐκ νεκρῶν ἀναστῆναι. 10 ἀπῆλθον οὖν πάλιν πρὸς
Him from (the) dead rise. went away Then again to

1438 3588 3101
ἑαυτοὺς οἱ μαθηταί.
themselves the disciples.

3137 1161 2476 4314 3588 3419 2799 1854 5613
11 Μαρία δὲ εἱστήκει πρὸς τὸ μνημεῖον κλαίουσα ἔξω· ὡς
Mary But stood at the tomb weeping outside. as

3767 2799 3879 1519 3588 3419 2532 2334 1417
οὖν ἔκλαιε, παρέκυψεν εἰς τὸ μνημεῖον, 12 καὶ θεωρεῖ δύο
Then she wept, she bent down into the tomb, and (she) beholds two

32 1722 3022 2516 1520 4314 3588 2776 2532
ἀγγέλους ἐν λευκοῖς καθεζομένους, ἕνα πρὸς τῇ κεφαλῇ, καὶ
angels in white sitting, one at the head, and

1520 4314 3588 4228 3699 2749 3588 4983 3588 2424 2532
ἕνα πρὸς τοῖς ποσίν, ὅπου ἔκειτο τὸ σῶμα τοῦ Ἰησοῦ. 13 καὶ
one at the feet, where had lain the body of Jesus. And

3004 846 1565 1135 5101 2799 3004 846 3754
λέγουσιν αὐτῇ ἐκεῖνοι, Γύναι, τί κλαίεις; λέγει αὐτοῖς, Ὅτι
say to her those, Woman, why do you weep? She says to them, because

stone taken away from the sepulchre.
2 Then she runneth, and cometh to Simon Peter, and to the other disciple, whom Jesus loved, and saith unto them, They have taken away the Lord out of the sepulchre, and we know not where they have laid him.
3 Peter therefore went forth, and that other disciple, and came to the sepulchre.
4 So they ran both together: and the other disciple did outrun Peter, and came first to the sepulchre.
5 And he stooping down, (and looking in), saw the linen clothes lying; yet went he not in.
6 Then cometh Simon Peter following him, and went into the sepulchre, and seeth the linen clothes lie,
7 And the napkin, that was about his head, not lying with the linen clothes, but wrapped together in a place by itself.
8 Then went in also that other disciple, which came first to the sepulchre, and he saw, and believed.
9 For as yet they knew not the scripture, that he must rise again from the dead.
10 Then the disciples went away again unto their own home.
11. But Mary stood without at the sepulchre weeping: and as she wept, she stooped down, (and looked) into the sepulchre,
12 And seeth two angels in white sitting, the one at the head, and the other at the feet, where the body of Jesus had lain.
13 And they say unto her, Woman, why weepest thou? She saith unto them, Because

Literal Translation

they moved my Lord, and I do not know where they put Him.
14 And saying these things, she turned to the rear and beholds Jesus standing, not knowing that it was Jesus.
15 Jesus says to her, Woman, why do you weep? Whom do you seek? That one thinking that it is the gardener, (she) says to Him, Sir, if you carried Him away, tell me where you put Him, and I will take Him away.
16 Jesus says to her, Mary! That one turning toward (Him), said to Him, Rabboni! That is to say, Teacher.

17 Jesus said to her, Do not touch Me, for I have not yet gone up to My Father. But go to My brothers, and say to them, I go up to My Father and your Father, and My God and your God.

18 Mary Magdalene came bringing word to the disciples that she has seen the Lord, and that He told her these things.

19. Then it being evening on that day, the first of the week, and the doors having been locked where the disciples were gathered together, because of fear of the Jews, Jesus came and stood in the midst and says to them, Peace to you.
20 And saying this, He showed them (His) hands and side. Then seeing the Lord, the disciples rejoiced.

21 Then Jesus said to them again, Peace to you. Even as has sent Me

John 20:14

142 3588 2962 3450 2532 3756 1492 4226 5087 846 2532
ἦραν τὸν Κύριόν μου, καὶ οὐκ οἶδα ποῦ ἔθηκαν αὐτόν. 14 καὶ
they moved the Lord of me, and not I know where they put Him. And

5023 2036 4762 1519 3588 3694 2532 2334 3588
ταῦτα εἰποῦσα ἐστράφη εἰς τὰ ὀπίσω, καὶ θεωρεῖ τὸν
these things saying, she turned to the rear, and beholds

2424 2476 2532 3756 1492 3754 3588 2424 2076 3004 846
Ἰησοῦν ἑστῶτα, καὶ οὐκ ᾔδει ὅτι ὁ Ἰησοῦς ἐστι. 15 λέγει αὐτῇ
Jesus standing, yet not knowing that Jesus it is. says to her

3588 2424 1135 5101 2799 5101 2212 1565 1380
ὁ Ἰησοῦς, Γύναι, τί κλαίεις; τίνα ζητεῖς; ἐκείνη, δοκοῦσα
Jesus, Woman, why do you weep? Whom do you seek? That one, thinking

3754 3588 2780 2076 3004 846 2962 1487 4771 941
ὅτι ὁ κηπουρός ἐστι, λέγει αὐτῷ, Κύριε, εἰ σὺ ἐβάστασας
that the gardener it is, says to Him, Sir, if you carried away

846 2036 3427 4226 846 5087 2504 846 142 3004
αὐτόν, εἰπέ μοι ποῦ αὐτὸν ἔθηκας, κἀγὼ αὐτὸν ἀρῶ. 16 λέγει
Him, tell me where Him you put, and I Him will take. says

846 3588 2424 3137 4762 1565 3004 846
αὐτῇ ὁ Ἰησοῦς, Μαρια. στραφεῖσα ἐκείνη λέγει αὐτῷ,
to her Jesus, Mary! turning That one says to Him,

4462 3739 3004 1320 3004 846 2424 3361
Ῥαββουνί· ὃ λέγεται Διδάσκαλε. 17 λέγει αὐτῇ Ἰησοῦς, Μή
Rabboni; that is to say, Teacher. says to her Jesus, Do not

3450 680 3768 1063 305 4314 3588 3962 3450
μου ἅπτου, οὔπω γὰρ ἀναβέβηκα πρὸς τὸν πατέρα μου·
Me touch, not yet for I have gone up to the Father of Me;

4198 1161 4314 3588 80 3450 2532 2036 846
πορεύου δὲ πρὸς τοὺς ἀδελφούς μου, καὶ εἰπὲ αὐτοῖς,
go but to the brothers of Me, and say to them,

305 4314 3588 3962 3450 2532 3962 5216 2532
Ἀναβαίνω πρὸς τὸν πατέρα μου καὶ πατέρα ὑμῶν, καὶ
I go up to the Father of Me and (the) Father of you, and

2316 3450 2532 2316 5216 2064 3137 3588 3094
Θεόν μου καὶ Θεὸν ὑμῶν. 18 ἔρχεται Μαρία ἡ Μαγδαληνὴ
the God of Me and the God of you. comes Mary the Magdalene

518 3588 3101 3754 3708 3588 2962 2532
ἀπαγγέλλουσα τοῖς μαθηταῖς ὅτι ἑώρακε τὸν Κύριον, καὶ
bringing word to the disciples, that she has seen the Lord, and

5023 2036 846
ταῦτα εἶπεν αὐτῇ.
these things He told to her.

5607 3767 3798 3588 2250 1565 3588 3391 3588 4521
19 Οὔσης οὖν ὀψίας, τῇ ἡμέρᾳ ἐκείνῃ τῇ μιᾷ τῶν σαββάτων,
it being Then evening day on that, the first of the week,

2532 3588 2374 2808 3699 2258 3588 3101 4863
καὶ τῶν θυρῶν κεκλεισμένων ὅπου ἦσαν οἱ μαθηταὶ συνηγ-
and the doors having been locked where were the disciples gathered

1223 3588 5401 3588 2453 2064 3588 2424 2532
μένοι, διὰ τὸν φόβον τῶν Ἰουδαίων, ἦλθεν ὁ Ἰησοῦς καὶ
together, because of the fear of the Jews, came Jesus and

2476 1519 3588 3319 2532 3004 846 1515 5213 2532 5124
ἔστη εἰς τὸ μέσον, καὶ λέγει αὐτοῖς, Εἰρήνη ὑμῖν. 20 καὶ τοῦτο
stood in the midst, and says to them, Peace to you! And this

2036 1166 846 3588 5495 2532 3588 4125 846
εἰπὼν ἔδειξεν αὐτοῖς τὰς χεῖρας καὶ τὴν πλευρὰν αὐτοῦ.
saying, He showed them the hands and the side of Him.

5463 3767 3588 3101 1492 3588 2962 2036 3767
ἐχάρησαν οὖν οἱ μαθηταὶ ἰδόντες τὸν Κύριον. 21 εἶπεν οὖν
rejoiced Then the disciples, seeing the Lord. said Then

846 3588 2424 3825 1515 5213 2531 649 3165 3588
αὐτοῖς ὁ Ἰησοῦς πάλιν, Εἰρήνη ὑμῖν· καθὼς ἀπέσταλκέ με ὁ
to them Jesus again, Peace to you! Even as has sent Me the

King James Version

they have taken away my Lord, and I know not where they have laid him.
14 And when she had thus said, she turned herself back, and saw Jesus standing, and knew not that it was Jesus.
15 Jesus saith unto her, Woman, why weepest thou? whom seekest thou? She, supposing him to be the gardener, saith unto him, Sir, if thou have borne him hence, tell me where thou hast laid him, and I will take him away.
16 Jesus saith unto her, Mary. She turned herself, and saith unto him, Rabboni; which is to say, Master.
17 Jesus saith unto her, Touch me not; for I am not yet ascended to my Father: but go to my brethren, and say unto them, I ascend unto my Father, and your Father; and (to) my God, and your God.

18 Mary Magdalene came and told the disciples that she had seen the Lord, and (that) he had spoken these things unto her.

19. Then the same day at evening, being the first (day) of the week, when the doors were shut where the disciples were assembled for fear of the Jews, came Jesus and stood in the midst, and saith unto them, Peace (be) unto you.

20 And when he had so said, he shewed unto them (his) hands and his side. Then were the disciples glad, when they saw the Lord.

21 Then said Jesus to them again, Peace (be) unto you: as (my) Father hath sent me,

Literal Translation

the Father, I also send you.
22 And having said this, He breathed on (them) and said to them, Receive (the) Holy Spirit.
23 Of whomever you forgive the sins, they are forgiven to them. Of whomever you hold, they have been held.

24. But Thomas, one of the Twelve, the (one) called Twin, was not with them when Jesus came.
25 Then the other disciples said to him, We have seen the Lord. But he said to them, If not I see the mark of the nails in His hands, and thrust my finger into the mark of the nails, and thrust my hand into His side, not at all will I believe.

26. And after eight days, His disciples were inside again, and Thomas (was) with them. The doors having been locked, Jesus came and stood in the midst, and said, Peace to you!

27 Then He said to Thomas, Bring your finger here and see My hands, and bring your hand, and thrust into My side, and become not unbelieving, but believing.
28 And Thomas answered, and said to Him, My Lord and my God!

29 Jesus said to him, Because you have seen Me, Thomas, you believed. Blessed (are) the (ones) not seeing and believing.

30. Then truly Jesus did many other miracles in the face of His disciples, which are not written in this book.

31 But these have been written that you may believe that

John 20:22

3962 2504 3992 5209 2532 5124 2036 1720 2532
πατήρ, κἀγὼ πέμπω ὑμᾶς. 22 καὶ τοῦτο εἰπὼν ἐνεφύσησε καὶ
Father, I also send you. And this having said, He breathed on and

3004 846 2983 4151 40 302 5100 863 3588
λέγει αὐτοῖς, Λάβετε Πνεῦμα Ἅγιον. 23 ἄν τινων ἀφῆτε τὰς
says to them, Receive (the) Spirit Holy. ever Of whom you forgive the

266 863 846 302 5100 2902 2902
ἁμαρτίας, ἀφίενται αὐτοῖς· ἄν τινων κρατῆτε, κεκράτηνται.
sins, they are forgiven to them; ever of whom you hold, they have been held.

2381 1161 1520 1537 3588 1427 3588 3004 1324 3756 2258
24 Θωμᾶς δέ, εἷς ἐκ τῶν δώδεκα, ὁ λεγόμενος Δίδυμος, οὐκ ἦν
Thomas But, one from the Twelve, the (one) being called Twin, not was

3326 846 3753 2064 3588 2424 3004 3767 846 3588 243
μετ' αὐτῶν ὅτε ἦλθεν ὁ Ἰησοῦς. 25 ἔλεγον οὖν αὐτῷ οἱ ἄλλοι
with them when came Jesus. said Then to him the other

3101 3708 3588 2962 3588 1161 2036 846 1437 3361
μαθηταί, Ἑωράκαμεν τὸν Κύριον. ὁ δὲ εἶπεν αὐτοῖς, Ἐὰν μὴ
disciples, We have seen the Lord. he But said to them, If not

1492 1722 3588 5495 846 3588 5179 3588 2247 2532 906
ἴδω ἐν ταῖς χερσὶν αὐτοῦ τὸν τύπον τῶν ἥλων, καὶ βάλω
I see in the hands of Him the mark of the nails, and thrust

3588 1147 3450 1519 3588 5179 3588 2247 2532 906 3588
τὸν δάκτυλόν μου εἰς τὸν τύπον τῶν ἥλων, καὶ βάλω τὴν
the finger of me into the mark of the nails, and thrust the

5495 3450 1519 3588 4125 846 3756 3361 4100
χεῖρά μου εἰς τὴν πλευρὰν αὐτοῦ, οὐ μὴ πιστεύσω.
hand of me into the side of Him, not at all will I believe.

2532 3326 2250 3638 3825 2258 2080 3588 3101 846
26 Καὶ μεθ' ἡμέρας ὀκτὼ πάλιν ἦσαν ἔσω οἱ μαθηταὶ αὐτοῦ,
And after days eight, again were inside the disciples of Him,

2532 2381 3326 846 2064 3588 2424 3588 2374
καὶ Θωμᾶς μετ' αὐτῶν. ἔρχεται ὁ Ἰησοῦς, τῶν θυρῶν
and Thomas with them. comes Jesus, the doors

2808 2532 2476 1519 3588 3319 2532 2036 1515 5213
κεκλεισμένων, καὶ ἔστη εἰς τὸ μέσον καὶ εἶπεν, Εἰρήνη ὑμῖν.
having been locked, and stood in the midst, and said, Peace to you!

1534 3004 3588 2381 5342 3588 1147 4675 5602 2532/1492/3588
27 εἶτα λέγει τῷ Θωμᾷ, Φέρε τὸν δάκτυλόν σου ὧδε, καὶ ἴδε τὰς
Then He says to Thomas, Bring the finger of you here, and see the

5495 3450 2532 5342 3588 5495 4675 2532 906 1519 3588 4125
χεῖράς μου· καὶ φέρε τὴν χεῖρά σου, καὶ βάλε εἰς τὴν πλευ-
hands of Me, and bring the hand of you, and thrust into the side

3450 2532 3361 1096 571 235 4103 2532 611
ράν μου· καὶ μὴ γίνου ἄπιστος, ἀλλὰ πιστός. 28 καὶ ἀπεκρίθη
of Me; and not become unbelieving, but believing. And answered

3588 2381 2532 2036 846 3588 2962 3450 2532 3588 2316 3450
ὁ Θωμᾶς, καὶ εἶπεν αὐτῷ, Ὁ Κύριός μου καὶ ὁ Θεός μου.
Thomas, and said to Him, The Lord of me and the God of me.

3004 846 3588 2424 3754 3708 3165 2381 4100
29 λέγει αὐτῷ ὁ Ἰησοῦς, Ὅτι ἑώρακάς με, Θωμᾶ, πεπίστευκας·
says to him Jesus, Because you have seen Me, Thomas, you believed.

3107 3588 3361 1492 2532 4100
μακάριοι οἱ μὴ ἰδόντες καὶ πιστεύσαντες.
Blessed the (ones) not seeing, and believing.

4183 3303 3767 2532 243 4592 4160 3588 2424 1799
30. Πολλὰ μὲν οὖν καὶ ἄλλα σημεῖα ἐποίησεν ὁ Ἰησοῦς ἐνώ-
many truly Then and other signs did Jesus in (the)

3588 3101 846 3739 3756 2076 1125 1722 3588
πιον τῶν μαθητῶν αὐτοῦ, ἃ οὐκ ἔστι γεγραμμένα ἐν τῷ
face of the disciples of Him, which not is written in

975 5129 5023 1161 1125 2443 4100 3754 3588
βιβλίῳ τούτῳ. 31 ταῦτα δὲ γέγραπται, ἵνα πιστεύσητε ὅτι ὁ
scroll this. these things But have been written that you believe that

King James Version

even so send I you.
22 And when he had said this, he breathed on (them), and saith unto them, Receive ye the Holy Ghost:
23 Whose soever sins ye remit, they are remitted unto them; (and) whose soever (sins) ye retain, they are retained.
24. But Thomas, one of the twelve, called Didymus, was not with them when Jesus came.
25 The other disciples therefore said unto him, We have seen the Lord. But he said unto them, Except I shall see in his hands the print of the nails, and put my finger into the print of the nails, and thrust my hand into his side, I will not believe.

26. And after eight days again his disciples were within, and Thomas with them: (then) came Jesus, the doors being shut, and stood in the midst, and said, Peace (be) unto you.

27 Then saith he to Thomas, Reach hither thy finger, and behold my hands; and reach hither thy hand, and thrust (it) into my side: and be not faithless, but believing.
28 And Thomas answered and said unto him, My Lord and my God.

29 Jesus saith unto him, Thomas, because thou hast seen me, thou hast believed: blessed (are) they that have not seen, and (yet) have believed.

30. And many other signs truly did Jesus in the presence of his disciples, which are not written in this book:

31 But these are written, that ye might believe that

Literal Translation

Jesus is the Christ, the Son of God, and that believing you may have life in His name.

John 21:1

2424 2076 3588 5547 3588 5207 3588 2316 2532 2443 4100
Ἰησοῦς ἐστιν ὁ Χριστὸς ὁ υἱὸς τοῦ Θεοῦ, καὶ ἵνα πιστεύοντες
Jesus is the Christ, the Son of God, and that believing
2222 2192 1722 3588 3686 846
ζωὴν ἔχητε ἐν τῷ ὀνόματι αὐτοῦ.
life you may have in the name of Him.

King James Version

Jesus is the Christ, the Son of God; and that believing ye might have life through his name.

John 21

1. After these things, Jesus revealed Himself again to the disciples at the Sea of Tiberias. And He revealed (Himself) in this way:

2 Simon Peter, and Thomas, being called Twin, and Nathanael from Cana of Galilee, and the (sons) of Zebedee, and two others of His disciples were together.

3 Simon Peter said to them, I am going out to fish. They said to him, We also are coming with you. They went and went up into the boat at once. And in that night, they caught nothing.

4 And it now becoming early morning, Jesus stood on the shore. However, the disciples did not know that it was Jesus.
5 Then Jesus said to them, Children, do you not have anything for eating? They answered Him, No.
6 And He said to them, Cast the net to the right parts of the boat and you will find.

7 Then they cast, and they no longer had (the) strength to draw it, from the multitude of the fish. Then the disciple whom Jesus loved said to Peter, It is the Lord. Then hearing that it is the Lord, Simon Peter having girded on (his) coat, for he was naked, and threw himself into the sea.
8 And the other disciples in the

John 21

3326 5023 5319 1438 3825 3588 2424 3588
1 Μετὰ ταῦτα ἐφανέρωσεν ἑαυτὸν πάλιν ὁ Ἰησοῦς τοῖς
After these things revealed Himself again Jesus to the
3101 1909 3588 2281 3588 5085 5319 1161
μαθηταῖς ἐπὶ τῆς θαλάσσης τῆς Τιβεριάδος· ἐφανέρωσε δὲ
disciples at the Sea of Tiberias. He revealed And
3779 2258 3674 4613 4074 2532 2381 3588 3004
οὕτως. 2 ἦσαν ὁμοῦ Σίμων Πέτρος, καὶ Θωμᾶς ὁ λεγόμενος
in this way: Were together Simon Peter, and Thomas being called
1324 2532 3482 3588 575 2580 3588 1056 2532 3588
Δίδυμος, καὶ Ναθαναὴλ ὁ ἀπὸ Κανᾶ τῆς Γαλιλαίας, καὶ οἱ
Twin, and Nathanael the (one) from Cana of Galilee, and those
3588 2199 2532 243 1537 3588 3101 846 1417
τοῦ Ζεβεδαίου, καὶ ἄλλοι ἐκ τῶν μαθητῶν αὐτοῦ δύο.
of Zebedee, and others from the disciples of Him two.
3004 846 4613 4074 5217 232 3004
3 λέγει αὐτοῖς Σίμων Πέτρος, Ὑπάγω ἁλιεύειν. λέγουσιν
says to them Simon Peter, I am going to fish. They say
846 2064 2532 2249 4862 4671 1831 2532 305
αὐτῷ, Ἐρχόμεθα καὶ ἡμεῖς σὺν σοί. ἐξῆλθον καὶ ἀνέβησαν
to him, are coming also We with you. They went and went up
1519 3588 4143 2117 2532 1722 1565 3588 3571 4084 3762
εἰς τὸ πλοῖον εὐθύς, καὶ ἐν ἐκείνῃ τῇ νυκτὶ ἐπίασαν οὐδέν.
into the boat at once. And in that night, they caught nothing.
4405 1161 2235 1096 2476 3588 2424 1519 3588 123
4 πρωΐας δὲ ἤδη γενομένης ἔστη ὁ Ἰησοῦς εἰς τὸν αἰγιαλόν·
early morn And now (it) becoming stood Jesus onto the shore.
3756 3305 1492 3588 3101 3754 2424 2076 3004 3767
οὐ μέντοι ᾔδεισαν οἱ μαθηταὶ ὅτι Ἰησοῦς ἐστι. 5 λέγει οὖν
not However knew the disciples that Jesus it is. says Then
846 3588 2424 3813 3361 5100 4371 2192 611
αὐτοῖς ὁ Ἰησοῦς, Παιδία, μή τι προσφάγιον ἔχετε; ἀπεκρί-
to them Jesus, Children, not anything for eating have you? They
846 3756 3588 1161 2036 846 906 1519 3588 1188
θησαν αὐτῷ, Οὔ. 6 ὁ δὲ εἶπεν αὐτοῖς, Βάλετε εἰς τὰ δεξιὰ
answered to Him, No. He And said to them, Cast to the right
3313 3588 4143 3588 1350 2532 2147 906 3767 2532
μέρη τοῦ πλοίου τὸ δίκτυον, καὶ εὑρήσετε. ἔβαλον οὖν, καὶ
parts of the boat the net, and you will find. they cast Then, and
3765 846 1670 2480 575 3588 4128 3588
οὐκέτι αὐτὸ ἑλκύσαι ἴσχυσαν ἀπὸ τοῦ πλήθους τῶν
no longer it to draw they had strength, from the multitude of the
2486 3004 3767 3588 3101 1565 3739 25 3588 2424
ἰχθύων. 7 λέγει οὖν ὁ μαθητὴς ἐκεῖνος ὃν ἠγάπα ὁ Ἰησοῦς
fish. says Then disciple that whom loved Jesus
3588 4074 3588 2962 2076 4613 3767 4074 191 3754 3588
τῷ Πέτρῳ, Ὁ Κύριός ἐστι. Σίμων οὖν Πέτρος, ἀκούσας ὅτι ὁ
to Peter, the Lord It is. Simon Then Peter, hearing that the
2962 2076 3588 1903 1241 2258 1063 1131 2532
Κύριός ἐστι, τὸν ἐπενδύτην διεζώσατο [ἦν γὰρ γυμνός], καὶ
Lord it is, the coat having girded on, he was for naked, and
906 1438 1519 3588 2281 3588 1161 243 3101 3588
ἔβαλεν ἑαυτὸν εἰς τὴν θάλασσαν· 8 οἱ δὲ ἄλλοι μαθηταὶ τῷ
threw himself into the sea. the And other disciples in the

John 21

1. After these things Jesus shewed himself again to the disciples at the sea of Tiberias; and on this wise shewed he (himself).

2 There were together Simon Peter, and Thomas called Didymus, and Nathanael of Cana in Galilee, and the (sons) of Zebedee, and two other of his disciples.

3 Simon Peter saith unto them, I go a fishing. They say unto him, We also go with thee. They went forth, and entered into a ship immediately; and that night they caught nothing.

4 But when the morning was now come, Jesus stood on the shore: but the disciples knew not that it was Jesus.
5 Then Jesus saith unto them, Children, have ye any meat? They answered him, No.

6 And he said unto them, Cast the net on the right side of the ship, and ye shall find. They cast therefore, and now they were not able to draw it for the multitude of fishes.

7 Therefore that disciple whom Jesus loved saith unto Peter, It is the Lord. Now when Simon Peter heard that it was the Lord, he girt (his) fisher's coat (unto him), (for he was naked,) and did cast himself into the sea.
8 And the other disciples

Literal Translation | **John 21:9** | **King James Version**

in the little boat came, for they were not far from the land, but from about two hundred cubits, dragging the net of the fish.

4142 2064 3756 1063 2258 3112 575 3588 1093 235
πλοιαρίῳ ἦλθον [οὐ γὰρ ἦσαν μακρὰν ἀπὸ τῆς γῆς, ἀλλ᾽
little boat came, not for they were far from the land, but
5613 575 4083 1250 4951 3588 1350 3588
ὡς ἀπὸ πηχῶν διακοσίων], σύροντες τὸ δίκτυον τῶν
about from cubits two hundred, dragging the net of the

came in a little ship; (for they were not far from land, but as it were two hundred cubits,) dragging the net with fishes.

9 Then when they went up onto the land, they saw a fire of coals lying, and a fish having been laid on (it), and bread.
10 Jesus said to them, Bring from the little fish which you caught now.

2486 5613 3767 576 1519 3588 1093 991 439
ἰχθύων. 9 ὡς οὖν ἀπέβησαν εἰς τὴν γῆν, βλέπουσιν ἀνθρακιὰν
fish. when Then they went up onto the land, they saw a fire of coals
2749 2532 3795 1945 2532 740 3004 846
κειμένην καὶ ὀψάριον ἐπικείμενον, καὶ ἄρτον. 10 λέγει αὐτοῖς
lying, and a fish having been laid on, and bread. says to them
3588 2424 5342 575 3588 3795 3739 4084 3568
ὁ Ἰησοῦς, Ἐνέγκατε ἀπὸ τῶν ὀψαρίων ὧν ἐπιάσατε νῦν.
Jesus, Bring from the little fish which you caught now.

9 As soon then as they were come to land, they saw a fire of coals there, and fish laid thereon, and bread.
10 Jesus saith unto them, Bring of the fish which ye have now caught.

11 Simon Peter went up, and dragged the net onto the land, full of big fish, a hundred and fifty three. And (though) being so many, the net was not torn.
12 Jesus said to them, Come, break fast. And no one of the disciples dared to ask Him, Who are You? knowing that it is the Lord.

305 4613 4074 2532 1670 3588 1350 1909 3588 1093
11 ἀνέβη Σίμων Πέτρος, καὶ εἵλκυσε τὸ δίκτυον ἐπὶ τῆς γῆς,
went up Simon Peter, and dragged the net onto the land,
3324 2486 3173 1540 4004 2532
μεστὸν ἰχθύων μεγάλων ἑκατὸν πεντηκοντατριῶν· καὶ
full fish of great, a hundred fifty three. And
5118 5607 3756 4977 3588 1350 3004 846 3588
τοσούτων ὄντων, οὐκ ἐσχίσθη τὸ δίκτυον. 12 λέγει αὐτοῖς ὁ
so many being, not was torn the net. says to them
2424 1205 709 3762 1161 5111 3588 3101
Ἰησοῦς, Δεῦτε ἀριστήσατε. οὐδεὶς δὲ ἐτόλμα τῶν μαθητῶν
Jesus, Come, break fast. no one And dared of the disciples
1833 846 4771 5101 1488 1492 3754 3588 2962 2076
ἐξετάσαι αὐτόν, Σὺ τίς εἶ; εἰδότες ὅτι ὁ Κύριός ἐστιν.
to question Him, You Who are? Knowing that the Lord it is.

11 Simon Peter went up, and drew the net to land full of great fishes, an hundred and fifty and three: and for all there were so many, yet was not the net broken.
12 Jesus saith unto them, Come (and) dine. And none of the disciples durst ask him, Who art thou? knowing that it was the Lord.

13 Then Jesus comes and takes the bread, and gives to them, and in the same way the little fish.
14 This now (is) the three times (that) Jesus was revealed to His disciples, (He) having been raised from (the) dead.

2064 3767 2424 2532 2983 3588 740 2532 1325
13 ἔρχεται οὖν Ἰησοῦς, καὶ λαμβάνει τὸν ἄρτον, καὶ δίδωσιν
comes Then Jesus, and takes the bread, and gives
846 2532 3588 3795 3668 5124 2235 5154 5319
αὐτοῖς, καὶ τὸ ὀψάριον ὁμοίως. 14 τοῦτο ἤδη τρίτον ἐφανερώθη
to them, and the little fish likewise. This now thrice was revealed
3588 2424 3588 3101 846 1453 1537 3498
ὁ Ἰησοῦς τοῖς μαθηταῖς αὐτοῦ, ἐγερθεὶς ἐκ νεκρῶν.
Jesus to the disciples of Him, having been raised from (the) dead.

13 Jesus then cometh, and taketh bread, and giveth them, and fish likewise.
14 This is now the third time that Jesus shewed himself to his disciples, after that he was risen from the dead.

15. Then when they broke fast, Jesus said to Simon Peter, Simon, (son) of Jonah, do you love Me more (than) these? He said to Him, Yes, Lord, You know that I love You. He said to him, Feed My lambs!
16 Again He says to him secondly, Simon, (son) of Jonah, do you love Me? He says to Him, Yes, Lord, You know that I love You. He says to him, Shepherd My sheep!
17 Thirdly, He said to him, Simon (son) of Jonah, do you love Me? Peter was grieved that He said to him a third (time), Do you love Me? And he said to him, Lord, You perceive all things, You know that

3753 3767 709 3004 3588 4613 4074 3588 2424
15 Ὅτε οὖν ἠρίστησαν, λέγει τῷ Σίμωνι Πέτρῳ ὁ Ἰησοῦς,
when Then they broke fast, says to Simon Peter Jesus,
4613 2495 25 3165 4119 5130 3004 846 3483
Σίμων Ἰωνᾶ, ἀγαπᾷς με πλεῖόν τούτων; λέγει αὐτῷ, Ναί,
Simon (son) of Jonah, do you love Me more (than) these? He says to Him, Yes,
2962 4771 1492 3754 5368 4571 3004 846 1006 3588 721 3450
Κύριε· σὺ οἶδας ὅτι φιλῶ σε. λέγει αὐτῷ, Βόσκε τὰ ἀρνία μου.
Lord, You know that I love You. He says to him, Feed the lambs of Me.
3004 846 3825 1208 4613 2495 25 3165 3004
16 λέγει αὐτῷ πάλιν δεύτερον, Σίμων Ἰωνᾶ, ἀγαπᾷς με; λέγει
He says to him again, secondly, Simon of Jonah, do you love Me? He says
846 3483 2962 4771 1492 3754 5368 4571 3004 846 4165
αὐτῷ, Ναὶ Κύριε· σὺ οἶδας ὅτι φιλῶ σε. λέγει αὐτῷ, Ποίμαινε
to Him, Yes, Lord, You know that I love You. He says to him, Shepherd
3588 4263 3450 3004 846 3588 5154 4613 2495 5368
τὰ πρόβατά μου. 17 λέγει αὐτῷ τὸ τρίτον, Σίμων Ἰωνᾶ, φιλεῖς
the sheep of Me. He says to him thirdly, Simon of Jonah, do you love
3165 3076 3588 4074 3754 2036 846 3588 5154 5368 3165
με; ἐλυπήθη ὁ Πέτρος ὅτι εἶπεν αὐτῷ τὸ τρίτον, φιλεῖς με;
Me? was grieved Peter because He said to him thirdly, Do you love Me?
2532 2036 846 2962 4771 3956 1492 4771 1097 3754
καὶ εἶπεν αὐτῷ, Κύριε, σὺ πάντα οἶδας, σὺ γινώσκεις ὅτι
And he said to Him, Lord, You all things perceive; You know that

15. So when they had dined, Jesus saith to Simon Peter, Simon, (son) of Jonas, lovest thou me more than these? He saith unto him, Yea, Lord; thou knowest that I love thee. He saith unto him, Feed my lambs.
16 He saith to him again the second time, Simon, (son) of Jonas, lovest thou me? He saith unto him, Yea, Lord; thou knowest that I love thee. He saith unto him, Feed my sheep.
17 He saith unto him the third time, Simon, (son) of Jonas, lovest thou me? Peter was grieved because he said unto him the third time, Lovest thou me? And he said unto him, Lord, thou knowest all things; thou knowest that

Literal Translation — **John 21:18** — **King James Version**

Literal Translation

I love You! Jesus says to him, Feed My sheep!

18 Truly, truly, I say to you, when you were younger, you girded yourself, and you walked where you desired. But when you grow old, you will stretch out your hands, and another will gird you, and will carry (you) where you do not desire.

19 But He said this, signifying by what death he will glorify God. And having said this, He told him, Follow Me.

20 But turning, Peter sees the disciple whom Jesus loved following, who also leaned on His breast at the Supper, and said, Lord, who is the (one) betraying You?

21 Seeing this one, Peter said to Jesus, Lord, and what (of) this one?

22 Jesus says to him, If I desire him to remain until I come, what (is that) to you? You follow Me.

23 Therefore, the word went out to the brothers that that disciple does not die. Yet Jesus did not say to him that he does not die, but, If I desire him to remain until I come, what (is that) to you?

24 This is the disciple witnessing about these other things, writing these things, and we know that his witness is true.

25 And many are the things whatever Jesus did, which if they were written singly, I suppose the world itself (could) not contain the scrolls having been written. Amen.

5368 4571 3004 846 3588 2424 1006 3588 4263 3450 281
φιλῶ σε. λέγει αὐτῷ ὁ Ἰησοῦς, Βόσκε τὰ πρόβατά μου. 18 ἀμὴν
I love You. says to him Jesus, Feed the sheep of Me. Truly,

281 3004 4671 3753 2258 3501 2224 4572 2532
ἀμὴν λέγω σοι, ὅτε ἦς νεώτερος, ἐζώννυες σεαυτόν, καὶ
truly, I say to you, when you were younger, you girded yourself, and

4043 3699 2309 3752 1161 1095 1614 3588
περιεπάτεις ὅπου ἤθελες· ὅταν δὲ γηράσῃς, ἐκτενεῖς τὰς
you walked where you desired, when but you grow old, you will stretch the

5495 4675 2532 243 4571 2224 2532 5342 3699 3756 2309
χεῖράς σου, καὶ ἄλλος σε ζώσει καὶ οἴσει ὅπου οὐ θέλεις.
hands of you, and another you will gird, and will carry where not you desire.

5124 1161 2036 4591 4169 2288 1392 3588 2316
19 τοῦτο δὲ εἶπε, σημαίνων ποίῳ θανάτῳ δοξάσει τὸν Θεόν.
this But He said, signifying by what death he will glorify God.

2532 5124 2036 3004 846 190 3427 1994
καὶ τοῦτο εἰπὼν λέγει αὐτῷ, Ἀκολούθει μοι. 20 Ἐπιστραφεὶς
And this having said He says to him, Follow Me. turning

1161 3588 4074 991 3588 3101 3739 25 3588 2424 190
δὲ ὁ Πέτρος βλέπει τὸν μαθητὴν ὃν ἠγάπα ὁ Ἰησοῦς ἀκολου-
And Peter sees the disciple whom loved Jesus following,

3739 2532 377 1722 3588 1173 1909 3588 4738 846
θοῦντα, ὃς καὶ ἀνέπεσεν ἐν τῷ δείπνῳ ἐπὶ τὸ στῆθος αὐτοῦ
who also leaned at the Supper on the breast of Him,

2532 2036 2962 5101 2076 3588 3860 4571 5126 1492 3588
καὶ εἶπε, Κύριε, τίς ἐστιν ὁ παραδιδούς σε; 21 τοῦτον ἰδὼν ὁ
and said, Lord, who is the (one) betraying You? this one seeing

4074 3004 3588 2424 2962 3778 1161 5101 3004 846 3588
Πέτρος λέγει τῷ Ἰησοῦ, Κύριε, οὗτος δὲ τί; 22 λέγει αὐτῷ ὁ
Peter says to Jesus, Lord, this one and what? says to him

2424 1437 846 2309 3306 2193 2064 5101 4314 4571
Ἰησοῦς, Ἐὰν αὐτὸν θέλω μένειν ἕως ἔρχομαι, τί πρός σε;
Jesus, If him I desire to remain until I come, what to you?

4771 190 3427 1831 3767 3588 3056 3778 1519 3588 80
σύ ἀκολούθει μοι. 23 ἐξῆλθεν οὖν ὁ λόγος οὗτος εἰς τοὺς ἀδελ-
You follow Me. went out Then word this to the brothers,

3754 3588 3101 1565 3756 599 2532 3756 2036
φούς, ὅτι ὁ μαθητὴς ἐκεῖνος οὐκ ἀποθνήσκει· καὶ οὐκ εἶπεν
that disciple that not does die. Yet not said

846 3588 2424 3754 3756 599 235 1437 846 2309
αὐτῷ ὁ Ἰησοῦς, ὅτι οὐκ ἀποθνήσκει· ἀλλ', Ἐὰν αὐτὸν θέλω
to him Jesus, that not he does die, but, If him I desire

3306 2193 2064 5101 4314 4571
μένειν ἕως ἔρχομαι, τί πρός σε;
to remain until I come, what to you?

3778 2076 3588 3101 3588 3140 4012 5130 2532
24. Οὗτός ἐστιν ὁ μαθητὴς ὁ μαρτυρῶν περὶ τούτων, καὶ
This is the disciple witnessing concerning these things, and

1125 5023 2532 1492 3754 227 2076 3588 3141
γράψας ταῦτα· καὶ οἴδαμεν ὅτι ἀληθὴς ἐστιν ἡ μαρτυρία
writing these things, and we know that true is the witness

846
αὐτοῦ.
of him.

2076 1161 2532 243 4183 3745 4160 3588 2424 3748
25. Ἔστι δὲ καὶ ἄλλα πολλὰ ὅσα ἐποίησεν ὁ Ἰησοῦς, ἅτινα
are And also the things many whatever did Jesus, which

1437 1125 2596 1520 3761 846 3633 3588 2889 5562
ἐὰν γράφηται καθ' ἕν, οὐδὲ αὐτὸν οἶμαι τὸν κόσμον χωρῆσαι
if they were written singly, not itself I suppose the world to contain

3588 1125 975 281
τὰ γραφόμενα βιβλία. Ἀμήν.
those having been written scrolls. Amen.

King James Version

I love thee. Jesus saith unto him, Feed my sheep.

18 Verily, verily, I say unto thee, When thou wast young, thou girdedst thyself, and walkedst whither thou wouldest: but when thou shalt be old, thou shalt stretch forth thy hands, and another shall gird thee, and carry (thee) whither thou wouldest not.

19 This spake he, signifying by what death he should glorify God. And when he had spoken this, he saith unto him, Follow me.

20 Then Peter, turning about, seeth the disciple whom Jesus loved following; which also leaned on his breast at supper, and said, Lord, which is he that betrayeth thee?

21 Peter seeing him saith to Jesus, Lord, and what (shall) this man (do)?

22 Jesus saith unto him, If I will that he tarry till I come, what (is that) to thee? follow thou me.

23 Then went this saying abroad among the brethren, that that disciple should not die: yet Jesus said not unto him, He shall not die; but, If I will that he tarry till I come, what (is that) to thee?

24 This is the disciple which testifieth of these things, and wrote these things: and we know that his testimony is true.

25 And there are also many other things which Jesus did, the which, if they should be written every one, I suppose that even the world itself could not contain the books that should be written. Amen.

Literal Translation

THE ACTS OF THE APOSTLES

Acts 1

1. Indeed, O Theophilus, I made the first account concerning all things which Jesus began both to do and to teach,
2 until which day He was taken up, having given directions to the apostles whom He chose out, through (the)' Holy Spirit,
3 to whom also He presented Himself living after His suffering, by many infallible proofs, being seen by them through forty days, and speaking the things concerning the kingdom of God.
4 And having met with them, He charged them not to depart from Jerusalem, but to await the promise of the Father, "which you heard of Me;
5 because John indeed baptized in water, but you will be baptized in (the) Holy Spirit not many days after these."
6 Then, indeed, coming together they questioned Him, saying, Lord, do You restore the kingdom to Israel at this time?
7 And He said to them, It is not yours to know times or seasons which the Father placed in His own authority;
8 but you will receive power, the Holy Spirit coming upon you, and you will be witnesses of Me both in Jerusalem, and in all Judea, and Samaria, and unto (the) end of (the) earth.
9 And saying these things, (as) they looked on, He was taken up, and a cloud

ΠΡΑΞΕΙΣ
ACTS
ΤΩΝ ΑΠΟΣΤΟΛΩΝ
OF THE APOSTLES

Acts 1

3588 3303 4413 3056 4160 4012 3956 5599
1 Τὸν μὲν πρῶτον λόγον ἐποιησάμην περὶ πάντων, ὦ
The indeed first account I made concerning all things, O

2321 3739 756 3588 2424 4160 5037 2532 1321 891
Θεόφιλε, ὧν ἤρξατο ὁ Ἰησοῦς ποιεῖν τε καὶ διδάσκειν, 2 ἄχρι
Theophilus, which began Jesus to do both and to teach, until

3739 2250 1781 3588 652 1223 4151
ἧς ἡμέρας, ἐντειλάμενος τοῖς ἀποστόλοις διὰ Πνεύματος
which day, having given directions to the apostles through (the) Spirit

40 3739 1586 353 3739 2532 3936 1438
Ἁγίου οὓς ἐξελέξατο, ἀνελήφθη· 3 οἷς καὶ παρέστησεν ἑαυτὸν
Holy whom He chose out, He was taken up; to whom also He showed Himself

2198 3326 3588 3958 846 1722 4183 5039 1223
ζῶντα μετὰ τὸ παθεῖν αὐτὸν ἐν πολλοῖς τεκμηρίοις, δι᾽
living after the suffering (of) Him by many infallible proofs, through

2250 5062 3700 846 2532 3004 3588
ἡμερῶν τεσσαράκοντα ὀπτανόμενος αὐτοῖς, καὶ λέγων τὰ
days forty being seen by' them, and saying the things

4012 3588 932 3588 2316 2532 4871 3326 846
περὶ τῆς βασιλείας τοῦ Θεοῦ. 4 καὶ συναλιζόμενος μετ᾽ αὐτῶν
about the kingdom of God. And having met with them

3853 846 575 2414 3361 5563
παρήγγειλεν αὐτοῖς ἀπὸ Ἱεροσολύμων μὴ χωρίζεσθαι,
He charged them from Jerusalem not to depart,

235 4037 3588 1860 3588 3962 3739 191
ἀλλὰ περιμένειν τὴν ἐπαγγελίαν τοῦ πατρός, ἣν ἠκούσατέ
but to await the promise of the Father, which you heard

3450 3754 2491 3303 907 5204 5210 1161 907
μου· 5 ὅτι Ἰωάννης μὲν ἐβάπτισεν ὕδατι, ὑμεῖς δὲ βαπτισθή-
of Me; because John indeed baptized in water, you but will be

1722 4151 40 3756 3326 4183 3778 2250
σεσθε ἐν Πνεύματι Ἁγίῳ οὐ μετὰ πολλὰς ταύτας ἡμέρας.
baptized in (the) Spirit Holy not after many these days.

3588 3303 3767 4905 1905 846 3004 2962
6. Οἱ μὲν οὖν συνελθόντες ἐπηρώτων αὐτὸν λέγοντες, Κύριε,
those Truly then coming together questioned Him saying, Lord,

1487 1722 3588 5550 5129 600 3588 932 3588
εἰ ἐν τῷ χρόνῳ τούτῳ ἀποκαθιστάνεις τὴν βασιλείαν τῷ
if at time this restore You the kingdom

2474 2036 1161 4314 846 3756 5216 2076 1097
Ἰσραήλ; 7 εἶπε δὲ πρὸς αὐτούς, Οὐχ ὑμῶν ἐστι γνῶναι
of Israel? He said And to them, Not of you it is to know

5550 2228 2540 3739 3588 3962 5087 1722 3588 2398 1849
χρόνους ἢ καιροὺς οὓς ὁ πατὴρ ἔθετο ἐν τῇ ἰδίᾳ ἐξουσίᾳ.
times or seasons which the Father placed in the own authority.

235 2983 1411 1904 3588 40 4151
8 ἀλλὰ λήψεσθε δύναμιν, ἐπελθόντος τοῦ Ἁγίου Πνεύματος
But you will receive power, coming the Holy Spirit

1909 5209 2532 2071 3427 3144 1722 5037 2419 2532 1722
ἐφ᾽ ὑμᾶς· καὶ ἔσεσθέ μοι μάρτυρες ἔν τε Ἱερουσαλήμ, καὶ ἐν
upon you; and you will be of Me witnesses in both Jerusalem and in

3956 3588 2449 2532 4540 2532 2193 2078 3588 1093
πάσῃ τῇ Ἰουδαίᾳ καὶ Σαμαρείᾳ, καὶ ἕως ἐσχάτου τῆς γῆς.
all Judea and Samaria, and unto (the) end of the earth.

2532 5023 2036 991 846 1869 2532 3507
9 καὶ ταῦτα εἰπών, βλεπόντων αὐτῶν ἐπήρθη, καὶ νεφέλη
And these things saying, watching them He was taken up and a cloud

King James Version

THE ACTS OF THE APOSTLES

Acts 1

1. The former treatise have I made, O Theophilus, of all that Jesus began both to do and teach,
2 Until the day in which he was taken up, after that he through the Holy Ghost had given commandments unto the apostles whom he had chosen:
3 To whom also he shewed himself alive after his passion by many infallible proofs, being seen of them forty days, and speaking of the things pertaining to the kingdom of God:
4 And, being assembled together with (them), commanded them that they should not depart from Jerusalem, but wait for the promise of the Father, which, (saith he), ye have heard of me.
5 For John truly baptized with water; but ye shall be baptized with the Holy Ghost not many days hence.
6 When they therefore were come together, they asked of him, saying, Lord, wilt thou at this time restore again the kingdom to Israel?
7 And he said unto them, It is not for you to know the times or the seasons, which the Father hath put in his own power.
8 But ye shall receive power, after that the Holy Ghost is come upon you: and ye shall be witnesses unto me both in Jerusalem, and in all Judaea, and in Samaria, and unto the uttermost part of the earth.
9 And when he had spoken these things, while they beheld, he was taken up; and a cloud

Literal Translation — **Acts 1:10** — **King James Version**

received Him from their eyes.
10 And as they were intently looking into the heaven, He having gone, even behold, two men in white clothing stood by them,

11 who also said, Men, Galileans, why do you stand looking up to the heaven? This Jesus, the (One) being taken from you into the heaven, will come in the way you saw Him going into the heaven.

5274 846 575 3588 3788 846 2532 5613 816
ὑπέλαβεν αὐτὸν ἀπὸ τῶν ὀφθαλμῶν αὐτῶν. 10 καὶ ὡς ἀτενί-
received Him from the eyes of them. And as gazing
2258 1519 3588 3772 4198 846 2532 2400
ζοντες ἦσαν εἰς τὸν οὐρανόν, πορευομένου αὐτοῦ, καὶ ἰδοὺ
they were into the heaven, having gone Him, and, behold!
435 1417 3936 846 1722 2066 3022 3739 2532
ἄνδρες δύο παρειστήκεισαν αὐτοῖς ἐν ἐσθῆτι λευκῇ, 11 οἳ καὶ
men Two stood by them in clothing white, who also
2036 435 1057 5101 2476 1689 1519 3588
εἶπον, Ἄνδρες Γαλιλαῖοι, τί ἑστήκατε ἐμβλέποντες εἰς τὸν
said, Men Galileans, why do you stand looking into the
3772 3778 3588 2424 3588 353 575 5216 1519 3588
οὐρανόν; οὗτος ὁ Ἰησοῦς, ὁ ἀναληφθεὶς ἀφ᾽ ὑμῶν εἰς τὸν
heaven? This Jesus, (the) One being taken up from you into the
3772 3779 2064 3739 5158 2300 846
οὐρανόν, οὕτως ἐλεύσεται ὃν τρόπον ἐθεάσασθε αὐτὸν
heaven, thus will come in (the) way you beheld Him
4198 1519 3588 3772
πορευόμενον εἰς τὸν οὐρανόν.
going into the heaven.

received him out of their sight.
10 And while they looked stedfastly toward heaven as he went up, behold, two men stood by them in white apparel;
11 Which also said, Ye men of Galilee, why stand ye gazing up into heaven? this same Jesus, which is taken up from you into heaven, shall so come in like manner as ye have seen him go into heaven.

12. Then they returned to Jerusalem from (the) mount being called Of Olive Grove, which is near Jerusalem, a sabbath's (journey) away.

13 And when they went in, they went up to the upper room where they were waiting: both Peter and James, and John and Andrew, Philip and Thomas, Bartholomew and Matthew, James (the son) of Alpheus and Simon the Zealot, and Judas (the brother) of James.

5119 5290 1519 2419 575 3735 3588 2564
12. Τοτε ὑπέστρεψαν εἰς Ἱερουσαλὴμ ἀπὸ ὄρους τοῦ καλου-
Then they returned into Jerusalem from (the) Mount being
1638 3739 2076 1451 2419 4521
μένου Ἐλαιῶνος, ὅ ἐστιν ἐγγὺς Ἱερουσαλήμ, σαββάτου
called Of Olives Grove, which is near Jerusalem, a sabbath's (journey)
2192 3598 2532 3753 1525 305 1519 3588 5253 3757
ἔχον ὁδόν. 13 καὶ ὅτε εἰσῆλθον, ἀνέβησαν εἰς τὸ ὑπερῷον οὗ
having a way. And when they entered, they went up to the upper room where
2258 2650 3588 5037 4074 2532 2385 2532 2491 2532
ἦσαν καταμένοντες, ὅ τε Πέτρος καὶ Ἰάκωβος καὶ Ἰωάννης καὶ
they were waiting, both Peter and James and John and
406 5376 2532 2381 918 2532 3156
Ἀνδρέας, Φίλιππος καὶ Θωμᾶς, Βαρθολομαῖος καὶ Ματθαῖος,
Andrew, Philip and Thomas, Bartholomew and Matthew,
2385 256 2532 4613 3588 2207 2532 2455 2385
Ἰάκωβος Ἁλφαίου καὶ Σίμων ὁ Ζηλωτής, καὶ Ἰούδας Ἰακώ-
James of Alpheus and Simon the Zealot, and Judas of James.

12. Then returned they unto Jerusalem from the mount called Olivet, which is from Jerusalem a sabbath day's journey.

13 And when they were come in, they went up into an upper room, where abode both Peter, and James, and John, and Andrew, Philip, and Thomas, Bartholomew, and Matthew, James (the son) of Alphaeus, and Simon Zelotes, and Judas (the brother) of James.

14 These all were continuing steadfastly in prayer and in supplication with one mind, with (the) women, and (with) Mary the mother of Jesus, and with His brothers.

3778 3956 2258 4342 3661 3588
βου. 14 οὗτοι πάντες ἦσαν προσκαρτεροῦντες ὁμοθυμαδὸν τῇ
These all were continuing steadfastly with one mind
4335 2532 3588 1162 4862 1135 2532 3137 3588 3384 3588
προσευχῇ καὶ τῇ δεήσει, σὺν γυναιξὶ καὶ Μαρίᾳ τῇ μητρὶ τοῦ
in prayer and in supplication, with (the) women and Mary the mother
2424 2532 4862 3588 80 846
Ἰησοῦ, καὶ σὺν τοῖς ἀδελφοῖς αὐτοῦ.
of Jesus, and with the brothers of Him.

14 These all continued with one accord in prayer and supplication, with the women, and Mary the mother of Jesus, and with his brethren.

15. And in these days, standing up in (the) middle of the disciples, (and (the) crowd of names together (being) about a hundred and twenty), Peter said,
16 Men, brothers, it behooved (for) this Scripture to be fulfilled which the Holy Spirit spoke before by David's mouth concerning Judas, the (one) having become guide to the (ones) seizing

2532 1722 3588 2250 3778 450 4074 1722 3319
15. Καὶ ἐν ταῖς ἡμέραις ταύταις ἀναστὰς Πέτρος ἐν μέσῳ
And in days these standing up Peter in (the) midst
3588 3101 2036 2258 5037 3793 3686 1909 3588 846 5613
τῶν μαθητῶν εἶπεν [ἦν τε ὄχλος ὀνομάτων ἐπὶ τὸ αὐτὸ ὡς
of the disciples said, was and(the) crowd of names together about
1540 1501 435 80 1163 4137 3588
ἑκατὸν εἴκοσιν], 16 Ἄνδρες ἀδελφοί, ἔδει πληρωθῆναι τὴν
a hundred twenty,, Men brothers, it behooved to be fulfilled
1124 3778 3739 4277 3588 4151 3588 40 1223 4750
γραφὴν ταύτην, ἣν προεῖπε τὸ Πνεῦμα τὸ Ἅγιον διὰ στόματος
Scripture this, which spoke before the Spirit Holy through mouth
1138 4012 2455 3588 1096 3595 3588 4815
Δαβὶδ περὶ Ἰούδα, τοῦ γενομένου ὁδηγοῦ τοῖς συλλαβοῦσι
David's concerning Judas, the (one) having been guide to the (ones) seizing

15. And in those days Peter stood up in the midst of the disciples, and said, (the number of names together were about an hundred and twenty,)
16 Men (and) brethren, this scripture must needs have been fulfilled, which the Holy Ghost by the mouth of David spake before concerning Judas, which was guide to them that

Acts 1:17

Literal Translation

Jesus;
17 for he was numbered with us, and obtained a portion of this ministry.
18 Indeed, then, this one bought a field out of the reward of unrighteousness; and beoming headlong, he burst in (the) middle, and poured out all his bowels.
19 And it became known to all those living in Jerusalem, so as that field to be called in the(ir) own dialect, Akeldama, that is, Field of Blood.

20 For it has been written in (the) scroll of Psalms, "Let his estate become forsaken, and he not be living in it." And, "Let another take his overseership." (Ps. 69:25; Ps. 109:8)

21 Therefore, must men being together with us all (the) time in which the Lord Jesus came in and went out among us,
22 beginning from the baptism of John until the day when He was taken from us, one of these to become a witness of His resurrection with us.

23 And they set out two: Joseph, he being called Barsabas, who was surnamed Justus, and Matthias.
24 And having prayed, they said, You, Lord, Heart-knower, show which one You chose out of these two,
25 to take the share of this ministry and apostleship, from which Judas fell, to go to (his) own place.

26 And they gave their lots. And the lot fell on Matthias; and he was numbered with the eleven apostles.

3588 2424 3754 2674 2258 4862 2254 2532 2975 3588
τὸν Ἰησοῦν. 17 ὅτι κατηριθμημένος ἦν σὺν ἡμῖν, καὶ ἔλαχε τὸν
Jesus; because being numbered he was with us, and obtained the

2819 3588 1248 3778 3778 3303 3767 2932
κλῆρον τῆς διακονίας ταύτης. 18 [οὗτος μὲν οὖν ἐκτήσατο
portion ministry this. this one indeed Then bought

5564 1537 3588 3408 3588 93 2532 4248 1096
χωρίον ἐκ τοῦ μισθοῦ τῆς ἀδικίας, καὶ πρηνὴς γενόμενος
a field out of the reward of unrighteousness, and headlong becoming

2997 3319 2532 1632 3956 3588 4698 846 2532
ἐλάκησε μέσος, καὶ ἐξεχύθη πάντα τὰ σπλάγχνα αὐτοῦ. 19 καὶ
he burst in (the) middle, and poured out all the bowels of him. And

1110 1096 3956 3588 2730 2419 5620
γνωστὸν ἐγένετο πᾶσι τοῖς κατοικοῦσιν Ἱερουσαλήμ, ὥστε
known it became to all those living in Jerusalem, so as

2564 3588 5564 1565 3588 2398 1258 846 184
κληθῆναι τὸ χωρίον ἐκεῖνο τῇ ἰδίᾳ διαλέκτῳ αὐτῶν Ἀκελ-
to be called field that in the own dialect of them, Akel-

5123 2076 5564 129 1125 1063 1722 976
δαμά, τοῦτ' ἔστι, χωρίον αἵματος.] 20 γέγραπται γὰρ ἐν βίβλῳ
dama, that is, Field of Blood. it has been written For in (the) scroll

5568 1096 3588 1886 846 2048 2532 3361 2077 3588
Ψαλμῶν, Γενηθήτω ἡ ἔπαυλις αὐτοῦ ἔρημος, καὶ μὴ ἔστω ὁ
of Psalms, Let become the estate of him forsaken, and not be he

2730 1722 846 2532 3588 1984 846 2983 2087
κατοικῶν ἐν αὐτῇ· καί, Τὴν ἐπισκοπὴν αὐτοῦ λάβοι ἕτερος.
living in it; and, The ovcrseership of him let take another.

1163 3767 3588 4905 2254 435 1722/3956/5550/1722/3739
21 δεῖ οὖν τῶν συνελθόντων ἡμῖν ἀνδρῶν ἐν παντὶ χρόνῳ ἐν ᾧ
must Then of the being together with us men in all (the) time in which

1525 2532 1831 1909 2248 3588 2962 2424 756
εἰσῆλθε καὶ ἐξῆλθεν ἐφ' ἡμᾶς ὁ Κύριος Ἰησοῦς, 22 ἀρξάμενος
came in and went out among us the Lord Jesus, beginning

575 3588 908 2491 2193 3588 2250 3739 353
ἀπὸ τοῦ βαπτίσματος Ἰωάννου, ἕως τῆς ἡμέρας ἧς ἀνελήφθη
from the baptism of John, until the day when He was taken

575 2257 3144 3588 386 846 1096 4862 2254
ἀφ' ἡμῶν, μάρτυρα τῆς ἀναστάσεως αὐτοῦ γενέσθαι σὺν ἡμῖν
from us, a witness of the resurrection of Him to become with us

1520 5130 2532 2476 1417 2501 3588 2564
ἕνα τούτων. 23 καὶ ἔστησαν δύο, Ἰωσὴφ τὸν καλούμενον
one of these. And they set two, Joseph the (one) being called

923 3739 1941 2459 2532 3159 2532
Βαρσαβᾶν, ὃς ἐπεκλήθη Ἰοῦστος, καὶ Ματθίαν. 24 καὶ προσ-
Barsabas, who was surnamed Justus, and Matthias. And having

4336 2036 4771 2962 2589 3956 322
ευξάμενοι εἶπον, Σὺ Κύριε καρδιογνῶστα πάντων, ἀνά-
prayed they said, You Lord Heart-knower of all, show

1537 5130 3588 1417 3739 1520 1586 2983 3588 2819
δειξον ἐκ τούτων τῶν δύο ὃν ἕνα ἐξελέξω, 25 λαβεῖν τὸν κλῆρον
out of these two which one You chose, to take the share

3588 1248 3778 2532 651 1537 3739 3845 2455
τῆς διακονίας ταύτης καὶ ἀποστολῆς, ἐξ ἧς παρέβη Ἰούδας,
of ministry this and apostleship, from which fell Judas,

4198 1519 3588 5117 3588 2398 2532 1325 2819
πορευθῆναι εἰς τὸν τόπον τὸν ἴδιον. 26 καὶ ἔδωκαν κλήρους
to go into the place own. And they gave lots

846 2532 4098 3588 2819 1909 3159 2532 4785
αὐτῶν, καὶ ἔπεσεν ὁ κλῆρος ἐπὶ Ματθίαν, καὶ συγκατεψη-
for them, and fell the lot on Matthias, and he was counted

3326 3588 1733 652
φίσθη μετὰ τῶν ἕνδεκα ἀποστόλων.
with the eleven apostles.

King James Version

took Jesus.
17 For he was numbered with us, and had obtained part of this ministry.
18 Now this man purchased a field with the reward of iniquity; and falling headlong, he burst asunder in the midst, and all his bowels gushed out.
19 And it was known unto all the dwellers at Jerusalem; insomuch as that field is called in their proper tongue, Aceldama, that is to say, The field of blood.

20 For it is written in the book of Psalms, Let his habitation be desolate, and let no man dwell therein: and his bishoprick let another take.

21 Wherefore of these men which have companied with us all the time that the Lord Jesus went in and out among us,
22 Beginning from the baptism of John, unto that same day that he was taken up from us, must one be ordained to be a witness with us of his resurrection.

23 And they appointed two, Joseph called Barsabas, who was surnamed Justus, and Matthias.
24 And they prayed, and said, Thou, Lord, which knowest the hearts of all (men), shew whether of these two thou hast chosen,
25 That he may take part of this ministry and apostleship, from which Judas by transgression fell, that he might go to his own place.
26 And they gave forth their lots; and the lot fell upon Matthias; and he was numbered with the eleven apostles.

Literal Translation

Acts 2

1. And in the fulfilling of the day of Pentecost, they were all with one mind on the same (place).
2 And suddenly came to be a sound out of the heaven, as being borne along by a violent wind! And it filled the whole of the house where they were sitting.
3 And tongues as of fire appeared to them, being distributed, and it sat on each of them.

4 And they were all filled of the Holy Spirit, and began to speak in other tongues, as the Spirit gave (ability) to them to speak.

5 And Jews were living in Jerusalem, devout men from every nation of those under the heaven.
6 But this sound occurring, the multitude came together and were confounded, because they each heard them speaking into (his) own dialect.

7 And all were amazed and marveled, saying to one another, Behold, are not all these, those speaking, Galileans?
8 And how do we hear each in our own dialect in which we were born,

9 Parthians, and Medes, and Elamites, and those living in Mesopotamia, both Judea and Cappadocia, Pontus and Asia,

10 both Phrygia and Pamphylia, Egypt, and the regions of Libya over against Cyrene, and the temporarily residing Romans, both Jews and proselytes,
11 Cretans and Arabians; we hear them speaking

Acts 2

2532 1722 3588 4845 3588 2250 3588 4005
1 Καὶ ἐν τῷ συμπληροῦσθαι τὴν ἡμέραν τῆς Πεντηκοστῆς,
And in the fulfilling of the Day of Pentecost,
2258 537 3661 1909 3588 846 2532 1096 869
ἦσαν ἅπαντες ὁμοθυμαδὸν ἐπὶ τὸ αὐτό. 2 καὶ ἐγένετο ἄφνω
they were all with one mind upon the same. And came to be suddenly
1537 3588 3772 2279 5618 5342 4157 972 2532
ἐκ τοῦ οὐρανοῦ ἦχος ὥσπερ φερομένης πνοῆς βιαίας, καὶ
out of the heaven a sound as being borne of a wind violent, and
4137 3650 3588 3624 3757 2258 2521 2532 3700
ἐπλήρωσεν ὅλον τὸν οἶκον οὗ ἦσαν καθήμενοι. 3 καὶ ὤφθησαν
it filled (the) whole of the house where they were sitting. And appeared
846 1266 1100 5616 4442 2523 5037 1909
αὐτοῖς διαμεριζόμεναι γλῶσσαι ὡσεὶ πυρός, ἐκάθισέ τε ἐφ'
to them being distributed tongues as of fire, it sat and on
1520 1538 846 2532 4130 537 4151
ἕνα ἕκαστον αὐτῶν. 4 καὶ ἐπλήσθησαν ἅπαντες Πνεύματος
one each of them. And they were filled all of (the) Spirit
40 2532 756 2980 2087 1100 2531 3588
Ἁγίου, καὶ ἤρξαντο λαλεῖν ἑτέραις γλώσσαις, καθὼς τὸ
Holy, and began to speak (in) other tongues, even as the
4151 1325 846 669
Πνεῦμα ἐδίδου αὐτοῖς ἀποφθέγγεσθαι.
Spirit gave to them to speak.

2258 1161 1722 2419 2730 2453 435
5 Ἦσαν δὲ ἐν Ἱερουσαλὴμ κατοικοῦντες Ἰουδαῖοι, ἄνδρες
were And in Jerusalem living Jews, men
2126 575 3956 1484 3588 5259 3588 3772 1096
εὐλαβεῖς, ἀπὸ παντὸς ἔθνους τῶν ὑπὸ τὸν οὐρανόν. 6 γενο-
devout, from every nation of those under the heaven. happen-
1161 3588 5456 3778 4905 3588 4128 2532 4797
μένης δὲ τῆς φωνῆς ταύτης, συνῆλθε τὸ πλῆθος καὶ συνεχύθη,
ing And sound this, came together the hrong and were confounded,
3754 191 1520 1538 3588 2398 1258 2980 846
ὅτι ἤκουον εἷς ἕκαστος τῇ ἰδίᾳ διαλέκτῳ λαλούντων αὐτῶν.
for they heard into each the own dialect speaking them.
1839 1161 3956 2532 2296 3004 4314 240
7 ἐξίσταντο δὲ πάντες καὶ ἐθαύμαζον, λέγοντες πρὸς ἀλλήλους,
were amazed And all and marveled, saying to one another,
3756 2400 3956 3778 1526 3588 2980 1057 2532
Οὐκ ἰδοὺ πάντες οὗτοί εἰσιν οἱ λαλοῦντες Γαλιλαῖοι; 8 καὶ
not Behold all these are those speaking Galileans? And
4459 2249 191 1538 3588 2398 1258 2257/1722/3739
πῶς ἡμεῖς ἀκούομεν ἕκαστος τῇ ἰδίᾳ διαλέκτῳ ἡμῶν ἐν ᾗ
how do we hear each the own dialect of us in which
1080 3934 2532 3370 2532 1639 2532 3588
ἐγεννήθημεν; 9 Πάρθοι καὶ Μῆδοι καὶ Ἐλαμῖται, καὶ οἱ
we were born? Parthians and Medes and Elamites, and those
2730 3588 3318 2449 5037 2532 2587
κατοικοῦντες τὴν Μεσοποταμίαν, Ἰουδαίαν τε καὶ Καπ-
living in Mesopotamia, Judea, both and Cappa-
4195 2532 3588 773 5435 5037 2532 3828
παδοκίαν, Πόντον καὶ τὴν Ἀσίαν, 10 Φρυγίαν τε καὶ Παμφυ-
docia, Pontus and Asia, Phrygia both and Pam-
125 2532 3588 3313 3588 3033 3588 2596 2957
λίαν, Αἴγυπτον καὶ τὰ μέρη τῆς Λιβύης τῆς κατὰ Κυρήνην,
philia, Egypt and the regions of Libya over against Cyrene,
2532 3588 1927 4514 2453 5037 2532 4339
καὶ οἱ ἐπιδημοῦντες Ῥωμαῖοι, 11 Ἰουδαῖοί τε καὶ προσήλυτοι,
and the temporarily residing Romans, Jews both and proselytes,
2912 2532 690 191 2980 846 3588
Κρῆτες καὶ Ἄραβες, ἀκούομεν λαλούντων αὐτῶν ταῖς
Cretans and Arabians, we hear speaking them (in)

King James Version

Acts 2

1. And when the day of Pentecost was fully come, they were all with one accord in one place.
2 And suddenly there came a sound from heaven as of a rushing mighty wind, and it filled all the house where they were sitting.
3 And there appeared unto them cloven tongues like as of fire, and it sat upon each of them.

4 And they were all filled with the Holy Ghost, and began to speak with other tongues, as the Spirit gave them utterance.

5 And there were dwelling at Jerusalem Jews, devout men, out of every nation under heaven.
6 Now when this was noised abroad, the multitude came together, and were confounded, because that every man heard them speak in his own language.

7 And they were all amazed and marvelled, saying one to another, Behold, are not all these which speak Galilaeans?
8 And how hear we every man in our own tongue, wherein we were born?
9 Parthians, and Medes, and Elamites, and the dwellers in Mesopotamia, and in Judaea, and Cappadocia, in Pontus, and Asia,

10 Phrygia, and Pamphylia, in Egypt, and in the parts of Libya about Cyrene, and strangers of Rome, Jews and proselytes,

11 Cretes and Arabians, we do hear them speak in

Acts 2:12

Literal Translation

(in) our languages the great deeds of God?
12 And all were amazed and puzzled, saying to one another, What would this wish to be?

13 But ridiculing, others said, They have been filled of sweet wine.

14. But standing up with the Eleven, Peter lifted up his voice and spoke out to them, Men, Jews, and all those living in Jerusalem, let this be known to you, and listen to my words:

15 For these are not drunk, as you imagine, for it is (the) third hour of the day.

16 But this is that having been spoken through the prophet Joel,
17 "And it shall be in the last days, says God, I will pour from My Spirit on all flesh, and your sons and your daughters will prophesy; and your young men will see visions, and your old men will dream dreams;

18 and I will pour out of My Spirit even on My slaves and slave-girls in those days, and they will prophesy.

19 And I will give wonders in the heaven above, and signs on the earth below, blood and fire and vapor of smoke.

20 The sun will be turned into darkness, and the moon into blood, before the coming of the great and glorious day of (the) Lord.
21 And it will be (that) everyone who shall call on (the) name of the Lord

2251 1100 3588 3167 3588 2316 1839 1161
ἡμετέραις γλώσσαις τὰ μεγαλεῖα τοῦ Θεοῦ. 12 ἐξίσταντο δὲ
our tongues the great deeds of God. were amazed And

3956 2532 1280 243 4314 243 3004 5101 302
πάντες καὶ διηπόρουν, ἄλλος πρὸς ἄλλον λέγοντες, Τί ἂν
all and were puzzled, other to other saying, What may

2309 5124 1511 2087 1161 5512 3004 3754
θέλοι τοῦτο εἶναι; 13 ἕτεροι δὲ χλευάζοντες ἔλεγον ὅτι
you wish this to be? others But ridiculing said because

1098 3325 1526
Γλεύκους μεμεστωμένοι εἰσί.
of new wine having been filled they are.

2476 1161 4074 4862 3588 1733 1869 3588 5456
14. Σταθεὶς δὲ Πέτρος σὺν τοῖς ἕνδεκα, ἐπῆρε τὴν φωνὴν αὐ-
standing But Peter with the Eleven, lifted up the voice of

846 2532 669 846 435 2453 2532 3588
τοῦ, καὶ ἀπεφθέγξατο αὐτοῖς, Ἄνδρες Ἰουδαῖοι, καὶ οἱ κατ-
him, and spoke out to them, Men Jews, and those

2730 2419 537 5124 5213 1110 2077
οικοῦντες Ἱερουσαλὴμ ἅπαντες, τοῦτο ὑμῖν γνωστὸν ἔστω,
living in Jerusalem all, this to you known let be,

2532 1801 3588 4487 3450 3756 1063 5613 5210 5274
καὶ ἐνωτίσασθε τὰ ῥήματά μου. 15 οὐ γάρ, ὡς ὑμεῖς ὑπολαμ-
and listen to the words of me. not For, as you imagine,

3778 3184 2076 1063 5610 5154 3588 2250
βάνετε, οὗτοι μεθύουσιν· ἔστι γὰρ ὥρα τρίτη τῆς ἡμέρας·
these are drunk; it is for hour (the) third of the day;

235 5124 2076 3588 2046 1223 3588 4396 2493
16 ἀλλὰ τοῦτό ἐστι τὸ εἰρημένον διὰ τοῦ προφήτου Ἰωήλ,
but this is that having been spoken through the prophet Joel,

2532 2071 1722 3588 2078 2250 3004 3588 2316 1632 575
17 Καὶ ἔσται ἐν ταῖς ἐσχάταις ἡμέραις, λέγει ὁ Θεός, ἐκχεῶ ἀπὸ
And it shall be in the last days, says God, I will pour from

3588 4151 3450 1909 3956 4561 2532 4395
τοῦ πνεύματός μου ἐπὶ πᾶσαν σάρκα· καὶ προφητεύσουσιν
the Spirit of Me on all flesh, and will prophesy

3588 5207 5216 2532 3588 2364 5216 2532 3588 3495 5216
οἱ υἱοὶ ὑμῶν καὶ αἱ θυγατέρες ὑμῶν, καὶ οἱ νεανίσκοι ὑμῶν
the sons of you and the daughters of you, and the young men of you

3706 3700 2532 3588 4245 5216 1798 1797
ὁράσεις ὄψονται, καὶ οἱ πρεσβύτεροι ὑμῶν ἐνύπνια ἐνυπνια-
visions will see, and the old men of you dreams will

2532 1065 1909 3588 1401 3450 2532 1909 3588 1399
σθήσονται· 18 καί γε ἐπὶ τοὺς δούλους μου καὶ ἐπὶ τὰς δούλας
dream, and even on the male slaves of Me and on the slave-girls

3450 1722 3588 2250 1565 1632 575 3588 4151 3450 2532
μου ἐν ταῖς ἡμέραις ἐκείναις ἐκχεῶ ἀπὸ τοῦ πνεύματός μου, καὶ
of Me in days those I will pour from the Spirit of Me, and

4395 2532 1325 5059 1722 3588 3772 507 2532
προφητεύσουσι. 19 καὶ δώσω τέρατα ἐν τῷ οὐρανῷ ἄνω, καὶ
they will prophesy. And I will give wonders in the heaven above, and

4592 1909 3588 1093 2736 129 2532 4442 2532 822 2586
σημεῖα ἐπὶ τῆς γῆς κάτω, αἷμα καὶ πῦρ καὶ ἀτμίδα καπνοῦ·
signs on the earth below, blood and fire and vapor of smoke;

3588 2246 3344 1519 4655 2532 3588 4582 1519
20 ὁ ἥλιος μεταστραφήσεται εἰς σκότος, καὶ ἡ σελήνη εἰς
the sun will be turned into darkness, and the moon into

129 4250 2228 2064 3588 2250 2962 3588 3173 2532
αἷμα, πρὶν ἢ ἐλθεῖν τὴν ἡμέραν Κυρίου τὴν μεγάλην καὶ
blood, before comes the day of (the) Lord great and

2016 2532 2071 3956 3739 302 1941 3588 3686 2962
ἐπιφανῆ· 21 καὶ ἔσται, πᾶς ὃς ἂν ἐπικαλέσηται τὸ ὄνομα Κυρίου
glorious. And it will be, everyone whoever calls on the name of (the) Lord

King James Version

our tongues the wonderful works of God.
12 And they were all amazed, and were in doubt, saying one to another, What meaneth this?

13 Others mocking said, These men are full of new wine.

14. But Peter, standing up with the eleven, lifted up his voice, and said unto them, Ye men of Judaea, and all (ye) that dwell at Jerusalem, be this known unto you, and hearken to my words:

15 For these are not drunken, as ye suppose, seeing it is (but) the third hour of the day.

16 But this is that which was spoken by the prophet Joel;
17 And it shall come to pass in the last days, saith God, I will pour out of my Spirit upon all flesh: and your sons and your daughters shall prophesy, and your young men shall see visions, and your old men shall dream dreams:

18 And on my servants and on my handmaidens I will pour out in those days of my Spirit; and they shall prophesy:

19 And I will shew wonders in heaven above, and signs in the earth beneath; blood, and fire, and vapour of smoke:

20 The sun shall be turned into darkness, and the moon into blood, before that great and notable day of the Lord come:
21 And it shall come to pass, (that) whosoever shall call on the name of the Lord

Literal Translation | **Acts 2:22** | ***King James Version***

will be saved." (Joel 3:15)
22 Men, Israelites, hear these words: Jesus the Nazarene, a man from God, having been approved among you by powerful deeds and wonders and signs, which God did through Him in your midst, as you yourselves also know,
23 this One given (to you) by the before-determined counsel and foreknowledge of God, (you) having taken through lawless hands, having crucified (Him), you put (Him) to death.
24 (But) God raised (Him) up, having loosed the pangs of death, because it was not possible for Him to be held by it.
25 For David said as to Him, "I foresaw the Lord before Me through all, because He is on My right (hand), that I not be moved.
26 For this reason My heart exulted, and My tongue was glad; and My flesh also will dwell on hope,
27 because You will not leave My soul in Hades, nor will You give Your Holy One to see corruption.
28 You revealed to Me paths of life; You will fill Me with joy with Your face." (Ps.16:8-11)
29 Men, brothers, it is permitted to say to you with plainness concerning the patriarch David, that he both died and was buried, and his tomb is among us until this day.
30 Then being a prophet, and knowing that God swore with an oath to him that of (the) fruit of his loin, as concerning flesh, to raise the Christ to sit on his throne, (see Ps. 132:11)
31 foreseeing,

4982 435 2475 191 3588 3056
σωθήσεται. 22 ἄνδρες Ἰσραηλῖται, ἀκούσατε τοὺς λόγους
will be saved. Men Israelites, hear words

5128 2424 3588 3480 435 575 3588 2316
τούτους· Ἰησοῦν τὸν Ναζωραῖον, ἄνδρα ἀπὸ τοῦ Θεοῦ
these; Jesus the Nazarene, a Man from God

584 1519 5209 1411 2532 5059 2532 4592
ἀποδεδειγμένον εἰς ὑμᾶς δυνάμεσι καὶ τέρασι καὶ σημείοις,
having been approved to you works of power and wonders and signs,

3739 4160 1223 846 3588 2316 1722 3319 5216 2531 2532 846
οἷς ἐποίησε δι' αὐτοῦ ὁ Θεὸς ἐν μέσῳ ὑμῶν, καθὼς καὶ αὐτοὶ
which did through Him God in (the) midst of you, even as also your(selves)

1492 5126 3588 3724 1012 2532 4268 3588 2316
οἴδατε, 23 τοῦτον τῇ ὡρισμένῃ βουλῇ καὶ προγνώσει τοῦ Θεοῦ
know, this (One) by the before counsel and foreknowledge of God

1560 2983 1223 5495 459 4362 337
ἔκδοτον λαβόντες, διὰ χειρῶν ἀνόμων προσπήξαντες ἀνείλ-
given up having taken, through hands lawless having curcified you

3739 3588 2316 450 3089 3588 5604 3588 2288
ετε· 24 ὃν ὁ Θεὸς ἀνέστησε, λύσας τὰς ὠδῖνας τοῦ θανάτου,
killed; whom God raised up, having loosed the pangs of death,

2530 3756 2258 1415 2902 846 5259 846 1138
καθότι οὐκ ἦν δυνατὸν κρατεῖσθαι αὐτὸν ὑπ' αὐτοῦ. 25 Δαβὶδ
because not was possible to be held Him by it. David

1063 3004 1519 846 4308 3588 2962 1799 3450
γὰρ λέγει εἰς αὐτόν, Προωρώμην τὸν Κύριον ἐνώπιόν μου
For says (as) to Him, I foresaw the Lord before me

1223 3956 3754 1537 1188 3450 2076 2443 3361 4531 1223
διὰ παντός· ὅτι ἐκ δεξιῶν μου ἐστίν, ἵνα μὴ σαλευθῶ· 26 διὰ
through all; because on (the) right of me He is, that not I be moved; because

5124 2165 3588 2588 3450 2532 21 3588 1100
τοῦτο εὐφράνθη ἡ καρδία μου, καὶ ἠγαλλιάσατο ἡ γλῶσσά
of this was glad the heart of me, and exulted the tongue

3450 2089 1161 2532 3588 4561 3450 2681 1909 1680 3754 3756
μου· ἔτι δὲ καὶ ἡ σάρξ μου κατασκηνώσει ἐπ' ἐλπίδι· 27 ὅτι οὐκ
of me, yet and also the flesh of me will dwell on hope; because not

1459 3588 5590 3450 1519 86 3761 1325 3588
ἐγκαταλείψεις τὴν ψυχήν μου εἰς ᾄδου, οὐδὲ δώσεις τὸν
You will leave the soul of Me in Hades, nor will You give the

3741 4675 1492 1312 1107 3427 3598 2222
ὅσιόν σου ἰδεῖν διαφθοράν. 28 ἐγνώρισάς μοι ὁδοὺς ζωῆς·
Holy One of You to see corruption. You revealed to Me paths of life;

4137 3165 2167 3326 3588 4383 4675 435
πληρώσεις με εὐφροσύνης μετὰ τοῦ προσώπου σου. 29 ἄνδρες
You will fill Me with joy with the face of you. Men

80 1832 2036 3326 3954 4314 5209 4012 3588
ἀδελφοί, ἐξὸν εἰπεῖν μετὰ παρρησίας πρὸς ὑμᾶς περὶ τοῦ
brothers, it is permitted to say with plainness to you concerning the

3966 1138 3754 2532 5053 2532 2290 2532 3588
πατριάρχου Δαβίδ, ὅτι καὶ ἐτελεύτησε καὶ ἐτάφη, καὶ τὸ
patriarch David, that both he died and was buried, and the

3418 846 2076 1722 2254 891 3588 2250 3778 4396
μνῆμα αὐτοῦ ἐστιν ἐν ἡμῖν ἄχρι τῆς ἡμέρας ταύτης. 30 προφή-
tomb of him is among us until day this. a prophet

3767 5225 2532 1492 3754 3727 3660 846 3588 2316
της οὖν ὑπάρχων, καὶ εἰδὼς ὅτι ὅρκῳ ὤμοσεν αὐτῷ ὁ Θεός,
Then being, and knowing that with an oath swore to him God,

1537 2590 3588 3751 846 3588 2596 4561 450
ἐκ καρποῦ τῆς ὀσφύος αὐτοῦ τὸ κατὰ σάρκα ἀναστήσειν
from (the) fruit of the loins of him according to flesh to raise up

3588 5547 2523 1909 3588 2362 846 4275
τὸν Χριστόν, καθίσαι ἐπὶ τοῦ θρόνου αὐτοῦ, 31 προϊδὼν
the Christ, to sit on the throne of him, foreseeing

shall be saved.
22 Ye men of Israel, hear these words; Jesus of Nazareth, a man approved of God among you by miracles and wonders and signs, which God did by him in the midst of you, as ye yourselves also know:
23 Him, being delivered by the determinate counsel and foreknowledge of God, ye have taken, and by wicked hands have crucified and slain:
24 Whom God hath raised up, having loosed the pains of death: because it was not possible that he should be holden of it.
25 For David speaketh concerning him, I foresaw the Lord always before my face, for he is on my right hand, that I should not be moved:
26 Therefore did my heart rejoice, and my tongue was glad; moreover also my flesh shall rest in hope:
27 Because thou wilt not leave my soul in hell, neither wilt thou suffer thine Holy One to see corruption.
28 Thou hast made known to me the ways of life; thou shalt make me full of joy with thy countenance.
29 Men (and) brethren, let me freely speak unto you of the patriarch David, that he is both dead and buried, and his sepulchre is with us unto this day.
30 Therefore being a prophet, and knowing that God had sworn with an oath to him, that of the fruit of his loins, according to the flesh, he would raise up Christ to sit on his throne;
31 He seeing

Literal Translation

he spoke about the resurrection of the Christ, that His soul was not left in Hades, nor did His flesh see corruption. (Ps.16:10)

32 This Jesus God raised up, of which we all are witnesses.

33 Then being exalted to the right of God, and receiving the promise of the Holy Spirit from the Father, He poured out this which you now see and hear.
34 For David did not ascend into Heaven, but he says, "The Lord said to my Lord, Sit at My right (hand)

35 until I place the hostile oes of You as a footstool to Your feet." (Ps.110:1)
36 Therefore assuredly, let all (the) house of Israel know that God made Him both Lord and Christ, this Jesus whom you crucified.

37. And having heard they were stabbed in the heart, and said to Peter and the rest of the apostles, Men, brothers, What shall we do?

38 And Peter said to them, Repent and be baptized, each of you on the name of Jesus Christ unto remission of sins. And you will receive the gift of the Holy Spirit.

39 For the promise is to you and to your children, even to all the (ones) at a distance, as many as (the) Lord our God shall call.

40 And with many other words he earnestly testified and exhorted, saying, Be saved from this perverse generation.

41. Then those who gladly welcoming

Acts 2:32

2980 4012 3588 386 3588 5547 3754 3756 2641
ἐλάλησε περὶ τῆς ἀναστάσεως τοῦ Χριστοῦ, ὅτι οὐ κατελείφθη
he spoke concerning the resurrection of the Christ, that not was left

3588 5590 846 1519 86 3761 3588 4561 846 1492 1312
ἡ ψυχὴ αὐτοῦ εἰς ᾅδου, οὐδὲ ἡ σὰρξ αὐτοῦ εἶδε διαφθοράν.
the soul of Him in Hades, nor the flesh of Him did see corruption.

5126 3588 2424 450 3588 2316 3739 3956 2249
32 τοῦτον τὸν Ἰησοῦν ἀνέστησεν ὁ Θεός, οὗ πάντες ἡμεῖς
This Jesus raised up God, of which all we

2070 3144 3588 1188 3767 3588 2316 5312 3588 5037
ἐσμεν μάρτυρες. 33 τῇ δεξιᾷ οὖν τοῦ Θεοῦ ὑψωθείς, τήν τε
are witnesses. to the right Then of God being exalted, the and

1860 3588 40 4151 2983 3844 3588 3962
ἐπαγγελίαν τοῦ Ἁγίου Πνεύματος λαβὼν παρὰ τοῦ πατρός,
promise of the Holy Spirit receiving from the Father,

1632 5124 3739 3568 5210 991 2532 191 3756 1063 1138
ἐξέχεε τοῦτο ὃ νῦν ὑμεῖς βλέπετε καὶ ἀκούετε. 34 οὐ γὰρ Δαβὶδ
He poured out this which now you see and hear. not For David

305 1519 3588 3772 3004 1161 846 2036 3588 2962 3588
ἀνέβη εἰς τοὺς οὐρανούς, λέγει δὲ αὐτός, Εἶπεν ὁ Κύριος τῷ
ascended into the heavens, says but he, said The Lord to the

2962 3450 2521 1537 1188 3450 2193 302 5087 3588 2190
Κυρίῳ μου, Κάθου ἐκ δεξιῶν μου, 35 ἕως ἂν θῶ τοὺς ἐχθρούς
Lord of Me, Sit at (the) right of Me, until I may place the hostile (ones)

4675 5286 3588 4228 4675 806 3767 1097 3956
σου ὑποπόδιον τῶν ποδῶν σου. 36 ἀσφαλῶς οὖν γινωσκέτω πᾶς
of You a footstool to the feet of You. assuredly Therefore let know all

3624 2474 3754 2532 2962 2532 5547 846 3588 2316
οἶκος Ἰσραήλ, ὅτι καὶ Κύριον καὶ Χριστὸν αὐτὸν ὁ Θεὸς
the house of Israel, that both Lord and Christ Him God

4160 5126 3588 2424 3739 5210 4717
ἐποίησε, τοῦτον τὸν Ἰησοῦν ὃν ὑμεῖς ἐσταυρώσατε.
made, this Jesus whom you crucified.

191 1161 2660 3588 2588 2036 5037 4314
37. Ἀκούσαντες δὲ κατενύγησαν τῇ καρδίᾳ, εἶπόν τε πρὸς
having heard And they were stabbed to the heart, said and to

3588 4074 2532 3588 3062 652 5101 4160
τὸν Πέτρον καὶ τοὺς λοιποὺς ἀποστόλους, Τί ποιήσομεν,
Peter and the remaining apostles, What may we do,

435 80 4074 1161 5346 4314 846 3340
ἄνδρες ἀδελφοί; 38 Πέτρος δὲ ἔφη πρὸς αὐτούς, Μετανοήσατε,
men brothers? Peter And said to them, Repent,

2532 907 1538 5216 1909 3588 3686 2424
καὶ βαπτισθήτω ἕκαστος ὑμῶν ἐπὶ τῷ ὀνόματι Ἰησοῦ
and be baptized each of you on the name of Jesus

5547 1519 859 266 2532 2983 3588 1431 3588
Χριστοῦ εἰς ἄφεσιν ἁμαρτιῶν, καὶ λήψεσθε τὴν δωρεὰν τοῦ
Christ unto remission of sins, and you will receive the gift of the

40 4151 5213 1063 2076 3588 1860 2532 3588
Ἁγίου Πνεύματος. 39 ὑμῖν γάρ ἐστιν ἡ ἐπαγγελία, καὶ τοῖς
Holy Spirit. to you For is the promise and to the

5043 5216 2532 3956 3588 1519 3112 3745 302 4341
τέκνοις ὑμῶν, καὶ πᾶσι τοῖς εἰς μακράν, ὅσους ἂν προσ-
children of you, even to all the (ones) at a distance, as many as shall call

2962 3588 2316 2257 2087 5037 3056 4119
καλέσηται Κύριος ὁ Θεὸς ἡμῶν. 40 ἑτέροις τε λόγοις πλείοσι
(the) Lord God of us. with other And words many

1263 2532 3870 3004 4982 575 3588 1074
διεμαρτύρετο καὶ παρεκάλει λέγων, Σώθητε ἀπὸ τῆς γενεᾶς
He earnestly testified and exhorted saying, Be saved from generation

3588 4646 3778 3588 3303 3767 780 588 3588
τῆς σκολιᾶς ταύτης. 41 οἱ μὲν οὖν ἀσμένως ἀποδεξάμενοι τὸν
perverse this. the (ones) Truly then gladly welcoming the

King James Version

this before spake of the resurrection of Christ, that his soul was not left in hell, neither his flesh did see corruption.

32 This Jesus hath God raised up, whereof we all are witnesses.

33 Therefore being by the right hand of God exalted, and having received of the Father the promise of the Holy Ghost, he hath shed forth this, which ye now see and hear.
34 For David is not ascended into the heavens: but he saith himself, The LORD said unto my Lord, Sit thou on my right hand,
35 Until I make thy foes thy footstool.
36 Therefore let all the house of Israel know assuredly, that God hath made that same Jesus, whom ye have crucified, both Lord and Christ.

37. Now when they heard (this), they were pricked in their heart, and said unto Peter and to the rest of the apostles, Men (and) brethren, what shall we do?
38 Then Peter said unto them, Repent, and be baptized every one of you in the name of Jesus Christ for the remission of sins, and ye shall receive the gift of the Holy Ghost.

39 For the promise is unto you, and to your children, and to all that are afar off, (even) as many as the Lord our God shall call.

40 And with many other words did he testify and exhort, saying, Save yourselves from this untoward generation.

41. Then they that gladly received

Literal Translation | **Acts 2:42** | **King James Version**

his words were baptized. And about three thousand souls were added that day.
42 And (they) were continuing steadfastly in the teaching of the apostles, and in the fellowship, and in the breaking of bread, and in the prayers.

3056 846 907 2532 4369 3588 2250
λόγον αὐτοῦ ἐβαπτίσθησαν· καὶ προσετέθησαν τῇ ἡμέρᾳ
word of him were baptized; and there were added day
1565 5590 5616 5153 2258 1161 4342
ἐκείνῃ ψυχαὶ ὡσεὶ τρισχίλιαι. 42 ἦσαν δὲ προσκαρτεροῦντες
that souls about three thousand. were And steadfastly continuing
3588 1322 3588 652 2532 3588 2842 2532 3588 2800
τῇ διδαχῇ τῶν ἀποστόλων καὶ τῇ κοινωνίᾳ, καὶ τῇ κλάσει
in the teaching of the apostles and in the fellowship, and in the breaking
3588 740 2532 3588 4335
τοῦ ἄρτου καὶ ταῖς προσευχαῖς.
of bread and in the prayers.

his word were baptized: and the same day there were added (unto them) about three thousand souls.
42 And they continued stedfastly in the apostles' doctrine and fellowship, and in breaking of bread, and in prayers.

43 And fear came to every soul, and many wonders and signs occurred through the apostles.
44 And all the believing ones were together and had all things common.
45 And they sold possessions and goods and distributed them to all, according as anyone had need.

1096 1161 3956 5590 5401 4183 5037 5059 2532
43 Ἐγένετο δὲ πάσῃ ψυχῇ φόβος, πολλά τε τέρατα καὶ
came And to every soul fear, many and wonders and
4592 1223 3588 652 1096 3956 1161 3588 4100
σημεῖα διὰ τῶν ἀποστόλων ἐγίνετο. 44 πάντες δὲ οἱ πιστεύ-
signs through the apostles occurred. all And the believing
2258 1909 3588 846 2532 2192 537 2839 2532 3588
οντες ἦσαν ἐπὶ τὸ αὐτό, καὶ εἶχον ἅπαντα κοινά, 45 καὶ τὰ
ones were together, and had all things common, and the
2933 2532 3588 5223 4097 2532 1266 846
κτήματα καὶ τὰς ὑπάρξεις ἐπίπρασκον, καὶ διεμέριζον αὐτὰ
goods and possessions they sold, and distributed them
3956 2530 302 5100 5532 2192 2596 2250 5037 4342
πᾶσι, καθότι ἄν τις χρείαν εἶχε. 46 καθ' ἡμέραν τε προσκαρτε-
to all, according as anyone need had. from day to day And continuing
3661 1722 3588 2411 2806 5037 2596 3624
ροῦντες ὁμοθυμαδὸν ἐν τῷ ἱερῷ, κλῶντές τε κατ' οἶκον
steadfastly with one mind in the temple, breaking and house to house
740 3335 5160 1722 20 2532 858
ἄρτον, μετελάμβανον τροφῆς ἐν ἀγαλλιάσει καὶ ἀφελότητι
bread, they shared food in gladness and simplicity
2588 134 3588 2316 2532 2192 5485 4314 3650
καρδίας, 47 αἰνοῦντες τὸν Θεόν, καὶ ἔχοντες χάριν πρὸς ὅλον
of heart, praising God, and having favor with all
3588 2992 3588 1161 2962 4369 3588 4982 2596
τὸν λαόν. ὁ δὲ Κύριος προσετίθει τοὺς σωζομένους καθ'
the people. the And Lord added the (ones) having been saved from
2250 3588 1577
ἡμέραν τῇ ἐκκλησίᾳ.
day to day to the church.

43 And fear came upon every soul: and many wonders and signs were done by the apostles.
44 And all that believed were together, and had all things common;
45 And sold their possessions and goods, and parted them to all (men), as every man had need.

46 And continuing steadfastly with one mind day to day in the temple, and breaking bread house to house, they shared food in gladness and simplicity of heart,
47 praising God, and having favor with all the people. And the Lord added to the church the (ones) having been saved from day to day.

46 And they, continuing daily with one accord in the temple, and breaking bread from house to house, did eat their meat with gladness and singleness of heart,
47 Praising God, and having favour with all the people. And the Lord added to the church daily such as should be saved.

Acts 3 | Acts 3 | Acts 3

1. And Peter and John were going up on the same (day) into the temple at the hour of prayer, the ninth.
2 And a certain man, being lame from his mother's womb, was being carried, whom day by day they put at the door of the temple, being called Beautiful, to ask alms from those going into the temple;

1909 3588 846 1161 4074 2532 2491 305 1519 3588
1 Ἐπὶ τὸ αὐτὸ δὲ Πέτρος καὶ Ἰωάννης ἀνέβαινον εἰς τὸ
on the same And Peter and John were going into the
2411 1909 3588 5610 3588 4335 3588 1766 2532 5100
ἱερὸν ἐπὶ τὴν ὥραν τῆς προσευχῆς τὴν ἐννάτην. 2 καί τις
temple at the hour of prayer the ninth. And a certain
435 5560 1537 2836 3384 846 5225 941
ἀνὴρ χωλὸς ἐκ κοιλίας μητρὸς αὐτοῦ ὑπάρχων ἐβαστάζετο·
man lame from womb mother's his being was being carried
3739 5087 2596 2250 4314 3588 2374 3588 2411 3588
ὃν ἐτίθουν καθ' ἡμέραν πρὸς τὴν θύραν τοῦ ἱεροῦ τὴν
whom they put from day to day at the door of the temple
3004 5611 3588 154 1654 3844 3588
λεγομένην Ὡραίαν, τοῦ αἰτεῖν ἐλεημοσύνην παρὰ τῶν
being called Beautiful, to ask alms from those
1531 1519 3588 2411 3739 1492 4074 2532 2491
εἰσπορευομένων εἰς τὸ ἱερόν. 3 ὃς ἰδὼν Πέτρον καὶ Ἰωάννην
going into the temple. Who seeing Peter and John

1. Now Peter and John went up together into the temple at the hour of prayer, (being) the ninth (hour).
2 And a certain man lame from his mother's womb was carried, whom they laid daily at the gate of the temple which is called Beautiful, to ask alms of them that entered into the temple;

3 who seeing Peter and John

3 Who seeing Peter and John

Literal Translation **Acts 3:4** *King James Version*

about to go into the temple, asked alms.
4 And with John, looking intently toward him, Peter said, Look to us!
5 And he attended to them, expecting to receive something from them.
6 But Peter said, There is no silver and gold to me, but what I have, this I give to you: In the name of Jesus Christ the Nazarene, rise up and walk!
7 And taking him by the right hand, he raised (him) up. And immediately his feet and ankle-bones were made firm.
8 And leaping up, he stood and walked about, and went with them into the temple, walking and leaping, and praising God.
9 And all the people saw him walking, and praising God.
10 And they recognized him, that it was the (one) having sat for alms at the Beautiful Gate of the temple. And they were filled with amazement and ecstasy at the thing having happened to him.

3195 1524 1519 3588 2411 2065 1654
μέλλοντας εἰσιέναι εἰς τὸ ἱερόν, ἠρώτα ἐλεημοσύνην.
being about to go into the temple, asked alms.

816 1161 4074 1519 846 4862 3588 2491 2036 991
4 ἀτενίσας δὲ Πέτρος εἰς αὐτὸν σὺν τῷ Ἰωάννῃ, εἶπε, Βλέψον
gazing intently But Peter at him with John, he said, Look

1519 2248 3588 1161 1907 846 4328 5100 3844 846
εἰς ἡμᾶς. 5 ὁ δὲ ἐπεῖχεν αὐτοῖς προσδοκῶν τι παρ' αὐτῶν
to us! he And attended to them expecting something from them

2983 2036 1161 4074 694 2532 5553 3756 5225
λαβεῖν. 6 εἶπε δὲ Πέτρος, Ἀργύριον καὶ χρυσίον οὐχ ὑπάρχει
to receive. said And Peter, Silver and gold not is

3427 3739 1161 2192 5124 4671 1325 1722 3588 3686 2424 5547
μοι· ὃ δὲ ἔχω, τοῦτό σοι δίδωμι. ἐν τῷ ὀνόματι Ἰησοῦ Χριστοῦ
to me; what but I have, this to you I give. In the name of Jesus Christ

3588 3480 1453 2532 4043 2532 4084 846 3588
τοῦ Ναζωραίου, ἔγειραι καὶ περιπάτει. 7 καὶ πιάσας αὐτὸν τῆς
the Nazarene, rise up and walk about. And taking him by the

1188 5495 1453 3916 1161 4732 846 3588
δεξιᾶς χειρὸς ἤγειρε· παραχρῆμα δὲ ἐστερεώθησαν αὐτοῦ αἱ
right hand he lifted up; immediately And were made strong of him the

939 2532 3588 4974 2532 1814 2476 2532 4043
βάσεις καὶ τὰ σφυρά. 8 καὶ ἐξαλλόμενος ἔστη καὶ περιεπάτει,
feet and the ankle-bones. And leaping up he stood and walked about,

2532 1525 4862 846 1519 3588 2411 4043 2532 242
καὶ εἰσῆλθε σὺν αὐτοῖς εἰς τὸ ἱερόν, περιπατῶν καὶ ἁλλόμενος
and went in with them into the temple, walking around and leaping

2532 134 3588 2316 2532 1492 846 3956 3588 2992 4043
καὶ αἰνῶν τὸν Θεόν. 9 καὶ εἶδεν αὐτὸν πᾶς ὁ λαὸς περιπα-
and praising God. And saw him all the people walking

2532 134 3588 2316 1921 5037 846 3754
τοῦντα καὶ αἰνοῦντα τὸν Θεόν· 10 ἐπεγίνωσκόν τε αὐτὸν ὅτι
around and praising God; they recognized And him that

3778 2258 3588 4314 3588 1654 2521 1909 3588 5611
οὗτος ἦν ὁ πρὸς τὴν ἐλεημοσύνην καθήμενος ἐπὶ τῇ Ὡραίᾳ
this was the (one) for alms having sat at the Beautiful

4439 3588 2411 2532 4130 2285 2532 1611
πύλῃ τοῦ ἱεροῦ· καὶ ἐπλήσθησαν θάμβους καὶ ἐκστάσεως
Gate of the temple; and they were filled (with) amazement and ecstasy

1909 3588 4819 846
ἐπὶ τῷ συμβεβηκότι αὐτῷ.
at the thing having happened to him.

about to go into the temple asked an alms.
4 And Peter, fastening his eyes upon him with John, said, Look on us.
5 And he gave heed unto them, expecting to receive something of them.
6 Then Peter said, Silver and gold have I none; but such as I have give I thee: In the name of Jesus Christ of Nazareth rise up and walk.
7 And he took him by the right hand, and lifted (him) up: and immediately his feet and ankle bones received strength.
8 And he leaping up stood, and walked, and entered with them into the temple, walking, and leaping, and praising God.
9 And all the people saw him walking and praising God:
10 And they knew that it was he which sat for alms at the Beautiful gate of the temple: and they were filled with wonder and amazement at that which had happened unto him.

11. And the healed lame (one) was holding to Peter and John, (and), all the people ran together to them on the porch being called Solomon's, greatly amazed.
12 And seeing (this), Peter answered to the people, Men, Israelites, why do you marvel at this one? Or why do you stare at us, as (if) by (our) own power or godliness we have made him to walk?
13 The God of Abraham and Isaac and Jacob, the God of our fathers, (Ex.3:15) glorified His

2902 1161 3588 2390 5560 3588 4074 2532
11. Κρατοῦντος δὲ τοῦ ἰαθέντος χωλοῦ τὸν Πέτρον καὶ
holding And the healed lame (one) Peter and

2491 4936 4314 846 3956 3588 2992 1909 3588 4745
Ἰωάννην, συνέδραμε πρὸς αὐτοὺς πᾶς ὁ λαὸς ἐπὶ τῇ στοᾷ
John, ran together to them all the people on the porch

3588 2564 4672 1569 1492 1161 4074
τῇ καλουμένῃ Σολομῶντος, ἔκθαμβοι. 12 ἰδὼν δὲ Πέτρος ἀπε-
being called Solomon's, greatly amazed. seeing And Peter

611 4314 3588 2992 435 2475 5101 2296
κρίνατο πρὸς τὸν λαόν, Ἄνδρες Ἰσραηλῖται, τί θαυμάζετε
answered to the people, Men Israelites, Why do you marvel

1909 5129 2228 2254 5101 816 5613 2398 1411 2228 2150
ἐπὶ τούτῳ, ἢ ἡμῖν τί ἀτενίζετε, ὡς ἰδίᾳ δυνάμει ἢ εὐσεβείᾳ
at this, or (at) us why do you stare, as by own power or goodness

4160 3588 4043 846 3588 2316 11 2532
πεποιηκόσι τοῦ περιπατεῖν αὐτόν; 13 ὁ Θεὸς Ἀβραὰμ καὶ
having made to walk about him? The God of Abraham and

2464 2532 2384 3588 2316 3588 3962 2257 1392 3588
Ἰσαὰκ καὶ Ἰακώβ, ὁ Θεὸς τῶν πατέρων ἡμῶν, ἐδόξασε τὸν
Isaac and Jacob, the God of the fathers of us, glorified the

11. And as the lame man which was healed held Peter and John, all the people ran together unto them in the porch that is called Solomon's, greatly wondering.
12 And when Peter saw (it), he answered unto the people, Ye men of Israel, why marvel ye at this? or why look ye so earnestly on us, as though by our own power or holiness we had made this man to walk?
13 The God of Abraham, and of Isaac, and of Jacob, the God of our fathers, hath glorified his

Literal Translation | **Acts 3:14** | **King James Version**

Servant Jesus, whom you delivered up, and denied Him in (the) presence of Pilate, that one having decided to set (Him) free.

14 But you denied the Holy and Righteous (One), and asked for a man, a murderer, to be granted to you.
15 And the Author of Life you killed, whom God raised up from (the) dead, of which we are witnesses.

16 And on the faith of His name, this one whom you behold and know was made strong (by) His name, and through faith in His name gave to him this complete soundness before you all.

17 And now, brothers, I know that you acted by way of ignorance, as also (did) your rulers.
18 But what things God before proclaimed through (the) mouth of all His prophets, (that) the Christ (was) to suffer, He fulfilled in this way.

19. Therefore repent and be converted, unto the blotting out of your sins, so that times of refreshing may come from (the) presence of the Lord,
20 and (that) He may send the (One) before proclaimed to you, Jesus Christ,
21 whom it is right Heaven truly to receive until the times of restoration of all things, of which God spoke through (the) mouth of all His holy prophets from (the) age.

22 For Moses truly said to the fathers, "(The) Lord your God will raise up to you a Prophet from your brothers, (One) like me; you shall hear Him according to all things, whatever (He) may speak

3816 846 2424 3739 5210 3860 2532 720
παῖδα αὐτοῦ Ἰησοῦν· ὃν ὑμεῖς παρεδώκατε, καὶ ἠρνήσασθε
Servant of Him Jesus; whom you delivered up, and denied

846 2596 4383 4091 2919 1565 630
αὐτὸν κατὰ πρόσωπον Πιλάτου, κρίναντος ἐκείνου ἀπο-
Him to (the) presence of Pilate, having decided that one to set

5210 1161 3588 40 2532 1342 720 2532 154
λύειν. 14 ὑμεῖς δὲ τὸν ἅγιον καὶ δίκαιον ἠρνήσασθε, καὶ ᾐτή-
free (Him). you But the holy and Righteous (One) denied, and

435 5406 5483 5213 3588 1161 747 3588
σασθε ἄνδρα φονέα χαρισθῆναι ὑμῖν, 15 τὸν δὲ ἀρχηγὸν τῆς
asked a man a murderer to be granted to you, the and Author

2222 615 3739 3588 2316 1453 1537 3498 3739 2249
ζωῆς ἀπεκτείνατε· ὃν ὁ Θεὸς ἤγειρεν ἐκ νεκρῶν, οὗ ἡμεῖς
of Life you killed; whom God raised up from (the) dead, of which we

3144 2070 2532 1909 3588 4102 3588 3686 846
μάρτυρές ἐσμεν. 16 καὶ ἐπὶ τῇ πίστει τοῦ ὀνόματος αὐτοῦ,
witnesses are. And on the faith of the name of Him,

5126 3739 2334 2532 1492 4732 3588 3686 846
τοῦτον ὃν θεωρεῖτε καὶ οἴδατε ἐστερέωσε τὸ ὄνομα αὐτοῦ·
this one whom you behold and know made strong the name of Him;

2532 3588 4102 3588 1223 846 1325 846 3588 3647
καὶ ἡ πίστις ἡ δι᾽ αὐτοῦ ἔδωκεν αὐτῷ τὴν ὁλοκληρίαν
and the faith through Him gave to him complete soundness

3778 561 3956 5216 2532 3568 80 1492 3754
ταύτην ἀπέναντι πάντων ὑμῶν. 17 καὶ νῦν, ἀδελφοί, οἶδα ὅτι
this before all of you. And now, brothers, I know that

2596 52 4238 5618 2532 3588 758 5216 3588 1161
κατὰ ἄγνοιαν ἐπράξατε, ὥσπερ καὶ οἱ ἄρχοντες ὑμῶν. 18 ὁ δὲ
by way of ignorance you acted, even as also the rulers of you. But

2316 3739 4293 1223 4750 3956 3588 4396
Θεὸς ἃ προκατήγγειλε διὰ στόματος πάντων τῶν προ-
God that before proclaimed through (the) mouth of all the

846 3958 3588 5547 4137 3779
φητῶν αὐτοῦ, παθεῖν τὸν Χριστὸν, ἐπλήρωσεν οὕτω.
prophets of Him, to suffer the Christ, He fulfilled this way.

3340 3767 2532 1994 1519 3588 1813 5216
19 μετανοήσατε οὖν καὶ ἐπιστρέψατε, εἰς τὸ ἐξαλειφθῆναι ὑμῶν
repent Therefore and be converted, unto the blotting out of you

3588 266 3704 302 2064 2540 403 575 4383
τὰς ἁμαρτίας, ὅπως ἂν ἔλθωσι καιροὶ ἀναψύξεως ἀπὸ προσ-
the sins, so as may come times of refreshing from the

3588 2962 2532 649 3588 4296
ώπου τοῦ Κυρίου, 20 καὶ ἀποστείλῃ τὸν προκεκηρυγμένον
presence of the Lord, and He may send the (One) before proclaimed

5213 2424 5547 3739 1163 3772 3303 1209 891
ὑμῖν Ἰησοῦν Χριστόν· 21 ὃν δεῖ οὐρανὸν μὲν δέξασθαι ἄχρι
to you Jesus Christ; whom it is right Heaven truly to receive until

5550 605 3956 3739 2980 3588 2316
χρόνων ἀποκαταστάσεως πάντων, ὧν ἐλάλησεν ὁ Θεὸς
(the) times of restoration of all things, which spoke God

1223 4750 3956 40 846 4396 575 165
διὰ στόματος πάντων ἁγίων αὐτοῦ προφητῶν ἀπ᾽ αἰῶνος.
through (the) mouth of all holy of Him prophets from (the) age.

3475 3303 1063 4314 3588 3962 2036 3754 4396
22 Μωσῆς μὲν γὰρ πρὸς τοὺς πατέρας εἶπεν ὅτι Προφήτην
Moses truly For to the fathers said, A Prophet

5213 450 2962 3588 2316 5216 1537 3588 80 5216
ὑμῖν ἀναστήσει Κύριος ὁ Θεὸς ὑμῶν ἐκ τῶν ἀδελφῶν ὑμῶν
to you will raise up (the) Lord God of you from the brothers of you

5613 1691 846 191 2596 3956 3745 302 2980 4314
ὡς ἐμέ· αὐτοῦ ἀκούσεσθε κατὰ πάντα ὅσα ἂν λαλήσῃ πρὸς
like me; Him you shall hear according to all whatever may speak to

Son Jesus; whom ye delivered up, and denied him in the presence of Pilate, when he was determined to let (him) go.

14 But ye denied the Holy One and the Just, and desired a murderer to be granted unto you;
15 And killed the Prince of life, whom God hath raised from the dead; whereof we are witnesses.

16 And his name through faith in his name hath made this man strong, whom ye see and know: yea, the faith which is by him hath given him this perfect soundness in the presence of you all.

17 And now, brethren, I wot that through ignorance ye did (it), as (did) also your rulers.
18 But those things, which God before had shewed by the mouth of all his prophets, that Christ should suffer, he hath so fulfilled.

19. Repent ye therefore, and be converted, that your sins may be blotted out, when the times of refreshing shall come from the presence of the Lord;
20 And he shall send Jesus Christ, which before was preached unto you:
21 Whom the heaven must receive until the times of restitution of all things, which God hath spoken by the mouth of all his holy prophets since the world began.

22. For Moses truly said unto the fathers, A prophet shall the Lord your God raise up unto you of your brethren, like unto me; him shall ye hear in all things whatsoever he shall say

Acts 3:23

Literal Translation

to you." (See Deut. 18:15-19)
23 And it shall be (that of) every soul, whoever should not hear that Prophet, shall be utterly destroyed from the people.
24 And also all the prophets, from Samuel and those in order, as many as spoke, also before proclaimed these days.
25 You are sons of the prophets and of the covenant which God appointed to our fathers, saying to Abraham, "Even in your Seed all the families of the earth shall be blessed." (Gen. 22:18)
26 Having raised up His Servant Jesus, God sent Him first to you, blessing you in turning away each one from your iniquities.

5209 2071 1161 3956 5590 3748 302 3361 191 3588 4396
ὑμᾶς. 23 ἔσται δὲ, πᾶσα ψυχὴ, ἥτις ἂν μὴ ἀκούσῃ τοῦ προφή-
you. it shall be And, every soul, whoever may not hear the prophet

1565 1842 1537 3588 2992 2532 3956 1161
του ἐκείνου, ἐξολοθρευθήσεται ἐκ τοῦ λαοῦ. 24 καὶ πάντες δὲ
that, will be utterly destroyed from the people. also all And

3588 4396 575 4545 2532 3588 2517 3745 2980
οἱ προφῆται ἀπὸ Σαμουὴλ καὶ τῶν καθεξῆς, ὅσοι ἐλάλησαν,
the prophets from Samuel and those in order, as many as spoke,

2532 4293 3588 2250 3778 5210 2075 5207 3588
καὶ προκατήγγειλαν τὰς ἡμέρας ταύτας. 25 ὑμεῖς ἐστε υἱοὶ τῶν
also before proclaimed days these. You are sons of the

4396 2532 3588 1242 3739 1303 3588 2316 4314 3588
προφητῶν, καὶ τῆς διαθήκης ἧς διέθετο ὁ Θεὸς πρὸς τοὺς
prophets, and of the covenant which appointed God to the

3962 2257 3004 4314 11 2532 3588 4690 4675
πατέρας ἡμῶν, λέγων πρὸς Ἀβραάμ, Καὶ τῷ σπέρματί σου
fathers of us, saying to Abraham, And in the Seed of you

1757 3956 3588 3965 3588 1093 5213 4412
ἐνευλογηθήσονται πᾶσαι αἱ πατριαὶ τῆς γῆς. 26 ὑμῖν πρῶτον
shall be blessed all the families of the earth. To you first

3588 2316 450 3588 3816 846 2424 649
ὁ Θεός, ἀναστήσας τὸν παῖδα αὐτοῦ Ἰησοῦν, ἀπέστειλεν
God, having raised up the Servant of Him Jesus, sent

846 2127 5209 1722 3588 654 1538 575
αὐτὸν εὐλογοῦντα ὑμᾶς, ἐν τῷ ἀποστρέφειν ἕκαστον ἀπὸ
Gun blessing you, in the turning away (of) each one from

3588 4189 5216
τῶν πονηριῶν ὑμῶν.
the iniquities of you.

King James Version

unto you.
23 And it shall come to pass, (that) every soul, which will not hear that prophet, shall be destroyed from among the people.
24 Yea, and all the prophets from Samuel and those that follow after, as many as have spoken, have likewise foretold of these days.
25 Ye are the children of the prophets, and of the covenant which God made with our fathers, saying unto Abraham, And in thy seed shall all the kindreds of the earth be blessed.

26 Unto you first God, having raised up his Son Jesus, sent him to bless you, in turning away every one of you from his iniquities.

Acts 4

1. And (as) they (were) speaking to the people, came upon them the priests, and the temple commander, and the Sadducees,

2 being greatly distressed because of their teaching the people, even to announce in Jesus the resurrection from (the) dead.

3 And they laid hands on them, and put (them) into custody until the morrow, for it was already evening.
4 But many of the (ones) hearing the Word believed; and the number of the men became about five thousand.

5. And it happened on the morrow the rulers and elders and scribes to be assembled into

2980 1161 846 4314 3588 2992 2186 846
1 Λαλούντων δὲ αὐτῶν πρὸς τὸν λαόν, ἐπέστησαν αὐτοῖς
speaking And they to the people, came upon them

3588 2409 2532 3588 4755 3588 2411 2532 3588 4523
οἱ ἱερεῖς καὶ ὁ στρατηγὸς τοῦ ἱεροῦ καὶ οἱ Σαδδουκαῖοι,
the priests and the commander of the temple and the Sadducees,

1278 1223 3588 1321 846 3588 2992 2532
2 διαπονούμενοι διὰ τὸ διδάσκειν αὐτοὺς τὸν λαόν, καὶ
being greatly distressed because of the teaching (of) them the people, even

2605 1722 3588 2424 3588 386 3588 1537 3498
καταγγέλλειν ἐν τῷ Ἰησοῦ τὴν ἀνάστασιν τὴν ἐκ νεκρῶν.
to announce in Jesus the resurrection from (the) dead.

2532 1911 846 3588 5495 2532 5087 1519 5084 1519
3 καὶ ἐπέβαλον αὐτοῖς τὰς χεῖρας, καὶ ἔθεντο εἰς τήρησιν εἰς
And they laid on them the hands, and put (them) into custody unto

3588 839 2258 1063 2073 2235 4183 1161 3588 191
τὴν αὔριον· ἦν γὰρ ἑσπέρα ἤδη. 4 πολλοὶ δὲ τῶν ἀκουσάντων
the morrow; it was for evening already. many But of those hearing

3588 3056 4100 2532 1096 3588 706 3588 435
τὸν λόγον ἐπίστευσαν· καὶ ἐγενήθη ὁ ἀριθμὸς τῶν ἀνδρῶν
the Word believed; and came to be the number of the men

5616 5505 4002
ὡσεὶ χιλιάδες πέντε.
about thousands five.

1096 1161 1909 3588 839 4863 846 3588
5. Ἐγένετο δὲ ἐπὶ τὴν αὔριον συναχθῆναι αὐτῶν τοὺς
it was And on the morrow to be assembled of them the

758 2532 4245 2532 1122 1519
ἄρχοντας καὶ πρεσβυτέρους καὶ γραμματεῖς εἰς
rulers and elders and scribes into

1. And as they spake unto the people, the priests, and the captain of the temple, and the Sadducees, came upon them,

2 Being grieved that they taught the people, and preached through Jesus the resurrection from the dead.

3 And they laid hands on them, and put (them) in hold unto the next day: for it was now eventide.
4 Howbeit many of them which heard the word believed; and the number of the men was about five thousand.

5. And it came to pass on the morrow, that their rulers, and elders, and scribes,

Literal Translation

Jerusalem;
6 also Annas the high priest, and Caiaphas, and John, and Alexander, and as many as were of (the) high priestly family.

7 And having stood them in the midst, (they) inquired, By what power, or in what name did you do this?

8 Then filled of (the) Holy Spirit, Peter said to them, Rulers of the people and elders of Israel,

9 if we are being examined today on a good work of an infirm man, by what this one has been healed,
10 let it be known to all of you, and to all the people of Israel, that in the name of Jesus Christ the Nazarene, whom, you crucified, whom God raised from (the) dead, in this (name) this one stands before you whole.

11 This (One) is the Stone counted worthless by you the builders, the (One) having become to (be) the Head of (the) Corner; (Ps. 118:22)
12 and there is salvation in no other One, for neither is there any other name under Heaven having been given among men by which we must be saved.

13. But beholding the boldness of Peter and John, and having perceived that they are untaught and untrained men, they marveled. And they recognized them, that they were with Jesus.
14 But seeing the man standing with them, the (one) having been healed, they had nothing to say against (him).
15 But commanding

Acts 4:6

2419 2532 452 3588 749 2532 2533 2532
·Ἰερουσαλήμ, 6 καὶ Ἄνναν τὸν ἀρχιερέα, καὶ Καιάφαν, καὶ
Jerusalem, also Annas the high priest, and Caiaphas, and

2491 2532 223 2532 3745 2258 1537 1085
Ἰωάννην, καὶ Ἀλέξανδρον, καὶ ὅσοι ἦσαν ἐκ γένους
John, and Alexander, and as many as were from (the) family

748 2532 2476 846 1722 3588 3319
ἀρχιερατικοῦ. 7 καὶ στήσαντες αὐτοὺς ἐν τῷ μέσῳ
high priestly. And having stood them in the middle

4441 1722 4169 1411 2228 1722 4169 3686 4160
ἐπυνθάνοντο, Ἐν ποίᾳ δυνάμει ἢ ἐν ποίῳ ὀνόματι ἐποιήσατε
(they) inquired, By what power or in what name did do

5124 5210 5119 4074 4130 4151 40 2036
τοῦτο ὑμεῖς; 8 τότε Πέτρος πλησθεὶς Πνεύματος Ἁγίου εἶπε
this you? Then Peter filled of (the) Spirit Holy said

4314 846 758 3588 2992 2532 4245 3588
πρὸς αὐτούς, Ἄρχοντες τοῦ λαοῦ καὶ πρεσβύτεροι τοῦ
to them, Rulers of the people and elders

2474 1487 2249 4594 350 1909 2108
Ἰσραήλ, 9 εἰ ἡμεῖς σήμερον ἀνακρινόμεθα ἐπὶ εὐεργεσίᾳ
of Israel, if we today are being examined on a good work

444 772 1722 5101 3778 4982 1110
ἀνθρώπου ἀσθενοῦς· ἐν τίνι οὗτος σέσωσται, 10 γνωστὸν
of a man infirm; by what this one has been healed, known

2077 3956 5213 2532 3956 3588 2992 2474 3754 1722 3588 3686
ἔστω πᾶσιν ὑμῖν καὶ παντὶ τῷ λαῷ Ἰσραήλ, ὅτι ἐν τῷ ὀνόματι
let it be to all of you and all the people of Israel, that in the name

2424 5547 3588 3480 3739 5210 4717 3739 3588
Ἰησοῦ Χριστοῦ τοῦ Ναζωραίου, ὃν ὑμεῖς ἐσταυρώσατε, ὃν ὁ
of Jesus Christ the Nazarene, whom you crucified, whom

2316 1453 1537 3498 1722 5129 3778 3936 1799
Θεὸς ἤγειρεν ἐκ νεκρῶν, ἐν τούτῳ οὗτος παρέστηκεν ἐνώπιον
God raised up from (the) dead, in this this one stands before

5216 5199 3778 2076 3588 3037 3588 1848 5259 5216
ὑμῶν ὑγιής. 11 οὗτός ἐστιν ὁ λίθος ὁ ἐξουθενηθεὶς ὑφ' ὑμῶν
you whole. This is the Stone counted worthless by you

3588 3618 3588 1096 1519 2776 1137 2532 3756
τῶν οἰκοδομούντων, ὁ γενόμενος εἰς κεφαλὴν γωνίας. 12 καὶ οὐκ
the builders, the (One) has become into (the) Head of th Corner. And not

2076 1722 243 3762 3588 4991 3777 1063 3686 2076 2087
ἔστιν ἐν ἄλλῳ οὐδενὶ ἡ σωτηρία· οὔτε γὰρ ὄνομά ἐστιν ἕτερον
is in other none the salvation; neither for name is another

5259 3588 3772 3588 1325 1722 444 1722 3739 1163 4982
ὑπὸ τὸν οὐρανὸν τὸ δεδομένον ἐν ἀνθρώποις, ἐν ᾧ δεῖ σωθῆναι
under Heaven having been given among men, by which must be saved

2248
ἡμᾶς.
us.

2334 1161 3588 3588 4074 3954 2532 2491
13 Θεωροῦντες δὲ τὴν τοῦ Πέτρου παρρησίαν καὶ Ἰωάννου,
beholding And the of Peter boldness and of John,

2532 2638 3754 444 62 1526 2532
καὶ καταλαβόμενοι ὅτι ἄνθρωποι ἀγράμματοί εἰσι καὶ
and having perceived that men unlettered they are and

2399 2296 1921 5037 846 3754 4862 3588
ἰδιῶται, ἐθαύμαζον, ἐπεγίνωσκόν τε αὐτοὺς ὅτι σὺν τῷ
untrained, they marveled, recognized and them that with

2424 2258 3588 1161 444 991 4862 846 2476
Ἰησοῦ ἦσαν. 14 τὸν δὲ ἄνθρωπον βλέποντες σὺν αὐτοῖς ἑστῶτα
Jesus they were. the But man seeing with them standing

3588 2323 3762 2192 471 2753 1161
τὸν τεθεραπευμένον, οὐδὲν εἶχον ἀντειπεῖν. 15 κελεύσαντες δὲ
the (one) having been healed, nothing they had to gainsay. commanding But

King James Version

Jerusalem.
6 And Annas the high priest, and Caiaphas, and John, and Alexander, and as many as were of the kindred of the high priest, were gathered together at Jerusalem.
7 And when they had set them in the midst, they asked, By what power, or by what name, have ye done this?

8 Then Peter, filled with the Holy Ghost, said unto them, Ye rulers of the people, and elders of Israel,

9 If we this day be examined of the good deed done to the impotent man, by what means he is made whole;
10 Be it known unto you all, and to all the people of Israel, that by the name of Jesus Christ of Nazareth, whom ye crucified, whom God raised from the dead, (even) by him doth this man stand here before you whole.

11 This is the stone which was set at nought of you builders, which is become the head of the corner.
12 Neither is there salvation in any other: for there is none other name under heaven given among men, whereby we must be saved.

13. Now when they saw the boldness of Peter and John, and perceived that they were unlearned and ignorant men, they marvelled; and they took knowledge of them, that they had been with Jesus.
14 And beholding the man which was healed standing with them, they could say nothing against it.
15 But when they had commanded

Literal Translation **Acts 4:16** *King James Version*

them to go outside the sanhedrin, they conferred with one another,

16 saying, What may we do to these men? For that a notable sign indeed has occurred through them is plain to all those living in Jerusalem, and we are not able to deny it.

17 But that it may not be more rumored about to the people, let us threaten them with a threat (that they) no longer speak on this name to any one of men.
18 And calling them, they ordered them not to speak at all, nor to teach on the name of Jesus.

19 But answering them Peter and John said, Whether it is right before God to listen to you rather than God, you judge.

20 For we are not able not to speak what we saw and heard.

21 But having threatened them again, they set them free, finding nothing (as to) how they might punish them, because of the people, because all glorified God on the thing occurring.

22 For the man on whom this sign of healing had occurred was more (than) forty years (of age).

23. And being set free, they came to (their) own and reported to them what the chief priests and elders said.
24 And having heard (they) with one passion lifted voice to God and said, Master, You (are) the God who made the heaven and the earth and the sea, and all the things in them, (Ex.20:11)
25 who through (the)

846 1854 3588 4892 565 4820 4314 240
αὐτοὺς ἔξω τοῦ συνεδρίου ἀπελθεῖν, συνέβαλον πρὸς ἀλλή-
them outside of the Sanhedrin to go, they conferred with one

3004 5101 4160 3588 444 5125 3754
λους, 16 λέγοντες, Τί ποιήσομεν τοῖς ἀνθρώποις τούτοις; ὅτι
another, saying, What may we do men to these? that

3303 1063 1110 4592 1096 1223 846 3956 3588 2730
μὲν γὰρ γνωστὸν σημεῖον γέγονε δι᾽ αὐτῶν, πᾶσι τοῖς κατοι-
indeed For a notable sign has occurred through them, to all those living

2419 5318 2532 3756 1410 720
κοῦσιν Ἱερουσαλὴμ φανερόν, καὶ οὐ δυνάμεθα ἀρνήσασθαι.
in Jerusalem (is) manifest, and not we are able to deny.

235 2443 3361 1909 4119 1268 1519 3588 2992 547
17 ἀλλ᾽ ἵνα μὴ ἐπὶ πλεῖον διανεμηθῇ εἰς τὸν λαόν, ἀπειλῇ
But that not on more it be rumored about to the people, with a threat

546 846 3371 2980 1909 3588 3686 5129
ἀπειλησώμεθα αὐτοῖς μηκέτι λαλεῖν ἐπὶ τῷ ὀνόματι τούτῳ
let us threaten them no longer to speak on name this

3367 444 2532 2564 846 3853
μηδενὶ ἀνθρώπων. 18 καὶ καλέσαντες αὐτούς, παρήγγειλαν
to no one of men. And calling them, they ordered

846 3588 2527 3361 5350 3366 1321 1909 3588
αὐτοῖς τὸ καθόλου μὴ φθέγγεσθαι μηδὲ διδάσκειν ἐπὶ τῷ
them at all not to speak nor to teach on the

3686 3588 2424 3588 1161 4074 2532 2491 611
ὀνόματι τοῦ Ἰησοῦ. 19 ὁ δὲ Πέτρος καὶ Ἰωάννης ἀποκριθέντες
name of Jesus. But Peter and John answering

4314 846 2036 1487 1342 2076 1799 3588 2316 5216
πρὸς αὐτοὺς εἶπον, Εἰ δίκαιόν ἐστιν ἐνώπιον τοῦ Θεοῦ ὑμῶν
to them said, If right it is before God you

191 3123 2228 3588 2316 2919 3756 1410 1063 2249
ἀκούειν μᾶλλον ἢ τοῦ Θεοῦ, κρίνατε. 20 οὐ δυνάμεθα γὰρ ἡμεῖς,
to hear rather than God, you judge. not are able For we,

3739 1492 2532 191 3361 2980 3588 1161 4324
ἃ εἴδομεν καὶ ἠκούσαμεν, μὴ λαλεῖν. 21 οἱ δὲ προσαπειλησά-
what we saw and heard, not to speak. they But having threatened

630 846 3367 2147 3588 4459 2849
μενοι ἀπέλυσαν αὐτούς, μηδὲν εὑρίσκοντες τὸ πῶς κολάσων-
again set free them, nothing finding how they might

846 1223 3588 2992 3754 3956 1392 3588 2316 1909
ται αὐτούς, διὰ τὸν λαόν, ὅτι πάντες ἐδόξαζον τὸν Θεὸν ἐπὶ
punish them, because of the people, for all glorified God on

3588 1096 2094 1063 2258 4119 5062 3588
τῷ γεγονότι. 22 ἐτῶν γὰρ ἦν πλειόνων τεσσαράκοντα ὁ
that occurring. of years For was more (than) forty the

444 1909 3739 1096 3588 4592 5124 3588 2392
ἄνθρωπος ἐφ᾽ ὃν ἐγεγόνει τὸ σημεῖον τοῦτο τῆς ἰάσεως.
man on whom had occurred sign this of healing.

630 1161 2064 4314 3588 2398 2532 518
23 Ἀπολυθέντες δὲ ἦλθον πρὸς τοὺς ἰδίους, καὶ ἀπήγγειλαν
being set free And they went to the own, and reported

3745 4314 846 3588 749 2532 3588 4245 2036 3588
ὅσα πρὸς αὐτοὺς οἱ ἀρχιερεῖς καὶ οἱ πρεσβύτεροι εἶπον. 24 οἱ
what to them the chief priests and the elders said. they

1161 191 3661 142 5456 4314 3588 2316 2532
δὲ ἀκούσαντες ὁμοθυμαδὸν ἦραν φωνὴν πρὸς τὸν Θεόν, καὶ
And having heard with one passion lifted voice to God, and

2036 1203 4771 3588 2316 4160 3588 3772 2532 3588
εἶπον, Δέσποτα, σὺ ὁ Θεὸς ποιήσας τὸν οὐρανὸν καὶ τὴν
said, Master, You the God who made the heaven and the

1093 2532 3588 2281 2532 3956 3588 1722 846 3588 1223
γῆν καὶ τὴν θάλασσαν καὶ πάντα τὰ ἐν αὐτοῖς· 25 ὁ διὰ στό-
earth and the sea and all the things in them; who through (the)

them to go aside out of the council, they conferred among themselves,

16 Saying, What shall we do to these men? for that indeed a notable miracle hath been done by them (is) manifest to all them that dwell in Jerusalem; and we cannot deny (it).

17 But that it spread no further among the people, let us straitly threaten them, that they speak henceforth to no man in this name.

18 And they called them, and commanded them not to speak at all nor teach in the name of Jesus.

19 But Peter and John answered and said unto them, Whether it be right in the sight of God to hearken unto you more than unto God, judge ye.
20 For we cannot but speak the things which we have seen and heard.

21 So when they had further threatened them, they let them go, finding nothing how they might punish them, because of the people: for all (men) glorified God for that which was done.

22 For the man was above forty years old, on whom this miracle of healing was shewed.

23. And being let go, they went to their own company, and reported all that the chief priests and elders had said unto them.
24 And when they heard that, they lifted up their voice to God with one accord, and said, Lord, thou (art) God, which hast made heaven, and earth, and the sea, and all that in them is:
25 Who by

Literal Translation

mouth of Your servant David said, "Why did the nations rage, and the people meditated foolish things.
26 The kings of the earth stood up, and the rulers were assembled on the same (day) against the Lord, yea, against His Christ." (Ps.2:1,2)
27 For on a truth both Herod and Pontius Pilate, with the nations and (the) peoples of Israel, were assemabled against Your holy child Jesus, whom You anointed,
28 to do whatever Your hand and Your counsel before-determined to be done.
29 And now, Lord, look upon their threatenings and give to Your slaves to speak Your Word with all boldness,
30 (that) You stretch out Your hand unto healing and signs and wonders to happen through the name of Your holy Servant Jesus.
31 And they having petitioned, the place in which they were gathered was shaken, and they were all filled with (the) Holy Spirit and spoke the Word of God. with boldness.
32. And of the multitude of those who had believed, the heart and the soul were one. And no one said any of the possessions to be (his) own, but all things were common to them.
33 And with great power the apostles gave the testimony of the resurrection of the Lord Jesus, and great grace was upon them all.
34 For neither was anyone needy among them, for as many as were owners of lands or houses, having sold (them), they bore

Acts 4:26

4750 1138 3588 3816 4675 2036 2444 5433 1484
ματος Δαβὶδ τοῦ παιδός σου εἰπών, Ἱνατί ἐφρύαξαν ἔθνη,
mouth of David the child of You said, Why did rage the nations,

2532 2992 3191 2756 3936 3588 935 3588 1093
καὶ λαοὶ ἐμελέτησαν κενά; 26 παρέστησαν οἱ βασιλεῖς τῆς γῆς,
and peoples meditated foolish things? stood up the kings of the earth,

2532 3588 758 4863 1909 3588 846 2596 3588 2962
καὶ οἱ ἄρχοντες συνήχθησαν ἐπὶ τὸ αὐτὸ κατὰ τοῦ Κυρίου,
and the rulers were assembled on the same against the Lord,

2532 2596 3588 5547 846 4863 1063 1909 225
καὶ κατὰ τοῦ Χριστοῦ αὐτοῦ· 27 συνήχθησαν γὰρ ἐπ' ἀληθείας
and against the Christ of Him; were assembled for on a truth

1909 3588 40 3816 4675 2424 3739 5548 2264 5037
ἐπὶ τὸν ἅγιον παῖδά σου Ἰησοῦν, ὃν ἔχρισας, Ἡρώδης τε
over the Holy Servant of You Jesus, whom You anointed, Herod both

2532 4194 4091 4862 1484 2532 2992 2474 4160
καὶ Πόντιος Πιλάτος, σὺν ἔθνεσι καὶ λαοῖς Ἰσραήλ, 28 ποιῆσαι
and Pontius Pilate, with nations and peoples of Israel, to do

3745 3588 5495 4675 2532 3588 1012 4675 4309 1096 2532
ὅσα ἡ χείρ σου καὶ ἡ βουλή σου προώρισε γενέσθαι. 29 καὶ
whatever the hand of You and the counsel of You predetermined to occur. And

3588 3568 2962 1896 1909 3588 547 846 2532 1325 3588
τὰ νῦν, Κύριε, ἔπιδε ἐπὶ τὰς ἀπειλὰς αὐτῶν, καὶ δὸς τοῖς
now, Lord, look upon the threatenings of them, and grant to the

1401 4675 3326 3954 3956 2980 3588 3056 4675
δούλοις σου μετὰ παρρησίας πάσης λαλεῖν τὸν λόγον σου,
slaves of You with boldness all to speak the Word of You,

1722 3588 3588 5495 4675 1614 4571 1519 2392 2532 4592 2532
30 ἐν τῷ τὴν χεῖρά σου ἐκτείνειν σε εἰς ἴασιν, καὶ σημεῖα καὶ
by the hand of You to stretch out You unto healing, and signs and

5059 1096 1223 3588 3686 3588 40 3816 4675
τέρατα γίνεσθαι διὰ τοῦ ὀνόματος τοῦ ἁγίου παιδός σου
wonders to happen through the name of the Holy Servant of You

2424 2532 1189 846 4531 3588 5117 1722/3739
Ἰησοῦ. 31 καὶ δεηθέντων αὐτῶν ἐσαλεύθη ὁ τόπος ἐν ᾧ
Jesus. And having petitioned they was shaken the place in which

2258 4863 2532 4130 537 4151
ἦσαν συνηγμένοι, καὶ ἐπλήσθησαν ἅπαντες Πνεύματος
they were gathered, and they were filled all with (the) Spirit

40 2532 2980 3588 3056 3588 2316 3326 3954
Ἁγίου, καὶ ἐλάλουν τὸν λόγον τοῦ Θεοῦ μετὰ παρρησίας.
Holy, and spoke the Word of God with boldness.

3588 1161 4128 3588 4100 2258 3588 2588 2532 3588
32 Τοῦ δὲ πλήθους τῶν πιστευσάντων ἦν ἡ καρδία καὶ ἡ
of the And multitude of those having believed was the heart and the

5590 3391 2532 3761 1520 5100 3588 5224 846 3004
ψυχὴ μία· καὶ οὐδ' εἷς τι τῶν ὑπαρχόντων αὐτῷ ἔλεγεν
soul one; and not one anything of the possessions to him he said

2398 1511 235 2258 846 537 2839 2532 3173
ἴδιον εἶναι, ἀλλ' ἦν αὐτοῖς ἅπαντα κοινά. 33 καὶ μεγάλη
(the) own to be, but were to them all things common. And with great

1411 591 3588 3142 3588 652 3588 386
δυμάμει ἀπεδίδουν τὸ μαρτύριον οἱ ἀπόστολοι τῆς ἀναστά-
power gave the testimony of the apostles of the resurrection

3588 2962 2424 5485 5037 3173 2258 1909 3956
σεως τοῦ Κυρίου Ἰησοῦ, χάρις τε μεγάλη ἦν ἐπὶ πάντας
of the Lord Jesus, grace and great was on all

846 3761 1063 1729 5100 5225 1722 846 3745 1063
αὐτούς. 34 οὐδὲ γὰρ ἐνδεής τις ὑπῆρχεν ἐν αὐτοῖς· ὅσοι γὰρ
of them. neither For needy anyone was among them; as many as For

2935 5564 2228 3614 5225 4453 5342 3588
κτήτορες χωρίων ἢ οἰκιῶν ὑπῆρχον, πωλοῦντες ἔφερον τὰς
owners of lands or houses were, having sold brought the

King James Version

the mouth of thy servant David hast said, Why did the heathen rage, and the people imagine vain things?
26 The kings of the earth stood up, and the rulers were gathered together against the Lord, and against his Christ.
27 For of a truth against thy holy child Jesus, whom thou hast anointed, both Herod, and Pontius Pilate, with the Gentiles, and the people of Israel, were gathered together,
28 For to do whatsoever thy hand and thy counsel determined before to be done.
29 And now, Lord, behold their threatenings: and grant unto thy servants, that with all boldness they may speak thy word,
30 By stretching forth thine hand to heal; and that signs and wonders may be done by the name of thy holy child Jesus.
31 And when they had prayed, the place was shaken where they were assembled together; and they were all filled with the Holy Ghost, and they spake the word of God with boldness.
32. And the multitude of them that believed were of one heart and of one soul: neither said any (of them) that ought of the things which he possessed was his own; but they had all things common.
33 And with great power gave the apostles witness of the resurrection of the Lord Jesus: and great grace was upon them all.
34 Neither was there any among them that lacked: for as many as were possessors of lands or houses sold them, and brought the

Acts 4:35

Literal Translation

the value of the (things) being sold,
35 and placed (them) beside the feet of the apostles. And it was distributed to each according as any may have had need.

5092 3588 4097 2532 5087 3844 3588 4228
τιμὰς τῶν πιπρασκομένων, 35 καὶ ἐτίθουν παρὰ τοὺς πόδας
values of those being sold, and placed beside the feet

3588 652 1239 1161 1538 2530 302 5100 5532
τῶν ἀποστόλων· διεδίδοτο δὲ ἑκάστῳ καθότι ἄν τις χρείαν
of the apostles; it was distributed and to each according as may any need

2192
εἶχεν.
to have had.

King James Version

prices of the things that were sold,
35 And laid (them) down at the apostles' feet: and distribution was made unto every man according as he had need.

36 And Joses, the (one) surnamed Barnabas by the apostles, having been translated is, Son of Consolation, a Levite, a Cypriot by race,

37 a field being his, having sold (it), he bore the money and placed (it) beside the feet of the apostles.

2500 1161 3588 1941 921 5259 3588 652
36 Ἰωσῆς δέ, ὁ ἐπικληθεὶς Βαρνάβας ὑπὸ τῶν ἀποστόλων
Joses And, the (one) surnamed Barnabas by the apostles,

3739 2076 3177 5207 3874 3019
[ὅ ἐστι, μεθερμηνευόμενον, υἱὸς παρακλήσεως], Λευίτης,
which is, having been translated, Son of Consolation, a Levite,

2953 3588 1085 5225 846 68 4453
Κύπριος τῷ γένει, 37 ὑπάρχοντος αὐτῷ ἀγροῦ, πωλήσας
a Cypriot by race, being to him a field, having sold

5342 3588 5536 2532 5087 3844 3588 4228 3588 652
ἤνεγκε τὸ χρῆμα, καὶ ἔθηκε παρά τοὺς πόδας τῶν ἀποστόλων.
brought the money, and placed by the feet of the apostles.

36 And Joses, who by the apostles was surnamed Barnabas, (which is, being interpreted, The son of consolation,) a Levite, (and) of the country of Cyprus,
37 Having land, sold (it), and brought the money, and laid (it) at the apostles' feet.

Acts 5

1. But a certain man named Ananias, with his wife Sapphira, sold a property,
2 and secretly kept back from the price, his wife also aware of (it), and bringing a certain part, (he) placed (it) beside the feet of the apostles.

3 But Peter said, Ananias, why did Satan fill your heart (for) you to lie to the Holy Spirit and to secretly keep back from the price of the land?

435 1161 5100 367 3686 4862 4551 3588 1135
1 Ἀνὴρ δέ τις Ἀνανίας ὀνόματι, σὺν Σαπφείρῃ τῇ γυναικὶ
man And a certain Ananias by name, with Sapphira the wife

846 4453 2933 2532 3557 575 3588 5092
αὐτοῦ, ἐπώλησε κτῆμα, 2 καὶ ἐνοσφίσατο ἀπὸ τῆς τιμῆς,
of him, sold a property, and secretly kept back from the price,

4894 2532 3588 1135 846 2532 5342 3313 5100
συνειδυίας καὶ τῆς γυναικὸς αὐτοῦ, καὶ ἐνέγκας μέρος τι
aware of (it) also the wife of him, and bringing part a certain

3844 3588 4228 3588 652 5087 2036 1161 4074
παρὰ τοὺς πόδας τῶν ἀποστόλων ἔθηκεν. 3 εἶπε δὲ Πέτρος,
beside the feet of the apostles placed (it). said But Peter,

367 1302 4137 3588 4567 3588 2588 4675
Ἀνανία, διατί ἐπλήρωσεν ὁ Σατανᾶς τὴν καρδίαν σου,
Ananias, why filled Satan the heart of you,

5574 4571 3588 4151 3588 40 2532 3557 575
ψεύσασθαί σε τὸ Πνεῦμα τὸ Ἅγιον, καὶ νοσφίσασθαι ἀπὸ
to deceive you the Spirit Holy, and to secretly keep back from

1. But a certain man named Ananias, with Sapphira his wife, sold a possession,
2 And kept back (part) of the price, his wife also being privy (to it), and brought a certain part, and laid (it) at the apostles' feet.

3 But Peter said, Ananias, why hath Satan filled thine heart to lie to the Holy Ghost, and to keep back (part) of the price of the land?

4 Remaining, did it not remain yours? And being sold, was it (not) in your authority? Why was this action put into your heart? You did not lie to men, but to God!

3588 5092 3588 5564 3780 3306 4671 3306 2532 4097 1722
τῆς τιμῆς τοῦ χωρίου; 4 οὐχὶ μένον σοὶ ἔμενε, καὶ πραθὲν ἐν
the price of the land? not Remaining to you did it remain, and sold in

3588 4674 1849 5225 5101 3754 5087 1722 3588 2588 4675 3588
τῇ σῇ ἐξουσίᾳ ὑπῆρχε; τί ὅτι ἔθου ἐν τῇ καρδίᾳ σου τὸ
your authority it was? Why was put in the heart of you

4229 5124 3756 5574 444 235 3588 2316
πρᾶγμα τοῦτο; οὐκ ἐψεύσω ἀνθρώποις, ἀλλὰ τῷ Θεῷ.
action this? not You lied to men, but to God.

4 Whiles it remained, was it not thine own? and after it was sold, was it not in thine own power? why hast thou conceived this thing in thine heart? thou hast not lied unto men, but unto God.

5 And hearing these words, falling down Ananias expired. And great fear came on all those hearing these things.

6 And the young men rising up, they wrapped him, and carrying out (they) buried (him).

191 1161 3588 367 3588 3056 5128 4098 1634
5 ἀκούων δὲ ὁ Ἀνανίας τοὺς λόγους τούτους, πεσὼν ἐξέψυξε·
hearing And Ananias words these, falling down expired;

2532 1096 5401 3173 1909 3956 3588 191
καὶ ἐγένετο φόβος μέγας ἐπὶ πάντας τοὺς ἀκούοντας
And came to be fear great on all those hearing

5023 450 1161 3588 3501 4958 846 2532
ταῦτα. 6 ἀναστάντες δὲ οἱ νεώτεροι συνέστειλαν αὐτόν, καὶ
these things. rising up And the young men they wrapped him, and

1627 2290
ἐξενέγκαντες ἔθαψαν.
carrying out (they) burried (him).

5 And Ananias hearing these words fell down, and gave up the ghost: and great fear came on all them that heard these things.

6 And the young men arose, wound him up, and carried (him) out, and buried (him).

Literal Translation

Acts 5:7

King James Version

7 And (it) was about three hours afterwards, his wife also entered, not knowing the (thing) happening.
8 And Peter answered her, Tell me if you gave over the land (for) so much? And she said, Yes, (for) so much.

9 And Peter said to her, Why (was it) that it was agreed with you to tempt the Spirit of (the) Lord? Behold, the feet of those burying your husband at the door! and they will carry you out.
10 And immediately she fell at his feet and expired. And entering, the young men found her dead, and carrying (her) out (they) buried her beside her husband.

11 And great fear came to be on all the church and on all those hearing these things.

1096 1161 5613 5610 5140 1292 2532 3588 1135 846
7 Ἐγένετο δὲ ὡς ὡρῶν τριῶν διάστημα, καὶ ἡ γυνὴ αὐτοῦ
(it) was And about hours three afterwards, and the wife of him
3361 1492 3588 1096 1525 611 1161 846 3588 4074
μὴ εἰδυῖα τὸ γεγονὸς εἰσῆλθεν. 8 ἀπεκρίθη δὲ αὐτῇ ὁ Πέτρος,
not knowing the happening came in. answered And her Peter,
2036 3427 1487 5118 3588 5564 591 3588 1161 2036 3483
Εἰπέ μοι, εἰ τοσούτου τὸ χωρίον ἀπέδοσθε. ἡ δὲ εἶπε, Ναί,
Tell me, if so much the land you gave over. she And said, Yes,
5118 3588 1161 4074 2036 4314 846 5101 3754 4856
τοσούτου. 9 ὁ δὲ Πέτρος εἶπε πρὸς αὐτήν, Τί ὅτι συνεφωνήθη
so much. And Peter said to her, Why was it agreed
5213 3985 3588 4151 2962 2400 3588 4228 3588 2290
ὑμῖν πειράσαι τὸ Πνεῦμα Κυρίου; ἰδού, οἱ πόδες τῶν θαψάν-
with you to tempt the Spirit of (the) Lord? Behold! The feet of those burying
3588 435 4675 1909 3588 2374 2532 1627 4571 4098 1161
των τὸν ἄνδρα σου ἐπὶ τῇ θύρᾳ, καὶ ἐξοίσουσί σε. 10 ἔπεσε δὲ
the husband of you at the door, and they will carry out you. she fell And
3916 3844 3588 4228 846 2532 1634 1525
παραχρῆμα παρὰ τοὺς πόδας αὐτοῦ, καὶ ἐξέψυξεν· εἰσελ-
immediately by the feet of him, and expired; coming
1161 3588 3495 2147 846 3498 2532 1627
θόντες δὲ οἱ νεανίσκοι εὗρον αὐτὴν νεκράν, καὶ ἐξενέγκαντες
And the young men found her dead, and carrying out
2290 4314 3588 435 846 2532 1096 5401 3173
ἔθαψαν πρὸς τὸν ἄνδρα αὐτῆς. 11 καὶ ἐγένετο φόβος μέγας
buried beside the husband of her. And came to be fear great
1909 3650 3588 1577 2532 1909 3956 3588 191
ἐφ᾽ ὅλην τὴν ἐκκλησίαν, καὶ ἐπὶ πάντας τοὺς ἀκούοντας
on all the assembly, and on all those hearing
5023
ταῦτα.
these things.

7 And it was about the space of three hours after, when his wife, not knowing what was done, came in.
8 And Peter answered unto her, Tell me whether ye sold the land for so much? And she said, Yea, for so much.
9 Then Peter said unto her, How is it that ye have agreed together to tempt the Spirit of the Lord? behold, the feet of them which have buried thy husband (are) at the door, and shall carry thee out.
10 Then fell she down straightway at his feet, and yielded up the ghost: and the young men came in, and found her dead, and, carrying (her) forth, buried (her) by her husband.
11 And great fear came upon all the church, and upon as many as heard these things.

12. And through the hands of the apostles many signs and wonders among the people occurred. And they were all with one passion in Solomon's Porch.
13 And of the rest, no one dared to be joined to them, but the people greatly magnified them.
14 And more believing ones were added to (the) Lord, multitudes of both men and of women,
15 so as to carry out the sick in the streets, and to place (them) on cots and mattresses, that (at the) coming of Peter, if even (his) shadow might overshadow some of them.
16 And also the multitude came together (from) the cities around Jerusalem, bearing sick ones and (those) being tormented by unclean spirits,

1223 1161 3588 5495 3588 652 1096 4592 2532
12 Διὰ δὲ τῶν χειρῶν τῶν ἀποστόλων ἐγίνετο σημεῖα καὶ
through And the hands of the apostles occurred signs and
5059 1722 3588 2992 4183 2532 2258 3661 537
τέρατα ἐν τῷ λαῷ πολλά· καὶ ἦσαν ὁμοθυμαδὸν ἅπαντες
wonders among the people many; and were with one mind all
1722 3588 4745 4672 3588 1161 3062 3762 5111
ἐν τῇ στοᾷ Σολομῶντος. 13 τῶν δὲ λοιπῶν οὐδεὶς ἐτόλμα
in the porch of Solomon. of the And rest no one dared
2853 846 235 3170 846 3588 2992 3123
κολλᾶσθαι αὐτοῖς, ἀλλ᾽ ἐμεγάλυνεν αὐτοὺς ὁ λαός· 14 μᾶλλον
to be joined to them, but magnified them the people; more
1161 4369 4100 3588 2962 4128 435 5037
δὲ προσετίθεντο πιστεύοντες τῷ Κυρίῳ, πλήθη ἀνδρῶν τε
and were added believing ones to the Lord, multitudes of men both
2532 1135 5620 2596 3588 4113 1627 3588
καὶ γυναικῶν· 15 ὥστε κατὰ τὰς πλατείας ἐκφέρειν τοὺς
and women; so as in the streets to carry out the
772 2532 5087 1909 2825 2532 2895 2443 2064
ἀσθενεῖς, καὶ τιθέναι ἐπὶ κλινῶν καὶ κραββάτων, ἵνα ἐρχο-
sick, and to place on cots and mattresses, that coming
4074 2579 3588 4639 1982 5100 846 4905
μένου Πέτρου κἂν ἡ σκιὰ ἐπισκιάσῃ τινὶ αὐτῶν. 16 συνήρχετο
Peter if even the shadow overshadow some of them. assembled
1161 2532 3588 4128 3588 4038 4172 1519 2419
δὲ καὶ τὸ πλῆθος τῶν πέριξ πόλεων εἰς Ἱερουσαλήμ,
And also the multitude of the round about cities to Jerusalem,
5342 772 2532 3791 5259 4151 169
φέροντες ἀσθενεῖς καὶ ὀχλουμένους ὑπὸ πνευμάτων ἀκαθάρ-
bearing sick ones and (those) being tormented by spirits unclean

12. And by the hands of the apostles were many signs and wonders wrought among the people; (and they were all with one accord in Solomon's porch.
13 And of the rest durst no man join himself to them: but the people magnified them.
14 And believers were the more added to the Lord, multitudes both of men and women.)
15 Insomuch that they brought forth the sick into the streets, and laid (them) on beds and couches, that at the least the shadow of Peter passing by might overshadow some of them.
16 There came also a multitude (out) of the cities round about unto Jerusalem, bringing sick folks, and them which were vexed with unclean spirits:

Literal Translation | **Acts 5:17** | *King James Version*

who were all healed.

17. And rising up, the high priest and all those with him, which is (the) sect of the Sadducees, were filled with jealousy,
18 and laid their hands on the apostles, and publicly put them in custody.

19 But by night an angel of (the) Lord opened the doors of the prison, and leading them out, he said,

20 Go! And standing in the temple, speak to the people all the words of this Life.
21 And having heard, they went into the temple about dawn and taught. But having come near, the high priest and those with him, he called together the Sanhedrin and all the elderhood of the sons of Israel. And (they) sent to the jail (for) them to be brought.

22 But having come near, the officers did not find them in the prison. And having returned, they reported,

23 saying, Indeed we found the jail having been shut with all security, and the guards outside standing before the doors. But opening it, we found no one inside.

24 And when they heard these words, both the priest and the temple commander and the chief priests were perplexed about them, what this might be.
25 But having come one reported to them, saying, Behold! The men whom you put in the prison are in the temple, standing and teaching the people.

3748 2323 537
των, οἵτινες ἐθεραπεύοντο ἅπαντες.
who were healed all.

450 1161 3588 749 2532 3956 3588 4862 846 3588 5607
17.᾽Αναστὰς δὲ ὁ ἀρχιερεὺς καὶ πάντες οἱ σὺν αὐτῷ [ἡ οὖσα
rising up And the chief priests and all those with him, which is

139 3588 4523 4130 2205 2532 1911
αἵρεσις τῶν Σαδδουκαίων], ἐπλήσθησαν ζήλου, 18 καὶ ἐπέ-
(the) sect of the Sadducees, were filled of jealousy, and laid

3588 5495 846 1909 3588 652 2532 5087
βαλον τὰς χεῖρας αὐτῶν ἐπὶ τοὺς ἀποστόλους, καὶ ἔθεντο
on the hands of them on the apostles, and put

846 1722 5084 1219 32 1161 2962 1223 3588
αὐτοὺς ἐν τηρήσει δημοσίᾳ. 19 ἄγγελος δὲ Κυρίου διὰ τῆς
them in custody publicly. an angel And of (the) Lord by

3571 455 3588 2374 3588 5438 1806 5037 846
νυκτὸς ἤνοίξε τὰς θύρας τῆς φυλακῆς, ἐξαγαγών τε αὐτοὺς
night opened the doors of the prison, leading out and them

2036 4198 2532 2476 2980 1722 3588 2411 3588 2992
εἶπε, 20 Πορεύεσθε, καὶ σταθέντες λαλεῖτε ἐν τῷ ἱερῷ τῷ λαῷ
said, Go, and standing speak in the temple to the people

3956 3588 4487 3588 2222 3778 191 1161 1525
πάντα τὰ ῥήματα τῆς ζωῆς ταύτης. 21 ἀκούσαντες δὲ εἰσῆλθον
all the words life of this. having heard And they went in

5259 3588 3722 1519 3588 2411 2532 1321 3854 1161
ὑπὸ τὸν ὄρθρον εἰς τὸ ἱερὸν, καὶ ἐδίδασκον. παραγενόμενος δὲ
about the dawn into the temple, and taught. having come near And

3588 749 2532 3588 4862 846 4779 3588 4892 2532
ὁ ἀρχιερεὺς καὶ οἱ σὺν αὐτῷ, συνεκάλεσαν τὸ συνέδριον καὶ
the chief priests and those with him, he called together the Sanhedrin and

3956 3588 1087 3588 5207 2474 2532 649 1519
πᾶσαν τὴν γερουσίαν τῶν υἱῶν ᾽Ισραήλ, καὶ ἀπέστειλαν εἰς
all the elderhood of the sons of Israel, and they sent to

3588 1201 71 846 3588 1161 5257 3854
τὸ δεσμωτήριον, ἀχθῆναι αὐτούς. 22 οἱ δὲ ὑπηρέται παρα-
the jail, to be brought them, the But under-officers having

3756 2147 846 1722 3588 5438 390
γενόμενοι οὐχ εὗρον αὐτοὺς ἐν τῇ φυλακῇ· ἀναστρέψαντες
come near not did find them in the prison; having returned

1161 518 3004 3754 3588 3303 1201 2147
δὲ ἀπήγγειλαν, 23 λέγοντες ὅτι Τὸ μὲν δεσμωτήριον εὕρομεν
and they reported, saying, the Indeed jail we found

2808 1722 3956 803 2532 3588 5441 1854
κεκλεισμένον ἐν πάσῃ ἀσφαλείᾳ, καὶ τοὺς φύλακας ἔξω
having been shut in all security, and the guards outside

2476 4253 3588 2374 455 1161 2080 3762 2147
ἑστῶτας πρὸ τῶν θυρῶν· ἀνοίξαντες δέ, ἔσω οὐδένα εὕρο-
standing at the doors; opening but, inside no one we

5613 1161 191 3588 3056 5128 3588/5037/2409/2532/3588
μεν. 24 ὡς δὲ ἤκουσαν τοὺς λόγους τούτους ὅ τε ἱερεὺς καὶ ὁ
found. as And heard words these the both priests and the

4755 3588 2411 2532 3588 749 1280 4012
στρατηγὸς τοῦ ἱεροῦ καὶ οἱ ἀρχιερεῖς, διηπόρουν περὶ
commander of the temple and the chief priests, were perplexed about

846 5101 302 1096 5124 3854 1161 5100 518
αὐτῶν, τί ἂν γένοιτο τοῦτο. 25 παραγενόμενος δέ τις ἀπήγ-
them, what might become this. having come And one re-

846 3004 3754 2400 3588 435 3739 5087 1722 3588
γειλεν αὐτοῖς λέγων ὅτι ᾽Ιδού, οἱ ἄνδρες οὓς ἔθεσθε ἐν τῇ
ported to them saying Behold! The men whom you put in the

5438 1526 1722 3588 2411 2476 2532 1321 3588 2992
φυλακῇ εἰσὶν ἐν τῷ ἱερῷ ἑστῶτες καὶ διδάσκοντες τὸν λαόν.
prison are in the temple standing and teaching the people.

---

and they were healed every one.

17. Then the high priest rose up, and all they that were with him, (which is the sect of the Sadducees,) and were filled with indignation,
18 And laid their hands on the apostles, and put them in the common prison.
19 But the angel of the Lord by night opened the prison doors, and brought them forth, and said,

20 Go, stand and speak in the temple to the people all the words of this life.
21 And when they heard (that), they entered into the temple early in the morning, and taught. But the high priest came, and they that were with him, and called the council together, and all the senate of the children of Israel, and sent to the prison to have them brought.

22 But when the officers came, and found them not in the prison, they returned, and told,

23 Saying, The prison truly found we shut with all safety, and the keepers standing without before the doors: but when we had opened, we found no man within.

24 Now when the high priest and the captain of the temple and the chief priests heard these things, they doubted of them whereunto this would grow.
25 Then came one and told them, saying, Behold, the men whom ye put in prison are standing in the temple, and teaching the people.

Literal Translation | **Acts 5:26** | **King James Version**

26 Then the commander going with the under-officers, (they) brought them, not with force, for they feared the people, that they not be stoned.
27 And bringing them, they stood in the sanhedrin. And the high priest questioned them,
28 saying, Did we not charge you by a charge (that) you not teach in this name? And, behold, you have filled Jerusalem with your teaching and intend to bring on us the blood of this man.

5119 565 3588 4755 4862 3588 5257 71
26 τότε ἀπελθὼν ὁ στρατηγὸς σὺν τοῖς ὑπηρέταις ἤγαγεν
Then going the commander with the under-officers brought

86 3756 3326 970 5399 1063 3588 2992 2443 3361
αὐτούς, οὐ μετὰ βίας, ἐφοβοῦντο γὰρ τὸν λαόν, ἵνα μὴ
them, not with force, they feared for the people, that not

3034 71 1161 846 2476 1722 3588 4892
λιθασθῶσιν. 27 ἀγαγόντες δὲ αὐτοὺς ἔστησαν ἐν τῷ συνεδρίῳ.
they be stoned. bringing And them they stood in the Sanhedrin.

2532 1905 846 3588 749 3004 3756 3852
καὶ ἐπηρώτησεν αὐτοὺς ὁ ἀρχιερεὺς, 28 λέγων, Οὐ παραγ-
And questioned them the high priest, saying, Not by a

3853 5213 3361 1321 1909 3588 3686
γελίᾳ παρηγγείλαμεν ὑμῖν μὴ διδάσκειν ἐπὶ τῷ ὀνόματι
charge did we charge you not to teach on name

5129 2532 2400 4137 3588 2419 3588
τούτῳ; καὶ ἰδοὺ πεπληρώκατε τὴν Ἱερουσαλὴμ τῆς δι-
this? And, behold, you have filled Jerusalem of the

1322 5216 2532 1014 1863 1909 2248 3588 129 3588
δαχῆς ὑμῶν, καὶ βούλεσθε ἐπαγαγεῖν ἐφ' ἡμᾶς τὸ αἷμα τοῦ
teaching of you, and purpose to bring on us the blood

444 5127 611 1161 3588 4074 2532 3588 652
ἀνθρώπου τούτου. 29 ἀποκριθεὶς δὲ ὁ Πέτρος καὶ οἱ ἀπόστολοι
man of this. answering But Peter and the apostles

26 Then went the captain with the officers, and brought them without violence: for they feared the people, lest they should have been stoned.
27 And when they had brought them, they set (them) before the council: and the high priest asked them,
28 Saying, Did not we straitly command you that ye should not teach in this name? and, behold, ye have filled Jerusalem with your doctrine, and intend to bring this man's blood upon us.

29 But answering Peter and the apostles said, It is right to obey God rather than man.
30 The God of our fathers raised up Jesus, whom you laid violent hands on, hanging (Him) on a tree.

31 This One God (has) exalted to His right (hand as) a Ruler and Savior, to give to Israel repentance and remission of sins.

32 And we are His witnesses of these words, and also the Holy Spirit, whom God gave to the (ones) obeying Him.

2036 3980 1163 2316 3123 2228 444 3588 2316 3588
εἶπον, Πειθαρχεῖν δεῖ Θεῷ μᾶλλον ἢ ἀνθρώποις. 30 ὁ Θεὸς τῶν
said, To obey it is right God rather than men. The God of the

3962 2257 1453 2424 3739 5210 1315
πατέρων ἡμῶν ἤγειρεν Ἰησοῦν, ὃν ὑμεῖς διεχειρίσασθε,
fathers of us raised up Jesus, whom you laid hands upon,

2910 1909 3586 5126 3588 2316 747 2532 4990
κρεμάσαντες ἐπὶ ξύλου. 31 τοῦτον ὁ Θεὸς ἀρχηγὸν καὶ σωτῆρα
hanging (Him) on a tree. This One God a Ruler and a Savior

5312 3588 1188 846 1325 3341 3588 2474 2532
ὕψωσε τῇ δεξιᾷ αὐτοῦ, δοῦναι μετάνοιαν τῷ Ἰσραὴλ καὶ
exalted to the right of Him, to give repentance to Israel and

859 266 2532 2249 2070 846 3144 3588
ἄφεσιν ἁμαρτιῶν. 32 καὶ ἡμεῖς ἐσμεν αὐτοῦ μάρτυρες τῶν
remission of sins. And we are of Him witnesses

4487 5130 2532 3588 4151 1161 3588 40 3739 1325 3588
ῥημάτων τούτων, καὶ τὸ Πνεῦμα δὲ τὸ Ἅγιον, ὃ ἔδωκεν ὁ
words of these, also the Spirit and Holy which gave

2316 3588 3980 846
Θεὸς τοῖς πειθαρχοῦσιν αὐτῷ.
God to the (ones) obeying Him.

29 Then Peter and the (other) apostles answered and said, We ought to obey God rather than men.
30 The God of our fathers raised up Jesus, whom ye slew and hanged on a tree.

31 Him hath God exalted with his right hand (to be) a Prince and a Saviour, for to give repentance to Israel, and forgiveness of sins.

32 And we are his witnesses of these things; and (so is) also the Holy Ghost, whom God hath given to them that obey him.

33. But those hearing were cut, and they took counsel to kill them.
34 But one standing up in the sanhedrin, a Pharisee named Gamaliel, a teacher of the Law honored by all the people, commanded to put the apostles outside a little (while).
35 And he said to them, Men, Israelites, take heed to yourselves what you intend to do to these men.

36 For before

3588 1161 191 1282 2532 1011 337
33. Οἱ δὲ ἀκούσαντες διεπρίοντο, καὶ ἐβουλεύοντο ἀνελεῖν
those And hearing were cut, and took counsel to kill

846 450 1161 5100 1722 3588 4892 5330 3686
αὐτούς. 34 ἀναστὰς δέ τις ἐν τῷ συνεδρίῳ Φαρισαῖος, ὀνό-
them. standing up But one in the Sanhedrin a Pharisee, by

1059 3547 5093 3956 3588 2992
ματι Γαμαλιήλ, νομοδιδάσκαλος, τίμιος παντὶ τῷ λαῷ,
name Gamaliel, a teacher of the Law, honored by all the people,

2753 1854 1024 5100 3588 652 4160 2036 5037
ἐκέλευσεν ἔξω βραχύ τι τοὺς αποστόλους ποιῆσαι. 35 εἶπέ τε
commanded outside a little the apostles to put. he said And

4314 846 435 2475 4337 1437 1909
πρὸς αὐτούς,"Ανδρες Ἰσραηλῖται, προσέχετε ἑαυτοῖς ἐπὶ
to them, Men Israelites, take heed to yourselves on

3588 444 5125 5101 3195 4238 4253 1063
τοῖς ἀνθρώποις τούτοις, τί μέλλετε πράσσειν. 36 πρὸ γὰρ
men these, what you intend to do. before For

33. When they heard (that), they were cut (to the heart), and took counsel to slay them.
34 Then stood there up one in the council, a Pharisee, named Gamaliel, a doctor of the law, had in reputation among all the people, and commanded to put the apostles forth a little space;
35 And said unto them, Ye men of Israel, take heed to yourselves what ye intend to do as touching these men.
36 For before

Literal Translation

Acts 5:37

these days Theudas stood up, saying himself to be somebody, to whom were joined a number of men, about four hundred, who was executed, and all, as many as obeyed him, were dispersed and came to nothing.

37 After this, Judas the Galilean stood up in the days of the Registration. And (he) drew away considerable people after him. Yet that one perished, and all were scattered, as many as obeyed him.

38 And now I say to you, draw away from these men and allow them; because if this counsel is of men, or this work, it will be destroyed.

39 But if it is from God, you will not be able to destroy it, lest you be found (to be) God-fighters.
40 And they obeyed him. And having called the apostles, (and) having beaten them, they charged (them) not to speak on the name of Jesus, and set them free.
41 Then indeed they departed from (the) presence of the Sanhedrin, rejoicing that they were deemed worthy to be dishonored on behalf of His name.
42 And every day they did not cease teaching and preaching the gospel (about) Jesus the Christ in the temple, and house to house.

5130 3588 2250 450 2333 3004 1511 5100
τούτων τῶν ἡμερῶν ἀνέστη Θευδᾶς, λέγων εἶναί τινα
these days stood up Theudas, saying to be someone

1438 3739 4347 706 435 5616 5071
ἑαυτόν, ᾧ προσεκολλήθη ἀριθμὸς ἀνδρῶν ὡσει τετρακοσίων·
himself, to whom were joined a number of men about four hundred;

3739 337 2532 3956 3745 3982 846 1262 2532
ὃς ἀνῃρέθη, καὶ πάντες ὅσοι ἐπείθοντο αὐτῷ διελύθησαν καὶ
who was executed, and all as many as obeyed him were dispersed and

1096 1519 3762 3326 5126 450 2455 3588 1057
ἐγένοντο εἰς οὐδέν. 37 μετὰ τοῦτον ἀνέστη Ἰούδας ὁ Γαλιλαῖος
came to nothing. After this stood up Judas the Galilean

1722 3588 2250 3588 582 2532 868 2992 2425
ἐν ταῖς ἡμέραις τῆς ἀπογραφῆς, καὶ ἀπέστησε λαὸν ἱκανόν
in the days of the registration, and drew away people much

3694 846 2548 622 2532 3956 3745 3982
ὀπίσω αὐτοῦ· κἀκεῖνος ἀπώλετο, καὶ πάντες ὅσοι ἐπείθοντο
after him; and that one perished, and all as many as obeyed

846 1287 2532 3588 3568 3004 5213 868
αὐτῷ διεσκορπίσθησαν. 38 καὶ τὰ νῦν λέγω ὑμῖν, ἀπόστητε
him were scattererd. And now I say to you, draw away

575 3588 444 5130 2532 1439 846 3754 1437 5600
ἀπὸ τῶν ἀνθρώπων τούτων, καὶ ἐάσατε αὐτούς· ὅτι ἐὰν ᾖ
from men these, and allow them; because if it be

1537 444 3588 1012 3778 2228 3588 2041 5124 2647
ἐξ ἀνθρώπων ἡ βουλὴ αὕτη ἢ τὸ ἔργον τοῦτο, καταλυθή-
of men counsel this or work this, it will be

1487/1161/1537 2316 2076 3756 1410 2647 846
σεται· 39 εἰ δὲ ἐκ Θεοῦ ἐστιν, οὐ δύνασθε καταλῦσαι αὐτό,
destroyed; if but from God it is, not you will be able to destroy it,

3379 2532 2314 2147 3982 1161 846 2532
μήποτε καὶ θεομάχοι εὑρεθῆτε. ἐπείσθησαν δὲ αὐτῷ, 40 καὶ
lest even God-fighters you will be found. they obeyed And him, and

4341 3588 652 1194 3853
προσκαλεσάμενοι τοὺς ἀποστόλους, δείραντες παρήγγειλαν
having called the apostles, having beaten (and) having charged

3361 2980 1909 3588 3686 3588 2424 2532 630 846
μὴ λαλεῖν ἐπὶ τῷ ὀνόματι τοῦ Ἰησοῦ, καὶ ἀπέλυσαν αὐτούς.
not to speak on the name of Jesus, and (they) set free them.

3588 3303 3767 4198 5463 575 4383 3588 4892
41 οἱ μὲν οὖν ἐπορεύοντο χαίροντες ἀπὸ προσώπου τοῦ συνεδ-
They indeed then departed rejoicing from (the) presence of the San-

3754 5228 3588 3686 846 2661 818
ρίου, ὅτι ὑπὲρ τοῦ ὀνόματος αὐτοῦ κατηξιώθησαν ἀτιμασθῆναι.
hedrin, for on behalf of name His they were deemed worthy to be dishonored.

3956 5037 2250 1722 3588 2411 2532 2596 3624 3756 3973
42 πᾶσάν τε ἡμέραν ἐν τῷ ἱερῷ καὶ κατ' οἶκον, οὐκ ἐπαύοντο
every And day in the temple and house to house, not they ceased

1321 2532 2097 2424 3588 5547
διδάσκοντες καὶ εὐαγγελιζόμενοι Ἰησοῦν τὸν Χριστόν.
teaching and preaching the gospel Jesus the Christ.

King James Version

these days rose up Theudas, boasting himself to be somebody; to whom a number of men, about four hundred, joined themselves: who was slain; and all, as many as obeyed him, were scattered, and brought to nought.

37 After this man rose up Judas of Galilee in the days of the taxing, and drew away much people after him: he also perished; and all, (even) as many as obeyed him, were dispersed.

38 And now I say unto you, Refrain from these men, and let them alone: for if this counsel or this work be of men, it will come to nought:

39 But if it be of God, ye cannot overthrow it; lest haply ye be found even to fight against God.
40 And to him they agreed: and when they had called the apostles, and beaten (them), they commanded that they should not speak in the name of Jesus, and let them go.

41 And they departed from the presence of the council, rejoicing that they were counted worthy to suffer shame for his name.
42 And daily in the temple, and in every house, they ceased not to teach and preach Jesus Christ.

Acts 6

1. But in these days, the disciples being multiplied, a murmuring of the Hellenists toward the Hebrews occurred, because their widows were being overlooked in the daily service.

1722 1161 3588 2250 3778 4129 3588 3101
1 Ἐν δὲ ταῖς ἡμέραις ταύταις, πληθυνόντων τῶν μαθητῶν,
in And days these, being multiplied the disciples,

1096 1112 3588 1675 4314 3588 1445
ἐγένετο γογγυσμὸς τῶν Ἑλληνιστῶν πρὸς τοὺς Ἑβραίους,
occurred a murmuring of the Hellenists against the Hebrews,

3754 3865 1722 3588 1248 3588 2522 3588 5503
ὅτι παρεθεωροῦντο ἐν τῇ διακονίᾳ τῇ καθημερινῇ αι χῆραι
because were overlooked in the service daily of the widows

1. And in those days, when the number of the disciples was multiplied, there arose a murmuring of the Grecians against the Hebrews, because their widows were neglected in the daily ministration.

Literal Translation

2 And having called near the multitude of the disciples, the Twelve said, It is not pleasing to us, having left the Word of God, to serve tables!
3 Then brothers, look out for men among you having been witnessed to, seven (men) full of (the) Holy Spirit and wisdom, whom we will appoint over this need.
4 But we shall continue steadfast in prayer and the service of the Word!
5 And the word (was) pleasing before all the multitude. And they chose out Stephen, a man full of faith and (the) Holy Spirit, and Philip, and Prochorus, and Nicanor, and Timon, and Parmenas, and Nicolas, a proselyte from Antioch,
6 (each of) whom they set before the apostles. And having prayed, they placed (their) hands on them.
7 And the Word of God increased, and the number of the disciples in Jerusalem was multiplying exceedingly. Even a great crowd of the priests obeyed the faith!
8. And Stephen, full of faith and power, was doing wonders and great signs among the people.
9 But some of those of the synagogue being called Libertines, rose up, also (some) Cyrenians and Alexandrians, and (some) of those from Cilicia and Asia Minor, disputing with Stephen.
10 And they had no strength to stand against the wisdom and the Spirit with which he spoke.
11 Then they suborned (some) men (to be) saying,

Acts 6:2

846 4341 1161 3588 1427 3588 4128 3588
αὐτῶν. 2 προσκαλεσάμενοι δὲ οἱ δώδεκα τὸ πλῆθος τῶν
of them. having called near And the twelve the multitude of the

3101 2036 3756 701 2076 2248 2641
μαθητῶν, εἶπον, Οὐκ ἀρεστόν ἐστιν ἡμᾶς, καταλείψαντας
disciples, they said, not pleasing It is to us having left

3588 3056 3588 2316 1247 5132 1980 3767
τὸν λόγον τοῦ Θεοῦ, διακονεῖν τραπέζαις. 3 ἐπισκέψασθε οὖν,
the Word of God, to serve tables. Look out, then,

80 435 1537 5216 3140 2033 4134
ἀδελφοί, ἄνδρας ἐξ ὑμῶν μαρτυρουμένους ἑπτά, πλήρεις
brothers, men from you having been witnessed to seven, full

4151 40 2532 4678 3739 2525 1909 3588
Πνεύματος Ἁγίου καὶ σοφίας, οὓς καταστήσομεν ἐπὶ τῆς
of (the) Spirit Holy and of wisdom, whom we will appoint over

5532 3778 2249 1161 3588 4335 2532 3588 1248 3588
χρείας ταύτης. 4 ἡμεῖς δὲ τῇ προσευχῇ καὶ τῇ διακονίᾳ τοῦ
duty this. we But to prayer and the service of the

3056 4342 2532 700 3588 3056 1799
λόγου προσκαρτερήσομεν. 5 καὶ ἤρεσεν ὁ λόγος ἐνώπιον
Word will continue steadfast. And was pleasing the word before

3956 3588 4128 2532 1586 4736 435 4134
παντὸς τοῦ πλήθους· καὶ ἐξελέξαντο Στέφανον, ἄνδρα πλήρη
all the multitude; and they chose out Stephen, a man full

4102 2532 4151 40 2532 5376 2532 4402
πίστεως καὶ Πνεύματος Ἁγίου, καὶ Φίλιππον, καὶ Πρόχο-
of faith and (the) Spirit Holy, and Philip, and Prochorus,

2532 3527 2532 5096 2532 3937 2532 3532
ρον, καὶ Νικάνορα, καὶ Τίμωνα, καὶ Παρμενᾶν, καὶ Νικόλαον
and Nicanor, and Timon, and Parmenas, and Nicolas

4339 491 3739 2476 1799 3588 652
προσήλυτον Ἀντιοχέα, 6 οὓς ἔστησαν ἐνώπιον τῶν ἀποστό-
a proselyte of Antioch, whom they set before the apostles;

2532 4336 2007 846 3588 5495
λων· καὶ προσευξάμενοι ἐπέθηκαν αὐτοῖς τὰς χεῖρας.
and having prayed they placed on them the hands.

2532 3588 3056 3588 2316 837 2532 4129 3588 706
7 Καὶ ὁ λόγος τοῦ Θεοῦ ηὔξανε, καὶ ἐπληθύνετο ὁ ἀριθμὸς
And the Word of God increased, and was multiplied the number

3588 3101 1722 2419 4970 4183 5037 3793 3588
τῶν μαθητῶν ἐν Ἱερουσαλὴμ σφόδρα, πολύς τε ὄχλος τῶν
of the disciples in Jerusalem exceedingly, a great even crowd of the

2409 5219 3588 4102
ἱερέων ὑπήκουον τῇ πίστει.
priests obeyed the faith.

4736 1161 4134 4102 2532 1411 4160 5059
8 Στέφανος δὲ πλήρης πίστεως καὶ δυνάμεως ἐποίει τέρατα
Stephen And full of faith and power did wonders

2532 4592 3137 1722 3588 2992 450 1161 5100 3588 1537
καὶ σημεῖα μεγάλα ἐν τῷ λαῷ. 9 ἀνέστησαν δέ τινες τῶν ἐκ
and signs great among the people. rose up But some of those of

3588 4864 3588 3004 3032 2532 2956
τῆς συναγωγῆς τῆς λεγομένης Λιβερτίνων, καὶ Κυρηναίων,
the synagogue being called of (the) Libertines, and of Cyrenians,

2532 221 2532 3588 575 2791 2532 773 4802
καὶ Ἀλεξανδρέων, καὶ τῶν ἀπὸ Κιλικίας καὶ Ἀσίας, συζη-
and of Alexandrians, also of those from Cilicia and Asia, dis-

3588 4736 2532 3756 2480 436 3588 4678
τοῦντες τῷ Στεφάνῳ. 10 καὶ οὐκ ἴσχυον ἀντιστῆναι τῇ σοφίᾳ
puting with Stephen. And not had strength to stand against the wisdom

2532 3588 4151 3739 2980 5119 5260 435 3004
καὶ τῷ πνεύματι ᾧ ἐλάλει. 11 τότε ὑπέβαλον ἄνδρας λέγοντας
and the spirit with which he spoke. Then they suborned men saying,

King James Version

2 Then the twelve called the multitude of the disciples (unto them), and said, It is not reason that we should leave the word of God, and serve tables.
3 Wherefore, brethren, look ye out among you seven men of honest report, full of the Holy Ghost and wisdom, whom we may appoint over this business.
4 But we will give ourselves continually to prayer, and to the ministry of the word.
5 And the saying pleased the whole multitude: and they chose Stephen, a man full of faith and of the Holy Ghost, and Philip, and Prochorus, and Nicanor, and Timon, and Parmenas, and Nicolas a proselyte of Antioch:
6 Whom they set before the apostles: and when they had prayed, they laid (their) hands on them.
7 And the word of God increased; and the number of the disciples multiplied in Jerusalem greatly; and a great company of the priests were obedient to the faith.
8.. And Stephen, full of faith and power, did great wonders and miracles among the people.
9 Then there arose certain of the synagogue, which is called (the synagogue) of the Libertines, and Cyrenians, and Alexandrians, and of them of Cilicia and of Asia, disputing with Stephen.
10 And they were not able to resist the wisdom and the spirit by which he spake.
11 Then they suborned men, which said,

Literal Translation

Acts 6:12

King James Version

We have heard him speaking blasphemous words against Moses and God!
12 And they stirred up the people and the elders and the scribes. And coming on, they seized him and led him into the Sanhedrin.

13 And they stood up false witnesses, (who were) saying, This man does not cease speaking blasphemous words against this holy place and the Law;

14 for we have heard him saying that Jesus the Nazarene, this One, will destroy this place and will change the customs which Moses delivered to us.
15 And having looked intently at him, all those having sat in the Sanhedrin, saw his face as if (it were the) face of an angel.

3754 191 846 2980 4487 989 1519
ὅτι Ἀκηκόαμεν αὐτοῦ λαλοῦντος ῥήματα βλάσφημα εἰς
We have heard him speaking words blasphemous against

3475 2532 3588 2316 4787 5037 3588 2992 2532 3588
Μωσῆν καὶ τὸν Θεόν. 12 συνεκίνησάν τε τὸν λαὸν καὶ τοὺς
Moses and God. they stirred up And the people and the

4245 2532 3588 1122 2532 2186
πρεσβυτέρους καὶ τοὺς γραμματεῖς, καὶ ἐπιστάντες συν-
elders and the scribes, and coming on they

4884 846 2532 71 1519 3588 4892 2476 5037
ἥρπασαν αὐτόν, καὶ ἤγαγον εἰς τὸ συνέδριον, 13 ἔστησάν τε
seized him, and led to the Sanhedrin. stood And

3144 5571 3004 3588 444 3778 3756 3973
μάρτυρας ψευδεῖς λέγοντας, Ὁ ἄνθρωπος οὗτος οὐ παύεται
witnesses false saying, man This not ceases

4487 989 2980 2596 3588 5117 3588 40
ῥήματα βλάσφημα λαλῶν κατὰ τοῦ τόπου τοῦ ἁγίου
words blasphemous speaking against place holy

5127 2532 3588 3551 191 1063 846 3004 3754
τούτου καὶ τοῦ νόμου· 14 ἀκηκόαμεν γὰρ αὐτοῦ λέγοντος ὅτι
this and the Law. we have heard For him saying,

2424 3588 3480 3778 2647 3588 5117 5126
Ἰησοῦς ὁ Ναζωραῖος οὗτος καταλύσει τὸν τόπον τοῦτον,
Jesus the Nazarene this One will destroy place this,

2532 236 3588 1485 3739 3860 2254 3475 2532 816
καὶ ἀλλάξει τὰ ἔθη ἃ παρέδωκεν ἡμῖν Μωϋσῆς. 15 καὶ ἀτενί-
and will change the customs which delivered to us Moses. And looking

1519 846 537 3588 2516 1722 3588 4892
σαντες εἰς αὐτὸν ἅπαντες οἱ καθεζόμενοι ἐν τῷ συνεδρίῳ,
intently at him all those having sat in the Sanhedrin,

1492 3588 4383 846 5616 4383 32
εἶδον τὸ πρόσωπον αὐτοῦ ὡσεὶ πρόσωπον ἀγγέλου.
saw the face of him as (if it were) the face of an angel.

We have heard him speak blasphemous words against Moses, and (against) God.
12 And they stirred up the people, and the elders, and the scribes, and came upon (him), and caught him, and brought (him) to the council,
13 And set up false witnesses, which said, This man ceaseth not to speak blasphemous words against this holy place, and the law:

14 For we have heard him say, that this Jesus of Nazareth shall destroy this place, and shall change the customs which Moses delivered us.
15 And all that sat in the council, looking stedfastly on him, saw his face as it had been the face of an angel.

Acts 7

1. And the high priest said, (Tell me) then if you thus hold these things?
2 And he said, Men, brothers, and fathers, listen! The God of glory appeared to our father Abraham, being in Mesopotamia before he lived in Haran,
3 and said to him, "Go out from your land and from your kindred, and come into a land which I will show to you." (Gen.12:1)

4 Then going out from (the) land of the Chaldeans, he lived in Haran. And after his father died, (God) moved him from there into this land in which you now live.

5 And He did not give to him an inheritance in

2036 1161 3588 749 1487 687 5023 3779 2192 3588 1161 5346
1 Εἶπε δὲ ὁ ἀρχιερεύς, Εἰ ἄρα ταῦτα οὕτως ἔχει; 2 ὁ δὲ ἔφη,
said And the high priest, If then these things thus hold? he And said,

435 80 2532 3962 191 3588 2316 3588 1391
Ἄνδρες ἀδελφοὶ καὶ πατέρες, ἀκούσατε. Ὁ Θεὸς τῆς δόξης
Men brothers and fathers, hear. The God of glory

3700 3588 3962 2257 11 5607 1722 3588 3318
ὤφθη τῷ πατρὶ ἡμῶν Ἀβραὰμ ὄντι ἐν τῇ Μεσοποταμίᾳ,
appeared to the father of us Abraham being in Mesopotamia,

4250 2228 2730 846 1722 5488 2532 2036 4314 846
πρὶν ἢ κατοικῆσαι αὐτὸν ἐν Χαρράν, 3 καὶ εἶπε πρὸς αὐτόν,
before lived he in Haran, and said to him,

1831 1537 3588 1093 4675 2532 1537 3588 4772 4675 2532 1204
Ἔξελθε ἐκ τῆς γῆς σου καὶ ἐκ τῆς συγγενείας σου, καὶ δεῦρο
Go out from the land of you and from the kindred of you, and come

1519 1093 3739 302 4671 1166 5119 1831 1722 1093 5466
εἰς γῆν ἣν ἄν σοι δείξω. 4 τότε ἐξελθὼν ἐκ γῆς Χαλδαίων
into a land which to you I will show. Then going out from (the) land of Chaldea

2730 1722 5488 2547 3326 3588 599 3588
κατῴκησεν ἐν Χαρράν· κἀκεῖθεν, μετὰ τὸ ἀποθανεῖν τὸν
he lived in Haran. And from there, after the dying of the

3962 846 3351 846 1519 3588 1093 3778 1519 3739
πατέρα αὐτοῦ, μετῴκισεν αὐτὸν εἰς τὴν γῆν ταύτην εἰς ἣν
father of him, (God) moved him into land this in which

5210 3568 2730 2532 3756 1325 846 2817 1722
ὑμεῖς νῦν κατοικεῖτε· 5 καὶ οὐκ ἔδωκεν αὐτῷ κληρονομίαν ἐν
you now live. And not He gave to him an inheritance in

1. Then said the high priest, Are these things so?
2 And he said, Men, brethren, and fathers, hearken; The God of glory appeared unto our father Abraham, when he was in Mesopotamia, before he dwelt in Charran,
3 And said unto him, Get thee out of thy country, and from thy kindred, and come into the land which I shall shew thee.
4 Then came he out of the land of the Chaldaeans, and dwelt in Charran: and from thence, when his father was dead, he removed him into this land, wherein ye now dwell.

5 And he gave him none inheritance in

Literal Translation

Acts 7:6

King James Version

it, not (even) a foot breadth. And (He) promised to give it to him for a possession and to his seed after him, there being no child to him.
6 And God spoke thus, that his seed would be a temporary resident in a strange land, and they would enslave it and oppress (it) four hundred years. (See Gen.15:13,17:8)
7 And God said, "I will judge the nation to whichever they may serve." And, "After these things they will come out and will do service to Me in this place." (Gen. 15:14; Ex. 3:12)
8 And He gave to him a covenant of circumcision; and so he fathered Isaac and circumcised him on the eighth day. And Isaac (fathered) Jacob, and Jacob the twelve patriarchs.

846 3761 968 4228 2532 1861 846 1325 1519
αὐτῇ, οὐδὲ βῆμα ποδός· καὶ ἐπηγγείλατο αὐτῷ δοῦναι εἰς
it, nor space of a foot; and promised him to give for
2697 846 2532 3588 4690 846 3326 846 3756
κατάσχεσιν αὐτὴν, καὶ τῷ σπέρματι αὐτοῦ μετ' αὐτόν, οὐκ
a possession it, and to the seed of him after him, not
5607 846 5043 2980 1161 3779 3588 2316 3754 2071 3588
ὄντος αὐτῷ τέκνου. 6 ἐλάλησε δὲ οὕτως ὁ Θεός, ὅτι ἔσται τὸ
being to him a child. spoke And thus God, that will be the
4690 846 3941 1722 1093 245 2532 1402
σπέρμα αὐτοῦ πάροικον ἐν γῇ ἀλλοτρίᾳ, καὶ δουλώσουσιν
seed of him a sojourner in a land strange, and they will enslave
846 2532 2559 2094 5071 2532 3588 1484 3739 1437
αὐτὸ καὶ κακώσουσιν, ἔτη τετρακόσια. 7 καὶ τὸ ἔθνος, ᾧ ἐὰν
it and will oppress, years four hundred. And the nation, whichever
1398 2919 1473 2036 3588 2316 2532 3326 5023
δουλεύσωσι, κρινῶ ἐγώ, εἶπεν ὁ Θεός· καὶ μετὰ ταῦτα
they may serve, will judge I, said God. And after these things
1831 2532 3000 3427 1722 3588 5117 5129 2532
ἐξελεύσονται καὶ λατρεύσουσί μοι ἐν τῷ τόπῳ τούτῳ. 8 καὶ
they will come out and will do service to Me in place this. And
1325 846 1242 4061 2532 3779 1080 3588
ἔδωκεν αὐτῷ διαθήκην περιτομῆς· καὶ οὕτως ἐγέννησε τὸν
He gave to him a covenant of circumcision; and so he fathered
2464 2532 4059 846 3588 2250 3588 3590 2532 3588
Ἰσαὰκ, καὶ περιέτεμεν αὐτὸν τῇ ἡμέρᾳ τῇ ὀγδόῃ· καὶ ὁ
Isaac, and circumcised him on the day eighth. And
2464 3588 2384 2532 3588 2384 3588 1427 3966
Ἰσαὰκ τὸν Ἰακώβ, καὶ ὁ Ἰακὼβ τοὺς δώδεκα πατριάρχας.
Isaac (fathered) Jacob, and Jacob the twelve patriarchs.

it, no, not (so much as) to set his foot on: yet he promised that he would give it to him for a possession, and to his seed after him, when (as yet) he had no child.
6 And God spake on this wise, That his seed should sojourn in a strange land; and that they should bring them into bondage, and entreat (them) evil four hundred years.
7 And the nation to whom they shall be in bondage will I judge, said God: and after that shall they come forth, and serve me in this place.
8 And he gave him the covenant of circumcision: and so (Abraham) begat Isaac, and circumcised him the eighth day; and Isaac (begat) Jacob; and Jacob (begat) the twelve patriarchs.

9 And being jealous of Joseph, the patriarchs sold (him) into Egypt. But God was with him,
10 and plucked him out from all his afflictions, and gave him favor and wisdom before Pharaoh (the) king of Egypt. And (Pharaoh) appointed him governor over Egypt and all his whole house.

2532 3588 3966 2206 3588 2501 591 1519
9 Καὶ οἱ πατριάρχαι ζηλώσαντες τὸν Ἰωσὴφ ἀπέδοντο εἰς
And the patriarchs being jealous Joseph gave over into
125 2532 2258 3588 2316 3326 846 2532 1807 846 1537
Αἴγυπτον· καὶ ἦν ὁ Θεὸς μετ' αὐτοῦ, 10 καὶ ἐξείλετο αὐτὸν ἐκ
Egypt; and was God with him, and plucked out him from
3956 3588 2347 846 2532 1325 846 5485 2532
πασῶν τῶν θλίψεων αὐτοῦ, καὶ ἔδωκεν αὐτῷ χάριν καὶ
all the afflictions of him; and gave him favor and
4678 1726 5328 935 125 2532 2525
σοφίαν ἐναντίον Φαραὼ βασιλέως Αἰγύπτου, καὶ κατέστησεν
wisdom before Pharaoh king of Egypt, and he appointed
846 2233 1909 125 2532 3650 3588 3624 846
αὐτὸν ἡγούμενον ἐπ' Αἴγυπτον καὶ ὅλον τὸν οἶκον αὐτοῦ.
him to be ruling over Egypt and whole the house of him.

9 And the patriarchs, moved with envy, sold Joseph into Egypt: but God was with him,
10 And delivered him out of all his afflictions, and gave him favour and wisdom in the sight of Pharaoh king of Egypt; and he made him governor over Egypt and all his house.

11 But a famine came over all the land of Egypt and Canaan, and great affliction. And our fathers did not find sustenance.
12 But having heard of grain being in Egypt, Jacob sent out our fathers first.
13 And at the second (time), Joseph was made known to his brothers, and Joseph's race came to be evident to Pharaoh.
14 And sending, Joseph called

2064 1161 3042 1909 3650 3588 1093 125 2532 5477 2532
11 ἦλθε δὲ λιμὸς ἐφ' ὅλην τὴν γῆν Αἴγυπτου καὶ Χαναάν, καὶ
came But a famine over whole the land of Egypt and Canaan, and
2347 3173 2532 3756 2147 5527 3588 3962
θλίψις μεγάλη· καὶ οὐχ εὕρισκον χορτάσματα οἱ πατέρες
affliction great; and not did find sustenance the fathers
2257 191 1161 2384 5607 4621 1722 125 1821
ἡμῶν. 12 ἀκούσας δὲ Ἰακὼβ ὄντα σῖτα ἐν Αἰγύπτῳ ἐξαπέστειλε
of us. having heard But Jacob being grain in Egypt he sent forth
3588 3962 2257 4412 2532/1722/3588/1208 319
τοὺς πατέρας ἡμῶν πρῶτον. 13 καὶ ἐν τῷ δευτέρῳ ἀνεγνωρίσθη
the fathers of us first. And in the second was made known
2501 3588 80 846 2532 5318 1096 3588 5328
Ἰωσὴφ τοῖς ἀδελφοῖς αὐτοῦ, καὶ φανερὸν ἐγένετο τῷ Φαραὼ
Joseph to the brothers of him, and evident came to be to Pharaoh
3588 1085 3588 2501 649 1161 2501 3333
τὸ γένος τοῦ Ἰωσήφ. 14 ἀποστείλας δὲ Ἰωσὴφ μετεκαλέσατο
the race of Joseph. having sent And Joseph called

11 Now there came a dearth over all the land of Egypt and Chanaan, and great affliction: and our fathers found no sustenance.
12 But when Jacob heard that there was corn in Egypt, he sent out our fathers first.
13 And at the second (time) Joseph was made known to his brethren; and Joseph's kindred was made known unto Pharaoh.
14 Then sent Joseph, and called

Literal Translation | **Acts 7:15** | **King James Version**

his father Jacob and all his kindred, seventy five souls in (all).

15 And Jacob went down into Egypt and he expired, he and our fathers.

16 And they were moved into Shechem, and were put in the tomb which Abraham bought (for) a price of silver from the sons of Hamor of Shechem.

17 But as the time of the promise drew near, which God swore to Abraham, the people increased and multiplied in Egypt,

18 until another king rose up who did not know Joseph. (Ex.1:8)

19 Having dealt slyly with our race, this one oppressed our fathers, causing their babes (to be) exposed (so as) not to being kept alive.

20 In which time Moses was generated and was beautiful to God; who was reared three months in his father's house.

21 And he being exposed, the daughter of Pharaoh took him up and reared him for a son to herself.

22 And Moses was instructed in all (the) wisdom of Egyptians and was powerful in words and in works.

23 But when a period of forty years was fulfilled to him, it arose in his heart to look upon his brothers, the sons of Israel.

24 And seeing one being wronged, he defended (him), and he did vengeance for the (one) having gotten the worse, striking the Egyptian.

25 And he thought his brothers (would) perceive that God would give them deliverance by his hand. But they did not

3588 3962 846 2384 2532 3956 3588 4772 846
τὸν πατέρα αὐτοῦ Ἰακώβ, καὶ πᾶσαν τὴν συγγένειαν αὐτοῦ,
the father of him Jacob, and all the kindred of him,

1722 5590 1440 4002 2597 1161 2384 1519 125
ἐν ψυχαῖς ἑβδομήκοντα πέντε. 15 κατέβη δὲ Ἰακὼβ εἰς Αἴγυπ-
in souls seventy five. went down And Jacob into Egypt

2532 5053 846 2532 3588 3962 2257 2532 3346
τον, καὶ ἐτελεύτησεν αὐτὸς καὶ οἱ πατέρες ἡμῶν· 16 καὶ μετετέ-
and expired he and the fathers of us; and they were

1519 4966 2532 5087 1722 3588 3418 3739 5608
θησαν εἰς Σιχέμ, καὶ ἐτέθησαν ἐν τῷ μνήματι ὃ ὠνήσατο
moved into Shechem, and were placed in the tomb which bought

11 5092 694 3844 3588 5207 1697 1722 4966
Ἀβραὰμ τιμῆς ἀργυρίου παρὰ τῶν υἱῶν Ἐμὸρ τοῦ Σιχέμ.
Abraham (for) a price of silver from the sons of Hamor in Shechem.

2531 1161 1448 3588 5550 3588 1860 3739 3660 3588 2316
17 Καθὼς δὲ ἤγγιζεν ὁ χρόνος τῆς ἐπαγγελίας ἧς ὤμοσεν ὁ Θεὸς
as And drew near the time of the promise which swore God

3588 11 837 3588 2992 2532 4129 1722 125
τῷ Ἀβραάμ, ηὔξησεν ὁ λαὸς καὶ ἐπληθύνθη ἐν Αἰγύπτῳ,
to Abraham, increased the people and multiplied in Egypt,

891 3757 450 935 2087 3739 3756 1492 3588 2501
18 ἄχρις οὗ ἀνέστη βασιλεὺς ἕτερος, ὃς οὐκ ᾔδει τὸν Ἰωσήφ.
until rose up king another, who not knew Joseph.

3778 2686 3588 1085 2257 2559 3588 3962
19 οὗτος κατασοφισάμενος τὸ γένος ἡμῶν, ἐκάκωσε τοὺς πατέ-
This one having dealt slyly with the race of us, oppressed the fathers

2257 3588 4160 1570 3588 1025 846 1519/3588 3361
ρας ἡμῶν, τοῦ ποιεῖν ἔκθετα τὰ βρέφη αὐτῶν, εἰς τὸ μὴ
of us, to make exposed the babes of them, unto not

2225 1722 3739 2540 1080 3475 2532 2258 791
ζωογονεῖσθαι. 20 ἐν ᾧ καιρῷ ἐγεννήθη Μωσῆς, καὶ ἦν ἀστεῖος
being kept alive. At which time was generated Moses, and he was beautiful

3588 2316 3739 397 3376 5140 1722 3588 3624 3588 3962
τῷ Θεῷ· ὃς ἀνετράφη μῆνας τρεῖς ἐν τῷ οἴκῳ τοῦ πατρός
to God; who was reared months three in the house of the father

846 1620 1161 846 337 846 3588 2364
αὐτοῦ. 21 ἐκτεθέντα δὲ αὐτόν, ἀνείλετο αὐτὸν ἡ θυγάτηρ
of him. being exposed And he, took up him the daughter

5328 2532 397 846 1438 1519 5207 2532 3811
Φαραώ, καὶ ἀνεθρέψατο αὐτὸν ἑαυτῇ εἰς υἱόν. 22 καὶ ἐπαιδεύθη
of Pharaoh, and reared him to herself for a son. And was instructed

3475 3956 4678 124 2258 1161 1415 1722 3056 2532
Μωσῆς πάσῃ σοφίᾳ Αἰγυπτίων· ἦν δὲ δυνατὸς ἐν λόγοις καὶ
Moses in all (the) wisdom of Egyptians; was and powerful in words and

1722 2041 5613 1161 4137 846 5063 5550
ἐν ἔργοις. 23 ὡς δὲ ἐπληροῦτο αὐτῷ τεσσαρακονταετὴς χρόνος,
in works. when But was fulfilled to him of forty years a time,

305 1909 3588 2588 846 1980 3588 80
ἀνέβη ἐπὶ τὴν καρδίαν αὐτοῦ ἐπισκέψασθαι τοὺς ἀδελφοὺς
it arose on the heart of him to look upon the brothers

846 3588 5207 2474 2532 1492 5100 91 292
αὐτοῦ τοὺς υἱοὺς Ἰσραήλ. 24 καὶ ἰδών τινα ἀδικούμενον, ἠμύ-
of him the sons of Israel And seeing one being wronged, he de-

2532 4160 1557 3588 2669 3960
νατο καὶ ἐποίησεν ἐκδίκησιν τῷ καταπονουμένῳ πατάξας
fended, and he did vengeance for the (one) having gotten the worse, striking

3588 124 3543 1161 4920 3588 80 846 3754
τὸν Αἰγύπτιον· 25 ἐνόμιζε δὲ συνιέναι τοὺς ἀδελφοὺς αὐτοῦ ὅτι
the Egyptian. he thought And to perceive the brothers of him that

3588 2316 1223 5495 846 1325 846 4991 3588 1161 3756
ὁ Θεὸς διὰ χειρὸς αὐτοῦ δίδωσιν αὐτοῖς σωτηρίαν· οἱ δὲ οὐ
God through (the) hand of him would give to them deliverance; they but not

his father Jacob to (him), and all his kindred, threescore and fifteen souls.

15 So Jacob went down into Egypt, and died, he, and our fathers,

16 And were carried over into Sychem, and laid in the sepulchre that Abraham bought for a sum of money of the sons of Emmor (the father) of Sychem.

17 But when the time of the promise drew nigh, which God had sworn to Abraham, the people grew and multiplied in Egypt,

18 Till another king arose, which knew not Joseph.

19 The same dealt subtilly with our kindred, and evil entreated our fathers, so that they cast out their young children, to the end they might not live.

20 In which time Moses was born, and was exceeding fair, and nourished up in his father's house three months:

21 And when he was cast out, Pharaoh's daughter took him up, and nourished him for her own son.

22 And Moses was learned in all the wisdom of the Egyptians, and was mighty in words and in deeds.

23 And when he was full forty years old, it came into his heart to visit his brethren the children of Israel.

24 And seeing one (of them) suffer wrong, he defended (him), and avenged him that was oppressed, and smote the Egyptian:

25 For he supposed his brethren would have understood how that God by his hand would deliver them: but they

Literal Translation | **Acts 7:26** | **King James Version**

perceive.
26 And the following day he appeared to them (while) fighting. And he constrained them to peace, saying, Men, you are brothers. Why do you wrong one another?
27 But the (one) wronging the neighbor thrust him away, saying, "Who appointed you a ruler and a judge over us?
28 Do you not want to do away with me (in the) way you did away with the Egyptian yesterday?" (Ex.2:14)
29 And Moses fled at this word. And he became a tenant in Midian land, where he fathered two sons. (Ex.2:13-15)
30 And forty years having been fulfilled, (the) Angel of (the) Lord appeared to him in a flame of fire (in) a bush in the desert of Mount Sinai.
31 And seeing, Moses marveled at the sight. And he coming up to look, a voice of (the) Lord came to him:
32 "I (am) the God of your fathers, the God of Abraham, and the God of Isaac, and the God of Jacob." (Ex. 3:6, 15) But coming to be trembling, Moses did not dare to look.
33 And the Lord said to him, "Loosen the sandal from your feet, for the place where you stand is holy ground.
34 I surely saw the affliction of My people in Egypt, and I have heard their groan, and I came down to pluck them out. And now, come, I will send you to Egypt." (Ex. 3:5 - 8a, 10a)
35 This Moses, whom they denied, saying, Who appointed you a ruler and a judge, this one God has sent as ruler and redeemer by (the) hand of (the) Angel

4920 3588 1161 1966 2250 3700 846 3164 2532
συνῆκαν. 26 τῇ δὲ ἐπιούσῃ ἡμέρᾳ ὤφθη αὐτοῖς μαχομένοις, καὶ
perceived. the But following day he appeared to them fighting, and
4900 846 1519 1515 2036 435 80 2075
συνήλασεν αὐτοὺς εἰς εἰρήνην, εἰπών, Ἄνδρες, ἀδελφοί ἐστε
constrained them to peace, saying, Men, brothers are
5210 2444 91 240 3588 1161 91 3588 4139
ὑμεῖς· ἱνατί ἀδικεῖτε ἀλλήλους; 27 ὁ δὲ ἀδικῶν τὸν πλησίον
you; why do you wrong one another? he But wronging the neighbor
683 846 2036 5101 4571 2525 758 2532
ἀπώσατο αὐτὸν, εἰπών, Τίς σε κατέστησεν ἄρχοντα καὶ
thrust away him, saying, Who you appointed a ruler and
1348 1909 2248 3361 337 3165 4771 2309 3739 5158
δικαστὴν ἐφ᾽ ἡμᾶς; 28 μὴ ἀνελεῖν με σὺ θέλεις, ὃν τρόπον
a judge over us? Not to do away me you desire, in the same way
337 5504 3588 124 5343 1161 3475 1722 3588 3056
ἀνεῖλες χθὲς τὸν Αἰγύπτιον; 29 ἔφυγε δὲ Μωσῆς ἐν τῷ λόγῳ
you did away yesterday the Egyptian? fled And Moses at word
5129 2532 1096 3941 1722 1093 3099 3757 1080 5207
τούτῳ, καὶ εγένετο πάροικος ἐν γῇ Μαδιάμ, οὗ ἐγέννησεν υἱοὺς
this, and came to be a tenant in land Midian, where he fathered sons
1417 2532 4137 2094 5062 3700 846 1722 3588
δύο. 30 Καὶ πληρωθέντων ἐτῶν τεσσαράκοντα ὤφθη αὐτῷ ἐν τῇ
two. And having been fulfilled years forty, appeared to him in the
2048 3588 3735 4614 32 2962 1722 5395 4442
ἐρήμῳ τοῦ ὄρους Σινᾶ ἄγγελος Κυρίου ἐν φλογὶ πυρὸς
desert of the Mount Sinai (the) Angel of (the) Lord in a flame of fire
942 3588 1161 3475 1492 2296 3588 3705 4334
βάτου. 31 ὁ δὲ Μωσῆς ἰδὼν ἐθαύμασε τὸ ὅραμα· προσερχο-
on a bush. And Moses seeing marveled at the sight. having come
1161 846 2657 1096 5456 2962 4314
μένου δὲ αὐτοῦ κατανοῆσαι, ἐγένετο φωνὴ Κυρίου πρὸς
up And he to look, occurred a voice of (the) Lord to
846 1473 3588 2316 3588 3962 4675 3588 2316 11 2532
αὐτόν, 32 Ἐγὼ ὁ Θεὸς τῶν πατέρων σου, ὁ Θεὸς Ἀβραὰμ καὶ
him, I (am) the God of the fathers of you, the God of Abraham and
3588 2316 2464 2532 3588 2316 2384 1790 1161 1096
ὁ Θεὸς Ἰσαὰκ και ὁ Θεὸς Ἰακώβ. ἔντρομος δὲ γενόμενος
the God of Isaac and the God of Jacob. trembling But becoming
3475 3756 5111 2657 2036 1161 846 3588 2962
Μωσῆς οὐκ ἐτόλμα κατανοῆσαι. 33 εἶπε δὲ αὐτῷ ὁ Κύριος,
Moses not did dare to look. said And to him the Lord,
3089 3588 5266 3588 4228 4675 3588 1063 5117 1722 3739
Λῦσον τὸ ὑπόδημα τῶν ποδῶν σου· ὁ γὰρ τόπος εν ᾧ
Loosen the sandal of the feet of you; the for place in which
2476 1093 40 2076 1492 1492 3588 2561 3588 2992
ἕστηκας γῆ ἁγία ἐστίν. 34 ἰδὼν εἶδον τὴν κάκωσιν τοῦ λαοῦ
you stand ground holy is. Seeing I saw the oppression of the people
3450 3588 1722 125 2532 3588 4726 846 191
μου τοῦ ἐν Αἰγύπτῳ, καὶ τοῦ στεναγμοῦ αὐτῶν ἤκουσα·
of Me in Egypt, and the groan of them I heard;
2532 2597 1807 846 2532 3568 1204 649 4571
καὶ κατέβην ἐξελέσθαι αὐτούς· καὶ νῦν δεῦρο, ἀποστελῶ σε
and I came down to pluck out them. And now come, I will send you
1519 125 5126 3588 3475 3739 720 2036
εἰς Αἴγυπτον. 35 Τοῦτον τὸν Μωϋσῆν ὃν ἠρνήσαντο εἰπόντες,
into Egypt. This Moses whom they denied saying,
5101 4571 2525 758 2532 1348 5126 3588 2316
Τίς σε κατέστησεν ἄρχοντα καὶ δικαστήν; τοῦτον ὁ Θεὸς
Who you appointed a ruler and a judge? This one God
758 2532 3086 649 1722 5495 32 3588
ἄρχοντα καὶ λυτρωτὴν ἀπέστειλεν ἐν χειρὶ ἀγγέλου τοῦ
a ruler and a deliverer has sent by (the) hand of (the) Angel

understood not.
26 And the next day he shewed himself unto them as they strove, and would have set them at one again, saying, Sirs, ye are brethren; why do ye wrong one to another?
27 But he that did his neighbour wrong thrust him away, saying, Who made thee a ruler and a judge over us?
28 Wilt thou kill me, as thou diddest the Egyptian yesterday?
29 Then fled Moses at this saying, and was a stranger in the land of Madian, where he begat two sons.
30 And when forty years were expired, there appeared to him in the wilderness of mount Sina an angel of the Lord in a flame of fire in a bush.
31 When Moses saw (it), he wondered at the sight: and as he drew near to behold (it), the voice of the Lord came unto him,
32 (Saying), I (am) the God of thy fathers, the God of Abraham, and the God of Isaac, and the God of Jacob. Then Moses trembled, and durst not behold.
33 Then said the Lord to him, Put off thy shoes from thy feet: for the place where thou standest is holy ground
34 I have seen, I have seen the affliction of my people which is in Egypt, and I have heard their groaning, and am come down to deliver them. And now come, I will send thee into Egypt.
35 This Moses whom they refused, saying, Who made thee a ruler and a judge? the same did God send (to be) a ruler and a deliverer by the hand of the angel

Literal Translation **Acts 7:36** **King James Version**

who appeared to him in the Bush.
36 This one led them out, having worked wonders and miracles in (the) land of Egypt and in (the) Sea of Reeds, and forty years in the wilderness.
37 This one is the Moses who said to the sons of Israel, "(The) Lord your God will raise up a Prophet to you from your brothers, (One) like me. You shall hear Him." (See Deu. 18:15)

38 This is the one having been in the assembly in the wilderness with the Angel speaking to him in Mount Sinai, and (with) our fathers, who received living words to give to us,

39 to whom our fathers did not desire to be subject, but thrust (him) away, and turned their hearts back to Egypt,

40 saying to Aaron, "Make for us gods which will go before us; for this Moses who led us out of (the) land of Egypt, we do not know what has happened to him." (Ex. 32:1)
41 And they made a calf in those days, and led a sacrifice up to the idol, and made merry in the works of their hands.

42 But God turned and gave them over to serve the host of the heaven, as it has been written in (the) scroll of the Prophets: "Did you bring victims and sacrifices to Me forty years in the wilderness, O house of Israel"?

43 And you took up the tent of Moloch, and the star of your god Remphan, the figures which you made in order to worship

3700 846 1722 3588 942 3778 1806 846
ὀφθέντος αὐτῷ ἐν τῇ βάτῳ. 36 οὗτος ἐξήγαγεν αὐτοὺς,
appearing to him in the Bush. This one led out them,

4160 5059 2532 4592 1722 1093 125 2532 1722 2063
ποιήσας τέρατα καὶ σημεῖα ἐν γῇ Αἰγύπτου καὶ ἐν Ἐρυθρᾷ
having done wonders and signs in (the) land of Egypt, and in of Reeds

2281 2532 1722 3588 2048 2094 5062 3778 2076
Θαλάσσῃ, καὶ ἐν τῇ ἐρήμῳ ἔτη τεσσαράκοντα. 37 οὗτός ἐστιν
(the) Sea, and in the desert years forty. This one is

3588 3475 3588 2036 3588 5207 2474 4396 5213
ὁ Μωυσῆς ὁ εἰπών τοῖς υἱοῖς Ἰσραήλ, Προφήτην ὑμῖν
the Moses saying to the sons of Israel, A Prophet for you

450 2962 3588 2316 5216 1537 3588 80 5216 5613 1691
ἀναστήσει Κύριος ὁ Θεὸς ὑμῶν ἐκ τῶν ἀδελφῶν ὑμῶν ὡς ἐμέ·
will raise up (the) Lord God of you from the brothers of you like me;

846 191 3778 2076 3588 1096 1722 3588 1577
αὐτοῦ ἀκούσεσθε. 38 οὗτός ἐστιν ὁ γενόμενος ἐν τῇ ἐκκλησίᾳ
Him you shall hear. This is (the) one having been in the assembly

1722 3588 2048 3326 3588 32 3588 2980 846 1722 3588
ἐν τῇ ἐρήμῳ μετὰ τοῦ ἀγγέλου τοῦ λαλοῦντος αὐτῷ ἐν τῷ
in the desert with the Angel speaking to him in the

3735 4614 2532 3588 3962 2257 3739 1209 3051 2198
ὄρει Σινᾶ καὶ τῶν πατέρων ἡμῶν· ὃς ἐδέξατο λόγια ζῶντα
Mount Sinai and (with) the fathers of us; who received words living

1325 2254 3739 3756 2309 5255 1096 3588 3962
δοῦναι ἡμῖν· 39 ᾧ οὐκ ἠθέλησαν ὑπήκοοι γενέσθαι οἱ πατέρες
to give to us; to whom not desired subject to be the fathers

2257 235 683 2532 4762 3588 2588 846
ἡμῶν, ἀλλ' ἀπώσαντο, καὶ ἐστράφησαν ταῖς καρδίαις αὐτῶν
of us, but thrust away, and turned away the hearts of them

1519 125 2036 3588 2 4160 2254 2316 3739
εἰς Αἴγυπτον, 40 εἰπόντες τῷ Ἀαρών, Ποίησον ἡμῖν θεοὺς οἳ
to Egypt, saying to Aaron, Make for us gods which

4313 2257 3588 1063 3475 3778 3739 1806
προπορεύσονται ἡμῶν· ὁ γὰρ Μωσῆς οὗτος, ὃς ἐξήγαγεν
will go before us; for Moses this, who led out

2248 1537 1093 125 3756 1492 5101 1096 846 2532
ἡμᾶς ἐκ γῆς Αἰγύπτου, οὐκ οἴδαμεν τί γέγονεν αὐτῷ. 41 καὶ
us from (the) land of Egypt, not we know what has occurred to him. And

3447 1722 3588 2250 1565 2532 321
ἐμοσχοποίησαν ἐν ταῖς ἡμέραις ἐκείναις, καὶ ἀνήγαγον
they made a calf in days those, and led up

2378 3588 1497 2532 2165 1722 3588 2041 3588
θυσίαν τῷ εἰδώλῳ, καὶ εὐφραίνοντο ἐν τοῖς ἔργοις τῶν
a sacrifice to the idol, and made merry in the works of the

5495 846 4762 1161 3588 2316 2532 3860 846
χειρῶν αὐτῶν. 42 ἔστρεψε δὲ ὁ Θεὸς, καὶ παρέδωκεν αὐτοὺς
hands of them. turned And God, and gave over them

3000 3588 4756 3588 3772 2531 1125 1722
λατρεύειν τῇ στρατιᾷ τοῦ οὐρανοῦ· καθὼς γέγραπται ἐν
to worship the host of the heaven, even as it has been written in

976 3588 4396 3361 4968 2532 2378 4374
βίβλῳ τῶν προφητῶν, Μὴ σφάγια καὶ θυσίας προσηνέγ-
(the) scroll of the prophets. Not victims and sacrifices you brought

3427 2094 5062 1722 3588 2048 3624 2474
κατέ μοι ἔτη τεσσαράκοντα ἐν τῇ ἐρήμῳ, οἶκος Ἰσραήλ;
to Me years forty in the desert, house of Israel?

2532 353 3588 4633 3588 3434 2532 3588 798 3588
43 καὶ ἀνελάβετε τὴν σκηνὴν τοῦ Μολόχ, καὶ τὸ ἄστρον τοῦ
And you took up the tent of Moloch, and the star of the

2316 5216 4481 3588 5179 3739 4160 4352
Θεοῦ ὑμῶν Ῥεμφάν, τοὺς τύπους οὓς ἐποιήσατε προσκυνεῖν
god of you Remphan, the figures which you made to worship

which appeared to him in the bush.
36 He brought them out, after that he had shewed wonders and signs in the land of Egypt, and in the Red sea, and in the wilderness forty years.
37 This is that Moses, which said unto the children of Israel, A prophet shall the Lord your God raise up unto you of your brethren, like unto me; him shall ye hear.

38 This is he, that was in the church in the wilderness with the angel which spake to him in the mount Sina, and (with) our fathers: who received the lively oracles to give unto us:

39 To whom our fathers would not obey, but thrust (him) from them, and in their hearts turned back again into Egypt,

40 Saying unto Aaron, Make us gods to go before us: for (as for) this Moses, which brought us out of the land of Egypt, we wot not what is become of him.
41 And they made a calf in those days, and offered sacrifice unto the idol, and rejoiced in the works of their own hands.

42 Then God turned, and gave them up to worship the host of heaven; as it is written in the book of the prophets, O ye house of Israel, have ye offered to me slain beasts and sacrifices (by the space of) forty years in the wilderness?

43 Yea, ye took up the tabernacle of Moloch, and the star of your god Remphan, figures which ye made to worship

Literal Translation | **Acts 7:44** | **King James Version**

them. And I will remove you beyond Babylon. (Amos 7:45)
44 The tabernacle of witness was among our fathers in the wilderness, as the (One) speaking to Moses commanded to make it according to the pattern which he had seen,
45 which also was brought in, our fathers having inherited with Joshua, in the possession of the nations, whom God drove out from the face of our fathers, until the days of David,

846 2532 3351 5209 1900 897 3588 4633
αὐτοῖς· καὶ μετοικιῶ ὑμᾶς ἐπέκεινα Βαβυλῶνος. 44 ἡ σκηνὴ
them; and I will remove you beyond Babylon. The tent
3588 3142 2258 3588 3962 2257 1722 3588 2048 2531
τοῦ μαρτυρίου ἦν τοῖς πατράσιν ἡμῶν ἐν τῇ ἐρήμῳ, καθὼς
of witness was to the fathers of us in the desert, even as
1299 3588 2980 3588 3475 4160 846 2596 3588
διετάξατο ὁ λαλῶν τῷ Μωσῇ, ποιῆσαι αὐτὴν κατὰ τὸν
commanded the (One) speaking to Moses, to make it according to the
5179 3739 3708 3739 2532 1521 1237 3588 3962
τύπον ὃν ἑωράκει. 45ἣν καὶ εἰσήγαγον διαδεξάμενοι οἱ πατέρες
pattern which he had seen. Which also was brought in having inherited the fathers
2257 3326 2424 1722 3588 2697 3588 1484 3739 1856 3588
ἡμῶν μετὰ Ἰησοῦ ἐν τῇ κατασχέσει τῶν ἐθνῶν, ὧν ἐξῶσεν ὁ
of us with Joshua in the possession of the nations, whom thrust out
2316 575 4383 3588 3962 2257 2193 3588 2250
Θεὸς ἀπὸ προσώπου τῶν πατέρων ἡμῶν, ἕως τῶν ἡμερῶν
God from the face of the fathers of us, until the days

them: and I will carry you away beyond Babylon.
44 Our fathers had the tabernacle of witness in the wilderness, as he had appointed, speaking unto Moses, that he should make it according to the fashion that he had seen.
45 Which also our fathers that came after brought in with Jesus into the possession of the Gentiles, whom God drave out before the face of our fathers, unto the days of David;

46 who found favor before God and asked to find a tabernacle for the God of Jacob;
47 but Solomon built Him a house.
48 But the Most High does not dwell in temples made by hand, as the prophet says,
49 "The heaven (is) My throne, and the earth a footstool of My feet; what sort of house will you build Me, says (the) Lord, or what (the) place of My rest?
50 Did not My hands make all these things?" (Isa. 66:1, 2)

1138 3739 2147 5485 1799 3588 2316 2532 154 2147
Δαβίδ· 46 ὃς εὗρε χάριν ἐνώπιον τοῦ Θεοῦ, καὶ ἠτήσατο εὑρεῖν
of David; who found favor before God, and asked to find
4638 3588 2316 2384 4672 1161 3618 846
σκήνωμα τῷ Θεῷ Ἰακώβ. 47 Σολομῶν δὲ ᾠκοδόμησεν αὐτῷ
a tent for the God of Jacob. Solomon And built for Him
3624 235 3756 3588 5310 1722 5499 3485 2730
οἶκον. 48 ἀλλ' οὐχ ὁ ὕψιστος ἐν χειροποιήτοις ναοῖς κατοικεῖ,
a house. But not the Most High in made-by-hand temples dwells,
2531 3588 4396 3004 3588 3772 3427 2362 3588 1161 1093
καθὼς ὁ προφήτης λέγει, 49 Ὁ οὐρανός μοι θρόνος, ἡ δὲ γῆ
even as the prophet says, The heaven (is) to Me a throne, the and earth
5286 3588 4228 3450 4169 3624 3618 3427
ὑποπόδιον τῶν ποδῶν μου· ποῖον οἶκον οἰκοδομήσετέ μοι;
a footstool of the feet of Me; what sort of house will you build for Me?
3004 2962 2228 5101 5117 3588 2663 3450 3780 3588
λέγει Κύριος· ἢ τίς τόπος τῆς καταπαύσεώς μου; 50 οὐχὶ ἡ
says (the) Lord; or what place of the rest of Me? Not the
5495 3450 4160 5023 3956
χείρ μου ἐποίησε ταῦτα πάντα;
hand of Me make these things all?

46 Who found favour before God, and desired to find a tabernacle for the God of Jacob.
47 But Solomon built him an house.
48 Howbeit the most High dwelleth not in temples made with hands; as saith the prophet,
49 Heaven (is) my throne, and earth (is) my footstool: what house will ye build me? saith the Lord: or what (is) the place of my rest?
50 Hath not my hand made all these things?

51. (Oh) stiffnecked and uncircumcised in the heart and in the ears! You always fell against the Holy Spirit. As your fathers (did), you also (did).

4644 2532 564 3588 2588 2532 3588
51. Σκληροτράχηλοι καὶ ἀπερίτμητοι τῇ καρδίᾳ καὶ τοῖς
Stiff-necked and uncircumcised in the hearts and in the
3775 5210 104 3588 4151 3588 40 496 5613 3588
ὠσίν, ὑμεῖς ἀεὶ τῷ Πνεύματι τῷ Ἁγίῳ ἀντιπίπτετε· ὡς οἱ
ears! You always the Spirit Holy fell against; as the
3962 5216 2532 5210 5101 3588 4396 3756 1377 3588
πατέρες ὑμῶν, καὶ ὑμεῖς. 52 τίνα τῶν προφητῶν οὐκ ἐδίωξαν οἱ
fathers of you, also you. Which of the prophets not persecuted the

51. Ye stiffnecked and uncircumcised in heart and ears, ye do always resist the Holy Ghost: as your fathers (did), so (do) ye.

52 Which of the prophets did your fathers not persecute? And they killed those who before proclaiming the coming of the Just One, of whom you now have become betrayers and murderers,

3962 5216 2532 615 3588 4293 4012
πατέρες ὑμῶν; καὶ ἀπέκτειναν τοὺς προκαταγγείλαντας περὶ
fathers of you? And they killed those before proclaiming concerning
3588 1660 3588 1342 3739 3568 5210 4273 2532 5406
τῆς ἐλεύσεως τοῦ δικαίου, οὗ νῦν ὑμεῖς προδόται καὶ φονεῖς
the coming of the Just One, of whom now you betrayers and murderers
1096 3748 2983 3588 3551 1519 1296 32
γεγένησθε· 53 οἵτινες ἐλάβετε τὸν νόμον εἰς διαταγὰς ἀγγέλων,
have become; who received the Law by disposition of angels,
2532 3756 5442
καὶ οὐκ ἐφυλάξατε.
and not did keep (it).

52 Which of the prophets have not your fathers persecuted? and they have slain them which shewed before of the coming of the Just One; of whom ye have been now the betrayers and murderers:

53 who received the Law by the disposition of angels and did not keep (it).

53 Who have received the law by the disposition of angels, and have not kept (it).

54. And hearing these things, they were cut to their hearts and

191 1161 5023 1282 3588 2588 846 2532
54 Ἀκούοντες δὲ ταῦτα, διεπρίοντο ταῖς καρδίαις αὐτῶν, καὶ
hearing And these things, they were cut to the hearts of them, and

54. When they heard these things, they were cut to the heart, and

Literal Translation

Acts 7:55

gnashed the teeth on him.
55 But being full of (the) Holy Spirit, looking intently into Heaven, he saw the glory of God, and Jesus standing at the right of God.
56 And (he) said, Behold, I see Heaven having been opened, and the Son of man standing at (the) right of God!
57 And crying out with a loud voice, they held their ears and rushed on him with one passion.
58 And throwing (him) outside the city, they stoned (him). And the witnesses put off their garments at the feet of a young man called Saul.
59 And they stoned Stephen, (he) invoking and saying, Lord Jesus, receive my spirit.
60 And placing the knees, he cried out with a loud voice, Lord, do not make stand this sin to them. And saying this, he fell asleep.

1031 3588 3599 1909 846 5225 1161 4134
ἔβρυχον τοὺς ὀδόντας ἐπ᾽ αὐτόν. 55 ὑπάρχων δὲ πλήρης
gnashed the teeth on him. being But full

4151 40 816 1519 3588 3772 1492 1391 2316
Πνεύματος Ἁγίου, ἀτενίσας εἰς τὸν οὐρανόν εἶδε δόξαν Θεοῦ,
of (the) Spirit Holy, looking intently into Heaven he saw (the) glory of God,

2532 2424 2476 1537 1188 3588 2316 2532 2036 2400
καὶ Ἰησοῦν ἑστῶτα ἐκ δεξιῶν τοῦ Θεοῦ, 56 καὶ εἶπεν, Ἰδού,
and Jesus standing at (the) right of God, and said, Behold,

2334 3588 3772 455 2532 3588 5207 3588 444
θεωρῶ τοὺς οὐρανοὺς ἀνεῳγμένους, καὶ τὸν υἱὸν τοῦ ἀνθρώ-
I see Heaven having been opened, and the Son of man

1537 1188 2479 3588 2316 2896 1161 5456 3173
που ἐκ δεξιῶν ἑστῶτα τοῦ Θεοῦ. 57 κράξαντες δὲ φωνῇ μεγάλῃ,
at (the) right standing of God. crying out And with a voice great,

4912 3588 3775 846 2532 3729 3661 1909
συνέσχον τὰ ὦτα αὐτῶν, καὶ ὥρμησαν ὁμοθυμαδὸν ἐπ᾽
they held the ears of them, and rushed with one passion on

846 2532 1544 1854 3588 4172 3036 2532 3588
αὐτόν· 58 καὶ ἐκβαλόντες ἔξω τῆς πόλεως, ἐλιθοβόλουν· καὶ οἱ
him; and throwing outside the city, they stoned (him). And the

3144 659 3588 2440 846 3844 3588 4228
μάρτυρες ἀπέθεντο τὰ ἱμάτια αὐτῶν παρὰ τοὺς πόδας
witnesses put off the garments of them beside the feet

3494 2564 4569 2532 3036 3588 4736
νεανίου καλουμένου Σαύλου. 59 καὶ ἐλιθοβόλουν τὸν Στέφανον,
of a young one being called Saul. And they stoned Stephen,

1941 2532 3004 2962 2424 1209 3588 4151
ἐπικαλούμενον καὶ λέγοντα, Κύριε Ἰησοῦ, δέξαι τὸ πνεῦμά
(he) invoking (God) and saying, Lord Jesus, receive the spirit

3450 5087 1161 3588 1119 2896 5456 3173 2962 3361
μου. 60 θεὶς δὲ τὰ γόνατα ἔκραξε φωνῇ μεγάλῃ, Κύριε, μὴ
of me. placing And the knees, he cried out with a voice great, Lord, not

2476 846 3588 266 3778 2532 5124 2036
στήσῃς αὐτοῖς τὴν ἁμαρτίαν ταύτην. καὶ τοῦτο εἰπὼν
make stand to them sin this. And this having said

2837
ἐκοιμήθη.
he fell asleep.

King James Version

they gnashed on him with (their) teeth.
55 But he, being full of the Holy Ghost, looked up stedfastly into heaven, and saw the glory of God, and Jesus standing on the right hand of God,
56 And said, Behold, I see the heavens opened, and the Son of man standing on the right hand of God.
57 Then they cried out with a loud voice, and stopped their ears, and ran upon him with one accord,
58 And cast (him) out of the city, and stoned (him): and the witnesses laid down their clothes at a young man's feet, whose name was Saul.
59 And they stoned Stephen, calling upon (God), and saying, Lord Jesus, receive my spirit.
60 And he kneeled down, and cried with a loud voice, Lord, lay not this sin to their charge. And when he had said this, he fell asleep.

Acts 8

1. And Saul was consenting to the doing away of him. And in that day a great persecution took place on the church in Jerusalem; and all were scattered throughout the regions of Judea and Samaria, except the apostles.
2 And devout men together carried Stephen and made a great lamentation over him.
3 But Saul ravaged the church, entering house by house,

4569 1161 2258 4909 3588 336 846
1 Σαῦλος δὲ ἦν συνευδοκῶν τῇ ἀναιρέσει αὐτοῦ.
Saul And was consenting to the doing away of him.

1096 1161 1722 1565 3588 2250 1375 3173 1909 3588
Ἐγένετο δὲ ἐν ἐκείνῃ τῇ ἡμέρᾳ διωγμὸς μέγας ἐπὶ τὴν
occurred And in that day a persecution great on the

1577 3588 1722 2414 3956 5037 1289
ἐκκλησίαν τὴν ἐν Ἱεροσολύμοις· πάντες τε διεσπάρησαν
church in Jerusalem; all and were scattered

2596 3588 5561 3588 2449 2532 4540 4133 3588
κατὰ τὰς χώρας τῆς Ἰουδαίας καὶ Σαμαρείας, πλὴν τῶν
through the countries of Judea and Samaria, except the

652 4792 1161 3588 4736 435 2126
ἀποστόλων. 2 συνεκόμισαν δὲ τὸν Στέφανον ἄνδρες εὐλαβεῖς,
apostles. together carried And Stephen men devout,

2532 4160 2870 3173 1909 846 4569 1161
καὶ ἐποιήσαντο κοπετὸν μέγαν ἐπ᾽ αὐτῷ. 3 Σαῦλος δὲ
and made a lamentation great over him. Saul And

3075 3588 1577 2596 3588 3624 1531
ἐλυμαίνετο τὴν ἐκκλησίαν, κατὰ τοὺς οἴκους εἰσπορευό-
ravaged the church, house by house having entered

Acts 8

1. And Saul was consenting unto his death. And at that time there was a great persecution against the church which was at Jerusalem; and they were all scattered abroad throughout the regions of Judaea and Samaria, except the apostles.
2 And devout men carried Stephen (to his burial), and made great lamentation over him.
3 As for Saul, he made havock of the church, entering into every house,

Literal Translation **Acts 8:4** *King James Version*

dragging both men and women, he delivered (them) to prison.
4 Then, indeed, the ones who had been scattered passed through, preaching the gospel (of) the Word.
5. And going down to a city of Samaria, Philip proclaimed Christ to them.
6 And with one passion the crowds heeded that being said by Philip when they heard and saw the many signs which he was doing.
7 For many came out from the (ones) having unclean spirits, crying with a loud voice. And many who had been paralyzed and lame were healed.
8 And great joy was in that city.
9 But a certain man named Simon had long been conjuring in the city and amazing the nation of Samaria, claiming himself to be someone great,
10 to whom all paid attention, from small to great, saying, This one is the great power of God.
11 And they were paying attention to him because for a long time he had amazed them (with his) conjuring.
12 But when they believed Philip preaching the gospel, the things concerning the kingdom of God, and the name of Jesus Christ, they were baptized, both men and women.
13 And Simon himself also believed, and being baptized was steadfastly continuing with Philip. And beholding works of power and signs happening, he was amazed
14. And the apostles in Jerusalem having heard that

4951 5037 435 2532 1135 3860 1519 5438
μενος, σύρων τε ἄνδρας καὶ γυναῖκας παρεδίδου εἰς φυλακήν.
dragging both men and women he delivered (them) to prison.

3588 3303 3767 1289 1330 2097 3588
4 Οἱ μὲν οὖν διασπαρέντες διῆλθον, εὐαγγελιζόμενοι τὸν
Those indeed then being scattered passed through, preaching the gospel the

3056 5376 1161 2718 1519 4172 3588 4540
λόγον. 5 Φίλιππος δὲ κατελθὼν εἰς πόλιν τῆς Σαμαρείας,
Word. Philip And going down to a city of Samaria,

2784 846 3588 5547 4337 5037 3588 3793 3588
ἐκήρυσσεν αὐτοῖς τὸν Χριστόν. 6 προσεῖχον τε οἱ ὄχλοι τοῖς
proclaimed to them the Christ. heeded And the crowds that

3004 5259 3588 5376 3661 1722 3588 191
λεγομένοις ὑπὸ τοῦ Φιλίππου ὁμοθυμαδὸν, ἐν τῷ ἀκούειν
being said by Philip with one passion, in the hearing

846 2532 991 3588 4592 3739 4160 4183 1063 3588
αὐτοὺς καὶ βλέπειν τὰ σημεῖα ἃ ἐποίει· 7 πολλῶν γὰρ τῶν
(of) them and seeing the signs which he was doing. many For of the

2192 4151 169 994 3173 5456
ἐχόντων πνεύματα ἀκάθαρτα, βοῶντα μεγάλῃ φωνῇ
(ones) having spirits unclean, crying with a great voice

1831 4183 1161 3886 2532 5560 2323
ἐξήρχετο· πολλοὶ δὲ παραλελυμένοι καὶ χωλοὶ ἐθεραπεύθη-
came out; many and having been paralyzed and lame were healed.

2532 1096 5479 3173 1722 3588 4172 1565
σαν. 8 καὶ ἐγένετο χαρὰ μεγάλη ἐν τῇ πόλει ἐκείνῃ.
And was joy great in city that.

435 1161 5100 3686 4613 4391 1722 3588 4172
9 Ἀνὴρ δέ τις ὀνόματι Σίμων προϋπῆρχεν ἐν τῇ πόλει
a man And certain by name Simon had been before in the city

3096 2532 1839 3588 1484 3588 4540 3004 1511
μαγεύων καὶ ἐξιστῶν τὸ ἔθνος τῆς Σαμαρείας, λέγων εἶναί
conjuring and amazing the nation of Samaria, saying to be

5100 1438 3173 3739 4337 3956 575 3398 2193
τινα ἑαυτὸν μέγαν· 10 ᾧ προσεῖχον πάντες ἀπὸ μικροῦ ἕως
someone himself great; to whom paid attention all from small unto

3173 3004 3778 2076 3588 1411 3588 2316 3588
μεγάλου, λέγοντες, Οὗτός ἐστιν ἡ δύναμις τοῦ Θεοῦ ἡ
great. saying. This one is the power of God

3173 4337 1161 846 1223 3588 2425 5550 3588
μεγάλη. 11 προσεῖχον δὲ αὐτῷ, διὰ τὸ ἱκανῷ χρόνῳ ταῖς
great. they were attending And to him, because for a long time with the

3095 1839 846 3753 1161 4100 3588 5376
μαγείαις ἐξεστακέναι αὐτούς. 12 ὅτε δὲ ἐπίστευσαν τῷ Φιλίππῳ
conjuring (he) had amazed them. when But they believed Philip

2097 3588 4012 3588 932 3588 2316 2532 3588
εὐαγγελιζομένῳ τὰ περὶ τῆς βασιλείας τοῦ Θεοῦ καὶ τοῦ
preaching the gospel, the things about the kingdom of God and the

3686 3588 2424 5547 907 435 5037 2532
ὀνόματος τοῦ Ἰησοῦ Χριστοῦ, ἐβαπτίζοντο ἄνδρες τε καὶ
name of Jesus Christ, they were baptized, men both and

1135 3588 1161 4613 2532 846 4100 2532 907
γυναῖκες. 13 ὁ δὲ Σίμων καὶ αὐτὸς ἐπίστευσε, καὶ βαπτισθεὶς
women. But Simon also himself believed, and being baptized

2258 4342 3588 5376 2334 5037 1411 2532
ἦν προσκαρτερῶν τῷ Φιλίππῳ· θεωρῶν τε δυνάμεις καὶ
was steadfastly continuing to Philip; beholding and works of power and

4592 1096 1839
σημεῖα γινομένα, ἐξίστατο.
signs happening, he was amazed.

191 1161 3588 1722 2414 652 3754
14 Ἀκούσαντες δὲ οἱ ἐν Ἱεροσολύμοις ἀπόστολοι ὅτι
having heard And the in Jerusalem apostles that

and haling men and women committed (them) to prison.
4 Therefore they that were scattered abroad went every where preaching the word.
5. Then Philip went down to the city of Samaria, and preached Christ unto them.
6 And the people with one accord gave heed unto those things which Philip spake, hearing and seeing the miracles which he did.
7 For unclean spirits, crying with loud voice, came out of many that were possessed (with them): and many taken with palsies, and that were lame, were healed.
8 And there was great joy in that city.
9 But there was a certain man, called Simon, which beforetime in the same city used sorcery, and bewitched the people of Samaria, giving out that himself was some great one:
10 To whom they all gave heed, from the least to the greatest, saying, This man is the great power of God.
11 And to him they had regard, because that of long time he had bewitched them with sorceries.
12 But when they believed Philip preaching the things concerning the kingdom of God, and the name of Jesus Christ, they were baptized, both men and women.
13 Then Simon himself believed also: and when he was baptized, he continued with Philip, and wondered, beholding the miracles and signs which were done.
14. Now when the apostles which were at Jerusalem heard that

Literal Translation **Acts 8:15** *King James Version*

Samaria had received the Word of God, they sent Peter and John to them,
15 who going down prayed concerning them so that they might receive (the) Holy Spirit.

16 For He was not yet fallen on any one of them, but they were only being baptized in the name of the Lord Jesus.

17 Then they laid hands on them, and they received (the) Holy Spirit.

18 But Simon having seen that the Holy Spirit is given through the laying on of the hands of the apostles, he offered them money,

19 saying, Also give to me this authority that to whomever I may lay on the hands he may receive (the) Holy Spirit.

20 But Peter said to him, Your silver be with you into perdition, because you thought to get the gift of God through money.

21 There is neither part nor lot to you in this matter, for your heart is not upright before the face of God.

22 Repent, then, from this wickedness of yours, and petition God if perhaps you will be forgiven the thought of your heart.

23 For I see you in (the) gall of bitterness and a bundle of unrighteousness.

24 And answering Simon said, You petition to the Lord on behalf of me, so that nothing of which you have spoken may come on me.

25 Then they indeed having earnestly testified and having spoken the Word

---

1209 3588 4540 3588 3056 3588 2316 649 4314
δέδεκται ἡ Σαμάρεια τὸν λόγον τοῦ Θεοῦ, ἀπέστειλαν πρὸς
has received Samaria the Word of God, they sent to

846 3588 4074 2532 2491 3748 2597
αὐτοὺς τὸν Πέτρον καὶ Ἰωάννην· 15 οἵτινες καταβάντες
them Peter and John; who going down

4336 4012 846 3704 2983 4151 40
προσηύξαντο περὶ αὐτῶν, ὅπως λάβωσι Πνεῦμα Ἅγιον·
prayed concerning them, so as they might receive (the) Spirit Holy;

3768 1063 2258 1909 3762 846 1968 3440 1161
16 οὔπω γὰρ ἦν ἐπ' οὐδενὶ αὐτῶν ἐπιπεπτωκός, μόνον δὲ
not yet for He was on no one of them fallen, only but

907 5225 1519 3588 3686 3588 2962 2424
βεβαπτισμένοι ὑπῆρχον εἰς τὸ ὄνομα τοῦ Κυρίου Ἰησοῦ.
being baptized they were into the name of the Lord Jesus.

5119 2007 3588 5495 1909 846 2532 2983
17 τότε ἐπετίθουν τὰς χεῖρας ἐπ' αὐτούς, καὶ ἐλάμβανον
Then they laid the hands on them, and they received

4151 40 2300 1161 3588 4613 3754 1223 3588 1936
Πνεῦμα Ἅγιον. 18 θεασάμενος δὲ ὁ Σίμων ὅτι διὰ τῆς ἐπιθέ-
(the) Spirit Holy. beholding And Simon that through the laying

3588 5495 3588 652 1325 3588 4151 3588
σεως τῶν χειρῶν τῶν ἀποστόλων δίδοται τὸ Πνεῦμα τὸ
on of the hands of the apostles is given the Spirit

40 4374 846 5536 3004 1325 2504
Ἅγιον, προσήνεγκεν αὐτοῖς χρήματα, 19 λέγων, Δότε κἀμοὶ
Holy, he offered them money, saying, Give also to me

3588 1849 3778 2443 3739 1437 2007 3588 5495 2983
τὴν ἐξουσίαν ταύτην, ἵνα ᾧ ἐὰν ἐπιθῶ τὰς χεῖρας, λαμβάνῃ
authority this, that to whomever I lay on the hands, he may receive

4151 40 4074 1161 2036 4314 846 3588 694 4675
Πνεῦμα Ἅγιον. 20 Πέτρος δὲ εἶπε πρὸς αὐτόν, Τὸ ἀργύριόν σου
(the) Spirit Holy. Peter But said to him, The silver of you

4862 4671 1498 1519 684 3754 3588 1431 3588 2316 3543
σὺν σοὶ εἴη εἰς ἀπώλειαν, ὅτι τὴν δωρεὰν τοῦ Θεοῦ ἐνόμισας
with you be into perdition, because the gift of God you thought

1223 5536 2932 3756 2076 4671 3310 3761 2819 1722
διὰ χρημάτων κτᾶσθαι. 21 οὐκ ἔστι σοι μερὶς οὐδὲ κλῆρος ἐν
through money to get. not There is to you part nor lot in

3588 3056 5129 3588 1063 2588 4675 3756 2076 2117 1799
τῷ λόγῳ τούτῳ. ἡ γὰρ καρδία σου οὐκ ἔστιν εὐθεῖα ἐνώπιον
matter this. the For heart of you not is upright before

3588 2316 3340 3767 575 3588 2549 4675 3778 2532
τοῦ θεοῦ. 22 μετανόησον οὖν ἀπὸ τῆς κακίας σου ταύτης, καὶ
God. Repent therefore from wickedness of you this, and

1189 3588 2316 1487 686 863 4671 3588 1963 3588
δεήθητι τοῦ Θεοῦ, εἰ ἄρα ἀφεθήσεταί σοι ἡ ἐπίνοια τῆς
petition God, if perhaps will be forgiven you the thought of the

2588 4675 1519 1063 5521 4088 2532 4886 93
καρδίας σου. 23 εἰς γὰρ χολὴν πικρίας καὶ σύνδεσμον ἀδικίας
heart of you. in For gall of bitterness and a bundle of unrighteousness

3708 4571 5607 611 1161 3588 4613 2036 1189 5210
ὁρῶ σε ὄντα. 24 ἀποκριθεὶς δὲ ὁ Σίμων εἶπε, Δεήθητε ὑμεῖς
I see you being. answering And Simon said, Petition you

5228 1700 4314 3588 2962 3704 3367 1904 1909 1691
ὑπὲρ ἐμοῦ πρὸς τὸν Κύριον, ὅπως μηδὲν ἐπέλθῃ ἐπ ἐμὲ
on behalf of me to the Lord, so as not one may come on me

3739 2046
ὧν εἰρήκατε.
of what you have spoken.

3588 3303 3767 1263 2532 2980 3588 3026
25. Οἱ μὲν οὖν διαμαρτυράμενοι καὶ λαλήσαντες τὸν λόγον
They indeed then having testified earnestly and having spoken the Word

---

Samaria had received the word of God, they sent unto them Peter and John:
15 Who, when they were come down, prayed for them, that they might receive the Holy Ghost:

16 (For as yet he was fallen upon none of them: only they were baptized in the name of the Lord Jesus.)

17 Then laid they (their) hands on them, and they received the Holy Ghost.

18 And when Simon saw that through laying on of the apostles' hands the Holy Ghost was given, he offered them money,

19 Saying, Give me also this power, that on whomsoever I lay hands, he may receive the Holy Ghost.

20 But Peter said unto him, Thy money perish with thee, because thou hast thought that the gift of God may be purchased with money.

21 Thou hast neither part nor lot in this matter: for thy heart is not right in the sight of God.

22 Repent therefore of this thy wickedness, and pray God, if perhaps the thought of thine heart may be forgiven thee.

23 For I perceive that thou art in the gall of bitterness, and (in) the bond of iniquity.

24 Then answered Simon, and said, Pray ye to the Lord for me, that none of these things which ye have spoken come upon me.

25 And they, when they had testified and preached the word

Literal Translation

of the Lord, they returned to Jerusalem, even having announced the gospel to many villages of the Samaritans.

26. But an angel of (the) Lord spoke to Philip, saying, Rise up, and go along south on the highway going down from Jerusalem to Gaza. This is (a) deserted (place).

27 And rising up he went. And, behold! An Ethiopian man, a eunuch, one in power (with) Candace the queen of Ethiopians, who was over all her treasure, who had come to Jerusalem to worship!
28 And (he) was returning. And sitting on his chariot, he read the prophet Isaiah.
29 And the Spirit said to Philip, Go near and join yourself to this chariot.

30 And running near Philip heard him reading the prophet Isaiah, and said, Indeed, do you know what you are reading?

31 But he said, For how should I be able except someone shall guide me? And he called Philip near coming up to sit with him.

32 And the content of the Scripture which he was reading was this: "He was led as a sheep onto slaughter, and as a voiceless lamb before the (one) shearing it, so He does not open His mouth.

33 In His humiliation His judgment was taken away; and who will recount His generation? Because His life is taken away from the earth." (Isa.53:7,8)
34 And answering the eunuch

Acts 8:26

3588 2962 5290 1519 2419 4183 5037 2968
τοῦ Κυρίου, ὑπέστρεψαν εἰς Ἱερουσαλήμ, πολλάς τε κώμας
of the Lord, returned to Jerusalem, (to) many and villages
3588 4541 2097
τῶν Σαμαρειτῶν εὐηγγελίσαντο.
of the Samaritans having preached the gospel.

32 1161 2962 2980 4314 5376 3004
26 Ἄγγελος δὲ Κυρίου ἐλάλησε πρὸς Φίλιππον, λέγων,
an angel And of (the) Lord spoke to Philip, saying,
450 2532 4198 2596 3314 1909 3588 3598 3588
Ἀνάστηθι καὶ πορεύου κατὰ μεσημβρίαν ἐπὶ τὴν ὁδὸν τὴν
Rise up and go along south on the way
2597 575 2419 1519 1048 3778 2076
καταβαίνουσαν ἀπὸ Ἱερουσαλὴμ εἰς Γάζαν· αὕτη ἐστὶν
going down from Jerusalem to Gaza; this is

2048 2532 450 4198 2532 2400 435 128
ἔρημος. 27 καὶ ἀναστὰς ἐπορεύθη· καὶ ἰδού, ἀνὴρ Αἰθίοψ
desert. And rising up he went.; And behold! A man Ethiopian
2135 1413 2582 3588 938 128 3739 2258
εὐνοῦχος δυνάστης Κανδάκης τῆς βασιλίσσης Αἰθιόπων, ὃς ἦν
a eunuch a power of Candace the queen of Ethiopians, who was
1909 3956 3588 1047 846 3739 2064 4352 1519
ἐπὶ πάσης τῆς γάζης αὐτῆς, ὃς ἐληλύθει προσκυνήσων εἰς
over all the treasure of her, who had come to worship into
2419 2258 5037 5290 2532 2521 1909 3588
Ἱερουσαλήμ, 28 ἦν τε ὑποστρέφων καὶ καθήμενος ἐπὶ τοῦ
Jerusalem, was and (he) returning and sitting on the
716 846 314 3588 4396 2268 2036 1161
ἅρματος αὐτοῦ, ἀνεγίνωσκε τὸν προφήτην Ἠσαΐαν. 29 εἶπε δὲ
chariot of him, he read the prophet Isaiah. said And
3588 4151 3588 5376 4334 2532 2853 3588 716
τὸ Πνεῦμα τῷ Φιλίππῳ, Πρόσελθε καὶ κολλήθητι τῷ ἅρματι
the Spirit to Philip, Go near and join yourself to chariot

5129 4370 1161 3588 5376 191 846
τούτῳ. 30 προσδραμὼν δὲ ὁ Φίλιππος ἤκουσεν αὐτοῦ
this. running near And Philip heard from him
314 3588 4396 2268 2532 2036 687
ἀναγινώσκοντος τὸν προφήτην Ἠσαΐαν, καὶ εἶπεν, Ἆρά
reading the prophet Isaiah, and said, Then
1065 1097 3739 314 3588 1161 2036 4459 1063 302 1410
γε γινώσκεις ἃ ἀναγινώσκεις; 31 ὁ δὲ εἶπε, Πῶς γὰρ ἂν δυναί-
indeed know you what you are reading? he And said, how For should I be
1437 3361 5100 3594 3165 3870 5037 3588 5376
μην, ἐὰν μή τις ὁδηγήσῃ με; παρεκάλεσέ τε τὸν Φίλιππον
able, if not someone shall guide me? he called near And Philip
305 2523 4862 846 3588 1161 4042 3588 1124 3739
ἀναβάντα καθίσαι σὺν αὐτῷ. 32 ἡ δὲ περιοχὴ τῆς γραφῆς ἣν
coming up to sit with him. the And content of the Scripture which
314 2258 3778 5613 4263 1909 4967 71 2532
ἀνεγίνωσκεν ἦν αὕτη, Ὡς πρόβατον ἐπὶ σφαγὴν ἤχθη, καὶ
he was reading was this, As a sheep onto slaughter He was led, and
5613 286 1726 3588 2751 846 880 3779 3756
ὡς ἀμνὸς ἐναντίον τοῦ κείροντος αὐτὸν ἄφωνος, οὕτως οὐκ
as a lamb before the (one) shearing it voiceless, so not

455 3588 4750 846 1722 3588 5014 846 3588 2920
ἀνοίγει τὸ στόμα αὐτοῦ. 33 Ἐν τῇ ταπεινώσει αὐτοῦ ἡ κρίσις
He opens the mouth of Him. In the humiliation of Him, the judgment
846 142 3588 1161 1074 846 5101 1334 3754
αὐτοῦ ἤρθη, τὴν δὲ γενεὰν αὐτοῦ τίς διηγήσεται; ὅτι
of Him was taken, the but generation of Him who will recount? For
142 575 3588 1093 3588 2222 846 611 1161 3588 2135
αἴρεται ἀπὸ τῆς γῆς ἡ ζωὴ αὐτοῦ. 34 ἀποκριθεὶς δὲ ὁ εὐνοῦχος
is taken from the earth the life of Him. answering And the eunuch

King James Version

of the Lord, returned to Jerusalem, and preached the gospel in many villages of the Samaritans.

26. And the angel of the Lord spake unto Philip, saying, Arise, and go toward the south unto the way that goeth down from Jerusalem unto Gaza, which is desert.

27 And he arose and went: and, behold, a man of Ethiopia, an eunuch of great authority under Candace queen of the Ethiopians, who had the charge of all her treasure, and had come to Jerusalem for to worship,
28 Was returning, and sitting in his chariot read Esaias the prophet.
29 Then the Spirit said unto Philip, Go near, and join thyself to this chariot.

30 And Philip ran thither to (him), and heard him read the prophet Esaias, and said, Understandest thou what thou readest?

31 And he said, How can I, except some man should guide me? And he desired Philip that he would come up and sit with him.

32 The place of the scripture which he read was this, He was led as a sheep to the slaughter; and like a lamb dumb before his shearer, so opened he not his mouth:

33 In his humiliation his judgment was taken away: and who shall declare his generation? for his life is taken from the earth.

34 And the eunuch answered

Acts 8:35

Literal Translation

said to Philip, I ask you,
about whom does the
prophet say this? About
himself, or about some
other one?
35 And opening his
mouth, and beginning
from this Scripture,
Philip preached the
gospel (of) Jesus to him.

36 And as they were go-
ing along the highway
they came on some
water. And the eunuch
said, Behold, water!
What prevents me
(from) being baptized?
37 And Philip said, If
you believe from all the
heart, it is lawful. And
answering he said, I be-
lieve Jesus Christ to be
the Son of God.

38 And he ordered the
chariot to stand still.
And both went down
into the water, both
Philip and the eunuch;
and he baptized him.

39 But when they came
up out of the water, (the)
Spirit of (the) Lord
caught away Philip.
And the eunuch saw
him no more; for he
went his way rejoicing.
40 And Philip was
found at Azotus. And
passing through he
preached the gospel to
all the cities until he
came to Caesarea.

3588 5376 2036 1189 4675 4012 5101 3588 4396 3004
τῷ Φιλίππῳ εἶπε, Δέομαί σου, περὶ τίνος ὁ προφήτης λέγει
to Philip said, I ask you, concerning whom the prophet says

5124 4012 1438 2228 4012 2087 5100 455 1161 3588
τοῦτο; περὶ ἑαυτοῦ, ἢ περὶ ἑτέρου τινός; 35 ἀνοίξας δὲ ὁ
this? Concerning himself, or concerning other someone? opening And

5376 3588 4750 846 2532 756 575 3588 1124
Φίλιππος τὸ στόμα αὐτοῦ, καὶ ἀρξάμενος ἀπὸ τῆς γραφῆς
Philip the mouth of him, and beginning from Scripture

3778 2097 846 3588 2424 5613 1161 4198
ταύτης, εὐηγγελίσατο αὐτῷ τὸν Ἰησοῦν. 36 ὡς δὲ ἐπορεύοντο
this, preached the gospel to him Jesus. as And they were going

2596 3588 3598 2064 1909 5100 5204 2532 5346 3588 2135
κατὰ τὴν ὁδόν, ἦλθον ἐπί τι ὕδωρ· καί φησιν ὁ εὐνοῦχος,
along the way, they came upon some water; and says the eunuch,

2400 5204 5101 2967 3165 907 2036 1161 3588 5376
Ἰδού, ὕδωρ· τί κωλύει με βαπτισθῆναι; 37 εἰπε δὲ ὁ Φίλιππος,
Behold, water! What prevents me to be baptized? said And Philip

1487 4100 1537 3650 3588 2588 1832 611 1161 2036
Εἰ πιστεύεις ἐξ ὅλης τῆς καρδίας, ἔξεστιν. ἀποκριθεὶς δὲ εἶπε,
If you believe from all the heart, it is lawful. answering And he said,

4100 3588 5207 3588 2316 1511 3588 2424 5547 2532
Πιστεύω τὸν υἱὸν τοῦ Θεοῦ εἶναι τὸν Ἰησοῦν Χριστόν. 38 καὶ
I believe the Son of God to be Jesus Christ. And

2753 2476 3588 716 2532 2597 297 1519 3588
ἐκέλευσε στῆναι τὸ ἅρμα· καὶ κατέβησαν ἀμφότεροι εἰς τὸ
he ordered to stand the chariot, and went down both into the

5204 3588 5037 5376 2532 3588 2135 2532 907 846
ὕδωρ, ὅ τε Φίλιππος καὶ ὁ εὐνοῦχος· καὶ ἐβάπτισεν αὐτόν.
water, both Philip and the eunuch; and he baptized him.

3753 1161 305 1537 3588 5204 4151 2962 726 3588
39 ὅτε δὲ ἀνέβησαν ἐκ τοῦ ὕδατος, Πνεῦμα Κυρίου ἥρπασε τὸν
when And they came up out of the water, (the) Spirit of (the) Lord caught away

5376 2532 3756 1492 846 3765 3588 2135 4198
Φίλιππον· καὶ οὐκ εἶδεν αὐτὸν οὐκέτι ὁ εὐνοῦχος, ἐπορεύετο
Philip; and not saw him no more the eunuch, he went

1063 3588 3598 846 5463 5376 1161 2147 1519
γὰρ τὴν ὁδὸν αὐτοῦ χαίρων. 40 Φίλιππος δὲ εὑρέθη εἰς
for the way of him rejoicing. Philip And was found at

108 2532 1330 2097 3588 4172 3956 2193
Ἄζωτον· καὶ διερχόμενος εὐηγγελίζετο τὰς πόλεις πάσας, ἕως
Azotus; and passing through he preached the gospel to the cities all, until

3588 2064 846 1519 2542
τοῦ ἐλθεῖν αὐτὸν εἰς Καισάρειαν.
the coming (of) him into Caesarea.

King James Version

Philip, and said, I pray
thee, of whom speaketh
the prophet this? of
himself, or of some
other man?
35 Then Philip opened
his mouth, and began at
the same scripture, and
preached unto him Je-
sus.

36 And as they went on
(their) way, they came
unto a certain water:
and the eunuch said,
See, (here is) water;
what doth hinder me to
be baptized?
37 And Philip said, If
thou believest with all
thine heart, thou
mayest. And he an-
swered and said, I be-
lieve that Jesus Christ is
the Son of God.
38 And he commanded
the chariot to stand still:
and they went down
both into the water, both
Philip and the eunuch;
and he baptized him.

39 And when they were
come up out of the
water, the Spirit of the
Lord caught away
Philip, that the eunuch
saw him no more: and
he went on his way re-
joicing.
40 But Philip was found
at Azotus: and passing
through he preached in
all the cities, till he came
to Caesarea.

Acts 9

1. But still breathing
threats and murder to-
ward the disciples of the
Lord, having come to
the high priest,
2 Saul asked from him
letters to Damascus, to
the synagogues, so that
if he found any being of
the Way, both men and
women, having bound
them he might bring
(them) to Jerusalem.

3 But in the going

3588 1161 4569 2089 1709 547 2532 5408 1519 3588
1 Ὁ δὲ Σαῦλος ἔτι ἐμπνέων ἀπειλῆς καὶ φόνου εἰς τοὺς
But Saul still breathing in threats and murder toward the

3101 3588 2962 4334 3588 749 154
μαθητὰς τοῦ Κυρίου, προσελθὼν τῷ ἀρχιερεῖ, 2 ᾐτήσατο
disciples of the Lord, having come to the High Priest, asked

3844 846 1992 1519 1154 4314 3588 4864
παρ' αὐτοῦ ἐπιστολὰς εἰς Δαμασκὸν πρὸς τὰς συναγωγάς,
from him letters to Damascus to the synagogues,

3704 1437 5100 2147 3588 3598 5607 435 5037 2532 1135
ὅπως ἐάν τινας εὕρῃ τῆς ὁδοῦ ὄντας ἄνδρας τε καὶ γυναῖκας,
so that if any he found of the Way being men both and women,

1210 71 1519 2419 1722 1161 3588 4198
δεδεμένους ἀγάγῃ εἰς Ἱερουσαλήμ. 3 ἐν δὲ τῷ πορεύεσθαι,
binding them he may bring to Jerusalem. in And the going,

1 . And Saul, yet
breathing out threaten-
ings and slaughter
against the disciples of
the Lord, went unto the
high priest,
2 And desired of him
letters to Damascus to
the synagogues, that if
he found any of this
way, whether they were
men or women, he
might bring them
bound unto Jerusalem.
3 And as he journeyed,

Literal Translation | **Acts 9:4** | *King James Version*

it happened! He drew near to Damascus, and suddenly a light from the heaven shone around him.
4 And falling on the earth he heard a voice saying to him, Saul, Saul! Why do you persecute Me?

1096 846 1448 3588 1154 2532 1810 4015
ἐγένετο αὐτὸν ἐγγίζειν τῇ Δαμασκῷ· καὶ ἐξαίφνης περι-
happened it he drew near to Damascus; and suddenly around
846 5457 575 3588 3772 2532 4098 1909 3588
ήστραψεν αὐτὸν φῶς ἀπὸ τοῦ οὐρανοῦ· 4 καὶ πεσὼν ἐπὶ τὴν
shone him a light out of the heaven; and falling on the
1093 191 5456 3004 846 4549 4549 5101 3165
γῆν ἤκουσε φωνὴν λέγουσαν αὐτῷ, Σαούλ, Σαούλ, τί με
earth he heard a voice saying to him, Saul, Saul, Why Me

he came near Damascus: and suddenly there shined round about him a light from heaven:
4 And he fell to the earth, and heard a voice saying unto him, Saul, Saul, why persecutest thou me?

5 And he said, Sir, who are you? And the Lord said, I am Jesus, whom you persecute; (it is) hard for you to kick against the prods.

1377 2036 1161 5101 1488 2962 3588 1161 2962 2036 1473 1510
διώκεις; 5 εἶπε δέ, Τίς εἶ, Κύριε; ὁ δε Κύριος εἶπεν, Ἐγώ εἰμι
you persecute? he said And, Who are you, Sir? the And Lord said, I am
2424 3739 4771 1377 4642 4671 4314 2759 2979
Ἰησοῦς ὃν σὺ διώκεις· σκληρόν σοι πρὸς κέντρα λακτίζειν.
Jesus whom you persecute; (it is) hard for you against (the) goads to kick.

5 And he said, Who art thou, Lord? And the Lord said, I am Jesus whom thou persecutest: (it is) hard for thee to kick against the pricks.

6 Both trembling and being astonished he said, Lord, what do you desire me to do? And the Lord (said) to him, Rise up and go into the city, and it will be told to you what you must do.
7 But the men traveling with him had been standing speechless, indeed hearing the voice, but seeing no one.

5141 5037 2532 2284 2036 2962 5101 3165 2309 4160 2532
6 τρέμων τε καὶ θαμβῶν εἶπε, Κύριε, τί με θέλεις ποιῆσαι; καὶ
trembling both And astonished he said, Lord, what me You desire to do? And
3588 2962 4314 846 450 2532 1525 1519 3588 4172
ὁ Κύριος πρὸς αὐτόν, ἀνάστηθι καὶ εἴσελθε εἰς τὴν πόλιν,
the Lord (said) to him, Rise up and go into the city,
2532 2980 4671 5101 4571 1163 4160 3588 1161 435 3588 4922
καὶ λαληθήσεταί σοι τί σε δεῖ ποιεῖν. 7 οἱ δὲ ἄνδρες οἱ συν-
and it will be told to you what you must do. the And men travel-
846 2476 1769 191 3303 3588
οδεύοντες αὐτῷ εἱστήκεισαν ἐννεοί, ἀκούοντες μὲν τῆς
ing with him had been standing speechless, hearing indeed the

6 And he trembling and astonished said, Lord, what wilt thou have me to do? And the Lord (said) unto him, Arise, and go into the city, and it shall be told thee what thou must do.
7 And the men which journeyed with him stood speechless, hearing a voice, but seeing no man.

8 And Saul was lifted up from the earth, but his eyes having been opened he saw no one. And leading him by the hand they brought (him) into Damascus.
9 And he was three days not seeing, and did not eat nor drink.

5456 3367 1161 2334 1453 1161 3588 4569 575 3588
φωνῆς, μηδένα δὲ θεωροῦντες. 8 ἠγέρθη δὲ ὁ Σαῦλος ἀπὸ τῆς
sound, no one but beholding. was lifted And Saul from the
1093 455 1161 3588 3788 846 3762 991
γῆς· ἀνεῳγμένων δὲ τῶν ὀφθαλμῶν αὐτοῦ, οὐδένα ἔβλεπε,
earth; having been opened but the eyes of him, no one he saw,
5496 1161 846 1521 1519 1154 2532 2258
χειραγωγοῦντες δὲ αὐτὸν εἰσήγαγον εἰς Δαμασκόν. 9 καὶ ἦν
leading by the hand and him they brought into Damascus. And he was
2250 5140 3361 991 2532 3756 5315 3761 4095
ἡμέρας τρεῖς μὴ βλέπων, καὶ οὐκ ἔφαγεν οὐδὲ ἔπιεν.
days three not seeing, and not did eat nor drink.

8 And Saul arose from the earth; and when his eyes were opened, he saw no man: but they led him by the hand, and brought (him) into Damascus.
9 And he was three days without sight, and neither did eat nor drink.

10. And there was a certain disciple in Damascus named Ananias. And the Lord said to him in a vision, Ananias! And he said, Lord, behold I.
11 And the Lord (said) to him, Rising up pass along on the street being called Straight and seek a Tarsian, Saul by name, in (the) house of Judas. For, behold, he is praying.

2258 1161 5100 3101 1722 1154 3686 367 2532
10 Ἦν δέ τις μαθητὴς ἐν Δαμασκῷ ὀνόματι Ἀνανίας, καὶ
was And a certain disciple in Damascus by name Ananias, and
2036 4314 846 3588 2962 1722 3705 367 3588 1161 2036
εἶπε πρὸς αὐτὸν ὁ Κύριος ἐν ὁράματι Ἀνανία. ὁ δὲ εἶπεν,
said to him the Lord in a vision, Ananias. he And said,
2400 1473 2962 3588 1161 2962 4314 846 450
Ἰδοὺ ἐγώ, Κύριε. 11 ὁ δὲ Κύριος πρὸς αὐτόν, Ἀναστὰς
Behold I, Lord. the And Lord (said) to him, Rising up
4198 1909 3588 4505 3588 2564 2117 2532 2212
πορεύθητι ἐπὶ τὴν ῥύμην τὴν καλουμένην Εὐθεῖαν, καὶ ζήτη-
pass along on the strreet having been called Straight, and seek
1722 3614 2455 4569 3686 5018 2400 1063
σον ἐν οἰκίᾳ Ἰούδα Σαῦλον ὀνόματι, Ταρσέα· ἰδοὺ γὰρ
in (the) house of Judas Saul by name, a Tarsian; behold for

10. And there was a certain disciple at Damascus, named Ananias; and to him said the Lord in a vision, Ananias. And he said, Behold, I (am here), Lord.
11 And the Lord (said) unto him, Arise, and go into the street which is called Straight, and enquire in the house of Judas for (one) called Saul, of Tarsus: for, behold, he prayeth,

12 And (he) has seen in a vision a man named Ananias coming in and putting a hand on him, so that he may see again.
13 And Ananias answered, Lord, I have heard from many about

4336 2532 1492 1722 3705 435 3686 367
προσεύχεται, 12 καὶ εἶδεν ἐν ὁράματι ἄνδρα ὀνόματι Ἀνανίαν
he is praying, and has seen in a vision a man by name Ananias
1525 2532 2007 846 5495 3704 308
εἰσελθόντα καὶ ἐπιθέντα αὐτῷ χεῖρα, ὅπως ἀναβλέψῃ.
coming in and putting on him a hand, so as he may see again.
611 1161 3588 367 2962 191 575 4183 4012
13 ἀπεκρίθη δὲ ὁ Ἀνανίας, Κύριε, ἀκήκοα ἀπὸ πολλῶν περὶ
answered And Ananias, Lord, I have heard from many about

12 And hath seen in a vision a man named Ananias coming in, and putting (his) hand on him, that he might receive his sight.
13 Then Ananias answered, Lord, I have heard by many of this

Literal Translation

this man, how many bad things he did to Your saints in Jerusalem.

14 And here he has authority from the chief priests to bind all the (ones) calling on Your name.

15 And the Lord said to him, Go, because this one is a vessel of election to Me, to bear My name before nations and kings and the sons of Israel.

16 For I will show him how much he must suffer for the sake of My name.

17 And Ananias went away and entered into the house. And putting hands on him (he) said, Brother Saul, the Lord has sent me, Jesus, the One who appeared to you in the highway on which you came, that you may see and be filled of (the) Holy Spirit.

18 And instantly it was as if scales fell away from his eyes, and instantly he saw again. And rising up, (he) was baptized.

19 And taking food (he) was strengthened. And Saul was with the disciples in Damascus some days.

20 And at once in the synagogues he proclaimed the Christ, that this One is the Son of God.

21 And all those hearing were amazed and said, Is this not the (one) destroying those who have called on this Name in Jerusalem, and he had come here for this, that binding them he might lead (them) before the chief priests?

22 But Saul was more filled with power, and (he) confounded the Jews living in Damascus,

Acts 9:14

3588 435 5127 3745 2556 4160 3588 40 4675 1722
τοῦ ἀνδρὸς τούτου, ὅσα κακὰ ἐποίησε τοῖς ἁγίοις σου ἐν
man this, how many bad things he did to the saints of You in

2419 2532 5602 2192 1849 3844 3588 749
Ἱερουσαλήμ· 14 καὶ ὧδε ἔχει ἐξουσίαν παρὰ τῶν ἀρχιερέων
Jerusalem; and here he has authority from the chief priests

1210 3956 3588 1941 3588 3686 4675 2036 1161
δῆσαι πάντας τοὺς ἐπικαλουμένους τὸ ὄνομά σου. 15 εἶπε δὲ
to bind all the (ones) having invoked the name of You. said But

4314 846 3588 2962 4198 3754 4632 1589 3427 2076
πρὸς αὐτὸν ὁ Κύριος, Πορεύου, ὅτι σκεῦος ἐκλογῆς μοι ἐστίν
to him the Lord, Go, because a vessel of election to Me is

3778 3588 941 3588 3686 3450 1799 1484 2532
οὗτος, τοῦ βαστάσαι τὸ ὄνομά μου ἐνώπιον ἐθνῶν καὶ
this one, to bear the name of Me before nations and

935 5207 5037 2474 1473 1063 5263 846 3745
βασιλέων, υἱῶν τε Ἰσραήλ· 16 ἐγὼ γὰρ ὑποδείξω αὐτῷ ὅσα
kings, sons and of Israel. I For will show him how many

1163 846 5228 3588 3686 3450 3958 565 1161
δεῖ αὐτὸν ὑπὲρ τοῦ ὀνόματός μου παθεῖν. 17 Ἀπῆλθε δὲ
must he on behalf of the name of Me suffer. went away And

367 2532 1525 1519 3588 3614 2532 2007 1909 846 3588
Ἀνανίας καὶ εἰσῆλθεν εἰς τὴν οἰκίαν, καὶ ἐπιθεὶς ἐπ' αὐτὸν τὰς
Ananias and entered into the house, and putting on him the

5495 2036 4549 80 3588 2962 649 3165 2424
χεῖρας εἶπε, Σαοὺλ ἀδελφέ, ὁ Κύριος ἀπέσταλκέ με, Ἰησοῦς
hands said, Saul Brother, the Lord has sent me, Jesus

3588 3700 4671 1722 3588 3598 3739 2064 3704 308 2532 4130
ὁ ὀφθείς σοι ἐν τῇ ὁδῷ ᾗ ἤρχου, ὅπως ἀναβλέψῃς καὶ πλη-
He appearing to you in the way which you came, so as you may see again and be

4151 40 2532 2112 634 575 3588
σθῇς Πνεύματος Ἁγίου. 18 καὶ εὐθέως ἀπέπεσον ἀπὸ τῶν
filled of (the) Spirit Holy. And instantly fell away from the

3788 846 5616 3013 308 5037 3916
ὀφθαλμῶν αὐτοῦ ὡσεὶ λεπίδες, ἀνέβλεψέ τε παραχρῆμα,
eyes of him as if scales, he saw again and instantly,

2532 450 907 2532 2983 5160 1765
καὶ ἀναστὰς ἐβαπτίσθη, 19 καὶ λαβὼν τροφὴν ἐνίσχυσεν.
and rising up was baptized, and taking food was strengthened.

1096 1161 3588 4569 3326 3588 1722 1154 3101
Ἐγένετο δὲ ὁ Σαῦλος μετὰ τῶν ἐν Δαμασκῷ μαθητῶν
was And Saul with the in Damascus disciples

2250 5100 2532 2112 1722 3588 4864 2784 3588
ἡμέρας τινάς, 20 καὶ εὐθέως ἐν ταῖς συναγωγαῖς ἐκήρυσσε τὸν
days some, and at once in the synagogues he proclaimed

5547 3754 3778 2076 3588 5207 3588 2316 1839 1161
Χριστόν, ὅτι οὗτός ἐστιν ὁ υἱὸς τοῦ Θεοῦ. 21 ἐξίσταντο δὲ
Christ, that this One is the Son of God. were amazed And

3956 3588 191 2532 3004 3756 3778 2076 3588 4199
πάντες οἱ ἀκούοντες καὶ ἔλεγον, Οὐχ οὗτός ἐστιν ὁ πορθήσας
all those hearing and said, Not this one is the (one) destroying

1722 2419 3588 1941 3588 3686 5124 2532
ἐν Ἱερουσαλὴμ τοὺς ἐπικαλουμένους τὸ ὄνομα τοῦτο, καὶ
in Jerusalem those having called on Name this and

5602 1519 5124 2064 2443 1210 846 71 1909
ὧδε εἰς τοῦτο ἐληλύθει ἵνα δεδεμένους αὐτοὺς ἀγάγῃ ἐπὶ
here for this he had come that binding them he may lead before

3588 749 4569 1161 3123 1743 2532 4797
τοὺς ἀρχιερεῖς; 22 Σαῦλος δὲ μᾶλλον ἐνεδυναμοῦτο, καὶ συνέ-
the chief priests? Saul And more was filled with power, and con-

3588 2453 3588 2730 1722 1154
χυνε τοὺς Ἰουδαίους τοὺς κατοικοῦντας ἐν Δαμασκῷ,
founded the Jews the (ones) living in Damascus,

King James Version

man, how much evil he hath done to thy saints at Jerusalem:

14 And here he hath authority from the chief priests to bind all that call on thy name.

15 But the Lord said unto him, Go thy way: for he is a chosen vessel unto me, to bear my name before the Gentiles, and kings, and the children of Israel:

16 For I will shew him how great things he must suffer for my name's sake.

17 And Ananias went his way, and entered into the house; and putting his hands on him said, Brother Saul, the Lord, (even) Jesus, that appeared unto thee in the way as thou camest, hath sent me, that thou mightest receive thy sight, and be filled with the Holy Ghost.

18 And immediately there fell from his eyes as it had been scales: and he received sight forthwith, and arose, and was baptized.

19 And when he had received meat, he was strengthened. Then was Saul certain days with the disciples which were at Damascus.

20 And straightway he preached Christ in the synagogues, that he is the Son of God.

21 But all that heard (him) were amazed, and said; Is not this he that destroyed them which called on this name in Jerusalem, and came hither for that intent, that he might bring them bound unto the chief priests?

22 But Saul increased the more in strength, and confounded the Jews which dwelt at Damascus,

Literal Translation **Acts 9:23** ***King James Version***

proving that this One is the Christ.

23. And when many days were fulfilled, the Jews plotted together to do away with him.
24 But their plot was known to Saul. And they carefully watched the gates both by day and by night so as to do away with him.
25 But taking (him) by night the disciples let (him) down through the wall, lowering (him) in a basket.

26 And Saul having arrived into Jerusalem, he tried to be joined to the disciples. And all feared him, not believing that he is a disciple.

27 But taking hold of him, Barnabas led (him) to the apostles and related to them how he saw the Lord in the highway, and that He spoke to him, and how in Damascus he spoke boldly in the name of Jesus.

28 And he was with them, going in and going out in Jerusalem, and speaking boldly in the name of the Lord Jesus.

29 Also he spoke and disputed with the Hellenists, and they took him in hand to do away with (him).
30 But knowing, the brothers led him down to Caesarea and sent him forth to Tarsus.

31 Then, indeed, the churches throughout all Judea, and Galilee, and Samaria, had peace, being built up and going on in the fear of the Lord. And (they) were multiplied (in) the comfort of the Holy Spirit.

4822 3754 3778 2076 3588 5547
συμβιβάζων ὅτι οὗτός ἐστιν ὁ Χριστός.
proving that this is the Christ.

5613 1161 4137 2250 2425 4823 3588
23 Ὡς δὲ ἐπληροῦντο ἡμέραι ἱκαναί, συνεβουλεύσαντο οἱ
when And were fulfilled days many, plotted together the

2453 337 846 1097 1161 3588 4569 3588 1917
Ἰουδαῖοι ἀνελεῖν αὐτόν· 24 ἐγνώσθη δὲ τῷ Σαύλῳ ἡ ἐπιβουλὴ
Jews to kill him; was known but to Saul the plot

846 3906 5037 3588 4439 2250 5037 2532 3571
αὐτῶν. παρετήρουν τε τὰς πύλας ἡμέρας τε καὶ νυκτὸς,
of them. they carefully watched And the gates by day both and by night,

3704 846 337 2983 1161 846 3588 3101 3571
ὅπως αὐτὸν ἀνέλωσι· 25 λαβόντες δὲ αὐτὸν οἱ μαθηταὶ νυκτὸς,
so that him they may kill; taking but him the disciples by night,

2524 1223 3588 5038 5465 1722 4711
καθῆκαν διὰ τοῦ τείχους, χαλάσαντες ἐν σπυρίδι.
let down through the wall, lowering (him) in a basket.

3854 1161 3588 4569 1519 2419 3987
26. Παραγενόμενος δὲ ὁ Σαῦλος εἰς Ἱερουσαλήμ, ἐπειρᾶτο
having arrived And Saul into Jerusalem, he tried

2853 3588 3101 2532 3956 5399 846 3361
κολλᾶσθαι τοῖς μαθηταῖς· καὶ πάντες ἐφοβοῦντο αὐτόν, μὴ
to be joined to the disciples; and all feared him, not

4100 3754 2076 3101 921 1161 1949
πιστεύοντες ὅτι ἐστὶ μαθητής. 27 Βαρνάβας δὲ ἐπιλαβόμενος
believing that he is a disciple. Barnabas But taking hold of

846 71 4314 3588 652 2532 1334 846
αὐτὸν ἤγαγε πρὸς τοὺς ἀποστόλους, καὶ διηγήσατο αὐτοῖς
him led (him) to the apostles, and related to them

4459 1722 3588 3598 1492 3588 2962 2532 3754 2980 846
πῶς ἐν τῇ ὁδῷ εἶδε τὸν Κύριον, καὶ ὅτι ἐλάλησεν αὐτῷ,
how in the way he saw the Lord, and that He spoke to him,

2532 4459 1722 1154 3955 1722 3588 3686 3588
καὶ πῶς ἐν Δαμασκῷ ἐπαρρησιάσατο ἐν τῷ ὀνόματι τοῦ
and how in Damascus he spoke boldly in the name

2424 2532 2258 3326 846 1531 2532 1607
Ἰησοῦ. 28 καὶ ἦν μετ' αὐτῶν εἰσπορευόμενος καὶ ἐκπορευό-
of Jesus. And he was with them having gone in and having gone

1722 2419 2532 3955 1722 3588 3686
μενος ἐν Ἱερουσαλήμ, καὶ παρρησιαζόμενος ἐν τῷ ὀνόματι
out in Jerusalem, and having spoken boldly in the name

3588 2962 2424 2980 5037 2532 4802 4314 3588
τοῦ Κυρίου Ἰησοῦ, 29 ἐλάλει τε καὶ συνεζήτει πρὸς τοὺς
of the Lord Jesus, he spoke and also debated with the

1675 3588 1161 2021 846 337 1921 1161
Ἑλληνιστάς· οἱ δὲ ἐπεχείρουν αὐτὸν ἀνελεῖν. 30 ἐπιγνόντες δὲ
Hellenists; they and took in hand him to kill. knowing But

3588 80 2609 846 1519 2542 2532 1821
οἱ ἀδελφοὶ κατήγαγον αὐτὸν εἰς Καισάρειαν, καὶ ἐξαπέ-
the brothers led down him to Caesarea, and sent

846 1519 5019 3588 3303 3767 1577 2596
στειλαν αὐτὸν εἰς Ταρσόν. 31 αἱ μὲν οὖν ἐκκλησίαι καθ'
forth him to Tarsus. the indeed Then churches throughout

3650 3588 2449 2532 1056 2532 4540 2192 1515
ὅλης τῆς Ἰουδαίας καὶ Γαλιλαίας καὶ Σαμαρείας εἶχον εἰρήνην
all Judea and Galilee and Samaria had peace

3618 2532 4198 3588 5401 3588 2962 2532
οἰκοδομούμεναι, καὶ πορευόμεναι τῷ φόβῳ τοῦ Κυρίου καὶ
being built up, and going on in the fear of the Lord and

3588 3874 3588 40 4151 4129
τῇ παρακλήσει τοῦ Ἁγίου Πνεύματος ἐπληθύνοντο.
the comfort of the Holy Spirit were multiplied.

proving that this is very Christ.

23. And after that many days were fulfilled, the Jews took counsel to kill him:
24 But their laying await was known of Saul. And they watched the gates day and night to kill him.

25 Then the discipl es took him by night, and let (him) down by the wall in a basket.

26 And when Saul was come to Jerusalem, he assayed to join himself to the disciples: but they were all afraid of him, and believed not that he was a disciple.
27 But Barnabas took him, and brought (him) to the apostles, and declared unto them how he had seen the Lord in the way, and that he had spoken to him, and how he had preached boldly at Damascus in the name of Jesus.

28 And he was with them coming in and going out at Jerusalem.

29 And he spake boldly in the name of the Lord Jesus, and disputed against the Grecians: but they went about to slay him.
30 (Which) when the brethren knew, they brought him down to Caesarea, and sent him forth to Tarsus.
31 Then had the churches rest throughout all Judaea and Galilee and Samaria, and were edified; and walking in the fear of the Lord, and in the comfort of the Holy Ghost, were multiplied.

Acts 9:32

Literal Translation

32. And it happened, passing through all, Peter also came down to the saints dwelling in Lydda.
33 And he found there a certain man named Aeneas who had been lying on a mattress eight years, having been paralyzed.
34 And Peter said to him, Aeneas! Jesus the Christ heals you; rise up and spread for yourself. And instantly he rose up.

35 And all those dwelling in Lydda and the Sharon (Plain) saw him, who (then) turned to the Lord.

1096 1161 4074 1330 1223 3956 2718
32 Ἐγένετο δὲ Πέτρον διερχόμενον διὰ πάντων κατελθεῖν
it happened And Peter passing through all came down
2532 4314 3588 40 3588 2730 3069 2147 1161
καὶ πρὸς τοὺς ἁγίους τοὺς κατοικοῦντας Λύδδαν. 33 εὗρε δὲ
also to the saints living in Lydda. he found And
1563 444 5100 132 3686 1537 2094 3638 2621
ἐκεῖ ἄνθρωπόν τινα Αἰνέαν ὀνόματι, ἐξ ἐτῶν ὀκτὼ κατακεί-
there man a certain Aeneas by name, of years eight having lain
1909 2895 3739 2258 3886 2532 2036 846 3588
μενον ἐπὶ κραββάτῳ, ὃς ἦν παραλελυμένος. 34 καὶ εἶπεν αὐτῷ ὁ
on a mattress, who was having been paralyzed. And said to him
4074 132 2390 4571 2424 3588 5547 450 2532
Πέτρος, Αἰνέα, ἰᾶταί σε Ἰησοῦς ὁ Χριστός· ἀνάστηθι καὶ
Peter, Aeneas, heals you Jesus Christ; rise up and
4766 4572 2532 2112 450 2532 1492 846
στρῶσον σεαυτῷ. καὶ εὐθέως ἀνέστη. 35 καὶ εἶδον αὐτὸν
spread for yourself. And at once he rose up. And saw him
3956 3588 2730 3069 2532 3588 4565 3748
πάντες οἱ κατοικοῦντες Λύδδαν καὶ τὸν Σάρωνα, οἵτινες
all those living in Lydda and the Sharon (plain), who
1994 1909 3588 2962
ἐπέστρεψαν ἐπὶ τὸν Κύριον.
turned to the Lord.

King James Version

32. And it came to pass, as Peter passed throughout all (quarters), he came down also to the saints which dwelt at Lydda.
33 And there he found a certain man named Aeneas, which had kept his bed eight years, and was sick of the palsy.
34 And Peter said unto him, Aeneas, Jesus Christ maketh thee whole: arise, and make thy bed. And he arose immediately.

35 And all that dwelt at Lydda and Saron saw him, and turned to the Lord.

36. And in Joppa was a certain disciple named Tabitha, which translated is called Dorcas (Gazelle). She was full of good works and of merciful deeds which she did.
37 And it happened in those days, having weakened she died. And having bathed her, they put (her) in an upper room.
38 And Lydda being near to Joppa, the disciples having heard that Peter is in it, they sent two men to him, begging (him) not to delay to come to them.

1722 2445 1161 5100 2258 3102 3686 5000 3739 1329
36 Ἐν Ἰόππῃ δέ τις ἦν μαθήτρια ὀνόματι Ταβιθά, ἣ διερμη-
in Joppa And a certain was disciple by name Tabitha, which being
3004 1393 3778 2258 4134 18 2041 2532
νευομένη λέγεται Δορκάς· αὕτη ἦν πλήρης ἀγαθῶν ἔργων καὶ
translated is called Dorcas; she was full of good works and
1654 3739 4160 1096 1161 1722 3588 2250 1565
ἐλεημοσυνῶν ὧν ἐποίει. 37 ἐγένετο δὲ ἐν ταῖς ἡμέραις ἐκείναις
merciful deeds which she did. it happened And in days those
770 846 599 3068 1161 846 5087
ἀσθενήσασαν αὐτὴν ἀποθανεῖν· λούσαντες δὲ αὐτὴν ἔθηκαν
having weakened she died. having bathed And her they put
1722 5253 1451 1161 5607 3069 3588 2445 3588 3101
ἐν ὑπερῴῳ. 38 ἐγγὺς δὲ οὔσης Λύδδης τῇ Ἰόππῃ, οἱ μαθηταὶ
in an upper room. near And being Lydda to Joppa, the disciples
191 3754 4074 2076 1722 846 649 1417
ἀκούσαντες ὅτι Πέτρος ἐστὶν ἐν αὐτῇ, ἀπέστειλαν δύο
having heard that Peter is in it, they sent two
435 4314 846 3870 3361 3635 1330
ἄνδρας πρὸς αὐτόν, παρακαλοῦντες μὴ ὀκνῆσαι διελθεῖν
men to him, begging (him) not to delay to come
2193 846 450 1161 4074 4905 846 3739
ἕως αὐτῶν. 39 ἀναστὰς δὲ Πέτρος συνῆλθεν αὐτοῖς· ὃν παρα-
unto them. rising up And Peter went with them; whom having

36. Now there was at Joppa a certain disciple named Tabitha, which by interpretation is called Dorcas: this woman was full of good works and almsdeeds which she did.
37 And it came to pass in those days, that she was sick, and died: whom when they had washed, they laid (her) in an upper chamber.
38 And forasmuch as Lydda was nigh to Joppa, and the disciples had heard that Peter was there, they sent unto him two men, desiring (him) that he would not delay to come to them.

39 And rising up Peter went with them, and having arrived they led up to the upper room. And all the widows stood by him, weeping and showing tunics and garments such as Dorcas made (while) being with them.
40 And putting all out, placing the knees Peter prayed. And turning to the body he said, Tabitha, Rise up! And she

3854 321 1519 3588 5253 2532 3936 846
γενόμενον ἀνήγαγον εἰς τὸ ὑπερῷον, καὶ παρέστησαν αὐτῷ
arrived they led up to the upper room, and stood by him
3956 3588 5503 2799 2532 1925 5509 2532
πᾶσαι αἱ χῆραι κλαίουσαι καὶ ἐπιδεικνύμεναι χιτῶνας καὶ
all the widows weeping and showing tunics and
2440 3745 4160 3326 846 5607 3588 1393 1544 1161
ἱμάτια ὅσα ἐποίει μετ' αὐτῶν οὖσα ἡ Δορκάς. 40 ἐκβαλὼν δὲ
garments such as made with them being Dorcas. thrusting out And
1854 3956 3588 4074 5087 3588 1119 4336 2532
ἔξω πάντας ὁ Πέτρος θεὶς τὰ γόνατα προσηύξατο· καὶ
outside all Peter placing the knees prayed; and
1994 4314 3588 4983 2036 5000 450 3588 1161
ἐπιστρέψας πρὸς τὸ σῶμα εἶπε, Ταβιθά, ἀνάστηθι. ἡ δὲ
turning to the body said, Tabitha, Rise up. she And

39 Then Peter arose and went with them. When he was come, they brought him into the upper chamber: and all the widows stood by him weeping, and shewing the coats and garments which Dorcas made, while she was with them.
40 But Peter put them all forth, and kneeled down, and prayed; and turning (him) to the body said, Tabitha, arise. And she

Literal Translation | **Acts 9:41** | **King James Version**

opened her eyes. And seeing Peter she sat up.

41 And giving her a hand he raised her up. And calling the saints and the widows he presented her living.

42 And it became known through all Joppa. And many believed on the Lord.

43 And it happened (that) he remained in Joppa considerable days with one Simon, a tanner.

455 3588 3788 846 2532 1492 3588 4074
ἤνοιξε τοὺς ὀφθαλμοὺς αὐτῆς· καὶ ἰδοῦσα τὸν Πέτρον,
opened the eyes of her; and seeing Peter,

339 1325 1161 846 5495 450 846 5455
ἀνεκάθισε. 41 δοὺς δὲ αὐτῇ χεῖρα, ἀνέστησεν αὐτήν· φωνήσας
she sat up. giving And her a hand, he raised up her; calling

1161 3588 40 2532 3588 5503 3936 846 2198
δὲ τοὺς ἁγίους καὶ τὰς χήρας, παρέστησεν αὐτὴν ζῶσαν.
and the saints and the widows, he presented her living.

1110 1161 1096 2596 3650 3588 2445 2532 4183
42 γνωστὸν δὲ ἐγένετο καθ' ὅλης τῆς Ἰόππης, καὶ πολλοὶ ἐπί-
known And it became through all Joppa, and many

4100 1909 3588 2962 1096 1161 2250 2425 3306
στευσαν ἐπὶ τὸν Κύριον. 43 Ἐγένετο δὲ ἡμέρας ἱκανὰς μεῖναι
believed on the Lord. it happened And days considerable remained

846 1722 2445 3844 5100 4613 1038
αὐτὸν ἐν Ἰόππῃ παρά τινι Σίμωνι βυρσεῖ.
he in Joppa with a certain Simon a tanner.

opened her eyes: and when she saw Peter, she sat up.

41 And he gave her (his) hand, and lifted her up, and when he had called the saints and widows, presented her alive.

42 And it was known throughout all Joppa; and many believed in the Lord.

43 And it came to pass, that he tarried many days in Joppa with one Simon a tanner.

Acts 10

Acts 10

1. But a certain man named Cornelius was in Caesarea, a centurion of a cohort being called Italian,

2 (one) devout and fearing God, with all his household, both doing many merciful deeds to the people and petitioning God through all.

3 About (the) ninth hour of the day, he saw plainly in a vision an angel of God coming to him, and saying to him, Cornelius!

4 And he was staring at him, and becoming terrified he said, What is it, Sir? And he said to him, Your prayers and your merciful deeds went up for a memorial before God.

5 And now send men to Joppa and call for Simon who is surnamed Peter.

6 This one is lodged with one Simon, a tanner, to whom is a house is beside (the) sea. He will tell you what you must do.

7 And as the angel speaking to Cornelius went away, having called two of his servants

435 1161 5100 2258 1722 2542 3686 2883 1543
1 Ἀνὴρ δέ τις ἦν ἐν Καισαρείᾳ ὀνόματι Κορνήλιος, ἑκατοντ-
man And a certain was in Caesarea by name Cornelius, a centurion

1537 4686 3588 2564 2483 2152 2532
άρχης ἐκ σπείρης τῆς καλουμένης Ἰταλικῆς, 2 εὐσεβὴς καὶ
from a cohort having been called Italian, a devout and

5399 3588 2316 4862 3956 3588 3624 846 4160 5037
φοβούμενος τὸν Θεὸν σὺν παντὶ τῷ οἴκῳ αὐτοῦ, ποιῶν τε
(one) fearing God with all the house of him, doing both

1654 4183 3588 2992 2532 1189 3588 2316 1275
ἐλεημοσύνας πολλὰς τῷ λαῷ, καὶ δεόμενος τοῦ Θεοῦ διὰ
merciful deeds many to the people, and petitioning God through

3956 1492 1722 3705 5320 5616 5610 1766 3588
παντός. 3 εἶδεν ἐν ὁράματι φανερῶς ὡσεὶ ὥραν ἐννάτην τῆς
all. He saw in a vision clearly about hour (the) ninth of the

2250 32 3588 2316 1525 4314 846 2532
ἡμέρας, ἄγγελον τοῦ Θεοῦ εἰσελθόντα πρὸς αὐτόν, καὶ
day, an angel of God coming in to him, and

2036 846 2883 3588 1161 816 846 2532 1719
εἰπόντα αὐτῷ, Κορνήλιε. 4 ὁ δὲ ἀτενίσας αὐτῷ καὶ ἔμφοβος
saying to him, Cornelius! he And was staring at him, and terrified

1096 2036 5101 2076 2962 2036 1161 846 3588 4335
γενόμενος εἶπε, Τί ἐστι, Κύριε; εἶπε δὲ αὐτῷ, Αἱ προσευχαί
becoming he said, What is it, Sir? he said And to him, The prayers

4675 2532 3588 1654 4675 305 1519 3422
σου καὶ αἱ ἐλεημοσύναι σου ἀνέβησαν εἰς μνημόσυνον
of you and the merciful deeds of you went up for a memorial

1799 3588 2316 2532 3568 3992 1519 2445 435 2532
ἐνώπιον τοῦ Θεοῦ. 5 καὶ νῦν πέμψον εἰς Ἰόππην ἄνδρας, καὶ
before God. And now send to Joppa men, and

3343 4613 3739 1941 4074 3778 3579
μετάπεμψαι Σίμωνά ὃς ἐπικαλεῖται Πέτρος· 6 οὗτος ξενίζεται
call for Simon who is surnamed Peter; this one is lodged

3844 5100 4613 1038 3739 2076 3614 3844 2281
παρά τινι Σίμωνι βυρσεῖ, ᾧ ἐστιν οἰκία παρὰ θάλασσαν·
with a certain Simon a tanner, to whom is a house beside (the) sea;

3778 2980 4671 5101 4571 1163 4160 5613 1161 565 3588
οὗτος λαλήσει σοι τί σε δεῖ ποιεῖν. 7 ὡς δὲ ἀπῆλθεν ὁ
this one will tell you what you must do. as And went away the

32 3588 2980 3588 2883 5455 1417 3588 3610
ἄγγελος ὁ λαλῶν τῷ Κορνηλίῳ, φωνήσας δύο τῶν οἰκετῶν
angel speaking to Cornelius, having called two of the servants

Acts 10

1. There was a certain man in Caesarea called Cornelius, a centurion of the band called the Italian (band),

2 (A) devout (man), and one that feared God with all his house, which gave much alms to the people, and prayed to God alway.

3 He saw in a vision evidently about the ninth hour of the day an angel of God coming in to him, and saying unto him, Cornelius.

4 And when he looked on him, he was afraid, and said, What is it, Lord? And he said unto him, Thy prayers and thine alms are come up for a memorial before God.

5 And now send men to Joppa, and call for (one) Simon, whose surname is Peter:

6 He lodgeth with one Simon a tanner, whose house is by the sea side: he shall tell thee what thou oughtest to do.

7 And when the angel which spake unto Cornelius was departed, he called two of his household servants,

Literal Translation | **Acts 10:8** | *King James Version*

and a devout soldier of those continually waiting on him,

8 and having explained all things to them, he sent away them to Joppa.

9. And on the morrow, these passing along on (the) road, and drawing near to the city, Peter went up on the roof to pray about (the) sixth hour.
10 And he became hungry and desired to taste (food). But as they were preparing, an ecstasy fell on him.

11 And he beholds the heaven having been opened and a certain vessel like a great sheet coming down on him, being tied by four corners, and let down onto the earth;
12 in which were all the four-footed animals of the earth, and the wild beasts, and the creeping things, and the birds of the heaven.
13 And a voice came to him, Rising up, Peter, slay and eat.
14 But Peter said, Not at all, Lord, because I never did eat anything common or unclean.

15 And again a voice (came) to him a second (time), What things God made clean, you do not make common.
16 And this happened three (times), and the vessel was taken up into the heaven again.

17 And as Peter was doubting within himself what the vision which he saw might be, even behold, the men who had been sent from Cornelius stood on the porch having asked out the house of Simon.
18 And calling out, they inquired if Simon being

---

846 2532 4757 2152 3588 4342 846
αὐτοῦ, καὶ στρατιώτην εὐσεβῆ τῶν προσκαρτερούντων αὐτῷ,
of him, and a soldier devout of those continually waiting on him,

2532 1834 846 537 649 846 1519 3588
8 καὶ ἐξηγησάμενος αὐτοῖς ἅπαντα, ἀπέστειλεν αὐτοὺς εἰς τὴν
and having explained to them all things, he sent away them to

2445
Ἰόππην.
Joppa.

3588 1161 1887 3596 1565 2532 3588 4172
9 Τῇ δὲ ἐπαύριον, ὁδοιπορούντων ἐκείνων καὶ τῇ πόλει
on the And morrow, passing along (the) road these and to the city

1448 305 4074 1909 3588 1430 4336 4012
ἐγγιζόντων, ἀνέβη Πέτρος ἐπὶ τὸ δῶμα προσεύξασθαι, περὶ
drawing near, went up Peter on the roof to pray, about

5610 1623 1096 1161 4361 2532 2309 1089
ὥραν ἕκτην· 10 ἐγένετο δὲ πρόσπεινος, καὶ ἤθελε γεύσασθαι·
hour sixth; he became and hungry, and desired to taste;

3903 1161 1565 1968 1909 846 1611
παρασκευαζόντων δὲ ἐκείνων, ἐπέπεσεν ἐπ᾽ αὐτὸν ἔκστασις,
preparing and they, fell on him an ecstasy,

2532 2334 3588 3772 455 2532 2597 1909
11 καὶ θεωρεῖ τὸν οὐρανὸν ἀνεῳγμένον, καὶ καταβαῖνον ἐπ᾽
and he beholds the heaven having been opened, and coming down on

846 4632 5100 5613 3607 3173 5064 746
αὐτὸν σκεῦός τι ὡς ὀθόνην μεγάλην, τέσσαρσιν ἀρχαῖς
him vessel a certain like sheet a great, at four corners

1210 2532 2524 1909 3588 1093 1722 3739 5225 3956
δεδεμένον, και καθιέμενον ἐπὶ τῆς γῆς· 12 ἐν ᾧ ὑπῆρχε πάντα
being tied, and being let down on the earth; in which were all

3588 5074 3588 1093 2532 3588 2342 2532 3588 2062 2532 3588
τὰ τετράποδα τῆς γῆς καὶ τὰ θηρία καὶ τὰ ἑρπετὰ καὶ τὰ
the quadrupeds of the earth, and the wild beasts and the reptiles and the

4071 3588 3772 2532 1096 5456 4314 846
πετεινὰ τοῦ οὐρανοῦ. 13 καὶ ἐγένετο φωνὴ πρὸς αὐτόν,
birds of the heaven. And came a voice to him,

450 4074 2380 2532 5315 3588 1161 4074 2036
Ἀναστάς, Πέτρε, θῦσον καὶ φάγε. 14 ὁ δὲ Πέτρος εἶπε,
Rising up, Peter, slay and eat. But Peter said,

3365 2962 3754 3763 5315 3956 2839 2228 169
Μηδαμῶς, Κύριε· ὅτι οὐδέποτε ἔφαγον πᾶν κοινὸν ἢ ἀκάθαρ-
Not at all, Lord; because never did I eat anything common or unclean.

2532 5456 3825 1537 1208 4314 846 3739 3588 2316
τον. 15 καὶ φωνὴ πάλιν ἐκ δευτέρου πρὸς αὐτόν, Ἃ ὁ Θεὸς
And a voice again from a second (time) to him, What things God

2511 4771 3361 2840 5124 1161 1096 1909 5151 2532
ἐκαθάρισε, σὺ μὴ κοίνου. 16 τοῦτο δὲ ἐγένετο ἐπὶ τρίς· καὶ
cleansed, you not make common. this And happened on three; and

3825 353 3588 4632 1519 3588 3772
πάλιν ἀνελήφθη τὸ σκεῦος εἰς τὸν οὐρανόν.
again was taken up the sheet into the heaven.

5613 1161 1722 1438 1280 3588 4074 5101 302 1498 3588 3705 3739
17. Ὡς δὲ ἐν ἑαυτῷ διηπόρει ὁ Πέτρος τί ἂν εἴη τὸ ὅραμα ὃ
as And in himself was doubting Peter what might be the vision which

1492 2532 2400 3588 435 3588 649 575 3588 2883
εἶδε, καὶ ἰδού οἱ ἄνδρες οἱ ἀπεσταλμένοι ἀπὸ τοῦ Κορνηλίου,
he saw, and behold, the men having been sent from Cornelius,

1331 3588 3614 4613 2186 1909 3588
διερωτήσαντες τὴν οἰκίαν Σίμωνος, ἐπέστησαν ἐπὶ τὸν
having asked out the house of Simon, stood on the

4440 2532 5455 4441 1487 4613 1941
πυλῶνα, 18 καὶ φωνήσαντες ἐπυνθάνοντο εἰ Σίμων, ὁ ἐπικαλού-
porch,. and calling they inquired if Simon, having been

---

and a devout soldier of them that waited on him continually;

8 And when he had declared all (these) things unto them, he sent them to Joppa.

9. On the morrow, as they went on their journey, and drew nigh unto the city, Peter went up upon the housetop to pray about the sixth hour:
10 And he became very hungry, and would have eaten: but while they made ready, he fell into a trance,

11 And saw heaven opened, and a certain vessel descending unto him, as it had been a great sheet knit at the four corners, and let down to the earth:
12 Wherein were all manner of fourfooted beasts of the earth, and wild beasts, and creeping things, and fowls of the air.

13 And there came a voice to him, Rise, Peter; kill, and eat.
14 But Peter said, Not so, Lord; for I have never eaten any thing that is common or unclean.

15 And the voice (spake) unto him again the second time, What God hath cleansed, (that) call not thou common.
16 This was done thrice: and the vessel was received up again into heaven.
17 Now while Peter doubted in himself what this vision which he had seen should mean, behold, the men which were sent from Cornelius had made enquiry for Simon's house, and stood before the gate,
18 And called, and asked whether Simon, which was

Literal Translation **Acts 10:19** ***King James Version***

Literal Translation

surnamed Peter is lodged here.
19 And (as) Peter pondered concerning the vision, the Spirit said to him, Behold, three men are seeking you.
20 But rising up, go down and go with them, not discriminating, because I have sent them.
21 And going down to the men, the (ones) having been sent from Cornelius to him, Peter said, Behold, I am he who you seek. What (is) the cause for which you are here?
22 And they said, Cornelius, a centurion, a just man and (one) fearing God, and having been testified to by all the nation of the Jews, was divinely warned by a holy angel to call you to his house and to hear words from you.
23 Then calling them in, he lodged (them). And on the morrow Peter went out with them. And some of the brothers from Joppa accompanied him.
24 And on the morrow they entered into Caesarea. And Cornelius was awaiting them, having called together his relatives and (his) intimate friends.
25 And as Peter was coming in, meeting him, Cornelius falling at (his) feet, worshiped.
26 But Peter lifted him up, saying, Stand up! I myself am also a man.
27 And conversing with him, he went in and found many having come together.
28 And he said to

4074 1759 3579 3588 1161 4074
μενος Πέτρος, ἐνθάδε ξενίζεται. 19 τοῦ δὲ Πέτρου
surnamed Peter, here is lodged. And Peter

1760 4012 3588 3705 2036 846 3588 4151 2400
ενθυμουμένου περὶ τοῦ ὁράματος, εἶπεν αὐτῷ τὸ Πνεῦμα, Ἰδού,
pondering about the vision, said to him the Spirit, Behold,

435 5140 2212 4571 235 450 2597 2532
ἄνδρες τρεῖς ζητοῦσί σε. 20 ἀλλὰ ἀναστὰς κατάβηθι, καὶ
men three are seeking you. But rising up go down, and

4198 4862 846 3367 1252 1360 1473 649
πορεύου σὺν αὐτοῖς, μηδὲν διακρινόμενος· διότι ἐγὼ ἀπέσταλκα
go with them, nothing discriminating; because I have sent

846 2597 1161 4074 4314 3588 435 3588 649
αὐτούς. 21 καταβὰς δὲ Πέτρος πρὸς τοὺς ἄνδρας τοὺς ἀπεσταλ-
them. going down And Peter to the men, those having been

575 3588 2883 4314 846 2036 2400 1473 1510 3739
μένους ἀπὸ τοῦ Κορνηλίου πρὸς αὐτόν, εἶπεν, Ἰδοὺ ἐγώ εἰμι ὅν
sent from Cornelius to him, said, Behold! I am whom

2212 5101 3588 156 1223 3739 3918 3588 1161 2036 2883
ζητεῖτε· τίς ἡ αἰτία δι' ἣν πάρεστε; 22 οἱ δὲ εἶπον, Κορνήλιος
you seek; what (is) the cause for which your are here? they And said, Cornelius,

1543 435 1342 2532 5399 3588 2316
ἑκατοντάρχης, ἀνὴρ δίκαιος καὶ φοβούμενος τὸν Θεὸν,
a centurion, a man just and (one) having feared God,

3140 5037 5259 3650 3588 1484 3588 2453
μαρτυρούμενός τε ὑπὸ ὅλου τοῦ ἔθνους τῶν Ἰουδαίων,
having been attested and by all the nation of the Jews,

5537 5259 32 40 3343 4571 1519 3588
ἐχρηματίσθη ὑπὸ ἀγγέλου ἁγίου μεταπέμψασθαί σε εἰς τὸν
was warned by an angel holy to call you to the

3624 846 2532 191 4487 3844 4675 1528
οἶκον αὐτοῦ, καὶ ἀκοῦσαι ῥήματα παρὰ σοῦ. 23 εἰσκαλεσάμενος
house of him, and to hear words from you. having called in

3767 846 3579
οὖν αὐτοὺς ἐξένισε.
Then them he lodged (them).

3588 1161 1887 3588 4074 1831 4862 846 2532 5100 3588
Τῇ δὲ ἐπαύριον ὁ Πέτρος ἐξῆλθε σὺν αὐτοῖς, καί τινες τῶν
on the And morrow Peter went out with them, and some of the

80 3588 575 3588 2445 4905 846 2532 3588
ἀδελφῶν τῶν ἀπὸ τῆς Ἰόππης συνῆλθον αὐτῷ. 24 καὶ τῇ
brothers from Joppa accompanied him. And on the

1887 1525 1519 3588 2542 3588 1161 2883 2258
ἐπαύριον εἰσῆλθον εἰς τὴν Καισάρειαν. ὁ δὲ Κορνήλιος ἦν
morrow they entered into Caesarea. And Cornelius was

4328 846 4779 3588 4773 846
προσδοκῶν αὐτούς, συγκαλεσάμενος τοὺς συγγενεῖς αὐτοῦ
awaiting them, having called together the relatives of him

2532 3588 316 5384 5613 1161 1096 1525 3588
καὶ τοὺς ἀναγκαίους φίλους. 25 ὡς δὲ ἐγένετο εἰσελθεῖν τὸν
and the intimate friends. when And was entering

4074 4876 846 3588 2883 4098 1909 3588
Πέτρον, συναντήσας αὐτῷ ὁ Κορνήλιος, πεσὼν ἐπὶ τοὺς
Peter, meeting him Cornelius, falling at the

4228 4352 3588 1161 4074 846 1453 3004
πόδας, προσεκύνησεν. 26 ὁ δὲ Πέτρος αὐτὸν ἤγειρε λέγων,
feet, worshiped. But Peter him lifted up saying,

450 2504 846 444 1510 2532 4926 846
Ἀνάστηθι· κἀγὼ αὐτὸς ἄνθρωπός εἰμι. 27 καὶ συνομιλῶν αὐτῷ
Stand up! I also (my)self a man am. And conversing with him

1525 2532 2147 4905 4183 5346 5037 4314
εἰσῆλθε, καὶ εὑρίσκει συνεληλυθότας πολλούς, 28 ἔφη τε πρὸς
he went in, and finds having come together many, said and to

King James Version

surnamed Peter, were lodged there.
19 While Peter thought on the vision, the Spirit said unto him, Behold, three men seek thee.
20 Arise therefore, and get thee down, and go with them, doubting nothing: for I have sent them.
21 Then Peter went down to the men which were sent unto him from Cornelius; and said, Behold, I am he whom ye seek: what (is) the cause wherefore ye are come?
22 And they said, Cornelius the centurion, a just man, and one that feareth God, and of good report among all the nation of the Jews, was warned from God by an holy angel to send for thee into his house, and to hear words of thee.
23 Then called he them in, and lodged (them). And on the morrow Peter went away with them, and certain brethren from Joppa accompanied him.
24 And the morrow after they entered into Caesarea. And Cornelius waited for them, and had called together his kinsmen and near friends.
25 And as Peter was coming in, Cornelius met him, and fell down at his feet, and worshipped (him).
26 But Peter took him up, saying, Stand up; I myself also am a man.
27 And as he talked with him, he went in, and found many that were come together.
28 And he said unto

Literal Translation | **Acts 10:29** | **King James Version**

them, You fully know how unlawful it is for a man, a Jew, to unite with or to come near to one of another race. Yet God showed to me not to call a man common or unclean.
29 Because of this, I also came without objection, being sent for. Then I ask for what reason did you send for me?
30 And Cornelius said, From (the) fourth day until this hour I was fasting, and the ninth hour I had been praying in my house. And, behold! A man stood before me in bright clothing.
31 And he said, Cornelius, your prayer was heard and your merciful deeds were remembered before God.
32 Therefore, send to Joppa and call for Simon who is surnamed Peter; this one is lodged in (the) house of Simon, a tanner, by (the) sea. Having come, (he) will speak to you.
33 Then at once I sent to you, and you did well (to) come. Now then, we are all present before God to hear all the things having been commanded you by God.
34. And opening (his) mouth, Peter said, Truly I perceive that God is not an accepter of faces,
35 but in every nation the (one) fearing Him and working righteousness is acceptable to Him.
36 The Word which He sent to the sons of Israel, preaching the gospel of peace through Jesus Christ, this One is Lord of all.
37 You know

846 5210 1987 5613 111 2076 435 2453
αὐτούς, Ὑμεῖς ἐπίστασθε ὡς ἀθέμιτόν ἐστιν ἀνδρὶ Ἰουδαίῳ
them, You fully know how unlawful it is (for) a man a Jew

2853 2228 4334 246 2532 1698 3588 2316
κολλᾶσθαι ἢ προσέρχεσθαι ἀλλοφύλῳ· καὶ ἐμοὶ ὁ Θεὸς
to unite with or to come near one of another race; and to me God

1166 3367 2839 2228 169 3004 444 1352 2532
ἔδειξε μηδένα κοινὸν ἢ ἀκάθαρτον λέγειν ἄνθρωπον· 29 διὸ καὶ
showed not one common or unclean to call a man. Because of this also

369 2064 3343 4441 3767 5101
ἀναντιρρήτως ἦλθον μεταπεμφθείς. πυνθάνομαι οὖν, τίνι
without objection I came being sent for. I ask Therefore, for what

3056 3343 3165 2532 3588 2883 5346 575 5067
λόγῳ μετεπέμψασθέ με; 30 καὶ ὁ Κορνήλιος ἔφη, Ἀπὸ τετάρτης
reason you sent for me? And Cornelius said, From (the) fourth

2250 3360 3778 3588 5610 2252 3522 2532 3588
ἡμέρας μέχρι ταύτης τῆς ὥρας ἤμην νηστεύων, καὶ τὴν
day until this hour I was fasting, and the

1766 5610 4336 1722 3588 3624 3450 2532 2400
ἐννάτην ὥραν προσευχόμενος ἐν τῷ οἴκῳ μου· καὶ ἰδού,
ninth hour had been praying in the house of me. And behold!

435 2476 1799 3450 1722 2066 2986 2532 5346
ἀνὴρ ἔστη ἐνώπιόν μου ἐν ἐσθῆτι λαμπρᾷ, 31 καὶ φησι,
A man stood before me in clothing bright, and says,

2883 1522 4675 3588 4335 2532 3588 1654
Κορνήλιε, εἰσηκούσθη σου ἡ προσευχὴ, καὶ αἱ ἐλεημοσύναι
Cornelius, was heard of you the prayer, and the merciful deeds

4675 3415 1799 3588 2316 3992 3767 1519 2445
σου ἐμνήσθησαν ἐνώπιον τοῦ Θεοῦ. 32 πέμψον οὖν εἰς Ἰόππην,
of you were remembered before God. send Therefore to Joppa,

2532 3333 4613 3739 1941 4074 3778 3579
καὶ μετακάλεσαι Σίμωνα ὃς ἐπικαλεῖται Πέτρος· οὗτος ξενί-
and call for Simon who is surnamed Peter; this one is

1722 3614 4613 1038 3844 2281 3739 3854
ζεται ἐν οἰκίᾳ Σίμωνος βυρσέως παρὰ θάλασσαν· ὃς παρα-
lodged in (the) house of Simon a tanner beside (the) sea; who having

2980 4671 1824 3767 3992 4314 4571 4771 5037
γενόμενος λαλήσει σοι. 33 ἐξαυτῆς οὖν ἔπεμψα πρὸς σέ· σύ τε
come will speak to you. At once then I sent to you; you and

2573 4160 3854 3568 3767 3956 2249 1799
καλῶς ἐποίησας παραγενόμενος. νῦν οὖν πάντες ἡμεῖς ἐνώ-
well did having come. Now then all we before

3588 2316 3918 191 3956 3588 4367
πιον τοῦ Θεοῦ πάρεσμεν ἀκοῦσαι πάντα τὰ προστεταγμένα
God are present to hear all the things being commanded

46715259 3588 2316 455 1161 4074 3588 4750 2036
σοι ὑπὸ τοῦ Θεοῦ. 34 ἀνοίξας δὲ Πέτρος τὸ στόμα εἶπεν,
you by God. opening And Peter the mouth said,

1909 225 2638 3754 3756 2076 4381
Ἐπ' ἀληθείας καταλαμβάνομαι ὅτι οὐκ ἔστι προσωπολή-
On truth I perceive that not is a receiver of

3588 2316 235 1722 3956 1484 3588 5399 846 2532
πτης ὁ Θεός· 35 ἀλλ' ἐν παντὶ ἔθνει ὁ φοβούμενος αὐτὸν καὶ
faces God; but in every nation the (one) fearing Him and

2038 1343 1184 846 2076 3588 3056 3739
ἐργαζόμενος δικαιοσύνην, δεκτὸς αὐτῷ ἐστι. 36 τὸν λόγον ὃν
working righteousness, acceptable to Him is. The Word which

649 3588 5207 2474 2097 1515 1223
ἀπέστειλε τοῖς υἱοῖς Ἰσραὴλ, εὐαγγελιζόμενος εἰρήνην διὰ
He sent to the sons of Israel, preaching the gospel peace through

2424 5547 3778 2076 3956 2962 5210 1492
Ἰησοῦ Χριστοῦ [οὗτός ἐστι πάντων Κύριος] 37 ὑμεῖς οἴδατε,
Jesus Christ, this One is of all Lord) you know,

them, Ye know how that it is an unlawful thing for a man that is a Jew to keep company, or come unto one of another nation; but God hath shewed me that I should not call any man common or unclean.
29 Therefore came I (unto you) without gainsaying, as soon as I was sent for: I ask therefore for what intent ye have sent for me?
30 And Cornelius said, Four days ago I was fasting until this hour; and at the ninth hour I prayed in my house, and, behold, a man stood before me in bright clothing,
31 And said, Cornelius, thy prayer is heard, and thine alms are had in remembrance in the sight of God.
32 Send therefore to Joppa, and call hither Simon, whose surname is Peter; he is lodged in the house of (one) Simon a tanner by the sea side: who, when he cometh, shall speak unto thee.
33 Immediately therefore I sent to thee; and thou hast well done that thou art come. Now therefore are we all here present before God, to hear all things that are commanded thee of God.
34. Then Peter opened (his) mouth, and said, Of a truth I perceive that God is no respecter of persons:
35 But in every nation he that feareth him, and worketh righteousness, is accepted with him.
36 The word which (God) sent unto the children of Israel, preaching peace by Jesus Christ: (he is Lord of all:)
37 That word, (I say), ye know,

Literal Translation | **Acts 10:38** | **King James Version**

the thing that happened throughout all Judea, beginning from Galilee after the baptism that John proclaimed,

3588 1096 4487 2596 3650 3588 2449 756 575
τὸ γενόμενον ῥῆμα καθ᾽ ὅλης τῆς Ἰουδαίας, ἀρξάμενον ἀπὸ
that had happened the thing through all of Judea, beginning from

3588 1056 3326 3588 908 3739 2784 2491
τῆς Γαλιλαίας, μετὰ τὸ βάπτισμα ὃ ἐκήρυξεν Ἰωάννης·
Galilee, after the baptism which proclaimed John;

which was published throughout all Judaea, and began from Galilee, after the baptism which John preached;

38 Jesus the (One) from Nazareth, how God anointed Him with (the) Holy Spirit and with power, who went about doing good, and healing all those having been oppressed by the Devil, because God was with Him.

2424 3588 575 3478 5613 5548 846 3588 2316 4151
38 Ἰησοῦν τὸν ἀπὸ Ναζαρέθ, ὡς ἔχρισεν αὐτὸν ὁ Θεὸς Πνεύ-
Jesus the (One) from Nazareth, how anointed Him God with (the)

40 2532 1411 3739 1330 2109 2532 2390
ματι Ἁγίῳ καὶ δυνάμει, ὃς διῆλθεν εὐεργετῶν καὶ ἰώμενος
Spirit Holy and with power, who went about doing good and healing

3956 3588 2616 5259 3588 1228 3754
πάντας τοὺς καταδυναστευομένους ὑπὸ τοῦ διαβόλου, ὅτι
all the (ones) having been oppressed by the devil, because

3588 2316 2258 3326 846
ὁ Θεὸς ἦν μετ᾽ αὐτοῦ.
God was with Him.

38 How God anointed Jesus of Nazareth with the Holy Ghost and with power: who went about doing good, and healing all that were oppressed of the devil; for God was with him.

39 And we are witnesses of all things which He did, both in the country of the Jews, and in Jerusalem, whom they did away with, hanging (Him) on a tree.

2532 2249 2070 3144 3956 3739
39 καὶ ἡμεῖς ἐσμεν μάρτυρες πάντων ὧν
And we are witnesses of all things which

4160 1722 5037 3588 5561 3588 2453 2532 1722 2419
ἐποίησεν ἔν τε τῇ χώρᾳ τῶν Ἰουδαίων καὶ ἐν Ἱερουσαλήμ·
He did in both the country of the Jews and in Jerusalem;

3739 337 2910 1909 3586
ὃν ἀνεῖλον κρεμάσαντες ἐπὶ ξύλου.
whom they killed hanging (Him) on a tree.

39 And we are witnesses of all things which he did both in the land of the Jews, and in Jerusalem; whom they slew and hanged on a tree:

40 God raised up this One the third day and gave to Him to become visible;

41 not to all the people, but to witnesses, the ones having been before hand-picked by God, to us who ate and drank with Him after His rising again from (the) dead.

5126 3588 2316 1453 3588
40 τοῦτον ὁ Θεὸς ἤγειρε τῇ
This (One) God raised up the

5154 2250 2532 1325 846 1717 1096 3756 3956
τρίτῃ ἡμέρᾳ, καὶ ἔδωκεν αὐτὸν ἐμφανῆ γενέσθαι, 41 οὐ παντὶ
third day, and gave Him visible to become, not to all

3588 2992 235 3144 3588 4401 5259 3588
τῷ λαῷ, ἀλλὰ μάρτυσι τοῖς προκεχειροτονημένοις ὑπὸ τοῦ
the people, but to witnesses those having been before hand-picked by

2316 2254 3748 4906 2532 4844 846
Θεοῦ, ἡμῖν, οἵτινες συνεφάγομεν καὶ συνεπίομεν αὐτῷ
God, to us, who ate with and drank with Him

3326 3588 450 846 1537 3498
μετὰ τὸ ἀναστῆναι αὐτὸν ἐκ νεκρῶν.
after the rising again of Him from (the) dead.

40 Him God raised up the third day, and shewed him openly;

41 Not to all the people, but unto witnesses chosen before of God, (even) to us, who did eat and drink with him after he rose from the dead.

42 And He commanded us to proclaim to the people and to witness solemnly that it is He who has been marked out by God (to be) Judge of (the) living and (the) dead.

2532 3853
42 καὶ παρήγγειλεν
And He commanded

2254 2784 3588 2992 2532 1263 3754 846
ἡμῖν κηρύξαι τῷ λαῷ, καὶ διαμαρτύρασθαι ὅτι οὗτός
us to proclaim to the people, and to solemnly witness that He

2076 3588 3724 5259 3588 2316 2923 2198 2532 3498
ἐστιν ὁ ὡρισμένος ὑπὸ τοῦ Θεοῦ κριτὴς ζώντων καὶ νεκρῶν.
it is who had been marked out by God (as) judge of living and of dead.

42 And he commanded us to preach unto the people, and to testify that it is he which was ordained of God (to be) the Judge of quick and dead.

43 To this One all the Prophets witness, (so that) through His name everyone believing into Him (will) receive remission of sins.

5129 3956 3588 4396 3140 859 266
43 τούτῳ πάντες οἱ προφῆται μαρτυροῦσιν, ἄφεσιν ἁμαρτιῶν
To this One all the prophets witness, remission of sins

2983 1223 3588 3686 846 3956 3588 4100
λαβεῖν διὰ τοῦ ὀνόματος αὐτοῦ πάντα τὸν πιστεύοντα
to receive through the name of Him everyone believing

1519 846
εἰς αὐτόν.
into Him.

43 To him give all the prophets witness, that through his name whosoever believeth in him shall receive remission of sins.

44. As Peter was yet speaking these words, the Holy Spirit fell on all the (ones) hearing the Word.

45 And the faithful of (the) circumcision were amazed, as many as came with Peter, because the gift of the Holy Spirit was poured out on the nations also.

2089 2980 3588 4074 3588 4487 5023 1968 3588
44 Ἔτι λαλοῦντος τοῦ Πέτρου τὰ ῥήματα ταῦτα, ἐπέπεσε τὸ
(As) yet speaking Peter words these, fell the

4151 3588 40 1909 3956 3588 191 3588 3056
Πνεῦμα τὸ Ἅγιον ἐπὶ πάντας τοὺς ἀκούοντας τὸν λόγον.
Spirit Holy on all the (ones) hearing the Word.

2532 1839 3588 1537 4061 4103 3745 4905 3588
45 καὶ ἐξέστησαν οἱ ἐκ περιτομῆς πιστοί, ὅσοι συνῆλθον τῷ
And were amazed those of circumcision faithful, as many as came with

4074 3754 2532 1909 3588 1484 3588 1431 3588 40 4151
Πέτρῳ, ὅτι καὶ ἐπὶ τὰ ἔθνη ἡ δωρεὰ τοῦ Ἁγίου Πνεύματος
Peter, because also on the nations the gift of the Holy Spirit

44. While Peter yet spake these words, the Holy Ghost fell on all them which heard the word.

45 And they of the circumcision which believed were astonished, as many as came with Peter, because that on the Gentiles also was poured out the gift of the Holy Ghost.

Acts 10:46

Literal Translation

46 For they heard them speaking in tongues and magnifying God. Then Peter answered,
47 Can anyone forbid the water that these not be baptized, who the Holy Spirit received, even as we also?

48 And he commanded them to be baptized in the name of the Lord. Then they asked him to remain some days.

1632 191 1063 846 2980 1100 2532
ἐκκέχυται· 46 ἤκουον γὰρ αὐτῶν λαλούντων γλώσσαις, καὶ
was poured out. they heard For them speaking in tongues, and

3170 3588 2316 5119 611 3588 4074 3385
μεγαλυνόντων τὸν Θεόν. τότε ἀπεκρίθη ὁ Πέτρος, 47 Μήτι
magnifying God. Then answered Peter, Not

3588 5204 2967 1410 5100 3588 3361 907 5128
τὸ ὕδωρ κωλῦσαι δύναταί τις, τοῦ μὴ βαπτισθῆναι τούτους,
the water forbid is able anyone, not to be baptized these,

3748 3588 4151 3588 40 2983 2531 2532 2249 4367
οἵτινες τὸ Πνεῦμα τὸ Ἅγιον ἔλαβον καθὼς καὶ ἡμεῖς; 48 προσ-
who the Spirit Holy received even as also we? he com-

5037 846 907 1722 3588 3686 3588 2962
έταξέ τε αὐτοὺς βαπτισθῆναι ἐν τῷ ὀνόματι τοῦ Κυρίου.
manded And them to be baptized in the name of the Lord.

5119 2065 846 1961 2250 5100
τότε ἠρώτησαν αὐτὸν ἐπιμεῖναι ἡμέρας τινάς.
Then they asked him to remain days some.

King James Version

46 For they heard them speak with tongues, and magnify God. Then answered Peter,
47 Can any man forbid water, that these should not be baptized, which have received the Holy Ghost as well as we?

48 And he commanded them to be baptized in the name of the Lord. Then prayed they him to tarry certain days.

Acts 11

Acts 11

1. And the apostles and the brothers being in Judea heard that the nations also received the Word of God.

2 And when Peter went up to Jerusalem, those of the circumcision disputed to him,
3 saying, You went in to men having uncircumcision and ate with them.
4 But beginning, Peter set out to them in order, saying,

5 I was in (the) city of Joppa, praying. And in an ecstasy, I saw a vision: a certain vessel (was) coming down, like a huge sheet, being let down by four corners out of the heaven; and it came as far as me.

6 gazing on (this), I perceived, and I saw the four-footed animals of the earth, and the wild beasts, and the creeping things, and the birds of the heaven.

7 And I heard a voice saying to me, Peter, rise up, slay and eat.
8 But I said, Not at all, Lord, because never (has) anything common or unclean entered into my mouth.
9 But answering me a voice

191 1161 3588 652 2532 3588 80 3588 5607 2596
1 Ἤκουσαν δὲ οἱ ἀπόστολοι καὶ οἱ ἀδελφοὶ οἱ ὄντες κατὰ
heard And the apostles and the brothers being throughout

3588 2449 3754 2532 3588 1484 1209 3588 3056 3588 2316
τὴν Ἰουδαίαν ὅτι καὶ τὰ ἔθνη ἐδέξαντο τὸν λόγον τοῦ Θεοῦ.
Judea that also the nations received the Word of God.

2532 3753 305 4074 1519 2414 1252 4314 846
2 καὶ ὅτε ἀνέβη Πέτρος εἰς Ἱεροσόλυμα, διεκρίνοντο πρὸς αὐ-
And when went Peter to Jerusalem, disputed with him

3588 1537 4061 3004 3754 4314 435 203
τὸν οἱ ἐκ περιτομῆς, 3 λέγοντες ὅτι Πρὸς ἄνδρας ἀκροβυστίαν
those of circumcision, saying, To men uncircumcision

2192 1525 2532 4906 846 756 1161 3588
ἔχοντας εἰσῆλθες, καὶ συνέφαγες αὐτοῖς. 4 ἀρξάμενος δὲ ὁ
having you went in, and you ate with them. beginning And

4074 1620 846 2517 3004 1473 2252 1722 4172
Πέτρος ἐξετίθετο αὐτοῖς καθεξῆς λέγων, 5 Ἐγὼ ἤμην ἐν πόλει
Peter set out to them in order saying, I was being in (the) city

2445 4336 2532 1492 1722 1611 3705 2597
Ἰόππῃ προσευχόμενος, καὶ εἶδον ἐν ἐκστάσει ὅραμα, κατα-
of Joppa praying, and I saw in an ecstasy a vision, coming

4632 5100 5613 3607 3173 5064 746
βαῖνον σκεῦός τι, ὡς ὀθόνην μεγάλην τέσσαρσιν ἀρχαῖς
down vessel a certain, as a sheet great by four corners

2524 1537 3588 3772 2532 2064 891 1700 1519 3739
καθιεμένην ἐκ τοῦ οὐρανοῦ, καὶ ἦλθεν ἄχρις ἐμοῦ· 6 εἰς ἣν
having been let down out of the heaven, and it came as far as me; into which

816 2657 2532 1492 3588 5074 3588 1093 2532
ἀτενίσας κατενόουν, καὶ εἶδον τὰ τετράποδα τῆς γῆς καὶ
gazing I perceived, and I saw the quadrupeds of the earth and

3588 2342 2532 3588 2062 2532 3588 4071 3588 3772 191
τὰ θηρία καὶ τὰ ἑρπετὰ καὶ τὰ πετεινὰ τοῦ οὐρανοῦ. 7 ἤκουσα
the wild beasts and the reptiles and the birds of the heaven. I heard

1161 5456 3004 3427 450 4074 2380 2532 5315
δὲ φωνῆς λεγούσης μοι, Ἀναστάς, Πέτρε, θῦσον καὶ φάγε.
And a voice saying to me, Rise up, Peter, slay and eat.

2036 1161 3365 2962 3754 3956 2839 2228 169
8 εἶπον δέ, Μηδαμῶς, Κύριε· ὅτι πᾶν κοινὸν ἢ ἀκάθαρτον
I said And, Not at all, Lord; because anything common or unclean

3763 1525 1519 3588 4750 3450 611 1161 3427 5456
οὐδέποτε εἰσῆλθεν εἰς τὸ στόμα μου. 9 ἀπεκρίθη δέ μοι φωνὴ
never entered into the mouth of me. answering But me a voice

Acts 11

1. And the apostles and brethren that were in Judaea heard that the Gentiles had also received the word of God.

2 And when Peter was come up to Jerusalem, they that were of the circumcision contended with him,
3 Saying, Thou wentest in to men uncircumcised, and didst eat with them.
4 But Peter rehearsed (the matter) from the beginning, and expounded (it) by order unto them, saying,
5 I was in the city of Joppa praying: and in a trance I saw a vision, A certain vessel descend, as it had been a great sheet, let down from heaven by four corners; and it came even to me:
6 Upon the which when I had fastened mine eyes, I considered, and saw fourfooted beasts of the earth, and wild beasts, and creeping things, and fowls of the air.
7 And I heard a voice saying unto me, Arise, Peter; slay and eat.
8 But I said, Not so, Lord: for nothing common or unclean hath at any time entered into my mouth.
9 But the voice answered me

Literal Translation

Acts 11:10

the second (time) out of the heaven, What things God has cleansed, you do not (make) common.
10 And this happened three (times), and all things were raised up into the heaven again.
11 And, behold! At once three men stood at the house in which I was, having been sent from Caesarea to me.
12 And the Spirit said to me to go with them, nothing discriminating. And these six brothers came with me, and we entered into the man's house.
13 And he reported to us how he saw the angel in his house, standing and saying to him, Send men to Joppa, and call for Simon the (one) being surnamed Peter,
14 who will speak words to you by which you and all your house will be saved.
15 And in my beginning to speak, the Holy Spirit fell on them, as also on us in (the) beginning.
16 And I remembered the Word of (the) Lord, how He said, John indeed baptized with water, but you will be baptized in (the) Holy Spirit.
17 Then if God gave the same gift as to them as also to us, having believed on the Lord Jesus Christ, and I, who was I to be able to prevent God?
18 And hearing these things, they rested and glorified God, saying, Then God also has given to the nations repentance unto life.
19. Then, indeed, they who were scattered from the oppression having occurred

1537 1208 1537 3588 3772 3739 3588 2316 2511 4771 3361
ἐκ δευτέρου ἐκ τοῦ οὐρανοῦ, Ἃ ὁ Θεὸς ἐκαθάρισε, σὺ μὴ
the second (time) out of the heaven, What things God has cleansed, you not

2840 5124 1161 1096 1909 5151 2532 3825 385
κοίνου. 10 τοῦτο δὲ ἐγένετο ἐπὶ τρίς, καὶ πάλιν ἀνεσπάσθη
(make) common. this And happened on three, and again were raised up

537 1519 3588 3772 2532 2400 1824 5140 435
ἅπαντα εἰς τὸν οὐρανόν. 11 καὶ ἰδού, ἐξαυτῆς τρεῖς ἄνδρες
all things into the heaven. And behold! At once three men

2186 1909 3588 3614 1722 3739 2252 649 575
ἐπέστησαν ἐπὶ τὴν οἰκίαν ἐν ᾗ ἤμην, ἀπεσταλμένοι ἀπὸ
stood at the house in which I was, having been sent from

2542 4314 3165 2036 1161 3427 3588 4151 4905
Καισαρείας πρός με. 12 εἶπε δὲ μοι τὸ Πνεῦμα συνελθεῖν
Caesarea to me. said And to me the Spirit to go with

846 3367 1252 2064 1161 4862 1698 2532 3588 1803
αὐτοῖς, μηδὲν διακρινόμενον. ἦλθον δὲ σὺν ἐμοὶ καὶ οἱ ἓξ
them, nothing discriminating. came And with me also six

80 3778 2532 1525 1519 3588 3624 3588 435
ἀδελφοὶ οὗτοι, καὶ εἰσήλθομεν εἰς τὸν οἶκον τοῦ ἀνδρός·
brothers these, and we entered into the house of the man.

518 5037 2254 4459 1492 3588 32 1722 3588 3624 846
13 ἀπήγγειλέ τε ἡμῖν πῶς εἶδε τὸν ἄγγελον ἐν τῷ οἴκῳ αὐτοῦ
he reported And to us how he saw the angel in the house of him

2476 2532 2036 846 649 1519 2445 435
σταθέντα, καὶ εἰπόντα αὐτῷ, Ἀπόστειλον εἰς Ἰόππην ἄνδρας,
standing, and saying to him, Send to Joppa men,

2532 3343 4613 3588 1941 4074 3739
καὶ μετάπεμψαι Σίμωνα, τὸν ἐπικαλούμενον Πέτρον, 14 ὃς
and call for Simon, the (one) having been surnamed Peter, who

2980 4487 4314 4571 1722 3739 4982 4771 2532 3956 3588
λαλήσει ῥήματα πρὸς σε, ἐν οἷς σωθήσῃ σὺ καὶ πᾶς ὁ
will speak words to you, by which will be saved you and all the

3624 4675 1722 1161 3588 756 3165 2980 1968 3588 4151
οἶκός σου. 15 ἐν δὲ τῷ ἄρξασθαί με λαλεῖν, ἐπέπεσε τὸ Πνεῦμα
house of you. in And beginning me to speak, fell on the Spirit

3588 40 1909 846 5618 2532 1909 2248 1722 746 3415
τὸ Ἅγιον ἐπ' αὐτούς, ὥσπερ καὶ ἐφ' ἡμᾶς ἐν ἀρχῇ. 16 ἐμνήσθην
Holy on them, as also on us in beginning. I remembered

1161 3588 4487 2962 5613 3004 2491 3303 907
δὲ τοῦ ῥήματος Κυρίου, ὡς ἔλεγεν, Ἰωάννης μὲν ἐβάπτισεν
And the word of (the) Lord, how He said, John indeed baptized

5204 5210 1161 907 1722 4151 40 1487 3767
ὕδατι, ὑμεῖς δὲ βαπτισθήσεσθε ἐν Πνεύματι Ἁγίῳ. 17 εἰ οὖν
with water, you but will be baptized in (the) Spirit Holy. If then

3588 2470 1431 1325 846 3588 2316 5613 2532 2254
τὴν ἴσην δωρεὰν ἔδωκεν αὐτοῖς ὁ Θεὸς ὡς καὶ ἡμῖν,
the same gift gave them God as also to us,

4100 1909 3588 2962 2424 5547 1473 1161 5101 2252
πιστεύσασιν ἐπὶ τὸν Κύριον Ἰησοῦν Χριστόν, ἐγὼ δὲ τίς ἤμην
having believed on the Lord Jesus Christ, I and who was

1415 2967 3588 2316 191 1161 5023 2270
δυνατὸς κωλῦσαι τὸν Θεόν; 18 ἀκούσαντες δὲ ταῦτα ἡσύχασαν,
able to prevent God? hearing And these things they rested,

2532 1392 3588 2316 3004 686 2532 3588 1484 3588
καὶ ἐδόξαζαν τὸν Θεὸν, λέγοντες, Ἄραγε καὶ τοῖς ἔθνεσιν ὁ
and glorified God, saying, Then also to the nations

2316 3588 3341 1325 1519 2222
Θεὸς τὴν μετάνοιαν ἔδωκεν εἰς ζωήν.
God repentance has given unto life.

3588 3303 3767 1289 575 3588 2347 3588 1096
19 Οἱ μὲν οὖν διασπαρέντες ἀπὸ τῆς θλίψεως τῆς γενομένης
they indeed Then who were dispersed from the affliction having occurred

King James Version

again from heaven, What God hath cleansed, (that) call not thou common.
10 And this was done three times: and all were drawn up again into heaven.
11 And, behold, immediately there were three men already come unto the house where I was, sent from Caesarea unto me.
12 And the Spirit bade me go with them, nothing doubting. Moreover these six brethren accompanied me, and we entered into the man's house:
13 And he shewed us how he had seen an angel in his house, which stood and said unto him, Send men to Joppa, and call for Simon, whose surname is Peter;
14 Who shall tell thee words, whereby thou and all thy house shall be saved.
15 And as I began to speak, the Holy Ghost fell on them, as on us at the beginning.
16 Then remembered I the word of the Lord, how that he said, John indeed baptized with water; but ye shall be baptized with the Holy Ghost.
17 Forasmuch then as God gave them the like gift as (he did) unto us, who believed on the Lord Jesus Christ; what was I, that I could withstand God?
18 When they heard these things, they held their peace, and glorified God, saying, Then hath God also to the Gentiles granted repentance unto life.
19. Now they which were scattered abroad upon the persecution that

Acts 11:20

Literal Translation

over Stephen passed through to Phoenicia and Cyprus and Antioch, speaking the Word to no one except only to Jews.

20 But some men from them, Cypriots and Cyrenians, who had come to Antioch, spoke to the Hellenists, announcing the gospel (of) the Lord Jesus.
21 And (the) hand of (the) Lord was with them, and a great number believing, (they) turned onto the Lord.

22. And the Word was heard in the ears of the church in Jerusalem concerning them. And they sent out Barnabas to go through as far as Antioch;
23 who having come, and seeing the grace of God, rejoiced. And he exhorted all with purpose of heart to abide near the Lord;

24 because he was a good man, and full of (the) Holy Spirit and of faith. And a considerable crowd was added to the Lord.

25 And Barnabas went out to Tarsus to seek Saul.
26 And finding him, he brought him to Antioch. And it happened to them were assembled in the church a whole year; and they taught a considerable crowd. And the disciples were first called Christians at Antioch.

27. And in these days prophets came down from Jerusalem to Antioch.
28 And one of them named Agabus having risen up, (he) signified through the Spirit that a great famine was about to be over all the inhabited earth, which also happened on

---

1909 4736 1330 2193 5403 2532 2954 2532
ἐπὶ Στεφάνῳ διῆλθον ἕως Φοινίκης καὶ Κύπρου καὶ
over Stephen passed through until Phoenicia and Cyprus and

490 3367 2980 3588 3056 1487 3361 3440
Ἀντιοχείας, μηδενὶ λαλοῦντες τὸν λόγον εἰ μὴ μόνον
Antioch, to no one speaking the Word except only

2453 2258 1161 5100 1537 846 435 2953 2532
Ἰουδαίοις. 20 ἦσαν δέ τινες ἐξ αὐτῶν ἄνδρες Κύπριοι καὶ
to Jews. were But some of them men Cypriots and

2956 3748 1525 1519 490 2980 4314
Κυρηναῖοι, οἵτινες εἰσελθόντες εἰς Ἀντιόχειαν, ἐλάλουν πρὸς
Cyrenians, who having come into Antioch, spoke to

3588 1675 2097 3588 2962 2424 2532
τοὺς Ἑλληνιστάς, εὐαγγελιζόμενοι τὸν Κύριον Ἰησοῦν. 21 καὶ
the Hellenists, preaching the gospel of the Lord Jesus. And

2258 5495 2962 3326 846 4183 5037 706 3588 4100 1994
ἦν χεὶρ Κυρίου μετ' αὐτῶν· πολύς τε ἀριθμὸς ὁ πιστεύσας ἐπέ-
was hand (the) Lord's with them; a much and number believing

1909 3588 2962 191 1161 3588 3056 1519 3588 3775 3588
στρεψεν ἐπὶ τὸν Κύριον. 22 ἠκούσθη δὲ ὁ λόγος εἰς τὰ ὦτα τῆς
turned onto the Lord. heard And the Word into the ears of the

1577 3588 1722 2414 4012 846 2532 1821
ἐκκλησίας τῆς ἐν Ἱεροσολύμοις περὶ αὐτῶν· καὶ ἐξαπέστειλαν
church in Jerusalem concerning them; and they sent out

921 1330 2193 490 3739 3854 2532
Βαρνάβαν διελθεῖν ἕως Ἀντιοχείας· 23 ὃς παραγενόμενος καὶ
Barnabas to go through until Antioch; who having come and

1492 3588 5485 3588 2316 5463 2532 3870 3956 3588
ἰδὼν τὴν χάριν τοῦ Θεοῦ ἐχάρη, καὶ παρεκάλει πάντας τῇ
seeing the grace of God rejoiced, and exhorted all

4286 3588 2588 4357 3588 2962 3754 2258 435
προθέσει τῆς καρδίας προσμένειν τῷ Κυρίῳ· 24 ὅτι ἦν ἀνὴρ
with purpose of heart to abide near the Lord; because he was a man

18 2532 4134 4151 40 2532 4102 2532
ἀγαθὸς καὶ πλήρης Πνεύματος Ἁγίου καὶ πίστεως· καὶ
good and full of (the) Spirit Holy and of faith. And

4369 3793 2425 3588 2962 1831 1161 1519 5019 3588
προσετέθη ὄχλος ἱκανὸς τῷ Κυρίῳ. 25 ἐξῆλθε δὲ εἰς Ταρσὸν ὁ
was added crowd a considerable to the Lord. went out And to Tarsus

921 327 4569 2532 2147 846 71
Βαρνάβας ἀναζητῆσαι Σαῦλον, 26 καὶ εὑρὼν αὐτὸν ἤγαγεν
Barnabas to seek Saul, and finding him he brought

846 1519 490 1096 1161 846 1763 3650
αὐτόν εἰς Ἀντιόχειαν. ἐγένετο δὲ αὐτοὺς ἐνιαυτὸν ὅλον
him into Antioch. it happened And to them a year whole

4863 1722 3588 1577 2532 1321 3793 2425
συναχθῆναι ἐν τῇ ἐκκλησίᾳ καὶ διδάξαι ὄχλον ἱκανόν, χρη-
were assembled in the church and taught crowd a considerable,

5537 5037 4412 1722 490 3588 3101 5546
ματίσαι τε πρῶτον ἐν Ἀντιοχείᾳ τοὺς μαθητὰς Χριστιανούς.
were called and first in Antioch the disciples Christians.

1722 3778 11613588 2250 2718 575 2414
27 Ἐν ταύταις δὲ ταῖς ἡμέραις κατῆλθον ἀπὸ Ἱεροσολύμων
in these And days came down from Jerusalem

4396 1519 490 ‘450 1161 1520 1537 846 3686
προφῆται εἰς Ἀντιόχειαν. 28 ἀναστὰς δὲ εἷς ἐξ αὐτῶν ὀνόματι
prophets to Antioch. having risen And one of them by name

13 4591 1223 3588 4151 3042 3173 3195
Ἄγαβος, ἐσήμανε διὰ τοῦ Πνεύματος λιμὸν μέγαν μέλλειν
Agabus, signified through the Spirit a famine great to be about

1510 1909 3650 3588 3625 3748 2532 1096 1909
ἔσεσθαι ἐφ' ὅλην τὴν οἰκουμένην· ὅστις καὶ ἐγένετο ἐπὶ
to be over all the inhabited earth; which also happened on

King James Version

arose about Stephen travelled as far as Phenice, and Cyprus, and Antioch, preaching the word to none but unto the Jews only.

20 And some of them were men of Cyprus and Cyrene, which, when they were come to Antioch, spake unto the Grecians, preaching the Lord Jesus.
21 And the hand of the Lord was with them: and a great number believed, and turned unto the Lord.

22. Then tidings of these things came unto the ears of the church which was in Jerusalem: and they sent forth Barnabas, that he should go as far as Antioch.
23 Who, when he came, and had seen the grace of God, was glad, and exhorted them all, that with purpose of heart they would cleave unto the Lord.
24 For he was a good man, and full of the Holy Ghost and of faith: and much people was added unto the Lord.

25 Then departed Barnabas to Tarsus, for to seek Saul:
26 And when he had found him, he brought him unto Antioch. And it came to pass, that a whole year they assembled themselves with the church, and taught much people. And the disciples were called Christians first in Antioch.

27. And in these days came prophets from Jerusalem unto Antioch.
28 And there stood up one of them named Agabus, and signified by the Spirit that there should be great dearth throughout all the world: which came to pass in the days of

Literal Translation

Claudius Caesar's (time).
29 And as any was prospered, the disciples, each of them, determined to send for ministry to those brothers living in Judea,
30 which they also did, sending to the elders through (the) hand of Barnabas and of Saul.

Acts 11:29

2804 2541 3588 1161 3101 2531 2141 5100
Κλαυδίου Καίσαρος. 29 τῶν δὲ μαθητῶν καθὼς ηὐπορεῖτό τις,
of Claudius Caesar's (time). the And disciples as was prospered any,

3724 1538 846 1519 1248 3992 3588 2730
ὥρισαν ἕκαστος αὐτῶν εἰς διακονίαν πέμψαι τοῖς κατοι-
determined each of them for ministration to send to those living

1722 3588 2449 80 3739 2532 4160 649
κοῦσιν ἐν τῇ Ἰουδαίᾳ ἀδελφοῖς· 30 ὃ καὶ ἐποίησαν ἀποστεί-
in Judea brothers; which also they did sending

4314 3588 4245 1223 5495 921 2532
λαντες πρὸς τοὺς πρεσβυτέρους διὰ χειρὸς Βαρνάβα καὶ
to the elders through (the) hand of Barnabas and

4569
Σαύλου.
of Saul.

King James Version

Claudius Caesar.
29 Then the disciples, every man according to his ability, determined to send relief unto the brethren which dwelt in Judaea:

30 Which also they did, and sent it to the elders by the hands of Barnabas and Saul.

Acts 12

1. And at that time Herod the king threw on the hands to oppress some of those from the church.
2 And with a sword he did away with James the brother of John.
3 And seeing that it was pleasing to the Jews, he added also to seize Peter, and they were (the) days of Unleavened (Bread)
4 whom also capturing, he put (him) into prison, delivering (him) to four sets of four soldiers to guard him, intending to bring him up to the people after the Passover.

5 Then Peter was indeed kept in the prison, but fervent prayer was being made by the church to God on his behalf.

6 But when Herod was about to lead him out, in that night Peter was sleeping between two soldiers, having been bound with two chains, also guards were keeping the prison before the door.

7 And, behold! An angel of (the) Lord stood by, and a light shone in the building. And striking Peter's side, he raised him up, saying, Rise up in haste! And the chains fell off

Acts 12

2596 1565 1161 3588 2540 1911 2264 3588 935
1. Κατ' ἐκεῖνον δὲ τὸν καιρὸν ἐπέβαλεν Ἡρῴδης ὁ βασιλεὺς
at that And time threw on Herod the king

3588 5495 2559 5100 3588 575 3588 1577 337 1161
τὰς χεῖρας κακῶσαί τινας τῶν ἀπὸ τῆς ἐκκλησίας. 2 ἀνεῖλε δὲ
the hands to oppress some of those from the church. he killed And

2385 3588 80 2491 3162 2532 1492 3754
Ἰάκωβον τὸν ἀδελφὸν Ἰωάννου μαχαίρᾳ. 3 καὶ ἰδὼν ὅτι ἀρε-
James the brother of John with a sword. And seeing that

701 2076 3588 2453 4369 4815 2532 4074
στόν ἐστι τοῖς Ἰουδαίοις, προσέθετο συλλαβεῖν καὶ Πέτρον·
pleasing it is to the Jews, he added to seize also Peter;

2258 1161 2250 3588 106 3739 2532 4084 5087 1519 5438
ἦσαν δὲ ἡμέραι τῶν ἀζύμων· 4 ὃν καὶ πιάσας ἔθετο εἰς φυλακήν,
were and days of unleaven; whom also capturing he put into prison,

3860 5064 5069 4757 5442
παραδοὺς τέσσαρσι τετραδίοις στρατιωτῶν φυλάσσειν
delivering (him) to four quaternions of soldiers to guard

846 1014 3326 3588 3957 321 846 3588
αὐτόν, βουλόμενος μετὰ τὸ πάσχα ἀναγαγεῖν αὐτὸν τῷ
him, intending after the Passover to bring up him to the

2992 3588 3303 3767 4074 5083 1722 3588 5438 4335
λαῷ. 5 ὁ μὲν οὖν Πέτρος ἐτηρεῖτο ἐν τῇ φυλακῇ· προσευχὴ
people. indeed Then Peter was being kept in the prison. prayer

1161 2258 1618 1096 5259 3588 1577 4314 3588 2316
δὲ ἦν ἐκτενὴς γινομένη ὑπὸ τῆς ἐκκλησίας πρὸς τὸν Θεὸν
But was earnestly being made by the church to God

5228 846 3753 1161 3195 846 4254 3588 2264 3588
ὑπὲρ αὐτοῦ. 6 ὅτε δὲ ἔμελλεν αὐτὸν προάγειν ὁ Ἡρῴδης, τῇ
on behalf of him. when And was about him to lead out Herod,

3571 1565 2258 3588 4074 2837 3342 1417 4757
νυκτὶ ἐκείνῃ ἦν ὁ Πέτρος κοιμώμενος μεταξὺ δύο στρατιω-
in night that was Peter sleeping between two soldiers,

1210 254 1417 5441 5037 4253 3588 2374
τῶν, δεδεμένος ἁλύσεσι δυσί· φύλακές τε πρὸ τῆς θύρας
having been bound with chains two; guards and before the door

5083 3588 5438 2532 2400 32 2962 2186 2532
ἐτήρουν τὴν φυλακήν. 7 καὶ ἰδού, ἄγγελος Κυρίου ἐπέστη, καὶ
were keeping the prison. And behold! An angel of (the) Lord stood by, and

5457 2989 1722 3588 3612 3960 1161 3588 4125 3588
φῶς ἔλαμψεν ἐν τῷ οἰκήματι· πατάξας δὲ τὴν πλευρὰν τοῦ
light shone in the building. striking And the side

4074 1453 846 3004 450 1722 5034 2532 1601
Πέτρου, ἤγειρεν αὐτὸν λέγων, Ἀνάστα ἐν τάχει. καὶ ἐξέπεσον
of Peter, he raised him saying, Rise up in haste! And fell off

Acts 12

1. Now about that time Herod the king stretched forth (his) hands to vex certain of the church.
2 And he killed James the brother of John with the sword.
3 And because he saw it pleased the Jews, he proceeded further to take Peter also. (Then were the days of unleavened bread.)
4 And when he had apprehended him, he put (him) in prison, and delivered (him) to four quaternions of soldiers to keep him; intending after Easter to bring him forth to the people.

5 Peter therefore was kept in prison: but prayer was made without ceasing of the church unto God for him.

6 And when Herod would have brought him forth, the same night Peter was sleeping between two soldiers, bound with two chains: and the keepers before the door kept the prison.

7 And, behold, the angel of the Lord came upon (him), and a light shined in the prison: and he smote Peter on the side, and raised him up, saying, Arise up quickly. And his chains fell off

Literal Translation

of him the chains from (his) hands.
8 And the angel said to him, Gird yourself, and bind under your sandals. And he did so. And he said to him, Throw around your garment and follow me.

9 And going out, he was following him, and did not know that this happening through the angel was true, but he thought he saw a vision.
10 And going through a first and a second guard, they came on the iron gate leading into the city, which opened to them of itself. And going out, they went on one street; and instantly the angel withdrew from him.

11 And having come, Peter said within himself, Now I know truly that (the) Lord sent out His angel and plucked me out of Herod's hand, and (out) of all the expectation of the people of the Jews.

12 And considering, he came onto the house of Mary the mother of John, the (one) being surnamed Mark, where many were gathered together, and praying.
13 And Peter (was) knocking (at) the door of the porch, (and) a slave-girl by name Rhoda came near to answer (the door).

14 And recognizing Peter's voice, from the joy she did not open the porch, but running in (she) reported Peter (was) standing before the porch.
15 But they said to her, You are raving. But she insisted, holding (it) to be so. And they said, It is his angel.

16 But Peter kept on

Acts 12:8

846 3588 254 1537 3588 5495 2036 5037 3588 32 4314
αὐτοῦ αἱ ἁλύσεις ἐκ τῶν χειρῶν. 8 εἶπέ τε ὁ ἄγγελος πρὸς
of him the chains from the hands. said And the angel to

846 4024 2532 5265 3588 4547 4675 4160
αὐτόν, Περίζωσαι καὶ ὑπόδησαι τὰ σανδάλιά σου. ἐποίησε
him, Gird yourself and bind under the sandals of you. he did

1161 3779 2532 3004 846 4016 3588 2440 4675 2532
δὲ οὕτω. καὶ λέγει αὐτῷ, Περιβαλοῦ τὸ ἱμάτιόν σου, καὶ
And so. And he says to him, Throw around the garment of you, and

190 3427 2532 1831 190 846 2532 3756 1492 3754
ἀκολούθει μοι. 9 καὶ ἐξελθὼν ἠκολούθει αὐτῷ· καὶ οὐκ ᾔδει ὅτι
follow me. And going out he was following him; and not knew that

227 2076 3588 1096 1223 3588 32 1380 1161 3705
ἀληθές ἐστι τὸ γινόμενον διὰ τοῦ ἀγγέλου, ἐδόκει δὲ ὅραμα
true it is that happening through the angel, he thought but a vision

991 1330 1161 4413 5438 2532 1208 2064
βλέπειν. 10 διελθόντες δὲ πρώτην φυλακὴν καὶ δευτέραν, ἦλθον
to see. going through And (the) first guard and (the) second, they came

1909 3588 4439 3588 4603 3588 5342 1519 3588 4172
ἐπὶ τὴν πύλην τὴν σιδηρᾶν, τὴν φέρουσαν εἰς τὴν πόλιν,
on the gate iron, leading into the city,

3748 844 455 846 2532 1831 4281
ἥτις αὐτομάτη ἠνοίχθη αὐτοῖς· καὶ ἐξελθόντες προῆλθον
which of itself opened to them. And going out they went on

4505 3391 2532 2112 868 3588 32 575 846 2532 3588
ῥύμην μίαν, καὶ εὐθέως ἀπέστη ὁ ἄγγελος ἀπ' αὐτοῦ. 11 καὶ ὁ
street one, and instantly withdrew the angel from him. And

4074 1096 1722 1438 2036 3568 1492 230 3754
Πέτρος, γενόμενος ἐν ἑαυτῷ, εἶπε, Νῦν οἶδα ἀληθῶς ὅτι
Peter, having come within himself, said, Now I know truly that

1821 2962 3588 32 846 2532 1807 3165 1537
ἐξαπέστειλε Κύριος τὸν ἄγγελον αὐτοῦ, καὶ ἐξείλετό με ἐκ
sent out (the) Lord the angel of Him, and plucked me out of

5495 2264 2532 3956 3588 4329 3588 2992 3588
χειρὸς Ἡρώδου καὶ πάσης τῆς προσδοκίας τοῦ λαοῦ τῶν
(the) hand of Herod, and of all the expectation of the people of the

2453 4894 5037 2064 1909 3588 3614 3137 3588
Ἰουδαίων. 12 συνιδών τε ἦλθεν ἐπὶ τὴν οἰκίαν Μαρίας τῆς
Jews. considering And he came onto the house of Mary the

3384 2491 3588 1941 3138 3757 2258
μητρὸς Ἰωάννου τοῦ ἐπικαλουμένου Μάρκου, οὗ ἦσαν
mother of John the (one) surnamed Mark where were

2425 4867 2532 4336 2925 1161
ἱκανοὶ συνηθροισμένοι καὶ προσευχόμενοι. 13 κρούσαντος δὲ
many gathered together and praying. knocking And

3588 4074 3588 2374 3588 4440 4334 3814
τοῦ Πέτρου τὴν θύραν τοῦ πυλῶνος, προσῆλθε παιδίσκη
Peter (at) the door of the porch, came near a slave-girl

5219 3686 4498 2532 1921 3588 5456 3588
ὑπακοῦσαι, ὀνόματι Ῥόδη. 14 καὶ ἐπιγνοῦσα τὴν φωνὴν τοῦ
to answer(the door),by name Rhoda. And recognizing the voice

4074 575 3588 5479 3756 455 3588 4440 1532
Πέτρου, ἀπὸ τῆς χαρᾶς οὐκ ἤνοιξε τὸν πυλῶνα, εἰσδραμοῦσα
of Peter, from the joy not she opened the porch, running

1161 518 2476 3588 4074 4253 3588 4440 3588 1161
δὲ ἀπήγγειλεν ἑστάναι τὸν Πέτρον πρὸ τοῦ πυλῶνος. 15 οἱ δὲ
but reported to stand Peter before the porch. they But

4314 846 2036 3105 3588 1161 1340 3779 2192
πρὸς αὐτὴν εἶπον, Μαίνῃ. ἡ δὲ διϊσχυρίζετο οὕτως ἔχειν.
to her said, You are raving. she But insisted so (it) to hold.

3588 1161 3004 3588 32 846 2076 3588 1161 4074 1961
οἱ δ' ἔλεγον, Ὁ ἄγγελος αὐτοῦ ἐστιν. 16 ὁ δὲ Πέτρος ἐπέμενε
they And said, The angel of him it is. But Peter kept on

King James Version

from (his) hands.
8 And the angel said unto him, Gird thyself, and bind on thy sandals. And so he did. And he saith unto him, Cast thy garment about thee, and follow me.

9 And he went out, and followed him; and wist not that it was true which was done by the angel; but thought he saw a vision.
10 When they were past the first and the second ward, they came unto the iron gate that leadeth unto the city; which opened to them of his own accord: and they went out, and passed on through one street; and forthwith the angel departed from him.
11 And when Peter was come to himself, he said, Now I know of a surety, that the Lord hath sent his angel, and hath delivered me out of the hand of Herod, and (from) all the expectation of the people of the Jews.

12. And when he had considered (the thing), he came to the house of Mary the mother of John, whose surname was Mark; where many were gathered together praying.
13 And as Peter knocked at the door of the gate, a damsel came to hearken, named Rhoda.

14 And when she knew Peter's voice, she opened not the gate for gladness, but ran in, and told how Peter stood before the gate.

15 And they said unto her, Thou art mad. But she constantly affirmed that it was even so. Then said they, It is his angel.

16 But Peter continued

Literal Translation **Acts 12:17** ***King James Version***

knocking. And having opened, they saw him and were amazed.
17 And signaling to them with the hand to be silent, he related to them how the Lord led him out of the prison. And he said, Report these things to James and the brothers. And going out, he went to another place.

18 And day having come, there was not a little tumult among the soldiers, What, then, had become of Peter?

19 And searching for him, and not finding (him), examining the guards, Herod commanded them to be led away. And going down from Judea to Caesarea, (he) stayed.

20. And Herod was in bitter hostility with (the) Tyrians and Sidonians. But with one passion they came to him. And persuading Blastus, the (one) over the king's bedroom, they begged peace, because their country was feeding from the royal (bounty).
21 And on a set day, having put on regal apparel, and sitting on the tribunal, Herod made a speech to them.

22 And the mass (of people) cried out, A voice of a god, and not of a man!
23 And immediately an angel of (the) Lord struck him, because he did not give the glory to God. And becoming worm-eaten, his soul went out.

24. But the Word of God grew and increased.
25 And Barnabas and Saul returned to Jerusalem, having fulfilled the service, and having taken with (them) John

2925 455 1161 1492 846 2532 1839 2678
κρούων· ἀνοίξαντες δὲ εἶδον αὐτὸν, καὶ ἐξέστησαν. 17 κατα-
knocking; having opened and they saw him, and were amazed. signal-

1161 846 3588 5495 4601 1334 846 4459 3588
σείσας δὲ αὐτοῖς τῇ χειρὶ σιγᾷν, διηγήσατο αὐτοῖς πῶς ὁ
ing And to them with the hand to be silent, he related to them how the

2962 846 1806 1537 3588 5438 2036 1161 518
Κύριος αὐτὸν ἐξήγαγεν ἐκ τῆς φυλακῆς. εἶπέ δέ, Ἀπαγγεί-
Lord him led out from the prison. he said And, Report

2385 2532 3588 80 5023 2532 1831 4198
λατε Ἰακώβῳ καὶ τοῖς ἀδελφοῖς ταῦτα. καὶ ἐξελθὼν ἐπορεύθη
to James and the brothers these things. And going out he went away

1519 2087 5117 1096 1161 2250 2258 5017 3756
εἰς ἕτερον τόπον. 18 γενομένης δὲ ἡμέρας, ἦν τάραχος οὐκ
to another place. having come And day there was tumult not

3641 1722 3588 4757 5101 686 3588 4074 1096
ὀλίγος ἐν τοῖς στρατιώταις, τί ἄρα ὁ Πέτρος ἐγένετο.
a little among the soldiers, what then (of) Peter had become.

2264 1161 1934 846 2532 3361 2147 350
19 Ἡρῴδης δὲ ἐπιζητήσας αὐτὸν καὶ μὴ εὑρών, ἀνακρίνας
Herod And searching for him and not finding, examining

3588 5441 2753 520 2532 2718 575 3588
τοὺς φύλακας, ἐκέλευσεν ἀπαχθῆναι. καὶ κατελθὼν ἀπὸ τῆς
the guards, commanded to be led away. And going down from

2449 1519 3588 2542 1304
Ἰουδαίας εἰς τὴν Καισάρειαν διέτριβεν.
Judea to Caesarea stayed.

2258 1161 3588 2264 2371 5183 2532 4606
20. Ἦν δὲ ὁ Ἡρώδης θυμομαχῶν Τυρίοις καὶ Σιδωνίοις·
was And Herod in bitter hostility with Tyrians and Sidonians.

3661 1161 3918 4314 846 2532 3982 986
ὁμοθυμαδὸν δὲ παρῆσαν πρὸς αὐτόν, καὶ πείσαντες Βλάστον
with one passion But they came to him, and persuading Blastus

3588 1909 3588 2846 3588 935 154 1515 1223 3588
τὸν ἐπὶ τοῦ κοιτῶνος τοῦ βασιλέως, ᾐτοῦντο εἰρήνην, διὰ τὸ
the (one) over the bedroom of the king, they asked peace, because of the

5142 846 3588 5561 575 3588 937 5002 1161
τρέφεσθαι αὐτῶν τὴν χώραν ἀπὸ τῆς βασιλικῆς. 21 τακτῇ δὲ
feeding of them the country from the royal (bounty). on a set And

2250 3588 2264 1746 2066 937 2532 2523
ἡμέρᾳ ὁ Ἡρώδης ἐνδυσάμενος ἐσθῆτα βασιλικὴν, καὶ καθίσας
day Herod having put on apparel regal, and sitting

1909 3588 968 1215 4314 846 3588 1161 1218
ἐπὶ τοῦ βήματος, ἐδημηγόρει πρὸς αὐτούς. 22 ὁ δὲ δῆμος
on the tribunal, made a speech to them. the And mass

2019 2316 5456 2532 3756 444 3916 1161
ἐπεφώνει, Θεοῦ φωνὴ καὶ οὐκ ἀνθρώπου. 23 παραχρῆμα δὲ
cried out, of a god A voice and not of a man. immediately And

3960 846 32 2962 473 3739 3756 1325 3588
ἐπάταξεν αὐτὸν ἄγγελος Κυρίου, ἀνθ' ὧν οὐκ ἔδωκε τὴν
struck him an angel of (the) Lord, because not he gave the

1391 3588 2316 2532 1096 4662 1634
δόξαν τῷ Θεῷ· καὶ γενόμενος σκωληκόβρωτος ἐξέψυξεν.
glory to God; and becoming worm-eaten his soul went out.

3588 1161 3056 3588 2316 837 2532 4129
24. Ὁ δὲ λόγος τοῦ Θεοῦ ηὔξανε καὶ ἐπληθύνετο.
the But Word of God grew and increased.

921 1161 2532 4569 5290 1519 2419
25. Βαρνάβας δὲ καὶ Σαῦλος ὑπέστρεψαν εἰς Ἱερουσαλήμ,
Barnabas And and Saul returned to Jerusalem,

4137 3588 1248 4838 2532 2491
πληρώσαντες τὴν διακονίαν, συμπαραλαβόντες καὶ Ἰωάννην
having fulfilled the ministry, having taken with (them) and John

knocking: and when they had opened (the door), and saw him, they were astonished.
17 But he, beckoning unto them with the hand to hold their peace, declared unto them how the Lord had brought him out of the prison. And he said, Go shew these things unto James, and to the brethren. And he departed, and went into another place.
18 Now as soon as it was day, there was no small stir among the soldiers, what was become of Peter.

19 And when Herod had sought for him, and found him not, he examined the keepers, and commanded that (they) should be put to death. And he went down from Judaea to Caesarea, and (there) abode.

20. And Herod was highly displeased with them of Tyre and Sidon: but they came with one accord to him, and, having made Blastus the king's chamberlain their friend, desired peace; because their country was nourished by the king's (country).
21 And upon a set day Herod, arrayed in royal apparel, sat upon his throne, and made an oration unto them.

22 And the people gave a shout, (saying, It is) the voice of a god, and not of a man.
23 And immediately the angel of the Lord smote him, because he gave not God the glory: and he was eaten of worms, and gave up the ghost.

24. But the word of God grew and multiplied.
25 And Barnabas and Saul returned from Jerusalem, when they had fulfilled (their) ministry, and took with them John,

Literal Translation | **Acts 13:1** | *King James Version*

the (one) being surnamed Mark.

3588 1941 3138
τὸν ἐπικληθέντα Μᾶρκον.
the (one) being surnamed Mark.

whose surname was Mark.

Acts 13

1. And in Antioch some among the existing church were prophets and teachers, both Barnabas and Simeon, he being called Niger, and Lucius the Cyrenian, and Manaen (the) foster-brother of Herod the tetrarch, and Saul.
2 And (as) they were serving the Lord and fasting, the Holy Spirit said, Now separate both Barnabas and Saul to Me, to the work to which I have called them.

3 Then, having fasted and having prayed, and placing hands on them, they let (them) go.

4. Then these indeed sent out by the Holy Spirit went down to Seleucia, and from there sailed away to Cyprus.

5 And having been in Salamis, they proclaimed the Word of God in the synagogues of the Jews. And they also had John as a helper.
6 And passing through the island as far as Paphos, they found a certain conjurer, a false prophet, a Jew named Bar-jesus.

7 (He) was with the proconsul, Sergius Paulus, an intelligent man. This one calling Barnabas and Saul to him, he sought to hear the Word of God.

8 But withstood them Elymas, the conjurer for so was translated

Acts 13

2258 1161 5100 1722 490 2596 3588 5607 1577
1. Ἦσαν δὲ τινες ἐν Ἀντιοχείᾳ κατὰ τὴν οὖσαν ἐκκλησίαν
were And some in Antioch among the existing church

4396 2532 1320 3588 5037 921 2532 4826 3588
προφῆται καὶ διδάσκαλοι ὅ τε Βαρνάβας καὶ Συμεὼν ὁ
prophets and teachers, both Barnabas and Simeon, he

2564 3526 2532 3066 3588 2956 3127 5037
καλούμενος Νίγερ, καὶ Λούκιος ὁ Κυρηναῖος, Μαναήν τε
having been called Niger, and Lucius the Cyrenian, Manaen and

2264 3588 5076 4939 2532 4569 3008
Ἡρώδου τοῦ τετράρχου σύντροφος, καὶ Σαῦλος. 2 λειτουρ-
of Herod the tetrarch foster-brother, and Saul. serving

1161 846 3588 2962 2532 3522 2036 3588
γούντων δὲ αὐτῶν τῷ Κυρίῳ καὶ νηστευόντων, εἶπε τὸ
And they the Lord and fasting, said the

4151 3588 40 873 1211 3427 3588 5037 921 2532 3588
Πνεῦμα τὸ Ἅγιον, Ἀφορίσατε δή μοι τόν τε Βαρνάβαν καὶ τὸν
Spirit Holy, separate Now to me both Barnabas and

4569 1519 3588 2041 3739 4341 846 5119 3522
Σαῦλον εἰς τὸ ἔργον ὃ προσκέκλημαι αὐτούς. 3 τότε νηστεύ-
Saul to the work to which I have called them. Then having

2532 4336 2532 2007 3588 5495 846
σαντες καὶ προσευξάμενοι καὶ ἐπιθέντες τὰς χεῖρας αὐτοῖς,
fasted and having prayed and placing on the hands to them,

630
ἀπέλυσαν.
they let them go.

3778 3303 3767 1599 5259 3588 4151 3588
4. Οὗτοι μὲν οὖν, ἐκπεμφθέντες ὑπὸ τοῦ Πνεύματος τοῦ
These indeed then, sent out by the Spirit

40 2718 1519 3588 4581 1564 5037 636
Ἁγίου, κατῆλθον εἰς τὴν Σελεύκειαν, ἐκεῖθέν τε ἀπέπλευσαν
Holy, went down to Seleucia, from there and sailed away

1519 3588 2954 2532 1096 1722 4529 2605 3588
εἰς τὴν Κύπρον. 5 καὶ γενόμενοι ἐν Σαλαμῖνι, κατήγγελλον τὸν
to Cyprus. And having come in Salamis, they proclaimed the

3056 3588 2316 1722 3588 4864 3588 2453 2192 1161
λόγον τοῦ Θεοῦ ἐν ταῖς συναγωγαῖς τῶν Ἰουδαίων· εἶχον δὲ
Word of God in the synagogues of the Jews. they had And

2532 2491 5257 1330 1161 3588 3520 891
καὶ Ἰωάννην ὑπηρέτην. 6 διελθόντες δὲ τὴν νῆσον ἄχρι
also John (as) assistant. passing through And the island as far as

3974 2147 5100 3097 5578 2453 3739
Πάφου εὗρόν τινα μάγον ψευδοπροφήτην Ἰουδαῖον, ᾧ
Paphos, they found a certain conjurer, a false prophet, a Jew, whose

3686 919 3739 2258 4862 3588 446 4588 3972
ὄνομα Βαριησοῦς, 7 ὃς ἦν σὺν τῷ ἀνθυπάτῳ Σεργίῳ Παύλῳ,
name (was) Bar-jesus, who was with the proconsul Sergius Paulus,

435 4908 3778 4341 921 2532
ἀνδρὶ συνετῷ. οὗτος προσκαλεσάμενος Βαρνάβαν καὶ
man an intelligent. This one calling to (him) Barnabas and

4569 1934 191 3588 3056 3588 2316 436
Σαῦλον ἐπεζήτησεν ἀκοῦσαι τὸν λόγον τοῦ Θεοῦ· 8 ἀνθίστατο
Saul sought to hear the Word of God. withstood

1161 846 1681 3588 3097 3779 1063 3177 3588
δὲ αὐτοῖς Ἐλύμας, ὁ μάγος (οὕτω γὰρ μεθερμηνεύεται τὸ
But them Elymas, the conjurer, so for was translated

Acts 13

1. Now there were in the church that was at Antioch certain prophets and teachers; as Barnabas, and Simeon that was called Niger, and Lucius of Cyrene, and Manaen, which had been brought up with Herod the tetrarch, and Saul.
2 As they ministered to the Lord, and fasted, the Holy Ghost said, Separate me Barnabas and Saul for the work whereunto I have called them.

3 And when they had fasted and prayed, and laid (their) hands on them, they sent (them) away.

4. So they, being sent forth by the Holy Ghost, departed unto Seleucia; and from thence they sailed to Cyprus.

5 And when they were at Salamis, they preached the word of God in the synagogues of the Jews: and they had also John to (their) minister.
6 And when they had gone through the isle unto Paphos, they found a certain sorcerer, a false prophet, a Jew, whose name (was) Barjesus:
7 Which was with the deputy of the country, Sergius Paulus, a prudent man; who called for Barnabas and Saul, and desired to hear the word of God.

8 But Elymas the sorcerer (for so is his name by interpretation)

Literal Translation

his name, seeking to turn awaythe proconsul from the faith.

9 But Saul, who (is) also (called) Paul, being filled with (the) Holy Spirit, and looking intently to him,
10 said, O son of the Devil, full of all guile and of all cunning, enemy of all righteousness, will you not stop perverting the right ways of (the) Lord?

11 And now, behold! (The) hand of the Lord (is) on you, and you will be blind, not seeing the sun until a time. And instantly a mist and darkness fell on him, and going about he sought (some to) lead (him) by the hand.

12 Then seeing the thing occurring, the proconsul believed, being astounded at the doctrine of the Lord.

13. And putting out from Paphos (with) those around (him), Paul came to Perga of Pamphylia. And departing from them, John returned to Jerusalem.
14. But going through from Perga, they arrived to Antioch-Pisidia, and going into the synagogue on the day of the sabbaths, they sat down.

15 And after the reading of the Law, and of the Prophets, the synagogue rulers sent to them, saying, Men, brothers, if there is a word of exhortation to the people, speak.

16 And rising up, and signaling with (his) hand, Paul said: Men, Israelites, and the ones fearing God, hear..

Acts 13:9

3686 846 2212 1294 3588 446 575 3588
ὄνομα αὐτοῦ], ζητῶν διαστρέψαι τὸν ἀνθύπατον ἀπὸ τῆς
name of him, seeking to turn away the proconsul from the

4102 4569 1161 3588 2532 3972 4130 4151
πίστεως. 9 Σαῦλος δέ, ὁ καὶ Παῦλος, πλησθεὶς Πνεύματος
faith. Saul But, who also (is) Paul, being filled with (the) Spirit

40 2532 816 1519 846 2036 5599 4134 3956
Ἁγίου, καὶ ἀτενίσας εἰς αὐτὸν 10 εἶπεν, Ὦ πλήρης παντὸς
Holy, and looking intently to him said, O full of all

1388 2532 3956 4468 5207 1228 2190 3956
δόλου καὶ πάσης ῥᾳδιουργίας, υἱὲ διαβόλου, ἐχθρὲ πάσης
deceit and of all cunning, son of the devil, enemy of all

1343 3756 3973 1294 3588 3598 2962 3588
δικαιοσύνης, οὐ παύσῃ διαστρέφων τὰς ὁδοὺς Κυρίου τὰς
righteousness, not will you cease turning away the ways of (the) Lord

2117 2532 3568 2400 5495 3588 2962 1909 4571 2532 2071
εὐθείας; 11 καὶ νῦν ἰδού, χεὶρ τοῦ Κυρίου ἐπὶ σέ, καὶ ἔσῃ
right? And now behold! hand of the Lord (is) on you, and you will be

5185 3361 991 3588 2246 891 2540 3916 1161
τυφλὸς, μὴ βλέπων τὸν ἥλιον ἄχρι καιροῦ. παραχρῆμά δὲ
blind, not seeing the sun until a time. instantly And

1968 1909 846 887 2532 4655 2532 4013 2212
ἐπέπεσεν ἐπ' αὐτὸν ἀχλὺς καὶ σκότος, καὶ περιάγων ἐζήτει
fell on him a mist and darkness, and going about he sought

5497 5119 1492 3588 446 3588 1096 4100
χειραγωγούς. 12 τότε ἰδὼν ὁ ἀνθύπατος τὸ γεγονὸς ἐπίστευσεν,
leaders by hand. Then seeing the proconsul the thing occurring believed,

1605 1909 3588 1322 3588 2962
ἐκπλησσόμενος ἐπὶ τῇ διδαχῇ τοῦ Κυρίου.
being astounded at the doctrine of the Lord.

321 1161 575 3588 3974 3588 4012 3588 3972 2064
13.'Αναχθέντες δὲ ἀπὸ τῆς Πάφου οἱ περὶ τὸν Παῦλον ἦλθον
setting sail And from Paphos those around Paul came

1519 4011 3588 3828 2491 1161 672 575
εἰς Πέργην τῆς Παμφυλίας. Ἰωάννης δὲ ἀποχωρήσας ἀπ'
to Perga of Pamphylia. John And departing from

846 5290 1519 2414 846 1161 1330 575
αὐτῶν ὑπέστρεψεν εἰς Ἱεροσόλυμα. 14 αὐτοὶ δὲ διελθόντες ἀπὸ
them returned to Jerusalem. they And going through from

3588 4011 3854 1519 490 3588 4099 2532
τῆς Πέργης, παρεγένοντο εἰς Ἀντιόχειαν τῆς Πισιδίας, καὶ
Perga, arrived to Antioch the Pisidian. And

1525 1519 3588 4864 3588 2250 3588 4521
εἰσελθόντες εἰς τὴν συναγωγὴν τῇ ἡμέρᾳ τῶν σαββάτων,
going into the synagogue on the day of the Sabbaths,

2523 3326 1161 3588 320 3588 3551 2532 3588
ἐκάθισαν. 15 μετὰ δὲ τὴν ἀνάγνωσιν τοῦ νόμου καὶ τῶν
sat down. after And the reading of the Law and of the

4396 649 3588 752 4314 846
προφητῶν, ἀπέστειλαν οἱ ἀρχισυνάγωγοι πρὸς αὐτούς,
Prophets, sent forth the synagogue rulers to them,

3004 435 80 1487 2076 3056 1722 5213 3874
λέγοντες, Ἄνδρες ἀδελφοί, ἐι ἔστι λόγος ἐν ὑμῖν παρα-
saying, Men brothers, if is a word among you of ex-

4314 3588 2992 3004 450 1161 3972 2532
κλήσεως πρὸς τὸν λαόν, λέγετε. 16 ἀναστὰς δὲ Παῦλος, καὶ
hortation to the people, say (it). rising up And Paul, and

2678 3588 5495 2036
κατασείσας τῇ χειρὶ, εἶπεν,
signaling with the hand, he said,

435 2475 2532 3588 5399 3588 2316 191
Ἄνδρες Ἰσραηλῖται, καὶ οἱ φοβούμενοι τὸν Θεόν, ἀκού-
Men Israelites, and those fearing God, hear.

King James Version

withstood them, seeking to turn away the deputy from the faith.

9 Then Saul, (who also (is called) Paul,) filled with the Holy Ghost, set his eyes on him,
10 And said, O full of all subtilty and all mischief, (thou) child of the devil, (thou) enemy of all righteousness, wilt thou not cease to pervert the right ways of the Lord?

11 And now, behold, the hand of the Lord (is) upon thee, and thou shalt be blind, not seeing the sun for a season. And immediately there fell on him a mist and a darkness; and he went about seeking some to lead him by the hand.

12 Then the deputy, when he saw what was done, believed, being astonished at the doctrine of the Lord.

13. Now when Paul and his company loosed from Paphos, they came to Perga in Pamphylia: and John departing from them returned to Jerusalem.
14. But when they departed from Perga, they came to Antioch in Pisidia, and went into the synagogue on the sabbath day, and sat down.

15 And after the reading of the law and the prophets the rulers of the synagogue sent unto them, saying, (Ye) men (and) brethren, if ye have any word of exhortation for the people, say on.

16 Then Paul stood up, and beckoning with (his) hand said, Men of Israel, and ye that fear God, give audience.

Literal Translation

17 The God of this people Israel chose out our fathers, and lifted up the people in (their) visitation in (the) land (of) Egypt. And with a high arm, He brought them out of it.
18 And as forty years time (passed), He tenderly bore them in the wilderness.
19 And having pulled down seven nations in Canaan land, (He) gave their land to them as an inheritance.
20 And after these things, as four hundred and fifty years (passed), He gave judges until Samuel the prophet.
21 And from there they asked (for) a king. And God gave Saul (the) son of Kish to them, a man of (the) tribe of Benjamin, (for) forty years.
22 And removing him, He raised up to them David for a king, to whom also He said, witnessing, "I found David the (son) of Jesse (to be) a man according to My (own) heart, who will do all My desires." (See 1 Samuel 13:14)
23 Of the seed of this one, according to promise, God raised up to Israel a Savior, Jesus;
24 John going before to proclaim before (the) face of His entrance a baptism of repentance to all the people of Israel.
25 And as John fulfilled the course, he said, Whom do you suppose me to be? I am not (He), but, behold! "He comes after me, of whom I am not worthy to loosen the sandal of (His) feet." (John 1:27)
26 Men, brothers, sons of (the) race of Abraham, and the ones among you fearing God, to you the word of this salvation was sent.
27 For those

Acts 13:17

3588 2316 3588 2992 5127 2474 1586 3588
σατε. 17 ὁ Θεὸς τοῦ λαοῦ τούτου Ἰσραὴλ ἐξελέξατο τοὺς
The God people of this Israel chose out the

3962 2257 2532 3588 2992 5312 1722 3588 3940 1722 1093
πατέρας ἡμῶν, καὶ τὸν λαὸν ὕψωσεν ἐν τῇ παροικίᾳ ἐν γῇ
fathers of us, and the people lifted up in the visitation in land

125 2532 3326 1023 5308 1806 846 1537
Αἰγύπτῳ, καὶ μετὰ βραχίονος ὑψηλοῦ ἐξήγαγεν αὐτοὺς ἐξ
(of) Egypt, and with an arm high he brought out them from

846 2532 5613 5063 5550 5159
αὐτῆς. 18 καὶ ὡς τεσσαρακονταετῆ χρόνον ἐτροποφόρησεν
it. And as (passed) forty years time He tenderly bore

846 1722 3588 2048 2532 2507 1484 2033 1722 1093 5477
αὐτοὺς ἐν τῇ ἐρήμῳ. 19 καὶ καθελὼν ἔθνη ἑπτὰ ἐν γῇ Χανάαν,
them in the desert. And having pulled down nations seven in land Canaan,

2624 846 3588 1093 846 2532 3326 5023
κατεκληροδότησεν αὐτοῖς τὴν γῆν αὐτῶν. 20 καὶ μετὰ ταῦτα,
(He) gave as an inheritance to them the land of them. And after these things,

5613 2094 5071 2532 4004 1325 2923 2193
ὡς ἔτεσι τετρακοσίοις καὶ πεντήκοντα, ἔδωκε κριτὰς ἕως
as years four hundred and fifty, He gave judges until

4545 3588 4396 2547 154 935 2532
Σαμουὴλ τοῦ προφήτου. 21 κἀκεῖθεν ᾐτήσαντο βασιλέα, καὶ
Samuel the prophet. And from there they asked a king, and

1325 846 3588 2316 3588 4549 5207 2797 435 1537 5443
ἔδωκεν αὐτοῖς ὁ Θεὸς τὸν Σαοὺλ υἱὸν Κίς, ἄνδρα ἐκ φυλῆς
gave them God Saul (the) son of Kish, a man of (the) tribe

958 2094 5062 2532 3179 846 1453
Βενιαμίν, ἔτη τεσσεράκοντα. 22 καὶ μεταστήσας αὐτὸν, ἤγειρεν
of Benjamin, years forty. And removing him, He raised

846 3588 1138 1519 935 3739 2532 2036 3140 2147
αὐτοῖς τὸν Δαβὶδ εἰς βασιλέα, ᾧ καὶ εἶπε μαρτυρήσας, Εὗρον
to them David for a king, to whom also He said witnessing, I found

1138 3588 3588 2421 435 2596 3588 2588 3450 3739
Δαβὶδ τὸν τοῦ Ἰεσσαί, ἄνδρα κατὰ τὴν καρδίαν μου, ὃς
David the (son) of Jesse, a man according to the heart of Me, who

4160 3956 3588 2307 3450 5127 3588 2316 575 3588
ποιήσει πάντα τὰ θελήματά μου. 23 τούτου ὁ Θεὸς ἀπὸ τοῦ
will do all the desires of Me. Of this one God from the

4690 2596 1860 1453 3588 2474 4990
σπέρματος κατ' ἐπαγγελίαν ἤγειρε τῷ Ἰσραὴλ σωτῆρα
seed according to promise raised to Israel a Savior

2424 4296 2491 4253 4383 3588
Ἰησοῦν, 24 προκηρύξαντος Ἰωάννου πρὸ προσώπου τῆς
Jesus, previously proclaiming John before (the) face of the

1529 846 908 3341 3956 3588 2992 2474
εἰσόδου αὐτοῦ βάπτισμα μετανοίας παντὶ τῷ λαῷ Ἰσραήλ.
coming of Him a baptism of repentance to all the people of Israel.

5613 1161 4137 3588 2491 3588 1408 3004 5101 3165
25 ὡς δὲ ἐπλήρου ὁ Ἰωάννης τὸν δρόμον, ἔλεγε, Τίνα με
as And fulfilled John the course, he said, Whom me

5282 1511 3756 1510 1473 235 2400 2064 3326 1691
ὑπονοεῖτε εἶναι; οὐκ εἰμὶ ἐγώ. ἀλλ' ἰδού, ἔρχεται μετ' ἐμέ,
do you suppose to be? not am I (He). But behold! He comes after me,

3739 3756 1510 514 3588 5266 3588 4228 3089 435
οὗ οὐκ εἰμὶ ἄξιος τὸ ὑπόδημα τῶν ποδῶν λῦσαι. 26 ἄνδρες
of whom not I am worthy the sandal of the feet to loosen. Men

80 5207 1085 11 2532 3588 1722 5213 5399 3588
ἀδελφοί, υἱοὶ γένους Ἀβραάμ, καὶ οἱ ἐν ὑμῖν φοβούμενοι τὸν
brothers, sons of (the) race of Abraham, and those among you fearing

2316 5213 3588 3056 3588 4991 3778 649 3588 1063
Θεόν, ὑμῖν ὁ λόγος τῆς σωτηρίας ταύτης ἀπεστάλη. 27 οἱ γὰρ
God, to you the word of salvation this was sent. those For

King James Version

17 The God of this people of Israel chose our fathers, and exalted the people when they dwelt as strangers in the land of Egypt, and with an high arm brought he them out of it.
18 And about the time of forty years suffered he their manners in the wilderness.
19 And when he had destroyed seven nations in the land of Chanaan, he divided their land to them by lot.
20 And after that he gave (unto them) judges about the space of four hundred and fifty years, until Samuel the prophet.
21 And afterward they desired a king: and God gave unto them Saul the son of Cis, a man of the tribe of Benjamin, by the space of forty years.
22 And when he had removed him, he raised up unto them David to be their king; to whom also he gave testimony, and said, I have found David the (son) of Jesse, a man after mine own heart, which shall fulfil all my will.
23 Of this man's seed hath God according to (his) promise raised unto Israel a Saviour, Jesus:
24 When John had first preached before his coming the baptism of repentance to all the people of Israel.
25 And as John fulfilled his course, he said, Whom think ye that I am? I am not (he). But, behold, there cometh one after me, whose shoes of (his) feet I am not worthy to loose.
26 Men (and) brethren, children of the stock of Abraham, and whosoever among you feareth God, to you is the word of this salvation sent.
27 For they

Literal Translation

dwelling in Jerusalem, and their rulers, not knowing this One, and the voices of the prophets being read throughout every sabbath, condemning (Him), they fulfilled (the Scriptures).
28 And having found not one cause of death, they asked Pilate to do away with Him.

29 And when they finished all the things having been written concerning Him, taking (Him) down from the tree, they laid (Him) in a tomb.
30 But God raised Him from (the) dead;
31 who appeared for many days to those coming up with Him from Galilee to Jerusalem, who are witnesses of Him to the people.
32. And we preach the gospel to you, the promise having come to the fathers,

33 that this (promise) God has fulfilled to us, their children, raising up Jesus; as also it has been written in the second Psalm, "You are My Son, today I have begotten You." (Psa. 2:7)
34 And that He raised Him from (the) dead, no more being about to return to corruption, so He has said, "I will give You the holy things of the faithful David." (Isa. 55:3)
35 So He also said in another, "You will not give Your Holy One to see corruption." (Psa. 16:10)
36 For having served (his) own generation by the counsel of God, David truly fell asleep and was added to his fathers and saw corruption.
37 But (He) whom God raised up, (this One) did not see corruption.
38 Then let it be known to you, men, brothers, that through this One to you remission of sins

Acts 13:28

2730 1722 2419 2532 3588 758 846 5126
κατοικοῦντες ἐν Ἰερουσαλὴμ καὶ οἱ ἄρχοντες αὐτῶν, τοῦτον
dwelling in Jerusalem and the rulers of them, this One

50 2532 3588 5456 3588 4396 3588 2596 3956
ἀγνοήσαντες, καὶ τὰς φωνὰς τῶν προφητῶν τὰς κατὰ πᾶν
not knowing, and the voices of the prophets throughout every

4521 314 2919 4137 2532
σάββατον ἀναγινωσκομένας κρίναντες ἐπλήρωσαν. 28 καὶ
sabbath being read, having judged (Him) they fulfilled. And

3367 156 2288 2147 154 4091
μηδεμίαν αἰτίαν θανάτου εὑρόντες, ᾐτήσαντο Πιλάτον
not one cause of death having found, they asked Pilate

337 846 5613 1161 5055 537 3588 4012 846
ἀναιρεθῆναι αὐτόν. 29 ὡς δὲ ἐτέλεσαν ἅπαντα τὰ περὶ αὐτοῦ
to do away with Him. when And they finished all the things about Him

1125 2507 575 3588 3586 5087 1519 3419
γεγραμμένα, καθελόντες ἀπὸ τοῦ ξύλου, ἔθηκαν εἰς μνημεῖον.
having been written, taking down from the tree, they laid into a tomb.

3588 1161 2316 1453 846 1537 3498 3739 3700 1909 2250
30 ὁ δὲ Θεὸς ἤγειρεν αὐτὸν ἐκ νεκρῶν· 31 ὃς ὤφθη ἐπὶ ἡμέρας
But God raised Him out of (the) dead; who appeared on days

4119 3588 4872 846 575 3588 1056 1519
πλείους τοῖς συναναβᾶσιν αὐτῷ ἀπὸ τῆς Γαλιλαίας εἰς
many to those having come up with Him from Galilee to

2419 3748 1526 3144 846 4314 3588 2992 2532
Ἰερουσαλήμ, οἵτινες εἰσι μάρτυρες αὐτοῦ πρὸς τὸν λαόν. 32 καὶ
Jerusalem, who were witnesses of Him to the people. And

2249 5209 2097 3588 4314 3588 3962 1860
ἡμεῖς ὑμᾶς εὐαγγελιζόμεθα τὴν πρὸς τοὺς πατέρας ἐπαγ-
we (to) you preach the gospel the to the fathers promise

1096 3754 3778 3588 2316 1603 3588
γελίαν γενομένην, 33 ὅτι ταύτην ὁ Θεὸς ἐκπεπλήρωκε τοῖς
having come, that this (promise) God has fulfilled to the

5043 846 2254 450 2424 5613 2532 1722 3588 5568
τέκνοις αὐτῶν ἡμῖν, ἀναστήσας Ἰησοῦν· ὡς καὶ ἐν τῷ ψαλμῷ
children of them to us, raising up Jesus, as also in the Psalm

3588 1208 1125 5207 3450 1488 4771 1473 4594
τῷ δευτέρῳ γέγραπται, Υἱός μου εἶ σύ, ἐγὼ σήμερον
second it has been written, Son of Me are You, I today

1080 4571 3754 1161 450 846 1537 3498 3371
γεγέννηκά σε. 34 ὅτι δὲ ἀνέστησεν αὐτὸν ἐκ νεκρῶν, μηκέτι
have begotten You. that And He raised up Him out of (the) dead, no more

3195 5290 1519 1312 3779 2046 3754
μέλλοντα ὑποστρέφειν εἰς διαφθοράν, οὕτως εἴρηκεν ὅτι
being about to return to corruption, so He has said,

1325 5213 3588 3741 1138 3588 4103 1352 2532 1722 2087 3004
Δώσω ὑμῖν τὰ ὅσια Δαβὶδ τὰ πιστά. 35 διὸ καὶ ἐν ἑτέρῳ λέγει,
I will give You the holy things of David the faithful. So also in another He says,

3756 1325 3588 3741 4675 1492 1312 1138 3303 1063
Οὐ δώσεις τὸν ὅσιόν σου ἰδεῖν διαφθοράν. 36 Δαβὶδ μὲν γὰρ
Not You will give the Holy One of You to see corruption. David indeed For

2398 1074 5256 3588 3588 2316 1012 2837 2532
ἰδίᾳ γενεᾷ ὑπηρετήσας τῇ τοῦ Θεοῦ βουλῇ ἐκοιμήθη, καὶ
own generation having served by the of God counsel fell asleep, and

4369 4314 3588 3962 846 2532 1492 1312 3739
προσετέθη πρὸς τοὺς πατέρας αὐτοῦ καὶ εἶδε διαφθοράν· 37 ὃν
was added to the fathers of Him and saw corruption. (He) whom

1161 3588 2316 1453 3756 1492 1312 1110 3767 2077
δὲ ὁ Θεὸς ἤγειρεν, οὐκ εἶδε διαφθοράν. 38 γνωστὸν οὖν ἔστω
but God raised up, not He did see corruption. known Therefore let it be

5213 435 80 3754 1223 5127 5213 859 266
ὑμῖν, ἄνδρες ἀδελφοί, ὅτι διὰ τούτου ὑμῖν ἄφεσις ἁμαρτιῶν
to you, men brothers, that through this One to you remission of sins

King James Version

that dwell at Jerusalem, and their rulers, because they knew him not, nor yet the voices of the prophets which are read every sabbath day, they have fulfilled (them) in condemning (him).
28 And though they found no cause of death (in him), yet desired they Pilate that he should be slain.

29 And when they had fulfilled all that was written of him, they took (him) down from the tree, and laid (him) in a sepulchre.

30 But God raised him from the dead:
31 And he was seen many days of them which came up with him from Galilee to Jerusalem, who are his witnesses unto the people.
32 And we declare unto you glad tidings, how that the promise which was made unto the fathers,
33 God hath fulfilled the same unto us their children, in that he hath raised up Jesus again; as it is also written in the second psalm, Thou art my Son, this day have I begotten thee.
34 And as concerning that he raised him up from the dead, (now) no more to return to corruption, he said on this wise, I will give you the sure mercies of David.
35 Wherefore he saith also in another (psalm), Thou shalt not suffer thine Holy One to see corruption.
36 For David, after he had served his own generation by the will of God, fell on sleep, and was laid unto his fathers, and saw corruption:
37 But he, whom God raised again, saw no corruption.
38 Be it known unto you therefore, men (and) brethren, that through this man is preached unto you the forgiveness of sins:

Literal Translation **Acts 13:39** ***King James Version***

is proclaimed to you. And from all things from which you could not be justified in the Law of Moses,

39. everyone believing in this One is justified.
40 Then watch (that) the thing spoken in the Prophets may not come on you:
41 "Behold, (you) despisers, and marvel, and perish, because I work a work in your days, a work which you would in no way believe, if anyone declares (it) to you." (Hab.1:5)

2605 2532 575 3956 3739 3756 1410 1722 3588
καταγγέλλεται· καὶ ἀπὸ πάντων ὧν οὐκ ἠδυνήθητε ἐν τῷ
is proclaimed. And from all things which not you could in the

3551 3475 1344 1722 5129 3956 3588 4100
νόμῳ Μωσέως δικαιωθῆναι, 39 ἐν τούτῳ πᾶς ὁ πιστεύων
Law of Moses be justified, in this One everyone believing

1344 991 3767 3361 1904 1909 5209 3588 2046 1722
δικαιοῦται. 40 βλέπετε οὖν μὴ ἐπέλθῃ ἐφ' ὑμᾶς τὸ εἰρημένον ἐν
is justified. watch Then not come upon you that being spoken in

3588 4396 1492 3588 2707 2532 2296
τοῖς προφήταις, 41 Ἴδετε, οἱ καταφρονηταί, καὶ θαυμάσατε,
the Prophets, See, the despisers and marvel,

2532 853 3754 2041 1473 2038 1722 3588 2250
καὶ ἀφανίσθητε· ὅτι ἔργον ἐγὼ ἐργάζομαι ἐν ταῖς ἡμέραις
and vanish; because a work I work in the days

5216 2041 3739 3756 3361 4100 1437 5100 1555 5213
ὑμῶν, ἔργον ᾧ οὐ μὴ πιστεύσητε, ἐάν τις ἐκδιηγῆται ὑμῖν.
of you, a work which not at all you believe, if anyone declares (it) to you.

39 And by him all that believe are justified from all things, from which ye could not be justified by the law of Moses.
40 Beware therefore, lest that come upon you, which is spoken of in the prophets;
41 Behold, ye despisers, and wonder, and perish: for I work a work in your days, a work which ye shall in no wise believe, though a man declare it unto you.

42. But the Jews going out of the synagogue, the nations begged that these words be spoken to them on the next sabbath.

43 And the synagogue being broken up, many of the Jews and of the devout proselytes followed Paul and Barnabas, who speaking to them persuaded them to continue in the grace of God.

1826 1161 1537 3588 4864 3588 2453 3870
42. Ἐξιόντων δε ἐκ τῆς συναγωγῆς τῶν Ἰουδαίων, παρεκά-
going out And from the synagogue of the Jews, begged

3588 1484 1519 3588 3342 4521 2980 846
λουν τὰ ἔθνη εἰς τὸ μεταξὺ σάββατον λαληθῆναι αὐτοῖς
the nations in the next sabbath to be spoken to them

3588 4487 5023 3089 1161 3588 4864 190
τὰ ῥήματα ταῦτα. 43 λυθείσης δὲ τῆς συναγωγῆς, ἠκολούθησαν
words these. being broken And the synagogue, followed

4183 3588 2453 2532 3588 4576 4339 3588
πολλοὶ τῶν Ἰουδαίων καὶ τῶν σεβομένων προσηλύτων τῷ
many ot the Jews and of the devout proselytes

3972 2532 3588 921 3748 4354 846
Παύλῳ καὶ τῷ Βαρνάβᾳ· οἵτινες προσλαλοῦντες αὐτοῖς,
Paul and Barnabas; who speaking to them,

3982 846 1961 3588 5485 3588 2316
ἔπειθον αὐτοὺς ἐπιμένειν τῇ χάριτι τοῦ Θεοῦ.
persuaded them to continue in the grace of God.

42. And when the Jews were gone out of the synagogue, the Gentiles besought that these words might be preached to them the next sabbath.
43 Now when the congregation was broken up, many of the Jews and religious proselytes followed Paul and Barnabas: who, speaking to them, persuaded them to continue in the grace of God.

44 And in the coming sabbath, almost all the city was gathered to hear the Word of God.
45 And the Jews seeing the crowds, they were filled with jealousy, and contradicted the things being spoken by Paul, contradicting and blaspheming.

3588 1161 2064 4521 4975 3956 3588 4172 4863
44. Τῷ δὲ ἐρχομένῳ σαββάτῳ σχεδὸν πᾶσα ἡ πόλις συνήχθη
in the And coming sabbath almost all the city was gathered

191 3588 3056 3588 2316 1492 1161 3588 2453 3588
ἀκοῦσαι τὸν λόγον τοῦ Θεοῦ. 45 ἰδόντες δὲ οἱ Ἰουδαῖοι τοὺς
to hear the Word of God. seeing And the Jews the

3793 4130 2205 2532 483 3588 5259 3588
ὄχλους ἐπλήσθησαν ζήλου, καὶ ἀντέλεγον τοῖς ὑπὸ τοῦ
crowds they were filled of jealousy, and contradicted the things by

3972 3004 483 2532 987
Παύλου λεγομένοις, ἀντιλέγοντες καὶ βλασφημοῦντες.
Paul being spoken, contradicting and blaspheming.

44 And the next sabbath day came almost the whole city together to hear the word of God.
45 But when the Jews saw the multitudes, they were filled with envy, and spake against those things which were spoken by Paul, contradicting and blaspheming.

46 But speaking boldly, Paul and Barnabas said, It was necessary (for) the Word of God to be spoken first to you; but since you indeed thrust it away and judge yourselves not worthy of everlasting life, behold, we turn to the nations.

47 For so the Lord has commanded us, "I have set You for a Light of nations,

3955 1161 3588 3972 2532 3588 921 2036 5213
46 παρρησιασάμενοι δὲ ὁ Παῦλος καὶ ὁ Βαρνάβας εἶπον, Ὑμῖν
speaking boldly But Paul and Barnabas said, To you

2258 316 4412 2980 3588 3056 3588 2316
ἦν ἀναγκαῖον πρῶτον λαληθῆναι τὸν λόγον τοῦ Θεοῦ.
it was necessary first to be spoken the Word of God.

1894 1161 683 846 2532 3756 514 2919 1438
ἐπειδὴ δὲ ἀπωθεῖσθε αὐτὸν, καὶ οὐκ ἀξίους κρίνετε ἑαυτοὺς
since then But you put away it, and not worthy judge yourselves

3588 166 2222 2400 4762 1519 3588 1484 3779 1063
τῆς αἰωνίου ζωῆς, ἰδοὺ στρεφόμεθα εἰς τὰ ἔθνη. 47 οὕτω γὰρ
of the everlasting life, behold, we turn to the nations. so For

1781 2254 3588 2962 5087 4571 1519 5457 1484 3588
ἐντέταλται ἡμῖν ὁ Κύριος, Τέθεικά σε εἰς φῶς ἐθνῶν, τοῦ
has commanded us the Lord, I have set you for a Light of (the) nations,

46 Then Paul and Barnabas waxed bold, and said, It was necessary that the word of God should first have been spoken to you: but seeing ye put it from you, and judge yourselves unworthy of everlasting life, lo, we turn to the Gentiles.
47 For so hath the Lord commanded us, (saying), I have set thee to be a light of the Gentiles,

Literal Translation

that You be for salvation to (the) end of the earth." (Isa.49:6)

48 And hearing, the nations rejoiced and glorified the Word of the Lord. And as many as had been appointed to eternal life believed.

49 And the Word of the Lord was carried through all the country.

50 But the Jews urged on the devout and honorable women, and the chief ones of the city, and raised up a persecution against Paul and Barnabas, and threw them out from their borders.

51 But these shaking off the dust of their feet on them, they came into Iconium.

52 And the disciples were filled with joy and (the) Holy Spirit.

Acts 14

1. And it happened in Iconium, they went in together into the synagogue of the Jews, and spoke so as for a huge multitude of both Jews and Greeks to believe.

2 But the disobeying Jews raised up and made malignant the souls of the nations against the brothers.

3 Then, indeed, they stayed a considerable time, speaking boldly on the Lord, witnessing to the Word of His grace, and (He) giving signs and wonders to occur through their hands.

4 An the multitude of the city was divided; and some were with the Jews, but others with the apostles.

5 And when a rush of the nations occurred, and both the Jews

Acts 13:48

1511 4571 1519 4991 2193 2078 3588 1093 191 1161 3588
εἶναί σε εἰς σωτηρίαν ἕως ἐσχάτου τῆς γῆς. 48 ἀκούοντα δὲ τὰ
to be you for salvation until the end of the earth. hearing And the
1484 5463 2532 1392 3588 3056 3588 2962 2532
ἔθνη ἔχαιρον, καὶ ἐδόξαζον τὸν λόγον τοῦ Κυρίου, καὶ
nations rejoiced, and glorified the Word of the Lord, and
4100 3745 2258 5021 1519 2222 166 1308
ἐπίστευσαν ὅσοι ἦσαν τεταγμένοι εἰς ζωὴν αἰώνιον· 49 διε-
believed as many as were appointed to life eternal. was
1161 3588 3056 3588 2962 1223 3650 3588 5561 3588 1161
φέρετο δὲ ὁ λόγος τοῦ Κυρίου δι᾽ ὅλης τῆς χώρας. 50 οἱ δὲ
carried And the Word of the Lord through all the country. the But
2453 3951 3588 4576 1135 2532 3588
Ἰουδαῖοι παρώτρυναν τὰς σεβομένας γυναῖκας καὶ τὰς
Jews urged on by the worshiping women and the
2158 2532 3588 4413 3588 4172 2532 1892
εὐσχήμονας καὶ τοὺς πρώτους τῆς πόλεως, καὶ ἐπήγειραν
honorable and the chief ones of the city, and raised up
1375 1909 3588 3972 2532 3588 921 2532 1544
διωγμὸν ἐπὶ τὸν Παῦλον καὶ τὸν Βαρνάβαν, καὶ ἐξέβαλον
persecution against Paul and Barnabas, and threw out
846 575 3588 3725 846 3588 1161 1621 3588
αὐτοὺς ἀπὸ τῶν ὁρίων αὐτῶν. 51 οἱ δὲ ἐκτιναξάμενοι τὸν
them from the borders of them. they And having shaken off the
2868 3588 4228 846 1909 846 2064 1519 2430
κονιορτὸν τῶν ποδῶν αὐτῶν ἐπ᾽ αὐτούς, ἦλθον εἰς Ἰκόνιον.
dust of the feet of them on them, they came into Iconium.
3588 1161 3101 4137 5479 2532 4151 40
52 οἱ δὲ μαθηταὶ ἐπληροῦντο χαρᾶς καὶ Πνεύματος Ἁγίου.
the And disciples were filled with joy and of (the) Spirit Holy.

Acts 14

1096 1161 1722 2430 2596 3588 846 1525 846 1519
1. Ἐγένετο δὲ ἐν Ἰκονίῳ, κατὰ τὸ αὐτὸ εἰσελθεῖν αὐτοὺς εἰς
it happened And in Iconium, together to enter them into
3588 4864 3588 2453 2532 2980 3779 5620
τὴν συναγωγὴν τῶν Ἰουδαίων, καὶ λαλῆσαι οὕτως ὥστε
the synagogue of the Jews, and to speak so as
4100 2453 5037 2532 1672 4183 4128 3588 1161
πιστεῦσαι Ἰουδαίων τε καὶ Ἑλλήνων πολὺ πλῆθος. 2 οἱ δὲ
to believe Jews both and Greeks a much multitude. the But
544 2453 1892 2532 2559 3588 5590 3588
ἀπειθοῦντες Ἰουδαῖοι ἐπήγειραν καὶ ἐκάκωσαν τὰς ψυχὰς τῶν
disobeying Jews raised up and embittered the souls of the
1484 2596 3588 80 2425 3303 3767 5550 1304
ἐθνῶν κατὰ τῶν ἀδελφῶν. 3 ἱκανὸν μὲν οὖν χρόνον διέτριψαν
nations against the brothers. a considerable indeed Then time they remained
3955 1909 3588 2962 3588 3140 3588 3056 3588
παρρησιαζόμενοι ἐπὶ τῷ Κυρίῳ τῷ μαρτυροῦντι τῷ λόγῳ τῆς
speaking boldly on the Lord witnessing to the Word
5485 846 2532 1325 4592 2532 5059 1096 1223
χάριτος αὐτοῦ, καὶ διδόντι σημεῖα καὶ τέρατα γίνεσθαι διὰ
of the grace of Him, and giving signs and wonders to occur through
3588 5495 846 4977 1161 3588 4128 3588 4172 2532
τῶν χειρῶν αὐτῶν. 4 ἐσχίσθη δὲ τὸ πλῆθος τῆς πόλεως· καὶ
the hands of them. was divided But the multitude of the city; and
3588 3303 2258 4862 3588 2453 3588 1161 4862 3588 652
οἱ μὲν ἦσαν σὺν τοῖς Ἰουδαίοις, οἱ δὲ σὺν τοῖς ἀποστόλοις.
some were with the Jews, others but with the apostles.
5613 1161 1096 3730 3588 1484 5037 2532 2453 4862 3588
5 ὡς δὲ ἐγένετο ὁρμὴ τῶν ἐθνῶν τε καὶ Ἰουδαίων σὺν τοῖς
as And occurred a rush of the nations and also Jews with the

King James Version

that thou shouldest be for salvation unto the ends of the earth.

48 And when the Gentiles heard this, they were glad, and glorified the word of the Lord: and as many as were ordained to eternal life believed.

49 And the word of the Lord was published throughout all the region.

50 But the Jews stirred up the devout and honourable women, and the chief men of the city, and raised persecution against Paul and Barnabas, and expelled them out of their coasts.

51 But they shook off the dust of their feet against them, and came unto Iconium.

52 And the disciples were filled with joy, and with the Holy Ghost.

Acts 14

1. And it came to pass in Iconium, that they went both together into the synagogue of the Jews, and so spake, that a great multitude both of the Jews and also of the Greeks believed.

2 But the unbelieving Jews stirred up the Gentiles, and made their minds evil affected against the brethren.

3 Long time therefore abode they speaking boldly in the Lord, which gave testimony unto the word of his grace, and granted signs and wonders to be done by their hands.

4 But the multitude of the city was divided: and part held with the Jews, and part with the apostles.

5 And when there was an assault made both of the Gentiles, and also of the Jews

Literal Translation **Acts 14:6** *King James Version*

and their rulers (came) to insult and to stone them,
6 perceiving (it) all, they fled to the cities of Lycaonia, Lystra and Derbe, and the surrounding country.
7 And they were preaching the gospel there.
8. And a certain man in Lystra sat powerless in the feet, being lame from his mother's womb, who had never walked.
9 This one was hearing Paul speaking, who, looking intently at him, and seeing that he had faith to be saved,
10 (he) said with a loud voice, Stand upright on your feet! And he leaped up and walked about.
11 And seeing what Paul did, the crowd lifted up their voice in Lycaonian, saying, The gods have come down to us, becoming like men.
12 And they called Barnabas, Zeus, and Paul, Hermes, because he was the (one) leading in the discourse.
13 But the priest of Zeus being before their city, carrying bulls and garlands to the gates, (he) wished to sacrifice along with the crowds.
14 But Paul and Barnabas, the apostles, having heard, tearing their garments, they leaped out into the crowd, crying out,
15 and saying, Men, why do you do these things? We also are men of like feelings to you, preaching the gospel to you to turn (you) from these vain (things) to the living God, who made the heaven and the earth and the sea, and all the things in them,
16 who in

758 846 5195 2532 3036 846 4894
ἄρχουσιν αὐτῶν, ὑβρίσαι καὶ λιθοβολῆσαι αὐτούς, 6 συνι-
rulers of them, to insult and to stone them, per-

2703 1519 3588 4172 3588 3071 3082
δόντες κατέφυγον εἰς τὰς πόλεις τῆς Λυκαονίας, Λύστραν
ceiving (it) all they fled into the cities of Lycaonia , Lystra

2532 1191 2532 3588 4066 2546 2258 2097
καὶ Δέρβην, καὶ τὴν περίχωρον· 7 κἀκεῖ ἦσαν εὐαγγελιζόμενοι.
and Derbe, and the neighborhood; and there they were preaching the gospel.

2532 5100 435 1722 3082 102 3588 4228 2521
8. Καί τις ἀνὴρ ἐν Λύστροις ἀδύνατος τοῖς ποσὶν ἐκάθητο,
And a certain man in Lystra powerless in the feet sat,

5560 1537 2836 3384 846 5225 3739 3763
χωλὸς ἐκ κοιλίας μητρὸς αὐτοῦ ὑπάρχων, ὃς οὐδέποτε
crippled from the womb of (the) mother of him being, who never

4043 3778 191 3588 3972 2980 3739
περιεπεπατήκει. 9 οὗτος ἤκουε τοῦ Παύλου λαλοῦντος· ὃς
had walked. This one was hearing Paul speaking; who

816 846 2532 1492 3754 4102 2192 3588 4982 2036
ἀτενίσας αὐτῷ, καὶ ἰδὼν ὅτι πίστιν ἔχει τοῦ σωθῆναι, 10 εἶπε
looking intently at him, and seeing that faith he has to be saved, said

3173 3588 5456 450 1909 3588 4228 4675 3717 2532
μεγάλῃ τῇ φωνῇ, Ἀνάστηθι ἐπὶ τοὺς πόδας σου ὀρθός. καὶ
with a great voice, Stand up on the feet of you erect. And

242 2532 4043 3588 1161 3793 1492 3739 4160 3588
ἥλλετο καὶ περιεπάτει. 11 οἱ δὲ ὄχλοι, ἰδόντες ὃ ἐποίησεν ὁ
he leaped and walked about. the And crowds, seeing what did

3972 1869 3588 5456 846 3072 3004 3588
Παῦλος ἐπῆραν τὴν φωνὴν αὐτῶν Λυκαονιστὶ λέγοντες, Οἱ
Paul lifted up the voice of them in Lycaonian saying, The

2316 3666 444 2597 4314 2248 2564
θεοὶ ὁμοιωθέντες ἀνθρώποις κατέβησαν πρὸς ἡμᾶς. 12 ἐκάλουν
gods have become like men having come down to us. they called

5037 3588 3303 921 2203 3588 1161 3972 2060 1894
τε τὸν μὲν Βαρνάβαν, Δία· τὸν δὲ Παῦλον, Ἑρμῆν, ἐπειδὴ
And indeed Barnabas, Zeus, and Paul, Hermes, since

846 2258 3588 2233 3588 3056 3588 1161 2409 3588 2203 3588
αὐτὸς ἦν ὁ ἡγούμενος τοῦ λόγου. 13 ὁ δὲ ἱερεὺς τοῦ Διὸς τοῦ
he was the (one) leading in the discourse. the But priest of Zeus

5607 4253 3588 4172 846 5022 2532 4725 1909 3588
ὄντος πρὸ τῆς πόλεως αὐτῶν, ταύρους καὶ στέμματα ἐπὶ τοὺς
being before the city of them, bulls and garlands to the

4440 5342 4862 3588 3793 2309 2380 191
πυλῶνας ἐνέγκας, σὺν τοῖς ὄχλοις ἤθελε θύειν. 14 ἀκούσαντες
gates bringing, with the crowds wished to sacrifice. having heard

1161 3588 652 921 2532 3972 1284 3588 2440
δὲ οἱ ἀπόστολοι Βαρνάβας καὶ Παῦλος, διαρρήξαντες τὰ ἱμάτια
And the apostles Barnabas and Paul, tearing the garments

846 1530 1519 3588 3793 2896 2532 3004
αὐτῶν, εἰσεπήδησαν εἰς τὸν ὄχλον, κράζοντες 15 καὶ λέγοντες,
of them, leaped out into the crowd, crying out and saying,

435 5101 5023 4160 2532 2249 3663 2070 5213
Ἄνδρες, τί ταῦτα ποιεῖτε; καὶ ἡμεῖς ὁμοιοπαθεῖς ἐσμεν ὑμῖν
Men, why these things do you? Also we of like feelings are to you

444 2097 5209 575 5130 3588 3152
ἄνθρωποι, εὐαγγελιζόμενοι ὑμᾶς ἀπὸ τούτων τῶν ματαίων
men, preaching the gospel to you from these vain (things)

1994 1909 3588 2316 3588 2198 3739 4160 3588 3772
ἐπιστρέφειν ἐπὶ τὸν Θεὸν τὸν ζῶντα, ὃς ἐποίησε τὸν οὐρανὸν
to turn to the God living, who made the heaven

2532 3588 1093 2532 3588 2281 2532 3956 3588 1722 846 3739 1722
καὶ τὴν γῆν καὶ τὴν θάλασσαν καὶ πάντα τὰ ἐν αὐτοῖς· 16 ὃς ἐν
and the earth and the sea and all the things in them; who in

with their rulers, to use (them) despitefully, and to stone them,
6 They were ware of (it), and fled unto Lystra and Derbe, cities of Lycaonia, and unto the region that lieth round about:
7 And there they preached the gospel.
8. And there sat a certain man at Lystra, impotent in his feet, being a cripple from his mother's womb, who never had walked:
9 The same heard Paul speak: who stedfastly beholding him, and perceiving that he had faith to be healed,
10 Said with a loud voice, Stand upright on thy feet. And he leaped and walked.
11 And when the people saw what Paul had done, they lifted up their voices, saying in the speech of Lycaonia, The gods are come down to us in the likeness of men.
12 And they called Barnabas, Jupiter; and Paul, Mercurius, because he was the chief speaker.
13 Then the priest of Jupiter, which was before their city, brought oxen and garlands unto the gates, and would have done sacrifice with the people.
14 (Which) when the apostles, Barnabas and Paul, heard (of), they rent their clothes, and ran in among the people, crying out,
15 And saying, Sirs, why do ye these things? We also are men of like passions with you, and preach unto you that ye should turn from these vanities unto the living God, which made heaven, and earth, and the sea, and all things that are therein:
16 Who in

Literal Translation

the generations having passed allowed all the nations to go in their ways,
17 And yet He did not leave Himself without witness, doing good, giving rain and fruit-bearing seasons to us from Heaven, filling our hearts (with) food and gladness.

18 And saying these things, they hardly stopped the crowds, (that they) not sacrifice to them.

19. But Jews came there from Antioch and Iconium, and persuading the crowds, and stoning Paul, they dragged (him) outside the city, supposing him to have died.
20 But the disciples surrounding him, arising he entered into the city. And on the morrow he went away with Barnabas to Derbe.
21 And having preached the gospel to that city, and having made many disciples, they returned to Lystra and Iconium and Antioch,

22 confirming the souls of the disciples, exhorting to continue in the faith, and that through many afflictions we must enter into the kingdom of God.

23 And having hand-picked elders for them in every church, having prayed with fastings, they committed them to the Lord into whom they had believed.

24 But having passed through Pisidia, they came into Pamphylia.
25 And having spoken the Word in Perga, they came down to Attalia,
26 and from there they sailed away to Antioch, from where they had been

Acts 14:17

3588 3944 1074 1439 3956 3588 1484 4198
ταῖς παρῳχημέναις γενεαῖς εἴασε πάντα τὰ ἔθνη πορεύεσθαι
the having passed by generations allowed all the nations to go

3588 3598 846 2532 2544 3756 267 1438 863
ταῖς ὁδοῖς αὐτῶν. 17 καί τοιγε οὐκ ἀμάρτυρον ἑαυτὸν ἀφῆκεν
the ways of them. And yet not untestified Himself left

15 3771 2254 5205 1325 2532 2540
ἀγαθοποιῶν, οὐρανόθεν ὑμῖν ὑετοὺς διδοὺς καὶ καιροὺς
doing good, from Heaven to us rain giving and seasons

2593 1705 5160 2532 2167 3588 2588
καρποφόρους, ἐμπιπλῶν τροφῆς καὶ εὐφροσύνης τὰς καρδίας
fruit-bearing, filling of food and of gladness the hearts

2257 2532 5023 3004 3433 2664 3588 3793
ἡμῶν. 18 καὶ ταῦτα λέγοντες, μόλις κατέπαυσαν τοὺς ὄχλους
of us. And these things saying, hardly they setttled down the crowds

3588 3361 2380 846
τοῦ μὴ θύειν αὐτοῖς.
not to sacrifice to them.

1904 1161 575 490 2532 2430 2453 2532
19. Ἐπῆλθον δὲ ἀπὸ Ἀντιοχείας καὶ Ἰκονίου Ἰουδαῖοι, καὶ
came over And from Antioch and Iconium Jews, and

3982 3588 3793 2532 3034 3588 3972 4951
πείσαντες τοὺς ὄχλους, καὶ λιθάσαντες τὸν Παῦλον, ἔσυρον
persuading the crowds, and stoning Paul, they dragged

1854 3588 4172 3543 846 2348 2944
ἔξω τῆς πόλεως, νομίσαντες αὐτὸν τεθνάναι. 20 κυκλωσάντων
outside the city, supposing him to have died. having surrounded

1161 846 3588 3101 450 1525 1519 3588 4172 2532
δὲ αὐτὸν τῶν μαθητῶν, ἀναστὰς εἰσῆλθεν εἰς τὴν πόλιν· καὶ
But him the disciples, rising up he entered into the city; and

3588 1887 1831 4862 3588 921 1519 1191 2097
τῇ ἐπαύριον ἐξῆλθε σὺν τῷ Βαρνάβᾳ εἰς Δέρβην. 21 Εὐαγγελι-
on the morrow he went with Barnabas into Derbe. preaching the

5037 3588 4172 1565 2532 3100 2425
σάμενοί τε τὴν πόλιν ἐκείνην, καὶ μαθητεύσαντες ἱκανούς,
gospel And city that, and having made disciples many,

5290 1519 3588 3082 2532 2430 2532 490
ὑπέστρεψαν εἰς τὴν Λύστραν καὶ Ἰκόνιον καὶ Ἀντιόχειαν,
they returned to Lystra and Iconium and Antioch,

1991 3588 5590 3588 3101 3870
22 ἐπιστηρίζοντες τὰς ψυχὰς τῶν μαθητῶν, παρακαλοῦντες
confirming the souls of the disciples, exhorting

1696 3588 4102 2532 3754 1223 4183 2347 1163 2248
ἐμμένειν τῇ πίστει, καὶ ὅτι διὰ πολλῶν θλίψεων δεῖ ἡμᾶς
to continue in the faith, and that through many oppressions must us

1525 1519 3588 932 3588 2316 5500 1161
εἰσελθεῖν εἰς τὴν βασιλείαν τοῦ Θεοῦ. 23 χειροτονήσαντες δὲ
enter into the kingdom of God. having hand-picked And

846 4245 2596 1577 4336 3326
αὐτοῖς πρεσβυτέρους κατ᾽ ἐκκλησίαν, προσευξάμενοι μετὰ
for them elders in (every) church, having prayed with

3521 3908 846 3588 2962 1519 3739 4100
νηστειῶν παρέθεντο αὐτοὺς τῷ Κυρίῳ εἰς ὃν πεπιστεύκεισαν.
fastings they committed them to the Lord into whom they had believed.

2532 1330 3588 4099 2064 1519 3828 2532
24 καὶ διελθόντες τὴν Πισιδίαν ἦλθον εἰς Παμφυλίαν. 25 καὶ
And passing through Pisidia they came into Pamphylia. And

2980 1722 4011 3588 3056 2597 1519 825
λαλήσαντες ἐν Πέργῃ τὸν λόγον, κατέβησαν εἰς Ἀττάλειαν·
having spoken in Perga the Word, they came down into Attalia;

2547 636 1519 490 3606 2258
26 κἀκεῖθεν ἀπέπλευσαν εἰς Ἀντιόχειαν, ὅθεν ἦσαν
and from there sailed away to Antioch, from where they were

King James Version

times past suffered all nations to walk in their own ways.

17 Nevertheless he left not himself without witness, in that he did good, and gave us rain from heaven, and fruitful seasons, filling our hearts with food and gladness.

18 And with these sayings scarce restrained they the people, that they had not done sacrifice unto them.

19. And there came thither (certain) Jews from Antioch and Iconium, who persuaded the people, and, having stoned Paul, drew (him) out of the city, supposing he had been dead.
20 Howbeit, as the disciples stood round about him, he rose up, and came into the city: and the next day he departed with Barnabas to Derbe.
21 And when they had preached the gospel to that city, and had taught many, they returned again to Lystra, and (to) Iconium, and Antioch,

22 Confirming the souls of the disciples, (and) exhorting them to continue in the faith, and that we must through much tribulation enter into the kingdom of God.
23 And when they had ordained them elders in every church, and had prayed with fasting, they commended them to the Lord, on whom they believed.
24 And after they had passed throughout Pisidia, they came to Pamphylia.
25 And when they had preached the word in Perga, they went down into Attalia:
26 And thence sailed to Antioch, from whence they had been

Literal Translation

committed to the grace of God for the work which they fulfilled.

27 And having arrived, and having assembled the church, they reported what things God had done with them and that He opened a door of faith to the nations.
28 And they continued there not a little time with the disciples.

Acts 14:27

3860 3588 5485 3588 2316 1519 3588 2041 3739 4137
παραδεδομένοι τῇ χάριτι τοῦ Θεοῦ εἰς τὸ ἔργον ὃ ἐπλή-
committed to the grace of God to the work which they

3854 1161 2532 4863 3588 1577
ρωσαν. 27 παραγενόμενοι δὲ καὶ συναγαγόντες τὴν ἐκκλησίαν,
fulfilled. having arrived And and having assembled the church,

312 3745 4160 3588 2316 3326 846 2532 3754 455
ἀνήγγειλαν ὅσα ἐποίησεν ὁ Θεὸς μετ᾽ αὐτῶν, καὶ ὅτι ἤνοιξε
they reported what things had done God with them, and that He opened

3588 1484 2374 4102 1304 1161 1563 5550 3756
τοῖς ἔθνεσι θύραν πίστεως. 28 διέτριβον δὲ ἐκεῖ χρόνον οὐκ
to the nations a door of faith. they continued And there a time not

3641 4862 3588 3101
ὀλίγον σὺν τοῖς μαθηταῖς.
little with the disciples.

King James Version

recommended to the grace of God for the work which they fulfilled.
27 And when they were come, and had gathered the church together, they rehearsed all that God had done with them, and how he had opened the door of faith unto the Gentiles.
28 And there they abode long time with the disciples.

Acts 15

1. And going down from Judea, some taught the brothers, (saying), If you are not circumcised (according) to the custom of Moses, you are not able to be saved.
2 Then discord and not a little disputation with them having occurred by Paul and Barnabas, they appointed Paul and Barnabas and some others of them to go up into Jerusalem to the apostles and elders concerning this question.

3 Then, indeed, having been sent forward by the church they passed through Phoenicia and Samaria, fully relating the conversion of the nations. And they were producing great joy (among) all the brothers.

4 And having arrived in Jerusalem, they were welcomed by the church and the apostles and the elders. And (they) reported what things God did with them.

5. But some of those rose up from the sect of the Pharisees who had believed, saying, It is necessary to circumcise them and to command (them) to keep the

Acts 15

2532 5100 2718 575 3588 2449 1321 3588
1. Καί τινες κατελθόντες ἀπὸ τῆς Ἰουδαίας, ἐδίδασκον τοὺς
And some going down from Judea, taught the

80 3754 1437 3361 4059 3588 1485 3475 3756
ἀδελφοὺς ὅτι Ἐὰν μὴ περιτέμνησθε τῷ ἔθει Μωϋσέως, οὐ
brothers, If not are circumcised by the custom of Moses, not

1410 4982 1096 3767 4714 2532 4803
δύνασθε σωθῆναι. 2 γενομένης οὖν στάσεως καὶ συζητήσεως
you are able to be saved. occurring Then discord and discussion

3756 3641 3588 3972 2532 3588 921 4314 846 5021
οὐκ ὀλίγης τῷ Παύλῳ καὶ τῷ Βαρνάβᾳ πρὸς αὐτούς, ἔταξαν
not a ltitle by Paul and Barnabas with them, they chose

305 3972 2532 921 2532 5100 243 1537
ἀναβαίνειν Παῦλον καὶ Βαρνάβαν καί τινας ἄλλους ἐξ
to go up Paul and Barnabas and some others from

846 4314 3588 652 2532 4245 1519 2419
αὐτῶν πρὸς τοὺς ἀποστόλους καὶ πρεσβυτέρους εἰς Ἱερου-
them to the apostles and elders to Jeru-

4012 3588 2213 5127 3588 3303 3767 4311
σαλὴμ περὶ τοῦ ζητήματος τούτου. 3 οἱ μὲν οὖν, προπεμ-
salem about question this. they indeed Then, being set

5259 3588 1577 1330 3588 5403 2532
φθέντες ὑπὸ τῆς ἐκκλησίας, διήρχοντο τὴν Φοινίκην καὶ
forward by the church, passed through Phoenicia and

4540 1555 3588 1995 3588 1484 2532
Σαμάρειαν, ἐκδιηγούμενοι τὴν ἐπιστροφὴν τῶν ἐθνῶν· καὶ
Samaria fully relating the conversion of the nations; and

4160 5479 3173 3956 3588 80 3854
ἐποίουν χαρὰν μεγάλην πᾶσι τοῖς ἀδελφοῖς. 4 παραγενό-
they caused joy great to all the brothers. having arrived

1161 1519 2419 588 5259 3588 1577
μενοι δὲ εἰς Ἱερουσαλήμ, ἀπεδέχθησαν ὑπὸ τῆς ἐκκλησίας
And into Jerusalem, they were welcomed by the church

2532 3588 652 2532 3588 4245 312 5037
καὶ τῶν ἀποστόλων καὶ τῶν πρεσβυτέρων, ἀνήγγειλάν τε
and the apostles and the elders, reported and

3745 3588 2316 4160 3326 846 1817 1161 5100 3588
ὅσα ὁ Θεὸς ἐποίησε μετ᾽ αὐτῶν. 5 ἐξανέστησαν δέ τινες τῶν
what things God did with them. rose up But some of those

575 3588 139 3588 5330 4100 3004
ἀπὸ τῆς αἱρέσεως τῶν Φαρισαίων πεπιστευκότες, λέγοντες
from the sect of the Pharisees having believed, saying,

3754 1163 4059 846 3853 5037 5083 3588
ὅτι Δεῖ περιτέμνειν αὐτούς, παραγγέλλειν τε τηρεῖν τὸν
It is necessary to circumcise them, to command and to keep the

Acts 15

1. And certain men which came down from Judaea taught the brethren, (and said), Except ye be circumcised after the manner of Moses, ye cannot be saved.
2 When therefore Paul and Barnabas had no small dissension and disputation with them, they determined that Paul and Barnabas, and certain other of them, should go up to Jerusalem unto the apostles and elders about this question.

3 And being brought on their way by the church, they passed through Phenice and Samaria, declaring the conversion of the Gentiles: and they caused great joy unto all the brethren.

4 And when they were come to Jerusalem, they were received of the church, and (of) the apostles and elders, and they declared all things that God had done with them.

5. But there rose up certain of the sect of the Pharisees which believed, saying, That it was needful to circumcise them, and to command (them) to keep the

Literal Translation

Acts 15:6

King James Version

Law of Moses.

6 And the apostles and the elders were assembled to see about this matter.
7 And much discussion having occurred, rising up Peter said to them: Men, brothers, you understand that from ancient days, God chose out among us (that) through my mouth the nations (should) hear the Word of the gospel, and to believe.

8 And the heart knowing God testified to them, giving them the Holy Spirit, even as also to us.

9 And He distinguished nothing between both us and them, having purified their hearts by faith.

10 Now, then, why do you test God by putting a yoke on the neck of the disciples which neither our fathers nor we had strength to bear?

11 But through the grace of (the) Lord Jesus Christ, we believe to be saved, according to which manner they also (believed).

12. And all the multitude kept silent and heard Barnabas and Paul relating what things God did through them among the nations, (even) the signs and wonders.
13. And after their silence, James answered, saying, Men, brothers, hear me:

14 Simeon has related (how) even as first God oversaw to take a people out from (among the) nations for His name.
15 And with this agree the words of the

3551 3475
νόμον Μωϋσέως.
Law of Moses.

4863 1161 3588 652 2532 3588 4245 1492
6. Συνήχθησαν δὲ οἱ ἀπόστολοι καὶ οἱ πρεσβύτεροι ἰδεῖν
were assembled And the apostles and the elders to see

4012 3588 3056 5127 4183 1161 4803 1096
περὶ τοῦ λόγου τούτου. 7 πολλῆς δὲ συζητήσεως γενομένης,
about matter this. much And discussion having occurred,

450 4074 2036 4314 846
ἀναστὰς Πέτρος εἶπε πρὸς αὐτούς,
rising up Peter said to them,

435 80 5210 1987 3754 575 2250 744
Ἄνδρες ἀδελφοί, ὑμεῖς ἐπίστασθε ὅτι ἀφ' ἡμερῶν ἀρχαίων
Men brothers, you understand that from days ancient

3588 2316 1722 2254 1586 1223 3588 4750 3450 191
ὁ Θεὸς ἐν ἡμῖν ἐξελέξατο, διὰ τοῦ στόματός μου ἀκοῦσαι
God among us chose out, through the mouth of me to hear

3588 1484 3588 3056 3588 2098 2532 4100 2532 3588
τὰ ἔθνη τὸν λόγον τοῦ εὐαγγελίου, καὶ πιστεῦσαι. 8 καὶ ὁ
the nations the Word of the gospel, and to believe. And the

2589 2316 3140 846 1325 846 3588
καρδιογνώστης Θεὸς ἐμαρτύρησεν αὐτοῖς, δοὺς αὐτοῖς τὸ
heart-knowing God testified to them, giving them the

4151 3588 40 2531 2532 2254 2532 3762 1252 3342
Πνεῦμα τὸ Ἅγιον, καθὼς καὶ ἡμῖν· 9 καὶ οὐδὲν διέκρινε μεταξὺ
Spirit Holy, even as also to us; and nothing distinguished between

2257 5037 2532 846 3588 4102 2511 3588 2588 846
ἡμῶν τε καὶ αὐτῶν, τῇ πίστει καθαρίσας τὰς καρδίας αὐτῶν.
us both and them, by faith having cleansed the hearts of them.

3568 3767 5101 3985 3588 2316 2007 2218 1909 3588
10 νῦν οὖν τί πειράζετε τὸν Θεόν, ἐπιθεῖναι ζυγὸν ἐπὶ τὸν
Now then why do you test God, to put a yoke on the

5137 3588 3101 3739 3777 3588 3962 2257 3777 2249
τράχηλον τῶν μαθητῶν, ὃν οὔτε οἱ πατέρες ἡμῶν οὔτε ἡμεῖς
neck of the disciples, which neither the fathers of us nor we

2480 941 235 1223 3588 5485 2962 2424
ἰσχύσαμεν βαστάσαι; 11 ἀλλὰ διὰ τῆς χάριτος Κυρίου Ἰησοῦ
had strength to bear? But through the grace of (the) Lord Jesus

5547 4100 4982 2596 3739 5158 2548
Χριστοῦ πιστεύομεν σωθῆναι, καθ' ὃν τρόπον κἀκεῖνοι.
Christ we believe to be saved, according to which way they also.

4601 1161 3956 3588 4128 2532 191 921 2532
12 Ἐσίγησε δὲ πᾶν τὸ πλῆθος, καὶ ἤκουον Βαρνάβα καὶ
was silent And all the multitude, and heard Barnabas and

3972 1834 3745 4160 3588 2316 4592 2532
Παύλου ἐξηγουμένων ὅσα ἐποίησεν ὁ Θεὸς σημεῖα καὶ
Paul relating what things did God signs and

5059 1722 3588 1484 1223 846 3326 1161 3588 4601 846
τέρατα ἐν τοῖς ἔθνεσι δι' αὐτῶν. 13 μετὰ δὲ τὸ σιγῆσαι αὐτούς,
wonders among the nations through them. after And the silence of them,

611 2385 3004
ἀπεκρίθη Ἰάκωβος λέγων,
answered James saying,

435 80 191 3450 4826 1834 2531
Ἄνδρες ἀδελφοί, ἀκούσατέ μου. 14 Συμεὼν ἐξηγήσατο καθὼς
Men brothers, hear me. Simeon has related even as

4412 3588 2316 1980 2983 1537 1484 2992 1909 3588
πρῶτον ὁ Θεὸς ἐπεσκέψατο λαβεῖν ἐξ ἐθνῶν λαὸν ἐπὶ τῷ
first God oversaw to take out of (the) nations a people for the

3686 846 2532 5129 4856 3588 3056 3588
ὀνόματι αὐτοῦ. 15 καὶ τούτῳ συμφωνοῦσιν οἱ λόγοι τῶν προ-
name of Him. And to this agree together the words of the

law of Moses.

6 And the apostles and elders came together for to consider of this matter.
7 And when there had been much disputing, Peter rose up, and said unto them, Men (and) brethren, ye know how that a good while ago God made choice among us, that the Gentiles by my mouth should hear the word of the gospel, and believe.

8 And God, which knoweth the hearts, bare them witness, giving them the Holy Ghost, even as (he did) unto us;

9 And put no difference between us and them, purifying their hearts by faith.

10 Now therefore why tempt ye God, to put a yoke upon the neck of the disciples, which neither our fathers nor we were able to bear?

11 But we believe that through the grace of the Lord Jesus Christ we shall be saved, even as they.

12. Then all the multitude kept silence, and gave audience to Barnabas and Paul, declaring what miracles and wonders God had wrought among the Gentiles by them.
13. And after they had held their peace, James answered, saying, Men (and) brethren, hearken unto me:

14 Simeon hath declared how God at the first did visit the Gentiles, to take out of them a people for his name.

15 And to this agree the words of the

Literal Translation **Acts 15:16** *King James Version*

prophets, as it has been
written,
16 "After these things I
will return and will
build again the taberna-
cle of David (which)
has fallen, and I will
build again the things
which have been de-
molished, and I will set
it up,
17 so as the rest of men
may seek the Lord,
even all the nations on
whom My name has
been called, says the
Lord, who is doing all
these things." (Amos
9:11,12)
18 All His works are
known to God from
eternity.
19 For this reason I
judge not to trouble
those from the nations
turning to God,

20 but to write to them
to hold back from the
pollutions of the idols,
and (from) fornication,
and that strangled, and
blood.

21 For in every city
from ancient genera-
tions Moses has those
proclaiming him, hav-
ing been read in the
synagogues on every
sabbath.

22. Then it seemed
(good) to the apostles
and the elders, with all
the church, to send men
having been chosen
from them to Antioch
with Paul and Barnabas,
Judas having been sur-
named Barsabas, and
Silas, leading men
among the brothers,

23 writing by their hand
these (things): The
apostles and the elders
and the brothers, to
those throughout Anti-
och, and Syria, and
Cilicia, brothers from
(the) nations: Greeting.

24 Since we heard that
some of us having gone
out

4396 2531 1125 3326 5023 390 2532
φητῶν, καθὼς γέγραπται, 16 Μετὰ ταῦτα ἀναστρέψω, καὶ
prophets even as it has been written, After these things I will return, and

456 3588 4633 1138 3588 4098 2532 3588
ἀνοικοδομήσω τὴν σκηνὴν Δαβὶδ τὴν πεπτωκυῖαν· καὶ τὰ
I will rebuild the tent of David having fallen; and that

2679 846 456 2532 461 846
κατεσκαμμένα αὐτῆς ἀνοικοδομήσω, καὶ ἀνορθώσω αὐτήν·
having been demolished of it I will rebuild, and I will set up it;

3704 302 1567 3588 2645 3588 444 3588
17 ὅπως ἂν ἐκζητήσωσιν οἱ κατάλοιποι τῶν ἀνθρώπων τὸν
so as may seek the rest of men the

2962 2532 3956 3588 1484 1909 3739 1941 3588 3686 3450
Κύριον, καὶ πάντα τὰ ἔθνη, ἐφ' οὓς ἐπικέκληται τὸ ὄνομά μου
Lord, even all the nations, on whom has been called the name of Me

1909 846 3004 2962 3588 4160 5023 3956 1110
ἐπ' αὐτούς, λέγει Κύριος ὁ ποιῶν ταῦτα πάντα. 18 γνωστὰ
on them, says (the) Lord who is doing these things all. Known

575 165 2076 3588 2316 3956 3588 2041 846 1352 1473
ἀπ' αἰῶνός ἐστι τῷ Θεῷ πάντα τὰ ἔργα αὐτοῦ. 19 διὸ ἐγὼ
from eternity are to God all the works of Him. Because I

2919 3361 3926 3588 575 3588 1484 1994
κρίνω μὴ παρενοχλεῖν τοῖς ἀπὸ τῶν ἐθνῶν ἐπιστρέφουσιν
judge not to trouble those from the nations turning

1909 3588 2316 235 1989 846 3588 567 575
ἐπὶ τὸν Θεόν· 20 ἀλλὰ ἐπιστεῖλαι αὐτοῖς τοῦ ἀπέχεσθαι ἀπὸ
to God; but to write to them to hold back from

3588 234 3588 1497 2532 3588 4202 2532 3588
τῶν ἀλισγημάτων τῶν εἰδώλων καὶ τῆς πορνείας καὶ τοῦ
pollutions of the idols and fornication and that

4156 2532 3588 129 3475 1063 1537 1074 744
πνικτοῦ καὶ τοῦ αἵματος. 21 Μωσῆς γὰρ ἐκ γενεῶν ἀρχαίων
strangled and blood. Moses For from generations ancient

2596 4172 3588 2784 846 2192 1722 3588 4864
κατὰ πόλιν τοὺς κηρύσσοντας αὐτὸν ἔχει, ἐν ταῖς συναγω-
in every city those proclaiming him he has, in the synagogues

2596 3956 4521 314
γαῖς κατὰ πᾶν σάββατον ἀναγινωσκόμενος.
on every sabbath having been read.

5119 1380 3588 652 2532 3588 4245 4862
22. Τότε ἔδοξε τοῖς ἀποστόλοις καὶ τοῖς πρεσβυτέροις σὺν
Then it seemed to the apostles and the elders with

3650 3588 1577 1586 435 1537 846 3992 1519
ὅλῃ τῇ ἐκκλησίᾳ, ἐκλεξαμένους ἄνδρας ἐξ αὐτῶν πέμψαι εἰς
all the church, having been chosen men from them to send to

490 4862 3588 3972 2532 921 2455 3588
Ἀντιόχειαν σὺν τῷ Παύλῳ καὶ Βαρνάβᾳ, Ἰούδαν τὸν
Antioch with Paul and Barnabas, Judas

1941 923 2532 4609 435 2233 1722
ἐπικαλούμενον Βαρσαβᾶν, καὶ Σίλαν, ἄνδρας ἡγουμένους ἐν
surnamed Barsabas, and Silas, men having led among

3588 80 1125 1223 5495 846 3592 3588
τοῖς ἀδελφοῖς, 23 γράψαντες διὰ χειρὸς αὐτῶν τάδε, Οἱ ἀπό-
the brothers, writing by (the) hand of them these (things): The

652 2532 3588 4245 2532 3588 80 3588 2596 3588
στολοι καὶ οἱ πρεσβύτεροι καὶ οἱ ἀδελφοὶ τοῖς κατὰ τὴν
apostles and the elders and the brothers to those throughout

490 2532 4947 2532 2791 80 3588 1537 1484
Ἀντιόχειαν καὶ Συρίαν καὶ Κιλικίαν ἀδελφοῖς τοῖς ἐξ ἐθνῶν,
Antioch and Syria and Cilicia, brothers from (the) nations,

5463 1894 191 3754 5100 1537 2257 1831
χαίρειν· 24 ἐπειδὴ ἠκούσαμεν ὅτι τινὲς ἐξ ἡμῶν ἐξελθόντες ἐτά-
Greeting. Since we heard that some of us having gone out

prophets; as it is written,
16 After this I will re-
turn, and will build
again the tabernacle of
David, which is fallen
down; and I will build
again the ruins thereof,
and I will set it up:

17 That the residue of
men might seek after
the Lord, and all the
Gentiles, upon whom
my name is called, saith
the Lord, who doeth all
these things.

18 Known unto God are
all his works from the
beginning of the world.
19 Wherefore my sen-
tence is, that we trouble
not them, which from
among the Gentiles are
turned to God:

20 But that we write
unto them, that they ab-
stain from pollutions of
idols, and (from) forni-
cation, and (from)
things strangled, and
(from) blood.
21 For Moses of old
time hath in every city
them that preach him,
being read in the syna-
gogues every sabbath
day.

22. Then pleased it the
apostles and elders, with
the whole church, to
send chosen men of
their own company to
Antioch with Paul and
Barnabas; (namely), Ju-
das surnamed
Barsabas, and Silas,
chief men among the
brethren:

23 And they wrote (let-
ters) by them after this
manner; The apostles
and elders and brethren
(send) greeting unto the
brethren which are of
the Gentiles in Antioch
and Syria and Cilicia:

24 Forasmuch as we
have heard, that certain
which went out

Literal Translation

have troubled you with words, unsettling your souls, saying, Be circumcised and keep the Law, to whom we gave no command;

25 it seemed (good) to us, having become of one mind, to send men having been chosen out to you along with our beloved Barnabas and Paul,
26 men who have given up their souls on behalf of the name of our Lord, Jesus Christ.

27 Therefore, we have sent Judas and Silas, they by word also announcing the same things.
28 For it seemed (good) to the Holy Spirit and to us to put on you not one greater burden than these necessary things:

29 To abstain from idol sacrifices, and blood, and (the things) strangled, and (from) fornication; from which continually keeping yourselves, you will do well. Be prospered.

30 Then indeed they being let go, they went to Antioch. And having assembled the multitude, (they) delivered the letter.
31 And having read (it), they rejoiced at the comfort.
32 And Judas and Silas, themselves also being prophets, exhorted the brothers through much speech, and confirmed (them).
33 And having continued for a time, they were let go with peace from the brothers to the apostles.

34 But it seemed (good) to Silas to remain.
35 And Paul and Barnabas with many others also stayed in Antioch, teaching and preaching the gospel, the Word of the

Acts 15:25

5015 5209 3056 384 3588 5590 5216
ραξαν ὑμᾶς λόγοις, ἀνασκευάζοντες τὰς ψυχὰς ὑμῶν,
troubled you with words, unsettling the souls of you,

3004 4059 2532 5083 3588 3551 3739 3756 1291
λέγοντες περιτέμνεσθαι καὶ τηρεῖν τὸν νόμον, οἷς οὐ διεστει-
saying, Be circumcised and keep the Law, to whom not we gave

1380 2254 1096 3661 1586
λάμεθα· 25 ἔδοξεν ἡμῖν γενομένοις ὁμοθυμαδόν, ἐκλεξαμένους
command; it seemed to us having become of one mind, having chosen out

435 3992 4314 5209 4862 3588 27 2257
ἄνδρας πέμψαι πρὸς ὑμᾶς, σὺν τοῖς ἀγαπητοῖς ἡμῶν
men to send to you, with the beloved of us

921 2532 3972 444 3860 3588 5590
Βαρνάβᾳ καὶ Παύλῳ, 26 ἀνθρώποις παραδεδωκόσι τὰς ψυχὰς
Barnabas and Paul, men having given up the souls

846 5228 3588 3686 3588 2962 2257 2424 5547
αὐτῶν ὑπὲρ τοῦ ὀνόματος τοῦ Κυρίου ἡμῶν Ἰησοῦ Χρι-
of them on behalf of the name of the Lord of us Jesus Christ.

649 3767 2455 2532 4609 2532 846 1223
στοῦ. 27 ἀπεστάλκαμεν οὖν Ἰούδαν καὶ Σίλαν, καὶ αὐτοὺς διὰ
we have sent Therefore Judas and Silas, and they through

3056 518 3588 846 1380 1063 3588 40
λόγου ἀπαγγέλλοντας τὰ αὐτά. 28 ἔδοξε γὰρ τῷ Ἁγίῳ
word proclaiming the same things. it seemed For to the Holy

4151 2532 2254 3367 4119 2007 5213 922
Πνεύματι, καὶ ἡμῖν, μηδὲν πλέον ἐπιτίθεσθαι ὑμῖν βάρος,
Spirit, and to us, nothing more to put on you burden

4133 3588 1876 5130 567 1494 2532
πλὴν τῶν ἐπάναγκες τούτων, 29 ἀπέχεσθαι εἰδωλοθύτων καὶ
than necessary things these, to abstain from idol sacrifices and

129 2532 4156 2532 4202 1537 3739 1301
αἵματος καὶ πνικτοῦ καὶ πορνείας· ἐξ ὧν διατηροῦντες
blood and (that) strangled and fornication; from which always keeping

1438 2095 4238 4517
ἑαυτούς, εὖ πράξετε. ἔρρωσθε.
yourselves, well you will do. Be prospered.

3588 3303 3767 630 2064 1519 490 2532 4863
30. Οἱ μὲν οὖν ἀπολυθέντες ἦλθον εἰς Ἀντιόχειαν· καὶ συν-
They indeed then being let go they went to Antioch; and having

3588 4128 1929 3588 1992 314
αγαγόντες τὸ πλῆθος, ἐπέδωκαν τὴν ἐπιστολήν. 31 ἀναγνόντες
assembled the multitude, delivered the letter. having read

1161 5463 1909 3588 3874 2455 1161 2532 4609 2532
δέ, ἐχάρησαν ἐπὶ τῇ παρακλήσει. 32 Ἰούδας δὲ καὶ Σίλας, καὶ
And, they rejoiced at the comfort. Judas And and Silas, also

846 4396 5607 1223 3056 4183 3870
αὐτοὶ προφῆται ὄντες, διὰ λόγου πολλοῦ παρεκάλεσαν
themselves prophets being, through speech much exhorted

3588 80 2532 1991 4160 1161 5550
τοὺς ἀδελφούς, καὶ ἐπεστήριξαν. 33 ποιήσαντες δὲ χρόνον,
the brothers, and confirmed. having continued And a time,

630 3326 1515 575 3588 80 4314 3588 652
ἀπελύθησαν μετ᾽ εἰρήνης ἀπὸ τῶν ἀδελφῶν πρὸς τοὺς αποσ-
they were let go with peace from the brothers to the apostles.

1380 1161 3588 4609 1961 846 3972 1161 2532
τόλους. 34 ἔδοξε δὲ τῷ Σίλᾳ ἐπιμεῖναι αὐτοῦ. 35 Παῦλος δὲ καὶ
it seemed But to Silas to remain there. Paul And and

921 1304 1722 490 1321 2532
Βαρνάβας διέτριβον ἐν Ἀντιοχείᾳ, διδάσκοντες καὶ
Barnabas stayed in Antioch, teaching and

2097 3326 2532 2087 4183 3588 3056 3588
εὐαγγελιζόμενοι, μετὰ καὶ ἑτέρων πολλῶν, τὸν λόγον τοῦ
preaching the gospel, with also others many, the Word of the

King James Version

from us have troubled you with words, subverting your souls, saying, (Ye must) be circumcised, and keep the law: to whom we gave no (such) commandment:
25 It seemed good unto us, being assembled with one accord, to send chosen men unto you with our beloved Barnabas and Paul,

26 Men that have hazarded their lives for the name of our Lord Jesus Christ.

27 We have sent therefore Judas and Silas, who shall also tell (you) the same things by mouth.
28 For it seemed good to the Holy Ghost, and to us, to lay upon you no greater burden than these necessary things;

29 That ye abstain from meats offered to idols, and from blood, and from things strangled, and from fornication: from which if ye keep yourselves, ye shall do well. Fare ye well.

30 So when they were dismissed, they came to Antioch: and when they had gathered the multitude together, they delivered the epistle:
31 (Which) when they had read, they rejoiced for the consolation.
32 And Judas and Silas, being prophets also themselves, exhorted the brethren with many words, and confirmed (them).
33 And after they had tarried (there) a space, they were let go in peace from the brethren unto the apostles.

34 Notwithstanding it pleased Silas to abide there still.
35 Paul also and Barnabas continued in Antioch, teaching and preaching the word of the

Literal Translation | **Acts 15:36** | *King James Version*

Lord.

36. And after some days Paul said to Barnabas, Indeed, having turned back, let us look after our brothers throughout every city in which we proclaimed the Word of the Lord, how they are holding (it).

37 But Barnabas purposed to take John with (them), the (one) being called Mark.
38 But Paul thought it well not to take that one with (them), (he) having withdrawn from them from Pamphylia, and not going with them to the work.

39 Then there was sharp feeling, so as to separate them from each other. And taking Mark, Barnabas sailed away to Cyprus.

40 But having chosen Silas, Paul went out, being commended to the grace of God by the brothers
41 And he went through Syria and Cilicia, making the churches strong.

2962
Κυρίου.
Lord.

3326 1161 5100 2250 2036 3972 4314 921
36. Μετὰ δέ τινας ἡμέρας εἶπε Παῦλος πρὸς Βαρνάβαν,
after And some days said Paul to Barnabas,

1994 1211 1980 3588 80 2257
Ἐπιστρέψαντες δὴ ἐπισκεψώμεθα τοὺς ἀδελφοὺς ἡμῶν
Having turned back indeed let us look after the brothers of us

2596 3956 4172 1722 3739 2605 3588 3056 3588
κατὰ πᾶσαν πόλιν, ἐν αἷς κατηγγείλαμεν τὸν λόγον τοῦ
throughout every city, in which we proclaimed the word of the

2962 4459 2192 921 1161 1011 4838
Κυρίου, πῶς ἔχουσι. 37 Βαρνάβας δὲ ἐβουλεύσατο συμπαραλα-
Lord, how they are holding. Barnabas And purposed to take with

3588 2491 3588 2564 3138 3972 1161
βεῖν τὸν Ἰωάννην, τὸν καλούμενον Μάρκον. 38 Παῦλος δὲ
(them) John, being called Mark. Paul But

515 3588 868 575 846 575 3828 2532 3361
ἠξίου, τὸν ἀποστάντα ἀπ' αὐτῶν ἀπὸ Παμφυλίας, καὶ μὴ
thought fit, (he) having withdrawn from them from Pamphilia, and not

4905 846 1519 3588 2041 3361 4838 5126
συνελθόντα αὐτοῖς εἰς τὸ ἔργον, μὴ συμπαραλαβεῖν τοῦτον.
going with them to the work, not to take with (them) that one.

1096 3767 3948 5620 673 846 575
39 ἐγένετο οὖν παροξυσμός, ὥστε ἀποχωρισθῆναι αὐτοὺς ἀπ'
there was Then sharp feeling, so as to separate them from

240 3588 5037 921 3880 3588 3138 1602
ἀλλήλων, τόν τε Βαρνάβαν παραλαβόντα τὸν Μάρκον ἐκπλεῦσαι
each other and Barnabas taking Mark to sail away

1519 2954 3972 1161 1951 4609 1831
εἰς Κύπρον· 40 Παῦλος δὲ ἐπιλεξάμενος Σίλαν ἐξῆλθε,
to Cyprus. Paul And having chosen Silas went out,

3860 3588 5485 3588 2316 5259 3588 80 1330
παραδοθεὶς τῇ χάριτι τοῦ Θεοῦ ὑπὸ τῶν ἀδελφῶν. 41 διήρχετο
being commended to the grace of God by the brothers. he went through

1161 3588 4947 2532 3588 2791 1991 3588 1577
δὲ τὴν Συρίαν καὶ Κιλικίαν, ἐπιστηρίζων τὰς ἐκκλησίας.
And Syria and Cilicia, making strong the churches.

Lord, with many others also.

36. And some days after Paul said unto Barnabas, Let us go again and visit our brethren in every city where we have preached the word of the Lord, (and see) how they do.

37 And Barnabas determined to take with them John, whose surname was Mark.
38 But Paul thought not good to take him with them, who departed from them from Pamphylia, and went not with them to the work.

39 And the contention was so sharp between them, that they departed asunder one from the other: and so Barnabas took Mark, and sailed unto Cyprus;
40 And Paul chose Silas, and departed, being recommended by the brethren unto the grace of God.
41 And he went through Syria and Cilicia, confirming the churches.

Acts 16

1. And he came down to Derbe and Lystra. And behold! A certain disciple named Timothy was there, (the) son of a certain faithful Jewish woman, but of a Greek father.
2 (This one) was testified to by the brothers in Lystra and Iconium.
3 Paul desired this one to go forth with him, and taking (him he) circumcised him, because of the Jews being in those places. For they all knew his father, that he was a Greek.

4 And as

2658 1161 1519 1191 2532 3082 2532 2400 3101
1. Κατήντησε δὲ εἰς Δέρβην καὶ Λύστραν· καὶ ἰδού, μαθητής
he came down And to Derbe and Lystra; and behold! A disciple

5100 2258 1563 3686 5095 5207 1135 5100 2453
τις ἦν ἐκεῖ, ὀνόματι Τιμόθεος, υἱὸς γυναικός τινος Ἰουδαίας
certain was there, by name Timothy, son woman certain Jewish

4103 3962 1161 1672 3739 3140 5259 3588 1722
πιστῆς, πατρὸς δὲ Ἕλληνος· 2 ὃς ἐμαρτυρεῖτο ὑπὸ τῶν ἐν
of a faithful, father but of a Greek; who was testified to by the in

3082 2532 2430 80 5126 2309 3588 3972
Λύστροις καὶ Ἰκονίῳ ἀδελφῶν. 3 τοῦτον ἠθέλησεν ὁ Παῦλος
Lystra and Iconium brothers. This one desired Paul

4862 846 1831 2532 2983 4059 846 1223 3588
σὺν αὐτῷ ἐξελθεῖν, καὶ λαβὼν περιέτεμεν αὐτόν, διὰ τοὺς
with him to go forth, and taking circumcised him, because of the

2453 3588 5607 1722 3588 5117 1565 1492 1063
Ἰουδαίους τοὺς ὄντας ἐν τοῖς τόποις ἐκείνοις· ᾔδεισαν γὰρ
Jews being in places those; they knew for

537 3588 3962 846 3754 1672 5225 5613 1161
ἅπαντες τὸν πατέρα αὐτοῦ, ὅτι Ἕλλην ὑπῆρχεν. 4 ὡς δὲ
all the father of him, that a Greek he was. as And

1. Then came he to Derbe and Lystra: and, behold, a certain disciple was there, named Timotheus, the son of a certain woman, which was a Jewess, and believed; but his father (was) a Greek:
2 Which was well reported of by the brethren that were at Lystra and Iconium.
3 Him would Paul have to go forth with him; and took and circumcised him because of the Jews which were in those quarters: for they knew all that his father was a Greek.
4 And as

Literal Translation

Acts 16:5

King James Version

they went through the cities, they delivered to them (the need) to keep the decrees, the things having been decided on by the apostles and the elders in Jerusalem.
5 Then indeed the churches were being made strong in the faith, and increased in number day by day.

6 And passing through the Phrygian and the Galatian country, being forbidden by the Holy Spirit to speak the Word in Asia,

7 having come down to Mysia, they attempted to go along Bithynia, and the Spirit did not allow them.

8 And passing by Mysia, they came down into Troas.
9. And a vision appeared to Paul during the night: a certain man of Macedonia (was) standing, entreating him and saying, Passing over into Macedonia, help us!
10 And when he saw the vision, we immediately sought to go out into Macedonia, concluding that the Lord had called us to preach the gospel to them.

11 Then setting sail from Troas, we ran a straight course into Samothrace, and on the morrow into Neapolis,
12 and from there into Philippi, which is the first city of that part of Macedonia, a colony. And we were in this city, staying some days.

13 And on the day of the sabbaths, we went outside the city beside a river, where it was customary (for) prayer to be (made). And sitting down, we spoke to the women who came together (there).
14. And a certain

1279 3588 4172 3860 846 5442 3588
διεπορεύοντο τὰς πόλεις, παρεδίδουν αὐτοῖς φυλάσσειν τὰ
they went through the cities, they delivered to them to keep the

1378 3588 2919 5259 3588 652 2532 3588 4245
δόγματα τὰ κεκριμένα ὑπὸ τῶν ἀποστόλων καὶ τῶν πρεσ-
decrees having been decided on by the apostles and the elders

3588 1722 2419 3588 3303 3767 1577 4732
βυτέρων τῶν ἐν Ἱερουσαλήμ. 5 αἱ μὲν οὖν ἐκκλησίαι ἐστερε-
in Jerusalem. the indeed Then churches were made

3588 4102 2532 4052 3588 706 2596 2250
οῦντο τῇ πίστει, καὶ ἐπερίσσευον τῷ ἀριθμῷ καθ' ἡμέραν.
strong in the faith, and increased in number day by day.

1330 1161 3588 5435 2532 3588 1054 5561
6. Διελθόντες δὲ τὴν Φρυγίαν καὶ τὴν Γαλατικὴν χώραν,
having passed through And the Phrygian and the Galatian country,

2967 5259 3588 40 4151 2980 3588 3056
κωλυθέντες ὑπὸ τοῦ Ἁγίου Πνεύματος λαλῆσαι τὸν λόγον
being prevented by the Holy Spirit to speak the Word

1722 3588 773 2064 2596 3588 3465 3985 2596 3588
ἐν τῇ Ἀσίᾳ, 7 ἐλθόντες κατὰ τὴν Μυσίαν ἐπείραζον κατὰ τὴν
in Asia, coming against Mysia they attempted along

978 4198 2532 3756 1439 846 3588 4151
Βιθυνίαν πορεύεσθαι· καὶ οὐκ εἴασεν αὐτοὺς τὸ Πνεῦμα·
Bithynia to go along; and not allowed them the Spirit.

3928 1161 3588 3465 2597 1519 5174 2532
8 παρελθόντες δὲ τὴν Μυσίαν κατέβησαν εἰς Τρωάδα. 9 καὶ
passing by And Mysia they came down to Troas. And

3705 1223 3588 3571 3700 3588 3972 435 5100 2258 3110
ὅραμα διὰ τῆς νυκτὸς ὤφθη τῷ Παύλῳ· ἀνήρ τις ἦν Μακεδὼν
a vision during the night appeared to Paul; man a certain was of Macedonia

2476 3870 846 2532 3004 1224 1519 3109
ἑστώς, παρακαλῶν αὐτὸν καὶ λέγων, Διαβὰς εἰς Μακεδονίαν,
standing, entreating him and saying, Passing over into Macedonia,

997 2254 5613 1161 3588 3705 1492 2112 2212
βοήθησον ἡμῖν. 10 ὡς δὲ τὸ ὅραμα εἶδεν, εὐθέως ἐζητήσαμεν
help us. as And the vision he saw, at once we sought

1831 1519 3588 3109 4822 3754 4341
ἐξελθεῖν εἰς τὴν Μακεδονίαν, συμβιβάζοντες ὅτι προσκέκλη-
to go out to Macedonia, concluding that has called

2248 3588 2962 2097 846
ται ἡμᾶς ὁ Κύριος εὐαγγελίσασθαι αὐτούς.
us the Lord to preach the gospel to them.

321 3767 575 3588 5174 2113 1519
11. Ἀναχθέντες οὖν ἀπὸ τῆς Τρωάδος, εὐθυδρομήσαμεν εἰς
setting sail Then from Troas, we ran a straight course to

4543 3588 5037 1966 1519 3496 1564 5037 1519
Σαμοθρᾴκην, τῇ τε ἐπιούσῃ εἰς Νεάπολιν, 12 ἐκεῖθέν τε εἰς
Samothrace, on the and next day to Neapolis, from there and to

5375 3748 2076 4413 3588 3310 3588 3109
Φιλίππους, ἥτις ἐστὶ πρώτη τῆς μερίδος τῆς Μακεδονίας
Philippi, which is (the) first of the part of Macedonia

4172 2862 2258 1161 1722 3778 3588 4172 1304
πόλις, κολωνία· ἦμεν δὲ ἐν ταύτῃ τῇ πόλει διατρίβοντες
city, a colony; we were and in this city remaining

2250 5100 3588 5037 2250 3588 4521 1831 1854 3588
ἡμέρας τινάς. 13 τῇ τε ἡμέρᾳ τῶν σαββάτων ἐξήλθομεν ἔξω τῆς
days some. on the And day of the sabbaths, we went out outside the

4172 3844 4215 3757 3543 4335 1511 2532
πόλεως παρὰ ποταμόν, οὗ ἐνομίζετο προσευχὴ εἶναι, καὶ
city beside a river, where was customary prayer to be, and

2523 2980 3588 4905 1135 2532 5100
καθίσαντες ἐλαλοῦμεν ταῖς συνελθούσαις γυναιξί. 14 καί τις
sitting down we spoke to the coming together women. And a certain

they went through the cities, they delivered them the decrees for to keep, that were ordained of the apostles and elders which were at Jerusalem.
5 And so were the churches established in the faith, and increased in number daily.

6 Now when they had gone throughout Phrygia and the region of Galatia, and were forbidden of the Holy Ghost to preach the word in Asia,
7 After they were come to Mysia, they assayed to go into Bithynia: but the Spirit suffered them not.

8 And they passing by Mysia came down to Troas.
9. And a vision appeared to Paul in the night; There stood a man of Macedonia, and prayed him, saying, Come over into Macedonia, and help us.

10 And after he had seen the vision, immediately we endeavoured to go into Macedonia, assuredly gathering that the Lord had called us for to preach the gospel unto them.

11 Therefore loosing from Troas, we came with a straight course to Samothracia, and the next (day) to Neapolis;
12 And from thence to Philippi, which is the chief city of that part of Macedonia, (and) a colony: and we were in that city abiding certain days.

13 And on the sabbath we went out of the city by a river side, where prayer was wont to be made; and we sat down, and spake unto the women which resorted (thither).
14 . And a certain

Literal Translation **Acts 16:15** ***King James Version***

woman named Lydia, a seller of purple of (the) city of Thyatira, (one) reverencing God, listened, whose heart the Lord opened thoroughly to pay attention to the things being spoken by Paul.
15 And as she and her house were baptized, she implored (Paul), saying, If you have judged me to be believing in the Lord, entering into my house, remain. And she strongly urged us.

1135 3686 3070 4211 4172 2363
γυνὴ ὀνόματι Λυδία, πορφυρόπωλις πόλεως Θυατείρων,
woman by name Lydia, a seller of purple of (the) city of Thyatira,

4576 3588 2316 191 3739 3588 2962 1272 3588 2588
σεβομένη τὸν Θεόν, ἤκουεν· ἧς ὁ Κύριος διήνοιξε τὴν καρδίαν,
reverencing God, heard; of whom the Lord opened the heart,

4337 3588 2980 5259 3588 3972 5613 1161 907
προσέχειν τοῖς λαλουμένοις ὑπὸ τοῦ Παύλου. 15 ὡς δὲ ἐβαπτί-
to attend to the things being spoken by Paul. when And she was

2532 3588 3624 846 3870 3004 1487 2919
σθη, καὶ ὁ οἶκος αὐτῆς, παρεκάλεσε λέγουσα, Εἰ κεκρίκατέ
baptized, and the house of her, she implored saying, If you have judged

3165 4103 3588 2962 1511 1525 1519 3588 3624 3450
με πιστὴν τῷ Κυρίῳ εἶναι, εἰσελθόντες εἰς τὸν οἶκόν μου,
me believing in the Lord to be, entering into the house of me,

3306 2532 3849 2248
μείνατε. καὶ παρεβιάσατο ἡμᾶς.
remain. And she urged us.

woman named Lydia, a seller of purple, of the city of Thyatira, which worshipped God, heard (us): whose heart the Lord opened, that she attended unto the things which were spoken of Paul.
15 And when she was baptized, and her household, she besought (us), saying, If ye have judged me to be faithful to the Lord, come into my house, and abide (there). And she constrained us.

16. And it happened, we having gone into (a place of) prayer, a certain slave-girl having a Pythonic spirit met us, whose divining brought much gain to her lords.

1096 1161 4198 2257 1519 4335 3814
16. Ἐγένετο δὲ πορευομένων ἡμῶν εἰς προσευχήν, παιδίσκην
it happened And having gone us into (a place of) prayer, a girl

5100 2192 4151 4436 528 2254 3748
τινὰ ἔχουσαν πνεῦμα Πύθωνος ἀπαντῆσαι ἡμῖν, ἥτις
certain having a spirit of Python met us, who

2039 4183 3930 3588 2962 846 3132
ἐργασίαν πολλὴν παρεῖχε τοῖς κυρίοις αὐτῆς, μαντευομένη.
gain much brought to the lords of her, divining.

16. And it came to pass, as we went to prayer, a certain damsel possessed with a spirit of divination met us, which brought her masters much gain by soothsaying:

17 Following after Paul and us, she cried out, saying, These men are slaves of the Most High God, who proclaim to us a way of salvation!

18 And she did this over many days. But becoming distressed, and turning to the (demonic) spirit, Paul said, In the name of Jesus Christ I command you to come out from her! And it came out in that same hour.

3778 2628 3588 3972 2532 2254 2896 3004
17 αὕτη κατακολουθήσασα τῷ Παύλῳ καὶ ἡμῖν, ἔκραζε λέγουσα,
She following after Paul and us, cried out saying,

3778 3588 444 1401 3588 2316 3588 5310 1526
Οὗτοι οἱ ἄνθρωποι δοῦλοι τοῦ Θεοῦ τοῦ ὑψίστου εἰσίν,
These men slaves of the God Most High are,

3748 2605 2254 3598 4991 5124 1161
οἵτινες καταγγέλλουσιν ἡμῖν ὁδὸν σωτηρίας. 18 τοῦτο δὲ
who proclaim to us a way of salvation. this And

4160 1909 4183 2250 1278 1161 3588 3972 2532
ἐποίει ἐπὶ πολλὰς ἡμέρας. διαπονηθεὶς δὲ ὁ Παῦλος, καὶ
she did over many days. becoming distressed But Paul, and

1994 3588 4151 2036 3853 4671 1722 3588
ἐπιστρέψας, τῷ πνεύματι εἶπε, Παραγγέλλω σοι ἐν τῷ
turning, to the spirit he said, I command you in the

3686 2424 5547 1831 575 846 2532 1831
ὀνόματι Ἰησοῦ Χριστοῦ, ἐξελθεῖν ἀπ' αὐτῆς. καὶ ἐξῆλθεν
name of Jesus Christ, to come out from her. And it came out

846 3588 5610
αὐτῇ τῇ ὥρᾳ.
in the same hour.

17 The same followed Paul and us, and cried, saying, These men are the servants of the most high God, which shew unto us the way of salvation.
18 And this did she many days. But Paul, being grieved, turned and said to the spirit, I command thee in the name of Jesus Christ to come out of her. And he came out the same hour.

19 And seeing that the hope of their gain went out, having seized Paul and Silas, her lords dragged (them) to the market before the magistrates.
20 And bringing them near to the magistrates, (they) said, These men are greatly disturbing our city, being Jews,

1492 1161 3588 2962 846 3754 1831 3588 1680 3588
19 ἰδόντες δὲ οἱ κύριοι αὐτῆς ὅτι ἐξῆλθεν ἡ ἐλπὶς τῆς
seeing And the lords of her that came out the hope of the

2039 846 1949 3588 3972 2532 3588 4609
ἐργασίας αὐτῶν, ἐπιλαβόμενοι τὸν Παῦλον καὶ τὸν Σίλαν,
gain of them, having seized Paul and Silas,

1670 1519 3588 58 1909 3588 758 2532 4317
εἵλκυσαν εἰς τὴν ἀγορὰν ἐπὶ τοὺς ἄρχοντας, 20 καὶ προσ-
dragged into the market before the rulers, and bringing

846 3588 4755 2036 3778 3588 444
αγαγόντες αὐτοὺς τοῖς στρατηγοῖς εἶπον, Οὗτοι οἱ ἄνθρω-
near them to the magistrates, (they) said, These men

1613 2257 3588 4172 2453 5225
ποι ἐκταράσσουσιν ἡμῶν τὴν πόλιν, Ἰουδαῖοι ὑπάρχοντες,
are greatly disturbing of us the city, Jews being,

19 And when her masters saw that the hope of their gains was gone, they caught Paul and Silas, and drew (them) into the marketplace unto the rulers,
20 And brought them to the magistrates, saying, These men, being Jews, do exceedingly trouble our city,

Literal Translation

21 and announce customs which it is not lawful for us to receive, nor to do, being Romans.
22 And together the crowd rose up against them. And tearing off their clothes, the magistrates ordered (men) to flog (them).

23 And laying on them many stripes, (they) threw (them) into prison, charging the jailer to keep them securely,

24 who, receiving such a charge, threw them into the inner prison, and made fast their feet in the stocks.

25. And about midnight, having prayed, Paul and Silas praised God in a hymn. And the prisoners listened to them.

26 And suddenly there was a great earthquake, so that the foundations of the jail (were) shaken. And immediately all the doors were opened, and all of the bonds were loosed.

27 And the jailer having become awake, and seeing that the doors of the prison had been opened, having drawn a sword, he was about to do away with himself, supposing the prisoners to have escaped.

28 But Paul called out with a loud voice, saying, Do no harm (to) yourself! For we are all here.
29 And asking for lights, he rushed in. And becoming trembly, he fell before Paul and Silas.
30 And leading them outside, he said, Sirs, what must I do that I may be saved?
31 And they said, Believe on the Lord Jesus Christ, and you will be saved,

Acts 16:21

2532 2605 1485 3739 3756 1832 2254 3858
21 καὶ καταγγέλλουσιν ἔθη ἃ οὐκ ἔξεστιν ἡμῖν παραδέχεσθαι
and they proclaim customs which not it is lawful for us to receive

3761 4160 4514 5607 2532 4911 3588 3793 2596
οὐδὲ ποιεῖν, Ῥωμαίοις οὖσι. 22 καὶ συνεπέστη ὁ ὄχλος κατ᾽
nor to do, Romans being. And rose together the crowd against

846 2532 3588 4755 4048 846 3588 2440
αὐτῶν, καὶ οἱ στρατηγοὶ περιρρήξαντες αὐτῶν τὰ ἱμάτια
them, and the magistrates tearing off of them the clothes

2753 4463 4183 5037 2007 846 4127
ἐκέλευον ῥαβδίζειν. 23 πολλάς τε ἐπιθέντες αὐτοῖς πληγὰς
ordered to flog. many And laying on them stripes

906 1519 5438 3853 3588 1200
ἔβαλον εἰς φυλακήν, παραγγείλαντες τῷ δεσμοφύλακι
threw into prison, charging the jailer

806 5083 846 3739 3852 5108 2983
ἀσφαλῶς τηρεῖν αὐτούς· 24 ὅς, παραγγελίαν τοιαύτην εἰληφώς,
securely to keep them; who a charge such having received,

906 846 1519 3588 2082 5438 2532 3588 4228
ἔβαλεν αὐτοὺς εἰς τὴν ἐσωτέραν φυλακήν, καὶ τοὺς πόδας
threw them into the inner prison, and the feet

846 805 1519 3588 3586 2596 1161 3588 3317
αὐτῶν ἠσφαλίσατο εἰς τὸ ξύλον. 25 κατὰ δὲ τὸ μεσονύκτιον
of them made fast in the stocks. about And midnight

3972 2532 4609 4336 5214 3588 2316
Παῦλος καὶ Σίλας προσευχόμενοι ὕμνουν τὸν Θεόν, ἐπη-
Paul and Silas having prayed hymned (the praise of) God,

1874 1161 846 3588 1198 869 1161 4578 1096
κροῶντο δὲ αὐτῶν οἱ δέσμιοι· 26 ἄφνω δὲ σεισμὸς ἐγένετο
listened and to them the prisoners. suddenly And earthquake occurred

3173 5620 4531 3588 2310 3588 1201
μέγας, ὥστε σαλευθῆναι τὰ θεμέλια τοῦ δεσμωτηρίου·
a great, so as to be shaken the foundations of the jail;

455 5037 3916 3588 2374 3956 2532 3956
ἀνεῴχθησάν τε παραχρῆμα αἱ θύραι πᾶσαι, καὶ πάντων
were opened and immediately the doors all, and of all

3588 1199 447 1853 1161 1096 3588 1200 2532
τὰ δεσμὰ ἀνέθη. 27 ἔξυπνος δὲ γενόμενος ὁ δεσμοφύλαξ, καὶ
the bonds were loosed. awake And having become the jailer, and

1492 455 3588 2374 3588 5438 4685
ἰδὼν ἀνεῳγμένας τὰς θύρας τῆς φυλακῆς, σπασάμενος
seeing having been opened the doors of the prison, having drawn

3162 3195 1438 337 3543 1628
μάχαιραν, ἔμελλεν ἑαυτὸν ἀναιρεῖν, νομίζων ἐκπεφευγέναι
a sword, was about himself to kill, supposing to have escaped

3588 1198 5455 1161 5456 3173 3588 3972 3004
τοὺς δεσμίους. 28 ἐφώνησε δὲ φωνῇ μεγάλῃ ὁ Παῦλος λέγων,
the prisoners. called But voice with a great Paul saying,

3367 4238 4572 2556 537 1063 2070 1759
Μηδὲν πράξῃς σεαυτῷ κακόν· ἅπαντες γάρ ἐσμεν ἐνθάδε.
nothing Do (to) yourself harm; all for we are here.

154 1161 5457 1530 2532 1790 1096
29 αἰτήσας δὲ φῶτα εἰσεπήδησε, καὶ ἔντρομος γενόμενος
asking And (for) lights he rushed in, and trembling having become

4363 3588 3972 2532 3588 4609 2532 4254 846
προσέπεσε τῷ Παύλῳ καὶ τῷ Σίλᾳ, 30 καὶ προαγαγὼν αὐτοὺς
he fell before Paul and Silas, and leading them

1854 5346 2962 5101 3165 1163 4160 2443 4982 3588 1161 2036
ἔξω ἔφη, Κύριοι, τί με δεῖ ποιεῖν ἵνα σωθῶ; 31 οἱ δὲ εἶπον,
outside said, Sirs, what me must do that I may be saved? they And said,

4100 1909 3588 2962 2424 5547 2532 4982
Πίστευσον ἐπὶ τὸν Κύριον Ἰησοῦν Χριστόν, καὶ σωθήσῃ
Believe on the Lord Jesus Christ and you will be saved

King James Version

21 And teach customs, which are not lawful for us to receive, neither to observe, being Romans.
22 And the multitude rose up together against them: and the magistrates rent off their clothes, and commanded to beat (them).
23 And when they had laid many stripes upon them, they cast (them) into prison, charging the jailor to keep them safely:

24 Who, having received such a charge, thrust them into the inner prison, and made their feet fast in the stocks.

25. And at midnight Paul and Silas prayed, and sang praises unto God: and the prisoners heard them.

26 And suddenly there was a great earthquake, so that the foundations of the prison were shaken: and immediately all the doors were opened, and every one's bands were loosed.

27 And the keeper of the prison awaking out of his sleep, and seeing the prison doors open, he drew out his sword, and would have killed himself, supposing that the prisoners had been fled.

28 But Paul cried with a loud voice, saying, Do thyself no harm: for we are all here.

29 Then he called for a light, and sprang in, and came trembling, and fell down before Paul and Silas,
30 And brought them out, and said, Sirs, what must I do to be saved?
31 And they said, Believe on the Lord Jesus Christ, and thou shalt be saved,

Literal Translation

Acts 16:32

King James Version

you and your house.
32 And they spoke the Word of the Lord to him, and to all those in his house.
33 And taking them in that hour of the night, he washed from (their) stripes. And he and all those of him were baptized at once.

34 And bringing them up to the house, he set a table before (them), and exulted whole-housely, having believed God.

35 And day having come, the magistrates sent the floggers, saying, set loose those men.

36 And the jailer announced these words to Paul, The magistrates have sent that you be set loose Now, then, going out, proceed in peace.
37 But Paul said to them, Having flogged us publicly, being Romans and uncondemned men, they threw (us) into prison. And now do they throw us out secretly? No, indeed! But coming themselves, let them bring us out.

38 And the floggers reported these words to the magistrates. And hearing that they were Romans, they were afraid.
39 And coming, they begged (them). And bringing (them) out, (they) asked (them) to go out of the city.
40 And going out from the prison, (they) went into the (house of) Lydia. And seeing the brothers, they exhorted them, and went out.

4771 2532 3588 3624 4675 2532 2980 846 3588 3056 3588
σὺ καὶ ὁ οἶκός σου. 32 καὶ ἐλάλησαν αὐτῷ τὸν λόγον τοῦ
you and the house of you. And they spoke to him the Word of the

2962 2532 3956 3588 1722 3588 3614 846 2532 3880
Κυρίου, καὶ πᾶσι τοῖς ἐν τῇ οἰκίᾳ αὐτοῦ. 33 καὶ παραλαβὼν
Lord, and all those in the house of him. And taking

846 1722 1565 3588 5610 3588 3571 3068 575 3588 4127
αὐτοὺς ἐν ἐκείνῃ τῇ ὥρᾳ τῆς νυκτὸς ἔλουσεν ἀπὸ τῶν πλη-
them in that hour of the night He washed from the stripes,

2532 907 846 2532 3588 846 3956 3916
γῶν, καὶ ἐβαπτίσθη αὐτὸς καὶ οἱ αὐτοῦ πάντες παραχρῆμα.
and was baptized he and those of him all at once.

321 5037 846 1519 3588 3624 846 3908 5132
34 ἀναγαγών τε αὐτοὺς εἰς τὸν οἶκον αὐτοῦ παρέθηκε τράπε-
bringing up And them to the house he set before a table,

2532 21 3832 4100 3588 2316
ζαν, καὶ ἠγαλλιάσατο πανοικὶ πεπιστευκὼς τῷ Θεῷ.
and exulted whole-housely having believed God.

2250 1161 1096 649 3588 4755 3588
35. Ἡμέρας δὲ γενομένης, ἀπέστειλαν οἱ στρατηγοὶ τοὺς
day And having come sent the magistrates the

4465 3004 630 3588 444 1565
ῥαβδούχους λέγοντες, Ἀπόλυσον τοὺς ἀνθρώπους ἐκείνους.
floggers saying, Set loose men those.

518 1161 3588 1200 3588 3056 5128 4314
36 ἀπήγγειλε δὲ ὁ δεσμοφύλαξ τοὺς λόγους τούτους πρὸς
announced And the jailer words these to

3588 3972 3754 649 3588 4755 2443 630
τὸν Παῦλον ὅτι Ἀπεστάλκασιν οἱ στρατηγοί, ἵνα ἀπολυθῆτε·
Paul, have sent The magistrates, that you be set loose;

3568 3767 1831 4198 1722 1515 3588 1161 3972
νῦν οὖν ἐξελθόντες πορεύεσθε ἐν εἰρήνῃ. 37 ὁ δὲ Παῦλος
now then going out proceed in peace. But Paul

5346 4314 846 1194 2248 1219 178
ἔφη πρὸς αὐτούς, Δείραντες ἡμᾶς δημοσίᾳ, ἀκατακρίτους,
said to them, Having flogged us publicly, uncondemned

444 4514 5225 906 1519 5438 2532
ἀνθρώπους Ῥωμαίους ὑπάρχοντας, ἔβαλον εἰς φυλακήν, καὶ
men, Romans being, they threw into prison, and

3568 2977 2248 1544 3756 1063 235 2064 846
νῦν λάθρα ἡμᾶς ἐκβάλλουσιν; οὐ γάρ· ἀλλὰ ἐλθόντες αὐτοὶ
now secretly us they throw out? No, indeed! But coming themselves

2248 1806 312 1161 3588 4755 3588
ἡμᾶς ἐξαγαγέτωσαν. 38 ἀνήγγειλαν δὲ τοῖς στρατηγοῖς οἱ
us let them bring out. reported And to the magistrates the

4465 3588 4487 5023 2532 5399 191
ῥαβδοῦχοι τὰ ῥήματα ταῦτα· καὶ ἐφοβήθησαν ἀκούσαντες
floggers words these. And they were afraid hearing

3754 4514 1526 2532 2064 3870 846 2532
ὅτι Ῥωμαῖοί εἰσι, 39 καὶ ἐλθόντες παρεκάλεσαν αὐτούς, καὶ
that Romans they are, and coming they begged them, and

1806 2065 1831 3588 4172 1831 1161 1537
ἐξαγαγόντες ἠρώτων ἐξελθεῖν τῆς πόλεως. 40 ἐξελθόντες δὲ ἐκ
bringing out asked to go out of the city. going out And from

3588 5438 1525 1519 3588 3070 2532 1492 3588 80
τῆς φυλακῆς εἰσῆλθον εἰς τὴν Λυδίαν· καὶ ἰδόντες τοὺς ἀδελ-
the prison entered into the (house of) Lydia; and seeing the brothers,

3870 846 2532 1831
φούς, παρεκάλεσαν αὐτούς, καὶ ἐξῆλθον.
they exhorted them, and went forth.

and thy house.
32 And they spake unto him the word of the Lord, and to all that were in his house.
33 And he took them the same hour of the night, and washed (their) stripes; and was baptized, he and all his, straightway.

34 And when he had brought them into his house, he set meat before them, and rejoiced, believing in God with all his house.

35 And when it was day, the magistrates sent the serjeants, saying, Let those men go.

36 And the keeper of the prison told this saying to Paul, The magistrates have sent to let you go: now therefore depart, and go in peace.
37 But Paul said unto them, They have beaten us openly uncondemned, being Romans, and have cast (us) into prison; and now do they thrust us out privily? nay verily; but let them come themselves and fetch us out.

38 And the serjeants told these words unto the magistrates: and they feared, when they heard that they were Romans.
39 And they came and besought them, and brought (them) out, and desired (them) to depart out of the city.
40 And they went out of the prison, and entered into (the house of) Lydia: and when they had seen the brethren, they comforted them, and departed.

Literal Translation

Acts 17

1. And traveling through Amphipolis and Apollonia, they came to Thessalonica, where there was a synagogue of the Jews.

2 And according to Paul's custom, he went in to them and reasoned with them from the Scriptures on three sabbaths,
3 opening and setting forth that the Christ must have suffered, and to have risen from (the) dead, and that this is the Christ, Jesus, whom I proclaim to you.

4 And some of them were persuaded and joined themselves to Paul and Silas, both a great multitude of the worshiping Greeks, and not a few of the leading women.

5. But becoming jealous, and having taken aside some wicked men of the market-loafers, and gathering a crowd, the disobeying Jews set the city into turmoil. And coming on the house of Jason, (they) sought to bring them on to the mob.
6 But not finding them, they dragged Jason and some brothers before the city judges, crying, Those having turned the habitable world upside down have come here, too;

7 whom Jason has received. And these all act contrary to the decrees of Caesar, saying there is another king, Jesus.

8 And hearing these things, they agitated the crowd and the city judges.
9 And taking security from Jason and the rest, they set them loose.

Acts 17

1353 1161 3588 295 2532 624 2064
1. Διοδεύσαντες δὲ τὴν Ἀμφίπολιν καὶ Ἀπολλωνίαν, ἦλθον
traveling through And Amphipolis and Apollonia, they came

1519 2332 3699 2258 3588 4864 3588 2453
εἰς Θεσσαλονίκην, ὅπου ἦν ἡ συναγωγὴ τῶν Ἰουδαίων·
into Thessalonica, where was a synagogue of the Jews.

2596 1161 3588 1486 3588 3972 1525 4314 846 2532 1909
2 κατὰ δὲ τὸ εἰωθὸς τῷ Παύλῳ εἰσῆλθε πρὸς αὐτούς, καὶ ἐπὶ
according to And the custom of Paul he went in to them, and on

4521 5140 1256 846 575 3588 1124 1272
σάββατα τρία διελέγετο αὐτοῖς ἀπὸ τῶν γραφῶν, 3 διανοίγων
sabbaths three he reasoned with them from the Scriptures, opening

2532 3908 3754 3588 5547 1163 3958 2532 450
καὶ παρατιθέμενος, ὅτι τὸν Χριστὸν ἔδει παθεῖν καὶ ἀναστῆ-
and setting forth, that the Christ must have suffered and to have

1537 3498 2532 3754 3778 2076 3588 5547 2424 3739 1473
ναι ἐκ νεκρῶν, καὶ ὅτι οὗτός ἐστιν ὁ Χριστὸς Ἰησοῦς, ὃν ἐγὼ
risen from (the) dead, and that this is the Christ, Jesus, whom I

2605 5213 2532 5100 1537 846 3982 2532
καταγγέλλω ὑμῖν. 4 καί τινες ἐξ αὐτῶν ἐπείσθησαν, καὶ
proclaim to you. And some of them were persuaded, and

4345 3588 3972 2532 3588 4609 3588 5037 4576
προσεκληρώθησαν τῷ Παύλῳ καὶ τῷ Σίλᾳ, τῶν τε σεβο-
joined themselves to Paul and Silas, of the both worship-

1672 4183 4128 1135 5037 3588 4413
μένων Ἑλλήνων πολὺ πλῆθος, γυναικῶν τε τῶν πρώτων
ing Greeks a great multitude, of women and the first (ones)

3756 3641 2206 1161 3588 544 2453 2532
οὐκ ὀλίγαι. 5 ζηλώσαντες δὲ οἱ ἀπειθοῦντες Ἰουδαῖοι, καὶ
not a few. becoming jealous But the disobeying Jews, and

4355 3588 60 5100 435 4190 2532
προσλαβόμενοι τῶν ἀγοραίων τινὰς ἄνδρας πονηρούς, καὶ
having taken aside the market-loafers some men wicked, and

3792 2350 3588 4172 2186 5037 3588
ὀχλοποιήσαντες, ἐθορύβουν τὴν πόλιν· ἐπιστάντες τε τῇ
gathering a crowd, set into turmoil the city. coming on And the

3614 2394 2212 846 71 1519 3588 1218 3361
οἰκίᾳ Ἰάσονος, ἐζήτουν αὐτοὺς ἀγαγεῖν εἰς τὸν δῆμον. 6 μὴ
house of Jason, sought them to bring on to the mob. not

2147 1161 846 4951 3588 2394 2532 5100 80
εὑρόντες δὲ αὐτούς, ἔσυρον τὸν Ἰάσονα καί τινας ἀδελφοὺς
finding But them, they dragged Jason and some brothers

1909 3588 4173 994 3754 3588 3588 3625
ἐπὶ τοὺς πολιτάρχας, βοῶντες ὅτι Οἱ τὴν οἰκουμένην
to the city judges, crying, Those the habitable world

387 3778 2532 1759 3918 3739 5264
ἀναστατώσαντες, οὗτοι καὶ ἐνθάδε πάρεισιν, 7 οὓς ὑποδέδε-
having turned upside down, these also here have come, whom has re-

2394 2532 3778 3956 561 3588 1378
κται Ἰάσων· καὶ οὗτοι πάντες ἀπέναντι τῶν δογμάτων
ceived Jason and these all contrary to the decrees

2541 4238 935 3004 2087 1511 2424
Καίσαρος πράττουσι, βασιλέα λέγοντες ἕτερον εἶναι, Ἰησοῦν.
of Caesar act, king saying another to be, Jesus.

5015 1161 3588 3793 2532 3588 4173 191
8 ἐτάραξαν δὲ τὸν ὄχλον καὶ τοὺς πολιτάρχας ἀκούοντας
they agitated And the crowd and the city judges hearing

5023 2532 2983 3588 2425 3844 3588 2394 2532 3588
ταῦτα. 9 καὶ λαβόντες τὸ ἱκανὸν παρὰ τοῦ Ἰάσονος καὶ τῶν
these things. And taking the security from Jason and the

3062 630 846
λοιπῶν, ἀπέλυσαν αὐτούς.
rest, they set loose them.

King James Version

Acts 17

1. Now when they had passed through Amphipolis and Apollonia, they came to Thessalonica, where was a synagogue of the Jews:

2 And Paul, as his manner was, went in unto them, and three sabbath days reasoned with them out of the scriptures,
3 Opening and alleging, that Christ must needs have suffered, and risen again from the dead; and that this Jesus, whom I preach unto you, is Christ.

4 And some of them believed, and consorted with Paul and Silas; and of the devout Greeks a great multitude, and of the chief women not a few.

5. But the Jews which believed not, moved with envy, took unto them certain lewd fellows of the baser sort, and gathered a company, and set all the city on an uproar, and assaulted the house of Jason, and sought to bring them out to the people.
6 And when they found them not, they drew Jason and certain brethren unto the rulers of the city, crying, These that have turned the world upside down are come hither also;

7 Whom Jason hath received: and these all do contrary to the decrees of Caesar, saying that there is another king, (one) Jesus.

8 And they troubled the people and the rulers of the city, when they heard these things.
9 And when they had taken security of Jason, and of the other, they let them go.

Literal Translation

10. But during the night at once the brothers sent both Paul and Silas to Berea; who having arrived went into the synagogue of the Jews.

11 And these were more noble than those in Thessalonica, for (they received) the Word with all readiness, daily examining the Scriptures if these things have (been so).

12 Then indeed many from among them believed, and not a few of the honorable Greek women and men.

13 But when the Jews from Thessalonica knew that the Word of God was also proclaimed in Berea by Paul, they came there also, shaking up the crowd.

14 And immediately, then, the brothers sent away Paul, to go on as toward the sea. But both Silas and Timothy remained there.

15 But those conducting Paul brought him as far as Athens. And having received a command to Silas and Timothy that they come to him quickly, they went out.

16. But awaiting them in Athens, Paul's spirit was pained within him, beholding the city being full of images.

17 Then, indeed, he addressed the Jews in the synagogue, and those worshiping, also in the market every day, to those happening to be (there).
18 And some of the

Acts 17:10

3588 1161 80 2112 1223 3588 3571 1599 3588 5037
10. Οἱ δὲ ἀδελφοὶ εὐθέως διὰ τῆς νυκτὸς ἐξέπεμψαν τόν τε
the But brothers at once during the night sent out both

3972 2532 3588 4609 1519 960 3748 3854
Παῦλον καὶ τὸν Σίλαν εἰς Βέροιαν· οἵτινες παραγενόμενοι
Paul and Silas to Berea, who having arrived

1519 3588 4864 3588 2453 549 3778 1161 2258
εἰς τὴν συναγωγὴν τῶν Ἰουδαίων ἀπῄεσαν. 11 οὗτοι δὲ ἦσαν
into the synagogue of the Jews went. these And were

2104 3588 1722 2332 3748 1209 3588
εὐγενέστεροι τῶν ἐν Θεσσαλονίκῃ, οἵτινες ἐδέξαντο τὸν
more noble (than) those in Thessalonica, who received the

3056 3326 3956 4288 3588 2596 2250 350
λόγον μετὰ πάσης προθυμίας, τὸ καθ' ἡμέραν ἀνακρίνοντες
Word with all readiness, day by day examining

3588 1124 1487 2192 5023 3779 4183 3303 3767 1537 846
τὰς γραφάς, εἰ ἔχοι ταῦτα οὕτως. 12 πολλοὶ μὲν οὖν ἐξ αὐτῶν
the Scriptures, if have (been) these things so. Many indeed then of them

4100 2532 3588 1674 1135 3588 2158
ἐπίστευσαν, καὶ τῶν Ἑλληνίδων γυναικῶν τῶν εὐσχη-
believed, and of the Greek women honorable

2532 435 3756 3641 5613 1161 1097 3588 575 3588
μόνων καὶ ἀνδρῶν οὐκ ὀλίγοι. 13 ὡς δὲ ἔγνωσαν οἱ ἀπὸ τῆς
and men not a few. when But knew the from

2332 2453 3754 2532 1722 3588 960 2605
Θεσσαλονίκης Ἰουδαῖοι ὅτι καὶ ἐν τῇ Βεροίᾳ κατηγγέλη
Thessalonica Jews that also in Berea was proclaimed

5259 3588 3972 3588 3056 3588 2316 2064 2546 4531
ὑπὸ τοῦ Παύλου ὁ λόγος τοῦ Θεοῦ, ἦλθον κἀκεῖ σαλεύοντες
by Paul the Word of God, they came there also shaking up

3588 3793 2112 1161 5119 3588 3972 1821 3588
τοὺς ὄχλους. 14 εὐθέως δὲ τότε τὸν Παῦλον ἐξαπέστειλαν οἱ
the crowd. at once And then Paul sent away the

80 4198 5613 1909 3588 2281 5278 1161 3588
ἀδελφοὶ πορεύεσθαι ὡς ἐπὶ τὴν θάλασσαν· ὑπέμενον δὲ ὅ
brothers to go on as toward ,the sea. remained But

5037 4609 2532 3588 5095 1563 3588 1161 2525 3588 3972
τε Σίλας καὶ ὁ Τιμόθεος ἐκεῖ. 15 οἱ δὲ καθιστῶντες τὸν Παῦλον,
both Silas and Timothy there. those And conducting Paul

71 846 2193 116 2532 2983 1785 4314
ἤγαγον αὐτὸν ἕως Ἀθηνῶν· καὶ λαβόντες ἐντολὴν πρὸς
brought him as far as Athens; and having received a command to

3588 4609 2532 5095 2443 5613 5033 2064 4314 846
τὸν Σίλαν καὶ Τιμόθεον, ἵνα ὡς τάχιστα ἔλθωσι πρὸς αὐτόν,
Silas and Timothy, that as quickly they come to him,

1826
ἐξῄεσαν.
they went out.

1722 1161 3588 116 1551 846 3588 3972
16. Ἐν δὲ ταῖς Ἀθήναις ἐκδεχομένου αὐτοὺς τοῦ Παύλου,
in And Athens awaiting them Paul,

3947 3588 4151 846 1722 846 2334 2712
παρωξύνετο τὸ πνεῦμα αὐτοῦ ἐν αὐτῷ, θεωροῦντι κατεί-
was pained the spirit of him within him, beholding full of

5607 3588 4172 1256 3303 3767 1722 3588 4864
δωλον οὖσαν τὴν πόλιν. 17 διελέγετο μὲν οὖν ἐν τῇ συναγωγῇ
images being the city. he addressed indeed Then in the synagogue

3588 2453 2532 3588 4576 2532 1722 3588 58 2596
τοῖς Ἰουδαίοις καὶ τοῖς σεβομένοις, καὶ ἐν τῇ ἀγορᾷ κατὰ
the Jews and those worshiping, also in the market

3956 2250 4314 3588 3909 5100 1161 3588
πᾶσαν ἡμέραν πρὸς τοὺς παρατυγχάνοντας. 18 τινὲς δὲ τῶν
every day to those happening to be (there). some And of the

King James Version

10. And the brethren immediately sent away Paul and Silas by night unto Berea: who coming (thither) went into the synagogue of the Jews.
11 These were more noble than those in Thessalonica, in that they received the word with all readiness of mind, and searched the scriptures daily, whether those things were so.

12 Therefore many of them believed; also of honourable women which were Greeks, and of men, not a few.

13 But when the Jews of Thessalonica had knowledge that the word of God was preached of Paul at Berea, they came thither also, and stirred up the people.

14 And then immediately the brethren sent away Paul to go as it were to the sea: but Silas and Timotheus abode there still.

15 And they that conducted Paul brought him unto Athens: and receiving a commandment unto Silas and Timotheus for to come to him with all speed, they departed.

16. Now while Paul waited for them at Athens, his spirit was stirred in him, when he saw the city wholly given to idolatry.

17 Therefore disputed he in the synagogue with the Jews, and with the devout persons, and in the market daily with them that met with him.
18 Then certain philosophers of the

Literal Translation — **Acts 17:19** — **King James Version**

Epicureans and of the Stoics, philosophers, fell in with him. And some said, What may this seed-scatterer wish to say? And these (others), He seems to be an announcer of foreign demons, (because he proclaimed Jesus and, the resurrection to them.
19 And taking hold of him, they led (him) to the Areopagus, saying, Are we able to know what (is) this new doctrine being spoken by you?

20 For you bring startling things to our ears. We are minded, then, to know what these things may wish to be.
21 And all Athenians and the strangers living (there) have leisure for nothing else than to say and to hear newer (things).

22. And standing in (the) middle of the Areopagus, Paul said, Men, Athenians, I behold you (are) god-fearers in everything;

23 for passing through and looking up at the objects of your worship, I also found an altar on which had been written, TO AN UNKNOWN GOD. Not knowing, then, whom you worship, this (One) I announce you.

24 The God who made the world and all things in it, this One being Lord of Heaven and of earth, does not dwell in handmade temples,

25 nor is served by hands of men, (as) having need of anything. (For) He is giving life and breath and all things to all.
26 And He made every nation of men of one blood, to live on all the face of the earth, ordaining

1946 2532 3588 4770 5386 4820 846
Ἐπικουρείων καὶ τῶν Στωϊκῶν φιλοσόφων συνέβαλλον αὐτῷ.
Epicureans and the Stoics philosophers fell in with him.

2532 5100 3004 5101 302 2309 3588 4691 3778 3004
καί τινες ἔλεγον, Τί ἂν θέλοι ὁ σπερμολόγος οὗτος λέγειν;
And some said, What may desire seed-picker this to say?

3588 1161 3581 1140 1380 2604 1511 3754 3588
οἱ δέ, Ξένων δαιμονίων δοκεῖ καταγγελεὺς εἶναι· ὅτι τὸν
these And, Of foreign demons he seems an announcer to be; because

2424 2532 3588 386 846 2097 1949
Ἰησοῦν καὶ τὴν ἀνάστασιν αὐτοῖς εὐηγγελίζετο. 19 ἐπιλα-
Jesus and the resurrection to them he proclaimed. taking

5037 846 1909 3588 697 697 71 3004
βόμενοί τε αὐτοῦ, ἐπὶ τὸν Ἄρειον πάγον ἤγαγον, λέγοντες,
hold of And him, onto the Areopagus led him, saying,

1410 1097 5101 3588 2537 3778 3588 5259 4675 2980
Δυνάμεθα γνῶναι, τίς ἡ καινὴ αὕτη ἡ ὑπὸ σοῦ λαλουμένη
Are we able to know what new this by you being spoken

1322 3579 1063 5100 1533 1519 3588 189 2257
διδαχή; 20 ξενίζοντα γάρ τινα εἰσφέρεις εἰς τὰς ἀκοὰς ἡμῶν·
doctrine (is)? startling things For some you bring to the ears of us;

1014 3767 1097 5101 302 2309 5023 1511 117
βουλόμεθα οὖν γνῶναι, τί ἂν θέλοι ταῦτα εἶναι. 21 [Ἀθηναῖοι
we are minded then to know that may wish these things to be. Athenians

1161 3956 2532 3588 1927 3581 1519 3762 2087 2119
δὲ πάντες καὶ οἱ ἐπιδημοῦντες ξένοι εἰς οὐδὲν ἕτερον εὐκαί-
And all and the dwelling strangers for nothing different have

2228 3004 5100 2532 191 2537
ρουν, ἢ λέγειν τι καὶ ἀκούειν καινότερον.]
leisure, either to say and to hear newer (things).

2476 1161 3588 3972 1722 3319 3588 697 697 5346
22. Σταθεὶς δὲ ὁ Παῦλος ἐν μέσῳ τοῦ Ἀρείου πάγου ἔφη,
standing And Paul in (the) midst of the Areopagus said,

435 117 2596 3956 5613 1174 5209
Ἄνδρες Ἀθηναῖοι, κατὰ πάντα ὡς δεισιδαιμονεστέρους ὑμᾶς
Men Athenians, in everything (how) very fearful of gods you

2334 1330 1063 2532 333 3588 4574
θεωρῶ. 23 διερχόμενος γὰρ καὶ ἀναθεωρῶν τὰ σεβάσματα
I behold. passing through For and looking up at the objects of worship

5216 2147 2532 1041 1722 3739 1924 57 2316
ὑμῶν, εὗρον καὶ βωμὸν ἐν ᾧ ἐπεγέγραπτο, Ἀγνώστῳ Θεῷ.
of you, I found also an altar in which had been written, To an Unknown God.

3739 3767 50 2151 5126 1473 2605 5213
ὃν οὖν ἀγνοοῦντες εὐσεβεῖτε, τοῦτον ἐγὼ καταγγέλλω ὑμῖν.
Whom, then, not knowing you worship, This One I announce to you.

3588 2316 3588 4160 3588 2889 2532 3956 3588 1722 846 3778
24 ὁ Θεὸς ὁ ποιήσας τὸν κόσμον καὶ πάντα τὰ ἐν αὐτῷ, οὗτος,
The God the One having made the world and all the things in it, this One

3772 2532 1093 2962 5225 3756 1722 5499
οὐρανοῦ καὶ γῆς κύριος ὑπάρχων, οὐκ ἐν χειροποιήτοις
of heaven and of earth Lord being, not in made by hand

3485 2730 3761 5259 5495 444 2323
ναοῖς κατοικεῖ, 25 οὐδὲ ὑπὸ χειρῶν ἀνθρώπων θεραπεύεται,
temples dwells, nor by (the) hands of men is served,

4326 5100 846 1325 3956 2222 2532 4157 2532
προσδεόμενός τινος, αὐτὸς διδοὺς πᾶσι ζωὴν καὶ πνοὴν καὶ
(nor) having need (of) anything, He is giving to all life and breath and

3588 3956 4160 5037 1537 1520 129 3956 1484 444
τὰ πάντα· 26 ἐποίησέ τε ἐξ ἑνὸς αἵματος πᾶν ἔθνος ἀνθρώπων,
things all. He made And of one blood every nation of men,

2730 1909 3956 3588 4383 3588 1093 3724 4384
κατοικεῖν ἐπὶ πᾶν τὸ πρόσωπον τῆς γῆς, ὁρίσας προτεταγ-
to dwell on all the face of the earth, ordaining (and) fore-

Epicureans, and of the Stoicks, encountered him. And some said, What will this babbler say? other some, He seemeth to be a setter forth of strange gods: because he preached unto them Jesus, and the resurrection.

19 And they took him, and brought him unto Areopagus, saying, May we know what this new doctrine, whereof thou speakest, (is)?

20 For thou bringest certain strange things to our ears: we would know therefore what these things mean.
21 (For all the Athenians and strangers which were there spent their time in nothing else, but either to tell, or to hear some new thing.)

22. Then Paul stood in the midst of Mars' hill, and said, (Ye) men of Athens, I perceive that in all things ye are too superstitious.

23 For as I passed by, and beheld your devotions, I found an altar with this inscription, TO THE UNKNOWN GOD. Whom therefore ye ignorantly worship, him declare I unto you.

24 God that made the world and all things therein, seeing that he is Lord of heaven and earth, dwelleth not in temples made with hands;
25 Neither is worshipped with men's hands, as though he needed any thing, seeing he giveth to all life, and breath, and all things;
26 And hath made of one blood all nations of men for to dwell on all the face of the earth, and hath determined the times before

Literal Translation

Acts 17:27

fore-appointed seasons and boundaries of their dwelling,

27 to seek the Lord, if perhaps they might feel after Him and might find Him, though indeed (He) being not far from each one of us.

28 For in Him we live and move and exist, as also some of the poets among you have said, For we are also His offspring.

29 Then being offspring of God, we ought not to suppose that the Godhead is like gold or silver or stone, engraved by art and the imagination of man.

30 Then truly, God having overlooked the times of ignorance, now strictly commands all men everywhere to repent,

31 because He set a day in which He is going to judge the habitable earth in righteousness, in a Man whom He appointed; having offered faith to all, having raised Him from (the) dead. (Ps.9:8)

32. And hearing (of) a resurrection of (the) dead, some indeed ridiculed, but (some) said, We will hear you again concerning this.

33 And so Paul went out from their midst.

34 But some men believed, adhering to him, among whom also (were) both Dionysius the Areopagite and a woman, Damaris by name, and others with them.

2540 2532 3588 3734 3588 2733 846
μένους καιροὺς καὶ τὰς ὁροθεσίας τῆς κατοικίας αὐτῶν,
appointed seasons and the boundaries of the dwelling of them,

2212 3588 2962 1487 686 5584 846 2532
27 ζητεῖν τὸν Κύριον, εἰ ἄραγε ψηλαφήσειαν αὐτὸν καὶ
to seek the Lord, if perhaps they might feel after Him and

2147 2544 3756 3112 575 1520 1538 2257
εὕροιεν, καίτοιγε οὐ μακρὰν ἀπὸ ἑνὸς ἑκάστου ἡμῶν
might find, even though not far from one each of us

5225 1722 846 1063 2198 2532 2795 2532 2070 5613
ὑπάρχοντα. 28 ἐν αὐτῷ γὰρ ζῶμεν καὶ κινούμεθα καὶ ἐσμέν· ὡς
being. in Him For we live and move and are; as

2532 5100 3588 2596 5209 4163 2046 3588 1063 2532 1085
καί τινες τῶν καθ' ὑμᾶς ποιητῶν εἰρήκασι, Τοῦ γὰρ καὶ γένος
also some of the among you poets have said, of Him For also offspring

2070 1085 3767 5225 3588 2316 3756 3784
ἐσμέν. 29 γένος οὖν ὑπάρχοντες τοῦ Θεοῦ, οὐκ ὀφείλομεν
we are. offspring Then being of God, not we ought

3543 5557 2228 696 2228 3037 5480 5078 2532
νομίζειν χρυσῷ ἢ ἀργύρῳ ἢ λίθῳ, χαράγματι τέχνης καὶ
to suppose to gold or to silver or to stone, to an engraving of art and

1761 444 3588 2304 1511 3664 3588 3303 3767
ἐνθυμήσεως ἀνθρώπου, τὸ θεῖον εἶναι ὅμοιον. 30 τοὺς μὲν οὖν
of imagination of man, the Godhood is like. the indeed Then

5550 3588 52 5237 3588 2316 3588 3568 3853 3588
χρόνους τῆς ἀγνοίας ὑπεριδὼν ὁ Θεὸς, τὰ νῦν παραγγέλλει τοῖς
times of ignorance having overlooked God, now commands

444 3956 3837 3340 1360 2476 2250
ἀνθρώποις πᾶσι πανταχοῦ μετανοεῖν· 31 διότι ἔστησεν ἡμέραν,
men all everywhere to repent; because He has set a day,

1722/3739/3195 2919 3588 3625 1722 1343 1722 435 3739
ἐν ᾗ μέλλει κρίνειν τὴν οἰκουμένην ἐν δικαιοσύνῃ, ἐν ἀνδρὶ ᾧ
in which He is going to judge the habitable earth in righteousness, by a man whom

3724 4102 3930 3956 450 846 1537 3498
ὥρισε, πίστιν παρασχὼν πᾶσιν, ἀναστήσας αὐτὸν ἐκ νεκρῶν.
appointed, faith having offered to all, having raised Him from (the) dead.

191 1161 386 3498 3588 3303 5512 3588
32. Ἀκούσαντες δὲ ἀνάστασιν νεκρῶν, οἱ μὲν ἐχλεύαζον· οἱ
hearing (of) And a resurrection of (the) dead, they indeed ridiculed;

1161 2036 191 4675 3825 4012 5127 2532 3779 3588
δὲ εἶπον, Ἀκουσόμεθά σου πάλιν περὶ τούτου. 33 καὶ οὕτως ὁ
but said, We will hear you again concerning this. And so

3972 1831 1537 3319 846 5100 1161 435
Παῦλος ἐξῆλθεν ἐκ μέσου αὐτῶν. 34 τινὲς δὲ ἄνδρες
Paul went out from (the) midst of them. some And men

2853 846 4100 1722 3739 2532 1354 3588
κολληθέντες αὐτῷ, ἐπίστευσαν· ἐν οἷς καὶ Διονύσιος ὁ
adhering to him, believed; among whom both Dionysius the

698 2532 1135 3686 1152 2532 2087 4862
Ἀρεοπαγίτης, καὶ γυνὴ ὀνόματι Δάμαρις, καὶ ἕτεροι σὺν
Areopagite, and a woman by name Damaris, and others with

846
αὐτοῖς.
them.

King James Version

appointed, and the bounds of their habitation;

27 That they should seek the Lord, if haply they might feel after him, and find him, though he be not far from every one of us:

28 For in him we live, and move, and have our being; as certain also of your own poets have said, For we are also his offspring.

29 Forasmuch then as we are the offspring of God, we ought not to think that the Godhead is like unto gold, or silver, or stone, graven by art and man's device.

30 And the times of this ignorance God winked at; but now commandeth all men every where to repent:

31 Because he hath appointed a day, in the which he will judge the world in righteousness by (that) man whom he hath ordained; (whereof) he hath given assurance unto all (men), in that he hath raised him from the dead.

32. And when they heard of the resurrection of the dead, some mocked: and others said, We will hear thee again of this (matter).

33 So Paul departed from among them.

34 Howbeit certain men clave unto him, and believed: among the which (was) Dionysius the Areopagite, and a woman named Damaris, and others with them.

Acts 18

1. And after these things, departing from Athens, Paul came to Corinth.

2 And finding a certain Jew named Aquila,

3326 1161 5023 5563 3588 3972 1537 3588 116 2064
1. Μετὰ δὲ ταῦτα χωρισθεὶς ὁ Παῦλος ἐκ τῶν Ἀθηνῶν ἦλθεν
after And these things departing Paul from Athens came

1519 2882 2532 2147 5100 2453 3686 207
εἰς Κόρινθον. 2 καὶ εὑρών τινα Ἰουδαῖον ὀνόματι Ἀκύλαν,
into Corinth. And finding a certain Jew by name Aquila,

1. After these things Paul departed from Athens, and came to Corinth;

2 And found a certain Jew named Aquila,

Acts 18:3

of Pontus by race, recently having come from Italy (with) his wife Priscilla, because Claudius had ordered all the Jews to leave Rome, he came to them.

3 And because of being of the same trade, he lived and worked with them; for they were tentmakers by trade.

4 And he reasoned in the synagogue on every sabbath persuading both Jews and Greeks.

5 And when both Silas and Timothy came down from Macedonia, Paul was pressed by the Spirit, earnestly testifying to the Jews (that) Jesus (is) the Christ.
6 But they resisting him, and blaspheming, having shaken (his) garments, he said to them, Your blood (be) on your head. I (am) pure (from it); from now on I will go to the nations.

7 And moving from there, he went into (the) house of one named Justus, (one) worshiping God, whose house being next door to the synagogue.
8 And Crispus, the synagogue ruler, believed the Lord along with all his house. And hearing, many of the Corinthians believed and were baptized.
9 And the Lord said to Paul through a vision in (the) night, Do not fear, but speak, and do not keep silence;

10 because I am with you, and no one shall set on you to oppress you; because there is much people to Me in

---

4193 3588 1085 4373 2064 575 3588 2482
Ποντικὸν τῷ γένει, προσφάτως ἐληλυθότα ἀπὸ τῆς Ἰταλίας,
of Pontus by race, recently having come from Italy,
2532 4252 1135 846 1223 3588 1299 2804
καὶ Πρίσκιλλαν γυναῖκα αὐτοῦ, διὰ τὸ διατεταχέναι Κλαυ-
and Priscilla (the) wife of him, because had ordered Claudius
5563 3956 3588 2453 1537 3588 4516
διον χωρίζεσθαι πάντας τοὺς Ἰουδαίους ἐκ τῆς Ῥώμης,
to depart all the Jews from Rome,

4334 846 2532 1223 3588 3673 1511 3306 3844
προσῆλθεν αὐτοῖς· 3 καὶ διὰ τὸ ὁμότεχνον εἶναι, ἔμενε παρ'
he came to them; and because of the same trade being, he abode with
846 2532 2038 2258 1063 4635 3588 5078
αὐτοῖς καὶ εἰργάζετο· ἦσαν γὰρ σκηνοποιοὶ τὴν τέχνην.
them and worked; they were for tentmakers by trade.
1256 1161 1722 3588 4864 2596 3956 4521 3982 5037
4 διελέγετο δὲ ἐν τῇ συναγωγῇ κατὰ πᾶν σάββατον, ἔπειθέ τε
he reasoned And in the synagogue on every sabbath, persuading both
2453 2532 1672
Ἰουδαίους καὶ Ἕλληνας.
Jews and Greeks.

5613 1161 2718 575 3588 3109 3588 5037 4609 2532 3588
5. Ὡς δὲ κατῆλθον ἀπὸ τῆς Μακεδονίας ὅ τε Σίλας καὶ ὁ
when And came down from Macedonia both Silas and
5095 4912 3588 4151 3588 3972 1263
Τιμόθεος, συνείχετο τῷ πνεύματι ὁ Παῦλος, διαμαρτυρό-
Timothy, was pressed by the Spirit Paul earnestly testifying
3588 2453 3588 5547 2424 498
μενος τοῖς Ἰουδαίοις τὸν Χριστὸν Ἰησοῦν. 6 ἀντιτασσο-
to the Jews the Christ Jesus (is). resisting
1161 846 2532 987 1621 3588
μένων δὲ αὐτῶν καὶ βλασφημούντων, ἐκτιναξάμενος τὰ
But him and blaspheming, having shaken the
2440 2036 4314 846 3588 129 5216 1909 3588 2776
ἱμάτια, εἶπε πρὸς αὐτούς, Τὸ αἷμα ὑμῶν ἐπὶ τὴν κεφαλὴν
garments, he said to them, The blood of you on the head
5216 2513 1473 575 3588 3568 1519 3588 1484 4198
ὑμῶν· καθαρὸς ἐγώ· ἀπὸ τοῦ νῦν εἰς τὰ ἔθνη πορεύσομαι.
of you (is); (being) pure I; from now to the nations I will go.

2532 3327 1564 2064 1519 3614 5100 3686 2459
7 καὶ μεταβὰς ἐκεῖθεν ἦλθεν εἰς οἰκίαν τινὸς ὀνόματι Ἰούστου,
And moving from there he went into (the) house of one by name Justus,
4576 3588 2316 3739 3588 3614 2258 4927 3588
σεβομένου τὸν Θεόν, οὗ ἡ οἰκία ἦν συνομοροῦσα τῇ
(one) worshiping God, of whom the house was being next door to the
4864 2921 1161 3588 752 4100 3588
συναγωγῇ. 8 Κρίσπος δὲ ὁ ἀρχισυνάγωγος ἐπίστευσε τῷ
synagogue. Crispus And the synagogue ruler believed the
2962 4862 3650 3588 3624 846 2532 4183 3588 2881
Κυρίῳ σὺν ὅλῳ τῷ οἴκῳ αὐτοῦ· καὶ πολλοὶ τῶν Κορινθίων
Lord with all the house of him; and many of the Corinthians
191 4100 2532 907 2036 1161 3588 2962 1223
ἀκούοντες ἐπίστευον καὶ ἐβαπτίζοντο. 9 εἶπε δὲ ὁ Κύριος δι'
hearing believed and were baptized. said And the Lord through
3705 1722 3571 3588 3972 3361 5399 235 2980 2532
ὁράματος ἐν νυκτὶ τῷ Παύλῳ, Μὴ φοβοῦ, ἀλλὰ λάλει καὶ
a vision in (the) night to Paul, Do not fear, but speak and
3361 4623 1360 1473 1510 3326 4675 2532 3762 2007
μὴ σιωπήσῃς· 10 διότι ἐγώ εἰμι μετὰ σοῦ, καὶ οὐδεὶς ἐπιθή-
not keep silence; because I am with you, and no one shall
4671 3588 2559 4571 1360 2992 2076 3427 4183 1722 3588
σεταί σοι τοῦ κακῶσαί σε· διότι λαός ἐστί μοι πολὺς ἐν τῇ
set on you to oppress you; because people is to Me much in

---

born in Pontus, lately come from Italy, with his wife Priscilla; (because that Claudius had commanded all Jews to depart from Rome:) and came unto them.

3 And because he was of the same craft, he abode with them, and wrought: for by their occupation they were tentmakers.

4 And he reasoned in the synagogue every sabbath, and persuaded the Jews and the Greeks.

5 And when Silas and Timotheus were come from Macedonia, Paul was pressed in the spirit, and testified to the Jews (that) Jesus (was) Christ.
6 And when they opposed themselves, and blasphemed, he shook (his) raiment, and said unto them, Your blood (be) upon your own heads; I (am) clean: from henceforth I will go unto the Gentiles.

7 And he departed thence, and entered into a certain (man's) house, named Justus, (one) that worshipped God, whose house joined hard to the synagogue.
8 And Crispus, the chief ruler of the synagogue, believed on the Lord with all his house; and many of the Corinthians hearing believed, and were baptized.
9 Then spake the Lord to Paul in the night by a vision, Be not afraid, but speak, and hold not thy peace:

10 For I am with thee, and no man shall set on thee to hurt thee: for I have much people in

Literal Translation

this city.
11 And he sat a year and six months teaching the Word of God among them.

12. But Gallio being proconsul of Achaia, the Jews rushed against Paul with one passion and brought him onto the tribunal,
13 saying, This one persuades men to worship God contrary to the Law.
14 But Paul being about to open (his) mouth, Gallio said to the Jews, If, indeed, then, it was some wrong or wicked criminality, O Jews, according to reason I would endure you.

15 But if it is a question about a word, and names, and the law according to you, you will see (to it) yourselves; for I do not wish to be a judge of these things.
16 And he drove them from the tribunal.

17 And all the Greeks having seized Sosthenes the ruler of the synagogue, they beat (him) before the tribunal. And not one of these things mattered to Gallio.

18. And having remained many days more, having taken leave (of) the brothers, Paul sailed to Syria, having shaved (his) head in Cenchrea, for he had a vow. And Priscilla and Aquila (were) with him.
19 And he came to Ephesus, and he left those there. But he entering into the synagogue, he reasoned with the Jews.
20 And they asking (him) to remain over a longer

Acts 18:11

4172 3778 2523 5037 1763 2532 3376 1803 1321
πόλει ταύτῃ. 11 ἐκάθισέ τε ἐνιαυτὸν καὶ μῆνας ἕξ, διδάσκων
city this. he sat And a year and months six, teaching

1722 846 3588 3056 3588 2316
ἐν αὐτοῖς τὸν λόγον τοῦ Θεοῦ.
among them the Word of God.

1058 1161 445 3588 882 2721
12. Γαλλίωνος δὲ ἀνθυπατεύοντος τῆς Ἀχαΐας, κατεπέστησαν
Gallio And being proconsul of Achaia, rushed against

3661 3588 2453 3588 3972 2532 71 846
ὁμοθυμαδὸν οἱ Ἰουδαῖοι τῷ Παύλῳ, καὶ ἤγαγον αὐτὸν
with one passion the Jews Paul, and brought him

1909 3588 968 3004 3754 3844 3588 3551 3778 374
ἐπὶ τὸ βῆμα, 13 λέγοντες ὅτι Παρὰ τὸν νόμον οὗτος ἀναπείθει
onto the tribunal, saying Contrary to the Law this one persuades

3588 444 4576 3588 2316 3195 1161 3588
τοὺς ἀνθρώπους σέβεσθαι τὸν Θεόν. 14 μέλλοντος δὲ τοῦ
men to worship God. being about And

3972 455 3588 4750 2036 3588 1058 4314 3588
Παύλου ἀνοίγειν τὸ στόμα, εἶπεν ὁ Γαλλίων πρὸς τοὺς
Paul to open the mouth, said Gallio to the

2453 1487 3303 3767 2258 92 5100 2228 4467
Ἰουδαίους, Εἰ μὲν οὖν ἦν ἀδίκημά τι ἢ ῥᾳδιούργημα
Jews, If indeed then it was wrong some or criminality

4190 5599 2453 2596 3056 302 430 5216
πονηρόν, ὦ Ἰουδαῖοι, κατὰ λόγον ἂν ἠνεσχόμην ὑμῶν·
wicked, O Jews, according to reason I would endure you;

1487 1161 2213 2076 4012 3056 2532 3686 2532 3551 3588
15 εἰ δὲ ζήτημά ἐστι περὶ λόγου καὶ ὀνομάτων καὶ νόμου τοῦ
if but a question it is concerning a word and names and law the

2596 5209 3700 846 2923 1063 1473 5130 3756
καθ' ὑμᾶς, ὄψεσθε αὐτοί· κριτὴς γὰρ ἐγὼ τούτων οὐ βού-
according to you, you will see selves; a judge for I of these things not intend

1014 1511 2532 556 846 575 3588 968
λομαι εἶναι. 16 καὶ ἀπήλασεν αὐτοὺς ἀπὸ τοῦ βήματος.
to be. And he drove them from the tribunal.

1949 1161 3956 3588 1672 4988 3588 752
17 ἐπιλαβόμενοι δὲ πάντες οἱ Ἕλληνες Σωσθένην τὸν ἀρχι-
having seized But all the Greeks Sosthenes the ruler

5180 1715 3588 968 2532 3762
συνάγωγον ἔτυπτον ἔμπροσθεν τοῦ βήματος. καὶ οὐδὲν
of (the) synagogue they beat (him) before the tribunal. And not one

5130 3588 1058 3199
τούτων τῷ Γαλλίωνι ἔμελεν.
of these things to Gallio mattered.

3588 1161 3972 2089 4357 2250 2425 3588
18. Ὁ δὲ Παῦλος ἔτι προσμείνας ἡμέρας ἱκανάς, τοῖς
And Paul yet having remained days many, to the

80 657 1602 1519 3588 4947 2532 4862 846
ἀδελφοῖς ἀποταξάμενος, ἐξέπλει εἰς τὴν Συρίαν, καὶ σὺν αὐτῷ
brothers having taken leave, he sailed into Syria, and with him

4252 2532 207 2751 3588 2776 1722 2747
Πρίσκιλλα καὶ Ἀκύλας, κειράμενος τὴν κεφαλὴν ἐν Κεγχρεαῖς·
Priscilla and Aquila, having shorn the head in Cenchrea;

2192 1063 2171 2658 1161 1519 2181 2548 2641
εἶχε γὰρ εὐχήν. 19 κατήντησε δὲ εἰς Ἔφεσον, κἀκείνους κατέ-
he had for a vow. he came down And to Ephesus, and those he

846 846 1161 1525 1519 3588 4864
λιπεν αὐτοῦ· αὐτὸς δὲ εἰσελθὼν εἰς τὴν συναγωγὴν διε-
left there; he but entering into the synagogue

1256 3588 2453 2065 1161 846 1909 4119
λέχθη τοῖς Ἰουδαίοις. 20 ἐρωτώντων δὲ αὐτῶν ἐπὶ πλείονα
reasoned with the Jews. asking And they over a longer

King James Version

this city.
11 And he continued (there) a year and six months, teaching the word of God among them.

12. And when Gallio was the deputy of Achaia, the Jews made insurrection with one accord against Paul, and brought him to the judgment seat,
13 Saying, This (fellow) persuadeth men to worship God contrary to the law.
14 And when Paul was now about to open (his) mouth, Gallio said unto the Jews, If it were a matter of wrong or wicked lewdness, O (ye) Jews, reason would that I should bear with you:

15 But if it be a question of words and names, and (of) your law, look ye (to it); for I will be no judge of such (matters).

16 And he drave them from the judgment seat.

17 Then all the Greeks took Sosthenes, the chief ruler of the synagogue, and beat (him) before the judgment seat. And Gallio cared for none of those things.

18. And Paul (after this) tarried (there) yet a good while, and then took his leave of the brethren, and sailed thence into Syria, and with him Priscilla and Aquila; having shorn (his) head in Cenchrea: for he had a vow.
19 And he came to Ephesus, and left them there: but he himself entered into the synagogue, and reasoned with the Jews.

20 When they desired (him) to tarry longer

Literal Translation **Acts 18:21** ***King James Version***

time with them, he did not agree,
21 but took leave of them, saying, By all means it is necessary for me to keep the coming feast at Jerusalem; but I will come again to you, God willing. And he sailed from Ephesus.

22 And having come down to Caesarea, having gone up and greeted the church, he went down to Antioch.

23 And some time having done, he went out, in order passing through the Galatian and Phrygian country, making strong all the disciples.

24. But a certain Jew named Apollos, an Alexandrian by race, an eloquent man, came to Ephesus, being powerful in the Scriptures.

25 This one having been taught by mouth in the way of the Lord, and (being) fervent in spirit, he spoke and taught accurately the things about the Lord, having understood only the baptism of John.

26 And this one began to speak boldly in the synagogue. And hearing him Priscilla and Aquila took him and more accurately expounded the way of God to him.

27 And he having purposed to go through into Achaia, having been encouraged, the brothers wrote to the disciples to welcome him; who, having arrived, much helped those believing through grace.

28 For he powerfully confuted the Jews publicly, proving through the Scriptures Jesus to be the

5550 3306 3844 846 3756 1962 235 657
χρόνον μεῖναι παρ' αὐτοῖς, οὐκ ἐπένευσεν· 21 ἀλλ' ἀπετάξατο
time to remain with them, not he agreed; but took leave

846 2036 1163 3165 3843 3588 1859 3588 2064 4160
αὐτοῖς εἰπών, Δεῖ με πάντως τὴν ἑορτὴν τὴν ἐρχομένην ποιῆ-
of them saying, Must me all the feast coming to keep

1519 2414 3825 1161 344 4314 5209 3588 2316
σαι εἰς Ἱεροσόλυμα· πάλιν δὲ ἀνακάμψω πρὸς ὑμᾶς, τοῦ Θεοῦ
at Jerusalem; again but I will come to you, God

2309 2532 321 575 3588 2181 2532 2718 1519
θέλοντος. καὶ ἀνήχθη ἀπὸ τῆς Ἐφέσου. 22 καὶ κατελθὼν εἰς
willing. And he sailed from Ephesus. And having come down at

2542 305 2532 782 3588 1577
Καισάρειαν, ἀναβὰς καὶ ἀσπασάμενος τὴν ἐκκλησίαν,
Caesarea, having gone up and having greeted the church,

2597 1519 490 2532 4160 5550 5100 1831
κατέβη εἰς Ἀντιόχειαν. 23 καὶ ποιήσας χρόνον τινὰ ἐξῆλθε,
he went down to Antioch. And having done time some he left,

1330 2517 3588 1054 5561 2532 5435
διερχόμενος καθεξῆς τὴν Γαλατικὴν χώραν καὶ Φρυγίαν,
passing through in order the Galatian country and Phrygia

1991 3956 3588 3101
ἐπιστηρίζων πάντας τοὺς μαθητάς.
strengthening all the disciples.

2453 1161 5100 625 3686 221 3588
24. Ἰουδαῖος δέ τις Ἀπολλὼς ὀνόματι, Ἀλεξανδρεὺς τῷ
Jew And a certain Apollos by name, an Alexandrian

1085 435 3052 2658 1519 2181 1415 5607 1722
γένει, ἀνὴρ λόγιος, κατήντησεν εἰς Ἔφεσον, δυνατὸς ὢν ἐν
by race, man an eloquent, came to Ephesus, powerful being in

3588 1124 3778 2258 2727 3588 3598 3588 2962
ταῖς γραφαῖς. 25 οὗτος ἦν κατηχημένος τὴν ὁδὸν τοῦ Κυρίου,
the Scriptures. This one was being orally taught the way of the Lord,

2532 2204 3588 4151 2980 2532 1321 199 3588 4012
καὶ ζέων τῷ πνεύματι ἐλάλει καὶ ἐδίδασκεν ἀκριβῶς τὰ περὶ
and fervent in spirit he spoke and taught accurately the things about

3588 2962 1987 3440 3588 908 2491
τοῦ Κυρίου, ἐπιστάμενος μόνον τὸ βάπτισμα Ἰωάννου·
the Lord, having understood only the baptism of John;

3778 5037 756 3955 1722 3588 4864 191
26 οὗτός τε ἤρξατο παρρησιάζεσθαι ἐν τῇ συναγωγῇ. ἀκού-
this one and began to speak boldly in the synagogue. hearing

191 1161 846 207 2532 4252 4355
σαντες δὲ αὐτοῦ Ἀκύλας καὶ Πρίσκιλλα, προσελάβοντο
And him Aquilla and Priscilla, took

846 2532 197 846 1620 3588 3588 2316 3598
αὐτόν, καὶ ἀκριβέστερον αὐτῷ ἐξέθεντο τὴν τοῦ Θεοῦ ὁδόν.
him, and more accurately to him expounded the of God way.

1014 1161 846 1330 1519 3588 882 4389
27 βουλομένου δὲ αὐτοῦ διελθεῖν εἰς τὴν Ἀχαΐαν, προτρεψά-
purposing And him to go through into Achaia, being encour-

3588 80 1125 3588 3101 588 846
μενοι οἱ ἀδελφοὶ ἔγραψαν τοῖς μαθηταῖς ἀποδέξασθαι αὐτόν·
aged, the brothers wrote to the disciples to welcome him;

3739 3854 4820 4183 3588 4100 1223
ὃς παραγενόμενος συνεβάλετο πολὺ τοῖς πεπιστευκόσι διὰ
who having arrived helped much those believing through

3588 5485 2159 1063 3588 2453 1246
τῆς χάριτος· 28 εὐτόνως γὰρ τοῖς Ἰουδαίοις διακατηλέγχετο
grace; powerfully for the Jews he confuted

1219 1925 1223 3588 1124 1511 3588 5547
δημοσίᾳ ἐπιδεικνὺς διὰ τῶν γραφῶν εἶναι τὸν Χριστὸν
publicly, proving through the Scriptures to be the Christ

time with them, he consented not;
21 But bade them farewell, saying, I must by all means keep this feast that cometh in Jerusalem: but I will return again unto you, if God will. And he sailed from Ephesus.

22 And when he had landed at Caesarea, and gone up, and saluted the church, he went down to Antioch.

23 And after he had spent some time (there), he departed, and went over (all) the country of Galatia and Phrygia in order, strengthening all the disciples.

24. And a certain Jew named Apollos, born at Alexandria, an eloquent man, (and) mighty in the scriptures, came to Ephesus.

25 This man was instructed in the way of the Lord; and being fervent in the spirit, he spake and taught diligently the things of the Lord, knowing only the baptism of John.

26 And he began to speak boldly in the synagogue: whom when Aquila and Priscilla had heard, they took him unto (them), and expounded unto him the way of God more perfectly.

27 And when he was disposed to pass into Achaia, the brethren wrote, exhorting the disciples to receive him: who, when he was come, helped them much which had believed through grace:

28 For he mightily convinced the Jews, (and that) publickly, shewing by the scriptures that Jesus

Literal Translation **Acts 19:1** *King James Version*

Christ.

2424
Ἰησοῦν.
Jesus.

was Christ.

Acts 19

1. And it happened, in the (time) Apollos was in Corinth, Paul (was) passing through the higher parts to come to Ephesus. And finding some disciples,
2 (he) said to them, Believing, did you receive (the) Holy Spirit? And they said to him, We did not even hear whether there is (the) Holy Spirit.
3 And he said to them, Then to what were you baptized? And they said, To the baptism of John.
4 And Paul said, John indeed baptized (with) a baptism of repentance, saying to the people that they should believe into the (One) coming after him, that is, into the Christ, Jesus.

5 And hearing, they were baptized into the name of the Lord Jesus.

6 And Paul laying hands on them, the Holy Spirit came on them, and they spoke in tongues and prophesied.

7 And all the men were about twelve.

Acts 19

1096 1161 1722 3588 3588 625 1511 1722 2882 3972
1.Ἐγένετο δέ, ἐν τῷ τὸν Ἀπολλὼ εἶναι ἐν Κορίνθῳ, Παῦλον
it happened And in the (time) Apollos was in Corinth, Paul

1330 3588 510 3313 2064 1519 2181 2532 2147
διελθόντα τὰ ἀνωτερικὰ μέρη ἐλθεῖν εἰς Ἔφεσον· καὶ εὑρών
passing through the higher parts came to Ephesus; and finding

5100 3101 2036 4314 846 1487 4151 40 2983
τινας μαθητὰς εἶπε πρὸς αὐτούς, 2 Εἰ Πνεῦμα Ἅγιον ἐλάβετε
some disciples, said to them, If (the) Spirit Holy you received

4100 3588 1161 2036 4314 846 235 3761 1487 4151
πιστεύσαντες; οἱ δὲ εἶπον πρὸς αὐτόν, Ἀλλ᾽ οὐδὲ εἰ Πνεῦμα
believing? they And said to him, But not even if (the) Spirit

40 2076 191 2036 5037 4314 846 1519 5101 3767
Ἅγιόν ἐστιν, ἠκούσαμεν. 3 εἶπέ τε πρὸς αὐτούς, Εἰς τί οὖν
Holy is we did hear. he said And to them, To what, then

907 3588 1161 2036 1519 3588 2491 908 2036
ἐβαπτίσθητε; οἱ δὲ εἶπον, Εἰς τὸ Ἰωάννου βάπτισμα. 4 εἶπε
were you baptized? they And said, To the of John baptism. said

1161 3972 2491 3303 907 908 3341 3588
δὲ Παῦλος, Ἰωάννης μὲν ἐβάπτισε βάπτισμα μετανοίας, τῷ
And Paul, John indeed baptized a baptism of repentance to the

2992 3004 1519 3588 2064 3326 846 2443 4100
λαῷ λέγων εἰς τὸν ἐρχόμενον μετ᾽ αὐτὸν ἵνα πιστεύσωσι,
people, saying into the (One) coming after him that they should believe,

2076 1519 3588 5547 2424 191 1161 907
τοῦτ᾽ ἔστιν, εἰς τὸν Χριστὸν Ἰησοῦν. 5 ἀκούσαντες δὲ ἐβαπτί-
this is, into the Christ Jesus. hearing And they were

1519 3588 3686 3588 2962 2424 2532 2007
σθησαν εἰς τὸ ὄνομα τοῦ Κυρίου Ἰησοῦ. 6 καὶ ἐπιθέντος
baptized into the name of the Lord Jesus. And laying on

846 3588 3972 3588 5495 2064 3588 4151 3588 40
αὐτοῖς τοῦ Παύλου τὰς χεῖρας, ἦλθε τὸ Πνεῦμα τὸ Ἅγιον
them Paul the hands, came the Spirit Holy

1909 846 2980 5037 1100 2532 4395 2258
ἐπ᾽ αὐτούς, ἐλάλουν τε γλώσσαις καὶ προεφήτευον. 7 ἦσαν
on them; the spoke and in tongues and prophesied. were

1161 3588 3956 435 5616 1177
δὲ οἱ πάντες ἄνδρες ὡσεὶ δεκαδύο.
And the all men about twelve.

Acts 19

1. And it came to pass, that, while Apollos was at Corinth, Paul having passed through the upper coasts came to Ephesus: and finding certain disciples,
2 He said unto them, Have ye received the Holy Ghost since ye believed? And they said unto him, We have not so much as heard whether there be any Holy Ghost.
3 And he said unto them, Unto what then were ye baptized? And they said, Unto John's baptism.
4 Then said Paul, John verily baptized with the baptism of repentance, saying unto the people, that they should believe on him which should come after him, that is, on Christ Jesus.
5 When they heard (this), they were baptized in the name of the Lord Jesus.
6 And when Paul had laid (his) hands upon them, the Holy Ghost came on them; and they spake with tongues, and prophesied.

7 And all the men were about twelve.

---

8 And going into the synagogue, he spoke boldly over three months, conversing with (them), and persuading concerning the things of the kingdom of God.
9 But as some were hardened, and did not obey, speaking evil of the Way before the multitude, departing from them, He separated the disciples, conversing day by day in the school of a certain Tyrannus.
10 And this happened over two years,

1525 1161 1519 3588 4864 3955 1909
8. Εἰσελθὼν δὲ εἰς τὴν συναγωγὴν ἐπαρρησιάζετο, ἐπὶ
entering And into the synagogue, he spoke boldly over

3376 5140 1256 2532 3982 3588 4012 3588 932
μῆνας τρεῖς διαλεγόμενος καὶ πείθων τὰ περὶ τῆς βασιλείας
months three conversing with and persuading the things concerning the kingdom

3588 2316 5613 1161 5100 4645 2532 544 2551
τοῦ Θεοῦ. 9 ὡς δέ τινες ἐσκληρύνοντο καὶ ἠπείθουν, κακολο-
of God. as But some were hardened and disobeyed, speaking

3588 3598 1799 3588 4128 868 575
γοῦντες τὴν ὁδὸν ἐνώπιον τοῦ πλήθους, ἀποστὰς ἀπ᾽
evil of the Way before the multitude, departing from

846 873 3588 3101 2596 2250 1256
αὐτῶν ἀφώρισε τοὺς μαθητάς, καθ᾽ ἡμέραν διαλεγόμενος
them, he separated the disciples, day by day conversing

1722 3588 4981 5181 5100 5124 1161 1096 1909 2094 1417
ἐν τῇ σχολῇ Τυράννου τινός. 10 τοῦτο δὲ ἐγένετο ἐπὶ ἔτη δύο,
in the school of Tyrannus a certain. this And happened over years two,

8 And he went into the synagogue, and spake boldly for the space of three months, disputing and persuading the things concerning the kingdom of God.
9 But when divers were hardened, and believed not, but spake evil of that way before the multitude, he departed from them, and separated the disciples, disputing daily in the school of one Tyrannus.

10 And this continued by the space of two years;

Literal Translation | **Acts 19:11** | *King James Version*

so as all those living in Asia heard the Word of the Lord Jesus, both Jews and Greeks.

5620 3956 3588 2730 3588 773 191 3588
ὥστε πάντας τοὺς κατοικοῦντας τὴν Ἀσίαν ἀκοῦσαι τὸν
so as all those living in Asia heard the
3056 3588 2962 2424 2453 5037 2532 1672
λόγον τοῦ Κυρίου Ἰησοῦ, Ἰουδαίους τε καὶ Ἕλληνας.
Word of the Lord Jesus, Jews both and Greeks.

so that all they which dwelt in Asia heard the word of the Lord Jesus, both Jews and Greeks.

11 And God did uncommon works of power through the hands of Paul,
12 so as even handkerchiefs or aprons from his skin to be brought onto those sick, and the diseases to be released from them, and the evil spirits to go out from them.

1411 5037 3756 3588 5177 4160 3588 2316 1223 3588 5495
11 δυνάμεις τε οὐ τὰς τυχούσας ἐποίει ὁ θεὸς διὰ τῶν χειρῶν
works of power And not the common did God through the hands
3972 5620 2532 1909 3588 770 2018 575
Παύλου, 12 ὥστε καὶ ἐπὶ τοὺς ἀσθενοῦντας ἐπιφέρεσθαι ἀπὸ
of Paul so as even onto those sick to be brought from
3588 5559 846 4676 2228 4612 2532 525
τοῦ χρωτὸς αὐτοῦ σουδάρια ἢ σιμικίνθια, καὶ ἀπαλλάσσε-
the skin of him handkerchiefs or aprons, and to be released
575 846 3588 3554 3588 5037 4151 3588 4190
σθαι ἀπ᾽ αὐτῶν τὰς νόσους, τά τε πνεύματα τὰ πονηρὰ
from them the diseases, the and spirits evil
1831 575 846
ἐξέρχεσθαι ἀπ᾽ αὐτῶν.
to go out from them.

11 And God wrought special miracles by the hands of Paul:
12 So that from his body were brought unto the sick handkerchiefs or aprons, and the diseases departed from them, and the evil spirits went out of them.

13. But some from the strolling Jews, exorcists, undertook to name the name of the Lord Jesus over those having evil spirits, saying, We adjure you (by) Jesus whom Paul proclaims.

2021 1161 5100 575 3588 4022
13 ἐπεχείρησαν δέ τινες ἀπὸ τῶν περιερ-
undertook But some from the strolling
2453 1845 3687 1909 3588 2192
χομένων Ἰουδαίων ἐξορκιστῶν ὀνομάζειν ἐπὶ τοὺς ἔχοντας
Jews exorcists to name over those having
3588 4151 3588 4190 3588 3686 3588 2962 2424 3004
τὰ πνεύματα τὰ πονηρὰ τὸ ὄνομα τοῦ Κυρίου Ἰησοῦ, λέγον-
the spirits evil the name of the Lord Jesus, saying,
3726 5209 3588 2424 3739 3588 3972 2784
τες, Ὁρκίζομεν ὑμᾶς τὸν Ἰησοῦν ὃν ὁ Παῦλος κηρύσσει.
we exorcise you (by) Jesus whom Paul proclaims.

13. Then certain of the vagabond Jews, exorcists, took upon them to call over them which had evil spirits the name of the Lord Jesus, saying, We adjure you by Jesus whom Paul preacheth.

14 And there were seven sons of Sceva, a Jewish chief priest, doing this.
15 But answering the evil spirit said, I know Jesus, and I comprehend Paul, but who are you?

2258 1161 5100 5207 4630 2453 749 2033 3588
14 ἦσαν δέ τινες υἱοὶ Σκευᾶ Ἰουδαίου ἀρχιερέως ἑπτὰ οἱ
were And of one sons, of Sceva, a Jewish chief priest, seven
5124 4160 611 1161 3588 4151 3588 4190
τοῦτο ποιοῦντες. 15 ἀποκριθὲν δὲ τὸ πνεῦμα τὸ πονηρὸν
this doing. answering And the spirit evil
2036 3588 2424 1097 2532 3588 3972 1987
εἶπε, Τὸν Ἰησοῦν γινώσκω, καὶ τὸν Παῦλον ἐπίσταμαι·
said, Jesus I know, and Paul I comprehend,
5210 1161 5101 2075
ὑμεῖς δὲ τίνες ἐστέ;
you but who are?

14 And there were seven sons of (one) Sceva, a Jew, (and) chief of the priests, which did so.
15 And the evil spirit answered and said, Jesus I know, and Paul I know; but who are ye?

16 And leaping on them the man in whom was the evil spirit, and overcoming them, he was strong against them, so as they having been wounded, (they) fled out of the house naked.

2532 2177 1909 846 3588 444
16 καὶ ἐφαλλόμενος ἐπ᾽ αὐτοὺς ὁ ἄνθρωπος
And leaping on them the man
1722 3739 2258 3588 4151 3588 4190 2532 2634 846
ἐν ᾧ ἦν τὸ πνεῦμα τὸ πονηρόν, καὶ κατακυριεύσας αὐτῶν,
in whom was the spirit evil, and overmastering them,
2480 2596 846 5620 1131 2532 5135
ἴσχυσε κατ᾽ αὐτῶν, ὥστε γυμνοὺς καὶ τετραυματισμένους
was strong against them, so as naked and having been wounded
1628 1537 3588 3624 1565
ἐκφυγεῖν ἐκ τοῦ οἴκου ἐκείνου.
to escape out of house that.

16 And the man in whom the evil spirit was leaped on them, and overcame them, and prevailed against them, so that they fled out of that house naked and wounded.

17 And this became known to all, both Jews and Greeks, those living in Ephesus. And fear fell on them all, and the name of the Lord Jesus was magnified.

5124 1161 1096 1110
17 τοῦτο δὲ ἐγένετο γνωστὸν
this And became known
3956 2453 5037 2532 1672 3588 2730 3588 2181
πᾶσιν Ἰουδαίοις τε καὶ Ἕλλησι τοῖς κατοικοῦσι τὴν Ἔφεσον,
to all, Jews both and Greeks, those living in Ephesus;
2532 1968 5401 1909 3956 846 2532 3170 3588
καὶ ἐπέπεσε φόβος ἐπὶ πάντας αὐτούς, καὶ ἐμεγαλύνετο τὸ
and fell on fear on all them, and was magnified the
3686 3588 2962 2424
ὄνομα τοῦ Κυρίου Ἰησοῦ.
name of the Lord Jesus.

17 And this was known to all the Jews and Greeks also dwelling at Ephesus; and fear fell on them all, and the name of the Lord Jesus was magnified.

18 And many of the (ones) having believed came confessing, and reporting the practices

4183 5037 3588 4100
18 πολλοί τε τῶν πεπιστευκότων
many And of those having believed
2064 1843 2532 312 3588 4234
ἤρχοντο, ἐξομολογούμενοι, καὶ ἀναγγέλλοντες τὰς πράξεις
came confessing and reporting the practices

18 And many that believed came, and confessed, and shewed

Literal Translation | **Acts 19:19** | **King James Version**

their deeds.
19 And many of the ones practicing the magical arts, bringing together the scrolls, burned (them) before all. And they counted the prices of them, and found (it to be) five ten thousands of silver.
20 So with might, the Word of the Lord increased and was strong.

21. And when these things were fulfilled, passing through Macedonia and Achaia, Paul purposed in the Spirit to go to Jerusalem, saying, After my coming there, I must also see Rome.

22 And sending into Macedonia two who ministered to him, Timothy and Erastus, he delayed a time in Asia.

23. And about that time there was not a little disturbance about the Way.
24 For one Demetrius, a silversmith, was making silver shrines of Artemis, (thus) providing no little trade (for) the craftsmen;

25 whom assembling also the workmen about such things, he said, Men, you understand that from this trade is the gain to us.
26 And you behold and hear that not only Ephesus, but almost all of Asia, persuading, this Paul perverted a huge crowd, saying that those being made by hands are not gods.

27 And not only this, the share to us is in danger to come into disrepute, but also the temple of the great goddess Artemis will be counted for nothing,

846 2425 1161 3588 3588 4021 4238 4851
αὐτῶν. 19 ἱκανοὶ δὲ τῶν τὰ περίεργα πραξάντων συνενέγκαν-
of them. many And of those the magical (arts) practicing bringing together

3588 976 2618 1799 3956 2532 4860
τες τὰς βίβλους κατέκαιον ἐνώπιον πάντων· καὶ συνεψήφισαν
the rolls burned (them) before all. And they counted

3588 5092 846 2532 2147 694 3461 4002 3779
τὰς τιμὰς αὐτῶν, καὶ εὗρον ἀργυρίου μυριάδας πέντε. 20 οὕτω
the prices of them, and found of silver ten thousands five. So

2596 2904 3588 3056 3588 2962 837 2532 2480
κατὰ κράτος ὁ λόγος τοῦ Κυρίου ηὔξανε καὶ ἴσχυεν.
with might the Word of the Lord increased and was strong.

5613 1161 4137 5023 5087 3588 3972 1722 3588 4151
21. Ὡς δὲ ἐπληρώθη ταῦτα, ἔθετο ὁ Παῦλος ἐν τῷ πνεύματι,
when And were fulfilled these things, purposed Paul in the Spirit,

1330 3588 3109 2532 882 4198 1519
διελθὼν τὴν Μακεδονίαν καὶ Ἀχαΐαν, πορεύεσθαι εἰς
passing through Macedonia and Achaia, to go to

2419 2036 3754 3326 3588 1096 3165 1563 1163 3165 2532
Ἱερουσαλήμ, εἰπὼν ὅτι Μετὰ τὸ γενέσθαι με ἐκεῖ, δεῖ με καὶ
Jerusalem, saying, After coming to be me there, must me also

4516 1492 649 1161 1519 3588 3109 1417 3588
Ῥώμην ἰδεῖν. 22 ἀποστείλας δὲ εἰς τὴν Μακεδονίαν δύο τῶν
Rome see. sending And into Macedonia two of those

1247 846 5095 2532 2037 846 1907
διακονούντων αὐτῷ, Τιμόθεον καὶ Ἔραστον, αὐτὸς ἐπέσχε
ministering to him, Timothy and Erastus, he delayed

5550 1519 3588 773
χρόνον εἰς τὴν Ἀσίαν.
a time in Asia.

1096 1161 2596 3588 2540 1565 5017 3756 3641
23. Ἐγένετο δὲ κατὰ τὸν καιρὸν ἐκεῖνον τάραχος οὐκ ὀλίγος
was And about time that disturbance not a little

4012 3588 3598 1216 1063 5100 3686 695
περὶ τῆς ὁδοῦ. 24 Δημήτριος γάρ τις ὀνόματι, ἀργυροκόπος,
concerning the Way. Demetrius For one by name, a silversmith,

4160 3485 693 735 3930 3588 5079
ποιῶν ναοὺς ἀργυροῦς Ἀρτέμιδος, παρείχετο τοῖς τεχνίταις
making shrines silver of Artemis, provided the craftsmen

2039 3756 3641 3739 4867 2532 3588 4012 3588
ἐργασίαν οὐκ ὀλίγην· 25 οὓς συναθροίσας, καὶ τοὺς περὶ τὰ
trade not a little; whom assembling, also the concerning

5108 2040 2036 435 1987 3754 1537 3778
τοιαῦτα ἐργάτας, εἶπεν, Ἄνδρες, ἐπίστασθε ὅτι ἐκ ταύτης
such things workmen, said, Men, you understand that from this

3588 2039 3588 2142 2257 2076 2532 2334 2532 191
τῆς ἐργασίας ἡ εὐπορία ἡμῶν ἐστι. 26 καὶ θεωρεῖτε καὶ ἀκούετε
trade the gain to us is. And you behold and hear

3754 3756 3440 2181 235 4975 3956 3588 773 3588
ὅτι οὐ μόνον Ἐφέσου, ἀλλὰ σχεδὸν πάσης τῆς Ἀσίας, ὁ
that not only Ephesus, but almost all Asia,

3972 3778 3982 3179 2425 3793 3004 3754
Παῦλος οὗτος πείσας μετέστησεν ἱκανὸν ὄχλον, λέγων ὅτι
Paul this persuading perverted a huge crowd, saying that

3756 1526 2316 3588 1223 5495 1096 3756 3440 1161 5124
οὐκ εἰσὶ θεοὶ οἱ διὰ χειρῶν γινόμενοι. 27 οὐ μόνον δὲ τοῦτο
not are gods those through hands having been made. not only And this

2793 2254 3588 3313 1519 557 2064 235 2532 3588
κινδυνεύει ἡμῖν τὸ μέρος εἰς ἀπελεγμὸν ἐλθεῖν, ἀλλὰ καὶ τὸ
is in danger to us the share into disrepute to come, but also the

3588 3173 2299 735 2411 1419 2762 3049
τῆς μεγάλης θεᾶς Ἀρτέμιδος ἱερὸν εἰς οὐδὲν λογισθῆναι,
of the great goddess Artemis temple for nothing will be counted,

their deeds.
19 Many of them also which used curious arts brought their books together, and burned them before all (men): and they counted the price of them, and found (it) fifty thousand (pieces) of silver.
20 So mightily grew the word of God and prevailed.

21. After these things were ended, Paul purposed in the spirit, when he had passed through Macedonia and Achaia, to go to Jerusalem, saying, After I have been there, I must also see Rome.

22 So he sent into Macedonia two of them that ministered unto him, Timotheus and Erastus; but he himself stayed in Asia for a season.

23. And the same time there arose no small stir about that way.

24 For a certain (man) named Demetrius, a silversmith, which made silver shrines for Diana, brought no small gain unto the craftsmen;

25 Whom he called together with the workmen of like occupation, and said, Sirs, ye know that by this craft we have our wealth.
26 Moreover ye see and hear, that not alone at Ephesus, but almost throughout all Asia, this Paul hath persuaded and turned away much people, saying that they be no gods, which are made with hands:

27 So that not only this our craft is in danger to be set at nought; but also that the temple of the great goddess Diana should be despised,

Literal Translation **Acts 19:28** ***King James Version***

and her greatness is also going to be diminished, whom all Asia and the habitable world worships.
28 And having heard, and having become full of anger, they cried out, saying, Great (is) Artemis of (the) Ephesians!
29 And all the city was filled with confusion. And they rushed with one passion into the theater, keeping a firm grip on Gaius and Aristarchus, Macedonians,, traveling companions of Paul.
30 And Paul intending to go in to the mob, the disciples did not allow him.
31 And also some of the Asiarchs, being his friends, sending to him begged (him) not to give himself into the theater.
32 Then others indeed cried out a different thing, for the assembly was confused, and the majority did not know on what account they came together.
33 But they dragged Alexander forward out of the crowd, the Jews thrusting him in front. And waving (his) hand, Alexander desired to defend himself to the mob.
34 But knowing that he is a Jew, one voice was from all, as (they were) crying out over two hours, Great (is) Artemis of (the) Ephesians!
35 And having quieted the crowd, the town clerk said, Men, Ephesians, for what man is there who does not know the city of the Ephesians (is) being temple-keeper of the great goddess Artemis, and of That Fallen From the Sky?
36 Then these things being undeniable, it is necessary for you, having been calmed, to be (so), and

3195 5037 2532 2507 3588 3168 846 3739 3650
μέλλειν τε καὶ καθαιρεῖσθαι τὴν μεγαλειότητα αὐτῆς, ἣν ὅλη
is going and also to be diminished the greatness of her, whom all

3588 773 2532 3588 3625 4576 191 1161 2532 1096
ἡ Ἀσία καὶ ἡ οἰκουμένη σέβεται. 28 ἀκούσαντες δὲ καὶ γενό-
Asia and the habitable world worships. having heard also And having

4134 2372 2896 3004 3173 3588 735
μενοι πλήρεις θυμοῦ, ἔκραζον λέγοντες, Μεγάλη ἡ Ἄρτεμις
become full of anger, they cried out saying, Great (is) Artemis

2180 2532 4130 3588 4172 3650 4799 3729 5037
Ἐφεσίων. 29 καὶ ἐπλήσθη ἡ πόλις ὅλη συγχύσεως· ὥρμησάν τε
of Ephesians! And was filled the city all of confusion. they rushed And

3661 1519 3588 2302 4884 1050 2532
ὁμοθυμαδὸν εἰς τὸ θέατρο, συναρπάσαντες Γάϊον καὶ
with one passion into the theater, keeping a firm grip on Gaius and

708 3110 4898 3588 3972 3588 1161
Ἀρίσταρχον Μακεδόνας, συνεκδήμους τοῦ Παύλου. 30 τοῦ δὲ
Aristarchus Macedonians, traveling companions of Paul. And

3972 1014 1525 1519 3588 1218 3756 1439 846
Παύλου βουλομένου εἰσελθεῖν εἰς τὸν δῆμον, οὐκ εἴων αὐτὸν
Paul having purposed to enter into the mob, not allowed him

3588 3101 5100 1161 2532 3588 775 5607 846 5384
οἱ μαθηταί. 31 τινὲς δὲ καὶ τῶν Ἀσιαρχῶν, ὄντες αὐτῷ φίλοι,
the disciples. some And also of the Asiarchs, being of him friends,

3992 4314 846 3870 3361 1325 1438 1519
πέμψαντες πρὸς αὐτὸν, παρεκάλουν μὴ δοῦναι ἑαυτὸν εἰς
sending to him, begged not to give himself into

3588 2302 243 3303 3767 243 5100 2896 2258 1063 3588
τὸ θέατρον. 32 ἄλλοι μὲν οὖν ἄλλο τι ἔκραζον· ἦν γὰρ ἡ
the theater. Others indeed then other some cried out,; was for the

1577 4797 2532 3588 4119 3756 1492 5101
ἐκκλησία συγκεχυμένη, καὶ οἱ πλείους οὐκ ᾔδεισαν τίνος
assembly confused, and the majority not did know of what

1752 4905 1537 1161 3588 3793 4264 223
ἕνεκεν συνεληλύθεισαν. 33 ἐκ δὲ τοῦ ὄχλου προεβίβασαν Ἀλέ-
on account they came together. out of But the crowd they dragged Alex-

4261 846 3588 2453 3588 1161 223
ξανδρον, προβαλλόντων αὐτὸν τῶν Ἰουδαίων. ὁ δὲ Ἀλέξαν-
ander, thrusting forward him the Jews. And Alexander,

2678 3588 5495 2309 626 3588 1218
δρος, κατασείσας τὴν χεῖρα, ἤθελεν ἀπολογεῖσθαι τῷ δήμῳ.
waving the hand desired to defend himself to the mob.

1921 1161 3754 2453 2076 5456 1096 3391 1537
34 ἐπιγνόντων δὲ ὅτι Ἰουδαῖός ἐστι, φωνὴ ἐγένετο μία ἐκ
knowing But that a Jew he is, voice there was one from

3956 5613 1909 5610 1417 2896 3173 3588 735
πάντων ὡς ἐπὶ ὥρας δύο κραζόντων, Μεγάλη ἡ Ἄρτεμις
all as over hours two screaming, Great (is) Artemis

2180 2687 1161 3588 1122 3588 3793 5346
Ἐφεσίων. 35 καταστείλας δὲ ὁ γραμματεὺς τὸν ὄχλον φησίν,
of Ephesians! having quieted And the town clerk the crowd he says,

435 2180 5101 1063 2076 444 3739 3756 1097
Ἄνδρες Ἐφέσιοι, τίς γάρ ἐστιν ἀνθρώπος ὃς οὐ γινώσκει
Men Ephesians, what for is man who not does know

3588 2180 4172 3511 5607 3588 3173 2299
τὴν Ἐφεσίων πόλιν νεωκόρον οὖσαν τῆς μεγάλης θεᾶς
the of (the) Ephesian city temple-keeper being of the great goddess

735 2532 3588 1356 368 3767 5607
Ἀρτέμιδος καὶ τοῦ Διοπετοῦς; 36 ἀναντιρρήτων οὖν ὄντων
Artemis and of that Fallen-from-the-sky? undeniable Then being

5130 1163 2076 5209 2687 5225 2532
τούτων, δέον ἐστὶν ὑμᾶς κατεσταλμένους ὑπάρχειν καὶ
these things, necessary it is you having been calmed to be (so), and

and her magnificence should be destroyed, whom all Asia and the world worshippeth.
28 And when they heard (these sayings), they were full of wrath, and cried out, saying, Great (is) Diana of the Ephesians.
29 And the whole city was filled with confusion: and having caught Gaius and Aristarchus, men of Macedonia, Paul's companions in travel, they rushed with one accord into the theatre.
30 And when Paul would have entered in unto the people, the disciples suffered him not.
31 And certain of the chief of Asia, which were his friends, sent unto him, desiring (him) that he would not adventure himself into the theatre.
32. Some therefore cried one thing, and some another: for the assembly was confused; and the more part knew not wherefore they were come together.
33 And they drew Alexander out of the multitude, the Jews putting him forward. And Alexander beckoned with the hand, and would have made his defence unto the people.
34 But when they knew that he was a Jew, all with one voice about the space of two hours cried out, Great (is) Diana of the Ephesians.
35 And when the townclerk had appeased the people, he said, (Ye) men of Ephesus, what man is there that knoweth not how that the city of the Ephesians is a worshipper of the great goddess Diana, and of the (image) which fell down from Jupiter?
36 Seeing then that these things cannot be spoken against, ye ought to be quiet, and

Literal Translation

to do nothing rash.
37 For you brought these men, (being) neither temple robbers nor blaspheming your goddess.

38 If then, indeed, Demetrius and those craftsmen with him have a matter against anyone, courts are being (held), and there are proconsuls. Let them accuse one another.
39 But if you seek concerning other things, it will be settled in a lawful assembly.
40 For also we are in danger to be accused of insurrection concerning today, there being no cause about which we will be able to give account of this crowding together.
41 And saying these things, he dismissed the assembly.

Acts 19:37

3367 4312 4238 71 1063 3588 435
μηδὲν προπετὲς πράττειν. 37 ἠγάγετε γὰρ τοὺς ἄνδρας
nothing rash to do. you brought For men

5128 3777 2417 3777 987 3588 2299
τούτους, οὔτε ἱεροσύλους οὔτε βλασφημοῦντας τὴν θεὰν
these, neither temple-robbers nor blaspheming the goddess

5216 1487 3303 3767 1216 2532 3588 4862 846 5079 4314
ὑμῶν. 38 εἰ μὲν οὖν Δημήτριος καὶ οἱ σὺν αὐτῷ τεχνῖται πρός
of you. If indeed then Demetrius and those with him craftsmen against

5100 3056 2192 60 71 2532 446
τινα λόγον ἔχουσιν, ἀγοραῖοι ἄγονται, καὶ ἀνθύπατοί
anyone a matter have, courts are being (held), and proconsuls

1526 1458 240 1487 1161 5100 4012 2087
εἰσιν· ἐγκαλείτωσαν ἀλλήλοις. 39 εἰ δέ τι περὶ ἑτέρων
there are; let them accuse one another. if But any about other things

1934 1722 3588 1772 1577 1956 2532 1063
ἐπιζητεῖτε, ἐν τῇ ἐννόμῳ ἐκκλησίᾳ ἐπιλυθήσεται. 40 καὶ γὰρ
you seek, in the lawful assembly it will be settled. also For

2793 1458 4714 4012 3588 4594 3367
κινδυνεύομεν ἐγκαλεῖσθαι στάσεως περὶ τῆς σήμερον, μηδενὸς
we are liable to be accused of insurrection concerning today, nothing

158 5225 4012 3739 1410 591 3056 3588
αἰτίου ὑπάρχοντος περὶ οὗ δυνησόμεθα ἀποδοῦναι λόγον τῆς
cause there being concerning which we will be able to give account

4963 3778 2532 5023 2036 630 3588 1577
συστροφῆς ταύτης. 41 καὶ ταῦτα εἰπών, ἀπέλυσε τὴν ἐκκλησίαν.
crowding together of this. And these things saying, he dismissed the assembly.

King James Version

to do nothing rashly.
37 For ye have brought hither these men, which are neither robbers of churches, nor yet blasphemers of your goddess.
38 Wherefore if Demetrius, and the craftsmen which are with him, have a matter against any man, the law is open, and there are deputies: let them implead one another.
39 But if ye enquire any thing concerning other matters, it shall be determined in a lawful assembly.
40 For we are in danger to be called in question for this day's uproar, there being no cause whereby we may give an account of this concourse.
41 And when he had thus spoken, he dismissed the assembly.

Acts 20

1. And after the ceasing of the tumult, having called the disciples, and having greeted (them), Paul went away to go into Macedonia.

2 And passing through those parts, and exhorting them with much speech, he came into Greece.
3 And spending three months, (there) having occurred a plot by the Jews (against) him, being about to sail away into Syria, he was minded to return through Macedonia.

4 And Sopater, a Berean; and Aristarchus and Secundus of the Thessalonians, and Gaius of Derbe, and Timothy, and Tychicus and Trophimus of Asia accompanied him as far as Asia.

5 These going forward, awaited us in Troas.

6 And we sailed away

Acts 20

3326 1161 3588 3973 3588 2351 4341
1. Μετὰ δὲ τὸ παύσασθαι τὸν θόρυβον, προσκαλεσάμενος
after And the ceasing of the tumult, having called

3588 3972 3588 3101 2532 782 1831 4198
ὁ Παῦλος τοὺς μαθητάς, καὶ ἀσπασάμενος, ἐξῆλθε πορευθῆναι
Paul the disciples, and having greeted (them), went away to go

1519 3588 3109 1330 1161 3588 3313 1565 2532 3870
εἰς τὴν Μακεδονίαν. 2 διελθὼν δὲ τὰ μέρη ἐκεῖνα, καὶ παρα-
into Macedonia. passing through And parts those, and having

846 3056 4183 2064 1519 3588 1671 4160
καλέσας αὐτοὺς λόγῳ πολλῷ, ἦλθεν εἰς τὴν Ἑλλάδα. 3 ποιή-
exhorted them with speech much, he came into Greece. spending

5037 3376 5140 1096 846 1917 5259 3588
σας τε μῆνας τρεῖς, γενομένης αὐτῷ ἐπιβουλῆς ὑπὸ τῶν
And months three, having occurred (against) him a plot by the

2453 3195 321 1519 3588 4947 1096
Ἰουδαίων μέλλοντι ἀνάγεσθαι εἰς τὴν Συρίαν, ἐγένετο
Jews being about to sail away into Syria, he was

1106 3588 5290 1223 3109 4902 1161
γνώμη τοῦ ὑποστρέφειν διὰ Μακεδονίας. 4 συνείπετο δὲ
minded to return through Macedonia. accompanied And

846 891 3588 773 4986 961 2331
αὐτῷ ἄχρι τῆς Ἀσιας Σώπατρος Βεροιαῖος· Θεσσαλονι-
him as far as Asia Sopater a Berean; of Thessalonians

1161 708 2532 4580 2532 1050 1190
κέων δὲ, Ἀρίσταρχος καὶ Σεκοῦνδος, καὶ Γάϊος Δερβαῖος,
and, Aristarchus and Secundus; and Gaius of Derbe,

2532 5095 774 1161 5190 2532 5161 3778
καὶ Τιμόθεος· Ἀσιανοὶ δέ, Τυχικὸς καὶ Τρόφιμος. 5 οὗτοι
and Timothy; of Asia and, Tychicus and Trophemus. These

4281 3306 2248 1722 5174 2249 1161 1602
προελθόντες ἔμενον ἡμᾶς ἐν Τρωάδι. 6 ἡμεῖς δὲ ἐξεπλεύσαμεν
going forward awaited us in Troas. we And sailed away

Acts 20

1. And after the uproar was ceased, Paul called unto (him) the disciples, and embraced (them), and departed for to go into Macedonia.

2 And when he had gone over those parts, and had given them much exhortation, he came into Greece,
3 And (there) abode three months. And when the Jews laid wait for him, as he was about to sail into Syria, he purposed to return through Macedonia.

4 And there accompanied him into Asia Sopater of Berea; and of the Thessalonians, Aristarchus and Secundus; and Gaius of Derbe, and Timotheus; and of Asia, Tychicus and Trophimus.

5 These going before tarried for us at Troas.

6 And we sailed away

Literal Translation

after the days of Unleavened (Bread) from Philippi, and came to them into Troas until five days, where we remained seven days.

7. And on the first of the week, the disciples having been gathered to break bread, being about to depart on the morrow, Paul reasoned to them. And he continued the discourse until midnight.

8 And many lamps were in the upper room where they were gathered.

9 And a certain young man named Eutychus (was) sitting on the window sill, being overborne by deep sleep, Paul reasoning for a longer time, being overborne by the sleep, he fell from the third floor down and was taken up dead.

10 But going down Paul fell on him, and having embraced (him), he said, Do not be terrified, for his soul is in him.

11 And going up, and breaking bread, and having tasted and conversing over a long (time), until dawn, he went out thus.

12 And they brought the boy living and were comforted not a little.

13. But going before onto the ship, we set sail for Assos, from there being about to take up Paul; for so it had been arranged, he intending to go on foot.

14 And when he met with us in Assos, taking him up we came to Mitylene.

15 And sailing away from there, on the next (day) we arrived

Acts 20:7

3326 3588 2250 3588 106 575 5375 2532 2064
μετὰ τὰς ἡμέρας τῶν ἀζύμων ἀπὸ Φιλίππων, καὶ ἤλθομεν
after the days of Unleavened from Philippi, and came
4314 846 1519 3588 5174 891 2250 4002 3757
πρὸς αὐτοὺς εἰς τὴν Τρῳάδα ἄχρις ἡμερῶν πέντε, οὗ
to them into Troas until days five, where
1304 2250 2033
διετρίψαμεν ἡμέρας ἑπτά.
we remained days seven.

1722 1161 3588 3391 3588 4521 4863 3588 3101
7. Ἐν δὲ τῇ μιᾷ τῶν σαββάτων, συνηγμένων τῶν μαθητῶν
in And the one of the sabbaths, having been gathered the disciples
3588 2806 740 3588 3972 1256 846 3195
τοῦ κλάσαι ἄρτον, ὁ Παῦλος διελέγετο αὐτοῖς, μέλλων
to break bread, Paul reasoned to them, being about
1826 3588 1887 3905 5037 3588 3056 3360 3317
ἐξιέναι τῇ ἐπαύριον, παρέτεινέ τε τὸν λόγον μέχρι μεσονυ-
to depart on the morrow, he continued and the discourse until midnight.
2258 1161 2985 2425 1722 3588 5253 3757 2258
κτίου. 8 ἦσαν δὲ λαμπάδες ἱκαναὶ ἐν τῷ ὑπερῴῳ οὗ ἦσαν
were And lamps many in the upper room where they were
4863 2521 1161 5100 3494 3686 2161 1909
συνηγμένοι. 9 καθήμενος δέ τις νεανίας ὀνόματι Εὔτυχος ἐπὶ
assembled. having sat And a certain youth by name Eutychus on
3588 2376 2702 5258 901 1256 3588
τῆς θυρίδος, καταφερόμενος ὕπνῳ βαθεῖ, διαλεγομένου τοῦ
the window sill, having been overborne by sleep deep, having reasoned
3972 1909 4119 2702 575 3588 5258 4098 575
Παύλου ἐπὶ πλεῖον, κατενεχθεὶς ἀπὸ τοῦ ὕπνου ἔπεσεν ἀπὸ
Paul (for) a longer (time), being overborne from the sleep he fell from
3588 5152 2736 2532 142 3498 2597 1161 3588 3972
τοῦ τριστέγου κάτω, καὶ ἤρθη νεκρός. 10 καταβὰς δὲ ὁ Παῦλος
the third floor down, and was taken up dead. going down But Paul
1968 846 2532 4843 2036 3361 2350
ἐπέπεσεν αὐτῷ, καὶ συμπεριλαβὼν εἶπε, Μὴ θορυβεῖσθε·
fell on him, and having embraced (him) said, Not be terrified;
3588 1063 5590 846 1722 846 2076 305 1161 2532 2806
ἡ γὰρ ψυχὴ αὐτοῦ ἐν αὐτῷ ἐστιν. 11 ἀναβὰς δὲ καὶ κλάσας
the for soul of him in him is. going up And and breaking
740 2532 1089 1909 2425 5037 3656 891 827
ἄρτον καὶ γευσάμενος, ἐφ᾽ ἱκανόν τε ὁμιλήσας ἄχρις αὐγῆς,
bread and having tasted, over a long (time) and conversing until dawn,
3779 1831 71 1161 3588 3816 2198 2532 3870
οὕτως ἐξῆλθεν. 12 ἤγαγον δὲ τὸν παῖδα ζῶντα, καὶ παρεκλήθη-
thus he went out. they brought And the boy living, and were comforted
3756 3357
σαν οὐ μετρίως.
not moderately.

2249 1161 4281 1909 3588 4143 321 1519 3588
13. Ἡμεῖς δὲ, προελθόντες ἐπὶ τὸ πλοῖον, ἀνήχθημεν εἰς τὴν
we And, going before onto the ship, set sail for
789 1564 3195 353 3588 3972 3779
Ἄσσον, ἐκεῖθεν μέλλοντες ἀναλαμβάνειν τὸν Παῦλον· οὕτω
Assos, from there being about to take up Paul; so
1063 2258 1299 3195 846 3978 5613 1161 4820
γὰρ ἦν διατεταγμένος, μέλλων αὐτὸς πεζεύειν. 14 ὡς δὲ συνέ-
for it was having been arranged, intending he to go on foot. when And he met
2254 1519 3588 789 353 846 2064 1519
βαλεν ἡμῖν εἰς τὴν Ἄσσον, ἀναλαβόντες αὐτὸν ἤλθομεν εἰς
with us in Assos, taking up him we came to
3412 2547 636 3588 1966 2658
Μιτυλήνην. 15 κἀκεῖθεν ἀποπλεύσαντες, τῇ ἐπιούσῃ κατηντή-
Mitylene. And from there sailing away, on the next (day) we arrived

King James Version

from Philippi after the days of unleavened bread, and came unto them to Troas in five days; where we abode seven days.

7. And upon the first (day) of the week, when the disciples came together to break bread, Paul preached unto them, ready to depart on the morrow; and continued his speech until midnight.

8 And there were many lights in the upper chamber, where they were gathered together.

9 And there sat in a window a certain young man named Eutychus, being fallen into a deep sleep: and as Paul was long preaching, he sunk down with sleep, and fell down from the third loft, and was taken up dead.

10 And Paul went down, and fell on him, and embracing (him) said, Trouble not yourselves; for his life is in him.

11 When he therefore was come up again, and had broken bread, and eaten, and talked a long while, even till break of day, so he departed.

12 And they brought the young man alive, and were not a little comforted.

13. And we went before to ship, and sailed unto Assos, there intending to take in Paul: for so had he appointed, minding himself to go afoot.

14 And when he met with us at Assos, we took him in, and came to Mitylene.

15 And we sailed thence, and came the next (day) over against Chios; and the next (day) we arrived

Literal Translation | **Acts 20:16** | *King James Version*

opposite Chios, and on the next we crossed to Samos. And having stayed at Trogyllium, the next (day) we came to Miletus.

481 5508 3588 1161 2087 3846 1519 4544 2532
σαμεν ἄντικρὺ Χίου· τῇ δὲ ἑτέρᾳ παρεβάλομεν εἰς Σάμον· καὶ
opposite Chios; on the and next we crossed to Samos; and

3306 1722 5175 3588 2192 2064 1519 3399
μείναντες ἐν Τρωγυλλίῳ, τῇ ἐχομένῃ ἤλθομεν εἰς Μίλητον.
having stayed in Trogyllium, the next (day) we came to Miletus.

over against Chios; and the next (day) we arrived at Samos, and tarried at Trogyllium; and the next (day) we came to Miletus.

16 For Paul had decided to sail by Ephesus, so as not happen to him to spend time in Asia; for he hastened if it was possible for him to be in Jerusalem (on) the day of Pentecost.

2919 1063 3588 3972 3896 3588 2181 3704 3361
16 ἔκρινε γὰρ ὁ Παῦλος παραπλεῦσαι τὴν Ἔφεσον, ὅπως μὴ
had decided For Paul to sail past Ephesus, so as not

1096 846 5551 1722 3588 773 4692 1063 1487
γένηται αὐτῷ χρονοτριβῆσαι ἐν τῇ Ἀσίᾳ· ἔσπευδε γάρ, εἰ
happen to him to spend time in Asia; he hastened for, if

1415 2258 846 3588 2250 3588 4005 1096
δυνατὸν ἦν αὐτῷ, τὴν ἡμέραν τῆς πεντηκοστῆς γενέσθαι
possible it was for him the day of Pentecost to be

1519 2414
εἰς Ἱεροσόλυμα.
into Jerusalem.

16 For Paul had determined to sail by Ephesus, because he would not spend the time in Asia: for he hasted, if it were possible for him, to be at Jerusalem the day of Pentecost.

17. And sending to Ephesus from Miletus, he called for the elders of the church.
18 And when they came to him, he said to them: You understand, from (the) first day (on) which I set foot in Asia, how I was with you all the time,

575 1161 3588 3399 3992 1519 2181 3333
17. Ἀπὸ δὲ τῆς Μιλήτου πέμψας εἰς Ἔφεσον μετεκαλέσατο
from And Miletus sending to Ephesus he called for

3588 4245 3588 1577 5613 1161 3854 4314
τοὺς πρεσβυτέρους τῆς ἐκκλησίας. 18 ὡς δὲ παρεγένοντο πρὸς
the elders of the church. when And they came to

846 2036 846
αὐτόν, εἶπεν αὐτοῖς,
him, he said to them,

5210 1987 575 4413 2250 575 3739 1910 1519
Ὑμεῖς ἐπίστασθε, ἀπὸ πρώτης ἡμέρας ἀφ' ἧς ἐπέβην εἰς
You understand, from (the) first day from which I set foot in

3588 773 4459 3326 5216 3588 3956 5550 1096
τὴν Ἀσίαν, πῶς μεθ' ὑμῶν τὸν πάντα χρόνον ἐγενόμην,
Asia, how with you the all time I was,

17. And from Miletus he sent to Ephesus, and called the elders of the church.
18 And when they were come to him, he said unto them, Ye know, from the first day that I came into Asia, after what manner I have been with you at all seasons,

19 serving the Lord with all humility, and many tears and trials happening to me by the plots of the Jews;

20 as I kept nothing back of the profitable (things), (so as) not to tell you, and to teach you publicly, and from house to house,

21 earnestly testifying (both) to Jews and to Greeks repentance toward God and faith toward our Lord Jesus Christ.

22 And now, behold, being bound by the Spirit, am going to Jerusalem, not knowing the things going to meet me in it,

23 but that the Holy Spirit testifies city by city saying that bonds and afflictions await me.

1398 3588 2962 3326 3956 5012 2532
19 δουλεύων τῷ Κυρίῳ μετὰ πάσης ταπεινοφροσύνης καὶ
serving the Lord with all humility and

4183 1144 2532 3986 3588 4819 3427 1722
πολλῶν δακρύων καὶ πειρασμῶν τῶν συμβάντων μοι ἐν
many tears and trials happening to me by

3588 1917 3588 2453 5613 3762 5288 3588
ταῖς ἐπιβουλαῖς τῶν Ἰουδαίων· 20 ὡς οὐδὲν ὑπεστειλάμην τῶν
the plots of the Jews; as nothing I kept back of the

4851 3588 3361 312 5213 2532 1321 5209
συμφερόντων, τοῦ μὴ ἀναγγεῖλαι ὑμῖν καὶ διδάξαι ὑμᾶς
profitable (things), not to tell you and to teach you

1219 2532 2596 3624 1263 2453 5037 2532
δημοσίᾳ καὶ κατ' οἴκους, 21 διαμαρτυρόμενος Ἰουδαίοις τε καὶ
publicly and house to house, earnestly testifying to Jews and also

1672 3588 1519 3588 2316 3341 2532 4102 3588 1519 3588
Ἕλλησι τὴν εἰς τὸν Θεὸν μετάνοιαν, καὶ πίστιν τὴν εἰς τὸν
to Greeks toward God repentance, and faith toward the

2962 2257 2424 5547 2532 3568 2400 1473 1210
Κύριον ἡμῶν Ἰησοῦν Χριστόν. 22 καὶ νῦν ἰδού, ἐγὼ δεδεμένος
Lord of us Jesus Christ. And now behold! I being bound

3588 4151 4198 1519 2419 3588 1722 846 4876
τῷ πνεύματι πορεύομαι εἰς Ἱερουσαλήμ, τὰ ἐν αὐτῇ συναντή-
by the Spirit am going to Jerusalem, the things in it going to

3427 3361 1492 4133 3754 3588 4151 3588 40 2596
σοντά μοι μὴ εἰδώς, 23 πλὴν ὅτι τὸ Πνεῦμα τὸ Ἅγιον κατὰ
meet me not knowing, but that the Spirit Holy city-

4172 1263 3004 3754 1199 3165 2532 2347 3306
πόλιν διαμαρτύρεται λέγον ὅτι δεσμά με καὶ θλίψεις μένουσιν.
by-city testifies saying that bonds me and afflictions await.

19 Serving the Lord with all humility of mind, and with many tears, and temptations, which befell me by the lying in wait of the Jews:

20 (And) how I kept back nothing that was profitable (unto you), but have shewed you, and have taught you publickly, and from house to house,

21 Testifying both to the Jews, and also to the Greeks, repentance toward God, and faith toward our Lord Jesus Christ.

22 And now, behold, I go bound in the spirit unto Jerusalem, not knowing the things that shall befall me there:

23 Save that the Holy Ghost witnesseth in every city, saying that bonds and afflictions abide me.

Literal Translation **Acts 20:24** ***King James Version***

24 But I make account of nothing, nor do I hold my life precious to myself, so that I might finish my course with joy, and the ministry which I received from the Lord Jesus, fully to testify the gospel of the grace of God.

235 3762 3056 4160 3761 2192 3588 5590 3450
24 ἀλλ᾽ οὐδενὸς λόγον ποιοῦμαι, οὐδὲ ἔχω τὴν ψυχήν μου
But of nothing account I make, nor I hold the life of me

5093 1683 5613 5048 3588 1408 3450 3326 5479
τιμίαν ἐμαυτῷ, ὡς τελειῶσαι τὸν δρόμον μου μετὰ χαρᾶς,
precious to myself, so as I may finish the course of me with joy,

2532 3588 1248 3739 2983 3844 3588 2962 2424
καὶ τὴν διακονίαν ἣν ἔλαβον παρὰ τοῦ Κυρίου Ἰησοῦ,
and the ministry which I received from the Lord Jesus,

1263 3588 2098 3588 5485 3588 2316 2532
διαμαρτύρασθαι τὸ εὐαγγέλιον τῆς χάριτος τοῦ Θεοῦ. 25 καὶ
to fully testify the gospel of the grace of God. And

24 But none of these things move me, neither count I my life dear unto myself, so that I might finish my course with joy, and the ministry, which I have received of the Lord Jesus, to testify the gospel of the grace of God.

25 And now, behold! I know that you all will see my face no more, among whom I went about proclaiming the kingdom of God.

3568 2400 1473 1492 3754 3765 3700 3588 4383 3450
νῦν ἰδού, ἐγὼ οἶδα ὅτι οὐκέτι ὄψεσθε τὸ πρόσωπόν μου
now behold! I know that no more will see the face of me

5210 3956 1722 3739 1330 2784 3588 932 3588
ὑμεῖς πάντες, ἐν οἷς διῆλθον κηρύσσων τὴν βασιλείαν τοῦ
you all, among whom I went about proclaiming the kingdom

2316
Θεοῦ.
of God.

25 And now, behold, I know that ye all, among whom I have gone preaching the kingdom of God, shall see my face no more.

26 Because of this I testify to you in this very day that I (am) pure from the blood of all.
27 For I did not keep back to declare to you all the counsel of God.
28 Therefore take heed to yourselves and to all the flock, in which the Holy Spirit placed you (as) overseers, to shepherd the church of God which He purchased through (His) own blood.

1352 3143 5213 1722 3588 4594 2250 3754
26 διὸ μαρτύρομαι ὑμῖν ἐν τῇ σήμερον ἡμέρᾳ, ὅτι
Therefore I testify to you in this very day, that

2513 1473 575 3588 129 3956 3756 1063 5288
καθαρός ἐγὼ ἀπὸ τοῦ αἵματος πάντων. 27 οὐ γὰρ ὑπεστειλάμην
clean I am from the blood of all. not For I kept back

3588 3361 312 5213 3956 3588 1012 3588 2316 4337
τοῦ μὴ ἀναγγεῖλαι ὑμῖν πᾶσαν τὴν βουλὴν τοῦ Θεοῦ. 28 προσ-
not to declare to you all the counsel of God. Take

3767 1438 2532 3956 3588 4168 1722 3739 5209 3588
έχετε οὖν ἑαυτοῖς καὶ παντὶ τῷ ποιμνίῳ, ἐν ᾧ ὑμᾶς τὸ
heed therefore to yourselves and to all the flock, in which you the

4151 3588 40 5087 1985 4165 3588 1577
Πνεῦμα τὸ Ἅγιον ἔθετο ἐπισκόπους, ποιμαίνειν τὴν ἐκκλη-
Spirit Holy placed overseers, to shepherd the church

3588 2316 3739 4046 1223 3588 2398 129
σίαν τοῦ Θεοῦ, ἣν περιεποιήσατο διὰ τοῦ ἰδίου αἵματος.
of God, which He purchased through the own blood.

26 Wherefore I take you to record this day, that I (am) pure from the blood of all (men).
27 For I have not shunned to declare unto you all the counsel of God.
28 Take heed therefore unto yourselves, and to all the flock, over the which the Holy Ghost hath made you overseers, to feed the church of God, which he hath purchased with his own blood.

29 For I know this, that after my departure grievous wolves will come in among you, not sparing the flock;
30 and from you yourselves will rise up men speaking perverted things, in order to draw away the disciples after themselves.
31 Because of this watch, remembering that I did not cease admonishing each one with tears night and day (for) three years.

1473 1063 1492 5124 3754 1525 3326 3588 867
29 ἐγὼ γὰρ οἶδα τοῦτο, ὅτι εἰσελεύσονται μετὰ τὴν ἄφιξίν
I For know this, that will come in after the departure

3450 3074 926 1519 5209 3361 5339 3588 4168 2532
μου λύκοι βαρεῖς εἰς ὑμᾶς, μὴ φειδόμενοι τοῦ ποιμνίου· 30 καὶ
of me wolves grievous into you, not sparing the flock; and

1537 5216 846 450 435 2980 1294
ἐξ ὑμῶν αὐτῶν ἀναστήσονται ἄνδρες λαλοῦντες διεστραμ-
from you (your)selves will rise up men speaking perverted

3588 645 3588 3101 3694 846 1352
μένα, τοῦ ἀποσπᾶν τοὺς μαθητὰς ὀπίσω αὐτῶν. 31 διὸ
things, to draw away the disciples after themselves. Therefore

1127 3421 3754 5148 3571 2532 2250
γρηγορεῖτε, μνημονεύοντες ὅτι τριετίαν νύκτα καὶ ἡμέραν
watch, remembering that three years night and day

3756 3973 3326 1144 3560 1520 1538 2532
οὐκ ἐπαυσάμην μετὰ δακρύων νουθετῶν ἕνα ἕκαστον. 32 καὶ
not I ceased with tears admonishing one each. And

29 For I know this, that after my departing shall grievous wolves enter in among you, not sparing the flock.
30 Also of your own selves shall men arise, speaking perverse things, to draw away disciples after them.

31 Therefore watch, and remember, that by the space of three years I ceased not to warn every one night and day with tears.

32 And now, brothers, I commend you to God and to the Word of His grace, which is able to build up and to give you inheritance among all those having been sanctified.

3588 3568 3908 5209 80 3588 2316 2532 3588 3056 3588
τὰ νῦν παρατίθεμαι ὑμᾶς, ἀδελφοί, τῷ Θεῷ καὶ τῷ λόγῳ τῆς
now I commend you, brothers, to God and to the Word

5485 846 3588 1410 2026 2532 1325
χάριτος αὐτοῦ, τῷ δυναμένῳ ἐποικοδομῆσαι, καὶ δοῦναι
of grace of Him, being able to build up, and to give

5213 2817 1722 3588 37 3956 694
ὑμῖν κληρονομίαν ἐν τοῖς ἡγιασμένοις πᾶσιν. 33 ἀργυ-
you inheritance among those having been sanctified all. Silver

32 And now, brethren, I commend you to God, and to the word of his grace, which is able to build you up, and to give you an inheritance among all them which are sanctified.

33 Silver

33 I have

Literal Translation

Acts 20:34

King James Version

or gold, or clothing of no one I desired.
34 But you yourselves know that these hands ministered to my needs, and to those who were with me.

35 I showed you all things, that working in this way we ought to help those being weak, and to remember the words of the Lord Jesus, that He said, Blessed it is to give than to receive.

36. And having said these things, placing his knees, he prayed with them all.
37 And there was much weeping of all, and falling on the neck of Paul, they ardently kissed him,

38 most of all grieving for the word which he said, that they are going to behold his face no more. And they escorted him to the ship.

2228 5553 2228 2441 3762 1937 846 1161
ρίου ἢ χρυσίου ἢ ἱματισμοῦ οὐδενὸς ἐπεθύμησα. 34 αὐτοὶ δὲ
or gold or clothing of no one I desired. (your)selves But

1097 3754 3588 5532 3450 2532 3588 5607 3326 1700
γινώσκετε ὅτι ταῖς χρείαις μου καὶ τοῖς οὖσι μετ᾽ ἐμοῦ
you know that to the needs of me and those being with me

5256 3588 5495 3778 3956 5263 5213 3754
ὑπηρέτησαν αἱ χεῖρες αὗται. 35 πάντα ὑπέδειξα ὑμῖν, ὅτι
ministered hands these. All things I showed to you, that

3779 2872 1163 482 3588 770
οὕτω κοπιῶντας δεῖ ἀντιλαμβάνεσθαι τῶν ἀσθενούντων,
thus working we ought to help those infirm (ones),

3421 5037 3588 3056 3588 2962 2424 3754 846
μνημονεύειν τε τῶν λόγων τοῦ Κυρίου Ἰησοῦ, ὅτι αὐτὸς
to remember and the words of the Lord Jesus, that He

2036 3107 2076 1325 3123 2228 2983
εἶπε, Μακάριόν ἐστι διδόναι μᾶλλον ἢ λαμβάνειν.
said, Blessed it is to give rather than to receive.

2532 5023 2036 5087 3588 1119 846 4862 3956
36. Καὶ ταῦτα εἰπών, θεὶς τὰ γόνατα αὐτοῦ, σὺν πᾶσιν
And these things having said, placing the knees of him, with all

846 4336 2425 1161 1096 2805 3956
αὐτοῖς προσηύξατο. 37 ἱκανὸς δὲ ἐγένετο κλαυθμὸς πάντων·
them he prayed. much And there was weeping of all;

2532 1968 1909 3588 5137 3588 3972 2705
καὶ ἐπιπεσόντες ἐπὶ τὸν τράχηλον τοῦ Παύλου κατεφίλουν
and falling on the neck of Paul they ardently kissed

846 3600 3122 1909 3588 3056 3739 2046 3754
αὐτόν, 38 ὀδυνώμενοι μάλιστα ἐπὶ τῷ λόγῳ ᾧ εἰρήκει, ὅτι
him, grieving most over the word which he said, that

3765 3195 3588 4383 846 2334 4311
οὐκέτι μέλλουσι τὸ πρόσωπον αὐτοῦ θεωρεῖν. προέπεμπον
no more they are going the face of him to behold. they escorted

1161 846 1519 3588 4143
δὲ αὐτὸν εἰς τὸ πλοῖον.
And him to the ship.

coveted no man's silver, or gold, or apparel.
34 Yea, ye yourselves know, that these hands have ministered unto my necessities, and to them that were with me.

35 I have shewed you all things, how that so labouring ye ought to support the weak, and to remember the words of the Lord Jesus, how he said, It is more blessed to give than to receive.

36. And when he had thus spoken, he kneeled down, and prayed with them all.
37 And they all wept sore, and fell on Paul's neck, and kissed him,

38 Sorrowing most of all for the words which he spake, that they should see his face no more. And they accompanied him unto the ship.

Acts 21

1. And when it was (time) to sail, we having been drawn away from them, having run direct we came to Cos, and on the next (day) to Rhodes, and from there to Patara.
2 And having found a ship crossing over to Phoenice, going on board we set sail:
3 and having sighted Cyprus, and leaving it on the left, we sailed to Syria, and came down to Tyre; for the ship was unloading the cargo there.

4 And having found disciples, we remained there seven days; who told Paul

Acts 21

5613 1161 1096 321 2248 645 575
1. Ὡς δὲ ἐγένετο ἀναχθῆναι ἡμᾶς ἀποσπασθέντας ἀπ᾽
when And it was (time) to sail away we having been withdrawn from

846 2113 2064 1519 3588 2972 3588 1161 1836
αὐτῶν, εὐθυδρομήσαντες ἤλθομεν εἰς τὴν Κῶν, τῇ δὲ ἑξῆς
them, having run direct we came to Coos, on the and next

1519 3588 4499 2547 1519 3959 2532 2147 4143
εἰς τὴν Ῥόδον, κἀκεῖθεν εἰς Πάταρα· 2 καὶ εὑρόντες πλοῖον
to Rhodes, and from there to Patara; and having found a ship

1276 1519 5403 1910 321 398
διαπερῶν εἰς Φοινίκην ἐπιβάντες ἀνήχθημεν. 3 ἀναφάναντες
crossing over to Phoenice, entering we set sail. having sighted

1161 3588 2954 2532 2641 846 2176 4126
δὲ τὴν Κύπρον, καὶ καταλιπόντες αὐτὴν εὐώνυμον ἐπλέομεν
And Cyprus, and leaving it on the left, we sailed

1519 4947 2532 2609 1519 5184 1566 1063 2258 3588
εἰς Συρίαν, καὶ κατήχθημεν εἰς Τύρον· ἐκεῖσε γὰρ ἦν τὸ
to Syria, and came down to Tyre; there for was the

4143 670 3588 1117 2532 429
πλοῖον ἀποφορτιζόμενον τὸν γόμον. 4 καὶ ἀνευρόντες
ship unloading the cargo. And having found

3101 1961 846 2250 2033 3748 3588 3972
μαθητάς, ἐπεμείναμεν αὐτοῦ ἡμέρας ἑπτά· οἵτινες τῷ Παύλῳ
disciples, we remained there days seven; who Paul

Acts 21

1. And it came to pass, that after we were gotten from them, and had launched, we came with a straight course unto Coos, and the (day) following unto Rhodes, and from thence unto Patara:
2 And finding a ship sailing over unto Phenicia, we went aboard, and set forth.
3 Now when we had discovered Cyprus, we left it on the left hand, and sailed into Syria, and landed at Tyre: for there the ship was to unlade her burden.

4 And finding disciples, we tarried there seven days: who said to Paul

Literal Translation

through the Spirit not to go up to Jerusalem.

5 But when it was (time for) us to complete the days, having set out, we traveled. (And they), with all (the) women and children went with us as far as outside the city. And placing the knees on the shore, praying,
6 and giving parting greetings to one another, we went up into the ship, and those went back to their own.

7 And completing the voyage from Tyre, we arrived at Ptolemais. And having greeted the brothers, we remained one day with them.

8 And on the morrow, those around (him) going out, Paul came to Caesarea. And going into the house of Philip the evangelist, (he) being of the Seven, we stayed with him.

9 And there were four virgin daughters to this one, who prophesied.
10 And we remaining more days, a certain prophet from Judea named Agabus came down.

11 And coming to us, and taking Paul's girdle, and binding his hands and feet, he said, The Holy Spirit says these (things): In Jerusalem the Jews will bind in this way the man whose girdle this is, and will deliver (him) up into the hands of (the) nations.

12 And when we heard these things, both we and the residents begged him not to go up to Jerusalem.

13 But Paul answered, What are you doing,

Acts 21:5

3004 1223 3588 4151 3361 305 1519 2419
ἔλεγον διὰ τοῦ Πνεύματος, μὴ ἀναβαίνειν εἰς Ἱερουσαλήμ.
told through the Spirit, not to go up to Jerusalem.

3753 1161 1096 2248 1822 3588 2250 1831 4198
5 ὅτε δὲ ἐγένετο ἡμᾶς ἐξαρτίσαι τὰς ἡμέρας, ἐξελθόντες ἐπο-
when But it was (time) us to complete the days, having set out we

4311 2248 3956 4862 1135 2532
ρευόμεθα, προπεμπόντων ἡμᾶς πάντων σὺν γυναιξὶ καὶ
traveled, accompanying us all with women and

5043 2193 1854 3588 4172 2532 5087 3588 1119 1909 3588
τέκνοις ἕως ἔξω τῆς πόλεως· καὶ θέντες τὰ γόνατα ἐπὶ τὸν
children as far as outside the city; and placing the knees on the

123 4336 2532 782 240 1910
αἰγιαλὸν προσηυξάμεθα, 6 καὶ ἀσπασάμενοι ἀλλήλους, ἐπέ-
shore praying, and giving parting greetings to each other, we

1519 3588 4143 1565 1161 5290 1519 3588 2398
βημεν εἰς τὸ πλοῖον, ἐκεῖνοι δὲ ὑπέστρεψαν εἰς τὰ ἴδια.
went up into the ship, those and went back to the own.

2249 1161 3588 4144 1274 575 5184 2658
7. Ἡμεῖς δέ, τὸν πλοῦν διανύσαντες ἀπὸ Τύρου, κατηντή-
we And, the voyage completing from Tyre, arrived

1519 4424 2532 782 3588 80 3306
σαμεν εἰς Πτολεμαΐδα, καὶ ἀσπασάμενοι τοὺς ἀδελφοὺς ἐμεί-
at Ptolemais, and having greeted the brothers we

3306 2250 3391 3844 846 3588 1161 1887 1831
ναμεν ἡμέραν μίαν παρ᾽ αὐτοῖς. 8 τῇ δὲ ἐπαύριον ἐξελθόντες
remained day one with them. on the And morrow going out

3588 4012 3588 3972 2064 1519 2542 2532 1525
οἱ περὶ τὸν Παῦλον ἤλθομεν εἰς Καισάρειαν· καὶ εἰσελθόντες
those around Paul came to Caesarea; and having gone

1519 3588 3624 5376 3588 2099 3588 5607 1537
εἰς τὸν οἶκον Φιλίππου τοῦ εὐαγγελιστοῦ, τοῦ ὄντος ἐκ
to the house of Philip the evangelist, being of

3588 2033 3306 3844 846 5129 1161 2258 2364
τῶν ἑπτά, ἐμείναμεν παρ᾽ αὐτῷ. 9 τούτῳ δὲ ἦσαν θυγατέρες
the Seven, we stayed with him. to this one And were daughters

3933 5064 4395 1961 1161 2257
παρθένοι τέσσαρες προφητεύουσαι. 10 ἐπιμενόντων δὲ ἡμῶν
virgin four prophesying. remaining And us

2250 4119 2718 5100 575 3588 2449 4396
ἡμέρας πλείους, κατῆλθέ τις ἀπὸ τῆς Ἰουδαίας προφήτης
days more, came down a certain from Judea prophet

3686 13 2532 2064 4314 2248 2532 142 3588 2223
ὀνόματι Ἄγαβος. 11 καὶ ἐλθὼν πρὸς ἡμᾶς, καὶ ἄρας τὴν ζώνην
by name Agabus. And coming to us, and taking the girdle

3588 3972 1210 5037 846 3588 5495 2532 3588 4228 2036
τοῦ Παύλου, δήσας τε αὐτοῦ τὰς χεῖρας καὶ τοὺς πόδας εἶπε,
of Paul, binding and of himself the hands and the feet he said,

3592 3004 3588 4151 3588 40 3588 435 3739 2076 3588 2223
Τάδε λέγει τὸ Πνεῦμα τὸ Ἅγιον, Τὸν ἄνδρα οὗ ἐστιν ἡ ζώνη
These things says the Spirit Holy, The man of whom is girdle

3778 3779 1210 1722 2419 3588 2453 2532
αὕτη, οὕτω δήσουσιν ἐν Ἱερουσαλὴμ οἱ Ἰουδαῖοι, καὶ
this, this way will bind in Jerusalem the Jews, and

3860 1519 5495 1484 5613 1161 191 5023
παραδώσουσιν εἰς χεῖρας ἐθνῶν. 12 ὡς δὲ ἠκούσαμεν ταῦτα,
will deliver up into (the) hands of nations. when And we heard these things,

3870 2249 5037 2532 3588 1786 3588 3361 305
παρεκαλοῦμεν ἡμεῖς τε καὶ οἱ ἐντόπιοι, τοῦ μὴ ἀναβαίνειν
begged we both and the residents not to go up

846 1519 2419 611 1161 3588 3972 5101 4160
αὐτὸν εἰς Ἱερουσαλήμ. 13 ἀπεκρίθη δὲ ὁ Παῦλος, Τί ποιεῖτε
him to Jerusalem. answered But Paul, What are you doing

King James Version

through the Spirit, that he should not go up to Jerusalem.

5 And when we had accomplished those days, we departed and went our way; and they all brought us on our way, with wives and children, till (we were) out of the city: and we kneeled down on the shore, and prayed.
6 And when we had taken our leave one of another, we took ship; and they returned home again.

7 And when we had finished (our) course from Tyre, we came to Ptolemais, and saluted the brethren, and abode with them one day.

8 And the next (day) we that were of Paul's company departed, and came unto Caesarea: and we entered into the house of Philip the evangelist, which was (one) of the seven; and abode with him.

9 And the same man had four daughters, virgins, which did prophesy.
10 And as we tarried (there) many days, there came down from Judaea a certain prophet, named Agabus.
11 And when he was come unto us, he took Paul's girdle, and bound his own hands and feet, and said, Thus saith the Holy Ghost, So shall the Jews at Jerusalem bind the man that owneth this girdle, and shall deliver (him) into the hands of the Gentiles.

12 And when we heard these things, both we, and they of that place, besought him not to go up to Jerusalem.

13 Then Paul answered, What mean

Literal Translation

Acts 21:14

King James Version

weeping and crushing my heart? For I not only am ready to be bound, but also to die at Jerusalem for the sake of the name of the Lord Jesus.

14 And he not being persuaded, we kept silence, saying, The will of the Lord be (done).

15 And after these days, having made ready, we went up to Jerusalem.

16 And also (some) of the disciples from Caesarea went with us, bringing Mnason, a certain Cypriot, an ancient disciple, with whom we might lodge.

17 And we being in Jerusalem, the brothers joyfully received us.

18 And on the next (day), Paul went in with us to James. And all the elders came.

19 And having greeted them, he related one by one what things God had worked among the nations through his ministry.

20 And hearing, they glorified the Lord, and said to him, You see, brother, how many myriads there are of Jews having believed, and all are zealous ones of the Law.

21 And they were informed about you, that you teach falling away from Moses, telling all the Jews throughout the nations not to circumcise (their) children, nor to walk in the customs.

22 What then is it? At all events, a multitude must come together, for they will hear that you have come.

2799 2532 4919 3450 3588 2588 1473 1063 3756
κλαίοντες καὶ συνθρύπτοντές μου τὴν καρδίαν; ἐγὼ γὰρ οὐ
weeping and crushing of me the heart? I For not

3440 1210 235 2532 599 1519 2419 2093
μόνον δεθῆναι, ἀλλὰ καὶ ἀποθανεῖν εἰς Ἱερουσαλὴμ ἑτοίμως
only to be bound, but also to die at Jerusalem readily

2192 5228 3588 3686 3588 2962 2424 3361 3982 1161
ἔχω ὑπὲρ τοῦ ὀνόματος τοῦ Κυρίου Ἰησοῦ. 14 μὴ πειθομένου δὲ
have because of the name of the Lord Jesus. not being persuaded And

846 2270 2036 3588 2307 3588 2962 1096
αὐτοῦ, ἡσυχάσαμεν εἰπόντες, Τὸ θέλημα τοῦ Κυρίου γενέσθω.
him, we kept silence saying, The will of the Lord let be (done).

3326 1161 3588 2250 3778 643 305
15. Μετὰ δὲ τὰς ἡμέρας ταύτας ἀποσκευασάμενοι ἀνε-
after And days these having made ready we

1519 2419 4905 1161 2532 3588 3101 575
βαίνομεν εἰς Ἱερουσαλήμ. 16 συνῆλθον δὲ καὶ τῶν μαθητῶν ἀπὸ
went up to Jerusalem. went And also the disciples from

2542 4862 2254 71 3844 3739 3579 3416
Καισαρείας σὺν ἡμῖν, ἄγοντες παρ᾽ ᾧ ξενισθῶμεν Μνάσωνί
Caesarea with us, bringing (one) with whom we may lodge, Mnason

5100 2953 744 3101
τινι Κυπρίῳ, ἀρχαίῳ μαθητῇ.
a certain Cypriot, an ancient disciple.

1096 1161 2257 1519 2414 780 1209
17. Γενομένων δὲ ἡμῶν εἰς Ἱεροσόλυμα, ἀσμένως ἐδέξαντο
being And us into Jerusalem, joyfully received

2248 3588 80 3588 1161 1966 1524 3588 3972 4862 2254
ἡμᾶς οἱ ἀδελφοί. 18 τῇ δὲ ἐπιούσῃ εἰσῄει ὁ Παῦλος σὺν ἡμῖν
us the brothers. on the And next went in Paul with us

4314 2385 3956 5037 3854 3588 4245 2532
πρὸς Ἰάκωβον, πάντες τε παρεγένοντο οἱ πρεσβύτεροι. 19 καὶ
to James, all and came the elders. And

782 846 1834 2596 1520 1538 3739 4160
ἀσπασάμενος αὐτούς, ἐξηγεῖτο καθ᾽ ἓν ἕκαστον ὧν ἐποίησεν
having greeted them, he related one by one of which did

3588 2316 1722 3588 1484 1223 3588 1248 846 3588 1161
ὁ Θεὸς ἐν τοῖς ἔθνεσι διὰ τῆς διακονίας αὐτοῦ. 20 οἱ δὲ ἀκού-
God among the nations through the ministry of him. they And

191 1392 3588 2962 2036 5037 846 2334 80
σαντες ἐδόξαζον τὸν Κύριον· εἶπόν τε αὐτῷ, Θεωρεῖς, ἀδελφέ,
hearing glorified the Lord; said and to him, You see, brother,

4214 3461 1526 2453 3588 4100 2532
πόσαι μυριάδες εἰσὶν Ἰουδαίων τῶν πεπιστευκότων· καὶ
how many myriads there are of Jews having believed; and

3956 2207 3588 3551 5225 2727 1161
πάντες ζηλωταὶ τοῦ νόμου ὑπάρχουσι· 21 κατηχήθησαν δὲ
all zealous of the Law are. they were informed And

4012 4675 3754 646 1321 575 3475 3588
περὶ σοῦ, ὅτι ἀποστασίαν διδάσκεις ἀπὸ Μωσέως τοὺς
about you, that falling away you teach from Moses

2596 3588 1484 3956 2453 3004 3361 4059
κατὰ τὰ ἔθνη πάντας Ἰουδαίους, λέγων μὴ περιτέμνειν
throughout the nations all Jews, saying not to circumcise

846 3588 5043 3366 3588 1485 4043 5101 3767 2076
αὐτοὺς τὰ τέκνα, μηδὲ τοῖς ἔθεσι περιπατεῖν. 22 τί οὖν ἐστι;
them the children, nor in the customs to walk. what Then is it?

3843 1163 4128 4905 191 1063 3754
πάντως δεῖ πλῆθος συνελθεῖν· ἀκούσονται γὰρ ὅτι
At all events must a multitude come together; they will hear for that

2064
ἐλήλυθας.
you have come.

ye to weep and to break mine heart? for I am ready not to be bound only, but also to die at Jerusalem for the name of the Lord Jesus.

14 And when he would not be persuaded, we ceased, saying, The will of the Lord be done.

15 And after those days we took up our carriages, and went up to Jerusalem.

16 There went with us also (certain) of the disciples of Caesarea, and brought with them one Mnason of Cyprus, an old disciple, with whom we should lodge.

17 And when we were come to Jerusalem, the brethren received us gladly.

18 And the (day) following Paul went in with us unto James; and all the elders were present.

19 And when he had saluted them, he declared particularly what things God had wrought among the Gentiles by his ministry.

20 And when they heard (it), they glorified the Lord, and said unto him, Thou seest, brother, how many thousands of Jews there are which believe; and they are all zealous of the law:

21 And they are informed of thee, that thou teachest all the Jews which are among the Gentiles to forsake Moses, saying that they ought not to circumcise (their) children, neither to walk after the customs.

22 What is it therefore? the multitude must needs come together: for they will hear that thou art come.

Literal Translation | **Acts 21:23** | **King James Version**

Literal Translation

23 Then do this, what we say to you: There are four men having a vow on themselves;
24 taking these, be purified with them, and be at expense on them, that they may shave the head. And all shall know that all what they have been told about you is nothing, but you yourself walk orderly, keeping the Law.

25 And concerning the believing nations, we joined in writing, judging them to observe no such thing, except to keep themselves both from idol sacrifice, and the blood, and a thing strangled, and (from) fornication.

26 Then taking the men on the next day, having been purified with them, Paul went into the temple, declaring the fulfillment of the days of the purification, until the offering should be offered for each one of them.

27 But as the seven days were going to be completed, having seen him in the temple, the Jews from Asia stirred up all the crowd, and threw on (their) hands on him,

28 crying out, Men, Israelites, help! This is the man teaching all everywhere against the people and the Law and this place. And even more, (he) also brought Greeks into the temple and has defiled this holy place.

29 For they had before seen Trophimus the Ephesian in

5124 3767 4160 3739 4671 3004 1526 2254 435
23 τοῦτο οὖν ποίησον ὅ σοι λέγομεν· εἰσὶν ἡμῖν ἄνδρες
this Then do which to you we say; there are to us men

5064 2171 2192 1909 1438 5128 3880
τέσσαρες εὐχὴν ἔχοντες ἐφ' ἑαυτῶν· 24 τούτους παραλαβὼν
four a vow having on themselves; these taking

48 4862 846 2532 1159 1909 846 2443
ἁγνίσθητι σὺν αὐτοῖς, καὶ δαπάνησον ἐπ' αὐτοῖς, ἵνα
be purified with them, and be at expense on them, that

3587 3588 2776 2532 1097 3956 3754 3739 2727
ξυρήσωνται τὴν κεφαλήν, καὶ γνῶσι πάντες ὅτι ὧν κατή-
they may shave the head, and may know all that of which they

4012 4675 3762 2076 235 4748 2532 846 3588
χηνται περὶ σοῦ οὐδέν ἐστιν, ἀλλὰ στοιχεῖς καὶ αὐτὸς τὸν
have been told about you nothing is, but you walk also yourself the

3551 5442 4012 1161 3588 4100 1484 2249
νόμον φυλάσσων. 25 περὶ δὲ τῶν πεπιστευκότων ἐθνῶν ἡμεῖς
Law keeping. concerning And the believing nations we

1989 2919 3367 5108 5083 846 1487
ἐπεστείλαμεν, κρίναντες μηδὲν τοιοῦτον τηρεῖν αὐτούς, εἰ
joined in writing, judging no such thing to observe them, if

3361 5442 846 3588 5037 1494 2532 3588 129 2532
μὴ φυλάσσεσθαι αὐτοὺς τό τε εἰδωλόθυτον καὶ τὸ αἷμα καὶ
not to keep from themselves the both idol sacrifice and the blood and

4156 2532 4202 5119 3588 3972 3880 3588
πνικτὸν καὶ πορνείαν. 26 τότε ὁ Παῦλος παραλαβὼν τοὺς
a thing strangled and fornication. Then Paul taking (to him) the

435 3588 2192 2250 4862 846 48 1524 1519
ἄνδρας, τῇ ἐχομένῃ ἡμέρᾳ σὺν αὐτοῖς ἁγνισθεὶς εἰσῄει εἰς
men, on the next day with them having been purified went into

3588 2411 1229 3588 1604 3588 2250 3588
τὸ ἱερόν, διαγγέλλων τὴν ἐκπλήρωσιν τῶν ἡμερῶν τοῦ
the temple, declaring the fulfillment of the days of the

49 2193 3757 4374 5228 1520 1538 846
ἁγνισμοῦ, ἕως οὗ προσηνέχθη ὑπὲρ ἑνὸς ἑκάστου αὐτῶν
purification, until should be offered on behalf of one each of them

3588 4376
ἡ προσφορά.
the offering.

5613 1161 3195 3588 2033 2250 4931 3588 575 3588
27. Ὡς δὲ ἔμελλον αἱ ἑπτὰ ἡμέραι συντελεῖσθαι, οἱ ἀπὸ τῆς
as But going to be the seven days completed, the from

773 2453 2300 846 1722 3588 2411 4797
Ἀσίας Ἰουδαῖοι, θεασάμενοι αὐτὸν ἐν τῷ ἱερῷ, συνέχεον
Asia Jews, having seen him in the temple, stirred up

3956 3588 3793 2532 1911 3588 5495 1909 846
πάντα τὸν ὄχλον, καὶ ἐπέβαλον τὰς χεῖρας ἐπ' αὐτόν,
all the crowd, and threw on the hands on him,

2896 435 2475 997 3778 2076 3588
28 κράζοντες, Ἄνδρες Ἰσραηλῖται, βοηθεῖτε. οὗτός ἐστιν ὁ
crying out, Men Israelites, help! This is the

444 3588 2596 3588 2992 2532 3588 3551 2532 3588 5117
ἄνθρωπος ὁ κατὰ τοῦ λαοῦ καὶ τοῦ νόμου καὶ τοῦ τόπου
man who against the people and the Law and place

5127 3956 3837 1321 2089 5037 2532 1672
τούτου πάντας πανταχοῦ διδάσκων· ἔτι τε καὶ Ἕλληνας
this all everywhere teaching; further and also Greeks

1521 1519 3588 2411 2532 2840 3588 40 5117
εἰσήγαγεν εἰς τὸ ἱερόν, καὶ κεκοίνωκε τὸν ἅγιον τόπον
brought into the temple, and has defiled holy place

5126 2258 1063 4308 5161 3588 2180 1722
τοῦτον. 29 ἦσαν γὰρ προεωρακότες Τρόφιμον τὸν Ἐφέσιον ἐν
this. were For before seen Trophimus the Ephesian in

King James Version

23 Do therefore this that we say to thee: We have four men which have a vow on them;
24 Them take, and purify thyself with them, and be at charges with them, that they may shave (their) heads: and all may know that those things, whereof they were informed concerning thee, are nothing; but (that) thou thyself also walkest orderly, and keepest the law.

25 As touching the Gentiles which believe, we have written (and) concluded that they observe no such thing, save only that they keep themselves from (things) offered to idols, and from blood, and from strangled, and from fornication.

26 Then Paul took the men, and the next day purifying himself with them entered into the temple, to signify the accomplishment of the days of purification, until that an offering should be offered for every one of them.

27 And when the seven days were almost ended, the Jews which were of Asia, when they saw him in the temple, stirred up all the people, and laid hands on him,

28 Crying out, Men of Israel, help: This is the man, that teacheth all (men) every where against the people, and the law, and this place: and further brought Greeks also into the temple, and hath polluted this holy place.

29 (For they had seen before with him in the city Trophimus an Ephesian, whom

Literal Translation

Acts 21:30

King James Version

the city with him, whom they supposed that Paul brought into the temple.

30 And the whole city was moved, and there was a running together of people. And having laid hold of Paul, they drew him outside of the temple, and at once the doors were shut.
31 But as they (were) seeking to kill him, a report came up to the chiliarch of the cohort, that all Jerusalem is in a tumult;
32 who immediately ran down to them, taking soldiers and centurions. And seeing the chiliarch and the soldiers, they stopped beating Paul.

33 Then going near, the chiliarch laid hold of him, and commanded (him) to be bound with two chains. And (he) asked who he may be, and what he is doing.
34 But others cried something else in the crowd, and not being able to know the certainty because of the uproar, he commanded him brought into the fortress.
35 But when he came on the stairs, it happened (for) him to be carried by the soldiers because of the violence of the crowd.
36 For the multitude of the people followed, crying out, Take him away!

37 And being about to be brought into the fortress, Paul said to the chiliarch, Is it lawful for me to say a thing to you? And he said, Do you know (to speak) in Greek?
38 Then are you not the Egyptian who before these days caused a riot, and the (one) leading out four thousand men of the assassins into the desert?
39 And

3588 4172 4862 846 3739 3543 3754 1519 3588 2411 1521
τῇ πόλει σὺν αὐτῷ, ὃν ἐνόμιζον ὅτι εἰς τὸ ἱερὸν εἰσήγαγεν
the city with him, whom they supposed that into the temple brought in

3588 3972 2795 5037/3588/4172/3650 2532 1096 4890
ὁ Παῦλος. 30 ἐκινήθη τε ἡ πόλις ὅλη, καὶ ἐγένετο συνδρομὴ
Paul. was moved And the city whole, and was a running together

3588 2992 2532 1949 3588 3972 1670 846 1854 3588
τοῦ λαοῦ· καὶ ἐπιλαβόμενοι τοῦ Παύλου εἷλκον αὐτὸν ἔξω τοῦ
of the people; and having seized Paul they drew him outside the

2411 2532 2112 2808 3588 2374 2212 1161
ἱεροῦ· καὶ εὐθέως ἐκλείσθησαν αἱ θύραι. 31 ζητούντων δὲ
temple; and at once were shut the doors. they seeking And

846 615 305 5334 3588 5506 3588 4686 3754
αὐτὸν ἀποκτεῖναι, ἀνέβη φάσις τῷ χιλιάρχῳ τῆς σπείρης, ὅτι
him to kill, came up a report to the chiliarch of the cohort, that

3650 4797 2419 3739 1824 3880
ὅλη συγκέχυται Ἱερουσαλήμ· 32 ὃς ἐξαυτῆς παραλαβὼν
all is in a tumult Jerusalem; who immediately having taken

4757 2532 1543 2701 1909 846
στρατιώτας καὶ ἑκατοντάρχους, κατέδραμεν ἐπ' αὐτούς·
soldiers and centurions ran down on them;

3588 1161 1492 3588 5506 2532 3588 4757 3973
οἱ δὲ, ἰδόντες τὸν χιλίαρχον καὶ τοὺς στρατιώτας, ἐπαύσαντο
they and, seeing the chiliarch and the soldiers, stopped

5180 3588 3972 5119 1448 3588 5506 1949
τύπτοντες τὸν Παῦλον. 33 τότε ἐγγίσας ὁ χιλίαρχος ἐπελάβετο
beating Paul. Then going near the chiliarch laid hold

846 2532 2753 1210 254 1417 2532 4441 5101
αὐτοῦ, καὶ ἐκέλευσε δεθῆναι ἁλύσεσι δυσι· καὶ ἐπυνθάνετο τίς
of him, and commanded to be bound with chains two; and asked what

302 1498 2532 5101 2076 4160 243 1161 243 5100 994 1722 3588
ἂν εἴη καὶ τί ἐστι πεποιηκώς. 34 ἄλλοι δὲ ἄλλο τι ἐβόων ἐν τῷ
may be, and what he is doing. others And else something cried in the

3793 3361 1410 1161 1097 3588 804 1223 3588 2351
ὄχλῳ· μὴ δυνάμενος δὲ γνῶναι τὸ ἀσφαλὲς διὰ τὸν θόρυβον,
crowd; not being able and to know the certainty because of the uproar,

2753 71 846 1519 3588 3925 3753 1161 1096
ἐκέλευσεν ἄγεσθαι αὐτὸν εἰς τὴν παρεμβολήν. 35 ὅτε δὲ ἐγένετο
he commanded to bring him into the fortress. when But he was

1909 3588 304 4819 941 846 5259 3588
ἐπὶ τοὺς ἀναβαθμούς, συνέβη βαστάζεσθαι αὐτὸν ὑπὸ τῶν
on the stairs, it happened to be carried him by the

4757 1223 3588 970 3588 3793 190 1063 3588
στρατιωτῶν διὰ τὴν βίαν τοῦ ὄχλου. 36 ἠκολούθει γὰρ τὸ
soldiers because of the violence of the crowd. followed For the

4128 3588 2992 2896 142 846
πλῆθος τοῦ λαοῦ κρᾶζον, Αἶρε αὐτόν.
multitude of the people crying out, Take away him!

3195 5037 1521 1519 3588 3925 3588 3972
37. Μέλλων τε εἰσάγεσθαι εἰς τὴν παρεμβολὴν ὁ Παῦλος
being about And to be brought into the fortress Paul

3004 3588 5506 1487 1832 3427 2036 5100 4314 4571 3588 1161/5346
λέγει τῷ χιλιάρχῳ, Εἰ ἔξεστί μοι εἰπεῖν τι πρός σε; ὁ δὲ ἔφη,
said to the chiliarch, If it is lawful for me to say a thing to you? he And said,

1676 1097 3756 68 4771 1488 3588 124 3588 4253
Ἑλληνιστὶ γινώσκεις; 38 οὐκ ἄρα σὺ εἶ ὁ Αἰγύπτιος ὁ πρὸ
in Greek Do you know? not Then you are the Egyptian, he before

5130 3588 2250 387 2532 1806 1519 3588
τούτων τῶν ἡμερῶν ἀναστατώσας καὶ ἐξαγαγὼν εἰς τὴν
these days caused a riot and leading out into the

2048 3588 5070 435 3588 4607 2036 1161
ἔρημον τοὺς τετρακισχιλίους ἄνδρας τῶν σικαρίων; 39 εἶπε δὲ
desert the four thousand men of the assassins? said And

---

they supposed that Paul had brought into the temple.)

30 And all the city was moved, and the people ran together: and they took Paul, and drew him out of the temple: and forthwith the doors were shut.
31 And as they went about to kill him, tidings came unto the chief captain of the band, that all Jerusalem was in an uproar.

32 Who immediately took soldiers and centurions, and ran down unto them: and when they saw the chief captain and the soldiers, they left beating of Paul.

33 Then the chief captain came near, and took him, and commanded (him) to be bound with two chains; and demanded who he was, and what he had done.
34 And some cried one thing, some another, among the multitude: and when he could not know the certainty for the tumult, he commanded him to be carried into the castle.
35 And when he came upon the stairs, so it was, that he was borne of the soldiers for the violence of the people.

36 For the multitude of the people followed after, crying, Away with him.

37 And as Paul was to be led into the castle, he said unto the chief captain, May I speak unto thee? Who said, Canst thou speak Greek?

38 Art not thou that Egyptian, which before these days madest an uproar, and leddest out into the wilderness four thousand men that were murderers?
39 But

Literal Translation

Paul said, Indeed I am a man, a Jew of Tarsus, of Cilicia, a citizen (of) no mean city. And I beg you, allow me to speak to the people.
40 And he having allowed him, standing on the stairs, Paul signaled with (his) hand to the people. And much silence having occurred, he spoke in the Hebrew dialect, saying,

Acts 21:40

3588 3972 1473 444 3303 1510 2453 5018 3588
ὁ Παῦλος, Ἐγὼ ἄνθρωπος μέν εἰμι Ἰουδαῖος, Ταρσεὺς τῆς
Paul, I a man indeed am, a Jew, a Tarsian
2791 3756 767 4172 4177 1189 1161 4675
Κιλικίας, οὐκ ἀσήμου πόλεως πολίτης· δέομαι δέ σου, ἐπί-
of Cilicia, not of a mean city a citizen; I beg and of you,
2010 3427 2980 4314 3588 2992 2010 1161 846
τρεψόν μοι λαλῆσαι πρὸς τὸν λαόν. 40 ἐπιτρέψαντος δὲ αὐτοῦ,
allow me to speak to the people. he having allowed And him,
3588 3972 2476 1909 3588 304 2678 3588 5495 3588
ὁ Παῦλος ἑστὼς ἐπὶ τῶν ἀναβαθμῶν κατέσεισε τῇ χειρὶ τῷ
Paul standing on the stairs signaled with the hand to the
2992 4183 1161 4602 1096 4377 3588 1446
λαῷ· πολλῆς δὲ σιγῆς γενομένης, προσεφώνησε τῇ Ἑβραΐδι
people; much and silence having occurred, he spoke in the Hebrew
1258 3004
διαλέκτῳ λέγων,
dialect saying,

King James Version

Paul said, I am a man (which am) a Jew of Tarsus, (a city) in Cilicia, a citizen of no mean city: and, I beseech thee, suffer me to speak unto the people.
40 And when he had given him licence, Paul stood on the stairs, and beckoned with the hand unto the people. And when there was made a great silence, he spake unto (them) in the Hebrew tongue, saying,

Acts 22

1. Men, brothers, and fathers, hear my defense now to you.

435 80 2532 3962 191 3450 3588 4314
1. Ἄνδρες ἀδελφοὶ καὶ πατέρες, ἀκούσατέ μου τῆς πρὸς
Men brothers and fathers, hear me the to
5209 3568 627
ὑμᾶς νῦν ἀπολογίας.
you now defense.

1. Men, brethren, and fathers, hear ye my defence (which I make) now unto you.

2 And hearing that he spoke in the Hebrew dialect to them, they showed more quietness. And he said:

191 1161 3754 3588 1446 1258 4377
2 Ἀκούσαντες δὲ ὅτι τῇ Ἑβραΐδι διαλέκτῳ προσεφώνει
hearing And that in the Hebrew dialect he spoke
846 3173 3930 2271 2532 5346
αὐτοῖς, μᾶλλον παρέσχον ἡσυχίαν. καὶ φησίν,
to them, more they showed quietness. And he says,

2 (And when they heard that he spake in the Hebrew tongue to them, they kept the more silence: and he saith,)

3 Indeed I am a man, a Jew, having been born in Tarsus of Cilicia, but having been brought up in this city at the feet of Gamaliel, having been trained according to the exactness of the ancestral law, being a zealous one of God, even as you all are today.

1473 3303 1510 435 2453 1080 1722 5019 3588
3 Ἐγὼ μέν εἰμι ἀνὴρ Ἰουδαῖος, γεγεννημένος ἐν Ταρσῷ τῆς
I truly am a man a Jew, having been born in Tarsus
2791 397 1161 1722 3588 4172 3778 3844 3588
Κιλικίας, ἀνατεθραμμένος δὲ ἐν τῇ πόλει ταύτῃ παρὰ τοὺς
of Cilicia, having been brought up and in city this at the
4228 1059 3811 2596 195 3588
πόδας Γαμαλιήλ, πεπαιδευμένος κατὰ ἀκρίβειαν τοῦ πα-
feet of Gamaliel, having been trained according to exactness of the an-
3971 3551 2207 5225 3588 2316 2531 3956
τρῴου νόμου, ζηλωτὴς ὑπάρχων τοῦ Θεοῦ, καθὼς πάντες
cestral Law, a zealous one being of God, even as all
5210 2075 4594 3739 3778 3588 3598 1377 891 2288
ὑμεῖς ἐστε σήμερον· 4 ὃς ταύτην τὴν ὁδὸν ἐδίωξα ἄχρι θανάτου,
you are today; who this Way persecuted as far as to death,
1195 2532 3860 1519 5438 435 5037 2532 1135
δεσμεύων καὶ παραδιδοὺς εἰς φυλακὰς ἄνδρας τε καὶ γυναῖκας,
binding and delivering up into prisons men both and women,

3 I am verily a man (which am) a Jew, born in Tarsus, (a city) in Cilicia, yet brought up in this city at the feet of Gamaliel, (and) taught according to the perfect manner of the law of the fathers, and was zealous toward God, as ye all are this day.

4 (I) persecuted this Way as far as death, binding and delivering up both men and women into prisons,

4 And I persecuted this way unto the death, binding and delivering into prisons both men and women.

5 as also the high priest and all the elderhood witnesses to me. And having received letters from (them) to the brothers, I traveled into Damascus leading also those being bound there to Jerusalem, in order that they might be punished.
6 And it happened to me, traveling

5613 2532 3588 749 3140 3427 2532 3956 3588 4244
5 ὡς καὶ ὁ ἀρχιερεὺς μαρτυρεῖ μοι, καὶ πᾶν τὸ πρεσβυτέριον·
as also the high priest witnesses to me, and all the elderhood;
3844 3739 2532 1992 1209 4314 3588 80 1519
παρ᾽ ὧν καὶ ἐπιστολὰς δεξάμενος πρὸς τοὺς ἀδελφούς, εἰς
from whom also letters having received to the brothers, into
1154 4198 71 2532 3588 1566 5607 1210
Δαμασκὸν ἐπορευόμην, ἄξων καὶ τοὺς ἐκεῖσε ὄντας δεδεμένους
Damascus I traveled, leading also those there being bound
1519 2419 2443 5097 1096 1161 3427 4198
εἰς Ἱερουσαλήμ, ἵνα τιμωρηθῶσιν. 6 ἐγένετο δέ μοι πορευο-
to Jerusalem, that they might be punished. it was And to me traveling

5 As also the high priest doth bear me witness, and all the estate of the elders: from whom also I received letters unto the brethren, and went to Damascus, to bring them which were there bound unto Jerusalem, for to be punished.
6 And it came to pass, that, as I made my journey,

Literal Translation

and drawing near to Damascus about midday, suddenly a great light out of the heaven shone around me.

7 And I fell to the ground, and heard a voice saying to me, Saul, Saul, why do you persecute Me?

8 And I answered, Who are you, Sir? And He said to me, I am Jesus the Nazarene whom you persecute.

9 But those being with me indeed beheld the light, and became alarmed, but did not hear His voice speaking to me.

10 And I said, What shall I do, Lord? And the Lord said to me, Rising up, go into Damascus, and there it will be told to you about all things which are appointed to you to do.

11 And as I did not see, from the glory of that light, being led by the hand by those being with me, I went into Damascus.

12 And a certain Ananias, a devout man according to the Law, having been testified to by all the Jews living (there),

13 coming to me and standing by, (he) said to me, Brother Saul, see again. And in the same hour I looked up to him.

14 And he said, The God of our fathers appointed you to know His will, and to see the Just One, and to hear a voice out of His mouth;

15 because you shall be a witness to Him to all men of what you have seen and heard.

16 And now what do you intend? Rising up, be baptized and wash away your sins, calling on the name of the

Acts 22:7

2532 1448 3588 1154 4012 3314 1810
μένῳ καὶ ἐγγίζοντι τῇ Δαμασκῷ, περὶ μεσημβρίαν, ἐξαίφνης
and drawing near to Damascus, about midday, suddenly

1537 3588 3772 4015 5457 2425 4012 1691 4098
ἐκ τοῦ οὐρανοῦ περιαστράψαι φῶς ἱκανὸν περὶ ἐμέ. 7 ἔπεσόν
out of the heaven shone light a great around me. I fell

5037 1519 3588 1475 2532 191 5456 3004 3427 4549
τε εἰς τὸ ἔδαφος, καὶ ἤκουσα φωνῆς λεγούσης μοι, Σαούλ,
And to the ground, and heard a voice saying to me, Saul

4549 5101 3165 1377 1473 1161 611 5101 1488 2962 2036
Σαούλ, τί με διώκεις; 8 ἐγὼ δὲ ἀπεκρίθην, Τίς εἶ, Κύριε; εἶπέ
Saul, why Me you persecute? I And answered, Who are you, Sir? He said

5037 4314 3165 1473 1510 2424 3588 3480 3739 4771 1377
τε πρός με, Ἐγώ εἰμι Ἰησοῦς ὁ Ναζωραῖος ὃν σὺ διώκεις.
And to me, I am Jesus the Nazarene whom you persecute.

3588 1161 4862 1698 5607 3588 3303 5457 2300 2532 1719
9 οἱ δὲ σὺν ἐμοὶ ὄντες τὸ μὲν φῶς ἐθεάσαντο, καὶ ἔμφοβοι
those But with me being the indeed light beheld, and alarmed

1096 3588 1161 5456 3756 191 3588 2980 3427
ἐγένοντο· τὴν δὲ φωνὴν οὐκ ἤκουσαν τοῦ λαλοῦντός μοι.
became; the but voice not they heard of Him speaking to me.

2036 1161 5101 4160 2962 3588 1161 2962 2036 4314 3165
10 εἶπον δέ, Τί ποιήσω, Κύριε; ὁ δὲ Κύριος εἶπε πρός με,
I said And, What shall I do, Lord? the And Lord said to me,

450 4198 1519 1154 2546 4671 2980
Ἀναστὰς πορεύου εἰς Δαμασκόν· κἀκεῖ σοι λαληθήσεται
Rising up go into Damascus; and there to you it will be said

4012 3956 3739 5021 4671 4160 5613 1161 3756 1689
περὶ πάντων ὧν τέτακταί σοι ποιῆσαι. 11 ὡς δὲ οὐκ ἐνέβλεπον
about all things which is appointed to you to do. as And not I saw again

575 3588 1391 3588 5457 1565 5496 5259
ἀπὸ τῆς δόξης τοῦ φωτὸς ἐκείνου, χειραγωγούμενος ὑπὸ
from the glory light of that, being led by the hand by

3588 4895 3427 2064 1519 1154 367 1161 5100
τῶν συνόντων μοι, ἦλθον εἰς Δαμασκόν. 12 Ἀνανίας δέ τις,
those being with me, I went into Damascus. Ananias And a certain,

435 2152 2596 3588 3551 3140 5259 3956
ἀνὴρ εὐσεβὴς κατὰ τὸν νόμον, μαρτυρούμενος ὑπὸ πάντων
a man devout according to the Law, having been testified to by all

3588 2730 2453 2064 4314 3165 2532 2186
τῶν κατοικούντων Ἰουδαίων, 13 ἐλθὼν πρός με καὶ ἐπιστὰς
the (ones) living (there) Jews, coming to me and standing by

2036 3427 4549 80 308 2504 846 3588 5610
εἰπέ μοι, Σαοὺλ ἀδελφέ, ἀνάβλεψον. κἀγὼ αὐτῇ τῇ ὥρᾳ
said to me, Saul Brother, see again. And I at the hour

308 1519 846 3588 1161 2036 3588 2316 3588 3962 2257
ἀνέβλεψα εἰς αὐτόν. 14 ὁ δὲ εἶπεν, Ὁ Θεὸς τῶν πατέρων ἡμῶν
looked up to him. he And said, The God ot the fathers of us

4400 4571 1097 3588 2307 846 2532 1492 3588
προεχειρίσατό σε γνῶναι τὸ θέλημα αὐτοῦ, καὶ ἰδεῖν τὸν
before appointed you to know the will of Him, and to see the

1342 2532 191 5456 1537 3588 4750 846 3754 2071
δίκαιον, καὶ ἀκοῦσαι φωνὴν ἐκ τοῦ στόματος αὐτοῦ. 15 ὅτι ἔσῃ
Just One, and to hear a voice out of the mouth of Him. For you will be

3144 846 4314 3956 444 3739 3708 2532
μάρτυς αὐτῷ πρὸς πάντας ἀνθρώπους ὧν ἑώρακας καὶ
a witness to Him to all men of which you have seen and

191 2532 3568 5101 3195 450 907 2532 628
ἤκουσας. 16 καὶ νῦν τί μέλλεις; ἀναστὰς βάπτισαι καὶ ἀπό-
heard. And now what intend you? Rising up be baptized and wash

3588 266 4675 1941 3588 3686 3588
λουσαι τὰς ἁμαρτίας σου, ἐπικαλεσάμενος τὸ ὄνομα τοῦ
away the sins of you, having called on the name of the

King James Version

and was come nigh unto Damascus about noon, suddenly there shone from heaven a great light round about me.

7 And I fell unto the ground, and heard a voice saying unto me, Saul, Saul, why persecutest thou me?

8 And I answered, Who art thou, Lord? And he said unto me, I am Jesus of Nazareth, whom thou persecutest.

9 And they that were with me saw indeed the light, and were afraid; but they heard not the voice of him that spake to me.

10 And I said, What shall I do, Lord? And the Lord said unto me, Arise, and go into Damascus; and there it shall be told thee of all things which are appointed for thee to do.

11 And when I could not see for the glory of that light, being led by the hand of them that were with me, I came into Damascus.

12 And one Ananias, a devout man according to the law, having a good report of all the Jews which dwelt (there),

13 Came unto me, and stood, and said unto me, Brother Saul, receive thy sight. And the same hour I looked up upon him.

14 And he said, The God of our fathers hath chosen thee, that thou shouldest know his will, and see that Just One, and shouldest hear the voice of his mouth.

15 For thou shalt be his witness unto all men of what thou hast seen and heard.

16 And now why tarriest thou? arise, and be baptized, and wash away thy sins, calling on the name of the

Literal Translation **Acts 22:17** ***King James Version***

Lord.
17 And it happened to me, having returned to Jerusalem and having prayed in the temple: I became in an ecstasy,
18 and I saw Him saying to me, Hurry and go out quickly from Jerusalem, because they will not receive your testimony concerning Me.

19 And I said, Lord, they understand that I was imprisoning and beating the ones believing on You throughout the synagogues.

20 And when the blood of Stephen Your witness was poured out, I myself also was standing by and consenting to his execution, and guarding the garments of those killing him.

21 And He said to me, Go, because I will send you to the nations afar off.

22. And they heard him as far as this word, and lifted up their voice, saying, Take such a one from the earth, for it is not fitting that he should live!
23 And they shouting, and tearing the garments, and throwing dust into the air,

24 the chiliarch ordered to bring him into the fortress, saying for him to be examined with scourges, that he may know for what crime they cried out so against him.
25 But as they stretched him with the thongs, Paul said to the centurion standing by, Is it lawful for you to flog a man, a Roman not found guilty?
26 And having heard, coming near the centurion reported to the chiliarch, saying,

2962 1096 1161 3427 5290 1519 2419 2532
Κυρίου. 17 ἐγένετο δέ μοι ὑποστρέψαντι εἰς Ἱερουσαλήμ, καὶ
Lord. it happened And to me having returned to Jerusalem, and

4336 3450 1722 3588 2411 1096 3165 1722 1611 2532
προσευχομένου μου ἐν τῷ ἱερῷ, γενέσθαι με ἐν ἐκστάσει, 18 καὶ
having prayed me in the temple, coming to be me in an ecstasy, and

1492 846 3004 3427 4692 2532 1831 1722 5034 1537
ἰδεῖν αὐτὸν λέγοντά μοι, Σπεῦσον καὶ ἔξελθε ἐν τάχει ἐξ
to see Him saying to me, Hurry and go out quickly out of

2419 1360 3756 3858 4675 3588 3141
Ἱερουσαλήμ· διότι οὐ παραδέξονταί σου τὴν μαρτυρίαν
Jerusalem; because not they will receive of you the testimony

4012 1700 2504 2036 2962 846 1987 3754 1473
περὶ ἐμοῦ. 19 κἀγὼ εἶπον, Κύριε, αὐτοὶ ἐπίστανται ὅτι ἐγὼ
concerning Me. And I said, Lord, they understand that I

2252 5439 2532 1194 2596 3588 4864 3588
ἤμην φυλακίζων καὶ δέρων κατὰ τὰς συναγωγὰς τοὺς
was imprisoning and beating throughout the synagogues those

4100 1909 4571 2532 3753 1632 3588 129 4736 3588
πιστεύοντας ἐπὶ σέ· 20 καὶ ὅτε ἐξεχεῖτο τὸ αἷμα Στεφάνου τοῦ
believing on You. And when was poured out the blood of Stephen the

3144 4675 2532 846 2252 2186 2532 4909 3588
μάρτυρός σου, καὶ αὐτὸς ἤμην ἐφεστὼς καὶ συνευδοκῶν τῇ
witness of You, also myself I was standing by and consenting to the

336 846 2532 5442 3588 2440 3588 337
ἀναιρέσει αὐτοῦ, καὶ φυλάσσων τὰ ἱμάτια τῶν ἀναιρούντων
execution of him, and guarding the garments of the (ones) killing

846 2532 2036 4314 3165 4198 3754 1473 1519 1484 3112
αὐτόν. 21 καὶ εἶπε πρός με, Πορεύου, ὅτι ἐγὼ εἰς ἔθνη μακρὰν
of him. And He said to me, Go, because I to the nations afar off

1821 4571
ἐξαποστελῶ σε.
will send you.

191 1161 846 891 5127 3588 3056 2532 1869
22. Ἤκουον δὲ αὐτοῦ ἄχρι τούτου τοῦ λόγου, καὶ ἐπῆραν
they heard And him as far as this word, and lifted up

3588 5456 846 3004 142 575 3588 1093 3588 5108
τὴν φωνὴν αὐτῶν λέγοντες, Αἶρε ἀπὸ τῆς γῆς τὸν τοιοῦτον·
the voice of them saying, Take away from the earth such a one;

3756 1063 2520 846 2198 2905 1161 846 2532
οὐ γὰρ καθῆκον αὐτὸν ζῆν. 23 κραυγαζόντων δὲ αὐτῶν, καὶ
not for it is fitting he should live. shouting And them, and

4495 3588 2440 2532 2868 906 1519 3588
ῥιπτούντων τὰ ἱμάτια, καὶ κονιορτὸν βαλλόντων εἰς τὸν
tearing the garments, and dust throwing into the

109 2753 846 3588 5506 71 1519 3588 3925
ἀέρα, 24 ἐκέλευσεν αὐτὸν ὁ χιλίαρχος ἄγεσθαι εἰς τὴν παρεμβο-
air, commanded him the chiliarch to bring into the fortress,

2036 3148 426 846 2443 1921 1223 3739
λήν, εἰπὼν μάστιξιν ἀνετάζεσθαι αὐτόν, ἵνα ἐπιγνῷ δι' ἣν
saying with scourges to be examined him, that he may know for what

156 3779 2019 846 5613 1161 4385 846 3588
αἰτίαν οὕτως ἐπεφώνουν αὐτῷ. 25 ὡς δὲ προέτειναν αὐτὸν τοῖς
cause thus they cried against him. as But they stretched him with the

2438 2036 4314 3588 2476 1543 3588 3972 1487
ἱμᾶσιν, εἶπεν πρὸς τὸν ἑστῶτα ἑκατόνταρχον ὁ Παῦλος, Εἰ
thongs, said to the standing by centurion Paul, If

444 4514 2532 178 1832 5213 3147
ἄνθρωπον Ῥωμαῖον καὶ ἀκατάκριτον ἔξεστιν ὑμῖν μαστίζειν;
a man a Roman and (one) not found guilty it is lawful for you to scourge?

191 1161 3588 1543 4334 518 3588
26 ἀκούσας δὲ ὁ ἑκατόνταρχος, προσελθὼν ἀπήγγειλε τῷ
hearing And the centurion, drawing near reported to the

Lord.
17 And it came to pass, that, when I was come again to Jerusalem, even while I prayed in the temple, I was in a trance;
18 And saw him saying unto me, Make haste, and get thee quickly out of Jerusalem: for they will not receive thy testimony concerning me.

19 And I said, Lord, they know that I imprisoned and beat in every synagogue them that believed on thee:

20 And when the blood of thy martyr Stephen was shed, I also was standing by, and consenting unto his death, and kept the raiment of them that slew him.

21 And he said unto me, Depart: for I will send thee far hence unto the Gentiles.

22. And they gave him audience unto this word, and (then) lifted up their voices, and said, Away with such a (fellow) from the earth: for it is not fit that he should live.
23 And as they cried out, and cast off (their) clothes, and threw dust into the air,

24 The chief captain commanded him to be brought into the castle, and bade that he should be examined by scourging; that he might know wherefore they cried so against him.
25 And as they bound him with thongs, Paul said unto the centurion that stood by, Is it lawful for you to scourge a man that is a Roman, and uncondemned?
26 When the centurion heard (that), he went and told the chief captain, saying,

Literal Translation | **Acts 22:27** | ***King James Version***

Watch what you are about to do, for this man is a Roman.

27 And having come up, the chiliarch said to him, Tell me, are you a Roman? And he said, Yes.

28 And the chiliarch answered, I bought this citizenship with a great sum. And Paul said, But I even have been born (free).

5506 3004 3708 5101 3195 4160 3588 1063 444
χιλιάρχῳ λέγων, Ὅρα τί μέλλεις ποιεῖν· ὁ γὰρ ἄνθρωπος
chiliarch saying, Watch what you are about to do; for man

3778 4514 2076 4334 1161/3588 5506 2036 846
οὗτος Ῥωμαῖός ἐστι. 27 προσελθὼν δὲ ὁ χιλίαρχος εἶπεν αὐτῷ,
this a Roman is. having come up And the chiliarch said to him,

3004 3427 1487 4771 4514 1488/3588/1161/5346/3483 611 5037 3588
Λέγε μοι, εἰ σὺ Ῥωμαῖος εἶ; ὁ δὲ ἔφη, Ναί. 28 ἀπεκρίθη τε ὁ
Tell me, you a Roman are? he And said, Yes. answered And the

5506 1473 4183 2774 3588 4174 3778
χιλίαρχος, Ἐγὼ πολλοῦ κεφαλαίου τὴν πολιτείαν ταύτην
chiliarch, I of a much sum citizenship this

2932 3588 1161 3972 5346 1473 1161 2532 1080
ἐκτησάμην. ὁ δὲ Παῦλος ἔφη, Ἐγὼ δὲ καὶ γεγέννημαι.
bought. And Paul said, I but even have been begotten.

Take heed what thou doest: for this man is a Roman.

27 Then the chief captain came, and said unto him, Tell me, art thou a Roman? He said, Yea.

28 And the chief captain answered, With a great sum obtained I this freedom. And Paul said, But I was (free) born.

29 Then at once those being about to examine him stood away from him. And the chiliarch also feared, fully knowing that he was a Roman, and that he had bound him.

2112 3767 868 575 846 3588 3195 846 426
29 εὐθέως οὖν ἀπέστησαν ἀπ' αὐτοῦ οἱ μέλλοντες αὐτὸν ἀνε-
At once then stood away from him those being about him to

2532 3588 5506 1161 5399 1921 3754 4514
τάζειν. καὶ ὁ χιλίαρχος δὲ ἐφοβήθη, ἐπιγνοὺς ὅτι Ῥωμαῖός
examine. also the chiliarch And feared, fully knowing that a Roman

2076 2532 3754 2258 846 1210
ἐστι, καὶ ὅτι ἦν αὐτὸν δεδεκώς.
he is, and that he was him he had bound.

29 Then straightway they departed from him which should have examined him: and the chief captain also was afraid, after he knew that he was a Roman, and because he had bound him.

30 And on the morrow, having purposed to know the certainty as to why he was accused by the Jews, he freed him from the bonds. And (he) commanded the chief priests and all their Sanhedrin to come. And bringing Paul down, (he) set (him) among them.

3588 1161 1887 1014 1097 3588 804 3588 5101
30. Τῇ δὲ ἐπαύριον βουλόμενος γνῶναι τὸ ἀσφαλές, τὸ τί
on the And morrow having purposed to know the certainty, why

2723 3844 3588 2453 3089 846 575 3588
κατηγορεῖται παρὰ τῶν Ἰουδαίων, ἔλυσεν αὐτόν ἀπὸ τῶν
he was accused by the Jews, he freed him from the

1199 2532 2753 2064 3588 749 2532 3650 3588
δεσμῶν, καὶ ἐκέλευσεν ἐλθεῖν τοὺς ἀρχιερεῖς καὶ ὅλον τὸ
bonds, and commanded to come the chief priests and all the

4892 846 2532 2609 3588 3972 2476 1519
συνέδριον αὐτῶν, καὶ καταγαγὼν τὸν Παῦλον ἔστησεν εἰς
Sanhedrin of them, and having brought Paul (he) set among

846
αὐτούς.
them.

30 On the morrow, because he would have known the certainty wherefore he was accused of the Jews, he loosed him from (his) bands, and commanded the chief priests and all their council to appear, and brought Paul down, and set him before them.

Acts 23

1. And havaing looked intently on the Sanhedrin, Paul said, Men, brothers, I in all good conscience have conducted myself toward God as far as this day.

2 But Ananias the high priest ordered those standing by him to strike his mouth.

3 Then Paul said to him, God is going to strike you, whitened wall! And do you sit judging me according to the Law, and contrary to the Law command me to be stricken?

4 And those standing by said, The high priest

Acts 23

816 1161 3588 3972 3588 4892 2036 435
1. Ἀτενίσας δὲ ὁ Παῦλος τῷ συνεδρίῳ εἶπεν, Ἄνδρες
having looked And Paul on the Sanhedrin said, Men

80 1473 3956 4893 18 4176 3588 2316
ἀδελφοί, ἐγὼ πάσῃ συνειδήσει ἀγαθῇ πεπολίτευμαι τῷ Θεῷ
brothers, I in all conscience good have lived to God

891 3778 3588 2250 3588 1161 749 367 2004
ἄχρι ταύτης τῆς ἡμέρας. 2 ὁ δὲ ἀρχιερεὺς Ἀνανίας ἐπέταξε
until this day. the And high priest, Ananias ordered

3588 3936 846 5180 846 3588 4750 5119 3588 3972
τοῖς παρεστῶσιν αὐτῷ τύπτειν αὐτοῦ τὸ στόμα. 3 τότε ὁ Παῦλος
those standing by him to strike of him the mouth. Then Paul

4314 846 2036 5180 4571 3195 3588 2316 5109 2867
πρὸς αὐτὸν εἶπε, Τύπτειν σε μέλλει ὁ Θεός, τοῖχε κεκονιαμένε·
to him said, to strike you is going God, wall whitened;

2532 4771 2521 2919 3165 2596 3588 3551 2532 3891
καὶ σὺ κάθῃ κρίνων με κατὰ τὸν νόμον, καὶ παρανομῶν
and you sit judging me according to the Law, and contrary to Law

2753 3165 5180 3588 1161 3936 2036 3588 749
κελεύεις με τύπτεσθαι; 4 οἱ δὲ παρεστῶτες εἶπον, Τὸν ἀρχιερέα
command me to be stricken? those And standing by said, The high priest

Acts 23

1. And Paul, earnestly beholding the council, said, Men (and) brethren, I have lived in all good conscience before God until this day.

2 And the high priest Ananias commanded them that stood by him to smite him on the mouth.

3 Then said Paul unto him, God shall smite thee, (thou) whited wall: for sittest thou to judge me after the law, and commandest me to be smitten contrary to the law?

4 And they that stood by said,

Literal Translation | **Acts 23:5** | ***King James Version***

of God do you revile?
5 And Paul said, Brothers, I did not know that he is high priest; for it has been written, "You shall not speak evilly of a ruler of your people." (Ex. 22:28)
6 But knowing that the one part consisted of Sadducees, and the other of Pharisees, Paul cried out in the Sanhedrin, Men, brothers, I am a Pharisee, a son of Pharisees; I am being judged concerning hope and resurrection of (the) dead!

3588 2316 3058 5346 5037 3588 3972 3756 1492 80
τοῦ Θεοῦ λοιδορεῖς; 5 ἔφη τε ὁ Παῦλος, Οὐκ ᾔδειν, ἀδελφοί,
of God do you revile? said And Paul, Not I knew, brothers,

3754 2076 749 1125 1063 758 3588 2992 4675
ὅτι ἐστὶν ἀρχιερεύς· γέγραπται γάρ, Ἄρχοντα τοῦ λαοῦ σου
that he is high priest; it has been written for, A ruler of the people of you

3756 2046 2560 1097 1161 3588 3972 3754 3588 1520 3313 2076
οὐκ ἐρεῖς κακῶς. 6 γνοὺς δὲ ὁ Παῦλος ὅτι τὸ ἓν μέρος ἐστὶ
not you shall speak evilly. knowing But Paul that the one part is

4523 3588 1161 2087 5330 2896 1722 3588
Σαδδουκαίων, τὸ δὲ ἕτερον Φαρισαίων, ἔκραξεν ἐν τῷ
Sadducees, the and other Pharisees, cried out in the

4892 435 80 1473 5330 1510 5207 5330
συνεδρίῳ, Ἄνδρες ἀδελφοί, ἐγὼ Φαρισαῖός εἰμι, υἱὸς Φαρι-
Sanhedrin, Men brothers, I a Pharisee am, a son of a

4012 1680 2532 386 3498 1473 2919
σαίου· περὶ ἐλπίδος καὶ ἀναστάσεως νεκρῶν ἐγὼ κρίνομαι.
Pharisee; concerning hope and resurrection of (the) dead I am being judged.

Revilest thou God's high priest?
5 Then said Paul, I wist not, brethren, that he was the high priest: for it is written, Thou shalt not speak evil of the ruler of thy people.
6 But when Paul perceived that the one part were Sadducees, and the other Pharisees, he cried out in the council, Men (and) brethren, I am a Pharisee, the son of a Pharisee: of the hope and resurrection of the dead I am called in question.

7 And he having spoken this, there was a discord between the Pharisees and the Sadducees; and the multitude was divided.
8 For the Sadducees indeed say there is no resurrection, nor angel, nor spirit. But Pharisees confess both.
9 And there was a great cry. And the scribes of the part of the Pharisees having risen up, they were contending, saying, We find nothing evil in this man. And, If a spirit spoke to him, or an angel, let us not fight against God.

5124 1161 846 2980 1096 4714 3588 5330
7 τοῦτο δὲ αὐτοῦ λαλήσαντος, ἐγένετο στάσις τῶν Φαρισαίων
this And him having spoken, occurred a discord of the Pharisees

2532 3588 4523 2532 4977 3588 4128 4523
καὶ τῶν Σαδδουκαίων, καὶ ἐσχίσθη τὸ πλῆθος. 8 Σαδδουκαῖοι
and the Sadducees, and was divided the multitude. Sadducees

3303 1063 3004 3361 1511 386 3366 32 3383
μὲν γὰρ λέγουσι μὴ εἶναι ἀνάστασιν, μηδὲ ἄγγελον, μήτε
truly For say not to be a resurrection, neither angel, nor

4151 5330 1161 3670 3588 297 1096 1161
πνεῦμα· Φαρισαῖοι δὲ ὁμολογοῦσι τὰ ἀμφότερα. 9 ἐγένετο δὲ
spirit. Pharisees But confess both. there was And

2906 3173 2532 450 3588 1122 3588 3313
κραυγὴ μεγάλη· καὶ ἀναστάντες οἱ γραμματεῖς τοῦ μέρους
a cry great, and having risen up the scribes of the part

3588 5330 1264 3004 3762 2556 2147
τῶν Φαρισαίων διεμάχοντο λέγοντες, Οὐδὲν κακὸν εὑρί-
the Pharisees, they were contending saying, Nothing evil we

1722 3588 444 5129 1487 1161 4151 2980
σκομεν ἐν τῷ ἀνθρώπῳ τούτῳ· εἰ δὲ πνεῦμα ἐλάλησεν
find in man this; if and a spirit spoke

846 2228 32 3361 2313 4183 1161 1096
αὐτῷ ἢ ἄγγελος, μὴ θεομαχῶμεν. 10 πολλῆς δὲ γινομένης
to him or an angel, not let us fight against God. much And having arisen

7 And when he had so said, there arose a dissension between the Pharisees and the Sadducees: and the multitude was divided.
8 For the Sadducees say that there is no resurrection, neither angel, nor spirit: but the Pharisees confess both.
9 And there arose a great cry: and the scribes (that were) of the Pharisees' part arose, and strove, saying, We find no evil in this man: but if a spirit or an angel hath spoken to him, let us not fight against God.

10 And discord having arisen, fearing lest Paul should be torn by them, the chiliarch commanded the soldiery to go down to seize him out of their midst, and to bring (him) into the fortress.

4714 2125 3588 5506 3361 1288 3588 3972 5259
στάσεως, εὐλαβηθεὶς ὁ χιλίαρχος μὴ διασπασθῇ ὁ Παῦλος ὑπ'
discord, fearing the chiliarch lest should be torn Paul by

846 2753 3588 4753 2597 726 846 1537
αὐτῶν, ἐκέλευσε τὸ στράτευμα καταβὰν ἁρπάσαι αὐτὸν ἐκ
them, commanded the soldiery going down to seize him out of (the)

3319 846 71 5037 1519 3588 3925
μέσου αὐτῶν, ἄγειν τε εἰς τὴν παρεμβολήν.
midst of them, to bring and into the fortress.

10 And when there arose a great dissension, the chief captain, fearing lest Paul should have been pulled in pieces of them, commanded the soldiers to go down, and to take him by force from among them, and to bring (him) into the castle.

11 And coming on to him in the following night the Lord said, Be cheered, Paul, for as you fully testified the things concerning Me in Jerusalem, so you must also testify at Rome.
12. And (it) becoming day, some of the Jews making

3588 1161 1966 3571 2186 846 3588 2962 2036 2293
11. Τῇ δὲ ἐπιούσῃ νυκτὶ ἐπιστὰς αὐτῷ ὁ Κύριος εἶπε, Θάρσει
in the And following night coming on to him the Lord said, Be cheered,

3972 5613 1063 1263 3588 4012 1700 1519 2419
Παῦλε· ὡς γὰρ διεμαρτύρω τὰ περὶ ἐμοῦ εἰς Ἱερουσαλήμ,
Paul; as for you fully testified the things about Me in Jerusalem,

3779 4571 1163 2532 1519 4516 3140
οὕτω σε δεῖ καὶ εἰς Ῥώμην μαρτυρῆσαι.
so you must also at Rome testify.

1096 1161 2250 4160 5100 3588 2453
12. Γενομένης δὲ ἡμέρας, ποιήσαντές τινες τῶν Ἰουδαίων
becoming And day, making some of the Jews

11 And the night following the Lord stood by him, and said, Be of good cheer, Paul: for as thou hast testified of me in Jerusalem, so must thou bear witness also at Rome.
12. And when it was day, certain of the Jews

Literal Translation **Acts 23:13** *King James Version*

a conspiracy cursed themselves, saying neither to eat nor to drink until they should kill Paul.
13 And those making this plot were more (than) forty;

14 who coming near to the chief priests and to the elders said, With a curse we have cursed ourselves to taste of nothing until we shall kill Paul..
15 Now, then, you with the sanhedrin inform the chiliarch, so that tomorrow he may bring him down to you, as intending to determine more accurately the things about him. And before his drawing near, we are ready to kill him.

16 But the son of Paul's sister having heard of the ambush, having come near, and entering into the fortress, reported to Paul.

17 And calling near one of the centurions, Paul said, Bring this young man to the chiliarch, for he has something to report to him.

18 Then indeed taking him, he brought (him) to the chiliarch and said, Paul the prisoner having called me near asked me to bring this young man to you, having a thing to tell you.

19 And laying hold of his hand, and drawing aside privately, the chiliarch asked, What is (it) that you have to report to me?
20 And he said, The Jews agreed to ask you so as tomorrow you bring down to the Sanhedrin

4963 332 1438 3004 3383 5315 3383
συστροφήν, ἀνεθεμάτισαν ἑαυτούς, λέγοντες μήτε φαγεῖν μήτε
a conspiracy, cursed themselves, saying neither to eat nor

4095 2193 3757 615 3588 3972 2258 1161 4119
πιεῖν ἕως οὗ ἀποκτείνωσι τὸν Παῦλον. 13 ἦσαν δὲ πλείους τεσ-
to drink until they should kill Paul. were And more (than)

5062 3588 3778 3588 4945 4160
σαράκοντα οἱ ταύτην τὴν συνωμοσίαν πεποιηκότες·
forty those this plot making;

3748 4334 3588 749 2532 3588 4245
14 οἵτινες προσελθόντες τοῖς ἀρχιερεῦσι καὶ τοῖς πρεσβυτέρ-
who having come near to the chief priests and to the elders

2036 331 332 1438 3367 1089
οις εἶπον, Ἀναθέματι ἀνεθεματίσαμεν ἑαυτούς, μηδενὸς γεύσα-
said, With a curse we cursed ourselves, of nothing to taste

2193 3757 615 3588 3972 3568 3767 5210
σθαι ἕως οὗ ἀποκτείνωμεν τὸν Παῦλον. 15 νῦν οὖν ὑμεῖς
until we may kill Paul. Now, then, you

1718 3588 5506 4862 3588 4892 3704 839 846
ἐμφανίσατε τῷ χιλιάρχῳ σὺν τῷ συνεδρίῳ, ὅπως αὔριον αὐτὸν
inform the chiliarch with the sanhedrin, so as tomorrow him

2609 4314 5209 5613 3195 1231 197
καταγάγῃ πρὸς ὑμᾶς, ὡς μέλλοντας διαγινώσκειν ἀκριβέ-
he bring down to you as intending to determine more

3588 4012 846 2249 1161 4253 3588 1448 846
στερον τὰ περὶ αὐτοῦ· ἡμεῖς δέ, πρὸ τοῦ ἐγγίσαι αὐτόν,
accurately that about him; we and before the drawing near of him

2092 2070 3588 337 846 191 1161 3588 5207 3588
ἕτοιμοί ἐσμεν τοῦ ἀνελεῖν αὐτόν. 16 ἀκούσας δὲ ὁ υἱὸς τῆς
ready are to kill him. having heard And the son of the

79 3972 3588 1749 3854 2532 1525
ἀδελφῆς Παύλου τὴν ἐνέδραν, παραγενόμενος καὶ εἰσελθὼν
sister of Paul of the ambush, having come near and entering

1519 3588 3925 518 3588 3972 4341
εἰς τὴν παρεμβολήν, ἀπήγγειλε τῷ Παύλῳ. 17 προσκαλεσά-
into the fortress reported to Paul. calling to (him)

1161 3588 3972 1520 3588 1543 5346 3588 3494
μενος δὲ ὁ Παῦλος ἕνα τῶν ἑκατονταρχῶν ἔφη, Τὸν νεανίαν
And Paul one of the centurions said, youth

5126 520 4314 3588 5506 2192 1063 5100 518
τοῦτον ἀπάγαγε πρὸς τὸν χιλίαρχον· ἔχει γάρ τι ἀπαγγεῖ-
This bring up to the chiliarch, he has for something to

846 3588 3303 3767 3880 846 71 4314 3588
λαί αὐτῷ. 18 ὁ μὲν οὖν παραλαβὼν αὐτὸν ἤγαγε πρὸς τὸν
report to him. he indeed Then taking him brought to the

5506 2532 5346 3588 1198 3972 4341
χιλίαρχον, καὶ φησίν, Ὁ δέσμιος Παῦλος προσκαλεσάμενός
chiliarch, and says The prisoner Paul having called (me) near

3165 2065 5126 3588 3494 71 4314 4571 2192 5100
με ἠρώτησε τοῦτον τὸν νεανίαν ἀγαγεῖν πρός σε, ἔχοντά τι
me asked this youth to bring to you, having a thing

2980 4671 1949 1161 3588 5495 846 3588 5506
λαλῆσαί σοι. 19 ἐπιλαβόμενος δὲ τῆς χειρὸς αὐτοῦ ὁ χιλίαρχος,
to tell you. laying hold And of the hand of him the chiliarch

2532 402 2596 2398 4441 5101 2076 3739 2192
καὶ ἀναχωρήσας κατ' ἰδίαν ἐπυνθάνετο, Τί ἐστιν ὃ ἔχεις
and having withdrawn privately asked, What is (it) which you

518 3427 2036 1161 3754 3588 2453 4934 3588
ἀπαγγεῖλαί μοι; 20 εἶπε δὲ ὅτι Οἱ Ἰουδαῖοι συνέθεντο τοῦ
to report to me? he said And, The Jews agreed

2065 4571 3704 839 1519 3588 4892 2609 3588
ἐρωτῆσαί σε, ὅπως αὔριον εἰς τὸ συνέδριον καταγάγῃς τον
to ask you so as tomorrow to the Sanhedrin you bring down

banded together, and bound themselves under a curse, saying that they would neither eat nor drink till they had killed Paul.
13 And they were more than forty which had made this conspiracy.

14 And they came to the chief priests and elders, and said, We have bound ourselves under a great curse, that we will eat nothing until we have slain Paul.
15 Now therefore ye with the council signify to the chief captain that he bring him down unto you to morrow, as though ye would enquire something more perfectly concerning him: and we, or ever he come near, are ready to kill him.

16 And when Paul's sister's son heard of their lying in wait, he went and entered into the castle, and told Paul.

17 Then Paul called one of the centurions unto (him), and said, Bring this young man unto the chief captain: for he hath a certain thing to tell him.

18 So he took him, and brought (him) to the chief captain, and said, Paul the prisoner called me unto (him), and prayed me to bring this young man unto thee, who hath something to say unto thee.

19 Then the chief captain took him by the hand, and went (with him) aside privately, and asked (him), What is that thou hast to tell me?
20 And he said, The Jews have agreed to desire thee that thou wouldest bring down

Literal Translation

Paul into the Sanhedrin, as being about to inquire more accurately concerning him.
21 Therefore, you (must) not be persuaded by them, for more than forty men of them lie in wait for him who put themselves under a curse neither to eat nor to drink until they kill him. And now they are ready, awaiting the promise from you.
22 Then the chiliarch dismissed the young man, charging (him), Tell no one that you reported these things to me.
23 And having called near a certain two of the centurions, he said, Get ready two hundred soldiers, so as they may go to Caesarea, and seventy horsemen, and two hundred spearmen, from the third hour of the night;
24 and animals to stand by, so that having set Paul on, they may bring (him) to Felix the governor.
25 (For he was) writing a letter, having this form:
26 Claudius Lysias to the most excellent governor, Felix, greeting:
27 This man having been seized by the Jews, and being about to be killed by them, coming on with the soldiers I rescued him, having learned that he was a Roman.
28 And being minded to know the charge for which they were accusing him, I brought him down to their Sanhedrin;
29 whom I found to be accused concerning questions of their law, and having nothing (as a) charge worthy of death or of bonds.
30 And it being revealed to me that a plot against the

Acts 23:21

3972 5613 3195 5100 197 4441 4012
Παῦλον, ὡς μέλλοντές τι ἀκριβέστερον πυνθάνεσθαι περὶ
Paul, as intending something more accurately to inquire concerning

846 4771 3767 3361 3982 846 1748 1063 846
αὐτοῦ. 21 σὺ οὖν μὴ πεισθῇς αὐτοῖς· ἐνεδρεύουσι γὰρ αὐτὸν
him. You, then, not be persuaded by them; lie in wait for for him

1537 846 435 4119 5062 3748 332
ἐξ αὐτῶν ἄνδρες πλείους τεσσαράκοντα, οἵτινες ἀνεθεμάτισαν
of them men more (than) forty, who cursed

1438 3383 5315 3383 4095 2193 3757 337 846 2532
ἑαυτοὺς μήτε φαγεῖν μήτε πιεῖν ἕως οὗ ἀνέλωσιν αὐτόν· καὶ
themselves neither to eat nor drink until they kill him, and

3568 2092 1526 4327 3588 575 4675 1860 3588
νῦν ἕτοιμοί εἰσι προσδεχόμενοι τὴν ἀπὸ σοῦ ἐπαγγελίαν. 22 ὁ
now ready they are, awaiting the from you promise. the

3303 3767 5506 630 3588 3494 3853 3367
μὲν οὖν χιλίαρχος ἀπέλυσε τὸν νεανίαν, παραγγείλας μηδενὶ
Then chiliarch dismissed the youth, charging (him) no one

1583 3754 5023 1718 4314 3165 2532 4341
ἐκλαλῆσαι ὅτι ταῦτα ἐνεφάνισας πρός με. 23 καὶ προσκαλεσά-
to tell that these things you reported to me. And calling near

1417 5100 3588 1543 2036 2090
μενος δύο τινὰς τῶν ἑκατοντάρχων εἶπεν, Ἑτοιμάσατε
two a certain of the centurions he said, Get ready

4757 1250 3704 4198 2193 2542
στρατιώτας διακοσίους ὅπως πορευθῶσιν ἕως Καισαρείας,
soldiers two hundred, so as they may go to Caesarea,

2532 2460 1440 2532 1187 1250 575
καὶ ἱππεῖς ἑβδομήκοντα, καὶ δεξιολάβους διακοσίους, ἀπὸ
and horsemen seventy, and spearmen two hundred, from

5154 5610 3588 3571 2934 5037 3936 2443 1913
τρίτης ὥρας τῆς νυκτός· 24 κτήνη τε παραστῆσαι, ἵνα ἐπιβιβά-
third hour of the night; beasts and to stand by, that having

3588 3972 1295 4314 5344 3588 2232
σαντες τὸν Παῦλον διασώσωσι πρὸς Φήλικα τὸν ἡγεμόνα·
set on Paul they may bring to Felix the governor;

1125 1992 4023 3588 5179 5126
25 γράψας ἐπιστολὴν περιέχουσαν τὸν τύπον τοῦτον·
having written a letter having form this:

2804 3079 3588 2903 2232 5344 5463
26 Κλαύδιος Λυσίας τῷ κρατίστῳ ἡγεμόνι Φήλικι χαίρειν.
Claudius Lysias to the most excellent governor, Felix, greeting.

3588 435 5126 4815 5259 3588 2453 2532
27 τὸν ἄνδρα τοῦτον συλληφθέντα ὑπὸ τῶν Ἰουδαίων, καὶ
man This having been seized by the Jews, and

3195 337 5259 846 2186 4862 3588 4753
μέλλοντα ἀναιρεῖσθαι ὑπ' αὐτῶν, ἐπιστὰς σὺν τῷ στρατεύ-
being about to be killed by them, coming on with the soldiery

1807 846 3129 3754 4514 2076 1014
ματι ἐξειλόμην αὐτόν, μαθὼν ὅτι Ῥωμαῖός ἐστι. 28 βουλόμενος
I rescued him, having learned that a Roman he is. being minded

1161 1097 3588 156 1223 3739 1458 846 2609
δὲ γνῶναι τὴν αἰτίαν δι' ἣν ἐνεκάλουν αὐτῷ, κατήγαγον
And to know the charge for which they were accusing him, I brought down

846 1519 3588 4892 846 3739 2147 1458 4012
αὐτὸν εἰς τὸ συνέδριον αὐτῶν· 29 ὃν εὗρον ἐγκαλούμενον περὶ
him to the Sanhedrin of them, whom I found being accused concerning

2213 3588 3551 846 3367 1161 514 2288 2228
ζητημάτων τοῦ νόμου αὐτῶν, μηδὲν δὲ ἄξιον θανάτου ἢ δεσ-
questions of the law of them, nothing and worthy of death or of

1199 1462 2192 3377 1161 3427 1917 1519 3588
μῶν ἔγκλημα ἔχοντα. 30 μηνυθείσης δέ μοι ἐπιβουλῆς εἰς τὸν
bonds charge having. being revealed And to me a plot against the

King James Version

Paul to morrow into the council, as though they would enquire somewhat of him more perfectly.
21 But do not thou yield unto them: for there lie in wait for him of them more than forty men, which have bound themselves with an oath, that they will neither eat nor drink till they have killed him: and now are they ready, looking for a promise from thee.
22 So the chief captain (then) let the young man depart, and charged (him, See thou) tell no man that thou hast shewed these things to me.
23 And he called unto (him) two centurions, saying, Make ready two hundred soldiers to go to Caesarea, and horsemen threescore and ten, and spearmen two hundred, at the third hour of the night;
24 And provide (them) beasts, that they may set Paul on, and bring (him) safe unto Felix the governor.
25 And he wrote a letter after this manner:
26 Claudius Lysias unto the most excellent governor Felix (sendeth) greeting.
27 This man was taken of the Jews, and should have been killed of them: then came I with an army, and rescued him, having understood that he was a Roman.
28 And when I would have known the cause wherefore they accused him, I brought him forth into their council:
29 Whom I perceived to be accused of questions of their law, but to have nothing laid to his charge worthy of death or of bonds.
30 And when it was told me how that the Jews laid wait for the

Literal Translation **Acts 23:31** *King James Version*

man being about to be (executed) by the Jews, I at once sent (him) to you, also commanding the accusers to say the things against him before you. Farewell.

435 3195 1510 5259 3588 2453 1824 3992
ἄνδρα μέλλειν ἔσεσθαι ὑπὸ τῶν Ἰουδαίων, ἐξαυτῆς ἔπεμψα
man being about to be by the Jews, at once I sent
4314 4571 3853 2532 3588 2725 3004 3588 4314
πρὸς σέ, παραγγείλας καὶ τοῖς κατηγόροις λέγειν τὰ πρὸς
to you, commanding also the accusers to say the things against
846 1909 4675 4517
αὐτὸν ἐπὶ σοῦ. ἔρρωσο.
him before you. Farewell.

man, I sent straightway to thee, and gave commandment to his accusers also to say before thee what (they had) against him. Farewell.

31 Then indeed taking up Paul according to the thing having been appointed to them, the soldiers brought (him) through the night to Antipatris.
32 And on the morrow, allowing the horsemen to go with him, they returned to the fortress.
33 (The others) having entered into Caesarea, and giving over the letter to the governor, (they) also presented Paul to him.
34 And having read (it), the governor asked from what province he is. And having learned that (he was) from Cilicia,

35 he said, I will hear you fully when also your accusers arrive. And (he) commanded him to be kept in the praetorium of Herod.

3588 3303 3767 4757 2596 3588 1299 846
31. Οἱ μὲν οὖν στρατιῶται, κατὰ τὸ διατεταγμένον αὐτοῖς,
the indeed Then soldiers, according to that having been set out to them,
353 3588 3972 71 1223 3588 3571 1519 3588
ἀναλαβόντες τὸν Παῦλον, ἤγαγον διὰ τῆς νυκτὸς εἰς τὴν
taking up Paul, brought through the night to
494 3588 1161 1887 1439 3588 2460 4198
Ἀντιπατρίδα. 32 τῇ δὲ ἐπαύριον ἐάσαντες τοὺς ἱππεῖς πορεύ-
Antipatris. on the And morrow allowing the horsemen to go
4862 846 5290 1519 3588 3925 3748
εσθαι σὺν αὐτῷ, ὑπέστρεψαν εἰς τὴν παρεμβολήν· 33 οἵτινες
with him, they returned to the fortress; who
1525 1519 3588 2542 2532 325 3588 1992
εἰσελθόντες εἰς τὴν Καισάρειαν καὶ ἀναδόντες τὴν ἐπιστολὴν
having entered into Caesarea and giving over the letter,
3588 2232 3936 2532 3588 3972 846 314
τῷ ἡγεμόνι, παρέστησαν καὶ τὸν Παῦλον αὐτῷ. 34 ἀναγνοὺς
to the governor, presented also Paul to him. having read
1161 3588 2232 2532 1905 1537 4169 1885 2076 2532
δὲ ὁ ἡγεμών, καὶ ἐπερωτήσας ἐκ ποίας ἐπαρχίας ἐστί, καὶ
And the governor, and asking from what province he is, and
4441 3754 575 2791 1251 4675 5346 3752 2532
πυθόμενος ὅτι ἀπὸ Κιλικίας, 35 Διακούσομαί σου, ἔφη, ὅταν καὶ
having learned that from Cilicia, I will hear you, he said, when also
3588 2725 4675 3854 2753 5037 846 1722 3588
οἱ κατήγοροί σου παραγένωνται. ἐκέλευσέ τε αὐτὸν ἐν τῷ
the accusers of you arrive; commanding and him in the
4232 3588 2264 5442
πραιτωρίῳ τοῦ Ἡρώδου φυλάσσεσθαι.
praetorium of Herod to be kept.

31 Then the soldiers, as it was commanded them, took Paul, and brought (him) by night to Antipatris.

32 On the morrow they left the horsemen to go with him, and returned to the castle:
33 Who, when they came to Caesarea, and delivered the epistle to the governor, presented Paul also before him.

34 And when the governor had read (the letter), he asked of what province he was. And when he understood that (he was) of Cilicia;

35 I will hear thee, said he, when thine accusers are also come. And he commanded him to be kept in Herod's judgment hall.

Acts 24

1. And after five days Ananias the high priest came down with the elders, and an orator, one Tertullus, who informed the governor against Paul.
2 And Tertullus being called, he began to accuse, saying, Obtaining much peace through you and excellent attainments having come to this nation through your forethought,

3 in every way and everywhere we welcome with all thankfulness, most excellent Felix.

3326 1161 4002 2250 2597 3588 749 367 3326
1. Μετὰ δὲ πέντε ἡμέρας κατέβη ὁ ἀρχιερεὺς Ἁνανίας μετὰ
after And five days came down the high priest Ananias, with
3588 4245 2532 4489 5061 5100 3748
τῶν πρεσβυτέρων καὶ ῥήτορος Τερτύλλου τινός, οἵτινες
the elders and an orator Tertullus one, who
1718 3588 2232 2596 3588 3972 2564 1161
ἐνεφάνισαν τῷ ἡγεμόνι κατὰ τοῦ Παύλου. 2 κληθέντος δὲ
informed the governor against Paul. being called And
846 756 2723 3588 5061 3004
αὐτοῦ, ἤρξατο κατηγορεῖν ὁ Τέρτυλλος λέγων,
him, began to accuse Tertullus saying,
4183 1515 5177 1223 4675 2532 2735
Πολλῆς εἰρήνης τυγχάνοντες διὰ σοῦ, καὶ κατορθωμάτων
Much peace obtaining through you, and excellent attainments
1096 3588 1484 5129 1223 3588 4674 4307 3839 5037
γινομένων τῷ ἔθνει τούτῳ διὰ τῆς σῆς προνοίας, 3 πάντῃ τε
having come to nation this through your forethought, in every way
2532 3837 588 2903 5344 3326 3956
καὶ πανταχοῦ ἀποδεχόμεθα, κράτιστε Φῆλιξ, μετὰ πάσης
also everywhere we welcome, most excellent Felix, with all

1. And after five days Ananias the high priest descended with the elders, and (with) a certain orator (named) Tertullus, who informed the governor against Paul.
2 And when he was called forth, Tertullus began to accuse (him), saying, Seeing that by thee we enjoy great quietness, and that very worthy deeds are done unto this nation by thy providence,

3 We accept (it) always, and in all places, most noble Felix, with all

Literal Translation

Acts 24:4

King James Version

4 But that I not hinder you longer, I beseech you to hear us briefly in your forbearance.
5 For having found this man pestilent and moving insurrection among all the Jews throughout the world, and a ringleader of the Nazarene sect;
6 who also attempted to profane the temple, whom we also seized and wished to judge according to our law;
7 but Lysias the chiliarch coming up with much force took (him) away out of our hands,
8 commanding his accusers to come to you, from whom you will be able yourself to know, having examined as to all these things of which we accuse him.
9 And the Jews also joined in, alleging these things to be so.
10. And the governor having signaled to him to speak, Paul answered: Understanding you as being a judge to this nation of many years, I cheerfully defend myself (as to) the things concerning myself,
11 you being able to know that not more than twelve days are to me from which I went worshiping in Jerusalem;
12 and neither did they find me reasoning with anyone in the temple, or making a riotous gathering of a crowd, neither in the synagogues, nor throughout the city;
13 nor are they able to prove that concerning which they now accuse

2169 2443 1161 3361 1909 4119 4571 1465 3870
εὐχαριστίας. 4 ἵνα δὲ μὴ ἐπὶ πλεῖόν σε ἐγκόπτω, παρακαλῶ
thankfulness. that But not to longer you I hinder, I beseech

191 4571 2257 4935 3588 4674 1932 2147 1063
ἀκοῦσαί σε ἡμῶν συντόμως τῇ σῇ ἐπιεικείᾳ. 5 εὑρόντες γὰρ
to hear you us briefly in your forbearance. having found For

3588 435 5126 3061 2532 2795 4714 3956 3588
τὸν ἄνδρα τοῦτον λοιμόν, καὶ κινοῦντα στάσιν πᾶσι τοῖς
man this pestilent, and moving insurrection among all the

2453 3588 2596 3588 3625 4414 5037 3588
Ἰουδαίοις τοῖς κατὰ τὴν οἰκουμένην, πρωτοστάτην τε τῆς
Jews throughout the habitable world, a ringleader and of the

3588 3480 139 3739 2532 3588 2411 3985 953
τῶν Ναζωραίων αἱρέσεως· 6 ὃς καὶ τὸ ἱερὸν ἐπείρασε βεβηλῶ-
Nazarene sect; who also the temple attempted to profane;

3739 2532 2902 2532 2596 3588 2251 3551 2309
σαι· ὃν καὶ ἐκρατήσαμεν καὶ κατὰ τὸν ἡμέτερον νόμον ἠθελή-
whom also we seized and according to our Law wished

2919 3928 1161 3079 3588 5506 3326 4183
σαμεν κρίνειν. 7 παρελθὼν δὲ Λυσίας ὁ χιλίαρχος μετὰ πολλῆς
to judge. coming up But Lysias the chiliarch with much

970 1537 3588 5495 2257 520 2753 3588 2725
βίας ἐκ τῶν χειρῶν ἡμῶν ἀπήγαγε, κελεύσας τοὺς κατηγό-
force out of the hands of us took, commanding the accusers

846 2064 1909 4571 3844 3739 1410 846 350
ρους αὐτοῦ ἔρχεσθαι ἐπὶ σέ· 8 παρ' οὗ δυνήσῃ, αὐτὸς ἀνα-
of him to come to you; from whom you can, yourself having

4012 3956 5130 1921 3739 2249 2723
κρίνας, περὶ πάντων τούτων ἐπιγνῶναι ὧν ἡμεῖς κατηγο-
examined, concerning all these things know fully of which we accuse

846 4934 1161 2532 3588 2453 5335
ροῦμεν αὐτοῦ. 9 συνέθεντο δὲ καὶ οἱ Ἰουδαῖοι, φάσκοντες
him. joined in And also the Jews, alleging

5023 3779 2192
ταῦτα οὕτως ἔχειν.
these things so to be.

611 1161 3588 3972 3506 846 3588 2232
10. Ἀπεκρίθη δὲ ὁ Παῦλος, νεύσαντος αὐτῷ τοῦ ἡγεμόνος
answered And Paul, having signaled to him the governor

3004
λέγειν,
to speak,

1537 4183 2094 5607 4571 2923 3588 1484 5129 1987
Ἐκ πολλῶν ἐτῶν ὄντα σε κριτὴν τῷ ἔθνει τούτῳ ἐπιστά-
Of many years being you a judge nation to this under-

2115 3588 4012 1683 626 1410
μενος, εὐθυμότερον τὰ περὶ ἐμαυτοῦ ἀπολογοῦμαι, 11 δυνα-
standing, cheerfully the things about myself I speak in my defense, being

4675 1097 3754 3756 4119 1526 3427 2250 2228 1177
μένου σου γνῶναι ὅτι οὐ πλείους εἰσί μοι ἡμέραι ἢ δεκαδύο,
able you to know that not more are to me days twelve

575 3739 305 4352 1722 2419 2532 3777 1722 3588
ἀφ' ἧς ἀνέβην προσκυνήσων ἐν Ἱερουσαλήμ· 12 καὶ οὔτε ἐν τῷ
from which I went worshiping in Jerusalem; and nothing in the

2411 2147 3165 4314 5100 1256 2228 1999
ἱερῷ εὗρόν με πρός τινα διαλεγόμενον ἢ ἐπισύστασιν
temple they found me with anyone reasoning or a riotous gathering

4160 3793 3777 1722 3588 4864 3777 2596 3588
ποιοῦντα ὄχλου, οὔτε ἐν ταῖς συναγωγαῖς, οὔτε κατὰ τὴν
making of a crowd, neither in the synagogues, nor throughout the

4172 3777 3936 1410 4012 3739 3568 2723
πόλιν. 13 οὔτε παραστῆσαι δύνανταί περὶ ὧν νῦν κατηγοροῦσί
city. Neither to prove are they able about which now they accuse

thankfulness.
4 Notwithstanding, that I be not further tedious unto thee, I pray thee that thou wouldest hear us of thy clemency a few words.
5 For we have found this man (a) pestilent (fellow), and a mover of sedition among all the Jews throughout the world, and a ringleader of the sect of the Nazarenes:
6 Who also hath gone about to profane the temple: whom we took, and would have judged according to our law.
7 But the chief captain Lysias came (upon us), and with great violence took (him) away out of our hands,
8 Commanding his accusers to come unto thee: by examining of whom thyself mayest take knowledge of all these things, whereof we accuse him.
9 And the Jews also assented, saying that these things were so.
10. Then Paul, after that the governor had beckoned unto him to speak, answered, Forasmuch as I know that thou hast been of many years a judge unto this nation, I do the more cheerfully answer for myself:
11 Because that thou mayest understand, that there are yet but twelve days since I went up to Jerusalem for to worship.
12 And they neither found me in the temple disputing with any man, neither raising up the people, neither in the synagogues, nor in the city:
13 Neither can they prove the things whereof they now accuse

Literal Translation

me.
14 But I confess this to you that according to the Way, which they say (is) a sect, this way I worship the ancestral God, believing all the things according to that having been written in the Law and the Prophets,

15 having hope toward God, which these themselves also admit, (of) a resurrection being about to be of (the) dead, both of just and unjust ones.
16 And in this I exercise myself to have always a blameless conscience toward God and men.
17 And after many years I arrived doing merciful deeds and offerings to my nation,

18 among which they found me purified in the temple, not with a crowd, nor with tumult, (but by) some Jews from Asia,
19 who it is right to be present before you and to accuse if they have anything against me.
20 Or these themselves say if they found anything unjust in me, I standing before the Sanhedrin,
21 than concerning this one voice which I cried out standing among them, that I am being judged today before you concerning a resurrection of (the) dead.

22. And having heard these things, Felix put them off, knowing more accurately about the Way, saying, When Lysias the chiliarch comes down, I will examine the things as to you.
23 And having ordered the centurion to keep Paul, and to have ease, and not to forbid anyone of his own to minister or to come to him, (he dismissed them).

Acts 24:14

3450 3670 1161 5124 4671 3754 2596 3588 3598 3739 3004
μου. 14 ὁμολογῶ δὲ τοῦτό σοι, ὅτι κατὰ τὴν ὁδὸν ἣν λέγουσιν
me. I confess But this to you, that according to the Way which they say

139 3779 3000 3588 3971 2316 4100 3956
αἵρεσιν, οὕτω λατρεύω τῷ πατρῴῳ Θεῷ, πιστεύων πᾶσι
a sect (is), this way I worship the ancestral God, believing all

3588 2596 3588 3551 2532 3588 4396 1125
τοῖς κατὰ τὸν νόμον καὶ τοῖς προφήταις γεγραμμένοις·
the things regarding the Law and the Prophets having been written;

1680 2192 1519 3588 2316 3739 2532 846 3778 4327
15 ἐλπίδα ἔχων εἰς τὸν Θεόν, ἣν καὶ αὐτοὶ οὗτοι προσδέχονται,
hope having toward God, which also themselves these admit,

386 3195 1510 3498 1342 5037 2532 94
ἀνάστασιν μέλλειν ἔσεσθαι νεκρῶν, δικαίων τε καὶ ἀδίκων.
a resurrection being about to be of (the) dead, of just both and unjust.

1722 5129 2532 846 778 677 4893 2192
16 ἐν τούτῳ καὶ αὐτὸς ἀσκῶ, ἀπρόσκοπον συνείδησιν ἔχειν
by this and myself I exercise, a blameless conscience to have

4314 3588 2316 2532 3588 444 1223 3956 1223 2094 1161
πρὸς τὸν Θεὸν καὶ τοὺς ἀνθρώπους διὰ παντός. 17 δι᾽ ἐτῶν δὲ
toward God and men through all. after years And

4119 3854 1654 4160 1519 3588 1484
πλειόνων παρεγενόμην ἐλεημοσύνας ποιήσων εἰς τὸ ἔθνος
many I arrived merciful deeds doing to the nation

3450 2532 4376 1722 3739 2147 3165 48 1722 3588 2411
μου καὶ προσφοράς· 18 ἐν οἷς εὗρόν με ἡγνισμένον ἐν τῷ ἱερῷ,
of me and offerings; among which they found me purified in the temple,

3756 3326 3793 3761 3326 2351 5100 575 3588 773
οὐ μετὰ ὄχλου οὐδὲ μετὰ θορύβου, 19 τινὲς ἀπὸ τῆς Ἀσίας
not with a crowd nor with tumult, some from Asia

2453 3739 1163 1909 4675 3918 2532 2723 1487 5100
Ἰουδαῖοι· οὓς ἔδει ἐπὶ σοῦ παρεῖναι καὶ κατηγορεῖν εἴ τι
Jews; whom it is right before you to be present and to accuse if anything

2192 4314 3165 2228 846 3778 2036 1487 5100 2147 1722
ἔχοιεν πρὸς με. 20 ἢ αὐτοὶ οὗτοι εἰπάτωσαν, εἴ τι εὗρον ἐν
they have against me. Or them these let say if anything they found in

1698 92 2476 3450 1909 3588 4892 2228 4012 3391
ἐμοὶ ἀδίκημα, στάντος μου ἐπὶ τοῦ συνεδρίου, 21 ἢ περὶ μιᾶς
me unjust, standing me before the Sanhedrin, than about one

3778 5456 3739 2896 2476 1722 846 3754 4012
ταύτης φωνῆς, ἧς ἔκραξα ἑστὼς ἐν αὐτοῖς, ὅτι Περὶ
this voice, which I cried out standing among them, Concerning

386 3498 1473 2919 4594 5259 5216
ἀναστάσεως νεκρῶν ἐγὼ κρίνομαι σήμερον ὑφ᾽ ὑμῶν.
a resurrection of (the) dead I am being judged today before you.

191 1161 5023 3588 5344 306 846 197
22. Ἀκούσας δὲ ταῦτα ὁ Φῆλιξ ἀνεβάλετο αὐτούς, ἀκριβέ-
having heard And these things Felix put off them, more

1492 3588 4012 3588 3598 2036 3752 3079 3588 5506
στερον εἰδὼς τὰ περὶ τῆς ὁδοῦ, εἰπών, Ὅταν Λυσίας ὁ χιλί-
accurately knowing the things about the Way, saying, When Lysias the chili-

2597 1231 3588 2596 5209 1299 5037
αρχος καταβῇ, διαγνώσομαι τὰ καθ᾽ ὑμᾶς· 23 διαταξάμενός τε
arch comes down I will examine the things as to you; having ordered and

3588 1543 5083 3588 3972 2192 5037 425 2532
τῷ ἑκατοντάρχῃ τηρεῖσθαι τὸν Παῦλον, ἔχειν τε ἄνεσιν, καὶ
the centurion to keep Paul, to have and ease, and

3367 2967 3588 2398 846 5256 2228 4334
μηδένα κωλύειν τῶν ἰδίων αὐτοῦ ὑπηρετεῖν ἢ προσέρχεσθαι
no one to forbid the own of him to minister or to come

846
αὐτῷ.
to him.

King James Version

me.
14 But this I confess unto thee, that after the way which they call heresy, so worship I the God of my fathers, believing all things which are written in the law and in the prophets:

15 And have hope toward God, which they themselves also allow, that there shall be a resurrection of the dead, both of the just and unjust.
16 And herein do I exercise myself, to have always a conscience void of offence toward God, and (toward) men.
17 Now after many years I came to bring alms to my nation, and offerings.

18 Whereupon certain Jews from Asia found me purified in the temple, neither with multitude, nor with tumult.
19 Who ought to have been here before thee, and object, if they had ought against me.

20 Or else let these same (here) say, if they have found any evil doing in me, while I stood before the council,
21 Except it be for this one voice, that I cried standing among them, Touching the resurrection of the dead I am called in question by you this day.

22. And when Felix heard these things, having more perfect knowledge of (that) way, he deferred them, and said, When Lysias the chief captain shall come down, I will know the uttermost of your matter.
23 And he commanded a centurion to keep Paul, and to let (him) have liberty, and that he should forbid none of his acquaintance to minister or come unto him.

Literal Translation

Acts 24:24

King James Version

24. And after some days, Felix having arrived with his wife Drusilla, (she) being a Jewess, he sent for Paul. And (he) heard him concerning the faith in Christ.

25 And (Paul) having reasoned concerning righteousness and self control, and the Judgment that is about to be, having become afraid, Felix answered, For the present, go; but taking time later, I will call for you;

26 and with it all also hoping that money will be given to him by Paul, that he might free him. Because of this (he) also more frequently sent for him (and) conversed with him.

27 But two years being completed, Felix received a successor, Porcius Festus. And wishing to show favors to the Jews, Felix left Paul being bound.

3326 1161 2250 5100 3854 3588 5344 4862
24 Μετὰ δὲ ἡμέρας τινάς παραγενόμενος ὁ Φῆλιξ σὺν
after And days some, having arrived Felix with

1409 3588 1135 846 5607 2453 3343
Δρουσίλλῃ τῇ γυναικὶ αὐτοῦ οὔσῃ Ἰουδαίᾳ, μετεπέμψατο
Drusilla the wife of him, being a Jewess, he sent for

3588 3972 2532 191 846 4012 3588 1519 5547
τὸν Παῦλον, καὶ ἤκουσεν αὐτοῦ περὶ τῆς εἰς Χριστὸν πί-
Paul, and heard him concerning the in Christ

4102 1256 1161 846 4012 1343 2532
στεως. 25 διαλεγομένου δὲ αὐτοῦ περὶ δικαιοσύνης καὶ
faith. having reasoned And him concerning righteousness and

1466 2532 3588 2917 3588 3195 1510 1719
ἐγκρατείας καὶ τοῦ κρίματος τοῦ μέλλοντος ἔσεσθαι, ἔμφοβος
self-control and the Judgment being about to be, afraid

1096 3588 5344 611 3588 3568 2192 4198 2540 1161
γενόμενος ὁ Φῆλιξ ἀπεκρίθη, Τὸ νῦν ἔχον πορεύου· καιρὸν δὲ
having become Felix answered, For the present go; time but

3335 3333 4571 260 1161 2532 1679 3754
μεταλαβὼν μετακαλέσομαί σε· 26 ἅμα δὲ καὶ ἐλπίζων ὅτι
taking later I will call for you; with it all but also hoping that

5536 1325 846 5259 3588 3972 3704 3089 846
χρήματα δοθήσεται αὐτῷ ὑπὸ τοῦ Παύλου, ὅπως λύσῃ αὐτόν·
money will be given to him by Paul, so that he might free him;

1352 2532 4437 846 3343 3656 846
διὸ καὶ πυκνότερον αὐτὸν μεταπεμπόμενος ὡμίλει αὐτῷ.
so also more frequently him having sent for he conversed with him.

1333 1161 4137 2983 1240 3588 5344 4201
27 διετίας δὲ πληρωθείσης, ἔλαβε διάδοχον ὁ Φῆλιξ Πόρκιον
two years And being completed, received a successor Felix Porcius

5347 2309 5037 5485 2698 3588 2453 3588 5344
Φῆστον· θέλων τε χάριτας καταθέσθαι τοῖς Ἰουδαίοις ὁ Φῆλιξ
Festus; wishing and favors to show to the Jews Felix

2641 3588 3972 1210
κατέλιπε τὸν Παῦλον δεδεμένον.
left Paul being bound.

24. And after certain days, when Felix came with his wife Drusilla, which was a Jewess, he sent for Paul, and heard him concerning the faith in Christ.

25 And as he reasoned of righteousness, temperance, and judgment to come, Felix trembled, and answered, Go thy way for this time; when I have a convenient season, I will call for thee.

26 He hoped also that money should have been given him of Paul, that he might loose him: wherefore he sent for him the oftener, and communed with him.

27 But after two years Porcius Festus came into Felix' room: and Felix, willing to shew the Jews a pleasure, left Paul bound.

Acts 25

1. Then entering the province, after three days Festus went up to Jerusalem from Caesarea.

2 And the high priest and the first ones of the Jews made a statement before him against Paul, and they entreated him,

3 asking a favor against him, so as he might send for him to Jerusalem, making a plot to kill him on the way.

4 Then indeed Festus answered that Paul (was) to be kept at Caesarea, he himself even being about to go shortly.

5 Then he said, those having power among you may go down

Acts 25

5347 3767 1910 3588 1885 3326 5140 2250 305
1. Φῆστος οὖν ἐπιβὰς τῇ ἐπαρχίᾳ, μετὰ τρεῖς ἡμέρας ἀνέβη
Festus Then entering the province, after three days went up

1519 2414 575 2542 1718 1161 846 3588
εἰς Ἱεροσόλυμα ἀπὸ Καισαρείας. 2 ἐνεφάνισαν δὲ αὐτῷ ὁ
to Jerusalem from Caesarea.. made a statement And to him the

749 2532 3588 4413 3588 2453 2596 3588 3972
ἀρχιερεὺς καὶ οἱ πρῶτοι τῶν Ἰουδαίων κατὰ τοῦ Παύλου,
chief priest and the first ones of the Jews against Paul,

2532 3870 846 154 5485 2596 846 3704
καὶ παρεκάλουν αὐτὸν, 3 αἰτούμενοι χάριν κατ' αὐτοῦ, ὅπως
and they entreated him, asking a favor against him, so as

3343 846 1519 2419 1747 4160
μεταπέμψηται αὐτὸν εἰς Ἱερουσαλήμ, ἐνέδραν ποιοῦντες
he might send for him to Jerusalem, a plot making

337 846 2596 3588 3598 3588 3303 3767 5347 611
ἀνελεῖν αὐτὸν κατὰ τὴν ὁδόν. 4 ὁ μὲν οὖν Φῆστος ἀπεκρίθη,
to kill him by the way. indeed Then Festus answered,

5083 3588 3972 1722 2542 1438 1161 3195 1722
τηρεῖσθαι τὸν Παῦλον ἐν Καισαρείᾳ, ἑαυτὸν δὲ μέλλειν ἐν
to be kept Paul in Caesarea, himself and being about in

5034 1607 3588 3767 1415 1722 5213 5346 4782
τάχει ἐκπορεύεσθαι. 5 οἱ οὖν δυνατοὶ ἐν ὑμῖν, φησί, συγκατα-
shortly to go forth. the Then able ones among you, he says, going down

Acts 25

1. Now when Festus was come into the province, after three days he ascended from Caesarea to Jerusalem.

2 Then the high priest and the chief of the Jews informed him against Paul, and besought him,

3 And desired favour against him, that he would send for him to Jerusalem, laying wait in the way to kill him.

4 But Festus answered, that Paul should be kept at Caesarea, and that he himself would depart shortly (thither).

5 Let them therefore, said he, which among you are able, go down

Literal Translation **Acts 25:6** ***King James Version***

with (me). If there is any thing amiss in this man, let them accuse him.

1487 5100 2076 824 1722 3588 435 5129 2723
βάντες, εἴ τί ἐστιν ἄτοπον ἐν τῷ ἀνδρὶ τούτῳ, κατηγορεί-
with (me), if anything is amiss in man this, let them

846
τωσαν αὐτοῦ.
accuse him.

with (me), and accuse this man, if there be any wickedness in him.

6 And having stayed among them more than ten days, going down to Caesarea, on the morrow sitting on the tribunal, he ordered Paul to be brought.
7 And he having arrived, the (ones) from Jerusalem, the Jews having come down stood around, also bringing many weighty charges against Paul, which they were not able to prove.

1304 1161 1722 846 2250 4119 2228 1176 2597
6. Διατρίψας δὲ ἐν αὐτοῖς ἡμέρας πλείους ἢ δέκα, καταβὰς
having stayed And among them days more than ten, going down

1519 2542 3588 1887 2523 1909 3588 968 2753
εἰς Καισάρειαν, τῇ ἐπαύριον καθίσας ἐπὶ τοῦ βήματος ἐκέ-
to Caesarea on the morrow sitting on the tribunal he

3588 3972 71 3854 1161 846
λευσε τὸν Παῦλον ἀχθῆναι. 7 παραγενομένου δὲ αὐτοῦ,
ordered Paul to be brought. having arrived And him,

4026 3588 575 2414 2597 2453
περιέστησαν οἱ ἀπὸ Ἱεροσολύμων καταβεβηκότες Ἰουδαῖοι,
stood around the ones from Jerusalem having come down Jews,

4183 2532 926 157 5342 2596 3588 3972 3739
πολλὰ καὶ βαρέα αἰτιάματα φέροντες κατὰ τοῦ Παύλου, ἃ
many and weighty accusations bringing against Paul, which

3756 2480 584 626 846 3754 3777 1519
οὐκ ἴσχυον ἀποδεῖξαι, 8 ἀπολογουμένου αὐτοῦ ὅτι Οὔτε εἰς
not they were able to prove, defending himself he said, Neither against

6 And when he had tarried among them more than ten days, he went down unto Caesarea; and the next day sitting on the judgment seat commanded Paul to be brought.
7 And when he was come, the Jews which came down from Jerusalem stood round about, and laid many and grievous complaints against Paul, which they could not prove.

8 Defending himself, (Paul) said, Neither against the Law of the Jews, nor against the temple, nor against Caesar have I sinned in a thing.
9. But wishing to show a favor to the Jews, answering Paul, Festus said, Do you desire to go up to Jerusalem to be judged before me there about these things?
10 But Paul said, I am standing before the tribunal of Caesar where I ought to be judged. I have wronged (the) Jews (in) nothingJews, as also you very well know.

3588 3551 3588 2453 3777 1519 3588 2411 3777 1519 2541
τὸν νόμον τῶν Ἰουδαίων, οὔτε εἰς τὸ ἱερὸν, οὔτε εἰς Καίσαρά
the Law of the Jews, nor against the temple, nor against Caesar

5100 264 3588 5347 1161 3588 2453 2309 5485
τι ἥμαρτον. 9 ὁ Φῆστος δὲ τοῖς Ἰουδαίοις θέλων χάριν
a thing I sinned. Festus But the Jews wishing a favor

2698 611 3588 3972 2036 2309 1519 2414
καταθέσθαι, ἀποκριθεὶς τῷ Παύλῳ εἶπε, Θέλεις εἰς Ἱεροσό-
to show, answering Paul said, Desire you to Jerusalem

305 1563 4012 5130 2919 1909 1700 2036 1161
λυμα ἀναβὰς, ἐκεῖ περὶ τούτων κρίνεσθαι ἐπ' ἐμοῦ; 10 εἶπε δὲ
to go up, there about these things to be judged before me? said And

3588 3972 1909 3588 968 2541 2476 1510 3757 3165 1163
ὁ Παῦλος, Ἐπὶ τοῦ βήματος Καίσαρος ἑστώς εἰμι, οὗ με δεῖ
Paul, Before the tribunal of Caesar standing I am, where me must

2919 2453 3762 91 5613 2532 4771 2566
κρίνεσθαι· Ἰουδαίους οὐδὲν ἠδίκησα, ὡς καὶ σὺ κάλλιον
be judged; Jews nothing I have wronged, as also you very well

1921
ἐπιγινώσκεις.
know.

8 While he answered for himself, Neither against the law of the Jews, neither against the temple, nor yet against Caesar, have I offended any thing at all.
9 But Festus, willing to do the Jews a pleasure, answered Paul, and said, Wilt thou go up to Jerusalem, and there be judged of these things before me?
10 Then said Paul, I stand at Caesar's judgment seat, where I ought to be judged: to the Jews have I done no wrong, as thou very well knowest.

11 For if I indeed do wrong and have done anything worthy of death, I do not refuse to die. But if there is nothing of which they accuse me, no one is able to give me up to them. I appeal to Caesar.

12 Then conferring with the Sanhedrin, Festus answered, You have appealed to Caesar; you shall go before Caesar.

1487 3303 1063 91 2532 514 2288 4238
11 εἰ μὲν γὰρ ἀδικῶ καὶ ἄξιον θανάτου πέπραχά
if indeed For I do wrong and worthy of death I have done

5100 3756 3868 3588 599 1487 1161 3762 2076 3739 3778
τι, οὐ παραιτοῦμαι τὸ ἀποθανεῖν· εἰ δὲ οὐδέν ἐστιν ὧν οὗτοι
a thing, not I refuse to die; if but not one is of which these

2723 3450 3762 3165 1410 846 5483
κατηγοροῦσί μου, οὐδείς με δύναται αὐτοῖς χαρίσασθαι.
accuse me, no one me is able to them to grant.

2541 1941 5119 3588 5347 4814 3326 3588
Καίσαρα ἐπικαλοῦμαι. 12 τότε ὁ Φῆστος συλλαλήσας μετὰ τοῦ
Caesar I appeal to. Then Festus having conferred with the

4824 611 2541 1941 1909 2541
συμβουλίου ἀπεκρίθη, Καίσαρα ἐπικέκλησαι; ἐπὶ Καίσαρα
Sanhedrin answered, Caesar you have appealed to; before Caesar

4198
πορεύσῃ.
you shall go.

11 For if I be an offender, or have committed any thing worthy of death, I refuse not to die: but if there be none of these things whereof these accuse me, no man may deliver me unto them. I appeal unto Caesar.
12 Then Festus, when he had conferred with the council, answered, Hast thou appealed unto Caesar? unto Caesar shalt thou go.

13. And some days having passed, Agrippa the king

2250 1161 1230 5100 67 3588 959
13. Ἡμερῶν δὲ διαγενομένων τινῶν, Ἀγρίππας ὁ βασιλεὺς
days And having passed some, Agrippa the king

13. And after certain days king Agrippa

Literal Translation

and Bernice arrived at Caesarea, greeting Festus.
14 And as they remained there more days, Festus set out to the king the things as to Paul, saying, A certain man having been left a prisoner by Felix,
15 about whom, on my being at Jerusalem, the chief priests and the elders of the Jews made a statement, asking judgment against him;
16 to whom I answered, It is not a custom with Romans to give up any man to destruction before the (one) being accused may have the accusers against (his) face, and may receive place of defense concerning the charge.
17 Then they coming together here, making no delay, sitting on the tribunal on the next (day), I commanded the man to be brought;
18 about whom, standing up, the accusers brought no charge of which I suspected,
19 but they had certain questions about (their) own demon worship, and about a certain Jesus having died, whom Paul claimed to live.
20 And being puzzled about this inquiry, I said, Did he desire to go to Jerusalem and to be judged there concerning these things?
21 But Paul having appealed for himself to be kept to the examination of Augustus, I commanded him to be held until I may send him to Caesar.
22. And Agrippa said to Festus, I also myself was minded to hear the man.

Acts 25:14

2532 959 2658 1519 2542 782 3588
καὶ Βερνίκη κατήντησαν εἰς Καισάρειαν, ἀσπασόμενοι τὸν
and Bernice arrived at Caesarea, greeting

5347 5613 1161 4119 2250 1304 1563 3588 5347 3588
Φῆστον. 14 ὡς δὲ πλείους ἡμέρας διέτριβον ἐκεῖ, ὁ Φῆστος τῷ
Festus. as And more days they remained there, Festus to the

935 394 3588 2596 3588 3972 3004 435 5100 2076
βασιλεῖ ἀνέθετο τὰ κατὰ τὸν Παῦλον, λέγων, Ἀνήρ τίς ἐστι
king set out the things (as to) Paul, saying, man A certain is

2641 5259 5344 1198 4012 3739 1096
καταλελειμμένος ὑπὸ Φήλικος δέσμιος, 15 περὶ οὗ γενομένου
having been left by Felix a prisoner, about whom having been

3450 1519 2414 1718 3588 749 2532 3588
μου εἰς Ἱεροσόλυμα ἐνεφάνισαν οἱ ἀρχιερεῖς καὶ οἱ πρεσ-
me at Jerusalem made a statement the chief priests and the elders

4245 3588 2453 154 2596 846 1349 4314
βύτεροι τῶν Ἰουδαίων, αἰτούμενοι κατ᾽ αὐτοῦ δίκην· 16 πρὸς
of the Jews, asking against him sentence; to

3739 611 3754 3756 2076 1985 4514 5483 5100
οὓς ἀπεκρίθην, ὅτι οὐκ ἔστιν ἔθος Ῥωμαίοις χαρίζεσθαί τινα
whom I answered, that not it is a custom with Romans to easily give any

444 1519 684 4250 2228 3588 2723 2596
ἄνθρωπον εἰς ἀπώλειαν, πρὶν ἢ ὁ κατηγορούμενος κατὰ
man into destruction before the (one) being accused against

4383 2192 3588 2725 5117 5037 627
πρόσωπον ἔχοι τοὺς κατηγόρους, τόπον τε ἀπολογίας
(his) face should have the accusers, place and of defense

2983 4012 3588 1462 4905 3767 846 1759
λάβοι περὶ τοῦ ἐγκλήματος. 17 συνελθόντων οὖν αὐτῶν ἐνθάδε,
receive concerning the charge. coming together Then they to here,

311 3367 4160 3588 1836 2523 1909 3588
ἀναβολὴν μηδεμίαν ποιησάμενος, τῇ ἑξῆς καθίσας ἐπὶ τοῦ
delay no having made, on the next sitting on the

968 2753 71 3588 435 4012 3739 2476 3588
βήματος, ἐκέλευσα ἀχθῆναι τὸν ἄνδρα· 18 περὶ οὗ σταθέντες οἱ
tribunal, I commanded to be brought the man; concerning whom standing the

2725 3762 156 2018 3739 5282 1473
κατήγοροι οὐδεμίαν αἰτίαν ἐπέφερον ὧν ὑπενόουν ἐγώ,
accusers no charge brought of which suspected I,

2213 1161 5100 4012 3588 2398 1175 2192 4314
19 ζητήματα δέ τινα περὶ τῆς ἰδίας δεισιδαιμονίας εἶχον πρὸς
questions but certain about the own demon-worship they had with

846 2532 4012 5100 2424 2348 3739 5335 3588 3972
αὐτὸν, καὶ περί τινος Ἰησοῦ τεθνηκότος, ὃν ἔφασκεν ὁ Παῦλος
him, and about a certain Jesus having died, whom claimed Paul

2198 639 1161 1473 1519 3588 4012 5127 2214
ζῆν. 20 ἀπορούμενος δὲ ἐγὼ εἰς τὴν περὶ τούτου ζήτησιν,
to live. being puzzled And I at the about this inquiry

3004 1487 1014 4198 1519 2419 2546 2919
ἔλεγον, εἰ βούλοιτο πορεύεσθαι εἰς Ἱερουσαλήμ, κἀκεῖ κρίνε-
said, if he desired to go to Jerusalem and there to be

4012 5130 3588 1161 3972 1941 5083
σθαι περὶ τούτων. 21 τοῦ δὲ Παύλου ἐπικαλεσαμένου τηρηθῆναι
judged about these things. But Paul having appealed to be kept

846 1519 3588 3588 4575 1233 2753 5083
αὐτὸν εἰς τὴν τοῦ Σεβαστοῦ διάγνωσιν, ἐκέλευσα τηρεῖσθαι
him to the of Augustine examination, I commanded to be kept

846 2193 3757 3992 846 4314 2541 67 1161
αὐτὸν, ἕως οὗ πέμψω αὐτὸν πρὸς Καίσαρα. 22 Ἀγρίππας δὲ
him, until I may send him to Caesar. Agrippa And

4314 3588 5347 5346 1014 2532 846 3588 444
πρὸς τὸν Φῆστον ἔφη, Ἐβουλόμην καὶ αὐτὸς τοῦ ἀνθρώπου
to Festus said, I was minded also myself the man

King James Version

and Bernice came unto Caesarea to salute Festus.
14 And when they had been there many days, Festus declared Paul's cause unto the king, saying, There is a certain man left in bonds by Felix:
15 About whom, when I was at Jerusalem, the chief priests and the elders of the Jews informed (me), desiring (to have) judgment against him.
16 To whom I answered, It is not the manner of the Romans to deliver any man to die, before that he which is accused have the accusers face to face, and have licence to answer for himself concerning the crime laid against him.
17 Therefore, when they were come hither, without any delay on the morrow I sat on the judgment seat, and commanded the man to be brought forth.
18 Against whom when the accusers stood up, they brought none accusation of such things as I supposed:
19 But had certain questions against him of their own superstition, and of one Jesus, which was dead, whom Paul affirmed to be alive.
20 And because I doubted of such manner of questions, I asked (him) whether he would go to Jerusalem, and there be judged of these matters.
21 But when Paul had appealed to be reserved unto the hearing of Augustus, I commanded him to be kept till I might send him to Caesar.
22 Then Agrippa said unto Festus, I would also hear the man myself.

Literal Translation | **Acts 25:23** | *King James Version*

And he says, Tomorrow you shall hear him.

191 3588 1161 839 5346 191 846
ἀκοῦσαι. ὁ δὲ Αὔριον, φησίν, ἀκούσῃ αὐτοῦ.
to hear. he And tomorrow, says, you shall hear him.

To morrow, said he, thou shalt hear him.

23 Then on the morrow, Agrippa and Bernice coming with much pomp and entering into the auditorium, with both the chiliarchs and the men of eminence being of the city, and Festus commanding, Paul was led out.

3588 3767 1887 2064 3588 67 2532 3588
23. Τῇ οὖν ἐπαύριον, ἐλθόντος τοῦ Ἀγρίππα καὶ τῆς
on the Then morrow, coming Agrippa and
959 3326 4183 5325 2532 1525 1519 3588
Βερνίκης μετὰ πολλῆς φαντασίας, καὶ εἰσελθόντων εἰς τὸ
Bernice with much pomp, and entering into the
201 4862 5037 3588 5506 2532 435 3588 2596
ἀκροατήριον, σύν τε τοῖς χιλιάρχοις καὶ ἀνδράσι τοῖς κατ'
auditorium, with both the chiliarchs and men the of
1851 5607 3588 4172 2532 2753 3588 5347 71 3588
ἐξοχὴν οὖσι τῆς πόλεως, καὶ κελεύσαντος τοῦ Φήστου, ἤχθη ὁ
eminence being of the city, and having commanded Festus, was brought
3972
Παῦλος.
Paul.

23 And on the morrow, when Agrippa was come, and Bernice, with great pomp, and was entered into the place of hearing, with the chief captains, and principal men of the city, at Festus' commandment Paul was brought forth.

24 And Festus said, King Agrippa, and all those men present with us, you behold this one about whom all the multitude of the Jews pleaded with me, both here and in Jerusalem, crying out that he ought to live no longer.

2532 5346 3588 5347 67 935 2532 3956
24 καί φησιν ὁ Φῆστος, Ἀγρίππα βασιλεῦ, καὶ πάντες
And says Festus, Agrippa King, and all
3588 4840 2254 435 2334 5126 4012 3739 3956 3588
οἱ συμπαρόντες ἡμῖν ἄνδρες, θεωρεῖτε τοῦτον περὶ οὗ πᾶν τὸ
those present with us men, you behold this one about whom all the
4128 3588 2453 1793 3427 1722 5037 2414 2532
πλῆθος τῶν Ἰουδαίων ἐνέτυχόν μοι ἔν τε Ἱεροσολύμοις καὶ
multitude of the Jews pleaded with me in both Jerusalem and
1759 1916 3361 1163 2198 846 3371
ἐνθάδε, ἐπιβοῶντες μὴ δεῖν ζῆν αὐτὸν μηκέτι.
here, crying out not ought to live him no longer.

24 And Festus said, King Agrippa, and all men which are here present with us, ye see this man, about whom all the multitude of the Jews have dealt with me, both at Jerusalem, and (also) here, crying that he ought not to live any longer.

25 But I having perceived nothing he had done worthy of death, also this one himself having appealed to Augustus, I decided to send him;

1473 1161
25 ἐγὼ δὲ
I But
2638 3367 514 2288 846 4238 2532
καταλαβόμενος μηδὲν ἄξιον θανάτου αὐτὸν πεπραχέναι, καὶ
having perceived nothing worthy of death he had done, also
846 1161 5127 1941 3588 4575 2919 3992
αὐτοῦ δὲ τούτου ἐπικαλεσαμένου τὸν Σεβαστόν, ἔκρινα πέμπειν
himself but this one having appealed to Augustus, I decided to send
846
αὐτόν.
him.

25 But when I found that he had committed nothing worthy of death, and that he himself hath appealed to Augustus, I have determined to send him.

26 about whom I have nothing certain to write to (my) lord. Because of this I brought him before you, and most of all before you, king Agrippa, so as the examination having occurred, I may have somewhat to write.

4012 3739 804 5100 1125 3588 2962 3756 2192 1352
26 περὶ οὗ ἀσφαλές τι γράψαι τῷ κυρίῳ οὐκ ἔχω. διὸ
About whom certain anything to write to the lord not I have. So
4254 846 1909 5216 2532 3122 1909 4675 935
προήγαγον αὐτὸν ἐφ' ὑμῶν, καὶ μάλιστα ἐπὶ σοῦ, βασιλεῦ
I brought forth him before you, and most before you, King
67 3704 3588 351 1096 2192 5100 1125
Ἀγρίππα, ὅπως τῆς ἀνακρίσεως γενομένης σχῶ τι γράψαι.
Agrippa, so that the examination having been I may have what I may write.

26 Of whom I have no certain thing to write unto my lord. Wherefore I have brought him forth before you, and specially before thee, O king Agrippa, that, after examination had, I might have somewhat to write.

27 For it seems unreasonable to me to send a prisoner, and not also to signify the charges against him.

249 1063 3427 1380 3992 1198 3361 2532 3588 2596
27 ἄλογον γάρ μοι δοκεῖ, πέμποντα δέσμιον, μὴ καὶ τὰς κατ'
unreasonable For to me it seems, sending a prisoner, not also the against
846 156 4591
αὐτοῦ αἰτίας σημᾶναι.
him charges to signify.

27 For it seemeth to me unreasonable to send a prisoner, and not withal to signify the crimes (laid) against him.

Acts 26

1. And Agrippa said to Paul, It is allowed for you yourself to speak. Then Paul made a defense, stretching out the hands:

67 1161 4314 3588 3972 5346 2010 4671
1. Ἀγρίππας δὲ πρὸς τὸν Παῦλον ἔφη, Ἐπιτρέπεταί σοι
Agrippa And to Paul said, It is allowed you
5228 4572 3004 5119 3588 3972 626 1614
ὑπὲρ σεαυτοῦ λέγειν. τότε ὁ Παῦλος ἀπελογεῖτο, ἐκτείνας
for yourself to speak. Then Paul made a defense, stretching
3588 5495
τὴν χεῖρα,
the hands,

1. Then Agrippa said unto Paul, Thou art permitted to speak for thyself. Then Paul stretched forth the hand, and answered for himself:

2. Concerning all of which I am accused by Jews, King

4012 3956 3739 1458 5259 2453 935
2 Περὶ πάντων ὧν ἐγκαλοῦμαι ὑπὸ Ἰουδαίων, βασιλεῦ
Concerning all things of which I am accused by Jews, King

2. I think myself happy, king

Literal Translation | **Acts 26:3** | **King James Version**

Agrippa, I count myself blessed being about to make defense before you today,
3 you being most of all expert, knowing of all the customs and questions also among the Jews. Because of this, I beg you patiently to hear me.
4 Indeed, then, all the Jews know my way of life from youth, from (the) beginning having been in my nation in Jerusalem,
5 who before knew me from the first, if they will to testify, that according to the most exact sect of our religion, I lived a Pharisee.
6 And now on hope of the promise having been made by God to the fathers, I stand being judged;
7 to which our twelve tribes hope to arrive, worshiping in earnestness night and day, concerning which hope I am accused by the Jews, king Agrippa.
8 Why is it judged unbelievable by you if God raises (the) dead?
9. Indeed, I then thought to myself that I ought to do many things contrary to the name of Jesus the Nazarene.
10 Which I also did in Jerusalem, I also shut up many of the saints in prisons, having received authority from the chief priests; and they being put to death, I cast a vote.
11 And often punishing them through all the synagogues, I compelled (them) to blaspheme. And being exceedingly furious against them, I even persecuted as far as the outside cities.
12. In which also having traveled

67 2233 1683 3107 3195 626
Ἀγρίππα, ἥγημαι ἐμαυτὸν μακάριον μέλλων ἀπολογεῖσθαι
Agrippa I count myself blessed being about to make defense

1909 4675 4594 3122 1109 5607 4571 1492 3956
ἐπὶ σοῦ σήμερον· 3 μάλιστα γνώστην ὄντα σε εἰδὼς πάντων
before you today; most of all expert being you knowing of all

3588 2596 2453 1485 5037 2532 2213 1352 1189 4675
τῶν κατὰ Ἰουδαίους ἐθῶν τε καὶ ζητημάτων· διὸ δέομαί σου,
the among Jews customs also and questions; therefore I beg you,

3116 191 3450 3588 3303 3767 981 3450 3588 1537
μακροθύμως ἀκοῦσαί μου. 4 τὴν μὲν οὖν βίωσίν μου τὴν ἐκ
patiently to hear me. the indeed Then way of life of me from

3503 3588 575 746 1096 1722 3588 1484 3450 1722
νεότητος τὴν ἀπ' ἀρχῆς γενομένην ἐν τῷ ἔθνει μου ἐν
youth from the beginning having been in the nation of me in

2414 2467 3956 3588 2453 4267
Ἱεροσολύμοις, ἴσασι πάντες οἱ Ἰουδαῖοι, 5 προγινώσκοντές
Jerusalem, know all the Jews, before knowing

3165 509 1437 2309 3140 3754 2596 3588 196
με ἄνωθεν, ἐὰν θέλωσι μαρτυρεῖν, ὅτι κατὰ τὴν ἀκριβεστά-
me from the first, if they will to testify, that according to the most exact

3588 139 3588 2251 2356 2198 5330 2532
την αἵρεσιν τῆς ἡμετέρας θρησκείας ἔζησα Φαρισαῖος. 6 καὶ
sect of our religion I lived a Pharisee. And

3568 1909 1680 3588 4314 3588 3962 1860 1096
νῦν ἐπ' ἐλπίδι τῆς πρὸς τοὺς πατέρας ἐπαγγελίας γενομένης
now on hope of the to the fathers promise having been

5259 3588 2316 2476 2919 1519 3739 3588 1429
ὑπὸ τοῦ Θεοῦ ἕστηκα κρινόμενος, 7 εἰς ἣν τὸ δωδεκάφυλον
by God I stand being judged, to which the twelve tribes

2257 1722 1616 3571 2532 2250 3000 1679 2658
ἡμῶν ἐν ἐκτενείᾳ νύκτα καὶ ἡμέραν λατρεῦον ἐλπίζει καταν-
of us in earnestness night and day worshiping hope to

4012 3739 1680 1458 935 67 5259
τῆσαι· περὶ ἧς ἐλπίδος ἐγκαλοῦμαι, βασιλεῦ Ἀγρίππα, ὑπὸ
arrive; concerning which hope I am accused, king Agrippa, by

3588 2453 5101 571 2919 3844 5213 1487 3588 2316
τῶν Ἰουδαίων. 8 τί ἄπιστον κρίνεται παρ' ὑμῖν, εἰ ὁ Θεὸς
the Jews. Why unbelievable is it judged by you if God

3498 1453 1473 3303 3767 1380 1683 4314 3588 3686
νεκροὺς ἐγείρει; 9 ἐγὼ μὲν οὖν ἔδοξα ἐμαυτῷ πρὸς τὸ ὄνομα
(the) dead raises? I indeed then thought to myself to the name

2424 3588 3480 1163 4183 1727 4238 3739 2532
Ἰησοῦ τοῦ Ναζωραίου δεῖν πολλὰ ἐναντία πρᾶξαι· 10 ὃ καὶ
of Jesus the Nazarene ought many things contrary to do; which also

4160 1722 2414 2532 4183 3588 40 1473 5438
ἐποίησα ἐν Ἱεροσολύμοις, καὶ πολλούς τῶν ἁγίων ἐγὼ φυλα-
I did in Jerusalem, and many of the saints I in

2623 3588 3844 3588 749 1849 2983
καῖς κατέκλεισα, τὴν παρὰ τῶν ἀρχιερέων ἐξουσίαν λαβών,
prison shut up, the from the chief priests authority receiving.

337 5037 846 2702 5586 2532 2596 3956
ἀναιρουμένων τε αὐτῶν κατήνεγκα ψῆφον. 11 καὶ κατὰ πάσας
being put to death And them I cast a vote. And through all

3588 4864 4178 5097 846 315
τὰς συναγωγὰς πολλάκις τιμωρῶν αὐτούς, ἠνάγκαζον
the synagogues often punishing them, I compelled

987 4057 5037 1693 846 1377
βλασφημεῖν· περισσῶς τε ἐμμαινόμενος αὐτοῖς, ἐδίωκον
to blaspheme. exceedingly and being furious against them, I persecuted

2193 2532 1519 3588 1854 4172 1722/3739/2532 4198
ἕως καὶ εἰς τὰς ἔξω πόλεις. 12 ἐν οἷς καὶ πορευόμενος
until even to the outside cities. In which also having traveled

Agrippa, because I shall answer for myself this day before thee touching all the things whereof I am accused of the Jews:
3 Especially (because I know) thee to be expert in all customs and questions which are among the Jews: wherefore I beseech thee to hear me patiently.
4 My manner of life from my youth, which was at the first among mine own nation at Jerusalem, know all the Jews;
5 Which knew me from the beginning, if they would testify, that after the most straitest sect of our religion I lived a Pharisee.
6 And now I stand and am judged for the hope of the promise made of God unto our fathers:
7 Unto which (promise) our twelve tribes, instantly serving (God) day and night, hope to come. For which hope's sake, king Agrippa, I am accused of the Jews.
8 Why should it be thought a thing incredible with you, that God should raise the dead?
9 I verily thought with myself, that I ought to do many things contrary to the name of Jesus of Nazareth.
10 Which thing I also did in Jerusalem: and many of the saints did I shut up in prison, having received authority from the chief priests; and when they were put to death, I gave my voice against (them).
11 And I punished them oft in every synagogue, and compelled (them) to blaspheme; and being exceedingly mad against them, I persecuted (them) even unto strange cities.
12. Whereupon as I went to

Acts 26:13

Literal Translation

to Damascus with authority and decision-power from the chief priests,

13 at midday along the highway, (O) king, I and those with me saw a light from heaven shining around me above the brightness of the sun.

14 And all of us falling to the ground, I heard a voice speaking to me, and saying in the Hebrew dialect, Saul, Saul why do you persecute Me? (It is) hard for you to kick against the goads.

15 And I said, Who are you, Sir? And He said, I am Jesus whom you persecute;

16 but rise up and stand on your feet, for (it is) for this reason I appeared to you, to appoint you a servant and a witness both of what you saw, and in what I shall appear to you,

17 delivering you from the people and the nations, to whom I now send you,

18 to open their eyes, and to turn (them) from darkness to light, and (from) the authority of Satan to God, in order that they (may) receive remission of sins, and an inheritance among those being sanctified by faith into Me.

19. From which, king Agrippa, I was not disobedient to the heavenly vision,

20 but to those first in Damascus, and Jerusalem, and to all the region of Judea, and to the nations, I proclaimed (the command) to repent and to turn to God, practicing works worthy of repentance.

21 Because of these things, having seized (me) in

1519 3588 1154 3326 1849 2532 2011 3588 3844 3588
εἰς τὴν Δαμασκὸν μετ' ἐξουσίας καὶ ἐπιτροπῆς τῆς παρὰ τῶν
to Damascus with authority and decision-power from the

749 2250 3319 2596 3588 3598 1492 935
ἀρχιερέων, 13 ἡμέρας μέσης, κατὰ τὴν ὁδὸν εἶδον, βασιλεῦ,
chief priests, at day mid- along the way I saw, king,

3771 5228 3588 2987 3588 2246 4034
οὐρανόθεν ὑπὲρ τὴν λαμπρότητα τοῦ ἡλίου, περιλάμψαν
from Heaven above the brightness of the sun, shining around

3165 5457 2532 3588 4862 1698 4198 3956 1161 2667
με φῶς καὶ τοὺς σὺν ἐμοὶ πορευομένους. 14 πάντων τε κατα-
me a light also those with me traveling. all And having

2257 1519 3588 1093 191 5456 2980 4314
πεσόντων ἡμῶν εἰς τὴν γῆν, ἤκουσα φωνὴν λαλοῦσαν πρός
fallen down us to the earth, I heard a voice speaking to

3165 2532 3004 3588 1446 1258 4549 4549 5101
με καὶ λεγουσαν τῇ Ἑβραΐδι διαλέκτῳ, Σαούλ, Σαούλ, τί
me and saying in the Hebrew dialect, Saul, Saul, why

3165 1377 4642 4671 4314 2759 2979 1473 1161
με διώκεις; σκληρόν σοι πρὸς κέντρα λακτίζειν. 15 ἐγὼ δὲ
Me persecute you? (it is) hard for you against the goads to kick. I And

2036 5101 1488 2962 3588 1161 2036 1473 1510 2424 3739 4771
εἶπον, Τίς εἶ, Κύριε; ὁ δὲ εἶπεν, Ἐγώ εἰμι Ἰησοῦς ὃν σὺ
said, Who are you, Sir? And He said, I am Jesus whom you

1377 235 450 2532 2476 1909 3588 4228 4675 1519
διώκεις 16 ἀλλὰ ἀνάστηθι, καὶ στῆθι ἐπὶ τοὺς πόδας σου· εἰς
persecute, But rise up, and stand on the feet of you; for

5124 1063 3700 4671 4400 4571 5257 2532
τοῦτο γὰρ ὤφθην σοι, προχειρίσασθαί σε ὑπηρέτην καὶ
this For I appeared to you, to appoint you a servant and

3144 3739 5037 1492 3739 5037 3700 4671 1807
μάρτυρα ὧν τε εἶδες ὧν τε ὀφθήσομαί σοι, 17 ἐξαιρούμενός
a witness of what both you saw in what and I shall appear to you, delivering

4571 1537 3588 2992 2532 3588 1484 1519 3739 3568 4571 649
σε ἐκ τοῦ λαοῦ καὶ τῶν ἐθνῶν, εἰς οὓς νῦν σε ἀποστέλλω,
you from the people and the nations, to whom now you I send,

455 3788 846 2532 1994 575 4655
18 ἀνοῖξαι ὀφθαλμοὺς αὐτῶν, καὶ ἐπιστρέψαι ἀπὸ σκότους
to open the eyes of them, and to turn from darkness

1519 5457 2532 3588 1849 3588 4567 1909 3588 2316 3588
εἰς φῶς καὶ τῆς ἐξουσίας τοῦ Σατανᾶ ἐπὶ τὸν Θεόν, τοῦ
to light and the authority of Satan to God,

2983 846 859 266 2532 2819 1722 3588 37
λαβεῖν αὐτοὺς ἄφεσιν ἁμαρτιῶν, καὶ κλῆρον ἐν τοῖς ἡγια-
to receive them remission of sins, and an inheritance among those being

4102 3588 1519 1691 3606 935 67 3756
σμένοις πίστει τῇ εἰς ἐμέ. 19 ὅθεν, βασιλεῦ Ἀγρίππα, οὐκ
sanctified by faith into Me. From which, king Agrippa, not

1096 545 3588 3770 3701 235 3588 1722
ἐγενόμην ἀπειθὴς τῇ οὐρανίῳ ὀπτασίᾳ· 20 ἀλλὰ τοῖς ἐν
I was disobedient to the heavenly vision; but to those in

1154 4412 2532 2414 1519 3956 5037 3588
Δαμασκῷ πρῶτόν καὶ Ἱεροσολύμοις, εἰς πᾶσάν τε τὴν
Damascus firstly, and (in) Jerusalem, to all and the

5561 3588 2449 2532 3588 1484 518 3340
χώραν τῆς Ἰουδαίας, καὶ τοῖς ἔθνεσιν, ἀπήγγελλον μετανοεῖν,
region of Judea, and to the nations, I proclaimed to repent,

2532 1994 1909 3588 2316 514 3588 3341 2041
καὶ ἐπιστρέφειν ἐπὶ τὸν Θεόν, ἄξια τῆς μετανοίας ἔργα
and to turn to God, worthy of repentance works

4238 1752 5130 3165 3588 2453 4815 1722
πράσσοντας. 21 ἕνεκα τούτων με οἱ Ἰουδαῖοι συλλαβόμενοι ἐν
practicing. Because of these things me the Jews having seized in

King James Version

Damascus with authority and commission from the chief priests,

13 At midday, O king, I saw in the way a light from heaven, above the brightness of the sun, shining round about me and them which journeyed with me.

14 And when we were all fallen to the earth, I heard a voice speaking unto me, and saying in the Hebrew tongue, Saul, Saul, why persecutest thou me? (it is) hard for thee to kick against the pricks.

15 And I said, Who art thou, Lord? And he said, I am Jesus whom thou persecutest.

16 But rise, and stand upon thy feet: for I have appeared unto thee for this purpose, to make thee a minister and a witness both of these things which thou hast seen, and of those things in the which I will appear unto thee;

17 Delivering thee from the people, and (from) the Gentiles, unto whom now I send thee,

18 To open their eyes, (and) to turn (them) from darkness to light, and (from) the power of Satan unto God, that they may receive forgiveness of sins, and inheritance among them which are sanctified by faith that is in me.

19 Whereupon, O king Agrippa, I was not disobedient unto the heavenly vision:

20 But shewed first unto them of Damascus, and at Jerusalem, and throughout all the coasts of Judaea, and (then) to the Gentiles, that they should repent and turn to God, and do works meet for repentance.

21 For these causes the Jews caught me in

Literal Translation | **Acts 26:22** | ***King James Version***

the temple, the Jews tried to kill (me).
22 Then obtaining help from God, I stand until this day having witnessed both to small and to great, saying nothing outside than what both the prophets and Moses said was going to happen:
23 if the Christ (was) liable to suffer, whether by a resurrection of (the) dead He was first going to proclaim light to the people and to the nations.

3588 2411 3987 1315 1947 3767 5177
τῷ ἱερῷ ἐπειρῶντο διαχειρίσασθαι. 22 ἐπικουρίας οὖν τυχὼν
the temple tried to kill (me). help Then obtaining
3588 3844 3588 2316 891 3588 2250 3778 2476
τῆς παρὰ τοῦ Θεοῦ, ἄχρι τῆς ἡμέρας ταύτης ἕστηκα
from God, until day this I stand
3140 3398 5037 2532 3173 3762 1622 3004 3739
μαρτυρούμενος μικρῷ τε καὶ μεγάλῳ, οὐδὲν ἐκτὸς λέγων ὧν
having witnessed to small and also to great, nothing outside of saying what
5037 3588 4396 2980 3195 1096 2532 3475 1487
τε οἱ προφῆται ἐλάλησαν μελλόντων γίνεσθαι καὶ Μωσῆς, 23 εἰ
both the prophets said was going to happen and Moses, whether
3805 3588 5547 1487 4413 1537 386 3498 5457
παθητὸς ὁ Χριστός, εἰ πρῶτος ἐξ ἀναστάσεως νεκρῶν φῶς
liable to suffer the Christ, whether first by a resurrection of (the) dead a light
3195 2605 3588 2992 2532 3588 1484
μέλλει καταγγέλλειν τῷ λαῷ καὶ τοῖς ἔθνεσι.
He is going to proclaim to the people and to the nations.

the temple, and went about to kill (me).
22 Having therefore obtained help of God, I continue unto this day, witnessing both to small and great, saying none other things than those which the prophets and Moses did say should come:
23 That Christ should suffer, (and) that he should be the first that should rise from the dead, and should shew light unto the people, and to the Gentiles.

24. And he having defended himself (with) these things, Festus said with a loud voice, Paul, You rave! Your many letters turn (you) into madness.
25 But he said, Not to madness, most excellent Festus, but I speak words of truth and sanity.
26 For the king understands concerning these things, to whom I speak, even being bold of speech. For I am persuaded not any of these things are hidden (from) him, nothing. For (the) doing of this is not in a corner.
27 King Agrippa, do you believe the Prophets? I know that you believe.
28 And Agrippa said to Paul, Do you persuade me to become a Christian in (but) a little?
29 And Paul said, I would pray to God, both in a little and in much, not only you, but also these hearing me today to become as I also am, except for these bonds.

5023 1161 846 626 3588 5347 3173 3588
24. Ταῦτα δὲ αὐτοῦ ἀπολογουμένου, ὁ Φῆστος μεγάλῃ τῇ
these things And him having defended himself, Festus great with the
5456 5346 3105 3972 3588 4183 4571 1121 1519 3130
φωνῇ ἔφη, Μαίνῃ, Παῦλε· τὰ πολλά σε γράμματα εἰς μανίαν
voice says, You rave, Paul; the many of you letters to madness
4062 3588 1161 3756 3105 5346 2903 5347 235
περιτρέπει. 25 ὁ δέ, Οὐ μαίνομαι, φησί, κράτιστε Φῆστε, ἀλλ'
turn (you). But, not to rave, he says, most excellent Festus, but
225 2532 4997 4487 669 1987
ἀληθείας καὶ σωφροσύνης ῥήματα ἀποφθέγγομαι. 26 ἐπίσταται
of truth and sanity words I declare. understands
1063 4012 5130 3588 935 4314 3739 2532 3955
γὰρ περὶ τούτων ὁ βασιλεύς, πρὸς ὃν καὶ παρρησιαζόμενος
For concerning these things the king, to whom even being bold of speech
2980 2990 1063 846 5100 5130 3756 3982 3762
λαλῶ· λανθάνειν γὰρ αὐτὸν τι τούτων οὐ πείθομαι οὐδέν·
I speak; to be hidden for from him any of these things not I am persuaded, nothing;
3756 1063 2076 1722 1137 4238 5124 4100
οὐ γάρ ἐστιν ἐν γωνίᾳ πεπραγμένον τοῦτο. 27 πιστεύεις,
not for is in a corner having been done (all) this. Do you believe,
935 67 3588 4396 1492 3754 4100 3588 1161
βασιλεῦ Ἀγρίππα, τοῖς προφήταις; οἶδα ὅτι πιστεύεις. 28 ὁ δὲ
king Agrippa, the Prophets? I know that you believe. And
67 4314 3588 3972 5346 1722 3641 3165 3982
Ἀγρίππας πρὸς τὸν Παῦλον ἔφη, Ἐν ὀλίγῳ με πείθεις
Agrippa to Paul said, In a little me you persuade
5546 1096 3588 1161 3972 2036 2172 302 3588
Χριστιανὸν γενέσθαι. 29 ὁ δὲ Παῦλος εἶπεν, Εὐξαίμην ἂν τῷ
a Christian to become. But Paul said, I would pray may
2316 2532 1722 3641 2532 1722 4183 3756 3440 4571 235 2532
Θεῷ, καὶ ἐν ὀλίγῳ καὶ ἐν πολλῷ οὐ μόνον σε, ἀλλὰ καὶ
God both in a little and in much not only you, but also
3956 3588 191 3450 4594 1096 5108
πάντας τοὺς ἀκούοντάς μου σήμερον, γενέσθαι τοιούτους
all those hearing me today, to become such
3697 2504 1510 3924 3588 1199 5130
ὁποῖος κἀγώ εἰμι, παρεκτὸς τῶν δεσμῶν τούτων.
as also I am, except bonds these.

24. And as he thus spake for himself, Festus said with a loud voice, Paul, thou art beside thyself; much learning doth make thee mad.
25 But he said, I am not mad, most noble Festus; but speak forth the words of truth and soberness.
26 For the king knoweth of these things, before whom also I speak freely: for I am persuaded that none of these things are hidden from him; for this thing was not done in a corner.
27 King Agrippa, believest thou the prophets? I know that thou believest.
28 Then Agrippa said unto Paul, Almost thou persuadest me to be a Christian.
29 And Paul said, I would to God, that not only thou, but also all that hear me this day, were both almost, and altogether such as I am, except these bonds.

30. And he saying these things, the king and the governor and Bernice rose up, and the (ones) who had sat with them.
31 And

2532 5023 2036 846 450 3588 935 2532 3588
30. Καὶ ταῦτα εἰπόντος αὐτοῦ, ἀνέστη ὁ βασιλεὺς καὶ ὁ
And these things having said he, rose up the king and the
2232 2228 5037 959 2532 3588 4775 846 2532
ἡγεμών, ἥ τε Βερνίκη, καὶ οἱ συγκαθήμενοι αὐτοῖς· 31 καὶ
governor, and Bernice, and those having sat with them; and

30. And when he had thus spoken, the king rose up, and the governor, and Bernice, and they that sat with them:
31 And

Literal Translation

having gone aside, they spoke to one another saying, This man does nothing worthy of death or of bonds.

32 And Agrippa said to Festus, This man was able to have been let go, if he had not appealed to Caesar.

Acts 26:32

402 2980 4314 240 3004 3754
ἀναχωρήσαντες ἐλάλουν πρὸς ἀλλήλους, λέγοντες ὅτι
having gone aside spoke to one another, saying,

3762 2288 514 2228 1199 4238 3588 444 3778
Οὐδὲν θανάτου ἄξιον ἢ δεσμῶν πράσσει ὁ ἄνθρωπος οὗτος.
Nothing of death worthy or of bonds does man this.

67 1161 3588 5347 5346 630 1410 3588
32 Ἀγρίππας δὲ τῷ Φήστῳ ἔφη, Ἀπολελύσθαι ἐδύνατο ὁ
Agrippa And to Festus said, To have been released was able

444 3778 1487 3361 1941 2541
ἄνθρωπος οὗτος, εἰ μὴ ἐπεκέκλητο Καίσαρα.
man this, if not he had appealed to Caesar.

King James Version

when they were gone aside, they talked between themselves, saying, This man doeth nothing worthy of death or of bonds.

32 Then said Agrippa unto Festus, This man might have been set at liberty, if he had not appealed unto Caesar.

Acts 27

1. And when it was decided for us to sail away to Italy, they delivered up both Paul and certain other prisoners to a centurion named Julius, of a cohort, (the) Augustan.
2 And embarking on a ship of Adramyttium being about to sail alongside Asian places, we set sail, Aristarchus a Macedonian of Thessalonica being with us.

3 And on the (next day) we landed at Sidon. And treating Paul kindly, Julius allowed (him) to go to (his) friends to obtain care.

4 And setting sail from there, we sailed close to Cyprus, because of the winds being contrary.

5 And sailing over the sea against Cilicia and Pamphylia, we came to Myra of Lycia.
6 And the centurion finding there an Alexandrian ship sailing to Italy, he put us into it.

7 And in many days, sailing slowly and with difficulty having come against Cnidus, the wind not allowing us, we sailed under the (lee) of Crete against Salmone.

8 And having sailed along it with difficulty, we came

Acts 27

5613 1161 2919 3588 636 2248 1519 3588 2482 3860
1. Ὡς δὲ ἐκρίθη τοῦ ἀποπλεῖν ἡμᾶς εἰς τὴν Ἰταλίαν, παρεδί-
when And it was decided to sail away us to Italy, they deliv-

3588 5037 3972 2532 5100 2087 1202 1543
δουν τόν τε Παῦλον καί τινας ἑτέρους δεσμώτας ἑκατοντάρχῃ,
ered both Paul and some other prisoners to a centurion,

3686 2457 4686 4575 1910 1161 4143
ὀνόματι Ἰουλίῳ, σπείρης Σεβαστῆς. 2 ἐπιβάντες δὲ πλοίῳ
by name Julius, of a cohort Augustan. embarking in And a ship

98 3195 4126 3588 2596 3588 773 5117
Ἀδραμυττηνῷ, μέλλοντες πλεῖν τοὺς κατὰ τὴν Ἀσίαν τόπους,
at Adramyttium, being about to sail alongside Asia places,

321 5607 4862 2254 708 3110
ἀνήχθημεν, ὄντος σὺν ἡμῖν Ἀριστάρχου Μακεδόνος
we set sail, being with us Aristarchus a Macedonian

2331 3588 5037 2087 2609 1519 4605 5364
Θεσσαλονικέως. 3 τῇ τε ἑτέρᾳ κατήχθημεν εἰς Σιδῶνα· φιλαν-
of Thessalonica. on the And next we were landed at Sidon; kindly

5037 3588 2457 3588 3972 5530 2010 4314
θρώπως τε ὁ Ἰούλιος τῷ Παύλῳ χρησάμενος ἐπέτρεψε πρὸς
and Juluis Paul treating allowed to

3588 5384 4198 1958 5177 2547 321
τοὺς φίλους πορευθέντα ἐπιμελείας τυχεῖν. 4 κἀκεῖθεν ἀναχθέν-
the friends going care to obtain. And from there setting

5284 3588 2954 1223 3588 3588 417 1511
τες ὑπεπλεύσαμεν τὴν Κύπρον, διὰ τὸ τοὺς ἀνέμους εἶναι
sail we sailed under the (lee) of Cyprus, because of the winds being

1727 3588 5037 3989 3588 2596 3588 2791 2532 3828
ἐναντίους. 5 τό τε πέλαγος τὸ κατὰ τὴν Κιλικίαν καὶ Παμφυ-
contrary. the And sea against Cilicia and Pamphy-

1277 2718 1519 3460 3588 3073 2546
λίαν διαπλεύσαντες, κατήλθομεν εἰς Μύρα τῆς Λυκίας. 6 κἀκεῖ
lia sailing through we came down to Myra of Lysia. And there

2147 3588 1543 4143 222 4126 1519 3588
εὑρὼν ὁ ἑκατόνταρχος πλοῖον Ἀλεξανδρῖνον πλέον εἰς τὴν
having found the centurion ship an Alexandrian sailing to

2482 1688 2248 1519 846 1722 2425 1161 2250
Ἰταλίαν ἐνεβίβασεν ἡμᾶς εἰς αὐτό. 7 ἐν ἱκαναῖς δὲ ἡμέραις
Italy, he put us into it. in many And days

1020 2532 3433 1096 2596 3588 2834 3361
βραδυπλοοῦντες, καὶ μόλις γενόμενοι κατὰ τὴν Κνίδον, μὴ
sailing slowly, and with difficulty having come against Cnidus, not

4330 2248 3588 417 5284 3588 2914
προσεῶντος ἡμᾶς τοῦ ἀνέμου, ὑπεπλεύσαμεν τὴν Κρήτην
allowing us the wind, we sailed under the (lee) of Crete

2596 4534 3433 5037 3881 846 2064
κατὰ Σαλμώνην· 8 μόλις τε παραλεγόμενοι αὐτὴν ἤλθομεν
against Salmone. with difficulty And having sailed along it we came

Acts 27

1. And when it was determined that we should sail into Italy, they delivered Paul and certain other prisoners unto (one) named Julius, a centurion of Augustus' band.
2 And entering into a ship of Adramyttium, we launched, meaning to sail by the coasts of Asia; (one) Aristarchus, a Macedonian of Thessalonica, being with us.

3 And the next (day) we touched at Sidon. And Julius courteously entreated Paul, and gave (him) liberty to go unto his friends to refresh himself.
4 And when we had launched from thence, we sailed under Cyprus, because the winds were contrary.

5 And when we had sailed over the sea of Cilicia and Pamphylia, we came to Myra, (a city) of Lycia.
6 And there the centurion found a ship of Alexandria sailing into Italy; and he put us therein.
7 And when we had sailed slowly many days, and scarce were come over against Cnidus, the wind not suffering us, we sailed under Crete, over against Salmone;

8 And, hardly passing it, came

Literal Translation | **Acts 27:9** | **King James Version**

to a certain place being called Fair Havens, near to which was a city, Lasea.

9 And much time having passed, and the voyage already being dangerous, because the Fast now had gone by, Paul advised (them),
10 saying, Men, I see that the voyage is about to be with injury and much loss, not only of the cargo and of the ship, but also of our lives.

11 But the centurion was rather persuaded by the helmsman and the ship-owner, than by the things spoken by Paul.

12 And the port not being fit for wintering, the most gave counsel to set sail from there, if somehow they may be able to pass the winter, having arrived at Phoenix, a port of Crete looking toward (the) southwest and toward (the) northwest.
13 And a south wind blowing gently, thinking to have gained the purpose, raising (anchor) they sailed along close by Crete.

14. And not much after, a typhonic wind having been called Euroclydon beat down (on) it.

15 And the ship being seized, and not being able to face against the wind, giving up we were borne along.
16 But running under an islet being called Clauda, we were hardly able to get mastery of the boat;

17 which taking, they used helps, undergirding the ship. And fearing

---

1519 5117 5100 2564 2568 2568 3739 1451 2258
εἰς τόπον τινὰ καλούμενον Καλοὺς Λιμένας, ᾧ ἐγγὺς ἦν
to place a certain being called Fair Havens, to which near was
4172 2996
πόλις Λασαία.
a city Lasea.

2425 1161 5550 1230 2532 5607 2235 2000
9. Ἱκανοῦ δὲ χρόνου διαγενομένου, καὶ ὄντος ἤδη ἐπισφα-
much And time having passed, and being now dangerous
3588 4144 1223 3588 2532 3588 3521 2235 3928
λοῦς τοῦ πλοός, διὰ τὸ καὶ τὴν νηστείαν ἤδη παρεληλυθέναι,
the voyage, because also the Fast now to have gone by,
3867 3588 3972 3004 846 435 2334 3754 3326
παρῄνει ὁ Παῦλος 10 λέγων αὐτοῖς, Ἄνδρες, θεωρῶ ὅτι μετὰ
advised Paul saying to them, Men, I perceive that with
5196 2532 4183 2209 3756 3440 3588 5414 2532 3588
ὕβρεως καὶ πολλῆς ζημίας, οὐ μόνον τοῦ φόρτου καὶ τοῦ
injury and much loss, not only the cargo and the
4143 235 2532 3588 5590 2257 3195 1510 3588 4144
πλοίου ἀλλὰ καὶ τῶν ψυχῶν ἡμῶν, μέλλειν ἔσεσθαι τὸν πλοῦν.
ship but also the lives of us, to be about to be the voyage.

3588 1161 1543 3588 2942 2532 3588 3490
11 ὁ δὲ ἑκατοντάρχος τῷ κυβερνήτῃ καὶ τῷ ναυκλήρῳ
the But centurion by the steersman and the ship-owner
3982 3123 2228 3588 5259 3588 3972 3004
ἐπείθετο μᾶλλον ἢ τοῖς ὑπὸ τοῦ Παύλου λεγομένοις.
was persuaded rather than the by Paul things said.

428 1161 3588 3040 5225 4314 3915
12 ἀνευθέτου δὲ τοῦ λιμένος ὑπάρχοντος πρὸς παραχειμασίαν,
not fit And the port being to wintering,
3588 4119 5087 1012 321 2547 1513 1410
οἱ πλείους ἔθεντο βουλὴν ἀναχθῆναι κἀκεῖθεν, εἴπως δύ-
the most gave counsel to set sail from there, if somehow they
2658 1519 5405 3914 3040 3588
ναιντο καταντήσαντες εἰς Φοίνικα παραχειμάσαι, λιμένα τῆς
may be able having arrived at Phoenice to pass the winter, a port
2914 991 2596 3047 2532 2596 5566 5285
Κρήτης βλέποντα κατὰ λίβα καὶ κατὰ χῶρον. 13 ὑποπνεύ-
of Crete looking toward southwest and toward northwest, blowing
1161 3558 1380 3588 4286 2902
σαντος δὲ νότου δόξαντες τῆς προθέσεως κεκρατηκέναι,
gently and a south wind, thinking the purpose to have gained,
142 788 3881 3588 2914 3326 3756 4183 1161
ἄραντες ᾆσσον παρελέγοντο τὴν Κρήτην. 14 μετ᾽ οὐ πολὺ δὲ
raising (anchor) close they sailed by Crete. after not much And
906 2596 846 417 5189 3588 2564 2148
ἔβαλε κατ᾽ αὐτῆς ἄνεμος τυφωνικὸς ὁ καλούμενος Εὐροκλύ-
beat down it wind a typhonic having been called Euroclydon;
4884 1161 3588 4143 2532 3361 1410
δων· 15 συναρπασθέντος δὲ τοῦ πλοίου, καὶ μὴ δυναμένου
being seized and the ship, and not being able
503 3588 417 1929 5342 3519 11615100
ἀντοφθαλμεῖν τῷ ἀνέμῳ, ἐπιδόντες ἐφερόμεθα. 16 νησίον δέ τι
to face the wind, giving up we were borne along. islet But an
5295 2564 2802 3433 2480 4031
ὑποδραμόντες καλούμενον Κλαύδην πόλις ἰσχύσαμεν περι-
running under being called Clauda hardly we had strength
1096 3588 4627 3739 142 996
κρατεῖς γενέσθαι τῆς σκάφης· 17 ἣν ἄραντες, βοηθείαις
mastery to get of the boat; which taking helps
5530 5269 3588 4143 5399 5037 3361 1519 3588
ἐχρῶντο, ὑποζωννύντες τὸ πλοῖον· φοβούμενοί τε μὴ εἰς τὴν
they used, undergirding the ship; fearing and not into

---

unto a place which is called The fair havens; nigh whereunto was the city (of) Lasea.

9 Now when much time was spent, and when sailing was now dangerous, because the fast was now already past, Paul admonished (them),
10 And said unto them, Sirs, I perceive that this voyage will be with hurt and much damage, not only of the lading and ship, but also of our lives.

11 Nevertheless the centurion believed the master and the owner of the ship, more than those things which were spoken by Paul.

12. And because the haven was not commodious to winter in, the more part advised to depart thence also, if by any means they might attain to Phenice, (and there) to winter; (which is) an haven of Crete, and lieth toward the south west and north west.
13 And when the south wind blew softly, supposing that they had obtained (their) purpose, loosing (thence), they sailed close by Crete.
14 But not long after there arose against it a tempestuous wind, called Euroclydon.

15 And when the ship was caught, and could not bear up into the wind, we let (her) drive.
16 And running under a certain island which is called Clauda, we had much work to come by the boat:

17 Which when they had taken up, they used helps, undergirding the ship; and, fearing

Literal Translation **Acts 27:18** *King James Version*

Syrtis they fall, lowering the tackle, so they were borne along.
18 But we having been exceedingly tempest-tossed, they made a casting on the next (day).
19 And on the third (day) they threw (out) the ship's tackle with their hands.
20 And neither sun nor stars appearing over many days, and no small tempest pressing hard, now all hope (for) us to be saved was taken away.
21 And there being much fasting, then standing up in their midst, Paul said, Truly, O men, being obedient to me (you) ought not to have set sail from Crete, and to have come by this injury and loss.
22 And now I exhort you to be cheered, for there will be no casting away of life from among you, but of the ship.

23 For this night stood by me an angel of God, whose I am, and whom I serve,
24 saying, Do not fear, Paul, You must stand before Caesar. And, behold! God has granted to you all those sailing with you.

25 So be cheered, men, for I believe God, that it will be so according to the way it was spoken to me.
26 But we must fall onto a certain island.

27. And as (the) fourteenth night came, we being carried about in the Adriatic Sea, toward (the) middle of the night the sailors supposed (us to) come near some country.
28 And sounding, they found twenty fathoms; and having moved a little and sounding again, they found fifteen fathoms.

29 And fearing lest onto

4950 1601 5465 3588 4632 3779 5342
σύρτιν ἐκπέσωσι, χαλάσαντες τὸ σκεῦος, οὕτως ἐφέροντο.
Syrtis they fall, lowering the tackle, thus they were borne.

4971 1161 5492 2257 3588 1836 1546 4160
18 σφοδρῶς δὲ χειμαζομένων ἡμῶν, τῇ ἑξῆς ἐκβολὴν ἐποιοῦντο·
exceedingly But being tempest-tossed we, on the next a casting out they made;

2532 3588 5154 849 3588 4631 3588 4143 4496
19 καὶ τῇ τρίτῃ αὐτόχειρες τὴν σκευὴν τοῦ πλοίου ἐρρίψαμεν.
and on the third with (our) hands the tackle of the ship they threw.

3383 1161 2246 3383 798 2014 1909 4119
20 μήτε δὲ ἡλίου μήτε ἄστρων ἐπιφαινόντων ἐπὶ πλείονας
neither And sun nor stars appearing over many

2250 5494 5037 3756 3641 1945 3063 4014
ἡμέρας, χειμῶνός τε οὐκ ὀλίγου ἐπικειμένου, λοιπὸν περιῃρεῖτο
days, tempest and no small pressing hard, now was taken away

3956 1680 3588 4982 2248 4183 1161 776
πᾶσα ἐλπὶς τοῦ σώζεσθαι ἡμᾶς. 21 πολλῆς δὲ ἀσιτίας
all hope to be saved us. much And fasting

5225 5119 2476 3588 3972 1722 3319 846 2036
ὑπαρχούσης, τότε σταθεὶς ὁ Παῦλος ἐν μέσῳ αὐτῶν εἶπεν,
being, then standing Paul in (the) midst of them said,

1163 3303 5599 435 3980 3427 3361 321 575 3588
Ἔδει μέν, ὦ ἄνδρες, πειθαρχήσαντάς μοι μὴ ἀνάγεσθαι ἀπὸ τῆς
(you) ought Truly, O men, having been obedient to me not to have set sail from

2914 2770 5037 3588 5196 3778 2532 3588 2209 2532
Κρήτης, κερδῆσαί τε τὴν ὕβριν ταύτην καὶ τὴν ζημίαν. 22 καὶ
Crete, to come by and injury this and loss. And

3588 3568 3867 5209 2114 580 1063 5590 3762
τὰ νῦν παραινῶ ὑμᾶς εὐθυμεῖν· ἀποβολὴ γὰρ ψυχῆς οὐδεμία
now I exhort you to be cheered; casting away for life no

2071 1537 5216 4133 3588 4143 3936 1063 3427 3588 3571
ἔσται ἐξ ὑμῶν, πλὴν τοῦ πλοίου. 23 παρέστη γάρ μοι τῇ νυκτὶ
will be of you, but of the ship. stood by For me night

3778 32 3588 2316 3739 1510 3739 2532 3000 3004 3361
ταύτῃ ἄγγελος τοῦ Θεοῦ οὗ εἰμι, ᾧ καὶ λατρεύω, 24 λέγων, Μὴ
this an angel of God, whose I am, whom also I serve, saying, Not

5399 3972 2541 4571 1163 3936 2532 2400 5483
φοβοῦ, Παῦλε· Καίσαρί σε δεῖ παραστῆναι· καὶ ἰδού, κεχάρισταί
do fear, Paul; Caesar you must stand before; and behold! has given

4671 3588 2316 3956 3588 4126 3326 4675 1352 2114
σοι ὁ Θεὸς πάντας τοὺς πλέοντας μετὰ σοῦ. 25 διὸ εὐθυμεῖτε
you God all those sailing with you. So be cheered

435 4100 1063 3588 2316 3754 3779 2071 2596 3739 5158
ἄνδρες· πιστεύω γὰρ τῷ Θεῷ ὅτι οὕτως ἔσται καθ' ὃν τρόπον
men; I believe for God that so it will be in the of which way

2980 3427 1519 3520 1161 5100 1163 2248 1601
λελάληταί μοι. 26 εἰς νῆσον δέ τινα δεῖ ἡμᾶς ἐκπεσεῖν.
it was spoken to me. onto island But a certain must we fall off.

5613 1161 5065 3571 1096 1308
27. Ὡς δὲ τεσσαρεσκαιδεκάτη νὺξ ἐγένετο, διαφερομένων
as And (the) fourteenth night came, being carried about

2257 1722 3588 99 2596 3319 3588 3571 5282 3588
ἡμῶν ἐν τῷ Ἀδρίᾳ, κατὰ μέσον τῆς νυκτὸς ὑπενόουν οἱ
we in the Adriatic, toward (the) middle of the night supposed the

3492 4317 5100 846 5561 2532 1001 2147
ναῦται προσάγειν τινὰ αὐτοῖς χώραν· 28 καὶ βολίσαντες εὗρον
sailers to come near some to them country. And sounding they found

3712 1501 1024 1161 1339 2532 3825 1001
ὀργυιὰς εἴκοσι· βραχὺ δὲ διαστήσαντες, καὶ πάλιν βολίσαντες,
fathoms twenty; a little and having moved, also again sounding,

2147 3712 1178 5399 5037 3381 1519
εὗρον ὀργυιὰς δεκαπέντε· 29 φοβούμενοί τε μήπως εἰς
they found fathoms fifteen; fearing and lest onto

lest they should fall into the quicksands, strake sail, and so were driven.
18 And we being exceedingly tossed with a tempest, the next (day) they lightened the ship;
19 And the third (day) we cast out with our own hands the tackling of the ship.
20 And when neither sun nor stars in many days appeared, and no small tempest lay on (us), all hope that we should be saved was then taken away.
21. But after long abstinence Paul stood forth in the midst of them, and said, Sirs, ye should have hearkened unto me, and not have loosed from Crete, and to have gained this harm and loss.

22 And now I exhort you to be of good cheer: for there shall be no loss of (any man's) life among you, but of the ship.

23 For there stood by me this night the angel of God, whose I am, and whom I serve,
24 Saying, Fear not, Paul; thou must be brought before Caesar: and, lo, God hath given thee all them that sail with thee.

25 Wherefore, sirs, be of good cheer: for I believe God, that it shall be even as it was told me.
26 Howbeit we must be cast upon a certain island.

27. But when the fourteenth night was come, as we were driven up and down in Adria, about midnight the shipmen deemed that they drew near to some country;
28 And sounded, and found (it) twenty fathoms: and when they had gone a little further, they sounded again, and found (it) fifteen fathoms.
29 Then fearing lest

Literal Translation

rough places they may fall out, and casting four anchors out of (the) stern, they wished day to come.
30 But the sailors seeking to flee out of the ship, and lowering the boat into the sea, pretending to be about to cast out anchors from (the) prow,

31 Paul said to the centurion, and to the soldiers, If not these remain in the ship, you are not able to be saved.

32 Then the soldiers cut away the ropes of the boat, and let it fall off.
33. And until day was about to come, Paul begged all to partake of food, saying, Today (is the) fourteenth day you continued waiting without food, having taken nothing.

34 Because of this I exhort you to take of food, for this is to your deliverance, for of no one of you a hair of your head will perish.

35 And saying these things, and taking bread, he gave thanks to God before all; and breaking, he began to eat.

36. And all having become cheerful, they also took food.

37 And we were, all the souls in the ship, two hundred seventy six.
38 And having been filled (with) food, they lightened the ship, throwing out the wheat into the sea.
39 And when day came, (they) did not recognize the land, but they noted a certain bay having a beach, into which they purposed, if they were able, to drive the

Acts 27:30

5138 5117 1601 1537 4403 4496 45
τραχεῖς τόπους ἐκπέσωμεν, ἐκ πρύμνης ῥίψαντες ἀγκύρας
rough places they may fall out, out of (the) stern throwing anchors

5064 2172 2250 1096 3588 1161 3492 2212
τέσσαρας, ηὔχοντο ἡμέραν γενέσθαι. 30 τῶν δὲ ναυτῶν ζητούν-
four, they wished day to come. the But sailors seeking

5343 1537 3588 4143 2532 5465 3588 4627 1519
των φυγεῖν ἐκ τοῦ πλοίου καὶ χαλασάντων τὴν σκάφην εἰς
to flee out of the ship, and lowering the boat into

3588 2281 4392 5613 1537 4408 3195 45
τὴν θάλασσαν, προφάσει ὡς ἐκ πρώρας μελλόντων ἀγκύρας
the sea, pretending as out of (the) prow being about anchors

1614 2036 3588 3972 3588 1543 2532 3588 4757
ἐκτείνειν, 31 εἶπεν ὁ Παῦλος τῷ ἑκατοντάρχῃ καὶ τοῖς στρατιώ-
to cast out, said Paul to the centurion and to the soldiers,

1437 3361 3778 3306 1722 3588 4143 5210 4982 3756
ταις, Ἐὰν μὴ οὗτοι μείνωσιν ἐν τῷ πλοίῳ, ὑμεῖς σωθῆναι οὐ
If not these remain in the ship, you to be saved not

1410 5119 3588 4757 609 3588 4979 3588
δύνασθε. 32 τότε οἱ στρατιῶται ἀπέκοψαν τὰ σχοινία τῆς
are able. Then the soldiers cut away the ropes of the

4627 2532 1439 846 1601 891 1161 3739 3195
σκάφης, καὶ εἴασαν αὐτὴν ἐκπεσεῖν. 33 ἄχρι δὲ οὗ ἔμελλεν
boat, and let it fall off. until And was about

2250 1096 3870 3588 3972 537 3335
ἡμέρα γίνεσθαι, παρεκάλει ὁ Παῦλος ἅπαντας μεταλαβεῖν
day to come, begged Paul all to partake

5160 3004 5065 4594 2250 4328
τροφῆς, λέγων, Τεσσαρεσκαιδεκάτην σήμερον ἡμέραν προσδο-
of food, saying, (the) fourteenth Today (is) day waiting

777 1300 3367 4355 1352
κῶντες ἄσιτοι διατελεῖτε, μηδὲν προσλαβόμενοι· 34 διὸ
without food you continued, nothing having taken. Therefore

3870 5209 4355 5160 5124 1063 4314 3588
παρακαλῶ ὑμᾶς προσλαβεῖν τροφῆς· τοῦτο γὰρ πρὸς τῆς
I exhort you to take of food; this for to

5212 4991 5225 3762 1063 5216 2359 1537 3588
ὑμετέρας σωτηρίας ὑπάρχει· οὐδενὸς γὰρ ὑμῶν θρὶξ ἐκ τῆς
your deliverance is; of no one for of you a hair from the

2776 4098 2036 1161 5023 2532 2983 740
κεφαλῆς πεσεῖται. 35 εἰπὼν δὲ ταῦτα καὶ λαβὼν ἄρτον,
head will be lost. saying and these things and taking bread,

2168 3588 2316 1799 3956 2532 2806 756
εὐχαρίστησε τῷ Θεῷ ἐνώπιον πάντων· καὶ κλάσας ἤρξατο
he gave thanks to God before all; and breaking began

2068 2115 1161 1096 3956 2532 846 4355
ἐσθίειν. 36 εὔθυμοι δὲ γενόμενοι πάντες καὶ αὐτοὶ προσελάβον-
to eat. cheerful And having become all, also they took

5160 2258 1161 1722 3588 4143 3588 3956 5590 1250
το τροφῆς. 37 ἦμεν δὲ ἐν τῷ πλοίῳ αἱ πᾶσαι ψυχαί, διακόσιαι
food. we were And in the ship the all souls, two hundred

1440 2880 1161 5160 2893 3588 4143
ἑβδομηκονταέξ. 38 κορεσθέντες δὲ τροφῆς ἐκούφιζον τὸ πλοῖον,
seventy-six. having been filled And of food they lightened the ship,

1544 3588 4621 1519 3588 2281 3753 1161 2250
ἐκβαλλόμενοι τὸν σῖτον εἰς τὴν θάλασσαν. 39 ὅτε δὲ ἡμέρα
throwing out the wheat into the sea. when And day

1096 3588 1093 3756 1921 2859 1161 5100 2657
ἐγένετο, τὴν γῆν οὐκ ἐπεγίνωσκον· κόλπον δέ τινα κατενόουν
came, the land not did recognize; bay but a certain they noted

2192 123 1519 3739 1011 1487 1410 1856 3588
ἔχοντα αἰγιαλὸν, εἰς ὃν ἐβουλεύσαντο εἰ δύναιντο ἐξῶσαι τὸ
having a beach, into which they purposed if they were able to drive the

King James Version

we should have fallen upon rocks, they cast four anchors out of the stern, and wished for the day.
30. And as the shipmen were about to flee out of the ship, when they had let down the boat into the sea, under colour as though they would have cast anchors out of the foreship,

31 Paul said to the centurion and to the soldiers, Except these abide in the ship, ye cannot be saved.

32 Then the soldiers cut off the ropes of the boat, and let her fall off.
33 And while the day was coming on, Paul besought (them) all to take meat, saying, This day is the fourteenth day that ye have tarried and continued fasting, having taken nothing.

34 Wherefore I pray you to take (some) meat: for this is for your health: for there shall not an hair fall from the head of any of you.

35 And when he had thus spoken, he took bread, and gave thanks to God in presence of them all: and when he had broken (it), he began to eat.
36 Then were they all of good cheer, and they also took (some) meat.
37 And we were in all in the ship two hundred threescore and sixteen souls.
38 And when they had eaten enough, they lightened the ship, and cast out the wheat into the sea.
39. And when it was day, they knew not the land: but they discovered a certain creek with a shore, into the which they were minded, if it were possible, to thrust in the

Literal Translation

Acts 27:40

King James Version

ship.
40 And having cast off the anchors, they left (them) in the sea, at the same time freeing the bands of the rudders, and raising the foresail to the breeze, they held to the beach.

41 And falling into a place between two seas, they drove the vessel. And indeed the prow having stuck firmly, (it) remained. But the stern was loosed by the violence of the waves.
42 And the mind of the soldiers was that they should kill the prisoners, lest any swimming out should escape.

43 But having purposed to save Paul, the centurion kept them back (from their) purpose and commanded those able to swim, casting (themselves) overboard first, to go out onto the land.

44 And the rest (went), some indeed on boards, and others on some of the things from the ship. And so it happened that all were saved on the land.

4143 2532 3588 45 4014 1439 1519 3588
πλοῖον. 40 καὶ τὰς ἀγκύρας περιελόντες εἴων εἰς τὴν
ship. And the anchors having cast off they left in the

2281 260 447 3588 2202 3588 4079 2532
θάλασσαν, ἅμα ἀνέντες τὰς ζευκτηρίας τῶν πηδαλίων· καὶ
sea, at the same time freeing the bands of the rudders; and

1869 3588 736 3588 4154 2722 1519 3588 123
ἐπάραντες τὸν ἀρτέμονα τῇ πνεούσῃ κατεῖχον εἰς τὸν αἰγιαλόν.
raising the foresail to the breeze, they held to the beach.

4045 1161 1519 5117 1337 2027 3588 3491
41 περιπεσόντες δὲ εἰς τόπον διθάλασσον ἐπώκειλαν τὴ ναῦν·
falling And into a place between two seas they drove in the vessel;

2532 3588 3303 4408 2043 3306 761 3588 1161 4403
καὶ ἡ μὲν πρώρα ἐρεισασα ἔμεινεν ἀσάλευτος, ἡ δὲ πρύμνα
and the indeed prow having stuck firmly (it) remained immovable, the but stern

3089 5259 3588 970 3588 2949 3588 1161 4757 1012
ἐλύετο ὑπὸ τῆς βίας τῶν κυμάτων. 42 τῶν δὲ στρατιωτῶν βουλὴ
was loosed by the violence of the waves. the And of (the) soldiers mind

1096 2443 3588 1202 615 3387 1579
ἐγένετο ἵνα τοὺς δεσμώτας ἀποκτείνωσι, μήτις ἐκκολυμβήσας
was that the prisoners they should kill, that not any swimming out

1309 3588 1161 1543 1014 1295 3588
διαφύγοι. 43 ὁ δὲ ἑκατόνταρχος, βουλόμενος διασῶσαι τὸν
should escape. the But centurion,. having purposed to save

3972 2967 846 3588 1013 2753 5037 3588
Παῦλον, ἐκώλυσεν αὐτοὺς τοῦ βουλήματος, ἐκέλευσέ τε τοὺς
Paul, kept back them (from) the purpose, commanded and those

1410 2860 641 4413 1909 3588 1093
δυναμένους κολυμβᾶν ἀπορρίψαντας πρώτους ἐπὶ τὴν γῆν
being able to swim throwing overboard first onto the land

1826 2532 3588 3062 3739 3303 1909 4548 3739 1161 1909
ἐξιέναι· 44 καὶ τοὺς λοιπούς, οὓς μὲν ἐπὶ σανίσιν, οὓς δὲ ἐπί
to go out; and the rest, some indeed on planks, some and onto

5100 3588 575 3588 4143 2532 3779 1096 3956
τινων τῶν ἀπὸ τοῦ πλοίου. καὶ οὕτως ἐγένετο πάντας
some of the things from the ship. And so it happened all

1295 1909 3588 1093
διασωθῆναι ἐπὶ τὴν γῆν.
to be saved on the land.

ship.
40 And when they had taken up the anchors, they committed (themselves) unto the sea, and loosed the rudder bands, and hoised up the mainsail to the wind, and made toward shore.

41 And falling into a place where two seas met, they ran the ship aground; and the forepart stuck fast, and remained unmoveable, but the hinder part was broken with the violence of the waves.
42 And the soldiers' counsel was to kill the prisoners, lest any of them should swim out, and escape.
43 But the centurion, willing to save Paul, kept them from (their) purpose; and commanded that they which could swim should cast (themselves) first (into the sea), and get to land:

44 And the rest, some on boards, and some on (broken pieces) of the ship. And so it came to pass, that they escaped all safe to land.

Acts 28

Acts 28

Acts 28

1. And having been saved, then they knew that the island is called Melita.

2 And the foreigners showed not the ordinary kindliness to us, for having lighted a fire because of the rain coming on, and because of the cold, they welcomed us all.
3 And Paul having gathered a bunch of sticks, and putting (them) on the fire, a snake coming out from the heat fastened on his hand.
4 And when the foreigners saw the beast hanging

2532 1295 5119 1921 3754 3194 3588 3520
1. Καὶ διασωθέντες, τότε ἐπέγνωσαν ὅτι Μελίτη ἡ νῆσος
And having been saved, then they knew that Melita the island

2564 3588 1161 915 3930 3756 3588 5177
καλεῖται. 2 οἱ δὲ βάρβαροι παρεῖχον οὐ τὴν τυχοῦσαν
is called. the And foreigners extended not the common

5363 2254 381 1063 4443 4355
φιλανθρωπίαν ἡμῖν· ἀνάψαντες γὰρ πυράν, προσελάβοντο
philanthropy us; having lighted for a fire, they welcomed

3956 2248 1223 3588 5205 3588 2186 2532 1223 3588 5592
πάντας ἡμᾶς, διὰ τὸν ὑετὸν τὸν ἐφεστῶτα, καὶ διὰ τὸ ψῦχος.
all us, because of the rain coming on, and due to the cold.

4962 1161 3588 3972 5434 4128 2532
3 συστρέψαντος δὲ τοῦ Παύλου φρυγάνων πλῆθος, καὶ
having gathered And Paul of sticks a bunch, and

2007 1909 3588 4443 2191 1537 3588 2329 1831
ἐπιθέντος ἐπὶ τὴν πυράν, ἔχιδνα ἐκ τῆς θέρμης ἐξελθοῦσα
putting on the fire, a snake from the heat coming out

2510 3588 5495 846 5613 1161 1492 3588 915 2910
καθῆψε τῆς χειρὸς αὐτοῦ. 4 ὡς δὲ εἶδον οἱ βάρβαροι κρεμά-
fastened on the hand of him. when And saw the foreigners hanging

1. And when they were escaped, then they knew that the island was called Melita.
2 And the barbarous people shewed us no little kindness: for they kindled a fire, and received us every one, because of the present rain, and because of the cold.

3 And when Paul had gathered a bundle of sticks, and laid (them) on the fire, there came a viper out of the heat, and fastened on his hand.
4 And when the barbarians saw the (venomous) beast hang

Literal Translation

from his hand, they said to one another, By all means this man is a murderer, whom being saved out of the sea, Justice did not permit to live.
5 Then he indeed shaking the beast off into the fire, (he) suffered no harm.
6 But they expected him to be about to swell up, or suddenly to fall down dead. But over much (time), they expecting and beholding nothing amiss happening to him, changing their minds, they said him to be a god.

7. And in the (parts) about that place were lands to the first man of the island, Publius by name, who having welcomed us, (he) hosted us three days in a friendly way.
8 And it happened the father of Publius was lying down, suffering from fevers and dysentery; to whom Paul, having entered and having prayed, having laid on his hands, healed him.

9 Then, this taking place, the rest of the (ones) having infirmities in the island also came to (him), and (they) were cured.

10 (They) also honored us with many honors. And on (our) setting sail, they laid on (us) the things for (our) needs..
11. And after three months we sailed in a ship which had wintered in the island, an Alexandrian with an ensign, Twin Brothers.
12 And having landed at Syracuse, we remained three days.
13 Going around from there, we arrived at Rhegium. And after one

Acts 28:5

3588 2342 1537 3588 5495 846 3004 4314 240
μενον τὸ θηρίον ἐκ τῆς χειρὸς αὐτοῦ, ἔλεγον πρὸς ἀλλήλους,
the beast from the hand of him, they said to one another,

3843 5406 2076 3588 444 3778 3739 1295 1537
Πάντως φονεύς ἐστιν ὁ ἄνθρωπος οὗτος, ὃν διασωθέντα ἐκ
By all means a murderer is man this, whom being saved out of

3588 2281 3588 1349 2198 3756 1439 3588 3303 3767 660
τῆς θαλάσσης ἡ Δίκη ζῆν οὐκ εἴασεν. 5 ὁ μὲν οὖν, ἀποτινάξας
the sea Justice to live not permitted. he indeed Then, shaking off

3588 2342 1519 3588 4442 3958 3762 2556 3588 1161 4328
τὸ θηρίον εἰς τὸ πῦρ, ἔπαθεν οὐδὲν κακόν. 6 οἱ δὲ προσεδόκων
the beast into the fire, suffered no harm. they But expected

846 3195 4092 2228 2667 869 3498 1909
αὐτὸν μέλλειν πίμπρασθαι ἢ καταπίπτειν ἄφνω νεκρόν· ἐπὶ
him being about to swell up or to fall down suddenly dead over

4183 1161 846 4328 2532 2334 3367
πολὺ δὲ αὐτῶν προσδοκώντων, καὶ θεωρούντων μηδὲν
much but they expecting, and beholding nothing

824 1519 846 1096 3328 3004 2316
ἄτοπον εἰς αὐτὸν γινόμενον, μεταβαλόμενοι ἔλεγον θεὸν
amiss to him having occurred, changing their minds they said a god

846 1511
αὐτὸν εἶναι.
him to be.

1722 1161 3588 4012 3588 5117 1565 5225 5564 3588
7 Ἐν δὲ τοῖς περὶ τὸν τόπον ἐκεῖνον ὑπῆρχε χωρία τῷ
in And the (parts) about place that were lands to the

4413 3588 3520 3686 4196 3739 324 2248
πρώτῳ τῆς νήσου, ὀνόματι Ποπλίῳ, ὃς ἀναδεξάμενος ἡμᾶς
first man of the island, by name Publius, who having welcomed us

5140 2250 5390 3579 1096 1161 3588 3962
τρεῖς ἡμέρας φιλοφρόνως ἐξένισεν. 8 ἐγένετο δὲ τὸν πατέρα
three days in a friendly way hosted. it happened And the father

3588 4196 4446 2532 1420 4912
τοῦ Ποπλίου πυρετοῖς καὶ δυσεντερίᾳ συνεχόμενον
of Publius fevers and dysentery having suffered

2621 4314 3739 3588 3972 1525 2532 4336
κατακεῖσθαι· πρὸς ὃν ὁ Παῦλος εἰσελθὼν, καὶ προσευξάμενος,
was lying down; to whom Paul having entered, and having prayed,

2007 3588 5495 846 2390 846 5127 3767 1096
ἐπιθεὶς τὰς χεῖρας αὐτῷ, ἰάσατο αὐτόν. 9 τούτου οὖν γενο-
laying on the hands him, healed him. this Then happening,

2532 3588 3062 3588 2192 769 1722 3588 3520
μένου, καὶ οἱ λοιποὶ οἱ ἔχοντες ἀσθενείας ἐν τῇ νήσῳ
also the rest of the (ones) having infirmities in the island

4334 2532 2323 3739 2532 4183 5092
προσήρχοντο καὶ ἐθεραπεύοντο· 10 οἳ καὶ πολλαῖς τιμαῖς
came to (him) and were cured; who also with many honors

5021 2248 2532 321 2007 3588 4314 3588 5532
ἐτίμησαν ἡμᾶς, καὶ ἀναγομένοις ἐπέθεντο τὰ πρὸς τὴν χρείαν.
honored us, and on our setting sail laid on the things for (our) needs.

3326 1161 5140 3376 321 1722 4143 3914
11. Μετὰ δὲ τρεῖς μῆνας ἀνήχθημεν ἐν πλοίῳ παρακεχει-
after And three months we set sail in a ship having

1722 3588 3520 222 3902 1359
μακότι ἐν τῇ νήσῳ, Ἀλεξανδρίνῳ, παρασήμῳ Διοσκούροις.
wintered in the island, an Alexandrian, with an ensign Twin Brothers.

2532 2609 1519 4946 1961 2250 5140
12 καὶ καταχθέντες εἰς Συρακούσας ἐπεμείναμεν ἡμέρας τρεῖς·
And having been landed at Syracuse we remained days three;

3606 4022 2658 1519 4484 2532 3326 3391
13 ὅθεν περιελθόντες κατηντήσαμεν εἰς Ῥήγιον, καὶ μετὰ μίαν
from where tacking we arrived at Rhegium, and after one

King James Version

on his hand, they said among themselves, No doubt this man is a murderer, whom, though he hath escaped the sea, yet vengeance suffereth not to live.
5 And he shook off the beast into the fire, and felt no harm.

6 Howbeit they looked when he should have swollen, or fallen down dead suddenly: but after they had looked a great while, and saw no harm come to him, they changed their minds, and said that he was a god.

7. In the same quarters were possessions of the chief man of the island, whose name was Publius; who received us, and lodged us three days courteously.
8 And it came to pass, that the father of Publius lay sick of a fever and of a bloody flux: to whom Paul entered in, and prayed, and laid his hands on him, and healed him.

9 So when this was done, others also, which had diseases in the island, came, and were healed:

10 Who also honoured us with many honours; and when we departed, they laded (us) with such things as were necessary.
11. And after three months we departed in a ship of Alexandria, which had wintered in the isle, whose sign was Castor and Pollux.
12 And landing at Syracuse, we tarried (there) three days.
13 And from thence we fetched a compass, and came to Rhegium: and after one

Literal Translation | **Acts 28:14** | **King James Version**

Literal Translation

day, a south wind having come on, on the second we came to Puteoli,

14 where having found brothers, we were entreated by them to remain seven days. And so we went toward Rome.

15 And the brothers from there having heard the things about us, (they) came out to meet us, as far as (the) marketplace of Appius, and Three Taverns; whom Paul seeing, having thanked God, he took courage.

16 And when we went into Rome, the centurion delivered the prisoners to the camp commander. But Paul was allowed to remain by himself, with the soldier guarding him.

17. And it was after three days Paul called together those being chief of the Jews. And they coming together, he said to them, Men, brothers, I did nothing contrary to the people, or to the ancestral customs. I was delivered a prisoner from Jerusalem into the hands of the Romans,

18 who having examined me were of a mind to let (me) go, because no cause of death was in me.

19 But the Jews speaking against (it), I was compelled to appeal to Caesar, not as having anything to accuse my nation.

20 Because of this, then, I called to you, to see and to speak to (you). For I have this chain around (me) for the sake of the hope of Israel.

21 And they said to him, We neither received letters concerning you

2250 1920 3558 1206 2064 1519 4223
ἡμέραν ἐπιγενομένου νότου, δευτεραῖοι ἤλθομεν εἰς Ποτιό-
day having come on a south wind, on the second we came to Puteoli;

3757 2147 80 3870 1909 846
λους· 14 οὗ εὑρόντες ἀδελφούς, παρεκλήθημεν ἐπ' αὐτοῖς
where having found brothers, we were entreated by them

1961 2250 2033 2532 3779 1519 3588 4516 2064
ἐπιμεῖναι ἡμέρας ἑπτά· καὶ οὕτως εἰς τὴν Ῥώμην ἤλθαμεν.
to remain days seven; and thus to Rome we went.

2547 3588 80 191 3588 4012 2257 1831 1519
15 κἀκεῖθεν οἱ ἀδελφοὶ ἀκούσαντες τὰ περὶ ἡμῶν, ἐξῆλθον εἰς
And from there the brothers having heard the things about us, came out to

529 2254 891 675 5410 2532 5140 4999
ἀπάντησιν ἡμῖν ἄχρις Ἀππίου Φόρου καὶ Τριῶν Ταβερνῶν·
meet us as far as Appii Forum and Three Taverns;

3739 1492 3588 3972 2168 3588 2316 2983 2294
οὓς ἰδὼν ὁ Παῦλος εὐχαριστήσας τῷ Θεῷ ἔλαβε θάρσος.
whom seeing Paul having thanked God he took courage.

3753 1161 2064 1519 4516 3588 1543 3860
16. Ὅτε δὲ ἤλθομεν εἰς Ῥώμην, ὁ ἑκατόνταρχος παρέδωκε
when And we went into Rome, the centurion delivered

3588 1198 3588 4759 3588 1161 3972 2010
τοὺς δεσμίους τῷ στρατοπεδάρχῃ· τῷ δὲ Παύλῳ ἐπετράπη
the prisoners to the camp commander; but Paul was allowed

3306 2596 1438 4862 3588 5442 846 4757
μένειν καθ' ἑαυτὸν, σὺν τῷ φυλάσσοντι αὐτὸν στρατιώτῃ.
to remain by himself, with the guarding him soldier.

1096 1161 3326 2250 5140 4779 3588 3972
17.Ἐγένετο δὲ μετὰ ἡμέρας τρεῖς συγκαλέσασθαι τὸν Παῦλον
it was And after days three called together Paul

3588 5607 3588 2453 4413 4905 1161 846
τοὺς ὄντας τῶν Ἰουδαίων πρώτους· συνελθόντων δὲ αὐτῶν,
those being of the Jews chief. coming together And them,

3004 4314 846 435 80 1473 3762 1727
ἔλεγε πρὸς αὐτούς, Ἄνδρες ἀδελφοί, ἐγὼ οὐδὲν ἐναντίον
he said to them, Men brothers, I nothing contrary

4160 3588 2992 2228 3588 1485 3588 3971 1198 1537
ποιήσας τῷ λαῷ ἢ τοῖς ἔθεσι τοῖς πατρῴοις, δέσμιος ἐξ
did to the people or to the customs ancestral, a prisoner from

2414 3860 1519 3588 5495 3588 4514
Ἱεροσολύμων παρεδόθην εἰς τὰς χεῖρας τῶν Ῥωμαίων,
Jerusalem I was delivered into the hands of the Romans,

3748 350 3165 1014 630 1223 3588 3367
18 οἵτινες ἀνακρίναντές με ἐβούλοντο ἀπολῦσαι, διὰ τὸ μηδε-
who having examined me were minded to let me go, because no

156 2288 5225 1722 1698 483 1161 3588
μίαν αἰτίαν θανάτου ὑπάρχειν ἐν ἐμοί. 19 ἀντιλεγόντων δὲ τῶν
cause of death to be in me. speaking against But the

2453 315 1941 2541 3756 5613 3588
Ἰουδαίων, ἠναγκάσθην ἐπικαλέσασθαι Καίσαρα, οὐχ ὡς τοῦ
Jews, I was compelled to appeal to Caesar; not as the

1484 3450 2192 5100 2723 1223 3778 3767 3588
ἔθνους μου ἔχων τι κατηγορῆσαι. 20 διὰ ταύτην οὖν τὴν
nation of me having anything to accuse. Because of this, then,

156 3870 5209 1492 2532 4354 1752 1063
αἰτίαν παρεκάλεσα ὑμᾶς ἰδεῖν καὶ προσλαλῆσαι· ἕνεκεν γὰρ
cause I called to you to see and to speak to; the sake of for

3588 1680 3588 2474 3588 254 3778 4029
τῆς ἐλπίδος τοῦ Ἰσραὴλ τὴν ἅλυσιν ταύτην περίκειμαι.
the hope of Israel, chain this I have around (me).

3588 1161 4314 846 2036 2249 3777 1121 4012 4675
21 οἱ δὲ πρὸς αὐτὸν εἶπον, Ἡμεῖς οὔτε γράμματα περὶ σοῦ
they And to him said, We neither letters concerning you

King James Version

day the south wind blew, and we came the next day to Puteoli:

14 Where we found brethren, and were desired to tarry with them seven days: and so we went toward Rome.

15 And from thence, when the brethren heard of us, they came to meet us as far as Appii forum, and The three taverns: whom when Paul saw, he thanked God, and took courage.

16 And when we came to Rome, the centurion delivered the prisoners to the captain of the guard: but Paul was suffered to dwell by himself with a soldier that kept him.

17. And it came to pass, that after three days Paul called the chief of the Jews together: and when they were come together, he said unto them, Men (and) brethren, though I have committed nothing against the people, or customs of our fathers, yet was I delivered prisoner from Jerusalem into the hands of the Romans.

18 Who, when they had examined me, would have let (me) go, because there was no cause of death in me.

19 But when the Jews spake against (it), I was constrained to appeal unto Caesar; not that I had ought to accuse my nation of.

20 For this cause therefore have I called for you, to see (you), and to speak with (you): because that for the hope of Israel I am bound with this chain.

21 And they said unto him, We neither received letters out of

Literal Translation | **Acts 28:22** | **King James Version**

from the Jews, nor having arrived has any one of the brothers reported or said anything evil concerning you.

22 But we think (it) fit into hear from you (as to) what you think; for indeed concerning this sect, it is known to us that it is spoken against everywhere.

23. And having appointed him a day, more came to him in the lodging, to whom he set out, earnestly testifying the kingdom of God and persuading them the things concerning Jesus, both from the law of Moses and the Prophets, from morning until evening.

24 And some indeed were persuaded by that being said, others disbelieved.
25 And being disagreed with one another, they were let go, Paul saying one word: Well did the Holy Spirit speak through the prophet Isaiah to our fathers,

26 saying, "Go to this people and say, Hearing you will hear, and not at all understand; and seeing you will see, and not at all perceive;

27 for the heart of this people was fattened, and they have heard with the ears heavily; and they closed their eyes lest at any time they see with (their) eyes, and hear with (their) ears, and understand with (their) heart, and be converted, and I should heal them." (Isa. 6:9, 10)
28 Then let it be known to you that the salvation of God was sent to the nations, and they will hear.
29 And

1209 575 3588 2449 3777 3854 5100 3588
ἐδεξάμεθα ἀπὸ τῆς Ἰουδαίας, οὔτε παραγενόμενός τις τῶν
received from the Jews, nor, having arrived anyone of the

80 518 2228 2980 5100 4012 4675 4190
ἀδελφῶν ἀπήγγειλεν ἢ ἐλάλησέ τι περὶ σοῦ πονηρόν.
brothers reported or said anything about you evil.

515 1161 3844 4675 191 3739 5426 4012 3303 1063 3588
22 ἀξιοῦμεν δὲ παρὰ σοῦ ἀκοῦσαι ἃ φρονεῖς· περὶ μὲν γὰρ τῆς
we think fit But from you to hear what you think; about indeed for

139 3778 1110 2076 2254 3754 3837 483
αἱρέσεως ταύτης γνωστόν ἐστιν ἡμῖν ὅτι πανταχοῦ ἀντιλέ-
sect this known is us, that everywhere it is

γεται.
spoken against.

5021 1161 846 2250 2240 4314 846 1519 3588
23. Ταξάμενοι δὲ αὐτῷ ἡμέραν, ἧκον πρὸς αὐτὸν εἰς τὴν
having appointed And him a day, came to him in the

3578 4119 3739 1620 1263 3588 932
ξενίαν πλείονες· οἷς ἐξετίθετο διαμαρτυρόμενος τὴν βασι-
lodging more, to whom he set forth earnestly testifying the king-

3588 2316 3982 5037 846 3588 4012 3588 2424 575
λείαν τοῦ Θεοῦ, πείθων τε αὐτοὺς τὰ περὶ τοῦ Ἰησοῦ, ἀπό
dom of God, persuading and them the things concerning Jesus from

5037 3588 3551 3475 2532 3588 4396 575 4404 2193
τε τοῦ νόμου Μωσέως καὶ τῶν προφητῶν, ἀπὸ πρωΐ ἕως
and the law of Moses and the Prophets. from morning until

2073 2532 3588 3303 3982 3588 3004 3588 1161
ἑσπέρας. 24 καὶ οἱ μὲν ἐπείθοντο τοῖς λεγομένοις, οἱ δὲ
evening. And some indeed were persuaded by that being said, others

569 800 1161 5607 4314 240 630
ἠπίστουν. 25 ἀσύμφωνοι δὲ ὄντες πρὸς ἀλλήλους ἀπελύοντο,
disbelieved. disagreed And being with one another, they were let go,

2036 3588 3972 4487 1520 3754 2573 3588 4151 3588 40
εἰπόντος τοῦ Παύλου ῥῆμα ἕν, ὅτι Καλῶς τὸ Πνεῦμα τὸ Ἅγιον
having said Paul word one, Well the Spirit Holy

2980 1223 2268 3588 4396 4314 3588 3962
ἐλάλησε διὰ Ἠσαΐου τοῦ προφήτου πρὸς τοὺς πατέρας
spoke through Isaiah the prophet to the fathers

2257 3004 4198 4314 3588 2992 5126 2532 2036
ἡμῶν, 26 λέγον, Πορεύθητι πρὸς τὸν λαὸν τοῦτον καὶ εἰπέ,
of us, saying, Go to people this and say:

189 191 2532 3756 3361 4920 2532 991 991
Ἀκοῇ ἀκούσετε, καὶ οὐ μὴ συνῆτε· καὶ βλέποντες βλέψετε,
in hearing you will hear, and not at all understand, and seeing you will see,

2532 3756 3361 1492 3975 1063 3588 2588 3588 2992 5127
καὶ οὐ μὴ ἴδητε· 27 ἐπαχύνθη γὰρ ἡ καρδία τοῦ λαοῦ τούτου,
and not at all perceive, was fattened for the heart people of this,

2532 3588 3775 917 191 2532 3588 3788 846
καὶ τοῖς ὠσὶ βαρέως ἤκουσαν, καὶ τοὺς ὀφθαλμοὺς αὐτῶν
and with the ears heavily they heard, and the eyes of them

2576 3379 1492 3588 3788 2532 3588 3775
ἐκάμμυσαν· μήποτε ἴδωσι τοῖς ὀφθαλμοῖς, καὶ τοῖς ὠσὶν
they closed, lest at any time they see with the eyes, and with the ears

191 2532 3588 2588 4920 2532 1994 2532
ἀκούσωσι, καὶ τῇ καρδίᾳ συνῶσι, καὶ ἐπιστρέψωσι, καὶ
hear, and with the heart understand, and be converted, and

2390 846 1110 3767 2077 5213 3754 3588 1484
ἰάσομαι αὐτούς. 28 γνωστὸν οὖν ἔστω ὑμῖν, ὅτι τοῖς ἔθνεσιν
I should heal them. Known, therefore, be it to you, that to the nations

649 3588 4992 3588 2316 846 2532 191 2532
ἀπεστάλη τὸ σωτήριον τοῦ Θεοῦ, αὐτοὶ καὶ ἀκούσονται. 29 καὶ
was sent the salvation of God, they and will hear. And

Judaea concerning thee, neither any of the brethren that came shewed or spake any harm of thee.

22 But we desire to hear of thee what thou thinkest: for as concerning this sect, we know that every where it is spoken against.

23. And when they had appointed him a day, there came many to him into (his) lodging; to whom he expounded and testified the kingdom of God, persuading them concerning Jesus, both out of the law of Moses, and (out of) the prophets, from morning till evening.

24 And some believed the things which were spoken, and some believed not.
25 And when they agreed not among themselves, they departed, after that Paul had spoken one word, Well spake the Holy Ghost by Esaias the prophet unto our fathers,

26 Saying, Go unto this people, and say, Hearing ye shall hear, and shall not understand; and seeing ye shall see, and not perceive:

27 For the heart of this people is waxed gross, and their ears are dull of hearing, and their eyes have they closed; lest they should see with (their) eyes, and hear with (their) ears, and understand with (their) heart, and should be converted, and I should heal them.

28 Be it known therefore unto you, that the salvation of God is sent unto the Gentiles, and (that) they will hear it.
29 And

Literal Translation | **Acts 28:30** | *King James Version*

he having said these things, the Jews went away, having much discussion among themselves.

5023 846 2036 565 3588 2453 4183 2192
ταῦτα αὐτοῦ εἰπόντος, ἀπῆλθον οἱ Ἰουδαῖοι, πολλὴν ἔχοντες
these things he having said, went away the Jews much having

1722 1438 4803
ἐν ἑαυτοῖς συζήτησιν.
among themselves discussion.

when he had said these words, the Jews departed, and had great reasoning among themselves.

30. And Paul remained two whole years in (his) own rented place, and he welcomed all those coming in to him,

3306 1161/3588 3972 1333 3650 1722 2398 3410 2532
30. Ἔμεινε δὲ ὁ Παῦλος διετίαν ὅλην ἐν ἰδίῳ μισθώματι, καὶ
remained And Paul two years a whole in (his) own rented place, and

588 3956 3588 1531 4314 846
ἀπεδέχετο πάντας τοὺς εἰσπορευομένους πρὸς αὐτόν,
welcomed all those coming in to him,

30. And Paul dwelt two whole years in his own hired house, and received all that came in unto him,

31 proclaiming the kingdom of God, and teaching the things concerning the Lord Jesus Christ with all freedom (and) without hindrance.

2784 3588 932 3588 2316 2532 1321 3588 4012
31 κηρύσσων τὴν βασιλείαν τοῦ Θεοῦ, καὶ διδάσκων τὰ περὶ
proclaiming the kingdom of God, and teaching the things about

3588 2962 2424 5547 3326 3956 3954
τοῦ Κυρίου Ἰησοῦ Χριστοῦ, μετὰ πάσης παρρησίας,
the Lord Jesus Christ, with all freedom,

209
ἀκωλύτως.
without hindrance.

31 Preaching the kingdom of God, and teaching those things which concern the Lord Jesus Christ, with all confidence, no man forbidding him.

Literal Translation

THE EPISTLE OF PAUL THE APOSTLE TO THE ROMANS

Romans 1

1. Paul, a slave of Jesus Christ, a called apostle, separated to the gospel of God,
2 which He promised before through His prophets in holy Scriptures,
3 concerning His Son whaving come out of the seed of David according to flesh,

4 (who was) marked out Son of God in power, according to (the) Spirit of Holiness, by resurrection of (the) dead, Jesus Christ our Lord;

5 through whom we received grace and apostleship to obedience of faith among all the nations, for His name's sake,
6 among whom are you also, called of Jesus Christ;
7 to all those being in Rome, beloved of God, called to (be) saints, Grace and peace to you from God our Father and (the) Lord Jesus Christ.

8 Firstly, I thank my God through Jesus Christ for you all, that your faith is being proclaimed in all the world.

9 For God is my witness, whom I serve in my spirit in the gospel of His Son, how without ceasing I make mention of you

10 always on my prayers, beseeching if by any means now at length I shall be blessed in the will of God to come to you.

11 For I long to see you, that I may impart some spiritual gift to you, for the

ΠΑΥΛΟΥ ΤΟΥ ΑΠΟΣΤΟΛΟΥ
PAUL THE APOSTLE

Η ΠΡΟΣ ΡΩΜΑΙΟΥΣ ΕΠΙΣΤΟΛΗ
TO (THE) ROMANS EPISTLE

Romans 1

3972 1401 2424 5547 2822 652
1 Παῦλος, δοῦλος Ἰησοῦ Χριστοῦ, κλητὸς ἀπόστολος,
Paul, a slave of Jesus Christ, a called apostle,

873 1519 2098 2316 3739 4279 1223
ἀφωρισμένος εἰς εὐαγγέλιον Θεοῦ, 2 ὃ προεπηγγείλατο διὰ
having been separated to (the) gospel of God, which He promised before through

3588 4396 846 1722 1124 40 4012 3588 5207
τῶν προφητῶν αὐτοῦ ἐν γραφαῖς ἁγίαις, 3 περὶ τοῦ υἱοῦ
the prophets of him in Scriptures holy, concerning the Son

846 3588 1096 1537 4690 1138 2596 4561
αὐτοῦ, τοῦ γενομένου ἐκ σπέρματος Δαβὶδ κατὰ σάρκα,
of Him, having come out of seed of David according to flesh,

3588 3724 5207 2316 1722 1411 2596 4151 42
4 τοῦ ὁρισθέντος υἱοῦ Θεοῦ ἐν δυνάμει, κατὰ πνεῦμα ἁγιω-
marked out Son of God in power, according to (the) Spirit of

1537 386 3498 2424 5547 3588 2962
σύνης, ἐξ ἀναστάσεως νεκρῶν, Ἰησοῦ Χριστοῦ τοῦ Κυρίου
holiness, by resurrection of (the) dead, Jesus Christ the Lord

2257 1223 3739 2983 5485 2532 651 1519 5218
ἡμῶν, 5 δι᾽ οὗ ἐλάβομεν χάριν καὶ ἀποστολὴν εἰς ὑπακοὴν
of us, through whom we received grace and apostleship to obedience

4100 1722 3956 3588 1484 5228 3588 3686 846 1722
πίστεως ἐν πᾶσι τοῖς ἔθνεσιν, ὑπὲρ τοῦ ὀνόματος αὐτοῦ, 6 ἐν
of faith among all the nations, for the sake of the name of Him, among

3739 2075 2532 5210 2822 2424 5547 3956 3588 5607
οἷς ἐστε καὶ ὑμεῖς, κλητοὶ Ἰησοῦ Χριστοῦ· 7 πᾶσι τοῖς οὖσιν
whom are also you, called of Jesus Christ; to all those being

1722 4516 27 2316 2822 40 5485 5213 2532
ἐν Ῥώμῃ ἀγαπητοῖς Θεοῦ, κλητοῖς ἁγίοις· χάρις ὑμῖν καὶ
in Rome beloved of God, called to (be) saints; grace to you and

1515 575 2316 3962 2257 2532 2962 2424 5547
εἰρήνη ἀπὸ Θεοῦ πατρὸς ἡμῶν καὶ Κυρίου Ἰησοῦ Χριστοῦ.
peace from God (the) Father of us and (the) Lord Jesus Christ.

4412 3303 2168 3588 2316 3450 1223 2424 5547
8. Πρῶτον μὲν εὐχαριστῶ τῷ Θεῷ μου διὰ Ἰησοῦ Χριστοῦ
Firstly truly I thank the God of me through Jesus Christ

5228 3956 5216 3754 3588 4102 5216 2605 1722
ὑπὲρ πάντων ὑμῶν, ὅτι ἡ πίστις ὑμῶν καταγγέλλεται ἐν
for all of you, that the faith of you is being proclaimed in

3650 3588 2889 3144 1063 3450 2076 3588 2316 3739 3000
ὅλῳ τῷ κόσμῳ. 9 μάρτυς γάρ μού ἐστιν ὁ Θεός, ᾧ λατρεύω
all the world. the witness For of me is God, whom I serve

1722 3588 4151 3450 1722 3588 2098 3588 5207 846 5613
ἐν τῷ πνεύματί μου ἐν τῷ εὐαγγελίῳ τοῦ υἱοῦ αὐτοῦ, ὡς
in the spirit of me in the gospel of the Son of Him, how

89 3417 5216 4160 3842 1909 3588
ἀδιαλείπτως μνείαν ὑμῶν ποιοῦμαι, 10 πάντοτε ἐπὶ τῶν
without ceasing mention of you I make, always on the

4335 3450 1189 1513 2235 4218 2137 1722 3588
προσευχῶν μου δεόμενος, εἴπως ἤδη ποτὲ εὐοδωθήσομαι ἐν τῷ
prayers of me beseeching, if at all now at length I shall be blessed in the

2307 3588 2316 2064 4314 5209 1971 1063 1492
θελήματι τοῦ Θεοῦ ἐλθεῖν πρὸς ὑμᾶς. 11 ἐπιποθῶ γὰρ ἰδεῖν
will of God to come to you. I long For to see

5209 2443 5100 3330 5486 5213 4152 1519 3588
ὑμᾶς, ἵνα τι μεταδῶ χάρισμα ὑμῖν πνευματικόν, εἰς τὸ
you, that some I may impart gift to you spiritual, for the

King James Version

THE EPISTLE OF PAUL THE APOSTLE TO THE ROMANS

Romans 1

1. Paul, a servant of Jesus Christ, called (to be) an apostle, separated unto the gospel of God,
2 (Which he had promised afore by his prophets in the holy scriptures,)
3 Concerning his Son Jesus Christ our Lord, which was made of the seed of David according to the flesh;

4 And declared (to be) the Son of God with power, according to the spirit of holiness, by the resurrection from the dead:

5 By whom we have received grace and apostleship, for obedience to the faith among all nations, for his name:
6 Among whom are ye also the called of Jesus Christ:
7 To all that be in Rome, beloved of God, called (to be) saints: Grace to you and peace from God our Father, and the Lord Jesus Christ.

8 First, I thank my God through Jesus Christ for you all, that your faith is spoken of throughout the whole world.

9 For God is my witness, whom I serve with my spirit in the gospel of his Son, that without ceasing I make mention of you always in my prayers;
10 Making request, if by any means now at length I might have a prosperous journey by the will of God to come unto you.

11 For I long to see you, that I may impart unto you some spiritual gift, to the

Literal Translation

ROMANS 1:12

King James Version

stablishing of you;
12 and this is to be comforted together among you, through the faith in one another, both yours and mine.
13 But I do not wish you to be ignorant, brothers, that often I purposed to come to you, and was prevented until the present, that I might have some fruit among you also, even as also among the other nations.
14 I am a debtor both to Greeks and to foreigners, both to wise, and to foolish,
15 so as far as in me (lies), I am eager to preach the gospel to you in Rome also.

16 For I am not ashamed of the gospel of Christ, for it is (the) power of God to salvation to everyone believing, both to Jew first, and to Greek;
17 for in it a righteousness of God is revealed from faith to faith; even as it has been written, "But the just shall live by faith." (Hab. 2:4)

18 For God's wrath is revealed from Heaven on all ungodliness and unrighteousness of men, holding fast the truth in unrighteousness,
19 because the thing known of God is clearly known within them, for God revealed (it) to them.
20 For the unseen things of Him from (the) creation of (the) world are clearly seen, being understood by the things made, both His eternal power and Godhead, for them to be without excuse.
21 Because having known God, they did not glorify Him as God, nor were thankful. But (they) became vain in their reasonings, and their undiscerning heart was darkened.

4741 5209 5124 1161 2076 4837 1722 5213
στηριχθῆναι ὑμᾶς, 12 τοῦτο δέ ἐστι συμπαρακληθῆναι ἐν ὑμῖν
establishing of you, this and is to be comforted together among you

1223 3588 1722 240 4102 5216 5037 2532 1700 3756 2309 1161
διὰ τῆς ἐν ἀλλήλοις πίστεως ὑμῶν τε καὶ ἐμοῦ. 13 οὐ θέλω δὲ
through the in one another faith of you and also of me. not I wish But

5209 50 80 3754 4178 4388 2064 4314
ὑμᾶς ἀγνοεῖν, ἀδελφοί, ὅτι πολλάκις προεθέμην ἐλθεῖν πρὸς
you to be ignorant, brothers, that often I purposed to come to

5209 2532 2967 891 3588 1204 2443 2590 5100 2192
ὑμᾶς [καὶ ἐκωλύθην ἄχρι τοῦ δεῦρο], ἵνα καρπὸν τινα σχῶ
you, and was prevented until the present, that fruit some I have

2532 1722 5213 2531 2532 1722 3588 3062 1484 1672 5037
καὶ ἐν ὑμῖν, καθὼς καὶ ἐν τοῖς λοιποῖς ἔθνεσιν. 14 Ἕλλησί τε
also among you, even as also in the remaining nations. to Greeks Both

2532 915 4680 5037 2532 453 3781 1510
καὶ βαρβάροις, σοφοῖς τε καὶ ἀνοήτοις ὀφειλέτης εἰμί·
and foreigners, to wise both and foolish a debtor I am;

3779 3588 2596 1691 4289 2532 5213 3588 1722 4516 2097
15 οὕτω τὸ κατ' ἐμὲ πρόθυμον καὶ ὑμῖν τοῖς ἐν Ῥώμῃ εὐαγγε-
so as to me I am eager also to you in Rome to preach

3756 1063 1870 3588 2098 3588 5547
λίσασθαι. 16 οὐ γὰρ ἐπαισχύνομαι τὸ εὐαγγέλιον τοῦ Χριστοῦ·
the gospel. not For I am ashamed of the gospel of Christ;

1411 1063 2316 2076 1519 4991 3956 3588 4100
δύναμις γὰρ Θεοῦ ἐστιν εἰς σωτηρίαν παντὶ τῷ πιστεύοντι,
power for of God it is to salvation to everyone believing,

2453 5037 4412 2532 1672 1343 1063 2316 1722
Ἰουδαίῳ τε πρῶτον καὶ Ἕλληνι. 17 δικαιοσύνη γὰρ Θεοῦ ἐν
Jew both firstly and to Greek. a righteousness For of God in

846 601 1537 4102 1519 4102 2531
αὐτῷ ἀποκαλύπτεται ἐκ πίστεως εἰς πίστιν, καθὼς
it is revealed from faith to faith, even as

1125 3588 1161 1342 1537 4102 2198
γέγραπται, Ὁ δὲ δίκαιος ἐκ πίστεως ζήσεται.
it has been written, the But just by faith shall live.

601 1063 3709 2316 575 3772 1909 3956
18 Ἀποκαλύπτεται γὰρ ὀργὴ Θεοῦ ἀπ' οὐρανοῦ ἐπὶ πᾶσαν
is revealed For the wrath of God from Heaven on all

763 2532 93 444 3588 3588 225 1722 93
ἀσέβειαν καὶ ἀδικίαν ἀνθρώπων τῶν τὴν ἀλήθειαν ἐν ἀδικίᾳ
ungodliness and unrighteousness of men the truth in unrighteousness

2722 1360 3588 1110 3588 2316 5318 2076 1722
κατεχόντων· 19 διότι τὸ γνωστὸν τοῦ Θεοῦ φανερόν ἐστιν ἐν
holding fast; because the thing known of God clearly known is in

846 3588 1063 2316 846 5319 3588 1063 517 846
αὐτοῖς· ὁ γὰρ Θεὸς αὐτοῖς ἐφανέρωσε. 20 τὰ γὰρ ἀόρατα αὐτοῦ
them; for God to them revealed (it). the things For unseen of Him

575 2937 2889 3588 4161 3539 2529
ἀπὸ κτίσεως κόσμου τοῖς ποιήμασι νοούμενα καθορᾶται,
from creation of (the) world by the things made being realized are clearly seen,

3588 5037 126 846 1411 2532 2305 1519 3588 1511 846
ἥ τε ἀΐδιος αὐτοῦ δύναμις καὶ θειότης, εἰς τὸ εἶναι αὐτοὺς
the both eternal of Him power and Godhead, for to be them

379 1360 1097 3588 2316 3756 5613 2316
ἀναπολογήτους· 21 διότι γνόντες τὸν Θεόν, οὐχ ὡς Θεὸν
without excuse; because having known God, not as God

1392 2228 2168 235 3154 1722 3588
ἐδόξασαν ἢ εὐχαρίστησαν, ἀλλ' ἐματαιώθησαν ἐν τοῖς
they glorified nor were thankful, but became vain in the

1261 846 2532 4654 3588 801 846
διαλογισμοῖς αὐτῶν, καὶ ἐσκοτίσθη ἡ ἀσύνετος αὐτῶν
reasonings of them, and was darkened the undiscerning of them

end ye may be established;
12 That is, that I may be comforted together with you by the mutual faith both of you and me.
13 Now I would not have you ignorant, brethren, that oftentimes I purposed to come unto you, (but was let hitherto,) that I might have some fruit among you also, even as among other Gentiles.
14 I am debtor both to the Greeks, and to the Barbarians; both to the wise, and to the unwise.
15 So, as much as in me is, I am ready to preach the gospel to you that are at Rome also.
16 For I am not ashamed of the gospel of Christ: for it is the power of God unto salvation to every one that believeth; to the Jew first, and also to the Greek.
17 For therein is the righteousness of God revealed from faith to faith: as it is written, The just shall live by faith.

18 For the wrath of God is revealed from heaven against all ungodliness and unrighteousness of men, who hold the truth in unrighteousness;

19 Because that which may be known of God is manifest in them; for God hath shewed (it) unto them.
20 For the invisible things of him from the creation of the world are clearly seen, being understood by the things that are made, (even) his eternal power and Godhead; so that they are without excuse:
21 Because that, when they knew God, they glorified (him) not as God, neither were thankful; but became vain in their imaginations, and their foolish heart was darkened.

Literal Translation

22 Professing to be
wise, they became fool-
ish
23 and changed the
glory of the incorrupt-
ible God in(to) a like-
ness of an image of cor-
ruptible man, and of
birds, and four-footed
animals, and creeping
things.
24 Because of this, God
gave them up to impu-
rity in the lusts of (their)
hearts, their bodies to be
dishonored among
themselves,
25 who changed the
truth of God into the lie,
and worshiped and
served the creature
rather than the Creator,
who is blessed forever.
Amen.
26 Because of this, God
gave them up to dishon-
orable passions, for
even their females
changed the natural use
to that contrary to na-
ture.
27 And likewise, the
males also having for-
saken the natural use of
the female burned in
their lust toward one an-
other, males with males
working out shameful-
ness, and receiving
back within themselves
the reward which was
fitting for their straying
away.
28 And even as they did
not think fit to have God
in (their) knowledge,
God gave them up to a
reprobate mind, to do
the things not being
right,
29 having been filled
with all unrighteous-
ness, fornication, de-
pravity, covetousness,
malignity, (being) full
of envy, murder, quar-
rels, deceit, evil habits,
(becoming) whisper-
ers, insolent,
30 slanderers, God-hat-
ers,

ROMANS 1:22

2588 5335 1511 4680 3471 2532
καρδία. 22 φάσκοντες εἶναι σοφοὶ ἐμωράνθησαν, 23 καὶ
heart. Professing to be wise they became foolish, and

236 3588 1391 3588 862 2316 1722 3667 1504
ἤλλαξαν τὴν δόξαν τοῦ ἀφθάρτου Θεοῦ ἐν ὁμοιώματι εἰκόνος
changed the glory of the incorruptible God in the likeness of an image

5349 444 2532 4071 2532 5074 2532 2062
φθαρτοῦ ἀνθρώπου καὶ πετεινῶν καὶ τετραπόδων καὶ ἑρπετῶν.
of corruptible man and birds and four-footed animals and reptiles.

1352 2532 3860 846 3588 2316 1722 3588 1939 3588
24 Διο καὶ παρέδωκεν αὐτοὺς ὁ Θεὸς ἐν ταῖς ἐπιθυμίαις τῶν
Therefore also gave up them God in the lusts of the

2588 846 1519 167 3588 818 3588 4983
καρδιῶν αὐτῶν εἰς ἀκαθαρσίαν, τοῦ ἀτιμάζεσθαι τὰ σώματα
hearts of them to impurity to be dishonored the bodies

846 1722 1438 3748 3337 3588 225 3588
αὐτῶν ἐν ἑαυτοῖς· 25 οἵτινες μετήλλαξαν τὴν ἀλήθειαν τοῦ
of the among themselves; who changed the truth

2316 1722 3588 5579 2532 4573 2532 3000 3588
Θεοῦ ἐν τῷ ψεύδει, καὶ ἐσεβάσθησαν καὶ ἐλάτρευσαν τῇ
of God in(to) the lie, and worshiped and served the

2937 3844 3588 2936 3739 2076 2128 1519 3588
κτίσει παρὰ τὸν κτίσαντα, ὅς ἐστιν εὐλογητὸς εἰς τοὺς
creature rather than the Creator, who is blessed to the

165 281
αἰῶνας. ἀμήν.
ages.

1223 5124 3860 846 3588 2316 1519 3806 819
26 διὰ τοῦτο παρέδωκεν αὐτοὺς ὁ Θεὸς εἰς πάθη ἀτιμίας·
Because of this gave up them God to passions of dishonor;

3588 5037 1063 2338 846 3337 3588 5446 5540
αἵ τε γὰρ θήλειαι αὐτῶν μετήλλαξαν τὴν φυσικὴν χρῆσιν
the even for females of them changed the natural use

1519 3588 3844 5449 3668 5037 2532 3588 730 863 3588
εἰς τὴν παρὰ φύσιν· 27 ὁμοίως τε καὶ οἱ ἄρσενες, ἀφέντες τὴν
to the (use) against nature; likewise and also the males, having forsaken the

5446 5540 3588 2338 1572 1722 3588 3715 846
φυσικὴν χρῆσιν τῆς θηλείας, ἐξεκαύθησαν ἐν τῇ ὀρέξει αὐτῶν
natural use of the female, burned in the lust of them

1519 240 730 1722 730 3588 808 2716
εἰς ἀλλήλους, ἄρσενες ἐν ἄρσεσι τὴν ἀσχημοσύνην κατερ-
toward one another, males among males the shamefulness working

2532 3588 489 3739 1163 3588 4106 846
γαζόμενοι, καὶ τὴν ἀντιμισθίαν ἣν ἔδει τῆς πλάνης αὐτῶν
out, and the reward which behoved the straying away of them

1722 1438 618
ἐν ἑαυτοῖς ἀπολαμβάνοντες.
in themselves receiving back.

2532 2531 3756 1381 3588 2316 2192 1722 1922
28 καὶ καθὼς οὐκ ἐδοκίμασαν τὸν Θεὸν ἔχειν ἐν ἐπιγνώσει,
And even as not they thought fit God to have in knowledge,

3860 846 3588 2316 1519 96 3563 4160 3588 3361
παρέδωκεν αὐτοὺς ὁ Θεὸς εἰς ἀδόκιμον νοῦν, ποιεῖν τὰ μὴ
gave up them God to a reprobate mind, to do the things not

2520 4137 3956 93 4202 4189
καθήκοντα, 29 πεπληρωμένους πάσῃ ἀδικίᾳ, πορνείᾳ, πονηρίᾳ.
being right, having been filled with all unrighteousness, fornication, malice,

4124 2549 3324 5355 5408 2054 1388
πλεονεξίᾳ, κακίᾳ· μεστοὺς φθόνου, φόνου, ἔριδος, δόλου,
covetousness, malignity; full of envy, murder, quarrels, deceit,

2550 5588 2637 2319 5197
κακοηθείας, ψιθυριστάς, 30 καταλάλους, θεοστυγεῖς, ὑβριστάς,
evil habits, whisperers, slanderers, God-haters, insolent,

King James Version

22 Professing them-
selves to be wise, they
became fools,
23 And changed the
glory of the uncorrup-
tible God into an image
made like to corruptible
man, and to birds, and
fourfooted beasts, and
creeping things.
24 Wherefore God also
gave them up to un-
cleanness through the
lusts of their own hearts,
to dishonour their own
bodies between them-
selves:
25 Who changed the
truth of God into a lie,
and worshipped and
served the creature
more than the Creator,
who is blessed for ever.
Amen.
26 For this cause God
gave them up unto vile
affections: for even
their women did change
the natural use into that
which is against nature:
27 And likewise also
the men, leaving the
natural use of the
woman, burned in their
lust one toward another;
men with men working
that which is unseemly,
and receiving in them-
selves that recompence
of their error which was
meet.
28 And even as they did
not like to retain God in
(their) knowledge, God
gave them over to a rep-
robate mind, to do those
things which are not
convenient;
29 Being filled with all
unrighteousness, forni-
cation, wickedness,
covetousness, mali-
ciousness; full of envy,
murder, debate, deceit,
malignity; whisperers,
30 Backbiters, haters

Romans 1:31

Literal Translation

proud, braggarts, devisers of evil things, disobedient to parents,
31 without discernment, perfidious, without natural affection, implacable, unmerciful,
32 who having known the righteous order of God, that those practicing such things are worthy of death, not only do them, but also applaud those practicing (them).

5244 213 2182 2556 1118 545
ὑπερηφάνους, ἀλαζόνας, ἐφευρετὰς κακῶν, γονεῦσιν ἀπει-
proud, braggarts, devisers of evil things, to parents dis-
801 802 794 786
θεῖς, 31 ἀσυνέτους, ἀσυνθέτους, ἀστόργους, ἀσπόνδους,
obedient, undiscerning, perfidious, without affection, implacable,
415 3748 3588 1345 3588 2316 1921 3754
ἀνελεήμονας· 32 οἵτινες τὸ δικαίωμα τοῦ Θεοῦ ἐπιγνόντες, ὅτι
unmerciful; who the righteous order of God having known, that
3588 3588 5108 4238 514 2288 1526 3756 3440 846
οἱ τὰ τοιαῦτα πράσσοντες ἄξιοι θανάτου εἰσίν, οὐ μόνον αὐτὰ
those such things practicing worthy of death are, not only them
4160 235 2532 4909 3588 4238
ποιοῦσιν, ἀλλὰ καὶ συνευδοκοῦσι τοῖς πράσσουσι.
do, but also approve those practicing (them).

King James Version

of God, despiteful, proud, boasters, inventors of evil things, disobedient to parents,
31 Without understanding, covenantbreakers, without natural affection, implacable, unmerciful:
32 Who knowing the judgment of God, that they which commit such things are worthy of death, not only do the same, but have pleasure in them that do them.

Romans 2

1. Therefore, O man, you are without excuse, everyone judging, for in that in which you judge the other, you condemn yourself; for you, the (ones) judging, practice the same things.
2 But we know that the judgment of God is according to truth on those that practice such things.
3 And, O man, the (one) judging those practicing such things, and doing them, do you think that you will escape the judgment of God?
4 Or do you despise the riches of His kindness, and the forbearance and the long-suffering, not knowing that the kindness of God leads you to repentance?
5 But according to your hardness and your impenitent heart, do you treasure up for yourself wrath in a day of wrath, and revelation of a righteous judgment of God,
6 who will give to each according to his works, (Ps.62:12)
7 to the (ones) truly by patience work good glory and honor and seeking incorruptibility, everlasting life ;
8 but to the (ones) even disobeying the truth, out of self-seeking, and obeying unrighteousness, (will be) anger and wrath,
9 trouble and pain on

Romans 2

1352 379 1488 5599 444 3956 3588 2919 1722 3739 1063
1 Διὸ ἀναπολόγητος εἶ, ὦ ἄνθρωπε πᾶς ὁ κρίνων· ἐν ᾧ γὰρ
Therefore without excuse are you, O man, everyone judging, in what for
2919 3588 2087 4572 2632 3588 1063 846 4238
κρίνεις τὸν ἕτερον, σεαυτὸν κατακρίνεις, τὰ γὰρ αὐτὰ πράσ-
you judge the other, yourself you condemn, the for same things you
3588 2919 1492 1161 3754 3588 2917 3588 2316 2076 2596
σεις ὁ κρίνων. 2 οἴδαμεν δὲ ὅτι τὸ κρίμα τοῦ Θεοῦ ἐστι κατὰ
practice those judging. we know But that the judgment of God is according to
225 1909 3588 3588 5108 4238 3049 1161 5124
ἀλήθειαν ἐπὶ τοὺς τὰ τοιαῦτα πράσσοντας. 3 λογίζῃ δὲ τοῦτο,
truth on the (ones) such things practicing. do you think And this,
5599 444 3588 2919 3588 3588 5108 4238 2532 4160
ὦ ἄνθρωπε ὁ κρίνων τοὺς τὰ τοιαῦτα πράσσοντας καὶ ποιῶν
O man the (one) judging those such things practicing' and doing
846 3754 4771 1628 3588 2917 3588 2316 2228 3588 4149
αὐτά, ὅτι σὺ ἐκφεύξῃ τὸ κρίμα τοῦ Θεοῦ; 4 ἢ τοῦ πλούτου
them, that you will escape the judgment of God? Or the riches
3588 5544 846 2532 3588 463 2532 3588 3115
τῆς χρηστότητος αὐτοῦ καὶ τῆς ἀνοχῆς καὶ τῆς μακροθυμίας
of the kindness of Him and the forbearance and the long-suffering
2706 50 3754 3588 5543 3588 2316 1519 3341
καταφρονεῖς, ἀγνοῶν ὅτι τὸ χρηστὸν τοῦ θεοῦ εἰς μετάνοιάν
do you despise, not knowing that the kindness of God to repentance
4571 71 2596 1161 3588 4643 4675 2532 279
σε ἄγει; 5 κατὰ δὲ τὴν σκληρότητά σου καὶ ἀμετανόητον
you leads? according to But the hardness of you and impenitent
2588 2343 4572 3709 1722 2250 3709 2532
καρδίαν θησαυρίζεις σεαυτῷ ὀργὴν ἐν ἡμέρᾳ ὀργῆς καὶ
heart do you treasure for yourself wrath in a day of wrath and
602 1341 3588 2316 3739 591 1538
ἀποκαλύψεως δικαιοκρισίας τοῦ θεου, 6 ὃς ἀποδώσει ἑκάστῳ
revelation of a righteous judgment of God, who will give to each
2596 3588 2041 846 3588 3303 2596 5281 2041 18
κατὰ τὰ ἔργα αὐτοῦ· 7 τοῖς μὲν καθ' ὑπομονὴν ἔργου ἀγαθοῦ
according to the works of him; to those truly by patience work good
1391 2532 5092 2532 861 2212 2222 166 3588
δόξαν καὶ τιμὴν καὶ ἀφθαρσίαν ζητοῦσι, ζωὴν αἰώνιον· 8 τοῖς
glory and honor and incorruptibility seeking, life everlasting; to those
1161 1537 2052 2532 544 3588 225 3982 1161
δὲ ἐξ ἐριθείας καὶ ἀπειθοῦσι μὲν τῇ ἀληθείᾳ, πειθομένοις δὲ
but of self-seeking and disobeying truly the truth, obeying and
3588 93 2372 2532 3709 2347 2532 4730 1909
τῇ ἀδικίᾳ, θυμὸς καὶ ὀργή, 9 θλίψις καὶ στενοχωρία, ἐπὶ
unrighteousness, anger and wrath, trouble and pain on

Romans 2

1. Therefore thou art inexcusable, O man, whosoever thou art that judgest: for wherein thou judgest another, thou condemnest thyself; for thou that judgest doest the same things.
2 But we are sure that the judgment of God is according to truth against them which commit such things.
3 And thinkest thou this, O man, that judgest them which do such things, and doest the same, that thou shalt escape the judgment of God?
4 Or despisest thou the riches of his goodness and forbearance and longsuffering; not knowing that the goodness of God leadeth thee to repentance?
5 But after thy hardness and impenitent heart treasurest up unto thyself wrath against the day of wrath and revelation of the righteous judgment of God;
6 Who will render to every man according to his deeds:
7 To them who by patient continuance in well doing seek for glory and honour and immortality, eternal life:
8 But unto them that are contentious, and do not obey the truth, but obey unrighteousness, indignation and wrath,
9 Tribulation and anguish, upon

Literal Translation **Romans 2:10** ***King James Version***

every soul of man hav-
ing worked out evil,
both of Jew firstly, and
of Greek.

10 But glory and honor
and peace (will be) to
everyone having
worked out good, both
to (the) Jew firstly, and
to (the) Greek.

11 For there is no re-
spect of persons with
God.
12 For as many as
sinned without Law
will also perish without
Law. And as many as
sinned within Law will
be judged through Law.
13 For not the hearers of
the Law are just with
God, but the doers of the
Law shall be justified.

14 For when nations not
having Law do by na-
ture the things of the
Law, they not having
Law are a law (to) them-
selves,

15 who demonstrate the
work of the law written
in their hearts, their con-
science witnessing with
(them), and the
thoughts between one
another accusing or
even excusing,

16 in a day when God
judges the hidden
things of men, accord-
ing to my gospel,
through Jesus Christ.

17 Behold! You are
called a Jew, and rest in
the Law, and boast in
God,
18 and know the will,
and approve the things
excelling, having been
instructed out of the
Law,
19 and having per-
suaded yourself to be a
guide of blind ones, a
light to those in dark-
ness,
20 an instructor of fool-
ish ones, a teacher of in-
fants, having the form
of knowledge and of the
truth in the Law.
21 Then the (one)
teaching

3956 5590 444 3588 2716 3588 2556
πᾶσαν ψυχὴν ἀνθρώπου τοῦ κατεργαζομένου τὸ κακόν,
every soul of man having worked out the evil,
2453 5037 4412 2532 1672 1391 1161 2532 5092 2532
Ἰουδαίου τε πρῶτον καὶ Ἕλληνος· 10 δόξα δὲ καὶ τιμὴ καὶ
of Jew both firstly and of Greek; glory but and honor and
1515 3956 3588 2038 3588 18 2453 5037 4412
εἰρήνη παντὶ τῷ ἐργαζομένῳ τὸ ἀγαθόν, Ἰουδαίῳ τε πρῶτον
peace to everyone having worked out the good, to Jew both firstly
2532 1672 3756 1063 2076 4382 3844 3588 2316
καὶ Ἕλληνι· 11 οὐ γάρ ἐστι προσωποληψία παρὰ τῷ Θεῷ.
and to Greek; not for is respect of persons with God.
3745 1063 460 264 460 2532 622 2532
12 ὅσοι γὰρ ἀνόμως ἥμαρτον, ἀνόμως καὶ ἀπολοῦνται· καὶ
as many as For without law sinned, without law also will perish; and
3745 1722 3551 264 1223 3551 2919 3756 1063 3588
ὅσοι ἐν νόμῳ ἥμαρτον, διὰ νόμου κριθήσονται· 13 οὐ γὰρ οἱ
as many as in law sinned, through law will be judged; not for the
202 3588 3551 1342 3844 3588 2316 235 3588 4163
ἀκροαταὶ τοῦ νόμου δίκαιοι παρὰ τῷ Θεῷ, ἀλλ' οἱ ποιηταὶ
hearers of the law (are) just with God, but the doers
3588 3551 1344 3752 1063 1484 3588 3361 3551
τοῦ νόμου δικαιωθήσονται. 14 ὅταν γὰρ ἔθνη τὰ μὴ νόμον
of the law shall be justified. when For nations not law
2192 5449 3588 3588 3551 4160 3778 3551 3361 2192
ἔχοντα φύσει τὰ τοῦ νόμου ποιῇ, οὗτοι, νόμον μὴ ἔχοντες,
having by nature the things of the law do, these, law not having,
1438 1526 3551 3748 1731 3588 2041 3588 3551
ἑαυτοῖς εἰσι νόμος· 15 οἵτινες ἐνδείκνυνται τὸ ἔργον τοῦ νόμου
themselves are a law; who demonstrate the work of the law
1123 1722 3588 2588 846 4828 846
γραπτὸν ἐν ταῖς καρδίαις αὐτῶν, συμμαρτυρούσης αὐτῶν
written in the hearts of them, witnessing with of them
3588 4893 2532 3342 240 3588 3053
τῆς συνειδήσεως, καὶ μεταξὺ ἀλλήλων τῶν λογισμῶν
the conscience, and between one another the thoughts
2723 2228 2532 626 1722 2250 3753 2919
κατηγορούντων ἢ καὶ ἀπολογουμένων, 16 ἐν ἡμέρᾳ ὅτε κρινεῖ
accusing or even excusing, in a day when judges
3588 2316 3588 2927 3588 444 2596 3588 2098 3450
ὁ Θεὸς τὰ κρυπτὰ τῶν ἀνθρώπων, κατὰ τὸ εὐαγγέλιόν μου,
God the hidden things of men, according to the gospel of me,
1223 2424 5547
διὰ Ἰησοῦ Χριστοῦ.
through Jesus Christ.

2396 4771 2453 2028 2532 1879 3588 3551
17 ἴδε σὺ Ἰουδαῖος ἐπονομάζῃ, καὶ ἐπαναπαύῃ τῷ νόμῳ,
Behold! You a Jew are named and rest in the Law,
2532 2744 1722 2316 2532 1097 3588 2307 2532
καὶ καυχᾶσαι ἐν Θεῷ, 18 καὶ γινώσκεις τὸ θέλημα, καὶ δοκι-
and boast in God, and know the will, and approve
1381 3588 1308 2727 1537 3588 3551 3982
μάζεις τὰ διαφέροντα, κατηχούμενος ἐκ τοῦ νόμου, 19 πέποιθάς
the things excelling, having been instructed out of the Law, having persuaded
5037 4572 3595 1511 5185 5457 3588 1722 4655 3810
τε σεαυτὸν ὁδηγὸν εἶναι τυφλῶν, φῶς τῶν ἐν σκότει, 20 παι-
and yourself a guide to be of blind ones, a light to those in darkness, an
878 1320 3516 2192 3588 3446
δευτὴν ἀφρόνων, διδάσκαλον νηπίων, ἔχοντα τὴν μόρφωσιν
instructor of foolish ones, a teacher of infants, having the form
3588 1108 2532 3588 225 1722/3588/3551 3588 3767 1321
τῆς γνώσεως καὶ τῆς ἀληθείας ἐν τῷ νόμῳ·21 ὁ οὖν διδάσκων
of knowledge and of the truth in the Law; the (one) then teaching

every soul of man that
doeth evil, of the Jew
first, and also of the
Gentile;
10 But glory, honour,
and peace, to every man
that worketh good, to
the Jew first, and also to
the Gentile:

11 For there is no re-
spect of persons with
God.

12 For as many as have
sinned without law
shall also perish without
law: and as many as
have sinned in the law
shall be judged by the
law;
13 (For not the hearers
of the law (are) just be-
fore God, but the doers
of the law shall be justi-
fied.
14 For when the Gen-
tiles, which have not the
law, do by nature the
things contained in the
law, these, having not
the law, are a law unto
themselves:
15 Which shew the
work of the law written
in their hearts, their con-
science also bearing
witness, and (their)
thoughts the mean
while accusing or else
excusing one another;)

16 In the day when God
shall judge the secrets of
men by Jesus Christ ac-
cording to my gospel.

17 Behold, thou art
called a Jew, and restest
in the law, and makest
thy boast of God,
18 And knowest (his)
will, and approvest the
things that are more ex-
cellent, being instructed
out of the law;
19 And art confident
that thou thyself art a
guide of the blind, a
light of them which are
in darkness,
20 An instructor of the
foolish, a teacher of
babes, which hast the
form of knowledge and
of the truth in the law.
21 Thou therefore
which teachest

Literal Translation

Romans 2:22

another, do you not teach yourself? The (one) preaching not to steal, do you steal?
22 The (one) saying not to commit adultery, do you commit adultery? The (one) detesting the idols, do you rob temples?
23 (You) who boast in Law, do you dishonor God through transgression of the Law?
24 For the name of God is blasphemed among the nations through you, even as it has been written: (Isa.52:5)
25 For indeed circumcision profits if you practice (the) Law, but if you are a transgressor of Law, your circumcision becomes uncircumcision.
26 If, then, the uncircumcision keeps the demands of the Law, (will) not his uncircumcision be counted for circumcision?
27 And will (not) the uncircumcision by nature (by) fulfilling the Law judge you, the (one who) through letter and circumcision (becomes) transgressor of Law?
28 For he is not a Jew that (is one) outwardly, nor (is) circumcision that outwardly in flesh;
29 but he (is) a Jew that (is one) inwardly, and circumcision (is) of heart, in spirit, not in letter; of whom the praise (is) not from men, but from God.

2087 4572 3756 1321 3588 2784 3361 2813
ἕτερον, σεαυτὸν οὐ διδάσκεις; ὁ κηρύσσων μὴ κλέπτειν,
another, yourself not do you teach? The (one) proclaiming not to steal,
2813 3588 3004 3361 3431 3431 3588 948
κλέπτεις; 22 ὁ λέγων μὴ μοιχεύειν, μοιχεύεις; ὁ βδελυσσόμενος
do you steal? He saying not to do adultery, do you do adultery? He detesting
3588 1497 2416 3739 1722 3551 2744 1223 3588
τὰ εἴδωλα, ἱεροσυλεῖς; 23 ὃς ἐν νόμῳ καυχᾶσαι, διὰ τῆς
the idols, do you rob temples? Who in Law boast, through the
3847 3588 3551 3588 2316 818 3588 1063 3686
παραβάσεως τοῦ νόμου τὸν Θεὸν ἀτιμάζεις; 24 τὸ γὰρ ὄνομα
transgression of the Law God do you dishonor? the For name
3588 2316 1223 5209 987 1722 3588 1484 2531 1125
τοῦ Θεοῦ δι᾽ ὑμᾶς βλασφημεῖται ἐν τοῖς ἔθνεσι, καθὼς γέγ-
of God through you is blasphemed among the nations, even as it has
4061 3303 1063 5623 1437 3551 4238
ραπται. 25 περιτομὴ μὲν γὰρ ὠφελεῖ, ἐὰν νόμον πράσσῃς·
been written. circumcision truly For profits, if Law you practice;
1437 1161 3848 3551 1510 3588 4061 4675 203
ἐὰν δὲ παραβάτης νόμου ᾖς, ἡ περιτομή σου ἀκροβυστία
if but a transgressor of Law you are, the circumcision of you uncircumcision
1096 1437 3767 3588 203 3588 1345 3588 3551
γέγονεν. 26 ἐὰν οὖν ἡ ἀκροβυστία τὰ δικαιώματα τοῦ νόμου
becomes. if Then the uncircumcision the ordinances of the law
5442 3780 3588 203 846 1519 4061 3049
φυλάσσῃ, οὐχὶ ἡ ἀκροβυστία αὐτοῦ εἰς περιτομὴν λογισθή-
keeps, (will) not the uncircumcision of him for circumcision be counted?
2532 2919 3588 1537 5449 203 3588 3551
σεται; 27 καὶ κρινεῖ ἡ ἐκ φύσεως ἀκροβυστία, τὸν νόμον
And will judge the by nature uncircumcision, the law
5055 4571 3588 1223 1121 2532 4061 3848
τελοῦσα σὲ τὸν διὰ γράμματος καὶ περιτομῆς παραβάτην
completing you the through letters and circumcision transgressor
3551 3756 1063 3588 1722 3588 5318 2453 2076/3761/3588/1722
νόμου; 28 οὐ γὰρ ὁ ἐν τῷ φανερῷ Ἰουδαῖός ἐστιν, οὐδὲ ἡ ἐν
of Law? not For the in the visible Jew he is, nor the in
3588 5318 1722 4561 4061 235/3588/1722/3588/2927 2453
τῷ φανερῷ ἐν σαρκὶ περιτομή· 29 ἀλλ᾽ ὁ ἐν τῷ κρυπτῷ Ἰουδαῖος,
the visible in flesh circumcision; but the in inwardly Jew (is),
2532 4061 2588 1722 4151 3756 1121 3739/3588
καὶ περιτομὴ καρδίας ἐν πνεύματι, οὐ γράμματι· οὗ ὁ
and circumcision (is) of heart, in spirit, not in letter; of whom the
1868 3756 1537 444 235 1537 3588 2316
ἔπαινος οὐκ ἐξ ἀνθρώπων, ἀλλ᾽ ἐκ τοῦ Θεοῦ.
praise (is) not from man, but from God.

King James Version

another, teachest thou not thyself? thou that preachest a man should not steal, dost thou steal?
22 Thou that sayest a man should not commit adultery, dost thou commit adultery? thou that abhorrest idols, dost thou commit sacrilege?
23 Thou that makest thy boast of the law, through breaking the law dishonourest thou God?
24 For the name of God is blasphemed among the Gentiles through you, as it is written.
25 For circumcision verily profiteth, if thou keep the law: but if thou be a breaker of the law, thy circumcision is made uncircumcision.
26 Therefore if the uncircumcision keep the righteousness of the law, shall not his uncircumcision be counted for circumcision?
27 And shall not uncircumcision which is by nature, if it fulfil the law, judge thee, who by the letter and circumcision dost transgress the law?
28 For he is not a Jew, which is one outwardly; neither (is that) circumcision, which is outward in the flesh:
29 But he (is) a Jew, which is one inwardly; and circumcision (is that) of the heart, in the spirit, (and) not in the letter; whose praise (is) not of men, but of God.

Romans 3

1. What then (is) the superiority of the Jew? Or what the profit of circumcision?
2 Much in every way. For first, indeed, that they were entrusted with the oracles of God.
3 For what if some did not believe? (Will) not their unbelief destroy the faith of God?

4 Let it not be! But let God be true, and every man

Romans 3

5101 3767 3588 4053 3588 2453 2228/5101/3588/5622 3588
1 Τί οὖν τὸ περισσὸν τοῦ Ἰουδαίου, ἢ τίς ἡ ὠφέλεια τῆς
What then the superiority of the Jew, or what the profit
4061 4183 2596 3956 5158 4412 3303 1063 3754
περιτομῆς; 2 πολὺ κατὰ πάντα τρόπον· πρῶτον μὲν γὰρ ὅτι
of circumcision? Much in every way; firstly truly for that
4100 3588 3051 3588 2316 5101 1063 1487 569
ἐπιστεύθησαν τὰ λόγια τοῦ Θεοῦ. 3 τί γὰρ εἰ ἠπίστησάν
they were entrusted with the oracles of God. what For if disbelieved
5100 3361 3588 570 846 3588 4102 3588 2316 2673
τινες; μὴ ἡ ἀπιστία αὐτῶν τὴν πίστιν τοῦ Θεοῦ καταργήσει;
some? Not the unbelief of them the faith of God destroy?
3361 1096 1096 1161/3588/2316 227 3956 1161 444
4 μὴ γένοιτο· γινέσθω δὲ ὁ Θεὸς ἀληθής, πᾶς δὲ ἄνθρωπος
Not let it be! let be But God be true, every and man

Romans 3

1. What advantage then hath the Jew? or what profit (is there) of circumcision?
2 Much every way: chiefly, because that unto them were committed the oracles of God.
3 For what if some did not believe? shall their unbelief make the faith of God without effect?
4 God forbid: yea, let God be true, but every man

Literal Translation | **Romans 3:5** | ***King James Version***

a liar; even as it has been written, "So as You should be justified in Your words, and will overcome in Your being judged." (Psa. 51:4)
5 But if our unrighteousness commends the righteousness of God, what shall we say? (Is) God unrighteous who lays on wrath? I speak according to man.
6 Let it not be! Otherwise, how will God judge the world?
7 For if in my lie the truth of God abounded to His glory, why am I yet judged as a sinner?
8 And not, as we are wrongly accused, and as some report us to say, Let us do bad things so that good things may come, (the) judgment of whom is just.

5583 2531 1125 3704 302 1344 1722 3588
ψεύστης, καθὼς γέγραπται, Ὅπως ἂν δικαιωθῇς ἐν τοῖς
a liar? even as it has been written, So as you may be justified in the

3056 4675 2532 3528 1722 3588 2919 4571 1487/1161/3588/93
λόγοις σου, καὶ νικήσεις ἐν τῷ κρίνεσθαί σε. 5 εἰ δὲ ἡ ἀδικία
sayings of you, and will overcome in the being judged of you. if But the unrighteousness

2257 2316 1343 4921 5101 2046 3361 94
ἡμῶν Θεοῦ δικαιοσύνην συνίστησι, τί ἐροῦμεν; μὴ ἄδικος
of us of God a righteousness commends, what shall we say? not unrighteous

3588 2316 3588 2018 3588 3709 2596 444 3004 3361
ὁ Θεὸς ὁ ἐπιφέρων τὴν ὀργήν; [κατὰ ἄνθρωπον λέγω]. 6 μὴ
(is) God inflicting wrath? - according to man I say -. Not

1096 1893 4459 2919 3588 2316 3588 2889 1487 1063 3588
γένοιτο· ἐπεὶ πῶς κρινεῖ ὁ Θεὸς τὸν κόσμον; 7 εἰ γὰρ ἡ
let it be! Otherwise how will judge God the world? If For the

225 3588 2316 1722 3588 1699 5582 4052 1519 3588
ἀλήθεια τοῦ Θεοῦ ἐν τῷ ἐμῷ ψεύσματι ἐπερίσσευσεν εἰς τὴν
truth of God by my lie abounded to the

1391 846 5101 2089 2504 5613 268 2919 2532 3361
δόξαν αὐτοῦ, τί ἔτι κἀγὼ ὡς ἁμαρτωλὸς κρίνομαι; 8 καὶ μή
glory of Him, why yet I also as a sinner am judged And not

2531 987 2532 2531 5346 5100 2248 3004
[καθὼς βλασφημούμεθα, καὶ καθώς φασί τινες ἡμᾶς λέγειν
as - we are wrongly accused, and even as report some of us to say-

3754 4160 3588 2556 2443 2064 3588 18 3739 3588
ὅτι], Ποιήσωμεν τὰ κακὰ ἵνα ἔλθῃ τὰ ἀγαθά; ὧν τὸ
Let us do things bad that may come things good? of whom the

2917 1738 2076
κρίμα ἔνδικόν ἐστι.
judgment just is.

a liar; as it is written, That thou mightest be justified in thy sayings, and mightest overcome when thou art judged.
5 But if our unrighteousness commend the righteousness of God, what shall we say? (Is) God unrighteous who taketh vengeance? (I speak as a man)
6 God forbid: for then how shall God judge the world?
7 For if the truth of God hath more abounded through my lie unto his glory; why yet am I also judged as a sinner?
8 And not (rather), (as we be slanderously reported, and as some affirm that we say,) Let us do evil, that good may come? whose damnation is just.

9 What then? Do we excel? Not at all! For before we have charged both Jews and Greeks, all to be under sin;
10 according as it has been written, There is none righteous, not one!
11 "There is none that understanding, there is not one that seeking after God." (Psa. 14:2)
12 All turned away, (they) became worthless together, "not (one is) doing kindness, not so much as one!" (Psa. 14:3)
13 "Their throat (is) an opened grave; they used deceit with their tongues;" (Psa. 5:9) "(the) poison of asps (is) under their lips;" (Psa. 140:3)
14 "whose mouth (is) full of cursing and bitterness." (Psa. 10:7)
15 "Their feet (are) swift to shed blood;
16 ruin and misery (are) in their way;
17 and they did not know a way of peace;" (Isa. 59:7,8)
18 "there is no fear of God before their eyes." (Psa. 36:1)

5101 3767 4284 3756 3843 4256 1063
9. Τί οὖν; προεχόμεθα; οὐ πάντως, προῃτιασάμεθα γὰρ
What then? Do we excel? Not at all, we before charged For

2453 5037 2532 1672 3956 5259 266 1511 2531
Ἰουδαίους τε καὶ Ἕλληνας πάντας ὑφ' ἁμαρτίαν εἶναι, 10 καθὼς
Jews both and Greeks all under sin to be, even as

1125 3754 3756 2076 1342 3761 1520 3756 2076 3588
γέγραπται ὅτι Οὐκ ἔστι δίκαιος οὐδὲ εἷς· 11 οὐκ ἔστιν ὁ
it has been written, Not is a righteous one, not one; not is (one)

4920 3756 2076 3588 1567 3588 2316 3956 1578
συνιῶν, οὐκ ἔστιν ὁ ἐκζητῶν τὸν Θεόν· 12 πάντες ἐξέκλιναν,
understanding, not is (one) seeking God; all turned away,

260 889 3756 2076 4160 5544 3756 2076 2193
ἅμα ἠχρεώθησαν· οὐκ ἔστι ποιῶν χρηστότητα, οὐκ ἔστιν ἕως
together became worthless; not is (one) doing kindness, not is so much as

1520 5028 455 3588 2995 846 3588 1100
ἑνός. 13 τάφος ἀνεῳγμένος ὁ λάρυγξ αὐτῶν, ταῖς γλώσσαις
one. A tomb having been opened the throat of them, with the tongues

846 1387 2447 785 5259 3588 5491 846 3739 3588
αὐτῶν ἐδολιοῦσαν· ἰὸς ἀσπίδων ὑπὸ τὰ χείλη αὐτῶν· 14 ὧν τὸ
of them they used deceit; of asps poison under the lips (is) of them;of whom the

4750 685 2532 4088 1073 3691 3588 4228 846 1632
στόμα ἀρᾶς καὶ πικρίας γέμει· 15 ὀξεῖς οἱ πόδες αὐτῶν ἐκχέαι
mouth of cursing and bitterness is full; swift of the feet of them to shed

129 4938 2532 5004 1722 3588 3598 846 2532
αἷμα· 16 σύντριμμα καὶ ταλαιπωρία ἐν ταῖς ὁδοῖς αὐτῶν, 17 καὶ
blood; ruin and misery in the way of them, and

3598 1515 3756 1097 3756 2076 5401 2316 561
ὁδὸν εἰρήνης οὐκ ἔγνωσαν· 18 οὐκ ἔστι φόβος Θεοῦ ἀπέναντι
a way of peace not they know; Not is fear of God before

3588 3788 846
τῶν ὀφθαλμῶν αὐτῶν.
the eyes of them.

9 What then? are we better (than they)? No, in no wise: for we have before proved both Jews and Gentiles, that they are all under sin;
10 As it is written, There is none righteous, no, not one:
11 There is none that understandeth, there is none that seeketh after God.
12 They are all gone out of the way, they are together become unprofitable; there is none that doeth good, no, not one.
13 Their throat (is) an open sepulchre; with their tongues they have used deceit; the poison of asps (is) under their lips:
14 Whose mouth (is) full of cursing and bitterness:
15 Their feet (are) swift to shed blood:
16 Destruction and misery (are) in their ways:
17 And the way of peace have they not known:
18 There is no fear of God before their eyes.

Literal Translation

19 But we know that
whatever the Law says,
it speaks to those within
the Law, so that every
mouth may be stopped,
and all the world be un-
der judgment to God.
20 Because by works of
law not (one of) all flesh
will be justified before
Him, for through law
(is) full knowledge of
sin.
21 But now a righteous-
ness of God has been re-
vealed apart from Law,
being witnessed by the
Law and the Prophets,
22 even the righteous-
ness of God through
faith of Jesus Christ to-
ward all and upon all the
(ones) believing; for
there is no difference,
23 for all sinned and
come short of the glory
of God,
24 having been justified
freely by His grace
through the redemption
in Christ Jesus,
25 whom God set forth
(as) a propitiation
through faith in His
blood, for a showing
forth of His righteous-
ness through the pass-
ing by of the sins that
had taken place before,
in the forbearance of
God,
26 for the showing forth
of His righteousness in
the present time, for His
being just and justifying
the (one that is) of (the)
faith of Jesus.
27 Then where (is) the
boasting? It was shut
out. Through what law?
Of works? No, but
through a law of faith.
28 Then we conclude a
man to be justified by
faith without works of
law.
29 Or (is He) the God of
Jews only? And not also
of the nations? Yes, of
the nations also,
30 since (it is) one God
who will justify circum-
cision by faith, and un-
circumcision through
faith.
31 Then do we destroy
law

Romans 3:19

1492 1161 3754 3745 3588 3551 3004 3588 1722 3588 3551 2980
19 Οἴδαμεν δὲ ὅτι ὅσα ὁ νόμος λέγει, τοῖς ἐν τῷ νόμῳ λαλεῖ,
we know But that what the law says, to those in the law it says,

2443 3956 4750 5420 2532 5267 1096 3956 3588 2889
ἵνα πᾶν στόμα φραγῇ, καὶ ὑπόδικος γένηται πᾶς ὁ κόσμος
that every mouth be stopped, and under judgment may become all the world

3588 2316 1360 1537 2041 3551 3756 1344 3956 4561
τῷ Θεῷ· 20 διότι ἐξ ἔργων νόμου οὐ δικαιωθήσεται πᾶσα σὰρξ
to God; because by works of law not will be justified all flesh

1799 846 1223 1063 3551 1922 266 3570 1161
ἐνώπιον αὐτοῦ· διὰ γὰρ νόμου ἐπίγνωσις ἁμαρτίας. 21 νυνὶ δὲ
before Him; through for law (is) full knowledge of sin. now But

5565 3551 1343 2316 5319 3140
χωρὶς νόμου δικαιοσύνη Θεοῦ πεφανέρωται, μαρτυρουμένη
apart from law a righteousness of God has been revealed, being witnessed

5259 3588 3551 2532 3588 4396 1343 1161 2316 1223
ὑπὸ τοῦ νόμου καὶ τῶν προφητῶν· 22 δικαιοσύνη δὲ Θεοῦ διὰ
by the Law and the Prophets; a righteousness and of God through

4102 2424 5547 1519 3956 2532 1909 3956 3588
πίστεως Ἰησοῦ Χριστοῦ εἰς πάντας καὶ ἐπὶ πάντας τοὺς
faith of Jesus Christ to all and upon all the (ones)

4100 3756 1063 2076 1293 3956 1063 264
πιστεύοντας· οὐ γάρ ἐστι διαστολή· 23 πάντες γὰρ ἥμαρτον
believing; not for there is a difference; all for sinned

2532 5302 3588 1391 3588 2316 1344 1432
καὶ ὑστεροῦνται τῆς δόξης τοῦ Θεοῦ, 24 δικαιούμενοι δωρεὰν
and come short of the glory of God, having been justified freely

3588 846 5485 1223 3588 629 3588 1722 5547
τῇ αὐτοῦ χάριτι διὰ τῆς ἀπολυτρώσεως τῆς ἐν Χριστῷ
by the of Him grace through the redemption in Christ

2424 3739 4388 3588 2316 2435 1223 3588 4102
Ἰησοῦ· 25 ὃν προέθετο ὁ Θεὸς ἱλαστήριον, διὰ τῆς πίστεως,
Jesus; whom set forth God a propitiation, through the faith,

1722 3588 846 129 1519 1732 3588 1343 846 1223
ἐν τῷ αὐτοῦ αἵματι, εἰς ἔνδειξιν τῆς δικαιοσύνης αὐτοῦ, διὰ
by the of Him blood, for a display of the righteousness of Him, through

3588 3929 3588 4266 265 1722 3588 463
τὴν πάρεσιν τῶν προγεγονότων ἁμαρτημάτων, 26 ἐν τῇ ἀνοχῇ
the passing by of the having before occurred sins, in the forbearance

3588 2316 4314 1732 3588 1343 846 1722 3588 3568
τοῦ Θεοῦ· πρὸς ἔνδειξιν τῆς δικαιοσύνης αὐτοῦ ἐν τῷ νῦν
of God; for the showing forth of the righteousness of Him in the present

2540 1519 3588 1511 846 1342 2532 1344 3588 1537
καιρῷ, εἰς τὸ εἶναι αὐτὸν δίκαιον καὶ δικαιοῦντα τὸν ἐκ
time, for the being of Him just and justifying the (one) of

4102 2424 4226 3767 3588 2746 1576 1223 4169
πίστεως Ἰησοῦ. 27 ποῦ οὖν ἡ καύχησις; ἐξεκλείσθη. διὰ ποίου
faith of Jesus. where Then the boasting? It was shut out. Through what

3551 3588 2041 3780 235 1223 3551 4102 3049
νόμου; τῶν ἔργων; οὐχί, ἀλλὰ διὰ νόμου πίστεως. 28 λογιζό-
law? Of works? No, but through a law of faith. We conclude

3767 4102 1344 444 5565 2041 3551
μεθα οὖν πίστει δικαιοῦσθαι ἄνθρωπον, χωρὶς ἔργων νόμου.
then by faith to be justified a man, without works of law.

2228 2453 3588 2316 3440 3780 1161 2532 1484 3483 2532
29 ἢ Ἰουδαίων ὁ Θεὸς μόνον; οὐχὶ δὲ καὶ ἐθνῶν; ναὶ καὶ
Or of Jews (is He) the God only? not And also of nations? Yes also

1484 1897 1520 3588 2316 3739 1344 4061 1537 4102
ἐθνῶν· 30 ἐπείπερ εἷς ὁ Θεός, ὃς δικαιώσει περιτομὴν ἐκ πί-
of nations; since (it is) one God, who will justify circumcision by

2532 203 1223 3588 4102 3551 3767 2673
στεως, καὶ ἀκροβυστίαν διὰ τῆς πίστεως. 31 νόμον οὖν καταρ-
faith, and uncircumcision through faith. law Then destroy

King James Version

19 Now we know that
what things soever the
law saith, it saith to them
who are under the law:
that every mouth may
be stopped, and all the
world may become
guilty before God.
20 Therefore by the
deeds of the law there
shall no flesh be justi-
fied in his sight: for by
the law (is) the knowl-
edge of sin.
21 But now the right-
eousness of God with-
out the law is mani-
fested, being witnessed
by the law and the
prophets;
22 Even the righteous-
ness of God (which is)
by faith of Jesus Christ
unto all and upon all
them that believe: for
there is no difference:
23 For all have sinned,
and come short of the
glory of God;
24 Being justified freely
by his grace through the
redemption that is in
Christ Jesus:
25 Whom God hath set
forth (to be) a propitia-
tion through faith in his
blood, to declare his
righteousness for the re-
mission of sins that are
past, through the for-
bearance of God;
26 To declare, (I say), at
this time his righteous-
ness: that he might be
just, and the justifier of
him which believeth in
Jesus.
27 Where (is) boasting
then? It is excluded. By
what law? of works?
Nay: but by the law of
faith.
28 Therefore we con-
clude that a man is jus-
tified by faith without
the deeds of the law.
29 (Is he) the God of the
Jews only? (is he) not
also of the Gentiles?
Yes, of the Gentiles
also:
30 Seeing (it is) one
God, which shall justify
the circumcision by
faith, and uncircumci-
sion through faith.
31 Do we then make
void the law

Literal Translation

of no effect through faith? Let it not be! But we establish law.

Romans 4:1

1223 3588 4102 3361 1096 235 3551 2476
γοῦμεν διὰ τῆς πίστεως; μὴ γένοιτο· ἀλλὰ νόμον ἱστῶμεν.
through the faith? Not let it be! But law we establish.

King James Version

through faith? God forbid: yea, we establish the law.

Romans 4

1. What then shall we say our father Abraham to have found according to flesh?
2 For if Abraham was justified by works, he has a boast, but not toward God.
3 For what does the Scripture say? "And Abraham believed God, and it was reckoned to him for righteousness." (Gen. 15:6)
4 Now (to one) working, the reward is not counted according to grace, but according to debt.
5 But to the (one) not working, but believing on the (One) justifying the ungodly, his faith is reckoned for righteousness.
6 Even as also David says of the blessedness of the man to whom God reckons righteousness apart from works:

7 "Blessed (are those) whose lawlessnesses are forgiven, and whose sins were covered;
8 blessed (the) man to whom (the) Lord will in no way charge sin." (Psa. 32:1,2)
9 (Is) this blessedness then on the circumcision, or also on the uncircumcision? For we say faith was reckoned to Abraham for righteousness.
10 How then was it reckoned? Being in circumcision, or in uncircumcision? Not in circumcision, but in uncircumcision!
11 And he received a sign of circumcision (as) a seal of the righteousness of faith (while) in uncircumcision, for him to be a father of the (ones) believing through uncircumcision, for righteousness to be reckoned to them also,
12 and

Romans 4

5101 3767 2046 11 3588 3962 2257 2147 2596
1 Τί οὖν ἐροῦμεν Ἀβραὰμ τὸν πατέρα ἡμῶν εὑρηκέναι κατὰ
What then shall we say Abraham the father of us to have found according to
4561 1487 1063 11 1537 2041 1344 2192 2745
σάρκα; 2 εἰ γὰρ Ἀβραὰμ ἐξ ἔργων ἐδικαιώθη, ἔχει καύχημα·
flesh? if For Abraham by works was justified, he has a boast;
235 3756 4314 3588 2316 5101 1063 3588 1124 3004 4100
ἀλλ' οὐ πρὸς τὸν Θεόν. 3 τί γὰρ ἡ γραφὴ λέγει; Ἐπίστευσε
but not toward God. what For the Scripture says? believed
1161 11 3588 2316 2532 3049 846 1519 1343 3588
δὲ Ἀβραὰμ τῷ Θεῷ, καὶ ἐλογίσθη αὐτῷ εἰς δικαιοσύνην. 4 τῷ
And Abraham God, and it was reckoned to him for righteousness.
1161 2038 3588 3408 3756 3049 2596 5485 235
δὲ ἐργαζομένῳ ὁ μισθὸς οὐ λογίζεται κατὰ χάριν, ἀλλὰ
But (one) working the reward not is reckoned according to grace, but
2596 3588 3783 3588 1161 3361 2038 4100 1161 1909
κατὰ τὸ ὀφείλημα. 5 τῷ δὲ μὴ ἐργαζομένῳ, πιστεύοντι δὲ ἐπὶ
according to debt. to the (one) But not working, believing but on
3588 1344 3588 765 3049 3588 4102 846 1519
τὸν δικαιοῦντα τὸν ἀσεβῆ, λογίζεται ἡ πίστις αὐτοῦ εἰς
the (One) justifying the ungodly, is reckoned the faith of him for
1343 2509 2532 1138 3004 3588 3108 3588
δικαιοσύνην, 6 καθάπερ καὶ Δαβὶδ λέγει τὸν μακαρισμὸν τοῦ
righteousness, even as also David says of the blessedness of the
444 3739 3588 2316 3049 1343 5565 2041
ἀνθρώπου, ᾧ ὁ Θεὸς λογίζεται δικαιοσύνην χωρὶς ἔργων,
man of whom God reckons righteousness apart from works,
3107 3739 863 3588 458 2532 3739 1943
7 Μακάριοι ὧν ἀφέθησαν αἱ ἀνομίαι, καὶ ὧν ἐπεκαλύφθησαν
Blessed of whom were remitted the lawlessness, and of whom were covered
3588 266 3107 435 3739 3756 3361 3049 2962
αἱ ἁμαρτίαι· 8 μακάριος ἀνὴρ ᾧ οὐ μὴ λογίσηται Κύριος
the sins; blessed (the) man to whom not at all will charge (the) Lord
266 3588 3108 3767 3778 1909 3588 4061 2228 2532
ἁμαρτίαν. 9 ὁ μακαρισμὸς οὖν οὗτος ἐπὶ τὴν περιτομήν, ἢ καὶ
sin. (Is) blessedness then this on the circumcision, or also
1909 3588 203 3004 1063 3754 3049 3588
ἐπὶ τὴν ἀκροβυστίαν; λέγομεν γὰρ ὅτι Ἐλογίσθη τῷ
on the uncircumcision? we say For was reckoned
11 3588 4102 1519 1343 4459 3767 3049 1722
Ἀβραὰμ ἡ πίστις εἰς δικαιοσύνην. 10 πῶς οὖν ἐλογίσθη; ἐν
to Abraham faith for righteousness. How then was it reckoned? In
4061 5607 2228 1722 203 3756 1722 4061 235 1722
περιτομῇ ὄντι, ἢ ἐν ἀκροβυστίᾳ; οὐκ ἐν περιτομῇ, ἀλλ' ἐν
circumcision being, or in uncircumcision? Not in circumcision, but in
203 2532 4592 2983 4061 4973 3588
ἀκροβυστίᾳ· 11 καὶ σημεῖον ἔλαβε περιτομῆς, σφραγῖδα τῆς
uncircumcision; and a sign he received of circumcision, a seal of the
1343 3588 4102 3588 1722 3588 203 1519 3588
δικαιοσύνης τῆς πίστεως τῆς ἐν τῇ ἀκροβυστίᾳ· εἰς τὸ
righteousness of the faith (while) in uncircumcision; for the
1511 846 3962 3956 3588 4100 1223 203
εἶναι αὐτὸν πατέρα πάντων τῶν πιστευόντων δι' ἀκροβυ-
being of him a father of all the (ones) believing through uncircum-
1519 3588 3049 2532 846 3588 1343 2532
στίας, εἰς τὸ λογισθῆναι καὶ αὐτοῖς τὴν δικαιοσύνην· 12 καὶ
cision, for to be reckoned also to them righteousness; and

Romans 4

1. What shall we say then that Abraham our father, as pertaining to the flesh, hath found?
2 For if Abraham were justified by works, he hath (whereof) to glory; but not before God.
3 For what saith the scripture? Abraham believed God, and it was counted unto him for righteousness.
4 Now to him that worketh is the reward not reckoned of grace, but of debt.
5 But to him that worketh not, but believeth on him that justifieth the ungodly, his faith is counted for righteousness.

6 Even as David also describeth the blessedness of the man, unto whom God imputeth righteousness without works,
7 (Saying), Blessed (are) they whose iniquities are forgiven, and whose sins are covered.
8 Blessed (is) the man to whom the Lord will not impute sin.
9 (Cometh) this blessedness then upon the circumcision (only), or upon the uncircumcision also? for we say that faith was reckoned to Abraham for righteousness.
10 How was it then reckoned? when he was in circumcision, or in uncircumcision? Not in circumcision, but in uncircumcision.
11 And he received the sign of circumcision, a seal of the righteousness of the faith which (he had yet) being uncircumcised: that he might be the father of all them that believe, though they be not circumcised; that righteousness might be imputed unto them also:
12 And

Literal Translation

a father of circumcision to those not of circumcision only, but also to those walking in the steps of the faith of our father Abraham during uncircumcision.

13 For the promise (was) not through Law to Abraham, or to his seed, (for) him to be the heir of the world, but through a righteousness of faith.
14 For if those of Law (are) heirs, faith has been voided, and the promise has been destroyed.

15 For the law works out wrath; for where no law is, neither (is) transgression.
16 Because of this, (it is) of faith, that (it be) according to grace, for the promise to be made sure to all the seed, not to the (seed) of the Law only, but also to that of (the) faith of Abraham, who is father of us all,

17 according as it has been written, "I have appointed you a father of many nations;" (Gen. 17:5) before God, whom he believed, the (One) making the dead live, and calling the things that are not as (if) being.

18 (He) against hope believed in hope, for the becoming (of) him a father of many nations, according to what has been said, "So shall your seed be." (Gen. 15:5)
19 And being about a hundred years (old), not weakening in faith, he did not consider his body to have died already, nor yet the death of Sarah's womb,

20 but at the promise of God (he) did not hesitate by unbelief, but was empowered by faith, giving glory to God,
21 and being fully persuaded that what He has promised,

Romans 4:13

3962 4061 3588 3756 1537 4061 3440 235 2532
πατέρα περιτομῆς τοῖς οὐκ ἐκ περιτομῆς μόνον, ἀλλὰ καὶ
a father of circumcision to those not of circumcision only, but also

3588 4748 3588 2487 3588 1722 3588 203 4102
τοῖς στοιχοῦσι τοῖς ἴχνεσι τῆς ἐν τῇ ἀκροβυστίᾳ πίστεως
to those walking in the steps of the during uncircumcision faith

3588 3962 2257 11 3756 1063 1223 3551 3588 1860
τοῦ πατρὸς ἡμῶν Ἀβραάμ. 13 οὐ γὰρ διὰ νόμου ἡ ἐπαγγελία
of the father of us Abraham. not For through Law the promise

3588 11 2228 3588 4690 846 3588 2818 846
τῷ Ἀβραὰμ ἢ τῷ σπέρματι αὐτοῦ, τὸ κληρονόμον αὐτὸν
to Abraham or to the seed of him, the heir him

1511 3588 2889 235 1223 1343 4102 1487 1063 3588
εἶναι τοῦ κόσμου, ἀλλὰ διὰ δικαιοσύνης πίστεως. 14 εἰ γὰρ οἱ
to be of the world, but through a righteousness of faith. if For those

1537 3551 2818 2758 3588 4102 2532 2673 3588
ἐκ νόμου κληρονόμοι, κεκένωται ἡ πίστις, καὶ κατήργηται ἡ
of Law (are) heirs, has been voided faith, and has been destroyed the

1860 3588 1063 3551 3709 2716 3757 1063 3756
ἐπαγγελία· 15 ὁ γὰρ νόμος ὀργὴν κατεργάζεται· οὗ γὰρ οὐκ
promise; the for law wrath works out, where for not

2076 3551 3761 3847 1223 5124 1537 4102 2443 2596
ἔστι νόμος, οὐδὲ παράβασις. 16 διὰ τοῦτο ἐκ πίστεως, ἵνα κατὰ
is law, neither (is) transgression. Because of this (it is) of faith, that (it may be)

5485 1519 3588 1511 949 3588 1860 3956 3588
χάριν, εἰς τὸ εἶναι βεβαίαν τὴν ἐπαγγελίαν παντὶ τῷ
according to grace, for the being made sure the promise to all the

4690 3756 3588 1537 3588 3551 3440 235 2532 3588 1537
σπέρματι, οὐ τῷ ἐκ τοῦ νόμου μόνον, ἀλλὰ καὶ τῷ ἐκ
seed, not to the of the law (seed) only, but also to (that) of

4102 11 3739 2076 3962 3956 2257 2531
πίστεως Ἀβραάμ, ὅς ἐστι πατὴρ πάντων ἡμῶν, 17 [καθὼς
(the) faith of Abraham, who is father of all of us - even as

1125 3754 3962 4183 1484 5087 4571 2713
γέγραπται ὅτι Πατέρα πολλῶν ἐθνῶν τέθεικά σε] κατέναντι
it has been written, a father of many nations I have appointed you - before

3739 4100 2316 3588 2227 3588 3498 2532
οὗ ἐπίστευσε Θεοῦ, τοῦ ζωοποιοῦντος τοὺς νεκρούς, καὶ
whom he believed God, the (One) making live the dead, and

2564 3588 3361 5607 5613 5607 3739 3844 1680 1909 1680
καλοῦντος τὰ μὴ ὄντα ὡς ὄντα. 18 ὃς παρ' ἐλπίδα ἐπ' ἐλπίδι
calling the things not being as being; who against hope on hope

4100 1519 3588 1096 846 3962 4183 1484
ἐπίστευσεν, εἰς τὸ γενέσθαι αὐτὸν πατέρα πολλῶν ἐθνῶν,
believed, for the becoming (of) him father of many nations,

2596 3588 2046 3779 2071 3588 4690 4675 2532 3361
κατὰ τὸ εἰρημένον, Οὕτως ἔσται τὸ σπέρμα σου. 19 καὶ μὴ
according to what was said, So shall be the seed of you. And not

770 3588 4102 3756 2657 3588 1438 4983 2235
ἀσθενήσας τῇ πίστει, οὐ κατενόησε τὸ ἑαυτοῦ σῶμα ἤδη
weakening in faith, not he considered the of himself body already

3499 1541 4225 5225 2532 3588
νενεκρωμένον [ἑκατονταέτης που ὑπάρχων], καὶ τὴν νέ-
having died - a hundred years about being -, and the

3500 3588 3388 4564 1519 1161 3588 1860 3588 2316
κρωσιν τῆς μήτρας Σάρρας· 20 εἰς δὲ τὴν ἐπαγγελίαν τοῦ Θεοῦ
death of the womb of Sarah; at but the promise of God

3756 1252 3588 570 235 1743 3588 4102 1325
οὐ διεκρίθη τῇ ἀπιστίᾳ, ἀλλ' ἐνεδυναμώθη τῇ πίστει, δοὺς
not hesitated by unbelief, but was empowered by faith, giving

1391 3588 2316 2532 4135 3754 3739 1861
δόξαν τῷ Θεῷ, 21 καὶ πληροφορηθεὶς ὅτι ὃ ἐπήγγελται,
glory to God, and being fully persuaded that what He has promised,

King James Version

the father of circumcision to them who are not of the circumcision only, but who also walk in the steps of that faith of our father Abraham, which (he had) being (yet) uncircumcised.
13 For the promise, that he should be the heir of the world, (was) not to Abraham, or to his seed, through the law, but through the righteousness of faith.
14 For if they which are of the law (be) heirs, faith is made void, and the promise made of none effect:

15 Because the law worketh wrath: for where no law is, (there is) no transgression.
16 Therefore (it is) of faith, that (it might be) by grace; to the end the promise might be sure to all the seed; not to that only which is of the law, but to that also which is of the faith of Abraham; who is the father of us all,
17 (As it is written, I have made thee a father of many nations,) before him whom he believed, (even) God, who quickeneth the dead, and calleth those things which be not as though they were.

18 Who against hope believed in hope, that he might become the father of many nations, according to that which was spoken, So shall thy seed be.
19 And being not weak in faith, he considered not his own body now dead, when he was about an hundred years old, neither yet the deadness of Sara's womb:

20 He staggered not at the promise of God through unbelief; but was strong in faith, giving glory to God;
21 And being fully persuaded that, what he had promised,

Literal Translation

He is also able to do.
22 Because of this, it was also counted to him for righteousness. (Gen.15:6)
23 But it was not written for him only, that it was reckoned to him,
24 but also on account of us, to whom it is about to be reckoned, to the (ones) believing on the (One) who has raised our Lord Jesus from (the) dead,
25 who was delivered because of our offenses and was raised for our justification.

Romans 4:22

1415 2076 2532 4160 1352 2532 3049 846 1519
δυνατός ἐστι καὶ ποιῆσαι. 22 διὸ καὶ ἐλογίσθη αὐτῷ εἰς
able He is also to do. Therefore also it was reckoned to him for

1343 3756 1125 1161 1223 846 3440 3754 3049
δικαιοσύνην. 23 Οὐκ ἐγράφη δὲ δι' αὐτὸν μόνον, ὅτι ἐλογίσθη
righteousness. not it was written But for him only, that it is reckoned

846 235 2532 1223 2248 3739 3195 3049 3588
αὐτῷ· 24 ἀλλὰ καὶ δι' ἡμᾶς, οἷς μέλλει λογίζεσθαι, τοῖς
to him; but also because of us, to whom it is going to be counted, to those

4100 1909 3588 1453 2424 3588 2962 2257 1537
πιστεύουσιν ἐπὶ τὸν ἐγείραντα Ἰησοῦν τὸν Κύριον ἡμῶν ἐκ
believing on the (One) having raised Jesus the Lord of us from

3498 3739 3860 1223 3588 3900 2257 2532 1453
νεκρῶν, 25 ὃς παρεδόθη διὰ τὰ παραπτώματα ἡμῶν, καὶ ἠγέρθη
(the) dead, who was delivered for the offenses of us, and was raised

1223 3588 1347 2257
διὰ τὴν δικαίωσιν ἡμῶν.
for the justification of us.

King James Version

he was able also to perform.
22 And therefore it was imputed to him for righteousness.
23 Now it was not written for his sake alone, that it was imputed to him;
24 But for us also, to whom it shall be imputed, if we believe on him that raised up Jesus our Lord from the dead;
25 Who was delivered for our offences, and was raised again for our justification.

Romans 5

1. Then having been justified by faith, we have peace with God through our Lord Jesus Christ,
2 through whom also we have had access by faith into this grace in which we stand, and we glory on (the) hope of the glory of God.
3 And not only so, but we glory also in afflictions, knowing that affliction works out patience,
4 and patience (works out) proven character; and proven character, hope.
5 And the hope does not put (us) to shame, because the love of God has been poured out in our hearts through (the) Holy Spirit given to us,
6 for we yet being without strength, in due time Christ died on behalf of ungodly (ones).
7 For hardly anyone will die on behalf of a just one, for perhaps one even dares to die on behalf of the good one.
8 But God commends His love to us in (this), that we being yet sinners, Christ died on behalf of us.
9 Much more then, having been justified now by

Romans 5

1344 3767 1537 4102 1515 2192 4314 3588
1 Δικαιωθέντες οὖν ἐκ πίστεως, εἰρήνην ἔχομεν πρὸς τὸν
having been justified Then by faith, peace we have with

2316 1223 3588 2962 2257 2424 5547 1223 3739 2532 3588
Θεὸν διὰ τοῦ Κυρίου ἡμῶν Ἰησοῦ Χριστοῦ, 2 δι' οὗ καὶ τὴν
God through the Lord of us Jesus Christ, through whom also the

4318 2192 3588 4102 1519 3588 5485 3778 1722
προσαγωγὴν ἐσχήκαμεν τῇ πίστει εἰς τὴν χάριν ταύτην ἐν
access we have had by faith into grace this in

3739 2476 2532 2744 1909 1680 3588 1391 3588 2316
ᾗ ἑστήκαμεν, καὶ καυχώμεθα ἐπ' ἐλπίδι τῆς δόξης τοῦ Θεοῦ.
which we stand, and glory on hope of the glory of God.

3756 3440 1161 235 2532 2744 1722 3588 2347 1492
3 οὐ μόνον δέ, ἀλλὰ καὶ καυχώμεθα ἐν ταῖς θλίψεσιν, εἰδότες
not only And (so), but also we glory in afflictions, knowing

3754 3588 2347 5281 2716 3588 1161 5281 1382
ὅτι ἡ θλῖψις ὑπομονὴν κατεργάζεται, 4 ἡ δὲ ὑπομονὴ δοκιμήν,
that affliction patience works out, and patience proof,

3588 1161 1382 1680 3588 1161 1680 3756 2617 3754 3588 26
ἡ δὲ δοκιμὴ ἐλπίδα· 5 ἡ δὲ ἐλπὶς οὐ καταισχύνει, ὅτι ἡ ἀγάπη
and proof hope; and hope not does put to shame, because the love

3588 2316 1632 1722 3588 2588 2257 1223 4151
τοῦ Θεοῦ ἐκκέχυται ἐν ταῖς καρδίαις ἡμῶν διὰ Πνεύματος
of God has been poured out in the hearts of us through (the) Spirit

40 3588 1325 2254 2089 1063 5547 5607 2257
Ἁγίου τοῦ δοθέντος ἡμῖν. 6 ἔτι γὰρ Χριστὸς, ὄντων ἡμῶν
Holy given to us. yet For Christ, being us

772 2596 2540 5228 765 599 3433 1063
ἀσθενῶν, κατὰ καιρὸν ὑπὲρ ἀσεβῶν ἀπέθανε. 7 μόλις γὰρ
without strength, in due time on behalf of ungodly (ones) died. hardly for

5228 1342 5100 599 5228 1063 3588 18 5029 5100
ὑπὲρ δικαίου τις ἀποθανεῖται· ὑπὲρ γὰρ τοῦ ἀγαθοῦ τάχα τις·
on behalf of a just one anyone will die; on behalf of for the good one perhaps one

2532 5111 599 4921 1161 3588 1438 26 1519
καὶ τολμᾷ ἀποθανεῖν. 8 συνίστησιν δὲ τὴν ἑαυτοῦ ἀγάπην εἰς
even dares to die. commends But the of Himself love to

2248 3588 2316 3754 2089 268 5607 2257 5547 5228
ἡμᾶς ὁ Θεός, ὅτι ἔτι ἁμαρτωλῶν ὄντων ἡμῶν Χριστὸς ὑπὲρ
us God, that yet sinners being us Christ on behalf of

2257 599 4183 3767 3123 1344 3568 1722/3588
ἡμῶν ἀπέθανε. 9 πολλῷ οὖν μᾶλλον, δικαιωθέντες νῦν ἐν τῷ
us died. much Then more, having been justified now by the

Romans 5

1. Therefore being justified by faith, we have peace with God through our Lord Jesus Christ:
2 By whom also we have access by faith into this grace wherein we stand, and rejoice in hope of the glory of God.
3 And not only (so), but we glory in tribulations also: knowing that tribulation worketh patience;
4 And patience, experience; and experience, hope:
5 And hope maketh not ashamed; because the love of God is shed abroad in our hearts by the Holy Ghost which is given unto us.
6 For when we were yet without strength, in due time Christ died for the ungodly.
7 For scarcely for a righteous man will one die: yet peradventure for a good man some would even dare to die.
8 But God commendeth his love toward us, in that, while we were yet sinners, Christ died for us.
9 Much more then, being now justified by

Literal Translation | **Romans 5:10** | ***King James Version***

His blood, we shall be saved from wrath through Him.
10 For if (while) being hostile (ones) we were reconciled to God through the death of His Son, much more having been reconciled, we shall be saved by His life;
11 and not only (so), but also glorying in God through our Lord Jesus Christ, through whom we now received the reconciliation.

129 846 4982 1223 846 575 3588 3709 1487
αἵματι αὐτοῦ, σωθησόμεθα δι᾽ αὐτοῦ ἀπὸ τῆς ὀργῆς. 10 εἰ
blood of Him, we shall be saved through Him from the wrath. if

1063 2190 5607 2644 3588 2316 1223 3588 2288
γὰρ ἐχθροὶ ὄντες κατηλλάγημεν τῷ Θεῷ διὰ τοῦ θανάτου
For hostile (ones) being we were reconciled to God through the death

3588 5207 846 4183 3123 2644 4982
τοῦ υἱοῦ αὐτοῦ, πολλῷ μᾶλλον καταλλαγέντες σωθησό-
of the Son of Him, much more having been reconciled we shall be

1722 3588 2222 846 3756 3440 1161 235 2532 2744 1722
μεθα ἐν τῇ ζωῇ αὐτοῦ· 11 οὐ μόνον δέ, ἀλλὰ καὶ καυχώμενοι ἐν
saved by the life of Him; not only (so) but, but also glorying in

3588 2316 1223 3588 2962 2257 2424 5547 1223 3739 3568 3588
τῷ Θεῷ διὰ τοῦ Κυρίου ἡμῶν Ἰησοῦ Χριστοῦ, δι᾽ οὗ νῦν τὴν
God through the Lord of us Jesus Christ, through whom now the

2643 2983
καταλλαγὴν ἐλάβομεν.
reconciliation we received.

his blood, we shall be saved from wrath through him.
10 For if, when we were enemies, we were reconciled to God by the death of his Son, much more, being reconciled, we shall be saved by his life.
11 And not only (so), but we also joy in God through our Lord Jesus Christ, by whom we have now received the atonement.

12 Because of this, even as sin entered into the world through one man, and death through sin, so also death passed to all men, inasmuch as all sinned.

1223 5124 5618 1223 1520 444 3588 266 1519 3588
12. Διὰ τοῦτο ὥσπερ δι᾽ ἑνὸς ἀνθρώπου ἡ ἁμαρτία εἰς τὸν
Because of this as through one man sin into the

2889 1525 2532 1223 3588 266 3588 2288 2532 3779
κόσμον εἰσῆλθε, καὶ διὰ τῆς ἁμαρτίας ὁ θάνατος, καὶ οὕτως
world entered, and through sin death, also so

1519 3956 444 3588 2288 1330 1909 3739 3956
εἰς πάντας ἀνθρώπους ὁ θάνατος διῆλθεν, ἐφ᾽ ᾧ πάντες
to all men death passed, inasmuch as all

12 Wherefore, as by one man sin entered into the world, and death by sin; and so death passed upon all men, for that all have sinned:

13 For sin was in (the) world until Law, but sin is not charged (if) there is no law;
14 but death reigned from Adam until Moses, even on the (ones) not sinning in the likeness of Adam's transgression, who is a type of the coming (One).

264 891 1063 3551 266 2258 1722 2889 266
ἥμαρτον· _ 13 ἄχρι γὰρ νόμου ἁμαρτία ἦν ἐν κόσμῳ· ἁμαρτία
sinned; - until for law sin was in (the) world; sin

1161 3756 1677 3361 5607 3551 235 936 3588
δὲ οὐκ ἐλλογεῖται, μὴ ὄντος νόμου. 14 ἀλλ᾽ ἐβασίλευσεν ὁ
but not is charged, there not being law. But reigned

2288 575 76 3360 3475 2532 1909 3588 3361 264
θάνατος ἀπὸ Ἀδὰμ μέχρι Μωσέως καὶ ἐπὶ τοὺς μὴ ἁμαρτή-
death from Adam until Moses even over those not sinning

1909 3588 3667 3588 3847 76 3739 2076
σαντας ἐπὶ τῷ ὁμοιώματι τῆς παραβάσεως Ἀδάμ, ὅς ἐστι
on the likeness of the transgression of Adam, who is

5179 3588 3195 235 3756 5613 3588 3900 3779
τύπος τοῦ μέλλοντος. 15 Ἀλλ᾽ οὐχ ὡς τὸ παράπτωμα, οὕτω
a type of the (One) coming. But not as the offense, so

13 (For until the law sin was in the world: but sin is not imputed when there is no law.
14 Nevertheless death reigned from Adam to Moses, even over them that had not sinned after the similitude of Adam's transgression, who is the figure of him that was to come.

15 But the free gift (shall) not (be) also like the offense. For if by the offense of the one the many died, much more the grace of God, and the gift in grace, which (is) of the one Man, Jesus Christ, did abound to the many.

2532 3588 5486 1487 1063 3588 3588 1520 3900 3588
καὶ τὸ χάρισμα. εἰ γὰρ τῷ τοῦ ἑνὸς παραπτώματι οἱ
also the free gift. if For by the of the one offense the

4183 599 4183 3123 3588 5485 3588 2316 2532 3588
πολλοὶ ἀπέθανον, πολλῷ μᾶλλον ἡ χάρις τοῦ Θεοῦ καὶ ἡ
many died, much more the grace of God and the

1431 1722 5485 3588 3588 1520 444 2424 5547 1519
δωρεὰ ἐν χάριτι τῇ τοῦ ἑνὸς ἀνθρώπου Ἰησοῦ Χριστοῦ εἰς
gift in grace of the one Man, Jesus Christ to

3588 4183 4052 2532 3756 5613 1223 1520 264
τοὺς πολλοὺς ἐπερίσσευσε. 16 καὶ οὐχ ὡς δι᾽ ἑνὸς ἁμαρτή-
the many abounded. And not as through one having sinned,

15 But not as the offence, so also (is) the free gift. For if through the offence of one many be dead, much more the grace of God, and the gift by grace, (which is) by one man, Jesus Christ, hath abounded unto many.

16 And the gift (shall) not (be) as through one having sinned; for indeed the judgment (was) of one to condemnation, but the free gift (is) of many offenses to justification.
17 For if by the offense of the one death reigned through

3588 1434 3588 3303 1063 2917 1537 1520 1519 2631
σαντος, τὸ δώρημα· τὸ μὲν γὰρ κρίμα ἐξ ἑνὸς εἰς κατάκριμα,
(be) the gift; the indeed for judgment of one to condemnation,

3588 1161 5486 1537 4183 3900 1519 1345 1487
τὸ δὲ χάρισμα ἐκ πολλῶν παραπτωμάτων εἰς δικαίωμα. 17 εἰ
the but free gift (is) of many offenses to justification. if

1063 3588 3588 1520 3900 3588 2288 936 1223
γὰρ τῷ τοῦ ἑνὸς παραπτώματι ὁ θάνατος ἐβασίλευσε διὰ
For the of the one offense death reigned through

16 And not as (it was) by one that sinned, (so) is) the gift: for the judgment (was) by one to condemnation, but the free gift (is) of many offences unto justification.
17 For if by one man's offence death reigned by one;

Literal Translation | **Romans 5:18** | **King James Version**

the one, much more the (ones) receiving the abundance of the grace and the gift of righteousness shall rule in life through the One, Jesus Christ.
18 So then, as through one offense (it was) toward all men to condemnation, so also through one accomplished righteousness toward all men to justification of life.

19 For as through the one man's disobedience the many were constituted sinners, so also through the obedience of the One the many shall be constituted righteous.

20 But Law came in besides, that the offense might abound. But where sin abounded, grace much more abounded,
21 that as sin ruled in death, so also grace might rule through righteousness to everlasting life, through Jesus Christ our Lord.

3588 1520 4183 3123 3588 3588 4050 3588 5485 2532
τοῦ ἑνός, πολλῷ μᾶλλον οἱ τὴν περισσείαν τῆς χάριτος καὶ
the one, much more the (ones) the abundance of the grace and

3588 1431 3588 1343 2983 1722 2222 936
τῆς δωρεᾶς τῆς δικαιοσύνης λαμβάνοντες ἐν ζωῇ βασιλεύ-
of the gift of righteousness receiving in life will

1223 3588 1520 2424 5547 686 3767 5613 1223 1520
σουσι διὰ τοῦ ἑνὸς Ἰησοῦ Χριστοῦ. 18 ἄρα οὖν ὡς δι᾽ ἑνὸς
reign through the One Jesus Christ. So then as through one

3900 1519 3956 444 1519 2631 3779
παραπτώματος εἰς πάντας ἀνθρώπους εἰς κατάκριμα, οὕτως
offense to all men to condemnation, so

2532 1223 1520 1345 1519 3956 444 1519 1347
καὶ δι᾽ ἑνὸς δικαιώματος εἰς πάντας ἀνθρώπους εἰς δικαίωσιν
also through one righteous act to all men to justification

2222 5618 1063 1223 3588 3876 3588 1520 444
ζωῆς. 19 ὥσπερ γὰρ διὰ τῆς παρακοῆς τοῦ ἑνὸς ἀνθρώπου
of life. as For through the disobedience of the one man

268 2525 3588 4183 3779 2532 1223 3588
ἁμαρτωλοὶ κατεστάθησαν οἱ πολλοί, οὕτω καὶ διὰ τῆς
sinners were constituted the many, so also through the

5218 3588 1520 1342 2525 3588 4183
ὑπακοῆς τοῦ ἑνὸς δίκαιοι κατασταθήσονται οἱ πολλοί.
obedience of the One righteous will be constituted the many.

3551 1161 3922 2443 4121 3588 3900 3757
20 νόμος δὲ παρεισῆλθεν, ἵνα πλεονάσῃ τὸ παράπτωμα· οὗ
Law But came in besides, that might abound the offense; where

1161 4121 3588 266 5248 3588 5485 2443
δὲ ἐπλεόνασεν ἡ ἁμαρτία, ὑπερεπερίσσευσεν ἡ χάρις· 21 ἵνα
but abounded the sin, more abounded grace; that

5618 936 3588 266 1722 3588 2288 3779 2532 3588
ὥσπερ ἐβασίλευσεν ἡ ἁμαρτία ἐν τῷ θανάτῳ, οὕτω καὶ ἡ
as reigned sin in death, so also

5485 936 1223 1343 1519 2222 166 1223
χάρις βασιλεύσῃ διὰ δικαιοσύνης εἰς ζωὴν αἰώνιον, διὰ
grace might reign through righteousness to life everlasting, through

2424 5547 3588 2962 2257
Ἰησοῦ Χριστοῦ τοῦ Κυρίου ἡμῶν.
Jesus Christ the Lord of us.

much more they which receive abundance of grace and of the gift of righteousness shall reign in life by one, Jesus Christ.)

18 Therefore as by the offence of one (judgment came) upon all men to condemnation; even so by the righteousness of one (the free gift came) upon all men unto justification of life.

19 For as by one man's disobedience many were made sinners, so by the obedience of one shall many be made righteous.

20 Moreover the law entered, that the offence might abound. But where sin abounded, grace did much more abound:
21 That as sin hath reigned unto death, even so might grace reign through righteousness unto eternal life by Jesus Christ our Lord.

Romans 6

1. What then shall we say? Shall we continue in sin that grace may abound?
2 Let it not be! We who died to sin, how shall we still live in it?
3 Or are you ignorant that all who were baptized into Christ Jesus were baptized into His death?

4 Therefore, we were buried with Him through baptism into death, that as Christ was raised up from (the) dead by the glory of the Father, so also we might walk in newness of life.

Romans 6

5101 3767 2046 1961 3588 266 2443 3588 5485
1. Τί οὖν ἐροῦμεν; ἐπιμενοῦμεν τῇ ἁμαρτίᾳ, ἵνα ἡ χάρις
What then shall we say? Shall we continue in sin, that grace

4121 3361 1096 3748 599 3588 266
πλεονάσῃ; 2 μὴ γένοιτο. οἵτινες ἀπεθάνομεν τῇ ἁμαρτίᾳ,
may abound? Not let it be! who We died to sin,

4459 2089 2198 1722 846 2228 50 3754 3745 907
πῶς ἔτι ζήσομεν ἐν αὐτῇ; 3 ἢ ἀγνοεῖτε ὅτι ὅσοι ἐβαπτίσθημεν
how still shall we live in it? Or are you ignorant that all who were baptized

1519 5547 2424 1519 3588 2288 846 907
εἰς Χριστὸν Ἰησοῦν, εἰς τὸν θάνατον αὐτοῦ ἐβαπτίσθημεν;
into Christ Jesus, into the death of Him were baptized?

4916 3767 846 1223 3588 908 1519 3588
4 συνετάφημεν οὖν αὐτῷ διὰ τοῦ βαπτίσματος εἰς τὸν
we were buried with Then Him through baptism into

2288 2443 5618 1453 5547 1537 3498 1223 3588
θάνατον· ἵνα ὥσπερ ἠγέρθη Χριστὸς ἐκ νεκρῶν διὰ τῆς
death; that as was raised Christ from (the) dead through the

1391 3588 3962 3779 2532 2249 1722 2538 2222
δόξης τοῦ πατρός, οὕτω καὶ ἡμεῖς ἐν καινότητι ζωῆς περι-
glory of the Father, so also we in newness of life might

Romans 6

1. What shall we say then? Shall we continue in sin, that grace may abound?
2 God forbid. How shall we, that are dead to sin, live any longer therein?
3 Know ye not, that so many of us as were baptized into Jesus Christ were baptized into his death?

4 Therefore we are buried with him by baptism into death: that like as Christ was raised up from the dead by the glory of the Father, even so we also should walk in newness of life.

Literal Translation **Romans 6:5** ***King James Version***

5 For if we have been planted together in the likeness of His death, so also shall we be in the resurrection,
6 knowing this, that our old man was crucified with (Him), that the body of sin might be done away, so that we no longer serve sin.

4043 1487 1063 4854 1096 3588 3667 3588
πατήσωμεν. 5 εἰ γὰρ σύμφυτοι γεγόναμεν τῷ ὁμοιώματι τοῦ
walk. if For planted together we have become in the likeness of the

2288 846 235 2532 3588 386 2071 5124
θανάτου αὐτοῦ, ἀλλὰ καὶ τῆς ἀναστάσεως ἐσόμεθα· 6 τοῦτο
death of Him, but also of (His) resurrection we shall be; this

1097 3754 3588 3820 2257 444 4957
γινώσκοντες, ὅτι ὁ παλαιὸς ἡμῶν ἄνθρωπος συνεσταυρώθη,
knowing, that the old of us man was crucified with (Him),

2443 2673 3588 4983 3588 266 3588 3371 1398
ἵνα καταργηθῇ τὸ σῶμα τῆς ἁμαρτίας, τοῦ μηκέτι δουλεύειν
that might be done away the body of sin, no longer to serve

5 For if we have been planted together in the likeness of his death, we shall be also (in the likeness) of (his) resurrection:
6 Knowing this, that our old man is crucified with (him), that the body of sin might be destroyed, that henceforth we should not serve sin.

7 For the (one) having died has been justified from sin.
8 But if we died with Christ, we believe that also we shall live with Him,
9 knowing that Christ having been raised from (the) dead dies no more; death no more lords it over Him.
10 For in that He died, He died to sin once for all; but in that He lives, He lives to God.

2248 3588 266 3588 1063 599 1344 575 3588
ἡμᾶς τῇ ἁμαρτίᾳ· 7 ὁ γὰρ ἀποθανὼν δεδικαίωται ἀπὸ τῆς
us sin; the (one) for having died has been justified from

266 1487 1161 599 4862 5547 4100 3754 2532
ἁμαρτίας. 8 εἰ δὲ ἀπεθάνομεν σὺν Χριστῷ, πιστεύομεν ὅτι καὶ
sin. if But we died with Christ, we believe that also

4800 846 1492 3754 5547 1453 1537
συζήσομεν αὐτῷ· 9 εἰδότες ὅτι Χριστὸς ἐγερθεὶς ἐκ νεκ-
we shall live with Him; knowing that Christ having been raised from (the)

3498 3765 599 2288 846 3765 2961 3739
ρῶν οὐκέτι ἀποθνήσκει· θάνατος αὐτοῦ οὐκέτι κυριεύει. 10 ὃ
dead no more dies; death Him no more lords it over. that

1063 599 3588 266 599 2178 3739 1161 2198 2198 3588
γὰρ ἀπέθανε, τῇ ἁμαρτίᾳ ἀπέθανεν ἐφάπαξ· ὃ δὲ ζῇ, ζῇ τῷ
For He died, to sin He died once for all; that but He lives He lives

7 For he that is dead is freed from sin.
8 Now if we be dead with Christ, we believe that we shall also live with him:
9 Knowing that Christ being raised from the dead dieth no more; death hath no more dominion over him.
10 For in that he died, he died unto sin once: but in that he liveth, he liveth unto God.

11 So also you count yourselves to be truly dead to sin, but alive to God in Christ Jesus our Lord.

2316 3779 2532 5210 3049 1438 3498 3303 1511 3588
Θεῷ. 11 οὕτω καὶ ὑμεῖς λογίζεσθε ἑαυτοὺς νεκροὺς μὲν εἶναι τῇ
to God. So also you count yourselves dead truly to be

266 2198 1161 3588 2316 1722 5547 2424 3588 2962
ἁμαρτίᾳ, ζῶντας δὲ τῷ Θεῷ ἐν Χριστῷ Ἰησοῦ τῷ Κυρίῳ
to sin, living but to God in Christ Jesus the Lord

2257
ἡμῶν.
of us.

11 Likewise reckon ye also yourselves to be dead indeed unto sin, but alive unto God through Jesus Christ our Lord.

12 Then do not let sin rule in your mortal body, to obey it in its lusts.
13 Neither present your members (as) instruments of unrighteousness to sin, but present yourselves to God as (one) living from (the) dead, and your members instruments of righteousness to God.
14 For sin shall not lord it over you, for you are not under law, but under grace.
15 What then? Shall we sin because we are not under law, but under grace? Let it not be!
16 Do you not know that to whom you present yourselves (as) slaves unto obedience, you are slaves to whom you obey, whether of sin

3361 3767 936 3588 266 1722 3588 2349 5216 4983
12. Μὴ οὖν βασιλευέτω ἡ ἁμαρτία ἐν τῷ θνητῷ ὑμῶν σώματι,
not Then let reign sin in the mortal of you body,

1519 3588 5219 846 1722 3588 1939 846 3366
εἰς τὸ ὑπακούειν αὐτῇ ἐν ταῖς ἐπιθυμίαις αὐτοῦ· 13 μηδὲ παρι-
to obey it in the lusts of it; neither present

3936 3588 3196 5216 3696 93 3588 266 235
στάνετε τὰ μέλη ὑμῶν ὅπλα ἀδικίας τῇ ἁμαρτίᾳ· ἀλλὰ
the members of you weapons of unrighteousness to sin; but

3936 1438 3588 2316 5613 1537 3498 2198 2532 3588
παραστήσατε ἑαυτοὺς τῷ Θεῷ ὡς ἐκ νεκρῶν ζῶντας, καὶ τὰ
present yourselves to God as from (the) dead living, and the

3196 5216 3696 1343 3588 2316 266 1063 5216
μέλη ὑμῶν ὅπλα δικαιοσύνης τῳ Θεῷ. 14 ἁμαρτία γὰρ ὑμῶν
members of you weapons of righteousness to God. sin for of you

3756 2961 3756 1063 2075 5259 3551 235 5259 5485
οὐ κυριεύσει· οὐ γάρ ἐστε ὑπὸ νόμον ἀλλ' ὑπὸ χάριν.
not shall lord it over; not for you are under law but under grace.

5101 3767 264 3754 3756 2070 5259 3551 235 5259
15. Τί οὖν; ἁμαρτήσομεν, ὅτι οὐκ ἐσμὲν ὑπὸ νόμον, ἀλλ' ὑπὸ
What then? Shall we sin, because not we are under law, but under

5485 3361 1096 3756 1492 3754 3739 3936 1438
χάριν; μὴ γένοιτο. 16 οὐκ οἴδατε ὅτι ᾧ παριστάνετε ἑαυτοὺς
grace? Not let it be! not Know you that to whom you present yourselves

1401 1519 5218 1401 2075 3739 5219 2273 266
δούλους εἰς ὑπακοήν, δοῦλοί ἐστε ᾧ ὑπακούετε, ἤτοι ἁμαρ-
slaves unto obedience, slaves you are to whom you obey, whether of sin

12 Let not sin therefore reign in your mortal body, that ye should obey it in the lusts thereof.
13 Neither yield ye your members (as) instruments of unrighteousness unto sin: but yield yourselves unto God, as those that are alive from the dead, and your members (as) instruments of righteousness unto God.
14 For sin shall not have dominion over you: for ye are not under the law, but under grace.
15 What then? shall we sin, because we are not under the law, but under grace? God forbid.
16 Know ye not, that to whom ye yield yourselves servants to obey, his servants ye are to whom ye obey; whether of sin

Romans 6:17

Literal Translation

to death, or obedience to righteousness?

17 But thanks (be) to God that you were slaves of sin, but you obeyed from (the) heart the form of doctrine to which you were delivered.

18 And having been set free from sin, you were enslaved to righteousness.

19 I speak as a man on account of the weakness of your flesh. For as you presented your members (as) slaves to impurity and to lawless act unto lawless act, so now yield your members (as) slaves to righteousness unto sanctification.

20 For when you were slaves of sin, you were free as to righteousness.

21 Therefore what fruit did you have then (in the things) over which you are now ashamed? For the end of those things (is) death.

22 But now being set free from sin, but having been enslaved to God, you have your fruit unto sanctification, and the end everlasting life.

23 For the wages of sin (is) death, but the free gift of God (is) everlasting life in Christ Jesus our Lord.

1519 2288 2228 5218 1519 1343 5485 1161 3588
τίας εἰς θάνατον, ἢ ὑπακοῆς εἰς δικαιοσύνην; 17 χάρις δὲ τῷ
unto death, or obedience unto righteousness? thanks But
2316 3754 2258 1401 3588 266 5219 1161 1537 2588
Θεῷ ὅτι ἦτε δοῦλοι τῆς ἁμαρτίας, ὑπηκούσατε δὲ ἐκ καρδίας
to God that you were slaves to sin, you obeyed but from (the) heart
1519 3739 3860 5179 1322 1659 1161 575
εἰς ὃν παρεδόθητε τύπον διδαχῆς· 18 ἐλευθερωθέντες δὲ ἀπὸ
to which you were delivered a form of doctrine; having been set free but from
3588 266 1402 3588 1343 442 3004
τῆς ἁμαρτίας, ἐδουλώθητε τῇ δικαιοσύνῃ. 19 ἀνθρώπινον λέγω
sin, you were enslaved to righteousness. as a man I speak
1223 3588 769 3588 4561 5216 5618 1063 3936
διὰ τὴν ἀσθένειαν τῆς σαρκὸς ὑμῶν· ὥσπερ γὰρ παρεστή-
because of the weakness of the flesh of you; as for you presented
3588 3196 5216 1401 3588 167 2532 3588 458 1519
σατε τὰ μέλη ὑμῶν δοῦλα τῇ ἀκαθαρσίᾳ καὶ τῇ ἀνομίᾳ εἰς
the members of you (as) slaves to impurity and to lawless act unto
3588 458 3779 3568 3936 3588 3196 5216 1401
τὴν ἀνομίαν, οὕτω νῦν παραστήσατε τὰ μέλη ὑμῶν δοῦλα
lawless act so now present the members of you (as) slaves
3588 1343 1519 38 3753 1063 1401 2258 3588
τῇ δικαιοσύνῃ εἰς ἁγιασμόν. 20 ὅτε γὰρ δοῦλοι ἦτε τῆς
to righteousness unto sanctification. when For slaves you were
266 1658 2258 3588 1343 5101 3767 2590
ἁμαρτίας, ἐλεύθεροι ἦτε τῇ δικαιοσύνῃ. 21 τίνα οὖν καρπὸν
of sin, free you were to righteousness. what Therefore fruit
2192 5119 1909 3739 3568 1870 3588 1063 5056 1565
εἴχετε τότε ἐφ᾽ οἷς νῦν ἐπαισχύνεσθε; τὸ γὰρ τέλος ἐκείνων
had you then over which now you are ashamed? For the end of those
2288 3570 1161 1659 575 3588 266 1402
θάνατος. 22 νυνὶ δέ, ἐλευθερωθέντες ἀπὸ τῆς ἁμαρτίας, δουλω-
(is) death. now But, having been set free from sin, having been
1161 3588 2316 2192 3588 2590 5216 1519 38 3588
θέντες δὲ τῷ Θεῷ, ἔχετε τὸν καρπὸν ὑμῶν εἰς ἁγιασμόν, τὸ
enslaved but to God, you have the fruit of you unto sanctification, the
1161 5056 2222 166 3588 1063 3800 3588 266
δὲ τέλος ζωὴν αἰώνιον. 23 τὰ γὰρ ὀψώνια τῆς ἁμαρτίας
and the end life everlasting. the For wages of sin
2288 3588 1161 5486 3588 2316 2222 166 1722 5547
θάνατος, τὸ δὲ χάρισμα τοῦ Θεοῦ ζωὴ αἰώνιος ἐν Χριστῷ
(is) death, the and gift of God life everlasting in Christ
2424 3588 2962 2257
Ἰησοῦ τῷ Κυρίῳ ἡμῶν.
Jesus the Lord of us.

King James Version

unto death, or of obedience unto righteousness?

17 But God be thanked, that ye were the servants of sin, but ye have obeyed from the heart that form of doctrine which was delivered you.

18 Being then made free from sin, ye became the servants of righteousness.

19 I speak after the manner of men because of the infirmity of your flesh: for as ye have yielded your members servants to uncleanness and to iniquity unto iniquity; even so now yield your members servants to righteousness unto holiness.

20 For when ye were the servants of sin, ye were free from righteousness.

21. What fruit had ye then in those things whereof ye are now ashamed? for the end of those things (is) death.

22 But now being made free from sin, and become servants to God, ye have your fruit unto holiness, and the end everlasting life.

23 For the wages of sin (is) death; but the gift of God (is) eternal life through Jesus Christ our Lord.

Romans 7

1. Or are you ignorant, brothers, for I speak to those knowing law, that the law lords it over the man for as long a time as he lives?

2 For the married woman was bound by law to the living husband; but if the husband dies, she is set free from the law of the husband.

3 So then, (if) the husband (is) living, she will be called an adulteress if

Romans 7

2228 50 80 1097 1063 3551 2980
1. Ἢ ἀγνοεῖτε, ἀδελφοί, [γινώσκουσι γὰρ νόμον λαλῶ],
Or are you ignorant, brothers, - to those knowing for law I speak -,
3754 3588 3551 2961 3588 444 1909 3745 5550 2198
ὅτι ὁ νόμος κυριεύει τοῦ ἀνθρώπου ἐφ᾽ ὅσον χρόνον ζῇ;
that the law lords it over the man over as long a time He lives?
3588 1063 5220 1135 3588 2198 435 1210 3551 1437 1161
2 ἡ γὰρ ὕπανδρος γυνὴ τῷ ζῶντι ἀνδρὶ δέδεται νόμῳ· ἐὰν δὲ
the For married woman to the living husband was bound by law; if but
599 3588 435 2673 575 3588 3551 3588 435
ἀποθάνῃ ὁ ἀνήρ, κατήργηται ἀπὸ τοῦ νόμου τοῦ ἀνδρός.
dies the husband, she is set free from the law of the husband.
686 3767 2198 3588 435 3428 5537 1437
3 ἄρα οὖν ζῶντος τοῦ ἀνδρὸς μοιχαλὶς χρηματίσει, ἐὰν
Therefore living the husband an adultress she will be called, if

Romans 7

1. Know ye not, brethren, (for I speak to them that know the law,) how that the law hath dominion over a man as long as he liveth?

2 For the woman which hath an husband is bound by the law to (her) husband so long as he liveth; but if the husband be dead, she is loosed from the law of (her) husband.

3 So then if, while (her) husband liveth, she be married to another man, she shall be called an adulteress: but if

Literal Translation | **Romans 7:4** | ***King James Version***

Literal Translation

she becomes another man's. But if the husband dies, she is free from the law, (so as for) her not to be an adulteress (by) becoming another man's.
4 So that, my brothers, you also were made dead to the law through the body of Christ, for you to become Another's, to the (One) having been raised from (the) dead, so that we may bear fruit to God.

5 For when we were in the flesh, the passions of sins were working in our members through the law for the bearing of fruit unto death.

6 But now we have been set free from the law, having died (to that) in which we were held, so as (for) us to serve in newness of spirit, and not (in) oldness of letter.

7 What shall we say then? (Is) the law sin? Let it not be! But I did not know sin except through law; for also I did not know lust except the law said, You shall not lust. (Ex.20:17)
8 But sin taking occasion through the commandment worked every lust in me; for apart from law, sin (is) dead.

9 And I was alive apart from law once, but the commandment coming sin came alive, and I died.
10 And the commandment unto life was found (to be) death to me;
11 for sin taking occasion through the commandment deceived me, and through it killed (me).
12 So indeed the law (is) holy, and the commandment

Romans 7:4

1096 435 2087 1437 1161 599 3588 435 1658
γένηται ἀνδρὶ ἑτέρῳ· ἐὰν δὲ ἀποθάνῃ ὁ ἀνήρ, ἐλευθέρα
she becomes man to another; if but dies the husband, free

2076 575 3588 3551 3588 3361 1511 846 3428 1096
ἐστὶν ἀπὸ τοῦ νόμου, τοῦ μὴ εἶναι αὐτὴν μοιχαλίδα, γενομέ-
she is from the law, not being her an adultress (if) becoming

435 2087 5620 80 3450 2532 5210 2289
νην ἀνδρὶ ἑτέρῳ. 4 ὥστε, ἀδελφοί μου, καὶ ὑμεῖς ἐθανατώθητε
(wife) man to another. So, brothers of me, also you were made dead

3588 3551 1223 3588 4983 3588 5547 1519 3588 1096
τῷ νόμῳ διὰ τοῦ σώματος τοῦ Χριστοῦ, εἰς τὸ γενέσθαι
to the law through the body of Christ, to come to be

5209 2087 3588 1537 3498 1453 2443 2592
ὑμᾶς ἑτέρῳ, τῷ ἐκ νεκρῶν ἐγερθέντι, ἵνα καρποφορ-
you to Another, to the (One) from (the) dead having been raised, that we may

3588 2316 3753 1063 2258 1722 3588 4561 3588 3804 3588
ήσωμεν τῷ Θεῷ. 5 ὅτε γὰρ ἦμεν ἐν τῇ σαρκί, τὰ παθήματα τῶν
bear fruit to God. when For we were in the flesh, the passions

266 3588 1223 3588 3551 1754 1722 3588 3196
ἁμαρτιῶν τὰ διὰ τοῦ νόμου ἐνηργεῖτο ἐν τοῖς μέλεσιν
of sins through the law working in the members

2257 1519 3588 2592 3588 2288 3570 1161 2673
ἡμῶν εἰς τὸ καρποφορῆσαι τῷ θανάτῳ. 6 νυνὶ δὲ κατηργήθη-
of us unto the bearing of fruit to death. now But we having been

575 3588 3551 599 1722 3739 2722 5620
μεν ἀπὸ τοῦ νόμου, ἀποθανόντες ἐν ᾧ κατειχόμεθα, ὥστε
set free from the law, having died (to that) in which we were held, so as

1398 2248 1722 2538 4151 2532 3756 3821
δουλεύειν ἡμᾶς ἐν καινότητι πνεύματος, καὶ οὐ παλαιότητι
to serve us in newness of spirit,

1121
γράμματος.
of letter.

5101 3767 2046 3588 3551 266 3361 1096 235 3588
7. Τί οὖν ἐροῦμεν; ὁ νόμος ἁμαρτία; μὴ γένοιτο· ἀλλὰ τὴν
What then shall we say? (Is) the law sin? Let it not be! But

266 3756 1097 1487 3361 1223 3551 3588 5037 1063 1939
ἁμαρτίαν οὐκ ἔγνων, εἰ μὴ διὰ νόμου· τήν τε γὰρ ἐπιθυμίαν
sin not I knew, if not through law; also for lust

3756 1492 1487 3361 3588 3551 3004 3756 1937 874
οὐκ ᾔδειν, εἰ μὴ ὁ νόμος ἔλεγεν, Οὐκ ἐπιθυμήσεις· 8 ἀφορμὴν
not I knew, if not the law said, not You shall lust; occasion

1161 2983 3588 266 1223 3588 1785 2716 1722
δὲ λαβοῦσα ἡ ἁμαρτία διὰ τῆς ἐντολῆς κατειργάσατο ἐν
but taking sin through the commandment worked in

1698 3956 1939 5565 1063 3551 266 3498
ἐμοὶ πᾶσαν ἐπιθυμίαν· χωρὶς γὰρ νόμου ἁμαρτία νεκρά.
me every lust; apart from for law sin (is) dead.

1473 1161 2198 5565 3551 4218 2064 1161 3588 1785
9 ἐγὼ δὲ ἔζων χωρὶς νόμου ποτέ· ἐλθούσης δὲ τῆς ἐντολῆς,
I And living apart from, law then; coming but the commandment,

3588 266 326 1473 1161 599 2532 2147 3427/3588
ἡ ἁμαρτία ἀνέζησεν, 10 ἐγὼ δὲ ἀπέθανον· καὶ εὑρέθη μοι ἡ
sin revived, I and died; and was found to me the

1785 3588 1519 2222 3778 1519 2288 3588 1063 266
ἐντολὴ ἡ εἰς ζωήν, αὕτη εἰς θάνατον· 11 ἡ γὰρ ἁμαρτία
commandment for life, this to death (was); for sin

874 2983 1223 3588 1785 1818 3165 2532 1223
ἀφορμὴν λαβοῦσα διὰ τῆς ἐντολῆς ἐξηπάτησέ με, καὶ δι'
occasion taking through the commandment deceived me, and through

846 615 5620 3588 3303 3551 40 2532 3588 1785
αὐτῆς ἀπέκτεινεν. 12 ὥστε ὁ μὲν νόμος ἅγιος, καὶ ἡ ἐντολὴ
it killed (me). So the indeed law (is) holy, and the commandment

King James Version

her husband be dead, she is free from that law; so that she is no adulteress, though she be married to another man.

4 Wherefore, my brethren, ye also are become dead to the law by the body of Christ; that ye should be married to another, (even) to him who is raised from the dead, that we should bring forth fruit unto God.

5 For when we were in the flesh, the motions of sins, which were by the law, did work in our members to bring forth fruit unto death.

6 But now we are delivered from the law, that being dead wherein we were held; that we should serve in newness of spirit, and not (in) the oldness of the letter.

7 What shall we say then? (Is) the law sin? God forbid. Nay, I had not known sin, but by the law: for I had not known lust, except the law had said, Thou shalt not covet.
8 But sin, taking occasion by the commandment, wrought in me all manner of concupiscence. For without the law sin (was) dead.

9 For I was alive without the law once: but when the commandment came, sin revived, and I died.
10 And the commandment, which (was ordained) to life, I found (to be) unto death.
11 For sin, taking occasion by the commandment, deceived me, and by it slew (me).

12 Wherefore the law (is) holy, and the commandment

Literal Translation **Romans 7:13** ***King James Version***

holy and just and good.
13 Then that (which is) good, (has it) become death to me? Let it not be! But sin, that it might appear (to be) sin, having worked out death to me through the good, in order that sin might become excessively sinful through the commandment.

14 For we know that the law is spiritual, but I fleshly, having been sold under sin.
15 For what I work out, I do not know. For what I do not will, this I do. But what I hate, this I do.

16 But if I do what I do not will, I agree with the law, that (it is) good.
17 But now I no longer work it out, but the sin dwelling in me.

18 For I know that in me, that is in my flesh, dwells no good. For to will is present to me, but to work out the good I do not find.

19 For what good I desire, I do not do. But the evil I do not desire, this I do.
20 But if I do what I do not desire, (it is) no longer I work it out, but sin dwelling in me.
21 I find then the law, (when) I desire to do the good, that evil is present with me.

22 For I delight in the law of God according to the inward man;

23 but I see another law in my members having warred against the law of my mind, and taking me captive by the law of sin being in my members.
24 O wretched man (that) I (am)! Who shall deliver me from this body

40 2532 1342 2532 18 3588 3767 18 1698 1096
ἁγία καὶ δικαία καὶ ἀγαθή. 13 τὸ οὖν ἀγαθὸν ἐμοὶ γέγονε
holy and just and good. the Then (has) good to me become
2288 3361 1096 235 3588 266 2443 5316 266
θάνατος; μὴ γένοιτο. ἀλλὰ ἡ ἁμαρτία, ἵνα φανῇ ἁμαρτία,
death? Let it not be! But sin, that it appear sin,
1223 3588 18 3427 2716 2288 2443 1096
διὰ τοῦ ἀγαθοῦ μοι κατεργαζομένη θάνατον, ἵνα γένηται
through the good to me having worked out death, that may become
2596 5236 268 3588 266 1223 3588 1785
καθ' ὑπερβολὴν ἁμαρτωλὸς ἡ ἁμαρτία διὰ τῆς ἐντολῆς.
excessively sinful sin through the commandment.

1492 1063 3754 3588 3551 4152 2076 1473 1161 4559
14 οἴδαμεν γὰρ ὅτι ὁ νόμος πνευματικός ἐστιν· ἐγὼ δὲ σάρκικός
we know For that the law spiritual is; I but fleshly
1510 4097 5259 3588 266 3739 1063 2716
εἰμι, πεπραμένος ὑπὸ τὴν ἁμαρτίαν. 15 ὃ γὰρ κατεργάζομαι
am, having been sold under sin. what For I work out,
3756 1097 3756 1063 3739 2309 5124 4238 235 3739 3404
οὐ γινώσκω· οὐ γὰρ ὃ θέλω, τοῦτο πράσσω· ἀλλ' ὃ μισῶ,
not I know; not For what I desire, this I practice,; but what I hate,
5124 4160 1487 1161 3739 3756 2309 5124 4160 4852 3588
τοῦτο ποιῶ. 16 εἰ δὲ ὃ οὐ θέλω, τοῦτο ποιῶ, σύμφημι τῷ
this I do. if But what not I desire, this I do, I agree with the
3551 3754 2570 3570 1161 3765 1473 2716 846
νόμῳ ὅτι καλός. 17 νυνὶ δὲ οὐκέτι ἐγὼ κατεργάζομαι αὐτό,
law that (it is) good. now But no longer I work out it,
235 3588 3611 1722 1698 266 1492 1063 3754 3756 3611 1722
ἀλλ' ἡ οἰκοῦσα ἐν ἐμοὶ ἁμαρτία. 18 οἶδα γὰρ ὅτι οὐκ οἰκεῖ ἐν
but the dwelling in me sin. I know For that not dwells in
1698 5123 5123 1722 3588 4561 3450 18 3588 1063 2309
ἐμοί, τοῦτ' ἔστιν ἐν τῇ σαρκί μου, ἀγαθόν· τὸ γὰρ θέλειν
me, this is in the flesh of me, the good; for to desire
3873 3427 3588 1161 2716 3588 2570 3756 2147
παράκειταί μοι, τὸ δὲ κατεργάζεσθαι τὸ καλὸν οὐχ εὑρίσκω.
is present to me, but to work out the good not I find.

3756 1063 3739 2309 4160 18 235 3739 3756 2309 2556 5124
19 οὐ γὰρ ὃ θέλω, ποιῶ ἀγαθόν· ἀλλ' ὃ οὐ θέλω κακὸν, τοῦτο
not For what I desire, I do good; but what not I desire evil, this
4238 1487 1161 3739 3756 2309 1473 5124 4160 3765 1473
πράσσω. 20 εἰ δὲ ὃ οὐ θέλω ἐγώ, τοῦτο ποιῶ, οὐκέτι ἐγὼ κατερ-
I practice. if But what not desire I, this I do, no longer I work
2716 846 235 3588 3611 1722 1698 266 2147 686
γάζομαι αὐτὸ, ἀλλ' ἡ οἰκοῦσα ἐν ἐμοὶ ἁμαρτία. 21 εὑρίσκω ἄρα
out it, but the dwelling in me sin. I find Then
3588 3551 3588 2309 1698 4160 3588 2570 3754 1698 3588 2556
τὸν νόμον τῷ θέλοντι ἐμοὶ ποιεῖν τὸ καλόν, ὅτι ἐμοὶ τὸ κακὸν
the law the (one) desiring me to do the good, that to me the evil
3873 4913 1063 3588 3551 3588 2316 2596 3588
παράκειται· 22 συνήδομαι γὰρ τῷ νόμῳ τοῦ Θεοῦ κατὰ τὸν
is present. delight For in the law of God according to the
2080 444 991 1161 2087 3551 1722 3588 3196 3450
ἔσω ἄνθρωπον· 23 βλέπω δὲ ἕτερον νόμον ἐν τοῖς μέλεσί μου
inner man; I see but another law in the members of me
497 3588 3551 3588 3563 3450 2532 163
ἀντιστρατευόμενον τῷ νόμῳ τοῦ νοός μου, καὶ αἰχμαλωτί-
having warred against the law of the mind of me, and taking captive
3165 3588 3551 3588 266 3588 5607 1722 3588 3196 3450
ζοντά με τῷ νόμῳ τῆς ἁμαρτίας τῷ ὄντι ἐν τοῖς μέλεσί μου.
me by the law of sin the (one) being in the members of me.
5005 1473 444 5101 3165 4506 1537 3588 4983
24 ταλαίπωρος ἐγὼ ἄνθρωπος· τίς με ῥύσεται ἐκ τοῦ σώματος
(O) wretched I man! Who me will deliver from body

holy, and just, and good.
13 Was then that which is good made death unto me? God forbid. But sin, that it might appear sin, working death in me by that which is good; that sin by the commandment might become exceeding sinful.

14. For we know that the law is spiritual: but I am carnal, sold under sin.
15 For that which I do I allow not: for what I would, that do I not; but what I hate, that do I.

16 If then I do that which I would not, I consent unto the law that (it is) good.
17 Now then it is no more I that do it, but sin that dwelleth in me.
18. For I know that in me (that is, in my flesh,) dwelleth no good thing: for to will is present with me; but (how) to perform that which is good I find not.

19 For the good that I would I do not: but the evil which I would not, that I do.
20 Now if I do that I would not, it is no more I that do it, but sin that dwelleth in me.
21 I find then a law, that, when I would do good, evil is present with me.

22 For I delight in the law of God after the inward man:

23. But I see another law in my members, warring against the law of my mind, and bringing me into captivity to the law of sin which is in my members.
24 O wretched man that I am! who shall deliver me from the body

Romans 7:25

Literal Translation

of death?
25 I thank God through Jesus Christ our Lord! So then I myself with the mind truly serve (the) law of God, and (with) the flesh (the) law of sin.

3588 2288 5127 2168 3588 2316 1223 2424
τοῦ θανάτου τούτου; 25 εὐχαριστῶ τῷ Θεῷ διὰ Ἰησοῦ
death this? I thank God through Jesus

5547 3588 2962 2257 686 3767 846 1473 3588 3303 3563
Χριστοῦ τοῦ Κυρίου ἡμῶν. ἄρα οὖν αὐτὸς ἐγὼ τῷ μὲν νοΐ
Christ the Lord of us. So then myself I truly with the mind

1398 3551 2316 3588 1161 4561 3551 266
δουλεύω νόμῳ Θεοῦ, τῇ δὲ σαρκὶ νόμῳ ἁμαρτίας.
serve (the) law of God, the and flesh (the) law of sin.

King James Version

of this death?
25 I thank God through Jesus Christ our Lord. So then with the mind I myself serve the law of God; but with the flesh the law of sin.

Romans 8

1. (There is) therefore now no condemnation to the (ones) in Christ Jesus, who do not walk according to flesh, but according to Spirit.
2 For the law of the Spirit of life in Christ Jesus set me free from the law of sin and of death.
3 For the law (being) powerless, in that it was weak through the flesh, God sending His own Son in (the) likeness of sinful flesh, and concerning sin condemned sin in the flesh,
4 So that the righteousness of the law might be fulfilled in us, the (ones) not walking according to flesh, but according to Spirit.
5 For the ones being according to flesh mind the things of the flesh, but the ones according to Spirit (mind) the things of the Spirit.
6 For the mind of the flesh (is) death, but the mind of the Spirit (is) life and peace;
7 because the mind of the flesh (is) enmity towards God; for it is not subject to the law of God, for neither can (it be).
8 And the (ones) being in (the) flesh are not able to please God.
9 But you are not in flesh, but in Spirit, if indeed (the) Spirit of God dwells in you. But if anyone has not (the) Spirit of Christ, this one is not His.
10 But if Christ (is) in you, the body indeed (is) dead

Romans 8

3762 686 3568 2631 3588 1722 5547 2424 3361
1. Οὐδὲν ἄρα νῦν κατάκριμα τοῖς ἐν Χριστῷ Ἰησοῦ, μὴ
no Therefore now condemnation to those in Christ Jesus, not

2596 4561 4043 235 2596 4151 3588 1063 3551
κατὰ σάρκα περιπατοῦσιν, ἀλλὰ κατὰ πνεῦμα. 2 ὁ γὰρ νόμος
according to flesh walking, but according to Spirit. the For law of the

3588 4151 3588 2222 1722 5547 2424 1659 3165 575
τοῦ πνεύματος τῆς ζωῆς ἐν Χριστῷ Ἰησοῦ ἠλευθέρωσέ με ἀπὸ
Spirit of life in Christ Jesus set free me from

3588 3551 3588 266 2532 3588 2288 3588 1063 102
τοῦ νόμου τῆς ἁμαρτίας καὶ τοῦ θανάτου. 3 τὸ γὰρ ἀδύνατον
the law of sin and of death. the For powerless

3588 3551 1722 3739 770 1223 3588 4561 3588 2316 3588
τοῦ νόμου, ἐν ᾧ ἠσθένει διὰ τῆς σαρκός, ὁ Θεὸς τὸν
law, in which it was weak through the flesh, God the

1438 5207 3992 1722 3667 4561 266 2532 4012
ἑαυτοῦ υἱὸν πέμψας ἐν ὁμοιώματι σαρκὸς ἁμαρτίας καὶ περὶ
of Himself Son sending in likeness of flesh of sin and concerning

266 2632 3588 266 1722 3588 4561 2443 3588 1345
ἁμαρτίας κατέκρινε τὴν ἁμαρτίαν ἐν τῇ σαρκί· 4 ἵνα τὸ δικαίω-
sin condemned sin in the flesh; that the righteous-

3588 3551 4137 1722 1254 3588 3361 2596 4561 4043
μα τοῦ νόμου πληρωθῇ ἐν ἡμῖν, τοῖς μὴ κατὰ σάρκα περιπατοῦ-
ness of the law may be fulfilled in us, the (ones) not according to flesh walking,

235 2596 4151 3588 1063 2596 4561 5607 3588/3588
σιν, ἀλλὰ κατὰ πνεῦμα. 5 οἱ γὰρ κατὰ σάρκα ὄντες τὰ τῆς
but according to Spirit. the (ones) For according to flesh being the things

4561 5426 3588 1161 2596 4151 3588 3588 4151 3588
σαρκὸς φρονοῦσιν· οἱ δὲ κατὰ πνεῦμα τὰ τοῦ πνεύματος. 6 τὸ
of flesh mind; the (ones) but according to Spirit the things of the Spirit. the

1063 5427 3588 4561 2288 3588 1161 5427 3588 4151
γὰρ φρόνημα τῆς σαρκὸς θάνατος· τὸ δὲ φρόνημα τοῦ πνεύμα-
For mind of the flesh (is) death; the but mind of the Spirit

2222 2532 1515 1360 3588 5427 3588 4561 2189 1519
τος ζωὴ καὶ εἰρήνη· 7 διότι τὸ φρόνημα τῆς σαρκὸς ἔχθρα εἰς
(is) life and peace; because the mind of the flesh (is) enmity toward

2316 3588 1063 3551 3588 2316 3756 5293 3761 1063
Θεόν, τῷ γὰρ νόμῳ τοῦ Θεοῦ οὐχ ὑποτάσσεται, οὐδὲ γὰρ
God, to the For law of God not it is subject, neither for

1410 3588 1161 1722 4561 5607 2316 700 3756 1410
δύναται· 8 οἱ δὲ ἐν σαρκὶ ὄντες Θεῷ ἀρέσαι οὐ δύνανται.
can it (be); the (ones) but in flesh being God to please not is able.

5210 1161 3756 2075 1722 4561 235 1722 4151 1512 4151
9 ὑμεῖς δὲ οὐκ ἐστὲ ἐν σαρκί, ἀλλ' ἐν πνεύματι, εἴπερ Πνεῦμα
you But not are in flesh, but in Spirit, if indeed (the) Spirit

2316 3611 1722 5213 1487 1161 5100 4151 5547 3756 2192 3778
Θεοῦ οἰκεῖ ἐν ὑμῖν. εἰ δέ τις Πνεῦμα Χριστοῦ οὐκ ἔχει, οὗτος
of God dwells in you. if But anyone (the) Spirit of Christ not has, this one

3756 2076 846 1487 1161 5547 1722 5213 3588 3303 4983 3498
οὐκ ἔστιν αὐτοῦ. 10 εἰ δὲ Χριστὸς ἐν ὑμῖν, τὸ μὲν σῶμα νεκρὸν
not is of Him. if But Christ (is) in you, the indeed body (is) dead

Romans 8

1. (There is) therefore now no condemnation to them which are in Christ Jesus, who walk not after the flesh, but after the Spirit.
2 For the law of the Spirit of life in Christ Jesus hath made me free from the law of sin and death.
3 For what the law could not do, in that it was weak through the flesh, God sending his own Son in the likeness of sinful flesh, and for sin, condemned sin in the flesh:
4 That the righteousness of the law might be fulfilled in us, who walk not after the flesh, but after the Spirit.
5 For they that are after the flesh do mind the things of the flesh; but they that are after the Spirit the things of the Spirit.
6 For to be carnally minded (is) death; but to be spiritually minded (is) life and peace.
7 Because the carnal mind (is) enmity against God: for it is not subject to the law of God, neither indeed can be.
8 So then they that are in the flesh cannot please God.
9 But ye are not in the flesh, but in the Spirit, if so be that the Spirit of God dwell in you. Now if any man have not the Spirit of Christ, he is none of his.
10 And if Christ (be) in you, the body (is) dead

Literal Translation **Romans 8:11** ***King James Version***

because of sin, but the Spirit (is) life because of righteousness.
11 But if the Spirit of the (One) having raised Jesus from (the) dead dwells in you, the (One) having raised the Christ from (the) dead will also make your mortal bodies live through the indwelling of His Spirit in you.

1223 266 3588 1161 4151 2222 1223 1343 1487/1161/3588
δι' ἁμαρτίαν, τὸ δὲ πνεῦμα ζωὴ διὰ δικαιοσύνην. 11 εἰ δὲ τὸ
because of sin, the but Spirit (is) life because of righteousness. if But the
4151 3588 1453 2424 1537 3498 3611 1722 5213 3588
Πνεῦμα τοῦ ἐγείραντος Ἰησοῦν ἐκ νεκρῶν οἰκεῖ ἐν ὑμῖν, ὁ
Spirit of the (One) having raised Jesus from (the) dead dwells in you, He
1453 3588 5547 1537 3498 2227 2532 3588 2349
ἐγείρας τὸν Χριστὸν ἐκ νεκρῶν ζῳοποιήσει καὶ τὰ θνητὰ
having raised Christ from (the) dead will make live also the mortal
4983 5216 1223 3588 1774 846 4151 1722
σώματα ὑμῶν, διὰ τοῦ ἐνοικοῦντος αὐτοῦ Πνεύματος ἐν
body of you, through the indwelling of Him Spirit in
5213
ὑμῖν.
you.

because of sin; but the Spirit (is) life because of righteousness.
11 But if the Spirit of him that raised up Jesus from the dead dwell in you, he that raised up Christ from the dead shall also quicken your mortal bodies by his Spirit that dwelleth in you.

12 So, then, brothers, we are debtors, not to the flesh, to live according to flesh;
13 for if you live according to flesh, you are going to die, but if by (the) Spirit you put to death the practices of the body, you will live.

686 3767 80 3781 2070 3756 3588 4561 3588 2596
12. Ἄρα οὖν, ἀδελφοί, ὀφειλέται ἐσμέν, οὐ τῇ σαρκὶ, τοῦ κατὰ
So then, brothers, debtors we are, not to the flesh, according to
4561 2198 1487 1063 2596 4561 2198 3195 599
σάρκα ζῆν· 13 εἰ γὰρ κατὰ σάρκα ζῆτε μέλλετε ἀποθνήσκειν,
flesh to live; if for according to flesh you live, you are going to die,
1487 1161 4151 3588 4234 3588 4983 2289 2198
εἰ δὲ πνεύματι τὰς πράξεις τοῦ σώματος θανατοῦτε, ζήσεσθε.
if but by(the) Spirit the practices of the body you put to death, you will live.

12 Therefore, brethren, we are debtors, not to the flesh, to live after the flesh.
13 For if ye live after the flesh, ye shall die: but if ye through the Spirit do mortify the deeds of the body, ye shall live.

14 For as many as are led by (the) Spirit of God, these are sons of God.
15 For you did not receive a spirit of slavery again to fear, but you received a Spirit of adoption by which we cry, Abba! Father!

16 The Spirit Himself witnesses with our spirit, that we are children of God.
17 And if children, also heirs; truly heirs of God, and joint-heirs of Christ, if indeed we suffer together, that we may also be glorified together.

3745 1063 4151 2316 71 3778 1526 5207 2316
14 ὅσοι γὰρ Πνεύματι Θεοῦ ἄγονται, οὗτοι εἰσιν υἱοὶ Θεοῦ.
as many as For by Spirit of God are led, these are sons of God.
3756 1063 2983 4151 1397 3825 1519 5401 235
15 οὐ γὰρ ἐλάβετε πνεῦμα δουλείας πάλιν εἰς φόβον, ἀλλ'
not For you received a spirit of slavery again to fear, but
2983 4151 5206 1722 3739 2896 5 3588 3962
ἐλάβετε πνεῦμα υἱοθεσίας, ἐν ᾧ κράζομεν, Αββα ὁ πατήρ·
you received a spirit of adoption, by which we cry, Abba, Father!
846 3588 4151 4828 3588 4151 2257 3754 2070
16 αὐτὸ τὸ Πνεῦμα συμμαρτυρεῖ τῷ πνεύματι ἡμῶν, ὅτι ἐσμὲν
itself The Spirit bears witness with the spirit of us, that we are
5043 2316 1487 1161 5043 2532 2818 2818 3303
τέκνα Θεοῦ. 17 εἰ δὲ τέκνα, καὶ κληρονόμοι· κληρονόμοι μὲν
children of God. if And children, also heirs; heirs truly
2316 4789 1161 5547 1512 4841 2443
Θεοῦ, συγκληρονόμοι δὲ Χριστοῦ· εἴπερ συμπάσχομεν, ἵνα
of God, joint-heirs and of Christ; if indeed we suffer together, that
2532 4888
καὶ συνδοξασθῶμεν.
also we may be glorified together.

14 For as many as are led by the Spirit of God, they are the sons of God.
15 For ye have not received the spirit of bondage again to fear; but ye have received the Spirit of adoption, whereby we cry, Abba, Father.
16 The Spirit itself beareth witness with our spirit, that we are the children of God:
17 And if children, then heirs; heirs of God, and joint-heirs with Christ; if so be that we suffer with (him), that we may be also glorified together.

18 For I calculate that the sufferings of the present time (are) not worthy (to compare to) the coming glory to be revealed in us.
19 For the earnest expectation of the creation is eagerly expecting the revelation of the sons of God.
20 For the creation was not willingly subjected to vanity, but through the (One) subjecting (it), on hope;
21 that also the creation itself will be freed from the slavery

3049 1063 3754 3756 514 3588 3804 3588 3568 2540
18. Λογίζομαι γὰρ ὅτι οὐκ ἄξια τὰ παθήματα τοῦ νῦν καιροῦ
I calculate For that not worthy the sufferings of the present time
4314 3588 3195 1391 601 1519 2248 3588 1063
πρὸς τὴν μέλλουσαν δόξαν ἀποκαλυφθῆναι εἰς ἡμᾶς. 19 ἡ γὰρ
to the coming glory to be revealed in us. the For
603 3588 2937 3588 602 3588 5207 3588
ἀποκαραδοκία τῆς κτίσεως τὴν ἀποκάλυψιν τῶν υἱῶν τοῦ
earnest expectation of the creation the revelation of the sons
2316 553 3588 1063 3153 3588 2937 5293
Θεοῦ ἀπεκδέχεται· 20 τῇ γὰρ ματαιότητι ἡ κτίσις ὑπετάγη,
of God is eagerly expecting; for to vanity the creation was subjected,
3756 1635 235 1223 3588 5293 1909 1680 3754 2532
οὐχ ἑκοῦσα, ἀλλὰ διὰ τὸν ὑποτάξαντα, ἐφ' ἐλπίδι· 21 ὅτι καὶ
not willingly, but through the (One) subjecting, on hope; that also
846 3588 2937 1659 575 3588 1397 3588
αὐτὴ ἡ κτίσις ἐλευθερωθήσεται ἀπὸ τῆς δουλείας τῆς
itself the creation will be set free from the slavery

18 For I reckon that the sufferings of this present time (are) not worthy (to be compared) with the glory which shall be revealed in us.
19 For the earnest expectation of the creature waiteth for the manifestation of the sons of God.
20 For the creature was made subject to vanity, not willingly, but by reason of him who hath subjected (the same) in hope,
21 Because the creature itself also shall be delivered from the bondage

Literal Translation **Romans 8:22** ***King James Version***

of corruption to the freedom of the glory of the children of God.

22 For we know that all the creation groans together and travails together until now.
23 And not only (so), but also we ourselves having the firstfruit of the Spirit, also we ourselves groan within ourselves, eagerly expecting adoption, the redemption of our body;

24 for we were saved by hope, but hope being seen is not hope; for what anyone sees, why does he also hope?
25 But if we hope for what we do not see, through patience we eagerly expect.
26 And likewise the Spirit also joins in to help our weaknesses. For we do not know what we should pray as we ought, but the Spirit Himself pleads our case on behalf of us with groanings that cannot be uttered.
27 But the (One) searching the hearts knows what (is the) mind of the Spirit, because He intercedes for (the) saints according to God.
28 But we know that God works together all things for good to the (ones) loving God, to the (ones) being called according to purpose;
29 because whom He foreknew, He also predestinated (to be) conformed to the image of His Son, for Him to be (the) First-born among many brothers;
30 and whom He predestinated, these He also called; and whom He called, these He also justified; but whom He justified, these He also glorified.
31 What then shall we say to these things? If God (be) for us, who (can be) against us?
32 Truly (He) who did not spare His own Son, but gave Him up for us all, how will

5356 1519 3588 1657 3588 1391 3588 5043 3588 2316
φθορᾶς εἰς τὴν ἐλευθερίαν τῆς δόξης τῶν τέκνων τοῦ Θεοῦ.
of corruption to the freedom of the glory of the children of God.

1492 1063 3754 3956 3588 2937 4959 2532 4944
22 οἴδαμεν γὰρ ὅτι πᾶσα ἡ κτίσις συστενάζει καὶ συνωδίνει
we know For that all the creation groans together and travails

891 3588 3568 3756 3440 1161 235 2532 846 3588 536
ἄχρι τοῦ νῦν· 23 οὐ μόνον δέ, ἀλλὰ καὶ αὐτοὶ τὴν ἀπαρχὴν
until the present; not only And (so), but also ourselves the firstfruit

3588 4151 2192 2532 2249 846 1722 1438 4727
τοῦ Πνεύματος ἔχοντες, καὶ ἡμεῖς αὐτοὶ ἐν ἑαυτοῖς στενά-
of the Spirit having, also we ourselves in ourselves groan,

5206 553 3588 629 3588
ζομεν, υἱοθεσίαν ἀπεκδεχόμενοι, τὴν ἀπολύτρωσιν τοῦ
adoption eagerly expecting, the redemption of the

4983 2257 3588 1063 1680 4982 1680 1161 991
σώματος ἡμῶν. 24 τῇ γὰρ ἐλπίδι ἐσώθημεν· ἐλπὶς δὲ βλεπομένη
body of us. For by hope we were being saved; hope but being seen

3756 2076 1680 3739 1063 991 5100 5101 2532 1679 1487 1161 3739
οὐκ ἔστιν ἐλπίς· ὃ γὰρ βλέπει τίς, τί καὶ ἐλπίζει; 25 εἰ δὲ ὃ
not is hope; what for sees anyone, why also does he hope? if But what

3756 991 1679 1223 5281 553
οὐ βλέπομεν ἐλπίζομεν, δι' ὑπομονῆς ἀπεκδεχόμεθα.
not we see we hope (for), through patience we eagerly expect.

5615 1161 2532 3588 4151 4873 3588
26. Ὡσαύτως δὲ καὶ τὸ Πνεῦμα συναντιλαμβάνεται ταῖς
likewise And also the Spirit joins in to help the

769 2257 3588 1063 5101 4336 2526 1163 3756
ἀσθενείαις ἡμῶν· τὸ γὰρ τί προσευξώμεθα καθὸ δεῖ, οὐκ
weaknesses of us; for what we may pray (for) as we ought, not

1492 235 846 3588 4151 5241 5228 2257
οἴδαμεν, ἀλλ' αὐτὸ τὸ πνεῦμα ὑπερεντυγχάνει ὑπὲρ ἡμῶν
we know, but itself the Spirit pleads our case on behalf of us

4726 215 3588 1161 2045 3588 2588 1492 5101 3588
στεναγμοῖς ἀλαλήτοις· 27 ὁ δὲ ἐραυνῶν τὰς καρδίας οἶδε τί τὸ
with groanings unutterable; the (One) but searching the hearts knows what

5427 3588 4151 3754 2596 2316 1793 5228
φρόνημα τοῦ Πνεύματος, ὅτι κατὰ Θεὸν ἐντυγχάνει ὑπὲρ
(is the) mind of the Spirit, because according to God He intercedes on behalf of

40 1492 1161 3754 3588 25 3588 2316 3956 4903
ἁγίων. 28 οἴδαμεν δὲ ὅτι τοῖς ἀγαπῶσι τὸν Θεὸν πάντα συν-
saints. we know And that the (ones) loving God all things

1519 18 3588 2596 4286 2822 5607 3754 3739
εργεῖ εἰς ἀγαθόν, τοῖς κατὰ πρόθεσιν κλητοῖς οὖσιν. 29 ὅτι οὓς
work together for good, those according to purpose called out being. For whom

4309 2532 4309 5656 3588 1504 3588 5207
προέγνω, καὶ προώρισε συμμόρφους τῆς εἰκόνος τοῦ υἱοῦ
He foreknew, also He predestinated conformed to the image of the Son

846 1519 3588 1511 846 4416 1722 4183 80
αὐτοῦ, εἰς τὸ εἶναι αὐτὸν πρωτότοκον ἐν πολλοῖς ἀδελφοῖς·
of Him, for to be Him First-born among many brothers;

3739 1161 4309 5128 2532 2564 2532 3739 2564
30 οὓς δὲ προώρισε, τούτους καὶ ἐκάλεσε· καὶ οὓς ἐκάλεσε, τού-
whom and He predestinated these also He called; and whom He called,

5128 2532 1344 3739 1161 1344 5128 2532 1392
τους καὶ ἐδικαίωσεν· οὓς δὲ ἐδικαίωσε, τούτους καὶ ἐδόξασε.
these also He justified; whom and He justified, these also He glorified.

5101 3767 2046 4314 5023 1487 3588 2316 5228 2257 5101
31. Τί οὖν ἐροῦμεν πρὸς ταῦτα; εἰ ὁ Θεὸς ὑπὲρ ἡμῶν, τίς
what Then shall we say to these things? If God (be) for us, who

2596 2257 3739 1065 3588 2398 5207 3756 5339 235 5228
καθ' ἡμῶν; 32 ὅς γε τοῦ ἰδίου υἱοῦ οὐκ ἐφείσατο, ἀλλ' ὑπὲρ
against us? (He) who truly the own Son not spared, but on behalf of

of corruption into the glorious liberty of the children of God.

22 For we know that the whole creation groaneth and travaileth in pain together until now.
23 And not only (they), but ourselves also, which have the firstfruits of the Spirit, even we ourselves groan within ourselves, waiting for the adoption, (to wit), the redemption of our body.
24 For we are saved by hope: but hope that is seen is not hope: for what a man seeth, why doth he yet hope for?
25 But if we hope for that we see not, (then) do we with patience wait for (it).

26 Likewise the Spirit also helpeth our infirmities: for we know not what we should pray for as we ought: but the Spirit itself maketh intercession for us with groanings which cannot be uttered.
27 And he that searcheth the hearts knoweth what (is) the mind of the Spirit, because he maketh intercession for the saints according to (the will of) God.
28 And we know that all things work together for good to them that love God, to them who are the called according to (his) purpose.
29 For whom he did foreknow, he also did predestinate (to be) conformed to the image of his Son, that he might be the firstborn among many brethren.
30 Moreover whom he did predestinate, them he also called: and whom he called, them he also justified: and whom he justified, them he also glorified.
31 What shall we then say to these things? If God (be) for us, who (can be) against us?
32 He that spared not his own Son, but delivered him up for us all, how shall

Literal Translation

He not freely give us all things with Him?

33 Who will bring (any) charge against God's elect? God (is) the (One) justifying!
34 Who (is) the (one) condemning? Christ (is) the (One) having died, but rather also (is He) having been raised, who also is at (the) right (hand) of God, who also intercedes on our behalf.
35 Who shall separate us from the love of Christ? (Shall) tribulation, or distress, or persecution, or famine, or nakedness, or danger, or sword?
36 Even as it has been written, "For Your sake we are killed all the day; we are counted as sheep of slaughter." (Psa. 44:22)
37 But in all these things we more than conquer through the (One) loving us.
38 For I have been persuaded that neither death, nor life, nor angels, nor rulers, nor powers, nor things present, nor things coming,
39 nor height, nor depth, nor any other creature will be able to separate us from the love of God in Christ Jesus, our Lord.

Romans 8:33

2257 3956 3860 846 4459 3780 2532 4862 846
ἡμῶν πάντων παρέδωκεν αὐτόν, πῶς οὐχὶ καὶ σὺν αὐτῷ
us all gave up Him, how not also with Him

3588 3956 2254 5483 5101 1458 2596 1588
τὰ πάντα ἡμῖν χαρίσεται; 33 τίς ἐγκαλέσει κατὰ ἐκλεκτῶν
all things to us will He freely give? Who will bring charge against the elect

2316 2316 3588 1344 5101 3588 2632 5547 3588
Θεοῦ; Θεὸς ὁ δικαιῶν· 34 τίς ὁ κατακρινῶν; Χριστὸς ὁ ἀπο-
of God? God (is) He justifying; who (is) he condemning? Christ (is) the (One)

599 3123 1161 2532 1453 3739 2532 2076 1722 1188 3588
θανών, μᾶλλον δὲ καὶ ἐγερθείς, ὃς καί ἐστιν ἐν δεξιᾷ τοῦ
having died, rather but also having been raised, who also is at (the) right

2316 3739 2532 1793 5228 2257 5101 2248 5563 575
Θεοῦ, ὃς καὶ ἐντυγχάνει ὑπὲρ ἡμῶν. 35 τίς ἡμᾶς χωρίσει ἀπὸ
of God, who also intercedes on behalf of us. Who us will separate from

3588 26 3588 5547 2347 2228 4730 2228 1375 2228
τῆς ἀγάπης τοῦ Χριστοῦ; θλῖψις, ἢ στενοχωρία, ἢ διωγμὸς, ἢ
the love of Christ? (Shall) trouble, or distress, or persecution, or

3042 2228 1132 2228 2794 2228 3162 2531 1125
λιμὸς, ἢ γυμνότης, ἢ κίνδυνος, ἢ μάχαιρα; 36 καθὼς γέγραπται
famine, or nakedness, or danger, or sword? Even as it has been written,

3754 1752 4675 2289 3650 3588 2250 3049
ὅτι Ἕνεκά σου θανατούμεθα ὅλην τὴν ἡμέραν· ἐλογίσθημεν
For the sake of You we are being killed all the day; we were counted

5613 4263 4967 235 1722 5125 3956 5245 1223
ὡς πρόβατα σφαγῆς. 37 ἀλλ ἐν τούτοις πᾶσιν ὑπερνικῶμεν διὰ
as sheep of slaughter. But in these things all we overconquer through

3588 25 2248 3982 1063 3754 3777 2288
τοῦ ἀγαπήσαντος ἡμᾶς. 38 πέπεισμαι γὰρ ὅτι οὔτε θάνατος
the (One) loving us. I have been persuaded For that not death

3777 2222 3777 32 3777 746 3777 1411 3777 1764
οὔτε ζωὴ οὔτε ἄγγελοι οὔτε ἀρχαὶ οὔτε δυνάμεις οὔτε ἐνεστῶτα
nor life nor angels nor rule rs nor powers nor things present

3777 3195 3777 5313 3777 899 3777 5100 2937 2087
οὔτε μέλλοντα 39 οὔτε ὕψωμα οὔτε βάθος οὔτε τις κτίσις ἑτέρα
nor things coming nor height nor depth nor any creature other

1410 2248 5563 575 3588 26 3588 2316 3588 1722
δυνήσεται ἡμᾶς χωρίσαι ἀπὸ τῆς ἀγάπης τοῦ Θεοῦ τῆς ἐν
will be able us to separate from the love of God in

5547 2424 3588 2962 2257
Χριστῷ Ἰησοῦ τῷ Κυρίῳ ἡμῶν.
Christ Jesus the Lord of us.

King James Version

he not with him also freely give us all things?

33 Who shall lay any thing to the charge of God's elect? (It is) God that justifieth.
34 Who (is) he that condemneth? (It is) Christ that died, yea rather, that is risen again, who is even at the right hand of God, who also maketh intercession for us.
35 Who shall separate us from the love of Christ? (shall) tribulation, or distress, or persecution, or famine, or nakedness, or peril, or sword?
36 As it is written, For thy sake we are killed all the day long; we are accounted as sheep for the slaughter.
37 Nay, in all these things we are more than conquerors through him that loved us.
38 For I am persuaded, that neither death, nor life, nor angels, nor principalities, nor powers, nor things present, nor things to come,
39 Nor height, nor depth, nor any other creature, shall be able to separate us from the love of God, which is in Christ Jesus our Lord.

Romans 9

1. I tell (the) truth in Christ, I do not lie, my conscience bearing witness with me in (the) Holy Spirit,
2 that my grief is great, and a never-ceasing pain (is) in my heart.
3 For I myself was wishing to be a curse from Christ on for the sake of my brothers, my kinsmen according to flesh,

4 who are Israelites, whose (is) the adoption, and the glory, and the covenants, and the

Romans 9

225 3004 1722 5547 3756 5547 4828
1. Ἀλήθειαν λέγω ἐν Χριστῷ, οὐ ψεύδομαι, συμμαρτυρούσης
(the) truth I tell in Christ, not I lie, bearing witness with

3427 3588 4893 3450 1722 4151 40 3754 3077 3427
μοι τῆς συνειδήσεώς μου ἐν Πνεύματι Ἁγίῳ, 2 ὅτι λύπη μοί
me the conscience of me in (the) Spirit Holy, that grief to me

2076 3173 2532 88 3601 3588 2588 3450 2172
ἐστι μεγάλη, καὶ ἀδιάλειπτος ὀδύνη τῇ καρδίᾳ μου. 3 ηὐχόμην
is great, and never-ceasing pain in the heart of me. was wishing

1063 846 1473 331 1511 575 3588 5547 5228 3588
γὰρ αὐτὸς ἐγὼ ἀνάθεμα εἶναι ἀπὸ τοῦ Χριστοῦ ὑπὲρ τῶν
For myself I a curse to be from Christ for the sake of the

80 3450 3588 4773 3450 2596 4561 3748 1526
ἀδελφῶν μου, τῶν συγγενῶν μου κατὰ σάρκα· 4 οἵτινές εἰσιν
brothers of me, the kinsmen of me according to flesh; who are.

2475 3739 3588 5206 2532 3588 1391 2532 3588 1242 2532 3588
Ἰσραηλῖται, ὧν ἡ υἱοθεσία καὶ ἡ δόξα καὶ αἱ διαθῆκαι καὶ ἡ
Israelites, of whom the adoption and the glory and the covenants and the

Romans 9

1. I say the truth in Christ, I lie not, my conscience also bearing me witness in the Holy Ghost,
2 That I have great heaviness and continual sorrow in my heart.
3 For I could wish that myself were accursed from Christ for my brethren, my kinsmen according to the flesh:

4 Who are Israelites; to whom (pertaineth) the adoption, and the glory, and the covenants, and the

Literal Translation **Romans 9:5** *King James Version*

Lawgiving, and the
service, and the prom-
ises;
5 whose (are) the fa-
thers, and from whom
(is) the Christ according
to flesh, He being God
over all, blessed to the
ages. Amen.
6 Not, however, that the
Word of God has failed.
For not all the (ones) of
Israel (are) Israel,
7 nor because they are
Abraham's seed (are)
all children, but "In
Isaac a Seed shall be
called to you." (Gen.,
21:12)
8 That is: Not the chil-
dren of flesh, these (are)
children of God, but the
children of the promise
(are) counted for a seed.
9 For the word of prom-
ise (is) this, "According
to this season I will
come, and a son will be
to Sarah." (Gen. 18:10)
10 And not only (so),
but also Rebekah hav-
ing in womb from one,
our father Isaac,
11 for (the children) not
yet having been gener-
ated, nor having done
any good or evil, that the
purpose of God accord-
ing to election might
stand, not of works, but
of the (One) calling,
12 it was said to her,
"The greater shall serve
the lesser;" (Gen.
25:23)
13 even as it has been
written, "I loved Jacob,
and I hated Esau."
(Mal. 1:2, 3)
14 What then shall we
say? (Is there) not un-
righteousness with
God? Let it not be!
15 For He said to
Moses, "I will have
mercy on whomever I
will have mercy, and I
will pity whomever I
will pity." (Ex. 33:19)
16 So, then, (it is) not of
the (one) willing, nor of
the (one) running, but of
the (One) having
mercy, of God.
17 For the Scripture
says to Pharaoh, "For
this very thing I raised
you up, so that I might
show forth My power in
you, and so that My
name might be pro-
claimed

3548 2532 3588 2999 2532 3588 1860 3739 3588 3962
νομοθεσία καὶ ἡ λατρεία καὶ αἱ ἐπαγγελίαι, 5 ὧν οἱ πατέρες,
law-giving and the service and the promises, of whom the fathers,

2532 1537 3739 3588 5547 3588 2596 4561 3588 5607 1909 3956 2316
καὶ ἐξ ὧν ὁ Χριστὸς τὸ κατὰ σάρκα, ὁ ὢν ἐπὶ πάντων, Θεὸς
and from whom the Christ according to flesh, He being over all, God

2128 1519 3588 165 281 3756 3634 1161 3754 1601
εὐλογητὸς εἰς τοὺς αἰῶνας, ἀμήν. 6 Οὐχ οἷον δὲ ὅτι ἐκπέπτωκεν
blessed to the ages, Amen. Not however that has failed

3588 3056 3588 2316 3756 1063 3956 3588 1537 2474 3778 2474
ὁ λόγος τοῦ Θεοῦ. οὐ γὰρ πάντες οἱ ἐξ Ἰσραήλ, οὗτοι Ἰσραήλ·
the Word of God. not For all the ones of Israel, these (are) Israel;

3761 3754 1526 4690 11 3956 5043 235 1722
7 οὐδ' ὅτι εἰσιν σπέρμα Ἀβραάμ, πάντες τέκνα, ἀλλ' Ἐν
nor because they are seed of Abraham (are) all children, but, In

2464 2564 4671 4690 5123 2076 3756 3588 5043 3588
Ἰσαὰκ κληθήσεταί σοι σπέρμα. 8 τοῦτ' ἔστιν, οὐ τὰ τέκνα τῆς
Isaac will be called to you a Seed. This is, not the children of the

4561 5023 5043 3588 2316 235 3588 5043 3588 1860
σαρκός, ταῦτα τέκνα τοῦ Θεοῦ· ἀλλὰ τὰ τέκνα τῆς ἐπαγγελίας
flesh, these children of God; but the children of the promise

3049 1519 4690 1860 1063 3588 3056 3778
λογίζεται εἰς σπέρμα. 9 ἐπαγγελίας γὰρ ὁ λόγος οὗτος,
(are) reckoned for a seed. of promise for the word this (is),

2596 3588 2540 5126 2064 2532 2071 3588 4564 5207
Κατὰ τὸν καιρὸν τοῦτον ἐλεύσομαι, καὶ ἔσται τῇ Σάρρᾳ υἱός.
According to time this I will come, and will be to Sarah a son.

3756 3440 1161 235 2532 4479 1537 1520 2845 2192
10 οὐ μόνον δέ, ἀλλὰ καὶ Ῥεβέκκα ἐξ ἑνὸς κοίτην ἔχουσα,
not only And (so), but also Rebekah from one in womb having,

2464 3588 3962 2257 3380 1063 1080 3366
Ἰσαὰκ τοῦ πατρὸς ἡμῶν -- 11 μήπω γὰρ γεννηθέντων, μηδὲ
Isaac the father of us not yet for having been generated, nor

4238 5100 18 2228 2556 2443 3588 2596 1589 3588 2316
πραξάντων τι ἀγαθὸν ἢ κακόν, ἵνα ἡ κατ' ἐκλογὴν τοῦ Θεοῦ
having practiced any good or evil,, that the according to election of God

4286 3306 3756 1537 2041 235 1537 3588 2564 4483
πρόθεσις μένῃ, 12 οὐκ ἐξ ἔργων, ἀλλ' ἐκ τοῦ καλοῦντος, ἐρρέθη
purpose might stand, not of works, but of the (One) calling, it was said

846 3754 3588 3187 1398 3588 1640 2531 1125
αὐτῇ ὅτι Ὁ μείζων δουλεύσει τῷ ἐλάσσονι· 13 καθὼς γέγραπται,
to her, The greater shall serve the lesser; even as it has been written,

3588 2384 25 3588 1161 2269 3404
Τὸν Ἰακὼβ ἠγάπησα, τὸν δὲ Ἠσαῦ ἐμίσησα.
Jacob I loved, and Esau I hated.

5101 3767 2046 3361 93 3844 3588 2316 3361 1096
14. Τί οὖν ἐροῦμεν; μὴ ἀδικία παρὰ τῷ Θεῷ; μὴ γένοιτο.
What then shall we say? Not unrighteousness with God? Not let it be!

3588 1063 3475 3004 1653 3739 302 1653 2532
15 τῷ γὰρ Μωσῇ λέγει, Ἐλεήσω ὃν ἂν ἐλεῶ, καὶ
For to Moses He says, I will have mercy on whomever I have mercy, and

3627 3739 302 3627 686 3767 3756 3588 2309 3761
οἰκτειρήσω ὃν ἂν οἰκτίρω. 16 ἄρα οὖν οὐ τοῦ θέλοντος, οὐδὲ
I will pity whomever I pity. so Therefore not of the (one) willing, nor

3588 5143 235 3588 1653 2316 3004 1063 3588 1124
τοῦ τρέχοντος, ἀλλὰ τοῦ ἐλεοῦντος Θεοῦ. 17 λέγει γὰρ ἡ γραφὴ
of the (one) running, but of the (one) having mercy God. says For the Scripture

3588 5328 3754 1519 846 5124 1825 4571 3704 1731
τῷ Φαραὼ ὅτι Εἰς αὐτὸ τοῦτο ἐξήγειρά σε, ὅπως ἐνδείξωμαι
to Pharaoh, For same this thing I raised up you, so that I may display

1722 4671 3588 1411 3450 2532 3704 1229 3588 3686
ἐν σοὶ τὴν δύναμίν μου, καὶ ὅπως διαγγελῇ τὸ ὄνομά
in you the power of Me, and so that may be proclaimed the name

giving of the law, and
the service (of God),
and the promises;
5 Whose (are) the fa-
thers, and of whom as
concerning the flesh
Christ (came), who is
over all, God blessed for
ever. Amen.
6 Not as though the
word of God hath taken
none effect. For they
(are) not all Israel,
which are of Israel:
7 Neither, because they
are the seed of Abra-
ham, (are they) all chil-
dren: but, In Isaac shall
thy seed be called.
8 That is, They which
are the children of the
flesh, these (are) not the
children of God: but the
children of the promise
are counted for the seed.
9 For this (is) the word
of promise, At this time
will I come, and Sara
shall have a son.
10 And not only (this);
but when Rebecca also
had conceived by one,
(even) by our father
Isaac;
11 (For (the children)
being not yet born, nei-
ther having done any
good or evil, that the
purpose of God accord-
ing to election might
stand, not of works, but
of him that calleth;)
12 It was said unto her,
The elder shall serve the
younger.
13 As it is written, Jacob
have I loved, but Esau
have I hated.
14 What shall we say
then? (Is there) un-
righteousness with
God? God forbid.
15 For he saith to
Moses, I will have
mercy on whom I will
have mercy, and I will
have compassion on
whom I will have com-
passion.
16 So then (it is) not of
him that willeth, nor of
him that runneth, but of
God that sheweth
mercy.
17 For the scripture
saith unto Pharaoh,
Even for this same pur-
pose have I raised thee
up, that I might shew
my power in thee, and
that my name might be
declared

Literal Translation | **Romans 9:18** | **King James Version**

in all the earth." (Ex. 9:16)
18 So, then, to whom He desires, He has mercy. And to whom He desires, He hardens.
19 You will then say to me, Why does He yet find fault? For who has resisted His purpose?
20 Yes, rather, O man, who are you answering against God? Shall the thing formed say to the (One) forming (it), Why did You make me this way?
21 Or has not the potter authority (over) the clay, out of the same lump indeed to make one vessel to honor, and one to dishonor?
22 But if God, desiring to show forth wrath, and to make His power known, endured in much long-suffering vessels of wrath having been fitted for destruction,
23 and that He make known the riches of His glory on vessels of mercy which He before prepared for glory,
24 whom He also called, not only us, of Jews, but also out of nations.
25 As also He says in Hosea, "I will call the Not My people, My people! And the Not Having-been Loved, Having-been Loved!"
26 And it shall be, in the place where it was said to them, You are not My people, there they will be called, "Sons of (the) living God." (Hos. 2:23)
27 But Isaiah cries on behalf of Israel, "If be the number of the sons of Israel as the sand of the sea, the remnant will be saved.
28 For (He is) finishing (the) matter and cutting short in righteousness, because (the) Lord will do a thing having been cut short on the earth." (Isa. 10:22, 23)
29 And as Isaiah has said before, "Except (the) Lord of Hosts

3450 1722 3956 3588 1093 686 3767 3739 2309 1653 3739
μου ἐν πάσῃ τῇ γῇ. 18 ἄρα οὖν ὃν θέλει ἐλεεῖ· ὃν
of Me in all the earth.So then to whom He desires He has mercy; whom

1161 2309 4645
δὲ θέλει σκληρύνει.
and He desires He hardens.

2046 3767 3427 5101 2089 3201 3588 1063 1013 846
19. Ἐρεῖς οὖν μοι, Τί ἔτι μέμφεται; τῷ γὰρ βουλήματι αὐτοῦ
You will say then to Me, Why yet He finds fault? the For purpose of Him

5101 436 3304 5599 444 4771/5101/1488/3588 470
τίς ἀνθέστηκε; 20 μενοῦνγε, ὦ ἄνθρωπε, σὺ τίς εἶ ὁ ἀνταπο-
who has resisted? Yes, rather, O man, you who are answering

3588 2316 3361 2046 3588 4110 3588 4111 5101/3165
κρινόμενος τῷ Θεῷ; μὴ ἐρεῖ τὸ πλάσμα τῷ πλάσαντι, Τί με
against God? Not will say the formed thing to Him forming, Why me

4160 3779 2228 3756 2192 1849 3588 2763 3588 4081
ἐποίησας οὕτως; 21 ἢ οὐκ ἔχει ἐξουσίαν ὁ κεραμεὺς τοῦ πηλοῦ,
You made this way? Or not has authority the potter of the clay,

1537 3588 846 5445 4160 3739 3303 1519 5092 4632 3739
ἐκ τοῦ αὐτοῦ φυράματος ποιῆσαι ὃ μὲν εἰς τιμὴν σκεῦος, ὃ
out of the same lump to make indeed one to honor vessel

1161 1519 819 1487 1161 2309 3588 2316 1731 3588 3709
δὲ εἰς ἀτιμίαν; 22 εἰ δὲ θέλων ὁ Θεὸς ἐνδείξασθαι τὴν ὀργὴν,
and one to dishonor? if But desiring God to show forth wrath,

2532 1107 3588 1415 846 5342 1722 4183 3115
καὶ γνωρίσαι τὸ δυνατὸν αὐτοῦ, ἤνεγκεν ἐν πολλῇ μα-
and to make known the power of Him, endured in much long-

4632 3709 2675 1519 684 2532 2443
κροθυμίᾳ σκεύη ὀργῆς κατηρτισμένα εἰς ἀπώλειαν· 23 καὶ ἵνα
suffering vessels of wrath having been fitted for destruction; and that

1107 3588 4149 3588 1391 846 1909 4632 1656
γνωρίσῃ τὸν πλοῦτον τῆς δόξης αὐτοῦ ἐπὶ σκεύη ἐλέους,
He make known the riches of the glory of Him on vessels of mercy,

3739 4282 1519 1391 3739 2532 2564 2248 3756 3440
ἃ προητοίμασεν εἰς δόξαν, 24 οὓς καὶ ἐκάλεσεν ἡμᾶς οὐ μόνον
which He before prepared for glory, whom also He called us not only

1537 2453 235 2532 1537 1484 5613/2532/1722/3588/5617/3004
ἐξ Ἰουδαίων, ἀλλὰ καὶ ἐξ ἐθνῶν; 25 ὡς καὶ ἐν τῷ Ὡσηὲ λέγει,
of Jews, but also of nations? As also in Hosea He says,

2564 3588 3756 2992 3450 2992 3450 2532 3588 3756 25
Καλέσω τὸν οὐ λαόν μου λαόν μου· καὶ τὴν οὐκ ἠγαπη-
I will call the Not People of Me a people of Me; and the (ones) Not Having- been

28 2532 2071 1722 3588 5117 3739 4483 846
μένην ἠγαπημένην. 26 καὶ ἔσται ἐν τῷ τόπῳ οὗ ἐρρέθη αὐτοῖς,
Loved Having-been Loved. And it shall be in the place where it was said to them,

3756 2992 3450 5210 1563 2564 5207 2316 2198
Οὐ λαός μου ὑμεῖς, ἐκεῖ κληθήσονται υἱοὶ Θεοῦ ζῶντος.
Not a people of Me you (are), there they will be called sons God of a living.

2268 1161 2896 5228 3588 2474 1437 5600 3588 706 3588
27 Ἠσαΐας δὲ κράζει ὑπὲρ τοῦ Ἰσραήλ, Ἐὰν ᾖ ὁ ἀριθμὸς τῶν
Isaiah And cries on behalf of Israel, If be the number of the

5207 2474 5613 3588 285 3588 2281 3588 2640
υἱῶν Ἰσραὴλ ὡς ἡ ἄμμος τῆς θαλάσσης, τὸ κατάλειμμα
sons of Israel as the sand of the sea, the remnant

4982 3056 1063 4931 2532 4932 1722 1343
σωθήσεται· 28 λόγον γὰρ συντελῶν καὶ συντέμνων ἐν δικαιο-
will be saved; (the) matter For (He is) finishing and cutting short in righteous-

3754 3056 4932 4160 2962 1909 3588
σύνῃ· ὅτι λόγον συντετμημένον ποιήσει Κύριος ἐπὶ τῆς
ness; because a thing having been cut short will do (the) Lord on the

1093 2532 2531 4280 2268 1487 3361 2962 4519
γῆς. 29 καὶ καθὼς προείρηκεν Ἠσαΐας, Εἰ μὴ Κύριος Σαβαὼθ
earth. And even as has been said before Isaiah, If not (the) Lord of Hosts

throughout all the earth.
18 Therefore hath he mercy on whom he will (have mercy), and whom he will he hardeneth.
19 Thou wilt say then unto me, Why doth he yet find fault? For who hath resisted his will?
20 Nay but, O man, who art thou that repliest against God? Shall the thing formed say to him that formed (it), Why hast thou made me thus?
21 Hath not the potter power over the clay, of the same lump to make one vessel unto honour, and another unto dishonour?
22 (What) if God, willing to shew (his) wrath, and to make his power known, endured with much longsuffering the vessels of wrath fitted to destruction:
23 And that he might make known the riches of his glory on the vessels of mercy, which he had afore prepared unto glory,
24 Even us, whom he hath called, not of the Jews only, but also of the Gentiles?
25 As he saith also in Osee, I will call them my people, which were not my people; and her beloved, which was not beloved.
26 And it shall come to pass, (that) in the place where it was said unto them, Ye (are) not my people; there shall they be called the children of the living God.
27 Esaias also crieth concerning Israel, Though the number of the children of Israel be as the sand of the sea, a remnant shall be saved:
28 For he will finish the work, and cut (it) short in righteousness: because a short work will the Lord make upon the earth.
29 And as Esaias said before, Except the Lord of Sabaoth

Literal Translation | **Romans 9:30** | *King James Version*

left a seed to us, we would have become as Sodom, and we would have become as Gomorrah." (Isa. 1:9)

1459 2254 4690 5613 4670 302 1096 2532 5613
ἐγκατέλιπεν ἡμῖν σπέρμα, ὡς Σόδομα ἂν ἐγενήθημεν, καὶ ὡς
left to us a seed, as Sodom we would have become, and as
1116 302 3666
Γόμορρα ἂν ὡμοιώθημεν.
Gomorrah we would have become.

had left us a seed, we had been as Sodoma, and been made like unto Gomorrha.

30 What then shall we say? That (the) nations, not following after righteousness had taken on righteousness, but a righteousness of faith;

31 but Israel, following after a law of righteousness did not arrive at a law of righteousness?

32 Why? Because (it was) not of faith, but as of works of Law. For they stumbled at the Stone-of-stumbling,

33 as it has been written, "Behold, I place in Zion a Stone-of-stumbling, and a Rock-of-offense, and everyone believing on Him will not be put to shame." (Isa. 28:16)

5101 3767 2046 3754 1484 3588 3361 1377 1343
30. Τί οὖν ἐροῦμεν; ὅτι ἔθνη, τὰ μὴ διώκοντα δικαιοσύνην,
What then shall we say? That nations, not following after righteousness,
2638 1343 1343 1161 3588 1537 4102
κατέλαβεν δικαιοσύνην, δικαιοσύνην δὲ τὴν ἐκ πίστεως·
had taken on righteousness, a righteousness but of faith;
2474 1161 1377 3551 1343 1519 3551
31 Ἰσραὴλ δέ, διώκων νόμον δικαιοσύνης εἰς νόμον
Israel but, following after a law of righteousness at a law
1343 3756 5348 1302 3754 3756 1537 4102 235 5613
δικαιοσύνης οὐκ ἔφθασε. 32 διατί; ὅτι οὐκ ἐκ πίστεως, ἀλλ' ὡς
of righteousness not did arrive. Why? Because not of faith, but as
1537 2041 3551 4350 1063 3588 3037 3588 4348
ἐξ ἔργων νόμου. προσέκοψαν γὰρ τῷ λίθῳ τοῦ προσκόμματος,
of works of law. they stumbled For at the Stone- of-stumbling,
2531 1125 2400 5087 1722 4622 3037 4348
33 καθὼς γέγραπται, Ἰδοὺ τίθημι ἐν Σιὼν λίθον προσκόμματος,
even as it has been written, Behold! I place in Zion a Stone-of-stumbling,
2532 4073 4625 2532 3956 3588 4100 1909 846 3756
καὶ πέτραν σκανδάλου· και πᾶς ὁ πιστεύων ἐπ' αὐτῷ οὐ καται-
and a Rock- of-offense; and everyone believing on Him not will be
2617
σχυνθήσεται.
ashamed.

30 What shall we say then? That the Gentiles, which followed not after righteousness, have attained to righteousness, even the righteousness which is of faith.
31 But Israel, which followed after the law of righteousness, hath not attained to the law of righteousness.
32 Wherefore? Because (they sought it) not by faith, but as it were by the works of the law. For they stumbled at that stumblingstone;
33 As it is written, Behold, I lay in Sion a stumblingstone and rock of offence: and whosoever believeth on him shall not be ashamed.

Romans 10 | Romans 10 | Romans 10

1. Brothers, truly my heart's pleasure and petition to God on behalf of Israel is for (it) to be saved.
2 For I testify to them that they have zeal to God, but not according to knowledge.

3 For being ignorant of the righteousness of God, and seeking to establish their own righteousness, they did not submit to the righteousness of God.

4 For Christ (is) the end of law for righteousness to everyone believing.
5 For Moses writes (of) the righteousness of the law: "The man doing these things shall live by them." (Lev. 18:5)

6 But the righteousness of faith says this: "Do not say in your heart, Who will go up into Heaven?"

80 3588 3303 2107 3588 1699 2588 2532 3588 1162 3588
1. Ἀδελφοί, ἡ μὲν εὐδοκία τῆς ἐμῆς καρδίας καὶ ἡ δέησις ἡ
Brothers, the truly pleasure of My heart and the petition
4314 3588 2316 5228 3588 2474 2076 1519 4991 3140
πρὸς τὸν Θεὸν ὑπὲρ τοῦ Ἰσραήλ ἐστιν εἰς σωτηρίαν. 2 μαρ-
to God on behalf of Israel is for (it) to be saved. I
1063 846 3754 2205 2316 2192 235 3756 2596
τυρῶ γὰρ αὐτοῖς ὅτι ζῆλον Θεοῦ ἔχουσιν, ἀλλ' οὐ κατ'
testify For to them that zeal to God they have, but not according to
1922 50 1063 3588 3588 2316 1343 2532
ἐπίγνωσιν. 3 ἀγνοοῦντες γὰρ τὴν τοῦ Θεοῦ δικαιοσύνην, καὶ
knowledge. being ignorant For the of God righteousness, and
3588 2398 1343 2212 2476 3588 1343 3588
τὴν ἰδίαν δικαιοσύνην ζητοῦντες στῆσαι, τῇ δικαιοσύνῃ τοῦ
the own righteousness seeking to establish, to the righteousness
2316 3756 5293 5056 1063 3551 5547 1519 1343
Θεοῦ οὐχ ὑπετάγησαν· 4 τέλος γὰρ νόμου Χριστὸς εἰς δικαιο-
of God not they submitted; the end for of law Christ (is) for righteous-
3956 3588 4100 3475 1063 1125 3588
σύνην παντὶ τῷ πιστεύοντι. 5 Μωσῆς γὰρ γράφει τὴν δι-
ness to everyone believing. Moses For writes: The
1343 3588 1537 3588 3551 3754 3588 4160 846 444
καιοσύνην τὴν ἐκ τοῦ νόμου, ὅτι ὁ ποιήσας αὐτὰ ἄνθρωπος
righteousness of the law, The doing of these things man
2198 1722 846 3588 1161 1537 4102 1343 3779 3004
ζήσεται ἐν αὐτοῖς. 6 ἡ δὲ ἐκ πίστεως δικαιοσύνη οὕτως λέγει,
shall live by them. the But of faith righteousness thus says,
3361 2036 1722 3588 2588 4675 5101 305 1519 3588 3772
Μὴ εἴπῃς ἐν τῇ καρδίᾳ σου, Τίς ἀναβήσεται εἰς τὸν οὐρανόν;
not Say in the heart of you, Who will go up into Heaven?

1. Brethren, my heart's desire and prayer to God for Israel is, that they might be saved.
2 For I bear them record that they have a zeal of God, but not according to knowledge.

3 For they being ignorant of God's righteousness, and going about to establish their own righteousness, have not submitted themselves unto the righteousness of God.
4 For Christ (is) the end of the law for righteousness to every one that believeth.
5 For Moses describeth the righteousness which is of the law, That the man which doeth those things shall live by them.
6 But the righteousness which is of faith speaketh on this wise, Say not in thine heart, Who shall ascend into heaven?

Literal Translation

that is, to bring down Christ;
7 or, "Who will go down into the abyss?" that is, to bring Christ up from (the) dead.
8 But what does it say? "The Word is near you, in your mouth and in your heart" that is, the Word of faith which we proclaim. (Deut. 9:4; 30:12 - 14).
9 Because if you confess (the) Lord Jesus with your mouth, and believe in your heart that God raised Him from (the) dead, you will be saved.
10 For with (the) heart (one) believes unto righteousness, and with (the) mouth (one) confesses unto salvation.
11 For the Scripture says, "Everyone believing on Him will not be put to shame." (Isa. 28:16)
12 For there is no difference both of Jew and of Greek, for the same Lord of all is rich toward all the (ones) calling on Him.
13 For everyone, "whoever may call on the name of (the) Lord will be saved." (Joel 3:5)
14 How then may they call on (One) in whom they have not believed? And how may they believe (One) of whom they have not heard? And how may they hear without preaching?
15 And how may they preach if they are not sent? Even as it has been written, "How beautiful the feet of those proclaiming the gospel of peace, of those proclaiming the gospel of good things." (Isa. 52:7)
16 But not all obeyed the gospel, for Isaiah says, "Lord, who has believed our report?" (Isa. 53:1)
17 Then faith (is) of hearing, and hearing through (the) Word of God.
18 But I say, Did they not at all hear? Yes, rather, "into all the earth their voice went out,

Romans 10:7

5124 2076 5547 2609 2228 5101 2597 1519
[τοῦτ' ἔστι Χριστὸν καταγαγεῖν·] 7 ἤ, Τίς καταβήσεται εἰς
- this is Christ to bring down' - or, Who will go down into

3588 12 5124 2076 5547 1537 3498 321
τὴν ἄβυσσον; [τοῦτ' ἔστι Χριστὸν ἐκ νεκρῶν ἀναγαγεῖν.]
the abyss, - this is Christ from (the) dead to bring up. -

235 5101 3004 1451 4675 3588 4487 2076 1722 3588 4750
8 ἀλλὰ τί λέγει; Ἐγγύς σου τὸ ῥῆμά ἐστιν, ἐν τῷ στόματί
But what says it? Near you the Word is, in the mouth

4675 2532 1722 3588 2588 4675 5124 2076 3588 4487 3588 4102
σου καὶ ἐν τῇ καρδίᾳ σου· τοῦτ' ἔστι τὸ ῥῆμα τῆς πίστεως
of you and in the heart of you; this is the word of faith

3739 2784 3754 1437 3670 1722 3588 4750 4675
ὃ κηρύσσομεν. 9 ὅτι ἐὰν ὁμολογήσῃς ἐν τῷ στόματί σου
which we proclaim. because if you confess with the mouth of you

2962 2424 2532 4100 1722 3588 2588 4675 3754 3588 2316
Κύριον Ἰησοῦν, καὶ πιστεύσῃς ἐν τῇ καρδίᾳ σου ὅτι ὁ Θεὸς
(the) Lord Jesus, and believe in the heart of you that God

846 1453 1537 3498 4982 2588 1063 4100
αὐτὸν ἤγειρεν ἐκ νεκρῶν, σωθήσῃ· 10 καρδίᾳ γὰρ πιστεύεται
Him raised from (the) dead, you will be saved; with heart for (one) believes

1519 1343 4750 1161 3670 1519 4991 3004
εἰς δικαιοσύνην, στόματι δὲ ὁμολογεῖται εἰς σωτηρίαν. 11 λέγει
unto righteousness, with mouth and (one) confesses unto salvation. says

1063 3588 1124 3956 3588 4100 1909 846 3756 2617
γὰρ ἡ γραφή, Πᾶς ὁ πιστεύων ἐπ' αὐτῷ οὐ καταισχυνθή-
For the Scripture, Everyone believing on Him not will be put to

3756 1063 2076 1293 2453 5037 2532 1672 3588
σεται. 12 οὐ γάρ ἐστι διαστολὴ Ἰουδαίου τε καὶ Ἕλληνος· ὁ
shame. not For is difference of Jew both and of Greek; the

1063 846 2962 3956 4147 1519 3956 3588
γὰρ αὐτὸς Κύριος πάντων, πλουτῶν εἰς πάντας τοὺς ἐπι-
for same Lord of all is rich to all the (ones)

1941 846 3956 1063 3739 302 1941 3588 3686
καλουμένους αὐτόν. 13 πᾶς γὰρ ὃς ἂν ἐπικαλέσηται τὸ ὄνομα
calling on Him. everyone For whoever calls on the name

2962 4982 4459 3767 1941 1519 3739 3756
Κυρίου σωθήσεται. 14 πῶς οὖν ἐπικαλέσωνται εἰς ὃν οὐκ ἐπί-
of (the) Lord will be saved. how Then may they call on (One) in whom not

4100 4459 1161 4100 3739 3756 191 4459 1161
στευσαν; πῶς δὲ πιστεύσωσιν οὗ οὐκ ἤκουσαν; πῶς δὲ
they believed? how And may they believe of whom not they heard? how And

191 5565 2784 4459 1161 2784 1437 3361
ἀκούσωσι χωρὶς κηρύσσοντος; 15 πῶς δὲ κηρύξωσιν ἐὰν μὴ
may they hear without preaching? how And may they preach if not

649 2531 1125 5613 5611 3588 4228 3588
ἀποσταλῶσι; καθὼς γέγραπται, Ὡς ὡραῖοι οἱ πόδες τῶν
they are sent? Even as it has been written, How beautiful the feet of those

2097 1515 3588 2097 3588 18
εὐαγγελιζομένων εἰρήνην, τῶν εὐαγγελιζομένων τὰ ἀγαθά.
preaching the gospel of peace, of those preaching the gospel of good things.

235 3756 3956 5219 3588 2098 2268 1063
16 Ἀλλ' οὐ πάντες ὑπήκουσαν τῷ εὐαγγελίῳ. Ἠσαΐας γὰρ
But not all obeyed the gospel. Isaiah For

3004 2962 1519 4100 3588 189 2257 686 3588 4102 1537
λέγει, Κύριε, τίς ἐπίστευσε τῇ ἀκοῇ ἡμῶν; 17 ἄρα ἡ πίστις ἐξ
says, Lord, who has believed the report of us? Then faith (is) of

189 3588 1161 189 1223 4487 2316 235 3004 3361 3756
ἀκοῆς, ἡ δὲ ἀκοὴ διὰ ῥήματος Θεοῦ. 18 ἀλλὰ λέγω, Μὴ οὐκ
hearing, the and hearing through a word of God. But I say, Not at all

191 3304 1519 3956 3588 1093 1831 3588 5353
ἤκουσαν; μενοῦνγε· εἰς πᾶσαν τὴν γῆν ἐξῆλθεν ὁ φθόγγος
did they hear? Yes, rather; into all the earth went out the voice

King James Version

(that is, to bring Christ down (from above):)
7 Or, Who shall descend into the deep? (that is, to bring up Christ again from the dead.)
8 But what saith it? The word is nigh thee, (even) in thy mouth, and in thy heart: that is, the word of faith, which we preach;
9 That if thou shalt confess with thy mouth the Lord Jesus, and shalt believe in thine heart that God hath raised him from the dead, thou shalt be saved.
10 For with the heart man believeth unto righteousness; and with the mouth confession is made unto salvation.
11 For the scripture saith, Whosoever believeth on him shall not be ashamed.
12 For there is no difference between the Jew and the Greek: for the same Lord over all is rich unto all that call upon him.
13 For whosoever shall call upon the name of the Lord shall be saved.
14 How then shall they call on him in whom they have not believed? and how shall they believe in him of whom they have not heard? and how shall they hear without a preacher?
15 And how shall they preach, except they be sent? as it is written, How beautiful are the feet of them that preach the gospel of peace, and bring glad tidings of good things!
16 But they have not all obeyed the gospel. For Esaias saith, Lord, who hath believed our report?
17 So then faith (cometh) by hearing, and hearing by the word of God.
18 But I say, Have they not heard? Yes verily, their sound went into all the earth,

Literal Translation | **Romans 10:19** | **King James Version**

and to the ends of the habitable world their words." (Psa.19:4)

19 But I say, Did not Israel know? First, Moses says, "I will provoke you to jealousy by a not-nation, by an unwise nation I will anger you." (Deut. 32:21)

20 But Isaiah (is) very bold and says, "I was found by those not seeking Me; I came to be revealed to those not inquiring after Me." (Isa. 65:1)

21 But to Israel He says, "All the day I stretched out My hands to a disobeying and gainsaying people." (Isa. 65:2)

846 2532 1519 3588 4009 3588 3625 3588 4487 846
αὐτῶν, καὶ εἰς τὰ πέρατα τῆς οἰκουμένης τὰ ῥήματα αὐτῶν.
of them, and into the ends of the habitable world the words of them.

235 3004 3361 3756 1097 2474 4413 3475 3004
19 ἀλλὰ λέγω, Μὴ οὐκ ἔγνω Ἰσραὴλ; πρῶτος Μωσῆς λέγει,
But I say, Not at all did know Israel? First Moses says,

1473 3863 5209 1909 3756 1484 1909 1484 801
Ἐγὼ παραζηλώσω ὑμᾶς ἐπ᾽ οὐκ ἔθνει, ἐπὶ ἔθνει ἀσυνέτῳ
I will provoke to jealousy you by not a nation, by a nation unwise

3949 5209 2268 1161 662 2532 3004 2147
παροργιῶ ὑμᾶς. 20 Ἠσαΐας δὲ ἀποτολμᾷ καὶ λέγει, Εὑρέθην
I will anger you. Isaiah And (is)I very bold and says, I was found

1722 3588 1691 3361 2212 1717 1096 3588 1691 3361 1905
ἐν τοῖς ἐμὲ μὴ ζητοῦσιν, ἐμφανὴς ἐγενόμην τοῖς ἐμὲ μὴ ἐπερω-
by those Me not seeking; revealed I came to be to those Me not inquiring

4314 1161 3588 2474 3004 3650 3588 2250 1600
τῶσι. 21 πρὸς δὲ τὸν Ἰσραὴλ λέγει, Ὅλην τὴν ἡμέραν ἐξεπέ-
after. to But Israel He says, All the day I stretched

3588 5495 3450 4314 2992 544 2532 483
τασα τὰς χεῖράς μου πρὸς λαὸν ἀπειθοῦντα καὶ ἀντιλέγοντα.
out the hand of Me to a people disobeying and gainsaying.

and their words unto the ends of the world.

19 But I say, Did not Israel know? First Moses saith, I will provoke you to jealousy by (them that are) no people, (and) by a foolish nation I will anger you.

20 But Esaias is very bold, and saith, I was found of them that sought me not; I was made manifest unto them that asked not after me.

21 But to Israel he saith, All day long I have stretched forth my hands unto a disobedient and gainsaying people.

Romans 11

1. I say then, Did not God thrust away His people? Let it not be! For I also am an Israelite, out of Abraham's seed, of (the) tribe of Benjamin.

2 God did not thrust away His people whom He foreknew. (Psa. 94:14) Or do you not know what the Scripture said in Elijah, how he pleaded with God against Israel, saying,

3 "Lord, they killed Your prophets, and they dug down Your altars, and I am left alone, and they seek my life." (1 Kings 19:10)

4 But what does the Divine answer say to him, "I reserved to Myself seven thousand men who did not bow a knee to Baal." (1 Kings 19:18)

5 So then, also in the present time a remnant according to election of grace has come into being.

6 But if by grace, no longer (is it) of works; else grace no longer becomes grace. But if of works, it is no longer grace; else work is no longer work.

7 What then? What Israel seeks,

Romans 11

3004 3767 3361 683 3588 2316 3588 2992 846 3361
1. Λέγω οὖν, Μὴ ἀπώσατο ὁ Θεὸς τὸν λαὸν αὐτοῦ; μὴ
I say Then, Did not thrust away God the people of Him? Not

1096 2532 1063 1473 2475 1510 1537 4690
γένοιτο, καὶ γὰρ ἐγὼ Ἰσραηλίτης εἰμί, ἐκ σπέρματος
let it be! ealso For I an Israelite am, out of (the) seed

11 5443 958 3756 683 3588 2316 3588 2992
Ἀβραάμ, φυλῆς Βενιαμίν. 2 οὐκ ἀπώσατο ὁ Θεὸς τὸν λαὸν
of Abraham, of tribe of Benjamin. not did thrust away God the people

846 3739 4267 2228 3756 1492 1722 2243 5101 3004 3588
αὐτοῦ ὃν προέγνω. ἢ οὐκ οἴδατε ἐν Ἠλίᾳ τί λέγει ἡ
of Him whom He foreknew. Or not did you know in Elijah what says the

1124 5613 1793 3588 2316 2596 3588 2474 3004 2962
γραφή; ὡς ἐντυγχάνει τῷ Θεῷ κατὰ τοῦ Ἰσραήλ, λέγων, 3 Κύριε,
Scripture? how he pleads with God against Israel, saying, Lord,

3588 4396 4675 615 2532 3588 2379 4675
τοὺς προφήτας σου ἀπέκτειναν, καὶ τὰ θυσιαστήριά σου
the prophets of You they killed, and the altars of You

2679 2504 5275 3441 2532 2212 3588
κατέσκαψαν· κἀγὼ ὑπελείφθην μόνος, καὶ ζητοῦσι τὴν
they dug down; and I am left alone, and they seek the

5590 3450 235 5101 3004 846 3588 5538 2641
ψυχήν μου. 4 ἀλλὰ τί λέγει αὐτῷ ὁ χρηματισμός; Κατέλιπον
life of me. But what says to him the divine answer? I reserved

1683 2035 435 3748 3756 2578 1119
ἐμαυτῷ ἑπτακισχιλίους ἄνδρας, οἵτινες οὐκ ἔκαμψαν γόνυ
to Myself seven thousand men, who not bowed (the) knee

3588 896 3779 3767 2532 1722 3588 3568 2540 3005 2596
τῇ Βάαλ. 5 οὕτως οὖν καὶ ἐν τῷ νῦν καιρῷ λεῖμμα κατ᾽
to Baal. So then also in the present time a remnant according to

1589 5485 1096 1487 1161 5485 3765 1537 2041
ἐκλογὴν χάριτος γέγονεν. 6 εἰ δὲ χάριτι, οὐκέτι ἐξ ἔργων,
election of grace has come to be. if And by grace, no longer of works,

1893 3588 5485 3765 1096 5485 1487 1161 1537 2041 3765 2076
ἐπεὶ ἡ χάρις οὐκέτι γίνεται χάρις. εἰ δὲ ἐξ ἔργων, οὐκέτι ἐστὶ
else grace no longer becomes grace. if But of works, no longer is it

5485 1893 3588 2041 3765 2076 2041 5101 3767 3739 1934
χάρις· ἐπεὶ τὸ ἔργον οὐκέτι ἐστὶν ἔργον. 7 τί οὖν; ὃ ἐπιζητεῖ
grace; else work no longer is work. What then? What seeks for

Romans 11

1. I say then, Hath God cast away his people? God forbid. For I also am an Israelite, of the seed of Abraham, (of) the tribe of Benjamin.

2 God hath not cast away his people which he foreknew. Wot ye not what the scripture saith of Elias? how he maketh intercession to God against Israel, saying,

3 Lord, they have killed thy prophets, and digged down thine altars; and I am left alone, and they seek my life.

4 But what saith the answer of God unto him? I have reserved to myself seven thousand men, who have not bowed the knee to (the image of) Baal.

5 Even so then at this present time also there is a remnant according to the election of grace.

6 And if by grace, then (is it) no more of works: otherwise grace is no more grace. But if (it be) of works, then is it no more grace: otherwise work is no more work.

7 What then? Israel hath not obtained that which he seeketh for;

Literal Translation

Romans 11:8

Israel, this it did not obtain, but the election obtained (it), and the rest were hardened;

8 even as it has been written, "God gave to them a spirit of slumber, eyes not to see and ears not to hear" until the present. (Isa. 29:10; Deut. 29:4)
9 And David said, "Let their table become for a snare and for a trap, and for a stumbling block, and for a repayment to them;
10 let their eyes be darkened, not to see, and their back bowing through all." (Psa. 69:22, 23)

11 I say, then, Did not they stumble that they fall? Let it not be! But by their slipping away (came) salvation to the nations, to provoke them to jealousy.

12 But if their slipping away (is the) riches of (the) world, and their loss (the) riches of (the) nations, how much more their fullness?

13 For I speak to you, the nations, since indeed I am an apostle of the nations, I glorify my ministry,
14 if somehow I may provoke to jealousy my flesh, and may save some of them.
15 For if their casting away (is the) reconciliation of (the) world, what the reception, if not life from (the) dead?
16 Now if the firstfruit (is) holy, also the lump. And if the root (is) holy, also the branches.
17 But if some of the branches were broken off, and you, being a wild olive tree were grafted in among them, and became a partaker of the root and the fatness of the olive tree,
18 do not boast against the branches. But if you do boast, (it is) not you (that)

2474 5127 3756 2013 3588 1161 1589 2013 3588 1161
Ἰσραήλ, τούτου οὐκ ἐπέτυχεν, ἡ δὲ ἐκλογὴ ἐπέτυχεν, οἱ δὲ
Israel, this not he obtained, the but election obtained (it), the and
3062 4456 2531 1125 1325 846 3588
λοιποὶ ἐπωρώθησαν· 8 καθὼς γέγραπται, Ἔδωκεν αὐτοῖς ὁ
rest were hardened; even as it has been written, gave to them
2316 4151 2659 3788 3588 3361 991 2532
Θεὸς πνεῦμα κατανύξεως, ὀφθαλμοὺς τοῦ μὴ βλέπειν, καὶ
God a spirit of slumber, eyes not to see, and
3775 3588 3361 191 2193 3588 4594 2250 2532 1138
ὦτα τοῦ μὴ ἀκούειν, ἕως τῆς σήμερον ἡμέρας. 9 καὶ Δαβὶδ
ears not to hear, until the present day. And David
3004 1096 3588 5132 846 1519 3803 2532 1519 2339
λέγει, Γενηθήτω ἡ τράπεζα αὐτῶν εἰς παγίδα, καὶ εἰς θήραν,
says, Let become the table of them for a snare, and for a trap
2532 1519 4625 2532 1519 468 846 4654
καὶ εἰς σκάνδαλον, καὶ εἰς ἀνταπόδομα αὐτοῖς· 10 σκοτισθή-
and for a stumbling-block, and for a repayment to them. to be darkened
3588 3788 846 3588 3361 991 2532 3588 3577
τωσαν οἱ ὀφθαλμοὶ αὐτῶν τοῦ μὴ βλέπειν, καὶ τὸν νῶτον
the eyes of them not to see, and the back

846 1223 3956 4781 3004 3767 3361 4417 2443
αὐτῶν διὰ παντὸς σύγκαμψον. 11 Λέγω οὖν, μὴ ἔπταισαν ἵνα
of them through all bowing. I say Then, not they stumble that
4098 3361 1096 235 3588 846 3900 3588
πέσωσι; μὴ γένοιτο· ἀλλὰ τῷ αὐτῶν παραπτώματι ἡ
they fall? Not let it be! But by the of the slipping away (came)
4991 3588 1484 1519 3588 3863 846 1487 1161 3588
σωτηρία τοῖς ἔθνεσιν, εἰς τὸ παραζηλῶσαι αὐτούς. 12 εἰ δὲ τὸ
salvation to the nations, in order to provoke to jealousy them. if But the
3900 846 4149 2889 2532 3588 2275 846
παράπτωμα αὐτῶν πλοῦτος κόσμου, καὶ τὸ ἥττημα αὐτῶν
slipping away of them (is the) riches of (the) world, and the loss of them
4149 1484 4214 3123 3588 4138 846
πλοῦτος ἐθνῶν, πόσῳ μᾶλλον τὸ πλήρωμα αὐτῶν;
(the) riches of nations, how much more the fullness of them?

5213 1063 3004 3588 1484 1909 3745 3303 1510 1473 1484
13. Ὑμῖν γὰρ λέγω τοῖς ἔθνεσιν. ἐφ' ὅσον μὲν εἰμι ἐγὼ ἐθνῶν
to you For I speak the nations. Since indeed am I of nations
652 3588 1248 1392 1487 4459 3863
ἀπόστολος, τὴν διακονίαν μου δοξάζω· 14 εἴ πως παραζη-
an apostle, the ministry of me I glorify; if (some)how I provoke to
3450 3588 4561 2532 4982 5100 1537 846 1487 1063 3588
λώσω μου τὴν σάρκα, καὶ σώσω τινὰς ἐξ αὐτῶν. 15 εἰ γὰρ ἡ
jealousy of me the flesh, and may save some of them. if For the
580 846 2643 2889 5101 3588 4356 1487 3361
ἀποβολὴ αὐτῶν καταλλαγὴ κόσμου, τίς ἡ πρόσληψις εἰ μὴ
casting away of them reconciliation of (the) world, what the reception, if not
2222 1537 3498 1487 1161 3588 536 40 2532 3588 5445 2532 1487
ζωὴ ἐκ νεκρῶν; 16 εἰ δὲ ἡ ἀπαρχὴ ἁγία, καὶ τὸ φύραμα· καὶ εἰ
life from (the) dead? if But the firstfruit (is) holy, also the lump; and if
3588 4491 40 2532 3588 2798 1487 1161 5100 3588 2798
ἡ ῥίζα ἁγία, καὶ οἱ κλάδοι. 17 Εἰ δέ τινες τῶν κλάδων ἐξε-
the root (is) holy, also the branches. if And some of the branches were
1575 4771 1161 65 5607 1461 1722 846 2532
κλάσθησαν, σὺ δὲ ἀγριέλαιος ὢν ἐνεκεντρίσθης ἐν αὐτοῖς, καὶ
broken off, you and a wild olive being were grafted in among them, and
4791 3588 4491 2532 3588 4096 3588 1636 1096
συγκοινωνὸς τῆς ῥίζης καὶ τῆς πιότητος τῆς ἐλαίας ἐγένου,
a partaker of the root and of the fatness of the olive tree became,
3361 2620 3588 2798 1487 1161 2620 3756 4771 3588
18 μὴ κατακαυχῶ τῶν κλάδων· εἰ δὲ κατακαυχᾶσαι, οὐ σὺ τὴν
not boast against the branches; if but you boast, not you the

King James Version

but the election hath obtained it, and the rest were blinded

8 (According as it is written, God hath given them the spirit of slumber, eyes that they should not see, and ears that they should not hear;) unto this day.
9 And David saith, Let their table be made a snare, and a trap, and a stumblingblock, and a recompence unto them:

10 Let their eyes be darkened, that they may not see, and bow down their back alway.

11 I say then, Have they stumbled that they should fall? God forbid: but (rather) through their fall salvation (is come) unto the Gentiles, for to provoke them to jealousy.
12 Now if the fall of them (be) the riches of the world, and the diminishing of them the riches of the Gentiles; how much more their fulness?
13 For I speak to you Gentiles, inasmuch as I am the apostle of the Gentiles, I magnify mine office:
14 If by any means I may provoke to emulation (them which are) my flesh, and might save some of them.
15 For if the casting away of them (be) the reconciling of the world, what (shall) the receiving (of them be), but life from the dead?
16 For if the firstfruit (be) holy, the lump (is) also (holy): and if the root (be) holy, so (are) the branches.
17 And if some of the branches be broken off, and thou, being a wild olive tree, wert graffed in among them, and with them partakest of the root and fatness of the olive tree;
18 Boast not against the branches. But if thou boast, thou bearest not

Literal Translation | **Romans 11:19** | **King James Version**

bears the root, but the root (bears) you.
19 You will say then, The branches were broken off that I might be grafted in.
20 Well! For unbelief they were broken off. And you stand by faith. Do not (be) high-minded, but fear.
21 For if God did not spare the natural branches, (fear) lest neither He will spare you.
22 Behold, then, (the) kindness and severity of God: Indeed on those having fallen, severity. But on you, kindness, if you continue in the kindness. Otherwise, you will also be cut off.

4491 941 235 3588 4491 4571 2046 3767 1575
ῥίζαν βαστάζεις, ἀλλὰ ἡ ῥίζα σέ. 19 ἐρεῖς οὖν, Ἐξεκλάσθησαν
root bears, but the root you. You will say then, were broken off

3588 2798 2443 1473 1461 2573 3588 570 1575
οἱ κλάδοι, ἵνα ἐγὼ ἐγκεντρισθῶ. 20 καλῶς· τῇ ἀπιστίᾳ ἐξεκλά-
the branches, that I might be grafted in. Well, for unbelief they were

4771 1161 3588 4102 2476 3361 5309 235
σθησαν, σὺ δὲ τῇ πίστει ἕστηκας. μὴ ὑψηλοφρόνει, ἀλλὰ
broken off, you and by faith stand. (Be) not high-minded, but

5399 1487 1063 3588 2316 3588 2596 5449 2798 3756 5339
φοβοῦ· 21 εἰ γὰρ ὁ Θεὸς τῶν κατὰ φύσιν κλάδων οὐκ ἐφείσατο,
fear; if for God the according to nature branches not did spare,

3381 3761 4675 5339 2396 3767 5544 2532 663
μήπως οὐδὲ σοῦ φείσεται. 22 ἴδε οὖν χρηστότητα καὶ ἀποτο-
lest neither you He will spare. Behold then (the) kindness and severity

2316 1909 3303 3588 4098 663 1909 1161 4571
μίαν Θεοῦ· ἐπὶ μὲν τοὺς πεσόντας, ἀποτομίαν· ἐπὶ δὲ σὲ
of God; on indeed the (ones) having fallen, severity; on but you

5544 1437 1961 3588 5544 1893 2532 4771
χρηστότητα, ἐὰν ἐπιμένῃς τῇ χρηστότητι· ἐπεὶ καὶ σὺ
kindness, if you continue in the kindness; otherwise also you

the root, but the root thee.
19 Thou wilt say then, The branches were broken off, that I might be graffed in.
20 Well; because of unbelief they were broken off, and thou standest by faith. Be not highminded, but fear:
21 For if God spared not the natural branches, (take heed) lest he also spare not thee.
22 Behold therefore the goodness and severity of God: on them which fell, severity; but toward thee, goodness, if thou continue in (his) goodness: otherwise thou also shalt be cut off.

23 And those also, if they do not continue in unbelief, will be grafted in. For God is able to graft them in again.

1581 2532 1565 1161 1437 3361 1961 3588 570
ἐκκοπήσῃ. 23 καὶ ἐκεῖνοι δέ, ἐὰν μὴ ἐπιμένωσιν τῇ ἀπιστίᾳ,
will be cut off. also those And, if not they continue in unbelief,

1461 1415 1063 2076 3588 2316 3825
ἐγκεντρισθήσονται· δυνατὸς γάρ ἐστιν ὁ Θεὸς πάλιν ἐγκεν-
will be grafted in; able for is God again to

23 And they also, if they abide not still in unbelief, shall be graffed in: for God is able to graff them in again.

24 For if you were cut out of the natural order wild olive (tree), and against nature were grafted into a good olive (tree), how much more these (being) according to nature will be grafted into (their) own olive tree?

1461 846 1487/1063/4771/1537/3588/2596 5449 1581 65
τρίσαι αὐτούς. 24 εἰ γὰρ σὺ ἐκ τῆς κατὰ φύσιν ἐξεκόπης ἀγρι-
graft in them. if For you out of the natural order were cut out wild

2532 3844 5449 1461 1519 2565 4214
ελαίου καὶ παρὰ φύσιν ἐνεκεντρίσθης εἰς καλλιέλαιον, πόσῳ
olive, and against nature were grafted in into a good olive, how much

3123 3778 3588 2596 5449 1461 3588 2398
μᾶλλον οὗτοι, οἱ κατὰ φύσιν, ἐγκεντρισθήσονται τῇ ἰδίᾳ
more these, those according to nature, will be grafted in the own

1636
ἐλαίᾳ.
olive tree?

24 For if thou wert cut out of the olive tree which is wild by nature, and wert graffed contrary to nature into a good olive tree: how much more shall these, which be the natural (branches), be graffed into their own olive tree?

25 For I do not want you to be ignorant (of) this mystery, brothers, so that you may not be wise within yourselves, that hardness in part has happened to Israel until the fullness of the nations comes in;
26 and so all Israel will be saved, even as it has been written, "The Deliverer will come out of Zion, and He will turn away ungodliness from Jacob.
27 And this (is) My covenant with them, when I take away their sins." (Isa.59:20,21)
28 Indeed, as regards the gospel, enemies for you, but as regards the election, beloved for the sake of the fathers.

3756 1063 2309 5209 50 80 3588 3466 5124
25. Οὐ γὰρ θέλω ὑμᾶς ἀγνοεῖν, ἀδελφοί, τὸ μυστήριον τοῦτο,
not For I wish you to be ignorant, brothers, (of) mystery this,

2443 3361 5600 3844 1438 5429 3754 4457 575 3313
ἵνα μὴ ἦτε παρ' ἑαυτοῖς φρόνιμοι, ὅτι πώρωσις ἀπὸ μέρους
that not you be within yourselves wise, that hardness from (in) part

3588 2474 1096 891 3757 3588 4138 3588 1484 1525
τῷ Ἰσραὴλ γέγονεν, ἄχρις οὗ τὸ πλήρωμα τῶν ἐθνῶν εἰσ-
to Israel has happened, until the fullness of the nations comes

2532 3779 3956 2474 4982 2531 1125
έλθῃ, 26 καὶ οὕτως πᾶς Ἰσραὴλ σωθήσεται· καθὼς γέγραπται,
in, and so all Israel will be saved; as it has been written,

2240 1537 4622 3588 4506 2532 654 763 575
Ἥξει ἐκ Σιὼν ὁ ῥυόμενος, καὶ ἀποστρέψει ἀσεβείας ἀπὸ
Will come out of Zion the Deliverer, and He will turn away ungodliness from

2384 2532 3778 846 3588 3844 1700 1242 3752 851
Ἰακώβ· 27 καὶ αὕτη αὐτοῖς ἡ παρ' ἐμοῦ διαθήκη, ὅταν ἀφέλω-
Jacob; and this (is) with them the from Me covenant, when I take

3588 266 846 2596 3303 3588 2098 2190 1223
μαι τὰς ἁμαρτίας αὐτῶν. 28 κατὰ μὲν τὸ εὐαγγέλιον, ἐχθροὶ δι'
away the sins of them. as regards Indeed the gospel, enemies for

5209 2596 1161 3588 1589 27 1223 3588 3962
ὑμᾶς· κατὰ δὲ τὴν ἐκλογήν, ἀγαπητοὶ διὰ τοὺς πατέρας.
you; as regards and the election, beloved for the sake of the fathers.

25 For I would not, brethren, that ye should be ignorant of this mystery, lest ye should be wise in your own conceits; that blindness in part is happened to Israel, until the fulness of the Gentiles be come in.
26 And so all Israel shall be saved: as it is written, There shall come out of Sion the Deliverer, and shall turn away ungodliness from Jacob:
27 For this (is) my covenant unto them, when I shall take away their sins.
28 As concerning the gospel, (they are) enemies for your sakes: but as touching the election, (they are) beloved for the fathers' sakes.

Literal Translation

29 For the free gifts and the calling of God (are) without repentance.

30 For as you then also disobeyed God, but now you have obtained mercy by the disobedience of these,
31 so also these now have disobeyed, so that they also may obtain mercy by your mercy.
32 For God shut up all in disobedience, that He may show mercy to all.

33 O (the) depth of (the) riches and of (the) wisdom and (the) knowledge of God! How unsearchable (are) His judgments and His ways past finding out!
34 For who has known the mind of (the) Lord? Or who became His counselor? (Isa. 40:13)
35 Or who first gave to Him, and it will be repaid to him?
36 Because of Him, and through Him, and to Him (are) all things. To Him be the glory to the ages. Amen.

Romans 11:29

278 1063 3588 5486 2532 3588 2821 3588 2316
29 ἀμεταμέλητα γὰρ τὰ χαρίσματα καὶ ἡ κλῆσις τοῦ Θεοῦ.
without repentance For the free gifts and the calling of God.

5618 1063 2532 5210 4218 544 3588 2316 3568 1161
30 ὥσπερ γὰρ καὶ ὑμεῖς ποτε ἠπειθήσατε τῷ Θεῷ, νῦν δὲ
as For also you then disobeyed God, now but

1653 3588 5130 543 3779 2532 3778 3568
ἠλεήθητε τῇ τούτων ἀπειθείᾳ· 31 οὕτω καὶ οὗτοι νῦν
you obtained mercy by the of these disobedience; so also these now

544 3588 5212 1656 2443 2532 846 1653 4788
ἠπείθησαν τῷ ὑμετέρῳ ἐλέει ἵνα καὶ αὐτοὶ ἐλεηθῶσιν· 32 συνέκ-
disobeyed by your mercy that also they may obtain mercy; shut

1063 3588 2316 3588 3956 1519 543 2443 3588 3956
λεισε γὰρ ὁ Θεὸς τοὺς πάντας εἰς ἀπείθειαν, ἵνα τοὺς πάντας
up for God all into disobedience that to all

1653
ἐλεήσῃ.
He may show mercy.

5599 899 4149 2532 4678 2532 1108 2316 5613
33. Ὦ βάθος πλούτου καὶ σοφίας καὶ γνώσεως Θεοῦ. ὡς
O (the) depth of (the) riches and of wisdom and knowledge of God! How

419 3588 2917 846 2532 421 3588 3598
ἀνεξεραύνητα τὰ κρίματα αὐτοῦ, καὶ ἀνεξιχνίαστοι αἱ ὁδοὶ
unsearchable the judgments of Him, and past finding out the ways

846 5101 1063 1097 3563 2962 2228 5101 4825 846
αὐτοῦ. 34 Τίς γὰρ ἔγνω νοῦν Κυρίου; ἢ τίς σύμβουλος αὐτοῦ
of Him. who For has known the mind of (the) Lord? Or who counselor of Him

1096 2228 5101 4272 846 2532 467
ἐγένετο; 35 ἢ τίς προέδωκεν αὐτῷ, καὶ ἀνταποδοθήσεται
has come to be? Or who first gave to Him, and it will be repaid

846 3754 1537 846 2532 1223 846 2532 1519 846 3588 3956
αὐτῷ; 36 ὅτι ἐξ αὐτοῦ καὶ δι' αὐτοῦ καὶ εἰς αὐτὸν τὰ πάντα·
to him? Because of Him and through Him and to Him (are) all things;

846 3588 1391 1519 3588 165 281
αὐτῷ ἡ δόξα εἰς τοὺς αἰῶνας· ἀμήν.
to Him be the glory to the ages; amen.

King James Version

29 For the gifts and calling of God (are) without repentance.

30 For as ye in times past have not believed God, yet have now obtained mercy through their unbelief:
31 Even so have these also now not believed, that through your mercy they also may obtain mercy.
32 For God hath concluded them all in unbelief, that he might have mercy upon all.

33 O the depth of the riches both of the wisdom and knowledge of God! how unsearchable (are) his judgments, and his ways past finding out!
34 For who hath known the mind of the Lord? or who hath been his counsellor?
35 Or who hath first given to him, and it shall be recompensed unto him again?
36 For of him, and through him, and to him, (are) all things: to whom (be) glory for ever. Amen.

Romans 12

Literal Translation

1. Therefore, brothers, I call on you through the compassions of God to present your bodies a living sacrifice, holy, well-pleasing to God, (which is) your reasonable service.
2 And be not conformed to this age, but be transformed by the renewing of your mind, in order (for you) to prove what (is) the good and well-pleasing and perfect will of God.

3 For through the grace given to me, I say to everyone being among you, not to have high thoughts beyond what is right to think.

Romans 12

3870 3767 5209 80 1223 3588 3628 3588
1. Παρακαλῶ οὖν ὑμᾶς, ἀδελφοί, διὰ τῶν οἰκτιρμῶν τοῦ
I call on Therefore you, brothers, through the compassions

2316 3936 3588 4983 5216 2316 2198 40
Θεοῦ, παραστῆσαι τὰ σώματα ὑμῶν θυσίαν ζῶσαν, ἁγίαν,
of God, to present the bodies of you sacrifice a living, holy

2101 3588 2316 3588 3050 2999 5216 2532 3361
εὐάρεστον τῷ Θεῷ, τὴν λογικὴν λατρείαν ὑμῶν. 2 καὶ μὴ
well-pleasing to God, the reasonable service of you. And not

4964 3588 165 5129 235 3339 3588
συσχηματίζεσθε τῷ αἶνι τούτῳ, ἀλλὰ μεταμορφοῦσθε τῇ
be conformed to age this, but be transformed by the

342 3588 3563 5216 1519 3588 1381 5209 5101 3588
ἀνακαινώσει τοῦ νοός ὑμῶν, εἰς τὸ δοκιμάζειν ὑμᾶς τί τὸ
renewing of the mind of you, to prove you what (is) the

2307 3588 2316 3588 18 2532 2101 2532 5046
θέλημα τοῦ Θεοῦ, τὸ ἀγαθὸν καὶ εὐάρεστον καὶ τέλειον.
will of God, the good and well-pleasing and perfect.

3004 1063 1223 3588 5485 3588 1325 3427 3956 3588
3 Λέγω γάρ, διὰ τῆς χάριτος τῆς δοθείσης μοι, παντὶ τῷ
I say For, through the grace given to me, to everyone

5607 1722 5213 3361 5252 3844 3739 1163 5426
ὄντι ἐν ὑμῖν, μὴ ὑπερφρονεῖν παρ' ὃ δεῖ φρονεῖν,
being among you, not to have high thoughts beyond what is right to think,

King James Version

1. I beseech you therefore, brethren, by the mercies of God, that ye present your bodies a living sacrifice, holy, acceptable unto God, (which is) your reasonable service.
2 And be not conformed to this world: but be ye transformed by the renewing of your mind, that ye may prove what (is) that good, and acceptable, and perfect, will of God.

3 For I say, through the grace given unto me, to every man that is among you, not to think (of himself) more highly than he ought to think;

Literal Translation

But set your mind to be sober-minded, even as God divided a measure of faith to each.
4 For even as we have many members in one body, but all members do not have the same function,
5 so we the many are one body in Christ, and each one members of one another.

6 But having different gifts according to the grace given to us, whether prophecy, according to the proportion of faith;
7 or ministry, in the ministry; or the (one) teaching, in the teaching;
8 or the (one) exhorting, in the exhortation; the (one) sharing, in simplicity; the (one) taking the lead, in diligence; the (one) showing mercy, in cheerfulness.
9 (Let) love (be) without dissimulation, shrinking from evil, cleaving to the good,
10 in brotherly love to one another, loving fervently, having gone before one another in honor;
11 in diligence, not slothful, fervent in spirit, serving the Lord;
12 in hope, rejoicing; in affliction, enduring; in prayer, steadfastly continuing;
13 imparting to the needs of the saints, pursuing hospitality.
14 Bless the (ones) persecuting you; bless, and do not curse.
15 Rejoice with rejoicing (ones), and weep with weeping (ones);
16 minding the same thing toward one another, not minding high things, but yielding to the lowly. Do not become wise within yourselves.
17 To no one evil returning evil. Providing for right things

Romans 12:4

235 5426 1519 3588 4993 1538 5613 3588 2316 3307
ἀλλὰ φρονεῖν εἰς τὸ σωφρονεῖν, ἑκάστῳ ὡς ὁ Θεὸς ἐμέρισε
but to think to be sober-minded, to each as God divided

3358 4102 2509 1063 1722 1520 4983 3196 4183
μέτρον πίστεως. 4 καθάπερ γὰρ ἐν ἑνὶ σώματι μέλη πολλὰ
a measure of faith. as For in one body members many

2192 3588 1161 3196 3956 3756 3588 846 2192 4234 3779 3588
ἔχομεν, τὰ δὲ μέλη πάντα οὐ τὴν αὐτὴν ἔχει πρᾶξιν, 5 οὕτως οἱ
we have, the but members all not the same have function, so the

4183 1722 4983 2070 1722 5547 3588 1161 2596 1520 240 3196
πολλοὶ ἓν σῶμά ἐσμεν ἐν Χριστῷ, τὸ δὲ καθ' εἷς ἀλλήλων μέλη.
many one body we are in Christ, and each one of one another members.

2192 1161 5486 2596 3588 5485 3588 1325 2254
6 ἔχοντες δὲ χαρίσματα κατὰ τὴν χάριν τὴν δοθεῖσαν ἡμῖν
having But gifts according to the grace given to us

1313 1535 4394 2596 3588 356 3588 4102
διάφορα, εἴτε προφητείαν κατὰ τὴν ἀναλογίαν τῆς πίστεως·
differing, whether prophecy, according to the proportion of faith;

1535 1248 1722 3588 1248 1535 3588 1321 1722 3588
7 εἴτε διακονίαν, ἐν τῇ διακονίᾳ· εἴτε ὁ διδάσκων, ἐν τῇ
or ministry, in the ministry; or the (one) teaching, in thet

1319 1535 3588 3870 1722 3588 3874 3588 3330
διδασκαλίᾳ· 8 εἴτε ὁ παρακαλῶν, ἐν τῇ παρακλήσει· ὁ μεταδι-
teaching; or the (one) exhorting, in the exhortation; he sharing,

1722 572 3588 4291 1722 4710 3588 1653
δοὺς, ἐν ἁπλότητι· ὁ προϊστάμενος, ἐν σπουδῇ, ὁ ἐλεῶν,
in simplicity; the (one) taking the lead, in diligence, he showing mercy,

1722 2432 3588 26 505 655 3588
ἐν ἱλαρότητι. 9 Ἡ ἀγάπη ἀνυπόκριτος. ἀποστυγοῦντες τὸ
in cheerfulness. (Let) love (be) without dissimulation; shrinking from the

4190 2853 3588 18 3588 5360 1519 240
πονηρόν, κολλώμενοι τῷ ἀγαθῷ. 10 τῇ φιλαδελφίᾳ εἰς ἀλλή-
evil, cleaving to the good; in brotherly love to one

5387 3588 5092 240 4285 3588
λους φιλόστοργοι· τῇ τιμῇ ἀλλήλους προηγούμενοι· 11 τῇ
another loving fervently; in honor one another having gone before;

4710 3361 3636 3588 4151 2204 3588 2540
σπουδῇ μὴ ὀκνηροί· τῷ πνεύματι ζέοντες, τῷ Κυρίῳ δου-
in diligence not slothful; in spirit burning, the Lord

1398 3588 1680 5463 3588 2347 5278 3588
λεύοντες, 12 τῇ ἐλπίδι χαίροντες· τῇ θλίψει ὑπομένοντες· τῇ
serving, in hope rejoicing; in trouble enduring;

4335 4342 3588 5532 3588 40
προσευχῇ προσκαρτεροῦντες· 13 ταῖς χρείαις τῶν ἁγίων
in prayer steadfastly continuing; to the needs of the saints

2841 3588 5381 1377 2127 3588
κοινωνοῦντες· τὴν φιλοξενίαν διώκοντες. 14 εὐλογεῖτε τοὺς
imparting; hospitality pursuing. Bless the (ones)

1377 5209 2127 2532 3361 2672 5463 3326
διώκοντας ὑμᾶς· εὐλογεῖτε καὶ μὴ καταρᾶσθε. 15 χαίρειν μετὰ
persecuting you; bless and not do curse. Rejoice with

5463 2799 2532 3326 2799 3588 846 1519 240
χαιρόντων, κλαίειν καὶ μετὰ κλαιόντων. 16 τὸ αὐτὸ εἰς ἀλλή-
rejoicing (ones), weep and with weeping (ones). The same toward one

5426 3361 3588 5308 5426 235 3588
λους φρονοῦντες· μὴ τὰ ὑψηλὰ φρονοῦντες, ἀλλὰ τοῖς
another minding; not the things high minding, but to the

5011 4879 3361 1096 5429 3844 1438
ταπεινοῖς συναπαγόμενοι. μὴ γίνεσθε φρόνιμοι παρ' ἑαυτοῖς.
lowly yielding. Not do become wise within yourselves.

3367 2556 473 2556 591 4306 2570
17 μηδενὶ κακὸν ἀντὶ κακοῦ ἀποδιδόντες. προνοούμενοι καλὰ
To no one evil for evil returning. Providing for right things

King James Version

but to think soberly, according as God hath dealt to every man the measure of faith.
4 For as we have many members in one body, and all members have not the same office:
5 So we, (being) many, are one body in Christ, and every one members one of another.

6 Having then gifts differing according to the grace that is given to us, whether prophecy, (let us prophesy) according to the proportion of faith;
7 Or ministry, (let us wait) on (our) ministering: or he that teacheth, on teaching;
8 Or he that exhorteth, on exhortation: he that giveth, (let him do it) with simplicity; he that ruleth, with diligence; he that sheweth mercy, with cheerfulness.
9 (Let) love be without dissimulation. Abhor that which is evil; cleave to that which is good.
10 (Be) kindly affectioned one to another with brotherly love; in honour preferring one another;
11 Not slothful in business; fervent in spirit; serving the Lord;
12 Rejoicing in hope; patient in tribulation; continuing instant in prayer;
13 Distributing to the necessity of saints; given to hospitality.
14 Bless them which persecute you: bless, and curse not.
15 Rejoice with them that do rejoice, and weep with them that weep.
16 (Be) of the same mind one toward another. Mind not high things, but condescend to men of low estate. Be not wise in your own conceits.
17 Recompense to no man evil for evil. Provide things

Literal Translation

before all men.
18 If possible, as to you, seeking peace with all men.

19 Not avenging yourselves, beloved, but give place to wrath, for it has been written, "Vengeance (is) Mine, I will repay, says (the) Lord." (Deut.32:35)
20 Then if your enemy hungers, feed him; if he thirsts, give him drink; for doing this you will heap coals of fire on his head. (Prov. 25:21, 22)

21 Do not be overcome by evil, but conquer the evil with good.

Romans 12:18

1799 3956 444 1487 1415 3588 1537 5216 3326
ἐνώπιον πάντων ἀνθρώπων. 18 εἰ δυνατόν, τὸ ἐξ ὑμῶν, μετὰ
before all men. If possible, as to you, with

3956 444 1514 3361 1438 1556
πάντων ἀνθρώπων εἰρηνεύοντες. 19 μὴ ἑαυτοὺς ἐκδικοῦντες,
all men seeking peace. Not yourselves avenging,

1556 235 1325 5117 3588 3709 1125 1063 1698
ἀγαπητοί, ἀλλὰ δότε τόπον τῇ ὀργῇ· γέγραπται γάρ, Ἐμοὶ
beloved, but give place to wrath; it has been written for, To Me

1557 1473 467 3004 2962 1437 3767 3983
ἐκδίκησις, ἐγὼ ἀνταποδώσω, λέγει Κύριος. 20 ἐὰν οὖν πεινᾷ
(is) vengeance, I will repay, says (the) Lord. if Then hungers

3588 2190 4675 5595 846 1437 1372 4222 846 5124
ὁ ἐχθρός σου, ψώμιζε αὐτόν· ἐὰν διψᾷ, πότιζε αὐτόν· τοῦτο
the enemy of you, feed him; if he thirsts, give drink to him; this

1063 4160 440 4442 4987 1909 3588 2776 846
γὰρ ποιῶν ἄνθρακας πυρὸς σωρεύσεις ἐπὶ τὴν κεφαλὴν αὐτοῦ.
for doing coals of fire you will heap on the head of him.

3361 3528 5259 3588 2556 235 3528/1722/3588/18 3588 2556
21 μὴ νικῶ ὑπὸ τοῦ κακοῦ, ἀλλὰ νίκα ἐν τῷ ἀγαθῷ τὸ κακόν.
Not be overcome by evil, but conquer with good the evil.

King James Version

honest in the sight of all men.
18 If it be possible, as much as lieth in you, live peaceably with all men.
19 Dearly beloved, avenge not yourselves, but (rather) give place unto wrath: for it is written, Vengeance (is) mine; I will repay, saith the Lord.
20 Therefore if thine enemy hunger, feed him; if he thirst, give him drink: for in so doing thou shalt heap coals of fire on his head.

21 Be not overcome of evil, but overcome evil with good.

Romans 13

1. Let every soul be subject to higher authorities, for there is no authority except from God, but the existing authorities have been ordained by God.
2 So that the (one) resisting the authority has opposed the ordinance of God, and the ones opposing will receive judgment to themselves.
3 For the rulers are not a terror to good works, but to the bad. And do you desire not to fear the authority? Do the good, and you will have praise from it;

4 for he is a servant of God to you for the good. But if you do the bad, be afraid; for he does not bear the sword in vain; for he is a servant of God, an avenger for wrath to the (one) practicing bad.

5 Because of this, (it is) necessary to be subject, not only because of wrath, but also because of conscience.
6 For because of this you also pay taxes, for they are ministers of God, for this very thing.

Romans 13

3956 5590 1849 5242 5293 3756
1. Πᾶσα ψυχὴ ἐξουσίαις ὑπερεχούσαις ὑποτασσέσθω· οὐ
Every soul authorities to higher let be subject to; not

1063 2076 1849 1487 3361 575 2316 3588 1161 5607 1849 5259
γὰρ ἔστιν ἐξουσία εἰ μὴ ἀπὸ Θεοῦ, αἱ δὲ οὖσαι ἐξουσίαι ὑπὸ
for there is authority except from God, the but existing authorities by

3588 2316 5021 1526 5620 3588 498 3588
τοῦ Θεοῦ τεταγμέναι εἰσίν. 2 ὥστε ὁ ἀντιτασσόμενος τῇ
God having been ordained are. So the (one) resisting the

1849 3588 3588 2316 1296 436 3588 1161 436
ἐξουσίᾳ, τῇ τοῦ Θεοῦ διαταγῇ ἀνθέστηκεν· οἱ δὲ ἀνθεστη-
authority the of God ordinance has opposed; the (ones) And having

1438 2917 2983 3588 1063 758 3756 1526
κότες ἑαυτοῖς κρίμα λήμψονται. 3 οἱ γὰρ ἄρχοντες οὐκ εἰσὶ
opposed to themselves judgment will receive. the For rulers not are

5401 3588 18 2041 235 3588 2556 2309 1161 3361
φόβος τῶν ἀγαθῶν ἔργων, ἀλλὰ τῷ κακῶν. θέλεις δὲ μὴ
a terror to good works, but to the bad. do you desire And not

5399 3588 1849 3588 18 4160 2532 2192 1868
φοβεῖσθαι τὴν ἐξουσίαν; τὸ ἀγαθὸν ποίει, καὶ ἕξεις ἔπαινον
to fear the authority? the good Do, and you will have praise

1537 846 2316 1063 1249 2076 4671 1519 3588 18 1437/1161
ἐξ αὐτῆς· 4 Θεοῦ γὰρ διάκονός ἐστι σοὶ εἰς τὸ ἀγαθόν. ἐὰν δὲ
from it; of God for a servant he is to you for the good. if But

3588 2556 4160 5399 3756 1063 1500 3588 3162 5409
τὸ κακὸν ποιῇς, φοβοῦ· οὐ γὰρ εἰκῇ τὴν μάχαιραν φορεῖ·
the bad you do, fear; not for in vain the sword he bears;

2316 1063 1249 2076 1558 1519 3709 3588 3588 2556
Θεοῦ γὰρ διάκονός ἐστιν, ἔκδικος εἰς ὀργὴν τῷ τὸ κακὸν
of God for a servant he is, an avenger for wrath to the (one) bad

4238 1352 318 5293 3756 3440 1223 3588
πράσσοντι. 5 διὸ ἀνάγκη ὑποτάσσεσθαι, οὐ μόνον διὰ τὴν
practicing Therefore it is necessary to be subject, not only because of

3709 235 2532 1223 3588 4893 1223 5124 1063/2532
ὀργήν, ἀλλὰ καὶ διὰ τὴν συνείδησιν. 6 διὰ τοῦτο γὰρ καὶ
wrath, but also because of conscience. on account of this For also

5411 5055 3011 1063 2316 1526 1519 846 5124
φόρους τελεῖτε· λειτουργοὶ γὰρ Θεοῦ εἰσιν, εἰς αὐτὸ τοῦτο
taxes you pay; ministers for of God are, for this very thing

Romans 13

1. Let every soul be subject unto the higher powers. For there is no power but of God: the powers that be are ordained of God.

2 Whosoever therefore resisteth the power, resisteth the ordinance of God: and they that resist shall receive to themselves damnation.

3 For rulers are not a terror to good works, but to the evil. Wilt thou then not be afraid of the power? do that which is good, and thou shalt have praise of the same:

4 For he is the minister of God to thee for good. But if thou do that which is evil, be afraid; for he beareth not the sword in vain: for he is the minister of God, a revenger to (execute) wrath upon him that doeth evil.
5 Wherefore (ye) must needs be subject, not only for wrath, but also for conscience sake.
6 For for this cause pay ye tribute also: for they are God's ministers, attending continually upon this very thing.

Literal Translation | **Romans 13:7** | *King James Version*

always giving attention. 7 Then give to all (their) dues: to the (one due) tax, the tax; to the (one due) tribute, the tribute; to the (one due) fear, the fear; to the (one due) honor, the honor.

4342 591 3767 3956 3588 3782 3588 3588
προσκαρτεροῦντες. 7 ἀπόδοτε οὖν πᾶσι τὰς ὀφειλάς, τῷ τὸν
always giving attention. give Then to all the dues; to the (one) the
5411 3588 5411 3588 3588 5056 3588 5056 3588 3588 5401 3588
φόρον τὸν φόρον, τῷ τὸ τέλος τὸ τέλος, τῷ τὸν φόβον τὸν
tax (due) the tax, to the (one) the tribute, the tribute, to the (one) the fear the
5401 3588 3588 5092 3588 5092
φόβον· τῷ τὴν τιμὴν τὴν τιμήν.
fear; to the (one) the honor the honor.

7 Render therefore to all their dues: tribute to whom tribute (is due); custom to whom custom; fear to whom fear; honour to whom honour.

8 Do not continue to owe anything, except to love one another. For the (one) loving the other has fulfilled law: 9 For, "Do not commit adultery, do not murder, do not steal, do not bear false witness, do not lust," and if (there is) any other commandment, it is summed up in this word in (this): "You shall love your neighbor as yourself." (Ex. 20:13 - 15; Lev. 19:18)

3367 3367 3784 1487 3361 3588 25 240 3588 1063
8. Μηδενὶ μηδὲν ὀφείλετε, εἰ μὴ τὸ ἀγαπᾶν ἀλλήλους· ὁ γὰρ
To no one nothing owe, except to love one another; he for
25 3588 2087 3551 4137 3588 1063 3756 3431
ἀγαπῶν τὸν ἕτερον, νόμον πεπλήρωκε. 9 τὸ γάρ, οὐ μοιχεύ-
loving the other, law has fulfilled. For: not do commit
3756 5407 3756 2813 3756 5576 3756
σεις, οὐ φονεύσεις, οὐ κλέψεις, οὐ ψευδομαρτυρήσεις, οὐκ
adultery, not do murder, not do steal, not do bear false witness, not
1937 2532 1487 5100 2087 1785 1722 5129 3588 3056
ἐπιθυμήσεις, καὶ εἴ τις ἑτέρα ἐντολή, ἐν τούτῳ τῷ λόγῳ
do lust, and if any other commandment, in this word
346 1722 3588 25 3588 4139 4675 5613
ἀνακεφαλαιοῦται, ἐν τῷ, Ἀγαπήσεις τὸν πλησίον σου ὡς
it is summed up, in (this), You shall love the neighbor of you as
1438 3588 26 3588 4139 2556 3756 2038
εαυτόν. 10 ἡ ἀγάπη τῷ πλησίον κακὸν οὐκ ἐργάζεται·
yourself. Love to the neighbor evil does not work;
4138 3767 3551 3588 26
πλήρωμα οὖν νόμου ἡ ἀγάπη.
fulfillment then of law (is) love.

8 Owe no man any thing, but to love one another: for he that loveth another hath fulfilled the law.
9 For this, Thou shalt not commit adultery, Thou shalt not kill, Thou shalt not steal, Thou shalt not bear false witness, Thou shalt not covet; and if (there be) any other commandment, it is briefly comprehended in this saying, namely, Thou shalt love thy neighbour as thyself.

10 Love does not work evil to the neighbor. Then love (is) the fulfillment of law.

10 Love worketh no ill to his neighbour: therefore love (is) the fulfilling of the law.

11 Also this, knowing the time, that (it is) now the hour for you to be aroused from sleep, for now our salvation (is) nearer than when we believed.
12 The night (is) far gone, and the day has drawn near; then let us cast off the works of darkness, and let us put on the weapons of the light.
13 Let us walk becomingly, as in (the) day, not in carousings and drunkennesses, not in cohabitation and lustful acts, not in fighting and envy.
14 But put on the Lord Jesus Christ, and do not make forethought for the lusts of the flesh.

2532 5124 1492 3588 2540 3754 5610 2248 2235 1537
11. Καὶ τοῦτο, εἰδότες τὸν καιρόν, ὅτι ὥρα ἡμᾶς ἤδη ἐξ
And this, knowing the time, that an hour we now out of
5258 1453 3568 1063 1452 2257 3588 4991 2228 3753
ὕπνου ἐγερθῆναι· νῦν γὰρ ἐγγύτερον ἡμῶν ἡ σωτηρία ἢ ὅτε
sleep to be raised; now for nearer of us the salvation than when
4100 3588 3571 4298 3588 1161 2250 1448
ἐπιστεύσαμεν. 12 ἡ νὺξ προέκοψεν, ἡ δὲ ἡμέρα ἤγγικεν·
we believed. The night (is) far gone, the and day has drawn near;
659 3767 3588 2041 3588 4655 2532 1746 3588 3696
ἀποθώμεθα οὖν τὰ ἔργα τοῦ σκότους, καὶ ἐνδυσώμεθα τὰ ὅπλα
let us cast off then the works of the darkness, and let us put on the weapons
3588 5457 5613 1722 2250 2156 4043 3361
τοῦ φωτός. 13 ὡς ἐν ἡμέρᾳ, εὐσχημόνως περιπατήσωμεν, μὴ
of the light. As in (the) day, becomingly let us walk, not
2970 2532 3178 3361 2845 2532 766 3361 2054
κώμοις καὶ μέθαις, μὴ κοίταις καὶ ἀσελγείαις, μὴ ἔριδι
in carousings and drinking, not in cohabitation and lustful acts, not in fighting
2532 2205 235 1746 3588 2962 2424 5547 2532
καὶ ζήλῳ. 14 ἀλλ ἐνδύσασθε τὸν Κύριον Ἰησοῦν Χριστόν, καὶ
and envy. But put on the Lord Jesus Christ, and
3588 4561 4307 3361 4160 1519 1939
τῆς σαρκὸς πρόνοιαν μὴ ποιεῖσθε εἰς ἐπιθυμίας.
of the flesh forethought not do make, for (its) lusts.

11 And that, knowing the time, that now (it is) high time to awake out of sleep: for now (is) our salvation nearer than when we believed.
12 The night is far spent, the day is at hand: let us therefore cast off the works of darkness, and let us put on the armour of light.
13 Let us walk honestly, as in the day; not in rioting and drunkenness, not in chambering and wantonness, not in strife and envying.
14 But put ye on the Lord Jesus Christ, and make not provision for the flesh, to (fulfil) the lusts (thereof).

Romans 14 | Romans 14 | Romans 14

1. And receive the (one) being weak in the faith, not to judgments of (your) thoughts.
2 One indeed believes to eat all things, one

3588 1161 770 3588 4102 4355 3361 1519
1. Τὸν δὲ ἀσθενοῦντα τῇ πίστει προσλαμβάνεσθε, μὴ εἰς
the (one) And being weak in the faith receive, not to
1253 1261 3739 3303 4100 5315 3956 3588
διακρίσεις διαλογισμῶν. 2 ὃς μὲν πιστεύει φαγεῖν πάντα, ὁ
judgments of thoughts. One indeed believies to eat all things, one

1. Him that is weak in the faith receive ye, (but) not to doubtful disputations.
2 For one believeth that he may eat all things: another,

Literal Translation | **Romans 14:3** | **King James Version**

but being weak, (another) one eats vegetables.
3 The (one) eating, do not despise the (one) not eating. And the (one) not eating, do not judge the (one) eating, for God received him.
4 Who are you judging another's servant? To his own master he stands or falls. But he will stand, for God is able to make him stand.
5 One indeed judges a day above (another) day; and (another) one judges every day (alike). Let each one be fully assured in (his) own mind.
6 The (one) minding the day, he minds (it) to (the) Lord. And the (one) not minding the day, he does not mind (it) to (the) Lord. The (one) eating, he eats to (the) Lord; for he gives thanks to God. And the (one) not eating, he does not eat to (the) Lord, and gives thanks to God.

1161 770 3001 2068 3588 2068 3588 3361 2068 3361
δὲ ἀσθενῶν λάχανα ἐσθίει. 3 ὁ ἐσθίων τὸν μὴ ἐσθίοντα μὴ
but being weak vegetables eats. The (one) eating the (one) not eating not

1848 2532 3588 3361 2068 3588 2068 3361 2919 3588
ἐξουθενείτω, καὶ ὁ μὴ ἐσθίων τὸν ἐσθίοντα μὴ κρινέτω· ὁ
do despise, and the (one) not eating the (one) eating not do judge;

2316 1063 846 4355 4771/5101/1488/3588/2919 245
Θεὸς γὰρ αὐτὸν προσελάβετο. 4 σὺ τίς εἶ ὁ κρίνων ἀλλότριον
God for him received. you Who are judging of another

3610 3588 2398 2962 4739 2228 4098 2476 1161
οἰκέτην; τῷ ἰδίῳ κυρίῳ στήκει ἢ πίπτει. σταθήσεται δέ,
a servant? To the own lord he stands or falls, he will stand But,

1415 1063 2076 3588 2316 2476 846 3739 3303 2919
δυνατὸς γάρ ἐστιν ὁ Θεὸς στῆσαι αὐτόν. 5 ὃς μὲν κρίνει
able for is God to stand him. One indeed judges

2250 3844 2250 3739 1161 2919 3956 2250 1538
ἡμέραν παρ' ἡμέραν, ὃς δὲ κρίνει πᾶσαν ἡμέραν· ἕκαστος
a day above a day, one and judges every day (alike); each

1722 3588 2398 3563 4135 3588 5426 3588 2250
ἐν τῷ ἰδίῳ νοι πληροφορείσθω. 6 ὁ φρονῶν τὴν ἡμέραν,
in the own mind let him be fully assured. The (one) minding the day,

2962 5426 2532 3588 3361 5426 3588 2250 2962 3756
Κυρίῳ φρονεῖ· καὶ ὁ μὴ θρονῶν τὴν ἡμέραν, Κυρίῳ οὐ
to (the) Lord he minds; and he not minding the day, to (the) Lord not

5426 3588 2068 2962 2068 2168 1063 3588 2316 2532
φρονεῖ, ὁ ἐσθίων Κυρίῳ ἐσθίει, εὐχαριστεῖ γὰρ τῷ Θεῷ· καὶ
he minds. He eating to (the) Lord he eats, he gives thanks for to God; and

3588 3361 2068 2962 3756 2068 2532 2168 3588 2316
ὁ μὴ ἐσθίων Κυρίῳ οὐκ ἐσθίει, καὶ εὐχαριστεῖ τῷ Θεῷ.
he not eating to (the) Lord not he eats, and gives thanks to God.

who is weak, eateth herbs.
3 Let not him that eateth despise him that eateth not; and let not him which eateth not judge him that eateth: for God hath received him.
4 Who art thou that judgest another man's servant? to his own master he standeth or falleth. Yea, he shall be holden up: for God is able to make him stand.
5 One man esteemeth one day above another: another esteemeth every day (alike). Let every man be fully persuaded in his own mind.
6 He that regardeth the day, regardeth (it) unto the Lord; and he that regardeth not the day, to the Lord he doth not regard (it). He that eateth, eateth to the Lord, for he giveth God thanks; and he that eateth not, to the Lord he eateth not, and giveth God thanks.

7 For no one of us lives to himself and no one dies to himself.
8 For both if we live, we live to (the) Lord; and if we die, we die to (the) Lord. Then if we live, and if we die, we are the Lord's.
9 For for this Christ both died and rose and lived again, that He might be Lord both of (the) dead and (the) living.

3762 1063 2257 1438 2198 2532 3762 1438 599
7 οὐδεὶς γὰρ ἡμῶν ἑαυτῷ ζῇ, καὶ οὐδεὶς ἑαυτῷ ἀποθνήσκει.
no one For of us to himself lives, and no one to himself dies.

1437 5037 1063 2198 3588 2962 2198 1437 5037 599
8 ἐάν τε γὰρ ζῶμεν, τῷ Κυρίῳ ζῶμεν· ἐάν τε ἀποθνήσκωμεν,
if both For we live, to (the) Lord we live; if and we die,

3588 2962 599 1437 5037 3767 2198 1437 5037 599
τῷ Κυρίῳ ἀποθνήσκωμεν· ἐάν τε οὖν ζῶμεν, ἐάν τε ἀποθνή-
to (the) Lord we die; if and then we live, if and we die,

3588 2962 2070 1519 5124 1063 5547 2532
σκωμεν, τοῦ Κυρίου ἐσμέν. 9 εἰς τοῦτο γὰρ Χριστὸς καὶ
of (the) Lord we are. for this For Christ also

599 2532 450 2532 326 2443 2532 3498 2532
ἀπέθανε καὶ ἀνέστη καὶ ἀνέζησεν, ἵνα καὶ νεκρῶν καὶ
died and rose (again) and lived (again), that both of dead and

7 For none of us liveth to himself, and no man dieth to himself.
8 For whether we live, we live unto the Lord; and whether we die, we die unto the Lord: whether we live therefore, or die, we are the Lord's.
9 For to this end Christ both died, and rose, and revived, that he might be Lord both of the dead and living.

10 But why do you judge your brother? Or why also do you despise your brother? For all shall stand before the judgment seat of Christ.
11 For it has been written, "(As) I live, says (the) Lord, that every knee will bow to Me, and every tongue will confess to God." (Isa. 49:18; 45:23)
12 So then each one of us will give account concerning himself to God.

2198 2961 4771 1161 5101 2919 3588 80 4675 2228
ζώντων κυριεύσῃ. 10 σὺ δὲ τί κρίνεις τὸν ἀδελφόν σου; ἢ
of living He might be Lord. you And why judge the brother of you? Or

2532 4771 5101 1848 3588 80 4675 3956 1063 3936
καὶ σὺ τί ἐξουθενεῖς τὸν ἀδελφόν σου; πάντες γὰρ παραστη-
also you why despise the brother of you? all For shall stand

3588 968 3588 5547 1125 1063 2198 1473
σόμεθα τῷ βήματι τοῦ Χριστοῦ. 11 γέγραπται γάρ, Ζῶ ἐγώ,
before the judgment seat of Christ. it has been written For, live (As) I,

3004 2962 3754 1698 2578 3956 1119 2532 3956 1100
λέγει Κύριος· ὅτι ἐμοὶ κάμψει πᾶν γόνυ, καὶ πᾶσα γλῶσσα
says (the) Lord; that to Me will bow every knee, and every tongue

1843 3588 2316 686 3767 1538 2257 4012
ἐξομολογήσεται τῷ Θεῷ. 12 ἄρα οὖν ἕκαστος ἡμῶν περὶ
will confess to God. So then each one of us concerning

1438 3056 1325 3588 2316
ἑαυτοῦ λόγον δώσει τῷ Θεῷ.
himself account will give to God.

10 But why dost thou judge thy brother? or why dost thou set at nought thy brother? for we shall all stand before the judgment seat of Christ.
11 For it is written, (As) I live, saith the Lord, every knee shall bow to me, and every tongue shall confess to God.
12 So then every one of us shall give account of himself to God.

Romans 14:13

Literal Translation

13 Then let us no longer judge one another, but rather judge this, not to put a stumbling-block or an offense toward a brother.

14 I know and am persuaded in (the) Lord Jesus that nothing by itself is common; except to the (one) counting anything to be common, (it is) common to that (one).
15 But if your brother is grieved because of (your) food, you no longer walk according to love. Do not by your food destroy that one for whom Christ died.
16 Then do not let your good be spoken evil of.
17 For the kingdom of God is not eating and drinking, but righteousness and peace and joy in (the) Holy Spirit.
18 For the (one) serving Christ in these things (is) well-pleasing to God, and approved by men.

19 So then let us pursue the things of peace, and the things for building up one another.
20 Do not by your food undo the work of God. Truly, all things (are) clean, but (it is) bad to the man eating through a stumbling-block.
21 (It is) good not to eat flesh, nor to drink wine, nor (anything) by which your brother stumbles, or is offended, or is weak.

22 Do you have faith? Have (it) to yourself before God. Blessed (is) the (one) not judging himself in what he approves.

23 But the (one) doubting, if he eats, (he) has been condemned, because (it is) not of faith; and all which (is) not of faith is sin.

3371 3767 240 2919 235 5124 2919
13. Μηκέτι οὖν ἀλλήλους κρίνωμεν· ἀλλὰ τοῦτο κρίνατε
No longer then one another let us judge; but this judge

3123 3588 3361 5087 4348 3588 80 2228 4625
μᾶλλον, τὸ μὴ τιθέναι πρόσκομμα τῷ ἀδελφῷ ἢ σκάνδαλον.
rather, not to put a stumbling-block to the brother or an offense.

1492 2532 3982 1722 2962 2424 3754 3762 2839 1223
14 οἶδα καὶ πέπεισμαι ἐν Κυρίῳ Ἰησοῦ, ὅτι οὐδὲν κοινὸν δι'
I know And am persuaded in (the) Lord Jesus, that nothing (is) common by

1438 1487 3361 3588 3049 5100 2839 1511 1565 2839
ἑαυτοῦ· εἰ μὴ τῷ λογιζομένῳ τι κοινὸν εἶναι, ἐκείνῳ κοινόν.
itself; except to the (one) deeming anything common to be, to that common (is).

1487 1161 1223 1033 3588 80 4675 3076 3765 2596 26
15 εἰ δὲ διὰ βρῶμα ὁ ἀδελφός σου λυπεῖται, οὐκέτι κατὰ ἀγάπην
if And because of food the brother of you is grieved, no longer according to love

4043 3361 3588 1033 4675 1565 622 5228 3739
περιπατεῖς. μὴ τῷ βρώματί σου ἐκεῖνον ἀπόλλυε, ὑπὲρ οὗ
do you walk. Not to the food of you that one destroy, for whom

5547 599 3361 987 3767 5216 3588 18
Χριστὸς ἀπέθανε. 16 μὴ βλασφημείσθω οὖν ὑμῶν τὸ ἀγαθόν·
Christ died. not let be spoken evil of Then of you the good;

3756 1063 2076 3588 932 3588 2316 1035 2532 4213 235
17 οὐ γάρ ἐστιν ἡ βασιλεία τοῦ Θεοῦ βρῶσις καὶ πόσις, ἀλλὰ
not for is the kingdom of God eating and drinking, but

1343 2532 1515 2532 5479 1722 4151 40 3588 1063
δικαιοσύνη καὶ εἰρήνη καὶ χαρὰ ἐν Πνεύματι Ἁγίῳ· 18 ὁ γὰρ
righteousness and peace and joy in (the) Spirit Holy. the (one) For

1722 5125 1398 3588 5547 2101 3588 2316 2532
ἐν τούτοις δουλεύων τῷ Χριστῷ εὐάρεστος τῷ Θεῷ, καὶ
in these serving Christ (is) well-pleasing to God, and

1384 3588 444 686 3767 3588 3588 1515 1377
δόκιμος τοῖς ἀνθρώποις. 19 ἄρα οὖν τὰ τῆς εἰρήνης διώκωμεν,
approved by men. So then the things of peace let us pursue,

2532 3588 3588 3619 3588 1519 240 3361 1752 1033
καὶ τὰ τῆς οἰκοδομῆς τῆς εἰς ἀλλήλους. 20 μὴ ἕνεκεν βρώματος
and the things for building up for one another. Not for the sake of food

2647 3588 2041 3588 2316 3956 3303 2513 235 2556
κατάλυε τὸ ἔργον τοῦ Θεοῦ. πάντα μὲν καθαρά, ἀλλὰ κακὸν
undo the work of God. all things Truly (are) clean, but bad

3588 444 3588 1223 4348 2068 2570 3588 3361
τῷ ἀνθρώπῳ τῷ διὰ προσκόμματος ἐσθίοντι. 21 καλὸν τὸ μὴ
to the man through a stumbling-block eating. (it is) good not

5315 2907 3366 4095 3631 3366 1722 3739 3588 80 4675
φαγεῖν κρέα, μηδὲ πιεῖν οἶνον, μηδὲ ἐν ᾧ ὁ ἀδελφός σου
to eat meat, not to drink wine, not (any) by which the brother of you

4350 2228 4624 2228 770 4771 4102 2192
προσκόπτει ἢ σκανδαλίζρται ἢ ἀσθενεῖ. 22 σὺ πίστιν ἔχεις;
stumbles or is offended or is weak. Do you faith have?

2596 4572 2192 1799 3588 2316 3107 3588 3361 2919
κατὰ σεαυτὸν ἔχε ἐνώπιον τοῦ Θεοῦ. μακάριος ὁ μὴ κρίνων
By yourself Have (it) before God. Blessed the (one) not judging

1438 1722 3739 1381 3588 1161 1252 1437 5315 2632
ἑαυτὸν ἐν ᾧ δοκιμάζει. 23 ὁ δὲ διακρινόμενος, ἐὰν φάγῃ, κατα-
himself in what he approves. the (one) But doubting , if he eats, has been

3754 3756 1537 4102 3956 1161 3739 3756 1537 4102
κέκριται, ὅτι οὐκ ἐκ πίστεως· πᾶν δὲ ὃ οὐκ ἐκ πίστεως
condemned, because not of faith; all and which (is) not of faith

266 2076
ἁμαρτία ἐστίν.
sin is.

King James Version

13 Let us not therefore judge one another any more: but judge this rather, that no man put a stumblingblock or an occasion to fall in (his) brother's way.
14 I know, and am persuaded by the Lord Jesus, that (there is) nothing unclean of itself: but to him that esteemeth any thing to be unclean, to him (it is) unclean.
15 But if thy brother be grieved with (thy) meat, now walkest thou not charitably. Destroy not him with thy meat, for whom Christ died.

16 Let not then your good be evil spoken of:

17 For the kingdom of God is not meat and drink; but righteousness, and peace, and joy in the Holy Ghost.
18 For he that in these things serveth Christ (is) acceptable to God, and approved of men.

19 Let us therefore follow after the things which make for peace, and things wherewith one may edify another.
20 For meat destroy not the work of God. All things indeed (are) pure; but (it is) evil for that man who eateth with offence.
21 (It is) good neither to eat flesh, nor to drink wine, nor (any thing) whereby thy brother stumbleth, or is offended, or is made weak.
22 Hast thou faith? have (it) to thyself before God. Happy (is) he that condemneth not himself in that thing which he alloweth.
23 And he that doubteth is damned if he eat, because (he eateth) not of faith: for whatsoever (is) not of faith is sin.

Literal Translation

Romans 15

1. But we, the power-
ful ones, ought to bear
the weaknesses of those
not powerful, and not to
please ourselves.
2 For each one of us let
him please (his) neigh-
bor for good, to building
up.
3 For also Christ did not
please Himself, but
even as it has been writ-
ten, "The reproaches of
those reproaching You
fell on Me." (Psa. 69:9)
4 For what things were
written (before) were
written for our instruc-
tion, that through pa-
tience and encourage-
ment of the Scriptures
we might have hope.
5 And may the God of
patience and encour-
agement give to you to
mind the same thing
among one another ac-
cording to Christ Jesus,
6 that with one accord
(and) with one mouth
you may glorify (the)
God and Father of our
Lord Jesus Christ.
7 Because of this, re-
ceive one another as
Christ also received us,
to (the) glory of God.
8 And I say, Jesus Christ
has become a minister
of circumcision for
(the) truth of God, to
confirm the promises of
the fathers,
9 and for the nations to
glorify God for mercy,
even as it has been writ-
ten, "Because of this I
will confess to You in
the nations, and I will
give praise to Your
name." (Psa. 18:49)
10 And again He says,
"Rejoice, nations, with
His people." (Deut.
32:43)
11 And again, "Praise
the Lord, all the nations,
and praise Him all the
peoples." (Psa. 117:1)
12 And again Isaiah
says, "The Root of
Jesse shall be, and the,
(One) rising up to rule
the nations;

Romans 15:1

3784 1161 2249 3588 1415 3588 771 3588 102
1. Ὀφείλομεν δὲ ἡμεῖς οἱ δυνατοὶ τὰ ἀσθενήματα τῶν ἀδυνά-
ought And we the powerful the weaknesses of the (ones) not
941 2532 3361 1438 700 1538 1063
των βαστάζειν, καὶ μὴ ἑαυτοῖς ἀρέσκειν. 2 ἕκαστος γὰρ
able to bear, and not (our)selves to please. each one For
2257 3588 4139 700 1519 3588 18 4314 3619
ἡμῶν τῷ πλησίον ἀρεσκέτω εἰς τὸ ἀγαθὸν πρὸς οἰκοδομήν·
of us the neighbor let him please for good to building up;
2532 1063 3588 5547 3756 1438 700 235 2531
3 καὶ γὰρ ὁ Χριστὸς οὐχ ἑαυτῷ ἤρεσεν, ἀλλὰ, καθὼς
even for Christ not Himself pleased, but, even as
1125 3588 3680 3588 3679 4571 1968
γέγραπται, Οἱ ὀνειδισμοὶ τῶν ὀνειδιζόντων σε ἐπέπεσον
it has been written, The reproaches of those reproaching You fell
1909 1691 3745 1063 4270 1519 3588 2251 1319
ἐπ' ἐμέ. 4 ὅσα γὰρ προεγράφη, εἰς τὴν ἡμετέραν διδασκαλίαν
on Me. what things For were written, for our instruction
4270 2443 1223 3588 5281 2532 3588 3874
προεγράφη, ἵνα διὰ τῆς ὑπομονῆς καὶ τῆς παρακλήσεως
were written, that through patience and encouragement
3588 1124 3588 1680 2192 3588 1161 2316 3588 5281
τῶν γραφῶν τὴν ἐλπίδα ἔχωμεν. 5 ὁ δὲ Θεὸς τῆς ὑπομονῆς
of the Scriptures hope we might have. the And God of patience
2532 3588 3874 1325 5213 3588 846 5426 1722 240
καὶ τῆς παρακλήσεως δῴη ὑμῖν τὸ αὐτὸ φρονεῖν ἐν ἀλλήλοις
and of encouragement give to you the same to mind among one another
2596 5547 2424 2443 3661 1722 1520 4750
κατὰ Χριστὸν Ἰησοῦν, 6 ἵνα ὁμοθυμαδὸν ἐν ἑνὶ στόματι
according to Christ Jesus, that with one accord with one mouth
1392 3588 2316 2532 3962 3588 2962 2257 2424
δοξάζητε τὸν Θεὸν καὶ πατέρα τοῦ Κυρίου ἡμῶν Ἰησοῦ
you may glorify the God and Father of the Lord osfus Jesus
5547 1352 4355 240 2531 2532/3588
Χριστοῦ. 7 διὸ προσλαμβάνεσθε ἀλλήλους, καθὼς καὶ ὁ Χρι-
Christ. Therefore receive one another, even as also Christ
5547 4355 2248 1519 1391 2316 3004 1161 2424
στὸς προσελάβετο ὑμᾶς, εἰς δόξαν Θεοῦ. 8 λέγω δὲ, Ἰησοῦν
received us, to (the) glory of God. I say And, Jesus
5547 1249 1096 4061 5228 225
Χριστὸν διάκονον γεγενῆσθαι περιτομῆς ὑπὲρ ἀληθείας
Chreist a minister has become of circumcision for (the) truth
2316 1519 3588 950 3588 1860 3588 3962 3588
Θεοῦ, εἰς τὸ βεβαιῶσαι τὰς ἐπαγγελίας τῶν πατέρων· 9 τὰ
of God to confirm the promises of the fathers; the
1161 1484 5228 1656 1392 3588 2316 2531 1125
δὲ ἔθνη ὑπὲρ ἐλέους δοξάσαι τὸν Θεόν, καθὼς γέγραπται,
and nations for mercy to glorify God, even as it has been written,
1223 5124 1843 4671 1722 1484 2532 3588 3686 4675
Διὰ τοῦτο ἐξομολογήσομαί σοι ἐν ἔθνεσι, καὶ τῷ ὀνοματί σου
Because of this I will confess to You among nations, and (to) the name of You
5567 2532 3825 3004 2165 1484 3326 3588 2992
ψαλῶ. 10 καὶ πάλιν λέγει, Εὐφράνθητε, ἔθνη, μετὰ τοῦ λαοῦ
I will praise. And again He says, Rejoice, nations, with the people
846 2532 3825 134 3588 2962 3956 3588 1484 2532
αὐτοῦ. 11 καὶ πάλιν, Αἰνεῖτε τὸν Κύριον πάντα τὰ ἔθνη, καὶ
of Him. And again, Praise the Lord all the nations, and
1867 846 3956 3588 2992 2532 3825 2268 3004
ἐπαινέσατε αὐτὸν πάντες οἱ λαοί. 12 καὶ πάλιν Ἡσαΐας λέγει,
praise Him all the peoples. And again Isaiah says,
2071 3588 4491 3588 2421 2532 3588 450 757 1484
Ἔσται ἡ ῥίζα τοῦ Ἰεσσαί, καὶ ὁ ἀνιστάμενος ἄρχειν ἐθνῶν·
shall be The root of Jesse, and the (One) rising up to rule (the) nations;

King James Version

Romans 15

1. We then that are
strong ought to bear the
infirmities of the weak,
and not to please our-
selves.
2 Let every one of us
please (his) neighbour
for (his) good to edifica-
tion.
3 For even Christ
pleased not himself;
but, as it is written, The
reproaches of them that
reproached thee fell on
me.
4 For whatsoever things
were written aforetime
were written for our
learning, that we
through patience and
comfort of the scrip-
tures might have hope.
5 Now the God of pa-
tience and consolation
grant you to be
likeminded one toward
another according to
Christ Jesus:
6 That ye may with one
mind (and) one mouth
glorify God, even the
Father of our Lord Jesus
Christ.
7 Wherefore receive ye
one another, as Christ
also received us to the
glory of God.
8 Now I say that Jesus
Christ was a minister of
the circumcision for the
truth of God, to confirm
the promises (made)
unto the fathers:
9 And that the Gentiles
might glorify God for
(his) mercy; as it is writ-
ten, For this cause I will
confess to thee among
the Gentiles, and sing
unto thy name.
10 And again he saith,
Rejoice, ye Gentiles,
with his people.
11 And again, Praise the
Lord, all ye Gentiles;
and laud him, all ye peo-
ple.
12 And again, Esaias
saith, There shall be a
root of Jesse, and he that
shall rise to reign over
the Gentiles;

Literal Translation

Romans 15:13

King James Version

on Him nations will hope." (Isa.11:10)
13 And may the God of hope fill you with all joy and peace in believing, for you to abound in hope, in power of (the) Holy Spirit.

14 But, my brothers, I am persuaded concerning you, even myself that you yourselves also are full of goodness, having been filled with all knowledge, being made able to warn one another.
15 But I wrote to you more boldly, brothers, as reminding you in part, because of the grace given to me by God,
16 for me to be a minister of Jesus Christ to the nations, sacredly ministering the gospel of God, that the offering of the nations might be acceptable, sanctified by (the) Holy Spirit.

17 Therefore I have glorying in Christ Jesus (as to) the things pertaining to God.
18 For I will not dare to speak of anything which Christ did not work out through me for (the) obedience of (the) nations in word and work,
19 in power of signs and wonders, in power of (the) Spirit of God, so as (for) me to have fulfilled (the preaching of) the gospel of Christ from Jerusalem and in a circuit as far as Illyricum.

20 And so eagerly striving to preach the gospel where Christ was not named, so that I should not build on another's foundation,

21 but even as it has been written, "They shall see, to whom nothing was announced concerning Him; and the ones that have not heard they shall understand." (Isa.52:15)

1909 846 1484 1679 3588 1161 2316 3588 1680 4137
ἐπ' αὐτῷ ἔθνη ἐλπιοῦσιν. 13 ὁ δὲ Θεὸς τῆς ἐλπίδος πληρώσαι
on Him nations will hope. the And God of hope fill

5209 3956 5479 2532 1515 1722 3588 4100 1519 3588 4052
ὑμᾶς πάσης χαρᾶς καὶ εἰρήνης ἐν τῷ πιστεύειν, εἰς τὸ περισ-
you of all joy and peace in believing, for to

5209 1722 3588 1680 1722 1411 4151 40
σεύειν ὑμᾶς ἐν τῇ ἐλπίδι, ἐν δυνάμει Πνεύματος Ἁγίου.
abound you in hope, in power of (the) Spirit Holy.

3982 1161 80 3450 2532 846 1473 4012 5216 3754
14. Πέπεισμαι δέ, ἀδελφοί μου, καὶ αὐτὸς ἐγὼ περὶ ὑμῶν, ὅτι
I am persuaded But, brothers of me, even myself I concerning you, that

2532 846 3324 2075 19 4137 3956
καὶ αὐτοὶ μεστοί ἐστε ἀγαθωσύνης, πεπληρωμένοι πάσης
also yourselves full you are of goodness, having been filled of all

1108 1410 2532 240 3560 5112
γνώσεως, δυνάμενοι καὶ ἀλλήλους νουθετεῖν. 15 τολμηρότερον
knowledge, being empowered also one another to warn, more boldly

1161 1125 5213 80 575 3313 5613 1878
δὲ ἔγραψα ὑμῖν, ἀδελφοι, ἀπὸ μέρους, ὡς ἐπαναμιμνήσκων
But I wrote you, brothers, in part, as reminding

5209 1223 3588 5485 3588 1325 3427 5259 3588 2316 1519 3588
ὑμᾶς, διὰ τὴν χάριν τὴν δοθεῖσάν μοι ὑπὸ τοῦ Θεοῦ, 16 εἰς τὸ
you, because of the grace given to me by God, for

1511 3165 3011 2424 5547 1519 3588 1484 2418
εἶναί με λειτουργὸν Ἰησοῦ Χριστοῦ εἰς τὰ ἔθνη, ἱερουρ-
to be me a minister of Jesus Christ to the nations, sacredly

3588 2098 3588 2316 2443 1096 3588 4376
γοῦντα τὸ εὐαγγέλιον τοῦ Θεοῦ, ἵνα γένηται ἡ προσφορὰ
minisering the gospel of God, that may become the offering

3588 1484 2144 37 1722 4151 40 2192
τῶν ἐθνῶν εὐπρόσδεκτος, ἡγιασμένη ἐν Πνεύματι Ἁγίῳ. 17 ἔχω
of the nations acceptable, sanctified by (the) Spirit Holy. I have

3767 2746 1722 5547 2424 3588 4314 2316 3756 1063
οὖν καύχησιν ἐν Χριστῷ Ἰησοῦ τὰ πρὸς Θεόν· 18 οὐ γὰρ
Therefore glorying in Christ Jesus the things with God; not for

5111 5100 2980 3739 3756 2716 5547 1223 1700
τολμήσω τι λαλεῖν ὧν οὐ κατειργάσατο Χριστὸς δι' ἐμοῦ,
I will dare anything to speak which not did work out Christ through me,

1519 5218 1484 3056 2532 2041 1722 1411 4592 2532
εἰς ὑπακοὴν ἐθνῶν, λόγῳ καὶ ἔργῳ, 19 ἐν δυνάμει σημείων καὶ
for obedience of (the) nations in word and work, in power of signs and

5059 1722 1411 4151 2316 5620 3165 575 2419
τεράτων, ἐν δυνάμει Πνεύματος Θεοῦ· ὥστε με ἀπὸ Ἱερου-
wonders, in power of (the) Spirit of God; so as me from Jeru-

2532 2945 3360 3588 2437 4137 3588
σαλὴμ καὶ κύκλῳ μέχρι τοῦ Ἰλλυρικοῦ πεπληρωκέναι τὸ
salem and in a circuit as far as Illyricum to have fulfilled the

2098 3588 5547 3779 1161 5389 2097
εὐαγγέλιον τοῦ Χριστοῦ· 20 οὕτω δὲ φιλοτιμούμενον εὐαγγελί-
Gospel of Christ; so and eagerly striving to preach

3756 3699 3687 5547 2443 3361 1909 245
ζεσθαι, οὐχ ὅπου ὠνομάσθη Χριστός, ἵνα μὴ ἐπ' ἀλλότριον
the gospel, not where was named Christ, that not on another's

2310 3618 235 2531 1125 3739 3756
θεμέλιον οἰκοδομῶ· 21 ἀλλὰ, καθὼς γέγραπται, Οἷς οὐκ
foundation I should build; but, even as it has been written, To whom not

312 4012 846 3700 2532 3739 3756 191
ἀνηγγέλη περὶ αὐτοῦ, ὄψονται, καὶ οἳ οὐκ ἀκηκόασι,
it was announced concerning Him, they shall see, and the (ones) not having heard,

4920
συνήσουσι.
they shall understand.

in him shall the Gentiles trust.
13 Now the God of hope fill you with all joy and peace in believing, that ye may abound in hope, through the power of the Holy Ghost.

14 And I myself also am persuaded of you, my brethren, that ye also are full of goodness, filled with all knowledge, able also to admonish one another.
15 Nevertheless, brethren, I have written the more boldly unto you in some sort, as putting you in mind, because of the grace that is given to me of God,
16 That I should be the minister of Jesus Christ to the Gentiles, ministering the gospel of God, that the offering up of the Gentiles might be acceptable, being sanctified by the Holy Ghost.

17 I have therefore whereof I may glory through Jesus Christ in those things which pertain to God.
18 For I will not dare to speak of any of those things which Christ hath not wrought by me, to make the Gentiles obedient, by word and deed,
19 Through mighty signs and wonders, by the power of the Spirit of God; so that from Jerusalem, and round about unto Illyricum, I have fully preached the gospel of Christ.

20 Yea, so have I strived to preach the gospel, not where Christ was named, lest I should build upon another man's foundation:

21 But as it is written, To whom he was not spoken of, they shall see: and they that have not heard shall understand.

Literal Translation

Romans 15:22

King James Version

22 Because of this I also was much hindered from coming to you,

23 but now having no more place in these regions, and having a longing to come to you for many years,

24 whenever I may go into Spain, I will come to you; for I hope (in) traveling through to see you and to be set forward there by you, if first I may be filled of you in part.

25 But now I am going to Jerusalem, doing service to the saints.

26 For Macedonia and Achaia thought it good to make certain gifts to the poor of the saints in Jerusalem.

27 For they thought it good, also being debtors of them; for if the nations shared in their spiritual things, they ought also to minister to them in the fleshly things.

28 Then having finished and having sealed this fruit to them, I will go through you into Spain.

29 And I know that I will come to you in the fullness of (the) blessing of the gospel of Christ (when) I come.

1352 2532 1465 3588 4183 3588 2064 4314 5209
22. Διὸ καὶ ἐνεκοπτόμην τὰ πολλὰ τοῦ ἐλθεῖν πρὸς ὑμᾶς·
Therefore also I was hindered much to come to you;

3570 1161 3371 5117 2192 1722 3588 2824 5125
23 νυνὶ δὲ μηκέτι τόπον ἔχων ἐν τοῖς κλίμασι τούτοις,
now but no longer place having in regions these,

1974 1161 2192 3588 2064 4314 5209 575 4183 2094
ἐπιποθίαν δὲ ἔχων τοῦ ἐλθεῖν πρὸς ὑμᾶς ἀπὸ πολλῶν ἐτῶν,
a longing and having to come to you from many years,

5613 1437 4198 1519 3588 4681 2064 4314 5209
24 ὡς ἐάν πορεύωμαι εἰς τὴν Σπανίαν, ἐλύσομαι πρὸς ὑμᾶς
whenever I shall go into Spain, I will come to you;

1679 1063 1279 2300 5209 2532 5259 5216
ἐλπίζω γὰρ διαπορευόμενος θεάσασθαι ὑμᾶς, καὶ ὑφ' ὑμῶν προ-
I hope for traveling through to behold you, and by you to be

4311 1563 1437 5216 4412 575 3313 1705
πεμφθῆναι ἐκεῖ, ἐὰν ὑμῶν πρῶτον ἀπὸ μέρους ἐμπλησθῶ.
set forward there, if of you firstly in part I may be filled.

3570 1161 4198 1519 2419 1247 3588 40
25 νυνὶ δὲ πορεύομαι εἰς Ἱερουσαλὴμ διακονῶν τοῖς ἁγίοις.
now And I am going to Jerusalem ministering to the saints.

2106 1063 3109 2532 882 2842 5100
26 εὐδόκησαν γὰρ Μακεδονία καὶ Ἀχαΐα κοινωνίαν τινὰ
thought it good For Macedonia and Achaia gifts certain

4160 1519 3588 4434 3588 40 3588 1722 2419
ποιήσασθαι εἰς τοὺς πτωχοὺς τῶν ἁγίων τῶν ἐν Ἱερου-
to make to th poor of the saints in Jeru-

2106 1063 2532 3781 846 1526 1487 1063
σαλήμ. 27 εὐδόκησαν γάρ, καὶ ὀφειλέται αὐτῶν εἰσὶν. εἰ γὰρ
salem. they thought it good For, and debtors of them are. if For

3588 4152 846 2841 3588 1484 3784
τοῖς πνευματικοῖς αὐτῶν ἐκοινώνησαν τὰ ἔθνη, ὀφείλουσι
in the spiritual things of them shared the nations, they ought

2532 1722 3588 4559 3008 846 5124 3767
καὶ ἐν τοῖς σαρκικοῖς λειτουργῆσαι αὐτοῖς. 28 τοῦτο οὖν
also in the fleshly things to minister to them. this Then

2005 2532 4972 846 3588 2590 5126
ἐπιτελέσας, καὶ σφραγισάμενος αὐτοῖς τὸν καρπὸν τοῦτον,
having finished, and having sealed to them fruit this,

565 1223 5216 1519 3588 4681 1492 1161 3754 2064
ἀπελεύσομαι δι' ὑμῶν εἰς τὴν Σπανίαν. 29 οἶδα δὲ ὅτι ἐρχό-
I will go away through you into Spain. I know And that coming

4314 5209 1722 4138 2129 3588 2098 3588
μενος πρὸς ὑμᾶς ἐν πληρώματι εὐλογίας τοῦ εὐαγγελίου τοῦ
to you in the fullness of (the) blessing of the gospel

5547 2064
Χριστοῦ ἐλεύσομαι.
of Christ I will come.

22 For which cause also I have been much hindered from coming to you.

23 But now having no more place in these parts, and having a great desire these many years to come unto you;

24 Whensoever I take my journey into Spain, I will come to you: for I trust to see you in my journey, and to be brought on my way thitherward by you, if first I be somewhat filled with your (company).

25 But now I go unto Jerusalem to minister unto the saints.

26 For it hath pleased them of Macedonia and Achaia to make a certain contribution for the poor saints which are at Jerusalem.

27 It hath pleased them verily; and their debtors they are. For if the Gentiles have been made partakers of their spiritual things, their duty is also to minister unto them in carnal things.

28 When therefore I have performed this, and have sealed to them this fruit, I will come by you into Spain.

29 And I am sure that, when I come unto you, I shall come in the fulness of the blessing of the gospel of Christ.

30 But I exhort you, brothers, by our Lord Jesus Christ, and by the love of the Spirit, to strive together with me in (your) prayers to God on my behalf,

31 that I be delivered from the (ones) disobeying in Judea, and that my ministry, which (is) to Jerusalem, may be acceptable to the

3870 1161 5209 80 1223 3588 2962 2257 2424
30. Παρακαλῶ δὲ ὑμᾶς, ἀδελφοί, διὰ τοῦ Κυρίου ἡμῶν Ἰησοῦ
I exhort And you, brothers, by the Lord of us Jesus

5547 2532 1223 3588 26 3588 4151 4865
Χριστοῦ, καὶ διὰ τῆς ἀγάπης τοῦ Πνεύματος, συναγωνί-
Christ, and through the love of the Spirit, to strive

3427 1722 3588 4335 5228 1700 4314 3588 2316
σασθαί μοι ἐν ταῖς προσευχαῖς ὑπὲρ ἐμοῦ πρὸς τὸν Θεόν·
together with me in the prayers on behalf of me to God;

2443 4506 575 3588 544 1722 3588 2449 2532 2443 3588
31 ἵνα ῥυσθῶ ἀπὸ τῶν ἀπειθούντων ἐν τῇ Ἰουδαίᾳ, καὶ ἵνα ἡ
that I be delivered from those disobeying in Judea, and that the

1248 3450 3588 1519 2419 2144 1096 3588
διακονία μου ἡ εἰς Ἱερουσαλὴμ εὐπρόσδεκτος γένηται τοῖς
ministry of me which (is) to Jerusalem acceptable will be to the

30 Now I beseech you, brethren, for the Lord Jesus Christ's sake, and for the love of the Spirit, that ye strive together with me in (your) prayers to God for me;

31 That I may be delivered from them that do not believe in Judaea; and that my service which (I have) for Jerusalem may be accepted of the

Literal Translation

saints,
32 that (I may) come to you in joy through (the) will of God, and that I may be refreshed with you.
33 And the God of peace (be) with all of you. Amen.

Romans 15:32

40 2443 1722 5479 2064 4314 5209 1223 2307 2316
ἁγίοις· 32 ἵνα ἐν χαρᾷ ἐλθὼ πρὸς ὑμᾶς διὰ θελήματος Θεοῦ,
saints; that in joy coming to you through (the) will of God,

2532 4875 5213 3588 1161 2316 3588 1515 3326
καὶ συναναπαύσωμαι ὑμῖν. 33 ὁ δὲ Θεὸς τῆς εἰρήνης μετὰ
and I may be refreshed with you. the And God of peace (be) with

3956 5216 281
πάντων ὑμῶν. ἀμήν.
all of you. Amen.

King James Version

saints
32 That I may come unto you with joy by the will of God, and may with you be refreshed.
33 Now the God of peace (be) with you all. Amen.

Romans 16

1. But I commend our sister Phoebe to you, being a servant of the church in Cenchrea,
2 that you may receive her in (the) Lord, (as is) worthy of the saints, and may assist her in whatever matter she may need of you. For she also became a helper of many, and of myself.

3 Greet Priscilla and Aquila, my fellow workers in Christ Jesus,

4 who laid down their neck on behalf of my life, to whom not only I give thanks, but also all the churches of the nations.

5 And (greet) the church at their house, and my beloved Epenetus, who is a firstfruit of Achaia for Christ.

6 Greet Mary, who did much labor for us.

7 Greet Andronicus and Junias, my kinsmen and fellow prisoners, noted among the apostles, who also were in Christ before me.

8 Greet Amplias my beloved in (the) Lord.

9 Greet Urbanus, our fellow-worker in Christ, and my beloved Stachys.
10 Greet Apelles,

Romans 16

4921 1161 5213 5402 3588 79 2257 5607
1. Συνίστημι δὲ ὑμῖν Φοίβην τὴν ἀδελφὴν ἡμῶν, οὖσαν
I command And you Phoebe the sister of us, being

1249 3588 1577 3588 1722 2747 2443 846 4327
διάκονον τῆς ἐκκλησίας τῆς ἐν Κεγχρεαῖς· 2 ἵνα αὐτὴν προσδέ-
a servant of the church in Cenchrea, that her you may

1722 2962 516 3588 40 2532 3936 846 1722 3739
ξησθε ἐν Κυρίῳ ἀξίως τῶν ἁγίων, καὶ παραστῆτε αὐτῇ ἐν ᾧ
receive in (the) Lord worthily of the saints, and may assist her in what-

302 5216 5535 4229 2532 1063 846 4368 4183
ἂν ὑμῶν χρῄζῃ πράγματι· καὶ γὰρ αὐτὴ προστάτις πολλῶν
ever of you she may need matter; also for she a helper of many

1096 2532 846 1700
ἐγενήθη, καὶ αὐτοῦ ἐμοῦ.
became, and myself of me.

782 4252 2532 207 3588 4904 3450
3. Ἀσπάσασθε Πρίσκιλλαν καὶ Ἀκύλαν τοὺς συνεργούς μου
Greet Priscilla and Aquila the fellow-workers of me

1722 5547 2424 3748 5228 3588 5590 3450 3588 1438
ἐν Χριστῷ Ἰησοῦ, 4 οἵτινες ὑπὲρ τῆς ψυχῆς μου τὸν ἑαυτῶν
in Christ Jesus, who on behalf of the life of me the of themselves

5137 5294 3739 3756 1473 3441 2168 235
τράχηλον ὑπέθηκαν, οἷς οὐκ ἐγὼ μόνος εὐχαριστῶ, ἀλλὰ
neck they laid down, to whom not I only give thanks, but

2532 3956 3588 1577 3588 1484 2532 3588 2596 3624 846
καὶ πᾶσαι αἱ ἐκκλησίαι τῶν ἐθνῶν, 5 καὶ τὴν κατ' οἶκον αὐτῶν
also all the churches of the nations, and the in house of them

1577 782 1866 3588 27 3450 3739
ἐκκλησίαν. ἀσπάσασθε Ἐπαίνετον τὸν ἀγαπητόν μου, ὅς
church. greet Epenetus the beloved of me, who

2076 536 3588 882 1519 5547 782 3137
ἐστιν ἀπαρχὴ τῆς Ἀχαΐας εἰς Χριστόν. 6 ἀσπάσασθε Μαριάμ,
is firstfruit of Achaia for Christ. Greet Mariam,

3748 4183 2872 1519 2248 782 408 2532
ἥτις πολλὰ ἐκοπίασεν εἰς ὑμᾶς. 7 ἀσπάσασθε Ἀνδρόνικον καὶ
who many things labored for you. Greet Andronicus and

2458 3588 4773 3450 2532 4869 3450
Ἰουνιᾶν τοὺς συγγενεῖς μου καὶ συναιχμαλώτους μου,
Junias the kinsmen of me and fellow-prisoners of me,

3748 1526 1978 1722 3588 652 3739 2532 4253 1700
οἵτινές εἰσιν ἐπίσημοι ἐν τοῖς ἀποστόλοις, οἳ καὶ πρὸ ἐμοῦ
who are notable among the apostles, who also before me

1096 1722 5547 782 291 3588 27
γεγόνασιν ἐν Χριστῷ. 8 ἀσπάσασθε Ἀμπλίαν τὸν ἀγαπητόν
were in Christ. Greet Amplias the beloved

3450 1722 2962 782 3773 3588 4904 2257 1722
μου ἐν Κυρίῳ. 9 ἀσπάσασθε Οὐρβανὸν τὸν συνεργὸν ἡμῶν ἐν
of me in (the) Lord. Greet Urbanus the fellow-worker of us in

5547 2532 4720 3588 27 3450 782 55
Χριστῷ, καὶ Στάχυν τὸν ἀγαπητόν μου. 10 ἀσπάσασθε Ἀπελ-
Christ, and Stachys the beloved of me. Greet Apelles

Romans 16

1. I commend unto you Phebe our sister, which is a servant of the church which is at Cenchrea:
2 That ye receive her in the Lord, as becometh saints, and that ye assist her in whatsoever business she hath need of you: for she hath been a succourer of many, and of myself also.

3 Greet Priscilla and Aquila my helpers in Christ Jesus:

4 Who have for my life laid down their own necks: unto whom not only I give thanks, but also all the churches of the Gentiles.

5 Likewise (greet) the church that is in their house. Salute my wellbeloved Epaenetus, who is the firstfruits of Achaia unto Christ.

6 Greet Mary, who bestowed much labour on us.

7 Salute Andronicus and Junia, my kinsmen, and my fellowprisoners, who are of note among the apostles, who also were in Christ before me.

8 Greet Amplias my beloved in the Lord.

9 Salute Urbane, our helper in Christ, and Stachys my beloved.
10 Salute Apelles

Literal Translation

Romans 16:11

King James Version

the approved in Christ; Greet those of Aristobulus.

11 Greet Herodion, my kinsman. Greet those of Narcissus, those being in (the) Lord.
12 Greet Tryphena and Tryphosa, those laboring in (the) Lord. Greet Persis the beloved, who has labored in many things in (the) Lord.

13 Greet Rufus, the elect in (the) Lord, and his mother and mine.

14 Greet Asyncritus, Phlegon, Hermas, Patrobas, Hermes, and the brothers with them.

15 Greet Philologus and Julias, Nereus and his sister, and Olympas, and all the saints with them.

16 Greet one another with a holy kiss. The churches of Christ greet you.

17 And brothers I exhort you to watch those making divisions and causes of stumbling contrary to the doctrine which you learned, and turn away from them.
18 For such ones do not serve our Lord Jesus Christ, but their own belly, and by smooth speech and eulogy (they) deceive the hearts of the guileless (ones).

19 For your obedience reached to all; therefore, I rejoice over you. But I desire you to be truly wise (as) to good, but simple toward evil.

20 And the God of peace shall bruise Satan under your

3588 1384 1722 5547 782 3588 1537 3588 711
λῆν τὸν δόκιμον ἐν Χριστῷ. ἀσπάσασθε τοὺς ἐκ τῶν Ἀριστο-
the approved in Christ. Greet those of Aristo-

782 2267 3588 4773 3450 782
βούλου. 11 ἀσπάσασθε Ἡρῳδίωνα τὸν συγγενῆ μου. ἀσπά-
bulus. Greet Herodian the kinsman of me. Greet

3588 1537 3588 3488 3588 5607 1722 2962 782
σασθε τοὺς ἐκ τῶν Ναρκίσσου, τοὺς ὄντας ἐν Κυρίῳ. 12 ἀσπά-
those of Narcissus, those being in (the) Lord. Greet

5170 2532 5173 3588 2872 1722 2962
σασθε Τρύφαιναν καὶ Τρυφῶσαν τὰς κοπιώσας ἐν Κυρίῳ.
Tryphena and Tryphosa the (ones) laboring in (the) Lord.

782 4069 3588 27 3748 4183 2872
ἀσπάσασθε Περσίδα τὴν ἀγαπητήν, ἥτις πολλὰ ἐκοπίασεν
Greet Persis the beloved, who many things labored

1722 2962 782 4504 3588 1588 1722 2962 2532
ἐν Κυρίῳ. 13 ἀσπάσασθε Ῥοῦφον τὸν ἐκλεκτὸν ἐν Κυρίῳ, καὶ
in (the) Lord. Greet Rufus the elect in (the) Lord, and

3588 3384 846 2532 1700 782 799
τὴν μητέρα αὐτοῦ καὶ ἐμοῦ. 14 ἀσπάσασθε Ἀσύγκριτον,
the mother of him and of me. Greet Asyncritus,

5393 2057 3969 2060 2532 3588 4862 846
Φλέγοντα, Ἑρμᾶν, Πατροβᾶν, Ἑρμῆν, καὶ τοὺς σὺν αὐτοῖς
Phlegan, Hermas, Patrobas, Hermes, and those with them

80 782 5378 2532 2456 3517 2532 3588
ἀδελφούς. 15 ἀσπάσασθε Φιλόλογον καὶ Ἰουλίαν, Νηρέα καὶ τὴν
brothers. Greet Philologus and Juliias, Nereus and the

79 846 2532 3652 2532 3588 4862 846 3956
ἀδελφὴν αὐτοῦ, καὶ Ὀλυμπᾶν, καὶ τοὺς σὺν αὐτοῖς πάντας
sister of him, and Olympas, and the with him all

40 782 240 1722 5370 40 782
ἁγίους. 16 ἀσπάσασθε ἀλλήλους ἐν φιλήματι ἁγίῳ. ἀσπάζονται
saints. Greet one another with a kiss holy. Greet

5209 3588 1577 3588 5547
ὑμᾶς αἱ ἐκκλησίαι τοῦ Χριστοῦ.
you the churches of Christ.

3870 1161 5209 80 4648 3588 3588 1370
17. Παρακαλῶ δὲ ὑμᾶς, ἀδελφοί, σκοπεῖν τοὺς τὰς διχοστα-
I exhort And you, brothers, to watch those the divisions

2532 3588 4625 3844 3588 1322 3739 5210 3129
σίας καὶ τὰ σκάνδαλα, παρὰ τὴν διδαχὴν ἣν ὑμεῖς ἐμάθετε,
and the offenses, against the doctrine which you learned,

4160 2532 1578 575 846 3588 1063 5108 3588
ποιοῦντας· καὶ ἐκκλίνατε ἀπ' αὐτῶν· 18 οἱ γὰρ τοιοῦτοι τῷ
making; and turn away from them; for such ones the

2962 2257 2424 5547 3756 1398 235 3588
Κυρίῳ ἡμῶν Ἰησοῦ Χριστῷ οὐ δουλεύουσιν, ἀλλὰ τῇ
Lord of us Jesus Christ not do serve, but the

1438 2836 2532 1223 3588 5542 2532 2129
ἑαυτῶν κοιλίᾳ· καὶ διὰ τῆς χρηστολογίας καὶ εὐλογίας
of themselves belly; and through smooth speech and eulogy

1818 3588 2588 3588 172 3588 1063 5216 5218
ἐξαπατῶσι τὰς καρδίας τῶν ἀκάκων. 19 ἡ γὰρ ὑμῶν ὑπακοὴ
deceive the hearts of the guileless. the For of you obedience

1519 3956 864 5463 3767 3588 1909 5213 2309 1161 5209
εἰς πάντας ἀφίκετο. χαίρω οὖν τὸ ἐφ' ὑμῖν· θέλω δὲ ὑμᾶς
to all reached. I rejoice Therefore over you; I desire and you

4680 3303 1511 1519 3588 18 185 1161 1519 3588 2556
σοφοὺς μὲν εἶναι εἰς τὸ ἀγαθόν, ἀκεραίους δὲ εἰς τὸ κακόν.
wise truly to be to the good, simple but toward the bad.

3588 1161 2316 3588 1515 4937 3588 4567 5259 3588
20 ὁ δὲ Θεὸς τῆς εἰρήνης συντρίψει τὸν Σατανᾶν ὑπὸ τοὺς
the And God of peace will crush Satan under the

approved in Christ. Salute them which are of Aristobulus' (household).
11 Salute Herodion my kinsman. Greet them that be of the (household) of Narcissus, which are in the Lord.
12 Salute Tryphena and Tryphosa, who labour in the Lord. Salute the beloved Persis, which laboured much in the Lord.

13 Salute Rufus chosen in the Lord, and his mother and mine.

14 Salute Asyncritus, Phlegon, Hermas, Patrobas, Hermes, and the brethren which are with them.

15 Salute Philologus, and Julia, Nereus, and his sister, and Olympas, and all the saints which are with them.

16 Salute one another with an holy kiss. The churches of Christ salute you.

17 Now I beseech you, brethren, mark them which cause divisions and offences contrary to the doctrine which ye have learned; and avoid them.
18 For they that are such serve not our Lord Jesus Christ, but their own belly; and by good words and fair speeches deceive the hearts of the simple.

19 For your obedience is come abroad unto all (men). I am glad therefore on your behalf: but yet I would have you wise unto that which is good, and simple concerning evil.
20 And the God of peace shall bruise Satan under your

Literal Translation **Romans 16:21** *King James Version*

4228 5216 1722 5034
πόδας ὑμῶν ἐν τάχει.
feet of you shortly.

feet shortly. The grace of our Lord Jesus Christ (be) with you. Amen.

3588 5485 3588 2962 2257 2424 5547 3326 5216
'Η χάρις τοῦ Κυρίου ἡμῶν 'Ιησοῦ Χριστοῦ μεθ' ὑμῶν.
The grace of the Lord of us Jesus Christ (be) with you.

281
ἀμήν.
Amen.

feet shortly. The grace of our Lord Jesus Christ (be) with you. Amen.

21 Timothy, my fellow-worker, and Lucius, and Jason, and Sosipater, my kinsmen, greet you.
22 I, Tertius, the (one) writing the epistle, greet you in (the) Lord.

782 5209 5095 3588 4904 3450 2532 3066
21.'Ασπάζονται ὑμᾶς Τιμόθεος ὁ συνεργός μου, καὶ Λούκιος
Greets you Timothy the fellow-worker of me, and Lucius

2532 2394 2532 4989 3588 4773 3450 782
καὶ 'Ιάσων καὶ Σωσίπατρος οἱ συγγενεῖς μου. 22 ἀσπάζομαι
and Jason and Sosipater the kinsmen of me. Greet

5209 1473 5060 3588 1125 3588 1992 1722 2962
ὑμᾶς ἐγὼ Τέρτιος, ὁ γράψας τὴν ἐπιστολὴν ἐν Κυρίῳ.
you I Tertius, the (one) writing the epistle in (the) Lord.

21 Timotheus my workfellow, and Lucius, and Jason, and Sosipater, my kinsmen, salute you.
22 I Tertius, who wrote (this) epistle, salute you in the Lord.

23 Gaius, the host of all the church and me, greets you. Erastus, the treasurer of the city, and Quartus the brother, greet you.

782 5209 1050 3588 3581 3450 2532 3588 1577 3650
23 ἀσπάζεται ὑμᾶς Γάιος ὁ ξένος μου καὶ τῆς ἐκκλησίας ὅλης.
greets you Gaius the host of me and the church of all.

782 5209 2037 3588 3623 3588 4172 2532
ἀσπάζεται ὑμᾶς Ἔραστος ὁ οἰκονόμος τῆς πόλεως, καὶ
greets you Erastus the treasurer of the city, and

2890 3588 80
Κούαρτος ὁ ἀδελφός.
Quartus the brother.

23 Gaius mine host, and of the whole church, saluteth you. Erastus the chamberlain of the city saluteth you, and Quartus a brother.

24 The grace of our Lord Jesus Christ (be) with you all. Amen.

3588 5485 3588 2962 2257 2424 5547 3326 3956
24 'Η χάρις τοῦ Κυριου ἡμῶν 'Ιησοῦ Χριστοῦ μετὰ πάντων
The grace of the Lord of us Jesus Christ (be) with all

5216 281
ὑμῶν. ἀμήν.
of you. Amen.

24 The grace of our Lord Jesus Christ (be) with you all. Amen.

25 Now to Him (who is) able to establish you according to my gospel, and the proclamation of Jesus Christ, according to the revelation of (the) mystery having been kept unvoiced during eternal times,
26 but now made plain, and by prophetic Scriptures, according to the commandment of the everlasting God, made known for obedience of faith to all the nations;

3588 1161 1410 5209 4741 2596 3588 2098 3456
25 Τῷ δὲ δυναμένῳ ὑμᾶς στηρίξαι κατὰ τὸ εὐαγγέλιόν μου
to the (one) And being able you to establish according to the gospel of me

2532 3588 2782 2424 5547 2596 602 3466
καὶ τὸ κήρυγμα 'Ιησοῦ Χριστοῦ, κατὰ ἀποκάλυψιν μυστη-
and the proclamation of Jesus Christ, according to (the) revelation of (the)

5550 166 4601 5319 1161 3568
ρίου χρόνοις αἰωνίοις σεσιγημένου, 26 φανερωθέντος δὲ νῦν,
mystery in times eternal having been kept unvoiced, made plain but now,

1223 5037 1124 4397 2596 2003 3588 166
διά τε γραφῶν προφητικῶν, κατ' ἐπιταγὴν τοῦ αἰωνίου
through and Scriptures prophetic, according to (the) command of the eternal

2316 1519 5218 4102 1519 3956 3588 1484 1107
Θεοῦ, εἰς ὑπακοὴν πίστεως εἰς πάντα τὰ ἔθνη γνωρισθέντος,
God, for obedience of faith to all the nations made known,

25 Now to him that is of power to stablish you according to my gospel, and the preaching of Jesus Christ, according to the revelation of the mystery, which was kept secret since the world began,
26 But now is made manifest, and by the scriptures of the prophets, according to the commandment of the everlasting God, made known to all nations for the obedience of faith:

27 to (the) only wise God through Jesus Christ, to whom (be) the glory forever. Amen.

3441 4680 2316 1223 2424 5547 3588 1391 1519 3588
27 μόνῳ σοφῷ Θεῷ, διὰ 'Ιησοῦ Χριστοῦ, ᾗ δόξα εἰς τοὺς
only wise to God through Jesus Christ, be glory to the

165 281
αἰῶνας. ἀμήν.
ages. Amen.

27 To God only wise, (be) glory through Jesus Christ for ever. Amen. (Written to the Romans from Corinthus, (and sent) by Phebe servant of the church at Cenchrea.)

Literal Translation

THE FIRST EPISTLE OF THE APOSTLE PAUL TO THE CORINTHIANS

ΠΑΥΛΟΥ ΤΟΥ ΑΠΟΣΤΟΛΟΥ Η ΠΡΟΣ
OF PAUL THE APOSTLE THE TO
ΚΟΡΙΝΘΙΟΥΣ ΕΠΙΣΤΟΛΗ ΠΡΩΤΗ
(THE) CORINTHIANS EPISTLE FIRST

King James Version

THE FIRST EPISTLE OF THE APOSTLE PAUL TO THE CORINTHIANS

1 Corinthians 1

1.Paul, a called apostle of Jesus Christ, by (the) will of God, and Sosthenes the brother,
2 to the church of God which is in Corinth, those having been sanctified in Christ Jesus, called-out saints, with all those calling on the name of our Lord Jesus Christ in every place, both theirs and ours:

3972 2822 652 2424 5547 1223 2307
1. Παῦλος κλητὸς ἀπόστολος Ἰησοῦ Χριστοῦ διὰ θελήματος
Paul a called apostle of Jesus Christ through (the) will
2316 2532 4988 3588 80 3588 1577 3588 2316 3588
Θεοῦ, καὶ Σωσθένης ὁ ἀδελφός, 2 τῇ ἐκκλησίᾳ τοῦ Θεοῦ τῇ
of God, and Sosthenes the brother, to the church of God
5607 1722 2882 37 1722 547 2424 2822
οὔσῃ ἐν Κορίνθῳ, ἡγιασμένοις ἐν Χριστῷ Ἰησοῦ, κλητοῖς
existing in Corinth, having been sanctified in Christ Jesus called out
40 4862 3956 3588 1941 3588 686 3588 2962
ἁγίοις, σὺν πᾶσι τοῖς ἐπικαλουμένοις τὸ ὄνομα τοῦ Κυρίου
saints, with all the ones calling on the name of the Lord
2257 2424 5547 1722 3956 5117 846 5037 2532 2257
ἡμῶν Ἰησοῦ Χριστοῦ ἐν παντὶ τόπῳ, αὐτῶν τε καὶ ἡμῶν·
of us Jesus Christ in every place, of them both and of us;

1. Paul, called (to be) an apostle of Jesus Christ through the will of God, and Sosthenes (our) brother,
2 Unto the church of God which is at Corinth, to them that are sanctified in Christ Jesus, called (to be) saints, with all that in every place call upon the name of Jesus Christ our Lord, both theirs and ours:

3 Grace to you, and peace, from God our Father and the Lord Jesus Christ.

5485 5213 2532 1515 575 2316 3962 2257 2532 2962
3 χάρις ὑμῖν καὶ εἰρήνη ἀπὸ Θεοῦ πατρὸς ἡμῶν καὶ Κυρίου
grace to you and peace from God (the) Father of us and (the) Lord
2424 5547
Ἰησοῦ Χριστō.
Jesus Christ.

3 Grace (be) unto you, and peace, from God our Father, and (from) the Lord Jesus Christ.

4 I give thanks to my God always concerning you (for) the grace of God having been given to you in Christ Jesus,
5 that in everything you were enriched in Him, (in) all discourse and all knowledge,
6 even as the testimony of Christ was confirmed in you,
7 so that you (are) not lacking in any gift, awaiting the revelation of our Lord, Jesus Christ,
8 who also will confirm you until (the) end, blameless in the day of our Lord Jesus Christ.
9 God (is) faithful, through whom you were called into (the) fellowship of His Son, Jesus Christ, our Lord.

2168 3588 2316 3450 3842 4012 5216 1909 3588
4. Εὐχαριστῶ τῷ Θεῷ μου πάντοτε περὶ ὑμῶν, ἐπὶ τῇ
I give thanks to God my always concerning you, on the
5485 3588 2316 3588 1325 5213 1722 5547 2424 3754 1722
χάριτι τοῦ Θεοῦ τῇ δοθείσῃ ὑμῖν ἐν Χριστῷ Ἰησοῦ, 5 ὅτι ἐν
grace of God having been given to you in Christ Jesus, that in
3956 4148 1722 846 1722 3956 3056 2532 3956
παντὶ ἐπλουτίσθητε ἐν αὐτῷ, ἐν παντὶ λόγῳ καὶ πάσῃ
everything you were enriched in Him, in all discourse and all
1108 2531 3588 3142 3588 5547 950 1722
γνώσει, 6 καθὼς τὸ μαρτύριον τοῦ Χριστοῦ ἐβεβαιώθη ἐν
knowledge, even as the testimony of Christ was confirmed in
5213 5620 5209 3361 5302 1722 3367 5486 553
ὑμῖν, 7 ὥστε ὑμᾶς μὴ ὑστερεῖσθαι ἐν μηδενὶ χαρίσματι, ἀπεκ-
you, so as you not to be lacking in no gift, having
3588 602 3588 2962 2257 2424
δεχομένους τὴν ἀποκάλυψιν τοῦ Κυρίου ἡμῶν Ἰησοῦ
been awaiting the revelation of the Lord of us Jesus
5547 3739 2532 950 5209 2193 5056 410 1722
Χριστοῦ, 8 ὃς καὶ βεβαιώσει ὑμᾶς ἕως τέλους, ἀνεγκλήτους ἐν
Christ, who also will confirm you until (the) end, blameless in
3588 2250 3588 2962 2257 2424 5547 4103 3588 2316
τῇ ἡμέρᾳ τοῦ Κυρίου ἡμῶν Ἰησοῦ Χριστοῦ. 9 πιστὸς ὁ Θεός
the day of the Lord of us Jesus Christ. Faithful (is) God
1223 3739 2564 1519 2842 3588 5207 846 2424
δι' οὗ ἐκλήθητε εἰς κοινωνίαν τοῦ υἱοῦ αὐτοῦ Ἰησοῦ
through whom you were called into fellowship of the Son of Him Jesus
5547 3588 2962 2257
Χριστοῦ τοῦ Κυρίου ἡμῶν.
Christ the Lord of us.

4 I thank my God always on your behalf, for the grace of God which is given you by Jesus Christ;
5 That in every thing ye are enriched by him, in all utterance, and (in) all knowledge;
6 Even as the testimony of Christ was confirmed in you:
7 So that ye come behind in no gift; waiting for the coming of our Lord Jesus Christ:
8 Who shall also confirm you unto the end, (that ye may be) blameless in the day of our Lord Jesus Christ.
9 God (is) faithful, by whom ye were called unto the fellowship of his Son Jesus Christ our Lord.

10 Now I exhort you, brothers, through the name of our Lord Jesus Christ (that) you all say the same thing,

3870 1161 5209 80 1223 3588 3686 3588
10. Παρακαλῶ δὲ ὑμᾶς, ἀδελφοί, διὰ τοῦ ὀνόματος τοῦ
I call upon And you, brothers, through the name of the
2962 2257 2424 5547 2443 3588 846 3004 3956
Κυρίου ἡμῶν Ἰησοῦ Χριστοῦ, ἵνα τὸ αὐτὸ λέγητε πάντες,
Lord of us Jesus Christ, that the same you say all,

10 Now I beseech you, brethren, by the name of our Lord Jesus Christ, that ye all speak the same thing,

Literal Translation

1 Corinthians 1:11

King James Version

and there be no divisions among you, but you be united in the same mind and in the same judgment.
11 For concerning you, my brothers, it was shown to me by those of Chloe that there are strifes among you.
12 But I say this, that each of you says, I am of Paul, and I of Apollos, and I of Cephas, and I of Christ.
13 Has Christ been divided? Was Paul crucified for you? Or were you baptized into the name of Paul?
14 I give thanks to God that I did not baptize one of you, except Crispus and Gaius,
15 that not anyone should say that you were baptized in my name.
16 And I also baptized the house of Stephanas. For the rest, I do not know if I baptized any other.
17 For Christ did not send me to baptize, but to preach the gospel, not in wisdom of words, lest the cross of Christ be nullified.
18 For the word of the cross is foolishness to those being lost, but to us being saved, (it) is (the) power of God.
19 For it has been written, "I will destroy the wisdom of the wise, and I will set aside the understanding of the understanding ones." (Isa. 29:14)
20 Where (is the) wise? Where (the) scribe? Where (the) lawyer of this world? Did God not make the wisdom of this world foolish?
21 For since in the wisdom of God the world (by) wisdom did not know God, God was pleased through the foolishness of preaching to save the ones believing.
22 And since Jews ask for a sign,

2532/3361/5600/1722/5213/4978 5600 1161 2675 1722/3588/846
καὶ μὴ ᾖ ἐν ὑμῖν σχίσματα, ἦτε δὲ κατηρτισμένοι ἐν τῷ αὐτῷ
and not be among you schisms, you be but (as) having been united in the same

3563 2532 1722 3588 846 1106 1213 1063 3427 4012 5216
νοι καὶ ἐν τῇ αὐτῇ γνώμῃ. 11 ἐδηλώθη γάρ μοι περὶ ὑμῶν,
mind and in the same judgment. it was shown For to me about you,

80 3450 5259 3588 5514 3754 2054 1722 5213 1526 3004
ἀδελφοί μου, ὑπὸ τῶν Χλόης, ὅτι ἔριδες ἐν ὑμῖν εἰσι. 12 λέγω
brothers of me, by those of Chloe, that strifes among you are. I say

1161 5124 3754 1538 5216 3004 1473 3303 1510 3972
δὲ τοῦτο, ὅτι ἕκαστος ὑμῶν λέγει, Ἐγὼ μέν εἰμι Παύλου,
And this, that each of you says, I indeed am of Paul,

1473 1161 625 1473 1161 2786 1473 1161 5547 3307
Ἐγὼ δὲ Ἀπολλῶ, Ἐγὼ δὲ Κηφᾶ, Ἐγὼ δὲ Χριστοῦ. 13 μεμέ-
I and of Apollos, I and of Cephas, I and of Christ. Has

3588 5547 3361 3972 4717 5228 5216 2228 1519
ρισται ὁ Χριστός; μὴ Παῦλος ἐσταυρώθη ὑπὲρ ὑμῶν, ἢ εἰς
been divided Christ? Not Paul was crucified on behalf of you, Or into

3588 3686 3972 907 2168 3588 2316 3754
τὸ ὄνομα Παύλου ἐβαπτίσθητε; 14 εὐχαριστῶ τῷ Θεῷ ὅτι
the name of Paul were you baptized? I give thanks to God that

3762 5216 907 1487 3361 2921 2532 1050 2443 3361 5100
οὐδένα ὑμῶν ἐβάπτισα, εἰ μὴ Κρίσπον καὶ Γάιον; 15 ἵνα μή τις
not one of you I baptized, except Crispus and Gaius; that not any

2036 3754 1519 3588 1699 3686 907 907 1161 2532 3588
εἴπῃ ὅτι εἰς τὸ ἐμὸν ὄνομα ἐβάπτισα. 16 ἐβάπτισα δὲ καὶ τὸν
should say that into my name you were baptized. I baptized But also the

4734 3624 3063 3756 1492 1487 5100 243 907 3756
Στεφανᾶ οἶκον· λοιπὸν οὐκ οἶδα εἴ τινα ἄλλον ἐβάπτισα. 17 οὐ
of Stephanus house; (for the) rest not I know if any other I baptized. not

1063 649 3165 5547 907 235 2097 3756
γὰρ ἀπέστειλέ με Χριστὸς βαπτίζειν, ἀλλ' εὐαγγελίζεσθαι, οὐκ
For sent me Christ to baptize, but to preach the gospel, not

1722 4678 3056 2443 3361 2758 3588 4716 3588 5547
ἐν σοφίᾳ λόγου, ἵνα μὴ κενωθῇ ὁ σταυρὸς τοῦ Χριστοῦ.
in wisdom of words, that not be nullified the cross of Christ.

3588 3056 1063 3588 3588 4716 3588 3303 622
18. Ὁ λόγος γὰρ ὁ τοῦ σταυροῦ τοῖς μὲν ἀπολλυμένοις
the Word For of the cross in those truly perishing

3472 2076 3588 1161 4982 2254 1411 2316 2076
μωρία ἐστί, τοῖς δὲ σῳζομένοις ἡμῖν δύναμις Θεοῦ ἐστι.
foolishness is, and being saved to us (the) power of God is.

1125 1063 622 3588 4678 3588 4680 2532 3588
19 γέγραπται γάρ, Ἀπολῶ τὴν σοφίαν τῶν σοφῶν, καὶ τὴν
it has been written For, I will destroy the wisdom of the wise, and the

4907 3588 4908 114 4226 4680 4226 1122
σύνεσιν τῶν συνετῶν ἀθετήσω. 20 ποῦ σοφός; ποῦ γραμ-
understanding of the perceiving I will set aside. Where (is the) wise? Where (the)

4226 4804 3588 165 5127 3780 3471
ματεύς; ποῦ συζητητὴς τοῦ αἰῶνος τούτου; οὐχὶ ἐμώ-
scribe? Where (the) disputer age of this? Did not make

3588 2316 3588 4678 3588 2889 5127 1894 1063
ρανεν ὁ Θεὸς τὴν σοφίαν τοῦ κόσμου τούτου; 21 ἐπειδὴ γὰρ
foolish God the wisdom world of this? since For

1722 3588 4678 3588 2316 3756 1097 3588 2889 1223 3588 4678 3588
ἐν τῇ σοφίᾳ τοῦ Θεοῦ οὐκ ἔγνω ὁ κόσμος διὰ τῆς σοφίας τὸν
in the wisdom of God not knew the world through the wisdom

2316 2106 3588 2316 1223 3588 3472 3588 2782
Θεόν, εὐδόκησεν ὁ Θεὸς διὰ τῆς μωρίας τοῦ κηρύγματος
God, was pleased God through the foolishness of preaching

4982 3588 4100 1894 2532 2453 4592
σῶσαι τοὺς πιστεύοντας. 22 ἐπειδὴ καὶ Ἰουδαῖοι σημεῖον
to save the ones) believing. since And Jews a sign

and (that) there be no divisions among you; but (that) ye be perfectly joined together in the same mind and in the same judgment.
11 For it hath been declared unto me of you, my brethren, by them (which are of the house) of Chloe, that there are contentions among you.
12 Now this I say, that every one of you saith, I am of Paul; and I of Apollos; and I of Cephas; and I of Christ.
13 Is Christ divided? was Paul crucified for you? or were ye baptized in the name of Paul?
14 I thank God that I baptized none of you, but Crispus and Gaius;
15 Lest any should say that I had baptized in mine own name.
16 And I baptized also the household of Stephanas: besides, I know not whether I baptized any other.
17 For Christ sent me not to baptize, but to preach the gospel: not with wisdom of words, lest the cross of Christ should be made of none effect.
18 For the preaching of the cross is to them that perish foolishness; but unto us which are saved it is the power of God.
19 For it is written, I will destroy the wisdom of the wise, and will bring to nothing the understanding of the prudent.
20 Where (is) the wise? where (is) the scribe? where (is) the disputer of this world? hath not God made foolish the wisdom of this world?
21 For after that in the wisdom of God the world by wisdom knew not God, it pleased God by the foolishness of preaching to save them that believe.
22 For the Jews require a sign,

Literal Translation

and Greeks seek wisdom,
23 we on the other hand preach Christ having been crucified (truly an offense to Jews, and foolishness to Greeks),

24 but to them, the called-out ones, both to Jews and to Greeks, Christ (is) the power of God and the wisdom of God;
25 because the foolish thing of God is wiser (than) men, and the weak thing of God is stronger (than) men.

1 Corinthians 1:23

154 2532 1672 4678 2212 2249 1161 2784
αἰτοῦσι, καὶ Ἕλληνες σοφίαν ζητοῦσιν· 23 ἡμεῖς δὲ κηρύσ-
ask, and Greeks wisdom seek; we but preach

5547 4717 2453 3303 4625
σομεν Χριστὸν ἐσταυρωμένον, Ἰουδαίοις μὲν σκάνδαλον,
Christ having been crucified, to Jews indeed an offense,

1672 1161 3472 846 1161 3588 2822 2453 5037 2532
Ἕλλησι δὲ μωρίαν· 24 αὐτοῖς δὲ τοῖς κλητοῖς, Ἰουδαίοις τε καὶ
to Greeks and foolishness; to them but the called out ones, to Jews both and

1672 5547 2316 1411 2532 2316 4678 3754 3588
Ἕλλησι, Χριστὸν Θεοῦ δύναμιν καὶ Θεοῦ σοφίαν. 25 ὅτι τὸ
to Greeks, Christ of God (the) power and of God (the) wisdom. For the

3474 3588 2316 4680 3588 444 2076 2532 3588 772
μωρὸν τοῦ Θεοῦ σοφώτερον τῶν ἀνθρώπων ἐστί, καὶ τὸ ἀσθενὲς
foolish thing of God wiser (than) men is, and the weak thing

3588 2316 2478 3588 444 2076
τοῦ Θεοῦ ἰσχυρότερον τῶν ἀνθρώπων ἐστι.
of God stronger (than) men is.

King James Version

and the Greeks seek after wisdom:
23 But we preach Christ crucified, unto the Jews a stumblingblock, and unto the Greeks foolishness;

24 But unto them which are called, both Jews and Greeks, Christ the power of God, and the wisdom of God.
25 Because the foolishness of God is wiser than men; and the weakness of God is stronger than men.

26 For you see your calling, brothers, that (there are) not many wise according to flesh, nor many powerful, not many wellborn.

27 But God chose the foolish things of the world that the wise might be shamed, and God chose the weak things of the world so that He might shame the strong things.
28 And God chose the low-born of the world, and the things despised, and the things that are not, so that He might nullify the things that are,
29 so that no flesh might glory in His presence.
30 But of Him, you are in Christ Jesus, who was made to us wisdom from God, both righteousness and sanctification and redemption,

31 so that even as it has been written, "He that glories, let him glory in (the) Lord." (Jer.9:24)

991 1063 3588 2821 5216 80 3754 3756 4183
26. Βλέπετε γὰρ τὴν κλῆσιν ὑμῶν, ἀδελφοί, ὅτι οὐ πολλοὶ
you see For the calling of you, brothers, that not many

4680 2596 4561 3756 4183 1415 3756 4183 2104
σοφοὶ κατὰ σάρκα, οὐ πολλοὶ δυνατοί, οὐ πολλοὶ εὐγενεῖς·
wise according to flesh, not many powerful, not many well-born;

235 3588 3474 3588 2889 1586 3588 2316 2443 3588
27 ἀλλὰ τὰ μωρὰ τοῦ κόσμου ἐξελέξατο ὁ Θεὸς, ἵνα τοὺς
but the foolish things of the world chose God, that the

4680 2617 2532 3588 772 3588 2889 1586 3588
σοφούς καταισχύνῃ· καὶ τὰ ἀσθενῆ τοῦ κόσμου ἐξελέξατο ὁ
wise might be shamed; and the weak things of the world chose

2316 2443 2617 3588 2478 2532 3588 36 3588 2889
Θεὸς, ἵνα καταισχύνῃ τὰ ἰσχυρά· 28 καὶ τὰ ἀγενῆ τοῦ κόσμου
God, that He might shame the strong things; and the low-born of the world

2532 3588 1848 1586 3588 2316 2532 3588 3361 5607
καὶ τὰ ἐξουθενημένα ἐξελέξατο ὁ Θεός, καὶ τὰ μὴ ὄντα,
and the things despised chose God, and the things not being,

2443 3588 5607 2673 3704 3361 2744 3956 4561
ἵνα τὰ ὄντα καταργήσῃ· 29 ὅπως μὴ καυχήσηται πᾶσα σὰρξ
that the things being He nullify; so as not might boast all flesh

1799 846 1537 846 1161 5210 2075 1722 5547 2424
ἐνώπιον αὐτοῦ. 30 ἐξ αὐτοῦ δὲ ὑμεῖς ἐστε ἐν Χριστῷ Ἰησοῦ,
before Him. of Him And you are in Christ Jesus,

3739 1096 2254 4678 575 2316 1343 5037 2532
ὃς ἐγενήθη ἡμῖν σοφία ἀπὸ Θεοῦ, δικαιοσύνη τε καὶ
who became to us wisdom from God, righteousness both and

38 2532 629 2443 2531 1125 3588
ἁγιασμὸς, καὶ ἀπολύτρωσις· 31 ἵνα καθὼς γέγραπται, Ὁ
sanctification, and redemption; that even as has been written, he

2744 1722 2962 2744
καυχώμενος ἐν Κυρίῳ καυχάσθω.
boasting in (the) Lord let him glory.

26 For ye see your calling, brethren, how that not many wise men after the flesh, not many mighty, not many noble, (are called):

27 But God hath chosen the foolish things of the world to confound the wise; and God hath chosen the weak things of the world to confound the things which are mighty;
28 And base things of the world, and things which are despised, hath God chosen, (yea), and things which are not, to bring to nought things that are:
29 That no flesh should glory in his presence.
30 But of him are ye in Christ Jesus, who of God is made unto us wisdom, and righteousness, and sanctification, and redemption:

31 That, according as it is written, He that glorieth, let him glory in the Lord.

1 Corinthians 2

1. And having come to you, brothers, I did not come with excellency of word or wisdom, proclaiming to you the testimony of God.
2 For I decided not to know anything among you except Jesus Christ,

1 Corinthians 2

2504 2064 4314 5209 80 2064 3756 2596 5247
1. Κἀγὼ ἐλθὼν πρὸς ὑμᾶς, ἀδελφοί, ἦλθον οὐ καθ' ὑπεροχὴν
And I having come to you, brothers, came not according to excellence

3056 2228 4678 2605 5213 3588 3142 3588 2316
λόγου ἢ σοφίας καταγγέλλων ὑμῖν τὸ μυστήριον τοῦ Θεοῦ.
of word or wisdom proclaiming to you the testimony of God.

3588 1063 2919 3588 1492 5100 1722 5213 1487 3361 2424 5547
2 οὐ γὰρ ἔκρινά τοῦ εἰδέναι τι ἐν ὑμῖν, εἰ μὴ Ἰησοῦν Χριστὸν,
not For I decided to know anything among you, except Jesus Christ,

1 Corinthians 2

1. And I, brethren, when I came to you, came not with excellency of speech or of wisdom, declaring unto you the testimony of God.
2 For I determined not to know any thing among you, save Jesus Christ,

Literal Translation

and this One having been crucified.
3 And I came to be with you in weakness, and in fear, and in much trembling.
4 And my word and my preaching (was) not in enticing words of human wisdom, but in proof of (the) Spirit and of power,
5 that your faith might not be in (the) wisdom of men, but in (the) power of God.

6 But we speak wisdom among the perfect, but not the wisdom of this age, nor of the rulers of this age, those being brought to nothing.

7 But we speak (the) wisdom of God in mystery, having been hidden, which God predetermined before the ages unto our glory,
8 which none of the rulers of this age has known. For if they had known, they would not have crucified the Lord of glory;

9 But even as it has been written, "Eye has not seen, and ear has not heard," nor has it risen up into the heart of man, "the things which God has prepared for the (ones) loving Him." (Isa.64:4)
10 But God revealed (them) to us by His Spirit, for the Spirit searches all things, even the depths of God.
11 For who among men knows the things of a man, if not the spirit of a man within him? So also no one has known the things of God except the Spirit of God.

12 But we did not receive the spirit of the world, but the Spirit from God, so that we might know the things that are freely given to us by God.
13 Which things we also speak, not in words taught in human

1 Corinthians 2:3

2532 5126 4717 2532 1473 1722 769 2532 1722
καὶ τοῦτον ἐσταυρωμένον. 3 καὶ ἐγὼ ἐν ἀσθενείᾳ καὶ ἐν
and this One having been crucified. And I in weakness and in

5401 2532 1722 5156 4183 1096 4314 5209 2532 3588 3056
φόβῳ καὶ ἐν τρόμῳ πολλῷ ἐγενόμην πρὸς ὑμᾶς. 4 καὶ ὁ λόγος
fear and in trembling much came to be with you. And the word

3450 2532 3588 2782 3450 3756 1722 3981 442 4678
μου καὶ τὸ κήρυγμά μου οὐκ ἐν πειθοῖς ἀνθρωπίνης σοφίας
of me and the preaching of me not in enticing of human wisdom

3056 235 1722 585 4151 2532 1411 2443 3588
λόγοις, ἀλλ᾽ ἐν ἀποδείξει πνεύματος καὶ δυνάμεως· 5 ἵνα ἡ
words, but in proof of (the) Spirit and of power; that the

4102 5216 33615600 1722 4678 444 235 1722 1411 2316
πίστις ὑμῶν μὴ ᾖ ἐν σοφίᾳ ἀνθρώπων, ἀλλ᾽ ἐν δυνάμει Θεοῦ.
faith of you not be in wisdom of men, but in (the) power of God.

4678 1161 2980 1722 3588 5046 4678 1161 3756 3588
6. Σοφίαν δὲ λαλοῦμεν ἐν τοῖς τελείοις· σοφίαν δὲ οὐ τοῦ
wisdom But we speak among the perfect; wisdom but not

165 5127 3761 3588 758 3588 165 5127
αἰῶνος τούτου, οὐδὲ τῶν ἀρχόντων τοῦ αἰῶνος τούτου,
age of this, neither of the rulers age of this,

3588 2673 235 2980 4678 2316 1722 3466
τῶν καταργουμένων· 7 ἀλλὰ λαλοῦμεν σοφίαν Θεοῦ ἐν μυστη-
those being brought to nothing; but we speak a wisdom of God in mystery,

3588 613 3739 4309 3588 2316 4253 3588
ρίῳ, τὴν ἀποκεκρυμμένην, ἣν προώρισεν ὁ Θεὸς πρὸ τῶν
having been hidden, which predetermined God before the

165 1519 1391 2257 3739 3762 3588 758 3588 165
αἰώνων εἰς δόξαν ἡμῶν· 8 ἣν οὐδεὶς τῶν ἀρχόντων τοῦ αἰῶνος
ages unto glory of us; which not one of the rulers age

5127 1097 1487 1063 1097 3756 302 3588 2962 3588
τούτου ἔγνωκεν· εἰ γὰρ ἔγνωσαν, οὐκ ἂν τὸν Κύριον τῆς
of this has known; if for they knew, not the Lord

1391 4717 235 2531 1125 3739 3788
δόξης ἐσταύρωσαν· 9 ἀλλὰ καθὼς γέγραπται, Ἃ ὀφθαλμὸς
of glory they would have crucified. But even as it has been written, Things which eye

3756 1492 2532 3775 3756 191 2532 1909 2588 444 3756
οὐκ εἶδε, καὶ οὖς οὐκ ἤκουσε, καὶ ἐπὶ καρδίαν ἀνθρώπου οὐκ
not did see, and ear not hear, and on (the) heart of man not

305 3739 2090 3588 2316 3588 25 846 2254/1161/3588
ἀνέβη, ἃ ἡτοίμασεν ὁ Θεὸς τοῖς ἀγαπῶσιν αὐτόν. 10 ἡμῖν δὲ ὁ
came up, things which prepared God the ones loving Him. to us But

2316 601 1223 3588 4151 846 3588 1063 4151
Θεὸς ἀπεκάλυψε διὰ τοῦ πνεύματος αὐτοῦ· τὸ γὰρ πνεῦμα
God revealed through the Spirit of Him; the for Spirit

3956 2045 2532 3588 899 3588 2316 5101 1063 1492 444
πάντα ἐραυνᾷ, καὶ τὰ βάθη τοῦ Θεοῦ. 11 τίς γὰρ οἶδεν ἀνθρώ-
all things searches, and the deep things of God. who For knows of man

3588 3588 444 1487 3361 3588 4151 3588 444 3588 1722
πων τὰ τοῦ ἀνθρώπου, εἰ μὴ τὸ πνεῦμα τοῦ ἀνθρώπου τὸ ἐν
the things of a man, if not the spirit of man within

846 3779 2532 3588 3588 2316 3762 1492 1487 3361 3588 4151
αὐτῷ; οὕτω καὶ τὰ τοῦ Θεοῦ οὐδεὶς οἶδεν, εἰ μὴ τὸ Πνεῦμα
him? So also the things of God no one has known, except the Spirit

3588 2316 2249 1161 3756 3588 4151 3588 2889 2983 235
τοῦ Θεοῦ. 12 ἡμεῖς δὲ οὐ τὸ πνεῦμα τοῦ κόσμου ἐλάβομεν, ἀλλὰ
of God. we And not the spirit of the world received, but

3588 4151 3588 1537 3588 2316 2443 1492 3588 5259 3588 2316
τὸ πνεῦμα τὸ ἐκ τοῦ Θεοῦ, ἵνα εἰδῶμεν τὰ ὑπὸ τοῦ Θεοῦ
the Spirit from God, that we may know the things by God

5483 2254 3739 2532 2980 3756 1722 1318 442
χαρισθέντα ἡμῖν· 13 ἃ καὶ λαλοῦμεν, οὐκ ἐν διδακτοῖς ἀνθρω-
freely given to us; which things also we speak, not in taught of human

King James Version

and him crucified.
3 And I was with you in weakness, and in fear, and in much trembling.

4 And my speech and my preaching (was) not with enticing words of man's wisdom, but in demonstration of the Spirit and of power:

5 That your faith should not stand in the wisdom of men, but in the power of God.

6 Howbeit we speak wisdom among them that are perfect: yet not the wisdom of this world, nor of the princes of this world, that come to nought:
7 But we speak the wisdom of God in a mystery, (even) the hidden (wisdom), which God ordained before the world unto our glory:
8 Which none of the princes of this world knew: for had they known (it), they would not have crucified the Lord of glory.

9 But as it is written, Eye hath not seen, nor ear heard, neither have entered into the heart of man, the things which God hath prepared for them that love him.
10 But God hath revealed (them) unto us by his Spirit: for the Spirit searcheth all things, yea, the deep things of God.

11 For what man knoweth the things of a man, save the spirit of man which is in him? even so the things of God knoweth no man, but the Spirit of God.

12 Now we have received, not the spirit of the world, but the spirit which is of God; that we might know the things that are freely given to us of God.
13 Which things also we speak, not in the words which man's wisdom teacheth,

Literal Translation

wisdom, but in (words) taught of the Holy Spirit, comparing spiritual things with spiritual things.
14 But a natural man does not receive the things of (the) Spirit of God, for they are foolishness to him, and he is not able to know (them), because they are spiritually discerned.

15 But indeed the spiritual one discerns all things, but he is discerned by no one.
16 For "who knew (the) mind of (the) Lord? Who will teach Him?" But we have (the) mind of Christ. (Isa.40:13)

1 Corinthians 2:14

4678 3056 235 1722 1318 4151 40
πίνης σοφίας λόγοις, ἀλλ' ἐν διδακτοῖς Πνεύματος Ἁγίου,
wisdom words, but in (words) taught of (the) Spirit Holy,

4152 4152 4793 5591 1161 444
πνευματικοῖς πνευματικὰ συγκρίνοντες. 14 ψυχικὸς δὲ ἄνθρω-
with spiritual things spiritual things comparing. a natural But man

3756 1209 3588 3588 4151 3588 2316 3472 1063
πος οὐ δέχεται τὰ τοῦ Πνεύματος τοῦ Θεοῦ· μωρία γὰρ
not receives the things of (the) Spirit of God; foolishness for

846 2076 2532 3756 1410 1097 3754 4153 350
αὐτῷ ἐστι, καὶ οὐ δύναται γνῶναι, ὅτι πνευματικῶς ἀνακρί-
to him they are, and not he is able to know, because spiritually they are

3588 1161 4152 350 3303 3956 846 1161 5259
νεται· 15 ὁ δὲ πνευματικὸς ἀνακρίνει μὲν πάντα, αὐτὸς δὲ ὑπ'
discerned. the But spiritual one discerns indeed all things, he but by

3762 350 5101 1063 1097 3563 2962 3739
οὐδενὸς ἀνακρίνεται. 16 τίς γὰρ ἔγνω νοῦν Κυρίου, ὃς
no one is discerned. who For knew (the) mind of (the) Lord, who

4822 846 2249 1161 3563 5547 2192
συμβιβάσει αὐτόν; ἡμεῖς δὲ νοῦν Χριστοῦ ἔχομεν.
will teach Him? we But (the) mind of Christ have.

King James Version

but which the Holy Ghost teacheth; comparing spiritual things with spiritual.
14 But the natural man receiveth not the things of the Spirit of God: for they are foolishness unto him: neither can he know (them), because they are spiritually discerned.

15 But he that is spiritual judgeth all things, yet he himself is judged of no man.
16 For who hath known the mind of the Lord, that he may instruct him? But we have the mind of Christ.

I Corinthians 3

1. And, brothers, I was not able to speak to you as to spiritual ones, but as to fleshly ones, as to babes in Christ.
2 I gave you milk to drink, and not food, for you were not then able, but neither yet are you yet able now.
3 For you are yet fleshly. For where among you (is) jealousy, and strife, and divisions, are you not fleshly and walk according to man?

4 For when one may say, Truly I am of Paul, and another, I of Apollos; are you not fleshly?
5 What then is Paul? And what (is) Apollos, but ministers through whom you believed, and to each as the Lord gave?

6 I planted, Apollos watered, but God made to grow.
7 So as neither the (one) planting is anything, nor the (one) watering, but God making to grow.
8 So the (one) planting and the (one) watering are one, and each one will receive (his) own reward according to (his) own labor.
9 For we are

1 Corinthians 3

2532 1473 80 3756 1410 2980 5213 5613 4152
1. Καὶ ἐγώ, ἀδελφοί, οὐκ ἠδυνήθην λαλῆσαι ὑμῖν ὡς πνευ-
And I, brothers, not was able to speak to you as to

235 5613 4556 5613 3516 1722 5547 1051
ματικοῖς, ἀλλ' ὡς σαρκικοῖς, ὡς νηπίοις ἐν Χριστῷ. 2 γάλα
spiritual ones, but as to fleshly, as to infants in Christ. milk

5209 4222 2532 3756 1033 3768 1063 1410 235
ὑμᾶς ἐπότισα, καὶ οὐ βρῶμα· οὔπω γὰρ ἠδύνασθε, ἀλλ'
you I gave to drink, and not food; not then for you were able, but

3777 2089 3568 1410 2089 1063 4559 2075 3699 1063 1722
οὐδὲ ἔτι νῦν δύνασθε· 3 ἔτι γὰρ σαρκικοί ἐστε· ὅπου γὰρ ἐν
neither yet now are you able; yet for fleshly you are; where for among

5213 2205 2532 2054 2532 1370 3780 4559 2075
ὑμῖν ζῆλος καὶ ἔρις καὶ διχοστασίαι, οὐχὶ σαρκικοί ἐστε,
you jealousy and strife and divisions, not fleshly you are,

2532 2596 444 4043 3752 1063 3004 5100 1473
καὶ κατὰ ἄνθρωπον περιπατεῖτε; 4 ὅταν γὰρ λέγῃ τις, Ἐγὼ
and according to man walk? when For may say one, I

3303 1510 3972 2087 1161 1473 625 3780 4559
μέν εἰμι Παύλου, ἕτερος δέ, Ἐγὼ Ἀπολλώ, οὐχὶ σαρκικοί
truly am of Paul, another and, I of Apollos, not fleshly

2075 5101 3767 2076 3972 5101 1161 625 235 2228 1249
ἐστε; 5 τίς οὖν ἐστι Παῦλος, τίς δὲ Ἀπολλώς; ἀλλ' ἢ διάκονοι
are you? What then is Paul, what and (is) Apollos? But servants

1223 3739 4100 2532 1538 5613 3588 2962 1325 1473
δι' ὧν ἐπιστεύσατε, καὶ ἑκάστῳ ὡς ὁ Κύριος ἔδωκεν; 6 ἐγὼ
through whom you believed, and to each as the Lord gave? I

5452 625 4222 235 3588 2316 837 5620
ἐφύτευσα, Ἀπολλὼς ἐπότισεν, ἀλλ' ὁ Θεὸς ηὔξανεν. 7 ὥστε
planted, Apollos watered, but God made to grow. So as

3777 3588 5452 2076 5100 3777 3588 4222 235 3588 837
οὔτε ὁ φυτεύων ἐστιν τι, οὔτε ὁ ποτίζων, ἀλλ' ὁ αὐξάνων
neither the (one) planting is anything, nor the (one) watering, but He making grow

2316 3588 5452 1161 2532 3588 4222 1722 1526 1538 1161 3588
Θεός. 8 ὁ φυτεύων δὲ καὶ ὁ ποτίζων ἕν εἰσιν· ἕκαστος δὲ τὸν
God. the (one) planting but and he watering one are; each one and the

2398 3408 2983 2596 3588 2398 2873 2316 1063
ἴδιον μισθὸν λήμψεται κατὰ τὸν ἴδιον κόπον. 9 Θεοῦ γάρ
own reward will receive according to the own labor. of God For

1 Corinthians 3

1 . And I, brethren, could not speak unto you as unto spiritual, but as unto carnal, (even) as unto babes in Christ.
2 I have fed you with milk, and not with meat: for hitherto ye were not able (to bear it), neither yet now are ye able.
3 For ye are yet carnal: for whereas (there is) among you envying, and strife, and divisions, are ye not carnal, and walk as men?

4 For while one saith, I am of Paul; and another, I (am) of Apollos; are ye not carnal?
5 Who then is Paul, and who (is) Apollos, but ministers by whom ye believed, even as the Lord gave to every man?

6 I have planted, Apollos watered; but God gave the increase.
7 So then neither is he that planteth any thing, neither he that watereth; but God that giveth the increase.
8 Now he that planteth and he that watereth are one: and every man shall receive his own reward according to his own labour.
9 For we are

1 Corinthains 3:10

Literal Translation

fellow workers of God, a field of God, (and) you are a building of God.

10 According to God's grace given to me, as a wise master builder, I laid a foundation, but another builds on (it). But let each one look how he builds on.

11 For no one is able to lay (any) other foundation beside the (One) being laid, who is Jesus the Christ.

12 And if anyone builds on this foundation gold, silver, precious stones, woods, grass, straw,

13 the work of each will be revealed; for the Day will make (it) known, because it is revealed in fire; and the fire will prove the work of each one, what sort it is.

14 If the work of anyone which he built remains, he will receive a reward.

15 If the work of anyone shall be consumed, he shall suffer loss; but he will be saved, but so as through fire.

16 Do you not know that you are a temple of God, and the Spirit of God dwells in you?
17 If anyone corrupts the temple of God, God will corrupt this one; for the temple of God is holy, which you are.

18 Let no one deceive himself, if anyone thinks to be wise among you in this age, let him become foolish, that he may become wise.
19 For the wisdom of this world is foolishness with God; for it has been written, "He is taking the wise in their (own) craftiness." (Job 5:13)
20 And again, "(The) Lord knows the reasonings

2070 4904 2316 1091 2316 3619 2075
ἐσμεν συνεργοί· Θεοῦ γεώργιον, Θεοῦ οἰκοδομή ἐστε.
we are fellow-workers; of God a field; of God a building you are.

2596 3588 5485 3588 2316 3588 1325 3427 5613 4680
10. Κατὰ τὴν χάριν τοῦ Θεοῦ τὴν δοθεῖσάν μοι, ὡς σοφὸς
According to the grace of God having been given to me, as a wise
753 2310 5087 243 1161 2026 1538
ἀρχιτέκτων θεμέλιον τέθεικα, ἄλλος δὲ ἐποικοδομεῖ. ἕκαστος
master builder a foundation I laid, another but builds on. each one
1161 991 4459 2026 2310 1063 243 3762
δὲ βλεπέτω πῶς ἐποικοδομεῖ· 11 θεμέλιον γὰρ ἄλλον οὐδεὶς
But let him look how he builds on. foundation For other no one
1410 5087 3844 3588 2749 3739 2076 2424 3588
δύναται θεῖναι παρὰ τὸν κείμενον, ὅς ἐστιν Ἰησοῦς ὁ
is able to lay beside the (One) being laid, who is Jesus the
5547 1487 1161 5100 2026 1909 3588 2310 5126
Χριστός. 12 εἰ δέ τις ἐποικοδομεῖ ἐπὶ τὸν θεμέλιον τοῦτον
Christ. if And anyone builds on foundation this
5557 696 3037 5093 3586 5528 2562
χρυσόν, ἄργυρον, λίθους τιμίους, ξύλα, χόρτον, καλάμην,
gold, silver, stones precious, woods, grass, straw,

1538 3588 2041 5318 1096 3588 1063 2250 1213
13 ἑκάστου τὸ ἔργον φανερὸν γενήσεται· ἡ γὰρ ἡμέρα δηλώσει,
of each one the work revealed will become; the for Day will reveal,
3754 1722 4442 601 2532 1538 3588 2041 3697
ὅτι ἐν πυρὶ ἀποκαλύπτεται; καὶ ἑκάστου τὸ ἔργον ὁποῖόν
because by fire it is revealed; and each one the work of what sort
2076 3588 4442 1381 1487 5100 3588 2041 3306 3739 2026
ἐστι τὸ πῦρ δοκιμάσει. 14 εἴ τινος τὸ ἔργον μενεῖ ὃ ἐπῳκοδό-
it is, the fire it will prove. If of anyone the work remains which he
3408 2983 1487 5100 3588 2041 2618
μησε, μισθὸν λήψεται. 15 εἴ τινος τὸ ἔργον κατακαήσεται,
built on, a reward he will receive. If anyone the work shall be consumed,
2210 846 1161 4982 3779 1161 5613 1223 4442
ζημιωθήσεται· αὐτὸς δὲ σωθήσεται, οὕτω δὲ ὡς διὰ πυρός.
he will suffer loss; he but will be saved, so but as through fire.

3756 1492 3754 3485 2316 2075 2532 3588 4151 3588 2316
16. οὐκ οἴδατε ὅτι ναὸς Θεοῦ ἐστε, καὶ τὸ Πνεῦμα τοῦ Θεοῦ
Do not you know that a temple of God you are, and the Spirit of God
3611 1722 5213 1487 5100 3588 3485 3588 2316 5351 5351
οἰκεῖ ἐν ὑμῖν; 17 εἴ τις τὸν ναὸν τοῦ Θεοῦ φθείρει, φθερεῖ
dwells in you? If anyone the temple of God corrupts, will corrupt
5126 3588 2316 3588 1063 3485 3588 2316 40 2076 3748
τοῦτον ὁ Θεός· ὁ γὰρ ναὸς τοῦ Θεοῦ ἅγιός ἐστιν, οἵτινές
this one God; the for temple of God holy is, who
2075 5210
ἐστε ὑμεῖς.
are you.

3367 1438 1818 1487 5100 1380 4680 1511 1722
18. Μηδεὶς ἑαυτὸν ἐξαπατάτω· εἴ τις δοκεῖ σοφὸς εἶναι ἐν
No one himself let deceive; if anyone thinks wise to be among
5213 1722 3588 165 5129 3474 1096 2443 1096 4680
ὑμῖν ἐν τῷ αἰῶνι τούτῳ, μωρὸς γενέσθω, ἵνα γένηται σοφός.
you in age this, foolish let him become, that he become wise.
3588 1063 4678 3588 2889 5127 3472 3844 3588 2316 2076
19 ἡ γὰρ σοφία τοῦ κόσμου τούτου μωρία παρὰ τῷ Θεῷ ἐστι.
the For wisdom world of this foolishness with God is.
1125 1063 3588 1405 3588 4680 1722 3588 3834
γέγραπται γάρ, Ὁ δρασσόμενος τοὺς σοφοὺς ἐν τῇ πανουρ-
it has been written For, He is taking the wise in the craftiness
846 2532 3825 2962 1097 3588 1261
γίᾳ αὐτῶν. 20 καὶ πάλιν, Κύριος γινώσκει τοὺς διαλογισμοὺς
of them. And again, (The) Lord knows the reasonings

King James Version

labourers together with God: ye are God's husbandry, (ye are) God's building.
10 According to the grace of God which is given unto me, as a wise masterbuilder, I have laid the foundation, and another buildeth thereon. But let every man take heed how he buildeth thereupon.
11 For other foundation can no man lay than that is laid, which is Jesus Christ.

12 Now if any man build upon this foundation gold, silver, precious stones, wood, hay, stubble;

13 Every man's work shall be made manifest: for the day shall declare it, because it shall be revealed by fire; and the fire shall try every man's work of what sort it is.
14 If any man's work abide which he hath built thereupon, he shall receive a reward.
15 If any man's work shall be burned, he shall suffer loss: but he himself shall be saved; yet so as by fire.

16 Know ye not that ye are the temple of God, and (that) the Spirit of God dwelleth in you?
17 If any man defile the temple of God, him shall God destroy; for the temple of God is holy, which (temple) ye are.

18 Let no man deceive himself. If any man among you seemeth to be wise in this world, let him become a fool, that he may be wise.

19 For the wisdom of this world is foolishness with God. For it is written, He taketh the wise in their own craftiness.

20 And again, The Lord knoweth the thoughts

Literal Translation — **1 Corinthians 3:21** — ***King James Version***

of the wise, that they are
worthless." (Psa. 94:
11)
21 So as let no one glory
in men; for all things are
yours,
22 whether Paul, or
Apollos, or Cephas, or
(the) world, or life, or
death, or things present,
or things to come; all
things are yours,
23 and you (are)
Christ's, and Christ (is)
God's.

3588 4680 3754 1526 3152 5620 3367 2744 1722
τῶν σοφῶν, ὅτι εἰσὶ μάταιοι. 21 ὥστε μηδεὶς καυχάσθω ἐν
of the wise, that they are worthless. So as no one let glory in
444 3956 1063 5216 2076 1535 3972 1535
ἀνθρώποις· πάντα γὰρ ὑμῶν ἐστιν, 22 εἴτε Παῦλος, εἴτε
men; all things for of you is, whether Paul, or
625 1535 2786 1535 2889 1535 2222 1535 2288
Ἀπολλῶς, εἴτε Κηφᾶς, εἴτε κόσμος, εἴτε ζωή, εἴτε θάνατος,
Apollos, or Cephas, or (the) world, or life, or death,
1535 1764 1535 3195 3956 5216 2076 5210 1161
εἴτε ἐνεστῶτα, εἴτε μέλλοντα· πάντα ὑμῶν ἐστιν, 23 ὑμεῖς δὲ
or things present, or things coming; all things of you are, you and
5547 5547 1161 2316
Χριστοῦ, Χριστὸς δὲ Θεοῦ.
of Christ, Christ and of God.

of the wise, that they are
vain.
21 Therefore let no man
glory in men. For all
things are yours;
22 Whether Paul, or
Apollos, or Cephas, or
the world, or life, or
death, or things present,
or things to come; all are
yours;
23 And ye are Christ's;
and Christ (is) God's.

I Corinthians 4 — 1 Corinthians 4 — 1 Corinthians 4

1. So let a man reckon
a man (to be) as under-
servants of Christ and
stewards of (the) mys-
teries of God.
2 And the rest, it is
sought among stewards
that one be found faith-
ful.
3 But to me it is a little
thing that I am judged
by you, or by a man's
day. But neither do I
judge myself.
4 For I know nothing in
myself, but I have not
been justified by this;
but He judging me is
(the) Lord.

5 Then do not judge
anything before time,
until the Lord shall
come, who will both
shed light on the hidden
things of darkness and
will reveal the counsels
of the hearts. And then
praise will be to each
one from God.

6 And, brothers, I trans-
ferred these things to
myself and Apollos be-
cause of you, that in us
you may learn not to
think above what has
been written, that you
not (be) puffed up one
against the other.
7 For who makes you to
differ? And what do
you have that you did
not receive? But also if
you received (it), why
do you boast as (if you)
did not receive?
8 You are already sated;

3779 2248 3049 444 5613 5257 5547
1. Οὕτως ἡμᾶς λογιζέσθω ἄνθρωπος, ὡς ὑπηρέτας Χριστοῦ
So us let count a man, as under-servants of Christ
2532 3623 3466 2316 3739 1161 3063 2212 1722
καὶ οἰκονόμους μυστηρίων Θεοῦ. 2 ὃ δὲ λοιπόν, ζητεῖται ἐν
and stewards of (the) mysteries of God. the And rest, it is sought among
3588 3623 2443 4103 5100 2147 1698 1161 1519 1646
τοῖς οἰκονόμοις, ἵνα πιστός τις εὑρεθῇ. 3 ἐμοὶ δὲ εἰς ἐλάχιστόν
the stewards, that faithful anyone be found. to me And for a little thing
2076 2443 5259 5216 350 2228 5259 442 2250
ἐστιν ἵνα ὑφ' ὑμῶν ἀνακριθῶ, ἢ ὑπὸ ἀνθρωπίνης ἡμέρας·
it is that by you I am judged, or by a man's day;
235 3761 1683 350 3762 1063 1683 4894
ἀλλ' οὐδὲ ἐμαυτὸν ἀνακρίνω. 4 οὐδὲν γὰρ ἐμαυτῷ σύνοιδα,
but neither myself I judge. nothing for in myself I know,
235 3756 1722 5129 1344 3588 1161 350 3165 2962
ἀλλ' οὐκ ἐν τούτῳ δεδικαίωμαι· ὁ δὲ ἀνακρίνων με Κύριός
but not by this have I been justified; He but judging me Lord
2076 5620 3361 4253 2540 5100 2919 2193 302 2064 3588 2962
ἐστιν. 5 ὥστε μὴ πρὸ καιροῦ τι κρίνετε, ἕως ἂν ἔλθῃ ὁ Κύριος,
is. So as not before time anything judge, until shall come the Lord,
3739 2532 5461 3588 2927 3588 4655 2532 5319
ὃς καὶ φωτίσει τὰ κρυπτὰ τοῦ σκότους, καὶ φανερώσει
who both will shed light on the hidden things of darkness, and will reveal
3588 1012 3588 2588 2532 5119 3588 1868 1096
τὰς βουλὰς τῶν καρδιῶν· καὶ τότε ὁ ἔπαινος γενήσεται
the counsels of the heart; and then the praise will be
1538 575 3588 2316
ἑκάστῳ ἀπὸ τοῦ Θεοῦ.
to each one from God.

5023 1161 80 3345 1519 1683 2532
6. Ταῦτα δέ, ἀδελφοί, μετεσχημάτισα εἰς ἐμαυτὸν καὶ
these things And, brothers, I transferred to myself and
625 1223 5209 2443 1722 2254 3129 3588 3361 5228 3739 1125
Ἀπολλὼ δι' ὑμᾶς, ἵνα ἐν ἡμῖν μάθητε τὸ μὴ ὑπὲρ ἃ γέγρα-
Apollos because of you, that in us you may learn not above what has been
5426 2443 3361 1520 5228 3588 1520 5448 2596 3588
πται φρονεῖν, ἵνα μὴ εἷς ὑπὲρ τοῦ ἑνὸς φυσιοῦσθε κατὰ τοῦ
written to think, that not one over one you are puffed up against the
2087 5101 1063 4571 1252 5101 1161 2192 3739 3756 2983 1487
ἑτέρου. 7 τίς γάρ σε διακρίνει; τί δὲ ἔχεις ὃ οὐκ ἔλαβες; εἰ
other: who For you makes differ? what And have you not you received? if
1161 2532 2983 5101 2744 5613 3361 2983 2235 2880
δὲ καὶ ἔλαβες, τί καυχᾶσαι ὡς μὴ λαβών; 8 ἤδη κεκορεσμένοι
But also you received, what boast you as not receiving? Already having been sated

1. Let a man so account
of us, as of the ministers
of Christ, and stewards
of the mysteries of God.
2 Moreover it is re-
quired in stewards, that
a man be found faithful.
3 But with me it is a very
small thing that I should
be judged of you, or of
man's judgment: yea, I
judge not mine own
self.

4 For I know nothing by
myself; yet am I not
hereby justified: but he
that judgeth me is the
Lord.
5 Therefore judge noth-
ing before the time, until
the Lord come, who
both will bring to light
the hidden things of
darkness, and will make
manifest the counsels of
the hearts: and then
shall every man have
praise of God.
6 And these things,
brethren, I have in a fig-
ure transferred to my-
self and (to) Apollos for
your sakes; that ye
might learn in us not to
think (of men) above
that which is written,
that no one of you be
puffed up for one
against another.
7 For who maketh thee
to differ (from an-
other)? and what hast
thou that thou didst not
receive? now if thou
didst receive (it), why
dost thou glory, as if
thou hadst not received
(it)?
8 Now ye are full,

Literal Translation **1 Corinthians 4:9** *King James Version*

already you became rich; you reigned without us, and oh that you really did reign, so that we also might reign with you!

9 For I think that God set us out last, the apostles, as appointed to death, because we became a spectacle to the world, even to angels and to men.
10 We (are) fools because of Christ, but you (are) prudent in Christ. We (are) weak, but you (are) strong. You (are) honored, but we not honored.
11 Until the present hour we both hunger and thirst, and are naked, and are buffeted, and wander homeless,

12 and labor, working with (our) own hands. Being cursed, we bless; persecuted, we bear;

13 being spoken evil of, we entreat; we have become as filth of the world, dirt wiped off by all until now.

14 I do not write these things shaming you, but warning (you) as my beloved children.
15 For if you should have myriads of trainers in Christ, yet not many fathers; for I fathered you in Christ Jesus through the gospel.
16 Then, I urge you, become imitators of me.

17 Because of this I sent Timothy to you, who is my beloved child, and faithful in (the) Lord, who will remind you (of) my ways in Christ, even as I teach everywhere in every church.
18 As to my not coming to you now, some were puffed up.
19 But if the Lord wills, I will come to you shortly.

2075 2235 4147 5565 2257 936 2532
ἐστε, ἤδη ἐπλουτήσατε, χωρὶς ἡμῶν ἐβασιλεύσατε· καὶ
you are, already you became rich, without us you reigned; and

3785 1065 936 2443 2532 2249 5213 4821
ὄφελόν γε ἐβασιλεύσατε· ἵνα καὶ ἡμεῖς ὑμῖν συμβασιλεύσω-
oh that really you did reign; that also we you might reign with.

1380 1063 3754 3588 2316 2248 3588 652 2078
μεν. 9 δοκῶ γὰρ ὅτι ὁ Θεὸς ἡμᾶς τοὺς ἀποστόλους ἐσχάτους
I think For that God us the apostles last

584 5613 1935 3754 2302 1096 3588
ἀπέδειξεν ὡς ἐπιθανατίους· ὅτι θέατρον ἐγενήθημεν τῷ
set out as appointed to death; because a spectacle we became to the

2889 2532 32 2532 444 2249 3474 1223
κόσμῳ, καὶ ἀγγέλοις καὶ ἀνθρώποις. 10 ἡμεῖς μωροὶ διὰ
world, even to angels and to men. We (are) fools because of

5547 5210 1161 5429 1722 5547 2249 772 5210
Χριστόν, ὑμεῖς δὲ φρόνιμοι ἐν Χριστῷ· ἡμεῖς ἀσθενεῖς, ὑμεῖς
Christ, you but prudent in Christ; we (are) weak, you

1161 2478 5210 1741 2249 1161 820 891 3588 737
δὲ ἰσχυροί· ὑμεῖς ἔνδοξοι, ἡμεῖς δὲ ἄτιμοι. 11 ἄχρι τῆς ἄρτι
but strong; you (are) honored, we but unhonored. Until the present

5610 2532 3983 2532 1372 2532 1130 2532
ὥρας καὶ πεινῶμεν καὶ διψῶμεν, καὶ γυμνιτεύομεν, καὶ
hour both we hunger, and thirst, and are naked, and

2852 2532 790 2532 2872 2038
κολαφιζόμεθα, καὶ ἀστατοῦμεν, 12 καὶ κοπιῶμεν ἐργαζόμενοι
are buffeted, and wander homeless, and labor working

3588 2398 5495 3058 2127 1377
ταῖς ἰδίαις χερσί· λοιδορούμενοι εὐλογοῦμεν, διωκόμενοι
with the own hands; being cursed we bless, being persecuted

430 987 3870 5613 4027
ἀνεχόμεθα· 13 βλασφημούμενοι παρακαλοῦμεν· ὡς περικαθάρ-
we bear; being spoken evil of we entreat; as filth

3588 2889 1096 3956 4067 2193 737
ματα τοῦ κόσμου ἐγενήθημεν, πάντων περίψημα, ἕως ἄρτι.
of the world we are become, of all dirt wiped off, until now.

3756 1788 5209 1125 5023 235 5613 5043 3450
14. Οὐκ ἐντρέπων ὑμᾶς γράφω ταῦτα, ἀλλ' ὡς τέκνα μου
Not shaming you I write these things, but as children of me

27 3560 1437 1063 3463 3807 2192 1722
ἀγαπητὰ νουθετῶ. 15 ἐὰν γὰρ μυρίους παιδαγωγοὺς ἔχητε ἐν
beloved warning. if For myriads of trainers you have in

5547 235 3756 4183 3962 1722 1063 5547 2424
Χριστῷ, ἀλλ' οὐ πολλοὺς πατέρας· ἐν γὰρ Χριστῷ Ἰησοῦ
Christ, but not many fathers; in for Christ Jesus

1223 3588 2098 1473 5209 1080 3870 3767
διὰ τοῦ εὐαγγελίου ἐγὼ ὑμᾶς ἐγέννησα. 16 παρακαλῶ οὖν
through the gospel I you fathered. I urge then

5209 3402 3450 1096 1223 5124 3992 5213 5095
ὑμᾶς, μιμηταί μου γίνεσθε. 17 διὰ τοῦτο ἔπεμψα ὑμῖν Τιμόθεον,
you, imitators of me you become. Because of this I sent to you Timothy,

3739 2076 5043 3450 27 2532 4103 1722 2962 3739 5209
ὅς ἐστίν τέκνον μου ἀγαπητὸν καὶ πιστὸν ἐν Κυρίῳ, ὃς ὑμᾶς
who is a child of me beloved and faithful in (the) Lord, who you

363 3588 3598 3450 3588 1722 5547 2531 3837
ἀναμνήσει τὰς ὁδούς μου τὰς ἐν Χριστῷ, καθὼς πανταχοῦ
will remind of the ways of me in Christ, even as everywhere

1722 3956 1577 1321 5613 3361 2064 1161 3450 4314
ἐν πάσῃ ἐκκλησίᾳ διδάσκω. 18 ὡς μὴ ἐρχομένου δέ μου πρὸς
in every church I teach. as for not coming And me to

5209 5448 5100 2064 1161 5030 4314 5209
ὑμᾶς ἐφυσιώθησάν τινες. 19 ἐλεύσομαι δὲ ταχέως πρὸς ὑμᾶς,
you were puffed up some. I will come But shortly to you,

now ye are rich, ye have reigned as kings without us: and I would to God ye did reign, that we also might reign with you.

9 For I think that God hath set forth us the apostles last, as it were appointed to death: for we are made a spectacle unto the world, and to angels, and to men.
10 We (are) fools for Christ's sake, but ye (are) wise in Christ; we (are) weak, but ye (are) strong; ye (are) honourable, but we (are) despised.
11 Even unto this present hour we both hunger, and thirst, and are naked, and are buffeted, and have no certain dwellingplace;

12 And labour, working with our own hands: being reviled, we bless; being persecuted, we suffer it:

13 Being defamed, we intreat: we are made as the filth of the world, (and are) the offscouring of all things unto this day.

14 I write not these things to shame you, but as my beloved sons I warn (you).
15 For though ye have ten thousand instructors in Christ, yet (have ye) not many fathers: for in Christ Jesus I have begotten you through the gospel.
16 Wherefore I beseech you, be ye followers of me.
17 For this cause have I sent unto you Timotheus, who is my beloved son, and faithful in the Lord, who shall bring you into remembrance of my ways which be in Christ, as I teach every where in every church.
18 Now some are puffed up, as though I would not come to you.
19 But I will come to you shortly,

Literal Translation

And I will not know the word of those who have been puffed up, but the power.
20 For the kingdom of God (is) not in word, but in power.
21 What do you desire? (Shall) I come to you with a rod, or (in) love and a spirit of meekness?

1 Corinthians 4:20

1437 3588 2962 2309 2532 1097 3756 3588 3056 3588
ἐὰν ὁ Κύριος θελήσῃ, καὶ γνώσομαι οὐ τὸν λόγον τῶν
if the Lord wills, and I will know not the word of those

5448 235 3588 1411 3756 1063 1722 3056 3588
πεφυσιωμένων, ἀλλὰ τὴν δύναμιν. 20 οὐ γὰρ ἐν λόγῳ ἡ
having been puffed up, but the power. not For in word the

932 3588 2316 235 1722 1411 5101 2309 1722 4464
βασιλεία τοῦ Θεοῦ, ἀλλ' ἐν δυνάμει. 21 τί θέλετε; ἐν ῥάβδῳ
kingdon of God, but in power. What desire you? With a rod

2064 4314 5209 2228 1722 26 4151 5037 4236
ἔλθω πρὸς ὑμᾶς, ἢ ἐν ἀγάπῃ πνεύματί τε πραΰτητος;
I come to you, or in love a spirit and of meekness?

King James Version

if the Lord will, and will know, not the speech of them which are puffed up, but the power.
20 For the kingdom of God (is) not in word, but in power.
21 What will ye? shall I come unto you with a rod, or in love, and (in) the spirit of meekness?

I Corinthians 5

1. Everywhere (it is) heard (that) fornication (is) among you, and such fornication which (is) not named among the nations, so as one to have (his) father's wife.
2 And you have been puffed up, and have not rather mourned, that the (one) that did this deed might be taken from your midst.

3 For indeed I being absent in body, but being present in spirit, (I) have already judged the (one) who has worked out this, as (if I were) present.
4 In the name of our Lord Jesus Christ, you being gathered together with my spirit also, with the power of our Lord Jesus Christ,

5 to deliver such a one to Satan for destruction of the flesh, that the spirit may be saved in the day of the Lord Jesus.

6 Your boast (is) not good. Do you not know that a little leaven leavens all the lump?

7 Then purge out the old leaven so that you may be a new lump, even as you are unleavened. For also Christ our Passover was sacrificed on our behalf.
8 So let us keep (the) feast, not with old leaven, nor with leaven of malice and of evil, but with unleavened (bread) of

1 Corinthians 5

3654 191 1722 5213 4202 2532 5108 4202
1. Ὅλως ἀκούεται ἐν ὑμῖν πορνεία, καὶ τοιαύτη πορνεία
Everywhere (it) is heard among you fornication, and such fornication

3748 3761 1722 3588 1484 3687 5620 1135 5100
ἥτις οὐδὲ ἐν τοῖς ἔθνεσιν ὀνομάζεται, ὥστε γυναῖκά τινα
which (is) not among the nations named, so as (the) wife someone

3588 3962 2192 2532 5210 5448 2075 2532 3780
τοῦ πατρὸς ἔχειν. 2 καὶ ὑμεῖς πεφυσιωμένοι ἐστέ, καὶ οὐχὶ
of the father to have. And you having been puffed up are, and not

3123 3996 2443 1808 1537 3319 5216 3588 3588 2041
μᾶλλον ἐπενθήσατε, ἵνα ἐξαρθῇ ἐκ μέσου ὑμῶν ὁ τὸ ἔργον
rather mourned, that might be taken from your midst the (one) deed

5124 4160 1473 3303 1063 5613 548 3588 4983 3918
τοῦτο ποιήσας. 3 ἐγὼ μὲν γάρ ὡς ἀπὼν τῷ σώματι παρὼν
this having done. I indeed For being absent in the body being present

1161 3588 4151 2235 2919 5613 3918 3588 3779 5124
δὲ τῷ πνεύματι, ἤδη κέκρικα ὡς παρὼν τὸν οὕτω τοῦτο
but in the spirit, already have judged as being present the (one) thus this

2716 1722 3588 3686 3588 2962 2257 2424
κατεργασάμενον, 4 ἐν τῷ ὀνόματι τοῦ Κυρίου ἡμῶν Ἰησοῦ
having worked out, in the name of the Lord of us Jesus

5547 4863 5216 2532 3588 1700 4151 4862
Χριστοῦ, συναχθέντων ὑμῶν καὶ τοῦ ἐμοῦ πνεύματος, σὺν
Christ, being assembled you also the of me spirit, with

3588 1411 3588 2962 2257 2424 5547 3860
τῇ δυνάμει τοῦ Κυρίου ἡμῶν Ἰησοῦ Χριστοῦ, 5 παραδοῦναι
the power of the Lord of us Jesus Christ, to deliver

3588 5108 3588 4567 1519 3639 3588 4561 2443 3588
τὸν τοιοῦτον τῷ Σατανᾷ εἰς ὄλεθρον τῆς σαρκός, ἵνα τὸ
such a one to Satan for destruction of the flesh, that the

4151 4982 1722 3588 2250 3588 2962 2424 3756 2570 3588
πνεῦμα σωθῇ ἐν τῇ ἡμέρᾳ τοῦ Κυρίου Ἰησοῦ. 6 Οὐ καλὸν τὸ
spirit may be saved in the day of the Lord Jesus. Not good (is) the

2745 5216 3756 1492 3754 3398 2219 3650 3588 5445
καύχημα ὑμῶν. οὐκ οἴδατε ὅτι μικρὰ ζύμη ὅλον τὸ φύραμα
boast of you. Do not you know that a little leaven all the lump

2220 1571 3767 3588 3820 2219 2443 5600 3501
ζυμοῖ; 7 ἐκκαθάρατε οὖν τὴν παλαιὰν ζύμην, ἵνα ἦτε νέον
leavens? purge out Then the old leaven, that you be a new

5445 2531 2075 106 2532 1063 3588 3957 2257 5228
φύραμα, καθώς ἐστε ἄζυμοι. καὶ γὰρ τὸ πάσχα ἡμῶν ὑπὲρ
lump, as you are unleavened. also For the Passover of us for

2257 2380 5547 5620 1858 3361 1722 2219 3820
ἡμῶν ἐθύθη Χριστός· 8 ὥστε ἑορτάζωμεν, μὴ ἐν ζύμῃ παλαιᾷ,
us was sacrificed Christ; so as let us keep feast, not with leaven old,

3366 1722 2219 2549 2532 4189 235 1722 106
μηδὲ ἐν ζύμῃ κακίας καὶ πονηρίας, ἀλλ' ἐν ἀζύμοις εἰλι-
not with leaven of malice and of evil, but with unleavened of

1 Corinthians 5

1. It is reported commonly (that there is) fornication among you, and such fornication as is not so much as named among the Gentiles, that one should have his father's wife.
2 And ye are puffed up, and have not rather mourned, that he that hath done this deed might be taken away from among you.
3 For I verily, as absent in body, but present in spirit, have judged already, as though I were present, (concerning) him that hath so done this deed,
4 In the name of our Lord Jesus Christ, when ye are gathered together, and my spirit, with the power of our Lord Jesus Christ,

5 To deliver such an one unto Satan for the destruction of the flesh, that the spirit may be saved in the day of the Lord Jesus.

6 Your glorying (is) not good. Know ye not that a little leaven leaveneth the whole lump?

7 Purge out therefore the old leaven, that ye may be a new lump, as ye are unleavened. For even Christ our passover is sacrificed for us:
8 Therefore let us keep the feast, not with old leaven, neither with the leaven of malice and wickedness; but with the unleavened (bread) of

Literal Translation

sincerity and truth.

9 I wrote to you in the
letter not to associate in-
timately with fornica-
tors;
10 and not altogether
with the fornicators of
this world, or with the
covetous, or with plun-
derers, or with idolaters,
since then you must go
out of the world.
11 But now I wrote to
you not to associate in-
timately; if anyone is
named a brother (and is)
either a fornicator, or a
covetous one, or an
idolater, or a reviler, or a
drunkard, or a plun-
derer, with such a one
not to eat.
12 For what (is it) to me
also to judge the ones
outside? Do you not
judge those inside?
13 But God will judge
the (ones) outside. And
you shall put out the evil
one from you.
(Deut.17:7)'

1 Corinthians 5:9

1505 2532 225
κρινείας καὶ ἀληθείας.
sincerity and truth.

1125 5213 1722 3588 1992 3361 4874
9. Ἔγραψα ὑμῖν ἐν τῇ ἐπιστολῇ μὴ συναναμίγνυσθαι
I wrote to you in the epistle not to associate intimately

4205 2532 3756 3843 3588 4205 3588 2889 5127
πόρνοις· 10 καὶ οὐ πάντως τοῖς πόρνοις τοῦ κόσμου τούτου,
with fornicators; and not altogether with the fornicators world of this,

2228 3588 4123 2228 727 2228 1496 1893
ἢ τοῖς πλεονέκταις, ἢ ἅρπαξιν, ἢ εἰδωλολάτραις· ἐπεὶ
or with the covetous, or with plunderers, or with idolaters; since

3784 686 1537 3588 2889 1831 3570 1161 1125 5213
ὀφείλετε ἄρα ἐκ τοῦ κόσμου ἐξελθεῖν. 11 νυνὶ δὲ ἔγραψα ὑμῖν
you ought then out of the world to go out. now But I wrote to you

3361 4874 1437 5100 80 3687 2228
μὴ συναναμίγνυσθαι, ἐάν τις ἀδελφὸς ὀνομαζόμενος ᾖ
not to associate intimately, if anyone a brother being named (is) either

4205 2228 4123 2228 1496 2228 3060 2228
πόρνος, ἢ πλεονέκτης, ἢ εἰδωλολάτρης, ἢ λοίδορος, ἢ
a fornicator, or a covetous one, or an idolater, or a reviler, or

3183 2228 727 3588 5108 3366 4906 5101 1063 3427
μέθυσος, ἢ ἅρπαξ· τῷ τοιούτῳ μηδὲ συνεσθίειν. 12 τί γάρ μοι
a drunkard, or a plunderer; with such a one not to eat. what For to me

2532 3588 1854 2919 3780 3588 2080 5210 2919 3588 1161
καὶ τοὺς ἔξω κρίνειν; οὐχὶ τοὺς ἔσω ὑμεῖς κρίνετε; 13 τοὺς δὲ
also the ones outside to judge? Not those inside you judge? the (ones) But

1854 3588 2316 2919 2532 1808 3588 4190 1537 5216 846
ἔξω ὁ Θεὸς κρινεῖ. καὶ ἐξάρεῖτε τὸν πονηρὸν ἐξ ὑμῶν αὐτῶν.
outside God will judge. And you shall put out the evil one from yourselves.

King James Version

sincerity and truth.

9 I wrote unto you in an
epistle not to company
with fornicators:
10 Yet not altogether
with the fornicators of
this world, or with the
covetous, or extortion-
ers, or with idolaters; for
then must ye needs go
out of the world.
11 But now I have writ-
ten unto you not to keep
company, if any man
that is called a brother
be a fornicator, or cov-
etous, or an idolater, or
a railer, or a drunkard, or
an extortioner; with
such an one no not to
eat.
12 For what have I to do
to judge them also that
are without? do not ye
judge them that are
within?
13 But them that are
without God judgeth.
Therefore put away
from among yourselves
that wicked person.

1 Corinthians 6

Literal Translation

1. Does anyone of you
having a matter against
another dare to be
judged before the un-
just, and not before the
saints?
2 Do you not know that
the saints will judge the
world? And if the world
is judged by you, are
you unworthy of small
judgments?
3 Do you not know that
we shall judge angels,
not (to speak) of this
life?
4 If, then, truly you have
judgments of this life,
those being least es-
teemed in the church,
you sit these
.**5** For I speak shame to
you. So, is there not a
wise one among you,
not even one who will
be able to discern his
brother in your midst?
6 But brother is judged
with brother, and this
before unbelievers!
7 Truly, then, there is al-
ready a failure with you
all,

5111 5100 5216 4229 2192 4314 3588 2087 2919
1. Τολμᾷ τις ὑμῶν, πρᾶγμα ἔχων πρὸς τὸν ἕτερον, κρίνεσθαι
Dares anyone of you, a matter having against the other, to be judged

1909 3588 94 2532 3780 1909 3588 40 3756 1492 3754 3588
ἐπὶ τῶν ἀδίκων, καὶ οὐχὶ ἐπὶ τῶν ἁγίων; 2 οὐκ οἴδατε ὅτι οἱ
before the unjust, and not before the saints? Do not you know that the

40 3588 2889 2919 2532 1487 1722 5213 2919 3588 2889
ἅγιοι τὸν κόσμον κρινοῦσι; καὶ εἰ ἐν ὑμῖν κρίνεται ὁ κόσμος,
saints the world will judge? And if by you is judged the world,

370 2075 2922 1646 3756 1492 3754 32
ἀνάξιοί ἐστε κριτηρίων ἐλαχίστων; 3 οὐκ οἴδατε ὅτι ἀγγέ-
unworthy are you judgments of small? Do not you know that angels

2919 3385 1065 982 982 3303 3767 2922
λους κρινοῦμεν; μήτι γε βιωτικά; 4 βιωτικὰ μὲν οὖν κριτήρια
we will judge? Not (to speak) of this life? Of this life truly then judgments

1437 2192 3588 1848 1722 3588 1577 5128
ἐὰν ἔχητε, τοὺς ἐξουθενημένους ἐν τῇ ἐκκλησίᾳ, τούτους
if you have, the ones being least esteemed in the church, these

2523 4314 1791 5213 3004 3779 3756 2076 1722
καθίζετε. 5 πρὸς ἐντροπὴν ὑμῖν λέγω. οὕτως οὐκ ἔστιν ἐν
sit you. For shame to you I say. So not is among

5213 4680 3761 1520 3739 1410 1252 303 3319 3588
ὑμῖν σοφὸς οὐδὲ εἷς, ὃς δυνήσεται διακρῖναι ἀνὰ μέσον τοῦ
you a wise one not even one, who will be able to discern in your midst the

80 846 235 80 3326 80 2919 2532
ἀδελφοῦ αὐτοῦ; 6 ἀλλὰ ἀδελφὸς μετὰ ἀδελφοῦ κρίνεται, καὶ
brother of him? But brother with brother is judged, and

5124 1909 571 2235 3303 3767 3654 2275 1722 5213 2076
τοῦτο ἐπὶ ἀπίστων; 7 ἤδη μὲν οὖν ὅλως ἥττημα ἐν ὑμῖν ἐστιν,
this before unbelievers? Already truly then all a failure with you is,

King James Version

1. Dare any of you,
having a matter against
another, go to law before
the unjust, and not be-
fore the saints?
2 Do ye not know that
the saints shall judge the
world? and if the world
shall be judged by you,
are ye unworthy to
judge the smallest mat-
ters?
3 Know ye not that we
shall judge angels? how
much more things that
pertain to this life?
4 If then ye have judg-
ments of things pertain-
ing to this life, set them
to judge who are least
esteemed in the church.
5 I speak to your shame.
Is it so, that there is not
a wise man among you?
no, not one that shall be
able to judge between
his brethren?
6 But brother goeth to
law with brother, and
that before the unbe-
lievers.
7 Now therefore there is
utterly a fault among
you,

1 Corinthians 6:8

Literal Translation

that you have lawsuits with yourselves. Why not instead be wronged? Why not instead be despoiled?
8 But you do wrong, and despoil, and these things (to) brothers!
9 Or do you not know that unjust ones will not inherit (the) kingdom of God? Do not be led astray, neither fornicators, nor idolaters, nor adulterers, nor abusers, nor homosexuals,

10 nor thieves, nor covetous ones, not drunkards, not revilers, not plunderers shall inherit (the) kingdom of God.

11 And some were these things, but you were washed, but you were sanctified, but you were justified in the name of the Lord Jesus, , and in the Spirit of our God.

12 All things (are) lawful to me, but not all things profit. All things (are) lawful to me, but I will not be ruled by any.
13 Foods for the belly, and the belly for foods, but God will destroy both this and these things. But the body (is) not for fornication, but for the Lord, and the Lord for the body.

14 And God both raised up the Lord, and (He) will raise up us through His power.

15 Do you not know that your bodies are members of Christ? Then having taken the members of Christ, shall I make (them) members of a harlot? Let it not be!
16 Or do you not know that he being joined to a harlot is one body? For He says, "The two (shall be) into one flesh." (Gen.2:24)
17 But he being joined to the Lord is one spirit.
18 Flee

3754 2917 2192 3326 1438 1302 3780 3123 91
ὅτι κρίματα ἔχετε μεθ᾽ ἑαυτῶν. διατί οὐχὶ μᾶλλον ἀδικεῖσθε;
that lawsuits you have with yourselves. Why not instead be wronged?

1302 3780 3123 650 235 5210 91 2532
διατί οὐχὶ μᾶλλον ἀποστερεῖσθε; 8 ἀλλὰ ὑμεῖς ἀδικεῖτε καὶ
Why not instead be despoiled? But you do wrong and

650 2532 5023 80 2228 3756 1492 3754 94
ἀποστερεῖτε, καὶ ταῦτα ἀδελφούς. 9 ἢ οὐκ οἴδατε ὅτι ἄδικοι
despoil, and these things (to) brothers. Or not you know that the unjust

932 2316 3756 2816 3361 4105 3777
βασιλείαν Θεοῦ οὐ κληρονομήσουσι; μὴ πλανᾶσθε· οὔτε
(the) kingdom of God not will inherit? not Be led astray; not

4205 3777 1496 3777 3432 3777 3120 3777
πόρνοι, οὔτε εἰδωλολάτραι, οὔτε μοιχοὶ, οὔτε μαλακοὶ, οὔτε
fornicators, nor idolaters, nor adulterers, nor effeminate, nor

733 3777 2812 3777 4123 3756 3183
ἀρσενοκοῖται, 10 οὔτε κλέπται, οὔτε πλεονέκται, οὔτε μέθυσοι,
homosexuals, nor thieves, nor covetous ones, nor drunkards,

3756 3060 3756 727 932 2316 3756 2816
οὐ λοίδοροι, οὐχ ἅρπαγες, βασιλείαν Θεοῦ οὐ κληρονομή-
not revilers, not plunderers, (the) kingdom of God not shall inherit.

2532 5023 5100 2258 235 628 235
σουσι. 11 καὶ ταῦτά τινες ἦτε· ἀλλὰ ἀπελούσασθε, ἀλλὰ
And these things some were; but you were washed, but

37 235 1344 1722 3588 3686 3588 2962
ἡγιάσθητε, ἀλλ᾽ ἐδικαιώθητε ἐν τῷ ὀνόματι τοῦ Κυρίου
you were sanctified, but you were justified in the name of the Lord

2424 2532 1722 3588 4151 3588 2316 2257
Ἰησοῦ, καὶ ἐν τῷ Πνεύματι τοῦ Θεοῦ ἡμῶν.
Jesus, and in the Spirit of the God of us.

3956 3427 1832 235 3756 3956 4851 3956 3427
12. Πάντα μοι ἔξεστιν, ἀλλ᾽ οὐ πάντα συμφέρει· πάντα μοι
All things to me (are) lawful, but not all things profit; all things to me

1832 235 3756 1473 1850 5259 5100 3588
ἔξεστιν, ἀλλ᾽ οὐκ ἐγὼ ἐξουσιασθήσομαι ὑπό τινος. 13 τὰ
(are) lawful, but not I will be ruled by any.

1033 3588 2836 2532 3588 2836 3588 1033 3588 1161 2316
βρώματα τῇ κοιλίᾳ, καὶ ἡ κοιλία τοῖς βρώμασιν· ὁ δὲ Θεὸς
Foods for the belly, and the belly for foods; but God

2532 3778 2532 5023 2673 3588 1161 4983 3756 3588
καὶ ταύτην καὶ ταῦτα καταργήσει. τὸ δὲ σῶμα οὐ τῇ
both this and these things will destroy. the But body not (is)

4202 235 3588 2962 2532 3588 2962 3588 4983 3588 1161
πορνείᾳ, ἀλλὰ τῷ Κυρίῳ, καὶ ὁ Κύριος τῷ σώματι· 14 ὁ δὲ
for fornication, but for the Lord, and the Lord for the body; and

2316 2532 3588 2962 1453 2532 2248 1825 1223 3588
Θεὸς καὶ τὸν Κύριον ἤγειρε, καὶ ἡμᾶς ἐξεγερεῖ διὰ τῆς
God also the Lord raised, and us will raise up through the

1411 846 3756 1492 3754 3588 4983 5216 3196
δυνάμεως αὐτοῦ. 15 οὐκ οἴδατε ὅτι τὰ σώματα ὑμῶν μέλη
power of Him. Do not you know that the bodies of you members

5547 2076 142 3767 3588 3196 3588 5547 4160
Χριστοῦ ἐστιν; ἄρας οὖν τὰ μέλη τοῦ Χριστοῦ ποιήσω
of Christ are? having taken Then the members of Christ shall I make

4204 3196 3361 1096 2228 3756 1492 3754 3588 2853 3588
πόρνης μέλη; μὴ γένοιτο. 16 ἢ οὐκ οἴδατε ὅτι ὁ κολλώμενος τῇ
of a harlot members? Not let it be! Or not you know that the (one) being joined

4204 1722 4983 2076 2071 1063 5346 3588 1417 1519 4561
πόρνῃ ἓν σῶμά ἐστιν; Ἔσονται γάρ, φησίν, οἱ δύο εἰς σάρκα
to a harlot one body is? will be For, He says, the two into flesh

3391 3588 1161 2853 3588 2962 1722 4151 2076 5343
μίαν. 17 ὁ δὲ κολλώμενος τῷ Κυρίῳ ἓν πνεῦμά ἐστι. 18 φεύγετε
one. the (one) But being joined to the Lord one spirit is. Flee

King James Version

because ye go to law one with another. Why do ye not rather take wrong? why do ye not rather (suffer yourselves to) be defrauded?
8 Nay, ye do wrong, and defraud, and that (your) brethren.
9 Know ye not that the unrighteous shall not inherit the kingdom of God? Be not deceived: neither fornicators, nor idolaters, nor adulterers, nor effeminate, nor abusers of themselves with mankind,

10 Nor thieves, nor covetous, nor drunkards, nor revilers, nor extortioners, shall inherit the kingdom of God.

11 And such were some of you: but ye are washed, but ye are sanctified, but ye are justified in the name of the Lord Jesus, and by the Spirit of our God.

12 All things are lawful unto me, but all things are not expedient: all things are lawful for me, but I will not be brought under the power of any.
13 Meats for the belly, and the belly for meats: but God shall destroy both it and them. Now the body (is) not for fornication, but for the Lord; and the Lord for the body.
14 And God hath both raised up the Lord, and will also raise up us by his own power.

15 Know ye not that your bodies are the members of Christ? shall I then take the members of Christ, and make (them) the members of an harlot? God forbid.
16 What? know ye not that he which is joined to an harlot is one body? for two, saith he, shall be one flesh.
17 But he that is joined unto the Lord is one spirit.
18 Flee

Literal Translation

fornication. Every sin which a man may do is outside the body, but he doing fornication sins against (his) own body.

19 Or do you not know that your body is a temple of (the) Holy Spirit, in you, which you have from God, and you are not of yourselves?

20 For you were bought with a price; then glorify God in your body, and in your spirit, which are of God.

1 Corinthians 6:19

3588 4202 3956 265 3739 1437 4160 444 1622
τὴν πορνείαν. πᾶν ἁμάρτημα ὃ ἐὰν ποιήσῃ ἄνθρωπος ἐκτὸς
fornication. Every sin which if may do a man outside

3588 4983 2076 3588 1161 4203 1519 3588 2398 4983
τοῦ σώματός ἐστιν· ὁ δὲ πορνεύων εἰς τὸ ἴδιον σῶμα
the body is; the (one) but doing fornication against the own body

5719 2228 3756 1492 3754 3588 4983 5216 3485 3588 1722 5213
ἁμαρτάνει. 19 ἢ οὐκ οἴδατε ὅτι τὸ σῶμα ὑμῶν ναὸς τοῦ ἐν ὑμῖν
sins. Or not you know that the body of you a temple of the in you

40 4151 2076 3739 2192 575 2316 2532 3756 2076
Ἁγίου Πνεύματός ἐστιν, οὗ ἔχετε ἀπὸ Θεοῦ, καὶ οὐκ ἐστὲ
Holy Spirit is, which you have from God, and not are you

1438 59 1063 5092 1392 1211 3588 2316 1722 3588
ἑαυτῶν, 20 ἠγοράσθητε γὰρ τιμῆς· δοξάσατε δὴ τὸν Θεὸν ἐν τῷ
of yourselves, you were bought for of a price; glorify then God in the

4983 5216 2532 1722 3588 4151 5216 3748 2076 3588 2316
σώματι ὑμῶν, καὶ ἐν τῷ πνεύματι ὑμῶν, ἅτινά ἐστι τοῦ θεοῦ.
body of you, and in the spirit of you, which are of God.

King James Version

fornication. Every sin that a man doeth is without the body; but he that committeth fornication sinneth against his own body.

19 What? know ye not that your body is the temple of the Holy Ghost (which is) in you, which ye have of God, and ye are not your own?

20 For ye are bought with a price: therefore glorify God in your body, and in your spirit, which are God's.

1 Corinthians 7

1. But concerning what you wrote to me, (it is) good for a man not to touch a woman;
2 but because of fornication, let each have his (own) wife, and let each have (her) own husband.
3 Let the husband give due kindness to the wife, and likewise the wife also to the husband.
4 The wife does not have authority of (her) own body, but the husband. And likewise also the husband does not have authority (over his) own body, but the wife.
5 Do not deprive one another, unless by agreement for a time, that you may be free for fasting and for prayer. And come together again on the same (place), that Satan may not tempt you through your incontinence.
6 But I say this by permission, not by command.

7 But I desire all men also to be as myself. But each has (his) own gift from God, one this way, and another this way.

8 But I say to the unmarried men, and to the widows, it is good for them

1 Corinthians 7

4012 1161 3739 1125 3427 2570 444 1135 3361
1. Περὶ δὲ ὧν ἐγράψατε μοι, καλὸν ἀνθρώπῳ γυναικὸς μὴ
concerning But what you wrote to me, (it is) good for a man a woman not

680 1223 1161 3588 4202 1538 3588 1438 1135
ἅπτεσθαι. 2 διὰ δὲ τὰς πορνείας ἕκαστος τὴν ἑαυτοῦ γυναῖκα
to touch. because of But the fornications each one the of himself wife

2192 2532 1538 3588 2398 435 2192 3588 1135 3588 435
ἐχέτω, καὶ ἑκάστη τὸν ἴδιον ἄνδρα ἐχέτω. 3 τῇ γυναικὶ ὁ ἀνὴρ
have; and each one the own husband have. To the wife the husband

3588 3784 2133 591 3668 1161 2532 3588 1135
τὴν ὀφειλομένην εὔνοιαν ἀποδιδότω· ὁμοίως δὲ καὶ ἡ γυνὴ
due kindness let give; likewise and also the wife

3588 435 3588 1135 3588 2398 4983 3756 1850 235
τῷ ἀνδρί. 4 ἡ γυνὴ τοῦ ἰδίου σώματος οὐκ ἐξουσιάζει, ἀλλ'
the husband. The wife of the own body not has authority, but

3588 435 3668 1161 2532 3588 435 3588 2398 4983 3756 1850
ὁ ἀνήρ· ὁμοίως δὲ καὶ ὁ ἀνὴρ τοῦ ἰδίου σώματος οὐκ ἐξου-
the husband; likewise and also the husband the own body no has

235 3588 1135 3361 650 240 1487 3361 5100 302
σιάζει, ἀλλ' ἡ γυνή. 5 μὴ ἀποστερεῖτε ἀλλήλους, εἰ μή τι ἂν
authority, but the wife. Not do deprive one another, unless may (be)

1537 4859 4314 2540 2443 4980 3588 3521 2532
ἐκ συμφώνου πρὸς καιρόν, ἵνα σχολάζητε τῇ νηστείᾳ καὶ
from agreement for a time, that you may be free for fasting and

3588 4335 2532 3825 1909 3588 846 4905 2443 3361
τῇ προσευχῇ, καὶ πάλιν ἐπὶ τὸ αὐτὸ συνέρχησθε, ἵνα μὴ
for prayer, and again on the same come together, that not

3985 5209 3588 4567 1223 3588 192 5216 5124 1161
πειράζῃ ὑμᾶς ὁ Σατανᾶς διὰ τὴν ἀκρασίαν ὑμῶν. 6 τοῦτο δὲ
may tempt you Satan through the incontinence of you. this And

3004 2596 4774 3756 2596 2003 2309 1063
λέγω κατὰ συγγνώμην, οὐ κατ' ἐπιταγήν. 7 θέλω γὰρ
I say by permission, not by command. I desire For

3956 444 1511 5613 2532 1683 235 1538 2398
πάντας ἀνθρώπους εἶναι ὡς καὶ ἐμαυτόν· ἀλλ' ἕκαστος ἴδιον
all men to be as also myself; but each one (the) own

5486 2192 1537 2316 3739 3303 3779 3739 1161 3779
χάρισμα ἔχει ἐκ Θεοῦ, ὃς μὲν οὕτως, ὃς δὲ οὕτως.
gift has from God, one this way, one and that way.

3004 1161 3588 22 2532 3588 5503 2570 846
8. Λέγω δὲ τοῖς ἀγάμοις καὶ ταῖς χήραις, καλὸν αὐτοῖς
I say And to the unmarried men and to the widows, good for them

1 Corinthians 7

1. Now concerning the things whereof ye wrote unto me: (It is) good for a man not to touch a woman.
2 Nevertheless, (to avoid) fornication, let every man have his own wife, and let every woman have her own husband.
3 Let the husband render unto the wife due benevolence: and likewise also the wife unto the husband.
4 The wife hath not power of her own body, but the husband: and likewise also the husband hath not power of his own body, but the wife.
5 Defraud ye not one the other, except (it be) with consent for a time, that ye may give yourselves to fasting and prayer; and come together again, that Satan tempt you not for your incontinency.
6 But I speak this by permission, (and) not of commandment.
7 For I would that all men were even as I myself. But every man hath his proper gift of God, one after this manner, and another after that.

8 I say therefore to the unmarried and widows, It is good for them

Literal Translation

1 Corinthians 7:9

if they also remain as I.
9 But if they do not have self control, let them marry; for it is better to marry than to be inflamed.

10 But I enjoin the ones having married, not I, but the Lord, a woman not to be separated from (her) husband;
11 but if indeed she is separated, remain unmarried, or be reconciled to the husband; and a husband not to leave (his) wife.
12 But to the rest I say, not the Lord, if any brother has an unbelieving wife, and she consents to live with him, let him not leave her.
13 And a woman who has an unbelieving husband, and he consents to live with her, let her not leave him.

14 For the unbelieving husband has been sanctified by the wife, and the unbelieving wife has been sanctified by the husband; else, then, your children are unclean, but now they are holy.
15 But if the unbelieving one separates, let (them) be separated; the brother or the sister is not in bondage in such (cases); but God has called us in peace.
16 For what do you know, wife, whether you will save the husband? Or what do you know, husband, whether you will save the wife?
17 Only as God has divided to each, each as the Lord has called, so let him walk. So I command in the churches.
18 (Was) anyone called having been circumcised? Do not be uncircumcised. Was anyone called in uncircumcision? Do not be circumcised.
19 Circumcision is nothing, and uncircumcision is nothing, but the keeping of God's commands.

2076 1437 3306 5613 2504 1487 1161 3756 1467
ἐστιν ἐὰν μείνωσιν ὡς κἀγώ· 9 εἰ δὲ οὐκ ἐγκρατεύονται,
it is if they remain as I also; if but not have self-control,

1060 2908 1063 2076 1060 2228 4448
γαμησάτωσαν· κρεῖσσον γάρ ἐστι γαμῆσαι ἢ πυροῦσθαι.
let them marry; better for it is to marry than to be inflamed.

3588 1161 1060 3853 3756 1473 235 3588 2962
10 τοῖς δὲ γεγαμηκόσι παραγγέλλω, οὐκ ἐγώ, ἀλλ' ὁ Κύριος,
to those But having married I enjoin, not I, but the Lord,

1135 575 435 3361 5563 1437 1161 2532 5563
γυναῖκα ἀπὸ ἀνδρὸς μὴ χωρισθῆναι 11 [ἐὰν δὲ καὶ χωρισθῇ,
a woman from (her) husband not to be separated. if But indeed she is separated,

3306 22 2228 3588 435 2644 2532 435
μενέτω ἄγαμος, ἢ τῷ ἀνδρὶ καταλλαγήτω]· καὶ ἄνδρα
remain unmarried, or to the husband be reconciled; and a husband

1135 3361 863 3588 1161 3062 1473 3004 3756 3588
γυναῖκα μὴ ἀφιέναι. 12 τοῖς δὲ λοιποῖς ἐγὼ λέγω, οὐχ ὁ
(his) wife not to leave. to the But rest I say, not the

2962 1487 5100 80 1135 2192 571 2532 846
Κύριος· εἴ τις ἀδελφὸς γυναῖκα ἔχει ἄπιστον, καὶ αὐτὴ
Lord; if any brother a wife has unbelieving, and she

4909 3611 3326 846 3361 863 846 2532 2532
συνευδοκεῖ οἰκεῖν μετ' αὐτοῦ, μὴ ἀφιέτω αὐτήν. 13 καὶ γυνὴ
consents to live with him, not let him leave her. And a wife

3748 2192 435 571 2532 846 4909 3611 3326
ἥτις ἔχει ἄνδρα ἄπιστον, καὶ αὐτὸς συνευδοκεῖ οἰκεῖν μετ'
who has a husband unbelieving, and he consents to live with

846 3361 863 846 37 1063 3588 435 3588 571
αὐτῆς, μὴ ἀφιέτω αὐτόν. 14 ἡγίασται γὰρ ὁ ἀνὴρ ὁ ἄπιστος
her, not let her leave him. has been sanctified For the husband unbelieving

1722 3588 1135 2532 37 3588 1135 3588 571 1722 3588 435
ἐν τῇ γυναικί, καὶ ἡγίασται ἡ γυνὴ ἡ ἄπιστος ἐν τῷ ἀνδρί·
by the wife, and has been sanctified the wife unbelieving by the husband;

1893 686 3588 5043 5216 169 2076 3568 1161 40 2076
ἐπεὶ ἄρα τὰ τέκνα ὑμῶν ἀκάθαρτά ἐστι, νῦν δὲ ἅγιά ἐστιν.
else then the children of you unclean is, now but holy they are.

1487 1161 3588 571 5563 5563 3756 1420 3588
15 εἰ δὲ ὁ ἄπιστος χωρίζεται, χωριζέσθω. οὐ δεδούλωται ὁ
if But the unbelieving separates, let be separated. Not is in bondage the

80 2228 3588 79 1722 3588 5108 1722 1161 1515 2564
ἀδελφὸς ἢ ἡ ἀδελφὴ ἐν τοῖς τοιούτοις· ἐν δὲ εἰρήνῃ κέκληκεν
brother of the sister in such (cases); in but peace has called

2248 3588 2316 5101 1063 1492 1135 1487 3588 435 4982 2228
ἡμᾶς ὁ Θεός. 16 τί γὰρ οἶδας, γύναι, ει' τὸν ἄνδρα σώσεις; ἢ
us God. what For do you know, wife, if the husband you will save? Or

5101 1492 435 1487 3588 1135 4982 1487 3361 1538 5613
τί οἶδας, ἄνερ, εἰ τὴν γυναῖκα σώσεις; 17 εἰ μὴ ἑκάστῳ ὡς
what know you, husband, if the wife you will save? Only to each as

3307 3588 2316 1538 5613 2564 3588 2962 3779
ἐμέρισεν ὁ Θεός, ἕκαστον ὡς κέκληκεν ὁ Κύριος, οὕτω
has apportioned God, each as has called the Lord, so

4043 2532 3779 1722 3588 1577 3956 1299
περιπατείτω. καὶ οὕτως ἐν ταῖς ἐκκλησίαις πάσαις διατάσσο-
let him walk. And so in the churches all I command.

4059 5100 2564 3361 1986 1722 203
μαι. 18 περιτετμημένος τις ἐκλήθη; μὴ ἐπισπάσθω. ἐν ἀκροβυσ-
Having been circumcised any was called? Not be uncircumcised. In uncir-

5100 2564 3361 4059 3588 4061 3762 2076
τίᾳ τις ἐκλήθη; μὴ περιτεμνέσθω. 19 ἡ περιτομὴ οὐδέν ἐστι,
cumcision any was called? Not be circumcised. Circumcision nothing is,

2532 3588 203 3762 2076 235 5084 1785 2316
καὶ ἡ ἀκροβυστία οὐδέν ἐστιν, ἀλλὰ τήρησις ἐντολῶν Θεοῦ.
and uncircumcision nothing is, but (the) keeping of the commands of God.

King James Version

if they abide even as I.
9 But if they cannot contain, let them marry: for it is better to marry than to burn.

10 And unto the married I command, (yet) not I, but the Lord, Let not the wife depart from (her) husband:
11 But and if she depart, let her remain unmarried, or be reconciled to (her) husband: and let not the husband put away (his) wife.
12 But to the rest speak I, not the Lord: If any brother hath a wife that believeth not, and she be pleased to dwell with him, let him not put her away.
13 And the woman which hath an husband that believeth not, and if he be pleased to dwell with her, let her not leave him.

14 For the unbelieving husband is sanctified by the wife, and the unbelieving wife is sanctified by the husband: else were your children unclean; but now are they holy.
15 But if the unbelieving depart, let him depart. A brother or a sister is not under bondage in such (cases): but God hath called us to peace.
16 For what knowest thou, O wife, whether thou shalt save (thy) husband? or how knowest thou, O man, whether thou shalt save (thy) wife?
17 But as God hath distributed to every man, as the Lord hath called every one, so let him walk. And so ordain I in all churches.
18 Is any man called being circumcised? let him not become uncircumcised. Is any called in uncircumcision? let him not be circumcised.
19 Circumcision is nothing, and uncircumcision is nothing, but the keeping of the commandments of God.

Literal Translation

20 Each one in the calling in which he was called, in this remain.
21 Were you called as a slave? It does not matter to you. But if you are able to be free, rather use (it).
22 For the (one) having been called a slave in (the) Lord is a freed man of (the) Lord. And likewise, the (one) having been called a free man is a slave of Christ.
23 You were redeemed with a price; do not become slaves of men.
24 Each in whatever (state) called, brothers, in this remain with God.

25 But about virgins, I have no command of (the) Lord. But I give judgment, as having received mercy by (the) Lord to be faithful.
26 Then I think this to be good, because of the present necessity: that (it is) good for a man to be thus.
27 Have you been bound to a wife? Do not seek release. Have you been loosed from a wife? Do not seek a wife.
28 But if you also marry, you do not sin. And if the virgin marries, she does not sin. But such will have trouble in the flesh. But I am sparing you.
29 But I say this, brothers, that the time has been cut short. For the rest is, that even the (ones) having wives be as not having,

30 and those weeping as not weeping, and those rejoicing as not rejoicing, and those buying as not possessing,
31 and those using this world as not abusing (it); for the mode of this world is passing away.

32 But I desire you to be without anxiety. The unmarried one cares for the things of the Lord, how to please the

1 Corinthians 7:20

1538 1722 3588 2821 3739 2564 1722 3778 3306 1401
20 ἕκαστος ἐν τῇ κλήσει ᾗ ἐκλήθη, ἐν ταύτῃ μενέτω. 21 δοῦλος
Each one in the calling in which he was called, in this remain. a slave

2564 3361 4671 3199 235 1487 2532 1410 1658
ἐκλήθης; μή σοι μελέτω· ἀλλ᾽ εἰ καὶ δύνασαι ἐλεύθερος
Were you called? Not to you it matters; but if also you are able free

1096 3123 5530 3588 1063 1722 2962 2564 1401
γενέσθαι, μᾶλλον χρῆσαι. 22 ὁ γὰρ ἐν Κυρίῳ κληθεὶς δοῦλος,
to become, rather use (it). the (one) For in (the) Lord having been called a slave,

558 2962 2076 3668 2532 3588 1658 2564
ἀπελεύθερος Κυρίου ἐστίν· ὁμοίως καὶ ὁ ἐλεύθερος κληθείς,
a freed man of (the) Lord is; likewise And he a free man having been called

1401 2076 5547 5092 59 3361 1096 1401
δοῦλός ἐστι Χριστοῦ. 23 τιμῆς ἠγοράσθητε· μὴ γίνεσθε δοῦλοι
a slave is of Christ. Of a price you were bought; not do become slaves

444 1538 1722 3739 2564 80 1722 5129 3306
ἀνθρώπων. 24 ἕκαστος ἐν ᾧ ἐκλήθη, ἀδελφοί, ἐν τούτῳ μενέτω
of men. Each one in whatever called, brothers, in this remain

3844 3588 2316
παρὰ τῷ Θεῷ.
with God.

4012 1161 3588 3933 2003 2962 3756 2192 1106
25. Περὶ δὲ τῶν παρθένων ἐπιταγὴν Κυρίου οὐκ ἔχω· γνώμην
concerning And the virgins a command of (the) Lord not I have; judgment

1161 1325 5613 1653 5259 2962 4103 1511 3543
δὲ δίδωμι ὡς ἠλεημένος ὑπὸ Κυρίου πιστὸς εἶναι. 26 νομίζω
but I give as having had mercy by (the) Lord faithful to be. I think

3767 5124 2570 5225 1223 3588 1764 318 3754
οὖν τοῦτο καλὸν ὑπάρχειν διὰ τὴν ἐνεστῶσαν ἀνάγκην, ὅτι
then this good to be because of the present necessity, that

2570 444 3588 3779 1511 1210 1135 3361 2212
καλὸν ἀνθρώπῳ τὸ οὕτως εἶναι. 27 δέδεσαι γυναικί; μὴ ζήτει
(it is) good for a man so to be. Have you been bound to a woman? Not seek

3080 3089 575 1135 3361 2212 1135 1437 1161 2532
λύσιν. λέλυσαι ἀπὸ γυναικός; μὴ ζήτει γυναῖκα. 28 ἐὰν δὲ καὶ
release. Have you been loosed from a wife? Not seek a wife. if But also

1060 3756 264 2532 1437 1060 3588 3933 3756 264
γήμῃς, οὐχ ἥμαρτες· καὶ ἐὰν γήμῃ ἡ παρθένος, οὐχ ἥμαρτε.
you marry, not you sin. And if marries the virgin, not she sinned.

2347 1161 3588 4561 2192 3588 5108 1473 1161 5216 5339
θλῖψιν δὲ τῇ σαρκὶ ἕξουσιν οἱ τοιοῦτοι· ἐγὼ δὲ ὑμῶν φείδομαι.
trouble But in the flesh will have such; I but you am sparing.

5124 1161 5346 80 3754 3588 2540 4958 3588
29 τοῦτο δέ φημι, ἀδελφοί, ὅτι ὁ καιρὸς συνεσταλμένος· τὸ
this But I say, brothers, that the time has been shortened. For

3063 2076 2443 2532 3588 2192 1135 5613 3361 2192 5600
λοιπὸν ἐστιν ἵνα καὶ οἱ ἔχοντες γυναῖκας ὡς μὴ ἔχοντες ὦσι·
the rest is that even those having wives, as not having be;

2532 3588 2799 5613 3361 2799 2532 3588 5463 5613 3361
30 καὶ οἱ κλαίοντες, ὡς μὴ κλαίοντες, καὶ οἱ χαίροντες· ὡς μὴ
And those weeping, as not weeping, and those rejoicing, as not

5463 2532 3588 59 5613 3361 2722 2532 3588
χαίροντες· καὶ οἱ ἀγοράζοντες, ὡς μὴ κατέχοντες· 31 καὶ οἱ
rejoicing; and those buying, as not possessing; and those

5530 3588 2889 5129 5613 3361 2710 3855
χρώμενοι τῷ κόσμῳ τούτῳ, ὡς μὴ καταχρώμενοι· παράγει
using world this, as not abusing (it); is passing away

1063 3588 4976 3588 2889 5127 2309 1161 5209 275
γὰρ τὸ σχῆμα τοῦ κόσμου τούτου. 32 θέλω δὲ ὑμᾶς ἀμερίμνους
for the mode world of this. I desire But you without anxiety

1511 3588 22 3309 3588 3588 2962 4459 700 3588
εἶναι. ὁ ἄγαμος μεριμνᾷ τὰ τοῦ Κυρίου, πῶς ἀρέσει τῷ
to be. The unmarried cares for the things of the Lord, how to please the

King James Version

20 Let every man abide in the same calling wherein he was called.
21 Art thou called (being) a servant? care not for it: but if thou mayest be made free, use (it) rather.
22 For he that is called in the Lord, (being) a servant, is the Lord's freeman: likewise also he that is called, (being) free, is Christ's servant.
23 Ye are bought with a price; be not ye the servants of men.

24 Brethren, let every man, wherein he is called, therein abide with God.
25 Now concerning virgins I have no commandment of the Lord: yet I give my judgment, as one that hath obtained mercy of the Lord to be faithful.
26 I suppose therefore that this is good for the present distress, (I say), that (it is) good for a man so to be.
27 Art thou bound unto a wife? seek not to be loosed. Art thou loosed from a wife? seek not a wife.
28 But and if thou marry, thou hast not sinned; and if a virgin marry, she hath not sinned. Nevertheless such shall have trouble in the flesh: but I spare you.
29 But this I say, brethren, the time (is) short: it remaineth, that both they that have wives be as though they had none;
30 And they that weep, as though they wept not; and they that rejoice, as though they rejoiced not; and they that buy, as though they possessed not;
31 And they that use this world, as not abusing (it): for the fashion of this world passeth away.
32 But I would have you without carefulness. He that is unmarried careth for the things that belong to the Lord, how he may please the

Literal Translation

Lord;
33 but the (one) having married cares for the things of the world, how to please the wife.
34 The wife and the virgin (are) different. The unmarried one cares for the things of the Lord, that she be holy in both body and spirit. But the married one cares for the things of the world, how to please the husband.
35 And I say this for your advantage, not that I put a snare (before) you, but for the fitting thing, and waiting on the Lord without distraction.
36 But if anyone thinks (it) behaving indecently toward his virgin, if he is beyond (his) prime, and so it ought to be, let him do what he desires; he does not sin; let them marry.

37 But (he) who stands firm in heart, not having necessity, but has authority as to (his) own will, and has judged this in his heart, to keep his virgin; he does well.

38 So that he that gives in marriage does well, and he that does not give in marriage does better.
39 A wife has been bound by law for as long a time as her husband lives; but if her husband sleeps, she is free to be married to whomever she desires, only in (the) Lord.

40 But she is happier if she remains so, according to my judgment. And I think I also have (the) Spirit of God.

1 Corinthians 7:33

2962 3588 1161 1060 3309 3588 3588 2889 4459 700
Κυρίῳ· 33 ὁ δὲ γαμήσας μεριμνᾷ τὰ τοῦ κόσμου, πῶς ἀρέσει
Lord; he but having married cares for the things of the world, how to please

3588 1135 3307 3588 1135 2532 3588 3933 3588 22
τῇ γυναικι. 34 μεμέρισται. ἡ γυνὴ καὶ ἡ παρθένος. ἡ ἄγαμος
the wife. Different (are) the wife and the virgin. The unmarried

3309 3588 3588 2962 2443 5600 40 2532 4983 2532 4151
μεριμνᾷ τὰ τοῦ Κυρίου, ἵνα ᾖ ἁγία καὶ σώματι καὶ πνεύματι·
cares for the things of the Lord, that she be holy both in body and in spirit;

3588 1161 1060 3309 3588 3588 2889 4459 700 3588
ἡ δὲ γαμήσασα μεριμνᾷ τὰ τοῦ κόσμου, πῶς ἀρέσει τῷ
the but married cares for the things of the world, how to please the

435 5124 1161 4314 3588 5216 846 4851 3004 3756
ἀνδρί. 35 τοῦτο δὲ πρὸς τὸ ὑμῶν αὐτῶν σύμφέρον λέγω· οὐχ
husband. this And for the of yourselves advantage I say; not

2443 1029 5213 1911 235 4314 3588 2158 2532
ἵνα βρόχον ὑμῖν ἐπιβάλω, ἀλλὰ πρὸς τὸ εὔσχημον καὶ
that a snare (before) you I put, but for the thing fitting and

2145 3588 2962 563 1487 1161 5100 807
εὐπρόσεδρον τῷ Κυρίῳ ἀπερισπάστως. 36 εἰ δέ τις ἀσχημονεῖν
waiting on the Lord without distraction. if But any to behave indecently

1909 3588 3933 846 3543 1437 5600 5230 2532 3779
ἐπὶ τὴν παρθένον αὐτοῦ νομίζει, ἐὰν ᾖ ὑπέρακμος, καὶ οὕτως
to the virgin of him thinks, if he is beyond (his) prime, and so

3784 1096 3739 2309 4160 3756 264 1060
ὀφείλει γίνεσθαι, ὃ θέλει ποιείτω· οὐχ ἁμαρτάνει· γαμείτω-
(it) ought to be, whatever he desires let him do; not he sins; let them

3739 1161 2476 1476 1722 3588 2588 3361 2192 318
σαν. 37 ὃς δὲ ἕστηκεν ἑδραῖος ἐν τῇ καρδίᾳ, μὴ ἔχων ἀνάγκην,
marry. (he) who but stands firm in the heart, not having necessity,

1849 1161 2192 4012 3588 2398 2307 2532 5124
ἐξουσίαν δὲ ἔχει περὶ τοῦ ἰδίου θελήματος, καὶ τοῦτο
authority but having concerning the own will, and this

2919 1722 3588 2588 846 3588 5083 3588 1438
κέκρικεν ἐν τῇ καρδίᾳ αὐτοῦ, τοῦ τηρεῖν τὴν ἑαυτοῦ
has judged in the heart of him, to keep the of himself

3933 2573 4160 5620 2532 3588 1547 2573 4160
παρθένον, καλῶς ποιεῖ. 38 ὥστε καὶ ὁ ἐκγαμίζων καλῶς ποιεῖ·
virgin, well he does. So as both he giving in marriage well does;

3588 1161 3361 1547 2908 4160 1135 1210 3551
ὁ δὲ μὴ ἐκγαμίζων κρεῖσσον ποιεῖ. 39 γυνὴ δέδεται νόμῳ
he and not giving in marriage better does. A wife has been bound by law

1909 3745 5550 2198 3588 435 846 1437 1161 2837 3588 435
ἐφ᾽ ὅσον χρόνον ζῇ ὁ ἀνὴρ αὐτῆς· ἐὰν δὲ κοιμηθῇ ὁ ἀνὴρ
for as long a time as lives the husband of her; if but sleeps the husband

846 1658 2076 3739 2309 1060 3440 1722 2962
αὐτῆς, ἐλευθέρα ἐστὶν ᾧ θέλει γαμηθῆναι, μόνον ἐν Κυρίῳ.
of her, free she is to whom she desires to be married, only in (the) Lord.

3107 1161 2076 1437 3779 3306 2596 3588 1699
40 μακαριωτέρα δέ ἐστιν ἐὰν οὕτω μείνῃ, κατὰ τὴν ἐμὴν
happier But she is if so she remains, according to my

1106 1380 1161 2504 4151 2316 2192
γνώμην· δοκῶ δὲ κἀγὼ Πνεῦμα Θεοῦ ἔχειν.
judgment; I think and I also (the) Spirit of God have.

King James Version

Lord:
33 But he that is married careth for the things that are of the world, how he may please (his) wife.
34 There is difference (also) between a wife and a virgin. The unmarried woman careth for the things of the Lord, that she may be holy both in body and in spirit: but she that is married careth for the things of the world, how she may please (her) husband.
35 And this I speak for your own profit; not that I may cast a snare upon you, but for that which is comely, and that ye may attend upon the Lord without distraction.
36 But if any man think that he behaveth himself uncomely toward his virgin, if she pass the flower of (her) age, and need so require, let him do what he will, he sinneth not: let them marry.
37 Nevertheless he that standeth stedfast in his heart, having no necessity, but hath power over his own will, and hath so decreed in his heart that he will keep his virgin, doeth well.

38 So then he that giveth (her) in marriage doeth well; but he that giveth (her) not in marriage doeth better.
39 The wife is bound by the law as long as her husband liveth; but if her husband be dead, she is at liberty to be married to whom she will; only in the Lord.

40 But she is happier if she so abide, after my judgment: and I think also that I have the Spirit of God.

1 Corinthians 8

1. But concerning the sacrifices to idols, we know that we all have knowledge. Knowledge puffs up, but love builds up.
2 But if anyone

1 Corinthians 8

4012 1161 3588 1494 1492 3754 3956 1108
1. Περὶ δὲ τῶν εἰδωλοθύτων, οἴδαμεν ὅτι πάντες γνῶσιν
concerning And the idolatrous sacrifices, we know that all knowledge

2192 3588 1108 5448 3588 1161 26 3618 1487 1161 5100
ἔχομεν. ἡ γνῶσις φυσιοῖ, ἡ δὲ ἀγάπη οἰκοδομεῖ. 2 εἰ δέ τις
we have. Knowledge puffs up, but love builds up. if But any

1 Corinthians 8

1. Now as touching things offered unto idols, we know that we all have knowledge. Knowledge puffeth up, but charity edifieth.
2 And if any

Literal Translation **1 Corinthians 8:3** ***King James Version***

thinks to know anything, he still has known nothing as he ought to know.
3 But if anyone loves God, he has been known by Him.
4 Then concerning the eating of things sacrificed to idols, we know that an idol (is) nothing in (the) world, and that (there) is no other God except One.
5 For even if (some) are called gods, either in Heaven or on the earth; even as there are many gods, and many lords;
6 but to us (is) one God, the Father, of whom (are) all things, and we for Him; and one Lord Jesus Christ, through whom (are) all things, and we through Him.
7 But the knowledge (is) not in all; but some being conscious of the idol eat as an idolatrous sacrifice until now; and their conscience being weak is defiled.
8 But food will not commend us to God. For neither if we eat do we excel, nor if we do not eat are we behind.
9 But watch lest this authority of yours become a cause of stumbling to the weak ones.
10 For if anyone sees you, the (one) having knowledge, sitting in an idol-temple, (will) not the weak one's conscience be built up so as to eat things sacrificed to idols?
11 And on your knowledge the weak brother is destroyed, (he) for whom Christ died.
12 And sinning in this way against (your) brothers, and wounding their conscience, being weak, you sin against Christ.
13 On account of this, if food offends my brother, I will not at all eat

1380 1492 5100 3764 3762 1097 2531 1163 1097
δοκεῖ εἰδέναι τι, οὐδέπω οὐδὲν ἔγνωκε καθὼς δεῖ γνῶναι·
thinks to know anything, nothing yet he has known as he ought to know;

1487 1161 5100 25 3588 2316 3778 1097 5259 846
3 εἰ δέ τις ἀγαπᾷ τὸν Θεόν, οὗτος ἔγνωσται ὑπ' αὐτοῦ.
if but anyone loves God, this one has been known by Him.

4012 3588 1035 3767 3588 1494 1492 3754 3762
4 περὶ τῆς βρώσεως οὖν τῶν εἰδωλοθύτων, οἴδαμεν ὅτι οὐδὲν
concerning the eating Then of the idolatrous sacrifices, we know that (is) not

1497 1722 2889 2532 3754 3762 2316 2087 1487 3361 1522
εἴδωλον ἐν κόσμῳ, καὶ ὅτι οὐδεὶς Θεὸς ἕτερος εἰ μὴ εἷς.
an idol in (the) world, and that (there is) no God other except One.

2532 1063 1512 1526 3004 2316 1535 1722 3772 1535 1909
5 καὶ γὰρ εἴπερ εἰσὶ λεγόμενοι θεοί, εἴτε ἐν οὐρανῷ, εἴτε ἐπὶ
even For if there are (that) called gods, either in Heaven, or upon

3588 1093 5618 1526 2316 4183 2532 2962 4183 235
τῆς γῆς· ὥσπερ εἰσὶ θεοὶ πολλοί, καὶ κύριοι πολλοί, 6 ἀλλ'
the earth; even as there are gods many, and lords many, but

2254 1520 2316 3588 3962 1537 3739 3588 3956 2532 2249 1519 846
ἡμῖν εἷς Θεὸς ὁ πατήρ, ἐξ οὗ τὰ πάντα καὶ ἡμεῖς εἰς αὐτόν·
to us one God the Father, of whom all things, and we for Him;

2532 1520 2962 2424 5547 1223 3739 3588 3956 2532 2249
καὶ εἷς Κύριος Ἰησοῦς Χριστός, δι' οὗ τὰ πάντα καὶ ἡμεῖς
and one Lord Jesus Christ, through whom all things, and we

1223 846 235 3756 1722 3956 3588 1108 5100 1161 3588 4893
δι' αὐτοῦ. 7 ἀλλ' οὐκ ἐν πᾶσιν ἡ γνῶσις· τινὲς δὲ τῇ συνειδήσει
through Him. But not in all (is) the knowledge; some and conscious

3588 1497 2193 737 5613 1494 2068 2532 3588
τοῦ εἰδώλου ἕως ἄρτι ὡς εἰδωλόθυτον ἐσθίουσι, καὶ ἡ
of the idol until now as an idolatrous sacrifice eat, and the

4893 846 772 5607 3435 1033 1161 2248
συνείδησις αὐτῶν ἀσθενὴς οὖσα μολύνεται. 8 βρῶμα δὲ ἡμᾶς
conscience of them weak being is defiled. food But us

3756 3936 3588 2316 3777 1063 1437 5315 4052
οὐ παρίστησι τῷ Θεῷ· οὔτε γὰρ ἐὰν φάγωμεν περισσεύο-
not will commend to God; neither for if we eat do we excel,

3777 1437 3361 5315 5302 991 1161 3381
μεν, οὔτε ἐὰν μὴ φάγωμεν ὑστερούμεθα. 9 βλέπετε δὲ μήπως
nor if not we eat are we lacking. watch But lest

3588 1849 5216 3778 4348 1096 3588 770
ἡ ἐξουσία ὑμῶν αὕτη πρόσκομμα γένηται τοῖς ἀσθενοῦσιν.
the authority of you this a stumbling block becomes to the weak ones.

1437 1063 5100 1492 4571 3588 2192 1108 1722 1493 2621
10 ἐὰν γάρ τις ἴδῃ σε τὸν ἔχοντα γνῶσιν ἐν εἰδωλείῳ κατακεί-
if For anyone sees you the (one) having knowledge in an idol temple

3780 3588 4893 846 772 5607 618
μενον, οὐχὶ ἡ συνείδησις αὐτοῦ ἀσθενοῦς ὄντος οἰκοδομηθή-
sitting, not the conscience of them weak being will be built up

1519 3588 3588 1494 2068 2532 622 3588 770
σεται εἰς τὸ τὰ εἰδωλόθυτα ἐσθίειν; 11 καὶ ἀπολεῖται ὁ ἀσθε-
so as the idolatrous sacrifice to eat? And is destroyed the weak

80 1909 3588 4674 1108 1223 3739 5547 599
νῶν ἀδελφὸς ἐπὶ τῇ σῇ γνώσει, δι' ὃν Χριστὸς ἀπέθανεν;
brother on the your knowledge, for whom Christ died?

3779 1161 264 1519 3588 80 2532 5180
12 οὕτω δὲ ἁμαρτάνοντες εἰς τοὺς ἀδελφούς, καὶ τύπτοντες
so And sinning against the brothers, and wounding

846 3588 4893 770 1519 5547 264
αὐτῶν τὴν συνείδησιν ἀσθενοῦσαν, εἰς Χριστὸν ἁμαρτάνετε.
of them the conscience being weak, against Christ you sin.

1355 1487 1033 4624 3588 80 3756 3588 3361 5315
13 διόπερ εἰ βρῶμα σκανδαλίζει τὸν ἀδελφόν μου, οὐ μὴ φάγω
Therefore if food causes to stumble the brother of me, not at all I eat

man think that he knoweth any thing, he knoweth nothing yet as he ought to know.
3 But if any man love God, the same is known of him.
4 As concerning therefore the eating of those things that are offered in sacrifice unto idols, we know that an idol (is) nothing in the world, and that (there is) none other God but one.
5 For though there be that are called gods, whether in heaven or in earth, (as there be gods many, and lords many,)
6 But to us (there is but) one God, the Father, of whom (are) all things, and we in him; and one Lord Jesus Christ, by whom (are) all things, and we by him.
7 Howbeit (there is) not in every man that knowledge: for some with conscience of the idol unto this hour eat (it) as a thing offered unto an idol; and their conscience being weak is defiled.
8 But meat commendeth us not to God: for neither, if we eat, are we the better; neither, if we eat not, are we the worse.
9 But take heed lest by any means this liberty of yours become a stumblingblock to them that are weak.
10 For if any man see thee which hast knowledge sit at meat in the idol's temple, shall not the conscience of him which is weak be emboldened to eat those things which are offered to idols;
11 And through thy knowledge shall the weak brother perish, for whom Christ died?
12 But when ye sin so against the brethren, and wound their weak conscience, ye sin against Christ.
13 Wherefore, if meat make my brother to offend, I will eat no

Literal Translation | **1 Corinthians 9:1** | ***King James Version***

flesh forever, so that I do not offend my brother.

2907 1519 3588 165 2443 3361 3588 80 3450 4624
κρέα εἰς τὸν αἰῶνα, ἵνα μὴ τὸν ἀδελφόν μου σκανδαλίσω.
flesh into the age, that not the brother of me I offend.

flesh while the world standeth, lest I make my brother to offend.

1 Corinthians 9

1. Am I not an apostle? Am I not free? Have I not seen our Lord Jesus Christ? Are you not my work in (the) Lord?
2 If I am not an apostle to others, yet I am indeed to you; for you are the seal of my apostleship in (the) Lord.
3 My defense to those examining me is this:
4 Have we not authority to eat and to drink?
5 Have we not authority to lead about a sister, a wife, as the rest of the apostles also, and Cephas, and the Lord's brothers (do)?
6 Or (is it) only Barnabas and I (who) have no authority to quit work?
7 Who serves as a soldier at (his) own wages at any time? Who plants a vineyard and does not eat of its fruit? Or who shepherds a flock and does not eat of the milk of the flock?
8 Do I speak these things according to man, or does not the Law say these things also?
9 For it has been written in the Law of Moses, "You shall not muzzle an ox threshing grain." (Deut.25:4) Is it (that) it matters to God (as to) oxen?
10 Or does He say (it) altogether because of us? It is written because of us, so that the (one) plowing ought to plow (in) hope, and the (one) threshing (in) hope to partake on hope.
11 If we have sowed spiritual things to you, (is it) a great thing if we shall reap of your fleshly things?
12 If others have a share of the authority (over) you,

1 Corinthians 9

3756 1510 652 3756 1510 1658 3780 2424
1. Οὐκ εἰμὶ ἀπόστολος; οὐκ εἰμὶ ἐλεύθερος; οὐχὶ Ἰησοῦν
Not am I an apostle? not Am I free? Not Jesus

5547 3588 2962 2257 3708 3756 3588 2041 3450 5210
Χριστὸν τὸν Κύριον ἡμῶν ἑώρακα; οὐ τὸ ἔργον μου ὑμεῖς
Christ the Lord of us I have seen? Not the work of me you

2075 1722 2962 1487 243 3756 1510 652 235 1065 5213
ἐστε ἐν Κυρίῳ; 2 εἰ ἄλλοις οὐκ εἰμὶ ἀπόστολος, ἀλλά γε ὑμῖν
are in (the) Lord? If to others not I am an apostle, yet indeed to you

1510 3588 1063 4973 3588 1699 651 5210 2075 1722 2962
εἰμι· ἡ γὰρ σφραγὶς τῆς ἐμῆς ἀποστολῆς ὑμεῖς ἐστε ἐν Κυρίῳ.
I am; the for seal of my apostleship you are in (the) Lord.

3588 1699 627 3588 1691 350 3778 2076 3361 3756
3 ἡ ἐμὴ ἀπολογία τοῖς ἐμὲ ἀνακρίνουσίν αὕτη ἐστί. 4 μὴ οὐκ
My defense to those me examining this is. Not

2192 1849 5315 2532 4095 3361 3756 2192 1849
ἔχομεν ἐξουσίαν φαγεῖν καὶ πιεῖν; 5 μὴ οὐκ ἔχομεν ἐξουσίαν
have we authority to eat and drink? not Have we authority

79 1135 4013 5613 2532 3588 3062 652
ἀδελφὴν γυναῖκα περιάγειν, ὡς καὶ οἱ λοιποὶ ἀπόστολοι,
a sister a wife to lead about, as also the rest (of the) apostles,

2532 3588 80 3588 2962 2532 2786 2228 3441 1473 2532
καὶ οἱ ἀδελφοὶ τοῦ Κυρίου, καὶ Κηφᾶς; 6 ἢ μόνος ἐγὼ καὶ
and the brothers of the Lord, and Cephas? Or only I and

921 3756 2192 1849 3588 2038 5101
Βαρνάβας οὐκ ἔχομεν ἐξουσίαν τοῦ μὴ ἐργάζεσθαι; 7 τίς
Barnabas not have we authority not to work? Who

4754 2398 3800 4218 5101 5452 490
στρατεύεται ἰδίοις ὀψωνίοις ποτέ; τίς φυτεύει ἀμπελῶνα,
soldiers at (his) own wages at any time? Who plants a vineyard,

2532 3588 2590 846 3756 2068 2228 5101 4165 4167
καὶ ἐκ τοῦ καρποῦ αὐτοῦ οὐκ ἐσθίει; ἢ τίς ποιμαίνει ποίμνην,
and of the fruit of it not eats? Or who shepherds a flock,

2532 1537 3588 1051 3588 4167 3756 2068 3361 2596 444
καὶ ἐκ τοῦ γάλακτος τῆς ποίμνης οὐκ ἐσθίει; 8 μὴ κατὰ ἄνθρω-
and of the milk of the flock not eats? Not according to man

5023 2980 2228 3780 2532 3588 3551 5023 3004 1722 1063
πον ταῦτα λαλῶ; ἢ οὐχὶ καὶ ὁ νόμος ταῦτα λέγει; 9 ἐν γὰρ
these things I speak? Or not also the Law these things says? in For

3588 3475 3551 1125 3756 5392 1016 248
τῷ Μωσέως νόμῳ γέγραπται, Οὐ φιμώσεις βοῦν ἀλοῶντα.
the of Moses Law it has been written, not You shall muzzle an ox threshing.

3361 3588 1016 3199 3588 2316 2228 1223 2248 3843 3004 1223
μὴ τῶν βοῶν μέλει τῷ Θεῷ; 10 ἢ δι' ἡμᾶς πάντως λέγει; δι'
Not of oxen matters it to God? Or because of us altogether He says? For

2248 1063 1125 3754 1909 1680 3784 3588 722
ἡμᾶς γὰρ ἐγράφη, ὅτι ἐπ' ἐλπίδι ὀφείλει ὁ ἀροτριῶν
us (it is) for it was written, that on hope ought the (one) plowing

772 2532 3588 248 3588 1680 846 3348 1909 1680
ἀροτριᾷν, καὶ ὁ ἀλοῶν τῆς ἐλπίδος αὐτοῦ μετέχειν ἐπ' ἐλπίδι.
to plow, and the threshing of the hope of him to partake on hope.

1487 2249 5213 3588 4152 4687 3173 1487 2249 5216
11 εἰ ἡμεῖς ὑμῖν τὰ πνευματικὰ ἐσπείραμεν, μέγα εἰ ἡμεῖς ὑμῶν
If we to you spiritual things sowed, (is it) a great thing if we of you

3588 4559 2325 1487 243 3588 1849 5216
τὰ σαρκικὰ θερίσομεν; 12 εἰ ἄλλοι τῆς ἐξουσίας ὑμῶν μετέ-
fleshly things shall reap? If others of the authority of you have a

1 Corinthians 9

1. Am I not an apostle? am I not free? have I not seen Jesus Christ our Lord? are not ye my work in the Lord?
2 If I be not an apostle unto others, yet doubtless I am to you: for the seal of mine apostleship are ye in the Lord.
3 Mine answer to them that do examine me is this,
4 Have we not power to eat and to drink?
5 Have we not power to lead about a sister, a wife, as well as other apostles, and (as) the brethren of the Lord, and Cephas?
6 Or I only and Barnabas, have not we power to forbear working?
7 Who goeth a warfare any time at his own charges? who planteth a vineyard, and eateth not of the fruit thereof? or who feedeth a flock, and eateth not of the milk of the flock?
8 Say I these things as a man? or saith not the law the same also?
9 For it is written in the law of Moses, Thou shalt not muzzle the mouth of the ox that treadeth out the corn. Doth God take care for oxen?
10 Or saith he (it) altogether for our sakes? For our sakes, no doubt, (this) is written: that he that ploweth should plow in hope; and that he that thresheth in hope should be partaker of his hope.
11 If we have sown unto you spiritual things, (is it) a great thing if we shall reap your carnal things?
12 If others be partakers of (this) power over you,

Literal Translation | **1 Corinthians 9:13** | *King James Version*

Literal Translation

(should) not rather we?
But we did not use this
authority, but we en-
dured all things, so that
we might not give a hin-
drance to the gospel of
Christ.
13 Do you not know
that those laboring
(about) holy things of
the temple eat? Those
attending (on) the altar
partake with the altar.

14 So also the Lord or-
dained those proclaim-
ing the gospel to live
from the gospel.

15 But I have not used
one of these. And I do
not write these things
that it should be so with
me. For (it is) good to
me rather to die than
that anyone nullify my
glorying.
16 For if I preach the
gospel, no glory is to
me; for necessity is laid
on me, and (it) is woe to
me if I do not preach the
gospel

17 For if I do this will-
ingly, I have a reward;
but if unwillingly, I am
entrusted with a stew-
ardship.

18 What then is my re-
ward? That preaching
the gospel I may make
the gospel of Christ
without charge, so as
not to use fully my
authority in the gospel.
19 For being free of all,
I enslaved myself to all,
that I might gain the
more.

20 And I became as a
Jew to the Jews, that I
might gain Jews; to
those under Law as un-
der Law, that I might
gain those under Law;
21 to those without Law
as without Law, not be-
ing without law of God,
but under (the) law of
Christ, that I might gain
(those) without Law.

22 I became to the weak
as weak, that I might
gain the weak.

3348 3756 3123 2249 235 3756 5530 3588 1849
χουσιν, οὐ μᾶλλον ἡμεῖς; Ἀλλ' οὐκ ἐχρησάμεθα τῇ ἐξουσίᾳ
a share, not rather we? But not we used authority

3778 235 3956 4722 2443 3361 1464 5100 1325
ταύτῃ· ἀλλὰ πάντα στέγομεν, ἵνα μὴ ἐγκοπήν τινα δῶμεν
this; but all things we endured, that not an obstacle anyone we give

3588 2098 3588 5547 3756 1492 3754 3588 3588 2413
τῷ εὐαγγελίῳ τοῦ Χριστοῦ. 13 οὐκ οἴδατε ὅτι οἱ τὰ ἱερὰ
to the gospel of Christ. Not you know that those holy things

2038 1537 3588 2411 2068 3588 3588 2379
ἐργαζόμενοι ἐκ τοῦ ἱεροῦ ἐσθίουσιν, οἱ τῷ θυσιαστηρίῳ
laboring (about) of the temple eat, those the altar

4332 3588 2379 4829 3779 2532
παρεδρεύοντες τῷ θυσιαστηρίῳ συμμερίζονται; 14 οὕτω καὶ
attending (on) the altar partake with? So also

3588 2962 1299 3588 3588 2098 2605 1537 3588
ὁ Κύριος διέταξε τοῖς τὸ εὐαγγέλιον καταγγέλλουσιν ἐκ τοῦ
the Lord ordained those of the gospel proclaiming of the

2098 2198 1473 1161 3762 5530 5130 3756
εὐαγγελίου ζῆν. 15 ἐγὼ δὲ οὐδενὶ ἐχρησάμην τούτων· οὐκ
gospel to live. I But not one have used of these; not

1125 1161 5023 2443 3779 1096 1722 1698 2570 1063 3427
ἔγραψα δὲ ταῦτα ἵνα οὕτω γένηται ἐν ἐμοί· καλὸν γάρ μοι
I write and these things that so it should be with me; good for to me

3123 599 2228 3588 2745 3450 2443 5100 2758 1437
μᾶλλον ἀποθανεῖν, ἢ τὸ καύχημά μου ἵνα τις κενώσῃ. 16 ἐὰν
rather to die, than the glorying of me that anyone nullify. if

1063 2097 3756 2076 3427 2745 318 1063
γὰρ εὐαγγελίζωμαι, οὐκ ἔστι μοι καύχημα· ἀνάγκη γάρ
For I preach the gospel, not is to me glory; necessity for

3427 1945 3759 1161 3427 2076 1437 3361 2097 1487
μοι ἐπίκειται· οὐαὶ δὲ μοι ἐστιν, ἐὰν μὴ εὐαγγελίζωμαι. 17 εἰ
me is laid on; woe and to me is, if not I preach the gospel. if

1063 1635 5124 4238 3408 2192 1487 1161 210 3622
γὰρ ἑκὼν τοῦτο πράσσω, μισθὸν ἔχω· εἰ δὲ ἄκων, οἰκονομίαν
For willingly this I do, a reward I have; if but unwillingly, a stewardship

4100 5101 3767 3427 2076 3588 3408 2443 2097
πεπίστευμαι. 18 τίς οὖν μοι ἐστιν ὁ μισθός; ἵνα εὐαγγελιζό-
I am entrusted with. What then of me is the reward? That preaching the

77 5087 3588 2098 3588 5547 1519 3588 3361
μενος ἀδάπανον θήσω τὸ εὐαγγέλιον τοῦ Χριστοῦ, εἰς τὸ μὴ
gospel without charge I lay down the gospel of Christ, so as not

2710 3588 1849 3450 1722 3588 2098 1658
καταχρήσασθαι τῇ ἐξουσίᾳ μου ἐν τῷ εὐαγγελίῳ. 19 Ἐλεύ-
to use to the full the authority of me in the gospel. free

1063 5607 1537 3956 3956 1683 1402 2443
θερος γὰρ ὢν ἐκ πάντων, πᾶσιν ἐμαυτὸν ἐδούλωσα, ἵνα
For being of all, to all myself I enslaved, that

3588 4119 2770 2532 1096 3588 2770 5613
τοὺς πλείονας κερδήσω. 20 καὶ ἐγενόμην τοῖς Ἰουδαίοις ὡς
the more I might gain. And I became to the Jews as

2453 2443 2453 2770 3588 5259 3551 5613 5259
Ἰουδαῖος, ἵνα Ἰουδαίους κερδήσω· τοῖς ὑπὸ νόμον ὡς ὑπὸ
a Jew, that Jews I might gain; to those under Law as under

3551 2443 3588 5259 3551 2770 3588 459 5613 459
νόμον, ἵνα τοὺς ὑπὸ νόμον κερδήσω· 21 τοῖς ἀνόμοις ὡς ἄνομος,
Law, that those under Law I might gain; to those without Law as without Law,

3361 5607 459 2316 235 1772 5547 2443 2770 459
μὴ ὢν ἄνομος Θεῷ ἀλλ' ἔννομος Χριστῷ, ἵνα κερδήσω ἀνόμους.
not beingwithout law ofGod but under law of Christ, that I might gain without Law;

1096 3588 772 5613 772 2443 3588 772
22 ἐγενόμην τοῖς ἀσθενέσιν ὡς ἀσθενής, ἵνα τοὺς ἀσθενεῖς
I became to the weak as weak, that the weak

King James Version

(are) not we rather?
Nevertheless we have
not used this power; but
suffer all things, lest we
should hinder the gos-
pel of Christ.

13 Do ye not know that
they which minister
about holy things live
(of the things) of the
temple? and they which
wait at the altar are par-
takers with the altar?
14 Even so hath the
Lord ordained that they
which preach the gos-
pel should live of the
gospel.

15 But I have used none
of these things: neither
have I written these
things, that it should be
so done unto me: for (it
were) better for me to
die, than that any man
should make my glory-
ing void.
16 For though I preach
the gospel, I have noth-
ing to glory of: for ne-
cessity is laid upon me;
yea, woe is unto me, if I
preach not the gospel!
17 For if I do this thing
willingly, I have a re-
ward: but if against my
will, a dispensation (of
the gospel) is commit-
ted unto me.
18 What is my reward
then? (Verily) that,
when I preach the gos-
pel, I may make the gos-
pel of Christ without
charge, that I abuse not
my power in the gospel.
19 For though I be free
from all (men), yet have
I made myself servant
unto all, that I might
gain the more.
20 And unto the Jews I
became as a Jew, that I
might gain the Jews; to
them that are under the
law, as under the law,
that I might gain them
that are under the law;
21 To them that are
without law, as without
law, (being not without
law to God, but under
the law to Christ,) that I
might gain them that are
without law.
22 To the weak became
I as weak, that I might
gain the weak:

Literal Translation

To all I have become all things, that by all means I might save some.

23 And I do this for the gospel, that I might become a fellow partaker of it.

24 Do you not know that those running in a stadium indeed all run, but one receives the prize? So run that you may obtain.

25 But everyone striving controls himself (in) all things. Then indeed those that they may receive a corruptible crown, but we an incorruptible.

26 So I run accordingly, as not uncertainly; so I fight, as not beating air;

27 but I buffet my body and lead (it) captive, lest proclaiming to others I myself might be disapproved.

1 Corinthians 9:23

2770 3588 3956 1096 3588 3956 2443 3843 5100
κερδήσω. τοῖς πᾶσι γέγονα τὰ πάντα, ἵνα πάντως τινὰς
I might gain. To all I have becomc all things, that by all means some

4982 5124 1161 4160 1223 3588 2098 2443 4791
σώσω. 23 τοῦτο δὲ ποιῶ διὰ τὸ εὐαγγέλιον, ἵνα συγκοινωνὸς
I might save. this And I do because of the gospel, that a fellow-partaker

846 1096 2756 1492 3754 3588 1722 4712 5143 3956
αὐτοῦ γένωμαι. 24 Οὐκ οἴδατε ὅτι οἱ ἐν σταδίῳ τρέχοντες πάν-
of it I might become. Not know you that those in a stadium running all

3303 5143 1520 1161 2983 3588 1017 3779
τες μὲν τρέχουσιν, εἷς δὲ λαμβάνει τὸ βραβεῖον; οὕτω
indeed run, one but receives the prize? So

5143 2443 2638 3956 1161 3588 75 3956
τρέχετε, ἵνα καταλάβητε. 25 πᾶς δὲ ὁ ἀγωνιζόμενος πάντα
run, that you may obtain. everyone And striving (in) all things

1467 1565 3303 3767 2443 5349 4735 2983
ἐγκρατεύεται· ἐκεῖνοι μὲν οὖν ἵνα φθαρτὸν στέφανον λάβω-
controls himself; those indeed then that a corruptible crown they may

2249 1161 862 1473 5106 3779 5143 5613 3756
σιν, ἡμεῖς δὲ ἄφθαρτον. 26 ἐγὼ τοίνυν οὕτω τρέχω ὡς οὐκ
receive, we but an incorruptible. I accordingly so run as not

84 3779 4438 5613 3756 109 1194 235 5299
ἀδήλως· οὕτω πυκτεύω, ὡς οὐκ ἀέρα δέρων· 27 ἀλλ' ὑπωπιάζω
uncertainly; so I fight, as not air beating; but I buffet

3450 3588 4983 2532 1396 3381 243 2784
μου τὸ σῶμα καὶ δουλαγωγῶ, μήπως, ἄλλοις κηρύξας
of me the body and lead (it) captive, that not to others proclaiming

846 96 1096
αὐτὸς ἀδόκιμος γένωμαι.
myself disapproved I may become.

King James Version

I am made all things to all (men), that I might by all means save some.

23 And this I do for the gospel's sake, that I might be partaker thereof with (you).

24 Know ye not that they which run in a race run all, but one receiveth the prize? So run, that ye may obtain.

25 And every man that striveth for the mastery is temperate in all things. Now they (do it) to obtain a corruptible crown; but we an incorruptible.

26 I therefore so run, not as uncertainly; so fight I, not as one that beateth the air:

27 But I keep under my body, and bring (it) into subjection: lest that by any means, when I have preached to others, I myself should be a castaway.

1 Corinthians 10

1. And I do not want you to be ignorant, brothers, that our fathers were all under the cloud, and all passed through the Sea.

2 And all were baptized to Moses in the cloud, and in the Sea,

3 and all ate the same spiritual food.

4 And all drank the same spiritual drink; for they drank of the spiritual rock following, and that Rock was Christ.

5 Yet God was not pleased with most of them, for they were scattered in the desert. (Num.14:16)

6 But these things became examples for us, so that we may not be lusters after bad things, even as those indeed lusted.

7 Neither be idolaters,

1 Corinthians 10

3756 2309 1161 5209 50 80 3754 3588 3962 2257
1. Οὐ θέλω δὲ ὑμᾶς ἀγνοεῖν, ἀδελφοί, ὅτι οἱ πατέρες ἡμῶν
not I desire And you to be ignorant, brothers, that the fathers of us

3956 5259 3588 3507 2258 2532 3956 1223 3588 2281
πάντες ὑπὸ τὴν νεφέλην ἦσαν, καὶ πάντες διὰ τῆς θαλάσσης
all under the cloud were, and all through the sea

1330 2532 3956 1519 3588 3475 907 1722 3588 3507
διῆλθον, 2 καὶ πάντες εἰς τὸν Μωσῆν ἐβαπτίσαντο ἐν τῇ νεφέλῃ
passed, and all to Moses were baptized in the cloud

2532 1722 3588 2281 2532 3956 3588 846 1033 4152
καὶ ἐν τῇ θαλάσσῃ, 3 καὶ πάντες τὸ αὐτὸ βρῶμα πνευματικὸν
and in the sea, and all the same food spiritual

3956 2532 3956 3588 846 4188 4152 4095
ἔφαγον, 4 καὶ πάντες τὸ αὐτο πόμὰ πνευματικὸν ἔπιον·
ate, and all the same drink spiritual drank;

4095 1063 1537 4152 190 4073 3588 1161
ἔπινον γὰρ ἐκ πνευματικῆς ἀκολουθούσης πέτρας· ἡ δὲ
they drank for of a spiritual following rock; the and

4073 2258 3588 5547 235 3756 1722 3588 4119 846
πέτρα ἦν ὁ Χριστός. 5 ἀλλ' οὐκ ἐν τοῖς πλείοσιν αὐτῶν
Rock was Christ. But not in the most of them

2106 3588 2316 2693 1063 1722 3588 2048 5023
εὐδόκησεν ὁ Θεός, κατεστρώθησαν γὰρ ἐν τῇ ἐρήμῳ. 6 ταῦτα
was well pleased God, they were scattered for in the desert. these things

1161 5179 2257 1096 1519 3588 3361 1511 2248 1938
δὲ τύποι ἡμῶν ἐγενήθησαν, εἰς τὸ μὴ εἶναι ἡμᾶς ἐπιθυμητὰς
And examples of us were, for not to be us lusters after

2956 2531 2548 1937 3366 1496
κακῶν, καθὼς κἀκεῖνοι ἐπεθύμησαν. 7 μηδὲ εἰδωλολάτραι
bad things, even as those indeed lusted. Neither idolaters

1 Corinthians 10

1. Moreover, brethren, I would not that ye should be ignorant, how that all our fathers were under the cloud, and all passed through the sea;

2 And were all baptized unto Moses in the cloud and in the sea;

3 And did all eat the same spiritual meat;

4 And did all drink the same spiritual drink: for they drank of that spiritual Rock that followed them: and that Rock was Christ.

5 But with many of them God was not well pleased: for they were overthrown in the wilderness.

6 Now these things were our examples, to the intent we should not lust after evil things, as they also lusted.

7 Neither be ye idolaters,

Literal Translation | **1 Corinthians 10:8** | **King James Version**

even as some of them, as it has been written, "The people sat down to eat and drink, and stood up to play." (Ex. 32:6)
8 Nor should we commit fornication, as some of them fornicated, and twenty three thousand fell in one day.

9 Neither over-tempt Christ, as some of them tempted, and were destroyed by serpents.

1096 2531 5100 846 5613 1125 2523 3588 2992
γίνεσθε, καθώς τινες αὐτῶν· ὡς γέγραπται, Ἐκάθισεν ὁ λαὸς
become, even as some of them; as it has been written, sat The people

5315 2532 4095 2532 450 3815 3366 4203
φαγεῖν καὶ πιεῖν, καὶ ἀνέστησαν παίζειν. 8 μηδὲ πορνεύωμεν,
to eat and to drink, and stood up to play. Neither do fornication,

2531 5100 846 4203 2532 4098 1722 3391 2250
καθώς τινες αὐτῶν ἐπόρνευσαν, καὶ ἔπεσον ἐν μιᾷ ἡμέρᾳ
even as some of them fornicated, and fell in one day

5140 5505 3366 1598 3588 5547 2531
εἰκοσιτρεῖς χιλιάδες. 9 μηδὲ ἐκπειράζωμεν τὸν Χριστόν, καθώς
twenty-three thousands. Neither overtempt the Christ, even as

2532 5100 846 3985 2532 5259 3588 3789 622
καί τινες αὐτῶν ἐπείρασαν, καὶ ὑπὸ τῶν ὄφεων ἀπώλοντο.
also some of them tempted, and by serpents were destroyed.

as (were) some of them; as it is written, The people sat down to eat and drink, and rose up to play.
8 Neither let us commit fornication, as some of them committed, and fell in one day three and twenty thousand.

9 Neither let us tempt Christ, as some of them also tempted, and were destroyed of serpents.

10 Neither should you murmur, as also some of them murmured, and were destroyed by the destroyer.
11 And all these things happened to those (as) examples, and (it) was written for our warning, on whom the ends of the ages have come.
12 So that he thinking to stand, let him watch that he not fall.
13 No temptation has taken you except (what is) human; but God (is) faithful, who will not allow you to be tempted above what you are able. But with the temptation, (He) will also make the way out, so as (for you) to be able to bear (it).

3366 1111 2531 2532 5100 846 1111 2532
10 μηδὲ γογγύζετε, καθὼς καὶ τινὲς αὐτῶν ἐγόγγυσαν, καὶ
Neither murmur, even as also some of them murmured, and

622 5259 3588 3644 5023 1161 3956 5179
ἀπώλοντο ὑπὸ τοῦ ὀλοθρευτοῦ. 11 ταῦτα δὲ πάντα τύποι
were destroyed by the destroyer. these things And all (as) examples

4819 1565 1125 1161 4314 3559 2257 1519
συνέβαινον ἐκείνοις· ἐγράφη δὲ πρὸς νουθεσίαν ἡμῶν, εἰς
happened to those; was written and for warning to us, to

3739 3588 5056 3588 165 2658 5620 3588 1380
οὓς τὰ τέλη τῶν αἰώνων κατήντηκεν. 12 ὥστε ὁ δοκῶν
whom the ends of the ages has arrived. So as he thinking

2476 991 3361 4098 3986 5209 3756 2983 1487
ἑστάναι βλεπέτω μὴ πέσῃ. 13 πειρασμὸς ὑμᾶς οὐκ εἴληφεν εἰ
to stand, let watch lest he falls. Temptation you not has taken ex-

3361 442 4103 1161 3588 2316 3739 3756 1439 5209
μὴ ἀνθρώπινος· πιστὸς δὲ ὁ Θεός, ὃς οὐκ ἐάσει ὑμᾶς πει-
cept (what is) human; faithful but (is) God, who not will allow you to

3985 5228 3739 1410 235 4160 4862 3588 3986
ρασθῆναι ὑπὲρ ὃ δύνασθε, ἀλλὰ ποιήσει σὺν τῷ πειρασμῷ
be tempted above what you are able, but will make with the temptation

2532 3588 1545 3588 1410 5297
καὶ τὴν ἔκβασιν τοῦ δύνασθαι ὑπενεγκεῖν.
also the way out, to be able to bear (it).

10 Neither murmur ye, as some of them also murmured, and were destroyed of the destroyer.
11 Now all these things happened unto them for ensamples: and they are written for our admonition, upon whom the ends of the world are come.
12 Wherefore let him that thinketh he standeth take heed lest he fall.
13 There hath no temptation taken you but such as is common to man: but God (is) faithful, who will not suffer you to be tempted above that ye are able; but will with the temptation also make a way to escape, that ye may be able to bear (it).

14 On account of this, flee from idolatry, my beloved.
15 I speak as to prudent ones; you judge what I say.
16 The cup of blessing which we bless, is it not a partaking of the blood of Christ? The bread which we break, is it not a partaking of the body of Christ?

17 Because we, the many, are one bread, one body, for we all partake of the one bread.
18 Look at Israel according to flesh; are not those eating the sacrifices partakers of the altar?
19 What then do I say, that

1355 27 3450 5343 575 3588 1495
14. Διόπερ, ἀγαπητοί μου, φεύγετε ἀπὸ τῆς εἰδωλολατρείας.
Therefore, beloved of me, flee from idolatry.

5613 5429 3004 2919 5210 3739 5346 3588 4221 3588
15 ὡς φρονίμοις λέγω, κρίνατε ὑμεῖς ὅ φημι. 16 τὸ ποτήριον τῆς
As to prudent ones I say, judge you what I say. The cup

2129 3739 2127 3780 2842 3588 129 3588
εὐλογίας ὃ εὐλογοῦμεν, οὐχὶ κοινωνία τοῦ αἵματος τοῦ
of blessing which we bless, not a partaking of the blood

5547 2076 3588 740 3739 2806 3780 2842 3588
Χριστοῦ ἐστί; τὸν ἄρτον ὃν κλῶμεν, οὐχὶ κοινωνία τοῦ
of Christ is? The bread which we break, not a partaking of the

4983 3588 5547 2076 3754 1520 740 1520 4983 3588
σώματος τοῦ Χριστοῦ ἐστιν; 17 ὅτι εἷς ἄρτος, ἓν σῶμα, οἱ
body of Christ is? Because one bread, one body, the

4183 2070 3588 1063 3956 1537 3588 1520 740 3348
πολλοί ἐσμεν· οἱ γὰρ πάντες ἐκ τοῦ ἑνὸς ἄρτου μετέχομεν.
many we are; for all of the one Bread we partake.

991 3588 2474 2596 4561 3780 3588 2068 3588
18 βλέπετε τὸν Ἰσραὴλ κατὰ σάρκα· οὐχὶ οἱ ἐσθίοντες τὰς
See Israel according to flesh; not those eating the

2378 2844 3588 2379 1526 5101 3767 5346 3754
θυσίας κοινωνοὶ τοῦ θυσιαστηρίου εἰσί; 19 τί οὖν φημι; ὅτι
sacrifices sharers of the altar are? What then do I say? That

14 Wherefore, my dearly beloved, flee from idolatry.
15 I speak as to wise men; judge ye what I say.
16 The cup of blessing which we bless, is it not the communion of the blood of Christ? The bread which we break, is it not the communion of the body of Christ?

17 For we (being) many are one bread, (and) one body: for we are all partakers of that one bread.

18 Behold Israel after the flesh: are not they which eat of the sacrifices partakers of the altar?
19 What say I then? that

Literal Translation | **1 Corinthians 10:20** | ***King James Version***

an idol is anything, or that an idolatrous sacrifice is anything?
20 But the things the nations sacrifice, (they) sacrifice to demons, and not to God. (Deut.32:17) But I do not want you to become sharers of demons;
21 you are not able to drink (the) cup of the Lord and a cup of demons; you are not able to partake of the table of (the) Lord, and a table of demons.
22 Or do we provoke the Lord to jealousy? Are we stronger (than) He?

23 All things are lawful to me, but not all things profit. All things are lawful to me, but not all things build up.
24 Let no one seek the thing of himself, but each one that of the other.
25 Eat everything being sold in a meat market, examining nothing because of conscience,
26 for "the earth (is) the Lord's, and the fullness of it." (Psa. 24:1)
27 And if any of the unbelievers invite you, and you desire to go, eat everything set before you, examining nothing because of conscience.

28 But if anyone tells you, This is slain in sacrifice, do not eat, because of that one pointing (it) out, and the conscience; for "the earth (is) the Lord's, and the fullness of it." (Psa. 24:1)
29 But I say conscience, not that of himself, but that of the other. For why is my freedom judged by another's conscience?
30 But if I partake by grace, why am I evil spoken of because of what I give thanks (for)?
31 Then whether you eat or drink, or whatever you do, do all things to the glory of God.
32 You be without offense both to Jews and to Greeks, and to the

1497 5100 2076 2228 3754 1494 5100 2076 235/3754/3739
εἴδωλόν τί ἐστιν; ἢ ὅτι εἰδωλοθυτόν τί ἐστιν; 20 ἀλλ᾽ ὅτι ἃ
an idol anything is? Or that an idol sacrifice anything is? But that what
2380 3588 1484 1140 2380 2532 3756 2316 3756 2309 1161 5209
θύει τὰ ἔθνη, δαιμονίοις θύει, καὶ οὐ Θεῷ· οὐ θέλω δὲ ὑμᾶς
sacrifice the nations, to demons sacrifice, and not to God; not I want but you
2844 3588 1140 1096 3756 1410 4221
κοινωνοὺς τῶν δαιμονίων γίνεσθαι. 21 οὐ δύνασθε ποτήριον
sharers of demons to become. not You are able a cup
2962 4095 2532 4221 1140 3756 1410 5132
Κυρίου πίνειν καὶ ποτήριον δαιμονίων· οὐ δύνασθε τραπέζης
of (the) Lord to drink and a cup of demons; not you are able a table
2962 3348 2532 5132 1140 2228 3863
Κυρίου μετέχειν καὶ τραπέζης δαιμονίων. 22 ἢ παραζηλοῦμεν
of (the) Lord to partake and a table of demons. Or do we make jealous
3588 2962 3361 2478 846 2070
τὸν Κύριον; μὴ ἰσχυρότεροι αὐτοῦ ἐσμεν;
the Lord? Not stronger (than) Him we are?

3956 3427 1832 235 3756 3956 4851 3956 3427
23. Πάντα μοι ἔξεστιν, ἀλλ᾽ οὐ πάντα συμφέρει. πάντα μοι
All things to me are lawful, but not all things profit. All things to me
1832 235 3756 3956 3618 3367 3588 1438 2212
ἔξεστιν, ἀλλ᾽ οὐ πάντα οἰκοδομεῖ. 24 μηδεὶς τὸ ἑαυτοῦ ζητείτω,
are lawful, but not all things build up. No one the thing of himself seeks,
235 3588 3588 2087 1538 3956 3588 1722 3111 4453
ἀλλὰ τὸ τοῦ ἑτέρου ἕκαστος. 25 πᾶν τὸ ἐν μακέλλῳ πωλού-
but the thing of the other each one. Everything in a meat market being
2068 3367 350 1223 3588 4893 3588
μενον ἐσθίετε μηδὲν ἀνακρίνοντες διὰ τὴν συνείδησιν· 26 τοῦ
sold eat nothing examining because of conscience; of the
1063 2962 3588 1093 2532 3588 4138 846 1487 1161 5100 2564
γὰρ Κυρίου ἡ γῆ καὶ τὸ πλήρωμα αὐτῆς. 27 εἰ δέ τις καλεῖ
for Lord the earth and the fullness of it (is). if But anyone invites
5209 3588 571 2532 2309 4198 3956 3588 3908
ὑμᾶς τῶν ἀπίστων, καὶ θέλετε πορεύεσθαι, πᾶν τὸ παρατιθέ-
you of the unbelievers, and you desire to go, everything set before
5213 2068 3367 350 1223 3588 4893
μενον ὑμῖν ἐσθίετε, μηδὲν ἀνακρίνοντες διὰ τὴν συνείδησιν.
you eat, nothing examining because of conscience.

1437 1161 5100 5213 2036 5124 1494 2076 3361 2068 1223
28 ἐὰν δέ τις ὑμῖν εἴπη, Τοῦτο εἰδωλόθυτόν ἐστι, μὴ ἐσθίετε, δι
if But anyone you tells, This slain in sacrifice is, not do eat, because
1565 3588 3377 2532 3588 4893 3588 1063 2962
ἐκεῖνον τὸν μηνύσαντα καὶ τὴν συνείδησιν· τοῦ γὰρ Κυριου
that one pointing out and conscience; the for (is the) Lord's
3588 1093 2532 3588 4138 846 4893 1161 3004 3780 3588
ἡ γῆ καὶ τὸ πλήρωμα αὐτῆς. 29 συνείδησιν δὲ λέγω, οὐχὶ τὴν
the earth and the fullness of it. conscience But I say, not he
1438 235 3588 3588 2087 2444 1063 3588 1657 3450
ἑαυτοῦ· ἀλλὰ τὴν τοῦ ἑτέρου· ἱνατί γὰρ ἡ ἐλευθερία μου
of himself; but the (one) of the other; why for the freedom of me
2919 5259 243 4893 1487 1161 1473 5485 3348 5101
κρίνεται ὑπὸ ἄλλης συνειδήσεως; 30 εἰ δὲ ἐγὼ χάριτι μετέχω, τί
is judged by another's conscience? if But I by grace partake, why
987 5228 3739 1473 2168 1535 3767 2068
βλασφημοῦμαι ὑπὲρ οὗ ἐγὼ εὐχαριστῶ; 31 εἴτε οὖν ἐσθίετε,
am I evil spoken of because of what I give thanks (for)? Whether then you eat,
1535 4095 1535 5100 4160 3956 1519 1391 2316 4160
εἴτε πίνετε, εἴτε τι ποιεῖτε, πάντα εἰς δόξαν Θεοῦ ποιεῖτε.
or drink, or what you do, all things to (the) glory of God do.
677 1096 2532 2453 2532 1672 2532 3588
32 ἀπρόσκοποι γίνεσθε καὶ Ἰουδαίοις καὶ Ἕλλησι καὶ τῇ
without offense you be both to Jews and to Greeks and to the

the idol is any thing, or that which is offered in sacrifice to idols is any thing?
20 But I (say), that the things which the Gentiles sacrifice, they sacrifice to devils, and not to God: and I would not that ye should have fellowship with devils.
21 Ye cannot drink the cup of the Lord, and the cup of devils: ye cannot be partakers of the Lord's table, and of the table of devils.
22 Do we provoke the Lord to jealousy? are we stronger than he?

23 All things are lawful for me, but all things are not expedient: all things are lawful for me, but all things edify not.
24 Let no man seek his own, but every man another's (wealth).
25 Whatsoever is sold in the shambles, (that) eat, asking no question for conscience sake:
26 For the earth (is) the Lord's, and the fulness thereof.
27 If any of them that believe not bid you (to a feast), and ye be disposed to go; whatsoever is set before you, eat, asking no question for conscience sake.

28 But if any man say unto you, This is offered in sacrifice unto idols, eat not for his sake that shewed it, and for conscience sake: for the earth (is) the Lord's, and the fulness thereof:
29 Conscience, I say, not thine own, but of the other: for why is my liberty judged of another (man's) conscience?
30 For if I by grace be a partaker, why am I evil spoken of for that for which I give thanks?
31 Whether therefore ye eat, or drink, or whatsoever ye do, do all to the glory of God.

32 Give none offence, neither to the Jews, nor to the Gentiles, nor to the

Literal Translation

church of God.
33 Even as I also please all in all things, not seeking my own advantage, but that of the many, that they may be saved.

1 Corinthians 10:33

1577 3588 2316 2531 2504 3956 3956 700 3361
ἐκκλησίᾳ τοῦ Θεοῦ· 33 καθὼς κἀγὼ πάντα πᾶσιν ἀρέσκω, μὴ
church of God; even as I also (in) all things all please, not

2212 3588 1683 4851 235 3588 3588 4183 2443
ζητῶν τὸ ἐμαυτοῦ σύμφέρον, ἀλλὰ τὸ τῶν πολλῶν, ἵνα
seeking the of myself advantage, but of the many, that

4982
σωθῶσι.
they may be saved.

King James Version

church of God:
33 Even as I please all (men) in all (things), not seeking mine own profit, but the (profit) of many, that they may be saved.

1 Corinthians 11

1. Become imitators of me, as I also of Christ.

2 But I praise you, brothers, because in all things you have remembered me, and even as I delivered to you, you hold fast the traditions.
3 But I want you to know that Christ is the Head of every man, and the man (is) the head of a woman, and God (is the) head of Christ.
4 Every man praying or prophesying, having (anything) down over (his) head shames his Head.
5 And every woman praying or prophesying with the head uncovered dishonors her head, for it is the same (as) being shaved.

6 For if a woman is not covered, let her also be shorn. But (if it) is shameful for a woman to be shorn, or to be shaved, let her be covered.
7 For truly a man ought not to have the head covered, being (the) image and glory of God; but woman is (the) glory of a man;
8 for man is not out of the woman, but woman out of man;
9 for also man was not created for the sake of the woman, but woman for the sake of the man.
10 Because of this, the woman ought to have authority on the head, because of the angels.
11 However, man is not apart from woman, nor

1 Corinthians 11

3402 3450 1096 2531 2504 5547
1. μιμηταί μου γίνεσθε, καθὼς κἀγὼ Χριστοῦ.
imitators of me Become, even as I also of Christ.

1867 1161 5209 80 3754 3956 3450 3415 2532
2. Ἐπαινῶ δὲ ὑμᾶς, ἀδελφοί, ὅτι πάντα μου μέμνησθε, καὶ
I praise But you, brothers, because all things of me you recalled, and

2531 3860 5213 3588 3862 2722 2309 1161
καθὼς παρέδωκα ὑμῖν τὰς παραδόσεις κατέχετε. 3 θέλω δὲ
even as I delivered to you the traditions you hold fast. I desire But

5209 1492 3754 3956 435 3588 2776 3588 5547 2076
ὑμᾶς εἰδέναι, ὅτι παντὸς ἀνδρὸς ἡ κεφαλὴ ὁ Χριστός ἐστι·
you to know, that of every man the head Christ is;

2776 1161 1135 3588 435 2776 1161 5547 3588 2316 3956
κεφαλὴ δὲ γυναικὸς ὁ ἀνήρ· κεφαλὴ δὲ Χριστοῦ, ὁ Θεός. 4 πᾶς
(the) head and of a woman the man; (the) head and of Christ, God. Every

435 4336 2228 4395 2596 2776 2192
ἀνὴρ προσευχόμενος ἢ προφητεύων, κατὰ κεφαλῆς ἔχων,
man praying or prophesying, down over (his) head having,

2617 3588 2776 846 3956 1161 1135 4336
καταισχύνει τὴν κεφαλὴν αὐτοῦ. 5 πᾶσα δὲ γυνὴ προσευχο-
shames the Head of him. every But woman praying

2228 4395 177 3588 2776 2617
μένη ἢ προφητεύουσα ἀκατακαλύπτῳ τῇ κεφαλῇ, καταισχύνει
or prophesying uncovered with the head, shames

3588 2776 1438 1520 1063 2076 2532 3588 846 3588 3587
τὴν κεφαλὴν εαὐτῆς· ἓν γάρ ἐστι καὶ τὸ αὐτὸ τῇ ἐξυρημένῃ.
the head of herself; one for it is and the same with being shaved.

1487 1063 3756 2619 1135 2532 2751 1487 1161 150
6 εἰ γὰρ οὐ κατακαλύπτεται γυνή, καὶ κειράσθω· εἰ δὲ αἰσχρὸν
if For not is covered a woman, also let her be shorn; if but shameful

1135 3588 2751 2228 3587 2619 2619
γυναικὶ τὸ κείρασθαι ἢ ξυρᾶσθαι, κατακαλυπτέσθω. 7 ἀνὴρ
for a woman to be shorn or to be shaved, let her be covered. a man

3303 1063 3756 3784 2619 3588 2776 1504 2532
μὲν γὰρ οὐκ ὀφείλει κατακαλύπτεσθαι τὴν κεφαλήν, εἰκὼν καὶ
indeed For not ought to be covered the head, (the) image and

1391 2316 5225 1135 1161 1391 435 2076 3756 1063
δόξα Θεοῦ ὑπάρχων· γυνὴ δὲ δόξα ἀνδρός ἐστιν. 8 οὐ γὰρ
glory of God being; the woman but glory of a man is. not For

2076 2076 1537 1135 235 1135 1537 435 2532 1063 3756
ἐστιν ἀνὴρ ἐκ γυναικός, ἀλλὰ γυνὴ ἐξ ἀνδρός· 9 καὶ γὰρ οὐκ
is man out of woman, but woman out of man; also for not

2936 435 1223 3588 1135 235 1135 1223 3588 435
ἐκτίσθη ἀνὴρ διὰ τὴν γυναῖκα, ἀλλὰ γυνὴ διὰ τὸν ἄνδρα·
was created man because of the woman, but woman because of the man;

1223 5124 3784 3588 1135 1849 2192 1909 3588 2776
10 διὰ τοῦτο ὀφείλει ἡ γυνὴ ἐξουσίαν ἔχειν ἐπὶ τῆς κεφαλῆς
Because of this ought the woman authority to have on the head

1223 3588 32 4133 3777 435 5565 1135 3777
διὰ τοὺς ἀγγέλους. 11 πλὴν οὔτε ἀνὴρ χωρὶς γυναικός, οὔτε
because of the angels. But neither man apart from woman, nor

1 Corinthians 11

1. Be ye followers of me, even as I also (am) of Christ.

2 Now I praise you, brethren, that ye remember me in all things, and keep the ordinances, as I delivered (them) to you.
3 But I would have you know, that the head of every man is Christ; and the head of the woman (is) the man; and the head of Christ (is) God.
4 Every man praying or prophesying, having (his) head covered, dishonoureth his head.

5 But every woman that prayeth or prophesieth with (her) head uncovered dishonoureth her head: for that is even all one as if she were shaven.

6 For if the woman be not covered, let her also be shorn: but if it be a shame for a woman to be shorn or shaven, let her be covered.
7 For a man indeed ought not to cover (his) head, forasmuch as he is the image and glory of God: but the woman is the glory of the man.
8 For the man is not of the woman; but the woman of the man.
9 Neither was the man created for the woman; but the woman for the man.
10 For this cause ought the woman to have power on (her) head because of the angels.
11 Nevertheless neither is the man without the woman, neither

Literal Translation

woman apart from man, in (the) Lord.
12 For as the woman (is) out of the man, so also the man through the woman; but all things from God.

13 Judge among yourselves: is it fitting (for) a woman to pray to God uncovered?
14 Or does not nature herself teach you that if a man indeed wears long hair, it is a dishonor to him?

15 But a woman if she wears hair long, it is a glory to her; because the hair has been given to her instead of a covering.
16 But if anyone thinks to be contentious, we do not have such a custom, neither the churches of God.

17 But enjoining this, I do not praise (you), because you come together not for the better, but for the worse.
18 Fot indeed, firstly, I hear divisions to be among you (when) you come together in the church. And I believe some part.
19 For there must also be heresies among you, so that the approved ones may become revealed among you.

20 Then you coming together into one place, it is not to eat (the) Lord's supper.
21 For each one takes (his) own supper first in the eating; and one is hungry, and another drunken.
22 For do you not have houses (in which) to eat and to drink? Or do you despise the church of God, and shame those who have not? What do I say to you? Shall I praise you for this? I do not praise.
23 For I received from the Lord what I also delivered to you, that the Lord Jesus

1 Corinthians 11:12

1135 5565 435 1722 2962 5618 1063 3588 1135 1722 3588
γυνὴ χωρὶς ἀνδρός, ἐν Κυρίῳ· 12 ὥσπερ γὰρ ἡ γυνὴ ἐκ τοῦ
woman apart from man, in (the) Lord; as for the woman out of the

435 3779 2532 3588 435 1223 3588 1135 3588 1161 3956
ἀνδρός, οὕτω καὶ ὁ ἀνὴρ διὰ τῆς γυναικός, τὰ δὲ πάντα
man, so also the man through the woman, but all things

1537 3588 2316 1722 5213 846 2919 4241 2076 1135
ἐκ τοῦ Θεοῦ. 13 ἐν ὑμῖν αὐτοῖς κρίνατε· πρέπον ἐστι γυναῖκα
from God. Among yourselves judge; fitting is it (for) a woman

177 3588 2316 4336 2228 3761 846 3588
ἀκατακάλυπτον τῷ Θεῷ προσεύχεσθαι; 14 ἢ οὐδὲ αὐτὴ ἡ
uncovered to God to pray? Not herself

5449 1321 5209 3754 435 3303 1437 2863 819
φύσις διδάσκει ὑμᾶς, ὅτι ἀνὴρ μὲν ἐὰν κομᾷ, ἀτιμία
nature teaches you, that a man indeed if he wears long hair, a dishonor

846 2076 1135 1161 1437 2863 1391 846 2076 3754
αὐτῷ ἐστι; 15 γυνὴ δὲ ἐὰν κομᾷ. δόξα αὐτῇ ἐστιν; ὅτι
to him it is? a woman But if she wears long hair a glory to her it is? Because

3588 2864 473 4018 1325 846 1487 1161 5100
ἡ κόμη ἀντὶ περιβολαίου δέδοται αὐτῇ. 16 εἰ δέ τις
the long hair instead of a covering has been given to her. if But anyone

1380 5380 1511 2249 5108 4914 3756 2192
δοκεῖ φιλόνεικος εἶναι, ἡμεῖς τοιαύτην συνήθειαν οὐκ ἔχομεν,
thinks contentious to be, we such a custom not do have,

3761 3588 1577 3588 2316
οὐδὲ αἱ ἐκκλησίαι τοῦ Θεοῦ.
neither the churches of God.

5124 1161 3853 3756 1867 3754 3756 1519 3588
17. Τοῦτο δὲ παραγγέλλων οὐκ ἐπαινῶ, ὅτι οὐκ εἰς τὸ
this But enjoining not I praise (you), because not for the

2909 235 1519 3588 2276 4905 4412 3303 1063
κρεῖττον ἀλλ᾽ εἰς τὸ ἧττον συνέρχεσθε. 18 πρῶτον μὲν γὰρ
better, but for the worse you come together. firstly indeed For

4905 5216 1722 3588 1577 191 4978 1722
συνερχομένων ὑμῶν ἐν τῃ ἐκκλησίᾳ, ἀκούω σχίσματα ἐν
coming together you in the church, I hear divisions among

5213 5225 2532 3313 5100 4100 1163 1063 2532 139 1722
ὑμῖν ὑπάρχειν, καὶ μέρος τι πιστεύω. 19 δεῖ γὰρ καὶ αἱρέσεις ἐν
you to be, and part some I believe. must For also heresies among

5213 1511 2443 3588 1384 5318 1096 1722 5213
ὑμῖν εἶναι, ἵνα οἱ δόκιμοι φανεροὶ γένωνται ἐν ὑμῖν.
you to be, that the approved ones revealed may become among you.

4905 3767 5216 1909 3588 846 3756 2076 2960
20 συνερχομένων οὖν ὑμῶν ἐπὶ τὸ αὐτὸ, οὐκ ἔστι Κυριακὸν
Coming together then you in one place, not it is of (the) Lord

1173 5315 1538 1063 3588 2398 1173 4301
δεῖπνον φαγεῖν. 21 ἕκαστος γὰρ τὸ ἴδιον δεῖπνον προλαμβάνει
a supper to eat. each one For the own supper takes first

1722 3588 5315 2532 3739 3303 3983 3739 1161 3184 3361 1063 3614
ἐν τῷ φαγεῖν, καὶ ὃς μὲν πεινᾷ, ὃς δὲ μεθύει. 22 μὴ γὰρ οἰκίας
in eating, and one hungers, another drunken. not For houses

3756 2192 1519 3588 2068 2532 4095 2228 3588 1577 3588 2316
οὐκ ἔχετε εἰς τὸ ἐσθίειν καὶ πίνειν; ἢ τῆς ἐκκλησίας τοῦ Θεοῦ
not you have in order to eat and to drink? Or the church of God

2706 2532 2617 3588 3361 2192 5101 5213 2036
καταφρονεῖτε, καὶ καταισχύνετε τοὺς μὴ ἔχοντας; τί ὑμῖν εἴπω;
do you despise, and shame those not having? What to you say I?

1867 5209 1722 5129 3756 1867 1473 1063 3880
ἐπαινέσω ὑμᾶς ἐν τούτῳ; οὐκ ἐπαινῶ. 23 Ἐγὼ γὰρ παρέλαβον
Shall I praise you in this? Not I praise. I For received

575 3588 2962 3739 2532 3860 5213 3754 3588 2962 S2424
ἀπὸ τοῦ Κυρίου, ὃ καὶ παρέδωκα ὑμῖν, ὅτι ὁ Κύριος Ἰησοῦς
from the Lord, what also I delivered to you, that the Lord Jesus

King James Version

the woman without the man, in the Lord.
12 For as the woman (is) of the man, even so (is) the man also by the woman; but all things of God.

13 Judge in yourselves: is it comely that a woman pray unto God uncovered?
14 Doth not even nature itself teach you, that, if a man have long hair, it is a shame unto him?

15 But if a woman have long hair, it is a glory to her: for (her) hair is given her for a covering.
16 But if any man seem to be contentious, we have no such custom, neither the churches of God.

17 Now in this that I declare (unto you) I praise (you) not, that ye come together not for the better, but for the worse.
18 For first of all, when ye come together in the church, I hear that there be divisions among you; and I partly believe it.
19 For there must be also heresies among you, that they which are approved may be made manifest among you.

20 When ye come together therefore into one place, (this) is not to eat the Lord's supper.
21 For in eating every one taketh before (other) his own supper: and one is hungry, and another is drunken.
22 What? have ye not houses to eat and to drink in? or despise ye the church of God, and shame them that have not? What shall I say to you? shall I praise you in this? I praise (you) not.
23 For I have received of the Lord that which also I delivered unto you, That the Lord Jesus

Literal Translation

1 Corinthians 11:24

King James Version

in the night in which He
was betrayed took
bread;
24 and giving thanks,
He broke and said,
"Take, eat; this is My
body which is broken
on behalf of you; this do
in remembrance of
Me."

25 In the same way the
cup, after the supping,
(He) said, "This cup is
the new covenant in My
blood; as often as you
may drink, do this in re-
membrance of Me."
(See Luke 22:19, 20)
26 For as often as you
may eat this bread, and
drink this cup, you sol-
emnly proclaim the
death of the Lord, until
He shall come.

27 So that whoever
should eat this bread, or
drink the cup of the
Lord, unworthily, (that
one) will be guilty of the
body and of the blood of
the Lord.
28 But let a man exam-
ine himself, and so let
him eat of the bread, and
let him drink of the cup;

29 for the (one) eating
and drinking un-
worthily eats and drinks
judgment to himself,
not discerning the body
of the Lord.
30 Because of this
many among you (are)
weak and feeble, and
many sleep.
31 For if we discerned
ourselves, we would
not be judged.
32 But being judged, we
are chastened by (the)
Lord, that we not be
condemned with the
world.
33 So that, my brothers,
coming together to eat,
wait for one another.
34 But if anyone hun-
gers, let him eat at
home, that you not
come together for judg-
ment. And the rest, I will
set in order whenever I
come.

1722 3588 3571 3739 3860 2983 740 2532 2168
ἐν τῇ νυκτὶ ᾗ παρεδίδοτο ἔλαβεν ἄρτον, 24 καὶ εὐχαριστήσας
in the night in which He was betrayed took bread, and giving thanks

2806 2532 2036 2983 5315 5124 3450 2076 3588 4983 3588
ἔκλασε, καὶ εἶπε, Λάβετε, φάγετε, τοῦτό μού ἐστι τὸ σῶμα τὸ
broke, and said, Take, eat, this of me is the body on

5228 5216 2806 5124 4160 1519 3588 1699 364
ὑπὲρ ὑμῶν κλώμενον· τοῦτο ποιεῖτε εἰς τὴν ἐμὴν ἀνάμνησιν.
behalf of you broken; this do for My remembrance.

5615 2532 3588 4221 3326 3588 1172 3004 5124
25 ὡσαύτως καὶ τὸ ποτήριον, μετὰ τὸ δειπνῆσαι, λέγων, Τοῦτο
in the same way And the cup, after the to sup, said, This

3588 4221 3588 2537 1242 2076 1722 3588 1699 129 5124
τὸ ποτήριον ἡ καινὴ διαθήκη ἐστὶν ἐν τῷ ἐμῷ αἵματι· τοῦτο
cup the new covenant is in My blood; this

4160 3740 302 4095 1519 3588 1699 364 3740
ποιεῖτε, ὁσάκις ἂν πίνητε, εἰς τὴν ἐμὴν ἀνάμνησιν. 26 ὁσάκις
do, as often as you may drink, for My remembrance. as often as

1063 302 2068 3588 740 5126 2532 3588 4221 5124
γὰρ ἂν ἐσθίητε τὸν ἄρτον τοῦτον, καὶ τὸ ποτήριον τοῦτο
For you may eat bread this, and cup this

4095 3588 2288 3588 2962 2605 891 3757 302
πίνητε, τὸν θάνατον τοῦ Κυρίου καταγγέλλετε ἄχρις ου ἂν
drink, the death of the Lord you proclaim until He may

2064 5620 3739 302 2068 3588 740 5126 2228 4095 3588
ἔλθῃ. 27 ὥστε ὃς ἂν ἐσθίῃ τὸν ἄρτον τοῦτον ἢ πίνῃ τὸ
come. So as whoever may eat bread this or drink the

4221 3588 2962 371 1777 2071 3588 4983 2532
ποτήριον τοῦ Κυρίου ἀναξίως, ἔνοχος ἔσται τοῦ σώματος καὶ
cup the Lord unworthily, guilty will be of the body and

129 3588 2962 1381 1161 444 1438 2532
αἵματος τοῦ Κυρίου. 28 δοκιμαζέτω δὲ ἄνθρωπος ἑαυτόν, καὶ
blood of the Lord. let examine But a man himself, and

3779 1537 3588 740 2068 2532 1537 3588 4221 4095
οὕτως ἐκ τοῦ ἄρτου ἐσθιέτω, καὶ ἐκ τοῦ ποτηρίου πινέτω.
so of the bread let him eat, and of the cup let him drink.

3588 1063 2068 2532 4095 371 2917 1437 2068 2532
29 ὁ γὰρ ἐσθίων καὶ πίνων ἀναξίως, κρίμα ἑαυτῷ ἐσθίει καὶ
the (one) For eating and drinking unworthily, judgment to himself eats and

4095 3361 1252 3588 4983 3588 2962 1223 5124 1722 5213
πίνει, μὴ διακρίνων τὸ σῶμα τοῦ Κυρίου. 30 διὰ τοῦτο ἐν ὑμῖν
drinks, not discerning the body of the Lord. Because of this among you

4183 772 2532 732 2532 2837 2425 1487 1063
πολλοὶ ἀσθενεῖς καὶ ἄρρωστοι, καὶ κοιμῶνται ἱκανοί. 31 εἰ γὰρ
(are) many weak and feeble, and sleep a number. if For

1438 1252 3756 302 2919 2919 1161
ἑαυτοὺς διεκρίνομεν, οὐκ ἂν ἐκρινόμεθα. 32 κρινόμενοι δέ,
ourselves we discerned, not we would be judged. being judged But,

5259 2962 3811 2443 3361 4862 3588 2889 2632
ὑπὸ Κυρίου παιδευομεθα, ἵνα μὴ σὺν τῷ κόσμῳ κατακριθῶμεν.
by (the) Lord we are chastened, that not with the world we are condemned.

5620 80 3450 4905 1519 3588 5315 240
33 ὥστε, ἀδελφοί μου, συνερχόμενοι εἰς τὸ φαγεῖν, ἀλλήλους
So as, brothers of me, coming together for the to eat, one another

1551 1487 1161 5100 3983 1722 3624 2068 2443 3361 1519 2917
ἐκδέχεσθε. 34 εἴ δὲ τις πεινᾷ, ἐν οἴκῳ ἐσθιέτω, ἵνα μὴ εἰς κρίμα
await. if And any hungers, at home let him eat, that not to judgment

4905 3588 1161 3062 5613 302 2064 1299
συνέρχησθε. τὰ δὲ λοιπά, ὡς ἂν ἔλθω, διατάξομαι.
you come together. the And rest, whenever I come, I will set in order.

the (same) night in
which he was betrayed
took bread:
24 And when he had
given thanks, he brake
(it), and said, Take, eat:
this is my body, which
is broken for you: this
do in remembrance of
me.

25 After the same man-
ner also (he took) the
cup, when he had
supped, saying, This
cup is the new testament
in my blood: this do ye,
as oft as ye drink (it), in
remembrance of me.
26 For as often as ye eat
this bread, and drink
this cup, ye do shew the
Lord's death till he
come.

27 Wherefore whoso-
ever shall eat this bread,
and drink (this) cup of
the Lord, unworthily,
shall be guilty of the
body and blood of the
Lord.
28 But let a man exam-
ine himself, and so let
him eat of (that) bread,
and drink of (that) cup.

29 For he that eateth and
drinketh unworthily,
eateth and drinketh
damnation to himself,
not discerning the
Lord's body.
30 For this cause many
(are) weak and sickly
among you, and many
sleep.
31 For if we would
judge ourselves, we
should not be judged.
32 But when we are
judged, we are chas-
tened of the Lord, that
we should not be con-
demned with the world.
33 Wherefore, my
brethren, when ye come
together to eat, tarry one
for another.
34 And if any man hun-
ger, let him eat at home;
that ye come not to-
gether unto condemna-
tion. And the rest will I
set in order when I
come.

Literal Translation

1 Corinthians 12

1. But concerning the
spiritual things, broth-
ers, I do not wish you to
be ignorant.
2 You know that being
led away, you nations
were led to dumb idols.
3 Because of this I make
known to you that no
one speaking by (the)
Spirit of God says, Je-
sus (is) a curse. And no
one is able to say Jesus
(is) Lord, except by
(the) Holy Spirit.

4 And there are differ-
ences of gifts, but the
same Spirit;
5 and there are differ-
ences of ministries, yet
the same Lord.

6 And there are differ-
ences of workings, but
the same God is work-
ing all things in all.
7 And to each one is
given the showing forth
of the Spirit to profit
(each).
8 For through the Spirit
is given to one a word of
wisdom, and to another
a word of knowledge,
according to the same
Spirit;
9 and to another, faith by
the same Spirit, and to
another, gifts of healing
by the same Spirit,
10 and to another,
workings of powers,
and to another, proph-
ecy, and to another, dis-
cerning of spirits, and to
another, kinds of lan-
guages, and to another,
interpretation of
tongues.

11 And the one and the
same Spirit works all
these things, distribut-
ing separately to each as
He purposes.

12 For even as the body
is one, and has many
members, but all the
members of the one
body, being many, (are)
one body, so also (is)
Christ.
13 For also we all were
baptized by one Spirit
into one body, whether
Jews or

1 Corinthians 12

4012 1161 3588 4152 80 3756 2309 5209 50
1. Περὶ δὲ τῶν πνευματικῶν, ἀδελφοί, οὐ θέλω ὑμᾶς ἀγνοεῖν.
concerning And the spiritual matters, brothers, not I wish you to be ignorant.

1492 3754 1484 2258 4314 3588 1497 3588 880 5613 302 71
2 οἴδατε ὅτι ἔθνη ἦτε πρὸς τὰ εἴδωλα τὰ ἄφωνα, ὡς ἂν ἤγεσθε
You know that nations you were to the idols voiceless, as you may be led

520 1352 1107 5213 3754 3762 1722 4151
ἀπαγόμενοι. 3 διὸ γνωρίζω ὑμῖν, ὅτι οὐδεὶς ἐν Πνεύματι
being led away. Therefore I make known to you, that no one by (the) Spirit

2316 2980 3004 331 2424 2532 3762 1410 2036
Θεοῦ λαλῶν λέγει ἀνάθεμα Ἰησοῦς· καὶ οὐδεὶς δύναται εἰπεῖ,
of God speaking says, A curse (is) Jesus; and no one is able to say,

2962 2424 1487 3361 1722 4151 40
Κύριος Ἰησοῦς, εἰ μὴ ἐν Πνεύματι Ἁγίῳ.
Lord Jesus. except by (the) Spirit Holy.

1243 1161 5486 1526 3588 1161 846 4151 2532
4. Διαιρέσεις δὲ χαρισμάτων εἰσί, τὸ δὲ αὐτὸ Πνεῦμα. 5 καὶ
differences But of gifts there are, the but same Spirit. And

1248 1526 1526 2532 3588 846 2962 2532 1243
διαιρέσεις διακονιῶν εἰσί, καὶ ὁ αὐτὸς Κύριος. 6 καὶ διαιρέ-
differences of ministries there are, and the same Lord. And differences

1755 1526 3588 1161 846 2076 2316 3588 1754 3588
σεις ἐνεργημάτων εἰσίν, ὁ δὲ αὐτὸς ἐστι Θεός, ὁ ἐνεργῶν τὰ
of workings there are, the and same is God, working

3956 1722 3956 1538 1161 1325 3588 5321 3588
πάντα ἐν πᾶσιν. 7 ἑκάστῳ δὲ δίδοται ἡ φανέρωσις τοῦ
all things in all. to each one But is given the showing forth of the

4151 4314 3588 4851 3739 3303 1063 1223 3588 4151
Πνεύματος πρὸς τὸ συμφέρον. 8 ᾧ μὲν γὰρ διὰ τοῦ Πνεύματος
Spirit to profit (each). to one For through the Spirit

1325 3056 4678 243 1161 3056 1108 2596 3588
δίδοται λόγος σοφίας, ἄλλῳ δὲ λόγος γνώσεως κατὰ τὸ
is given a word of wisdom, to another and a word of knowledge according to the

846 4151 2087 1161 4102 1722 3588 846 4151 243 1161
αὐτὸ Πνεῦμα, 9 ἑτέρῳ δὲ πίστις, ἐν τῷ αὐτῷ Πνεύματι, ἄλλῳ δὲ
same Spirit, to another and faith, by the same Spirit, to another and

5486 2386 1722 3588 846 4151 243 1161 1755
χαρίσματα ἰαμάτων, ἐν τῷ αὐτῷ Πνεύματι· 10 ἄλλῳ δὲ ἐνεργή-
gifts of healing, by the same Spirit; to another and workings

1411 243 1161 4394 243 1161 1253
ματα δυνάμεων, ἄλλῳ δὲ προφητεία, ἄλλῳ δὲ διακρίσεις
of powers, to another and prophecy, to another and discernings

4151 2087 1161 1085 1100 243 1161 2058
πνευμάτων, ἑτέρῳ δὲ γένη γλωσσῶν, ἄλλῳ δὲ ἑρμηνεία
of spirits, to another and kinds of tongues, to another and interpretation

1100 3956 1161 5023 1754 3588 1722 2532 3588 846 4151
γλωσσῶν· 11 πάντα δὲ ταῦτα ἐνεργεῖ τὸ ἓν καὶ τὸ αὐτὸ Πνεῦμα,
of tongues; all and these things works the one and the same Spirit,

1244 2398 1538 2531 1014
διαιροῦν ἰδίᾳ ἑκάστῳ καθὼς βούλεται.
distributing separately to each as He purposes.

2509 1063 3588 4983 1520 2076 2532 3196 2192 4183
12. Καθάπερ γὰρ τὸ σῶμα ἕν ἐστι, καὶ μέλη ἔχει πολλά,
even as For the body one is, and members has many,

3956 1161 3588 3196 3588 4983 3588 1520 4183 5607 1520
πάντα δὲ τὰ μέλη τοῦ σώματος τοῦ ἑνός, πολλὰ ὄντα, ἕν
all but the members of the body one, many being, one

2076 4983 3779 2532 3588 5547 2532 1063 1722 1520 4151
ἐστι σῶμα, οὕτω καὶ ὁ Χριστός. 13 καὶ γὰρ ἐν ἑνὶ Πνεύματι
is body, so also the Christ. also For by one Spirit

2249 3956 1519 1722 4983 907 1535 2453 1535
ἡμεῖς πάντες εἰς ἓν σῶμα ἐβαπτίσθημεν, εἴτε Ἰουδαῖοι εἴτε
we all into one body were baptized, whether Jews or

King James Version

1 Corinthians 12

1. Now concerning
spiritual (gifts), breth-
ren, I would not have
you ignorant.
2 Ye know that ye were
Gentiles, carried away
unto these dumb idols,
even as ye were led.
3 Wherefore I give you
to understand, that no
man speaking by the
Spirit of God calleth Je-
sus accursed: and (that)
no man can say that Je-
sus is the Lord, but by
the Holy Ghost.

4 Now there are diver-
sities of gifts, but the
same Spirit.
5 And there are differ-
ences of administra-
tions, but the same
Lord.
6 And there are diversi-
ties of operations, but it
is the same God which
worketh all in all.
7 But the manifestation
of the Spirit is given to
every man to profit
withal.
8 For to one is given by
the Spirit the word of
wisdom; to another the
word of knowledge by
the same Spirit;

9 To another faith by the
same Spirit; to another
the gifts of healing by
the same Spirit;
10 To another the work-
ing of miracles; to an-
other prophecy; to an-
other discerning of spir-
its; to another (divers)
kinds of tongues; to an-
other the interpretation
of tongues:

11 But all these worketh
that one and the self-
same Spirit, dividing to
every man severally as
he will.

12 For as the body is
one, and hath many
members, and all the
members of that one
body, being many, are
one body: so also (is)
Christ.
13 For by one Spirit are
we all baptized into one
body, whether (we be)
Jews or

Literal Translation | **1 Corinthians 12:14** | **King James Version**

Greeks, whether slaves
or free, even all were
given to drink into one
Spirit.
14 For also the body is
not one member, but
many.
15 If the foot says, Be-
cause I am not a hand, I
am not of the body, on
account of this, is it not
of the body?
16 And if the ear says,
Because I am not an
eye, I am not of the
body, on account of this,
is it not of the body?
17 If all the body (were)
an eye, where (would
be) the hearing? If all
hearing, where the
smelling?
18 But now God set the
members, each one of
them, in the body, even
as He desired.
19 But if all was one
member, where
(would) the body (be)?
20 But now, indeed,
many (are) the mem-
bers, but one body.
21 And the eye is not
able to say to the hand, I
have no need of you; or
again the head to the
feet, I have no need of
you.
22 But much rather the
members of the body
seeming to be weaker
are necessary.
23 And those of the
body we think to be less
honorable, to these we
put more abundant
honor around (them).
And our unpresentable
(members) have more
abundant propriety.
24 But our presentable
(members) have no
need. But God tem-
pered the body together,
having given more
abundant honor to the
(member) having need,
25 that there not be divi-
sion in the body, but
(that) the members
might have the same
care for one another.
26 And if one member
suffers, all the members
suffer with (it). If one
member is glorified, all
the members rejoice
with (it).

1672 1535 1401 1535 1658 2532 3956 1519 1520 4151
Ἕλληνες, εἴτε δοῦλοι εἴτε ἐλεύθεροι· καὶ πάντες εἰς ἓν Πνεῦμα
Greeks, whether slaves or free; and all into one Spirit

4222 2532 1063 3588 4983 3756 2076 1520 3196 235
ἐποτίσθημεν. 14 καὶ γὰρ τὸ σῶμα οὐκ ἔστιν ἓν μέλος, ἀλλὰ
were given to drink. also For the body not is one member, but

4183 1437 2036 3588 4228 3754 3756 1510 5495 3756 1510 1537 3588
πολλά. 15 ἐὰν εἴπῃ ὁ πούς, Ὅτι οὐκ εἰμὶ χείρ, οὐκ εἰμὶ ἐκ τοῦ
many. If says the foot, Because not I am a hand, not I am of the

4983 3756 3844 5124 3756 2076 1537 3588 4983 2532
σώματος· οὐ παρὰ τοῦτο οὐκ ἔστιν ἐκ τοῦ σώματος; 16 καὶ
body; not on account of this not is (it) of the body? And

1437 2036 3588 3775 3754 3756 1510 3788 3756 1510 1537 3588
ἐὰν εἴπῃ τὸ οὖς, Ὅτι οὐκ εἰμὶ ὀφθαλμός, οὐκ εἰμὶ ἐκ τοῦ
if says the ear, Because not I am an eye, not I am of the

4983 3756 3844 5124 3756 2076 1537 3588 4983 1487
σώματος· οὐ παρὰ τοῦτο οὐκ ἔστιν ἐκ τοῦ σώματος; 17 εἰ
body; not on account of this not is (it) of the body? If

3650 3588 4983 3788 4226 3588 189 1487 3650 189 4226
ὅλον τὸ σῶμα ὀφθαλμός, ποῦ ἡ ἀκοή; εἰ ὅλον ἀκοή, ποῦ
all the body (was) an eye, where the hearing? If all hearing, where

3588 3750 3570/1161/3588/2316/5087 3588 3196 1520 1538 846
ἡ ὄσφρησις; 18 νυνὶ δὲ ὁ Θεὸς ἔθετο τὰ μέλη ἓν ἕκαστον αὐτῶν,
the smelling? now But God set the members one each of them,

1722 3588 4983 2531 2309 1487/1161/2258/3588/3956/1520/3196
ἐν τῷ σώματι καθὼς ἠθέλησεν. 19 εἰ δὲ ἦν τὰ πάντα ἓν μέλος,
in the body even as He desired. if And was all one member,

4226 3588 4983 3568 1161 4183 3303 3196 1520 1161 4983 3756
ποῦ τὸ σῶμα; 20 νῦν δὲ πολλὰ μὲν μέλη, ἓν δὲ σῶμα. 21 οὐ
where the body? now But many indeed members, one but body. not

1410 1161 3588 3788 2036 3588 5495 5532 4675 3756 2192
δύναται δὲ ὁ ὀφθαλμὸς εἰπεῖν τῇ χειρί, Χρείαν σου οὐκ ἔχω·
is able And the eye to say to the hand, Need of you not I have;

2228 3825 3588 2776 3588 4228 5532 5216 3756 2192 235
ἢ πάλιν ἡ κεφαλὴ τοῖς ποσί, Χρείαν ὑμῶν οὐκ ἔχω. 22 ἀλλὰ
or again the head to the feet, Need of you not I have. But

4183 3123 3588 1380 3196 3588 4983 772
πολλῷ μᾶλλον τὰ δοκοῦντα μέλη τοῦ σώματος ἀσθενέ-
by much more the seeming members of the body weaker

5225 316 2076 2532 3739 1380 820
στερα ὑπάρχειν, ἀναγκαῖά ἐστι, 23 καὶ ἃ δοκοῦμεν ἀτιμότερα
to be, necessary is, and which we think less honorable

1511 3588 4983 5125 5092 4053 4060
εἶναι τοῦ σώματος, τούτοις τιμὴν περισσοτέραν περιτίθεμεν·
to be of the body, to these honor more abundant we put around;

2532 3588 809 2257 2157 4053 2192
καὶ τὰ ἀσχήμονα ἡμῶν εὐσχημοσύνην περισσοτέραν ἔχει·
and the unpresentable of us propriety more abundant has;

3588 1161 2158 2257 3756 5532 2192 235 3588 2316 4786
24 τὰ δὲ εὐσχήμονα ἡμῶν οὐ χρείαν ἔχει· ἀλλ᾽ ὁ Θεὸς συνε-
the but presentable of us not need has; but God tempered

3588 4983 3588 5302 4053 1325 5092
κέρασε τὸ σῶμα, τῷ ὑστεροῦντι περισσοτέραν δοὺς τιμήν,
together the body, to the (one) lacking more abundant having given honor,

2443 3361 5600 4978 1722 3588 4983 235 3588 846 5228 240
25 ἵνα μὴ ᾖ σχίσμα ἐν τῷ σώματι, ἀλλὰ τὸ αὐτὸ ὑπὲρ ἀλλήλων
that not be division in the body, but the same for one another

3309 3588 3196 2532 1535 3958 1520 3196 4841
μεριμνῶσι τὰ μέλη. 26 καὶ εἴτε πάσχει ἓν μέλος, συμπάσχει
might care the members. And whether suffers one member, suffers with (it)

3956 3588 3196 1535 1392 1520 3196 4796 3956
πάντα τὰ μέλη· εἴτε δοξάζεται ἓν μέλος, συγχαίρει πάντα
all the members; or is glorified one member, rejoices with (it)I all

Gentiles, whether (we
be) bond or free; and
have been all made to
drink into one Spirit.
14 For the body is not
one member, but many.
15 If the foot shall say,
Because I am not the
hand, I am not of the
body; is it therefore not
of the body?
16 And if the ear shall
say, Because I am not
the eye, I am not of the
body; is it therefore not
of the body?
17 If the whole body
(were) an eye, where
(were) the hearing? If
the whole (were) hear-
ing, where (were) the
smelling?
18 But now hath God
set the members every
one of them in the body,
as it hath pleased him.
19 And if they were all
one member, where
(were) the body?
20 But now (are they)
many members, yet but
one body.
21 And the eye cannot
say unto the hand, I
have no need of thee:
nor again the head to the
feet, I have no need of
you.
22 Nay, much more
those members of the
body, which seem to be
more feeble, are neces-
sary:
23 And those (mem-
bers) of the body, which
we think to be less hon-
ourable, upon these we
bestow more abundant
honour; and our un-
comely (parts) have
more abundant comeli-
ness.
24 For our comely
(parts) have no need:
but God hath tempered
the body together, hav-
ing given more abun-
dant honour to that
(part) which lacked:
25 That there should be
no schism in the body;
but (that) the members
should have the same
care one for another.
26 And whether one
member suffer, all the
members suffer with it;
or one member be hon-
oured, all the members
rejoice with it.

Literal Translation

27 And you are Christ's body, and members in part.

28 And God placed some in the church: firstly apostles; secondly, prophets; thirdly, teachers; then works of power; then gifts of healing, helps, governings, kinds of languages.

29 (Are) all apostles? All prophets? All teachers? All workers of power?
30 Do all have gifts of healing? Do all speak languages? Do all interpret?

31 But fervently desire the better gifts. And yet I show you a way according to excellence:

1 Corinthians 12:27

3588 3196 5210 1161 2075 4983 5547 2532 3196 1537 3313
τὰ μέλη. 27 ὑμεῖς δέ ἐστε σῶμα Χριστοῦ, καὶ μέλη ἐκ μέρους.
the members. you And are a body of Christ, and members in part.

2532 3739 3303 5087 3588 2316 1722 3588 1577 4412 652
28 καὶ οὓς μὲν ἔθετο ὁ Θεὸς ἐν τῇ ἐκκλησίᾳ πρῶτον ἀποστόλ-
And some placed God in the church firstly apostles

1208 4396 5154 1320 1899 1411
ους, δεύτερον προφήτας, τρίτον διδασκάλους, ἔπειτα δυνάμεις,
secondly prophets, thirdly teachers, then works of power,

1534 5486 2386 484 2941 1085
εἶτα χαρίσματα ἰαμάτων, ἀντιλήψεις, κυβερνήσεις, γένη
then gifts of healing, helps, governings, kinds

1100 3361 3956 652 3361 3956 4396
γλωσσῶν. 29 μὴ πάντες ἀπόστολοι; μὴ πάντες προφῆται;
of tongues. Not all (are) apostles? Not all (are) prophets?

3361 3956 1320 3361 3956 1411 3361 3956
μὴ πάντες διδάσκαλοι; μὴ πάντες δυνάμεις; 30 μὴ πάντες
Not all (are) teachers;? Not all workers of power? Not all

5486 2192 2386 3361 3956 1100 2980
χαρίσματα ἔχουσιν ἰαμάτων; μὴ πάντες γλώσσαις λαλοῦσι;
gifts have of healing? Not all tongues speak?

3361 3956 1329 2206 1161 3588 5486 3588
μὴ πάντες διερμηνεύουσι; 31 ζηλοῦτε δὲ τὰ χαρίσματα τὰ
Not all interpret? fervently desire But the gifts

2909 2532 2089 2596 5236 3598 5213 1166
κρείττονα. καὶ ἔτι καθ' ὑπερβολὴν ὁδὸν ὑμῖν δείκνυμι.
better. And yet according to excellence a way to you I show.

King James Version

27 Now ye are the body of Christ, and members in particular.

28 And God hath set some in the church, first apostles, secondarily prophets, thirdly teachers, after that miracles, then gifts of healings, helps, governments, diversities of tongues.

29 (Are) all apostles? (are) all prophets? (are) all teachers? (are) all workers of miracles?
30 Have all the gifts of healing? do all speak with tongues? do all interpret?

31 But covet earnestly the best gifts: and yet shew I unto you a more excellent way.

1 Corinthians 13

1. If I speak in the tongues of men and of angels, but I do not have love, I have become (as) sounding brass or a clanging cymbal.

2 And if I have prophecies, and know all mysteries and all knowledge, and if I have all faith so as to move mountains, but do not have love, I am nothing.

3 And if I give out all my goods, and if I deliver my body that I be burned, but I do not have love, I am profited not a thing.

4 Love has patience, is kind; love is not envious; love does not vaunt (itself), is not puffed up;
5 does not behave indecently, does not seek its own things, is not easily provoked, thinks no evil;
6 does not rejoice over the wrong,, but rejoices in the

1 Corinthians 13

1437 3588 1100 3588 444 2980 2532 3588
1. Ἐὰν ταῖς γλώσσαις τῶν ἀνθρώπων λαλῶ καὶ τῶν
If in the tongues of men I speak even

32 26 1161 3361 2192 1096 5475 2278/2228
ἀγγέλων, ἀγάπην δὲ μὴ ἔχω, γέγονα χαλκὸς ἠχῶν ἢ
of angels, love but not I have, I have become brass sounding, or

2950 214 2532 1437 2192 4394 2532 1492 3588
κύμβαλον ἀλαλάζον. 2 καὶ ἐὰν ἔχω προφητείαν καὶ εἰδῶ τὰ
a cymbal clanging. And if I have prophecies and know

3466 3956 2532 3956 3588 1108 2532 1437 2192 3956
μυστήρια πάντα καὶ πᾶσαν τὴν γνῶσιν, καὶ ἐὰν ἔχω πᾶσαν
mysteries all and all knowledge, and if I have all

3588 4102 5620 3735 3179 26 1161 3361 2192 3762
τὴν πίστιν, ὥστε ὄρη μεθιστάνειν, ἀγάπην δὲ μὴ ἔχω, οὐδέν
faith, so as mountains to move, love but not I have, nothing

1510 2532 1437 5595 3956 3588 5224 3450 2532 1437
εἰμι. 3 καὶ ἐὰν ψωμίσω πάντα τὰ ὑπάρχοντά μου, καὶ ἐὰν
I am. And if I give out all the goods of me, and if

3860 3588 4983 3450 2443 2545 26 1161 3361 2192
παραδῶ τὸ σῶμά μου ἵνα καυθήσωμαι, ἀγάπην δὲ μὴ ἔχω,
I deliver the body of me that I be burned, love but not I have,

3762 5623 3588 26 3114 5541 3588
οὐδὲν ὠφελοῦμαι. 4 ἡ ἀγάπη μακροθυμεῖ, χρηστεύεται· ἡ
nothing I am profited. Love suffers long, is kind;

26 3756 2206 3588 26 3756 4068 3756 5448
ἀγάπη οὐ ζηλοῖ· ἡ ἀγάπη οὐ περπερεύεται, οὐ φυσιοῦται,
love not is envious; love not vaunts itself, not is puffed up,

3756 807 3756 2212 3588 1438 3756 3947 3756
5 οὐκ ἀσχημονεῖ, οὐ ζητεῖ τὰ ἑαυτῆς, οὐ παροξύνεται, οὐ
not behaves indecently, not seeks the things of itself, not is provoked, not

3049 3588 2556 3756 5463 1909 3588 93 4796 1161 3588
λογίζεται τὸ κακόν, 6 οὐ χαίρει ἐπὶ τῇ ἀδικίᾳ, συγχαίρει δὲ τῇ
thinks the evil, not rejoices over the wrong, rejoices with but the

1 Corinthians 13

1. Though I speak with the tongues of men and of angels, and have not charity, I am become (as) sounding brass, or a tinkling cymbal.

2 And though I have (the gift of) prophecy, and understand all mysteries, and all knowledge; and though I have all faith, so that I could remove mountains, and have not charity, I am nothing.

3 And though I bestow all my goods to feed (the poor), and though I give my body to be burned, and have not charity, it profiteth me nothing.

4 Charity suffereth long, (and) is kind; charity envieth not; charity vaunteth not itself, is not puffed up,
5 Doth not behave itself unseemly, seeketh not her own, is not easily provoked, thinketh no evil;
6 Rejoiceth not in iniquity, but rejoiceth in the

Literal Translation

truth.
7 (Love) quietly covers all things, believes all things, hopes all things, endures all things.
8 Love never fails. But if (there are) prophecies, they will be abolished; if tongues, they shall cease; if knowledge, it will be caused to cease
9 For we know in part, and we prophesy in part;
10 but when the perfect thing comes, then that (which is) in part will be caused to cease.
11 When I was an infant, I spoke as an infant, I thought as an infant, I reasoned as an infant. But when I became a man, I caused to cease the things of the infant.
12 For now we see through a mirror in obscurity, but then face to face. Now I know in part, but then I will fully know even as I also was fully known.

13 But now faith, hope, and love, these three things remain; but the greatest of these (is) love.

1 Corinthians 13:7

225 3956 4722 3956 4100 3956 1679
ἀληθείᾳ· 7 πάντα στέγει, πάντα πιστεύει, πάντα ἐλπίζει,
truth; all things quietly covers, all things believes, all things hopes,

3956 5278 3588 26 3763 1601 1535 1161 4394
πάντα ὑπομένει. 8 ἡ ἀγάπη οὐδέποτε ἐκπίπτει· εἴτε δὲ προφη-
all things endures. Love never fails; whether but proph-

2673 1535 1100 3973 1535
τεῖαι, καταργηθήσονται· εἴτε γλῶσσαι, παύσονται· εἴτε
esies, they will be caused to cease; if tongues, they shall cease; if

1108 2673 1537 3313 1063 1097 2532/1537
γνῶσις, καταργηθήσεται. 9 ἐκ μέρους γὰρ γινώσκομεν, καὶ ἐκ
knowledge, it will be caused to cease. in part For we know, and in

3313 4395 3752 1161 2064 3588 5046 5119 3588 1537
μέρους προφητεύομεν· 10 ὅταν δὲ ἔλθῃ τὸ τέλειον, τότε τὸ ἐκ
part we prophesy; when but comes the perfect thing, then that in

3313 2673 3753 2252 3516 5613 3516
μέρους καταργηθήσεται. 11 ὅτε ἤμην νήπιος, ὡς νήπιος
part will be caused to cease. When I was an infant, as an infant

2980 5613 3516 5426 5613 3516 3049 3753 1161
ἐλάλουν, ὡς νήπιος ἐφρόνουν, ὡς νήπιος ἐλογιζόμην· ὅτε δὲ
I spoke, as an infant I thought, as an infant I reasoned; when but

1096 435 2673 3588 3588 3516 991 1063
γέγονα ἀνήρ, κατήργηκα τὰ τοῦ νηπίου. 12 βλέπομεν γὰρ
I became a man, I did away with the things of the infant. we see For

737 1223 2072 1722 135 5119 1161 4383 4314
ἄρτι δι᾽ ἐσόπτρου ἐν αἰνίγματι, τότε δὲ πρόσωπον πρὸς
yet through a mirror in obscurity, then but face to

4383 737 1097 1537 3313 5119 1161 1921
πρόσωπον· ἄρτι γινώσκω ἐκ μέρους, τότε δὲ ἐπιγνώσομαι
face; now I know in part, then but I will fully know

2531 2532 1921 3570 1161 3306 4102 1680 26
καθὼς καὶ ἐπεγνώσθην. 13 νυνὶ δὲ μένει πίστις, ἐλπίς, ἀγάπη,
even as also I was fully known. now But remains faith, hope, love,

3588 5140 5023 3187 1161 5130 3588 26
τὰ τρία ταῦτα· μείζων δὲ τούτων ἡ ἀγάπη.
three these things; greater and of these (is) love.

King James Version

truth;
7 Beareth all things, believeth all things, hopeth all things, endureth all things.
8 Charity never faileth: but whether (there be) prophecies, they shall fail; whether (there be) tongues, they shall cease; whether (there be) knowledge, it shall vanish away.
9 For we know in part, and we prophesy in part.
10 But when that which is perfect is come, then that which is in part shall be done away.
11 When I was a child, I spake as a child, I understood as a child, I thought as a child: but when I became a man, I put away childish things.
12 For now we see through a glass, darkly; but then face to face: now I know in part; but then shall I know even as also I am known.

13 And now abideth faith, hope, charity, these three; but the greatest of these (is) charity.

1 Corinthians 14

1. Pursue love, and seek eagerly the spiritual things, but rather that you may prophesy.
2 For the (one) speaking in a tongue does not speak to men, but to God, for no one hears, but in spirit he speaks mysteries.
3 But the (one) prophesying to men speaks (for) building up, and encouragement, and comfort.
4 The (one) speaking in a tongue builds himself up, but he prophesying builds up a church.
5 And I desire all of you to speak in tongues, but rather that you may prophesy. For the (one) prophesying (is) greater than the (one) speaking in tongues, unless he interpret

1 Corinthians 14

1377 3588 26 2206 1161 3588 4152 3123
1. Διώκετε τὴν ἀγάπην· ζηλοῦτε δὲ τὰ πνευματικά, μᾶλλον
Pursue love; seek eagerly and the spiritual things, rather

1161 2443 4395 3588 1063 2980 1100 3756 444
δὲ ἵνα προφητεύητε. 2 ὁ γὰρ λαλῶν γλώσσῃ οὐκ ἀνθρώποις
but that you may prophesy. the (one) For speaking in a tongue not to men

2980 235 3588 2316 3762 1063 191 4151 1161 2980
λαλεῖ, ἀλλὰ τῷ Θεῷ· οὐδεὶς γὰρ ἀκούει, πνεύματι δὲ λαλεῖ
speaks, but to God; no one for hears, in spirit but he speaks

3466 3588 1161 4395 444 2980 3619 2532
μυστήρια. 3 ὁ δὲ προφητεύων ἀνθρώποις λαλεῖ οἰκοδομὴν καὶ
mysteries. the (one) But prophesying to men speaks for building up and

3874 2532 3889 3588 2980 1100 1438 3618
παράκλησιν καὶ παραμυθίαν. 4 ὁ λαλῶν γλώσσῃ ἑαυτὸν οἰκο-
encouragement and comfort. The (one) speaking in a tongue himself builds

3588 1161 4395 1577 3618 2309 1161 3956
δομεῖ, ὁ δὲ προφητεύων ἐκκλησίαν οἰκοδομεῖ. 5 θέλω δὲ πάντας
up, the (one) but prophesying a church builds up. I desire And all

5209 2980 1100 3123 1161 2443 4395 3187
ὑμᾶς λαλεῖν γλώσσαις, μᾶλλον δὲ ἵνα προφητεύητε· μείζων
of you to speak in tongues, rather but that you may prophesy; greater

1063 3588 4395 2228 3588 2980 1100 1622/1487/3361 1329
γὰρ ὁ προφητεύων ἢ ὁ λαλῶν γλώσσαις, ἐκτὸς εἰ μὴ διερμη-
for the (one) prophesying than he speaking in tongues, unless he interprets.

1 Corinthians 14

1. Follow after charity, and desire spiritual (gifts), but rather that ye may prophesy.
2 For he that speaketh in an (unknown) tongue speaketh not unto men, but unto God: for no man understandeth (him); howbeit in the spirit he speaketh mysteries.
3 But he that prophesieth speaketh unto men (to) edification, and exhortation, and comfort.
4 He that speaketh in an (unknown) tongue edifieth himself; but he that prophesieth edifieth the church.
5 I would that ye all spake with tongues, but rather that ye prophesied: for greater (is) he that prophesieth than he that speaketh with tongues, except he interpret,

Literal Translation

that the church may receive building up.

6 But now, brothers, if I come to you speaking in tongues, what will I profit you, except I speak to you either in revelation, or in knowledge, or in prophecy, or in teaching?

7 Yet lifeless things giving a sound, whether pipe or harp, if they do not give a distinction to the sound, how will it be known the thing being piped or the thing being harped?

8 For also if a trumpet gives an uncertain sound, who will get himself ready to war?

9 So also you, if you do not give a clear word through the tongue, how will it be known the thing being said? For you will be speaking into air.

10 So it may be many kinds of sounds are in (the) world, and not one (is) without (distinct) sound.

11 If, then, I do not know the power of the sound, I will be a foreigner to the (one) speaking, and he speaking in me a foreigner.

12 So also you, since you are zealots of spiritual things, seek to build up the church that you may abound.

13 So then, the (one) speaking in a tongue, let him pray that he may interpret.

14 For if I pray in a tongue, my spirit prays, but my mind is unfruitful.

15 What then is it? I will pray with the spirit, and I will also pray with the mind; I will sing with the spirit, and also I will sing with the mind.

16 Else, if you bless in the spirit, the one occupying the place of the unlearned, how will he say the amen at your giving of thanks, since what he says, he does not know?

1 Corinthains 14:6

2443/3588 1577 3619 2983 3570 1161 80 1437
νεύῃ, ἵνα ἡ ἐκκλησία οἰκοδομὴν λάβῃ. 6 νυνὶ δέ, ἀδελφοί, ἐὰν
that the church building up may receive. now But, brothers, if

2064 4314 5209 1100 2980 5101 5209 5623 1437 3361
ἔλθω πρὸς ὑμᾶς γλώσσαις λαλῶν, τί ὑμᾶς ὠφελήσω, ἐὰν μὴ
I come to you in tongues speaking, what you will I profit, if not

5213 2980 2228 1722 602 2228 1722 1108 2228 1722 4394
ὑμῖν λαλήσω ἢ ἐν ἀποκαλύψει, ἢ ἐν γνώσει, ἢ ἐν προφητείᾳ,
to you I speak either in revelation, or in knowledge, or in prophecy,

2228 1722 1322 3676 3588 895 5456 1325 1535 836
ἢ ἐν διδαχῇ; 7 ὅμως τὰ ἄψυχα φωνὴν διδόντα, εἴτε αὐλὸς,
or in teaching? Yet lifeless things a sound giving, whether pipe,

1535 2788 1437 1293 3588 5353 3361 1325 4459
εἴτε κιθάρα, ἐὰν διαστολὴν τοῖς φθόγγοις μὴ δῷ, πῶς
or harp, if a distinction to the sound not they give, how

1097 3588 832 2228 3588 2789 2532 1063
γνωσθήσεται τὸ αὐλούμενον ἢ τὸ κιθαριζόμενον; 8 καὶ γὰρ
will it be known the thing being piped or the thing being harped? indeed For

1437 82 5456 4536 1325 5101 3903 1519
ἐὰν ἄδηλον φωνὴν σάλπιγξ δῷ, τίς παρασκευάσεται εἰς
if an uncertain sound a trumpet gives, who will get himself ready to

4171 3779 2532 5210 1223 3588 1100 1437 3361 2154
πόλεμον; 9 οὕτω καὶ ὑμεῖς διὰ τῆς γλώσσης ἐὰν μὴ εὔσημον
war? So also you through the tongue if not a clear

3056 1325 4459 1097 3588 2980 2071 1063
λόγον δῶτε, πῶς γνωσθήσεται τὸ λαλούμενον; ἔσεσθε γὰρ
word give, how will it be known the thing being said? you will be For

1519 109 2980 5118 1487 5177 1085 5456 2076
εἰς ἀέρα λαλοῦντες. 10 τοσαῦτα, εἰ τύχοι, γένη φωνῶν ἐστὶν
into air speaking. So many, if may be, kinds of sounds are

1722 2889 2532 3762 880 1437 3767 3361 1492 3588 1411
ἐν κόσμῳ, καὶ οὐδὲν ἄφωνον. 11 ἐὰν οὖν μὴ εἰδῶ τὴν δύναμιν
in (the) world, and not one is voiceless. If then not I know the power

3588 5456 2071 3588 2980 915 2532 3588 2980 1722
τῆς φωνῆς, ἔσομαι τῷ λαλοῦντι βάρβαρος, καὶ ὁ λαλῶν ἐν
of the sound, I will be to the (one) speaking a foreigner, and he speaking in

1698 915 3779 2532 5210 1893 2207 2075 4151
ἐμοὶ βάρβαρος. 12 οὕτω καὶ ὑμεῖς, ἐπεὶ ζηλωταί ἐστε πνευ-
me a foreigner. So also you, since zealots you are of

4314 3588 3619 3588 1577 2212 2443 4052
μάτων, πρὸς τὴν οἰκοδομὴν τῆς ἐκκλησίας ζητεῖτε ἵνα περισ-
spiritual things, to the building up of the church seek that you may

1355 3588 2980 1100 4336 2443 1329
σεύητε. 13 διόπερ ὁ λαλῶν γλώσσῃ προσευχέσθω ἵνα διερμη-
abound. Therefore he speaking in a tongue let him pray that he may

1437 1063 4336 1100 3588 4151 3450
νεύῃ. 14 ἐὰν γὰρ προσεύχωμαι γλώσσῃ, τὸ πνεῦμά μου
interpret. if For I pray in a tongue, the spirit of me

4336 3588 1161 3563 3450 175 2076 5101 3767 2076
προσεύχεται, ὁ δὲ νοῦς μου ἄκαρπός ἐστι. 15 τί οὖν ἐστι;
prays, the but mind of me unfruitful is. What then is it?

4336 3588 4151 4336 1161 2532 3588 3563 5567
προσεύξομαι τῷ πνεύματι, προσεύξομαι δὲ καὶ τῷ νοΐ· ψαλῶ
I will pray with the spirit, I will pray and also with the mind; I sing

3588 4151 5567 1161 2532 3588 3563 1893 1437 2127 3588
τῷ πνεύματι, ψαλῶ δὲ καὶ τῷ νοΐ. 16 ἐπεὶ ἐὰν εὐλογήσῃς τῷ
with the spirit, I sing and also with the mind. Else if you bless in the

4151 3588 378 3588 5117 3588 2399 4459 2046
πνεύματι, ὁ ἀναπληρῶν τὸν τόπον τοῦ ἰδιώτου πῶς ἐρεῖ
spirit, the (one) occupying the place of the unlearned how will he say

3588 281 1909 3588 4674 2169 1894 5101 3004 3756 1492
τὸ ἀμήν ἐπὶ τῇ σῇ εὐχαριστίᾳ, ἐπειδὴ τί λέγεις οὐκ οἶδε;
the amen at your giving thanks, since what he says not he knows?

King James Version

that the church may receive edifying.

6 Now, brethren, if I come unto you speaking with tongues, what shall I profit you, except I shall speak to you either by revelation, or by knowledge, or by prophesying, or by doctrine?

7 And even things without life giving sound, whether pipe or harp, except they give a distinction in the sounds, how shall it be known what is piped or harped?

8 For if the trumpet give an uncertain sound, who shall prepare himself to the battle?

9 So likewise ye, except ye utter by the tongue words easy to be understood, how shall it be known what is spoken? for ye shall speak into the air.

10 There are, it may be, so many kinds of voices in the world, and none of them (is) without signification.

11 Therefore if I know not the meaning of the voice, I shall be unto him that speaketh a barbarian, and he that speaketh (shall be) a barbarian unto me.

12 Even so ye, forasmuch as ye are zealous of spiritual (gifts), seek that ye may excel to the edifying of the church.

13 Wherefore let him that speaketh in an (unknown) tongue pray that he may interpret.

14 For if I pray in an (unknown) tongue, my spirit prayeth, but my understanding is unfruitful.

15 What is it then? I will pray with the spirit, and I will pray with the understanding also: I will sing with the spirit, and I will sing with the understanding also.

16 Else when thou shalt bless with the spirit, how shall he that occupieth the room of the unlearned say Amen at thy giving of thanks, seeing he understandeth not what thou sayest?

Literal Translation

17 For you truly give thanks well, but the other is not built up.

18 I thank my God (that) I speak more languages than all of you.
19 But in a church I desire to speak five words with my mind, that I may also instruct others, than myriads of words in a tongue.

20 Brothers, do not be children in (your) minds, but in malice be like infants, and in (your) minds be mature.
21 It has been written in the Law, "By other tongues and in other lips I will speak to this people, and even so they will not hear Me, says (the) Lord." (Isa. 28:11, 12)

22 So that tongues are not a sign to the (ones) believing, but to the (ones) not believing. But prophecy (is) not to the (ones) not believing, but to the (ones) believing.
23 Then if the whole church assembles together, and all speak in tongues, and uninstructed ones or unbelievers come in, will they not say that you rave?

24 But if all prophesy, and some unbeliever or one not instructed comes in, he is convicted by all, he is judged by all.

25 And so the secrets of his heart become revealed; and so, falling on (his) face, he will worship God, declaring that God is truly among you.

26 Then what is it, brothers? When you come together, each one of you has a psalm, he has a teaching, he has a tongue, he has a revelation, he has

1 Corinthians 14:17

4771 3303 1063 2573 2168 235 3588 2087 3756 3618
17 σὺ μὲν γὰρ καλως εὐχαριστεῖς, ἀλλ' ὁ ἕτερος οὐκ οἰκοδο-
you truly for well give thanks, but the other not is built

2168 3588 2316 3450 3956 5216 3123
μεῖται. 18 εὐχαριστῶ τῷ Θεῷ μου, πάντων ὑμῶν μᾶλλον
up. I thank the God of me, all of you more than

1100 2980 235 1722 1577 2309 4002 3056 1223
γλώσσαις λαλῶν· 19 ἀλλ' ἐν ἐκκλησίᾳ θέλω πέντε λόγους διὰ
in languages I speak, but in a church I desire five words with

3588 3563 3450 2980 2443 2532 243 2727 2228 3463
τοῦ νοός μου λαλῆσαι, ἵνα καὶ ἄλλους κατηχήσω, ἢ μυρίους
the mind of me to speak, that also others I may instruct, than myriads

3056 1722 1100
λόγους ἐν γλώσσῃ.
of words in a tongue.

80 3361 3813 1096 3588 5424 235 3588 2549
20. 'Αδελφοί, μὴ παιδία γίνεσθε ταῖς φρεσίν· ἀλλὰ τῇ κακίᾳ
Brothers, not children be in the minds, but in malice

3515 3588 1161 5424 5046 1096 1722 3588 3551
νηπιάζετε, ταῖς δὲ φρεσὶ τέλειοι γίνεσθε. 21 ἐν τῷ νόμῳ
be like infants, in the and minds mature be. In the Law

1125 3754 1722 2084 2532 1722 5491 2087
γέγραπται ὅτι 'Εν ἑτερογλώσσοις καὶ ἐν χείλεσιν ἑτέροις
it has been written, In other tongues and in lips other

2980 3588 2992 5129 2532 3761 3779 1522 3450
λαλήσω τῷ λαῷ τούτῳ, καὶ οὐδ' οὕτως εἰσακούσονταί μου,
I will speak people to this, and not so will they hear Me,

3004 2962 5620 3588 1100 1519 4592 1526 3756 3588
λέγει Κύριος. 22 ὥστε αἱ γλῶσσαι εἰς σημεῖόν εἰσιν, οὐ τοῖς
says (the) Lord. So as tongues for a sign are, not to the

4100 235 3588 571 3588 1161 4394 3756 3588
πιστεύουσιν, ἀλλὰ τοῖς ἀπίστοις· ἡ δὲ προφητεία, οὐ τοῖς
(ones) believing, but to the unbelieving; and prophecy, not to the

571 235 3588 4100 1437 3767 4905 3588
ἀπίστοις, ἀλλὰ τοῖς πιστεύουσιν. 23 'Εὰν οὖν συνέλθῃ ἡ
unbelieving, but to the (ones) believing. if Then assembles the

1577 3650 1909 3588 846 2532 3956 1100 2980
ἐκκλησία ὅλη ἐπὶ τὸ αὐτὸ, καὶ πάντες γλώσσαις λαλῶσιν,
church whole together, and all in tongues speak,

1525 1161 2399 2228 571 3756 2046 3754 3105
εἰσέλθωσι δὲ ἰδιῶται ἢ ἄπιστοι, οὐκ ἐροῦσιν ὅτι μαίνεσθε;
come in and uninstructed or unbelievers, not will they say that you rave?

1437 1161 3956 4395 1525 1161 5100 571 2228
24 ἐὰν δὲ πάντες προφητεύωσιν, εἰσέλθῃ δέ τις ἄπιστος ἢ
if And all prophesy, comes in and some unbeliever or

2399 1651 5259 3956 350 5259 3956
ἰδιώτης, ἐλέγχεται ὑπὸ πάντων, ἀνακρίνεται ὑπὸ πάντων,
uninstructed, he is convicted by all, he is judged by all,

2532 3779 3588 2927 3588 2588 846 5318 1096 2532
25 καὶ οὕτω τὰ κρυπτὰ τῆς καρδίας αὐτοῦ φανερὰ γίνεται· καὶ
and so the secrets of the heart of him revealed become; and

3779 4098 1909 4383 4352 3588 2316 518
οὕτω πεσὼν ἐπὶ πρόσωπον προσκυνήσει τῷ Θεῷ ἀπαγ-
so falling on (his) face he will worship God, declaring

3754/3588/2316/3689 1722 5213 2076
γέλλων ὅτι ὁ Θεὸς ὄντως ἐν ὑμῖν ἐστι.
that God truly among you is.

5101 3767 2076 80 3752 4905 1538 5216
26. Τί οὖν ἐστιν, ἀδελφοί; ὅταν συνέρχησθε, ἕκαστος ὑμῶν
What then is it, brothers? When you come together, each one of you

5568 2192 1322 2192 1100 2192 602 2192
ψαλμὸν ἔχει, διδαχὴν ἔχει, γλῶσσαν ἔχει, ἀποκάλυψιν ἔχει,
a psalm has, a teaching he has, a tongue he has, a revelation he has,

King James Version

17 For thou verily givest thanks well, but the other is not edified.

18 I thank my God, I speak with tongues more than ye all:
19 Yet in the church I had rather speak five words with my understanding, that (by my voice) I might teach others also, than ten thousand words in an (unknown) tongue.

20 Brethren, be not children in understanding: howbeit in malice be ye children, but in understanding be men.
21 In the law it is written, With (men of) other tongues and other lips will I speak unto this people; and yet for all that will they not hear me, saith the Lord.

22 Wherefore tongues are for a sign, not to them that believe, but to them that believe not: but prophesying (serveth) not for them that believe not, but for them which believe.
23 If therefore the whole church be come together into one place, and all speak with tongues, and there come in (those that are) unlearned, or unbelievers, will they not say that ye are mad?

24 But if all prophesy, and there come in one that believeth not, or (one) unlearned, he is convinced of all, he is judged of all:

25 And thus are the secrets of his heart made manifest; and so falling down on (his) face he will worship God, and report that God is in you of a truth.

26 How is it then, brethren? when ye come together, every one of you hath a psalm, hath a doctrine, hath a tongue, hath a revelation, hath an

Literal Translation

1 Corinthians 14:27

King James Version

an interpretation. Let all
things be for building
up.
27 If one speaks in a
tongue, (let it be) by two
or three (at) the most,
and in turn, also let one
interpret.
28 And if there is no in-
terpreter, let him be si-
lent in church, and let
him speak to himself
and to God.
29 And (if there are) two
or three prophets, let
them speak, and the oth-
ers let them discern.
30 But if (a revelation)
is revealed to another
sitting by, let the first be
silent.
31 For you are all able
to prophesy one by one,
that all may learn, and
all may be encouraged.
32 And the spirits of
prophets (are) subject to
prophets.
33 For God is not (God)
of confusion, but of
peace, as in all the
churches of the saints.

2058 2192 3956 4314 3619 1096 1535
ἑρμηνείαν ἔχει. πάντα πρὸς οἰκοδομὴν γινέσθω. 27 εἴτε
an interpretation he has. all things for building up Let be. If
1100 5100 2980 2596 1417/2228/3588/4118 5140 2532 303 3313
γλώσσῃ τις λαλεῖ, κατὰ δύο ἢ τὸ πλεῖστον τρεῖς, καὶ ἀνὰ μέρος,
in a tongue one speaks, by two or the most three, and in turn,
2532 1520 1329 1437 1161 3361 5600 1328 4601
καὶ εἷς διερμηνευέτω· 28 ἐὰν δὲ μὴ ᾖ διερμηνευτής, σιγάτω
and one let interpret; if but not an interpreter, be silent
1722 1577 1438 1161 2980 2532 3588 2316 4396 1161
ἐν ἐκκλησίᾳ· ἑαυτῷ δὲ λαλείτω καὶ τῷ Θεῷ. 29 προφῆται δὲ
in church; to himself and let him speak and to God. prophets And
1417 2228 5140 2980 2532 3588 243 1252 1437 1161
δύο ἢ τρεῖς λαλείτωσαν, καὶ οἱ ἄλλοι διακρινέτωσαν. 30 ἐὰν δὲ
two or three let them speak, and the others let them discern. if And
243 601 2521 3588 4413 4601 1410
ἄλλῳ ἀποκαλυφθῇ καθημένῳ, ὁ πρῶτος σιγάτω. 31 δύνασθε
to another is revealed sitting, the first let be silent. you are able
1063 2596 1520 3956 4395 2443 3956 3129
γὰρ καθ' ἕνα πάντες προφητεύειν, ἵνα πάντες μανθάνωσι,
For one by one all to prophesy, that all may learn,
2532 3956 3870 2532 4151 4396 4396
καὶ πάντες παρακαλῶνται· 32 καὶ πνεύματα προφητῶν προφή-
and all may be encouraged; and (the) spirits of prophets to prophets
5293 3756 1063 2076 181 3588 2316 235
ταις ὑποτάσσεται· 33 οὐ γάρ ἐστιν ἀκαταστασίας ὁ Θεός, ἀλλ'
(are) subject; not for is of confusion God, but
1515 5613 1722 3956 3588 1577 3588 40
εἰρήνης ὡς ἐν πάσαις ταῖς ἐκκλησίαις τῶν ἁγίων,
of peace as in all the churches of the saints,

interpretation. Let all
things be done unto edi-
fying.
27 If any man speak in
an (unknown) tongue,
(let it be) by two, or at
the most (by) three, and
(that) by course; and let
one interpret.
28 But if there be no in-
terpreter, let him keep
silence in the church;
and let him speak to
himself, and to God.
29 Let the prophets
speak two or three, and
let the other judge.
30 If (any thing) be re-
vealed to another that
sitteth by, let the first
hold his peace.
31 For ye may all
prophesy one by one,
that all may learn, and
all may be comforted.
32 And the spirits of the
prophets are subject to
the prophets.
33 For God is not (the
author) of confusion,
but of peace, as in all
churches of the saints.

34 Let the women in
the churches be silent,
for it is not allowed to
them to speak, let them
be subject, as also the
Law says.
35 But if they desire to
learn anything, let them
question (their) hus-
bands at home; for it is
a shame for a woman to
speak in a church.
36 Or did the Word of
God go out from you?
Or did it reach only to
you?

3588 1135 5216 1722 3588 1577 4601 3756 1063
34 αἱ γυναῖκες ὑμῶν ἐν ταῖς ἐκκλησίαις σιγάτωσαν, οὐ γὰρ
Let the women of you in the churches be silent, not for
2010 846 2980 235 5293 2531 2532
ἐπιτέτραπται αὐταῖς λαλεῖν, ἀλλ' ὑποτάσσεσθαι, καθὼς καὶ
it is allowed to them to speak, but let them be subject, even as also
3588 3551 3004 1487 1161 5100 3129 2309 1722 3624 3588
ὁ νόμος λέγει. 35 εἰ δέ τι μαθεῖν θέλουσιν, ἐν οἴκῳ τοὺς
the Law says. if But anything to learn they desire, at home the
2398 435 1905 150 1063 2076 1135 1722
ἰδίους ἄνδρας ἐπερωτάτωσαν· αἰσχρὸν γάρ ἐστι γυναιξὶν ἐν
own husbands let them question; a shame for it is for women in
1577 2980 2228 575 5216 3588 3056 3588 2316 1831 2228
ἐκκλησίᾳ λαλεῖν. 36 ἢ ἀφ' ὑμῶν ὁ λόγος τοῦ Θεοῦ ἐξῆλθεν; ἢ
a church to speak. Or from you the Word of God go out? Or
1519 5209 3441 2658
εἰς ὑμᾶς μόνους κατήντησεν;
to you only did it reach?

34 Let your women
keep silence in the
churches: for it is not
permitted unto them to
speak; but (they are
commanded) to be un-
der obedience, as also
saith the law.
35 And if they will learn
any thing, let them ask
their husbands at home:
for it is a shame for
women to speak in the
church.
36 What? came the
word of God out from
you? or came it unto
you only?

37 If anyone thinks to be
a prophet, or a spiritual
one, let him recognize
what things I write to
you, that they are a com-
mand of the Lord.
38 But if any be igno-
rant, let him be ignorant.
39 So then, brothers,
eagerly seek to proph-
esy, and do not forbid to
speak in languages.
40 And let all things be
done decently and in or-
der.

1487 5100 1380 4396 1511 2228 4152 1921
37. Εἴ τις δοκεῖ προφήτης εἶναι ἢ πνευματικός, ἐπιγι-
If anyone thinks a prophet to be or a spiritual one, let him
3739 1125 5213 3754 3588 2962 1526 1785 1487
νωσκέτω ἃ γράφω ὑμῖν, ὅτι τοῦ Κυρίου εἰσὶν ἐντολαί. 38 εἰ
recognize what I write to you, that of the Lord they are a command. if
1161 5100 50 50
δέ τις ἀγνοεῖ, ἀγνοείτω.
But any be ignorant, let him be ignorant.
5620 80 2206 3588 4395 2532 3588 2980
39 ὥστε, ἀδελφοί, ζηλοῦτε τὸ προφητεύειν, καὶ τὸ λαλεῖν
So as, brothers, eagerly seek to prophesy, and to speak
1100 3361 2967 3956 2156 2532 2596 5010
γλώσσαις μὴ κωλύετε. 40 πάντα εὐσχημόνως καὶ κατὰ τάξιν
in languages not do forbid. All things decently and according to order

37 If any man think
himself to be a prophet,
or spiritual, let him ac-
knowledge that the
things that I write unto
you are the command-
ments of the Lord.
38 But if any man be ig-
norant, let him be igno-
rant.
39 Wherefore, breth-
ren, covet to prophesy,
and forbid not to speak
with tongues.
40 Let all things be done
decently and in order.

Literal Translation **1 Corinthians 15:1** *King James Version*

1096
γινέσθω.
let be done.

1 Corinthians 15

1. But, brothers, I make known to you the gospel which I preached to you, which also you received, in which also you stand,
2 by which also you are being kept safe, if you hold fast the word which I preached to you, except (it was) not in vain (that) you believed.
3 For among first things I delivered to you that which I also received, that Christ died on behalf of our sins, according to the Scriptures,
4 and that He was buried, and that He was raised the third day, according to the Scriptures,
5 and that He appeared to Cephas, and then to the Twelve.
6 Then He appeared to over five hundred brothers at one time, of whom the most remain until now, but some also fell asleep.
7 Then He appeared to James, then to all the apostles;
8 and last of all, even as if to an untimely birth, He also appeared to me.
9 For I am the least of the apostles, who am not sufficient to be called an apostle, because I persecuted the church of God.
10 But by (the) grace of God I am what I am, and His grace which (was) toward me has not been without fruit, but I labored more abundantly (than) all (of them), yet not I, but the grace of God with me.
11 Then whether I or those, so we preach, and so you believed.
12 But if Christ is proclaimed, that He has been raised from (the) dead, how do some among you say that there is not a resurrection of (the) dead?
13 But if

1 Corinthians 15

1107 1161 5213 80 3588 2098 3739 2097
1. Γνωρίζω δὲ ὑμῖν, ἀδελφοί, τὸ εὐαγγέλιον ὃ εὐηγγελισάμην
I make known And to you, brothers, the gospel which I preached
5213 3739 2532 3880 1722/3739/2532 2476 1223 3739 2532
ὑμῖν, ὃ καὶ παρελάβετε, ἐν ᾧ καὶ ἑστήκατε, 2 δι᾽ οὗ καὶ
to you, which also you received, in which also you stand, through which also
4982 5100 3056 2097 5213 1487 2722 1622 1487
σῴζεσθε, τίνι λόγῳ εὐηγγελισάμην ὑμῖν, εἰ κατέχετε, ἐκτὸς εἰ
you are saved, what word I preached to you, if you hold fast, except if
3361 1500 4100 3860 1063 5213 1722 4413 3739
μὴ εἰκῇ ἐπιστεύσατε. 3 παρέδωκα γὰρ ὑμῖν ἐν πρώτοις, ὃ
not in vain you believed. I delivered For to you among first things, which
2532 3880 3754 5547 599 5228 3588 266 2257
καὶ παρέλαβον, ὅτι Χριστὸς ἀπέθανεν ὑπὲρ τῶν ἁμαρτιῶν ἡμῶν
also I received, that Christ died on behalf of the sins of us
2596 3588 1124 2532 3754 2290 2532 3754 1453
κατὰ τὰς γραφάς· 4 καὶ ὅτι ἐτάφη· καὶ ὅτι ἐγήγερται
according to the Scriptures; and that He was buried; and that He has been raised
3588 5154 2250 2596 3588 1124 2532 3754 3700 2786 1534
τῇ τρίτῃ ἡμέρᾳ κατὰ τὰς γραφάς· 5 καὶ ὅτι ὤφθη Κηφᾷ, εἶτα
third day according to the Scriptures; and that He appeared to Cephas, then
3588 1427 1899 3700 1883 4001 80
τοῖς δώδεκα· 6 ἔπειτα ὤφθη ἐπάνω πεντακοσίοις ἀδελφοῖς
to the Twelve; afterward He appeared to over five hundred brothers
2178 1537/3739/3588 4119 3306 2193 737 5100 1161 2532 2837
ἐφάπαξ, ἐξ ὧν οἱ πλείους μένουσιν ἕως ἄρτι, τινὲς δὲ καὶ εκοι-
at one time, of whom the most remain until now, some but also fell
1899 3700 2385 1534 3588 652 3956
μήθησαν· 7 ἔπειτα ὤφθη Ἰακώβῳ, εἶτα τοῖς ἀποστόλοις πᾶσιν·
asleep; afterward He appeared to James, then the apostles to all;
2078 1161 3956 5619 3588 1626 3700 2504
8 ἔσχατον δὲ πάντων, ὡσπερεὶ τῷ ἐκτρώματι, ὤφθη κἀμοί
last and of all, even as if to an untimely birth, He appeared to me also.
1473 1063 1510 3588 1646 3588 652 3739 3756 1510 2425
9 ἐγὼ γάρ εἰμι ὁ ἐλάχιστος τῶν ἀποστόλων, ὃς οὐκ εἰμὶ ἱκανὸς
I For am the least of the apostles, who not am sufficient
2564 652 1360 1377 3588 1577 3588 2316
καλεῖσθαι ἀπόστολος, διότι ἐδίωξα τὴν ἐκκλησίαν τοῦ Θεοῦ.
to be called an apostle, because I persecuted the church of God.
5485 1161 2316 1510/3739/1510/2532/3588/5485/846/3588/1519/1691/3756
10 χάριτι δὲ Θεοῦ εἰμι ὅ εἰμι, καὶ ἡ χάρις αὐτοῦ ἡ εἰς ἐμὲ οὐ
by grace But of God I am what I am, and the grace of Him to me not
2756 1096 235 4053 846 3956 2872
κενὴ ἐγενήθη, ἀλλὰ περισσότερον αὐτῶν πάντων ἐκοπίασα·
fruitless was, but more abundantly (than) them all I labored;
3756 1473 1161 235/3588/5485/3588/2316/3588/4862/1698 1535 3767 1473
οὐκ ἐγὼ δέ, ἀλλ᾽ ἡ χάρις τοῦ Θεοῦ ἡ σὺν ἐμοί. 11 εἴτε οὖν ἐγώ,
not I and, but the grace of God with me. Whether then I,
1535 1565 3779 2784 2532 3779 4100
εἴτε ἐκεῖνοι, οὕτω κηρύσσομεν, καὶ οὕτως ἐπιστεύσατε.
or those, so we proclaim, and so you believed.
1487 1161 5547 2784 3754 1537 3498 1453 4459
12. Εἰ δὲ Χριστὸς κηρύσσεται ὅτι ἐκ νεκρῶν ἐγήγερται, πῶς
if But Christ is proclaimed that from dead He has been raised, how
3004 5100 1722 5213 3754 386 3498 3756 2076 1487/1161
λέγουσι τινες ἐν ὑμῖν ὅτι ἀνάστασις νεκρῶν οὐκ ἔστιν; 13 εἰ δὲ
say some among you that a resurrection of dead ones not is? if But

1 Corinthians 15

1. Moreover, brethren, I declare unto you the gospel which I preached unto you, which also ye have received, and wherein ye stand;
2 By which also ye are saved, if ye keep in memory what I preached unto you, unless ye have believed in vain.
3 For I delivered unto you first of all that which I also received, how that Christ died for our sins according to the scriptures;
4 And that he was buried, and that he rose again the third day according to the scriptures:
5 And that he was seen of Cephas, then of the twelve:
6 After that, he was seen of above five hundred brethren at once; of whom the greater part remain unto this present, but some are fallen asleep.
7 After that, he was seen of James; then of all the apostles.
8 And last of all he was seen of me also, as of one born out of due time.
9 For I am the least of the apostles, that am not meet to be called an apostle, because I persecuted the church of God.
10 But by the grace of God I am what I am: and his grace which (was bestowed) upon me was not in vain; but I laboured more abundantly than they all: yet not I, but the grace of God which was with me.
11 Therefore whether (it were) I or they, so we preach, and so ye believed.
12 Now if Christ be preached that he rose from the dead, how say some among you that there is no resurrection of the dead?
13 But if

Literal Translation | **1 Corinthians 15:14** | ***King James Version***

there is not a resurrection of (the) dead, neither has Christ been raised.

14 But if Christ has not been raised, then our proclamation (is) worthless, and your faith is also worthless.
15 And also we are found (to be) false witnesses of God, because we witnessed according to God that He raised Christ, whom He did not raise, if then dead ones are not raised.
16 For if dead ones are not raised, neither has Christ been raised
.17 But if Christ has not been raised, your faith (is) foolish; you are still in your sins.
18 Then also the (ones) having fallen asleep in Christ were lost.
19 If we only have hope in Christ in this life, of all men we are more miserable.

386 3498 3756 2076 3761 5547 1453
ἀνάστασις νεκρῶν οὐκ ἔστιν, οὐδὲ Χριστὸς ἐγήγερται·
a resurrection of dead ones not is, neither Christ has been raised;

1487 1161 5547 3756 1453 2756 686 3588 2782
14 εἰ δὲ Χριστὸς οὐκ ἐγήγερται, κενὸν ἄρα τὸ κήρυγμα
if But Christ not has been raised, worthless then the proclamation

2257 2756 1161/2532/3588/4102/5216 2147 1161 2532 5575
ἡμῶν, κενὴ δὲ καὶ ἡ πίστις ὑμῶν, 15 εὑρισκόμεθα δὲ καὶ ψευδο-
of us, worthless and also the faith of you, we are found and also false

3588 2316 3754 3140 2596 3588 2316 3754
μάρτυρες τοῦ Θεοῦ, ὅτι ἐμαρτυρήσαμεν κατὰ τοῦ Θεοῦ ὅτι
witnesses of God, because we witnessed according to God that

1453 3588 5547 3739 3756 1453 1512 686 3498 3756
ἤγειρε τὸν Χριστόν, ὃν οὐκ ἤγειρεν εἴπερ ἄρα νεκροὶ οὐκ
He raised Christ, whom not He raised if then dead ones not

1453 1487 1063 3498 3756 1453 3761 5547
ἐγείρονται. 16 εἰ γὰρ νεκροὶ οὐκ ἐγείρονται, οὐδὲ Χριστὸς
are raised. if For dead ones not are raised, neither Christ

1453 1487/1161 5547 3756 1453 3152 3588 4102
ἐγήγερται· 17 εἰ δὲ Χριστὸς οὐκ ἐγήγερται, ματαία ἡ πίστις
has been raised; if but Christ not has been raised, foolish the faith

5216 2089 2075 1722 3588 266 5216 686/2532/3588 2837
ὑμῶν· ἔτι ἐστὲ ἐν ταῖς ἁμαρτίαις ὑμῶν. 18 ἄρα καὶ οἱ κοιμη-
of you; still you are in the sins of you. Then also those having

1722 5547 622 1487/1722/3588/2222/3778 1679
θέντες ἐν Χριστῷ ἀπώλοντο. 19 εἰ ἐν τῇ ζωῇ ταύτῃ ἠλπικότες
fallen asleep in Christ were lost. If in life this having hoped

2070 1722 5547 3440 1652 3956 444
ἐσμὲν ἐν Χριστῷ μόνον, ἐλεεινότεροι πάντων ἀνθρώπων
we are in Christ only, more miserable of all men

2070
ἐσμέν.
we are.

there be no resurrection of the dead, then is Christ not risen:

14 And if Christ be not risen, then (is) our preaching vain, and your faith (is) also vain.
15 Yea, and we are found false witnesses of God; because we have testified of God that he raised up Christ: whom he raised not up, if so be that the dead rise not.

16 For if the dead rise not, then is not Christ raised:

17 And if Christ be not raised, your faith (is) vain; ye are yet in your sins.
18 Then they also which are fallen asleep in Christ are perished.
19 If in this life only we have hope in Christ, we are of all men most miserable.

20 But now Christ has been raised from (the) dead; He became the firstfruit of the (ones) having fallen asleep.
21 For since death (is) through man, also through a Man (is) a resurrection of (the) dead;
22 for as in Adam all die, so also in Christ all' will be made alive.

23 But each in (his) own order: Christ, the firstfruit, afterward those of Christ at His coming.

24 Then (is) the end, when He delivers the kingdom to God, even the Father, when He makes to cease all rule and all authority and power.
25 for it is right for Him to reign until He shall have put all the enemies under His feet; (Psa. 110:1)
26 (The) last

3570 1161 5547 1453 1537 3498 536 3588
20. Νυνὶ δὲ Χριστὸς ἐγήγερται ἐκ νεκρῶν, ἀπαρχὴ τῶν
now But Christ has been raised from (the) dead, first fruit of those

2837 1096 1894 1063 1223 444 3588 2288
κεκοιμημένων ἐγένετο. 21 ἐπειδὴ γὰρ δι' ἀνθρώπου ὁ θάνατος,
having fallen asleep He became. since For through man (is) death,

2532 1223 444 386 3498 5618 1063 1722 3588
καὶ δι' ἀνθρώπου ἀνάστασις νεκρῶν· 22 ὥσπερ γὰρ ἐν τῷ
and through a Man a resurrection of (the) dead; as For in

76 3956 599 3779 2532 1722 3588 5547
Ἀδὰμ πάντες ἀποθνῄσκουσιν, οὕτω καὶ ἐν τῷ Χριστῷ
Adam all die, so also in Christ

3956 2227 1538 1161 1722 3588 2398 5001
πάντες ζῳοποιηθήσονται. 23 ἕκαστος δὲ ἐν τῷ ἰδίῳ τάγματι·
all will be made alive. each But in the own order;

536 5547 1899 3588 5547 1722 3588 3952 846
ἀπαρχὴ Χριστός, ἔπειτα οἱ Χριστοῦ ἐν τῇ παρουσίᾳ αὐτοῦ·
(the) firstfruit Christ, afterward those of Christ in the coming of Him;

1534 3588 5056 3752 3860 3588 932 3588 2316 2532
24 εἶτα τὸ τέλος, ὅταν παραδῷ τὴν βασιλείαν τῷ Θεῷ καὶ
Then the end, when He delivers the kingdom of God even

3962 3752 2673 3956 746 2532 3956 1849
πατρί, ὅταν καταργήσῃ πᾶσαν ἀρχὴν καὶ πᾶσαν ἐξουσίαν
(the) Father, when He makes to cease all rule and all authority

2532 1411 1163 1063 846 936 891 3757 302
καὶ δύναμιν. 25 δεῖ γὰρ αὐτὸν βασιλεύειν, ἄχρις οὗ ἂν
and power. it is right For Him to reign, until He shall have

5087 3956 3588 2190 5259 3588 4228 846 2078
θῇ πάντας τοὺς ἐχθροὺς ὑπὸ τοὺς πόδας αὐτοῦ. 26 ἔσχατος
put all the enemies under the feet of Him. (The) last

20 But now is Christ risen from the dead, (and) become the firstfruits of them that slept.
21 For since by man (came) death, by man (came) also the resurrection of the dead.
22 For as in Adam all die, even so in Christ shall all be made alive.

23 But every man in his own order: Christ the firstfruits; afterward they that are Christ's at his coming.

24 Then (cometh) the end, when he shall have delivered up the kingdom to God, even the Father; when he shall have put down all rule and all authority and power.
25 For he must reign, till he hath put all enemies under his feet.
26 The last

Literal Translation | **1 Corinthians 15:27** | **King James Version**

enemy made to cease (is) death.
27 For He subjected all things under His feet; but when He says, All things have been subjected, (it is) plain that (it) excepts the (One) who has subjected all things to Him. (Psa.8:6)
28 But when all things are subjected to Him, then the Son Himself also will be subjected to the (One) who has subjected all things to Him, that God may be all things in all.

2190 2673 3588 2288 3956 1063 5293 5259
ἐχθρὸς καταργεῖται ὁ θάνατος· 27 πάντα γὰρ ὑπέταξεν ὑπὸ
enemy made to cease (is) death; all things For He subjected under

3588 4228 846 3752 1161 2036 3754 3956 5293
τοὺς πόδας αὐτοῦ. ὅταν δὲ εἴπῃ ὅτι Πάντα ὑποτέτακται,
the feet of Him. when But He says, All things have been subjected,

1212 3754 1622 3588 5293 846 3588 3956 3752
δῆλον ὅτι ἐκτὸς τοῦ ὑποτάξαντος αὐτῷ τὰ πάντα. 28 ὅταν
(it is) plain that except (the) One having subjected to Him all things. when

1161 5293 846 3588 3956 5119 2532 846 3588 5207 5293
δὲ ὑποταγῇ αὐτῷ τὰ πάντα, τότε καὶ αὐτὸς ὁ υἱὸς ὑποταγή-
But is subjected to Him all things, then also Himself the Son will be sub-

3588 5293 846 3588 3956 2443/5600/3588/2316/3588
σεται τῷ ὑποτάξαντι αὐτῷ τὰ πάντα, ἵνα ᾖ ὁ Θεὸς τὰ
jected to the (One) having subjected to Him all things, that may be God

3956 1722 3956
πάντα ἐν πᾶσιν.
all things in all.

enemy (that) shall be destroyed (is) death.
27 For he hath put all things under his feet. But when he saith all things are put under (him, it is) manifest that he is excepted, which did put all things under him.
28 And when all things shall be subdued unto him, then shall the Son also himself be subject unto him that put all things under him, that God may be all in all.

29 Otherwise, what will they do, the (ones) having been baptized on behalf of the dead? If (the) dead are not at all raised, why indeed are they baptized on behalf of (the) dead?
30 Why are we also in danger every hour?
31 Day by day I die, by your glorying, which I have in Christ Jesus our Lord.
32 If according to man I fought with beasts in Ephesus, what (is) the profit to me if dead ones are not raised? "Let us eat and drink, for tomorrow we die." (Isa. 22:13)

1893 5101 4160 3588 907 5228 3588 3498
29.'Επεὶ τί ποιήσουσιν οἱ βαπτιζόμενοι ὑπὲρ τῶν νεκρῶν;
Otherwise what will they do those having been baptized for the dead;

1487 3654 3498 3756 1453 5101 2532 907 5228 3588
εἰ ὅλως νεκροὶ οὐκ ἐγείρονται, τί καὶ βαπτίζονται ὑπὲρ τῶν
if at all dead ones not are raised, why indeed are they baptized for the

3498 5101 2532 2249 2793 3956 5610 2596
νεκρῶν; 30 τί καὶ ἡμεῖς κινδυνεύομεν πᾶσαν ὥραν; 31 καθ'
dead? Why also we are in danger every hour? (Day

2250 599 3513 3588 2251 2746 3739 2192 1722
ἡμέραν ἀποθνήσκω, νὴ τὴν ὑμετέραν καύχησιν, ἣν ἔχω ἐν
by) day I die, by your glorying, which I have in

5547 2424 3588 2962 2257 1487 2596 444
Χριστῷ Ἰησοῦ τῷ Κυρίῳ ἡμῶν. 32 εἰ κατὰ ἄνθρωπον
Christ Jesus the Lord of us. If according to man

2341 1722 2181 5101 3427 3588 3786 1487 3498 3756
ἐθηριομάχησα ἐν Ἐφέσῳ, τί μοι τὸ ὄφελος, εἰ νεκροὶ οὐκ
I fought with beasts in Ephesus, what to me the profit, if dead ones not

1453 5315 2532 4095 839 1063 599
ἐγείρονται; φάγωμεν καὶ πίωμεν, αὔριον γὰρ ἀποθνήσκομεν.
are raised? Let us eat and drink, tomorrow for we die.

29 Else what shall they do which are baptized for the dead, if the dead rise not at all? why are they then baptized for the dead?
30 And why stand we in jeopardy every hour?
31 I protest by your rejoicing which I have in Christ Jesus our Lord, I die daily.
32 If after the manner of men I have fought with beasts at Ephesus, what advantageth it me, if the dead rise not? let us eat and drink; for to morrow we die.

33 Do not be led astray; bad companionships corrupt good habits.
34 Be righteously awake, and do not sin; for some have ignorance of God. I speak to you for shame.

3361 4105 5351 2239 5543 3657 2556
33 μὴ πλανᾶσθε· Φθείρουσιν ἤθη χρήσθ' ὁμιλίαι κακαί.
not Be led astray; will corrupt habits good companionships bad.

1594 1346 2532 3361 264 56 1063 2316
34 ἐκνήψατε δικαίως, καὶ μὴ ἁμαρτάνετε· ἀγνωσίαν γὰρ Θεοῦ
You be aroused righteously, and not sin; ignorance for of God

5100 2192 4314 1791 5213 3004
τινὲς ἔχουσι· πρὸς ἐντροπὴν ὑμῖν λέγω.
some have; for shame to you I speak.

33 Be not deceived: evil communications corrupt good manners.
34 Awake to righteousness, and sin not; for some have not the knowledge of God: I speak (this) to your shame.

35 But someone will say, How are (the) dead raised? And with what body do they come?
36 Foolish ones! What you sow is not made alive if it does not die.
37 And what you sow, you do not sow the body that (is) going to be, but a bare grain, it may be of wheat, or of some of the rest,
38 and God gives it a body according as He desired, and

235 2046 5100 4459 1453 3588 3498 4169 1161 4983
35. 'Αλλ' ἐρεῖ τις, Πῶς ἐγείρονται οἱ νεκροί; ποίῳ δὲ σώματι
But will say someone, How are raised the dead ones? with what And body

2064 878 4771 3739 4687 3756 2227 1437 3361
ἔρχονται; 36 ἄφρων, σὺ ὃ σπείρεις, οὐ ζῳοποιεῖται ἐὰν μὴ
do they come? Foolish ones, you what you sow, not is made alive if not

599 2532 3588 4687 3756 3588 4983 3588 1096
ἀποθάνῃ· 37 καὶ ὃ σπείρεις, οὐ τὸ σῶμα τὸ γενησόμενον
it dies; and what sow, not the body (which) is going to be

4687 235 1131 2848 1487 5177 4621 2228 5100 3588
σπείρεις, ἀλλὰ γυμνὸν κόκκον, εἰ τύχοι, σίτου ἤ τινος τῶν
(that) you sow, but a naked grain, it may be, of wheat or some of the

3062 3588 1161 2316 846 1325 4983 2531 2309 2532
λοιπῶν· 38 ὁ δὲ Θεὸς αὐτῷ δίδωσι σῶμα καθὼς ἠθέλησε, καὶ
rest; but God to it gives a body as He desired, and

35 But some (man) will say, How are the dead raised up? and with what body do they come?
36 (Thou) fool, that which thou sowest is not quickened, except it die:
37 And that which thou sowest, thou sowest not that body that shall be, but bare grain, it may chance of wheat, or of some other (grain):
38 But God giveth it a body as it hath pleased him, and

Literal Translation

to each of the seeds its own body.
39 Not every flesh (is) the same flesh, but indeed other (one) flesh of men, and another flesh of beasts, and another of fish, and another (the) flesh of birds.
40 And (there are) heavenly bodies, and earthly bodies. But the glory of the heavenly (is) truly different, and that of the earthly different;
41 one glory of (the) sun, and another glory of (the) moon, and another glory of (the) stars; for star differs from star in glory.
42 So also the resurrection of the dead. It is sown in corruption, it is raised in incorruption.
43 It is sown in dishonor, it is raised in glory. It is sown in weakness, it is raised in power.

44 It is sown a natural body, it is raised a spiritual body; there is a natural body, and there is a spiritual body.

45 So also it has been written, "The first man, Adam, became a living soul;" the last Adam a life-giving Spirit. (Gen. 2:7)

46 But not firstly the spiritual, but the natural; afterward the spiritual.

47 The first man (was) out of earth, earthy. The second Man (was) the Lord out of Heaven. (Gen.2:7)
48 Such the earthy (man), such also the earthy ones. And such the heavenly Man, such also the heavenly ones.
49 And as we bore the image of the earthy man, we shall also bear the image of the heavenly Man.
50 And I say this, brothers, that flesh and blood is not able to inherit (the) kingdom of God, nor does corruption inherit incorruption.

1 Corinthians 15:39

1538 3588 4690 3588 2398 4983 3756 3956 4561 3588
ἑκάστῳ τῶν σπερμάτων τὸ ἴδιον σῶμα. 39 οὐ πᾶσα σὰρξ ἡ
to each of the seeds the own body. (is) not All flesh the
846 4561 235 243 3303 4561 444 243 1161 4561
αὐτὴ σάρξ· ἀλλὰ ἄλλη μὲν σὰρξ ἀνθρώπων, ἄλλη δὲ σὰρξ
same flesh; but other indeed flesh of men, other and flesh
2934 243 1161 2486 243 1161 4561 4421 2532 4983
κτηνῶν, ἄλλη δὲ ἰχθύων, ἄλλη δὲ σὰρξ πτηνῶν. 40 καὶ σώματα
of animals, other and of fish, other and flesh of birds. And (are) bodies
2032 2532 4983 1919 235 2087 3303 3588 3588
ἐπουράνια, καὶ σώματα ἐπίγεια· ἀλλ' ἑτέρα μὲν ἡ τῶν ἐπου-
heavenly, and bodies earthly; but other truly (is) of the
2032 1391 2087 1161 3588 3588 1919 243 1391 2246 2532
ρανίων δόξα, ἑτέρα δὲ ἡ τῶν ἐπιγείων. 41 ἄλλη δόξα ἡλίου, καὶ
heavenly glory, other and that of the earthly. (There is) other glory of sun, and
243 1391 4582 2532 243 1391 792 792 1063
ἄλλη δόξα σελήνης, καὶ ἄλλη δόξα ἀστέρων· ἀστὴρ γὰρ
other glory of moon, and other glory of stars; star for
792 1308 1722 1391 3779 2532 3588 386 3588
ἀστέρος διαφέρει ἐν δόξῃ. 42 Οὕτω καὶ ἡ ἀνάστασις τῶν
from star differs in glory. So also the resurrection of the
3498 4687 1722 5356 1453 1722 861 4687
νεκρῶν. σπείρεται ἐν φθορᾷ, ἐγείρεται ἐν ἀφθαρσίᾳ· 43 σπεί-
dead. It is sown in corruption, it is raised in incorruption; It is
1722 819 1453 1722 1391 4687 1722 769
ρεται ἐν ἀτιμίᾳ, ἐγείρεται ἐν δόξῃ· σπείρεται ἐν ἀσθενείᾳ,
sown in dishonor, it is raised in glory; it is sown in weakness,
1453 1722 1411 4687 4983 5591 1453
ἐγείρεται ἐν δυνάμει· 44 σπείρεται σῶμα ψυχικόν, ἐγείρεται
it is raised in power; it is sown a body natural, it is raised
4983 4152 2076 4983 5591 2532 2076 4983
σῶμα πνευματικόν. ἔστι σῶμα ψυχικόν, καὶ ἔστι σῶμα
a body spiritual. There is a body natural, and there is a body
4152 3779 2532 1125 1096 3588 4413
πνευματικόν. 45 οὕτω καὶ γέγραπται, Ἐγένετο ὁ πρῶτος
spiritual. So also it has been written, became The first
444 76 1519 5590 2198 3588 2078 76 1519
ἄνθρωπος Ἀδὰμ εἰς ψυχὴν ζῶσαν· ὁ ἔσχατος Ἀδὰμ εἰς
man Adam into soul a living; the last Adam
4151 2227 235 3756 4412 3588 4152 235
πνεῦμα ζωοποιοῦν. 46 ἀλλ' οὐ πρῶτον τὸ πνευματικόν, ἀλλὰ
spirit a life-giving. But not firstly the spiritual (body), but
3588 5591 1899 3588 4152 3588 4413 444 1537
τὸ ψυχικόν, ἔπειτα τὸ πνευματικόν. 47 ὁ πρῶτος ἄνθρωπος ἐκ
the natural afterward the spiritual. The first man (was) out of
1093 5517 3588 1208 444 3588 2962 1537 3772
γῆς, χοϊκός, ὁ δεύτερος ἄνθρωπος, ὁ Κύριος ἐξ οὐρανοῦ.
earth, earthy, the second Man, the Lord out of Heaven.
3634 3588 5517 5108 2532 3588 5517 2532 3634 3588 2032
48 οἷος ὁ χοικός, τοιοῦτοι καὶ οἱ χοικοι· καὶ οἷος ὁ ἐπουράνιος,
Such the earthy (man), such also the earthy ones; and such the heavenly Man,
5108 2532 3588 2032 2532 2531 5409 3588
τοιοῦτοι καὶ οἱ ἐπουράνιοι· 49 καὶ καθὼς ἐφορέσαμεν τὴν
such also the heavenly ones; and even as we bore the
1504 3588 5517 5409 2532 3588 1504 3588 2032
εἰκόνα τοῦ χοϊκοῦ, φορέσομεν καὶ τὴν εἰκόνα τοῦ ἐπουρανίου.
image of the earthy man, we shall bear also the image of the heavenly Man.
5124 1161 5346 80 3754 4561 2532 129 932
50. Τοῦτο δέ φημι, ἀδελφοί, ὅτι σὰρξ καὶ αἷμα βασιλείαν
this And I say, brothers, that flesh and blood (the) kingdom
2316 2816 3756 1410 3761 3588 5356 3588 861
Θεοῦ κληρονομῆσαι οὐ δύναται, οὐδὲ ἡ φθορὰ τὴν ἀφθαρ-
of God inherit not is able, nor corruption incorruption

King James Version

to every seed his own body.
39 All flesh (is) not the same flesh: but (there is) one (kind of) flesh of men, another flesh of beasts, another of fishes, (and) another of birds.
40 (There are) also celestial bodies, and bodies terrestrial: but the glory of the celestial (is) one, and the (glory) of the terrestrial (is) another.
41 (There is) one glory of the sun, and another glory of the moon, and another glory of the stars: for (one) star differeth from (another) star in glory.
42 So also (is) the resurrection of the dead. It is sown in corruption; it is raised in incorruption:
43 It is sown in dishonour; it is raised in glory: it is sown in weakness; it is raised in power:

44 It is sown a natural body; it is raised a spiritual body. There is a natural body, and there is a spiritual body.

45 And so it is written, The first man Adam was made a living soul; the last Adam (was made) a quickening spirit.

46 Howbeit that (was) not first which is spiritual, but that which is natural; and afterward that which is spiritual.
47 The first man (is) of the earth, earthy: the second man (is) the Lord from heaven.
48 As (is) the earthy, such (are) they also that are earthy: and as (is) the heavenly, such (are) they also that are heavenly.
49 And as we have borne the image of the earthy, we shall also bear the image of the heavenly.
50 Now this I say, brethren, that flesh and blood cannot inherit the kingdom of God; neither doth corruption inherit incorruption.

1 Corinthians 15:51

Literal Translation

51 Behold! I speak a mystery to you: indeed we shall not all fall asleep, but we shall all be changed.

52 In a moment, in a blink of an eye, at the last trumpet; for a trumpet will sound, and the dead will be raised incorruptible, and we shall all be changed.

53 For this corruptible must put on incorruption, and this mortal (must) put on immortality.

54 And when this corruptible shall put on incorruption, and this mortal shall put on immortality, then will occur the word that has been written, "Death was swallowed up in victory." (Isa. 25:8)

55 "O death, where (is your) sting? Hades, where (is your) victory?" (Hos.13:14)

56 And the sting of death (is) sin, and the power of sin (is) the law;

57 but thanks (be) to God giving to us the victory through our Lord Jesus Christ!

58 So as, my beloved brothers, (you) be firm, immovable, abounding in the work of the Lord always, knowing that your labor is not without fruit in (the) Lord.

2816 2400 3466 5213 3004 3956 3303 3756
σίαν κληρονομεῖ. 51 ἰδού, μυστήριον ὑμῖν λέγω· Πάντες μὲν οὐ
inherit. Behold! A mystery to you I speak; all indeed not

2837 3956 1161 236 1722 823 1722 4493
κοιμηθησόμεθα, πάντες δὲ ἀλλαγησόμεθα, 52 ἐν ἀτόμῳ, ἐν ῥιπῇ
we shall fall asleep, all but shall be changed, in a moment, in a blink

3788 1722 3588 2078 4536 4537 1063 2532 3588
ὀφθαλμοῦ, ἐν τῇ ἐσχάτῃ σάλπιγγι· σαλπίσει γάρ, καὶ οἱ
of the eye, at the last trumpet; a trumpet will sound for, and the

3498 1453 862 2532 2249 236
νεκροὶ ἐγερθήσονται ἄφθαρτοι, καὶ ἡμεῖς ἀλλαγησόμεθα.
dead ones will be raised incorruptible, and we shall be changed.

1163 1063 3588 5349 5124 1746 861 2532/3588
53 δεῖ γὰρ τὸ φθαρτὸν τοῦτο ἐνδύσασθαι ἀφθαρσίαν, καὶ τὸ
must For corruptible this put on incorruption, and

2349 5124 1746 110 3752 1161 3588 5349
θνητὸν τοῦτο ἐνδύσασθαι ἀθανασίαν. 54 ὅταν δὲ τὸ φθαρτὸν
mortal this put on immortality. when And corruptible

5124 1746 861 2532 3588 2349 5124 1746
τοῦτο ἐνδύσηται ἀφθαρσίαν, καὶ τὸ θνητὸν τοῦτο ἐνδύσηται
this shall put on incorruption, and mortal this put on

110 5119 1096 3588 3056 3588 1125 2666
ἀθανασίαν, τότε γενήσεται ὁ λόγος ὁ γεγραμμένος, Κατε-
immortality, then will occur the word having been written, was

3588 2288 1519 3534 4226 4675 2288 3588 2759 4226
πόθη ὁ θάνατος εἰς νῖκος. 55 ποῦ σου, θάνατε, τὸ κέντρον; ποῦ
swallowed Death in victory. Where of you, death, the sting; where

4675 86 3588 3534 3588 1161 2759 3588 2288 3588 266 3588
σου, ᾅδη, τὸ νῖκος; 56 τὸ δὲ κέντρον τοῦ θανάτου ἡ ἁμαρτία· ἡ
of you, Hades, the victory? the And sting of death (is) sin; the

1161 1411 3588 266 3588 3551 3588 1161 2316 5485 3588
δὲ δύναμις τῆς ἁμαρτίας ὁ νόμος· 57 τῷ δὲ Θεῷ χάρις τῷ
and power of sin (is) the law; But to God thanks He

1325 2254 3588 3534 1223 3588 2962 2257 2424 5547
διδόντι ἡμῖν τὸ νῖκος διὰ τοῦ Κυρίου ἡμῶν Ἰησοῦ Χριστοῦ.
giving to us the victory through the Lord of us Jesus Christ.

5620 80 3450 27 1476 1096 277
58 ὥστε, ἀδελφοί μου ἀγαπητοί, ἑδραῖοι γίνεσθε, ἀμετακίνητοι,
So as, brothers of me beloved, firm be, immovable,

4052 1722 3588 2041 3588 2962 3842 1492 3754
περισσεύοντες ἐν τῷ ἔργῳ τοῦ Κυρίου πάντοτε, εἰδότες ὅτι
abounding in the work of the Lord always, knowing that

3588 2873 5216 3756 2076 2756 1722 2962
ὁ κόπος ὑμῶν οὐκ ἔστι κενὸς ἐν Κυρίῳ.
the labor of you not is fruitless in (the) Lord.

King James Version

51 Behold, I shew you a mystery; We shall not all sleep, but we shall all be changed,

52 In a moment, in the twinkling of an eye, at the last trump: for the trumpet shall sound, and the dead shall be raised incorruptible, and we shall be changed.

53 For this corruptible must put on incorruption, and this mortal (must) put on immortality.

54 So when this corruptible shall have put on incorruption, and this mortal shall have put on immortality, then shall be brought to pass the saying that is written, Death is swallowed up in victory.

55 O death, where (is) thy sting? O grave, where (is) thy victory?

56 The sting of death (is) sin; and the strength of sin (is) the law.

57 But thanks (be) to God, which giveth us the victory through our Lord Jesus Christ.

58 Therefore, my beloved brethren, be ye stedfast, unmoveable, always abounding in the work of the Lord, forasmuch as ye know that your labour is not in vain in the Lord

1 Corinthians 16

Literal Translation

1. And about the collection for the saints, as I charged the churches of Galatia, so also you do.

2 On the first of a week, let each of you put by himself, storing up whatever he is prospered, that there not be collections then when I come.

3 And when I arrive, whomever you approve through these epistles,

4012 1161 3588 3048 3588 1519 3588 40 5618 1299
1. Περὶ δὲ τῆς λογίας τῆς εἰς τοὺς ἁγίους, ὥσπερ διέταξα
concerning And the collection for the saints, as I charged

3588 1577 3588 1053 3779 2532 5210 4160 2596
ταῖς ἐκκλησίαις τῆς Γαλατίας, οὕτω καὶ ὑμεῖς ποιήσατε. 2 κατὰ
the churches of Galatia, so also you do. On

3391 4521 1538 5216 3844 1438 5087 2343 3739
μίαν σαββάτων ἕκαστος ὑμῶν παρ' ἑαυτῷ τιθέτω, θησαυρίζων ὅ
one of sabbaths each of you by himself let him put, storing up

5100 302 2137 2443 3361 3752 2064 5119 3048 1096 3752
τι ἂν εὐοδῶται, ἵνα μή, ὅταν ἔλθω, τότε λογίαι γίνωνται. 3 ὅταν
whatever he is prospered, that not when I come, then collections there be. when

1161 3854 3739 1437 1381 1223 1992 5128
δὲ παραγένωμαι, οὓς ἐὰν δοκιμάσητε δι' ἐπιστολῶν, τούτους
And I arrive, whomever you approve through epistles, these

King James Version

1. Now concerning the collection for the saints, as I have given order to the churches of Galatia, even so do ye.

2 Upon the first (day) of the week let every one of you lay by him in store, as (God) hath prospered him, that there be no gatherings when I come.

3 And when I come, whomsoever ye shall approve by (your) letters, them

Literal Translation

I will send to carry your grace to Jerusalem.
4 And if it is suitable for me to go also, they shall go with me.
5 But I will come to you when I go through Macedonia. For I am going through Macedonia.
6 And possibly I will stay with you, or even spend the winter, that you may set me forward wherever I may go.
7 For I do not desire to see you now in passage, but I am hoping to remain some time with you, if the Lord permits.
8 But I will remain in Ephesus until Pentecost.
9 For a door opened to me, great and effective, and many (are) opposing.
10 But if Timothy comes, see that he is with you without fear; for he works the work of the Lord, even as I.
11 Then do not let any despise him, but set him forward in peace, that he may come to me; for I am waiting for him with the brothers.
12 And concerning the brother Apollos, I much urged him that he come to you with the brothers, but it was not altogether (his) will that he come now. But he will come when he has opportunity.
13 Watch! Stand fast in the faith! Be men! Be strong!
14 Let all your things be in love.
15 But I exhort you, brothers. You know the house of Stephanas, that it is the firstfruit of Achaia, and they appointed themselves to ministry to the saints.
16 (See) that you also may submit to such ones,

1 Corinthians 16:4

3992 667 3588 5485 5216 1519 2419 1437 1161 5600
πέμψω ἀπενεγκεῖν τὴν χάριν ὑμῶν εἰς Ἱερουσαλήμ· 4 ἐὰν δὲ ᾖ
I will send to carry the grace of you to Jerusalem; if but it is

514 3588 2504 4198 4862 1698 4198 2064
ἄξιον τοῦ κἀμὲ πορεύεσθαι, σὺν ἐμοὶ πορεύσονται. 5 ἐλεύσομαι
suitable me also to go, with me they shall go. I will come

1161 4314 5209 3752 3109 1330 3109 1063
δὲ πρὸς ὑμᾶς, ὅταν Μακεδονίαν διέλθω· Μακεδονίαν γὰρ
And to you, when Macedonia I go through; Macedonia for

1330 4314 5209 1161 5177 3887 2228 2532 3914
διέρχομαι· 6 πρὸς ὑμᾶς δὲ τυχὸν παραμενῶ, ἢ καὶ παραχειμάσω,
I am going through, with you and possibly I will stay, or even spend the winter,

2443 5210 3165 4311 3757 1437 4198 3756 2309 1063
ἵνα ὑμεῖς με προπέμψητε οὗ ἐὰν πορεύωμαι. 7 οὐ θέλω γὰρ
that you me may set forward wherever I may go. not I desire For

5209 737 1722 3938 1492 1679 1161 5550 5100 1961
ὑμᾶς ἄρτι ἐν παρόδῳ ἰδεῖν· ἐλπίζω δὲ χρόνον τινὰ ἐπιμεῖναι
you yet in passage to see; I am hoping but time some to remain

4314 5209 1437 3588 2962 2010 1961 1161 1722 2181 2193
πρὸς ὑμᾶς, ἐὰν ὁ Κύριος ἐπιτρέπῃ. 8 ἐπιμενῶ δὲ ἐν Ἐφέσῳ ἕως
with you, if the Lord permits. I will remain But in Ephesus until

3588 4005 2374 1063 3427 455 3173 2532 1756
τῆς Πεντηκοστῆς· 9 θύρα γάρ μοι ἀνέῳγε μεγάλη καὶ ἐνεργής,
Pentecost; a door for to me opened great and effective,

2532 480 4183
καὶ ἀντικείμενοι πολλοί.
and (are) opposing many.

1437 1161 2064 5095 991 2443 870 1096 4314
10. Ἐὰν δὲ ἔλθῃ Τιμόθεος, βλέπετε ἵνα ἀφόβως γένηται πρὸς
if But comes Timothy, see that without fear he may be with

5209 3588 1063 2041 2962 2038 5613 2532 1473 3361 5100
ὑμᾶς· τὸ γὰρ ἔργον Κυρίου ἐργάζεται ὡς καὶ ἐγώ. 11 μή τις
you; for (the) works of (the) Lord he works as also I. Let not any

3767 846 1848 4311 1161 846 1722 1515 2443
οὖν αὐτὸν ἐξουθενήσῃ· προπέμψατε δὲ αὐτὸν ἐν εἰρήνῃ, ἵνα
then him despise; set forward but him in peace, that

2064 4314 3165 1551 1063 846 3326 3588 80 4012
ἔλθῃ πρός με· ἐκδέχομαι γὰρ αὐτὸν μετὰ τῶν ἀδελφῶν. 12 περὶ
he come to me; I am awaiting for him with the brothers. concerning

1161 625 3588 80 4183 3870 846 2443
δὲ Ἀπολλὼ τοῦ ἀδελφοῦ, πολλὰ παρεκάλεσα αὐτὸν ἵνα
And Apollos the brother, much I urged him that

2064 4314 5209 3326 3588 80 2532 3843 3756 2258
ἔλθῃ πρὸς ὑμᾶς μετὰ τῶν ἀδελφῶν· καὶ πάντως οὐκ ἦν
he come to you with the brothers; and altogether not it was

2307 2443 3568 2064 2064 1161 3752 2119
θέλημα ἵνα νῦν ἔλθῃ, ἐλεύσεται δὲ ὅταν εὐκαιρήσῃ.
(his) will that now he come, he will come but when he has opportunity.

1127 4739 1722 3588 4102 407 2901
13. Γρηγορεῖτε, στήκετε ἐν τῇ πίστει, ἀνδρίζεσθε, κραταιοῦ-
Watch! Stand in the faith! Be men! Be strong!

3956 5216 1722 26 1096
σθε· 14 πάντα ὑμῶν ἐν ἀγάπῃ γινέσθω.
All things of you in love let be.

3870 1161 5209 80 1492 3588 3614 4734
15. Παρακαλῶ δὲ ὑμᾶς, ἀδελφοί [οἴδατε τὴν οἰκίαν Στεφανᾶ,
I exhort And you, brothers, you know the house of Stephanas,

3754 2076 536 3588 882 2532 1519 1248 3588 40
ὅτι ἐστὶν ἀπαρχὴ τῆς Ἀχαΐας, καὶ εἰς διακονίαν τοῖς ἁγίοις
that it is firstfruit of Achaia, and to ministry to the saints

5021 1438 2443 2532 5210 5293 3588 5108
ἔταξαν ἑαυτούς] 16 ἵνα καὶ ὑμεῖς ὑποτάσσησθε τοῖς τοιούτοις,
they set themselves, that also you may subnit to such ones,

King James Version

will I send to bring your liberality unto Jerusalem.
4 And if it be meet that I go also, they shall go with me.
5 Now I will come unto you, when I shall pass through Macedonia: for I do pass through Macedonia.
6 And it may be that I will abide, yea, and winter with you, that ye may bring me on my journey whithersoever I go.
7 For I will not see you now by the way; but I trust to tarry a while with you, if the Lord permit.
8 But I will tarry at Ephesus until Pentecost.
9 For a great door and effectual is opened unto me, and (there are) many adversaries.
10 Now if Timotheus come, see that he may be with you without fear: for he worketh the work of the Lord, as I also (do).
11 Let no man therefore despise him: but conduct him forth in peace, that he may come unto me: for I look for him with the brethren.
12 As touching (our) brother Apollos, I greatly desired him to come unto you with the brethren: but his will was not at all to come at this time; but he will come when he shall have convenient time.
13 Watch ye, stand fast in the faith, quit you like men, be strong.
14 Let all your things be done with charity.
15 I beseech you, brethren, (ye know the house of Stephanas, that it is the firstfruits of Achaia, and (that) they have addicted themselves to the ministry of the saints,)
16 That ye submit yourselves unto such,

Literal Translation **1 Corinthians 16:17** ***King James Version***

and to everyone working and laboring with (me).
17 And I rejoice at the coming of Stephanas, and of Fortunatus and Achaicus, because these supplied your lack.
18 For they refreshed my spirit and yours. Therefore recognize such ones.

19 The churches of Asia greet you. Aquila and Priscilla much greet you in (the) Lord, with the church in their house.

20 The brothers all greet you. Greet one another with a holy kiss.

21 The greeting with my hand, Paul.
22 If anyone does not love the Lord Jesus Christ, let him be a curse. Our Lord comes!
23 The grace of the Lord Jesus Christ (be) with you.
24 My love (be) with all of you in Christ Jesus. Amen.

2532 3956 3588 4903 2532 2872 5463 1161 1909 3588
καὶ παντὶ τῷ συνεργοῦντι καὶ κοπιῶντι. 17 χαίρω δὲ ἐπὶ τῇ
and to everyone working with (me) and laboring. I rejoice And at the

3952 4734 2532 5415 2532 883 3754 3588
παρουσίᾳ Στεφανᾶ καὶ Φορτουνάτου καὶ Ἀχαϊκοῦ, ὅτι τὸ
presence of Stephanas and of Fortunatus and of Achaicus, that

5216 5303 3778 378 373 1063 3588 1699
ὑμῶν υστέρημα οὗτοι ἀνεπλήρωσαν. 18 ἀνέπαυσαν γὰρ τὸ ἐμὸν
your lack these supplied; they refreshed for my

4151 2532 3588 5216 1921 3767 3588 5108
πνεῦμα καὶ τὸ ὑμῶν· ἐπιγινώσκετε οὖν τοὺς τοιούτους.
spirit and of you; recognize therefore such ones.

782 5209 3588 1577 3588 773 782
19. Ἀσπάζονται ὑμᾶς αἱ ἐκκλησίαι τῆς Ἀσίας· ἀσπάζονται
Greet you the churches of Asia. Greets

5209 1722 2962 4183 207 2532 4252 4862 3588 2596
ὑμᾶς ἐν Κυρίῳ πολλὰ Ἀκύλας καὶ Πρίσκιλλα, σὺν τῇ κατ'
you in (the) Lord much Aquila and Priscilla, with the in

3624 846 1577 782 5209 3588 80
οἶκον αὐτῶν ἐκκλησίᾳ. 20 ἀσπάζονται ὑμᾶς οἱ ἀδελφοὶ
(the) house of them church. Greet you the brothers

3956 782 240 1722 5370 40
πάντες. Ἀσπάσασθε ἀλλήλους ἐν φιλήματι ἁγίῳ.
all. Greet one another with kiss a holy.

3588 783 3588 1699 5495 3972 1487 5100 3756 5368 3588
21. Ὁ ἀσπασμὸς τῇ ἐμῇ χειρὶ Παύλου. 22 εἴ τις οὐ φιλεῖ τὸν
The greeting with my hand of Paul. If anyone not love the

2962 2424 5547 2277 331 3134 3134 3588 5485
Κύριον Ἰησοῦν Χριστόν, ἤτω ἀνάθεμα. Μαραν ἀθά. 23 ἡ χάρις
Lord Jesus Christ, let him be a curse. Our Lord comes. The grace

3588 2962 2424 5547 3326 5216 3588 26 3450 3326
τοῦ Κυρίου Ἰησοῦ Χριστοῦ μεθ' ὑμῶν. 24 ἡ ἀγάπη μου μετὰ
of the Lord Jesus Christ (be) with you. The love of me with

3956 5216 1722 5547 2424 281
πάντων ὑμῶν ἐν Χριστῷ Ἰησοῦ. ἀμήν.
all of you in Christ Jesus. Amen.

and to every one that helpeth with (us), and laboureth.
17 I am glad of the coming of Stephanas and Fortunatus and Achaicus: for that which was lacking on your part they have supplied.
18 For they have refreshed my spirit and yours: therefore acknowledge ye them that are such.
19 The churches of Asia salute you. Aquila and Priscilla salute you much in the Lord, with the church that is in their house.

20 All the brethren greet you. Greet ye one another with an holy kiss.

21 The salutation of (me) Paul with mine own hand.
22 If any man love not the Lord Jesus Christ, let him be Anathema Maranatha.
23 The grace of our Lord Jesus Christ (be) with you.
24 My love (be) with you all in Christ Jesus. Amen. (The first (epistle) to the Corinthians was written from Philippi by Stephanas and Fortunatus and Achaicus and Timotheus.)

Literal Translation

THE SECOND EPISTLE OF THE APOSTLE PAUL TO THE CORINTHIANS

2 Corinthians 1

1. Paul, an apostle of Jesus Christ, through (the) will of God, and Timothy the brother, to the church of God being in Corinth, with all the saints being in all Achaia,

2 Grace to you and peace from God our Father and (the) Lord Jesus Christ.

3 Blessed (be) the God and Father of our Lord Jesus Christ, the Father of compassions and God of all comfort,

4 the (One) comforting us on all our affliction, for us to be able to comfort those in every affliction, through the comfort by which we ourselves are comforted by God.

5 Because as the sufferings of Christ abound in us, so also our comfort abounds through Christ.
6 But if we are troubled, (it is) for your comfort and salvation, being worked out in (the) endurance of the same sufferings which we also suffer. If we are comforted, (it is) for your comfort and salvation;

7 and our hope for you (is) certain, knowing that even as you are sharers of the sufferings, so also of the comfort.
8 For, brothers, we do not want you to be ignorant as to our trouble having happened to us in

ΠΑΥΛΟΥ ΤΟΥ ΑΠΟΣΤΟΛΟΥ Η ΠΡΟΣ
OF PAUL THE APOSTLE THE TO

ΚΟΡΙΝΘΙΟΥΣ ΕΠΙΣΤΟΛΗ ΔΕΥΤΕΡΑ
CORINTHIANS EPISTLE SECOND

2 Corinthians 1

3972 652 2424 5547 1223 2307 2316
1. Παῦλος ἀπόστολος Ἰησοῦ Χριστοῦ διὰ θελήματος Θεοῦ,
Paul an apostle of Jesus Christ through (the) will of God,
2532 5095 3588 80 3588 1577 3588 2316 3588 5607 1722
καὶ Τιμόθεος ὁ ἀδελφός, τῇ ἐκκλησίᾳ τοῦ Θεοῦ τῇ οὔσῃ ἐν
and Timothy the brother, to the church God being in
2882 4862 3588 40 3956 3588 5607 1722 3650 3588 882
Κορίνθῳ, σὺν τοῖς ἁγίοις πᾶσιν τοῖς οὖσιν ἐν ὅλῃ τῇ Ἀχαΐᾳ·
Corinth, with the saints all being in all Achaia;
5485 5213 2532 1515 575 2316 3962 2257 2532 2962
2 χάρις ὑμῖν καὶ εἰρήνη ἀπὸ Θεοῦ πατρὸς ἡμῶν καὶ Κυρίου
Grace to you and peace from God (the) Father of us and (the) Lord
2424 5547
Ἰησοῦ Χριστοῦ.
Jesus Christ.

2128 3588 2316 2532 3962 3588 2962 2257 2424
3. Εὐλογητὸς ὁ Θεὸς καὶ πατὴρ τοῦ Κυρίου ἡμῶν Ἰησοῦ
Blessed (be) the God and Father of the Lord of us Jesus
5547 3588 3962 3588 3628 2532 2316 3956 3874
Χριστοῦ, ὁ πατὴρ τῶν οἰκτιρμῶν καὶ Θεὸς πάσης παρα-
Christ, the Father of compassions and (the) God of all comfort,
3588 3870 2248 1909 3956 3588 2347 3257
κλήσεως, 4 ὁ παρακαλῶν ἡμᾶς ἐπὶ πάσῃ τῇ θλίψει ἡμῶν,
the (One) comforting us on all the trouble of us,
1519 3588 1410 2248 3870 3588 1722 3956 2347 1223
εἰς τὸ δύνασθαι ἡμᾶς παρακαλεῖν τοὺς ἐν πάσῃ θλίψει, διὰ
for to be able us to comfort the (ones) in every trouble, through
3588 3874 3739 3870 846 5259 3588 2316
τῆς παρακλήσεως ἧς παρακαλούμεθα αὐτοὶ ὑπὸ τοῦ Θεοῦ.
the comfort of which we are comforted ourselves by God.
3754 2531 4052 3588 3804 3588 5547 1519 2248
5 ὅτι καθὼς περισσεύει τὰ παθήματα τοῦ Χριστοῦ εἰς ἡμᾶς,
Because even as abounds the sufferings of Christ in us,
3779 1223 5547 4052 2532/3588 3874 2257 1535
οὕτω διὰ Χριστοῦ περισσεύει καὶ ἡ παράκλησις ἡμῶν. 6 εἴτε
so through Christ abounds also the comfort of us. whether
1161 2346 5228 3588 5216 3874 2532 4991
δὲ θλιβόμεθα, ὑπὲρ τῆς ὑμῶν παρακλήσεως καὶ σωτηρίας,
And we are troubled, for the of you comfort and salvation,
3588 1745 1722 5281 3588 846 3804 3739
τῆς ἐνεργουμένης ἐν ὑπομονῇ τῶν αὐτῶν παθημάτων ὧν
being worked out in (the) endurance of the same sufferings which
2532 2249 3958 1535 3870 5228 3588 5216
καὶ ἡμεῖς πάσχομεν· εἴτε παρακαλούμεθα, ὑπὲρ τῆς ὑμῶν
also we suffer; whether we are comforted, (it is) for your
3874 2532 4991 2532 3588 1680 2257 949 5216
παρακλήσεως καὶ σωτηρίας· 7 καὶ ἡ ἐλπὶς ἡμῶν βεβαία ὑπὲρ
comfort and salvation; and the hope of us (is) firm for
5216 1492 3754 5618 2844 2075 3588 3804
ὑμῶν· εἰδότες ὅτι ὥσπερ κοινωνοί ἐστε τῶν παθημάτων,
you; knowing that as sharers you are of the suffering,
3779 2532 3588 3874 3756 1063 2309 5209 50
οὕτω καὶ τῆς παρακλήσεως. 8 οὐ γὰρ θέλομεν ὑμᾶς ἀγνοεῖν,
so also of the comfort. not For we desire you to be ignorant,
80 5228 3588 2347 2257 3588 1096 2254 1722 3588
ἀδελφοί, ὑπὲρ τῆς θλίψεως ἡμῶν τῆς γενομένης ἡμῖν ἐν τῇ
brothers, as to the trouble of us having happened to us in

King James Version

THE SECOND EPISTLE OF THE APOSTLE PAUL TO THE CORINTHIANS

2 Corinthians 1

1. Paul, an apostle of Jesus Christ by the will of God, and Timothy (our) brother, unto the church of God which is at Corinth, with all the saints which are in all Achaia:

2 Grace (be) to you and peace from God our Father, and (from) the Lord Jesus Christ.

3 Blessed (be) God, even the Father of our Lord Jesus Christ, the Father of mercies, and the God of all comfort;

4 Who comforteth us in all our tribulation, that we may be able to comfort them which are in any trouble, by the comfort wherewith we ourselves are comforted of God.

5 For as the sufferings of Christ abound in us, so our consolation also aboundeth by Christ.
6 And whether we be afflicted, (it is) for your consolation and salvation, which is effectual in the enduring of the same sufferings which we also suffer: or whether we be comforted, (it is) for your consolation and salvation.

7 And our hope of you (is) stedfast, knowing, that as ye are partakers of the sufferings, so (shall ye be) also of the consolation.

8 For we would not, brethren, have you ignorant of our trouble which came to us in

Literal Translation | **2 Corinthians 1:9** | ***King James Version***

Asia, that we were excessively burdened beyond (our) power, so as for us even to despair to live.
9 But we (our)selves have the sentence of death in ourselves, that we should not trust on ourselves, but on God, the (One) raising the dead,
10 who delivered us from so great a death, and does deliver; in whom we have hope that even yet He will deliver (us),
11 you also laboring together on behalf of us in prayer, that the gracious gift by many persons be (the cause of) thanksgiving through many for us.

773 3754 2596 5236 916 5228 1411 5620
Ἀσίᾳ, ὅτι καθ᾽ ὑπερβολὴν ἐβαρήθημεν ὑπὲρ δύναμιν, ὥστε
Asia, that excessively we were burdened beyond ability, so as
1820 2248 2532 3588 2198 235 846 1722 1438 3588
ἐξαπορηθῆναι ἡμᾶς καὶ τοῦ ζῆν. 9 ἀλλὰ αὐτοὶ ἐν ἑαυτοῖς τὸ
to despair us even to live. But (our)selves in ourselves the
610 3588 2288 2192 2443 3361 3982 5600
ἀπόκριμα τοῦ θανάτου ἐσχήκαμεν, ἵνα μὴ πεποιθότες ὦμεν
sentence of death we have, that not should trust we
1909 1438 235 1909 3588 2316 3588 1453 3588 3498 3739
ἐφ᾽ ἑαυτοῖς, ἀλλ᾽ ἐπὶ τῷ Θεῷ τῷ ἐγείροντι τοὺς νεκρούς· 10 ὃς
on ourselves, but on God the (One) raising the dead; who
1537 5082 2288 4506 2248 2532 4506 1519 3939
ἐκ τηλικούτου θανάτου ἐρρύσατο ἡμᾶς καὶ ῥύσεται, εἰς ὃν
out of so great a death delivered us and does deliver, in whom
1679 3754 2532 2089 4506 4943 2532 5216
ἠλπίκαμεν ὅτι καὶ ἔτι ῥύσεται· 11 συνυπουργούντων καὶ ὑμῶν
we have hope that even yet He will deliver. laboring together also you
5228 2257 3588 1162 2443 1537 4183 4383 3588 1519
ὑπὲρ ἡμῶν τῇ δεήσει, ἵνα ἐκ πολλῶν προσώπων τὸ εἰς
on behalf of us in prayer, that by many persons the for
2248 5486 1223 4183 2168 5228 2257
ἡμᾶς χάρισμα διὰ πολλῶν εὐχαριστηθῇ ὑπὲρ ἡμῶν.
us gift through many thanks may be given on behalf of us.

Asia, that we were pressed out of measure, above strength, insomuch that we despaired even of life:
9 But we had the sentence of death in ourselves, that we should not trust in ourselves, but in God which raiseth the dead:
10 Who delivered us from so great a death, and doth deliver: in whom we trust that he will yet deliver (us);
11 Ye also helping together by prayer for us, that for the gift (bestowed) upon us by the means of many persons thanks may be given by many on our behalf.

12. For our glorying is this, the testimony of our conscience, that we behaved in the world in simplicity and sincerity of God, not in fleshly wisdom, but in (the) grace of God, and more abundantly toward you.
13 For we do not write other (things) to you than what you read or even recognize; and I hope that you will recognize even to (the) end,
14 even as you also (in) part recognized us, that we are your glorying, even as also you (are) ours in the day of the Lord Jesus.

3588 1063 2746 2257 3778 2076 3588 3142 3588
12. Ἡ γὰρ καύχησις ἡμῶν αὕτη ἐστί, τὸ μαρτύριον τῆς
the For glorying of us this is, the testimony of the
3142 2257 3754 1722 572 2532 1505 2316
συνειδήσεως ἡμῶν, ὅτι ἐν ἁπλότητι καὶ εἰλικρινείᾳ Θεοῦ,
conscience of us, that in simplicity and sincerity of God,
3756 1722 4678 4559 235 1722 5485 2316 390
οὐκ ἐν σοφίᾳ σαρκικῇ, ἀλλ᾽ ἐν χάριτι Θεοῦ, ἀνεστράφημεν
not in wisdom fleshly, but in (the) grace of God, we behaved
1722 3588 2889 4056 1161 4314 5209 3756 1063 243
ἐν τῷ κόσμῳ, περισσοτέρως δὲ πρὸς ὑμᾶς. 13 οὐ γὰρ ἄλλα
in the world, more abundantly and toward you. not For other things
1125 5213 235 2228 3739 314 2228 2532 1921
γράφομεν ὑμῖν, ἀλλ᾽ ἢ ἃ ἀναγινώσκετε ἢ καὶ ἐπιγινώσκετε,
we write to you, other than what you read, or even perceive,
1679 1161/ 3754/2532/2193 5056 1921 2531 2532 1921
ἐλπίζω δὲ ὅτι καὶ ἕως τέλους ἐπιγνώσεσθε· 14 καθὼς καὶ ἐπέ-
I hope and that also until the end you will perceive; even as also you
2248 575 3313 3754 2745 5216 2070 2509
γνωτε ἡμᾶς ἀπὸ μέρους, ὅτι καύχημα ὑμῶν ἐσμεν, καθάπερ
perceived us from (in) part, because glorying of you we are, even as
2532 5210 2257 1722 3588 2250 3588 2962 2424
καὶ ὑμεῖς ἡμῶν, ἐν τῇ ἡμέρᾳ τοῦ Κυρίου Ἰησοῦ.
also you of us, in the day of the Lord Jesus.

12. For our rejoicing is this, the testimony of our conscience, that in simplicity and godly sincerity, not with fleshly wisdom, but by the grace of God, we have had our conversation in the world, and more abundantly to you-ward.
13 For we write none other things unto you, than what ye read or acknowledge; and I trust ye shall acknowledge even to the end;
14 As also ye have acknowledged us in part, that we are your rejoicing, even as ye also (are) ours in the day of the Lord Jesus.

15. And in this confidence, I purposed to come to you before now, that you might have a second benefit,
16 and to go through you into Macedonia, and again from Macedonia to come to you and to be set forward by you to Judea.
17 Then purposing this, did I indeed use lightness? Or what I

2532 3778 3588 4006 1014 4314 5209 2064
15. Καὶ ταύτῃ τῇ πεποιθήσει ἐβουλόμην πρὸς ὑμᾶς ἐλθεῖν
And in this confidence I purposed to you to come
4386 2443 1208 5485 2192 2532 1223 5216 1330
πρότερον, ἵνα δευτέραν χάριν ἔχητε, 16 καὶ δι᾽ ὑμῶν διελθεῖν
previously, that a second benefit you have, and through you to go through
1519 3109 2532 3825 575 3109 2064 4314 5209
εἰς Μακεδονίαν, καὶ πάλιν ἀπὸ Μακεδονίας ἐλθεῖν πρὸς ὑμᾶς,
into Macedonia, and again from Macedonia to come to you,
2532 5259 5216 4311 1519 3588 2449 5124 3767
καὶ ὑφ᾽ ὑμῶν προπεμφθῆναι εἰς τὴν Ἰουδαίαν. 17 τοῦτο οὖν
and by you to be set forward to Judea. This then
1011 3361 5100 687 3588 1644 5530 2228 3739 1011
βουλόμενος, μή τι ἄρα τῇ ἐλαφρίᾳ ἐχρησάμην; ἢ ἃ βου-
having purposed, not indeed lightness I used, or what I

15. And in this confidence I was minded to come unto you before, that ye might have a second benefit;
16 And to pass by you into Macedonia, and to come again out of Macedonia unto you, and of you to be brought on my way toward Judaea.
17 When I therefore was thus minded, did I use lightness? or the things that I

Literal Translation

purposed, did I purpose according to flesh, that may be with me yes, yes, and no, no?

18 But God (is) faithful, that our word to you did not become Yes and No.

19 For Jesus Christ the Son of God, the (One) proclaimed among you by us, through me and Silvanus and Timothy, not became Yes and No, but has been Yes in Him.

20 For as many promises as (are) of God, in Him (they are) Yes, and in Him (are) Amen, for glory to God through us.

21 But He confirming us and anointing us with you in Christ (is) God,

22 even He having sealed us, and having given the earnest of the Spirit in our hearts.

23 And I call God (as) witness to my soul that to spare you I came no more to Corinth.

24 Not that we rule over your faith, but we are fellow-workers of your joy. For by faith you stand.

2 Corinthians 1:18

2596 4561 1011 244/5600/3844/1698/3588/3483/3483
λεύομαι κατὰ σάρκα βουλεύομαι, ἵνα ᾖ παρ' ἐμοὶ τὸ ναὶ ναὶ
purposed according to flesh I purpose, that may be with me the Yes Yes

2532 3588 3756 3756 4103 1161 3588 2316 3754 3588 3056 2257 3588 4314
καὶ τὸ οὒ οὔ; 18 πιστὸς δὲ ὁ Θεὸς, ὅτι ὁ λόγος ἡμῶν ὁ πρὸς
and the No No; faithful But (is) God, that the word of us to

5209 3756 1096 3483 2532 3756 3588 1063 3588 2316 5207 2424
ὑμᾶς οὐκ ἐγένετο ναὶ καὶ οὔ. 19 ο γὰρ τοῦ Θεοῦ υἱὸς Ἰησοῦς
you not became Yes and No. the of God For Son Jesus

5547 3588 1722 5213 1223 2257 2784 1223 1700 2532 4610
Χριστὸς ὁ ἐν ὑμῖν δι' ἡμῶν κηρυχθείς, δι' ἐμοῦ καὶ Σιλουανοῦ
Christ, the (One) among you by us proclaimed, through me and Silvanus

2532 5095 3756 1096 3483 2532 3756 235 3483 1722 846
καὶ Τιμοθέου, οὐκ ἐγένετο ναὶ καὶ οὔ, ἀλλὰ ναὶ ἐν αὐτῷ
and Timothy, not became Yes and No, but Yes in Him

1096 3745 1063 1860 2316 1722 846/3588/3483/2532/1722
γέγονεν. 20 ὅσαι γὰρ ἐπαγγελίαι Θεοῦ, ἐν αὐτῷ τὸ ναί, καὶ ἐν
has been. as many as For (are) promises of God, in Him the Yes, and in

846 3588 281 3588 2316 4314 1391 1223 2257 3588 1161 950
αὐτῷ τὸ Ἀμήν, τῷ Θεῷ πρὸς δόξαν δι' ἡμῶν. 21 ὁ δὲ βεβαιῶν
Him the Amen to God unto glory through us. He But confirming

2248 4862 5213 1519 5547 2532 5548 2248 2316 3588 2532
ἡμᾶς σὺν ὑμῖν εἰς Χριστὸν, καὶ χρίσας ἡμᾶς, Θεός· 22 ὁ καὶ
us with you in Christ, and anointing us, God; He and

4972 2248 2532 1325 3588 728 3588 4151
σφραγισάμενος ἡμᾶς, καὶ δοὺς τὸν ἀρραβῶνα τοῦ Πνεύ-
having sealed us, and having given the earnest of the Spirit

1722 3588 2588 2257
ματος ἐν ταῖς καρδίαις ἡμῶν.
in the hearts of us.

1473 1161 3144 3588 2316 1941 1909 3588 1699
23. Ἐγὼ δὲ μάρτυρα τὸν Θεὸν ἐπικαλοῦμαι ἐπὶ τὴν ἐμὴν
I And (as) witness God call on my

5590 3754 5339 5216 3765 2064 1519 2882 3756
ψυχήν, ὅτι φειδόμενος ὑμῶν οὐκέτι ἦλθον εἰς Κόρινθον. 24 οὐχ
soul, that sparing you no more I came to Corinth. Not

3754 2961 5216 3588 4102 235 4904 2070 3588
ὅτι κυριεύομεν ὑμῶν τῆς πίστεως, ἀλλὰ συνεργοί ἐσμεν τῆς
that we rule over of you the faith, but fellow-workers we are of the

5479 5216 3588 1063 4102 2476
χαρᾶς ὑμῶν, τῇ γὰρ πίστει ἑστήκατε.
joy of you, for by faith you stand.

King James Version

purpose, do I purpose according to the flesh, that with me there should be yea yea, and nay nay?

18 But (as) God (is) true, our word toward you was not yea and nay.

19 For the Son of God, Jesus Christ, who was preached among you by us, (even) by me and Silvanus and Timotheus, was not yea and nay, but in him was yea.

20 For all the promises of God in him (are) yea, and in him Amen, unto the glory of God by us.

21 Now he which stablisheth us with you in Christ, and hath anointed us, (is) God;

22 Who hath also sealed us, and given the earnest of the Spirit in our hearts.

23 Moreover I call God for a record upon my soul, that to spare you I came not as yet unto Corinth.

24 Not for that we have dominion over your faith, but are helpers of your joy: for by faith ye stand.

2 Corinthians 2

1. But I decided this within myself, not to come to you again in grief.

2 For if I grieve you, who yet will be making me glad, if not the (one) being grieved by me?

3 And I wrote this same thing to you, lest having come I might have grief from (those) of whom I ought to rejoice, trusting in you all that my joy is (the joy) of all of you.

4 For out of much trouble and agony

2 Corinthians 2

2919 1063 1683 5124 3588 3361 3825 2064 1722 2077 4314
1. ἔκρινα δὲ ἐμαυτῷ τοῦτο, τὸ μὴ πάλιν ἐλθεῖν ἐν λύπῃ πρὸς
I decided But in myself this, not again to come in grief to

5209 1487 1063 1473 3076 5209 2532 5101 2076 3588 2165
ὑμᾶς. 2 εἰ γὰρ ἐγὼ λυπῶ ὑμᾶς, καὶ τίς ἐστιν ὁ εὐφραίνων
you. if For I grieve you, even who is (it) making glad

3165 1508 3588 3076 1537 1700 2532 1125 5213 5124
με, εἰ μὴ ὁ λυπούμενος ἐξ ἐμοῦ; 3 καὶ ἔγραψα ὑμῖν τοῦτο
me, if not Him being grieved of me? And I wrote to you this

846 2443 3361 2064 3077 2192 575 3739 1163 3165 5463
αὐτό, ἵνα μὴ ἐλθὼν λύπην ἔχω ἀφ' ὧν ἔδει με χαίρειν,
same thing, lest having come grief I may have from whom ought me to rejoice,

3982 1909 3956 5209 3754 3588 699 5479 3956 5216
πεποιθὼς ἐπὶ πάντας ὑμᾶς, ὅτι ἡ ἐμὴ χαρὰ πάντων ὑμῶν
trusting in all (of) you, that my joy all of you

2076 1537 1063 4183 2347 2532 4928
ἐστιν. 4 ἐκ γὰρ πολλῆς θλίψεως καὶ συνοχῆς
is out of For much trouble and anxiety

2 Corinthians 2

1. But I determined this with myself, that I would not come again to you in heaviness.

2 For if I make you sorry, who is he then that maketh me glad, but the same which is made sorry by me?

3 And I wrote this same unto you, lest, when I came, I should have sorrow from them of whom I ought to rejoice; having confidence in you all, that my joy is (the joy) of you all.

4 For out of much affliction and anguish

Literal Translation

of heart I wrote to you, through many tears, not that you be grieved, but that you know the love which I have more abundantly toward you.

5. But if anyone has grieved, he has not grieved me, but (in) part, that I not overbear all of you.
6 This censure by the majority (is) enough (for) such a one.
7 So as on the contrary, rather you should forgive and comfort such a one, that (he) not be swallowed up (by) the overflowing grief.
8 So I beseech you to confirm (your) love to him.

9 For to this I also wrote, that I might know the proof of you, if you are obedient in all things.
10 But to whom you forgive anything, I also. For also if I have forgiven anything, of whom I have forgiven (it, it is) for you, in Christ's person,
11 so that we should not be overreached by Satan, for we are not ignorant of his devices.

12. And having come into Troas for the gospel of Christ, and a door having been opened to me in (the) Lord,
13 I had no ease in my spirit at my not finding my brother Titus, but having taken leave of them, I went out to Macedonia.
14 But thanks (be) to God, the (One) always leading us in triumph in Christ, and the (One) revealing through us the odor of the knowledge of Him in every place.
15 For we are a sweet smell to God because of Christ in the (ones) being saved, and in the (ones) being lost;

16 to the one, an odor of death unto death,

2 Corinthians 2:5

2588 1125 5213 1223 4183 1144 3756 2443
καρδίας ἔγραψα ὑμῖν διὰ πολλῶν δακρύων, οὐχ ἵνα
of heart I wrote to you through many tears, not that

3076 235 3588 26 2443 1097 3739 2192 4056
λυπηθῆτε, ἀλλὰ τὴν ἀγάπην ἵνα γνῶτε ἣν ἔχω περισ-
you be grieved, but the love that you know which I have more

1519 5209
σοτέρως εἰς ὑμᾶς.
abundantly toward you.

1487 1161 5100 3076 3756 1691 3076 235 575 3313
5. Εἰ δέ τις λελύπηκεν, οὐκ ἐμὲ λελύπηκεν, ἀλλ' ἀπὸ μέρους,
if But anyone has grieved, not me he has grieved, but from (in) part,

2443 3361 1912 3956 5209 2425 3588 5108 3588 2009
ἵνα μὴ ἐπιβαρῶ πάντας ὑμᾶς. 6 ἱκανὸν τῷ τοιούτῳ ἡ ἐπιτιμία
that not I overbear all of you. Enough (for) such a one censure

3778 3588 5259 3588 4119 5620 5121 3123 5209
αὕτη ἡ ὑπὸ τῶν πλειόνων· 7 ὥστε τοὐναντίον μᾶλλον ὑμᾶς
this by the majority; so as on the contrary rather you

5483 2532 3870 3361 4459 3588 4055
χαρίσασθαι καὶ παρακαλέσαι, μή πως τῇ περισσοτέρᾳ
to forgive and to comfort, lest (some)how the overflowing

3077 2666 3588 5108 1352 3870 5209 2964
λύπῃ καταποθῇ ὁ τοιοῦτος. 8 διὸ παρακαλῶ ὑμᾶς κυρῶσαι
grief swallow such a one. Therefore I beseech you to confirm

1519 846 26 1519 5124 1063 2532 1125 2443 1097
εἰς αὐτὸν ἀγάπην. 9 εἰς τοῦτο γὰρ καὶ ἔγραψα ἵνα γνῶ
to him (your) love. to this For also I wrote that I might know

3588 1382 5216 1487 1519 3956 5255 2075 3739/1161/5100
τὴν δοκιμὴν ὑμῶν, εἰ εἰς πάντα ὑπήκοοί ἐστε. 10 ᾧ δέ τι
the proof of you, if in all things obedient you are. to whom But anything

5483 2532 1473 2532 1063 1473 1487 5100 5483 3739 5483
χαρίζεσθε, καὶ ἐγώ· καὶ γὰρ ἐγὼ εἴ τι κεχάρισμαι, ᾧ κεχάρισ-
you forgive, also I; also for I if anything I have forgiven, of whom I

1223 5209 1722 4383 5547 2443 3361 4122
μαι, δι' ὑμᾶς ἐν προσώπῳ Χριστοῦ, 11 ἵνα μὴ πλεονεκτη-
have forgiven, for you in (the) person of Christ, that not we be over-

5259 3588 4567 3756 1063 846 3588 3540 50
θῶμεν ὑπὸ τοῦ Σατανᾶ· οὐ γὰρ αὐτοῦ τὰ νοήματα ἀγνοοῦμεν.
reached by Satan; not for of him the devices we are ignorant.

2064 1161 1519 3588 5174 1519 3588 2098 3588 5547
12.'Ελθὼν δὲ εἰς τὴν Τρῳάδα εἰς τὸ εὐαγγέλιον τοῦ Χριστοῦ,
having come And to Troas in the gospel of Christ,

2532 2374 3427 455 1722 2962 3756 2192 425 3588
καὶ θύρας μοι ἀνεῳγμένης ἐν Κυρίῳ, 13 οὐκ ἔσχηκα ἄνεσιν τῷ
and a door to me having been opened in (the) Lord, not I had rest to the

4151 3450 3588 3361 2147 3165 5103 3588 80 3450 235
πνεύματί μου, τῷ μὴ εὑρεῖν με Τίτον τὸν ἀδελφόν μου· ἀλλὰ
spirit of me, in the not to find me Titus the brother of me; but

657 846 1831 1519 3109 3588 1161 2316
ἀποταξάμενος αὐτοῖς ἐξῆλθον εἰς Μακεδονίαν. 14 Τῷ δὲ Θεῷ
having taken leave of them I went out to Macedonia. But to God

5485 3588 3842 2358 2248 1722 3588 5547 2532 3588
χάρις τῷ πάντοτε θριαμβεύοντι ἡμᾶς ἐν τῷ Χριστῷ, καὶ τὴν
thanks the (One) always leading in triumph us in Christ, and the

3744 3588 1108 846 5319 1223 2257 1722 3956
ὀσμὴν τῆς γνώσεως αὐτοῦ φανεροῦντι δι' ἡμῶν ἐν παντὶ
odor of the knowledge of Him revealing through us in every

5117 3754 5547 2175 2070 3588 2316 1722 3588 4982
τόπῳ· 15 ὅτι Χριστοῦ εὐωδία ἐσμὲν τῷ Θεῷ ἐν τοῖς σῳζομένοις
place; because of Christ a sweet smell we are to God in those being saved

2532/1722/3588 622 3739 3303 3744 2288 1519 2288
καὶ ἐν τοῖς ἀπολλυμένοις, 16 οἷς μὲν ὀσμὴ θανάτου εἰς θάνατον,
and in those being lost; to the one an odor of death unto death,

King James Version

of heart I wrote unto you with many tears; not that ye should be grieved, but that ye might know the love which I have more abundantly unto you.

5. But if any have caused grief, he hath not grieved me, but in part: that I may not overcharge you all.
6 Sufficient to such a man (is) this punishment, which (was inflicted) of many.
7 So that contrariwise ye (ought) rather to forgive (him), and comfort (him), lest perhaps such a one should be swallowed up with overmuch sorrow.
8 Wherefore I beseech you that ye would confirm (your) love toward him.
9 For to this end also did I write, that I might know the proof of you, whether ye be obedient in all things.
10 To whom ye forgive any thing, I (forgive) also: for if I forgave any thing, to whom I forgave (it), for your sakes (forgave I it) in the person of Christ;
11 Lest Satan should get an advantage of us: for we are not ignorant of his devices.
12. Furthermore, when I came to Troas to (preach) Christ's gospel, and a door was opened unto me of the Lord,
13 I had no rest in my spirit, because I found not Titus my brother: but taking my leave of them, I went from thence into Macedonia.
14 Now thanks (be) unto God, which always causeth us to triumph in Christ, and maketh manifest the savour of his knowledge by us in every place.
15 For we are unto God a sweet savour of Christ, in them that are saved, and in them that perish:
16 To the one (we are) the savour of death unto death;

Literal Translation | **2 Corinthians 2:17** | ***King James Version***

and to the other, an odor of life unto life. And who is sufficient for these things?
17 For we are not as the many, hawking the Word of God; but as of sincerity, but as of God. We speak in Christ, in the sight of God.

3739 1161 3744 2222 1519 2222 2532 4314 5023 5101 2425
οἷς δὲ ὀσμὴ ζωῆς εἰς ζωήν. καὶ πρὸς ταῦτα τίς ἱκανός;
to the other but an odor of life unto life. And for these things who (is) enough?
3756 1063 2070 5613 3588 4183 2585 3588 3056 3588
17 οὐ γάρ ἐσμεν ὡς οἱ πολλοὶ, καπηλεύοντες τὸν λόγον τοῦ
not For we are as the many, hawking the Word
2316 235 5613 1537 1505 235 5613 1537 2316 2714
Θεοῦ· ἀλλ' ὡς ἐξ εἰλικρινείας, ἀλλ' ὡς ἐκ Θεοῦ, κατένώπιον
of God; but as of sincerity, but as of God, in the sight of
3588 2316 1722 5547 2980
τοῦ Θεοῦ, ἐν Χριστῷ λαλοῦμεν.
God, in Christ we speak.

and to the other the savour of life unto life. And who (is) sufficient for these things?
17 For we are not as many, which corrupt the word of God: but as of sincerity, but as of God, in the sight of God speak we in Christ.

2 Corinthians 3

1. Do we begin again to commend ourselves? Or do we, as some, need commendatory letters to you, or commendatory (ones) from you?

2 You are our letter, having been inscribed in our hearts, being known and being read by all men,

3 (it) being made plain that you are Christ's letter, ministered by us, not having been inscribed by ink, but by (the) Spirit of (the) living God, not in tables of stone, but in fleshly tables of (the) heart.

4 And we have such confidence through Christ toward God;

5 not that we are sufficient of ourselves to reason out anything as out of ourselves, but our sufficiency (is) of God,

6 who also made us sufficient (as) ministers of a new covenant, not of letter, but of Spirit. For the letter kills, but the Spirit makes alive.

7 But if the ministry of death having been engraved in letters in stone was with glory, so as the sons of Israel not to be able to gaze into the face of Moses because of the glory of his face,

756 3825 1438 4921 2228 3361 5535
1. Ἀρχόμεθα πάλιν ἑαυτοὺς συνιστάνειν; ἢ μὴ χρήζομεν ὥς
Do we begin again ourselves to commend? Or not need we as
5613 5100 4956 1992 4314 5209 2228 1537 5216
τινες, συστατικῶν ἐπιστολῶν πρὸς ὑμᾶς, ἢ ἐξ ὑμῶν
some commendatory epistles to you or from you
4956 3588 1992 2257 5210 2075 1449
συστατικῶν; 2 ἡ ἐπιστολὴ ἡμῶν ὑμεῖς ἐστε, ἐγγεγραμμένη
commendatory (ones)? The epistle of us you are, having been inscribed
1722 3588 2588 2257 1097 2532 314
ἐν ταῖς καρδίαις ἡμῶν, γινωσκομένη καὶ ἀναγινωσκομένη
in the hearts of us, being known and being read
5259 3956 444 5319 3754 2075 1992
ὑπὸ πάντων ἀνθρώπων· 3 φανερούμενοι ὅτι ἐστὲ ἐπιστολὴ
by all men; being manifested that you are an epistle
5547 1247 5259 2257 1449 3756 3188
Χριστοῦ διακονηθεῖσα ὑφ' ἡμῶν, ἐγγεγραμμένη οὐ μέλανι,
of Christ ministered by us, having been inscribed not by ink,
235 4151 2316 2198 3756 1722 4109 3035 235 1722
ἀλλὰ Πνεύματι Θεοῦ ζῶντος, οὐκ ἐν πλαξὶ λιθίναις, ἀλλ' ἐν
but by (the) Spirit of God a living, not in tables of stone, but in
4109 2588 4560 4006 1161 5108 2192
πλαξὶ καρδίαις σαρκίναις. 4 πεποίθησιν δὲ τοιαύτην ἔχομεν
tables (of the) heart fleshly. confidence And such we have
1223 3588 5547 4314 3588 2316 3756 3754 2425 2070 575
διὰ τοῦ Χριστοῦ πρὸς τὸν Θεόν. 5 οὐχ ὅτι ἱκανοί ἐσμεν ἀφ'
through Christ toward God. Not that sufficient we are of
1438 3049 5100 5613 1537 1438 235 3588 2426 2257
ἑαυτῶν λογίσασθαί τι ὡς ἐξ ἑαυτῶν, ἀλλ' ἡ ἱκανότης ἡμῶν
ourselves to reason out anything as of ourselves, but the sufficiency of us
1537 3588 2316 3739 2532 2427 2248 1249 2537
ἐκ τοῦ Θεοῦ· 6 ὃς καὶ ἱκάνωσεν ἡμᾶς διακόνους καινῆς
(is) of God; who also made sufficient us (as) ministers of a new
1242 3756 1121 235 4151 3588 1063 1121
διαθήκης, οὐ γράμματος, ἀλλὰ πνεύματος· τὸ γὰρ γράμμα
covenant, not of letter, but of Spirit; the for letter
615 3588 1161 4151 2227 1487 1161 3588 1248 3588
ἀποκτείνει, τὸ δὲ πνεῦμα ζῳοποιεῖ. 7 εἰ δὲ ἡ διακονία τοῦ
kills, the but Spirit makes alive. if And the ministry
2288 1722 1121 1795 1722 3037 1096 1722
θανάτου ἐν γράμμασιν ἐντετυπωμένη ἐν λίθοις, ἐγενήθη ἐν
of death in letter having been engraved in stone, was in
1391 5620 3361 1410 816 3588 5207 2474 1519 3588
δόξῃ, ὥστε μὴ δύνασθαι ἀτενίσαι τοὺς υἱοὺς Ἰσραὴλ εἰς τὸ
glory, so as not to be able to gaze the sons of Israel to the
4383 3475 1223 3588 1391 3588 4383 846
πρόσωπον Μωσέως διὰ τὴν δόξαν τοῦ προσώπου αὐτοῦ,
face of Moses because of the glory of the face of him,

1. Do we begin again to commend ourselves? or need we, as some (others), epistles of commendation to you, or (letters) of commendation from you?
2 Ye are our epistle written in our hearts, known and read of all men:

3 (Forasmuch as ye are) manifestly declared to be the epistle of Christ ministered by us, written not with ink, but with the Spirit of the living God; not in tables of stone, but in fleshy tables of the heart.

4 And such trust have we through Christ to God-ward:

5 Not that we are sufficient of ourselves to think any thing as of ourselves; but our sufficiency (is) of God;

6 Who also hath made us able ministers of the new testament; not of the letter, but of the spirit: for the letter killeth, but the spirit giveth life.
7 But if the ministration of death, written (and) engraven in stones, was glorious, so that the children of Israel could not stedfastly behold the face of Moses for the glory of his countenance;

Literal Translation **2 Corinthians 3:8** ***King James Version***

which is being done away, (Ex.34:34)
8 how much rather the ministry of the Spirit will be in glory!
9 For if the ministry of condemnation (was) glory, much rather the ministry of righteousness abounds in glory.

10 For neither indeed has been glorified the (thing) having been glorified in this respect, because of the surpassing glory.
11 For if the thing being done away (was) through glory, much rather the (thing) remaining (is) in glory.
12. Therefore having such hope, we use much boldness.
13 And not as Moses, (who) put a veil over his face, for the sons of Israel not to gaze at the end of the (thing) being done away. (Ex.34:35)

14 But their thoughts were hardened, for until the present the same veil remains on the reading of the old covenant, not being unveiled, that it is being done away in Christ.

15 But until today (when) Moses is being read, a veil lies on their heart.

16 But whenever it turns to (the) Lord, the veil is taken away.

17 And the Lord is the Spirit; and where the Spirit of (the) Lord (is), there (is) freedom.
18 But we all with unveiled face beholding in a mirror the glory of (the) Lord are being changed (into) the same image from glory to glory, as from (the) Lord Spirit.

3588 2673 4459 3780 3123 3588 1248 3588 4151
τὴν καταργουμένην, 8 πῶς οὐχὶ μᾶλλον ἡ διακονία τοῦ πνεύ-
being done away, how not rather the ministry of the Spirit

2071 1722 1391 1487/1063/3588 1248 3588 2633 1722
ματος ἔσται ἐν δόξῃ; 9 εἰ γὰρ ἡ διακονίᾳ τῆς κατακρίσεως ἐν
will be in glory? if For the ministry of condemnation in

1391 4183 3123 4052 3588 1248 3588 1343
δόξα, πολλῷ μᾶλλον περισσεύει ἡ διακονία τῆς δικαιοσύνης
glory (was), much rather abounds the ministry of righteousness

1391 2532 1063 3761 1392 3588 1392 1722 5129
δόξῃ. 10 καὶ γὰρ οὐδὲ δεδόξασται τὸ δεδοξασμένον ἐν τούτῳ
(in) glory. indeed For neither has been glorified the (thing) having been glorified in this

3588 3313 1752 3588 5235 1391 1487 1063 3588
τῷ μέρει ἕνεκεν τῆς ὑπερβαλλούσης δόξης. 11 εἰ γὰρ τὸ κατ-
respect because of the surpassing glory. if For the (thing)

2673 1223 1391 4183 3123 3588 3306 1722 1391
αργούμενον διὰ δόξης, πολλῷ μᾶλλον τὸ μένον, ἐν δόξῃ.
being done away through glory, much rather the (thing) remaining in glory.

2192 3767 5108 1680 4183 3954 5530
12. Ἔχοντες οὖν τοιαύτην ἐλπίδα, πολλῇ παρρησίᾳ χρώ-
having Therefore such hope, much boldness we

2532 3756 2509 3475 5087 2571 1909 3588 4383
μεθα, 13 καὶ οὐ καθάπερ Μωσῆς ἐτίθει κάλυμμα ἐπὶ τὸ πρόσω-
use, and not as Moses put a veil over the face

1438 4314 3588 3361 816 3588 5207 2474 1519 3588
πον ἑαυτοῦ, πρὸς τὸ μὴ ἀτενίσαι τοὺς υἱοὺς Ἰσραὴλ εἰς τὸ
of himself, for not to gaze the sons of Israel at the

73 3588 2673 235 4456 3588 3540
τέλος τοῦ καταργουμένου· 14 ἀλλ᾽ ἐπωρώθη τὰ νοήματα
end of the (thing) being done away; but were hardened the thoughts

846 891 1063 3588 4594 3588 846 2571 1909 3588
αὐτῶν· ἄχρι γὰρ τῆς σήμερον τὸ αὐτὸ κάλυμμα ἐπὶ τῇ
of them; until for the present the same veil on the

320 3588 3820 1242 3306 3361 343
ἀναγνώσει τῆς παλαιᾶς διαθήκης μένει μὴ ἀνακαλυπτόμενον,
reading of the old covenant remains not being unveiled,

3739 5100 1722 5547 2673 235 2193 4594 2259
ὅ τι ἐν Χριστῷ καταργεῖται. 15 ἀλλ᾽ ἕως σήμερον, ἡνίκα
which in Christ is being done away. But until today, when

314 3475 2571 1909 3588 2588 846 2749
ἀναγινώσκηται Μωσῆς, κάλυμμα ἐπὶ τὴν καρδίαν αὐτῶν κεῖται·
is being read Moses, a veil on the heart of them lies;

2259 1161 302 1994 4314 2962 4014 3588
16 ἡνίκα δ᾽ ἂν ἐπιστρέψῃ πρὸς Κύριον, περιαιρεῖται τὸ
when but ever it turns to (the) Lord, is taken away the

2571 3588 1161 2962 3588 4151 2076 3757/1161/3588/4151
κάλυμμα. 17 ὁ δὲ Κύριος τὸ Πνεῦμά ἐστιν· οὗ δὲ τὸ Πνεῦμα
veil. the And Lord the Spirit is, where and the Spirit of

2962 1563 1657 2249 1161 3956 343
Κυρίου, ἐκεῖ ἐλευθερία. 18 ἡμεῖς δὲ πάντες, ἀνακεκαλυμμένῳ
(the) Lord (is), there freedom (is). we But all having been unveiled

4383 3588 1391 2962 2734 3588 846
προσώπῳ τὴν δόξαν Κυρίου κατοπτριζόμενοι, τὴν αὐτὴν
with face the glory of (the) Lord beholding in a mirror, the same

1504 3339 575 1391 1519 1391 2509 575
εἰκόνα μεταμορφούμεθα ἀπὸ δόξης εἰς δόξαν, καθάπερ ἀπὸ
image are being changed (into) from glory to glory, even as from

2962 4151
Κυρίου Πνεύματος.
of (the) Lord Spirit.

which (glory) was to be done away:
8 How shall not the ministration of the spirit be rather glorious?
9 For if the ministration of condemnation (be) glory, much more doth the ministration of righteousness exceed in glory.

10 For even that which was made glorious had no glory in this respect, by reason of the glory that excelleth.
11 For if that which is done away (was) glorious, much more that which remaineth (is) glorious.

12. Seeing then that we have such hope, we use great plainness of speech:
13 And not as Moses, (which) put a vail over his face, that the children of Israel could not stedfastly look to the end of that which is abolished:
14 But their minds were blinded: for until this day remaineth the same vail untaken away in the reading of the old testament; which (vail) is done away in Christ.

15 But even unto this day, when Moses is read, the vail is upon their heart.

16 Nevertheless when it shall turn to the Lord, the vail shall be taken away.
17 Now the Lord is that Spirit: and where the Spirit of the Lord (is), there (is) liberty.
18 But we all, with open face beholding as in a glass the glory of the Lord, are changed into the same image from glory to glory, (even) as by the Spirit of the Lord.

Literal Translation

2 Corinthians 4

1. Because of this having this ministry, even as we obtained mercy, we do not faint.
2 But we have renounced the hidden things of shame, not walking in craftiness, nor adulterating the Word of God, but (by) the revelation of the truth commending ourselves to every conscience of men before God.

3 But if indeed our gospel is being hidden, it is hidden in the (ones) being lost,
4 in whom the god of this age has blinded the thoughts of the unbelieving, so that the brightness of the gospel of the glory of Christ, who is the image of God, should not dawn on them.

5 For we do not proclaim ourselves, but Christ Jesus (as) Lord, and ourselves your slaves for the sake of Jesus.

6 Because God (is) the (One) saying, Out of darkness Light shall shine, who shone in our hearts to (give the) brightness of the knowledge of the glory of God in (the) face of Jesus Christ.

7 But we have this treasure in earthen vessels, so that the excellence of the power may be of God, and not from us;

8. in every (way) being troubled, but not being hemmed in; being perplexed, but not utterly at a loss;
9 being persecuted, but not being forsaken; being cast down, but not destroyed;
10 always bearing about the dying of the Lord Jesus in the body,

2 Corinthians 4

1223 5124 2192 3588 1248 3778 2531 1653
1. Διὰ τοῦτο ἔχοντες τὴν διακονίαν ταύτην, καθὼς ἠλεήθη-
Because of this having ministry this, even as we obtained,

3756 1573 235 550 3588 2927 3588
μεν, οὐκ εκκακοῦμεν· 2 ἀλλ ' ἀπειπάμεθα τὰ κρυπτὰ τῆς
mercy, not we faint; but we have renounced the hidden things

152 3361 4043 1722 3834 3366 1389
αἰσχύνης, μὴ περιπατοῦντες ἐν πανουργίᾳ μηδὲ δολοῦντες
of shame, not walking in craftiness nor adulterating

3588 3056 3588 2316 235 3588 5321 3588 225
τὸν λόγον τοῦ Θεοῦ, ἀλλὰ τῇ φανερώσει τῆς ἀληθείας
the Word of God, but the revelation of the truth

4921 1438 4314 3956 4893 444
συνιστῶντες ἑαυτοὺς πρὸς πᾶσαν συνείδησιν ἀνθρώπων
commending ourselves to every conscience of men

1799 3588 2316 1487 1161 2532 2076 2572 3588 2098
ἐνώπιον τοῦ Θεοῦ. 3 εἰ δὲ καὶ ἔστι κεκαλυμμένον τὸ εὐαγγέλιον
before God. if But indeed is being hidden the gospel

2257 1722 3588 622 2076 2572 1722/3739/3588/2316
ἡμῶν, ἐν τοῖς ἀπολλυμένοις ἐστὶ κεκαλυμμένον, 4 ἐν οἷς ὁ θεὸς
of us, in the (ones) being lost it is being hidden, in whom the god

3588 165 5127 5186 3588 3540 3588 571
τοῦ αἰῶνος τούτου ἐτύφλωσε τὰ νοήματα τῶν ἀπίστων,
age of this has blinded the thoughts of the unbelieving,

1519 3588 3361 826 846 3588 5462 3588 2098
εἰς τὸ μὴ αὐγάσαι αὐτοῖς τὸν φωτισμὸν τοῦ εὐαγγελίου
for the not to dawn on them the brightness of the gospel

3588 1391 3588 5547 3739 2076 1504 3588 2316 3756 1063
τῆς δόξης τοῦ Χριστοῦ, ὅς ἐστιν εἰκὼν τοῦ Θεοῦ. 5 οὐ γὰρ
of the glory of Christ, who is (the) image of God. not For

1438 2784 235 5547 2424 2962
ἑαυτοὺς κηρύσσομεν, ἀλλὰ Χριστὸν Ἰησοῦν Κύριον·
ourselves we proclaim, but Christ Jesus (as) Lord;

1438 1161 1401 5216 1223 2424 3754 3588 2316 3588 2036
ἑαυτοὺς δὲ δούλους ὑμῶν διὰ Ἰησοῦν. 6 ὅτι ὁ Θεὸς ὁ εἰπὼν
ourselves but slaves of you on behalf of Jesus. Because God the (One) saying:

1537 4655 5457 2989 3739 2989 1722 3588 2588 2257
ἐκ σκότους φῶς λάμψει, ὃς ἔλαμψεν ἐν ταῖς καρδίαις ἡμῶν,
Out of darkness Light shall shine, who shone in the hearts of us,

4314 5462 3588 1108 3588 1391 3588 2316 1722
πρὸς φωτισμὸν τῆς γνώσεως τῆς δόξης τοῦ Θεοῦ ἐν
to (give the) brightness of the knowledge of the glory of God in

4383 2424 5547
προσώπῳ Ἰησοῦ Χριστοῦ.
(the) face of Jesus Christ.

2192 1161 3588 2344 5126 1722 3749 4632
7. Ἔχομεν δὲ τὸν θησαυρὸν τοῦτον ἐν ὀστρακίνοις σκεύεσιν,
we have And treasure this in earthen vessels,

2443 3588 5236 3588 1411 5600 3588 2316 2532 3361 1537 2257
ἵνα ἡ ὑπερβολὴ τῆς δυνάμεως ᾖ τοῦ Θεοῦ, καὶ μὴ ἐξ ἡμῶν·
that the excellence of the power may be of God, and not of us;

1722 3956 2346 235 3756 4729 639
8 ἐν παντὶ θλιβόμενοι, ἀλλ' οὐ στενοχωρούμενοι· ἀπορού-
in every (way) being troubled, but not being hemmed in; being per-

235 3756 1820 1377 235 3756 1459
μενοι, ἀλλ' οὐκ ἐξαπορούμενοι· 9 διωκόμενοι, ἀλλ' οὐκ ἐγκατα-
plexed, but not utterly at a loss; being persecuted, but not forsaken,

2598 235 3756 622 3842
λειπόμενοι, καταβαλλόμενοι, ἀλλ' οὐκ ἀπολλύμενοι, 10 πάν-
being cast down, but not destroyed, always

3588 3500 3588 2962 2424 1722 3588 4983 4064
τοτε τὴν νέκρωσιν τοῦ Κυρίου Ἰησοῦ ἐν τῷ σώματι περιφέ-
the dying of the Lord Jesus in the body bearing

King James Version

2 Corinthians 4

1. Therefore seeing we have this ministry, as we have received mercy, we faint not;
2 But have renounced the hidden things of dishonesty, not walking in craftiness, nor handling the word of God deceitfully; but by manifestation of the truth commending ourselves to every man's conscience in the sight of God.

3 But if our gospel be hid, it is hid to them that are lost:

4 In whom the god of this world hath blinded the minds of them which believe not, lest the light of the glorious gospel of Christ, who is the image of God, should shine unto them.

5 For we preach not ourselves, but Christ Jesus the Lord; and ourselves your servants for Jesus' sake.

6 For God, who commanded the light to shine out of darkness, hath shined in our hearts, to (give) the light of the knowledge of the glory of God in the face of Jesus Christ.

7 But we have this treasure in earthen vessels, that the excellency of the power may be of God, and not of us.

8. (We are) troubled on every side, yet not distressed; (we are) perplexed, but not in despair;
9 Persecuted, but not forsaken; cast down, but not destroyed;
10 Always bearing about in the body the dying of the Lord Jesus,

Literal Translation

2 Corinthians 4:11

King James Version

that also the life of Jesus may be revealed in our body.

11 For we who live are always being delivered up to death on account of Jesus, that also the life of Jesus may be revealed in our mortal flesh;
12 so that death indeed works in us, and life in you.
13. But having the same spirit of faith, according to (that) having been written, "I believed, therefore I spoke," we also believe, and therefore we speak, (Psa. 116:10)
14 knowing that He having raised the Lord Jesus will also raise us through Jesus, and will present (us) with you.

15 For all things (are) for your sake, that the grace may superabound through the thanksgiving of the greater number, to the glory of God.

2443 2532 3588 2222 3588 2424 1722 3588 4983 2257
ροντες, ἵνα καὶ ἡ ζωὴ τοῦ Ἰησοῦ ἐν τῷ σώματι ἡμῶν
about, that also the life of Jesus in the body of us

5319 104 1063 2249 3588 2198 1519 2288 3860
φανερωθῇ. 11 ἀεὶ γὰρ ἡμεῖς οἱ ζῶντες εἰς θάνατον παραδιδό-
may be revealed. always For we the (ones) living to death are being deliv-

1223 2424 2443 2532 3588 2222 3588 2424 5319 1722 3588
μεθα διὰ Ἰησοῦν, ἵνα καὶ ἡ ζωὴ τοῦ Ἰησοῦ φανερωθῇ ἐν τῇ
ered because of Jesus, that also the life of Jesus may be revealed in the

2349 4561 2257 5620/3588/3303 2288 1722 2254 1754
θνητῇ σαρκὶ ἡμῶν. 12 ὥστε ὁ μὲν θάνατος ἐν ἡμῖν ἐνεργεῖται,
mortal flesh of us.. So as indeed death in us works,

3588/1161/2222/1722/5213 2192 1161 3588 846 4151 3588 4102
ἡ δὲ ζωὴ ἐν ὑμῖν. 13 ἔχοντες δὲ τὸ αὐτὸ πνεῦμα τῆς πίστεως,
and life in you. having But the same spirit of faith,

2596 3588 1125 4100 1352 2980 2532 2249
κατὰ τὸ γεγραμμένον, Ἐπίστευσα, διὸ ἐλάλησα, καὶ ἡμεῖς
according to (that) having been written, I believed, so I spoke, also we

4100 1352 2532 2980 1492 3754 3588 1453 3588
πιστεύομεν, διὸ καὶ λαλοῦμεν· 14 εἰδότες ὅτι ὁ ἐγείρας τὸν
believe, therefore and we speak; knowing that He having raised the

2962 2424 2532 2248 1223 2424 1453 2532 3936
Κύριον Ἰησοῦν καὶ ἡμᾶς διὰ Ἰησοῦ ἐγερεῖ, καὶ παραστήσει
Lord Jesus also us through Jesus will raise, and will present (us)

4862 5213 3588 1063 3956 1223 5209 2443 3588 5485 4121
σὺν ὑμῖν. 15 τὰ γὰρ πάντα δι' ὑμᾶς, ἵνα ἡ χάρις πλεονάσασα
with you. For all things (are) for you, that grace may superabound

1223 3588 4119 3588 2169 4052 1519 3588
διὰ τῶν πλειόνων τὴν εὐχαριστίαν περισσεύσῃ εἰς τὴν
through the greater number the thanksgiving may cause to abound to the

1391 3588 2316
δόξαν τοῦ Θεοῦ.
glory of God.

that the life also of Jesus might be made manifest in our body.

11 For we which live are alway delivered unto death for Jesus' sake, that the life also of Jesus might be made manifest in our mortal flesh.

12 So then death worketh in us, but life in you.
13. We having the same spirit of faith, according as it is written, I believed, and therefore have I spoken; we also believe, and therefore speak;
14 Knowing that he which raised up the Lord Jesus shall raise up us also by Jesus, and shall present (us) with you.

15 For all things (are) for your sakes, that the abundant grace might through the thanksgiving of many redound to the glory of God.

16 Because of this, we do not faint, but if indeed our outward man is being decayed, yet the inward (man) is being renewed day by day.

17 For the lightness of our present affliction works out for us an eternal weight of glory, surpassing (moment) by surpassing (moment);

18 we not considering the things being seen, but the things not being seen; for the things being seen (are) not lasting, but the things not being seen (are) everlasting.

1352 3756 1573 235 1487 2532 3588 1854 2257 444
16. Διὸ οὐκ ἐγκακοῦμεν· ἀλλ' εἰ καὶ ὁ ἔξω ἡμῶν ἄνθρωπος
Therefore not we faint; but if indeed the outward of us man

1311 235 3588 2081 341 2250 2532 2250
διαφθείρεται, ἀλλ' ὁ ἔσωθεν ἀνακαινοῦται ἡμέρᾳ καὶ ἡμέρᾳ.
is being decayed, yet the inward (man) is being renewed day (by) day.

3588 1063 3910 1645 3588 2347 2257 2596 5236
17 τὸ γὰρ παραυτίκα ἐλαφρὸν τῆς θλίψεως ἡμῶν καθ' ὑπερ-
the For present lightness of the affliction of us surpassing

1519 5236 166 922 1391 2716
βολὴν εἰς ὑπερβολὴν αἰώνιον βάρος δόξης κατεργάζεται
(moment) by surpassing (moment) an eternal weight of glory works

2254 3361 4648 2257 3588 991 235 3588 3361
ἡμῖν, 18 μὴ σκοπούντων ἡμῶν τὰ βλεπόμενα, ἀλλὰ τὰ μὴ
for us, not considering us the things being seen, but the things not

991 3588 1063 991 4340 3588 1161 3361 991
βλεπόμενα· τὰ γὰρ βλεπόμενα πρόσκαιρα· τὰ δὲ μὴ βλεπό-
being seen; the things For being seen (are) not lasting; the things but not being

166
μενα αἰώνια.
seen (are) everlasting.

16 For which cause we faint not; but though our outward man perish, yet the inward (man) is renewed day by day.

17 For our light affliction, which is but for a moment, worketh for us a far more exceeding (and) eternal weight of glory;

18 While we look not at the things which are seen, but at the things which are not seen: for the things which are seen (are) temporal; but the things which are not seen (are) eternal.

2 Corinthians 5

1. For we know that if our earthly house of (this) tabernacle is taken down, we have a building from God, a house not made by hands,

2 Corinthians 5

1492 1063 3754 1437 3588 1919 2257 3614 3588 4636
1. Οἴδαμεν γὰρ ὅτι ἐὰν ἡ ἐπίγειος ἡμῶν οἰκία τοῦ σκήνους
we know For that if the earthly of us house of the tabernacle

2647 3619 1537 2316 2192 3614 886
καταλυθῇ, οἰκοδομὴν ἐκ Θεοῦ ἔχομεν, οἰκίαν ἀχειροποίητον,
is taken down, a building of God we have, a house not made by hands,

2 Corinthians 5

1. For we know that if our earthly house of (this) tabernacle were dissolved, we have a building of God, an house not made with hands,

2 Corinthians 5:2

Literal Translation

eternal in Heaven.
2 For also in this we groan, greatly desiring to be clothed with our dwelling place from Heaven,

3 if indeed (in) being clothed, we shall not be found naked.
4 For indeed, being in the tabernacle, we groan, having been weighed down, inasmuch as we do not wish to be unclothed, but to be clothed, so that the mortal may be swallowed up by the life.
5 And the (One) having worked in us for this same thing (is) God, who also (is) giving to us the earnest of the Spirit.
6 Then always being fully assured, and knowing that being at home in the body we are away from home from the Lord,
7 for we walk by faith, not by sight,
8 even we are fully assured, and think it good rather to go away from home out of the body, and to come home to the Lord.
9. Because of this, we also are striving to be well-pleasing to Him, whether being at home, or being away from home.
10 For we all must appear before the Judgment seat of Christ, so that each one may receive the things (done) through the body, according to what he did, whether good or bad.

11 Then knowing the fear of the Lord, we persuade men, and we have been known to God; and I also hope to have been known in your consciences.
12 For we do not again commend ourselves to you, but are giving you occasion of glorying on our behalf, that you may have (it) toward those boasting in appearance and not

166 1722 3588 3772 2532 1063 1722 5129 4727 3588
αἰώνιον ἐν τοῖς οὐρανοῖς. 2 καὶ γὰρ ἐν τούτῳ στενάζομεν, τὸ
eternal in Heaven. also For in this we groan, the

3613 2257 3588 1537 3772 1902 1971
οἰκητήριον ἡμῶν τὸ ἐξ οὐρανοῦ ἐπενδύσασθαι ἐπιποθοῦντες·
the dwelling place of us from Heaven to put on greatly desiring;

-1489- 2532 1746 3756 1131 2147 2532/1063/3588
3 εἴ γε καὶ ἐνδυσάμενοι οὐ γυμνοὶ εὑρεθησόμεθα. 4 καὶ γὰρ οἱ
if indeed being clothed, not naked we shall be found. indeed For

5607 1722 3588 4636 4727 916 1909/3739/3756/2309
ὄντες ἐν τῷ σκήνει στενάζομεν βαρούμενοι· ἐφ' ᾧ οὐ θέλομεν
being in the tabernacle, we groan being burdened; since not we wish

1562 235 1902 2443 2666 3588 2349
ἐκδύσασθαι ἀλλ' ἐπενδύσασθαι, ἵνα καταποθῇ τὸ θνητὸν
to be unclothed, but to be clothed, that may be swallowed the mortal

5259 3588 2222 3588 1161 2716 2248 1519 846 5124
ὑπὸ τῆς ζωῆς. 5 ὁ δὲ κατεργασάμενος ἡμᾶς εἰς αὐτὸ τοῦτο
by the life. the (One) And having worked iu us for same thing

2316 3588 2532 1325 2254 3588 728 3588 4151
Θεός, ὁ καὶ δοὺς ἡμῖν τὸν ἀρραβῶνα τοῦ Πνεύματος.
(is) God, He also giving to us the earnest of the Spirit.

2292 3767 3842 2532 1492 3754 1736 1722 3588
6 θαρροῦντες οὖν πάντοτε, καὶ εἰδότες ὅτι ἐνδημοῦντες ἐν τῷ
being assured Then always, and knowing that being at home in the

4983 1553 575 3588 2962 1223 4102 1063
σώματι ἐκδημοῦμεν ἀπὸ τοῦ Κυρίου, 7 [διὰ πίστεως γὰρ
body we are away from the Lord, through faith for

4043 3756 1223 1491 2292 1161 2532 2106
περιπατοῦμεν οὐ διὰ εἴδους], 8 θαρροῦμεν δὲ, καὶ εὐδοκοῦμεν
we walk, not through sight, we are assured even, and think it good

3123 1553 1537 3588 4983 2532 1736 4314 3588
μᾶλλον ἐκδημῆσαι ἐκ τοῦ σώματος, καὶ ἐνδημῆσαι πρὸς τὸν
rather to go away from home out of the body, and to come home to the

2962 1352 2532 5389 1535 1736 1535 1553
Κύριον. 9 διὸ καὶ φιλοτιμούμεθα, εἴτε ἐνδημοῦντες, εἴτε ἐκδη-
Lord. Therefore also we are striving, whether being at home, or being away

2101 846 1511 3588 1063 3956 2248
μοῦντες, εὐάρεστοι αὐτῷ εἶναι. 10 τοὺς γὰρ πάντας ἡμᾶς
from home, well-pleasing to Him to be. For all us

5319 1163 1715 3588 968 3588 5547 2443
φανερωθῆναι δεῖ ἔμπροσθεν τοῦ βήματος τοῦ Χριστοῦ, ἵνα
to be revealed must before the Judgment-seat of Christ, that

2865 1538 3588 1223 3588 4983 4314 3739 4238
κομίσηται ἕκαστος τὰ διὰ τοῦ σώματος, πρὸς ἃ ἔπραξεν,
may receive each one the things through the body, according to what he did,

1535 18 1535 2556
εἴτε ἀγαθὸν, εἴτε κακόν.
whether good, or bad.

1492 3767 3588 5401 3588 2962 444 3982
11. Εἰδότες οὖν τὸν φόβον τοῦ Κυρίου ἀνθρώπους πείθομεν,
knowing Then the fear of the Lord men we persuade,

2316 1161 5319 1679 1161 2532 1722 3588 4893
Θεῳ δὲ πεφανερώμεθα· ἐλπίζω δὲ καὶ ἐν ταῖς συνειδήσεσιν
to God and we have been known; I hope and also in the consciences

5216 5319 3756 1063 3825 1438 4921
ὑμῶν πεφανερῶσθαι. 12 οὐ γὰρ πάλιν ἑαυτοὺς συνιστάνομεν
of you to have been known. not For again ourselves we commend

5213 235 874 1325 5213 2745 5228 2257
ὑμῖν, ἀλλὰ ἀφορμὴν διδόντες ὑμῖν καυχήματος ὑπὲρ ἡμῶν,
to you, but an occasion giving to you of boasting on behalf of us,

2443 2197 4314 3588 1722 4383 2744 2532 3756
ἵνα ἔχητε πρὸς τοὺς ἐν προσώπῳ καυχωμένους, καὶ οὐ
that you may have toward those in appearance boasting, and not

King James Version

eternal in the heavens.
2 For in this we groan, earnestly desiring to be clothed upon with our house which is from heaven:

3 If so be that being clothed we shall not be found naked.
4 For we that are in (this) tabernacle do groan, being burdened: not for that we would be unclothed, but clothed upon, that mortality might be swallowed up of life.
5 Now he that hath wrought us for the selfsame thing (is) God, who also hath given unto us the earnest of the Spirit.

6 Therefore (we are) always confident, knowing that, whilst we are at home in the body, we are absent from the Lord:
7 (For we walk by faith, not by sight:)
8 We are confident, (I say), and willing rather to be absent from the body, and to be present with the Lord.

9. Wherefore we labour, that, whether present or absent, we may be accepted of him.
10 For we must all appear before the judgment seat of Christ; that every one may receive the things (done) in (his) body, according to that he hath done, whether (it be) good or bad.

11 Knowing therefore the terror of the Lord, we persuade men; but we are made manifest unto God; and I trust also are made manifest in your consciences.
12 For we commend not ourselves again unto you, but give you occasion to glory on our behalf, that ye may have somewhat to (answer) them which glory in appearance, and not

Literal Translation

2 Corinthians 5:13

King James Version

in heart.
13 For if we are insane, (it is) to God; or (if) we are clear-minded, (it is) for you.
14 For the love of Christ constrains us, having judged this, that if One died on behalf of all, then the all died;
15 and He died for all, that the living ones may live no more to themselves, but to the (One) having died for them and having been raised.
16. So as we now know no one according to flesh, but even if we have known Christ according to flesh, yet now we no longer know (Him so).
17 So that if anyone (is) in Christ, (that one) is a new creation; the old things passed away; behold! All things have become new!
18 And all things (are) of God, the (One) having reconciled us to Himself through Jesus Christ, and having given to us the ministry of reconciliation,
19 as that God was in Christ reconciling (the) world to Himself, not charging their trespasses to them, and having put the word of reconciliation in us.

2588 1535 1063 1839 2316 1535 4993 5213
καρδίᾳ. 13 εἴτε γὰρ ἐξέστημεν, Θεῷ· εἴτε σωφρονοῦμεν, ὑμῖν.
in heart. whether For we are insane, to God; or we are clear-minded, to you (it is).

3588 1063 26 3588 5547 4912 2248 2919 5124
14 ἡ γὰρ ἀγάπη τοῦ Χριστοῦ συνέχει ἡμᾶς, κρίναντας τοῦτο,
the For love of Christ constrains us, having judged this,

3754 1487 1519 5228 3956 599 686 3588 3956 599
ὅτι εἰ εἷς ὑπὲρ πάντων ἀπέθανεν, ἄρα οἱ πάντες ἀπέθανον·
that if One on behalf of all died, then the all died;

2532 5228 3956 599 2443 3588 2198 3371 1438
15 καὶ ὑπὲρ πάντων ἀπέθανεν, ἵνα οἱ ζῶντες μηκέτι ἑαυτοῖς
and on behalf of all He died, that those living no more to themselves

2198 235 3588 5228 846 599 2532 1453 5620
ζῶσιν, ἀλλὰ τῷ ὑπὲρ αὐτῶν ἀποθανόντι, καὶ ἐγερθέντι. 16 ωστε
live, but the (One) for them having died, and having been raised. So as

2249 575 3588 3568 3762 1492 2596 4561 1487 1161 2532
ἡμεῖς ἀπὸ τοῦ νῦν οὐδένα οἴδαμεν κατὰ σάρκα· εἰ δὲ καὶ
we from now no one know according to flesh; if but even

1097 2596 4561 5547 235 3568 3765 1097
ἐγνώκαμεν κατὰ σάρκα Χριστόν, ἀλλὰ νῦν οὐκέτι γινώ-
we have known according to flesh Christ, but now no more we know.

5620 1487 5100 1722 5547 2537 2937 3588 744
σκομεν. 17 ὥστε εἴ τις ἐν Χριστῷ, καινὴ κτίσις· τὰ ἀρχαῖα
So as if anyone in Christ (is), a new creature; the old things

3928 2400 1096 2537 3588 3956 3588 1161 3956 1537
παρῆλθεν, ἰδοὺ γέγονε καινά τὰ πάντα. 18 τὰ δὲ πάντα ἐκ
passed away, behold! have become new All things. the things and all (are) from

3588 2316 3588 2644 2248 1438 1223 2424
τοῦ Θεοῦ, τοῦ καταλλάξαντος ἡμᾶς ἑαυτῷ διὰ Ἰησοῦ
God, the (one) having reconciled us to Himself through Jesus

5547 2532 1325 2254 3588 1248 3588 2643 5613
Χριστοῦ, καὶ δόντος ἡμῖν τὴν διακονίαν τῆς καταλλαγῆς, 19 ὡς
Christ and having given us the ministry of reconciliation, as

3754 2316 2258 1722 5547 2889 2644 1438 3361
ὅτι Θεὸς ἦν ἐν Χριστῷ κόσμον καταλλάσσων ἑαυτῷ, μὴ
that God was in Christ (the) world reconciling to Himself, not

3049 846 3588 3900 846 2532 5087 1722
λογιζόμενος αὐτοῖς τὰ παραπτώματα αὐτῶν, καὶ θέμενος ἐν
charging to them the trespasses of them, and having put in

2254 3588 3056 3588 2643
ἡμῖν τὸν λόγον τῆς καταλλαγῆς.
us the word of reconciliation.

in heart.
13 For whether we be beside ourselves, (it is) to God: or whether we be sober, (it is) for your cause.
14 For the love of Christ constraineth us; because we thus judge, that if one died for all, then were all dead:
15 And (that) he died for all, that they which live should not henceforth live unto themselves, but unto him which died for them, and rose again.
16. Wherefore henceforth know we no man after the flesh: yea, though we have known Christ after the flesh, yet now henceforth know we (him) no more.
17 Therefore if any man (be) in Christ, (he is) a new creature: old things are passed away; behold, all things are become new.
18 And all things (are) of God, who hath reconciled us to himself by Jesus Christ, and hath given to us the ministry of reconciliation;
19 To wit, that God was in Christ, reconciling the world unto himself, not imputing their trespasses unto them; and hath committed unto us the word of reconciliation.

20 Then on behalf of Christ, we are ambassadors, as God (is) exhorting through us, we beseech on behalf of Christ, Be reconciled to God.
21 For He made the (One) who knew no sin (to be) sin on our behalf, that we might become (the) righteousness of God in Him.

5228 5547 3767 4243 5613 3588 2316 3870
20 Ὑπὲρ Χριστοῦ οὖν πρεσβεύομεν ὡς τοῦ Θεοῦ παρακαλ-
on behalf of Christ Then we are ambassadors as God exhorting

1223 2257 1189 5228 5547 2644 3588
οῦντος δι' ἡμῶν· δεόμεθα ὑπὲρ Χριστοῦ, καταλλάγητε τῷ
through us; we beseech on behalf of Christ, be reconciled

2316 3588 1063 3361 1097 266 5228 2257 266
Θεῷ. 21 τὸν γὰρ μὴ γνόντα ἁμαρτίαν, ὑπὲρ ἡμῶν ἁμαρτίαν
God. the (One) For not knowing sin, on behalf of us sin

4160 2443 2249 1096 1343 2316 1722 846
ἐποίησεν, ἵνα ἡμεῖς γενώμεθα δικαιοσύνη Θεοῦ ἐν αὐτῷ.
He made, that we might become (the) righteousness of God in Him.

20 Now then we are ambassadors for Christ, as though God did beseech (you) by us: we pray (you) in Christ's stead, be ye reconciled to God.
21 For he hath made him (to be) sin for us, who knew no sin; that we might be made the righteousness of God in him.

2 Corinthians 6

1. But working together we also call on you not to receive the grace of God in vain.
2 For He says, "In an acceptable time

4903 1161 2532 3870 3361 1519 2756 3588
1. συνεργοῦντες δὲ καὶ παρακαλοῦμεν μὴ εἰς κενὸν τὴν
working together And also we exhort not in vain the

5485 3588 2316 1209 5209 3004 1063 2540 1184
χάριν τοῦ Θεοῦ δέξασθαι ὑμᾶς 2 [λέγει γάρ, Καιρῷ δεκτῷ
grace of God to receive you, He says for, in a time acceptable

1. We then, (as) workers together (with him), beseech (you) also that ye receive not the grace of God in vain.
2 (For he saith, I have heard thee in a time accepted,

Literal Translation

I heard you, and in a day of salvation I helped you." Behold! Now (is) the acceptable time! Behold! Now (is the) day of salvation! (Isa. 49:8)
3 (We are) not giving a cause of stumbling, in nothing, that the ministry may not be blamed,
4 but in everything commending ourselves as God's ministers, in much patience, in afflictions, in emergencies, in difficulties,
5 in stripes, in imprisonments, in riots, in labors, in watchings, in fastings,
6 in pureness, in knowledge, in long-suffering, in kindness, in the Holy Spirit, in unfeigned love,
7 in (the) word of truth, in (the) power of God, through the weapons of righteousness on the right (hand) and on the left,
8 through glory and dishonor, through evil report and good report; as deceivers, and (yet) true;
9 as unknown, and (yet) well known, as dying, and (yet), look, we live; as flogged, and (yet) not put to death;
10 as grieved, yet always rejoicing; as poor, yet enriching many; as having nothing, yet possessing all things.

11. Our mouth is opened to you, Corinthians, our heart has been made larger.
12 You are not restrained in us, but you are restrained in your (own) bowels.
13 But for the same reward, I speak as to children, you also be made larger.
14 Do not be unequally yoked (with) unbelievers. For what partnership

2 Corinthians 6:3

1873 4675 2532 1722 2250 4991 997 4671 2400 3568
ἐπήκουσά σου, καὶ ἐν ἡμέρᾳ σωτηρίας ἐβοήθησά σοι· ἰδού, νῦν
I heard you, and in a day of salvation I helped you; behold, now

2540 2144 2400 3568 2250 4991 3367 1722
καιρὸς εὐπρόσδεκτος, ἰδού, νῦν ἡμέρα σωτηρίας] 3 μηδεμίαν ἐν
(is) a time acceptable, behold, now a day of salvation; not one in

3367 1325 4349 2443 3361 3469 3588 1248 235
μηδενὶ διδόντες προσκοπήν, ἵνα μὴ μωμηθῇ ἡ διακονία· 4 ἀλλ'
nothing giving cause of stumbling, that not be blamed the ministry; but

1722 3956 4921 1438 5613 2316 1249 1722 5281
ἐν παντὶ συνιστῶντες ἑαυτοὺς ὡς Θεοῦ διάκονοι, ἐν ὑπομονῇ
in everything commending ourselves as of God ministers, in patience

4183 1722 2347 1722 318 1722 4730 1722 4127
πολλῇ, ἐν θλίψεσιν, ἐν ἀνάγκαις, ἐν στενοχωρίαις, 5 ἐν πλη-
much, in troubles, in emergencies, in difficulties, in stripes,

1722 5438 1722 181 1722 2873 1722 70
γαῖς, ἐν φυλακαῖς, ἐν ἀκαταστασίαις, ἐν κόποις, ἐν ἀγρυ-
in imprisonments, in riots, in labors, in watch-

1722 3521 1722 54 1722 1108 1722
πνίαις, ἐν νηστείαις, 6 ἐν ἁγνότητι, ἐν γνώσει, ἐν μα-
ings, in fastings, in pureness, in knowledge, in long-

3115 1722 5544 1722 4151 40 1722 26
κροθυμίᾳ, ἐν χρηστότητι, ἐν Πνεύματι Ἁγίῳ, ἐν ἀγάπῃ
suffering, in kindness, in Spirit Holy, in love

505 1722 3056 225 1722 1411 2316 1223 3588
ἀνυποκρίτῳ, 7 ἐν λόγῳ ἀληθείας, ἐν δυνάμει Θεοῦ, διὰ τῶν
unfeigned, in a word of truth, in (the) power of God, through the

3696 3588 1343 3588 1188 2532 710 1223
ὅπλων τῆς δικαιοσύνης τῶν δεξιῶν καὶ ἀριστερῶν, 8 διὰ
weapons of righteousness on the right and on (the) left, through

1391 2532 819 1223 1426 2532 2162 5613 4108
δόξης καὶ ἀτιμίας, διὰ δυσφημίας καὶ εὐφημίας· ὡς πλάνοι,
glory and dishonor, through evil report and good report; as deceivers

2532 227 5613 50 2532 1921 5613
καὶ ἀληθεῖς· 9 ὡς ἀγνοούμενοι καὶ ἐπιγινωσκόμενοι· ὡς
and (yet) true; as unknown and (yet) well-known; as

599 2532 2400 2198 5613 3811 2532 3361
ἀποθνήσκοντες, καὶ ἰδού, ζῶμεν· ὡς παιδευόμενοι, καὶ μὴ
dying, and behold, we live; as flogged, and not

2289 5613 3076 104 1161 5463 5613 4434
θανατούμενοι· 10 ὡς λυπούμενοι, ἀεὶ δὲ χαίροντες· ὡς πτωχοί,
put to death; as grieved, always but rejoicing; as poor

4183 1161 4148 5613 3367 2192 2532 3956
πολλοὺς δὲ πλουτίζοντες· ὡς μηδὲν ἔχοντες, καὶ πάντα
many but enriching; as nothing having, yet all things

2722
κατέχοντες.
possessing.

3588 4750 2257 455 4314 5209 2881 3588 2588
11. Τὸ στόμα ἡμῶν ἀνέῳγεν πρὸς ὑμᾶς, Κορίνθιοι, ἡ καρδία
The mouth of us is opened to you, Corinthians, the heart

2257 4115 3756 4729 1722 2254 4729
ἡμῶν πεπλάτυνται. 12 οὐ στενοχωρεῖσθε ἐν ἡμῖν, στενοχω-
of us has been made larger. not You are restrained in us, you are

1161 1722 3588 4698 5216 3588 1161 846
ρεῖσθε δὲ ἐν τοῖς σπλάγχνοις ὑμῶν. 13 τὴν δὲ αὐτὴν
restrained but in the bowels of you. the But same

489 5613 5043 3004 4115 2532 5210
ἀντιμισθίαν [ὡς τέκνοις λέγω], πλατύνθητε καὶ ὑμεῖς.
reward, as children I speak, be enlarged also you.

3361 1096 2086 571 5101 1063 3352
14. Μὴ γίνεσθε ἑτεροζυγοῦντες ἀπίστοις· τίς γὰρ μετοχὴ
Do not become unequally yoked (with) unbelievers; what for partnership

King James Version

and in the day of salvation have I succoured thee: behold, now (is) the accepted time; behold, now (is) the day of salvation.)
3 Giving no offence in any thing, that the ministry be not blamed:
4 But in all (things) approving ourselves as the ministers of God, in much patience, in afflictions, in necessities, in distresses,
5 In stripes, in imprisonments, in tumults, in labours, in watchings, in fastings;
6 By pureness, by knowledge, by longsuffering, by kindness, by the Holy Ghost, by love unfeigned,
7 By the word of truth, by the power of God, by the armour of righteousness on the right hand and on the left,
8 By honour and dishonour, by evil report and good report: as deceivers, and (yet) true;
9 As unknown, and (yet) well known; as dying, and, behold, we live; as chastened, and not killed;
10 As sorrowful, yet alway rejoicing; as poor, yet making many rich; as having nothing, and (yet) possessing all things.
11. O (ye) Corinthians, our mouth is open unto you, our heart is enlarged.
12 Ye are not straitened in us, but ye are straitened in your own bowels.
13 Now for a recompence in the same, (I speak as unto (my) children,) be ye also enlarged.
14 Be ye not unequally yoked together with unbelievers: for what fellowship

Literal Translation

does righteousness (have) with lawlessness? And what fellowship does light (have) with darkness?
15 And what agreement does Christ (have) with Belial? Or what part does a believer (have) with an unbeliever?
16 And what union does a temple of God (have) with idols? For you are a temple of (the) living God, even as God' said, "I will dwell in them and walk among (them), and I will be their God, and they shall be My people." (Lev. 26:12; Ezek. 37:27)
17 Because of this, come out from among them and be separated, says (the) Lord, and do not touch (the) unclean thing, and I will receive you. (Isa.52:11)
18 And I will be a Father to you, and you will be sons and daughters to Me, says (the) Lord Almighty. (2 Sam.7:8,14)

2 Corinthians 6:15

1343 2532 458 2228 5101 2842 5457 4314 4655
δικαιοσύνη καὶ ἀνομίᾳ; τίς δὲ κοινωνία φωτὶ πρὸς σκότος;
righteousness and lawlessness? what and fellowship light with darkness?

5101 1161 4857 5547 4314 955 2228 5101 3310 4103
15 τίς δὲ συμφώνησις Χριστοῦ πρὸς Βελιαλ; ἢ τίς μερὶς πιστῷ
what And agreement (has) Christ with Belial? Or what part a believer

3326 571 5101 1161 4783 3485 2316 3326 1497
μετὰ ἀπίστου; 16 τίς δὲ συγκατάθεσις ναῷ Θεοῦ μετὰ εἰδώλων;
with an unbeliever? what And union (has) a temple of God with idols?

5210 1063 3485 2316 2075 2198 2531 2036 3588 2316 3754
ὑμεῖς γὰρ ναὸς Θεοῦ ἐστε ζῶντος, καθὼς εἶπεν ὁ Θεὸς ὅτι
you For a temple of God are of a living, even as said God,

1774 1722 846 2532 1704 2532 2071 846
Ἐνοικήσω ἐν αὐτοῖς, καὶ ἐμπεριπατήσω· καὶ ἔσομαι αὐτῶν
I will dwell in them, and I will walk among (them); and I will be of them

2316 2532 846 2071 3427 2992 1352 1831 1722 3319
Θεός, καὶ αὐτοὶ ἔσονταί μοι λαός. 17 διὸ ἐξέλθατε ἐκ μέσου
God, and they shall be to me a people. Therefore come out from amidst

846 2532 873 3004 2962 2532 169 3361
αὐτῶν καὶ ἀφορίσθητε, λέγει Κύριος, καὶ ἀκαθάρτου μὴ
them and be separated, says (the) Lord, and an unclean thing not

680 2504 1523 5209 2532 2071 5213 1519 3962
ἅπτεσθε· κἀγὼ εἰσδέξομαι ὑμᾶς, 18 καὶ ἔσομαι ὑμῖν εἰς πατέρα,
touch; and I will receive you, and I will be to you for a Father,

2532 5210 2071 3427 1519 5207 2532 2364 3004 2962
καὶ ὑμεῖς ἔσεσθέ μοι εἰς υἱοὺς καὶ θυγατέρας, λέγει Κύριος
and you will be to Me for sons and daughters, says (the) Lord

3841
παντοκράτωρ.
Almighty.

King James Version

hath righteousness with unrighteousness? and what communion hath light with darkness?
15 And what concord hath Christ with Belial? or what part hath he that believeth with an infidel?
16 And what agreement hath the temple of God with idols? for ye are the temple of the living God; as God hath said, I will dwell in them, and walk in (them); and I will be their God, and they shall be my people.
17 Wherefore come out from among them, and be ye separate, saith the Lord, and touch not the unclean (thing); and I will receive you,
18 And will be a Father unto you, and ye shall be my sons and daughters, saith the Lord Almighty.

2 Corinthians 7

1. Then having these promises, beloved, let us purify ourselves from all defilement of flesh and of spirit, perfecting holiness in (the) fear of God.

2 Make room for us. We wronged no one, we corrupted no one, we overreached no one.
3 I do not speak to condemnation, for I have said before that you are in our hearts, for (us) to die together and to live together.
4 My boldness toward you (is) great. My glorying on your behalf (is) much. I have been filled with comfort; I overflow with joy on all our trouble.

5. For, indeed, we having come into Macedonia, no one of us had rest (in) our flesh,

2 Corinthians 7

3778 3767 2192 3588 1860 27
1. ταύτας οὖν ἔχοντες τὰς ἐπαγγελίας, ἀγαπητοί,
these Then having promises, beloved,

2511 1438 575 3956 3436 4561 2532
καθαρίσωμεν ἑαυτοὺς ἀπὸ παντὸς μολυσμοῦ σαρκὸς καὶ
let us purify ourselves from all defilement of flesh and

4151 2005 42 1722 5401 2316
πνεύματος, ἐπιτελοῦντες ἁγιωσύνην ἐν φόβῳ Θεοῦ.
of spirit, perfecting holiness in (the) fear of God.

5562 2248 3762 91 3762 5351
2. Χωρήσατε ἡμᾶς· οὐδένα ἠδικήσαμεν, οὐδένα ἐφθείραμεν,
Make room for us; no one we wronged, no one we corrupted,

3762 4122 3756 4314 2633 3004 4280
οὐδένα ἐπλεονεκτήσαμεν. 3 οὐ πρὸς κατάκρισιν λέγω· προεί-
no one we overreached. Not for condemnation I speak; I have said

1063 3754 1722 3588 2588 2257 2075 1519 3588 4880
ρηκα γάρ, ὅτι ἐν ταῖς καρδίαις ἡμῶν ἐστε εἰς τὸ συναποθα-
before for, that in the hearts of us you are for to die with

2532 4800 4183 3427 3954 4314 5209 4183 3427
νεῖν καὶ συζῆν. 4 πολλή μοι παρρησία πρὸς ὑμᾶς, πολλή μοι
(you) and to live with. Much to me boldness toward you, much to me

2746 5228 5216 4137 3588 3874 5258
καύχησις ὑπὲρ ὑμῶν· πεπλήρωμαι τῇ παρακλήσει, ὑπερ-
glorying on behalf of you; I have been filled with comfort, I

3588 5479 1063 3956 3588 2347 2257
περισσεύομαι τῇ χαρᾷ ἐπὶ πάσῃ τῇ θλίψει ἡμῶν.
overflow with joy on all the trouble of us.

2532 1063 2064 2257 1519 3109 3762 2192
5. Καὶ γὰρ ἐλθόντων ἡμῶν εἰς Μακεδονίαν οὐδεμίαν ἔσχηκεν
indeed For having come us into Macedonia no one has had

2 Corinthians 7

1. Having therefore these promises, dearly beloved, let us cleanse ourselves from all filthiness of the flesh and spirit, perfecting holiness in the fear of God.

2 Receive us; we have wronged no man, we have corrupted no man, we have defrauded no man.
3 I speak not (this) to condemn (you): for I have said before, that ye are in our hearts to die and live with (you).
4 Great (is) my boldness of speech toward you, great (is) my glorying of you: I am filled with comfort, I am exceeding joyful in all our tribulation.

5. For, when we were come into Macedonia, our flesh had no

Literal Translation

2 Corinthians 7:6

King James Version

but being troubled in every way, (with) fightings (on the) outside and fears (on the) inside.
6 But the (One) comforting the lowly comforted us by the coming of Titus.
7 And not only by his coming, but also by the comfort with which he was comforted over you, relating to us your longing, your mourning, your zeal on my behalf, so as for me to rejoice more.
8 Because even if I grieved you in the letter, I do not regret, if indeed I did regret, for I see that letter grieved you, if indeed for an hour.
9 Now I rejoice, not that you were grieved, but that you were grieved to repentance. For you grieved according to God, that you might suffer loss in nothing by us.
10 For the grief according to God works repentance to salvation, not to be regretted. But the grief of the world works death.
11 For behold! This same thing, you being grieved according to God, how much it fully worked earnestness in you, but (also) defense, but (also) indignation, but (also) fear, but (also) desire, but (also) zeal, but (also) vengeance! In everything you commended yourselves to be clear in the matter.
12. Then even if I wrote to you, (it was) not for the sake of the (one) who did wrong, nor for the sake of the (one) having suffered wrong, but for the sake of revealing our earnestness on your behalf, (for) you before God.
13 For this reason we have been comforted

425 3588 4561 2257 235 1722 3956 2346 1855 3163
ἄνεσιν ἡ σὰρξ ἡμῶν, ἀλλ' ἐν παντὶ θλιβόμενοι· ἔξωθεν μάχαι,
rest the flesh of us, but in every way being troubled; without fightings,

2081 5401 235 3588 3870 3588 5011
ἔσωθεν φόβοι. 6 'αλλ' ὁ παρακαλῶν τοὺς ταπεινοὺς παρε-
within fears. But the (One) comforting the lowly

3870 2248 3588 2316 1722 3588 3952 5103 3753/3440/1161/1722
κάλεσεν ἡμᾶς, ὁ Θεὸς, ἐν τῇ παρουσίᾳ Τίτου· 7 οὐ μόνον δὲ ἐν
comforted us, God, by the coming of Titus; not only And by

3588 3952 846 235 2532 1722 3588 3874 3739 3870
τῇ παρουσίᾳ αὐτοῦ, ἀλλὰ καὶ ἐν τῇ παρακλήσει ᾗ παρεκλήθη
the coming of him, but also by the comfort with which he was eased

1909 5213 312 2254 3588 5216 1972 3588 5216
ἐφ' ὑμῖν, ἀναγγέλλων ἡμῖν τὴν ὑμῶν ἐπιπόθησιν, τὸν ὑμῶν
over you, relating to us the of you longing, the of you

3602 3588 5216 2205 5228 1700 5620 3165 3123
ὀδυρμόν, τὸν ὑμῶν ζῆλον ὑπὲρ ἐμοῦ, ὥστε με μᾶλλον
mourning, the of you zeal on behalf of me, so as me more

5463 3754/1487/2532 3076 5209 1722 3588 1992 3756 3338
χαρῆναι. 8 ὅτι εἰ καὶ ἐλύπησα ὑμᾶς ἐν τῇ ἐπιστολῇ, οὐ μετα-
to rejoice. Because if even I grieved you by the epistle, not I

1487 2532 3338 991 1063 3754 3588 1992
μέλομαι, εἰ καὶ μετεμελόμην βλέπω γὰρ ὅτι ἡ ἐπιστολὴ
regret, if indeed I regretted; I see for that epistle

1565 1487 2532 4314 5610 3076 5209 3568 5463 3756
ἐκείνη, εἰ καὶ πρὸς ὥραν, ἐλύπησεν ὑμᾶς, 9 νῦν χαίρω, οὐχ
that, if indeed for an hour, it grieved you, now I rejocie, not

3754 3076 235 3754 3076 1519 3341 3076
ὅτι ἐλυπήθητε, ἀλλ' ὅτι ἐλυπήθητε εἰς μετάνοιαν· ἐλυπήθητε
that you were grieved, but that you were grieved unto repentance; you grieved

1063 2596 2316 2443 1722 3367 2210 1537 2257 3588 1063
γὰρ κατὰ Θεόν, ἵνα ἐν μηδενὶ ζημιωθῆτε ἐξ ἡμῶν. 10 ἡ γὰρ
for according to God, that in nothing you might suffer loss by us. the For

2596 2316 3077 3341 1519 4991 278
κατὰ Θεὸν λύπη μετάνοιαν εἰς σωτηρίαν ἀμεταμέλητον
according to God grief repentance to salvation unregrettable

2716 3588 1161 3588 2889 3077 2288 2716
κατεργάζεται· ἡ δὲ τοῦ κόσμου λύπη θάνατον κατεργά-
works; the but of the world grief death works.

2400 1063 846 5124 3588 2596 2316 3076 5209
ζεται. 11 ἰδοὺ γάρ, αὐτὸ τοῦτο, τὸ κατὰ Θεὸν λυπηθῆναι ὑμᾶς,
behold For, same (thing) this, the according to God to be grieved you,

4214 2716 5213 4710 235 627
πόσην κατειργάσατο ὑμῖν σπουδήν, ἀλλὰ ἀπολογίαν,
how much it fully worked in you earnestness, but defense,

235 24 235 5401 235 1972 235
ἀλλὰ ἀγανάκτησιν, ἀλλὰ φόβον, ἀλλὰ ἐπιπόθησιν, ἀλλὰ
but indignation, but fear, but eager desire, but

2205 235 1557 1722 3956 4921 1438 53
ζῆλον, ἀλλὰ ἐκδίκησιν. ἐν παντὶ συνεστήσατε ἑαυτοὺς ἁγνοὺς
zeal, but vengeance. In everything you commended yourselves clear

1511 1722 3588 4229 686 1487 2532 1125 5213 3756 1752
εἶναι ἐν τῷ πράγματι. 12 ἄρα εἰ καὶ ἔγραψα ὑμῖν, οὐχ εἵνεκεν
to be in the affair. Then if even I wrote to you, not (it was) for

3588 91 3761 1752 3588 91 235 1752
τοῦ ἀδικήσαντος, οὐδὲ εἵνεκεν τοῦ ἀδικηθέντος, ἀλλ εἵνεκεν
the (one) doing wrong, nor for the (one) being wronged, but for

3588 5319 3588 4710 5216 3588 5228 2257 4314
τοῦ φανερωθῆναι τὴν σπουδὴν ἡμῶν τὴν ὑπὲρ ὑμῶν πρὸς
to be revealed the earnestness of us on behalf of you toward

5209 1799 3588 2316 1223 5124 3870 1909 3588
ὑμᾶς ἐνώπιον τοῦ Θεοῦ. 13 διὰ τοῦτο παρακεκλήμεθα ἐπὶ τῇ
you before God. Because of this we have been comforted over the

rest, but we were troubled on every side; without (were) fightings, within (were) fears.
6 Nevertheless God, that comforteth those that are cast down, comforted us by the coming of Titus;
7 And not by his coming only, but by the consolation wherewith he was comforted in you, when he told us your earnest desire, your mourning, your fervent mind toward me; so that I rejoiced the more.
8 For though I made you sorry with a letter, I do not repent, though I did repent: for I perceive that the same epistle hath made you sorry, though (it were) but for a season.
9 Now I rejoice, not that ye were made sorry, but that ye sorrowed to repentance: for ye were made sorry after a godly manner, that ye might receive damage by us in nothing.
10 For godly sorrow worketh repentance to salvation not to be repented of: but the sorrow of the world worketh death.
11 For behold this selfsame thing, that ye sorrowed after a godly sort, what carefulness it wrought in you, yea, (what) clearing of yourselves, yea, (what) indignation, yea, (what) fear, yea, (what) vehement desire, yea, (what) zeal, yea, (what) revenge! In all (things) ye have approved yourselves to be clear in this matter.
12. Wherefore, though I wrote unto you, (I did it) not for his cause that had done the wrong, nor for his cause that suffered wrong, but that our care for you in the sight of God might appear unto you.
13 Therefore we were comforted

Literal Translation

over your comfort, and we rather rejoice more abundantly over the joy of Titus, because his spirit has been refreshed by all of you.

14 Because if I have boasted anything to him about you, I was not ashamed. But as we spoke all things in truth to you, so also our boasting as to Titus became truth.
15 And his tender feelings are abundant toward you, remembering the obedience of all of you, as you received him with fear and trembling.

16 Therefore, I rejoice, that in everything I am fully assured in you.

2 Corinthians 8

1. But, brothers, we make known to you the grace of God having been given among the churches of Macedonia,
2 that in much testing of trouble, the overflowing of their joy and the depth of their poverty abounded to the riches of their sincerity.

3 For I testify (that) according to (their) ability and beyond (their) ability, (they) willingly (gave),
4 with much entreating, begging us (that they might) receive of us the grace and the fellowship of the ministry to the saints.
5 And not as we hoped, but (they) first gave themselves to the Lord and to us through (the) will of God,

6 for us to call on Titus, that even as he began before, so also he might complete this grace to you also.
7. But even as you abound in everything, in faith, and in word, and

2 Corinthians 7:14

3874 5216 4056 1161 3123 5463 1909 3588
παρακλήσει ὑμῶν περισσοτέρως δὲ μᾶλλον ἐχάρημεν ἐπὶ τῇ
comfort of you abundantly and rather we rejoice over the

5479 5103 3754 373 3588 4151 846 575 3956
χαρᾷ Τίτου, ὅτι ἀναπέπαυται τὸ πνεῦμα αὐτοῦ ἀπὸ πάντων
joy of Titus, because has been rested the spirit of him from all

5216 3754 1487 5100 846 5228 5216 2744 3756 2617
ὑμῶν. 14 ὅτι εἴ τι αὐτῷ ὑπὲρ ὑμῶν κεκαύχημαι, οὐ κατησχύν-
you. Because if anything to him for you I have boasted, not I was ashamed;

235 5613 3956 1722 225 2980 5213 3779/2532/3588
θην· ἀλλ' ὡς πάντα ἐν ἀληθείᾳ ἐλαλήσαμεν ὑμῖν, οὕτω καὶ ἡ
but as all things in truth we spoke to you, so also the

2746 2257/3588/1909/5103 225 1096 2532 3588 4698
καύχησις ἡμῶν, ἡ ἐπὶ Τίτου, ἀλήθεια ἐγενήθη. 15 καὶ τὰ σπλάγ-
glorying of us, (which) to Titus, truth became. And the bowels

846 4056 1519 5209 2076 363
χνα αὐτοῦ περισσοτέρως εἰς ὑμᾶς ἐστιν ἀναμιμνῃσκομένου
of him abundantly toward you are, remembering

3588 3956 5216 5218 5613 3326 5401 2532 5156
τὴν πάντων ὑμῶν ὑπακοήν, ὡς μετὰ φόβου καὶ τρόμου
the all of you obedience, as with fear and trembling

1209 846 5463 3767 3754 1722 3956 2292 1722 5213
ἐδέξασθε αὐτόν. 16 χαίρω οὖν ὅτι ἐν παντὶ θαρρῶ ἐν ὑμῖν.
you received him. I rejoice Then that in everything I am assured in you.

2 Corinthians 8

1107 1161 5213 80 3588 5485 3588 2316 3588
1. Γνωρίζομεν δὲ ὑμῖν, ἀδελφοί, τὴν χάριν τοῦ Θεοῦ τὴν
we make known But to you, brothers, the grace of God

1325 1722 3588 1577 3588 3109 3754 1722 4183
δεδομένην ἐν ταῖς ἐκκλησίαις τῆς Μακεδονίας, 2 ὅτι ἐν πολλῇ
having been given among the churches of Macedonia, that in much

1382 2347 3588 4050 3588 5479 846 2532 3588 2596
δοκιμῇ θλίψεως ἡ περισσεία τῆς χαρᾶς αὐτῶν καὶ ἡ κατὰ
testing of trouble the overflowing of the joy of them and the due to

899 4432 846 4052 1519 3588 4149 3588
βάθους πτωχεία αὐτῶν ἐπερίσσευσεν εἰς τὸ πλοῦτος τῆς
(the) depth (of the) poverty of them abounded to the riches of the

572 846 3754 2596 1411 3140 2532 5228
ἁπλότητος αὐτῶν. 3 ὅτι κατὰ δύναμιν, μαρτυρῶ, καὶ ὑπὲρ
sincerity of them. Because according to ability, I witness, and beyond

1411 830 3326 4183 3874 1189
δύναμιν, αὐθαίρετοι, 4 μετὰ πολλῆς παρακλήσεως δεόμενοι
ability, willingly, with much entreating begging

2257 3588 5485 2532 3588 2842 3588 1248 3588 1519
ἡμῶν τὴν χάριν καὶ τὴν κοινωνίαν τῆς διακονίας τῆς εἰς
us the grace and the fellowship of the ministry to

3588 40 1209 2248 2532 3756 2531 1679 235
τοὺς ἁγίους δέξασθαι ἡμᾶς· 5 καὶ οὐ καθὼς ἠλπίσαμεν, ἀλλ'
the saints to receive of us; and not as we hoped, but

1438 1325 4412 3588 2962 2532 2254 1223 2307
ἑαυτοὺς ἔδωκαν πρῶτον τῷ Κυρίῳ, καὶ ἡμῖν διὰ θελήματος
themselves gave firstly to the Lord, and to us through the will

2316 1519 3588 3870 2248 5103 2443 2531 4278
Θεοῦ, 6 εἰς τὸ παρακαλέσαι ἡμᾶς Τίτον, ἵνα καθὼς προενήρ-
of God, For to call on us Titus, that even as he began,

3779 2532 2005 1519 5209 2532 3588 5485 3778
ξατο, οὕτω καὶ ἐπιτελέσῃ εἰς ὑμᾶς καὶ τὴν χάριν ταύτην.
before, so also he should complete to you also grace this.

235 5618 1722 3956 4052 4102 2532 3056 2532
7 ἀλλ' ὥσπερ ἐν παντὶ περισσεύετε, πίστει, καὶ λόγῳ, καὶ
But as in everything you abound, in faith, and in word, and

King James Version

in your comfort: yea, and exceedingly the more joyed we for the joy of Titus, because his spirit was refreshed by you all.

14 For if I have boasted any thing to him of you, I am not ashamed; but as we spake all things to you in truth, even so our boasting, which (I made) before Titus, is found a truth.
15 And his inward affection is more abundant toward you, whilst he remembereth the obedience of you all, how with fear and trembling ye received him.

16 I rejoice therefore that I have confidence in you in all (things).

2 Corinthians 8

1. Moreover, brethren, we do you to wit of the grace of God bestowed on the churches of Macedonia;
2 How that in a great trial of affliction the abundance of their joy and their deep poverty abounded unto the riches of their liberality.

3 For to (their) power, I bear record, yea, and beyond (their) power (they were) willing of themselves;
4 Praying us with much intreaty that we would receive the gift, and (take upon us) the fellowship of the ministering to the saints.
5 And (this they did), not as we hoped, but first gave their own selves to the Lord, and unto us by the will of God.
6 Insomuch that we desired Titus, that as he had begun, so he would also finish in you the same grace also.
7 . Therefore, as ye abound in every (thing, in) faith, and utterance, and

Literal Translation

in knowledge, and in all earnestness, and in your love in us, that you also should abound in this grace.
8 I do not speak by command, but through the earnestness of others and testing the trueness of your love.

9 For you know the grace of our Lord Jesus Christ, that being rich because of you He became poor, so that you might become rich by the poverty of that One.
10. And I give judgment in this, for this to be profitable to you, who began before not only to do, but also to be willing from last year.

11 But now also complete the doing (of it), so that even as (there was) the eagerness (in) the willing, so also the completing, (giving) out of (what you) have.
12 For if the eagerness is present, (it is) acceptable according to (what) anyone has, not according to (what) one does not have.
13 For (it is) not that (there may be) ease to others, but trouble (to) you;
14 but of equality in the present time, your abundance for their need; but also that their abundance may be for your need, so as may be equality;
15 even as it has been written, "He (gathering) much, he had nothing left over, and he (gathering) little had no less." (Ex. 16:18)

16. But thanks (be) to God, giving the same earnestness for you in the heart of Titus.
17 For truly he received the entreating, but being more earnest, he went out to you of his own accord.
18 But we sent with him the brother whose praise (is) in the

2 Corinthians 8:8

1108 2532 3956 4710 2532 3588 1537 5216 1722 2254 26
γνώσει, καὶ πάσῃ σπουδῇ, καὶ τῇ ἐξ ὑμῶν ἐν ἡμῖν ἀγάπῃ,
in knowledge, and in all earnestness, and the of you in us love,

2443 2532 1722 3778 3588 5485 4052 3756 2596 2003
ἵνα καὶ ἐν ταύτῃ τῇ χάριτι περισσεύητε. 8 οὐ κατ' ἐπιταγὴν
that also in this grace you abound. Not by command

3004 235 1223 3588 2087 4710 2532 3588 3588 5212
λέγω, ἀλλὰ διὰ τῆς ἑτέρων σπουδῆς καὶ τὸ τῆς ὑμετέρας
I say, but through the of others earnestness also the of your

26 1103 1381 1097 1063 3588 5485 3588
ἀγάπης γνήσιον δοκιμάζων. 9 γινώσκετε γὰρ τὴν χάριν τοῦ
love trueness testing. you know For the grace of the

2962 2257 2424 5547 3754 1223 5209 4433
Κυρίου ἡμῶν Ἰησοῦ Χριστοῦ, ὅτι δι' ὑμᾶς ἐπτώχευσε,
Lord of us Jesus Christ, that because of you He became poor,

4145 5607 2443 5210 3588 1565 4432 4147 2532
πλούσιος ὤν, ἵνα ὑμεῖς τῇ ἐκείνου πτωχείᾳ πλουτήσητε. 10 καὶ
rich being, that you by the of that One poverty might become rich. And

1106 1722 5129 1325 5124 1063 5213 4851 3748
γνώμην ἐν τούτῳ δίδωμι· τοῦτο γὰρ ὑμῖν συμφέρει, οἵτινες
judgment in this I give; this for to you to be profitable, who

3756 3440 3588 4160 235 2532 3588 2309 4278 575
οὐ μόνον τὸ ποιῆσαι ἀλλὰ καὶ τὸ θέλειν προενήρξασθε ἀπὸ
not only the to do but also the to will you before began from

4070 3570 1161 2532 3588 4160 2005 3704 2509
πέρυσι. 11 νυνὶ δὲ καὶ τὸ ποιῆσαι ἐπιτελέσατε, ὅπως, καθάπερ
last year. now But also the to do (of it) complete, so as, even as

3588 4288 3588 2309 3779 2532 3588 2005 1537 3588 2192
ἡ προθυμία τοῦ θέλειν, οὕτω καὶ τὸ ἐπιτελέσαι ἐκ τοῦ ἔχειν.
the eagerness of the to will, so also to complete from the to have.

1487 1063 3588 4288 4295 2526 1437 2192 5100 2144
12 εἰ γὰρ ἡ προθυμία πρόκειται, καθὸ ἐὰν ἔχῃ τις, εὐπρόσδε-
if For the eagerness is present, according as may have anyone, (he is)

3756 2526 3756 2192 3756 1063 2443 243 425 5213 1161
κτος, οὐ καθὸ οὐκ ἔχει. 13 οὐ γὰρ ἵνα ἄλλοις ἄνεσις, ὑμῖν δὲ
acceptable, not as (one) not has. not For that to others ease, you but

2347 235 1537 2471 1722 3588 3568 2540 3588 5216 4051
θλῖψις· ἀλλ' ἐξ ἰσότητος 14 ἐν τῷ νῦν καιρῷ τὸ ὑμῶν περίσ-
trouble; but of equality, in the present time the of you abun-

1519 3588 1565 5303 2443 2532 3588 1565 4051
σευμα εἰς τὸ ἐκείνων ὑστέρημα, ἵνα καὶ τὸ ἐκείνων περίσσευμα
dance for the of those need, that also the of those abundance

1096 1519 3588 5216 5303 3704 1096 2471
γένηται εἰς τὸ ὑμῶν ὑστέρημα· ὅπως γένηται ἰσότης,
may be for the of you need; so as may be equality,

2531 1125 3588 3588 4183 3756 4121 2532/3588/3588
15 καθὼς γέγραπται, Ὁ τὸ πολὺ, οὐκ ἐπλεόνασε· καὶ ὁ τὸ
even as it has been written, He (taking) much, not he had over; and he the

3641 3756 1641
ὀλίγον οὐκ ἠλαττόνησε.
little not had less.

5485 1161 3588 2316 3588 1325 3588 846 4710 5228
16. Χάρις δὲ τῷ Θεῷ τῷ διδόντι τὴν αὐτὴν σπουδὴν ὑπὲρ
thanks But to God giving the same earnestness for

5216 1722 3588 2588 5103 3754 3588 3303 3874 1209
ὑμῶν ἐν τῇ καρδίᾳ Τίτου, 17 ὅτι τὴν μὲν παράκλησιν ἐδέξατο,
you in the heart of Titus, because the indeed entreating he received,

4705 1161 5225 830 1831 4314 5209
σπουδαιότερος δὲ ὑπάρχων αὐθαίρετος ἐξῆλθεν πρὸς ὑμᾶς.
more earnest and being, of his own accord he went out to you.

4842 1161 3326 846 3588 80 3739 3588 1868 1722 3588
18 συνεπέμψαμεν δὲ μετ' αὐτοῦ τὸν ἀδελφόν, οὗ ὁ ἔπαινος ἐν τῷ
we sent and with him the brother, of whom the praise is in the

King James Version

knowledge, and (in) all diligence, and (in) your love to us, (see) that ye abound in this grace also.
8 I speak not by commandment, but by occasion of the forwardness of others, and to prove the sincerity of your love.

9 For ye know the grace of our Lord Jesus Christ, that, though he was rich, yet for your sakes he became poor, that ye through his poverty might be rich.
10. And herein I give (my) advice: for this is expedient for you, who have begun before, not only to do, but also to be forward a year ago.

11 Now therefore perform the doing (of it); that as (there was) a readiness to will, so (there may be) a performance also out of that which ye have.
12 For if there be first a willing mind, (it is) accepted according to that a man hath, (and) not according to that he hath not.
13 For (I mean) not that other men be eased, and ye burdened:
14 But by an equality, (that) now at this time your abundance (may be a supply) for their want, that their abundance also may be (a supply) for your want: that there may be equality:
15 As it is written, He that (had gathered) much had nothing over; and he that (had gathered) little had no lack.
16. But thanks (be) to God, which put the same earnest care into the heart of Titus for you.
17 For indeed he accepted the exhortation; but being more forward, of his own accord he went unto you.
18 And we have sent with him the brother, whose praise (is) in the

Literal Translation | **2 Corinthians 8:19** | ***King James Version***

gospel throughout all the churches,
19 and not only (so), but also he having been chosen by the churches (as) a traveling companion to us with this gift, being ministered by us to the glory of the Lord Himself, and your eagerness,
20 avoiding this, lest anyone should blame us in this bounty being ministered by us;
21 providing right things not only before (the) Lord, but also before men.
22 And we sent with them our brother whom we often proved in many things to be earnest, and now much more earnest by the great assurance which (I have) toward you.
23 Whether as to Titus, (he is) my partner and a fellow-worker for you; or (about) our brothers, (they are) messengers of the churches, (the) glory of Christ.
24 Then show them a proof of your love and of our boasting on your behalf, even in (the) sight of the churches.

2098 1223 3956 3588 1577 3756 3440 1161 235
εὐαγγελίῳ διὰ πασῶν τῶν ἐκκλησιῶν· 19 οὐ μόνον δὲ, ἀλλὰ
gospel throughout all the churches; not only and, but

2532 5500 5259 3588 1577 4898 2257
καὶ χειροτονηθεὶς ὑπὸ τῶν ἐκκλησιῶν συνέκδημος ἡμῶν
also having been chosen by the churches a traveling companion to us

4862 3588 5485 3778 3588 1247 5259 2257 4314 3588
σὺν τῇ χάριτι ταύτῃ τῇ διακονουμένῃ ὑφ' ἡμῶν πρὸς τὴν
with gift this, being ministered by us to the

846 3588 2962 1391 2532 4288 5216 4724
αὐτοῦ τοῦ Κυρίου δόξαν, καὶ προθυμίαν ὑμῶν· 20 στελλόμενοι
Himself of the Lord glory, and (the) eagerness of you; avoiding

5124 3361 5100 2248 3469 1722 3588 100 3778/3588
τοῦτο, μή τις ἡμᾶς μωμήσηται ἐν τῇ ἁδρότητι ταύτῃ τῇ
this, lest anyone us should blame in bounty this

1247 5259 2257 4306 2570 3756 3440
διακονουμένῃ ὑφ' ἡμῶν· 21 προνοοῦμεν καλὰ οὐ μόνον
being ministered by us; providing right things not only

1799 2962 235 2532 1799 444 4842
ἐνώπιον Κυρίου ἀλλὰ καὶ ἐνώπιον ἀνθρώπων. 22 συνεπέμψα-
before (the) Lord but also before men. we sent with

1161 846 3588 80 2257 3739 1381 1722 4183
μεν δὲ αὐτοῖς τὸν ἀδελφὸν ἡμῶν, ὃν ἐδοκιμάσαμεν ἐν πολλοῖς
And them the brother of us, whom we proved in many things

4178 4705 5607 3570 1161 4183 4706
πολλάκις σπουδαῖον ὄντα, νυνὶ δὲ πολὺ σπουδαιότερον,
many times earnest being, now and much more earnest,

4006 4183 3588 1519 5209 1535 5228 5103 2844
πεποιθήσει πολλῇ τῇ εἰς ὑμᾶς. 23 εἴτε ὑπὲρ Τίτου, κοινωνὸς
in assurance much toward you. Whether as to Titus, partner

1699 2532 1519 5209 4904 1535 80 2257 652
ἐμὸς καὶ εἰς ὑμᾶς συνεργός· εἴτε ἀδελφοὶ ἡμῶν, ἀπόστολοι
my and for you fellow-worker; or brothers of us, messengers

1577 1391 5547 3588 3767 1732 3588 26
ἐκκλησιῶν, δόξα Χριστοῦ. 24 τὴν οὖν ἔνδειξιν τῆς ἀγάπης
of churches, (the) glory of Christ. the Therefore proof of the love

5216 2532 2257 2746 5228 5216 1519 846 1731
ὑμῶν, καὶ ἡμῶν καυχήσεως ὑπὲρ ὑμῶν, εἰς αὐτοὺς ἐνδείξασθε
of you, and of us the boasting on behalf of you, to them showing forth

2532 1519 4383 3588 1577
καὶ εἰς πρόσωπον τῶν ἐκκλησιῶν.
and in (the) sight of the churches.

gospel throughout all the churches;
19 And not (that) only, but who was also chosen of the churches to travel with us with this grace, which is administered by us to the glory of the same Lord, and (declaration of) your ready mind:
20 Avoiding this, that no man should blame us in this abundance which is administered by us:
21 Providing for honest things, not only in the sight of the Lord, but also in the sight of men.
22 And we have sent with them our brother, whom we have oftentimes proved diligent in many things, but now much more diligent, upon the great confidence which (I have) in you.
23 Whether (any do enquire) of Titus, (he is) my partner and fellowhelper concerning you: or our brethren (be enquired of, they are) the messengers of the churches, (and) the glory of Christ.
24 Wherefore shew ye to them, and before the churches, the proof of your love, and of our boasting on your behalf.

2 Corinthians 9

1. For indeed concerning the ministry to the saints, it is surperfluous for me to write to you.
2 For I know your eagerness, of which I boast to Macedonia on your behalf, that Achaia has made ready from last year, and your zeal arouses the greater number.
3 But I sent the brothers that our boasting which (is) on your behalf should not be in vain in this respect, that as I said, you

2 Corinthians 9

4012 3303 1063 3588 1248 3588 1519 3588 40 4053
1. Περὶ μὲν γὰρ τῆς διακονίας τῆς εἰς τοὺς ἁγίους περισσόν
concerning indeed For the ministry to the saints superfluous

3427 2076 3588 1125 5213 1492 1063 3588 4288 5216 3736
μοί ἐστι τὸ γράφειν ὑμῖν, 2 οἶδα γὰρ τὴν προθυμίαν ὑμῶν, ἣν
to me it is to write to you, I know for the eagerness of you, which

5228 5216 2744 3110 3754 882 3903
ὑπὲρ ὑμῶν καυχῶμαι Μακεδόσιν, ὅτι Ἀχαΐα παρεσκεύασται
on behalf of you I boast to Macedonia, that Achaia has made ready

575 4070 2532 3588 1537 5216 2205 2042 3588 4119
ἀπὸ πέρυσι· καὶ ὁ ἐξ ὑμῶν ζῆλος ἠρέθισε τοὺς πλείονας.
from last yeaar; and the of you zeal arouses the greater number.

3992 1161 3588 80 2443 3361 3588 2745 2257 3588 5228
3 ἔπεμψα δὲ τοὺς ἀδελφούς, ἵνα μὴ τὸ καύχημα ἡμῶν τὸ ὑπὲρ
I sent And the brothers, that not the boast of us on behalf of

5216 2758 1722 3588 3313 5129 2443 2531 3004
ὑμῶν κενωθῇ ἐν τῷ μέρει τούτῳ· ἵνα καθὼς ἔλεγον, παρε-
you may be in vain in respect this; that even as I said having

2 Corinthians 9

1. For as touching the ministering to the saints, it is superfluous for me to write to you:
2 For I know the forwardness of your mind, for which I boast of you to them of Macedonia, that Achaia was ready a year ago; and your zeal hath provoked very many.
3 Yet have I sent the brethren, lest our boasting of you should be in vain in this behalf; that, as I said, ye may

Literal Translation

were ready;
4 lest if Macedonians come with me and find you not ready, that we, we do not say you, should be ashamed in this assurance of boasting.

5 Therefore, I thought (it) necessary to exhort the brothers, that they go forward to you and arrange beforehand your promised blessing, this to be ready, thus as a blessing and not as greediness.

6. And this: the (one) sowing sparingly will also reap sparingly, and the (one) sowing on (hope of) blessings will also reap on blessings.
7 Each one as he purposes in (his) heart, not out of grief or out of necessity, for God loves a cheerful giver.
8 And God (is) able to make all grace to abound toward you, that in everything, always having all self sufficiency, you may abound to every good work;

9 even as it has been written, "He scattered, he gave to the poor, his righteousness abides forever." (Psa. 112:9)
10 Now He that supplies seed to the sower and bread for eating, may He supply and multiply your seed and increase the fruits of your righteousness,

11 in everything (you) being enriched to all sincerity, which works out thanksgiving to God through us.

12 Because the ministry of this service is not only making up the things lacking of the

2 Corinthians 9:4

3903 5600 -3381- 1437 2064 4862 1698 3110
σκευασμένοι ἦτε· 4 μή πως, ἐὰν ἔλθωσι σὺν ἐμοὶ Μακεδόνες
been ready you were; not (some)how, if come with me Macedonians

2532 2147 5209 532 2617 2249 2443
καὶ εὕρωσιν ὑμᾶς ἀπαρασκευάστους, καταισχυνθῶμεν ἡμεῖς [ἵνα
and find you not ready, should be ashamed we, that

3361 3004 5210 1722 3588 5287 3778 3588 2746
μὴ λέγωμεν ὑμεῖς] ἐν τῇ ὑποστάσει ταύτῃ τῆς καυχήσεως.
not we say you, in assurance this of boasting.

316 3767 2233 3870 3588 80 2443
5 ἀναγκαῖον οὖν ἡγησάμην παρακαλέσαι τοὺς ἀδελφούς, ἵνα
necessary Therefore I thought (it) to exhort the brothers, that

4281 1519 5209 2532 4294 3588 4293
προέλθωσιν εἰς ὑμᾶς, καὶ προκαταρτίσωσι τὴν προκατηγ-
they go forward to you, and arrange beforehand the having been

2129 5216 3778 2092 1511 3779 5613
γελμένην εὐλογίαν ὑμῶν, ταύτην ἑτοίμην εἶναι, οὕτως ὡς
promised blessing of you, this ready to be, so as

2129 2532 3361 5618 4124
εὐλογίαν καὶ μὴ ὥσπερ πλεονεξίαν.
a blessing and not as greediness.

5124 1161 3588 4687 5340 5340 2532 2325
6. Τοῦτο δέ, ὁ σπείρων φειδομένως, φειδομένως καὶ θερίσει·
this And, the (one) sowing sparingly, sparingly also will reap;

2532 3588 4687 1909 2129 1909 2129 2532 2325
καὶ ὁ σπείρων ἐπ' εὐλογίαις, ἐπ' εὐλογίαις καὶ θερίσει.
and the (one) sowing on (hope of) blessing, on blessing also will reap.

1538 2531 4255 3588 2588 3361/1537/3077/2228/1537
7 ἕκαστος καθὼς προαιρεῖται τῇ καρδίᾳ· μὴ ἐκ λύπης ἢ ἐξ
Each one as he purposes in the heart; not of grief or of

318 2431 1063 1395 25 3588 2316 1415 1161 3588
ἀνάγκης· ἱλαρὸν γὰρ δότην ἀγαπᾷ ὁ Θεός. 8 δυνατος δὲ ὁ
necessity; a cheerful for giver loves God. is able And

2316 3956 5485 4052 1519 5209 2443 1722 3956
Θεὸς πᾶσαν χάριν περισσεῦσαι εἰς ὑμᾶς, ἵνα ἐν παντὶ
God all grace to abound to you, that in everything

3842 3956 841 2192 4052 1519 3956
πάντοτε πᾶσαν αὐτάρκειαν ἔχοντες περισσεύητε εἰς πᾶν
always all self-sufficiency having you may abound to every

2041 18 2531 1125 4650 1325 3588
ἔργον ἀγαθόν, 9 καθὼς γέγραπται, Ἐσκόρπισεν, ἔδωκε τοῖς
work good, even as it has been written, He scattered, he gave to the

3993 3588 1343 846 3306 1519 3588 165 3588 1161
πένησιν, ἡ δικαιοσύνη αὐτοῦ μένει εἰς τὸν αἰῶνα. 10 ὁ δὲ
poor, the righteousness of him remains to the age. he And

2023 4690 3588 4687 2532 740 1519 1035
ἐπιχορηγῶν σπέρμα τῷ σπείροντι, καὶ ἄρτον εἰς βρῶσιν
that supplies seed to the sower, and bread for eating

5524 2532 4129 3588 4703 5216 2532 837
χορηγήσαι, καὶ πληθυναι τὸν σπόρον ὑμῶν, καὶ αὐξήσαι
may He supply, and multiply the seed of you, and increase

3588 1081 3588 1343 5216 1722 3956 4148
τὰ γεννήματα τῆς δικαιοσύνης ὑμῶν· 11 ἐν παντὶ πλουτι-
the fruits of the righteousness of you; in everything being

1519 3956 572 3748 2716 1223 2257
ζόμενοι εἰς πᾶσαν ἁπλότητα, ἥτις κατεργάζεται δι' ἡμῶν
enriched to all sincerity, which works out through us

2169 3588 2316 3754 3588 1248 3588 3009 3778
εὐχαριστίαν τῷ Θεῷ. 12 ὅτι ἡ διακονία τῆς λειτουργίας ταύτης
thanksgiving to God. Because the ministry service of this

3588 3440 2076 4322 3588 5303 3588
οὐ μόνον ἐστὶ προσαναπληροῦσα τὰ ὑστερήματα τῶν
not only is making up the things lacking of the

King James Version

be ready:
4 Lest haply if they of Macedonia come with me, and find you unprepared, we (that we say not, ye) should be ashamed in this same confident boasting.

5 Therefore I thought it necessary to exhort the brethren, that they would go before unto you, and make up beforehand your bounty, whereof ye had notice before, that the same might be ready, as (a matter of) bounty, and not as (of) covetousness.

6. But this (I say), He which soweth sparingly shall reap also sparingly; and he which soweth bountifully shall reap also bountifully.
7 Every man according as he purposeth in his heart, (so let him give); not grudgingly, or of necessity: for God loveth a cheerful giver.
8 And God (is) able to make all grace abound toward you; that ye, always having all sufficiency in all (things), may abound to every good work:

9 (As it is written, He hath dispersed abroad; he hath given to the poor: his righteousness remaineth for ever.
10 Now he that ministereth seed to the sower both minister bread for (your) food, and multiply your seed sown, and increase the fruits of your righteousness;)

11 Being enriched in every thing to all bountifulness, which causeth through us thanksgiving to God.

12 For the administration of this service not only supplieth the want of the

Literal Translation

2 Corinthians 9:13

King James Version

saints, but also multiplying through many thanksgivings to God,

13 through the proof of this service, (they) glorifying God by your confession on the submission to the gospel of Christ, and the sincerity of the fellowship toward them and toward all;

14 and with their petition for you, a longing after you, because of the surpassing grace of God on you.

15 But thanks (be) to God for His unspeakable gift.

40 235 2532 4052 1223 4183 2169
ἁγίων, ἀλλὰ καὶ περισσεύουσα διὰ πολλῶν εὐχαριστιῶν
saints, but also abounding through many thanksgivings

3588 2316 1223 3588 1382 3588 1248 3778 1392
τῷ Θεῷ· 13 διὰ τῆς δοκιμῆς τῆς διακονίας ταύτης δοξάζοντες
to God; through the proof ministry of this glorifying

3588 2316 1909 3588 5292 3588 3671 5216 1519 3588
τὸν Θεὸν ἐπὶ τῇ ὑποταγῇ τῆς ὁμολογίας ὑμῶν εἰς τὸ
God on the submission by the confession of you to the

2098 3588 5547 2532 572 3588 2842 1519
εὐαγγέλιον τοῦ Χριστοῦ, καὶ ἁπλότητι τῆς κοινωνίας εἰς
gospel of Christ, and (the) sincerity of the fellowship toward

846 2532 1519 3956 2532 846 1162 5228 5216
αὐτοὺς καὶ εἰς πάντας· 14 καὶ αὐτῶν δεήσει ὑπὲρ ὑμῶν
them and toward all; and them with petition for you

1971 5209 1223 3588 5235 5485 3588
ἐπιποθούντων ὑμᾶς διὰ τὴν ὑπερβάλλουσαν χάριν τοῦ
longing after you because of the surpassing grace

2316 1909 5213 5485 1161 3588 2316 1909 3588 411 846
Θεοῦ ἐφ' ὑμῖν. 15 χάρις δὲ τῷ Θεῷ ἐπὶ τῇ ἀνεκδιηγήτῳ αὐτοῦ
of God on you. thanks But to God on the unspeakable of Him

1431
δωρεᾷ.
gift.

saints, but is abundant also by many thanksgivings unto God;

13 Whiles by the experiment of this ministration they glorify God for your professed subjection unto the gospel of Christ, and for (your) liberal distribution unto them, and unto all (men);

14 And by their prayer for you, which long after you for the exceeding grace of God in you.

15 Thanks (be) unto God for his unspeakable gift.

2 Corinthians 10

1. And I myself, Paul, call on you through the meekness and forbearance of Christ - I, who indeed to look upon am lowly among you, but being absent am bold toward you;

2 but I ask, not being present, that I may be bold with the confidence which I think to be daring toward some, those reckoning us as walking according to flesh.

3 For walking about in flesh, we do not wage war according to flesh;

4 for the weapons of our warfare (are) not fleshly, but powerful to God in order to pull down strongholds,

5 pulling down imaginations and every high thing lifting up (itself) against the knowledge of God, and bringing into captivity every thought into the obedience of Christ,

6 and having readiness to avenge all disobedience, whenever your obedience is fulfilled.

7. Do you look at things

2 Corinthians 10

846 1161 1473 3972 3870 5209 1223 3588 4236
1. Αὐτὸς δὲ ἐγὼ Παῦλος παρακαλῶ ὑμᾶς διὰ τῆς πρᾳότητος
myself And I Paul call on you through the meekness

2532 1932 3588 5547 3739 2596 4383 3303 5011
καὶ ἐπιεικείας τοῦ Χριστοῦ, ὃς κατὰ πρόσωπον μὲν ταπεινὸς
and forbearance of Christ, who according to face indeed lowly

1722 5213 548 1161 2292 1519 5209 1189 1161 3588 3361 3918
ἐν ὑμῖν, ἀπὼν δὲ θαρρῶ εἰς ὑμᾶς· 2 δέομαι δέ, τὸ μὴ παρὼν
among you, being absent but bold toward you; I ask but, not being present,

2292 3588 4006 3739 3049 5111 1909 5100
θαρρῆσαι τῇ πεποιθήσει ᾗ λογίζομαι τολμῆσαι ἐπί τινας
to be bold in the confidence which I think to be daring toward some

3588 3049 2248 5613 2596 4561 4043
τοὺς λογιζομένους ἡμᾶς ὡς κατὰ σάρκα περιπατοῦντας.
the (ones) reckoning us as according to flesh walking.

1722 4561 1063 4043 3756 2596 4561 4754
3 ἐν σαρκὶ γὰρ περιπατοῦντες, οὐ κατὰ σάρκα στρατευόμεθα
in flesh For walking, not according to flesh we wage war

3588 1063 3696 3588 4752 2257 3756 4559 235
4 [τὰ γὰρ ὅπλα τῆς στρατείας ἡμῶν οὐ σαρκικά, ἀλλὰ
the for weapons of the warfare of us (are) not fleshly, but

1415 3588 2316 4314 2506 3794 3053
δυνατὰ τῷ Θεῷ πρὸς καθαίρεσιν ὀχυρωμάτων], λογισμοὺς
powerful to God in order to demolish strongholds; imaginations

2507 2532 3956 5313 1869 2596 3588 1108
καθαιροῦντες 5 καὶ πᾶν ὕψωμα ἐπαιρόμενον κατὰ τῆς γνώσεως
demolishing and every high thing exalting (itself) against the knowledge

3588 2316 2532 163 3956 3540 1519 3588 5218
τοῦ Θεοῦ, καὶ αἰχμαλωτίζοντες πᾶν νόημα εἰς τὴν ὑπακοὴν
of God, and bringing into captivity every thought into the obedience

3588 5547 2532 1722 2092 2192 1556 3956
τοῦ Χριστοῦ, 6 καὶ ἐν ἑτοίμῳ ἔχοντες ἐκδικῆσαι πᾶσαν
of Christ, and in readiness having to avenge all

3876 3752 4137 5216 3588 5218 3588 2596
παρακοήν, ὅταν πληρωθῇ ὑμῶν ἡ ὑπακοή. 7 Τὰ κατὰ
disobedience, whenever is fulfilled of you the obedience. The things as to

2 Corinthians 10

1. Now I Paul myself beseech you by the meekness and gentleness of Christ, who in presence (am) base among you, but being absent am bold toward you:

2 But I beseech (you), that I may not be bold when I am present with that confidence, wherewith I think to be bold against some, which think of us as if we walked according to the flesh.

3 For though we walk in the flesh, we do not war after the flesh:

4 (For the weapons of our warfare (are) not carnal, but mighty through God to the pulling down of strong holds;)

5 Casting down imaginations, and every high thing that exalteth itself against the knowledge of God, and bringing into captivity every thought to the obedience of Christ;

6 And having in a readiness to revenge all disobedience, when your obedience is fulfilled.

7. Do ye look on things after the

Literal Translation | **2 Corinthians 10:8** | ***King James Version***

according to appearance? If anyone has persuaded himself to be of Christ, let him think this again as to himself, that as he (is) of Christ, so also we (are) of Christ.

8 For even if I also somewhat more fully should boast about our authority, which the Lord gave us for building up and not for pulling you down, I will not be put to shame;

9 so that I not seem to scare you by epistles.

10 Because, they say, the epistles (are) weighty and strong, but the bodily presence (is) weak, and (his) speech being despised.

11 Let such a one think this, that such as we (are) in word through epistles, being absent, such (we are) also being present in deed.

12. For we dare not to rank or compare ourselves with some of those commending themselves, but they measuring themselves among themselves and comparing themselves to themselves, (are) not perceptive.

13 But we will not boast beyond measure, but according to measure of the rule which the God of measure distributed to us, to reach even to you.

14 For we do not overstretch ourselves as (if) not reaching to you, for we also came to you in the gospel of Christ,

15 not boasting beyond measure in the labors of others, but having hope that the growing faith among you will be magnified according to our rule, to overflowing,

16 in order to preach the gospel (in the things beyond you, not

---

4383 991 1487 5100 3982 1438 5547 1511
πρόσωπον βλέπετε; εἴ τις πέποιθεν ἑαυτῷ Χριστοῦ εἶναι,
appearance you look (at)? If anyone has persuaded himself of Christ to be,

5124 3049 3825 575 1438 3754 2531 846
τοῦτο λογιζέσθω πάλιν ἀφ' ἑαυτοῦ, ὅτι καθὼς αὐτὸς
this let him think again as to himself, that even as he (is)

5547 3779 2532 2249 5547 1437 5037 1063 2532 4053
Χριστοῦ, οὕτω καὶ ἡμεῖς Χριστοῦ. 8 ἐάν τε γὰρ καὶ περισσό-
of Christ, so also we (are) of Christ. if even For also more abun-

5100 2744 4012 3588 1849 2257 3739 1325 3588
τερόν τι καυχήσωμαι περὶ τῆς ἐξουσίας ἡμῶν, [ἧς ἔδωκεν ὁ
dantly somewhat I may more fully boast about the authority of us, which gave the

2962 2254 1519 3619 2532 3756 1519 2506 5216
Κύριος ἡμῖν εἰς οἰκοδομήν, καὶ οὐκ εἰς καθαίρεσιν ὑμῶν],
Lord to us for building up, and not for pulling down of you,

3756 153 2443 3361 1380 5613 302 1629 5209 1223
οὐκ αἰσχυνθήσομαι· 9 ἵνα μὴ δόξω ὡς ἂν ἐκφοβεῖν ὑμᾶς διὰ
not I will be put to shame; that not I seem as though to scare you through

3588 1992 3754 3588 3303 1992 5346 926 2532
τῶν ἐπιστολῶν. 10 ὅτι Αἱ μὲν ἐπιστολαί, φησί, βαρεῖαι καὶ
the epistles. Because the indeed epistles, he says, (are) weighty and

2478 3588 1161 3952 3588 4983 772 2532 3588 3056
ἰσχυραί· ἡ δὲ παρουσία τοῦ σώματος ἀσθενής, καὶ ὁ λόγος
strong; the but presence of the body (is) weak, and the speech

1848 5124 3049 3588 5108 3754 3634 2070
ἐξουθενημένος. 11 τοῦτο λογιζέσθω ὁ τοιοῦτος, ὅτι οἷοί ἐσμεν
being despised. this Let think such a one, that such as we are

3588 3056 1223 1992 548 5108 2532 3818
τῷ λόγῳ δι' ἐπιστολῶν ἀπόντες, τοιοῦτοι καὶ παρόντες
in word through epistles being absent, such also being present

3588 2041 3756 1063 5111 1469 2228 4793 1438
τῷ ἔργῳ. 12 οὐ γὰρ τολμῶμεν ἐγκρῖναι ἢ συγκρῖναι ἑαυτούς
in work. not For we dare to rank with or to compare ourselves

5100 3588 1438 4921 235 846 1722 1438
τισι τῶν ἑαυτοὺς συνιστανόντων· ἀλλὰ αὐτοὶ ἐν ἑαυτοῖς
with some of those themselves commending; but they among themselves

1438 3354 2532 4793 1438 1438 3756
ἑαυτοὺς μετροῦντες, καὶ συγκρίνοντες ἑαυτοὺς ἑαυτοῖς, οὐ
themselves measuring, and comparing themselves to themselves, not

4920 2249 1161 3780 1519 3588 280 2744 235
συνιοῦσιν. 13 ἡμεῖς δὲ οὐχὶ εἰς τὰ ἄμετρα καυχησόμεθα, ἀλλὰ
(are) perceptive. we But not beyond measure will boast, but

2596 3588 3358 3588 2583 3739 3307 2254 3588 2316 3358
κατὰ τὸ μέτρον τοῦ κανόνος οὗ ἐμέρισεν ἡμῖν ὁ Θεός, μέτρου
according to measure of the rule which divided to us the God of measure,

2185 891 2532 5216 3756 1063 5613 3361 2185 1519 5209
ἐφικέσθαι ἄχρι καὶ ὑμῶν. 14 οὐ γὰρ ὡς μὴ ἐφικνούμενοι εἰς ὑμᾶς
to reach as far as even you. not For as not having reached to you

5239 1438 891 1063 2532 5216 5348 1722 3588
ὑπερεκτείνομεν ἑαυτούς· ἄχρι γὰρ καὶ ὑμῶν ἐφθάσαμεν ἐν τῷ
do we overstretch ourselves; as far as for even you we came in the

2098 3588 5547 3756 1519 3588 280 2744 1722
εὐαγγελίῳ τοῦ Χριστοῦ· 15 οὐκ εἰς τὰ ἄμετρα καυχώμενοι, ἐν
gospel of Christ; not beyond measure boasting, in

245 2873 1680 1161 2192 837 3588
ἀλλοτρίοις κόποις, ἐλπίδα δὲ ἔχοντες, αὐξανομένης τῆς
others (the) labors, hope but having, growing the

4102 5216 1722 5213 3170 2596 3588 2583 2257 1519
πίστεως ὑμῶν, ἐν ὑμῖν μεγαλυνθῆναι κατὰ τὸν κανόνα ἡμῶν εἰς
faith of you, among you to be magnified according to the rule of us to

4050 1519 3588 5238 5216 2097 3756
περισσείαν, 16 εἰς τὰ ὑπερέκεινα ὑμῶν εὐαγγελίσασθαι, οὐκ
overflowing, in the things beyond you to preach the gospel, not

---

after the outward appearance? If any man trust to himself that he is Christ's, let him of himself think this again, that, as he (is) Christ's, even so (are) we Christ's.

8 For though I should boast somewhat more of our authority, which the Lord hath given us for edification, and not for your destruction, I should not be ashamed:

9 That I may not seem as if I would terrify you by letters.

10 For (his) letters, say they, (are) weighty and powerful; but (his) bodily presence (is) weak, and (his) speech contemptible.

11 Let such an one think this, that, such as we are in word by letters when we are absent, such (will we be) also in deed when we are present.

12. For we dare not make ourselves of the number, or compare ourselves with some that commend themselves: but they measuring themselves by themselves, and comparing themselves among themselves, are not wise.

13 But we will not boast of things without (our) measure, but according to the measure of the rule which God hath distributed to us, a measure to reach even unto you.

14 For we stretch not ourselves beyond (our measure), as though we reached not unto you: for we are come as far as to you also in (preaching) the gospel of Christ:

15 Not boasting of things without (our) measure, (that is), of other men's labours; but having hope, when your faith is increased, that we shall be enlarged by you according to our rule abundantly,

16 To preach the gospel in the (regions) beyond you,

Literal Translation

to boast in another's rule (as) to things ready.
17 But the (one) glorying, let him glory in (the) Lord.
18 For not the (one) commending himself is the one approved, but (the one) whom the Lord commends.

2 Corinthians 10:17

1722 245 2583 1519 3588 2092 2744 3588 1161 2744
ἐν ἀλλοτρίῳ κανόνι εἰς τὰ ἕτοιμα καυχήσασθαι. 17 ὁ δὲ καυχώ-
in another's rule (as) to things ready to boast. the But glorying,

1722 2962 2744 3756 1063 3588 1438 4921
μενος, ἐν Κυρίῳ καυχάσθω. 18 οὐ γὰρ ὁ ἑαυτὸν συνιστῶν,
in (the) Lord let him glory. not For he himself commending,

1565 2076 1384 235 3739/3588/2962 4921
ἐκεῖνός ἐστι δόκιμος, ἀλλ' ὃν ὁ Κύριος συνίστησιν.
that one is approved, but whom the Lord commends.

King James Version

(and) not to boast in another man's line of things made ready to our hand.
17 But he that glorieth, let him glory in the Lord.
18 For not he that commendeth himself is approved, but whom the Lord commendeth.

2 Corinthians 11

1. I would that you endured me a little in foolishness; but, indeed, bear with me.
2 For I am jealous (over) you with a jealousy of God. For I have promised you to one Man, to present (you) a pure virgin to Christ.
3 But I fear lest somehow, as the serpent deceived Eve in his craftiness, so your thoughts should be corrupted from the purity which (is due) to Christ.
4 For if, indeed, the (one) coming proclaims another Jesus, whom we have not proclaimed, or (if) you receive another spirit which you have not received, or another gospel which you never accepted, you might well endure (these).
5. For I judge (myself) to have come behind the highest apostles (in) nothing.
6 But even if (I am) unskilled in speech, yet not in knowledge. But in every way (I) have been clearly revealed to you in all things.
7 Or did I commit sin, humbling myself that you might be exalted, because I preached the gospel of God to you without charge?
8 I stripped other churches, receiving wages for the serving of you.
9 And being present with you and lacking, I was not a burden to anyone. The brothers coming from Macedonia completely made up for my lack. And in every way I kept myself without burden (to you),

2 Corinthians 11

3784 430 3450 3397 3588 877 235 2532
1. Ὄφελον ἀνείχεσθέ μου μικρὸν τῇ ἀφροσύνῃ· ἀλλὰ καὶ
I would that you endured me a little of foolishness; but indeed

430 3450 2206 1063 5209 2316 2205 718 1063
ἀνέχεσθέ μου. 2 ζηλῶ γὰρ ὑμᾶς Θεοῦ ζήλῳ· ἡρμοσάμην γὰρ
endure me. I (am) jealous For (of) you of God with a jealousy; I joined for

5209 1520 435 3933 53 3936 3588 5547
ὑμᾶς ἑνὶ ἀνδρὶ παρθένον ἁγνὴν παραστῆσαι τῷ Χριστῷ.
you to one Man a virgin pure to present to Christ.

5399 1161 33614459 5613 3588 3789 2096 1818 1722 3588
3 φοβοῦμαι δὲ μή πως ὡς ὁ ὄφις Εὔαν ἐξηπάτησεν ἐν τῇ
I fear But lest somehow, as the serpent Eve deceived in the

3834 846 3779 5351 3588 3540 5216 575 3588
πανουργίᾳ αὐτοῦ, οὕτω φθαρῇ τὰ νοήματα ὑμῶν ἀπὸ τῆς ἁπλό-
craftiness of him, so may be spoiled the thoughts of you from the simplicity

572 3588 1519 3588 5547 1487 3303 1063 3588 2064 243
τητος τῆς εἰς τὸν Χριστόν. 4 εἰ μὲν γὰρ ὁ ἐρχόμενος ἄλλον
(due) to Christ. if indeed For he coming another

2424 2784 3739 3756 2784 2228 4151 2087
Ἰησοῦν κηρύσσει ὃν οὐκ ἐκηρύξαμεν, ἢ πνεῦμα ἕτερον λαμ-
Jesus proclaims whom not we have proclaimed, or spirit another you

2983 3739 3756 2983 2228 2098 2087 3739 3756 1209
βάνετε ὃ οὐκ ἐλάβετε, ἢ εὐαγγέλιον ἕτερον ὃ οὐκ ἐδέξασθε,
receive which not you received, or gospel another which not you accepted,

2573 430 3049 1063 3367 5302 3588
καλῶς ἠνείχεσθε. 5 λογίζομαι γὰρ μηδὲν ὑστερηκέναι τῶν
(these) well you endure. I judge For nothing to have come behind the

5228 3029 652 1487 1161 2532 2399 3588 3056 235 3756
ὑπὲρ λίαν ἀποστόλων. 6 εἰ δὲ καὶ ἰδιώτης τῷ λόγῳ, ἀλλ' οὐ
highest apostles. if But even unskilled in speech, but not

3588 1108 235 1722 3956 5319 1722 3956 1519 5209 2228
τῇ γνώσει· ἀλλ' ἐν παντὶ φανερωθέντες ἐν πᾶσιν εἰς ὑμᾶς. 7 ἢ
in knowledge; but in every way having been revealed in all things to you. Or

266 4160 1683 5013 2443 5210 5312
ἁμαρτίαν ἐποίησα ἐμαυτὸν ταπεινῶν ἵνα ὑμεῖς ὑψωθῆτε,
sin did I commit myself humbling that you may be exalted,

3754 1432 3588 3588 2316 2098 2097 5213
ὅτι δωρεὰν τὸ τοῦ Θεοῦ εὐαγγέλιον εὐηγγελισάμην ὑμῖν;
because freely the of God gospel I preached to you?

243 1577 4813 2983 3800 4314 3588 521
8 ἄλλας ἐκκλησίας ἐσύλησα, λαβὼν ὀψώνιον πρὸς τὴν ὑμῶν
Other churches I stripped, having received wages for the of you

1248 2532 3918 4314 5209 2532 5302 3756 2655
διακονίαν· 9 καὶ παρὼν πρὸς ὑμᾶς καὶ ὑστερηθείς οὐ κατενάρ-
ministry; and being present with you and lacking not I was a

3762 3588 1063 5303 3450 4322
κησα οὐδενός· τὸ γὰρ ὑστέρημά μου προσανεπλήρωσαν
burden of no one; the for lack of me made up completely

3588 80 2064 575 3109 2532 1722 3956 4
οἱ ἀδελφοί, ἐλθόντες ἀπὸ Μακεδονίας· καὶ ἐν παντὶ ἀβαρῆ
the brothers, having come from Macedonia; and in every way no burden

2 Corinthians 11

1. Would to God ye could bear with me a little in (my) folly: and indeed bear with me.
2 For I am jealous over you with godly jealousy: for I have espoused you to one husband, that I may present (you as) a chaste virgin to Christ.
3 But I fear, lest by any means, as the serpent beguiled Eve through his subtilty, so your minds should be corrupted from the simplicity that is in Christ.
4 For if he that cometh preacheth another Jesus, whom we have not preached, or (if) ye receive another spirit, which ye have not received, or another gospel, which ye have not accepted, ye might well bear with (him).
5. For I suppose I was not a whit behind the very chiefest apostles.
6 But though (I be) rude in speech, yet not in knowledge; but we have been throughly made manifest among you in all things.
7 Have I committed an offence in abasing myself that ye might be exalted, because I have preached to you the gospel of God freely?
8 I robbed other churches, taking wages (of them), to do you service.
9 And when I was present with you, and wanted, I was chargeable to no man: for that which was lacking to me the brethren which came from Macedonia supplied: and in all (things) I have kept myself from being burdensome

Literal Translation

and I will keep (myself).
10 The truth of Christ is in me, that this boasting shall not be silenced in me in the regions of Achaia.

11 Why? Because I do not love you? God knows.

12 But what I do, I also will do, that I may cut off the occasion of those desiring an occasion, so that in that which they boast, they be found also as we.
13 For such ones (are) false apostles, deceitful workers transforming themselves into apostles of Christ.
14 For did not Satan marvelously transform himself into an angel of light?

15 (It is) not a great thing, then, if also his ministers transform themselves as ministers of righteousness, whose end will be according to their works.

16. Again I say, let not anyone think me to be foolish. But if otherwise, even if as foolish, receive me, that I also may boast a little.
17 What I speak, I speak not according to (the) Lord, but as in foolishness, in this boldness of boasting.
18 Since many boast according to the flesh, I also will boast.
19 For you gladly endure fools, being wise.

20 For you endure if anyone enslaves you, if anyone devours, if anyone takes away (from you), if anyone exalts (self), if anyone beats you in the face.
21 I speak according to dishonor, as if we have been weak. But in whatever anyone dares (I say it in foolishness), I also dare.
22. Are they Hebrews? I also. Are they Israelites?

2 Corinthians 11:10

5213 1683 5083 2532 5083 2076 225 5547
ὑμῖν ἐμαυτὸν ἐτήρησα καὶ τηρήσω. 10 ἔστιν ἀλήθεια Χριστοῦ
to you myself I kept and I will keep. is (The) truth of Christ
1722 1698 3754 3588 2746 3778 3756 4972 1519 1691 1722 3588
ἐν ἐμοί ὅτι ἡ καύχησις αὕτη οὐ φραγήσεται εἰς ἐμὲ ἐν τοῖς
in me that boasting this not shall be silenced in me in the
2824 3588 882 1302 3754 3756 25 5209 3588 2316
κλίμασι τῆς Ἀχαΐας. 11 διατί; ὅτι οὐκ ἀγαπῶ ὑμᾶς; ὁ Θεὸς
regions of Achaia. Why? Because not I love you? God
1492 3588 1161 4160 2532 4160 2443 1581 3588 874 3588
οἶδεν. 12 ὃ δὲ ποιῶ, καὶ ποιήσω, ἵνα ἐκκόψω τὴν ἀφορμὴν τῶν
knows what But I do, also I will do, that I may cut off the occasion of those
2309 874 2443 1722 3739 2744 2147 2531
θελόντων ἀφορμήν, ἵνα ἐν ᾧ καυχῶνται, εὑρεθῶσι καθὼς
desiring an occasion, that in which they boast, they be found even as
2532 2249 3588 1063 5108 5570 2040 1386
καὶ ἡμεῖς. 13 οἱ γὰρ τοιοῦτοι ψευδαπόστολοι, ἐργάται δόλιοι,
also we (are). For such (are) false apostles, workers deceitful,
3345 1519 652 5547 2532 3756
μετασχηματιζόμενοι εἰς ἀποστόλους Χριστοῦ. 14 καὶ οὐ
having transformed themselves into apostles of Christ, And not
2298 846 1063 3588 4567 3345 1519
θαυμαστόν· αὐτὸς γὰρ ὁ Σατανᾶς μετασχηματίζεται εἰς
marvelously himself for Satan transforms himself into
32 5457 3756 3173 3767 1487 2532 3588 1249 846
ἄγγελον φωτός. 15 οὐ μέγα οὖν εἰ καὶ οἱ διάκονοι αὐτοῦ
an angel of light. not a great thing Then if also the servants of him
3345 5613 1249 1343 3739 3588 5056
μετασχηματίζονται ὡς διάκονοι δικαιοσύνης, ὧν τὸ τέλος
transform themselves as ministers of righteousness, of whom the end
2071 2596 3588 2041 846
ἔσται κατὰ τὰ ἔργα αὐτῶν.
will be according to the works of them.

3825 3004 3361 5100 3165 1380 878 1511 1487 1161-3361- 2579
16. Πάλιν λέγω, μή τίς με δόξῃ ἄφρονα εἶναι· εἰ δὲ μή γε, κἂν
Again I say, not anyone me think foolish to be; if but otherwise, even
5613 878 1209 3165 2443 3397 5100 2504 2744 3739
ὡς ἄφρονα δέξασθέ με, ἵνα μικρόν τι κἀγὼ καυχήσωμαι. 17 ὃ
as foolish receive me, that little some I also may boast. What
2980 3756 2980 2596 2962 235 5613 1722 877 1722 3778
λαλῶ, οὐ λαλῶ κατὰ Κύριον, ἀλλ' ὡς ἐν ἀφροσύνῃ, ἐν ταύτῃ
I speak, not I speak according to (the) Lord, but as in foolishness, in this
3588 5287 3588 2746 1893 4183 2744 2596
τῇ ὑποστάσει τῆς καυχήσεως. 18 ἐπεὶ πολλοὶ καυχῶνται κατὰ
boldness of boasting. Since many boast according to
3588 4561 2504 2744 2234 1063 430 3588
τὴν σάρκα, κἀγὼ καυχήσομαι. 19 ἡδέως γὰρ ἀνέχεσθε τῶν
the flesh, I also will boast. gladly For you endure
878 5429 5607 430 1063 1487 5100 5209 2615
ἀφρόνων, φρόνιμοι ὄντες. 20 ἀνέχεσθε γάρ, εἴ τις ὑμᾶς κατα-
fools, wise being. you endure For, if anyone you enslaves,
1487 5100 2719 1487 5100 2983 1487 5100 1869 1487
δουλοῖ, εἴ τις κατεσθίει, εἴ τις λαμβάνει, εἴ τις ἐπαίρεται, εἴ
if anyone devours, if anyone receives (you), if anyone lifts himself, if
5100 5209 1519 4383 1194 2596 819 3004 5613 3754
τις ὑμᾶς εἰς πρόσωπον δέρει. 21 κατὰ ἀτιμίαν λέγω, ὡς ὅτι
anyone you in the face beats. According to dishonor I say, as that
2249 770 1722 3739 1161 302 5100 5111 1722 877
ἡμεῖς ἠσθενήσαμεν· ἐν ᾧ δ' ἂν τις τολμᾷ [ἐν ἀφροσύνῃ
we have been weak; in what but ever anyone dares, in foolishness
3004 5111 2504 1445 1526 2504 2475
λέγω], τολμῶ κἀγώ. 22 Ἑβραῖοί εἰσι; κἀγώ· Ἰσραηλῖταί
I speak, dare I also. Hebrews are they? I also! Israelites

King James Version

unto you, and (so) will I keep (myself).
10 As the truth of Christ is in me, no man shall stop me of this boasting in the regions of Achaia.

11 Wherefore? because I love you not? God knoweth.

12 But what I do, that I will do, that I may cut off occasion from them which desire occasion; that wherein they glory, they may be found even as we.
13 For such (are) false apostles, deceitful workers, transforming themselves into the apostles of Christ.
14 And no marvel; for Satan himself is transformed into an angel of light.

15 Therefore (it is) no great thing if his ministers also be transformed as the ministers of righteousness; whose end shall be according to their works.

16. I say again, Let no man think me a fool; if otherwise, yet as a fool receive me, that I may boast myself a little.
17 That which I speak, I speak (it) not after the Lord, but as it were foolishly, in this confidence of boasting.
18 Seeing that many glory after the flesh, I will glory also.
19 For ye suffer fools gladly, seeing ye (yourselves) are wise.
20 For ye suffer, if a man bring you into bondage, if a man devour (you), if a man take (of you), if a man exalt himself, if a man smite you on the face.
21 I speak as concerning reproach, as though we had been weak. Howbeit whereinsoever any is bold, (I speak foolishly,) I am bold also.
22. Are they Hebrews? so (am) I. Are they Israelites?

Literal Translation

2 Corinthians 11:23

King James Version

I also. Are they Abraham's seed? I also.
23 Are they ministers of Christ? I speak as beside myself, I (being) beyond (them): in labors, more abundantly; in stripes, beyond measure; in prisons, much more; in deaths, many times.
24 Five times I received forty (stripes) minus one from the Jews.
25 I was flogged three times; I was stoned once; I was shipwrecked three times; I have spent a night and a day in the deep.
26 (I have been) in travels often, in dangers of rivers, in dangers of robbers, in dangers from (my) race, in dangers from (the) nations, in dangers in (the) city, in dangers in (the) desert, in dangers in (the) sea, in dangers among false brothers,
27 in hardship and toil, often in watchings, in hunger and thirst, often in fastings, in cold and nakedness.
28 Apart from the things outside conspiring against me day by day, the care of all the churches.
29 Who is weak, and I am not weak? Who is caused to stumble, and I do not burn?
30 If it is right to boast, I will boast (of) the things of my infirmity.
31 The God and Father of our Lord Jesus Christ knows, He being blessed to the ages, that I am not lying.
32 In Damascus, the ethnarch of Aretas the king guarded the city of (the) Damascenes, desiring to seize me.
33 And I was let down through a window through the wall in a basket and escaped their hands.

1526 2504 4690 11 1526 2504 1249 5547
εἰσι; κἀγώ. σπέρμα Ἀβραάμ εἰσι; κἀγώ· 23 διάκονοι Χριστοῦ
are they? I also. Seed of Abraham are they? I also. Ministers of Christ

1526 3912 5723 5228 1473 1722 2873 4056
εἰσι; [παραφρονῶν λαλῶ] ὑπὲρ ἐγώ· ἐν κόποις περισσοτέ-
are they? As beside myself I speak, beyond I in labors more abundantly,

1722 4127 5234 1722 5438 4056
ρως, ἐν πληγαῖς ὑπερβαλλόντως, ἐν φυλακαῖς περισσοτέρως,
in stripes surpassing measure, in prisons more abundantly,

1722 2288 4178 5259 2453 3999 5062
εν θανάτοις πολλάκις. 24 ὑπὸ Ἰουδαίων πεντάκις τεσσερά-
in deaths many times. By Jews five times forty

3844 3391 2983 5151 4463 530 3034
κοντα παρὰ μίαν ἔλαβον. 25 τρὶς ἐρραβδίσθην, ἅπαξ ἐλιθάσθην,
(stripes) less one I received. thrice I was flogged, once I was stoned,

5151 3489 3574 1722 3588 1037 4160
τρὶς ἐναυάγησα, νυχθήμερον ἐν τῷ βυθῷ πεποίηκα·
thrice I was shipwrecked, a night and a day in the deep I have done;

3597 4178 2794 4215 2794
26 ὁδοιπορίαις πολλάκις, κινδύνοις ποταμῶν, κινδύνοις λῃ-
in travels many times, in dangers of rivers, in dangers of

3027 2794 1537 1085 2794 1537 1484 2794 1722
στῶν, κινδύνοις ἐκ γένους, κινδύνοις ἐξ ἐθνῶν, κινδύνοις ἐν
robbers, in dangers from (my) race, in dangers from nations, in dangers in

4172 2794 1722 2047 2794 1722 2281 2794
πόλει, κινδύνοις ἐν ἐρημίᾳ, κινδύνοις ἐν θαλάσσῃ, κινδύνοις
a city, in dangers in a desert, in dangers in (the) sea, in dangers

1722 5569 1722 2873 2532 3449 1722 70
ἐν ψευδαδέλφοις· 27 ἐν κόπῳ καὶ μόχθῳ, ἐν ἀγρυπνίαις
among false brothers; in labor and hardship, in watchings

4178 1722 3042 2532 1373 1722 3521 4178 1722 5592
πολλάκις, ἐν λιμῷ καὶ δίψει, ἐν νηστείαις πολλάκις, ἐν ψύχει
many times, in hunger and thirst, in fastings many times, in cold

2532 1132 5565 3588 3924 3588 1999 3450
καὶ γυμνότητι. 28 χωρὶς τῶν παρεκτός, ἡ ἐπισύστασίς μου
and nakedness;. Apart from the things outside, the conspiring against me

3588 2596 2250 3588 3308 3956 3588 1577 5101
ἡ καθ᾽ ἡμέραν, ἡ μέριμνα πασῶν τῶν ἐκκλησιῶν. 29 τίς
day by day, the care of all the churches. Who

770 2532 3756 770 5101 4624 2532 3756 1473
ἀσθενεῖ, καὶ οὐκ ἀσθενῶ; τίς σκανδαλίζεται, καὶ οὐκ ἐγὼ
is weak, and not I am weak? Who is caused to stumble, and not I

4448 1487 2744 1163 3588 3588 769 3450 2744
πυροῦμαι; 30 εἰ καυχᾶσθαι δεῖ, τὰ τῆς ἀσθενείας μου καυχήσο-
burn? If to boast is right, the things of the infirmity of me I will

3588 2316 2532 3962 3588 2962 2257 2424 5547
μαι. 31 ὁ Θεὸς καὶ πατὴρ τοῦ Κυρίου ἡμῶν Ἰησοῦ Χριστοῦ
boast. The God and Father of the Lord of us Jesus Christ

1492 3588 5607 2128 1519 3588 165 3754 3756 5574 1722
οἶδεν, ὁ ὢν εὐλογητὸς εἰς τοὺς αἰῶνας, ὅτι οὐ ψεύδομαι. 32 ἐν
knows, He being blessed to the ages, that not I am lying. In

1154 3588 1481 702 3588 935 5432 3588
Δαμασκῷ ὁ ἐθνάρχης Ἀρέτα τοῦ βασιλέως ἐφρούρει τὴν
Damascus the ethnarch of Aretas the king guarded the

1153 4172 4084 3165 2309 2532 1223 2376 1722
Δαμασκηνῶν πόλιν, πιάσαι με θέλων· 33 καὶ διὰ θυρίδος ἐν
Damascenes city, to seize me desiring; and through a window in

4553 5465 1223 3588 5038 2532 1628 3588
σαργάνῃ ἐχαλάσθην διὰ τοῦ τείχους, καὶ ἐξέφυγον τὰς
a basket I was lowered through the wall, and escaped the

5495 846
χεῖρας αὐτοῦ.
hands of them.

so (am) I. Are they the seed of Abraham? so (am) I.
23 Are they ministers of Christ? (I speak as a fool) I (am) more; in labours more abundant, in stripes above measure, in prisons more frequent, in deaths oft.
24 Of the Jews five times received I forty (stripes) save one.
25 Thrice was I beaten with rods, once was I stoned, thrice I suffered shipwreck, a night and a day I have been in the deep;
26 (In) journeyings often, (in) perils of waters, (in) perils of robbers, (in) perils by (mine own) countrymen, (in) perils by the heathen, (in) perils in the city, (in) perils in the wilderness, (in) perils in the sea, (in) perils among false brethren;
27 In weariness and painfulness, in watchings often, in hunger and thirst, in fastings often, in cold and nakedness.
28 Beside those things that are without, that which cometh upon me daily, the care of all the churches.
29 Who is weak, and I am not weak? who is offended, and I burn not?
30 If I must needs glory, I will glory of the things which concern mine infirmities.
31 The God and Father of our Lord Jesus Christ, which is blessed for evermore, knoweth that I lie not.
32 In Damascus the governor under Aretas the king kept the city of the Damascenes with a garrison, desirous to apprehend me:
33 And through a window in a basket was I let down by the wall, and escaped his hands.

Literal Translation

2 Corinthians 12

1. To boast really not (is) profitable to me, for I will come to visions and revelations of (the) Lord.
2 I know a man in Christ fourteen years before, whether in (the) body, I do not know, or out of (the) body, I do not know, God knows, such a one (was) caught up to (the) third Heaven.

3 And I know such a man, whether in (the) body or out of the body, I do not know; God knows,

4 that he was caught up into Paradise and heard unspeakable words which a man is not permitted to speak.
5 On behalf of such a one I will boast. But I will not boast on my behalf, except in my weaknesses.
6 For if I desire to boast, I will not be foolish, for I speak the truth. But I spare, lest anyone reckons me (to be) beyond what he sees me or hears anything of me.
7. And by superabundance of the revelations, that I not be made arrogant, a thorn in the flesh was given to me, a messenger of Satan, that he might buffet me, that I not be made haughty.

8 Beyond this I entreated the Lord three times, that it depart from me.
9 And He said to me, My grace is sufficient for you, for My power is perfected in weakness. Therefore, I will rather gladly boast in my weaknesses, that the power of Christ may overshadow me.

10 Because of this, I am pleased in weaknesses, in insults, in dire needs, in persecutions, in distresses, for the sake of Christ. For when I may be weak, then I am powerful.

2 Corinthians 12

2744 1211 3756 4851 3427 2064 1063 1519 3701
1. Καυχᾶσθαι δὴ οὐ συμφέρει μοι· ἐλεύσομαι γὰρ εἰς ὀπτα-
To boast really not is profitable to me; I will come for to visions

2532 602 2962 1492 444 1722 2962
σίας καὶ ἀποκαλύψεις Κυρίου. 2 οἶδα ἄνθρωπον ἐν Χριστῷ
and revelations of (the) Lord. I know a man in Christ

4253 2094 1180 1535 1722 4983 3756 1492 1535 1622
πρὸ ἐτῶν δεκατεσσάρων [εἴτε ἐν σώματι, οὐκ οἶδα· εἴτε ἐκτὸς
before years fourteen, whether in (the) body, not I know; or outside

3588 4983 3756 1492 3588 2316 1492 726 3588 5108
τοῦ σώματος, οὐκ οἶδα· ὁ Θεὸς οἶδεν], ἁρπαγέντα τὸν τοιοῦ-
the body, not I know; God knows, caught up such

2193 5154 3772 2532 1492 3588 5108 444
τον ἕως τρίτου οὐρανοῦ. 3 καὶ οἶδα τὸν τοιοῦτον ἄνθρωπον
a one to (the) third heaven. And I know such a man,

1535 1722 4983 1535 1622 3588 4983 3756 1492 3588 2316
[εἴτε ἐν σώματι, εἴτε ἐκτὸς τοῦ σώματος, οὐκ οἶδα· ὁ Θεὸς
whether in (the) body, or outside the body, not I know; God

1492 3754 726 1519 3588 3857 2532 191 731
οἶδεν], 4 ὅτι ἡρπάγη εἰς τὸν παράδεισον, καὶ ἤκουσεν ἄρρητα
knows, that he was caught into Paradise, and heard unspeakable

4487 3739 3756 1832 444 2980 5228 3588 5108
ῥήματα ἃ οὐκ ἐξὸν ἀνθρώπῳ λαλῆσαι. 5 ὑπὲρ τοῦ τοιούτου
words which not is permitted a man to speak. On behalf of such a one

2744 5228 1161 1683 3756 2744 1487 3361 1722 3588
καυχήσομα, ὑπὲρ δὲ ἐμαυτοῦ οὐ καυχήσομαι, εἰ μὴ ἐν ταῖς
I will boast; on behalf of but myself not I will boast, except in the

769 3450 1437 1063 2309 2744 3756 2071
ἀσθενείαις μου· 6 ἐὰν γὰρ θελήσω καυχήσασθαι, οὐκ ἔσομαι
weaknesses of me; if for I should desire to boast, not I will be

878 225 1063 2046 5339 1161 3361 5100 1519 1691 3049
ἄφρων· ἀλήθειαν γὰρ ἐρῶ· φείδομαι δέ, μή τις εἰς ἐμὲ λογίση-
foolish; truth for I will speak; I spare but, lest anyone to me reckons

5228 3739 991 3165 2228 191 5100 1537 1700 2532 3588 5236
ται ὑπὲρ ὃ βλέπει με, ἢ ἀκούει τι ἐξ ἐμοῦ. 7 καὶ τῇ ὑπερ-
beyond what he sees me, or hears anything of me. And the superabund-

3588 602 2443 3361 5229 1325 3427
βολῃ τῶν ἀποκαλύψεων ἵνα μὴ ὑπεραίρωμαι, ἐδόθη μοι
ance of the revelations that not I be made arrogant, was given to me

4647 3588 4561 32 4566 2443 3165 3852 2443 3361
σκόλοψ τῇ σαρκί, ἄγγελος Σατᾶν ἵνα με κολαφίζῃ, ἵνα μὴ
a thorn in the flesh, a messenger of Satan that me he might buffet, that not

5229 5228 5127 5151 3588 2962 3870 2443
ὑπεραίρωμαι. 8 ὑπὲρ τούτου τρὶς τὸν Κύριον παρεκάλεσα, ἵνα
I be made arrogant. As to this three times the Lord I sought, that

868 575 1700 2532 2046 3427 714 4671 3588 5485 3450
ἀποστῇ ἀπ' ἐμοῦ. 9 καὶ εἴρηκέ μοι, Ἀρκεῖ σοι ἡ χάρις μου·
it depart from me. And He said to me, Enough for you (is) the grace of Me;

3588 1063 1411 3450 1722 769 5048 2236 3767
ἡ γὰρ δύναμίς μου ἐν ἀσθενείᾳ τελειοῦται. ἥδιστα οὖν
the for power of Me in weakness is perfected. greatly Therefore

3123 2744 1722 3588 769 3450 2443 1981
μᾶλλον καυχήσομαι ἐν ταῖς ἀσθενείαις μου, ἵνα ἐπισκηνώσῃ
rather I will boast in the weaknesses of me, that may overshadow

1909 1691 3588 1411 3588 5547 1352 2106 1722 769 1722
ἐπ' ἐμὲ ἡ δύναμις τοῦ Χριστοῦ. 10 διὸ εὐδοκῶ ἐν ἀσθενείαις, ἐν
over me the power of Christ. Because of this I delight in weaknesses, in

5196 1722 318 1722 1375 1722 4730 5228
ὕβρεσιν, ἐν ἀνάγκαις, ἐν διωγμοῖς, ἐν στενοχωρίαις, ὑπὲρ
insults, in dire needs, in persecutions, in distresses, for the sake of

5547 3752 1063 770 5119 1415 1510
Χριστοῦ· ὅταν γὰρ ἀσθενῶ, τότε δυνατός εἰμι.
Christ; when for I am weak, then powerful I am.

King James Version

2 Corinthians 12

1. It is not expedient for me doubtless to glory. I will come to visions and revelations of the Lord.
2 I knew a man in Christ above fourteen years ago, (whether in the body, I cannot tell; or whether out of the body, I cannot tell: God knoweth;) such an one caught up to the third heaven.

3 And I knew such a man, (whether in the body, or out of the body, I cannot tell: God knoweth;)

4 How that he was caught up into paradise, and heard unspeakable words, which it is not lawful for a man to utter.
5 Of such an one will I glory: yet of myself I will not glory, but in mine infirmities.

6 For though I would desire to glory, I shall not be a fool; for I will say the truth: but (now) I forbear, lest any man should think of me above that which he seeth me (to be), or (that) he heareth of me.
7. And lest I should be exalted above measure through the abundance of the revelations, there was given to me a thorn in the flesh, the messenger of Satan to buffet me, lest I should be exalted above measure.
8 For this thing I besought the Lord thrice, that it might depart from me.
9 And he said unto me, My grace is sufficient for thee: for my strength is made perfect in weakness. Most gladly therefore will I rather glory in my infirmities, that the power of Christ may rest upon me.
10 Therefore I take pleasure in infirmities, in reproaches, in necessities, in persecutions, in distresses for Christ's sake: for when I am weak, then am I strong.

Literal Translation

2 Corinthians 12:11

King James Version

11. Boasting, I have become foolish. You compelled me. For I ought to be commended by you, for I lacked nothing of the highest apostles, even though I am nothing.
12 Truly the signs of the apostle were worked out among you in all patience, in signs, and in wonders, and by works of power.
13 For what is it in which you were less than the rest of (the) churches, except that I myself did not burden you? Forgive me this wrong.

14 Behold! I hold (myself) ready to come to you a third (time). And I will not burden you, for I do not seek your things, but you. For the children ought not to lay up treasure for the parents, but the parents for the children.
15 But I will most gladly spend and be spent on behalf of your souls, even if loving you more and more, I am loved (the) less.

16 But let it be so, I did not burden you; but being crafty, I took you with bait.

17 By any whom I have sent to you, did I overreach you by him?

18 I besought Titus and sent the brother with (him). Did Titus overreach you? Did we not walk in the same spirit? Did we not (walk) in the same steps?

19 Again, do you think that we are defending to you? We speak before God in Christ, but in all things for your building up, beloved.
20 For I fear lest somehow coming I not

1096 878 2744 5210 3165 315 1473 1063
11. Γέγονα ἄφρων καυχώμενος· ὑμεῖς με ἠναγκάσατε· ἐγὼ γὰρ
I have become foolish boasting; you me compelled; I for

3784 5259 5216 4921 3762 1063 5302 3588
ὤφειλον ὑφ' ὑμῶν συνίστασθαι· οὐδὲν γὰρ ὑστέρησα τῶν
ought by you to be commended; nothing for I lacked of the

5228 3029 652 1487 2532 3762 1510 3588 3303 4592 3588
ὑπερ λίαν ἀποστόλων, εἰ καὶ οὐδέν εἰμι. 12 τὰ μὲν σημεῖα τοῦ
highest very apostles, if even nothing I am. the Indeed signs of the

652 2716 1722 5213 1722 3956 5281 1722 4592
ἀποστόλου κατειργάσθη ἐν ὑμῖν ἐν πάσῃ ὑπομονῇ, ἐν σημείοις
apostle were worked out in you in all patience, in signs

2532 5059 2532 1411 5101 1063 2076 3739 2274 5228 3588
καὶ τέρασι καὶ δυνάμεσι. 13 τί γάρ ἐστιν ὃ ἡττήθητε ὑπὲρ τὰς
and wonders and works of power. what For is it which you were less than the

3062 1577 1487 3361 3754 846 1473 3756 2655 5216
λοιπὰς ἐκκλησίας, εἰ μὴ ὅτι αὐτὸς ἐγὼ οὐ κατενάρκησα ὑμῶν;
rest (of the) churches, if not that myself I not burdened you?

5483 3427 3588 93 3778
χαρίσασθέ μοι τὴν ἀδικίαν ταύτην.
Forgive me wrong this.

2400 5154 2093 2192 2064 4314 5209 2532/3756
14. Ἰδοὺ τρίτον ἑτοίμως ἔχω ἐλθεῖν πρὸς ὑμᾶς, καὶ οὐ
Behold! A third (time) ready I hold (myself) to come to you, and not

2655 5216 3756 1063 2212 3588 5216 235 5209 3756
καταναρκήσω ὑμῶν· οὐ γὰρ ζητῶ τὰ ὑμῶν, ἀλλ' ὑμᾶς· οὐ
I will burden you; not for I seek the things of you, but you; not

1063 3784 3588 5043 3588 1118 2343 235 3588
γὰρ ὀφείλει τὰ τέκνα τοῖς γονεῦσι θησαυρίζειν, ἀλλ' οἱ
for ought the children for the parents to lay up treasure, but the

1118 3588 5043 1473 1161 2236 1159 2532
γονεῖς τοῖς τέκνοις. 15 ἐγὼ δὲ ἥδιστα δαπανήσω καὶ ἐκδα-
parents for the children. I But most gladly will spend and be

1550 5228 3588 5590 5216 1487 2532 4056
πανηθήσομαι ὑπὲρ τῶν ψυχῶν ὑμῶν, εἰ καὶ περισσοτέρως
spent on behalf of the souls of you, if even more abundantly

5209 25 2276 25 2077 1161 1473 3756 2599
ὑμᾶς ἀγαπῶν, ἧττον ἀγαπῶμαι. 16 ἔστω δέ, ἐγὼ οὐ κατε-
you I love, (the) less I am loved. let it be But, I not

5209 235 5225 3835 1388 5209
βάρησα ὑμᾶς· ἀλλ' ὑπάρχων πανοῦργος, δόλῳ ὑμᾶς
burdened you; but being crafty, with guile you

2983 3361 5100 3739 649 4314 5209 1223 846 4122
ἔλαβον. 17 μή τινα ὧν ἀπέσταλκα πρὸς ὑμᾶς, δι' αὐτοῦ ἐπλε-
I took. Not anyone whom I have sent to you, through him did I

5209 3870 5103 2532 4882 3588
ονέκτησα ὑμᾶς; 18 παρεκάλεσα Τίτον, καὶ συναπέστειλα τὸν
overreach you? I besought Titus, and sent with (him) the

80 3361 5100 4122 5209 5103 3756 3588 846 4151
ἀδελφόν· μή τι ἐπλεονέκτησεν ὑμᾶς Τίτος; οὐ τῷ αὐτῷ Πνεύματι
brother; not overreached you Titus? not in the same Spirit

4043 3756 3588 846 2487
περιεπατήσαμεν; οὐ τοῖς αὐτοῖς ἴχνεσι;
we walk? not in the same steps (we walk)?

3825 1380 3754 5213 626 2714 3588
19. Πάλιν δοκεῖτε ὅτι ὑμῖν ἀπολογούμεθα; κατενώπιον τοῦ
Again do you think that to you we are defending? Before

2316 1722 5547 2980 3588 1161 3956 27 5228
Θεοῦ ἐν Χριστῷ λαλοῦμεν· τὰ δὲ πάντα, ἀγαπητοί, ὑπὲρ
God in Christ we speak; the things but in all, beloved, on behalf of

3588 5216 3619 5399 1063 3361 4459 2064 3756
τῆς ὑμῶν οἰκοδομῆς. 20 φοβοῦμαι γάρ, μή πως ἐλθὼν οὐχ
the of you building up. I fear For lest coming not

11. I am become a fool in glorying; ye have compelled me: for I ought to have been commended of you: for in nothing am I behind the very chiefest apostles, though I be nothing.
12 Truly the signs of an apostle were wrought among you in all patience, in signs, and wonders, and mighty deeds.
13 For what is it wherein ye were inferior to other churches, except (it be) that I myself was not burdensome to you? forgive me this wrong.

14 Behold, the third time I am ready to come to you; and I will not be burdensome to you: for I seek not yours, but you: for the children ought not to lay up for the parents, but the parents for the children.

15 And I will very gladly spend and be spent for you; though the more abundantly I love you, the less I be loved.

16 But be it so, I did not burden you: nevertheless, being crafty, I caught you with guile.

17 Did I make a gain of you by any of them whom I sent unto you?

18 I desired Titus, and with (him) I sent a brother. Did Titus make a gain of you? walked we not in the same spirit? (walked we) not in the same steps?

19 Again, think ye that we excuse ourselves unto you? we speak before God in Christ: but (we do) all things, dearly beloved, for your edifying.
20 For I fear, lest, when I come, I shall not

2 Corinthians 12:21

Literal Translation

find you as I wish, and I be found by you such as you do not wish; lest somehow (there be) strifes, envyings, angers, rivalries, evil speakings, whisperings, puffings up, disturbances;
21 that not (in) my having come again, my God may not humble me with you, and I shall mourn many of those having sinned before and not having repented over the uncleanness and fornication and lustfulness which they have practiced.

3634 2309 2147 5209 2504 2147 5213 3634 3756 2309 3361
οἵους θέλω εὕρω ὑμᾶς, κἀγὼ εὑρεθῶ ὑμῖν οἷον οὐ θέλετε· μή
such as I wish I find you, and I am found by you such as not you wish; lest
4459 2054 2205 2372 2052 2636 5587
πως ἔρεις, ζῆλοι, θυμοί, ἐριθεῖαι, καταλαλιαί, ψιθυρισμοί,
(be) strifes, envyings, angers, rivalries, evil speakings, whisperings,
5450 181 3361 3825 2064 3165 5013
φυσιώσεις, ἀκαταστασίαι· 21 μὴ πάλιν ἐλθόντα με ταπεινώσῃ
puffings up, disturbances; not again having come me may humble
3588 2316 3450 4314 5209 2532 3996 4183 3588 4258
ὁ Θεός μου πρὸς ὑμᾶς, καὶ πενθήσω πολλοὺς τῶν προη-
the God of me with you, and I shall mourn many of those having
2532 3361 3340 1909 3588 167 2532
μαρτηκότων, καὶ μὴ μετανοησάντων ἐπὶ τῇ ἀκαθαρσίᾳ καὶ
previously sinned, and not having repented over the uncleanness and
4202 2532 766 3739 4238
πορνείᾳ καὶ ἀσελγείᾳ ᾗ ἔπραξαν.
fornication and lustfulness which they have practiced.

King James Version

find you such as I would, and (that) I shall be found unto you such as ye would not: lest (there be) debates, envyings, wraths, strifes, backbitings, whisperings, swellings, tumults:
21 (And) lest, when I come again, my God will humble me among you, and (that) I shall bewail many which have sinned already, and have not repented of the uncleanness and fornication and lasciviousness which they have committed.

2 Corinthians 13

1. I am coming to you this third (time). "In the mouth of two or three witnesses every matter shall be established." (Deut.19:15)
2 I said before, and I say beforehand, as being present the second (time) and being absent now. I write to those having sinned before, and all the rest, that if I come again I will not spare;
3 since you seek a proof of Christ speaking in me, who is not weak toward you, but is powerful in you,
4 for even if He was crucified out of weakness, yet He lives by (the) power of God. For even we are weak in Him, yet we shall live by (the) power of God toward you.
5 Examine yourselves, whether you are in the faith, test yourselves. Or do you not yourselves perceive that Jesus Christ is in you, unless you are reprobates?
6 And I hope you will know that we are not reprobates.
7. But I pray to God (for) you not to do evil, none. (It is) not that we may appear approved, but that you

5154 5124 2064 4314 5209 1909 4750 1417
1. Τρίτον τοῦτο ἔρχομαι πρὸς ὑμᾶς. ἐπὶ στόματος δύο
third (time) This I am coming to you. On (the) mouth of two
3144 2532 5140 2476 3956 4487 4280 2532
μαρτύρων καὶ τριῶν σταθήσεται πᾶν ῥῆμα. 2 προείρηκα καὶ
witnesses and of three shall be settled every matter. I said before and
4302 5613 3918 3588 1208 2532 548 3568 1125
προλέγω, ὡς παρὼν τὸ δεύτερον, καὶ ἀπὼν νῦν γράφω
I say beforehand, as being present the second, and being absent now I write
3588 4258 2532 3588 3062 3956 3754 1437 2064
τοῖς προημαρτηκόσι καὶ τοῖς λοιποῖς πᾶσιν, ὅτι ἐὰν ἔλθω
to those having before sinned and the rest all, that if I come
1519 3588 3825 3756 5339 1893 1382 2212 3588 1722 1698
εἰς τὸ πάλιν, οὐ φείσομαι· 3 ἐπεὶ δοκιμὴν ζητεῖτε τοῦ ἐν ἐμοὶ
to (you) again, not I will spare; since a proof you seek in me
2980 5547 3739 1519 5209 3756 770 235 1414
λαλοῦντος Χριστοῦ, ὃς εἰς ὑμᾶς οὐκ ἀσθενεῖ, ἀλλὰ δυνατεῖ
speaking of Christ, who toward you not is weak, but powerful
1722 5213 2532 1063 1487 4717 1537 769 235 2198 1537
ἐν ὑμῖν· 4 καὶ γὰρ εἰ ἐσταυρώθη ἐξ ἀσθενείας, ἀλλὰ ζῇ ἐκ
in you; even For if He was crucified out of weakness, but He lives by
1411 2316 2532 1063 2532 2249 770 1722 846 235
δυνάμεως Θεοῦ. καὶ γὰρ καὶ ἡμεῖς ἀσθενοῦμεν ἐν αὐτῷ, ἀλλὰ
(the) power of God. indeed For even we are weak in Him, but
2198 4862 846 1537 1411 2316 1519 5209 1438
ζησόμεθα σὺν αὐτῷ ἐκ δυνάμεως Θεοῦ εἰς ὑμᾶς. 5 ἑαυτοὺς
we shall live with Him by (the) power of God toward you. Yourselves
3985 1487 2075 1722 3588 4102 1438 1381 2228 3756
πειράζετε εἰ ἐστὲ ἐν τῇ πίστει, ἑαυτοὺς δοκιμάζετε. ἢ οὐκ
examine whether you are in the faith, yourselves test. Or not
1921 1438 3754 2424 5547 1722 5213 2076
ἐπιγινώσκετε ἑαυτούς, ὅτι Ἰησοῦς Χριστὸς ἐν ὑμῖν ἐστίν;
you perceive yourselves, that Jesus Christ in you is?
1487/3361/5100/96 2075 1679 1161 3754 1097 3754 2249 3756
εἰ μή τι ἀδόκιμοί ἐστε. 6 ἐλπίζω δὲ ὅτι γνώσεσθε ὅτι ἡμεῖς οὐκ
if not reprobates you are. I hope And that you will know that we not
2070 96 2172 1161 4314 3588 2316 3361 4160 5209
ἐσμὲν ἀδόκιμοι. 7 εὔχομαι δὲ πρὸς τὸν Θεόν, μὴ ποιῆσαι ὑμᾶς
are reprobates. I pray And to God, not to do you
2556 3367 3756 2443 2249 1384 5316 235 2443 5210
κακὸν μηδέν, οὐχ ἵνα ἡμεῖς δόκιμοι φανῶμεν, ἀλλ' ἵνα ὑμεῖς
evil not any, not that we approved may appear, but that you

2 Corinthians 13

1. This (is) the third (time) I am coming to you. In the mouth of two or three witnesses shall every word be established.
2 I told you before, and foretell you, as if I were present, the second time; and being absent now I write to them which heretofore have sinned, and to all other, that, if I come again, I will not spare:
3 Since ye seek a proof of Christ speaking in me, which to you-ward is not weak, but is mighty in you.
4 For though he was crucified through weakness, yet he liveth by the power of God. For we also are weak in him, but we shall live with him by the power of God toward you.
5 Examine yourselves, whether ye be in the faith; prove your own selves. Know ye not your own selves, how that Jesus Christ is in you, except ye be reprobates?
6 But I trust that ye shall know that we are not reprobates.
7. Now I pray to God that ye do no evil; not that we should appear approved, but that ye

Literal Translation

2 Corinthians 13:8

King James Version

may do the good, and
we may be reprobates.
8 For we cannot do any-
thing against the truth,
but on behalf of the
truth.

9 For we rejoice when
we are weak and you
are powerful. But we
pray for this also, your
perfection.
10 Because of this, I
write these things while
absent, that being pre-
sent I may not deal
sharply (with you) ac-
cording to the authority
which the Lord gave me
for building up and not
for pulling down.

11. For the rest, broth-
ers, rejoice! Perfect
yourselves; encourage
yourselves, mind the
same thing, be at peace;
and the God of love and
of peace will be with
you.
12 Greet one another
with a holy kiss.

13 All the saints greet
you.

14 The grace of (the)
Lord Jesus Christ and
the love of God and the
fellowship of the Holy
Spirit (be) with you all.
Amen.

3588 2570 4160 2249 1161 5613 96 5600 3756 1063 1410
τὸ καλὸν ποιῆτε, ἡμεῖς δὲ ὡς ἀδόκιμοι ὦμεν. 8 οὐ γὰρ δυνά-
the good may do, we and as reprobates may be. not For we can

5100 2596 3588 225 235 5228 3588 225
μεθά τι κατὰ τῆς ἀληθείας, ἀλλ' ὑπὲρ τῆς ἀληθείας.
do anything against the truth, but on behalf of the truth.

5463 1063 3752 2249 770 5210 1161 1415 5600
9 χαίρομεν γὰρ ὅταν ἡμεῖς ἀσθενῶμεν, ὑμεῖς δὲ δυνατοὶ ἦτε·
we rejoice For when we are weak, you and powerful are;

5124 1161 2532 2172 3588 5216 2676 1223 5124
τοῦτο δὲ καὶ εὐχόμεθα, τὴν ὑμῶν κατάρτισιν. 10 διὰ τοῦτο
this and also we pray, the of you perfection. Because of this

5023 548 1125 2443 3918 3361 664 5667
ταῦτα ἀπὼν γράφω, ἵνα παρὼν μὴ ἀποτόμως χρήσωμαι,
these things being absent I write, that being present not sharply I may deal,

2598 3588 1849 3739 1325 3427 3588 2962 1519 3619 2532
κατὰ τὴν ἐξουσίαν ἣν ἔδοκέ μοι ὁ Κύριος εἰς οἰκοδομήν, καὶ
according to the authority which gave me the Lord for building up, and

3756 1519 2506
οὐκ εἰς καθαίρεσιν.
not for pulling down.

3063 80 5463 2675 3870
11. Λοιπόν, ἀδελφοί, χαίρετε· καταρτίζεσθε, παρακαλεῖσθε,
For the rest, brothers, rejoice; perfect yourselves, encourage yourselves,

358 846 5426 1514 2532 3588 2316 3588 26 2532
τὸ αὐτὸ φρονεῖτε, εἰρηνεύετε· καὶ ὁ Θεὸς τῆς ἀγάπης καὶ
the same thing mind, be at peace; and the God of love and

1515 2071 3326 5216 782 240 1722 40
εἰρήνης ἔσται μεθ' ὑμῶν. 12 ἀσπάσασθε ἀλλήλους ἐν ἁγίῳ
peace will be with you. Greet one another with a holy

5370
φιλήματι.
kiss.

782 5209 3588 40 3956
'Ασπάζονται ὑμᾶς οἱ ἅγιοι πάντες.
Greet you the saints all.

3588 5485 3588 2962 2424 5547 2532 3588 26 3588
13. Ἡ χάρις τοῦ Κυρίου Ἰησοῦ Χριστοῦ, καὶ ἡ ἀγάπη τοῦ
The grace of (the) Lord Jesus Christ, and the love

2316 2532 3588 2842 3588 40 4151 3326 3956
Θεοῦ, καὶ ἡ κοινωνία τοῦ Ἁγίου Πνεύματος μετὰ πάντων
of God, and the fellowship of the Holy Spirit (be) with all

5216 5216
ὑμῶν. ἀμήν.
of you. Amen.

should do that which is
honest, though we be as
reprobates.
8 For we can do nothing
against the truth, but for
the truth.

9 For we are glad, when
we are weak, and ye are
strong: and this also we
wish, (even) your per-
fection.
10 Therefore I write
these things being ab-
sent, lest being present I
should use sharpness,
according to the power
which the Lord hath
given me to edification,
and not to destruction.

11. Finally, brethren,
farewell. Be perfect, be
of good comfort, be of
one mind, live in peace;
and the God of love and
peace shall be with you.

12 Greet one another
with an holy kiss.

13 All the saints salute
you.
14 The grace of the
Lord Jesus Christ, and
the love of God, and the
communion of the Holy
Ghost, (be) with you all.
Amen. (The second
(epistle) to the Corin-
thians was written from
Philippi, (a city) of
Macedonia, by Titus
and Lucas.)

Literal Translation

THE EPISTLE OF PAUL THE APOSTLE TO THE GALATIANS

Galatians 1

1. Paul, an apostle, not from men nor through man, but through Jesus Christ and God (the) Father, the (One) having raised Him from (the) dead,

2 and all the brothers with me, to the churches of Galatia.

3 Grace to you and peace from God (the) Father and our Lord Jesus Christ,

4 who gave Himself for our sins, so that He might deliver us out of the present evil age, according to the will of our God and Father,

5 to whom (be) the glory forever and ever. Amen.

6 I wonder that you are so quickly being transferred from Him having called you by (the) grace of Christ to another gospel,

7 which is not another; only there are some troubling you and desiring to pervert the gospel of Christ.

8 But even if we, or an angel out of Heaven, should preach a gospel to you beside that which we preached to you, let him be accursed.

9 As we have said before, and now I say again, If anyone preaches a gospel to you beside what you received, let him be accursed.

10 For do I now persuade men or God? Or do I seek to please men? For if I yet pleased men, I would not be a slave of Christ.

ΠΑΥΛΟΥ Η ΠΡΟΣ
OF PAUL THE TO

ΓΑΛΑΤΑΣ ΕΠΙΣΤΟΛΗ
GALATIANS EPISTLE

Galatians 1

3972 652 3756 575 444 3761 1223 444
1. Παῦλος ἀπόστολος [οὐκ ἀπ' ἀνθρώπων, οὐδὲ δι' ἀνθρώ-
Paul an apostle, not from men, nor through

235 1223 2424 5547 2532 2316 3962 3588
που, ἀλλὰ διὰ Ἰησοῦ Χριστοῦ, καὶ Θεοῦ πατρὸς τοῦ
men, but through Jesus Christ, and God (the) Father the (One)

1453 846 1537 3498 2532 3588 4862 1698 3956
ἐγείραντος αὐτὸν ἐκ νεκρῶν], 2 καὶ οἱ σὺν ἐμοὶ πάντες
having raised Him from (the) dead, and those with me all

80 3588 1577 3588 1053 5485 5213 2532
ἀδελφοί, ταῖς ἐκκλησίαις τῆς Γαλατίας· 3 χάρις ὑμῖν καὶ
brothers, to the churches of Galatia; grace to you and

1515 575 2316 3962 2532 2962 2257 2424 5547
εἰρήνη ἀπὸ Θεοῦ πατρός, καὶ Κυρίου ἡμῶν Ἰησοῦ Χριστοῦ,
peace from God (the) Father, and (the) Lord of us Jesus Christ,

3588 1325 1438 5228 3588 266 2257 3704 1807
4 τοῦ δόντος ἑαυτὸν ὑπὲρ τῶν ἁμαρτιῶν ἡμῶν, ὅπως ἐξέληται
He having given Himself for the sins of us, so as He might deliver

2248 1537 3588 1764 165 4190 2596 3588 2307 3588
ἡμᾶς ἐκ τοῦ ἐνεστῶτος αἰῶνος πονηροῦ, κατὰ τὸ θέλημα τοῦ
us out of the present age of evil, according to the will of the

2316 2532 3962 2257 3739/3588/1391/1519 3588 165 3588
Θεοῦ καὶ πατρὸς ἡμῶν· 5 ᾧ ἡ δόξα εἰς τοὺς αἰῶνας τῶν
God and Father of us; whose (is) the glory to the ages of the

165 281
αἰώνων. ἀμήν.
ages. Amen.

2296 3754 3779 5030 3346 575 3588 2564
6. Θαυμάζω ὅτι οὕτω ταχέως μετατίθεσθε ἀπὸ τοῦ καλέ-
I wonder that so quickly you are turned back from the (One who)

5209 1722 5485 5547 1519 2087 2098 3739
σαντος ὑμᾶς ἐν χάριτι Χριστοῦ εἰς ἕτερον εὐαγγέλιον· 7 ὃ
has called you by (the) grace of Christ to another gospel; which

3756 2076 243 1487 3361 5100 1526 3588 5015 5209 2532
οὐκ ἔστιν ἄλλο, εἰ μή τινές εἰσιν οἱ ταράσσοντες ὑμᾶς καὶ
not is another, only some there are who trouble you and

2309 3344 3588 2098 3588 5547 235
θέλοντες μεταστρέψαι τὸ εὐαγγέλιον τοῦ Χριστοῦ. 8 ἀλλὰ
desire to pervert the gospel of Christ. But

2532 1437 2249 2228 32 1537 3772 2097 5213 3844
καὶ ἐὰν ἡμεῖς ἢ ἄγγελος ἐξ οὐρανοῦ εὐαγγελίζηται ὑμῖν παρ'
even if we or an angel out of Heaven preach a gospel to you beside

3739 2097 5213 331 2077 5613 4280
ὃ εὐηγγελισάμεθα ὑμῖν, ἀνάθεμα ἔστω. 9 ὡς προειρήκαμεν,
which we preached to you, accursed let him be. As we have said before,

2532 737 3825 3004 1487 5100 5209 2097 3844 3739
καὶ ἄρτι πάλιν λέγω, εἴ τις ὑμᾶς εὐαγγελίζεται παρ ' ὃ
and now again say, if anyone (to) you preaches a gospel beside what

3880 331 2077 737 1063 444 3982
παρελάβετε, ἀνάθεμα ἔστω. 10 ἄρτι γὰρ ἀνθρώπους πείθω
you received, accursed let him be. now For men do I persuade

2228/3588/2316 2228 2212 444 700 1487 1063 2089 444
ἢ τὸν Θεόν; ἢ ζητῶ ἀνθρώποις ἀρέσκειν; εἰ γὰρ ἔτι ἀνθρώ-
or God? Or do I seek men to please? if For yet men

700 5547 1401 3756 302 2252
ποις ἤρεσκον, Χριστοῦ δοῦλος οὐκ ἂν ἤμην.
I pleased, of Christ a slave not I would be.

King James Version

THE EPISTLE OF PAUL THE APOSTLE TO THE GALATIANS

Galatians 1

1. Paul, an apostle, (not of men, neither by man, but by Jesus Christ, and God the Father, who raised him from the dead;)

2 And all the brethren which are with me, unto the churches of Galatia:

3 Grace (be) to you and peace from God the Father, and (from) our Lord Jesus Christ,

4 Who gave himself for our sins, that he might deliver us from this present evil world, according to the will of God and our Father:

5 To whom (be) glory for ever and ever. Amen.

6 I marvel that ye are so soon removed from him that called you into the grace of Christ unto another gospel:

7 Which is not another; but there be some that trouble you, and would pervert the gospel of Christ.

8 But though we, or an angel from heaven, preach any other gospel unto you than that which we have preached unto you, let him be accursed.

9 As we said before, so say I now again, If any (man) preach any other gospel unto you than that ye have received, let him be accursed.

10 For do I now persuade men, or God? or do I seek to please men? for if I yet pleased men, I should not be the servant of Christ.

Galatians 1:11

Literal Translation

11 And, brothers, I make known to you the gospel preached by me, that it is not according to man.
12 For I did not receive it from man, nor was I taught (it), but by a revelation of Jesus Christ.

13 For you heard my way of life when (I was) in Judaism, that with surpassing (zeal) I persecuted the church of God and ravaged it.
14 And (I) progressed in Judaism beyond many contemporaries in my race, being much more a zealot of the traditions of my ancestors.

15 But when God was pleased, He having separated me from my mother's belly and having called through His grace,

16 to reveal His Son in me, that I might preach Him among the nations, immediately I did not confer with flesh and blood,

17 nor did I go up to Jerusalem to the apostles before me, but I went away into Arabia and returned again to Damascus.

18 Then after three years, I went up to Jerusalem to learn from Peter and remained with him fifteen days.
19 But I saw (no) other of the apostles except James the brother of the Lord.

20 And what I write to you, behold, before God I do not lie.
21 Then I went into the regions of Syria and of Cilicia,
22 but I was not known by face to the

1107 1161 5213 80 3588 2098 3588 2097
11. Γνωρίζω δὲ ὑμῖν, ἀδελφοί, τὸ εὐαγγέλιον τὸ εὐαγγελισθὲν
I make known And to you, brothers, the gospel preached

5259 1700 3754 3756 2076 2596 444 3761 1063 1473 3844
ὑπ' ἐμοῦ, ὅτι οὐκ ἔστι κατὰ ἄνθρωπον. 12 οὐδὲ γὰρ ἐγὼ παρὰ
by me, that not it is according to man. not For I from

444 3880 846 3777 1321 235 1223
ἀνθρώπου παρέλαβον αὐτό, οὔτε ἐδιδάχθην, ἀλλὰ δι'
man received it, nor was I taught, but through

602 2424 5547 191 1063 3588 1699
ἀποκαλύψεως Ἰησοῦ Χριστοῦ. 13 ἠκούσατε γὰρ τὴν ἐμὴν
a revelation of Jesus Christ. you heard For my

391 4218 1722 3588 2454 3754 2596 5236 1377
ἀναστροφήν ποτε ἐν τῷ Ἰουδαϊσμῷ, ὅτι καθ' ὑπερβολὴν ἐδίω-
way of life when in Judaism, that with surpassing (zeal) I

3588 1577 3588 2316 2532 4199 846 2532
κον τὴν ἐκκλησίαν τοῦ Θεοῦ, καὶ ἐπόρθουν αὐτήν· 14 καὶ
persecuted the church of God, and ravaged it; and

4298 1722 3588 2454 5228 4183 4915
προέκοπτον ἐν τῷ Ἰουδαϊσμῷ ὑπὲρ πολλοὺς συνηλικιώτας
progressed in Judaism beyond many contemporaries

1722 3588 1085 3450 4056 2207 5225 3588
ἐν τῷ γένει μου, περισσοτέρως ζηλωτὴς ὑπάρχων τῶν
in the race of me, much more a zealot being of the

3967 3450 3862 3753 1161 2106 3588 2316 3588
πατρικῶν μου παραδόσεων. 15 ὅτε δὲ εὐδόκησεν ὁ Θεός, ὁ
ancestral of me traditions. when But was pleased God, He

873 3165 1537 2836 3384 3450 2532 2564 1223 3588
ἀφορίσας με ἐκ κοιλίας μητρός μου καὶ καλέσας διὰ τῆς
separating me from belly mother's my and calling through the

5485 846 601 3588 5207 846 1722 1698 2443
χάριτος αὐτοῦ, 16 ἀποκαλύψαι τὸν υἱὸν αὐτοῦ ἐν ἐμοί, ἵνα
grace of Him, to reveal the Son of Him in me, that

2097 846 1722 3588 1484 2112 3756 4323
εὐαγγελίζωμαι αὐτὸν ἐν τοῖς ἔθνεσιν, εὐθέως οὐ προσανε-
I might preach Him among the nations, immediately not I conferred

4561 2532 129 3761 424 1519 2414 4314
θέμην σαρκὶ καὶ αἵματι· 17 οὐδὲ ἀνῆλθον εἰς Ἱεροσόλυμα πρὸς
with flesh and blood; neither did I go up to Jerusalem to

3588 4253 1700 652 235 565 1519 688 2532
τοὺς πρὸ ἐμοῦ ἀποστόλους, ἀλλ' ἀπῆλθον εἰς Ἀραβίαν, καὶ
the before me apostles, but I went away into Arabia, and

3825 5290 1519 1154
πάλιν ὑπέστρεψα εἰς Δαμασκόν.
again returned to Damascus.

1899 3326 2094 5140 424 1519 2414 2477
18. Ἔπειτα μετὰ ἔτη τρία ἀνῆλθον εἰς Ἱεροσόλυμα ἱστορῆσαι
Then after years three I went up to Jerusalem to learn from

4074 2532 1961 4314 846 2250 1178 2087
Πέτρον, καὶ ἐπέμεινα πρὸς αὐτὸν ἡμέρας δεκαπέντε. 19 ἕτερον
Peter, and remained with him days fifteen. other

1161 3588 652 3756 1492 1487 3361 2385 3588 80
δὲ τῶν ἀποστόλων οὐκ εἶδον, εἰ μὴ Ἰάκωβον τὸν ἀδελφὸν
But of the apostles not I saw, except James the brother

3588 2962 3739 1161 1125 5213 2400 1799 3588 2316 3754
τοῦ Κυρίου. 20 ἃ δὲ γράφω ὑμῖν, ἰδοὺ ἐνώπιον τοῦ Θεοῦ, ὅτι
of the Lord. what And I write to you, behold before God, that

3756 5574 1899 2064 1519 3588 2824 3588 4947 2532
οὐ ψεύδομαι. 21 ἔπειτα ἦλθον εἰς τὰ κλίματα τῆς Συρίας καὶ
not I lie. Then I went into the regions of Syria and

3588 2791 2252 1161 50 3588 4383 3588
τῆς Κιλικίας. 22 ἤμην δὲ ἀγνοούμενος τῷ προσώπῳ ταῖς
of Cilicia. I was And unknown by face to the

King James Version

11 But I certify you, brethren, that the gospel which was preached of me is not after man.
12 For I neither received it of man, neither was I taught (it), but by the revelation of Jesus Christ.

13 For ye have heard of my conversation in time past in the Jews' religion, how that beyond measure I persecuted the church of God, and wasted it:
14 And profited in the Jews' religion above many my equals in mine own nation, being more exceedingly zealous of the traditions of my fathers.

15 But when it pleased God, who separated me from my mother's womb, and called (me) by his grace,

16 To reveal his Son in me, that I might preach him among the heathen; immediately I conferred not with flesh and blood:

17 Neither went I up to Jerusalem to them which were apostles before me; but I went into Arabia, and returned again unto Damascus.

18 Then after three years I went up to Jerusalem to see Peter, and abode with him fifteen days.
19 But other of the apostles saw I none, save James the Lord's brother.

20 Now the things which I write unto you, behold, before God, I lie not.
21 Afterwards I came into the regions of Syria and Cilicia;
22 And was unknown by face unto the

Literal Translation

churches of Judea in Christ.
23 But only they were hearing that he who (was) persecuting us then, now preaches the gospel, the faith which he then ravaged;
24 and they glorified God in me.

Galatians 2

1. Then through fourteen years, I again went up to Jerusalem with Barnabas, also taking Titus with (me).
2 And I went up according to revelation. And I put before them the gospel which I proclaim in the nations, but privately to the ones seeming (to be pillars), lest I run, or I ran, into vanity.
3 But not even Titus, the (one) with me, a Greek, was compelled to be circumcised.
4 But (it was) because of those false brothers stealing in, who stole in to spy on our freedom which we have in Christ Jesus, they desiring to enslave us,
5 to whom not even for an hour we yielded in subjection, that the truth of the gospel might continue with you.
6 But from those seeming to be something, of what kind they were then does not matter to me; God does not accept the face of man, for those seeming (important) conferred nothing to me;
7 but on the contrary, seeing that I have been entrusted (with) the gospel of the uncircumcision, even as Peter to the circumcision,
8 for He working in Peter to an apostleship of the circumcision, also worked in me to the nations,
9 and knowing the grace given to me, James and

Galatians 1:23

1577 3588 2449 3588 1722 5547 3440 1161
ἐκκλησίαις τῆς Ἰουδαίας ταῖς ἐν Χριστῷ· 23 μόνον δὲ
churches of Judea in Christ; only but

191 2258 3754 3588 1377 2248 4218 3568 2097
ἀκούοντες ἦσαν ὅτι Ὁ διώκων ἡμᾶς ποτέ, νῦν εὐαγγελίζεται
hearing they were that the (one) persecuting us then, now preaches the gospel

3588 4102 3739 4218 4199 2532 1392 1722 1698 3588 2316
τὴν πίστιν ἥν ποτε ἐπόρθει. 24 καὶ ἐδόξαζον ἐν ἐμοὶ τὸν Θεόν.
the faith which then he ravaged. And they glorified in me God.

Galatians 2

1899 1223 1180 2094 3825 305 1519 2414
1. Ἔπειτα διὰ δεκατεσσάρων ἐτῶν πάλιν ἀνέβην εἰς Ἱεροσό-
Then through fourteen years again I went up to Jerusalem

3326 921 4838 2532 5103 305 1161
λυμα μετὰ Βαρνάβα, συμπαραλαβὼν καὶ Τίτον. 2 ἀνέβην δὲ
with Barnabas, taking with (me) also Titus. I went up And

2596 602 2532 394 846 3588 2098 3739
κατὰ ἀποκάλυψιν, καὶ ἀνεθέμην αὐτοῖς τὸ εὐαγγέλιον ὃ
according to a revelation, and I put before them the gospel which

2784 1722 3588 1484 2596 2398 1161 3588 1380 -3381- 1519
κηρύσσω ἐν τοῖς ἔθνεσι, κατ' ἰδίαν δὲ τοῖς δοκοῦσι, μή πως εἰς
I proclaim in the nations, privately but to those seeming, lest into

2756 5143 2228 5143 235 3761 5103 3588 4862 1698 1672
κενὸν τρέχω ἢ ἔδραμον. 3 ἀλλ' οὐδὲ Τίτος ὁ σὺν ἐμοί, Ἕλλην
vanity I run or I ran. But not even Titus he with me, a Greek

5607 315 4059 1223 1161 3588 3920
ὤν, ἠναγκάσθη περιτμηθῆναι· 4 διὰ δὲ τοὺς παρεισάκτους
being, was compelled to be circumcised; because of but those stealing in

5569 3748 3922 2684 3588
ψευδαδέλφους, οἵτινες παρεισῆλθον κατασκοπῆσαι τὴν
false brothers, who stole in to spy on the

1657 2257 3739 2192 1722 5547 2424 2443 2248
ἐλευθερίαν ἡμῶν ἣν ἔχομεν ἐν Χριστῷ Ἰησοῦ, ἵνα ἡμᾶς
freedom of us which we have in Christ Jesus, that us

2615 3739 3761 4314 5610 1502 3588 5292
καταδουλώσωνται· 5 οἷς οὐδὲ πρὸς ὥραν εἴξαμεν τῇ ὑποταγῇ,
they desire to enslave; to whom not for an hour we yielded in subjection,

2443 3588 225 3588 2098 1265 4314 5209 575 1161
ἵνα ἡ ἀλήθεια τοῦ εὐαγγελίου διαμείνῃ πρὸς ὑμᾶς. 6 ἀπὸ δὲ
that the truth of the gospel might continue with you. from But

3588 1380 1511 5100 3697 4218 2258 3762 3427
τῶν δοκούντων εἶναί τι [ὁποῖοί ποτε ἦσαν οὐδέν μοι
those seeming to be something, of what kind then they were nothing to me

1308 4383 2316 444 3756 2983 1698
διαφέρει· πρόσωπον Θεὸς ἀνθρώπου οὐ λαμβάνει] - ἐμοὶ
matters; the face God of man not does accept, to me

1063 3588 1380 3762 4323 235 5121
γὰρ οἱ δοκοῦντες οὐδὲν προσανέθεντο· 7 ἀλλὰ τοὐναντίον,
for those seeming nothing conferred; but on the contrary,

1492 3754 4100 3588 2098 3588 203
ἰδόντες ὅτι πεπίστευμαι τὸ εὐαγγέλιον τῆς ἀκροβυστίας,
knowing that I have been entrusted (with) the gospel of the uncircumcision,

2531 4074 3588 4061 3588 1063 1754 4074 1519
καθὼς Πέτρος τῆς περιτομῆς 8 [ὁ γὰρ ἐνεργήσας Πέτρῳ εἰς
even as Peter to the circumcision, the (one) for working in Peter to

651 3588 4061 1754 2532 1698 1519 3588 1484
ἀποστολὴν τῆς περιτομῆς, ἐνήργησε καὶ ἐμοὶ εἰς τὰ ἔθνη],
an apostleship of the circumcision, worked also to me to the nations,

2532 1097 3588 5485 3588 1325 3427 2385 2532
9 καὶ γνόντες τὴν χάριν τὴν δοθεῖσάν μοι, Ἰάκωβος καὶ
and knowing the grace given to me, James and

King James Version

churches of Judaea which were in Christ:
23 But they had heard only, That he which persecuted us in times past now preacheth the faith which once he destroyed.
24 And they glorified God in me.

Galatians 2

1. Then fourteen years after I went up again to Jerusalem with Barnabas, and took Titus with (me) also.
2 And I went up by revelation, and communicated unto them that gospel which I preach among the Gentiles, but privately to them which were of reputation, lest by any means I should run, or had run, in vain.
3 But neither Titus, who was with me, being a Greek, was compelled to be circumcised:
4 And that because of false brethren unawares brought in, who came in privily to spy out our liberty which we have in Christ Jesus, that they might bring us into bondage:
5 To whom we gave place by subjection, no, not for an hour; that the truth of the gospel might continue with you.
6 But of these who seemed to be somewhat, (whatsoever they were, it maketh no matter to me: God accepteth no man's person:) for they who seemed (to be somewhat) in conference added nothing to me:
7 But contrariwise, when they saw that the gospel of the uncircumcision was committed unto me, as (the gospel) of the circumcision (was) unto Peter;
8 (For he that wrought effectually in Peter to the apostleship of the circumcision, the same was mighty in me toward the Gentiles:)
9 And when James, Cephas, and John, who seemed to be pillars, perceived the grace that was given unto me,

Literal Translation | **Galatians 2:10** | ***King James Version***

Cephas and John, those seeming to be pillars, gave right hands of fellowship to Barnabas and to me, that we (go) to the nations, but they to the circumcision;

10 only that we might remember the poor, which same thing I was eager to do.

11 But when Peter came to Antioch, I opposed (him) to his face, because he was to be blamed.
12 For before some came from James, he ate with the nations. But when they came, he drew back and separated himself, being afraid of those of the circumcision.

13 And also the rest of the Jews dissembled with him, so as even Barnabas was led away with their dissembling.
14 But when I saw that they did not walk uprightly with the truth of the gospel, I said to Peter before all, If you being a Jew, live (as) a non-Jew and not (as the) Jews, why do you compel (the) nations to Judaize?

15 We, Jews by nature, and not sinners of the nations,
16 knowing that a man is not justified by works of law, if not through faith of Jesus Christ, we also believed in Christ Jesus, that we may be justified by faith of Christ and not by works of law, because all flesh will not be justified by works of law.

17 But if seeking to be justified in Christ, we ourselves also were found (to be) sinners, (is) Christ then a minister of sin? Let it not be!

18 For if I

2786 2532 2491 3588 1380 4769 1511 1188
Κηφᾶς καὶ Ἰωάννης, οἱ δοκοῦντες στύλοι εἶναι, δεξιὰς
Cephas and John, those seeming pillars to be, right (hands)

1325 1698 2532 921 2842 2443 2249 1519 3588 1484
ἔδωκαν ἐμοὶ καὶ Βαρνάβᾳ κοινωνίας, ἵνα ἡμεῖς εἰς τὰ ἔθνη,
gave to me and Barnabas of fellowship, that we to the nations,

846 1161 1519 3588 4061 3440 3588 4434 2443 3421
αὐτοὶ δὲ εἰς τὴν περιτομήν· 10 μόνον τῶν πτωχῶν ἵνα μνημο-
they but to the circumcision; only the poor that we might

3739 2532 4704 846 5124 4160
νεύωμεν, ὃ καὶ ἐσπούδασα αὐτὸ τοῦτο ποιῆσαι.
remember, which indeed I was eager the same this to do.

3753 1161 2064 4074 1519 490 2596 4383
11. Ὅτε δὲ ἦλθε Πέτρος εἰς Ἀντιόχειαν, κατὰ πρόσωπον
when But came Peter to Antioch, against face

846 436 3754 2607 2258 4253 3588 1063 2064
αὐτῷ ἀντέστην, ὅτι κατεγνωσμένος ἦν. 12 πρὸ τοῦ γὰρ ἐλθεῖν
to him I opposed, because to be condemned he was. before the For coming

5100 575 2385 3326 3588 1484 4906 3753 1161
τινὰς ἀπὸ Ἰακώβου, μετὰ τῶν ἐθνῶν συνήσθιεν· ὅτε δὲ
some from James, with the nations he ate; when but

2064 5288 2532 873 1438 5399 3588 1537
ἦλθον, ὑπέστελλε καὶ ἀφώριζεν ἑαυτόν, φοβούμενος τοὺς ἐκ
they came, he drew back and separated himself, being afraid of those of

4061 2532 4942 846 2532 3588 3062 2453
περιτομῆς. 13 καὶ συνυπεκρίθησαν αὐτῷ καὶ οἱ λοιποὶ Ἰουδαῖοι,
circumcision. And dissembled with him also the rest of the Jews,

5620 2532 921 4879 846 3588 5272 235
ὥστε καὶ Βαρνάβας συναπήχθη αὐτῶν τῇ ὑποκρίσει. 14 ἀλλ᾽
so as even Barnabas was led away with of them the dissembling. But

3753 1492 3754 3756 3716 4314 3588 225 3588
ὅτε εἶδον ὅτι οὐκ ὀρθοποδοῦσι πρὸς τὴν ἀλήθειαν τοῦ
then I saw that not they walked uprightly with the truth of the

2098 2036 3588 4074 1715 3956 1487 4771
εὐαγγελίου, εἶπον τῷ Πέτρῳ ἔμπροσθεν πάντων, Εἰ σύ
gospel, I said to Peter in front of all, If you

2453 5225 1483 2198 2532 3756 2452 5101 3588
Ἰουδαῖος ὑπάρχων, ἐθνικῶς ζῇς καὶ οὐκ Ἰουδαϊκῶς, τί τὰ
a Jew being, heathen-like live and not (as the) Jews, why the

1484 315 2450 2249 5449 2453 2532 3756
ἔθνη ἀναγκάζεις Ἰουδαΐζειν; 15 ἡμεῖς φύσει Ἰουδαῖοι, καὶ οὐκ
nations you compel to Judaize? We by nature Jews, and not

1537 1484 268 1492 3754 3756 1344 444
ἐξ ἐθνῶν ἁμαρτωλοί, 16 εἰδότες ὅτι οὐ δικαιοῦται ἄνθρωπος
of (the) heathen sinners, knowing that not is justified a man

1537 2041 3551 1437 3361 1223 4102 2424 5547 2532
ἐξ ἔργων νόμου, ἐὰν μὴ διὰ πίστεως Ἰησοῦ Χριστοῦ, καὶ
by works of law, except through faith of Jesus Christ, even

2249 1519 5547 2424 4100 2443 1344 1537
ἡμεῖς εἰς Χριστὸν Ἰησοῦν ἐπιστεύσαμεν, ἵνα δικαιωθῶμεν ἐκ
we in Christ Jesus believed, that we may be justified by

4102 5547 2532 3756 1537 2041 3551 1360 3756 1344
πίστεως Χριστοῦ, καὶ οὐκ ἐξ ἔργων νόμου· διότι οὐ δικαιωθή-
faith of Christ, and not of works of law; because not will be justi-

1537 2041 3551 3956 4561 1487 1161 2212 1344
σεται ἐξ ἔργων νόμου πᾶσα σάρξ. 17 εἰ δέ, ζητοῦντες δικαιωθῆ-
fied by works of law all flesh. if But, seeking to be justified

1722 5547 2147 2532 846 268 687
ναι ἐν Χριστῷ, εὑρέθημεν καὶ αὐτοὶ ἁμαρτωλοί, ἆρα
in Christ, we were found also ourselves sinners, then

5547 266 1249 3361 1096 1487/1063/3739 2647
Χριστὸς ἁμαρτίας διάκονος; μὴ γένοιτο. 18 εἰ γὰρ ἃ κατέλυσα,
(is) Christ of sin a minister? Not let it be! if For what I destroyed,

---

they gave to me and Barnabas the right hands of fellowship; that we (should go) unto the heathen, and they unto the circumcision.

10 Only (they would) that we should remember the poor; the same which I also was forward to do.

11 But when Peter was come to Antioch, I withstood him to the face, because he was to be blamed.
12 For before that certain came from James, he did eat with the Gentiles: but when they were come, he withdrew and separated himself, fearing them which were of the circumcision.
13 And the other Jews dissembled likewise with him; insomuch that Barnabas also was carried away with their dissimulation.
14 But when I saw that they walked not uprightly according to the truth of the gospel, I said unto Peter before (them) all, If thou, being a Jew, livest after the manner of Gentiles, and not as do the Jews, why compellest thou the Gentiles to live as do the Jews?
15 We (who are) Jews by nature, and not sinners of the Gentiles,
16 Knowing that a man is not justified by the works of the law, but by the faith of Jesus Christ, even we have believed in Jesus Christ, that we might be justified by the faith of Christ, and not by the works of the law: for by the works of the law shall no flesh be justified.

17 But if, while we seek to be justified by Christ, we ourselves also are found sinners, (is) therefore Christ the minister of sin? God forbid.
18 For if I

Literal Translation

build again these things which I destroyed, I confirm myself (as) a transgressor.
19 For through law I died to law, that I might live to God.
20 I have been crucified with Christ, and I live; (yet) no longer I, but Christ lives in me. And the (life) I now live in the flesh, I live by faith toward the Son of God, the (One) loving me and giving Himself over on my behalf.
21 I do not set aside the grace of God; for if righteousness (is) through law, then Christ died without cause.

Galatians 2:19

5023 3825 3618 3848 1683 4921 1473
ταῦτα πάλιν οἰκοδομῶ, παραβάτην ἐμαυτὸν συνίστημι. 19 ἐγὼ
these things again I build, a transgressor myself I establish. I
1063 1223 3551 3551 599 2443 2316 2198 5547
γὰρ διὰ νόμου νόμῳ ἀπέθανον, ἵνα Θεῷ ζήσω. Χριστῷ
For through law to law died, that to God I might live. With Christ
4957 2198 1161 3765 1473 2198 1161 1722 1698 5547
συνεσταύρωμαι· 20 ζῶ δὲ, οὐκέτι ἐγώ, ζῇ δὲ ἐν ἐμοὶ Χριστός·
I have been crucified; I live and, no longer I, lives but in me Christ;
3739 1161 3568 2198 1722 4561 1722 4102 2198 3588 3588 5207 3588 2316
ὃ δὲ νῦν ζῶ ἐν σαρκί, ἐν πίστει ζῶ τῇ τοῦ υἱοῦ τοῦ Θεοῦ,
what and now I live in flesh, in faith I live to the Son of God,
3588 25 3165 2532 3860 1438 5228 1700 3756
τοῦ ἀγαπήσαντός με καὶ παραδόντος ἑαυτὸν ὑπὲρ ἐμοῦ. 21 οὐκ
the (One) loving me and giving over Himself on behalf of me. not
114 3588 5485 3588 2316 1487 1063 1223 3551 1343
ἀθετῶ τὴν χάριν τοῦ Θεοῦ· εἰ γὰρ διὰ νόμου δικαιοσύνη,
I set aside the grace of God; if for through law righteousness,
686 5547 1432 599
ἄρα Χριστὸς δωρεὰν ἀπέθανεν.
then Christ without cause died.

King James Version

build again the things which I destroyed, I make myself a transgressor.
19 For I through the law am dead to the law, that I might live unto God.
20 I am crucified with Christ: nevertheless I live; yet not I, but Christ liveth in me: and the life which I now live in the flesh I live by the faith of the Son of God, who loved me, and gave himself for me.
21 I do not frustrate the grace of God: for if righteousness (come) by the law, then Christ is dead in vain.

Galatians 3

1. O foolish Galatians, who bewitched you not to obey the truth, to whom before (your) eyes Jesus Christ was publicly portrayed among you crucified?
2 This only I desire to learn from you: Did you receive the Spirit by works of law or by hearing of faith?
3 Are you so foolish? Having begun in (the) Spirit, do you now perfect (yourself) in the flesh?
4 Did you suffer so much vainly, if indeed (it) also (was) vainly?
5 Then He supplying the Spirit to you and working works of power in you, (is it) by works of law, or by hearing of faith?
6 Even as Abraham believed God, and it was counted to him for righteousness.
7 Know, then, that those of faith, these are sons of Abraham.
8 And the Scripture foreseeing that God would justify the nations by faith, preached the gospel before to Abraham: "All the nations will be blessed in you." (Gen.12:3)
9 So that those of faith are blessed with

Galatians 3

5599 453 1052 5101 5209 940 3588 225 3361
1. Ὦ ἀνόητοι Γαλάται, τίς ὑμᾶς ἐβάσκανε τῇ ἀληθείᾳ μὴ
O foolish Galatians, who you bewitched the truth not
3982 3739 2596 3788 2424 5547 4270
πείθεσθαι, οἷς κατ' ὀφθαλμοὺς Ἰησοῦς Χριστὸς προεγράφη
to obey, to whom before the eyes of Jesus Christ was written afore
1722 5213 4717 5124 3440 2309 3129 575 5216
ἐν ὑμῖν ἐσταυρωμένος; 2 τοῦτο μόνον θέλω μαθεῖν ἀφ' ὑμῶν,
among you crucified? This only I desire to learn from you,
1537 2041 3551 3588 4151 2983 2228 1537 189 4102
ἐξ ἔργων νόμου τὸ Πνεῦμα ἐλάβετε, ἢ ἐξ ἀκοῆς πίστεως;
by works of law the Spirit did you receive, or by hearing of faith?
3779 453 2075 1728 4151 3568 4561
3 οὕτως ἀνόητοί ἐστε; ἐναρξάμενοι Πνεύματι, νῦν σαρκὶ
so foolish Are you? having begun in (the) Spirit, now (in) flesh
2005 5118 3958 1500 -1489- 2532 1500 3588 3767
ἐπιτελεῖσθε; 4 τοσαῦτα ἐπάθετε εἰκῇ; εἴ γε καὶ εἰκῇ. 5 ὁ οὖν
do you perfect? So much suffered you vainly? If indeed even vainly. He then
2023 5213 3588 4151 2532 1754 1411 1722 5213
ἐπιχορηγῶν ὑμῖν τὸ Πνεῦμα καὶ ἐνεργῶν δυνάμεις ἐν ὑμῖν,
supplying to you the Spirit and working works of power in you,
1537 2041 3551 2228 1537 189 4102 2531 11
ἐξ ἔργων νόμου, ἢ ἐξ ἀκοῆς πίστεως; 6 καθὼς Ἀβραὰμ ἐπί-
by works of law, or by hearing of faith? Even as Abraham
4100 3588 2316 2532 3049 846 1519 1343 1097
στευσε τῷ Θεῷ, καὶ ἐλογίσθη αὐτῷ εἰς δικαιοσύνην. 7 γινώ-
believed God, and it was counted to him for righteousness. Know
686 3754 3588 1537 4102 3778 1526 5207 11
σκετε ἄρα ὅτι οἱ ἐκ πίστεως, οὗτοί εἰσιν υἱοὶ Ἀβραάμ.
then that those of faith, these are sons of Abraham.
4275 1161 3588 1124 3754 1537 4102 1344 3588 1484 3588
8 προϊδοῦσα δὲ ἡ γραφὴ ὅτι ἐκ πίστεως δικαιοῖ τὰ ἔθνη ὁ
foreseeing And the Scripture that by faith would justify the nations
2316 4283 3588 11 3754 2127
Θεός, προευηγγελίσατο τῷ Ἀβραὰμ ὅτι Εὐλογηθήσονται
God, preached the gospel before to Abraham that will be blessed
1722 4671 3956 3588 1484 5620 3588 1537 4102 2127 4862
ἐν σοὶ πάντα τὰ ἔθνη. 9 ὥστε οἱ ἐκ πίστεως εὐλογοῦνται σὺν
in you all the nations. So as those of faith are blessed with

Galatians 3

1. O foolish Galatians, who hath bewitched you, that ye should not obey the truth, before whose eyes Jesus Christ hath been evidently set forth, crucified among you?
2 This only would I learn of you, Received ye the Spirit by the works of the law, or by the hearing of faith?
3 Are ye so foolish? having begun in the Spirit, are ye now made perfect by the flesh?
4 Have ye suffered so many things in vain? if (it be) yet in vain.
5 He therefore that ministereth to you the Spirit, and worketh miracles among you, (doeth he it) by the works of the law, or by the hearing of faith?
6 Even as Abraham believed God, and it was accounted to him for righteousness.
7 Know ye therefore that they which are of faith, the same are the children of Abraham.
8 And the scripture, foreseeing that God would justify the heathen through faith, preached before the gospel unto Abraham, (saying), In thee shall all nations be blessed.
9 So then they which be of faith are blessed with

Literal Translation **Galatians 3:10** ***King James Version***

the faithful Abraham.
10 For as many as are out of works of law, (these) are under a curse. For it has been written, "Cursed (is) everyone who does not continue in all the things having been written in the book of the Law, to do them." (Deut. 27:26)
11 And that no one is justified by law before God (is) clear because, "The just shall live by faith." (Hab. 2:4)
12 But the Law is not of faith, but, "The man doing these things shall live in them." (Lev. 18:5)
13 Christ redeemed us from the curse of the law, having become a curse for us; for it has been written, "Cursed (is) everyone having been hung on a tree;" (Deut. 21:23)
14 that the blessing of Abraham might be to the nations in Christ Jesus, that we might receive the promise of the Spirit through faith.

3588 4103 11 3745 1063 1537 2041 3551 1526 5259
τῷ πιστῷ 'Αβραάμ. 10 ὅσοι γὰρ ἐξ ἔργων νόμου εἰσίν, ὑπὸ
the faithful Abraham. as many as For out of works of law are, under

2671 1526 1125 1063 1944 3956 3739 3756
κατάραν εἰσί· γέγραπται γάρ, 'Επικατάρατος πᾶς ὃς οὐκ
a curse are; it has been written for, Cursed (is) everyone who not

1696 1722 3956 3588 1125 1722 3588 975 3588 3551
ἐμμένει ἐν πᾶσι τοῖς γεγραμμένοις ἐν τῷ βιβλίῳ τοῦ νόμου,
continues in all the things having been written in the roll of the law,

3588 4160 846 3754 1161 1722 3551 3762 1344 3844
τοῦ ποιῆσαι αὐτά. 11 ὅτι δὲ ἐν νόμῳ οὐδεὶς δικαιοῦται παρὰ
to do them. that And by law no one is justified before

3588 2316 1212 3754 3588 1342 1537 4102 2198 3588 1161
τῷ Θεῷ, δῆλον· ὅτι 'Ο δίκαιος ἐκ πίστεως ζήσεται· 12 ὁ δὲ
God, (is) clear; because, The just one by faith will live; the and

3551 3756 2076 1537 4102 235 3588 4160 846 444
νόμος οὐκ ἔστιν ἐκ πίστεως, ἀλλ' 'Ο ποιήσας αὐτὰ ἄνθρωπος
law not is of faith, but, The having done these things man

2198 1722 846 5547 2248 1805 1537 3588
ζήσεται ἐν αὐτοῖς. 13 Χριστὸς ἡμᾶς ἐξηγόρασεν ἐκ τῆς
shall live in them. Christ us redeemed out of the

2671 3588 3551 1096 5228 2257 2671 1125
κατάρας τοῦ νόμου, γενόμενος ὑπὲρ ἡμῶν κατάρα· γέγραπται
curse of the law, having become for us a curse; it has been written

1063 1944 3956 3588 2910 1909 3586 2443 1519 3588
γάρ, 'Επικατάρατος πᾶς ὁ κρεμάμενος ἐπὶ ξύλου· 14 ἵνα εἰς τὰ
for, Cursed (is) everyone who has been hung on a tree; that to the

1484 3588 2129 3588 11 1096 1722 5547 2424 2443 3588
ἔθνη ἡ εὐλογία τοῦ 'Αβραὰμ γένηται ἐν Χριστῷ 'Ιησοῦ, ἵνα τὴν
nations the blessing of Abraham might be in Christ Jesus, that the

1860 3588 4151 2983 1223 3588 4102
ἐπαγγελίαν τοῦ Πνεύματος λάβωμεν διὰ τῆς πίστεως.
promise of the Spirit we might receive through the faith.

faithful Abraham.
10 For as many as are of the works of the law are under the curse: for it is written, Cursed (is) every one that continueth not in all things which are written in the book of the law to do them.
11 But that no man is justified by the law in the sight of God, (it is) evident: for, The just shall live by faith.
12 And the law is not of faith: but, The man that doeth them shall live in them.
13 Christ hath redeemed us from the curse of the law, being made a curse for us: for it is written, Cursed (is) every one that hangeth on a tree:
14 That the blessing of Abraham might come on the Gentiles through Jesus Christ; that we might receive the promise of the Spirit through faith.

15 Brothers, I speak according to man, a covenant having been ratified, even (among) mankind, no one sets aside or adds to (it).
16 But the promises were spoken to Abraham and to his Seed (it does not say, And to seeds, as of many, but as of one, "And to your Seed," which is Christ). (Gen. 12:7, 13, 15; 24:7)
17 And I say this, A covenant having been ratified before to Christ by God, (the) Law coming into being four hundred and thirty years after, does not annul the promise, so as to abolish (it).
18 For if the inheritance (is) of law, (it is) no more of promise; but God has given (it) to Abraham through promise.
19 Why the Law then? It was added because of transgressions,

80 2596 444 3004 3676 444 2964
15. 'Αδελφοί, κατὰ ἄνθρωπον λέγω· ὅμως ἀνθρώπου κεκυρω-
Brothers, according to man I say; even of man having been

1242 3762 114 2228 1928 3588 1161
μένην διαθήκην οὐδεὶς ἀθετεῖ ἢ ἐπιδιατάσσεται. 16 τῷ δὲ
ratified a covenant no one sets aside or adds to (it). And

11 4483 3588 1860 2532 3588 4690 846
'Αβραὰμ ἐρρήθησαν αἱ ἐπαγγελίαι, καὶ τῷ σπέρματι αὐτοῦ.
to Abraham were spoken the promises, and to the Seed of him.

3756 3004 2532 3588 4690 5613 1909 4183 235 5613 1909
οὐ λέγει, Καὶ τοῖς σπέρμασιν, ὡς ἐπὶ πολλῶν, ἀλλ' ὡς ἐφ'
Not it says, And to the seeds, as upon many, but as upon

1520 2532 3588 4690 4675 3739 2076 5547 5124 1161 3004
ἑνός, Καὶ τῷ σπέρματί σου, ὅς ἐστι Χριστός. 17 τοῦτο δὲ λέγω,
One, And to the Seed of you, who is Christ. this And I say,

1242 4300 5259 3588 2316 1519 5547 3588 3326
διαθήκην προκεκυρωμένην ὑπὸ τοῦ Θεοῦ εἰς Χριστὸν ὁ μετὰ
A covenant having been ratified before by God to Christ the after

2094 5071 2532 5144 1096 3551 3756 208 1519
ἔτη τετρακόσια καὶ τριάκοντα γεγονὼς νόμος οὐκ ἀκυροῖ, εἰς
years four hundred and thirty coming into being Law not annuls, so

3588 2673 3588 1860 1487 1063 1537 3551 3588 2817
τὸ καταργῆσαι τὴν ἐπαγγελίαν. 18 εἰ γὰρ ἐκ νόμου ἡ κληρονο-
as to abolish the promise. if For of law the inheritance

3765 1537 1860 3588 1161 11 1223 1860
μία, οὐκέτι ἐξ ἐπαγγελίας· τῷ δὲ 'Αβραὰμ δι' ἐπαγγελίας
(is), no more (is it) of promise; but to Abraham through promise

5483 3588 2316 5101 3767 3588 3551 3588 3847 5484
κεχάρισται ὁ Θεός. 19 τί οὖν ὁ νόμος; τῶν παραβάσεων χάριν
has given (it) God. Why then the Law? the transgressions For the sake of

15 Brethren, I speak after the manner of men; Though (it be) but a man's covenant, yet (if it be) confirmed, no man disannulleth, or addeth thereto.
16 Now to Abraham and his seed were the promises made. He saith not, And to seeds, as of many; but as of one, And to thy seed, which is Christ.
17 And this I say, (that) the covenant, that was confirmed before of God in Christ, the law, which was four hundred and thirty years after, cannot disannul, that it should make the promise of none effect.
18 For if the inheritance (be) of the law, (it is) no more of promise: but God gave (it) to Abraham by promise.
19 Wherefore then (serveth) the law? It was added because of transgressions,

Literal Translation | **Galatians 3:20** | ***King James Version***

Literal Translation

until the Seed should have come, to whom it had been promised, being ordained through angels in a mediator's hand.
20 But the Mediator is not of one, but God is one.
21 Then is the Law against the promises of God? Let it not be! For if a law had been given which had been able to make alive, indeed righteousness would have been out of law.
22 But the Scripture locked up all under sin, that the promise by faith of Jesus Christ might be given to the ones believing.

23 But before the coming of faith, we were guarded under law, having been locked up to the faith being about to be revealed.

24 So that the Law has become a trainer of us (until) Christ, that we might be justified by faith.
25 But faith having come, we are no longer under a trainer.
26 For you are all sons of God through faith in Christ Jesus.
27 For as many as were baptized into Christ, you put on Christ.
28 There is not Jew nor Greek, there is no slave nor freeman, there is no male and female; for you are all one in Christ Jesus.

29 And if you (are) of Christ, then you are a seed of Abraham, even heirs according to promise.

4369 891 3757 2064 3588 4690 3739 1861 1299
προσετέθη, ἄχρις οὗ ἔλθῃ τὸ σπέρμα ᾧ ἐπήγγελται, διατα-
it was added, until should have come the Seed to whom it has been made, having

1223 32 1722 5495 3316 3588 1161 3316 1520 3756
γεὶς δι' ἀγγέλων ἐν χειρὶ μεσίτου. 20 ὁ δὲ μεσίτης ἑνὸς οὐκ
been ordained through angels in hand a mediator's. the But mediator of one not

2076 3588 1161 2316 1520 2076 3588 3767 3551 2596 3588 1860
ἔστιν, ὁ δὲ Θεὸς εἷς ἐστίν. 21 ὁ οὖν νόμος κατὰ τῶν ἐπαγγελιῶν
is, but God one is. the Then Law against the promises

3588 2316 3361 1096 1487 1063 1325 3551 3588 1410
τοῦ Θεοῦ; μὴ γένοιτο. εἰ γὰρ ἐδόθη νόμος ὁ δυνάμενος
of God (is)? Not let it be! if For has been given a law which was able

2227 3689 302 1537 3551 2258 3588 1343 235
ζωοποιῆσαι, ὄντως ἂν ἐκ νόμου ἦν ἡ δικαιοσύνη. 22 ἀλλὰ
to make alive, indeed would out of law been the righteousness. But

4788 3588 1124 3588 3956 5259 266 2443/3588
συνέκλεισεν ἡ γραφὴ τὰ πάντα ὑπὸ ἁμαρτίαν, ἵνα ἡ
locked up the Scriptures all under sin, that the

1860 1537 4102 2424 5547 1325 3588 4100
ἐπαγγελία ἐκ πίστεως Ἰησοῦ Χριστοῦ δοθῇ τοῖς πιστεύουσι.
promise by faith of Jesus Christ might be given to those believing.

4253 3588 1161 2064 3588 4102 5259 3551 5432
23 Πρὸ τοῦ δὲ ἐλθεῖν τὴν πίστιν, ὑπὸ νόμον ἐφρουρούμεθα,
before the But coming of faith, under law we were guarded,

4788 1519 3588 3195 4102 601
συγκεκλεισμένοι εἰς τὴν μέλλουσαν πίστιν ἀποκαλυφθῆναι.
having been locked up to the being about faith to be revealed.

5620 3588 3551 3807 2257 1096 1519 5547 2443
24 ὥστε ὁ νόμος παιδαγωγὸς ἡμῶν γέγονεν εἰς Χριστόν, ἵνα
So as the law a trainer of us has become (until) Christ, that

1537 4102 1344 2064 1161 3588 4102 3765
ἐκ πίστεως δικαιωθῶμεν. 25 ἐλθούσης δὲ τῆς πίστεως, οὐκέτι
by faith we might be justified. having come But faith, no more

5259 3807 2070 3956 1063 5207 2316 2075 1223 3588
ὑπὸ παιδαγωγόν ἐσμεν. 26 πάντες γὰρ υἱοὶ Θεοῦ ἐστε διὰ τῆς
under a trainer we are. all For sons of God you are through

4102 1722 5547 2424 3745 1063 1519 5547 907
πίστεως ἐν Χριστῷ Ἰησοῦ. 27 ὅσοι γὰρ εἰς Χριστὸν ἐβαπτί-
faith in Christ Jesus. as many as For into Christ were

5547 1746 3756 1762 2453 3761 1672
σθητε, Χριστὸν ἐνεδύσασθε. 28 οὐκ ἔνι Ἰουδαῖος οὐδὲ Ἕλλην,
baptized, Christ you put on. not There is Jew nor Greek,

3756 1762 1401 3761 1658 3756 1762 730 2532 2338 3956
οὐκ ἔνι δοῦλος οὐδὲ ἐλεύθερος, οὐκ ἔνι ἄρσεν καὶ θῆλυ· πάντες
not there is slave nor freeman, not there is male and female; all

1063 5210 1519 2075 1722 5547 2424 1487 1161 5210 5547
γὰρ ὑμεῖς εἷς ἐστε ἐν Χριστῷ Ἰησοῦ. 29 εἰ δὲ ὑμεῖς Χριστοῦ,
for you one are in Christ Jesus. if And you (are) of Christ,

686 3588 11 4690 2075 2532 2596 1860 2818
ἄρα τοῦ Ἀβραὰμ σπέρμα ἐστέ, καὶ κατ' ἐπαγγελίαν κληρονό-
then of Abraham a seed you are, even according to promise heirs.

μοι.

King James Version

till the seed should come to whom the promise was made; (and it was) ordained by angels in the hand of a mediator.
20 Now a mediator is not (a mediator) of one, but God is one.
21 (Is) the law then against the promises of God? God forbid: for if there had been a law given which could have given life, verily righteousness should have been by the law.
22 But the scripture hath concluded all under sin, that the promise by faith of Jesus Christ might be given to them that believe.

23 But before faith came, we were kept under the law, shut up unto the faith which should afterwards be revealed.

24 Wherefore the law was our schoolmaster (to bring us) unto Christ, that we might be justified by faith.
25 But after that faith is come, we are no longer under a schoolmaster.
26 For ye are all the children of God by faith in Christ Jesus.
27 For as many of you as have been baptized into Christ have put on Christ.
28 There is neither Jew nor Greek, there is neither bond nor free, there is neither male nor female: for ye are all one in Christ Jesus.
29 And if ye (be) Christ's, then are ye Abraham's seed, and heirs according to the promise.

Galatians 4

Literal Translation

1. But I say, Over so long a time the heir is an infant, he being lord of all does not differ from a slave,
2 but is under

3004 1161 1909 3745 5550 3588 2818 3516 2076
1. Λέγω δέ, ἐφ' ὅσον χρόνον ὁ κληρονόμος νήπιός ἐστιν,
I say But, over so long a time the heir an infant is,

3762 1308 1401 2962 3956 5607 235 5259
οὐδὲν διαφέρει δούλου, κύριος πάντων ὤν· 2 ἀλλὰ ὑπὸ
nothing he differs (from) a slave, lord of all being; but under

King James Version

1. Now I say, (That) the heir, as long as he is a child, differeth nothing from a servant, though he be lord of all;
2 But is under

Literal Translation

Galatians 4:3

guardians and house-
masters until the (term)
set before by the father.

3 So we also, when we
were infants, we were
under the elements of
the world, being en-
slaved.
4 But when the fullness
of the time came, God
sent forth His Son, hav-
ing become out of a
woman, having come
under Law,
5 that He might redeem
the ones under law, that
we might receive the
adoption of sons.
6 And because you are
sons, God sent forth the
Spirit of His Son into
your hearts, crying,
Abba! Father!

7 So that you no more
are a slave, but a son,
and if a son, also an heir
of God through Christ.

8 But then, indeed, not
knowing God, you
served as slaves (to) the
(ones) not by nature be-
ing gods.
9 But now, knowing
God, but rather being
known by God, how do
you turn again to the
weak and poor ele-
ments to which you de-
sire again to slave
anew?
10 You observe days
and months and sea-
sons and years.

11 I fear (for) you, lest
somehow I have la-
bored among you in
vain.
12 Brothers, I beg of
you, be as I (am), be-
cause I (am) as you. You
wronged me (in) noth-
ing.
13 But you know that
because of weakness of
the flesh, I preached the
gospel to you before;
14 and you did not de-
spise my temptation in
my flesh nor disdained
(it), but you received
me as an angel of God,
as Christ Jesus.

2012 2076 2532 3623 891 3588 4287 3588
ἐπιτρόπους ἐστὶ καὶ οἰκονόμους, ἄχρι τῆς προθεσμίας τοῦ
guardians is and housemasters, until the (term) set before by the

3962 3779 2532 2249 3753 2258 3516 5259 3588 4747
πατρός. 3 οὕτω καὶ ἡμεῖς, ὅτε ἦμεν νήπιοι, ὑπὸ τὰ στοιχεῖα
father. So also we, when we were infants, under the elements

3588 2889 2258 1402 3753 1161 2064 3588 4138
τοῦ κόσμου ἦμεν δεδουλωμένοι· 4 ὅτε δὲ ἦλθε τὸ πλήρωμα
of the world we were having been enslaved. when But came the fullness

3588 5550 1821 3588 2316 3588 5207 846 1096
τοῦ χρόνου, ἐξαπέστειλεν ὁ Θεὸς τὸν υἱὸν αὐτοῦ, γενό-
of the time, sent forth God the Son of Him, having

1537 1135 1096 5259 3551 2443 3588 5259
μενον ἐκ γυναικός, γενόμενον ὑπὸ νόμον, 5 ἵνα τοὺς ὑπὸ
become of a woman, having become under law, that those under

3551 1805 2443 3588 5206 618 3754 1161
νόμον ἐξαγοράσῃ, ἵνα τὴν υἱοθεσίαν ἀπολάβωμεν. 6 ὅτι δέ
law He might redeem, that the adoption of sons we may receive. because And

2075 5207 1821 3588 2316 3588 4151 3588 5207 846
ἐστε υἱοί, ἐξαπέστειλεν ὁ Θεὸς τὸ Πνεῦμα τοῦ υἱοῦ αὐτοῦ
you are sons, sent forth God the Spirit of the Son of Him

1519 3588 2588 5216 2896 5 3588 3962 5620 3765
εἰς τὰς καρδίας ὑμῶν, κρᾶζον, Ἀββᾶ, ὁ πατήρ. 7 ὥστε οὐκέτι
into the hearts of you, crying, Abba, Father! So as no more

1488 1401 235 5207 1487 1161 5207 2532 2818 2316 1223
εἶ δοῦλος, ἀλλ' υἱός· εἰ δὲ υἱός, καὶ κληρονόμος Θεοῦ διὰ
are you a slave, but a son; if and a son, also an heir of God through

5547
Χριστοῦ.
Christ.

235 5119 3303 3756 1492 2316 1398 3588 3361
8. Ἀλλὰ τότε μέν, οὐκ εἰδότες Θεόν, ἐδουλεύσατε τοῖς μὴ
But then indeed, not knowing God, you served as slaves those not

5449 5607 2316 3568 1161 1097 2316 3123 1161 1097
φύσει οὖσι θεοῖς· 9 νῦν δέ, γνόντες Θεόν, μᾶλλον δὲ γνωσθέντες
by nature being gods; now but, knowing God, rather but being known

5259 2316 4459 1994 3825 1909 3588 772 2532
ὑπὸ Θεοῦ, πῶς ἐπιστρέφετε πάλιν ἐπὶ τὰ ἀσθενῆ καὶ
by God, how do you turn again upon the weak and

4434 4747 3739 3825 509 1398 2309 2250
πτωχὰ στοιχεῖα, οἷς πάλιν ἄνωθεν δουλεύειν θέλετε; 10 ἡμέρας
poor elements, which again anew to enslave you desire? days

3906 2532 3376 2532 2540 2532 1763
παρατηρεῖσθε, καὶ μῆνας, καὶ καιρούς, καὶ ἐνιαυτούς.
You observe, and months, and seasons, and years.

5399 5209 3361 3381 1500 2872 1519 5209
11 φοβοῦμαι ὑμᾶς, μή πως εἰκῇ κεκοπίακα εἰς ὑμᾶς.
I fear (for) you, lest somehow in vain I have labored among you.

1096 5613 1473 3754 2504 5613 5210 80 1189 5216
12. Γίνεσθε ὡς ἐγώ, ὅτι κἀγὼ ὡς ὑμεῖς, ἀδελφοί, δέομαι ὑμῶν.
Be as I, because I also as you, brothers, I beg of you.

3762 3165 91 1492 1161 3754 1223 769 3588 4561
οὐδέν με ἠδικήσατε· 13 οἴδατε δὲ ὅτι δι' ἀσθένειαν τῆς σαρκὸς
Nothing me you wronged; you know and that because weakness of the flesh

2097 5213 3588 4386 2532 3588 3986 3450
εὐηγγελισάμην ὑμῖν τὸ πρότερον. 14 καὶ τὸν πειρασμόν μου
I preached the gospel to you before. And the temptation of me

3588 1722 3588 4561 3450 3756 1848 3761 1609
τὸν ἐν τῇ σαρκί μου οὐκ ἐξουθενήσατε οὐδὲ ἐξεπτύσατε,
in the flesh of me not you despised nor disdained,

235 5613 32 2316 1209 3165 5613 5547 2424
ἀλλ' ὡς ἄγγελον Θεοῦ ἐδέξασθέ με, ὡς Χριστὸν Ἰησοῦν.
but as an angel of God you received me, as Christ Jesus.

King James Version

tutors and governors
until the time appointed
of the father.

3 *Even* so we, when we
were children, were in
bondage under the ele-
ments of the world:
4 But when the fulness
of the time was come,
God sent forth his Son,
made of a woman,
made under the law,

5 To redeem them that
were under the law, that
we might receive the
adoption of sons.
6 And because ye are
sons, God hath sent
forth the Spirit of his
Son into your hearts,
crying, Abba, Father.

7 Wherefore thou art no
more a servant, but a
son; and if a son, then an
heir of God through
Christ.

8 Howbeit then, when
ye knew not God, ye did
service unto them
which by nature are no
gods.
9 But now, after that ye
have known God, or
rather are known of
God, how turn ye again
to the weak and beg-
garly elements, where-
unto ye desire again to
be in bondage?
10 Ye observe days, and
months, and times, and
years.

11 I am afraid of you,
lest I have bestowed
upon you labour in vain.
12. Brethren, I beseech
you, be as I (am); for I
(am) as ye (are): ye have
not injured me at all.
13 Ye know how
through infirmity of the
flesh I preached the
gospel unto you at the
first.
14 And my temptation
which was in my flesh
ye despised not, nor re-
jected; but received me
as an angel of God,
(even) as Christ Jesus.

Literal Translation

Galatians 4:15

King James Version

15 What then was your
blessedness? For I tes-
tify to you that if you
were able, plucking out
your eyes, (you) would
have given (them) to
me.
16 So then did I become
your enemy speaking
truth to you?
17 They are zealous for
you, (but) not well; but
they (only) desire to
shut you out, that you be
zealous to them.
18 But (it is) good to be
zealous always in (a)
good thing and not only
in my being present
with you.
19 My children, (for)
whom I again travail
until Christ should be
formed to you,
20 even now I desired to
be present with you and
to change my voice, for
I am in doubt (as) to
you.

21 Tell me, those desir-
ing to be under Law, do
you not hear the Law?
22 For it has been writ-
ten, Abraham had two
sons, one out of the
slave woman and one
out of the free woman.
23 But, indeed, he of the
slave woman has been
born according to flesh,
and he out of the free
woman through the
promise,
24 which things are be-
ing allegorized, for
these are two cove-
nants, one, indeed, from
Mount Sinai bringing
forth to slavery (which
is Hagar,
25 for Hagar is Mount
Sinai in Arabia and cor-
responds to the present
Jerusalem, and she
slaves with her chil-
dren),
26 but the Jerusalem
(from) above is free,
who is the mother of us
all;
27 for it has been writ-
ten, "Be glad, barren
(one) not bearing; break
forth and shout, the
(one) not travailing; for
more (are) the children
of the desolate rather
than she having the

5101 3767 2258 3588 3108 5216 3140 1063 5213/3754/1487
15 τίς οὖν ἦν ὁ μακαρισμὸς ὑμῶν; μαρτυρῶ γὰρ ὑμῖν ὅτι, εἰ
What then was the blessedness of you? I witness For to you that, if
1415 3588 3788 5216 1846 302 1325 3427
δυνατὸν, τοὺς ὀφθαλμοὺς ὑμῶν ἐξορύξαντες ἂν ἐδώκατέ μοι.
you were able, the eyes of you plucking out would have given to me.
5620 2190 5216 1096 226 5213 2206 5209
16 ὥστε ἐχθρὸς ὑμῶν γέγονα ἀληθεύων ὑμῖν; 17 ζηλοῦσιν ὑμᾶς
So then an enemy of you became I speaking truth to you? They are zealous for you
3756 2573 235 1576 5209 2309 2443 846 2206
οὐ καλῶς, ἀλλὰ ἐκκλεῖσαι ὑμᾶς θέλουσιν, ἵνα αὐτοὺς ζηλοῦτε.
not well, but to shut out you they desire, that to them you be zealous.
2570 1161/3588 2206 1722 2570 3842 2532 3361 3440
18 καλὸν δὲ τὸ ζηλοῦσθαι ἐν καλῷ πάντοτε, καὶ μὴ μόνον
(it is) good But to be zealous in a good thing always, and not only
1722 3588 3918 3165 4314 5209 5040 3450 3739 3825 5605
ἐν τῷ παρεῖναί με πρὸς ὑμᾶς. 19 τεκνία μου, οὓς πάλιν ὠδίνω,
in being present me with you, children of me, (for) whom again I travail,
891 3757 3445 5547 1722 5213 2309 1161 3918 4314
ἄχρις οὗ μορφωθῇ Χριστὸς ἐν ὑμῖν, 20 ἤθελον δὲ παρεῖναι πρὸς
until should be formed Christ in you, I desired and to be present with
5209 737 2532 236 3588 5456 3450 3754 639 1722
ὑμᾶς ἄρτι, καὶ ἀλλάξαι τὴν φωνήν μου, ὅτι ἀποροῦμαι ἐν
you now, and to change the voice of me, because I am in doubt in
5213
ὑμῖν.
you.

3004 3427 3588 5259 3551 2309 1511 3588 3551 3756
21. Λέγετέ μοι, οἱ ὑπὸ νόμον θέλοντες εἶναι, τὸν νόμον οὐκ
Tell me, those under law desiring to be, the law not
191 1125 1063 3754 11 1417 5207 2192 1520
ἀκούετε; 22 γέγραπται γάρ, ὅτι Ἀβραὰμ δύο υἱοὺς ἔσχεν· ἕνα
you hear? It has been written For, Abraham two sons had; one
1537 3588 3814 2532 1520 1537 3588 1658 235/3588/3303/1537/3588
ἐκ τῆς παιδίσκης καὶ ἕνα ἐκ τῆς ἐλευθέρας. 23 ἀλλʼ ὁ μὲν ἐκ τῆς
out of the slave-woman and one out of the free woman. But he indeed of the
3814 2596 4561 1080 3588 1161 1537 3588 1658 1223
παιδίσκης κατὰ σάρκα γεγέννηται, ὁ δὲ ἐκ τῆς ἐλευθέρας διὰ
slave-woman according to flesh has been born, he and of the free woman by
3588 1860 3748 2076 238 3778 1063
τῆς ἐπαγγελίας. 24 ἅτινά ἐστιν ἀλληγορούμενα· αὗται γάρ
the promise. Which things is being allegorized; these for
1526 3588 1417 1242 3391 3303 575 3735 4614 1519 1397
εἰσιν αἱ δύο διαθῆκαι· μία μὲν ἀπὸ ὄρους Σινᾶ, εἰς δουλείαν
are two covenants; one indeed from Mount Sinai to slavery
1080 3748 2076 28 3588 1063 28 4614 3735 2076 1722
γεννῶσα, ἥτις ἐστὶν Ἄγαρ. 25 τὸ γὰρ Ἄγαρ Σινᾶ ὄρος ἐστὶν ἐν
generating, which is Hagar. the For Hagar Sinai Mount is in
3588 688 4960 1161 3588 3568 2419 1398 1161 3326
τῇ Ἀραβίᾳ, συστοιχεῖ δὲ τῇ νῦν Ἱερουσαλήμ, δουλεύει δὲ μετὰ
Arabia, corresponds and to the now Jerusalem, she slaves and with
3588 5043 846 3588 1161 507 2419 1658 2076
τῶν τέκνων αὐτῆς. 26 ἡ δὲ ἄνω Ἱερουσαλὴμ ἐλευθέρα ἐστίν,
the children of her. the But above Jerusalem free is,
3748 2076 3384 3956 2257 1125 1063 2165
ἥτις ἐστὶ μήτηρ πάντων ἡμῶν. 27 γέγραπται γάρ, Εὐφράνθητι
who is mother of all of us. it has been written For, Be glad
4723 3588 3756 5088 4486 2532 994 3588 3756 5605
στεῖρα ἡ οὐ τίκτουσα· ῥῆξον καὶ βόησον ἡ οὐκ ὠδίνουσα·
barren (one) not bearing; break forth and shout the (one) not travailing;
3754 4183 3588 5043 3588 2048 3123 2228 3588 2192 3588
ὅτι πολλὰ τὰ τέκνα τῆς ἐρήμου μᾶλλον ἢ τῆς ἐχούσης τὸν
because more the children of the desolate rather than she having the

15 Where is then the
blessedness ye spake
of? for I bear you re-
cord, that, if (it had
been) possible, ye
would have plucked out
your own eyes, and
have given them to me.
16 Am I therefore be-
come your enemy, be-
cause I tell you the
truth?
17 They zealously af-
fect you, (but) not well;
yea, they would ex-
clude you, that ye might
affect them.
18 But (it is) good to be
zealously affected al-
ways in (a) good
(thing), and not only
when I am present with
you.
19 My little children, of
whom I travail in birth
again until Christ be
formed in you,
20 I desire to be present
with you now, and to
change my voice; for I
stand in doubt of you.

21 Tell me, ye that de-
sire to be under the law,
do ye not hear the law?
22 For it is written, that
Abraham had two sons,
the one by a bondmaid,
the other by a free-
woman.
23 But he (who was) of
the bondwoman was
born after the flesh; but
he of the freewoman
(was) by promise.

24 Which things are an
allegory: for these are
the two covenants; the
one from the mount Si-
nai, which gendereth to
bondage, which is
Agar.
25 For this Agar is
mount Sinai in Arabia,
and answereth to Jeru-
salem which now is,
and is in bondage with
her children.

26 But Jerusalem which
is above is free, which is
the mother of us all.
27 For it is written, Re-
joice, (thou) barren that
bearest not; break forth
and cry, thou that tra-
vailest not: for the deso-
late hath many more
children than she which
hath an

Literal Translation

Galatians 4:28

husband." (Isa. 54:1)
28 But, brothers, we are children of promise according to Isaac.
29 But then, even as he born according to flesh persecuted the (one) according to Spirit, so also now.
30 But what says the Scripture? "Cast out the slave woman and her son, for in no way shall the son of the slave (woman) inherit with the son of the free." (Gen. 21:10)
31 Then, brothers, we are not children of a slave woman but of the free woman.

435 2249 1161 80 2596 2464 1860 5043
ἄνδρα. 28 ἡμεῖς δέ, ἀδελφοί, κατὰ Ἰσαὰκ, ἐπαγγελίας τέκνα
husband. we But, brothers, according to Isaac, of promise children

2070 235 5618 5119 3588 2596 4561 1080 1377 3588
ἐσμέν. 29 ἀλλ' ὥσπερ τότε ὁ κατὰ σάρκα γεννηθεὶς ἐδίωκε τὸν
we are. But even as then he according to flesh generated persecuted him

2596 4151 3779 2532 3568 235 5101 3004 3588 1124 1544
κατὰ Πνεῦμα, οὕτω καὶ νῦν. 30 ἀλλὰ τί λέγει ἡ γραφή; Ἔκβαλε
according to Spirit, so also now. But what says the Scripture? Cast out

3588 3814 2532 3588 5207 846 3756 1063 3361 2816
τὴν παιδίσκην καὶ τὸν υἱὸν αὐτῆς, οὐ γὰρ μὴ κληρονομήσῃ
the slave-woman and the son of her, not for at all shall inherit

3588 5207 3588 3814 3326 3588 5207 3588 1658 686
ὁ υἱὸς τῆς παιδίσκης μετὰ τοῦ υἱοῦ τῆς ἐλευθέρας. 31 ἄρα,
the son of the slave-woman with the son of the free woman. Then

80 3756 2070 3814 5043 235 3588 1658
ἀδελφοί, οὐκ ἐσμὲν παιδίσκης τέκνα, ἀλλὰ τῆς ἐλευθέρας.
brothers, not we are of a slave-woman children, but of the free woman.

King James Version

husband.
28 Now we, brethren, as Isaac was, are the children of promise.
29 But as then he that was born after the flesh persecuted him (that was born) after the Spirit, even so (it is) now.
30 Nevertheless what saith the scripture? Cast out the bondwoman and her son: for the son of the bondwoman shall not be heir with the son of the freewoman.
31 So then, brethren, we are not children of the bondwoman, but of the free.

Galatians 5

1. Then stand firm in the freedom with which Christ made us free and do not be held again with a yoke of slavery.
2 Behold! I, Paul, say to you that if you are circumcised, Christ will profit you nothing.
3 And I testify again to every man being circumcised, that he is a debtor to do all the Law,
4 you who are justified by law are loosed from from Christ, you fell from grace.
5 For we through (the) Spirit eagerly wait for (the) hope of righteousness out of faith.
6 For in Christ Jesus, neither circumcision nor uncircumcision has any strength, but faith working through love.
7 You were running well; who held you back (that) you do not obey the truth?
8 The persuasion (is) not from Him calling you.
9 A little leaven leavens all the lump.
10 I trust as to you in (the) Lord that you will think nothing else, but that the (one) troubling you shall bear the judgment, whoever he may be.
11 But I, brothers, if

3588 1657 3767 3739 5547 2248 1659 4739
1. τῇ ἐλευθερίᾳ οὖν ᾗ Χριστὸς ἡμᾶς ἠλευθέρωσε, στήκετε,
in the freedom Then with which Christ us made free, stand firm,

2532 3361 3825 2218 1397 1758
καὶ μὴ πάλιν ζυγῷ δουλείας ἐνέχεσθε.
and not again with a yoke of slavery be held.

2396 1473 3972 3004 5213 3754 1437 4059 5547
2. Ἴδε, ἐγὼ Παῦλος λέγω ὑμῖν, ὅτι ἐὰν περιτέμνησθε, Χριστὸς
Behold! I Paul say to you, that if you are circumcised, Christ

5209 3762 5623 3143 1161 3825 3956 444
ὑμᾶς οὐδὲν ὠφελήσει. 3 μαρτύρομαι δὲ πάλιν παντὶ ἀνθρώπῳ
you nothing will profit. I testify And again to every man

4059 3754 3781 2076 3650 3588 3551 4160
περιτεμνομένῳ, ὅτι ὀφειλέτης ἐστὶν ὅλον τὸν νόμον ποιῆσαι.
being circumcised, that a debtor he is all the law to do.

2673 575 3588 5547 3748 1722 3551 1344
4 κατηργήθητε ἀπὸ τοῦ Χριστοῦ, οἵτινες ἐν νόμῳ δικαιοῦ-
You were loosed from the Christ, whoever by law are justified;

3588 5485 1601 2249 1063 4151 1537 4102
σθε· τῆς χάριτος ἐξεπέσατε. 5 ἡμεῖς γὰρ Πνεύματι ἐκ πίστεως
grace you fell from. we For by (the) Spirit from faith

1680 1343 553 1722 1063 5547 2424
ἐλπίδα δικαιοσύνης ἀπεκδεχόμεθα. 6 ἐν γὰρ Χριστῷ Ἰησοῦ
(the) hope of righteousness eagerly await. in For Christ Jesus

3777 4061 5100 2480 3777 203 235 4102 1223
οὔτε περιτομή τι ἰσχύει, οὔτε ἀκροβυστία, ἀλλὰ πίστις δι'
neither circumcision any strength (has), nor uncircumcision, but faith through

26 1754 5143 2573 5101 5209 348 3588
ἀγάπης ἐνεργουμένη. 7 ἐτρέχετε καλῶς· τίς ὑμᾶς ἀνέκοψε τῇ
love working. You were running well; who you held back the

225 3361 3982 3588 3988 3756 1537 3588 2564
ἀληθείᾳ μὴ πείθεσθαι; 8 ἡ πεισμονὴ οὐκ ἐκ τοῦ καλοῦντος
truth not you obey? The persuasion (is) not from the (one) calling

5209 3398 2219 3650 3588 5445 2220 1473 3982 1519
ὑμᾶς. 9 μικρὰ ζύμη ὅλον τὸ φύραμα ζυμοῖ. 10 ἐγὼ πέποιθα εἰς
you. A little leaven all the lump leavens. I trust as to

5209 1722 2962 3754 3762 243 5426 3588 1161 5015
ὑμᾶς ἐν Κυρίῳ, ὅτι οὐδὲν ἄλλο φρονήσετε· ὁ δὲ ταράσσων
you in (the) Lord, that nothing other you will think; the (one) but troubling

5209 941 3588 2917 3748 302 5600 1473 1161 80 1487
ὑμᾶς βαστάσει τὸ κρίμα, ὅστις ἂν ᾖ. 11 ἐγὼ δέ, ἀδελφοί, εἰ
you shall hear the Judgment, whoever he may be. I But, brothers, if

Galatians 5

1.. Stand fast therefore in the liberty wherewith Christ hath made us free, and be not entangled again with the yoke of bondage.
2 Behold, I Paul say unto you, that if ye be circumcised, Christ shall profit you nothing.
3 For I testify again to every man that is circumcised, that he is a debtor to do the whole law.
4 Christ is become of no effect unto you, whosoever of you are justified by the law; ye are fallen from grace.
5 For we through the Spirit wait for the hope of righteousness by faith.
6 For in Jesus Christ neither circumcision availeth any thing, nor uncircumcision; but faith which worketh by love.
7. Ye did run well; who did hinder you that ye should not obey the truth?
8 This persuasion (cometh) not of him that calleth you.
9 A little leaven leaveneth the whole lump.
10 I have confidence in you through the Lord, that ye will be none otherwise minded: but he that troubleth you shall bear his judgment, whosoever he be.
11 And I, brethren, if

Literal Translation

I proclaim circumcision, why am I still persecuted? Then the offense of the Cross has passed away.
12 I would that the (ones) causing you to doubt will cut themselves off.

Galatians 5:12

4061 2089 2784 5101 2089 1377 686 2673
περιτομὴν ἔτι κηρύσσω, τί ἔτι διώκομαι; ἄρα κατήργηται
circumcision still proclaim, why yet am I persecuted? Then has passed away
3588 4625 3588 4716 3785 2532 609
τὸ σκάνδαλον τοῦ σταυροῦ. 12 ὄφελον καὶ ἀποκόψονται
the offense of the cross. Would that also will sever themselves
3588 387 5209
οἱ ἀναστατοῦντες ὑμᾶς.
those causing to doubt you.

King James Version

I yet preach circumcision, why do I yet suffer persecution? then is the offence of the cross ceased.
12 I would they were even cut off which trouble you.

---

13 For, brothers, you were called to freedom. Only do not (use) the freedom for (an) opening to the flesh. But through love serve one another.
14 For the whole law is fulfilled in one word, in (this): "You shall love your neighbor as yourself." (Lev.19:18)
15 But if you bite and devour one another, be careful that you are not consumed by one another.

5210 1063 1909 1657 2564 80 3440 3361 3588
13. Ὑμεῖς γὰρ ἐπ' ἐλευθερίᾳ ἐκλήθητε, ἀδελφοί· μόνον μὴ τὴν
you For for freedom were called, brothers; only not the
1657 1519 874 3588 4561 235 1223 3588 26
ἐλευθερίαν εἰς ἀφορμὴν τῇ σαρκί, ἀλλὰ διὰ τῆς ἀγάπης
freedom for gain to the flesh, but through love
1398 240 3588 1063 3956 3551 1722 1520 3056 4137
δουλεύετε ἀλλήλοις. 14 ὁ γὰρ πᾶς νόμος ἐν ἑνὶ λόγῳ πληροῦται,
slaves to one another. the For whole law in one word is fulfilled,
1722 3588 25 3588 4139 4675 5613 1438 1487/1161
ἐν τῷ, Ἀγαπήσεις τὸν πλησίον σου ὡς ἑαυτόν. 15 εἰ δὲ
in the (word), You shall love the neighbor of you as yourself. if But
240 1143 2532 2719 991 3361 5259 240
ἀλλήλους δάκνετε καὶ κατεσθίετε, βλέπετε μὴ ὑπὸ ἀλλήλων
one another you bite and devour, watch lest by one another
355
ἀναλωθῆτε.
you are consumed.

13 For, brethren, ye have been called unto liberty; only (use) not liberty for an occasion to the flesh, but by love serve one another.
14 For all the law is fulfilled in one word, (even) in this; Thou shalt love thy neighbour as thyself.
15 But if ye bite and devour one another, take heed that ye be not consumed one of another.

---

16 But I say, Walk in (the) Spirit, and you will not fulfill (the) lust of (the) flesh.
17 For the flesh lusts against the Spirit, and the Spirit against the flesh; and these are contrary to one another; lest whatever you may will, these things you do.
18 But if you are led by (the) Spirit, you are not under law.
19 Now the works of the flesh are clearly revealed, which are: adultery, fornication, uncleanness, lustfulness,
20 idolatry, sorcery, hatreds, fightings, jealousies, angers, rivalries, divisions, heresies,
21 envyings, murders, drunkennesses, wild parties, and things like these; of which I tell you beforehand, as I also said before, that the ones practicing such things will not inherit (the) kingdom of God.
22 But the fruit of the Spirit is: love, joy, peace, long-suffering, kindness, goodness, faith,
23 meekness,

3004 1161 4151 4043 2532 1939 4561 3756
16. Λέγω δέ, Πνεύματι περιπατεῖτε, καὶ ἐπιθυμίαν σαρκὸς οὐ
I say And, in (the) Spirit walk, and (the) lust of (the) flesh not
3361 5055 3588 1063 4561 1937 2596 3588 4151 3588
μὴ τελέσητε. 17 ἡ γὰρ σὰρξ ἐπιθυμεῖ κατὰ τοῦ Πνεύματος, τὸ
at all you will fulfill. the For flesh lusts against the Spirit, the
1161 4151 2596 3588 4561 5023 1161 480 240
δὲ Πνεῦμα κατὰ τῆς σαρκός· ταῦτα δὲ ἀντίκειται ἀλλήλοις,
and Spirit against the flesh; these things and (are) contrary to one another,
2443/3361/3739/302/2309 5023 4160 1487 1161 4151 71
ἵνα μὴ ἃ ἂν θέλητε, ταῦτα ποιῆτε. 18 εἰ δὲ Πνεύματι ἄγεσθε,
that not whatever you will, these things you do. if But by (the) Spirit you are led,
3756 2075 5259 3551 5318 1161 2076 3588 2041 3588 4561
οὐκ ἐστὲ ὑπὸ νόμον. 19 φανερὰ δέ ἐστι τὰ ἔργα τῆς σαρκός,
not you are under Law. clearly revealed Now are the works of the flesh,
3748 2076 3430 4202 167 766 1495
ἅτινά ἐστι μοιχεία, πορνεία, ἀκαθαρσία, ἀσέλγεια, 20 εἰδω-
which are adultery, fornication, uncleanness, lustfulness, idol
5331 2189 2054 2205 2372 2052
λολατρεία, φαρμακεία, ἔχθραι, ἔρεις, ζῆλοι, θυμοί, ἐριθεῖαι,
service, sorcery, enmities, fightings, jealousies, angers, rivalries,
1370 139 5355 5408 3178 2970 2532 3588
διχοστασίαι, αἱρέσεις, 21 φθόνοι, φόνοι, μέθαι, κῶμοι, καὶ τὰ
divisions, heresies, envyings, murders, drunkennesses, revelings, and
3664 5125 3739 4302 5213 2531 2532 4277 3754
ὅμοια τούτοις· ἃ προλέγω ὑμῖν, καθὼς καὶ προεῖπον, ὅτι
like things to these; which I tell before you, even as also I said previously, that
3588 3588 5108 4238 932 2316 3756 2816
οἱ τὰ τοιαῦτα πράσσοντες βασιλείαν Θεοῦ οὐ κληρονομή-
those things such practicing (the) kingdom of God not will inherit.
3588 1161 2590 3588 4151 2076 26 5479
σουσιν. 22 ὁ δὲ καρπὸς τοῦ Πνεύματός ἐστιν ἀγάπη, χαρά,
the But fruit of the Spirit is love, joy,
1515 3115 5544 19 4102 4236
εἰρήνη, μακροθυμία, χρηστότης, ἀγαθωσύνη, πίστις, 23 πρᾳό-
peace, long-suffering, kindness, goodness, faith, meekness,

16 (This) I say then, Walk in the Spirit, and ye shall not fulfil the lust of the flesh.
17 For the flesh lusteth against the Spirit, and the Spirit against the flesh: and these are contrary the one to the other: so that ye cannot do the things that ye would.
18 But if ye be led of the Spirit, ye are not under the law.
19 Now the works of the flesh are manifest, which are (these); Adultery, fornication, uncleanness, lasciviousness,
20 Idolatry, witchcraft, hatred, variance, emulations, wrath, strife, seditions, heresies,
21 Envyings, murders, drunkenness, revellings, and such like: of the which I tell you before, as I have also told (you) in time past, that they which do such things shall not inherit the kingdom of God.
22 But the fruit of the Spirit is love, joy, peace, longsuffering, gentleness, goodness, faith,
23 Meekness,

Literal Translation

Galatians 5:24

King James Version

self-control. Against such things there is not a law.
24 But the ones belonging to Christ crucified the flesh with (its) passions and the lusts.

1466 2596 3588 5108 3756 2076 3551 3588 1161
της, ἐγκράτεια· κατὰ τῶν τοιούτων οὐκ ἔστι νόμος. 24 οἱ δὲ
self-control; against such things not is a law. those And

3588 5547 3588 4561 4717 4862 3588 3804
τοῦ Χριστοῦ, τὴν σάρκα ἐσταύρωσαν σὺν τοῖς παθήμασι
of Christ, the flesh crucified with the passions

2532 3588 1939
καὶ ταῖς ἐπιθυμίαις.
and the lusts.

temperance: against such there is no law.
24 And they that are Christ's have crucified the flesh with the affections and lusts.

25 If we live in (the) Spirit, let us also walk in (the) Spirit.
26 Let us not become glory-seeking ones, provoking one another, envying one another.

1487 2198 4151 4151 2532 4748 3361 1096
25 Εἰ ζῶμεν Πνεύματι, Πνεύματι καὶ στοιχῶμεν. 26 μὴ γινώ-
If we live in (the) Spirit, in (the) Spirit also let us walk. Not let us

2755 240 4292 240 5354
μεθα κενόδοξοι, ἀλλήλους προκαλούμενοι, ἀλλήλοις φθονοῦν-
be vainglorious, one another provoking, one another envying.

τες.

25 If we live in the Spirit, let us also walk in the Spirit.
26 Let us not be desirous of vain glory, provoking one another, envying one another.

Galatians 6

1. Brothers, if a man is taken in some fault, you, the spiritual ones, restore such a one in the spirit of meekness, considering yourself, that you not also be tempted.

80 1437 2532 4301 444 1722 5100 3900
1. Ἀδελφοί, ἐὰν καὶ προληφθῇ ἄνθρωπος ἔν τινι παραπτώ-
Brothers, if indeed is overtaken a man in some fault,

5210 3588 4152 2675 3588 5108 1722
ματι, ὑμεῖς οἱ πνευματικοὶ καταρτίζετε τὸν τοιοῦτον ἐν
you the spiritual ones restore such a one in

4151 4236 4648 4572 3361 2532 4771 3985
πνεύματι πρᾳότητος, σκοπῶν σεαυτὸν μὴ καὶ σὺ πειρασθῇς.
(the) spirit of meekness, considering yourself lest also you be tempted.

1. Brethren, if a man be overtaken in a fault, ye which are spiritual, restore such an one in the spirit of meekness; considering thyself, lest thou also be tempted.

2 Bear one another's burdens, and so you will fulfill the law of Christ.
3 For if anyone thinks to be something, he deceives himself, being nothing.
4 But let each one prove his work, and then he alone will have a boast in himself and not as to another.
5 For each one will bear (his) own load.

240 3588 922 941 2532 3779 378 3588
2 ἀλλήλων τὰ βάρη βαστάζετε, καὶ οὕτως ἀναπληρώσατε τὸν
Of one another the burdens bear, and so you will fulfill the

3551 3588 5547 1487 1063 1380 5100 1511 5100 3367
νόμον τοῦ Χριστοῦ. 3 εἰ γὰρ δοκεῖ τις εἶναί τι, μηδὲν
law of Christ. if For thinks anyone to be something, nothing

5607 1438 5422 3588 1161 2041 1438 1381
ὤν, ἑαυτὸν φρεναπατᾷ. 4 τὸ δὲ ἔργον ἑαυτοῦ δοκιμαζέτω
being, himself he deceives. the But work of himself let prove

1538 2532 5119 1519 1438 3441 3588 2745 2192 2532 3756 1519
ἕκαστος, καὶ τότε εἰς ἑαυτὸν μόνον τὸ καύχημα ἕξει, καὶ οὐκ εἰς
each one, and then to himself alone the boast he will have, and not to

3588 2087 1538 1063 3588 2398 5413 941
τὸν ἕτερον. 5 ἕκαστος γὰρ τὸ ἴδιον φορτίον βαστάσει.
the other. each one For the own load will bear.

2 Bear ye one another's burdens, and so fulfil the law of Christ.
3 For if a man think himself to be something, when he is nothing, he deceiveth himself.
4 But let every man prove his own work, and then shall he have rejoicing in himself alone, and not in another.
5 For every man shall bear his own burden.

6 But let the (one) being taught in the Word share with the (one) teaching, in all good things.
7 Do not be deceived, God is not mocked. For whatever a man may sow, that he also will reap.
8 For the (one) sowing to his flesh will reap corruption of the flesh. But the (one) sowing to the Spirit will reap everlasting life from the Spirit.

2841 1161 3588 2727 3588 3056 3588 2727
6 Κοινωνείτω δὲ ὁ κατηχούμενος τὸν λόγον τῷ κατηχοῦντι
let him share And the (one) being taught in the Word with the (one) teaching

1722 3956 18 3361 4105 2316 3756 3456 3588 1063
ἐν πᾶσιν ἀγαθοῖς. 7 μὴ πλανᾶσθε, Θεὸς οὐ μυκτηρίζεται· ὃ γὰρ
in all good things. Not be led astray, God not is mocked; what for

1437 4687 444 5124 2532 2325 3754 3588 4687 1519
ἐὰν σπείρῃ ἄνθρωπος, τοῦτο καὶ θερίσει. 8 ὅτι ὁ σπείρων εἰς
ever may sow a man, this also he will reap. Because he sowing to

3588 4561 1438 1537 3588 4561 2325 5356 3588 1161 4687
τὴν σάρκα ἑαυτοῦ, ἐκ τῆς σαρκὸς θερίσει φθοράν· ὁ δὲ σπεί-
the flesh of himself, of the flesh will reap corruption; he but sowing

1519 3588 4151 1537 3588 4151 2325 2222 166
ρων εἰς τὸ Πνεῦμα, ἐκ τοῦ Πνεύματος θερίσει ζωὴν αἰώνιον.
to the Spirit, of the Spirit will reap life everlasting.

6 Let him that is taug ht in the word communicate unto him that teacheth in all good things.
7 Be not deceived; God is not mocked: for whatsoever a man soweth, that shall he also reap.
8 For he that soweth to his flesh shall of the flesh reap corruption; but he that soweth to the Spirit shall of the Spirit reap life everlasting.

9 But we should not weaken in doing good, for in due time we shall

3588 1161 2570 4160 3361 1573 2540 1063 2398 2325
9 τὸ δὲ καλὸν ποιοῦντες μὴ ἐκκακῶμεν· καιρῷ γὰρ ἰδίῳ θερίσο-
the And good doing not let us weaken; in time for its own we shall

9 And let us not be weary in well doing: for in due season we shall

Literal Translation | **Galatians 6:10** | *King James Version*

reap, if (we) do not faint.
10 So then, as we have time, let us work good toward all, and especially toward the household of the faith.

3361 1590 686 3767 5613 2540 2192 2038
μεν, μὴ ἐκλυόμενοι. 10 ἄρα οὖν ὡς καιρὸν ἔχομεν, ἐργαζώμεθα
reap, not fainting. So then as time we have, let us work
3588 18 4314 3956 3122 1161 4314 3588 3609 3588
τὸ ἀγαθὸν πρὸς πάντας, μάλιστα δὲ πρὸς τοὺς οἰκείους τῆς
the good to all, most of all and to the household of the
4102
πίστεως.
faith.

reap, if we faint not.
10 As we have therefore opportunity, let us do good unto all (men), especially unto them who are of the household of faith.

11 See in what large letters I write to you with my hand.
12 As many as desire to look well in (the) flesh, these compel you to be circumcised, only that they may not be persecuted for the cross of Christ.
13 For they themselves having been circumcised do not even keep (the) Law, but they desire you to be circumcised so that they may boast in your flesh.
14 But may it never be for me to boast, except in the cross of our Lord Jesus Christ, through whom the world has been crucified to me, and I to the world.
15 For in Christ Jesus neither circumcision (has) any strength nor uncircumcision, but a new creation.
16 And as many as shall walk by this rule, peace and mercy (be) on them and on the Israel of God.

1492 4080 5213 1121 1125 3588 1699 5495
11. Ἴδετε πηλίκοις ὑμῖν γράμμασιν ἔγραψα τῇ ἐμῇ χειρί.
See in how large to you letters I write with my hand.
3745 2309 2146 1722 4561 3778 315
12 ὅσοι θέλουσιν εὐπροσωπῆσαι ἐν σαρκί, οὗτοι ἀναγκάζουσιν
As many as desire to look well in (the) flesh, these compel
5209 4059 3440 2443 3361 3588 4716 3588 5547
ὑμᾶς περιτέμνεσθαι, μόνον ἵνα μὴ τῷ σταυρῷ τοῦ Χριστοῦ
you to be circumcised, only that not for the cross of Christ
1377 3761 1063 3588 4059 846 3551
διώκωνται. 13 οὐδὲ γὰρ οἱ περιτεμνόμενοι αὐτοὶ νόμον
they are persecuted. neither For those being circumcised themselves law
5442 235 2309 5209 4059 2443 1722 3588
φυλάσσουσιν· ἀλλὰ θέλουσιν ὑμᾶς περιτέμνεσθαι, ἵνα ἐν τῇ
keep; but they desire you to be circumcised, that in
5212 4561 2744 1698 1161 3361 1096 2744 1487
ὑμετέρᾳ σαρκὶ καυχήσωνται. 14 ἐμοὶ δὲ μὴ γένοιτο καυχᾶσθαι εἰ
your flesh they may boast. to me But not it may be to boast if
3361 1722 3588 4716 3588 2962 2257 2424 5547 1223/3739/1698
μὴ ἐν τῷ σταυρῷ τοῦ Κυρίου ἡμῶν Ἰησοῦ Χριστοῦ· δι' οὗ ἐμοὶ
not in the cross of the Lord of us Jesus Christ; through whom to me
2889 4717 2504 3588 2889 1722 1063 5547 2424
κόσμος ἐσταύρωται, κἀγὼ τῷ κόσμῳ. 15 ἐν γὰρ Χριστῷ Ἰησοῦ
(the) world has been crucified, and I to the world. in For Christ Jesus
3777 4061 5100 2480 3777 203 235 2537
οὔτε περιτομή τι ἰσχύει, οὔτε ἀκροβυστία, ἀλλὰ καινὴ
neither circumcision any strength (has), nor uncircumcision, but a new
2937 2532 3745 3588 2583 5129 4748 1515 1909
κτίσις. 16 καὶ ὅσοι τῷ κανόνι τούτῳ στοιχήσουσιν, εἰρήνη ἐπ'
creation. And as many as by rule this shall walk, peace on
846 2532 1656 2532 1909 3588 2474 3588 2316
αὐτούς καὶ ἔλεος, καὶ ἐπὶ τὸν Ἰσραὴλ τοῦ Θεοῦ.
them and mercy, and on the Israel of God.

11 Ye see how large a letter I have written unto you with mine own hand.
12. As many as desire to make a fair shew in the flesh, they constrain you to be circumcised; only lest they should suffer persecution for the cross of Christ.
13 For neither they themselves who are circumcised keep the law; but desire to have you circumcised, that they may glory in your flesh.
14 But God forbid that I should glory, save in the cross of our Lord Jesus Christ, by whom the world is crucified unto me, and I unto the world.
15 For in Christ Jesus neither circumcision availeth any thing, nor uncircumcision, but a new creature.
16 And as many as walk according to this rule, peace (be) on them, and mercy, and upon the Israel of God.

17 For the rest, let no one cause troubles to me, for I bear in my body the brands of the Lord Jesus.

3588 3064 287. 3427 3367 3930 1473/1063/3588
17. Τοῦ λοιποῦ, κόπους μοι μηδεὶς παρεχέτω· ἐγὼ γὰρ τὰ
For the rest, troubles to me no one let cause; I For the
4742 3588 2962 2424 1722 3588 4983 3450 941
στίγματα τοῦ Κυρίου Ἰησοῦ ἐν τῷ σώματί μου βαστάζω.
brands of the Lord Jesus in the body of me bear.

17 From henceforth let no man trouble me: for I bear in my body the marks of the Lord Jesus.

18 The grace of our Lord Jesus Christ (be) with your spirit, brothers. Amen.

3588 5485 3588 2962 2257 2424 5547 3326 3588
18. Ἡ χάρις τοῦ Κυρίου ἡμῶν Ἰησοῦ Χριστοῦ μετὰ τοῦ
The grace of the Lord of us Jesus Christ (be) with the
4151 5216 80 281
πνεύματος ὑμῶν, ἀδελφοί. ἀμήν.
spirit of you, brothers. Amen.

18 Brethren, the grace of our Lord Jesus Christ (be) with your spirit. Amen. (To (the) Galatians written from Rome.)

Literal Translation

THE EPISTLE OF PAUL THE APOSTLE TO THE EPHESIANS

Ephesians 1

1. Paul, (an) apostle of Jesus Christ through (the) will of God, to the saints being in Ephesus and faithful in Christ Jesus:

2 Grace to you and peace from God our Father and (the) Lord Jesus Christ.

3 Blessed (is) the God and Father of our Lord Jesus Christ, who blessed us with every spiritual blessing in the heavenlies with Christ,

4 even as He chose us in Him before (the) foundation of (the) world, for us to be holy and without blemish before Him in love,

5 predestinating us to adoption through Jesus Christ to Himself, according to the good pleasure of His will,

6 to (the) praise of (the) glory of His grace in which He favored us in the (One) having been loved,
7 in whom we have redemption through His blood, the remission of trespasses, according to the riches of His grace

8 which He caused to abound toward us in all wisdom and understanding,
9 making known to us the mystery of His will, according to His good pleasure which He purposed in Himself,
10 for the administration of the fullness of the times to head up all things in Christ, both the things in the heavens, and the things on earth,

ΠΑΥΛΟΥ ΤΟΥ ΑΠΟΣΤΟΛΟΥ
OF PAUL THE APOSTLE
Η ΠΡΟΣ ΕΦΕΣΙΟΥΣ ΕΠΙΣΤΟΛΗ
THE TO EPHESIANS EPISTLE

Ephesians 1

3972 652 2424 5547 1223 2307 2316
1. Παῦλος ἀπόστολος Ἰησοῦ Χριστοῦ διὰ θελήματος Θεοῦ,
Paul an apostle of Jesus Christ through (the) will of God,

3588 40 3588 5607 1722 2181 2532 4103 1722 5547
τοῖς ἁγίοις τοῖς οὖσιν ἐν Ἐφέσῳ καὶ πιστοῖς ἐν Χριστῷ
to the saints being in Ephesus and faithful in Christ

2424 5485 5213 2532 1515 575 2316 3962 2257 2532
Ἰησοῦ· 2 χάρις ὑμῖν καὶ εἰρήνη ἀπὸ Θεοῦ πατρὸς ἡμῶν καὶ
Jesus grace to you and peace from God (the) Father of us and

2962 2424 5547
Κυρίου Ἰησοῦ Χριστοῦ.
(the) Lord Jesus Christ.

2128 3588 2316 2532 3962 3588 2962 2257 2424
3. Εὐλογητὸς ὁ Θεὸς καὶ πατὴρ τοῦ Κυρίου ἡμῶν Ἰησοῦ
Blessed is the God and Father of the Lord of us Jesus

5547 3588 2127 2248 1722 3956 2129 4152
Χριστοῦ, ὁ εὐλογήσας ἡμᾶς ἐν πάσῃ εὐλογίᾳ πνευματικῇ
Christ, who blessed us with every blessing spiritual

1722 3588 2032 1722 5547 2531 1586 2248 1722
ἐν τοῖς ἐπουρανίοις ἐν Χριστῷ· 4 καθὼς ἐξελέξατο ἡμᾶς ἐν
in the heavenlies in Christ; even as He chose us in

846 4253 2602 2889 1511 2248 40 2532
αὐτῷ πρὸ καταβολῆς κόσμου, εἶναι ἡμᾶς ἁγίους καὶ
Him before (the) foundation of (the) world, to be us holy and

299 2714 846 1722 26 4309 2248 1519
ἀμώμους κατενώπιον αὐτοῦ ἐν ἀγάπῃ, 5 προορίσας ἡμᾶς εἰς
unblemished before Him in love, predestinating us to

5206 1223 2424 5547 1519 846 2596 3588 2107
υἱοθεσίαν διὰ Ἰησοῦ Χριστοῦ εἰς αὐτόν, κατὰ τὴν εὐδοκίαν
adoption through Jesus Christ to Himself, according to the good pleasure

3588 2307 846 1519 1868 1391 3588 5485 846
τοῦ θελήματος αὐτοῦ, 6 εἰς ἔπαινον δόξης τῆς χάριτος αὐτοῦ,
of the will of Him, to (the) praise of (the) glory of the grace of Him

1722 3739 5487 2248 1722 3588 25 1722 3739 2192 3588
ἐν ᾗ ἐχαρίτωσεν ἡμᾶς ἐν τῷ ἠγαπημένῳ· 7 ἐν ᾧ ἔχομεν τὴν
with which He favored us in the (One) having been loved; in whom we have the

629 1223 3588 129 846 3588 859 3588
ἀπολύτρωσιν διὰ τοῦ αἵματος αὐτõ, τὴν ἄφεσιν τῶν
redemption through the blood of Him, the remission

3900 2596 3588 4149 3588 5485 846
παραπτωμάτων, κατὰ τὸν πλοῦτον τῆς χάριτος αὐτοῦ,
of trespasses, according to the riches of the grace of Him,

3739 4052 1519 2248 1722 3956 4678 2532 5428
8 ἧς ἐπερίσσευσεν εἰς ἡμᾶς ἐν πάσῃ σοφίᾳ καὶ φρονήσει,
which He caused to abound to us in all wisdom and intelligence,

1107 2254 3588 3466 3588 2307 846 2596
9 γνωρίσας ἡμῖν τὸ μυστήριον τοῦ θελήματος αὐτοῦ, κατὰ
making known to us the mystery of the will of Him, according to

3588 2107 846 3739 4388 1722 846 1519 3622
τὴν εὐδοκίαν αὐτοῦ, ἣν προέθετο ἐν αὐτῷ 10 εἰς οἰκονομίαν
the good pleasure of Him, which He purposed in Himself for stewardship

3588 4138 3588 2540 346 3588 3956
τοῦ πληρώματος τῶν καιρῶν, ἀνακεφαλαιώσασθαι τὰ πάντα
of the fullness of the times, to head up all things

1722 3588 5547 3588 5037 1722 3588 3772 2532 3588 1909 3588 1093
ἐν τῷ Χριστῷ, τὰ τε ἐν τοῖς οὐρανοῖς καὶ τὰ ἐπὶ τῆς γῆς·
in Christ, the things both in the heavens and the things on the earth;

King James Version

THE EPISTLE OF PAUL THE APOSTLE TO THE EPHESIANS

Ephesians 1

1. Paul, an apostle of Jesus Christ by the will of God, to the saints which are at Ephesus, and to the faithful in Christ Jesus:

2 Grace (be) to you, and peace, from God our Father, and (from) the Lord Jesus Christ.

3 Blessed (be) the God and Father of our Lord Jesus Christ, who hath blessed us with all spiritual blessings in heavenly (places) in Christ:

4 According as he hath chosen us in him before the foundation of the world, that we should be holy and without blame before him in love:
5 Having predestinated us unto the adoption of children by Jesus Christ to himself, according to the good pleasure of his will,

6 To the praise of the glory of his grace, wherein he hath made us accepted in the beloved.
7 In whom we have redemption through his blood, the forgiveness of sins, according to the riches of his grace;

8 Wherein he hath abounded toward us in all wisdom and prudence;
9 Having made known unto us the mystery of his will, according to his good pleasure which he hath purposed in himself:
10 That in the dispensation of the fulness of times he might gather together in one all things in Christ, both which are in heaven, and which are on earth;

Literal Translation

in Him,
11 in whom we also have been chosen to an inheritance, being predestinated according to (the) purpose of the (One) working all things according to the counsel of His (own) will,
12 for us to be to (the) praise of His glory, the ones having previously trusted in Christ;
13 in whom also you, hearing the Word of truth, the gospel of your salvation, in whom also believing you were sealed with the Holy Spirit of promise,

14 who is an earnest of our inheritance, to (the) redemption of the purchased possession, to (the) praise of His glory.

15 Because of this, I also hearing of the faith among you in the Lord Jesus and love toward all the saints,

16 do not cease giving thanks on your behalf, making mention of you in my prayers,
17 that the God of our Lord Jesus Christ, the Father of glory, may give to you a spirit of wisdom and revelation in (the) full knowledge of Him,
18 the eyes of your mind having been enlightened, for you to know what is the hope of His calling, and what the riches of the glory of His inheritance in the saints,

19 and what (is) the surpassing greatness of His power toward us, the (ones) believing according to the working of the might of His strength

20 which He worked in Christ having raised Him from (the) dead;

Ephesians 1:11

1722 846 1722 3739 2532 2820 4309 2596
ἐν αὐτῷ, 11 ἐν ᾧ καὶ ἐκληρώθημεν, προορισθέντες κατὰ
in Him, in whom also we have been chosen to an inheritance, being predestinated according to

4286 3588 3588 3956 1754 2596 3588 1012 3588
πρόθεσιν τοῦ τὰ πάντα ἐνεργοῦντος κατὰ τὴν βουλὴν τοῦ
(the) purpose of the (One) all things working according to the counsel of the

2307 846 1519 3588 1511 2248 1519 1868 3588 1391
θελήματος αὐτοῦ, 12 εἰς τὸ εἶναι ἡμᾶς εἰς ἔπαινον τῆς δόξης
will of Him, for to be us to (the) praise of the glory

846 3588 4276 1722 3588 5547 1722 3739 2532 5210
αὐτοῦ, τοὺς προηλπικότας ἐν τῷ Χριστῷ· 13 ἐν ᾧ καὶ ὑμεῖς,
of Him, those having previously trusted in Christ; in whom also you,

191 3588 3056 3588 225 3588 2098 3588
ἀκούσαντες τὸν λόγον τῆς ἀληθείας, τὸ εὐαγγέλιον τῆς
hearing the Word of truth, the gospel of the

4991 5216 1722 3739/2532 4100 4972 3588
σωτηρίας ὑμῶν, ἐν ᾧ καὶ πιστεύσαντες ἐσφραγίσθητε τῷ
salvation of you, in whom also believing you were sealed with the

4151 3588 1860 3588 40 3739 2076 728 3588
Πνεύματι τῆς ἐπαγγελίας τῷ Ἁγίῳ, 14 ὅς ἐστιν ἀρραβὼν τῆς
Spirit of promise the Holy, who is an earnest of the

2817 2257 1519 629 3588 4047 1519
κληρονομίας ἡμῶν, εἰς ἀπολύτρωσιν τῆς περιποιήσεως, εἰς
inheritance of us, until (the) redemption of the possession, to

1868 3588 1391 846
ἔπαινον τῆς δόξης αὐτοῦ.
(the) praise of the glory of Him.

1223 5124 2504 191 3588 2596 5209 4102/1722/3588
15. Διὰ τοῦτο κἀγώ, ἀκούσας τὴν καθ᾽ ὑμᾶς πίστιν ἐν τῷ
Because of this I also, hearing the among you faith in the

2962 2424 2532 3588 26 3588 1519 3956 3588 40
Κυρίῳ Ἰησοῦ καὶ τὴν ἀγάπην τὴν εἰς πάντας τοὺς ἁγίους,
Lord Jesus and the love to all the saints,

3756 3973 2168 5228 5216 3417 5216 4160
16 οὐ παύομαι εὐχαριστῶν ὑπὲρ ὑμῶν, μνείαν ὑμῶν ποιού-
not do cease giving thanks on behalf of you, mention of you having

1909 3588 4335 3450 2443 3588 2316 3588 2962 2257
μενος ἐπὶ τῶν προσευχῶν μου· 17 ἵνα ὁ Θεὸς τοῦ Κυρίου ἡμῶν
made on the prayers of me; that the God of the Lord of us

2424 5547 3588 3962 3588 1391 1325 5213 4151
Ἰησοῦ Χριστοῦ, ὁ πατὴρ τῆς δόξης, δῴη ὑμῖν πνεῦμα
Jesus Christ, the Father of glory, may give to you a spirit

4678 2532 602 1722 1922 846 5461
σοφίας καὶ ἀποκαλύψεως, ἐν ἐπιγνώσει αὐτοῦ· 18 πεφωτι-
of wisdom and revelation, in (the) knowledge of Him; having been

3588 3788 3588 1271 5216 1519 3588 1492
σμένους τοὺς ὀφθαλμοὺς τῆς διανοίας ὑμῶν, εἰς τὸ εἰδέναι
enlightened the eyes of the mind of you, for to know

5209 5101 2076 3588 1680 3588 2821 846 2532 5101 3588 4149
ὑμᾶς τίς ἐστιν ἡ ἐλπὶς τῆς κλήσεως αὐτοῦ, καὶ τίς ὁ πλοῦτος
you what is the hope of the calling of Him, and what the riches

3588 1391 3588 2817 846 1722 3588 40 2532/5101/3588
τῆς δόξης τῆς κληρονομίας αὐτοῦ ἐν τοῖς ἁγίοις, 19 καὶ τί τὸ
of the glory of the inheritance of Him in the saints, and what the

5235 3174 3588 1411 846 1519 2248 3588
ὑπερβάλλον μέγεθος τῆς δυνάμεως αὐτοῦ εἰς ἡμᾶς τοὺς
surpassing greatness of the power of Him toward us the (ones)

4100 2596 3588 1753 3588 2904 3588 2479
πιστεύοντας, κατὰ τὴν ἐνέργειαν τοῦ κράτους τῆς ἰσχύος
believing, according to the working of the might of the strength

846 3739 1754 1722 3588 5547 1453 846 1537 3498
αὐτοῦ 20 ἣν ἐνήργησεν ἐν τῷ Χριστῷ, ἐγείρας αὐτὸν ἐκ νεκρῶν,
of Him, which He worked in Christ, having raised Him from (the) dead,

King James Version

(even) in him:
11 In whom also we have obtained an inheritance, being predestinated according to the purpose of him who worketh all things after the counsel of his own will:
12 That we should be to the praise of his glory, who first trusted in Christ.
13 In whom ye also (trusted), after that ye heard the word of truth, the gospel of your salvation: in whom also after that ye believed, ye were sealed with that holy Spirit of promise,

14 Which is the earnest of our inheritance until the redemption of the purchased possession, unto the praise of his glory.

15 Wherefore I also, after I heard of your faith in the Lord Jesus, and love unto all the saints,

16 Cease not to give thanks for you, making mention of you in my prayers;
17 That the God of our Lord Jesus Christ, the Father of glory, may give unto you the spirit of wisdom and revelation in the knowledge of him:
18 The eyes of your understanding being enlightened; that ye may know what is the hope of his calling, and what the riches of the glory of his inheritance in the saints,

19 And what (is) the exceeding greatness of his power to us-ward who believe, according to the working of his mighty power,

20 Which he wrought in Christ, when he raised him from the dead,

Ephesians 1:21

Literal Translation

yea, (He) seated (Him) at His right in the heavenlies,
21 far above all rule, and authority, and power, and lordship, and every name having been named, not only in this age, but also in the coming (age);

22 and He put all (things) under His feet and gave Him (to be) Head over all (things) to the church,

23 which is His body: the fullness of Him filling all things in all;

2532 2523 1722 1188 846 1722 3588 2032 5231
καὶ ἐκάθισεν ἐν δεξιᾷ αὐτοῦ ἐν τοῖς ἐπουρανίοις, 21 ὑπερ-
and He seated (Him) at (the) right of Him in the heavenlies, far

3956 746 2532 1849 2532 1411 2532 2963
άνω πάσης ἀρχῆς καὶ ἐξουσίας καὶ δυνάμεως καὶ κυριό-
above all rule and authority and power and lordship,

2532 3956 3686 3687 3756 3440 1722 3588
τητος, καὶ παντὸς ὀνόματος ὀνομαζομένου οὐ μόνον ἐν τῷ
and every name having been named not only in

165 5129 235 2532 1722 3588 3195 2532 3956 5293
αἰῶνι τούτῳ, ἀλλὰ καὶ ἐν τῷ μέλλοντι· 22 καὶ πάντα ὑπέταξεν
age this, but also in the coming (age); and all things subjected

5259 3588 4228 846 2532 846 1325 2776 5228 3956 3588
ὑπὸ τοὺς πόδας αὐτοῦ, καὶ αὐτὸν ἔδωκε κεφαλὴν ὑπὲρ πάντα τῇ
under the feet of Him, and Him gave (to be) Head over all things to the

1577 3748 2076 3588 4983 846 3588 4138 3588
ἐκκλησίᾳ, 23 ἥτις ἐστὶ τὸ σῶμα αὐτοῦ, τὸ πλήρωμα τοῦ
church, which is the body of Him, the fullness of the (One)

3956 1722 3956 4137
πάντα ἐν πᾶσι πληρουμένου.
all things in all filling.

King James Version

and set (him) at his own right hand in the heavenly (places),
21 Far above all principality, and power, and might, and dominion, and every name that is named, not only in this world, but also in that which is to come:

22 And hath put all (things) under his feet, and gave him (to be) the head over all (things) to the church,

23 Which is his body, the fulness of him that filleth all in all.

Ephesians 2

Literal Translation

1. and (He worked in) you being dead in trespasses and sins,
2 in which you walked then according to the age of this world, according to the ruler of the authority of the air, the spirit now working in the sons of disobedience,

3 among whom also we all conducted ourselves formerly in the lusts of our flesh, doing the things willed of the flesh and of the understandings, and were by nature the children of wrath, even as the rest.

4 But God, being rich in mercy, because of His great love (with) which He loved us,
5 even we being dead in sins, (He) made us alive together with Christ, by grace you are being saved,

6 and raised (us) up together and seated (us) together in the heavenlies in Christ Jesus,
7 that He might show in the coming ages the exceeding great riches of His

2532 5209 5607 3498 3588 3900 2532 3588
1. Καὶ ὑμᾶς ὄντας νεκροὺς τοῖς παραπτώμασι καὶ ταῖς
And you being dead in the trespasses and in the

266 1722 3739 4218 4043 2596 3588 165 3588
ἁμαρτίαις, 2 ἐν αἷς ποτὲ περιεπατήσατε κατὰ τὸν αἰῶνα τοῦ
sins, in which then you walked according to the age

2889 5127 2596 3588 758 3588 1849 3588 109
κόσμου τούτου, κατὰ τὸν ἄρχοντα τῆς ἐξουσίας τοῦ ἀέρος,
world of this, according to the ruler of the authority of the air,

3588 4151 3588 3568 1754 1722 3588 5207 3588 543
τοῦ πνεύματος τοῦ νῦν ἐνεργοῦντος ἐν τοῖς υἱοῖς τῆς ἀπει-
the spirit now working in the sons of dis-

1722 3739 2532 2249 3956 390 4218 1722 3588
θείας· 3 ἐν οἷς καὶ ἡμεῖς πάντες ἀνεστράφημέν ποτε ἐν ταῖς
obedience; among whom also we all conducted ourselves then in the

1939 3588 4561 2257 4160 3588 2307 3588
ἐπιθυμίαις τῆς σαρκὸς ἡμῶν, ποιοῦντες τὰ θελήματα τῆς
lusts of the flesh of us, doing the things willed of the

4561 2532 3588 1271 2532 2258 5043 5449 3709 5613
σαρκὸς καὶ τῶν διανοιῶν, καὶ ἦμεν τέκνα φύσει ὀργῆς, ὡς
flesh and of the understandings, and were children by nature of wrath, as

2532 3588 3062 3588 1161 2316 4145 5607 1722 1656 1223 3588
καὶ οἱ λοιποί· 4 ὁ δὲ Θεὸς, πλούσιος ὢν ἐν ἐλέει, διὰ τὴν
even the rest; but God, rich being in mercy, because of the

4183 26 846 3739 25 2248 2532 5607 2248
πολλὴν ἀγάπην αὐτοῦ ἣν ἠγάπησεν ἡμᾶς, 5 καὶ ὄντας ἡμᾶς
much love of Him (with) which He loved us, even being us

3498 3588 3900 4806 3588 5547
νεκροὺς τοῖς παραπτώμασι συνεζωοποίησε τῷ Χριστῷ
dead in trespasses (He) made us alive with Christ,

5485 2075 4982 2532 4891 2532 4776
[χάριτί ἐστε σεσωσμένοι], 6 καὶ συνήγειρε, καὶ συνεκάθισεν
by grace you are saved, and (us) raised together, and seated together

1722 3588 2032 1722 5547 2424 2443 1731 1722 3588
ἐν τοῖς ἐπουρανίοις ἐν Χριστῷ Ἰησοῦ· 7 ἵνα ἐνδείξηται ἐν τοῖς
in the heavenlies in Christ Jesus, that He might show in the

165 3588 1904 3588 5235 4149 3588
αἰῶσι τοῖς ἐπερχομένοις τὸν ὑπερβάλλοντα πλοῦτον τῆς
ages coming on the surpassing riches of the

King James Version

1. And you (hath he quickened), who were dead in trespasses and sins;
2 Wherein in time past ye walked according to the course of this world, according to the prince of the power of the air, the spirit that now worketh in the children of disobedience:

3 Among whom also we all had our conversation in times past in the lusts of our flesh, fulfilling the desires of the flesh and of the mind; and were by nature the children of wrath, even as others.

4 But God, who is rich in mercy, for his great love wherewith he loved us,
5 Even when we were dead in sins, hath quickened us together with Christ, (by grace ye are saved;)

6 And hath raised (us) up together, and made (us) sit together in heavenly (places) in Christ Jesus:
7 That in the ages to come he might shew the exceeding riches of his

Literal Translation

Ephesians 2:8

King James Version

grace in kindness toward us in Christ Jesus.

8 For by grace you are saved, through faith, and this not of yourselves; (it is) the gift of God;
9 not of works, that not anyone should boast;
10 for we are (His) workmanship, created in Christ Jesus unto good works, which God before prepared that we should walk in them.

11 Because of this, remember that you, the nations, (were) then in (the) flesh (those having been called Uncircumcision by those having been called Circumcision in (the) flesh made by hand)
12 that at that time you were without Christ, alienated from the commonwealth of Israel and strangers of the covenants of promise, having no hope and without God in the world.
13 But now in Christ Jesus you, the (ones) then being afar off came to be near by the blood of Christ.

14 For He is our peace, the (One) making us both one, and having broken down the middle wall of partition,

15 in His flesh causing to cease the enmity, the Law of the commandments in decrees, that He might in Himself create the two into one new man, making peace,
16 and might reconcile both in one body to God through the cross, slaying the enmity in Himself.

17 And coming, (He) proclaimed peace to you, the (ones) afar off, and to the (ones) near.
18 For through Him

5485 846 1722 5544 1909 2248 1722 5547 2424
χάριτος αὐτοῦ ἐν χρηστότητι ἐφ' ἡμᾶς ἐν Χριστῷ Ἰησοῦ·
grace of Him in kindness toward us in Christ Jesus;

3588 1063 5485 2075 4982 1223 3588 4102 2532 5124
8 τῇ γὰρ χάριτί ἐστε σεσωσμένοι διὰ τῆς πίστεως, καὶ τοῦτο
for by grace you are saved through faith, and this

3756 1537 5216 2316 3588 1435 3756 1537 2041 2443 3361 5100
οὐκ ἐξ ὑμῶν· θεοῦ τὸ δῶρον· 9 οὐκ ἐξ ἔργων, ἵνα μή τις
not of you; of God (is) the gift; not of works, that not anyone

2744 846 1063 2070 4161 2936 1722 5547
καυχήσηται. 10 αὐτοῦ γάρ ἐσμεν ποίημα, κτισθέντες ἐν Χριστῷ
should boast. of Him For we are (His) workmanship, created in Christ

2424 1909 2041 18 3739 4282 3588 2316 2443
Ἰησοῦ ἐπὶ ἔργοις ἀγαθοῖς, οἷς προητοίμασεν ὁ θεός, ἵνα
Jesus unto works good, which before prepared God, that

1722 846 4043
ἐν αὐτοῖς περιπατήσωμεν.
in them we should walk.

1352 3421 3754 5210 4218 3588 1484 1722 4561 3588
11. Διὸ μνημονεύετε, ὅτι ὑμεῖς ποτὲ τὰ ἔθνη ἐν σαρκί, οἱ
Therefore remember, that you then the nations in (the) flesh, the

3004 203 5259 3588 3004 4061 1722
λεγόμενοι ἀκροβυστία ὑπὸ τῆς λεγομένης περιτομῆς ἐν
(ones) being called uncircumcision by the (ones) being called circumcision in

4561 5499 3754 2258 1722 3588 2540 1565 5565
σαρκὶ χειροποιήτου, 12 ὅτι ἦτε ἐν τῷ καιρῷ ἐκείνῳ χωρὶς
(the) flesh made by hand, because you were at time that without

5547 526 3588 4174 3588 2474 2532
Χριστοῦ, ἀπηλλοτριωμένοι τῆς πολιτείας τοῦ Ἰσραήλ, καὶ
Christ, having been alienated from the commonwealth of Israel, and

3581 3588 1242 3588 1860 1680 3361 2192
ξένοι τῶν διαθηκῶν τῆς ἐπαγγελίας, ἐλπίδα μὴ ἔχοντες,
strangers of the covenants of promise, hope not having,

2532 112 1722 3588 2889 3570 1161 1722 5547 2424 5210 3588
καὶ ἄθεοι ἐν τῷ κόσμῳ. 13 νυνὶ δὲ ἐν Χριστῷ Ἰησοῦ ὑμεῖς οἱ
and godless in the world. now But in Christ Jesus you the (ones)

4218 5607 3112 1451 1096 1722 3588 129 3588
ποτὲ ὄντες μακρὰν ἐγγὺς ἐγενήθητε ἐν τῷ αἵματι τοῦ
then being afar off near came to be by the blood

5547 846 1063 2076 3588 1515 2257 3588 4160 3588
Χριστοῦ. 14 αὐτὸς γάρ ἐστιν ἡ εἰρήνη ἡμῶν, ὁ ποιήσας τὰ
of Christ. He For is the peace of us, the (One) making

297 1520 2532 3588 3320 3588 5418 3089 3588
ἀμφότερα ἕν, καὶ τὸ μεσότοιχον τοῦ φραγμοῦ λύσας, τὴν
both one, and the middle wall of partition having broken, the

2189 1722 3588 4561 846 3588 3551 3588 1785 1722
ἔχθραν ἐν τῇ σαρκὶ αὐτοῦ, 15 τὸν νόμον τῶν ἐντολῶν ἐν
enmity in the flesh of Him, the law of the commandments in

1378 2673 2443 3588 1417 2936 1722 1438 1519 1522
δόγμασι, καταργήσας· ἵνα τοὺς δύο κτίσῃ ἐν ἑαυτῷ εἰς ἕνα
decrees, having made to cease; that the two He create in Himself into one

2537 444 4160 1515 2532 604 3588
καινὸν ἄνθρωπον, ποιῶν εἰρήνην, 16 καὶ ἀποκαταλλάξῃ τοὺς
new man, making peace, and might reconcile

297 1722 1520 4983 3588 2316 1223 3588 4716
ἀμφοτέρους ἐν ἑνὶ σώματι τῷ Θεῷ διὰ τοῦ σταυροῦ,
both in one body to God through the cross

615 3588 2189 1722 846 2532 2064 2097
ἀποκτείνας τὴν ἔχθραν ἐν αὐτῷ· 17 καὶ ἐλθὼν εὐηγγελίσατο
slaying the enmity in Himself; and coming proclaimed

1515 5213 3588 3112 2532 3588 1451 3754 1223 846
εἰρήνην ὑμῖν τοῖς μακρὰν καὶ τοῖς ἐγγύς· 18 ὅτι δι' αὐτοῦ
peace to you those afar off and to those near; because through Him

grace in (his) kindness toward us through Christ Jesus.

8 For by grace are ye saved through faith; and that not of yourselves: (it is) the gift of God:
9 Not of works, lest any man should boast.

10 For we are his workmanship, created in Christ Jesus unto good works, which God hath before ordained that we should walk in them.

11 Wherefore remember, that ye (being) in time past Gentiles in the flesh, who are called Uncircumcision by that which is called the Circumcision in the flesh made by hands;
12 That at that time ye were without Christ, being aliens from the commonwealth of Israel, and strangers from the covenants of promise, having no hope, and without God in the world:

13 But now in Christ Jesus ye who sometimes were far off are made nigh by the blood of Christ.

14 For he is our peace, who hath made both one, and hath broken down the middle wall of partition (between us);

15 Having abolished in his flesh the enmity, (even) the law of commandments (contained) in ordinances; for to make in himself of twain one new man, (so) making peace;
16 And that he might reconcile both unto God in one body by the cross, having slain the enmity thereby:

17 And came and preached peace to you which were afar off, and to them that were nigh.
18 For through him

Literal Translation

we both have access by one Spirit to the Father.
19 So, then, you are no longer strangers and tenants, but (you are) fellow citizens of the saints and (of the) household of God,
20 having been built up on the foundation of the apostles and prophets, Jesus Christ Himself being (the) cornerstone,
21 in whom all the building being fitted together grows into a holy temple in (the) Lord,
22 in whom you also are being built together into a dwelling place of God in (the) Spirit.

Ephesians 2:19

2192 3588 4318 3588 297 1722 1520 4151 4314
ἔχομεν τὴν προσαγωγὴν οἱ ἀμφότεροι ἐν ἑνὶ Πνεύματι πρὸς
we have access both by one Spirit unto

3588 3962 686 3767 3765 2075 3581 2532 3941 235
τὸν πατέρα. 19 ἄρα οὖν οὐκέτι ἐστὲ ξένοι καὶ πάροικοι, ἀλλὰ
the Father. Then therefore no more you are strangers and tenants, but

4847 3588 40 2532 3609 3588 2316 2026
συμπολῖται τῶν ἁγίων καὶ οἰκεῖοι τοῦ Θεοῦ, 20 ἐποικοδομη-
fellow-citizens of the saints and (of the) household of God, having been

1909 3588 2310 3588 652 2532 4396 5607
θέντες ἐπὶ τῷ θεμελίῳ τῶν ἀποστόλων καὶ προφητῶν, ὄντος
built on the foundation of the apostles and prophets, being

204 846 2424 5547 1722/3739/3956/3588 3619
ἀκρογωνιαίου αὐτοῦ Ἰησοῦ Χριστοῦ, 21 ἐν ᾧ πᾶσα ἡ οἰκοδομὴ
(the) cornerstone (Him)self Jesus Christ, in whom all the building

4883 837 1519 3485 40 1722 2962 1722/3739
συναρμολογουμένη αὔξει εἰς ναὸν ἅγιον ἐν Κυρίῳ, 22 ἐν ᾧ
being fitted together grows into a temple holy in (the) Lord, in whom

2532 5210 4925 1519 2732 3588 2316 1722
καὶ ὑμεῖς συνοικοδομεῖσθε εἰς κατοικητήριον τοῦ Θεοῦ ἐν
also you are being built together into a dwelling-place of God in

4151
Πνεύματι.
(the) Spirit.

King James Version

we both have access by one Spirit unto the Father.
19 Now therefore ye are no more strangers and foreigners, but fellowcitizens with the saints, and of the household of God;
20 And are built upon the foundation of the apostles and prophets, Jesus Christ himself being the chief corner (stone);
21 In whom all the building fitly framed together groweth unto an holy temple in the Lord:
22 In whom ye also are builded together for an habitation of God through the Spirit.

Ephesians 3

1. Because of this , I, Paul, the prisoner of Christ Jesus on behalf of you, the nations,
2 if, indeed, you heard of the stewardship of the grace of God given to me for you,
3 that by revelation was made known to me the mystery, as I wrote before in brief,
4 by the reading of which you are able to realize my understanding in the mystery of Christ,
5 which was not made known to the sons of men in other generations, as it now it was revealed to His holy apostles and prophets in (the) Spirit,
6 (for) the nations to be joint-heirs, and a joint-body and joint-sharers of His promise in Christ through the gospel,
7 of which I was made a minister according to the gift of the grace of God given to me, according to the working of His

Ephesians 3

5127 5484 1473 3972 3588 1198 3588 5547 2424
1. Τούτου χάριν ἐγὼ Παῦλος ὁ δέσμιος τοῦ Χριστοῦ Ἰησοῦ
this Because of I Paul the prisoner of Christ Jesus

5228 5216 3588 1484 1489 191 3588 3622 3588
ὑπὲρ ὑμῶν τῶν ἐθνῶν, 2 εἴγε ἠκούσατε τὴν οἰκονομίαν τῆς
on behalf of you the nations, if indeed you heard of the stewardship of the

5485 3588 2316 3588 1325 3427 1519 5209 3754 2596
χάριτος τοῦ Θεοῦ τῆς δοθείσης μοι εἰς ὑμᾶς, 3 ὅτι κατὰ
grace of God given to me for you, that by way of

602 1107 3427 3588 3466 2531 4270
ἀποκάλυψιν ἐγνώρισέ μοι τὸ μυστήριον, καθὼς προέγραψα
revelation was made known to me the mystery even as I wrote before

1722 3641 4314 3739 1410 314 3539 3588
ἐν ὀλίγῳ, 4 πρὸς ὃ δύνασθε ἀναγινώσκοντες νοῆσαι τὴν
in brief, by which you are able reading to realize the

4907 3450 1722 3588 3466 3588 5547 3739 1722 2087
σύνεσίν μου ἐν τῷ μυστηρίῳ τοῦ Χριστοῦ· 5 ὃ ἐν ἑτέραις
understanding of me in the mystery of Christ; which in other

1074 3756 1107 3588 5207 3588 444 5613 3568
γενεαῖς οὐκ ἐγνωρίσθη τοῖς υἱοῖς τῶν ἀνθρώπων, ὡς νῦν
generations not was made known to the sons of men, as now

601 3588 40 652 846 2532 4396
ἀπεκαλύφθη τοῖς ἁγίοις ἀποστόλοις αὐτοῦ καὶ προφήταις
it was revealed to the holy apostles of Him and prophets

1722 4151 1511 3588 1484 4789 2532 4954 2532
ἐν Πνεύματι· 6 εἶναι τὰ ἔθνη συγκληρονόμα καὶ σύσσωμα καὶ
in (the) Spirit; to be the nations joint-heirs and a joint-body and

4830 3588 1860 846 1722 3588 5547 1223 3588
συμμέτοχα τῆς ἐπαγγελίας αὐτοῦ ἐν τῷ Χριστῷ διὰ τοῦ
joint-sharers of the promise of Him in Christ through the

2098 3739 1096 1249 2596 3588 1431 3588
εὐαγγελίου, 7 οὗ ἐγενόμην διάκονος κατὰ τὴν δωρεὰν τῆς
gospel, of which I became a minister according to the gift of the

5485 3588 2316 3588 1325 3427 2596 3588 1753 3588
χάριτος τοῦ Θεοῦ, τὴν δοθεῖσάν μοι κατὰ τὴν ἐνέργειαν τῆς
grace of God, given to me according to the working of the

Ephesians 3

1. For this cause I Paul, the prisoner of Jesus Christ for you Gentiles,
2 If ye have heard of the dispensation of the grace of God which is given me to you-ward:
3 How that by revelation he made known unto me the mystery; (as I wrote afore in few words,
4 Whereby, when ye read, ye may understand my knowledge in the mystery of Christ)
5 Which in other ages was not made known unto the sons of men, as it is now revealed unto his holy apostles and prophets by the Spirit;
6 That the Gentiles should be fellowheirs, and of the same body, and partakers of his promise in Christ by the gospel:
7 Whereof I was made a minister, according to the gift of the grace of God given unto me by the effectual working of his

Ephesians 3:8

Literal Translation

power.
8 This grace was given to me, less than the least of all the saints, to preach the gospel of the unsearchable riches of Christ among the nations,
9 and to bring to light all, what (is) the fellowship of the mystery having been hidden from eternity in God, the (One) creating all things through Jesus Christ,
10 so that now to the rulers and to the authorities in the heavenlies might be made known through the church the manifold wisdom of God,
11 according to (the) purpose of the ages which He accomplished in Christ Jesus our Lord,
12 in whom we have boldness and access in confidence through His faith.
13 Therefore, I ask (you) not to faint at my troubles on your behalf, which is your glory.
14 Because of this I bow my knees to the Father of our Lord Jesus Christ,
15 of whom every family in Heaven and on earth is named,
16 that He may give you, according to the riches of His glory, by (His) power to become mighty in the inward man through His Spirit,
17 that through faith Christ may dwell in your hearts, having been rooted and having been founded in love,
18 that you may be given strength to grasp, with all the saints, what (is) the breadth and length and depth and height,
19 and to know the surpassing knowledge and love of Christ,

1411 846 1698 3588 1647 3956 3588
δυνάμεως αὐτοῦ. 8 ἐμοὶ τῷ ἐλαχιστοτέρῳ πάντων τῶν
power of Him. To me the less than the least of all the

40 1325 3588 5485 3778 1722 3588 1484 2097
ἁγίων ἐδόθη ἡ χάρις αὕτη, ἐν τοῖς ἔθνεσιν εὐαγγελίσασθαι
saints was given grace this, in the nations to preach the gospel

3588 2097 4149 3588 5547 2532 5461
τὸν ἀνεξιχνίαστον πλοῦτον τοῦ Χριστοῦ, 9 καὶ φωτίσαι
the unsearchable riches of Christ, and to bring to light

3956 5101 3588 2842 3588 3466 3588 613
πάντας τίς ἡ κοινωνία τοῦ μυστηρίου τοῦ ἀποκεκρυμμένου
all what (is) the fellowship of the mystery having been hidden

575 3588 165 1722 3588 2316 3588 3588 3956 2936 1223
ἀπὸ τῶν αἰώνων ἐν τῷ Θεῷ τῷ τὰ πάντα κτίσαντι διὰ
from the eternity in God the (One) all things having created by

2424 5547 2443 1107 3568 3588 746 2532 3588
Ἰησοῦ Χριστοῦ, 10 ἵνα γνωρισθῇ νῦν ταῖς ἀρχαῖς καὶ ταῖς
Jesus Christ, that might be revealed now to the rulers and to the

1849 1722 3588 2032 1223 3588 1577 3588 4182
ἐξουσίαις ἐν τοῖς ἐπουρανίοις διὰ τῆς ἐκκλησίας ἡ πολυποί-
authorities in the heavenlies through the church the manifold

4678 3588 2316 2596 4286 3588 165 3739 4160
κιλος σοφία τοῦ Θεοῦ, 11 κατὰ πρόθεσιν τῶν αἰώνων ἣν ἐποίη-
wisdom of God, according to (the) purpose of the ages which He

1722 5547 2424 3588 2962 2257 1722 3739 2192 3588
σεν ἐν Χριστῷ Ἰησοῦ τῷ Κυρίῳ ἡμῶν· 12 ἐν ᾧ ἔχομεν τὴν
made in Christ Jesus the Lord of us; in which we have

3954 2532 3588 4318 1722 4006 1223 3588
παρρησίαν καὶ τὴν προσαγωγὴν ἐν πεποιθήσει διὰ τῆς
boldness and access in confidence through the

4102 846 1352 154 3361 1573 1722 3588 2347
πίστεως αὐτοῦ. 13 διὸ αἰτοῦμαι μὴ ἐκκακεῖν ἐν ταῖς θλίψεσί
faith of Him. Therefore I ask (you) not to faint at the troubles

3450 5228 5216 3748 2076 1391 5216
μου ὑπὲρ ὑμῶν, ἥτις ἐστὶ δόξα ὑμῶν.
of me on behalf of you, which is glory of you.

5127 5484 2578 3588 1119 3450 4314 3588 3962
14. Τούτου χάριν κάμπτω τὰ γόνατά μου πρὸς τὸν πατέρα
this Because of I bow the knees of me to the Father

3588 2962 2257 2424 5547 1537 3739 3956 3965 1722
τοῦ Κυρίου ἡμῶν Ἰησοῦ Χριστοῦ, 15 ἐξ οὗ πᾶσα πατριὰ ἐν οὐ-
of the Lord of us Jesus Christ, of whom every family in

3772 2532 1909 1093 3687 2443 1325 5213 2596 3588 4149
ρανοῖς καὶ ἐπὶ γῆς ὀνομάζεται, 16 ἵνα δώῃ ὑμῖν, κατὰ τὸν πλοῦ-
Heaven and on earth is named, that He may give you, according to the

3588 1391 846 1411 2901 1223 3588 4151
τον τῆς δόξης αὐτοῦ, δυνάμει κραταιωθῆναι διὰ τοῦ Πνεύ-
riches of the glory of Him, by power to become mighty through the Spirit

846 1519 3588 2080 444 2730 3588 5547
ματος αὐτοῦ εἰς τὸν ἔσω ἄνθρωπον, 17 κατοικῆσαι τὸν Χριστὸν
of Him into the inward man, to dwell Christ

1223 3588 4102 1722 3588 2588 5216 1722 26 4492
διὰ τῆς πίστεως ἐν ταῖς καρδίαις ὑμῶν· ἐν ἀγάπῃ ἐρριζω-
through faith in the hearts of you; in love having been

2532 2311 2443 1840 2638 4862
μένοι καὶ τεθεμελιωμένοι 18 ἵνα ἐξισχύσητε καταλαβέσθαι σὺν
rooted and having been founded that you be strengthened to grasp with

3956 3588 40 5101 3588 4114 2532 3372 2532 899 2532 5311
πᾶσι τοῖς ἁγίοις, τί τὸ πλάτος καὶ μῆκος καὶ βάθος καὶ ὕψος,
all the saints, what (is) the breadth and length and depth and height,

1097 5037 3588 5235 3588 1108 26 3588
19 γνῶναί τε τὴν ὑπερβάλλουσαν τῆς γνώσεως ἀγάπην τοῦ
to know and the surpassing knowledge love

King James Version

power.
8 Unto me, who am less than the least of all saints, is this grace given, that I should preach among the Gentiles the unsearchable riches of Christ;
9 And to make all (men) see what (is) the fellowship of the mystery, which from the beginning of the world hath been hid in God, who created all things by Jesus Christ:
10 To the intent that now unto the principalities and powers in heavenly (places) might be known by the church the manifold wisdom of God,
11 According to the eternal purpose which he purposed in Christ Jesus our Lord:
12 In whom we have boldness and access with confidence by the faith of him.
13 Wherefore I desire that ye faint not at my tribulations for you, which is your glory.
14 For this cause I bow my knees unto the Father of our Lord Jesus Christ,
15 Of whom the whole family in heaven and earth is named,
16 That he would grant you, according to the riches of his glory, to be strengthened with might by his Spirit in the inner man;
17 That Christ may dwell in your hearts by faith; that ye, being rooted and grounded in love,
18 May be able to comprehend with all saints what (is) the breadth, and length, and depth, and height;
19 And to know the love of Christ, which passeth knowledge,

Literal Translation | **Ephesians 3:20** | ***King James Version***

that you may be filled to all the fullness of God.

20 Now to Him being able beyond all things to do exceedingly above all that we ask or think, according to the power working in us,

21 to Him (be) the glory in the church in Christ Jesus, to all the generations of the age of the ages. Amen.

5547 2443 4137 1519 3956 3588 4138 3588 2316
Χριστοῦ, ἵνα πληρωθῆτε εἰς πᾶν τὸ πλήρωμα τοῦ Θεοῦ.
of Christ, that you may be fitted to all the fullness of God.

3588 1161 1410 5228 3956 4160 5228 1537 4053
20. Τῷ δὲ δυναμένῳ ὑπὲρ πάντα ποιῆσαι ὑπὲρ ἐκ περισσοῦ
to the (One) But being able beyond all things to do exceedingly above

3739 154 2228 3539 2596 3588 1411 3588 1754
ὧν αἰτούμεθα ἢ νοοῦμεν, κατὰ τὴν δύναμιν τὴν ἐνεργου-
what we ask or think, according to the power working

1722 2254 846 3588 1391 1722 3588 1577 1722 5547 2424
μένην ἐν ἡμῖν, 21 αὐτῷ ἡ δόξα ἐν τῇ ἐκκλησίᾳ ἐν Χριστῷ Ἰησοῦ
in us, to Him (be) the glory in the church in Christ Jesus

1519 3956 3588 1074 3588 165 3588 165 281
εἰς πάσας τὰς γενεὰς τοῦ αἰῶνος τῶν αἰώνων. ἀμήν.
to all the generations of the age of the ages. Amen.

that ye might be filled with all the fulness of God.

20 Now unto him that is able to do exceeding abundantly above all that we ask or think, according to the power that worketh in us,

21 Unto him (be) glory in the church by Christ Jesus throughout all ages, world without end. Amen.

Ephesians 4

1. Then I, the prisoner in (the) Lord, exhort you to walk worthily of the calling in which you were called,

2 with all humility and meekness, with long-suffering, bearing with one another in love,

3 being eager to keep the unity of the Spirit in the bond of peace.

4 (There is) one body and one Spirit, even as you also were called in one hope of your calling;

5 one Lord, one faith, one baptism,

6 one God and Father of all, He above all and through all and in you all.

7 But to each one of us was given grace according to the measure of the gift of Christ.

8 Because of this, He says, "Having gone up on high, He led captivity captive, and gave gifts to men." (Psa. 68:18)

9 But that He went up, what is it except that He also first went down into the lower parts of the earth?

10 the (One) coming down Himself also is the (One) going up above all the heavens, that He might fill all things.

11 And indeed He gave some (to be) apostles;

Ephesians 4

3870 3767 5209 1473 3588 1198 1722 2962 516
1. Παρακαλῶ οὖν ὑμᾶς ἐγώ, ὁ δέσμιος ἐν Κυρίῳ, ἀξίως
exhort Therefore you I, the prisoner in (the) Lord worthily

4043 3588 2821 3739 2564 3326 3956
περιπατῆσαι τῆς κλήσεως ἧς ἐκλήθητε, 2 μετὰ πάσης ταπει-
to walk of the calling of which you were called, with all

5012 2532 4236 3326 3115 430
νοφροσύνης καὶ πρᾳότητος, μετὰ μακροθυμίας, ἀνεχό-
humility and meekness, with long-suffering, bearing

240 1722 26 4704 5083 3588 1775
μενοι ἀλλήλων ἐν ἀγάπῃ, 3 σπουδάζοντες τηρεῖν τὴν ἑνότητα
with one another in love, being eager to keep the unity

3588 4151 1722 3588 4886 3588 1515 1722 4983 2532
τοῦ Πνεύματος ἐν τῷ συνδέσμῳ τῆς εἰρήνης. 4 ἓν σῶμα καὶ
of the Spirit in the bond of peace. One body and

1520 4151 2531 2532 2564 1722 3391 1680 3588 2821
ἓν Πνεῦμα, καθὼς καὶ ἐκλήθητε ἐν μιᾷ ἐλπίδι τῆς κλήσεως
one Spirit, even as also you were called in one hope of the calling

5216 1520 2962 3391 4102 1520 908 1520 2316 2532
ὑμῶν· 5 εἷς Κύριος, μία πίστις, ἓν βάπτισμα, 6 εἷς Θεὸς καὶ
of you; one Lord, one faith, one baptism, one God and

3962 3956 3588 1909 3956 2532 1223 3956 2532 1722
πατὴρ πάντων, ὁ ἐπὶ πάντων, καὶ διὰ πάντων, καὶ ἐν
Father of all, the (One) above all, and through all, and in

3956 5213 1520 1161 1538 2257 1325 3588 5485 2596 3588
πᾶσιν ὑμῖν. 7 ἑνὶ δὲ ἑκάστῳ ἡμῶν ἐδόθη ἡ χάρις κατὰ τὸ
all of you. to one But each of us was given grace according to the

3358 3588 1431 3588 5547 1352 3004 305 1519
μέτρον τῆς δωρεᾶς τοῦ Χριστοῦ. 8 διὸ λέγει, Ἀναβὰς εἰς
measure of the gift of Christ. Therefore He says, Having gone up on

5311 162 161 2532 1325 1390 3588
ὕψος ᾐχμαλώτευσεν αἰχμαλωσίαν, καὶ ἔδωκε δόματα τοῖς
high He led captive captivity, and gave gifts

444 3588 1161 305 5101 2076 1487 3361 3754 2532 2597
ἀνθρώποις. 9 [τὸ δέ, Ἀνέβη, τί ἐστιν εἰ μὴ ὅτι καὶ κατέβη
to men. that But, He went up, what is it except that also He went down

4412 1519 3588 2737 3313 3588 1093 3588 2597 846
πρῶτον εἰς τὰ κατώτερα μέρη τῆς γῆς; 10 ὁ καταβάς, αὐτός
first into the lower parts of the earth? The (One) coming down, Himself

2076 2532 3588 305 5231 3956 3588 3772 2443
ἐστι καὶ ὁ ἀναβὰς ὑπεράνω πάντων τῶν οὐρανῶν, ἵνα
is also the (One) going up far above all the heavens, that

4137 3588 3956 2532 846 1325 3588 3303 652
πληρώσῃ τὰ πάντα.] 11 καὶ αὐτὸς ἔδωκε τοὺς μὲν ἀποστό-
He might fill all things. And He gave some apostles,

Ephesians 4

1. I therefore, the prisoner of the Lord, beseech you that ye walk worthy of the vocation wherewith ye are called,

2 With all lowliness and meekness, with longsuffering, forbearing one another in love;

3 Endeavouring to keep the unity of the Spirit in the bond of peace.

4 (There is) one body, and one Spirit, even as ye are called in one hope of your calling;

5 One Lord, one faith, one baptism,

6 One God and Father of all, who (is) above all, and through all, and in you all.

7 But unto every one of us is given grace according to the measure of the gift of Christ.

8 Wherefore he saith, When he ascended up on high, he led captivity captive, and gave gifts unto men.

9 (Now that he ascended, what is it but that he also descended first into the lower parts of the earth?

10 He that descended is the same also that ascended up far above all heavens, that he might fill all things.)

11 And he gave some, apostles;

Literal Translation | **Ephesians 4:12** | ***King James Version***

and some prophets; and
some evangelists; and
some pastors and teach-
ers;
12 with a view to the
perfecting of the saints
for the work of the min-
istry, for the building up
of the body of Christ,

3588 1161 4396 3588 1161 2099 3588 1161
λους, τοὺς δὲ προφήτας, τοὺς δὲ εὐαγγελιστάς, τοὺς δὲ
some and prophets, some and evangelists, some and
4166 2532 1320 4314 3588 2677 3588
ποιμένας καὶ διδασκάλους, 12 πρὸς τὸν καταρτισμὸν τῶν
pastors and teachers, for the perfecting of the
40 1519 2041 1248 1519 3619 3588 4983 3588
ἁγίων, εἰς ἔργον διακονίας, εἰς οἰκοδομὴν τοῦ σώματος τοῦ
saints, for (the) work of ministry, to building up of the body
5547 3360 2658 3588 3956 1519 3588 1775
Χριστοῦ· 13 μέχρι καταντήσωμεν οἱ πάντες εἰς τὴν ἑνότητα
of Christ; until we may come all to the unity

and some, prophets;
and some, evangelists;
and some, pastors and
teachers;
12 For the perfecting of
the saints, for the work
of the ministry, for the
edifying of the body of
Christ:

13 until we all may
come to the unity of the
faith and of the full
knowledge of the Son
of God, to a full-grown
man, to (the) measure of
(the) stature of the full-
ness of Christ,

3588 4102 2532 3588 1922 3588 5207 3588 2316 1519
τῆς πίστεως καὶ τῆς ἐπιγνώσεως τοῦ υἱοῦ τοῦ Θεοῦ, εἰς
of the faith and of the full knowledge of the Son of God, to
435 5046 1519 3358 2244 3588 4138 3588
ἄνδρα τέλειον, εἰς μέτρον ἡλικίας τοῦ πληρώματος τοῦ
a man full-grown, to (the) measure of (the) stature of the fullness
5547 2443 3371 5600 3516 2831 2532
Χριστοῦ· 14 ἵνα μηκέτι ὦμεν νήπιοι, κλυδωνιζόμενοι καὶ
of Christ; that no longer we may be infants, being blown and

13 Till we all come in
the unity of the faith,
and of the knowledge of
the Son of God, unto a
perfect man, unto the
measure of the stature
of the fulness of Christ:

14 so that we may no
longer be infants, being
blown and carried to
and fro by every wind of
doctrine, to the sleight
of men, in craftiness to
the trickery of error,

4064 3956 417 3588 1319 1722 3588 2940
περιφερόμενοι παντὶ ἀνέμῳ τῆς διδασκαλίας, ἐν τῇ κυβείᾳ
being carried about by every wind of doctrine, to the sleight
3588 444 1722 3834 4314 3588 3180 3588
τῶν ἀνθρώπων, ἐν πανουργίᾳ, πρὸς τὴν μεθοδείαν τῆς
of men, in craftiness to the trickery
4106 226 1161 1722 26 837 1519 846 3588
πλάνης· 15 ἀληθεύοντες δὲ ἐν ἀγάπῃ αὐξήσωμεν εἰς αὐτὸν τὰ
of error; speaking truth but in love we may grow into Him (in)

14 That we (hence-
forth) be no more chil-
dren, tossed to and fro,
and carried about with
every wind of doctrine,
by the sleight of men,
(and) cunning crafti-
ness, whereby they lie
in wait to deceive;

15 but speaking truth in
love, we may grow up
into Him in all things,
who is the Head, the
Christ,
16 from whom all the
body, being fitted and
compacted together
through every assisting
bond, according to (the)
effectual working of
one measure (in) each
part, producing the
growth of the body to
the building up of itself
in love.

3956 3739 2076 3588 2776 3588 5547 1537 3739 3956 3588 4983
πάντα, ὅς ἐστιν ἡ κεφαλή, ὁ Χριστός, 16 ἐξ οὗ πᾶν τὸ σῶμα
all things, who is the Head, the Christ, of whom all the body
4883 2532 4822 1223 3956 860
συναρμολογούμενον καὶ συμβιβαζόμενον διὰ πάσης ἁφῆς
being fitted together and being compacted together through every bond
3588 2024 2596 1753 1722 3358 1520 1538
τῆς ἐπιχορηγίας κατ' ἐνέργειαν ἐν μέτρῳ ἑνὸς ἑκάστου
of assistance according to (the) working in measure of one each
3313 3588 838 3588 4983 4160 1519 3619
μέρους, τὴν αὔξησιν τοῦ σώματος ποιεῖται εἰς οἰκοδομὴν
part, the growth of the body producing to the building up
1438 1722 26
ἑαυτοῦ ἐν ἀγάπῃ.
of itself in love.

15 But speaking the
truth in love, may grow
up into him in all things,
which is the head,
(even) Christ:
16 From whom the
whole body fitly joined
together and com-
pacted by that which
every joint supplieth,
according to the effec-
tual working in the
measure of every part,
maketh increase of the
body unto the edifying
of itself in love.

17 Therefore, I say this,
and testify in (the) Lord,
that you no longer walk
even as also the rest (of
the) nations walk, in
(the) vanity of their
mind,
18 having been dark-
ened in the intellect,
having been alienated
(from) the life of God
because of the igno-
rance being in them be-
cause of the hardness of
their heart,
19 who, having cast off
all feeling, gave them-
selves up to lust, for
(the)

5124 3767 3004 2532 3143 1722 2962 3371 5209
17. Τοῦτο οὖν λέγω καὶ μαρτύρομαι ἐν Κυρίῳ, μηκέτι ὑμᾶς
this Therefore I say and testify in (the) Lord, no longer you
4043 2531 2532 3588 3062 1484 4043 1722 3153
περιπατεῖν, καθὼς καὶ τὰ λοιπὰ ἔθνη περιπατεῖ ἐν ματαιό-
walk, even as also the rest (of the) nations walk in vanity
3588 3563 846 4654 3588 1271 5607
τητι τοῦ νοὸς αὐτῶν, 18 ἐσκοτισμένοι τῇ διανοίᾳ, ὄντες
of the mind of them, having been darkened in the intellect, being
526 3588 2222 3588 2316 1223 3588 52 3588
ἀπηλλοτριωμένοι τῆς ζωῆς τοῦ Θεοῦ διὰ τὴν ἄγνοιαν τὴν
alienated (from) the life of God because of the ignorance
5607 1722 846 1223 3588 4457 3588 2588 846
οὖσαν ἐν αὐτοῖς, διὰ τὴν πώρωσιν τῆς καρδίας αὐτῶν·
being in them, because of the hardness of the heart of them;
3748 524 1438 3860 3588 766 1519
19 οἵτινες ἀπηλγηκότες ἑαυτοὺς παρέδωκαν τῇ ἀσελγείᾳ, εἰς
who having cast off all feeling themselves gave up to lust, to

17 This I say therefore,
and testify in the Lord,
that ye henceforth walk
not as other Gentiles
walk, in the vanity of
their mind,
18 Having the under-
standing darkened, be-
ing alienated from the
life of God through the
ignorance that is in
them, because of the
blindness of their heart:
19 Who being past feel-
ing have given them-
selves over unto lascivi-
ousness, to

Ephesians 4:20

Literal Translation

working of all uncleanness with greediness.
20 But you have not so learned Christ,
21 if indeed you heard Him and were taught in Him, as (the) truth is in Jesus.

22 for you have put off the old man, as regards the former behavior, having been corrupted according to the deceitful lusts,

23 and to be renewed in the spirit of your mind,

24 and to put on the new man, (which) according to God (was) created in righteousness and true holiness.

25 Therefore, having put off the false, speak truth each with his neighbor, because we are members of one another.
26 Be angry but do not sin; do not let the sun go down on your wrath,

27 nor give place to the devil.
28 The one stealing, let him steal no more, but rather let him labor, working what (is) good with the hands, that he may have (something) to give to the (one) having need.
29 Let not any rotten word go out of your mouth, but if any (is) good to building up (in respect to) the need, that it may give grace to the ones hearing.
30 And do not grieve the Holy Spirit of God, by whom you were sealed to (the) day of redemption.
31 Let all bitterness, and anger, and wrath, and tumult, and evil speaking be put away from you, along with all badness.
32 And be kind to one another, tenderhearted, having forgiven yourselves, even as also God in Christ forgave

2039 167 3956 1722 4124 5210 1161 3756
ἐργασίαν ἀκαθαρσίας πάσης ἐν πλεονεξίᾳ. 20 ὑμεῖς δὲ οὐχ
(the) working of uncleanness all in greediness. you But not
3779 3129 3588 5547 1489 846 191 2532 1722
οὕτως ἐμάθετε τὸν Χριστόν, 21 εἴγε αὐτὸν ἠκούσατε καὶ ἐν
so learned Christ, if indeed Him you heard and by
846 1321 2531 2076 225 1722 3588 2424
αὐτῷ ἐδιδάχθητε, καθώς ἐστιν ἀλήθεια ἐν τῷ Ἰησοῦ·
Him were taught, even as is (the) truth in Jesus;

659 5209 2596 3588 4387 391 3588
22 ἀποθέσθαι ὑμᾶς, κατὰ τὴν προτέραν ἀναστροφήν, τὸν
to put off you, as regards the former behavior, of the
3820 444 3588 5351 2596 3588 1939
παλαιὸν ἄνθρωπον, τὸν φθειρόμενον κατὰ τὰς ἐπιθυμίας
old man, having been corrupted according to the lusts
3588 539 365 1161 3588 4151 3588 3563 5216
τῆς ἀπάτης· 23 ἀνανεοῦσθαι δὲ τῷ πνεύματι τοῦ νοὸς ὑμῶν,
of deceit; to be renewed and in the spirit of the mind of you,
2532 1746 3588 2537 444 3588 2596 2316
24 καὶ ἐνδύσασθαι τὸν καινὸν ἄνθρωπον, τὸν κατὰ Θεὸν κτι-
and to put on the new man, according to God
2936 1722 1343 2532 3742 3588 225
σθέντα ἐν δικαιοσύνῃ καὶ ὁσιότητι τῆς ἀληθείας.
created in righteousness and holiness of truth.

1352 659 3588 5579 2980 225 1538
25. Διὸ ἀποθέμενοι τὸ ψεῦδος λαλεῖτε ἀλήθειαν ἕκαστος
Therefore having put off the lie speak truth each
3326 3588 4139 846 3754 2070 240 3196 3710
μετὰ τοῦ πλησίον αὐτοῦ· ὅτι ἐσμὲν ἀλλήλων μέλη. 26 ὀργίζεσθε
with the neighbor of him; because we are of one another members. Be angry
2532 3361 264 3588 2246 3361 1931 1909 3588 3950
καὶ μὴ ἁμαρτάνετε· ὁ ἥλιος μὴ ἐπιδυέτω ἐπὶ τῷ παροργισμῷ
but not do sin; the sun not let set on the wrath
5216 3383 1325 5117 3588 1228 3588 2813 3371
ὑμῶν· 27 μήτε δίδοτε τόπον τῷ διαβόλῳ. 28 ὁ κλέπτων μηκέτι
of you; nor give place to the devil. The (one) stealing no more
2813 3123 1161 2872 2038 3588 18 3588
κλεπτέτω· μᾶλλον δὲ κοπιάτω, ἐργαζόμενος τὸ ἀγαθὸν ταῖς
let him steal; rather but let him labor, working the good with the
5532 2443 2192 3330 3588 5532 2192 3956 3056
χερσίν, ἵνα ἔχῃ μεταδιδόναι τῷ χρείαν ἔχοντι. 29 πᾶς λόγος
hands, that he may have to give to the (one) need having. Every word
4550 1537 3588 4750 5216 3361 1607 235 1487 5100
σαπρὸς ἐκ τοῦ στόματος ὑμῶν μὴ ἐκπορευέσθω, ἀλλ' εἴ τις
rotten out of the mouth of you not let go, but if any
18 4314 3619 3588 5532 2443 1325 5485 3588 191
ἀγαθὸς πρὸς οἰκοδομὴν τῆς χρείας, ἵνα δῷ χάριν τοῖς ἀκού-
(is) good to building up the need, that it may give grace to those
2532 3361 3076 3588 4151 3588 40 3588 2316 1722 3739
ουσι. 30 καὶ μὴ λυπεῖτε τὸ Πνεῦμα τὸ Ἅγιον τοῦ Θεοῦ, ἐν ᾧ
hearing. And not do grieve the Spirit Holy of God, by whom
4972 1519 2250 629 3956 4088 2532
ἐσφραγίσθητε εἰς ἡμέραν ἀπολυτρώσεως. 31 πᾶσα πικρία καὶ
you were sealed to a day of redemption. All bitterness and
2372 2532 3709 2532 2906 2532 988 142 575 5216
θυμὸς καὶ ὀργὴ καὶ κραυγὴ καὶ βλασφημία ἀρθήτω ἀφ' ὑμῶν,
anger and wrath and tumult and evil speaking put away from you,
4862 3956 2549 1096 1161 1519 240 5543 2155
σὺν πάσῃ κακίᾳ· 32 γίνεσθε δὲ εἰς ἀλλήλους χρηστοί, εὔσπλαγ-
with all badness; become and to one another kind, tender-
5483 1438 2531 2532/3588/2316/1722/5547 5483
χνοι, χαριζόμενοι ἑαυτοῖς, καθὼς καὶ ὁ Θεὸς ἐν Χριστῷ ἐχαρί-
hearted, having forgiven yourselves, even as also God in Christ forgave

King James Version

work all uncleanness with greediness.
20 But ye have not so learned Christ;
21 If so be that ye have heard him, and have been taught by him, as the truth is in Jesus:

22 That ye put off concerning the former conversation the old man, which is corrupt according to the deceitful lusts;

23 And be renewed in the spirit of your mind;

24 And that ye put on the new man, which after God is created in righteousness and true holiness.

25 Wherefore putting away lying, speak every man truth with his neighbour: for we are members one of another.
26 Be ye angry, and sin not: let not the sun go down upon your wrath:

27 Neither give place to the devil.
28 Let him that stole steal no more: but rather let him labour, working with (his) hands the thing which is good, that he may have to give to him that needeth.
29 Let no corrupt communication proceed out of your mouth, but that which is good to the use of edifying, that it may minister grace unto the hearers.
30 And grieve not the holy Spirit of God, whereby ye are sealed unto the day of redemption.
31 Let all bitterness, and wrath, and anger, and clamour, and evil speaking, be put away from you, with all malice:
32 And be ye kind one to another, tenderhearted, forgiving one another, even as God for Christ's sake hath forgiven

Literal Translation

you.

Ephesians 5

1. Then become imitators of God, as beloved children,
2 and walk in love, even as Christ also loved us and gave up Himself on our behalf, an offering and a sacrifice for an odor of a sweet smell to God.
3 But let not fornication, and all uncleanness, or greediness, be named among you, as is fitting for saints;

4 also shamefulness, and foolish talking, or joking, the things not becoming, but rather thanksgiving.
5 For be knowing this, that every fornicator, or unclean one, or covetous (one), who is an idolater, has no inheritance in the kingdom of Christ and of God.

6 Let no one deceive you with empty words, for through these the wrath of God is coming on the sons of disobedience.

7 Then do not be partners with them;
8 for you then were darkness, but now light in (the) Lord; walk as children of light.

9 For the fruit of the Spirit (is) in all goodness and righteousness and truth,
10 proving what is well-pleasing to (the) Lord.
11 And have no fellowship with the unfruitful works of darkness, but rather even reprove (them).
12 For it is shameful even to speak of the secret things being done by them.
13 But all things being exposed by the light are clearly revealed, for everything

Ephesians 5:1

5483 5213
σατο ὑμῖν.
you.

Ephesians 5

1096 3767 3402 3588 2316 5613 5043 27 2532
1. Γίνεσθε οὖν μιμηταὶ τοῦ Θεοῦ, ὡς τέκνα ἀγαπητά· 2 καὶ
become Then imitators of God, as children beloved; and
4043 1722 26 2531 2532 3588 5547 25 2248
περιπατεῖτε ἐν ἀγάπῃ, καθὼς καὶ ὁ Χριστὸς ἠγάπησεν ἡμᾶς,
walk in love, even as also Christ loved us,
2532 3860 1438 5228 2257 4376 2532 2378
καὶ παρέδωκεν ἑαυτὸν ὑπὲρ ἡμῶν προσφορὰν καὶ θυσίαν
and gave up Himself on behalf of us an offering and a sacrifice
3588 2316 1519 3744 2175 4202 1161 2532 3956 167
τῷ Θεῷ εἰς ὀσμὴν εὐωδίας. 3 πορνεία δὲ καὶ πᾶσα ἀκαθαρσία
to God for an odor of sweet smell. fornication But and all uncleanness
2228 4124 3366 3687 1722 5213 2531 4241 40
ἢ πλεονεξία μηδὲ ὀνομαζέσθω ἐν ὑμῖν, καθὼς πρέπει ἁγίοις·
or greediness not let be named among you, even as is fitting for saints;
2532 151 2532 3473 2228 2160 3588 3756
4 καὶ αἰσχρότης καὶ μωρολογία ἢ εὐτραπελία, τὰ οὐκ ἀνή-
also shamefulness and foolish talking or joking, the things not
433 235 3123 2169 5124 1063 2075
κοντα· ἀλλὰ μᾶλλον εὐχαριστία. 5 τοῦτο γὰρ ἔστε γινώ-
becoming, but rather thanksgiving. this For be knowing,
1097 3754 3956 4205 2228 169 2228 4123 3739 2076
σκοντες, ὅτι πᾶς πόρνος, ἢ ἀκάθαρτος, ἢ πλεονέκτης, ὅς ἐστιν
that every fornicator, or unclean one, or covetous one, who is
1496 3756 2192 2817 1722 3588 932 3588
εἰδωλολάτρης, οὐκ ἔχει κληρονομίαν ἐν τῇ βασιλείᾳ τοῦ
an idolator, not has inheritance in the kingdom
5547 2532 2316 3367 5209 538 2756 3056
Χριστοῦ καὶ Θεοῦ. 6 μηδεὶς ὑμᾶς ἀπατάτω κενοῖς λόγοις·
of Christ and of God. Let no one you deceive with empty words;
1223 5023 1063 2064 3588 3709 3588 2316 1909 3588 5207
διὰ ταῦτα γὰρ ἔρχεται ἡ ὀργὴ τοῦ Θεοῦ ἐπὶ τοὺς υἱοὺς
through these for is coming the wrath of God on the sons
3588 543 3361 3767 1096 4830 846 2258 1063
τῆς ἀπειθείας. 7 μὴ οὖν γίνεσθε συμμέτοχοι αὐτῶν· 8 ἦτε γὰρ
of disobedience. not Then become sharers with them; you were for
4218 4655 3568 1161 5457 1722 2962 5613 5043 5457 4043
ποτε σκότος, νῦν δὲ φῶς ἐν Κυρίῳ· ὡς τέκνα φωτὸς περι-
then darkness, now but light in (the) Lord; as children of light walk,
3588 1063 2590 3588 4151 1722 3956 19
πατεῖτε 9 ὁ γὰρ καρπὸς τοῦ Πνεύματος ἐν πάσῃ ἀγαθωσύνῃ
the for fruit of the Spirit (is) in all goodness
2532 1343 2532 225 1381 5101 2076 2101
καὶ δικαιοσύνῃ καὶ ἀληθείᾳ, 10 δοκιμάζοντες τί ἐστιν εὐάρε-
and righteousness and truth, proving what is well-
3588 2962 2532 3361 4790 3588 2041 3588
στον τῷ Κυρίῳ· 11 καὶ μὴ συγκοινωνεῖτε τοῖς ἔργοις τοῖς
pleasing to (the) Lord; and not do have fellowship with the works
175 3588 4655 3123 1161 2532 1651 3588 1063
ἀκάρποις τοῦ σκότους, μᾶλλον δὲ καὶ ἐλέγχετε· 12 τὰ γὰρ
unfruitful of darkness, rather but even reprove; the things for
2931 1096 5259 846 150 2076 2532 3004 3588 1161
κρυφῇ γινόμενα ὑπ' αὐτῶν αἰσχρόν ἐστι καὶ λέγειν. 13 τὰ δὲ
hidden being done by them shameful it is even to speak. But
3956 1651 5259 3588 5457 5319 3956 1063
πάντα ἐλεγχόμενα ὑπὸ τοῦ φωτὸς φανεροῦται· πᾶν γὰρ
all things being reproved by the light is revealed; everything for

King James Version

you.

Ephesians 5

1. Be ye therefore followers of God, as dear children;
2 And walk in love, as Christ also hath loved us, and hath given himself for us an offering and a sacrifice to God for a sweetsmelling savour.
3 But fornication, and all uncleanness, or covetousness, let it not be once named among you, as becometh saints;

4 Neither filthiness, nor foolish talking, nor jesting, which are not convenient: but rather giving of thanks.
5 For this ye know, that no whoremonger, nor unclean person, nor covetous man, who is an idolater, hath any inheritance in the kingdom of Christ and of God.

6 Let no man deceive you with vain words: for because of these things cometh the wrath of God upon the children of disobedience.

7 Be not ye therefore partakers with them.
8 For ye were sometimes darkness, but now (are ye) light in the Lord: walk as children of light:
9 (For the fruit of the Spirit (is) in all goodness and righteousness and truth;)
10 Proving what is acceptable unto the Lord.

11 And have no fellowship with the unfruitful works of darkness, but rather reprove (them).
12 For it is a shame even to speak of those things which are done of them in secret.
13 But all things that are reproved are made manifest by the light: for whatsoever

Literal Translation

having been revealed is light.
14 Because of this, He says, "Arise, sleeping (one) and stand up from the dead, and Christ will shine on you."

15 Then watch how carefully you walk, not as unwise, but as wise ones,
16 redeeming the time, because the days are evil.
17 Because of this do not be foolish, but understanding what the will of the Lord (is).
18 And do not be drunk with wine, in which is debauchery, but be filled with (the) Spirit,
19 speaking to yourselves in psalms and hymns and spiritual songs, singing and praising in your heart to the Lord,
20 giving thanks at all times for all things in the name of our Lord Jesus Christ, even to God (the) Father,

21 having been subject to one another in (the) fear of God.

22 Wives, subject yourselves to (your) own husbands, as to the Lord,
23 because a husband is head of the wife, as also Christ (is) Head of the church, and He is Savior of the body.

24 But even as the church is subject to Christ, so also the wives to (their) own husbands in everything.
25 Husbands, love your wives, even as Christ also loved the church and gave Himself up on its behalf,

26 that He might sanctify it, cleansing (it) by the washing of the water in (the) Word,
27 that He might present it to Himself (as) the glorious church,

Ephesians 5:14

3588 5319 5457 2076 1352 3004 1453 3588 2518
τὸ φανερούμενον φῶς ἐστί.14 διὸ λέγει, Ἔγειραι ὁ καθεύδων
having been revealed light is. Therefore He says, Arise sleeping (one)

2532 450 1537 3588 3498 2532 2017 4671 3588 5547
καὶ ἀνάστα ἐκ τῶν νεκρῶν, καὶ ἐπιφαύσει σοι ὁ Χριστός.
and stand up from the dead, and will shine on you Christ.

991 3767 4459 199 4043 3361 5613 781
15. Βλέπετε οὖν πῶς ἀκριβῶς περιπατεῖτε, μὴ ὡς ἄσοφοι,
watch Therefore how carefully you walk, not as unwise,

235 5613 4680 1805 3588 2540 3754 3588 2250
ἀλλ᾽ ὡς σοφοί, 16 ἐξαγοραζόμενοι τὸν καιρόν, ὅτι αἱ ἡμέραι
but as wise, redeeming the time, because the days

4190 1526 1223 5124 3361 1096 878 235 4920
πονηραί εἰσι. 17 διὰ τοῦτο μὴ γίνεσθε ἄφρονες, ἀλλὰ συνιέντες
evil are. Because of this not do become foolish, but understanding

5101 3588 2307 3588 2962 2532 3361 3182 3631 1722 3739
τί τὸ θέλημα τοῦ Κυρίου. 18 καὶ μὴ μεθύσκεσθε οἴνῳ, ἐν ᾧ
what the will of the Lord (is). And not do be drunk with wine, in which

2076 810 235 4137 1722 4151 2980
ἐστὶν ἀσωτία, ἀλλὰ πληροῦσθε ἐν Πνεύματι, 19 λαλοῦντες
is debauchery, but be filled with (the) Spirit, speaking

1438 5568 2532 5215 2532 5603 4152 103
ἑαυτοῖς ψαλμοῖς καὶ ὕμνοις καὶ ᾠδαῖς πνευματικαῖς, ᾄδοντες
to yourselves in psalms and hymns and songs spiritual, singing

2532 5567 1722 3588 2588 5216 3588 2962 2168
καὶ ψάλλοντες ἐν τῇ καρδίᾳ ὑμῶν τῷ Κυρίῳ, 20 εὐχαριστοῦντες
and psalming in the heart of you to the Lord, giving thanks

3842 5228 3956 1722 3686 3588 2962 2257 2424
πάντοτε ὑπὲρ πάντων ἐν ὀνόματι τοῦ Κυρίου ἡμῶν Ἰησοῦ
always for all things in (the) name of the Lord of us Jesus

5547 3588 2316 2532 3962 5293 240 1722
Χριστοῦ τῷ Θεῷ καὶ πατρί, 21 ὑποτασσόμενοι ἀλλήλοις ἐν
Christ to God and (the) Father, being subject one another in

5401 2316
φόβῳ Θεοῦ.
(the) fear of God.

3588 1135 3588 2398 435 5293 5613 3588
22. Αἱ γυναῖκες, τοῖς ἰδίοις ἀνδράσιν ὑποτάσσεσθε, ὡς τῷ
The wives, to the own husbands subject yourselves, as to the

2962 3754 3588 435 2076 2776 3588 1135 5613 2532 3588
Κυρίῳ, 23 ὅτι ὁ ἀνήρ ἐστι κεφαλὴ τῆς γυναικός, ὡς καὶ ὁ
Lord, because a husband is head of the wife, as also

5547 2776 3588 1577 2532 846 2076 4990 3588
Χριστὸς κεφαλὴ τῆς ἐκκλησίας, καὶ αὐτός ἐστι σωτὴρ τοῦ
Christ (is) Head of the church, and He is Savior of the

4983 235 5618 3588 1577 5293 3588 5547
σώματος. 24 ἀλλ᾽ ὥσπερ ἡ ἐκκλησία ὑποτάσσεται τῷ Χριστῷ,
body. But as the church is subject to Christ,

3779 2532 3588 1135 3588 2398 435 1722 3956 3588
οὕτω καὶ αἱ γυναῖκες τοῖς ἰδίοις ἀνδράσιν ἐν παντί. 25 οἱ
so also the wives to the own husbands in everything. The

435 25 3588 1135 1438 2531 2532 3588 5547
ἄνδρες, ἀγαπᾶτε τὰς γυναῖκας ἑαυτῶν, καθὼς καὶ ὁ Χριστὸς
husbands, love the wives (of) yourselves, even as also Christ

25 3588 1577 2532 1438 3860 5228 846
ἠγάπησε τὴν ἐκκλησίαν, καὶ ἑαυτὸν παρέδωκεν ὑπὲρ αὐτῆς·
loved the church, and Himself gave up on behalf of it;

2443 846 37 2511 3588 3067 3588 5204 1722
26 ἵνα αὐτὴν ἁγιάσῃ, καθαρίσας τῷ λουτρῷ τοῦ ὕδατος ἐν
that it He might sanctify, cleansing by the washing of the water by

4487 2443 3936 846 1438 1741 3588 1577
ῥήματι, 27 ἵνα παραστήσῃ αὐτὴν ἑαυτῷ ἔνδοξον τὴν ἐκκλη-
(the) Word, that He might present it to Himself glorious the church

King James Version

doth make manifest is light.
14 Wherefore he saith, Awake thou that sleepest, and arise from the dead, and Christ shall give thee light.

15 See then that ye walk circumspectly, not as fools, but as wise,

16 Redeeming the time, because the days are evil.
17 Wherefore be ye not unwise, but understanding what the will of the Lord (is).
18 And be not drunk with wine, wherein is excess; but be filled with the Spirit;
19 Speaking to yourselves in psalms and hymns and spiritual songs, singing and making melody in your heart to the Lord;
20 Giving thanks always for all things unto God and the Father in the name of our Lord Jesus Christ;

21 Submitting yourselves one to another in the fear of God.

22 Wives, submit yourselves unto your own husbands, as unto the Lord.
23 For the husband is the head of the wife, even as Christ is the head of the church: and he is the saviour of the body.

24 Therefore as the church is subject unto Christ, so (let) the wives (be) to their own husbands in every thing.
25 Husbands, love your wives, even as Christ also loved the church, and gave himself for it;

26 That he might sanctify and cleanse it with the washing of water by the word,
27 That he might present it to himself a glorious church,

Literal Translation

not having spot or wrinkle, or any such things, but that it be holy and without blemish.

28 So, husbands ought to love their wives as their (own) bodies, he loving his wife loves himself,

29 for then no one hated his (own) flesh, but nourishes and cherishes it, even as also the Lord the church.

30 For we are members of His body, of His flesh, and of His bones.

31 "For this a man shall leave his father and mother, and shall cleave to his wife, and the two shall be one flesh." (Gen.2:24)

32 This mystery is great, but I speak as to Christ and as to the church.

33 However, you also, everyone, let each love his wife as himself, and the wife, that she give deference to the husband.

Epheisans 5:28

3361 2192 4696 2228 4512 2228 5100 3588 5108 235
σίαν, μὴ ἔχουσαν σπίλον ἢ ῥυτίδα ἤ τι τῶν τοιούτων, ἀλλ'
not having spot or wrinkle or any of such things, but

2443 5600 40 2532 299 3779 3784 3588 435 25
ἵνα ᾖ ἁγία καὶ ἄμωμος. 28 οὕτως ὀφείλουσιν οἱ ἄνδρες ἀγαπᾶν
that it be holy and unblemished. So ought the husbands to love

3588 1438 1135 5613 3588 1438 4983 3588 25 3588
τὰς ἑαυτῶν γυναῖκας ὡς τὰ ἑαυτῶν σώματα. ὁ ἀγαπῶν τὴν
the of themselves wives as the of themselves bodies. The (one) loving the

1438 1135 1438 25 3762 1063 4218 3588 1438
ἑαυτοῦ γυναῖκα ἑαυτὸν ἀγαπᾷ· 29 οὐδεὶς γάρ ποτε τὴν ἑαυτοῦ
of himself wife himself loves; no one for then the of himself

4561 3404 235 1625 2532 2282 846 2531 2532
σάρκα ἐμίσησεν, ἀλλ' ἐκτρέφει καὶ θάλπει αὐτήν, καθὼς καὶ
flesh hates, but nourishes and cherishes it, even as also

3588 2962 3588 1577 3754 3196 2070 3588 4983 846
ὁ Κύριος τὴν ἐκκλησίαν· 30 ὅτι μέλη ἐσμὲν τοῦ σώματος αὐτοῦ,
the Lord the church; because members we are of the body of Him,

1537 3588 4561 846 2532 1537 3588 3747 846 473 5127
ἐκ τῆς σαρκὸς αὐτοῦ καὶ ἐκ τῶν ὀστέων αὐτοῦ. 31 Ἀντὶ τού-
of the flesh of Him and of the bones of Him. Because of this

2641 444 3588 3962 846 2532 3588
του καταλείψει ἄνθρωπος τὸν πατέρα αὐτοῦ καὶ τὴν
shall leave a man the father of Him and the

3384 2532 4347 4314 3588 1135 846
μητέρα, καὶ προσκολληθήσεται πρὸς τὴν γυναῖκα αὐτοῦ,
mother, and shall cleave to the wife of him,

2532 2071 3588 1417 1519 4561 3391 3588 3466 5124 3173
καὶ ἔσονται οἱ δύο εἰς σάρκα μίαν. 32 τὸ μυστήριον τοῦτο μέγα
and shall be the two into flesh one. mystery This great

2076 1473 1161 3004 1519 5547 2532 1519 3588 1577 4133
ἐστίν· ἐγὼ δὲ λέγω εἰς Χριστόν, καὶ εἰς τὴν ἐκκλησίαν. 33 πλὴν
is; I but say as to Christ, and as to the church. But

2532 5210 3588 2596 1520 1538 3588 1438 1135 3779
καὶ ὑμεῖς οἱ καθ' ἕνα, ἕκαστος τὴν ἑαυτοῦ γυναῖκα οὕτως
also you one by one, each the of himself wife so

25 5613 1438 3588 1161 1135 2443 5399 3588 435
ἀγαπάτω ὡς ἑαυτόν· ἡ δὲ γυνὴ ἵνα φοβῆται τὸν ἄνδρα.
let him love as himself, the and wife that she defer to the husband.

King James Version

not having spot, or wrinkle, or any such thing; but that it should be holy and without blemish.

28 So ought men to love their wives as their own bodies. He that loveth his wife loveth himself.

29 For no man ever yet hated his own flesh; but nourisheth and cherisheth it, even as the Lord the church:

30 For we are members of his body, of his flesh, and of his bones.

31 For this cause shall a man leave his father and mother, and shall be joined unto his wife, and they two shall be one flesh.

32 This is a great mystery: but I speak concerning Christ and the church.

33 Nevertheless let every one of you in particular so love his wife even as himself; and the wife (see) that she reverence (her) husband.

Ephesians 6

1. Children, obey your parents in (the) Lord, for this is right.

2 Honor your father and mother, which is (the) first commandment with a promise, (Ex. 20:12)

3 that it may be well with you, and you may be long-lived on the earth.

4 And fathers, do not provoke your children, but nurture them in (the) discipline and admonition of (the) Lord.

5 Slaves, obey (your) lords according to flesh, with fear

Ephesians 6

3588 5043 5219 3588 1118 5216 1722 2962 5124
1. Τὰ τέκνα, ὑπακούετε τοῖς γονεῦσιν ὑμῶν ἐν Κυρίῳ· τοῦτο
The children obey the parents of you in (the) Lord; this

1063 2076 1342 5091 3588 3962 4675 2532 3588 3384
γάρ ἐστι δίκαιον. 2 Τίμα τὸν πατέρα σου καὶ τὴν μητέρα
for is right. Honor the father of you and the mother,

3748 2076 1785 4413 1722 1860 2443 2095 4671
[ἥτις ἐστὶν ἐντολὴ πρώτη ἐν ἐπαγγελίᾳ], 3 ἵνα εὖ σοι
which is commandment (the) first with a promise, that well with you

1096 2532 2071 3118 1909 3588 1093 2532 3588 3962
γένηται, καὶ ἔσῃ μακροχρόνιος ἐπὶ τῆς γῆς. 4 καὶ οἱ πατέρες,
it may be, and you may be long-lived on the earth. And the fathers,

3361 3949 3588 5043 5216 235 1625 846 1722
μὴ παροργίζετε τὰ τέκνα ὑμῶν, ἀλλ' ἐκτρέφετε αὐτὰ ἐν
not do provoke the children of you, but nurture them in

3809 2532 3559 2962
παιδείᾳ καὶ νουθεσίᾳ Κυρίου.
(the) discipline and admonition of (the) Lord.

3588 1401 5219 3588 2962 2596 4561 3326 5401
5. Οἱ δοῦλοι, ὑπακούετε τοῖς κυρίοις κατὰ σάρκα μετὰ φόβου
The slaves, obey the lords according to flesh with fear

Ephesians 6

1. Children, obey your parents in the Lord: for this is right.

2 Honour thy father and mother; (which is the first commandment with promise;)

3 That it may be well with thee, and thou mayest live long on the earth.

4 And, ye fathers, provoke not your children to wrath: but bring them up in the nurture and admonition of the Lord.

5 Servants, be obedient to them that are (your) masters according to the flesh, with fear

Ephesians 6:6

Literal Translation

and trembling, in singleness of your heart, as to Christ;

6 not by way of eye-service as men-pleasers, but as slaves of Christ doing the will of God from (the) soul,
7 serving as slaves with good will as to the Lord, and not (as to) men,

8 each one knowing that whatever good thing he does, this he shall receive from the Lord, whether a slave or a freeman.
9 And lords, do the same things toward them, forbearing threatening, knowing that the Lord of you and of them is in Heaven, and there is no respect of persons with Him.

10 For the rest, my brothers, be made powerful in (the) Lord and in the might of His strength.
11 Put on all the armor of God, for you to be able to stand against the wiles of the devil,

12 because wrestling against flesh and blood is not to us, but against the rulers, against the authorities, against the world's rulers, of the darkness of this age, against the spiritual (powers) of evil in the heavenlies.

13 Because of this, take up the whole armor of God that you may be able to resist in the evil day, and having worked out all things, to stand.

14 Then stand firm, having girded your loins about with truth and having put on the breastplate of righteousness,
15 and having shod the feet with (the) preparation of the gospel

2532 5156 1722 572 3588 2588 5216 5613 3588 5547
καὶ τρόμου, ἐν ἁπλότητι τῆς καρδίας ὑμῶν, ὡς τῷ Χριστῷ·
and trembling, in singleness of the heart of you, as to Christ;

3361 2596 3787 5613 441 235 5613 1401
6 μὴ κατ' ὀφθαλμοδουλείαν ὡς ἀνθρωπάρεσκοι, ἀλλ' ὡς δοῦλοι
not by way of eye-service as men-pleasers, but as slaves

3588 5547 4160 3588 2307 3588 2316 1537 5590 3326
τοῦ Χριστοῦ, ποιοῦντες τὸ θέλημα τοῦ Θεοῦ ἐκ ψυχῆς, 7 μετ'
of Christ, doing the will of God from (the) soul, with

2133 1398 5623 3588 2962 2532 3756 444
εὐνοίας δουλεύοντες ὡς τῷ Κυρίῳ καὶ οὐκ ἀνθρώποις·
good will serving as slaves as to the Lord, and not (as to) men,

1492 3754/3739/1437/5100/1538 4160 18 5124 2865
8 εἰδότες ὅτι ὃ ἐάν τι ἕκαστος ποιήσῃ ἀγαθόν, τοῦτο κομιεῖται
knowing that whatever each one does good thing, this he will get

3844 3588 2962 1535 1401 1535 1658 2532 3588 2962
παρὰ τοῦ Κυρίου, εἴτε δοῦλος, εἴτε ἐλεύθερος. 9 καὶ οἱ κύριοι,
from the Lord, whether a slave or a freeman. And the lords,

3588 846 4160 4314 846 447 3588 547 1492
τὰ αὐτὰ ποιεῖτε πρὸς αὐτούς, ἀνιέντες τὴν ἀπειλήν· εἰδότες
the same things do toward them, forbearing the threatening; knowing

3754 2532 5216 846 3588 2962 2076 1722 3772 2532 4382
ὅτι καὶ ὑμῶν αὐτῶν ὁ Κύριός ἐστιν ἐν οὐρανοῖς, καὶ προσω-
that also of you of them the Lord is in Heaven, and respect

3756 2076 3844 846
ποληψία οὐκ ἔστι παρ' αὐτῷ.
of persons not is with Him.

3588 3063 80 3450 1743 1722 2962 2532 1722
10. Τὸ λοιπόν, ἀδελφοί μου, ἐνδυναμοῦσθε ἐν Κυρίῳ, καὶ ἐν
For the rest, brothers of me, be empowered in (the) Lord, and in

3588 2904 3588 2479 846 1746 3588 3833 3588
τῷ κράτει τῆς ἰσχύος αὐτοῦ. 11 ἐνδύσασθε τὴν πανοπλίαν τοῦ
the might of the strength of Him. Put on the whole armor

2316 4314 3588 1410 5209 2476 4314 3588 3180 3588
Θεοῦ, πρὸς τὸ δύνασθαι ὑμᾶς στῆναι πρὸς τὰς μεθοδείας τοῦ
of God, in order to be able you to stand against the wiles of the

1228 3754 3756 2076 2254/3588/3823 4314 129 2532 4561
διαβόλου. 12 ὅτι οὐκ ἔστιν ἡμῖν ἡ πάλη πρὸς αἷμα καὶ σάρκα,
devil. Because not is to us wrestling against blood and flesh,

235 4314 3588 746 4314 3588 1849 4314 3588
ἀλλὰ πρὸς τὰς ἀρχάς, πρὸς τὰς ἐξουσίας, πρὸς τοὺς κο-
but against the rulers, against the authorities, against the world's

2888 3588 4655 3588 165 5127 4314 3588
σμοκράτορας τοῦ σκότους τοῦ αἰῶνος τούτου, πρὸς τὰ
rulers of the darkness age of this, against the

4152 3588 4189 1722 3588 2032 1223 5124
πνευματικὰ τῆς πονηρίας ἐν τοῖς ἐπουρανίοις. 13 διὰ τοῦτο
spiritual (powers) of evil in the heavenlies. Because of this

353 3588 3833 3588 2316 2443 1410 436
ἀναλάβετε τὴν πανοπλίαν τοῦ Θεοῦ, ἵνα δυνηθῆτε ἀντιστῆ-
take up the whole armor of God, that you be able to resist

1722 3588 2250 3588 4190 2532 537 2716
ναι ἐν τῇ ἡμέρᾳ τῇ πονηρᾷ καὶ ἅπαντα κατεργασάμενοι
in the day of evil and all things having worked out

2476 2476 3767 4024 3588 3751 5216 1722
στῆναι. 14 στῆτε οὖν περιζωσάμενοι τὴν ὀσφὺν ὑμῶν ἐν
to stand. stand Therefore having girded about the loins of you with

225 2532 1746 3588 2382 3588 1343 2532
ἀληθείᾳ, καὶ ἐνδυσάμενοι τὸν θώρακα τῆς δικαιοσύνης, 15 καὶ
truth, and having put on the breastplace of the righteousness, and

5265 3588 4228 1722 2091 3588 2098 3588
ὑποδησάμενοι τοὺς πόδας ἐν ἑτοιμασίᾳ τοῦ εὐαγγελίου τῆς
having shod the feet with (the) preparation of the gospel

King James Version

and trembling, in singleness of your heart, as unto Christ;

6 Not with eyeservice, as menpleasers; but as the servants of Christ, doing the will of God from the heart;
7 With good will doing service, as to the Lord, and not to men:

8 Knowing that whatsoever good thing any man doeth, the same shall he receive of the Lord, whether (he be) bond or free.
9 And, ye masters, do the same things unto them, forbearing threatening: knowing that your Master also is in heaven; neither is there respect of persons with him.

10 Finally, my brethren, be strong in the Lord, and in the power of his might.
11 Put on the whole armour of God, that ye may be able to stand against the wiles of the devil.

12 For we wrestle not against flesh and blood, but against principalities, against powers, against the rulers of the darkness of this world, against spiritual wickedness in high (places).

13 Wherefore take unto you the whole armour of God, that ye may be able to withstand in the evil day, and having done all, to stand.

14 Stand therefore, having your loins girt about with truth, and having on the breastplate of righteousness;
15 And your feet shod with the preparation of the gospel

Epheisans 6:16

Literal Translation

of peace.
16 Above all, taking up the shield of faith, with which you will be able to quench all the darts of the evil one, having been made fiery.

17 Also, take the helmet of salvation, and the sword of the Spirit which is the Word of God;
18 through all prayer and petition, praying at every time in (the) Spirit, and watching to this same thing with all perseverance and petition concerning all the saints.

19 (Pray) also on my behalf, that to me may be given speech in (the) opening of my mouth with boldness to make known the mystery of the gospel,

20 for which I am an ambassador in a chain, that in it I may speak boldly as it is right for me to speak.

21 But that you also may know the things about me, what I am doing, Tychicus, the beloved brother and faithful minister in (the) Lord, will make known all things to you,
22 whom I sent to you for this same thing, that you might know the things about us, and (he) may comfort your hearts.

23 Peace to the brothers, and love with faith, from God (the) Father and (the) Lord Jesus Christ.
24 Grace (be) with all those that love our Lord Jesus Christ in incorruptibility. Amen.

1515 1909 3956 353 3588 2375 3588 4102
εἰρήνης· 16 ἐπὶ πᾶσιν ἀναλαβόντες τὸν θυρεὸν τῆς πίστεως,
of peace; above all having taken up the shield of faith,

1722 3739 1410 3956 3588 956 3588 4190 3588 4448
ἐν ᾧ δυνήσεσθε πάντα τὰ βέλη τοῦ πονηροῦ τὰ πεπυρωμένα
by which you will be able all the darts of the evil one having been made fiery

4570 2532 3588 4030 3588 4992 1209 2532
σβέσαι. 17 καὶ τὴν περικεφαλαίαν τοῦ σωτηρίου δέξασθε, καὶ
to quench. And the helmet of salvation take, and

3588 3162 3588 4151 3739 2076 4487 2316 1223 3956
τὴν μάχαιραν τοῦ Πνεύματος, ὅ ἐστι ῥῆμα Θεοῦ· 18 διὰ πάσης
the sword of the Spirit, which is the Word of God; through all

4335 2532 1162 4336 1722 3956 2540 1722
προσευχῆς καὶ δεήσεως προσευχόμενοι ἐν παντὶ καιρῷ ἐν
prayer and petition praying at every time in

4151 2532 1519 846 5124 69 1722 3956
Πνεύματι, καὶ εἰς αὐτὸ τοῦτο ἀγρυπνοῦντες ἐν πάσῃ
(the) Spirit, and to same thing this watching in all

4343 2532 1162 4012 3956 3588 40 2532
προσκαρτερήσει καὶ δεήσει περὶ πάντων τῶν ἁγίων, 19 καὶ
perseverance and petition concerning all the saints, and

5228 1700 2443 3427 1325 3056 1722 457 3588 4750
ὑπὲρ ἐμοῦ, ἵνα μοι δοθείη λόγος ἐν ἀνοίξει τοῦ στόματός
on behalf of me, that to me may be given speech in opening of the mouth

3450 1722 3954 1107 3588 3466 3588 2098
μου ἐν παρρησίᾳ, γνωρίσαι τὸ μυστήριον τοῦ εὐαγγελίου,
of me in boldness, to make known the mystery of the gospel

5228 3739 4243 1722 254 2443 1722 846 3955
20 ὑπὲρ οὗ πρεσβεύω ἐν ἁλύσει, ἵνα ἐν αὐτῷ παρρησιάσωμαι,
for which I am ambassador in a chain, that in it I may speak boldly,

5613 1163 3165 2980
ὡς δεῖ με λαλῆσαι.
as it behooves me to speak.

2443 1161 1492 2532 5210 3588 2596 1691 5101 4238 3956
21. Ἵνα δὲ εἰδῆτε καὶ ὑμεῖς τὰ κατ' ἐμέ, τί πράσσω, πάντα
that But may know also you the things about me, what I am doing, all things

5213 1107 5190 3588 27 80 2532 4103
ὑμῖν γνωρίσει Τυχικὸς ὁ ἀγαπητὸς ἀδελφὸς καὶ πιστὸς
to you will make known Tychicus the beloved brother and faithful

1249 1722 2962 3739 3992 4314 5209 1519 846 5124
διάκονος ἐν Κυρίῳ· 22 ὃν ἔπεμψα πρὸς ὑμᾶς εἰς αὐτὸ τοῦτο,
minister in (the) Lord; whom I sent to you for same thing this,

2443 1097 3588 4012 2257 2532 3870 3588 2588
ἵνα γνῶτε τὰ περὶ ἡμῶν, καὶ παρακαλέσῃ τὰς καρδίας
that you may know the things about us, and may comfort the hearts

5216
ὑμῶν.
of you.

1515 3588 80 2532 26 3326 4102 575 2316
23. Εἰρήνη τοῖς ἀδελφοῖς καὶ ἀγάπη μετὰ πίστεως ἀπὸ Θεοῦ
Peace to the brothers and love with faith from God

3962 2532 2962 2424 5547 3588 5485 3326 3956
πατρὸς καὶ Κυρίου Ἰησοῦ Χριστοῦ. 24 ἡ χάρις μετὰ πάντων
(the) Father and (the) Lord Jesus Christ. Grace (be) with all

3588 25 3588 2962 2257 2424 5547 1722
τῶν ἀγαπώντων τὸν Κύριον ἡμῶν Ἰησοῦν Χριστὸν ἐν
those loving the Lord of us Jesus Christ in

861
ἀφθαρσίᾳ.
incorruptibility.

King James Version

of peace;
16 Above all, taking the shield of faith, wherewith ye shall be able to quench all the fiery darts of the wicked.

17 And take the helmet of salvation, and the sword of the Spirit, which is the word of God:
18 Praying always with all prayer and supplication in the Spirit, and watching thereunto with all perseverance and supplication for all saints;

19 And for me, that utterance may be given unto me, that I may open my mouth boldly, to make known the mystery of the gospel,

20 For which I am an ambassador in bonds: that therein I may speak boldly, as I ought to speak.

21 But that ye also may know my affairs, (and) how I do, Tychicus, a beloved brother and faithful minister in the Lord, shall make known to you all things:
22 Whom I have sent unto you for the same purpose, that ye might know our affairs, and (that) he might comfort your hearts.

23 Peace (be) to the brethren, and love with faith, from God the Father and the Lord Jesus Christ.
24 Grace (be) with all them that love our Lord Jesus Christ in sincerity. Amen. (To (the) Ephesians written from Rome, by Tychicus.)

Literal Translation

THE EPISTLE OF PAUL THE APOSTLE TO THE PHILIPPIANS

Philippians 1

1. Paul, and Timothy, slaves of Jesus Christ, to all the saints in Christ Jesus who are in Philippi, with the overseers and ministers:

2 Grace to you and peace from God our Father and (the) Lord Jesus Christ.

3 I thank my God on all the remembrance of you,
4 always in my every petition on your behalf making (my) petition with joy

5 over your fellowship in the gospel, from (the) first day until now,

6 being persuaded of this very thing, that the (One) having begun a good work in you will complete (it) until (the) day of Jesus Christ;
7 as it is righteous for me to think this on behalf of you all because you have me in (your) heart, both in my bonds and in the defense and confirmation of the gospel, you are all sharers of the grace with me.

8 For God is my witness as I long after you all in (the) bowels of Jesus Christ.
9 And this I pray, that your love may yet abound more and more in full knowledge and all perception,

10 for you (to) distinguish (between) differing things, that you may be sincere and without blame unto (the) day of Christ,

11 having been filled

ΠΑΥΛΟΥ ΤΟΥ ΑΠΟΣΤΟΛΟΥ
PAUL THE APOSTLE

Η ΗΡΟΣ ΦΙΛΙΠΠΗΣΙΟΥΣ ΕΠΙΣΤΟΛΗ
TO (THE) PHILIPPIANS EPISTLE

Philippians 1

3972 2532 5095 1401 2424 5547 3956 3588
1. Παῦλος καὶ Τιμόθεος, δοῦλοι Ἰησοῦ Χριστοῦ, πᾶσι τοῖς
Paul and Timothy, slaves of Jesus Christ, to all the
40 1722 5547 2424 3588 5607 1722 5375 4862 1985
ἁγίοις ἐν Χριστῷ Ἰησοῦ τοῖς οὖσιν ἐν Φιλίπποις, σὺν ἐπι-
saints in Christ Jesus being in Philippi, with over-
2532 1249 5485 5213 2532 1515 575 2316
σκόποις καὶ διακόνοις· 2 χάρις ὑμῖν καὶ εἰρήνη ἀπὸ Θεοῦ
seers and ministers; grace to you and peace from God
3962 2257 2532 2962 2424 5547
πατρὸς ἡμῶν καὶ Κυρίου Ἰησοῦ Χριστοῦ.
(the) Father of us and (the) Lord Jesus Christ.

2168 3588 2316 3450 1909 3956 3588 3417 5216 3842
3. Εὐχαριστῶ τῷ Θεῷ μου ἐπὶ πάσῃ τῇ μνείᾳ ὑμῶν, 4 πάντοτε
I thank the God of me on all the remembrance of you, always
1722 3956 1162 3450 5228 3956 5216 3326 5479 3588
ἐν πάσῃ δεήσει μου ὑπὲρ πάντων ὑμῶν μετὰ χαρᾶς τὴν
in every petition of me on behalf of all of you with joy the
1162 4160 1909 3588 2842 5216 1519 3588 2098
δέησιν ποιούμενος, 5 ἐπὶ τῇ κοινωνίᾳ ὑμῶν εἰς τὸ εὐαγγέλιον,
petition making, over the fellowship of you in the gospel,
575 4413 2250 891 3588 3568 3982 846 5124
ἀπὸ πρώτης ἡμέρας ἄχρι τοῦ νῦν· 6 πεποιθὼς αὐτὸ τοῦτο,
from (the) first day until now; being persuaded very thing this,

3754 3588 1728 1722 5213 2041 18 2005 891
ὅτι ὁ ἐναρξάμενος ἐν ὑμῖν ἔργον ἀγαθὸν ἐπιτελέσει ἄχρις
that the (One) having begun in you a work good will complete (it) until
2250 2424 5547 2531 2076 1342 1698 5124
ἡμέρας Ἰησοῦ Χριστοῦ· 7 καθώς ἐστι δίκαιον ἐμοὶ τοῦτο
(the) day of Jesus Christ; even as it is righteous for me this
5426 5228 3956 5216 1223 3588 2192 3165 1722 3588 2588
φρονεῖν ὑπὲρ πάντων ὑμῶν, διὰ τὸ ἔχειν με ἐν τῇ καρδίᾳ
to think on behalf of all of you, because of having me in the heart
5209 1722 5037 3588 1199 3450 2532 1722 3588 627 2532 951
ὑμᾶς, ἔν τε τοῖς δεσμοῖς μου καὶ ἐν τῇ ἀπολογίᾳ καὶ βεβαιώσει
of you, in both the bonds of me and in the defense and confirmation
3588 2098 4791 3450 3588 5485 3956
τοῦ εὐαγγελίου, συγκοινωνούς μου τῆς χάριτος πάντας
of the gospel, sharers with me of the grace all

5209 5607 3144 1063 3450 2076 3588 2316 5613 1971
ὑμᾶς ὄντας. 8 μάρτυς γάρ μου ἐστιν ὁ Θεός, ὡς ἐπιποθῶ
you being. witness For of me is God, as I long after
3956 5209 1722 4698 2424 5547 2532 5124
πάντας ὑμᾶς ἐν σπλάγχνοις Ἰησοῦ Χριστοῦ. 9 καὶ τοῦτο
all you in (the) bowels of Jesus Christ. And this
4336 2443 3588 26 5216 2089 3123 2532 3123
προσεύχομαι, ἵνα ἡ ἀγάπη ὑμῶν ἔτι μᾶλλον καὶ μᾶλλον
I pray, that the love of you yet more and more
4052 1722 1922 2532 3956 144 1519 3588
περισσεύῃ ἐν ἐπιγνώσει καὶ πάσῃ αἰσθήσει, 10 εἰς τὸ
may abound in full knowledge and all perception, for the
1381 5209 3588 1308 2443 5600 1506 2532
δοκιμάζειν ὑμᾶς τὰ διαφέροντα, ἵνα ἦτε εἰλικρινεῖς καὶ
approving of you the things differing, that you be sincere and
677 1519 2250 5547 4137 2590
ἀπρόσκοποι εἰς ἡμέραν Χριστοῦ, 11 πεπληρωμένοι καρπῶν
without blame unto (the) day of Christ, having been filled (with) fruits

King James Version

THE EPISTLE OF PAUL THE APOSTLE TO THE PHILIPPIANS

Philippians 1

1. Paul and Timotheus, the servants of Jesus Christ, to all the saints in Christ Jesus which are at Philippi, with the bishops and deacons:

2 Grace (be) unto you, and peace, from God our Father, and (from) the Lord Jesus Christ.

3 I thank my God upon every remembrance of you,
4 Always in every prayer of mine for you all making request with joy,

5 For your fellowship in the gospel from the first day until now;

6 Being confident of this very thing, that he which hath begun a good work in you will perform (it) until the day of Jesus Christ:
7 Even as it is meet for me to think this of you all, because I have you in my heart; inasmuch as both in my bonds, and in the defence and confirmation of the gospel, ye all are partakers of my grace.

8 For God is my record, how greatly I long after you all in the bowels of Jesus Christ.
9 And this I pray, that your love may abound yet more and more in knowledge and (in) all judgment;

10 That ye may approve things that are excellent; that ye may be sincere and without offence till the day of Christ;

11 Being filled with the

Literal Translation

of righteousness through Jesus Christ, to (the) glory and praise of God.

12 But I want you to know, brothers, that the things concerning me have more fully come to (the) advancement of the gospel,
13 so that in all the praetorium, and to all the rest, my bonds have become clearly revealed (to be) in Christ.
14 And the most of the brothers in (the) Lord, being confident in my bonds, more exceedingly dare to speak the Word fearlessly.

15 Some, indeed, even preach Christ because of envy and strife, but some also because of good will.

16 These, indeed, proclaim Christ out of party spirit, not sincerely, thinking to bring affliction to my bonds.
17 But these (others) out of love, knowing that I am set for defense of the gospel.
18 For what? Yet in every way, whether in pretense or in truth, Christ is proclaimed, and I rejoice in this; yet also I will rejoice.

19 For I know that this will go on to deliverance to me through your petition and (the) supply of (the) Spirit of Jesus Christ,

20 according to my earnest expectation and hope, that in nothing I shall be ashamed, but as always in all boldness even now Christ will be magnified in my body, whether through life or through death.

21 For to me to live (is) Christ, and to die (is) gain.
22 But if (I) live in (the) flesh, this to me

Philippians 1:12

1343 3588 1223 2424 5547 1519 1391 2532 1868
δικαιοσύνης τῶν διὰ Ἰησοῦ Χριστοῦ, εἰς δόξαν καὶ ἔπαινον
of righteousness through Jesus Christ, to (the) glory and praise
2316
Θεοῦ.
of God.

1097 1161 5209 1014 80 3754 3588 2596 1691
12. Γινώσκειν δὲ ὑμᾶς βούλομαι, ἀδελφοί, ὅτι τὰ κατ᾽ ἐμὲ
to know And you I want, brothers, that the things about me,
3123 1519 4297 3588 2098 2064 5620 3588
μᾶλλον εἰς προκοπὴν τοῦ εὐαγγελίου ἐλήλυθεν· 13 ὥστε τοὺς
rather to (the) advance of the gospel has come; so as the
1199 3450 5318 1722 5547 1096 1722 3650 3588 4232
δεσμούς μου φανεροὺς ἐν Χριστῷ γενέσθαι ἐν ὅλῳ τῷ πραι-
bonds of me clearly revealed in Christ become in all the prae-
2532 3588 3062 3956 2532 3588 4119 3588 80
τωρίῳ καὶ τοῖς λοιποῖς πᾶσι, 14 καὶ τοὺς πλείονας τῶν ἀδελφῶν
torium, and to the rest all, and the most of the brothers
1722 2962 3982 3588 1199 3450 4056
ἐν Κυρίῳ πεποιθότας τοῖς δεσμοῖς μου, περισσοτέρως
in (the) Lord being confident in the bonds of me more exceedingly
5111 870 3588 3056 2980 5100 3303 2532 1223 5355
τολμᾶν ἀφόβως τὸν λόγον λαλεῖν. 15 τινὲς μὲν καὶ διὰ φθόνον
to dare fearlessly the Word to speak. Some indeed even through envy
2532 2054 5100 1161/2532/1223 2107 3588 5547 2784
καὶ ἔριν, τινὲς δὲ καὶ δι᾽ εὐδοκίαν τὸν Χριστὸν κηρύσσουσιν·
and strife, some but also because of good will Christ preach;
3588 3303 1537 2052 3588 5547 2605 3756 55
16 οἱ μὲν ἐξ ἐριθείας τὸν Χριστὸν καταγγέλλουσιν, οὐχ ἁγνῶς,
these indeed out of rivalry Christ proclaim, not sincerely,
3633 2347 2018 3588 1199 3450 3588 1161 1537 26
οἰόμενοι θλίψιν ἐπιφέρειν τοῖς δεσμοῖς μου· 17 οἱ δὲ ἐξ ἀγάπης,
thinking trouble to bring to the bonds of me; these but out of love,
1492 3754 1519 627 3588 2098 2749 5101 1063
εἰδότες ὅτι εἰς ἀπολογίαν τοῦ εὐαγγελίου κεῖμαι. 18 τί γάρ;
knowing that for defense of the gospel I am set. what For?
4133 3956 5158 1535 4392 1535 225 5547
πλὴν παντὶ τρόπῳ, εἴτε προφάσει εἴτε ἀληθείᾳ, Χριστὸς
Yet in every way, whether in pretense or in truth, Christ
2605 2532 1722 5129 5463 235 2532 5463
καταγγέλλεται· καὶ ἐν τούτῳ χαίρω, ἀλλὰ καὶ χαρήσομαι.
is proclaimed; and in this I rejoice, yet also I will rejoice.
1492 1063 3754 5124 3427 576 1519 4991 1223 3588
19 οἶδα γὰρ ὅτι τοῦτό μοι ἀποβήσεται εἰς σωτηρίαν διὰ τῆς
I know For that this to me will go on to salvation through the
5216 1162 2532 2024 3588 4151 2424
ὑμῶν δεήσεως, καὶ ἐπιχορηγίας τοῦ Πνεύματος Ἰησοῦ
of you petition, and supply of the Spirit of Jesus
5547 2596 3588 603 2532 1680 3450 3754 1722
Χριστοῦ, 20 κατὰ τὴν ἀποκαραδοκίαν καὶ ἐλπίδα μου, ὅτι ἐν
Christ, according to the earnest expectation and hope of me, that in
3762 153 235 1722 3956 3954 5613 3842
οὐδενὶ αἰσχυνθήσομαι, ἀλλ᾽ ἐν πάσῃ παρρησίᾳ, ὡς πάν-
nothing I shall be ashamed, but in all boldness, as always
2532 3568 3170 5547 1722 3588 4983 3450
τοτε, καὶ νῦν μεγαλυνθήσεται Χριστὸς ἐν τῷ σώματί μου,
and now will be magnified Christ in the body of me,
1535 1223 2222 1535 1223 2288 1698 1063 3588 2198 5547
εἴτε διὰ ζωῆς εἴτε διὰ θανάτου. 21 ἐμοὶ γὰρ τὸ ζῆν, Χριστὸς·
whether through life or through death. to me For to live, Christ;
2532 3588 599 2771 1487/1161/3588/2198/1722/4561 5124 3427
καὶ τὸ ἀποθανεῖν κέρδος. 22 εἰ δὲ τὸ ζῆν ἐν σαρκί, τοῦτό μοι
and to die is gain. if But to live in (the) flesh, this to me

King James Version

of righteousness, which are by Jesus Christ, unto the glory and praise of God.

12 But I would ye should understand, brethren, that the things (which happened) unto me have fallen out rather unto the furtherance of the gospel;
13 So that my bonds in Christ are manifest in all the palace, and in all other (places);
14 And many of the brethren in the Lord, waxing confident by my bonds, are much more bold to speak the word without fear.

15 Some indeed preach Christ even of envy and strife; and some also of good will:

16 The one preach Christ of contention, not sincerely, supposing to add affliction to my bonds:
17 But the other of love, knowing that I am set for the defence of the gospel.
18 What then? notwithstanding, every way, whether in pretence, or in truth, Christ is preached; and I therein do rejoice, yea, and will rejoice.

19 For I know that this shall turn to my salvation through your prayer, and the supply of the Spirit of Jesus Christ,

20 According to my earnest expectation and (my) hope, that in nothing I shall be ashamed, but (that) with all boldness, as always, (so) now also Christ shall be magnified in my body, whether (it be) by life, or by death.
21 For to me to live (is) Christ, and to die (is) gain.
22 But if I live in the flesh, this

Philippians 1:23

Literal Translation

(is) fruit of (my) labor, and what I shall choose I do not know.
23 For I am constrained by the two: having the desire to depart and be with Christ, (which is) rather much better,
24 but to remain in the flesh (is) more necessary on account of you.
25 And being assured of this, I know that I will remain and will continue with you all for your advancement and joy of faith,

26 so that your glorying may abound in Christ Jesus in me through my presence with you again.

27 Only conduct yourself worthily of the gospel of Christ, so that whether coming and seeing you, or being absent, I hear the things concerning you, that you stand firm in one spirit, and one soul, striving together in the faith of the gospel,
28 and in nothing being terrified by the (ones) opposing, which to them truly is a proof of destruction, but to you of salvation, and this from God;

29 because it was granted to you on behalf of Christ not only to believe into Him, but also to suffer on His behalf,
30 having the same struggle which you saw in me and now hear (to be) in me.

2590 2041 2532 5101 138 3756 1107 4912
καρπὸς ἔργου· καὶ τί αἱρήσομαι οὐ γνωρίζω. 23 συνέχομαι
(is) fruit of (my) work; and what I shall choose not I know. I am constrained

1063 1537 3588 1417 3588 1939 2192 1519 3588 360 2532 4862
γὰρ ἐκ τῶν δύο, τὴν ἐπιθυμίαν ἔχων εἰς τὸ ἀναλῦσαι καὶ σὺν
For by the two, the desire having to depart and with

5547 1511 4183 3123 2909 3588 1161 1961 1722
Χριστῷ εἶναι, πολλῷ μᾶλλον κρεῖσσον· 24 τὸ δὲ ἐπιμένειν ἐν
Christ be, much rather better; but to remain in

3588 4561 316 1223 5209 2532 5124 3982
τῇ σαρκὶ ἀναγκαιότερον δι' ὑμᾶς. 25 καὶ τοῦτο πεποιθὼς
the flesh (is) more necessary on account of you. And this being assured

1492 3754 3306 2532 4839 3956 5213 1519 3588 5216
οἶδα ὅτι μενῶ, καὶ συμπαραμενῶ πᾶσιν ὑμῖν εἰς τὴν ὑμῶν
I know that I will stay, and will continue with all of you to the of you

4297 2532 5479 3588 4102 2443 3588 2745 5216
προκοπὴν καὶ χαρὰν τῆς πίστεως, 26 ἵνα τὸ καύχημα ὑμῶν
advancement and joy of the faith, that the glorying of you

4052 1722 5547 2424 1722 1698 1223 3588 1699 3952
περισσεύῃ ἐν Χριστῷ Ἰησοῦ ἐν ἐμοὶ, διὰ τῆς ἐμῆς παρου-
may abound in Christ Jesus in me, through my presence

3825 4314 5209 3440 516 3588 2098 3588
σίας πάλιν πρὸς ὑμᾶς. 27 μόνον ἀξίως τοῦ εὐαγγελίου τοῦ
again with you. Only worthily of the gospel

5547 4176 2443 1535 2064 2532 1492 5209 1535
Χριστοῦ πολιτεύεσθε, ἵνα εἴτε ἐλθὼν καὶ ἰδὼν ὑμᾶς, εἴτε
of Christ conduct yourselves, that whether coming and seeing you, or,

548 191 3588 4012 5216 3754 4739 1722 1520 4151
ἀπών, ἀκούσω τὰ περὶ ὑμῶν, ὅτι στήκετε ἐν ἑνὶ πνεύματι,
being absent, I hear the things about you, that you stand in one spirit,

3391 5590 4866 3588 4102 3588 2098 2532 3361
μιᾷ ψυχῇ συναθλοῦντες τῇ πίστει τοῦ εὐαγγελίου, 28 καὶ μὴ
with one soul striving together in the faith of the gospel, and not

4426 1722 3367 5259 3588 480 3748 846
πτυρόμενοι ἐν μηδενὶ ὑπὸ τῶν ἀντικειμένων· ἥτις αὐτοῖς
being terrified in nothing by the (ones) opposing; which to them

3303 2076 1732 684 5213 1161 4991 2532 5124
μέν ἐστιν ἔνδειξις ἀπωλείας, ὑμῖν δὲ σωτηρίας, καὶ τοῦτο
truly is a proof of destruction, to you but salvation, and this

575 2316 3754 5213 5483 3588 5228 5547 3756 3440 3588
ἀπὸ Θεοῦ· 29 ὅτι ὑμῖν ἐχαρίσθη τὸ ὑπὲρ Χριστοῦ, οὐ μόνον τὸ
from God; because to you it was granted on behalf of Christ, not only

1519 846 4100 235 2532 3588 5228 846 3958 3588
εἰς αὐτὸν πιστεύειν, ἀλλὰ καὶ τὸ ὑπὲρ αὐτοῦ πάσχειν· 30 τὸν
into Him to believe, but also on behalf of Him to suffer; the

846 73 2192 3634 1492 1722 1698 2532 3568 191 1722
αὐτὸν ἀγῶνα ἔχοντες οἷον εἴδετε ἐν ἐμοὶ, καὶ νῦν ἀκούετε ἐν
same struggle having which you saw in me, and now hear in

1698
ἐμοί.
me.

King James Version

(is) the fruit of my labour: yet what I shall choose I wot not.
23 For I am in a strait betwixt two, having a desire to depart, and to be with Christ; which is far better:
24 Nevertheless to abide in the flesh (is) more needful for you.

25 And having this confidence, I know that I shall abide and continue with you all for your furtherance and joy of faith;

26 That your rejoicing may be more abundant in Jesus Christ for me by my coming to you again.

27 Only let your conversation be as it becometh the gospel of Christ: that whether I come and see you, or else be absent, I may hear of your affairs, that ye stand fast in one spirit, with one mind striving together for the faith of the gospel;
28 And in nothing terrified by your adversaries: which is to them an evident token of perdition, but to you of salvation, and that of God.

29 For unto you it is given in the behalf of Christ, not only to believe on him, but also to suffer for his sake;
30 Having the same conflict which ye saw in me, and now hear (to be) in me.

Philippians 2

Philippians 2

1. Then if (there is) any comfort in Christ, if any consolation of love, if any fellowship of (the) Spirit, if any tendernesses and compassions,
2 fulfill my joy, that you think the same,

Philippians 2

1487 5100 3767 3874 1722 5547 1487 5100 3890
1. Εἴ τις οὖν παράκλησις ἐν Χριστῷ, εἴ τι παραμύθιον
if (is) any Then comfort in Christ, if any consolation

26 1487 5100 2842 4151 1487 5100 4698 2532
ἀγάπης, εἴ τις κοινωνία Πνεύματος, εἴ τινα σπλάγχνα καὶ
of love, if any fellowship of (the) Spirit, if any compassions and

3628 4137 3450 3588 5479 2443 3588 846 5426
οἰκτιρμοί, 2 πληρώσατέ μου τὴν χαράν, ἵνα τὸ αὐτὸ φρονῆτε,
compassions, fulfill of me the joy, that the same you think,

Philippians 2

1. If (there be) therefore any consolation in Christ, if any comfort of love, if any fellowship of the Spirit, if any bowels and mercies,
2 Fulfil ye my joy, that ye be likeminded,

Literal Translation

having the same love,
one in soul, minding the
one thing,
3 (doing) nothing ac-
cording to party spirit or
self-glory, but in humil-
ity, esteeming one an-
other to surpass them-
selves;
4 each not looking at
their own things, but
each also (at the) things
of others.
5 For think this among
you which (mind was)
also in Christ Jesus,
6 who subsisting in
(the) form of God
thought (it) not robbery
to be equal with God,
7 but emptied Himself,
taking (the) form of a
slave, becoming in (the)
likeness of men
8 and being found in
fashion as a man, He
humbled Himself, be-
coming obedient until
death, even (the) death
of a cross.
9 Because of this also
God highly exalted
Him, and gave to Him a
name above every
name,
10 that at the name of Je-
sus every knee should
bow, of heavenly (be-
ings) and earthly (be-
ings), and (beings) un-
der (the) earth,
11 and every tongue
should confess that Je-
sus Christ (is) Lord, to
(the) glory of God (the)
Father.
12 So as, my beloved,
even as you always
obeyed, not as in my
presence only, but now
much rather in my ab-
sence, cultivate your
salvation with fear and
trembling,
13 for God is the (One)
working in you both to
will and to work for the
sake of (His) good
pleasure.
14 Do all things without
murmurings and dis-
putings,
15 that you may be
blameless and harm-
less, children of God,
without fault in the
midst of a crooked

Philippians 2:3

3588 846 26 2192 4861 3588 1520 5426
τὴν αὐτὴν ἀγάπην ἔχοντες, σύμψυχοι, τὸ ἓν φρονοῦντες.
the same love having, one in soul, the one thing minding.

3367 2596 2052 2228 2754 235 3588 5012
3 μηδὲν κατ’ ἐριθείαν ἢ κενοδοξίαν, ἀλλὰ τῇ ταπεινοφροσύνῃ
nothng according to rivalry or self-glory, but in humility

240 2233 5242 1438 3361 3588 1438
ἀλλήλους ἡγούμενοι ὑπερέχοντας ἑαυτῶν· 4 μὴ τὰ ἑαυτῶν
one another esteeming surpassing themselves; not the things of themselves

1538 4648 235 2532 3588 2087 1538 5124 1063
ἕκαστος σκοπεῖτε, ἀλλὰ καὶ τὰ ἑτέρων ἕκαστος. 5 τοῦτο γὰρ
each looking at, but also the things of others each. this For

5426 1722 5213 3739 2532 1722 5547 2424 3739 1722 3444
φρονείσθω ἐν ὑμῖν ὃ καὶ ἐν Χριστῷ Ἰησοῦ, 6 ὃς ἐν μορφῇ
think among you which also (was) in Christ Jesus, who in (the) form

2316 5225 3756 725 2233 3588 1511 2470 2316 235
Θεοῦ ὑπάρχων οὐχ ἁρπαγμὸν ἡγήσατο τὸ εἶναι ἴσα Θεῷ, 7 ἀλλ’
of God subsisting, not robbery thought (it) to be equal with God, but

1438 2758 3444 1401 2983 1722 3667 444
ἑαυτὸν ἐκένωσε, μορφὴν δούλου λαβών, ἐν ὁμοιώματι ἀνθρώ-
Himself emptied, (the) form of a slave taking, in likeness of men

1096 2532 4976 2147 5613 444 5013
πων γενόμενος· καὶ σχήματι εὑρεθεὶς ὡς ἄνθρωπος, 8 ἐταπείνω-
becoming; and in fashion being found as a man, He humbled

1438 1096 5255 3360 2288 2288 1161
σεν ἑαυτόν, γενόμενος ὑπήκοος μέχρι θανάτου, θανάτου δὲ
Himself, becoming obedient until death, (the) death even

4716 1352 2532 3588 2316 846 5251 2532 5483
σταυροῦ. 9 διὸ καὶ ὁ Θεὸς αὐτὸν ὑπερύψωσε, καὶ ἐχαρίσατο
of a cross. Because of this also God Him highly exalted, and gave

846 3686 3588 5228 3956 3686 2443 1722 3588 3686 2424
αὐτῷ ὄνομα τὸ ὑπὲρ πᾶν ὄνομα· 10 ἵνα ἐν τῷ ὀνόματι Ἰησοῦ
to Him a name above every name; that at the name of Jesus

3956 1119 2578 2032 2532 1919 2532 2709
πᾶν γόνυ κάμψῃ ἐπουρανίων καὶ ἐπιγείων καὶ καταχθο-
every knee should bow of heavenly (beings) and of earthly (beings), and (beings)

2532 3956 1100 1843 3754 2962
νίων, 11 καὶ πᾶσα γλῶσσα ἐξομολογήσηται ὅτι Κύριος
under the earth, and every tongue should confess that Lord (is)

2424 5547 1519 1391 2316 3962
Ἰησοῦς Χριστός, εἰς δόξαν Θεοῦ πατρός.
Jesus Christ, to (the) glory of God (the) Father.

5620 27 3450 2531 3842 5219 3361 5613
12. Ὥστε, ἀγαπητοί μου, καθὼς πάντοτε ὑπηκούσατε, μὴ ὡς
So as, beloved of me, even as always you obeyed, not as

1722 3588 3952 3450 3440 235 3568 4183 3123 1722 3588
ἐν τῇ παρουσίᾳ μου μόνον, ἀλλὰ νῦν πολλῷ μᾶλλον ἐν τῇ
in the presence of me only, but now much rather in the

666 3450 3326 5401 2532 5156 3588 1438 4991
ἀπουσίᾳ μου, μετὰ φόβου καὶ τρόμου τὴν ἑαυτῶν σωτηρίαν
absence of me, with fear and trembling the of yourselves salvation

2716 3588 2316 1063 2076 3588 1754 1722 5213 2532 3588
κατεργάζεσθε· 13 ὁ Θεὸς γάρ ἐστιν ὁ ἐνεργῶν ἐν ὑμῖν καὶ τὸ
cultivate; God for is the (One) working in you both

2309 2532 3588 1754 5228 3588 2107 3956 4160
θέλειν καὶ τὸ ἐνεργεῖν ὑπὲρ τῆς εὐδοκίας. 14 πάντα ποιεῖτε
to will and to work for the sake of (His) good pleasure. All things do

5565 1112 2532 1261 2443 1096 273
χωρὶς γογγυσμῶν καὶ διαλογισμῶν, 15 ἵνα γένησθε ἄμεμπτοι
without murmurings and disputings, that you may be blameless

2532 185 5043 2316 298 1722 3319 1074 4646
καὶ ἀκέραιοι, τέκνα Θεοῦ ἀμώμητα ἐν μέσῳ γενεᾶς σκολιᾶς
and harmless, children of God faultless in (the) midst of a generation crooked

King James Version

having the same love,
(being) of one accord,
of one mind.
3 (Let) nothing (be
done) through strife or
vainglory; but in lowli-
ness of mind let each es-
teem other better than
themselves.
4 Look not every man
on his own things, but
every man also on the
things of others.
5 Let this mind be in
you, which was also in
Christ Jesus:
6 Who, being in the
form of God, thought it
not robbery to be equal
with God:
7 But made himself of
no reputation, and took
upon him the form of a
servant, and was made
in the likeness of men:
8 And being found in
fashion as a man, he
humbled himself, and
became obedient unto
death, even the death of
the cross.
9 Wherefore God also
hath highly exalted him,
and given him a name
which is above every
name:
10 That at the name of
Jesus every knee should
bow, of (things) in
heaven, and (things) in
earth, and (things) un-
der the earth;
11 And (that) every
tongue should confess
that Jesus Christ (is)
Lord, to the glory of
God the Father.
12 Wherefore, my be-
loved, as ye have al-
ways obeyed, not as in
my presence only, but
now much more in my
absence, work out your
own salvation with fear
and trembling.
13 For it is God which
worketh in you both to
will and to do of (his)
good pleasure.
14 Do all things without
murmurings and dis-
putings:
15 That ye may be
blameless and harm-
less, the sons of God,
without rebuke, in the
midst of a crooked

Philippians 2:16

Literal Translation

generation, even having been perverted, among whom you shine as luminaries in (the) world,
16 holding up a word of life, for a glorying to me in (the) day of Christ, that I ran not in vain, nor labored in vain.

17 But if indeed I am poured out on the sacrifice and service of your faith, I rejoice; yea, I rejoice with you all.
18 And you also rejoice (in) the same and rejoice with me.

19 But I hope in the Lord Jesus to send Timothy to you soon, that I may also be cheered, knowing the things about you.
20 For I have no one like-minded, (one) who genuinely will care for the things about you.
21 For all seek their own things, not the things of Christ Jesus.
22 But you know the proof of him, that as a child to a father, he served with me for the gospel.
23 Then I hope to send this one at once, whenever I shall see the things about me.
24 But I trust in (the) Lord that I myself also will come shortly.
25 But I thought it needful to send to you Epaphroditus, the brother and fellow-worker, and my fellow-soldier, and your messenger and minister of my need,

26 since he was longing for you all and has been troubled because you heard that he was sick.
27 For indeed he was sick, near to death; but God had mercy on him, and not only on him, but also on me, that not I should have grief on grief.

28 Therefore, I sent him more eagerly, that seeing him again

2532 1294 1722 3739 5316 5613 5458 1722 2889
καὶ διεστραμμένης, ἐν οἷς φαίνεσθε ὡς φωστῆρες ἐν κόσμῳ,
and having been perverted, among whom you shine as luminaries in (the) world,

3056 2222 1907 1519 2745 1698 1519 2250
16 λόγον ζωῆς ἐπέχοντες, εἰς καύχημα ἐμοὶ εἰς ἡμέραν
a word of life holding up, for a glorying to me in (the) day

5547 3754 3756 1519 2756 5143 3761 1519 2756 2872
Χριστοῦ, ὅτι οὐκ εἰς κενὸν ἔδραμον, οὐδὲ εἰς κενὸν ἐκοπίασα.
of Christ, that not in vain I ran, nor in vain labored.

235 1487 2532 4689 1909 3588 2378 2532 3009 3588
17 ἀλλ' εἰ καὶ σπένδομαι ἐπὶ τῇ θυσίᾳ καὶ λειτουργίᾳ τῆς
But if indeed I am poured out on the sacrifice and service of the

4102 5216 5463 2532 4796 3956 5213 3588 1161 846
πίστεως ὑμῶν, χαίρω καὶ συγχαίρω πᾶσιν ὑμῖν· 18 τὸ δ' αὐτὸ
faith of you, I rejoice and I rejoice with all you; the and same

2532 5210 5463 2532 4796 3427
καὶ ὑμεῖς χαίρετε καὶ συγχαίρετέ μοι.
also you rejoice and rejoice with me.

1679 1161 1722 2962 2424 5095 5030 3992
19. Ἐλπίζω δὲ ἐν Κυρίῳ Ἰησοῦ, Τιμόθεον ταχέως πέμψαι
I hope But in (the) Lord Jesus, Timothy shortly to send

5213 2443 2504 2174 1097 3588 4012 5216 3762 1063 2192
ὑμῖν, ἵνα κἀγὼ εὐψυχῶ, γνοὺς τὰ περὶ ὑμῶν. 20 οὐδένα γὰρ ἔχω
to you, that I also may be cheered, knowing the things about you. no one For I have

2473 3748 1104 3588 4012 5216 3309 3588 3956
ἰσόψυχον, ὅστις γνησίως τὰ περὶ ὑμῶν μεριμνήσει. 21 οἱ πάντες
like-minded, who genuinely the things about you will care for. all

1063 3588 1438 2212 3756 3588 3588 5547 2424 3588
γὰρ τὰ ἑαυτῶν ζητοῦσιν, οὐ τὰ τοῦ Χριστοῦ Ἰησοῦ. 22 τὴν
For the things of themselves seek, not the things of Christ Jesus. the

1161 1382 846 1097 3754 5613 3962 5043 4862 1698
δὲ δοκιμὴν αὐτοῦ γινώσκετε, ὅτι ὡς πατρὶ τέκνον, σὺν ἐμοὶ
But proof of him you know, that as to a father a child, with me

1398 1519 3588 2098 5126 3303 3767 1679
ἐδούλευσεν εἰς τὸ εὐαγγέλιον. 23 τοῦτον μὲν οὖν ἐλπίζω
he served for the gospel. This one truly then I hope

3992 5613 302 872 3588 4012 1691 1824 3982 1161
πέμψαι, ὡς ἂν ἀπίδω τὰ περὶ ἐμὲ, ἐξαυτῆς· 24 πέποιθα δὲ
to send, as I shall have seen the things about me, at once; I trust but

1722 2962 3754 2532 846 5030 2064 316 1161
ἐν Κυρίῳ, ὅτι καὶ αὐτὸς ταχέως ἐλεύσομαι. 25 ἀναγκαῖον δὲ
in (the) Lord, that also myself shortly I will come. necessary But

2233 1891 3588 80 2532 4904 2532
ἡγησάμην Ἐπαφρόδιτον τὸν ἀδελφὸν καὶ συνεργὸν καὶ
I thought (it) Epaphroditus the brother and fellow-worker and

4961 3450 5216 1161 652 2532 3011 3588
συστρατιώτην μου, ὑμῶν δὲ ἀπόστολον, καὶ λειτουργὸν τῆς
fellow-soldier of me, of you and messenger, and minister of the

5532 3450 3992 4314 5209 1894 1971 2258 3956
χρείας μου, πέμψαι πρὸς ὑμᾶς· 26 ἐπειδὴ ἐπιποθῶν ἦν πάντας
need of me, to send to you; since longing after he was all

5209 2532 85 1360 191 3754 770 2532 1063
ὑμᾶς, καὶ ἀδημονῶν, διότι ἠκούσατε ὅτι ἠσθένησε· 27 καὶ γὰρ
you, and being troubled, because you heard that he was sick; indeed for

770 3897 2288 235 3588 2316 846 1653
ἠσθένησε παραπλήσιον θανάτῳ· ἀλλ' ὁ Θεὸς αὐτόν ἠλέησεν,
he was sick near to death; but God him had mercy on,

3756 846 1161 3440 235 2532 1691 2443 3361 3077 1909 3077 2192
οὐκ αὐτὸν δὲ μόνον, ἀλλὰ καὶ ἐμέ, ἵνα μὴ λύπην ἐπὶ λύπῃ σχῶ.
not on him and only, but also on me, that not grief on grief I may have.

4708 3767 3992 846 2443 1492 846 3825
28 σπουδαιοτέρως οὖν ἔπεμψα αὐτόν, ἵνα, ἰδόντες αὐτὸν πάλιν,
more eagerly Therefore I sent him, that seeing him again,

King James Version

and perverse nation, among whom ye shine as lights in the world;
16 Holding forth the word of life; that I may rejoice in the day of Christ, that I have not run in vain, neither laboured in vain.

17 Yea, and if I be offered upon the sacrifice and service of your faith, I joy, and rejoice with you all.
18 For the same cause also do ye joy, and rejoice with me.

19 But I trust in the Lord Jesus to send Timotheus shortly unto you, that I also may be of good comfort, when I know your state.
20 For I have no man likeminded, who will naturally care for your state.
21 For all seek their own, not the things which are Jesus Christ's.
22 But ye know the proof of him, that, as a son with the father, he hath served with me in the gospel.
23 Him therefore I hope to send presently, so soon as I shall see how it will go with me.
24 But I trust in the Lord that I also myself shall come shortly.
25 Yet I supposed it necessary to send to you Epaphroditus, my brother, and companion in labour, and fellowsoldier, but your messenger, and he that ministered to my wants.

26 For he longed after you all, and was full of heaviness, because that ye had heard that he had been sick.
27 For indeed he was sick nigh unto death: but God had mercy on him; and not on him only, but on me also, lest I should have sorrow upon sorrow.

28 I sent him therefore the more carefully, that, when ye see him again,

Philippians 2:29

Literal Translation

you may rejoice, and I may be less grieved.
29 Then receive him in (the) Lord with all joy and hold such in honor,
30 that through the work of Christ he drew near as far as to death, (his) life having been exposed, that he may fill up your lack of service toward me.

5463 2504 253 5600 4327 3767 846 1722
χαρῆτε, κἀγὼ ἀλυπότερος ὦ. 29 προσδέχεσθε οὖν αὐτὸν ἐν
you may rejoice, and I less grieved may be. receive Therefore him in
2962 3326 3956 5479 2532 3588 5108 1784 2192
Κυρίῳ μετὰ πάσης χαρᾶς, καὶ τοὺς τοιούτους ἐντίμους ἔχετε·
(the) Lord with all joy, and such ones honored hold;
3754 1223 3588 2041 3588 5547 3360 2288 1448
30 ὅτι διὰ τὸ ἔργον τοῦ Χριστοῦ μέχρι θανάτου ἤγγισε,
that through the work of Christ as far as death he drew near,
3851 3588 5590 2443 378 3588 5216
παραβολευσάμενος τῇ ψυχῇ, ἵνα ἀναπληρώσῃ τὸ ὑμῶν
having been exposed the life, that he might fill up the of you
5303 3588 4314 3165 3009
ὑστέρημα τῆς πρός με λειτουργίας.
lack toward me of service.

King James Version

ye may rejoice, and that I may be the less sorrowful.
29 Receive him therefore in the Lord with all gladness; and hold such in reputation:
30 Because for the work of Christ he was nigh unto death, not regarding his life, to supply your lack of service toward me.

Philippians 3

Philippians 3

1. For the rest my brothers, rejoice in (the) Lord. To write the same things to you truly (is) not tiresome to me, but safe for you.
2 Look out (for) the dogs, look out (for) the evil workers, look out (for) the concision (party).
3 For we are the circumcision, the (ones) worshiping by the Spirit of God, and glorying in Christ Jesus, and not trusting in flesh.
4 Though I also having trust in flesh; if any other thinks to trust in flesh, I more;
5 in circumcision, (the) eighth day, of (the) race of Israel, (the) tribe of Benjamin, a Hebrew of the Hebrews; according to Law, a Pharisee;
6 according to zeal, persecuting the church; according to righteousness in Law, being blameless.
7 But what things were gain to me, these I have counted loss because of Christ.
8 But, nay, rather I also count all things to be loss because of the excellency of the knowledge of Christ Jesus my Lord, for whose sake I have suffered the loss of all things and count (them to be) trash, that I might gain Christ
9 and be found in Him; not having my own righteousness

Philippians 3

3588 3063 80 3450 5463 1722 2962 3588 846
1. Τὸ λοιπόν, ἀδελφοί μου, χαίρετε ἐν Κυρίῳ. τὰ αὐτὰ
For the rest, brothers of me, rejoice in (the) Lord. The same things
1125 5213 1698 3303 3756 3636 5213 1161 804 991
γράφειν ὑμῖν ἐμοὶ μὲν οὐκ ὀκνηρόν, ὑμῖν δὲ ἀσφαλές. 2 Βλέπετε
I write to you for me truly not (is) tiresome, for you but safe. Look (to)
3588 2965 991 3588 2556 2040 991 3588
τοὺς κύνας, βλέπετε τοὺς κακοὺς ἐργάτας, βλέπετε τὴν
the dogs, look (to) the evil workers, look (to) the
2699 2249 1063 2070 3588 4061 3588 4151 2316
κατατομήν· 3 ἡμεῖς γάρ ἐσμεν ἡ περιτομή, οἱ Πνεύματι Θεῷ
concision; we for are the circumcision, those by Spirit of God
3000 2532 2744 1722 5547 2424 2532 3756 1722
λατρεύοντες, καὶ καυχώμενοι ἐν Χριστῷ Ἰησοῦ, καὶ οὐκ ἐν
worshiping, and glorying in Christ Jesus, and not in
4561 3982 2539 1473 2192 4006 2532 1722 4561
σαρκὶ πεποιθότες· 4 καίπερ ἐγὼ ἔχων πεποίθησιν καὶ ἐν σαρκι·
flesh trusting; even though I having trust also in flesh;
1487 5100 1380 243 3982 1722 4561 1473 3123 4061
εἴ τις δοκεῖ ἄλλος πεποιθέναι ἐν σαρκί, ἐγὼ μᾶλλον· 5 περιτομῇ
if any think other to trust in flesh, I more; in circumcision
3637 1537 1085 2474 5443 958 1445 1537
ὀκταήμερος, ἐκ γένους Ἰσραήλ, φυλῆς Βενιαμίν, Ἑβραῖος ἐξ
(the) eighth day; of (the) race of Israel, (the) tribe of Benjamin, a Hebrew of
1445 2596 3551 5330 2596 2205 1377 3588
Ἑβραίων, κατὰ νόμον Φαρισαῖος, 6 κατὰ ζῆλον διώκων τὴν
Hebrews; according to Law a Pharisee, according to zeal persecuting the
1577 2596 1343 3588 1722 3551 1096 273
ἐκκλησίαν, κατὰ δικαιοσύνην τὴν ἐν νόμῳ γενόμενος ἄμεμ-
church, according to righteousness in (the) Law being blame-
235 3748 2258 3427 2771 5023 2233 1223 3588 5547
πτος. 7 ἀλλ᾽ ἅτινα ἦν μοι κέρδη, ταῦτα ἥγημαι διὰ τὸν Χριστὸν
less. But what things were to me gain, these I have counted because of Christ
2209 235 3304 2532 2233 3956 2209 1511 1223
ζημίαν. 8 ἀλλὰ μενοῦνγε καὶ ἡγοῦμαι πάντα ζημίαν εἶναι διὰ
loss. But nay, rather also I count all things loss to be because
3588 5242 3588 1108 5547 2424 3588 2962 3450
τὸ ὑπερέχον τῆς γνώσεως Χριστοῦ Ἰησοῦ τοῦ Κυρίου μου·
of the excellency of the knowledge of Christ Jesus the Lord of me;
1223 3739 3588 3956 2210 2532 2233 4657 1511 2443
δι᾽ ὃν τὰ πάντα ἐζημιώθην, καὶ ἡγοῦμαι σκύβαλα εἶναι, ἵνα
for whose sake all things I suffered loss, and count trash to be, that
5547 2770 2532 2147 1722 846 3361 2192 1699 1343
Χριστὸν κερδήσω, 9 καὶ εὑρεθῶ ἐν αὐτῷ, μὴ ἔχων ἐμὴν δικαιο-
Christ I might gain, and be found in Him, not having my righteousness

Philippians 3

1. Finally, my brethren, rejoice in the Lord. To write the same things to you, to me indeed (is) not grievous, but for you (it is) safe.
2 Beware of dogs, beware of evil workers, beware of the concision.
3 For we are the circumcision, which worship God in the spirit, and rejoice in Christ Jesus, and have no confidence in the flesh.
4 Though I might also have confidence in the flesh. If any other man thinketh that he hath whereof he might trust in the flesh, I more:
5 Circumcised the eighth day, of the stock of Israel, (of) the tribe of Benjamin, an Hebrew of the Hebrews; as touching the law, a Pharisee;
6 Concerning zeal, persecuting the church; touching the righteousness which is in the law, blameless.
7 But what things were gain to me, those I counted loss for Christ.
8 Yea doubtless, and I count all things (but) loss for the excellency of the knowledge of Christ Jesus my Lord: for whom I have suffered the loss of all things, and do count them (but) dung, that I may win Christ,
9 And be found in him, not having mine own righteousness,

Literal Translation

Philippians 3:10

of Law, but through
(the) faith of Christ,
(having) the righteous-
ness of God on faith,

10 to know Him and the
power of His resurrec-
tion, and the fellowship
of His sufferings, hav-
ing been conformed to
His death,

11 if somehow I may at-
tain to a resurrection out
of the dead.
12 Not that already I
(have) received or al-
ready been perfected,
but I press on, if I also
may lay hold, inasmuch
as I also was laid hold of
by Christ Jesus.
13 Brothers, I do not
count myself to have
laid hold, but one (thing
I do), forgetting the
things behind, and
stretching forward to
(those) before,
14 I press on after a
mark for the prize of
the high calling of God
in Christ Jesus.

15 Then as many as
(are) perfect, let us think
this; and if you think any
other thing, God will
also reveal this to you.
16 Yet (as) to where we
have arrived, walk by
the same rule, (being) of
the same mind.

17 Be fellow-imitators
of me, brothers, and
mark those walking this
way, even as you have
us (for) a pattern.
18 For many walk (as)
the enemies of the cross
of Christ, of whom I
often told you, and now
even weeping I say it,

19 whose end (is) de-
struction, whose god
(is) the belly, and who
glory in their shame,
(those) minding
earthly things.

20 For our citizenship is
in Heaven, from where
we also wait for a Sav-
ior, (the) Lord Jesus
Christ,
21 who will transform
our body of humili-
ation,

3588 1537 3551 235 3588 1223 4102 5547 3588 1537
σύνην τὴν ἐκ νόμου, ἀλλὰ τὴν διὰ πίστεως Χριστοῦ, τὴν ἐκ
of Law, but the through faith of Christ, the of

2316 1343 1909 3588 4102 3588 1097 846 2532
Θεοῦ δικαιοσύνην ἐπὶ τῇ πίστει· 10 τοῦ γνῶναι αὐτὸν, καὶ
God righteousness (based) on faith; to know Him, and

3588 1411 3588 386 846 2532 3588 2842 3588
τὴν δύναμιν τῆς ἀναστάσεως αὐτοῦ, καὶ τὴν κοινωνίαν τῶν
the power of the resurrection of Him, and the fellowship of the

3804 846 4833 3588 2288 846 1487
παθημάτων αὐτοῦ, συμμορφούμενος τῷ θανάτῳ αὐτοῦ, 11 εἴ
sufferings of Him, being conformed to the death of Him, if

4459 2658 1519 3588 1815 3588 3498 3756 3754
πως καταντήσω εἰς τὴν ἐξανάστασιν τῶν νεκρῶν. 12 οὐχ ὅτι
somehow I might attain to the resurrection out of (the) dead. Not that

2235 2983 2228 2235 5048 1377 1161 1487 2532 2638
ἤδη ἔλαβον, ἢ ἤδη τετελείωμαι· διώκω δὲ, εἰ καὶ καταλάβω
already I received, or already been perfected; I press on but, if also I may lay hold

1909 3739 2532 2638 5259 3588 5547 2424 80
ἐφ' ᾧ καὶ κατελήμφθην ὑπὸ τοῦ Χριστοῦ Ἰησοῦ. 13 ἀδελφοί,
for that also I was laid hold of by Christ Jesus. Brothers,

1473 1683 3756 3049 2638 1520 1161 3588 3303 3694
ἐγὼ ἐμαυτὸν οὐ λογίζομαι κατειληφέναι· ἓν δέ, τὰ μὲν ὀπίσω
I myself not reckon to have laid hold; one but, the things behind

1950 3588 1161 1715 1901 2596
ἐπιλανθανόμενος, τοῖς δὲ ἔμπροσθεν ἐπεκτεινόμενος, 14 κατὰ
forgetting, the things and before stretching forward to (those), after

4649 1377 1909 3588 1017 3588 507 2821 3588 2316
σκοπὸν διώκω ἐπὶ τὸ βραβεῖον τῆς ἄνω κλήσεως τοῦ Θεοῦ
a mark I press on for the prize of the high calling of God

1722 5547 2424 3745 3767 5046 5124 5426 2532 1487
ἐν Χριστῷ Ἰησοῦ. 15 Ὅσοι οὖν τέλειοι, τοῦτο φρονῶμεν· καὶ εἴ
in Christ Jesus. as many as Then (are) perfect, this let us think; and if

5100 2088 5426 2532 5124 3588 2316 5213 601 4133
τι ἑτέρως φρονεῖτε, καὶ τοῦτο ὁ Θεὸς ὑμῖν ἀποκαλύψει· 16 πλὴν
anything other you think, even this God to you will reveal; yet

1519 3739 5348 3588 846 4748 2583 3588 846 5426
εἰς ὃ ἐφθάσαμεν, τῷ αὐτῷ στοιχεῖν κανόνι, τὸ αὐτὸ φρονεῖν.
to what we arrived, by the same to walk rule, of the same mind.

4831 3450 1096 80 2532 4648 3588 3779
17. Συμμιμηταί μου γίνεσθε, ἀδελφοί, καὶ σκοπεῖτε τοὺς οὕτω
fellow-imitators of me Become, brothers, and mark those thus

4043 2531 2192 5179 2248 4183 1063 4043
περιπατοῦντας καθὼς ἔχετε τύπον ἡμᾶς. 18 πολλοὶ γὰρ περι-
walking, even as you have a pattern us. many For walk,

3739 4178 3004 5213 3568 1161 2532 2799 3004
πατοῦσιν, οὓς πολλάκις ἔλεγον ὑμῖν, νῦν δὲ καὶ κλαίων λέγω,
of whom often I said to you, now and even weeping I say,

3588 2190 3588 4716 3588 5547 3739 3588 5056 684
τοὺς ἐχθροὺς τοῦ σταυροῦ τοῦ Χριστοῦ· 19 ὧν τὸ τέλος ἀπώ-
(as) the enemies of the cross of Christ; of whom the end (is) ruin,

3739/3588/2316/3588/2836/2532/3588/1391/1722/3588/152 846 3588
λεια, ὧν ὁ θεὸς ἡ κοιλία, καὶ ἡ δόξα ἐν τῇ αἰσχύνῃ αὐτῶν, οἱ
of whom the god the belly (is), and the glory in the shame of them, those

3588 1919 5426 2257 1063 3588 4175 1722 3772
τὰ ἐπίγεια φρονοῦντες. 20 ἡμῶν γὰρ τὸ πολίτευμα ἐν οὐρανοῖς
the earthly things thinking. of us For the citizenship in Heaven

5225 1537 3739 2532 4990 553 2962 2424
ὑπάρχει, ἐξ οὗ καὶ Σωτῆρα ἀπεκδεχόμεθα, Κύριον Ἰησοῦν
is, from where also a Savior we await, (the) Lord Jesus

5547 3739 3345 3588 4983 3588 5014
Χριστόν· 21 ὃς μετασχηματίσει τὸ σῶμα τῆς ταπεινώσεως
Christ; who will transform the body of the humiliation

King James Version

which is of the law, but
that which is through
the faith of Christ, the
righteousness which is
of God by faith:
10 That I may know
him, and the power of
his resurrection, and the
fellowship of his suffer-
ings, being made con-
formable unto his
death;
11 If by any means I
might attain unto the
resurrection of the dead.
12 Not as though I had
already attained, either
were already perfect:
but I follow after, if that
I may apprehend that
for which also I am ap-
prehended of Christ Je-
sus.
13 Brethren, I count not
myself to have appre-
hended: but (this) one
thing (I do), forgetting
those things which are
behind, and reaching
forth unto those things
which are before,
14 I press toward the
mark for the prize of the
high calling of God in
Christ Jesus.
15 Let us therefore, as
many as be perfect, be
thus minded: and if in
any thing ye be other-
wise minded, God shall
reveal even this unto
you.
16 Nevertheless,
whereto we have al-
ready attained, let us
walk by the same rule,
let us mind the same
thing.
17 Brethren, be follow-
ers together of me, and
mark them which walk
so as ye have us for an
ensample.
18 (For many walk, of
whom I have told you
often, and now tell you
even weeping, (that
they are) the enemies of
the cross of Christ:
19 Whose end (is) de-
struction, whose God
(is their) belly, and
(whose) glory (is) in
their shame, who mind
earthly things.)
20 For our conversation
is in heaven; from
whence also we look for
the Saviour, the Lord
Jesus Christ:
21 Who shall change
our vile body,

Literal Translation

Philippians 4:1

King James Version

for it to be conformed to His body of glory, according to the working of His power, even to subject all things to Himself.

2257 1519 3588 1096 846 4832 3588 4983 3588 1391
ἡμῶν, εἰς τὸ γενέσθαι αὐτὸ σύμμορφον τῷ σώματι τῆς δόξης
of us, for to be it conformed to the body of the glory

846 2596 3588 1753 3588 1410 846 2532 5293
αὐτοῦ, κατὰ τὴν ἐνέργειαν τοῦ δύνασθαι αὐτὸν καὶ ὑποτάξαι
of Him, according to the working of the ability (of) Him even to subject

1438 3588 3956
ἑαυτῷ τὰ πάντα.
to Himself all things.

that it may be fashioned like unto his glorious body, according to the working whereby he is able even to subdue all things unto himself.

Philippians 4

1. So as, my brothers, beloved and longed for, my joy and crown, so stand firm in (the) Lord, beloved.

2 I entreat Euodias, and I entreat Syntyche, to think the same in (the) Lord.

3 And I also ask you, true yoke-fellow, help those who struggled along with me and with Clement in the gospel, and the rest, fellow-workers with me, whose names (are) in the Scroll of Life.

4 Rejoice in (the) Lord always. Again I say, Rejoice!

5 Let your reasonableness be known to all men. The Lord (is) near.

6 Be anxious of nothing, but in everything by prayer and by petition with thanksgivings, let your requests be made known to God;

7 and the peace of God which surpasses all understanding will keep your hearts and your minds in Christ Jesus.

8 For the rest, brothers, whatever is true, whatever honorable, whatever (is) just, whatever pure, whatever lovely, whatever of good report, if (of) any virtue, and if (of) any praise, meditate (on) these things.

9 And what things you learned and received and heard and saw in me, practice these things, and

Philippians 4

5620 80 3450 27 2532 1973 5479 2532
1. Ὥστε, ἀδελφοί μου ἀγαπητοὶ καὶ ἐπιπόθητοι, χαρὰ καὶ
So as, brothers of me beloved and longed for, joy and

4735 3450 3779 4739 1722 2962 27
στέφανός μου, οὕτω στήκετε ἐν Κυρίῳ, ἀγαπητοί.
crown of me, so stand in (the) Lord, beloved.

2136 3870 2532 4941 3870 3588 846
2. Εὐοδίαν παρακαλῶ, καὶ Συντύχην παρακαλῶ, τὸ αὐτὸ
Euodia I entreat, and Syntyche I entreat, the same

5426 1722 2962 2532 2065 2532 4571 4805 1103 4815
φρονεῖν ἐν Κυρίῳ. 3 καὶ ἐρωτῶ καὶ σέ, σύζυγε γνήσιε, συλ-
think in (the) Lord. And I ask also you, yoke-fellow true, help

846 3748 1722 3588 2098 4866 3427
λαμβάνου αὐταῖς, αἵτινες ἐν τῷ εὐαγγελίῳ συνήθλησάν μοι,
them, who in the gospel struggled with me,

3326 2532 2815 2532 3588 3062 4904 3450 3739
μετὰ καὶ Κλήμεντος, καὶ τῶν λοιπῶν συνεργῶν μου, ὧν
with and Clement, and the rest fellow-workers of me, of whom

3588 3686 1722 976 2222
τὰ ὀνόματα ἐν βίβλῳ ζωῆς.
the names (are) in (the) Scroll of life.

5463 1722 2962 3842 3825 2046 5463 3588
4 Χαίρετε ἐν Κυρίῳ πάντοτε· πάλιν ἐρῶ, χαίρετε. 5 τὸ
Rejoice in (the) Lord always; again I will say, Rejoice. The

1933 5216 1097 3956 444 3588 2962 1451
ἐπιεικὲς ὑμῶν γνωσθήτω πᾶσιν ἀνθρώποις. ὁ Κύριος ἐγγύς.
reasonableness of you let be known to all men. The Lord (is) near.

3367 3309 235 1722 3956 3588 4335 2532 3588 1162
6 μηδὲν μεριμνᾶτε, ἀλλ' ἐν παντὶ τῇ προσευχῇ καὶ τῇ δεήσει
nothing be anxious about, but in everything by prayer and petition

3326 2169 3588 155 5216 1107 4314 3588 2316
μετὰ εὐχαριστίας τὰ αἰτήματα ὑμῶν γνωριζέσθω πρὸς τὸν Θεόν.
with thanksgivings the requests of you let be made known to God.

2532 3588 1515 3588 2316 3588 5242 3956 3563 5432
7 καὶ ἡ εἰρήνη τοῦ Θεοῦ, ἡ ὑπερέχουσα πάντα νοῦν, φρουρήσει
And the peace of God, which surpasses all understanding, will keep

3588 2588 5216 2532 3588 3540 5216 1722 5547 2424
τὰς καρδίας ὑμῶν καὶ τὰ νοήματα ὑμῶν ἐν Χριστῷ Ἰησοῦ.
the hearts of you and the minds of you in Christ Jesus.

3588 3063 80 3745 2076 227 3745 4586 3745
8. Τὸ λοιπόν, ἀδελφοί, ὅσα ἐστὶν ἀληθῆ, ὅσα σεμνά, ὅσα
(For) the rest, brothers, whatever is true, whatever honorable, whatever

1342 3745 53 3745 4375 3745 2163 1487 5100 703
δίκαια, ὅσα ἁγνά, ὅσα προσφιλῆ, ὅσα εὔφημα, εἴ τις ἀρετὴ
just, whatever pure, whatever lovely, whatever of good report, if any virtue

2532 1487 5100 1868 5023 3049 3739 2532 3129 2532
καὶ εἴ τις ἔπαινος, ταῦτα λογίζεσθε. 9 ἃ καὶ ἐμάθετε καὶ παρε-
and if any praise, (on) these things meditate. Which things both you learned and

3880 2532 191 2532 1492 1722 1698 5023 4238 2532
λάβετε καὶ ἠκούσατε καὶ εἴδετε ἐν ἐμοί, ταῦτα πράσσετε· καὶ
received and heard and saw in me, these things practice; and

Philippians 4

1. Therefore, my brethren dearly beloved and longed for, my joy and crown, so stand fast in the Lord, (my) dearly beloved.

2 I beseech Euodias, and beseech Syntyche, that they be of the same mind in the Lord.

3 And I intreat thee also, true yokefellow, help those women which laboured with me in the gospel, with Clement also, and (with) other my fellowlabourers, whose names (are) in the book of life.

4 Rejoice in the Lord alway: (and) again I say, Rejoice.

5 Let your moderation be known unto all men. The Lord (is) at hand.

6 Be careful for nothing; but in every thing by prayer and supplication with thanksgiving let your requests be made known unto God.

7 And the peace of God, which passeth all understanding, shall keep your hearts and minds through Christ Jesus.

8 Finally, brethren, whatsoever things are true, whatsoever things (are) honest, whatsoever things (are) just, whatsoever things (are) pure, whatsoever things (are) lovely, whatsoever things (are) of good report; if (there be) any virtue, and if (there be) any praise, think on these things.

9 Those things, which ye have both learned, and received, and heard, and seen in me, do: and

Literal Translation | **Philippians 4:10** | ***King James Version***

the God of peace will be with you.

10 But I rejoiced in (the) Lord greatly that now at last you revived (your) thinking on my behalf, although you indeed did think, but lacked opportunity).
11 Not that I speak as to need, for I have learned to be contented in whatever (state) I am.
12 But I know to be humbled, and I know to abound; in everything, and in all things, I am taught both to be filled and to hunger, both to abound, and to lack.
13 I have strength to do all things through Christ, the (One) strengthening me.
14 Yet you did well in sharing my troubles.
15 And you know also, Philippians, that in (the) beginning of the gospel, when I went out from Macedonia, not one church shared with me in (the) matter of giving and receiving, except you only.
16 Because truly in Thessalonica you sent to my need, both once and twice.
17 Not that I seek a gift, but I seek the fruit multiplying to your account.
18 But I have all things and more than enough; I have been filled, receiving from Epaphroditus the things from you, an odor of sweet smell, an acceptable sacrifice, pleasing to God.
19 And my God will fill your every need according to His riches in glory in Christ Jesus.
20 Now may glory (be) to our God and Father to the ages of the ages. Amen.
21 Greet every saint in Christ Jesus.

3588 2316 3588 1515 2071 3326 5216
ὁ Θεὸς τῆς εἰρήνης ἔσται μεθ’ ὑμῶν.
the God of peace will be with you.

5463 1161 1722 2962 3171 3754 2235 4218 330 3588
10. Ἐχάρην δὲ ἐν Κυρίῳ μεγάλως, ὅτι ἤδη ποτὲ ἀνεθάλετε τὸ
I rejoiced And in (the) Lord greatly, that now at last you revived

5228 1700 5426 1909 3739 2532 5426 170 1161 3756
ὑπὲρ ἐμοῦ φρονεῖν· ἐφ’ ᾧ καὶ ἐφρονεῖτε, ἠκαιρεῖσθε δέ. 11 οὐχ
on behalf of me thinking; although also you thought, lacked opportunity but. Not

3754 2596 5304 3004 1473 1063 3129 1722 3739 1510
ὅτι καθ ’ ὑστέρησιν λέγω· ἐγὼ γὰρ ἔμαθον, ἐν οἷς εἰμι,
that by way of need I speak; I for learned, in what (state) I am,

842 1511 1492 2532 5013 1492 2532 4052
αὐτάρκης εἶναι. 12 οἶδα καὶ ταπεινοῦσθαι, οἶδα καὶ περισ-
contented to be. I know And to be humbled, I know and to

1722 3956 2532 1722 3956 3453 2532 5526 2532
σεύειν· ἐν παντὶ καὶ ἐν πᾶσι μεμύημαι καὶ χορτάζεσθαι καὶ
abound; in everything and in all things I am taught both to be filled and

3983 2532 4052 2532 5302 3956 2480 1722
πεινᾶν, καὶ περισσεύειν καὶ ὑστερεῖσθαι. 13 πάντα ἰσχύω ἐν
to hunger, both to abound and to lack. All things I can do in

3588 1743 3165 5547 4133 2573 4160
τῷ ἐνδυναμοῦντί με Χριστῷ. 14 πλὴν καλῶς ἐποιήσατε
the (One) strengthening me Christ. Yet well you did

4790 3450 3588 2347 1492 1161 2532 5210
συγκοινωνήσαντές μου τῇ θλίψει. 15 οἴδατε δὲ καὶ ὑμεῖς,
sharing in of me the troubles. know And also you,

5374 3754 1722 746 3588 2098 3753 1831
Φιλιππήσιοι, ὅτι ἐν ἀρχῇ τοῦ εὐαγγελίου, ὅτε ἐξῆλθον
Philippians, that in (the) beginning of the gospel, when I went out

575 3109 3762 3427 1577 2841 1519
ἀπὸ Μακεδονίας, οὐδεμία μοι ἐκκλησία ἐκοινώνησεν εἰς
from Macedonia, not one me church shared with in

3056 1394 2532 3028 1487 3361 5210 3441 3754 2532 1722
λόγον δόσεως καὶ λήψεως, εἰ μὴ ὑμεῖς μόνοι· 16 ὅτι καὶ ἐν
(the) matter of giving and receiving, except you only; because even in

2332 2532 530 2532 1364 1519 3588 5532 3427 3992
Θεσσαλονίκῃ καὶ ἅπαξ καὶ δὶς εἰς τὴν χρείαν μοι ἐπέμψατε.
Thessalonica both once and twice to the need of me you sent.

3756 3754 1934 3588 1390 235 1934 3588 2590 3588
17 οὐχ ὅτι ἐπιζητῶ τὸ δόμα, ἀλλ’ ἐπιζητῶ τὸν καρπὸν τὸν
Not that I seek the gift, but I seek the fruit

4121 1519 3056 5216 568 1161 3956 2532 4052
πλεονάζοντα εἰς λόγον ὑμῶν. 18 ἀπέχω δὲ πάντα καὶ περισ-
multiplying to (the) account of you. I have But all things and abound;

4137 1209 3844 1891 3588 3844
σεύω· πεπλήρωμαι, δεξάμενος παρὰ Ἐπαφροδίτου τὰ παρ’
I have been filled, receiving from Epaphroditus the things from

5216 3744 2175 2378 1184 2101 3588 2316
ὑμῶν, ὀσμὴν εὐωδίας, θυσίαν δεκτήν, εὐάρεστον τῷ Θεῷ.
you, an odor of sweet smell, a sacrifice acceptable, well-pleasing to God.

3588 1161 2316 3450 4137 3956 5532 5216 2596 3588
19 ὁ δὲ Θεός μου πληρώσει πᾶσαν χρείαν ὑμῶν κατὰ τὸν
the And God of me will fill every need of you according to the

4149 846 1722 1391 1722 5547 2424 3588 1161 2316 2532
πλοῦτον αὐτοῦ ἐν δόξῃ ἐν Χριστῷ Ἰησοῦ. 20 τῷ δὲ Θεῷ καὶ
riches of Him in glory in Christ Jesus. to the Now God and

3962 2257 3588 1391 1519 3588 165 3588 165 281
πατρὶ ἡμῶν ἡ δόξα εἰς τοὺς αἰῶνας τῶν αἰώνων· ἀμήν.
Father of you (be) the glory to the ages of the ages; Amen.

782 3956 40 1722 5547 2424 782
21. Ἀσπάσασθε πάντα ἅγιον ἐν Χριστῷ Ἰησοῦ. ἀσπά-
Greet every saint in Christ Jesus. Greet

the God of peace shall be with you.

10 But I rejoiced in the Lord greatly, that now at the last your care of me hath flourished again; wherein ye were also careful, but ye lacked opportunity.
11 Not that I speak in respect of want: for I have learned, in whatsoever state I am, (therewith) to be content.
12 I know both how to be abased, and I know how to abound: every where and in all things I am instructed both to be full and to be hungry, both to abound and to suffer need.
13 I can do all things through Christ which strengtheneth me.
14 Notwithstanding ye have well done, that ye did communicate with my affliction.
15 Now ye Philippians know also, that in the beginning of the gospel, when I departed from Macedonia, no church communicated with me as concerning giving and receiving, but ye only.
16 For even in Thessalonica ye sent once and again unto my necessity.
17 Not because I desire a gift: but I desire fruit that may abound to your account.
18 But I have all, and abound: I am full, having received of Epaphroditus the things (which were sent) from you, an odour of a sweet smell, a sacrifice acceptable, wellpleasing to God.
19 But my God shall supply all your need according to his riches in glory by Christ Jesus.
20 Now unto God and our Father (be) glory for ever and ever. Amen.
21 Salute every saint in Christ Jesus.

Literal Translation

Philippians 4:22

King James Version

The brothers with me greet you.
22 All the saints greet you, most of all those of Caesar's house.

23 The grace of our Lord Jesus Christ (be) with all of you. Amen.

5209 3588 4862 1698 80 782 5209 3956
ζονται ὑμᾶς οἱ σὺν ἐμοὶ ἀδελφοί. 22 ἀσπάζονται ὑμᾶς πάντες
you the with me brothers. Greet you all

3588 40 3122 1161 3588 1537 3588 2541 3614
οἱ ἅγιοι, μάλιστα δὲ οἱ ἐκ τῆς Καίσαρος οἰκίας.
the saints, most of all but those of the of Caesar house.

3588 5485 3588 2962 2257 2424 5547 3326 3956
23 Ἡ χάρις τοῦ Κυρίου ἡμῶν Ἰησοῦ Χριστοῦ μετὰ πάντων
The grace of the Lord of us Jesus Christ (be) with all

5216 281
ὑμῶν. ἀμήν.
of you. Amen.

The brethren which are with me greet you.
22 All the saints salute you, chiefly they that are of Caesar's household.

23 The grace of our Lord Jesus Christ (be) with you all. Amen. (To (the) Philippians written from Rome, by Epaphroditus.)

Literal Translation

THE EPISTLE OF PAUL THE APOSTLE TO THE COLOSSIANS

ΠΑΥΛΟΥ ΤΟΥ ΑΠΟΣΤΟΛΟΥ
OF PAUL THE APOSTLE

Η ΠΡΟΣ ΚΟΛΟΣΣΑΕΙΣ ΕΠΙΣΤΟΛΗ
THE TO COLOSSIANS EPISTLE

King James Version

THE EPISTLE OF PAUL THE APOSTLE TO THE COLOSSIANS

Colossians 1

1. Paul, (an) apostle of Jesus Christ through the will of God, and Timothy the brother,
2 to the saints and faithful brothers in Christ in Colosse: Grace and peace to you from God our Father and (the) Lord Jesus Christ.

3 We give thanks to God and (the) Father of our Lord Jesus Christ, praying continually concerning you,
4 hearing of your faith in Christ Jesus and the love toward all the saints,

5 because of the hope being laid up for you in Heaven, which you heard before in the Word of the truth of the gospel,

6 coming to you, as also in all the world, and it is bearing fruit even also among you, from the day in which you heard and fully knew the grace of God in truth;

7 even as you also learned from Epaphras our beloved fellow-slave, who is a faithful minister of Christ for you,

8 he also showing to us your love in (the) Spirit.

9 Because of this also, from the day in which we heard, we do not cease praying on your behalf, and asking that you may be filled (with) the full knowledge of His will in all wisdom

Colossians 1

3972 652 2424 5547 1223 2307 2316
1. Παῦλος ἀπόστολος Ἰησοῦ Χριστοῦ διὰ θελήματος Θεοῦ,
Paul an apostle of Jesus Christ through the will of God,

2532 5095 3588 80 3588 1722 2857 40 2532
καὶ Τιμόθεος ὁ ἀδελφός, 2 τοῖς ἐν Κολοσσαῖς ἁγίοις καὶ
and Timothy the brother, to the in Colosse saints and

4103 80 1722 5547 5485 5213 2532 1515 575 2316
πιστοῖς ἀδελφοῖς ἐν Χριστῷ· χάρις ὑμῖν καὶ εἰρήνη ἀπὸ Θεοῦ
faithful brothers in Christ; Grace to you and peace from God

3962 2257 2532 2962 2424 5547
πατρὸς ἡμῶν καὶ Κυρίου Ἰησοῦ Χριστοῦ.
(the) Father of us and (the) Lord Jesus Christ.

2168 3588 2316 2532 3962 3588 2962 2257
3. Εὐχαριστοῦμεν τῷ Θεῷ καὶ πατρὶ τοῦ Κυρίου ἡμῶν
We give thanks to God and Father of the Lord of us

2424 5547 3842 4012 5216 4336 191
Ἰησοῦ Χριστοῦ, πάντοτε περὶ ὑμῶν προσευχόμενοι, 4 ἀκού-
Jesus Christ, always concerning you praying, having

3588 4102 5216 1722 5547 2424 2532 3588 26
σαντες τὴν πίστιν ὑμῶν ἐν Χριστῷ Ἰησοῦ, καὶ τὴν ἀγάπην
heard the faith of you in Christ Jesus, and the love

3588 1519 3956 3588 40 1223 3588 1680 3588 606
τὴν εἰς πάντας τοὺς ἁγίους, 5 διὰ τὴν ἐλπίδα τὴν ἀποκειμένην
toward all the saints, because of the hope being laid up

5213 1722 3588 3772 3739 4257 1722 3588 3056 3588
ὑμῖν ἐν τοῖς οὐρανοῖς, ἣν προηκούσατε ἐν τῷ λόγῳ τῆς
for you in Heaven, which you heard before in the Word of the

225 3588 2098 3588 3918 1519 5209 2531 2532
ἀληθείας τοῦ εὐαγγελίου, 6 τοῦ παρόντος εἰς ὑμᾶς, καθὼς καὶ
truth of the gospel, (which is) coming to you, even as also

1722 3956 3588 2889 2532 2076 2592 2531 2532
ἐν παντὶ τῷ κόσμῳ, καὶ ἔστὶ καρποφορούμενον, καθὼς καὶ
in all the world, and it is bearing fruit, even as also

1722 5213 575 3739 2250 191 2532 1921 3588 5485 3588
ἐν ὑμῖν, ἀφ' ἧς ἡμέρας ἠκούσατε καὶ ἐπέγνωτε τὴν χάριν τοῦ
among you, from which day you heard and fully knew the grace

2316 1722 225 2531 2532 3129 575 1889 3588
Θεοῦ ἐν ἀληθείᾳ· 7 καθὼς καὶ ἐμάθετε ἀπὸ Ἐπαφρᾶ τοῦ
of God in truth; as also you learned from Epaphras the

27 4889 2257 3739 2076 4103 5228 5216
ἀγαπητοῦ συνδούλου ἡμῶν, ὅς ἐστι πιστὸς ὑπὲρ ὑμῶν
beloved fellow-slave of us, who is a faithful on behalf of you

1249 3588 5547 3588 2532 1213 2254 3588 5216 26
διάκονος τοῦ Χριστοῦ, 8 ὁ καὶ δηλώσας ἡμῖν τὴν ὑμῶν ἀγάπην
minister of Christ, he also showing us the of you love

1722 4151
ἐν Πνεύματι.
in (the) Spirit.

1223 5124 2532 2249 575 3739 2250 191 3756 3973
9. Διὰ τοῦτο καὶ ἡμεῖς, ἀφ' ἧς ἡμέρας ἠκούσαμεν, οὐ παυό-
Because of this also we, from which day we heard, do not cease

5228 5216 4336 2532 154 2443 4137
μεθα ὑπὲρ ὑμῶν προσευχόμενοι, καὶ αἰτούμενοι ἵνα πληρω-
on behalf of you praying, and asking that you may

3588 1922 3588 2307 846 1722 3956 4678
θῆτε τὴν ἐπίγνωσιν τοῦ θελήματος αὐτοῦ ἐν πάσῃ σοφίᾳ
be filled (with) the knowledge of the will of Him in all wisdom

Colossians 1

1. Paul, an apostle of Jesus Christ by the will of God, and Timotheus (our) brother,
2 To the saints and faithful brethren in Christ which are at Colosse: Grace (be) unto you, and peace, from God our Father and the Lord Jesus Christ.

3 We give thanks to God and the Father of our Lord Jesus Christ, praying always for you,
4 Since we heard of your faith in Christ Jesus, and of the love (which ye have) to all the saints,

5 For the hope which is laid up for you in heaven, whereof ye heard before in the word of the truth of the gospel;

6 Which is come unto you, as (it is) in all the world; and bringeth forth fruit, as (it doth) also in you, since the day ye heard (of it), and knew the grace of God in truth:

7 As ye also learned of Epaphras our dear fellowservant, who is for you a faithful minister of Christ;

8 Who also declared unto us your love in the Spirit.

9 For this cause we also, since the day we heard (it), do not cease to pray for you, and to desire that ye might be filled with the knowledge of his will in all wisdom

Literal Translation

Colossians 1:10

King James Version

and spiritual understanding,
10 (for) you to walk worthily of the Lord to all pleasing, bearing fruit in every good work and growing into the full knowledge of God;

11 being empowered with all power according to the might of His glory, to all patience and longsuffering with joy;

12 giving thanks to the Father, who has made us fit for a share of the inheritance of the saints in light,
13 who delivered us out of the authority of darkness, and translated (us) into the kingdom of the Son of His love,

14 in whom we have redemption through His blood, the remission of sins;
15 who is (the) image of the invisible God, (the) First-born of all creation.
16 For all things were created in Him, the things in the heavens, and the things on the earth, the visible and the invisible; whether thrones, or lordships, or rulers, or authorities, all things have been created through Him and for Him.

17 And He is before all things, and all things has subsisted in Him.
18 And He is the Head of the body, the church, who is (the) Beginning, (the) Firstborn from (the) dead, that He may be preeminent in all things;
19 because all the fullness was pleased to dwell in Him,

20 and through Him making peace by the blood of His cross, to reconcile all things to Himself; through Him, whether the things on the earth, or the things in

2532 4907 4152 4043 5209 516 3588
καὶ συνέσει πνευματικῇ, 10 περιπατῆσαι ὑμᾶς ἀξίως τοῦ
and understanding spiritual, to walk you worthily of the

2962 1519 3956 699 1722 3956 2041 18
Κυρίου εἰς πᾶσαν ἀρεσκείαν, ἐν παντὶ ἔργῳ ἀγαθῷ
Lord to all pleasing, in every work good

2592 2532 837 1519 3588 1922 3588 2316
καρποφοροῦντες καὶ αὐξανόμενοι εἰς τὴν ἐπίγνωσιν τοῦ Θεοῦ·
bearing fruit and growing into the full knowledge of God;

1722 3956 1411 1412 2596 3588 2904 3588 1391
11 ἐν πάσῃ δυνάμει δυναμούμενοι, κατὰ τὸ κράτος τῆς δόξης
with all power being empowered, according to the might of the glory

846 1519 3956 5281 2532 3115 3326 5479
αὐτοῦ, εἰς πᾶσαν ὑπομονὴν καὶ μακροθυμίαν, μετὰ χαρᾶς·
of Him, to all patience and long-suffering, with joy;

2168 3588 3962 3588 2427 2248 1519 3588 3310
12 εὐχαριστοῦντες τῷ πατρὶ τῷ ἱκανώσαντι ἡμᾶς εἰς τὴν μερίδα
giving thanks to the Father having made fit us for the share

3588 2819 3588 40 1722 3588 5457 3739 4506 2248 1537 3588
τοῦ κλήρου τῶν ἁγίων ἐν τῷ φωτί, 13 ὃς ἐρρύσατο ἡμᾶς ἐκ τῆς
of the inheritance of the saints in light, who delivered us out of the

1849 3588 4655 2532 3179 1519 3588 932 3588
ἐξουσίας τοῦ σκότους, καὶ μετέστησεν εἰς τὴν βασιλείαν τοῦ
authority of darkness, and translated (us) into the kingdom of the

5207 3588 26 846 1722 3739 2192 3588 629 1223
υἱοῦ τῆς ἀγάπης αὐτοῦ, 14 ἐν ᾧ ἔχομεν τὴν ἀπολύτρωσιν διὰ
Son of the love of Him, in whom we have redemption through

3588 129 846 3588 859 3588 266 3739 2076 1504
τοῦ αἵματος αὐτοῦ, τὴν ἄφεσιν τῶν ἁμαρτιῶν· 15 ὅς ἐστιν εἰκὼν
the blood of Him, the remission of sins; who is (the) image

3588 2316 3588 517 4416 3956 2937 3754
τοῦ Θεοῦ τοῦ ἀοράτου, πρωτότοκος πάσης κτίσεως· 16 ὅτι
of God the invisible, the First-born of all creation; because

1722 846 2936 3588 3956 3588 1722 3588 3772 2532 3588 1909
ἐν αὐτῷ ἐκτίσθη τὰ πάντα, τὰ ἐν τοῖς οὐρανοῖς καὶ τὰ ἐπὶ
in Him were created the things all, the things in the heavens and the things on

3588 1093 3588 3707 2532 3588 517 1535 2362 1535 2963
τῆς γῆς, τὰ ὁρατὰ καὶ τὰ ἀόρατα, εἴτε θρόνοι, εἴτε κυριό-
the earth, the visible and the invisible, whether thrones, or lordships,

1535 746 1535 1849 3588 3956 1223 846 2532 1519
τητες, εἴτε ἀρχαί, εἴτε ἐξουσίαι· τὰ πάντα δι' αὐτοῦ καὶ εἰς
whether rulers, or authorities; all things through Him and for

846 2936 2532 846 2076 4253 3956 2532 3588 3956
αὐτὸν ἔκτισται· 17 καὶ αὐτός ἐστι πρὸ πάντων, καὶ τὰ πάντα
Him have been created; and He is before all things, and all things

1722 846 4921 2532 846 2076 3588 2776 3588 4983
ἐν αὐτῷ συνέστηκε. 18 καὶ αὐτός ἐστιν ἡ κεφαλὴ τοῦ σώματος,
in Him has subsisted. And He is the Head of the body,

3588 1577 3739 2076 746 4416 1537 3588 3498
τῆς ἐκκλησίας· ὅς ἐστιν ἀρχή, πρωτότοκος ἐκ τῶν νεκρῶν,
the church; who is (the) Beginning, First-born from the dead,

2443 1096 1722 3956 846 4409 3754 1722 846 2106
ἵνα γένηται ἐν πᾶσιν αὐτὸς πρωτεύων· 19 ὅτι ἐν αὐτῷ εὐδόκησε
that may be in all things He pre-eminent; because in Him was pleased

3956 3588 4138 2730 2532 1223 846 604
πᾶν τὸ πλήρωμα κατοικῆσαι, 20 καὶ δι' αὐτοῦ ἀποκαταλλάξαι
all the fullness to dwell, and through Him to reconcile

3588 3956 1519 846 1517 1223 3588 129 3588
τὰ πάντα εἰς αὐτόν, εἰρηνοποιήσας διὰ τοῦ αἵματος τοῦ
all things to Himself, making peace through the blood of the

4716 846 1223 846 1535 3588 1909 3588 1093 1535 3588 1722
σταυροῦ αὐτοῦ, δι' αὐτοῦ, εἴτε τὰ ἐπὶ τῆς γῆς, εἴτε τὰ ἐν
cross of Him, through Him, whether the things on the earth, or the things in

and spiritual understanding;
10 That ye might walk worthy of the Lord unto all pleasing, being fruitful in every good work, and increasing in the knowledge of God;

11 Strengthened with all might, according to his glorious power, unto all patience and longsuffering with joyfulness;

12 Giving thanks unto the Father, which hath made us meet to be partakers of the inheritance of the saints in light:
13 Who hath delivered us from the power of darkness, and hath translated (us) into the kingdom of his dear Son:
14 In whom we have redemption through his blood, (even) the forgiveness of sins:
15 Who is the image of the invisible God, the firstborn of every creature:
16 For by him were all things created, that are in heaven, and that are in earth, visible and invisible, whether (they be) thrones, or dominions, or principalities, or powers: all things were created by him, and for him:

17 And he is before all things, and by him all things consist.
18 And he is the head of the body, the church: who is the beginning, the firstborn from the dead; that in all (things) he might have the preeminence.
19 For it pleased (the Father) that in him should all fulness dwell;

20 And, having made peace through the blood of his cross, by him to reconcile all things unto himself; by him, (I say), whether (they be) things in earth, or things in

Colossians 1:21

Literal Translation

the heavens.
21 And you then being alienated and hostile ones in (your) mind by evil works, yet now He reconciled
22 in the body of His flesh, through (His) death, to present you holy and without blemish and without charge before Him,
23 if indeed you continue in the faith grounded and settled and not being moved away from the hope of the gospel which you heard proclaimed in all the creation under the heaven, of which I, Paul, became a minister.
24 who now rejoice in my sufferings on your behalf and fill up in my flesh the things lacking of the afflictions of Christ on behalf of His body, which (is) the church,
25 of which I became a minister, according to the administration of God given to me for you, to fulfill the Word of God,
26 the mystery having been hidden from the ages and from the generations, but now was revealed to His saints;
27 to whom God willed to make known what (are) the riches of the glory of this mystery among the nations, who is Christ in you, the hope of glory;
28 whom we proclaim, warning every man and teaching every man in all wisdom, that we may present every man

3588 3772 2532 5209 4218 5607 526 2532
τοῖς οὐρανοῖς. 21 καὶ ὑμᾶς ποτὲ ὄντας ἀπηλλοτριωμένους καὶ
the heavens. And you then being alienated and

2190 3588 1271 1722 3588 2041 3588 4190 3570/ 1161
ἐχθροὺς τῇ διανοίᾳ ἐν τοῖς ἔργοις τοῖς πονηροῖς, νυνὶ δὲ
hostile ones in the mind by (your) works evil, now but

604 1722 3588 4983 3588 4561 846 1223 3588
ἀποκατήλλαξεν 22 ἐν τῷ σώματι τῆς σαρκὸς αὐτοῦ διὰ τοῦ
He reconciled in the body of the flesh of Him through the

2288 3936 5209 40 2532 299 2532
θανάτου, παραστῆσαι ὑμᾶς ἁγίους καὶ ἀμώμους καὶ
death (of Him), to present you holy and without blemish and

410 2714 846 1489 1961 3588 4102
ἀνεγκλήτους κατενώπιον αὐτοῦ· 23 εἴγε ἐπιμένετε τῇ πίστει
without charge before Him; if indeed you continue in the faith

2311 2532 1476 2532 3361 3334 575 3588
τεθεμελιωμένοι καὶ ἑδραῖοι, καὶ μὴ μετακινούμενοι ἀπὸ τῆς
having been founded and steadfast, and not being moved away from the

1680 3588 2098 3739 191 3588 2784 1722
ἐλπίδος τοῦ εὐαγγελίου οὗ ἠκούσατε, τοῦ κηρυχθέντος ἐν
hope of the gospel which you heard, proclaimed in

3956 3588 2937 3588 5259 3588 3772 3739 1096 1473
πάσῃ τῇ κτίσει τῇ ὑπὸ τὸν οὐρανόν, οὗ ἐγενόμην ἐγὼ
all the creation under the heaven, of which became I

3972 1249
Παῦλος διάκονος.
Paul a minister.

3739 3568 5463 1722 3588 3804 3450 5228 5216 2532
24. Ὃς νῦν χαίρω ἐν τοῖς παθήμασί μου ὑπὲρ ὑμῶν, καὶ
Who now rejoice in the sufferings of me on behalf of you, and

466 3588 5303 3588 2347 3588 5547
ἀνταναπληρῶ τὰ ὑστερήματα τῶν θλίψεων τοῦ Χριστοῦ
fill up the things lacking of the afflictions of Christ

1722 3588 4561 3450 5228 3588 4983 846 3739 2076 3588
ἐν τῇ σαρκί μου ὑπὲρ τοῦ σώματος αὐτοῦ, ὅ ἐστιν ἡ
in the flesh of me on behalf of the body of Him, which is the

1577 3739 1096 1473 1249 2596 3588 3622
ἐκκλησία· 25 ἧς ἐγενόμην ἐγὼ διάκονος, κατὰ τὴν οἰκονομίαν
church; of which became I a minister, as regards the stewardship

3588 2316 3588 1325 3427 1519 5209 4137 3588 3056
τοῦ Θεοῦ τὴν δοθεῖσάν μοι εἰς ὑμᾶς, πληρῶσαι τὸν λόγον
of God given to me for you, to fulfill the Word

3588 2316 3588 3466 3588 613 575 3588
τοῦ Θεοῦ, 26 τὸ μυστήριον τὸ ἀποκεκρυμμένον ἀπὸ τῶν
of God, the mystery having been hidden from the

165 2532 575 3588 1074 3570 1161 5319 3588 40
αἰώνων καὶ ἀπὸ τῶν γενεῶν· νυνὶ δὲ ἐφανερώθη τοῖς ἁγίοις
ages and from the generations; now but was revealed to the saints

846 3739 2309 3588 2316 1107 5101 3588 4149 3588
αὐτοῦ, 27 οἷς ἠθέλησεν ὁ Θεὸς γνωρίσαι τίς ὁ πλοῦτος τῆς
of Him, to whom desired God to make known what (are) the riches of the

1391 3588 3466 5127 1722 3588 1484 3739 2076 5547
δόξης τοῦ μυστηρίου τούτου ἐν τοῖς ἔθνεσιν, ὅς ἐστι Χριστὸς
glory mystery of this among the nations, who is Christ

1722 5213 3588 1680 3588 1391 3739 2249 2605
ἐν ὑμῖν, ἡ ἐλπὶς τῆς δόξης· 28 ὃν ἡμεῖς καταγγέλλομεν, νου-
in us, the hope of glory; whom we proclaim,

3560 3956 444 2532 1321 3956 444
θετοῦντες πάντα ἄνθρωπον, καὶ διδάσκοντες πάντα ἄνθρω-
warning every man, and teaching every man

1722 3956 4678 2443 3936 3956 444
πον ἐν πάσῃ σοφίᾳ, ἵνα παραστήσωμεν πάντα ἄνθρωπον
in all wisdom, that we may present every man

King James Version

heaven.
21 And you, that were sometime alienated and enemies in (your) mind by wicked works, yet now hath he reconciled
22 In the body of his flesh through death, to present you holy and unblameable and unreproveable in his sight:
23 If ye continue in the faith grounded and settled, and (be) not moved away from the hope of the gospel, which ye have heard, (and) which was preached to every creature which is under heaven; whereof I Paul am made a minister;
24 Who now rejoice in my sufferings for you, and fill up that which is behind of the afflictions of Christ in my flesh for his body's sake, which is the church:
25 Whereof I am made a minister, according to the dispensation of God which is given to me for you, to fulfil the word of God;
26 (Even) the mystery which hath been hid from ages and from generations, but now is made manifest to his saints:
27 To whom God would make known what (is) the riches of the glory of this mystery among the Gentiles; which is Christ in you, the hope of glory:
28 Whom we preach, warning every man, and teaching every man in all wisdom; that we may present every man

Literal Translation

Colossians 1:29

King James Version

full-grown in Christ Jesus,
29 for which also I labor, struggling according to the working of Him who works in me in power.

5046 1722 5547 2424 1519 3739 2532 2872 75
τέλειον ἐν Χριστῷ Ἰησοῦ· 29 εἰς ὃ καὶ κοπιῶ, ἀγωνιζόμενος
full-grown in Christ Jesus; for which also I labor, struggling
2596 3588 1753 846 3588 1754 1722 1698 1722
κατὰ τὴν ἐνέργειαν αὐτοῦ, τὴν ἐνεργουμένην ἐν ἐμοὶ ἐν
according to the working of Him, the (one) working in me in
1411
δυνάμει.
power.

perfect in Christ Jesus:
29 hereunto I also labour, striving according to his working, which worketh in me mightily.

Colossians 2

1. For I want you to know how great a struggle I have concerning you, and those in Laodicea, and as many as have not seen my face in (the) flesh,
2 that their hearts may be comforted, being joined together in love, and to all riches of the full assurance of the understanding, to (the) full knowledge of the mystery of God, even of (the) Father and of Christ,
3 in whom are hidden all the treasures of wisdom and of knowledge.
4 And I say this that no one may beguile you with persuasive words.
5 For though I am indeed absent in the flesh, yet I am with you in spirit, rejoicing and seeing your order and the firmness of (your) faith in Christ.

2309 1063 5209 1492 2245 73 2192 4012 5216 2532
1. Θέλω γὰρ ὑμᾶς εἰδέναι ἡλίκον ἀγῶνα ἔχω περὶ ὑμῶν καὶ
I want For you to know how great a struggle I have as to you and
3588 1722 2993 2532 3745 3756 3708 3588 4383 3450
τῶν ἐν Λαοδικείᾳ, καὶ ὅσοι οὐχ ἑωράκασι τὸ πρόσωπόν μου
those in Laodicea, and as many as not have seen the face of me
1722 4561 2443 3870 3588 2588 846 4822
ἐν σαρκί, 2 ἵνα παρακληθῶσιν αἱ καρδίαι αὐτῶν, συμβιβασθέν-
in (the) flesh, that may be comforted the hearts of them, being joined to-
1722 26 2532 1519 3956 4149 3588 4136 3588
των ἐν ἀγάπῃ, καὶ εἰς πάντα πλοῦτον τῆς πληροφορίας τῆς
gether in love, and to all riches of the full assurance of the
4907 1519 1922 3588 3466 3588 2316 2532 3962
συνέσεως, εἰς ἐπίγνωσιν τοῦ μυστηρίου τοῦ Θεοῦ καὶ πατρὸς
understanding, to (the) full knowledge of the mystery of God and of father
2532 3588 5547 1722 3739 1526 3956 3588 2344 3588 4678
καὶ τοῦ Χριστοῦ, 3 ἐν ᾧ εἰσὶ πάντες οἱ θησαυροὶ τῆς σοφίας
and of Christ, in whom are all the treasures of wisdom
2532 3588 1108 614 5124 1161 3004 2443 3361 5100 5209
καὶ τῆς γνώσεως ἀπόκρυφοι. 4 Τοῦτο δὲ λέγω, ἵνα μή τις ὑμᾶς
and knowledge hidden. this And I say, that not anyone you
3884 1722 4086 1487 1063 2532 3588 4561 548
παραλογίζηται ἐν πιθανολογίᾳ. 5 εἰ γὰρ καὶ τῇ σαρκὶ ἄπειμι,
beguile by persuasive words. if For indeed in the flesh I am,
235 3588 4151 4862 5213 1510 5463 2532 991 5216
ἀλλὰ τῷ πνεύματι σὺν ὑμῖν εἰμί, χαίρων καὶ βλέπων ὑμῶν
yet in the spirit with you I am, rejoicing and seeing of you
3588 5010 2532 3588 4733 3588 1519 5547 4102 5216
τὴν τάξιν, καὶ τὸ στερέωμα τῆς εἰς Χριστὸν πίστεως ὑμῶν.
the order, and the firmness of the in Christ faith of you.

1. For I would that ye knew what great conflict I have for you, and (for) them at Laodicea, and (for) as many as have not seen my face in the flesh;
2 That their hearts might be comforted, being knit together in love, and unto all riches of the full assurance of understanding, to the acknowledgement of the mystery of God, and of the Father, and of Christ;
3 In whom are hid all the treasures of wisdom and knowledge.
4 And this I say, lest any man should beguile you with enticing words.
5 For though I be absent in the flesh, yet am I with you in the spirit, joying and beholding your order, and the stedfastness of your faith in Christ.

6 Therefore, as you received Christ Jesus the Lord, walk in Him,
7 having been rooted and built up in Him, and having been confirmed in the faith, even as you were taught, abounding in it with thanksgiving.

5613 3767 3880 3588 5547 2424 3588 2962 1722
6. Ὡς οὖν παρελάβετε τὸν Χριστὸν Ἰησοῦν τὸν Κύριον, ἐν
As therefore you received Christ Jesus the Lord, in
846 4043 4492 2532 2026 1722
αὐτῷ περιπατεῖτε, 7 ἐρριζωμένοι καὶ ἐποικοδομούμενοι ἐν
Him walk, having been rooted and having been built up in
846 2532 950 3588 4102 2531 1321
αὐτῷ, καὶ βεβαιούμενοι τῇ πίστει, καθὼς ἐδιδάχθητε,
Him, and being confirmed in the faith, even as you were taught,
4052 1722 846 1722 2169
περισσεύοντες ἐν αὐτῇ ἐν εὐχαριστίᾳ.
abounding in it in thanksgiving.

6 As ye have therefore received Christ Jesus the Lord, (so) walk ye in him:
7 Rooted and built up in him, and stablished in the faith, as ye have been taught, abounding therein with thanksgiving.

8 Watch that there not be one robbing you through philosophy and empty deceit, according to the tradition of men, according to the elements of the world, and not according to Christ.
9 For in

991 3361 5100 5209 2071 3588 4812 1223 3588 5385
8. βλέπετε μή τις ὑμᾶς ἔσται ὁ συλαγωγῶν διὰ τῆς φιλοσο-
Watch, lest anyone you shall be robbing through philosophy
2532 2756 539 2596 3588 3862 3588 444
φίας καὶ κενῆς ἀπάτης, κατὰ τὴν παράδοσιν τῶν ἀνθρώπων,
and vain deceit, according to the tradition of men,
2596 3588 4747 3588 2889 2532 3756 2596 5547 3754 1722
κατὰ τὰ στοιχεῖα τοῦ κόσμου, καὶ οὐ κατὰ Χριστόν· 9 ὅτι ἐν
according to the elements of the world, and not according to Christ; because in

8 Beware lest any man spoil you through philosophy and vain deceit, after the tradition of men, after the rudiments of the world, and not after Christ.
9 For in

Colossians 2:10

Literal Translation

Him dwells all the fullness of the Godhead bodily;

10 and having been filled, you are in Him, who is the Head of all rule and authority,
11 in whom also you were circumcised with a circumcision not made by hand, in the putting off of the body of the sins of the flesh, by the circumcision of Christ,
12 being buried with Him in baptism, in whom also you were raised through the faith of the working of God, having raised Him from the dead.

13 And you, being dead in the offenses and the uncircumcision of your flesh, He made alive together with Him, having remitted all your offenses,
14 blotting out the handwriting in the ordinances against us, which was contrary to us, even (He) has taken it out of the midst, having nailed it to the cross;
15 having stripped the rulers and the authorities, He made a show (of them) in public, triumphing (over) them in it.

16 Then do not let anyone judge you in eating, or in drinking, or in respect of a feast, or the new moon, or of sabbaths,
17 which (are) a shadow of coming things, but the body (is) of Christ.
18 Let no one condemn you, delighting in humility and worship of the angels, pushing into things which he has not seen, (being) puffed up by the mind of his flesh without a cause,
19 and not holding fast the Head, from whom all the body, being supplied

---

846 2730 3956 3588 4138 3588 2320 4985
αὐτῷ κατοικεῖ πᾶν τὸ πλήρωμα τῆς θεότητος σωματικῶς,
Him dwells all the fullness of the Godhead bodily,

2532 2075 1722 846 4137 3739 2076 3588 2776 3956
10 καὶ ἐστε ἐν αὐτῷ πεπληρωμένοι, ὅς ἐστιν ἡ κεφαλὴ πάσης
and you are in Him having been filled, who is the Head of all

746 2532 1849 1722 3739 2532 4059 4061
ἀρχῆς καὶ ἐξουσίας· 11 ἐν ᾧ καὶ περιετμήθητε περιτομῇ
rule and authority; in whom also you were circumcised with a circumcision

886 1722 3588 555 3588 4983 3588 266
ἀχειροποιήτῳ, ἐν τῇ ἀπεκδύσει τοῦ σώματος τῶν ἁμαρτιῶν
not made by hand, in the putting off of the body of the sins

3588 4561 1722 3588 4061 3588 5547 4916 846
τῆς σαρκός, ἐν τῇ περιτομῇ τοῦ Χριστοῦ, 12 συνταφέντες αὐτῷ
of the flesh, by the circumcision of Christ, co-buried with Him

1722 3588 908 1722 3739 2532 4891 1223 3588 4102 3588
ἐν τῷ βαπτίσματι, ἐν ᾧ καὶ συνηγέρθητε διὰ τῆς πίστεως τῆς
in the baptism, in whom also you were raised through the faith of the

1753 3588 2316 3588 1453 846 1537 3588 3498
ἐνεργείας τοῦ Θεοῦ, τοῦ ἐγείραντος αὐτὸν ἐκ τῶν νεκρῶν.
working of God, having raised Him from the dead.

2532 5209 3498 5607 1722 3588 3900 2532 3588 203
13 καὶ ὑμᾶς, νεκροὺς ὄντας ἐν τοῖς παραπτώμασι καὶ τῇ ἀκρο-
And you dead being in the offenses and the uncir-

3588 4561 5216 4806 4862 846 5483
βυστίᾳ τῆς σαρκὸς ὑμῶν, συνεζωοποίησε σὺν αὐτῷ, χαρισά-
cumcision of the flesh of you, He made alive with Him, having

5213 3956 3588 3900 1813 3588 2596 2257
μενος ὑμῖν πάντα τὰ παραπτώματα, 14 ἐξαλείψας τὸ καθ᾽ ἡμῶν
remitted of you all the offenses, blotting out the against us

5498 3588 1378 3739 2258 5227 2254 2532 846
χειρόγραφον τοῖς δόγμασιν, ὃ ἦν ὑπεναντίον ἡμῖν· καὶ αὐτὸ
handwriting in ordinances, which were contrary to us; and it

142 1537 3588 3319 4338 846 3588 4716 554
ἦρκεν ἐκ τοῦ μέσου, προσηλώσας αὐτὸ τῷ σταυρῷ· 15 ἀπεκδυ-
has taken out of the midst, having nailed it to the cross; having

3588 746 2532 3588 1849 1165 1722
σάμενος τὰς ἀρχὰς καὶ τὰς ἐξουσίας, ἐδειγμάτισεν ἐν
stripped the rulers and the authorities, He made show (of them) in

3954 2358 846 1722 846
παρρησίᾳ, θριαμβεύσας αὐτοὺς ἐν αὐτῷ.
public, triumphing (over) them in it.

3361 3767 5100 5209 2919 1722 1035 2228 1722 4213 2228 1722
16. Μὴ οὖν τις ὑμᾶς κρινέτω ἐν βρώσει ἢ ἐν πόσει, ἢ ἐν
Not therefore anyone you let judge in eating or in drinking, or in

3313 1859 2228 3561 2228 4521 3739 2076 4639 3588
μέρει ἑορτῆς ἢ νευμηνίας ἢ σαββάτων· 17 ἅ ἐστι σκιὰ τῶν
respect of a feast or a new moon or of sabbaths; which is a shadow of things

3195 3588 1161 4983 3588 5547 3367 5209
μελλόντων, τὸ δὲ σῶμα τοῦ Χριστοῦ. 18 μηδεὶς ὑμᾶς
coming, the but body (is) of Christ. No one you

2603 2309 1722 5012 2532 2356 3588
καταβραβευέτω θέλων ἐν ταπεινοφροσύνῃ καὶ θρησκείᾳ τῶν
let give judgment willing in humility and worship of the

32 3739 3361 3708 1687 1500 5448 5259 3588
ἀγγέλων, ἃ μὴ ἑώρακεν ἐμβατεύων, εἰκῇ φυσιούμενος ὑπὸ τοῦ
angels, things which not he has seen pushing into, without a cause puffed up bythe

3563 3588 4561 846 2532 3756 2902 3588 2776 1537/3739
νοὸς τῆς σαρκὸς αὐτοῦ, 19 καὶ οὐ κρατῶν τὴν κεφαλήν, ἐξ οὗ
mind of the flesh of him, and not holding the Head, from whom

3956 3588 4983 1223 3588 860 2532 4886 2023
πᾶν τὸ σῶμα, διὰ τῶν ἁφῶν καὶ συνδέσμων ἐπιχορηγούμενον
all the body, through the joints and bands being supplied

King James Version

him dwelleth all the fulness of the Godhead bodily.

10 And ye are complete in him, which is the head of all principality and power:
11 In whom also ye are circumcised with the circumcision made without hands, in putting off the body of the sins of the flesh by the circumcision of Christ:
12 Buried with him in baptism, wherein also ye are risen with (him) through the faith of the operation of God, who hath raised him from the dead.

13 And you, being dead in your sins and the uncircumcision of your flesh, hath he quickened together with him, having forgiven you all trespasses;
14 Blotting out the handwriting of ordinances that was against us, which was contrary to us, and took it out of the way, nailing it to his cross;
15 (And) having spoiled principalities and powers, he made a shew of them openly, triumphing over them in it.

16 Let no man therefore judge you in meat, or in drink, or in respect of an holyday, or of the new moon, or of the sabbath (days):
17 Which are a shadow of things to come; but the body (is) of Christ.
18 Let no man beguile you of your reward in a voluntary humility and worshipping of angels, intruding into those things which he hath not seen, vainly puffed up by his fleshly mind,
19 And not holding the Head, from which all the body by joints and bands having nourishment ministered,

Literal Translation

and having been joined together through the joints and bands, will grow with the growth of God.
20 If, then, you died with Christ from the elements of the world, why are you under (its) decrees, as living in (the) world?
21 Do not handle, do not taste, do not touch,
22 (These) things are all to r corruption in the using, according to the injunctions and teachings of men.
23 Which things indeed have a repute of wisdom in self-imposed worship and humility, and unsparing (abuse) of (the) body, not in any honor with respect to gratification of the flesh.

Colossians 2:20

2532 4822 837 3588 838 3588 2316
καὶ συμβιβαζόμενον, αὔξει τὴν αὔξησιν τοῦ Θεοῦ.
and having been joined, will grow with the growth of God.

1487 3767 599 4862 3588 5547 575 3588 4747
20. Εἰ οὖν ἀπεθάνετε σὺν τῷ Χριστῷ ἀπὸ τῶν στοιχείων
If then you died with Christ from the elements

3588 2889 5101 5613 2198 1722 2889 1379 3361
τοῦ κόσμου, τί, ὡς ζῶντες ἐν κόσμῳ, δογματίζεσθε, 21 Μὴ
of the world, why, as living in (the) world, are you under decrees, Not

680 3366 1089 3366 2345 3739 2076 3956 1519 5356/3588
ἅψῃ, μηδὲ γεύσῃ, μηδὲ θίγῃς, 22 [ἅ ἐστι πάντα εἰς φθορὰν τῇ
touch, nor taste, nor handle, which things are all for corruption in the

671 2596 3588 1778 2532 1319 3588
ἀποχρήσει], κατὰ τὰ ἐντάλματα καὶ διδασκαλίας τῶν
using, according to the injunctions and doctrines of the

444 3748 2076 3056 3303 2192 4678 1722
ἀνθρώπων; 23 ἅτινά ἐστι λόγον μὲν ἔχοντα σοφίας ἐν ἐθε-
of men? Which things is a repute indeed having of wisdom in self-

1479 2532 5012 2532 857 4983 3756
λοθρησκείᾳ καὶ ταπεινοφροσύνῃ καὶ ἀφειδίᾳ σώματος, οὐκ
imposed worship and humility and unsparing (abuse) of body, not

1722 5092 5100 4314 4140 3588 4561
ἐν τιμῇ τινὶ πρὸς πλησμονὴν τῆς σαρκός.
in honor any for gratification of the flesh.

King James Version

and knit together, increaseth with the increase of God.
20 Wherefore if ye be dead with Christ from the rudiments of the world, why, as though living in the world, are ye subject to ordinances,
21 (Touch not; taste not; handle not;
22 Which all are to perish with the using;) after the commandments and doctrines of men?
23 Which things have indeed a shew of wisdom in will worship, and humility, and neglecting of the body; not in any honour to the satisfying of the flesh.

Colossians 3

1. If, then, you were raised with Christ, seek the things above, where Christ is sitting at (the) right of God;
2 mind the things above, not the things on the earth,
3 For you died, and your life has been hidden with Christ in God.
4 Whenever Christ our life is revealed, then also you will be revealed with Him in glory.

Colossians 3

1487 3767 4891 3588 5547 3588 507 2212 3757/3588
1. Εἰ οὖν συνηγέρθητε τῷ Χριστῷ, τὰ ἄνω ζητεῖτε, οὗ ὁ
If then you were raised with Christ, the things above seek, where

5547 2076 1722 1188 3588 2316 2521 3588 507
Χριστός ἐστιν ἐν δεξιᾷ τοῦ Θεοῦ καθήμενος. 2 τὰ ἄνω
Christ is at (the) right of God sitting the things above

5426 3361 3588 1909 3588 1093 599 1063 2532 3588 2222 5216
φρονεῖτε, μὴ τὰ ἐπὶ τῆς γῆς. 3 ἀπεθάνετε γάρ, καὶ ἡ ζωὴ ὑμῶν
Mind, not the things on the earth. you died For, and the life of you

2928 4862 3588 5547 1722 3588 2316 3752 3588 5547
κέκρυπται σὺν τῷ Χριστῷ ἐν τῷ θεῷ. 4 ὅταν ὁ Χριστὸς
has been hidden with Christ in God. Whenever Christ

5319 3588 2222 2257 5119 2532 5210 4862 846
φανερωθῇ, ἡ ζωὴ ἡμῶν, τότε καὶ ὑμεῖς σὺν αὐτῷ
is revealed, the life of us, then also you with Him

5319 1722 1391
φανερωθήσεσθε ἐν δόξῃ.
will be revealed in glory.

Colossians 3

1. If ye then be risen with Christ, seek those things which are above, where Christ sitteth on the right hand of God.
2 Set your affection on things above, not on things on the earth.
3 For ye are dead, and your life is hid with Christ in God.
4 When Christ, (who is) our life, shall appear, then shall ye also appear with him in glory.

5 Then put to death your members which (are) on the earth: fornication; uncleanness; passion; evil lust; and covetousness, which is idolatry;
6 on account of which things the wrath of God is coming on the sons of disobedience,
7 among whom you also walked at one time, when you lived in these.
8 But now, you also, put off all (these) things: wrath, anger, malice, evil-speaking, shameful speech

3499 3767 3588 3196 5216 3588 1909 3588 1093 4202
5. Νεκρώσατε οὖν τὰ μέλη ὑμῶν τὰ ἐπὶ τῆς γῆς, πορνείαν,
put to death Therefore the members of you on the earth, fornication,

167 3806 1939 2556 2532 3588 4124
ἀκαθαρσίαν, πάθος, ἐπιθυμίαν κακήν, καὶ τὴν πλεονεξίαν,
uncleanness, passion, lust evil, and covetousness,

3748 2076 1495 1223 3739 2064 3588 3709 3588 2316
ἥτις ἐστὶν εἰδωλολατρεία, 6 δι' ἃ ἔρχεται ἡ ὀργὴ τοῦ Θεοῦ
which is idolatry; because of which is coming the wrath of God

1909 3588 5207 3588 543 1722 3739 2532 5210 4043
ἐπὶ τοὺς υἱοὺς τῆς ἀπειθείας· 7 ἐν οἷς καὶ ὑμεῖς περιεπατήσατέ
on the sons of disobedience; among whom also you walked

4218 3753 2198 1722 846 3570 1161 659 2532 5210 3588
ποτε, ὅτε ἐζῆτε ἐν αὐτοῖς. 8 νυνὶ δὲ ἀπόθεσθε καὶ ὑμεῖς τὰ
then, when you lived in these. now But put off also you

3956 3709 2372 2549 988 148
πάντα, ὀργήν, θυμόν, κακίαν, βλασφημίαν, αἰσχρολογίαν
all things, wrath anger, malice, evil speaking, shameful speech

5 Mortify therefore your members which are upon the earth; fornication, uncleanness, inordinate affection, evil concupiscence, and covetousness, which is idolatry:
6 For which things' sake the wrath of God cometh on the children of disobedience:
7 In the which ye also walked some time, when ye lived in them.
8 But now ye also put off all these; anger, wrath, malice, blasphemy, filthy communication

Literal Translation | **Colossians 3:9** | *King James Version*

Literal Translation

out of your mouth.
9 Do not lie to one another, having put off the old man with his practices,

10 and having put on the new, having been renewed in full knowledge according to (the) image of the (One) creating him,
11 where there is no Greek and Jew, circumcision and uncircumcision, foreigner, Scythian, slave (or) freeman, but Christ (is) all things and in all.

12 Then put on as elect ones of God, holy and beloved, bowels of compassions, kindness, humility, meekness, long-suffering,

13 bearing with one another and forgiving yourselves, if anyone has a complaint against any; even as Christ forgave you, so also you (should forgive).
14 And above all these, (add) love, which is (the) bond of perfectness.

15 And let the peace of God rule in your hearts, to which you also were called in one body, and be thankful.
16 Let the Word of Christ dwell in you richly, in all wisdom teaching and exhorting yourselves in psalms and hymns and spiritual songs, singing with grace in your hearts to the Lord.

17 And everything, whatever you do in word or in work, (do) all things in the name of (the) Lord Jesus, giving thanks to God and (the) Father through Him.

18 Wives, be subject to (your) own husbands, as is becoming

1537 3588 4750 5216 3361 5574 1519 240 554
ἐκ τοῦ στόματος ὑμῶν· 9 μὴ ψεύδεσθε εἰς ἀλλήλους, ἀπεκδυσά-
out of the mouth of you; Not do lie to one another, having put

3588 3820 444 4862 3588 4234 846
μενοι τὸν παλαιὸν ἄνθρωπον σὺν ταῖς πράξεσιν αὐτοῦ,
off the old man with the practices of him,

2532 1746 3588 3501 3588 341 1519
10 καὶ ἐνδυσάμενοι τὸν νέον, τὸν ἀνακαινούμενον εἰς
and having put on the new (man), being renewed in

1922 2596 1504 3588 2936 846 3699 3756 1762
ἐπίγνωσιν κατ' εἰκόνα τοῦ κτίσαντος αὐτόν· 11 ὅπου οὐκ ἔνι
knowledge according to image of the (One) creating him; where not there is

1672 2532 2453 4061 2532 203 915
Ἕλλην καὶ Ἰουδαῖος, περιτομὴ καὶ ἀκροβυστία, βάρβαρος,
Greek and Jew, circumcision and uncircumcision, foreigner,

4658 1401 1658 235 3588 3956 2532 1722 3956 5547
Σκύθης, δοῦλος, ἐλεύθερος· ἀλλὰ τὰ πάντα καὶ ἐν πᾶσι Χριστός.
Scythian, slave, (or) freeman; but all things and in all Christ (is).

1746 3767 5613 1588 3588 2316 40 2532
12. Ἐνδύσασθε οὖν, ὡς ἐκλεκτοὶ τοῦ θεοῦ, ἅγιοι καὶ
put on Therefore, as elect ones of God, holy and

25 4698 3628 5544 5012
ἠγαπημένοι, σπλάγχνα οἰκτιρμῶν, χρηστότητα, ταπεινο-
having been loved, bowels of compassions, kindness, humility,

4236 3115 430 240
φροσύνην, πρᾳότητα, μακροθυμίαν· 13 ἀνεχόμενοι ἀλλήλων,
meekness, long-suffering; forbearing one another,

2532 5483 1438 1437 5100 4314 5100 2192 3437 2531
καὶ χαριζόμενοι ἑαυτοῖς, ἐάν τις πρός τινα ἔχῃ μομφήν· καθὼς
and forgiving yourselves, if anyone against any has a complaint; as

2532 3588 5547 5483 5213 3779 2532 5210 1909 3956 1161
καὶ ὁ Χριστὸς ἐχαρίσατο ὑμῖν, οὕτω καὶ ὑμεῖς· 14 ἐπὶ πᾶσι δὲ
indeed Christ forgave you, so also you; above all and

5125 3588 26 3748 2076 4886 3588 5047
τούτοις τὴν ἀγάπην, ἥτις ἐστὶ σύνδεσμος τῆς τελειότητος.
these things love, which is (the) bond of perfectness.

2532 3588 1515 3588 2316 1018 1722 3588 2588 5216
15 καὶ ἡ εἰρήνη τοῦ Θεοῦ βραβευέτω ἐν ταῖς καρδίαις ὑμῶν,
And the peace of God let rule in the hearts of you,

1519 3739 2532 2564 1722 1520 4983 2532 2170 1096 3588
εἰς ἣν καὶ ἐκλήθητε ἐν ἑνὶ σώματι· καὶ εὐχάριστοι γίνεσθε. 16 ὁ
to which also you were called in one body; and thankful be. The

3056 3588 5547 1774 1722 5213 4146 1722 3956
λόγος τοῦ Χριστοῦ ἐνοικείτω ἐν ὑμῖν πλουσίως ἐν πάσῃ
Word of Christ let dwell in you richly in all

4678 1321 2532 3560 1438 5568 2532
σοφίᾳ· διδάσκοντες καὶ νουθετοῦντες ἑαυτούς, ψαλμοῖς, καὶ
wisdom teaching and exhorting yourselves, in Psalms, and

5215 2532 5603 4152 1722 5485 103 1722/3588
ὕμνοις, καὶ ᾠδαῖς πνευματικαῖς, ἐν χάριτι ᾄδοντες ἐν τῇ
hymns, and songs spiritual, with grace singing in the

2588 5216 3588 2962 2532 3956 3739 5100 302 4160 1722
καρδίᾳ ὑμῶν τῷ Κυρίῳ. 17 καὶ πᾶν ὅ τι ἂν ποιῆτε, ἐν
hearts of you to the Lord. And everything whatever you do, in

3056 2228 1722 2041 3956 1722 3686 2962 2424
λόγῳ ἢ ἐν ἔργῳ, πάντα ἐν ὀνόματι Κυρίου Ἰησοῦ,
word or in work, all things in (the) name of (the) Lord Jesus,

2168 3588 2316 2532 3962 1223 846
εὐχαριστοῦντες τῷ Θεῷ καὶ πατρὶ δι' αὐτοῦ.
giving thanks to God and (the) Father through Him.

3588 1135 5293 3588 2398 435 5613
18. Αἱ γυναῖκες, ὑποτάσσεσθε τοῖς ἰδίοις ἀνδράσιν, ὡς
The wives, be subject to the own husbands, as

King James Version

out of your mouth.
9 Lie not one to another, seeing that ye have put off the old man with his deeds;

10 And have put on the new (man), which is renewed in knowledge after the image of him that created him:
11 Where there is neither Greek nor Jew, circumcision nor uncircumcision, Barbarian, Scythian, bond (nor) free: but Christ (is) all, and in all.

12 Put on therefore, as the elect of God, holy and beloved, bowels of mercies, kindness, humbleness of mind, meekness, longsuffering;
13 Forbearing one another, and forgiving one another, if any man have a quarrel against any: even as Christ forgave you, so also (do) ye.
14 And above all these things (put on) charity, which is the bond of perfectness.

15 And let the peace of God rule in your hearts, to the which also ye are called in one body; and be ye thankful.
16 Let the word of Christ dwell in you richly in all wisdom; teaching and admonishing one another in psalms and hymns and spiritual songs, singing with grace in your hearts to the Lord.

17 And whatsoever ye do in word or deed, (do) all in the name of the Lord Jesus, giving thanks to God and the Father by him.

18 Wives, submit yourselves unto your own husbands, as it is fit

Colossians 3:19

Literal Translation

in (the) Lord.
19 Husbands, love the wives and do not be bitter against them.
20 Children, obey the parents in all things, for this is pleasing to the Lord.
21 Fathers, do not provoke your children, that they may not be disheartened.
22 Slaves, obey the lords according to flesh in all thingss, not with eye-service as men-pleasers, but in singleness of heart, fearing God.

23 And (in) everything, whatever you may do, work from the soul as to the Lord and not to men,
24 knowing that from the Lord you shall receive the reward of the inheritance. For you serve the Lord Christ.

25 But the (one) doing wrong will receive what he did wrong, and there is no respect of persons.

433 1722 2962 3588 435 25 3588 1135 2532 3361
ἀνῆκεν ἐν Κυρίῳ. 19 οἱ ἄνδρες, ἀγαπᾶτε τὰς γυναῖκας, καὶ μὴ
fitting in (the) Lord. The husbands, love the wives, and not
4087 4314 846 3588 5043 5219 3588 1118
πικραίνεσθε πρὸς αὐτάς. 20 τὰ τέκνα, ὑπακούετε τοῖς γονεῦσι
be bitter against them. The children, obey the parents
2596 3956 5124 1063 2076 2101 3588 2962 3588
κατὰ πάντα· τοῦτο γάρ ἐστιν εὐάρεστον τῷ Κυρίῳ. 21 οἱ
according to all; this for is well-pleasing to the Lord. The
3962 3361 2042 3588 5043 5216 2443 3361 120 3588
πατέρες, μὴ ἐρεθίζετε τὰ τέκνα ὑμῶν, ἵνα μὴ ἀθυμῶσιν. 22 οἱ
fathers, not do provoke the children of you, that not they be dispirited. The
1401 5219 2596 3956 3588 2596 4561 2962 3361/1722
δοῦλοι, ὑπακούετε κατὰ πάντα τοῖς κατὰ σάρκα κυρίοις, μὴ ἐν
slaves, obey according to all things those according to flesh lords, not with
3787 5613 441 235 1722 572 2588
ὀφθαλμοδουλείαις ὡς ἀνθρωπάρεσκοι, ἀλλ᾽ ἐν ἁπλότητι καρ-
eye-service as men-pleasers, but in singleness of heart,
5399 3588 2316 2532 3956 3739 5100 1437 4160 1537
δίας, φοβούμενοι τὸν Θεόν· 23 καὶ πᾶν ὅ τι ἐὰν ποιῆτε, ἐκ
fearing God. And (in)everything whatever you do, from
5590 2038 5613 3588 2962 2532 3756 444 1492
ψυχῆς ἐργάζεσθε, ὡς τῷ Κυρίῳ καὶ οὐκ ἀνθρώποις· 24 εἰδότες
(the) soul work, as to the Lord and not to men; knowing
3754 575 2962 618 3588 469 3588 2817
ὅτι ἀπὸ Κυρίου ἀπολήψεσθε τὴν ἀνταπόδοσιν τῆς κληρονο-
that from (the) Lord you will receive the reward of the inheritance;
3588 1063 2962 5547 1398 3588 1063 91
μίας· τῷ γὰρ Κυρίῳ Χριστῷ δουλεύετε. 25 ὁ δὲ ἀδικῶν
the For Lord Christ you serve. he And doing wrong
2865 3739 91 2532 3756 2076 4382
κομιεῖται ὃ ἠδίκησε· καὶ οὐκ ἔστι προσωποληψία.
will receive what he did wrong; and not (is) respect of persons.

King James Version

in the Lord.
19 Husbands, love (your) wives, and be not bitter against them.
20 Children, obey (your) parents in all things: for this is well pleasing unto the Lord.
21 Fathers, provoke not your children (to anger), lest they be discouraged.
22 Servants, obey in all things (your) masters according to the flesh; not with eyeservice, as menpleasers; but in singleness of heart, fearing God:

23 And whatsoever ye do, do (it) heartily, as to the Lord, and not unto men;
24 Knowing that of the Lord ye shall receive the reward of the inheritance: for ye serve the Lord Christ.

25 But he that doeth wrong shall receive for the wrong which he hath done: and there is no respect of persons.

Colossians 4

1. Lords, give the just thing and supply equality to the slaves, knowing that you have a Lord in Heaven also.

2 Steadfastly continue in prayer, watching in it with thanksgiving,
3 praying together about us also, that God may open to us a door of the Word, to speak the mystery of Christ, on account of which I also have been bound,
4 that I may make it clear, as I ought to speak.
5 Walk in wisdom toward the ones outside, redeeming the time.
6 Let your speech (be) always with grace, having been seasoned with salt, to know how you ought to answer each one.

Colossians 4

3588 2962 3588 1342 2532 3588 2471 3588 1401
1. οἱ κύριοι, τὸ δίκαιον καὶ τὴν ἰσότητα τοῖς δούλοις
The lords, the just thing and the equality to the slaves
3930 1492 3754 2532 5210 2192 2962 1722 3772
παρέχεσθε, εἰδότες ὅτι καὶ ὑμεῖς ἔχετε Κύριον ἐν οὐρανοῖς.
supply, knowing that also you have a Lord in Heaven.
3588 4335 4342 1127 1722 846 1722
2. Τῇ προσευχῇ προσκαρτερεῖτε, γρηγοροῦντες ἐν αὐτῇ ἐν
In the prayer steadfastly continue, watching in it with
2169 4336 260 2532 4012 2257 2443 3588 2316
εὐχαριστίᾳ· 3 προσευχόμενοι ἅμα καὶ περὶ ἡμῶν, ἵνα ὁ Θεὸς
thanksgiving; praying together also about us, that God
455 2254 2374 3588 3056 2980 3588 3466 3588
ἀνοίξῃ ἡμῖν θύραν τοῦ λόγου, λαλῆσαι τὸ μυστήριον τοῦ
may open to us a door of the Word, to speak the mystery
5547 1223 3739 2532 1210 2443 5319 846 5613 1163 3165
Χριστοῦ, δι᾽ ὃ καὶ δέδεμαι· 4 ἵνα φανερώσω αὐτό, ὡς δεῖ με
of Christ, for which also I have been bound; that I may reveal it, as ought me
2980 1722 4678 4043 4314 3588 1854 3588 2540
λαλῆσαι. 5 ἐν σοφίᾳ περιπατεῖτε πρὸς τοὺς ἔξω, τὸν καιρὸν
to speak. In wisdom Walk toward those outside, the time
1805 3588 3056 5216 3842 1722 5485 217
ἐξαγοραζόμενοι. 6 ὁ λόγος ὑμῶν πάντοτε ἐν χάριτι, ἅλατι
redeeming. The speech of you always (let be) with grace, with salt
741 1492 4459 1163 5209 1520 1538 611
ἠρτυμένος, εἰδέναι πῶς δεῖ ὑμᾶς ἑνὶ ἑκάστῳ ἀποκρίνεσθαι.
being seasoned, to know how ought you one each to answer.

Colossians 4

1. Masters, give unto (your) servants that which is just and equal; knowing that ye also have a Master in heaven.

2 Continue in prayer, and watch in the same with thanksgiving;
3 Withal praying also for us, that God would open unto us a door of utterance, to speak the mystery of Christ, for which I am also in bonds:
4 That I may make it manifest, as I ought to speak.
5 Walk in wisdom toward them that are without, redeeming the time.
6 Let your speech (be) alway with grace, seasoned with salt, that ye may know how ye ought to answer every man.

Colossians 4:7

Literal Translation

7 All the things about me, Tychicus the beloved brother and faithful minister and fellow-slave in (the) Lord, will make known to you,
8 whom I sent to you for this very thing, that he know the things about you, and that he might comfort your hearts,
9 with Onesimus the faithful and beloved brother, who is of you. They will make known to you all the things here.

10 Aristarchus, my fellow prisoner, greets you, also Mark the cousin of Barnabas, about whom you received orders. If he comes to you, receive him.
11 And Jesus, the (one) being called Justus, those being of the circumcision, (greet you), these only fellow-workers for the kingdom of God, who became a comfort to me.

12 Epaphras greets you, he of you, a slave of Christ, always striving on your behalf in prayers, that you may stand full-grown and being complete in every will of God.

13 For I bear witness to him, that he has much zeal on your behalf, and those in Laodicea, and those in Hierapolis.

14 Luke the beloved physician greets you, also Demas.

15 Greet the brothers in Laodicea, and Nymphas and the church in his house.
16 And when this letter is read before you, cause that

3588 2596 1691 3956 1107 5213 5190 3588 27
7. Τὰ κατ᾽ ἐμὲ πάντα γνωρίσει ὑμῖν Τυχικός, ὁ ἀγαπητὸς
The things about me all will make known to you Tychicus, the beloved

80 2532 4103 1249 2532 4889 1722 2962 3739
ἀδελφὸς καὶ πιστὸς διάκονος καὶ σύνδουλος ἐν Κυρίῳ· 8 ὃν
brother and faithful minister and fellow-slave in (the) Lord; whom

3992 4314 5209 1519 846 5124 2443 1097 3588 4012 5216
ἔπεμψα πρὸς ὑμᾶς εἰς αὐτὸ τοῦτο, ἵνα γνῷ τὰ περὶ ὑμῶν
I sent to you for this same thing, that he know the things about you

2532 3870 3588 2588 5216 4862 3682 3588
καὶ παρακαλέσῃ τὰς καρδίας ὑμῶν· 9 σὺν Ὀνησίμῳ τῷ
and he might comfort the hearts of you; with Onesimus the

4103 2532 27 80 3739 2076 1537 5216 3956 5213
πιστῷ καὶ ἀγαπητῷ ἀδελφῷ, ὅς ἐστιν ἐξ ὑμῶν. πάντα ὑμῖν
faithful and beloved brother, who is of you. all things to you

1107 3588 5602
γνωριοῦσι τὰ ὧδε.
They will make known the things here.

782 5209 708 3588 4869 3450
10. Ἀσπάζεται ὑμᾶς Ἀρίσταρχος ὁ συναιχμάλωτός μου,
Greets you Aristarchus the fellow-captive of me,

2532 3138 3588 431 921 4012 3739 2983 1785
καὶ Μάρκος ὁ ἀνεψιὸς Βαρνάβα [περὶ οὗ ἐλάβετε ἐντολάς·
and Mark the cousin of Barnabas, about whom you received orders;

1437 2064 4314 5209 1209 846 2532 2424 3588 3004
ἐὰν ἔλθῃ πρὸς ὑμᾶς, δέξασθε αὐτόν], 11 καὶ Ἰησοῦς ὁ λεγό-
if he comes to you, receive him, and Jesus he named

2459 3588 5607 1537 4061 3778 3441 4904
μενος Ἰοῦστος, οἱ ὄντες ἐκ περιτομῆς· οὗτοι μόνοι συνεργοὶ
Justus, those being of the circumcision; these only fellow-workers

1519 3588 932 3588 2316 3748 1096 3427
εἰς τὴν βασιλείαν τοῦ Θεοῦ, οἵτινες ἐγενήθησάν μοι
for the kingdom of God, who became to me

3931 782 5209 1889 3588 1537 5216 1401
παρηγορία. 12 ἀσπάζεται ὑμᾶς Ἐπαφρᾶς ὁ ἐξ ὑμῶν, δοῦλος
a comfort. Greets you Epaphras he of you, a slave

5547 3842 75 5228 5216 1722 3588 4335
Χριστοῦ, πάντοτε ἀγωνιζόμενος ὑπὲρ ὑμῶν ἐν ταῖς προσ-
of Christ, always struggling on behalf of you in the

2443 2476 5046 2532 4137 1722 3956
ευχαῖς, ἵνα στῆτε τέλειοι καὶ πεπληρωμένοι ἐν παντὶ
prayers, that you may stand mature and being complete in all

2307 3588 2316 3140 1063 846 3754 2192 2205
θελήματι τοῦ Θεοῦ. 13 μαρτυρῶ γὰρ αὐτῷ ὅτι ἔχει ζῆλον
(the) will of God. I testify For to him that he has zeal

4183 5228 5216 2532 3588 1722 2993 2532 3588 1722 2404
πολὺν ὑπὲρ ὑμῶν καὶ τῶν ἐν Λαοδικείᾳ καὶ τῶν ἐν Ἱεραπό-
much on behalf of you and those in Laodicea and those in Hierapolis.

782 5209 3065 3588 2395 3588 27 2532
λει. 14 ἀσπάζεται ὑμᾶς Λουκᾶς ὁ ἰατρὸς ὁ ἀγαπητός, καὶ
Greets you Luke the physician beloved, and

1214 782 3588 1722 2993 80 2532 3564
Δημᾶς. 15 ἀσπάσασθε τοὺς ἐν Λαοδικείᾳ ἀδελφούς, καὶ Νυμφᾶν,
Demas. Greet the in Laodicea brothers, and Nymphas,

2532 3588 2596 3624 846 1577 2532 3752 314
καὶ τὴν κατ᾽ οἶκον αὐτοῦ ἐκκλησίαν. 16 καὶ ὅταν ἀναγνωσθῇ
and the at (the) house of him church. And when is read

3844 5213 3588 1992 4160 2443 2532 1722 3588 2994
παρ᾽ ὑμῖν ἡ ἐπιστολή, ποιήσατε ἵνα καὶ ἐν τῇ Λαοδικέων
before you the epistle, cause that also in the Laodicean

1577 314 2532 3588 1537 2993 2443 2532
ἐκκλησίᾳ ἀναγνωσθῇ, καὶ τὴν ἐκ Λαοδικείας ἵνα καὶ
church it is read, and the (one) of Laodicea that also

King James Version

7 All my state shall Tychicus declare unto you, (who is) a beloved brother, and a faithful minister and fellowservant in the Lord:
8 Whom I have sent unto you for the same purpose, that he might know your estate, and comfort your hearts;
9 With Onesimus, a faithful and beloved brother, who is (one) of you. They shall make known unto you all things which (are done) here.

10 Aristarchus my fellowprisoner saluteth you, and Marcus, sister's son to Barnabas, (touching whom ye received commandments: if he come unto you, receive him;)
11 And Jesus, which is called Justus, who are of the circumcision. These only (are my) fellowworkers unto the kingdom of God, which have been a comfort unto me.

12 Epaphras, who is (one) of you, a servant of Christ, saluteth you, always labouring fervently for you in prayers, that ye may stand perfect and complete in all the will of God.

13 For I bear him record, that he hath a great zeal for you, and them (that are) in Laodicea, and them in Hierapolis.

14 Luke, the beloved physician, and Demas, greet you.

15 Salute the brethren which are in Laodicea, and Nymphas, and the church which is in his house.
16 And when this epistle is read among you, cause that

Literal Translation

it be read also in the Laodicean church, and that you also read the (one) of Laodicea.
17 And say to Archippus, Look to the ministry which you received in (the) Lord, that you may fulfill it.
18 The greeting by my hand, Paul. Remember my bonds. Grace (be) with you. Amen.

Colossians 4:17

5210 314 2532 2036 751 991 3588 1248
ὑμεῖς ἀναγνῶτε. 17 καὶ εἴπατε Ἀρχίππῳ, Βλέπε τὴν διακονίαν
you read. And say to Archippus, Look (to) the ministry

3739 3880 1722 2962 2443 846 4137
ἣν παρέλαβες ἐν Κυρίῳ, ἵνα αὐτὴν πληροῖς.
which you received in (the) Lord, that it you may fulfill.

3588 783 3588 1699 5495 3972 3421 3450 3588
18. Ὁ ἀσπασμὸς τῇ ἐμῇ χειρὶ Παύλου. μνημονεύετέ μου τῶν
The greeting by my hand Paul. Remember of me the

1199 3588 5485 3326 5216 281
δεσμῶν. ἡ χάρις μεθ' ὑμῶν. ἀμήν.
bonds. Grace (be) with you. Amen.

King James Version

it be read also in the church of the Laodiceans; and that ye likewise read the (epistle) from Laodicea.
17 And say to Archippus, Take heed to the ministry which thou hast received in the Lord, that thou fulfil it.
18 The salutation by the hand of me Paul. Remember my bonds. Grace (be) with you. Amen. (Written from Rome to Colossians by Tychicus and Onesimus.)

Literal Translation

THE FIRST EPISTLE OF PAUL THE APOSTLE TO THE THESSALONIANS

1 Thessalonians 1

1. Paul and Silvanus and Timothy to the church of Thessalonians in God (the) Father and (the) Lord Jesus Christ: Grace and peace to you from God our Father and (the) Lord Jesus Christ.

2 We give thanks to God always concerning you all, making mention of you on our prayers,

3 remembering without ceasing your work of faith and labor of love, and the patience of hope of our Lord Jesus Christ before our God and Father,

4 knowing, brothers having been loved, your election by God.
5 For our gospel did not come to you in word only, but also in power, and in (the) Holy Spirit, and in much assurance, even as you know what kind we were among you for your sake.

6 And you became imitators of us and of the Lord, welcoming the Word in much affliction with joy of (the) Holy Spirit.

7 So as you became examples to all those believing in Macedonia and Achaia.
8 For the Word of the Lord sounded out from you not only in Macedonia

ΠΑΥΛΟΥ ΤΟΥ ΑΠΟΣΤΟΛΟΥ Η ΠΡΟΣ ΘΕΣΣΑΛΟΝΙΚΕΙΣ ΕΠΙΣΤΟΛΗ ΠΡΩΤΗ

OF PAUL THE APOSTLE THE TO THESSALONIANS EPISTLE FIRST

1 Thessalonians 1

3972 2532 4610 2532 5095 3588 1577 2331
1. Παῦλος καὶ Σιλουανὸς καὶ Τιμόθεος, τῇ ἐκκλησίᾳ Θεσ-
Paul and Silvanus and Timothy, to the church of Thes-

1722 2316 3962 2532 2962 2424 5547 5485
σαλονικέων ἐν Θεῷ πατρὶ, καὶ Κυρίῳ Ἰησοῦ Χριστῷ· χάρις
salonians in God (the) Father, and (the) Lord Jesus Christ; grace

5213 2532 1515 575 2316 3962 2257 2532 2962 2424
ὑμῖν καὶ εἰρήνη ἀπό θεοῦ πατρὸς ἡμῶν καὶ Κυρίου Ἰησοῦ
to you and peace from God (the) Father of us and (the) Lord Jesus

5547
Χριστοῦ.
Christ.

2168 3588 2316 3842 4012 3956 5216
2. Εὐχαριστοῦμεν τῷ Θεῷ πάντοτε περὶ πάντων ὑμῶν,
We give thanks to God always concerning all you,

3417 5216 4160 1909 3588 4335 2257 89
μνείαν ὑμῶν ποιούμενοι ἐπὶ τῶν προσευχῶν ἡμῶν, ἀδια-
mention of you making on the prayers of us, un-

3421 5216 3588 2041 3588 4102 2532
λείπτως 3 μνημονεύοντες ὑμῶν τοῦ ἔργου τῆς πίστεως, καὶ
ceasingly remembering of you the work of faith, and

3588 2873 3588 26 2532 3588 5281 3588 1680 3588
τοῦ κόπου τῆς ἀγάπης, καὶ τῆς ὑπομονῆς τῆς ἐλπίδος τοῦ
the labor of love, and the patience of hope of the

2962 2257 2424 5547 1715 3588 2316 2532
Κυρίου ἡμῶν Ἰησοῦ Χριστοῦ, ἔμπροσθεν τοῦ Θεοῦ καὶ
Lord of us Jesus Christ, before the God and

3962 2257 1492 80 25 5259 2316 3588
πατρὸς ἡμῶν· 4 εἰδότες, ἀδελφοὶ ἠγαπημένοι, ὑπὸ Θεοῦ τὴν
Father of us; knowing, brothers having been loved, by God the

1589 5216 3754 3588 2098 2257 3756 1096 1519 5209
ἐκλογὴν ὑμῶν, 5 ὅτι τὸ εὐαγγέλιον ἡμῶν οὐκ ἐγενήθη εἰς ὑμᾶς
election of you, because the gospel of us not came to you

1722 3056 3440 235 2532 1722 1411 2532 1722 4151 40
ἐν λόγῳ μόνον, ἀλλὰ καὶ ἐν δυνάμει, καὶ ἐν Πνεύματι Ἁγίῳ,
in word only, but also in power, and in (the) Spirit Holy,

2532 1722 4136 4183 2531 1492 3634 1096 1722
καὶ ἐν πληροφορίᾳ πολλῇ, καθὼς οἴδατε οἷοι ἐγενήθημεν ἐν
and in assurance much, even as you know what kind we were among

5213 1223 5209 2532 5210 3402 2257 1096 2532 3588
ὑμῖν δι᾽ ὑμᾶς. 6 καὶ ὑμεῖς μιμηταὶ ἡμῶν ἐγενήθητε καὶ τοῦ
you because of you. And you imitators of us became and of the

2962 1209 3588 3056 1722 2347 4183 3326 5479
Κυρίου, δεξάμενοι τὸν λόγον ἐν θλίψει πολλῇ μετὰ χαρᾶς
Lord, welcoming the Word in affliction much with joy

4151 40 5620 1096 5209 5179 3956 3588
Πνεύματος Ἁγίου, 7 ὥστε γενέσθαι ὑμᾶς τύπους πᾶσι τοῖς
of (the) Spirit Holy, so as to become you examples to all those

4100 1722 3588 3109 2532 1722 3588 882 575 5216 1063
πιστεύουσιν ἐν τῇ Μακεδονίᾳ καὶ ἐν τῇ Ἀχαΐᾳ. 8 ἀφ ὑμῶν γὰρ
believing in Macedonia and in Achaia. from you For

1837 3588 3056 3588 2962 3756 3440 1722 3588 3109
ἐξήχηται ὁ λόγος τοῦ Κυρίου οὐ μόνον ἐν τῇ Μακεδονίᾳ
sounded the Word of the Lord not only in Macedonia

King James Version

THE FIRST EPISTLE OF PAUL THE APOSTLE TO THE THESSALONIANS

1 Thessalonians 1

1. Paul, and Silvanus, and Timotheus, unto the church of the Thessalonians (which is) in God the Father and (in) the Lord Jesus Christ: Grace (be) unto you, and peace, from God our Father, and the Lord Jesus Christ.

2 We give thanks to God always for you all, making mention of you in our prayers;

3 Remembering without ceasing your work of faith, and labour of love, and patience of hope in our Lord Jesus Christ, in the sight of God and our Father;

4 Knowing, brethren beloved, your election of God.
5 For our gospel came not unto you in word only, but also in power, and in the Holy Ghost, and in much assurance; as ye know what manner of men we were among you for your sake.

6 And ye became followers of us, and of the Lord, having received the word in much affliction, with joy of the Holy Ghost:

7 So that ye were ensamples to all that believe in Macedonia and Achaia.
8 For from you sounded out the word of the Lord not only in Macedonia

Literal Translation

and Achaia, but also in every place your faith toward God has gone out, so that there is no need for us to have to say anything.

9 For they themselves announce about us what kind of entrance we have to you, and how you turned to God from the idols, to serve (the) true and living God,
10 and to await His Son from Heaven, whom He raised from (the) dead, Jesus, the (One) delivering us from the coming wrath.

1 Thessalonians 1:9

2532 882 235 2532 1722 3956 5117 3588 4102 5216 3588
καὶ Ἀχαΐᾳ, ἀλλα καὶ ἐν παντὶ τόπῳ ἡ πίστις ὑμῶν ἡ
and Achaia, but also in every place the faith of you

4314 3588 2316 1831 5620 3361 5532 2219 2248 2980
πρὸς τὸν Θεὸν ἐξελήλυθεν, ὥστε μὴ χρείαν ἡμᾶς ἔχειν λαλεῖν
toward God has gone out, so as not need (for) us to have to say

5100 846 1063 4012 2257 518 3697 1529 2192
τι· 9 αὐτοὶ γὰρ περὶ ἡμῶν ἀπαγγέλλουσιν ὁποίαν εἴσοδον ἔσχο-
anything; themselves for about us announce what kind of entrance we

4314 5209 2532 4459 1994 4314 3588 2316 575 3588
μεν πρὸς ὑμᾶς, καὶ πῶς ἐπεστρέψατε πρὸς τὸν Θεὸν ἀπὸ τῶν
have to you, and how you turned to God from the

1497 1398 2316 2198 2532 228 2532 362
εἰδώλων δουλεύειν Θεῷ ζῶντι καὶ ἀληθινῷ, 10 καὶ ἀναμένειν
idols to serve God living and true, and to await

3588 5207 846 1537 3588 3772 3739 1453 1537 3498
τὸν υἱὸν αὐτοῦ ἐκ τῶν οὐρανῶν, ὃν ἤγειρεν ἐκ νεκρῶν,
the Son of Him from Heaven, whom He raised from (the) dead,

2424 3588 4506 2248 575 3588 3709 3588 2064
Ἰησοῦν, τὸν ῥυόμενον ἡμᾶς ἀπὸ τῆς ὀργῆς τῆς ἐρχομένης.
Jesus, the (One) delivering us from the wrath coming.

King James Version

and Achaia, but also in every place your faith to God-ward is spread abroad; so that we need not to speak any thing.

9For they themselves shew of us what manner of entering in we had unto you, and how ye turned to God from idols to serve the living and true God;
10And to wait for his Son from heaven, whom he raised from the dead, (even) Jesus, which delivered us from the wrath to come.

1 Thessalonians 2

1. For brothers, you yourselves know our entrance to you, that it has not been in vain.
2 But also having suffered before and having been insulted in Philippi, as you know, we were bold in our God to speak the gospel of God to you in much agony.

3 For our exhortation (was) not of error, nor of uncleanness, nor in guile;
4 but even as we have been approved by God to be entrusted (with) the gospel, so we speak, not as pleasing men, but God, the (One) trying our hearts.

5 For neither were we then (found) with word of flattery, even as you know, nor with pretext of covetousness; God (is) witness,

6 nor seeking glory from men, neither from you, nor from others, being able to be in heaviness, as apostles of Christ.
7 But we were gentle in

1 Thessalonians 2

846 1063 1492 80 3588 1529 2257 3588 4314
1. Αὐτοὶ γὰρ οἴδατε, ἀδελφοί, τὴν εἴσοδον ἡμῶν τὴν πρὸς
yourselves For know, brothers, the entrance of us to

5209 3754 3756 2756 1096 235 2532 4310
ὑμᾶς, ὅτι οὐ κενὴ γέγονεν· 2 ἀλλα καὶ προπαθόντες
you, that not in vain it has been; but also having before suffered

2532 5195 2531 1492 1722 5375 3955
καὶ ὑβρισθέντες, καθὼς οἴδατε, ἐν Φιλίπποις ἐπαρρησιασάμεθα
and having been insulted, even as you know, in Phillipi we were bold

1722 3588 2316 2257 2980 4314 5209 3588 2098 3588
ἐν τῷ Θεῷ ἡμῶν λαλῆσαι πρὸς ὑμᾶς τὸ εὐαγγέλιον τοῦ
in the God of us to speak to you the gospel

2316 1722 4183 73 3588 1063 3874 2257 3756 1537
Θεοῦ ἐν πολλῷ ἀγῶνι. 3 ἡ γὰρ παράκλησις ἡμῶν οὐκ ἐκ
of God in much agony. the For exhortation of us not of

4106 3761 1537 167 3777 1722 1388 235 2531
πλάνης, οὐδὲ ἐξ ἀκαθαρσίας, οὐδὲ ἐν δόλῳ, 4 ἀλλὰ καθὼς
error, nor of uncleanness, nor in guile, but as

1381 5259 3588 2316 4100 3588 2098
δεδοκιμάσμεθα ὑπὸ τοῦ Θεοῦ πιστευθῆναι τὸ εὐαγγέλιον,
we have been approved by God to be entrusted (with) the gospel,

3779 2980 3756 5613 444 700 235 3588 2316
οὕτω λαλοῦμεν, οὐχ ὡς ἀνθρώποις ἀρέσκοντες, ἀλλα τῷ Θεῷ
so we speak, not as men pleasing, but God

3588 1381 3588 2588 2257 3777 1063 4218 1722 3056
τῷ δοκιμάζοντι τὰς καρδίας ἡμῶν. 5 οὔτε γάρ ποτε ἐν λόγῳ
the (One) trying the hearts of us. neither For then with word

2850 1096 2531 1492 3777 1722 4392
κολακείας ἐγενήθημεν, καθὼς οἴδατε, οὔτε ἐν προφάσει
of flattery were we, as you know, nor in pretext

4124 2316 3144 3777 2212 1537 444
πλεονεξίας· θεὸς μάρτυς· 6 οὔτε ζητοῦντες ἐξ ἀνθρώπων
of covetousness; God (is) witness; not seeking from men

1391 3777 575 5216 3777 575 243 1410 1722 922
δόξαν, οὔτε ἀφ᾽ ὑμῶν οὔτε ἀπ᾽ ἄλλων, 7 δυνάμενοι ἐν βάρει
glory, neither from you nor from others, being able in heaviness

1511 5613 5547 652 235 1096 2261 1722
εἶναι, ὡς Χριστοῦ ἀπόστολοι, ἀλλ᾽ ἐγενήθημεν ἤπιοι ἐν
to be, as of Christ apostles, but we were gentle in

1 Thessalonians 2

1. For yourselves, brethren, know our entrance in unto you, that it was not in vain:
2But even after that we had suffered before, and were shamefully entreated, as ye know, at Philippi, we were bold in our God to speak unto you the gospel of God with much contention.

3For our exhortation (was) not of deceit, nor of uncleanness, nor in guile:
4But as we were allowed of God to be put in trust with the gospel, even so we speak; not as pleasing men, but God, which trieth our hearts.

5For neither at any time used we flattering words, as ye know, nor a cloke of covetousness; God (is) witness:

6Nor of men sought we glory, neither of you, nor (yet) of others, when we might have been burdensome, as the apostles of Christ.
7But we were gentle

Literal Translation | **1 Thessalonians 2:8** | ***King James Version***

Literal Translation

your midst, as if a nurse should warmly cherish her children;
8 so yearning over you, we were well-pleased to impart to you not only the gospel of God, but also our own souls, because you have become beloved to us.
9 For, brothers, you remember our labor and the toil, for night and day working in order to not put a burden on anyone of you, we proclaimed to you the gospel of God.

10 You and God (are) witnesses how holily and righteously and blamelessly we were to you, the (ones) believing;

11 even as you know how (I was to) each one of you, as a father (to) his children, exhorting and consoling you,
12 testifying for you to walk worthily of God, He calling you to His kingdom and glory.

13 And because of this we give thanks to God without ceasing, that having received (the) Word of hearing from us, you welcomed (it) of God, not (as) a word of men, but as it is, truly (the) Word of God, which also works in you, the (ones) believing.

14 For, brothers, you became imitators of the churches of God being in Judea in Christ Jesus, because you also suffered these things by (your) own fellow countrymen, as they also by the Jews,

15 who both killed the Lord Jesus and their own prophets, also having driven

3319 5216 5613 302 5162 2282 3588 1438 5043 3779
μέσῳ ὑμῶν, ὡς ἂν τροφὸς θάλπῃ τὰ ἑαυτῆς τέκνα· 8 οὕτως
(the) midst of you, as if a nurse should cherish the of herself children; so

2442 5216 2106 3330 5213 3756 3440 3588
ἱμειρόμενοι ὑμῶν, εὐδοκοῦμεν μεταδοῦναι ὑμῖν οὐ μόνον τὸ
yearning over you we were well-pleased to impart to you not only the

2098 3588 2316 235 2532 3588 1438 5590 1360
εὐαγγέλιον τοῦ Θεοῦ, ἀλλὰ καὶ τὰς ἑαυτῶν ψυχάς, διότι
gospel of God, but also the of ourselves souls, because

27 2254 1096 3421 1063 80 3588
ἀγαπητοὶ ἡμῖν γεγένησθε. 9 μνημονεύετε γάρ, ἀδελφοί, τὸν
beloved to us you have become. you remember For, brothers, the

2873 2257 2532 3588 3449 3571 1063 2532 2250 2038
κόπον ἡμῶν καὶ τὸν μόχθον· νυκτὸς γὰρ καὶ ἡμέρας ἐργαζό-
labor of us and the toil; night for and day working,

4314 3588 3361 1912 5100 5216 2784 1519
μενοι, πρὸς τὸ μὴ ἐπιβαρῆσαί τινα ὑμῶν, ἐκηρύξαμεν εἰς
in order to not put a burden on anyone of you, we proclaimed to

5209 3588 2098 3588 2316 5210 3144 2532 3588 2316
ὑμᾶς τὸ εὐαγγέλιον τοῦ Θεοῦ. 10 ὑμεῖς μάρτυρες καὶ ὁ Θεός,
you the gospel of God. You (are) witnesses and God,

5613 3743 2532 1346 2532 274 5213 3588 4100
ὡς ὁσίως καὶ δικαίως καὶ ἀμέμπτως ὑμῖν τοῖς πιστεύουσιν
how holily and righteously and blamelessly to you the (ones) believing

1096 2509 1492 5613 1520 1538 5216 5613 3962
ἐγενήθημεν· 11 καθάπερ οἴδατε ὡς ἕνα ἕκαστον ὑμῶν, ὡς πατὴρ
we were; even as you know how one each of you, as a father

5043 1438 3870 5209 2532 3888 2532
τέκνα ἑαυτοῦ, 12 παρακαλοῦντες ὑμᾶς καὶ παραμυθούμενοι καὶ
children of himself, exhorting you and consoling and

3140 1519 3588 4043 5209 516 3588 2316
μαρτυρόμενοι, εἰς τὸ περιπατῆσαι ὑμᾶς ἀξίως τοῦ Θεοῦ
testifying, for to have walked you worthily of God

3588 2564 5209 1519 3588 1438 932 2532 1391
τοῦ καλοῦντος ὑμᾶς εἰς τὴν ἑαυτοῦ βασιλείαν καὶ δόξαν.
the (One) calling you into the of Himself kingdom and glory.

1223 5124 2532 2249 2168 3588 2316 89
13. Διὰ τοῦτο καὶ ἡμεῖς εὐχαριστοῦμεν τῷ Θεῷ ἀδιαλείπτως,
Because of this also we give thanks to God without ceasing,

3754 3880 3056 189 3844 2257 3588 2316
ὅτι παραλαβόντες λόγον ἀκοῆς παρ᾽ ἡμῶν τοῦ Θεοῦ,
that having received (the) Word of hearing from us of God,

1209 3756 3056 444 235 2531 2076 230
ἐδέξασθε οὐ λόγον ἀνθρώπων, ἀλλὰ καθώς ἐστιν ἀληθῶς
you welcomed not (as) a word of men, but as it is truly,

3056 2316 3739 2532 1754 1722 5213 3588 4100
λόγον θεοῦ, ὃς καὶ ἐνεργεῖται ἐν ὑμῖν τοῖς πιστεύουσιν.
(the) Word of God, which also works in you the (ones) believing.

5210 1063 3402 1096 80 3588 1577 3588
14 ὑμεῖς γὰρ μιμηταὶ ἐγενήθητε, ἀδελφοί, τῶν ἐκκλησιων τοῦ
you For imitators became, brothers, of the churches

2316 3588 5607 1722 3588 2449 1722 5547 2424 3754 5024
Θεοῦ τῶν οὐσῶν ἐν τῇ Ἰουδαίᾳ ἐν Χριστῷ Ἰησοῦ· ὅτι ταυτὰ
of God being in Judea in Christ Jesus; for these things

3958 2532 5210 5259 3588 2398 4853 2531 2532
ἐπάθετε καὶ ὑμεῖς ὑπὸ τῶν ἰδίων συμφυλετῶν, καθὼς καὶ
suffered also you by the own countrymen, as also

846 5259 3588 2453 3588 2532 3588 2962 615
αὐτοὶ ὑπὸ τῶν Ἰουδαίων, 15 τῶν καὶ τὸν Κύριον ἀποκτεινάν-
they by the Jews, the (ones) both the Lord killing

2424 2532 3588 2398 4396 2532 5209 1559
των Ἰησοῦν καὶ τοὺς ἰδίους προφήτας, καὶ ἡμᾶς ἐκδιωξάν-
Jesus and the own prophets, and us having driven out

King James Version

among you, even as a nurse cherisheth her children:
8 So being affectionately desirous of you, we were willing to have imparted unto you, not the gospel of God only, but also our own souls, because ye were dear unto us.
9 For ye remember, brethren, our labour and travail: for labouring night and day, because we would not be chargeable unto any of you, we preached unto you the gospel of God.

10 Ye (are) witnesses, and God (also), how holily and justly and unblameably we behaved ourselves among you that believe:

11 As ye know how we exhorted and comforted and charged every one of you, as a father (doth) his children,
12 That ye would walk worthy of God, who hath called you unto his kingdom and glory.

13 For this cause also thank we God without ceasing, because, when ye received the word of God which ye heard of us, ye received (it) not (as) the word of men, but as it is in truth, the word of God, which effectually worketh also in you that believe.

14 For ye, brethren, became followers of the churches of God which in Judaea are in Christ Jesus: for ye also have suffered like things of your own countrymen, even as they (have) of the Jews:

15 Who both killed the Lord Jesus, and their own prophets, and have persecuted us;

Literal Translation | **1 Thessalonians 2:16** | **King James Version**

us out, and not pleasing God, and (being) contrary to all men,
16 hindering us (from) speaking to the nations in order that they be saved, for to fill up their sins always. But the wrath has come on them to (the) end.

2532 2316 3361 700 2532 3956
των, καὶ Θεῷ μὴ ἀρεσκόντων, καὶ πᾶσιν
and God not pleasing, and to all

444 1727 2967 2248 3588 1484 2980
ἀνθρώποις ἐναντίων, 16 κωλυόντων ἡμᾶς τοῖς ἔθνεσι λαλῆσαι
men contrary, hindering us to the nations to speak

2443 4982 1519 3588 378 846 3588 266 3842
ἵνα σωθῶσιν, εἰς τὸ ἀναπληρῶσαι αὐτῶν τὰς ἁμαρτίας πάντοτε·
that they be saved, for the to fill up of them the sins always;

5348 1161 1909 846 3588 3709 1519 5056
ἔφθασε δὲ ἐπ' αὐτοὺς ἡ ὀργὴ εἰς τέλος.
is come but on them the wrath to (the) end.

and they please not God, and are contrary to all men:
16 Forbidding us to speak to the Gentiles that they might be saved, to fill up their sins alway: for the wrath is come upon them to the uttermost.

17 But, brothers, we being taken away from you for an hour's time, in presence, not in heart, more abundantly we were eager with much desire to see your face.
18 Because of this, we desired to come to you, truly I, Paul, both once and twice; but Satan hindered us.

2249 1161 80 642 575 5216 4314
17. Ἡμεῖς δέ, ἀδελφοί, ἀπορφανισθέντες ἀφ' ὑμῶν πρὸς
we But, brothers, being taken away from you for

2540 5610 4383 3756 2588 4056 4704
καιρὸν ὥρας, προσώπῳ οὐ καρδίᾳ, περισσοτέρως ἐσπουδάσαμεν
time of an hour, in presence not in heart, more abundantly were eager

3588 4383 5216 1492 1722 4183 1939 1352 2309
τὸ πρόσωπον ὑμῶν ἰδεῖν ἐν πολλῇ ἐπιθυμίᾳ. 18 διὸ ἠθελήσαμεν
the face of you to see with much desire. Therefore we desired

2064 4314 5209 1473 3303 3972 2532 530 2532 1364 2532
ἐλθεῖν πρὸς ὑμᾶς, ἐγὼ μὲν Παῦλος καὶ ἅπαξ καὶ δίς, καὶ ἐνέ-
to come to you, I truly Paul both once and twice, and

1465 2248 3588 4567 5101 1063 2257 1680 2228 5479 2228
κοψεν ἡμᾶς ὁ Σατανᾶς. 19 τίς γὰρ ἡμῶν ἐλπὶς ἢ χαρὰ ἢ στέ-
hindered us Satan. what For of us hope or joy or crown

17 But we, brethren, being taken from you for a short time in presence, not in heart, endeavoured the more abundantly to see your face with great desire.
18 Wherefore we would have come unto you, even I Paul, once and again; but Satan hindered us.

19 For what (is) our hope, or joy, or crown of glorying? (Is it) not even you (to be) before our Lord Jesus Christ at His coming?

20 For you are our glory and joy.

4735 2746 2228 3780 2532 5210 1715 3588 2962
φανος καυχήσεως; ἢ οὐχὶ καὶ ὑμεῖς, ἔμπροσθεν τοῦ Κυρίου
of glorying? Not even you, before the Lord

2257 2424 5547 1722 3588 846 3952 5210 1063
ἡμῶν Ἰησοῦ Χριστοῦ ἐν τῇ αὐτοῦ παρουσίᾳ; 20 ὑμεῖς γάρ
of us Jesus Christ at the of Him coming? you For

2075 3588 1391 2257 2532 3588 5479
ἐστε ἡ δόξα ἡμῶν καὶ ἡ χαρά.
are the glory of us and the joy.

19 For what (is) our hope, or joy, or crown of rejoicing? (Are) not even ye in the presence of our Lord Jesus Christ at his coming?

20 For ye are our glory and joy.

1 Thessalonians 3

1. So no longer enduring, we were pleased to be left in Athens alone,
2 and sent Timothy, our brother and minister of God, and our fellow worker in the gospel of Christ, in order to establish you and to encourage you concerning your faith,

1352 3371 4722 2106 2641 1722
1. Διὸ μηκέτι στέγοντες εὐδοκήσαμεν καταλειφθῆναι ἐν
So no longer enduring we were pleased to be left in

116 3441 2532 3992 5095 3588 80 2257
Ἀθήναις μόνοι, 2 καὶ ἐπέμψαμεν Τιμόθεον, τὸν ἀδελφὸν ἡμῶν
Athens alone, and sent Timothy, the brother of us

2532 1249 3588 2316 2532 4904 2257 1722 3588 2098
καὶ διάκονον τοῦ Θεοῦ καὶ συνεργὸν ἡμῶν ἐν τῷ εὐαγγελίῳ
and minister of God and fellow-worker of us in the gospel

3588 5547 1519 3588 4741 5209 2532 3870 5209 4012
τοῦ Χριστοῦ, εἰς τὸ στηρίξαι ὑμᾶς καὶ παρακαλέσαι ὑμᾶς περι
of Christ, for the to establish you and to encourage you concerning

1. Wherefore when we could no longer forbear, we thought it good to be left at Athens alone;
2 And sent Timotheus, our brother, and minister of God, and our fellowlabourer in the gospel of Christ, to establish you, and to comfort you concerning your faith:

3 that no one be drawn aside by these afflictions. For you yourselves know that we are appointed to this.
4 For even when we were with you, we said to you before that we are about to be afflicted, as it also happened, even you know.
5 Because of this

3588 4102 5216 3588 3367 4525 1722 3588 2347
τῆς πίστεως ὑμῶν, 3 τὸ μηδένα σαίνεσθαι ἐν ταῖς θλίψεσι
the faith of you, no one to be drawn aside by afflictions

3778 846 1063 1492 3754 1519 5124 2749 2532 1063
ταύταις· αὐτοὶ γὰρ οἴδατε ὅτι εἰς τοῦτο κείμεθα. 4 καὶ γὰρ
these; yourselves for know that to this we are appointed. even For

3753 4314 5209 2258 4302 5213 3754 3195 2346
ὅτε πρὸς ὑμᾶς ἦμεν, προελέγομεν ὑμῖν ὅτι μέλλομεν θλί-
when with you we were, we said before to you that we are about to be

2531 2532 1096 2532 1492 1223 5124 2504
βεσθαι, καθὼς καὶ ἐγένετο καὶ οἴδατε. 5 διὰ τοῦτο κἀγὼ
afflicted, even as also it happened even you know. Because of this I also

3 That no man should be moved by these afflictions: for yourselves know that we are appointed thereunto.
4 For verily, when we were with you, we told you before that we should suffer tribulation; even as it came to pass, and ye know.
5 For

Literal Translation

1 Thessalonians 3:6

King James Version

no longer enduring, I also sent to know your faith, lest perhaps the tempting (one) did tempt you, and our labor should come to be in vain.

6 But now Timothy coming to us from you, and announcing good news to us (of) your love and faith, and that you have good remembrance of us always, longing to see us, even as also we (long to see) you.

7 Because of this we were comforted over you, brothers, on all our affliction and distress through your faith,

8 because now we live, if you stand firm in (the) Lord.

9 For what thanks are we able to return to God concerning you, over all the joy (with) which we rejoice because of you before our God,

10 night and day super-abundantly petitioning to see your face, and to complete the things lacking in your faith?

11 But may our God and Father Himself, and our Lord Jesus Christ, direct our way to you.

12 And may the Lord make you to increase and to abound in love toward one another and toward all, even as we also toward you,

13 in order to establish your hearts blameless in holiness before our God and our Father at the coming of our Lord Jesus Christ with all His saints.

3371 4722 3992 1519 3588 1097 3588 4102 5216
μηκέτι στέγων, ἔπεμψα εἰς τὸ γνῶναι τὴν πίστιν ὑμῶν,
no longer enduring, sent for the to know the faith of you,

3361 3381 3985 5209 3588 3985 2532 1519 2756 1096 3588
μή πως ἐπείρασεν ὑμᾶς ὁ πειράζων, καὶ εἰς κενὸν γένηται ὁ
lest perhaps did tempt you the tempting (one), and in vain came to be the

2873 2257 737 1161 2064 5095 4314 2248 575
όκόπος ἡμῶν. 6 ἄρτι δὲ ἐλθόντος Τιμοθέου πρὸς ἡμᾶς ἀφ'
labor of us. now But havng come Timothy to us from

5216 2532 2097 2254 3588 4102 2532 3588 26
ὑμῶν, καὶ εὐαγγελισαμένου ἡμῖν τὴν πίστιν καὶ τὴν ἀγάπην
you, and announcing good news to us (of) the faith and the love

5216 2532 3754 2192 3417 2257 18 3842 1971
ὑμῶν, καὶ ὅτι ἔχετε μνείαν ἡμῶν ἀγαθὴν πάντοτε, ἐπιπο-
of you, and that you have remembrance of us good always, longing

2248 1492 2509 2532 2249 5209 1223 5124
θοῦντες ἡμᾶς ἰδεῖν, καθάπερ καὶ ἡμεῖς ὑμᾶς· 7 διὰ τοῦτο
us to see, even as also we you; because of this

3870 80 1909 5213 1909 3956 3588 2347 2532
παρεκλήθημεν, ἀδελφοί, ἐφ' ὑμῖν ἐπὶ πάσῃ τῇ θλίψει καὶ
we were comforted, brothers, over you on all the affliction and

318 2257 1223 3588 5216 4102 3754 3568 2198 1437
ἀνάγκῃ ἡμῶν διὰ τῆς ὑμῶν πίστεως· 8 ὅτι νῦν ζῶμεν, ἐὰν
distress of us through the of you faith; because now we live, if

5210 4739 1722 2962 5101 1063 2169 1410 3588
ὑμεῖς στήκετε ἐν Κυρίῳ. 9 τίνα γὰρ εὐχαριστίαν δυνάμεθα τῷ
you stand firm in (the) Lord. what For thanks are we able

2316 467 4012 5216 1909 3956 3588 5479 3739
Θεῷ ἀνταποδοῦναι περὶ ὑμῶν, ἐπὶ πάσῃ τῇ χαρᾷ ᾗ χαί-
to God to return concerning you, over all the joy (with) which

5463 1223 5209 1715 3588 2316 2257 3571 2532 2250
ρομεν δι' ὑμᾶς ἔμπροσθεν τοῦ Θεοῦ ἡμῶν, 10 νυκτὸς καὶ ἡμέρας
we rejoice because of you before the God of us, night and day

5228 4057 1189 1519 3588 1492 5216 3588 4383
ὑπὲρ ἐκ περισσοῦ δεόμενοι εἰς τὸ ἰδεῖν ὑμῶν τὸ πρόσωπον,
super-abundantly petitioning for the to see of you the face,

2532 2675 3588 5303 3588 4102 5216
καὶ καταρτίσαι τὰ ὑστερήματα τῆς πίστεως ὑμῶν;
and to complete the things lacking in the faith of you?

846 1161 3588 2316 2532 3962 2257 2532 3588 2962 2257
11. Αὐτὸς δὲ ὁ Θεὸς καὶ πατὴρ ἡμῶν, καὶ ὁ Κύριος ἡμῶν
Himself And the God and Father of us, and the Lord of us

2424 5547 2720 3588 3598 2257 4314 5209 5209
Ἰησοῦς Χριστός, κατευθύναι τὴν ὁδὸν ἡμῶν πρὸς ὑμᾶς· 12 ὑμᾶς
Jesus Christ, may He direct the way of us to you; you

1161 3588 2962 4121 2532 4052 3588 26 1519 240
δὲ ὁ Κύριος πλεονάσαι καὶ περισσεύσαι τῇ ἀγάπῃ εἰς ἀλλή-
and the Lord make to exceed and to abound in love toward one

2532 1519 3956 2509 2532 2249 1519 5209 1519 3588
λους καὶ εἰς πάντας, καθάπερ καὶ ἡμεῖς εἰς ὑμᾶς, 13 εἰς τὸ
another and toward all, even as also we toward you, to

4741 5216 3588 2588 273 1722 42
στηρίξαι ὑμῶν τὰς καρδίας ἀμέμπτους ἐν ἁγιωσύνῃ,
establish of you the hearts blameless in holiness,

1715 3588 2316 2532 3962 2257 1722 3588 3952 3588
ἔμπροσθεν τοῦ Θεοῦ καὶ πατρὸς ἡμῶν, ἐν τῇ παρουσίᾳ τοῦ
before the God and Father of us, in the coming of the

2962 2257 2424 5547 3326 3956 3588 40
Κυρίου ἡμῶν Ἰησοῦ Χριστοῦ μετὰ πάντων τῶν ἁγίων
Lord of us Jesus Christ with all the saints

846
αὐτοῦ.
of Him.

this cause, when I could no longer forbear, I sent to know your faith, lest by some means the tempter have tempted you, and our labour be in vain.

6 But now when Timotheus came from you unto us, and brought us good tidings of your faith and charity, and that ye have good remembrance of us always, desiring greatly to see us, as we also (to-see) you:

7 Therefore, brethren, we were comforted over you in all our affliction and distress by your faith:

8 For now we live, if ye stand fast in the Lord.

9 For what thanks can we render to God again for you, for all the joy wherewith we joy for your sakes before our God;

10 Night and day praying exceedingly that we might see your face, and might perfect that which is lacking in your faith?

11 Now God himself and our Father, and our Lord Jesus Christ, direct our way unto you.

12 And the Lord make you to increase and abound in love one toward another, and toward all (men), even as we (do) toward you:

13 To the end he may stablish your hearts unblameable in holiness before God, even our Father, at the coming of our Lord Jesus Christ with all his saints.

Literal Translation

1 Thessalonians 4
1. For the rest then, brothers, we beseech you and we exhort in (the) Lord Jesus, even as you received from us how you ought to walk and to please God, that you abound more.
2 For you know what injunctions we gave you through the Lord Jesus.
3 For this is God's will, your sanctification, (for) you to abstain from fornication,
4 each one of you to know to possess his vessel in purity and honor,
5 not in passion of lust, even as also the nations (do), not knowing God;
6 not to go beyond and to overreach his brother in the matter, because (the) avenger concerning all these (is) the Lord, even as indeed we told you before, and solemnly witnessed.
7 For God did not call us to uncleaness, but in purity.
8 Therefore, the (one) that despises does not despise man, but God, even the (One) giving His Holy Spirit to us.
9 But concerning brotherly love, you have no need (for me) to write to you, for you yourselves are taught by God to love one another.
10 For you indeed do it toward the brothers in all Macedonia. But, brothers, we exhort you to abound more,
11 And to try earnestly to be quiet, and to practice (your) own things, and to work with (your) own hands, even as we enjoined you,
12 that you may walk becomingly toward those outside, and

1 Thessalonians 4:1

3063 3767 80 2065 5209 2532 3870
1. Λοιπὸν οὖν, ἀδελφοί, ἐρωτῶμεν ὑμᾶς καὶ παρακαλοῦ-
For the rest then, brothers, we beseech you and we exhort

1722 2962 2424 2531 3880 3844 2257 3588 4459
μεν ἐν Κυρίῳ Ἰησοῦ, καθὼς παρελάβετε παρ' ἡμῶν τὸ πῶς
in (the) Lord Jesus, even as you received from us how

1163 5209 4043 2532 700 2316 2443 4052
δεῖ ὑμᾶς περιπατεῖν καὶ ἀρέσκειν Θεῷ, ἵνα περισσεύητε
ought you to walk and to please God, that you abound

3123 1492 1063 5101 3852 1325 5213 1223
μᾶλλον. 2 οἴδατε γὰρ τίνας παραγγελίας ἐδώκαμεν ὑμῖν διὰ
more. you know For what injunctions we gave you through

3588 2962 2424 5124 1063 2076 2307 3588 2316 3588
τοῦ Κυρίου Ἰησοῦ. 3 τοῦτο γάρ ἐστι θέλημα τοῦ Θεοῦ, ὁ
the Lord Jesus. this For is (the) will of God, the

38 5216 567 5209 575 3588 4202 1492
ἁγιασμὸς ὑμῶν, ἀπέχεσθαι ὑμᾶς ἀπὸ τῆς πορνείας· 4 εἰδέναι
sanctification of you, to abstain you from fornication; to know

1538 5216 3588 1438 4632 2932 1722 38 2532 5092
ἕκαστον ὑμῶν τὸ ἑαυτοῦ σκεῦος κτᾶσθαι ἐν ἁγιασμῷ καὶ τιμῇ,
each one of you the of himself vessel to possess in purity and honor,

3361 1722 3806 1939 2509 2532 3588 1484 3588 3361 1492 3588
5 μὴ ἐν πάθει ἐπιθυμίας, καθάπερ καὶ τὰ ἔθνη τὰ μὴ εἰδότα τὸν
not in passion of lust, even as also the nations not knowing

2316 3588 3361 5233 2532 4122 1722 3588 4229
Θεόν· 6 τὸ μὴ ὑπερβαίνειν καὶ πλεονεκτεῖν ἐν τῷ πράγματι
God; not to go beyond and to overreach in the matter

3588 80 846 1360 1558 3588 2962 4012 3956
τὸν ἀδελφὸν αὐτοῦ· διότι ἔκδικος ὁ Κύριος περὶ πάντων
the brother of him; because (the) avenger (is) the Lord concerning all

5130 2531 2532 4277 5213 2532 1263
τούτων, καθὼς καὶ προείπαμεν ὑμῖν καὶ διεμαρτυράμεθα.
these, even as indeed we before told you and solemnly witnessed.

3756 1063 2564 2248 3588 2316 1909 167 235 1722
7 οὐ γὰρ ἐκάλεσεν ἡμᾶς ὁ Θεὸς ἐπὶ ἀκαθαρσίᾳ ἀλλ' ἐν
not For called us God to uncleanness, but in

38 5105 3588 114 3756 444 114 235
ἁγιασμῷ. 8 τοιγαροῦν ὁ ἀθετῶν οὐκ ἄνθρωπον ἀθετεῖ, ἀλλὰ
purity. Therefore the (one) despising not man despises, but

3588 2316 3588 2532 1325 3588 4151 846 3588 40 1519 2248
τὸν Θεὸν τὸν καὶ δόντα τὸ Πνεῦμα αὐτοῦ τὸ Ἅγιον εἰς ἡμᾶς.
God, the (One) also having given the Spirit of Him the Holy to us.

4012 1161 3588 5360 3756 5532 2192 1125 5213
9. Περὶ δὲ τῆς φιλαδελφίας οὐ χρείαν ἔχετε γράφειν ὑμῖν·
concerning But brotherly love no need you have to write to you;

846 1063 5210 2312 2075 1519 3588 25 240
αὐτοὶ γὰρ ὑμεῖς θεοδίδακτοί ἐστε εἰς τὸ ἀγαπᾶν ἀλλήλους·
yourselves for you taught by God are for the to love one another;

2532 1063 4160 846 1519 3956 3588 80 3588/1722/3650
10 καὶ γὰρ ποιεῖτε αὐτὸ εἰς πάντας τοὺς ἀδελφοὺς τοὺς ἐν ὅλῃ
indeed for you do it toward all the brothers in all

3588 3109 3870 1161 5209 80 4052
τῇ Μακεδονίᾳ. παρακαλοῦμεν δὲ ὑμᾶς, ἀδελφοί, περισσεύειν
Macedonia. we exhort But you, brothers, to abound

3123 2532 5389 2270 2532 4238 3588 2398
μᾶλλον, 11 καὶ φιλοτιμεῖσθαι ἡσυχάζειν καὶ πράσσειν τὰ ἴδια,
more, and to try earnestly to be quiet and to practice the own,

2532 2038 3588 2398 5495 5216 2531 5213 3853
καὶ ἐργάζεσθαι ταῖς ἰδίαις χερσὶν ὑμῶν, καθὼς ὑμῖν παρηγ-
and to work with the own hands of you, even as you we

2443 4043 2156 4314 3588 1854 2532
γείλαμεν· 12 ἵνα περιπατῆτε εὐσχημόνως πρὸς τοὺς ἔξω, καὶ
enjoined; that you may walk becomingly toward those outside, and

King James Version

1 Thessalonians 4
1. Furthermore then we beseech you, brethren, and exhort (you) by the Lord Jesus, that as ye have received of us how ye ought to walk and to please God, (so) ye would abound more and more.
2 For ye know what commandments we gave you by the Lord Jesus.
3 For this is the will of God, (even) your sanctification, that ye should abstain from fornication:
4 That every one of you should know how to possess his vessel in sanctification and honour;
5 Not in the lust of concupiscence, even as the Gentiles which know not God:
6 That no (man) go beyond and defraud his brother in (any) matter: because that the Lord (is) the avenger of all such, as we also have forewarned you and testified.
7 For God hath not called us unto uncleanness, but unto holiness.
8 He therefore that despiseth, despiseth not man, but God, who hath also given unto us his holy Spirit.
9 But as touching brotherly love ye need not that I write unto you: for ye yourselves are taught of God to love one another.
10 And indeed ye do it toward all the brethren which are in all Macedonia: but we beseech you, brethren, that ye increase more and more;
11 And that ye study to be quiet, and to do your own business, and to work with your own hands, as we commanded you;
12 That ye may walk honestly toward them that are without, and

1 Thessalonians 4:13

Literal Translation

(that) you may have need of nothing.

13 But I do not desire you to be ignorant, brothers, concerning those having slept, that you not grieve, as the rest also, not having hope.
14 For if we believe that Jesus died and rose again, even so God will also bring with Him all those who have fallen asleep through Jesus.
15 For we say this to you in (the) Word of (the) Lord, that we the living who remain to the coming of the Lord not at all will go before those who have fallen asleep.
16 Because the Lord Himself shall come down from Heaven with a trumpet-call of an archangel's voice, and with God's trumpet. And the dead in Christ will rise again first.
17 Then we the living, the (ones) remaining will be caught up together with them in (the) clouds to a meeting of the Lord in (the) air. And so we will always be with (the) Lord.
18 So, then, comfort one another with these words.

3367 5532 2192
μηδενὸς χρείαν ἔχητε.
of nothing need you may have.

3756 2309 1161 5209 50 80 4012 3588 2837
13. Οὐ θέλω δὲ ὑμᾶς ἀγνοεῖν, ἀδελφοί, περὶ τῶν κεκοιμη-
not I desire But you to be ignorant, brothers, concerning those having

2443 3361 3076 2531 2532 3588 3062 3588 3361 2192
μένων, ἵνα μὴ λυπῆσθε, καθὼς καὶ οἱ λοιποὶ οἱ μὴ ἔχοντες
slept, that not you grieve, even as also the rest not having

1680 1487 1063 4100 3754 2424 599 2532 450
ἐλπίδα. 14 εἰ γὰρ πιστεύομεν ὅτι Ἰησοῦς ἀπέθανε καὶ ἀνέστη,
hope. if For we believe that Jesus died and rose again,

846 2532 3588 2316 3588 2837 1223 3588 2424 71 4862
οὕτω καὶ ὁ Θεὸς τοὺς κοιμηθέντας διὰ τοῦ Ἰησοῦ ἄξει σὺν
so even God the (ones) having slept through Jesus will bring with

846 5124 1063 5213 3004 1722 3056 2962 3754 2249 3588
αὐτῷ. 15 τοῦτο γὰρ ὑμῖν λέγομεν ἐν λόγῳ Κυρίου, ὅτι ἡμεῖς οἱ
Him. this For to you we say in (the) Word of (the) Lord, that we the

2198 3588 4035 1519 3588 3952 3588 2962 3756
ζῶντες οἱ περιλειπόμενοι εἰς τὴν παρουσίαν τοῦ Κυρίου, οὐ
living remaining to the coming of the Lord, not

3361 5348 3588 2837 3754 846 3588 296 1722
μὴ φθάσωμεν τοὺς κοιμηθέντας. 16 ὅτι αὐτὸς ὁ Κύριος ἐν
at all may go before those having slept. Because Himself the Lord in

2752 1722 5456 743 2532 1722 4536 2316
κελεύσματι, ἐν φωνῇ ἀρχαγγέλου, καὶ ἐν σάλπιγγι Θεοῦ
a trumpet-call, by a voice of an archangel, and with a trumpet of God

2597 575 3772 2532 3588 3498 1722 5547 450
καταβήσεται ἀπ' οὐρανοῦ, καὶ οἱ νεκροὶ ἐν Χριστῷ ἀναστή-
will come down from Heaven, and the dead in Christ will rise

4412 1899 2249 3588 2198 3588 4035
σονται πρῶτον· 17 ἔπειτα ἡμεῖς οἱ ζῶντες, οἱ περιλειπόμενοι,
again first; then we the living, the (ones) remaining,

260 4862 846 726 1722 3507 1519 529
ἅμα σὺν αὐτοῖς ἁρπαγησόμεθα ἐν νεφέλαις εἰς ἀπάντησιν
together with them will be caught up in clouds to a meeting

3588 2962 1519 109 2532 3779 3842 4862 2962 2071
τοῦ Κυρίου εἰς ἀέρα· καὶ οὕτω πάντοτε σὺν Κυρίῳ ἐσόμεθα.
of the Lord into (the) air, and so always with (the) Lord we will be.

5620 3870 240 1722 3588 3056 5125
18 ὥστε παρακαλεῖτε ἀλλήλους ἐν τοῖς λόγοις τούτοις.
So then comfort one another in words these.

King James Version

(that) ye may have lack of nothing.

13 But I would not have you to be ignorant, brethren, concerning them which are asleep, that ye sorrow not, even as others which have no hope.
14 For if we believe that Jesus died and rose again, even so them also which sleep in Jesus will God bring with him.
15 For this we say unto you by the word of the Lord, that we which are alive (and) remain unto the coming of the Lord shall not prevent them which are asleep.
16 For the Lord himself shall descend from heaven with a shout, with the voice of the archangel, and with the trump of God: and the dead in Christ shall rise first:
17 Then we which are alive (and) remain shall be caught up together with them in the clouds, to meet the Lord in the air: and so shall we ever be with the Lord.
18 Wherefore comfort one another with these words.

1 Thessalonians 5

Literal Translation

1. But concerning the times and the seasons, brothers, you have no need (for it) to be written.
2 For you yourselves know accurately that the day of (the) Lord as a thief in the night, so it comes.
3 For when they say, Peace and safety! Then sudden destruction comes upon them, like travail to the (one) in womb having, and not at all they shall escape.
4 But you, brothers, are not in darkness, that

4012 1161 3588 5550 2532 3588 2540 80 3756 5532
1. Περὶ δὲ τῶν χρόνων καὶ τῶν καιρῶν, ἀδελφοί, οὐ χρείαν
concerning But the times and the seasons, brothers, not need

2192 5213 1125 846 1063 199 1492 3754 3588 2250
ἔχετε ὑμῖν γράφεσθαι, 2 αὐτοὶ γὰρ ἀκριβῶς οἴδατε ὅτι ἡ ἡμέρα
have you to be written, yourselves for accurately you know that (the) day

2962 5613 2812 1722 3571 3779 2064 3752 1063
Κυρίου ὡς κλέπτης ἐν νυκτὶ οὕτως ἔρχεται· 3 ὅταν γὰρ
of (the) Lord as a thief in (the) night so it comes; when for

3004 1515 2532 803 5119 160 846
λέγωσιν, Εἰρήνη καὶ ἀσφάλεια, τότε αἰφνίδιος αὐτοῖς
they say, Peace and safety! Then sudden them

2186 3639 5618 3588 5604 3588 1722 1064 2192 2532
ἐφίσταται ὄλεθρος ὥσπερ ἡ ὠδὶν τῇ ἐν γαστρὶ ἐχούσῃ, καὶ
comes on destruction as the travail to the (one) in womb having, and

3756 3361 1628 5210 1161 80 3756 2075 1722 4655 2443
οὐ μὴ ἐκφύγωσιν. 4 ὑμεῖ δέ, ἀδελφοί, οὐκ ἐστὲ ἐν σκότει, ἵνα
not at all they may escape. you But, brothers, not are in darkness, that

King James Version

1. But of the times and the seasons, brethren, ye have no need that I write unto you.
2 For yourselves know perfectly that the day of the Lord so cometh as a thief in the night.
3 For when they shall say, Peace and safety; then sudden destruction cometh upon them, as travail upon a woman with child; and they shall not escape.
4 But ye, brethren, are not in darkness, that

Literal Translation

the Day should overtake you as a thief.
5 You are all sons of light and sons of day; we are not of night, nor of darkness.
6 So then, let us not sleep, as the rest also (do), but let us watch and be sober.
7 For the (ones) sleeping sleep by night, and the (ones) having been drunk are drunk by night.
8 But we being of day, let us be sober, having put on (the) breastplate of faith and love, and (the) hope of salvation (as) a helmet;
9 because God has not appointed us to wrath, but to obtainment of salvation through our Lord Jesus Christ,
10 the (One) having died on our behalf, so that whether we watch or we sleep, we may live together with Him.
11 Therefore, encourage one another, and build up one another, as you also do.
12 But, brothers, we entreat you to know the (ones) laboring among you, and taking the lead of you in (the) Lord, and warning you,
13 even esteem them most exceedingly in love because of their work. Be at peace among yourselves.
14 And we exhort you, brothers, to warn the disorderly, comfort the (ones) (that are) fainthearted, cleave to the weak, be long-suffering towards all.
15 See (that) not anyone returns evil for evil to anyone, but always pursue the good, both towards one another and towards all.
16 Rejoice always!
17 Pray without ceasing.
18 In everything

1 Thessalonians 5:5

3588 2250 5209 5613 2812 2638 3956 5210 5207 5457
ἡ ἡμέρα ὑμᾶς ὡς κλέπτης καταλάβῃ· 5 πάντες ὑμεῖς υἱοὶ φωτός
the day you as a thief should overtake; all you sons of light

2075 2532 5207 2250 3756 2070 3571 3761 4655 686
ἐστε καὶ υἱοὶ ἡμέρας· οὐκ ἐσμὲν νυκτὸς οὐδὲ σκότους· 6 ἄρα
are and sons of day; not we are of night nor of darkness; So

3767 3361 2518 5613 2532 3588 3062 235 1127 2532
οὖν μὴ καθεύδωμεν ὡς καὶ οἱ λοιποί, ἀλλὰ γρηγορῶμεν καὶ
then not let us sleep as also the rest, but let us watch and

3525 3588 1063 2518 3571 2518 2532 3588
νήφωμεν. 7 οἱ γὰρ καθεύδοντες νυκτὸς καθεύδουσι· καὶ οἱ
be sober. the (ones) For sleeping by night sleep; and (the) ones

3182 3571 3184 2249 1161 2250 5607
μεθυσκόμενοι νυκτὸς μεθύουσιν· 8 ἡμεῖς δέ, ἡμέρας ὄντες,
being drunk by night are drunk; we but, of day being,

3525 1746 2382 4102 2532 26 2532
νήφωμεν, ἐνδυσάμενοι θώρακα πίστεως καὶ ἀγάπης, καὶ
let us be sober, having put on a breastplate of faith and love, and

4030 1680 4991 3754 3756 5087 2248 3588 2316
περικεφαλαίαν, ἐλπίδα σωτηρίας. 9 ὅτι οὐκ ἔθετο ἡμᾶς ὁ Θεὸς
a helmet, hope of salvation. because not appointed us God

1519 3709 235 1519 4047 4991 1223 3588 2962 2257
εἰς ὀργὴν, ἀλλ' εἰς περιποίησιν σωτηρίας διὰ τοῦ Κυρίου ἡμῶν
to wrath, but to obtainment of salvation through the Lord of us

2424 5547 3588 599 5228 2257 2443 1535
Ἰησοῦ Χριστοῦ, 10 τοῦ ποθανόντος ὑπὲρ ἡμῶν, ἵνα, εἴτε
Jesus Christ, the (One) having died on behalf of us, that, whether

1127 1535 2518 260 4862 846 2198 1352
γρηγορῶμεν εἴτε καθεύδωμεν, ἅμα σὺν αὐτῷ ζήσωμεν. 11 διὸ
we watch or we sleep, together with Him we may live. So

3870 240 2532 3618 1520 3588 1520 2531
παρακαλεῖτε ἀλλήλους, καὶ οἰκοδομεῖτε εἷς τὸν ἕνα, καθὼς
encourage one another, and build up one the other, even as

2532 4160
καὶ ποιεῖτε.
also you do.

2065 1161 5209 80 1492 3588 2872 1722
12. Ἐρωτῶμεν δὲ ὑμᾶς, ἀδελφοί, εἰδέναι τοὺς κοπιῶντας ἐν
we entreat And you, brothers, to know the (ones) laboring among

5213 2532 4291 5216 1722 2962 2532 3560
ὑμῖν, καὶ προϊσταμένους ὑμῶν ἐν Κυρίῳ, καὶ νουθετοῦντας
you, and taking the lead of you in (the)Lord, and warning

5209 2532 2233 846 5228 1537 4057 1722 26 1223
ὑμᾶς, 13 καὶ ἡγεῖσθαι αὐτοὺς ὑπὲρ ἐκ περισσοῦ ἐν ἀγάπῃ διὰ
you, even to esteem them most exceedingly in love because of

3588 2041 846 1514 1722 1438 3870 1161
τὸ ἔργον αὐτῶν. εἰρηνεύετε ἐν ἑαυτοῖς. 14 παρακαλοῦμεν δὲ
the work of them. Be at peace among yourselves. we exhort And

5209 80 3560 3588 813 3888 3588
ὑμᾶς, ἀδελφοί, νουθετεῖτε τοὺς ἀτάκτους, παραμυθεῖσθε τοὺς
you, brothers, warn the disorderly, comfort the

3642 472 3588 772 3114 4314
ὀλιγοψύχους, ἀντέχεσθε τῶν ἀσθενῶν, μακροθυμεῖτε πρὸς
faint-hearted, cleave to the (ones) being weak, be long-suffering to

3956 3708 3361 5100 2556 473 2556 5100 591 235
πάντας. 15 ὁρᾶτε μή τις κακὸν ἀντὶ κακοῦ τινι ἀποδῷ· ἀλλὰ
all. See (that) not anyone evil for evil to anyone returns; but

3842 3588 18 1377 2532 1519 240 2532 1519 3956
πάντοτε τὸ ἀγαθὸν διώκετε καὶ εἰς ἀλλήλους καὶ εἰς πάντας.
always the good pursue even toward one another and toward all.

3842 5463 89 4336 1722 3956
16 Πάντοτε χαίρετε· 17 ἀδιαλείπτως προσεύχεσθε· 18 ἐν παντὶ
always Rejoice. without ceasing Pray. In everything

King James Version

that day should overtake you as a thief.
5 Ye are all the children of light, and the children of the day: we are not of the night, nor of darkness.
6 Therefore let us not sleep, as (do) others; but let us watch and be sober.
7 For they that sleep sleep in the night; and they that be drunken are drunken in the night.
8 But let us, who are of the day, be sober, putting on the breastplate of faith and love; and for an helmet, the hope of salvation.
9 For God hath not appointed us to wrath, but to obtain salvation by our Lord Jesus Christ,
10 Who died for us, that, whether we wake or sleep, we should live together with him.
11 Wherefore comfort yourselves together, and edify one another, even as also ye do.
12 And we beseech you, brethren, to know them which labour among you, and are over you in the Lord, and admonish you;
13 And to esteem them very highly in love for their work's sake. (And) be at peace among yourselves.
14 Now we exhort you, brethren, warn them that are unruly, comfort the feebleminded, support the weak, be patient toward all (men).
15 See that none render evil for evil unto any (man); but ever follow that which is good, both among yourselves, and to all (men).
16.Rejoice evermore.
17 Pray without ceasing.
18 In every thing

Literal Translation

give thanks, for this (is the) will of God in Christ Jesus toward you.
19 Do not quench the Spirit.
20 Do not despise prophecies.
21 Test all things, hold fast to the good.
22 Keep back from every appearance of evil.

23 And may the God of peace Himself fully sanctify you, and may your whole spirit and soul and body be kept blamelessly at the coming of our Lord Jesus Christ.

24 He who calls you (is) faithful, who also will perform (it).

25 Brothers, pray concerning us.

26 Greet all the brothers with a holy kiss.

27 I charge you by the Lord that this letter be read to all the holy brothers.

28 The grace of our Lord Jesus Christ (be) with you. Amen.

1 Thessalonians 5:19

2168 5124 1063 2307 2316 1722 5547 2424 1519
εὐχαριστεῖτε· τοῦτο γὰρ θέλημα Θεοῦ ἐν Χριστῷ Ἰησοῦ εἰς
give thanks; this for (is the) will of God in Christ Jesus to

5209 3588 4151 3361 4570 4394 3361 1848
ὑμᾶς. 19 τὸ Πνεῦμα μὴ σβέννυτε· 20 προφητείας μὴ ἐξουθενεῖτε·
you. The Spirit not do quench; prophecies not despise;

3956 1381 3588 2570 2722 575 3956 1491
21 πάντα δοκιμάζετε· τὸ καλὸν κατέχετε·22 ἀπὸ παντὸς εἴδους
all things test; the good hold fast; from every appearance

4190 567
πονηροῦ ἀπέχεσθε.
of evil keep back.

846 1161 3588 2316 3588 1515 37 5209 3651
23. Αὐτὸς δὲ ὁ Θεὸς τῆς εἰρήνης ἁγιάσαι ὑμᾶς ὁλοτελεῖς·
Himself And the God of peace may He sanctify you fully.

2532 3648 5216 3588 4151 2532 3588 5590 2532 3588 4983
καὶ ὁλόκληρον ὑμῶν τὸ πνεῦμα καὶ ἡ ψυχὴ καὶ τὸ σῶμα
And whole of you the spirit and the soul and the body

274 1722 3588 3952 3588 2962 2257 2424 5547
ἀμέμπτως ἐν τῇ παρουσίᾳ τοῦ Κυρίου ἡμῶν Ἰησοῦ Χριστοῦ
blamelessly at the coming of the Lord of us Jesus Christ

5083
τηρηθείη.
may be kept.

4103 3588 2564 5209 3739 2532 4160
24 πιστὸς ὁ καλῶν ὑμᾶς, ὃς καὶ ποιήσει.
Faithful (is) He calling you, who also will perform (it).

80 4336 4012 2257
25. Ἀδελφοί, προσεύχεσθε περὶ ἡμῶν.
Brothers, pray concerning us.

782 3588 80 3956 1722 5370 40
26. Ἀσπάσασθε τοὺς ἀδελφοὺς πάντας ἐν φιλήματι ἁγίῳ.
Greet the brothers all with a kiss holy.

3726 5209 3588 2962 314 3588 1992
27 ορκίζω ὑμᾶς τὸν Κύριον ἀναγνωσθῆναι τὴν ἐπιστολὴν
I charge you by the Lord to be read the epistle

3956 3588 40 80
πᾶσι τοῖς ἁγίοις ἀδελφοῖς.
to all the holy brothers.

3588 5485 3588 2962 2257 2424 5547 3326 5216
28. Ἡ χάρις τοῦ Κυρίου ἡμῶν Ἰησοῦ Χριστοῦ μεθ' ὑμῶν.
The grace of the Lord of us Jesus Christ (be) with you.

281
ἀμήν.
Amen.

King James Version

give thanks: for this is the will of God in Christ Jesus concerning you.
19 Quench not the Spirit.
20 Despise not prophesyings.
21 Prove all things; hold fast that which is good.
22 Abstain from all appearance of evil.

23 And the very God of peace sanctify you wholly; and (I pray God) your whole spirit and soul and body be preserved blameless unto the coming of our Lord Jesus Christ.

24 Faithful (is) he that calleth you, who also will do (it).

25 Brethren, pray for us.

26 Greet all the brethren with an holy kiss.

27 I charge you by the Lord that this epistle be read unto all the holy brethren.

28 The grace of our Lord Jesus Christ (be) with you. Amen. (The first (epistle) to the Thessalonians was written from Athens.)

Literal Translation

THE SECOND EPISTLE OF THE APOSTLE PAUL TO THE THESSALONIANS

2 Thessalonians 1

1. Paul and Silvanus and Timothy to the church of Thessalonians in God our Father and (the) Lord Jesus Christ:

2 Grace to you and peace from God our Father and (the) Lord Jesus Christ.

3 Brothers, we are bound to give thanks to God always concerning you, even as it is right, because your faith grows exceedingly, and the love of each one of you multiplies toward one another,

4 so as for us to boast ourselves in you among the churches of God for your patience and faith in all your persecutions, and the afflictions which you endure,

5 a clear token of the just judgment of God, for you to be counted worthy of the kingdom of God, for which you indeed suffer;

6 since (it is) a just thing with God to pay back affliction to the ones afflicting you,

7 and to (give) you, those being afflicted, rest with us at the revelation of the Lord Jesus from Heaven with angels of His power,

8 in flaming fire giving full vengeance to those not knowing God, and to those not obeying the gospel of our Lord Jesus Christ,

9 who will pay the penalty: everlasting destruction from the

ΠΑΥΛΟΥ ΤΟΥ ΑΠΟΣΤΟΛΟΥ Η ΗΡΟΣ ΘΕΣΣΑΛΟΝΙΚΕΙΣ ΕΠΙΣΤΟΛΗ ΔΕΥΤΕΡΑ

OF PAUL THE APOSTLE THE TO THESSALONIANS EPISTLE SECOND

2 Thessalonians 1

3972 2532 4610 2532 5095 3588 1577 2331
1. Παῦλος καὶ Σιλουανὸς καὶ Τιμόθεος τῇ ἐκκλησίᾳ Θεσσα-
Paul and Silvanus and Timothy to the church of Thes-
1722 2316 3962 2257 2532 2962 2424 5547
λονικέων ἐν Θεῷ πατρὶ ἡμῶν καὶ Κυρίῳ Ἰησοῦ Χριστῷ·
salonians in God (the) Father of us and (the) Lord Jesus Christ:
5485 5213 2532 1515 575 2316 3962 2257 2532 2962
2 χάρις ὑμῖν καὶ εἰρήνη ἀπὸ Θεοῦ πατρὸς ἡμῶν καὶ Κυρίου
Grace to you and peace from God (the) Father of us and (the) Lord
2424 5547
Ἰησοῦ Χριστοῦ.
Jesus Christ.

2168 3784 3588 2316 3842 4012 5216
3. Εὐχαριστεῖν ὀφείλομεν τῷ Θεῷ πάντοτε περὶ ὑμῶν,
to give thanks We ought to God always concerning you,
80 2531 514 2076 3754 5232 3588 4102 5216
ἀδελφοί, καθὼς ἄξιόν ἐστιν, ὅτι ὑπεραυξάνει ἡ πίστις ὑμῶν,
brothers, even as right it is, because grows exceedingly the faith of you,
2532 4121 3588 26 1520 1538 3956 5216 1519 240
καὶ πλεονάζει ἡ ἀγάπη ἑνὸς ἑκάστου πάντων ὑμῶν εἰς ἀλλή-
and multiplies the love one of each all of you to one
5620 2248 846 1722 5213 2744 1722 3588
λους· 4 ὥστε ἡμᾶς αὐτοὺς ἐν ὑμῖν ἐγκαυχᾶσθαι ἐν ταῖς
another; so as us ourselves in you to boast among the
1577 3588 2316 5228 3588 5281 5216 2532 4102 1722
ἐκκλησίαις τοῦ Θεοῦ ὑπὲρ τῆς ὑπομονῆς ὑμῶν καὶ πίστεως ἐν
churches of God for the patience of you and faith in
3956 3588 1375 5216 2532 3588 2347 3739 430
πᾶσι τοῖς διωγμοῖς ὑμῶν καὶ ταῖς θλίψεσιν αἷς ἀνέχεσθε·
all the persecutions of you and the afflictions which you endure;

1730 3588 1342 2920 3588 2316 1519 3588 2661
5 ἔνδειγμα τῆς δικαίας κρίσεως τοῦ Θεοῦ, εἰς τὸ καταξιωθῆναι
a clear token of the just judgment of God, for to be counted worthy
5209 3588 932 3588 2316 5228 3739 2532 3958 1512
ὑμᾶς τῆς βασιλείας τοῦ Θεοῦ, ὑπὲρ ἧς καὶ πάσχετε· 6 εἴπερ
you of the kingdom of God, for which indeed you suffer; since
1342 3844 2316 467 3588 2346 5209 2347
δίκαιον παρὰ Θεῷ ἀνταποδοῦναι τοῖς θλίβουσιν ὑμᾶς θλίψιν,
a just thing with God to repay to the (ones) afflicting you affliction,
2532 5213 3588 2346 425 3326 2257 1722 3588 602
7 καὶ ὑμῖν τοῖς θλιβομένοις ἄνεσιν μεθ' ἡμῶν, ἐν τῇ ἀποκαλύψει
and to you those being afflicted rest with us, at the revelation
3588 2962 2424 575 3772 3326 32 1411 846
τοῦ Κυρίου Ἰησοῦ ἀπ' οὐρανοῦ μετ' ἀγγέλων δυνάμεως αὐτοῦ,
of the Lord Jesus from Heaven with angels of power of Him,
1722 4442 5395 1325 1557 3588 3361 1492 2316 2532
8 ἐν πυρὶ φλογός, διδόντος ἐκδίκησιν τοῖς μὴ εἰδόσι Θεόν, καὶ
in fire of flame, giving full vengeance to those not knowing God, and
3588 3361 5219 3588 2098 3588 2962 2257 2424
τοῖς μὴ ὑπακούουσι τῷ εὐαγγελίῳ τοῦ Κυρίου ἡμῶν Ἰησοῦ
to those not obeying the gospel of the Lord of us Jesus
5547 3748 1349 5099 3639 166 575 4383
Χριστοῦ· 9 οἵτινες δίκην τίσουσιν, ὄλεθρον αἰώνιον ἀπὸ προσ-
Christ; who (the) penalty will pay, destruction eternal from (the)

King James Version

THE SECOND EPISTLE OF THE APOSTLE PAUL TO THE THESSALONIANS

2 Thessalonians 1

1. Paul, and Silvanus, and Timotheus, unto the church of the Thessalonians in God our Father and the Lord Jesus Christ:

2 Grace unto you, and peace, from God our Father and the Lord Jesus Christ.

3 We are bound to thank God always for you, brethren, as it is meet, because that your faith groweth exceedingly, and the charity of every one of you all toward each other aboundeth;

4 So that we ourselves glory in you in the churches of God for your patience and faith in all your persecutions and tribulations that ye endure:

5 (Which is) a manifest token of the righteous judgment of God, that ye may be counted worthy of the kingdom of God, for which ye also suffer:

6 Seeing (it is) a righteous thing with God to recompense tribulation to them that trouble you;

7 And to you who are troubled rest with us, when the Lord Jesus shall be revealed from heaven with his mighty angels,

8 In flaming fire taking vengeance on them that know not God, and that obey not the gospel of our Lord Jesus Christ:

9 Who shall be punished with everlasting destruction from the

Literal Translation

2 Thessalonians 1:10

face of the Lord, and from the glory of His strength,

10 when He comes to be glorified in His saints, and to be admired in all the (ones) believing in that Day, because our testimony to you was believed.

11 For which we also continually pray concerning you, that our God may deem you worthy of the calling, and may fulfill all the good pleasure of (His) goodness, and work of faith in power,

12 so that the name of our Lord Jesus Christ may be glorified in you, and you in Him, according to the grace of our God and of (the) Lord Jesus Christ.

3588 2962 2532 575 3588 1391 3588 2479 846
ώπου τοῦ Κυρίου καὶ ἀπὸ τῆς δόξης τῆς ἰσχύος αὐτοῦ,
face of the Lord and from the glory of the strength of Him,

3752 2064 1740 1722 3588 40 846 2532
10 ὅταν ἔλθῃ ἐνδοξασθῆναι ἐν τοῖς ἁγίοις αὐτοῦ, καὶ
when He comes to be glorified in the saints of Him, and

2296 1722 3956 3588 4100 3754 4100 3588
θαυμασθῆναι ἐν πᾶσι τοῖς πιστεύουσιν [ὅτι ἐπιστεύθη τὸ
to be admired in all the (ones) believing, because was believed the

3142 2257 1909 5209 1722 3588 2250 1565 1519 3739 2532
μαρτύριον ἡμῶν ἐφ᾽ ὑμᾶς] ἐν τῇ ἡμέρᾳ ἐκείνῃ. 11 εἰς ὃ καὶ
testimony of us to you, in day that. For which also

4336 3842 4012 5216 2443 5209 515 3588 2821
προσευχόμεθ πάντοτε περὶ ὑμῶν, ἵνα ὑμᾶς ἀξιώσῃ τῆς κλήσεως
we pray always concerning you, that you may deem worthy of the calling

3588 2316 2257 2532 4137 3956 2107 19 2532
ὁ Θεὸς ἡμῶν, καὶ πληρώσῃ πᾶσαν εὐδοκίαν ἀγαθωσύνης καὶ
the God of us, and may fulfill every pleasure of goodness and

2041 4102 1722 1411 3704 1740 3588 3686 3588
ἔργον πίστεως ἐν δυνάμει· 12 ὅπως ἐνδοξασθῇ τὸ ὄνομα τοῦ
work of faith in power; so as may be glorified the name of the

2962 2257 2424 5547 1722 5213 2532 5210 1722 846
Κυρίου ἡμῶν Ἰησοῦ Χριστοῦ ἐν ὑμῖν, καὶ ὑμεῖς ἐν αὐτῷ,
Lord of us Jesus Christ in you, and you in Him,

2596 3588 5485 3588 2316 2257 2532 2962 2424 5547
κατὰ τὴν χάριν τοῦ Θεοῦ ἡμῶν καὶ Κυρίου Ἰησοῦ Χριστοῦ.
according to the grace of the God of us and (the) Lord Jesus Christ.

King James Version

presence of the Lord, and from the glory of his power;

10 When he shall come to be glorified in his saints, and to be admired in all them that believe, because our testimony among you was believed in that day.

11 Wherefore also we pray always for you, that our God would count you worthy of (this) calling, and fulfil all the good pleasure of (his) goodness, and the work of faith with power:

12 That the name of our Lord Jesus Christ may be glorified in you, and ye in him, according to the grace of our God and the Lord Jesus Christ.

2 Thessalonians 2

1. And, brothers, we entreat you, by the coming of our Lord Jesus Christ, and of our gathering together to Him,

2 for you not to be quickly shaken (in) the mind, nor to be disturbed, neither through a spirit, nor through speech, nor through letter, as through us, as (if) the Day of Christ has come.

3 Do not let anyone deceive you (in any) way, because that Day will not come if not first comes the falling away, and the man of sin is revealed, the son of perdition,

4 the (one) opposing and exalting himself over everything being called God, or object of worship, so as for him to sit in the temple of God as God, setting forth that he himself is God.

5 Do you not remember that I told

2065 1161 5209 80 5228 3588 3952 3588
1. Ἐρωτῶμεν δὲ ὑμᾶς, ἀδελφοί, ὑπὲρ τῆς παρουσίας τοῦ
we entreat And you, brothers, by the coming of the

2962 2257 2424 5547 2532 2257 1997 1909
Κυρίου ἡμῶν Ἰησοῦ Χριστοῦ, καὶ ἡμῶν ἐπισυναγωγῆς ἐπ᾽
Lord of us Jesus Christ, and of us gathering together to

846 1519 3588 3361 5030 4531 5209 575 3588 3563
αὐτόν, 2 εἰς τὸ μὴ ταχέως σαλευθῆναι ὑμᾶς ἀπὸ τοῦ νοός,
Him, for not quickly to be shaken you from the mind,

3383 2360 3383 1223 4151 3383 1223 1223 3056 3383
μήτε θροεῖσθαι, μήτε διὰ πνεύματος, μήτε διὰ λόγου, μήτε δι᾽
nor to be disturbed, neither through a spirit, nor through speech, nor through

1992 5613 1223 2257 5613 3754 1764 3588 2250 3588 5547
ἐπιστολῆς ὡς δι᾽ ἡμῶν, ὡς ὅτι ἐνέστηκεν ἡ ἡμέρα τοῦ Χριστοῦ·
epistle, as through us, as that is come the day of the Christ;

3361 5100 5209 1818 2596 3367 5158 3754 1437 3361 2064
3 μή τις ὑμᾶς ἐξαπατήσῃ κατὰ μηδένα τρόπον· ὅτι ἐὰν μὴ ἔλθῃ
Let not anyone you deceive, by no way; because if not comes

3588 646 4412 2532 601 3588 444 3588
ἡ ἀποστασία πρῶτον, καὶ ἀποκαλυφθῇ ὁ ἄνθρωπος τῆς
the falling away first, and is revealed the man

266 3588 5207 3588 684 3588 480 2532
ἁμαρτίας, ὁ υἱὸς τῆς ἀπωλείας, 4 ὁ ἀντικείμενος καὶ
of sin, the son of perdition, the (one) opposing even

5229 1909 3956 3004 2316 2228 4574 5620
ὑπεραιρόμενος ἐπὶ πᾶν λεγόμενον Θεὸν ἢ σέβασμα, ὥστε
exalting himself over everything being called God or object of worship, so as

846 1519 3588 3485 3588 2316 5613 2316 2523 584
αὐτὸν εἰς τὸν ναὸν τοῦ Θεοῦ ὡς Θεὸν καθίσαι, ἀποδεικνύντα
him in the temple of God as God to sit, setting forth

1438 3754 2076 2316 3756 3421 3754 2089 5607 4314
ἑαυτὸν ὅτι ἔστι Θεός. 5 οὐ μνημονεύετε ὅτι ἔτι ὢν πρὸς
himself that he is God. Do not you remember that yet being with

2 Thessalonians 2

1. Now we beseech you, brethren, by the coming of our Lord Jesus Christ, and (by) our gathering together unto him,

2 That ye be not soon shaken in mind, or be troubled, neither by spirit, nor by word, nor by letter as from us, as that the day of Christ is at hand.

3 Let no man deceive you by any means: for (that day shall not come), except there come a falling away first, and that man of sin be revealed, the son of perdition;

4 Who opposeth and exalteth himself above all that is called God, or that is worshipped; so that he as God sitteth in the temple of God, shewing himself that he is God.

5 Remember ye not, that, when I was yet with

2 Thessalonians 2:6

Literal Translation

you these things, I yet being with you?
6 And now you know the thing holding back, for him to be revealed in his time.
7 For the mystery of lawlessness already is working, only he (is) holding back now, until it comes out of (the) midst.
8 And then the Lawless One will be revealed, whom the Lord will consume by the spirit of His mouth, and (He will) bring to nought by the brightness of His coming;
9 whose is the coming according to the working of Satan in all power and signs and wonders of a lie,
10 and in all deceit of unrighteousness in the (ones) being lost, because they did not receive the love of the truth for them to be saved.
11 And because of this, God will send to them a working of error, for them to believe the lie,
12 that all may be judged, those not having believed the truth, but having had delight in unrighteousness.
13 But we ought to thank God always concerning you, brothers, having been loved by (the) Lord, because God chose you from (the) beginning to salvation in sanctification of (the) Spirit and belief of (the) truth,
14 to which He called you through our gospel, to obtainment of (the) glory of our Lord Jesus Christ.
15 So, then, brothers, stand firm and hold fast the traditions you were taught, whether by word or by our epistle.
16 And may our Lord Himself, Jesus Christ, and our God and

5209 5023 3004 5213 2532 3568 3588 2722 1492 1519
ὑμᾶς ταῦτα ἔλεγον ὑμῖν; 6 καὶ νῦν τὸ κατέχον οἴδατε, εἰς
you, these things I told you? And now the thing holding back you know, for

3588 601 846 1722 3588 1438 2540 3588 1063
τὸ ἀποκαλυφθῆναι αὐτὸν ἐν τῷ ἑαυτοῦ καιρῷ. 7 τὸ γὰρ
the to be revealed him in the of him time. the For

3466 2235 1754 3588 458 3440 3588 2722 737
μυστήριον ἤδη ἐνεργεῖται τῆς ἀνομίας· μόνον ὁ κατέχων ἄρτι,
mystery already works of lawlessness, only he holding back now,

2193 1537 3319 1096 2532 5119 601 3588
ἕως ἐκ μέσου γένηται. 8 καὶ τότε ἀποκαλυφθήσεται ὁ
until out of (the) midst it comes. And then will be revealed the

459 3739 3588 2962 355 3588 4151 3588 4750 846
ἄνομος, ὃν ὁ Κύριος ἀνελώσει τῷ πνεύματι τοῦ στόματος αὐτοῦ,
lawless one, whom the Lord will consume by the spirit of the mouth of Him,

2532 2673 3588 2015 3588 3952 846 3739
καὶ καταργήσει τῇ ἐπιφανείᾳ τῆς παρουσίας αὐτοῦ· 9 οὗ
and bring to nothing by the brightness of the coming of Him; of whom

2076 3588 3952 2596 1753 3588 4567 1722 3956 1411
ἐστιν ἡ παρουσία κατ᾽ ἐνέργειαν τοῦ Σατανᾶ ἐν πάσῃ δυνάμει
is the coming according to the working of Satan in all power

2532 4592 2532 5059 5579 2532 1722 3956 539 3588
καὶ σημείοις καὶ τέρασι ψεύδους, 10 καὶ ἐν πάσῃ ἀπάτῃ τῆς
and signs and wonders of a lie, and with all deceit of

93 1722 3588 622 473 3739 3588 26 3588
ἀδικίας ἐν τοῖς ἀπολλυμένοις, ἀνθ᾽ ὧν τὴν ἀγάπην τῆς
unrighteousness in those being lost, because that the love of the

225 3756 1209 1519 3588 4982 846 2532 1223 5124
ἀληθείας οὐκ ἐδέξαντο εἰς τὸ σωθῆναι αὐτούς. 11 καὶ διὰ τοῦτο
truth not they received for to be saved them. And because of

3992 846 3588 2316 1753 4106 1519 3588 4100
πέμψει αὐτοῖς ὁ Θεὸς ἐνέργειαν πλάνης, εἰς τὸ πιστεῦσαι
this will send to them God a working of error, for to believe

846 3588 5579 2443 2919 3956 3588 3361 4100
αὐτοὺς τῷ ψεύδει· 12 ἵνα κριθῶσι πάντες οἱ μὴ πιστεύσαντες
them the lie; that may be judged all those not having believed

3588 225 235 2106 3588 93
τῇ ἀληθείᾳ, ἀλλ᾽ εὐδοκήσαντες τῇ ἀδικίᾳ.
the truth, but having had delight in unrighteousness.

2249 1161 3784 2168 3588 2316 3842 4012
13. Ἡμεῖς δὲ ὀφείλομεν εὐχαριστεῖν τῷ Θεῷ πάντοτε περὶ
we But ought to thank God always about

5216 80 25 5259 2962 3754 138 5209
ὑμῶν, ἀδελφοὶ ἠγαπημένοι ὑπὸ Κυρίου, ὅτι εἵλετο ὑμᾶς
you, brothers, having been loved by (the) Lord, because chose you

3588 2316 575 746 1519 4991 1722 38 4151 2532
ὁ Θεὸς ἀπ᾽ ἀρχῆς εἰς σωτηρίαν ἐν ἁγιασμῷ Πνεύματος καὶ
God from (the) beginning to salvation in sanctification of (the) Spirit and

4102 225 1519 3739 2564 5209 1223 3588 2098
πίστει ἀληθείας· 14 εἰς ὃ ἐκάλεσεν ὑμᾶς διὰ τοῦ εὐαγγελίου
belief of (the) truth; to which He called you through the gospel

2257 1519 4047 1391 3588 2962 2257 2424
ἡμῶν, εἰς περιποίησιν δόξης τοῦ Κυρίου ἡμῶν Ἰησοῦ
of us, to obtainment of (the) glory of the Lord of us Jesus

5547 686 3767 80 4739 2532 2902 3588 3862
Χριστοῦ. 15 ἄρα οὖν, ἀδελφοί, στήκετε, καὶ κρατεῖτε τὰς παρα-
Christ. So then, brothers, stand firm, and hold fast the tra-

3739 1321 1535 1223 3056 1535 1223 1992 2257
δόσεις ἃς ἐδιδάχθητε εἴτε διὰ λόγου εἴτε δι᾽ ἐπιστολῆς ἡμῶν.
ditions which you were taught either by word or through an epistle of us.

846 1161 3588 2962 2257 2424 5547 2532 3588 2316 2532
16 Αὐτὸς δὲ ὁ Κύριος ἡμῶν Ἰησοῦς Χριστὸς, καὶ ὁ Θεὸς καὶ
Himself And the Lord of us, Jesus Christ and the God and

King James Version

you, I told you these things?
6 And now ye know what withholdeth that he might be revealed in his time.
7 For the mystery of iniquity doth already work: only he who now letteth (will let), until he be taken out of the way.
8 And then shall that Wicked be revealed, whom the Lord shall consume with the spirit of his mouth, and shall destroy with the brightness of his coming:
9 (Even him), whose coming is after the working of Satan with all power and signs and lying wonders,
10 And with all deceivableness of unrighteousness in them that perish; because they received not the love of the truth, that they might be saved.
11 And for this cause God shall send them strong delusion, that they should believe a lie:
12 That they all might be damned who believed not the truth, but had pleasure in unrighteousness.
13 But we are bound to give thanks alway to God for you, brethren beloved of the Lord, because God hath from the beginning chosen you to salvation through sanctification of the Spirit and belief of the truth:
14 Whereunto he called you by our gospel, to the obtaining of the glory of our Lord Jesus Christ.
15 Therefore, brethren, stand fast, and hold the traditions which ye have been taught, whether by word, or our epistle.
16 Now our Lord Jesus Christ himself, and God, even our

Literal Translation

2 Thessalonians 2:17

King James Version

Father, the (One) loving and gives us everlasting comfort and a good hope by grace,
17 Comfort your hearts, and may He establish you in every good word and work.

3962 2257 3588 25 2248 2532 1325 3874 166
πατὴρ ἡμῶν, ὁ ἀγαπήσας ἡμᾶς καὶ δοὺς παράκλησιν αἰωνίαν
Father of us the (One) having loved us and having given comfort everlasting

2532 1680 18 1722 5485 3870 5216 3588
καὶ ἐλπίδα ἀγαθὴν ἐν χάριτι, 17 παρακαλέσαι ὑμῶν τὰς
and hope a good by grace, may He comfort of you the

2588 2532 4741 5209 1722 3956 3056 2532 2041 18
καρδίας καὶ στηρίξαι ὑμᾶς ἐν παντι λόγῳ καὶ ἔργῳ ἀγαθῷ.
hearts and establish you in ever y word and work good.

Father, which hath loved us, and hath given (us) everlasting consolation and good hope through grace,
17 Comfort your hearts, and stablish you in every good word and work.

2 Thessalonians 3

1. For the rest, brothers, pray concerning us, that the Word of the Lord may run and be glorified, even as also (it has) with you,
2 and that we may be delivered from perverse and evil men. For all do not have the faith.

3 But the Lord is faithful who will establish and will guard (you) from the evil.
4 But we are persuaded in (the) Lord as to you, that whatever things we have enjoined you, you both do and you will do.

5 And the Lord direct your hearts into the love of God and into the patience of Christ.

3588 3063 4336 80 4012 2257 2443 3588 3056
1. Τὸ λοιπὸν προσεύχεσθε, ἀδελφοί, περὶ ἡμῶν, ἵνα ὁ λόγος
For the rest, pray, brothers, concerning us, that the word

3588 2962 5143 2532 1392 2531 2532 4314 5209 2532
τοῦ Κυρίου τρέχῃ καὶ δοξάζηται, καθὼς καὶ πρὸς ὑμᾶς, 2 καὶ
of the Lord may run and be glorified, as also with you, and

2443 4506 575 3588 824 2532 4190 444
ἵνα ῥυσθῶμεν ἀπὸ τῶν ἀτόπων καὶ πονηρῶν ἀνθρώπων·
that we be delivered from perverse and evil men;

3756 1063 3956 3588 4102 4103 1161 2076 3588 2962 3739
οὐ γὰρ πάντων ἡ πίστις. 3 πιστὸς δέ ἐστιν ὁ Κύριος, ὃς
is not for of all the faith. faithful But is the Lord, who

4741 5209 2532 5442 575 3588 4190 3982
στηρίξει ὑμᾶς καὶ φυλάξει ἀπὸ τοῦ πονηροῦ. 4 πεποίθαμεν
will establish you and will guard from the evil. we are persuaded

1161 1722 2962 1909 5209 3754 3739 3853 5213 2532
δὲ ἐν Κυρίῳ ἐφ᾽ ὑμᾶς, ὅτι ἃ παραγγέλλομεν ὑμῖν καὶ
But in (the) Lord as to you, that what things we enjoin you both

4160 2532 4160 3588 1161 2962 2720 5216 3588
ποιεῖτε καὶ ποιήσετε. 5 ὁ δὲ Κύριος κατευθύναι ὑμῶν τὰς
you do and will do. the And Lord direct of you the

2588 1519 3588 26 3588 2316 2532 1519 3588 5281 3588
καρδίας εἰς τὴν ἀγάπην τοῦ Θεοῦ, καὶ εἰς τὴν ὑπομονὴν τοῦ
hearts into the love of God, and into the patience

5547
Χριστοῦ.
of Christ.

1. Finally, brethren, pray for us, that the word of the Lord may have (free) course, and be glorified, even as (it is) with you:
2 And that we may be delivered from unreasonable and wicked men: for all (men) have not faith.
3 But the Lord is faithful, who shall stablish you, and keep (you) from evil.
4 And we have confidence in the Lord touching you, that ye both do and will do the things which we command you.
5 And the Lord direct your hearts into the love of God, and into the patient waiting for Christ.

6 And we enjoin you, brothers, in the name of our Lord Jesus Christ, to draw yourselves back from every brother walking disorderly, and not according to the tradition which you received from us.

7 For you yourselves know how it is right to imitate us, because we were not disorderly among you;
8 nor did we eat bread freely from anyone, but by labor and toil, working night and day in order not to burden anyone of you.
9 Not that we do not have authority, but that we give ourselves (as) an example

3853 1161 5213 80 1722 3686 3588 2962
6. Παραγγέλλομεν δὲ ὑμῖν, ἀδελφοί, ἐν ὀνόματι τοῦ Κυρίου
we enjoin And you, brothers, in the name of the Lord

2257 2424 5547 4724 5209 575 3956 80
ἡμῶν Ἰησοῦ Χριστοῦ, στέλλεσθαι ὑμᾶς ἀπὸ παντὸς ἀδελφοῦ
of us, Jesus Christ, to draw back you from every brother

814 4043 2532 3361 2596 3588 3862 3739
ἀτάκτως περιπατοῦντος, καὶ μὴ κατὰ τὴν παράδοσιν ἣν
insubordinately walking, and not according to the tradition which

3880 3844 2257 846 1063 1492 4459 1163 3401
παρέλαβε παρ᾽ ἡμῶν. 7 αὐτοὶ γὰρ οἴδατε πῶς δεῖ μιμεῖσθαι
you received from us. yourselves For you know how it is right to imitate

2248 3754 3756 812 1722 5213 3761 1432 740
ἡμᾶς, ὅτι οὐκ ἠτακτήσαμεν ἐν ὑμῖν, 8 οὐδὲ δωρεὰν ἄρτον
us, because not we were disorderly among you, nor freely bread

5315 3844 5100 235 1722 2873 2532 3449 3571 2532
ἐφάγομεν παρά τινος, ἀλλ᾽ ἐν κόπῳ καὶ μόχθῳ, νύκτα καὶ
ate from anyone, but by labor and toil, night and

2250 2038 4314 3588 3361 1912 5100 5216
ἡμέραν ἐργαζόμενοι, πρὸς τὸ μὴ ἐπιβαρῆσαί τινα ὑμῶν·
day working to not to burden anyone of you;

3756 3754 3756 2192 1849 235 2443 1438 5179 1325
9 οὐχ ὅτι οὐκ ἔχομεν ἐξουσίαν, ἀλλ᾽ ἵνα ἑαυτοὺς τύπον δῶμεν
not that not we have authority, but that ourselves an example we give

6 Now we command you, brethren, in the name of our Lord Jesus Christ, that ye withdraw yourselves from every brother that walketh disorderly, and not after the tradition which he received of us.

7 For yourselves know how ye ought to follow us: for we behaved not ourselves disorderly among you;
8 Neither did we eat any man's bread for nought; but wrought with labour and travail night and day, that we might not be chargeable to any of you:
9 Not because we have not power, but to make ourselves an ensample

2 Thessalonians 3:10

Literal Translation

to you, for you to imitate us.
10 For even when we were with you, we enjoined this to you: If anyone does not desire to work, neither let him eat.
11 For we hear some are walking in a disorderly way among you, not working at all, but being busybodies.
12 And we command such and exhort through our Lord Jesus Christ that working with quietness, they may eat their own bread.

13 And you, brothers, do not lose heart in well doing.

14 But if anyone does not obey our word through the epistle, mark that one, and do not associate with him, that he be shamed.

15 But do not count (him) an enemy, but warn him as a brother.

16 And may the Lord of peace Himself through all give peace to you in every way. The Lord (be) with all of you.

17 The greeting of Paul by my hand which is (the) sign in every epistle; so I write.
18 The grace of our Lord Jesus Christ (be) with you all. Amen.

5213 1519 3588 3401 2248 2532 1063 3753 2258 4314 5209
ὑμῖν εἰς τὸ μιμεῖσθαι ἡμᾶς. 10 καὶ γὰρ ὅτε ἦμεν πρὸς ὑμᾶς,
to you for to imitate us. even For when we were with you,

5124 3853 5213/3754/1487/5100/3756/2309 2309 3366
τοῦτο παρηγγέλλομεν ὑμῖν ὅτι Εἴ τις οὐ θέλει ἐργάζεσθαι, μηδὲ
this we enjoined you, If anyone not desires to work, not

2068 191 1063 5100 4043 1722 5213
ἐσθιέτω. 11 ἀκούομεν γάρ τινας περιπατοῦντας ἐν ὑμῖν
let him eat. we hear (of) For some walking among you

814 3367 2038 235 4020 3588
ἀτάκτως, μηδὲν ἐργαζομένους, ἀλλὰ περιεργαζομένους. 12 τοῖς
disorderly, nothing working, but working all about.

1161 5108 3853 2532 3870 1223 3588
δὲ τοιούτοις παραγγέλλομεν καὶ παρακαλοῦμεν διὰ τοῦ
And such we enjoin and exhort through the

2962 2257 2424 5547 2443 3326 2271 2038
Κυρίω ἡμῶν, Ἰησοῦ Χριστοῦ, ἵνα μετὰ ἡσυχίας ἐργαζόμενοι
Lord of us, Jesus Christ, that with quietness working

3588 1438 740 2068 5210 1161 80 3361
τὸν ἑαυτῶν ἄρτον ἐσθίωσιν. 13 ὑμεῖς δέ, ἀδελφοί, μὴ
the of themselves bread they may eat. you And, brothers, not

1573 2569 1487 1161 5100 3756 5219 3588 3056
ἐγκακήσητε καλοποιοῦντες. 14 εἰ δέ τις οὐχ ὑπακούει τῷ λόγῳ
do lose heart (in) well doing. if And any not obeys the word

2257 1223 3588 1992 5126 4593 2532 3361
ἡμῶν διὰ τῆς ἐπιστολῆς, τοῦτον σημειοῦσθε, καὶ μὴ
of us through the epistle, this one mark, and not

4874 846 2443 1788 2532 3361 5613 2190
συναναμίγνυσθε αὐτῷ, ἵνα ἐντραπῇ· 15 καὶ μὴ ὡς ἐχθρὸν
do associate with him, that he be shamed; and not as an enemy

2233 235 3560 5613 80
ἡγεῖσθε, ἀλλὰ νουθετεῖτε ὡς ἀδελφόν.
count (him), but warn as a brother.

846 1161 3588 2962 3588 1515 1325 5213 3588 1515
16. Αὐτὸς δὲ ὁ Κύριος τῆς εἰρήνης δῴη ὑμῖν τὴν εἰρήνην
Himself And the Lord of peace give to you the peace

1223 3956 1722 3956 5158 3588 2962 3326 3956 5216
διὰ παντὸς ἐν παντὶ τρόπῳ. ὁ Κύριος μετὰ πάντων ὑμῶν.
through all in every way. The Lord (be) with all you.

3588 783 3588 1699 5495 3972 3739 2076 4592 1722
17. Ὁ ἀσπασμὸς τῇ ἐμῇ χειρὶ Παύλου, ὅ ἐστιν σημεῖον ἐν
The greeting by my hand of Paul, which is a sign in

3956 1992 3779 1125 3588 5485 3588 2962 2257
πάσῃ ἐπιστολῇ· οὕτω γράφω. 18 ἡ χάρις τοῦ Κυρίου ἡμῶν
every epistle; so I write. The grace of the Lord of us.

2424 5547 3326 3956 5216 281
Ἰησοῦ Χριστοῦ μετὰ πάντων ὑμῶν. ἀμήν.
Jesus Christ (be) with all you. Amen.

King James Version

unto you to follow us.
10 For even when we were with you, this we commanded you, that if any would not work, neither should he eat.

11 For we hear that there are some which walk among you disorderly, working not at all, but are busybodies.
12 Now them that are such we command and exhort by our Lord Jesus Christ, that with quietness they work, and eat their own bread.

13 But ye, brethren, be not weary in well doing.

14 And if any man obey not our word by this epistle, note that man, and have no company with him, that he may be ashamed.

15 Yet count (him) not as an enemy, but admonish (him) as a brother.

16 Now the Lord of peace himself give you peace always by all means. The Lord (be) with you all.

17 The salutation of Paul with mine own hand, which is the token in every epistle: so I write.
18 The grace of our Lord Jesus Christ (be) with you all. Amen.
(The second (epistle)) to the Thessalonians was written from Athens.)

Literal Translation

THE FIRST EPISTLE OF PAUL TO TIMOTHY

1 Timothy 1

1. Paul an apostle of Jesus Christ according to a command of God our Savior, even (the) Lord Jesus Christ, (our) Hope,

2 to Timothy, a true child in (the) faith: Grace, mercy, peace from God our Father and our Lord Jesus Christ.

3 Even as I called on you to remain (in) Ephesus, I going to Macedonia, that you might charge some not to teach other doctrines,

4 nor to give heed to fables and to endless genealogies, which occasion doubts, rather than the nurture of God in faith.

5 But the end of the commandment is love out of a pure heart and a good conscience, and faith not pretended,

6 from which having missed the mark, some turned aside to empty talking,
7 wishing to be teachers of law, neither understanding what they say, nor about that which they confidently affirm.
8 And we know that the Law (is) good, if anyone uses it lawfully,
9 knowing this, that law (is) not laid down for a righteous one, but for lawless and undisciplined ones, for ungodly and sinful ones, for unholy and profane ones, for slayers of fathers and slayers of mothers, for murderers,
10 for fornicators, for homosexuals, for slave-traders, for liars, for perjurers, and if any

ΠΑΥΛΟΥ ΤΟΥ ΑΠΟΣΤΟΛΟΥ Η ΗΡΟΣ
OF PAUL THE APOSTLE THE TO

ΤΙΜΟΘΕΟΝ ΕΠΙΣΤΟΛΗ ΠΡΩΤΗ
TIMOTHY EPISTLE FIRST

1 Timothy 1

3972 652 2424 5547 2596 2003 2316
1. Παῦλος ἀπόστολος Ἰησοῦ Χριστοῦ κατ' ἐπιταγὴν Θεοῦ
Paul an apostle of Jesus Christ according to a command of God

4990 2257 2532 2962 2424 5547 3588 1680
σωτῆρος ἡμῶν, καὶ Κυρίου Ἰησοῦ Χριστοῦ τῆς ἐλπίδος
the Savior of us, even (the) Lord Jesus Christ the hope

2257 5095 1103 5043 1722 4102 5485 1656 1515
ἡμῶν, 2 Τιμοθέῳ γνησίῳ τέκνῳ ἐν πίστει· χάρις, ἔλεος, εἰρήνη
of us, to Timothy a true child in (the) faith; Grace, mercy, peace

575 2316 3962 2257 2532 2424 5547 3588 2962
ἀπὸ Θεοῦ πατρὸς ἡμῶν καὶ Ἰησοῦ Χριστοῦ τοῦ Κυρίου
from God (the) Father of us and Jesus Christ the Lord

2257
ἡμῶν.
of us.

2531 3870 4571 4357 1722 2181 4198
3. Καθὼς παρεκάλεσά σε προσμεῖναι ἐν Ἐφέσῳ, πορευό-
As I besought you to remain in Ephesus, (I) going

1519 3109 2443 3853 5100 3361 2085
μενος εἰς Μακεδονίαν, ἵνα παραγγείλῃς τισὶ μὴ ἑτεροδιδα-
into Macedonia, that you might enjoin some not to teach

3366 4337 3454 2532 1076 562
σκαλεῖν, 4 μηδὲ προσέχειν μύθοις καὶ γενεαλογίαις ἀπεράντοις,
other doctrines, nor to attend to tales and to genealogies endless,

3748 2214 3930 3123 2228 3622 2316 3588
αἵτινες ζητήσεις παρέχουσι μᾶλλον ἢ οἰκοδομίαν Θεοῦ τὴν
which doubts provide rather than a stewardship of God

1722 4102 3588 1161 5056 3588 3852 2076 26 1537
ἐν πίστει. 5 τὸ δὲ τέλος τῆς παραγγελίας ἐστὶν ἀγάπη ἐκ
in faith. the But end of the commandment is love out of

2513 2588 2532 4893 18 2532 4102
καθαρᾶς καρδίας καὶ συνειδήσεως ἀγαθῆς καὶ πίστεως
a pure heart and a conscience good and faith

505 3739 5100 795 1624 1519
ἀνυποκρίτου· 6 ὧν τινες ἀστοχήσαντες ἐξετράπησαν εἰς
unpretended; which some missing the mark turned aside to

3150 2309 1511 3547 3361 3539
ματαιολογίαν, 7 θέλοντες εἶναι νομοδιδάσκαλοι, μὴ νοοῦντες
empty talking, wishing to be teachers of law, not understanding

3383 3739 3004 3383 4012 5101 1226 1492
μήτε ἃ λέγουσι, μήτε περὶ τίνων διαβεβαιοῦνται. 8 οἴδαμεν
either what they say, or about what things they strongly affirm. we know

1161 3754 2570 3588 3551 1437 5100 846 3545 5530 1492
δὲ ὅτι καλὸς ὁ νόμος, ἐάν τις αὐτῷ νομίμως χρῆται, 9 εἰδὼς
But that (is) good the law, if anyone it lawfully uses, knowing

5124 3754 1342 3551 3756 2749 459 1161 2532 506
τοῦτο, ὅτι δικαίῳ νόμος οὐ κεῖται, ἀνόμοις δὲ καὶ ἀνυπο-
this, that for a just one law not is laid down, for lawless but and insubordi-

765 2532 268 462 2532 952
τάκτοις, ἀσεβέσι καὶ ἁμαρτωλοῖς, ἀνοσίοις καὶ βεβήλοις,
nate, for ungodly and sinful ones, for unholy and profane ones,

3964 2532 3389 409 4205 733
πατρολῴαις καὶ μητραλῴαις, ἀνδροφόνοις, 10 πόρνοις, ἀρσενο-
for father-slayers and mother-slayers, for men-slayers, for fornicators, for homo-

405 5583 1965 2532 1487 5100
κοίταις, ἀνδραποδισταῖς, ψεύσταις, ἐπιόρκοις, καὶ εἴ τι
sexuals, for slave-traders, for liars, for perjurers, and if any

King James Version

THE FIRST EPISTLE OF PAUL TO TIMOTHY

1 Timothy 1

1. Paul, an apostle of Jesus Christ by the commandment of God our Saviour, and Lord Jesus Christ, (which is) our hope;

2 Unto Timothy, (my) own son in the faith: Grace, mercy, (and) peace, from God our Father and Jesus Christ our Lord.

3 As I besought thee to abide still at Ephesus, when I went into Macedonia, that thou mightest charge some that they teach no other doctrine,
4 Neither give heed to fables and endless genealogies, which minister questions, rather than godly edifying which is in faith: (so do).
5 Now the end of the commandment is charity out of a pure heart, and (of) a good conscience, and (of) faith unfeigned:
6 From which some having swerved have turned aside unto vain jangling;
7 Desiring to be teachers of the law; understanding neither what they say, nor whereof they affirm.
8 But we know that the law (is) good, if a man use it lawfully;
9 Knowing this, that the law is not made for a righteous man, but for the lawless and disobedient, for the ungodly and for sinners, for unholy and profane, for murderers of fathers and murderers of mothers, for manslayers,
10 For whoremongers, for them that defile themselves with mankind, for menstealers, for liars, for perjured persons, and if there be any

1 Timothy 1:11

Literal Translation

other thing opposes sound doctrine,
11 according to the gospel of the glory of the blessed God (with) which I was entrusted.

12 And I have thanks to Him empowering me, our Lord Jesus Christ, because He counted me faithful, putting (me) into the ministry,

13 the (one) who before was a blasphemer, and a persecutor, and insolent; but I received mercy, because being ignorant I did (it) in unbelief.
14 (But) the grace of our Lord abounded exceedingly with faith and love in Christ Jesus.
15 Faithful (is) the Word and worthy of all acceptance, that Christ Jesus came into the world to save sinners, of whom I am chief.
16 But for this reason I received mercy, that in me first Jesus Christ might show forth all long-suffering, for an example to those being about to believe on Him to everlasting life.

17 Now to the King eternal, incorruptible, invisible, (the) only wise God, (be) honor and glory forever and ever. Amen.

18 This charge I commit to you, (my) child Timothy, according to the prophecies going before (as to) you, that you might war the good warfare by them,
19 having faith and a good conscience, which some having thrust away, made shipwreck concerning the faith,
20 of whom are Hymenaeus and Alexander, whom

2087 3588 5198 1319 480 2596 3588
ἕτερον τῇ ὑγιαινούσῃ διδασκαλίᾳ ἀντίκειται, 11 κατὰ τὸ
other thing the sound teaching opposes, according to the

2098 3588 1391 3588 3107 2316 3739 4100
εὐαγγέλιον τῆς δόξης τοῦ μακαρίου Θεοῦ, ὃ ἐπιστεύθην
gospel of the glory of the blessed God, which was entrusted

1473
ἐγώ.
I.

2532 5485 2192 3588 1743 3165 5547 2424 3588
12. Καὶ χάριν ἔχω τῷ ἐνδυναμώσαντί με Χριστῷ Ἰησοῦ τῷ
And thanks I have to the (One) empowering me Christ Jesus the

2962 2257 3754 4103 3165 2233 5087 1519 1248
Κυρίῳ ἡμῶν, ὅτι πιστόν με ἡγήσατο, θέμενος εἰς διακονίαν,
Lord of us, because faithful me He counted, putting (me) into ministry,

3588 4386 5607 989 2532 1376 2532 5197
13 τὸ πρότερον ὄντα βλάσφημον καὶ διώκτην καὶ ὑβριστήν·
the (one) before being a blasphemer and a persecutor and insolent;

235 1653 3754 50 4160 1722 570 5250
ἀλλ᾽ ἠλεήθην, ὅτι ἀγνοῶν ἐποίησα ἐν ἀπιστίᾳ· 14 ὑπερ-
but I obtained mercy, because being ignorant I did (it) in unbelief; super-

1161 3588 5485 3588 2962 2257 3326 4102 2532
επλεόνασε δὲ ἡ χάρις τοῦ Κυρίου ἡμῶν μετὰ πίστεως καὶ
abounded but the grace of the Lord of us with faith and

26 3588 1722 5547 2424 4103 3588 3056 2532 3956
ἀγάπης τῆς ἐν Χριστῷ Ἰησοῦ. 15 πιστὸς ὁ λόγος καὶ πάσης
love in Christ Jesus. Faithful (is) the Word and of all

594 514 3754 5547 2424 2064 1519 3588 2889
ἀποδοχῆς ἄξιος, ὅτι Χριστὸς Ἰησοῦς ἦλθεν εἰς τὸν κόσμον
acceptance worthy, that Christ Jesus came into the world

268 4982 3739 4413 1510 1473 235 1223 5124
ἁμαρτωλοὺς σῶσαι, ὧν πρῶτός εἰμι ἐγώ· 16 ἀλλὰ διὰ τοῦτο
sinners to save, of whom chief am I; but because of this

1653 2443 1722 1698 4413 1731 2424 5547 3588
ἠλεήθην, ἵνα ἐν ἐμοὶ πρώτῳ ἐνδείξηται Ἰησοῦς Χριστὸς τὴν
I obtained mercy, that in me first might show forth Jesus Christ

3956 3115 4314 5296 3588 3195
πᾶσαν μακροθυμίαν, πρὸς ὑποτύπωσιν τῶν μελλόντων
all long-suffering, for a pattern to the (ones) being about

4100 1909 846 1519 2222 166 3588 1161 935 3588
πιστεύειν ἐπ᾽ αὐτῷ εἰς ζωὴν αἰώνιον. 17 τῷ δὲ βασιλεῖ τῶν
to believe on Him for life everlasting. to the But King of the

165 862 517 3441 4680 2316 5092 2532 1391
αἰώνων, ἀφθάρτῳ, ἀοράτῳ, μόνῳ σοφῷ Θεῷ, τιμὴ καὶ δόξα
ages, incorruptible, invisible, (the) only wise God, (be) honor and glory

1519 3588 165 3588 165 281
εἰς τοὺς αἰῶνας τῶν αἰώνων. ἀμήν.
to the ages of the ages. Amen.

3778 3588 3852 3908 4671 5043
18. Ταύτην τὴν παραγγελίαν παρατίθεμαί σοι, τέκνον
This charge I commit to you, child

5095 2596 3588 4254 1909 4571 4394 2443
Τιμόθεε, κατὰ τὰς προαγούσας ἐπὶ σὲ προφητείας, ἵνα
Timothy, according to the going before as to you prophecies, that

4754 1722 846 3588 2570 4752 2192 4102 2532
στρατεύῃ ἐν αὐταῖς τὴν καλὴν στρατείαν, 19 ἔχων πίστιν καὶ
you might war by them the good warfare, having faith and

18 4893 3739 5100 683 4012 3588 4102
ἀγαθὴν συνείδησιν, ἥν τινες ἀπωσάμενοι περὶ τὴν πίστιν
a good conscience, which some having thrust away concerning the faith

3489 3739 2076 5211 2532 223 3739
ἐναυάγησαν· 20 ὧν ἐστιν Ὑμέναιος καὶ Ἀλέξανδρος, οὓς
made shipwreck; of whom is Hymenaeus and Alexander, whom

King James Version

other thing that is contrary to sound doctrine;
11 According to the glorious gospel of the blessed God, which was committed to my trust.

12 And I thank Christ Jesus our Lord, who hath enabled me, for that he counted me faithful, putting me into the ministry;

13 Who was before a blasphemer, and a persecutor, and injurious: but I obtained mercy, because I did (it) ignorantly in unbelief.
14 And the grace of our Lord was exceeding abundant with faith and love which is in Christ Jesus.
15 This (is) a faithful saying, and worthy of all acceptation, that Christ Jesus came into the world to save sinners; of whom I am chief.
16 Howbeit for this cause I obtained mercy, that in me first Jesus Christ might shew forth all longsuffering, for a pattern to them which should hereafter believe on him to life everlasting.

17 Now unto the King eternal, immortal, invisible, the only wise God, (be) honour and glory for ever and ever. Amen.

18 This charge I commit unto thee, son Timothy, according to the prophecies which went before on thee, that thou by them mightest war a good warfare;
19 Holding faith, and a good conscience; which some having put away concerning faith have made shipwreck:
20 Of whom is Hymenaeus and Alexander; whom

Literal Translation

I delivered to Satan, that they may be taught not to blaspheme.

1 Timothy 2:1

3860 3588 4567 2443 3811 3361 987
παρέδωκα τῷ Σατανᾷ, ἵνα παιδευθῶσιν μὴ βλασφημεῖν.
I delivered to Satan, that they may be taught not to blaspheme.

King James Version

I have delivered unto Satan, that they may learn not to blaspheme.

1 Timothy 2

Literal Translation

1. First of all then, I exhort (that) petitions, prayers, intercessions, (and) thanksgivings be made on behalf of all men,
2 for kings and all the ones being in high position, that we may lead a tranquil and quiet existence in all godliness and dignity.
3 For this (is) good and acceptable before God our deliverer,
4 who desires all men to be delivered and to come to a full knowledge of truth.
5 For God (is) one, also (there is) one Mediator of God and of men, (the) Man Christ Jesus,
6 the (One) having given Himself a ransom on behalf of all, the testimony (to be given) in its own times,
7 to which I was appointed a herald and apostle (I speak the truth in Christ, I do not lie), a teacher of (the) nations, in faith and truth.
8 Therefore, I desire the men to pray in every place, lifting up holy hands without wrath and doubting.
9 So also the women to adorn themselves in proper clothing, with modesty and sensibleness, not with plaiting, or gold, or pearls, or expensive garments,
10 but what becomes women professing fear of God, through good works.
11 Let a woman learn in silence, in all subjection.
12 And I do not allow a woman

1 Timothy 2

3870 3767 4412 3956 4160 1162 4335
1. Παρακαλῶ οὖν πρῶτον πάντων ποιεῖσθαι δεήσεις, προσ-
I exhort Therefore firstly of all to be made petitions, prayers,
1783 2169 5228 3956 444
ευχάς, ἐντεύξεις, εὐχαριστίας, ὑπὲρ πάντων ἀνθρώπων·
intercessions, thanksgivings, on behalf of all men;
5228 935 2532 3956 3588 1722 5247 5607 2443
2 ὑπὲρ βασιλέων καὶ πάντων τῶν ἐν ὑπεροχῇ ὄντων, ἵνα
for kings and all the (ones) in high position being, that
2263 2532 2272 979 1236 1722 3956 2150 2532
ἤρεμον καὶ ἡσύχιον βίον διάγωμεν ἐν πάσῃ εὐσεβείᾳ καὶ
a tranquil and quiet existence we may lead in all godliness and
4587 5124 1063 2570 2532 587 1799 3588
σεμνότητι. 3 τοῦτο γὰρ καλὸν καὶ ἀπόδεκτον ἐνώπιον τοῦ
reverence. this For (is) good and acceptable before the
4990 2257 2316 3739 3956 444 2309 4982
σωτῆρος ἡμῶν Θεοῦ, 4 ὃς πάντας ἀνθρώπους θέλει σωθῆναι
Savior of us God, who all (sorts) of men desires to be saved
2532 1519 1922 225 2064 1520 1063 2316 1520 2532
καὶ εἰς ἐπίγνωσιν ἀληθείας ἐλθεῖν. 5 εἷς γὰρ Θεός, εἷς καὶ
and to a full knowledge of truth to come. one For God (is), one also
3316 2316 2532 444 444 5547 2424
μεσίτης Θεοῦ καὶ ἀνθρώπων, ἄνθρωπος Χριστὸς Ἰησοῦς,
Mediator of God and of men, (the) man Christ Jesus,
3588 1325 1438 487 5228 3956 3588 3142
6 ὁ δοὺς ἑαυτὸν ἀντίλυτρον ὑπὲρ πάντων, τὸ μαρτύριον
He having given Himself a ransom on behalf of all, the testimony
2540 2398 1519 3739 5087 1473 2783 2532 652 225
καιροῖς ἰδίοις, 7 εἰς ὃ ἐτέθην ἐγὼ κῆρυξ καὶ ἀπόστολος [ἀλή-
in its time own, to which was appointed I a herald and apostle, truth
3004 1722 5547 3756 5574 1320 1484 1722
θειαν λέγω ἐν Χριστῷ, οὐ ψεύδομαι], διδάσκαλος ἐθνῶν ἐν
I say in Christ, not I do lie, a teacher of nations in
4102 2532 225
πίστει καὶ ἀληθείᾳ.
faith and truth.

1014 3767 4336 3588 435 1722 3956 5117
8. Βούλομαι οὖν προσεύχεσθαι τοὺς ἄνδρας ἐν παντὶ τόπῳ,
I purpose Therefore to pray the men in every place,
1869 3741 5495 5565 3709 2532 1261
ἐπαίροντας ὁσίους χεῖρας, χωρὶς ὀργῆς καὶ διαλογισμοῦ.
lifting up holy hands, without wrath and doubting.
5615 2532 3588 1135 1722 2689 2887 3326 127
9 ὡσαύτως καὶ τὰς γυναῖκας ἐν καταστολῇ κοσμίῳ, μετὰ αἰδοῦς
Likewise also the women in clothing decent, with modesty
2532 4997 2885 1438 3361 1722 4117 2228 5557 2228
καὶ σωφροσύνης, κοσμεῖν ἑαυτάς, μὴ ἐν πλέγμασιν, ἢ χρυσίῳ, ἢ
and sensibleness, to adorn themselves, not with plaiting, or gold, or
3135 2228 2441 4185 235 3739 4241
μαργαρίταις, ἢ ἱματισμῷ πολυτελεῖ, 10 ἀλλ' [ὃ πρέπει
pearls, or garments expensive, but what becomes
1135 1861 2317 1223 2041 18
γυναιξὶν ἐπαγγελλομέναις θεοσέβειαν] δι' ἔργων ἀγαθῶν.
women professing fear of God, by means of works good.
1135 1722 2271 3129 1722 3956 5292 1135 1161
11 γυνὴ ἐν ἡσυχίᾳ μανθανέτω ἐν πάσῃ ὑποταγῇ. 12 γυναικὶ δὲ
a woman in silence Let learn in all subjection. a woman But

King James Version

1 Timothy 2

1. I exhort therefore, that, first of all, supplications, prayers, intercessions, (and) giving of thanks, be made for all men;
2 For kings, and (for) all that are in authority; that we may lead a quiet and peaceable life in all godliness and honesty.
3 For this (is) good and acceptable in the sight of God our Saviour;
4 Who will have all men to be saved, and to come unto the knowledge of the truth.
5 For (there is) one God, and one mediator between God and men, the man Christ Jesus;
6 Who gave himself a ransom for all, to be testified in due time.
7 Whereunto I am ordained a preacher, and an apostle, (I speak the truth in Christ, (and) lie not;) a teacher of the Gentiles in faith and verity.
8 I will therefore that men pray every where, lifting up holy hands, without wrath and doubting.
9 In like manner also, that women adorn themselves in modest apparel, with shamefacedness and sobriety; not with broided hair, or gold, or pearls, or costly array;
10 But (which becometh women professing godliness) with good works.
11 Let the woman learn in silence with all subjection.
12 But I suffer not a woman

1 Timothy 2:13

Literal Translation

to teach nor to exercise authority (over) a man, but to be in silence.
13 For Adam was formed first, then Eve.
14 And Adam was not deceived, but (the) woman being deceived has become in transgression;
15 but she will be kept safe through the childbearing, if they continue in faith and love and holiness, with sensibleness.

1321 3756 2010 3761 831 435 235 1511
διδάσκειν οὐκ ἐπιτρέπω, οὐδὲ αὐθεντεῖν ἀνδρός, ἀλλ' εἶναι
to teach not I allow, nor to exercise authority of a man, but to be

1722 2271 76 1063 4413 4111 1534 2096 2532
ἐν ἡσυχίᾳ. 13 Ἀδὰμ γὰρ πρῶτος ἐπλάσθη, εἶτα Εὔα· 14 καὶ
in silence. Adam For first was formed, then Eve; and

76 3756 538 3588 1161 1135 538 1722 3847
Ἀδὰμ οὐκ ἠπατήθη, ἡ δὲ γυνὴ ἀπατηθεῖσα ἐν παραβάσει
Adam not was deceived, the but woman being deceived in transgression

1096 4982 1161 1223 3588 5042 1437 3306 1722
γέγονε· 15 σωθήσεται δὲ διὰ τῆς τεκνογονίας, ἐὰν μείνωσιν ἐν
has become; she will be saved but through the childbearing, if they remain in

4102 2532 26 2532 38 3326 4997
πίστει καὶ ἀγάπῃ καὶ ἁγιασμῷ μετὰ σωφροσύνης.
faith and love and holiness with sensibleness.

King James Version

to teach, nor to usurp authority over the man, but to be in silence.
13 For Adam was first formed, then Eve.
14 And Adam was not deceived, but the woman being deceived was in the transgression.
15 Notwithstanding she shall be saved in childbearing, if they continue in faith and charity and holiness with sobriety.

1 Timothy 3

Literal Translation

1. Faithful (is) the Word: If anyone reaches out to overseership, he desires a good work.
2 Then it behooves the overseer to be blameless, husband of one wife, temperate, sensible, well-ordered, hospitable, apt at teaching;
3 not a drinker, not a contentious one, not greedy of ill gain, but gentle, not quarrelsome, not loving money;
4 ruling his own house well, having children in subjection with all respect.
5 But if anyone does not know to rule (his) own house, how will he care for a church of God?
6 (He should) not (be) a novice, lest being puffed up he may fall into the Devil's judgment.
7 But he must also have a good witness from those outside, that he not fall into reproach and (into) a snare of the Devil.
8 Likewise, deacons (to be) reverent, not double-tongued, not addicted to much wine, not greedy of ill gain,
9 having the mystery of the faith with a pure conscience.
10 And also let these be tested first, then let them minister, being without reproach.
11 Likewise, (their) wives

1 Timothy 3

4103 3588 3056 1487 5100 1984 3713 2570 2041
1. Πιστὸς ὁ λόγος· εἴ τις ἐπισκοπῆς ὀρέγεται, καλοῦ ἔργου
Faithful (is) the Word; if anyone to overseership aspires, a good work

1937 1163 3767 3588 1985 423 1511 3391
ἐπιθυμεῖ. 2 δεῖ οὖν τὸν ἐπίσκοπον ἀνεπίληπτον εἶναι, μιᾶς
he desires. it behooves Then the overseer blameless to be, of one

1135 435 3524 4998 2887 5382
γυναικὸς ἄνδρα, νηφάλιον, σώφρονα, κόσμιον, φιλόξενον,
wife husband, temperate, sensible, orderly, hospitable,

1317 3361 3943 3361 4131 3361 146
διδακτικόν· 3 μὴ πάροινον, μὴ πλήκτην, μὴ αἰσχροκερδῆ,
apt at teaching; not a drinker, not a striker, not greedy of ill gain,

235 1933 269 866 3588 2398 3624 2573
ἀλλ' ἐπιεικῆ, ἄμαχον, ἀφιλάργυρον· 4 τοῦ ἰδίου οἴκου καλῶς
but gentle, not quarrelsome, not avaricious, the own house well

4291 5043 2192 1722 5292 3326 3956
προϊστάμενον, τέκνα ἔχοντα ἐν ὑποταγῇ μετὰ πάσης
ruling, children having in subjection with all

4587 1487 1161 5100 3588 2398 3624 4291 3756 1492
σεμνότητος 5 [εἰ δέ τις τοῦ ἰδίου οἴκου προστῆναι οὐκ οἶδε,
reverence, if but anyone the own house to rule not knows,

4459 1577 2316 1959 3361 3504 2443 3361
πῶς ἐκκλησίας Θεοῦ ἐπιμελήσεται;] 6 μὴ νεόφυτον, ἵνα μὴ
how a church of God will he care for? Not a novice, that not

5187 1519 2917 1706 3588 1228 1163 1161 846 2532
τυφωθεὶς εἰς κρίμα ἐμπέσῃ τοῦ διαβόλου. 7 δεῖ δε αὐτὸν καὶ
being puffed up into judgment fall of the devil. it behooves And him also

3141 2570 2192 575 3588 1855 2443 3361 1519 3680
μαρτυρίαν καλὴν ἔχειν ἀπὸ τῶν ἔξωθεν, ἵνα μὴ εἰς ὀνειδισμὸν
a witness good to have from those outside, that not into reproach

1706 2532 3803 3588 1228 1249 5615
ἐμπέσῃ καὶ παγίδα τοῦ διαβόλου. 8 διακόνους ὡσαύτως
he fall, and (into) a snare of the devil. deacons Likewise

4586 3361 1351 3361 3631 4183 4337 3361
σεμνούς, μὴ διλόγους, μὴ οἴνῳ πολλῷ προσέχοντας, μὴ
(to be) reverent, not double-tongued, not wine to much addicted, not

146 2192 3588 3466 3588 4102 1722 2513
αἰσχροκερδεῖς, 9 ἔχοντας τὸ μυστήριον τῆς πίστεως ἐν καθαρᾷ
greedy of ill gain, having the mystery of the faith with a clean

4893 2532 3778 1161 1381 4412 1534
συνειδήσει. 10 καὶ οὗτοι δὲ δοκιμαζέσθωσαν πρῶτον, εἶτα
conscience. also these And let be tested first, then

1247 410 5607 1135 5615
διακονείτωσαν ἀνέγκλητοι ὄντες. 11 γυναῖκας ὡσαύτως
let them minister without reproach being. wives Likewise

1 Timothy 3

1. This (is) a true saying, If a man desire the office of a bishop, he desireth a good work.
2 A bishop then must be blameless, the husband of one wife, vigilant, sober, of good behaviour, given to hospitality, apt to teach;
3 Not given to wine, no striker, not greedy of filthy lucre; but patient, not a brawler, not covetous;
4 One that ruleth well his own house, having his children in subjection with all gravity;
5 (For if a man know not how to rule his own house, how shall he take care of the church of God?)
6 Not a novice, lest being lifted up with pride he fall into the condemnation of the devil.
7 Moreover he must have a good report of them which are without; lest he fall into reproach and the snare of the devil.
8. Likewise (must) the deacons (be) grave, not doubletongued, not given to much wine, not greedy of filthy lucre;
9 Holding the mystery of the faith in a pure conscience.
10 And let these also first be proved; then let them use the office of a deacon, being (found) blameless.
11 Even so (must their) wives

Literal Translation **1 Timothy 3:12** ***King James Version***

(to be) reverent, not slanderers, temperate, faithful in all things.
12 Let deacons be husbands of one wife, ruling (their) own households and children well.

13 For those having served well gain a good grade for themselves and much boldness in faith, the (boldness which is) in Christ Jesus.

4586 3361 1228 3524 4103 1722 3956 1249
σεμνάς, μὴ διαβόλους, νηφαλίους, πιστὰς ἐν πᾶσι. 12 διάκονοι
reverent, not slanderers, temperate, faithful in all. deacons

2077 3391 1135 435 5043 2573 4291
ἔστωσαν μιᾶς γυναικὸς ἄνδρες, τέκνων καλῶς προϊστάμενοι
Let be of one wife husbands, children well ruling

2532 3588 2398 3624 3588 1063 2573 1247 898
καὶ τῶν ἰδίων οἴκων. 13 οἱ γὰρ καλῶς διακονήσαντες βαθμὸν
and the own households. those For well having ministered a grade

1438 2570 4046 2532 4183 3954 1722
ἑαυτοῖς καλὸν περιποιοῦνται, καὶ πολλὴν παρρησίαν ἐν
for themselves good acquire, and much boldness in

4102 3588 1722 5547 2424
πίστει τῇ ἐν Χριστῷ Ἰησοῦ.
faith the (one) in Christ Jesus.

(be) grave, not slanderers, sober, faithful in all things.
12 Let the deacons be the husbands of one wife, ruling their children and their own houses well.
13 For they that have used the office of a deacon well purchase to themselves a good degree, and great boldness in the faith which is in Christ Jesus.

14 I write these things to you, hoping to come to you shortly.
15 But if I delay, that you may know how to behave in the house of God, which is (the) church of the living God, (the) pillar and foundation of the truth.

16 And confessedly, great is the mystery of godliness: God was manifested in flesh, was justified in Spirit, was seen by angels, was proclaimed among nations, was believed on in (the) world, was taken up in glory.

5023 4671 1125 1679 2064 4314 4571 5032 1437
14. Ταῦτά σοι γράφω, ἐλπίζων ἐλθεῖν πρὸς σὲ τάχιον· 15 ἐὰν
These things to you I write, hoping to come to you shortly; if

1161 1019 2443 1492 4459 1163 1722 3624 2316 390
δὲ βραδύνω, ἵνα εἰδῇς πῶς δεῖ ἐν οἴκῳ Θεοῦ ἀναστρέ-
but I delay, that you may know how must in (the) house of God to behave,

3748 2076 1577 2316 2198 4769 2532
φεσθαι, ἥτις ἐστὶν ἐκκλησία Θεοῦ ζῶντος, στύλος καὶ
which is (the) church of God (the) living pillar and

1477 3588 225 2532 3672 3173 2076 3588
ἑδραίωμα τῆς ἀληθείας. 16 καὶ ὁμολογουμένως μέγα ἐστὶ τὸ
foundation of the truth. And confessedly great is the

3588 2150 3466 2316 5319 1722 4561 1344
τῆς εὐσεβείας μυστήριον· Θεος ἐφανερώθη ἐν σαρκί, ἐδικαιώθη
of godliness mystery; God was manifested in flesh, was justified

1722 4151 3700 32 2784 1722 1484
ἐν πνεύματι, ὤφθη ἀγγέλοις, ἐκηρύχθη ἐν ἔθνεσιν,
in spirit, was seen by angels, was proclaimed among nations,

4100 1722 2889 353 1722 1391
ἐπιστεύθη ἐν κόσμῳ, ἀνελήμφθη ἐν δόξῃ.
was believe in (the) world, was taken up in glory.

14 These things write I unto thee, hoping to come unto thee shortly:
15 But if I tarry long, that thou mayest know how thou oughtest to behave thyself in the house of God, which is the church of the living God, the pillar and ground of the truth.
16 And without controversy great is the mystery of godliness: God was manifest in the flesh, justified in the Spirit, seen of angels, preached unto the Gentiles, believed on in the world, received up into glory.

1 Timothy 4 — 1 Timothy 4 — 1 Timothy 4

1. But the Spirit expressly says that in latter times some will depart from the faith, cleaving to deceiving spirits and teachings of demons,

2 in lying hypocrisy being seared in (their) own conscience,

3 forbidding to marry, (saying) to abstain from foods, which God created for partaking with thanksgiving by the believers and (those) knowing the truth.

4 Because every creature of God (is) good, and nothing to be thrust away, but having been received with thanksgiving;
5 for through

3588 1161 4151 4490 3004 3754 1722 5306 2540
1. Τὸ δὲ Πνεῦμα ῥητῶς λέγει, ὅτι ἐν ὑστέροις καιροῖς
the But Spirit in words says, that in latter times

868 5100 3588 4102 4337 4151
ἀποστήσονταί τινες τῆς πίστεως, προσέχοντες πνεύμασι
will depart from some the faith, adhering to spirits

4108 2532 1319 1140 1722 5272
πλάνοις καὶ διδασκαλίαις δαιμονίων, 2 ἐν ὑποκρίσει
deceiving and doctrines of demons, in hypocrisy

5573 2743 3588 2398 4893 2967
ψευδολόγων, κεκαυτηριασμένων τὴν ἰδίαν συνείδησιν, 3 κωλυό-
of liars, having been seared the own conscience, forbidding

1060 567 1033 3739 3588 2316 2936 1519
ντων γαμεῖν, ἀπέχεσθαι βρωμάτων, ἃ ὁ Θεὸς ἔκτισεν εἰς
to marry, (saying) to abstain from foods, which God created for

3336 3326 2169 3588 4103 2532 1921
μετάληψιν μετὰ εὐχαριστίας τοῖς πιστοῖς καὶ ἐπεγνωκόσι
partaking with thanksgiving by the believers and (those) knowing

3588 225 3754 3956 2938 2316 2570 2532 3762
τὴν ἀλήθειαν. 4 ὅτι πᾶν κτίσμα Θεοῦ καλόν, καὶ οὐδὲν
the truth. Because every creature of God (is) good, and nothing

579 3326 2169 2983 37 1063
ἀπόβλητον, μετὰ εὐχαριστίας λαμβανόμενον· 5 ἁγιάζεται γὰρ
to be put away, with thanksgiving having been received; it is sanctified for

1. Now the Spirit speaketh expressly, that in the latter times some shall depart from the faith, giving heed to seducing spirits, and doctrines of devils;
2 Speaking lies in hypocrisy; having their conscience seared with a hot iron;
3 Forbidding to marry, (and commanding) to abstain from meats, which God hath created to be received with thanksgiving of them which believe and know the truth.

4 For every creature of God (is) good, and nothing to be refused, if it be received with thanksgiving:
5 For it is sanctified

1 Timothy 4:6

Literal Translation

God's Word and prayerful intercession, it is sanctified.

6 Having laid down these things to the brothers, you will be a good servant of Jesus Christ, having been nourished by the words of faith, and of the good doctrine which you have followed.
7 But refuse the profane and old-womanish tales. And exercise yourself to godliness.

8 For bodily exercise is profitable to a little, but godliness is profitable to all things, having promise of the present life and of that coming.

9 Faithful (is) the Word and worthy of all acceptance;

10 for to this we also labor and (are) reproached, because we hope on (the) living God, who is deliverer of all men, especially of believers.
11 Enjoin and teach these things.

12 Let no one despise your youth, but become an example of the believers in word, in conduct, in love, in spirit, in faith, in purity.

13 Until I come, attend to reading, to exhortation, to teaching.

14 Do not be neglectful of the gift in you, which was given to you through prophecy, with laying on of the hands of the elders.

15 Give care to these things; be in these things in order that your progress may be plain in all.
16 Give attention to yourself and to the doctrine; continue in them, for doing this, you will both save yourself and those hearing you.

Greek Interlinear

1223 3056 2316 2532 1783
διὰ λόγου Θεοῦ καὶ ἐντεύξεως.
through a word of God and prayerful intercession.

5023 5294 3588 80 2570 2071 1249
6. Ταῦτα ὑποτιθέμενος τοῖς ἀδελφοῖς καλὸς ἔσῃ διάκονος
These things having suggested to the brothers, good you will be minister

2424 5547 1789 3588 3056 3588 4102 2532
Ἰησοῦ Χριστοῦ, ἐντρεφόμενος τοῖς λόγοις τῆς πίστεως, καὶ
of Jesus Christ, being nourished by the words of the faith, and

3588 2570 1319 3739 3877 3588 1161 952
τῆς καλῆς διδασκαλίας ᾗ παρηκολούθηκας. 7 τοὺς δὲ βεβήλους
by the good teaching which you have followed. the But profane

2532 1126 3454 3868 1128 1161 4572 4314
καὶ γραώδεις μύθους παραιτοῦ. γύμναζε δὲ σεαυτὸν πρὸς
and old-womanish tales refuse. exercise And yourself to

2150 3588 1063 4984 1129 4314 3641 2076
εὐσέβειαν· 8 ἡ γὰρ σωματικὴ γυμνασία πρὸς ὀλίγον ἐστὶν
godliness; for bodily exercise for a little is

5624 3588 1161 2150 4314 3956 5624 2076 1860
ὠφέλιμος· ἡ δὲ εὐσέβεια πρὸς πάντα ὠφέλιμός ἐστιν, ἐπαγ-
profitable; but godliness to all things profitable is, promise

2192 2222 3588 3568 2532 3588 3195 4103 3588
γελίαν ἔχουσα ζωῆς τῆς νῦν καὶ τῆς μελλούσης. 9 πιστὸς ὁ
having life of the now and the coming. Faithful the

3056 2532 3956 594 514 1519 5124 1063 2532 2872
λόγος καὶ πάσης ἀποδοχῆς ἄξιος. 10 εἰς τοῦτο γὰρ καὶ κοπιῶ-
Word and of all acceptance worthy;. to this For also we labor

2532 3679 3754 1679 1909 2316 2198 3739 2076
μεν καὶ ὀνειδιζόμεθα, ὅτι ἠλπίκαμεν ἐπὶ Θεῷ ζῶντι, ὅς ἐστι
and (are) reproached, because we have set hope on God (the) living, who is

4990 3956 444 3122 4103 3853
σωτὴρ πάντων ἀνθρώπων, μάλιστα πιστῶν. 11 παράγγελλε
Savior of all (sorts) of men, especially of believers. Enjoin

5023 2532 1321 3367 4675 3588 3503 2706
ταῦτα καὶ δίδασκε. 12 μηδείς σου τῆς νεότητος καταφρονείτω,
these things and teach. No one of you the youth let despise,

235 5179 1096 3588 4103 1722 3056 1722 391 1722
ἀλλὰ τύπος γίνου τῶν πιστῶν ἐν λόγῳ, ἐν ἀναστροφῇ, ἐν
but an example become of the believers in word, in conduct, in

26 1722 4151 1722 4102 1722 47 2193 2064
ἀγάπῃ, ἐν πνεύματι, ἐν πίστει, ἐν ἁγνείᾳ. 13 ἕως ἔρχομαι
love, in spirit, in faith, in purity. Until I come,

4337 3588 320 3588 3874 3588 1319 3361
πρόσεχε τῇ ἀναγνώσει, τῇ παρακλήσει, τῇ διδασκαλίᾳ. 14 μὴ
attend to the reading, to the exhortation, to the teaching. Not

272 3588 1722 4671 5486 3739 1325 4671 1223 4394
ἀμέλει τοῦ ἐν σοὶ χαρίσματος, ὃ ἐδόθη σοι διὰ προφητείας
be neglectful of the in you gift, which was given you through prophecy

3326 1936 3588 5495 3588 4244 5023 3191
μετὰ ἐπιθέσεως τῶν χειρῶν τοῦ πρεσβυτερίου. 15 ταῦτα μελέτα,
with laying on of the hands of the elders. These things attend to,

1722 5125 2468 2443 4675 3588 4297 5318 5600 1722 3956 1907
ἐν τούτοις ἴσθι, ἵνα σου ἡ προκοπὴ φανερὰ ᾖ ἐν πᾶσιν. 16 ἔπεχε
in these things be, that of you the progress plain may be in all. Hold on

4572 2532 3588 1319 1961 846 5124 1063 4160
σεαυτῷ καὶ τῇ διδασκαλίᾳ. ἐπίμενε αὐτοῖς· τοῦτο γὰρ ποιῶν
to yourself and to the doctrine. Continue in them; this for doing

2532 4572 4982 2532 3588 191 4675
καὶ σεαυτὸν σώσεις καὶ τοὺς ἀκούοντάς σου.
and yourself you will save and those hearing you.

King James Version

by the word of God and prayer.

6 If thou put the brethren in remembrance of these things, thou shalt be a good minister of Jesus Christ, nourished up in the words of faith and of good doctrine, whereunto thou hast attained.
7 But refuse profane and old wives' fables, and exercise thyself (rather) unto godliness.

8 For bodily exercise profiteth little: but godliness is profitable unto all things, having promise of the life that now is, and of that which is to come.
9 This (is) a faithful saying and worthy of all acceptation.

10 For therefore we both labour and suffer reproach, because we trust in the living God, who is the Saviour of all men, specially of those that believe.
11 These things command and teach.

12 Let no man despise thy youth; but be thou an example of the believers, in word, in conversation, in charity, in spirit, in faith, in purity.

13 Till I come, give attendance to reading, to exhortation, to doctrine.

14 Neglect not the gift that is in thee, which was given thee by prophecy, with the laying on of the hands of the presbytery.

15 Meditate upon these things; give thyself wholly to them; that thy profiting may appear to all.
16 Take heed unto thyself, and unto the doctrine; continue in them: for in doing this thou shalt both save thyself, and them that hear thee.

Literal Translation

1 Timothy 5

1. Do not sharply rebuke an elder, but exhort as a father; (and) younger ones as brothers,
2 older (women) as mothers, younger (women) as sisters, in all purity.
3 Honor widows, the (ones) really being widows.
4 But if any widow has children or grandchildren, let them learn first to be godly to their own house and to make a return payment to (those) born before, for this is good and pleasing before God.
5 But (honor) the (one) being really a widow, even having been left alone, (who) has set (her) hope on God and continues in petitions and prayers night and day.
6 But she who lives in self-pleasure has died while living.
7 And enjoin these things that they may be blameless.
8 But if anyone does not provide for (his) own, and especially (his) family, he has denied the faith and is worse than an unbeliever.
9 Let a widow be enrolled having become not less than sixty years, (the) wife of one man,
10 being witnessed by good works, if she brought up children, if she hosted strangers, if she washed the feet of saints, if she relieved afflicted ones, if she followed after every good work.
11 But refuse younger widows; for whenever they grow lustful against Christ, they desire to marry,
12 having guilt because they set aside the first faith;
13 and with it all, they also learn (to be) idle, going around the houses, and not only idle, but also gossips and busybodies, speaking the things not proper.
14 Therefore, I desire the young women to marry, to bear children,

1 Timothy 5:1

4245 3361 1969 235 3870 5613 3962
1. Πρεσβυτέρῳ μὴ ἐπιπλήξῃς, ἀλλὰ παρακάλει ὡς πατέρα·
an elder man not Rebuke, but exhort as a father;

3501 5613 80 4245 5613 3384 3501
νεωτέρους, ὡς ἀδελφούς· 2 πρεσβυτέρας, ὡς μητέρας· νεωτέρας,
younger ones, as brothers; older women, as mothers; younger women,

5613 79 1722 3956 47 5503 5091 3588 3689 5503
ὡς ἀδελφάς, ἐν πάσῃ ἁγνείᾳ. 3 χήρας τίμα τὰς ὄντως χήρας.
as sisters, in all purity. widows Honor, those being true widows.

1487 1161 5100 5503 5043 2228 1549 2192 3129 4412
4 εἰ δέ τις χήρα τέκνα ἢ ἔκγονα ἔχει, μανθανέτωσαν πρῶτον
if But any widow children or grandchildren has, let them learn firstly

3588 2398 3624 2151 2532 287 591 3588 4269
τὸν ἴδιον οἶκον εὐσεβεῖν, καὶ ἀμοιβὰς ἀποδιδόναι τοῖς προγό-
the own house to be godly to, and repayments to return to the fore-

5124 1063 2076 2570 2532 587 1799 3588 2316
νοις· τοῦτο γάρ ἐστι καλὸν καὶ ἀπόδεκτον ἐνώπιον τοῦ Θεοῦ.
bears; this for is good and acceptable before God.

3588 1161 3689 5503 2532 3443 1679 1909 3588 2316
5 ἡ δὲ ὄντως χήρα καὶ μεμονωμένη ἤλπικεν ἐπὶ τὸν Θεόν,
the But being true widow even having been left has set hope on God,

2532 4357 3588 1162 2532 3588 4335 3571 2532
καὶ προσμένει ταῖς δεήσεσι καὶ ταῖς προσευχαῖς νυκτὸς καὶ
and continues in the petitions and the prayers night and

2250 3588 1161 4684 2198 2348 2532 5023 3853
ἡμέρας. 6 ἡ δὲ σπαταλῶσα ζῶσα τέθνηκε. 7 καὶ ταῦτα παράγ-
day. the (one) But living for self-pleasure (while) living has died. And these things enjoin,

2443 423 5600 1487 1161 5100 3588 2398 2532
γελλε, ἵνα ἀνεπίληπτοι ὦσιν. 8 εἰ δέ τις τῶν ἰδίων καὶ
that without reproach they may be. if But anyone the own and

3122 3588 3609 3756 4306 3588 4102 720 2532
μάλιστα τῶν οἰκείων οὐ προνοεῖ, τὴν πίστιν ἤρνηται, καὶ
especially the family not provides for, the faith he has denied, and

2076 571 5501 5503 2639 3361 1640 2094
ἔστιν ἀπίστου χείρων. 9 χήρα καταλεγέσθω μὴ ἔλαττον ἐτῶν
is an unbeliever worse than. A widow let be enrolled not less (than) years

1835 1096 1520 435 1135 1722 2041 2570
ἑξήκοντα, γεγονυῖα ἑνὸς ἀνδρὸς γυνή, 10 ἐν ἔργοις καλοῖς
sixty, having become of one husband wife, in works good

3140 1487 5044 1487 3580 1487 40
μαρτυρουμένη, εἰ ἐτεκνοτρόφησεν, εἰ ἐξενοδόχησεν, εἰ ἁγίων
being witnessed, if she nurtured children, if she hosted strangers, if of saints

4228 3538 1487 2346 1884 1487 3956 2041
πόδας ἔνιψεν, εἰ θλιβομένοις ἐπήρκεσεν, εἰ παντὶ ἔργῳ
feet she washed, if afflicted ones she relieved, if every work

18 1872 3501 1161 5503 3868 3752
ἀγαθῷ ἐπηκολούθησεν. 11 νεωτέρας δὲ χήρας παραιτοῦ· ὅταν
good she followed after. younger But widows refuse; when

1063 2691 3588 5547 1060 2309
γὰρ καταστρηνιάσωσι τοῦ Χριστοῦ, γαμεῖν θέλουσιν,
for they grow lustful against Christ, to marry they desire,

2192 2917 3754 3588 4413 4102 114 260 1161
12 ἔχουσαι κρίμα, ὅτι τὴν πρώτην πίστιν ἠθέτησαν· 13 ἅμα δὲ
having (a) judgment, because the first faith they set aside; withal and

2532 692 3129 4022 3588 3614 3756 3440
καὶ ἀργαὶ μανθάνουσι, περιερχόμεναι τὰς οἰκίας, οὐ μόνον
also idle they learn (to be), going around the houses, not only

1161 692 235 2532 5397 2532 4021 2980 3588
δὲ ἀργαί, ἀλλὰ καὶ φλύαροι καὶ περίεργοι, λαλοῦσαι τὰ
and idle, but also gossips and busybodies, speaking the things

3361 1163 1014 3767 3501 1060 5041
μὴ δέοντα. 14 βούλομαι οὖν νεωτέρας γαμεῖν, τεκνογονεῖν,
not proper. I will Therefore younger women to marry, to bear children,

King James Version

1 Timothy 5

1. Rebuke not an elder, but intreat (him) as a father; (and) the younger men as brethren;
2 The elder women as mothers; the younger as sisters, with all purity.
3 Honour widows that are widows indeed.
4 But if any widow have children or nephews, let them learn first to shew piety at home, and to requite their parents: for that is good and acceptable before God.
5 Now she that is a widow indeed, and desolate, trusteth in God, and continueth in supplications and prayers night and day.
6 But she that liveth in pleasure is dead while she liveth.
7 And these things give in charge, that they may be blameless.
8 But if any provide not for his own, and specially for those of his own house, he hath denied the faith, and is worse than an infidel.
9 Let not a widow be taken into the number under threescore years old, having been the wife of one man,
10 Well reported of for good works; if she have brought up children, if she have lodged strangers, if she have washed the saints' feet, if she have relieved the afflicted, if she have diligently followed every good work.
11 But the younger widows refuse: for when they have begun to wax wanton against Christ, they will marry;
12 Having damnation, because they have cast off their first faith.
13 And withal they learn (to be) idle, wandering about from house to house; and not only idle, but tattlers also and busybodies, speaking things which they ought not.
14 I will therefore that the younger women marry, bear children,

Literal Translation | **1 Timothy 5:15** | ***King James Version***

to rule the house, giving no occasion to the adversary on account of reproach.
15 For some already have turned aside behind Satan.

16 If any believing man or believing woman has widows, let (them) relieve them, and do not burden the church, that it may relieve those being really widows.

17 Let the elders who take the lead well be counted worthy of double honor, especially those laboring in word and teaching.

18 For the Scripture says, "You shall not muzzle an ox treading out grain," and, "The laborer is worthy of his pay." (Deut.25:4)
19 Do not receive an accusation against an elder unless on (the testimony of) two or three witnesses.
20 The ones sinning before all, rebuke, that the rest also may have fear.
21 I solemnly witness before God and (the) Lord Jesus Christ and the elect angels, that you should guard these things without prejudice, doing nothing by way of partiality.

22 Lay hands quickly on no one, nor share in (the) sins of others. Keep yourself pure.
23 No longer drink water, but use a little wine on account of your stomach and your frequent infirmities.

24 The sins of some men are plain before, going before to judgment, but indeed some they follow after.

25 Likewise, also the good works are plain beforehand, and those otherwise cannot be hidden.

3616 3367 874 1325 3588 480
οἰκοδεσποτεῖν, μηδεμίαν ἀφορμὴν διδόναι τῷ ἀντικειμένῳ
to rule the house, no occasion to give to the (one) opposing

3059 5484 2235 1063 5100 1624 3694 3588
λοιδορίας χάριν. 15 ἤδη γάρ τινες ἐξετράπησαν ὀπίσω τοῦ
reproach on account of. already For some turned aside behind

4567 1487 5100 4103 2228 4103 2192 5503 1884 846
Σατανᾶ. 16 εἴ τις πιστὸς ἢ πιστὴ ἔχει χήρας, ἐπαρκείτω αὐταῖς,
Satan. If any believing man or believing woman has widows, let relieve them,

2532 3361 916 3588 1577 2443 3588 3689 5503 1884
καὶ μὴ βαρείσθω ἡ ἐκκλησία, ἵνα ταῖς ὄντως χήραις ἐπαρ-
and not burden the church, that those being true widows it may

κέσῃ.
relieve.

3588 2573 4291 4245 1362 5092 515
17. Οἱ καλῶς προεστῶτες πρεσβύτεροι διπλῆς τιμῆς ἀξιού-
The well ruling elders of double honor count

3122 3588 2872 1722 3056 2532 1319
σθωσαν, μάλιστα οἱ κοπιῶντες ἐν λόγῳ καὶ διδασκαλίᾳ.
worthy, especially the (ones) laboring in word and teaching.

3004 1063 3588 1124 1016 248 3756 5392 2532 514
18 λέγει γὰρ ἡ γραφή, Βοῦν ἀλοῶντα οὐ φιμώσεις. καί, Ἄξιος
says For the Scripture, An ox threshing not you shall muzzle. And., Worthy

3588 2040 3588 3408 846 2596 4245
ὁ ἐργάτης τοῦ μισθοῦ αὐτοῦ. 19 κατὰ πρεσβυτέρου κατη-
the workman of the pay of him. Against an elder

2724 3361 3858 1622 1487 3361 1909 1417 2228 5140 3144
γορίαν μὴ παραδέχου, ἐκτὸς εἰ μὴ ἐπὶ δύο ἢ τριῶν μαρτύ-
accusation not do receive, unless on two or three witnesses.

3588 264 1799 3956 1651 2443 2532
ρων. 20 τοὺς ἁμαρτάνοντας ἐνώπιον πάντων ἔλεγχε, ἵνα καὶ
Those sinning before all reprove, that also

3588 3062 5401 2192 1263 1799 3588 2316
οἱ λοιποὶ φόβον ἔχωσι. 21 διαμαρτύρομαι ἐνώπιον τοῦ Θεοῦ
the rest fear may have. I solemnly witness before God

2532 2962 2424 5547 2532 3588 1588 32 2443
καὶ Κυρίου Ἰησοῦ Χριστοῦ καὶ τῶν ἐκλεκτῶν ἀγγέλων, ἵνα
and (the) Lord Jesus Christ and the elect angels, that

5023 5442 5565 4299 3367 4160 2596
ταῦτα φυλάξῃς χωρὶς προκρίματος, μηδὲν ποιῶν κατὰ
these things you guard without prejudice, nothing doing by way of

4346 5495 5030 3367 2007 3366 2841
πρόσκλισιν. 22 χεῖρας ταχέως μηδενὶ ἐπιτίθει, μηδὲ κοινώνει
partiality. hands quickly no one Lay on, nor share in

266 245 4572 53 5083 3371 5202
ἁμαρτίαις ἀλλοτρίαις· σεαυτὸν ἁγνὸν τήρει. 23 μηκέτι ὑδροπό-
(the) sins of others; yourself pure keep. No longer drink

235 3631 3641 5530 1223 3588 4751 4675 2532 3588
τει, ἀλλ᾽ οἴνῳ ὀλίγῳ χρῶ, διὰ τὸν στόμαχον σου καὶ τὰς
water, but wine a little use, because of the stomach of you and the

4437 4675 769 5100 444 3588 266
πυκνάς σου ἀσθενείας. 24 Τινῶ1ν ἀνθρώπων αἱ ἁμαρτίαι
frequent of you weaknesses. of some men The sins

4271 1526 4254 1519 2920 5100 1161 2532 1872
πρόδηλοί εἰσι, προάγουσαι εἰς κρίσιν· τισὶ δὲ καὶ ἐπακο-
plain before are, going before to judgment; some but indeed they

5615 2532 3588 2570 2041 4271 2076 2532
λουθοῦσιν· 25 ὡσαύτως καὶ τὰ καλὰ ἔργα πρόδηλα ἐστι· καὶ
follow on; likewise also the good works plain before are; and

3588 247 2192 2928 3756 1410
τὰ ἄλλως ἔχοντα κρυβῆναι οὐ δύνανται.
those otherwise having to be hidden not cannot.

guide the house, give none occasion to the adversary to speak reproachfully.
15 For some are already turned aside after Satan.

16 If any man or woman that believeth have widows, let them relieve them, and let not the church be charged; that it may relieve them that are widows indeed.

17 Let the elders that rule well be counted worthy of double honour, especially they who labour in the word and doctrine.

18 For the scripture saith, Thou shalt not muzzle the ox that treadeth out the corn. And, The labourer (is) worthy of his reward.
19 Against an elder receive not an accusation, but before two or three witnesses.

20 Them that sin rebuke before all, that others also may fear.
21 I charge (thee) before God, and the Lord Jesus Christ, and the elect angels, that thou observe these things without preferring one before another, doing nothing by partiality.

22 Lay hands suddenly on no man, neither be partaker of other men's sins: keep thyself pure.
23 Drink no longer water, but use a little wine for thy stomach's sake and thine often infirmities.

24 Some men's sins are open beforehand, going before to judgment; and some (men) they follow after.

25 Likewise also the good works (of some) are manifest beforehand; and they that are otherwise cannot be hid.

Literal Translation

1 Timothy 6

1. Let as many as are slaves under a yoke count their own masters worthy of all honor, that the name and teaching of God may not be blasphemed.
2 And those having believing masters, let them not despise (them), because they are brothers, but rather let them serve as slaves, because they are believing and beloved ones, those receiving of the good service in return. Teach and exhort these things.

3 If anyone teaches differently, and does not consent to sound words, those of our Lord Jesus Christ and the doctrine according to godliness,

4 he has been puffed up, understanding nothing, but (is) sick concerning doubts and arguments, out of which comes envy, strife, evil-speakings, evil suspicions,
5 idle uselessness, of men whose mind has been corrupted and deprived of the truth, supposing gain to be godliness. Withdraw from such (persons).

6 But godliness with contentment is great gain.

7 For we have brought nothing into the world, (and it is) plain that neither can we carry anything out.
8 But having food and clothing, we will be satisfied with these.
9 But those having purposed to be rich fall into temptation and a snare, and many foolish and hurtful lusts, which plunge men into damnation and loss.

10 For the love of money is a root of all evils, (by means) of which some having lusted after (it) were seduced

1 Timothy 6:1

3745 1526 5259 2218 1401 3588 2398 1203
1. Ὅσοι εἰσὶν ὑπὸ ζυγὸν δοῦλοι, τοὺς ἰδίους δεσπότας
As many as are under a yoke slaves, the own masters

3956 5092 514 2233 2443 3361 3588 3686 3588 2316/2532
πάσης τιμῆς ἀξίους ἡγείσθωσαν, ἵνα μὴ τὸ ὄνομα τοῦ Θεοῦ καὶ
of all honor worthy esteem, that not the name of God and

3588 1319 987 3588 1161 4103 2192 1203
ἡ διδασκαλία βλασφημῆται. 2 οἱ δὲ πιστοὺς ἔχοντες δεσπότας
the teaching be blasphemed. those And believing having masters

3361 2706 3754 80 1526 235 3123 1398
μὴ καταφρονείτωσαν, ὅτι ἀδελφοί εἰσιν· ἀλλὰ μᾶλλον δου-
not let them despise, because brothers they are; but rather let them

3754 4103 1526 2532 27 3588 3588 2108
λευέτωσαν, ὅτι πιστοί εἰσι καὶ ἀγαπητοὶ οἱ τῆς εὐεργεσίας
serve as slaves, because believing are and beloved those of the good service

482 5023 1321 2532 3870
ἀντιλαμβανόμενοι. ταῦτα δίδασκε καὶ παρακάλει.
receiving in return. These things teach and exhort.

1487 5100 2085 2532 3361 4334 5198
3 εἴ τις ἑτεροδιδασκαλεῖ, καὶ μὴ προσέρχεται ὑγιαίνουσι
If anyone teaches differently, and not consents to sound

3056 3588 3588 2962 2257 2424 5547 2532 3588 2596
λόγοις, τοῖς τοῦ Κυρίου ἡμῶν Ἰησοῦ Χριστοῦ, καὶ τῇ κατ'
words, those of the Lord of us Jesus Christ, and to the according to

2150 1319 5187 3367 1987 235
εὐσέβειαν διδασκαλίᾳ, 4 τετύφωται, μηδὲν ἐπιστάμενος, ἀλλὰ
godliness teaching, he has been puffed up, nothing understanding, but

3552 4012 2214 2532 3055 1537 3739 1096 5355
νοσῶν περὶ ζητήσεις καὶ λογομαχίας, ἐξ ὧν γίνεται φθόνος,
is sick concerning doubts and arguments, out of which comes envy,

2054 988 5283 4190 3859 1311
ἔρις, βλασφημίαι, ὑπόνοιαι πονηραί, 5 παραδιατριβαὶ διε-
strife, evil speakings, suspicions evil, idle uselessness, having

444 3588 3563 2532 650 3588
φθαρμένων ἀνθρώπων τὸν νοῦν, καὶ ἀπεστερημένων τῆς
been corrupted of men the mind, and deprived of the

225 3543 4200 1511 3588 2150 868
ἀληθείας, νομιζόντων πορισμὸν εἶναι τὴν εὐσέβειαν. ἀφί-
truth, supposing gain to be godliness. Withdraw

575 3588 5108 2076 1161 4200 3173 3588 2150
στασο ἀπὸ τῶν τοιούτων. 6 ἔστι δὲ πορισμὸς μέγας ἡ εὐσέβεια
from such. is But gain great godliness

3326 841 3762 1063 1533 1519 3588 2889
μετὰ αὐταρκείας· 7 οὐδὲν γὰρ εἰσηνέγκαμεν εἰς τὸν κόσμον,
with contentment; nothing for we have brought into the world,

1212 3754 3761 1627 5100 1410 2192 1161 1305
δῆλον ὅτι οὐδὲ ἐξενεγκεῖν τι δυνάμεθα· 8 ἔχοντες δὲ διατροφὰς
(it is) plain that neither to carry out anything are we able; having but foods

2532 4629 5125 714 3588 1161 1014
καὶ σκεπάσματα, τούτοις ἀρκεσθησόμεθα. 9 οἱ δὲ βουλόμενοι
and clothings, with these things we will be satisfied. those But purposing

4147 1706 1519 3986 2532 3803 2532 1939
πλουτεῖν ἐμπίπτουσιν εἰς πειρασμὸν καὶ παγίδα καὶ ἐπιθυ-
to be rich fall into temptation and a snare and lusts

4183 453 2532 983 3748 1036 3588
μίας πολλὰς ἀνοήτους καὶ βλαβεράς, αἵτινες βυθίζουσι τοὺς
many foolish and hurtful, which cause to sink

444 1519 3639 2532 684 4491 1063 3956 3588
ἀνθρώπους εἰς ὄλεθρον καὶ ἀπώλειαν. 10 ῥίζα γὰρ πάντων τῶν
men into ruin and destruction. a root For of all

2556 2076 3588 5365 3739 5100 3713 635
κακῶν ἐστιν ἡ φιλαργυρία, ἧς τινες ὀρεγόμενοι ἀπεπλανήθη-
evils is the love of money, of which some lusting after were seduced

King James Version

1 Timothy 6

1. Let as many servants as are under the yoke count their own masters worthy of all honour, that the name of God and (his) doctrine be not blasphemed.
2 And they that have believing masters, let them not despise (them), because they are brethren; but rather do (them) service, because they are faithful and beloved, partakers of the benefit. These things teach and exhort.

3 If any man teach otherwise, and consent not to wholesome words, (even) the words of our Lord Jesus Christ, and to the doctrine which is according to godliness;
4 He is proud, knowing nothing, but doting about questions and strifes of words, whereof cometh envy, strife, railings, evil surmisings,
5 Perverse disputings of men of corrupt minds, and destitute of the truth, supposing that gain is godliness: from such withdraw thyself.

6 But godliness with contentment is great gain.

7 For we brought nothing into (this) world, (and it is) certain we can carry nothing out.
8 And having food and raiment let us be therewith content.
9 But they that will be rich fall into temptation and a snare, and (into) many foolish and hurtful lusts, which drown men in destruction and perdition.

10 For the love of money is the root of all evil: which while some coveted after,

Literal Translation

from the faith, and they themselves pierced through by many pains.

11 But you, O man of God, flee these things and pursue righteousness, godliness, faith, love, patience, and meekness.

12 Fight the good fight of faith. Lay hold on eternal life, to which you were also called, and confessed the good confession before many witnesses.

13 I charge you before God, He making all things alive, and (before) Christ Jesus, He witnessing the good confession to Pontius' Pilate,

14 that you keep the commandment spotless, blameless, until the appearing of our Lord Jesus Christ,
15 who in His own time will reveal the blessed and only Potentate, the King of the ones reigning and Lord of the ones lording,
16 the only (One) having immortality, living in light that cannot be approached, whom no one of men saw, nor can see; to whom be honor and everlasting might. Amen.

17 Charge the rich in the present age not to be high-minded, nor to set hope on the uncertainty of riches, but in the living God, He offering to us richly all things for enjoyment;

18 to do good, to be rich in good works, to be ready to share, generous,
19 treasuring up

1 Timothy 6:11

575 3588 4102 2532 1438 4044 3601
σαν ἀπὸ τῆς πίστεως καὶ ἑαυτοὺς περιέπειραν ὀδύναις
from the faith, and themselves pierced around pains

4183
πολλαῖς.
by many.

4771 1161 5599 444 2316 5023 5343 1377 1161 1343
11. Σὺ δέ, ὦ ἄνθρωπε Θεοῦ, ταῦτα φεῦγε· δίωκε δὲ δικαιο-
you But, O man of God, these things flee; pursue and righteous-

2150 4102 26 5281 4236
σύνην, εὐσέβειαν, πίστιν, ἀγάπην, ὑπομονήν, πρᾳότητα.
ness, godliness, faith, love, patience, meekness.

75 3588 2570 73 3588 4102 1949 3588
12 ἀγωνίζου τὸν καλὸν ἀγῶνα τῆς πίστεως, ἐπιλαβοῦ τῆς
Fight the good fight of faith. Lay hold on

166 2222 1519 3739 2532 2564 2532 3670 3588 2570
αἰωνίου ζωῆς, εἰς ἣν καὶ ἐκλήθης καὶ ὡμολόγησας τὴν καλὴν
everlasting life, to which also you were called and confessed the good

3671 1799 4183 3144 3853 4671
ὁμολογίαν ἐνώπιον πολλῶν μαρτύρων. 13 παραγγέλλω σοι
confession before many witnesses. I charge you

1799 3588 2316 3588 2227 3588 3956 2532 5547
ἐνώπιον τοῦ Θεοῦ τοῦ ζῳογονοῦντος τὰ πάντα, καὶ Χριστοῦ
before God the (One) making alive all things, and Christ

2424 3588 3140 1909 4194 4091 3588 2570
Ἰησοῦ τοῦ μαρτυρήσαντος ἐπὶ Ποντίου Πιλάτου τὴν καλὴν
Jesus the (One) having witnessed on Pontius Pilate the good

3671 5083 4571 3588 1785 784 423
ὁμολογίαν, 14 τηρῆσαί σε τὴν ἐντολὴν ἄσπιλον, ἀνεπίληπτον,
confession, to keep you the commandment unspotted, irreproachable,

3360 3588 2015 3588 2962 2257 2424 5547 3739
μέχρι τῆς ἐπιφανείας τοῦ Κυρίου ἡμῶν Ἰησοῦ Χριστοῦ, 15 ἣν
until the appearing of the Lord of us Jesus Christ, which

2540 2398 1166 3588 3107 2532 3441 1413 3588 935
καιροῖς ἰδίοις δείξει ὁ μακάριος καὶ μόνος δυνάστης, ὁ βασι-
in time its own will reveal the blessed and only Potentate, the King

3588 936 2532 2962 3588 2961 3588
λεὺς τῶν βασιλευόντων καὶ Κύριος τῶν κυριευόντων, 16 ὁ
of the (ones) reigning and Lord of the (ones) ruling, the

3441 2192 110 5457 3611 676 3739 1492 3762
μόνος ἔχων ἀθανασίαν, φῶς οἰκῶν ἀπρόσιτον, ὃν εἶδεν οὐδεὶς
only (One) having immortality, light living in unapproachable, whom saw no one

444 3761 1492 1410 3739 5092 2532 2904 166
ἀνθρώπων, οὐδὲ ἰδεῖν δύναται· ᾧ τιμὴ καὶ κράτος αἰώνιον·
of men, nor see are able; to whom(be) honor and might everlasting.

281
ἀμήν.
Amen.

3588 4145 1722 3588 3568 165 3853 3361 5309
17. Τοῖς πλουσίοις ἐν τῷ νῦν αἰῶνι παράγγελλε, μὴ ὑψη-
The rich in the present age enjoin not to be

3366 1679 1909 4149 83 235 1722
λοφρονεῖν, μηδὲ ἠλπικέναι ἐπὶ πλούτου ἀδηλότητι, ἀλλ' ἐν
high-minded, nor to set hope on of riches (the) uncertainty, but in

3588 2316 3588 2198 3588 3930 2254 4146 3956
τῷ Θεῷ τῷ ζῶντι, τῷ παρέχοντι ἡμῖν πλουσίως πάντα
God the living, the (One) offering to us richly all things

1519 619 14 4147 1722 2041 2570
εἰς ἀπόλαυσιν· 18 ἀγαθοεργεῖν, πλουτεῖν ἐν ἔργοις καλοῖς,
for enjoyment; to work good, to be rich in works good,

2130 1511 2843 597
εὐμεταδότους εἶναι, κοινωνικούς, 19 ἀποθησαυρίζοντας
ready to impart to be, generous, treasuring away

King James Version

they have erred from the faith, and pierced themselves through with many sorrows.

11 But thou, O man of God, flee these things; and follow after righteousness, godliness, faith, love, patience, meekness.

12 Fight the good fight of faith, lay hold on eternal life, whereunto thou art also called, and hast professed a good profession before many witnesses.

13 I give thee charge in the sight of God, who quickeneth all things, and (before) Christ Jesus, who before Pontius Pilate witnessed a good confession;

14 That thou keep (this) commandment without spot, unrebukeable, until the appearing of our Lord Jesus Christ:
15 Which in his times he shall shew, (who is) the blessed and only Potentate, the King of kings, and Lord of lords;
16 Who only hath immortality, dwelling in the light which no man can approach unto; whom no man hath seen, nor can see: to whom (be) honour and power everlasting. Amen.

17 Charge them that are rich in this world, that they be not highminded, nor trust in uncertain riches, but in the living God, who giveth us richly all things to enjoy;

18 That they do good, that they be rich in good works, ready to distribute, willing to communicate;
19 Laying up in store

Literal Translation

for themselves a good foundation for the coming (age), that they may lay hold on everlasting life.

20 O Timothy, guard the Deposit, having turned away from the profane empty babblings and opposing theories of the falsely named knowledge,
21 which some having asserted have missed the mark concerning the faith. Grace (be) with you. Amen.

1 Timothy 6:20

1438 2310 2570 1519 3588 3195 2443 1949 3588
ἑαυτοῖς θεμέλιον καλὸν εἰς τὸ μέλλον, ἵνα ἐπιλάβωνται τῆς
for themselves foundation a good for the coming (age), that they lay hold on

166 2222
αἰωνίου ζωῆς.
everlasting life.

5599 5095 3588 3872 5442 1624
20. Ὦ Τιμόθεε, τὴν παρακαταθήκην φύλαξον, ἐκτρεπόμενος
O Timothy, the Deposit guard, having turned from

3588 952 2757 2532 477 3588 5581
τὰς βεβήλους κενοφωνίας καὶ ἀντιθέσεις τῆς ψευδωνύμου
the profane empty babblings and opposing theories of the falsely named

1108 3739 5100 1861 4012 3588 4102
γνώσεως, 21 ἥν τινες ἐπαγγελλόμενοι περὶ τὴν πίστιν
knowledge; which some asserting concerning the faith

795
ἠστόχησαν.
have missed the mark.

3588 5485 3326 4675 281
Ἡ χάρις μετά σοῦ. ἀμήν.
Grace (be) with you. Amen.

King James Version

for themselves a good foundation against the time to come, that they may lay hold on eternal life.

20 O Timothy, keep that which is committed to thy trust, avoiding profane (and) vain babblings, and oppositions of science falsely so called:
21 Which some professing have erred concerning the faith. Grace (be) with thee. Amen.
(The first to Timothy was written from Laodicea, which is the chiefest city of Phrygia Pacatiana.)

Literal Translation

The Second Epistle of Paul to Timothy

2 Timothy 1

1. Paul an apostle of Jesus Christ through (the) will of God according to a promise of life (which is) in Christ Jesus,
2 to (my) beloved child Timothy: Grace, mercy, peace from God (the) Father and Christ Jesus our Lord.

3 I have thanks to God, whom I worship from (my) forebears in a pure conscience, how unceasingly I have remembrance concerning you in my petitions night and day,
4 longing to see you, being reminded of your tears, that I may be filled with joy,
5 taking recollection of the unpretended faith in you, which first dwelt in your grandmother Lois and (in) your mother Eunice, and I am assured that (it is) also in you.

6 For which cause I remind you to fan into flame the gift of God which is in you through the laying on of my hands.

7 For God did not give a spirit of cowardice to us, but of power and of love, and of self-control.

8 Therefore you should not be ashamed of the testimony of our Lord, nor (of) me, His prisoner. But suffer hardship with the gospel, according to (the) power of God,
9 He having saved us and having called (us) with a holy calling, not according to our works, but according to (His) own purpose and grace given to us in Christ Jesus

ΠΑΥΛΟΥ ΤΟΥ ΑΠΟΣΤΟΛΟΥ Η ΗΡΟΣ
OF PAUL THE APOSTLE THE TO

ΤΙΜΟΘΕΟΝ ΕΠΙΣΤΟΛΗ ΔΕΥΤΕΡΑ
TIMOTHY EPISTLE SECOND

2 Timothy 1

3972 652 2424 5547 1223 2307 2316
1. Παῦλος ἀπόστολος Ἰησοῦ Χριστοῦ διὰ θελήματος Θεοῦ
Paul an apostle of Jesus Christ through (the) will of God

2596 1860 2222 3588 1722 5547 2424 5095
κατ᾽ ἐπαγγελίαν ζωῆς τῆς ἐν Χριστῷ Ἰησοῦ, 2 Τιμοθέῳ
by way of a promise of life in Christ Jesus, to Timothy

27 5043 5485 1656 1515 575 2316 3962 2532
ἀγαπητῷ τέκνῳ· χάρις, ἔλεος, εἰρήνη ἀπὸ Θεοῦ πατρὸς καὶ
beloved child; Grace, mercy, peace from God (the) Father and

5547 2424 3588 2962 2257
Χριστοῦ Ἰησοῦ τοῦ Κυρίου ἡμῶν.
Christ Jesus the Lord of us.

5485 2192 3588 2316 3739 3000 575 4269 1722 2513
3. Χάριν ἔχω τῷ Θεῷ, ᾧ λατρεύω ἀπὸ προγόνων ἐν καθαρᾷ
Thanks I have to God, whom I worship from (my) forebears in a pure

4893 5613 88 2192 3588 4012 4675 3417 1722 3588
συνειδήσει, ὡς ἀδιάλειπτον ἔχω τὴν περὶ σοῦ μνείαν ἐν ταῖς
conscience, as without ceasing I have the about you remembrance in the

1162 3450 3571 2532 2250 1971 4571 1492 3415
δεήσεσί μου νυκτὸς καὶ ἡμέρας, 4 ἐπιποθῶν σε ἰδεῖν, μεμνη-
petitions of me night and day, longing you to see, being

4675 3588 1144 2443 5479 4137 5280
μένος σου τῶν δακρύων, ἵνα χαρᾶς πληρωθῶ, 5 ὑπόμνησιν
reminded of you the tears, that (with) joy I may be filled, recollection

2983 3588 1722 4671 505 4102 3748 1774
λαμβάνων τῆς ἐν σοὶ ἀνυποκρίτου πίστεως, ἥτις ἐνῴκησε
taking of the in you unpretended faith, which indwelt

4412 1722 3588 3125 4675 3090 2532 3588 3384 4675 2131
πρῶτον ἐν τῇ μάμμῃ σου Λωΐδι καὶ τῇ μητρί σου Εὐνίκῃ,
firstly in the grandmother of you Lois and (in) the mother of you Eunice,

3982 1161 3754 2532 1722 4671 1223 3739 156 363 4571
πέπεισμαι δὲ ὅτι καὶ ἐν σοί. 6 δι᾽ ἣν αἰτίαν ἀναμιμνήσκω σε
I am assured and that also in you (is). For which cause I remind you

329 3588 5486 3588 2316 3739 2076 1722 4671 1223 3588
ἀναζωπυρεῖν τὸ χάρισμα τοῦ Θεοῦ, ὅ ἐστιν ἐν σοὶ διὰ τῆς
to fan the flame of the gift of God, which is in you through the

1936 3588 5495 3450 3756 1063 1325 2254 3588 2316
ἐπιθέσεως τῶν χειρῶν μου. 7 οὐ γὰρ ἔδωκεν ἡμῖν ὁ Θεὸς
laying on the hands of me. not For gave to us God

4151 1167 235 1411 2532 26 2532 4995
πνεῦμα δειλίας, ἀλλὰ δυνάμεως καὶ ἀγάπης καὶ σωφρονι-
a spirit of cowardice, but of power and of love and of self-

3361 3767 1870 3588 3142 3588 2962 2257
σμοῦ. 8 μὴ οὖν ἐπαισχυνθῇς τὸ μαρτύριον τοῦ Κυρίου ἡμῶν,
control. not Therefore be ashamed of the testimony of the Lord of us,

3366 1691 3588 1198 846 235 4777 3588
μηδὲ ἐμὲ τὸν δέσμιον αὐτοῦ· ἀλλὰ συγκακοπάθησον τῷ
nor (of) me the prisoner of Him; but suffer hardship with the

2098 2596 1411 2316 3588 4982 2248 2532
εὐαγγελίῳ κατὰ δύναμιν Θεοῦ, 9 τοῦ σώσαντος ἡμᾶς καὶ
gospel according to (the) power of God, the (One) having saved us and

2564 2821 40 3756 2596 3588 2041 2257 235 2596
καλέσαντος κλήσει ἁγίᾳ, οὐ κατὰ τὰ ἔργα ἡμῶν, ἀλλὰ κατ᾽
having called calling with a holy, not according to works of us, but by

2398 4286 2532 5485 3588 1325 2254 1722 5547 2424
ἰδίαν πρόθεσιν καὶ χάριν τὴν δοθεῖσαν ἡμῖν ἐν Χριστῷ Ἰησοῦ
(His) own purpose and grace having been given to us in Christ Jesus

King James Version

The Second Epistle of Paul to Timothy

2 Timothy 1

1. Paul, an apostle of Jesus Christ by the will of God, according to the promise of life which is in Christ Jesus,
2 To Timothy, (my) dearly beloved son: Grace, mercy, (and) peace, from God the Father and Christ Jesus our Lord.

3 I thank God, whom I serve from (my) forefathers with pure conscience, that without ceasing I have remembrance of thee in my prayers night and day;
4 Greatly desiring to see thee, being mindful of thy tears, that I may be filled with joy;
5 When I call to remembrance the unfeigned faith that is in thee, which dwelt first in thy grandmother Lois, and thy mother Eunice; and I am persuaded that in thee also.

6 Wherefore I put thee in remembrance that thou stir up the gift of God, which is in thee by the putting on of my hands.

7 For God hath not given us the spirit of fear; but of power, and of love, and of a sound mind.

8 Be not thou therefore ashamed of the testimony of our Lord, nor of me his prisoner: but be thou partaker of the afflictions of the gospel according to the power of God;
9 Who hath saved us, and called (us) with an holy calling, not according to our works, but according to his own purpose and grace, which was given us in Christ Jesus

Literal Translation

before eternal times,
10 but now having been revealed through the appearance of our Savior, Jesus Christ, making death of no effect, bringing life and incorruptibility to light through the gospel,

11 for which I was appointed a herald and apostle and a teacher of nations.
12 For which cause I also suffer these things. But I am not ashamed, for I know whom I have believed, and I am persuaded that He is able to guard my deposit until that Day.

13 Hold a pattern of sound words which you heard from me, in faith and love in Christ Jesus.
14 Guard the good Deposit (given) through (the) Holy Spirit indwelling in us.

2 Timothy 1:10

4253 5550 166 5319 1161 3568 1223 3588
πρὸ χρόνων αἰωνίων, 10 φανερωθεῖσαν δὲ νῦν διὰ τῆς ἐπι-
before times eternal, having been revealed and now through the

2015 3588 4990 2257 2424 5547 2673
φανείας τοῦ σωτῆρος ἡμῶν Ἰησοῦ Χριστοῦ, καταργήσαντος
appearance of the Savior of us Jesus Christ, having made of no effect

3303 3588 2288 5461 1161 2222 2532 861 1223 3588
μὲν τὸν θάνατον, φωτίσαντος δὲ ζωὴν καὶ ἀφθαρσίαν διὰ τοῦ
truly death, having brought to light and life and incorruption through the

2098 1519 3739 5087 1473 2783 2532 652 2532
εὐαγγελίου, 11 εἰς ὃ ἐτέθην ἐγὼ κήρυξ καὶ ἀπόστολος καὶ
gospel for which was appointed I a herald and apostle and

1320 1484 1223 3739 156 2532 5023 3958 235 3756
διδάσκαλος ἐθνων. 12 δι' ἣν αἰτίαν καὶ ταῦτα πάσχω, ἀλλ' οὐκ
a teacher of nations. for which cause also these things I suffer, but not

1870 1492 1063 3739 4100 2532 3982 3754
ἐπαισχύνομαν, οἶδα γὰρ ᾧ πεπίστευκα, καὶ πέπεισμαι ὅτι
I am ashamed, I know for whom I have believed, and I am persuaded that

1415 2076 3588 3866 3450 5442 1519 1565 3588
δυνατός ἐστι τὴν παραθήκην μου φυλάξαι εἰς ἐκείνην τὴν
able He is the deposit of me to guard unto that

2250 5296 2192 5198 3056 3739 3844 1700
ἡμέραν. 13 ὑποτύπωσιν ἔχε ὑγιαινόντων λόγων ὧν παρ' ἐμοῦ
Day. a pattern Have of sound words which from me

191 1722 4102 2532 26 3588 1722 5547 2424 3588
ἤκουσας, ἐν πίστει καὶ ἀγάπῃ τῇ ἐν Χριστῷ Ἰησοῦ. 14 τὴν
you heard, in faith and love in Christ Jesus. the

2570 3872 5442 1223 4151 40 3588
καλὴν παρακαταθήκην φύλαξον διὰ Πνεύματος Ἁγίου τοῦ
good Deposit Guard through (the) Spirit Holy

1774 1722 2254
ἐνοικοῦντος ἐν ἡμῖν.
indwelling in us.

King James Version

before the world began,
10 But is now made manifest by the appearing of our Saviour Jesus Christ, who hath abolished death, and hath brought life and immortality to light through the gospel:

11 Whereunto I am appointed a preacher, and an apostle, and a teacher of the Gentiles.
12 For the which cause I also suffer these things: nevertheless I am not ashamed: for I know whom I have believed, and am persuaded that he is able to keep that which I have committed unto him against that day.
13 Hold fast the form of sound words, which thou hast heard of me, in faith and love which is in Christ Jesus.
14 That good thing which was committed unto thee keep by the Holy Ghost which dwelleth in us.

15 You know this, that all those in Asia turned away from me, of whom are Phygellus and Hermogenes.
16 May the Lord give mercy to the house of Onesiphorus, because he often refreshed me, and he was not ashamed of my chain,
17 but having come to Rome, he more diligently sought and found (me).
18 May the Lord give to him to find mercy from (the) Lord in that Day. And what things he served in Ephesus, you know very well.

1492 5124 3754 654 3165 3956 3588/1722/3588
15. Οἶδας τοῦτο, ὅτι ἀπεστράφησάν με πάντες οἱ ἐν τῇ
You know this, that turned away from me all those in

773 3739 2076 5436 2532 2061 1325 1656 3588 2962
Ἀσίᾳ, ὧν ἐστι Φύγελος καὶ Ἑρμογένης. 16 δῴη ἔλεος ὁ Κύριος
Asia, of whom is Phygellus and Hermogenes. May give mercy the Lord

3588 3683 3624 3754 4178 3165 404 2532 3588 254
τῷ Ὀνησιφόρου οἴκῳ· ὅτι πολλάκις με ἀνέψυξε καὶ τὴν ἅλυσίν
to the of Onesiphorus house; because often me he refreshed and the chain

3450 3756 1870 235 1096 1722 4516 4706
μου οὐκ ἐπαισχύνθη, 17 ἀλλὰ γενόμενος ἐν Ῥώμῃ σπουδαιό-
of me not he was ashamed, but having come in Rome more

2212 31652532 2147 1325 846 3588 2962 2147 1656
τερον ἐζήτησέ με καὶ εὗρε 18 [δῴη αὐτῷ ὁ Κύριος εὑρεῖν ἔλεος
diligently he sought me and found; may give to him the Lord to find mercy

3844 2962 1722 1565 3588 2250 2532 3745 1722 2181
παρὰ Κυρίου ἐν ἐκείνῃ τῇ ἡμέρᾳ]· καὶ ὅσα ἐν Ἐφέσῳ
from (the) Lord in that Day; and what things in Ephesus

1247 957 4771 1097
διηκόνησε, βέλτιον σὺ γινώσκεις.
he served, very well you know.

15 This thou knowest, that all they which are in Asia be turned away from me; of whom are Phygellus and Hermogenes.
16 The Lord give mercy unto the house of Onesiphorus; for he oft refreshed me, and was not ashamed of my chain:
17 But, when he was in Rome, he sought me out very diligently, and found (me).
18 The Lord grant unto him that he may find mercy of the Lord in that day: and in how many things he ministered unto me at Ephesus, thou knowest very well.

2 Timothy 2

1. Then my child, you be empowered by grace in Christ Jesus.
2 And what things you heard from me through many witnesses,

2 Timothy 2

4771 3767 5043 3450 1743 1722 3588 5485 3588 1722 5547
1. Σὺ οὖν, τέκνον μου, ἐνδυναμοῦ ἐν τῇ χάριτι τῇ ἐν Χριστῷ
you Therefore, child of me, be empowered by grace in Christ

2424 2532 3739 191 3844 1700 1223 4183 3144
Ἰησοῦ, 2 καὶ ἃ ἤκουσας παρ' ἐμοῦ διὰ πολλῶν μαρτύρων,
Jesus, and what things you heard from me through many witnesses,

2 Timothy 2

1. Thou therefore, my son, be strong in the grace that is in Christ Jesus.
2 And the things that thou hast heard of me among many witnesses,

Literal Translation

commit these things to faithful men, such as will be competent also to teach others.
3 Then you suffer hardship as a good soldier of Jesus Christ.
4 No one serving as a soldier entangles (himself) with the affairs of (this) life, so that he might please the (one) enlisting (him).
5 And also if anyone competes, he is not crowned unless he competes lawfully.
6 (It is) right the laboring farmer to partake first of the fruits.
7 Consider what I say, for the Lord will give you understanding in all things.
8 Remember Jesus Christ, having been raised from (the) dead, of (the) seed of David, according to my gospel,
9 in which I suffer ill as an evildoer, unto bonds; but the Word of God has not been bound.
10 Because of this, I endure all things on account of the elect, that they also may obtain salvation in Christ Jesus, with everlasting glory.
11 Faithful (is) the Word: for if we died with (Him), we also shall live with (Him);
12 if we endure, we shall also reign with (Him); if we deny (Him), that One will deny us;
13 if we are unfaithful, that One remains faithful; He is not able to deny Himself.
14 Remind (them of) these things, solemnly testifying before the Lord not to dispute about words for nothing useful, to (the) throwing down (of) those hearing.
15 Be eager to present yourself approved to God, a workman unashamed, rightly dividing the Word of Truth.
16 But shun profane, empty babblings, for

2 Timothy 2:3

5023 3908 4103 444 3748 2425 2071
ταῦτα παράθου πιστοῖς ἀνθρώποις, οἵτινες ἱκανοὶ ἔσονται
these things commit to faithful men, who competent will be

2532 2087 1321 4771/3767 2553 5613 2570 4757
καὶ ἑτέρους διδάξαι. 3 συ οὖν κακοπάθησον ὡς καλὸς στρατιώ-
also others to teach. you Then suffer hardship as a good soldier

2424 5547 3762 4754 1707 3588
της Ἰησοῦ Χριστοῦ. 4 οὐδεὶς στρατευόμενος ἐμπλέκεται ταῖς
of Jesus Christ. No one serving as a soldier tangles with the

3588 979 4230 2443 3588 4758 700
τοῦ βίου πραγματείαις, ἵνα τῷ στρατολογήσαντι ἀρέσῃ.
of life affairs, that the (One) having enlisted (him) he please.

1437 1161 2532 118 5100 3756 4737 1437 3361 3545 118
5 ἐὰν δὲ καὶ ἀθλῇ τις, οὐ στεφανοῦται ἐὰν μὴ νομίμως ἀθλήσῃ.
if And also competes any not he is crowned if not lawfully he competes.

3588 2872 1092 1163 4412 3588 2590 3335
6 τὸν κοπιῶντα γεωργὸν δεῖ πρῶτον τῶν καρπῶν μετα-
The laboring farmer it behooves firstly of the fruits to

3539 3739 3004 1325 1063 4671 3588 2962 4907 1722
λαμβάνειν. 7 νόει ὃ λέγω· δῴη γάρ σοι ὁ Κύριος σύνεσιν ἐν
partake. Consider what I say; will give for you the Lord understanding in

3956 3421 2424 5547 1453 1537 3498
πᾶσι. 8 μνημόνευε Ἰησοῦν Χριστὸν ἐγηγερμένον ἐκ νεκρῶν,
all. Remember Jesus Christ having been raised from (the) dead;

1537 4690 1138 2596 3588 2098 3450 1722 3739 2553
ἐκ σπέρματος Δαβίδ, κατὰ τὸ εὐαγγέλιόν μου· 9 ἐν ᾧ κακο-
of (the) seed of David, according to the gospel of me; in which I

3360 1199 5613 2557 235 3588 3056 3588 2316
παθῶ μέχρι δεσμῶν, ὡς κακοῦργος· ἀλλὰ ὁ λόγος τοῦ Θεοῦ
suffer ill unto bonds, as an evildoer; but the Word of God

3756 1210 1223 5124 3956 5278 1223 3588 1588
οὐ δέδεται. 10 διὰ τοῦτο πάντα ὑπομένω διὰ τοὺς ἐκλεκτούς,
not (is) bound. Because of this all things I endure on account of the elect,

2443 2532 846 4991 5177 3588 1722 5547 2424 3326
ἵνα καὶ αὐτοὶ σωτηρίας τύχωσι τῆς ἐν Χριστῷ Ἰησοῦ, μετὰ
that also they salvation may obtain in Christ Jesus, with

1391 166 4103 3588 3056 14871063 4880 2532
δόξης αἰωνίου. 11 πιστὸς ὁ λόγος· Εἰ γὰρ συναπεθάνομεν, καὶ
glory everlasting. Faithful (is) the Word; if for we died with (Him), also

4800 1487 5278 2532 4821 1487 720
συζήσομεν· 12 εἰ ὑπομένομεν, καὶ συμβασιλεύσομεν· εἰ ἀρνού-
we shall live; if we endure, also we shall reign with (Him); if we deny

2548 720 2248 1487 569 1565
μεθα, κἀκεῖνος ἀρνήσεται ἡμᾶς· 13 εἰ ἀπιστοῦμεν, ἐκεῖνος
(Him), that One will deny us; if we are unfaithful, that One

4103 3306 720 1063 1438 3756 1410
πιστὸς μένει· ἀρνήσασθαι γὰρ ἑαυτὸν οὐ δύναται.
faithful remains; to deny for Himself not He is able.

5023 5279 1263 1799 3588
14. Ταῦτα ὑπομίμνῃσκε, διαμαρτυρόμενος ἐνώπιον τοῦ
These things remind (them), solemnly testifying before the

2962 3361 3054 1519 3762 5539 1909 2692
Κυριου μὴ λογομαχεῖν εἰς οὐδὲν χρήσιμον, ἐπὶ καταστροφῇ
Lord not to dispute about words for nothing useful, to throwing down

3588 191 4704 4572 1384 3936
τῶν ἀκουόντων. 15 σπούδασον σεαυτὸν δόκιμον παραστῆσαι
the (ones) hearing. Be eager to present yourself approved to show

3588 2316 2040 422 3718 3588 3056
τῷ Θεῷ, ἐργάτην ἀνεπαίσχυντον, ὀρθοτομοῦντα τὸν λόγον
to God, a workman unashamed, rightly dividing the Word

3588 225 3588 1161 952 2757 4026 1909
τῆς ἀληθείας. 16 τὰς δὲ βεβήλους κενοφωνίας περιΐστασο· ἐπὶ
of truth. the But profane empty babblings shun; to

King James Version

the same commit thou to faithful men, who shall be able to teach others also.
3 Thou therefore endure hardness, as a good soldier of Jesus Christ.
4 No man that warreth entangleth himself with the affairs of (this) life; that he may please him who hath chosen him to be a soldier.
5 And if a man also strive for masteries, (yet) is he not crowned, except he strive lawfully.
6 The husbandman that laboureth must be first partaker of the fruits.
7 Consider what I say; and the Lord give thee understanding in all things.
8 Remember that Jesus Christ of the seed of David was raised from the dead according to my gospel:
9 Wherein I suffer trouble, as an evil doer, (even) unto bonds; but the word of God is not bound.
10 Therefore I endure all things for the elect's sakes, that they may also obtain the salvation which is in Christ Jesus with eternal glory.
11 (It is) a faithful saying: For if we be dead with (him), we shall also live with (him):
12 If we suffer, we shall also reign with (him): if we deny (him), he also will deny us:
13 If we believe not, (yet) he abideth faithful: he cannot deny himself.
14 Of these things put (them) in remembrance, charging (them) before the Lord that they strive not about words to no profit, (but) to the subverting of the hearers.
15 Study to shew thyself approved unto God, a workman that needeth not to be ashamed, rightly dividing the word of truth.
16 But shun profane (and) vain babblings: for

Literal Translation

they will go on to more
ungodliness,
17 and their word will
have growth like gan-
grene, of whom (are)
Hymenaeus and
Philetus,

18 who missed the
mark concerning the
truth, saying the resur-
rection already has
come, and overturn the
faith of some.

19 However, the foun-
dation of God stands
firm, having this seal,
"(The) Lord knew
those being His;" (see
Num.16:5,70), also,
"Let everyone naming
the name of Christ de-
part from unrighteous-
ness."
20 But in a great house
not only are there ves-
sels of gold and silver,
but also of wood and of
earth, and some to
honor and some to dis-
honor.
21 Then if anyone puri-
fies himself from these,
he will be a vessel to
honor, having been
sanctified and made
useful to the Master,
having been prepared to
every good work.
22 But flee youthful
lusts and pursue right-
eousness, faith, love,
peace, with the (ones)
calling on the Lord out
of a pure heart.
23 But refuse the fool-
ish and uninstructed
questionings, knowing
that they generate quar-
rels.

24 But a slave of (the)
Lord ought not to quar-
rel, but to be gentle to-
wards all, apt to teach,
forbearing,
25 in meekness teach-
ing those who have op-
posed, if perhaps God
may give them repen-
tance for a full knowl-
edge of (the) truth,
26 and they may awake
out of the snare of the
devil, having been
taken captive by him, in
order to (do) the will of
that one.

2 Timothy 2:17

4119 1063 4298 763 2532 3588 3056 846 5613
πλεῖον γὰρ προκόψουσιν ἀσεβείας, 17 καὶ ὁ λόγος αὐτῶν ὡς
more for they will advance ungodliness, and the word of them as

1044 3542 2192 3739 2076 5211 2532 5372
γάγγραινα νομὴν ἕξει· ὧν ἐστιν Ὑμέναιος καὶ Φίλητος·
gangrene feeding will have of whom is Hymenaeus and Philetus;

3748 4012 3588 225 795 3004 3588
18 οἵτινες περὶ τὴν ἀλήθειαν ἠστόχησαν, λέγοντες τὴν
who concerning the truth missed the mark, saying the

386 2235 1096 2532 396 3588 5100 4102
ἀνάστασιν ἤδη γεγονέναι, καὶ ἀνατρέπουσι τήν τινων πίστιν.
resurrection already to have come, and overturn the of some faith.

3588 3305 4731 2310 3588 2316 2476 2192 3588
19 ὁ μέντοι στερεὸς θεμέλιος τοῦ Θεοῦ ἕστηκεν, ἔχων τὴν
the However firm foundation of God stands, having

4973 3778 1097 2962 3588 5607 846 2532
σφραγῖδα ταύτην, Ἔγνω Κύριος τοὺς ὄντας αὐτοῦ, καί,
seal this, knew (The) Lord the (ones) being His, and,

868 575 93 3956 3588 3687 3588 3686 5547 1722
Ἀποστήτω ἀπὸ ἀδικίας πᾶς ὁ ὀνομάζων τὸ ὄνομα Χριστοῦ. 20 ἐν
Let depart from iniquity everyone naming the name of Christ. in

3173 1161 3614 3756 2076 3440 4632 5552 2532 693 235
μεγάλῃ δὲ οἰκίᾳ οὐκ ἔστι μόνον σκεύη χρυσᾶ καὶ ἀργυρᾶ, ἀλλὰ
a great But house not is there only vessels golden and silver, but

2532 3585 2532 3749 2532 3739 3303 1519 5092 3739 1161 1519 819
καὶ ξύλινα καὶ ὀστράκινα, καὶ ἃ μὲν εἰς τιμὴν, ἃ δὲ εἰς ἀτιμίαν.
also wooden and earthen; and some to honor, and some to dishonor.

1437 3767 5100 1571 1438 575 5130 2071 4632 1519
21 ἐὰν οὖν τις ἐκκαθάρῃ ἑαυτὸν ἀπὸ τούτων, ἔσται σκεῦος εἰς
If therefore any cleanses himself from these, he will be a vessel to

5092 37 2532 2173 3588 1203 1519 3956
τιμήν, ἡγιασμένον, καὶ εὔχρηστον τῷ δεσπότῃ, εἰς πᾶν
honor, having been sanctified, and useful to the master, to every

2041 18 2090 3588 1161 3512 1939
ἔργον ἀγαθὸν ἡτοιμασμένον. 22 τὰς δὲ νεωτερικὰς ἐπιθυμίας
work good having been prepared. the And youthful lusts;

5343 1377 1161 1343 4102 26 1515 3326
φεῦγε· δίωκε δὲ δικαιοσύνην, πίστιν, ἀγάπην, εἰρήνην, μετὰ
flee; pursue and righteousness, faith, love, peace, with

3588 1941 3588 2962 1537 2513 2588 3588 1161
τῶν ἐπικαλουμένων τὸν Κύριον ἐκ καθαρᾶς καρδίας. 23 τὰς δὲ
the (ones) calling on the Lord out of a pure heart. the But

3474 2532 521 2214 3868 1492 3754
μωρὰς καὶ ἀπαιδεύτους ζητήσεις παραιτοῦ, εἰδὼς ὅτι
foolish and uninstructed questionings refuse, knowing that

1080 3163 1401 1161 2962 3756 1163 3164 235
γεννῶσι μάχας. 24 δοῦλον δὲ Κυρίου οὐ δεῖ μάχεσθαι, ἀλλ᾽
they generate quarrels. a slave And of (the) Lord not must quarrel, but

2261 1511 4314 3956 1317 420 1722 4236
ἤπιον εἶναι πρὸς πάντας, διδακτικόν, ἀνεξίκακον, 25 ἐν πρᾳό-
gentle to be toward all, apt to teach, forbearing, in meek-

3811 3588 475 3379 1325 846
τητι παιδεύοντα τοὺς ἀντιδιατιθεμένους· μήποτε δῷ αὐτοῖς
ness teaching the (ones) opposing; (if) perhaps may give them

3588 2316 3341 1519 1922 225 2532 366
ὁ Θεὸς μετάνοιαν εἰς ἐπίγνωσιν ἀληθείας, 26 καὶ ἀνανήψωσιν
God repentance unto a full knowledge of truth; and they regain senses

1537 3588 3588 1228 3803 2221 5259 846 1519 3588
ἐκ τῆς τοῦ διαβόλου παγίδος, ἐζωγρημένοι ὑπ᾽ αὐτοῦ εἰς τὸ
from the of the devil snare, having been captured by him to (do) the

1565 2307
ἐκείνου θέλημα.
of that one will.

King James Version

they will increase unto
more ungodliness.
17 And their word will
eat as doth a canker: of
whom is Hymenaeus
and Philetus;

18 Who concerning the
truth have erred, saying
that the resurrection is
past already; and over-
throw the faith of some.

19 Nevertheless the
foundation of God stan-
deth sure, having this
seal, The Lord knoweth
them that are his. And,
Let every one that
nameth the name of
Christ depart from iniq-
uity.
20 But in a great house
there are not only ves-
sels of gold and of sil-
ver, but also of wood
and of earth; and some
to honour, and some to
dishonour.

21 If a man therefore
purge himself from
these, he shall be a ves-
sel unto honour, sancti-
fied, and meet for the
master's use, (and) pre-
pared unto every good
work.
22 Flee also youthful
lusts: but follow right-
eousness, faith, charity,
peace, with them that
call on the Lord out of a
pure heart.
23 But foolish and un-
learned questions
avoid, knowing that
they do gender strifes.

24 And the servant of
the Lord must not
strive; but be gentle
unto all (men), apt to
teach, patient,
25 In meekness in-
structing those that op-
pose themselves; if God
peradventure will give
them repentance to the
acknowledging of the
truth;
26 And (that) they may
recover themselves out
of the snare of the devil,
who are taken captive
by him at his will.

Literal Translation

2 Timothy 3

1. But know this, that in (the) last days grievous times will be at hand.
2 For men will be lovers of themselves, lovers of money, braggarts, arrogant, blasphemers, disobedient to parents, unthankful, unholy,
3 without natural feeling, unyielding, slanderers, without self-control, savage, haters of good,
4 betrayers, reckless, puffed up, lovers of pleasure rather than lovers of God,
5 having a form of godliness, but denying the power of it; even turn away from these.

6 For of these are those creeping into houses and leading silly women captive, (the ones) having been heaped with sins, being led away by various lusts,
7 always learning, but never being able to come to a full knowledge of (the) truth.
8 But in the way Jannes and Jambres withstood Moses, so also these withstand the truth, men having been corrupted (in) mind, found worthless as to the faith.

9 But they will not go further, for their foolishness will be plain to all, as also that of those became.

10 But you have closely followed my doctrine, the conduct, the purpose, the faith, the long-suffering, the love, the patient endurance,

11 the persecutions, the sufferings, such as happened to me in Antioch, in Iconium, in Lystra, what persecutions I bore. And the Lord delivered me out of all.

12 And, indeed, all desiring to live godly in Christ

2 Timothy 3:1

5124 1161 1097 3754 1722 2078 2250 1764
1. Τοῦτο δὲ γίνωσκε, ὅτι ἐν ἐσχάταις ἡμέραις ἐνστήσονται
this And know, that in (the) last days will be at hand

2540 5467 2071 1063 3588 444 5367 5366
καιροὶ χαλεποί. 2 ἔσονται γὰρ οἱ ἄνθρωποι φίλαυτοι, φιλ-
times grievous. will be For men self-lovers, money-

213 5244 989 1118 545
άργυροι, ἀλαζόνες, ὑπερήφανοι, βλάσφημοι, γονεῦσιν ἀπει-
lovers, braggarts, arrogant, blasphemers, to parents dis-

884 462 794 786 1228
θεῖς, ἀχάριστοι, ἀνόσιοι, 3 ἄστοργοι, ἄσπονδοι, διάβολοι,
obedient, unthankful, unholy, without natural feeling, implacable, slanderers,

193 434 865 4273 4312 5187
ἀκρατεῖς, ἀνήμεροι, ἀφιλάγαθοι, 4 προδόται, προπετεῖς, τετυ-
without self-control, savage, haters of good, betrayers, reckless, puffed

5187 5369 3123 2228 5377 2192 3446
φωμένοι, φιλήδονοι μᾶλλον ἢ φιλόθεοι, 5 ἔχοντες μόρφωσιν
up, pleasure-lovers rather than God-lovers, having a form

2150 3588 1161 1411 846 720 2532 5128
εὐσεβείας, τὴν δὲ δύναμιν αὐτῆς ἠρνημένοι· καὶ τούτους
of godliness, the but power of it having denied; even these

665 1537 5130 1063 1526 3588 1744 1519 3588 3614
ἀποτρέπου. 6 ἐκ τούτων γάρ εἰσιν οἱ ἐνδύνοντες εἰς τὰς οἰκίας,
turn awaya from. of these For are those creeping into houses,

2532 162 3588 1133 4987 266
καὶ αἰχμαλωτίζοντες τὰ γυναικάρια σεσωρευμένα ἁμαρ-
and leading captive silly women having been heaped with

71 1939 4164 3842 3129
τίαις, ἀγόμενα ἐπιθυμίαις ποικίλαις, 7 πάντοτε μανθάνοντα
sins, being led lusts by various, always learning

2532 3368 1519 1922 225 2064 1410 3739
καὶ μηδέποτε εἰς ἐπίγνωσιν ἀληθείας ἐλθεῖν δυνάμενα. 8 ὃν
and never to a full knowledge of truth to come being able. by

5158 1161 2389 2532 2387 436 3475 3779
τρόπον δὲ Ἰάννης καὶ Ἰαμβρῆς ἀντέστησαν Μωϋσεῖ, οὕτω
what way And Jannes and Jambres opposed Moses, so

2532 3778 436 3588 225 444 2704
καὶ οὗτοι ἀνθίστανται τῇ ἀληθείᾳ, ἄνθρωποι κατεφθαρ-
also these oppose the truth, men having been

3588 3563 96 4012 3588 4102 235 3756 4298
μένοι τὸν νοῦν, ἀδόκιμοι περὶ τὴν πίστιν. 9 ἀλλ' οὐ προκό-
corrupted the mind, reprobate concerning the faith. But not they will

1909 4119 3588 1063 454 846 1552 2071 3956
ψουσιν ἐπὶ πλεῖον· ἡ γὰρ ἄνοια αὐτῶν ἔκδηλος ἔσται πᾶσιν,
advance to more; the for folly of them plain will be to all,

5613 2532 3588 1565 1096 4771 1161 3877 3450 3588
ὡς καὶ ἡ ἐκείνων ἐγένετο. 10 σὺ δὲ παρηκολούθησάς μου τῇ
as also the (folly) of those became. you But have clearly followed of me the

1319 3588 72 3588 4286 3588 4102 3588
διδασκαλίᾳ, τῇ ἀγωγῇ, τῇ προθέσει, τῇ πίστει, τῇ μα-
teaching, the conduct, the purpose, the faith, the long-

3115 3588 26 3588 5281 3588 1375 3588 3804
κροθυμίᾳ, τῇ ἀγάπῃ, τῇ ὑπομονῇ, 11 τοῖς διωγμοῖς, τοῖς παθή-
suffering, the love, the patience, the persecutions, the sufferings,

3634 3427 1096 1722 490 1722 2430 1722 3082
μασιν, οἷά μοι ἐγένετο ἐν Ἀντιοχείᾳ, ἐν Ἰκονίῳ, ἐν Λύστροις,
which to me happened in Antioch, in Iconium, in Lystra,

3634 1375 5297 2532 1537 3956 3165 4506 3588
οἵους διωγμοὺς ὑπήνεγκα· καὶ ἐκ πάντων με ἐρρύσατο ὁ
what persecutions I bore; yet out of all me delivered the

2962 2532 3956 1161 3588 2309 2153 2198 1722 5547
Κύριος. 12 καὶ πάντες δὲ οἱ θέλοντες εὐσεβῶς ζῆν ἐν Χριστῷ
Lord. indeed all And those desiring godly to live in Christ

King James Version

2 Timothy 3

1. This know also, that in the last days perilous times shall come.
2 For men shall be lovers of their own selves, covetous, boasters, proud, blasphemers, disobedient to parents, unthankful, unholy,

3 Without natural affection, trucebreakers, false accusers, incontinent, fierce, despisers of those that are good,
4 Traitors, heady, highminded, lovers of pleasures more than lovers of God;
5 Having a form of godliness, but denying the power thereof: from such turn away.

6 For of this sort are they which creep into houses, and lead captive silly women laden with sins, led away with divers lusts,

7 Ever learning, and never able to come to the knowledge of the truth.
8 Now as Jannes and Jambres withstood Moses, so do these also resist the truth: men of corrupt minds, reprobate concerning the faith.

9 But they shall proceed no further: for their folly shall be manifest unto all (men), as theirs also was.

10 But thou hast fully known my doctrine, manner of life, purpose, faith, longsuffering, charity, patience,

11 Persecutions, afflictions, which came unto me at Antioch, at Iconium, at Lystra; what persecutions I endured: but out of (them) all the Lord delivered me.

12 Yea, and all that will live godly in Christ

Literal Translation

Jesus will be persecuted.
13 But evil men and pretenders will go forward to the worse, leading astray and being led astray.

14 But you keep on in what you learned and were assured of, knowing from whom you learned,
15 and that from a babe you know the Holy Scriptures, those being able to make you wise to salvation through belief in Christ Jesus.
16 Every Scripture (is) God-breathed and profitable for doctrine, for reproof, for correction, for instruction in righteousness,

17 so that the man of God may be complete, fully furnished for every good work.

2 Timothy 3:13

2424 1377 4190 1161 444 2532 1114
Ἰησοῦ διωχθήσονται. 13 πονηροὶ δὲ ἄνθρωποι καὶ γόητες
Jesus will be persecuted. evil But men and pretenders

4298 1909 3588 5501 4105 2532 4105
προκόψουσιν ἐπὶ τὸ χεῖρον, πλανῶντες καὶ πλανώμενοι.
will go forward to worse, deceiving and being deceived.

4771 1161 3306 1722 3739 3129 2532 4104 1492 3844 5101
14 σὺ δὲ μένε ἐν οἷς ἔμαθες καὶ ἐπιστώθης, εἰδὼς παρὰ τίνος
you But continue in what you learned and were assured of, knowing from whom

3129 2532 3754 575 1025 3588 2413 1121 1492 3588
ἔμαθες, 15 καὶ ὅτι ἀπὸ βρέφους τὰ ἱερὰ γράμματα οἶδας, τὰ
you learned, and that from a babe the Holy Scripture you know, those

1410 4571 4679 1519 4991 1223 4102 3588 1722
δυνάμενά σε σοφίσαι εἰς σωτηρίαν διὰ πίστεως τῆς ἐν
being able you to make wise to salvation through belief in

5547 2424 3956 1124 2315 2532 5624
Χριστῷ Ἰησοῦ. 16 πᾶσα γραφὴ θεόπνευστος καὶ ὠφέλιμος
Christ Jesus. Every Scripture (is) God-breathed and profitable

4314 1319 4314 1650 4314 1882 4314
πρὸς διδασκαλίαν, πρὸς ἐλεγμόν, πρὸς ἐπανόρθωσιν, πρὸς
for teaching, for reproof, for correction, for

3809 3588 1722 1343 2443 739 5600/3588/3588/2316
παιδείαν τὴν ἐν δικαιοσύνῃ· 17 ἵνα ἄρτιος ᾖ ὁ τοῦ Θεοῦ
instruction in righteousness; that fitted may be the of God

444 4314 3956 2041 18 1822
ἄνθρωπος, πρὸς πᾶν ἔργον ἀγαθὸν ἐξηρτισμένος.
man, for every work good having been furnished.

King James Version

Jesus shall suffer persecution.
13 But evil men and seducers shall wax worse and worse, deceiving, and being deceived.

14 But continue thou in the things which thou hast learned and hast been assured of, knowing of whom thou hast learned (them);
15 And that from a child thou hast known the holy scriptures, which are able to make thee wise unto salvation through faith which is in Christ Jesus.
16 All scripture (is) given by inspiration of God, and (is) profitable for doctrine, for reproof, for correction, for instruction in righteousness:
17 That the man of God may be perfect, throughly furnished unto all good works.

2 Timothy 4

2 Timothy 4

1. Then I solemnly witness before God and the Lord Jesus Christ, He being about to judge living and dead (at) His appearance and His kingdom:

2 preach the Word, be urgent, in season, out of season, convict, warn, encourage with all long-suffering and teaching.

3 For a time will be when they will not endure sound doctrine, but according to their own lusts, they will heap up to themselves teachers tickling the ear;

4 and (they) will turn away the ear from the truth and will be turned aside to myths.
5 But you be clear-minded in all, suffer hardship, do (the) work of an evangelist, fully carry out your ministry.

1263 3767 1473 1799 3588 2316 2532 3588
1. Διαμαρτύρομαι οὖν ἐγὼ ἐνώπιον τοῦ Θεοῦ, και τοῦ
solemnly witness Then I before God, and the

2962 2424 5547 3588 3195 2919 2198 2532
Κυρίου Ἰησοῦ Χριστοῦ, τοῦ μέλλοντος κρίνειν ζῶντας καὶ
Lord Jesus Christ, the (One) being about to judge living and

3498 2596 3588 2015 846 2532 3588 932
νεκρούς κατὰ τὴν ἐπιφάνειαν αὐτοῦ καὶ τὴν βασιλείαν
dead according to the appearance of Him and the kingdom

846 2784 3588 3056 2186 2122 171
αὐτοῦ, 2 κήρυξον τὸν λόγον, ἐπίστηθι εὐκαίρως, ἀκαίρως,
of Him, proclaim the Word, be urgent in season, out of season,

1651 2008 3870 1722 3956 3115
ἔλεγξον, ἐπιτίμησον, παρακάλεσον, ἐν πάσῃ μακροθυμίᾳ
reprove, warn encourage, with all long-suffering

2532 1322 2071 1063 2540 3753 3588 5198 1319
καὶ διδαχῇ. 3 ἔσται γὰρ καιρὸς ὅτε τῆς ὑγιαινούσης διδα-
and teaching. there will be For a time when sound doctrine

3756 430 235 2596 3588 1939 3588 2398
σκαλίας οὐκ ἀνέξονται, ἀλλὰ κατὰ τὰς ἐπιθυμίας τὰς ἰδίας
not they will bear, but according to the lusts the own

1438 2002 1320 2833 3588 189
ἑαυτοῖς ἐπισωρεύσουσι διδασκάλους, κνηθόμενοι τὴν ἀκοήν·
to themselves they will heap up teachers, tickling the ear;

2532 575 3303 3588 225 3588 189 654 1909
4 καὶ ἀπὸ μὲν τῆς ἀληθείας τὴν ἀκοὴν ἀποστρέψουσιν, ἐπὶ
and from indeed the truth the ear will turn away, to

11613588 3454 1624 4771 1161/3525 1722 3956 2553
δὲ τοὺς μύθους ἐκτραπήσονται. 5 σὺ δὲ νῆφε ἐν πᾶσι, κακοπά-
and myths will be turned. you But be sober in all, suffer

2041 4160 2099 3588 1248 4675
θησον, ἔργον ποίησον εὐαγγελιστοῦ, τὴν διακονίαν σου
evil, (the) work do of an evangelist, the ministry of you

2 Timothy 4

1. I charge (thee) therefore before God, and the Lord Jesus Christ, who shall judge the quick and the dead at his appearing and his kingdom;

2 Preach the word; be instant in season, out of season; reprove, rebuke, exhort with all longsuffering and doctrine.

3 For the time will come when they will not endure sound doctrine; but after their own lusts shall they heap to themselves teachers, having itching ears;

4 And they shall turn away (their) ears from the truth, and shall be turned unto fables.
5 But watch thou in all things, endure afflictions, do the work of an evangelist, make full proof of thy ministry.

Literal Translation

2 Timothy 4:6

King James Version

6 For I am already being poured out, and the time of my release has arrived.
7 I have fought the good fight. I have finished the course. I have kept the faith.
8 For the rest, the crown of righteousness is laid up for me, which the Lord, the righteous Judge, will give to me in that Day, and not only to me, but also to all the ones loving His appearance.

9 Make haste to come to me shortly.
10 For Demas deserted me, loving the present age, and (he) went to Thessalonica. Crescens (went) to Galatia, Titus to Dalmatia.

11 Only Luke is with me. Taking Mark, bring (him) with you, for he is useful to me for ministry.
12 But I sent Tychicus to Ephesus.
13 When you come, bring the cloak which I left in Troas with Carpus, and the scrolls, especially the parchments.

14 Alexander the coppersmith demonstrated many evil things to me. The Lord will give back to him according to his works.
15 You also guard against (him), for he greatly withstood our words.
16 In my first defense no one was beside me, but all deserted me. May it not be reckoned to them.
17 But the Lord stood with me and gave me power, that through me the preaching might be fulfilled, and all the nations might hear. And I was delivered out of

4135 1473 1063 2235 4689 2532 3588 2540 3588
πληροφόρησον. 6 ἐγὼ γὰρ ἤδη σπένδομαι, καὶ ὁ καιρὸς τῆς
fulfill. I For already am being poured out, and the time

1699 359 2186 3588 73 3588 2570 75
ἐμῆς ἀναλύσεώς ἐφέστηκε. 7 τὸν ἀγῶνα τὸν καλὸν ἠγώνισμαι,
my of departure has arrived. The fight good I have fought,

3588 1408 5055 3588 4102 5083 3063
τὸν δρόμον τετέλεκα, τὴν πίστιν τετήρηκα· 8 λοιπὸν,
the course I have finished, the faith I have kept; for the rest,

606 3427 3588 3588 1343 4735 3739 591
ἀπόκειταί μοι ὁ τῆς δικαιοσύνης στέφανος, ὃν ἀποδώσει
is laid up for me the of righteousness crown which will give

3427 3588 2962 1722 1565 3588 2250 3588 1342 2923 3756
μοι ὁ Κύριος ἐν ἐκείνῃ τῇ ἡμέρᾳ, ὁ δίκαιος κριτής· οὐ
to me the Lord in that Day, the righteous Judge; not

3450 1161 1698 235 2532 3956 3588 25 3588 2015
μόνον δὲ ἐμοὶ ἀλλὰ καὶ πᾶσι τοῖς ἠγαπηκόσι τὴν ἐπιφάνειαν
only and to me but also all the (ones) loving the appearance

846
αὐτοῦ.
of Him.

4704 2064 4314 3165 5030 1214 1063 3165
9. Σπούδασον ἐλθεῖν πρός με ταχέως· 10 Δημᾶς γάρ με
Make haste to come to me shortly; Demas For me

1459 25 3588 3568 165 2532 4198 1519 2332
ἐγκατέλιπεν ἀγαπήσας τὸν νῦν αἰῶνα, καὶ ἐπορεύθη εἰς Θεσ-
deserted loving the present age, and went to Thes-

2913 1519 1053 5103 1519 1149
σαλονίκην· Κρήσκης εἰς Γαλατίαν, Τίτος εἰς Δαλματίαν.
salonica; Crescens to Galatia, Titus to Dalmatia.

3065 2076 3441 3326 1700 3138 353 71 3326
11 Λουκᾶς ἐστι μόνος μετ' ἐμοῦ. Μάρκον ἀναλαβὼν ἄγε μετὰ
Luke is Only with me. Mark having taken bring with

4572 2076 1063 3427 2173 1519 1248 5190 1161
σεαυτοῦ· ἔστι γάρ μοι εὔχρηστος εἰς διακονίαν. 12 Τυχικὸν δὲ
yourself; he is for to me useful for ministry. Tychicus And

649 1519 2181 3588 5341 3739 620 1722 5174
ἀπέστειλα εἰς Ἔφεσον. 13 τὸν φελόνην ὃν ἀπέλιπον ἐν Τρῳάδι
I sent to Ephesus. The cloak which I left in Troas

3844 2591 2064 5342 2532 3588 975 3122 3588
παρὰ Κάρπῳ, ἐρχόμενος φέρε, καὶ τὰ βιβλία, μάλιστα τὰς
with Carpus, coming bring and the scrolls, especially the

3200 223 3588 5471 4183 3427 2556 1731
μεμβράνας. 14 Ἀλέξανδρος ὁ χαλκεὺς πολλά μοι κακὰ ἐνεδεί-
parchments. Alexander the coppersmith much to me evils showed;

591 846 3588 2962 2596 3588 2041 846 3739 2532
ξατο· ἀποδῴη αὐτῷ ὁ Κύριος κατὰ τὰ ἔργα αὐτοῦ· 15 ὃν καὶ
will give to him the Lord according to the works of him; whom also

4771 5442 3029 1063 436 3588 2251 3056
σὺ φυλάσσου, λίαν γὰρ ἀνθέστηκε τοῖς ἡμετέροις λόγοις.
you guard (against), greatly for he opposed our words.

1722 3588 4413 3450 627 3762 3427 4836 235
16 Ἐν τῇ πρώτῃ μου ἀπολογίᾳ οὐδείς μοι συμπαρεγένετο, ἀλλὰ
At the first of me defense no one me came to (my) aid, but

3956 3165 1459 3361 846 3049 3588 1161 2962
πάντες με ἐγκατέλιπον· μὴ αὐτοῖς λογισθείη· 17 ὁ δὲ Κύριός
all me deserted; not to them may it be reckoned; the but Lord

3427 3936 2532 1743 3165 2443 1223 1700 3588 2782
μοι παρέστη, καὶ ἐνεδυνάμωσέ με, ἵνα δι' ἐμοῦ τὸ κήρυγμα
me stood with, and empowered me, that through me the preaching

4135 2532 191 3956 3588 1484 2532 4506 1537
πληροφορηθῇ, καὶ ἀκούσῃ πάντα τὰ ἔθνη· καὶ ἐρρύσθην ἐκ
might be fulfilled, and might hear all the nations; and I was delivered out of

6 For I am now ready to be offered, and the time of my departure is at hand.
7 I have fought a good fight, I have finished (my) course, I have kept the faith:
8 Henceforth there is laid up for me a crown of righteousness, which the Lord, the righteous judge, shall give me at that day: and not to me only, but unto all them also that love his appearing.

9 Do thy diligence to come shortly unto me:
10 For Demas hath forsaken me, having loved this present world, and is departed unto Thessalonica; Crescens to Galatia, Titus unto Dalmatia.

11 Only Luke is with me. Take Mark, and bring him with thee: for he is profitable to me for the ministry.
12 And Tychicus have I sent to Ephesus.
13 The cloke that I left at Troas with Carpus, when thou comest, bring (with thee), and the books, (but) especially the parchments.
14 Alexander the coppersmith did me much evil: the Lord reward him according to his works:
15 Of whom be thou ware also; for he hath greatly withstood our words.
16 At my first answer no man stood with me, but all (men) forsook me: (I pray God) that it may not be laid to their charge.
17 Notwithstanding the Lord stood with me, and strengthened me; that by me the preaching might be fully known, and (that) all the Gentiles might hear: and I was delivered out of

Literal Translation

(the) mouth of the lion.
18 And the Lord will
deliver me from every
wicked work and will
save (me) into His
heavenly kingdom; to
whom (be) the glory
forever and ever.
Amen.

19 Greet Prisca and
Aquila and the house of
Onesiphorus.

20 Erastus remained in
Corinth, but I left Tro-
phimus sick in Miletus.
21 Try to come before
winter. Eubulus greets
you, and Pudens, and
Linus, and Claudia, and
all the brothers.

22 The Lord Jesus
Christ (be) with your
spirit. Grace (be) with
you. Amen.

2 Timothy 4:18

4750 3023 2532 4506 3165 3588 2962 575 3956
στόματος λέοντος. 18 καὶ ῥύσεταί με ὁ Κύριος ἀπὸ παντὸς
(the) mouth of (the) lion. And will deliver me the Lord from every

2041 4190 2532 4982 1519 3588 932 846 3588
ἔργου πονηροῦ, καὶ σώσει εἰς τὴν βασιλείαν αὐτοῦ τὴν
work wicked, and will save to the kingdom of Him

2032 3739 3588 1391 1519 3588 165 3588 165 281
ἐπουράνιον· ᾧ ἡ δόξα εἰς τοὺς αἰῶνας τῶν αἰώνων. ἀμήν.
heavenly; to whom (be) the glory to the ages of the ages. Amen.

782 4251 2532 207 2532 3588 3683
19. Ἄσπασαι Πρίσκαν καὶ Ἀκύλαν καὶ τὸν Ὀνησιφόρου
Greet Priscilla and Aquila, and the of Onesiphorus

3624 2037 3306 1722 2882 5161 1161 620
οἶκον. 20 Ἔραστος ἔμεινεν ἐν Κορίνθῳ· Τρόφιμον δὲ ἀπέλιπον
house. Erastus remained in Corinth; Trophimus but I left

1722 3399 770 4704 4253 5494 2064
ἐν Μιλήτῳ ἀσθενοῦντα. 21 σπούδασον πρὸ χειμῶνος ἐλθεῖν.
in Miletus sick. Make haste before winter to come.

782 4571 2103 2532 4227 2532 3044 2532 2803
Ἀσπάζεταί σε Εὔβουλος, καὶ Πούδης, καὶ Λίνος, καὶ Κλαυδία,
Greets you Eubulus, and Pudens, and Linus, and Claudia,

2532 3588 80 3956
καὶ οἱ ἀδελφοὶ πάντες.
and the brothers all.

3588 2962 2424 5547 3326 3588 4151 4675 3588
22 Ὁ Κύριος Ἰησοῦς Χριστὸς μετὰ τοῦ πνεύματός σου. ἡ
The Lord Jesus Christ (be) with the spirit of you.

5485 3326 5216 281
χάρις μεθ' ὑμῶν. ἀμήν.
Grace (be) with you. Amen.

King James Version

the mouth of the lion.
18 And the Lord shall
deliver me from every
evil work, and will pre-
serve (me) unto his
heavenly kingdom: to
whom (be) glory for
ever and ever. Amen.

19 Salute Prisca and
Aquila, and the house-
hold of Onesiphorus.

20 Erastus abode at
Corinth: but Trophimus
have I left at Miletum
sick.
21 Do thy diligence to
come before winter.
Eubulus greeteth thee,
and Pudens, and Linus,
and Claudia, and all the
brethren.

22 The Lord Jesus
Christ (be) with thy
spirit. Grace (be) with
you. Amen. (The sec-
ond (epistle) unto Ti-
motheus, ordained the
first bishop of the
church of the Ephe-
sians, was written from
Rome, when Paul was
brought before Nero the
second time.)

Literal Translation

THE EPISTLE OF PAUL TO TITUS

Titus 1

1. Paul, a slave of God and an apostle of Jesus Christ according to (the) faith of (the) elect of God and full knowledge of (the) truth according to godliness,
2 on hope of eternal life which the never-lying God promised before (the) eternal times,
3 but revealed His Word in its own times in a proclamation (with) which I was entrusted by (the) command of our Savior God:

4 to Titus, a true child according to (our) common faith; grace, mercy, peace from God (the) Father and (the) Lord Jesus Christ our Savior.

5 For this cause I left you in Crete, that you might set in order the things lacking and appoint elders in every city, as I ordered you:

6 If anyone is blameless, husband of one wife, having faithful children, not in accusation of loose behavior, or insubordinate,

7 for it behooves the overseer to be blameless as a steward of God), not self-pleasing, not prone to anger, not given to wine, not a quarreler, not greedy of ill gain;
8 but hospitable, a lover of good, discreet, just, holy, temperate,
9 clinging to the faithful Word according to the teaching, that he may be able both to encourage by sound doctrine and to convict the (ones) contradicting.

ΠΑΥΛΟΥ Η ΗΡΟΣ
OF PAUL THE TO

ΤΙΤΟΝ ΕΠΙΣΤΟΛΗ
TITUS EPISTLE

Titus 1

3972 1401 2316 652 1161 2424 5547 2596
1. Παῦλος, δοῦλος Θεοῦ, ἀπόστολος δὲ Ἰησοῦ Χριστοῦ, κατὰ
Paul, a slave of God, apostle and of Jesus Christ, according to
4102 1588 2316 2532 1922 225 3588 2596
πίστιν ἐκλεκτῶν θεοῦ καὶ ἐπίγνωσιν ἀληθείας τῆς κατ᾽
(the) faith of (the) elect of God and full knowledge of (the) truth according to
2150 1909 1680 2222 166 3739 1861 3588
εὐσέβειαν, 2 ἐπ᾽ ἐλπίδι ζωῆς αἰωνίου, ἣν ἐπηγγείλατο ὁ
godliness, on hope of life eternal, which promised the
893 2316 4253 5550 166 5319 1161 2540
ἀψευδὴς Θεὸς πρὸ χρόνων αἰωνίων, 3 ἐφανέρωσε δὲ καιροῖς
never-lying God before times eternal, revealed but times
2398 3588 3056 846 1722 2782 3739 4100 1473 2596
ἰδίοις τὸν λόγον αὐτοῦ ἐν κηρύγματι ὃ ἐπιστεύθην ἐγὼ κατ᾽
(in its) own the Word of Him in a proclamation which was entrusted I by
2003 3588 4990 2257 2316 5103 1103 5043
ἐπιταγὴν τοῦ σωτῆρος ἡμῶν Θεοῦ, 4 Τίτῳ γνησίῳ τέκνῳ
(the) command of the Savior of us God, to Titus a true child
2596 2839 4102 5485 1656 1515 575 2316 3962
κατὰ κοινὴν πίστιν· χάρις, ἔλεος, εἰρήνη ἀπὸ Θεοῦ πατρὸς,
according to a common faith; grace, mercy, peace from God (the) Father,
2532 2962 2424 5549 3588 4990 2257
καὶ κυρίου Ἰησοῦ Χριστοῦ τοῦ σωτῆρος ἡμῶν.
and (the) Lord Jesus Christ the Savior of us.

5127 5484 2641 4571 1722 2914 2443 3588 3007
5. Τούτου χάριν κατέλιπόν σε ἐν Κρήτῃ, ἵνα τὰ λείποντα
For this cause I left you in Crete, that the things lacking
1930 2532 2525 2596 4172 4245
ἐπιδιορθώσῃ, καὶ καταστήσῃς κατὰ πόλιν πρεσβυτέρους,
you should set in order, and appoint in each city elders,
5613 1473 4671 1299 1487 5100 2076 410 3391
ὡς ἐγώ σοι διεταξάμην· 6 εἴ τίς ἐστιν ἀνέγκλητος, μιᾶς
as I you ordered; if anyone is blameless, of one
1135 435 5043 2192 4103 3361 1722 2724 810
γυναικὸς ἀνήρ, τέκνα ἔχων πιστά, μὴ ἐν κατηγορίᾳ ἀσωτίας
wife husband, children having believing, not in accusation of looseness
2228 506 1163 1063 3588 1985 410 1511
ἢ ἀνυπότακτα. 7 δεῖ γὰρ τὸν ἐπίσκοπον ἀνέγκλητον εἶναι,
or insubordinate. it behooves For the overseer blameless to be,
5613 2316 3623 3361 829 3361 3711 3361 3943
ὡς Θεοῦ οἰκονόμον· μὴ αὐθάδη, μὴ ὀργίλον, μὴ πάροινον,
as of God a steward; not self-pleasing, not easily angered, not given to wine,
3361 4131 3361 146 235 5382 5358
μὴ πλήκτην, μὴ αἰσχροκερδῆ, 8 ἀλλὰ φιλόξενον, φιλάγαθον,
not a quarreler, not greedy of ill gain,, but hospitable, a lover of good,
4998 1342 3741 1468 472 3588 2596
σώφρονα, δίκαιον, ὅσιον, ἐγκρατῆ, 9 ἀντεχόμενον τοῦ κατὰ
discreet, just, holy, temperate, clinging to the according to
3588 1322 4103 3056 2443 1415 5600 2532 3870
τὴν διδαχὴν πιστοῦ λόγου, ἵνα δυνατὸς ᾖ καὶ παρακαλεῖν
the teaching faithful Word, that able he may be both to exhort
1722 3588 1319 3588 5198 2532 3588 483
ἐν τῇ διδασκαλίᾳ τῇ ὑγιαινούσῃ, καὶ τοὺς ἀντιλέγοντας
in the doctrine sound, and the (ones) contradicting
1651
ἐλέγχειν.
to convict.

King James Version

THE EPISTLE OF PAUL TO TITUS

Titus 1

1. Paul, a servant of God, and an apostle of Jesus Christ, according to the faith of God's elect, and the acknowledging of the truth which is after godliness;
2 In hope of eternal life, which God, that cannot lie, promised before the world began;
3 But hath in due times manifested his word through preaching, which is committed unto me according to the commandment of God our Saviour;
4 To Titus, (mine) own son after the common faith: Grace, mercy, (and) peace, from God the Father and the Lord Jesus Christ our Saviour.

5 For this cause left I thee in Crete, that thou shouldest set in order the things that are wanting, and ordain elders in every city, as I had appointed thee:
6 If any be blameless, the husband of one wife, having faithful children not accused of riot or unruly.

7 For a bishop must be blameless, as the steward of God; not selfwilled, not soon angry, not given to wine, no striker, not given to filthy lucre;
8 But a lover of hospitality, a lover of good men, sober, just, holy, temperate;
9 Holding fast the faithful word as he hath been taught, that he may be able by sound doctrine both to exhort and to convince the gainsayers.

Literal Translation

Titus 1:10

10 For there are indeed many insubordinate men, empty talkers and mind-deluders, especially those of (the) circumcision,
11 (whose) mouths (you) must silence, who overturn whole houses, teaching things which (they) ought not for the sake of ill gain.
12 One of them, a prophet of their own, said: Cretans (are) always liars, evil beasts, idle gluttons.
13 This testimony is true; for which cause convict them severely, that they may be sound in the faith,
14 not listening to Jewish myths and commandments of men, having turned away from the truth.
15 Truly, all things (are) pure to the pure, but to the (ones) having been defiled and unbelieving, nothing (is) pure, but even their mind and conscience has been defiled.
16 They profess to know God, but by (their) works they deny (Him), being abominable and disobedient, and worthless to every good work.

1526 1063 4183 2532 506 3151 2532
10. Εἰσὶ γὰρ πολλοὶ καὶ ἀνυπότακτοι, ματαιολόγοι καὶ
there are For many indeed insubordinate men, empty talkers and
5423 3122 3588 1537 4061 3739 1163 1993
φρεναπάται, μάλιστα οἱ ἐκ περιτομῆς, 11 οὓς δεῖ ἐπιστομίζειν·
mind-deluders, especially those of circumcision, of whom you must silence;
3748 3650 3624 396 1321 3739 3361 1163
οἵτινες ὅλους οἴκους ἀνατρέπουσι, διδάσκοντες ἃ μὴ δεῖ,
who whole houses overturn, teaching things not right,
150 2771 5484 2036 5100 1537 846 2398 846
αἰσχροῦ κέρδους χάριν. 12 εἶπέ τις ἐξ αὐτῶν, ἴδιος αὐτῶν
ill gain for the sake of. said One of them, an own of them
4396 2912 104 5583 2556 2342 1064 692
προφήτης, Κρῆτες ἀεὶ ψεῦσται, κακὰ θηρία, γαστέρε ἀργαί.
prophet, Cretans always (are) liars, evil beasts, gluttons, idle.
3588 3141 3778 2076 227 1223 3739 156 1651 846
13 ἡ μαρτυρία αὕτη ἐστὶν ἀληθής. δι' ἣν αἰτίαν ἔλεγχε αὐτοὺς
testimony This is true. For which cause convict them
664 2443 5198 1722 3588 4102 3361 4337
ἀποτόμως, ἵνα ὑγιαίνωσιν ἐν τῇ πίστει, 14 μὴ προσέχοντες
severely, that they may be sound in the faith, not listening
2451 3454 2532 1785 444 654
Ἰουδαϊκοῖς μύθοις καὶ ἐντολαῖς ἀνθρώπων ἀποστρεφομένων
to Jewish myths and commandments of men having turned away from
3588 225 3956 3303 2513 3588 2513 3588 1161
τὴν ἀλήθειαν· 15 πάντα μὲν καθαρὰ τοῖς καθαροῖς· τοῖς δὲ
the truth; all things indeed (are) pure to the pure; to those but
3392 2532 571 3762 2513 235 3392
μεμιασμένοις καὶ ἀπίστοις οὐδὲν καθαρόν· ἀλλὰ μεμίανται
having been defiled and unbelieving nothing (is) pure; but has been defiled
846 2532 3588 3563 2532 3588 4893 2316 3670
αὐτῶν καὶ ὁ νοῦς καὶ ἡ συνείδησις. 16 Θεὸν ὁμολογοῦσιν
of them even the mind and the conscience. God they profess
1492 3588 1161 2041 720 947 5607 2532
εἰδέναι, τοῖς δὲ ἔργοις ἀρνοῦνται, βδελυκτοὶ ὄντες καὶ
to know, by the but works they deny (Him), abominable being and
545 2532 4314 3956 2041 18 96
ἀπειθεῖς καὶ πρὸς πᾶν ἔργον ἀγαθὸν ἀδόκιμοι.
disobedient and to every work good reprobate.

King James Version

10 For there are many unruly and vain talkers and deceivers, specially they of the circumcision:
11 Whose mouths must be stopped, who subvert whole houses, teaching things which they ought not, for filthy lucre's sake.
12 One of themselves, (even) a prophet of their own, said, The Cretians (are) alway liars, evil beasts, slow bellies.
13 This witness is true. Wherefore rebuke them sharply, that they may be sound in the faith;
14 Not giving heed to Jewish fables, and commandments of men, that turn from the truth.
15 Unto the pure all things (are) pure: but unto them that are defiled and unbelieving (is) nothing pure; but even their mind and conscience is defiled.
16 They profess that they know God; but in works they deny (him), being abominable, and disobedient, and unto every good work reprobate.

Titus 2

1. But you speak things which (are) fitting to sound doctrine:
2 aged men to be temperate, sensible, discreet, sound in the faith, in love, in patience;
3 aged (women) likewise reverent in behavior, not slanderers, not having been enslaved by much wine, teachers of good,
4 that they might train the young (women) to be lovers of husbands, lovers of children,
5 discreet, chaste, house-workers, good, subject to (their) own husbands, so that

4771 1161 2980 3739 4241 3588 5198 1319 4246
1. Σὺ δὲ λάλει ἃ πρέπει τῇ ὑγιαινούσῃ διδασκαλίᾳ· 2 πρεσ-
you But speak things which become sound doctrine; aged
3524 1511 4586 4998 5198 3588
βύτας νηφαλίους εἶναι, σεμνούς, σώφρονας, ὑγιαίνοντας τῇ
men temperate to be, sensible, discreet, sound in the
4102 3588 26 3588 5281 4247 5615 1722
πίστει, τῇ ἀγάπῃ, τῇ ὑπομονῇ· 3 πρεσβύτιδας ὡσαύτως ἐν
faith; in love, in patience; aged women likewise in
2688 2412 3361 1228 3361 3631 4183
καταστήματι ἱεροπρεπεῖς, μὴ διαβόλους, μὴ οἴνῳ πολλῷ
behavior reverent, not slanderers, not wine by much
1402 2567 2443 4994 3588 3501
δεδουλωμένας, καλοδιδασκάλους, 4 ἵνα σωφρονίζωσι τὰς νέας
having been enslaved, teachers of good, that they may train the young
5362 1511 5388 4998 53
φιλάνδρους εἶναι, φιλοτέκνους, 5 σώφρονας, ἁγνάς,
husband-lovers to be, child-lovers, discreet, chaste,
3626 18 5293 3588 2398 435 2443
οἰκουρούς, ἀγαθάς, ὑποτασσομένας τοῖς ἰδίοις ἀνδράσιν, ἵνα
house workers, good, being subject to the own husbands, that

1. But speak thou the things which become sound doctrine:
2 That the aged men be sober, grave, temperate, sound in faith, in charity, in patience.
3 The aged women likewise, that (they be) in behaviour as becometh holiness, not false accusers, not given to much wine, teachers of good things;
4 That they may teach the young women to be sober, to love their husbands, to love their children,
5 (To be) discreet, chaste, keepers at home, good, obedient to their own husbands, that

Literal Translation

the word of God may not be blasphemed.
6 The younger men in the same way exhort to be discreet;
7 having holding forth yourself a pattern of good works about all things, in the doctrine, in purity, sensibleness, incorruption,

8 (in) sound speech, not to be condemned; that the (one) in opposition may be ashamed, having nothing bad to say about you.
9 Slaves, be subject to (their) own masters, well-pleasing in everything, not speaking against (them),
10 not stealing, but showing all good fidelity, that they may adorn the doctrine of our Savior God in everything.

11For the saving grace of God appeared to all (sorts of) men,

12 instructing us that having denied ungodliness and worldly lusts, we should live discreetly and righteously and godly in the present age,
13 looking for the blessed hope and appearance of the glory of our great God and Savior Jesus Christ,

14 who gave Himself on our behalf, that He might redeem us from all iniquity and purify a special people for His own possession, zealous of good works. (Ps.130:8; Eze.37:23; Deut.14:2)

15 Speak these things and exhort and convict with all authority. Let no one despise you.

Titus 2:6

3361/3588/3056/3588/2316 987 3588 3501 5615
μὴ ὁ λόγος τοῦ Θεοῦ βλασφημῆται· 6 τοὺς νεωτέρους ὡσαύτως
not the Word of God be blasphemed; the younger men likewise

3870 4993 4012 3956 4572 3930
παρακάλει σωφρονεῖν· 7 περὶ πάντα σεαυτὸν παρεχόμενος
exhort to be discreet; concerning all things yourself holding forth

5179 2570 2041 1722 3588 1319 90 4587
τύπον καλῶν ἔργων, ἐν τῇ διδασκαλίᾳ ἀδιαφθορίαν, σεμνότητα,
a pattern of good works, in the teaching in purity, sensibleness,

861 3056 5199 176 2443 3588 1537 1727
ἀφθαρσίαν, 8 λόγον ὑγιῆ, ἀκατάγνωστον, ἵνα ὁ ἐξ ἐναντίας
incorruption, speech sound without condemnation, that he of opposition

1788 3367 2192 4012 5216 3004 5337 1401 2398
ἐντραπῇ, μηδὲν ἔχων περὶ ὑμῶν λέγειν φαῦλον. 9 δούλους ἰδίοις
be ashamed, nothing having about you to say bad. Slaves to own

1203 5293 1722 3956 2101 1511 3361
δεσπόταις ὑποτάσσεσθαι, ἐν πᾶσιν εὐαρέστους εἶναι, μὴ
masters to be subject, in everything well-pleasing to be, not

483 3361 3557 235 3956 4102 1732
ἀντιλέγοντας, 10 μὴ νοσφιζομένους, ἀλλὰ πίστιν πᾶσαν ἐνδει-
contradicting, not stealing, but fidelity all showing

18 2443 3588 1319 3588 4990 2257
κνυμένους ἀγαθήν, ἵνα τὴν διδασκαλίαν τοῦ σωτῆρος ἡμῶν
good, that the doctrine of the Savior of us

2316 2885 1722 3956 2014 1063 3588 5485 3588 2316 3588
Θεοῦ κοσμῶσιν ἐν πᾶσιν. 11 ἐπεφάνη γὰρ ἡ χάρις τοῦ Θεοῦ ἡ
God they may adorn in everything. appeared For the grace of God

4992 3956 444 3811 2248 2443 720
σωτήριος πᾶσιν ἀνθρώποις, 12 παιδεύουσα ἡμᾶς ἵνα, ἀρνησά-
saving to all (sorts) of men, instructing us that, having

3588 763 2532 3588 2886 1939 4996 2532
μενοι τὴν ἀσέβειαν καὶ τὰς κοσμικὰς ἐπιθυμίας, σωφρόνως καὶ
denied ungodliness and worldly lust, discreetly and

1346 2532 2153 2198 1722 3588 3568 165 4327
δικαίως καὶ εὐσεβῶς ζήσωμεν ἐν τῷ νῦν αἰῶνι, 13 προσδεχό-
righteously and godly we might live in the present age, expecting

3588 3107 1680 2532 2015 3588 1391 3588
μενοι τὴν μακαρίαν ἐλπίδα καὶ ἐπιφάνειαν τῆς δόξης τοῦ
the blessed hope and appearance of the glory of the

3173 2316 2532 4990 2257 2424 5547 3739 1325
μεγάλου Θεοῦ καὶ σωτῆρος ἡμῶν Ἰησοῦ Χριστοῦ, 14 ὃς ἔδωκεν
great God and Savior of us Jesus Christ, who gave

1438 5228 2257 2443 3084 2248 575 3956
ἑαυτὸν ὑπὲρ ἡμῶν, ἵνα λυτρώσηται ἡμᾶς ἀπὸ πάσης
Himself on behalf of us, that He might redeem us from all

458 2532 2511 1438 2992 4041 2207
ἀνομίας, καὶ καθαρίσῃ ἑαυτῷ λαὸν περιούσιον, ζηλωτὴν
lawlessness, and purify for Himself a people special, zealous

2570 2041
καλῶν ἔργων.
of good works.

5023 2980 2532 3870 2532 1651 3326 3956
15. Ταῦτα λάλει, καὶ παρακάλει, καὶ ἔλεγχε μετὰ πάσης
These things speak, and exhort, and convict with all

2003 3367 4675 4065
ἐπιταγῆς. μηδείς σου περιφρονείτω.
authority no one you Let despise.

King James Version

the word of God be not blasphemed.
6 Young men likewise exhort to be sober minded.
7 In all things shewing thyself a pattern of good works: in doctrine (shewing) uncorruptness, gravity, sincerity,

8 Sound speech, that cannot be condemned; that he that is of the contrary part may be ashamed, having no evil thing to say of you.
9 (Exhort) servants to be obedient unto their own masters, (and) to please (them) well in all (things); not answering again;
10 Not purloining, but shewing all good fidelity; that they may adorn the doctrine of God our Saviour in all things.
11 For the grace of God that bringeth salvation hath appeared to all men,
12 Teaching us that, denying ungodliness and worldly lusts, we should live soberly, righteously, and godly, in this present world;

13 Looking for that blessed hope, and the glorious appearing of the great God and our Saviour Jesus Christ;

14 Who gave himself for us, that he might redeem us from all iniquity, and purify unto himself a peculiar people, zealous of good works.

15 These things speak, and exhort, and rebuke with all authority. Let no man despise thee.

Titus 3

Literal Translation

1. Remind them to be subject to rulers and authorities,

Titus 3

5279 846 746 2532 1849 5293
1. Ὑπομίμνησκε αὐτοὺς ἀρχαῖς καὶ ἐξουσίαις ὑποτάσσεσθαι,
Remind them to rulers and authorities to be subject,

King James Version

Titus 3

1. Put them in mind to be subject to principalities and powers,

Literal Translation

to be obedient, to be ready in every good work,

2 to speak evil of no one, not quarrelsome, (but) forbearing, showing forth all meekness to all men.

3 For we also once were senseless, disobedient, led astray, slaving for various lusts and pleasures, living in malice and envy, hateful, hating one another.

4 But when the kindness and love of God our Savior toward man appeared,

5 not by works in righteousness which we had done, but according to His mercy, He saved us through (the) washing of regeneration and renewal of (the) Holy Spirit,

6 whom He poured out on us richly through Jesus Christ, our Savior;

7 that being justified by the grace of that One, we should become heirs according to (the) hope of eternal life.

8 Faithful (is) the Word, and concerning these things I desire you to strongly affirm that the (ones) having believed God should take thought to maintain good works. These are the things good and profitable to men.

9 But keep back from foolish questionings and genealogies and arguments and quarrels of law, for they are unprofitable and vain.

10 After the first and second warning, avoid a man of heresy,

11 knowing that such a one has been perverted and sins, being self-condemned.

12 When I shall send Artemas to you or Tychicus, hasten to

Titus 3:2

3980 4314 3956 2041 18 2092 1511 3367
πειθαρχεῖν, πρὸς πᾶν ἔργον ἀγαθὸν ἑτοίμους εἶναι, 2 μηδένα
to be obedient. to every work good ready to be, no one

987 269 1511 1933 3956 1731
βλασφημεῖν, ἀμάχους εἶναι, ἐπιεικεῖς, πᾶσαν ἐνδεικνυμένους
to speak evil of, not quarrelsome to be, forbearing, all showing forth

4236 4314 3956 444 2258 1063 4218 2532
πρᾳότητα πρὸς πάντας ἀνθρώπους. 3 ἦμεν γάρ ποτε καὶ
meekness to all men. were For then also

2249 453 545 4105 1398 1939
ἡμεῖς ἀνόητοι, ἀπειθεῖς, πλανώμενοι, δουλεύοντες ἐπιθυμίαις
we senseless, disobedient, being led astray, slaving for lusts

2532 2237 4164 1722 2549 2532 5355 1236
καὶ ἡδοναῖς ποικίλαις, ἐν κακίᾳ καὶ φθόνῳ διάγοντες,
and pleasures various, in malice and envy living,

4767 3404 240 3753 1161 3588 5544 2532 3588
στυγητοί, μισοῦντες ἀλλήλους. 4 ὅτε δὲ ἡ χρηστότης καὶ ἡ
hateful, hating one another. when But the kindness and

5363 2014 3588 4990 2257 2316 3756 1537
φιλανθρωπία ἐπεφάνη τοῦ σωτῆρος ἡμῶν Θεοῦ, 5 οὐκ ἐξ
love toward man appeared of the Savior of us God, not by

2041 3588 1722 1343 3739 4160 2249 235 2596
ἔργων τῶν ἐν δικαιοσύνῃ ὧν ἐποιήσαμεν ἡμεῖς, ἀλλὰ κατὰ
works in righteousness which had done we, but according to

3588 846 1656 4982 2248 1223 3067 3824
τὸν αὐτοῦ ἔλεον ἔσωσεν ἡμᾶς, διὰ λουτροῦ παλιγγενεσίας
the of Him mercy He saved us, through (the) washing of regeneration

2532 342 4151 40 3739 1632 1909 2248
καὶ ἀνακαινώσεως Πνεύματος Ἁγίου, 6 οὗ ἐξέχεεν ἐφ' ἡμᾶς
and renewal of (the) Spirit Holy, which He poured on us

4146 1223 2424 5547 3588 4990 2257 2443
πλουσίως, διὰ Ἰησοῦ Χριστοῦ τοῦ σωτῆρος ἡμῶν, 7 ἵνα
richly, through Jesus Christ the Savior of us, that

1344 3588 1565 5485 2818 1096 2596
δικαιωθέντες τῇ ἐκείνου χάριτι, κληρονόμοι γενώμεθα κατ'
being justified by the of that One grace, heirs we might become according to

1680 2222 166 4103 3588 3056 2532 4012 5130
ἐλπίδα ζωῆς αἰωνίου. 8 πιστὸς ὁ λόγος, καὶ περὶ τούτων
(the) hope of life eternal. Faithful (is) the Word, and as to these things

1014 4571 1226 2443 5431 2570 2041
βούλομαί σε διαβεβαιοῦσθαι, ἵνα φροντίζωσι καλῶν ἔργων
I desire you to strongly affirm, that may take thought of good works

4291 3588 4100 3588 2316 5023 2076 3588
προΐστασθαι οἱ πεπιστευκότες τῷ Θεῷ. ταῦτά ἐστι τὰ
to maintain the (ones) having believed God. These are the things

2570 2532 5624 3588 444 3474 1161 2214 2532
καλὰ καὶ ὠφέλιμα τοῖς ἀνθρώποις· 9 μωρὰς δὲ ζητήσεις καὶ
good and profitable to men; foolish but questionings and

1076 2532 2054 2532 3163 3544 4026 1526
γενεαλογίας καὶ ἔρεις καὶ μάχας νομικὰς περιΐστασο· εἰσὶ
genealogies and arguments and quarrels of law keep back from; are

1063 512 2532 3152 141 444 3326 3391
γὰρ ἀνωφελεῖς καὶ μάταιοι. 10 αἱρετικὸν ἄνθρωπον μετὰ μίαν
for unprofitable and vain. A heretical man after one

2532 1208 3559 3868 1492 3754 1612 3588
καὶ δευτέραν νουθεσίαν παραιτοῦ, 11 εἰδὼς ὅτι ἐξέστραπται ὁ
and a second warning avoid, knowing that has been perverted

5108 2532 264 5607 843
τοιοῦτος, καὶ ἁμαρτάνει, ὢν αὐτοκατάκριτος.
such a one, and sins, being self-condemned.

3752 3992 734 4314 4571 2228 5190 4704
12. Ὅταν πέμψω Ἀρτεμᾶν πρὸς σὲ ἢ Τυχικόν, σπούδασον
When I shall send Artemas to you or Tychicus, make haste

King James Version

to obey magistrates, to be ready to every good work,

2 To speak evil of no man, to be no brawlers, (but) gentle, shewing all meekness unto all men.

3 For we ourselves also were sometimes foolish, disobedient, deceived, serving divers lusts and pleasures, living in malice and envy, hateful, (and) hating one another.

4 But after that the kindness and love of God our Saviour toward man appeared,

5 Not by works of righteousness which we have done, but according to his mercy he saved us, by the washing of regeneration, and renewing of the Holy Ghost;

6 Which he shed on us abundantly through Jesus Christ our Saviour;

7 That being justified by his grace, we should be made heirs according to the hope of eternal life.

8 (This is) a faithful saying, and these things I will that thou affirm constantly, that they which have believed in God might be careful to maintain good works. These things are good and profitable unto men.

9 But avoid foolish questions, and genealogies, and contentions, and strivings about the law; for they are unprofitable and vain.

10 A man that is an heretick after the first and second admonition reject;

11 Knowing that he that is such is subverted, and sinneth, being condemned of himself.

12 When I shall send Artemas unto thee, or Tychicus, be diligent

Literal Translation

come to me at Nicopolis. For I have decided to winter there.

13 Diligently set forward Zenas the lawyer and Apollos, that nothing be lacking to them.
14 And let ours also learn to maintain good works for necessary uses, that they may not be without fruit.

15 All those with me greet you. Greet those who love us in (the) faith.

Grace (be) with you all. Amen.

Titus 3:13

2064 4314 3165 1519 3533 1563 1063 2919 3914
ἐλθεῖν πρός με εἰς Νικόπολιν· ἐκεῖ γὰρ κέκρικα παραχειμάσαι.
to come to me at Nicopolis; there for I have decided to winter.

2211 3588 3544 2532 625 4709 4311
13 Ζηνᾶν τὸν νομικὸν καὶ ᾿Απολλῶ σπουδαίως πρόπεμψον,
Zenas the lawyer and Apollos diligently set forward,

2443 3367 846 3007 3129 1161 2532 3588 2251
ἵνα μηδὲν αὐτοῖς λείπῃ. 14 μανθανέτωσαν δὲ καὶ οἱ ἡμέτεροι
that nothing to them be lacking. let learn And also our (own)

2570 2041 4291 1519 3588 316 5532 2443 3361
καλῶν ἔργων προΐστασθαι εἰς τὰς ἀναγκαίας χρείας, ἵνα μὴ
of good works to maintain for necessary uses, that not

5600 175
ὦσιν ἄκαρποι.
they be without fruit.

782 4571 3588 3326 1700 3956 782 3588
15. ᾿Ασπάζονταί σε οἱ μετ᾿ ἐμοῦ πάντες. ἄσπασαι τοὺς
Greet you those with me all. Greet those

5368 2248 1722 4102
φιλοῦντας ἡμᾶς ἐν πίστει.
loving us in faith.

3588 5485 3326 3956 5216 281
῾Η χάρις μετὰ πάντων ὑμῶν. ἀμήν.
Grace (be) with all of you. Amen.

King James Version

to come unto me to Nicopolis: for I have determined there to winter.
13 Bring Zenas the lawyer and Apollos on their journey diligently, that nothing be wanting unto them.
14 And let ours also learn to maintain good works for necessary uses, that they be not unfruitful.

15 All that are with me salute thee. Greet them that love us in the faith. Grace (be) with you all. Amen. (It was written to Titus, ordained the first bishop of the church of the Cretians, from Nicopolis of Macedonia.)

Literal Translation

The Epistle of Paul to Philemon

Philemon 1

1. Paul, a prisoner of Christ Jesus, and Timothy the brother, to Philemon the beloved and our fellow-worker,
2 and to Apphia the beloved, and to Archippus our fellow-soldier, and to the church in your house:
3 Grace to you and peace from God our Father and (the) Lord Jesus Christ.

4 I thank my God always making mention of you in my prayers,

5 hearing of your love and faith which you have toward the Lord Jesus, and toward all the saints,

6 so that the fellowship of your faith may operate in a full knowledge of every good thing in you for Jesus Christ.

7 For we have much joy and encouragement over your love, in that the hearts of the saints have been refreshed through you, brother.

8. Because of this, having much boldness in Christ to enjoin you (to do) what (is) becoming,
9 rather because of love I entreat, being such a one as Paul (the) aged, and now also a prisoner of Jesus Christ;
10 I entreat you concerning my child Onesimus, whom I fathered in my bonds,
11 the (one) once useless to you, but now useful to you and to me; whom I sent back to you.
12 Even receive him, this

ΠΑΥΛΟΥ Η ΠΡΟΣ
OF PAUL THE TO

ΦΙΛΗΜΟΝΑ ΕΠΙΣΤΟΛΗ
PHILEMON EPISTLE

Philemon 1

3972 1198 5547 2424 2532 5095 3588 80
1. Παῦλος δέσμιος Χριστοῦ Ἰησοῦ, καὶ Τιμόθεος ὁ ἀδελφός,
Paul a prisoner of Christ Jesus, and Timothy the brother,
5371 3588 27 2532 4904 2257 2532 682 3588
Φιλήμονι τῷ ἀγαπητῷ καὶ συνεργῷ ἡμῶν, 2 καὶ Ἀπφίᾳ τῇ
to Philemon the beloved and fellow-worker of us, and to Apphia the
27 2532 751 3588 4961 2257 2532 3588
ἀγαπητῇ, καὶ Ἀρχίππῳ τῷ συστρατιώτῃ ἡμῶν, καὶ τῇ
beloved, and to Archippus the fellow-soldier of us, and to the
2596 3624 4675 1577 5485 5213 2532 1515 575 2316
κατ' οἶκόν σου ἐκκλησίᾳ· 3 χάρις ὑμῖν καὶ εἰρήνη ἀπὸ Θεοῦ
at house of you church: Grace to you and peace from God
3962 2257 2532 2962 2424 5547
πατρὸς ἡμῶν καὶ Κυρίου Ἰησοῦ Χριστοῦ.
(the) Father of us and (the) Lord Jesus Christ.

2168 3588 2316 3450 3842 3417 4675 4160
4. Εὐχαριστῶ τῷ Θεῷ μου, πάντοτε μνείαν σου ποιούμενος
I thank the God of me, always mention of you making
1909 3588 4335 3450 191 467 3588 26 2532 3588
ἐπὶ τῶν προσευχῶν μου, 5 ἀκούων σου τὴν ἀγάπην, καὶ τὴν
at the prayers of me, hearing of you the love, and the
4102 3739 2192 4314 3588 2962 2424 2532 1519 3956 3588
πίστιν ἣν ἔχεις πρὸς τὸν Κύριον Ἰησοῦν καὶ εἰς πάντας τοὺς
faith which you have to the Lord Jesus and to all the
40 3704 3588 2842 3588 4102 4675 1756 1096
ἁγίους, 6 ὅπως ἡ κοινωνία τῆς πίστεώς σου ἐνεργὴς γένηται
saints, so as the fellowship of the faith of you effective may be
1722 1922 3956 18 3588 1722 5213 1519 5547 2424
ἐν ἐπιγνώσει παντὸς ἀγαθοῦ τοῦ ἐν ὑμῖν εἰς Χριστὸν Ἰησοῦν.
in a full knowledge of every good (which is) in you for Christ Jesus.
5485 1063 2192 4183 2532 3874 1909 3588 26
7 χαρὰν γὰρ ἔχομεν πολλὴν καὶ παράκλησιν ἐπὶ τῇ ἀγάπῃ
joy For we have much and encouragement over the love
4675 3754 3588 4698 3588 40 373 1223 4675
σου, ὅτι τὰ σπλάγχνα τῶν ἁγίων ἀναπέπαυται διὰ σοῦ,
of you, that the bowels of the saints have been refreshed through you,
80
ἀδελφέ.
brother.

1352 4183 1722 5547 3954 2192 2004 4671
8. Διὸ πολλὴν ἐν Χριστῷ παρρησίαν ἔχων ἐπιτάσσειν σοι
Therefore much in Christ boldness having to enjoin you
3588 433 1223 3588 26 3123 3870 5108
τὸ ἀνῆκον, 9 διὰ τὴν ἀγάπην μᾶλλον παρακαλῶ, τοιοῦτος
the thing fitting, because of love rather I entreat, such a one
5607 5613 3972 4246 3570 1161 2532 1198 2424
ὢν ὡς Παῦλος πρεσβύτης, νυνὶ δὲ καὶ δέσμιος Ἰησοῦ
being as Paul (the) aged one, now and also a prisoner of Jesus
5547 3870 4571 4012 3588 1700 5043 3739 1080 1722
Χριστοῦ. 10 παρακαλῶ σε περὶ τοῦ ἐμοῦ τέκνου, ὃν ἐγέννησα ἐν
Christ. I beseech you concerning the of me child, whom I fathered in
3588 1199 3450 3682 3588 4218 4671 890 3570 1161
τοῖς δεσμοῖς μου, Ὀνήσιμον, 11 τόν ποτέ σοι ἄχρηστον, νυνὶ δὲ
the bonds of me, Onesimus, the (one) then to you useless, now but
4671 2532 1698 2173 3739 375 4771 1161 846 5123
σοὶ καὶ ἐμοὶ εὔχρηστον, 12 ὃν ἀνέπεμψα· σὺ δὲ αὐτόν, τοῦτ'
to you and to me useful, whom I sent back; to you even him, this

King James Version

The Epistle of Paul to Philemon

Philemon 1

1. Paul, a prisoner of Jesus Christ, and Timothy (our) brother, unto Philemon our dearly beloved, and fellowlabourer,
2 And to (our) beloved Apphia, and Archippus our fellowsoldier, and to the church in thy house:
3 Grace to you, and peace, from God our Father and the Lord Jesus Christ.

4 I thank my God, making mention of thee always in my prayers,

5 Hearing of thy love and faith, which thou hast toward the Lord Jesus, and toward all saints;

6 That the communication of thy faith may become effectual by the acknowledging of every good thing which is in you in Christ Jesus.

7 For we have great joy and consolation in thy love, because the bowels of the saints are refreshed by thee, brother.

8. Wherefore, though I might be much bold in Christ to enjoin thee that which is convenient,
9 Yet for love's sake I rather beseech (thee), being such an one as Paul the aged, and now also a prisoner of Jesus Christ.
10 I beseech thee for my son Onesimus, whom I have begotten in my bonds:
11 Which in time past was to thee unprofitable, but now profitable to thee and to me:
12 Whom I have sent again: thou

Literal Translation

is, my bowels;
13 Whom I purposed to
hold with myself, that
for you he minister to
me in the bonds of the
gospel.

14 But I was willing to
do nothing without your
consent, that your good
might not be by way of
necessity, but by way of
willingness.

15. For perhaps for this
he was separated for an
hour, that you might re-
ceive him eternally;
16 no longer as a slave,
but beyond a slave, a be-
loved brother, espe-
cially to me, and how
much more to you, both
in (the) flesh and in (the)
Lord.
17 Then if you have me
as a partner, receive him
as me.
18 And if he wronged
you (in) anything, or
owes, reckon this to me.
19 I, Paul, wrote with
my hand; I will repay
(that I not say to you that
you even owe yourself
to me also).

20 Yes, brother, (that) I
may have your help in
(the) Lord, refresh my
bowels in (the) Lord.
21 Trusting to your obe-
dience, I wrote to you,
knowing that you will
do even beyond what I
say.
22 But at once prepare
lodging for me; for I
hope that through your
prayers I shall be given
to you.

23. Epaphras, my fel-
low-captive in Christ
Jesus, greets you,

24 (also) my fellow-
workers Mark, Aristar-
chus, Demas, (and)
Luke.

25 The grace of our
Lord Jesus Christ (be)
with your spirit. Amen.

Philemon 1:13

2076 3588 1699 4698 4355 3739 1473 1014 4314
ἔστι τὰ ἐμὰ σπλάγχνα, προσλαβοῦ· 13 ὃν ἐγὼ ἐβουλόμην πρὸς
is the of me bowels, receive (him); whom I purposed with

1683 2722 2443 5228 4675 1247 3427 1722 3588 1199
ἐμαυτὸν κατέχειν, ἵνα ὑπὲρ σοῦ διακονῇ μοι ἐν τοῖς δεσμοῖς
myself to hold that on behalf of you he minister to me in the bonds

3588 2098 5565 1161 3588 4674 1106 3762 2309
τοῦ εὐαγγελίου· 14 χωρὶς δὲ τῆς σῆς γνώμης οὐδὲν ἠθέλησα
of the gospel; without but your consent nothing I was willing

4160 2443 3361 5613 2596 318 3588 18 4675 5600 235
ποιῆσαι, ἵνα μὴ ὡς κατὰ ἀνάγκην τὸ ἀγαθόν σου ᾖ, ἀλλὰ
to do, that not as by way of necessity the good of you be, but

2596 1595 5029 1063 1223 5124 5563 4314 5610
κατὰ ἑκούσιον. 15 τάχα γὰρ διὰ τοῦτο ἐχωρίσθη πρὸς ὥραν,
by way of willingness. perhaps For because of this he was separated for an hour,

2443 166 846 568 3765 5613 1401 235 5228
ἵνα αἰώνιον αὐτὸν ἀπέχῃς· 16 οὐκέτι ὡς δοῦλον, ἀλλ' ὑπὲρ
at eternally him you receive; no longer as a slave, but beyond

1401 80 27 3122 1698 4214 1161 3123
δοῦλον, ἀδελφὸν ἀγαπητόν, μάλιστα ἐμοί, πόσῳ δὲ μᾶλλον
a slave, a brother beloved, especially to me, how much and more

4671 2532 1722 4561 2532 1722 2962 1487 3767 1691 2192 2844
σοὶ καὶ ἐν σαρκὶ καὶ ἐν Κυρίῳ. 17 εἰ οὖν ἐμὲ ἔχεις κοινωνόν,
to you both in flesh and in (the) Lord. if Then me you have a partner,

4355 846 5613 1691 1487 1161 5100 91 4571 2228 3784
προσλαβοῦ αὐτὸν ὡς ἐμέ. 18 εἰ δέ τι ἠδίκησέ σε ἢ ὀφείλει,
receive him as me. if And anything he wronged you or owes,

5124 1698 1677 1473 3972 1125 3588 1699 5495 1473
τοῦτο ἐμοὶ ἐλλόγει· 19 ἐγὼ Παῦλος ἔγραψα τῇ ἐμῇ χειρί, ἐγὼ
this to me reckon; I Paul wrote with my hand, I

661 2443 3361 3004 4671 3754 2532 4572 3427 4359
ἀποτίσω· ἵνα μὴ λέγω σοι ὅτι καὶ σεαυτόν μοι προσοφείλεις.
will repay; that not I say to you that truly yourself to me you owe also.

3483 80 1473 4675 3685 1722 2962 373 3450 3588
20 ναί, ἀδελφέ, ἐγώ σου ὀναίμην ἐν Κυρίῳ· ἀνάπαυσόν μου τὰ
Yes, brother, I of you may have help in (the) Lord; refresh of me the

4698 1722 2962 2982 3588 5218 4675 1125
σπλάγχνα ἐν Κυρίῳ. 21 πεποιθὼς τῇ ὑπακοῇ σου ἔγραψά
bowels in (the) Lord. Having trusted in the obedience of you I wrote

4671 1492 3754 2532 5228 3739 3004 4160 260 1161 2532 2090
σοι, εἰδὼς ὅτι καὶ ὑπὲρ ὃ λέγω ποιήσεις. 22 ἅμα δὲ καὶ ἑτοί-
to you, knowing that even above what I say you will do. withal But also prepare

3427 3578 1679 1063 3754 1223 3588 4335 5216
μαζέ μοι ξενίαν· ἐλπίζω γὰρ ὅτι διὰ τῶν προσευχῶν ὑμῶν
for me lodging; I hope for that through the prayers of you

5483 5213
χαρισθήσομαι ὑμῖν.
I will be given to you.

782 4571 1889 3588 4869 3450 1722
23. Ἀσπάζονταί σε Ἐπαφρᾶς ὁ συναιχμάλωτός μου ἐν
Greet you Epaphras the fellow-captive of me in

5547 2424 3138 708 1214 3065 3588
Χριστῷ Ἰησοῦ, 24 Μᾶρκος, Ἀρίσταρχος, Δημᾶς, Λουκᾶς, οἱ
Christ Jesus, Mark, Aristarchus, Demas, Luke, the

4904 3450
συνεργοί μου.
fellow-workers of me.

3588 5485 3588 2962 2257 2424 5547 3326 3588
25 Ἡ χάρις τοῦ Κυρίου ἡμῶν Ἰησοῦ Χριστοῦ μετὰ τοῦ
The grace of the Lord of us Jesus Christ (be) with the

4151 5216 281
πνεύματος ὑμῶν. ἀμήν.
spirit of you. Amen.

King James Version

therefore receive him,
that is, mine own bow-
els:
13 Whom I would have
retained with me, that in
thy stead he might have
ministered unto me in
the bonds of the gospel:

14 But without thy mind
would I do nothing; that
thy benefit should not
be as it were of neces-
sity, but willingly.

15. For perhaps he
therefore departed for a
season, that thou
shouldest receive him
for ever;
16 Not now as a servant,
but above a servant, a
brother beloved, spe-
cially to me, but how
much more unto thee,
both in the flesh, and in
the Lord?
17 If thou count me
therefore a partner, re-
ceive him as myself.
18 If he hath wronged
thee, or oweth (thee)
ought, put that on mine
account;
19 I Paul have written
(it) with mine own
hand, I will repay (it):
albeit I do not say to thee
how thou owest unto
me even thine own self
besides.
20 Yea, brother, let me
have joy of thee in the
Lord: refresh my bow-
els in the Lord.
21 Having confidence
in thy obedience I wrote
unto thee, knowing that
thou wilt also do more
than I say.
22 But withal prepare
me also a lodging: for I
trust that through your
prayers I shall be given
unto you.

23. There salute thee
Epaphras, my fellow-
prisoner in Christ Jesus;

24 Marcus, Aristar-
chus, Demas, Lucas,
my fellowlabourers.

25 The grace of our
Lord Jesus Christ (be)
with your spirit. Amen.
(Written from Rome to
Philemon, by One-
simus a servant.)

Literal Translation

THE EPISTLE OF PAUL THE APOSTLE T0 THE HEBREWS
Hebrews 1

1. In many parts and in many ways of old, God spoke to the fathers in the prophets;
2 in these last days (He) spoke to us in (the) Son, whom He appointed heir of all; through whom He also made the ages;

3 who being the shining splendor of (His) glory, and the express image of His essence, and upholding all things by the word of His power, having made purification of our sins through Himself, (He) sat down on (the) right of the Majesty on high, (Psa.110:1)

4 having become so much better than the angels, He has inherited a name more excellent than they.

5 For to which of the angels did He ever say, "You are My Son; today I have begotten You"? And again, "I will be a Father to Him, and He shall be a Son to Me." (Psa.2:7;2 Sam. 7:16)
6 And again, when He brings the First-born into the habitable world, He says, "And let all (the) angels of God worship Him." (Deut. 32:43)
7 And as to the angels, He says, "Who makes His angels spirits, and His ministers a flame of fire;" (Psa.104:4)

8 but as to the Son, "Your throne, (O) God, (is) to the age of the age. A scepter of righteousness (is) the scepter of Your kingdom;
9 You loved righteousness and hated lawlessness; because of this God, Your God, has anointed You

ΠΑΥΛΟΥ ΤΟΥ ΑΠΟΣΤΟΛΟΥ Η ΗΡΟΣ
OF PAUL THE APOSTLE THE TO
ΕΒΡΑΙΟΥΣ ΕΠΙΣΤΟΛΗ
HEBREWS EPISTLE
Hebrews 1

4181 2532 4187 3819 3588 2316 2980 3588
1. Πολυμερῶς καὶ πολυτρόπως πάλαι ὁ θεὸς λαλήσας τοῖς
In many parts and in many ways of old God having spoken to the
4396 1722 3588 3962 1909 2078 3588 2250 3778
πατράσιν ἐν τοῖς προφήταις, 2 ἐπ' ἐσχάτου τῶν ἡμερῶν τού-
fathers by the prophets, in (the) last days of
2980 2254 1722 5207 3739 5087 2818 3956 1223
των ἐλάλησεν ἡμῖν ἐν υἱῷ, ὃν ἔθηκε κληρονόμον πάντων, δι'
these spoke to us in (the) Son, whom He appointed heir of all, through
3739 2532 3588 165 4160 3739 5607 541 3588 1391
οὗ καὶ τοὺς αἰῶνας ἐποίησεν, 3 ὃς ὢν ἀπαύγασμα τῆς δόξης
whom also the ages He made, who being (the) radiance of the glory
2532 5481 3588 5287 846 5342 5037 3588 3956
καὶ χαρακτὴρ τῆς ὑποστάσεως αὐτοῦ, φέρων τε τὰ πάντα
and the express image of the essence of Him, upholding and all things
3588 4487 3588 1411 846 1223 1438 2512
τῷ ῥήματι τῆς δυνάμεως αὐτοῦ, δι' ἑαυτοῦ καθαρισμὸν
by the word of the power of Him, through Himself purification
4160 3588 266 2257 2523 1722 1180 3588
ποιησάμενος τῶν ἁμαρτιῶν ἡμῶν, ἐκάθισεν ἐν δεξιᾷ τῆς
having made of the sins of us, sat down on (the) right of the
3172 1722 5308 5118 2909 1096 3588
μεγαλωσύνης ἐν ὑψηλοῖς, 4 τοσούτῳ κρείττων γενόμενος τῶν
Majesty on high, by so much better having become (than) the
32 3745 1313 3844 846 2816
ἀγγέλων, ὅσῳ διαφορώτερον παρ' αὐτοὺς κεκληρονόμηκεν
angels, as a more excellent than them he has inherited
3686 5101 1063 2036 4218 3588 32 5207 3450 1488 4771 1473
ὄνομα. 5 τίνι γὰρ εἶπέ ποτε τῶν ἀγγέλων, Υἱός μου εἶ σύ, ἐγὼ
name. to which For said He ever of the angels, Son of Me are you, I
4594 1080 4571 2532 3825 1473 2071 846 1519
σήμερον γεγέννηκά σε; καὶ πάλιν, Ἐγὼ ἔσομαι αὐτῷ εἰς
today have begotten you? And again, I will be to Him for
3960 2532 846 2071 3427 1519 5207 3752 1161 3825 1521
πατέρα, καὶ αὐτὸς ἔσται μοι εἰς υἱόν; 6 ὅταν δὲ πάλιν εἰσα-
a Father, and He will be to Me for a Son? when And again He
3588 4416 1519 3588 3625 3004 2532 4352
γάγῃ τὸν πρωτότοκον εἰς τὴν οἰκουμένην, λέγει, Καὶ προσ-
brings the First-born into the habitable world, He says, And let
846 3956 32 2316 2532 4314 3303 3588
κυνησάτωσαν αὐτῷ πάντες ἄγγελοι Θεοῦ. 7 καὶ πρὸς μὲν τοὺς
worship Him all angels of God. And as to indeed the
32 3004 3588 4160 3588 32 846 4151
ἀγγέλους λέγει, Ὁ ποιῶν τοὺς ἀγγέλους αὐτοῦ πνεύματα,
angels He says, Who is making the angels of Him spirits,
2532 3588 3011 846 4442 5395 4314 1161 3588 5207
καὶ τοὺς λειτουργοὺς αὐτοῦ πυρὸς φλόγα· 8 πρὸς δὲ τὸν υἱόν,
and the ministers of Him of fire a flame; as to but the Son
3588 2362 4675 3588 2316 1519 3588 165 3588 165 4464
Ὁ θρόνος σου, ὁ θεός, εἰς τὸν αἰῶνα τοῦ αἰῶνος· ῥάβδος
The throne of You, God, (is) to the age of the age; (the) scepter
2118 3588 4464 3588 932 4675 25 1343
εὐθύτητος ἡ ῥάβδος τῆς βασιλείας σου. 9 ἠγάπησας δικαιο-
of uprightness (is) the scepter of the kingdom of You. You loved righteous-
2532 3403 458 1223 5124 5548 4571 3588 2316 3588
σύνην, καὶ ἐμίσησας ἀνομίαν· διὰ τοῦτο ἔχρισέ σε ὁ Θεός, ὁ
ness, and hated lawlessness; because of this anointed You God, the

King James Version

THE EPISTLE OF PAUL THE APOSTLE TO THE HEBREWS
Hebrews 1

1. God, who at sundry times and in divers manners spake in time past unto the fathers by the prophets,
2 Hath in these last days spoken unto us by (his) Son, whom he hath appointed heir of all things, by whom also he made the worlds;
3 Who being the brightness of (his) glory, and the express image of his person, and upholding all things by the word of his power, when he had by himself purged our sins, sat down on the right hand of the Majesty on high;

4 Being made so much better than the angels, as he hath by inheritance obtained a more excellent name than they.

5 For unto which of the angels said he at any time, Thou art my Son, this day have I begotten thee? And again, I will be to him a Father, and he shall be to me a Son?
6 And again, when he bringeth in the firstbegotten into the world, he saith, And let all the angels of God worship him.

7 And of the angels he saith, Who maketh his angels spirits, and his ministers a flame of fire.

8 But unto the Son (he saith), Thy throne, O God, (is) for ever and ever: a sceptre of righteousness (is) the sceptre of thy kingdom.
9 Thou hast loved righteousness, and hated iniquity; therefore God, (even) thy God, hath anointed thee

Literal Translation | **Hebrews 1:10** | ***King James Version***

(with) the oil of gladness above Your fellows." (Psa.45:6,7)
10 And, "You, Lord, founded the earth at (the) beginning, and the heavens are works of Your hands.
11 They will vanish away, but You will continue; and (they) will all become old, like a garment,
12 and You shall fold them up like a covering, and (they) shall be changed. But You are the same, and Your years shall not fail." (Psa. 102:25 - 27)
13 But to which of the angels did He ever say, "Sit at My right (hand) until I place Your enemies (as) a footstool of Your feet?" (Psa.110:1)
14 Are they not all ministering spirits for service, being sent out because of the (ones) being about to inherit salvation?

2316 4675 1637 20 3844 3588 3353 4675 2532
θεός σου, ἔλαιον ἀγαλλιάσεως παρὰ τοὺς μετόχους σου. 10 καί,
God of You, (with) oil of gladness above the partners of You. And

4771 2596 746 2962 3588 1093 2311 2532 2041 3588
Σὺ κατ᾽ ἀρχάς, Κύριε, τὴν γῆν ἐθεμελίωσας, καὶ ἔργα τῶν
You at(the) beginning, Lord, the earth founded, and works of the

5495 4675 1526 3588 3772 846 622 4771 1161 1265
χειρῶν σού εἰσιν οἱ οὐρανοί· 11 αὐτοὶ ἀπολοῦνται, σὺ δὲ δια-
hands of You are the heavens; they will vanish away, You but will

2532 3956 5613 2440 3822 2532 5616
μένεις· καὶ πάντες ὡς ἱμάτιον παλαιωθήσονται, 12 καὶ ὡσεὶ
remain; and all as a garment shall become old, and as

4018 1667 846 2532 236 4771 1161 846
περιβόλαιον ἑλίξεις αὐτούς καὶ ἀλλαγήσονται· σὺ δὲ ὁ αὐτὸς
a covering You shall roll them and shall be changed; You but the same

1488 2532 3588 2094 4675 3756 1587 4314 5101 1161 3588
εἶ, καὶ τὰ ἔτη σου οὐκ ἐκλείψουσι. 13 πρὸς τίνα δὲ τῶν
are, and the years of You not shall fail. to which But of the

32 2046 4218 2521 1537 1188 3450 2193 302 5087 3588
ἀγγέλων εἴρηκέ ποτε, Κάθου ἐκ δεξιῶν μου, ἕως ἂν θῶ τοὺς
angels has He said at any time, Sit off (the) right of Me, until I may put the

2190 4675 5086 3588 4228 4675 3780 3956 1526
ἐχθρούς σου ὑποπόδιον τῶν ποδῶν σου; 14 οὐχὶ πάντες εἰσὶ
enemies of You a footstool of the feet of You? not all Are they

3010 4151 1519 1248 649 1223
λειτουργικὰ πνεύματα, εἰς διακονίαν ἀποστελλόμενα διὰ
ministering spirits, for service being sent forth because of

3588 3195 2816 4991
τοὺς μέλλοντας κληρονομεῖν σωτηρίαν;
the (ones) being about to inherit salvation?

with the oil of gladness above thy fellows.
10 And, Thou, Lord, in the beginning hast laid the foundation of the earth; and the heavens are the works of thine hands:
11 They shall perish; but thou remainest; and they all shall wax old as doth a garment;
12 And as a vesture shalt thou fold them up, and they shall be changed: but thou art the same, and thy years shall not fail.
13 But to which of the angels said he at any time, Sit on my right hand, until I make thine enemies thy footstool?
14 Are they not all ministering spirits, sent forth to minister for them who shall be heirs of salvation?

Hebrews 2

Hebrews 2

Hebrews 2

1. Because of this we ought to give the more earnest heed to the things having been heard, lest we should not slip away at any time.
2 For if the word spoken through angels was confirmed, and every transgression and disobedience received a just repayment;
3 how shall we escape, having neglected so great a salvation? Which having received a beginning to be spoken through the Lord, was confirmed to us by the (ones) having heard,
4 God bearing witness with (them) by both signs and wonders, and by various works of power, even by distribution (of the) Holy Spirit, according to His will.

5 For He did not put the coming world under angels,

1223 5124 1163 4065 2248 4337 3588 191
1. Διὰ τοῦτο δεῖ περισσοτέρως ἡμᾶς προσέχειν τοῖς ἀκου-
Because of this ought more earnest us to give heed to the things

3379 3901 1487 1063 3588 1223 32
σθεῖσι, μήποτε παραρυῶμεν. 2 εἰ γὰρ ὁ δι᾽ ἀγγέλων
having been heard, lest we should slip away. if For the through angels

2980 3056 1096 949 2532 3956 3847 2532
λαληθεὶς λόγος ἐγένετο βέβαιος, καὶ πᾶσα παράβασις καὶ
having been spoken Word was confirmed, and every transgression and

3876 2983 1738 3405 4459 2249 1628
παρακοὴ ἔλαβεν ἔνδικον μισθαποδοσίαν, 3 πῶς ἡμεῖς ἐκφευ-
disobedience received a just recompense, how we shall escape

5082 272 4991 3748 746
ξόμεθα τηλικαύτης ἀμελήσαντες σωτηρίας; ἥτις, ἀρχὴν
so great having neglected a salvation? Which a beginning

2983 2980 1223 3588 2962 5259 3588 191
λαβοῦσα λαλεῖσθαι διὰ τοῦ Κυρίου, ὑπὸ τῶν ἀκουσάντων
having received to be spoken through the Lord, by the (ones) having heard

1519 2248 950 4901 3588 2316 4592
εἰς ἡμᾶς ἐβεβαιώθη, 4 συνεπιμαρτυροῦντος τοῦ Θεοῦ σημείοις
to us was confirmed, bearing witness with God by signs

5037 2532 5059 2532 4164 1411 2532 4151 40
τε καὶ τέρασι καὶ ποικίλαις δυνάμεσι, καὶ Πνεύματος Ἁγίου
both and wonders, and by various works of power, and (the) Spirit Holy

3311 2596 3588 846 2308
μερισμοῖς, κατὰ τὴν αὐτοῦ θέλησιν.
by distribution, according to the of Him will.

3756 1063 32 5293 3588 3625 3588 3195
5. Οὐ γὰρ ἀγγέλοις ὑπέταξεν τὴν οἰκουμένην τὴν μέλλουσαν,
not For to angels He subjected the habitable world coming,

1. Therefore we ought to give the more earnest heed to the things which we have heard, lest at any time we should let (them) slip.
2 For if the word spoken by angels was stedfast, and every transgression and disobedience received a just recompence of reward;
3 How shall we escape, if we neglect so great salvation; which at the first began to be spoken by the Lord, and was confirmed unto us by them that heard (him);
4 God also bearing (them) witness, both with signs and wonders, and with divers miracles, and gifts of the Holy Ghost, according to his own will?

5 For unto the angels hath he not put in subjection the world to come,

Literal Translation **Hebrews 2:6** ***King James Version***

about which we speak,
6 but one fully testified somewhere, saying, "What is man, that You are mindful of him; or the son of man, that You look upon him"?

7 You made him a little less than (the) angels; You crowned him with glory and honor; and You set him over the works of Your hands;

8 "You subjected all things under his feet." (Psa. 8:4-6) For in order to subject to Him all things, He left nothing not subjected to him. But now we do not yet see all things having been subjected to him.

9 But we do see Jesus crowned with glory and honor, who on account of the suffering of death (was) made a little less than the angels, so that by (the) grace of God He might taste of death for every (son).

10 For it was fitting for Him, because of whom (are) all things, and through whom (are) all things, bringing many sons to glory, to perfect (Him) as the Author of their salvation through sufferings.
11 For both He sanctifying and the (ones) being sanctified (are) all of one; for which cause He is not ashamed to call them brothers,
12 saying, "I will announce Your name to My brothers; I will hymn to You in (the) midst of the assembly." (Psa. 22:22)
13 And again, "I will be trusting on Him." And again, "Behold, I and the children whom God gave to Me." (Isa. 8:17, 18)
14 Since, then, the children have partaken of flesh and blood, in like manner He Himself also shared the same things, that through death He might cause to cease the (one) having the power

4012 3739 2980 1263 1161 4225 5100 3004 5100
περὶ ἧς λαλοῦμεν. 6 διεμαρτύρατο δέ πού τις λέγων, Τί
about which we speak. solemnly witnessed But somewhere one saying, What

2076 444 3754 3403 846 2228 5207 444
ἐστιν ἄνθρωπος, ὅτι μιμνήσκῃ αὐτοῦ; ἢ υἱὸς ἀνθρώπου,
is man, that You are mindful of him? Or (the) son of man,

3754 1980 846 1642 846 1024 5100 3844
ὅτι ἐπισκέπτῃ αὐτόν; 7 ἠλάττωσας αὐτὸν βραχύ τι παρ᾽
that You look upon him? You made less him a little than

32 1391 2532 5092 4737 846 2532 2525
ἀγγέλους· δόξῃ καὶ τιμῇ ἐστεφάνωσας αὐτόν, καὶ κατέ-
the angels with glory and with honor You crowned him, and You

846 1909 3588 2041 3588 5495 4675 3956 5293
στησας αὐτὸν ἐπὶ τὰ ἔργα τῶν χειρῶν σου· 8 πάντα ὑπέταξας
set him over the works of the hands of You; all things You subjected

5270 3588 4228 846 1722 1063 3588 5293 846
ὑποκάτω τῶν ποδῶν αὐτοῦ. ἐν γὰρ τῷ ὑποτάξαι αὐτῷ
under the feet of him. in order For to subject to him

3588 3956 3762 863 846 506 3568 1161 3768
τὰ πάντα, οὐδὲν ἀφῆκεν αὐτῷ ἀνυπότακτον. νῦν δὲ οὔπω
all things, nothing He left to him not subjected. now But not yet

3708 846 3588 3956 5293 3588 1161 1024 5100
ὁρῶμεν αὐτῷ τὰ πάντα ὑποτεταγμένα. 9 τὸν δὲ βραχύ τι
do we see to him all things having been subjected. the (one) But a little

3844 32 1642 991 2424 1223 3588
παρ᾽ ἀγγέλους ἠλαττωμένον βλέπομεν Ἰησοῦν, διὰ τὸ
than the angels having been made less we see Jesus, because of the

3804 3588 2288 1391 2532 5092 4737 3704
πάθημα τοῦ θανάτου δόξῃ καὶ τιμῇ ἐστεφανωμένον, ὅπως
suffering of death with glory and with honor having been crowned, so as

5485 2316 5228 3956 1089 2288 4241 1063
χάριτι Θεοῦ ὑπὲρ παντὸς γεύσηται θανάτου. 10 ἔπρεπε γὰρ
by grace of God on behalf of every (son) He might taste of death. it was fitting For

846 1223 3739 3588 3956 2532 1223 3739 3588 3956 4183
αὐτῷ, δι᾽ ὃν τὰ πάντα, καὶ δι᾽ οὗ τὰ πάντα, πολλοὺς
Him because of whom all things, and through whom (are) all things, many

5207 1519 1391 71 3588 747 3588 4991 846
υἱοὺς εἰς δόξαν ἀγαγόντα, τὸν ἀρχηγὸν τῆς σωτηρίας αὐτῶν
sons to glory having brought, the Author of the salvation of them

1223 3804 5048 3588 5037 1063 37 2532 3588 37
διὰ παθημάτων τελειῶσαι. 11 ὅ τε γὰρ ἁγιάζων καὶ οἱ ἁγιαζό-
through sufferings to perfect. He both For sanctifying and the being sanc-
ones

1537 1520 3956 1223 3739 156 3756 1870 80
μενοι, ἐξ ἑνὸς πάντες· δι᾽ ἣν αἰτίαν οὐκ ἐπαισχύνεται ἀδελ-
tified, of one all (are); for which cause not He is ashamed brothers

846 2564 3004 518 3588 3686 4675 3588
φοὺς αὐτοὺς καλεῖν, 12 λέγων, Ἀπαγγελῶ τὸ ὄνομά σου τοῖς
them to call, saying, I will announce the name of You to the

80 3450 1722 3319 1577 5214 4571 2532 3825 1473
ἀδελφοῖς μου, ἐν μέσῳ ἐκκλησίας ὑμνήσω σε. 13 καὶ πάλιν, Ἐγὼ
the brothers of Me, in amidst (the) church I will hymn you. And again, I

2071 3982 1909 846 2532 3825 2400 1473 2532/3588
ἔσομαι πεποιθὼς ἐπ᾽ αὐτῷ. καὶ πάλιν, Ἰδοὺ ἐγὼ καὶ τὰ
will be trusting on Him. And again, Behold! I and the

3813 3739/3427/1325 3588 2316 1893 3767 3588 3813 2841
παιδία ἅ μοι ἔδωκεν ὁ Θεός. 14 ἐπεὶ οὖν τὰ παιδία κεκοινώ-
children whom to Me gave God. Since then the children have

4561 2532 129 2532 846 3898 3348
νηκεν σαρκὸς καὶ αἵματος, καὶ αὐτὸς παραπλησίως μετέσχε
partaken of flesh and blood, also Himself in like manner He shared

3588 846 2443 1223 3588 2288 2673 3588 3588 2904
τῶν αὐτῶν, ἵνα διὰ τοῦ θανάτου καταργήσῃ τὸν τὸ κράτος
the same things, that through the death He might annul the the (one) power

whereof we speak.
6 But one in a certain place testified, saying, What is man, that thou art mindful of him? or the son of man, that thou visitest him?

7 Thou madest him a little lower than the angels; thou crownedst him with glory and honour, and didst set him over the works of thy hands:
8 Thou hast put all things in subjection under his feet. For in that he put all in subjection under him, he left nothing (that is) not put under him. But now we see not yet all things put under him.

9 But we see Jesus, who was made a little lower than the angels for the suffering of death, crowned with glory and honour; that he by the grace of God should taste death for every man.

10 For it became him, for whom (are) all things, and by whom (are) all things, in bringing many sons unto glory, to make the captain of their salvation perfect through sufferings.

11 For both he that sanctifieth and they who are sanctified (are) all of one: for which cause he is not ashamed to call them brethren,

12 Saying, I will declare thy name unto my brethren, in the midst of the church will I sing praise unto thee.
13 And again, I will put my trust in him. And again, Behold I and the children which God hath given me.

14 Forasmuch then as the children are partakers of flesh and blood, he also himself likewise took part of the same; that through death he might destroy him that had the power

Literal Translation

Hebrews 2:15

King James Version

of death, (that is, the Devil);
15 and might set these free, as many as by fear of death were subject to slavery through all the (time) to live.

16 For indeed He does not take hold of angels, but He takes hold of (the) seed of Abraham.

17 For this reason He ought by all means to become like (His) brothers, that He might become a merciful and faithful high priest in the things respecting God, in order to make propitiation for the sins of (His) people.
18 For being tried in what He has suffered, He is able to help those having been tried.

2192 3588 2288 1523 2076 3588 1228 2532 525
ἔχοντα τοῦ θανάτου, τοῦτ᾿ ἔστι τὸν διάβολον, 15 καὶ ἀπαλ-
having of death, this is the devil, and might set
5128 3745 5401 2288 1223 3956 3588 2198
λάξῃ τούτους, ὅσοι φόβῳ θανάτου διὰ παντὸς τοῦ ζῆν
free these, as many as by fear of death through all the (time) to live
1777 2258 1397 3756 1063 1222 32 1949
ἔνοχοι ἦσαν δουλείας. 16 οὐ γὰρ δήπου ἀγγέλων ἐπιλαμβά-
subject were to slavery. not For indeed of angels He takes hold,
235 4690 11 1949 3606 3784
νεται, ἀλλὰ σπέρματος Ἀβραὰμ ἐπιλαμβάνεται. 17 ὅθεν ὤφειλε
but of (the) seed of Abraham He takes hold. Therefore He ought
2596 3956 3588 80 3666 2443 1655 1096
κατὰ πάντα τοῖς ἀδελφοῖς ὁμοιωθῆναι, ἵνα ἐλεήμων γένηται
by all means to the brothers to become like, that a merciful He might be
2532 4103 749 3588 4314 3588 2316 1519 3588 2433
καὶ πιστὸς ἀρχιερεὺς τὰ πρὸς τὸν Θεόν, εἰς τὸ ἱλάσκεσ-
and faithful High Priest (in) the things as to God, for the to propitiate
3588 266 3588 2992 1722 3739 1063 3958 846 3985
θαι τὰς ἁμαρτίας τοῦ λαοῦ. 18 ἐν ᾧ γὰρ πέπονθεν αὐτὸς πειρα-
the sins of the people. in what For has suffered He having been
1410 3588 3985 997
σθείς, δύναται τοῖς πειραζομένοις βοηθῆσαι.
tried, He is able those being tried to help.

of death, that is, the devil;
15 And deliver them who through fear of death were all their lifetime subject to bondage.

16 For verily he took not on (him the nature of) angels; but he took on (him) the seed of Abraham.
17 Wherefore in all things it behoved him to be made like unto (his) brethren, that he might be a merciful and faithful high priest in things (pertaining) to God, to make reconciliation for the sins of the people.
18 For in that he himself hath suffered being tempted, he is able to succour them that are tempted.

Hebrews 3

1. For which reason, holy brothers, called (to be) partakers of a heavenly (calling), consider the Apostle and High Priest of our confession, Christ Jesus,
2 being faithful to Him who appointed Him, as also Moses in all His house. (Num.12:7)
3 For He was counted worthy of more glory than Moses, by so much as the (one) having built the house has more honor than the house.

4 For every house is built by someone; but He who built all things (is) God.
5 And Moses truly (was) faithful in all His house as a ministering servant, for a testimony of the things having been spoken;
6 but Christ as Son over His house, whose house we are, if truly we hold fast the confidence and glory of the hope firm to the end.

7 Because of this, even as the Holy Spirit says, "Today, if

Hebrews 3

3606 80 40 2821 2032 3353
1. Ὅθεν, ἀδελφοὶ ἅγιοι, κλήσεως ἐπουρανίου μέτοχοι,
Therefore, brothers holy, calling of a heavenly sharers,
2657 3588 652 2532 749 3588 3671
κατανοήσατε τὸν ἀπόστολον καὶ ἀρχιερέα τῆς ὁμολογίας
consider the Apostle and High Priest of the confession
2257 5547 2424 4103 5607 3588 4160 846
ἡμῶν Χριστὸν Ἰησοῦν, 2 πιστὸν ὄντα τῷ ποιήσαντι αὐτόν,
of us Christ Jesus, faithful being to the (One) making Him,
5613 2532 3475 1722 3650 3588 3624 846 4119 1063 1391
ὡς καὶ Μωσῆς ἐν ὅλῳ τῷ οἴκῳ αὐτοῦ. 3 πλείονος γὰρ δόξης
as also Moses in all the house of him. of more For glory
3778 3844 3475 515 2596 3745 4119 5092 2192
οὗτος παρὰ Μωσῆν ἠξίωται, καθ᾿ ὅσον πλείονα τιμὴν ἔχει
this One than Moses has been counted worthy by so much as more honor has
3588 3624 3588 2680 846 3956 1063 3624 2680
τοῦ οἴκου ὁ κατασκευάσας αὐτόν. 4 πᾶς γὰρ οἶκος κατασκευά-
(than) the house of him having built it. every For house is prepared
5259 5100 3588 1161 3588 3956 2680 2316 2532
ζεται ὑπό τινος· ὁ δὲ τὰ πάντα κατασκευάσας, Θεός. 5 καὶ
by someone; He but all things having built, (is) God. And
3475 3303 4103 1722 3650 3588 3624 846 5613 2324 1519
Μωσῆς μὲν πιστὸς ἐν ὅλῳ τῷ οἴκῳ αὐτοῦ ὡς θεράπων, εἰς
Moses indeed (was) faithful in all the house of him as a servant, for
3142 3588 2980 5547 1161 5613 5207 1909 3588
μαρτύριον τῶν λαληθησομένων· 6 Χριστὸς δὲ ὡς υἱὸς ἐπὶ τὸν
a testimony of the things having been spoken; Christ but as a Son over the
3624 846 3739 3624 2070 2249 1437 3588 3954 2532
οἶκον αὐτοῦ· οὗ οἶκός ἐσμεν ἡμεῖς, ἐάνπερ τὴν παρρησίαν καὶ
house of Him; of whom a house are we, if truly the confidence and
3588 2745 3588 1680 3360 5056 949 2722
τὸ καύχημα τῆς ἐλπίδος μέχρι τέλους βεβαίν κατάσχωμεν.
the glory of the hope until (the) end firm we hold fast.
1352 2531 3004 3588 4151 3588 40 4594 1437 3588
7 διό, καθὼς λέγει τὸ Πνεῦμα τὸ Ἅγιον, Σήμερον ἐὰν τῆς
Therefore, even as says the Spirit Holy, Today, if the

Hebrews 3

1 . Wherefore, holy brethren, partakers of the heavenly calling, consider the Apostle and High Priest of our profession, Christ Jesus;
2 Who was faithful to him that appointed him, as also Moses (was faithful) in all his house.
3 For this (man) was counted worthy of more glory than Moses, inasmuch as he who hath builded the house hath more honour than the house.
4 For every house is builded by some (man); but he that built all things (is) God.
5 And Moses verily (was) faithful in all his house, as a servant, for a testimony of those things which were to be spoken after;
6 But Christ as a son over his own house; whose house are we, if we hold fast the confidence and the rejoicing of the hope firm unto the end.

7 Wherefore (as the Holy Ghost saith, To day if

Literal Translation | **Hebrews 3:8** | **King James Version**

Literal Translation

you hear His voice,

8 do not harden your hearts, as in the provocation, in the day of temptation in the wilderness,

9 there where your fathers tempted Me, testing Me, and saw My works forty years.

10 Because of this, I was angry with that generation and said, They always go astray in heart; and they did not know My ways;

11 so I swore in My wrath, They shall not enter into My rest." (Psa.95:11)

12 Watch, brothers, lest perhaps shall be in any one of you an evil heart of unbelief in falling away from (the) living God.

13 But exhort yourselves each day, as long as it is being called today, that not any of you be hardened by (the) deceit of sin.

14 For we have become partakers of Christ, if truly we hold the beginning of the assurance firm to (the) end;

15 while it is said, "Today, if you hear His voice, do not harden your hearts, as in the provocation." (Psa 94:7, 8)

16 For having heard, some provoked (Him), but not all those having come out of Egypt through Moses.

17 But with whom was He angry forty years? (Was it) not with the ones having sinned, whose corpses fell in the wilderness?

18 And to whom did He swear (they would) not enter into His rest, except to those not having obeyed?

19 And we see that they were not able to enter in because of unbelief.

Hebrews 3:8

5456 846 191 3361 4645 3588 2588 5216
φωνῆς αὐτοῦ ἀκούσητε, 8 μὴ σκληρύνητε τὰς καρδίας ὑμῶν,
voice of Him you hear, not do harden the heart of you,

5613 1722 3588 3894 2596 3588 2250 3588 3986
ὡς ἐν τῷ παραπικρασμῷ, κατὰ τὴν ἡμέραν τοῦ πειρασμοῦ
as in the provocation, in the day of the temptation

1722/3588/2048 3757 3985 3165 3588 3962 5216 1381
ἐν τῇ ἐρήμῳ, 9 οὗ ἐπείρασαν με οἱ πατέρες ὑμῶν, ἐδοκίμασάν
in the wilderness, where tempted Me the fathers of you, testing

3165 2532 1492 3588 2041 3450 5062 2094 1352 4360
με, καὶ εἶδον τὰ ἔργα μου τεσσεράκοντα ἔτη. 10 διὸ προσ-
Me and saw the works of Me forty years. Therefore I was

3588 1074 1565 2532 2036 104 4105 3588 2588
ώχθισα τῇ γενεᾷ ἐκείνῃ, καὶ εἶπον, Ἀεὶ πλανῶνται τῇ καρδίᾳ·
angry with generation this, and I said, Always they err in the heart;

846 1161 3756 1097 3588 3598 3450 5613 3660 1722 3588 3709
αὐτοὶ δὲ οὐκ ἔγνωσαν τὰς ὁδούς μου· 11 ὡς ὤμοσα ἐν τῇ ὀργῇ
they and not did know the ways of Me; as I swore in the wrath

3450 1487 1525 1519 3588 2663 3450 991
μου, Εἰ εἰσελεύσονται εἰς τὴν κατάπαυσίν μου. 12 Βλέπετε,
of Me, If they shall enter into the rest of Me. Watch,

80 3361 4218 2071 1722 5100 5216 2588 4190 570
ἀδελφοί, μή ποτε ἔσται ἔν τινι ὑμῶν καρδία πονηρὰ ἀπιστίας
brothers, not perhaps shall be in anyone of you a heart evil of unbelief

1722 3588 868 575 2316 2198 235 3870
ἐν τῷ ἀποστῆναι ἀπὸ θεοῦ ζῶντος· 13 ἀλλὰ παρακαλεῖτε
in falling away from God (the) living; but exhort

1438 2596 1538 2250 891 3757 3588 4594 2564
ἑαυτοὺς καθ᾽ ἑκάστην ἡμέραν, ἄχρις οὗ τὸ σήμερον καλεῖται,
yourselves each day, while today it is being called,

2443 3361 4645 5100 1537 5216 539 3588 266 3353
ἵνα μὴ κληρυνθῇ τις ἐξ ὑμῶν ἀπάτῃ τῆς ἁμαρτίας· 14 μέτοχοι
that not be hardened anyone of you by (the) deceit of sin; partakers

1063 1096 3588 5547 1437 3588 746 3588 5287
γὰρ γεγόναμεν τοῦ Χριστοῦ, ἐάνπερ τὴν ἀρχὴν τῆς ὑπο-
for we have become of Christ, if truly the beginning of the

3360 5056 949 2722 1722 3588 3004
στάσεως μέχρι τέλους βεβαίαν κατάσχωμεν· 15 ἐν τῷ λέγεσθαι,
assurance until (the) end firm we hold fast; in the to be said,

4594 1437 3588 5456 846 191 3361 4645 3588
Σήμερον ἐὰν τῆς φωνῆς αὐτοῦ ἀκούσητε, μὴ σκληρύνητε τὰς
Today if the voice of Him you hear, no do harden the

2588 5216 5613 1722 3588 3894 5100 1063 191
καρδίας ὑμῶν ὡς ἐν τῷ παραπικρασμῷ. 16 τίνες γὰρ ἀκού-
hearts of you, as in the provocation. some For having

3893 235 3756 3956 3588 1831 1537
σαντες παρεπίκραναν, ἀλλ᾽ οὐ πάντες οἱ ἐξελθόντες ἐξ
heard provoked, but not all the (ones) having come out of

125 1223 3475 5101 1161 4360 5062
Αἰγύπτου διὰ Μωσέως. 17 τίσι δὲ προσώχθισε τεσσεράκοντα
Egypt through Moses. with whom But was He angry forty

2094 3780 3588 264 3739 3588 2966 4098 1722 3588
ἔτη; οὐχὶ τοῖς ἁμαρτήσασιν, ὧν τὰ κῶλα ἔπεσεν ἐν τῇ
years? Not with those having sinned, of whom the corpses fell in the

2048 5101 1161 3660 3361 1525 1519 3588 2663
ἐρήμῳ; 18 τίσι δὲ ὤμοσε μὴ εἰσελεύσεσθαι εἰς τὴν κατάπαυσιν
desert? to whom And swore He not to enter into the rest

846 1487/3361/3588 544 2532 991 3754 3756 1410
αὐτοῦ, εἰ μὴ τοῖς ἀπειθήσασι; 19 καὶ βλέπομεν ὅτι οὐκ ἠδυνή-
of Him, if not those not having obeyed? And we see that not they were

1525 1223 570
θησαν εἰσελθεῖν δι᾽ ἀπιστίαν.
able to enter in because of unbelief.

King James Version

ye will hear his voice,

8 Harden not your hearts, as in the provocation, in the day of temptation in the wilderness:

9 When your fathers tempted me, proved me, and saw my works forty years.

10 Wherefore I was grieved with that generation, and said, They do alway err in (their) heart; and they have not known my ways.

11 So I sware in my wrath, They shall not enter into my rest.)

12 Take heed, brethren, lest there be in any of you an evil heart of unbelief, in departing from the living God.

13 But exhort one another daily, while it is called To day; lest any of you be hardened through the deceitfulness of sin.

14 For we are made partakers of Christ, if we hold the beginning of our confidence stedfast unto the end;

15 While it is said, To day if ye will hear his voice, harden not your hearts, as in the provocation.

16 For some, when they had heard, did provoke: howbeit not all that came out of Egypt by Moses.

17 But with whom was he grieved forty years? (was it) not with them that had sinned, whose carcases fell in the wilderness?

18 And to whom sware he that they should not enter into his rest, but to them that believed not?

19 So we see that they could not enter in because of unbelief.

Literal Translation

Hebrews 4

1. Then let us fear lest perhaps in any way a promise being left to enter into His rest, (that) any of you may seem to come short.

2 For, indeed, we have had the gospel preached (to us), even as they also; but the word did not profit those hearing (it), not having been mixed with faith in the (ones) having heard.
3 For we, the (ones) having believed, enter into the rest, even as He said, "As I swore in My wrath, they shall not enter into My rest," though the works having come into being from (the) foundation of the world. (Psa. 95:11)

4 For He has spoken somewhere about the seventh (day) this way, "And God rested from all His works in the seventh day." (Gen. 2:2)

5 And in this (place) again, "They shall not enter into My rest." (Psa. 95:11)
6 Therefore, since it remains (for) some to enter into it, and those who formerly had the gospel preached did not enter in because of disobedience,
7 He again marks out a certain day, saying in David, "Today," after such a time, according as He has said, "Today, if you hear His voice, do not harden your hearts." (Psa. 95:7,8)

8 For if Joshua gave them rest, then He would not have afterwards spoken about another day.
9 So, then, there remains a sabbath rest to the people of God.
10 For He entering into His rest, (He) Himself also rested from His works, as God (had rested) from His own.

11 Therefore, let us be eager to enter into that

Hebrews 4

5399 3767 3379 2641 1860
1. Φοβηθῶμεν οὖν μήποτε καταλειπομένης ἐπαγγελίας
let us fear Therefore lest perhaps being left a promise

1525 1519 3588 2663 846 1380 5100 1537 5216
εἰσελθεῖν εἰς τὴν κατάπαυσιν αὐτοῦ, δοκῇ τις ἐξ ὑμῶν
to enter into the rest of Him, seems anyone of you

5302 2532 1063 2070 2097 2509
ὑστερηκέναι. 2 καὶ γάρ ἐσμεν εὐηγγελισμένοι καθάπερ
to come short. indeed For we are having had the gospel preached as

2548 235 3756 5623 3588 3056 3588 189 1565 3361
κἀκεῖνοι, ἀλλ' οὐκ ὠφέλησεν ὁ λόγος τῆς ἀκοῆς ἐκείνους, μὴ
those also, but not did profit the Word of hearing those, not

4786 3588 4102 3588 191 1525 1063
συγκεκραμένος τῇ πίστει τοῖς ἀκούσασιν. 3 εἰσερχόμεθα γὰρ
having been mixed with faith in those having heard. we enter For

1519 3588 2663 3588 4100 2531 2046 5613
εἰς τὴν κατάπαυσιν οἱ πιστεύσαντες, καθὼς εἴρηκεν, Ὡς
into the rest the (ones) having believed, even as He said, As

3660 1722 3588 3709 3450 1487 1525 1519 3588 2663
ὤμοσα ἐν τῇ ὀργῇ μου, Εἰ εἰσελεύσονται εἰς τὴν κατά-
I swore in the wrath of Me, If they shall enter into the rest

3450 2543 3588 2041 575 2663 2889
παυσίν μου· καίτοι τῶν ἔργων ἀπὸ καταβολῆς κόσμου
of Me; though the works from (the) foundation of world

1096 2046 1063 4225 4012 3588 1442 3779
γενηθέντων. 4 εἴρηκε γάρ που περὶ τῆς ἑβδόμης οὕτω,
having come into being. He has said For somewhere about the seventh (day) thus,

2532 2664 3588 2316 1722 3588 2250 3588 1442 575 3956
Καὶ κατέπαυσεν ὁ Θεὸς ἐν τῇ ἡμέρᾳ τῇ ἑβδόμῃ ἀπὸ πάντων
And rested God in the day seventh from all

3588 2041 846 2532 1722 5129 3825 1487 1525 1519
τῶν ἔργων αὐτοῦ· 5 καὶ ἐν τούτῳ πάλιν, Εἰ εἰσελεύσονται εἰς
the works of Him; and in this (place) again, If they shall enter into

3588 2663 3450 1893 3767 620 5100 1525
τὴν κατάπαυσίν μου. 6 ἐπεὶ οὖν ἀπολείπεται τινὰς εἰσελθεῖν
the rest of Me. Since then it remains (for) some to enter

1519 846 2532 3588 4386 2097 3756 1525 1223
εἰς αὐτήν, καὶ οἱ πρότερον εὐαγγελισθέντες οὐκ εἰσῆλθον δι'
into it, and those before having had the gospel preached not entered for

543 3825 5100 3724 2250 4594 1722 1138
ἀπείθειαν, 7 πάλιν τινὰ ὁρίζει ἡμέραν, Σήμερον, ἐν Δαβὶδ
disobedience, again a certain marks out day, Today, in David

3004 3326 5118 5550 2531 2046 4594 1437
λέγων, μετὰ τοσοῦτον χρόνον, καθὼς εἴρηται, Σήμερον ἐὰν
saying, after such a time, as He has said, Today if

3588 5456 846 191 3361 4645 3588 2588
τῆς φωνῆς αὐτοῦ ἀκούσητε, μὴ σκληρύνητε τὰς καρδίας
the voice of Him you hear, not do harden the hearts

5216 1487 1063 846 2424 2664 3756 302 4012 243
ὑμῶν. 8 εἰ γὰρ αὐτοὺς Ἰησοῦς κατέπαυσεν, οὐκ ἂν περὶ ἄλλης
of you. if For them (Joshua) rested, not concerning another

2980 3326 5023 2250 686 620 4520
ἐλάλει μετὰ ταῦτα ἡμέρας. 9 ἄρα ἀπολείπεται σαββατισμὸς
He was speaking after these things day. Then remains a sabbath rest

3588 2992 3588 2316 3588 1063 1525 1519 3588 2663 846
τῷ λαῷ τοῦ Θεοῦ. 10 ὁ γὰρ εἰσελθὼν εἰς τὴν κατάπαυσιν αὐτοῦ
to the people of God. He For having entered into the rest of Him

2532 846 2664 575 3588 2041 846 5618 575 3588
καὶ αὐτὸς κατέπαυσεν ἀπὸ τῶν ἔργων αὐτοῦ, ὥσπερ ἀπὸ τῶν
also Himself rested from the works of Him, as from the

2398 3588 2316 4704 3767 1525 1519 1565 3588
ἰδίων ὁ Θεός. 11 σπουδάσωμεν οὖν εἰσελθεῖν εἰς ἐκείνην τὴν
own (did) God. Let us be eager therefore to enter into that

King James Version

Hebrews 4

1. Let us therefore fear, lest, a promise being left (us) of entering into his rest, any of you should seem to come short of it.

2 For unto us was the gospel preached, as well as unto them: but the word preached did not profit them, not being mixed with faith in them that heard (it).
3 For we which have believed do enter into rest, as he said, As I have sworn in my wrath, if they shall enter into my rest: although the works were finished from the foundation of the world.

4 For he spake in a certain place of the seventh (day) on this wise, And God did rest the seventh day from all his works.

5 And in this (place) again, If they shall enter into my rest.
6 Seeing therefore it remaineth that some must enter therein, and they to whom it was first preached entered not in because of unbelief:

7 Again, he limiteth a certain day, saying in David, To day, after so long a time; as it is said, To day if ye will hear his voice, harden not your hearts.

8 For if Jesus had given them rest, then would he not afterward have spoken of another day.
9 There remaineth therefore a rest to the people of God.
10 For he that is entered into his rest, he also hath ceased from his own works, as God (did) from his.

11 Let us labour therefore to enter into that

Hebrews 4:12

Literal Translation

rest, that not anyone fall in the same example of disobedience.

12 For the Word of God (is) living, and powerfully working, and sharper than every two-edged sword, and piercing as far as (the) division of both soul and spirit, of both joints and marrow, and able to judge of the thoughts and intentions of the heart;
13 and there is no creature unrevealed before Him; but all things (are) naked and laid open to His eyes, with whom (is) our account.

2663 2443 3361 1722 3588 846 5100 5262 4098 3588
κατάπαυσιν, ἵνα μὴ ἐν τῷ αὐτῷ τις ὑποδείγματι πέσῃ τῆς
rest, that not in the same anyone example may fall

543 2198 1063 3588 3056 3588 2316 2532 1756 2532
ἀπειθείας. 12 ζῶν γὰρ ὁ λόγος τοῦ Θεοῦ, καὶ ἐνεργὴς, καὶ
of disobedience. (is) living For the Word of God, and working, and

5114 5228 3956 3162 1366 2532 1338
τομώτερος ὑπὲρ πᾶσαν μάχαιραν δίστομον, καὶ διϊκνού-
sharper than every sword two-mouthed, and piercing

891 3311 5590 5037 2532 4151 719 5037 2532
μενος ἄχρι μερισμοῦ ψυχῆς τε καὶ πνεύματος, ἁρμῶν τε καὶ
as far as (the) division of soul both and spirit, of joints both and

3452 2532 2924 1761 2532 1771 2588 2532
μυελῶν, καὶ κριτικὸς ἐνθυμήσεων καὶ ἐννοιῶν καρδίας. 13 καὶ
of marrow, and able to judge of thoughts and intentions of a heart. And

3756 2076 2937 852 1799 846 3956 1161 1131 2532
οὐκ ἔστι κτίσις ἀφανὴς ἐνώπιον αὐτοῦ· πάντα δὲ γυμνὰ καὶ
not there is (a) creature unrevealed before Him; all things but (are) naked and

5136 3588 3788 846 4314 3739 2254 3588 3056
τετραχηλισμένα τοῖς ὀφθαλμοῖς αὐτοῦ πρὸς ὃν ἡμῖν ὁ λόγος.
having been laid open to the eyes of Him with whom to us (is) the account.

King James Version

rest, lest any man fall after the same example of unbelief.

12 For the word of God (is) quick, and powerful, and sharper than any twoedged sword, piercing even to the dividing asunder of soul and spirit, and of the joints and marrow, and (is) a discerner of the thoughts and intents of the heart.
13 Neither is there any creature that is not manifest in his sight: but all things (are) naked and opened unto the eyes of him with whom we have to do.

---

14 Then having a great High Priest who has passed through the heavens, Jesus the Son of God, let us hold fast the confession.

15 For we do not have a high priest not being able to sympathize with our weaknesses, but (One) having been tried in all respects according to (our) likeness, apart from sin.
16 Therefore, let us draw near with confidence to the throne of grace, that we may receive mercy, and we may find grace for help in time of need.

2192 3767 749 3173 1330 3588
14. Ἔχοντες οὖν ἀρχιερέα μέγαν, διεληλυθότα τοὺς
having Therefore a High Priest great, having passed through the

3772 2424 3588 5207 3588 2316 2902 3588 3671
οὐρανούς, Ἰησοῦν τὸν υἱὸν τοῦ Θεοῦ, κρατῶμεν τῆς ὁμολογίας.
heavens, Jesus the Son of God, let us hold fast the confession.

3756 1063 2192 749 3361 1410 4834 3588
15 οὐ γὰρ ἔχομεν ἀρχιερέα μὴ δυνάμενον συμπαθῆσαι ταῖς
not For we have a high priest not being able to sympathize with the

769 2257 3987 1161 2596 3956 2596 3665
ἀσθενείαις ἡμῶν, πεπειρασμένον δὲ κατὰ πάντα καθ' ὁμοιό-
weaknesses of us, having been tempted but (One) in all according to (our) like-

5565 266 4334 3767 3326 3954 3588
τητα, χωρὶς ἁμαρτίας. 16 προσερχώμεθα οὖν μετὰ παρρησίας τῷ
ness apart from sin. Let us draw near then with confidence to the

2362 3588 5485 2443 2983 1656 2532 5485 2147 1519
θρόνῳ τῆς χάριτος, ἵνα λάβωμεν ἔλεον καὶ χάριν εὕρωμεν εἰς
throne of grace, that we may receive mercy and grace we may find for

2121 996
εὔκαιρον βοήθειαν.
timely help.

14 Seeing then that we have a great high priest, that is passed into the heavens, Jesus the Son of God, let us hold fast (our) profession.

15 For we have not an high priest which cannot be touched with the feeling of our infirmities; but was in all points tempted like as (we are, yet) without sin.

16 Let us therefore come boldly unto the throne of grace, that we may obtain mercy, and find grace to help in time of need.

Hebrews 5

1. For every high priest being taken from men is appointed on behalf of men in the things respecting God, that he may offer both gifts and sacrifices for sins;
2 being able to feel in due measure for those not knowing and having been led astray, since he also is circled about (with) weakness.
3 And because of this he ought to offer for sins as concerning the people, so also concerning himself.
4 And no one takes the honor to himself,

Hebrews 5

3956 1063 749 1537 444 2983 5528
1. Πᾶς γὰρ ἀρχιερεὺς, ἐξ ἀνθρώπων λαμβανόμενος, ὑπὲρ
every For high priest, of men having been taken, on behalf of

444 2525 3588 4314 3588 2316 2443 4374
ἀνθρώπων καθίσταται τὰ πρὸς τὸν Θεόν, ἵνα προσφέρῃ
men is appointed (in) the things as to God, that he may offer

1435 5037 2532 2378 5228 266 3356 1410
δῶρά τε καὶ θυσίας ὑπὲρ ἁμαρτιῶν, 2 μετριοπαθεῖν δυνάμενος
gifts both and sacrifices on behalf of sins, to suffer in measure being able

3588 50 2532 4105 1893 2532 846 4029
τοῖς ἀγνοοῦσιν καὶ πλανωμένοις, ἐπεὶ καὶ αὐτὸς περίκειται
for those not knowing and being led astray, since also he is encompassed

769 2532 1223 3778 3784 2531 4012 3588 2992 3779
ἀσθένειαν· 3 καὶ διὰ ταύτην ὀφείλει, καθὼς περὶ τοῦ λαοῦ, οὕτω
(with) weakness; and because of this he ought, as concerning the people, so

2532 4012 1438 4374 5228 266 2532 3756 1438
καὶ περὶ ἑαυτοῦ, προσφέρειν ὑπερ ἁμαρτιῶν. 4 καὶ οὐχ ἑαυτῷ
also concerning himself, to offer on behalf of sins. And not to himself

Hebrews 5

1. For every high priest taken from among men is ordained for men in things (pertaining) to God, that he may offer both gifts and sacrifices for sins:
2 Who can have compassion on the ignorant, and on them that are out of the way; for that he himself also is compassed with infirmity.
3 And by reason hereof he ought, as for the people, so also for himself, to offer for sins.
4 And no man taketh this honour unto himself, but he that is called of God, as (was) Aaron.
5 So also Christ glorified not himself to

Literal Translation

the honor, but the (one) having been called by God, even as indeed Aaron. So also the Christ not glorified Himself to become a high priest, but the (One) having spoken to Him, "You are My Son; today I have generated You." (Psa.2:7)

6 As He also says in another, "You (are) a priest forever according to the order of Melchizedek," (Psa. 110:4)

7 who in the days of His flesh having offered both petitions and entreaties to Him being able to save Him from death, with strong crying and tears, and having been heard from (His) godly fear;

8 though being a Son, He learned obedience from the things which He suffered;
9 and having been perfected, He became (the) cause of eternal salvation to all the (ones) obeying Him,

10 having been called out by God (as) a High Priest according to the order of Melchizedek.

11 Concerning whom we (have) much to say, and hard to interpret since you have become dull in hearing.
12 For indeed because of the time (you are) due to be teachers, (yet) you need to have someone to teach you again the rudiments of the beginning of the oracles of God, and you became (in) need of milk, and not of solid food;

13 for everyone partaking of milk (is) without experience (in the) word of righteousness, for he is an infant.
14 But solid food is for (the) full grown, having exercised the faculties

Hebrews 5:6

5100 2983 3588 5092 235 3588 2564 5259 3588 2316
τις λαμβάνει τὴν τιμήν, ἀλλὰ ὁ καλούμενος ὑπὸ τοῦ Θεοῦ,
anyone takes the honor, but the (one) having been called by God,

2509 2532 3588 2 3779 2532 3588 5547 3756 1438
καθάπερ καὶ ὁ Ἀαρών. 5 οὕτω καὶ ὁ Χριστὸς οὐχ ἑαυτὸν
even as indeed Aaron. So also the Christ not Himself

1392 1096 749 235 3588 2980 4314 846
ἐδόξασε γενηθῆναι ἀρχιερέα, ἀλλ' ὁ λαλήσας πρὸς αὐτόν,
glorified to become a high priest, but the (One) having spoken to Him,

5207 3450 1488 4771 1473 4594 1080 4571 2531 2532 1722
Υἱός μου εἶ σύ, ἐγὼ σήμερον γεγέννηκά σε. 6 καθὼς καὶ ἐν
Son of Me are you, I today have generated You. Even as also in

2087 3004 4771 2409 1519 3588 165 2596 3588 5010
ἑτέρῳ λέγει, Σὺ ἱερεὺς εἰς τὸν αἰῶνα κατὰ τὴν τάξιν
another He says, You (are) a priest to the age according to the order

3198 3739 1722 3588 2250 3588 4561 846 1162 5037
Μελχισέδεκ. 7 ὃς ἐν ταῖς ἡμέραις τῆς σαρκὸς αὐτοῦ, δεήσεις τε
of Melchisedek. Who in the days of the flesh of him, petitions both

2532 2428 4314 3588 1410 4982 846 1537 2288
καὶ ἱκετηρίας πρὸς τὸν δυνάμενον σώζειν αὐτὸν ἐκ θανάτου
and entreaties to the (one) being able to save Him out of death

3326 2906 2478 2532 1144 4374 2532
μετὰ κραυγῆς ἰσχυρᾶς καὶ δακρύων προσενέγκας, καὶ
with crying strong and tears having offered, and

1522 575 3588 2124 2539 5607 5207 3129
εἰσακουσθεὶς ἀπὸ τῆς εὐλαβείας, 8 καίπερ ὢν υἱός ἔμαθεν
having been heard from the godly fear, though being a Son He learned

575 3739 3958 3588 5218 2532 5048
ἀφ' ὧν ἔπαθε τὴν ὑπακοήν, 9 καὶ τελειωθεὶς
from the things which He suffered obedience, and having been perfected

1096 3588 5219 846 3956 159
ἐγένετο τοῖς ὑπακούουσιν αὐτῷ πᾶσιν αἴτιος
He became to the (ones) obeying Him to all (the) cause

4991 166 4316 5259 3588 2316
σωτηρίας αἰωνίου· 10 προσαγορευθεὶς ὑπὸ τοῦ Θεοῦ
of salvation eternal; having been called out by God

749 2596 3588 5010 3198
ἀρχιερεὺς κατὰ τὴν τάξιν Μελχισέδεκ.
a High Priest according to the order of Melchizedek.

4012 3739 4183 2254 3588 3056 2532 1421 3004
11. Περὶ οὗ πολὺς ἡμῖν ὁ λόγος καὶ δυσερμήνευτος λέγειν,
Concerning whom much to us the Word and hard to interpret to say,

1893 3576 1096 3588 189 2532 1063 3784 1511
ἐπεὶ νωθροὶ γεγόνατε ταῖς ἀκοαῖς. 12 καὶ γὰρ ὀφείλοντες εἶναι
since dully you have become in the hearings. indeed For being due to be

1320 1223 3588 5550 3825 5532 2192 3588 1321
διδάσκαλοι διὰ τὸν χρόνον, πάλιν χρείαν ἔχετε τοῦ διδά-
teachers because of the time, again need you have to

5209 5101 3588 4747 3588 746 3588 3051 3588 2316
σκειν ὑμᾶς, τινὰ τὰ στοιχεῖα τῆς ἀρχῆς τῶν λογίων τοῦ Θεοῦ·
teach you, someone the rudiments of the beginning of the oracles of God;

2532 1096 5532 2192 1051 2532 3756 4731
καὶ γεγόνατε χρείαν ἔχοντες γάλακτος, καὶ οὐ στερεᾶς
and you became (in) need having of milk, and not of solid

5160 3956 1063 3588 3348 1051 552 3056
τροφῆς. 13 πᾶς γὰρ ὁ μετέχων γάλακτος ἄπειρος λόγου
food. everyone For partaking of milk (is) unskilled (in) the Word

1343 3516 1063 2076 5046 1161 2076 3588 4731
δικαιοσύνης· νήπιος γάρ ἐστι. 14 τελείων δέ ἐστιν ἡ στερεὰ
of righteousness; an infant for he is. for full-grown But is solid

5160 3588 1223 3588 1838 3588 145 1128
τροφή, τῶν διὰ τὴν ἕξιν τὰ αἰσθητήρια γεγυμνασμένα
food, of those through habit the faculties having exercised

King James Version

be made an high priest; but he that said unto him, Thou art my Son, to day have I begotten thee.

6 As he saith also in another (place), Thou (art) a priest for ever after the order of Melchisedec.

7 Who in the days of his flesh, when he had offered up prayers and supplications with strong crying and tears unto him that was able to save him from death, and was heard in that he feared;

8 Though he were a Son, yet learned he obedience by the things which he suffered;
9 And being made perfect, he became the author of eternal salvation unto all them that obey him;

10 Called of God an high priest after the order of Melchisedec.

11 Of whom we have many things to say, and hard to be uttered, seeing ye are dull of hearing.
12 For when for the time ye ought to be teachers, ye have need that one teach you again which (be) the first principles of the oracles of God; and are become such as have need of milk, and not of strong meat.
13 For every one that useth milk (is) unskilful in the word of righteousness: for he is a babe.
14 But strong meat belongeth to them that are of full age, (even) those who by reason of use have their senses exercised

Literal Translation **Hebrews 6:1** ***King James Version***

through habit, for distinction of both good and bad.

2192 4314 1253 2570 5037 2532 2556
ἐχόντων πρὸς διάκρισιν καλοῦ τε καὶ κακοῦ.
having for distinction of good both and bad.

to discern both good and evil.

Hebrews 6

1. Because of this, having left the discourse of the beginning of Christ, let us be borne on to full growth, not laying down again a foundation of repentance from dead works, and of faith upon God,
2 of (the) baptisms, of doctrine, and of laying on of hands, and of resurrection of dead ones, and of eternal judgment.
3 And this we will do, if indeed God permits.

4 For (it is) impossible for those once having been enlightened, and having tasted of the heavenly gift, and having become partakers of (the) Holy Spirit,
5 and having tasted (the) good Word of God, and (the) works of power of a coming age,
6 and having fallen away, again to renew to repentance, crucifying again for themselves the Son of God, and putting (Him) to open shame.
7 For the earth drinking in the rain often coming upon it, and producing vegetation fit for those for whom it is also worked, receives blessing from God;

8 but bearing thorns and thistles, (it is) deemed unfit and near a curse, of which the end (is) for burning.

Hebrews 6

1352 863 3588 3588 746 3588 5547 3056 1909 3588
1. Διὸ ἀφέντες τὸν τῆς ἀρχῆς τοῦ Χριστοῦ λόγον, ἐπὶ τὴν
Therefore having left the of the beginning of Christ discourse, on to
5047 5342 3361 3825 2310 2598
τελειότητα φερώμεθα, μὴ πάλιν θεμέλιον καταβαλλόμενοι
full growth let us be borne, not again a foundation laying down
3341 575 3498 2041 2532 4102 1909 2316 909
μετανοίας ἀπὸ νεκρῶν ἔργων, καὶ πίστεως ἐπὶ Θεόν, 2 βαπτι-
of repentance from dead works, and of faith upon God, of baptisms
1322 1936 5037 5495 386 5037 3498
σμῶν διδαχῆς, ἐπιθέσεώς τε χειρῶν, ἀναστάσεώς τε νεκρῶν,
of doctrine, of laying on and of hands, of resurrection and of the dead,
2532 2917 166 2532 5124 4160 1437 2010
καὶ κρίματος αἰωνίου. 3 καὶ τοῦτο ποιήσομεν, ἐάνπερ ἐπι-
and judgment of eternal. And this we will do, if indeed
3588 2316 102 1063 3588 530 5461
τρέπῃ ὁ Θεός. 4 ἀδύνατον γὰρ, τοὺς ἅπαξ φωτισθέντας,
permits God. (it is) impossible For (for) those once being enlightened,
1089 5037 3588 1431 3588 2032 2532 3353
γευσαμένους τε τῆς δωρεᾶς τῆς ἐπουρανίου, καὶ μετόχους
having tasted and of the gift heavenly, and partakers
1096 4151 40 2532 2570 1089 2316
γενηθέντας Πνεύματος Ἁγίου, 5 καὶ καλὸν γευσαμένους Θεοῦ
having become of (the) Spirit Holy, and (the) good having tasted of God
4487 1411 5037 3195 165 2532 3895
ῥῆμα, δυνάμεις τε μέλλοντος αἰῶνος, 6 καὶ παραπεσόντας,
Word, works of power and of a coming age, and having fallen away,
3825 340 1519 3341 388 1438
πάλιν ἀνακαινίζειν εἰς μετάνοιαν, ἀνασταυροῦντας ἑαυτοῖς
again to renew to repentance, crucifying again for themselves
3588 5207 3588 2316 2532 3856 1093 1063 3588
τὸν υἱὸν τοῦ Θεοῦ καὶ παραδειγματίζοντας. 7 γῆ γὰρ ἡ
the Son of God and putting (Him) to open shame. earth For
4095 3588 1909 846 4178 2064 5205 2532
πιοῦσα τὸν ἐπ᾽ αὐτῆς πολλάκις ἐρχόμενον ὑετόν, καὶ
drinking the upon it often coming rain, and
5088 1008 2111 1565 1223 3739 2532 1090
τίκτουσα βοτάνην εὔθετον ἐκείνοις δι᾽ οὓς καὶ γεωργεῖται,
producing vegetation suitable for those for whom indeed it is worked,
3335 2129 575 3588 2316 1627 1161 173
μεταλαμβάνει εὐλογίας ἀπὸ τοῦ Θεοῦ· 8 ἐκφέρουσα δὲ ἀκάνθας
receives blessing from God; bringing forth but thorns
2532 5146 96 2532 2671 1451 3739 3588 5056 1519
καὶ τριβόλους, ἀδόκιμος καὶ κατάρας ἐγγύς, ἧς τὸ τέλος εἰς
and thistles, (it is) disapproved and a curse near, of which the end (is) for
2740
καῦσιν.
burning.

Hebrews 6

1. Therefore leaving the principles of the doctrine of Christ, let us go on unto perfection; not laying again the foundation of repentance from dead works, and of faith toward God,
2 Of the doctrine of baptisms, and of laying on of hands, and of resurrection of the dead, and of eternal judgment.

3 And this will we do, if God permit.

4 For (it is) impossible for those who were once enlightened, and have tasted of the heavenly gift, and were made partakers of the Holy Ghost,
5 And have tasted the good word of God, and the powers of the world to come,
6 If they shall fall away, to renew them again unto repentance; seeing they crucify to themselves the Son of God afresh, and put (him) to an open shame.
7 For the earth which drinketh in the rain that cometh oft upon it, and bringeth forth herbs meet for them by whom it is dressed, receiveth blessing from God:

8 But that which beareth thorns and briers (is) rejected, and (is) nigh unto cursing; whose end (is) to be burned.

9 But, loved ones, even if we indeed speak so, we have been persuaded better things concerning you, even holding fast salvation.
10 For God (is) not unjust, to forget your work and the labor

3982 1161 4012 5216 27 3588 2909 2532
9. Πεπείσμεθα δὲ περὶ ὑμῶν, ἀγαπητοί, τὰ κρείττονα καὶ
we have been persuaded But about you, loved ones, the things better even
2192 4991 1487 2532 3779 2980 3756 1063 94 3588
ἐχόμενα σωτηρίας, εἰ καὶ οὕτω λαλοῦμεν· 10 οὐ γὰρ ἄδικος ὁ
holding fast salvation, if indeed so we speak; not for unjust
2316 1950 3588 2041 5216 2532 3588 2873 3588
Θεὸς ἐπιλαθέσθαι τοῦ ἔργου ὑμῶν, καὶ τοῦ κόπου τῆς
God (is) to be forgetful of the work of you, and the labor

9 But, beloved, we are persuaded better things of you, and things that accompany salvation, though we thus speak.
10 For God (is) not unrighteous to forget your work and labour

Literal Translation

of love which you showed to His name, ministering to the saints, and (now are) ministering.
11 But we desire each of you to show the same eagerness, to the full assurance of the hope to (the) end;
12 that you not become dull, but imitators of those who through faith and long-suffering (are) inheriting the promises.

13 For God having made promise to Abraham, since He had no greater to swear by, (He) swore by Himself,
14 saying, "Surely blessing I will bless you, and multiplying I will multiply you." (Gen. 22:16,17)
15 And so, being long-suffering, he obtained the promise.
16 For men indeed swear by the greater, and an oath to make things sure (is) to them the end of all gainsaying.
17 In which way, God purposing to more fully declare to the heirs of the promise the unchangeableness of His counsel, He interposed by an oath,

18 that through two unchangeable things, in which (it was) not possible (for) God to lie, we might have a strong consolation, those having fled to lay hold on the hope set before (us),
19 which we have as an anchor of the soul, both certain and sure, and entering into the inner (side) of the veil,
20 where Jesus entered as forerunner for us, having become a High Priest forever, according to the order of Melchizedek.

Hebrews 6:11

26 3739 1731 1519 3588 3686 846 1247
ἀγάπης ἧς ἐνεδείξασθε εἰς τὸ ὄνομα αὐτοῦ, διακονήσαντες
of love which you showed to the name of Him, having ministered

3588 40 2532 1247 1937 1161 1538 5216
τοῖς ἁγίοις καὶ διακονοῦντες. 11 ἐπιθυμοῦμεν δὲ ἕκαστον ὑμῶν
to the saints and (now) ministering. we desire But each one of you

3588 846 1731 4710 4314 2532 4136 3588
τὴν αὐτὴν ἐνδείκνυσθαι σπουδὴν πρὸς τὴν πληροφορίαν τῆς
the same to show eagerness to the full assurance of the

1680 891 5056 2443 3361 3576 1096 3402 1161
ἐλπίδος ἄχρι τέλους· 12 ἵνα μὴ νωθροὶ γένησθε, μιμηταὶ δὲ
hope unto (the) end; that not dull you become, imitators but

3588 1223 4102 2532 3115 2816 3588
τῶν διὰ πίστεως καὶ μακροθυμίας κληρονομούντων τὰς
of those through faith and long-suffering (are) inheriting the

1860
ἐπαγγελίας.
promises.

3588 1063 11 1861 3588 2316 1893 2596
13. Τῷ γὰρ Ἀβραὰμ ἐπαγγειλάμενος ὁ Θεός, ἐπεὶ κατ'
For to Abraham having made promise God, since by

3762 2192 3173 3660 3660 2596 1438 3004
οὐδενὸς εἶχε μείζονος ὀμόσαι, ὤμοσε καθ' ἑαυτοῦ, 14 λέγων,
no one He had greater to swear, (He) swore by Himself, saying,

2229 3375 2127 2127 1161 2532 4129 4129 4571
Ἠ μὴν εὐλογῶν εὐλογήσω σε, καὶ πληθύνων πληθυνῶ σε.
Surely blessing I will bless you, and multiplying I will multiply you.

2532 3779 3314 2013 3588 1860 444
15 καὶ οὕτω μακροθυμήσας ἐπέτυχε τῆς ἐπαγγελίας. 16 ἄνθρ-
And so being long-suffering he obtained the promise. men

3303 1063 2596 3588 3173 3660 2532 3956 846
ωποι μὲν γὰρ κατὰ τοῦ μείζονος ὀμνύουσι, καὶ πάσης αὐτοῖς
indeed For by the greater swear, and of all (is) to them

485 4009 1519 951 3588 3727 1722 3739 4054
ἀντιλογίας πέρας εἰς βεβαίωσιν ὁ ὅρκος· 17 ἐν ᾧ περισσότερον
gainsaying an end for confirmation the oath; in which more fully

1014 3588 2316 1925 3588 2818 3588 1860
βουλόμενος ὁ Θεὸς ἐπιδεῖξαι τοῖς κληρονόμοις τῆς ἐπαγ-
purposing God to show the heirs of the promise

3588 276 3588 1012 846 3315 3727
γελίας τὸ ἀμετάθετον τῆς βουλῆς αὐτοῦ, ἐμεσίτευσεν ὅρκῳ,
the unchangeableness of the counsel of Him, He interposed by an oath,

2443 1223 1417 4229 276 1722 3739 102
18 ἵνα διὰ δύο πραγμάτων ἀμεταθέτων, ἐν οἷς ἀδύνατον
that through two things unchangeable, in which (it was) impossible

5574 2316 2478 3874 2192 3588 2703
ψεύσασθαι Θεόν, ἰσχυρὰν παράκλησιν ἔχωμεν οἱ κατα-
to lie God, a strong consolation we might have the (ones)

2902 3588 4295 1680 3739 5613 45
φυγόντες κρατῆσαι τῆς προκειμένης ἐλπίδος· 19 ἣν ὡς ἄγκυραν
having fled to lay hold of the set before (us) hope; which as an anchor

2192 3588 5590 804 5037 2532 949 2532 1525
ἔχομεν τῆς ψυχῆς, ἀσφαλῆ τε καὶ βεβαίαν, καὶ εἰσερχομένην
we have of the soul, secure both and firm, and entering

1519 3588 2082 3588 2665 3699 4274 5228
εἰς τὸ ἐσώτερον τοῦ καταπετάσματος· 20 ὅπου πρόδρομος ὑπὲρ
into the inner (side) of the veil; where a Forerunner on behalf of

2257 1525 2424 2596 3588 5010 3198 749
ἡμῶν εἰσῆλθεν Ἰησοῦς, κατὰ τὴν τάξιν Μελχισέδεκ ἀρχιερεὺς
us entered Jesus, according to the order of Melchizedek a High Priest

1096 1519 3588 165
γενόμενος εἰς τὸν αἰῶνα.
having become to the age.

King James Version

of love, which ye have shewed toward his name, in that ye have ministered to the saints, and do minister.
11 And we desire that every one of you do shew the same diligence to the full assurance of hope unto the end:
12 That ye be not slothful, but followers of them who through faith and patience inherit the promises.

13 For when God made promise to Abraham, because he could swear by no greater, he sware by himself,
14 Saying, Surely blessing I will bless thee, and multiplying I will multiply thee.
15 And so, after he had patiently endured, he obtained the promise.
16 For men verily swear by the greater: and an oath for confirmation (is) to them an end of all strife.
17 Wherein God, willing more abundantly to shew unto the heirs of promise the immutability of his counsel, confirmed (it) by an oath:

18 That by two immutable things, in which (it was) impossible for God to lie, we might have a strong consolation, who have fled for refuge to lay hold upon the hope set before us:
19 Which (hope) we have as an anchor of the soul, both sure and stedfast, and which entereth into that within the veil;
20 Whither the forerunner is for us entered, (even) Jesus, made an high priest for ever after the order of Melchisedec.

Literal Translation

Hebrews 7

1. For this Melchizedek, king of Salem, priest of the most high God, the (one) having met Abraham returning from the slaughter of the kings, and having blessed him;
2 to whom also Abraham divided a tenth from all (first being interpreted, king of righteousness; and then also king of Salem, which is, king of peace, (Gen. 14:17-20)

3 without father, without mother, without genealogy, nor beginning of days, nor having end of life, but having been made like the Son of God, (he) remains a priest in perpetuity).

4 Now behold how great this (one was), to whom even the patriarch Abraham gave a tenth of the spoils;
5 and indeed those of the sons of Levi receiving the priesthood have a command to tithe the people according to Law, (that is, from their brothers, though coming forth out of Abraham's loins),

6 but he not counting (his) genealogy from them has tithed Abraham, and has blessed the (one) having the promises.

7 But without contradiction, the lesser is blessed by the better.
8 And here dying men indeed receive tithes, but there (it) having been witnessed that he lives;

9 and as a word to say, through Abraham Levi also, the (one) receiving tithes, has been tithed.
10 For he was yet in his father's loins when Melchizedek met him.

11 Truly, then, if perfection was through the Levitical priestly office (for the

Hebrews 7

3778 1063 3588 3198 935 4532 2409 3588
1. Οὗτος γὰρ ὁ Μελχισέδεκ, βασιλεὺς Σαλήμ, ἱερεὺς τοῦ
this For Melchizedek, king of Salem, priest

2316 3588 5310 3588 4876 11 5290 575
Θεοῦ τοῦ ὑψίστου, ὁ συναντήσας Ἀβραὰμ ὑποστρέφοντι ἀπὸ
of God the Most High, the (one) having met Abraham returning from

3588 2871 3588 935 2532 2127 846 3739 2532 1181
τῆς κοπῆς τῶν βασιλέων καὶ εὐλογήσας αὐτόν, 2 ᾧ καὶ δεκάτην
the slaughter of the kings and having blessed him, to whom also a tenth

575 3956 3307 11 4412 3303 2059
ἀπὸ πάντων ἐμέρισεν Ἀβραάμ [πρῶτον μὲν ἑρμηνευόμενος
from all divided Abraham, firstly indeed being interpreted

935 1343 1899 1161 2532 935 4532 3739 2076
βασιλεὺς δικαιοσύνης, ἔπειτα δὲ καὶ βασιλεὺς Σαλήμ, ὅ ἐστι
king of righteousness, then and also king of Salem, which is

935 1515 540 282 35 3383
βασιλεὺς εἰρήνης· 3 ἀπάτωρ, ἀμήτωρ, ἀγενεαλόγητος, μήτε
king of peace; without father, without mother, without pedigree, nor

746 2250 3383 2222 5056 219 871 1161 3588
ἀρχὴν ἡμερῶν μήτε ζωῆς τέλος ἔχων, ἀφωμοιωμένος δὲ τῷ
beginning of days nor of life end having, having been made like but the

5207 3588 2316 3306 2409 1519 3588 1336
υἱῷ τοῦ θεοῦ, μένει ἱερεὺς εἰς τὸ διηνεκές.
Son of God, remains a priest to perpetuity.

2334 1161 4080 3778 3739 2532 1181 11 1325
4. Θεωρεῖτε δὲ πηλίκος οὗτος, ᾧ καὶ δεκάτην Ἀβραὰμ ἔδωκεν
behold And how great this (one), to whom even a tenth Abraham gave

1537 3588 205 3588 3966 2532 3588 3303 1537 3588 5207
ἐκ τῶν ἀκροθινίων ὁ πατριάρχης. 5 καὶ οἱ μὲν ἐκ τῶν υἱῶν
of the spoils the patriarch. And those indeed of the sons

3017 3588 2405 2983 1785 2192 586
Λευὶ τὴν ἱερατείαν λαμβάνοντες ἐντολὴν ἔχουσιν ἀποδεκα-
of Levi the priesthood receiving a commandment have to tithe

3588 2992 2596 3588 3551 5123 2076 3588 80
τοῦν τὸν λαὸν κατὰ τὸν νόμον, τοῦτ᾽ ἔστι τοὺς ἀδελφοὺς
the people according to the Law, this is the brothers

846 2539 1831 1537 3588 3751 11 3588 1161
αὐτῶν, καίπερ ἐξεληλυθότας ἐκ τῆς ὀσφύος Ἀβραάμ· 6 ὁ δὲ
of them, though having come forth out of the loins of Abraham; he but

3361 1075 1537 846 1183 3588 11 2532
μὴ γενεαλογούμενος ἐξ αὐτῶν δεδεκάτωκε τὸν Ἀβραάμ, καὶ
not counting (his) pedigree from them has tithed Abraham, and

3588 2192 3588 1860 2127 5565 1161 3956 485
τὸν ἔχοντα τὰς ἐπαγγελίας εὐλόγηκε. 7 χωρὶς δὲ πάσης ἀντι-
the (one) having the promises (this one) blessed. without And all contra-

3588 1640 5259 3588 2909 2127 2532 5602
λογίας, τὸ ἔλαττον ὑπὸ τοῦ κρείττονος εὐλογεῖται. 8 καὶ ὧδε
diction, the lesser by the better is blessed. And here

3303 1181 599 444 2983 1563 1161
μὲν δεκάτας ἀποθνήσκοντες ἄνθρωποι λαμβάνουσιν· ἐκεῖ δέ,
truly tithes dying men receive; there but,

444 3754 2198 2532 5613 2031 2036 1223 11 2532
μαρτυρούμενος ὅτι ζῇ. 9 καί, ὡς ἔπος εἰπεῖν, διὰ Ἀβραὰμ καὶ
being witnessed that he lives. And, as a word to say, through Abraham also

3017 3588 1181 2983 1183 2089 1063 1722 3588 3751
Λευὶ ὁ δεκάτας λαμβάνων δεδεκάτωται· 10 ἔτι γὰρ ἐν τῇ ὀσφύϊ
Levi the (one) tithes receiving has been tithed; yet for in the loins

3588 3962 2258 3753 4876 846 3588 3198
τοῦ πατρὸς ἦν, ὅτε συνήντησεν αὐτῷ ὁ Μελχισέδεκ.
of the father he was, when met him Melchizedek.

1487 3303 3767 5050 1223 3588 3020 2420 2258 3588
11. Εἰ μὲν οὖν τελείωσις διὰ τῆς Λευιτικῆς ἱερωσύνης ἦν [ὁ
If therefore perfection through the Levitical priestly office was, the

King James Version

Hebrews 7

1. For this Melchisedec, king of Salem, priest of the most high God, who met Abraham returning from the slaughter of the kings, and blessed him;
2 To whom also Abraham gave a tenth part of all; first being by interpretation King of righteousness, and after that also King of Salem, which is, King of peace;

3 Without father, without mother, without descent, having neither beginning of days, nor end of life; but made like unto the Son of God; abideth a priest continually.

4 Now consider how great this man (was), unto whom even the patriarch Abraham gave the tenth of the spoils.
5 And verily they that are of the sons of Levi, who receive the office of the priesthood, have a commandment to take tithes of the people according to the law, that is, of their brethren, though they come out of the loins of Abraham:
6 But he whose descent is not counted from them received tithes of Abraham, and blessed him that had the promises.

7 And without all contradiction the less is blessed of the better.
8 And here men that die receive tithes; but there he (receiveth them), of whom it is witnessed that he liveth.

9 And as I may so say, Levi also, who receiveth tithes, payed tithes in Abraham.
10 For he was yet in the loins of his father, when Melchisedec met him.

11 If therefore perfection were by the Levitical priesthood, (for

Literal Translation

people has been given
Law under it, why yet
need (for) another priest
to arise according to the
order of Melchizedek
and not to be called ac-
cording to the order of
Aaron?
12 For the priestly of-
fice being changed, of
necessity a change of
law also occurs.
13 For the (One) of
whom these things are
said has partaken of an-
other tribe, from which
no one has given devo-
tion at the altar.
14 For (it is) clear that
our Lord has risen out of
Judah, as to which tribe
Moses spoke nothing
concerning priesthood.
15 And it is still more
abundantly clear if an-
other priest arises ac-
cording to the likeness
of Melchizedek,
16 who has not become
(so) according to a law
of a fleshly command,
but according to (the)
power of an indissol-
uble life.
17 For it is testified,
"You (are) a priest for-
ever according to the or-
der of Melchizedek."
(Psa. 110:4)
18 For indeed an annul-
ment of (the) preceding
command comes about
because of it is weakly
and unprofitable.
19 For the Law per-
fected nothing, but a
bringing in of a better
hope, through which
we draw near to God.
20 And by how much (it
was) not apart from
oath-taking;
21 for they having be-
come priests apart from
oath-taking, but He
with oath-taking
through Him who says
to Him, "(The) Lord
swore, and will not care
(to change) afterward,
You (are) a priest to the
age according to the or-
der of Melchizedek;"
(Psa. 110:4)
22 by so much Jesus has
become Surety of a bet-
ter covenant.
23 And they indeed are
many priests, being pre-
vented from continuing
because of death;
24 but He has the

Hebrews 7:12

2992 1063 1909 846 3549 5101 2089 5532 2596 3588
λαὸς γὰρ ἐπ' αὐτῇ νενομοθέτητο], τίς ἔτι χρεία κατὰ, τὴν
people for under it has been given Law, why yet need according to the
5010 3198 2087 450 2409 2532 3756 2596 3588
τάξιν Μελχισέδεκ ἕτερον ἀνίστασθαι ἱερέα, καὶ οὐ κατὰ τὴν
order of Melchizedek another to rise priest, and not according to the
5010 2 3004 3346 1063 3588 2420
τάξιν 'Ααρὼν λέγεσθαι; 12 μετατιθεμένης γὰρ τῆς ἱερωσύνης,
order of Aaron to be called? being changed For the priestly office,
1537 318 2532 3551 3331 1096 1909 3739 1063 3004
ἐξ ἀνάγκης καὶ νόμου μετάθεσις γίνεται. 13 ἐφ' ὃν γὰρ λέγεται
of necessity also of law a change occurs. with whom For are said
5023 5443 2087 3348 575 3739 3762 4337
ταῦτα, φυλῆς ἑτέρας μετέσχηκεν, ἀφ' ἧς οὐδεὶς προσέσχηκε
these things, tribe of another has partaken, from which no one has given devotion
3588 2379 4271 1063 3754 1537 2448 393
τῷ θυσιαστηρίῳ· 14 πρόδηλον γὰρ ὅτι ἐξ 'Ιούδα ἀνατέταλκεν
at the altar; it is clear for that out of Judah has risen
3588 2962 2257 1519 3739 5443 3762 4012 2420 3475
ὁ Κύριος ἡμῶν, εἰς ἣν φυλὴν οὐδὲν περὶ ἱερωσύνης Μωσῆς
the Lord of us, as to which tribe nothing concerning priesthood Moses
2980 2532 4054 2089 2612 2076 1487 2596 3588
ἐλάλησε. 15 καὶ περισσότερον ἔτι κατάδηλόν ἐστιν, εἰ κατὰ τὴν
spoke. And more abundantly still quite clear it is, if according to the
3665 3198 450 2409 2087 3739 3756 2596
ὁμοιότητα Μελχισέδεκ ἀνίσταται ἱερεὺς ἕτερος, 16 ὃς οὐ κατὰ
likeness of Melchizedek arises priest another, who not according to
3551 1785 4559 1096 235 2596 1411 2222
νόμον ἐντολῆς σαρκικῆς γέγονεν, ἀλλὰ κατὰ δύναμιν ζωῆς
a law of command fleshly has become, but according to (the) power life
179 3140 1063 3754 4771 2409 1519 3588 165 2596
ἀκαταλύτου· 17 μαρτυρεῖ γὰρ ὅτι Σὺ ἱερεὺς εἰς τὸν αἰῶνα κατὰ
of an indissoluble; it is testified for, You (are) a priest to the age according to
3588 5010 3198 115 3303 1063 1096 4254
τὴν τάξιν Μελχισέδεκ. 18 ἀθέτησις μὲν γὰρ γίνεται προαγού-
the order of Melchizedek. an annulment indeed For comes to be of (the)
1785 1223 3588 846 772 2532 512 3762
σης ἐντολῆς, διὰ τὸ αὐτῆς ἀσθενὲς καὶ ἀνωφελές, 19 οὐδὲν
before command, because of the of it weak(ness) and unprofitable(ness), nothing
1063 5048 3588 3551 1898 1161 2909 1680 1223
γὰρ ἐτελείωσεν ὁ νόμος, ἐπεισαγωγὴ δὲ κρείττονος ἐλπίδος, δι'
for perfected the Law, a bringing in but of a better hope, through
3739 1448 3588 2316 2532 2596 3745 3756 5565 3728
ἧς ἐγγίζομεν τῷ θεῷ. 20 Καὶ καθ' ὅσον οὐ χωρὶς ὁρκωμοσίας,
which we draw near to God. And by how much not without oath-taking,
3588 3303 1063 5565 3728 1526 2409 1096 3588
[οἱ μὲν γὰρ χωρὶς ὁρκωμοσίας εἰσὶν ἱερεῖς γεγονότες, 21 ὁ
those truly for without oath-taking are priests having become, He
1161 3326 3728 1223 3588 3004 4314 846 3660
δὲ μετὰ ὁρκωμοσίας, διὰ τοῦ λέγοντος πρὸς αὐτόν, Ὤμοσε
but with oath-taking, through the (One) saying to Him, Swore
2962 2532 3756 3338 4771 2409 1519 3588 165 2596
Κύριος, καὶ οὐ μεταμεληθήσεται, Σὺ ἱερεὺς εἰς τὸν αἰῶνα κατὰ
(the) Lord, and not will care (to change), You a priest to the age according to
3588 5010 3198 2596 5118 2909 1242
τὴν τάξιν Μελχισεδέκ]· 22 κατὰ τοσοῦτον κρείττονος διαθήκης
the order of Melchizedek; by so much of a better covenant
1096 1450 2424 2532 3588 3303 4119 1526 1096
γέγονεν ἔγγυος 'Ιησοῦς. 23 καὶ οἱ μὲν πλείονές εἰσι γεγονότες
has become surety Jesus. And those indeed many are having become
2409 1223 3588 3306 2967 3887 3588 1161 1223 3588
ἱερεῖς, διὰ τὸ θανάτῳ κωλύεσθαι παραμένειν· 24 ὁ δὲ, διὰ τὸ
priests, because of by death being prevented to continue; He but, because of

King James Version

under it the people re-
ceived the law,) what
further need (was there)
that another priest
should rise after the or-
der of Melchisedec, and
not be called after the
order of Aaron?
12 For the priesthood
being changed, there is
made of necessity a
change also of the law.
13 For he of whom
these things are spoken
pertaineth to another
tribe, of which no man
gave attendance at the
altar.
14 For (it is) evident that
our Lord sprang out of
Juda; of which tribe
Moses spake nothing
concerning priesthood.
15 And it is yet far more
evident: for that after the
similitude of Mel-
chisedec there ariseth
another priest,
16 Who is made, not af-
ter the law of a carnal
commandment, but af-
ter the power of an end-
less life.
17 For he testifieth,
Thou (art) a priest for
ever after the order of
Melchisedec.
18 For there is verily a
disannulling of the
commandment going
before for the weakness
and unprofitableness
thereof.
19 For the law made
nothing perfect, but the
bringing in of a better
hope (did); by the which
we draw nigh unto God.
20 And inasmuch as not
without an oath (he was
made priest):
21 (For those priests
were made without an
oath; but this with an
oath by him that said
unto him, The Lord
sware and will not re-
pent, Thou (art) a priest
for ever after the order
of Melchisedec:)
22 By so much was Je-
sus made a surety of a
better testament.
23 And they truly were
many priests, because
they were not suffered
to continue by reason of
death:
24 But this (man), be-
cause

Literal Translation

Hebrews 7:25

King James Version

priesthood not to be passed on, because of His remaining to the age.

25 And from this He is able to save to perfection those who come to God through Him, ever living to intercede on their behalf.

26 For such a High Priest was fitting for us: holy, without evil, undefiled, having been separated from sinners, and having become higher than the heavens;
27 who has no need, as do the high priests, to offer sacrifices day by day, first on behalf of His own sins, then (for) those of the people. For He did this once for all, having offered up Himself.

28 For the Law appoints men high priests who have infirmity, but the word of the swearing of an oath, after the Law, (appoints the) Son to the age, having been perfected.

3306 846 1519 3588 165 531 2192 3588 2420
μένειν αὐτὸν εἰς τὸν αἰῶνα, ἀπαράβατον ἔχει τὴν ἱερωσύνην.
to remain Him to the age, not to be passed on has the priestly office.

3606 2532 4982 1519 3588 3838 1410 3588 3842
25 ὅθεν καὶ σῴζειν εἰς τὸ παντελὲς δύναται τοὺς προσερχο-
from this And to save to perfection He is able the (ones) drawing

1223 846 3588 2316 3842 2198 1519 3588 1793
μένους δι' αὐτοῦ τῷ Θεῷ, πάντοτε ζῶν εἰς τὸ ἐντυγχάνειν
near through Him to God, ever living for the intercede

5228 846
ὑπὲρ αὐτῶν.
on behalf of them.

5108 1063 2254 4334 749 3741 172
26. Τοιοῦτος γὰρ ἡμῖν ἔπρεπεν ἀρχιερεύς, ὅσιος, ἄκακος,
such For to us was fitting a High Priest, holy, without evil,

283 5563 575 3588 268 2532 5308
ἀμίαντος, κεχωρισμένος ἀπὸ τῶν ἁμαρτωλῶν, καὶ ὑψηλό-
undefiled, having been separated from sinners, and higher

3588 3772 1096 3739 3756 2192 2596 2250
τερος τῶν οὐρανῶν γενόμενος· 27 ὃς οὐκ ἔχει καθ' ἡμέραν
than the heavens having become; who not has (day by) day

318 5618 3588 749 4386 5228 3588 2398
ἀνάγκην, ὥσπερ οἱ ἀρχιερεῖς, πρότερον ὑπὲρ τῶν ἰδίων
need, as the high priests, firstly on behalf of the own

266 2378 399 1899 3588 3588 2992 5124
ἁμαρτιῶν θυσίας ἀναφέρειν, ἔπειτα τῶν τοῦ λαοῦ· τοῦτο
sins sacrifices to offer up, then (for) those of the people; this

1063 4160 2178 1438 399 3588 3551 1063
γὰρ ἐποίησεν ἐφάπαξ, ἑαυτὸν ἀνενέγκας. 28 ὁ νόμος γὰρ
for He did once for all, Himself having offered up. the law For

444 2525 749 2192 769 3588
ἀνθρώπους καθίστησιν ἀρχιερεῖς, ἔχοντας ἀσθένειαν· ὁ
men appoints high priests, having infirmity; the

3056 1161 3588 3728 3588 3326 3588 3551 5207 1519
λόγος δὲ τῆς ὁρκωμοσίας τῆς μετὰ τὸν νόμον υἱὸν εἰς
word but of the oath-taking after the law (appoints) a Son to

3588 165 5048
τὸν αἰῶνα τετελειωμένον.
the age having been perfected.

he continueth ever, hath an unchangeable priesthood.

25 Wherefore he is able also to save them to the uttermost that come unto God by him, seeing he ever liveth to make intercession for them.

26 For such an high priest became us, (who is) holy, harmless, undefiled, separate from sinners, and made higher than the heavens;
27 Who needeth not daily, as those high priests, to offer up sacrifice, first for his own sins, and then for the people's: for this he did once, when he offered up himself.

28 For the law maketh men high priests which have infirmity; but the word of the oath, which was since the law, (maketh) the Son, who is consecrated for evermore.

Hebrews 8

1. Now a summary over the things being said: We have such a High Priest, who sat down on (the) right of the throne of the Majesty in Heaven,
2 Minister of the (Holy of) Holies, and of the true tabernacle which the Lord raised up, and not man.
3 For every high priest is set in place to offer both gifts and sacrifices; from which (it is) necessary (for) this One also to have something which He may offer.
4 For if indeed He were on earth, He would not (even) be a priest, there being those priests

Hebrews 8

2774 1161 1909 3588 3004 5108 2192
1. Κεφάλαιον δὲ ἐπὶ τοῖς λεγομένοις· τοιοῦτον ἔχομεν
a summary Now over the things being spoken of; such we have

749 3739 2523 1722 1188 3588 2362 3588 3172
ἀρχιερέα, ὃς ἐκάθισεν ἐν δεξιᾷ τοῦ θρόνου τῆς μεγαλωσύνης
a High Priest, who sat at (the) right of the throne of the Majesty

1722 3588 3772 3588 39 3011 2532 3588 4633 3588
ἐν τοῖς οὐρανοῖς, 2 τῶν ἁγίων λειτουργός, καὶ τῆς σκηνῆς τῆς
in Heaven, of the holies a minister, and of the tabernacle

228 3739 4078 3588 2962 2532 3756 444 3956 1063
ἀληθινῆς, ἣν ἔπηξεν ὁ Κύριος, καὶ οὐκ ἄνθρωπος. 3 πᾶς γὰρ
true, which raised up the Lord, and not man. every For

749 1519 3588 4374 1435 5037 2532 2378 2525
ἀρχιερεὺς εἰς τὸ προσφέρειν δῶρά τε καὶ θυσίας καθίσταται·
high priest to the to offer gifts both and sacrifices is appointed;

3606 316 2192 5100 2532 5126 3739 4374 1487
ὅθεν ἀναγκαῖον ἔχειν τι καὶ τοῦτον ὃ προσενέγκῃ. 4 εἰ
from which it is needful to have something also this One which He may offer. if

3303/1063/2258/1909/1093 3761 302 2258 2409 5607 3588 2409 3588
μὲν γὰρ ἦν ἐπὶ γῆς, οὐδ' ἂν ἦν ἱερεύς, ὄντων τῶν ἱερέων τῶν
truly For He were on earth, not He would be a priest, being those priests

Hebrews 8

1. Now of the things which we have spoken (this is) the sum: We have such an high priest, who is set on the right hand of the throne of the Majesty in the heavens;
2 A minister of the sanctuary, and of the true tabernacle, which the Lord pitched, and not man.
3 For every high priest is ordained to offer gifts and sacrifices: wherefore (it is) of necessity that this man have somewhat also to offer.
4 For if he were on earth, he should not be a priest, seeing that there are priests

Literal Translation

offering gifts according to the Law,
5 who serve the pattern of and shadow of heavenly things, even as Moses was (divinely) warned, being about to make the tabernacle: For He says, "See (that) you make all things according to the pattern having been shown to you in the mount." (Exo. 25:40)

6 But now He has gotten a more excellent ministry, also by so much as He is a mediator of a better covenant, which has been enacted on better promises.

7 For if that first was faultless, place would not have been sought for a second.
8 For finding fault, He said to them, "Behold, days are coming, says (the) Lord, and I will bring to fulfilment a new covenant on the house of Israel and on the house of Judah;
9 not according to the covenant which I made with their fathers in (the) day of My taking hold of their hand to lead them out of the land of Egypt;" because they did not continue in My covenant, and I did not regard them, says (the) Lord.
10 "Because this (is) the covenant which I will covenant with the house of Israel after those days, says (the) Lord, giving My laws into their mind, and I will write them on their hearts, and I will be their God, and they shall be My people.

11 And they shall no more teach each one his neighbor, and each one their brother, saying, Know the Lord; because all shall know Me, from the least of them to their great ones.

12 For I will be merciful to their unrighteousnesses,

Hebrews 8:5

4374 2596 3588 3551 3588 1435 3748 5262
προσφερόντων κατὰ τὸν νόμον τὰ δῶρα, 5 οἵτινες ὑποδείγματι
offering according to the Law the gifts, who an example

2532 4639 3000 3588 2032 2531 5537
καὶ σκιᾷ λατρεύουσι τῶν ἐπουρανίων, καθὼς κεχρημάτισται
and a shadow serve of the heavenly things, even as has been warned

3475 3195 2005 3588 4633 3708 1063 5346
Μωσῆς μέλλων ἐπιτελεῖν τὴν σκηνήν, Ὅρα, γάρ φησί,
Moses being about to make the tabernacle, See, For He says,

4160 3956 2596 3588 5179 3588 1166 4671 1722 3588 3735
ποιήσῃς πάντα κατὰ τὸν τύπον τὸν δειχθέντα σοι ἐν τῷ ὄρει.
you make all things according to the pattern being shown to you in the mount.

3570 1161 1313 5177 3009 3745 2532 2909
6 νυνὶ δὲ διαφορωτέρας τέτευχε λειτουργίας, ὅσῳ καὶ κρείτ-
now And a more excellent He has gotten ministry, by so much also of a

2076 1242 3316 3748 1909 2909 1860
τονός ἐστι διαθήκης μεσίτης, ἥτις ἐπὶ κρείττοσιν ἐπαγγελίαις
better He is covenant Mediator, which on better promises

3549 1487 1063 3588 4413 1565 2258 273 3756 302
νενομοθέτηται. 7 Εἰ γὰρ ἡ πρώτη ἐκείνη ἦν ἄμεμπτος, οὐκ ἂν
has been enacted. if For first that was faultless, not would

1208 2212 5117 3201 1063 846 3004 2400
δευτέρας ἐζητεῖτο τόπος. 8 μεμφόμενος γὰρ αὐτοὺς λέγει, Ἰδού,
of a second been sought place. finding fault For them He says, Behold!

2250 2064 3004 2962 2532 4931 1909 3588 3624
ἡμέραι ἔρχονται, λέγει Κύριος, καὶ συντελέσω ἐπὶ τὸν οἶκον
Days are coming, says (the) Lord, and I will bring to fulfilment on the house

2474 2532 1909 3588 3624 2448 1242 2537 3756 2596
Ἰσραὴλ καὶ ἐπὶ τὸν οἶκον Ἰούδα διαθήκην καινήν· 9 οὐ κατὰ
of Israel and on the house of Judah covenant a new; not according to

3588 1242 3739 4160 3588 3962 846 1722 2250
τὴν διαθήκην ἣν ἐποίησα τοῖς πατράσιν αὐτῶν ἐν ἡμέρᾳ
the covenant which I made with the fathers of them in (the) day

1949 3450 3588 5495 846 1806 846 1537
ἐπιλαβομένου μου τῆς χειρὸς αὐτῶν ἐξαγαγεῖν αὐτοὺς ἐκ
taking hold Me the hands of them to lead forth them out of

1093 125 3754 846 3756 1696 1722 3588 1242 3450
γῆς Αἰγύπτου· ὅτι αὐτοὶ οὐκ ἐνέμειναν ἐν τῇ διαθήκῃ μου,
land of Egypt; because they not continued in the covenant of Me,

2504 1696 846 3004 2962 3754 3778 3588 1242 3739
κἀγὼ ἠμέλησα αὐτῶν, λέγει Κύριος. 10 ὅτι αὕτη ἡ διαθήκη ἣν
and I not regarded them, says (the) Lord. Because this the covenant which

1303 3588 3624 2474 3326 3588 2250 1565 3004
διαθήσομαι τῷ οἴκῳ Ἰσραὴλ μετὰ τὰς ἡμέρας ἐκείνας, λέγει
I will covenant with the house of Israel after days these, says

2962 1325 3551 3450 1519 3588 1271 846 2532 1909
Κύριος, διδοὺς νόμους μου εἰς τὴν διάνοιαν αὐτῶν, καὶ ἐπὶ
(the) Lord, giving laws of Me into the minds of them, and on

2588 846 1924 846 2532 2071 846 1519 2316
καρδίας αὐτῶν ἐπιγράψω αὐτούς· καὶ ἔσομαι αὐτοῖς εἰς Θεόν,
(the) hearts of them I will write them; and I will be to them for God,

2532 846 2071 3427 1519 2992 2532 3756 3361 1321 1538
καὶ αὐτοὶ ἔσονταί μοι εἰς λαόν. 11 καὶ οὐ μὴ διδάξωσιν ἕκαστος
and they will be to Me for a people. And not at all may they teach each one

3588 4139 846 2532 1538 3588 80 846 3004
τὸν πολίτην αὐτοῦ, καὶ ἕκαστος τὸν ἀδελφὸν αὐτοῦ, λέγων,
the neighbor of them, and each one the brother of them, saying,

1097 3588 2962 3754 3956 1492 3165 575 3398 846
Γνῶθι τὸν Κύριον· ὅτι πάντες εἰδήσουσί με, ἀπὸ μικροῦ αὐτῶν
Know the Lord; because all will know Me from little of them

2193 3173 846 3754 2436 2071 3588 93
ἕως μεγάλου αὐτῶν. 12 ὅτι ἵλεως ἔσομαι ταῖς ἀδικίαις
until great of them. Because merciful I will be to the unrighteousnesses

King James Version

that offer gifts according to the law:
5 Who serve unto the example and shadow of heavenly things, as Moses was admonished of God when he was about to make the tabernacle: for, See, saith he, (that) thou make all things according to the pattern shewed to thee in the mount.

6 But now hath he obtained a more excellent ministry, by how much also he is the mediator of a better covenant, which was established upon better promises.

7 For if that first (covenant) had been faultless, then should no place have been sought for the second.
8 For finding fault with them, he saith, Behold, the days come, saith the Lord, when I will make a new covenant with the house of Israel and with the house of Judah:
9 Not according to the covenant that I made with their fathers in the day when I took them by the hand to lead them out of the land of Egypt; because they continued not in my covenant, and I regarded them not, saith the Lord.

10 For this (is) the covenant that I will make with the house of Israel after those days, saith the Lord; I will put my laws into their mind, and write them in their hearts: and I will be to them a God, and they shall be to me a people:

11 And they shall not teach every man his neighbour, and every man his brother, saying, Know the Lord: for all shall know me, from the least to the greatest.

12 For I will be merciful to their unrighteousness,

Literal Translation

and I will not at all still remember their sins and their lawlessnesses." (Jer. 31:31 - 34)
13 In the saying, "New," He has made the first old. And the thing having been made old and growing aged (is) near disappearing.

Hebrews 8:13

846 2532 3588 266 846 2532 3588 458 846
αὐτῶν, καὶ τῶν ἁμαρτιῶν αὐτῶν καὶ τῶν ἀνομιῶν αὐτῶν
of them and the sins of them and the lawlessnesses of them

3756 3361 3415 2089 1722 3588 3004 2537 3822
οὐ μὴ μνησθῶ ἔτι. 13 ἐν τῷ λέγειν, Καινὴν, πεπαλαίωκε
not at all I will remember still. In the to say, New, He has made old

3588 4413 3588 1161 3822 2532 1095 1451 854
τὴν πρώτην. τὸ δὲ παλαιούμενον καὶ γηράσκον, ἐγγὺς ἀφανι-
the first. the thing And being made old and growing aged, near dis-

σμοῦ.
appearing (is).

King James Version

and their sins and their iniquities will I remember no more.
13 In that he saith, A new (covenant), he hath made the first old. Now that which decayeth and waxeth old (is) ready to vanish away.

Hebrews 9

1. Truly, then, the first (tabernacle) also had ordinances of service, and the earthly holy place.
2 For the first tabernacle was prepared, in which (was) both the lampstand and the table, and the setting out of the loaves, which is called holy.
3 But behind the second veil (is) a tabernacle, that called Holy of Holies,
4 having a golden altar of incense, and the ark of the covenant covered around on all sides with gold, in which (was) the golden pot having the manna, and Aaron's rod that budded, and the tablets of the covenant;
5 and above it (the) Cherubs of Glory overshadowing the mercy-seat, about which now is not (time) to speak piece by piece.
6 And these having been prepared thus, the priests go into the first tabernacle through all, completing the services.
7 But into the second the high priest (goes) alone once (in) the year, not without blood, which he offers for himself and the ignorances of the people;
8 the Holy Spirit signifying (by) this (that) the way of the Holies has not yet been made manifest, the first tabernacle

Hebrews 9

2192 3303 3767 2532 3588 4413 1345 2999 3588 5037
1. Εἶχε μὲν οὖν καὶ ἡ πρώτη δικαιώματα λατρείας, τό τε
had Truly then also the first ordinances of service, the and

39 2886 4633 1063 2680 3588/4413/ 1722/3739/3588
ἅγιον κοσμικόν. 2 σκηνὴ γὰρ κατεσκευάσθη ἡ πρώτη, ἐν ᾗ ἥ
holy place worldly. a tabernacle For was prepared the first, in which the

5037 3087 2532 3588 5132 2532 3588 4286 3588 740 3748
τε λυχνία καὶ ἡ τράπεζα καὶ ἡ πρόθεσις τῶν ἄρτων, ἥτις
both lampstand and the table and the setting out of the loaves, which

3004 39 3326 1161 3588 1208 2665 4633 3588
λέγεται ἅγια· 3 μετὰ δὲ τὸ δεύτερον καταπέτασμα σκηνὴ ἡ
is called holy; after and the second veil a tabernacle that

3004 39 39 5552 2192 2369 2532
λεγομένη ἅγια ἁγίων, 4 χρυσοῦν ἔχουσα θυμιατήριον, καὶ
being called Holy of Holies, golden having an altar, and

3588 2787 3588 1242 4028 3840
τὴν κιβωτὸν τῆς διαθήκης περικεκαλυμμένην πάντοθεν
the Ark of the Covenant having been covered around on all sides

5553 1722 3739 4713 5552 2192 3588 3131 2532 3588 4464
χρυσίῳ, ἐν ᾗ στάμνος χρυσῆ ἔχουσα τὸ μάννα, καὶ ἡ ῥάβδος
with gold, in which a pot golden having the manna, and the rod

2 3588 985 2532 3588 4109 3588 1242 5231
Ἀαρὼν ἡ βλαστήσασα, καὶ αἱ πλάκες τῆς διαθήκης· 5 ὑπερ-
of Aaron budded, and the tablets of the covenant; above

1161 846 5502 1391 2683 3588 2435
άνω δὲ αὐτῆς Χερουβὶμ δόξης κατασκιάζοντα τὸ ἱλαστή-
and it (the) Cherubs of Glory overshadowing the Mercy-

4012 3739 3756 2076 3568 3004 2596 3313 5130 1161 3779
ριον· περὶ ὧν οὐκ ἔστι νῦν λέγειν κατὰ μέρος. 6 Τούτων δὲ οὕτω
seat; about which not is now to speak piece by piece. these And thus

2680 1519 3303 3588 4413 4633 1223 3956
κατεσκευασμένων, εἰς μὲν τὴν πρώτην σκηνὴν διὰ παντὸς
having been prepared, into indeed the first tabernacle through all

1524 3588 2409 3588 2999 2005 1519 1161 3588
εἰσίασιν οἱ ἱερεῖς, τὰς λατρείας ἐπιτελοῦντες; 7 εἰς δὲ τὴν
go in the priest, the services completing; into but the

1208 530 3588 1763 3441 3588 749 3756 5565
δευτέραν ἅπαξ τοῦ ἐνιαυτοῦ μόνος ὁ ἀρχιερεύς, οὐ χωρὶς
second once (in) the year alone (goes) the high priest, not without

129 3588 4374 5228 1438 2532 3588 3588 2992 51
αἵματος, ὃ προσφέρει ὑπὲρ ἑαυτοῦ καὶ τῶν τοῦ λαοῦ ἀγνοη-
blood, which he offers on behalf of himself and the of the people igno-

5124 1213 3588 4151 3588 40 3380
μάτων· 8 τοῦτο δηλοῦντος τοῦ Πνεύματος τοῦ Ἁγίου, μήπω
rances; this showing the Spirit Holy, not yet

5319 3588 3588 39 3598 2089 3588 4413 4633
πεφανερῶσθαι τὴν τῶν ἁγίων ὁδὸν, ἔτι τῆς πρώτης σκηνῆς
to have been revealed the of the Holies way, yet the first tabernacle

Hebrews 9

1. Then verily the first (covenant) had also ordinances of divine service, and a worldly sanctuary.
2 For there was a tabernacle made; the first, wherein (was) the candlestick, and the table, and the shewbread; which is called the sanctuary.
3 And after the second veil, the tabernacle which is called the Holiest of all;
4 Which had the golden censer, and the ark of the covenant overlaid round about with gold, wherein (was) the golden pot that had manna, and Aaron's rod that budded, and the tables of the covenant;
5 And over it the cherubims of glory shadowing the mercyseat; of which we cannot now speak particularly.
6 Now when these things were thus ordained, the priests went always into the first tabernacle, accomplishing the service (of God).
7 But into the second (went) the high priest alone once every year, not without blood, which he offered for himself, and (for) the errors of the people:
8 The Holy Ghost this signifying, that the way into the holiest of all was not yet made manifest, while as the first tabernacle

Literal Translation

still having standing;
9 which (was) a parable for the present time, according to which both gifts and sacrifices are offered, (but) as regards conscience, not being able to perfect the (one) serving,
10 only on foods and drinks, and various washings, and fleshly ordinances, until (the) time of setting things right has been imposed.

11 But Christ having appeared (as) a High Priest of the coming good things, through the greater and more perfect tabernacle not made by hand, that is, not of this creation,
12 nor through the blood of goats and of calves, but through (His) own blood, (He) entered once for all into the (Holy of) Holies, having procured eternal redemption.

13 For if the blood of bulls and goats, and ashes of a heifer sprinkling those having been defiled, sanctifies to the purity of the flesh,

14 by how much more the blood of Christ (who through (the) eternal Spirit offered Himself without blemish to God), will purify your conscience from dead works so as to serve (the) living God!

15 And because of this He is Mediator of a new covenant, so that, death having occurred for redemption of transgressions under the first covenant, those having been called out might receive the promise of the eternal inheritance.
16 For where a covenant (is), the death of him having covenanted must be offered.
17 For a covenant (is) firm over (those) dead, since it never has force when he who has covenanted (is) living.

Hebrews 9:9

2192 4714 3748 3850 1519 3588 2540 3588 1764
ἐχούσης στάσιν· 9 ἥτις παραβολὴ εἰς τὸν καιρὸν τὸν ἐνεστη-
having standing; which (was) a parable for the time present,

2596 3739 1435 5037 2532 2378 4374 3361 1410
κότα, καθ' ὃν δῶρά τε καὶ θυσίαι προσφέρονται μὴ δυνά-
according to which gifts both and sacrifices are being offered, not being

2596 4893 5048 3588 3000 3440
μεναι κατὰ συνείδησιν τελειῶσαι τὸν λατρεύοντα, 10 μόνον
able as to conscience to perfect the (one) serving, only

1909 1033 2532 4188 2532 1313 909 2532
ἐπὶ βρώμασι καὶ πόμασι καὶ διαφόροις βαπτισμοῖς καὶ
on foods and drinks and various washings even

1345 4561 3360 2540 1357 1945
δικαιώμασι σαρκὸς μέχρι καιροῦ διορθώσεως ἐπικείμενα.
prdinances of flesh until a time of setting things right being imposed.

5547 1161 3854 749 3588 3195
11. Χριστὸς δὲ παραγενόμενος ἀρχιερεὺς τῶν μελλοντων
Christ But having appeared (as) a High Priest of the coming

18 1223 3588 3173 2532 5046 4633 3756
ἀγαθῶν, διὰ τῆς μείζονος καὶ τελειοτέρας σκηνῆς, οὐ
good things, through the greater and more perfect tabernacle, not

5499 5123 2076 3756 3778 3588 2937 3761 1223
χειροποιήτου, τοῦτ' ἔστιν, οὐ ταύτης τῆς κτίσεως, 12 οὐδὲ δι'
made with hands, this is, not of this creation, nor through

129 5131 2532 3448 1223 1161 3588 2398 129
αἵματος τράγων καὶ μόσχων, διὰ δὲ τοῦ ἰδίου αἵματος,
blood of goats and of calves, through but the own blood,

1525 2178 1519 3588 39 166 3085 2147
εἰσῆλθεν ἐφάπαξ εἰς τὰ ἅγια, αἰωνίαν λύτρωσιν εὑράμενος.
entered once for all into the Holies, eternal redemption having found.

1487 1063 3588 129 5022 2532 5131 2532 4700 1151
13 εἰ γὰρ τὸ αἷμα ταύρων καὶ τράγων, καὶ σποδὸς δαμάλεως
if For the blood of bulls and goats, and ashes of a heifer

4472 3588 2840 37 4314 3588 3588
ῥαντίζουσα τοὺς κεκοινωμένους, ἁγιάζει πρὸς τὴν τῆς
sprinkling the (ones) having been polluted, sanctifies to the of the

4561 2514 4214 3123 3588 129 3588 5547
σαρκὸς καθαρότητα, 14 πόσῳ μᾶλλον τὸ αἷμα τοῦ Χριστοῦ,
flesh cleanness, by how much more the blood Christ,

3739 1223 4151 166 1438 4374 299 3588
ὃς διὰ Πνεύματος αἰωνίου ἑαυτὸν προσήνεγκεν ἄμωμον τῷ
who through (the) Spirit Eternal Himself offered without spot

2316 2511 3588 4893 5216 575 3498 2041 1519
Θεῷ, καθαριεῖ τὴν συνείδησιν ἡμῶν ἀπὸ νεκρῶν ἔργων, εἰς
to God, will cleanse the conscience of you from dead works, for

3588 3000 2316 2198 2532 1223 5124 1242 2537
τὸ λατρεύειν θεῷ ζῶντι; 15 καὶ διὰ τοῦτο διαθήκης καινῆς
the to serve God (the) Living? And because of this covenant of a new

3316 2076 3704 2288 1096 1519 629
μεσίτης ἐστίν, ὅπως, θανάτου γενομένου εἰς ἀπολύτρωσιν
Mediator He is, so as, death having occurred for redemption

3588 1909 3588 4413 1242 3847 3588 1860
τῶν ἐπὶ τῇ πρώτῃ διαθήκῃ παραβάσεων, τὴν ἐπαγγελίαν
of the under the first covenant transgressions, the promise

2983 3588 2564 3588 166 2817 3699 1063
λάβωσιν οἱ κεκλημένοι τῆς αἰωνίου κληρονομίας. 16 ὅπου γὰρ
may receive those being called of the eternal inheritance. where (is) For

1242 2288 318 5342 3588 1303 1242
διαθήκη, θάνατον ἀνάγκη φέρεσθαι τοῦ διαθεμένου· 17 διαθήκη
a covenant, death (is) needful to be offered to the (one) covenanting; a covenant

1063 1909 3498 949 1893 3361 4218 2480 3753 2198 3588
γὰρ ἐπὶ νεκροῖς βεβαία, ἐπεὶ μή ποτε ἰσχύει ὅτε ζῇ ὁ
for over (those) dead (is) firm, since not ever has it strength when living he

King James Version

was yet standing:
9 Which (was) a figure for the time then present, in which were offered both gifts and sacrifices, that could not make him that did the service perfect, as pertaining to the conscience;
10 (Which stood) only in meats and drinks, and divers washings, and carnal ordinances, imposed (on them) until the time of reformation.

11 But Christ being come an high priest of good things to come, by a greater and more perfect tabernacle, not made with hands, that is to say, not of this building;
12 Neither by the blood of goats and calves, but by his own blood he entered in once into the holy place, having obtained eternal redemption (for us).

13 For if the blood of bulls and of goats, and the ashes of an heifer sprinkling the unclean, sanctifieth to the purifying of the flesh:

14 How much more shall the blood of Christ, who through the eternal Spirit offered himself without spot to God, purge your conscience from dead works to serve the living God?

15 And for this cause he is the mediator of the new testament, that by means of death, for the redemption of the transgressions (that were) under the first testament, they which are called might receive the promise of eternal inheritance.
16 For where a testament (is), there must also of necessity be the death of the testator.
17 For a testament (is) of force after men are dead: otherwise it is of no strength at all while the testator liveth.

Literal Translation | **Hebrews 9:18** | **King James Version**

18 From which neither the first (covenant) was dedicated without blood.
19 For (when) every command had been spoken according to Law by Moses to all the people, having taken the blood of the calves and goats, with water and scarlet wool and hyssop, and he sprinkled both the scroll and all the people,
20 saying, "This (is) the blood of the covenant which God enjoined to you." (Exo. 24:8)
21 And he likewise sprinkled both the tabernacle and all the service vessels with the blood.
22 And almost all things are cleansed by blood according to the Law; and apart from shedding of blood no remission occurs.

23 Then (it was) needful for the examples of the things in the heavens to be cleansed (with) these; but the heavenly things themselves by better sacrifices than these.
24 For Christ did not enter into (the) (Holy of) Holies made by hands, antitypes of the true things, but into Heaven itself, now to appear in the presence of God on our behalf,

25 not that often He should offer Himself even as the high priest enters into the (Holy of) Holies year by year with blood of others;
26 since He must often have suffered from (the) foundation of the world. But now once, at the completion of the ages, He has been revealed for putting away of sin through the sacrifice of Himself.
27 And as it is reserved to men once to die, and after this Judgment;
28 so Christ, having been once offered of many

1303 3606 3761 3588 4413 5565 129 1457
διαθέμενος. 18 ὅθεν οὐδὲ ἡ πρώτη χωρὶς αἵματος ἐγκεκαι-
having covenanted. from which neither the first without blood was dedicated;

2980 1063 3956 1785 2596 3588 3551 5259
νισται· 19 λαληθείσης γὰρ πάσης ἐντολῆς κατὰ τὸν νόμον ὑπὸ
having been spoken for every command according to the Law by

3475 3956 3588 2992 2983 3588 129 3588 3448 2532
Μωσέως παντὶ τῷ λαῷ, λαβὼν τὸ αἷμα τῶν μόσχων καὶ
Moses to all the people having taken the blood of the calves and

5131 3326 5204 2532 2053 2847 2532 5301 846 5037
τράγων, μετὰ ὕδατος καὶ ἐρίου κοκκίνου καὶ ὑσσώπου αὐτό τε
of goats, with water and wool scarlet and hyssop it(self) both

3588 975 2532 3956 3588 2992 4472 3004 5124 3588
τὸ βιβλίον καὶ πάντα τὸν λαὸν ἐράντισε, 20 λέγων, Τοῦτο τὸ
the scroll and all the people he sprinkled, saying, This (is) the

129 3588 1242 3739 1781 4314 5209 3588 2316 2532 3588
αἷμα τῆς διαθήκης ἧς ἐνετείλατο πρὸς ὑμᾶς ὁ Θεός. 21 καὶ τὴν
blood of the covenant which enjoined to you God. both the

4632 1161 2532 3956 3588 4632 3588 3009 3588 129
σκηνὴν δὲ καὶ πάντα τὰ σκεύη τῆς λειτουργίας τῷ αἵματι
tabernacle And also all the vessels of the service with the blood

3668 4472 2532 4975 1722 129 3956 2511
ὁμοίως ἐράντισε. 22 καὶ σχεδὸν ἐν αἵματι πάντα καθαρίζεται
likewise he sprinkled. And almost by blood all things are cleansed

2596 3588 3551 2532 5565 130 3756 1096 859
κατὰ τὸν νόμον, καὶ χωρὶς αἱματεκχυσίας οὐ γίνεται ἄφεσις.
according to the Law, and without the shedding of blood not occurs remission.

318 3767 3588 3303 5262 3588/1722/3588 3772
23. Ἀνάγκη οὖν τὰ μὲν ὑποδείγματα τῶν ἐν τοῖς οὐρανοῖς,
(It was) needful then the things truly examples of the in the heavens,

5125 2511 846 1161 3588 2032 2909
τούτοις καθαρίζεσθαι, αὐτὰ δὲ τὰ ἐπουράνια κρείττοσι
these to be cleansed, them(selves) but the heavenly things by better

2378 3844 3778 3756 1063 1519 5499 39 1525
θυσίαις παρὰ ταύτας. 24 οὐ γὰρ εἰς χειροποίητα ἅγια εἰσῆλθεν
sacrifices than these. not For into made by hands Holies entered

3588 5547 499 3588 228 235 1519 846 3588
ὁ Χριστός, ἀντίτυπα τῶν ἀληθινῶν, ἀλλ' εἰς αὐτὸν τὸν
Christ antitypes of the true things, but into it(self)

3772 3568 1718 3588 4383 3588 2316 5228
οὐρανόν, νῦν ἐμφανισθῆναι τῷ προσώπῳ τοῦ Θεοῦ ὑπὲρ
Heaven, now to appear in the presence of God on behalf of

2257 3761 2443 4178 4374 1438 5618 3588
ἡμῶν· 25 οὐδ' ἵνα πολλάκις προσφέρῃ ἑαυτόν, ὥσπερ ὁ
us; not that often He should offer Himself, even as the

749 1525 1519 3588 39 2596 1763 1722 129
ἀρχιερεὺς εἰσέρχεται εἰς τὰ ἅγια κατ' ἐνιαυτὸν ἐν αἵματι
high priest enters into the Holies (year by) year with blood

245 1893 1163 846 4178 3958 575 2602
ἀλλοτρίῳ· 26 ἐπεὶ ἔδει αὐτὸν πολλάκις παθεῖν ἀπὸ καταβολῆς
of others; since must He often to have suffered from foundation

2889 3586 1161 530 1909 4930 3588 165 1519 115
κόσμου· νῦν δὲ ἅπαξ ἐπὶ συντελείᾳ τῶν αἰώνων εἰς ἀθέτησιν
of (the) world; now but once at (the) completion of the ages for putting away

266 1223 3588 2378 846 5319 2532 2596 3745
ἁμαρτίας διὰ τῆς θυσίας αὐτοῦ πεφανέρωται. 27 καὶ καθ' ὅσον
of sin through the sacrifice of Him He has been revealed. And for as much as

606 3588 444 530 599 3326 1161 5124
ἀπόκειται τοῖς ἀνθρώποις ἅπαξ ἀποθανεῖν, μετὰ δὲ τοῦτο
it is reserved to men once to die, after and this

2920 3779 3588 5547 530 4374 1519 3588 4183
κρίσις· 28 οὕτως ὁ Χριστός, ἅπαξ προσενεχθεὶς εἰς τὸ πολλῶν
Judgment; so Christ, once having been offered for of many

18 Whereupon neither the first (testament) was dedicated without blood.
19 For when Moses had spoken every precept to all the people according to the law, he took the blood of calves and of goats, with water, and scarlet wool, and hyssop, and sprinkled both the book, and all the people,
20 Saying, This (is) the blood of the testament which God hath enjoined unto you.
21 Moreover he sprinkled with blood both the tabernacle, and all the vessels of the ministry.

22 And almost all things are by the law purged with blood; and without shedding of blood is no remission.

23 (It was) therefore necessary that the patterns of things in the heavens should be purified with these; but the heavenly things themselves with better sacrifices than these.
24 For Christ is not entered into the holy places made with hands, (which are) the figures of the true; but into heaven itself, now to appear in the presence of God for us:

25 Nor yet that he should offer himself often, as the high priest entereth into the holy place every year with blood of others;
26 For then must he often have suffered since the foundation of the world: but now once in the end of the world hath he appeared to put away sin by the sacrifice of himself.
27 And as it is appointed unto men once to die, but after this the judgment:

28 So Christ was once offered

Literal Translation

to bear (the) sins, (He) shall appear a second (time) without sin to the (ones) expecting Him for salvation.

Hebrews 10:1

399 266 1537 1208 5565 266 3700
ἀνενεγκεῖν ἁμαρτίας, ἐκ δευτέρου χωρὶς ἁμαρτίας ὀφθήσεται
to bear (the) sins, a second time without sin will appear to

3588 846 553 1519 4991
τοῖς αὐτὸν ἀπεκδεχομένοις εἰς σωτηρίαν.
to the (ones) Him expecting for salvation.

King James Version

to bear the sins of many; and unto them that look for him shall he appear the second time without sin unto salvation.

Hebrews 10

1. For the Law had a shadow of the coming good things, not the image (itself) of (those) things. (Appearing) year by year with the same sacrifices, which they offer continually, they never are able to perfect the ones drawing near.

2 Otherwise, would they not have ceased to be offered, because those serving did not still have conscience of sins, having once for all been cleansed?

3 But in these (there is) a remembrance of sins year by year,

4 for (it is) not possible for the blood of bulls and goats to take away sins.

5 For this reason, coming into the world, He says, "Sacrifice and offering You did not desire, but You prepared a body for Me.

6 You did not delight in burnt offerings and (sacrifices) concerning sins.

7 Then I said, Lo, I come, (in the) heading of the Book, it was written concerning Me, to do Your will, O God." (Psa. 39:6 - 9 LXX; Psa. 40:6 - 8 Masoretic)

8 Above, saying, "You did not desire nor were pleased (with) sacrifice and offering and burnt offerings and (sacrifices) concerning sins," which are offered according to the Law,

9 then He said, "Lo, I come to do Your will, O God." He takes away the first in order that He may set up the second;

10 by which will we are sanctified through the offering of the body

Hebrews 10

4639 1063 2192 3588 3551 3588 3195 18 3756
1. Σκιὰν γὰρ ἔχων ὁ νόμος τῶν μελλόντων ἀγαθῶν, οὐκ
a shadow For having the Law of the coming good things, not

846 3588 1504 3588 4229 2596 1763 3588
αὐτὴν τὴν εἰκόνα τῶν πραγμάτων, κατ' ἐνιαυτὸν ταῖς
it (self) the image of those things, (year by) year with the

846 2378 3739 4374 1519 3588 1336 3763
αὐταῖς θυσίαις ἃς προσφέρουσιν εἰς τὸ διηνεκές, οὐδέποτε
same sacrifices which they offer continually, never

1410 3588 4334 5048 1893 3756 302
δύναται τοὺς προσερχομένους τελειῶσαι. 2 ἐπεὶ οὐκ ἂν
are able the (ones) drawing near to perfect. Since not would

3973 4374 1223 3588 3367 2192 2089 4893
ἐπαύσαντο προσφερόμεναι, διὰ τὸ μηδεμίαν ἔχειν ἔτι συνείδη-
they have ceased being offered, because of not to have still conscience

266 3588 3000 530 2508 235
σιν ἁμαρτιῶν τοὺς λατρεύοντας, ἅπαξ κεκαθαρισμένους; 3 ἀλλ'
of sins those serving, once having been cleansed? But

1722 846 364 266 2596 1763 102 1063
ἐν αὐταῖς ἀνάμνησις ἁμαρτιῶν κατ' ἐνιαυτόν· 4 ἀδύνατον γὰρ
in them a remembrance of sins (year by) year; it is impossible for

129 5022 2532 5131 851 266 1352 1525
αἷμα ταύρων καὶ τράγων ἀφαιρεῖν ἁμαρτίας. 5 διὸ εἰσερχό-
blood of bulls and goats to take away sins. Therefore entering

1519 3588 2889 3004 2378 2532 4376 3756
μενος εἰς τὸν κόσμον λέγει, Θυσίαν καὶ προσφορὰν οὐκ
into the world He says, Sacrifice and offering not

2309 4983 1161 2675 3427 3646 2532 4012
ἠθέλησας, σῶμα δὲ κατηρτίσω μοι· 6 ὁλοκαυτώματα καὶ περὶ
You desired, a body but You prepared for Me; burnt offerings and as to (sacrifices)

266 3756 2106 5119 2036 2400 2240 1722 2777
ἁμαρτίας οὐκ εὐδόκησας. 7 τότε εἶπον, Ἰδοὺ, ἥκω [ἐν κεφαλίδι
sins not You were pleased. Then I said, Behold, I come, in the heading

975 1125 4012 1700 3588 4160 3588 2316 3588
βιβλίου γέγραπται περὶ ἐμοῦ] τοῦ ποιῆσαι, ὁ Θεός, τὸ
of (the) Book it was written about Me, to do God, the

2307 4675 511 3004 3754 2378 2532 4376
θέλημά σου. 8 ἀνώτερον λέγων ὅτι Θυσίαν καὶ προσφορὰν
will of You. Above saying that sacrifice and offering

2532 3646 2532 4012 266 3756 2309 3761
καὶ ὁλοκαυτώματα καὶ περὶ ἁμαρτίας οὐκ ἠθέλησας, οὐδὲ
and burnt offerings and (sacrifices) as to sins not You desired, nor

2106 3748 2596 3588 3551 4374 5119
εὐδόκησας [αἵτινες κατὰ τὸν νόμον προσφέρονται], 9 τότε
were pleased, which according to the Law are offered, then

2046 2400 2240 3588 4160 3588 2316 3588 2307 4675
εἴρηκεν, Ἰδοὺ, ἥκω τοῦ ποιῆσαι, ὁ Θεός, τὸ θέλημά σου.
He said, Behold, I come to do, God. the will of You.

337 3588 4413 2443 3588 1208 2476 1722 3739 2307
ἀναιρεῖ τὸ πρῶτον, ἵνα τὸ δεύτερον στήσῃ. 10 ἐν ᾧ θελήματι
He takes away the first, that the second He may set up. By which will

37 2070 3588 3588 4376 3588 4983 3588
ἡγιασμένοι ἐσμὲν διὰ τῆς προσφορᾶς τοῦ σώματος τοῦ
sanctified we are through the offering of the body

Hebrews 10

1. For the law having a shadow of good things to come, (and) not the very image of the things, can never with those sacrifices which they offered year by year continually make the comers thereunto perfect.

2 For then would they not have ceased to be offered? because that the worshippers once purged should have had no more conscience of sins.

3 But in those (sacrifices there is) a remembrance again (made) of sins every year.

4 For (it is) not possible that the blood of bulls and of goats should take away sins.

5 Wherefore when he cometh into the world, he saith, Sacrifice and offering thou wouldest not, but a body hast thou prepared me:

6 In burnt offerings and (sacrifices) for sin thou hast had no pleasure.

7 Then said I, Lo, I come (in the volume of the book it is written of me,) to do thy will, O God.

8 Above when he said, Sacrifice and offering and burnt offerings and (offering) for sin thou wouldest not, neither hadst pleasure (therein); which are offered by the law;

9 Then said he, Lo, I come to do thy will, O God. He taketh away the first, that he may establish the second.

10 By the which will we are sanctified through the offering of the body

Literal Translation | **Hebrews 10:11** | ***King James Version***

of Jesus Christ once for all.

11. And indeed every priest stands day by day ministering, and often offering the same sacrifices, which can never take away sins.

2424 5547 2178 2532 3956 3303 2409 2476 2596
Ἰησοῦ Χριστοῦ ἐφάπαξ. 11 καὶ πᾶς μὲν ἱερεὺς ἕστηκε καθ᾽
of Jesus Christ once for all. And every indeed priest stands (day by)

2250 3008 2532 3588 846 4178 4374
ἡμέραν λειτουργῶν καὶ τὰς αὐτὰς πολλάκις προσφέρων
day ministering and the same often offering

2378 3748 3763 1410 4014 266
θυσίας, αἵτινες οὐδέποτε δύνανται περιελεῖν ἁμαρτίας·
sacrifices, which never is able to take away sins;

Jesus Christ once (for all).

11. And every priest standeth daily ministering and offering oftentimes the same sacrifices, which can never take away sins:

12 But He, offering but one sacrifice for sins, sat down in perpetuity (at the) right (hand) of God,
13 from then on expecting until His enemies are placed (as) a footstool of His feet.

846 1161 3391 5228 266 4374 2378 1519 3588
12 αὐτὸς δὲ μίαν ὑπὲρ ἁμαρτιῶν προσενέγκας θυσίαν εἰς τὸ
He but one on behalf of sins having offered sacrifice in

1336 2523 1722 1188 3588 2316 3588 3063 1551
διηνεκὲς ἐκάθισεν ἐν δεξιᾷ τοῦ Θεοῦ, 13 τὸ λοιπὸν ἐκδεχόμενος
perpetuity sat down at (the) right of God, from then on expecting

2193 5087 3588 2190 846 5286 3588 4228 846
ἕως τεθῶσιν οἱ ἐχθροὶ αὐτοῦ ὑποπόδιον τῶν ποδῶν αὐτοῦ.
until are put the enemies of Him (as) a footstool of the feet of Him.

12 But this man, after he had offered one sacrifice for sins for ever, sat down on the right hand of God;
13 From henceforth expecting till his enemies be made his footstool.

14 For by one offering He has perfected in perpetuity the ones being sanctified.
15 And the Holy Spirit witnesses to us also. For after having said before,
16 "This (is) the covenant which I will covenant to them after those days," says (the) Lord: "Giving My laws on their hearts, and I will write them on their minds;"

3391 1063 4376 5048 1519 3588 1336 3588 37
14 μιᾷ γὰρ προσφορᾷ τετελείωκεν εἰς τὸ διηνεκὲς τοὺς ἁγιαζο-
by one For offering He has perfected in perpetuity the (ones) being

3140 1161 2254 2532 3588 4151 3588 40 3326 1063
μένους. 15 μαρτυρεῖ δὲ ἡμῖν καὶ τὸ Πνεῦμα τὸ Ἅγιον· μετὰ γὰρ
sanctified. witnesses And to us also the Spirit Holy; after for

3588 4280 3778 3588 1242 3739 1303 4314
τὸ προειρηκέναι, 16 Αὕτη ἡ διαθήκη ἣν διαθήσομαι πρὸς
to have said before, This (is) the covenant which I will covenant to

846 3326 3588 2250 1565 3004 2962 1325 3551
αὐτοὺς μετὰ τὰς ἡμέρας ἐκείνας, λέγει Κύριος, διδοὺς νόμους
them after days those, says (the) Lord, Giving laws

3450 1909 2588 846 2532 1909 3588 1271 846
μου ἐπὶ καρδίας αὐτῶν, καὶ ἐπὶ τὴν διάνοιῶν αὐτῶν
of Me on hearts of them, also on the minds of them

14 For by one offering he hath perfected for ever them that are sanctified.
15 (Whereof) the Holy Ghost also is a witness to us: for after that he had said before,
16 This (is) the covenant that I will make with them after those days, saith the Lord, I will put my laws into their hearts, and in their minds will I write them;

17 also (He adds), "I will not at all still remember their sins and their lawless deeds." (Jer. 31:33, 34)
18 But where remission of these (is), there (is) no longer offering concerning sins.

1924 846 2532 3588 266 846 2532 3588
ἐπιγράψω αὐτούς· 17 καὶ τῶν ἁμαρτιῶν αὐτῶν καὶ τῶν
I will write them; and the sins of them and the

458 846 3756 3361 3415 2089 3699 1161 859
ἀνομιῶν αὐτῶν οὐ μὴ μνησθῶ ἔτι. 18 ὅπου δὲ ἄφεσις
lawlessnesses of them not at all I will remember still. where And remission

5130 3756 4376 4012 266
τούτων, οὐκέτι προσφορὰ περὶ ἁμαρτίας.
of these (is), no longer (is) offering concerning sins.

17 And their sins and iniquities will I remember no more.
18 Now where remission of these (is, there is) no more offering for sin.

19. Then, brothers, having confidence for the entering of the (Holy of) Holies by the blood of Jesus,
20 which He consecrated for us, a new and living way through the veil; that is, His flesh;
21 and (having) a Great Priest over the house of God,
22 let us draw near with a true heart in full assurance of faith, our hearts having been sprinkled from an evil conscience, and (our) body having been washed in pure water;
23 let us hold

2192 3767 80 3954 1519 3588 1529 3588
19. Ἔχοντες οὖν, ἀδελφοί, παρρησίαν εἰς τὴν εἴσοδον τῶν
having Therefore, brothers, confidence for the entering of the

39 1722 3588 129 2424 3739 1457 2254 3598
ἁγίων ἐν τῷ αἵματι Ἰησοῦ, 20 ἣν ἐνεκαίνισεν ἡμῖν ὁδὸν
Holies by the blood of Jesus, which He consecrated for us a way

4372 2532 2198 1223 3588 2665 5123
πρόσφατον καὶ ζῶσαν, διὰ τοῦ καταπετάσματος, τοῦτ᾽
new and living, through the veil, this

2076 3588 4561 846 2532 2409 3173 1909 3588 3624 3588
ἔστι, τῆς σαρκὸς αὐτοῦ, 21 καὶ ἱερέα μέγαν ἐπὶ τὸν οἶκον τοῦ
is, the flesh of Him, and (having) priest a great over the house

2316 4334 3326 228 2588 1722 4136
Θεοῦ, 22 προσερχώμεθα μετὰ ἀληθινῆς καρδίας ἐν πληρο-
of God, let us draw near with a true heart in full

4102 4472 3588 2588 575 4893
φορίᾳ πίστεως, ἐρραντισμένοι τὰς καρδίας ἀπὸ συνειδήσεως
assurance of faith, having been sprinkled the hearts from a conscience

4190 2532 3068 3588 4983 5204 2513 2722
πονηρᾶς, καὶ λελουσμένοι τὸ σῶμα ὕδατι καθαρῷ· 23 κατέχω-
evil, and having been washed the body water in clean; let us hold

19. Having therefore, brethren, boldness to enter into the holiest by the blood of Jesus,
20 By a new and living way, which he hath consecrated for us, through the veil, that is to say, his flesh;
21 And (having) an high priest over the house of God;
22 Let us draw near with a true heart in full assurance of faith, having our hearts sprinkled from an evil conscience, and our bodies washed with pure water.
23 Let us hold fast

Literal Translation **Hebrews 10:24** ***King James Version***

fast the confession of the hope without yielding, for He who has promised is faithful.
24 And let us consider one another, to incitement of love and of good works,
25 not forsaking the assembling together of ourselves, as (is the) custom of some, but exhorting, and by so much more as you see the Day drawing near.

26 For (if) we (are) willfully sinning after receiving the full knowledge of the truth, there remains no more sacrifice concerning sins,
27 but a certain fearful expectation of judgment and zealous fire being about to consume the adversaries.
28 (If) anyone did not regard (the) Law of Moses, (that one) dies without pities on (the word of) two or three witnesses. (Deut.17:6)
29 How much worse punishment do you think will be thought worthy (to receive), the (one) trampling the Son of God, and having counted common the blood of the covenant in which he was sanctified, and having insulted the Spirit of grace?
30 For we know Him who has said, "Vengeance (belongs) to Me; I will repay, says (the) Lord." And again, "The Lord will judge His people."
31 (It is) a fearful thing to fall into (the) hands of (the) living God. (Deut. 32:35, 36)

32. But call to mind the former days in which being enlightened you endured much conflict of sufferings;
33 indeed being exposed both to reproaches and to afflictions; and having become sharers of those so living.
34 For indeed

3588 3671 3588 1680 186 4103 1063 3588
μεν τὴν ὁμολογίαν τῆς ἐλπίδος ἀκλινῆ, πιστὸς γὰρ ὁ
the confession of the hope unyieldingly faithful for (is) He
1861 2532 2657 240 1519 3948
ἐπαγγειλάμενος· 24 καὶ κατανοῶμεν ἀλλήλους εἰς παροξυσμὸν
having promised; and let us consider one another in incitement
26 2532 2570 2041 3361 1459 3588 1997
ἀγάπης καὶ καλῶν ἔργων, 25 μὴ ἐγκαταλείποντες τὴν ἐπισυν-
of love and of good works, not forsaking the assembling
1438 2531 1485 5100 235 3870
αγωγὴν ἑαυτῶν, καθὼς ἔθος τισίν, ἀλλὰ παρακαλοῦντες,
of ourselves, as the) custom of some (is), but exhorting,
2532 5118 3123 3745 991 1448 3588 2250
καὶ τοσούτῳ μᾶλλον, ὅσῳ βλέπετε ἐγγίζουσαν τὴν ἡμέραν.
and by so much more, as you see drawing near the Day.

1569 1063 264 2257 3326 3358 2983 3588
26. Ἑκουσίως γὰρ ἁμαρτανόντων ἡμῶν μετὰ τὸ λαβεῖν τὴν
willfully For sinning us after to receive the
1922 3588 225 3756 4012 266 620
ἐπίγνωσιν τῆς ἀληθείας, οὐκέτι περὶ ἁμαρτιῶν ἀπολείπεται
full knowledge of the truth, no more concerning sins remains
2378 5398 1161 5100 1561 2920 2532 4442 2205
θυσία, 27 φοβερὰ δέ τις ἐκδοχὴ κρίσεως, καὶ πυρὸς ζῆλος
a sacrifice, fearful but some expectation of judgment, and of fire zeal
2068 3195 3588 5227 114 5100 3551
ἐσθίειν μέλλοντος τοὺς ὑπεναντίους. 28 ἀθετήσας τις νόμον
to consume being about the adversaries. having disregarded Anyone Law
3475 5565 3628 1909 1417 2228 5140 3144
Μωσέως χωρὶς οἰκτιρμῶν ἐπὶ δυσὶν ἢ τρισὶ μάρτυσιν
of Moses without pities on (the word) of two or three witnesses
599 4214 1380 5501 515 5098
ἀποθνήσκει· 29 πόσῳ δοκεῖτε, χείρονος ἀξιωθήσεται τιμω-
dies; by how much think you, of worse shall be thought worthy (of)
3588 3588 5207 3588 2316 2662 2532 3588 129
ρίας ὁ τὸν υἱὸν τοῦ Θεοῦ καταπατήσας, καὶ τὸ αἷμα
punishment he the Son of God having trampled, and the blood
3588 1242 2839 2233 1722 3739 37 2532 3588
τῆς διαθήκης κοινὸν ἡγησάμενος ἐν ᾧ ἡγιάσθη, καὶ τὸ
of the covenant common having deemed by which he was sanctified, and the
4151 3588 5485 1796 1492 1063 3588 2036
Πνεῦμα τῆς χάριτος ἐνυβρίσας; 30 οἴδαμεν γὰρ τὸν εἰπόντα,
Spirit of grace insulted? we know For the (One) having said
1698 1557 1473 467 3004 2962 2532 3825
Ἐμοὶ ἐκδίκησις, ἐγὼ ἀνταποδώσω, λέγει Κύριος· καὶ πάλιν,
To Me (is) vengeance, I will repay, says (the) Lord; and again,
2962 2919 3588 2992 846 5398 3588 1706 1519
Κύριος κρινεῖ τὸν λαὸν αὐτοῦ. 31 φοβερὸν τὸ ἐμπεσεῖν εἰς
(The) Lord will judge the people of Him. A fearful thing (it is) to fall into
5495 2316 2198
χεῖρας Θεοῦ ζῶντος.
(the) hands God of (the) Living.

363 1161 3588 4386 2250 1722 3739 5461
32. Ἀναμιμνήσκεσθε δὲ τὰς πρότερον ἡμέρας, ἐν αἷς φωτι-
call to mind But the former days, in which having
4183 119 5278 3804 5124 3303
σθέντες πολλὴν ἄθλησιν ὑπεμείνατε παθημάτων· 33 τοῦτο μὲν,
been enlightened much conflict you endured of sufferings; this partly,
3680 5037 2532 2374 2301 5124 1161 2844
ὀνειδισμοῖς τε καὶ θλίψεσι θεατριζόμενοι, τοῦτο δε, κοινωνοὶ
to reproaches both and to afflictions being exposed, (partly) and, sharers
3588 3779 390 1096 2532 1063 3588
τῶν οὕτως ἀναστρεφομένων γενηθέντες. 34 καὶ γὰρ τοῖς
of those so living having become. indeed For in the

the profession of (our) faith without wavering; (for he (is) faithful that promised;)
24 And let us consider one another to provoke unto love and to good works:
25 Not forsaking the assembling of ourselves together, as the manner of some (is); but exhorting (one another): and so much the more, as ye see the day approaching.

26. For if we sin wilfully after that we have received the knowledge of the truth, there remaineth no more sacrifice for sins,
27 But a certain fearful looking for of judgment and fiery indignation, which shall devour the adversaries.
28 He that despised Moses' law died without mercy under two or three witnesses:
29 Of how much sorer punishment, suppose ye, shall he be thought worthy, who hath trodden under foot the Son of God, and hath counted the blood of the covenant, wherewith he was sanctified, an unholy thing, and hath done despite unto the Spirit of grace?
30 For we know him that hath said, Vengeance (belongeth) unto me, I will recompense, saith the Lord. And again, The Lord shall judge his people.
31 (It is) a fearful thing to fall into the hands of the living God.
32. But call to remembrance the former days, in which, after ye were illuminated, ye endured a great fight of afflictions;
33 Partly, whilst ye were made a gazingstock both by reproaches and afflictions; and partly, whilst ye became companions of them that were so used.
34 For ye had

Literal Translation

Hebrews 10:35

you suffered together in my bonds; and you accepted the seizure of your possessions with joy, knowing yourselves to have a better and abiding possession in Heaven.
35 Then do not throw away your confidence, which has great reward.

36 For you have need of patience, that having done the will of God you may obtain the promise.
37 For, "yet a very little (and) the (One) coming will come, and will not delay." (Hab. 2:3)
38 "But the just shall live by faith; and if he draws back, My soul is not pleased in him." (Hab. 2:4)
39 But we are not of (those) withdrawing to destruction, but of faith, to (the) preservation of (the) soul.

1199 3450 4834 2532 3588 724 3588 5224
δεσμοῖς μου συνεπαθήσατε, καὶ τὴν ἁρπαγὴν τῶν ὑπαρχόν-
bonds of me you suffered together, and the seizure of the possessions

5216 3326 5479 4327 1097 2192 1722
των ὑμῶν μετὰ χαρᾶς προσεδέξασθε, γινώσκοντες ἔχειν ἐν
of you with joy you accepted, knowing to have in

1438 2909 5223 1722 3772 2532 3306 3361
ἑαυτοῖς κρείττονα ὕπαρξιν ἐν οὐρανοῖς καὶ μένουσαν. 35 μὴ
yourselves a better possession in Heaven and abiding. not

577 3767 3588 3954 5216 3748 2192 3405
ἀποβάλητε οὖν τὴν παρρησίαν ὑμῶν, ἥτις ἔχει μισθαποδο-
do cast away Therefore the confidence of you, which has reward

3173 5281 1063 2192 5532 2443 3588 2307
σίαν μεγάλην. 36 ὑπομονῆς γὰρ ἔχετε χρείαν, ἵνα τὸ θέλημα
great. of patience For you have need, that the will

3588 2316 3954 2865 3588 1860 2089 1063
τοῦ Θεοῦ ποιήσαντες κομίσησθε τὴν ἐπαγγελίαν. 37 ἔτι γὰρ
of God having don you may obtain the promise. yet For

3397 3745 3745 3588 2064 2240 2532 3756 5549 3588 1161
μικρὸν ὅσον ὅσον, ὁ ἐρχόμενος ἥξει, καὶ οὐ χρονιεῖ. 38 ὁ δὲ
little a very, the coming One will come, and not delay. the But

1342 3450 1537 4102 2198 2532 1437 5288 3756
δίκαιός ἐκ πίστεως ζήσεται· καὶ ἐὰν ὑποστείληται, οὐκ
just by faith shall live; and if he draws back, not

2106 3588 5590 3450 1722 846 2249 1161 3756 2070 5289
εὐδοκεῖ ἡ ψυχή μου ἐν αὐτῷ. 39 ἡμεῖς δὲ οὐκ ἐσμὲν ὑποστολῆς
is pleased the soul of Me in him. we But not are (of those) drawing

1519 684 235 4102 1519 4047 5590
εἰς ἀπώλειαν, ἀλλὰ πίστεως εἰς περιποίησιν ψυχῆς.
to destruction, but of faith to preservation of (the) soul.

King James Version

compassion of me in my bonds, and took joyfully the spoiling of your goods, knowing in yourselves that ye have in heaven a better and an enduring substance.
35 Cast not away therefore your confidence, which hath great recompence of reward.

36 For ye have need of patience, that, after ye have done the will of God, ye might receive the promise.
37 For yet a little while, and he that shall come will come, and will not tarry.
38 Now the just shall live by faith: but if (any man) draw back, my soul shall have no pleasure in him.
39 But we are not of them who draw back unto perdition; but of them that believe to the saving of the soul.

Hebrews 11

1. Now faith is (the) substance of things having been hoped, (the) evidence of things not having been seen.
2 For by this the elders obtained witness.
3 By faith we understand the ages to have been framed by (the) word of God, so that the things seen (should) not come into being out of things that appear.
4. By faith Abel offered a greater sacrifice to God than Cain, by which he obtained witness to be righteous, God testifying over his gifts; and through it, having died, he yet speaks.
5 By faith Enoch was translated (so as) not to see death, and was not found, because God translated him. For before his translation, he had obtained witness to have been pleasing to God. (Gen.5:24)
6 But without

2076 1161 4102 1679 5287 4229
1. Ἔστι δὲ πίστις ἐλπιζομένων ὑπόστασις, πραγμάτων
is Now faith of things being hoped (the) substance of things

1650 3756 991 1722 3778 1063 3140 3588
ἔλεγχος οὐ βλεπομένων. 2 ἐν ταύτῃ γὰρ ἐμαρτυρήθησαν οἱ
(the) evidence not being seen. by this For obtained witness the

4245 4102 3539 2675 3588 165
πρεσβύτεροι. 3 Πίστει νοοῦμεν κατηρτίσθαι τοὺς αἰῶνας
elders. By faith we understand to have been framed the ages

4487 2316 1519 3588 3361 1537 5316 3588 991 1096
ῥήματι Θεοῦ, εἰς τὸ μὴ ἐκ φαινομένων τά βλεπόμενα γεγονέ-
by a word of God, so as not out of things appearing the things being seen to have

4102 4119 2316 6 3844 2535 4374 3588
ναι. 4 πίστει πλείονα θυσίαν Ἄβελ παρὰ Κάϊν προσήνεγκε τῷ
become. By faith a greater sacrifice Abel than Cain offered

2316 1223 3739 3140 1511 1342 3140 1909 3588
Θεῷ, δι᾽ ἧς ἐμαρτυρήθη εἶναι δίκαιος, μαρτυροῦντος ἐπὶ τοῖς
to God by which he was testified to be righteous, tesifying over the

1435 846 3588 2316 2532 1223 846 599 2089 2980
δώροις αὐτοῦ τοῦ Θεοῦ, καὶ δι᾽ αὐτῆς ἀποθανὼν ἔτι λαλεῖ.
gifts of him God, and through it having died yet he speaks.

4102 1802 3346 3588 3361 1492 2288 2532 3756
5 πίστει Ἐνὼχ μετετέθη τοῦ μὴ ἰδεῖν θάνατον, καὶ οὐχ
By faith Enoch was translated not to see death, and not

2147 1360 3346 846 3588 2316 4253 1063 3588 3331
εὑρίσκετο, διότι μετέθηκεν αὐτὸν ὁ θεός· πρὸ γὰρ τῆς μεταθέ-
was found, because translated him God; before for the translating

846 3140 2100 3588 2316 5565 1161
σεως αὐτοῦ μεμαρτύρηται εὐαρεστηκέναι τῷ Θεῷ· 6 χωρὶς δὲ
of him he obtained witness to have been pleasing to God; without but

1. Now faith is the substance of things hoped for, the evidence of things not seen.
2 For by it the elders obtained a good report.
3 Through faith we understand that the worlds were framed by the word of God, so that things which are seen were not made of things which do appear.
4. By faith Abel offered unto God a more excellent sacrifice than Cain, by which he obtained witness that he was righteous, God testifying of his gifts: and by it he being dead yet speaketh.
5 By faith Enoch was translated that he should not see death; and was not found, because God had translated him: for before his translation he had this testimony, that he pleased God.
6 But without

Literal Translation

Hebrews 11:7

King James Version

faith (it is) impossible to please (God). For it is right (that) the (one) drawing near to God should believe that He is, and (that) He becomes a rewarder to the ones seeking Him out.
7 Being divinely warned about the things not yet having been seen, moved with fear, by faith Noah prepared an ark for (the) salvation of his house; through which he condemned the world and became heir of the righteousness according to faith.
8. Having been called out by faith, Abraham obeyed to go forth to a place which he was going to receive for an inheritance; and (he) went out not understanding where he went.

9 By faith he tenanted as a foreigner in a land of promise, living in tents with Isaac and Jacob, the joint-heirs of the same promise;

10 for he looked forward to a city having the foundations of which the builder and maker is God.
11 Also by faith Sarah herself received power for conception of seed even beyond (the) time of age, (and) gave birth; since she deemed the (One) having promised (to be) faithful.
12 Because of this even from one (and that (from) one (man they) were generated, and these (of) one having been dead, (seed) even as the stars of the heaven in multitude and countless as sand by the seaside. (Gen.22:17)
13 These all died by way of faith, not having received the promises, but havng seen them from afar, and having been persuaded, and having embraced and having confessed that they are strangers and pilgrims.

4102 102 2100 4100 1063 1163 3588
πίστεως ἀδύνατον εὐαρεστῆσαι, πιστεῦσαι γὰρ δεῖ τὸν
faith (it is) impossible to please (God), to believe for must the (one)

4334 3588 2316 3754 2076 2532 3588 1567 846
προσερχόμενον τῷ Θεῷ, ὅτι ἔστι καὶ τοις ἐκζητοῦσιν αὐτὸν
drawing near to God, that He is and to the (ones) seeking out Him

3406 1096 4102 5537 3575 4012 3588
μισθαποδότης γίνεται. 7 πίστει χρηματισθεὶς Νῶε περὶ τῶν
a rewarder He becomes. By faith having been warned Noah about the things

3369 991 2125 2680 2787 1519
μηδέπω βλεπομένων, εὐλαβηθεὶς κατεσκεύασε κιβωτὸν εἰς
not yet being seen, being moved with fear (he) prepared an ark for

4991 3588 3624 846 1223 3739 2632 3588 2889 2532
σωτηρίαν τοῦ οἴκου αὐτοῦ, δι' ἧς κατέκρινε τὸν κόσμον, καὶ
(the) salvation of the house of him, by which he condemned the world, and

3588 2596 4102 1343 1096 2818 4102
τῆς κατὰ πίστιν δικαιοσύνης ἐγένετο κληρονόμος. 8 πίστει
of the according to faith righteousness became heir. By faith

2564 11 5219 1831 1519 3588 5117 3739
καλούμενος Ἀβραὰμ ὑπήκουσεν ἐξελθεῖν εἰς τὸν τόπον ὃν
being called Abraham obeyed to go forth into a place which

3195 2983 1519 2817 2532 1831 3361 1987
ἤμελλε λαμβάνειν εἰς κληρονομίαν, καὶ ἐξῆλθε μὴ ἐπιστά-
he going to receive for an inheritance, and went out not under-

4226 2064 4102 3939 1519 3588 1093 3588 1860
μενος ποῦ ἔρχεται. 9 πίστει παρῴκησεν εἰς τὴν γῆν τῆς ἐπαγ-
standing where he went. By faith he tenanted (the) land of

5613 245 1722 4633 2730 3326 2464
γελίας, ὡς ἀλλοτρίαν, ἐν σκηναῖς κατοικήσας μετὰ Ἰσαὰκ
promise, as a foreigner, in tents dwelling with Isaac

2532 2384 3588 4789 3588 1860 3588 846
καὶ Ἰακὼβ, τῶν συγκληρονόμων τῆς ἐπαγγελίας τῆς αὐτῆς·
and Jacob, the co-heirs of the promise same;

1551 1063 3588 3588 2310 2192 4172 3739
10 ἐξεδέχετο γὰρ τὴν τοὺς θεμελίους ἔχουσαν πόλιν, ἧς
he looked forward for to the the foundations having city, of which

5079 2532 1217 3588 2316 4102 2532 846 4564
τεχνίτης καὶ δημιουργὸς ὁ Θεός. 11 πίστει καὶ αὐτὴ Σάρρα
(the) builder and maker (was) God. By faith also her(self) Sarah

1411 1519 2602 4690 2983 2532 3844 2540
δύναμιν εἰς καταβολὴν σπέρματος ἔλαβε καὶ παρὰ καιρὸν
power for conception of seed received even beyond time

2244 5088 1983 4103 2233 3588 1861
ἡλικίας ἔτεκεν, ἐπεὶ πιστὸν ἡγήσατο τὸν ἐπαγγειλάμενον.
of age gave birth, since faithful she deemed the (One) having promised.

1352 2532 575 1520 1080 2532 5023 3499
12 διὸ καὶ ἀφ' ἑνὸς ἐγεννήθησαν, καὶ ταῦτα νενεκρωμένου,
Therefore even from one were generated, and these (of) one having died,

2531 3588 798 3588 3772 3588 4128 2532 5616 285 3588 3844
καθὼς τὰ ἄστρα τοῦ οὐρανοῦ τῷ πλήθει, καὶ ὡσεὶ ἄμμος ἡ παρὰ
even as the stars of the heaven in multitude, and as sand by

3588 5491 3588 2281 3588 382
τὸ χεῖλος τῆς θαλάσσης ἡ ἀναρίθμητος.
the lip of the sea countless.

2596 4102 599 3778 3956 3361 2983 3588
13. Κατὰ πίστιν ἀπέθανον οὗτοι πάντες, μὴ λαβόντες τὰς
By way of faith died these all, not having received the

1860 235 4207 846 1492 2532 3982
ἐπαγγελίας, ἀλλὰ πόρρωθεν αὐτὰς ἰδόντες, καὶ πεισθεντες,
promises, but from afar them having seen, and being perusaded,

2532 782 2532 3670 3754 3581 2532 3927
καὶ ἀσπασάμενοι, καὶ ὁμολογήσαντες ὅτι ξένοι καὶ παρ-
and having embraced, and having confessed that strangers and pilgrims

faith (it is) impossible to please (him): for he that cometh to God must believe that he is, and (that) he is a rewarder of them that diligently seek him.

7 By faith Noah, being warned of God of things not seen as yet, moved with fear, prepared an ark to the saving of his house; by the which he condemned the world, and became heir of the righteousness which is by faith.

8. By faith Abraham, when he was called to go out into a place which he should after receive for an inheritance, obeyed; and he went out, not knowing whither he went.

9 By faith he sojourned in the land of promise, as (in) a strange country, dwelling in tabernacles with Isaac and Jacob, the heirs with him of the same promise:

10 For he looked for a city which hath foundations, whose builder and maker (is) God.
11 Through faith also Sara herself received strength to conceive seed, and was delivered of a child when she was past age, because she judged him faithful who had promised.

12 Therefore sprang there even of one, and him as good as dead, (so many) as the stars of the sky in multitude, and as the sand which is by the sea shore innumerable.

13 These all died in faith, not having received the promises, but having seen them afar off, and were persuaded of (them), and embraced (them), and confessed that they were strangers and pilgrims

Literal Translation

Hebrews 11:14

King James Version

of the earth.
14 For those saying such things make clear that they seek a fatherland.
15 And truly if they remembered that from which they came out, they had time to return.

16 But now they stretch forth to a better, that is, a heavenly (land). Therefore, God is not ashamed (of) them, to be called their God; for He prepared a city for them.

17 By faith, being tested, Abraham offered up Isaac; and he receiving the promises was offering up the only begotten,

18 as to whom it was said, "In Isaac your Seed shall be called;" (Gen. 21:12)
19 reckoning that God (was) able to raise even from (the) dead; from where indeed he obtained him in a parable.
20. By faith concerning things to come Isaac blessed Jacob and Esau.

21 By faith dying Jacob blessed each of the sons of Joseph, and worshiped on the top of his staff.

22 Dying Joseph by faith made mention of the Exodus of the sons of Israel, and (he) gave orders concerning his bones.
23 Being born, Moses was by faith hidden by his parents three months, because they saw the child (was) fair; and they did not fear the king's decree.
24 Having become great, Moses by faith refused to be called (the) son of Pharaoh's daughter,
25 having chosen rather to suffer affliction with the people of God than for a time to have

1526 1909 3588 1093 3588 1063 5108 3004
επίδημοί εἰσιν ἐπὶ τῆς γῆς. 14 οἱ γὰρ τοιαῦτα λέγοντες
they are on the earth. the (ones) For such things saying

1718 3754 3968 1934 2532 1487 3303 1565
ἐμφανίζουσιν ὅτι πατρίδα ἐπιζητοῦσι. 15 καὶ εἰ μὲν ἐκείνης
make clear that a fatherland they seek. And if indeed that

3421 575 3739 1831 2192 302 2540 344
ἐμνημόνευον ἀφ' ἧς ἐξῆλθον, εἶχον ἂν καιρὸν ἀνακάμψαι.
they remembered from which they came out, they might have had time to return.

3570 1161 2909 3713 5123 2076 2032 1352
16 νυνὶ δὲ κρείττονος ὀρέγονται, τοῦτ' ἔστιν, ἐπουρανίου· διὸ
now But (to) a better stretch forth to, this is a heavenly; so then

3756 1941 846 3588 2316 2316 1941 846
οὐκ ἐπαισχύνεται αὐτοὺς ὁ Θεὸς, Θεὸς ἐπικαλεῖσθαι αὐτῶν·
not is ashamed (of) them God, God to be called of them;

2090 1063 846 4172
ἡτοίμασε γὰρ αὐτοῖς πόλιν.
He prepared for them a city.

4102 4374 11 3588 2464 3985
17. Πίστει προσενήνοχεν 'Αβραὰμ τὸν 'Ισαὰκ πειραζόμενος,
By faith offered up Abraham Isaac being tested,

2532 3588 3439 4374 3588 3588 1860 324
καὶ τὸν μονογενῆ προσέφερεν ὁ τὰς ἐπαγγελίας ἀναδεξά-
and the only-begotten was offering up the (one) the promises having

4314 3739 2980 3754 1722 2464 2564 4671
μενος, 18 πρὸς ὃν ἐλαλήθη ὅτι 'Εν 'Ισαὰκ κληθήσεταί σοι
received, as to whom it was spoken, In Isaac shall be called of you

4690 3049 3754 2532 1537 3498 1453 1415 3588
σπέρμα, 19 λογισάμενος ὅτι καὶ ἐκ νεκρῶν ἐγείρειν δυνατὸς ὁ
seed, having reckoned that even from (the) dead to raise (was) able

2316 3606 846 2532 1722 3850 2865 4102 4012
Θεός· ὅθεν αὐτὸν καὶ ἐν παραβολῇ ἐκομίσατο. 20 πίστει περὶ
God; from where him indeed in a parable he obtained. By faith as to

3195 2127 2464 3588 2384 2532 3588 2269
μελλόντων εὐλόγησεν 'Ισαὰκ τὸν 'Ιακὼβ καὶ τὸν 'Ησαῦ.
coming things blessed Isaac Jacob and Esau.

4102 2384 599 1538 3588 5207 2501
21 πίστει 'Ιακὼβ ἀποθνήσκων ἕκαστον τῶν υἱῶν 'Ιωσὴφ
By faith Jacob dying each of the sons of Joseph

2127 2532 4352 1909 3588 206 3588 4464 846
εὐλόγησε, καὶ προσεκύνησεν ἐπὶ τὸ ἄκρον τῆς ῥάβδου αὐτοῦ.
blessed, and worshiped on the top of the staff of him.

4102 2501 5053 4012 3588 1841 3588 5207 2474
22 Πίστει 'Ιωσὴφ τελευτῶν περὶ τῆς ἐξόδου τῶν υἱῶν 'Ισραὴλ
By faith Joseph dying concerning the exodus of the sons of Israel

3421 2532 4012 3588 3747 846 1781 4101
ἐμνημόνευσε, καὶ περὶ τῶν ὀστέων αὐτοῦ ἐνετείλατο. 23 πίστει
remembered, and concerning the bones of him gave command. By faith

3475 1080 2928 5150 5259 3588 3962
Μωσῆς γεννηθεὶς ἐκρύβη τρίμηνον ὑπὸ τῶν πατέρων
Moses having been generated was hidden three months by the parents

846 1360 1492 791 3588 3913 2532 3756 5399
αὐτοῦ, διότι εἶδον ἀστεῖον τὸ παιδίον· καὶ οὐκ ἐφοβήθησαν
of him, because they saw (was) handsome the child; and not they feared

3588 1297 3588 935 4102 3475 3173 1096
τὸ διάταγμα τοῦ βασιλέως. 24 πίστει Μωσῆς μέγας γενόμενος
the decree of the king. By faith Moses great having become

720 3004 5207 2364 5328 3123 138
ἠρνήσατο λέγεσθαι υἱὸς θυγατρὸς Φαραώ, 25 μᾶλλον ἑλόμενος
refused to be called son of (the) daughter of Pharaoh, rather choosing

4778 3588 2992 3588 2316 2228 4340 2192
συγκακουχεῖσθαι τῷ λαῷ τοῦ Θεοῦ ἢ πρόσκαιρον ἔχειν
to suffer affliction with the people of God than for a time to have

on the earth.
14 For the (ones) saying such things made clear that they seek a country.

15 And truly, if they had been mindful of that (country) from whence they came out, they might have had time to have returned.
16 But now they stretch forth to a better (country), that is, a heavenly: so then God is not ashamed to be called their God: for he prepared for them a city.

17 By faith Abraham being tested offered up Isaac: and he who had received the promises was offering up his only begotten (son),

18 Of whom it was said, In Isaac shall your seed be called:
19 having reckoned that God (was) able to raise (him) up, even from (the) dead; from where also he received him in a figure.
20. By faith Isaac blessed Jacob and Esau concerning things to come.

21 By faith dying Jacob, blessed both the sons of Joseph; and worshiped, (leaning) upon the top of his staff.
22 By faith dying Joseph remembered concerning the exodus of the children of Israel; and gave commandment concerning his bones.
23 By faith Moses, having been generated, was hid three months by his parents, because they saw (he was) a handsome child; and they were not afraid of the king's decree.
24 By faith Moses having become great refused to be called the son of Pharaoh's daughter;
25 having chosen rather to suffer affliction with the people of God, than to have enjoyment

Literal Translation **Hebrews 11:26** ***King James Version***

of sin;

26 having esteemed the reproach of Christ greater riches (than) the treasures (of) Egypt, for he was looking to the reward.

27 By faith he left Egypt, not fearing the wrath of the king; for he kept on as seeing the Invisible (One).

28 By faith he made the Passover, and the sprinkling of blood, that the (one) destroying of the first-born might not touch them.

29 By faith they passed through the Red Sea, as through dry (land); by which attempt having taken the Egyptians were swallowed up.

30 By faith the walls of Jericho fell down, having been circled during seven days.

31 By faith Rahab the harlot did not perish with those having disobeyed, having received the spies with peace.

32 And what more may I say? For the times will fail me telling about Gideon, Barak, and also Samson and Jephthah, and also David and Samuel, and the prophets,

33 who through faith overcame kingdoms, worked out righteousness, obtained promises, stopped (the) mouths of lions,

34 quenched (the) power of fire, escaped the mouths of (the) sword, acquired power from weakness, became strong in war, armies of foreigners being made to yield.

35 Women received their dead by resurrection; but others were beaten to death, not accepting deliverance, that they might obtain a better resurrection.

36 And others received trial of mockings

266 619 3173 4149 2233 3588
ἁμαρτίας ἀπόλαυσιν· 26 μείζονα πλοῦτον ἡγησάμενος τῶν
of sin enjoyment; greater riches having esteemed(than) the

1722 125 2344 3588 3680 3588 5547 578
ἐν Αἰγύπτῳ θησαυρῶν τὸν ὀνειδισμὸν τοῦ Χριστοῦ, ἀπέ-
(of) Egypt treasures the reproach of Christ, he was

1063 1519 3588 3405 4102 2641
βλεπε γὰρ εἰς τὴν μισθαποδοσίαν. 27 πίστει κατέλιπεν
looking for to the reward. By faith he left

125 3361 5399 3588 2372 3588 935 3588 1063
Αἴγυπτον, μὴ φοβηθεὶς τὸν θυμὸν τοῦ βασιλέως· τὸν γὰρ
Egypt, not fearing the wrath of the king; the for

517 5613 3708 2594 4102 4160 3588 3957
ἀόρατον ὡς ὁρῶν ἐκαρτέρησε. 28 πίστει πεποίηκε τὸ πάσχα
invisible (One) as seeing he kept on. By faith he made the Passover

2532 3588 4378 3588 129 2443 3361 3588 3645 3588
καὶ τὴν πρόσχυσιν τοῦ αἵματος, ἵνα μὴ ὁ ὀλοθρεύων τὰ
and the sprinkling of blood, that not the (one) destroying the

4416 2345 846 4102 1224 3588 2063
πρωτότοκα θίγῃ αὐτῶν. 29 πίστει διέβησαν τὴν Ἐρυθρὰν
first-born should touch them. By faith they went through the Red

2281 5613 1223 3584 3739 3984 2983 3588 124
θάλασσαν ὡς διὰ ξηρᾶς· ἧς πεῖραν λαβόντες οἱ Αἰγύπτιοι
Sea as through dry (land); which trial having taken the Egyptians

2666 4102 3588 5038 2410 4098 2944
κατεπόθησαν. 30 πίστει τὰ τείχη Ἱεριχὼ ἔπεσε, κυκλωθέντα
were swallowed. By faith the walls of Jericho fell, having been circled

1909 2033 2250 4102 4460 3588 4204 3756 4881
ἐπὶ ἑπτὰ ἡμέρας. 31 πίστει Ῥαὰβ ἡ πόρνη οὐ συναπώλετο
during seven days. By faith Rahab the harlot not did perish

3588 544 1209 3588 2685 3326 1515
τοῖς ἀπειθήσασι, δεξαμένη τοὺς κατασκόπους μετ' εἰρήνης.
with those having disobeyed, receiving the spies with peace.

2532 5101 5037 3004 1952 1063 3165 1334 3588 5550 4012
32 καὶ τί ἔτι λέγω; ἐπιλείψει γάρ με διηγούμενον ὁ χρόνος περὶ
And what yet may I say? will fail For me relating the times about

1066 913 5037 2532 4564 2532 2422 1138 5037 2532
Γεδεών, Βαράκ τε καὶ Σαμψών καὶ Ἰεφθάε, Δαβίδ τε καὶ
Gideon, Barak both and Samson and Jephthah, David both and

4545 2532 3588 4396 3739 1223 4102 2610
Σαμουὴλ καὶ τῶν προφητῶν· 33 οἳ διὰ πίστεως κατηγωνίσαντο
Samuel and the prophets; who through faith overcame

932 2038 1343 2013 1860
βασιλείας, εἰργάσαντο δικαιοσύνην, ἐπέτυχον ἐπαγγελιῶν,
kingdoms, worked out righteousness, obtained promises,

5420 4750 3023 4570 1411 4442 5343
ἔφραξαν στόματα λέντων, 34 ἔσβεσαν δύναμιν πυρός, ἔφυγον
stopped (the) mouths of lions, quenched (the) power of fire, escaped

4750 3162 1743 575 769 1096
στόματα μαχαίρας, ἐνεδυναμώθησαν ἀπὸ ἀσθενείας, ἐγενή-
(the) mouths of swords, acquired power from weakness, became

2478 1722 4171 3925 2827 245
θησαν ἰσχυροὶ ἐν πολέμῳ, παρεμβολὰς ἔκλιναν ἀλλοτρίων.
strong in war, armies (being) made to yield of foreigners.

2983 1135 1537 386 3588 3498 846 243
35 ἔλαβον γυναῖκες ἐξ ἀναστάσεως τοὺς νεκροὺς αὐτῶν· ἄλλοι
received Women by resurrection the dead of them; others

1161 5178 3756 4327 3588 629
δὲ ἐτυμπανίσθησαν, οὐ προσδεξάμενοι τὴν ἀπολύτρωσιν,
but were beaten to death, not having accepted deliverance,

2443 2909 386 5177 2087 1161 1701
ἵνα κρείττονος ἀναστάσεως τύχωσιν· 36 ἕτεροι δὲ ἐμπαιγμῶν
that a better resurrection they might obtain; others and of mockings

the pleasures of sin for a season;

26 Esteeming the reproach of Christ greater riches than the treasures in Egypt: for he had respect unto the recompence of the reward.

27 By faith he forsook Egypt, not fearing the wrath of the king: for he endured, as seeing him who is invisible.

28 Through faith he kept the passover, and the sprinkling of blood, lest he that destroyed the firstborn should touch them.

29 By faith they passed through the Red sea as by dry (land): which the Egyptians assaying to do were drowned.

30 By faith the walls of Jericho fell down, after they were compassed about seven days.

31 By faith the harlot Rahab perished not with them that believed not, when she had received the spies with peace.

32. And what shall I more say? for the time would fail me to tell of Gedeon, and (of) Barak, and (of) Samson, and (of) Jephthae; (of) David also, and Samuel, and (of) the prophets:

33 Who through faith subdued kingdoms, wrought righteousness, obtained promises, stopped the mouths of lions,

34 Quenched the violence of fire, escaped the edge of the sword, out of weakness were made strong, waxed valiant in fight, turned to flight the armies of the aliens.

35 Women received their dead raised to life again: and others were tortured, not accepting deliverance; that they might obtain a better resurrection:

36 And others had trial of (cruel) mockings

Literal Translation

Hebrews 11:37

King James Version

and of floggings; yea, more, of bonds and of prison:

37 they were stoned; they were tried; they were sawn in two; they died by murder of sword; they went about in sheepskins and in goatskins, being in need, being afflicted, being ill-treated
38 of whom the world was not worthy, wandering in deserted places, and mountains, and caves, and the holes of the earth.
39 And having obtained witness through the faith, these all did not obtain the promise,
40 God having foreseen something better concerning us, that they should not be perfected apart from us.

2532 3148 3984 2983 2089 1161 1199 2532 5438
καὶ μαστίγων πεῖραν ἔλαβον, ἔτι δὲ δεσμῶν καὶ φυλακῆς·
and floggings trial received, more and bonds and of prison;

3034 4249 3985 1722 5408 3162
37 ἐλιθάσθησαν, ἐπρίσθησαν, ἐπειράσθησαν, ἐν φόνῳ μαχαίρης
they were stoned, they were tried, they were sawn apart, by murder of sword

599 4022 1722 3374 1722 122 1192
ἀπέθανον· περιῆλθον ἐν μηλωταῖς, ἐν αἰγείοις δέρμασιν,
they died; they went about in sheepskins, in goat skins,

5302 2346 2558 3739 3756 2258 514
ὑστερούμενοι, θλιβόμενοι, κακουχούμενοι, 38 [ὧν οὐκ ἦν ἄξιος
being in need, being afflicted, being ill-treated, of whom not was worthy

3588 2889 1722 2047 4105 2532 3735 2532 4693
ὁ κόσμος], ἐν ἐρημίαις πλανώμενοι καὶ ὄρεσι καὶ σπηλαίοις
the world, in deserted places wandering and moutains and caves

2532 3588 3692 3588 1093 2532 3778 3956 3140
καὶ ταῖς ὀπαῖς τῆς γῆς. 39 καὶ οὗτοι πάντες, μαρτυρηθέντες
and the holes of the earth. And these all, having obtained witness

1223 3588 4102 3756 2865 3588 1860 3588
διὰ τῆς πίστεως οὐκ ἐκομίσαντο τὴν ἐπαγγελίαν, 40 τοῦ
through the faith not did obtain the promise,

2316 4012 2257 2909 5100 4265 2443 3361 5565
Θεοῦ περὶ ἡμῶν κρεῖττόν τι προβλεψαμένου, ἵνα μὴ χωρὶς
God concerning us better something having foreseen, that not without

2257 5048
ἡμῶν τελειωθῶσιν.
us they should be perfected.

and scourgings, yea, moreover of bonds and imprisonment:

37 They were stoned, they were sawn asunder, were tempted, were slain with the sword: they wandered about in sheepskins and goatskins; being destitute, afflicted, tormented;
38 (Of whom the world was not worthy:) they wandered in deserts, and (in) mountains, and (in) dens and caves of the earth.
39 And these all, having obtained a good report through faith, received not the promise:
40 God having provided some better thing for us, that they without us should not be made perfect.

Hebrews 12

1. So therefore we also, having so great a cloud of witnesses lying around us, having laid aside every weight and the easily surrounding sin, through patience let us also run the race set before us,

2 looking to the Author and Finisher of (our) faith, Jesus, who for the joy set before Him endured (the) cross, having despised the shame, and sat down at (the) right of the throne of God.

3 For consider Him who had endured such gainsaying of sinners against Himself, that you do not grow weary, fainting in your souls.
4 You did not yet resist unto blood, wrestling against sin.

5 And you have forgotten the exhortation which (He) speaks with you, as with sons,

5105 2532 2249 5118 2192 4029 2254
1. Τοιγαροῦν καὶ ἡμεῖς, τοσοῦτον ἔχοντες περικείμενον ἡμῖν
So therefore also we, such having lying around us

3509 3144 3591 659 3956 2532 3588 2139
νέφος μαρτύρων, ὄγκον ἀποθέμενοι πάντα καὶ τὴν εὐπερί-
a cloud of witnesses, weight having laid aside every and the easily

266 1223 5281 5143 3588 4295
στατον ἁμαρτίαν, δι' ὑπομονῆς τρέχωμεν τὸν προκείμενον
surrounding sin, through patince let us run the set before

2254 73 872 1519 3588 3588 4102 747 2532
ἡμῖν ἀγῶνα, 2 ἀφορῶντες εἰς τὸν τῆς πίστεως ἀρχηγὸν καὶ
us race, looking to the of the faith Author and

5051 2424 3739 473 3588 4295 846 5479
τελειωτὴν Ἰησοῦν, ὃς, ἀντὶ τῆς προκειμένης αὐτῷ χαρᾶς
Finisher Jesus, who because of the set before Him joy

5278 4716 152 2706 1722 1188 5037 3588
ὑπέμεινε σταυρὸν, αἰσχύνης καταφρονήσας, ἐν δεξιᾷ τε τοῦ
endured (the) cross, (the) shame having despised, at (the) right and of the

2362 3588 2316 2523 357 1063 3588 5108
θρόνου τοῦ Θεοῦ ἐκάθισεν. 3 ἀναλογίσασθε γὰρ τὸν τοιαύτην
throne of God sat down. consider For the (One) such

5278 5259 3588 268 1519 846 485
ὑπομεμενηκότα ὑπὸ τῶν ἁμαρτωλῶν εἰς αὐτὸν ἀντιλογίαν,
having endured by of sinners against Himself gainsaying,

2443 3361 2577 3588 5590 5216 1590 3768 3360
ἵνα μὴ κάμητε ταῖς ψυχαῖς ὑμῶν ἐκλυόμενοι. 4 οὔπω μέχρις
that not you grow weary in the souls of you fainting. Not yet unto

129 464 4314 3588 266 464
αἵματος ἀντικατέστητε πρὸς τὴν ἁμαρτίαν ἀνταγωνιζόμε-
blood you resisted against sin wrestling;

2532 1585 3588 3874 3748 5213 5613 5207
νοι· 5 καὶ ἐκλέλησθε τῆς παρακλήσεως, ἥτις ὑμῖν ὡς υἱοῖς
and you have forgotten the exhortation, which with you as with sons

1. Wherefore seeing we also are compassed about with so great a cloud of witnesses, let us lay aside every weight, and the sin which doth so easily beset (us), and let us run with patience the race that is set before us,

2 Looking unto Jesus the author and finisher of (our) faith; who for the joy that was set before him endured the cross, despising the shame, and is set down at the right hand of the throne of God.

3 For consider him that endured such contradiction of sinners against himself, lest ye be wearied and faint in your minds.

4 Ye have not yet resisted unto blood, striving against sin.

5 And ye have forgotten the exhortation which speaketh unto you as unto children,

Literal Translation

“My sons, do not de-
spise the chastening of
(the) Lord, nor faint
(while) being corrected
by Him.
6 For whom (the) Lord
loves, He disciplines,
and whips every son
whom He receives.”
(Prov. 3:11,12)
7 If you endure disci-
pline, God is dealing
with you as with sons;
for who is (the) son
whom a father does not
discipline?
8 But if you are without
discipline, of which all
have become sharers,
then you are bastards,
and not sons.

9 Furthermore, indeed
we have had fathers of
our flesh (as) correc-
tors, and we respected
(them). Shall we not
much more be subject
to the Father of spirits,
and we shall live?
10 For they truly disci-
plined (us) for a few
days according to the
thing seeming good to
them; but He for (our)
profit, (in order for us)
to partake of His holi-
ness.

11 And all discipline for
the present indeed does
not seem to be joyous,
but grievous; but after-
ward it gives back
peaceable fruit of right-
eousness to the (ones)
having been exercised
by it.
12. Because of this,
straighten the hands
hanging alongside, and
the having been enfee-
bled knees;
13 and make straight
tracks for your feet, that
the lame not be turned
aside, but rather healed.
(Isa.35:3; Prov.4:26)

14 Eagerly pursue
peace with all, and holi-
ness, without which no
one will see the Lord,
15 watching diligently
that not any lack from
the grace of God, that no
root of bitterness grow-
ing up may crowd in (on
you), and through this
many be defiled;
16 lest

Hebrews 12:6

1256 5207 3450 3361 3643 3809 2962 3366
διαλέγεται, Υἱέ μου, μὴ ὀλιγώρει παιδείας Κυρίου, μηδὲ
(He) speaks, Son of Me, not do despise (the) chastening of (the) Lord, nor

1590 5259 846 1651 3739 1063 25 2962
ἐκλύου ὑπ᾽ αὐτοῦ ἐλεγχόμενος· 6. ὃν γὰρ ἀγαπᾷ Κύριος
faint by Him being corrected; whom for loves (the) Lord

3811 3146 1161 3956 5207 3739 3858 1487
παιδεύει· μαστιγοῖ δὲ πάντα υἱὸν ὃν παραδέχεται. 7 εἰ
He disciplines; whips and every son whom He receives. If

3809 5278 5613 5207 5213 4374 3588 2316 5101
παιδείαν ὑπομένετε, ὡς υἱοῖς ὑμῖν προσφέρεται ὁ Θεός· τίς
discipline you endure, as with sons with you is dealing God; who

1063 2076 5207 3739 3756 3811 3962 1487 1161 5565 2075
γάρ ἐστιν υἱὸς ὃν οὐ παιδεύει πατήρ; 8 εἰ δὲ χωρίς ἐστε
for is a son whom not disciplines a father? if But without you are

3809 3739 3353 1096 3956 686 3541 2075 2532
παιδείας, ἧς μέτοχοι γεγόνασι πάντες, ἄρα νόθοι ἐστε καὶ
discipline, of which sharers have become all, then bastards you are and

3756 5207 1534 3588 3303 3588 4561 2257 3962 2192
οὐχ υἱοί. 9 εἶτα τοὺς μὲν τῆς σαρκὸς ἡμῶν πατέρας εἴχομεν
not sons. Furthermore the indeed the flesh of us fathers we had

3810 2532 1788 3756 4183 3123 5293
παιδευτάς, καὶ ἐνετρεπόμεθα· οὐ πολλῷ μᾶλλον ὑποταγησό-
(as) correctors, and we respected (them); not much more shall we be subject

3588 3962 3588 4151 2532 2198 3588 3303 1063
μεθα τῷ πατρὶ τῶν πνευμάτων, καὶ ζήσομεν; 10 οἱ μὲν γὰρ
to the Father of spirits, and we shall live? they truly For

4314 3641 2250 2596 3588 1380 846 3811 3588
πρὸς ὀλίγας ἡμέρας κατὰ τὸ δοκοῦν αὐτοῖς ἐπαίδευον· ὁ
for a few days according to that seeming (good) to them disciplined (us); He

1161/1909/3588 4851 1519 3588 3335 3588 41 846
δὲ ἐπὶ τὸ συμφέρον, εἰς τὸ μεταλαβεῖν τῆς ἁγιότητος αὐτοῦ.
but for the profit, to the to partake of the holiness of Him.

3956 1161 3809 4314 3303 3588 3918 3756 1380 5479 1511
11 πᾶσα δὲ παιδεία πρὸς μὲν τὸ παρὸν οὐ δοκεῖ χαρᾶς εἶναι,
all And discipline for indeed the present not seems of joy to be,

235 3077 5305 1161 2590 1516 3588 1223 846
ἀλλὰ λύπης· ὕστερον δὲ καρπὸν εἰρηνικὸν τοῖς δι᾽ αὐτῆς
but of grief; afterward but fruit peacable to the (ones) through it

1128 591 1343 1352 3588 3935
γεγυμνασμένοις ἀποδίδωσι δικαιοσύνης. 12 διὸ τὰς παρειμένας
having been exercised it gives back of righteousness. Therefore the hanging alongside

5495 2532 3588 3886 1119 461 2532
χεῖρας καὶ τὰ παραλελυμένα γόνατα ἀνορθώσατε· 13 καὶ
hands and the having been enfeebled knees straighten up; and

5163 3717 4160 3588 4228 5216 2443 3361 3588 5560
τροχιὰς ὀρθὰς ποιήσατε τοῖς ποσὶν ὑμῶν, ἵνα μὴ τὸ χωλὸν
tracks straight make for the feet of you, that not the lame

1624 2390 1161 3123
ἐκτραπῇ, ἰαθῇ δὲ μᾶλλον.
be turned aside, be healed but rather.

1515 1377 3326 3956 2532 3588 38 3739
14. Εἰρήνην διώκετε μετὰ πάντων, καὶ τὸν ἁγιασμόν, οὗ
peace Follow with all, and holiness, which

5565 3762 3700 3588 2962 1983 3361 5100
χωρὶς οὐδεὶς ὄψεται τὸν Κύριον· 15 ἐπισκοποῦντες μή τις
without no one will see the Lord; watching diligently lest any

5302 575 3588 5485 3588 2316 3361 5100 4491 4088
ὑστερῶν ἀπὸ τῆς χάριτος τοῦ θεοῦ· μή τις ῥίζα πικρίας
lacking from the grace of God; lest any root of bitterness

507 5453 1776 2532 1223 3778 3392 4183 3361
ἄνω φύουσα ἐνοχλῇ, καὶ διὰ ταύτης μιανθῶσι πολλοί· 16 μή
up growing disturb, and through this be defiled many; lest

King James Version

My son, despise not
thou the chastening of
the Lord, nor faint when
thou art rebuked of him:

6 For whom the Lord
loveth he chasteneth,
and scourgeth every
son whom he receiveth.
7 If ye endure chasten-
ing, God dealeth with
you as with sons; for
what son is he whom the
father chasteneth not?

8 But if ye be without
chastisement, whereof
all are partakers, then
are ye bastards, and not
sons.

9 Furthermore we have
had fathers of our flesh
which corrected (us),
and we gave (them)
reverence: shall we not
much rather be in sub-
jection unto the Father
of spirits, and live?
10 For they verily for a
few days chastened (us)
after their own pleasure;
but he for (our) profit,
that (we) might be par-
takers of his holiness.

11 Now no chastening
for the present seemeth
to be joyous, but griev-
ous: nevertheless after-
ward it yieldeth the
peaceable fruit of right-
eousness unto them
which are exercised
thereby.
12. Wherefore lift up
the hands which hang
down, and the feeble
knees;
13 And make straight
paths for your feet, lest
that which is lame be
turned out of the way;
but let it rather be
healed.

14 Follow peace with
all (men), and holiness,
without which no man
shall see the Lord:
15 Looking diligently
lest any man fail of the
grace of God; lest any
root of bitterness
springing up trouble
(you), and thereby
many be defiled;
16 Lest

Literal Translation

any fornicator, or pro-
fane one, as Esau, who
for one feeding gave up
his birthright;

17 for you know also
that afterwards desiring
to inherit the blessing,
he was rejected, for he
found no place of re-
pentance, though hav-
ing sought it with tears.
(Gen. 27:36 - 39)

18. For you have not
drawn near to (the)
mountain having been
touched, and having
been lit with fire, and to
gloom, and darkness,
and of tempest,
19 and to a sound of
trumpet, and to a voice
of words, which those
having heard begged
that not a word be added
to them;
20 for they could not
bear the thing enjoined:
"Even if a beast touches
the mountain, it will be
stoned, or shot through
with a dart." (Ex. 19:12,
13)
21 And so fearful was
the thing appearing,
Moses said, "I am terri-
fied and trembling."
(Deut. 9:19)
22 But you have drawn
near Mount Zion, even
(the) city of (the) living
God, to a heavenly Je-
rusalem, and to myriads
of angels,
23 and to an assembly,
a church of the first-
born ones having been
enrolled in Heaven; and
to God (the) judge of all,
and to spirits of just
ones who have been
perfected;
24 and to Jesus the Me-
diator of a new cove-
nant, and to blood of
sprinkling, speaking
better things than (that)
of Abel.
25 Watch (that) you do
not refuse the (One)
speaking; for if these
did not escape who re-
fused Him who di-
vinely warned (them)
on earth, much rather
we, those turning away
from Heaven;
26 whose voice shook
the earth then, but now
He has promised, say-
ing, "Yet once

Hebrews 12:17

5100 4205 2228 952 5613 2269 3739 473 1035 3391
τις πόρνος, ἢ βέβηλος, ὡς Ἠσαῦ, ὃς ἀντὶ βρώσεως μιᾶς
any fornicator, or profane one, as Esau, who for the sake of feeding one

591 3588 4415 846 2467 1063 3754 2532 3341
ἀπέδοτο τὰ πρωτοτόκια αὐτοῦ. 17 ἴστε γὰρ ὅτι καὶ μετέπειτα
gave up the birthright of him. you know For that indeed afterwards

2309 2816 3588 2129 593 3341
θέλων κληρονομῆσαι τὴν εὐλογίαν, ἀπεδοκιμάσθη· μετανοίας
desiring to inherit the blessing, he was rejected; of repentance

1063 5117 3756 2147 2539 3326 1144 1567 846
γὰρ τόπον οὐχ εὗρε, καίπερ μετὰ δακρύων ἐκζητήσας αὐτήν.
for place not he found, though with tears having sought it.

3756 1063 4334 5584 3735 2532 2545
18. Οὐ γὰρ προσεληλύθατε ψηλαφωμένῳ ὄρει, καὶ κεκαυ-
not For you have drawn near being touched (the) mountain, and been

4442 2532 1105 2532 4655 2532 2366 2532 4536
μένῳ πυρί, καὶ γνόφῳ, καὶ ζόφῳ, καὶ θυέλλῃ, 19 καὶ σάλπιγ-
lit with fire, and to gloom, and darkness, and tempest, and of trumpet

2279 2532 5456 4487 3739 3588 191 3868
γος ἤχῳ, καὶ φωνῇ ῥημάτων, ἧς οἱ ἀκούσαντες παρῃτή-
to a sound, and to a voice of words, which the (ones) having heard begged

3361 4369 846 3056 3756 5342 1063/3588
σαντο μὴ προστεθῆναι αὐτοῖς λόγον· 20 οὐκ ἔφερον γὰρ τὸ
not to be added to them a word; not they bore for that

1291 2579 2342 2345 3588 3735 3036
διαστελλόμενον, Κἂν θηρίον θίγῃ τοῦ ὄρους, λιθοβοληθή-
being enjoined, If even a beast touches the mountain, it will be stoned

2228 1002 2700 2532 3779 5398 2258/3588
σεται ἢ βολίδι κατατοξευθήσεται· 21 καί, οὕτω φοβερὸν ἦν τὸ
or with a dart shot through; and, so fearful was (it)

5324 3475 2036 1630 1510 2532 1790
φανταζόμενον, Μωσῆς εἶπεν, Ἔκφοβός εἰμι καὶ ἔντρομος.
appearing, (that) Moses said, terrified I am and trembling.

235 4334 4622 3735 2532 4172 2316 2198
22 ἀλλὰ προσεληλύθατε Σιὼν ὄρει, καὶ πόλει Θεοῦ ζῶντος,
But you have drawn near Zion Mount, and a city God of (the) living,

2419 2032 2532 3461 32 3831
Ἰερουσαλὴμ ἐπουρανίῳ, καὶ μυριάσιν ἀγγέλων, πανηγύρει
Jerusalem to a heavenly, and to myriads of angels, to an assembly

2532 1577 4416 1722 3772 583
23 καὶ ἐκκλησίᾳ πρωτοτόκων ἐν οὐρανοῖς ἀπογεγραμμένων,
and a church of first-born ones in Heaven having been enrolled,

2532 2923 2316 3956 2532 4151 1342 5048
καὶ κριτῇ Θεῷ πάντων, καὶ πνεύμασι δικαίων τετελειω-
and (the) Judge God of all, and to spirits of just ones having been

2532 1242 3501 3316 2424 2532 129 4473
μένων, 24 καὶ διαθήκης νέας μεσίτῃ Ἰησοῦ, καὶ αἵματι ῥαντι-
perfected, and covenant of a new mediator Jesus, and to blood of

2909 2980 3844 3588 6 991 3361
σμοῦ κρείττονα λαλοῦντι παρὰ τὸ Ἄβελ. 25 Βλέπετε μὴ
sprinkling better things speaking than (that) of Abel. Watch (that) not

3868 3588 2980 1487 1063 1565 3756 5343 3588
παραιτήσησθε τὸν λαλοῦντα. εἰ γὰρ ἐκεῖνοι οὐκ ἔφυγον, τὸν
you refuse the (One) speaking. if For these not escaped,

1909 3588 1093 3868 5537 4183 3123
ἐπὶ τῆς γῆς παραιτησάμενοι χρηματίζοντα, πολλῷ μᾶλλον
on the earth having refused (the One) divinely warning, much rather

2249 3588 3588 575 3772 654 3739 3588 5456 3588
ἡμεῖς οἱ τὸν ἀπ' οὐρανῶν ἀποστρεφόμενοι· 26 οὗ ἡ φωνὴ τὴν
we the (ones) from Heaven turning away; of whom the voice the

1093 4531 5119 3568 1161 1861 3004 2089 530
γῆν ἐσάλευσε τότε, νῦν δὲ ἐπήγγελται, λέγων, Ἔτι ἅπαξ
earth shook then, now but He has promised, saying, Yet once

King James Version

there (be) any fornica-
tor, or profane person,
as Esau, who for one
morsel of meat sold his
birthright.
17 For ye know how
that afterward, when he
would have inherited
the blessing, he was re-
jected: for he found no
place of repentance,
though he sought it
carefully with tears.

18. For ye are not come
unto the mount that
might be touched, and
that burned with fire, nor
unto blackness, and
darkness, and tempest,
19 And the sound of a
trumpet, and the voice
of words; which (voice)
they that heard intreated
that the word should not
be spoken to them any
more:
20 (For they could not
endure that which was
commanded, And if so
much as a beast touch
the mountain, it shall be
stoned, or thrust
through with a dart:
21 And so terrible was
the sight, (that) Moses
said, I exceedingly fear
and quake:)
22 But ye are come unto
mount Sion, and unto
the city of the living
God, the heavenly Jeru-
salem, and to an innu-
merable company of
angels,
23 To the general as-
sembly and church of
the firstborn, which are
written in heaven, and
to God the Judge of all,
and to the spirits of just
men made perfect,
24 And to Jesus the me-
diator of the new cove-
nant, and to the blood of
sprinkling, that
speaketh better things
than (that of) Abel.
25 See that ye refuse not
him that speaketh. For if
they escaped not who
refused him that spake
on earth, much more
(shall not) we (escape),
if we turn away from
him that (speaketh)
from heaven:
26 Whose voice then
shook the earth: but
now he hath promised,
saying, Yet once

Hebrews 12:27

Literal Translation

I will shake not only the earth, but also the heaven." (Hag. 2:6)
27 Now the (words), "Yet once" make clear the removal of the things being shaken, as having been made, so that the things not shaken may remain.
28 For this reason, receiving an unshakable kingdom, let us have grace, by which we may serve God well-pleasingly, with reverence and awe;
29 for indeed, "Our God (is) a consuming fire." (Deut. 4:24)

1473 4579 3756 3440 3588 1093 235 2532 3588 3772 3588 1161
ἐγὼ σείω οὐ μόνον τὴν γῆν, ἀλλὰ καὶ τὸν οὐρανόν. 27 τὸ δέ,
I shake not only the earth, but also the heaven. the (words) Now,

2089 530 1213 3588 4531 3588 3331 5613
Ἔτι ἅπαξ, δηλοῖ τῶν σαλευομένων τὴν μετάθεσιν, ὡς
Yet once, makes clear of the (things) being shaken the removal, as

4160 2443 3306 3588 3361 4531 1352
πεποιημένων, ἵνα μείνῃ τὰ μὴ σαλευόμενα. 28 διὸ βασι-
having been made, that may remain the things not shaken. Therefore

932 761 3880 2192 5485 1223 3739
λείαν ἀσάλευτον παραλαμβάνοντες, ἔχωμεν χάριν, δι᾽ ἧς λα-
kingdom an unshakable receiving, let us have grace, through which

3000 2102 3588 2316 3326 127 2532 2124 2532
τρεύωμεν εὐαρέστως τῷ Θεῷ μετὰ αἰδοῦς καὶ εὐλαβείας· 29 καὶ
we may serve well-pleasingly God with reverence and fear; indeed

1063 3588 2316 2257 4442 2654
γὰρ ὁ θεὸς ἡμῶν πῦρ καταναλίσκον.
for the God of us fire a consuming (is).

King James Version

more I shake not the earth only, but also heaven.
27 And this (word), Yet once more, signifieth the removing of those things that are shaken, as of things that are made, that those things which cannot be shaken may remain.
28 Wherefore we receiving a kingdom which cannot be moved, let us have grace, whereby we may serve God acceptably with reverence and godly fear:
29 For our God (is) a consuming fire.

Hebrews 13

Literal Translation

1. Let brotherly love continue.
2 Do not forget hospitality, for by this some unknowingly hosted angels.
3 Be mindful of the prisoners, as having been bound with (them); of those ill-treated, as also being in the body yourselves.
4 Marriage (is) honorable in all, and the bed undefiled; but God will judge fornicators and adulterers.
5 (Set your) way of life without money-loving, being satisfied with present things; for He has said, "Not will I leave you, nor will I forsake you, never!" (Deut. 31:6)
6 So that we may confidently say, "(The) Lord (is) my helper, and I will not be afraid. What shall man do to me?" (Psa.118:6)

7. Remember your leaders who spoke the Word of God to you, considering the issue of (their) conduct, imitate (their) faith:
8 Jesus Christ, the same yesterday and today, even to the ages.

9 Do not be carried away by various and strange doctrines; for (it is) good (that) the heart be confirmed by grace

3588 5360 3306 3588 5381 3361 1950
1. Ἡ φιλαδελφία μενέτω. 2 τῆς φιλοξενίας μὴ ἐπιλανθάνεσθε,
brotherly love let remain. of hospitality (Be) not forgetful;

1223 3778 1063 2990 5100 3579 32 3403
διὰ ταύτης γὰρ ἔλαθόν τινες ξενίσαντες ἀγγέλους. 3 μιμνή-
because of this for unknowingly some hosted angels. Be

3588 1198 5613 4887 3588 2558
σκεσθε τῶν δεσμίων, ὡς συνδεδεμένοι· τῶν κακουχουμένων,
mindful of the prisoners, as being bound with (them); of those being ill-treated,

5613/2532/846 5607 1722 4983 5093 3588 1062 1722 3956 2532 3588
ὡς καὶ αὐτοὶ ὄντες ἐν σώματι. 4 τίμιος ὁ γάμος ἐν πᾶσι, καὶ ἡ
as also yourselves being in the body. honorable Marriage (is) in all, and the

2845 283 4205 1161 2532 3432 2919 3588 2316 866
κοίτη ἀμίαντος, πόρνους δὲ καὶ μοιχοὺς κρινεῖ ὁ Θεός. 5 ἀφιλ-
bed undefiled, fornicators but and adulterers will judge God. With-

3588 5158 714 3588 3918 846
άργυρος ὁ τρόπος, ἀρκούμενοι τοῖς παροῦσιν· αὐτὸς
out money-loving (be) the way of life, being satisfied with the things present; He

1063 2046 3756 3361 4571 44 3761 3756 3361 4571 1459 5620
γὰρ εἴρηκεν, Οὐ μή σε ἀνῶ, οὐδ᾽ οὐ μή σε ἐγκαταλίπω. 6 ὥστε
for has said, Not at all you I will leave, not at all you I will forsake. So as

2292 2248 3004 2962 1698 998 2532 3756 5399
θαρροῦντας ἡμᾶς λέγειν, Κύριος ἐμοὶ βοηθός, καὶ οὐ φοβηθή-
may confidently we say, (The) Lord of me (is) a helper, and not I will be

5101 4160 3427 444
σομαι τί ποιήσει μοι ἄνθρωπος;
afraid what will do to me men?

3421 3588 2233 5216 3748 2980 5213
7. Μνημονεύετε τῶν ἡγουμένων ὑμῶν, οἵτινες ἐλάλησαν ὑμῖν
Remember the leaders of you, who spoke to you

3588 3056 3588 2316 3739 333 3588 1545 3588
τὸν λόγον τοῦ Θεοῦ· ὧν ἀναθεωροῦντες τὴν ἔκβασιν τῆς
the Word of God; of whom considering the issue of the

391 3401 3588 4102 2424 5547 5504 2532
ἀναστροφῆς, μιμεῖσθε τὴν πίστιν. 8 Ἰησοῦς Χριστὸς χθὲς καὶ
behavior, imitate (their) faith. Jesus Christ yesterday and

4594 3588 846 2532 1519 3588 165 1322 4164 2532
σήμερον ὁ αὐτός, καὶ εἰς τοὺς αἰῶνας. 9 διδαχαῖς ποικίλαις καὶ
today (is) the same, even to the ages. doctrines By various and

3581 3361 4064 2570 1063 5485 950 3588
ξέναις μὴ περαφέρεσθε· καλὸν γὰρ χάριτι βεβαιοῦσθαι τὴν
strange not be carried away; good for by grace to be confirmed the

King James Version

1. Let brotherly love continue.
2 Be not forgetful to entertain strangers: for thereby some have entertained angels unawares.
3 Remember them that are in bonds, as bound with them; (and) them which suffer adversity, as being yourselves also in the body.
4 Marriage (is) honourable in all, and the bed undefiled: but whoremongers and adulterers God will judge.
5 (Let your) conversation (be) without covetousness; (and be) content with such things as ye have: for he hath said, I will never leave thee, nor forsake thee.
6 So that we may boldly say, The Lord (is) my helper, and I will not fear what man shall do unto me.

7. Remember them which have the rule over you, who have spoken unto you the word of God: whose faith follow, consider-ing the end of (their) conversation.
8 Jesus Christ the same yesterday, and to day, and for ever.
9 Be not carried about with divers and strange doctrines. For (it is) a good thing that the heart be established

Literal Translation **Hebrews 13:9** ***King James Version***

not by foods, in which those walking (in them) were not profited.

10 We have an altar of which those serving the tabernacle have no authority to eat.
11 For of the animals (whose) blood is brought by the high priest into the Holies concerning sins, of these the bodies are burned outside the camp.
12 Because of this also, in order that He might, sanctify the people by (His) own blood, Jesus suffered outside the gate.
13 So let us go forth to Him outside the camp bearing His reproach.
14 For we do not have here a continuing city, but we seek the (one) coming.
15 Then through Him let us offer up a sacrifice of praise to God always, that is, (the) fruit of the lips, confessing to His name.

16. But do not be forgetful of doing good and sharing, for God is well pleased with such sacrifices.
17 Yield to those taking the lead of you, and submit, for they watch for your souls, giving an account, that they may do this with joy, and not (with) grieving; for this (would be) no profit to you.

18 Pray for us, for we are persuaded that we have a good conscience, in all things wishing to behave well.

19 But I much more urge (you) to do this that I may sooner be restored to you.

2588 3756 1033 1722 3739 3756 5623 3588 4043
καρδίαν, οὐ βρώμασιν, ἐν οἷς οὐκ ὠφελήθησαν οἱ περιπατή-
heart, not by foods, by which not were profited the (ones) having

2192 2379 1537 3739 5315 3756 2192
σαντες. 10 ἔχομεν θυσιαστήριον, ἐξ οὗ φαγεῖν οὐκ ἔχουσιν
walked (in these). We have an altar, of which to eat not have

1849 3588 3588 4633 3000 3739 1063 1533 2226
ἐξουσίαν οἱ τῇ σκηνῇ λατρεύοντες. 11 ὧν γὰρ εἰσφέρεται ζώων
authority those in the tabernacle serving. of what For is brought animals

3588 129 4012 266 1519 3588 39 1223 3588 749 5130
τὸ αἷμα περὶ ἁμαρτίας εἰς τὰ ἅγια διὰ τοῦ ἀρχιερέως, τούτων
the blood concerning sins into the Holies through the high priest, of these

3588 4983 2618 1854 3588 3925 1352 2532
τὰ σώματα κατακαίεται ἔξω τῆς παρεμβολῆς. 12 διὸ καὶ
the bodies are burned outside the camp. Because of this also

2424 2443 37 1223 3588 2398 129 3588 2992 1854
Ἰησοῦς, ἵνα ἁγιάσῃ διὰ τοῦ ἰδίου αἵματος τὸν λαόν, ἔξω
Jesus, that He might sanctify through the own blood the people, outside

3588 4439 3958 5106 1831 4314 846 1854 3588
τῆς πύλης ἔπαθε. 13 τοίνυν ἐξερχώμεθα πρὸς αὐτὸν ἔξω τῆς
the gate suffered. So let us go forth to Him outside the

3925 3588 3680 846 5342 3756 1063 2192
παρεμβολῆς, τὸν ὀνειδισμὸν αὐτοῦ φέροντες. 14 οὐ γὰρ ἔχομεν
camp, the reproach of Him bearing. not For we have

5602 3306 4172 235 3588 3195 1934 1223
ὧδε μένουσαν πόλιν, ἀλλὰ τὴν μέλλουσαν ἐπιζητοῦμεν. 15 δι'
here a continuing city, but the (one) coming we seek. Through

846 3767 399 2378 133 1223 3956 3588 2316
αὐτοῦ οὖν ἀναφέρωμεν θυσίαν αἰνέσεως διὰ παντὸς τῷ Θεῷ,
Him, therefore, let us offer up a sacrifice of praise through all to God,

5123 2076 2590 5491 3670 3588 3686
τοῦτ' ἔστι καρπὸν χειλέων ὁμολογούντων τῷ ὀνόματι
this is (the) fruit of the lips confessing to the name

846 3588 1161 2140 2532 2842 3361 2100
αὐτοῦ. 16 τῆς δὲ εὐποιΐας καὶ κοινωνίας μὴ ἐπιλανθάνεσθε·
of Him. of the But doing good and sharing not be forgetful;

5108 1063 2378 2100 3588 2316 3982 3588
τοιαύταις γὰρ θυσίαις εὐαρεστεῖται ὁ Θεός. 17 πείθεσθε τοῖς
with such for sacrifices is well-pleased God. Obey those

2233 5216 2532 5226 846 1063 69
ἡγουμένοις ὑμῶν, καὶ ὑπείκετε· αὐτοὶ γὰρ ἀγρυπνοῦσιν
taking the lead of you, and submit to (them); they for watch

5228 3588 5590 5216 5613 3056 591 2443 3326
ὑπὲρ τῶν ψυχῶν ὑμῶν, ὡς λόγον ἀποδώσοντες· ἵνα μετὰ
on behalf of the souls of you, as an account giving; that with

5479 5124 4160 2532 3361 4727 255 1063
χαρᾶς τοῦτο ποιῶσι, καὶ μὴ στενάζοντες· ἀλυσιτελὲς γὰρ
joy this they may do, and not (with) grieving; profitless for

5213 5124
ὑμῖν τοῦτο.
to you this (would be).

4336 4012 2257 3982 1063 3754 2570
18. Προσεύχεσθε περὶ ἡμῶν· πεποίθαμεν γὰρ ὅτι καλὴν
Pray concerning us; we are persuaded for that a good

4893 2192 1722 3956 2573 2309 390
συνείδησιν ἔχομεν, ἐν πᾶσι καλῶς θέλοντες ἀναστρέφεσθαι.
conscience we have, in all well desiring to conduct (ourselves).

4056 1161 3870 5124 4160 2443 5032
19 περισσοτέρως δὲ παρακαλῶ τοῦτο ποιῆσαι, ἵνα τάχιον
more abundantly But I exhort (you) this to do, that sooner

600 5213
ἀποκατασταθῶ ὑμῖν.
I may be restored to you.

with grace; not with meats, which have not profited them that have been occupied therein.

10 We have an altar, whereof they have no right to eat which serve the tabernacle.
11 For the bodies of those beasts, whose blood is brought into the sanctuary by the high priest for sin, are burned without the camp.
12 Wherefore Jesus also, that he might sanctify the people with his own blood, suffered without the gate.

13 Let us go forth therefore unto him without the camp, bearing his reproach.
14 For here have we no continuing city, but we seek one to come.
15 By him therefore let us offer the sacrifice of praise to God continually, that is, the fruit of (our) lips giving thanks to his name.

16. But to do good and to communicate forget not: for with such sacrifices God is well pleased.
17 Obey them that have the rule over you, and submit yourselves: for they watch for your souls, as they that must give account, that they may do it with joy, and not with grief: for that (is) unprofitable for you.

18 Pray for us: for we trust we have a good conscience, in all things willing to live honestly.

19 But I beseech (you) the rather to do this, that I may be restored to you the sooner.

Literal Translation

Hebrews 13:20

King James Version

20 Now the God of peace, He having led up out of (the) dead, the great Shepherd of the sheep, in (the) blood of (the) everlasting covenant, our Lord Jesus,
21 perfect you in every good work, in order to do His will, doing in you that (which) is pleasing before Him, through Jesus Christ, to whom (be) the glory to the ages of the ages. Amen.

3588 1161 2316 3588 1515 3588 321 1537 3498
20. Ὁ δὲ Θεὸς τῆς εἰρήνης, ὁ ἀναγαγὼν ἐκ νεκρῶν
the Now God of peace, the (One) having led out of (the) dead
3588 4166 3588 4263 3588 3173 1722 129 1242
τὸν ποιμένα τῶν προβάτων τὸν μέγαν ἐν αἵματι διαθήκης
the Shepherd of the sheep great in (the) blood of the covenant
166 3588 2962 2257 2424 2675 5209 1722
αἰωνίου, τὸν Κύριον ἡμῶν Ἰησοῦν, 21 καταρτίσαι ὑμᾶς ἐν
eternal, the Lord of us Jesus, perfect you in
3956 2041 18 1519 3588 4160 3588 2307 846 4160
παντὶ ἔργῳ ἀγαθῷ εἰς τὸ ποιῆσαι τὸ θέλημα αὐτοῦ, ποιῶν
every work good for the to do the will of Him, doing
1722 5213 3588 2101 1799 846 1223 2424 5547
ἐν ἡμῖν τὸ εὐάρεστον ἐνώπιον αὐτοῦ, διὰ Ἰησοῦ Χριστοῦ·
in you the thing pleasing before Him, through Jesus Christ;
3739 3588 1391 1515 3588 165 3588 165 281
ᾧ ἡ δόξα εἰς τοὺς αἰῶνας τῶν αἰώνων. ἀμήν.
to whom (be) the glory to the ages of the ages. Amen.

20 Now the God of peace, that brought again from the dead our Lord Jesus, that great shepherd of the sheep, through the blood of the everlasting covenant,
21 Make you perfect in every good work to do his will, working in you that which is wellpleasing in his sight, through Jesus Christ; to whom (be) glory for ever and ever. Amen.

22. And, brothers, I exhort you, endure the word of exhortation, for I indeed wrote to you by (a) few (words).
23 You know the brother, Timothy, having been freed, with whom if he comes sooner, I will see you.

3870 1161 5209 80 430 3588 3056 3588
22. Παρακαλῶ δὲ ὑμᾶς, ἀδελφοί, ἀνέχεσθε τοῦ λόγου τῆς
I exhort And you, brothers, endure the word
3875 2532 1063 1223 1024 1989 5213 1097
παρακλήσεως· καὶ γὰρ διὰ βραχέων ἐπέστειλα ὑμῖν. 23 γινώ-
of exhortation; indeed for through few (words) I wrote to you. Know
3588 80 5095 630 3326 3739 1437 5032
σκετε τὸν ἀδελφὸν Τιμόθεον ἀπολελυμένον, μεθ' οὗ, ἐὰν τάχιον
the brother Timothy, having been freed, with whom, if sooner
2064 3700 5209
ἔρχηται, ὄψομαι ὑμᾶς.
he comes, I will see you.

22. And I beseech you, brethren, suffer the word of exhortation: for I have written a letter unto you in few words.
23 Know ye that (our) brother Timothy is set at liberty; with whom, if he come shortly, I will see you.

24 Greet all those leading you, also all the saints. Those from Italy greet you.

782 3956 3588 2233 5216 2532 3956
24. Ἀσπάσασθε πάντας τοὺς ἡγουμένους ὑμῶν, καὶ πάντας
Greet all the (ones) leading of you, and all
3588 40 782 5209 3588 575 3588 2482
τοὺς ἁγίους. ἀσπάζονται ὑμᾶς οἱ ἀπὸ τῆς Ἰταλίας.
the saints. greet you Those from Italy.

24 Salute all them that have the rule over you, and all the saints. They of Italy salute you.

25 Grace (be) with you all. Amen.

3588 5485 3326 3956 5216 281
25 Ἡ χάρις μετὰ πάντων ὑμῶν. ἀμήν.
Grace (be) with all of you. Amen.

25 Grace (be) with you all. Amen. (Written to the Hebrews from Italy, by Timothy.)

Literal Translation

THE GENERAL EPISTLE OF JAMES

James 1

1. James, a slave of God and of (the) Lord Jesus Christ, to the twelve tribes in the Dispersion, greeting:

2 My brothers count (it) all joy when you fall into various trials,

3 knowing that the proving of your faith works patience.
4 But let patience have its perfective work, that you may be perfect and complete, lacking nothing.

5 But if any of you lacks wisdom, let him ask from God, (who) gives to all freely and not reproaching, and it will be given to him.

6 But let him ask in faith, doubting nothing. For the (one) who doubts is like a wave of (the) sea, being driven by wind and being tossed;

7 for do not let that man suppose that he will receive anything from the Lord;
8 (he is) a double-minded man, not dependable in all his ways.

9 But let (the) lowly brother rejoice in his exaltation;
10 and the rich one (rejoice) in his humiliation, because he will pass away like the flower of the grass.
11 For the sun rose with the hot wind and dried out the grass, and its flower fell out, and the beauty of its appearance perished; so also the rich one

ΙΑΚΩΒΟΥ
OF JAMES
ΕΠΙΣΤΟΛΗ ΚΑΘΟΛΙΚΗ
EPISTLE GENERAL

James 1

2385 2316 2532 2962 2424 5547 1401 3588
1. Ἰάκωβος, Θεοῦ καὶ Κυρίου Ἰησοῦ Χριστοῦ δοῦλος, ταῖς
James, of God and of (the) Lord Jesus Christ, a slave, to the
1427 5443 3588 1722 3588 1290 5463
δώδεκα φυλαῖς ταῖς ἐν τῃ διασπορᾷ, χαίρειν.
twelve tribes in the Dispersion, to greet.

3956 5479 2233 80 3450 3752 3986
2. Πᾶσαν χαρὰν ἡγήσασθε, ἀδελφοί μου, ὅταν πειρασμοῖς
all joy Count (it), brothers of me, when temptations
4045 4164 1097 3754 3588 1383 5216 3588
περιπέσητε ποικίλοις, 3 γινώσκοντες ὅτι τὸ δοκίμιον ὑμῶν τῆς
you fall into various, knowing that the proving of you the
4102 2716 5281 3588 1161 5281 2041
πίστεως κατεργάζεται ὑπομονήν· 4 ἡ δὲ ὑπομονὴ ἔργον
faith works patience; and patience work
5046 2192 2443 5600 5046 2532 3648 1722 3367
τέλειον ἐχέτω, ἵνα ἦτε τέλειοι καὶ ὁλόκληροι, ἐν μηδενὶ
perfective let it have, that you may be perfect and complete, in nothing
3007
λειπόμενοι.
having lacked.

1487/1161/5100/5216 3007 4678 154 3844 3588 1325
5 Εἰ δέ τις ὑμῶν λείπεται σοφίας, αἰτείτω παρὰ τοῦ διδόντος
if But any of you lacks wisdom, let him ask from giving
2316 3956 574 2532 3361 3679 2532 1325 846
θεοῦ πᾶσιν ἁπλῶς, καὶ μὴ ὀνειδίζοντος, καὶ δοθήσεται αὐτῷ.
God to all freely, and not reproaching, and it will be given to him.
154 1161 1722 4102 3367 1252 3588 1063 1252
6 αἰτείτω δὲ ἐν πίστει, μηδὲν διακρινόμενος· ὁ γὰρ διακρινό-
let him ask But in faith, nothing doubting; the (one) for doubting
1503 2830 2281 416 2532 4494
μενος ἔοικε κλύδωνι θαλάσσης ἀνεμιζομένῳ καὶ ῥιπιζομένῳ.
(is) like a wave of (the) sea, being driven by wind and being tossed.
3361 1063 3663 3588 444 1565 3754 2983 5100 3844
7 μὴ γὰρ οἰέσθω ὁ ἄνθρωπος ἐκεῖνος ὅτι λήψεταί τι παρὰ
not For let suppose man that that he will receive anything from
3588 2962 435 1374 182 1722 3956 3588
τοῦ Κυρίου. 8 ἀνὴρ δίψυχος, ἀκατάστατος ἐν πάσαις ταῖς
the Lord. (He is) a man double-minded, undependable in all the
3598 846
ὁδοῖς αὐτοῦ.
ways of him.

2744 1161 3588 80 3588 5011 1722 3588 5311 846 3588
9. Καυχάσθω δὲ ὁ ἀδελφὸς ὁ ταπεινὸς ἐν τῷ ὕψει αὐτοῦ· 10 ὁ
let boast But the brother lowly in the exaltation of him; the
1161 4145 1722 3588 5014 846 3754 5613 438 5528
δὲ πλούσιος ἐν τῇ ταπεινώσει αὐτοῦ· ὅτι ὡς ἄνθος χόρτου
and rich one in the humiliation of him; because as a flower of grass
3928 393 1063 3588 2246 4862 3588 2742 2532
παρελεύσεται. 11 ἀνέτειλε γὰρ ὁ ἥλιος σὺν τῷ καύσωνι, καὶ
he will pass away. rose For the sun with the hot wind, and
3583 3588 5528 2532 3588 438 846 1601 2532 3588 2143
ἐξήρανε τὸν χόρτον, καὶ τὸ ἄνθος αὐτοῦ ἐξέπεσε, καὶ ἡ εὐπρέ-
dried out the grass, and the flower of it fell out, and the beauty
3588 4383 846 622 3779 2532 3588 4145
πεια τοῦ προσώπου αὐτοῦ ἀπώλετο· οὕτω καὶ ὁ πλούσιος
of the appearance of it perished; so also the rich one

King James Version

THE GENERAL EPISTLE OF JAMES

James 1

1. James, a servant of God and of the Lord Jesus Christ, to the twelve tribes which are scattered abroad, greeting.

2 My brethren, count it all joy when ye fall into divers temptations;

3 Knowing (this), that the trying of your faith worketh patience.
4 But let patience have (her) perfect work, that ye may be perfect and entire, wanting nothing.

5 If any of you lack wisdom, let him ask of God, that giveth to all (men) liberally, and upbraideth not; and it shall be given him.

6 But let him ask in faith, nothing wavering. For he that wavereth is like a wave of the sea driven with the wind and tossed.

7 For let not that man think that he shall receive any thing of the Lord.
8 A double minded man (is) unstable in all his ways.

9 Let the brother of low degree rejoice in that he is exalted:
10 But the rich, in that he is made low: because as the flower of the grass he shall pass away.
11 For the sun is no sooner risen with a burning heat, but it withereth the grass, and the flower thereof falleth, and the grace of the fashion of it perisheth: so also shall the rich man

Literal Translation | **James 1:12** | **King James Version**

Literal Translation

will fade away in his
ways. (Isa.40:6,7)

12. Blessed (is) the
man who endures temp-
tation, because having
been approved he will
receive the crown of
life, which the Lord
promised to the ones
loving Him.
13 Let no one being
tempted say, I am
tempted from God. For
God is not tempted by
evils, and He tempts no
one.

14 But each one is
tempted by his own
lusts, having been
drawn out and having
been seduced (by
them).
15 Then being con-
ceived, lust brings forth
sin. And sin being fully
formed brings forth
death.
16 Do not go astray, my
beloved brothers,
17 every (act of) good
giving and every per-
fect gift is from above,
coming down from the
Father of lights, with
whom is no variation or
shadow of turning.
18 Having purposed,
He brought us forth by
(the) Word of truth, for
us to be a certain first-
fruit of His creatures.

19. So that, my be-
loved brothers, let every
man be swift to hear,
slow to speak, slow to
wrath.
20 For (the) wrath of
man does not work out
(the) righteousness of
God.
21 On account of this,
putting away all filthi-
ness and overflowing of
evil, in meekness re-
ceive the implanted
Word being able to save
your souls.
22. But become doers
of (the) Word, and not
hearers only, deceiving
yourselves.
23 Because if anyone
(is) a hearer

James 1:12

1722 3588 4197 846 3313
ἐν ταῖς πορείαις αὐτοῦ μαρανθήσεται.
in the ways of him will fade away.

3107 435 3739 5278 3986 3754 1384
12. Μακάριος ἀνὴρ ὃς ὑπομένει πειρασμόν· ὅτι δόκιμος
Blessed (the) man who endures temptation; because approved
1096 2983 3588 4735 3588 2222 3739 1861 3588
γενόμενος λήψεται τὸν στέφανον τῆς ζωῆς, ὃν ἐπηγγείλατο ὁ
having become he will receive the crown of life, which promised the
2962 3588 25 846 3367 3985 3004
Κύριος τοῖς ἀγαπῶσιν αὐτόν. 13 μηδεὶς πειραζόμενος λεγέτω
Lord to the (ones) loving Him. no one being tempted Let say,
3754 575 3588 2316 3985 3588 1063 2316 551 2076
ὅτι Ἀπὸ τοῦ Θεοῦ πειράζομαι· ὁ γὰρ Θεὸς ἀπείραστός ἐστι
I am of God tempted; for God not tempted is
2556 3985 1161 846 3762 1538 1161 3985
κακῶν, πειράζει δὲ αὐτὸς οὐδένα· 14 ἕκαστος δὲ πειράζεται,
by evils, tempts and He no one; each one but is tempted,
5259 3588 2398 1939 1828 2532 1185 1534
ὑπὸ τῆς ἰδίας ἐπιθυμίας ἐξελκόμενος καὶ δελεαζόμενος· 15 εἶτα
by the own lusts being drawn out and being seduced; then
3588 1939 4815 5088 266 3588 1161 266
ἡ ἐπιθυμία συλλαβοῦσα τίκτει ἁμαρτίαν· ἡ δὲ ἁμαρτία
lust having conceived produces sin; and sin
658 616 2288 3361 4105 80
ἀποτελεσθεῖσα ἀποκύει θάνατον. 16 μὴ πλανᾶσθε, ἀδελφοί
being fully formed brings forth death. not Do go astray, brothers
3450 27 3956 1394 18 2532 3956 1434 5046
μου ἀγαπητοί. 17 πᾶσα δόσις ἀγαθὴ καὶ πᾶν δώρημα τέλειον
of me beloved. Every giving good and every gift perfect
509 2076 2597 575 3588 3962 3588 5457 3844
ἄνωθέν ἐστι, καταβαῖνον ἀπὸ τοῦ πατρὸς τῶν φώτων, παρ᾽
from above is, coming down from the Father of lights, with
3739 3756 1762 3883 2228 5157 644 1014
ᾧ οὐκ ἔνι παραλλαγή, ἢ τροπῆς ἀποσκίασμα. 18 βουληθεὶς
whom not is variation, or of turning shadow. Having purposed
616 2248 3056 225 1519 3588 1511 2248 536
ἀπεκύησεν ἡμᾶς λόγῳ ἀληθείας, εἰς τὸ εἶναι ἡμᾶς ἀπαρχήν
He brought forth us by a Word of truth, for to be us firstfruit
5100 3588 846 2938
τινα τῶν αὐτοῦ κτισμάτων.
a certain of the of Him creatures.

5620 80 3450 27 2077 3956 444 5036
19. Ὥστε, ἀδελφοί μου ἀγαπητοί, ἔστω πᾶς ἄνθρωπος ταχὺς
So that, brothers of me beloved, let be every man swift
1519 3588 191 1021 1519 3588 2980 1021 1519 3709
εἰς τὸ ἀκοῦσαι, βραδὺς εἰς τὸ λαλῆσαι, βραδὺς εἰς ὀργήν·
for to hear, slow for to speak, slow to wrath;
3709 1063 435 1343 2316 3756 2716 1352
20 ὀργὴ γὰρ ἀνδρὸς δικαιοσύνην θεοῦ οὐ κατεργάζεται. 21 διὸ
(the) wrath for of man (the) righteousness of God not works. Therefore
659 3956 4507 2532 4050 2549 1722 4240
ἀποθέμενοι πᾶσαν ῥυπαρίαν καὶ περισσείαν κακίας, ἐν πραΰ-
putting away all filthiness and overflowing of evil, in meek-
1209 3588 1721 3056 3588 1410 4982 3588
τητι δέξασθε τὸν ἔμφυτον λόγον, τὸν δυνάμενον σῶσαι τὰς
ness receive the implanted Word, being able to save the
5590 5216 1096 1161 4163 3056 2532 3361 3440
ψυχὰς ὑμῶν. 22 γίνεσθε δὲ ποιηταὶ λόγου, καὶ μὴ μόνον
soul of you. become And doers of the Word, and not only
202 3884 1438 3754 1487 5100 202
ἀκροαταὶ παραλογιζόμενοι ἑαυτούς. 23 ὅτι εἴ τις ἀκροατὴς
hearers, deceiving yourselves. Because if anyone a hearer

King James Version

fade away in his ways.

12. Blessed (is) the
man that endureth
temptation: for when he
is tried, he shall receive
the crown of life, which
the Lord hath promised
to them that love him.

13 Let no man say when
he is tempted, I am
tempted of God: for
God cannot be tempted
with evil, neither temp-
teth he any man:

14 But every man is
tempted, when he is
drawn away of his own
lust, and enticed.
15 Then when lust hath
conceived, it bringeth
forth sin: and sin, when
it is finished, bringeth
forth death.

16 Do not err, my be-
loved brethren.

17 Every good gift and
every perfect gift is
from above, and
cometh down from the
Father of lights, with
whom is no variable-
ness, neither shadow of
turning.
18 Of his own will begat
he us with the word of
truth, that we should be
a kind of firstfruits of his
creatures.

19. Wherefore, my be-
loved brethren, let every
man be swift to hear,
slow to speak, slow to
wrath:

20 For the wrath of man
worketh not the right-
eousness of God.
21 Wherefore lay apart
all filthiness and super-
fluity of naught-iness,
and receive with meek-
ness the engrafted
word, which is able to
save your souls.

22. But be ye doers of
the word, and not hear-
ers only, deceiving your
own selves.
23 For if any be a hearer

James 1:24

Literal Translation

of (the) Word, and not a doer, this one is like a man considering his natural face in a mirror; 24 for he considered himself, and has gone away, and immediately (he) forgot of what kind he was.

25 But the (one) looking into the perfect law of freedom, and continuing (in it), this one not having become a forgetful hearer, but a doer of (the) work, this one will be blessed in his doing.

26. If anyone thinks to be religious among you, (yet) not bridling his tongue, but deceiving his heart, this one's religion (is) vain.

27 Pure and undefiled religion before God and (the) Father (is) this: to visit orphans and widows in their afflictions, (and) to keep oneself unspotted from the world.

3056 2076 2532 3756 4163 3778 1503 435 2657
λόγου ἐστὶ καὶ οὐ ποιητής, οὗτος ἔοικεν ἀνδρὶ κατανοοῦντι
of (the) Word is and not a doer, this one is like a man considering

3588 4383 3588 1078 846 1722 2072 2657
τὸ πρόσωπον τῆς γενέσεως αὐτοῦ ἐν ἐσόπτρῳ· 24 κατενόησε
the face of the natural of him in a mirror; he considered

1063 1438 2532 565 2532 2112 1953 3697 2258
γὰρ ἑαυτὸν καὶ ἀπελήλυθε, καὶ εὐθέως ἐπελάθετο ὁποῖος ἦν.
for himself and has gone away, and immediately forgot what sort he was.

3588 1161 3879 1519 3551 5046 3588 3588 1657 2532
25 ὁ δὲ παρακύψας εἰς νόμον τέλειον τὸν τῆς ἐλευθερίας καὶ
he But having looked into law perfect the of freedom and

3887 3778 3756 202 1953 1096
παραμείνας, οὗτος οὐκ ἀκροατὴς ἐπιλησμονῆς γενόμενος
continuing, this one not a hearer of forgetfulness having been

235 4163 2041 3778 3107 1722 3588 4162 846
ἀλλὰ ποιητὴς ἔργου, οὗτος μακάριος ἐν τῇ ποιήσει αὐτοῦ
but a doer of (the) work, this one blessed in the doing of him

2071 1487 5100 1380 2357 1511 1722 5213 3361 5468
ἔσται. 26 εἴ τις δοκεῖ θρῆσκος εἶναι ἐν ὑμῖν, μὴ χαλιναγωγῶν
is. If anyone thinks religious to be among you, not bridling

1100 846 235 538 2588 846 5127
γλῶσσαν αὐτοῦ, ἀλλ' ἀπατῶν καρδίαν αὐτοῦ, τούτου
the tongue of him, but deceiving (the) heart of himself, this one's

3152 3588 2356 2356 2513 2532 283 3844
μάταιος ἡ θρησκεία. 27 θρησκεία καθαρὰ καὶ ἀμίαντος παρὰ
vain the religion (is) religion Pure and undefiled before

3588 2316 2532 3962 3778 2076 1980 3737 2532
τῷ Θεῷ καὶ πατρὶ αὕτη ἐστίν, ἐπισκέπτεσθαι ὀρφανοὺς καὶ
the God and Father this is, to visit orphans and

5503 1722 3588 2347 846 784 1438 5083 575 3588
χήρας ἐν τῇ θλίψει αὐτῶν, ἄσπιλον ἑαυτὸν τηρεῖν ἀπὸ τοῦ
widows in the affliction of them, unspotted himself to keep from the

2889
κόσμου.
world.

King James Version

of the word, and not a doer, he is like unto a man beholding his natural face in a glass: 24 For he beholdeth himself, and goeth his way, and straightway forgetteth what manner of man he was.

25 But whoso looketh into the perfect law of liberty, and continueth (therein), he being not a forgetful hearer, but a doer of the work, this man shall be blessed in his deed.

26. If any man among you seem to be religious, and bridleth not his tongue, but deceiveth his own heart, this man's religion (is) vain.

27 Pure religion and undefiled before God and the Father is this, To visit the fatherless and widows in their affliction, (and) to keep himself unspotted from the world.

James 2

Literal Translation

1. My brothers, do not with partiality have the faith of our Lord Jesus Christ, the (Lord) of glory.
2 For if a gold-fingered man in splendid clothing comes into your synagogue, and also a poor one in shabby clothing also comes in;

3 and you look on the one wearing the splendid clothing, and say to him, You sit here comfortably; and to the poor one you say, You stand there, or, Sit here under my footstool;
4 did you not even make a difference among yourselves and become judges

80 3450 3361 1722 4382 2192 3588 4102
1. Ἀδελφοί μου, μὴ ἐν προσωποληψίαις ἔχετε τὴν πίστιν
Brothers of me, not in partiality to have the faith

3588 2962 2257 2424 5547 3588 1391 1437 1063 1525
τοῦ Κυρίου ἡμῶν Ἰησοῦ Χριστοῦ τῆς δόξης. 2 ἐὰν γὰρ εἰσ-
of the Lord of us Jesus Christ of the (Lord) of glory. if For

1519 3588 4864 5216 435 5554 1722
έλθῃ εἰς τὴν συναγωγὴν ὑμῶν ἀνὴρ χρυσοδακτύλιος ἐν
comes into the synagogue of you a man gold-fingered in

2066 2986 1525 1161 2532 4434 1722 4508 2066
ἐσθῆτι λαμπρᾷ, εἰσέλθῃ δὲ καὶ πτωχὸς ἐν ῥυπαρᾷ ἐσθῆτι,
clothing splendid, comes in and also a poor one in shabby clothing,

2532 1914 1909 3588 5409 3588 2066 3588 2986
3 καὶ ἐπιβλέψητε ἐπὶ τὸν φοροῦντα τὴν ἐσθῆτα τὴν λαμπρὰν,
and you look on the (one) wearing the clothing splendid,

2532 2036 846 4771 2521 5602 2573 2532 3588 4434
καὶ εἴπητε αὐτῷ, Σὺ κάθου ὧδε καλῶς, καὶ τῷ πτωχῷ
and say to him, You sit here well, and to the poor one

2036 4771 2476 1563 2228 2521 5602 5259 3588 5286 3450
εἴπητε, Σὺ στῆθι ἐκεῖ, ἢ κάθου ὧδε ὑπὸ τὸ ὑποπόδιόν μου·
you say, You stand there, or sit here under the footstool of me;

2532 3756 1252 1722 1438 2532 1096 2923
4 καὶ οὐ διεκρίθητε ἐν ἑαυτοῖς, καὶ ἐγένεσθε κριταὶ
even did not make a difference among yourselves, and became judges

King James Version

1. My brethren, have not the faith of our Lord Jesus Christ, (the Lord) of glory, with respect of persons.
2 For if there come unto your assembly a man with a gold ring, in goodly apparel, and there come in also a poor man in vile raiment;

3 And ye have respect to him that weareth the gay clothing, and say unto him, Sit thou here in a good place; and say to the poor, Stand thou there, or sit here under my footstool:

4 Are ye not then partial in yourselves, and are become judges

Literal Translation | **James 2:5** | **King James Version**

(with) evil thoughts?

5 Hear, my beloved brothers, did not God choose out the poor of this world to be rich in faith, and heirs of the kingdom which He promised to the ones loving Him?

6 But you dishonored the poor one. Do not the rich ones oppress you, and they drag you to judgment seats?

7 Do they not blaspheme the good Name called on you?

8 If you truly fulfill (the) royal law according to the Scripture, "You shall love your neighbor as yourself," you do well. (Lev. 19:18)

9 But if you show partiality (to persons), you work sin, having been found guilty as transgressors by the law.

10 For whoever shall keep the whole law, but stumbles in one, he has become guilty of all.

11 For He who said, "You shall not commit adultery," also said, "You shall not murder." (Ex. 20:13, 14) But if you do not commit adultery, but commit murder, you have become a transgressor of (the) law.

12 So speak and so do as being about to be judged by (the) law of liberty.

13 For the judgment (will be) without mercy to the (one) not doing mercy. And mercy rejoices over judgment.

14. My brothers, what (is) the gain if anyone says he has faith, but he does not have works? Is faith able to save him?

15 But if a brother or a sister is naked and may be lacking in daily food,

16 and any one of you say to them, Go in peace, be warmed and filled, but does not give them

---

1261 4190 191 80 3450 27 3756
διαλογισμῶν πονηρῶν; 5 ἀκούσατε, ἀδελφοί μου ἀγαπητοί. οὐχ
thoughts of evil? Hear, brothers of me beloved. Not

3588 2316 1586 3588 4434 3588 2889 5127 4145
ὁ Θεὸς ἐξελέξατο τοὺς πτωχοὺς τοῦ κόσμου τούτου, πλουσίους
did God choose out the poor world of this, rich

1722 4102 2532 2818 3588 932 3739 1861
ἐν πίστει, καὶ κληρονόμους τῆς βασιλείας ἧς ἐπηγγείλατο
in faith, and heirs of the kingdom which He promised

3588 25 846 5210 1161 818 3588 4434 3756
τοῖς ἀγαπῶσιν αὐτόν; 6 ὑμεῖς δὲ ἠτιμάσατε τὸν πτωχόν. οὐχ
to those loving Him? you But dishonored the poor one. Not

3588 4145 2616 5216 2532 846 1670
οἱ πλούσιοι καταδυναστεύουσιν ὑμῶν, καὶ αὐτοὶ ἕλκουσιν
the rich ones do oppress you, and they drag

5209 1519 2922 3756 846 987 3588 2570 3686
ὑμᾶς εἰς κριτήρια; 7 οὐκ αὐτοὶ βλασφημοῦσι τὸ καλὸν ὄνομα
you to judgment seats? Not they do blaspheme the good name

3588 1941 1909 5209 1487 3305 3551 5055 937
τὸ ἐπικληθὲν ἐφ᾽ ὑμᾶς; 8 εἰ μέντοι νόμον τελεῖτε βασιλικόν,
called upon you? If indeed law you fulfill a royal,

2596 3588 1124 25 3588 4139 4675 5613 4572
κατὰ τὴν γραφήν, Ἀγαπήσεις τὸν πλησίον σου ὡς σεαυ-
according to the Scripture, You shall love the neighbor of you as your-

2573 4160 1487 1161 4380 266 2038
τόν, καλῶς ποιεῖτε· 9 εἰ δὲ προσωποληπτεῖτε, ἁμαρτίαν ἐργά-
self, well you do; if But show partiality, sin you work,

1651 5259 3588 3551 5613 3848 3748 1063
ζεσθε, ἐλεγχόμενοι ὑπὸ τοῦ νόμου ὡς παραβάται. 10 ὅστις γὰρ
being reproved by the law as transgressors. who For

3650 3588 3650 5083 4417 1161 1722 1520 1096 3956
ὅλον τὸν νόμον τηρήσει, πταίσει δὲ ἐν ἑνί, γέγονε πάντων
whole the law keeps, stumbles but in one, he has become of all

1777 3588 1063 2036 3361 3431 2036 2532 3361 5407
ἔνοχος. 11 ὁ γὰρ εἰπών, Μὴ μοιχεύσῃς, εἶπε καί, Μὴ φονεύσῃς·
guilty. the (one) For saying, Not commit adultery, said also, Not do murder;

1487 1161 3756 3431 5407 1161 1096 3848 3551
εἰ δὲ οὐ μοιχεύσεις, φονεύσεις δέ, γέγονας παραβάτης νόμου.
if but not you do adultery, murder but, you have become a transgressor of law.

3779 2980 2532 3779 4160 5613 1223 3551 1657
12 οὕτω λαλεῖτε καὶ οὕτω ποιεῖτε, ὡς διὰ νόμου ἐλευθερίας
So speak and so do, as through a law of freedom

3195 2919 3588 1063 2920 448 3588
μέλλοντες κρίνεσθαι. 13 ἡ γὰρ κρίσις ἀνέλεως τῷ
being about to be judged. the For Judgment (will be) unmerciful to Him

3361 4160 1656 2532 2620 1656 2920
μὴ ποιήσαντι ἔλεος· καὶ κατακαυχᾶται ἔλεος κρίσεως.
not having done mercy; and exults over mercy judgment.

5101 3588 3786 80 3450 1437 4102 3004 5100 2192
14. Τί τὸ ὄφελος, ἀδελφοί μου, ἐὰν πίστιν λέγῃ τις ἔχειν,
What (is) the profit, brothers of me, if faith says anyone to have

2041 1161 3361 2192 3361 1410 3588 4102 4982 846 1437 1161
ἔργα δὲ μὴ ἔχῃ; μὴ δύναται ἡ πίστις σῶσαι αὐτόν; 15 ἐὰν δὲ
works but not has? Not is able the faith to save him? if But

80 2228 79 1131 5225 2532 3007 5600
ἀδελφὸς ἢ ἀδελφὴ γυμνοὶ ὑπάρχωσι καὶ λειπόμενοι ὦσι
a brother or a sister naked are and lacking may be

3588 2184 5160 2036 1161 5100 846 1537 5216 5217
τῆς ἐφημέρου τροφῆς, 16 εἴπῃ δέ τις αὐτοῖς ἐξ ὑμῶν, Ὑπάγετε
of daily food, says and anyone to them of you, Go

1722 1515 2328 2532 5526 3361 1325 1161 846
ἐν εἰρήνῃ, θερμαίνεσθε καὶ χορτάζεσθε, μὴ δῶτε δὲ αὐτοῖς
in peace, be warmed and filled, not you give but them

---

of evil thoughts?

5 Hearken, my beloved brethren, Hath not God chosen the poor of this world rich in faith, and heirs of the kingdom which he hath promised to them that love him?

6 But ye have despised the poor. Do not rich men oppress you, and draw you before the judgment seats?

7 Do not they blaspheme that worthy name by the which ye are called?

8 If ye fulfil the royal law according to the scripture, Thou shalt love thy neighbour as thyself, ye do well:

9 But if ye have respect to persons, ye commit sin, and are convinced of the law as transgressors.

10 For whosoever shall keep the whole law, and yet offend in one (point), he is guilty of all.

11 For he that said, Do not commit adultery, said also, Do not kill. Now if thou commit no adultery, yet if thou kill, thou art become a transgressor of the law.

12 So speak ye, and so do, as they that shall be judged by the law of liberty.

13 For he shall have judgment without mercy, that hath shewed no mercy; and mercy rejoiceth against judgment.

14. What (doth it) profit, my brethren, though a man say he hath faith, and have not works? can faith save him?

15 If a brother or sister be naked, and destitute of daily food,

16 And one of you say unto them, Depart in peace, be (ye) warmed and filled; notwithstanding ye give them

Literal Translation **James 2:17** *King James Version*

the things the body needs, what gain (is it)?
17 So also faith, if it does not have works, is dead (being) by itself.
18 But someone will say, You have faith, and I have works. Show me your faith apart from your works, and I will show you my faith from my works.

19 You believe that God is one. You do well; even the demons believe and tremble.
20 But are you willing to know, O vain man, that faith apart from works is dead?

21 Was not our father Abraham justified by works offering up his son Isaac on the altar? (Gen.22:9)

22 Do you see that faith worked with his works; and out of the works the faith was perfected.
23 And the Scripture was fulfilled, saying, "And Abraham believed God, and it was counted for righteousness to him;" and he was called, "Friend of God." (Gen. 15:6; Isa. 41:8)
24 You see, then, that a man is justified out of works, and not out of faith only.

25 But in the same way Rahab the harlot was also justified out of works, having received the messengers, and sending them out by another way.
26 For as the body apart from the spirit is dead, so also faith apart from works is dead.

3588 2006 3588 4983 5101 3588 3786 3779 2532 3588 4102
τὰ ἐπιτήδεια τοῦ σώματος, τί τὸ ὄφελος; 17 οὕτω καὶ ἡ πίστις,
the necessities of the body, what (is) the profit? So also faith,

1437 3361 2041 2192 3498 2076 2596 1438 235 2046 5100 4771
ἐὰν μὴ ἔργα ἔχῃ, νεκρά ἐστι καθ' ἑαυτήν. 18 ἀλλ' ἐρεῖ τις, Σὺ
if not works has, dead it is by itself. But will say one, You

4102 2192 2504 2041 2192 1166 3427 3588 4102 4675
πίστιν ἔχεις, κἀγὼ ἔργα ἔχω· δεῖξόν μοι τὴν πίστιν σου
faith have, and I works have; show me the faith of you

5665 3588 2041 4675 2504 1166 4671 1537 3588 2041 3450
χωρὶς τῶν ἔργων σου, κἀγώ δείξω σοι ἐκ τῶν ἔργων μου
without the works of you, and I will show you from the works of me

3588 4102 3450 4771 4100 3754 3588 2316 1520 2076 2573
τὴν πίστιν μου. 19 σὺ πιστεύεις ὅτι ὁ θεός εἷς ἐστί· καλῶς
the faith of me. You believe that God one is; well

4160 2532 3588 1140 4100 2532 5425 2309
ποιεῖς· καὶ τὰ δαιμόνια πιστεύουσι, καὶ φρίσσουσι. 20 θέλεις
you do; even the demons believe, and tremble. are you willing

1161 1097 5599 444 2756 3754 3588 4102 5565 3588 2041
δὲ γνῶναι, ὦ ἄνθρωπε κενέ, ὅτι ἡ πίστις χωρὶς τῶν ἔργων
But to know, O man vain, that faith without works

3498 2076 11 3588 3962 2257 3756 1537 2041 1344
νεκρά ἐστιν; 21 Ἀβραὰμ ὁ πατὴρ ἡμῶν οὐκ ἐξ ἔργων ἐδικαιώθη,
dead is? Abraham the father of us not by works Was justified,

399 2464 3588 5207 846 1909 3588 2379
ἀνενέγκας Ἰσαὰκ τὸν υἱὸν αὐτοῦ ἐπὶ τὸ θυσιαστήριον;
offering up Issac the son of him on the altar?

991 3754 3588 4102 4903 3588 2041 846 2532/1537/3588
22 βλέπεις ὅτι ἡ πίστις συνήργει τοῖς ἔργοις αὐτοῦ, καὶ ἐκ τῶν
(Do) you see that faith worked with the works of him, and from the

2041 3588 4102 5048 2532 4137 3588 1124 3588
ἔργων ἡ πίστις ἐτελειώθη; 23 καὶ ἐπληρώθη ἡ γραφὴ ἡ
works the faith was perfected? and was faithful the Scripture

3004 4100 1161 11 3588 2316 2532 3049
λέγουσα, Ἐπίστευσε δὲ Ἀβραὰμ τῷ Θεῷ, καὶ ἐλογίσθη
saying, believed And Abraham God, and it was counted

846 1519 1343 2532 5384 2316 2564 3708 5106
αὐτῷ εἰς δικαιοσύνην, καὶ φίλος Θεοῦ ἐκλήθη. 24 ὁρᾶτε τοίνυν
to him for righteousness, and friend of God he was called. You see then

3754 1537 2041 1344 444 2532 3756 1537 4102 3440
ὅτι ἐξ ἔργων δικαιοῦται ἄνθρωπος, καὶ οὐκ ἐκ πίστεως μόνον.
that from works is justified a man, and not from faith alone.

3668 1161 2532 4460 3588 4204 3756 1537 2041 1344 5264
25 ὁμοίως δὲ καὶ Ῥαὰβ ἡ πόρνη οὐκ ἐξ ἔργων ἐδικαιώθη, ὑποδε-
likewise And also Rahab the harlot not from works was justified, enter-

3588 32 2532 2087 3598 1544 5618
ξαμένη τοὺς ἀγγέλους, καὶ ἑτέρᾳ ὁδῷ ἐκβαλοῦσα; 26 ὥσπερ
taining the messengers, and by another way sending out (them)? as

1063 3588 4983 5565 4151 3498 2076 3779 2532 3588
γὰρ τὸ σῶμα χωρὶς πνεύματος νεκρόν ἐστιν, οὕτω καὶ ἡ
For the body without spirit dead is, so also

4102 5565 3588 2041 3498 2076
πίστις χωρὶς τῶν ἔργων νεκρά ἐστι.
faith without the works dead is.

not those things which are needful to the body; what (doth it) profit?
17 Even so faith, if it hath not works, is dead, being alone.
18 Yea, a man may say, Thou hast faith, and I have works: shew me thy faith without thy works, and I will shew thee my faith by my works.

19 Thou believest that there is one God; thou doest well: the devils also believe, and tremble.
20 But wilt thou know, O vain man, that faith without works is dead?

21 Was not Abraham our father justified by works, when he had offered Isaac his son upon the altar?

22 Seest thou how faith wrought with his works, and by works was faith made perfect?
23 And the scripture was fulfilled which saith, Abraham believed God, and it was imputed unto him for righteousness: and he was called the Friend of God.
24 Ye see then how that by works a man is justified, and not by faith only.

25 Likewise also was not Rahab the harlot justified by works, when she had received the messengers, and had sent (them) out another way?
26 For as the body without the spirit is dead, so faith without works is dead also.

James 3

1. My brothers do not be many teachers, knowing that we will receive greater judgment.
2 For we all stumble (in) many (ways). If

James 3

3361 4183 1320 1096 80 3450 1492 3754
1. Μὴ πολλοὶ διδάσκαλοι γίνεσθε, ἀδελφοί μου, εἰδότες ὅτι
not many teachers Become, brothers of me, knowing that

3187 2917 2983 4183 1063 4417 537 1487
μεῖζον κρίμα ληψόμεθα. 2 πολλὰ γὰρ πταίομεν ἅπαντες. εἴ
greater judgment we will receive. (in) many (ways) For we stumble all. If

James 3

1. My brethren, be not many masters, knowing that we shall receive the greater condemnation.
2 For in many things we offend all. If

Literal Translation

any one does not stumble in word, this (one is) a mature man, able also to bridle the whole body.
3 Behold, we put bits in the mouths of the horses, for them to obey us; and we turn about their whole body.
4 Behold, the ships also, being so great, and being driven by violent winds, (they are) directed by a very small rudder, where the impulse of the (one) steering purposes.
5 So also the tongue is a little member, and boasts great things. Behold, how little a fire kindles how large (a) forest!
6 And the tongue (is) a fire, the world of iniquity. So the tongue is set among our members, spotting all the body, and inflaming the course of nature, and having been inflamed by Hell.
7 For every species of beasts, both indeed of birds, of creeping things, and of sea animals, is tamed, and has been tamed by the human (species);
8 but no one of men is able to tame the tongue; (it is) an evil that cannot be restrained, full of death-dealing poison.
9 By this we bless God and (the) Father; and by this we curse men having come into being according to (the) image of God.
10 Out of the same mouth comes forth blessing and cursing. My brothers it is not fitting (for) these things to be so.
11 (Does) the fountain out of the same hole send forth the sweet and the bitter?
12 My brothers, is a fig tree able to produce olives,

James 3:3

5100 1722 3056 3756 4417 3778 5046 435 1415 5468
τις ἐν λόγῳ οὐ πταίει, οὗτος τέλειος ἀνήρ, δυνατὸς χαλιν-
anyone in word not stumbles, this (is) a mature man, able to

2532 3650 3588 4983 2400 3588 2462 3588 5469
αγωγῆσαι καὶ ὅλον τὸ σῶμα. 3 ἰδού, τῶν ἵππων τοὺς χαλι-
bridle also whole the body. Behold, of the horses the bits

1519 3588 4750 906 4314 3588 3982 846
νοὺς εἰς τὰ στόματα βάλλομεν πρὸς τὸ πείθεσθαι αὐτοὺς
into the mouths we put for to obey them

2254 2532 3650 3588 4983 846 3329 2400 2532 3588
ἡμῖν, καὶ ὅλον τὸ σῶμα αὐτῶν μετάγομεν. 4 ἰδού, καὶ τὰ
us, and whole body of them we turn about. Behold, also the

4143 5082 5607 2532 5259 4642 417 1643
πλοῖα, τηλικαῦτα ὄντα, καὶ ὑπὸ σκληρῶν ἀνέμων ἐλαυνό-
ships, so great being, and by hard winds being

3329 5259 1646 4079 3699 302 3588 3730
μενα, μετάγεται ὑπὸ ἐλαχίστου πηδαλίου, ὅπου ἂν ἡ ὁρμὴ
driven, is directed by a very little rudder, wherever the impulse

3588 2116 1014 3779 2532 3588 1100 3398 3196
τοῦ εὐθύνοντος βούληται. 5 οὕτω καὶ ἡ γλῶσσα μικρὸν μέλος
of the (one) steering purposes. So also the tongue a little member

2076 2532 3166 2400 3641 4442 2245 5208
ἐστὶ, καὶ μεγαλαυχεῖ. Ἰδού, ὀλίγον πῦρ ἡλίκην ὕλην
is, and great things boasts. Behold, how little a fire how great forest

381 2532 3588 1100 4442 3588 2889 3588 93 3779
ἀνάπτει. 6 καὶ ἡ γλῶσσα πῦρ, ὁ κόσμος τῆς ἀδικίας· οὕτως
kindles. Yea, the tongue (is) a fire, the world of iniquity; so

3588 1100 2525 1722 3588 3196 2257 3588 4695
ἡ γλῶσσα καθίσταται ἐν τοῖς μέλεσιν ἡμῶν, ἡ σπιλοῦσα
the tongue is set among the members of us, spotting

3650 3588 4983 2532 5394 3588 5164 3588 1078
ὅλον τὸ σῶμα, καὶ φλογίζουσα τὸν τροχὸν τῆς γενέσεως,
all the body, and inflaming the course of nature,

2532 5394 5259 3588 1067 3956 1063 5449 2342
καὶ φλογιζομένη ὑπὸ τῆς γεέννης. 7 πᾶσα γὰρ φύσις θηρίων
and being inflamed by Gehenna. every For nature of beasts

5037 2532 4071' 2062 5037 2532 1724 1150 2532
τε καὶ πετεινῶν, ἑρπετῶν τε καὶ ἐναλίων, δαμάζεται καὶ
both and of birds, of reptiles both and of sea animals, is tamed and

1150 3588 5449 3588 442 3588 1161 1100
δεδάμασται τῇ φύσει τῇ ἀνθρωπίνῃ· 8 τὴν δὲ γλῶσσαν
has been tamed by the nature human. the But tongue

3762 1410 444 1150 183 2556
οὐδεὶς δύναται ἀνθρώπων δαμάσαι· ἀκατάσχετον κακόν,
no one is able of men to tame; (it is) an unrestrainable evil,

3324 2447 2287 1722 846 2127 3588 2316 2532
μεστὴ ἰοῦ θανατηφόρου. 9 ἐν αὐτῇ εὐλογοῦμεν τὸν Θεὸν καὶ
full of poison death-dealing. By this we bless God and

3962 2532 1722 846 2672 3588 444 3588 2596
πατέρα, καὶ ἐν αὐτῇ καταρώμεθα τοὺς ἀνθρώπους τοὺς καθ'
(the) Father, and by this we curse men according to

3669 2316 1096 1537 3588 846 4750 1831
ὁμοίωσιν Θεοῦ γεγονότας· 10 ἐκ τοῦ αὐτοῦ στόματος ἐξέρχεται
(the) image of God having become; out of the same mouth comes forth

2129 2532 2671 3756 5534 80 3450 5023 3779
εὐλογία καὶ κατάρα. οὐ χρή, ἀδελφοί μου, ταῦτα οὕτω
blessing and cursing. not It is fitting, brothers of me, these things so

1096 3385 3588 4077 1537 3588 846 3692 1032 3588 1099
γίνεσθαι. 11 μήτι ἡ πηγὴ ἐκ τῆς αὐτῆς ὀπῆς βρύει τὸ γλυκὺ
to be. (Does) not the fountain from the same hole send out the sweet

2532 3588 4089 3361 1410 80 3450 4808 1636
καὶ τὸ πικρόν; 12 μὴ δύναται, ἀδελφοί μου, συκῆ ἐλαίας
and the bitter? Not is able, brothers of me, a fig-tree olives

King James Version

any man offend not in word, the same (is) a perfect man, (and) able also to bridle the whole body.
3 Behold, we put bits in the horses' mouths, that they may obey us; and we turn about their whole body.
4 Behold also the ships, which though (they be) so great, and (are) driven of fierce winds, yet are they turned about with a very small helm, whithersoever the governor listeth.
5 Even so the tongue is a little member, and boasteth great things. Behold, how great a matter a little fire kindleth!
6 And the tongue (is) a fire, a world of iniquity: so is the tongue among our members, that it defileth the whole body, and setteth on fire the course of nature; and it is set on fire of hell.
7 For every kind of beasts, and of birds, and of serpents, and of things in the sea, is tamed, and hath been tamed of mankind:
8 But the tongue can no man tame; (it is) an unruly evil, full of deadly poison.
9 Therewith bless we God, even the Father; and therewith curse we men, which are made after the similitude of God.
10 Out of the same mouth proceedeth blessing and cursing. My brethren, these things ought not so to be.
11 Doth a fountain send forth at the same place sweet (water) and bitter?
12 Can the fig tree, my brethren, bear olive

Literal Translation | **James 3:13** | ***King James Version***

or a vine figs? So neither (can) a fountain produce both salt and sweet water.

4160 2228 288 4810 3779 3762 4077 252 2532
ποιῆσαι, ἢ ἄμπελος σῦκα; οὕτως οὐδεμία πηγὴ ἁλυκὸν καὶ
to produce, or a vine figs; so neither a fountain salt and
1099 4160 5204
γλυκὺ ποιῆσαι ὕδωρ.
sweet to produce water.

berries? either a vine, figs? so (can) no fountain both yield salt water and fresh.

13. Who (is) wise and knowing among you? Let him show his works by (his) good behavior, in meekness of wisdom.
14 But if you have bitter jealousy and contention in your heart, do not boast and lie against the truth.
15 This is not the wisdom coming down from above, but (is) earthly, beastly, devilish.

5101 4680 2532 1990 1722 5213 1166 1537 3588 2570
13. Τίς σοφὸς καὶ ἐπιστήμων ἐν ὑμῖν; δειξάτω ἐκ τῆς καλῆς
Who (is) wise and knowing among you? Let him show by the good
391 3588 2041 846 1722 4240 4678 1487 1161 2205
ἀναστροφῆς τὰ ἔργα αὐτοῦ ἐν πραΰτητι σοφίας. 14 εἰ δὲ ζῆλον
behavior the works of him in meekness of wisdom. if But jealousy
4089 2192 2532 2052 1722 3588 2588 5216 3361 2620
πικρὸν ἔχετε καὶ ἐρίθειαν ἐν τῇ καρδίᾳ ὑμῶν, μὴ κατα-
bitter you have and contention in the heart of you, not do exult
2532 5574 2596 3588 225 3756 2076 3778 3588
καυχᾶσθε καὶ ψεύδεσθε κατὰ τῆς ἀληθείας. 15 οὐκ ἔστιν αὕτη ἡ
over and lie against the truth. not is This the
4678 509 2718 235 1919 5591 1141
σοφία ἄνωθεν κατερχομένη, ἀλλ ' ἐπίγειος, ψυχική, δαι-
wisdom from above coming down, but (is) earthly, beastly,

13. Who (is) a wise man and endued with knowledge among you? let him shew out of a good conversation his works with meekness of wisdom.
14 But if ye have bitter envying and strife in your hearts, glory not, and lie not against the truth.
15 This wisdom descendeth not from above, but (is) earthly, sensual, devilish.

16 For where jealousy and contention (are), there (is) confusion and every foul deed.
17 But the wisdom from above is firstly truly pure, then peaceable, forbearing, yielding, full of mercy and of good fruits, not partial and not pretended.
18 And (the) fruit of righteousness is sown in peace for the (ones) making peace.

3699 1063 2205 2532 2052 1563 181 2532
μονιώδης. 16 ὅπου γὰρ ζῆλος καὶ ἐρίθεια, ἐκεῖ ἀκαταστασία καὶ
devilish. where For jealousy and contention, there (is) confusion and
3956 5337 4229 3588 1161 509 4678 4412 3303 53
πᾶν φαῦλον πρᾶγμα. 17 ἡ δὲ ἄνωθεν σοφία πρῶτον μὲν ἁγνή
every foul deed. the But from above wisdom firstly truly pure
2076 1899 1516 1933 2138 3324 1656 2532
ἐστιν, ἔπειτα εἰρηνική, ἐπιεικής, εὐπειθής, μεστὴ ἐλέους καὶ
is, then peaceable, forbearing, yielding, full of mercy and
2590 18 87 2532 505 2590 1161 3588
καρπῶν ἀγαθῶν, ἀδιάκριτος καὶ ἀνυπόκριτος. 18 καρπὸς δὲ τῆς
fruits of good, not partial and not pretended. (the) fruit And the
1343 1722 1515 4687 3588 4160 1515
δικαιοσύνης ἐν εἰρήνῃ σπείρεται τοῖς ποιοῦσιν εἰρήνην.
of righteousness in peace is sown for the (ones) making peace.

16 For where envying and strife (is), there (is) confusion and every evil work.
17 But the wisdom that is from above is first pure, then peaceable, gentle, (and) easy to be intreated, full of mercy and good fruits, without partiality, and without hypocrisy.
18 And the fruit of righteousness is sown in peace of them that make peace.

James 4

1. From where do wars and fightings among you (come)? (Is it) not from this, from your lusts warring in your members?
2 You desire greatly and do not have. You murder, and are jealous, and are not able to obtain. You fight and you war, and you do not have, because you do not ask (God).
3 You ask, and do not receive, because you ask wrongly, in order that you may spend on your lusts.
4 Adulterers and adulteresses! Do you not know that the friendship of the world is enmity (to) God? Whoever, then, purposes to be a friend of the world

4159 4171 2532 3163 1722 5213 3756 1782 1537 3588
1. Πόθεν πόλεμοι καὶ μάχαι ἐν ὑμῖν; οὐκ ἐντεῦθεν, ἐκ τῶν
From where (are) wars and fights among you? Not from this, from the
2237 5216 3588 4754 1722 3588 3196 5216
ἡδονῶν ὑμῶν τῶν στρατευομένων ἐν τοῖς μέλεσιν ὑμῶν;
lusts of you warring in the members of you?
1937 2532 3756 2192 5407 2532 2206 2532 3756 1410
2 ἐπιθυμεῖτε, καὶ οὐκ ἔχετε· φονεύετε καὶ ζηλοῦτε, καὶ οὐ δύνα-
You desire, and not have; you murder and are jealous, and not are
2013 3164 2532 4170 3756 2192 1161 1223 3588 3361
σθε ἐπιτυχεῖν· μάχεσθε καὶ πολεμεῖτε, οὐκ ἔχετε δέ, διὰ τὸ μὴ
able to obtain; you fight and you war, not have but, because not
154 5209 154 2532 3756 2983 1360 2560
αἰτεῖσθαι ὑμᾶς· 3 αἰτεῖτε, καὶ οὐ λαμβάνετε, διότι κακῶς
ask you; you ask, and not you receive, because wrongly
154 2443 1722 3588 2237 5216 1159 3432 2532
αἰτεῖσθε, ἵνα ἐν ταῖς ἡδοναῖς ὑμῶν δαπανήσητε. 4 μοιχοὶ καὶ
you ask, that on the lusts of you you may spend. Adulterers and
3428 3756 1492 3754 3588 5373 3588 2889 2189 3588
μοιχαλίδες, οὐκ οἴδατε ὅτι ἡ φιλία τοῦ κόσμου ἔχθρα τοῦ
adulteresses, not know that the friendship of the world enmity
2316 2076 3739 302 3767 1014 5384 1511 3588 2889
Θεοῦ ἐστιν; ὃς ἂν οὖν βουληθῇ φίλος εἶναι τοῦ κόσμου,
of God is? Whoever then purposes a friend to be of the world,

1. From whence (come) wars and fightings among you? (come they) not hence, (even) of your lusts that war in your members?
2 Ye lust, and have not: ye kill, and desire to have, and cannot obtain: ye fight and war, yet ye have not, because ye ask not.
3 Ye ask, and receive not, because ye ask amiss, that ye may consume (it) upon your lusts.
4 Ye adulterers and adulteresses, know ye not that the friendship of the world is enmity with God? whosoever therefore will be a friend of the world

Literal Translation

is put down (as) an enemy of God.
5 Or do you think that vainly the Scripture says, "The spirit which has dwelt in us yearns to envy"?
6 But He gives greater grace. Because of this it says, "God sets (Himself) against proud ones, but He gives grace to humble ones." (Prov. 3:34)
7 Then be subject to God. Resist the Devil, and he will flee from you.
8 Draw near to God, and He will draw near to you. Cleanse (your) hands, sinners! And purify (your) hearts, double-minded ones!
9 Be distressed, and mourn, and weep. Let your laughter be turned to mourning, and (your) joy into shame.
10 Be humbled before the Lord, and He will exalt you.

11. Do not speak against one another, brothers. The (one) slandering a brother, and judging a brother, (he) speaks against law, and judges law. But if you judge law, you are not a doer of law, but a judge.
12 One is the Lawgiver, who is able to save and to destroy. Who are you who judges another?

13 Come now, those saying, Today or tomorrow we will go into this city, and we will spend one year there, and we will trade and will make a profit,
14 who do not know of the morrow. For what (is) your life? For it is a mist, which for a little (while) appears, and then disappears.

15 Instead of you to say, If the Lord wills, even we will live, and we will do

James 4:5

2190 3588 2316 2525 2228 1380 3754 2761 3588 1124
ἐχθρὸς τοῦ Θεοῦ καθίσταται. 5 ἢ δοκεῖτε ὅτι κενῶς ἡ γραφὴ
an enemy of God is put down (as). Or do you think that vainly the Scripture
3004 4314 5355 1971 3588 4151 3739 2730 1722 2254
λέγει, Πρὸς φθόνον ἐπιποθεῖ τὸ πνεῦμα ὃ κατῴκισεν ἐν ἡμῖν;
says, to envy yearns the spirit which has dwelt in us?
3187 1161 1325 5485 1352 3004 3588 2316 5244
6 μείζονα δὲ δίδωσι χάριν· διὸ λέγει, Ὁ Θεὸς ὑπερηφάνοις
greater But He gives grace; therefore it says, God proud ones
498 5011 1161 1325 5485 5293 3767
ἀντιτάσσεται, ταπεινοῖς δὲ δίδωσι χάριν. 7 ὑποτάγητε οὖν
sets Himself against, to the humble but He gives grace be subject Therefore
3588 2316 436 3588 1228 2532 5343 575 5216
τῷ θεῷ· ἀντίστητε τῷ διαβόλῳ, καὶ φεύξεται ἀφ' ὑμῶν·
to God; oppose the devil, and he will flee from you;
1448 3588 2316 2532 1448 5213 2511 5495
8 ἐγγίσατε τῷ Θεῷ, καὶ ἐγγιεῖ ὑμῖν· καθαρίσατε χεῖρας,
Draw near to God, and He will draw near to you; cleanse (the) hands,
268 2532 48 2588 1374 5003
ἁμαρτωλοί, καὶ ἁγνίσατε καρδίας, δίψυχοι. 9 ταλαιπωρή-
sinners, and purify (your) hearts, double-minded ones. Be distressed
2532 3996 2532 2799 3588 1071 5216 1519 3997
σατε καὶ πενθήσατε καὶ κλαύσατε· ὁ γέλως ὑμῶν εἰς πένθος
and mourn and weep, the laughter of you to mourning
3344 2532 3588 5479 1519 2726 5013
μετατραφήτω, καὶ ἡ χαρὰ εἰς κατήφειαν. 10 ταπεινώθητε
let be turned and the joy into shame. Be humbled
1799 3588 2962 2532 5312 5209
ἐνώπιον τοῦ Κυρίου, καὶ ὑψώσει ὑμᾶς.
before the Lord, and He will exalt you.

3361 2635 240 80 3588 2635
11. Μὴ καταλαλεῖτε ἀλλήλων, ἀδελφοί. ὁ καταλαλῶν
Not do speak against one another, brothers. The (one) slandering
80 2532 2919 3588 80 846 2635 3551
ἀδελφοῦ, καὶ κρίνων τὸν ἀδελφὸν αὐτοῦ, καταλαλεῖ νόμου,
a brother, and judging the brother of him, speaks against law,
2532 2919 3551 1487 1161 3551 2919 3756 1488 4163 3551
καὶ κρίνει νόμον· εἰ δὲ νόμον κρίνεις, οὐκ εἶ ποιητὴς νόμου,
and judges law; if and law you judge, not you are a doer of law
235 2923 1520 2076 3588 3550 3588 1410 4982 2532
ἀλλὰ κριτής. 12 εἷς ἐστιν ὁ νομοθέτης, ὁ δυνάμενος σῶσαι καὶ
but a judge. One is the Lawgiver, who is able to save and
622 4771 5101 1488 3739 2919 3588 2087
ἀπολέσαι· σὺ τίς εἶ ὃς κρίνεις τὸν ἕτερον;
to destroy; you whose are who judges the other?

33 3568 3588 3004 4594 3588 839 4198 1519
13. Ἄγε νῦν οἱ λέγοντες, Σήμερον ἢ αὔριον πορευσόμεθα εἰς
Come now those saying, Today or tomorrow we will go into
3592 3588 4172 2532 4160 1563 1763 1520 2532
τήνδε τὴν πόλιν, καὶ ποιήσομεν ἐκεῖ ἐνιαυτὸν ἕνα, καὶ
this city, and we will spend there year one, and
1710 2532 2770 3748 3756 1987 3588
ἐμπορευσόμεθα, καὶ κερδήσομεν· 14 οἵτινες οὐκ ἐπίστασθε τὸ
we will trade, and will make a profit; (you) who not do know of the
3588 839 4169 1063 3588 2222 5216 822 1063 2076 3588 4314
τῆς αὔριον. ποία γὰρ ἡ ζωὴ ὑμῶν; ἀτμὶς γάρ ἐστιν ἡ πρὸς
morrow. what For the life of you? a mist For it is, which for
3641 5316 1899 2532 853 473 3588 3004
ὀλίγον φαινομένη, ἔπειτα καὶ ἀφανιζομένη. 15 ἀντὶ τοῦ λέγειν
a little (while) appears, then and disappears. Instead of to say
5209 1437 3588 2962 2309 2532 2198 2532 4160
ὑμᾶς, Ἐὰν ὁ Κύριος θελήσῃ, καὶ ζήσομεν, καὶ ποιήσομεν
you, If the Lord wills, even we will live, and we will do

King James Version

is the enemy of God.
5 Do ye think that the scripture saith in vain, The spirit that dwelleth in us lusteth to envy?
6 But he giveth more grace. Wherefore he saith, God resisteth the proud, but giveth grace unto the humble.
7 Submit yourselves therefore to God. Resist the devil, and he will flee from you.
8 Draw nigh to God, and he will draw nigh to you. Cleanse (your) hands, (ye) sinners; and purify (your) hearts, (ye) double minded.
9 Be afflicted, and mourn, and weep: let your laughter be turned to mourning, and (your) joy to heaviness.
10 Humble yourselves in the sight of the Lord, and he shall lift you up.

11. Speak not evil one of another, brethren. He that speaketh evil of (his) brother, and judgeth his brother, speaketh evil of the law, and judgeth the law: but if thou judge the law, thou art not a doer of the law, but a judge.
12 There is one lawgiver, who is able to save and to destroy: who art thou that judgest another?

13 Go to now, ye that say, To day or to morrow we will go into such a city, and continue there a year, and buy and sell, and get gain:
14 Whereas ye know not what (shall be) on the morrow. For what (is) your life? It is even a vapour, that appeareth for a little time, and then vanisheth away.
15 For that ye (ought) to say, If the Lord will, we shall live, and do

James 4:16

Literal Translation

this or that;
16 but now you boast in your arrogances. All such boasting is evil.

17 Therefore, to (anyone) knowing to do good, and not doing (it), it is sin to him.

5124 2228 1565 3568 1161 2744 1722 3588 212 5216
τοῦτο ἢ ἐκεῖνο. 16 νῦν δὲ καυχᾶσθε ἐν ταῖς ἀλαζονείαις ὑμῶν·
this or that. now But you boast in the arrogances of you;
3956 2746 5108 4190 2076 1492 3767 2570
πᾶσα καύχησις τοιαύτη πονηρά ἐστιν. 17 εἰδότι οὖν καλὸν
all boastings such evil are. To (one) knowing then good
4160 2532 3361 4160 266 846 2076
ποιεῖν καὶ μὴ ποιοῦντι, ἁμαρτία αὐτῷ ἐστιν.
to do and not doing (it) sin to him it is.

King James Version

this, or that.
16 But now ye rejoice in your boastings: all such rejoicing is evil.

17 Therefore to him that knoweth to do good, and doeth (it) not, to him it is sin.

James 5

1. Come now, rich ones, weep, howling over your miseries coming on.
2 Your riches have rotted, and your garments have become moth-eaten.
3 Your gold and silver have rusted over, and their poison will be a testimony to you, and will eat your flesh as fire. You heaped treasure in (the) last days.

33 3568 3588 4145 2799 3649 1909 3588
1. Ἄγε νῦν οἱ πλούσιοι, κλαύσατε ὀλολύζοντες ἐπὶ ταῖς
Come now the (ones) rich, weep crying aloud over the
5004 5216 3588 1904 3588 4149 5216
ταλαιπωρίαις ὑμῶν ταῖς ἐπερχομέναις. 2 ὁ πλοῦτος ὑμῶν
miseries of you coming on. The riches of you
4595 2532 3588 2440 5216 4598 1096 3588 5557
σέσηπε, καὶ τὰ ἱμάτια ὑμῶν σητόβρωτα γέγονεν· 3 ὁ χρυσὸς
have rotted, and the garments of you moth-eaten have become; the gold
5216 2532 3588 696 2728 2532 3588 2447 846 1519 3142
ὑμῶν καὶ ὁ ἄργυρος κατίωται, καὶ ὁ ἰὸς αὐτῶν εἰς μαρτύ-
of you and the silver have rusted over, and the poison of them for a testimony
5213 2071 2532 5315 3588 4561 5216 5613 4442
ριον ὑμῖν ἔσται, καὶ φάγεται τὰς σάρκας ὑμῶν ὡς πῦρ.
to you will be, and will eat the flesh of you as fire.

1. Go to now, (ye) rich men, weep and howl for your miseries that shall come upon (you).
2 Your riches are corrupted, and your garments are motheaten.
3 Your gold and silver is cankered; and the rust of them shall be a witness against you, and shall eat your flesh as it were fire. Ye have heaped treasure together for the last days.

4 Behold! The wages of the workmen who have reaped your fields cry out, being kept back from you. And the cries of the (ones) who have reaped have entered into the ears of (the) Lord of Hosts.

5 You lived luxuriously on the earth, and lived in self-gratification; you nourished your hearts as in a day of slaughter;

6 you condemned; you murdered the righteous; he does not resist you.

2343 1722 2078 2250 2400 3588 3408 3588
ἐθησαυρίσατε ἐν ἐσχάταις ἡμέραις. 4 ἰδοὺ ὁ μισθὸς τῶν
You heaped treasure in (the) last days. Behold! The wages of the
2040 3588 270 3588 5561 5216 3588 650
ἐργατῶν τῶν ἀμησάντων τὰς χώρας ὑμῶν, ὁ ἀπεστερη-
workers having reaped the fields of you, being kept
575 5216 2896 2532 3588 995 3588 2325 1519 3588
μένος ἀφ' ὑμῶν, κράζει· καὶ αἱ βοαὶ τῶν θερισάντων εἰς τὰ
back from you, cries out; and the cries of the (ones) having reaped into the
3775 2962 4519 1525 5171 1909 3588
ὦτα Κυρίου Σαβαὼθ εἰσεληλύθασιν. 5 ἐτρυφήσατε ἐπὶ τῆς
ears of (the) Lord of Hosts have entered. You lived luxuriously on the
1093 2532 4684 5142 3588 2588 5216 5613 1722
γῆς καὶ ἐσπαταλήσατε· ἐθρέψατε τὰς καρδίας ὑμῶν ὡς ἐν
earth and lived wantonly; you nourished the hearts of you as in
2250 4967 2613 5407 3588 1342 3756
ἡμέρᾳ σφαγῆς. 6 κατεδικάσατε, ἐφονεύσατε τὸν δίκαιον· οὐκ
a day of slaughter. You condemned, you murdered the righteous; not
498 5213
ἀντιτάσσεται ὑμῖν.
he resists you.

4 Behold, the hire of the labourers who have reaped down your fields, which is of you kept back by fraud, crieth: and the cries of them which have reaped are entered into the ears of the Lord of sabaoth.

5 Ye have lived in pleasure on the earth, and been wanton; ye have nourished your hearts, as in a day of slaughter.

6 Ye have condemned (and) killed the just; (and) he doth not resist you.

7. Therefore, brothers, be long-suffering until the coming of the Lord. Behold, the farmer waits for the precious fruit of the earth, being long-suffering over it until it may receive (the) early and the latter rain.
8 You also be long-suffering. Set your hearts firmly, because the coming of the Lord is near.
9 Do not murmur against

3114 3767 80 2193 3588 3952 3588
7. Μακροθυμήσατε οὖν, ἀδελφοί, ἕως τῆς παρουσίας τοῦ
be long-suffering Then, brothers, until the coming of the
2962 2400 3588 1092 1551 3588 5093 2590 3588
Κυρίου. ἰδού, ὁ γεωργὸς ἐκδέχεται τὸν τίμιον καρπὸν τῆς
Lord. Behold! The farmer awaits the precious fruit of the
1093 3114 1909 846 2193 302 2983 5205 4406 2532
γῆς, μακροθυμῶν ἐπ' αὐτῷ, ἕως ἂν λάβῃ ὑετὸν πρώϊμον καὶ
earth, being long-suffering over it, until it may receive rain (the) early and
3797 3114 2532 5210 4741 3588 2588
ὄψιμον. 8 μακροθυμήσατε καὶ ὑμεῖς, στηρίξατε τὰς καρδίας
latter. Be long-suffering also you, establish the hearts
5216 3754 3588 3952 3588 2962 1448 3361 4727 2596
ὑμῶν, ὅτι ἡ παρουσία τοῦ Κυρίου ἤγγικε. 9 μὴ στενάζετε κατ'
of you, because the coming of the Lord is near. not Murmur against

7. Be patient therefore, brethren, unto the coming of the Lord. Behold, the husbandman waiteth for the precious fruit of the earth, and hath long patience for it, until he receive the early and latter rain.
8 Be ye also patient; stablish your hearts: for the coming of the Lord draweth nigh.
9 Grudge not one against

Literal Translation

James 5:10

King James Version

one another, brothers, that you not be condemned. Behold, (the) Judge stands before the door.
10 My brothers, (as) an example of suffering ill, and of long-suffering, take the prophets who spoke in the name of (the) Lord.
11 Behold! We esteem the (ones) blessed who endure. You have heard of the patience of Job, and you saw (the) end of the Lord, that the Lord is full of compassion and pitying.

12. But before all things, my brothers, do not swear, neither by the heaven, nor by the earth, nor any other oath. But let (your) yes be yes, and the no, no, that you may not fall under judgment.

13 Does anyone suffer ill among you? Let him pray. Is anyone cheerful? Let him praise in song.
14 Is any among you sick? Let him call the elders of the church, and let them pray over him, anointing him with oil in the name of the Lord.
15 And the prayer of faith will cure those being sick, and the Lord will raise him up. And if he may have committed sins, it will be forgiven him.

16 Confess offenses to one another, and pray for one another, that you may be healed. (The) prayer of a righteous one (has) great strength, having been made effective.
17 Elijah was a man of like feeling to us, and he prayed in prayer (for it) not to rain; and it did not rain on the earth three years and six months.
18 And he prayed again,

240 80 2443 3361 2632 2400 3588 2923 4253
ἀλλήλων, ἀδελφοί, ἵνα μὴ κατακριθῆτε· ἰδού, ὁ κριτὴς πρὸ
one another, brothers, that not you be judged; behold, the Judge before

3588 2374 2476 5262 2983 3588 2552
τῶν θυρῶν ἕστηκεν. 10 ὑπόδειγμα λάβετε τῆς κακοπαθείας,
the door stands. an example Take of suffering ill,

80 3450 2532 3588 3115 3588 4396 3739
ἀδελφοί μου, καὶ τῆς μακροθυμίας, τοὺς προφήτας οἳ
brothers of me, and of long-suffering, the prophets who

2980 3588 3686 2962 2400 3106 3588
ἐλάλησαν τῷ ὀνόματι Κυρίου. 11 ἰδού, μακαρίζομεν τοὺς
spoke in the name of (the) Lord. Behold! We esteem blessed those

5278 3588 5281 2492 191 2532 3588 5056
ὑπομένοντας· τὴν ὑπομονὴν Ἰὼβ ἠκούσατε, καὶ τὸ τέλος
enduring; the patience of Job you heard, and the end

2962 1492 3754 4184 2076 3588 2962 2532
Κυρίου εἴδετε, ὅτι πολύσπλαγχνός ἐστιν ὁ Κύριος καὶ
of (the) Lord you saw, that full of compassion is the Lord and

3629
οἰκτίρμων.
pitying.

4253 3956 1161 80 3450 3361 3660 3383 3588
12. Πρὸ πάντων δέ, ἀδελφοί μου, μὴ ὀμνύετε, μήτε τὸν
before all things But, brothers of me, not do swear, neither by the

3772 3383 3588 1093 3383 243 5100 3727 2277 1161
οὐρανόν, μήτε τὴν γῆν, μήτε ἄλλον τινὰ ὅρκον· ἤτω δὲ
heaven, nor by the earth, nor other any oath; let be but

5216 3588 3483 3483 2532 3588 3756 3756 2443 3361 5259 2920 4098
ὑμῶν τὸ ναί, ναί, καὶ τὸ οὔ, οὔ· ἵνα μὴ ὑπὸ κρίσιν πέσητε.
of you the yes, yes, and the no, no; that not under judgment you fall.

2553 5100 1722 5213 4336 2114 5100
13. Κακοπαθεῖ τις ἐν ὑμῖν; προσευχέσθω. εὐθυμεῖ τις;
suffer ill Do any among you? Let him pray. Is cheerful any?

5567 770 5100 1722 5213 4341 3588 4245
ψαλλέτω. 14 ἀσθενεῖ τις ἐν ὑμῖν; προσκαλεσάσθω τοὺς πρεσ-
Let him sing. Is infirm any among you? Let him summon the elders

3588 1577 2532 4336 1909 846
βυτέρους τῆς ἐκκλησίας, καὶ προσευξάσθωσαν ἐπ' αὐτόν,
of the church, and let them pray over him,

218 846 1637 1722 3588 3686 3588 2962 2532/3588
ἀλείψαντες αὐτὸν ἐλαίῳ ἐν τῷ ὀνόματι τοῦ Κυρίου· 15 καὶ ἡ
having anointed him with oil in the name of the Lord; And the

2171 3588 4102 4982 3588 2577 2532 1453 846 3588
εὐχὴ τῆς πίστεως σώσει τὸν κάμνοντα, καὶ ἐγερεῖ αὐτὸν ὁ
prayer of faith will cure the (one) being sick, and will raise him the

2962 2579 266 5600 4160 863 846
Κύριος· κἂν ἁμαρτίας ᾖ πεποιηκώς, ἀφεθήσεται αὐτῷ.
Lord; and if sin he be (one) having done, it will be forgiven him.

1843 240 3588 3900 2532 2172
16 ἐξομολογεῖσθε ἀλλήλοις τὰ παραπτώματα, καὶ εὔχεσθε
Confess to one another the offenses, and pray

5228 240 3704 2390 4183 2480 1162 1342
ὑπὲρ ἀλλήλων, ὅπως ἰαθῆτε. πολὺ ἰσχύει δέησις δικαίου
for one another, so as you may be healed. very strong (is) (the) petition of one righteous

1754 2243 444 2258 3663 2254 2532
ἐνεργουμένη. 17 Ἠλίας ἄνθρωπος ἦν ὁμοιοπαθὴς ἡμῖν, καὶ
being made effective. Elijah a man was of like feeling to us, and

4335 4336 3588 3361 1026 2532 3756 1026 1909
προσευχῇ προσηύξατο τοῦ μὴ βρέξαι· καὶ οὐκ ἔβρεξεν ἐπὶ
in prayer he prayed not to rain; and not it rained on

3588 1093 1763 5140 2532 3376 1803 2532 3825
τῆς γῆς ἐνιαυτοὺς τρεῖς καὶ μῆνας ἕξ. 18 καὶ πάλιν
the earth years three and months six. And again

another, brethren, lest ye be condemned: behold, the judge standeth before the door.
10 Take, my brethren, the prophets, who have spoken in the name of the Lord, for an example of suffering affliction, and of patience.

11 Behold, we count them happy which endure. Ye have heard of the patience of Job, and have seen the end of the Lord; that the Lord is very pitiful, and of tender mercy.

12. But above all things, my brethren, swear not, neither by heaven, neither by the earth, neither by any other oath: but let your yea be yea; and (your) nay, nay; lest ye fall into condemnation.

13 Is any among you afflicted? let him pray. Is any merry? let him sing psalms.
14 Is any sick among you? let him call for the elders of the church; and let them pray over him, anointing him with oil in the name of the Lord:
15 And the prayer of faith shall save the sick, and the Lord shall raise him up; and if he have committed sins, they shall be forgiven him.

16 Confess (your) faults one to another, and pray one for another, that ye may be healed. The effectual fervent prayer of a righteous man availeth much.
17 Elias was a man subject to like passions as we are, and he prayed earnestly that it might not rain: and it rained not on the earth by the space of three years and six months.
18 And he prayed again,

Literal Translation | **James 5:19** | *King James Version*

and the heaven gave rain, and the earth caused its fruit to sprout.

4336 2532 3588 3772 5205 1325 2532 3588 1093
προσηύξατο, καὶ ὁ οὐρανὸς ὑετὸν ἔδωκε, καὶ ἡ γῆ
he prayed, and the heaven rain gave, and the earth

985 3588 2590 846
ἐβλάστησε τὸν καρπὸν αὐτῆς.
caused to sprout the fruit of it.

and the heaven gave rain, and the earth brought forth her fruit.

19. If anyone among you errs from the truth, brothers, and anyone turns him back,
20 know that the (one) turning a sinner from (the) error of his way will save (the) soul from death, and will hide a multitude of sins.

80 1437 5100 1722 5213 4105 575 3588 225 2532
19. Ἀδελφοί, ἐάν τις ἐν ὑμῖν πλανηθῇ ἀπὸ τῆς ἀληθείας, καὶ
Brothers, if anyone among you errs from the truth, and

1994 5100 846 1097 3754 3588 1994 268
ἐπιστρέψῃ τις αὐτόν, 20 γινωσκέτω ὅτι ὁ ἐπιστρέψας ἁμαρ-
turns anyone him, know that the (one) having turned a

1537 4106 3598 846 4982 5590 1537 2288 2532
τωλὸν ἐκ πλάνης ὁδοῦ αὐτοῦ σώσει ψυχὴν ἐκ θανάτου, καὶ
sinner from (the) error way of him will save (the) soul from death, and

2572 4128 266
καλύψει πλῆθος ἁμαρτιῶν.
will cover a multitude of sins.

19. Brethren, if any of you do err from the truth, and one convert him;
20 Let him know, that he which converteth the sinner from the error of his way shall save a soul from death, and shall hide a multitude of sins.

Literal Translation

THE FIRST GENERAL EPISTLE OF PETER

1 Peter 1

1. Peter, an apostle of Jesus Christ, to (the) elect pilgrims of (the) dispersion of Pontus, of Galatia, of Cappadocia, of Asia, and of Bithynia,

2 according to the foreknowledge of God (the) Father, in sanctification of (the) Spirit to obedience and sprinkling of (the) blood of Jesus Christ: Grace and peace be multiplied to you.

3 Blessed (be) the God and Father of our Lord Jesus Christ, He according to His great mercy having regenerated us to a living hope through (the) resurrection of Jesus Christ from (the) dead,

4 to an inheritance incorruptible and undefiled, and unfading, having been kept in Heaven for you
5 by (the) power of God, having been guarded through faith to a salvation ready to be revealed in (the) last time;
6 in which you exult; yet a little (while), if need be, grieving in manifold trials,
7 so that the proving of your faith, much more precious than perishing gold, but having been proved through fire, may be found to praise and honor and glory at (the) revelation of Jesus Christ;

8 whom having not seen, you love; in whom not yet seeing, but believing, you exult with unspeakable joy and having been glorified,
9 obtaining the end of your faith, (the) salvation of (your) souls.

ΠΕΤΡΟΥ
OF PETER

ΕΠΙΣΤΟΛΗ ΚΑΘΟΛΙΚΗ ΠΡΩΤΗ
EPISTLE GENERAL FIRST

1 Peter 1

4074 652 2424 5547 3927 3927
1. Πέτρος, ἀπόστολος Ἰησοῦ Χριστοῦ, ἐκλεκτοῖς παρεπιδή-
Peter, an apostle of Jesus Christ, to (the) elect pilgrims
1270 4195 1053 2587 2587
μοις διασπορᾶς Πόντου, Γαλατίας, Καππαδοκίας, Ἀσίας,
of (the) dispersion of Pontus, of Galatia, of Cappadocia, of Asia,
2532 978 2596 4268 2316 3962 1722
καὶ Βιθυνίας, 2 κατὰ πρόγνωσιν Θεοῦ πατρός, ἐν
and Bithynia, according to (the) foreknowledge of God (the) Father, in
38 4151 1519 5218 2532 4473 129 2424
ἁγιασμῷ Πνεύματος, εἰς ὑπακοὴν καὶ ῥαντισμὸν αἵματος Ἰησοῦ
sanctification of (the) Spirit, to obedience and sprinkling of blood of Jesus
5547 5485 5213 2532 1515 4129
Χριστοῦ· χάρις ὑμῖν καὶ εἰρήνη πληθυνθείη.
Christ; grace to you and peace be multiplied.

2128 3588 2316 2532 3962 3588 2962 2257 2424
3. Εὐλογητὸς ὁ Θεὸς καὶ πατὴρ τοῦ Κυρίου ἡμῶν Ἰησοῦ
Blessed (be) the God and Father of the Lord of us Jesus
5547 3588 2596 3588 4183 846 1656 313 2248
Χριστοῦ, ὁ κατὰ τὸ πολὺ αὐτοῦ ἔλεος ἀναγεννήσας ἡμᾶς
Christ, the (One) according to much of Him mercy, having regenerated us
1519 1680 2198 1223 386 2424 5547 1537 3498
εἰς ἐλπίδα ζῶσαν δι' ἀναστάσεως Ἰησοῦ Χριστοῦ ἐκ νεκρῶν,
to a hope living through (the) resurrection of Jesus Christ from (the) dead,
1519 2817 862 2532 283 2532 263
4 εἰς κληρονομίαν ἄφθαρτον καὶ ἀμίαντον καὶ ἀμάραντον,
to an inheritance incorruptible and undefiled and unfading,
5083 1722 3772 1519 2248 3588 1722 1411 2316
τετηρημένην ἐν οὐρανοῖς εἰς ὑμᾶς, 5 τοὺς ἐν δυνάμει Θεοῦ
having been kept in Heaven for you, by (the) power of God
5432 1223 4102 1519 4991 2092 601
φρουρουμένους διὰ πίστεως εἰς σωτηρίαν ἑτοίμην ἀποκαλυ-
being guarded through faith to a salvation ready to be revealed
1722 2540 2078 1722 3739 21 3641 737
φθῆναι ἐν καιρῷ ἐσχάτῳ. 6 ἐν ᾧ ἀγαλλιᾶσθε, ὀλίγον ἄρτι,
in time (the) last. In which you exult, a little yet
1487 1163 2076 3076 1722 4164 3986 2443 3588
εἰ δέον ἐστί, λυπηθέντες ἐν ποικίλοις πειρασμοῖς, 7 ἵνα τὸ
if needful it is, grieving by manifold trials, that the
1383 5216 3588 4102 4183 5093 5553 3588
δοκίμιον ὑμῶν τῆς πίστεως πολυ τιμιώτερον χρυσίου τοῦ
proving of you of the faith, much more precious than gold
622 1223 4442 1161 1381 2147 1519
ἀπολλυμένου, διὰ πυρὸς δὲ δοκιμαζομένου, εὑρεθῇ εἰς
of perishing, through fire yet being proved, may be found to
1868 2532 5092 2532 1391 1722 622 2424 5547
ἔπαινον καὶ τιμὴν καὶ δόξαν ἐν ἀποκαλύψει Ἰησοῦ Χριστοῦ·
praise and honor and glory at (the) revelation of Jesus Christ;
3739 3756 1492 25 1519 3739 737 3361 3708 4100
8 ὃν οὐκ ἰδόντες ἀγαπᾶτε, εἰς ὃν ἄρτι μὴ ὁρῶντες, πιστεύοντες
whom not having seen you love, into whom yet not seeing believing
1161 21 5479 412 2532 1392 2865
δὲ, ἀγαλλιᾶσθε χαρᾷ ἀνεκλαλήτῳ καὶ δεδοξασμένῃ, 9 κομιζό-
but, you exult with joy unspeakable and having been glorified, obtaining
3588 5056 3588 4102 5216 4991 5590
μενοι τὸ τέλος τῆς πίστεως ὑμῶν, σωτηρίαν ψυχῶν.
the end of the faith of you, (the) salvation of (your) souls.

King James Version

THE FIRST GENERAL EPISTLE OF PETER

1 Peter 1

1. Peter, an apostle of Jesus Christ, to the strangers scattered throughout Pontus, Galatia, Cappadocia, Asia, and Bithynia,

2 Elect according to the foreknowledge of God the Father, through sanctification of the Spirit, unto obedience and sprinkling of the blood of Jesus Christ: Grace unto you, and peace, be multiplied.

3 Blessed (be) the God and Father of our Lord Jesus Christ, which according to his abundant mercy hath begotten us again unto a lively hope by the resurrection of Jesus Christ from the dead,

4 To an inheritance incorruptible, and undefiled, and that fadeth not away, reserved in heaven for you,
5 Who are kept by the power of God through faith unto salvation ready to be revealed in the last time.
6 Wherein ye greatly rejoice, though now for a season, if need be, ye are in heaviness through manifold temptations:
7 That the trial of your faith, being much more precious than of gold that perisheth, though it be tried with fire, might be found unto praise and honour and glory at the appearing of Jesus Christ:
8 Whom having not seen, ye love; in whom, though now ye see (him) not, yet believing, ye rejoice with joy unspeakable and full of glory:
9 Receiving the end of your faith, (even) the salvation of (your) souls.

Literal Translation

10. About which salvation the prophets sought out and searched out, prophesying concerning the grace for you,
11 searching for what, or what sort of time the Spirit of Christ made clear within them; testifying beforehand of the sufferings (belonging) to Christ, and the glories after these.
12 To whom it was revealed that not to themselves, but to us they ministered the same things, which now were announced to you by those having preached the gospel to you in (the) Holy Spirit sent from Heaven; into which things angels long to bow to look.

13. Because of this, having girded up the loins of your mind, being sober, perfectly hope on the grace being brought to you at (the) revelation of Jesus Christ,
14 as children of obedience, not fashioning yourselves to your former lusts in your ignorance,
15 but according to the Holy One who has called you, you also become holy in all conduct;
16 because it has been written, "Be holy, because I am holy." (Lev. 19:2)
17. And if you call on (the) Father, the (One) judging according to the work of each one without respect to persons, pass the time of your pilgrimage in fear,
18 knowing that not with corruptible things, silver or gold, you were redeemed from your worthless way of life handed down from (your) fathers,
19 but with precious blood of Christ, as of an unblemished and unspotted lamb,
20 indeed having been foreknown before (the) foundation of (the) world, but revealed in

1 Peter 1:10

4012 3739 4991 1567 2532 1567 4396
10 περὶ ἧς σωτηρίας ἐξεζήτησαν καὶ ἐξηρεύνησαν προφῆται
About which salvation sought out and searched out prophets

3588 4012 3588 1519 5209 5485 4395 2045
οἱ περὶ τῆς εἰς ὑμᾶς χάριτος προφητεύσαντες· 11 ἐρευνῶντες
the concerning the for you grace prophesying; searching

1519 5101 2228 4169 2540 1213 3588 1722 846 4151 5547
εἰς τίνα ἢ ποῖον καιρὸν ἐδήλου τὸ ἐν αὐτοῖς Πνεῦμα Χριστοῦ,
for what or what sort of time made clear the in them Spirit of Christ,

4303 3588 1519 5547 3804 2532 3588 3326
προμαρτυρόμενον τὰ εἰς Χριστὸν παθήματα καὶ τὰς μετὰ
testifying beforehand of the (belonging) to Christ sufferings and the after

5023 1391 3739 601 3754 3756 1438 2254 1161
ταῦτα δόξας. 12 οἷς ἀπεκαλύφθη ὅτι οὐχ ἑαυτοῖς, ἡμῖν δὲ
these glories. to whom it was revealed that not to themselves, to us but

1247 846 3739 3568 312 5213 1223 3588 2097
διηκόνουν αὐτά, ἃ νῦν ἀνηγγέλη ὑμῖν διὰ τῶν εὐαγ-
they ministered the same which now were proclaimed to you through those having

5209 1722 4151 40 649 575
γελισαμένων ὑμᾶς ἐν Πνεύματι Ἁγίῳ ἀποσταλέντι ἀπ᾽
preached the gospel to you in (the) Spirit Holy sent from

3772 1519 3739 1937 32 3879
οὐρανοῦ, εἰς ἃ ἐπιθυμοῦσιν ἄγγελοι παρακύψαι.
Heaven, into which things long angels to look into.

1352 328 3588 3751 3588 1271 5216
13. Διὸ ἀναζωσάμενοι τὰς ὀσφύας τῆς διανοίας ὑμῶν,
Therefore girding up the loins of the mind of you,

3525 5049 1679 1909 3588 5342 5213 5485
νήφοντες, τελείως ἐλπίσατε ἐπὶ τὴν φερομένην ὑμῖν χάριν
being sober, perfectly hope on the being brought to you grace

1722 602 2424 5547 5613 5043 5218 3361
ἐν ἀποκαλύψει Ἰησοῦ Χριστοῦ· 14 ὡς τέκνα ὑπακοῆς, μὴ
at (the) revelation of Jesus Christ; as children of obedience, not

4964 3588 4386 1722 3588 52 5216 1939
συσχηματιζόμενοι ταῖς πρότερον ἐν τῇ ἀγνοίᾳ ὑμῶν ἐπιθυ-
fashioning yourselves to the formerly in the ignorance of you lusts,

235 2596 3588 2564 5209 40 2532 846 40
μίαις, 15 ἀλλὰ κατὰ τὸν καλέσαντα ὑμᾶς ἅγιον καὶ αὐτοὶ ἅγιοι
but according to the having called you Holy (One) also yourselves holy

1722 3956 391 1096 1360 1125 40
ἐν πάσῃ ἀναστροφῇ γενήθητε· 16 διότι γέγραπται, Ἅγιοι
in all conduct become. Because it has been written, holy

1096 3754 1473 40 1510 2532 1487 3962 1941 3588
γένεσθε, ὅτι ἐγὼ ἅγιός εἰμι. 17 Καὶ εἰ πατέρα ἐπικαλεῖσθε τὸν
Be, because I holy am. And if (as) Father you call on (Him) He

678 2919 2596 3588 1538 2041 1722
ἀπροσωπολήπτως κρίνοντα κατὰ τὸ ἑκάστου ἔργον, ἐν
without respect of persons judging according to the of each one work, in

5401 3588 3588 3940 5216 5550 390 1492
φόβῳ τὸν τῆς παροικίας ὑμῶν χρόνον ἀναστράφητε· 18 εἰδότες
fear the of the pilgrimage of you time pass; knowing

3754 3756 5349 694 2228 5553 3084 1537 3588
ὅτι οὐ φθαρτοῖς, ἀργυρίῳ ἢ χρυσίῳ, ἐλυτρώθητε ἐκ τῆς
that not by corruptible things, silver or gold, you were redeemed from the

3152 5216 391 3970 235 5093
ματαίας ὑμῶν ἀναστροφῆς πατροπαραδότου, 19 ἀλλὰ τιμίῳ
worthless of you way of life handed down from fathers, but with precious

129 5613 286 299 2532 784 5547 4267
αἵματι ὡς ἀμνοῦ ἀμώμου καὶ ἀσπίλου Χριστοῦ, 20 προεγνω-
blood as of a lamb unblemished and unspotted, of Christ, having been

3303 4253 2602 2889 5319 1161 1909
σμένου μὲν πρὸ καταβολῆς κόσμου, φανερωθέντος δὲ ἐπ᾽
foreknown truly before (the) foundation of the world, revealed but in

King James Version

10. Of which salvation the prophets have enquired and searched diligently, who prophesied of the grace (that should come) unto you:
11 Searching what, or what manner of time the Spirit of Christ which was in them did signify, when it testified beforehand the sufferings of Christ, and the glory that should follow.
12 Unto whom it was revealed, that not unto themselves, but unto us they did minister the things, which are now reported unto you by them that have preached the gospel unto you with the Holy Ghost sent down from heaven; which things the angels desire to look into.

13. Wherefore gird up the loins of your mind, be sober, and hope to the end for the grace that is to be brought unto you at the revelation of Jesus Christ;
14 As obedient children, not fashioning yourselves according to the former lusts in your ignorance:

15 But as he which hath called you is holy, so be ye holy in all manner of conversation;
16 Because it is written, Be ye holy; for I am holy.
17. And if ye call on the Father, who without respect of persons judgeth according to every man's work, pass the time of your sojourning (here) in fear:
18 Forasmuch as ye know that ye were not redeemed with corruptible things, (as) silver and gold, from your vain conversation (received) by tradition from your fathers;
19 But with the precious blood of Christ, as of a lamb without blemish and without spot:
20 Who verily was foreordained before the foundation of the world, but was manifest in

Literal Translation

(the) last times because of you,
21 the (ones) believing in God through Him, the (One) raising Him from (the) dead, and giving glory to Him so that your faith and hope may be in God.
22 Having purified your souls in the obedience of the truth through the Spirit to unpretended brotherly love, love one another fervently out of a pure heart,

23 having been regenerated, not by corruptible seed, but incorruptible, through (the) living word of God, and remaining to the age.

24 Because all flesh (is) as grass, and all (the) glory of men as (the) flower of grass; the grass was dried, and its flower fell out,

25 but (the) Word of (the) Lord remains to the age. And this is the Word preached as gospel to you.
(Isa. 40:68)

1 Peter 1:21

5550 3588 5550 1223 5209 3588 1223 846 4100
ἐσχάτου τῶν χρόνων δι᾽ ὑμᾶς, 21 τοὺς δι᾽ αὐτοῦ πιστεύοντας
(the) last of the times because of you, the (ones) through Him believing

1519 2316 3588 1453 846 1537 3498 2532 1391 846
εἰς Θεὸν, τὸν ἐγείραντα αὐτὸν ἐκ νεκρῶν, καὶ δόξαν αὐτῷ
into God, the (One) having raised Him from (the) dead, and glory to Him

1325 5620 3588 4102 5216 2532 1680 1511 1519 2316 3588
δόντα, ὥστε τὴν πίστιν ὑμῶν καὶ ἐλπίδα εἶναι εἰς Θεόν. 22 τὰς
having given, so as the faith of you and hope to be in God. The

5590 5216 48 1722 3588 5218 3588 225 1223 4151
ψυχὰς ὑμῶν ἡγνικότες ἐν τῇ ὑπακοῇ τῆς ἀληθείας διὰ Πνεύ-
souls of you having purified in the obedience of the truth through (the)

1519 5360 505 1537 2513 2588
ματος εἰς φιλαδελφίαν ἀνυπόκριτον, ἐκ καθαρᾶς καρδίας
Spirit to brotherly love unpretended, from (the) pure heart

240 25 1619 313 3756 1537
ἀλλήλους ἀγαπήσατε ἐκτενῶς· 23 ἀναγεγεννημένοι οὐκ ἐκ
one another love fervently; having been regenerated not by

4701 5349 235 862 1223 3056 2198 2316
σπορᾶς φθαρτῆς, ἀλλὰ ἀφθάρτου, διὰ λόγου ζῶντος Θεοῦ
seed corruptible, but incorruptible, through Word (the) living of God

2532 3306 1519 3588 165 1360 3956 4561 5613 5528
καὶ μένοντος εἰς τὸν αἰῶνα. 24 διότι πᾶσα σὰρξ ὡς χόρτος,
and remaining to the age. Because all flesh (is) as grass,

2532 3956 1391 444 5613 438 5528 3583 3588
καὶ πᾶσα δόξα ἀνθρώπου ὡς ἄνθος χόρτου· ἐξηράνθη ὁ
and all (the) glory of man as (the) flower of grass; was dried out the

5528 2532 3588 438 846 1601 3588 1161 4487 2962
χόρτος, καὶ τὸ ἄνθος αὐτοῦ ἐξέπεσε· 25 τὸ δὲ ῥῆμα Κυρίου
grass, and the flower of it fell out; the but Word of (the) Lord

3306 1519 3588 165 5124 1161 2076 3588 4487 3588 2097
μένει εἰς τὸν αἰῶνα. τοῦτο δέ ἐστι τὸ ῥῆμα τὸ εὐαγγελισθὲν
remains to the age. this And is the Word preached as gospel

1519 5209
εἰς ὑμᾶς.
to you.

King James Version

these last times for you,
21 Who by him do believe in God, that raised him up from the dead, and gave him glory; that your faith and hope might be in God.

22 Seeing ye have purified your souls in obeying the truth through the Spirit unto unfeigned love of the brethren, (see that ye) love one another with a pure heart fervently:

23 Being born again, not of corruptible seed, but of incorruptible, by the word of God, which liveth and abideth for ever.

24 For all flesh (is) as grass, and all the glory of man as the flower of grass. The grass withereth, and the flower thereof falleth away:
25 But the word of the Lord endureth for ever. And this is the word which by the gospel is preached unto you.

1 Peter 2

1. Then laying aside all malice, and all guile, and hypocrisies, and envies, and all evil words,
2 as newborn babes desire the pure soul-nourishing milk, that you may grow by it;

3 if indeed you tasted that the Lord is good; (Psa.34:8)

4 to whom drawing near, a living Stone, indeed having been rejected by men, but elect by God, precious;
5 you also as living stones are being built a spiritual house, a holy priesthood, to offer spiritual sacrifices acceptable

1 Peter 2

659 3767 3956 2549 2532 3956 1388 2532
1. Ἀποθέμενοι οὖν πᾶσαν κακίαν καὶ πάντα δόλον καὶ
laying aside Then all malice and all guile and

5272 2532 5355 2532 3956 2636 5613 738
ὑποκρίσεις καὶ φθόνους καὶ πάσας καταλαλιάς, 2 ὡς ἀρτιγέν-
hypocrisies and envies and all evil words, as newborn

1025 3588 3050 97 1051 1971 2443 1722
νητα βρέφη, τὸ λογικὸν ἄδολον γάλα ἐπιποθήσατε, ἵνα ἐν
babes, the soul-nourishing pure milk desire, that by

846 837 1512 1089 3754 5543 3588 2962
αὐτῷ αὐξηθῆτε, 3 εἴπερ ἐγεύσασθε ὅτι χρηστὸς ὁ Κύριος·
it you may grow, if indeed you tasted that good the Lord (is);

4314 3739 4334 3037 2198 5259 444 3303
4 πρὸς ὃν προσερχόμενοι, λίθον ζῶντα, ὑπὸ ἀνθρώπων μὲν
to whom drawing near, a Stone living, by men indeed

593 3844 1161 2316 1588 1784 2532 846
ἀποδεδοκιμασμένον, παρὰ δὲ Θεῷ ἐκλεκτὸν, ἔντιμον, 5 καὶ αὐτοὶ
having been rejected, by but God elect, precious, also yourselves

5613 3037 2198 3618 3624 4152 2406
ὡς λίθοι ζῶντες οἰκοδομεῖσθε οἶκος πνευματικὸς, ἱεράτευμα
as stones living are being built a house spiritual, a priesthood

40 399 4152 2378 2144 3588
ἅγιον, ἀνενέγκαι πνευματικὰς θυσίας εὐπροσδέκτους τῷ
holy, to offer spiritual sacrifices acceptable

1 Peter 2

1 . Wherefore laying aside all malice, and all guile, and hypocrisies, and envies, and all evil speakings,
2 As newborn babes, desire the sincere milk of the word, that ye may grow thereby:

3 If so be ye have tasted that the Lord (is) gracious.

4 To whom coming, (as unto) a living stone, disallowed indeed of men, but chosen of God, (and) precious,
5 Ye also, as lively stones, are built up a spiritual house, an holy priesthood, to offer up spiritual sacrifices, acceptable

1 Peter 2:6

Literal Translation

to God through Jesus Christ.
6 Because of this, it is also contained in the Scripture: "Behold, I lay in Zion an elect, precious Stone, a Corner-foundation; and the one believing on Him shall never in any way be ashamed." (Isa. 28:16)
7 Then to you who believe (belongs) the honor. But to disobeying ones, (He is the) Stone which those building rejected; this One became (the) Head-of-the-corner,
8 and a Stone-of-stumbling, and a Rock-of-offense to those disobeying, stumbling at the Word, to which they were also appointed. (Psa.118:22; Isa.8:14)
9 But you (are) an elect race, a royal priesthood, a holy nation, a people for possession, so that you may openly speak of the virtues of the (One) who has called you out of darkness into His marvelous light;

10 (you) who then were not a people, but now (are) the people of God; the one not pitied (then), but now pitied. (Ex. 23:22; Isa. 43:20,21; Hos. 1:6,9)
11. Beloved, I exhort (you) as (temporary) pilgrims and strangers to abstain from fleshly lusts which war against the soul;

12 having your behavior good among the nations, in that which they speak against you as evildoers; by observing (your) good works, they may glorify God in a day of visitation.

13. Then be in obedience to every ordinance of men because of the Lord; whether to a king, as being supreme;
14 or to governors, as through Him having indeed been sent for vengeance (on) evildoers, but praise

2316 1223 2424 5547 1352 2532 4023 1722 3588 1124
Θεῷ διὰ Ἰησοῦ Χριστοῦ. 6 διὸ καὶ περιέχει ἐν τῇ γραφῇ,
to God through Jesus Christ. Because also it is contained in the Scripture,

2400 5087 1722 4622 3037 204 1588 1784
Ἰδοὺ, τίθημι ἐν Σιὼν λίθον ἀκρογωνιαῖον, ἐκλεκτὸν, ἔντιμον·
Behold! I lay in Zion a Stone Corner-foundation, elect, precious;

2532 3588 4100 1909 846 3756 3361 2617 5213 3767 3588
καὶ ὁ πιστεύων ἐπ' αὐτῷ οὐ μὴ καταισχυνθῇ. 7 ὑμῖν οὖν ἡ
and the (one) believing on Him not at all shall be ashamed. to you, then, the

5092 3588 4100 544 1161 3037 3739 593
τιμὴ τοῖς πιστεύουσιν· ἀπειθοῦσι δὲ, λίθος ὃν ἀπεδοκί-
honor, the (ones) believing; to disobeying ones but a Stone which rejected

3588 3618 3778 1096 1519 2776 1137
μασαν οἱ οἰκοδομοῦντες, οὗτος ἐγενήθη εἰς κεφαλὴν γωνίας,
the (ones) building, this (One) came to be for Head of (the) corner,

2532 3037 4348 2532 4073 4625 3739 4350
8 καὶ, λίθος προσκόμματος καὶ πέτρα σκανδάλου· οἳ προσ-
and, a Stone-of Stumbling and a Rock-of-Offense to the (ones)

3588 3056 544 1519 3739 2532 5087 5210
κόπτουσι τῷ λόγῳ ἀπειθοῦντες, εἰς ὃ καὶ ἐτέθησαν· 9 ὑμεῖς
stumbling at the Word being disobedient, to which truly they were appointed. you

1161 1085 1588 934 2406 1484 40 2992
δὲ γένος ἐκλεκτόν, βασίλειον ἱεράτευμα, ἔθνος ἅγιον, λαὸς
But a race elect, a royal priesthood, a nation holy, a people

1519 4047 3704 3588 703 1804 3588 1537
εἰς περιποίησιν, ὅπως τὰς ἀρετὰς ἐξαγγείλητε τοῦ ἐκ
for possession, so as the virtues you may tell out the (One) from

4655 5209 2564 1519 3588 2298 846 5457
σκότους ὑμᾶς καλέσαντος εἰς τὸ θαυμαστὸν αὐτοῦ φῶς·
darkness you having called into the marvelous of Him light;

3588 4218 3756 2992 3568 1161 2992 2316 3588 3756 1653 3568
10. οἵ ποτε οὐ λαὸς, νῦν δὲ λαὸς Θεοῦ· οἱ οὐκ ἠλεημένοι νῦν
who then not a people, now but a people of God; the (ones) not pitied, now

1161 1653
δὲ ἐλεηθέντες.
but pitied.

27 3870 5613 3941 2532 3927
11. Ἀγαπητοί, παρακαλῶ ὡς παροίκους καὶ παρεπιδή-
Beloved, I exhort (you) as pilgrims and strangers

567 3588 4559 1939 3748 4754
μους ἀπέχεσθαι τῶν σαρκικῶν ἐπιθυμιῶ, αἵτινες στρατεύον-
to abstain from fleshly lusts, which war

2596 3588 5590 3588 391 5216 1722 3588 1484
ται κατὰ τῆς ψυχῆς· 12 τὴν ἀναστροφὴν ὑμῶν ἐν τοῖς ἔθνεσιν
against the soul; the behavior of you among the nations

2192 2570 2443 1722 3739 2635 5216 5613 2555
ἔχοντες καλήν, ἵνα, ἐν ᾧ καταλαλοῦσιν, ὑμῶν ὡς κακοποιῶν,
having good, that, in which they speak against you as evildoers,

1537 3588 2570 2041 2029 1392 3588 2316
ἐκ τῶν καλῶν ἔργων, ἐποπτεύσαντες δοξάσωσι τὸν Θεὸν
by the good works, having witnessed they may glorify God

1722 2250 1984
ἐν ἡμέρᾳ ἐπισκοπῆς.
in a day of visitation.

5293 3767 3956 442 2937 1223 3588 2962
13. Ὑποτάγητε οὖν πάσῃ ἀνθρωπίνῃ κτίσει διὰ τὸν Κύριον·
Be obedient then to every of man creation because of the Lord;

1535 935 5613 5242 1535 2232 5613 1223 846
εἴτε βασιλεῖ, ὡς ὑπερέχοντι· 14 εἴτε ἡγεμόσιν, ὡς δι' αὐτοῦ
whether to a king as being supreme; or to governors, as through Him

3992 1519 1557 3303 2555 1868 1161
πεμπομένοις εἰς ἐκδίκησιν μὲν κακοποιῶν, ἔπαινον δὲ
having been sent for vengeance indeed (on) evildoers, praise but

King James Version

to God by Jesus Christ.
6 Wherefore also it is contained in the scripture, Behold, I lay in Sion a chief corner stone, elect, precious: and he that believeth on him shall not be confounded.
7 Unto you therefore which believe (he is) precious: but unto them which be disobedient, the stone which the builders disallowed, the same is made the head of the corner,

8 And a stone of stumbling, and a rock of offence, (even to them) which stumble at the word, being disobedient: whereunto also they were appointed.
9 But ye (are) a chosen generation, a royal priesthood, an holy nation, a peculiar people; that ye should shew forth the praises of him who hath called you out of darkness into his marvellous light:

10 Which in time past (were) not a people, but (are) now the people of God: which had not obtained mercy, but now have obtained mercy.

11. Dearly beloved, I beseech (you) as strangers and pilgrims, abstain from fleshly lusts, which war against the soul;

12 Having your conversation honest among the Gentiles: that, whereas they speak against you as evildoers, they may by (your) good works, which they shall be-hold, glorify God in the day of visitation.

13. Submit yourselves to every ordinance of man for the Lord's sake: whether it be to the king, as supreme;
14 Or unto governors, as unto them that are sent by him for the punishment of evildoers, and for the praise

Literal Translation | **1 Peter 2:15** | *King James Version*

of well-doers.
15 Because so is the will of God, doing good to silence the ignorance of foolish men;

15 3754 3779 2076 3588 2307 3588 2316 17
ἀγαθοποιῶν. 15 ὅτι οὕτως ἐστὶ τὸ θέλημα τοῦ Θεοῦ, ἀγαθο-
of well-doers. Bcause so is the will of God, doing

5392 3588 3588 878 444 56
ποιοῦντας φιμοῦν τὴν τῶν ἀφρόνων ἀνθρώπων ἀγνωσίαν·
good to silence the of foolish men ignorance;

of them that do well.
15 For so is the will of God, that with well doing ye may put to silence the ignorance of foolish men:

16 as free, and not having freedom as a cover of evil, but as slaves of God.
17 Honor all, love the brotherhood, fear God, honor the king.

5613 1658 2532 3361 5613 1942 2192 3588 2549 3588
16 ὡς ἐλεύθεροι, καὶ μὴ ὡς ἐπικάλυμμα ἔχοντες τῆς κακίας τὴν
as free, and not as a cover having of evil

1657 235 5613 2316 1401 3956 5091 3588
ἐλευθερίαν, ἀλλ' ὡς δοῦλοι Θεοῦ. 17 πάντας τιμήσατε. τὴν
freedom, but as of God slaves. all Honor. the

81 25 3588 2316 5399 3588 935
ἀδελφότητα ἀγαπᾶτε. τὸν Θεὸν φοβεῖσθε. τὸν βασιλέα
brotherhood Love. God Fear. the king

5091
τιμᾶτε.
Honor.

16 As free, and not using (your) liberty for a cloke of maliciousness, but as the servants of God.
17 Honour all (men). Love the brotherhood. Fear God. Honour the king.

18. Servants, (be) obedient to (your) masters in all fear, not only to those good and forbearing, but also to the perverse (ones).
19 For this (is) a grace, if because of conscience (toward) God anyone bears grief, suffering unjustly.
20 For what glory (is it) if you patiently endure (while) sinning and being buffeted? But if you (are) suffering (while) doing good, and patiently endure, this (is) a grace from God.
21 For you were called to this, for even Christ suffered on our behalf, leaving behind an example for us, that you should follow His steps;

3588 3610 5293 1722 3956 5401 3588 1203
18. Οἱ οἰκέται, ὑποτασσόμενοι ἐν παντὶ φόβῳ τοῖς δεσπό-
Servants, being subject in all fear to the masters,

3756 3440 3588 18 2532 1933 235 2532 3588
ταις, οὐ μόνον τοῖς ἀγαθοῖς καὶ ἐπιεικέσιν, ἀλλὰ καὶ τοῖς
not only to the good and forbearing, but also to those

4646 5124 1063 5485 1487 1223 4893 2316 5297
σκολιοῖς. 19 τοῦτο γὰρ χάρις εἰ διὰ συνείδησιν Θεοῦ ὑποφέρει
perverse. this For (is) a grace, if because of conscience of God bears

5100 3077 3958 95 4169 1063 2811 1487 264
τις λύπας πάσχων ἀδίκως. 20 ποῖον γὰρ κλέος, εἰ ἁμαρτάνοντες
anyone grief suffering unjustly. what For glory (is it), if sinning

2532 2852 5278 235 1487 15 2532
καὶ κολαφιζόμενοι ὑπομενεῖτε; ἀλλ' εἰ ἀγαθοποιοῦντες καὶ
and being buffeted you patiently endure? But if doing good and

3958 5278 5124 5485 3844 2316 1519 5124
πάσχοντες ὑπομενεῖτε, τοῦτο χάρις παρὰ Θεῷ. 21 εἰς τοῦτο
suffering you patiently endure, this (is) a grace from God. to this

1063 2564 3754 2532 5547 3958 5228 2257 2254
γὰρ ἐκλήθητε, ὅτι καὶ Χριστὸς ἔπαθεν ὑπὲρ ἡμῶν, ἡμῖν
For you were called, because also Christ suffered on behalf of us, for us

5277 5261 2443 1872 3588
ὑπολιμπάνων ὑπογραμμόν, ἵνα ἐπακολουθήσητε τοῖς
leaving behind an example, that you should follow the

18. Servants, (be) subject to (your) masters with all fear; not only to the good and gentle, but also to the froward.
19 For this (is) thankworthy, if a man for conscience toward God endure grief, suffering wrongfully.
20 For what glory (is it), if, when ye be buffeted for your faults, ye shall take it patiently? but if, when ye do well, and suffer (for it), ye take it patiently, this (is) acceptable with God.
21 For even hereunto were ye called: because Christ also suffered for us, leaving us an example, that ye should follow his steps:

22 who did not sin, nor was guile found in His mouth; (Isa.53:9)
23 who, being reviled, did not revile in return; suffering, He did not threaten, but gave (Himself) up to Him who (was) judging righteously;
24 who Himself bore in His body our sins onto the tree; that dying to sins, we might live to righteousness; of whom, by His wound, you were healed.

2487 846 3739 266 3756 4160 3761 2147 1388
ἴχνεσιν αὐτοῦ· 22 ὃς ἁμαρτίαν οὐκ ἐποίησεν, οὐδὲ εὑρέθη δόλος
steps of Him; who sin not did do, nor was found guile

1722 3588 4750 846 3739 3058 3756 486
ἐν τῷ στόματι αὐτοῦ· 23 ὃς λοιδορούμενος οὐκ ἀντελοιδόρει,
in the mouth of Him; who being reviled not reviled in return,

3958 3756 546 3860 1161 3588 2919 1346 3739
πάσχων οὐκ ἠπείλει, παρεδίδου δὲ τῷ κρίνοντι δικαίως· 24 ὃς
suffering not He threatened, gave (Himself) but to Him judging righteously; who

3588 266 2257 846 399 1722 3588 4983 846
τὰς ἁμαρτίας ἡμῶν αὐτὸς ἀνήνεγκεν ἐν τῷ σώματι αὐτοῦ
the sins of us Himself carried up in the body of Him

1909 3588 3586 2443 3588 266 581 3588 1343
ἐπὶ τὸ ξύλον, ἵνα ταῖς ἁμαρτίαις ἀπογενόμενοι τῇ δικαιο-
onto the tree, that to sins dying, to righteousness

2198 3739 3588 3468 846 2390 2258 1063 5613
σύνῃ ζήσωμεν· οὗ τῷ μώλωπι αὐτοῦ ἰάθητε. 25 ἦτε γὰρ ὡς
we might live; of whom the wound of Him you were healed. you were For as

4263 4105 235 1994 3568 1909 3588
πρόβατα πλανώμενα· ἀλλ' ἐπεστράφητε νῦν ἐπὶ τὸν ποι-
sheep wandering; but you turned now to the

22 Who did no sin, neither was guile found in his mouth:
23 Who, when he was reviled, reviled not again; when he suffered, he threatened not; but committed (himself) to him that judgeth righteously:
24 Who his own self bare our sins in his own body on the tree, that we, being dead to sins, should live unto righteousness: by whose stripes ye were healed.

25 For you were straying sheep, but now you are turned to the

25 For ye were as sheep going astray; but are now returned unto

Literal Translation

Shepherd and Overseer of your souls.

1 Peter 3:1

4166 2532 1985 3588 5590 5216
μένα καὶ ἐπίσκοπον τῶν ψυχῶν ὑμῶν.
Shepherd and Overseer of the souls of you.

King James Version

the Shepherd and Bishop of your souls.

1 Peter 3

Literal Translation

1. Likewise, wives, submitting yourselves to (your) own husbands, that even if any disobey the word, through the behavior of the wives, without a word they will be won,
2 observing your pure behavior in fear.

3 Of whom let it not be the outward (act) of braiding of hairs, and of putting gold around, or of clothing of adornment.
4 but the hidden man of the heart, in the incorruptible (adornment) of the meek and quiet spirit, which is of great value before God.

5 For so then indeed the holy women (who were) hoping on God adorned themselves, submitting themselves to their own husbands,

6 as Sarah obeyed Abraham, calling him lord; whose children you became, doing good, and not fearing terror, not one. (Gen.18:12)

7 Likewise, husbands, dwelling together according to knowledge, as with a weaker vessel, the female, bestowing honor, as truly (being) co-heirs of (the) grace of life, not cutting off your prayers.

8. And, finally, (be) all of one mind, sympathetic, loving the brothers, tenderhearted, friendly,
9 not giving back evil for evil, or reviling against reviling; but, on the contrary, (give) blessing;

3668 3588 1135 5293 3588 2398 435
1. Ὁμοίως, αἱ γυναῖκες, ὑποτασσόμεναι τοῖς ἰδίοις ἀν-
Likewise, wives, submitting yourselves to the own

2443 2532 1487 5100 544 3588 3056 1223 3588 3588
δράσιν, ἵνα, καὶ εἴ τινες ἀπειθοῦσι τῷ λόγῳ, διὰ τῆς τῶν
husbands, that, even if any disobey the Word, through the of the

1135 391 427 3056 2770 2029
γυναικῶν ἀναστροφῆς ἄνευ λόγου κερδηθήσωνται, 2 ἐπο-
wives behavior without a word they will be won, having

3588 1722 5401 53 391 5216 3739
πτεύσαντες τὴν ἐν φόβῳ ἁγνὴν ἀναστροφὴν ὑμῶν. 3 ὧν
witnessed the in fear pure behavior of you. Of whom

2077 3756 3588 1855 1708 2359 2532 4025 5553
ἔστω οὐχ ὁ ἔξωθεν ἐμπλοκῆς τριχῶν, καὶ περιθέσεως χρυσίων,
let it be not the outward of braiding of hairs, and of putting around gold,

2228 1745 2440 2889 235 3588 2927 3588 2588
ἢ ἐνδύσεως ἱματίων κόσμος· 4 ἀλλ' ὁ κρυπτὸς τῆς καρδίας
or of clothing of garments adornment; but the hidden of the heart

444 1722 3588 862 3588 4239 2532 2272 4151
ἄνθρωπος, ἐν τῷ ἀφθάρτῳ τοῦ πραέος καὶ ἡσυχίου πνεύ-
man, in the incorruptible of the meek and quiet spirit,

3739 2076 1799 3588 2316 4185 3779 1063 4218
ματος, ὅ ἐστιν ἐνώπιον τοῦ Θεοῦ πολυτελές. 5 οὕτω γάρ ποτε
which is before God of great value. so For then

2532 3588 40 1135 3588 1679 1909 3588 2316 2885
καὶ αἱ ἅγιαι γυναῖκες αἱ ἐλπίζουσαι ἐπὶ τὸν Θεὸν ἐκόσμουν
also the holy women hoping on God adornment

1438 5293 3588 2398 435 5613 4564
ἑαυτάς, ὑποτασσόμεναι τοῖς ἰδίοις ἀνδράσιν· 6 ὡς Σάρρα
(of) themselves, submitting to the own husbands; as Sarah

5219 3588 11 2962 846 2564 3739 1096
ὑπήκουσε τῷ Ἀβραάμ, κύριον αὐτὸν καλοῦσα, ἧς ἐγενήθητε
obeyed Abraham, lord him calling, of whom you became

5043 15 2532 3361 5399 3367 4423
τέκνα, ἀγαθοποιοῦσαι καὶ μὴ φοβούμεναι μηδεμίαν πτόησιν.
children, doing good and not fearing no one terror.

3588 435 3668 4924 2596 1108 5613 772
7. Οἱ ἄνδρες ὁμοίως, συνοικοῦντες κατὰ γνῶσιν, ὡς ἀσ-
Husbands likewise, dwelling together according to knowledge, as with

4632 3588 1134 632 5092 5613 2532
θενεστέρῳ σκεύει τῷ γυναικείῳ ἀπονέμοντες τιμήν, ὡς καὶ
a weaker vessel the female bestowing honor, as also

4789 5485 2222 1519 3588 3361 1581 3588
συγκληρονόμοι χάριτος ζωῆς, εἰς τὸ μὴ ἐκκόπτεσθαι τὰς
co-heirs of (the) grace of life, unto not cutting off the

4335 5216
προσευχὰς ὑμῶν.
prayers of you.

3588 1161 5056 3956 3675 4835 5361
8. Τὸ δὲ τέλος, πάντες ὁμόφρονες, συμπαθεῖς, φιλάδελφοι,
And finally, all of one mind, sympathetic, loving brothers,

2155 5391 3361 591 2556 473 2556
εὔσπλαγχνοι, φιλόφρονες· 9 μὴ ἀποδιδόντες κακὸν ἀντὶ κακοῦ,
tenderhearted, friendly; not giving back evil against evil,

2228 3059 473 3059 5121 1161 2127
ἢ λοιδορίαν ἀντὶ λοιδορίας· τοὐναντίον δὲ εὐλογοῦντες,
or reviling against reviling; on the contrary but blessing,

King James Version

1. Likewise, ye wives, (be) in subjection to your own husbands; that, if any obey not the word, they also may without the word be won by the conversation of the wives;
2 While they behold your chaste conversation (coupled) with fear.
3 Whose adorning let it not be that outward (adorning) of plaiting the hair, and of wearing of gold, or of putting on of apparel;

4 But (let it be) the hidden man of the heart, in that which is not corruptible, (even the ornament) of a meek and quiet spirit, which is in the sight of God of great price.
5 For after this manner in the old time the holy women also, who trusted in God, adorned themselves, being in subjection unto their own husbands:
6 Even as Sara obeyed Abraham, calling him lord: whose daughters ye are, as long as ye do well, and are not afraid with any amazement.

7 Likewise, ye husbands, dwell with (them) according to knowledge, giving honour unto the wife, as unto the weaker vessel, and as being heirs together of the grace of life; that your prayers be not hindered.

8. Finally, (be ye) all of one mind, having compassion one of another, love as brethren, (be) pitiful, (be) courteous:
9 Not rendering evil for evil, or railing for railing: but contrariwise blessing;

Literal Translation

knowing that you were called to this in order that you might inherit blessing.
10 For the (one) desiring to love life, and to see good days, let him restrain his tongue from evil, even his lips not to speak guile.

11 Let him turn aside from evil, and let him do good. Let him seek peace, and pursue it;
12 because the eyes of (the) Lord (are) on the righteous, and His ears (open) to their prayer. But (the) face of (the) Lord (is) against (any) doing evil things. (Psa.34:12-16)

13 And who (is) the (one) harming you if you become imitators of the good?
14. But if you truly suffer because of righteousness, blessed (are you). But do not fear their fear, nor be troubled. (Isa.8:12,13)
15 But sanctify the Lord God in your hearts, and always (be) ready to (give) an answer to everyone asking you a reason concerning the hope in you, with meekness and fear,
16 having a good conscience, that while they speak against you as evildoers, they may be shamed, those falsely accusing your good behavior in Christ.

17 For (it is) better, if the will of God wills (it), to suffer (for) doing good than (for) doing evil.
18 Because even Christ once suffered concerning sins, the just for the unjust, that He might bring us to God; indeed being put to death in (the) flesh, but made alive in the Spirit;

19 in which also, going in to the spirits in prison, He then proclaimed
20 to disobeying ones, when once

1 Peter 3:10

1492 3754 1519 5124 2564 2443 2129 2816
εἰδότες ὅτι εἰς τοῦτο ἐκλήθητε, ἵνα εὐλογίαν κληρονομήσητε.
knowing that to this you were called, that blessing you might inherit.

3588 1063 2309 2222 25 2532 1492 2250 18
10 ὁ γὰρ θέλων ζωὴν ἀγαπᾶν. καὶ ἰδεῖν ἡμέρας ἀγαθάς,
the (one) For desiring life to love, and to see days good,

3973 3588 1100 846 575 2556 2532 5491 846
παυσάτω τὴν γλῶσσαν αὐτοῦ ἀπὸ κακοῦ, καὶ χείλη αὐτοῦ
hold back the tongue of him from evil, and (the) lips of him

3588 3361 2980 1388 1578 575 2556 2532 4160
τοῦ μὴ λαλῆσαι δόλον· 11 ἐκκλινάτω ἀπὸ κακοῦ, καὶ ποιησάτω
not to speak guile; let him turn away from evil, and let him do

18 2212 1515 2532 1377 846 3754 3588
ἀγαθόν· ζητησάτω εἰρήνην, καὶ διωξάτω αὐτήν. 12 ὅτι οἱ
good; let him seek peace, and pursue it. Because the

3778 2962 1909 1342 2532 3775 846 1519 1162
ὀφθαλμοὶ Κυρίου ἐπὶ δικαίους καὶ ὦτα αὐτοῦ εἰς δέησιν
eyes of (the) Lord on the righteous, and ears of Him (open) to petition

846 4383 1161 2962 1909 4160 2556
αὐτῶν· πρόσωπον δὲ Κυρίου ἐπὶ ποιοῦντας κακά.
of them; (the) face but of (the) Lord against doing evil things.

2532 5101 3588 2559 5209 1437 3588 18 3402 1096
13. Καὶ τίς ὁ κακώσων ὑμᾶς, ἐὰν τοῦ ἀγαθοῦ μιμηταὶ γένη-
And who (is) he harming you, if of the good imitators you come

235 1487 2532 3958 1223 1343 3107 3588 1161
σθε; 14 ἀλλ' εἰ καὶ πάσχοιτε διὰ δικαιοσύνην, μακάριοι· τὸν δὲ
to be? But if also you suffer because of righteousness, blessed (are you); but

5401 846 3361 5399 3366 5015 2962 1161 3588
φόβον αὐτῶν μὴ φοβηθῆτε, μηδὲ ταραχθῆτε· 15 Κύριον δὲ τὸν
fear of them not fear, nor be troubled; Lord but the

2316 37 1722 3588 2588 5216 2092 1161 104 4314
Θεὸν ἁγιάσατε ἐν ταῖς καρδίαις ὑμῶν· ἕτοιμοι δὲ ἀεὶ πρὸς
God sanctify in the hearts of you; ready and always to

627 3956 3588 154 5209 3056 4012 3588 1722 5213
ἀπολογίαν παντὶ τῷ αἰτοῦντι ὑμᾶς λόγον περὶ τῆς ἐν ὑμῖν
give a reason to everyone asking you a word concerning the in you

1680 3326 4240 2532 5401 4983 2192
ἐλπίδος, 16 μετὰ πραΰτητος καὶ φόβου· συνείδησιν ἔχοντες
hope, with meekness and fear; conscience having

18 2443 1722 3739 2635 5216 5613 2555
ἀγαθήν, ἵνα ἐν ᾧ καταλαλῶσιν ὑμῶν ὡς κακοποιῶν,
a good, that in which they speak against you as evildoers,

2617 3588 1908 5216 3588 18 1722
καταισχυνθῶσιν οἱ ἐπηρεάζοντες ὑμῶν τὴν ἀγαθὴν ἐν
they may be shamed, the (ones) abusing of you the good in

5547 391 2909 1063 15 1487
Χριστῷ ἀναστροφήν. 17 κρεῖττον γὰρ ἀγαθοποιοῦντας, εἰ
Christ behavior. it is better For doing good, if

2309 3588 2307 3588 2316 3958 2228 2554 3754
θέλει τὸ θέλημα τοῦ Θεοῦ, πάσχειν, ἢ κακοποιοῦντας. 18 ὅτι
wills the will of God, to suffer, than (for) doing evil. Because

2532 5547 530 4012 266 3958 1342 5228
καὶ Χριστὸς ἅπαξ περὶ ἁμαρτιῶν ἔπαθε, δίκαιος ὑπὲρ
even Christ once concerning sins suffered, the just on behalf of

94 2443 2248 4317 3588 2316 2289 3303
ἀδίκων, ἵνα ἡμᾶς προσαγάγῃ τῷ Θεῷ, θανατωθεὶς μὲν
(the) unjust, that us He may bring to God, being put to death truly

4561 2227 1161 3588 4151 1722 3739 2532 3588 1722 5438
σαρκὶ, ζῳοποιηθεὶς δὲ τῷ πνεύματι, 19 ἐν ᾧ καὶ τοῖς ἐν φυλακῇ
in (the) flesh, made alive but in the spirit, in which also to the in prison

4151 4198 2784 544 4218 3753 530
πνεύμασι πορευθεὶς ἐκήρυξεν, 20 ἀπειθήσασί ποτε, ὅτε ἅπαξ
spirits going He proclaimed, to disobeying ones then, when once

King James Version

knowing that ye are thereunto called, that ye should inherit a blessing.
10 For he that will love life, and see good days, let him refrain his tongue from evil, and his lips that they speak no guile:

11 Let him eschew evil, and do good; let him seek peace, and ensue it.
12 For the eyes of the Lord (are) over the righteous, and his ears (are open) unto their prayers: but the face of the Lord (is) against them that do evil.

13 And who (is) he that will harm you, if ye be followers of that which is good?
14. But and if ye suffer for righteousness' sake, happy (are ye): and be not afraid of their terror, neither be troubled;
15 But sanctify the Lord God in your hearts: and (be) ready always to (give) an answer to every man that asketh you a reason of the hope that is in you with meekness and fear:

16 Having a good conscience; that, whereas they speak evil of you, as of evildoers, they may be ashamed that falsely accuse your good conversation in Christ.

17 For (it is) better, if the will of God be so, that ye suffer for well doing, than for evil doing.
18 For Christ also hath once suffered for sins, the just for the unjust, that he might bring us to God, being put to death in the flesh, but quickened by the Spirit:

19 By which also he went and preached unto the spirits in prison;
20 Which sometime were disobedient, when once

1 Peter 3:21

Literal Translation

the long-suffering of God waited in (the) days of Noah, an ark having been prepared in which a few, that is, eight souls, were saved through water.
21 Which antitype now also saves us, baptism (not a putting away of (the) filth of (the) flesh, but (the) answer of a good conscience toward God through (the) resurrection of Jesus Christ;

22 who, having gone into Heaven is at (the) right of God, (the) angels, and authorities, and powers being subjected to Him).

1551 3588 3588 2316 3115 1722 2250 3575 2680
ἐξεδέχετο ἡ τοῦ Θεοῦ μακροθυμία ἐν ἡμέραις Νῶε, κατα-
waited the of God long-suffering in (the) days of Noah, having

2787 1519 3739 3641 5123 2076 3638
σκευαζομένης κιβωτοῦ, εἰς ἣν ὀλίγαι, τοῦτ᾽ ἔστιν ὀκτὼ
been prepared an ark, into which a few, this is eight

5590 1295 1223 5204 3739 2532 2248 499 3568
ψυχαί, διεσώθησαν δι᾽ ὕδατος· 21 ᾧ καὶ ἡμᾶς ἀντίτυπον νῦν
souls, were saved through water; which also us antitype now

4982 908 3756 4561 595 4509 235 4893
σῴζει βάπτισμα, οὐ σαρκὸς ἀπόθεσις ῥύπου, ἀλλὰ συνει-
saves baptism, not of (the) flesh removal of (the) filth, but conscience

18 1906 1519 2316 1223 386 2424
δήσεως ἀγαθῆς ἐπερώτημα εἰς Θεόν, δι᾽ ἀναστάσεως Ἰησοῦ
of a good an answer toward God, through (the) resurrection of Jesus

5547 3739 2076 1722 1188 3588 2316 4198 1519 3772
Χριστοῦ, 22 ὅς ἐστιν ἐν δεξιᾷ τοῦ Θεοῦ, πορευθεὶς εἰς οὐρ-
Christ, who is at (the) right of God, having gone into Heaven,

5293 846 32 2532 1849 2532 1411
ανόν, ὑποταγέντων αὐτῷ ἀγγέλων καὶ ἐξουσιῶν καὶ δυνάμεων.
being subjected to Him angels and authorities and powers.

King James Version

the longsuffering of God waited in the days of Noah, while the ark was a preparing, wherein few, that is, eight souls were saved by water.
21 The like figure whereunto (even) baptism doth also now save us (not the putting away of the filth of the flesh, but the answer of a good conscience toward God,) by the resurrection of Jesus Christ:

22 Who is gone into heaven, and is on the right hand of God; angels and authorities and powers being made subject unto him.

1 Peter 4

Literal Translation

1. Therefore, Christ having suffered in behalf of us in (the) flesh, also you arm yourselves (with) the same thought, that he suffering in (the) flesh has been made to rest from sin,
2 for (him) no longer to live in (the) lusts of men, but (to live) the remaining time in (the) flesh in (the) will of God.
3 For (the) time of life having passed is sufficient for us to have worked out the will of the nations, having gone on in wantonness, lusts, drunkenness, parties, carousings, and unlawful idolatries;
4 in which they are surprised, you not running with (them) into the same overflow of unsavedness, blaspheming;
5 who will give account to the (One) having readiness to judge (the) living and dead.
6 For to this (end) also the gospel was preached to (the) dead, that they might be judged according to men in (the) flesh, but might live according to God in (the) Spirit.
7. But the end of all things has drawn near. Then be disciplined and

5547 3767 3958 5228 2257 4561 2532 5210 3588
1. Χριστοῦ οὖν παθόντος ὑπὲρ ἡμῶν σαρκί, καὶ ὑμεῖς τὴν
Christ Therefore having suffered for us in (the) flesh, also you the

846 1771 3695 3754 3588 3958 1722 4561 3973
αὐτὴν ἔννοιαν ὁπλίσασθε· ὅτι ὁ παθὼν ἐν σαρκί, πέπαυται
same thought arm yourselves; because he suffering in (the) flesh, has ceased

266 1519 3588 3371 444 1939 235 2307
ἁμαρτίας· 2 εἰς τὸ μηκέτι ἀνθρώπων ἐπιθυμίαις, ἀλλὰ θελή-
from sin; for the no longer of men in (the) lusts, but in (the)

2316 3588 1939 1722 4561 980 5550 713
ματι Θεοῦ τὸν ἐπίλοιπον ἐν σαρκὶ βιῶσαι χρόνον. 3 ἀρκετὸς
will of God the remaining in (the) flesh to live time. sufficient

1063 2254 3588 3928 5550 3588 979 3588 2307 3588
γὰρ ἡμῖν ὁ παρεληλυθὼς χρόνος τοῦ βίου τὸ θέλημα τῶν
For to us the having passed away time of life the will of the

1484 2716 4198 1722 766 1939
ἐθνῶν κατεργάσασθαι, πεπορευμένους ἐν ἀσελγείαις, ἐπιθυ-
nations being worked out, having gone (on) in wantonness, lusts,

3632 2970 4224 2532 766 1495
μίαις, οἰνοφλυγίαις, κώμοις, πότοις, καὶ ἀθεμίτοις εἰδωλο-
drunkennesses, parties, carousings, and unlawful idolatries;

1722 3739 3579 3361 4936 5216 1519 3588
λατρείαις· 4 ἐν ᾧ ξενίζονται, μὴ συντρεχόντων ὑμῶν εἰς τὴν
in which they are surprised, not running with you into the

846 3588 810 401 987 3739 591
αὐτὴν τῆς ἀσωτίας ἀνάχυσιν, βλασφημοῦντες· 5 οἳ ἀποδώ-
same of unsavedness overflow, blaspheming; who will give

3056 3588 2093 2192 2919 2198 2532 3498
σουσι λόγον τῷ ἑτοίμως ἔχοντι κρῖναι ζῶντας καὶ νεκρούς.
account to the (One) ready having to judge living and dead.

1519 5124 1063 2532 3498 2097 2443 2919 3303
6 εἰς τοῦτο γὰρ καὶ νεκροῖς εὐηγγελίσθη, ἵνα κριθῶσι μὲν
for this For also to dead ones was preached the gospel, that they might be judged truly

2596 444 4561 2198 1161 2596 2316 4151
κατὰ ἀνθρώπους σαρκί, ζῶσι δὲ κατὰ Θεὸν πνεύματι.
according to men in (the) flesh, might live but according to God in (the) Spirit.

3956 1161 3588 5056 1448 4993 3767 2532
7. Πάντων δὲ τὸ τέλος ἤγγικε· σωφρονήσατε οὖν καὶ
of all things But the end has drawn near; be disciplined then and

King James Version

1. Forasmuch then as Christ hath suffered for us in the flesh, arm yourselves likewise with the same mind: for he that hath suffered in the flesh hath ceased from sin;
2 That he no longer should live the rest of (his) time in the flesh to the lusts of men, but to the will of God.
3 For the time past of (our) life may suffice us to have wrought the will of the Gentiles, when we walked in lasciviousness, lusts, excess of wine, revellings, banquetings, and abominable idolatries:

4 Wherein they think it strange that ye run not with (them) to the same excess of riot, speaking evil of (you):
5 Who shall give account to him that is ready to judge the quick and the dead.
6 For for this cause was the gospel preached also to them that are dead, that they might be judged according to men in the flesh, but live according to God in the spirit.
7. But the end of all things is at hand: be ye therefore sober, and

Literal Translation

be sensible to prayers;
8 and before all things having fervent love to yourselves, because love will cover a multitude of sins. (Prov. 10:12)

9 Be hospitable to one another without murmurings,
10 each one as he received a gift, ministering it to yourselves as good stewards of the manifold grace of God.
11 If anyone speaks, (let it be) as (the) words of God; if anyone ministers, as by strength which God supplies, that in all things God may be glorified through Jesus Christ; to whom is the glory and the might forever and ever. Amen.

1 Peter 4:8

3525 1519 3588 4335 4253 3956 1161 3588 1519 1438
νήψατε εἰς τὰς προσευχάς· 8 πρὸ πάντων δὲ τὴν εἰς ἑαυτοὺς
be sensible to prayers; before all things and to yourselves

26 1618 2192 3754 3588 26 2572 4128
ἀγάπην ἐκτενῆ ἔχοντες, ὅτι ἡ ἀγάπη καλύψει πλῆθος
love fervent having, because love will cover a multitude

266 5382 1519 240 427 1112
ἁμαρτιῶν· 9 φιλόξενοι εἰς ἀλλήλους ἄνευ γογγυσμῶν·
of sins; Be hospitable to one another without murmuring;

1538 2531 2983 5486 1519 1438 846 1247
10 ἕκαστος καθὼς ἔλαβε χάρισμα, εἰς ἑαυτοὺς αὐτὸ διακονοῦν-
each one as he received a gift, to yourselves it ministering,

5613 2570 3623 4164 5485 2316 1487 5100 2980
τες, ὡς καλοὶ οἰκονόμοι ποικίλης χάριτος Θεοῦ· 11 εἴ τις λαλεῖ,
as good stewards of (the) manifold grace of God; if any speaks,

5613 3051 2316 1487 5100 1247 5613 1537 2479 3739 5524 3588
ὡς λόγια Θεοῦ· εἴ τις διακονεῖ, ὡς ἐξ ἰσχύος ἧς χορηγεῖ ὁ
as (the) words of God; if any ministers, as by strength which supplies

2316 2443 1722 3956 1392 3588 2316 1223 2424 5547 3739
Θεός· ἵνα ἐν πᾶσι δοξάζηται ὁ Θεὸς διὰ Ἰησοῦ Χριστοῦ, ᾧ
God; that in all things may be glorified God through Jesus Christ, to whom

2076 3588 1391 2532 3588 2904 1519 3588 165 3588 165
ἐστιν ἡ δόξα καὶ τὸ κράτος εἰς τοὺς αἰῶνας τῶν αἰώνων.
is the glory and the might to the ages of the ages.

281
ἀμήν.
Amen

King James Version

watch unto prayer.
8 And above all things have fervent charity among yourselves: for charity shall cover the multitude of sins.

9 Use hospitality one to another without grudging.
10 As every man hath received the gift, (even so) minister the same one to another, as good stewards of the manifold grace of God.
11 If any man speak, (let him speak) as the oracles of God; if any man minister, (let him do it) as of the ability which God giveth: that God in all things may be glorified through Jesus Christ, to whom be praise and dominion for ever and ever. Amen.

12. Beloved, do not be astonished at the fiery trial happening to you for (your) testing, as (if) a surprise (were) occurring to you;
13 but according as you share the sufferings of Christ, rejoice; so that you may rejoice exulting at the revelation of His glory.
14 If you are reviled in (the) name of Christ, (you are) blessed, because the Spirit of God and of glory rests on you. Truly, according to them, He is blasphemed; but according to you, He is glorified. (Isa.11:2)
15 For do not let any of you suffer as a murderer, or a thief, or an evildoer, or as a meddler in the affairs of others.
16 But if (one suffers) as a Christian, do not let him be ashamed, but to glorify God in this respect.
17 Because the time (has come) to begin the judgment from the house of God; and if firstly from us, what (will be) the end of the ones disobeying the gospel of God?

27 3361 3579 3588 1722 5213 4451 4314 3986
12. Ἀγαπητοί, μὴ ξενίζεσθε τῇ ἐν ὑμῖν πυρώσει πρὸς πειρα-
Beloved, not be astonished among you fiery trial for trial

5213 1096 5613 3581 5213 4819 235 2526
σμὸν ὑμῖν γινομένῃ, ὡς ξένου ὑμῖν συμβαίνοντος· 13 ἀλλὰ καθὸ
of you happening, as a surprise to you occurring; but as

2841 3588 3588 5547 3804 5463 2443 2532 1722
κοινωνεῖτε τοῖς τοῦ Χριστοῦ παθήμασι, χαίρετε, ἵνα καὶ ἐν
you share the of Christ sufferings, rejoice, that also at

3588 602 3588 1391 846 5463 21 1487
τῇ ἀποκαλύψει τῆς δόξης αὐτοῦ χαρῆτε ἀγαλλιώμενοι. 14 εἰ
the revelation of the glory of Him you may rejoice exulting. If

3679 1722 3686 5547 3107 3754 3588 3588 1391
ὀνειδίζεσθε ἐν ὀνόματι Χριστοῦ, μακάριοι· ὅτι τὸ τῆς δόξης
you are reviled in (the) name of Christ, blessed (are you); because the glory

2532 3588 3588 2316 4151 1909 5209 373 2596 3303
καὶ τὸ τοῦ Θεοῦ Πνεῦμα ἐφ᾽ ὑμᾶς ἀναπαύεται· κατὰ μὲν
and the of the God Spirit on you rests; according to truly

846 987 2596 1161 5209 1392 3361 1063 5100
αὐτοὺς βλασφημεῖται, κατὰ δὲ ὑμᾶς δοξάζεται. 15 μὴ γάρ τις
them, He is blasphemed, according but to you He is glorified. not For any

5216 3958 5613 5406 2228 2812 2228 2555 2228 5613
ὑμῶν πασχέτω ὡς φονεύς, ἢ κλέπτης, ἢ κακοποιός, ἢ ὡς
of you let suffer as a murderer, or a thief, or an evildoer, or as

244 1487 1161 5613 5546 3361 153
ἀλλοτριοεπίσκοπος· 16 εἰ δὲ ὡς Χριστιανός, μὴ αἰσχυνέσθω,
a meddler; if but as a Christian, not be ashamed,

1392 1161 3588 2316 1722 3588 3313 5129 3754 3588 2540 3588
δοξαζέτω δὲ τὸν Θεὸν ἐν τῷ μέρει τούτῳ. 17 ὅτι ὁ καιρὸς τοῦ
to glorify but God in respect this. Because the time

756 3588 2917 575 3588 3624 3588 2316 1487 1161 4412
ἄρξασθαι τὸ κρίμα ἀπὸ τοῦ οἴκου τοῦ Θεοῦ· εἰ δὲ πρῶτον
to begin the judgment from the house of God; if and firstly

575 2257 5101 3588 5056 3588 544 3588 3588 2316
ἀφ᾽ ἡμῶν, τί τὸ τέλος τῶν ἀπειθούντων τῷ τοῦ Θεοῦ
from us, what (will be) the end of the (ones) disobeying the of God

12. Beloved, think it not strange concerning the fiery trial which is to try you, as though some strange thing happened unto you:
13 But rejoice, inasmuch as ye are partakers of Christ's sufferings; that, when his glory shall be revealed, ye may be glad also with exceeding joy.
14 If ye be reproached for the name of Christ, happy (are ye); for the spirit of glory and of God resteth upon you: on their part he is evil spoken of, but on your part he is glorified.
15 But let none of you suffer as a murderer, or (as) a thief, or (as) an evildoer, or as a busybody in other men's matters.
16 Yet if (any man suffer) as a Christian, let him not be ashamed; but let him glorify God on this behalf.
17 For the time (is come) that judgment must begin at the house of God: and if (it) first (begin) at us, what shall the end (be) of them that obey not the gospel of God?

Literal Translation

18 And if the righteous is scarcely saved, where will the ungodly and sinner appear? (Prov. 11;31)
19 So as indeed the (ones) suffering according to the will of God, let them commit their souls as to a faithful Creator in well-doing.

1 Peter 4:18

2098 2532 1487 3588 1342 3433 4982 3588 765 2532
εὐαγγελίῳ; 18 καὶ εἰ ὁ δίκαιος μόλις σῴζεται, ὁ ἀσεβὴς καὶ
gospel? And if the righteous scarcely is saved, the ungodly and

268 4226 5316 5620 2532 3588 3958 2596 3588
ἁμαρτωλὸς ποῦ φανεῖται; 19 ὥστε καὶ οἱ πάσχοντες κατὰ τὸ
sinner where will appear? So as indeed those suffering according to the

2307 3588 2316 5613 4103 2939 3908 3588
θέλημα τοῦ Θεοῦ ὡς πιστῷ κτίστῃ παρατιθέσθωσαν τὰς
will of God as to a faithful Creator let them commit the

5590 1438 1722 16
ψυχὰς ἑαυτῶν ἐν ἀγαθοποιΐᾳ.
souls of themselves in well-doing.

King James Version

18 And if the righteous scarcely be saved, where shall the ungodly and the sinner appear?
19 Wherefore let them that suffer according to the will of God commit the keeping of their souls (to him) in well doing, as unto a faithful Creator.

1 Peter 5

1. I, a fellow elder, exhort the elders among you, I being also witness of the sufferings of Christ, and (being) sharer of the glory about to be revealed:
2 Shepherd the flock of God among you, exercising oversight, not by compulsion, but willingly; nor eagerly for base gain, but readily;
3 nor as exercising lordship over the ones allotted (to you), but becoming examples of the flock.
4 And (at) the appearing of the Chief Shepherd, you will receive the never-fading crown of glory.
5. Likewise, younger ones be subject to older ones; and all being subject to one another. Put on humility, because God sets (Himself) against proud ones, but He gives grace to humble ones. (Prov. 3:34; James 4:6)
6 Then be humbled under the mighty hand of God, that He may exalt you in time;
7 casting all your anxiety onto Him, because it matters to Him concerning you.
8 Be sensible, watch, because your adversary (the) devil walks about as a roaring lion, seeking someone he may devour;
9 whom firmly resist in the faith,

1 Peter 5

4245 3588 1722 5213 3870 3588 4850
1. Πρεσβυτέρους τοὺς ἐν ὑμῖν παρακαλῶ ὁ συμπρεσβύτερος
elders The among you I exhort (I) a fellow-elder (being)

2532 3144 3588 3588 5547 3804 3588 2532 3588 3195
καὶ μάρτυς τῶν τοῦ Χριστοῦ παθημάτων, ὁ καὶ τῆς μελλού-
and witness of the of Christ sufferings, the also of the being

601 1391 2844 4165 3588 1722 5213
σης ἀποκαλύπτεσθαι δόξης κοινωνός· 2 ποιμάνατε τὸ ἐν ὑμῖν
about to be revealed glory sharer; shepherd the among you

4168 3588 2316 1983 3361 317 235
ποίμνιον τοῦ Θεοῦ, ἐπισκοποῦντες μὴ ἀναγκαστῶς, ἀλλ᾽
flock of God, exercising oversight not by compulsion, but

1596 3366 147 235 4290 3366 5613
ἑκουσίως· μηδὲ αἰσχροκερδῶς, ἀλλὰ προθύμως· 3 μηδ᾽ ὡς
willingly; nor eagerly for base gain, but readily; nor as

2634 3588 2819 235 5179 1096 3588
κατακυριεύοντες τῶν κλήρων, ἀλλὰ τύποι γινόμενοι τοῦ
exercising lordship of the allotment, but examples becoming of the

4168 2532 5319 3588 750 2865 3588
ποιμνίου. 4 καὶ φανερωθέντος τοῦ ἀρχιποίμενος, κομιεῖσθε τὸν
flock. And at the appearing of the chief Shepherd, you will receive the

262 3588 1391 4735 3668 3501 5293
ἀμαράντινον τῆς δόξης στέφανον. 5 ὁμοίως, νεώτεροι, ὑποτά-
unfading of glory crown. Likewise, younger ones, be

4245 3956 1161 240 5293 3588
γητε πρεσβυτέροις· πάντες δὲ ἀλλήλοις ὑποτασσόμενοι, τὴν
subject to older ones; all and to one another being subject,

5012 1463 3754 3588 2316 5244
ταπεινοφροσύνην ἐγκομβώσασθε· ὅτι ὁ Θεὸς ὑπερηφάνοις
humility put on, because God proud ones

498 5011 1161 1325 5485 5013
ἀντιτάσσεται, ταπεινοῖς δὲ δίδωσι χάριν. 6 ταπεινώθητε
sets (Himself) against, to humble ones but He gives grace. Be humbled

3767 5259 3588 2900 5495 3588 2316 2443 5209 5312 1722
οὖν ὑπὸ τὴν κραταιὰν χεῖρα τοῦ Θεοῦ, ἵνα ὑμᾶς ὑψώσῃ ἐν
then under the mighty hand of God, that you He may exalt in

2540 3956 3588 3308 5216 1977 1909 846
καιρῷ, 7 πᾶσαν τὴν μέριμναν ὑμῶν ἐπιρρίψαντες ἐπ᾽ αὐτόν,
time, all the anxiety of you casting onto Him,

3754 846 3199 4012 5216 3525 1127 3754 3588
ὅτι αὐτῷ μέλει περὶ ὑμῶν. 8 νήψατε, γρηγορήσατε, ὅτι ὁ
because to Him it matters about you. Be sensible, watch, because the

476 5216 1228 5613 3023 5612 4043
ἀντίδικος ὑμῶν διάβολος ὡς λέων ὠρυόμενος, περιπατεῖ
adversary of you (the) devil as a lion roaring walks about

2212 5101 2666 3739 436 4731 3588 4102
ζητῶν τινα καταπίῃ· 9 ᾧ ἀντίστητε στερεοὶ τῇ πίστει,
seeking someone he may devour; whom resist firm in the faith,

1 Peter 5

1. The elders which are among you I exhort, who am also an elder, and a witness of the sufferings of Christ, and also a partaker of the glory that shall be revealed:
2 Feed the flock of God which is among you, taking the oversight (thereof), not by constraint, but willingly; not for filthy lucre, but of a ready mind;
3 Neither as being lords over (God's) heritage, but being ensamples to the flock.
4 And when the chief Shepherd shall appear, ye shall receive a crown of glory that fadeth not away.
5. Likewise, ye younger, submit yourselves unto the elder. Yea, all (of you) be subject one to another, and be clothed with humility: for God resisteth the proud, and giveth grace to the humble.
6 Humble yourselves therefore under the mighty hand of God, that he may exalt you in due time:
7 Casting all your care upon him; for he careth for you.
8 Be sober, be vigilant; because your adversary the devil, as a roaring lion, walketh about, seeking whom he may devour:
9 Whom resist stedfast in the faith,

Literal Translation

knowing the same sufferings are being completed in your brotherhood in (the) world.

10. Now the God of all grace, the (One) calling us to His eternal glory in Christ Jesus, you having suffered a little, (He) Himself will perfect, confirm, strengthen, establish (you).

11 To Him (be) the glory and the might to the ages of the ages. Amen.

12 I wrote to you by a few (words) by way of Silvanus the faithful brother, as I reckon, exhorting and witnessing this to be (the) true grace of God, in which you stand.
13 The fellow-elected in Babylon greet you; also Mark my son.

14 Greet one another with a kiss of love. Peace (be) to you, all those in Christ Jesus. Amen.

1 Peter 5:10

1492 3588 846 3588 3804 3588 1722 2889 5216 81
εἰδότες τὰ αὐτὰ τῶν παθημάτων τῇ ἐν κόσμῳ ὑμῶν ἀδελ-
knowing the same sufferings in the in (the) world of you brother-

2005 3588 1161 2316 3956 5485 3588 2564
φότητι ἐπιτελεῖσθαι. 10 Ὁ δὲ Θεὸς πάσης χάριτος, ὁ καλέσας
hood are being completed. the And God of all grace, the (One) calling

2248 1519 3588 166 846 1391 1722 5547 2424 3641
ἡμᾶς εἰς τὴν αἰώνιον αὐτοῦ δόξαν ἐν Χριστῷ Ἰησοῦ, ὀλίγον
us to the everlasting of Him glory in Christ Jesus, a little

3958 846 2675 5209 4741 4599
παθόντας αὐτὸς καταρτίσαι ὑμᾶς, στηρίξαι, σθενώσαι,
having suffered Himself will perfect you, confirm, strengthen,

2311 846 3588 1391 2532 3588 2904 1519 3588 165 3588
θεμελιώσαι. 11 αὐτῷ ἡ δόξα καὶ τὸ κράτος εἰς τοὺς αἰῶνας τῶν
establish (you). To Him the glory and the might to the ages of the

165 281
αἰώνων. ἀμήν.
ages Amen.

1223 4610 5213 3588 4103 80 5613 3049
12. Διὰ Σιλουανοῦ ὑμῖν τοῦ πιστοῦ ἀδελφοῦ, ὡς λογίζομαι,
Through Silvanus to you the faithful brother, as I reckon,

1223 3641 1125 3870 2532 1957 3778
δι᾽ ὀλίγων ἔγραψα, παρακαλῶν καὶ ἐπιμαρτυρῶν ταύτην
through a few (words) I wrote, exhorting and witnessing this

1511 227 5485 3588 2316 1519 3739 2476 782
εἶναι ἀληθῆ χάριν τοῦ Θεοῦ εἰς ἣν ἑστηκατε. 13 ἀσπάζεται
to be (the) true grace of God in which you stand. Greets

5209 3588 1722 897 4899 2532 3138 3588 5207 3450
ὑμᾶς ἡ ἐν Βαβυλῶνι συνεκλεκτή, καὶ Μᾶρκος ὁ υἱός μου.
you the in Babylon fellow-elected, and Mark the son of me.

782 240 1722 5370 26
14 ἀσπάσασθε ἀλλήλους ἐν φιλήματι ἀγάπης.
Greet one another with a kiss of love.

1515 5213 3956 3588 1722 5547 2424 281
Εἰρήνη ὑμῖν πᾶσι τοῖς ἐν Χριστῷ Ἰησοῦ. ἀμήν.
Peace to you all the (ones) in Christ Jesus. Amen.

King James Version

knowing that the same afflictions are accomplished in your brethren that are in the world.

10. But the God of all grace, who hath called us unto his eternal glory by Christ Jesus, after that ye have suffered a while, make you perfect, stablish, strengthen, settle (you).

11 To him (be) glory and dominion for ever and ever. Amen.

12 By Silvanus, a faithful brother unto you, as I suppose, I have written briefly, exhorting, and testifying that this is the true grace of God wherein ye stand.
13 The (church that is) at Babylon, elected together with (you), saluteth you; and (so doth) Marcus my son.

14 Greet ye one another with a kiss of charity. Peace (be) with you all that are in Christ Jesus. Amen.

Literal Translation

THE SECOND GENERAL EPISTLE OF PETER

2 Peter 1

1. Simon Peter, a slave and apostle of Jesus Christ, to those equally precious with us, having obtained faith in (the) righteousness of our God and our Savior, Jesus Christ:
2 Grace to you, and peace be multiplied by a full knowledge of God, and of Jesus our Lord.

3 As His divine power has given to us all things (pertaining) to life and godliness through the full knowledge of the (One) having called us through glory and virtue,
4 by which means He has given to us the very great and precious promises, so that through these you might be partakers of (the) divine nature, escaping from the corruption in (the) world by lust.
5. But also in this very thing, having brought in all diligence, fully supplying in your faith (with) virtue; and virtue (with) knowledge;
6 and knowledge (with) self-control; and self-control (with) patience; and patience (with) godliness;

7 and godliness (with) brotherly love; and brotherly love (with) love.
8 For these things being in you, and abounding, (they will) make you not idle, not unfruitful in the full knowledge of our Lord Jesus Christ.

9 For the one in whom these things (are) not present is blind, being shortsighted, taking on forgetfulness of the cleansing of his sins in time past.
10. On account of this,

ΠΕΤΡΟΥ
OF PETER
ΕΠΙΣΤΟΛΗ ΚΑΘΟΛΙΚΗ ΔΕΥΤΕΡΑ
EPISTLE GENERAL SECOND

2 Peter 1

4826 4074 1401 2532 652 2424 5547
1. Σίμων Πέτρος, δοῦλος καὶ ἀπόστολος Ἰησοῦ Χριστοῦ,
Simon Peter, a slave and apostle of Jesus Christ,

3588 2472 2254 2975 4102 1722 1343 2532 2316
τοῖς ἰσότιμον ἡμῖν λαχοῦσιν πίστιν ἐν δικαιοσύνῃ τοῦ Θεοῦ
those equally precious with us having obtained faith in (the) righteousness of the God

2257 2532 4990 2257 2424 5547 5485 5213 2532
ἡμῶν καὶ σωτῆρος ἡμῶν Ἰησοῦ Χριστοῦ· 2 χάρις ὑμῖν καὶ
of us and Savior of us Jesus Christ; grace to you and

1515 4129 1722 1922 3588 2316 2532 2424 3588
εἰρήνη πληθυνθείη ἐν ἐπιγνώσει τοῦ Θεοῦ καὶ Ἰησοῦ τοῦ
peace be multiplied by a full knowledge of God and of Jesus the

2962 2257 5613 3956 2254 3588 2304 1411 846 3588
Κυρίου ἡμῶν. 3 ὡς πάντα ἡμῖν τῆς θείας δυνάμεως αὐτοῦ τὰ
Lord of us. As all things to us the divine power of Him

4314 2222 2532 2150 1433 1223 3588 1922
πρὸς ζωὴν καὶ εὐσέβειαν δεδωρημένης, διὰ τῆς ἐπιγνώσεως
as to life and godliness having been given, through the full knowledge

3588 2564 2248 1223 1391 2532 703 1223/3739/3588/3176
τοῦ καλέσαντος ἡμᾶς διὰ δόξης καὶ ἀρετῆς· 4 δι' ὧν τὰ μέγ-
of the (One) having called us through glory and virtue, through which the very

2254 3588 5093 1862 1433 2443 1223 5130
ιστα ἡμῖν καὶ τίμια ἐπαγγέλματα δεδώρηται, ἵνα διὰ τούτων
to us and precious promises He has given, that through these

1096 2304 2844 5449 668 3588 1722 2889
γένησθε θείας κοινωνοὶ φύσεως, ἀποφυγόντες τῆς ἐν κόσμῳ
you might be of divine partakers nature, escaping from the in (the) world

1722 1939 5356 2532 846 5124 1161 4710 3956
ἐν ἐπιθυμίᾳ φθορᾶς. 5 καὶ αὐτὸ τοῦτο δέ, σπουδὴν πᾶσαν
by lust corruption. also same in this thing But, diligence all

3923 2023 1722 3588 4102 5216 3588
παρεισενέγκαντες, ἐπιχορηγήσατε ἐν τῇ πίστει ὑμῶν τὴν
having brought in, (to) supply in the faith of you

703 1722 1161 3588 703 3588 1108 1722 1161 3588 1108 3588
ἀρετήν, ἐν δὲ τῇ ἀρετῇ τὴν γνῶσιν, 6 ἐν δὲ τῇ γνώσει τὴν
virtue, with and virtue knowledge, with and knowledge

1466 1722 1161 3588 1466 3588 5281 1722 116 3588
ἐγκράτειαν, ἐν δὲ τῇ ἐγκρατείᾳ τὴν ὑπομονήν, ἐν δὲ τῇ
self-control, with and self-control patience, with and

5281 3588 2150 1722/1161/3588 2150 3588 5360
ὑπομονῇ τὴν εὐσέβειαν, 7 ἐν δὲ τῇ εὐσεβείᾳ τὴν φιλαδελφίαν,
patience godliness, with and godliness brotherly love,

1722/1161/3588 5360 3588 26 5023 1063 5213 5225
ἐν δὲ τῇ φιλαδελφίᾳ τὴν ἀγάπην. 8 ταῦτα γὰρ ὑμῖν ὑπάρ-
with and brotherly love love. these things For in you being

2532 4121 3756 692 3761 175 2525
χοντα καὶ πλεονάζοντα, οὐκ ἀργοὺς οὐδὲ ἀκάρπους καθί-
and abounding, not idle nor unfruitful (makes)

1519 3588 3588 2962 2257 2424 5547 1922
στησιν εἰς τὴν τοῦ Κυρίου ἡμῶν Ἰησοῦ Χριστοῦ ἐπίγνωσιν.
(you) to be in the of the Lord of us Jesus Christ full knowledge.

3739 1063 3361 3918 5023 5185 2076 3467 3024
9 ᾧ γὰρ μὴ πάρεστι ταῦτα, τυφλός ἐστι, μυωπάζων, λήθην
(he) in whom For not is present these things, blind is, being short-sighted, forgetfulness

2983 3588 2512 3588 3819 846 266 1352
λαβὼν τοῦ καθαρισμοῦ τῶν πάλαι αὐτοῦ ἁμαρτιῶν. 10 διὸ
taking on the cleansing of the in time past of him sins. Therefore

King James Version

THE SECOND GENERAL EPISTLE OF PETER

2 Peter 1

1. Simon Peter, a servant and an apostle of Jesus Christ, to them that have obtained like precious faith with us through the righteousness of God and our Saviour Jesus Christ:
2 Grace and peace be multiplied unto you through the knowledge of God, and of Jesus our Lord,

3 According as his divine power hath given unto us all things that (pertain) unto life and godliness, through the knowledge of him that hath called us to glory and virtue:
4 Whereby are given unto us exceeding great and precious promises: that by these ye might be partakers of the divine nature, having escaped the corruption that is in the world through lust.

5 And beside this, giving all diligence, add to your faith virtue; and to virtue knowledge;

6 And to knowledge temperance; and to temperance patience; and to patience godliness;

7 And to godliness brotherly kindness; and to brotherly kindness charity.
8 For if these things be in you, and abound, they make (you that ye shall) neither (be) barren nor unfruitful in the knowledge of our Lord Jesus Christ.

9 But he that lacketh these things is blind, and cannot see afar off, and hath forgotten that he was purged from his old sins.
10 Wherefore

Literal Translation | **2 Peter 1:11** | **King James Version**

brothers, rather be diligent to make sure of your calling and election; for doing these things, you will not ever fall (into sin).

11 For so will be richly furnished to you the entrance into the everlasting kingdom of our Lord and Savior, Jesus Christ.

3123 80 4704 949 5216 3588 2821
μᾶλλον, ἀδελφοί, σπουδάσατε βεβαίαν ὑμῶν τὴν κλῆσιν
rather, brothers, be diligent sure of you the calling
2532 1589 4160 5023 1063 4160 3756 3361 4417
καὶ ἐκλογὴν ποιεῖσθαι· ταῦτα γὰρ ποιοῦντες οὐ μὴ πταίσητέ
and election to make; these things for doing not at all will fall
4218 3779 1063 4146 2023 5213 3588 1529
ποτε· 11 οὕτω γὰρ πλουσίως ἐπιχορηγηθήσεται ὑμῖν ἡ εἴσοδος
ever. so For richly will be furnished to you the entrance
1519 3588 166 932 3588 2962 2257 2532 4990
εἰς τὴν αἰώνιον βασιλείαν τοῦ Κυρίου ἡμῶν καὶ σωτῆρος
into the everlasting kingdom of the Lord of us and Savior
2424 5547
Ἰησοῦ Χριστοῦ.
Jesus Christ.

the rather, brethren, give diligence to make your calling and election sure: for if ye do these things, ye shall never fall:

11 For so an entrance shall be ministered unto you abundantly into the everlasting kingdom of our Lord and Saviour Jesus Christ.

12. For this reason I will not neglect to cause you to remember always concerning these things, though (you) know and have been confirmed in the present truth.
13 But I deem (it) right, so long as I am in this tabernacle, to stir you up by a reminder,
14 knowing that the putting off of my tabernacle is soon, as indeed our Lord Jesus Christ made clear to me.
15 And I will also be diligent to cause you always to have memory of these things after my departure.

1352 3756 272 5209 104 5279 4012 5130
12. Διὸ οὐκ ἀμελήσω ὑμᾶς ἀεὶ ὑπομιμνήσκειν περὶ τούτων,
Therefore not I will neglect you always to cause to remember about these,
2539 1492 2532 4741 1722 3588 3918 225
καίπερ εἰδότας, καὶ ἐστηριγμένους ἐν τῇ παρούσῃ ἀληθείᾳ.
though knowing, and having been confirmed in the present truth.
1342 1161 2233 1909 3745 1510 1722 5129 3588 4638
13 δίκαιον δὲ ἡγοῦμαι, ἐφ' ὅσον εἰμὶ ἐν τούτῳ τῷ σκηνώματι,
right And I deem (it), so long as I am in this tabernacle,
1326 5209 1722 5280 1492 3754 5031 2076 3588
διεγείρειν ὑμᾶς ἐν ὑπομνήσει· 14 εἰδὼς ὅτι ταχινή ἐστιν ἡ
to arouse you by a reminder; knowing that soon is the
595 3588 4638 3450 2531 2532 3588 2962 2257
ἀπόθεσις τοῦ σκηνώματός μου, καθὼς καὶ ὁ Κύριος ἡμῶν
putting off of the tabernacle of me, even as also the Lord of us
2424 5547 1213 3427 4704 1161 2532 1539
Ἰησοῦς Χριστὸς ἐδήλωσέ μοι. 15 σπουδάσω δὲ καὶ ἑκάστοτε
Jesus Christ made clear to me. I will be diligent And also always
2192 5209 3326 3588 1699 1841 3588 5130 3420
ἔχειν ὑμᾶς μετὰ τὴν ἐμὴν ἔξοδον τὴν τούτων μνήμην
to have you after my departure the of these things memory
4160 3756 1063 4679 3454 1811
ποιεῖσθαι. 16 οὐ γὰρ σεσοφισμένοις μύθοις ἐξακολουθήσαντες
to cause. not For having been cleverly devised fables having followed

12. Wherefore I will not be negligent to put you always in remembrance of these things, though ye know (them), and be established in the present truth.
13 Yea, I think it meet, as long as I am in this tabernacle, to stir you up by putting (you) in remembrance;
14 Knowing that shortly I must put off (this) my tabernacle, even as our Lord Jesus Christ hath shewed me.
15 Moreover I will endeavour that ye may be able after my decease to have these things always in remembrance.

16. For not having followed fables which had been cleverly devised, we made known to you the power and coming of our Lord Jesus Christ, but having become eyewitnesses of the majesty of that (One).

17 For having received honor and glory from God (the) Father, such a voice having been borne to Him from the magnificent glory, "This is My Son, the Beloved, in whom I found delight," (Matt. 17:5)

18 even we heard this voice having been borne out of Heaven, being with Him in the holy mountain,
19 and we have the more established prophetic word, in which

1107 5213 3588 3588 2962 2257 2424 5547
ἐγνωρίσαμεν ὑμῖν τὴν τοῦ Κυρίου ἡμῶν Ἰησοῦ Χριστοῦ
we made known to you the of the Lord of us Jesus Christ
1411 2532 3952 235 2030 1096 3588
δύναμιν καὶ παρουσίαν, ἀλλ' ἐπόπται γενηθέντες τῆς
power and coming, but eyewitnesses having become of the
1565 3168 2983 1063 3844 2316 3962
ἐκείνου μεγαλειότητος. 17 λαβὼν γὰρ παρὰ Θεοῦ πατρὸς
of that (One) majesty. having received For from God (the) Father
5092 2532 1391 5456 5342 846 5107 5259 3588
τιμὴν καὶ δόξαν, φωνῆς ἐνεχθείσης αὐτῷ τοιᾶσδε ὑπὸ τῆς
honor and glory, a voice having been borne to Him such from the
3169 1391 3778 2076 3588 5207 3450 3588 27
μεγαλοπρεποῦς δόξης, Οὗτός ἐστιν ὁ υἱός μου ὁ ἀγαπητός,
magnificent glory, This is the Son of Me the Beloved,
1519 3739 1473 2106 2532 3778 3588 5456 2249 191
εἰς ὃν ἐγὼ εὐδόκησα· 18 καὶ ταύτην τὴν φωνὴν ἡμεῖς ἠκού-
in whom I am well-pleased; and this voice we heard
1537 3772 5342 4862 846 5607 1722 3588 3735 3588
σαμεν ἐξ οὐρανοῦ ἐνεχθεῖσαν, σὺν αὐτῷ ὄντες ἐν τῷ ὄρει τῷ
out of Heaven having been borne, with Him being in the mountain
40 2532 2192 949 3588 4397 3056 3739
ἁγίῳ. 19 καὶ ἔχομεν βεβαιότερον τὸν προφητικὸν λόγον, ᾧ
holy. And we have more firm the prophetic Word, in which

16. For we have not followed cunningly devised fables, when we made known unto you the power and coming of our Lord Jesus Christ, but were eyewitnesses of his majesty.

17 For he received from God the Father honour and glory, when there came such a voice to him from the excellent glory, This is my beloved Son, in whom I am well pleased.

18 And this voice which came from heaven we heard, when we were with him in the holy mount.
19 We have also a more sure word of prophecy; whereunto

Literal Translation

you do well to take heed, as to a lamp shining in a murky place, until day dawns and the Daystar rises in your hearts;

20 knowing this first, that every prophecy of Scripture did not come into being of (its) own interpretation;

21 for prophecy was not at any time borne by (the) will of man, but having been borne along by (the) Holy Spirit, holy men of God spoke.

2 Peter 1:20

2573 4160 4337 5613 3088 5316 1722 850
καλῶς ποιεῖτε προσέχοντες, ὡς λύχνῳ φαίνοντι ἐν αὐχμηρῷ
well you do taking heed, as to a lamp shining in a murky

5117 2193 3757 2250 1306 2532 5459 393 1722
τόπῳ, ἕως οὗ ἡμέρα διαυγάσῃ, καὶ φωσφόρος ἀνατείλῃ ἐν
place, until day dawns, and (the) Daystar rises in

3588 2588 5216 5124 4412 1097 3754 3956
ταῖς καρδίαις ὑμῶν· 20 τοῦτο πρῶτον γινώσκοντες, ὅτι πᾶσα
the hearts of you; this firstly knowing, that every

4394 1124 2398 1955 3756 1096 3756 1063
προφητεία γραφῆς ἰδίας ἐπιλύσεως οὐ γίνεται. 21 οὐ γὰρ
prophecy of Scripture of (its) own unloosing not came into being. not For

2307 444 5342 4218 4394 235 5259
θελήματι ἀνθρώπου ἠνέχθη ποτὲ προφητεία, ἀλλ' ὑπὸ
by (the) will of man was borne at any time prophecy, but by

4151 40 5342 2980 40 2316 444
Πνεύματος Ἁγίου φερόμενοι ἐλάλησαν ἅγιοι Θεοῦ ἄνθρωποι.
(the) Spirit Holy being borne along spoke (the) holy of God men.

King James Version

ye do well that ye take heed, as unto a light that shineth in a dark place, until the day dawn, and the day star arise in your hearts:

20 Knowing this first, that no prophecy of the scripture is of any private interpretation.

21 For the prophecy came not in old time by the will of man: but holy men of God spake (as they were) moved by the Holy Ghost.

2 Peter 2

1. But false prophets were also among the people, as also false teachers will be among you, who will secretly bring in destructive heresies, and denying the Master who has bought them, bringing swift destruction on themselves.

2 And many will follow their destructive ways, by whom the way of truth will be evil spoken of.

3 And by covetousness, with well-turned words, they will use you for gain, for whom judgment of old does not linger, and their destruction does not slumber.

4. For if God did not spare sinning angels, but delivered (them) to chains of darkness, thrust down into Tartarus, having been kept to judgment;

5 and did not spare (the) ancient world, but preserved Noah (the) eighth, a herald of righteousness, bringing a flood on a world of ungodly ones;

6 and covering the cities (of) Sodom and Gomorrah with ashes, (He) condemned (them) with an overthrow, setting an example to (men) intending to live ungodly.

7 And

2 Peter 2

1096 1161 2532 5578 1722 3588 2992 5613 2532 1722
1. Ἐγένοντο δὲ καὶ ψευδοπροφῆται ἐν τῷ λαῷ, ὡς καὶ ἐν
there were But also false prophets among the people, as also among

5213 2071 5572 3748 3919
ὑμῖν ἔσονται ψευδοδιδάσκαλοι, οἵτινες παρεισάξουσιν
you will be false teachers, who will secretly. bring in

139 684 2532 3588 59 846 1203
αἱρέσεις ἀπωλείας, καὶ τὸν ἀγοράσαντα αὐτοὺς δεσπότην
heresies of destruction, and the having bought them Master

720 1863 1438 5031 684 2532
ἀρνούμενοι, ἐπάγοντες ἑαυτοῖς ταχινὴν ἀπώλειαν. 2 καὶ
denying, bringing on themselves swift destructon. And

4183 1811 846 3588 684 1223 3739
πολλοὶ ἐξακολουθήσουσιν αὐτῶν ταῖς ἀπωλείαις, δι' οὓς
many will follow of them the destructive ways, by whom

3588 3598 3588 225 987 2532 1722 4124
ἡ ὁδὸς τῆς ἀληθείας βλασφημηθήσεται. 3 καὶ ἐν πλεονεξίᾳ
the way of the truth will be evil spoken of. And by covetousness

4112 3056 5209 1710 3739 3588 2917 1597
πλαστοῖς λόγοις ὑμᾶς ἐμπορεύσονται· οἷς τὸ κρίμα ἔκπαλαι
with well-turned words you they will use for gain; for whom the judgment of old

3756 691 2532 3588 684 846 3756 3573 1487 1063 3588
οὐκ ἀργεῖ, καὶ ἡ ἀπώλεια αὐτῶν οὐ νυστάζει. 4 εἰ γὰρ ὁ
not lingers, and the destruction of them not slumbers. if For

2316 32 264 3756 5339 235 4577
Θεὸς ἀγγέλων ἁμαρτησάντων οὐκ ἐφείσατο, ἀλλὰ σειραῖς
God angels sinning not did spare, but by chains

2217 5020 3860 1519 2920 5083 2532
ζόφου ταρταρώσας παρέδωκεν εἰς κρίσιν τετηρημένους· 5 καὶ
of darkness thrust down into Tartarus delivered (them) to judgment having been kept; and

744 2889 3756 5339 235 3590 3575 1343
ἀρχαίου κόσμου οὐκ ἐφείσατο, ἀλλ' ὄγδοον Νῶε δικαιοσύνης
(the) ancient world not spared, but (the) eighth Noah of righteousness

2783 5442 2627 2889 765 1863 2532
κήρυκα ἐφύλαξε, κατακλυσμὸν κόσμῳ ἀσεβῶν ἐπάξας· 6 καὶ
a herald preserved, a flood a world of ungodly ones bringing on; and

4172 4670 2532 1116 5077 2692
πόλεις Σοδόμων καὶ Γομόρρας τεφρώσας καταστροφῇ
the cities Sodom and Gomorrah covering with ashes by an overthrow

2632 5262 3195 764 5087 2532
κατέκρινεν, ὑπόδειγμα μελλόντων ἀσεβεῖν τεθεικώς· 7 καὶ
condemned, an example of men intending to live ungodly setting; and

2 Peter 2

1. But there were false prophets also among the people, even as there shall be false teachers among you, who privily shall bring in damnable heresies, even denying the Lord that bought them, and bring upon themselves swift destruction.

2 And many shall follow their pernicious ways; by reason of whom the way of truth shall be evil spoken of.

3 And through covetousness shall they with feigned words make merchandise of you: whose judgment now of a long time lingereth not, and their damnation slumbereth not.

4 For if God spared not the angels that sinned, but cast (them) down to hell, and delivered (them) into chains of darkness, to be reserved unto judgment;

5 And spared not the old world, but saved Noah the eighth (person), a preacher of righteousness, bringing in the flood upon the world of the ungodly;

6 And turning the cities of Sodom and Gomorrha into ashes condemned (them) with an overthrow, making (them) an ensample unto those that after should live ungodly;

7 And

Literal Translation

He delivered righteous Lot, who had been oppressed by the behavior of the lawless in lustfulness.
8 For that righteous one living among them day after day, in seeing and in hearing, (his) righteous soul (was) tormented with (their) lawless works.
9. (But the) Lord knows to deliver the godly out of temptation, and to keep the unjust for a day of judgment, being punished,
10 and most of all those going after flesh in (the)_ lust of defilement, and despising dominion, darers, self-pleasing; they do not tremble (at) glories, speaking evil;

11 where angels being greater in strength and power do not bring against them a slandering charge before (the) Lord.
12 But these as unreasoning natural beasts, having been born for capture and corruption, speaking evil in that (of) which they are ignorant, they shall utterly perish in their corruption,
13 being about to receive (the) wages of unrighteousness, deeming indulgence in the day (to be) pleasure; spots and blemishes reveling (in) their deceits, feasting along with you,
14 having eyes full of an adulteress, and never ceasing from sin; alluring unsettled souls; having a heart busied (with) covetousness; cursed children;

15 forsaking a straight way, they went astray, following the way of Balaam the (son) of Beor, who loved (the) wages of unrighteousness,
16 but had reproof of (his) own transgression, the dumb ass speaking in a man's voice

2 Peter 2:8

1342 3091 2669 5259 3588 3588 113 1722
δίκαιον Λώτ, καταπονούμενον ὑπὸ τῆς τῶν ἀθέσμων ἐν
righteous Lot, having been oppressed by the of the lawless in

766 391 4506 990 1063 2532 189 3588
ἀσελγείᾳ ἀναστροφῆς ἐρρύσατο· 8 [βλέμματι γὰρ καὶ ἀκοῇ ὁ
lustfulness behavior delivered; in seeing for and hearing the

1342 1460 1722 846 2250 1537 2250 5590
δίκαιος ἐγκατοικῶν ἐν αὐτοῖς, ἡμέραν ἐξ ἡμέρας ψυχὴν
righteous one living among them, day after day (his) soul

1342 459 2041 928 1492 2962 2152
δικαίαν ἀνόμοις ἔργοις ἐβασάνιζεν]· 9 οἶδε Κύριος εὐσεβεῖς
righteous with lawless works tormented; knows (the) Lord (the) godly

1537 3986 4506 94 1161 1519 2250 2920 2849
ἐκ πειρασμῶν ῥύεσθαι, ἀδίκους δὲ εἰς ἡμέραν κρίσεως κολαζο-
out of temptation to deliver, the unjust But for a day of judgment being

5083 3122 1161 3588 3694 4561 1722 1939
μένους τηρεῖν, 10 μάλιστα δὲ τοὺς ὀπίσω σαρκὸς ἐν ἐπιθυμίᾳ
punished to keep, most of all and the after flesh in lust

3394 4198 2532 2963 2706
μιασμοῦ πορευομένους, καὶ κυριότητος καταφρονοῦντας.
of defilement (ones) going, and dominion despising.

5113 829 1391 3756 5141 987
τολμηταί, αὐθάδεις, δόξας οὐ τρέμουσι βλασφημοῦντες·
darers, self-pleasing, glories, not they tremble (at) speaking evil;

3699 32 2479 2532 1411 3173 5607 3756 5342
11 ὅπου ἄγγελοι, ἰσχύϊ καὶ δυνάμει μείζονες ὄντες, οὐ φέρουσι
where angels, in strength and power greater being, not do bring

2596 846 3844 2962 989 2920 3778 1161 5613
κατ᾽ αὐτῶν παρὰ Κυρίῳ βλάσφημον κρίσιν. 12 οὗτοι δέ, ὡς
against them before (the) Lord a slandering charge. these But, as

249 2226 5446 1080 1519 259 2532 5356 1722
ἄλογα ζῷα φυσικὰ γεγενημένα εἰς ἅλωσιν καὶ φθοράν, ἐν
unreasoning beasts natural having been born for capture and corruption, in

3739 50 987 1722 3588 5356 846 2704
οἷς ἀγνοοῦσι βλασφημοῦντες, ἐν τῇ φθορᾷ αὐτῶν καταφθαρή-
which they are ignorant speaking evil, in the corruption of them will utterly

2865 3408 93 2237 2233 3588
σονται, 13 κομιούμενοι μισθὸν ἀδικίας, ἡδονὴν ἡγούμενοι τὴν
perish, being about to receive wages of wrong, (as) pleasure deeming

1722 2250 5172 4696 2532 3470 1792 1722 3588
ἐν ἡμέρᾳ τρυφήν, σπίλοι καὶ μῶμοι, ἐντρυφῶντες ἐν ταῖς
in (the) day indulgence, spots and blemishes, reveling (in) in the

539 846 4910 5213 3788 2192
ἀπάταις αὐτῶν συνευωχούμενοι ὑμῖν, 14 ὀφθαλμοὺς ἔχοντες
deceits of them feasting along with you, eyes having

3324 3428 2532 180 266 1185
μεστοὺς μοιχαλίδος καὶ ἀκαταπαύστους ἁμαρτίας, δελεά-
full of an adulteress and not ceasing from sin, alluring

5590 793 2588 1128 4124
ζοντες ψυχὰς ἀστηρίκτους, καρδίαν γεγυμνασμένην πλεονε-
souls unsettled, a heart having been busied covetous-

2192 2671 5043 2641 3588 2117
ξίαις ἔχοντες, κατάρας τέκνα· 15καταλιπόντες τὴν εὐθεῖαν
ness having, of curse children; forsaking the straight

3598 4105 1811 3588 3598 3588 903 3588
ὁδὸν ἐπλανήθησαν, ἐξακολουθήσαντες τῇ ὁδῷ τοῦ Βαλαὰμ τοῦ
way they went astray, following the way of Balaam

1007 3739 3408 93 25 1649 1161 2192 2398
Βοσόρ, ὃς μισθὸν ἀδικίας ἠγάπησεν, 16 ἔλεγξιν δὲ ἔσχεν ἰδίας
(son of) Beor, who wages of wrong loved, reproof and had of own

3892 5268 880 1722 444 5456 5350
παρανομίας· ὑποζύγιον ἄφωνον ἐν ἀνθρώπου φωνῇ φθεγξά-
transgression; ass a dumb with of a man voice speaking

King James Version

delivered just Lot, vexed with the filthy conversation of the wicked:
8 (For that righteous man dwelling among them, in seeing and hearing, vexed (his) righteous soul from day to day with (their) unlawful deeds;)
9 The Lord knoweth how to deliver the godly out of temptations, and to reserve the unjust unto the day of judgment to be punished:
10. But chiefly them that walk after the flesh in the lust of uncleanness, and despise government. Presumptuous (are they), selfwilled, they are not afraid to speak evil of dignities.

11 Whereas angels, which are greater in power and might, bring not railing accusation against them before the Lord.
12 But these, as natural brute beasts, made to be taken and destroyed, speak evil of the things that they understand not; and shall utterly perish in their own corruption;
13 And shall receive the reward of unrighteousness, (as) they that count it pleasure to riot in the day time. Spots (they are) and blemishes, sporting themselves with their own deceivings while they feast with you;
14 Having eyes full of adultery, and that cannot cease from sin; beguiling unstable souls: an heart they have exercised with covetous practices; cursed children:
15 Which have forsaken the right way, and are gone astray, following the way of Balaam (the son) of Bosor, who loved the wages of unrighteousness;
16 But was rebuked for his iniquity: the dumb ass speaking with man's voice

Literal Translation

held back the madness of the prophet.
17. These are springs without water, clouds being driven by tempest, for whom the blackness of darkness has been kept to the ages.
18 For speaking overswollen (words) of vanity, by (the) lusts of the flesh, by unbridled lusts, they allure those indeed escaping the ones living in error,

19 promising them freedom, (though) themselves being slaves of corruption, for by whom anyone has been subdued, even to this one he has been enslaved.
20 For if by a full knowledge of the Lord and Savior, Jesus Christ, (they) have escaped the defilements of the world, and again being entangled (they) have been subdued by these, (then their) last things have become worse (than) the first.
21 For it was better for them not to have fully known the way of righteousness, than fully knowing to turn from the holy commandment delivered to them.

22 But (the) word of the true proverb has happened to them: (The) dog having returned to (his) own vomit; also, (the) sow having been washed to wallowing (in) mud. (Prov. 26:11)

2 Peter 2:17

2967 3588 3588 4396 3913 3778 1526
μενον, ἐκώλυσε τὴν τοῦ προφήτου παραφρονίαν. 17 οὗτοί εἰσι
restrained the of the prophet madness. These are

4077 504 3507 5259 2978 1643 3739 3588
πηγαὶ ἄνυδροι, νεφέλαι ὑπὸ λαίλαπος ἐλαυνόμεναι, οἷς ὁ
springs without water, clouds by tempest being driven, for whom the

2217 3588 4655 1519 165 5083 5246 1063
ζόφος τοῦ σκότους εἰς αἰῶνα τετήρηται. 18 ὑπέρογκα γὰρ
blackness of darkness to (the) ages has been kept. overswollen (words) for

3153 5350 1185 1722 1939 4561
ματαιότητος φθεγγόμενοι, δελεάζουσιν ἐν ἐπιθυμίαις σαρκός,
of vanity speaking, they allure by (the) lusts of (the) flesh,

1722 1939 3588 3689 668 3588 1722 4106
ἐν ἀσελγείαις, τοὺς οντως ἀποφυγόντας τοὺς ἐν πλάνῃ
in unbridled lusts, the (ones) indeed escaping the (ones) in error

390 1657 846 1861 846
ἀναστρεφομένους, 19 ἐλευθερίαν αὐτοῖς ἐπαγγελλόμενοι, αὐτοὶ
living, freedom to them promising, themselves

1401 5225 3588 5356 3739 1063 5100 2274
δοῦλοι ὑπάρχοντες τῆς φθορᾶς· ᾧ γάρ τις ἥττηται,
slaves being of corruption; by whom for any has been subdued,

5129 2532 1402 1487 1063 668 3588 3393 3588
τούτῳ καὶ δεδούλωται. 20 εἰ γὰρ ἀποφυγόντες τὰ μιάσματα τοῦ
to this one also he has been enslaved. if For having escaped the defilements of the

2889 1722 1922 3588 2962 2532 4990 2424 5547
κόσμου ἐν ἐπιγνώσει τοῦ Κυρίου καὶ σωτῆρος Ἰησοῦ Χρι-
world by a full knowledge of the Lord and Savior Jesus Christ,

5125 1161 3825 1707 2274 1096 846
στοῦ, τούτοις δὲ πάλιν ἐμπλακέντες ἡττῶνται, γέγονεν αὐτοῖς
by these and again being entangled they are subdued, has become to them

3588 2078 5501 3588 4413 2909 1063 2258 846
τὰ ἔσχατα χείρονα τῶν πρώτων. 21 κρεῖττον γὰρ ἦν αὐτοῖς
the last things worse (than) the first. better For it was for them

3361 1921 3588 3598 3588 1343 2228 1921
μὴ ἐπεγνωκέναι τὴν ὁδὸν τῆς δικαιοσύνης, ἢ ἐπιγνοῦσιν
not to have fully known the way of righteousness, than fully knowing

1994 1537 3588 3860 846 40 1785
ἐπιστρέψαι ἐκ τῆς παραδοθείσης αὐτοῖς ἁγίας ἐντολῆς.
to turn from the delivered to them holy commandment.

4819 1161 846 3588 3588 227 3942 2965
22 συμβέβηκε δὲ αὐτοῖς τὸ τῆς ἀληθοῦς παροιμίας, Κύων
has happened to them the (word) of The true proverb, (The) dog

1994 1909 3588 2398 1829 2532 5300 3068 1519
ἐπιστρέψας ἐπὶ τὸ ἴδιον ἐξέραμα, καί, ὗς λουσαμένη εἰς
having returned to the own vomit, and, (the) sow washed to

2946 1004
κύλισμα βορβόρου.
wallowing of mud.

King James Version

forbad the madness of the prophet.
17. These are wells without water, clouds that are carried with a tempest; to whom the mist of darkness is reserved for ever.
18 For when they speak great swelling (words) of vanity, they allure through the lusts of the flesh, (through much) wantonness, those that were clean escaped from them who live in error.

19 While they promise them liberty, they themselves are the servants of corruption: for of whom a man is overcome, of the same is he brought in bondage.
20 For if after they have escaped the pollutions of the world through the knowledge of the Lord and Saviour Jesus Christ, they are again entangled therein, and overcome, the latter end is worse with them than the beginning.

21 For it had been better for them not to have known the way of righteousness, than, after they have known (it), to turn from the holy commandment delivered unto them.

22 But it is happened unto them according to the true proverb, The dog (is) turned to his own vomit again; and the sow that was washed to her wallowing in the mire.

2 Peter 3

1. Beloved, I now write to you this second epistle, in which by reminder I stir up your sincere mind to remember

2 the words having been spoken before by the holy prophets, and the command of the

2 Peter 3

3778 2235 27 1208 5213 1125 1992
1. Ταύτην ἤδη, ἀγαπητοί, δευτέραν ὑμῖν γράφω ἐπιστολήν,
This now, beloved, second to you I write epistle,

1722 3739 1326 5216 1722 5280 3588 1506 1271
ἐν αἷς διεγείρω ὑμῶν ἐν ὑπομνήσει τὴν εἰλικρινῆ διάνοιαν,
in which I stir up you by reminder the sincere mind,

3415 3588 4280 4487 5259 3588 40
2 μνησθῆναι τῶν προειρημένων ῥημάτων ὑπὸ τῶν ἁγίων
to remember the having been spoken words by the holy

4396 2532 3588 3588 652 2257 1785 3588
προφητῶν, καὶ τῆς τῶν ἀποστόλων ἡμῶν ἐντολῆς τοῦ
prophets, and the of the apostles of us command of the

2 Peter 3

1. This second epistle, beloved, I now write unto you; in (both) which I stir up your pure minds by way of remembrance:
2 That ye may be mindful of the words which were spoken before by the holy prophets, and of the commandment of us the apostles of the

Literal Translation

Lord and Savior by us,
the apostles;
3 firstly, knowing this,
that during (the) last
days scoffers will come
walking according to
their own lusts,

4 and saying, Where is
the promise of His com-
ing? For from which
(the) fathers fell asleep,
all things remain so
from the beginning of
creation.

5. For this is hidden
from them (by their)
willing (it so), that heav-
ens were of old, and
earth by water, and
through water, having
subsisted by the Word of
God,
6 through which the
world which then was,
being flooded by water,
perished.
7 But the heavens and
the earth now, having
been stored up by the
same Word, are being
kept for fire to a day of
judgment and destruc-
tion of ungodly men.

8. But let not this one
thing be hidden (from)
you, beloved, that one
day with (the) Lord (is)
as a thousand years, and
a thousand years as one
day.
9 The Lord is not slow
(concerning) the prom-
ise, as some deem slow-
ness, but is long-suffer-
ing toward us, not hav-
ing purposed any (of us)
to perish, but all (of us)
to come to repentance.
10 But (the) day of (the)
Lord will come as a
thief in (the) night, in
which the heavens will
pass away with rushing
sound, and burning,
(the) elements will be
dissolved, and earth and
the works in it will be
burned up.
11. Then all these be-
ing (about) to be dis-
solved, what sort ought
you to be in holy behav-
ior and godliness,

12 looking for and

2 Peter 3:3

2962 2532 4990 5124 4412 1097 3754
Κυρίου καὶ σωτῆρος· 3 τοῦτο πρῶτον γινώσκοντες, ὅτι
Lord and Savior; this firstly knowing, that

2064 1909 2078 3588 2250 1703 2596 3588
ἐλεύσονται ἐπ᾽ ἐσχάτου τῶν ἡμερῶν ἐμπαῖκται, κατὰ τὰς
will come during (the) last of the days scoffers, according to the

2398 846 1939 4198 2532 3004 4226
ἰδίας αὐτῶν ἐπιθυμίας πορευόμενοι, 4 καὶ λέγοντες, Ποῦ
own of them lusts going and saying, Where

2076 3588 1860 3588 3952 846 575 3739 1063 3588
ἐστιν ἡ ἐπαγγελία τῆς παρουσίας αὐτοῦ; ἀφ᾽ ἧς γὰρ οἱ
is the promise of the coming of Him? from which For the

3962 2837 3956 3779 1265 575 746
πατέρες ἐκοιμήθησαν, πάντα οὕτω διαμένει ἀπ᾽ ἀρχῆς
fathers fell asleep, all things so remain from (the) beginning

2937 2990 1063 846 5124 2309 3754 3772
κτίσεως. 5 λανθάνει γὰρ αὐτοὺς τοῦτο θέλοντας, ὅτι οὐρανοὶ
of creation. is hidden For them this (by their) willing, that heavens

2258 1597 2532 1093 1537 5204 2532 1223 5204 4921
ἦσαν ἔκπαλαι, καὶ γῆ ἐξ ὕδατος, καὶ δι᾽ ὕδατος συνεστῶσα,
were of old, and earth by water, and through water having subsisted,

3588 3588 2316 3056 1223 3739 3588 5119 2889 5204 2626
τῷ τοῦ Θεοῦ λόγῳ, 6 δι᾽ ὧν ὁ τότε κόσμος ὕδατι κατακλυ-
by the of God Word, by which the then world by water being

622 3588 1161 3568 3772 2532 3588 1093 3588 846 3056
σθεὶς ἀπώλετο· 7 οἱ δὲ νῦν οὐρανοὶ καὶ ἡ γῆ τῷ αὐτῷ λόγῳ
flooded perished. the But now heavens and the earth by the same Word

2343 1526 4442 5083 1519 2250 2920
τεθησαυρισμένοι εἰσί, πυρι, τηρούμενοι εἰς ἡμέραν κρίσεως
having been stored up are, for fire, being kept unto a day of judgment

2532 684 3588 765 444
καὶ ἀπωλείας τῶν ἀσεβῶν ἀνθρώπων.
and (the) destruction of ungodly men

1722 1161 5124 3361 2990 5209 27 3754 3391
8. Ἓν δὲ τοῦτο μὴ λανθανέτω ὑμᾶς, ἀγαπητοί, ὅτι μία
one But this thing not let be hidden from you, beloved, that one

2250 3844 2962 5613 5507 2094 2532 5507 2094 5613 2250
ἡμέρα παρὰ Κυρίῳ ὡς χίλια ἔτη, καὶ χίλια ἔτη ὡς ἡμέρα
day with (the) Lord (is) as a thousand years and a thousand years as day

3391 3756 1019 3588 2962 3588 1860 5613 5100 1022
μία. 9 οὐ βραδύνει ὁ Κύριος τῆς ἐπαγγελίας, ὥς τινες βραδυ-
one. Not is slow the Lord of the promise, as some slowness

2233 235 3114 1519 2248 3361 1014
τητα ἡγοῦνται· ἀλλὰ μακροθυμεῖ εἰς ἡμᾶς, μὴ βουλόμενός
deem; but is long-suffering toward us, not purposing

5100 622 235 3956 1519 3341 5562 2240
τινας ἀπολέσθαι, ἀλλὰ πάντας εἰς μετάνοιαν χωρῆσαι. 10 ἥξει
any (of us) to perish, but all (of us) to repentance to come. will come

1161 3588 2250 2962 5613 2812 1722 3571 1722 3739 3588 3772
δὲ ἡ ἡμέρα Κυρίου ὡς κλέπτης ἐν νυκτι, ἐν ᾗ οἱ οὐρανοὶ
But (the) day of (the) Lord as a thief in (the) night, in which the heavens

4500 3928 4747 1161 2741 3089
ῥοιζηδὸν παρελεύσονται, στοιχεῖα δὲ καυσούμενα λυθή-
with rushing sound will pass away, (the) elements and burning will be

2532 1093 2532 3588 1722 846 2041 2618 5130
σονται, καὶ γῆ καὶ τὰ ἐν αὐτῇ ἔργα κατακαήσεται. 11 τούτων
dissolved, and earth and the in it works will be burned up. these things

3767 3956 3089 4217 1163 5225 5209 1722
οὖν πάντων λυομένων, ποταποὺς δεῖ ὑπάρχειν ὑμᾶς ἐν
Then all being dissolved, what sort ought to be you in

40 391 2532 2150 4328 2532
ἁγίαις ἀναστροφαῖς καὶ εὐσεβείαις, 12 προσδοκῶντας καὶ
holy behavior and godliness, looking for and

King James Version

Lord and Saviour:
3 Knowing this first,
that there shall come in
the last days scoffers,
walking after their own
lusts,

4 And saying, Where is
the promise of his com-
ing? for since the fathers
fell asleep, all things
continue as (they were)
from the beginning of
the creation.

5. For this they will-
ingly are ignorant of,
that by the word of God
the heavens were of old,
and the earth standing
out of the water and in
the water:
6 Whereby the world
that then was, being
overflowed with water,
perished:
7 But the heavens and
the earth, which are
now, by the same word
are kept in store, re-
served unto fire against
the day of judgment and
perdition of ungodly
men.

8 But, beloved, be not
ignorant of this one
thing, that one day (is)
with the Lord as a thou-
sand years, and a thou-
sand years as one day.
9 The Lord is not slack
concerning his prom-
ise, as some men count
slackness; but is long-
suffering to us-ward,
not willing that any
should perish, but that
all should come to re-
pentance.
10 But the day of the
Lord will come as a
thief in the night; in the
which the heavens shall
pass away with a great
noise, and the elements
shall melt with fervent
heat, the earth also and
the works that are
therein shall be burned
up.
11. (Seeing) then (that)
all these things shall be
dissolved, what manner
(of persons) ought ye to
be in (all) holy conver-
sation and godliness,
12 Looking for and

Literal Translation

hastening the coming of the Day of God, through which (the) heavens having been set afire will be dissolved; and burning, (the) elements will melt?
13 But according to His promise, we look for new heavens and a new earth, in which righteousness dwells.

14. Because of this, beloved, looking for these things, be diligent, spotless, and without blemish, to be found in peace by Him.
15 And think of the long-suffering of our Lord (as) salvation, as also our beloved brother Paul wrote to you, according to the wisdom given to him;

16 as also in all his epistles, speaking in them concerning these things, in which are some things hard to understand, which the unlearned and unsettled pervert, as also (they do) the rest of the Scriptures, to (their) own destruction.
17. Then beloved, you knowing beforehand, watch lest being led away by the error of the lawless you fall from (your) own steadfastness.

18 But grow in grace and knowledge of our Lord and Savior, Jesus Christ. To Him (be) the glory, both now and to (the) day of eternity. Amen.

2 Peter 3:13

4692 3588 3952 3588 3588 2316 2250 1223 3739
σπεύδοντας τὴν παρουσίαν τῆς τοῦ Θεοῦ ἡμέρας, δι᾽ ἣν
hastening the coming of the of God Day, for which

3772 4448 3089 2532 4747 2741
οὐρανοὶ πυρούμενοι λυθήσονται, καὶ στοιχεῖα καυσούμενα
(the) heavens having been fired will be dissolved, and (the) elements burning

5080 2537 1161 3772 2532 1093 2537 2596 3588
τήκεται. 13 καινοὺς δὲ οὐρανοὺς καὶ γῆν καινὴν κατὰ τὸ
will melt. new But heavens and earth new according to the

1862 846 4328 1722 3739 1343 2730
ἐπάγγελμα αὐτοῦ προσδοκῶμεν, ἐν οἷς δικαιοσύνη κατοικεῖ.
promise of Him we look for, in which righteousness dwells.

1352 27 5023 4328 4704
14. Διό, ἀγαπητοί, ταῦτα προσδοκῶντες σπουδάσατε
Therefore, beloved, these things looking for be diligent

784 2532 298 846 2147 1722 1515 2532 3588
ἄσπιλοι καὶ ἀμώμητοι αὐτῷ εὑρεθῆναι ἐν εἰρήνῃ. 15 καὶ τὴν
spotless and without blemish, by Him to be found in peace. And the

3588 2962 2257 3115 4991 2233 2531
τοῦ Κυρίου ἡμῶν μακροθυμίαν σωτηρίαν ἡγεῖσθε, καθὼς
of the Lord of us long-suffering salvation deem, even as

2532 3588 27 2257 80 3972 2596 3588 846
καὶ ὁ ἀγαπητὸς ἡμῶν ἀδελφὸς Παῦλος κατὰ τὴν αὐτῷ
also the beloved of us brother Paul according to the of him

1325 4678 1125 5213 5613 2532 1722 3956 3588
δοθεῖσαν σοφίαν ἔγραψεν ὑμῖν· 16 ὡς καὶ ἐν πάσαις ταῖς
given wisdom wrote to you; as also in all (his)

1992 2980 1722 846 4012 5130 1722 3739 2076 1425
ἐπιστολαῖς, λαλῶν ἐν αὐταῖς περὶ τούτων· ἐν οἷς ἐστι δυσνόη-
epistles, speaking in them concerning these; in which are hard to under-

5100 3739 3588 261 2532 793 4761 5613 2532 3588
τά τινα, ἃ οἱ ἀμαθεῖς καὶ ἀστήρικτοι στρεβλοῦσιν, ὡς καὶ τὰς
stand some, which the unlearned and unsettled pervert, as also the

3062 1124 4314 3588 2398 846 684 5210 3767
λοιπὰς γραφάς, πρὸς τὴν ἰδίαν αὐτῶν ἀπώλειαν. 17 ὑμεῖς οὖν,
remaining Scriptures, to the own of them destruction. You then,

27 4267 5442 2443 3361 3588 3588
ἀγαπητοί, προγινώσκοντες φυλάσσεσθε, ἵνα μή, τῇ τῶν
beloved, knowing beforehand watch, that not by the of the

113 4106 4879 1601 3588 2398 4740
ἀθέσμων πλάνῃ συναπαχθέντες, ἐκπέσητε τοῦ ἰδίου στηριγ-
lawless error being led away, you fall from the own steadfast-

837 1161 1722 5485 2532 1108 3588 2962 2257 2532
μοῦ. 18 αὐξάνετε δὲ ἐν χάριτι καὶ γνώσει τοῦ Κυρίου ἡμῶν καὶ
ness. grow But in grace and knowledge of the Lord of us and

4990 2424 5547 846 3588 1391 2532 3568 2532 1519
σωτῆρος Ἰησοῦ Χριστοῦ. αὐτῷ ἡ δόξα καὶ νῦν καὶ εἰς
Savior Jesus Christ. To Him (be) the glory both now and to

2250 165 281
ἡμέραν αἰῶνος. ἀμήν.
a day of eternity. Amen.

King James Version

hasting unto the coming of the day of God, wherein the heavens being on fire shall be dissolved, and the elements shall melt with fervent heat?
13 Nevertheless we, according to his promise, look for new heavens and a new earth, wherein dwelleth righteousness.

14 Wherefore, beloved, seeing that ye look for such things, be diligent that ye may be found of him in peace, without spot, and blameless.
15 And account (that) the longsuffering of our Lord (is) salvation; even as our beloved brother Paul also according to the wisdom given unto him hath written unto you;
16 As also in all (his) epistles, speaking in them of these things; in which are some things hard to be understood, which they that are unlearned and unstable wrest, as (they do) also the other scriptures, unto their own destruction.
17 Ye therefore, beloved, seeing ye know (these things) before, beware lest ye also, being led away with the error of the wicked, fall from your own stedfastness.

18 But grow in grace, and (in) the knowledge of our Lord and Saviour Jesus Christ. To him (be) glory both now and for ever. Amen.

THE FIRST GENERAL EPISTLE OF JOHN

1 John 1

1. (We announce to you) what was from the beginning, what we have heard, what we have seen with our eyes, what we beheld, and (what) our hands touched, concerning the Word of Life.
2 And the Life was revealed, and we have seen, and we bear witness, and we proclaim to you the everlasting Life which was with the Father, and was revealed to us.

3 We proclaim to you what we have seen, and (what) we have heard, that you also may have fellowship with us. And truly our fellowship (is) with the Father and with His Son, Jesus Christ.

4 And we write these things to you, that your joy may be full.

5. And this is the message which we have heard from Him, and we proclaim to you: God is light, and no darkness is in Him, none!

6 If we say that we have fellowship with Him, and we walk in the darkness, we lie and are not practicing the truth.

7 But if we walk in the light, as He is in the light, we have fellowship with one another, and the blood of His Son Jesus Christ cleanses us from all sin.

8 If we say that we have no sin, we deceive ourselves, and the truth is not in us.
9 If

ΙΩΑΝΝΟΥ
OF JOHN
ΕΠΙΣΤΟΛΗ ΚΑΘΟΛΙΚΗ ΠΡΩΤΗ
EPISTLE GENERAL FIRST

1 John 1

3739 2258 575 746 3739 191 3739 3708 3588
1. Ὃ ἦν ἀπ' ἀρχῆς, ὃ ἀκηκόαμεν, ὃ ἑωράκαμεν τοῖς
What was from (the) beginning, what we have heard, what we have seen

3788 2257 3739 2300 2532 3588 5495 2257
ὀφθαλμοῖς ἡμῶν, ὃ ἐθεασάμεθα, καὶ αἱ χεῖρες ἡμῶν
with the eyes of us, what we beheld, and the hands of us

5584 4012 3588 3056 3588 2222 2532 3588 2222 5319
ἐψηλάφησαν περὶ τοῦ λόγου τῆς ζωῆς 2 [καὶ ἡ ζωὴ ἐφανε-
touched concerning the Word of life, and the Life was

2532 3708 2532 3140 2532 518
ρώθη, καὶ ἑωράκαμεν, καὶ μαρτυροῦμεν, καὶ ἀπαγγέλλομεν
revealed, and we have seen, and we bear witness, and proclaim

5213 3588 2222 3588 166 3748 2258 4314 3588 3962 2532
ὑμῖν τὴν ζωὴν τὴν αἰώνιον, ἥτις ἦν πρὸς τὸν πατέρα, καὶ
to you the Life everlasting, which was with the Father, and

5319 2254 3739 3708 2532 191 518
ἐφανερώθη ἡμῖν]· 3 ὃ ἑωράκαμεν καὶ ἀκηκόαμεν, ἀπαγ-
was revealed to us; what we have seen and we have heard, we

5213 2443 2532 5210 2842 2192 3326 2257 2532
γέλλομεν ὑμῖν, ἵνα καὶ ὑμεῖς κοινωνίαν ἔχητε μεθ' ἡμῶν· καὶ
proclaim to you, that also you fellowship may have with us; indeed

3588 2842 1161 3588 2251 3326 3588 3962 2532 3326 3588 5207
ἡ κοινωνία δὲ ἡ ἡμετέρα μετὰ τοῦ πατρὸς καὶ μετὰ τοῦ υἱοῦ
fellowship and our (is) with the Father and with the Son

846 2424 5547 2532 5023 1125 5213 2443 3588 5479
αὐτοῦ Ἰησοῦ Χριστοῦ· 4 καὶ ταῦτα γράφομεν ὑμῖν, ἵνα ἡ χαρὰ
of Him Jesus Christ. And these things we write to you, that the joy

5216 3588 4137
ὑμῶν ᾖ πεπληρωμένη.
of you be fulfilled.

2532 3778 2076 3588 1860 3739 191 575 846 2532
5. Καὶ αὕτη ἐστὶν ἡ ἀγγελία ἣν ἀκηκόαμεν ἀπ' αὐτοῦ καὶ
And this is the message which we have heard from Him and

312 5213 3754 3588 2316 5457 2076 2532 4653 1722 846
ἀναγγέλλομεν ὑμῖν, ὅτι ὁ Θεὸς φῶς ἐστί, καὶ σκοτία ἐν αὐτῷ
we proclaim to you, that God light is, and darkness in Him

3756 2076 3762 1437 2036 3754 2842 2192 3326
οὐκ ἔστιν οὐδεμία. 6 ἐὰν εἴπωμεν ὅτι κοινωνίαν ἔχομεν μετ'
not is, none. If we say that fellowship we have with

846 2532 1722 3588 4655 4043 5574 2532 3756
αὐτοῦ, καὶ ἐν τῷ σκότει περιπατῶμεν, ψευδόμεθα, καὶ οὐ
Him, and in the darkness we walk, we lie, and not

4160 3588 225 225 1161 1722 3588 5457 4043
ποιοῦμεν τὴν ἀλήθειαν· 7 ἐὰν δὲ ἐν τῷ φωτὶ περιπατῶμεν,
are practicing the truth; if But in the light we walk,

5613 846 2076 1722 3588 5457 2842 2192 3326 240
ὡς αὐτός ἐστιν ἐν τῷ φωτί, κοινωνίαν ἔχομεν μετ' ἀλλήλων,
as He is in the light, fellowship we have with one another,

2532 3588 129 2424 5547 3588 5207 846 2511 2248
καὶ τὸ αἷμα Ἰησοῦ Χριστοῦ τοῦ υἱοῦ αὐτοῦ καθαρίζει ἡμᾶς
and the blood of Jesus Christ the Son of Him cleanses us

575 3956 266 1437 2036 3754 266 3756 2192
ἀπὸ πάσης ἁμαρτίας. 8 ἐὰν εἴπωμεν ὅτι ἁμαρτίαν οὐκ ἔχομεν,
from all sin. If we say that sin not we have,

1438 4105 2532 3588 225 3756 2076 1722 2254 1437
ἑαυτοὺς πλανῶμεν, καὶ ἡ ἀλήθεια οὐκ ἔστιν ἐν ἡμῖν. 9 ἐὰν
ourselves we deceive, and the truth not is in us. If

THE FIRST GENERAL EPISTLE OF JOHN

1 John 1

1 . That which was from the beginning, which we have heard, which we have seen with our eyes, which we have looked upon, and our hands have handled, of the Word of life;
2 (For the life was manifested, and we have seen (it), and bear witness, and shew unto you that eternal life, which was with the Father, and was manifested unto us;)

3 That which we have seen and heard declare we unto you, that ye also may have fellowship with us: and truly our fellowship (is) with the Father, and with his Son Jesus Christ.

4 And these things write we unto you, that your joy may be full.

5. This then is the message which we have heard of him, and declare unto you, that God is light, and in him is no darkness at all.

6 If we say that we have fellowship with him, and walk in darkness, we lie, and do not the truth:

7 But if we walk in the light, as he is in the light, we have fellowship one with another, and the blood of Jesus Christ his Son cleanseth us from all sin.

8 If we say that we have no sin, we deceive ourselves, and the truth is not in us.
9 If

Literal Translation

we confess our sins, He is faithful and righteous that He may forgive us the sins, and may cleanse us from all unrighteousness.

10 If we say that we have not sinned, we make Him a liar, and His word is not in us.

1 John 1:10

3670 3588 266 2257 4103 2076 2532 1342
ὁμολογῶμεν τὰς ἁμαρτίας ἡμῶν, πιστός ἐστι καὶ δίκαιος
we confess the sins of us, faithful He is and righteous

2443 863 2254 3588 266 2532 2511 2248 575 3956
ἵνα ἀφῇ ἡμῖν τὰς ἁμαρτίας, καὶ καθαρίσῃ ἡμᾶς ἀπὸ πάσης
that He may forgive us the sins, and may cleanse us from all

93 1437 2036 3754 3756 264 5583
ἀδικίας. 10 ἐὰν εἴπωμεν ὅτι οὐχ ἡμαρτήκαμεν, ψεύστην
unrighteousness. If we say that not we have sinned, a liar

4160 846 2532 3588 3056 846 3756 2076 1722 2254
ποιοῦμεν αὐτόν, καὶ ὁ λόγος αὐτοῦ οὐκ ἔστιν ἐν ἡμῖν.
we make Him, and the Word of Him not is in us.

King James Version

we confess our sins, he is faithful and just to forgive us (our) sins, and to cleanse us from all unrighteousness.

10 If we say that we have not sinned, we make him a liar, and his word is not in us.

1 John 2

1. My little children, I write these things to you so that you do not sin. And if anyone sins, we have an Advocate with the Father, Jesus Christ (the) righteous.
2 And He is (the) propitiation relating to our sins, and not relating to ours only, but also relating to all the world.

3. And by this we know that we have known Him, if we keep His commandments.
4 The (one) saying, I have known Him, and not keeping His commandments is a liar, and the truth is not in that one.
5 But whoever keeps His word, truly in this one the love of God has been perfected. By this we know that we are in Him.

6 The (one) saying to abide in Him ought so to walk himself as that (One) walked.
7 Brothers, I do not write a new commandment to you, but an old commandment which you had from (the) beginning. The old commandment is the Word which you heard from (the) beginning.
8 Again I write a new commandment to you what is true in Him and in you, because the darkness is passing away, and the true Light already shines.
9 The (one) saying to be in the light,

I John 2

5040 3450 5023 1125 5213 2443 3361 264 2532 1437
1. Τεκνία μου, ταῦτα γράφω ὑμῖν, ἵνα μὴ ἁμάρτητε. καὶ ἐάν
Little children of me, these things I write to you, that not you sin. And if

5100 264 3875 2192 4314 3588 3962 2424
τις ἁμάρτῃ, παράκλητον ἔχομεν πρὸς τὸν πατέρα, Ἰησοῦν
anyone sins, an advocate we have with the Father, Jesus

5547 1342 2532 846 2434 2076 4012 3588 266
Χριστὸν δίκαιον· 2 καὶ αὐτὸς ἱλασμός ἐστι περὶ τῶν ἁμαρτιῶν
Christ (the) righteous; and He a propitiation is concerning the sins

2257 3756 4012 3588 2251 1161 3440 235 2532 4012 3650
ἡμῶν· οὐ περὶ τῶν ἡμετέρων δὲ μόνον, ἀλλὰ καὶ περὶ ὅλου
of us; not concerning ours but only, but also concerning all

3588 2889 2532 1722 5129 1097 3754 1097 846
τοῦ κόσμου. 3 καὶ ἐν τούτῳ γινώσκομεν ὅτι ἐγνώκαμεν αὐτόν,
the world. And by this we know that we have known Him,

1437 3588 1785 846 5083 3588 3004 1097 846
ἐὰν τὰς ἐντολὰς αὐτοῦ τηρῶμεν. 4 ὁ λέγων, Ἔγνωκα αὐτόν,
if the commandments of Him we keep. The (one) saying, I have known Him,

2532 3588 1785 846 3361 5083 5583 2076 2532 1722 5129
καὶ τὰς ἐντολὰς αὐτοῦ μὴ τηρῶν, ψεύστης ἐστί, καὶ ἐν τούτῳ
and the commandments of Him not keeping, a liar is, and in this one

3588 225 3756 2076 3739 1161 302 5083 846 3588 3056 230
ἡ ἀλήθεια οὐκ ἔστιν· 5 ὃς δ' ἂν τηρῇ αὐτοῦ τὸν λόγον, ἀληθῶς
the truth not is; whoever keeps of Him the Word, truly

1722 5129 3588 26 3588 2316 5048 1722 5129 1097
ἐν τούτῳ ἡ ἀγάπη τοῦ Θεοῦ τετελείωται. ἐν τούτῳ γινώ-
in this one the love of God has been perfected. By this we know

3754 1722 846 2070 3588 3004 1722 846 3306 3784
σκομεν ὅτι ἐν αὐτῷ ἐσμέν· 6 ὁ λέγων ἐν αὐτῷ μένειν ὀφείλει,
that in Him we are; the (one) saying in Him to abide ought,

2531 1565 4043 2532 846 3779 4043
καθὼς ἐκεῖνος περιεπάτησε, καὶ αὐτὸς οὕτω περιπατεῖν.
even as that One walked, also himself so to walk.

80 3756 1785 2537 1125 5213 235 1785
7. Ἀδελφοί, οὐκ ἐντολὴν καινὴν γράφω ὑμῖν, ἀλλ' ἐντολὴν
Brothers, not a commandment new I write to you, but a commandment

3820 3739 2192 575 746 3588 1785 3588 3820 2076 3588
παλαιάν, ἣν εἴχετε ἀπ' ἀρχῆς· ἡ ἐντολὴ ἡ παλαιά ἐστιν ὁ
old, which you had from beginning; the commandment old is the

3056 3739 191 575 746 3825 1785 2537 1125
λόγος ὃν ἠκούσατε ἀπ' ἀρχῆς. 8 πάλιν ἐντολὴν καινὴν γράφω
Word which you have heard from beginning. Again commandment new I write

5213 3739 2076 227 1722 846 2532 1722 5213 3754 3588 4653 3855
ὑμῖν, ὅ ἐστιν ἀληθὲς ἐν αὐτῷ καὶ ἐν ὑμῖν· ὅτι ἡ σκοτία παρ-
to you, what is true in Him and in you; because the darkness is

2532/3588/5457/3588 228 2235 5316 3588 3004 1722 3588 5457
άγεται καὶ τὸ φῶς τὸ ἀληθινὸν ἤδη φαίνει. 9 ὁ λέγων ἐν τῷ φωτὶ
passing away and the light true already shines. He saying in the light

1 John 2

1. My little children, these things write I unto you, that ye sin not. And if any man sin, we have an advocate with the Father, Jesus Christ the righteous:
2 And he is the propitiation for our sins: and not for ours only, but also for (the sins of) the whole world.

3. And hereby we do know that we know him, if we keep his commandments.
4 He that saith, I know him, and keepeth not his commandments, is a liar, and the truth is not in him.

5 But whoso keepeth his word, in him verily is the love of God perfected: hereby know we that we are in him.

6 He that saith he abideth in him ought himself also so to walk, even as he walked.
7 Brethren, I write no new commandment unto you, but an old commandment which ye had from the beginning. The old commandment is the word which ye have heard from the beginning.
8 Again, a new commandment I write unto you, which thing is true in him and in you: because the darkness is past, and the true light now shineth.
9 He that saith he is in the light,

Literal Translation | **1 John 2:10** | **King James Version**

and hating his brother, is in the darkness until now.

10 The (one) loving his brother abides in the light, and no offense is in him.

11 But the (one) hating his brother is in the darkness, and walks in the darkness, and does not know where he is going, because the darkness blinded his eyes.

12. Little children, I write to you because you have been forgiven (your) sins through His name.

13 Fathers, I write to you because you have known Him from (the) beginning. I write to you, young men, because you overcome the evil. I write to you, young ones, because you have known the Father.

14 Fathers, I have written to you because you have known Him from (the) beginning. I have written to you, young men, because you are strong, and the word of God abides in you, and you have overcome the evil one.

15. Do not love the world nor the things in the world. If anyone loves the world, the love of the Father is not in him,

16 because all that (that is) in the world: the lust of the flesh, and the lust of the eyes, and the pride of life, is not of the Father, but is of the world.

17 And the world is passing away, and its lust. But the (one) doing the will of God abides to the age.

18. Young ones, it is a last hour, and as you heard that the antichrist is coming, even now many antichrists have come,

1511 2532 3588 80 846 3404 1722 3588 4653 2076 2193
εἶναι καὶ τὸν ἀδελφὸν αὐτοῦ μισῶν, ἐν τῇ σκοτίᾳ ἐστὶν ἕως
to be and the brother of him hating, in the darkness is until

737 3588 25 3588 80 846 1722 3588 5457 3404 2532
ἄρτι. 10 ὁ ἀγαπῶν τὸν ἀδελφὸν αὐτοῦ ἐν τῷ φωτὶ μένει, καὶ
now. The (one) loving the brother of him in the light abides, and

4625 1722 846 3756 2076 3588 1161 3404 3588 80
σκάνδαλον ἐν αὐτῷ οὐκ ἔστιν. 11 ὁ δὲ μισῶν τὸν ἀδελφὸν
offense in him not is. the (one) But hating the brother

846 1722 3588 4653 2076 2532 1722 3588 4653 4043 2532 3756
αὐτοῦ ἐν τῇ σκοτίᾳ ἐστί, καὶ ἐν τῇ σκοτίᾳ περιπατεῖ, καὶ οὐκ
of him in the darkness is, and in the darkness walks, and not

1492 4225 5217 3754 3588 4653 5186 3588 3788
οἶδε ποῦ ὑπάγει, ὅτι ἡ σκοτία ἐτύφλωσε τοὺς ὀφθαλμοὺς
knows where he is going, because the darkness blinded the eyes

846
αὐτοῦ.
of him.

1125 5213 5040 3754 863 5213 3588 266
12. Γράφω ὑμῖν, τεκνία, ὅτι ἀφέωνται ὑμῖν αἱ ἁμαρτίαι
I write to you, little children, for have been forgiven you the sins

1223 3588 3686 846 1125 5213 3962 3754 1097 3588
διὰ τὸ ὄνομα αὐτοῦ. 13 γράφω ὑμῖν, πατέρες, ὅτι ἐγνώκατε τὸν
because of the name of Him. I write to you, fathers, because you have known Him

575 746 1125 5213 3495 3754 3528 3588 4190
ἀπ᾽ ἀρχῆς. γράφω ὑμῖν, νεανίσκοι, ὅτι νενικήκατε τὸν πονη-
from beginning. I write to you, young men, because you have overcome the evil.

1125 5213 3813 3754 1097 3588 3962 1125
ρόν. 14 γράφω ὑμῖν, παιδία, ὅτι ἐγνώκατε τὸν πατέρα. ἔγραψα
I write to you little children, for you have known the father. I wrote

5213 3962 3754 1097 3588 575 746 1125 5213
ὑμῖν, πατέρες, ὅτι ἐγνώκατε τὸν ἀπ᾽ ἀρχῆς. ἔγραψα ὑμῖν,
to you, fathers, because you have known Him from beginning. I wrote to you,

3495 3754 2478 2075 2532 3588 3056 3588 2316 1722 5213
νεανίσκοι, ὅτι ἰσχυροί ἐστε, καὶ ὁ λόγος τοῦ Θεοῦ ἐν ὑμῖν
young men, because strong you are, and the Word of God in you

3306 2532 3528 3588 4190 3361 25 3588 2889
μένει, καὶ νενικήκατε τὸν πονηρόν. 15 μὴ ἀγαπᾶτε τὸν κόσμον,
abides, and you have overcome the evil. Not do love the world,

3366 3588 1722 3588 2889 1437 5100 25 3588 2889 3756 2076
μηδὲ τὰ ἐν τῷ κόσμῳ. ἐάν τις ἀγαπᾷ τὸν κόσμον, οὐκ ἔστιν
nor the things in the world. If anyone loves the world, not is

3588 26 3588 3962 1722 846 3754 3956 3588 1722 3588 2889 3588
ἡ ἀγάπη τοῦ πατρὸς ἐν αὐτῷ. 16 ὅτι πᾶν τὸ ἐν τῷ κόσμῳ, ἡ
the love of the Father in him. Because all (that is) in the world, the

1939 3588 4561 2532 3588 1939 3588 3788 2532 3588
ἐπιθυμία τῆς σαρκός, καὶ ἡ ἐπιθυμία τῶν ὀφθαλμῶν, καὶ ἡ
lust of the flesh, and the lust of the eyes, and the

212 3588 979 3756 2076 1537 3588 3962 235 1537 3588
ἀλαζονεία τοῦ βίου, οὐκ ἔστιν ἐκ τοῦ πατρός, ἀλλ᾽ ἐκ τοῦ
pride of life, not is of the Father, but of the

2889 2076 2532 3588 2889 3855 2532 3588 1939 846
κόσμου ἐστί. 17 καὶ ὁ κόσμος παράγεται, καὶ ἡ ἐπιθυμία αὐτοῦ·
world is. And the world is passing away, and the lust of it;

3588 1161 4160 3588 2307 3588 2316 3306 1519 3588 165
ὁ δὲ ποιῶν τὸ θέλημα τοῦ Θεοῦ μένει εἰς τὸν αἰῶνα.
the (one) but doing the will of God abides to the age.

3713 2078 5610 2076 2532 2531 191 3754 3588
18. Παιδία, ἐσχάτη ὥρα ἐστί· καὶ καθὼς ἠκούσατε ὅτι ὁ
Little children, (the) last hour it is; and as you heard that the

500 2064 2532 3568 500 4183 1096
ἀντίχριστος ἔρχεται, καὶ νῦν ἀντίχριστοι πολλοὶ γεγόνασιν·
antichrist is coming, and now antichrists many have come

and hateth his brother, is in darkness even until now.

10 He that loveth his brother abideth in the light, and there is none occasion of stumbling in him.

11 But he that hateth his brother is in darkness, and walketh in darkness, and knoweth not whither he goeth, because that darkness hath blinded his eyes.

12. I write unto you, little children, because your sins are forgiven you for his name's sake.

13 I write unto you, fathers, because ye have known him (that is) from the beginning. I write unto you, young men, because ye have overcome the wicked one. I write unto you, little children, because ye have known the Father.

14 I have written unto you, fathers, because ye have known him (that is) from the beginning. I have written unto you, young men, because ye are strong, and the word of God abideth in you, and ye have overcome the wicked one.

15. Love not the world, neither the things (that are) in the world. If any man love the world, the love of the Father is not in him.

16 For all that (is) in the world, the lust of the flesh, and the lust of the eyes, and the pride of life, is not of the Father, but is of the world.

17 And the world passeth away, and the lust thereof: but he that doeth the will of God abideth for ever.

18. Little children, it is the last time: and as ye have heard that antichrist shall come, even now are there many antichrists;

Literal Translation **2 John 2:19** ***King James Version***

from which you know that it is a last hour.
19 They went out from us, but they were not of us. For if they were of us, they would have remained with us; but (they left) so that it might be revealed that they all are not of us.

20 And you have an anointing from the Holy One, and you know all things.
21 I did not write to you because you do not know the truth, but because you know it, and because every lie is not of the truth.
22 Who is the liar, except the (one) denying, (saying) that Jesus is not the Christ? This is the antichrist, the (one) denying the Father and the Son.
23 Everyone denying the Son does not have the Father. The (one) confessing the Son also has the Father.

24. Then what you heard from (the) beginning, let it abide in you. If what you heard from (the) beginning abides in you, you will abide both in the Son and in the Father.
25 And this is the promise which He promised us: everlasting life.
26 I wrote these things to you concerning the ones leading you astray.
27 And the anointing which you received from Him abides in you, and you have no need that anyone teach you. But as His anointing teaches you concerning all things, and is true, and is not a lie, and as He taught you, abide in Him.

28 And now, little children, abide in Him, that when He is revealed we may have confidence, and not be shamed from Him in His coming.

29 If you know

3606 1097 3754 2078 5610 2076 1537 2257 1831
ὅθεν γινώσκομεν ὅτι ἐσχάτη ὥρα ἐστίν. 19 ἐξ ἡμῶν ἐξῆλθον,
from which you know that a last hour it is. From us they went out

235 3756 2258 1537 2257 1487 1063 2258 1537 2257 3306
ἀλλ' οὐκ ἦσαν ἐξ ἡμῶν· εἰ γὰρ ἦσαν ἐξ ἡμῶν, μεμενήκεισαν
but not they were of us; if for they were of us, they have remained

302 3326 2257 235 2443 5319 3754 3756 1526 3956
ἂν μεθ' ἡμῶν· ἀλλ' ἵνα φανερωθῶσιν ὅτι οὐκ εἰσὶ πάντες
would with us; but that it may be revealed that not they are all

1537 2257 2532 5210 5545 2192 575 3588 40 2532 1492
ἐξ ἡμῶν. 20 καὶ ὑμεῖς χρίσμα ἔχετε ἀπὸ τοῦ ἁγίου, καὶ οἴδατε
of us. And you an anointing have from the Holy One, and you know

3956 3756 1125 5210 3754 3756 1492 3588 225 235
πάντα. 21 οὐκ ἔγραψα ὑμῖν, ὅτι οὐκ οἴδατε τὴν ἀλήθειαν, ἀλλ'
all things. Not I wrote to you, because not you know the truth, but

3754 1492 846 2532 3754 3956 5579 1537 3588 225 3756
ὅτι οἴδατε αὐτήν, καὶ ὅτι πᾶν ψεῦδος ἐκ τῆς ἀληθείας οὐκ
because you know it, and because every lie of the truth not

2076 5100 2076 3588 5583 1487 3361 3588 720 3754 2424
ἔστι. 22 τίς ἐστιν ὁ ψεύστης, εἰ μὴ ὁ ἀρνούμενος ὅτι Ἰησοῦς
is. Who is the liar, except the (one) denying that Jesus

3756 2076 3588 5547 3778 2076 3588 500 3588 720
οὐκ ἔστιν ὁ Χριστός; οὗτός ἐστιν ὁ ἀντίχριστος, ὁ ἀρνούμενος
not is the Christ? This is the antichrist, the (one) denying

3588 3962 2532 3588 5207 3956 3588 720 3588 5207 3761
τὸν πατέρα καὶ τὸν υἱόν. 23 πᾶς ὁ ἀρνούμενος τὸν υἱὸν οὐδὲ
the Father and the Son. Everyone denying the Son neither

3588 3962 2192 3588 3671 3588 5207 2532 3588 3962 2192
τὸν πατέρα ἔχει· ὁ ὁμολογῶν τὸν υἱὸν καὶ τὸν πατέρα ἔχει.
the Father has; the (one) confessing the Son also the Father has.

5210 3767 3739 191 575 746 1722 5213 3306 1437 1722
24 ὑμεῖς οὖν ὃ ἠκούσατε ἀπ' ἀρχῆς, ἐν ὑμῖν μενέτω. ἐὰν ἐν
you then What you heard from beginning, in you let it abide. If in

5213 3306 3739 575 746 191 2532 5210 1722 3588 5207 2532
ὑμῖν μείνῃ ὃ ἀπ' ἀρχῆς ἠκούσατε, καὶ ὑμεῖς ἐν τῷ υἱῷ καὶ
you remains what from beginning you heard, both you in the Son and

1722 3588 3962 3306 2532 846 2076 3588 1860 3739 846
ἐν τῷ πατρὶ μενεῖτε. 25 καὶ αὕτη ἐστὶν ἡ ἐπαγγελία ἣν αὐτὸς
in the Father remains. And this is the promise which He

1861 2254 3588 2222 3588 166 5023 1125
ἐπηγγείλατο ἡμῖν, τὴν ζωὴν τὴν αἰώνιον. 26 ταῦτα ἔγραψα
promised us, the life everlasting. these things I wrote

5213 4012 3588 4105 5209 2532 5210 3588 5545 3739
ὑμῖν περὶ τῶν πλανώντων ὑμᾶς. 27 καὶ ὑμεῖς, τὸ χρίσμα ὃ
to you concerning those leading astray you. And you, the anointing which

2983 575 846 1722 5213 3306 2532 3756 5532 2192 2443 5100
ἐλάβετε ἀπ' αὐτοῦ ἐν ὑμῖν μένει, καὶ οὐ χρείαν ἔχετε ἵνα τις
you received from Him in you abides, and no need you have that any

1321 5209 235 5613 3588 846 5545 1321 5209 4012
διδάσκῃ ὑμᾶς· ἀλλ' ὡς τὸ αὐτὸ χρίσμα διδάσκει ὑμᾶς περὶ
teach you; but as the of Him anointing teaches you about

3956 2532 227 2076 2532 3756 2076 5579 2532 2531
πάντων, καὶ ἀληθές ἐστι, καὶ οὐκ ἔστι ψεῦδος, καὶ καθὼς
all things, an true is, and not is a lie, and even as

1321 5209 3306 1722 846 2532 3568 5040 3306 1722
ἐδίδαξεν ὑμᾶς, μενεῖτε ἐν αὐτῷ. 28 καὶ νῦν, τεκνία, μένετε ἐν
He taught you, abide in Him. And now, little children, abide in

846 2443 3752 5319 2192 3954 2532 3361
αὐτῷ· ἵνα ὅταν φανερωθῇ, εχωμεν παρρησίαν, καὶ μὴ
Him; that when He is revealed, we may have confidence, and not

153 575 846 1722 3588 3952 846 1437 1492
αἰσχυνθῶμεν ἀπ' αὐτοῦ ἐν τῇ παρουσίᾳ αὐτοῦ. 29 ἐὰν εἰδῆτε
be shamed from Him in the coming of Him. If you know

whereby we know that it is the last time.
19 They went out from us, but they were not of us; for if they had been of us, they would (no doubt) have continued with us: but (they went out), that they might be made manifest that they were not all of us.

20 But ye have an unction from the Holy One, and ye know all things.
21 I have not written unto you because ye know not the truth, but because ye know it, and that no lie is of the truth.

22 Who is a liar but he that denieth that Jesus is the Christ? He is antichrist, that denieth the Father and the Son.

23 Whosoever denieth the Son, the same hath not the Father: ((but) he that acknowledgeth the Son hath the Father also).

24. Let that therefore abide in you, which ye have heard from the beginning. If that which ye have heard from the beginning shall remain in you, ye also shall continue in the Son, and in the Father.
25 And this is the promise that he hath promised us, (even) eternal life.
26 These (things) have I written unto you concerning them that seduce you.
27 But the anointing which ye have received of him abideth in you, and ye need not that any man teach you: but as the same anointing teacheth you of all things, and is truth, and is no lie, and even as it hath taught you, ye shall abide in him.
28 And now, little children, abide in him; that, when he shall appear, we may have confidence, and not be ashamed before him at his coming.
29 If ye know

Literal Translation

that He is righteous, know that everyone doing righteousness has been generated from Him.

1 John 3:1

3754 1342 2076 1097 3754 3956 3588 4160 3588 1343
ὅτι δίκαιός ἐστι, γινώσκετε ὅτι πᾶς ὁ ποιῶν τὴν δικαιοσύνην
that righteous He is, know that everyone doing righteousness
1537 846 1080
ἐξ αὐτοῦ γεγέννηται.
from Him has been generated.

King James Version

that he is righteous, ye know that every one that doeth righteousness is born of him.

1 John 3

1. See what manner of love the Father has given us, that we may be called children of God. For this reason the world does not know us, because it did not know Him.
2 Beloved, now we are the children of God, and it was not yet revealed what we shall be. But we know that if He is revealed, we shall be like Him, because we shall see Him as He is.
3. And everyone having this hope on Him purifies himself even as that (One) is pure.

4 Everyone practicing sin also practices lawlessness, and sin is lawlessness.
5 And you know that He was revealed that He might take away our sins, and sin is not in Him.

6 Everyone abiding in Him does not sin. Everyone sinning has not seen Him, nor known Him.

7 Little children, let no one lead you astray; the (one) practicing righteousness is righteous, even as that One is righteous.
8 The (one) practicing sin is of the Devil, because the Devil sins from (the) beginning. For this the Son of God was revealed, that He undo the works of the Devil.
9 Everyone who has been generated of God does not sin, because His seed abides in him, and he is not able to sin, because he has been generated of God.
10 By this

1 John 3

1492 4217 26 1325 2254 3588 3962 2443 5043
1. ἴδετε ποταπὴν ἀγάπην δέδωκεν ἡμῖν ὁ πατήρ, ἵνα τέκνα
See what manner of love has given us the Father, that children
2316 2564 1223 5124 3588 2889 3756 1097 2248 3754
Θεοῦ κληθῶμεν. διὰ τοῦτο ὁ κόσμος οὐ γινώσκει ἡμᾶς, ὅτι
of God we may be called. Therefore the world not knows us because
3756 1097 846 27 3568 5043 2316 2070 2532 3768
οὐκ ἔγνω αὐτόν. 2 ἀγαπητοί, νῦν τέκνα Θεοῦ ἐσμέν, καὶ οὔπω
not it knew Him. Beloved, now children of God we are, and not yet
5319 5100 2071 1492 1161 3754 1437 5319 3664
ἐφανερώθη τί ἐσόμεθα· οἴδαμεν δὲ ὅτι ἐὰν φανερωθῇ, ὅμοιοι
was it revealed what we shall be; we know but that if He is revealed, like
846 2071 3754 3700 846 2531 2076 2532 3956 3588
αὐτῷ ἐσόμεθα, ὅτι ὀψόμεθα αὐτὸν καθώς ἐστι. 3 καὶ πᾶς ὁ
Him we will be, bccause we will see Him as He is. And everyone
2192 3588 1680 3778 1909 846 48 1438 2531
ἔχων τὴν ἐλπίδα ταύτην ἐπ᾽ αὐτῷ ἁγνίζει ἑαυτόν, καθὼς
having hope this on him purifies himself, even as
1565 53 2076 3956 3588 4160 3588 266 2532 3588
ἐκεῖνος ἁγνός ἐστι. 4 πᾶς ὁ ποιῶν τὴν ἁμαρτίαν, καὶ τὴν
that One pure is. Everyone practicing sin, also
458 4160 2532 3588 266 2076 3588 458 2532 1492 3754
ἀνομίαν ποιεῖ· καὶ ἡ ἁμαρτία ἐστὶν ἡ ἀνομία. 5 καὶ οἴδατε ὅτι
lawlessness practices; and sin is lawlessness. And you know that
1565 5319 2443 5100 266 2257 142 2532 264
ἐκεῖνος ἐφανερώθη, ἵνα τὰς ἁμαρτίας ἡμῶν ἄρῃ· καὶ ἁμαρτία
that (one) was revealed, that the sins of us He might take away; and sin
1722 846 3756 2076 3956/3588/1722/846 3306 3756 264 3956/3588
ἐν αὐτῷ οὐκ ἔστι. 6 πᾶς ὁ ἐν αὐτῷ μένων οὐχ ἁμαρτάνει· πᾶς ὁ
in Him not is. Everyone in Him abiding not sins; evcryone
264 3756 3708 846 3761 1097 846
ἁμαρτάνων οὐχ ἑώρακεν αὐτόν, οὐδὲ ἔγνωκεν αὐτόν.
sinning not has seen Him, nor known Him.

5040 3367 4105 5209 3588 4160 3588 1343
7 τεκνία, μηδεὶς πλανάτω ὑμᾶς· ὁ ποιῶν τὴν δικαιοσύνην
Little children, no one let lead astray you; the (one) practicing righteousness
1342 2076 2531 1565 1342 2076 3588 4160 3588
δίκαιός ἐστι, καθὼς ἐκεῖνος δίκαιός ἐστιν· 8 ὁ ποιῶν τὴν
righteous is, even as that (One) righteous is; the (one) practicing
266 1537 3588 1228 2076 3754 575 746 3588 1228
ἁμαρτίαν ἐκ τοῦ διαβόλου ἐστίν, ὅτι ἀπ᾽ ἀρχῆς ὁ διάβολος
sin of the devil is, because from beginning the devil
264 1519 5124 5319 3588 5207 3588 2316 2443 3089
ἁμαρτάνει. εἰς τοῦτο ἐφανερώθη ὁ υἱὸς τοῦ Θεοῦ, ἵνα λύσῃ
sins. For this was revealed the Son of God, that He undo
3588 2041 3588 1228 3956 3588 1080 1537 3588 2316
τὰ ἔργα τοῦ διαβόλου. 9 πᾶς ὁ γεγεννημένος ἐκ τοῦ Θεοῦ
the works of the devil. Everyone having been generated of God
266 3756 4160 3754 4690 846 1722 846 3306 2532 3756
ἁμαρτίαν οὐ ποιεῖ, ὅτι σπέρμα αὐτοῦ ἐν αὐτῷ μένει· καὶ οὐ
sin not does, because seed of Him in him abides; and not
1410 264 3754 1537 3588 2316 1080 1722 5129
δύναται ἁμαρτάνειν, ὅτι ἐκ τοῦ Θεοῦ γεγέννηται. 10 ἐν τούτῳ
he is able to sin, because of God he has been generated. By this

1 John 3

1. Behold, what manner of love the Father hath bestowed upon us, that we should be called the sons of God: therefore the world knoweth us not, because it knew him not.
2 Beloved, now are we the sons of God, and it doth not yet appear what we shall be: but we know that, when he shall appear, we shall be like him; for we shall see him as he is.
3. And every man that hath this hope in him purifieth himself, even as he is pure.

4 Whosoever committeth sin transgresseth also the law: for sin is the transgression of the law.
5 And ye know that he was manifested to take away our sins; and in him is no sin.

6 Whosoever abideth in him sinneth not: whosoever sinneth hath not seen him, neither known him.

7 Little children, let no man deceive you: he that doeth righteousness is righteous, even as he is righteous.
8 He that committeth sin is of the devil; for the devil sinneth from the beginning. For this purpose the Son of God was manifested, that he might destroy the works of the devil.

9 Whosoever is born of God doth not commit sin; for his seed remaineth in him: and he cannot sin, because he is born of God.

10 In this

Literal Translation

the children of God and
the children of the Devil
are revealed: Everyone
not practicing right-
eousness is not of God;
also the (one) not loving
his brother.
11. Because this is the
message which you
heard from (the) begin-
ning, that we should
love one another,
12 not as Cain was of
the evil, and killed his
brother. And for what
did he kill him? Be-
cause his works were
evil, but the things of his
brother (were) right-
eous.

13 Do not marvel, my
brothers, if the world
hates you.
14 We know that we
have passed from death
to life because we love
the brothers. The (one)
not loving the brother
remains in death.

15 Everyone hating the
brother is a murderer,
and you know that
every murderer does
not have everlasting life
abiding in him.

16. By this we have
known the love of God,
because that (One) laid
down His life on behalf
of us; and on behalf of
the brothers we ought to
lay down (our) lives.

17 Whoever has the
means of life of the
world, and sees his
brother having need,
and shuts up his bowels
from him, how does the
love of God abide in
him?

18 My little children, let
us not love in word, or
in tongue, but in deed
and in truth.
19 And in this we shall
know that we are of the
truth, and shall per-
suade our hearts before
Him,

1 John 3:11

5318 2076 3588 5043 3588 2316 2532 3588 5043 3588 1228
φανερά ἐστι τὰ τέκνα τοῦ Θεοῦ καὶ τὰ τέκνα τοῦ διαβόλου·
revealed are the children of God and the children of the devil;

3956 3588 3361 4160 1343 3756 2076 1537 3588 2316 2532 3588 3361
πᾶς ὁ μὴ ποιῶν δικαιοσύνην οὐκ ἔστιν ἐκ τοῦ Θεοῦ, καὶ ὁ μὴ
everyone not practicing righteousness not is of God, also he not

25 3588 80 846 3754 3778 2076 3588 31 3739
ἀγαπῶν τὸν ἀδελφὸν αὐτοῦ. 11 ὅτι αὕτη ἐστὶν ἡ ἀγγελία ἣν
loving the brother of him. Because this is the message which

191 575 746 2443 25 240 3756 2531
ἠκούσατε ἀπ' ἀρχῆς, ἵνα ἀγαπῶμεν ἀλλήλους· 12 οὐ καθὼς
you heard from beginning, that we should love one another; not as

2535 1537 3588 4190 2258 2532 4969 3588 80 846 2532
Κάϊν ἐκ τοῦ πονηροῦ ἦν, καὶ ἔσφαξε τὸν ἀδελφὸν αὐτοῦ. καὶ
Cain of the evil was, and killed the brother of him. And

5484 5101 4969 846 3754 3588 2041 846 4190 2258
χάριν τίνος ἔσφαξεν αὐτόν; ὅτι τὰ ἔργα αὐτοῦ πονηρὰ ἦν,
for what did he kill him? Because the works of him evil were,

3588 1161 3588 80 846 1342
τὰ δὲ τοῦ ἀδελφοῦ αὐτοῦ δίκαια.
the things but of the brother of him (were) righteous.

3361 2296 80 3450 1487 3404 5209 3588 2889
13. Μὴ θαυμάζετε, ἀδελφοί μου, εἰ μισεῖ ὑμᾶς ὁ κόσμος·
Not do marvel, brothers of me, if hates you the world;

2249 1492 3754 3327 1537 3588 2288 1519 3588
14 ἡμεῖς οἴδαμεν ὅτι μεταβεβήκαμεν ἐκ τοῦ θανάτου εἰς τὴν
We know that we have passed from death into

2222 3754 25 3588 80 3588 3361 25 3588 80
ζωήν, ὅτι ἀγαπῶμεν τοὺς ἀδελφούς. ὁ μὴ ἀγαπῶν τὸν ἀδελφόν,
life, because we love the brothers. The (one) not loving the brother,

3306 1722 3588 2288 3956 3588 3404 3588 80 846 80
μένει ἐν τῷ θανάτῳ. 15 πᾶς ὁ μισῶν τὸν ἀδελφὸν αὐτοῦ ἀνθρω-
remains in death. Everyone hating the brother of him a murderer

2076 2532 1492 3754 3956 443 3756 2192
ποκτόνος ἐστί· καὶ οἴδατε ὅτι πᾶς ἀνθρωποκτόνος οὐκ ἔχει
is; and you know that every murderer not has

2222 166 1722 846 3306 1722 5129 1097 3588
ζωὴν αἰώνιον ἐν αὐτῷ μένουσαν. 16 ἐν τούτῳ ἐγνώκαμεν τὴν
life everlasting in him abiding. By this we have known the

26 3588 2316 3754 1565 5228 2257 3588 5590 846
ἀγάπην τοῦ Θεοῦ, ὅτι ἐκεῖνος ὑπὲρ ἡμῶν τὴν ψυχὴν αὐτοῦ
love of God, because that (One) on behalf of us the life of Him

5087 2532 2249 3784 5228 3588 3784 3588 5590
ἔθηκε· καὶ ἡμεῖς ὀφείλομεν ὑπὲρ τῶν ἀδελφῶν τὰς ψυχὰς
laid down; and we ought on behalf of the brothers the lives

5087 3739 1161 302 2192 3588 979 3588 2889 2532 2334 3588
τιθέναι. 17 ὃς δ' ἂν ἔχῃ τὸν βίον τοῦ κόσμου, καὶ θεωρῇ τὸν
lay down. Whoever has the means of life of the world, and beholds the

80 846 5532 2192 2532 2808 3588 4698
ἀδελφὸν αὐτοῦ χρείαν ἔχοντα, καὶ κλείσῃ τὰ σπλάγχνα
brother of him need having, and shuts up the bowels

846 575 846 4459 3588 26 3588 2316 3306 1722 846
αὐτοῦ ἀπ' αὐτοῦ, πῶς ἡ ἀγάπη τοῦ Θεοῦ μένει ἐν αὐτῷ;
of him from him, how the love of God abides in him?

5040 3450 3361 25 3056 3366 1100 235 2041
18 τεκνία μου, μὴ ἀγαπῶμεν λόγῳ μηδὲ γλώσσῃ, ἀλλ' ἔργῳ
Little children of me, not let us love in word nor in tongue, but in deed

2532 225 2532 1722 5129 1097 3754 1537 3588 225
καὶ ἀληθείᾳ. 19 καὶ ἐν τούτῳ γινώσκομεν ὅτι ἐκ τῆς ἀληθείας
and in truth. And in this we shall know that of the truth

2070 2532 1715 846 3982 3588 2588 2257
ἐσμέν, καὶ ἔμπροσθεν αὐτοῦ πείσομεν τὰς καρδίας ἡμῶν,
we are, and before Him shall persuade the heart of us,

King James Version

the children of God are
manifest, and the chil-
dren of the devil: who-
soever doeth not right-
eousness is not of God,
neither he that loveth
not his brother.
11. For this is the mes-
sage that ye heard from
the beginning, that we
should love one another.
12 Not as Cain, (who)
was of that wicked one,
and slew his brother.
And wherefore slew he
him? Because his own
works were evil, and his
brother's righteous.

13 Marvel not, my
brethren, if the world
hate you.
14 We know that we
have passed from death
unto life, because we
love the brethren. He
that loveth not (his)
brother abideth in
death.
15 Whosoever hateth
his brother is a mur-
derer: and ye know that
no murderer hath eter-
nal life abiding in him.

16. Hereby perceive
we the love (of God),
because he laid down
his life for us: and we
ought to lay down (our)
lives for the brethren.

17 But whoso hath this
world's good, and seeth
his brother have need,
and shutteth up his
bowels (of compas-
sion) from him, how
dwelleth the love of
God in him?

18 My little children, let
us not love in word, nei-
ther in tongue; but in
deed and in truth.
19 And hereby we
know that we are of the
truth, and shall assure
our hearts before him.

Literal Translation **1 John 3:20** ***King James Version***

20 that if our heart accuses us, (we know) that God is greater than our heart and knows all things.
21 Beloved, if our heart does not accuse us, we have confidence with God.

3754 1437 2607 2257 3588 2588 3754 3187 2076 3588
20 ὅτι ἐὰν καταγινώσκῃ ἡμῶν ἡ καρδία, ὅτι μείζων ἐστὶν ὁ
that if accuses of us the heart, that greater is

2316 3588 2588 2257 2532 1097 3956 27
Θεὸς τῆς καρδίας ἡμῶν, καὶ γινώσκει πάντα. 21 ἀγαπητοί,
God (than) the heart of us, and knows all things. Beloved,

1437 3588 2588 2257 3361 2607 2257 3954
ἐὰν ἡ καρδία ἡμῶν μὴ καταγινώσκῃ ἡμῶν, παρρησίαν
if the heart of us not accuses us, confidence

2192 4314 3588 2316 2532 3739 1437 154 2983 3844
ἔχομεν πρὸς τὸν Θεόν, 22 καὶ ὃ ἐὰν αἰτῶμεν, λαμβάνομεν παρ'
we have with God, and whatever we ask, we receive from

20 For if our heart condemn us, God is greater than our heart, and knoweth all things.
21 Beloved, if our heart condemn us not, (then) have we confidence toward God.

22. And whatever we ask, we receive from Him, because we keep His commandments, and we do the things pleasing before Him.
23 And this is His commandment, that we should believe (on) the name of His Son, Jesus Christ, and love one another, even as He gave command to us.

846 3754 3588 1785 846 5083 2532 3588 701
αὐτοῦ, ὅτι τὰς ἐντολὰς αὐτοῦ τηροῦμεν, καὶ τὰ ἀρεστὰ
Him, because the commandments of Him we keep, and the things pleasing

1799 846 4160 2532 3778 2076 3588 1785 846
ἐνώπιον αὐτοῦ ποιοῦμεν. 23 καὶ αὕτη ἐστὶν ἡ ἐντολὴ αὐτοῦ,
before Him we do. And this is the commandment of Him,

2443 4100 3588 3686 3588 5207 846 2424 5547
ἵνα πιστεύσωμεν τῷ ὀνόματι τοῦ υἱοῦ αὐτοῦ Ἰησοῦ Χρι-
that we should believe (on) the name of the Son of Him Jesus Christ,

2532 25 240 2531 1325 1785 2254
στοῦ, καὶ ἀγαπῶμεν ἀλλήλους, καθὼς ἔδωκεν ἐντολὴν ἡμῖν.
and love one another, even as He gave command to us.

22. And whatsoever we ask, we receive of him, because we keep his commandments, and do those things that are pleasing in his sight.
23 And this is his commandment, That we should believe on the name of his Son Jesus Christ, and love one another, as he gave us commandment.

24 And the (one) keeping His commandments abides in Him, and He in him. And by this we know that He abides in us, by the Spirit which He gave to us.

2532 3588 5083 3588 1785 846 1722 846 3306 2532 846 1722
24 καὶ ὁ τηρῶν τὰς ἐντολὰς αὐτοῦ ἐν αὐτῷ μένει, καὶ αὐτὸς ἐν
and (the) one keeping the comandments of Him in Him abides, and He in

846 2532 1722 5129 1097 3754 3306 1722 2254 1537 3588
αὐτῷ. καὶ ἐν τούτῳ γινώσκομεν ὅτι μένει ἐν ἡμῖν, ἐκ τοῦ
him. And by this we know that He abides in us, by the

4151 3739 2254 1325
Πνεύματος οὗ ἡμῖν ἔδωκεν.
Spirit which to us He gave.

24 And he that keepeth his commandments dwelleth in him, and he in him. And hereby we know that he abideth in us, by the Spirit which he hath given us.

1 John 4

1. Beloved, do not believe every spirit, but test the spirits, whether they are from God; for many false prophets have gone forth into the world.
2 By this know the Spirit of God: every spirit which confesses that Jesus Christ has come in (the) flesh is from God.

27 3361 3956 4151 4100 235 1381
1. Ἀγαπητοί, μὴ παντὶ πνεύματι πιστεύετε, ἀλλὰ δοκι-
Beloved not every spirit believe, but test

3588 4151 1487 1537 3588 2316 2076 3754 4183
μάζετε τὰ πνεύματα, εἰ ἐκ τοῦ Θεοῦ ἐστίν· ὅτι πολλοὶ
the spirits, whether of God they are; because many

5578 1831 1519 3588 2889 1722 5129
ψευδοπροφῆται ἐξεληλύθασιν εἰς τὸν κόσμον. 2 ἐν τούτῳ
false prophets have gone forth into the world. By this

1097 3588 4151 3588 2316 3956 5141 3739 3670
γινώσκετε τὸ Πνεῦμα τοῦ Θεοῦ· πᾶν πνεῦμα ὃ ὁμολογεῖ
know the Spirit of God; every spirit which confesses

2424 5547 1722 4561 2064 1537 3588 2316 2076
Ἰησοῦν Χριστὸν ἐν σαρκὶ ἐληλυθότα ἐκ τοῦ Θεοῦ ἐστί·
Jesus Christ in (the) flesh having come of God is;

1. Beloved, believe not every spirit, but try the spirits whether they are of God: because many false prophets are gone out into the world.
2 Hereby know ye the Spirit of God: Every spirit that confesseth that Jesus Christ is come in the flesh is of God:

3 And every spirit which does not confess that Jesus Christ has come in (the) flesh is not from God; and this is the antichrist which you heard is coming, and now is already in the world.
4 Little children, you are of God and

2532 3956 4151 3739 3361 3670 3588 2424 5547 1722
3 καὶ πᾶν πνεῦμα ὃ μὴ ὁμολογεῖ τὸν Ἰησοῦν Χριστὸν ἐν
and every spirit which not confesses Jesus Christ in

4561 2064 1537 3588 2316 3756 2076 2532 5124 2076 3588
σαρκὶ ἐληλυθότα, ἐκ τοῦ Θεοῦ οὐκ ἔστι· καὶ τοῦτό ἐστι τὸ
flesh having come, of God not is; and this is the (spirit)

3588 500 3588 191 3754 2064 2532 3568 1722 3588
τοῦ ἀντιχρίστου, ὃ ἀκηκόατε ὅτι ἔρχεται, καὶ νῦν ἐν τῷ
of the antichrist, which you heard that it is coming, and now in the

2889 2076 2235 5210 1537 3588 2316 2075 5040 2532
κόσμῳ ἐστὶν ἤδη. 4 ὑμεῖς ἐκ τοῦ Θεοῦ ἐστέ, τεκνία, καὶ
world is already. You of God are, little children and

3 And every spirit that confesseth not that Jesus Christ is come in the flesh is not of God: and this is that (spirit) of antichrist, whereof ye have heard that it should come; and even now already is it in the world.
4 Ye are of God, little children,

Literal Translation

have overcome them, because He in you is greater than he in the world.
5 They are of the world; because of this they speak of the world, and the world hears them.

6 We are of God; the (one) knowing God hears us. Whoever is not of God does not hear us. From this we know the spirit of truth and the spirit of error.

7. Beloved, let us love one another, because love is of God, and everyone who loves has been born of God, and knows God.
8 The (one) who does not love has not known God, because God is love.
9 By this the love of God was revealed in us, because His Son, the Only begotten, God has sent into the world that we might live through Him.
10 In this is love, not that we loved God, but that He loved us, and sent His Son (to be) a propitiation relating to our sins.

11 Beloved, if God so loved us, we also ought to love one another.

12 No one has beheld God at any time. If we love one another, God abides in us, and His love having been perfected is in us.

13 By this we know that we abide in Him, and He in us, because of His Spirit He has given to us.
14. And we have beheld and bear witness that the Father has sent

1 John 4:5

3528 846 3754 3187 2075 3588 1722 5213 2228 3588 1722 3588
νενικήκατε αὐτούς· ὅτι μείζων ἐστὶν ὁ ἐν ὑμῖν ἢ ὁ ἐν τῷ
have overcome them; because greater is the (One) in you (than) he in the

2889 846 1537 3588 2889 1526 1223 5124 1537 3588 2889
κόσμῳ. 5 αὐτοὶ ἐκ τοῦ κόσμου εἰσί· διὰ τοῦτο ἐκ τοῦ κόσμου
world. They of the world are; because of this of the world

2980 2532 3588 2889 846 191 2249 1537 3588 2316
λαλοῦσι, καὶ ὁ κόσμος αὐτῶν ἀκούει. 6 ἡμεῖς ἐκ τοῦ Θεοῦ
they speak, and the world them hears. We of God

2070 3588 1097 3588 2316 191 2257 3739 3756 2076 1537
ἐσμέν· ὁ γινώσκων τὸν Θεόν, ἀκούει ἡμῶν· ὃς οὐκ ἔστιν ἐκ
are; the (one) knowing God, hears us; (he) who not is of

3588 2316 3756 191 2257 1537 5127 1097 3588
τοῦ Θεοῦ, οὐκ ἀκούει ἡμῶν. ἐκ τούτου γινώσκομεν τὸ
God, not hears us. From this we know the

4151 3588 225 2532 3588 4151 3588 4106
πνεῦμα τῆς ἀληθείας καὶ τὸ πνεῦμα τῆς πλάνης.
spirit of truth and the spirit or error.

27 25 240 3754 3588 26 1537 3588
7. Ἀγαπητοί, ἀγαπῶμεν ἀλλήλους· ὅτι ἡ ἀγάπη ἐκ τοῦ
Beloved, let us love on another; because love of

2316 2076 2532 3956 3588 25 1537 3588 2316 1080 2532
Θεοῦ ἐστί, καὶ πᾶς ὁ ἀγαπῶν ἐκ τοῦ Θεοῦ γεγέννηται, καὶ
God is, and everyone loving of God has been generated, and

1097 3588 2316 3588 3361 25 3756 1097 3588 2316 3754
γινώσκει τὸν Θεόν. 8 ὁ μὴ ἀγαπῶν οὐκ ἔγνω τὸν Θεόν· ὅτι
knows God. The (one) not loving not knew God; because

3588 2316 26 2076 1722 5129 5319 3588 26 3588
ὁ Θεὸς ἀγάπη ἐστίν. 9 ἐν τούτῳ ἐφανερώθη ἡ ἀγάπη τοῦ
God love is. By this was revealed the love

2316 1722 2254 3754 3588 5207 846 3588 3439 649
Θεοῦ ἐν ἡμῖν, ὅτι τὸν υἱὸν αὐτοῦ τὸν μονογενῆ ἀπέσταλκεν
of God in us, because the Son of Him the only-begotten has sent

3588 2316 1722 3588 2889 2443 2198 1223 846 1722 5129
ὁ Θεὸς εἰς τὸν κόσμον, ἵνα ζήσωμεν δι' αὐτοῦ. 10 ἐν τούτῳ
God into the world, that we might live through Him. In this

2076 3588 26 3756 3754 2249 25 3588 2316 235
ἐστὶν ἡ ἀγάπη, οὐχ ὅτι ἡμεῖς ἠγαπήσαμεν τὸν Θεόν, ἀλλ'
is love, not that we loved God, but

3754 846 25 2248 2532 649 3588 5207 846
ὅτι αὐτὸς ἠγάπησεν ἡμᾶς, καὶ ἀπέστειλε τὸν υἱὸν αὐτοῦ
that He loved us, and sent the Son of Him

2434 4012 3588 266 2257 27 1487 3779 3588
ἱλασμὸν περὶ τῶν ἁμαρτιῶν ἡμῶν. 11 ἀγαπητοί, εἰ οὕτως ὁ
a propitiation concerning the sins of us. Beloved, if so

2316 25 2248 2532 2249 3784 240 25
Θεὸς ἠγάπησεν ἡμᾶς, καὶ ἡμεῖς ὀφείλομεν ἀλλήλους ἀγαπᾷν.
God loved us, also we ought one another to love.

2316 3762 4455 2300 1437 25 240
12 Θεὸν οὐδεὶς πώποτε τεθέαται· ἐὰν ἀγαπῶμεν ἀλλήλους,
God No one ever has beheld; if we love one another,

3588 2316 1722 2254 3306 2532 3588 26 846 5048
ὁ Θεὸς ἐν ἡμῖν μένει, καὶ ἡ ἀγάπη αὐτοῦ τετελειωμένη
God in us abides, and the love of Him having been perfected

2076 1722 2254 1722 5129 1097 3754 1722 846 3306 2532
ἐστιν ἐν ἡμῖν. 13 ἐν τούτῳ γινώσκομεν ὅτι ἐν αὐτῷ μένομεν καὶ
is in us. By this we know that in Him we abide and

846 1722 2254 3754 1537 3588 4151 846 1325 2254
αὐτὸς ἐν ἡμῖν, ὅτι ἐκ τοῦ Πνεύματος αὐτοῦ δέδωκεν ἡμῖν.
He in us, because of the Spirit of Him He has given to us.

2532 2249 2300 2532 3140 3754 3588 3962 649
14 καὶ ἡμεῖς τεθεάμεθα καὶ μαρτυροῦμεν ὅτι ὁ πατὴρ ἀπέσταλκε
And we have beheld and bear witness that the Father has sent

King James Version

and have overcome them: because greater is he that is in you, than he that is in the world.
5 They are of the world: therefore speak they of the world, and the world heareth them.

6 We are of God: he that knoweth God heareth us; he that is not of God heareth not us. Hereby know we the spirit of truth, and the spirit of error.

7. Beloved, let us love one another: for love is of God; and every one that loveth is born of God, and knoweth God.
8 He that loveth not knoweth not God; for God is love.
9 In this was manifested the love of God toward us, because that God sent his only begotten Son into the world, that we might live through him.
10 Herein is love, not that we loved God, but that he loved us, and sent his Son (to be) the propitiation for our sins.

11 Beloved, if God so loved us, we ought also to love one another.

12 No man hath seen God at any time. If we love one another, God dwelleth in us, and his love is perfected in us.

13 Hereby know we that we dwell in him, and he in us, because he hath given us of his Spirit.
14. And we have seen and do testify that the Father sent

1 John 4:15

Literal Translation

the Son (as) Savior of the world.
15 Whoever confesses that Jesus is the Son of God, God abides in him, and he in God.

16 And we have known and have believed the love which God has in us. God is love, and the one abiding in love abides in God, and God in him.
17 By this love has been perfected with us, that we have confidence in the day of judgment, that as He is, we are also in this world.

18 There is no fear in love, but perfect love casts out fear, because fear has punishment; and the (one) fearing has not been perfected in love.

19 We love Him because He first loved us.

20 If anyone says, I love God, and hates his brother, he is a liar. For the (one) not loving his brother whom he has seen, how is he able to love God whom he has not seen?
21 And we have this commandment from Him, that the (one) who loves God also loves his brother.

3588 5207 4990 3588 2889 3739 302 3670 3754 2424
τὸν υἱὸν σωτῆρα τοῦ κόσμου. 15 ὃς ἂν ὁμολογήσῃ ὅτι Ἰησοῦς
the Son (as) Savior of the world. Whoever confesses that Jesus

2076 3588 5207 3588 2316 3588 2316 1722 846 3306 2532 846 1722
ἐστιν ὁ υἱὸς τοῦ Θεοῦ, ὁ Θεὸς ἐν αὐτῷ μένει, καὶ αὐτὸς ἐν
is the Son of God, God in him abides, and he in

3588 2316 2532 2249 1097 2532 4100 3588 26
τῷ Θεῷ. 16 καὶ ἡμεῖς ἐγνώκαμεν καὶ πεπιστεύκαμεν τὴν ἀγάπην
God. And we have known and have believed the love

3739 2192 3588 2316 1722/2254/3588/2316 26 2076 2532/3588/3306/1722/3588
ἣν ἔχει ὁ Θεὸς ἐν ἡμῖν. ὁ Θεὸς ἀγάπη ἐστί, καὶ ὁ μένων ἐν τῇ
which has God in us. God love is, and he abiding in

26 1722 3588 2316 3306 2532 3588 2316 1722 846 1722 5129 5048
ἀγάπῃ, ἐν τῷ Θεῷ μένει, καὶ ὁ Θεὸς ἐν αὐτῷ. 17 ἐν τούτῳ τετε-
love, in God abides, and God in him. By this has

3588 26 3326 2257 2443 3954 2192 1722 3588
λείωται ἡ ἀγάπη μεθ' ἡμῶν, ἵνα παρρησίαν ἔχωμεν ἐν τῇ
been perfected love with us, that confidence we have in the

2250 3588 2920 3754 2531 1565 2076 2532 2249 2070 1722
ἡμέρᾳ τῆς κρίσεως, ὅτι καθὼς ἐκεῖνός ἐστι, καὶ ἡμεῖς ἐσμὲν ἐν
day of judgment, that as that (One) is, also we are in

3588 2889 5129 5401 3756 2076 1722 3588 26 235 3588
τῷ κόσμῳ τούτῳ. 18 φόβος οὐκ ἔστιν ἐν τῇ ἀγάπῃ, ἀλλ' ἡ
world this. Fear not is in love, but

5046 26 1854 906 3588 5401 3754 3588 5401 2851
τελεία ἀγάπη ἔξω βάλλει τὸν φόβον, ὅτι ὁ φόβος κόλασιν
perfect love out casts fear, because fear punishment

2192 3588 1161 5399 3756 5048 1722 3588 26
ἔχει· ὁ δὲ φοβούμενος οὐ τετελείωται ἐν τῇ ἀγάπῃ.
has; the (one) and fearing not has been perfected in love.

2249 25 846 3754 846 4413 25 2248
19 ἡμεῖς ἀγαπῶμεν αὐτόν, ὅτι αὐτὸς πρῶτος ἠγάπησεν ἡμᾶς.
We love Him, because He first loved us.

1437 5100 2036 3754 25 3588 2316 2532 3588 80 846
20 ἐάν τις εἴπῃ ὅτι Ἀγαπῶ τὸν Θεόν, καὶ τὸν ἀδελφὸν αὐτοῦ
If anyone says, I love God, and the brother of him

3404 5583 2076 3588 1063 3361 25 3588 80 846 3739
μισῇ, ψεύστης ἐστίν· ὁ γὰρ μὴ ἀγαπῶν τὸν ἀδελφὸν αὐτοῦ ὃν
hates, a liar he is; the (one) for not loving the brother of him whom

3708 3588 2316 3739 3756 3708 4459 1410 25 2532
ἑώρακε, τὸν Θεὸν ὃν οὐχ ἑώρακε πῶς δύναται ἀγαπᾶν; 21 καὶ
he has seen, God whom not he has seen how is he able to love? And

3778 3588 1785 2192 575 846 2443 3588 25 3588 2316
ταύτην τὴν ἐντολὴν ἔχομεν ἀπ' αὐτοῦ, ἵνα ὁ ἀγαπῶν τὸν θεόν,
this commandment we have from Him, that the (one) loving God,

25 2532 3588 80 846
ἀγαπᾷ καὶ τὸν ἀδελφὸν αὐτοῦ.
loves also the brother of him.

King James Version

the Son (to be) the Saviour of the world.
15 Whosoever shall confess that Jesus is the Son of God, God dwelleth in him, and he in God.
16 And we have known and believed the love that God hath to us. God is love; and he that dwelleth in love dwelleth in God, and God in him.
17 Herein is our love made perfect, that we may have boldness in the day of judgment: because as he is, so are we in this world.

18 There is no fear in love; but perfect love casteth out fear: because fear hath torment. He that feareth is not made perfect in love.

19 We love him, because he first loved us.

20 If a man say, I love God, and hateth his brother, he is a liar: for he that loveth not his brother whom he hath seen, how can he love God whom he hath not seen?
21 And this commandment have we from him, That he who loveth God love his brother also.

1 John 5

1 John 5 (Literal Translation)

1. Everyone who believes that Jesus is the Christ has been generated of God. And everyone loving the (one) generating also loves the (one) who has been generated of Him.
2 By this we know that we love the children of God: when we love God

3956 3588 4100 3754 2424 2076 3588 5547 1537 3588 2316
1. Πᾶς ὁ πιστεύων ὅτι Ἰησοῦς ἐστὶν ὁ Χριστός, ἐκ τοῦ Θεοῦ
Everyone believing that Jesus is the Christ, of God

1080 2532 3956 3588 25 3588 1080 25
γεγέννηται· καὶ πᾶς ὁ ἀγαπῶν τὸν γεννήσαντα ἀγαπᾷ
has been generated; and everyone loving the (One) generating loves

2532 3588 1080 1537 846 1722 5129 1097 3754
καὶ τὸν γεγεννημένον ἐξ αὐτοῦ. 2 ἐν τούτῳ γινώσκομεν ὅτι
also him having been generated of Him. By this we know that

25 3588 5043 3588 2316 3752 3588 2316 25
ἀγαπῶμεν τὰ τέκνα τοῦ Θεοῦ, ὅταν τὸν Θεὸν ἀγαπῶμεν,
we love the children of God, whenever God we love,

1 John 5 (King James Version)

1. Whosoever believeth that Jesus is the Christ is born of God: and every one that loveth him that begat loveth him also that is begotten of him.

2 By this we know that we love the children of God, when we love God,

Literal Translation

and practice His commandments.
3 For this is the love of God, that we keep His commandments; and His commandments are not heavy.
4 Because everything having been generated of God overcomes the world, and this is the victory overcoming the world, our faith.

5 Who is the (one) overcoming the world except the (one) who believes that Jesus is the Son of God?
6. This is the (One) coming through water and blood, Jesus Christ; not by the water only, but by the water and the blood. And the Spirit is the (One) witnessing, because the Spirit is the truth.
7 For there are three bearing witness in Heaven: the Father the Word, and the Holy Spirit; and these three are one.

8 And there are three who bear witness on the earth: The Spirit, and the water, and the blood; and the three are to the one.

9. If we receive the witness of men, the witness of God is greater; because this is the witness of God which He has witnessed about His Son:

10 The (one) believing into the Son of God has the witness in himself. The (one) not believing God has made Him a liar, because he has not believed in the witness which God has witnessed concerning His Son.

11 And this is the witness: that God gave us everlasting life, and this life is in His Son.

12 The (one) having the Son has life.

1 John 5:3

2532 3588 1785 846 5083 3778 1063 2076 3588 26
καὶ τὰς ἐντολὰς αὐτοῦ τηρῶμεν. 3 αὕτη γάρ ἐστιν ἡ ἀγάπη
and the commandments of Him we keep. this For is the love

3588 2316 2443 3588 1785 846 5083 2532 3588 1785
τοῦ Θεοῦ, ἵνα τὰς ἐντολὰς αὐτοῦ τηρῶμεν· καὶ αἱ ἐντολαὶ
of God, that the commandments of Him we keep; and the commands

846 926 3756 1526 3754 3956 3588 1080 1537 3588
αὐτοῦ βαρεῖαι οὐκ εἰσίν.4 ὅτι πᾶν τὸ γεγεννημένον ἐκ τοῦ
of Him heavy not are. Because everyone having been generated of

2316 3528 3588 2889 2532 3778 2076 3588 3529 3588 3528 3588
Θεοῦ νικᾷ τὸν κόσμον· καὶ αὕτη ἐστὶν ἡ νίκη ἡ νικήσασα τὸν
God overcomes the world; and this is the victory overcoming the

2889 3588 4102 2257 5100 2076 3588 3528 3588 2889 1487/3361/3588
κόσμον, ἡ πίστις ἡμῶν. 5 τίς ἐστιν ὁ νικῶν τὸν κόσμον, εἰ μὴ ὁ
world, the faith of us. Who is the (one) overcoming the world, if not he

4100 3754 2424 2076 3588 5207 3588 2316 3778 2076 3588
πιστεύων ὅτι Ἰησοῦς ἐστιν ὁ υἱὸς τοῦ Θεοῦ; 6 οὗτός ἐστιν ὁ
believing that Jesus is the Son of God? This is the (One)

2064 1223 5204 2532 129 2424 3588 5547 3756 1722 3588
ἐλθὼν δι' ὕδατος καὶ αἵματος, Ἰησοῦς ὁ Χριστός· οὐκ ἐν τῷ
coming through water and blood, Jesus Christ; not by the

5204 3440 235 1722 3588 5204 2532 3588 129 2532 3588 4151
ὕδατι μόνον, ἀλλ' ἐν τῷ ὕδατι καὶ τῷ αἵματι. καὶ τὸ Πνεῦμά
water only, but by the water and the blood. And the Spirit

2076 3588 3140 3754 3588 4151 2076 3588 225 3754 5140
ἐστι τὸ μαρτυροῦν, ὅτι τὸ Πνεῦμά ἐστιν ἡ ἀλήθεια. 7 ὅτι τρεῖς
is the (One) witnessing, because the Spirit is the truth. Because three

1526 3588 3140 1722 3588 3772 3588 3962 3588 3056 2532
εἰσιν οἱ μαρτυροῦντες ἐν τῷ οὐρανῷ, ὁ πατήρ, ὁ λόγος, καὶ
there are bearing witness in Heaven, the Father, the Word, and

3588 40 4151 2532 3778 3588 5140 1520 1526 2532 5140 1526
τὸ Ἅγιον Πνεῦμα· καὶ οὗτοι οἱ τρεῖς ἕν εισι. 8 καὶ τρεῖς εἰσὶν
the Holy Spirit; and these three One is. And three there are

3588 3140 1722 358 1093 3588 4151 2532 3588 5204 2532 3588
οἱ μαρτυροῦντες ἐν τῇ γῇ, τὸ Πνεῦμα, καὶ τὸ ὕδωρ, καὶ τὸ
who bear witness on the earth, the Spirit, and the water, and the

129 2532 3588 5140 1519 3588 1520 1526 1487 3588 3141 3588
αἷμα· καὶ οἱ τρεῖς εἰς τὸ ἕν εἰσιν. 9 εἰ τὴν μαρτυρίαν τῶν
blood; and the three to the one are. If the witness

444 2983 3588 3141 3588 2316 3187 2076
ἀνθρώπων λαμβάνομεν, ἡ μαρτυρία τοῦ Θεοῦ μείζων ἐστίν·
of men we receive, the witness of God greater is;

3754 3778 2076 3588 3141 3588 2316 3739 3140 4012
ὅτι αὕτη ἐστὶν ἡ μαρτυρία τοῦ Θεοῦ, ἣν μεμαρτύρηκε περὶ
because this is the witness of God, which He has witnessed about

3588 5207 846 3588 4100 1519 3588 5207 3588 2316 2192 3588
τοῦ υἱοῦ αὐτοῦ. 10 ὁ πιστεύων εἰς τὸν υἱὸν τοῦ Θεοῦ ἔχει τὴν
the Son of Him. The (one) believing into the Son of God has the

3141 1722 1438 3588 3361 4100 3588 2316 5583 4160
μαρτυρίαν ἐν ἑαυτῷ· ὁ μὴ πιστεύων τῷ Θεῷ ψεύστην πεποί-
witness in himself; the (one) not believing God a liar has

846 3754 3756 4100 1519 3588 3141 3739
ηκεν αὐτόν, ὅτι οὐ πεπίστευκεν εἰς τὴν μαρτυρίαν, ἣν
made Him, because not he has believed in the witness, which

3140 3588 2316 4012 3588 5207 846 2532 3778 2076
μεμαρτύρηκεν ὁ Θεὸς περὶ τοῦ υἱοῦ αὐτοῦ. 11 καὶ αὕτη ἐστὶν
has witnessed God concerning the Son of Him. And this is

3588 3141 3754 2222 166 1325 2254 3588 2316 2532 3778
ἡ μαρτυρία, ὅτι ζωὴν αἰώνιον ἔδωκεν ἡμῖν ὁ Θεός, καὶ αὕτη
the witness, that life everlasting gave us God, and this

3588/2222/1722/3588/5207/ 846/ 2076 3588 2192 3588 5207 2192 3588 5207
ἡ ζωὴ ἐν τῷ υἱῷ αὐτοῦ ἐστίν. 12 ὁ ἔχων τὸν υἱὸν ἔχει τὴν ζωήν·
life in the Son of Him is. The (one) having the Son has life;

King James Version

and keep his commandments.
3 For this is the love of God, that we keep his commandments: and his commandments are not grievous.
4 For whatsoever is born of God overcometh the world: and this is the victory that overcometh the world, (even) our faith.

5 Who is he that overcometh the world, but he that believeth that Jesus is the Son of God?
6. This is he that came by water and blood, (even) Jesus Christ; not by water only, but by water and blood. And it is the Spirit that beareth witness, because the Spirit is truth.

7 For there are three that bear record in heaven, the Father, the Word, and the Holy Ghost: and these three are one.

8 And there are three that bear witness in earth, the Spirit, and the water, and the blood: and these three agree in one.

9. If we receive the witness of men, the witness of God is greater: for this is the witness of God which he hath testified of his Son.

10 He that believeth on the Son of God hath the witness in himself: he that believeth not God hath made him a liar; because he believeth not the record that God gave of his Son.

11 And this is the record, that God hath given to us eternal life, and this life is in his Son.

12 He that hath the Son hath life;

1 John 5:13

Literal Translation

The (one) not having the Son of God does not have life.

13. I wrote these things to you, the ones believing in the name of the Son of God, that you may know that you have everlasting life, and that you may believe in the name of the Son of God.
14 And this is the confidence we have toward Him, that if we ask anything according to His will, He hears us.

15 And if we know that He hears us, whatever we ask, we know that we have the requests which we have asked from Him.

16 If anyone sees his brother sinning a sin not unto death, he shall ask; and He shall give life to him, to the ones not sinning unto death. There is a sin unto death. I do not say that he should ask about that.

17 All unrighteousness is sin, and there is a sin not unto death.

18. We know that everyone having been generated of God does not sin, but the one generated of God keeps himself, and the evil does not touch him.
19 We know that we are of God, and the whole world lies in evil.

20 And we know that the Son of God has come, and (He) has given to us an understanding that we may know the true (One), and we are in the true (One), in His Son Jesus Christ. This is the true God and the life everlasting.

21 Little children, guard yourselves from idols. Amen.

3588 3361 2192 3588 5207 3588 2316 3588 2222 3756 2192
ὁ μὴ ἔχων τὸν υἱὸν τοῦ Θεοῦ τὴν ζωὴν οὐκ ἔχει.
the (one) not having the Son of God life not has.
5023 1125 5213 3588 4100 1519 3588 3686 3588
13. Ταῦτα ἔγραψα ὑμῖν τοῖς πιστεύουσιν εἰς τὸ ὄνομα τοῦ
These things I wrote to you, the (ones) believing in the name of the
5207 3588 2316 2443 1492 3754 2222 2192 166 2532 2443
υἱοῦ τοῦ Θεοῦ, ἵνα εἰδῆτε ὅτι ζωὴν ἔχετε αἰώνιον, καὶ ἵνα
Son of God, that you may know that life you have everlasting, and that
4100 1519 3588 3686 3588 5207 3588 2316 2532 3778 2076
πιστεύητε εἰς τὸ ὄνομα τοῦ υἱοῦ τοῦ Θεοῦ. 14 καὶ αὕτη ἐστὶν
you may believe in the name of the Son of God. And this is
3588 3954 3739 2192 4314 846 3754 1437 5100 154 2596
ἡ παρρησία ἣν ἔχομεν πρὸς αὐτόν, ὅτι ἐάν τι αἰτώμεθα κατὰ
the confidence which we have toward Him, that if anything we ask according to
3588 2307 846 191 2257 2532 1437 1492 3754 191
τὸ θέλημα αὐτοῦ, ἀκούει ἡμῶν· 15 καὶ ἐὰν οἴδαμεν ὅτι ἀκούει
the will of Him, He hears us; and if we know that He hears
2257 3739 302 154 1492 3754 2192 3588 155 3739
ἡμῶν, ὃ ἂν αἰτώμεθα, οἴδαμεν ὅτι ἔχομεν τὰ αἰτήματα ἃ
us, whatever we ask, we know that we have the requests which
154 3844 846 1437 5100 1492 3588 80 846
ᾐτήκαμεν παρ᾿ αὐτοῦ. 16 ἐάν τις ἴδῃ τὸν ἀδελφὸν αὐτοῦ
we have asked from Him. If anyone sees the brother of him
264 266 3361 4314 2288 154 2532 1325
ἁμαρτάνοντα ἁμαρτίαν μὴ πρὸς θάνατον, αἰτήσει, καὶ δώσει
sinning a sin not unto death, he shall ask, and He will give
846 2222 3588 264 3361 4314 2288 2076 266
αὐτῷ ζωὴν τοῖς ἁμαρτάνουσι μὴ πρὸς θάνατον. ἔστιν ἁμαρτία
to him life to the (one) sinning not unto death. There is a sin
4314 2288 3756 4012 1565 3004 2443 2065 3956
πρὸς θάνατον· οὐ περὶ ἐκείνης λέγω ἵνα ἐρωτήσῃ. 17 πᾶσα
unto death; not concerning that I say that he should ask. All
93 266 2076 2532 2076 266 3756 4314 2288
ἀδικία ἁμαρτία ἐστί· καὶ ἔστιν ἁμαρτία οὐ πρὸς θάνατον.
unrighteousness sin is; and there is a sin not unto death.

1492 3754 3956 3588 1080 1537 3588 2316 3756
18. Οἴδαμεν ὅτι πᾶς ὁ γεγεννημένος ἐκ τοῦ Θεοῦ οὐχ
We know that everyone having been generated of God not
264 235 3588 1080 1537 3588 2316 5083 1438 2532/3588
ἁμαρτάνει· ἀλλ᾿ ὁ γεννηθεὶς ἐκ τοῦ Θεοῦ τηρεῖ ἑαυτόν, καὶ ὁ
sins; but the (one) generated of God keeps himself, and the
4190 3756 680 846 1492 3754 1537 3588 2316
πονηρὸς οὐχ ἅπτεται αὐτοῦ. 19 οἴδαμεν ὅτι ἐκ τοῦ Θεοῦ
evil not touches him. We know that of God
2070 2532 3588 2889 3650 1722 3588 4190 2749 1492 1161
ἐσμέν, καὶ ὁ κόσμος ὅλος ἐν τῷ πονηρῷ κεῖται. 20 οἴδαμεν δὲ
we are, and the world whole in evil lies. we know And
3754/3588/5207/3588 2316 2240 2532 1325 2254 1271 2443
ὅτι ὁ υἱὸς τοῦ Θεοῦ ἥκει, καὶ δέδωκεν ἡμῖν διάνοιαν ἵνα
that the Son of God is come, and has given to us an understanding that
1097 3588 228 2532 2070 1722 3588 228 1722 3588
γινώσκωμεν τὸν ἀληθινόν· καί ἐσμὲν ἐν τῷ ἀληθινῷ, ἐν τῷ
we might know the true (One); and we are in the true (One), in the
5207 846 2424 5547 3778 2076 3588 228 2316
υἱῷ αὐτοῦ Ἰησοῦ Χριστῷ. οὗτός ἐστιν ὁ ἀληθινὸς Θεός,
Son of Him Jesus Christ. This is the true God,
2532 3588 2222 166 5040 5442 1438 575 3588
και ἡ ζωὴ αἰώνιος. 21 τεκνία, φυλάξατε ἑαυτοὺς ἀπὸ τῶν
and the life everlasting. Little children, guard yourselves from the
1497 281
εἰδώλων. ἀμήν.
idols. Amen.

King James Version

(and) he that hath not the Son of God hath not life.

13. These things have I written unto you that believe on the name of the Son of God; that ye may know that ye have eternal life, and that ye may believe on the name of the Son of God.
14 And this is the confidence that we have in him, that, if we ask any thing according to his will, he heareth us:

15 And if we know that he hear us, whatsoever we ask, we know that we have the petitions that we desired of him.

16 If any man see his brother sin a sin (which is) not unto death, he shall ask, and he shall give him life for them that sin not unto death. There is a sin unto death: I do not say that he shall pray for it.

17 All unrighteousness is sin: and there is a sin not unto death.

18. We know that whosoever is born of God sinneth not; but he that is begotten of God keepeth himself, and that wicked one toucheth him not.
19 (And) we know that we are of God, and the whole world lieth in wickedness.
20 And we know that the Son of God is come, and hath given us an understanding, that we may know him that is true, and we are in him that is true, (even) in his Son Jesus Christ. This is the true God, and eternal life.

21 Little children, keep yourselves from idols. Amen.

ΙΩΑΝΝΟΥ
OF JOHN
ΕΠΙΣΤΟΛΗ ΔΕΥΤΕΡΑ
EPISTLE SECOND

Literal Translation

THE SECOND EPISTLE OF JOHN

2 John

1. The elder to (the) elect lady and her children, whom I love in truth; and not I only, but also all those who have known the truth,

2 because of the truth remaining among us, and will be with us to the age.
3 Grace, mercy, peace will be with you from God (the) Father and from (the) Lord Jesus Christ, the Son of the Father, in truth and love.

4. I rejoiced greatly because I found your children walking in truth, as we received command from the Father.

5 And I now request you, lady, not writing to you as a new commandment, but (one) which we had from (the) beginning, that we should love one another.
6 And this is love, that we should walk according to His commandments. This is the commandment, even as you heard from (the) beginning, that you should walk in it.
7. Because many deceivers went out into the world, those not confessing Jesus Christ to have come in (the) flesh, this is the deceiver and the antichrist.
8 Watch yourselves, that we may not lose the things we worked out, but that we may receive a full reward.
9 Everyone transgressing and not abiding in the doctrine of Christ does not have God. The (one) abiding in the

2 John

3588 4245 1588 2959 2532 3588 5043 846
1. Ὁ πρεσβύτερος ἐκλεκτῇ κυρίᾳ καὶ τοῖς τέκνοις αὐτῆς,
The elder to (the) elect lady and the children of her,

3739 1473 25 1722 225 2532 3756 1473 3441 235 2532
οὓς ἐγὼ ἀγαπῶ ἐν ἀληθείᾳ, καὶ οὐκ ἐγὼ μόνος, ἀλλὰ καὶ
whom I love in truth, and not I only, but also

3956 2588 1097 3588 225 1223 3588 225 3588
πάντες οἱ ἐγνωκότες τὴν ἀλήθειαν, 2 διὰ τὴν ἀλήθειαν τὴν
all those who have known the truth, because of the truth

3306 1722 2254 2532 3326 2257 2071 1519 3588 165 2071
μένουσαν ἐν ἡμῖν, καὶ μεθ' ἡμῶν ἔσται εἰς τὸν αἰῶνα· 3 ἔσται
remaining among us, and with us will be to the age; will be

3326 5216 5485 1656 1515 3844 2316 3962 2532 3844
μεθ' ὑμῶν χάρις, ἔλεος, εἰρήνη παρὰ Θεοῦ πατρός, καὶ παρὰ
with you Grace, mercy, peace from God (the) Father, and from

2962 2424 5547 3588 5207 3588 3962 1722 225 2532
Κυρίου Ἰησοῦ Χριστοῦ τοῦ υἱοῦ τοῦ πατρός, ἐν ἀληθείᾳ καὶ
(the) Lord Jesus Christ the Son of the Father, in truth and

26
ἀγάπῃ.
love.

5463 3029 3754 2147 1537 3588 5043 4675 4043
4. Ἐχάρην λίαν ὅτι εὕρηκα ἐκ τῶν τέκνων σου περιπατοῦν-
I rejoiced greatly because I found of the children of you walking

1722 225 2531 1785 2983 3844 3588 3962
τας ἐν ἀληθείᾳ, καθὼς ἐντολὴν ἐλάβομεν παρὰ τοῦ πατρός.
in truth, as commandment was received from the Father.

2532 3568 2065 4571 2959 3756 5613 1785 1125 4671 2537
5 καὶ νῦν ἐρωτῶ σε, κυρία, οὐχ ὡς ἐντολὴν γράφων σοι καινὴν,
And now I request you, lady, not as a command writing to you a new,

235 3739 2192 575 746 2443 25 240 2532
ἀλλὰ ἣν εἴχομεν ἀπ' ἀρχῆς, ἵνα ἀγαπῶμεν ἀλλήλους. 6 καὶ
but which we had from beginning, that we should love one another. And

3778 2076 3588 26 2443 4043 2596 3588 1785
αὕτη ἐστὶν ἡ ἀγάπη, ἵνα περιπατῶμεν κατὰ τὰς ἐντολὰς
this is love, that we should walk according to the commands

846 3778 2076 3588 1785 2531 191 575 746
αὐτοῦ. αὕτη ἐστιν ἡ ἐντολή, καθὼς ἠκούσατε ἀπ' ἀρχῆς,
of Him. This is the command, even as you heard from beginning,

2443 1722 846 4043 3754 4183 4108 1525 1519 3588
ἵνα ἐν αὐτῇ περιπατῆτε. 7 ὅτι πολλοὶ πλάνοι εισῆλθον εἰς τὸν
that in it you should walk. Because many deceivers went out into the

2889 3588 3361 3670 2424 5547 2064 1722
κόσμον, οἱ μὴ ὁμολογοῦντες Ἰησοῦν Χριστὸν ἐρχόμενον ἐν
world, those not confessing Jesus Christ coming in

4561 3778 2076 3588 4108 2532 3588 500 991
σαρκί. οὗτός ἐστιν ὁ πλάνος καὶ ὁ ἀντίχριστος. 8 βλέπετε
(the) flesh. This is the deceiver and the antichrist. Watch

1438 2443 3361 622 3739 2038 235 3408
ἑαυτούς, ἵνα μὴ ἀπολέσωμεν ἃ εἰργασάμεθα, ἀλλὰ μισθὸν
yourselves, that not we may lose the things we worked out, but a reward

4134 618 3956 3588 3845 2532 3361 3306 1722
πλήρη ἀπολάβωμεν. 9 πᾶς ὁ παραβαίνων καὶ μὴ μένων ἐν
full we should receive. Everyone transgressing and not abiding in

3588 1322 3588 5547 2316 3756 2192 3588 3306 1722 3588
τῇ διδαχῇ τοῦ Χριστοῦ, Θεὸν οὐκ ἔχει· ὁ μένων ἐν τῇ
the doctrine of Christ, God not has; the (one) abiding in the

King James Version

THE SECOND EPISTLE OF JOHN

2 John

1. The elder unto the elect lady and her children, whom I love in the truth; and not I only, but also all they that have known the truth;

2 For the truth's sake, which dwelleth in us, and shall be with us for ever.
3 Grace be with you, mercy, (and) peace, from God the Father, and from the Lord Jesus Christ, the Son of the Father, in truth and love.

4. I rejoiced greatly that I found of thy children walking in truth, as we have received a commandment from the Father.

5 And now I beseech thee, lady, not as though I wrote a new commandment unto thee, but that which we had from the beginning, that we love one another.
6 And this is love, that we walk after his commandments. This is the commandment, That, as ye have heard from the beginning, ye should walk in it.
7. For many deceivers are entered into the world, who confess not that Jesus Christ is come in the flesh. This is a deceiver and an antichrist.

8 Look to yourselves, that we lose not those things which we have wrought, but that we receive a full reward.
9 Whosoever transgresseth, and abideth not in the doctrine of Christ, hath not God. He that abideth in the

Literal Translation | **2 John 10** | **King James Version**

doctrine of Christ, even this one has the Father and the Son.

10 If anyone comes to you and does not bear this doctrine, do not receive him into (the) house, and do not speak a greeting to him.

11 For the (one) speaking a greeting shares in his evil works.

1322 3588 5547 3778 2532 3588 3962 2532 3588 5207
διδαχῇ τοῦ Χριστοῦ, οὗτος καὶ τὸν πατέρα καὶ τὸν υἱὸν
doctrine of Christ, this one even the Father and the Son
2192 1487 5100 2064 4314 5209 2532 3778 3588 1322 3756
ἔχει. 10 εἴ τις ἔρχεται πρὸς ὑμᾶς, καὶ ταύτην τὴν διδαχὴν οὐ
has. If anyone comes to you, and this doctrine not
5342 3361 2983 846 1519 3614 2532 5463 846 3361
φέρει, μὴ λαμβάνετε αὐτὸν εἰς οἰκίαν, καὶ χαίρειν αὐτῷ μὴ
speaks, not do receive him into (the) house, and a greeting to him not
3004 3588 1063 3004 846 5463 2841 3588 2041
λέγετε· 11 ὁ γὰρ λέγων αὐτῷ χαίρειν κοινωνεῖ τοῖς ἔργοις
do speak; the (one) for speaking to him a greeting shares in the works
846 3588 4190
αὐτοῦ τοῖς πονηροῖς.
of him evil.

doctrine of Christ, he hath both the Father and the Son.

10 If there come any unto you, and bring not this doctrine, receive him not into (your) house, neither bid him God speed:

11 For he that biddeth him God speed is partaker of his evil deeds.

12. Having many things to write to you, I do not intend (to speak) by means of paper and ink, but I am hoping to come to you, and to speak mouth to mouth, that our joy may be fulfilled.
13 The children of your elect sister greet you. Amen.

4183 2192 5213 1125 3756 1014 1223 5489
12. Πολλὰ ἔχων ὑμῖν γράφειν οὐκ ἠβουλήθην διὰ χάρτου
Many things having to you to write not I intend by means of paper
2532 3188 235 1679 2064 4314 5209 2532 4750 4314
καὶ μέλανος· ἀλλὰ ἐλπίζω ἐλθεῖν πρὸς ὑμᾶς, καὶ στόμα πρὸς
and ink; but I am hoping to come to you, and mouth to
4750 2980 2443 3588 5479 2557 5600 4137 782
στόμα λαλῆσαι, ἵνα ἡ χαρὰ ἡμῶν ᾖ πεπληρωμένη. 13 ἀσπά-
mouth to speak, that the joy of us may be fulfilled. Greet
4571 3588 5043 3588 79 4675 3588 1588 281
ζεταί σε τὰ τέκνα τῆς ἀδελφῆς σου τῆς ἐκλεκτῆς. ἀμήν.
you the children of the sister of you elect. Amen.

12. Having many things to write unto you, I would not (write) with paper and ink: but I trust to come unto you, and speak face to face, that our joy may be full.
13 The children of thy elect sister greet thee. Amen.

Literal Translation

THE THIRD EPISTLE OF JOHN

3 John

1. The elder to Gaius
the beloved, whom I
love in truth.

2 Beloved, in regard to
all things, I pray (for)
you to do well and to be
in health, as your soul
does well.
3 For I rejoiced greatly
(at the) coming of (the)
brothers, also bearing
witness of you in the
truth, as you walk in
truth.
4 I have no greater joy
than these things, that I
hear my children are
walking in truth.

5 Beloved, you do faith-
fully whatever you
work for the brothers
and for the strangers,
6 who in love bore wit-
ness of you before (the)
church, whom you will
do well to send forward
worthily of God.

7 For on behalf of His
name they went out,
taking nothing from the
nations.
8 Therefore, we ought
to welcome such (men),
that we may become
co-workers in the truth.

9. I wrote to the church,
but he loving to be first
of them, Diotrephes,
does not receive us.
10 Because of this, if I
come, I will recall his
works which he does,
ranting against us with
evil words. And not be-
ing satisfied (with)
these, neither does he
receive the brothers;
and those purposing
(so) he prevents, and

ΙΩΑΝΝΟΥ
OF JOHN

ΕΠΙΣΤΟΛΗ ΤΡΙΤΗ
EPISTLE THIRD

3 John

3588 4245 1050 3588 27 3739 1473 25 1722
1. Ὁ πρεσβύτερος Γαΐῳ τῷ ἀγαπητῷ, ὃν ἐγὼ ἀγαπῶ ἐν
The elder to Gaius the beloved, whom I love in

225
ἀληθείᾳ.
truth.

27 4012 3956 2172 4571 2137 2532
2. Ἀγαπητέ, περὶ πάντων εὔχομαί σε εὐοδοῦσθαι καὶ
Beloved, concerning all things I pray you to do well and

5198 2531 2137 4675 3588 5590 5463 1063 3029
ὑγιαίνειν, καθὼς εὐοδοῦταί σου ἡ ψυχή. 3 ἐχάρην γὰρ λίαν,
to be in health, even as does well of you the soul. I rejoiced For greatly,

2064 80 2532 3140 4675 3588 225
ἐρχομένων ἀδελφῶν καὶ μαρτυρούντων σου τῇ ἀληθείᾳ,
coming (the) brothers and bearing witness of you in the truth,

2531 4771 1722 225 4043 3186 5130 3756
καθὼς σὺ ἐν ἀληθείᾳ περιπατεῖς. 4 μειζοτέραν τούτων οὐκ
as you in truth walk. Greater (than) these things not

2192 5479 2443 191 3588 1699 5043 1722 225 4043
ἔχω χαράν, ἵνα ἀκούω τὰ ἐμὰ τέκνα ἐν ἀληθείᾳ περι-
I have joy, that I hear my children in (the) truth are

πατοῦντα.
walking.

27 4103 4160 3739 1437 2038 1519 3588 80
5. Ἀγαπητέ, πιστὸν ποιεῖς ὃ ἐὰν ἐργάσῃ εἰς τοὺς ἀδελφοὺς
Beloved, faithfully you do whatever you work for the brothers

2532 1519 3588 3581 3739 3140 4675 3588 26 1799
καὶ εἰς τοὺς ξένους, 6 οἳ ἐμαρτύρησάν σου τῇ ἀγάπῃ ἐνώπιον
and for the strangers, who bore witness of you in love before

1577 3739 2573 4160 4311 516 3588 2316
ἐκκλησίας· οὓς καλῶς ποιήσεις προπέμψας ἀξίως τοῦ Θεοῦ.
(the) church; whom well you will do sending forward worthily of God.

5228 1063 3588 3686 846 1831 3367 2983
7 ὑπὲρ γὰρ τοῦ ὀνόματος αὐτοῦ ἐξῆλθον μηδὲν λαμβάνοντες
in behalf of For the name of Him they went out nothing taking

575 3588 1484 2249 3767 3784 618 3588
ἀπὸ τῶν ἐθνῶν. 8 ἡμεῖς οὖν ὀφείλομεν ἀπολαμβάνειν τοὺς
from the nations. We therefore ought to welcome the

5108 2443 4904 1096 3588 225
τοιούτους, ἵνα συνεργοὶ γινώμεθα τῇ ἀληθείᾳ.
such (men), that co-workers we may become in the truth.

1125 3588 1577 235 3588 5383 846 1361
9. Ἔγραψα τῇ ἐκκλησίᾳ· ἀλλ' ὁ φιλοπρωτεύων αὐτῶν Διοτ-
I wrote to the church; but the (one) loving to be first of them Diot-

3756 1926 2248 1223 5124 1437 2064 5279
ρέφης οὐκ ἐπιδέχεται ἡμᾶς. 10 διὰ τοῦτο, ἐὰν ἔλθω, ὑπο-
rephes not receives us. Because of this, if I come, I will

846 3588 2041 3739 4160 3056 4190 5396
μνήσω αὐτοῦ τὰ ἔργα ἃ ποιεῖ, λόγοις πονηροῖς φλυαρῶν
recall of him the works which he does, with words evil babbling against

2248 2532 3361 714 1909 5125 3777 846 1926
ἡμᾶς· καὶ μὴ ἀρκούμενος ἐπὶ τούτοις, οὔτε αὐτὸς ἐπιδέχεται
us; and not being satisfied on these, neither he receives

3588 80 2532 3588 1014 2967 2532 1537 3588
τοὺς ἀδελφούς, καὶ τοὺς βουλομένους κωλύει, καὶ ἐκ τῆς
the brothers, and those purposing (so) he prevents, and from the

King James Version

THE THIRD EPISTLE OF JOHN

3 John

1. The elder unto the
well beloved Gaius,
whom I love in the truth.

2 Beloved, I wish above
all things that thou
mayest prosper and be
in health, even as thy
soul prospereth.
3 For I rejoiced greatly,
when the brethren came
and testified of the truth
that is in thee, even as
thou walkest in the
truth.
4 I have no greater joy
than to hear that my
children walk in truth.

5 Beloved, thou doest
faithfully whatsoever
thou doest to the breth-
ren, and to strangers;
6 Which have borne
witness of thy charity
before the church:
whom if thou bring for-
ward on their journey
after a godly sort, thou
shalt do well:
7 Because that for his
name's sake they went
forth, taking nothing of
the Gentiles.
8 We therefore ought to
receive such, that we
might be fellowhelpers
to the truth.

9. I wrote unto the
church: but Diotrephes,
who loveth to have the
preeminence among
them, receiveth us not.
10 Wherefore, if I
come, I will remember
his deeds which he
doeth, prating against
us with malicious
words: and not content
therewith, neither doth
he himself receive the
brethren, and forbid-
deth them that would,
and

Literal Translation

thrusts (them) out from the church.
11 Beloved, do not imitate the bad, but the good. The (one) doing good is of God; but the (one) doing bad has not seen God.
12 Witness has been borne to Demetrius by all, and by the truth itself. And we also bear witness, and you know that our witness is true.

13. I had many things to write, but I do not desire to write by means of pen and ink.
14 But I am hoping to see you at once, and we will speak mouth to mouth.
15 Peace to you. The friends greet you. Greet the friends by name.

(Note: Some manuscripts show verse 15 as verse 14.)

3 John 11

1577 1544 27 3361 3401 3588 2556 235 3588
ἐκκλησίας ἐκβάλλει. 11 ἀγαπητέ, μὴ μιμοῦ τὸ κακὸν, ἀλλὰ τὸ
church (them) thrusts out. Beloved, not do imitate the bad, but the

18 3588 15 1537 3588 2316 2076 3588 1161 2554
ἀγαθόν. ὁ ἀγαθοποιῶν ἐκ τοῦ Θεοῦ ἐστιν· ὁ δὲ κακοποιῶν
good. The (one) doing good of God is; the (one) but doing bad

3756 3708 3588 2316 1216 3140 5259
οὐχ ἑώρακε τὸν Θεόν. 12 Δημητρίῳ μεμαρτύρηται ὑπὸ
not has seen God. To Demetrius witness has been borne by

3956 2532 5259 846 3588 225 2532 2249 1161 3140
πάντων, καὶ ὑπ' αὐτῆς τῆς ἀληθείας· καὶ ἡμεῖς δὲ μαρτυροῦ-
all, and by itself the truth; also we and bear witness,

2532 1492 3754 3588 3141 2257 227 2076
μεν, καὶ οἴδατι ὅτι ἡ μαρτυρία ἡμῶν ἀληθής ἐστι.
and you know that the witness of us true is.

4183 2192 1125 235 3756 2309 1223 3188 2532
13. Πολλὰ εἶχον γράφειν, ἀλλ' οὐ θέλω διὰ μέλανος καὶ
Many things I had to write, but not I desire through ink and

2563 4671 1125 1679 1161 2112 1492 4571 2532 4750
καλάμου σοι γράψαι· 14 ἐλπίζω δὲ εὐθέως ἰδεῖν σε, καὶ στόμα
pen to you to write; I am hoping but at once to see you, and mouth

4314 4750 2980 1515 4671 782 4571 3588
πρὸς στόμα λαλήσομεν. 15 εἰρήνη σοι. ἀσπάζονταί σε οἱ
to mouth will speak. Peace to you. Greet you the

5384 782 3588 5384 2596 3686
φίλοι. ἀσπάζου τοὺς φίλους κατ' ὄνομα.
friends. Greet the friends by name.

King James Version

casteth (them) out of the church.
11 Beloved, follow not that which is evil, but that which is good. He that doeth good is of God: but he that doeth evil hath not seen God.
12 Demetrius hath good report of all (men), and of the truth itself: yea, and we (also) bear record; and ye know that our record is true.

13. I had many things to write, but I will not with ink and pen write unto thee:
14 But I trust I shall shortly see thee, and we shall speak face to face. Peace (be) to thee. (Our) friends salute thee. Greet the friends by name.

ΙΟΥΔΑ
JUDE

ΕΠΙΣΤΟΛΗ ΚΑΘΟΛΙΚΗ
EPISTLE GENERAL

THE EPISTLE OF JUDE

Jude

1. Jude, a slave of Jesus Christ, and brother of James, to the (ones) called in God the Father, having been set apart, and having been kept to Jesus Christ:
2 mercy and peace and love be multiplied to you.

3 Beloved, making all diligence to write to you about the common salvation, I had need to write to you exhorting (you) to contend earnestly for the faith once delivered to the saints.

4 For certain men stole in , those of old having been written before to this judgment, ungodly ones perverting the grace of God (it) into unbridled lust, and denying the only Master, God, even our Lord Jesus Christ.

5. But I purpose to remind you, you once knowing these things, that the Lord having saved a people out of the land of Egypt, in the second place He destroyed the ones not believing.
6 And those angels not having kept their first place, but having deserted their dwelling-place, He has kept in everlasting chains under darkness for the Judgment of a great day;

7 as Sodom and Gomorrah, and the cities around them, in like manner to these, committing fornication, and going away after other flesh, set before an example, undergoing vengeance of everlasting fire.
8 . Likewise, indeed, also these ,

Jude

2455 2424 5547 1401 80 1161 2385
1. Ἰούδας Ἰησοῦ Χριστοῦ δοῦλος, ἀδελφὸς δὲ Ἰακώβου,
Jude of Jesus Christ a slave, brother and of James,

3588 1722 2316 3962 37 2532 2424 5547 5083
τοῖς ἐν Θεῷ πατρὶ ἡγιασμένοις, καὶ Ἰησοῦ Χριστῷ τετηρη-
to those in God (the) Father having been set apart, and to Jesus Christ having been

2822 1656 5213 2532 1515 2532 26 4129
μένοις, κλητοῖς· 2 ἔλεος ὑμῖν καὶ εἰρήνη καὶ ἀγάπη πληθυνθείη.
kept, called; mercy to you and peace and love, be multiplied.

27 3956 4710 4160 1125 5213 4012
3. Ἀγαπητοί, πᾶσαν σπουδὴν ποιούμενος γράφειν ὑμῖν περὶ
Beloved, all diligence making to write to you about

3588 2839 4991 318 2192 1125 5213 3870
τῆς κοινῆς σωτηρίας, ἀνάγκην ἔσχον γράψαι ὑμῖν, παρα-
the common salvation, need I had to write to you, ex-

1864 3588 530 3860 3588 40
καλῶν ἐπαγωνίζεσθαι τῇ ἅπαξ παραδοθείσῃ τοῖς ἁγίοις
horting to earnestly contend for the once delivered to the saints

4102 3921 1063 5100 444 3588 3819 4270
πίστει. 4 παρεισέδυσαν γάρ τινες ἄνθρωποι, οἱ πάλαι προγε-
faith. stole in For certain men, those of old having

1519 5124 3588 2917 765 3588 3588 2316 2257
γραμμένοι εἰς τοῦτο τὸ κρίμα, ἀσεβεῖς, τὴν τοῦ Θεοῦ ἡμῶν
been written before to this judgment, ungodly (ones), the of the God of us

5485 3346 1519 766 2532 3588 3441 1203
χάριν μετατιθέντες εἰς ἀσέλγειαν, καὶ τὸν μόνον δεσπότην
grace perverting (it) into unbridled lust, and the only Master

2316 2532 2962 2257 2424 5547 720
Θεόν, καὶ Κύριον ἡμῶν Ἰησοῦν Χριστὸν ἀρνούμενοι.
God, and Lord of us Jesus Christ denying

5279 1161 5209 1014 1491 5209 530 5124
5. Ὑπομνῆσαι δὲ ὑμᾶς βούλομαι, εἰδότας ὑμᾶς ἅπαξ τοῦτο,
to remind And you I purpose, knowing you once this,

3754 3588 2962 2992 1537 1093 125 4982 3588 1208
ὅτι ὁ Κύριος, λαὸν ἐκ γῆς Αἰγύπτου σώσας, τὸ δεύτερον
that the Lord, a people out of land of Egypt having saved, in the second place

3588 3361 4100 622 32 5037 3588 3361
τοὺς μὴ πιστεύσαντας ἀπώλεσεν. 6 ἀγγέλους τε τοὺς μὴ
those not believing He destroyed. angels And those not

5083 3588 1438 746 235 620 3588
τηρήσαντας τὴν ἑαυτῶν ἀρχήν, ἀλλὰ ἀπολιπόντας τὸ
having kept the of themselves first place, but having deserted the

2398 3613 1519 2920 3173 2250 1199 126
ἴδιον οἰκητήριον, εἰς κρίσιν μεγάλης ἡμέρας δεσμοῖς ἀϊδίοις
own dwelling place, for (the) Judgment of a great day in chains eternal

5259 2217 5083 5613 4670 2532 1116 2532 3588 4012
ὑπὸ ζόφον τετήρηκεν. 7 ὡς Σόδομα καὶ Γόμορρα, καὶ αἱ περὶ
under blackness He has kept. As Sodom and Gomorrah, and those around

846 4172 3588 3664 5125 5158 1608
αὐτὰς πόλεις, τὸν ὅμοιον τούτοις τρόπον ἐκπορνεύσασαι,
them cities, in the similar to these manner committing fornication,

2532 565 3694 4561 2087 4295 1164
καὶ ἀπελθοῦσαι ὀπίσω σαρκὸς ἑτέρας, πρόκεινται δεῖγμα,
and going away after flesh other, set before an example,

4442 166 1399 5254 3668 3305 2532 3778
πυρὸς αἰωνίου δίκην ὑπέχουσαι. 8 ὁμοίως μέντοι καὶ οὗτοι
of fire everlasting vengeance undergoing. Likewise indeed also these

THE EPISTLE OF JUDE

Jude

1. Jude, the servant of Jesus Christ, and brother of James, to them that are sanctified by God the Father, and preserved in Jesus Christ, (and) called:
2 Mercy unto you, and peace, and love, be multiplied.

3 Beloved, when I gave all diligence to write unto you of the common salvation, it was needful for me to write unto you, and exhort (you) that ye should earnestly contend for the faith which was once delivered unto the saints.
4 For there are certain men crept in unawares, who were before of old ordained to this condemnation, ungodly men, turning the grace of our God into lasciviousness, and denying the only Lord God, and our Lord Jesus Christ.

5. I will therefore put you in remembrance, though ye once knew this, how that the Lord, having saved the people out of the land of Egypt, afterward destroyed them that believed not.
6 And the angels which kept not their first estate, but left their own habitation, he hath reserved in everlasting chains under darkness unto the judgment of the great day.

7 Even as Sodom and Gomorrha, and the cities about them in like manner, giving themselves over to fornication, and going after strange flesh, are set forth for an example, suffering the vengeance of eternal fire.

8. Likewise also these

Literal Translation

dreaming (ones) flesh even defile, and despise lordship, and speak evil of glories.
9 But Michael the archangel, when contending with the devil, he argued about the body of Moses; he dared not bring a judgment of blasphemy, but said, Let the Lord rebuke you! (Zech.3:2)

10 But what things they do not know, they speak evil of these. And what things they understand naturally, like the animals without reason, they are corrupted by these.
11 Woe to them, because they went the way of Cain, and gave themselves up to the error of Balaam for reward, and perished in the gainsaying of Korah!
12 These are rocky reefs in your love feasts, feasting together with you, feeding themselves without fear, waterless clouds being carried about by winds, fruitless autumn trees, having died twice, having been plucked up by the roots;

13 wild waves of the sea foaming up their shames, wandering stars for whom blackness of darkness has been kept to the age.

14 And the seventh from Adam, Enoch, also prophesied to these men, saying, Behold, the Lord came with myriads of His saints,

15 to do judgment against all, and to rebuke all the ungodly of them concerning all their ungodly works which they ungodly did, and concerning all the hard things ungodly sinners spoke against Him.

16 These are murmurers, complainers, according to

Jude 9

1797 4561 3303 3392 2963 1161 114
ἐνυπνιαζόμενοι σάρκα μὲν μιαίνουσι, κυριότητα δὲ ἀθετοῦσι,
dreaming (ones) flesh even defile, lordship and despise,

1391 1161 987 3588 1161 3413 3588 743 3753 3588
δόξας δὲ βλασφημοῦσιν. 9 ὁ δὲ Μιχαὴλ ὁ ἀρχάγγελος, ὅτε τῷ
glories and speak evil of. But Michael the archangel, when with the

1228 1252 1256 4012 3588 3475 4983
διαβόλῳ διακρινόμενος διελέγετο περὶ τοῦ Μωσέως σώ-
devil contending he argued about the of Moses body,

3756 5111 2920 2018 988 235
ματος, οὐκ ἐτόλμησε κρίσιν ἐπενεγκεῖν βλασφημίας, ἀλλ᾽
not he dared a judgment to bring of blasphemy, but

2036 2008 4671 2962 3778 1161 3745 3303 3756 1492
εἶπεν, Ἐπιτιμήσαι σοι Κύριος. 10 οὗτοι δὲ ὅσα μὲν οὐκ οἴδασι
said, Let rebuke you (the) Lord. these But what things not they know

987 3745 1161 5447 5613 3588 249 2226 1987
βλασφημοῦσιν· ὅσα δὲ φυσικῶς, ὡς τὰ ἄλογα ζῷα, ἐπί-
they speak evil of; what things and naturally, as the unreasoning animals, they

1722 5125 5351 3759 846 3754 3588 3598 3588
στανται, ἐν τούτοις φθείρονται. 11 οὐαὶ αὐτοῖς· ὅτι τῇ ὁδῷ τοῦ
understand, by these they are corrupted. Woe to them; because in the way

2535 4198 2532 3588 4106 3588 903 3408
Κάϊν ἐπορεύθησαν, καὶ τῇ πλάνῃ τοῦ Βαλαὰμ μισθοῦ
of Cain they went, and to the error of Balaam (for) reward

1632 2532 3588 485 3588 2879 622 3778
ἐξεχύθησαν, καὶ τῇ ἀντιλογίᾳ τοῦ Κορὲ ἀπώλοντο. 12 οὗτοί
gave themselves, and in the gainsaying of Korah perished. These

1526 1722 3588 26 5216 4694 4910 5213
εἰσιν ἐν ταῖς ἀγάπαις ὑμῶν σπιλάδες, συνευωχούμενοι ὑμῖν,
are in the love-feasts of you rocky reefs, feasting together with you,

870 1438 4165 3507 504 5259
ἀφόβως ἑαυτοὺς ποιμαίνοντες· νεφέλαι ἄνυδροι, ὑπὸ
without fear themselves feeding; clouds waterless by

417 4064 1186 5352 175 1364
ἀνέμων περιφερόμεναι· δένδρα φθινοπωρινά, ἄκαρπα, δὶς
winds having been carried about; trees autumn, without fruit, twice

599 1610 2949 66 2281 1890
ἀποθανόντα, ἐκριζωθέντα· 13 κύματα ἄγρια θαλάσσης, ἐπ-
dying, having been uprooted; waves wild of (the) sea,

3588 1438 152 792 4107 3739 3588
αφρίζοντα τὰς ἑαυτῶν αἰσχύνας· ἀστέρες πλανῆται, οἷς ὁ
foaming up the of themselves shames; stars wandering, for whom

2217 3588 4655 1519 3588 165 5083 4395
ζόφος τοῦ σκότους εἰς τὸν αἰῶνα τετήρηται. 14 προεφήτευσε
blackness of darkness to the age has been kept. prophesied

1161 2532 5125 1442 575 76 1802 3004 2400
δὲ καὶ τούτοις ἕβδομος ἀπὸ Ἀδὰμ Ἐνώχ, λέγων, Ἰδού,
And also to these (the) seventh from Adam, Enoch, saying, Behold!

2064 2962 1722 3461 40 846 4160 2920 2596
ἦλθε Κύριος ἐν μυριάσιν ἁγίαις αὐτοῦ, 15 ποιῆσαι κρίσιν κατὰ
came (The) Lord with myriads saints of Him, to do judgment against

3956 2532 1827 3956 3588 765 846 4012 3956
πάντων, καὶ ἐξελέγξαι πάντας τοὺς ἀσεβεῖς αὐτῶν περὶ πάντων
all, and to rebuke all the ungodly of them concerning all

3588 2041 763 846 3739 764 2532 4012 3956
τῶν ἔργων ἀσεβείας αὐτῶν ὧν ἠσέβησαν, καὶ περὶ πάντων
the works ungodly of them which they ungodly did, and concerning all

3588 4642 3739 2980 2596 846 268 765
τῶν σκληρῶν ὧν ἐλάλησαν κατ᾽ αὐτοῦ ἁμαρτωλοὶ ἀσεβεῖς.
the hard things which spoke against Him sinners ungodly.

3778 1526 1113 3202 2596 3588
16 οὗτοί εἰσι γογγυσταί, μεμψίμοιροι, κατὰ τὰς
These are murmurers, complainers, according to the

King James Version

(filthy) dreamers defile the flesh, despise dominion, and speak evil of dignities.
9 Yet Michael the archangel, when contending with the devil he disputed about the body of Moses, durst not bring against him a railing accusation, but said, The Lord rebuke thee.

10 But these speak evil of those things which they know not: but what they know naturally, as brute beasts, in those things they corrupt themselves.
11 Woe unto them! for they have gone in the way of Cain, and ran greedily after the error of Balaam for reward, and perished in the gainsaying of Core.
12 These are spots in your feasts of charity, when they feast with you, feeding themselves without fear: clouds (they are) without water, carried about of winds; trees whose fruit withereth, without fruit, twice dead, plucked up by the roots;

13 Raging waves of the sea, foaming out their own shame; wandering stars, to whom is reserved the blackness of darkness for ever.

14 And Enoch also, the seventh from Adam, prophesied of these, saying, Behold, the Lord cometh with ten thousands of his saints,

15 To execute judgment upon all, and to convince all that are ungodly among them of all their ungodly deeds which they have ungodly committed, and of all their hard (speeches) which ungodly sinners have spoken against him.

16 These are murmurers, complainers, walking after

Literal Translation

their lusts going, and their mouth speaks proud things, admiring faces for the sake of gain.

17. But you, beloved, remember the words spoken before by the apostles of our Lord Jesus Christ,

18 because they told you that at (the) last time there will be mockers going after ungodlinesses according to their lusts.

19 These are the ones setting themselves apart, animal-like ones, not having the Spirit.

20 But you, beloved, building yourselves up by your most holy faith, praying in the Holy Spirit,

21 keep yourselves in the love of God, eagerly awaiting the mercy of our Lord Jesus Christ to everlasting life.

22 And truly pity some, making a distinction.

23 But save others with fear, snatching (them) out of the fire, hating even the garment having been stained from the flesh.

24. Now to Him being able to keep you without stumbling, and to set you before His glory without blemish, with exultation;

25 to the only wise God, our Savior, (be) glory and majesty and might and authority, even now and to all the ages. Amen.

Jude 17

1939 846 4198 2532 3588 4750 846 2980
ἐπιθυμίας αὐτῶν πορευόμενοι, καὶ τὸ στόμα αὐτῶν λαλεῖ
lusts of them going, and the mouth of them speaks

5246 2296 4383 5622 5484
ὑπέρογκα, θαυμάζοντες πρόσωπα ὠφελείας χάριν.
proud things, admiring faces gain for the sake of.

5210 1161 27 3415 3588 4487 3588
17. Ὑμεῖς δέ, ἀγαπητοί, μνήσθητε τῶν ῥημάτων τῶν
you But, beloved, remember the words

4280 5259 3588 652 3588 2962 2257
προειρημένων ὑπὸ τῶν ἀποστόλων τοῦ Κυρίου ἡμῶν
spoken before by the apostles of the Lord of us

2424 5547 3754 3004 5213 3754 1722 2078 5550
Ἰησοῦ Χριστοῦ· 18 ὅτι ἔλεγον ὑμῖν, ὅτι ἐν ἐσχάτῳ χρόνῳ
Jesus Christ; because they told you, that at (the) last time

2071 1703 2596 3588 1438 1939 4198
ἔσονται ἐμπαῖκται, κατὰ τὰς ἑαυτῶν ἐπιθυμίας πορευό-
will be mockers, according to the of themselves lusts going

3588 763 3778 1526 3588 592 1438
μενοι τῶν ἀσεβειῶν. 19 οὗτοί εἰσιν οἱ ἀποδιορίζοντες ἑαυτούς,
after the ungodlinesses. These are they dividing apart themselves,

5591 4151 3361 2192 5210 1161 27 3588 40
ψυχικοί, Πνεῦμα μὴ ἔχοντες. 20 ὑμεῖς δέ, ἀγαπητοί, τῇ ἁγιω-
animal-like, (the) Spirit not having. you But, beloved, in the most

5216 4102 2026 1438 1722 4151
τάτῃ ὑμῶν πίστει ἐποικοδομοῦντες ἑαυτούς, ἐν Πνεύματι
holy of you faith building up yourselves, in (the) Spirit

40 4336 1438 1722 26 2316 5083
Ἁγίῳ προσευχόμενοι, 21 ἑαυτοὺς ἐν ἀγάπῃ Θεοῦ τηρήσατε,
Holy praying, yourselves in (the) love of God keep,

4327 3588 1656 3588 2962 2257 2424 5547
προσδεχόμενοι τὸ ἔλεος τοῦ Κυρίου ἡμῶν Ἰησοῦ Χριστοῦ
eagerly awaiting the mercy of the Lord of us Jesus Christ

1519 2222 166 2532 3739 3303 1653 1252 3739
εἰς ζωὴν αἰώνιον. 22 καὶ οὓς μὲν ἐλεεῖτε διακρινομένοι· 23 οὓς
to life everlasting. And some truly pity making a distinction,; others

1161 1722 5401 4982 1537 3588 4442 726 3404 2532
δὲ ἐν φόβῳ σώζετε, ἐκ τοῦ πυρὸς ἁρπάζοντες, μισοῦντες καὶ
but with fear save, out of the fire snatching (them), hating even

3588 575 3588 4561 4695 5509
τὸν ἀπὸ τῆς σαρκὸς ἐσπιλωμένον χιτῶνα.
the from the flesh stained garment.

3588 1161 1410 5442 5209 679 2532 2476
24. Τῷ δὲ δυναμένῳ φυλάξαι ὑμᾶς ἀπταίστους, καὶ στῆσαι
to Him Now being able to keep you without stumbling, and to set

2714 3588 1391 846 299 1722 20
κατενώπιον τῆς δόξης αὐτοῦ ἀμώμους ἐν ἀγαλλιάσει,
(you) before the glory of Him without blemish with exultation,

3441 4680 2316 4990 2257 1391 2532 3172
25 μόνῳ σοφῷ Θεῷ σωτῆρι ἡμῶν, δόξα καὶ μεγαλωσύνη,
to (the) only wise God Savior of us, (be) glory and greatness,

2904 2532 1849 2532 3568 2532 1519 3956 3588 165
κράτος καὶ ἐξουσία, καὶ νῦν καὶ εἰς πάντας τοὺς αἰῶνας.
might and authority, even now and to all the ages.

281
ἀμήν.
Amen.

King James Version

their own lusts; and their mouth speaketh great swelling (words), having men's persons in admiration because of advantage.

17. But, beloved, remember ye the words which were spoken before of the apostles of our Lord Jesus Christ;

18 How that they told you there should be mockers in the last time, who should walk after their own ungodly lusts.

19 These be they who separate themselves, sensual, having not the Spirit.

20 But ye, beloved, building up yourselves on your most holy faith, praying in the Holy Ghost,

21 Keep yourselves in the love of God, looking for the mercy of our Lord Jesus Christ unto eternal life.

22 And of some have compassion, making a difference:

23 And others save with fear, pulling (them) out of the fire; hating even the garment spotted by the flesh.

24. Now unto him that is able to keep you from falling, and to present (you) faultless before the presence of his glory with exceeding joy,

25 To the only wise God our Saviour, (be) glory and majesty, dominion and power, both now and ever. Amen.

Literal Translation

THE HOLY REVELATION OF JOHN THE DIVINE

Revelation 1

1. A Revelation of Jesus Christ, which God gave to Him to show to His slaves things which must occur quickly. And He signified (by) sending through His angel to His slave, John,

2 who testified of the Word of God and the witness of Jesus Christ, even as many things as he saw.
3 Blessed (is) the (one) reading, and those hearing the words of this prophecy, and keeping the things having been written; for the time (is) near.

4. John to the seven churches in Asia: Grace to you, and peace, from the (One) who is, and who was, and who (is) coming, and from the seven spirits which are before His throne;

5 even from Jesus Christ the faithful witness, the First-born out of the dead, and the Ruler of the kings of the earth. To Him loving us and washing us from our sins by His blood,

6 and made us kings and priests to God, even His Father. To Him (is) the glory and the might forever and ever. Amen.

7 Behold, He comes with the clouds, and every eye will see Him, and the ones who pierced Him, and all the tribes of the earth will wail on account of Him. Yes, Amen.

ΑΠΟΚΑΛΥΨΙΣ ΤΟΥ ΑΓΙΟΥ
REVELATION THE HOLY
ΙΩΑΝΝΟΥ ΤΟΥ ΘΕΟΛΟΓΟΥ
OF JOHN THE DIVINE

Revelation 1

602 2424 5547 3739 1325 846 3588 2316
1. Ἀποκάλυψις Ἰησοῦ Χριστοῦ, ἣν ἔδωκεν αὐτῷ ὁ Θεός,
A revelation of Jesus Christ, which gave to Him God
1161 3588 1401 846 3739 1163 1096 1722 5034 2532 4591
δεῖξαι τοῖς δούλοις αὐτου, ἃ δεῖ γενέσθαι ἐν τάχει, καὶ ἐσή-
to show to the slaves of Him things which must occur with speed, and He
649 1223 3588 32 846 3588 1401 846
μανεν ἀποστείλας διὰ τοῦ ἀγγέλου αὐτοῦ τῷ δούλῳ αὐτοῦ
signified sending through the angel of Him to the slave of Him
2491 3739 3140 3588 3056 3588 2316 2532 3588 3141
Ἰωάννῃ, 2 ὃς ἐμαρτύρησε τὸν λόγον τοῦ Θεοῦ καὶ τὴν μαρτυ-
John, who testified of the Word of God and the witness
2424 5547 3745 5037 1492 3107 3588 314
ρίαν Ἰησοῦ Χριστοῦ, ὅσα τε εἶδε. 3 μακάριος ὁ ἀναγινώσκων,
Jesus Christ, as many as even he saw. Blessed the (one) reading,
2532 3588 191 3588 3056 3588 4394 2532 5083
καὶ οἱ ἀκούοντες τοὺς λόγους τῆς προφητείας καὶ τηροῦντες
and the (ones) hearing the words of the prophecy and keeping
3588 1722 846 1125 3588 1063 2540 1451
τὰ ἐν αὐτῇ γεγραμμένα· ὁ γὰρ καιρὸς ἐγγύς.
the things in it having been written; the for time is near.

2491 3588 2033 1577 3588 1722 3588 773 5485
4. Ἰωάννης ταῖς ἑπτὰ ἐκκλησίαις ταῖς ἐν τῇ Ἀσίᾳ· χάρις
John to the seven churches in Asia; Grace
5213 2532 1515 575 3588 3588 5607 2532 3588 2258 2532 3588 2064
ὑμῖν καὶ εἰρήνη ἀπὸ τοῦ ὁ ὢν καὶ ὁ ἦν καὶ ὁ ἐρχόμενος·
to you and peace from the (One) being and who was and who is coming;
2532 575 3588 2033 4151 3739 2076 1799 3588 2392
καὶ ἀπὸ τῶν ἑπτὰ πνευμάτων ἃ ἐστιν ἐνώπιον τοῦ θρόνου
and from the seven Spirits which are before the throne
846 2532 575 2424 5547 3588 3144 3588 4103 3588
αὐτοῦ· 5 καὶ ἀπὸ Ἰησοῦ Χριστοῦ, ὁ μάρτυς ὁ πιστός, ὁ
of Him; and from Jesus Christ, the witness faithful, the
4416 1537 3588 3498 2532 3588 758 3588 935 3588 1093
πρωτότοκος ἐκ τῶν νεκρῶν, καὶ ὁ ἄρχων τῶν βασιλέων τῆς γῆς.
First-born out of the dead, and the Ruler of the kings of the earth.
3588 25 2248 2532 3068 2248 575 3588 266
τῷ ἀγαπήσαντι ἡμᾶς, καὶ λούσαντι ἡμᾶς ἀπὸ τῶν ἁμαρτιῶν
To the (One) loving us, and washed us from the sins
2257 1722 3588 129 846 2532 4160 2248 935 2532
ἡμῶν ἐν τῷ αἵματι αὐτοῦ· 6 καὶ ἐποίησεν ἡμᾶς βασιλεῖς καὶ
of us in the blood of Him; and made us kings and
2409 3588 2316 2532 3962 846 846 3588 1391 2532 3588 2904
ἱερεῖς τῷ Θεῷ καὶ πατρὶ αὐτου· αὐτῷ ἡ δόξα καὶ τὸ κράτος
priests to the God and Father of Him; to Him (is) the glory and the might
1519 3588 165 3588 165 281 2400 2064 3326 3588
εἰς τοὺς αἰῶνας τῶν αἰώνων. ἀμήν. 7 ἰδού, ἔρχεται μετὰ τῶν
to the ages of the ages. Amen. Behold! He comes with the
3507 2532 3700 846 3956 3788 2532 3748 846
νεφελῶν, καὶ ὄψεται αὐτὸν πᾶς ὀφθαλμός, καὶ οἵτινες αὐτὸν
clouds, and will see Him every eye, and those with Him
1574 2532 2875 1909 846 3956 3588 5443 3588
ἐξεκέντησαν· καὶ κόψονται ἐπ' αὐτὸν πᾶσαι αἱ φυλαὶ τῆς
pierced; and will wail over Him all the tribes of the
1093 3483 281
γῆς. ναί, ἀμήν.
earth. Yes, amen.

King James Version

THE HOLY REVELATION OF JOHN THE DIVINE

Revelation 1

1. The Revelation of Jesus Christ, which God gave unto him, to shew unto his servants things which must shortly come to pass; and he sent and signified (it) by his angel unto his servant John:

2 Who bare record of the word of God, and of the testimony of Jesus Christ, and of all things that he saw.
3 Blessed (is) he that readeth, and they that hear the words of this prophecy, and keep those things which are written therein: for the time (is) at hand.

4. John to the seven churches which are in Asia: Grace (be) unto you, and peace, from him which is, and which was, and which is to come; and from the seven Spirits which are before his throne;

5 And from Jesus Christ, (who is) the faithful witness, (and) the first begotten of the dead, and the prince of the kings of the earth. Unto him that loved us, and washed us from our sins in his own blood,

6 And hath made us kings and priests unto God and his Father; to him (be) glory and dominion for ever and ever. Amen.

7 Behold, he cometh with clouds; and every eye shall see him, and they (also) which pierced him: and all kindreds of the earth shall wail because of him. Even so, Amen.

Literal Translation

8 I am the Alpha and the Omega, (the) Beginning and (the) Ending, says the Lord, the (One) who is, and who was, and who (is) coming, the Almighty.

9. I, even your brother John, and co-sharer in the affliction, and in the kingdom and patience of Jesus Christ, came to be in the island being called Patmos, because of the Word of God and because of the witness of Jesus Christ.

10 I came to be in (the) Spirit on the Lord's day, and I heard behind me a great voice, as of a trumpet,

11 saying, I am the Alpha and the Omega, the First and the Last; also, What you see, write in a scroll, and send to the seven churches of Asia: to Ephesus, and to Smyrna, and to Pergamos, and to Thyatira, and to Sardis, and to Philadelphia, and to Laodicea.

12. And I turned to see the voice which spoke with me. And having turned, I saw seven golden lampstands,

13 and in (the) midst of the seven lampstands (One) like (the) Son of man, having been clothed to (the) feet, and having been girded with a golden girdle at the breasts.

14 And the hairs of His head (were) white as white wool, as snow, and His eyes as a flame of fire;

15 and His feet like burnished brass having been fired in a furnace; and His voice as a sound of many waters;

16 and having in His right hand seven stars; and a sharp, two-edged sword proceeding out of

Revelation 1:8

1473 1510 3588 1/ 2532/3588/5598/746 2532 5056 3004 3588
8. Ἐγώ εἰμι τὸ Α καὶ τὸ Ω, ἀρχὴ καὶ τέλος, λέγει ὁ
I am the Alpha and the Omega, Beginning and Ending, says the

2962 3588/5607/2532/3588/2258/2532/3588 2064 3588 3841
Κύριος, ὁ ὢν καὶ ὁ ἦν καὶ ὁ ἐρχόμενος, ὁ παντοκράτωρ.
Lord, the (One) being and who was and is coming, the Almighty.

1473 2491 3588 2532 80 5216 2532 4791 1722
9. Ἐγὼ Ἰωάννης, ὁ καὶ ἀδελφὸς ὑμῶν καὶ συγκοινωνὸς ἐν
I John, the even brother of you and co-sharer in

3588 2347 2532 1722 3588 932 2532 5281 2424 5547
τῇ θλίψει και ἐν τῇ βασιλείᾳ καὶ ὑπομονῇ Ἰησοῦ Χριστοῦ,
the affliction and in the kingdom and patience of Jesus Christ,

1096 1722 3588 3520 3588 2564 3963 1223 3588 3056
ἐγενόμην ἐν τῇ νήσῳ τῇ καλουμένῃ Πάτμῳ, διὰ τὸν λόγον
came to be in the island being called Patmos, for the Word

3588 2316 2532 1223 3588 3141 2424 5547 1096
τοῦ Θεοῦ και διὰ τὴν μαρτυρίαν Ἰησοῦ Χριστοῦ. 10 ἐγενόμην
of God and because of the witness of Jesus Christ. I came to be

1722 4151 1722 3588 2960 2250 2532 191 3694 3450
ἐν Πνεύματι ἐν τῇ Κυριακῇ ἡμέρᾳ· καὶ ἤκουσα ὀπίσω μου
in (the) Spirit in the Lord's day; and I heard behind me

5465 3173 5613 4536 3004 1473 1510 3588 1 2532
φωνὴν μεγάλην ὡς σάλπιγγος, 11 λεγούσης, Ἐγώ εἰμι τὸ Α καὶ
a voice great as a trumpet, saying, I am the Alpha and

3588 5598 3588 4413 2532 3588 2078 2532 3739 991 1125 1519
τὸ Ω, ὁ πρῶτος καὶ ὁ ἔσχατος· καί, Ὃ βλέπεις γράψον εἰς
the Omega, the First and the Last; and, What you see write into

975 2532 3992 3588 2033 1577 3588 1722 773 1519
βιβλίον, καὶ πέμψον ταῖς ἑπτὰ ἐκκλησίαις ταῖς ἐν' Ασιᾳ, εἰς
a scroll, and send to the seven churhes in Asia, to

2181 2532 1519 4667 2532 1519 4010 2532 1519 2363
Ἔφεσον, καὶ εἰς Σμύρναν, καὶ εἰς Πέργαμον, καὶ εἰς Θυάτειρα,
Ephesus, and to Smyrna, and to Pergamos, and to Thyatira,

2532 1519 4554 2532 1519 5359 2532 1519 2993
καὶ εἰς Σάρδεις, καὶ εἰς Φιλαδέλφειαν, καὶ εἰς Λαοδίκειαν.
and to Sardis, and to Philadelphia, and to Laodicea.

2532 1994 991 3588 5456 3748 2980 3326 1700
12 καὶ ἐπέστρεψα βλέπειν τὴν φωνὴν ἥτις ἐλάλησε μετ' ἐμοῦ.
And I turned to see the voice which spoke with me.

2532 1994 1492 2033 3087 5552 2532 1722 3319
καὶ ἐπιστρέψας εἶδον ἑπτὰ λυχνίας χρυσᾶς, 13 καὶ ἐν μέσῳ
And having turned I saw seven lampstands of gold, and in (the) midst

3588 2033 3087 3664 5207 444 1746
τῶν ἑπτὰ λυχνιῶν ὅμοιον υἱῷ ἀνθρώπου, ἐνδεδυμένον
of the seven lampstands (One) like (the) Son of man, having been clothed

4158 2532 4024 4314 3588 3149 2223
ποδήρη, καὶ περιεζωσμένον πρὸς τοῖς μαστοῖς ζώνην
to (the) feet, and having been girded with at the breasts a girdle

5552 3588 1161 2776 846 2532 3588 2359 3022 5616 2053
χρυσῆν. 14 ἡ δὲ κεφαλὴ αὐτοῦ καὶ αἱ τρίχες λευκαὶ ὡσεὶ ἔριον
of gold. the And head of Him and the hairs white as wool

3022 5613 5510 2532 3588 3788 846 5613 5395 4442
λευκόν, ὡς χιών· καὶ οἱ ὀφθαλμοὶ αὐτοῦ ὡς φλὸξ πυρός·
white, as snow; and the eyes of Him as a flame of fire;

2532 3588 4228 846 3664 5474 5613 1722 2575
15 καὶ οἱ πόδες αὐτοῦ ὅμοιοι χαλκολιβάνῳ, ὡς ἐν καμίνῳ
And the feet of Him like burnished brass, as in a furnace

4448 2532 3588 5456 846 5613 5456 5204 4183
πεπυρωμένοι· καὶ ἡ φωνὴ αὐτοῦ ὡς φωνὴ ὑδάτων πολλῶν,
having been fired; and the voice of Him as a sound of waters many,

2532 2192 1722 3588 1188 846 5495 792 2033 2532 1537 3588
16 καὶ ἔχων ἐν τῇ δεξιᾷ αὐτοῦ χειρὶ ἀστέρας ἑπτά· καὶ ἐκ τοῦ
and having in the right of Him hand stars seven; and out of the

King James Version

8 I am Alpha and Omega, the beginning and the ending, saith the Lord, which is, and which was, and which is to come, the Almighty.

9. I John, who also am your brother, and companion in tribulation, and in the kingdom and patience of Jesus Christ, was in the isle that is called Patmos, for the word of God, and for the testimony of Jesus Christ.

10 I was in the Spirit on the Lord's day, and heard behind me a great voice, as of a trumpet,

11 Saying, I am Alpha and Omega, the first and the last: and, What thou seest, write in a book, and send (it) unto the seven churches which are in Asia; unto Ephesus, and unto Smyrna, and unto Pergamos, and unto Thyatira, and unto Sardis, and unto Philadelphia, and unto Laodicea.

12. And I turned to see the voice that spake with me. And being turned, I saw seven golden candlesticks;

13 And in the midst of the seven candlesticks (one) like unto the Son of man, clothed with a garment down to the foot, and girt about the paps with a golden girdle.

14 His head and (his) hairs (were) white like wool, as white as snow; and his eyes (were) as a flame of fire;

15 And his feet like unto fine brass, as if they burned in a furnace; and his voice as the sound of many waters.

16 And he had in his right hand seven stars: and out of

Literal Translation

His mouth, and His face
shining as the sun in its
power.

17 And when I saw
Him, I fell at His feet, as
dead. And He put His
right hand on me, say-
ing to me, Do not fear. I
am the First and the
Last,

18 and the Living One;
and I became dead; and,
behold, I am living to
the ages of the ages.
Amen. And I have the
keys to Hades, and of
death.

19 Write what things
you saw, and what
things are, and what
things are about to oc-
cur after these things.
20 The mystery of the
seven stars which you
saw on My right, and
the seven golden lamp-
stands: the seven stars
are angels of the seven
churches, and the seven
lampstands you saw are
seven churches.

Revelation 1:17

4750 846 4501 1366 3691 1607 2532
στόματος αὐτοῦ ῥομφαία δίστομος ὀξεῖα ἐκπορευομένη, καὶ
mouth of Him a sword two-mouthed sharp proceeding, and

3588 3799 846 5613 3588 2246 5316 1722 3588 1411 846 2532
ἡ ὄψις αὐτοῦ, ὡς ὁ ἥλιος φαίνει ἐν τῇ δυνάμει αὐτοῦ. 17 καὶ
the face of Him, as the sun shines in the power of it. And

3753 1492 846 4098 4314 3588 4228 846 5613 3498 2532
ὅτε εἶδον αὐτόν, ἔπεσα πρὸς τοὺς πόδας αὐτοῦ ὡς νεκρός· καὶ
when I saw Him, I fell at the feet of Him as dead; and

2007 3588 1188 846 5495 1909 1691 3004 3427 3361
ἐπέθηκε τὴν δεξιὰν αὐτοῦ χεῖρα ἐπ' ἐμὲ, λέγων μοι, Μὴ
He placed the right of Him hand on me, saying to me, Not

5399 1473 1510 3588 4413 2532 3588 2078 2532 3588 2198
φοβοῦ· ἐγώ εἰμι ὁ πρῶτος καὶ ὁ ἔσχατος, 18 καὶ ὁ ζῶν,
do fear; I am the First and the Last, and the Living One

2532 1096 3498 2532 2400 2198 1510 1519 3588 165 3588
καὶ ἐγενόμην νεκρὸς, καὶ ἰδοὺ, ζῶν εἰμι εἰς τοὺς αἰῶνας τῶν
and I became dead, and behold, living I am to the ages of the

165 281 2532 2192 3588 2807 3588 86 2532 3588 2288
αἰώνων, ἀμήν· καὶ ἔχω τὰς κλεῖς τοῦ ᾅδου καὶ τοῦ θανάτου.
ages, Amen. And I have the keys of Hades and of death.

1125 3739 1492 2532 3739 1526 2532 3739 3195 1096
19 γράψον ἃ εἶδες, καὶ ἃ εἰσί, καὶ ἃ μέλλει γενέσθαι
Write things which you saw, and things which are, and things that are about to be

3326 5023 3588 3466 3588 2033 792 3739 1492 1909 3588
μετὰ ταῦτα· 20 τὸ μυστήριον τῶν ἑπτὰ ἀστέρων ὧν εἶδες ἐπὶ τῆς
after these things; the mystery of the seven stars which you saw on the

1188 3450 2532 3588 2033 3087 3588 5552 3588 2033 792
δεξιᾶς μου, καὶ τὰς ἑπτὰ λυχνίας τὰς χρυσᾶς, οἱ ἑπτὰ ἀστέρες
right of me, and the seven lampstands of gold, the seven stars

32 3588 2033 1577 1526 2532 3588 2033 3087 3739
ἄγγελοι τῶν ἑπτὰ ἐκκλησιῶν εἰσι· καὶ αἱ ἑπτὰ λυχνίαι ἃς
angels of the seven churches are; and the seven lampstands which

1492 2033 1577 1526
εἶδες ἑπτὰ ἐκκλησίαι εἰσί.
you saw seven churches are.

King James Version

his mouth went a sharp
twoedged sword: and
his countenance (was)
as the sun shineth in his
strength.

17 And when I saw him,
I fell at his feet as dead.
And he laid his right
hand upon me, saying
unto me, Fear not; I am
the first and the last:

18 I (am) he that liveth,
and was dead; and, be-
hold, I am alive for ev-
ermore, Amen; and
have the keys of hell and
of death.

19 Write the things
which thou hast seen,
and the things which
are, and the things
which shall be hereaf-
ter;
20 The mystery of the
seven stars which thou
sawest in my right hand,
and the seven golden
candlesticks. The seven
stars are the angels of
the seven churches: and
the seven candlesticks
which thou sawest are
the seven churches.

Revelation 2

1. To the angel of the
Ephesian church, write:
These things says the
(One) holding the seven
stars in His right (hand),
He walking in (the)
midst of the seven gold-
en lampstands:

2 I know your works,
and your labor, and your
patience, and that you
cannot bear evil ones;
and (you) tried those
pretending to be apos-
tles and are not, and
found them (to be) liars.
3 And (I know you)
bore up and have pa-
tience and on account of
My name you have la-
bored and have not
wearied,
4 But I have

Revelation 2

3588 32 3588 2179 15777 1125
1. Τῷ ἀγγέλῳ τῆς Ἐφεσίνης ἐκκλησίας γράψον·
To the angel of the Ephesian church write;

3592 3004 3588 2902 3588 2033 792 1722 3588 1188
Τάδε λέγει ὁ κρατῶν τοὺς ἑπτὰ ἀστέρας ἐν τῇ δεξιᾷ
These things says the (One) holding the seven stars in the right

846 3588 4043 1722 3319 3588 2033 3087 3588
αὐτοῦ, ὁ περιπατῶν ἐν μέσῳ τῶν ἑπτὰ λυχνιῶν τῶν
of Him, the (one) walking in (the) midst of the seven lampstands

5552 1492 3588 2041 4675 2532 3588 2873 4675 2532 3588
χρυσῶν· 2 Οἶδα τὰ ἔργα σου, καὶ τὸν κόπον σου, καὶ τὴν
of gold; I know the works of you, and the labor of you, and the

5281 4675 2532 3754 3756 1410 941 2556 2532
ὑπομονήν σου, καὶ ὅτι οὐ δύνῃ βαστάσαι κακούς, καὶ
patience of you, and that you cannot bear evil ones, and

3985 3588 5335 1511 652 2532 3756 1526
ἐπείρασω τοὺς φάσλπμτας εἶναι ἀποστόλους καὶ οὐκ εἰσί,
(you) tried the (ones) pretending to be apostles and not are,

2532 2147 846 5571 2532 941 2532 5281 2192
καὶ εὗρες αὐτοὺς ψευδεῖς· 3 και ἐβάστασας καὶ ὑπομονὴν ἔχεις,
and found them liars; and you bore up and patience have,

2532 1223 3588 3686 3450 2872 2532 3756 2577 235 2192
καὶ διὰ τὸ ὄνομά μου κεκοπίακας καὶ οὐ κέκμηκας. 4 ἀλλ' ἔχω
even due to the name of Me you have labored and not have wearied. But I have

Revelation 2

1. Unto the angel of the
church of Ephesus
write; These things saith
he that holdeth the seven
stars in his right hand,
who walketh in the
midst of the seven gold-
en candlesticks;

2 I know thy works, and
thy labour, and thy pa-
tience, and how thou
canst not bear them
which are evil: and thou
hast tried them which
say they are apostles,
and are not, and hast
found them liars:
3 And hast borne, and
hast patience, and for
my name's sake hast la-
boured, and hast not
fainted.
4 Nevertheless I have

Literal Translation | **Revelation 2:5** | **King James Version**

against you that you left your first love.
5 Then remember from where you have fallen, and repent, and do the first works. And if not, I am coming to you quickly, and will remove your lampstand from its place, unless you repent.

6 But you have this, that you hate the works of the Nicolaitans, which I also hate.

7 The (one) who has an ear, hear what the Spirit says to the churches. To the (one) overcoming, I will give to him to eat of the Tree of Life which is in (the) midst of the Paradise of God.

8. And to the angel of the church of Smyrna, write: These things says the First and the Last, who became dead, and lived:

9 I know your works, and the affliction, and the poverty; but you are rich. And (I know) the evil speaking of those saying themselves to be Jews, and they are not, but (are) a synagogue of Satan.

10 Do not at all fear what you are about to suffer. Behold, the Devil is about to throw (some) of you into prison, so that you may be tried; and you will have affliction ten days. Be faithful until death, and I will give you the crown of life.
11 The (one) who has an ear, hear what the Spirit says to the churches. The (one) overcoming will not at all be hurt by the second death.

12. And to the angel of the church in Pergamos, write: These things says the (One) having the sharp, two-edged sword:

2596 4675 3754 3588 26 4675 3588 4413 863 3421
κατὰ σοῦ, ὅτι τὴν ἀγάπην σου τὴν πρώτην ἀφῆκας. 5 μνημό-
against you, that the love of you the first you left. Remember

3767 4159 1601 2532 3340 2532 3588 4413
νευε οὖν πόθεν ἐκπέπτωκας, καὶ μετανόησον, καὶ τὰ πρῶτα
therefore from where you have falled, and repent, and the first

2041 4160 1487 1161 3361 2064 4671 5034 2532 2795 3588
ἔργα ποίησον· εἰ δὲ μή, ἔρχομαί σοι ταχύ, καὶ κινήσω τὴν
works do; if and not, I am coming to you quickly, and will move the

3087 4675 1537 3588 5117 846 1437 3361 3340 235
λυχνίαν σου ἐκ τοῦ τόπου αὐτῆς, ἐὰν μὴ μετανοήσῃς. 6 ἀλλὰ
lampstand of you from the place of it, if not you repent. But

5117 2192 3754 3404 3588 2041 3588 3531 3739 2504
τοῦτο ἔχεις, ὅτι μισεῖς τὰ ἔργα τῶν Νικολαιτῶν, ἃ κἀγὼ
this you have, that you hate the works of the Nicolaitans, which I also

3404 3588 2192 3775 191 5101 3588 4151 3004 3588 1577
μισῶ. 7 ὁ ἔχων οὖς ἀκουσάτω τί τὸ Πνεῦμα λέγει ταῖς ἐκκλη-
hate. The (one) having an ear hear what the Spirit says to he churches.

3588 3528 1325 846 5315 1537 3588 3586 3588
σίαις. τῷ νικῶντι δώσω αὐτῷ φαγεῖν ἐκ τοῦ ξύλου τῆς
To the (one) overcoming I will give to him to eat of the Tree

2222 3588 2076 1722 3319 3588 3857 3588 2316
ζωῆς, ὅ ἐστιν ἐν μέσῳ τοῦ παραδείσου τοῦ Θεοῦ.
of Life, which is in (the) midst of the Paradise of God

2532 3588 32 3588 1577 4668 1125
8. Καὶ τῷ ἀγγέλῳ τῆς ἐκκλησίας Σμυρναίων γράψον·
And to the angel of the church of Smyrna write;

3592 3004 3588 4413 2532 3588 2078 3739 1096 3498 2532
Τάδε λέγει ὁ πρῶτος καὶ ὁ ἔσχατος, ὃς ἐγένετο νεκρὸς καὶ
These things says the First and the Last, who became dead and

2198 1492 4675 3588 2041 2532 3588 2347 2532 3588 4432
ἔζησεν· 9 Οἶδά σου τὰ ἔργα καὶ τὴν θλῖψιν καὶ τὴν πτωχείαν
lived; I know of you the works and the affliction and the poverty,

4145 1161 1488 2532 3588 988 3588 3004 3004
[πλούσιος δὲ εἶ], καὶ τὴν βλασφημίαν τῶν λεγόντων Ἰου-
rich but you are, and the evil speaking of those saying Jews

1511 1438 2532 3756 1526 235 2453 3588
δαίους εἶναι ἑαυτούς, καὶ οὐκ εἰσὶν, ἀλλὰ συναγωγὴ τοῦ
to be themselves, and not they are, but a synagogue

4567 3367 5399 3739 3195 3958 2400 3195 906
Σατανᾶ. 10 μηδὲν φοβοῦ ἃ μέλλεις πάσχειν· ἰδοὺ, μέλλει βάλειν
of Satan. Not at all fear what you are about to suffer; behold, is about to cast

1537 5216 3588 1228 1519 5438 2443 3985 2532 2192
ἐξ ὑμῶν ὁ διάβολος εἰς φυλακὴν, ἵνα πειρασθῆτε· καὶ ἕξετε
(some) of you the devil into prison, that you may be tried; and you will have

2347 2250 1176 1096 4103 891 2288 2532 1325
θλῖψιν ἡμερῶν δέκα. γίνου πιστὸς ἄχρι θανάτου, καὶ δώσω
affliction days ten. Be faithful until death, and I will give

4671 3588 4735 3588 2222 3588 2192 3775 191 5101 3588
σοι τὸν στέφανον τῆς ζωῆς. 11 ὁ ἔχων οὖς ἀκουσάτω τί τὸ
you the crown of life. The (one) having an ear to hear what the

4151 3004 3588 1577 3588 3528 3756 3361 91 1537
Πνεῦμα λέγει ταῖς ἐκκλησίαις. ὁ νικῶν οὐ μὴ ἀδικηθῇ ἐκ
Spirit has to the churches. The (one) overcoming not ever will be hurt by

3588 2288 3588 1208
τοῦ θανάτου τοῦ δευτέρου.
the death second.

2532 3588 32 3588 4010 1577 1125
12. Καὶ τῷ ἀγγέλῳ τῆς Περγάμῳ ἐκκλησίας γράψον,
And to the angel of the Peramos church write,

3592 3004 3588 2192 3588 4501 3588 1366 3588
Τάδε λέγει ὁ ἔχων τὴν ῥομφαίαν τὴν δίστομον τὴν
These things says the (One) having the sword two-mouthed

(somewhat) against thee, because thou hast left thy first love.
5 Remember therefore from whence thou art fallen, and repent, and do the first works; or else I will come unto thee quickly, and will remove thy candlestick out of his place, except thou repent.

6 But this thou hast, that thou hatest the deeds of the Nicolaitans, which I also hate.

7 He that hath an ear, let him hear what the Spirit saith unto the churches; To him that overcometh will I give to eat of the tree of life, which is in the midst of the paradise of God.

8. And unto the angel of the church in Smyrna write; These things saith the first and the last, which was dead, and is alive;

9 I know thy works, and tribulation, and poverty, (but thou art rich) and (I know) the blasphemy of them which say they are Jews, and are not, but (are) the synagogue of Satan.

10 Fear none of those things which thou shalt suffer: behold, the devil shall cast (some) of you into prison, that ye may be tried; and ye shall have tribulation ten days: be thou faithful unto death, and I will give thee a crown of life.

11 He that hath an ear, let him hear what the Spirit saith unto the churches; He that overcometh shall not be hurt of the second death.

12. And to the angel of the church in Pergamos write; These things saith he which hath the sharp sword with two edges;

Literal Translation | **Revelation 2:13** | ***King James Version***

3691 1492 3588 2041 4675 2532 4226 2730 3699 3588
ὀξεῖαν· 13 Οἶδα τὰ ἔργα σου καὶ ποῦ κατοικεῖς, ὅπου ὁ
sharp I know the works of you and where you dwell, where the

2362 3588 4567 2532 2902 3588 3686 3450 2532 3756 720
θρόνος τοῦ Σατανᾶ, καὶ κρατεῖς τὸ ὄνομά μου, καὶ οὐκ ἠρνήσω
throne (is) of Satan, and you hold the name of Me, and not denied

3588 4102 3450 2532 1722 3588 2250 1722 3739 493 3588 3144
τὴν πίστιν μου καὶ ἐν ταῖς ἡμέραις ἐν αἷς Ἀντιπᾶς ὁ μάρτυς
the faith of Me even in the days in which (was) Antipas the witness

3450 3588 4103 3739 615 3844 5213 3699 2730 3588
μου, ὁ πιστός, ὃς ἀπεκτάνθη παρ᾽ ὑμῖν, ὅπου κατοικεῖ ὁ
of Me, faithful, who was killed alongside you, where dwells

4567 235 2192 2596 4675 3641 3754 2192 1563
Σατανᾶς. 14 ἀλλ᾽ ἔχω κατὰ σοῦ ὀλίγα, ὅτι ἔχεις ἐκεῖ
Satan. But I have against you a few things, for you have there

13 I know your works, and where you dwell, where the throne of Satan (is). And you hold My name, and did not deny My faith even in the days in which Antipas (was) My faithful witness; who was killed alongside you, where Satan dwells.

13 I know thy works, and where thou dwellest, (even) where Satan's seat (is): and thou holdest fast my name, and hast not denied my faith, even in those days wherein Antipas (was) my faithful martyr, who was slain among you, where Satan dwelleth.

2902 3588 1322 903 3739 1321 3588 904 906
κρατοῦντας τὴν διδαχὴν Βαλαάμ, ὃς ἐδίδασκε τὸν Βαλὰκ βαλεῖν
those holding the teaching of Balaam, who taught Balak to throw

4625 1799 3588 5207 2474 5315 1494 2532
σκάνδαλον ἐνώπιον τῶν υἱῶν Ἰσραήλ, φαγεῖν εἰδωλόθυτα καὶ
a snare before the sons of Israel, to eat idol sacrifices and

4203 3779 2192 2532 4771 2902 3588 1322
πορνεῦσαι. 15 οὕτως ἔχεις καὶ σὺ κρατοῦντας τὴν διδαχὴν
to do fornication. So have also you those holding to the teaching

3588 3531 3739 3404 3340 1487 1161 3361 2064 4671
τῶν Νικολαϊτῶν ὃ μισῶ. 16 μετανόησον· εἰ δὲ μή, ἔρχομαί σοι
of the Nicolaitans; which I hate. Repent! if But not, I will come to you

5035 2532 4170 3326 846 1722 3588 4501 3588 4750
ταχύ, καὶ πολεμήσω μετ᾽ αὐτῶν ἐν τῇ ῥομφαίᾳ τοῦ στό-
quickly, and I will make war with them by the sword of the mouth

3450 3588 2192 3775 191 5101 3588 4151 3004 3588
ματός μου. 17 ὁ ἔχων οὖς ἀκουσάτω τί τὸ Πνεῦμα λέγει ταῖς
of Me.The (one) having an ear hear what the Spirit says to the

14 But I have a few things against you, that you have there those holding the teachings of Balaam, who taught Balak to throw a stumbling-block before the sons of Israel, to eat idol sacrifices, and to commit fornication.

15 So you also have those holding the teaching of the Nicolaitans, which thing I hate.
16 Repent! But if not, I will come to you quickly, and I will make war with them by the sword of My mouth.

14 But I have a few things against thee, because thou hast there them that hold the doctrine of Balaam, who taught Balac to cast a stumbling block before the children of Israel, to eat things sacrificed unto idols, and to commit fornication.
15 So hast thou also them that hold the doctrine of the Nicolaitans, which thing I hate.
16 Repent; or else I will come unto thee quickly, and will fight against them with the sword of my mouth.

1577 3588 3528 1325 846 5315 575 3588
ἐκκλησίαις. τῷ νικῶντι δώσω αὐτῷ φαγεῖν ἀπὸ τοῦ
churches. To the (one) overcoming I will give him to eat from the

3131 3588 2928 2532 1325 846 5586 3022 2532
μάννα τοῦ κεκρυμμένου, καὶ δώσω αὐτῷ ψῆφον λευκήν, καὶ
manna hidden, and I will give him a stone white, and

1909 3588 5586 3686 2537 1125 3739 3762 1097
ἐπὶ τὴν ψῆφον ὄνομα καινὸν γεγραμμένον, ὃ οὐδεὶς ἔγνω
on the stone name a new being written which no one knows

1487/3361/3588 2983
εἰ μὴ ὁ λαμβάνων.
except the (one) receiving (it)

17 The (one) who has an ear, hear what the Spirit says to the churches. To the (one) overcoming, I will give him to eat from the hidden manna. And I will give to him a white stone, and on the stone a new name having been written, which no one knows except the (one) receiving (it).

17 He that hath an ear, let him hear what the Spirit saith unto the churches; To him that overcometh will I give to eat of the hidden manna, and will give him a white stone, and in the stone a new name written, which no man knoweth saving he that receiveth (it).

2532 3588 32 3588 1722 2363 1577 1125
18. Καὶ τῷ ἀγγέλῳ τῆς ἐν Θυατείροις ἐκκλησίας γράψον,
And to the angel of the in Thyatira church write,

3592 3004 3588 5207 3588 2316 3588 2192 3588 3788 846
Τάδε λέγει ὁ υἱὸς τοῦ Θεοῦ, ὁ ἔχων τοὺς ὀφθαλμοὺς αὐτοῦ
These things says the Son of God, He having the eyes of Him

5613 5395 4442 2532 3588 4228 846 3664 5474
ὡς φλόγα πυρός, καὶ οἱ πόδες αὐτοῦ ὅμοιοι χαλκολιβάνῳ·
as a flame of fire, and the feet of Him like burnished brass;

18. And to the angel of the church in Thyatira, write: These things says the Son of God, the (One) having His eyes as a flame of fire, and His feet like burnished brass:

18. And unto the angel of the church in Thyatira write; These things saith the Son of God, who hath his eyes like unto a flame of fire, and his feet (are) like fine brass;

1492 4675 3588 2041 2532 3588 26 2532 3588 1248 2532
19 Οἶδά σου τὰ ἔργα, καὶ τὴν ἀγάπην καὶ τὴν διακονίαν, καὶ
I know of you the works, and the love and the ministry, and

3588 4102 2532 3588 5281 4675 2532 3588 2041 4675 2532 3588
τὴν πίστιν καὶ τὴν ὑπομονήν σου, καὶ τὰ ἔργα σου, καὶ τὰ
the faith and the patience of you, and the works of you, and the

2078 4119 3588 4413 235 2192 2596 4675 3641
ἔσχατα πλείονα τῶν πρώτων. 20 ἀλλὰ ἔχω κατὰ σοῦ ὀλίγα
last more than the first. But I have against you a few things

19 I know your works, and the love, and the ministry, and the faith, and your patience, and your works; and the last more than the first.
20 But I have a few things against you,

19 I know thy works, and charity, and service, and faith, and thy patience, and thy works; and the last (to be) more than the first.
20 Notwithstanding I have a few things against thee,

Literal Translation

that you allow the woman Jezebel to teach, the (one) saying herself (to be) a prophetess, and to cause My slaves to go astray, and to commit fornication, and to eat idol sacrifices.
21 And I gave time to her that she might repent of her fornication. And she did not repent.
22 Behold, I am throwing her into a bed, and into great affliction those committing adultery with her, unless they repent of their works.
23 And I will kill her children with death; and all the churches will know that I am the (One) searching the inner parts and hearts. And I will give to each of you according to your works.

24 But I say to you and to the rest in Thyatira, as many as do not have this teaching, and who did not know the deep things of Satan, as they say: I am not casting another burden on you;

25 but what you have, hold until I shall come.

26 And the (one) overcoming, and the (one) keeping My works until (the) end, I will give to him authority over the nations,

27 and he will shepherd them with an iron staff; they are broken to pieces like clay vessels; as I also have received from My Father.
28 And I will give to him the morning star.

29 The (one) who has an ear, hear what the Spirit says to the churches.

Revelation 3

1. And to the angel of the church in Sardis, write: These things says the (One) having the seven Spirits of God, and the

Revelation 2:21

3754 1439 3588 1135 2403 3588 3004 1438 4398
ὅτι ἐᾷς τὴν γυναῖκα Ἰεζάβελ, ἡ λέγουσα ἑαυτὴν προφῆ-
that you allow the woman Jezabel, the (one) saying herself a prophet-

1321 2532 4105 1699 1401 4203 2532
τιν, διδάσκειν καὶ πλανᾶσθαι τοὺς ἐμοὺς δούλους πορνεῦσαι καὶ
ess, to teach and to cause to err My slaves to do fornication and

1494 5315 2532 1325 846 5550 2443 3340
εἰδωλόθυτα φαγεῖν. 21 καὶ ἔδωκα αὐτῇ χρόνον ἵνα μετανοήσῃ,
idol sacrifices to eat. And I gave to her time that she may repent,

1537 3588 4202 846 2532 3756 3340 2400 1473 906
ἐκ τῆς πορνείας αὐτῆς, καὶ οὐ μετανόησεν. 22 ἰδού, ἐγὼ βάλλω
of the fornication of her, and not she repented. Behold! I am casting

846 1519 2825 2532 3588 3431 3326 846 1519 2347
αὐτὴν εἰς κλίνην, καὶ τοὺς μοιχεύοντας μετ' αὐτῆς εἰς θλῖψιν
her into a bed, and those committing adultery with her into affliction

3173 1437 3361 3340 1537 3588 2041 846 2532 3588
μεγάλην, ἐὰν μὴ μετανοήσωσιν ἐκ τῶν ἔργων αὐτῶν· 23 καὶ τὰ
great, if not they may repent of the works of them; And the

5043 846 615 1722 2288 2532 1097 3956
τέκνα αὐτῆς ἀποκτενῶ ἐν θανάτῳ· καὶ γνώσονται πᾶσαι
children of her I will kill with death; and will know all

3588 1577 3754 1473 1510 3588 2045 3510 2532 2588
αἱ ἐκκλησίαι ὅτι ἐγώ εἰμι ὁ ἐραυνῶν νεφροὺς καὶ καρδίας·
the churches that I am the (One) searching kidneys and hearts;

2532 1325 5213 1538 2596 3588 2041 5216 5213 1161
καὶ δώσω ὑμῖν ἑκάστῳ κατὰ τὰ ἔργα ὑμῶν. 24 ὑμῖν δὲ
and I will give to you each according to the works of you. to you But

3004 2532 3062 3588 1722 2363 3745 3756 2192 3588
λέγω καὶ λοιποῖς τοῖς ἐν Θυατείροις, ὅσοι οὐκ ἔχουσι τὴν
I say and to the rest in Thyatira, as many as not have

1322 3778 2532 3748 3756 1097 3588 899 3588
διδαχὴν ταύτην, καὶ οἵτινες οὐκ ἔγνωσαν τὰ βάθη τοῦ
teaching this, and who not knew the deep things

4567 5613 3004 3756 906 1909 5209 243 922 4133
Σατανᾶ, ὡς λέγουσιν, οὐ βαλῶ ἐφ' ὑμᾶς ἄλλο βάρος. 25 πλὴν
of Satan, as they say, not I am casting on you another load, but

3739 2192 2902 891 3757/302/2240 2532 3588 3528 2532
ὃ ἔχετε κρατήσατε, ἄχρις οὗ ἂν ἥξω. 26 καὶ ὁ νικῶν καὶ
what you have hold, until I shall come. And he overcoming and

3588 5083 891 5056 3588 2041 3450 1325 846 1849 1909
ὁ τηρῶν ἄχρι τέλους τὰ ἔργα μου, δώσω αὐτῷ ἐξουσίαν ἐπὶ
he keeping until (the) end the works of Me, I will give him authority over

3588 1484 2532 4165 846 1722 4464 4603 5613 3588
τῶν ἐθνῶν· 27 καὶ ποιμανεῖ αὐτοὺς ἐν ῥάβδῳ σιδηρᾷ, ὡς τὰ
the nations; and he will shepherd them with a staff iron, as

4632 3588 2764 4937 5613 2504 2983 3844 3588
σκεύη τὰ κεραμικὰ συντρίβεται· 28 ὡς κἀγὼ εἴληφα παρὰ τοῦ
vessels clay they are broken; as I also have received from the

3962 3450 2532 1325 846 3588 792 3588 4407
πατρός μου· καὶ δώσω αὐτῷ τὸν ἀστέρα τὸν πρωινόν.
Father of Me; and I will give him the star morning.

3588 2192 3775 191 5101 3588 4151 3004 3588 1577
29 ὁ ἔχων οὖς ἀκουσάτω τί τὸ Πνεῦμα λέγει ταῖς ἐκκλησίαις.
the (one) having an ear hear what the Spirit says to the churches.

Revelation 3

2532 3588 32 3588 1722 4554 1577 1125
1. Καὶ τῷ ἀγγέλῳ τῆς ἐν Σάρδεσιν ἐκκλησίας γράψον,
And to the angel of the inn Sardis church write,

3592 3004 3588 2192 3588 2033 4151 3588 2316 2532 3588
Τάδε λέγει ὁ ἔχων τὰ ἑπτὰ πνεύματα τοῦ Θεοῦ καὶ τοὺς
These things says He having the seven Spirits of God and the

King James Version

because thou sufferest that woman Jezebel, which calleth herself a prophetess, to teach and to seduce my servants to commit fornication, and to eat things sacrificed unto idols.
21 And I gave her space to repent of her fornication; and she repented not.
22 Behold, I will cast her into a bed, and them that commit adultery with her into great tribulation, except they repent of their deeds.
23 And I will kill her children with death; and all the churches shall know that I am he which searcheth the reins and hearts: and I will give unto every one of you according to your works.

24 But unto you I say, and unto the rest in Thyatira, as many as have not this doctrine, and which have not known the depths of Satan, as they speak; I will put upon you none other burden.

25 But that which ye have (already) hold fast till I come.
26 And he that overcometh, and keepeth my works unto the end, to him will I give power over the nations:

27 And he shall rule them with a rod of iron; as the vessels of a potter shall they be broken to shivers: even as I received of my Father.
28 And I will give him the morning star.

29 He that hath an ear, let him hear what the Spirit saith unto the churches.

Revelation 3

1. And unto the angel of the church in Sardis write; These things saith he that hath the seven Spirits of God, and the

Literal Translation **Revelation 3:2** ***King James Version***

seven stars: I know your works, that you have the name that you live, and are dead.

2 Be watching, and establish the things left, which are about to die. For I have not found your works being fulfilled before God.

3 Then remember how you received and heard, and keep, and repent. If, then, you do not watch, I will come upon you like a thief, and you will not at all know what hour I come upon you.

4 You also have a few names in Sardis which did not defile their robes, and they shall walk with Me in white because they are worthy.

5 The (one) overcoming, this (one) shall be clothed in white garments, and I will not at all blot his name out of the Scroll of Life; and I will acknowledge his name before My Father, and before His angels.

6 The (one) who has an ear, hear what the Spirit says to the churches.

7. And to the angel of the church in Philadelphia, write: These things says the Holy One, the True One, the (One) having the key of David, the (One) opening, and no one shuts; and shuts, and no one opens:

8 I know your works. Behold! I have given a door being opened before you, and no one is able to shut it, because you have a little power and have kept My word, and have not denied My name.

9 Behold, I give out of the synagogue of Satan, those saying themselves to be Jews, and they are not, but

2033 792 1492 4675 3588 2041 3754 3588 3686 2192 3754
ἑπτὰ ἀστέρας· Οἶδά σου τὰ ἔργα, ὅτι τὸ ὄνομα ἔχεις ὅτι
seven stars; I know of you the works, that the name you have that

2198 2532 3498 1488 1096 1127 2532 4741 3588 3062
ζῇς, καὶ νεκρὸς εἶ. 2 γίνου γρηγορῶν, καὶ στήρισον τὰ λοιπὰ
you live, and dead are. Be watching, and establish the things left

3739 3195 599 3756 1063 2147 4675 3588 2041 4137
ἃ μέλλει ἀποθανεῖν· οὐ γὰρ εὕρηκά σου τὰ ἔργα πεπληρω-
which are about to die; not for I have found of you the works being

1799 3588 2316 3421 3767 4459 2983 2532
μένα ἐνώπιον τοῦ Θεοῦ. 3 μνημόνευε οὖν πῶς εἴληφας καὶ
fulfilled before God. Remember then how you received and

191 2532 5083 2532 3340 1437 3767 3361 1127
ἤκουσας, καὶ τήρει, καὶ μετανόησον. ἐὰν οὖν μὴ γρηγορή-
heard, and keep, and repent. If then not you watch,

2240 1909 1161 5613 2812 2532 3756 3361 1097 4169 5610
σῃς, ἥξω ἐπί σε ὡς κλέπτης, καὶ οὐ μὴ γνῷς ποίαν ὥραν
I will come on you as a thief, and not at all you know what hour

2240 1909 4571 2192 3641 3686 2532 1722 4554 3739 3756
ἥξω ἐπὶ σέ. 4 ἔχεις ὀλίγα ὀνόματα καὶ ἐν Σάρδεσιν, ἃ οὐκ
I come on you. You have a few names also in Sardis, which not

3435 3588 2440 846 2532 4043 3326 1700 1722
ἐμόλυναν τὰ ἱμάτια αὐτῶν· καὶ περιπατήσουσι μετ' ἐμοῦ ἐν
defile the garments of them; and they shall walk with Me in

3022 3754 514 1526 3588 3528 3778 4016 1722
λευκοῖς, ὅτι ἄξιοί εἰσιν. 5 ὁ νικῶν, οὗτος περιβαλεῖται ἐν
white, because worthy they are. The (one) overcoming, he shall be clothed in

2440 3022 2532 3756 3361 1813 3588 3686 846 1537 3588
ἱματίοις λευκοῖς· καὶ οὐ μὴ ἐξαλείψω τὸ ὄνομα αὐτοῦ ἐκ τῆς
garments white; and not at all will I blot the name of him out of the

976 3588 2222 2532 1843 3588 3686 846
βίβλου τῆς ζωῆς, καὶ ἐξομολογήσομαι τὸ ὄνομα αὐτοῦ
Scroll of Life, and I will acknowledge the name of him

1799 3588 3962 3450 2532 1799 3588 32 846
ἐνώπιον τοῦ πατρός μου, καὶ ἐνώπιον τῶν ἀγγέλων αὐτοῦ.
before the Father of Me, and before the angels of Him.

3588 2192 3775 191 5101 3588 4151 3004 3588 1577
6 ὁ ἔχων οὖς ἀκουσάτω τί τὸ Πνεῦμα λέγει ταῖς ἐκκλησίαις.
The (one) having an ear hear what the Spirit says to the churches.

2532 3588 32 3588 1722 5359 1577 1125
7. Καὶ τῷ ἀγγέλῳ τῆς ἐν Φιλαδελφείᾳ ἐκκλησίας γράψον·
And to the angel of the in Philadelphia church write;

3592 3004 3588 40 3588 228 3588 2192 3588 2807 3588
Τάδε λέγει ὁ ἅγιος, ὁ ἀληθινός, ὁ ἔχων τὴν κλεῖδα τοῦ
These things says the Holy One, the True One, the (One) having the key

1138 3588 455 2532 3762 2808 2532 2808 2532 3762
Δαβίδ, ὁ ἀνοίγων καὶ οὐδεὶς κλείει, καὶ κλείει καὶ οὐδεὶς
of David, the (One) opening and no one shuts, and shuts and no one

455 1492 4675 3588 2041 2400 1325 1799 4675 2374
ἀνοίγει· 8 Οἶδά σου τὰ ἔργα [ἰδοὺ, δέδωκα ἐνώπιόν σου θύραν
opens; I know of you the works, Behold! I have given before you a door

455 2532 3762 1410 2808 846 3754 3398
ἀνεῳγμένην, καὶ οὐδεὶς δύναται κλεῖσαι αὐτήν], ὅτι μικρὰν
being opened, and no one is able to shut it, because a little

2192 1411 2532 5083 3450 3588 3056 2532 3756 720
ἔχεις δύναμιν, καὶ ἐτήρησάς μου τὸν λόγον, καὶ οὐκ ἠρνήσω
you have power, and have kept of Me the Word, and not denied

3588 3686 3450 2400 1325 1537 3588 4864 3588 4567
τὸ ὄνομά μου. 9 ἰδοὺ, δίδωμι ἐκ τῆς συναγωγῆς τοῦ Σατανᾶ,
the name of Me. Behold! I give out of the synagogue of Satan,

3588 3004 1438 2453 1511 2532 3756 1526 235
τῶν λεγόντων ἑαυτοὺς Ἰουδαίους εἶναι, καὶ οὐκ εἰσὶν, ἀλλὰ
those saying themselves Jews to be, and not are, but

seven stars; I know thy works, that thou hast a name that thou livest, and art dead.

2 Be watchful, and strengthen the things which remain, that are ready to die: for I have not found thy works perfect before God.

3 Remember therefore how thou hast received and heard, and hold fast, and repent. If therefore thou shalt not watch, I will come on thee as a thief, and thou shalt not know what hour I will come upon thee.

4 Thou hast a few names even in Sardis which have not defiled their garments; and they shall walk with me in white: for they are worthy.

5 He that overcometh, the same shall be clothed in white raiment; and I will not blot out his name out of the book of life, but I will confess his name before my Father, and before his angels.

6 He that hath an ear, let him hear what the Spirit saith unto the churches.

7. And to the angel of the church in Philadelphia write; These things saith he that is holy, he that is true, he that hath the key of David, he that openeth, and no man shutteth; and shutteth, and no man openeth;

8 I know thy works: behold, I have set before thee an open door, and no man can shut it: for thou hast a little strength, and hast kept my word, and hast not denied my name.

9 Behold, I will make them of the synagogue of Satan, which say they are Jews, and are not, but

Literal Translation | **Revelation 3:10** | **King James Version**

they lie; behold, I will make them come and bow down before your feet, and they shall know that I loved you.

10 Because you kept the word of My patience, I also will keep you out of the hour of trial which is about to come on all the habitable world, in order to try those dwelling on the earth.

11 Behold, I am coming quickly. Hold what you have that no one take your crown.
12 The (one) overcoming, I will make him a pillar in the temple of My God, and he shall not at all go out any more. And I will write the name of My God on him, and the name of the city of My God, the new Jerusalem, which comes down out of Heaven from My God, and My new name.

13 The (one) who has an ear, hear what the Spirit says to the churches.

14. And to the angel of the church of Laodicea, write: These things says the Amen, the faithful and true Witness, the Head of the creation of God:
15 I know your works, that you are neither cold nor hot. I would that you were cold or hot.
16 So, because you are lukewarm, and neither cold nor hot, I am about to vomit you out of My mouth.

17 Because you say, I am rich, and I am made rich, and I have need of nothing, and do not know that you are the wretched (one) and miserable and poor and blind and

5574 2400 4160 846 2443 2240 2532 4352
ψεύδονται· ἰδού, ποιήσω αὐτοὺς ἵνα ἥξουσι καὶ προσκυνή-
they lie; behold, I will make them that they shall come and shall bow

1799 3588 4228 4675 2532 1097 3754 1473
σωσιν ἐνώπιον τῶν ποδῶν σου, καὶ γνῶσιν ὅτι ἐγὼ
before the feet of you, and they shall know that I

25 4571 3754 5083 3588 3056 3588 5281 3450
ἠγάπησά σε. 10 ὅτι ἐτήρησας τὸν λόγον τῆς ὑπομονῆς μου,
loved you. Because you kept the Word of the patience of Me,

2504 1161 5083 1537 3588 5610 3588 3986 3588 3195
κἀγώ σε τηρήσω ἐκ τῆς ὥρας τοῦ πειρασμοῦ, τῆς μελλούσης
and I you will keep out of the hour of trial, being about

2064 1909 3588 3625 3650 3985 3588 2730
ἔρχεσθαι ἐπὶ τῆς οἰκουμένης ὅλης, πειράσαι τοὺς κατοι-
to come on the habitable world all, to try the (ones) dwelling

1909 3588 1093 2400 2064 5035 2902 3739 2192 2443
κοῦντας ἐπὶ τῆς γῆς. 11 ἰδού, ἔρχομαι ταχύ· κράτει ὃ ἔχεις, ἵνα
on the earth. Behold! I am coming quickly; hold what you have that

3367 2983 3588 4735 4675 3588 3528 4160
μηδεὶς λάβῃ τὸν στέφανόν σου. 12 ὁ νικῶν, ποιήσω
no one take the crown of you. The (one) overcoming, I will make

846 4769 1722 3588 3485 3588 2316 3450 2532 1854 3756 3361 1831
αὐτὸν στῦλον ἐν τῷ ναῷ τοῦ Θεοῦ μου, καὶ ἔξω οὐ μὴ ἐξέλθῃ
him a pillar in the temple of the God of Me, and out not at all he will go

2089 2532 1125 1909 846 3588 3686 3588 2316 3450 2532 3588
ἔτι, καὶ γράψω ἐπ' αὐτὸν τὸ ὄνομα τοῦ Θεοῦ μου, καὶ τὸ
yet, and I will write on him the name the God of Me, and the

3686 3588 4172 3588 2316 3450 3588 2537 2419 3588
ὄνομα τῆς πόλεως τοῦ Θεοῦ μου, τῆς καινῆς Ἱερουσαλήμ, ἣ
name of the city of the God of Me, the new Jerusalem, which

2597 1537 3588 3772 575 3588 2316 3450 2532 3588 3686
καταβαίνει ἐκ τοῦ οὐρανοῦ ἀπὸ τοῦ Θεοῦ μου, καὶ τὸ ὄνομά
comes down out of Heaven from the God of Me, and the name

3450 3588 2537 3588 2192 3775 191 5101 3588 4151 3004 3588
μου τὸ καινόν. 13 ὁ ἔχων οὖς ἀκουσάτω τί τὸ Πνεῦμα λέγει ταῖς
of Me new. The (one) having an ear hear what the Spirit says to the

1577
ἐκκλησίαις.
churches.

2532 3588 32 3588 1722 1577 2994 1125
14. Καὶ τῷ ἀγγέλῳ τῆς ἐκκλησίας Λαοδικεων γράψον,
And to the angel of the church Laodicea write,

3592 3004 3588 281 3588 3144 3588 4103 2532 228 3588
Τάδε λέγει ὁ Ἀμήν, ὁ μάρτυς ὁ πιστὸς καὶ ἀληθινός, ἡ
These things says the Amen, the Witness faithful and true, the

746 3588 2937 3588 2316 1492 4675 3588 2041 3754 3777
ἀρχὴ τῆς κτίσεως τοῦ Θεοῦ· 15 Οἶδά σου τὰ ἔργα, ὅτι οὔτε
Head of the creation of God; I know of you the works, that neither

5593 1488 3777 2200 3785 5593 1498 2228 2200 3779
ψυχρὸς εἶ οὔτε ζεστός· ὄφελον ψυχρὸς εἴης ἢ ζεστός. 16 οὕτως
cold are you nor hot; I would that cold you were or hot. So

3754 5513 1488 2532 3777 2200 3777 2200 3195 4571 1692
ὅτι χλιαρὸς εἶ καὶ οὔτε ψυχρὸς οὔτε ζεστὸς, μέλλω σε ἐμέσαι
because luke-warm you are and neither cold nor hot, I am about you to vomit

1537 3588 4750 3450 3754 3004 3754 4145 1510 2532
ἐκ τοῦ στόματός μου. 17 ὅτι λέγεις ὅτι Πλούσιός εἰμι, καὶ
out of the mouth of Me. Because you say rich I am, and

4147 2532 3762 5532 2192 2532 3756 1492 3754 4771
πεπλούτηκα καὶ οὐδενὸς χρείαν ἔχω, καὶ οὐκ οἶδας ὅτι σὺ
I am made rich, and of nothing need I have, and not know that you

1488 3588 5005 2532 1652 2532 4434 2532 5185 2532
εἶ ὁ ταλαίπωρος καὶ ἐλεεινὸς καὶ πτωχὸς καὶ τυφλὸς καὶ
are the wretched (one) and miserable and poor and blind and

do lie; behold, I will make them to come and worship before thy feet, and to know that I have loved thee.

10 Because thou hast kept the word of my patience, I also will keep thee from the hour of temptation, which shall come upon all the world, to try them that dwell upon the earth.

11 Behold, I come quickly: hold that fast which thou hast, that no man take thy crown.
12 Him that overcometh will I make a pillar in the temple of my God, and he shall go no more out: and I will write upon him the name of my God, and the name of the city of my God, (which is) new Jerusalem, which cometh down out of heaven from my God: and (I will write upon him) my new name.

13 He that hath an ear, let him hear what the Spirit saith unto the churches.

14. And unto the angel of the church of the Laodiceans write; These things saith the Amen, the faithful and true witness, the beginning of the creation of God;
15 I know thy works, that thou art neither cold nor hot: I would thou wert cold or hot.
16 So then because thou art lukewarm, and neither cold nor hot, I will spue thee out of my mouth.
17 Because thou sayest, I am rich, and increased with goods, and have need of nothing; and knowest not that thou art wretched, and miserable, and poor, and blind, and

Literal Translation — **Revelation 3:18** — *King James Version*

naked.
18 I advise you to buy from Me gold having been fired by fire, that you may be rich; and white garments, that you may be clothed, and your shame and nakedness may not be revealed. And anoint your eyes with eye salve, that you may see.

1131 4823 4671 59 3844 1700 5553 4448
γυμνός· 18 συμβουλεύω σοι ἀγοράσαι παρ' ἐμοῦ χρυσίον πεπυ-
naked; I counsel you to buy from Me gold having

1537 4442 2443 4147 2532 2440 3022
ρωμένον ἐκ πυρὸς, ἵνα πλουτήσῃς, καὶ ἱμάτια λευκὰ,
been fired by fire, that you may be rich, and garments white,

2443 4016 2532 3361 5319 3588 152 3588 1132
ἵνα περιβάλῃ, καὶ μὴ φανερωθῇ, ἡ αἰσχύνη τῆς γυμνότητός
that you be clothed, and not may be revealed the shame of the nakedness

4675 2532 2854 1472 3588 3778 4675 2443
σου· καὶ κολλούριον ἔγχρισον τοὺς ὀφθαλμούς σου, ἵνα
of you; and with eyesalve anoint the eyes of you, that

naked:
18 I counsel thee to buy of me gold tried in the fire, that thou mayest be rich; and white raiment, that thou mayest be clothed, and (that) the shame of thy nakedness do not appear; and anoint thine eyes with eyesalve, that thou mayest see.

19 I, as many as I love, I rebuke and I chasten. Be zealous, then, and repent.
20 Behold, I stand at the door and knock: If anyone hears My voice and opens the door, I will enter to him, and I will dine with him, and he with Me.

991 1473 3745 1437 5368 1651 2532 3811 2206
βλέπῃς. 19 ἐγὼ ὅσους ἐὰν φιλῶ, ἐλέγχω καὶ παιδεύω· ζήλωσον
you may see. I as many as I love, I rebuke and I chasten; be zealous

3767 2532 3340 2400 2476 1909 3588 2374 2532 2925
οὖν καὶ μετανόησον. 20 ἰδοὺ, ἕστηκα ἐπὶ τὴν θύραν καὶ κρούω·
then and repent. Behold! I stand at the door and knock;

1437 5100 191 3588 5456 3450 2532 455 3588 2374
ἐάν τις ἀκούσῃ τῆς φωνῆς μου, καὶ ἀνοίξῃ τὴν θύραν,
If anyone hears the voice of Me, and opens the door,

1525 4314 846 2532 1172 3326 846 2532
εἰσελεύσομαι πρὸς αὐτὸν. καὶ δειπνήσω μετ' αὐτοῦ, καὶ
I will come in to him. And I will dine with him, and

846 3326 1700 3588 3528 1325 846 2523 3326 1700
αὐτὸς μετ' ἐμοῦ. 21 ὁ νικῶν, δώσω αὐτῷ καθίσαι μετ' ἐμοῦ
he with Me. The (one) overcoming I will give him to sit with Me

1722 3588 2362 3450 5613 2504 3528 2532 2523 3326 3588
ἐν τῷ θρόνῳ μου, ὡς κἀγὼ ἐνίκησα καὶ ἐκάθισα μετὰ τοῦ
in the throne of Me, as I also overcame and sat with the

3962 3450 1722 3588 2362 846 3588 2192 3775 191 5101
πατρός μου ἐν τῷ θρόνῳ αὐτοῦ. 22 ὁ ἔχων οὖς ἀκουσάτω τί
Father of Me in the throne of Him. The (one) having an ear hear what

3588 4151 3004 3588 1577
τὸ Πνεῦμα λέγει ταῖς ἐκκλησίαις.
the Spirit says to the churches.

19 As many as I love, I rebuke and chasten: be zealous therefore, and repent.
20 Behold, I stand at the door, and knock: if any man hear my voice, and open the door, I will come in to him, and will sup with him, and he with me.

21 The (one) overcoming, I will give to him to sit with Me in My throne, as I also overcame and sat with My Father in His throne.

22 The (one) who has an ear, hear what the Spirit says to the churches.

21 To him that overcometh will I grant to sit with me in my throne, even as I also overcame, and am set down with my Father in his throne.

22 He that hath an ear, let him hear what the Spirit saith unto the churches.

Revelation 4

1. After these things I saw. And behold, a door having been opened in Heaven! And I heard the first voice as a trumpet speaking with me, saying, Come up here, and I will show you what must happen after these things.

3326 5023 1492 2532 2400 2374 455 1722 3588
1. Μετὰ ταῦτα εἶδον, καὶ ἰδοὺ, θύρα ἠνεῳγμένη ἐν τῷ
After these things I saw, and behold, a door having been opened in

3772 2532 3588 5456 3588 4413 3739 191 5613 4536
οὐρανῷ, καὶ ἡ φωνὴ ἡ πρώτη ἣν ἤκουσα ὡς σάλπιγγος
Heaven, and the voice first which I heard as a trumpet

2980 3326 1700 3004 305 5602 2532 1166 4671
λαλούσης μετ' ἐμοῦ, λέγουσα, Ἀνάβα ὧδε, καὶ δείξω σοι
speaking with Me, saying, Come up here, and I will show you

3739 1163 1096 3326 5023 2532 2112 1096 1722 4151
ἃ δεῖ γενέσθαι μετὰ ταῦτα. 2 καὶ εὐθέως ἐγενόμην ἐν πνεύματι·
what must happen after these things. And at once I became in spirit;

1. After this I looked, and, behold, a door (was) opened in heaven: and the first voice which I heard (was) as it were of a trumpet talking with me; which said, Come up hither, and I will shew thee things which must be hereafter.

2 And at once I became in spirit. And, behold! A throne was set in Heaven, and (One) sitting on the throne.
3 And the (One) sitting was in appearance like a jasper stone, and a sardius; and a rainbow was around the throne, in appearance (like) an emerald.
4 And around the throne (I saw) twenty-four thrones,

2532 2400 2362 2749 1722 3588 3772 2532 1909 3588 2362
καὶ ἰδοὺ, θρόνος ἔκειτο ἐν τῷ οὐρανῷ, καὶ ἐπὶ τοῦ θρόνου
And, behold! A throne was set in Heaven, and on the throne

2521 2532 3588 2521 2258 3664 3706 3037 2393
καθήμενος, 3 καὶ ὁ καθήμενος ἦν ὅμοιος ὁράσει λίθῳ ἰάσπιδι
(One) sitting, And the (one) sitting was like in appearance a stone jasper

2532 4555 2532 2463 2943 3588 2362 3664 3706
καὶ σαρδίνῳ· καὶ ἶρις κυκλόθεν τοῦ θρόνου ὅμοιος ὁράσει
and a sardius; and a rainbow (was) around the throne like in appearance

4664 2532 2943 3588 2362 2362 1501 2532
σμαραγδίνῳ. 4 καὶ κυκλόθεν τοῦ θρόνου θρόνοι εἴκοσι καὶ
to an emerald. And around the throne (were) thrones twenty and

2 And immediately I was in the spirit: and, behold, a throne was set in heaven, and (one) sat on the throne.
3 And he that sat was to look upon like a jasper and a sardine stone: and (there was) a rainbow round about the throne, in sight like unto an emerald.
4 And round about the throne (were) four and twenty seats:

Revelation 4:5

Literal Translation

and on the thrones I saw twenty-four elders sitting, having been clothed in white garments. And they had golden crowns on their heads.

5 And out of the throne come forth lightnings and thunders and voices. And seven lamps of fire (are) burning before the throne, which are the seven Spirits of God;

6 and a glassy sea before the throne, like crystal. And in (the) midst of the throne and around the throne (were) four living creatures, full of eyes before and behind.
7 And the first living creature (was) like a lion; and the second living creature like a calf; and the third living creature having a face like a man; and the fourth living creature like an eagle flying.

8 And (the) four living creatures each one had six wings all around, and within being full of eyes. And they had no rest day and night, saying, Holy, holy, holy, Lord God Almighty, the (One who) was, and is, and the coming (One)!

9. And when ever the living creatures shall give glory and honor and thanks to the (One) sitting on the throne, to the (One) living forever and ever,

10 the twenty-four elders will fall down before Him sitting on the throne; and they will worship the (One) living forever and ever, and will throw

5064 2532 1909 3588 2362 1492 3588 1501 5064
τέσσαρες· καὶ ἐπὶ τοὺς θρόνους εἶδον τοὺς εἴκοσι τέσσαρας
four; and on the throne I saw the twenty four

4245 2521 4016 1722 2440
πρεσβυτέρους καθημένους περιβεβλημένους ἐν ἱματίοις
elders sitting having been clothed in garments

3022 2532 2192 1909 3588 2776 846 4735
λευκοῖς, καὶ ἔσχον ἐπὶ τὰς κεφαλὰς αὐτῶν στεφάνους
white, and they had on the heads of them crowns

5552 2532 1537 3588 2362 1607 796 2532
χρυσοῦς. 5 καὶ ἐκ τοῦ θρόνου ἐκπορεύονται ἀστραπαὶ καὶ
of gold. And out of the throne came forth lightnings and

1027 2532 5456 2532 2033 2985 4442 2545
βρονταί καὶ φωναι. καὶ ἑπτὰ λαμπάδες πυρὸς καιόμεναι
thunders and voices. And seven lamps of fire (are) burning

1799 3588 2362 3739 1526 3588 2033 4151 3588 2316
ἐνώπιον τοῦ θρόνου, αἵ εἰσι τὰ ἑπτὰ πνεύματα τοῦ Θεοῦ·
before the throne, which are the seven Spirits of God;

2532 1799 3588 2362 2281 5193 3664 2930
6 καὶ ἐνώπιον τοῦ θρόνου θάλασσα ὑαλίνη, ὁμοία κρυσ-
And before the throne sea a glassy, like to

2532 1722 3319 3588 2362 2532 2945 3588 2362 5064
τάλλῳ. καὶ ἐν μέσῳ τοῦ θρόνου καὶ κύκλῳ τοῦ θρόνου τέσσαρα
crystal. And in (the) midst of the throne and around the throne four

2226 1073 3788 1715 2532 3693 2532 3588
ζῷα γέμοντα ὀφθαλμῶν ἔμπροσθεν καὶ ὄπισθεν· 7 καὶ τὸ
living creatures full of eyes before and behind; and the

2226 3588 4413 3664 3023 2532 3588 1208 2226 3664
ζῷον τὸ πρῶτον ὅμοιον λέοντι, καὶ τὸ δεύτερον ζῷον ὅμοιον
living creature first like a lion, and the second living creature like

3448 2532 3588 5154 2226 2192 3588 4383 5613 444
μόσχῳ, καὶ τὸ τρίτον ζῷον ἔχον τὸ πρόσωπον ὡς ἀνθρώπος,
a calf, and the third living creature having a face as of a man,

2532 3588 5067 2226 3664 105 4072 2532 4072
καὶ τὸ τέταρτον ζῷον ὅμοιον ἀετῷ πετομένῳ. 8 καὶ τέσσαρα
and the fourth living creature like an eagle flying. And (the) four

2226 1520 2596 1438 2192 303 4420 1803 2943 2532
ζῷα, ἓν καθ᾽ ἑαυτὸ εἶχον ἀνὰ πτέρυγας ἕξ, κυκλόθεν, καὶ
living creatures one by one having each wings six all around, and

2081 1073 3788 2532 372 3756 2192
ἔσωθεν γέμοτα ὀφθαλμῶν, καὶ ἀνάπαυσιν οὐκ ἔχουσιν
within being full of eyes, and respite not they have

2250 2532 3571 3004 40 40 40 2962 3588
ἡμέρας καὶ νυκτὸς, λέγοντα, Ἅγιος ἅγιος ἅγιος Κύριος ὁ
day and night, saying, Holy holy holy Lord

2316 3588 3841 3588 2258 2532 3588 5607 2532 3588 2064 2532
Θεὸς ὁ παντοκράτωρ, ὁ ἦν καὶ ὁ ὢν καὶ ὁ ἐρχόμενος. 9 καὶ
God the Almighty, the (One) (who) was and is and the coming (One). And

3752 1325 3588 2226 1391 2532 5092 2532 2169 3588
ὅταν δώσουσι τὰ ζῷα δόξαν καὶ τιμὴν καὶ εὐχαριστίαν τῷ
when shall give the living creature glory and honor and thanks to Him

2521 1909 3588 2362 3588 2198 1519 3588 165 3588
καθημένῳ ἐπὶ τοῦ θρόνου, τῷ ζῶντι εἰς τοὺς αἰῶνας τῶν
sitting on the throne to the (One) living to the ages of the

165 4098 3588 1501 5064 4245
αἰώνων, 10 πεσοῦνται οἱ εἴκοσι τέσσαρες πρεσβύτεροι
ages, will fall down the twenty four elders

1799 3588 2521 1909 3588 2362 2532 4352 3588
ἐνώπιον τοῦ καθημένου ἐπὶ τοῦ θρόνου, καὶ προσκυνησοῦσι τῷ
before the (One) sitting on the throne, and they will worship Him

2198 1519 3588 165 3588 165 2532 906 3588
ζῶντι εἰς τοὺς αἰῶνας τῶν αἰώνων, καὶ βαλλοῦσι τοὺς
living to the ages of the ages, and will cast the

King James Version

and upon the seats I saw four and twenty elders sitting, clothed in white raiment; and they had on their heads crowns of gold.

5 And out of the throne proceeded lightnings and thunderings and voices: and (there were) seven lamps of fire burning before the throne, which are the seven Spirits of God.

6 And before the throne (there was) a sea of glass like unto crystal: and in the midst of the throne, and round about the throne, (were) four beasts full of eyes before and behind.
7 And the first beast (was) like a lion, and the second beast like a calf, and the third beast had a face as a man, and the fourth beast (was) like a flying eagle.

8 And the four beasts had each of them six wings about (him); and (they were) full of eyes within: and they rest not day and night, saying, Holy, holy, holy, Lord God Almighty, which was, and is, and is to come.

9. And when those beasts give glory and honour and thanks to him that sat on the throne, who liveth for ever and ever,

10 The four and twenty elders fall down before him that sat on the throne, and worship him that liveth for ever and ever, and cast

Literal Translation

Revelation 4:11

King James Version

their crowns before the throne, saying,
11 Lord, You are worthy to receive the glory and the honor and the power, because You created all things, and through Your will they exist and were created.

4735 846 1799 3588 2362 3004 514 1488
στεφάνους αὐτῶν ἐνώπιον τοῦ θρόνου, λέγοντες, 11 Ἄξιος εἶ,
crowns of them before the throne, saying, Worthy are you,

2962 2983 3588 1391 2532 3588 5092 2532 3588 1411 3754 4771
Κύριε, λαβεῖν τὴν δόξαν καὶ τὴν τιμὴν καὶ τὴν δύναμιν· ὅτι σὺ
Lord, to receive the glory and the honor and the power; because you

2936 3588 3956 2532 1223 3588 2307 4675 1526 2532 2936
ἔκτισας τὰ πάντα, καὶ διὰ τὸ θέλημά σου εἰσὶ καὶ ἐκτίσθησαν.
created all things, and because of the will of you they are and were created.

their crowns before the throne, saying,
11 Thou art worthy, O Lord, to receive glory and honour and power: for thou hast created all things, and for thy pleasure they are and were created.

Revelation 5

1. And I saw on the right of the (One) sitting on the throne a scroll having been written within and on the back, having been sealed with seven seals.
2 And I saw a strong angel proclaiming with a great voice: Who is worthy to open the scroll, and to loosen its seals?

3 And no one in Heaven was able to open the scroll nor to see it, neither on the earth, nor underneath the earth.

4 And I wept much, because no one worthy was found to open and to read the scroll, nor to see it.

5 And one of the elders said to me, Do not weep, Behold, the Lion being of the tribe of Judah, the Root of David, overcame (so as) to open the scroll, and to loose its seven seals.

6 And I saw, and behold, in (the) midst of the throne, and of the four living creatures, and in (the) midst of the elders, (was) a Lamb standing, as having been slain, having seven horns and seven eyes, which are the seven Spirits of God, having been sent out into all the earth.
7 And He came and took the scroll out of the right (hand) of Him sitting on the throne.
8. And when He took the scroll, the

Revelation 5

2532 1492 1909 3588 1188 3588 2521 1909 3588 2362
1. Καὶ εἶδον ἐπὶ τὴν δεξιὰν τοῦ καθημένου ἐπὶ τοῦ θρόνου
And I saw on the right of the (One) sitting on the throne

975 1125 2081 2532 3693 2696
βιβλίον γεγραμμένον ἔσωθεν καὶ ὄπισθεν, κατεσφραγισμένον
a scroll having been written within and on the back, having been sealed

4973 2033 2532 1492 32 2478 2784
σφραγῖσιν ἑπτά. 2 καὶ εἶδον ἄγγελον ἰσχυρὸν κηρύσσοντα
with seals seven. And I saw an angel strong proclaiming

5456 3173 5101 2076 514 455 3588 975 2532 3089
φωνῇ μεγάλῃ, Τίς ἐστιν ἄξιος ἀνοῖξαι τὸ βιβλίον, καὶ λῦσαι
with a voice great, Who is worthy to open the scroll and to loosen

3588 4973 846 2532 3762 1410 1722 3588 3772
τὰς σφραγῖδας αὐτοῦ; 3 καὶ οὐδεὶς ἠδύνατο ἐν τῷ οὐρανῷ
the seals of it? And no one was able in Heaven

3761 1909 3588 1093 3761 5270 3588 1093 455 3588 975
οὐδὲ ἐπὶ τῆς γῆς, οὐδὲ ὑποκάτω τῆς γῆς ἀνοῖξαι τὸ βιβλίον,
nor on the earth, nor underneath the earth to open the scroll,

3761 991 846 2532 1473 2799 4183 3754 3762 514
οὔδε βλέπειν αὐτό. 4 καὶ ἐγὼ ἔκλαιον πολλά, ὅτι οὐδεὶς ἄξιος
nor to see it. And I wept much, because no one worthy

2147 455 2532 314 3588 975 3777 991 846
εὑρέθη ἀνοῖξαι καὶ ἀναγνῶναι τὸ βιβλίον, οὔτε βλέπειν αὐτό.
was found to open and to read the scroll, nor to see it.

2532 1520 1537 3588 4245 3004 3427 3361 2799 2400
5 καὶ εἷς ἐκ τῶν πρεσβυτέρων λέγει μοι, Μὴ κλαῖε· ἰδού,
And one of the elders said to me, Not do weep; behold,

3528 3588 3023 3588 5607 1537 3588 5443 2448 3588 4491 1138
ἐνίκησεν ὁ λέων ὁ ὢν ἐκ τῆς φυλῆς Ἰούδα, ἡ ῥίζα Δαβίδ,
overcame the Lion being of the tribe of Judah, the Root of David,

455 3588 975 2532 3089 3588 2033 4973 846
ἀνοῖξαι τὸ βιβλίον καὶ λῦσαι τὰς ἑπτὰ σφραγῖδας αὐτοῦ.
to open the scroll and to loose the seven seals of it.

2532 1492 2532 2400 1722 3319 3588 2362 2532 3588 5064
6 καὶ εἶδον, καὶ ιδού, ἐν μέσῳ τοῦ θρόνου καὶ τῶν τεσσάρων
And I saw, and behold, in (the) midst of the throne and of the four

2226 2532 1722 3319 3588 4245 721 2476 5613
ζώων, καὶ ἐν μέσῳ τῶν πρεσβυτέρων, ἀρνίον ἑστηκὸς ὡς
living creatures, and amidst the elders, a Lamb standing as

4969 2192 2768 2033 2532 3788 2033 3739 1526
ἐσφαγμένον, ἔχον κέρατα ἑπτὰ καὶ ὀφθαλμοὺς ἑπτά, οἵ εἰσι
having been slain, having horns seven and eyes seven, which are

3588 2033 3588 2316 4151 649 1519 3956 3588
τὰ ἑπτὰ τοῦ Θεοῦ πνεύματα ἀπεσταλμένα εἰς πᾶσαν τὴν
the seven of God Spirits. having been sent out into all the

1093 2532 2064 2532 2983 3588 975 1537 3588 1188 3588
γῆν. 7 καὶ ἦλθε, καὶ εἴληφε τὸ βιβλίον ἐκ τῆς δεξιᾶς τοῦ
earth. And He came, and took the scroll out of the right of the

2521 1909 3588 2362 2532 3753 2983 3588 975 3588
καθημένου ἐπὶ τοῦ θρόνου. 8 καὶ ὅτε ἔλαβε τὸ βιβλίον, τὰ
(One) sitting on the throne. And when He took the scroll, the

Revelation 5

1. And I saw in the right hand of him that sat on the throne a book written within and on the backside, sealed with seven seals.

2 And I saw a strong angel proclaiming with a loud voice, Who is worthy to open the book, and to loose the seals thereof?

3 And no man in heaven, nor in earth, neither under the earth, was able to open the book, neither to look thereon.

4 And I wept much, because no man was found worthy to open and to read the book, neither to look thereon.

5 And one of the elders saith unto me, Weep not: behold, the Lion of the tribe of Juda, the Root of David, hath prevailed to open the book, and to loose the seven seals thereof.

6 And I beheld, and, lo, in the midst of the throne and of the four beasts, and in the midst of the elders, stood a Lamb as it had been slain, having seven horns and seven eyes, which are the seven Spirits of God sent forth into all the earth.

7 And he came and took the book out of the right hand of him that sat upon the throne.
8. And when he had taken the book, the

Revelation 5:9

Literal Translation

four living creatures and the twenty-four elders fell down before the Lamb, each one having harps, and golden bowls full of incenses, which are the prayers of the saints.

9 And they sing a new song, saying, Worthy are You to receive the scroll, and to open its seals, because You were slain, and by Your blood purchased us to God out of every tribe and tongue and people and nation,
10 and made us kings and priests to our God; and we shall reign over the earth.
11 And I saw, and I heard a sound of many angels around the throne, and the living creatures, and the elders, and their number was myriads of myriads, and thousands of thousands,

12 saying with a great voice, Worthy is the Lamb having been slain to receive the power and riches and wisdom and strength and honor and glory and blessing.

13 And every creature which is in Heaven, and in the earth, and underneath the earth, and the things that are on the sea, and the things in all of them, I heard saying: To the (One) sitting on the throne, and to the Lamb, (be) the blessing and the honor and the glory and the might to the ages of the ages..

14 And the four living creatures said, Amen. And the twenty-four elders fell down and worshiped (the) One living to (the) ages of the ages.

5064 2226 2532 3588 1501 4245 4098
τέσσαρα ζῶα καὶ οἱ εἰκοσιτέσσαρες πρεσβύτεροι ἔπεσον
four living creatures and the twenty-four elders fell down

1799 3588 721 2192 1538 2788 2532 5357
ἐνώπιον τοῦ ἀρνίου, ἔχοντες ἕκαστος κιθάρας, καὶ φιάλας
before the Lamb, having each one harps, and bowls

5552 1073 2368 3739 1526 3588 4335 3588
χρυσᾶς γεμούσας θυμιαμάτων, αἵ εἰσιν αἱ προσευχαὶ τῶν
of gold full of incenses, whihc are the prayers of the

40 2532 103 5603 2537 3004 514 1488 2983
ἁγίων. 9 καὶ ᾄδουσιν ᾠδὴν καινὴν, λέγοντες, Ἄξιος εἶ λαβεῖν
saints. And they sing a song new, saying, Worthy are You to receive

3588 975 2532 455 3588 4973 846 3754 4969
τὸ βιβλίον, καὶ ἀνοῖξαι τὰς σφραγῖδας αὐτοῦ· ὅτι ἐσφάγης,
the scroll, and to open the seals of it; because You were slain

2532 59 3588 2316 2248 1722 3588 129 4675 1537 3956 5443
καὶ ἠγόρασας τῷ Θεῷ ἡμᾶς ἐν τῷ αἵματί σου ἐκ πάσης φυλῆς
and purchased the to God us by the blood of You out of every tribe

2532 1100 2532 2992 2532 1484 2532 4160 2248 3588 2316
καὶ γλώσσης καὶ λαοῦ καὶ ἔθνους, 10 καὶ ἐποίησας ἡμᾶς τῷ Θεῷ
and tongue and people and nation, and made us to the God

2257 935 2532 2409 2532 936 1909 3588 1093 2532
ἡμῶν βασιλεῖς καὶ ἱερεῖς, καὶ βασιλεύσομεν ἐπὶ τῆς γῆς. 11 καὶ
of us kings and priests, and we shall reign over the earth. And

1492 2532 191 5456 32 4183 2943 3588
εἶδον, καὶ ἤκουσα φωνὴν ἀγγέλων πολλῶν κύκλῳ τοῦ
I saw, and I heard a sound of angels many around the

2362 2532 3588 2226 2532 3588 4245 2532 2258 3588
θρόνου καὶ τῶν ζῴων καὶ τῶν πρεσβυτέρων· καὶ ἦν ὁ
throne and the living creatures and of the elders; and was the

706 846 3463 3463 2532 5505 5505
ἀριθμὸς αὐτῶν μυριάδες μυριάδων, καὶ χιλιάδες χιλιάδων,
number of them myriads of myriads, and thousands of thousands

3004 5456 3173 514 2076 3588 721 3588 4969
12 λέγοντες φωνῇ μεγάλῃ, Ἄξιόν ἐστι τὸ ἀρνίον τὸ ἐσφαγ-
saying with a voice great, Worthy is the Lamb having been

2983 3588 1411 2532 4149 2532 4678 2532
μένον λαβεῖν τὴν δύναμιν καὶ πλοῦτον καὶ σοφίαν καὶ
slain to receive the power and riches and wisdom and

2479 2532 5092 2532 1391 2532 2129 2532 3956 2938 3739
ἰσχὺν καὶ τιμὴν καὶ δόξαν καὶ εὐλογίαν. 13 καὶ πᾶν κτίσμα ὅ
strength and honor and glory and blesssing. And every creature which

2076 1722 3588 3772 2532 1722 3588 1093 2532 5270 3588 1093 2532
ἐστιν ἐν τῷ οὐρανῷ καὶ ἐν τῇ γῇ, καὶ ὑποκάτω τῆς γῆς, καὶ
is in Heaven and in the earth, and underneath the earth, and

1909 3588 2281 3739 2076 2532 3588 1722 846 3956 191
ἐπὶ τῆς θαλάσσης ἅ ἐστι, καὶ τὰ ἐν αὐτοῖς πάντα, ἤκουσα
on the sea the things that are, and the things in them all, I heard

3004 3588 2521 1909 3588 2362 2532 3588 721 3588
λέγοντας, Τῷ καθημένῳ ἐπὶ τοῦ θρόνῳ καὶ τῷ ἀρνίῳ ἡ
saying to the (One) sitting on the throne and to the Lamb the

2129 2532 3588 5092 2532 3588 1391 2532 3588 2904 1519 3588 165
εὐλογία καὶ ἡ τιμὴ καὶ ἡ δόξα καὶ τὸ κράτος εἰς τοὺς αἰῶνας
blessing and the honor and the glory and the might to the ages

3588 165 2532 3588 5064 2226 3004 281 2532 3588
τῶν αἰώνων. 14 καὶ τὰ τέσσαρα ζῶα ἔλεγον, Ἀμήν. καὶ οἱ
of the ages. And the four living creatures said, Amen. And the

1501 4245 4098 2532 4352
εἰκοσιτέσσαρες πρεσβύτεροι ἔπεσαν καὶ προσεκύνησαν
twenty-four elders fell down and worshiped

2198 1519 3588 165 3588 165
ζῶντι εἰς τοὺς αἰῶνας τῶν αἰώνων.
(the) living One to (the) ages of the ages.

King James Version

four beasts and four (and) twenty elders fell down before the Lamb, having every one of them harps, and golden vials full of odours, which are the prayers of saints.

9 And they sung a new song, saying, Thou art worthy to take the book, and to open the seals thereof: for thou wast slain, and hast redeemed us to God by thy blood out of every kindred, and tongue, and people, and nation;
10 And hast made us unto our God kings and priests: and we shall reign on the earth.
11 And I beheld, and I heard the voice of many angels round about the throne and the beasts and the elders: and the number of them was ten thousand times ten thousand, and thousands of thousands;

12 Saying with a loud voice, Worthy is the Lamb that was slain to receive power, and riches, and wisdom, and strength, and honour, and glory, and blessing.
13 And every creature which is in heaven, and on the earth, and under the earth, and such as are in the sea, and all that are in them, heard I saying, Blessing, and honour, and glory, and power, (be) unto him that sitteth upon the throne, and unto the Lamb for ever and ever.

14 And the four beasts said, Amen. And the four (and) twenty elders fell down and worshipped him that liveth for ever and ever.

Literal Translation

Revelation 6

1. And I saw when the Lamb opened one of the seals. And I heard one of the four living creatures, like a sound of thunder, saying, Come and see.
2 And I saw, and behold, a white horse! And the (one) sitting on it had a bow. And a crown was given to him, and he went out overcoming, and that he might overcome.

3 And when He opened the second seal, I heard the second living creature saying, Come and see.
4 And another horse went out, red. And it was given to the (one) sitting on (it) to take peace from the earth, and that they should slay one another. And a large sword was given to him.

5 And when He opened the third seal, I heard the third living creature saying, Come and see. And I saw, and behold, a black horse, and the (one) sitting on it having a balance in his hand.

6 And I heard a voice in (the) midst of the four living creatures saying, A choenix of wheat (for) a denarius, and three choenixes of barley (for) a denarius; and do not harm the oil and the wine.

7 And when He opened the fourth seal, I heard a voice of the fourth living creature saying, Come and see.
8 And I saw, and behold, a pale green horse, and the name of the (one) sitting on it (was) Death; and Hades followed with him. And authority was given to them to kill over the fourth

Revelation 6

2532 1492 3753 455 3588 721 3391 1537 3588 4973
1. Καὶ εἶδον ὅτε ἤνοιξε τὸ ἀρνίον μίαν ἐκ τῶν σφραγίδων,
And I saw when opened the Lamb one of the seals,

2532 191 1520 1537 3588 5064 2226 3004 5613 5456
καὶ ἤκουσα ἑνὸς ἐκ τῶν τεσσάρων ζῴων λέγοντος, ὡς φωνῆς
and I heard one of the four living creatures saying, as a sound

1027 2064 2532 991 2532 1492 2532 2400 2462
βροντῆς, Ἔρχου καὶ βλέπε. 2 καὶ εἶδον, καὶ ἰδού, ἵππος
of thunder, Come and see. And I saw, and behold! a horse

3022 2532 3588 2521 1909 846 2192 5115 2532 1325
λευκός, καὶ ὁ καθήμενος ἐπ' αὐτῷ ἔχων τόξον· καὶ ἐδόθη
white, and the (one) sitting on it having a bow; and was given

846 4735 2532 1831 3528 2532 2443 3528
αὐτῷ στέφανος, καὶ ἐξῆλθε νικῶν. καὶ ἵνα νικήσῃ.
to it a crown, and he went out overcoming and that he might overcome.

2532 3753 455 3588 1208 4973 191 3588
3. Καὶ ὅτε ἤνοιξε τὴν δευτέραν σφραγῖδα, ἤκουσα τοῦ
And when He opened the second seal, I heard the

1208 2226 3004 2064 2532 991 2532 1831
δευτέρου ζῴου λέγοντος, Ἔρχου καὶ βλέπε. 4 καὶ ἐξῆλθεν
second living creature saying, Come and see. And went out

243 2462 4450 2532 3588 2521 1909 846 1325
ἄλλος ἵππος πυρρός· καὶ τῷ καθημένῳ ἐπ' αὐτῷ ἐδόθη
another horse red; and the (one) sitting on it was given

846 2983 3588 1515 575 3588 1093 2532 2443 240
αὐτῷ λαβεῖν τὴν εἰρήνην ἀπὸ τῆς γῆς, καὶ ἵνα ἀλλήλους
to him to take the peace from the earth, and that one another

4969 2532 1325 846 3162 3173
σφάξωσι· καὶ ἐδόθη αὐτῷ μάχαιρα μεγάλη.
they shall slay; and was given to him a sword large.

2532 3753 455 3588 5154 4973 191 3588 5154
5. Καὶ ὅτε ἤνοιξε τὴν τρίτην σφραγῖδα, ἤκουσα τοῦ τρίτου
And when He opened the third seal, I heard the third

2226 3004 2064 2532 991 2532 1492 2532 2400 2462
ζῴου λέγοντος, Ἔρχου καὶ βλέπε. καὶ εἶδον, καὶ ἰδού, ἵππος
living creature saying, Come and see. And I saw, and behold! horse

3189 2532 3588 2521 1909 846 2192 2218 1722 3588 5495
μέλας, καὶ ὁ καθήμενος ἐπ' αὐτῷ ἔχων ζυγὸν ἐν τῇ χειρὶ
A black, and the (one) sitting on it having a balance in the hand

846 2532 191 5456 1722 3319 3588 5064 2226
αὐτοῦ. 6 καὶ ἤκουσα φωνὴν ἐν μέσῳ τῶν τεσσάρων ζῴων
of him. And I heard a voice in (the) midst of the four living creatures

3004 5518 4621 1220 2532 5140 5518 2915
λέγουσαν, Χοῖνιξ σίτου δηναρίου, καὶ τρεῖς χοίνικες κριθῆς
saying, A choenix of wheat (for) a denarius, and three choenixes of barley

1220 2532 3588 1637 2532 3588 3631 3361 91
δηναρίου· καὶ τὸ ἔλαιον καὶ τὸν οἶνον μὴ ἀδικήσῃς.
(for) a denarius; and the oil and the wine not harm.

2532 3753 455 3588 4973 3588 5067 191
7. Καὶ ὅτε ἤνοιξε τὴν σφραγῖδα τὴν τετάρτην, ἤκουσα
And when He opened the seal fourth, I heard

5456 3588 5067 2226 3004 2064 2532 991 2532
φωνὴν τοῦ τετάρτου ζῴου λέγουσαν, Ἔρχου καὶ βλέπε. 8 καὶ
(the) voice of the fourth living creature saying, Come and see. And

1492 2532 2400 2462 5515 2532 3588 2521 1883
εἶδον, καὶ ἰδού, ἵππος χλωρός, καὶ ὁ καθήμενος ἐπάνω
I saw, and behold, horse a pale green, and the one) sitting on

846 3686 846 3588 2288 2532 3588 86 190 3326
αὐτοῦ, ὄνομα αὐτῷ ὁ θάνατος, καὶ ὁ ᾅδης ἀκολουθεῖ μετ'
it, (the) name to it (was) death, and Hades followed with

846 2532 1325 846 1849 615 1909 3588 5067
αὐτοῦ· καὶ ἐδόθη αὐτοῖς ἐξουσία ἀποκτεῖναι ἐπὶ τὸ τέταρτον
him; and was given to them authority to kill over the fourth

King James Version

Revelation 6

1. And I saw when the Lamb opened one of the seals, and I heard, as it were the noise of thunder, one of the four beasts saying, Come and see.
2 And I saw, and behold a white horse: and he that sat on him had a bow; and a crown was given unto him: and he went forth conquering, and to conquer.

3 And when he had opened the second seal, I heard the second beast say, Come and see.
4 And there went out another horse (that was) red: and (power) was given to him that sat thereon to take peace from the earth, and that they should kill one another: and there was given unto him a great sword.

5 And when he had opened the third seal, I heard the third beast say, Come and see. And I beheld, and lo a black horse; and he that sat on him had a pair of balances in his hand.

6 And I heard a voice in the midst of the four beasts say, A measure of wheat for a penny, and three measures of barley for a penny; and (see) thou hurt not the oil and the wine.

7 And when he had opened the fourth seal, I heard the voice of the fourth beast say, Come and see.
8 And I looked, and behold a pale horse: and his name that sat on him was Death, and Hell followed with him. And power was given unto them over the fourth

Revelation 6:9

Literal Translation

of the earth with sword, and with famine, and with death, and by the wild beasts of the earth.

9. And when He opened the fifth seal, I saw under the altar the souls of those having been slain for the Word of God, and for the witness which they had.
10 And they cried with a great voice, saying, Until when, holy and true Master, do You not judge and avenge (for) our blood, from those dwelling on the earth?

11 And there was given to each one a white robe. And it was said to them that they should rest yet a little time, until might be fulfilled also (the number) of their fellow-slaves and their brothers, those being about to be killed, even as they.

12. And I saw when He opened the sixth seal. And behold, a great earthquake occurred. And the sun became black as sackcloth made of hair; and the moon became as blood;
13 and the stars of the heaven fell to the earth, as a fig tree being shaken by a great wind casts its unripe figs.

14 And (the) heaven departed like a scroll being rolled up. And every mountain and island were moved out of their places.

15 And the kings of the earth, and the great ones, and the rich ones, and the chiliarchs, and the powerful ones, and the slave, and every freeman, hid themselves in the caves and in the rocks of the mountains.

16 And they say

3588 1093 1722 4501 2532 1722 3042 2532 1722 2288 2532 5259 3588
τῆς γῆς ἐν ῥομφαίᾳ καὶ ἐν λιμῷ, καὶ ἐν θανάτῳ, καὶ ὑπὸ τῶν
of the earth with sword and with famine, and with death, and by the

2342 3588 1093
θηρίων τῆς γῆς.
wild beasts of the earth.

2532 3753 455 3588 3991 4973 1492 5270
9. Καὶ ὅτε ἤνοιξε τὴν πέμπτην σφραγῖδα, εἶδον ὑποκάτω
And when He opened the fifth seal, I saw underneath

3588 2379 3588 5590 3588 4969 1223 3588 3056
τοῦ θυσιαστηρίου τὰς ψυχὰς τῶν ἐσφαγμένων διὰ τὸν λόγον
the altar the souls of those having been slain for the Word

3588 2316 2532 1223 3588 3141 3739 2192 2532 2896 5456
τοῦ Θεοῦ, καὶ διὰ τὴν μαρτυρίαν ἣν εἶχον, 10 καὶ ἔκραξαν φωνῇ
of God, and for the witness which they had, and they cried with a voice

3173 3004 2193 4219 3588 1203 3588 40 2532 3588
μεγάλῃ, λέγοντες, Ἕως πότε, ὁ δεσπότης ὁ ἅγιος καὶ ὁ ἀλη-
great. saying, Until when, Master, holy and true,

228 3756 2919 2532 1556 3588 129 2257 575 3588 2730
θινός, οὐ κρίνεις καὶ ἐκδικεῖς τὸ αἷμα ἡμῶν ἀπὸ τῶν κατοι-
not do You judge and avenge the blood of us from those living

1909 3588 1093 2532 1325 1538 4749 3022
κούντων ἐπὶ τῆς γῆς; 11 καὶ ἐδόθησαν ἑκάστοις στολαὶ λευκαί,
on the earth? And was given to each one a robe white,

2532 4483 846 2443 373 2089 5550 3398 2193
καὶ ἐρρέθη αὐτοῖς ἵνα ἀναπαύσωνται ἔτι χρόνον μικρόν, ἕως
and it was said to them that they should rest yet time a little, until

3757 4137 2532 3588 4889 846 2532 3588 80
οὗ πληρώσονται καὶ οἱ σύνδουλοι αὐτῶν καὶ οἱ ἀδελφοὶ
should be fulfilled also the fellow-slaves of them and the brothers

846 3588 3195 615 5613 2532 846
αὐτῶν, οἱ μέλλοντες ἀποκτείνεσθαι ὡς καὶ αὐτοί.
of them, those being about to be killed as also they.

2532 1492 3753 455 3588 4973 3588 1623 2532 2400
12. Καὶ εἶδον ὅτε ἤνοιξε τὴν σφραγῖδα τὴν ἕκτην, καὶ ἰδού,
And I saw when He opened the seal sixth, and behold!

4578 3173 1096 2532 3588 2246 1096 3189 5613 4526
σεισμὸς μέγας ἐγένετο, καὶ ὁ ἥλιος ἐγένετο μέλας ὡς σάκκος
An earthquake great occurred, and the sun became black as sackcloth

5155 2532 3588 4582 1096 5613 129 2532 3588 792 3588
τρίχινος, καὶ ἡ σελήνη ἐγένετο ὡς αἷμα, 13 καὶ οἱ ἀστέρες τοῦ
made of hair, and the moon became as blood, and the stars of the

3772 4098 1519 3588 1093 5613 4808 906 3588 3653
οὐρανοῦ ἔπεσαν εἰς τὴν γῆν, ὡς συκῆ βάλλει τοὺς ὀλύνθους
heaven fell to the earth, as a fig-treee casts the unripe figs

846 5259 3173 417 4579 2532 3772 673
αὐτῆς ὑπὸ μεγάλου ἀνέμου σειομένη, 14 καὶ οὐρανὸς ἀπεχω-
of it, by a great wind being shaken, and (the) heaven departed

5613 975 1507 2532 3956 3735 2532 3520 1537
ρίσθη ὡς βιβλίον ἑλισσόμενον, καὶ πᾶν ὄρος καὶ νῆσος ἐκ
as a scroll being rolled up, and every mountain and island from

3588 5117 846 2795 2532 3588 935 3588 1093 2532
τῶν τόπων αὐτῶν ἐκινήθησαν. 15 καὶ οἱ βασιλεῖς τῆς γῆς καὶ
the places of them were moved. And the kings of the earth and

3588 3175 2532 3588 4145 2532 3588 5506 2532 3588
οἱ μεγιστᾶνες, καὶ οἱ πλούσιοι, καὶ οἱ χιλίαρχοι, καὶ οἱ
the great ones, and the rich, and the chiliarchs, and the

1415 2532 3956 1401 2532 3956 1658 2928 1438
δυνατοί, καὶ πᾶς δοῦλος καὶ πᾶς ἐλεύθερος, ἔκρυψαν ἑαυτοὺς
powerful, and the slave, and every freeman, hid themselves

1519 3588 4693 2532 1519 3588 4073 3588 3735 2532 3004
εἰς τὰ σπήλαια καὶ εἰς τὰς πέτρας τῶν ὀρέων, 16 καὶ λέγουσι
in the caves and in the rocks of the mountains, and they say

King James Version

part of the earth, to kill with sword, and with hunger, and with death, and with the beasts of the earth.

9. And when he had opened the fifth seal, I saw under the altar the souls of them that were slain for the word of God, and for the testimony which they held:
10 And they cried with a loud voice, saying, How long, O Lord, holy and true, dost thou not judge and avenge our blood on them that dwell on the earth?

11 And white robes were given unto every one of them; and it was said unto them, that they should rest yet for a little season, until their fellowservants also and their brethren, that should be killed as they (were), should be fulfilled.

12. And I beheld when he had opened the sixth seal, and, lo, there was a great earthquake; and the sun became black as sackcloth of hair, and the moon became as blood;
13 And the stars of heaven fell unto the earth, even as a fig tree casteth her untimely figs, when she is shaken of a mighty wind.
14 And the heaven departed as a scroll when it is rolled together; and every mountain and island were moved out of their places.

15 And the kings of the earth, and the great men, and the rich men, and the chief captains, and the mighty men, and every bondman, and every free man, hid themselves in the dens and in the rocks of the mountains;

16 And said

Literal Translation

Revelation 6:17

King James Version

to the mountains and to the rocks, Fall on us, and hide us from (the) face of the (One) sitting on the throne, even from the wrath of the Lamb,
17 because the great day of His wrath has come; and who is able to stand?

3588 3735 2523 3588 4073 4098 1909 2248 2532 2928
τοῖς ὄρεσι καὶ ταῖς πέτραις, Πέσετε ἐφ' ἡμᾶς, καὶ κρύψατε
to the mountains and to the rocks, Fall on us, and hide

2248 575 4383 3588 2521 1909 3588 2362 2532
ἡμᾶς ἀπὸ προσώπου τοῦ καθημένου ἐπὶ τοῦ θρόνου, καὶ
us from (the) face of the (One) sitting on the throne, even

575 3588 3709 3588 721 3754 2064 3588 2250 3588 3173
ἀπὸ τῆς ὀργῆς τοῦ ἀρνίου· 17 ὅτι ἦλθεν ἡ ἡμέρα ἡ μεγάλη
from the wrath of the Lamb; because came the day great

3588 3709 846 2532 5101 1410 2476
τῆς ὀργῆς αὐτοῦ, καὶ τίς δύναται σταθῆναι;
of the wrath of Him, and who is able to stand?

to the mountains and rocks, Fall on us, and hide us from the face of him that sitteth on the throne, and from the wrath of the Lamb:
17 For the great day of his wrath is come; and who shall be able to stand?

Revelation 7

1. And after these things I saw four angels standing on the four corners of the earth, holding the four winds of the earth, that wind should not blow on the earth, nor on the sea, nor on every tree.

2532 3326 5023 1492 5064 32 2476 1909 3588
1. Καὶ μετὰ ταῦτα εἶδον τέσσαρας ἀγγέλους ἑστῶτας ἐπὶ τὰς
And after these things I saw four angels standing on the

5064 1137 3588 1093 2902 3588 5064
τέσσαρας γωνίας τῆς γῆς, κρατοῦντας τοὺς τέσσαρας
four corners of the earth, holding the four

417 3588 1093 2443 3361 4154 417 1909 3588 1093 3383 1909
ἀνέμους τῆς γῆς, ἵνα μὴ πνέῃ ἄνεμος ἐπὶ τῆς γῆς, μήτε ἐπὶ
winds of the earth, that not should blow wind on the earth, nor on

3588 2281 3383 1909 3956 1186 2532 1492 243
τῆς θαλάσσης, μήτε ἐπὶ πᾶν δένδρον. 2 καὶ εἶδον ἄλλον
the sea, nor on every tree. And I saw another

1. And after these things I saw four angels standing on the four corners of the earth, holding the four winds of the earth, that the wind should not blow on the earth, nor on the sea, nor on any tree.

2 And I saw another angel coming up from the rising of the sun, having a seal of (the) living God. And he cried (with) a great voice to the four angels to whom it was given to them to harm the earth and the sea, saying,

32 305 575 395 2246 2192 4973
ἄγγελον ἀναβαίνοντα ἀπὸ ἀνατολῆς ἡλίου, ἔχοντα σφρα-
angel coming up from (the) rising of (the) sun, having a

2316 2198 2532 2896 5456 3173 3588 5064
γῖδα Θεοῦ ζῶντος· καὶ ἔκραξε φωνῇ μεγάλῃ τοῖς τέσσαρσιν
seal of God (the) living; and he cried (with) voice a great to the four

32 3739 1325 846 91 3588 1093 2532 3588
ἀγγέλοις, οἷς ἐδόθη αὐτοῖς ἀδικῆσαι τὴν γῆν καὶ τὴν
angels, to whom it was given to them to harm the earth and the

2281 3004 3361 91 3588 1093 3383 3588 2281
θάλασσαν, 3 λέγων, Μὴ ἀδικήσητε τὴν γῆν μήτε τὴν θάλασ-
sea, saying, Not do harm the earth nor the sea,

2 And I saw another angel ascending from the east, having the seal of the living God: and he cried with a loud voice to the four angels, to whom it was given to hurt the earth and the sea,

3 Do not harm the earth, nor the sea, nor the trees, until we seal the slaves of our God on their foreheads.

3383 3588 1186 891 3757 4972 3588 1401
σαν, μήτε τὰ δένδρα, ἄχρι οὗ σφραγίσωμεν τοὺς δούλους
nor the trees, until we may seal the slaves

3588 2316 2257 1909 3588 3359 846 2532 191 3588
τοῦ Θεοῦ ἡμῶν ἐπὶ τῶν μετώπων αὐτῶν. 4 καὶ ἤκουσα τὸν
of the God of us on the foreheads of them. And I heard the

3 Saying, Hurt not the earth, neither the sea, nor the trees, till we have sealed the servants of our God in their foreheads.

4 And I heard the number of those having been sealed: one hundred forty-four thousands, having been sealed out of every tribe of the sons of Israel:

706 3588 4972 1540 5505 4972
ἀριθμὸν τῶν ἐσφραγισμένων, ρμδ' χιλιάδες, ἐσφραγισμένοι
number of the(ones) having been sealed, 144 thousands, having been sealed

1537 3956 5443 5207 2474
ἐκ πάσης φυλῆς υἱῶν Ἰσραήλ·
out of every tribe of (the) sons of Israel;

4 And I heard the number of them which were sealed: (and there were) sealed an hundred (and) forty (and) four thousand of all the tribes of the children of Israel.

5 Out of the tribe of Judah, twelve thousand having been sealed. Out of the tribe of Reuben, twelve thousand having been sealed. Out of the tribe of Gad, twelve thousand having been sealed.

1537 5443 2448 1427 5505 4972
5. Ἐκ φυλῆς Ἰούδα, ιβ' χιλιάδες ἐσφραγισμένοι·
Of (the) tribe of Judah, 12 thousands having been sealed;

1537 5443 4502 1427 5505 4972
Ἐκ φυλῆς Ῥουβὴν ιβ' χιλιάδες ἐσφραγισμένοι·
Of (the) tribe of Reuben 12 thousands having been sealed;

1537 5443 1045 1427 5505 4972
Ἐκ φυλῆς Γὰδ ιβ' χιλιάδες ἐσφραγισμένοι·
Of (the) tribe of Gad 12 thousands having been sealed;

5 Of the tribe of Juda (were) sealed twelve thousand. Of the tribe of Reuben (were) sealed twelve thousand. Of the tribe of Gad (were) sealed twelve thousand.

6 Out of the tribe of Asher, twelve thousand having been sealed.

1537 5443 768 1427 5505 4972
6. Ἐκ φυλῆς Ἀσὴρ ιβ' χιλιάδες ἐσφραγισμένοι·
Of (the) tribe of Asher 12 thousands having been sealed;

6 Of the tribe of Aser (were) sealed twelve thousand.

Literal Translation

Revelation 7:7

King James Version

Out of the tribe of Naphtali, twelve thousand having been sealed. Out of the tribe of Manasseh, twelve thousand having been sealed.
7 Out of the tribe of Simeon, twelve thousand having been sealed. Out of the tribe of Levi, twelve thousand having been sealed. Out of the tribe of Issachar, twelve thousand having been sealed.
8 Out of the tribe of Zebulun, twelve thousand having been sealed. Out of the tribe of Joseph, twelve thousand having been sealed. Out of the tribe of Benjamin, twelve thousand having been sealed.

1537 5443 3508 1427 5505 4972
Ἐκ φυλῆς Νεφθαλὶμ, ιβ´ χιλιάδες ἐσφραγισμένοι·
Of (the) tribe of Naphtali 12 thousands having been sealed;

1537 5443 3128 1427 5505 4972
Ἐκ φυλῆς Μανασσῆ, ιβ´ χιλιάδες ἐσφραγισμένοι·
Of (the) tribe of Manasseh 12 thousands having been sealed;

1537 5443 4826 1427 5505 4972
7. Ἐκ φυλῆς Συμεὼν, ιβ´ χιλιάδες ἐσφραγισμένοι·
Of (the) tribe of Simeon, 12 thousands having been sealed;

1537 5443 3017 1427 5505 4972
Ἐκ φυλῆς Λευὶ, ιβ´ χιλιάδες ἐσφραγισμένοι·
Of (the) tribe of Levi, 12 thousands having been sealed;

1537 5443 2466 1427 5505 4972
Ἐκ φυλῆς Ἰσαχὰρ, ιβ´ χιλιάδες ἐσφραγισμένοι·
of (the) tribe of Issachar, 12 thousands having been sealed;

1537 5443 2194 1427 5505 4972
8. Ἐκ φυλῆς Ζαβουλὼν, ιβ´ χιλιάδες ἐσφραγισμένοι·
Of (the) tribe of Zebulun, 12 thousands having been sealed;

1537 5443 2501 1427 5505 4972
Ἐκ φυλῆς Ἰωσὴφ, ιβ´ χιλιάδες ἐσφραγισμένοι·
Of (he) tribe of Joseph, 12 thousands having been sealed;

1537 5443 958 1427 5505 4972
Ἐκ φυλῆς Βενιαμὶν, ιβ´ χιλιάδες ἐσφραγισμένοι.
Of (the) tribe of Benjamin, 12 thousands having been sealed.

Of the tribe of Nepthalim (were) sealed twelve thousand. Of the tribe of Man-asses (were) sealed twelve thousand.

7 Of the tribe of Simeon (were) sealed twelve thousand. Of the tribe of Levi (were) sealed twelve thousand. Of the tribe of Issachar (were) sealed twelve thousand.

8 Of the tribe of Zabulon (were) sealed twelve thousand. Of the tribe of Joseph (were) sealed twelve thousand. Of the tribe of Benjamin (were) sealed twelve thousand.

9. After these things I saw, and behold! A huge crowd which no one was able to number them, out of every nation, even tribes and peoples and tongues standing in front of the throne, and before the Lamb, having been clothed with white robes, and palms in their hands.

3326 5023 1492 2532 2400 3793 4183 3739 705
9. Μετὰ ταῦτα εἶδον, καὶ ἰδοὺ, ὄχλος πολύς, ὃν ἀριθμῆσαι
After these things I saw, and behold! crowd A huge, which to number

846 3762 1410 1537 3956 1484 2532 5443 2532
αὐτὸν οὐδεὶς ἠδύνατο, ἐκ παντὸς ἔθνους καὶ φυλῶν καὶ
them no one was able out of every nation and tribes and

2992 2532 1100 2476 1799 3588 2362 2532
λαῶν καὶ γλωσσῶν, ἑστῶτες ἐνώπιον τοῦ θρόνου καὶ
peoples and tongues, standing before the throne and

1799 3588 721 4016 4749 3022 2532
ἐνώπιον τοῦ ἀρνίου, περιβεβλημένους στολὰς λευκάς, καὶ
before the Lamb, having been clothed (with) robes white, and

5404 1722 3588 5495 846 2532 2896 5456 3173
φοίνικες ἐν ταῖς χερσὶν αὐτῶν· 10 καὶ κράζοντες φωνῇ μεγάλῃ,
palms in the hands of them; and they cry (with) voice a great,

3004 3588 4991 3588 2316 2257 3588 2521 1909 3588
λέγοντες, Ἡ σωτηρία τῷ Θεῷ ἡμῶν τῷ καθημένῳ ἐπὶ τοῦ
saying, Salvation to the God of us sitting on the

2362 2532 3588 721 2532 3956 3588 32 2476
θρόνου, καὶ τῷ ἀρνίῳ. 11 καὶ πάντες οἱ ἄγγελοι εἱστήκεσαν
throne, and to the Lamb. And all the angels stood

2945 3588 2362 2532 3588 4245 2532 3588 5064
κύκλῳ τοῦ θρόνου καὶ τῶν πρεσβυτέρων καὶ τῶν τεσ-
around the throne and the elders and of the four

2226 2532 4098 1799 3588 2362 1909 4383
σάρων ζῴων, καὶ ἔπεσαν ἐνώπιον τοῦ θρόνου ἐπὶ πρόσωπον
living creatues, and they fell before the throne on (the) face

846 2532 4352 3588 2316 3004 281 3588
αὐτῶν, καὶ προσεκύνησαν τῷ Θεῷ, 12 λέγοντες, Ἀμήν· ἡ
of them, and worshiped God, saying, Amen;

2129 2532 3588 1391 2532 3588 4678 2532 3588 2169 2532/3588/5092
εὐλογία καὶ ἡ δόξα καὶ ἡ σοφία καὶ ἡ εὐχαριστία καὶ ἡ τιμὴ
blessing and glory and wisdom and thanksgiving and honor

2532/3588/1411 2532 3588 2479 3588 2316 2257 1519 3588 165 3588
καὶ ἡ δύναμις καὶ ἡ ἰσχὺς τῷ Θεῷ ἡμῶν εἰς τοὺς αἰῶνας τῶν
and power and strength to the God of us to the ages of the

165 281
αἰώνων. ἀμήν.
ages. Amen.

9. After this I beheld, and, lo, a great multitude, which no man could number, of all nations, and kindreds, and people, and tongues, stood before the throne, and before the Lamb, clothed with white robes, and palms in their hands;

10 And they cry with a great voice, saying, Salvation to our God sitting on the throne, and to the Lamb.

10 And cried with a loud voice, saying, Salvation to our God which sitteth upon the throne, and unto the Lamb.

11 And all the angels and of the elders and of the four living creatures stood around the throne. And they fell before the throne on their faces, and worshiped God,

11 And all the angels stood round about the throne, and (about) the elders and the four beasts, and fell before the throne on their faces, and worshipped God,

12 saying, Amen. Blessing and glory and wisdom and thanksgiving and honor and power and strength to our God to the ages of the ages. Amen.

12 Saying, Amen: Blessing, and glory, and wisdom, and thanksgiving, and honour, and power, and might, (be) unto our God for ever and ever. Amen.

Literal Translation

13. And one of the elders answered, saying to me, These, the ones having been clothed (in) the white robes, who are they, and from where did they come?
14 And I said to him, Sir, you know. And he said to me, These are the (ones) coming out of the great tribulation; and they washed their robes and whitened them in the blood of the Lamb.

15 Because of this they are before the throne of God, and serve Him day and night in His temple. And the (One) sitting on the throne (spread His) tabernacle over them.
16 And they will not hunger still, nor will they thirst still, nor at all shall fall on them the sun, nor any kind of heat.

17 Because the Lamb in the midst of the throne will shepherd them, and will lead them on (the) living fountains of waters; and God will wipe off every tear from their eyes.

Revelation 7:13

2532 611 1520 1537 3588 4245 3004 3427 3778
13. Καὶ ἀπεκρίθη εἷς ἐκ τῶν πρεσβυτέρων, λέγων μοι, Οὗτοι
And answered one ot the elders, saying to me, These
3588 4016 3588 4749 3588 3022 5101 1526 2532 4159
οἱ περιβεβλημένοι τὰς στολὰς τὰς λευκάς, τίνες εἰσὶ, καὶ πόθεν
the (ones) having been clothed (in) robes the white, who are they, and whence
2064 2532 2046 846 2962 4771 1492 2532 2036 3427 3778
ἦλθον; 14 καὶ εἴρηκα αὐτῷ, Κύριέ, σὺ οἶδας. καὶ εἶπέ μοι, Οὗτοί
came they? And I said to him, Sir, you know. And he said to me, These
1526 3588 2064 1537 3588 2347 3588 3173 2532 4150
εἰσιν οἱ ἐρχόμενοι ἐκ τῆς θλίψεως τῆς μεγάλης, καὶ ἔπλυναν
are the (ones) coming out of the affliction great, and they washed
3588 4749 846 2532 3021 846 1722 3588 129 3588
τὰς στολὰς αὐτῶν, καὶ ἐλεύκαναν αὐτὰς ἐν τῷ αἵματι τοῦ
the robes of them, and whitened them in the blood of the
721 1223 5124 1526 1799 3588 2362 3588 2316
ἀρνίου. 15 διὰ τοῦτό εἰσιν ἐνώπιον τοῦ θρόνου τοῦ Θεοῦ,
Lamb. Because of this they are before the throne of God,
2532 3000 846 2250 2532 3571 1722 3588 3485 846
καὶ λατρεύουσιν αὐτῷ ἡμέρας καὶ νυκτὸς ἐν τῷ ναῷ αὐτοῦ·
and serve Him day and night in the temple of Him;
2532 3588 2521 1909 3588 2362 4637 1909 846 3756
καὶ ὁ καθήμενος ἐπὶ τοῦ θρόνου σκηνώσει ἐπ' αὐτούς. 16 οὐ
and the (one) sitting on the throne tabernacled over them. not
3983 2089 3761 1372 2089 3761 3361 4098 1909
πεινάσουσιν ἔτι, οὐδὲ διψήσουσιν ἔτι, οὐδὲ μὴ πέσῃ ἐπ'
they will hunger longer, nor will they thirst longer, nor not shall fall on
846 3588 2246 3761 3956 2738 3754 3588 721 3588 303
αὐτοὺς ὁ ἥλιος, οὐδὲ πᾶν καῦμα· 17 ὅτι τὸ ἀρνίον τὸ ἀνα-
them the sun, nor every (kind of) heat; because the Lamb in the midst
3588 2362 4165 846 2532 3594 846 1909
μέσον τοῦ θρόνου ποιμανεῖ αὐτούς, καὶ ὁδηγήσει αὐτοὺς ἐπὶ
of the throne will shepherd them, and will lead them on
2198 4077 5204 2532 1813 3588 2316 3956 1144
ζώσας πηγὰς ὑδάτων, καὶ ἐξαλείψει ὁ Θεὸς πᾶν δάκρυον
living fountains of waters, and will wipe off God every tear
575 3588 3788 846
ἀπὸ τῶν ὀφθαλμῶν αὐτῶν.
from the eyes of them.

King James Version

13. And one of the elders answered, saying unto me, What are these which are arrayed in white robes? and whence came they?

14 And I said unto him, Sir, thou knowest. And he said to me, These are they which came out of great tribulation, and have washed their robes, and made them white in the blood of the Lamb.

15 Therefore are they before the throne of God, and serve him day and night in his temple: and he that sitteth on the throne shall dwell among them.
16 They shall hunger no more, neither thirst any more; neither shall the sun light on them, nor any heat.

17 For the Lamb which is in the midst of the throne shall feed them, and shall lead them unto living fountains of waters: and God shall wipe away all tears from their eyes.

Revelation 8

1. And when He opened the seventh seal, a silence occurred in Heaven, about a half hour.
2 And I saw the seven angels who stood before God, and seven trumpets were given to them.

3 And another angel came and stood at the altar, having a golden censer. And many incenses were given to him, that he give with the prayers of all the saints on the golden altar

Revelation 8

2532 3753 455 3588 4973 3588 1442 1096 4602
1. Καὶ ὅταν ἤνοιξε τὴν σφραγῖδα τὴν ἑβδόμην, ἐγένετο σιγὴ
And when He opened the seal seventh, occurred a silence
1722 3588 3772 5613 2256 2532 1492 3588 2033 32 3739
ἐν τῷ οὐρανῷ ὡς ἡμιώριον. 2 καὶ εἶδον τοὺς ἑπτὰ ἀγγέλους οἳ
in Heaven about a half hour. And I saw the seven angels who
1799 3588 2316 2476 2532 1325 846 2033
ἐνώπιον τοῦ Θεοῦ ἑστήκασι, καὶ ἐδόθησαν αὐτοῖς ἑπτὰ
before God stood, and were given to them seven
4536
σάλπιγγες.
trumpets.

2532 243 32 2064 2532 2476 1909 3588 2379
3. Καὶ ἄλλος ἄγγελος ἦλθε, καὶ ἐστάθη ἐπὶ τὸ θυσιαστηρίον,
And another angel came, and stood at the altar,
2192 3031 5552 2532 1325 846 2368 4183
ἔχων λιβανωτὸν χρυσοῦν· καὶ ἐδόθη αὐτῷ θυμιάματα πολλὰ,
having a censer of gold; amd was given to him incenses many,
2443 1325 3588 4335 3588 40 3956 1909 3588 2362
ἵνα δώσει ταῖς προσευχαῖς τῶν ἁγίων πάντων ἐπὶ τὸ θυσια-
that he give with the prayers of the souls all at the altar

Revelation 8

1. And when he had opened the seventh seal, there was silence in heaven about the space of half an hour.
2 And I saw the seven angels which stood before God; and to them were given seven trumpets.

3 And another angel came and stood at the altar, having a golden censer; and there was given unto him much incense, that he should offer (it) with the prayers of all saints upon the golden altar

Literal Translation

before the throne.
4 And the smoke of the incenses went up with the prayers of the saints out of the hand of the angel before God.

5 And the angel has taken the censer, and has filled it from the fire of the altar, and cast (it) into the earth; and sounds and thunders and lightnings and an earthquake occurred.

6 And the seven angels having the seven trumpets prepared themselves, that they might trumpet.

7. And the first angel trumpeted. And hail and fire mixed with blood occurred. And it was cast onto the earth; and the third (part) of the trees was burned down; and all green grass was burned down.

8 And the second angel trumpeted. And as a great mountain burning with fire was thrown into the sea. And the third (part) of the sea became blood;
9 and the third (part) of the creatures having souls died in the sea; and the third part of the ships was destroyed.

10 And the third angel trumpeted. And a great burning star, like a lamp, fell out of the heaven. And it fell onto the third (part) of the rivers, and onto the fountains of waters.
11 And the name of the star is said (to be) Wormwood. And the third (part) of the waters became changed into wormwood. And many men died from the

Revelation 8:4

3588 40 3588 1799 3588 2362 2532 305 3588
στήριον τὸ χρυσουν τὸ ἐνώπιον τοῦ θρόνου. 4 καὶ ἀνέβη ὁ
of gold before the throne. And went up the

2586 3588 2368 3588 4335 3588 40 1537
καπνὸς τῶν θυμιαμάτων ταῖς προσευχαῖς τῶν ἁγίων ἐκ
smoke of the incenses with the prayers of the saints out of

5495 3588 32 1799 3588 2316 2532 2983 3588
χειρὸς τοῦ ἀγγέλου ἐνώπιον τοῦ Θεοῦ. 5 καὶ εἴληφεν ὁ
(the) hand of the angel before God. And has taken the

32 3588 3031 2532 1072 846 1537 3588 4442 3588
ἄγγελος τὸν λιβανωτόν, καὶ ἐγέμισεν αὐτὸ ἐκ τοῦ πυρὸς τοῦ
angel the censer, and filled it from the fire of the

2379 2532 906 1519 3588 1093 2532 1096 5456 2532
θυσιαστηρίου, καὶ ἔβαλεν εἰς τὴν γῆν· καὶ ἐγένοντο φωναὶ καὶ
altar, and cast (it) into the earth; and occurred sounds and

1027 2532 796 2532 4578
βρονταὶ καὶ ἀστραπαὶ καὶ σεισμός.
thunders and lightnings and an earthquake.

2532 3588 2033 32 3588 2192 3588 2033 4536
6. Καὶ οἱ ἑπτὰ ἄγγελοι οἱ ἔχοντες τὰς ἑπτὰ σάλπιγγας
And the seven angels having the seven trumpets

2090 1438 2443 4537
ἡτοίμασαν ἑαυτοὺς ἵνα σαλπίσωσι.
prepared themselves that they might trumpet.

2532 3588 4413 32 4537 · 2532 1096 5464 2532
7. Καὶ ὁ πρῶτος ἄγγελος ἐσάλπισε, καὶ ἐγένετο χάλαζα καὶ
And the first angel trumpeted, and occurred hail and

4442 3396 129 2532 906 1519 3588 1093 2532 3588
πῦρ μεμιγμένα αἵματι, καὶ ἐβλήθη εἰς τὴν γῆν· καὶ τὸ
fire being mixed with blood, and it was cast onto the earth; and the

5154 3588 1186 2618 2532/3956 5528 5515 2618
τρίτον τῶν δένδρων κατεκάη, καὶ πᾶς χόρτος χλωρὸς κατεκάη.
third (part) of the trees was burned, and all grass greeen was burned.

2532 3588 1208 32 4537 2532/5613/3735 3173
8. Καὶ ὁ δεύτερος ἄγγελος ἐσάλπισε, καὶ ὡς ὄρος μέγα
And the second angel trumpeted, and as a mountain great

4442 2545 906 1519 3588 2281 2532 1096 3588
πυρὶ καιόμενον ἐβλήθη εἰς τὴν θάλασσαν· καὶ ἐγένετο τὸ
with fire burning was cast into the sea; and became the

5154 3588 2281 129 2532 559 3588 5154 3588
τρίτον τῆς θαλάσσης αἷμα· 9 καὶ ἀπέθανε τὸ τρίτον τῶν
third (part) of the sea blood; and died the third (part) of the

2938 3588 1722 3588 2281 3588 2192 5590 2532 3588 5154
κτισμάτων τῶν ἐν τῇ θαλάσσῃ, τὰ ἔχοντα ψυχάς, καὶ τὸ τρίτον
creatures in the sea, the (ones) having souls, and the third (part)

3588 4143 1311
τῶν πλοίων διεφθάρη.
of the ships were destroyed.

2532 3588 5154 32 4537 2532 4098 1537 3588
10. Καὶ ὁ τρίτος ἄγγελος ἐσάλπισε, καὶ ἔπεσεν ἐκ τοῦ
And the third angel trumpeted, and fell out of the

3772 792 3173 2545 5613 2985 2532 4098 1909 3588
οὐρανοῦ ἀστὴρ μέγας καιόμενος ὡς λαμπάς, καὶ ἔπεσεν ἐπὶ τὸ
heaven a star great burning like a lamp, and it fell onto the

5154 3588 4215 2532 1909 3588 4077 5204 2532 3588 3686
τρίτον τῶν ποταμῶν, καὶ ἐπὶ τὰς πηγὰς ὑδάτων. 11 καὶ τὸ ὄνομα
third (part) of the rivers, and onto the fountains of waters. And the name

3588 792 3004 894 2532 1096 3588 5154 3588
τοῦ ἀστέρος λέγεται Ἄψινθος· καὶ γίνεται τὸ τρίτον τῶν
of the star is said (to be) Wormwood; and became the third (part) of the

5204 1519 894 2532 4183 444 599 1537 3588
ὑδάτων εἰς ἄψινθον, καὶ πολλοὶ ἀνθρώπων ἀπέθανον ἐκ τῶν
waters into wormwood, and many of men died from the

King James Version

which was before the throne.
4 And the smoke of the incense, (which came) with the prayers of the saints, ascended up before God out of the angel's hand.
5 And the angel took the censer, and filled it with fire of the altar, and cast (it) into the earth: and there were voices, and thunderings, and lightnings, and an earthquake.

6 And the seven angels which had the seven trumpets prepared themselves to sound.

7. The first angel sounded, and there followed hail and fire mingled with blood, and they were cast upon the earth: and the third part of trees was burnt up, and all green grass was burnt up.

8 And the second angel sounded, and as it were a great mountain burning with fire was cast into the sea: and the third part of the sea became blood;
9 And the third part of the creatures which were in the sea, and had life, died; and the third part of the ships were destroyed.

10 And the third angel sounded, and there fell a great star from heaven, burning as it were a lamp, and it fell upon the third part of the rivers, and upon the fountains of waters;
11 And the name of the star is called Wormwood: and the third part of the waters became wormwood; and many men died of the

Literal Translation

Revelation 8:12

King James Version

waters, because they were bitter.

5204 3754 4087
ὑδάτων, ὅτι ἐπικράνθησαν.
waters, because they were bitter.

waters, because they were made bitter.

12 And the fourth angel trumpeted. And the third (part) of the sun, and the third (part) of the moon, and the third (part) of the stars, was struck, that the third (part) of them might be darkened, and the third (part) of the day might not appear; and in the same way the night.

2532 3588 5067 32 4537 2532 4141 3588 5154
12. Καὶ ὁ τέταρτος ἄγγελος ἐσάλπισε, καὶ ἐπλήγη τὸ τρίτον
And the fourth angel trumpeted, and was struck the third
3588 2246 2532 3588 5154 3588 4582 2532 3588 5154 3588
τοῦ ἡλίου καὶ τὸ τρίτον τῆς σελήνης καὶ τὸ τρίτον τῶν
of the sun and the third (part) of the moon and the third (part) of the
792 2443 4654 3588 5154 846 2532 3588 2250 3361
ἀστέρων, ἵνα σκοτισθῇ τὸ τρίτον αὐτῶν, καὶ ἡ ἡμέρα μὴ
stars, that might be darkened the third of them, and the day not
5316 3588 5154 846 2532/3588/3571/3668
φαίνῃ τὸ τρίτον αὐτῆς, καὶ ἡ νὺξ ὁμοίως.
appear the third (part) of it, and the night likewise.

12 And the fourth angel sounded, and the third part of the sun was smitten, and the third part of the moon, and the third part of the stars; so as the third part of them was darkened, and the day shone not for a third part of it, and the night likewise.

13 And I saw, and I heard one angel flying in mid-heaven, saying with a great voice, Woe! Woe! Woe to those dwelling on the earth, from the rest of (the) voices of the trumpet of the three angels being about to trumpet!

2532 1492 2532 191 1520 32 4072 1722 3321
13. Καὶ εἶδον, καὶ ἤκουσα ἑνὸς ἀγγέλου πετωμένου ἐν μεσου-
And I saw, and I heard one angel flying in mid-
3004 5456 3173 3759 3759 3759 3588
ρανήματι, λέγοντος φωνῇ μεγάλῃ, Οὐαὶ, οὐαὶ, οὐαὶ τοῖς
heaven, saying, with a voice great, Woe! Woe! Woe to those
2730 1909 3588 1093 1537 3588 3062 5456 3588 4536
κατοικοῦντας ἐπὶ τῆς γῆς, ἐκ τῶν λοιπῶν φωνῶν τῆς σάλ-
dwelling on the earth, from the rest of (the) voices of the
3588 5140 32 3588 3195 4537
πιγγος τῶν τριῶν ἀγγέλων τῶν μελλόντων σαλπίζειν.
trumpet of the three angels being about to trumpet!

13 And I beheld, and heard an angel flying through the midst of heaven, saying with a loud voice, Woe, woe, woe, to the inhabiters of the earth by reason of the other voices of the trumpet of the three angels, which are yet to sound!

Revelation 9

1. And the fifth angel trumpeted. And I saw a star out of the heaven having fallen onto the earth. And the key to the pit of the abyss was given to it.
2 And he opened the pit of the abyss. And smoke went up out of the pit, like smoke of a great furnace. And the sun was darkened, and the air, from the smoke of the pit.

3 And out of the smoke locusts came forth to the earth. And authority was given to them, as the scorpions of the earth have authority.

4 And it was said to them that they should not harm the grass of the earth, nor every green thing, nor every tree, except only the men who do not have the seal of God on their foreheads.
5 And it was given to them that they should not

2532 3588 3991 32 4537 2532 1492 792 1537 3588
1. Καὶ ὁ πέμπτος ἄγγελος ἐσάλπισε, καὶ εἶδον ἀστέρα ἐκ τοῦ
And the fifth angel trumpeted, and I saw a star out of the
3772 4098 1519 3588 1093 2532 1325 846 3588 2807
οὐρανοῦ πεπτωκότα εἰς τὴν γῆν, καὶ ἐδόθη αὐτῷ ἡ κλεὶς
heaven having fallen onto the earth, and was given to it the key
3588 5421 3588 12 2532 455 3588 5421 3588 12
τοῦ φρέατος τῆς ἀβύσσου. 2 καὶ ἤνοιξε τὸ φρέαρ τῆς ἀβύσσου,
to the pit of the abyss. And he opened the pit of the abyss,
2532 305 2586 1537 3588 5421 5613 2586 2575
καὶ ἀνέβη καπνὸς ἐκ τοῦ φρέατος ὡς καπνὸς καμίνου
and went up a smoke out of the pit as smoke of a furnace
3173 2532 4654 3588 2246 2532 3588 109 1537 3588 2586
μεγάλης, καὶ ἐσκοτίσθη ὁ ἥλιος καὶ ὁ ἀὴρ ἐκ τοῦ καπνοῦ
great, and was darkened the sun and the air from the smoke
3588 5421 2532/1537/3588/2586 1831 200 1519 3588 1093
τοῦ φρέατος. 3 καὶ ἐκ τοῦ καπνοῦ ἐξῆλθον ἀκρίδες εἰς τὴν γῆν,
of the pit. And out of the smoke came forth locusts to the earth,
2532 1325 846 1849 5613 2192 1849 3588 4651
καὶ ἐδόθη αὐταῖς ἐξουσία ὡς ἔχουσιν ἐξουσίαν οἱ σκορπίοι
and was given to them authority, as have authority the scorpions
3588 1093 2532 4483 846 2443 3361 91 3588 5528 3588
τῆς γῆς. 4 καὶ ἐρρέθη αὐταῖς ἵνα μὴ ἀδικήσωσι τὸν χόρτον
of the earth. And it was said to them that not they would harm the grass
3588 1093 3761 3956 5515 3761 3956 1186 1487/3361/3588
τῆς γῆς, οὐδὲ πᾶν χλωρόν, οὐδὲ πᾶν δένδρον, εἰ μὴ τοὺς
of the earth, nor every green thing, nor every tree, except the
444 3441 3748 3756 2192 3588 4973 3588
ἀνθρώπους μόνους οἵτινες οὐκ ἔχουσι τὴν σφραγῖδα τοῦ
men only who not have the seal
2316 1909 3588 3359 846 2532 1325 846 2443 3361
Θεοῦ ἐπὶ τῶν μετώπων αὐτῶν. 5 καὶ ἐδόθη αὐταῖς ἵνα μὴ
of God on the foreheads of them. And was given to them that not

1. And the fifth angel sounded, and I saw a star fall from heaven unto the earth: and to him was given the key of the bottomless pit.

2 And he opened the bottomless pit; and there arose a smoke out of the pit, as the smoke of a great furnace; and the sun and the air were darkened by reason of the smoke of the pit.

3 And there came out of the smoke locusts upon the earth: and unto them was given power, as the scorpions of the earth have power.

4 And it was commanded them that they should not hurt the grass of the earth, neither any green thing, neither any tree; but only those men which have not the seal of God in their foreheads.
5 And to them it was given that they should not

Literal Translation — **Revelation 9:6** — *King James Version*

Literal Translation

kill them, but that they be tormented five months. And their torment (is) as the torment of a scorpion when it stings a man.

6 And in those days men will seek death, and they will not find it. And they will long to die, yet death will flee from them.

7 And the likenesses of the locusts (were) like horses having been prepared for war; and on their heads as crowns, like gold; and their faces like the faces of men.

8 And they had hairs like the hairs of women; and their teeth were like those of lions.
9 And they had breastplates like iron breastplates; and the sound of their wings (was) like the sound of chariots with many horses running to war.

10 And they have tails like scorpions, and their stings were in their tails; and their authority (is) to harm men five months.

11 And they have a king over them, the angel of the abyss. In Hebrew his name (was) Abaddon, and in Greek he (has) the name Apollyon.
12 The first woe has departed; behold, after these things come two woes.

13. And the sixth angel trumpeted. And I heard one voice out of the four horns of the golden altar before God,

14 saying to the sixth angel who had

615 846 235 2443 928 3376 4002
ἀποκτείνωσιν αὐτούς, ἀλλ' ἵνα βασανισθῶσι μῆνας πέντε·
they should kill them, but that they be tormented months five;

2532 3588 929 846 5613 929 4651 3752
καὶ ὁ βασανισμὸς αὐτῶν ὡς βασανισμὸς σκορπίου, ὅταν
and the torment of them (is) as (the) torment of a scorpion when

3817 444 2532/1722/3588 2250 1565 2212
παίσῃ ἄνθρωπον. 6 καὶ ἐν ταῖς ἡμέραις ἐκείναις ζητήσουσιν
it stings a man. And in days those will seek

3588 444 3588 2288 2532 3756 2147 846
οἱ ἄνθρωποι τὸν θάνατον, καὶ οὐχ εὑρήσουσιν αὐτόν·
men death, and not they will find it;

2532 1937 599 2532 5343 3588 2288 575
καὶ ἐπιθυμήσουσιν ἀποθανεῖν, καὶ φεύξεται ὁ θάνατος ἀπ'
and they will long to die, and will flee death from

846 2532 3588 3667 3588 200 3664 2462 2090
αὐτῶν. 7 καὶ τὰ ὁμοιώματα τῶν ἀκρίδων ὅμοια ἵπποις ἡτοι-
them. And the likenesses of the locusts like horses having

1519 4171 2532 1909 3588 2776 846 5613
μασμένοις εἰς πόλεμον, καὶ ἐπὶ τὰς κεφαλὰς αὐτῶν ὡς
been prepared for war, and on the heads of them as

4735 3664 5557 2532 3588 4383 846 5613
στέφανοι ὅμοιοι χρυσῷ, καὶ τὰ πρόσωπα αὐτῶν ὡς
crowns like gold, and the faces of them as

4383 444 2532 2192 2359 5613 2359 1135
πρόσωπα ἀνθρώπων, 8 καὶ εἶχον τρίχας ὡς τρίχας γυναικῶν,
the faces of men, and they had hairs as hairs of a woman,

2532 3588 3599 846 5613 3023 2258 2532 2192 2382
καὶ οἱ ὀδόντες αὐτῶν ὡς λεόντων ἦσαν, 9 καὶ εἶχον θώρακας
and the teeth of them as of lions were, and they had breastplates

5613 2382 4603 2532 3588 5456 3588 4420 846
ὡς θώρακας σιδηροῦς, καὶ ἡ φωνὴ τῶν πτερύγων αὐτῶν
as breastplates iron, and the sound of the wings of them

5613 5456 716 2462 4183 5143 1519 4171
ὡς φωνὴ ἁρμάτων ἵππων πολλῶν τρεχόντων εἰς πόλεμον.
as (the) sound chariots of horses many running to war.

2532 2192 3769 3664 4651 2532 3759 2258 1722 3588
10 καὶ ἔχουσιν οὐρὰς ὁμοίας σκορπίοις, καὶ κέντρα, ἦν ἐν ταῖς
And they have tails like scorpions, and stings were in the

3769 846 2532 3588 1849 846 91 3588 444
οὐραῖς αὐτῶν καὶ ἡ ἐξουσία αὐτῶν ἀδικῆσαι τοὺς ἀνθρώ-
tails of them and the authority of them (is) to harm men

3376 4002 2532 2192 1909 846 935 3588
πους μῆνας πέντε. 11 καὶ ἔχουσιν ἐπ' αὐτῶν βασιλέα τὸν
months five. And they have over them a king, the

32 3588 12 3686 846 1447 3
ἄγγελον τῆς ἀβύσσου· ὄνομα αὐτῷ Ἑβραϊστὶ Ἀβαδδὼν,
angel of the abyss; name to him in Hebrew Abaddon,

2532 1722 3588 1673 3686 2192 623 3588 3759 3588 3391
καὶ ἐν τῇ Ἑλληνικῇ ὄνομα ἔχει Ἀπολλύων. 12 ἡ οὐαὶ ἡ μία
and in the Greek (the) name he has (is) Apollyon. The woe one

565 2400 2064 2089/1417/3759 3326 5023
ἀπῆλθεν· ἰδοὺ, ἔρχονται ἔτι δύο οὐαὶ μετὰ ταῦτα.
has departed; behold, comes yet two woes after these things.

2532 3588 1623 32 4537 2532 191 5456 3391 1537
13. Καὶ ὁ ἕκτος ἄγγελος ἐσάλπισε, καὶ ἤκουσα φωνὴν μίαν ἐκ
And the sixth angel trumpeted, and I heard a voice one from

3588 5064 2768 3588 2379 3588 5552
τῶν τεσσάρων κεράτων τοῦ θυσιαστηρίου τοῦ χρυσοῦ
the four horns of the altar of gold

3588 1799 3588 2316 3004 3588 1623 32 3739 2192
τοῦ ἐνώπιον τοῦ Θεοῦ, 14 λέγουσαν τῷ ἕκτῳ ἀγγέλῳ ὃς εἶχε
before God, saying to the sixth angel who had

King James Version

kill them, but that they should be tormented five months: and their torment (was) as the torment of a scorpion, when he striketh a man.

6 And in those days shall men seek death, and shall not find it; and shall desire to die, and death shall flee from them.

7 And the shapes of the locusts (were) like unto horses prepared unto battle; and on their heads (were) as it were crowns like gold, and their faces (were) as the faces of men.

8 And they had hair as the hair of women, and their teeth were as (the teeth) of lions.
9 And they had breastplates, as it were breastplates of iron; and the sound of their wings (was) as the sound of chariots of many horses running to battle.

10 And they had tails like unto scorpions, and there were stings in their tails: and their power (was) to hurt men five months.

11 And they had a king over them, (which is) the angel of the bottomless pit, whose name in the Hebrew tongue (is) Abaddon, but in the Greek tongue hath (his) name Apollyon.
12 One woe is past; (and), behold, there come two woes more hereafter.

13. And the sixth angel sounded, and I heard a voice from the four horns of the golden altar which is before God,

14 Saying to the sixth angel which had

Literal Translation

Revelation 9:15

the trumpet, Release the four angels, those having been bound at the great river Euphrates.

15 And the four angels were released, those having been prepared for the hour and day and month and year, that they should kill the third (part) of men.

16 And the number of the armies of the cavalry (was) two myriads of myriads; and I heard their number.
17 And so I saw in the vision the horses, and those sitting on them, having fire-colored breastplates, even dusky red and brimstone-like; and the heads of the horses as heads of lions; and out of their mouths come fire and smoke and brimstone.

18 By these three were killed the third (part) of men, by the fire, and by the smoke, and by the brimstone coming out of their mouths.
19 For their authority is in their mouth, and in their tails; for their tails (are) like snakes, having heads, and they do harm with them.

20 And the rest of men, those not killed by these plagues, did not repent of the works of their hands, that they will not worship demons, and golden idols, and silver, and bronze, and stone, and wooden idols, which neither are able to see, nor to hear, nor to walk.

21 And they did not repent of

3588 4536 3089 3588 5064 32 3588 1210
τὴν σάλπιγγα, Λῦσον τοὺς τέσσαρας ἀγγέλους τοὺς δεδε-
the trumpet, Loose the four angels the (ones) having

1909 3588 4215 3588 3173 2166 2532 3089
μένους ἐπὶ τῷ ποταμῷ τῷ μεγάλῳ Εὐφράτῃ. 15 καὶ ἐλύθησαν
been bound at the river great Euphrates. And were loosed

3588 5064 32 3588 2090 1519 3588 5610 2532
οἱ τέσσαρες ἄγγελοι οἱ ἡτοιμασμένοι εἰς τὴν ὥραν καὶ
the four angels the (ones) having been prepared for the hour and

2250 2532 3376 2532 1763 2443 615 3588 5154
ἡμέραν καὶ μῆνα καὶ ἐνιαυτόν, ἵνα ἀποκτείνωσι τὸ τρίτον
day and month and year, that they should kill the third (part)

3588 444 2532 3588 706 4753 3588 2461
τῶν ἀνθρώπων. 16 καὶ ὁ ἀριθμὸς στρατευμάτων τοῦ ἱππικοῦ
of men. And the number of the armies of the cavalry

1417 3461 3461 2532 191 3588 706 846 2532
δύο μυριάδες μυριάδων· καὶ ἤκουσα τὸν ἀριθμὸν αὐτῶν. 17 καὶ
two myriads of myriads; and I heard the number of them. And

3779 1492 3588 2462 1722/3588 3706 2532 3588 2521
οὕτως εἶδον τοὺς ἵππους ἐν τῇ ὁράσει, καὶ τοὺς καθημένους
so I saw the horses in the vision, and those sitting

1909 846 2192 2382 4447 2532 5191
ἐπ᾽ αὐτῶν, ἔχοντας θώρακας πυρίνους καὶ ὑακινθίνους
on them having breastplates fire-colored and dusky red

2532 2306 2532 3588 2776 3588 2462 5613 2776 3023
καὶ θειώδεις· καὶ αἱ κεφαλαὶ τῶν ἵππων ὡς κεφαλαὶ λεόντων,
and brimstone-like; and the heads of the horses as heads of lions,

2532 1537 3588 4750 846 1607 4442 2532 2586
καὶ ἐκ τῶν στομάτων αὐτῶν ἐκπορεύεται πῦρ καὶ καπνὸς
and out of the mouths of them comes out fire and smoke

2532 2303 5259 3588 5140 5130 615 3588 5154
καὶ θεῖον. 18 ὑπὸ τῶν τριῶν τούτων ἀπεκτάνθησαν τὸ τρίτον
and brimstone. By three these were killed the third (part)

3588 444 1537 3588 4442 2532 1537 3588 2586 2532 1537 3588
τῶν ἀνθρώπων, ἐκ τοῦ πυρὸς καὶ ἐκ τοῦ καπνοῦ καὶ ἐκ τοῦ
of men from the fire and from the smoke and from the

2316 3588 1607 1537 3588 4750 846 3588 1063
θείου τοῦ ἐκπορευομένου ἐκ τῶν στομάτων αὐτῶν. 19 ἡ γὰρ
brimstone coming out from the mouths of them. the For

1849 846 1722 3588 4750 846 1526 2532 1722 3588 3769
ἐξουσία αὐτῶν ἐν τῷ στόματι αὐτῶν ἐστι, καὶ ἐν ταῖς οὐραῖς
authority of them in the mouth of them is, and in the tails

846 3588 1063 3769 846 3664 3789 2192 2776
αὐτῶν· αἱ γὰρ οὐραὶ αὐτῶν ὅμοιαι ὄφεσιν, ἔχουσαι κεφαλάς,
of them; the for tails of them (are) like snakes, having heads,

2532 1722 846 91 2532 3588 3062 3588 444 3739 3756
καὶ ἐν αὐταῖς ἀδικοῦσι. 20 καὶ οἱ λοιποὶ τῶν ἀνθρώπων, οἳ οὐκ
and with them they do harm. And the rest men, who not

615 1722 3588 4127 3778 3756 3340 1537
ἀπεκτάνθησαν ἐν ταῖς πληγαῖς ταύταις, οὐ μετενόησαν ἐκ
were killed by plagues these, not repented of

3588 2041 3588 5495 846 2443 3361 4352 3588
τῶν ἔργων τῶν χειρῶν αὐτῶν, ἵνα μὴ προσκυνήσωσι τὰ
the works of the hands of them, that not they will worship

1140 2532 1497 3588 5552 2532 3588 693 2532 3588
δαιμόνια, καὶ εἴδωλα τὰ χρυσᾶ καὶ τὰ ἀργυρᾶ καὶ τὰ
demons, and idols golden and silver and

5470 2532 3588 3035 2532 3588 3585 3739 3777 991 1410
χαλκᾶ καὶ τὰ λίθινα καὶ τὰ ξύλινα, ἃ οὔτε βλέπειν δύναται,
bronze and stone and wood, which neither see are able,

3777 191 3777 4043 2532 3756 3340 1537 3588
οὔτε ἀκούειν, οὔτε περιπατεῖν, 21 καὶ οὐ μετενόησαν ἐκ τῶν
nor to hear, nor to walk, and not they repented of the

King James Version

the trumpet, Loose the four angels which are bound in the great river Euphrates.

15 And the four angels were loosed, which were prepared for an hour, and a day, and a month, and a year, for to slay the third part of men.

16 And the number of the army of the horsemen (were) two hundred thousand thousand: and I heard the number of them.
17 And thus I saw the horses in the vision, and them that sat on them, having breastplates of fire, and of jacinth, and brimstone: and the heads of the horses (were) as the heads of lions; and out of their mouths issued fire and smoke and brimstone.

18 By these three was the third part of men killed, by the fire, and by the smoke, and by the brimstone, which issued out of their mouths.
19 For their power is in their mouth, and in their tails: for their tails (were) like unto serpents, and had heads, and with them they do hurt.

20 And the rest of the men which were not killed by these plagues yet repented not of the works of their hands, that they should not worship devils, and idols of gold, and silver, and brass, and stone, and of wood: which neither can see, nor hear, nor walk:

21 Neither repented they of

Literal Translation

their murders, nor of their sorceries, nor of their fornications, nor of their thefts.

Revelation 10:1

5408 846 3777 1537 3588 5331 846 3777 1537 3588
φόνων αὐτῶν, οὔτε ἐκ τῶν φαρμακειῶν αὐτῶν, οὔτε ἐκ τῆς
murders of them, nor of the sorceries of them, nor of the

4202 846 3777 1537 3588 2809 846
πορνείας αὐτῶν, οὔτε ἐκ τῶν κλεμμάτων αὐτῶν.
fornications of them, nor of the thefts of them.

King James Version

their murders, nor of their sorceries, nor of their fornication, nor of their thefts.

Revelation 10

1. And I saw another strong angel coming down out of the heaven, having been clothed with a cloud, and a rainbow on the head; and his face as the sun, and his feet as pillars of fire.

2 And he had in his hand a little scroll having been opened. And he placed his right foot on the sea, and the left on the land,

3 and cried with a great voice, as a lion roars. And when he cried, the seven thunders spoke their voices.

4 And when the seven thunders spoke their voices, I was about to write. And I heard a voice out of Heaven saying to me, Seal what things the seven thunders spoke, and do not write these things.

5 And the angel whom I saw standing on the sea and on the land lifted his hand to Heaven,

6 and swore by Him living forever and ever, who created the heaven and the things in it, and the earth and the things in it, and the sea and the things in it, that time shall no longer be;

7 but in the days of the voice of the seventh angel, whenever he is about to trumpet, and should be ended the mystery of God, as He

Revelation 10

2532 1492 243 32 2478 2597 1537 3588
1. Καὶ εἶδον ἄλλον ἄγγελον ἰσχυρὸν καταβαίνοντα ἐκ τοῦ
And I saw another angel strong coming down out of the

3772 4016 3507 2532 3588 2463 1909 3588 2776
οὐρανοῦ, περιβεβλημένον νεφέλην, καὶ ἡ ἶρις ἐπὶ τῆς κεφαλῆς,
heaven, having been clothed (with) a cloud, and a rainbow on the head,

2532 3588 4383 846 5613 3588 2246 2532 3588 4228 846 5613
καὶ τὸ πρόσωπον αὐτοῦ ὡς ὁ ἥλιος, καὶ οἱ πόδες αὐτοῦ ὡς
and the face of him as the sun, and the feet of him as

4769 4442 2532 2192 1722 3588 5495 846 974
στῦλοι πυρός, 2 καὶ ἔιχεν ἐν τῇ χειρὶ αὐτοῦ βιβλαρίδιον
pillars of fire, and he had in the hand of hm a little scroll

455 2532 5087 3588 4228 846 3588 1188 1909 3588
ἀνεῳγμένον· καὶ ἔθηκε τὸν πόδα αὐτοῦ τὸν δεξιὸν ἐπὶ τὴν
having been opened; and he placed the foot of him the right on the

228 3588 1161 2176 1909 3588 1093 2532 2896 5456
θαλάσσαν, τὸν δὲ εὐώνυμον ἐπὶ τὴν γῆν, 3 καὶ ἔκραξε φωνῇ
sea, the and left on the land, and cried with a voice

3173 5618 3023 3455 2532 3753 2896 2980 3588
μεγάλῃ ὥσπερ λέων μυκᾶται. καὶ ὅτε ἔκραξεν, ἐλάλησαν αἱ
great as a lion roars. And when he cried out, spoke the

2033 1027 3588 1438 5456 2532 3753 2980 3588 2033
ἑπτὰ βρονταὶ τὰς ἑαυτῶν φωνάς. 4 καὶ ὅτε ἐλάλησαν αἱ ἑπτὰ
seven thunders the of themselves voices. And when spoke the seven

1027 3588 5456 1438 3195 1125 2532 191
βρονται τὰς φωνὰς ἑαυτῶν, ἔμελλον γράφειν· καὶ ἤκουσα
thunders the voices of themselves, I was going to write; and I heard

5456 1537 3588 3772 3004 3427 4972 3739 2980
φωνὴν ἐκ τοῦ οὐρανοῦ, λέγουσαν μοι, Σφράγισον ἃ ἐλάλησαν
a voice out of Heaven, saying to me, Seal what things spoke

3588 2033 1027 2532 3361 5023 1125 2532 3588 32 3739
αἱ ἑπτὰ βρονταί, καὶ μὴ ταῦτα γράψῃς. 5 καὶ ὁ ἄγγελος ὃν
the seven thunders, and not these things write. And the angel whom

1492 2476 1909 3588 2281 2532 1909 3588 1093 142 3588 5495
εἶδον ἑστῶτα ἐπὶ τῆς θαλάσσης καὶ ἐπὶ τῆς γῆς ἦρε τὴν χεῖρα
I saw standing on the sea and on the land lifted the hand

846 1519 3588 3772 2532 3660 1722 3588 2198 1519 3588
αὐτοῦ εἰς τὸν οὐρανὸν, 6 καὶ ὤμοσεν ἐν τῷ ζῶντι εἰς τοὺς
of him toward Heaven, and swore by the (One) living to the

165 3588 165 3739 39362198 3588 3772 2532 3588 1722
αἰῶνας τῶν αἰώνων, ὃς ἔκτισε τὸν οὐρανὸν καὶ τὰ ἐν
ages of the ages, who created the heaven and the things in

846 2532 3588 1093 2532 3588 1722 846 2532 3588 2281 2532
αὐτῷ, καὶ τὴν γῆν καὶ τὰ ἐν αὐτῇ, καὶ τὴν θάλασσαν καὶ
it, and the earth and the things in it, and the sea and

3588 1722 846 3754 5550 3756 2071 2089 235 1722 3588
τὰ ἐν αὐτῇ, ὅτι χρόνος οὐκ ἔσται ἔτι, 7 ἀλλ' ἐν ταῖς
the things in it, that time not shall be longer, but in the

2250 3588 5456 3588 1442 32 3752 3195
ἡμέραις τῆς φωνῆς τοῦ ἑβδόμου ἀγγέλου, ὅταν μέλλῃ
days of the voice of the seventh angel, whenever he is about

4537 2532 5055 3588 3466 3588 2316 5613 2097
σαλπίζειν, καὶ τελεσθῇ τὸ μυστήριον τοῦ Θεοῦ, ὡς εὐηγ-
to trumpet, and may be ended the mystery of God, as He

Revelation 10

1. And I saw another mighty angel come down from heaven, clothed with a cloud: and a rainbow (was) upon his head, and his face (was) as it were the sun, and his feet as pillars of fire:

2 And he had in his hand a little book open: and he set his right foot upon the sea, and (his) left (foot) on the earth,

3 And cried with a loud voice, as (when) a lion roareth: and when he had cried, seven thunders uttered their voices.

4 And when the seven thunders had uttered their voices, I was about to write: and I heard a voice from heaven saying unto me, Seal up those things which the seven thunders uttered, and write them not.

5 And the angel which I saw stand upon the sea and upon the earth lifted up his hand to heaven,

6 And sware by him that liveth for ever and ever, who created heaven, and the things that therein are, and the earth, and the things that therein are, and the sea, and the things which are therein, that there should be time no longer:

7 But in the days of the voice of the seventh angel, when he shall begin to sound, the mystery of God should be finished, as he

Literal Translation — **Revelation 10:8** — *King James Version*

proclaimed to His slaves, the prophets.
8. And the voice which I heard out of Heaven was again speaking to me, and saying, Go, take the little scroll having been opened in the hand of the angel standing on the sea and on the land.

3588 1438 1401 3588 4396 2532 3588 5456 3739
γέλισε τοῖς ἑαυτοῦ δούλοις τοῖς προφήταις. 8 καὶ ἡ φωνὴ ἣν
proclaimed to the of Himself slaves the prophets. And the voice which

191 1537 3588 3772 3825 2980 3326 1700 2532
ἤκουσα ἐκ τοῦ οὐρανοῦ, πάλιν λαλοῦσα μετ᾽ ἐμοῦ, καὶ
I heard out of Heaven, again spoke with me, and

3004 5217 2983 3588 974 3588 455 1722
λέγουσα, Ὕπαγε, λάβε τὸ βιβλαρίδιον τὸ ἠνεῳγμένον ἐν
saying, Go, take the little scroll having been opened in

3588 5495 32 3588 2476 1909 3588 2281 2532 1909
τῇ χειρὶ ἀγγέλου τοῦ ἑστῶτος ἐπὶ τῆς θαλάσσης καὶ ἐπὶ
the hand of the angel standing on the sea and on

3588 1093 2532 565 4314 3588 32 3004 846 1325
τῆς γῆς. 9 καὶ ἀπῆλθον πρὸς τὸν ἄγγελον, λέγων αὐτῷ, Δός
the land. And I went away to the angel, saying to him, Give

3427 3588 974 2532 3004 3427 2983 2532 2719 846
μοι τὸ βιβλαρίδιον. καὶ λέγει μοι, Λάβε καὶ κατάφαγε αὐτό·
me the little scroll. And he said to me, Take and eat up it;

2532 4087 4675 3588 2836 235 1722 3588 4750 4675 2071
καὶ πικρανεῖ σου τὴν κοιλίαν, ἀλλ᾽ ἐν τῷ στόματί σου ἔσται
and it will embitter of you the belly, but in the mouth of you it will be

1099 5613 3192 2532 2983 3588 974 1537 3588 5495 3588
γλυκὺ ὡς μέλι. 10 καὶ ἔλαβον τὸ βιβλαρίδιον ἐκ τῆς χειρὸς τοῦ
sweet as honey. And I took the little scroll out of the hand of the

32 2532 2719 846 2532 2258 1722 3588 4750 3450
ἀγγέλου, καὶ κατέφαγον αὐτό, καὶ ἦν ἐν τῷ στόματί μου
angel, and ate it, and it was in the mouth of me

5613 3192 1099 2532 3753 5315 846 4087 3588 2836
ὡς μέλι, γλυκύ· καὶ ὅτε ἔφαγον αὐτό, ἐπικράνθη ἡ κοιλία
as honey, sweet; and when I ate it, was made bitter the belly

3450 2532 3004 3427 1163 1161 3825 4395 1909 2992 2532
μου. 11 καὶ λέγει μοι, Δεῖ σε πάλιν προφητεῦσαι ἐπὶ λαοις καὶ
of me. And he says to me, must You again prophesy as to peoples and

1484 2532 1100 2532 935 4183
ἔθνεσι καὶ γλώσσαις καὶ βασιλεῦσι πολλοῖς.
nations and tongues and kings many.

hath declared to his servants the prophets.
8. And the voice which I heard from heaven spake unto me again, and said, Go (and) take the little book which is open in the hand of the angel which standeth upon the sea and upon the earth.

9 And I went away toward the angel, say-ing to him, Give the little scroll to me. And he said to me, Take and eat it up, and it will make your belly bitter, but it will be sweet as honey in your mouth.

9 And I went unto the angel, and said unto him, Give me the little book. And he said unto me, Take (it), and eat it up; and it shall make thy belly bitter, but it shall be in thy mouth sweet as honey.

10 And I took the little scroll out of the angel's hand, and ate it. And it was sweet like honey in my mouth; and when I ate it, my belly was made bitter.

10 And I took the little book out of the angel's hand, and ate it up; and it was in my mouth sweet as honey: and as soon as I had eaten it, my belly was bitter.

11 And he said to me, You must again prophesy as to peoples and nations and tongues and many kings.

11 And he said unto me, Thou must prophesy again before many peoples, and nations, and tongues, and kings.

Revelation 11

1. And a reed like a staff was given to me, and the angel stood, saying, Rise and measure the temple of God and the altar, and those worshiping in it.
2 And cast aside the outside court of the temple, and do not measure it. For it was given to the nations, and they will trample the holy city forty-two months.

2532 1325 3427 2563 3664 4464 2532 3588 32
1. Καὶ ἐδόθη μοι κάλαμος ὅμοιος ῥάβδῳ, καὶ ὁ ἄγγελος
And was given to me a reed like a staff, and the angel

2476 3004 1453 2532 3354 3588 3485 3588 2316
εἱστήκει, λέγων, Ἔγειραι, καὶ μέτρησον τὸν ναὸν τοῦ Θεοῦ,
stood, saying, Rise, and measure the temple of God

2532 3588 2379 2532 3588 4352 1722 846 2532
καὶ τὸ θυσιαστήριον καὶ τοὺς προσκυνοῦντας ἐν αὐτῷ. 2 καὶ
and the altar and those worshiping in it. And

3588 833 3588 2081 3588 3485 1544 1854 2532 3361 846
τὴν αὐλὴν τὴν ἔξωθεν τοῦ ναοῦ ἔκβαλε ἔξω, καὶ μὴ αὐτὴν
the court outside of the temple cast outside, and not it

3354 3754 1325 3588 1484 2532 3588 4172 3588 40
μετρήσῃς, ὅτι ἐδόθη τοῖς ἔθνεσι· καὶ τὴν πόλιν τὴν ἁγίαν
measure, because it was given to the nations; and the city holy

3961 3376 5062 1417 2532 1325 3588 1417
πατήσουσι μῆνας τεσσεράκοντα δύο. 3 καὶ δώσω τοῖς δυσὶ
they will trample months forty two. And I will give to the two

3144 3450 2532 4395 2250 5507 1250
μάρτυσί μου, καὶ προφητεύσουσιν ἡμέρας χιλίας διακοσίας
witnesses of Me, and they will prophesy days a thousand two-hundred

1835 40 4526 3778 1526 3588 1417 1636
ἑξήκοντα περιβεβλημένοι σάκκους. 4 οὗτοί εἰσιν αἱ δύο ἐλαῖαι,
sixty having been clothed (in) sackcloth. These are the two olive-trees,

1. And there was given me a reed like unto a rod: and the angel stood, saying, Rise, and measure the temple of God, and the altar, and them that worship therein.
2 But the court which is without the temple leave out, and measure it not; for it is given unto the Gentiles: and the holy city shall they tread under foot forty (and) two months.

3. And I will give to My two witnesses, and they will prophesy a thousand, two hundred and sixty days, dressed (in) sackcloth.
4 These are the two olive trees,

3. And I will give (power) unto my two witnesses, and they shall prophesy a thousand two hundred (and) threescore days, clothed in sackcloth.
4 These are the two olive trees,

Literal Translation **Revelation 11:5** ***King James Version***

and the two lampstands, standing before the God of the earth.

5 And if anyone desires to harm them, fire comes out of their mouth and consumes their enemies. And if anyone desires to harm them, so ought him to be killed.

6 These have the authority to shut up the heaven, that no rain may rain in the days of their prophecy. And they have authority over the waters, to turn them into blood, and to strike the earth with every plague, as often as they desire.
7 And when they complete their witness, the beast coming up out of the abyss will make war with them, and will overcome them, and will kill them.

8 And their bodies (will be) on the street of the great city, which spiritually is called Sodom and Egypt, where indeed our Lord was crucified.

9 And some from the peoples and tribes and tongues and nations will see their dead bodies three days and a half; and they do not allow their dead bodies to be put in tombs.

10 And those living on the earth will rejoice over them, and will make merry. And they will send one another gifts, because these two prophets tormented those living on the earth.

11 And after three days and a half, a spirit of life from God entered into them, and they stood on

2532 3588 1417 3087 3588 1799 3588 2316 3588/1093 2476
καὶ αἱ δύο λυχνίαι αἱ ἐνώπιον τοῦ Θεοῦ τῆς γῆς ἑστῶσαι.
and the two lampstands before God of the earth standing.

2532 1487 5100 846 2309 91 4442 1607 1537 3588
5 καὶ εἴ τις αὐτοὺς θέλῃ ἀδικῆσαι, πῦρ ἐκπορεύεται ἐκ τοῦ
And if anyone them desires to harm, fire will come out from the

4750 846 2532 2719 3588 2190 846 2532/1487
στόματος αὐτῶν, καὶ κατεσθίει τοὺς ἐχθροὺς αὐτῶν· καὶ εἴ
mouths of them, and consumes the enemies of them; and if

5100 846 2309 91 3779 1163 846 615
τις αὐτοὺς θέλῃ ἀδικῆσαι, οὕτω δεῖ αὐτὸν ἀποκτανθῆναι.
anyone them desires to harm, so ought him to be killed.

3778 2192 1849 2808 3588 3772 2443 3361 1026
6 οὗτοι ἔχουσιν ἐξουσίαν κλεῖσαι τὸν οὐρανόν, ἵνα μὴ βρέχῃ
These have authority to shut the heaven, that not may rain

5205 1722 2250 846 3588 4394 2532 1849 2192
ὑετὸς ἐν ἡμέραις αὐτῶν τῆς προφητείας· καὶ ἐξουσίαν ἔχου-
rain in days of them ofthe prophecy, and authority they

1909 3588 5204 4762 846 1519 129 2532 3960
σιν ἐπὶ τῶν ὑδάτων, στρέφειν αὐτὰ εἰς αἷμα, καὶ πατάξαι
have over the waters, to turn them into blood, and to strike

3588 1093 1722 3956 4127 3740 1437 2309 2532 3752
τὴν γῆν ἐν πάσῃ πληγῇ, ὁσάκις ἐὰν θελήσωσι. 7 καὶ ὅταν
the earth with every plague, as often as if they desire. And when

5055 3588 3141 846 3588 2342 3588 305 1537
τελέσωσι τὴν μαρτυρίαν αὐτῶν, τὸ θηρίον τὸ ἀναβαῖνον ἐκ
they finish the witness of them, the beast coming up out of

3588 12 4160 4171 3326 846 2532 3528
τῆς ἀβύσσου ποιήσει πόλεμον μετ᾽ αὐτῶν, καὶ νικήσει
the abyss will make war with them, and will overcome

846 2532 615 846 2532 3588 4430 846 1909
αὐτούς, καὶ ἀποκτενεῖ αὐτούς. 8 καὶ τὸ πτώματα αὐτῶν ἐπὶ
them, and will kill them. And the bodies of them on

3588 4113 4172 3588 3173 3748 2564 4153
τῆς πλατείας πόλεως τῆς μεγάλης, ἥτις καλεῖται πνευ-
the street of city the of great, which is called spirit-

4670 2532 125 3699 2532 3588 2962 2257
ματικῶς Σόδομα καὶ Αἴγυπτος, ὅπου καὶ ὁ Κύριος ἡμῶν
ually Sodom and Egypt, where indeed the Lord of us

4717 2532 991 1537 3588 2992 2532 5443 2532
ἐσταυρώθη. 9 καὶ βλέψουσιν ἐκ τῶν λαῶν καὶ φυλῶν καὶ
was crucified. And will see (some) of the peoples and tribes and

1100 2532 1484 3588 4430 846 2250 5140 2532
γλωσσῶν καὶ ἐθνῶν τὰ πτώματα αὐτῶν ἡμέρας τρεῖς καὶ
tongues and nations the bodies of them days three and

2255 2532 3588 4430 846 3756 863 5087 1519
ἥμισυ, καὶ τὰ πτώματα αὐτῶν οὐκ ἀφήσουσι τεθῆναι εἰς
a half, and the bodies of them not they allow to be placed into

3418 2532 3588 2730 1909 3588 1093 5463 1909
μνήματα. 10 καὶ οἱ κατοικοῦντες ἐπὶ τῆς γῆς χαροῦσιν ἐπ᾽
tombs. And those dwelling on the earth will rejoice over

846 2532 2165 2532 1435 3992 240
αὐτοῖς, καὶ εὐφρανθήσονται, καὶ δῶρα πέμψουσιν ἀλλήλοις,
them, and will make merry, and gifts they will send one another,

3754 3778 3588 1417 4396 928 3588 2730
ὅτι οὗτοι οἱ δύο προφῆται ἐβασάνισαν τοὺς κατοικοῦντας
because these two prophets tormented the (ones) dwelling

1909 3588 1093 2532 3326 3588 5140 2250 2532 2255 4151
ἐπὶ τῆς γῆς. 11 καὶ μετὰ τὰς τρεῖς ἡμέρας καὶ ἥμισυ, πνεῦμα
on the earth. And after three days and a half a spirit

2222 1537 3588 2316 1525 1909 846 2532 2476 1909
ζωῆς ἐκ τοῦ Θεοῦ εἰσῆλθεν ἐπ᾽ αὐτούς, καὶ ἔστησαν ἐπὶ
of life from God entered them, and they stood on

and the two candlesticks standing before the God of the earth.

5 And if any man will hurt them, fire proceedeth out of their mouth, and devoureth their enemies: and if any man will hurt them, he must in this manner be killed.

6 These have power to shut heaven, that it rain not in the days of their prophecy: and have power over waters to turn them to blood, and to smite the earth with all plagues, as often as they will.

7 And when they shall have finished their testimony, the beast that ascendeth out of the bottomless pit shall make war against them, and shall overcome them, and kill them.

8 And their dead bodies (shall lie) in the street of the great city, which spiritually is called Sodom and Egypt, where also our Lord was crucified.

9 And they of the people and kindreds and tongues and nations shall see their dead bodies three days and an half, and shall not suffer their dead bodies to be put in graves.

10 And they that dwell upon the earth shall rejoice over them, and make merry, and shall send gifts one to another; because these two prophets tormented them that dwelt on the earth.

11 And after three days and a half the Spirit of life from God entered into them, and they stood upon

Literal Translation | **Revelation 11:12** | *King James Version*

their feet. And great fear fell on the ones beholding them.

3588 4228 846 2532 5401 3173 4098 1909 3588 2334
τοὺς πόδας αὐτῶν, καὶ φόβος μέγας ἔπεσεν ἐπὶ τοὺς θεωρουν-
the feet of them, and fear great fell on the (ones) beholding
846 2532 191 5456 3173 1537 3588 3772
τας αὐτούς. 12 καὶ ἤκουσαν φωνὴν μεγάλην ἐκ τοῦ οὐρανοῦ,
them. And they heard a voice great from Heaven,

their feet; and great fear fell upon them which saw them.

12 And they heard a great voice out of Heaven saying to them, Come up here. And they went up into the heaven in the cloud. And their enemies saw them.

3004 846 305 5602 2532 305 1519 3588
λέγουσαν αὐτοῖς, 'Ανάβητε ὧδε. καὶ ἀνέβησαν εἰς τὸν
saying to them, Come up here. And they went up into the
3772 1722 3588 3507 2532 2334 846 3588 2190
οὐρανὸν ἐν τῇ νεφέλῃ, καὶ ἐθεώρησαν αὐτοὺς οἱ ἐχθροὶ
Heaven in the cloud; and beheld them the enemies
846
αὐτῶν.
of them.

12 And they heard a great voice from heaven saying unto them, Come up hither. And they ascended up to heaven in a cloud; and their enemies beheld them.

13 And in that hour a great earthquake occurred, and the tenth (part) of the city fell. And there were killed in the earthquake seven thousand names of men. And the rest became terrified, and gave glory to the God of Heaven.

2532 1722 1565 3588 5610 1096 4578 3173 2532 3588
13 καὶ ἐν ἐκείνῃ τῇ ὥρᾳ ἐγένετο σεισμὸς μέγας, καὶ τὸ
And in that hour occurred earthquake a great, and the
1182 3588 4172 4098 2532 615 1722 3588 4578
δέκατον τῆς πόλεως ἔπεσε, καὶ ἀπεκτάνθησαν ἐν τῷ σεισμῷ
tenth (part) of the city fell, and were killed in the earthquake
3686 444 5505 2033 2532 3588 3062 1719
ὀνόματα ἀνθρώπων, χιλιάδες ἑπτά, καὶ οἱ λοιποὶ ἔμφοβοι
names of men, thousands seven, and the rest terrified
1096 2532 1325 1391 3588 2316 3588 3772
ἐγένοντο, καὶ ἔδωκαν δόξαν τῷ Θεῷ τοῦ οὐρανοῦ.
became, and gave glory to the God of Heaven.

13 And the same hour was there a great earthquake, and the tenth part of the city fell, and in the earthquake were slain of men seven thousand: and the remnant were affrighted, and gave glory to the God of heaven.

14. The second woe passed away. And, behold, the third woe is coming quickly.

3588 3759 3588 1208 565 2532 2400 3588 3759 3588 5154
14. Ἡ οὐαὶ ἡ δευτέρα ἀπῆλθεν· καὶ ἰδού, ἡ οὐαὶ ἡ τρίτη
The woe second passed away. And behold! The woe third
2064 5035
ἔρχεται ταχύ.
is coming quickly.

14. The second woe is past; (and), behold, the third woe cometh quickly.

15 And the seventh angel trumpeted. And there were great voices in Heaven, saying, The kingdoms of the world became our Lord's, even of His Christ; and He shall reign to the ages of the ages..

2532 3588 1442 32 4537 2532 1096 5456
15. Καὶ ὁ ἕβδομος ἄγγελος ἐσάλπισε, καὶ ἐγένοντο φωναὶ
And the seventh angel trumpeted, and there were voices
3173 1722 3588 3772 3004 1096 3588 932
μεγάλαι ἐν τῷ οὐρανῷ, λέγουσαι, Ἐγένοντο αἱ βασιλεῖαι
great in Heaven, saying, became the kingdoms
3588 2889 3588 2962 2257 2532 3588 5547 846 2532
τοῦ κόσμου, τοῦ Κυρίου ἡμῶν, καὶ τοῦ Χριστοῦ αὐτοῦ, καὶ
of the world, of the Lord of us, and the Christ of Him, and
936 1519 3588 165 3588 165
βασιλεύσει εἰς τοὺς αἰῶνας τῶν αἰώνων.
He shall reign to the ages of the ages.

15 And the seventh angel sounded; and there were great voices in heaven, saying, The kingdoms of this world are become (the kingdoms) of our Lord, and of his Christ; and he shall reign for ever and ever.

16 And the twenty-four elders sitting before God on His throne fell on their faces and worshiped God,

2532 3588 1501 2532
16 καὶ οἱ εἴκοσι καὶ
And the twenty and
5064 4245 3588 1799 3588 2316 2521 1909
τέσσαρες πρεσβύτεροι οἱ ἐνώπιον τοῦ Θεοῦ καθήμενοι ἐπὶ
four elders before God sitting on
3588 2362 846 4098 1909 3588 4383 846 2532
τοὺς θρόνους αὐτῶν, ἔπεσαν ἐπὶ τὰ πρόσωπα αὐτῶν, καὶ
the throne of Him, fell on the faces of them, and
4352 3588 2316
προσεκύνησαν τῷ Θεῷ,
worshiped God,

16 And the four and twenty elders, which sat before God on their seats, fell upon their faces, and worshipped God,

17 saying, We thank You, Lord God Almighty, the (One) who is, and who was, and who is coming, because You took Your great power and reigned.

3004 2168 4671 2962
17 λέγοντες, Εὐχαριστοῦμέν σοι, Κύριε
saying, We thank You, Lord
3588 2316 3588 3841 3588 5607 2532 3588 2258 2532 3588 2064
ὁ Θεὸς ὁ παντοκράτωρ, ὁ ὢν καὶ ὁ ἦν καὶ ὁ ἐρχόμενος,
God Almighty, the (One) being and who was and who (is) coming,
3754 2983 3588 1411 4675 3588 3173 2532 936
ὅτι εἴληφας τὴν δύναμίν σου τὴν μεγάλην, καὶ ἐβασίλευσας·
because you took the power of You great, and' reigned;

17 Saying, We give thee thanks, O Lord God Almighty, which art, and wast, and art to come; because thou hast taken to thee thy great power, and hast reigned.

18 And the nations were full of wrath; and Your wrath came, and the time of the judging of the dead, and to give the reward to

2532 3588 1484 3710 2532 2064 3588 3709 4675 2532 3588
18 καὶ τὰ ἔθνη ὠργίσθησαν, καὶ ἦλθεν ἡ ὀργή σου, καὶ ὁ
And the nations were wrathful, and came the wrath of You, and the
2540 3588 3498 2919 2532 1325 3588 3408 3588
καιρὸς τῶν νεκρῶν κριθῆναι, καὶ δοῦναι τὸν μισθὸν τοῖς
time of the dead to be judged, and to give the reward to the

18 And the nations were angry, and thy wrath is come, and the time of the dead, that they should be judged, and that thou shouldest give reward unto

Revelation 11:19

Literal Translation

Your slaves, to the prophets, and to the saints, and to the ones fearing Your name, to the small and to the great, and to destroy those destroying the earth.

19 And the temple of God in Heaven was opened, and the ark of His covenant was seen in His temple, and lightnings, and voices, and thunders, and earthquake, and a great hail occurred.

1401 4675 3588 4396 2532 3588 40 2532 3588 5399
δούλοις σου τοῖς προφήταις καὶ τοῖς ἁγίοις καὶ τοῖς φοβου-
slaves of You to the prophets and to the saints and to those fearing

3588 3686 4675 3588 3398 2532 3588 3173 2532
μένοις τὸ ὄνομά σου, τοῖς μικροῖς καὶ τοῖς μεγάλοις, καὶ
the name of You, to the small and to the great, and

1311 3588 1311 3588 1093
διαφθεῖραι τοὺς διαφθείροντας τὴν γῆν.
to destroy the (ones) destroying the earth.

2532 455 3588 3485 3588 2316 1722 3588 3772 2532 3700 3588
19 καὶ ἠνοίγη ὁ ναὸς τοῦ Θεοῦ ἐν τῷ οὐρανῷ, καὶ ὤφθη ἡ
And was opened the temple of God in Heaven, and was seen the

2787 3588 1242 846 1722 3588 3485 846 2532 1096
κιβωτὸς τῆς διαθήκης αὐτοῦ ἐν τῷ ναῷ αὐτοῦ· καὶ ἐγένοντο
ark of the covenant of Him in the temple of Him; and occurred

796 2532 5456 2532 1027 2532 4578 2532 5464
ἀστραπαὶ καὶ φωναὶ καὶ βρονταὶ καὶ σεισμὸς καὶ χάλαζα
lightnings and sounds and thunders and an earthquake and a hail

3173
μεγάλη.
great.

King James Version

thy servants the prophets, and to the saints, and them that fear thy name, small and great; and shouldest destroy them which destroy the earth.

19 And the temple of God was opened in heaven, and there was seen in his temple the ark of his testament: and there were lightnings, and voices, and thunderings, and an earthquake, and great hail.

Revelation 12

1. And a great sign was seen in the heavens, a woman having been clothed with the sun, and the moon was underneath her feet; and on her head a crown of twelve stars;

2 and having (a babe) in womb. She cries, being in labor, and having been distressed to bear.

3 And another sign was seen in the heavens. And, behold! A great red dragon having seven heads and ten horns! And on his heads were seven diadems,

4 and his tail drew the third (part) of the stars of the heaven, and he throws them to the earth. And the dragon stood before the woman being about to bear, so that when she bears he might devour her child.

5 And she bore a son, a male, who is going to shepherd all the nations with an iron staff. And her child was seized to God, and (to) His throne.

6 And the

Revelation 12

2532 4592 3173 3700 1722 3588 3772 1135 4016
1. Καὶ σημεῖον μέγα ὤφθη ἐν τῷ οὐρανῷ, γυνὴ περιβεβλη-
And a sign great was seen in the heavens, a woman having been

3588 2246 2532 3588 4582 5270 3588 4228 846
μένη τὸν ἥλιον, καὶ ἡ σελήνη ὑποκάτω τῶν ποδῶν αὐτῆς,
clothed (with) the sun, and the moon underneath the feet of her,

2532 1909 3588 2776 846 4735 792 1427 2532
καὶ ἐπὶ τῆς κεφαλῆς αὐτῆς στέφανος ἀστέρων δώδεκα· 2 καὶ
and on the head of her a crown of stars twelve; and

1722 1064 2192 2896 5605 2532 928
ἐν γαστρὶ ἔχουσα, κράζει ὠδίνουσα, καὶ βασανιζομένη
in womb having, she cries being in travail, and being distressed

5088 2532 3700 243 4592 1722 3588 3772 2532 2400
τεκεῖν. 3 καὶ ὤφθη ἄλλο σημεῖον ἐν τῷ οὐρανῷ, καὶ ἰδού,
to bear. And was seen another sign in the heaven, and behold!

1404 3173 4450 2192 2776 2033 2532 2768
δράκων μέγας πυρρός, ἔχων κεφαλὰς ἑπτὰ καὶ κέρατα
dragon A great red, having heads seven and horns

1176 2532 1909 3588 2776 846 1238 2033 2532 3588 3769
δέκα, καὶ ἐπὶ τὰς κεφαλὰς αὐτοῦ διαδήματα ἑπτά. 4 καὶ ἡ οὐρὰ
ten, and on the heads of him diadems seven. And the tail

846 4951 3588 5154 3588 792 3588 3772 2532
αὐτοῦ σύρει τὸ τρίτον τῶν ἀστέρων τοῦ οὐρανοῦ, καὶ
of him draws the third (part) of the stars of the heaven, and

906 846 1519 3588 1093 2532 3588 1404 2476 1799
ἔβαλεν αὐτοὺς εἰς τὴν γῆν· καὶ ὁ δράκων ἕστηκεν ἐνώπιον
throws them onto the earth; and the dragon stood before

3588 1135 3588 3195 5088 2443 3752 5088 3588 5043
τῆς γυναικὸς τῆς μελλούσης τεκεῖν, ἵνα, ὅταν τέκῃ τὸ τέκνον
the woman being about to bear, that, when she bears the child

846 2719 2532 5088 5207 730 3739 3195 4165
αὐτῆς καταφάγῃ. 5 καὶ ἔτεκεν υἱόν ἄρρενα, ὃς μέλλει ποι-
of her he may devour. And she bore a son, a male, who is going to

3956 3588 1484 1722 4464 4603 2532 726 3588
μαίνειν πάντα τὰ ἔθνη ἐν ῥάβδῳ σιδηρᾷ· καὶ ἡρπάσθη τὸ
shepherd all the nations with staff an iron and was seized the

5043 846 4314 3588 2316 2532 3588 2362 846 2532 3588
τέκνον αὐτῆς πρὸς τὸν Θεὸν καὶ τὸν θρόνον αὐτοῦ. 6 καὶ ἡ
child of her to God and the throne of Him. And the

Revelation 12

1. And there appeared a great wonder in heaven; a woman clothed with the sun, and the moon under her feet, and upon her head a crown of twelve stars:

2 And she being with child cried, travailing in birth, and pained to be delivered.

3 And there appeared another wonder in heaven; and behold a great red dragon, having seven heads and ten horns, and seven crowns upon his heads.

4 And his tail drew the third part of the stars of heaven, and did cast them to the earth: and the dragon stood before the woman which was ready to be delivered, for to devour her child as soon as it was born.

5 And she brought forth a man child, who was to rule all nations with a rod of iron: and her child was caught up unto God, and (to) his throne.

6 And the

Literal Translation — **Revelation 12:7** — ***King James Version***

woman fled into the wilderness, where she has a place having been prepared from God, that there they might nourish her a thousand two hundred and sixty days.

1135 5343 1722 3588 2048 3699 2192 5117 2090
γυνὴ ἔφυγεν εἰς τὴν ἔρημον, ὅπου ἔχει τόπον ἡτοιμασμένον
woman fled into the wildereness, where she has a place having been readied
575 3588 2316 2443 1563 5142 846 2250 5507
ἀπὸ τοῦ Θεοῦ, ἵνα ἐκεῖ τρέφωσιν αὐτὴν ἡμέρας χιλίας
from God, that there they might nourish her days a thousand
1250 1835
διακοσίας ἑξήκοντα.
two hundred (and) sixty.

woman fled into the wilderness, where she hath a place prepared of God, that they should feed her there a thousand two hundred (and) threescore days.

7. And war occurred in Heaven, Michael and His angels making war against the dragon. And the dragon and his angels made war,
8 but they did not have strength, nor yet was place found for them in Heaven.
9 And the great dragon was cast out, the old serpent being called Devil and Satan; he deceiving the whole habitable world was cast out onto the earth, and his angels were cast out with him.

2532 1096 4171 1722 3588 3772 3588 3413 2532 3588
7. Καὶ ἐγένετο πόλεμος ἐν τῷ οὐρανῷ, ὁ Μιχαὴλ καὶ οἱ
And occurred war in Heaven, Michael and the
32 846 4170 2596 3588 1404 2532 3588
ἄγγελοι αὐτοῦ ἐπολέμησαν κατὰ τοῦ δράκοντος· καὶ ὁ
angels of Him made war against the dragon; and the
1404 4170 2532 3588 32 846 2532 3756 2480
δράκων ἐπολέμησε, καὶ οἱ ἄγγελοι αὐτοῦ, 8 καὶ οὐκ ἴσχυσαν,
dragon warred, and the angels of him, and not they prevailed,
3777 5117 2147 846 2089 1722 3588 3772 2532 906
οὔτε τόπος εὑρέθη αὐτῶν ἔτι ἐν τῷ οὐρανῷ. 9 καὶ ἐβλήθη
nor place was found of them yet in Heaven. And was cast
3588 1404 3588 3173 3588 3789 3588 744 3588 2564 1228
ὁ δράκων ὁ μέγας, ὁ ὄφις ὁ ἀρχαῖος, ὁ καλούμενος διάβολος
the dragon great, the serpent old, being called devil
2532 3588 4567 3588 4105 3588 3625 3650 906
καὶ ὁ Σατανᾶς, ὁ πλανῶν τὴν οἰκουμένην ὅλην· ἐβλήθη
and Satan, the (one) deceiving the habitable world whole; was cast
1519 3588 1093 2532 3588 32 846 3326 846 906
εἰς τὴν γῆν, καὶ οἱ ἄγγελοι αὐτοῦ μετ' αὐτοῦ ἐβλήθησαν.
to the earth, and the angels of him with him were cast.

7. And there was war in heaven: Michael and his angels fought against the dragon; and the dragon fought and his angels,
8 And prevailed not; neither was their place found any more in heaven.
9 And the great dragon was cast out, that old serpent, called the Devil, and Satan, which deceiveth the whole world: he was cast out into the earth, and his angels were cast out with him.

10 And I heard a great voice saying in Heaven, Now has come the salvation and power and the kingdom of our God, and the authority of His Christ, because the accuser of our brothers is thrown down, the (one) accusing them before our God day and night.

2532 191 5456 3173 3004 1722/3588 3772 737
10 καὶ ἤκουσα φωνὴν μεγάλην λεγουσαν ἐν τῷ οὐρανῷ, Ἄρτι
And I heard voice a great saying in Heaven, Now
1096 3588 4991 2532/3588 1411 2532 3588 932 3588 2316
ἐγένετο ἡ σωτηρία καὶ ἡ δύναμις καὶ ἡ βασιλεία τοῦ Θεοῦ
has come the salvation and the power and the kingdom of the God
2257 2532 3588 1849 3588 5547 846 3754 2598
ἡμῶν καὶ ἡ ἐξουσία τοῦ Χριστοῦ αὐτοῦ· ὅτι κατεβλήθη
of us and the authority of the Christ of Him; because is cast down
3588 2725 3588 80 2257 3588 2723 846
ὁ κατήγορος τῶν ἀδελφῶν ἡμῶν, ὁ κατηγορῶν αὐτῶν
the accuser of the brothers of us, the (one) accusing them
1799 3588 2316 2257 2250 2532 3571
ἐνώπιον τοῦ Θεοῦ ἡμῶν ἡμέρας καὶ νυκτός.
before the God of us day and night.

10 And I heard a loud voice saying in heaven, Now is come salvation, and strength, and the kingdom of our God, and the power of his Christ: for the accuser of our brethren is cast down, which accused them before our God day and night.

11 And they overcame him because of the blood of the Lamb, and because of the word of their testimony. And they did not love their soul even until death.

2532 846
11 καὶ αὐτοὶ
And they
3528 846 1223 3588 129 3588 721 2532 1223 3588 3056
ἐνίκησαν αὐτὸν διὰ τὸ αἷμα τοῦ ἀρνίου, καὶ διὰ τὸν λόγον
overcame him because of the blood of the Lamb, and because of the Word
3588 3141 846 2532 3756 25 3588 5590 846
τῆς μαρτυρίας αὐτῶν, καὶ οὐκ ἠγάπησαν τὴν ψυχὴν αὐτῶν
of the witness of them, and not they loved the life of them
891 2288
ἄχρι θανάτου.
until death.

11 And they overcame him by the blood of the Lamb, and by the word of their testimony; and they loved not their lives unto the death.

12. Because of this, be glad, the heavens and those tabernacling in them. Woe to the (ones) dwelling on the earth, and in the sea, because the Devil came down to you having great anger, knowing that he has a little time!

1223 5124 2165 3588 3772 2532/3588/1722
12 διὰ τοῦτο εὐφραίνεσθε, οἱ οὐρανοὶ καὶ οἱ ἐν
Because of this be glad, the heavens and those in
846 4637 3759 3588 2730 3588 1093 2532 3588
αὐτοῖς σκηνοῦντες· οὐαὶ τοῖς κατοικοῦσι τὴν γῆν καὶ τὴν
them tabernacling; woe to (the) ones inhabiting the earth and the
2281 3754 2597 3588 1228 4314 5209 2192 2372
θάλασσαν, ὅτι κατέβη ὁ διάβολος πρὸς ὑμᾶς ἔχων θυμὸν
sea, because came down the devil to you having anger
3173 1492 3754 3641 2540 2192
μέγαν, εἰδὼς ὅτι ὀλίγον καιρὸν ἔχει.
great, knowing that a little time he has.

12. Therefore rejoice, (ye) heavens, and ye that dwell in them. Woe to the inhabiters of the earth and of the sea! for the devil is come down unto you, having great wrath, because he knoweth that he hath but a short time.

Literal Translation

13 And when the dragon saw that he was cast out onto the earth, he chased the woman who bore the male.
14 And two wings of the great eagle were given to the woman, that she might fly into the wilderness, to her place, where she is nourished there a time, and times, and half a time, away from the serpent's face.
15 And the serpent threw water out of his mouth like a river after the woman, that he might cause her to be carried off by the river.

16 And the earth helped the woman, and the earth opened its mouth and swallowed the river which the dragon threw out of his mouth.

17 And the dragon was enraged over the woman, and went away to make war with the rest of her seed, those keeping the commandments of God, and having the testimony of Jesus Christ.

Revelation 12:13

2532 3753 1492 3588 1404 3754 906 1519 3588 1093 1377
13. Καὶ ὅτε εἶδεν ὁ δράκων ὅτι ἐβλήθη εἰς τὴν γῆν, ἐδίωξε
And when saw the dragon that he was cast into the earth, he chased

3588 1135 3748 5088 3588 730 2532 1325 3588 1135
τὴν γυναῖκα ἥτις ἔτεκε τὸν ἄρρενα. 14 καὶ ἐδόθησαν τῇ γυναικὶ
the woman who bore the male. And were given to the woman

1417 4420 3588 105 3588 3173 2443 4072 1519 3588
δύο πτέρυγες τοῦ ἀετοῦ τοῦ μεγάλου, ἵνα πέτηται εἰς τὴν
two wings of the eagle great, that she may fly into the

2048 1519 3588 5117 846 3699 5142 1563 2540 2532
ἔρημον εἰς τὸν τόπον αὐτῆς, ὅπου τρέφεται ἐκεῖ καιρόν, καὶ
wilderness to the place of her, where she is nourished there a time, and

2540 2532 2255 2540 575 4383 3588 3789 2532
καιρούς καὶ ἥμισυ καιροῦ, ἀπὸ προσώπου τοῦ ὄφεως. 15 καὶ
times and half a time, from (the) face of the serpent. And

906 3588 3789 3694 3588 1135 1537 3588 4750 846
ἔβαλεν ὁ ὄφις ὀπίσω τῆς γυναικὸς ἐκ τοῦ στόματος αὐτοῦ
threw the serpent after the woman out of the mouth of him

5204 5613 4215 2443 3778 4216 4160
ὕδωρ ὡς ποταμόν, ἵνα ταύτην ποταμοφόρητον ποιήσῃ.
water as a river, that her carried off by the river he might make.

2532 997 3588 1093 3588 1135 2532 455 3588 1093 3588 4750
16 καὶ ἐβοήθησεν ἡ γῆ τῇ γυναικί, καὶ ἤνοιξεν ἡ γῆ τὸ στόμα
And helped the earth the woman, and opened the earth the mouth

846 2532 2666 3588 4215 3739 906 3588 1404 1537 3588
αὐτῆς, καὶ κατέπιε τὸν ποταμὸν ὃν ἔβαλεν ὁ δράκων ἐκ τοῦ
of it, and swallowed the river which cast the dragon out of the

4750 846 2532 3710 3588 1404 1909 3588 1135 2532
στόματος αὐτοῦ. 17 καὶ ὠργίσθη ὁ δράκων ἐπὶ τῇ γυναικί, καὶ
mouth of him. And was enraged the dragon over the woman, and

565 4160 4171 3326 3588 3062 3588 4690
ἀπῆλθε ποιῆσαι πόλεμον μετὰ τῶν λοιπῶν τοῦ σπέρματος
went away to make war with the rest of the seed

846 3588 5083 3588 1785 3588 2316 2532 2192
αὐτῆς, τῶν τηρούντων τὰς ἐντολὰς τοῦ θεοῦ καὶ ἐχόντων
of her, the (ones) keeping the commandments of God and having

3588 3141 3588 2424 5547 2532 2476 1909 3588
τὴν μαρτυρίαν τοῦ Ἰησοῦ Χριστοῦ· 18 καὶ ἐστάθην ἐπὶ τὴν
the witness of Jesus Christ. And I stood on the

285 3588 2281
ἄμμον τῆς θαλάσσης. (Note some manuscripts show verse 18 as
sand of the sea.

Revelation 13:1.)

King James Version

13 And when the dragon saw that he was cast unto the earth, he persecuted the woman which brought forth the man (child).
14 And to the woman were given two wings of a great eagle, that she might fly into the wilderness, into her place, where she is nourished for a time, and times, and half a time, from the face of the serpent.
15 And the serpent cast out of his mouth water as a flood after the woman, that he might cause her to be carried away of the flood.

16 And the earth helped the woman, and the earth opened her mouth, and swallowed up the flood which the dragon cast out of his mouth.
17 And the dragon was wroth with the woman, and went to make war with the remnant of her seed, which keep the commandments of God, and have the testimony of Jesus Christ.

Revelation 13

1. And I stood on the sand of the sea. And I saw a beast coming up out of the sea, having seven heads and ten horns, and on his horns ten diadems, and on its heads names of blasphemy.

2 And the beast which I saw was like a leopard, and its feet as of a bear, and its mouth as a lion's mouth.

Revelation 13

2532 1492 1537 3588 2281 2342 305 2192
1. Καὶ εἶδον ἐκ τῆς θαλάσσης θηρίον ἀναβαῖνον, ἔχον
And I saw out of the sea a beast coming up, having

2776 2033 2532 2768 1176 2532 1909 3588 2768 846 1176
κεφαλὰς ἑπτὰ καὶ κέρατα δέκα, καὶ ἐπὶ τῶν κεράτων αὐτοῦ δέκα
heads seven and horns ten, and on the horns of it ten

1238 2532 1909 3588 2776 846 3686 988
διαδήματα, καὶ ἐπὶ τὰς κεφαλὰς αὐτοῦ ὀνόμα βλασφημίας.
diadems, and on the heads of it names of blasphemy.

2532 3588 2342 3739 1492 2258 3664 3917 2532 3588 4228
2 καὶ τὸ θηρίον, ὃ εἶδον, ἦν ὅμοιον παρδάλει, καὶ οἱ πόδες
And the beast, which I saw, was like a leopard, and the feet

846 5613 715 2532 3588 4750 846 5613 4750 3023
αὐτοῦ ὡς ἄρκτου, καὶ τὸ στόμα αὐτοῦ ὡς στόμα λέοντος·
of it as of a bear, and the mouth of it as (the) mouth of a lion;

Revelation 13

1. And I stood upon the sand of the sea, and saw a beast rise up out of the sea, having seven heads and ten horns, and upon his horns ten crowns, and upon his heads the name of blasphemy.

2 And the beast which I saw was like unto a leopard, and his feet were as (the feet) of a bear, and his mouth as the mouth of a lion:

Literal Translation

Revelation 13:3

King James Version

And the dragon gave its power to it, and its throne, and great authority.
3 And I saw one of its heads, as having been slain to death, and its deadly wound was healed. And all the earth marveled after the beast.

4 And they worshiped the dragon who gave authority to the beast; and they worshiped the beast, saying, Who (is) like the beast; who is able to make war with it?

5 And a mouth speaking great things and blasphemies was given to it. And authority to act forty-two months was given to it.
6 And it opened its mouth in blasphemy toward God, to blaspheme His name and His tabernacle, and those tabernacling in Heaven.

7 And it was given to it to war with the saints, and to overcome them. And authority was given to it over every tribe and tongue and nation.

8 And all those dwelling in the earth will worship it, of whom the names had not been written in the Book of Life of the Lamb having been slain from (the) foundation of the world.
9 If anyone has an ear, let him hear.

10 If anyone gathers captivity, into captivity he goes. If anyone will kill by a sword, by a sword he must be killed. Here is the patience and the faith of the saints.

2532 1325 846 3588 1404 3588 1411 846 2532 3588
καὶ ἔδωκεν αὐτῷ ὁ δράκων τὴν δύναμιν αὐτοῦ, καὶ τὸν
and gave to it the dragon the power of it and the
2362 846 2532 1849 3137 2532 1492 3391 3588
θρόνον αὐτοῦ, καὶ ἐξουσίαν μεγάλην. 3 καὶ εἶδον μίαν τῶν
throne of it, and authority great. And I saw one of the
2776 846 5613 4969 1519 2288 2532 3588 4127 3588
κεφαλῶν αὐτοῦ ὡς ἐσφαγμένην εἰς θάνατον· καὶ ἡ πληγὴ τοῦ
heads of it as having been slain to death; and the wound of the
2288 846 2323 2532 2296 3650 3588 1093 3694
θανάτου αὐτοῦ ἐθεραπεύθη· καὶ ἐθαύμασεη ὅλη ἡ γῆ ὀπίσω
death of it was healed; and marveled all the earth after

3588 2342 2532 4352 3588 1404 3739 1325
τοῦ θηρίου· 4 καὶ προσεκύνησαν τὸν δράκοντα ὃς ἔδωκεν
the beast; and they worshiped the dragon who gave
1849 3588 2342 2532 4352 3588 2342 3004
ἐξουσίαν τῷ θηρίῳ, καὶ προσεκύνησαν τὸ θηρίον, λέγοντες,
authority to the beast, and they worshiped the beast, saying,
5101 3664 3588 2342 5101 1410 4170 3326 846
Τίς ὅμοιος τῷ θηρίῳ, τίς δύναται πολεμῆσαι μετ' αὐτοῦ;
Who (is) like the beast, who is able to make war with it?

2532 1325 846 4750 2980 3173 2532 988 2532
5 καὶ ἐδόθη αὐτῷ στόμα λαλοῦν μεγάλα καὶ βλασφημίας· καὶ
And was given to it a mouth speaking great things and blasphemies; and
1325 846 1849 4160 3376 5062 1417 2532
ἐδόθη αὐτῷ ἐξουσία ποιῆσαι μῆνας τεσσεράκοντα δύο. 6 καὶ
was given to it authority to perform months forty two. And
455 3588 4750 846 1519 987 4314 3588 2316
ἤνοιξε τὸ στόμα αὐτοῦ εἰς βλασφημίαν πρὸς τὸν Θεόν,
it opened the mouth of it in blasphemy toward God,
987 3588 3686 846 2532 3588 4633 846 2532
βλασφημῆσαι τὸ ὄνομα αὐτοῦ, καὶ τὴν σκηνὴν αὐτοῦ, καὶ
to blaspheme the name of Him, and the tabernacle of Him, and
3588 1722 3588 3772 4637 2532 1325 846 4171
τοὺς ἐν τῷ οὐρανῷ σκηνοῦντας. 7 καὶ ἐδόθη αὐτῷ πόλεμον
those in Heaven tabernacling. And was given to it war
4160 3326 3588 40 2532 3528 846 2532 1325
ποιῆσαι μετὰ τῶν ἁγίων καὶ νικῆσαι αὐτούς· καὶ ἐδόθη
to make with the saints and to overcome them; and was given
846 1849 1909 3956 5443 2532 1100 2532 1484
αὐτῷ ἐξουσία ἐπὶ πᾶσαν φυλὴν καὶ γλῶσσαν καὶ ἔθνος.
to it authority over every tribe and tongue and nation.

2532 4352 846 3956 3588 2730 1909 3588
8 καὶ προσκυνήσουσιν αὐτόν πάντες οἱ κατοικοῦντες ἐπὶ τῆς
And will worship it all the (ones) dwelling on the
1093 3739 3756 1125 3588 3686 1722 3588 976 3588 2222
γῆς, ὧν οὐ γέγραπται τὰ ὀνόματα ἐν τῇ βιβλίῳ τῆς ζωῆς
earth, of whom not was written the names in the Scroll of Life
3588 721 4969 575 2602 2889 1487 5100 2192
τοῦ ἀρνίου ἐσφαγμένου ἀπὸ καταβολῆς κόσμου. 9 εἴ τις ἔχει
of the Lamb having been slain from (the) foundation world's. If anyone has
3775 191 1487 5100 161 4863 1487 161
οὖς, ἀκουσάτω. 10 εἴ τις αἰχμαλωσίαν συνάγει, εἰς αἰχμαλω-
an ear, let him hear. If anyone captivity gathers into captivity
5217 1487 5100 1722 3162 615 1163 846 1722
σίαν ὑπάγει· εἴ τις ἐν μαχαίρᾳ ἀποκτενεῖ, δεῖ αὐτὸν ἐν
he goes; if anyone by a sword will kill, must he by
3162 615 5602 2076 3588 5281 2532 3588 4102
μαχαίρα ἀποκτανθῆναι. ὧδέ ἐστιν ἡ ὑπομονὴ καὶ ἡ πίστις
a sword be killed. Here is the patience and the faith
3588 40
τῶν ἁγίων.
of the saints.

and the dragon gave him his power, and his seat, and great authority.
3 And I saw one of his heads as it were wounded to death; and his deadly wound was healed: and all the world wondered after the beast.

4 And they worshipped the dragon which gave power unto the beast: and they worshipped the beast, saying, Who (is) like unto the beast? who is able to make war with him?

5 And there was given unto him a mouth speaking great things and blasphemies; and power was given unto him to continue forty (and) two months.
6 And he opened his mouth in blasphemy against God, to blaspheme his name, and his tabernacle, and them that dwell in heaven.
7 And it was given unto him to make war with the saints, and to overcome them: and power was given him over all kindreds, and tongues, and nations.

8 And all that dwell upon the earth shall worship him, whose names are not written in the book of life of the Lamb slain from the foundation of the world.
9 If any man have an ear, let him hear.

10 He that leadeth into captivity shall go into captivity: he that killeth with the sword must be killed with the sword. Here is the patience and the faith of the saints.

Literal Translation

11. And I saw another beast coming up out of the earth. And it had two horns like a lamb, but spoke like a dragon.
12 And it executes all the authority of the first beast before it. And it causes that the earth and those dwelling in it should worship the first beast, of which was healed its deadly wound.

13 And it does great signs, that even fire it causes to come down out of the heaven onto the earth before men.

14 And it deceives those dwelling on the earth, because of the signs which were given to it to do before the beast, saying to those dwelling on the earth to make an image to the beast who has the wound of the sword, and lived.

15 And was given to it to give a spirit to the image of the beast, so that the image of the beast might even speak, and might cause as many as would not worship the image of the beast to be killed.

16 And the small and the great, and the rich and the poor, and the freemen and the slaves, it causes that they give to them all a mark on their right hand, or on their foreheads,

17 even that not any could buy or sell, except the one having the mark, or the name of the beast, or the number of its name.

18 Here is wisdom: Let the one having reason count the number of

Revelation 13:11

2532 1492 243 2342 305 1537/3588/1093/2532 2192
11. Καὶ εἶδον ἄλλο θηρίον ἀναβαῖνον ἐκ τῆς γῆς, καὶ εἶχε
And I saw another beast coming up out of the earth, and it had

2768 1417 3664 721 2532 2980 5613 1404 2532 3588
κέρατα δύο ὅμοια ἀρνίῳ, καὶ ἐλάλει ὡς δράκων. 12 καὶ τὴν
horns two like a lamb, and it spoke as a dragon. And the

1849 3588 4413 2342 3956 4160 1799 846
ἐξουσίαν τοῦ πρώτου θηρίου πᾶσαν ποιεῖ ἐνώπιον αὐτοῦ.
authority of the first beast all it does before it.

2532 4160 3588 1093 2532 3588 2730 1722 846 2443
καὶ ποιεῖ τὴν γῆν καὶ τοὺς κατοικοῦντας ἐν αὐτῇ ἵνα
And it makes the earth and the (ones) dwelling in it that

4352 3588 2342 3588 4413 3739 2323 3588
προσκυνήσουσι τὸ θηρίον τὸ πρῶτον, οὗ ἐθεραπεύθη ἡ
they should worship the beast first, of which was healed the

4127 3588 2288 846 2532 4160 4592 3173 2443
πληγὴ τοῦ θανάτου αὐτοῦ. 13 καὶ ποιεῖ σημεῖα μεγάλα, ἵνα
wound of death of it. And it does signs great, that

2532 4442 4160 2597 1537 3588 3772 1519 3588 1093
καὶ πῦρ ποιῇ καταβαίνειν ἐκ τοῦ οὐρανοῦ εἰς τὴν γῆν
even fire it makes to come down out of the heaven onto the earth

1799 3588 444 2532 4105 3588 2730
ἐνώπιον τῶν ἀνθρώπων. 14 καὶ πλανᾷ τοὺς κατοικοῦντας
before men. And it deceives those dwelling

1909 3588 1093 1223 3588 4592 3739 1325 846 4160 1799
ἐπὶ τῆς γῆς διὰ τὰ σημεῖα ἃ ἐδόθη αὐτῷ ποιῆσαι ἐνώπιον
on the earth because of the signs which were given to it to do before

3588 2342 3004 3588 2730 1909 3588 1093 4160
τοῦ θηρίου, λέγων τοῖς κατοικοῦσιν ἐπὶ τῆς γῆς ποιῆσαι
the beast, saying to those dwelling on the earth to make

1504 3588 2342 3739 2192 3588 4127 3588 3162 2532 2198
εἰκόνα τῷ θηρίῳ ὃ ἔχει τὴν πληγὴν τῆς μαχαίρας καὶ ἔζησε.
an image to the beast who has the wound of the sword and lived.

2532 1325 846 1325 4151 3588 1504 3588 2342 2443/2532
15 καὶ ἐδόθη αὐτῷ δοῦναι πνεῦμα τῇ εἰκόνι τοῦ θηρίου, ἵνα καὶ
And was given to it to give a spirit to the image of the beast, that even

2980 3588 1504 3588 2342 2532 4160 3745 302 3361
λαλήσῃ ἡ εἰκὼν τοῦ θηρίου, καὶ ποιήσῃ, ὅσοι ἂν μὴ
might speak the image of the beast, and might make, as many as would not

4352 3588 1504 3588 2342 2443 615
προσκυνήσωσι τὴν εἰκόνα τοῦ θηρίου, ἵνα ἀποκτανθῶσι.
worship the image of the beast, that (they) be killed.

2532 4160 3956 3588 3398 2532 3588 3173 2532 3588
16 καὶ ποιεῖ πάντας, τοὺς μικροὺς καὶ τοὺς μεγάλους, καὶ τοὺς
And it makes all, the small and the great, and the

4145 2532 3588 4434 2532 3588 1658 2532 3588
πλουσίους καὶ τοὺς πτωχούς, καὶ τοὺς ἐλευθέρους καὶ τοὺς
rich and the poor, and the freemen and the

1401 2443 1325 846 5480 1909 3588 5495 846
δούλους, ἵνα δώσῃ αὐτοῖς χάραγμα ἐπὶ τῆς χειρὸς αὐτῶν
slave, that it may give to them a mark on the hand of them

3588 1188 2228 1909 3588 3359 846 2532 2443 3361 5100
τῆς δεξιᾶς, ἢ ἐπὶ τῶν μετώπων αὐτῶν, 17 καὶ ἵνα μή τις
right, or on the foreheads of them, and that not anyone

1410 59 2228 4453 1487 3361 3588 2192 3588 5480 2228
δύνηται ἀγοράσαι ἢ πωλῆσαι, εἰ μὴ ὁ ἔχων τὸ χάραγμα ἤ
could buy or sell, if not he having the mark, or

3588 3686 3588 2342 2228 3588 706 3588 3686 846 5602
τὸ ὄνομα τοῦ θηρίου ἢ τὸν ἀριθμὸν τοῦ ὀνόματος αὐτοῦ. 18 ὧδε
the name of the beast, or the number of the name of it. Here

3588 4678 2076 3588 2192 3588 3563 5585 3588 706 3588
ἡ σοφία ἐστίν. ὁ ἔχων τὸν νοῦν ψηφισάτω τὸν ἀριθμὸν τοῦ
wisdom is. The (one) having reason let him count the number of the

King James Version

11. And I beheld another beast coming up out of the earth; and he had two horns like a lamb, and he spake as a dragon.
12 And he exerciseth all the power of the first beast before him, and causeth the earth and them which dwell therein to worship the first beast, whose deadly wound was healed.

13 And he doeth great wonders, so that he maketh fire come down from heaven on the earth in the sight of men,

14 And deceiveth them that dwell on the earth by (the means of) those miracles which he had power to do in the sight of the beast; saying to them that dwell on the earth, that they should make an image to the beast, which had the wound by a sword, and did live.

15 And he had power to give life unto the image of the beast, that the image of the beast should both speak, and cause that as many as would not worship the image of the beast should be killed.

16 And he causeth all, both small and great, rich and poor, free and bond, to receive a mark in their right hand, or in their foreheads:

17 And that no man might buy or sell, save he that had the mark, or the name of the beast, or the number of his name.

18 Here is wisdom. Let him that hath understanding count the number of the

Literal Translation

the beast, for it is the number of a man and its number (is) 666.

Revelation 14

1. And I saw, and behold, the Lamb standing on Mount Zion! And with Him were a hundred (and) forty-four thousands, with the name of His Father having been written on their foreheads.

2 And I heard a sound out of Heaven, as a sound of many waters, and as a sound of great thunder. Also I heard a sound of harpers harping on their harps.
3 And they sing as a new song before the throne, and before the four living creatures and the elders. And no one was able to learn the song except the hundred (and) forty-four thousands, those having been redeemed from the earth.

4 These are the ones who were not defiled with women, for they are virgins. These are the ones following the Lamb wherever He may go. These were redeemed from among men as (a) firstfruit to God and to the Lamb.

5 And no guile was found in their mouth, for they are without blemish before the throne of God.

6. And I saw another angel flying in mid-heaven, having an everlasting gospel to proclaim to those dwelling on the earth, even to every nation and tribe and tongue and people,

7 saying in a great voice, Fear God, and give glory to Him,

Revelation 14:1

2342 706 1063 444 2076 2532/3588/706 846 5516
θηρίου· ἀριθμὸς γὰρ ἀνθρώπου ἐστί, καὶ ὁ ἀριθμὸς αὐτοῦ Χξς.
beast (the) number for of a man it is, and the number of it 666.

Revelation 14

2532 1492 2532 2400 721 2476 1909 3588 3735 4622 2532
1. Καὶ εἶδον, καὶ ἰδου, ἀρνίον ἑστηκὸς ἐπὶ τὸ ὄρος Σιών, καὶ
And I saw, and behold! (The) Lamb standing on the mount Zion, and

3326 846 1540 5062 5064 5505 2192
μετ αὐτοῦ ἑκατὸν τεσσεράκοντα τέσσαρες χιλιάδες, ἔχουσαι
with Him a hundred (and) forty four thousands, having

3588 3686 3588 3962 846 1125 1909 3588 3359
τὸ ὄνομα τοῦ πατρὸς αὐτοῦ γεγραμμένον ἐπὶ τῶν μετώπων
the name of the Father of Him having been written on the foreheads

846 2532 191 5456 1537 3588 3772 5613 5456 5204
αὐτῶν. 2 καὶ ἤκουσα φωνὴν ἐκ τοῦ οὐρανοῦ, ὡς φωνὴν ὑδάτων
of them. And I heard a sound out of Heaven, as a sound of waters

4183 2532 5613 5456 1027 3173 2532 5456 191
πολλῶν, καὶ ὡς φωνὴν βροντῆς μεγάλης· καὶ φωνὴν ἤκουσα
many, and as a sound of thunder great; abd a sound I heard

2790 2789 1722 3588 2788 846 2532
κιθαρῳδῶν κιθαριζόντων ἐν ταῖς κιθάραις αὐτῶν. 3 καὶ
of harpers harping on the harps of them. And

103 5613 5603 2537 1799 3588 2362 2532 1799
ᾄδουσιν ὡς ᾠδὴν καινὴν ἐνώπιον τοῦ θρόνου, καὶ ἐνώπιον
they sang as a song new before the throne, and before

3588 5064 2226 2532 3588 4245 2532 3762 1410
τῶν τεσσάρων ζῴων καὶ τῶν πρεσβυτέρων· καὶ οὐδεὶς ἠδύ-
the four living creatures and the elders; and no one was

3129 3588 5603 1487 3361 3588 1540 5062 5064
νατο μαθεῖν τὴν ᾠδήν, εἰ μὴ αἱ ἑκατὸν τεσσεράκοντατέσ-
able to learn the song, except the hundred forty-four

5505 3588 59 575 3588 1093 3778 1526 3739
σαρες χιλιάδες, οἱ ἠγορασμένοι ἀπὸ τῆς γῆς. 4 οὗτοί εἰσιν οἳ
thousands, those being redeemed from the earth. These are who

3326 1135 3756 3435 3933 1063 1526 3778
μετὰ γυναικῶν οὐκ ἐμολύνθησαν, παρθένοι γάρ εἰσιν. οὗτοι
with women not were defiled, virgins for they are. These

1526 3588 190 3588 721 3699 302 5217 3778
εἰσιν οἱ ἀκολουθοῦντες τῷ ἀρνίῳ ὅπου ἂν ὑπάγῃ. οὗτοι
are those following the Lamb wherever He may go. These

59 575 3588 444 536 3588 2316 2532 3588
ἠγοράσθησαν ἀπὸ τῶν ἀνθρώπων, ἀπαρχὴ τῷ Θεῷ καὶ τῷ
were redeemed from men, firstfruit to God and to the

721 2532 1722 3588 4750 846 3756 2147 1388 299
ἀρνίῳ, 5 καὶ ἐν τῷ στόματι αὐτῶν οὐχ εὑρέθη δόλος· ἄμωμοι
Lamb, and in the mouth of them not was found guile; unmarked

1063 1526 1799 3588 2362 3588 2316
γὰρ εἰσιν ἐνώπιον τοῦ θρόνου τοῦ Θεοῦ.
for they are before the throne of God.

2532 1492 243 32 4072 1722 3321
6. Καὶ εἶδον ἄλλον ἄγγελον πετόμενον ἐν μεσουρανήματι,
And I saw another angel flying in mid-heaven,

2192 2098 166 2097 3588 2730
ἔχοντα εὐαγγέλιον αἰώνιον, εὐαγγελίσαι τοὺς κατοικοῦντας
having a gospel everlasting, to proclaim to those dwelling

1909 3588 1093 2532 3956 1484 2532 5543 2532 1100 2532 2992
ἐπὶ τῆς γῆς, καὶ πᾶν ἔθνος καὶ φυλὴν καὶ γλῶσσαν καὶ λαόν,
on the earth, and every nation and tribe and tongue and people,

3004 1722 5456 3173 5399 3588 2316 2532 1325 846
7 λέγοντα ἐν φωνῇ μεγάλῃ, Φοβήθητε τὸν Θεὸν, καὶ δότε αὐτῷ
saying in a voice great, Fear God, and give to Him

King James Version

beast: for it is the number of a man; and his number (is) Six hundred threescore (and) six.

Revelation 14

1. And I looked, and, lo, a Lamb stood on the mount Sion, and with him an hundred forty (and) four thousand, having his Father's name written in their foreheads.

2 And I heard a voice from heaven, as the voice of many waters, and as the voice of a great thunder: and I heard the voice of harpers harping with their harps:
3 And they sung as it were a new song before the throne, and before the four beasts, and the elders: and no man could learn that song but the hundred (and) forty (and) four thousand, which were redeemed from the earth.

4 These are they which were not defiled with women; for they are virgins. These are they which follow the Lamb whithersoever he goeth. These were redeemed from among men, (being) the firstfruits unto God and to the Lamb.

5 And in their mouth was found no guile: for they are without fault before the throne of God.

6. And I saw another angel fly in the midst of heaven, having the everlasting gospel to preach unto them that dwell on the earth, and to every nation, and kindred, and tongue, and people,
7 Saying with a loud voice, Fear God, and give glory to him;

Literal Translation | **Revelation 14:8** | *King James Version*

because the hour of His judgment has come; also, Worship Him who has made the heaven, and the earth, and the sea, and (the) fountains of waters.

1391 3754 2064 3588 5610 3588 2920 846 2532 4352
δόξαν, ὅτι ἦλθεν ἡ ὥρα τῆς κρίσεως αὐτοῦ, καὶ προσκυνή-
glory, because came the hour of the judgment of Him, and worship
3588 4160 3588 2281 2532 3588 1093 2532 2281
σατε τῷ ποιήσαντι τὸν οὐρανὸν καὶ τὴν γῆν καὶ θάλασ-
the (One) having made the heaven and the earth and (the) sea
2532 4077 5204
σαν καὶ πηγὰς ὑδάτων.
and fountains of waters.

for the hour of his judgment is come: and worship him that made heaven, and earth, and the sea, and the fountains of waters.

8 And another angel followed, saying, The great city, Babylon, has fallen, has fallen; because of the wine of the anger of her fornication, she made all nations to drink.

2532 243 32 190 3004 4098 4098
8. Καὶ ἄλλος ἄγγελος ἠκολούθησε, λέγων, Ἔπεσεν, ἔπεσε
And another angel followed, saying, has fallen, has fallen,
897 3588 4172 3588 3173 3754 1537 3588 3631 3588 2372
Βαβυλὼν ἡ πόλις ἡ μεγάλη, ὅτι ἐκ τοῦ οἴνου τοῦ θυμοῦ
Babylon the city great, because of the wine of the anger
3588 4202 846 4222 3956 1484
τῆς πορνείας αὐτῆς πεπότικε πάντα ἔθνη.
of the fornication of her she made to drink all nations.

8 And there followed another angel, saying, Babylon is fallen, is fallen, that great city, because she made all nations drink of the wine of the wrath of her fornication.

9 And a third angel followed them, saying in a great voice, If anyone worships the beast and its image, and receives a mark on his forehead, or in his hand,

2532 5154 32 190 846 3004 1722 5456
9. Καὶ τρίτος ἄγγελος ἠκολούθησεν αὐτοῖς, λέγων ἐν φωνῇ
And a third angel followed them, saying in voice
3173 1487 5100 3588 2342 4352 2532 3588 1504 846
μεγάλῃ, Εἴ τις τὸ θηρίον προσκυνεῖ καὶ τὴν εἰκόνα αὐτοῦ,
a great, If anyone the beast worships and the image of it,
2532 2983 5480 1909 3588 3359 846 2228 1909 3588
καὶ λαμβάνει χάραγμα ἐπὶ τοῦ μετώπου αὐτοῦ, ἢ ἐπὶ τὴν
and receives a mark on the forehead of him, or on the
5495 846 2532 846 4095 1537 3588 3631 3588 2372 3588
χεῖρα αὐτοῦ, 10 καὶ αὐτὸς πίεται ἐκ τοῦ οἴνου τοῦ θυμοῦ τοῦ
hand of him, even he shall drink of the wine of the anger

9 And the third angel followed them, saying with a loud voice, If any man worship the beast and his image, and receive (his) mark in his forehead, or in his hand,

10 he also shall drink of the wine of the anger of God having been mixed undiluted in the cup of His wrath. And he will be tormented in fire and brimstone before the holy angels and before the Lamb.

11 And the smoke of their torment goes up to ages of ages. And those worshiping the beast and its image have no rest night and day, even if anyone receives the mark of its name.

2316 3588 2767 194 1722 3588 4221 3588 3709
Θεοῦ, τοῦ κεκερασμένου ἀκράτου ἐν τῷ ποτηρίῳ τῆς ὀργῆς
of God, having been mixed undiluted in the cup of the wrath
846 2532 928 1722 4442 2532 2303 1799 3588
αὐτοῦ, καὶ βασανισθήσεται ἐν πυρὶ καὶ θείῳ ἐνώπιον τῶν
of Him, and will be tormented in fire and brimstone beforre the
40 32 2532 1799 3588 721 2532/3588 2586 3588
ἁγίων ἀγγέλων, καὶ ἐνώπιον τοῦ ἀρνίου. 11 καὶ ὁ καπνὸς τοῦ
holy angels, and before the Lamb. And the smoke of the
929 846 305 1519 165 165 2532 3756
βασανισμοῦ αὐτῶν ἀναβαίνει εἰς αἰῶνας αἰώνων· καὶ οὐκ
torment of them goes up to ages of ages; and not
2192 372 2250 2532 3571 3588 4352 3588
ἔχουσιν ἀνάπαυσιν ἡμέρας καὶ νυκτός, οἱ προσκυνοῦντες τὸ
have rest day and night, the (ones) worshiping the
2342 2532 3588 1504 846 2532 1487 5100 2983 3588 5480
θηρίον καὶ τὴν εἰκόνα αὐτοῦ, καὶ εἴ τις λαμβάνει τὸ χάραγμα
beast and the image of him, and if anyone receives the mark
3588 3686 846 5602 5281 3588 40 2076 5602
τοῦ ὀνόματος αὐτοῦ. 12 ὧδε ὑπομονὴ τῶν ἁγίων ἐστίν· ὧδε
of the name of it. Here (the) patience of the saints is; here

10 The same shall drink of the wine of the wrath of God, which is poured out without mixture into the cup of his indignation; and he shall be tormented with fire and brimstone in the presence of the holy angels, and in the presence of the Lamb:

11 And the smoke of their torment ascendeth up for ever and ever: and they have no rest day nor night, who worship the beast and his image, and whosoever receiveth the mark of his name.

12 Here is the patience of the saints; here (are) the (ones) keeping the commands of God, and the faith of Jesus.

3588 5083 3588 1785 3588 2316 2532 3588 4102 2424
οἱ τηροῦντες τὰς ἐντολὰς τοῦ Θεοῦ καὶ τὴν πίστιν Ἰησοῦ.
the (ones) keeping the commandments of God and the faith of Jesus.

12 Here is the patience of the saints: here (are) they that keep the commandments of God, and the faith of Jesus.

13 And I heard a voice out of Heaven saying to me, Write: Blessed (are) the dead, the (ones) dying in the Lord from now. Yes, says the Spirit, they shall rest from their labors,

2532 191 5456 1537 3588 3772 3004 3427
13. Καὶ ἤκουσα φωνῆς ἐκ τοῦ οὐρανοῦ λεγούσης μοι,
And I heard a voice out of Heaven saying to me,
1125 3107 3588 3498 3588 1722 2962 599 575
Γράψον, Μακάριοι οἱ νεκροὶ οἱ ἐν Κυρίῳ ἀποθνήσκοντες ἀπ'
Write, Blessed (are) the dead, those in (the) Lord dying from
737 3483 3004 3588 4151 2443 373 1537 3588 2873
ἄρτι. ναί, λέγει τὸ Πνεῦμα, ἵνα ἀναπαύσωνται ἐκ τῶν κόπων
now. Yes, says the Spirit, that they shall rest from the labors

13 And I heard a voice from heaven saying unto me, Write, Blessed (are) the dead which die in the Lord from henceforth: Yea, saith the Spirit, that they may rest from their labours;

Literal Translation | **Revelation 14:14** | *King James Version*

and their works follow with them.

846 3588 1161 2041 846 190 3326 846
αὐτῶν· τὰ δὲ ἔργα αὐτῶν ἀκολουθεῖ μετ' αὐτῶν.
of them; the and works of them follow with them.

and their works do follow them.

14. And I saw; and behold, a white cloud and on the cloud (One) sitting, like (the) Son of man, having on His head a golden crown, and in His hand a sharp sickle.

2532 1492 2532 2400 3507 3507 2532 1909 3588 3507
14. Καὶ εἶδον, καὶ ἰδοὺ, νεφέλη λευκή, καὶ ἐπὶ τὴν νεφέλην
And I saw, and behold! cloud A white, and on the cloud

2521 3664 5207 444 2192 1909 3588 2776
καθήμενος ὅμοιος υἱῷ ἀνθρώπου, ἔχων ἐπὶ τῆς κεφαλῆς
(One) sitting like (the) Son of man, having on the head

846 4735 5552 2532 1722 3588 5495 846 1407
αὐτοῦ στέφανον χρυσοῦν, καὶ ἐν τῇ χειρὶ αὐτοῦ δρέπανον
of him a crown of gold, and in the hand of him a sickle

3691
ὀξύ.
sharp.

14. And I looked, and behold a white cloud, and upon the cloud (one) sat like unto the Son of man, having on his head a golden crown, and in his hand a sharp sickle.

15 And another angel went forth out of the temple, crying in a great voice to the (One) sitting on the cloud, Send Your sickle and reap, because Your hour to reap has come, because the harvest of the earth has(become) withered.

16 And the (One) sitting on the cloud thrust His sickle onto the earth, and the earth was reaped.

2532 243 32 1831 1537 3588 3485 2896 1722
15 καὶ ἄλλος ἄγγελος ἐξῆλθεν ἐκ τοῦ ναοῦ, κράζων ἐν
And another angel went forth out of the temple, crying in

3173 5456 3588 2521 1909 3588 3507 3992 3588
μεγάλῃ φωνῇ τῷ καθημένῳ ἐπὶ τῆς νεφέλης, Πέμψον τὸ
a great voice to the (One) sitting on the cloud, Send the

1407 4675 2532 2325 3754 2064 4671 3588 5610 3588 2325
δρέπανόν σου καὶ θέρισον· ὅτι ἦλθε σοι ἡ ὥρα τοῦ θερίσαι,
sickle of You and reap; because came You the hour to reap,

3754 3583 3588 2326 3588 1093 2532 906 3588 2521
ὅτι ἐξηράνθη ὁ θερισμὸς τῆς γῆς. 16 καὶ ἔβαλεν ὁ καθήμενος
because was dried the harvest of the earth. And thrust the (One) sitting

1909 3588 3507 3588 1407 846 1909 3588 1093 2532
ἐπὶ τὴν νεφέλην τὸ δρέπανον αὐτοῦ ἐπὶ τὴν γῆν, καὶ
on the cloud the sickle of Him on the earth, and

2325 3588 1093
ἐθερίσθη ἡ γῆ.
was reaped the earth.

15 And another angel came out of the temple, crying with a loud voice to him that sat on the cloud, Thrust in thy sickle, and reap: for the time is come for thee to reap; for the harvest of the earth is ripe.

16 And he that sat on the cloud thrust in his sickle on the earth; and the earth was reaped.

17 And another angel went forth out of the temple in Heaven, he also having a sharp sickle.

18 And another angel went forth out of the altar having authority over the fire. And he spoke with a great cry to the one having the sharp sickle, saying, Send your sharp sickle and gather the clusters of the vine of the earth, because its grapes are ripened.

2532 243 32 1831 1537 3588 3485 3588 1722 3588
17. Καὶ ἄλλος ἄγγελος ἐξῆλθεν ἐκ τοῦ ναοῦ τοῦ ἐν τῷ
And another angel went forth out of the temple in

3772 2192 2532 846 1407 3691 2532 243 32
οὐρανῷ, ἔχων καὶ αὐτὸς δρέπανον ὀξύ. 18 καὶ ἄλλος ἄγγελος
Heaven, having also he a sickle sharp. And another angel

1831 1537 3588 2379 2192 1849 1909 3588 4443
ἐξῆλθεν ἐκ τοῦ θυσιαστηρίου, ἔχων ἐξουσίαν ἐπὶ τοῦ πυρός,
went forth out of the Altar, having authority over the fire,

2532 5455 2906 3173 3588 2192 3588 1407 3588 3691
καὶ ἐφώνησε κραυγῇ μεγάλῃ τῷ ἔχοντι τὸ δρέπανον τὸ ὀξὺ,
and he spoke cry with a great to him having the sickle sharp,

3004 3992 4675 3588 1407 3588 3691 2532 5166 3588
λέγων, Πέμψον σου τὸ δρέπανον τὸ ὀξὺ καὶ τρύγησον τοὺς
saying, Send of you the sickle sharp and gather the

1009 3588 288 3588 1093 3754 187 3588 4718
βότρυας τῆς ἀμπέλου τῆς γῆς, ὅτι ἤκμασαν αἱ σταφυλαὶ
clusters of the vine of the earth, because are ripened the grapes

846
αὐτῆς.
of it.

17 And another angel came out of the temple which is in heaven, he also having a sharp sickle.

18 And another angel came out from the altar, which had power over fire; and cried with a loud cry to him that had the sharp sickle, saying, Thrust in thy sharp sickle, and gather the clusters of the vine of the earth; for her grapes are fully ripe.

19 And the angel thrust his sickle into the earth and gathered the vine of the earth, and threw into the great winepress of the anger of God.

20 And the winepress was trodden outside the city, and blood went out of the winepress as far as the bridles of the horses, from a thousand six hundred stadia.

2532 906 3588 32 3588 1407 846 1519 3588 1093
19 καὶ ἔβαλεν ὁ ἄγγελος τὸ δρέπανον αὐτοῦ εἰς τὴν γῆν,
And thrust the angel the sickle of him into the earth,

2532 5166 3588 288 3588 1093 2532 906 1519 3588 3025
καὶ ἐτρύγησε τὴν ἄμπελον τῆς γῆς, καὶ ἔβαλεν εἰς τὴν ληνὸν
and gathered the vine of the earth, and threw into the winepress

3588 2372 3588 2316 3588 3173 2532 3961 3588 3025
τοῦ θυμοῦ τοῦ Θεοῦ τὸν μέγαλην. 20 καὶ ἐπατήθη ἡ ληνὸς
of the anger of God great. And was trodden the winepress

1854 3588 4172 2532 1831 129 1537 3588 3025 891 3588
ἔξω τῆς πόλεως, καὶ ἐξῆλθεν αἷμα ἐκ τῆς ληνοῦ ἄχρι τῶν
outside the city, and came forth blood out of the winepress as far as the

5469 3588 2462 575 4712 5507 1812
χαλινῶν τῶν ἵππων, ἀπὸ σταδίων χιλίων ἑξακοσίων.
bridles of the horses, from stadia a thousand six hundred.

19 And the angel thrust in his sickle into the earth, and gathered the vine of the earth, and cast (it) into the great winepress of the wrath of God.

20 And the winepress was trodden without the city, and blood came out of the winepress, even unto the horse bridles, by the space of a thousand (and) six hundred furlongs.

Literal Translation

Revelation 15

1. And I saw another sign in Heaven, great and marvelous: seven angels having the last seven plagues, because the anger of God was completed in them.

2 And I saw, as a glassy sea having been mixed with fire. And the (ones) overcoming the beast, and its image, and its mark, of the number of its name, (were) standing on the glassy sea, having harps of God.

3 And they sing the song of Moses the slave of God, and the song of the Lamb, saying, Great and marvelous (are) Your works, Lord God Almighty, righteous and true (are) Your ways, the King of the saints.

4 Who (will) not at all fear You, Lord, and glorify Your name? Because (You) only (are) holy. Because all the nations will come and will worship before You, because Your righteousnesses were revealed.

5. And after these things I saw; and behold! The temple of the tabernacle of the testimony in Heaven was opened!

6 And the seven angels having the seven plagues came forth out of the temple, having been clothed in clean and bright linen, and golden bands having been girded around the breasts.

7 And one of the four living creatures gave to the seven angels seven golden bowls filled (with) the anger of God living to the ages of the ages.

8 And

Revelation 15

2532 1492 243 4592 1722 3588 3772 3173 2532 2298
1. Καὶ εἶδον ἄλλο σημεῖον ἐν τῷ οὐρανῷ μέγα καὶ θαυμα-
And I saw another sign in Heaven great and marvelous
32 2033 2192 4127 2033 3588 2078
στόν, ἀγγέλους ἑπτὰ ἔχοντας πληγὰς ἑπτὰ τὰς ἐσχάτας,
angels seven having plagues seven the last,
3754 1722 846 5055 3588 2372 3588 2316
ὅτι ἐν αὐταῖς ἐτελέσθη ὁ θυμὸς τοῦ Θεοῦ.
because in them was completed the anger of God.

2532 1492 5613 2281 5193 3396 4442
2. Καὶ εἶδον ὡς θάλασσαν ὑαλίνην μεμιγμένην πυρί,
And I saw as a sea glassy having been mixed with fire,
2532 3588 3528 1537 3588 2342 2532 1537 3588 1504 846
καὶ τοὺς νικῶντας ἐκ τοῦ θηρίου καὶ ἐκ τῆς εἰκόνος αὐτοῦ
and the (ones) overcoming of the beast and of the image of it
2532 1537 3588 5480 846 1537 3588 706 3588 3686
καὶ ἐκ τοῦ χαράγματος αὐτοῦ, ἐκ τοῦ ἀριθμοῦ τοῦ ὀνόματος
and of the mark of it, of the number of the name
846 2476 1909 3588 2281 3588 5193 2192
αὐτοῦ, ἑστῶτας ἐπὶ τὴν θάλασσαν τὴν ὑαλίνην, ἔχοντας
of it, standing on the sea glassy, having
2788 3588 2316 2532 103 3588 5603 3475 3588 1401
κιθάρας τοῦ Θεοῦ. 3 καὶ ᾄδουσι τὴν ᾠδὴν Μωσέως τοῦ δούλου
harps of God. And they sing the song of Moses the slave
3588 2316 2532 3588 5603 3588 721 3004 3173
τοῦ Θεοῦ, καὶ τὴν ᾠδὴν τοῦ ἀρνίου, λέγοντες, Μεγάλα
of God, and the song of the Lamb, saying, Great
2532 2298 3588 2041 4675 2962 3588 2316 3588 3841
καὶ θαυμαστὰ τὰ ἔργα σου, Κύριε ὁ Θεὸς ὁ παντοκράτωρ·
and marvelous the works of You, Lord God Almighty;
1342 2532 228 3588 3598 4675 3588 935 3588 40 5101
δίκαιαι καὶ ἀληθιναὶ αἱ ὁδοί σου, ὁ βασιλεὺς τῶν ἁγιῶν. 4 τίς
righteous and true the ways of You, the King of the saints. Who
3756 3361 5399 1161 2962 2532 1392 3588 3686 4675 3754
οὐ μὴ φοβηθῇ σε, Κύριε, καὶ δοξάσῃ τὸ ὄνομά σου; ὅτι
in no way fear You, Lord, and glorify the name of You? For
3441 3741 3754 3956 3588 1484 2240 2532 4352
μόνος ὅσιος· ὅτι πάντα τὰ ἔθνη ἥξουσι καὶ προσκυνή-
(You) only (are) holy; because all the nations will come and will worship
1799 4675 3754 3588 1345 4675 5319
σουσιν ἐνώπιόν σου, ὅτι τὰ δικαιώματά σου ἐφανερώθησαν.
before You, because the righteousnesses of You were revealed.

2532 3326 5023 1492 2532 2400 455 3588 3485 3588 4633
5. Καὶ μετὰ ταῦτα εἶδον, καὶ ἰδού, ἠνοίγη ὁ ναὸς τῆς σκηνῆς
And after these things I saw, and behold! was opened The temple of the tent
3588 3142 1722 3588 3772 2532 1831 3588 2033 32
τοῦ μαρτυρίου ἐν τῷ οὐρανῷ· 6 καὶ ἐξῆλθον οἱ ἑπτὰ ἄγγελοι
of the testimony in Heaven; and came forth the seven angels
2192 3588 2033 4127 1537 3588 3485 1746 3043
ἔχοντες τὰς ἑπτὰ πληγὰς ἐκ τοῦ ναοῦ, ἐνδεδυμένοι λίνον
having the seven plagues out of the temple, being clothed (in) linen
2513 2532 2986 2532 4024 4012 3588 4738
καθαρὸν καὶ λαμπρόν, καὶ περιεζωσμένοι περὶ τὰ στήθη
clean and bright, and having been girded around the breasts
2223 5552 2532 1520 1537 3588 5064 2226 1325 3588
ζώνας χρυσᾶς. 7 καὶ ἓν ἐκ τῶν τεσσάρων ζῴων ἔδωκε τοῖς
(with) girdles of gold. And one of the four living creatures gave to the
2033 32 2033 5357 5552 1073 3588 2372
ἑπτὰ ἀγγέλοις ἑπτὰ φιάλας χρυσᾶς γεμούσας τοῦ θυμοῦ
seven angels seven bowls of gold filled of the anger
3588 2316 3588 2198 1519 3588 165 3588 165 2532
τοῦ Θεοῦ τοῦ ζῶντος εἰς τοὺς αἰῶνας τῶν αἰώνων. 8 καὶ
of God the living to the ages of the ages. And

King James Version

Revelation 15

1. And I saw another sign in heaven, great and marvellous, seven angels having the seven last plagues; for in them is filled up the wrath of God.

2 And I saw as it were a sea of glass mingled with fire: and them that had gotten the victory over the beast, and over his image, and over his mark, (and) over the number of his name, stand on the sea of glass, having the harps of God.

3 And they sing the song of Moses the servant of God, and the song of the Lamb, saying, Great and marvellous (are) thy works, Lord God Almighty; just and true (are) thy ways, thou King of saints.

4 Who shall not fear thee, O Lord, and glorify thy name? for (thou) only (art) holy: for all nations shall come and worship before thee; for thy judgments are made manifest.

5. And after that I looked, and, behold, the temple of the tabernacle of the testimony in heaven was opened:

6 And the seven angels came out of the temple, having the seven plagues, clothed in pure and white linen, and having their breasts girded with golden girdles.

7 And one of the four beasts gave unto the seven angels seven golden vials full of the wrath of God, who liveth for ever and ever.

8 And

Literal Translation

the temple was filled (with) the smoke of the glory of God, and (with) His power. And no one was able to enter into the temple until the seven plagues of the seven angels should be completed.

Revelation 16:1

1072 3588 3485 2586 1537 3588 1391 3588 2316 2532 1537 3588
ἐγεμίσθη ὁ ναὸς καπνοῦ ἐκ τῆς δόξης τοῦ Θεοῦ, καὶ ἐκ τῆς
was filled the temple of smoke of the glory of God, and of the

1411 846 2532 3762 1410 1525 1519 3588 3485
δυνάμεως αὐτοῦ· καὶ οὐδεὶς ἠδύνατο εἰσελθεῖν εἰς τὸν ναόν,
power of Him; and no one was able to enter into the temple,

891 5055 3588/2033 4127 3588 2033 32
ἄχρι τελεσθῶσιν αἱ ἑπτὰ πληγαὶ τῶν ἑπτὰ ἀγγέλων.
until should be finished the seven plagues of the seven angels.

King James Version

the temple was filled with smoke from the glory of God, and from his power; and no man was able to enter into the temple, till the seven plagues of the seven angels were fulfilled.

Revelation 16

1. And I heard a great voice out of the temple saying to the seven angels: Go and pour out the bowls of the anger of God onto the earth.

2532 191 3173 5456 1537 3588 3485 3004 3588
1. Καὶ ἤκουσα φωνῆς μεγάλης ἐκ τοῦ ναοῦ, λεγούσης τοῖς
And I heard voice a great out of the temple, saying to the

2033 32 5217 2532 1632 3588 5357 3588 2372
ἑπτὰ ἀγγέλοις, Ὑπάγετε, καὶ ἐκχέατε τὰς φιάλας τοῦ θυμοῦ
seven angels, Go, and pour out the bowls of the anger

3588 2316 1519 3588 1093
τοῦ Θεοῦ εἰς τὴν γῆν.
of God onto the earth.

1. And I heard a great voice out of the temple saying to the seven angels, Go your ways, and pour out the vials of the wrath of God upon the earth.

2 And the first went away and poured out his bowl onto the earth. And it became a bad and evil sore onto the men, the (ones) having the mark of the beast, and the (ones) worshiping its image.

2532 565 3588 4413 2532 1632 3588 5357 846 1909
2. Καὶ ἀπῆλθεν ὁ πρῶτος καὶ ἐξέχεε τὴν φιάλην αὐτοῦ ἐπὶ
And went away the first and poured out the bowl of him on

3588 1093 2532 1096 1688 2556 2532 4190 1519 3588
τὴν γῆν· καὶ ἐγένετο ἕλκος κακὸν καὶ πονηρὸν ἐπὶ τοὺς
the earth; and it became sore a bad and evil on the

444 3588 2192 3588 5480 3588 2342 2532 3588
ἀνθρώπους τοὺς ἔχοντας τὸ χάραγμα τοῦ θηρίου, καὶ τοὺς
men the (ones) having the mark of the beast, and the (ones)

3588 1504 846 4352
τῇ εἰκόνι αὐτοῦ προσκυνοῦντας.
the image of him worshiping.

2 And the first went, and poured out his vial upon the earth; and there fell a noisome and grievous sore upon the men which had the mark of the beast, and (upon) them which worshipped his image.

3 And the second angel poured out his bowl onto the sea. And it became blood, as of a dead one, and every soul of life died in the sea.

2532 3588 1208 32 1632 3588 5357 846 1519 3588
3. Καὶ ὁ δεύτερος ἄγγελος ἐξέχεε τὴν φιάλην αὐτοῦ εἰς τὴν
And the second angel poured out the bowl of him onto the

2281 2532 1096 129 5613 3498 2532 3956 5590
θάλασσαν· καὶ ἐγένετο αἷμα ὡς νεκροῦ, καὶ πᾶσα ψυχὴ
sea; and it became blood as of a dead one, and every soul

2198 599 1722 3588 2281
ζῶσα ἀπέθανεν ἐν τῇ θαλάσσῃ.
living died in the sea.

3 And the second angel poured out his vial upon the sea; and it became as the blood of a dead (man): and every living soul died in the sea.

4 And the third angel poured out his bowl onto the rivers, and onto the fountains of the waters; and it became blood.
5 And I heard the angel of the waters saying, You are righteous, Lord, the (One) who is, and who was, and who will be, because You judged these things,
6 since they poured out the blood of (the) saints and of (the) prophets; and You gave blood to them to drink, for they are deserving.
7 And I heard another out of the altar saying, Yes, Lord God Almighty,

2532 3588 5154 32 1632 3588 5357 846 1519 3588
4. Καὶ ὁ τρίτος ἄγγελος ἐξέχεε τὴν φιάλην αὐτοῦ εἰς τοὺς
And the third angel poured out the bowl of him onto the

4215 2532 1519 3588 4077 3588 5204 2532 1096 129
ποταμοὺς καὶ εἰς τὰς πηγὰς τῶν ὑδάτων· καὶ ἐγένετο αἷμα.
rivers and onto the fountains of the waters; and it became blood.

2532 191 3588 32 3588 5204 3004 1342
5 καὶ ἤκουσα τοῦ ἀγγέλου τῶν ὑδάτων λέγοντος, Δίκαιος,
And I heard the angel of the waters saying, Righteous,

2962 1488 3588 5607 2532/3588/2258/2532/3588 3741 3754 5023
Κύριε, εἶ, ὁ ὢν καὶ ὁ ἦν καὶ ὁ ἐσόμενος, ὅτι ταῦτα
Lord, You are the (One) being, and who was and who will be, because these things

2919 3754 129 40 2532 4396 1632 2532 129
ἔκρινας· 6 ὅτι αἷμα ἁγίων καὶ προφητῶν ἐξέχεαν, καὶ αἷμα
You judged; since (the) blood of saints and prophets they poured out, and blood

846 1325 4095 514 1063 1526 2532 191 243 1537
αὐτοῖς ἔδωκας πιεῖν· ἄξιοί γάρ εἰσι. 7 καὶ ἤκουσα ἄλλου ἐκ
of them You gave to drink; deserving for they are. And I heard another out of

3588 2379 3004 3483 2962 3588 2316 3588 341
τοῦ θυσιαστηρίου λέγοντος, Ναί, Κύριε ὁ Θεὸς ὁ παντοκράτωρ,
the altar saying, Yes, Lord God Almighty,

4 And the third angel poured out his vial upon the rivers and fountains of waters; and they became blood.
5 And I heard the angel of the waters say, Thou art righteous, O Lord, which art, and wast, and shalt be, because thou hast judged thus.
6 For they have shed the blood of saints and prophets, and thou hast given them blood to drink; for they are worthy.
7 And I heard another out of the altar say, Even so, Lord God Almighty,

Literal Translation **Revelation 16:8** *King James Version*

Your judgments (are) true and righteous.

228 2532 1342 3588 2920 4675
ἀληθιναὶ καὶ δίκαιαι αἱ κρίσεις σου.
true and righteous the judgments of You.

true and righteous (are) thy judgments.

8. And the fourth angel poured out his bowl onto the sun. And it was given to him to burn men with fire.

2532 3588 5067 32 1632 3588 5357 846 1909 3588
8. Καὶ ὁ τέταρτος ἄγγελος ἐξέχεε τὴν φιάλην αὐτοῦ ἐπὶ τὸν
And the fourth angel poured out the bowl of him on the
2246 2532 1325 846 2739 3588 444 1722 4442
ἥλιον· καὶ ἐδόθη αὐτῷ καυματίσαι τοὺς ἀνθρώπους ἐν πυρί.
sun; and it was given to it to burn men with fire.

8. And the fourth angel poured out his vial upon the sun; and power was given unto him to scorch men with fire.

9 And men were burned with great heat. And they blasphemed the name of God, the (One) having authority over these plagues and they did not repent to give Him glory.

2532 2739 3588 444 2738 3173 2532 987
9 καὶ ἐκαυματίσθησαν οἱ ἄνθρωποι καῦμα μέγα, καὶ ἐβλασφή-
And were burned men (with) heat great, and they blas-
3588 3686 3588 2316 3588 2192 1849 1909 3588
μησαν τὸ ὄνομα τοῦ Θεοῦ τοῦ ἔχοντος ἐξουσίαν ἐπὶ τὰς
phemed the name God the (One) having authority over
4127 3778 2532 3756 3340 1325 846 1391
πληγὰς ταύτας, καὶ οὐ μετενόησαν δοῦναι αὐτῷ δόξαν.
plagues these, and not they repented to give Him glory.

9 And men were scorched with great heat, and blasphemed the name of God, which hath power over these plagues: and they repented not to give him glory.

10 And the fifth angel poured out his bowl onto the throne of the beast. And its kingdom became darkened; and they gnawed their tongues from the pain.

2532 3588 3991 32 1632 3588 5357 846 1909 3588
10. Καὶ ὁ πέμπτος ἄγγελος ἐξέχεε τὴν φιάλην αὐτοῦ ἐπὶ τὸν
And the fifth angel poured out the bowl of him onto the
2362 3588 2342 2532 1096 3588 932 846 4656
θρόνον τοῦ θηρίου· καὶ ἐγένετο ἡ βασιλεία αὐτοῦ ἐσκοτω-
throne of the beast; and became the kingdom of it darkened;
2532 3145 3588 1100 846 1537 3588 4192
μένη· καὶ ἐμασσῶντο τὰς γλώσσας αὐτῶν ἐκ τοῦ πόνου,
and they gnawed the tongue of them from the pain;

10 And the fifth angel poured out his vial upon the seat of the beast; and his kingdom was full of darkness; and they gnawed their tongues for pain,

11 And they blasphemed the God of Heaven, from their pains and from their sores. And they did not repent of their works.

2532 987 3588 2316 3588 3772 1537 3588 4192
11 καὶ ἐβλασφήμησαν τὸν Θεὸν τοῦ οὐρανοῦ ἐκ τῶν πόνων
and they blasphemed the God of Heaven from the pains
846 2532 1537 3588 1668 846 2532 3756 3340 1537 3588
αὐτῶν καὶ ἐκ τῶν ἑλκῶν αὐτῶν, καὶ οὐ μετενόησαν ἐκ τῶν
of them and from the sores of them, and not they repented from the
2041 846
ἔργων αὐτῶν.
works of them.

11 And blasphemed the God of heaven because of their pains and their sores, and repented not of their deeds.

12. And the sixth angel poured out his bowl onto the great river Euphrates, and its water was dried up so that might be prepared the way of the kings from (the) rising of (the) sun.

2532 3588 1623 32 1632 3588 5357 846 1909 3588
12. Καὶ ὁ ἕκτος ἄγγελος ἐξέχεε τὴν φιάλην αὐτοῦ ἐπὶ τὸν
And the sixth angel poured out the bowl of him onto the
4215 3588 3173 3588 2166 2532 3583 3588 5204
ποταμὸν τὸν μέγαν τὸν Εὐφράτην· καὶ ἐξηράνθη τὸ ὕδωρ
river great Euphrates, and was dried up the water
846 2443 2090 3588 3598 3588 935 3588 575
αὐτοῦ, ἵνα ἑτοιμασθῇ ἡ ὁδὸς τῶν βασιλέων τῶν ἀπὸ
of it, that might be prepared the way of the kings from
395 2246
ἀνατολῶν ἡλίου.
(the) rising of (the) sun.

12. And the sixth angel poured out his vial upon the great river Euphrates; and the water thereof was dried up, that the way of the kings of the east might be prepared.

13 And I saw three unclean spirits like frogs (come) out of the mouth of the dragon, and out of the mouth of the beast, and out of the mouth of the false prophet.

2532 1492 1537 3588 4750 3588 1404
13 καὶ εἶδον ἐκ τοῦ στόματος τοῦ δράκοντος,
And I saw out of the mouth of the dragon,
2532 1537 3588 4750 3588 2342 2532 1537 3588 4750 3588
καὶ ἐκ τοῦ στόματος τοῦ θηρίου, καὶ ἐκ τοῦ στόματος τοῦ
and out of the mouth of the beast, and out of the mouth of the
5578 4151 5140 169 3664 944
ψευδοπροφήτου, πνεύματα τρία ἀκάθαρτα ὅμοια βατρά-
false prophet, spirits three unclean like frogs;
χοις·

13 And I saw three unclean spirits like frogs (come) out of the mouth of the dragon, and out of the mouth of the beast, and out of the mouth of the false prophet.

14 For they are spirits of demons doing signs, (which) go forth to the kings of the earth, even of the whole habitable world, to assemble them to the war of that day,

1526 1063 4151 1142 4160 4592 3739
14 εἰσιν γὰρ πνεύματα δαιμόνων ποιοῦντα σημεῖα, ἃ
they are For spirits of demons doing signs, which
1607 1909 3588 935 3588 1093 2532 3588 3625
ἐκπορεύεται ἐπὶ τοὺς βασιλεῖς τῆς γῆς καὶ τῆς οἰκουμένης
go forth to the kings of the earth even of the habitable world
3650 4863 846 1519 3588 4171 3588 2250 1565
ὅλης, συναγαγεῖν αὐτοὺς εἰς τὸν πόλεμον τῆς ἡμέρας ἐκείνης
whole, to assemble them to the war of day that

14 For they are the spirits of devils, working miracles, (which) go forth unto the kings of the earth and of the whole world, to gather them to the battle of that great day

Literal Translation **Revelation 16:15** ***King James Version***

the great (Day) of God Almighty.
15 Behold, I am coming as a thief. Blessed (is) the (one) watching and keeping his garments, that he does not walk naked, and they may see his shame.

16 And He assembled them in the place having been called in Hebrew, Armageddon.

17. And the seventh angel poured out his bowl into the air, and a great voice came from the throne from the temple of Heaven, saying, It has happened!
18 And voices and thunders and lightnings occurred. And a great earthquake occurred, such as did not occur since man came into being on the earth, such a huge earthquake, so great!

19 And the great city came to be into three parts, and the cities of the nations fell. And Babylon the great was remembered before God, to give to her the cup of the wine of the anger of His wrath.

20 And every island fled away, and mountains were not found.

21 And a great hail, as the size of a talent, came down out of the heaven upon men. And men blasphemed God from the plague of the hail, because its plague is exceedingly great.

3588 3173 3588 2316 3588 3841 2400
τῆς μεγάλης τοῦ Θεοῦ τοῦ παντοκράτορος. 15 [Ἰδού,
the great (Day) of God the Almighty. Behold!
2064 5613 3107 2812 3588 1127 2532 5083 3588
ἔρχομαι ὡς κλέπτης. μακάριος ὁ γρηγορῶν καὶ τηρῶν τὰ
I am coming as a thief; blessed (is) the (one) watching and keeping the
2440 846 2443 3361 1131 4043 2532 991 3588
ἱμάτια αὐτοῦ, ἵνα μὴ γυμνὸς περιπατῇ, καὶ βλέπωσι τὴν
garments of him, that not naked he may walk, and they may see the
808 846 2532 4863 846 1519 3588 5117
ἀσχημοσύνην αὐτοῦ.] 16 καὶ συνήγαγεν αὐτοὺς εἰς τὸν τόπον
shame of him. And he assembled them in the place
3588 2564 1447 717
τὸν καλούμενον Ἑβραϊστὶ Ἀρμαγεδδών.
having been called in Hebrew Armageddon.
2532 3588 1442 32 1632 3588 5357 846 1519 3588
17. Καὶ ὁ ἕβδομος ἄγγελος ἐξέχεε τὴν φιάλην αὐτου εἰς τὸν
And the seventh angel poured out the bowl of him into the
109 2532 1831 5456 3173 575 3588 3485 3588 3772
ἀέρα· καὶ ἐξῆλθε φωνὴ μεγάλη ἀπὸ τοῦ ναοῦ τοῦ οὐρανοῦ,
air; and came a voice great from the temple of Heaven,
575 3588 2362 3004 1096 2532 1096 5456 2532
ἀπὸ τοῦ θρόνου, λέγουσα, Γέγονε. 18 καὶ ἐγένοντο φωναὶ καὶ
from the throne, saying, It has happened. And occurred voices and
1027 2532 796 2532 4578 1096 3173 3634 3756
βρονταί καὶ ἀστραπαί, καὶ σεισμὸς ἐγένετο μέγας, οἷος οὐκ
thunders and lightnings, and an earthquake occurred great, such as not
1096 575 3739 3588 444 1096 1909 3588 1093 5082
ἐγένετο ἀφ' οὗ οἱ ἄνθρωποι ἐγένοντο ἐπὶ τῆς γῆς, τηλι-
did occur from when man came into being on the earth, such a
4578 3779 3173 2532 1096 3588 4172 3588 3173
κοῦτος σεισμός, οὕτω μέγας. 19 καὶ ἐγένετο ἡ πόλις ἡ μεγάλη
huge earthquake, so great. And came to be the city great
1519 5140 3313 2532 3588 4172 3588 1484 4098 2532 897
εἰς τρία μέρη, καὶ αἱ πόλεις τῶν ἐθνῶν ἔπεσον· καὶ Βαβυλὼν
into three parts, and the cities of the nations fell; and Babylon
3588 3173 3415 1799 3588 2316 1325 846 3588 4221
ἡ μεγάλη ἐμνήσθη ἐνώπιον τοῦ Θεοῦ, δοῦναι αὐτῇ τὸ ποτή-
the great was remembered before God, to give to her the cup
3588 3631 3588 2372 3588 3709 846 2532 3956 3520
ριον τοῦ οἴνου τοῦ θυμοῦ τῆς ὀργῆς αὐτοῦ. 20 καὶ πᾶσα νῆσος
of the wine of the anger of the wrath of Him. And every island
5343 2532 3735 3756 2147 2532 5464 3173 5613 5006
ἔφυγε, καὶ ὄρη οὐχ εὑρέθησαν. 21 καὶ χάλαζα μεγάλη, ὡς ταλαν-
fled, and mountains not were found. And a hail great, as talent-
2597 1537 3588 3772 1909 3588 444 2532
τιαία, καταβαίνει ἐκ τοῦ οὐρανοῦ ἐπὶ τοὺς ἀνθρώπους· καὶ
sized, comes down out of the heaven on man; and
987 3588 444 3588 2316 1537 3588 4127
ἐβλασφήμησαν οἱ ἄνθρωποι τὸν Θεὸν ἐκ τῆς πληγῆς
blasphemed men God from the plague
3588 5464 3754 3173 2076 3588 4127 846 4970
τῆς χαλάζης· ὅτι μεγάλη ἐστὶν ἡ πληγὴ αὐτῆς σφόδρα.
of the hail, because great is the plague of it exceedingly.

of God Almighty.
15 Behold, I come as a thief. Blessed (is) he that watcheth, and keepeth his garments, lest he walk naked, and they see his shame.

16 And he gathered them together into a place called in the Hebrew tongue Armageddon.

17. And the seventh angel poured out his vial into the air; and there came a great voice out of the temple of heaven, from the throne, saying, It is done.
18 And there were voices, and thunders, and lightnings; and there was a great earthquake, such as was not since men were upon the earth, so mighty an earthquake, (and) so great.

19 And the great city was divided into three parts, and the cities of the nations fell: and great Babylon came in remembrance before God, to give unto her the cup of the wine of the fierceness of his wrath.

20 And every island fled away, and the mountains were not found.
21 And there fell upon men a great hail out of heaven, (every stone) about the weight of a talent: and men blasphemed God because of the plague of the hail; for the plague thereof was exceeding great.

Revelation 17

1. And one of the seven angels having the seven bowls came and spoke with me, saying to me, Come, I will show

2532 2064 1520 1537 3588 2033 32 3588 2192 3588
1. Καὶ ἦλθεν εἷς ἐκ τῶν ἑπτὰ ἀγγέλων τῶν ἐχόντων τὰς
And came one of the seven angels having the
2033 5357 2532 2980 3326 1700 3004 3427 1204 1166
ἑπτὰ φιάλας, καὶ ἐλάλησε μετ' ἐμοῦ, λέγων μοι, Δεῦρο, δείξω
seven bowls, and spoke with me, saying to me, Come, I will show

1. And there came one of the seven angels which had the seven vials, and talked with me, saying unto me, Come hither; I will shew

Literal Translation | **Revelation 17:2** | *King James Version*

you the judgment of the great harlot sitting on the many waters,

2 with whom the kings of the earth committed fornication, and the (ones) inhabiting the earth became drunk from the wine of her fornication.
3 And he carried me away into a desert, by (the) Spirit. And I saw a woman sitting on a scarlet beast, filled with names of blasphemy, having seven heads and ten horns.

4 And the woman was clothed (in) purple and scarlet, and having been gilded with gold and precious stone and pearls, having a golden cup in her hand, filled with abominations and uncleanness of her fornication.

5 And on her forehead was a name having been written: MYSTERY, BABYLON THE GREAT. THE MOTHER OF THE HARLOTS AND OF THE ABOMINATIONS OF THE EARTH.
6 And I saw the woman being drunk from the blood of the saints, and from the blood of the witnesses of Jesus. And I marveled, seeing her with a great marveling.
7. And the angel said to me, Why did you marvel? I will tell you the mystery of the woman, and of the beast sustaining her, the one having the seven heads and the ten horns.

8 The beast which you saw was, and is not, and is about to come up out of the abyss, and goes to perdition. And those dwelling on the earth will marvel, the ones whose names have not been written on the Scroll

4671 3588 2917 3588 4204 3588 3173 3588 2521 1909 3588
σοι τὸ κρίμα τῆς πόρνης τῆς μεγάλης, τῆς καθημένης ἐπὶ τῶν
you the judgment of the harlot great, sitting on the
5204 3588 4183 3326 3739 4203 3588 935 3588
ὑδάτων τῶν πολλῶν· 2 μεθ' ἧς ἐπόρνευσαν οἱ βασιλεῖς τῆς
waters many; with whom do fornication the kings of the
1093 2532 3184 1537 3588 3631 3588 4202 846 3588
γῆς, καὶ ἐμεθύσθησαν ἐκ τοῦ οἴνου τῆς πορνείας αὐτῆς οἱ
earth, and became drunk from the wine of the fornication of her those
2730 3588 1093 2532 667 3165 1519 2048 1722
κατοικοῦντες τὴν γῆν. 3 καὶ ἀπήνεγκέ με εἰς ἔρημον ἐν
inhabiting the earth. And he carried away me into a desert by
4151 2532 1492 1135 2521 1909 2342 2847
Πνεύματι· καὶ εἶδον γυναῖκα καθημένην ἐπὶ θηρίον κόκκινον,
(the) Spirit; and I saw a woman sitting on beast a scarlet,
1073 3686 988 2192 2776 2033 2532 2768
γέμον ὀνομάτων βλασφημίας, ἔχον κεφαλὰς ἑπτὰ καὶ κέρατα
full of names of blasphemy, having heads seven and horns
1176 2532 3588 1135 2258 4016 4209 2532 2847
δέκα. 4 καὶ ἡ γυνὴ ἦν περιβεβλημένη πορφύρᾳ καὶ κοκκίνῳ,
ten. And the woman was having been clothed (in) purple and scarlet,
2532 5558 5557 2532 3037 5093 2532 3135
καὶ κεχρυσωμένη χρυσῷ καὶ λίθῳ τιμίῳ καὶ μαργαρίταις,
and having been gilded with gold and stone precious and pearls,
2192 5552 4221 1722 3588 5495 846 1073 946
ἔχουσα χρυσοῦν ποτήριον ἐν τῇ χειρὶ αὐτῆς, γέμον βδε-
having a golden cup in the hand of her, full of abom-
2532 168 4202 846 2532 1909 3588
λυγμάτων καὶ ἀκαθάρτητος πορνείας αὐτῆς, 5 καὶ ἐπὶ τὸ
inations and uncleanness of (the) fornication of her, and on the
3359 846 3686 1125 3466 897
μέτωπον αὐτῆς ὄνομα γεγραμμένον, Μυστήριον, Βαβυλὼν
forehead of her a name having been written, MYSTERY, BABYLON
3588 3173 3588 3384 3588 4204 2532 3588 946 3588
ἡ μεγάλη, ἡ μήτηρ τῶν πορνῶν καὶ τῶν βδελυγμάτων τῆς
THE GREAT, the Mother of the Harlots and of the abominations of the
1093 2532 1492 3588 1135 3184 1537 3588 129 3588
γῆς. 6 καὶ εἶδον τὴν γυναῖκα μεθύουσαν ἐκ τοῦ αἵματος τῶν
earth. And I saw the woman being drunk from the blood of the
40 2532 1537 3588 129 3588 3144 2424 2532
ἁγίων, καὶ ἐκ τοῦ αἵματος τῶν μαρτύρων Ἰησοῦ. καὶ
saints, and from the blood of the witnesses of Jesus. And
2296 1492 846 2295 3173 2532 2036 3427 3588
ἐθαύμασα, ἰδὼν αὐτήν, θαῦμα μέγα. 7 καὶ εἶπέ μοι ὁ
I marveled, seeing her, marvel a great. And said to me the
32 1302 2296 1473 4671 2046 3588 3466 3588
ἄγγελος, Διατί ἐθαύμασας; ἐγώ σοι ἐρῶ τὸ μυστήριον τῆς
angel, Why did you marvel? I you will tell the mystery of the
1135 2532 3588 2342 3588 941 846 3588
γυναικός, καὶ τοῦ θηρίου τοῦ βαστάζοντος αὐτήν, τοῦ
woman, and of the beast sustaining her, the (one)
2192 3588 2033 2776 2532 3588 1176 2768 3588 2342 3739
ἔχοντος τὰς ἑπτὰ κεφαλὰς καὶ τὰ δέκα κέρατα· 8 τὸ θηρίον, ὃ
having the seven heads and the ten horns. The beast, which
1492 2258 2532 3756 2076 2532 3195 305 1537 3588 12
εἶδες, ἦν, καὶ οὐκ ἔστι, καὶ μέλλει ἀναβαίνειν ἐκ τῆς ἀβύσσου,
you saw, was, and not is, and is about to come up from the abyss,
2532 1519 684 5217 2532 2296 3588 2730
καὶ εἰς ἀπώλειαν ὑπάγειν. καὶ θαυμάσονται οἱ κατοικοῦντες
and to perdition goes. And will marvel those dwelling
1909 3588 1093 3739 3756 1125 3588 3686 1909 3588 975
ἐπὶ τῆς γῆς, ὧν οὐ γέγραπται τὰ ὀνόματα ἐπὶ τὸ βιβλίον
on the earth, of whom not has been written the names on the Scroll

unto thee the judgment of the great whore that sitteth upon many waters:
2 With whom the kings of the earth have committed fornication, and the inhabitants of the earth have been made drunk with the wine of her fornication.
3 So he carried me away in the spirit into the wilderness: and I saw a woman sit upon a scarlet coloured beast, full of names of blasphemy, having seven heads and ten horns.

4 And the woman was arrayed in purple and scarlet colour, and decked with gold and precious stones and pearls, having a golden cup in her hand full of abominations and filthiness of her fornication:

5 And upon her forehead (was) a name written, MYSTERY, BABYLON THE GREAT, THE MOTHER OF HARLOTS AND ABOMINATIONS OF THE EARTH.
6 And I saw the woman drunken with the blood of the saints, and with the blood of the martyrs of Jesus: and when I saw her, I wondered with great admiration.
7. And the angel said unto me, Wherefore didst thou marvel? I will tell thee the mystery of the woman, and of the beast that carrieth her, which hath the seven heads and ten horns.

8 The beast that thou sawest was, and is not; and shall ascend out of the bottomless pit, and go into perdition: and they that dwell on the earth shall wonder, whose names were not written in the book

Literal Translation

of Life from (the) foundation of the world, seeing the beast, that it was a thing, and is not, yet now is.
9 Here (is) the mind having wisdom: the seven heads are seven mountains, where the woman sits on them.

10 And the kings are seven. The five fell, and the one is, (and) the other has not yet come. And when he does come, he must remain a little.
11 And the beast which was, and is not, even he is the eighth, and is of the seven, and goes to perdition.
12 And the ten horns you saw are ten kings who have not yet received a kingdom, but will receive authority as kings one hour with the beast.

13 These have one mind, and their power and authority they shall give up to the beast.

14 These will make war with the Lamb, and the Lamb will overcome them, because He is Lord of lords and King of kings, and the ones with Him (are the) called and elect and faithful ones.
15. And he says to me, The waters which you saw, where the harlot sits, are peoples and crowds and nations and tongues.
16 And the ten horns which you saw on the beast, these will hate the harlot, and will make her (to be) laid waste and naked. And they will eat her flesh, and will burn her down with fire.
17 For God gave into their hearts to do His mind, and to act in one mind, and to give their kingdom

Revelation 17:9

3588 2222 575 2602 2889 991 3588 2342 3739
τῆς ζωῆς ἀπὸ καταβολῆς κόσμου, βλέποντες τὸ θηρίον ὅ,
of Life from (the) foundation of (the) world, seeing the beast that,
5100 2258 2532 3756 2076 2539 2076 5602/3588/3563/3588/2192 4678
τι ἦν, καὶ οὐκ ἔστι, καίπερ εστιν. 9 ὧδε ὁ νοῦς ὁ ἔχων σοφίαν.
a thing it was, and not is, although it is. Here (is) the mind having wisdom.
2033 2776 3735 1526 2033 3699 3588 1135 2521 1909
αἱ ἑπτά κεφαλαὶ ὄρη εἰσὶν ἑπτά, ὅπου ἡ γυνὴ κάθηται ἐπ'
The seven heads mountains are seven, where the woman sits on
846 2532 935 2033 1526 3588 4002 4098 2532 3588
αὐτῶν. καὶ βασιλεῖς ἑπτά εἰσιν· 10 οἱ πέντε ἔπεσον, καὶ ὁ
them. And kings seven are; the five fell, and the
1520 2076 3588 243 3768 2064 2532 3752 2064 3641 846 1163
εἷς ἔστιν, ὁ ἄλλος οὔπω ἦλθε· καὶ, ὅταν ἔλθῃ, ὀλίγον αὐτὸν δεῖ
one is, the other not yet come; and, when he comes, a little he must
3306 2532 3588 2342 /739/2258/2532/3756/2076 2532 846 3590
μεῖναι. 11 καὶ τὸ θηρίον ὃ ἦν, καὶ οὐκ ἔστι, καὶ αὐτὸς ὄγδοός
remain. And the beast which was, and not is, even he eighth
2076 2532 1537 3588 2033 2076 2532 1519 684 5217 2532 3588
ἐστι, καὶ ἐκ τῶν ἑπτά ἐστι, καὶ εἰς ἀπώλειαν ὑπάγει. 12 καὶ τὰ
is, and of the seven is, and to perdition goes. And the
1176 2768 3739 1492 1176 935 1526 3748 932
δέκα κέρατα, ἃ εἶδες, δέκα βασιλεῖς εἰσίν, οἵτινες βασιλείαν
ten horns, which you saw, ten kings are, who a kingdom
3768 2983 235 1849 5613 935 3391 5610 2983
οὔπω ἔλαβον, ἀλλ' ἐξουσίαν ὡς βασιλεῖς μίαν ὥραν λαμβά-
not yet received, but authority as kings one hour receive
3326 3588 2342 3778 3391 1096 2192 2532 3588
νουσι μετὰ τοῦ θηρίου. 13 οὗτοι μίαν γνώμην ἔχουσι, καὶ τὴν
with the beast. These one mind have, and the
1411 2532 3588 1849 1438 3588 2342 1239
δύναμιν καὶ τὴν ἐξουσίαν ἑαυτῶν τῷ θηρίῳ διαδιδώουσιν.
power and the authority of themselves to the beast they shall give up.
3778 3326 3588 721 4170 2532 3588 721 3528
14 οὗτοι μετὰ τοῦ ἀρνίου πολεμήσουσι, καὶ τὸ ἀρνίον νικήσει
These with the Lamb will make war, and the Lamb will overcome
846 3754 2962 2962 2076 2532 935 935 2532
αὐτούς, ὅτι Κύριος κυρίων ἐστὶ καὶ βασιλεὺς βασιλέων, καὶ
them, because Lord of lords is and King of kings, and
3588 3326 846 2822 2532 1588 2532 4103 2532 3004 3427
οἱ μετ' αὐτοῦ, κλητοὶ καὶ ἐκλεκτοὶ καὶ πιστοί. 15 Καὶ λέγει μοι,
those with him, (the) called and elect and faithful. And he says to me,
3588 5204 3739 1492 3757 3588 4204 2521 2992 2532 3793
Τὰ ὕδατα, ἃ εἶδες, οὗ ἡ πόρνη κάθηται, λαοὶ καὶ ὄχλοι
The waters, which you saw, where the harlot sits, peoples and crowds
1526 2532 1484 2532 1100 2532 3588 1176 2768 3739 1492 1909
εἰσί, καὶ ἔθνη καὶ γλῶσσαι. 16 καὶ τὰ δέκα κέρατα, ἃ εἶδες, ἐπὶ
are, and nations and tongues. And the ten horns, which you saw, on
2588 2342 3778 3404 3588 4204 2532 2049
τὸ θηρίον, οὗτοι μισήσουσι τὴν πόρνην, καὶ ἠρημωμένην
the beast, these will hate the harlot, and laid waste
4160 846 2532 1131 2532 3588 4561 846
ποιήσουσιν αὐτὴν καὶ γυμνήν, καὶ τὰς σάρκας αὐτῆς
will make her and naked, and the flesh of her
5315 2532 846 2618 1722 4442 3588 1063 2316
φάγονται, καὶ αὐτὴν κατακαύσουσιν ἐν πυρί. 17 ὁ γὰρ Θεὸς
they will eat, and her will burn down with fire. For God
1325 1519 3588 2588 846 4160 3588 1106 846
ἔδωκεν εἰς τὰς καρδίας αὐτῶν ποιῆσαι τὴν γνώμην αὐτοῦ,
gave into the hearts of them to do the mind of Him,
2532 4160 3391 1106 2532 1325 3588 932 846
καὶ ποιῆσαι μίαν γνώμην, καὶ δοῦναι τὴν βασιλείαν αὐτῶν
and to do one mind, and to give the kingdom of them

King James Version

of life from the foundation of the world, when they behold the beast that was, and is not, and yet is.
9 And here (is) the mind which hath wisdom. The seven heads are seven mountains, on which the woman sitteth.
10 And there are seven kings: five are fallen, and one is, (and) the other is not yet come; and when he cometh, he must continue a short space.
11 And the beast that was, and is not, even he is the eighth, and is of the seven, and goeth into perdition.
12 And the ten horns which thou sawest are ten kings, which have received no kingdom as yet; but receive power as kings one hour with the beast.

13 These have one mind, and shall give their power and strength unto the beast.

14 These shall make war with the Lamb, and the Lamb shall overcome them: for he is Lord of lords, and King of kings: and they that are with him (are) called, and chosen, and faithful.
15. And he saith unto me, The waters which thou sawest, where the whore sitteth, are peoples, and multitudes, and nations, and tongues.
16 And the ten horns which thou sawest upon the beast, these shall hate the whore, and shall make her desolate and naked, and shall eat her flesh, and burn her with fire.
17 For God hath put in their hearts to fulfil his will, and to agree, and give their kingdom

Literal Translation | **Revelation 17:18** | ***King James Version***

to the beast, until the words of God shall be fulfilled.
18 And the woman whom you saw is the great city, having a kingdom over the kings of the earth.

3588 2342 891 5055 3588 4487 3588 2316 2532/3588
τῷ θηρίῳ, ἄχρι τελεσθῇ τὰ ῥήματα τοῦ Θεοῦ. 18 καὶ ἡ
to the beast, until shall be completed the words of God. And the

1135 3739 1492 2076 3588 4172 3588 3173 3588 2192 932
γυνή, ἣν εἶδες, ἐστὶν ἡ πόλις ἡ μεγάλη, ἡ ἔχουσα βασιλείαν
woman whom you saw, is the city great, having a kingdom

1909 3588 935 3588 1093
ἐπὶ τῶν βασιλέων τῆς γῆς.
over the kings of the earth.

unto the beast, until the words of God shall be fulfilled.
18 And the woman which thou sawest is that great city, which reigneth over the kings of the earth.

Revelation 18

1. And after these things I saw another angel coming down out of Heaven having great authority, and the earth was lighted up from his glory.
2 And he cried in a strong, great voice, saying, Babylon the great has fallen! It has fallen, and it has become a dwelling-place of demons, and a prison of every unclean spirit, and a prison of every unclean bird, even having been hated,
3 because of the wine of the anger of her fornication which all the nations have drunk, even the kings of the earth have committed fornication with her; and the merchants of the earth became rich from the power of her luxury.
4 And I heard another voice out of Heaven saying, My people, come out of her, that you may not share in her sins, and that you may not receive of her plagues;
5 because her sins joined together, even up to Heaven, and God remembered her unjust deeds.
6 Give back to her as also she gave back to you, and double to her double, according to her works. In the cup which she mixed, mix

Revelation 18

2532 3326 5023 1492 243 32 2597 1537
1. Καὶ μετὰ ταῦτα εἶδον ἄλλον ἄγγελον καταβαίνοντα ἐκ
And after these things I saw another angel coming down out of

3588 3772 2192 1849 3173 2532 3588 1093 5461
τοῦ οὐρανοῦ, ἔχοντα ἐξουσίαν μεγάλην· καὶ ἡ γῆ ἐφωτίσθη
Heaven, having authority great; and the earth was lighted

1537 3588 1391 846 2532 2896 1722 2479 5456 3173
ἐκ τῆς δόξης αὐτοῦ. 2 καὶ ἔκραξεν ἐν ἰσχύϊ, φωνῇ μεγάλῃ,
from the glory of him. And he cried in a strong, voice great,

3004 4098 4098 897 3588 3173 2532 1096
λέγων, Ἔπεσεν, ἔπεσεν Βαβυλὼν ἡ μεγάλη, καὶ ἐγένετο
saying, Has fallen, has fallen Babylon the great, and has become

2732 1142 2532 5438 3956 4151
κατοικητήριον δαιμόνων, καὶ φυλακὴ παντὸς πνεύματος
a dwelling-place of demons, and a prison of every spirit

169 2532 5438 3956 3732 169 2532
ἀκαθάρτου, καὶ φυλακὴ παντὸς ὀρνέου ἀκαθάρτου καὶ
unclean, and a prison of every bird unclean, and

3404 3754 1537 3588 3631 3588 2372 3588 4202 846
μεμισημένου. 3 ὅτι ἐκ τοῦ οἴνου τοῦ θυμοῦ τῆς πορνείας αὐτῆς
having been hated. Because of the wine of the anger of the fornication of her

4095 3956 3588/1484 2532/3588 935 3588 1093 3326 846
πέπωκε πάντα τὰ ἔθνη, καὶ οἱ βασιλεῖς τῆς γῆς μετ᾽ αὐτῆς
have drunk all the nations, and the kings of the earth with her

4203 2532 3588 1713 3588/1093/1537/3588 1411 3588
ἐπόρνευσαν, καὶ οἱ ἔμποροι τῆς γῆς ἐκ τῆς δυνάμεως τοῦ
committed fornication, and the merchants of the earth from the power of the

4764 846 4147
στρήνους αὐτῆς ἐπλούτησαν.
luxury of her became rich.

2532 191 243 5456 1537 3588 3772 3004
4. Καὶ ἤκουσα ἄλλην φωνὴν ἐκ τοῦ οὐρανοῦ, λέγουσαν,
And I heard another voice out of Heaven, saying,

1831 1537 846 3588 2992 3450 2443 3361 4790 3588
Ἐξέλθετε ἐξ αὐτῆς ὁ λαός μου, ἵνα μὴ συγκοινωνήσητε ταῖς
Come out of her people of Me, that not you share the

266 846 2532 2443 3361 2983 1537 3588 4127 846
ἁμαρτίαις αὐτῆς, καὶ ἵνα μὴ λάβητε ἐκ τῶν πληγῶν αὐτῆς·
sins of her, and that not you receive of the plagues of her;

3754 190 846 3588 266 891 3588 3772 2532
5. ὅτι ἐκολλήθησαν αὐτῆς αἱ ἁμαρτίαι ἄχρι τοῦ οὐρανοῦ, καὶ
because joined together of her the sins up to Heaven, and

3421 3588 2316 3588 92 846 591 846
ἐμνημόνευσεν ὁ Θεὸς τὰ ἀδικήματα αὐτῆς. 6 ἀπόδοτε αὐτῇ
remembered God the unjust deeds of her. Return to her

5613 2532 846 591 5213 2532 1363 846 1362
ὡς καὶ αὐτὴ ἀπέδωκεν ὑμῖν, καὶ διπλώσατε αὐτῇ διπλᾶ
as also she returned to you, and double to her double

2596 3588 2041 846 1722 3588 4221 3739 2767 2767
κατὰ τὰ ἔργα αὐτῆς· ἐν τῷ ποτηρίῳ ᾧ ἐκέρασε κεράσατε
according to the works of her; in the cup in which she mixed, mix

Revelation 18

1. And after these things I saw another angel come down from heaven, having great power; and the earth was lightened with his glory.
2 And he cried mightily with a strong voice, saying, Babylon the great is fallen, is fallen, and is become the habitation of devils, and the hold of every foul spirit, and a cage of every unclean and hateful bird.
3 For all nations have drunk of the wine of the wrath of her fornication, and the kings of the earth have committed fornication with her, and the merchants of the earth are waxed rich through the abundance of her delicacies.
4 And I heard another voice from heaven, saying, Come out of her, my people, that ye be not partakers of her sins, and that ye receive not of her plagues.
5 For her sins have reached unto heaven, and God hath remembered her iniquities.
6 Reward her even as she rewarded you, and double unto her double according to her works: in the cup which she hath filled fill

Literal Translation

to her double.
7 By what things she glorified herself, and luxuriated, by so much give back to her torment and mourning. Because she says in her heart, I sit as a queen, and I am not a widow; and I do not see mourning at all.

8 Because of this, in one day her plagues shall come: death, and mourning, and famine; and she will be consumed with fire, for strong (is the) Lord God judging her.

9. And the kings of the earth will weep for her, and will wail over her, those having fornicated and having luxuriated with her, when they see the smoke of her burning;
10 standing from afar because of the fear of her torment, saying, Woe! Woe to the great city, Babylon, the strong city! For in one hour your judgment came.

11 And the merchants of the earth weep and mourn over her, because no one buys their cargo any more,

12 cargo of gold, and silver, and of precious stone, and of pearls, and of fine linen, and of purple, and of silk, and of scarlet, and all sandarac wood, and every ivory vessel, and every vessel of very precious wood, and of bronze, and of iron, and of marble,

13 and cinnamon, and incenses, and ointment, and frankincense, and wine, and oil, and fine meal, and wheat, and beasts, and sheep, and horses, and chariots, and of bodies and souls of men.

14 And the

Revelation 18:7

846 1362 3745 1392 1438 2532 4763
αὐτῇ διπλοῦν. 7 ὅσα ἐδόξασεν ἑαυτὴν καὶ ἐστρηνίασε,
to her double. By what things she glorified herself and luxuriated,

5118 1325 846 929 2532 3997 3754 1722 3588
τοσοῦτον δότε αὐτῇ βασανισμὸν καὶ πένθος· ὅτι ἐν τῇ
such give to her torment and mourning; because in the

2588 846 3004 2521 938 2532 5503 3756 1510
καρδίᾳ αὐτῆς λέγει, Κάθημαι βασίλισσα, καὶ χήρα οὐκ εἰμί,
heart of her she says, I sit a queen, and a widow not I am,

2532 3997 3756 3361 1492 1223 5124 1722 3391 2250 2240 3588
καὶ πένθος οὐ μὴ ἴδω. 8 διὰ τοῦτο ἐν μιᾷ ἡμέρᾳ ἥξουσιν αἱ
and mourning not at all I see. Because of this in one day shall come the

4127 846 2288 2532 3997 2532 3042 2532 1722 4442
πληγαὶ αὐτῆς, θάνατος καὶ πένθος καὶ λιμός, καὶ ἐν πυρὶ
plagues of her, death and mourning and famine, and with fire

2618 3754 2478 2962 3588 2316 3588 2919 846
κατακαυθήσεται, ὅτι ἰσχυρὸς Κύριος ὁ Θεὸς ὁ κρίνων αὐτήν.
she will be burned up, because strong (is the) Lord God judging her.

2532 2799 846 2532 2875 1909 846 3588 935 3588
9 καὶ κλαύσονται αὐτήν, καὶ κόψονται ἐπ' αὐτῇ οἱ βασιλεῖς τῆς
And will weep for her, and will wail over her the kings of the

1093 3588 3326 846 4203 2532 4763 3752
γῆς οἱ μετ' αὐτῆς πορνεύσαντες καὶ στρηνιάσαντες, ὅταν
earth, those with her having fornicated and having luxuriated, when

991 3588 2586 3588 4451 846 575 3113
βλέπωσι τὸν καπνὸν τῆς πυρώσεως αὐτῆς, 10 ἀπὸ μακρόθεν
they see the smoke of the burning of her, from afar

2476 1223 3588 5401 3588 929 846 3004
ἑστηκότες διὰ τὸν φόβον τοῦ βασανισμοῦ αὐτῆς, λέγοντες,
standing because of the fear of the torment of her, saying,

3759 3759 3588 4172 3588 3173 897 3588 4172 3588 2478
Οὐαί, οὐαί, ἡ πόλις ἡ μεγάλη Βαβυλών, ἡ πόλις ἡ ἰσχυρά,
Woe! Woe, to the city great Babylon, the city strong,

3754 1722/3391/5610 2064 3588 2920 4675 2532 3588 1713 3588
ὅτι ἐν μιᾷ ὥρᾳ ἦλθεν ἡ κρίσις σου. 11 καὶ οἱ ἔμποροι τῆς
because in one hour came the judgment of you! And the merchants of the

1093 2799 2532 3996 1909 846 3754 3588 1117 846
γῆς κλαίουσι καὶ πενθοῦσιν ἐπ' αὐτῇ, ὅτι τὸν γόμον αὐτῶν
earth weep and mourn over her, because the cargo of them

3762 59 3765 1117 5557 2532 696 2532
οὐδεὶς ἀγοράζει οὐκέτι· 12 γόμον χρυσοῦ, καὶ ἀργύρου, καὶ
no one buys no more; cargo of gold, and of silver, and

3037 5093 2532 3135 2532 1040 2532 4209
λίθου τιμίου, καὶ μαργαρίτου, καὶ βύσσου, καὶ πορφύρας,
of stone precious, and of pearls, and of fine linen, and of purple,

2532 4596 2532 2847 2532 3956 3586 2367 2532 3956
καὶ σηρικοῦ, καὶ κοκκίνου· καὶ πᾶν ξύλον θύϊνον, καὶ πᾶν
and of silk, and of scarlet; and all wood sandarac, and every

4632 1661 2532 3956 4632 1537 3586 5093
σκεῦος ἐλεφάντινον, καὶ πᾶν σκεῦος ἐκ ξύλου τιμιωτάτου,
vessel ivory, and every vessel of wood very precious,

2532 5475 2532 4604 2532 3139 2532 2792 2532
καὶ χαλκοῦ, καὶ σιδήρου, καὶ μαρμάρου· 13 καὶ κινάμωμον, καὶ
and of bronze, and of iron, and of marble; and cinnamon, and

2368 2532 3464 2532 3030 2532 3631 2532 1637
θυμιάματα, καὶ μύρον, καὶ λίβανον, καὶ οἶνον, καὶ ἔλαιον,
incenses, and ointment, and frankincense, and wine, and oil,

2532 4585 2532 4621 2532 2934 2532 4263 2532 2462
καὶ σεμίδαλιν, καὶ σῖτον, καὶ κτήνη, καὶ πρόβατα· καὶ ἵππων,
and fine meal, and wheat, and beasts, and sheep; and horses,

2532 4480 2532 4983 2532 5590 444 2532 3588
καὶ ῥεδῶν, καὶ σωμάτων· καὶ ψυχὰς ἀνθρώπων. 14 καὶ ἡ
and chariots, and bodies; and souls of men. And the

King James Version

to her double.
7 How much she hath glorified herself, and lived deliciously, so much torment and sorrow give her: for she saith in her heart, I sit a queen, and am no widow, and shall see no sorrow.

8 Therefore shall her plagues come in one day, death, and mourning, and famine; and she shall be utterly burned with fire: for strong (is) the Lord God who judgeth her.

9. And the kings of the earth, who have committed fornication and lived deliciously with her, shall bewail her, and lament for her, when they shall see the smoke of her burning,
10 Standing afar off for the fear of her torment, saying, Alas, alas, that great city Babylon, that mighty city! for in one hour is thy judgment come.

11 And the merchants of the earth shall weep and mourn over her; for no man buyeth their merchandise any more:

12 The merchandise of gold, and silver, and precious stones, and of pearls, and fine linen, and purple, and silk, and scarlet, and all thyine wood, and all manner vessels of ivory, and all manner vessels of most precious wood, and of brass, and iron, and marble,

13 And cinnamon, and odours, and ointments, and frankincense, and wine, and oil, and fine flour, and wheat, and beasts, and sheep, and horses, and chariots, and slaves, and souls of men.

14 And the

Literal Translation

ripe fruits of the lust of
your soul went away
from you, and all the fat
things, and the bright
things went away from
you, and you will find
them no more, not at all.
15 The merchants of
these things, the ones
being enriched from
her, will stand from afar
because of the fear of
her torment, weeping
and mourning;
16 and saying, Woe!
Woe to the great city
having been clothed in
linen and purple and
scarlet, and having been
gilded with gold and
precious stone, and
pearls!
17 For in one hour such
great wealth was deso-
lated. And every ship-
pilot and all company
on the ships, and sailors,
and as many as work the
sea, stood from afar,
18 and cried out, seeing
the smoke of her burn-
ing, saying, What (is)
like the great city?
19 And they threw dust
on their heads, and cried
out, weeping and
mourning, saying,
Woe! Woe to the great
city, by which all those
having ships in the sea
were rich, from her
costliness, because in
one hour she was ru-
ined.
20. Be glad over her,
Heaven, and the holy
apostles, and the proph-
ets, because God judged
your judgment on her.
21 And one strong an-
gel lifted a stone like a
great millstone, and
threw (it) into the sea,
saying, This way, on a
violent impulse, Baby-
lon the great city will be
thrown down, and it
will never more still be
found.
22 And

Revelation 18:15

3703 3588 1939 3588 5590 4675 565 575 4675 2532
ὀπώρα τῆς ἐπιθυμίας τῆς ψυχῆς σου ἀπῆλθεν ἀπὸ σοῦ, καὶ
ripe fruits of the lust of the soul of you went away from you, and

3956 3588 3045 2532 3588 2986 565 575 4675 2532
πάντα τὰ λιπαρὰ καὶ τὰ λαμπρὰ ἀπῆλθεν ἀπὸ σοῦ, καὶ
all the fat things and the bright things went away from you, and

3765 3756 3361 2147 846 3588 1713 5130 3588 4147
οὐκέτι οὐ μὴ εὑρήσῃς αὐτά. 15 οἱ ἔμποροι τούτων, οἱ πλουτή-
no more not at all you will find them. The merchants of these, those being

575 846 575 3113 2476 1223 3588 5401
σαντες ἀπ' αὐτῆς, ἀπὸ μακρόθεν στήσονται διὰ τὸν φόβον
enriched from her, from afar will stand because of the fear

3588 929 846 2799 2532 3996 2532
τοῦ βασανισμοῦ αὐτῆς, κλαίοντες καὶ πενθοῦντες, 16 καὶ
of the torment of her, weeping and mourning, and

3004 3759 3759 3588 4172 3588 3173 3588 4016
λέγοντες, Οὐαί, οὐαί, ἡ πόλις ἡ μεγάλη, ἡ περιβεβλημένη
saying, Woe! Woe, the city great, having been clothed in

1039 2532 4210 2532 2847 2532 5558 1722
βύσσινον καὶ πορφυροῦν καὶ κόκκινον, καὶ κεχρυσωμένη ἐν
linen and purple and scarlet, and having been gilded in

5557 2532 3037 5093 2532 3135 3754 3391 5610 2049
χρυσῷ καὶ λίθῳ τιμίῳ καὶ μαργαρίταις· 17 ὅτι μιᾷ ὥρᾳ ἠρη-
gold and stone precious and pearls; because in one hour was

3588 5118 4149 2532 3956 2942 2532 3956 1909
μώθη ὁ τοσοῦτος πλοῦτος. καὶ πᾶς κυβερνήτης, καὶ πᾶς ἐπὶ
desolated such great wealth! And every helmsman, and all on

3588 4143 3588 3658 2532 3492 2532 3745 3588 2281
τῶν πλοίων ὁ ὅμιλος, καὶ ναῦται, καὶ ὅσοι τὴν θάλασσαν
the ships the company, and sailors, and as many as the sea

2038 575 3113 2476 2532 2896 3708
ἐργάζονται, ἀπὸ μακρόθεν ἔστησαν, 18 καὶ ἔκραζον, ὁρῶντες
work, from afar stood, and cried out, seeing

3588 2586 3588 4451 846 3004 5101 3664 3588
τὸν καπνὸν τῆς πυρώσεως αὐτῆς, λέγοντες, Τίς ὁμοία τῇ
the smoke of the burning of her, saying, What (is) like the

4172 3588 3173 2532 906 5522 1909 3588 2776 846
πόλει τῇ μεγάλῃ; 19 καὶ ἔβαλον χοῦν ἐπὶ τὰς κεφαλὰς αὐτῶν,
city great? and they threw dust on the heads of them,

2532 2896 2799 2532 3996 3004 3759 3759
καὶ ἔκραζον κλαίοντες καὶ πενθοῦντες, λέγοντες, Οὐαί, οὐαί,
and cried out weeping and mourning, saying, Woe! Woe,

3588 4172 3588 3173 1722 3739 4147 3956 3588 2192 4143
ἡ πόλις ἡ μεγάλη, ἐν ᾗ ἐπλούτησαν πάντες οἱ ἔχοντες πλοῖα
(to) the city great, by which were enriched all the (ones) having ships

1722 3588 2281 1537 3588 5094 846 3754 3391 5610 2049
ἐν τῇ θαλάσσῃ ἐκ τῆς τιμιότητος αὐτῆς, ὅτι μιᾷ ὥρᾳ ἠρη-
in the sea from the costliness of her, because in one hour was

2165 1909 846 3772 2532/3588 40 652
μώθη. 20 εὐφραίνου ἐπ' αὐτήν, οὐρανέ, καὶ οἱ ἅγιοι ἀπόστολοι,
she ruined! Be glad over her, Heaven, and the holy apostles,

2532 3588 4396 3754 2919 3588 2316 3588 2917 5216 1537 846
καὶ οἱ προφῆται, ὅτι ἔκρινεν ὁ Θεὸς τὸ κρίμα ὑμῶν ἐξ αὐτῆς.
and the prophets, because judged God the judgment of you on her.

2532 142 1520 32 2478 3037 5613 3458 3173 2532
21. Καὶ ἦρεν εἷς ἄγγελος ἰσχυρὸς λίθον ὡς μύλον μέγαν, καὶ
And lifted one angel strong a stone as a millstone great, and

906 1519 3588 2281 3004 3779 3731 906
ἔβαλεν εἰς τὴν θάλασσαν, λέγων, Οὕτως ὁρμήματι βληθή-
threw (it) into the sea, saying, Thus on an impulse will be

897 3588 3173 4172 2532/3756/3361 2147 2089 2532
σεται Βαβυλὼν ἡ μεγάλη πόλις, καὶ οὐ μὴ εὑρεθῇ ἔτι. 22 καὶ
thrown Babylon the great city, and not at all will be found yet. And

King James Version

fruits that thy soul lusted
after are departed from
thee, and all things
which were dainty and
goodly are departed
from thee, and thou
shalt find them no more
at all.
15 The merchants of
these things, which
were made rich by her,
shall stand afar off for
the fear of her torment,
weeping and wailing,
16 And saying, Alas,
alas, that great city, that
was clothed in fine
linen, and purple, and
scarlet, and decked with
gold, and precious
stones, and pearls!
17 For in one hour so
great riches is come to
nought. And every
shipmaster, and all the
company in ships, and
sailors, and as many as
trade by sea, stood afar
off,
18 And cried when they
saw the smoke of her
burning, saying, What
(city is) like unto this
great city!
19 And they cast dust on
their heads, and cried,
weeping and wailing,
saying, Alas, alas, that
great city, wherein were
made rich all that had
ships in the sea by rea-
son of her costliness! for
in one hour is she made
desolate.
20. Rejoice over her,
(thou) heaven, and (ye)
holy apostles and
prophets; for God hath
avenged you on her.
21 And a mighty angel
took up a stone like a
great millstone, and cast
(it) into the sea, saying,
Thus with violence
shall that great city
Babylon be thrown
down, and shall be
found no more at all.
22 And

Literal Translation

Revelation 18:23

King James Version

the sound of harpers, and of musicians, and flutists, and of trumpeters will not at all still be heard in you. And every craftsman of every craft will not at all still be found in you. And the sound of a mill will not at all still be heard in you.

23 And the light of a lamp will not all still shine in you. And the voice of the bridegroom and bride will not at all still be heard in you. For your merchants were the great ones of the earth, for by your sorcery all the nations were misled.

24 And in her was found the blood of prophets, and of saints, and of all the (ones) having been slain on the earth.

5456 2790 2532 3451 2532 834 2532 4538
φωνὴ κιθαρῳδῶν καὶ μουσικῶν καὶ αὐλητῶν καὶ σαλπιστῶν
sound of harpers and of musicians and flutists and of trumpeters

3756 3361 191 1722/4671/2089/2532/3956 5079 3956 5078
οὐ μὴ ἀκουσθῇ ἐν σοὶ ἔτι, καὶ πᾶς τεχνίτης πάσης τέχνης
not at all will be heard in you still, and every craftsman of every craft

3756 3361 2147 1722/4671/2089/2532 5456 3458 3756 3361 191 1722
οὐ μὴ εὑρεθῇ ἐν σοὶ ἔτι, καὶ φωνὴ μύλου οὐ μὴ ἀκουσθῇ ἐν
not at all will be found in you still,and a sound of a mill not at all will be heard in

4671 2089 2532 5457 3088 3756 3361 5316 1722 4671 2089 2532 5456
σοὶ ἔτι, 23 καὶ φῶς λύχνου οὐ μὴ φάνῃ ἐν σοὶ ἔτι, καὶ φωνὴ
you still, and light of a lamp not at all (shall) shine in you still, and voice

3566 2532 3565 3756 3361 191 1722 4671 2089 3754 3588 1713
νυμφίου καὶ νύμφης οὐ μὴ ἀκουσθῇ ἐν σοὶ ἔτι· ὅτι οἱ ἔμποροί
of groom and bride not at all will be heard in you still; for the merchants

4675 2258 3588 3175 3588 1093 3754 1722 3588 5331 4675
σου ἦσαν οἱ μεγιστᾶνες τῆς γῆς, ὅτι ἐν τῇ φαρμακείᾳ σου
of you were the great ones of the earth, for by the sorceries of you

4105 3956 3588 1484 2532 1722 846 129 4396
ἐπλανήθησαν πάντα τὰ ἔθνη. 24 καὶ ἐν αὐτῇ αἷμα προφητῶν
were led astray all the nations,. And in her (the) blood of prophets

2532 40 2147 2532 3956 3588 4969 1909 3588 1093
καὶ ἁγίων εὑρέθη, καὶ πάντων τῶν ἐσφαγμένων ἐπὶ τῆς γῆς.
and saints were found, and of all the (ones) having been slain on the earth.

the voice of harpers, and musicians, and of pipers, and trumpeters, shall be heard no more at all in thee; and no craftsman, of whatsoever craft (he be), shall be found any more in thee; and the sound of a millstone shall be heard no more at all in thee;

23 And the light of a candle shall shine no more at all in thee; and the voice of the bridegroom and of the bride shall be heard no more at all in thee: for thy merchants were the great men of the earth; for by thy sorceries were all nations deceived.

24 And in her was found the blood of prophets, and of saints, and of all that were slain upon the earth.

Revelation 19

Revelation 19

1. And after these things, I heard a great voice of a numerous crowd in Heaven, saying, Hallelujah! The salvation and the glory and the honor and the power of the Lord our God!

2 For true and righteous (are) His judgments, because He judged the great harlot who defiled the earth with her fornication. And He avenged the blood of His slaves out of her hand.

2532 3326 5023 191 5456 3793 4183 3173
1. Καὶ μετὰ ταῦτα ἤκουσα φωνὴν ὄχλου πολλοῦ μεγάλην
And after these things I heard a voice of a multitude many great

1722 3588 3772 3004 239 3588 4991 2532 3588
ἐν τῷ οὐρανῷ, λεγόντος, Ἀλληλούϊ· ἡ σωτηρία καὶ ἡ
in Heaven, saying, Hallelujah! The salvation and the

1391 2532 3588 5092 2532 3588 1411 2962 3588 2316 2257 3754
δόξα καὶ ἡ τιμὴ καὶ ἡ δύναμις Κυρίῳ τῷ Θεῷ ἡμῶν· 2 ὅτι
glory and the honor and the power of (the) Lord God of us,; because

228 2532 1342 3588 2920 846 3754 2919 3588 4204
ἀληθιναὶ καὶ δίκαιαι αἱ κρίσεις αὐτοῦ· ὅτι ἔκρινε τὴν πόρνην
true and righteous the judgments of Him; for He judged the harlot

3588 3173 3748 5351 3588 1093 1722 3588 4202 846
τὴν μεγάλην, ἥτις ἔφθειρε τὴν γῆν ἐν τῇ πορνείᾳ αὐτῆς,
Great, who defiled the earth by the fornication of her,

2532 1556 3588 129 3588 1401 846 1537 3588 5495 846
καὶ ἐξεδίκησε τὸ αἷμα τῶν δούλων αὐτοῦ ἐκ τῆς χειρὸς αὐτῆς.
and He avenged the blood of the slaves of Him out of the hands of her.

Revelation 19

1. And after these things I heard a great voice of much people in heaven, saying, Alleluia; Salvation, and glory, and honour, and power, unto the Lord our God:

2 For true and righteous (are) his judgments: for he hath judged the great whore, which did corrupt the earth with her fornication, and hath avenged the blood of his servants at her hand.

3 And secondly they said, Hallelujah! Also her smoke goes up to the ages of the ages.

4 And the twenty-four elders, and the four living creatures fell down and worshiped God sitting on the throne, saying, Amen! Hallelujah!

2532 1208 2046 239 2532 3588 2586 846
3 καὶ δεύτερον εἴρηκαν, Ἀλληλούϊα· καὶ ὁ καπνὸς αὐτῆς
And secondly they said, Hallelujah! And the smoke of her

305 1519 3588 165 3588 165 2532 4098 3588
ἀναβαίνει εἰς τοὺς αἰῶνας τῶν αἰώνων. 4 καὶ ἔπεσαν οἱ
goes up to the ages of the ages. And fell down the

4245 3588 1501 2532 5064 2532 3588 5064
πρεσβύτεροι οἱ εἴκοσι καὶ τέσσαρες, καὶ τὰ τέσσαρα
elders twenty and four, and the four

2226 2532 4352 3588 16 3588 2521 1909 3588 2362
ζῶα, καὶ προσεκύνησαν τῷ Θεῷ τῷ καθημένῳ ἐπὶ τῷ θρόνου,
living creatures and worshiped God sitting on the throne,

3004 281 239 2532 5456 1537 3588 2362
λέγοντες, Ἀμήν· Ἀλληλούϊα. 5 καὶ φωνὴ ἐκ τοῦ θρόνου
saying, Amen; Hallelujah! And a voice from the throne

1831 3004 134 3588 2316 2257 3956 3588 1401
ἐξῆλθε, λέγουσα, Αἰνεῖτε τὸν Θεὸν ἡμῶν, πάντες οἱ δοῦλοι
came out, saying, Praise the God of us, all the slaves

3 And again they said, Alleluia. And her smoke rose up for ever and ever.

4 And the four and twenty elders and the four beasts fell down and worshipped God that sat on the throne, saying, Amen; Alleluia.

5 And a voice came out from the throne, saying, Praise our God, all His slaves,

5 And a voice came out of the throne, saying, Praise our God, all ye his servants,

Revelation 19:6

Literal Translation

and the (ones) fearing Him, the small and the great.

6 And I heard as a sound of a huge crowd, and as a sound of many waters, and as a sound of strong thunders, saying, Hallelujah! Because (the), Lord God Almighty reigned.

7 Let us rejoice and let us exult, and we will give the glory to Him, because the marriage of the Lamb came, and His wife prepared herself.

8 And it was given to her that she be clothed (with) fine linen, clean and bright; for the fine linen is the righteousnesses of the saints.

9 And he says to me, Write: Blessed (are) the (ones) having been called to the supper of the marriage of the Lamb. And he says to me, These words of God are true.

10 And I fell before his feet to worship him, but he said to me, See, do not (do it)! I am a fellow-slave of yours, and of your brothers, having the testimony of Jesus. Worship God. For the testimony of Jesus is the spirit of prophecy.

11. And I saw Heaven having been opened. And, behold! A white horse, and He sitting on it having been called Faithful and True. And He judges and wars in righteousness.

12 And His eyes (were) as a flame of fire, and on His head many diadems, having a name that had been written, which no one knows except Himself;

13 and having been clothed in a garment having been dipped in blood. And

---

846 2532 3588 5399 846 2532 3588 3398 2532 3588 3173
αὐτοῦ, καὶ οἱ φοβούμενοι αὐτόν, καὶ οἱ μικροὶ καὶ οἱ μεγάλοι.
of Him, and those fearing Him, even the small and the great.

2532 191 5613 5456 3793 4183 2532 5613 5456 5204
6 καὶ ἤκουσα ὡς φωνὴν ὄχλου πολλοῦ, καὶ ὡς φωνὴν ὑδάτων
And I heard as a sound of a crowd huge, and as a sound of waters

4183 2532 5613 5456 1027 2478 3004
πολλῶν, καὶ ὡς φωνὴν βροντῶν ἰσχυρῶν, λεγόντας,
many, and as a sound thunders of strong, saying,

239 3754 936 2962 3588 2316 3588 3841
Ἀλληλουϊά· ὅτι ἐβασίλευσε Κύριος ὁ Θεὸς ὁ παντοκράτωρ.
Hallelujah! Because reigned (the) Lord God Almighty.

5463 2532 21 2532 1325 3588 1391 846
7 χαίρωμεν καὶ ἀγαλλιώμεθα, καὶ δώμεν τὴν δόξαν αὐτῷ·
Let us rejoice and let us exult, and we will give the glory to Him;

3754 2064 3588 1062 3588 721 2532 3588 1135 846 2090
ὅτι ἦλθεν ὁ γάμος τοῦ ἀρνίου, καὶ ἡ γυνὴ αὐτοῦ ἡτοίμασεν
because came the marriage of the Lamb, and the wife of Him prepared

1438 2532 1325 846 2443 4016 1039 2513
ἑαυτήν. 8 καὶ ἐδόθη αὐτῇ ἵνα περιβάληται βύσσινον καθαρὸν
herself. And it was given to her that she be clothed (with) fine linen clean

2532 2986 3588 1063 1039 3588 1345 2076 3588
καὶ λαμπρόν· τὸ γὰρ βύσσινον τὰ δικαιώματά ἐστι τῶν
and bright; the for fine linen the righteousness is of the

40 2532 3004 3427 1125 3107 3588 1519 3588 1173
ἁγίων. 9 καὶ λέγει μοι, Γράψον· Μακάριοι οἱ εἰς τὸ δεῖπνον
saints. And he says to me, Write; Blessed the (ones) to the supper

3588 1062 3588 721 2564 2532 3004 3427 3778 3588
τοῦ γάμου τοῦ ἀρνίου κεκλημένοι. καὶ λέγει μοι, Οὗτοι οἱ
of the marriage of the Lamb having been called. And he says to me, These

3056 228 1526 3588 2316 2532 4098 1715 3588
λόγοι ἀληθινοί εἰσι τοῦ Θεοῦ. 10 καὶ ἔπεσον ἔμπροσθεν τῶν
words true are of God. And I fell before the

4228 846 4352 846 2532 3004 3427 3708 3361
ποδῶν αὐτοῦ προσκυνῆσαι αὐτῷ· καὶ λέγει μοι, Ὅρα μή·
feet of him to worship him; and he says to me, See, not do;

4889 4675 1510 2532 3588 80 4675 3588 2192 3588
σύνδουλός σου εἰμὶ καὶ τῶν ἀδελφῶν σου τῶν ἐχόντων τὴν
A fellow-slave of you I am and of the brothers of you having the

3141 3588 2424 3588 2316 4352 3588 1063
μαρτυρίαν τοῦ Ἰησοῦ· τῷ Θεῷ προσκύνησον· ἡ γὰρ
witness of Jesus; to God give worship; the for

3141 3588 2424 2076 3588 4151 3588 4394
μαρτυρία τοῦ Ἰησοῦ ἐστι τὸ πνεῦμα τῆς προφητείας.
witness of Jesus is the spirit of prophecy.

2532 1492 3588 3772 455 2532 2400 2462
11. Καὶ εἶδον τὸν οὐρανὸν ἀνεῳγμένον, καὶ ἰδού, ἵππος
And I saw Heaven having been opened, and behold! A horse

3022 2532 3588 2521 1909 846 2564 4103 2532
λευκός, καὶ ὁ καθήμενος ἐπ᾽ αὐτόν, καλούμενος πιστὸς καὶ
white, and the (One) sitting on it being called faithful and

228 2532 1722 1343 2919 2532 4170 3588 1161
ἀληθινός, καὶ ἐν δικαιοσύνῃ κρίνει καὶ πολεμεῖ. 12 οἱ δὲ
true, and in righteousness He judges and wars. the And

3788 846 5613 5395 4442 2532 1909 3588 2776 846
ὀφθαλμοὶ αὐτοῦ ὡς φλὸξ πυρός, καὶ ἐπὶ τὴν κεφαλὴν αὐτοῦ
eyes of Him as a flame of fire, and on the head of Him

1238 4183 2192 3686 1125 3739 3762 1492 1487 3361
διαδήματα πολλά· ἔχων ὄνομα γεγραμμένον ὃ οὐδεὶς οἶδεν εἰ μὴ
diadems many having a name having been written which no one knows if not

846 2532 4016 2440 911 129
αὐτός, 13 καὶ περιβεβλημένος ἱμάτιον βεβαμμένον αἵματι·
Him, and being clothed (in) a garment having been dipped in blood;

King James Version

and ye that fear him, both small and great.

6 And I heard as it were the voice of a great multitude, and as the voice of many waters, and as the voice of mighty thunderings, saying, Alleluia: for the Lord God omnipotent reigneth.

7 Let us be glad and rejoice, and give honour to him: for the marriage of the Lamb is come, and his wife hath made herself ready.

8 And to her was granted that she should be arrayed in fine linen, clean and white: for the fine linen is the righteousness of saints.

9 And he saith unto me, Write, Blessed (are) they which are called unto the marriage supper of the Lamb. And he saith unto me, These are the true sayings of God.

10 And I fell at his feet to worship him. And he said unto me, See (thou do it) not: I am thy fellowservant, and of thy brethren that have the testimony of Jesus: worship God: for the testimony of Jesus is the spirit of prophecy.

11. And I saw heaven opened, and behold a white horse; and he that sat upon him (was) called Faithful and True, and in righteousness he doth judge and make war.

12 His eyes (were) as a flame of fire, and on his head (were) many crowns; and he had a name written, that no man knew, but he himself.

13 And he (was) clothed with a vesture dipped in blood: and

Literal Translation | **Revelation 19:14** | *King James Version*

His name is called The Word of God.
14 And the armies in Heaven followed Him on white horses, being dressed in fine linen, white and clean.

15 And out of His mouth goes forth a sharp sword, that with it He might smite the nations. And He will shepherd them with an iron rod. And He treads the winepress of the wine of the anger and of the wrath of God Almighty.

16 And He has on (His) garment and on His thigh a name having been written: KING OF KINGS AND LORD OF LORDS.

17 And I saw one angel standing in the sun. And he cried with a great voice, saying to all the birds flying in mid-heaven, Come and gather together to the supper of the great God,

18 that you may eat the flesh of kings, and (the) flesh of commanders, and (the) flesh of strong ones, and (the) flesh of horses, and of the (ones) sitting on them, and (the) flesh of all, both freemen and slaves, even of the small and great.

19 And I saw the beast and the kings of the earth, and their armies being assembled to make war with the (One) sitting on the horse, and with His army.

20 And the beast was seized, and with this (one) the false prophet doing signs before it, by which he led astray those

2532 2564 3588 3686 846 3588 3056 3588 2316 2532 /3588
καὶ καλεῖται τὸ ὄνομα αὐτοῦ, Ὁ λόγος τοῦ Θεοῦ. 14 καὶ τὰ
and is called the name of Him, The Word of God. And the

4753 3588/1722/3588 3772 190 846 1909 2462
στρατεύματα τὰ ἐν τῷ οὐρανῷ ἠκολούθει αὐτῷ ἐφ' ἵπποις
armies in Heaven followed Him on horses

3022 1746 1039 3022 2532 2513 2532 1537
λευκοῖς, ἐνδεδυμένοι βύσσινον λευκὸν καὶ καθαρόν. 15 καὶ ἐκ
white, having been dressed (in) fine linen white and clean. And from

3588 4750 846 1607 4501 3691 2443 1722 846
τοῦ στόματος αὐτοῦ ἐκπορεύεται ῥομφαία ὀξεῖα, ἵνα ἐν αὐτῇ
the mouth of Him goes forth a sword sharp, that with it

3960 3588 1484 2532 846 4165 846 1722 4464 4603
πατάσσῃ τὰ ἔθνη· καὶ αὐτὸς ποιμανεῖ αὐτοὺς ἐν ῥάβδῳ σιδηρᾷ·
He may smite the nations; and He will shepherd them with a rod iron;

2532 846 3961 3588 3025 3588 3631 3588 2372 2532 3588 3709
καὶ αὐτὸς πατεῖ τὴν ληνὸν τοῦ οἴνου τοῦ θυμοῦ καὶ τῆς ὀργῆς
and He treads the press of the wine of the anger and of the wrath

3588 2316 3588 3841 2532 2192 1909 3588 2440 2532 1909
τοῦ Θεοῦ τοῦ παντοκράτορος. 16 καὶ ἔχει ἐπὶ τὸ ἱμάτιον καὶ ἐπὶ
of God Almighty. And He has on the garment and on

3588 3382 846 3686 1125 935 935 2532
τὸν μηρὸν αὐτοῦ ὄνομα γεγραμμένον, Βασιλεὺς βασιλέων καὶ
the thigh of Him a name having been written, KING OF KINGS AND

2962 2962
Κύριος κυρίων.
LORD OF LORDS.

2532 1492 1520 32 2476 1722 3588 2246 2532 2896
17. Καὶ εἶδον ἕνα ἄγγελον ἑστῶτα ἐν τῷ ἡλίῳ· καὶ ἔκραξε
And I saw one angel standing in the sun and he cried

5456 3173 3004 3956 3588 3732 3588 4072 1722
φωνῇ μεγάλῃ, λέγων πᾶσι τοῖς ὀρνέοις τοῖς πετωμένοις ἐν
voice with a great, saying to all the birds flying in

3321 1205 2532 4863 1519 3588 1173 3588
μεσουρανήματι, Δεῦτε καὶ συνάγεσθε εἰς τὸ δεῖπνον τοῦ
mid-heaven, Come and gather together to the supper of the

3173 2316 2443 5315 4561 935 2532 4561
μεγάλου Θεοῦ, 18 ἵνα φάγητε σάρκας βασιλέων, καὶ σάρκας
great God, that you may eat (the) flesh of kings, and (the) flesh

5506 2532 4561 2478 2532 4561 2462 2532 3588
χιλιάρχων, καὶ σάρκας ἰσχυρῶν, καὶ σάρκας ἵππων καὶ τῶν
of chiliarchs, and (the) flesh of strong ones, and (the) flesh of horses and of those

2521 1909 846 2532 4561 3956 1658 5037 2532
καθημένων ἐπ' αὐτῶν, καὶ σάρκας πάντων, ἐλευθέρων τε καὶ
sitting on them, and (the) flesh of all, freemen both and

1401 2532 3398 2532 3173
δούλων, καὶ μικρῶν καὶ μεγάλων.
slaves, even of small and great.

2532 1492 3588 2342 2532 3588 935 3588 1093 2532 3588
19 Καὶ εἶδον τὸ θηρίον, καὶ τοὺς βασιλεῖς τῆς γῆς, καὶ τὰ
And I saw the beast, and the kings of the earth, and the

4753 846 4863 4160 4171 3326 3588
στρατεύματα αὐτῶν συνηγμένα ποιῆσαι πόλεμον μετὰ τοῦ
armies of them being assembled to make war with the (One)

2521 1909 3588 2462 2532 3326 3588 4753 846
καθημένου ἐπὶ τοῦ ἵππου, καὶ μετὰ τοῦ στρατεύματος αὐτοῦ.
sitting on the horse, and with the army of Him.

2532 4084 3588 2342 2532 3326 5127 3588 5578 3588
20 καὶ ἐπιάσθη τὸ θηρίον, καὶ μετὰ τούτου ὁ ψευδοπροφήτης ὁ
And was seized the beast, and with this (one) the false prophet

4160 3588 4592 1799 846 1722 3739 4105 3588
ποιήσας τὰ σημεῖα ἐνώπιον αὐτοῦ, ἐν οἷς ἐπλάνησε τοὺς
doing the signs before it, by which he led astray those

his name is called The Word of God.
14 And the armies (which were) in heaven followed him upon white horses, clothed in fine linen, white and clean.
15 And out of his mouth goeth a sharp sword, that with it he should smite the nations: and he shall rule them with a rod of iron: and he treadeth the winepress of the fierceness and wrath of Almighty God.

16 And he hath on (his) vesture and on his thigh a name written, KING OF KINGS, AND LORD OF LORDS.

17 And I saw an angel standing in the sun; and he cried with a loud voice, saying to all the fowls that fly in the midst of heaven, Come and gather yourselves together unto the supper of the great God;

18 That ye may eat the flesh of kings, and the flesh of captains, and the flesh of mighty men, and the flesh of horses, and of them that sit on them, and the flesh of all (men, both) free and bond, both small and great.

19 And I saw the beast, and the kings of the earth, and their armies, gathered together to make war against him that sat on the horse, and against his army.

20 And the beast was taken, and with him the false prophet that wrought miracles before him, with which he deceived them

Literal Translation | **Revelation 19:21** | ***King James Version***

having received the mark of the beast, and those worshiping its image. The two were thrown alive into the Lake of Fire burning with brimstone.
21 And the rest were killed with the sword of the (One) sitting on the horse, it having gone out of His mouth. And all the birds were filled from their flesh.

2983 3588 5480 3588 2342 2532 3588 4352
λαβόντας τὸ χάραγμα τοῦ θηρίου, καὶ τοὺς προσκυνοῦντας
having received the mark of the beast, and those worshiping

3588 1504 846 2198 906 3588 1417 1519 3588 3041 3588
τῇ εἰκόνι αὐτοῦ· ζῶντες ἐβλήθησαν οἱ δύο εἰς τὴν λίμνην τοῦ
the image of it; living were thrown the two into the Lake

4442 3588 2545 1722 3588 2303 2532 3588 3062 615
πυρὸς τὴν καιομένην ἐν τῷ θείῳ· 21 καὶ οἱ λοιποὶ ἀπεκτάν-
of Fire burning with brimstone; and the rest were killed

1722 3588 4501 3588 2521 1909 3588 2462 3588
θησαν ἐν τῇ ῥομφαίᾳ τοῦ καθημένου ἐπὶ τοῦ ἵππου, τῇ
with the sword of the (One) sitting on the horse,

1607 1537 3588 4750 846 2532 3956 3588 3732
ἐκπορευομένῃ ἐκ τοῦ στόματος αὐτοῦ· καὶ πάντα τὰ ὄρνεα
having gone forth from the mouth of Him; and all the birds

5526 1537 3588 4561 846
ἐχορτάσθησαν ἐκ τῶν σαρκῶν αὐτῶν.
were filled from the flesh of them.

that had received the mark of the beast, and them that worshipped his image. These both were cast alive into a lake of fire burning with brimstone.
21 And the remnant were slain with the sword of him that sat upon the horse, which (sword) proceeded out of his mouth: and all the fowls were filled with their flesh.

Revelation 20 | Revelation 20 | Revelation 20

1. And I saw an angel coming down out of Heaven, having the key of the abyss, and a great chain on his hand.

2 And he laid hold of the dragon, the old serpent who is (the) devil and Satan, and bound him a thousand years,

3 and threw him into the abyss, and shut him up, and sealed over him, that he should not still lead astray the nations, until the thousand years are ended. And after these things, he must be set loose a little time.

4. And I saw thrones, and they sat on them. And judgment was given to them, and the souls of the ones having been beheaded because of the witness of Jesus, and because of the Word of God, and who had not worshiped the beast nor its image, and had not received the mark on their forehead and on their hand. And they lived and reigned with

2532 1492 32 2597 1537 3588 3772
1. Καὶ εἶδον ἄγγελον καταβαίνοντα ἐκ τοῦ οὐρανοῦ,
And I saw an angel coming down out of Heaven

2192 3588 2807 3588 12 2532 254 3173 1909
ἔχοντα τὴν κλεῖδα τῆς ἀβύσσου, καὶ ἅλυσιν μεγάλην ἐπὶ
having the key of the abyss, and a chain great on

3588 5495 846 2532 2902 3588 1404 3588 3789 3588
τὴν χεῖρα αὐτοῦ. 2 καὶ ἐκράτησε τὸν δράκοντα, τὸν ὄφιν τὸν
the hand of him. And he laid hold of the dragon, the serpent

744 3739 2076 1228 2532 4567 2532 1210 846
ἀρχαῖον, ὅς ἐστι διάβολος καὶ Σατανᾶς, καὶ ἔδησεν αὐτὸν
old, who is devil and Satan, and bound' him

5507 2094 2532 906 846 1519 3588 12 2532 2808
χίλια ἔτη, 3 καὶ ἔβαλεν αὐτὸν εἰς τὴν ἄβυσσον, καὶ ἔκλεισεν
a thousand years, and threw him into the abyss, and shut up

846 2532 4972 1883 846 2443 3361 4105
αὐτόν, καὶ ἐσφράγισεν ἐπάνω αὐτοῦ, ἵνα μὴ πλανήσῃ
him, and sealed over him, that not he might mislead

3588 1484 2089 891 5055 3588 5507 2094 2532 3326 5023 1163
τὰ ἔθνη ἔτι, ἄχρι τελεσθῇ τὰ χίλια ἔτη· καὶ μετὰ ταῦτα δεῖ
the nations still, until are ended the thousand years; and after these things must

846 3089 3398 5550
αὐτὸν λυθῆναι μικρὸν χρόνον.
he be loosed a little time.

2532 1492 2362 2532 2523 1909 846 2532 2917
4. Καὶ εἶδον θρόνους, καὶ ἐκάθισαν ἐπ᾽ αὐτούς, καὶ κρίμα
And I saw thrones, and they sat on them, and judgment

1325 846 2532 3588 5590 3588 3990 1223 3588
ἐδόθη αὐτοῖς· καὶ τὰς ψυχὰς τῶν πεπελεκισμένων διὰ τὴν
was given to them; and the souls of those having been beheaded due to the

3141 2424 2532 1223 3588 3056 3588 2316 2532 3748
μαρτυρίαν Ἰησοῦ, καὶ διὰ τὸν λόγον τοῦ Θεοῦ, καὶ οἵτινες
witness of Jesus, and because of the Word of God, and who

3756 4352 3588 2342 3777 3588 1504 846 2532
οὐ προσεκύνησαν τῷ θηρίῳ, οὔτε τὴν εἰκόνα αὐτοῦ, καὶ
not had worshiped the beast, nor the image of him, and

3756 2983 3588 5480 1909 3588 3359 846 2532 1909
οὐκ ἔλαβον τὸ χάραγμα ἐπὶ τὸ μέτωπον αὐτῶν, καὶ ἐπὶ
not received the mark on the forehead of them, and on

3588 5495 846 2532 2198 2532 936 3326
τὴν χεῖρα αὐτῶν· καὶ ἔζησαν, καὶ ἐβασίλευσαν μετὰ
the hand of them; and they lived, and reigned with

1. And I saw an angel come down from heaven, having the key of the bottomless pit and a great chain in his hand.

2 And he laid hold on the dragon, that old serpent, which is the Devil, and Satan, and bound him a thousand years,

3 And cast him into the bottomless pit, and shut him up, and set a seal upon him, that he should deceive the nations no more, till the thousand years should be fulfilled: and after that he must be loosed a little season.

4. And I saw thrones, and they sat upon them, and judgment was given unto them: and (I saw) the souls of them that were beheaded for the witness of Jesus, and for the word of God, and which had not worshipped the beast, neither his image, neither had received (his) mark upon their foreheads, or in their hands; and they lived and reigned with

Literal Translation

Revelation 20:5

King James Version

Christ a thousand years.
5 But the rest of the dead did not live again until the thousand years were ended. This (is) the first resurrection.

5547 5507 2094 3588 1161 3062 3588 3498 3756 326
Χριστοῦ χίλια ἔτη. 5 οἱ δὲ λοιποὶ τῶν νεκρῶν οὐκ ἀνέζησαν
Christ a thousand years. the But rest of the dead not lived again
2193 5055 3588 5507 2094 3778 3588 386 3588 4413
ἕως τελεσθῇ τὰ χίλια ἔτη. αὕτη ἡ ἀνάστασις ἡ πρώτη.
until were ended the thousand years. This (is) the resurrection first.

Christ a thousand years.
5 But the rest of the dead lived not again until the thousand years were finished. This (is) the first resurrection.

6 Blessed and holy (is) the (one) having part in the first resurrection. The second death has no authority over these, but they will be priests of God and of Christ, and will reign with Him a thousand years.

3107 2532 40 3588 2192 3313 1722 3588 386 3588 4413
6 μακάριος καὶ ἅγιος ὁ ἔχων μέρος ἐν τῇ ἀναστάσει τῇ πρώτη·
Blessed and holy he having part in the resurrection first;
1909 5130 3588 2288 3588 1208 3756 2192 1849 235
ἐπὶ τούτων ὁ θάνατος ὁ δεύτερος οὐκ ἔχει ἐξουσίαν, ἀλλ᾽
over these the death second not has authority, but
2071 2409 3588 2316 2532 3588 5547 2532 936
ἔσονται ἱερεῖς τοῦ Θεοῦ καὶ τοῦ Χριστοῦ, καὶ βασιλεύσουσι
they will be priests of God and of Christ, and will reign
3326 846 5507 2094
μετ᾽ αὐτοῦ χίλια ἔτη.
with Him a thousand years.

6 Blessed and holy (is) he that hath part in the first resurrection: on such the second death hath no power, but they shall be priests of God and of Christ, and shall reign with him a thousand years.

7. And whenever the thousand years are ended, Satan will be set loose out of his prison,
8 and he will go out to lead astray the nations in the four corners of the earth, Gog and Magog, to assemble them in war, whose number (is) as the sand of the sea.

2532 3752 5055 3588 5507 2094 3089 3588 4567 1537
7. Καὶ ὅταν τελεσθῇ τὰ χίλια ἔτη, λυθήσεται ὁ Σατανᾶς ἐκ
And when are finished the thousand years, will be loosed Satan from
3588 5438 846 2532 1831 4105 3588 1484 3588
τῆς φυλακῆς αὐτοῦ, 8 καὶ ἐξελεύσεται πλανῆσαι τὰ ἔθνη τὰ
the prison of him, and he will go out to lead astray the nations
1722 3588 5064 1137 3588 1093 3588 1136 2532 3098
ἐν ταῖς τέσσαρσι γωνίαις τῆς γῆς, τὸν Γὼγ καὶ Μαγώγ,
in the four corners of the earth, Gog and Magog,
4863 846 1519 4171 3739 3588 706 5613 3588 285
συναγαγεῖν αὐτοὺς εἰς πόλεμον· ὧν ὁ ἀριθμὸς ὡς ἡ ἄμμος
to assemble them in war; of whom the numbers (is) as the sand
3588 2281
τῆς θαλάσσης.
of the sea.

7. And when the thousand years are expired, Satan shall be loosed out of his prison,
8 And shall go out to deceive the nations which are in the four quarters of the earth, Gog and Magog, to gather them together to battle: the number of whom (is) as the sand of the sea.

9 And they went up over the breadth of the land and encircled the camp of the saints, and the beloved city. And fire from God came down out of Heaven and burned them down.

2532 305 1909 3588 4114 3588 1093 2532
9 καὶ ἀνέβησαν ἐπὶ τὸ πλάτος τῆς γῆς καὶ
And they went up over the breadth of the land and
2944 3588 3925 2532 40 2532 3588 4172 3588
ἐκύκλωσαν τὴν παρεμβολὴν τῶν ἁγίων καὶ τὴν πόλιν τὴν
encircled the camp of the saints and the city
25 2532 2597 4442 575 3588 2316 1537/3588 3772
ἠγαπημένην· καὶ κατέβη πῦρ ἀπὸ τοῦ Θεοῦ ἐκ τοῦ οὐρανοῦ,
beloved; and came down fire from God out of Heaven,
2532 2719 846
καὶ κατέφαγεν αὐτούς.
and burned down them.

9 And they went up on the breadth of the earth, and compassed the camp of the saints about, and the beloved city: and fire came down from God out of heaven, and devoured them.

10 And the devil leading them astray was thrown into the Lake of Fire and Brimstone, where the beast and the false prophet (are). And they were tormented day and night to the ages of the ages.

2532/3588 1228 3588 4105 846
10 καὶ ὁ διάβολος ὁ πλανῶν αὐτοὺς
And the devil leading astray them
906 1519 3588 3041 3588 4442 2532 2303 3699 3588 2342
ἐβλήθη εἰς τὴν λίμνην τοῦ πυρὸς καὶ θείου, ὅπου τὸ θηρίον
was thrown into the Lake of Fire and Brimstone, where the beast
2532 3588 5578 2532 928 2250 2532
καὶ ὁ ψευδοπροφήτης· καὶ βασανισθήσονται ἡμέρας καὶ
and the false prophet (are); and they will be tormented day and
3571 1519 3588 165 3588 165
νυκτὸς εἰς τοὺς αἰῶνας τῶν αἰώνων.
night to the ages of the ages.

10 And the devil that deceived them was cast into the lake of fire and brimstone, where the beast and the false prophet (are), and shall be tormented day and night for ever and ever.

11. And I saw a great white throne, and the (One) sitting on it, from whose face the earth and the heaven fled; and a place was not found for them.
12 And I saw the dead, (the) small and the great, standing before God. And scrolls were opened.

2532 1492 2362 3022 3173 2532 3588 2521 1909
11. Καὶ εἶδον θρόνον λευκὸν μέγαν, καὶ τὸν καθήμενον ἐπ᾽
And I saw a throne white great, and the (One) sitting on
846 3739 575 3588 4383 5343 3588 1093 2532 3588 3772 2532
αὐτοῦ οὗ ἀπὸ τοῦ προσώπου ἔφυγεν ἡ γῆ καὶ ὁ οὐρανός, καὶ
it of whom from the face fled the earth and the heaven, and
5117 3756 2147 846 2532 1492 3588 3498 3398
τόπος οὐχ εὑρέθη αὐτοῖς. 12 καὶ εἶδον τοὺς νεκρούς, μικροὺς
a place not was found for them. And I saw the dead, (the) small
2532 3173 2476 1799 3588 2316 2532 975 455
καὶ μεγάλους, ἑστῶτας ἐνώπιον τοῦ Θεοῦ, καὶ βιβλία ἠνεῴχθη-
and great, standing before God, and scrolls were opened;

11. And I saw a great white throne, and him that sat on it, from whose face the earth and the heaven fled away; and there was found no place for them.
12 And I saw the dead, small and great, stand before God; and the books were opened:

Revelation 20:13

Literal Translation

And another Scroll was opened, (which is) the (Scroll) of Life. And the dead were judged out of the things having been written in the scrolls, according to their works.
13 And the sea gave up the dead in it. And death and Hades gave up the dead in them. And they were each judged according to their works.
14 And death and Hades were thrown into the Lake of Fire. This is the second death.

15 And if anyone was not found having been written in the Scroll of Life, he was thrown into the Lake of Fire.

2532 975 243 455 3739 2076 3588 2222 2532 2919
σαν· καὶ βιβλίον ἄλλο ἠνεῴχθη, ὅ ἐστι τῆς ζωῆς· καὶ ἐκρί-
and scroll another was opened, which is the (Scroll) of Life; and were
3588 3498 1537 3588 1125 1722 3588 975 2596
θησαν οἱ νεκροὶ ἐκ τῶν γεγραμμένων ἐν τοῖς βιβλίοις, κατὰ
judged the dead out of those having been written in the scrolls, according to
3588 2041 846 2532 1325 3588 2281 3588 1722 846 3498
τὰ ἔργα αὐτῶν. 13 καὶ ἔδωκεν ἡ θάλασσα τοὺς ἐν αὐτῇ νεκροὺς,
the works of them. And gave the sea the in it dead,
2532 3588 2288 2532/3588/86 1325 3588 1722 846 3498 2532
καὶ ὁ θάνατος καὶ ὁ ᾅδης ἔδωκαν τοὺς ἐν αὐτοῖς νεκρούς· καὶ
and death and Hades gave the in them dead; and
2919 1538 2596 3588 2041 846 2532 3588 2288 2532
ἐκρίθησαν ἕκαστος κατὰ τὰ ἔργα αὐτῶν. 14 καὶ ὁ θάνατος καὶ
they were judged each according to the works of them. And death and
3588 86 906 1519 3588 3041 3588 4442 3778 2076 3588
ὁ ᾅδης ἐβλήθησαν εἰς τὴν λίμνην τοῦ πυρός· οὗτος ἐστιν ὁ
Hades were thrown into the Lake of Fire; This is the
1208 2288 2532 1487 5100 3756 2147 1722 3588 976 3588
δεύτερος θάνατος. 15 καὶ εἴ τις οὐχ εὑρέθη ἐν τῇ βίβλῳ τῆς
second death. And if anyone not was found in the Scroll
2222 1125 906 1519 3588 3041 3588 4442
ζωῆς γεγραμμένος, ἐβλήθη εἰς τὴν λίμνην τοῦ πυρός.
of Life having been written, he was thrown into the Lake of Fire.

King James Version

and another book was opened, which is (the book) of life: and the dead were judged out of those things which were written in the books, according to their works.
13 And the sea gave up the dead which were in it; and death and hell delivered up the dead which were in them: and they were judged every man according to their works.
14 And death and hell were cast into the lake of fire. This is the second death.

15 And whosoever was not found written in the book of life was cast into the lake of fire.

Revelation 21

1. And I saw a new heaven and a new earth, for the first heaven and the first earth passed away, and the sea is no more.

2 And I, John, saw the holy city, New Jerusalem, coming down out of Heaven from God, having been prepared as a bride, having been adorned for her Husband.
3 And I heard a great voice out of Heaven, saying, Behold, the tabernacle of God with men! And He will tabernacle with them, and they will be His peoples, and God Himself will be with them as their God.

4 And God will wipe away every tear from their eyes. And death will be no longer, nor mourning, nor outcry, nor pain will be no longer; for the first things passed away.
5 And the (One) sitting on the throne said, Behold,

2532 1492 3772 2537 2532 1093 2537 3588 1063 4413
1. Καὶ εἶδον οὐρανὸν καινὸν καὶ γῆν καινήν· ὁ γὰρ πρῶτος
And I saw heaven a new and earth new; the for first
3772 2532 3588 4413 1093 3928 2532 3588 2281 3756 2076
οὐρανὸς καὶ ἡ πρώτη γῆ παρῆλθε, καὶ ἡ θάλασσα οὐκ ἔστιν
heaven and the first earth passed away, and the sea not is
2089 2532 1473 2491 1492 3588 4172 3588 40 2419
ἔτι. 2 καὶ ἐγὼ Ἰωάννης εἶδον τὴν πόλιν τὴν ἁγίαν Ἱερουσαλὴμ
yet. And I John saw the city holy Jerusalem
2537 2597 575 3588 2316 1537 3588 3772 2090
καινὴν, καταβαίνουσαν ἀπὸ τοῦ Θεοῦ ἐκ τοῦ οὐρανοῦ, ἡτοι-
New, coming down from God out of Heaven, having
5613 3565 2885 3588 435 846 2532
μασμένην ὡς νύμφην κεκοσμημένην τῷ ἀνδρὶ αὐτῆς. 3 καὶ
been prepared as a bride having been adorned for the Husband of her. And
191 5456 3173 1537 3588 3772 3004 2400 3588
ἤκουσα φωνῆς μεγάλης ἐκ τοῦ οὐρανοῦ, λεγούσης, Ἰδού, ἡ
I heard a voice great out of Heaven, saying, Behold! The
4633 3588 2316 3326 3588 444 2532 4637 3326
σκηνὴ τοῦ Θεοῦ μετὰ τῶν ἀνθρώπων, καὶ σκηνώσει μετ᾽
tabernacle of God with men, and He will tabernacle with
846 2532 846 2992 846 2071 2532 846 3588 2316 2071
αὐτῶν, καὶ αὐτοὶ λαοὶ αὐτοῦ ἔσονται, καὶ αὐτὸς ὁ Θεὸς ἔσται
them, and they peoples of Him will be, and Himself God will be
3326 846 2316 846 2532 1813 3588 2316 3956 1144
μετ᾽ αὐτῶν, Θεὸς αὐτῶν. 4 καὶ ἐξαλείψει ὁ Θεὸς πᾶν δάκρυον
with them, (the) God of them. And will wipe away God every tear
575 3588 3788 846 2532 3588 2288 3756 2071 2089 3777
ἀπὸ τῶν ὀφθαλμῶν αὐτῶν, καὶ ὁ θάνατος οὐκ ἔσται ἔτι· οὔτε
from the eyes of them, and death not will be longer; nor
3997 3777 2906 3777 4192 3756 2071 2089 3754 3588 4413
πένθος, οὔτε κραυγή, οὔτε πόνος οὐκ ἔσται ἔτι· ὅτι τὰ πρῶτα
mourning, nor outcry, nor pain not will be longer; for the first things
565 2532 2036 3588 2521 1909 3588 2362 2400
ἀπῆλθον. 5 καὶ εἶπεν ὁ καθήμενος ἐπὶ τοῦ θρόνου, Ἰδοὺ,
passed away. And said the (One) sitting on the throne, Behold!

1. And I saw a new heaven and a new earth: for the first heaven and the first earth were passed away; and there was no more sea.

2 And I John saw the holy city, new Jerusalem, coming down from God out of heaven, prepared as a bride adorned for her husband.
3 And I heard a great voice out of heaven saying, Behold, the tabernacle of God (is) with men, and he will dwell with them, and they shall be his people, and God himself shall be with them, (and be) their God.

4 And God shall wipe away all tears from their eyes; and there shall be no more death, neither sorrow, nor crying, neither shall there be any more pain: for the former things are pass-ed away.
5 And he that sat upon the throne said, Behold,

Literal Translation | **Revelation 21:6** | ***King James Version***

I make all things new. And He says to me, Write, because these words are faithful and true.
6 And He said to me, It is done! I am the Alpha and the Omega, the Head and the Ending. To (the one) thirsting, I will freely give of the fountain of the water of life.
7 The (one) overcoming will inherit all things, and I will be God to him, and he will be the son to Me.
8 But for the cowardly and unbelieving, and disgusting (ones), and murderers, and fornicators, and sorcerers, and idolaters, and all the lying ones, their part will be in the Lake burning with fire and brimstone, which is (the) second death.

2537 3956 4160 2532 3004 3427 1125 3754 3778 3588 3056
καινὰ πάντα ποιῶ. καὶ λέγει μοι, Γράψον· ὅτι οὗτοι οἱ λόγοι
new all things I make. And He says to me, Write; because these words

228 2532 4103 1526 2532 2036 3427 1096 1473 1510 3588
ἀληθινοὶ καὶ πιστοί εἰσι. 6 καὶ εἶπέ μοι, Γέγονε. ἐγώ εἰμι τὸ
true and faithful are. And He said to me, It is done. I am the

1 2532 3588 5598 3588 746 2532 3588 5056 1473 3588 1372
Α καὶ τὸ Ω, ἡ ἀρχὴ καὶ τὸ τέλος. ἐγὼ τῷ διψῶντι
Alpha and the Omega, the Head and the End. I to (the one) thirsting

1325 1537 3588 4077 3588 5204 3588 2222 1432 3588
δώσω ἐκ τῆς πηγῆς τοῦ ὕδατος τῆς ζωῆς δωρεάν. 7 ὁ
will give of the fountain of the water of life freely. The (one)

3528 2816 3956 2532 2071 846 2316 2532 846
νικῶν κληρονομήσει πάντα, καὶ ἔσομαι αὐτῷ Θεὸς, καὶ αὐτὸς
overcoming will inherit all things, and I will be to him God, and he

2071 3427/3588/5207 1169 1161 2532 571 2532 948
ἔσται μοι ὁ υἱός. 8 δειλοῖς δὲ καὶ ἀπίστοις καὶ ἐβδελυγμένοις
will be to me the son. to cowardly But and unbelieving and disgusting (ones)

2532 5406 2532 4205 2532 5332 2532 1496 2532
καὶ φονεῦσι καὶ πόρνοις καὶ φαρμακεῦσι καὶ εἰδωλολάτραις, καὶ
and murderers and fornicators and sorcerers and idolaters, and

3956 3588 5571 3588 3313 846 1722 3588 3041 3588 2545
πᾶσι τοῖς ψευδέσι, τὸ μέρος αὐτῶν ἐν τῇ λίμνῃ τῇ καιομένῃ
all the lying ones, the part of them in the Lake burning

4442 2532 2303 3739 2076 1208 2288
πυρὶ καὶ θείῳ, ὅ ἐστι δεύτερος θάνατος.
with fire and with brimstone, which is (the) second death.

I make all things new. And he said unto me, Write: for these words are true and faithful.
6 And he said unto me, It is done. I am Alpha and Omega, the beginning and the end. I will give unto him that is athirst of the fountain of the water of life freely.
7 He that overcometh shall inherit all things; and I will be his God, and he shall be my son.
8 But the fearful, and unbelieving, and the abominable, and murderers, and whoremongers, and sorcerers, and idolaters, and all liars, shall have their part in the lake which burneth with fire and brimstone: which is the second death.

9. And one of the seven angels came to me, he having the seven bowls being filled with the seven last plagues, and spoke with me, saying, Come, I will show you the bride, the wife of the Lamb.
10 And he carried me in Spirit on to a great and high mountain, and showed me the great city, Holy Jerusalem, coming down out of Heaven from God,
11 having the glory of God. And its light (was) like a very precious stone, as a jasper stone, being clear as crystal,
12 and having a great and high wall, having twelve gates, and twelve angels on the gates, and names having been inscribed, which are of the twelve tribes of the sons of Israel.
13 From (the) east, three gates; from (the) north, three gates;

2532 2064 4314 3165 1520 3588 2033 32 3588 2192 3588
9. Καὶ ἦλθε πρός με εἷς τῶν ἑπτὰ ἀγγέλων τῶν ἐχόντων τὰς
And came to me one of the seven angels the (one) having the

2033 5357 3588 1073 3588 2033 4127 3588 2078
ἑπτὰ φιάλας τὰς γεμούσας τῶν ἑπτὰ πληγῶν τῶν ἐσχάτων,
seven bowls being filled of the seven plagues last,

2532 2980 3326 1700 3004 1204 1161 4671 3588 3565
καὶ ἐλάλησε μετ᾽ ἐμοῦ, λέγων, Δεῦρο, δείξω σοι τὴν νύμφην
and (he) spoke with me, saying, Come, I will show you the bride

3588 721 3588 1135 2532 667 3165 1722 4151 1909
τοῦ ἀρνίου τὴν γυναῖκα. 10 καὶ ἀπήνεγκέ με ἐν Πνεύματι ἐπ᾽
of the Lamb the wife. And he carried me in Spirit onto

3735 3173 2532 5308 2532 1166 3427 3588 4172 3173
ὄρος μέγα καὶ ὑψηλόν, καὶ ἔδειξέ μοι τὴν πόλιν μεγάλην,
mount a great and high, and showed to me the city great,

3588 40 2419 2597 1537 3588 3772 575
τὴν ἁγίαν Ἱερουσαλήμ, καταβαίνουσαν ἐκ τοῦ οὐρανοῦ ἀπὸ
Holy Jerusalem, coming down out of Heaven from

3588 2316 2192 3588 1391 3588 2316 2532 3588 5458 846
τοῦ Θεοῦ, 11 ἔχουσαν τὴν δόξαν τοῦ Θεοῦ· καὶ ὁ φωστὴρ αὐτῆς
God, having the glory of God; and the light of it

3664 3037 5093 5613 3037 2393 2929
ὅμοιος λίθῳ τιμιωτάτῳ, ὡς λίθῳ ἰάσπιδι κρυσταλλίζοντι·
(was) like a stone very precious, as stone a jasper being clear as crystal;

2192 5037 5038 3173 2532 5308 2192 4440
12 ἔχουσαν τε τεῖχος μέγα καὶ ὑψηλόν, ἔχουσαν πυλῶνας
having and wall a great and high, having gates

1427 2532 1909 3588 4440 32 1427 2532 3686
δώδεκα, καὶ ἐπὶ τοῖς πυλῶσιν ἀγγέλους δώδεκα, καὶ ὀνόματα
twelve, and on the gates angels twelve, and names

1924 3739 2076 3588 1427 5443 3588 5207 2474
ἐπιγεγραμμένα, ἅ ἐστι τῶν δώδεκα φυλῶν τῶν υἱῶν Ἰσραήλ.
having been inscribed, which are the twelve tribes of the sons of Israel.

575 395 4440 5140 575 1005 4440 5140
13 ἀπ᾽ ἀνατολῆς, πυλῶνες τρεῖς· ἀπὸ βορρᾶ, πυλῶνες τρεῖς·
From (the) east, gates three; from (the) north, gates three;

9. And there came unto me one of the seven angels which had the seven vials full of the seven last plagues, and talked with me, saying, Come hither, I will shew thee the bride, the Lamb's wife.
10 And he carried me away in the spirit to a great and high mountain, and shewed me that great city, the holy Jerusalem, descending out of heaven from God,
11 Having the glory of God: and her light (was) like unto a stone most precious, even like a jasper stone, clear as crystal;
12 And had a wall great and high, (and) had twelve gates, and at the gates twelve angels, and names written thereon, which are (the names) of the twelve tribes of the children of Israel:
13 On the east three gates; on the north three gates;

Revelation 21:14

Literal Translation

from the south, three gates; and from the west, three gates.

14 And the wall of the city had twelve foundations, and in them the names of the twelve apostles of the Lamb.
15 And he speaking with me had a golden reed, that he may measure the city, and its gates and its wall.
16 And the city lies four-cornered, even its length as much as the width also. And he measured the city with the reed at twelve thousand stadia; its length and width and height are equal.

17 And he measured its wall, a hundred (and) forty-four cubits, a measure of a man, which is of an angel.

18 And the structure of its wall was jasper; and the city (was) pure gold, like pure glass.

19 And the foundation of the wall of the city having been adorned with every precious stone: The first foundation, jasper; the second, sapphire; the third, chalcedony; the fourth, emerald;
20 the fifth, sardonyx; the sixth, sardius; the seventh, chrysolite; the eighth, beryl; the ninth, topaz; the tenth, chrysoprasus; the eleventh, hyacinth; the twelfth, amethyst.

21 And the twelve gates (were) twelve pearls; respectively each one of the gates was of one pearl. And the street of the city was pure gold, as transparent glass.

575 3558 4440 5140 2532 575 1424 4440 5140
ἀπὸ νότου, πυλῶνες τρεῖς· καὶ ἀπὸ δυσμῶν, πυλῶνες τρεῖς.
from (the) south, gates three; and from (the) west, gates three.

2532 3588 5038 3588 4172 2192 2310 1427 2532 1722
14 καὶ τὸ τεῖχος τῆς πόλεως ἔχον θεμελίους δώδεκα, καὶ ἐν
And the wall of the city having foundations twelve, and in

846 3686 3588 1427 652 3588 721 2532
αὐτοῖς ὀνόματα τῶν δώδεκα ἀποστόλων τοῦ ἀρνίου. 15 καὶ
them names of the twelve apostles of the Lamb. And

3588 2980 3326 1700 2192 2563 5552 2443 3354 3588
ὁ λαλῶν μετ' ἐμοῦ εἶχε κάλαμον χρυσοῦν, ἵνα μετρήσῃ τὴν
he speaking with me had a reed of gold, that he may measure the

4172 2532 3588 4440 846 2532 3588 5038 846 2532
πόλιν, καὶ τοὺς πυλῶνας αὐτῆς, καὶ τὸ τεῖχος αὐτῆς. 16 καὶ
city, and the gates of it, and the wall of it. And

3588 4172 5068 2749 2532/3588/3372 846 5118
ἡ πόλις τετράγωνος κεῖται, καὶ τὸ μῆκος αὐτῆς τοσοῦτόν
the city four-cornered lies, and the length of it so much

2076 3745 2532 3588 4114 2532 3354 3588 4172 3588
ἐστιν ὅσον καὶ τὸ πλάτος. καὶ ἐμέτρησε τὴν πόλιν τῷ
is as much as also the width. And he measured the city with the

2563 1909 4712 1427 5505 3588 3372 2532 3588
καλάμῳ ἐπὶ σταδίων δώδεκα χιλιάδων· τὸ μῆκος καὶ τὸ
reed at stadia twelve thousands; the length and the

4114 2532 3588 5311 846 2470 2076 2532 3354 3588 5038
πλάτος καὶ τὸ ὕψος αὐτῆς ἴσα ἐστί. 17 καὶ ἐμέτρησε τὸ τεῖχος
width and the height of it equal are. And he measured the wall

846 1540 5062 5064 4083 3358
αὐτῆς ἑκατὸν τεσσαράκοντα τεσσάρων πηχῶν, μέτρον
of it a hundred (and) forty four cubits, a meausre

444 3739 2076 32 2532 2258 3588 1739 3588 5038
ἀνθρώπου, ὅ ἐστιν ἀγγέλου. 18 καὶ ἦν ἡ ἐνδόμησις τοῦ τείχους
of a man, which is of an angel. And was the structure of the wall

846 2393 2532 3588 4172 5553 2513 3664 5194
αὐτῆς, ἴασπις· καὶ ἡ πόλις χρυσίον καθαρόν, ὁμοία ὑάλῳ
of it, jasper; and the city (was) gold clean, like glass

2513 2532 3588 2310 3588 5038 3588 4172 3956 3037
καθαρῷ. 19 καὶ οἱ θεμέλιοι τοῦ τείχους τῆς πόλεως παντὶ λίθῳ
clean. And the foundations of the wall of the city with every stone

5093 2885 3588 2310 3588 4413 2393 3588 1208
τιμίῳ κεκοσμημένοι. ὁ θεμέλιος ὁ πρῶτος, ἴασπις· ὁ δεύτερος,
precious was adorned. The foundation first, jasper; the second,

4552 3588 5154 5472 3588 5067 4665 3588
σάπφειρος· ὁ τρίτος, χαλκηδών· ὁ τέταρτος, σμάραγδος· 20 ὁ
sapphire; the third, chalcedony; the fourth, emerald; the

3991 4557 3588/1623 4556 3588 1442 5555
πέμπτος, σαρδόνυξ· ὁ ἕκτος, σάρδιος· ὁ ἕβδομος, χρυσόλιθος·
fifth, sardonyx; the sixth, sardius; the seventh, chrysolite;

3588 3590 969 3588 1766 5116 3588 1182
ὁ ὄγδοος, βήρυλλος· ὁ ἔννατος, τοπάζιον· ὁ δέκατος,
the eighth, beryl; the ninth, topaz; the tenth,

5556 3588 1734 5192 3588 1428 271
χρυσόπρασος· ὁ ἑνδέκατος, ὑάκινθος· ὁ δωδέκατος, ἀμέ-
chrysoprasus; the eleventh, hyacinch; the twelfth,

2532/3588 1427 4440 1427 3135 303
θυστος. 21 καὶ οἱ δώδεκα πυλῶνες, δώδεκα μαργαρῖται ἀνὰ
amethyst. And the twelve gates, (were) twelve pearls; respectively

1520 1538 3588 4440 2258 1537 1520 3135 2532 3588
εἷς ἕκαστος τῶν πυλώνων ἦν ἐξ ἑνὸς μαργαρίτου· καὶ ἡ
one each of the gates was of one pearl; and the

4113 3588 4172 5553 2513 5613 5194 1307
πλατεῖα τῆς πόλεως χρυσίον καθαρὸν, ὡς ὕαλος διαφανής.
street of the city (was) of gold pure, as glass transparent.

King James Version

on the south three gates; and on the west three gates.

14 And the wall of the city had twelve foundations, and in them the names of the twelve apostles of the Lamb.
15 And he that talked with me had a golden reed to measure the city, and the gates thereof, and the wall thereof.
16 And the city lieth foursquare, and the length is as large as the breadth: and he measured the city with the reed, twelve thousand furlongs. The length and the breadth and the height of it are equal.

17 And he measured the wall thereof, an hundred (and) forty (and) four cubits, (according to) the measure of a man, that is, of the angel.
18 And the building of the wall of it was (of) jasper: and the city (was) pure gold, like unto clear glass.

19 And the foundations of the wall of the city (were) garnished with all manner of precious stones. The first foundation (was) jasper; the second, sapphire; the third, a chalcedony; the fourth, an emerald;
20 The fifth, sardonyx; the sixth, sardius; the seventh, chrysolite; the eighth, beryl; the ninth, a topaz; the tenth, a chrysoprasus; the eleventh, a jacinth; the twelfth, an amethyst.

21 And the twelve gates (were) twelve pearls; every several gate was of one pearl: and the street of the city (was) pure gold, as it were transparent glass.

Literal Translation

Revelation 21:22

King James Version

22. And I saw no temple in it, for the Lord God Almighty is its temple, even the Lamb.
23 And the city had no need of the sun, nor of the moon, that they might shine in it, for the glory of God illuminated it, even its lamp (is) the Lamb.

24 And the nations of the (ones) saved will walk in its light; and the kings of the earth bring their glory and honor into it.

25 And its gates may not at all be shut by day, for no night will be there.
26 And they will bring the glory and the honor of the nations into it.
27 And all profaning may not at all enter into it, or (any) making an abomination or a lie; except the (ones) having been written in the Scroll of Life of the Lamb.

2532 3485 3756 1492 1722 846 3588 1063 2962 3588 2316 3588 3841
22 καὶ ναὸν οὐκ εἶδον ἐν αὐτῇ· ὁ γὰρ Κύριος ὁ Θεὸς ὁ παντο-
And a temple not I saw in it; the for Lord God Almighty

3485 846 2076 2532 3588 721 2532 3588 4172 3756
κράτωρ ναὸς αὐτῆς ἐστι, καὶ τὸ ἀρνίον. 23 καὶ ἡ πόλις οὐ
temple of it is, even the Lamb. And the city not

5532 2192 3588 2246 3761 3588 4582 2443 5316 1722
χρείαν ἔχει τοῦ ἡλίου, οὐδὲ τῆς σελήνης, ἵνα φαίνωσιν ἐν
need had of the sun, nor of the moon, that they may shine in

846 3588 1063 1391 3588 2316 5461 846 2532 3588 3088
αὐτῇ· ἡ γὰρ δόξα τοῦ Θεοῦ ἐφώτισεν αὐτήν, καὶ ὁ λύχνος
it; the for (the) glory of God illuminated it, even the lamp

846 3588 721 2532 3588 1484 3588 4982 1722 3588 5457
αὐτῆς τὸ ἀρνίον. 24 καὶ τὰ ἔθνη τῶν σωζομένων ἐν τῷ φωτὶ
of it (is) the Lamb. And the nations of those saved in the light

846 4043 2532 3588 935 3588 1093 5342 3588
αὐτῆς περιπατήσουσι· καὶ οἱ βασιλεῖς τῆς γῆς φέρουσι τὴν
of it will walk; and the kings of the earth bring the

1391 2532 3588 5092 846 1519 846 2532 3588 4440
δόξαν καὶ τὴν τιμὴν αὐτῶν εἰς αὐτήν· 25 καὶ οἱ πυλῶνες
glory and the honor of them into it. and the gates

846 3756 3361 2808 2250 3571 1063 3756 2071 1563 2532
αὐτῆς οὐ μὴ κλεισθῶσιν ἡμέρας [νὺξ γὰρ οὐκ ἔσται ἐκεῖ]· 26 καὶ
of it not at all may be shut by day -- night for not is there; -- and

5342 3588 1391 2532 3588 5092 3588 1484 1519 846 2532
οἴσουσι τὴν δόξαν καὶ τὴν τιμὴν τῶν ἐθνῶν εἰς αὐτήν. 27 καὶ
they will bring the glory and the honor of the nations into it. And

3756 3361 1525 1519 846 3956 2840 2532 4160 946
οὐ μὴ εἰσέλθῃ εἰς αὐτὴν πᾶν κοινοῦν, καὶ ποιοῦν βδέλ-
not at all may enter into it all profaning, and (any) making an

2532 5579 1487 3361 3588 1125 1722 3588 975 3588
υγμα καὶ ψεῦδος· εἰ μὴ οἱ γεγραμμένοι ἐν τῷ βιβλίῳ τῆς
abomination and a lie; except those having been written in the Scroll

2222 3588 721
ζωῆς τοῦ ἀρνίου.
of Life of the Lamb.

22. And I saw no temple therein: for the Lord God Almighty and the Lamb are the temple of it.
23 And the city had no need of the sun, neither of the moon, to shine in it: for the glory of God did lighten it, and the Lamb (is) the light thereof.

24 And the nations of them which are saved shall walk in the light of it: and the kings of the earth do bring their glory and honour into it.

25 And the gates of it shall not be shut at all by day: for there shall be no night there.
26 And they shall bring the glory and honour of the nations into it.
27 And there shall in no wise enter into it any thing that defileth, neither (whatsoever) worketh abomination, or (maketh) a lie: but they which are written in the Lamb's book of life.

Revelation 22

Revelation 22

Revelation 22

1. And he showed me a pure river of water of life, bright as crystal, coming forth out of the throne of God and of the Lamb.

2 In the midst of its street and of the river, from here and from there, (was) a tree of life producing twelve fruits: according to one month each yielding its fruit. And the leaves of the tree (will be) for healing of the nations.

3 And every curse will no longer be. And the throne of God and the Lamb will be in it; and His slaves will serve

2532 1166 3427 2513 4215 5204 2222 2986
1. Καὶ ἔδειξέ μοι καθαρὸν ποταμὸν ὕδατος ζωῆς, λαμ-
And he showed me a clean river of water of life, bright

5613 2930 1607 1537 3588 2362 3588 2316
πρὸν ὡς κρύσταλλον, ἐκπορευόμενον ἐκ τοῦ θρόνου τοῦ Θεοῦ
as crystal, coming forth out of the throne of God

2532 3588 721 1722 3319 3588 4113 846 2532 3588
καὶ τοῦ ἀρνίου. 2 ἐν μέσῳ τῆς πλατείας αὐτῆς, καὶ τοῦ
and the Lamb. In (the) midst of the street of it, and of the

4215 1782 2532 1782 3586 2222 4160 2590
ποταμοῦ ἐντεῦθεν καὶ εντεῦθεν, ξύλον ζωῆς, ποιοῦν καρποὺς
river from here and from there, a tree of life, producing fruits

1427 2596 3376 1520 1538 591 3588 2590
δώδεκα, κατὰ μῆνα ἕνα ἕκαστον ἀποδιδοῦν τὸν καρπὸν
twelve, according to month one each yielding the fruit

846 2532 3588 5444 3588 3586 1519 2322 3588 1484
αὐτοῦ, καὶ τὰ φύλλα τοῦ ξύλου εἰς θεραπείαν τῶν ἐθνῶν.
of it, and the leaves of the tree (will be) for healing of the nations.

2532 3956 2652 3756 2071 2089 2532 3588 2362 3588 2316 2532
3 καὶ πᾶν κατανάθεμα οὐκ ἔσται ἔτι· καὶ ὁ θρόνος τοῦ Θεοῦ καὶ
And every curse not will be still; and the throne of God and

3588 721 1722 846 2071 2532 3588 1401 846 3000
τοῦ ἀρνίου ἐν αὐτῇ ἔσται· καὶ οἱ δοῦλοι αὐτοῦ λατρεύσουσιν
the Lamb in it will be; and the slaves of Him will serve

1. And he shewed me a pure river of water of life, clear as crystal, proceeding out of the throne of God and of the Lamb.

2 In the midst of the street of it, and on either side of the river, (was there) the tree of life, which bare twelve (manner of) fruits, (and) yielded her fruit every month: and the leaves of the tree (were) for the healing of the nations.

3 And there shall be no more curse: but the throne of God and of the Lamb shall be in it; and his servants shall serve

Literal Translation — **Revelation 22:4** — ***King James Version***

Literal Translation

Him.
4 And they will see His face; and His name (will be) on their foreheads.

5 And night will not be there; and they have no need of a lamp (or) a light of the sun, because the Lord God will enlighten them. And they shall reign to the ages of the ages..

6. And he said to me, These words (are) faithful and true. And the Lord God of the holy prophets sent His angel to show His slaves what must happen quickly.

7 Behold, I am coming quickly. Blessed (is) the (one) keeping the words of the prophecy of this Scroll.

8 And I, John, (was) the (one) seeing and hearing these things. And when I heard and saw, I fell down to worship before the feet of the angel showing me these things.
9 And he says to me, See, do not (do it)! For I am your fellow-slave, and of your brothers the prophets, and of the ones keeping the words of this Book. Do worship to God.

10 And he said to me, Do not seal the words of the prophecy of this Scroll, because the time is near.
11 The one acting unjustly, let him still act unjustly; and the filthy, let him still be filthy; and the righteous, let him still do righteousness; and the (one) holy, let him still be holy.
12 And, behold, I am coming quickly, and My reward (is) with Me, to give

846 2532 3700 3588 4383 846 2532 3588 3686
αὐτῷ, 4 καὶ ὄψονται τὸ πρόσωπον αὐτοῦ· καὶ τὸ ὄνομα
to Him, and they will see the face of Him; and the name

846 1909 3588 3359 846 2532 3571 3756 2071 1563 2532
αὐτοῦ ἐπὶ τῶν μετώπων αὐτῶν. 5 καὶ νὺξ οὐκ ἔσται ἐκεῖ, καὶ
of Him (will be) on the foreheads of them. And night not will be there, and

5532 3756 2192 3088 2532 5457 2246 3754
χρείαν οὐκ ἔχουσι λύχνου καὶ φωτὸς ἡλίου, ὅτι
need not they have of a lamp and a light of (the) sun, because

2962 3588/2316 5461 846 2532 936 1519 3588
Κύριος ὁ Θεὸς φωτίζει αὐτούς· καὶ βασιλεύσουσιν εἰς τοὺς
(the) Lord God will enlighten them; and they will reign to the

165 3588 165
αἰῶνας τῶν αἰώνων.
ages of the ages..

2532 2036 3427 3778 3588 3056 4103 2532 228 2532
6. Καὶ εἶπέ μοι, Οὗτοι οἱ λόγοι πιστοὶ καὶ ἀληθινοί· καὶ
And he said to me, These words (are) faithful and true; and

2962 3588 2316 3588 40 4396 649 3588 32
Κύριος ὁ Θεὸς τῶν ἁγίων προφητῶν ἀπέστειλε τὸν ἄγγελον
(the) Lord God of the holy prophets sent the angel

846 1166 3588 1401 846 3739/1163 1096 1722 5034
αὐτοῦ δεῖξαι τοῖς δούλοις αὐτοῦ ἃ δεῖ γενέσθαι ἐν τάχει.
of Him to show the slaves of Him what must happen quickly.

2400 2064 5035 3107 3588 5083 3588 3056 3588
7 ἰδού, ἔρχομαι ταχύ. μακάριος ὁ τηρῶν τοὺς λόγους τῆς
Behold! I am coming quickly. Blessed the (one) keeping the words of the

4394 3588 975 5127
προφητείας τοῦ βιβλίου τούτου.
prophecy Scroll of this.

2532 1473 2491 3588 991 5023 2532 191 2532 3753
8. Καὶ ἐγὼ Ἰωάννης ὁ βλέπων ταῦτα καὶ ἀκούων. καὶ ὅτε
And I John the (one) seeing these things and hearing, and when

191 2532 991 4098 4352 1715 3588
ἤκουσα καὶ ἔβλεψα, ἔπεσα προσκυνῆσαι ἔμπροσθεν τῶν
I heard and saw, I fell down to worship before the

4228 3588 32 3588 1166 3427 5023 2532 3004
ποδῶν τοῦ ἀγγέλου τοῦ δεικνύοντός μοι ταῦτα. 9 καὶ λέγει
feet of the angel showing me these things. And he says

3427 3708 3361 4889 4675 1063 1510 2532 3588 80 4675
μοι, Ὅρα μή· σύνδουλός σου γάρ εἰμι, καὶ τῶν ἀδελφῶν σου
to me, See not (do it); a fellow-slave of you for I am, and the brothers of you

3588 4396 2532 3588 5083 3588 3056 3588
τῶν προφητῶν, καὶ τῶν τηρούντων τοὺς λόγους τοῦ
the prophets, and of the (ones) keeping the words

975 5127 3588/2316 4352
βιβλίου τούτου· τῷ Θεῷ προσκύνησον.
Scroll of this; to God do worship.

2532 3004 3427 3361 4972 3588 3056 3588
10. Καὶ λέγει μοι, Μὴ σφραγίσῃς τοὺς λόγους τῆς
And he says to me, Not do seal the words of the

4394 3588 975 5127 3754/3588/2540 1451 2076
προφητείας τοῦ βιβλίου τούτου· ὅτι ὁ καιρὸς ἐγγύς ἐστιν.
prophecy Scroll of this; because the time near is.

3588 91 91 2089 2532 3588 4510 4510 2089/2532/3588
11 ὁ ἀδικῶν ἀδικησάτω ἔτι· καὶ ὁ ῥυπῶν ῥυπωσάτω ἔτι· καὶ ὁ
He doing unjustly let him do unjustly still; and he filthy let be filthy still. and he

1342 1344 2089 2532/3588 40 37 2089 2532
δίκαιος δικαιωθήτω ἔτι· καὶ ὁ ἅγιος ἁγιασθήτω ἔτι. 12 καὶ
righteous do righteousness still; and he holy, let him be holy still. And

2400 2064 5035 2532 3588 3408 3450 3326 1700 591
Ἰδού, ἔρχομαι ταχύ, καὶ ὁ μισθός μου μετ' ἐμοῦ, ἀποδοῦναι
behold! I am coming quickly, and the reward of Me with Me, to give

King James Version

him:
4 And they shall see his face; and his name (shall be) in their foreheads.
5 And there shall be no night there; and they need no candle, neither light of the sun; for the Lord God giveth them light: and they shall reign for ever and ever.

6. And he said unto me, These sayings (are) faithful and true: and the Lord God of the holy prophets sent his angel to shew unto his servants the things which must shortly be done.

7 Behold, I come quickly: blessed (is) he that keepeth the sayings of the prophecy of this book.

8 And I John saw these things, and heard (them). And when I had heard and seen, I fell down to worship before the feet of the angel which shewed me these things.
9 Then saith he unto me, See (thou do it) not: for I am thy fellowservant, and of thy brethren the prophets, and of them which keep the sayings of this book: worship God.

10 And he saith unto me, Seal not the sayings of the prophecy of this book: for the time is at hand.
11 He that is unjust, let him be unjust still: and he which is filthy, let him be filthy still: and he that is righteous, let him be righteous still: and he that is holy, let him be holy still.
12 And, behold, I come quickly; and my reward (is) with me, to give

Literal Translation **Revelation 22:13** ***King James Version***

to each as his work is.
13 I am the Alpha and the Omega, the Beginning and the Ending, the First and the Last.
14 Blessed (are) the (ones) doing His commands, that their authority will be over the Tree of Life, and by the gates they may enter into the city.

15 But outside (are) the dogs and the sorcerers, and the fornicators, and the murderers, and the idolaters, and everyone loving and making a lie.
16 I, Jesus, sent My angel to witness these things to you over the churches. I am the Root and Offspring of David, the bright and morning Star.

17 And the Spirit and the bride say, Come! And the (one) hearing, let him say, Come! And the (one) thirsting, let him come; and the (one) desiring, let him take of the water of life freely.

18 For I testify together everyone hearing the words of the prophecy of this Scroll: If anyone adds to these things, God will add upon him the plagues having been written in this Scroll.

19 And if anyone will take away from the words of (the) Scroll of this prophecy, God will take away his part from (the) Scroll of Life, and out of the holy city, and of the things having been written in this Scroll.

20. The (One) testifying these things says, Yes, I am coming quickly. Amen. Yes, come, Lord Jesus!

1538 5613 3588 2041 846 2071 1473/1510/3588/1/2532/3588
ἑκάστῳ ὡς τὸ ἔργον αὐτοῦ ἔσται. 13 ἐγώ εἰμι τὸ Α καὶ τὸ
to each as the work of him is. I am the Alpha and the

5598 746 2532 5056 3588 4413 2532/3588/2078 3107 3588
Ω, ἀρχὴ καὶ τέλος, ὁ πρῶτος καὶ ὁ ἔσχατος. 14 μακάριοι οἱ
Omega, Beginning and Ending, the First and the Last. Blessed (are) those

4160 3588 1785 846 2443 2071 3588 1849 846 1909 3588
ποιοῦντες τὰς ἐντολὰς αὐτοῦ, ἵνα ἔσται ἡ ἐξουσία αὐτῶν ἐπὶ τὸ
doing the commands of Him, that will be the authority of Him over the

3586 3588 2222 2532 3588 4440 1525 1519 3588
ξύλον τῆς ζωῆς, καὶ τοῖς πυλῶσιν εἰσέλθωσιν εἰς τὴν
tree of life, and by the gates they may enter into the

4172 1854 1161/3588/2965/2532/3588 5333 2532/3588/4205/2532/3588
πόλιν. 15 ἔξω δὲ οἱ κύνες καὶ οἱ φαρμακοί καὶ οἱ πόρνοι καὶ οἱ
city. (are) outside But the dogs and the sorcerers and the fornicators and the

5406 2532 3588 1496 2532/3956/3588/5368/2532 4160 5579
φονεῖς καὶ οἱ εἰδωλολάτραι, καὶ πᾶς ὁ φιλῶν καὶ ποιῶν ψεῦδος.
murderers and the idolaters, and everyone loving and making a lie.

1473 2424 3992 3588 32 3450 3140
16. Ἐγὼ Ἰησοῦς ἔπεμψα τὸν ἄγγελόν μου μαρτυρῆσαι
I Jesus sent the angel of Me to witness

5213 5023 1909 3588 1577 1473 1510 3588 4491 2532 3588
ὑμῖν ταῦτα ἐπὶ ταῖς ἐκκλησίαις. ἐγώ εἰμι ἡ ῥίζα καὶ τὸ
to you these things over the churches. I am the Root and the

1085 3588 1138 3588 792 3588 2986 2532 3720
γένος τοῦ Δαβίδ, ὁ ἀστὴρ ὁ λαμπρὸς καὶ ὀρθρινός.
Offspring of David, the Star bright and morning.

2532 3588 4151 2532 3588 3565 3004 2064 2532 3588 191
17. Καὶ τὸ Πνεῦμα καὶ ἡ νύμφη λέγουσιν, Ἐλθέ. καὶ ὁ ἀκούων
And the Spirit and the bride say, Come. And he hearing

2036 2064 2532 3588 1372 2064 2532 3588 2309 2983
εἰπάτω, Ἐλθέ. καὶ ὁ διψῶν ἐλθέτω· καὶ ὁ θέλων λαμβανέτω
let him say, Come. And he thirsting let him come; and he willing, let him take

3588 5204 2222 1432
τὸ ὕδωρ ζωῆς δωρεάν.
the water of life freely.

4828 1063 3956 191 3588 3056 3588
18. Συμμαρτυροῦμαι γὰρ παντὶ ἀκούοντι τοὺς λόγους τῆς
I testify together For everyone hearing the words of the

4394 3588 975 5127 1437 5100 2007 4314
προφητείας τοῦ βιβλίου τούτου, Ἐάν τις ἐπιτιθῇ πρὸς
prophecy Scroll of this, if anyone adds to

5023 2007 3588 2316 1909 846 3588 4127 3588 1125
ταῦτα, ἐπιθήσει ὁ Θεὸς ἐπ' αὐτὸν τὰς πληγὰς τὰς γεγραμ-
these things, will add God on him the plagues having been

1722 975 5129 2532 1437 5100 851 575 3588 3056
μένας ἐν βιβλίῳ τούτῳ· 19 καὶ ἐάν τις ἀφαιρῇ ἀπὸ τῶν λόγων
written in Scroll this; and if anyone will take away from the words

976 3588 4394 3778 851 3588 2316 3588 3313
βίβλου τῆς προφητείας ταύτης, ἀφαιρήσει ὁ Θεὸς τὸ μέρος
of (the) Scroll of prophecy this, will take away God the part

846 575 976 3588 2222 2532/1537/3588 4172 3588 40
αὐτοῦ ἀπὸ βίβλου τῆς ζωῆς, καὶ ἐκ τῆς πόλεως τῆς ἁγίας,
of him from (the) Scroll of Life, and out of the city holy,

2532 3588 1125 1722 975 5129
καὶ τῶν γεγραμμένων ἐν βιβλίῳ τούτῳ.
and of the things having been written in Scroll this.

3004 3588 3140 5023 3483 2064 5035 281
20. Λέγει ὁ μαρτυρῶν ταῦτα, Ναί, ἔρχομαι ταχύ. ἀμήν.
Says the (One) testifying these things, Yes, I am coming quickly. Amen.

3483 2064 2962 2424
Ναί, ἔρχου, Κύριε Ἰησοῦ.
Yes, come, Lord Jesus.

---

every man according as his work shall be.
13 I am Alpha and Omega, the beginning and the end, the first and the last.
14 Blessed (are) they that do his commandments, that they may have right to the tree of life, and may enter in through the gates into the city.

15 For without (are) dogs, and sorcerers, and whoremongers, and murderers, and idolaters, and whosoever loveth and maketh a lie.

16 I Jesus have sent mine angel to testify unto you these things in the churches. I am the root and the offspring of David, (and) the bright and morning star.

17 And the Spirit and the bride say, Come. And let him that heareth say, Come. And let him that is athirst come. And whosoever will, let him take the water of life freely.

18 For I testify unto every man that heareth the words of the prophecy of this book, If any man shall add unto these things, God shall add unto him the plagues that are written in this book:

19 And if any man shall take away from the words of the book of this prophecy, God shall take away his part out of the book of life, and out of the holy city, and (from) the things which are written in this book.

20. He which testifieth these things saith, Surely I come quickly. Amen. Even so, come, Lord Jesus.

Literal Translation

21 The grace of our Lord Jesus Christ (be) with all of you. Amen.

Revelation 22:21

3588	5485	3588	2962	2257	2424	5547	3326	3956
21.῾Η	χάρις	τοῦ	Κυρίου	ἡμῶν	᾿Ιησοῦ	Χριστοῦ	μετὰ	πάντων
The	grace	of the	Lord	of us	Jesus	Christ	(be) with	all

5216	281
ὑμῶν.	ἀμήν.
of you.	Amen.

King James Version

21 The grace of our Lord Jesus Christ (be) with you all. Amen.

Jay P. Green, Sr., is an ardent Bible student with several publications to his credit, including an interlinear Bible and a Bible translation.